P R E S E N T E D

To

Millard Pettit

By

On

THE
MacArthur
student
BIBLE

JOHN MACARTHUR
AUTHOR AND GENERAL EDITOR

NKJV
NEW
KING
JAMES
VERSION

WORD PUBLISHING
NASHVILLE
A Thomas Nelson Company

TABLE OF CONTENTS

TABLE OF ABBREVIATIONS

A.D.	in the year of our Lord	NT	New Testament
B.C.	before Christ	NU	the most prominent modern Critical Text of the Greek New Testament, published in the twenty-seventh edition of the Nestle-Aland *Greek New Testament* and in the fourth edition of the United Bible Societies' *Greek New Testament* (see Preface, "The New Testament Text")
e.g.	for example		
f., ff.	following verse, following verses		
Gr.	Greek		
Heb.	Hebrew		
i.e.	that is		
Kt.	Kethib (literally, in Aramaic, "written")—the written words of the Hebrew Old Testament preserved by the Masoretes (see "Qr.")		
		OT	Old Testament
Lat.	Latin	Qr.	Qere (literally, in Aramaic, "read")—certain words read aloud, differing from the written words, in the Masoretic tradition of the Hebrew Old Testament (see "Kt.")
lit.	literally		
LXX	Septuagint—an ancient translation of the Old Testament into Greek		
M	Majority Text (See Preface, "The New Testament Text")		
		TR	Textus Receptus or Received Text (see Preface, "The New Testament Text")
ms., mss.	manuscript, manuscripts		
MT	Masoretic Text—the traditional Hebrew Old Testament (see Preface, "The Old Testament Text")	v., vv.	verse, verses
		vss.	versions—ancient translations of the Bible

INTRODUCTION
TO THE BIBLE

The Bible is a collection of 66 documents inspired by God. These documents are gathered into two testaments, the Old (39) and the New (27). Prophets, priests, kings, and leaders from the nation of Israel wrote the Old Testament books in Hebrew (with two passages in Aramaic). The apostles and their associates wrote the New Testament books in Greek.

The Old Testament begins with the creation of the universe and closes about 400 years before the birth of Jesus Christ.

The history of the Old Testament flows in the following order:

- Creation of the universe
- Fall of man
- Flood over the whole earth
- Abraham, Isaac, and Jacob (Israel)—fathers of the chosen nation
- The history of Israel
  - Exile in Egypt—430 years
  - Exodus and wilderness wanderings—40 years
  - Conquest of Canaan—7 years
  - Era of Judges—350 years
  - United Kingdom—Saul, David, Solomon—110 years
  - Divided Kingdom—Judah/Israel—350 years
  - Exile in Babylon—70 years
  - Return and rebuilding the land—140 years

The details of this history are explained in the 39 books, which are divided into 5 categories:

- The Law—5 (Genesis–Deuteronomy)
- History—12 (Joshua–Esther)
- Wisdom—5 (Job–Song of Solomon)
- Major Prophets—5 (Isaiah–Daniel)
- Minor Prophets—12 (Hosea–Malachi)

After the completion of the Old Testament, there were 400 years of silence, during which God did not speak or inspire any Scripture. That silence was broken by the arrival of John the Baptist, who announced that the promised Savior had come.

While the 39 Old Testament books focus on the history of Israel and the promise of the coming Savior, the 27 New Testament books focus on the person of Christ and the establishment of the church. The four gospels give the record of His birth, life, death, resurrection, and ascension. Each of the four writers views the greatest and most important event in history, the life of Jesus Christ, from a different perspective. Matthew looks at Him through the perspective of His kingdom; Mark through the perspective of His servanthood; Luke through the perspective of His humanness; and John through the perspective of His deity.

The Book of Acts tells the story of the impact of the life, death, and resurrection of Jesus Christ—His ascension, the coming of the Holy Spirit, the birth of the church, and the early years of gospel preaching by the apostles and their associates.

The 21 epistles (or letters) were written to churches and individuals to teach about the person and work of Jesus Christ and how to live and witness until He returns.

The New Testament closes with Revelation, which begins by addressing the current church age and culminates with the prophecies of Christ's return, when He will establish His earthly kingdom, bring judgment on the ungodly, and bless His believers. Following Christ's millennial reign will be the last judgment, in which all believers of all time will enter the ultimate eternal glory prepared for them, and all the ungodly will be consigned to eternal punishment in hell.

The one, unifying theme unfolding throughout the whole Bible is that for His own glory, God has chosen to create and gather to Himself a group of people, who will live in His eternal kingdom, to praise, honor, and serve Him forever, and through whom He will display His wisdom, power, mercy, grace, and glory. To gather His chosen ones, God must redeem them from sin. The Bible reveals God's plan for this redemption, from its origin in eternity past to its completion in eternity future. All covenants and eras are secondary to the one continuous plan of redemption.

There is one God, who is Creator and Lord. The Bible is one book. It offers one plan of grace, recorded from its initiation in Creation, through its fulfillment in Christ, to its completion in Revelation. The Bible is the story of God's redeeming His chosen people for His glory.

As God's redemptive purposes and plan unfold in Scripture, five recurring motifs are constantly emphasized:

- the character of God
- the judgment for sin and disobedience
- the blessing for faith and obedience
- the sacrifice of the Lord Savior for sin
- the glory of the coming kingdom

Everything revealed in both the Old Testament and New Testament falls into these five categories. As one studies Scripture, it is essential to grasp these recurring themes which shape all of the passages, and to recognize that what is introduced in the Old Testament is also clarified in the New Testament.

1. The Revelation of the Character of God

Above all else, Scripture is God's self-revelation. In that self-revelation is established His standard of absolute holiness because of His holy character. From Adam and Eve, the standard of righteousness was established and is sustained through the last page of the New Testament.

2. The Revelation of Divine Judgment for Sin and Disobedience

Scripture repeatedly deals with the matter of man's sin. Of the 1,189 chapters in the Bible, only four do not involve a fallen world: the first two and the last two—before the Fall in Eden and after the creation of the new heaven and new earth. The rest is the chronicle of the tragedy of sin.

In the Old Testament, God showed the disaster of sin—starting with Adam and Eve to Cain and Abel, the relentless record shows the continual devastation produced by sin. In the New Testament, the tragedy of sin becomes clearer as Jesus issues a call to repentance. Disobedience is even more flagrant than in the Old Testament because it involves the rejection of the Lord Jesus Christ in the brighter light of New Testament truth.

3. The Revelation of Divine Blessing for Faith and Obedience

Scripture repeatedly promises wonderful rewards, in this life and in eternity, to those who trust and seek to obey God. In the Old Testament, God showed the blessings of repentance, faith, and obedience—as seen in the lives of Abel, the patriarchs, the remnant in Israel, and even Gentiles who believed, such as the people of Nineveh. In the New Testament, God showed the blessedness of redemption for those who responded to the preach-

ing of John the Baptist, Jesus, and the apostles. To all those and to all who will believe through all of history, there is blessing promised in this world and the world to come.

4. The Revelation of the Savior and His Sacrifice for Sin

This is the heart of both the Old Testament and the New Testament. The promise of blessing is dependent upon grace and mercy for the sinner. Such forgiveness is dependent upon a payment of sin's penalty to satisfy God's holy justice. That requires a substitute— one to die in the sinner's place. God's chosen substitute—the only one who qualified—is Jesus. Salvation is always by the same gracious means, whether during Old Testament or New Testament times. When any sinner repents, convinced he has no power to save himself from the judgment he deserves, and pleads for mercy, God grants him forgiveness. God then declares him righteous because Christ's sacrifice covers him. In the Old Testament, God justified sinners that same way, in anticipation of Christ's atoning work. Therefore, there is a continuity of grace and salvation through all of redemptive history. Having fulfilled all righteousness by His perfect life, Christ fulfilled justice by His death. Thus God Himself atoned for our sin, at a very high price. That is what Scripture means when it speaks of salvation by grace.

5. The Glory of Christ and His Kingdom

As in any book, how the story ends is the most crucial and compelling part—so with the Bible. Redemptive history is controlled by God, so as to culminate in His eternal glory. Scripture notes several very specific features of the end planned by God.

The Old Testament repeatedly mentions an earthly kingdom ruled by the Messiah, accompanied by the salvation of Israel, the salvation of Gentiles, the renewal of the earth from the effects of the curse, and the bodily resurrection of God's people who have died. Finally, the Old Testament predicts the creation of a new heaven and new earth—which will be the eternal state of the godly—and a final hell for the ungodly. In the New Testament, these features are clarified and expanded. The King will return in glory, bringing judgment, resurrection, and His kingdom for all who believe. The Lord will reign in the renewed earth, exercising power over the whole world and receiving due honor and worship. Following that kingdom will come the dissolution of the renewed, but still sin-stained creation, and the subsequent creation of a new heaven and new earth—which will be the eternal state of those who believe.

To understand these five themes reveals the glorious pattern of the Bible. With these in mind, the Bible will unfold, not as 66 separate documents, or even two separate testaments—but as one book, by one divine Author, who wrote it all with one overarching theme.

My prayer is that the magnificent and overwhelming theme of the redemption of sinners for the glory of God will carry every reader with captivating interest from beginning to end of the story. Christian—this is your story. It is from God for you—about you. It tells what He planned for you, why He made you, what you were, what you have become in Christ, and what He has prepared for you in eternal glory.

JOHN MACARTHUR

Considering the human tendency to doubt God, it is common for a person to be skeptical of the authenticity of the Bible, considering its bold claims to be the only, true Word of God. Many minds have struggled with valid questions, such as these:

- Where did the Bible come from?
- Who wrote the Bible—God or man?
- Has Scripture been protected from human tampering over the centuries?
- How close to the original manuscripts are today's translations?
- How did the Bible get to our time and in our language?
- If the Scriptures were written over a period of 1,500 years (about 1405 B.C. to A.D. 95), passed down since then for almost 2,000 years, and translated into several thousand languages, what prevented the Bible from being changed by the carelessness or ill motives of men?

A study of the Scriptures alone settles all questions to the extent that someone need never be bothered by them again. Scripture gives this assurance.

Scripture's Self Claims

Take the Bible and let it speak for itself. Does it claim to be God's Word? Yes! Over 2,000 times in the Old Testament alone, the Bible asserts that God spoke what is written within its pages. From the beginning (Gen. 1:3) to the end (Mal. 4:3) and continually throughout, this is what Scripture claims.

Passages in Scripture make powerful statements about the Bible, setting it apart from any other religious instruction ever known in the history of mankind. Its content marks it as "sacred" (2 Tim. 3:15) and "holy" (Rom. 1:2). The Bible claims ultimate spiritual authority in doctrine, correction, and instruction because it represents the inspired Word of Almighty God. Scripture asserts its spiritual sufficiency, so much so that it claims exclusivity for its teaching (see Is. 55:11; 2 Pet. 1:3,4).

God's Word declares that it is *inerrant* (Pss. 12:6; 119:140; Prov. 30:5a; John 10:35) and *infallible* (2 Tim. 3:16,17). In other words, it is true and therefore trustworthy. All of these qualities are dependent on the fact that the Scriptures are God-given (2 Tim. 3:16; 2 Pet. 1:20,21), which guarantees its quality at the Source and at its original writing.

The Publishing Process

The Bible does not expect its reader to speculate on how divine qualities were transferred from God to His Word, but rather anticipates the questions with convincing answers. Every generation of skeptics has assailed the self-claims of the Bible, but its own explanations and answers have been more than equal to the challenge. The Bible has gone through God's publishing process in being given to and distributed among the human race. Its several features are discussed below.

Revelation

God took the initiative to reveal Himself to mankind (Heb. 1:1), sometimes through the created order, visions/dreams, or speaking prophets. However, the most complete and understandable self-disclosures were through the propositions of Scripture (1 Cor. 2:6–16). The revealed and written Word of God is unique in that it is the only revelation of God that is complete and that so clearly declares man's sinfulness and God's provision of the Savior.

Inspiration

The revelation of God was captured in the writings of Scripture by means of "inspiration." "All Scripture *is* given by inspiration of God. . ." (2 Tim. 3:16). Peter explains the process, ". . .knowing this first, that no prophecy of Scripture is of any private interpretation, for prophecy never came by the will of man, but holy men of God spoke *as they were moved by the Holy Spirit*" (2 Pet. 1:20,21). Through the work of the Holy Spirit, the Word of God was protected from human error.

Canonicity

We must understand that the Bible is actually one book with one Divine Author, though it was written over a period of 1,500 years through the pens of almost 40 human writers. The Bible began with the creation account of Genesis 1–2, written by Moses about 1405 B.C., and extends to the eternity future account of Revelation 21–22, written by the Apostle John about A.D. 95. But this raises a significant question: How do we know which sacred writings were to be included in the canon of Scripture and which ones were to be excluded?

Over the centuries, three widely recognized principles were used to validate those writings that were divinely inspired. First, the writing had to have a recognized prophet or apostle as its author (or one associated with them, as in the case of Mark, Luke, Hebrews, James, and Jude). Second, the writing could not disagree with or contradict previous Scripture. Third, the writing had to have general consensus by the church as an inspired book.

Preservation

God anticipated man's and Satan's malice towards the Scripture with divine promises to preserve His Word. The very continued existence of Scripture is guaranteed in Isaiah 40:8, "The grass withers, the flower fades, but the word of our God stands forever" (see 1 Pet. 1:25). This even means that no inspired Scripture has been lost in the past and still awaits rediscovery. The battle for the Bible rages, but Scripture has and will continue to outlast its enemies.

> So shall My word be that goes forth from My mouth; it shall not return to Me void, but it shall accomplish what I please, and it shall prosper *in the thing* for which I sent it.
>
> (Isaiah 55:11).

Transmission

Through the centuries, the practitioners of textual criticism, a precise science, have discovered, preserved, catalogued, evaluated, and published an amazing array of biblical manuscripts from both the Old and New Testaments. In fact, the number of existing biblical manuscripts dramatically outdistances the existing fragments of any other ancient literature. By comparing text with text, the textual critic can confidently determine what the original prophetic/apostolic, inspired writing contained. For example, the discovery of the Dead Sea Scrolls in 1947–1956 (manuscripts that are dated about 200–100 B.C.) proved to be monumentally important. After comparing the earlier Hebrew texts with the later ones, only a few slight variants were discovered, none of which changed the meaning of any passage. Although the Old Testament had been translated and copied for centuries, the latest version was essentially the same as the earlier ones.

The New Testament findings are even more decisive because a much larger amount of material is available for study; there are over 5,000 Greek New Testament manuscripts that range from the whole testament to scraps of papyri which contain as little as part of one verse. A few existing fragments date back to within 25–50 years of the original writing. New Testament textual scholars have generally concluded that 1) 99.99 percent of the original writings have been reclaimed, and 2) of the remaining one hundredth of one percent, there are no variants substantially affecting any Christian doctrine.

Summing It Up

God intended His Word to abide forever (preservation). Therefore His written self-disclosure (revelation) was protected from error in its original writing (inspiration) and collected in 66 books of the Old and New Testaments (canonicity).

Through the centuries, tens of thousands of copies and thousands of translations have been made (transmission) which did introduce some minute error. Because there is an abundance of existing ancient Old Testament and New Testament manuscripts, however, the exacting science of textual criticism has been able to reclaim the content of the original writings (revelation and inspiration) to the extreme degree of 99.99 percent, with the remaining one hundredth of one percent having no effect on its content (preservation).

The sacred book which we read and obey deserves to unreservedly be called The Bible, since its author is God and it bears the qualities of total truth and complete trustworthiness that also characterizes its divine source.

Is There More To Come?

How do we know that God will not amend our current Bible with a 67th inspired book? Or, in other words, "Is the canon forever closed?" The most compelling text on the closed canon is the Scripture to which nothing has been added for 1,900 years.

> For I testify to everyone who hears the words of the prophecy of this book: If anyone adds to these things, God will add to him the plagues that are written in this book; and if anyone takes away from the words of the book of this prophecy, God shall take away his part from the Book of Life, from the holy city, and *from* the things which are written in this book.
>
> Revelation 22:18,19

The Bible

This Book contains the mind of God, the state of man, the way of salvation, the doom of sinners, and the happiness of believers.

Read it to be wise, believe it to be saved, and practice it to be holy.

It contains light to direct you, food to support you, and comfort to cheer you. It is the traveler's map, the pilgrim's staff, the pilot's compass, the soldier's sword, and the Christian's charter.

It should fill the memory, rule the heart, and guide the feet.

Read it slowly, frequently, and prayerfully.

> For this reason we also thank God without ceasing, because when you received the word of God which you heard from us, you welcomed *it* not *as* the word of men, but as it is in truth, the word of God, which also effectively works in you who believe.
>
> 1 Thessalonians 2:13

HOW TO
STUDY THE BIBLE

Why is God's Word so important? Because it contains God's will for your life (2 Tim. 3:16,17). The Bible is the only source of absolute, divine authority for you as a servant of Jesus Christ. Consider the following descriptive claims from Scripture:

- "The law of the LORD is perfect, converting the soul; the testimony of the LORD is sure, making wise the simple" (Ps. 19:7).
- "Every word of God is pure; He *is* a shield to those who put their trust in Him. Do not add to His words, lest He rebuke you, and you be found a liar" (Prov. 30:5,6).
- "For I testify to everyone who hears the words of the prophecy of this book: If anyone adds to these things, God will add to him the plagues that are written in this book; and if anyone takes away from the words of the book of this prophecy, God shall take away his part from the Book of Life, from the holy city, and *from* the things which are written in this book" (Rev. 22:18,19).
- "So shall My word be that goes forth from My mouth; it shall not return to Me void, but it shall accomplish what I please, and it shall prosper *in the thing* for which I sent it" (Is. 55:11).

What Are the Basics of Bible Study?

The idea of personal Bible study is simple but requires discipline and long-term goals. I want to share with you five steps for Bible study that will give you a pattern to follow.

STEP 1—Reading. Develop a plan on how you will approach reading through the Bible. Unlike most books, you will probably not read it straight through from cover to cover. You can find several Bible reading plans in the back of this Bible, and many other plans are good, as well. Read a passage of Scripture repeatedly until you understand its theme, meaning the main truth of the passage.

For example, in the Old Testament I would suggest you read it straight through, spread over time. Since that is a significant reading project, do not feel overwhelmed. Simply try to find the truths that God has revealed for you to learn. In the New Testament, you may want to take a more repetitious approach. You can read one book numerous times in a row so that you will retain what you have read. If you want to try this, begin with a short book, such as 1 John, and read its five chapters carefully through in one sitting. After you have finished, begin again, reading 1 John every day for thirty days. At the end of that time, you will really know what is in the book.

STEP 2—Interpreting. As you read Scripture, always keep in mind one simple question: What does this mean? Let the Holy Spirit be your teacher (1 John 2:27), for this is the Book that He authored. Pray for wisdom to understand the meaning, and read diligently.

As you interpret Scripture, several common errors should be avoided.

1. Do not draw any conclusions at the price of proper interpretation. That is, do not make the Bible say what you want it to say, but rather let it say what God intended.

2. Avoid superficial interpretation. You have heard people say, "To me, this passage means," or "I feel it is saying. . . ." Recognize that between your time and the biblical times, you must bridge cultural, geographical, and historical gaps. These gaps do not invalidate biblical truth, but you will understand the message much more clearly if you understand the context in which it was written.

3. Do not spiritualize the passage. Interpret and understand the passage in its normal, literal, historical, grammatical sense, just as you would understand any other piece of literature you were reading today.

Four principles should guide us as we interpret the Bible: literal, historical, grammatical, and synthesis.

1. *The Literal Principle*. Scripture should be understood in its literal, normal, and natural sense. While the Bible does contain figures of speech and symbols, they were intended to convey literal truth. In general, the Bible speaks in literal terms, and we must allow it to speak for itself.

2. *The Historical Principle*. We must ask what the text meant to the people to whom it was first written. In this way we can develop a proper contextual understanding of the original intent of Scripture.

3. *The Grammatical Principle*. Ask simple questions about the basic structure. To whom do the pronouns refer? What is the tense of the main verb? Simple details like these make the meaning of the text clearer.

4. *The Synthesis Principle*. The Reformers called this *analogia scriptura*, meaning that the Bible does not contradict itself. If an interpretation of one passage contradicts a truth taught elsewhere in the Scriptures, our interpretation cannot be correct. Scripture must be compared with Scripture to discover its full meaning.

STEP 3—Evaluating. At times you will find it helpful to consult others to ensure that you have interpreted the Bible correctly. Read Bible introductions, commentaries, and background books to enrich your thinking. In your evaluation, be a true seeker. Accept the truth of God's Word even though it may cause you to change what you have always believed or it may require you to alter your life pattern.

STEP 4—Applying. Studying Scripture without allowing it to penetrate the depths of your soul would be like preparing a banquet without sitting down to eat and enjoy it. Ask the ultimate question: How do the divine truths apply to my attitude and actions?

Jesus made this promise to those who would carry their personal Bible study through to this point: "If you know these things, blessed are you if you do them" (John 13:17).

Having read and interpreted the Bible, you should have a basic understanding of what the Bible says and what it means by what it says. But studying the Bible does not stop there. The ultimate goal should be to hear its message and to grow spiritually. That requires personal application.

Bible study is not complete until we ask ourselves, "What does this mean for my life, and how can I practically apply it?" We must take the knowledge we have gained from our reading and draw out the practical principles that apply to our personal lives.

If there is a command to be obeyed, we obey it. If there is a promise to be embraced, we claim it. If there is a warning to be followed, we heed it. This is the ultimate step: We submit to Scripture and let it transform our lives. If you skip this step, you will never enjoy your Bible study, and the Bible will never change your life.

STEP 5—Correlating. Finally, make connections between the doctrine you have learned in a particular passage with divine truths and principles taught elsewhere in the Bible to form the big picture. Always keep in mind that the Bible is a single book in 66 parts, and its truths are taught over and over again in a variety of stories and principles. By correlating and cross-referencing, you will begin to build a sound doctrinal foundation.

What Now?

It is not enough just to study the Bible. We must meditate upon it and immerse ourselves in the purifying solution of God's Word.

> This Book of the Law shall not depart from your mouth, but you shall meditate in it day and night, that you may observe to do according to all that is written in it. For then you will make your way prosperous, and then you will have good success.
>
> Joshua 1:8

Purpose

In the preface to the 1611 edition, the translators of the Authorized Version, known popularly as the King James Bible, state that it was not their purpose "to make a new translation . . . but to make a good one better." Indebted to the earlier work of William Tyndale and others, they saw their best contribution to consist in revising and enhancing the excellence of the English versions which had sprung from the Reformation of the sixteenth century. In harmony with the purpose of the King James scholars, the translators and editors of the present work have not pursued a goal of innovation. They have perceived the Holy Bible, New King James Version, as a continuation of the labors of the earlier translators, thus unlocking for today's readers the spiritual treasures found especially in the Authorized Version of the Holy Scriptures.

A Living Legacy

For nearly four hundred years, and throughout several revisions of its English form, the King James Bible has been deeply revered among the English-speaking peoples of the world. The precision of translation for which it is historically renowned, and its majesty of style, have enabled that monumental version of the Word of God to become the mainspring of the religion, language, and legal foundations of our civilization.

Although the Elizabethan period and our own era share in zeal for technical advance, the former period was more aggressively devoted to classical learning. Along with this awakened concern for the classics came a flourishing companion interest in the Scriptures, an interest that was enlivened by the conviction that the manuscripts were providentially handed down and were a trustworthy record of the inspired Word of God. The King James translators were committed to producing an English Bible that would be a precise translation, and by no means a paraphrase or a broadly approximate rendering. On the one hand, the scholars were almost as familiar with the original languages of the Bible as with their native English. On the other hand, their reverence for the divine Author and His Word assured a translation of the Scriptures in which only a principle of utmost accuracy could be accepted.

In 1786 Catholic scholar Alexander Geddes said of the King James Bible, "If accuracy and strictest attention to the letter of the text be supposed to constitute an excellent version, this is of all versions the most excellent." George Bernard Shaw became a literary legend in our century because of his severe and often humorous criticisms of our most cherished values. Surprisingly, however, Shaw pays the following tribute to the scholars commissioned by King James: "The translation was extraordinarily well done because to the translators what they were translating was not merely a curious collection of ancient books written by different authors in different stages of culture, but the Word of God divinely revealed through His chosen and expressly inspired scribes. In this conviction they carried out their work with boundless reverence and care and achieved a beautifully artistic result." History agrees with these estimates. Therefore, while seeking to unveil the excellent *form* of the traditional English Bible, special care has also been taken in the present edition to preserve the work of *precision* which is the legacy of the 1611 translators.

Complete Equivalence in Translation

Where new translation has been necessary in the New King James Version, the most complete representation of the original has been rendered by considering the history of usage and etymology of words in their contexts. This principle of complete equivalence seeks to preserve *all* of the information in the text, while presenting it in good literary form. Dynamic equivalence, a recent procedure in Bible translation, commonly results in

paraphrasing where a more literal rendering is needed to reflect a specific and vital sense. For example, complete equivalence truly renders the original text in expressions such as "lifted her voice and wept" (Gen. 21:16); "I gave you cleanness of teeth" (Amos 4:6); "Jesus met them, saying, 'Rejoice!' " (Matt. 28:9); and "Woman, what does your concern have to do with Me?" (John 2:4). Complete equivalence translates fully, in order to provide an English text that is both accurate and readable.

In keeping with the principle of complete equivalence, it is the policy to translate interjections which are commonly omitted in modern language renderings of the Bible. As an example, the interjection *behold*, in the older King James editions, continues to have a place in English usage, especially in dramatically calling attention to a spectacular scene, or an event of profound importance such as the Immanuel prophecy of Isaiah 7:14. Consequently, *behold* is retained for these occasions in the present edition. However, the Hebrew and Greek originals for this word can be translated variously, depending on the circumstances in the passage. Therefore, in addition to *behold*, words such as *indeed*, *look*, *see*, and *surely* are also rendered to convey the appropriate sense suggested by the context in each case.

In faithfulness to God and to our readers, it was deemed appropriate that all participating scholars sign a statement affirming their belief in the verbal and plenary inspiration of Scripture, and in the inerrancy of the original autographs.

Devotional Quality

The King James scholars readily appreciated the intrinsic beauty of divine revelation. They accordingly disciplined their talents to render well-chosen English words of their time, as well as a graceful, often musical arrangement of language, which has stirred the hearts of Bible readers through the years. The translators, the committees, and the editors of the present edition, while sensitive to the late-twentieth-century English idiom, and while adhering faithfully to the Hebrew, Aramaic, and Greek texts, have sought to maintain those lyrical and devotional qualities that are so highly regarded in the Authorized Version. This devotional quality is especially apparent in the poetic and prophetic books, although even the relatively plain style of the Gospels and Epistles cannot strictly be likened, as sometimes suggested, to modern newspaper style. The Koine Greek of the New Testament is influenced by the Hebrew background of the writers, for whom even the Gospel narratives were not merely flat utterance, but often sung in various degrees of rhythm.

The Style

Students of the Bible applaud the timeless devotional character of our historic Bible. Yet it is also universally understood that our language, like all living languages, has undergone profound change since 1611. Subsequent revisions of the King James Bible have sought to keep abreast of changes in English speech. The present work is a further step toward this objective. Where obsolescence and other reading difficulties exist, present-day vocabulary, punctuation, and grammar have been carefully integrated. Words representing ancient objects, such as *chariot* and *phylactery*, have no modern substitutes and are therefore retained.

A special feature of the New King James Version is its conformity to the thought flow of the 1611 Bible. The reader discovers that the sequence and selection of words, phrases, and clauses of the new edition, while much clearer, are so close to the traditional that there is remarkable ease in listening to the reading of either edition while following with the other.

In the discipline of translating biblical and other ancient languages, a standard method of transliteration, that is, the English spelling of untranslated words, such as names of persons and places, has never been commonly adopted. In keeping with the design of the present work, the King James spelling of untranslated words is retained, although made uniform throughout. For example, instead of the spellings *Isaiah* and *Elijah* in the Old Testament, and *Esaias* and *Elias* in the New Testament, *Isaiah* and *Elijah* now appear in both Testaments.

King James doctrinal and theological terms, for example, *propitiation, justification,* and

sanctification, are generally familiar to English-speaking peoples. Such terms have been retained except where the original language indicates need for a more precise translation.

Readers of the Authorized Version will immediately be struck by the absence of several pronouns: *thee, thou,* and *ye* are replaced by the simple *you,* while *your* and *yours* are substituted for *thy* and *thine* as applicable. *Thee, thou, thy* and *thine* were once forms of address to express a special relationship to human as well as divine persons. These pronouns are no longer part of our language. However, reverence for God in the present work is preserved by capitalizing pronouns, including *You, Your,* and *Yours,* which refer to Him. Additionally, capitalization of these pronouns benefits the reader by clearly distinguishing divine and human persons referred to in a passage. Without such capitalization the distinction is often obscure, because the antecedent of a pronoun is not always clear in the English translation.

In addition to the pronoun usages of the seventeenth century, the *-eth* and *-est* verb endings, so familiar in the earlier King James editions, are now obsolete. Unless a speaker is schooled in these verb endings, there is common difficulty in selecting the correct form to be used with a given subject of the verb in vocal prayer. That is, should we use *love, loveth,* or *lovest? do, doeth, doest,* or *dost? have, hath,* or *hast?* Because these forms are obsolete, contemporary English usage has been substituted for the previous verb endings.

In older editions of the King James Version, the frequency of the connective *and* far exceeded the limits of present English usage. Also, biblical linguists agree that the Hebrew and Greek original words for this conjunction may commonly be translated otherwise, depending on the immediate context. Therefore, instead of *and,* alternatives such as *also, but, however, now, so, then,* and *thus* are accordingly rendered in the present edition, when the original language permits.

The real character of the Authorized Version does not reside in its archaic pronouns or verbs or other grammatical forms of the seventeenth century, but rather in the care taken by its scholars to impart the letter and spirit of the original text in a majestic and reverent style.

The Format

The format of the New King James Version is designed to enhance the vividness and devotional quality of the Holy Scriptures:

- Subject headings assist the reader to identify topics and transitions in the biblical content.
- Words or phrases in *italics* indicate expressions in the original language which require clarification by additional English words, as also done throughout the history of the King James Bible.
- Verse numbers within a paragraph are easily distinguishable.
- *Oblique type* in the New Testament indicates a quotation from the Old Testament.
- Prose is divided into paragraphs to indicate the structure of thought.
- Poetry is structured as contemporary verse to reflect the poetic form and beauty of the passage in the original language.
- The covenant name of God was usually translated from the Hebrew as "LORD" or "GOD" (using capital letters as shown) in the King James Old Testament. This tradition is maintained. In the present edition the name is so capitalized whenever the covenant name is quoted in the New Testament from a passage in the Old Testament.

The Old Testament Text

The Hebrew Bible has come down to us through the scrupulous care of ancient scribes who copied the original text in successive generations. By the sixth century A.D. the scribes were succeeded by a group known as the Masoretes, who continued to preserve the sacred Scriptures for another five hundred years in a form known as the Masoretic Text. Babylonia, Palestine, and Tiberias were the main centers of Masoretic activity; but by the

tenth century A.D. the Masoretes of Tiberias, led by the family of ben Asher, gained the ascendancy. Through subsequent editions, the ben Asher text became in the twelfth century the only recognized form of the Hebrew Scriptures.

Daniel Bomberg printed the first Rabbinic Bible in 1516–17; that work was followed in 1524–25 by a second edition prepared by Jacob ben Chayyim and also published by Bomberg. The text of ben Chayyim was adopted in most subsequent Hebrew Bibles, including those used by the King James translators. The ben Chayyim text was also used for the first two editions of Rudolph Kittel's *Biblia Hebraica* of 1906 and 1912. In 1937 Paul Kahle published a third edition of *Biblia Hebraica*. This edition was based on the oldest dated manuscript of the ben Asher text, the Leningrad Manuscript B19a (A.D. 1008), which Kahle regarded as superior to that used by ben Chayyim.

For the New King James Version the text used was the 1967/1977 Stuttgart edition of the *Biblia Hebraica*, with frequent comparisons being made with the Bomberg edition of 1524–25. The Septuagint (Greek) Version of the Old Testament and the Latin Vulgate also were consulted. In addition to referring to a variety of ancient versions of the Hebrew Scriptures, the New King James Version draws on the resources of relevant manuscripts from the Dead Sea caves. In the few places where the Hebrew was so obscure that the 1611 King James was compelled to follow one of the versions, but where information is now available to resolve the problems, the New King James Version follows the Hebrew text. Significant variations are recorded in footnotes.

The New Testament Text

There is more manuscript support for the New Testament than for any other body of ancient literature. Over five thousand Greek, eight thousand Latin, and many more manuscripts in other languages attest the integrity of the New Testament. There is only one basic New Testament used by Protestants, Roman Catholics, and Orthodox, by conservatives and liberals. Minor variations in hand copying have appeared through the centuries, before mechanical printing began about A.D. 1450.

Some variations exist in the spelling of Greek words, in word order, and in similar details. These ordinarily do not show up in translation and do not affect the sense of the text in any way.

Other manuscript differences such as omission or inclusion of a word or a clause, and two paragraphs in the Gospels, should not overshadow the overwhelming degree of *agreement* which exists among the ancient records. Bible readers may be assured that the most important differences in English New Testaments of today are due, not to manuscript divergence, but to the way in which translators view the task of translation: How literally should the text be rendered? How does the translator view the matter of biblical inspiration? Does the translator adopt a paraphrase when a literal rendering would be quite clear and more to the point? The New King James Version follows the historic precedent of the Authorized Version in maintaining a literal approach to translation, except where the idiom of the original language cannot be translated directly into our tongue.

The King James New Testament was based on the traditional text of the Greek-speaking churches, first published in 1516, and later called the Textus Receptus or Received Text. Although based on the relatively few available manuscripts, these were representative of many more which existed at the time but only became known later. In the late nineteenth century, B. Westcott and F. Hort taught that this text had been officially edited by the fourth-century church, but a total lack of historical evidence for this event has forced a revision of the theory. It is now widely held that the Byzantine Text that largely supports the Textus Receptus has as much right as the Alexandrian or any other tradition to be weighed in determining the text of the New Testament.

Since the 1880s most contemporary translations of the New Testament have relied upon a relatively few manuscripts discovered chiefly in the late nineteenth and early twentieth centuries. Such translations depend primarily on two manuscripts, Codex Vaticanus and Codex Sinaiticus, because of their greater age. The Greek text obtained by using these

sources and the related papyri (our most ancient manuscripts) is known as the Alexandrian Text. However, some scholars have grounds for doubting the faithfulness of Vaticanus and Sinaiticus, since they often disagree with one another, and Sinaiticus exhibits excessive omission.

A third viewpoint of New Testament scholarship holds that the best text is based on the consensus of the majority of existing Greek manuscripts. This text is called the Majority Text. Most of these manuscripts are in substantial agreement. Even though many are late, and none is earlier than the fifth century, usually their readings are verified by papyri, ancient versions, quotations from the early church fathers, or a combination of these. The Majority Text is similar to the Textus Receptus, but it corrects those readings which have little or no support in the Greek manuscript tradition.

Today, scholars agree that the science of New Testament textual criticism is in a state of flux. Very few scholars still favor the Textus Receptus as such, and then often for its historical prestige as the text of Luther, Calvin, Tyndale, and the King James Version. For about a century most have followed a Critical Text (so called because it is edited according to specific principles of textual criticism) which depends heavily upon the Alexandrian type of text. More recently many have abandoned this Critical Text (which is quite similar to the one edited by Westcott and Hort) for one that is more eclectic. Finally, a small but growing number of scholars prefer the Majority Text, which is close to the traditional text except in the Revelation.

In light of these facts, and also because the New King James Version is the fifth revision of a historic document translated from specific Greek texts, the editors decided to retain the traditional text in the body of the New Testament. It is most important to emphasize that fully eighty-five percent of the New Testament text is the same in the Textus Receptus, the Alexandrian Text, and the Majority Text.

New King James Footnotes

Significant explanatory notes, alternate translations, and cross-references, as well as New Testament citations of Old Testament passages, are supplied in the footnotes.

Important textual variants in the Old Testament are identified in a standard form.

The textual notes in the present edition of the New Testament make no evaluation of readings, but do clearly indicate the manuscript sources of readings. They objectively present the facts without such tendentious remarks as "the best manuscripts omit" or "the most reliable manuscripts read." Such notes are value judgments that differ according to varying viewpoints on the text. By giving a clearly defined set of variants the New King James Version benefits readers of all textual persuasions.

Where significant variations occur in the New Testament Greek manuscripts, textual notes are classified as follows:

NU-Text

These variations from the traditional text generally represent the Alexandrian or Egyptian type of text described previously in "The New Testament Text." They are found in the Critical Text published in the twenty-sixth edition of the Nestle-Aland Greek New Testament (N) and in the United Bible Societies' fourth edition (U), hence the acronym, "NU-Text."

M-Text

This symbol indicates points of variation in the Majority Text from the traditional text, as also previously discussed in "The New Testament Text." It should be noted that M stands for whatever reading is printed in the published *Greek New Testament According to the Majority Text*, whether supported by overwhelming, strong, or only a divided majority textual tradition.

The textual notes reflect the scholarship of the past 150 years and will assist the reader to observe the variations between the different manuscript traditions of the New Testament. Such information is generally not available in English translations of the New Testament.

The first five books of the Bible—Genesis, Exodus, Leviticus, Numbers, and Deuteronomy—form a unified literary unit called the Pentateuch, meaning "five rolls." The five independent books were written as a unified historical sequence, with each succeeding book beginning where the former left off.

Genesis' first words, "In the beginning God created . . ." (Gen. 1:1) imply God's eternal existence and announce the spectacular transition into time and space. While the exact date of creation cannot be determined, it certainly would be estimated to be thousands of years ago, not millions. Starting with Abraham (about 2166 B.C.) in Gen. 11, this book spans more than 300 hundred years until the death of Joseph in Egypt (about 1804 B.C.). Another 300-year gap separates the death of Joseph from the birth of Moses in Egypt (about 1525 B.C.; Ex. 2).

Exodus begins with the words "Now these are the names" (Ex. 1:1), listing Jacob's family members who went down to Egypt to be with Joseph near the end of Gen. 46:8. The second book of the Pentateuch records the escape of the Israelites from Egypt and concludes when the cloud that led the people through the wilderness descends upon the newly constructed tabernacle.

That the Hebrew words of Leviticus may be translated "Now the LORD called to Moses" (Lev. 1:1) from the cloud of God's Presence in the tabernacle of meeting, God summons Moses to give the Israelites their law that told Israel how they must approach their Holy Lord. Leviticus concludes with, "These are the commandments which the LORD commanded Moses for the children of Israel on Mount Sinai" (Lev. 27:34).

Numbers begins as God commissions Moses to take a census in preparation for war against Israel's enemies. The book's title in the Hebrew Bible accurately reflects the content—"Wilderness." Due to their lack of faith, Israel was afraid to fight their enemies in order to claim the Promised Land. After 40 years in the wilderness as punishment for their rebellion, Israel arrived on the plains of Moab.

Moses preached the Book of Deuteronomy as a sermon on the Plains of Moab in preparation for God's people to enter the land of covenant promise (2Ch. 1:1–4:3). The title Deuteronomy is from the Greek phrase deuteros nomos, meaning "second law." The book restates and reapplies the law to Israel's new circumstances.

Moses was the human author of the Pentateuch (Ex. 17:14; 24:4; Num. 33:1, 2; Deut. 31:9; Josh. 1:8; 1Kin. 2:3), thus, another title for the collection is "The Books of Moses." Through Moses, God revealed Himself, his former works, Israel's family history, and its role in His plan of redemption for mankind. The Pentateuch is foundational to all the rest of Scripture.

The Pentateuch was Israel's first inspired body of Scripture. For many years, it alone was Israel's Bible. Another common title for this section of Scripture is Torah or Law. The Israelites were to meditate upon it (Josh. 1:8), teach it to their children (Deut. 6:4–9), and read it publicly (Neh. 8:1ff).

Because the Israelites' knowledge of the world came through the Scriptures and their ancestors the Mesopotamians, they needed clarification about the creation of the world, how it developed, and how Israel had come into existence (Genesis 1:1) helped Israel understand the origin and nature of creation, human labor, sin, marriage, murder, death, bigamy, judgment, the multiplicity of languages, cultures, etc. These chapters established the worldview that explained the remainder of the Pentateuch.

In Gen. 12:1–3, God appeared to Abraham and made a three-fold promise to give them a land, descendants, and blessing. Years later God restates the three-fold promise into a cov-

INTRODUCTION TO THE PENTATEUCH

The first five books of the Bible (Genesis, Exodus, Leviticus, Numbers, and Deuteronomy) form a complete literary unit called the Pentateuch, meaning "five scrolls." The five independent books were written as a unified historical sequence, with each succeeding book beginning where the former left off.

Genesis' first words, "In the beginning God created . . . " (Gen. 1:1) imply God's eternal existence and announce the spectacular transition into time and space. While the exact date of creation cannot be determined, it certainly would be estimated to be thousands of years ago, not millions. Starting with Abraham (about 2165–1990 B.C.) in Gen. 11, this book spans more than 300 hundred years until the death of Joseph in Egypt (about 1804 B.C.). Another 300-year gap separates the death of Joseph from the birth of Moses in Egypt (about 1525 B.C.; Ex. 2).

Exodus begins with the words "Now these *are* the names" (Ex. 1:1), listing Jacob's family members who went down to Egypt to be with Joseph near the end of Gen. (Gen. 46ff.). The second book of the Pentateuch records the escape of the Israelites from Egypt and concludes when the cloud that led the people through the wilderness descends upon the newly constructed tabernacle.

The first Hebrew words of Leviticus may be translated, "Now the LORD called to Moses" (Lev. 1:1). From the cloud of God's Presence in the tabernacle of meeting, God summons Moses to give him the ceremonial law that told Israel how they must approach their Holy Lord. Leviticus concludes with, "These *are* the commandments which the LORD commanded Moses for the children of Israel on Mount Sinai" (Lev. 27:34).

Numbers, begins as God commissions Moses to take a census in preparation for war against Israel's enemies. The book's title in the Hebrew Bible accurately reflects the content—"Wilderness." Due to their lack of faith, Israel was afraid to fight their enemies in order to claim the Promised Land. After 40 years in the wilderness as punishment for their rebellion, Israel arrived on the plains of Moab.

Moses preached the Book of Deuteronomy as a sermon on the Plains of Moab in preparation for God's people to enter the land of covenant promise (Gen. 12:1–3). The title Deuteronomy is from the Greek phrase *deuteros nomos*, meaning "second law." The book restates and reapplies the law to Israel's new circumstances.

Moses was the human author of the Pentateuch (Ex. 17:14; 24:4; Num. 33:1,2; Deut. 31:9; Josh. 1:8; 2 Kin. 21:8); thus, another title for the collection is "The Books of Moses." Through Moses, God revealed Himself, His former works, Israel's family history, and its role in His plan of redemption for mankind. The Pentateuch is foundational to all the rest of Scripture.

The Pentateuch was Israel's first inspired body of Scripture. For many years, it alone was Israel's Bible. Another common title for this section of Scripture is *Torah* or Law. The Israelites were to meditate upon it (Josh. 1:8), teach it to their children (Deut. 6:4–8), and read it publicly (Neh. 8:1ff.).

Because the Israelites' knowledge of the world came through the Egyptians and their ancestors the Mesopotamians, they needed clarification about the creation of the world, how it developed, and how Israel had come into existence. Genesis 1–11 helped Israel understand the origin and nature of creation, human labor, sin, marriage, murder, death, bigamy, judgment, the multiplicity of languages, cultures, etc. These chapters established the worldview that explained the remainder of the Pentateuch.

In Gen. 12:1–3, God appeared to Abraham and made a three-fold promise to give them a land, descendants, and blessing. Years later, God recast the three-fold promise into a cov-

enant (Gen. 15:7ff.). The remainder of Genesis treats the fulfillment of all three promises but focuses especially on the seed, or descendants. The barrenness of each of the patriarchs' chosen wives taught Israel the importance of trust and patience as they waited for God to fulfill His promise.

The rest of the Pentateuch expounds on the fulfillment of the Abrahamic Covenant. In Exodus, Israel meets the God of their fathers as He leads them forth from Egypt to the Promised Land. Leviticus emphasizes the meticulous care with which the people and priests were to approach God in worship and daily living. Holiness and cleanliness unite in simple and practical ways. Numbers and Deuteronomy focus on the journey to and preparation for the Land. But the underlying theme of the Pentateuch is the initial, unfolding fulfillment of God's promises made to Abraham.

INTRODUCTION TO THE PROPHETS

The writing prophets of the Old Testament fall into two groups: the four major prophets—Isaiah, Jeremiah, Ezekiel, and Daniel—and the 12 minor prophets—Hosea, Joel, Amos, Obadiah, Jonah, Micah, Nahum, Habakkuk, Zephaniah, Haggai, Zechariah, and Malachi. The Book of Lamentations falls into the major-prophet grouping because of its connection with Jeremiah.

In addition to these, the Old Testament regarded others as prophets as well. Prophets such as Gad, Nathan, Elijah, and Elisha were typical of the nonwriting prophets. In a sense, John the Baptist as a forerunner of Jesus was a prophet who belonged to the Old Testament era.

The following table gives the sequence, approximate dates, and direction of ministry for the writing prophets, with "Israel" designating the northern kingdom and "Judah" the southern:

PROPHETS ORGANIZED BY DATE AND DIRECTION OF MINISTRY

Prophet	Ministered To	In the Years
Obadiah	Edom	850–840 B.C.
Joel	Judah	835–796 B.C.
Jonah	Nineveh	784–774 B.C.
Amos	Israel	763–755 B.C.
Hosea	Israel	755–710 B.C.
Isaiah	Judah	739–680 B.C.
Micah	Judah	735–710 B.C.
Nahum	Nineveh	650–630 B.C.
Zephaniah	Judah	635–625 B.C.
Jeremiah	Judah	627–570 B.C.
Habakkuk	Judah	620–605 B.C.
Daniel	Babylon	605–536 B.C.
Ezekiel	Babylon	593–570 B.C.
Haggai	Judah	520–505 B.C.
Zechariah	Judah	520–470 B.C.
Malachi	Judah	437–417 B.C.

Another way to categorize the writing prophets relates them chronologically to the captivities of Israel (about 722 B.C.) and Judah (about 586 B.C.):

PROPHETS ORGANIZED BY WRITING DATE AND CAPTIVITY

Pre-Exilic		Exilic	Post-Exilic
Obadiah	Micah	Daniel	Haggai
Joel	Nahum	Ezekiel	Zechariah
Jonah	Zephaniah		Malachi
Amos	Jeremiah		
Hosea	Habakkuk		
Isaiah			

The writing prophets' messages sometimes related to the immediate future (Is. 7:1–11) and sometimes to the distant future (Is. 7:12–14). They made frequent predictions about the coming Messiah and saw Him in two roles: that of a suffering Messiah (Is. 53) and that of a reigning Messiah (Is. 11). Even the prophets were unable to fully comprehend how these two aspects of the Messiah's future ministry would fit together (1 Pet. 1:10–12).

God's dealings with Israel dominate the pages of the major and minor prophets, but several books—Daniel, Obadiah, Jonah, and Nahum—show God working in Gentile world history. The other prophetic books look beyond Israel from time to time to note how God's chosen nation will impact the rest of the nations (for example, Is. 52:10,15) or how God will judge the nations.

The period of the writing prophets ended roughly 400 years before the coming of Christ. No official declaration marked the end of Old Testament prophecy, but the people of Israel gradually realized that no prophet had appeared in Israel for a considerable period of time. From the perspective of later times, it is obvious that the great prophetic movement of the Old Testament ended and thus began the 400 "silent years," followed by the written ministries of New Testament apostles and prophets.

GENESIS

God started everything. The Bible doesn't begin with an argument for God's existence; it begins by accepting that our existence depends on God. The ancient Greek translation of the Old Testament (also called the Septuagint, or LXX) titled this first book "Genesis," meaning "origins." Eventually, English translators borrowed the word directly. The title used in Hebrew texts simply highlights the very first word of the book, which means "in the beginning."

AUTHOR AND DATE

Genesis was written by Moses, approximately 1445 to 1405 B.C.

Although Genesis does not name its author, and the events described in the text end almost three centuries before his birth, both the Old Testament and the New Testament designate Moses as the author (see below). In addition, Moses' educational background makes him the likely candidate (Acts 7:22). Further, no compelling reasons have been forthcoming to challenge Mosaic authorship.

Genesis was written after the Exodus (about 1445 B.C.), but before Moses' death (about 1405 B.C.).

Old Testament witnesses to Moses' authorship of Genesis: Exodus 17:14; Numbers 33:2; Joshua 8:31; 1 Kings 2:3; 2 Kings 14:6; Ezra 6:18; Nehemiah 13:1; Daniel 9:11,13; Malachi 4:4.

New Testament witnesses to Moses' authorship of Genesis: Matthew 8:4; Mark 12:26; Luke 16:29; 24:27,44; John 5:46; 7:22; Acts 15:1; Romans 10:19; 1 Corinthians 9:9; 2 Corinthians 3:15.

BACKGROUND AND SETTING

The initial setting for Genesis is eternity past. God, by willful act and divine Word, spoke all creation into existence, furnished it, and finally breathed life into a lump of dirt that He fashioned in His image to become Adam. Shortly thereafter God created Eve. He made this couple the crowning point of His creation; that is, companions who would enjoy fellowship with Him and bring glory to His name.

Genesis has three distinct and sequential geographical settings: (1) Mesopotamia (chapters 1–11); (2) the Promised Land (chapters 12–36); (3) Egypt (chapters 37–50). The time frames of these three segments are: (1) Creation to 2090 B.C.; (2) 2090 to 1897 B.C.; and (3) 1897 to 1804 B.C. Genesis covers more time than all the remaining books of the Bible combined.

In this book of beginnings, God revealed His nature and His worldview to Israel. Usually, this contrasted sharply with the gods and worldviews of Israel's neighbors. Writing under the inspiration of the Holy Spirit, Moses made no attempt to defend the existence of God or to present a systematic discussion of God's person and works. Instead, God was revealed clearly and dramatically through His words and actions.

In addition to God's nature, Genesis introduces these foundations of biblical theology: God the Father, God the Son, God the Holy Spirit, human beings and human nature, sin, redemption, covenant, Satan and angels, kingdom, revelation, Israel, judgment, and blessing. Particular attention is given to God's abundant grace as Genesis shows Him responding to the willful disobedience of humankind. Persistent human sinfulness and persistent godly grace stand as opposites. Yet, in later biblical words, the more sin abounded the more did God's grace abound (Romans 5:20).

The original publication of Genesis came at a crucial time in history. Because God's people were preparing to enter Canaan to claim the land and dispossess the Canaanite inhabitants of their homes and property, God explained their enemies' background. They needed to understand God's reasons for the war they were about to wage

GENESIS OFFERED THE JEWISH NATION AN UNDERSTANDING OF THEIR PLACE IN WORLD HISTORY AND IN GOD'S PLANS.

because God had already declared the immorality of killing. The war brought by the Israelites was God's judgment on the Canaanites. Genesis establishes a consistent moral standard with the other four books (Exodus, Leviticus, Numbers, and Deuteronomy) that Moses was writing.

Genesis offered the Jewish nation an understanding of their place in world history and in God's plans. It tells of God's choice of Abraham and God's promise to build a nation through him. That nation, approaching the Promised Land under Joshua's leadership, was part of the fulfillment of God's promise to Abraham. God's three-fold promise—descendants (seed), land, and blessing—were formalized in a covenant between God and Abraham (Genesis 15:1–20). The rest of Scripture bears out the fulfillment of this promise.

One other theme highlights both the theological and historical significance of Genesis in Scripture. No other book in the Bible corresponds so closely with Revelation, the final book. In Revelation, the paradise that was lost in Genesis will be regained. All of the world's problems began with sin and God's curse (Genesis 3). We can almost hear the excitement in John's own words, as he exults, "And there shall be no more curse" (Revelation 22:3). Not surprisingly, in the final chapter of God's Word, believers will find themselves back in the Garden of Eden, the eternal paradise of God, eating from the tree of life (Revelation 22:1–14).

OUTLINE

Genesis can be divided into two basic sections: (1) Primitive history (Genesis 1–11) and (2) Patriarchal history (Genesis 12–50).

Primitive history includes four major events: (A) Creation (Genesis 1–2); (B) the Fall into sin (Genesis 3–5); (C) the Flood (Genesis 6–9); and (D) the Dispersion of Peoples (Genesis 10–11). Patriarchal history spotlights 4 great men: (A) Abraham (Genesis 12:1–25:8); (B) Isaac (Genesis 21:1–35:29); (C) Jacob (Genesis 25:21–50:14); and (D) Joseph (Genesis 30:22–50:26).

I. PRIMITIVE HISTORY—FOUR MAJOR EVENTS (1–11)
    A. Creation (1,2)
    B. The Fall into Sin (3–5)
    C. The Flood (6–9)
    D. The Dispersion of Peoples (10,11)

II. PATRIARCHAL HISTORY—FOUR GREAT MEN (12–50)
    A. Abraham (12:1–25:8)
    B. Isaac (21:1–35:29)
    C. Jacob (25:21–50:14)
    D. Joseph (30:22–50:26)

The History of Creation

1 In the beginning God created the heavens and the earth. ²The earth was without form, and void; and darkness *was^a* on the face of the deep. And the Spirit of God was hovering over the face of the waters.

³Then God said, "Let there be light"; and there was light. ⁴And God saw the light, that *it was* good; and God divided the light from the darkness. ⁵God called the light Day, and the darkness He called Night. So the evening and the morning were the first day.

> **1:5 first day.** God completed the creation in 7 days, which constituted a complete week. Scholars differ on their interpretation of the length of this week. One "day" can refer to: (1) the light portion of a 24 hour period (1:5,14); (2) an extended period of time (2:4); or (3) the whole 24 hour period while the earth completes a full rotation on its axis. Each "day" in Genesis refers to a 24 hour period. The cycle of light and dark means that the earth was rotating on its axis, receiving light from a source on one side of the earth, even though the sun was not yet created (v. 16).

⁶Then God said, "Let there be a firmament in the midst of the waters, and let it divide the waters from the waters." ⁷Thus God made the firmament, and divided the waters which *were* under the firmament from the waters which *were* above the firmament; and it was so. ⁸And God called the firmament Heaven. So the evening and the morning were the second day.

⁹Then God said, "Let the waters under the heavens be gathered together into one place, and let the dry *land* appear"; and it was so. ¹⁰And God called the dry *land* Earth, and the gathering together of the waters He called Seas. And God saw that *it was* good.

¹¹Then God said, "Let the earth bring forth grass, the herb *that* yields seed, *and* the fruit tree *that* yields fruit according to its kind, whose seed *is* in itself, on the earth"; and it was so. ¹²And the earth brought forth grass, the herb *that* yields seed according to its kind, and the tree *that* yields fruit, whose seed *is* in itself according to its kind. And God saw that *it was* good. ¹³So the evening and the morning were the third day.

¹⁴Then God said, "Let there be lights in the firmament of the heavens to divide the day from the night; and let them be for signs and seasons, and for days and years; ¹⁵and let them be for lights in the firmament of the heavens to give light on the earth"; and it was so. ¹⁶Then God made two great lights: the greater light to rule the

---

1:2 ^aWords in italic type have been added for clarity. They are not found in the original Hebrew or Aramaic.

How does the Bible challenge or agree with current scientific theories?

Scientific theories, by their very definition, are subject to change and adjustment. Scripture remains as God's revealed unchanging declaration of truth. The Bible was not written as a challenge to any particular scientific theory, but scientific theories have often been designed to challenge or undermine biblical statements. They either agree with scripture or are mistaken.

The description in Genesis 1:1 that "God created the heavens and the earth" yields three basic conclusions: (1) creation was a recent event measured in thousands not millions of years ago; (2) creation was *ex nihilo*, meaning that God created out of nothing; (3) creation was special, with light and time being the first of God's creative acts, since the day-count (Genesis 1:5) began before the creation of sun and moon (Genesis 1:16).

One key in evaluating scientific theories depends on our understanding of the biblical word "created." Although the Hebrew word used in Genesis 1:1 can be used to describe the act of shaping or altering existent matter (Isaiah 65:18), such is not the case with the Bible's first words. God spoke the heavens and the earth into existence. Both context and the rest of Scripture bear witness to God's creativity without use of any pre-existing material (Isaiah 40:28; 45:8,12,18; 48:13; Jeremiah 10:16; Acts 17:24).

day, and the lesser light to rule the night. *He made* the stars also. [17]God set them in the firmament of the heavens to give light on the earth, [18]and to rule over the day and over the night, and to divide the light from the darkness. And God saw that *it was* good. [19]So the evening and the morning were the fourth day.

[20]Then God said, "Let the waters abound with an abundance of living creatures, and let birds fly above the earth across the face of the firmament of the heavens." [21]So God created great sea creatures and every living thing that moves, with which the waters abounded, according to their kind, and every winged bird according to its kind. And God saw that *it was* good. [22]And God blessed them, saying, "Be fruitful and multiply, and fill the waters in the seas, and let birds multiply on the earth." [23]So the evening and the morning were the fifth day.

[24]Then God said, "Let the earth bring forth the living creature according to its kind: cattle and creeping thing and beast of the earth, *each* according to its kind"; and it was so. [25]And God made the beast of the earth according to its kind, cattle according to its kind, and everything that creeps on the earth according to its kind. And God saw that *it was* good.

[26]Then God said, "Let Us make man in Our image, according to Our likeness; let them have dominion over the fish of the sea, over the birds of the air, and over the cattle, over all[a] the earth and over every creeping thing that creeps on the earth." [27]So God created man in His *own* image; in the image of God He created him; male and female He created them. [28]Then God blessed them, and God said to them, "Be fruitful and multiply; fill the earth and subdue it; have dominion over the fish of the sea, over the birds of the air, and over every living thing that moves on the earth."

[29]And God said, "See, I have given you every herb *that* yields seed which *is* on the face of all the earth, and every tree whose fruit yields seed; to you it shall be for food. [30]Also, to every beast of the earth, to every bird of the air, and to everything that creeps on the earth, in which *there is* life, *I have given* every green herb for food"; and it was so. [31]Then God saw everything that He had made, and indeed *it was* very good. So the evening and the morning were the sixth day.

2 Thus the heavens and the earth, and all the host of them, were finished. [2]And on the seventh day God ended His work which He had done, and He rested on the seventh day from all His work which He had done. [3]Then God blessed the seventh day and sanctified it, because in it He rested from all His work which God had created and made.

> **2:2 ended ... rested.** On the seventh day of creation God rested—not due to weariness but rather to establish the pattern for man's work cycle. God modeled the ideal for man: six days of work followed by one day of rest. Later, God ordained the Sabbath as a sacred day to set aside for worship and rest. In the NT, the church began worshiping on the first day of the week (Sunday) rather than on the last (Saturday) to commemorate the resurrection of Christ (Acts 20:7).

[4]This *is* the history[a] of the heavens and the earth when they were created, in the day that the LORD God made the earth and the heavens, [5]before any plant of the field was in the earth and before any herb of the field had grown. For the LORD God had not caused it to rain on the earth, and *there was* no man to till the ground; [6]but a mist went up from the earth and watered the whole face of the ground.

[7]And the LORD God formed man *of* the dust of the ground, and breathed into his nostrils the breath of life; and man became a living being.

> **1:26 Us ... Our.** The first clear reference to the three-person nature of God, as the Father, the Son, and the Holy Spirit. This unique relationship is called the triunity of God. Even the very name of God, Elohim (1:1), is a plural form of El. **man.** The masterpiece of creation, a human being, was made in God's image to rule creation. **Our image.** This phrase defined man's unique relation to God and set him apart from the animals. He was like God in that he could reason and had intellect, will, and emotion. When he was first created, he was like God because he was good and sinless.

1:26 [a]Syriac reads *all the wild animals of.*　　2:4 [a]Hebrew *toledoth,* literally *generations*

Life in God's Garden

[8]The LORD God planted a garden eastward in Eden, and there He put the man whom He had formed. [9]And out of the ground the LORD God made every tree grow that is pleasant to the sight and good for food. The tree of life *was* also in the midst of the garden, and the tree of the knowledge of good and evil.

> **2:9 tree of life.** The tree of life was a real tree located in the center of the Garden of Eden. It had special properties to sustain eternal life, and Adam may have eaten its fruit, thus sustaining his life (2:16). Such a tree, symbolic of eternal life, will be in the new heavens and new earth (see Rev. 22:2,14). **tree of the knowledge of good and evil.** See 2:16; 3:1–6, 11,22. Perhaps God gave it this name because it was a test of whether or not Adam and Eve would obey God.

[10]Now a river went out of Eden to water the garden, and from there it parted and became four riverheads. [11]The name of the first *is* Pishon; it *is* the one which skirts the whole land of Havilah, where *there is* gold. [12]And the gold of that land *is* good. Bdellium and the onyx stone *are* there. [13]The name of the second river *is* Gihon; it *is* the one which goes around the whole land of Cush. [14]The name of the third river *is* Hiddekel;[a] it *is* the one which goes toward the east of Assyria. The fourth river *is* the Euphrates.

[15]Then the LORD God took the man and put him in the garden of Eden to tend and keep it. [16]And the LORD God commanded the man, saying, "Of every tree of the garden you may freely eat; [17]but of the tree of the knowledge of good and evil you shall not eat, for in the day that you eat of it you shall surely die."

[18]And the LORD God said, "*It is* not good that man should be alone; I will make him a helper comparable to him." [19]Out of the ground the LORD God formed every beast of the field and every bird of the air, and brought *them* to Adam to see what he would call them. And whatever Adam called each living creature, that *was* its name. [20]So Adam gave names to all cattle, to the birds of the air, and to every beast of the field. But for Adam there was not found a helper comparable to him.

[21]And the LORD God caused a deep sleep to fall on Adam, and he slept; and He took one of his ribs, and closed up the flesh in its place. [22]Then the rib which the LORD God had taken from man He made into a woman, and He brought her to the man. [23]And Adam said:

> "This *is* now bone of my bones
> And flesh of my flesh;
> She shall be called Woman,
> Because she was taken out of Man."

[24]Therefore a man shall leave his father and mother and be joined to his wife, and they shall become one flesh.

[25]And they were both naked, the man and his wife, and were not ashamed.

> **2:23 bone of my bones.** Adam's short poem gives a name to his new companion, who is the delight of his heart. The man (ish) names her "woman" (isha) because she had been made from part of his own flesh and bones. The English words "man" and "woman" sustain the same relationship as the Hebrew words, hinting at that original creation of the woman.

The Temptation and Fall of Man

3 Now the serpent was more cunning than any beast of the field which the LORD God had made. And he said to the woman, "Has God indeed said, 'You shall not eat of every tree of the garden'?"

[2]And the woman said to the serpent, "We may eat the fruit of the trees of the garden; [3]but of the fruit of the tree which *is* in the midst of the garden, God has said, 'You shall not eat it, nor shall you touch it, lest you die.' "

[4]Then the serpent said to the woman, "You will not surely die. [5]For God knows that in the day you eat of it your eyes will be opened, and you will be like God, knowing good and evil."

[6]So when the woman saw that the tree *was* good for food, that it *was* pleasant to the eyes, and a tree desirable to make *one* wise, she took of its fruit and ate. She also

---

2:14 [a]Or *Tigris*

gave to her husband with her, and he ate. ⁷Then the eyes of both of them were opened, and they knew that they *were* naked; and they sewed fig leaves together and made themselves coverings.

⁸And they heard the sound of the LORD God walking in the garden in the cool of the day, and Adam and his wife hid themselves from the presence of the LORD God among the trees of the garden.

⁹Then the LORD God called to Adam and said to him, "Where *are* you?"

3:9 "Where *are* you?" God asked Adam this question not because He did not know where he was but because He was forcing him to explain why he was hiding. Adam and Eve hid because they felt shame, remorse, confusion, guilt, and fear. There was no place to hide; there never is. (See Ps. 139:1–12.)

¹⁰So he said, "I heard Your voice in the garden, and I was afraid because I was naked; and I hid myself."

¹¹And He said, "Who told you that you *were* naked? Have you eaten from the tree of which I commanded you that you should not eat?"

¹²Then the man said, "The woman whom You gave *to be* with me, she gave me of the tree, and I ate."

¹³And the LORD God said to the woman, "What *is* this you have done?"

The woman said, "The serpent deceived me, and I ate."

¹⁴So the LORD God said to the serpent:

" Because you have done this,
You *are* cursed more than all cattle,
And more than every beast of the field;
On your belly you shall go,
And you shall eat dust
All the days of your life.
15   And I will put enmity
Between you and the woman,
And between your seed and her
Seed;
He shall bruise your head,
And you shall bruise His heel."

3:15 bruise your head … bruise His heel. This is the first Messianic prophecy, foretelling the coming of Jesus Christ. Ever since the Fall, Satan's "seed" (Satan and unbelievers, who are called the Devil's children in John 8:44) has struggled against the woman's seed (Christ, a descendant of Eve, and His children). In the midst of this curse passage, God gives a message of hope—"He" is Christ, who will one day defeat Satan completely. Satan could only "bruise" Christ's heel (cause Him to suffer), while Christ will bruise Satan's head (destroy him with a fatal blow).

¹⁶To the woman He said:

"I will greatly multiply your sorrow
and your conception;

What do Christians mean when they talk about the Fall?

The Fall refers to that moment in time when human beings first disobeyed God. Genesis 3 tells the painful episode. What Eve set into motion, Adam confirmed and completed by joining her. They sinned together. The willful decision of Adam and Eve created a state of rebellion between the creation and her Creator.

The expression "the fall" comes from the Bible itself. The apostle Paul uses the word in summarizing the human condition in Romans 3:23, "... for all have sinned and fall short of the glory of God."

The word "fall" carries with it the sense of defeat and destruction. Great cities fell. So did people. But another fall preceded all these; the fall of the angel Lucifer, who became known as Satan (Isaiah 14:12–15). In the Fall, our first ancestors declared us on Satan's side.

The Bible makes it clear that the Fall brought sin into every subsequent person's life: "Therefore, just as through one man sin entered the world, and death through sin, and thus death spread to all men, because all sinned" (Romans 5:12). Our capacity for sin is inborn. We are sinners before we have the opportunity to sin. Not only are we sinners because we sin; we first sin because we are sinners. Why? Because we have all inherited the effects of Adam's fall.

In pain you shall bring forth children;
Your desire *shall be* for your husband,
And he shall rule over you."

[17]Then to Adam He said, "Because you have heeded the voice of your wife, and have eaten from the tree of which I commanded you, saying, 'You shall not eat of it':

"Cursed *is* the ground for your sake;
In toil you shall eat *of* it
All the days of your life.
[18]   Both thorns and thistles it shall bring
forth for you,
And you shall eat the herb of the field.
[19]   In the sweat of your face you shall eat
bread
Till you return to the ground,
For out of it you were taken;
For dust you *are*,
And to dust you shall return."

[20]And Adam called his wife's name Eve, because she was the mother of all living. [21]Also for Adam and his wife the LORD God made tunics of skin, and clothed them. [22]Then the LORD God said, "Behold, the man has become like one of Us, to know good and evil. And now, lest he put out his hand and take also of the tree of life, and eat, and live forever"— [23]therefore the LORD God sent him out of the garden of Eden to till the ground from which he was taken. [24]So He drove out the man; and He placed cherubim at the east of the garden of Eden, and a flaming sword which turned every way, to guard the way to the tree of life.

Cain Murders Abel

4 Now Adam knew Eve his wife, and she conceived and bore Cain, and said, "I have acquired a man from the LORD." [2]Then she bore again, this time his brother Abel. Now Abel was a keeper of sheep, but Cain was a tiller of the ground. [3]And in the process of time it came to pass that Cain brought an offering of the fruit of the ground to the LORD. [4]Abel also brought of the firstborn of his flock and of their fat. And the LORD respected Abel and his offering, [5]but He did not respect Cain and his of-

fering. And Cain was very angry, and his countenance fell.

4:4,5 Abel's offering was acceptable (see Heb. 11:4), because it was in every way obediently given according to what God must have revealed, though the revelation is not recorded in Genesis. Abel's offering was an animal, it was the very best of what he had, and it was the culmination of a zealous heart for God. Cain, however, disdained the divine instruction and just brought what he wanted to bring: some of his crop.

[6]So the LORD said to Cain, "Why are you angry? And why has your countenance fallen? [7]If you do well, will you not be accepted? And if you do not do well, sin lies at the door. And its desire *is* for you, but you should rule over it."

[8]Now Cain talked with Abel his brother;[a] and it came to pass, when they were in the field, that Cain rose up against Abel his brother and killed him.

[9]Then the LORD said to Cain, "Where *is* Abel your brother?"

He said, "I do not know. *Am* I my brother's keeper?"

[10]And He said, "What have you done? The voice of your brother's blood cries out to Me from the ground. [11]So now you *are* cursed from the earth, which has opened its mouth to receive your brother's blood from your hand. [12]When you till the ground, it shall no longer yield its strength to you. A fugitive and a vagabond you shall be on the earth."

[13]And Cain said to the LORD, "My punishment *is* greater than I can bear! [14]Surely You have driven me out this day from the face of the ground; I shall be hidden from Your face; I shall be a fugitive and a vagabond on the earth, and it will happen *that* anyone who finds me will kill me."

[15]And the LORD said to him, "Therefore,[a] whoever kills Cain, vengeance shall be taken on him sevenfold." And the LORD set a mark on Cain, lest anyone finding him should kill him.

The Family of Cain

[16]Then Cain went out from the presence of the LORD and dwelt in the land of Nod

---

4:8 [a]Samaritan Pentateuch, Septuagint, Syriac, and Vulgate add *"Let us go out to the field."*
4:15 [a]Following Masoretic Text and Targum; Septuagint, Syriac, and Vulgate read *Not so.*

on the east of Eden. ¹⁷And Cain knew his wife, and she conceived and bore Enoch. And he built a city, and called the name of the city after the name of his son—Enoch. ¹⁸To Enoch was born Irad; and Irad begot Mehujael, and Mehujael begot Methushael, and Methushael begot Lamech.

¹⁹Then Lamech took for himself two wives: the name of one *was* Adah, and the name of the second *was* Zillah. ²⁰And Adah bore Jabal. He was the father of those who dwell in tents and have livestock. ²¹His brother's name *was* Jubal. He was the father of all those who play the harp and flute. ²²And as for Zillah, she also bore Tubal-Cain, an instructor of every craftsman in bronze and iron. And the sister of Tubal-Cain *was* Naamah.

²³Then Lamech said to his wives:

"Adah and Zillah, hear my voice;
  Wives of Lamech, listen to my
    speech!
  For I have killed a man for wounding
    me,
  Even a young man for hurting me.
²⁴ If Cain shall be avenged sevenfold,
    Then Lamech seventy-sevenfold."

A New Son

²⁵And Adam knew his wife again, and she bore a son and named him Seth, "For God has appointed another seed for me instead of Abel, whom Cain killed." ²⁶And as for Seth, to him also a son was born; and he named him Enosh.ᵃ Then *men* began to call on the name of the LORD.

The Family of Adam

5 This is the book of the genealogy of Adam. In the day that God created man, He made him in the likeness of God. ²He created them male and female, and blessed them and called them Mankind in the day they were created. ³And Adam lived one hundred and thirty years, and begot *a son* in his own likeness, after his image, and named him Seth. ⁴After he begot Seth, the days of Adam were eight hundred years; and he had sons and daughters. ⁵So all the days that Adam lived were nine hundred and thirty years; and he died.

⁶Seth lived one hundred and five years, and begot Enosh. ⁷After he begot Enosh, Seth lived eight hundred and seven years, and had sons and daughters. ⁸So all the days of Seth were nine hundred and twelve years; and he died.

⁹Enosh lived ninety years, and begot Cainan.ᵃ ¹⁰After he begot Cainan, Enosh lived eight hundred and fifteen years, and had sons and daughters. ¹¹So all the days of Enosh were nine hundred and five years; and he died.

¹²Cainan lived seventy years, and begot Mahalalel. ¹³After he begot Mahalalel, Cainan lived eight hundred and forty years, and had sons and daughters. ¹⁴So all the days of Cainan were nine hundred and ten years; and he died.

¹⁵Mahalalel lived sixty-five years, and begot Jared. ¹⁶After he begot Jared, Mahalalel lived eight hundred and thirty years, and had sons and daughters. ¹⁷So all the days of Mahalalel were eight hundred and ninety-five years; and he died.

¹⁸Jared lived one hundred and sixty-two years, and begot Enoch. ¹⁹After he begot Enoch, Jared lived eight hundred years, and had sons and daughters. ²⁰So all the days of Jared were nine hundred and sixty-two years; and he died.

²¹Enoch lived sixty-five years, and begot Methuselah. ²²After he begot Methuselah, Enoch walked with God three hundred years, and had sons and daughters. ²³So all the days of Enoch were three hundred and sixty-five years. ²⁴And Enoch walked with God; and he *was* not, for God took him.

5:24 walked with God ... *was* not, for God took him. Enoch is the only exception in the chapter from the repeated comment, "and he died" (see 4:17,18; 1 Chr. 1:3; Luke 3:37; Heb. 11:5; Jude 14). Only one other man, Noah, has enjoyed this intimacy of a relationship of walking with God (6:9). Enoch was taken to heaven alive by God, as Elijah was later (2 Kin. 2:1–12).

²⁵Methuselah lived one hundred and eighty-seven years, and begot Lamech. ²⁶After he begot Lamech, Methuselah lived seven hundred and eighty-two years, and had sons and daughters. ²⁷So all the days of

4:26 ᵃGreek *Enos*   5:9 ᵃHebrew *Qenan*

Methuselah were nine hundred and sixty-nine years; and he died.

> **5:25–27 Methuselah.** The man who lived the longest life on record. He died the year of the Flood (see 7:6).

²⁸Lamech lived one hundred and eighty-two years, and had a son. ²⁹And he called his name Noah, saying, "This *one* will comfort us concerning our work and the toil of our hands, because of the ground which the LORD has cursed." ³⁰After he begot Noah, Lamech lived five hundred and ninety-five years, and had sons and daughters. ³¹So all the days of Lamech were seven hundred and seventy-seven years; and he died.

³²And Noah was five hundred years old, and Noah begot Shem, Ham, and Japheth.

The Wickedness and Judgment of Man

6 Now it came to pass, when men began to multiply on the face of the earth, and daughters were born to them, ²that the sons of God saw the daughters of men, that they *were* beautiful; and they took wives for themselves of all whom they chose.

> **6:2 the sons of God saw the daughters of men.** The sons of God, identified elsewhere as angels (Job 1:6; 2:1; 38:7), saw and took human wives. This violated the God-ordained order of human marriage and procreation (Gen. 2:24). The passage strongly emphasizes the angelic vs. human contrast. The NT identifies these as fallen angels who indwelt men, for in order to procreate physically, they had to possess human, male bodies.

³And the LORD said, "My Spirit shall not strive*ª* with man forever, for he *is* indeed flesh; yet his days shall be one hundred and twenty years." ⁴There were giants on the earth in those days, and also afterward, when the sons of God came in to the daughters of men and they bore *children* to them. Those *were* the mighty men who *were* of old, men of renown.

⁵Then the LORD*ª* saw that the wickedness of man *was* great in the earth, and *that* every intent of the thoughts of his heart *was* only evil continually. ⁶And the LORD was sorry that He had made man on the earth, and He was grieved in His heart. ⁷So the LORD said, "I will destroy man whom I have created from the face of the earth, both man and beast, creeping thing and birds of the air, for I am sorry that I have made them." ⁸But Noah found grace in the eyes of the LORD.

Noah Pleases God

⁹This is the genealogy of Noah. Noah was a just man, perfect in his generations. Noah walked with God. ¹⁰And Noah begot three sons: Shem, Ham, and Japheth. ¹¹The earth also was corrupt before God, and the earth was filled with violence. ¹²So God looked upon the earth, and indeed it was corrupt; for all flesh had corrupted their way on the earth.

The Ark Prepared

¹³And God said to Noah, "The end of all flesh has come before Me, for the earth is filled with violence through them; and behold, I will destroy them with the earth. ¹⁴Make yourself an ark of gopherwood; make rooms in the ark, and cover it inside and outside with pitch. ¹⁵And this is how you shall make it: The length of the ark *shall be* three hundred cubits, its width fifty cubits, and its height thirty cubits. ¹⁶You shall make a window for the ark, and you shall finish it to a cubit from above; and set the door of the ark in its side. You

> **6:15,16** The ark was not designed for beauty or speed, but these dimensions provided extraordinary stability in the tumultuous floodwaters. A cubit was about 18 inches long, which made the ark 450 feet long, 75 feet wide, and 45 feet high. A gigantic box of that size would be very stable in the water and impossible to capsize. The volume of space in the ark was 1.4 million cubic feet, equal to the capacity of 522 standard railroad box cars. It had 3 stories, each 15 feet high; each deck was equipped with rooms (lit. "nests"). "Pitch" was a resin substance to seal the seams and cracks in the wood. The "window" may have actually been a low wall around the flat roof to catch water for all on the ark.

6:3 *ª*Septuagint, Syriac, Targum, and Vulgate read *abide.*   6:5 *ª*Following Masoretic Text and Targum; Vulgate reads *God*; Septuagint reads *LORD God.*

shall make it *with* lower, second, and third *decks*. ¹⁷And behold, I Myself am bringing floodwaters on the earth, to destroy from under heaven all flesh in which *is* the breath of life; everything that *is* on the earth shall die. ¹⁸But I will establish My covenant with you; and you shall go into the ark—you, your sons, your wife, and your sons' wives with you. ¹⁹And of every living thing of all flesh you shall bring two of every *sort* into the ark, to keep *them* alive with you; they shall be male and female. ²⁰Of the birds after their kind, of animals after their kind, and of every creeping thing of the earth after its kind, two of every *kind* will come to you to keep *them* alive. ²¹And you shall take for yourself of all food that is eaten, and you shall gather *it* to yourself; and it shall be food for you and for them."

²²Thus Noah did; according to all that God commanded him, so he did.

The Great Flood

7 Then the LORD said to Noah, "Come into the ark, you and all your household, because I have seen *that* you *are* righteous before Me in this generation. ²You shall take with you seven each of every clean animal, a male and his female; two each of animals that *are* unclean, a male and his female; ³also seven each of birds of the air, male and female, to keep the species alive on the face of all the earth. ⁴For after seven more days I will cause it to rain on the earth forty days and forty nights, and I will destroy from the face of the earth all living things that I have made." ⁵And Noah did according to all that the LORD commanded him. ⁶Noah *was* six hundred years old when the floodwaters were on the earth.

⁷So Noah, with his sons, his wife, and his sons' wives, went into the ark because of the waters of the flood. ⁸Of clean animals, of animals that *are* unclean, of birds, and of everything that creeps on the earth, ⁹two by two they went into the ark to Noah, male and female, as God had commanded Noah. ¹⁰And it came to pass after seven days that the waters of the flood were on the earth. ¹¹In the six hundredth year of Noah's life, in the second month, the seventeenth day of the month, on that day all the fountains of

7:11 all the fountains of the great deep were broken up. The subterranean waters sprang up from deep fountains inside the earth to form the seas and rivers (1:10; 2:10–14), which were not produced by rainfall, since it never rained before the Flood. **the windows of heaven.** The celestial waters in the canopy encircling the globe were dumped on the earth and joined with the terrestrial and the subterranean waters (see 1:7). The Flood ended the water canopy surrounding the earth and unleashed the water in the earth. Thus began the earth's cycle of hydrology, with rain and evaporation (see Job 26:8; Eccl. 1:7; Is. 55:10; Amos 9:6).

How significant is the Flood in the overall biblical history?

The Bible treats the Flood as a worldwide event directly brought by God as a judgment on the sin of humanity. The Flood hangs like a warning cloud over all of subsequent history. Fortunately, that cloud also holds a rainbow of God's promised grace.

Conditions in Noah's day were ripe for judgment. "Then the LORD saw that the wickedness of man was great in the earth, and that every intent of the thoughts of his heart was only evil continually" (Genesis 6:5). This verse provides one of the strongest and clearest statements about man's sinful nature. Many other verses make it clear that God had every reason for radical action: Jeremiah 17:9,10; Matthew 12:34,35; 15:18,19; Mark 7:21; Luke 6:45. Other notable Scriptures on the worldwide flood brought by God include Job 12:15; 22:16; Psalms 29:10; 104:6–9; Isaiah 54:9; Matthew 24:37–39; Luke 17:26,27; Hebrews 11:7; 1 Peter 3:20; 2 Peter 2:5; 3:5,6.

The Flood illustrates several important aspects of God's character and God's relationship with His creation: (1) God retains ultimate control of world events; (2) God can and will judge sin; (3) God can and does exercise grace even in judgment; (4) An even more universal and final judgment will be carried out on the world based on God's timetable.

the great deep were broken up, and the windows of heaven were opened. ¹²And the rain was on the earth forty days and forty nights.

¹³On the very same day Noah and Noah's sons, Shem, Ham, and Japheth, and Noah's wife and the three wives of his sons with them, entered the ark— ¹⁴they and every beast after its kind, all cattle after their kind, every creeping thing that creeps on the earth after its kind, and every bird after its kind, every bird of every sort. ¹⁵And they went into the ark to Noah, two by two, of all flesh in which *is* the breath of life. ¹⁶So those that entered, male and female of all flesh, went in as God had commanded him; and the LORD shut him in.

¹⁷Now the flood was on the earth forty days. The waters increased and lifted up the ark, and it rose high above the earth. ¹⁸The waters prevailed and greatly increased on the earth, and the ark moved about on the surface of the waters. ¹⁹And the waters prevailed exceedingly on the earth, and all the high hills under the whole heaven were covered. ²⁰The waters prevailed fifteen cubits upward, and the mountains were covered. ²¹And all flesh died that moved on the earth: birds and cattle and beasts and every creeping thing that creeps on the earth, and every man. ²²All in whose nostrils *was* the breath of the spirit*ᵃ* of life,

all that *was* on the dry *land,* died. ²³So He destroyed all living things which were on the face of the ground: both man and cattle, creeping thing and bird of the air. They were destroyed from the earth. Only Noah and those who *were* with him in the ark remained *alive.* ²⁴And the waters prevailed on the earth one hundred and fifty days.

7:24 one hundred and fifty days. These 150 days included the 40 day and night period of rain (7:12,17). At the end of this period, the Flood had risen to its peak (see 8:3). After this period, 2½ months passed before the water receded to reveal other mountain peaks (8:4,5), 4½ months passed before the dove could find dry land (8:8–12), and almost 8 months passed before the occupants could leave the ark (8:14).

Noah's Deliverance

8 Then God remembered Noah, and every living thing, and all the animals that *were* with him in the ark. And God made a wind to pass over the earth, and the

8:1 Then God remembered Noah. God's covenant with Noah meant that He would provide for and protect Noah in the midst of severe judgment. God preserved a remnant for Himself as He initiated steps to reestablish the created order on earth. **the waters subsided.** God used the wind to dry the ground, and water evaporated into the atmosphere.

7:22 *ᵃ*Septuagint and Vulgate omit *of the spirit.*

THE FLOOD CHRONOLOGY

1. In the 600th year of Noah (second month, tenth day), Noah entered the ark (Genesis 7:4,10,11).
2. In the 600th year of Noah (second month, seventeenth day), the Flood began (Genesis 7:11).
3. The waters flooded the earth for 150 days (5 months of 30 days each), including the 40 days and 40 nights of rain (Genesis 7:12,17,24; 8:1).
4. In the 600th year of Noah (seventh month, seventh day), the waters began to recede (7:24; 8:1).
5. The waters later receded to the point that (600th year, seventh month, seventeenth day) the ark rested on Ararat (Genesis 8:3,4).
6. The waters continued to abate so that (600th year, tenth month, first day) the tops of the mountains were visible (Genesis 8:5).
7. Forty days later (600th year, eleventh month, tenth day) Noah sent out a raven and a dove (Genesis 8:6). Over the next 14 days, Noah sent out two more doves (Genesis 8:10,12). In all, this took 61 days or two months and one day.
8. By Noah's 601st year on the first month, the first day, the water had dried up (Genesis 8:12,13).
9. Noah waited one month and twenty-six days before he disembarked in the second month, the 27th day of his 601st year. From beginning to end, the Flood lasted one year and ten days from Genesis 7:11 to Genesis 8:14.

waters subsided. ²The fountains of the deep and the windows of heaven were also stopped, and the rain from heaven was restrained. ³And the waters receded continually from the earth. At the end of the hundred and fifty days the waters decreased. ⁴Then the ark rested in the seventh month, the seventeenth day of the month, on the mountains of Ararat. ⁵And the waters decreased continually until the tenth month. In the tenth *month,* on the first *day* of the month, the tops of the mountains were seen.

⁶So it came to pass, at the end of forty days, that Noah opened the window of the ark which he had made. ⁷Then he sent out a raven, which kept going to and fro until the waters had dried up from the earth. ⁸He also sent out from himself a dove, to see if the waters had receded from the face of the ground. ⁹But the dove found no resting place for the sole of her foot, and she returned into the ark to him, for the waters *were* on the face of the whole earth. So he put out his hand and took her, and drew her into the ark to himself. ¹⁰And he waited yet another seven days, and again he sent the dove out from the ark. ¹¹Then the dove came to him in the evening, and behold, a freshly plucked olive leaf *was* in her mouth; and Noah knew that the waters had receded from the earth. ¹²So he waited yet another seven days and sent out the dove, which did not return again to him anymore.

¹³And it came to pass in the six hundred and first year, in the first *month,* the first *day* of the month, that the waters were dried up from the earth; and Noah removed the covering of the ark and looked, and indeed the surface of the ground was dry. ¹⁴And in the second month, on the twenty-seventh day of the month, the earth was dried.

¹⁵Then God spoke to Noah, saying, ¹⁶"Go out of the ark, you and your wife, and your sons and your sons' wives with you. ¹⁷Bring out with you every living thing of all flesh that *is* with you: birds and cattle and every creeping thing that creeps on the earth, so that they may abound on the earth, and be fruitful and multiply on the earth." ¹⁸So Noah went out, and his sons and his wife and his sons' wives with him. ¹⁹Every animal, every creeping thing, every bird, *and* whatever creeps on the earth, according to their families, went out of the ark.

8:17–19 be fruitful and multiply. As God began to replenish the created order that He had destroyed, He repeated the words of the blessing that He had put upon non-human creatures (1:22). After the Flood, Noah faced a very different world, where longevity of life began to decline, and the earth was subject to storms, severe weather, blazing heat, freezing cold, seismic action, and natural disasters.

God's Covenant with Creation

²⁰Then Noah built an altar to the LORD, and took of every clean animal and of every clean bird, and offered burnt offerings on the altar. ²¹And the LORD smelled a soothing aroma. Then the LORD said in His heart, "I will never again curse the ground for man's sake, although the imagination of man's heart *is* evil from his youth; nor will I again destroy every living thing as I have done.

²² "While the earth remains,
Seedtime and harvest,
Cold and heat,
Winter and summer,
And day and night
Shall not cease."

9 So God blessed Noah and his sons, and said to them: "Be fruitful and multiply, and fill the earth.ᵃ ²And the fear of you and the dread of you shall be on every beast of the earth, on every bird of the air, on all that move *on* the earth, and on all the fish of the sea. They are given into your hand. ³Every moving thing that lives shall be food for you. I have given you all things, even as the green herbs. ⁴But you shall not eat flesh with its life, *that is,* its blood. ⁵Surely for your lifeblood I will demand *a reckoning*; from the hand of every beast I will require it, and from the hand of man. From the

9:5 beast ... man. Capital punishment was invoked upon every animal (Ex. 21:28) or man who took human life unlawfully. (See John 19:11; Acts 25:11; Rom. 13:4 for NT support for this punishment.)

9:1 ᵃCompare Genesis 1:28

hand of every man's brother I will require the life of man.

6   "Whoever sheds man's blood,
     By man his blood shall be shed;
     For in the image of God
     He made man.
7   And as for you, be fruitful and
       multiply;
     Bring forth abundantly in the earth
     And multiply in it."

> **9:6 For in the image of God.** The reason man could kill animals, but neither animals nor man could kill man, is because man alone was created in God's image.

8Then God spoke to Noah and to his sons with him, saying: 9"And as for Me, behold, I establish My covenant with you and with your descendants*a* after you, 10and with every living creature that *is* with you: the birds, the cattle, and every beast of the earth with you, of all that go out of the ark, every beast of the earth. 11Thus I establish My covenant with you: Never again shall all flesh be cut off by the waters of the flood; never again shall there be a flood to destroy the earth."

12And God said: "This *is* the sign of the covenant which I make between Me and you, and every living creature that *is* with you, for perpetual generations: 13I set My rainbow in the cloud, and it shall be for the sign of the covenant between Me and the earth. 14It shall be, when I bring a cloud over the earth, that the rainbow shall be seen in the cloud; 15and I will remember My covenant which *is* between Me and you and every living creature of all flesh; the waters shall never again become a flood to destroy all flesh. 16The rainbow shall be in the

> **9:16 the everlasting covenant.** This covenant with Noah is the first of five divinely originated covenants that are described as "everlasting." The term "everlasting" can mean either (1) to the end of time and/or (2) through eternity future. It does not include eternity past. The other four such covenants include the following: (1) Abrahamic (Gen. 17:7); (2) Priestly (Num. 25:10–13); (3) Davidic (2 Sam. 23:5); and (4) New (Jer. 32:40).

cloud, and I will look on it to remember the everlasting covenant between God and every living creature of all flesh that *is* on the earth." 17And God said to Noah, "This *is* the sign of the covenant which I have established between Me and all flesh that *is* on the earth."

Noah and His Sons

18Now the sons of Noah who went out of the ark were Shem, Ham, and Japheth. And Ham *was* the father of Canaan. 19These three *were* the sons of Noah, and from these the whole earth was populated.

20And Noah began *to be* a farmer, and he planted a vineyard. 21Then he drank of the wine and was drunk, and became uncovered in his tent. 22And Ham, the father of Canaan, saw the nakedness of his father, and told his two brothers outside. 23But Shem and Japheth took a garment, laid *it* on both their shoulders, and went backward and covered the nakedness of their father. Their faces *were* turned away, and they did not see their father's nakedness.

24So Noah awoke from his wine, and knew what his younger son had done to him. 25Then he said:

   "Cursed *be* Canaan;
     A servant of servants
     He shall be to his brethren."

26And he said:

   "Blessed *be* the LORD,
     The God of Shem,
     And may Canaan be his servant.
27   May God enlarge Japheth,
     And may he dwell in the tents of Shem;
     And may Canaan be his servant."

28And Noah lived after the flood three hundred and fifty years. 29So all the days of Noah were nine hundred and fifty years; and he died.

Nations Descended from Noah

10 Now this *is* the genealogy of the sons of Noah: Shem, Ham, and Japheth. And sons were born to them after the flood.

9:9 *a*Literally *seed*

²The sons of Japheth *were* Gomer, Magog, Madai, Javan, Tubal, Meshech, and Tiras. ³The sons of Gomer *were* Ashkenaz, Riphath,*ᵃ* and Togarmah. ⁴The sons of Javan *were* Elishah, Tarshish, Kittim, and Dodanim.*ᵃ* ⁵From these the coastland *peoples* of the Gentiles were separated into their lands, everyone according to his language, according to their families, into their nations.

⁶The sons of Ham *were* Cush, Mizraim, Put,*ᵃ* and Canaan. ⁷The sons of Cush *were* Seba, Havilah, Sabtah, Raamah, and Sabtechah; and the sons of Raamah *were* Sheba and Dedan.

⁸Cush begot Nimrod; he began to be a mighty one on the earth. ⁹He was a mighty hunter before the Lᴏʀᴅ; therefore it is said, "Like Nimrod the mighty hunter before the Lᴏʀᴅ." ¹⁰And the beginning of his kingdom was Babel, Erech, Accad, and Calneh, in the land of Shinar. ¹¹From that land he went to Assyria and built Nineveh, Rehoboth Ir, Calah, ¹²and Resen between Nineveh and Calah (that *is* the principal city).

¹³Mizraim begot Ludim, Anamim, Lehabim, Naphtuhim, ¹⁴Pathrusim, and Casluhim (from whom came the Philistines and Caphtorim).

¹⁵Canaan begot Sidon his firstborn, and Heth; ¹⁶the Jebusite, the Amorite, and the Girgashite; ¹⁷the Hivite, the Arkite, and the Sinite; ¹⁸the Arvadite, the Zemarite, and the Hamathite. Afterward the families of the Canaanites were dispersed. ¹⁹And the border of the Canaanites was from Sidon as you go toward Gerar, as far as Gaza; then as you go toward Sodom, Gomorrah, Admah, and Zeboiim, as far as Lasha. ²⁰These *were* the sons of Ham, according to their families, according to their languages, in their lands *and* in their nations.

²¹And *children* were born also to Shem, the father of all the children of Eber, the brother of Japheth the elder. ²²The sons of Shem *were* Elam, Asshur, Arphaxad, Lud, and Aram. ²³The sons of Aram *were* Uz,

10:3 *ᵃ*Spelled *Diphath* in 1 Chronicles 1:6   10:4 *ᵃ*Spelled *Rodanim* in Samaritan Pentateuch and 1 Chronicles 1:7   10:6 *ᵃ*Or *Phut*

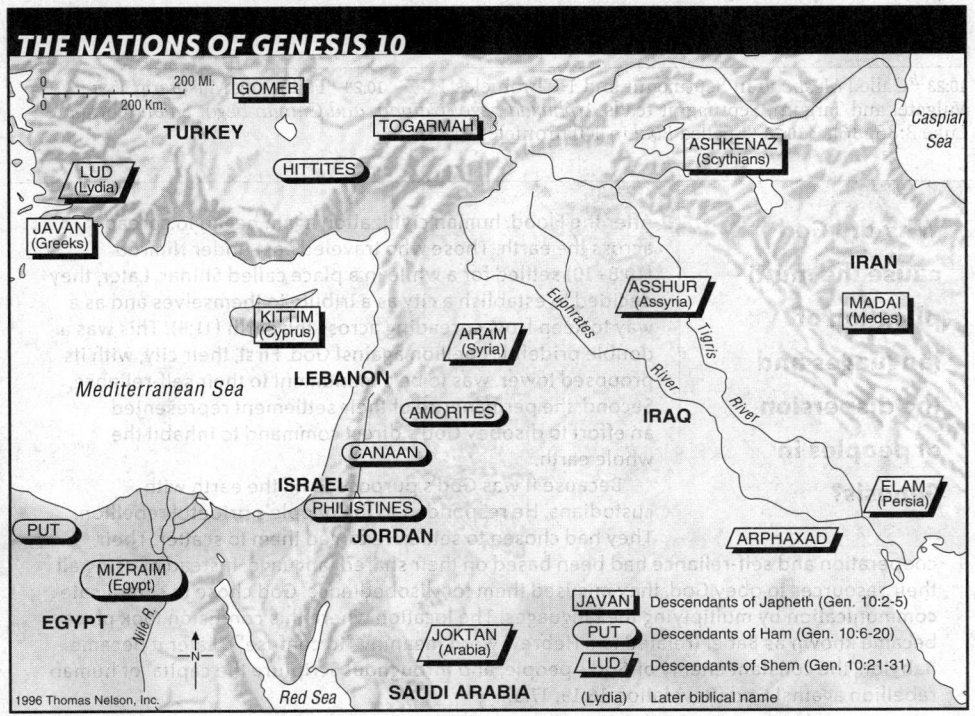

THE NATIONS OF GENESIS 10

1996 Thomas Nelson, Inc.

Hul, Gether, and Mash.*a* ²⁴Arphaxad begot Salah,*a* and Salah begot Eber. ²⁵To Eber were born two sons: the name of one *was* Peleg, for in his days the earth was divided; and his brother's name *was* Joktan. ²⁶Joktan begot Almodad, Sheleph, Hazarmaveth, Jerah, ²⁷Hadoram, Uzal, Diklah, ²⁸Obal,*a* Abimael, Sheba, ²⁹Ophir, Havilah, and Jobab. All these *were* the sons of Joktan. ³⁰And their dwelling place was from Mesha as you go toward Sephar, the mountain of the east. ³¹These *were* the sons of Shem, according to their families, according to their languages, in their lands, according to their nations.

³²These *were* the families of the sons of Noah, according to their generations, in their nations; and from these the nations were divided on the earth after the flood.

The Tower of Babel

11 Now the whole earth had one language and one speech. ²And it came to pass, as they journeyed from the east, that they found a plain in the land of Shinar, and they dwelt there. ³Then they said to one another, "Come, let us make bricks and bake *them* thoroughly." They had brick for stone, and they had asphalt for mortar. ⁴And they said, "Come, let us build ourselves a city, and a tower whose top *is* in the heavens; let us make a name for ourselves, lest we be scattered abroad over the face of the whole earth."

> **11:3,4 build ourselves a city.** After God commanded the people to scatter to fill the earth, the people, under the leadership of the powerful Nimrod, disobeyed God's command to disperse. They stopped to build a city and tower in their own honor. The tower itself was not the singular act of rebellion. Rather, human pride caused them to rebel against

⁵But the LORD came down to see the city and the tower which the sons of men had built. ⁶And the LORD said, "Indeed the people *are* one and they all have one language, and this is what they begin to do; now nothing that they propose to do will be withheld from them. ⁷Come, let Us go down and there confuse their language, that they may not understand one another's speech." ⁸So the LORD scattered them abroad from there over the face of all the earth, and they ceased building the city. ⁹Therefore its name is called Babel, because there the LORD confused the language of all the earth; and from there the LORD scattered them abroad over the face of all the earth.

10:23 *a*Called *Meshech* in Septuagint and 1 Chronicles 1:17   10:24 *a*Following Masoretic Text, Vulgate, and Targum; Septuagint reads *Arphaxad begot Cainan, and Cainan begot Salah* (compare Luke 3:35, 36).   10:28 *a*Spelled *Ebal* in 1 Chronicles 1:22

Why did God cause the multiplication of languages and the dispersion of peoples in Genesis?

After the Flood, human civilization again began to spread across the earth. Those who traveled east under Nimrod (10:8–10) settled for a while in a place called Shinar. Later, they decided to establish a city as a tribute to themselves and as a way to keep from spreading across the earth (11:4). This was a double prideful rebellion against God. First, their city, with its proposed tower, was to be a monument to their self-reliance. Second, the permanence of their settlement represented an effort to disobey God's direct command to inhabit the whole earth.

Because it was God's purpose to fill the earth with custodians, He responded to the people's prideful rebellion. They had chosen to settle; He forced them to scatter. Their cooperation and self-reliance had been based on their shared language. Instead of using all their resources to obey God, they misused them for disobedience. God chose to complicate communication by multiplying the languages. The location where this confusion took place became known as Babel (related to a Hebrew word meaning "to confuse"). Later it became Babylon, the constant enemy of God's people, and throughout Scripture the capital of human rebellion against God (Revelation 16:19; 17:5).

Shem's Descendants

¹⁰This *is* the genealogy of Shem: Shem *was* one hundred years old, and begot Arphaxad two years after the flood. ¹¹After he begot Arphaxad, Shem lived five hundred years, and begot sons and daughters.

¹²Arphaxad lived thirty-five years, and begot Salah. ¹³After he begot Salah, Arphaxad lived four hundred and three years, and begot sons and daughters.

¹⁴Salah lived thirty years, and begot Eber. ¹⁵After he begot Eber, Salah lived four hundred and three years, and begot sons and daughters.

¹⁶Eber lived thirty-four years, and begot Peleg. ¹⁷After he begot Peleg, Eber lived four hundred and thirty years, and begot sons and daughters.

¹⁸Peleg lived thirty years, and begot Reu. ¹⁹After he begot Reu, Peleg lived two hundred and nine years, and begot sons and daughters.

²⁰Reu lived thirty-two years, and begot Serug. ²¹After he begot Serug, Reu lived two hundred and seven years, and begot sons and daughters.

²²Serug lived thirty years, and begot Nahor. ²³After he begot Nahor, Serug lived two hundred years, and begot sons and daughters.

²⁴Nahor lived twenty-nine years, and begot Terah. ²⁵After he begot Terah, Nahor lived one hundred and nineteen years, and begot sons and daughters.

²⁶Now Terah lived seventy years, and begot Abram, Nahor, and Haran.

Terah's Descendants

²⁷This *is* the genealogy of Terah: Terah begot Abram, Nahor, and Haran. Haran begot Lot. ²⁸And Haran died before his father Terah in his native land, in Ur of the Chaldeans. ²⁹Then Abram and Nahor took wives: the name of Abram's wife *was* Sarai, and the name of Nahor's wife, Milcah, the daughter of Haran the father of Milcah and the father of Iscah. ³⁰But Sarai was barren; she had no child.

11:27 Abram. The name means "exalted father." See 17:5.

---

³¹And Terah took his son Abram and his grandson Lot, the son of Haran, and his daughter-in-law Sarai, his son Abram's wife, and they went out with them from Ur of the Chaldeans to go to the land of Canaan; and they came to Haran and dwelt there. ³²So the days of Terah were two hundred and five years, and Terah died in Haran.

Promises to Abram

12 Now the LORD had said to Abram:

" Get out of your country,
From your family
And from your father's house,
To a land that I will show you.
² I will make you a great nation;
I will bless you
And make your name great;
And you shall be a blessing.
³ I will bless those who bless you,
And I will curse him who curses you;
And in you all the families of the
earth shall be blessed."

12:1–3 the LORD...to Abram. This passage contains the promise whose fulfillment extends all through Scripture. It is an everlasting covenant which includes four components: (1) seed (see Gal. 3:8,16, referring to Christ); (2) land (15:18–21; 17:8); (3) a nation (12:2; 17:4); and (4) divine blessing and protection (12:3). The covenant is unconditional in the sense of its ultimate fulfillment of a kingdom and salvation. It has great national importance to Israel, as magnified by repeated references in the OT, and great spiritual importance to all believers.

---

⁴So Abram departed as the LORD had spoken to him, and Lot went with him. And Abram *was* seventy-five years old when he departed from Haran. ⁵Then Abram took Sarai his wife and Lot his brother's son, and all their possessions that they had gathered, and the people whom they had acquired in Haran, and they departed to go to the land of Canaan. So they came to the land of Canaan. ⁶Abram passed through the land to the place of Shechem, as far as the terebinth tree of Moreh.^a And the Canaanites *were* then in the land. ⁷Then the LORD appeared to Abram and said, "To your descendants I will give this

---

land." And there he built an altar to the LORD, who had appeared to him. [8]And he moved from there to the mountain east of Bethel, and he pitched his tent *with* Bethel on the west and Ai on the east; there he built an altar to the LORD and called on the name of the LORD. [9]So Abram journeyed, going on still toward the South.[a]

Abram in Egypt

[10]Now there was a famine in the land, and Abram went down to Egypt to dwell there, for the famine *was* severe in the land. [11]And it came to pass, when he was close to entering Egypt, that he said to Sarai his wife, "Indeed I know that you *are* a woman of beautiful countenance. [12]Therefore it will happen, when the Egyptians see you, that they will say, 'This *is* his wife'; and they will kill me, but they will let you live. [13]Please say you *are* my sister, that it may be well with me for your sake, and that I[a] may live because of you."

> **12:12,13 his wife...my sister.** Because Abram was afraid that Pharaoh would take Sarai into his harem and kill him, he disguised his true relationship to her (although Sarai was Abram's half-sister, see 20:12). Abram sought to protect himself on his own rather than trusting God to fulfill His promises.

[14]So it was, when Abram came into Egypt, that the Egyptians saw the woman, that she *was* very beautiful. [15]The princes of Pharaoh also saw her and commended her to Pharaoh. And the woman was taken to Pharaoh's house. [16]He treated Abram well for her sake. He had sheep, oxen, male donkeys, male and female servants, female donkeys, and camels.

[17]But the LORD plagued Pharaoh and his house with great plagues because of Sarai, Abram's wife. [18]And Pharaoh called Abram and said, "What *is* this you have done to me? Why did you not tell me that she *was* your wife? [19]Why did you say, 'She *is* my sister'? I might have taken her as my wife. Now therefore, here is your wife; take *her* and go your way." [20]So Pharaoh commanded *his* men concerning him; and they sent him away, with his wife and all that he had.

Abram Inherits Canaan

13 Then Abram went up from Egypt, he and his wife and all that he had, and Lot with him, to the South.[a] [2]Abram *was* very rich in livestock, in silver, and in gold. [3]And he went on his journey from the South as far as Bethel, to the place where his tent had been at the beginning, between Bethel and Ai, [4]to the place of the altar which he had made there at first. And there Abram called on the name of the LORD.

[5]Lot also, who went with Abram, had flocks and herds and tents. [6]Now the land was not able to support them, that they might dwell together, for their possessions were so great that they could not dwell together. [7]And there was strife between the herdsmen of Abram's livestock and the herdsmen of Lot's livestock. The Canaanites and the Perizzites then dwelt in the land.

[8]So Abram said to Lot, "Please let there be no strife between you and me, and between my herdsmen and your herdsmen; for we *are* brethren. [9]*Is* not the whole land before you? Please separate from me. If *you take* the left, then I will go to the right; or, if *you go* to the right, then I will go to the left."

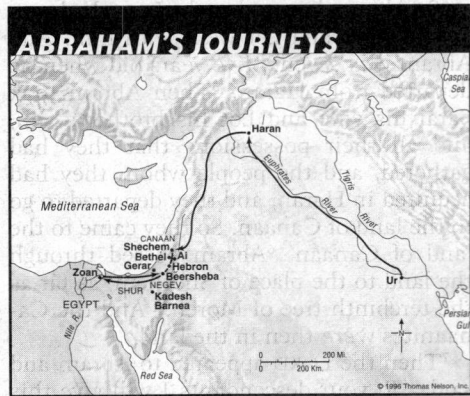

ABRAHAM'S JOURNEYS

> **13:8 we are brethren.** Abram's reaction to the conflict showed a whole new attitude from the self-centered one he portrayed in Egypt. Waiving his right to seniority, he gave the choice of land to his nephew, Lot.

¹⁰And Lot lifted his eyes and saw all the plain of Jordan, that it *was* well watered everywhere (before the LORD destroyed Sodom and Gomorrah) like the garden of the LORD, like the land of Egypt as you go toward Zoar. ¹¹Then Lot chose for himself all the plain of Jordan, and Lot journeyed east. And they separated from each other. ¹²Abram dwelt in the land of Canaan, and Lot dwelt in the cities of the plain and pitched *his* tent even as far as Sodom. ¹³But the men of Sodom *were* exceedingly wicked and sinful against the LORD.

¹⁴And the LORD said to Abram, after Lot had separated from him: "Lift your eyes now and look from the place where you are—northward, southward, eastward, and westward; ¹⁵for all the land which you see I give to you and your descendants*ᵃ* forever. ¹⁶And I will make your descendants as the dust of the earth; so that if a man could number the dust of the earth, *then* your descendants also could be numbered. ¹⁷Arise, walk in the land through its length and its width, for I give it to you."

¹⁸Then Abram moved *his* tent, and went and dwelt by the terebinth trees of Mamre,*ᵃ* which *are* in Hebron, and built an altar there to the LORD.

Lot's Captivity and Rescue

14And it came to pass in the days of Amraphel king of Shinar, Arioch king of Ellasar, Chedorlaomer king of Elam, and Tidal king of nations,*ᵃ* ²*that* they made war with Bera king of Sodom, Birsha king of Gomorrah, Shinab king of Admah, Shemeber king of Zeboiim, and the king of Bela (that is, Zoar). ³All these joined together in the Valley of Siddim (that is, the Salt Sea). ⁴Twelve years they served Chedorlaomer, and in the thirteenth year they rebelled.

⁵In the fourteenth year Chedorlaomer and the kings that *were* with him came and attacked the Rephaim in Ashteroth Karnaim, the Zuzim in Ham, the Emim in Shaveh Kiriathaim, ⁶and the Horites in their mountain of Seir, as far as El Paran, which *is* by the wilderness. ⁷Then they turned back and came to En Mishpat (that *is,* Kadesh), and attacked all the country of the Amalekites, and also the Amorites who dwelt in Hazezon Tamar.

⁸And the king of Sodom, the king of Gomorrah, the king of Admah, the king of Zeboiim, and the king of Bela (that *is,* Zoar) went out and joined together in battle in the Valley of Siddim ⁹against Chedorlaomer king of Elam, Tidal king of nations,*ᵃ* Amraphel king of Shinar, and Arioch king of Ellasar—four kings against five. ¹⁰Now the Valley of Siddim *was full of* asphalt pits; and the kings of Sodom and Gomorrah fled; *some* fell there, and the remainder fled to the mountains. ¹¹Then they took all the goods of Sodom and Gomorrah, and all their provisions, and went their way. ¹²They also took Lot, Abram's brother's son who dwelt in Sodom, and his goods, and departed.

¹³Then one who had escaped came and told Abram the Hebrew, for he dwelt by the terebinth trees of Mamre*ᵃ* the Amorite, brother of Eshcol and brother of Aner; and they *were* allies with Abram. ¹⁴Now when Abram heard that his brother was taken captive, he armed his three hundred and eighteen trained *servants* who were born in his own house, and went in pursuit as far as Dan. ¹⁵He divided his forces against them by night, and he and his servants attacked them and pursued them as far as Hobah, which *is* north of Damascus. ¹⁶So he brought back all the goods, and also brought back his brother Lot and his goods, as well as the women and the people.

¹⁷And the king of Sodom went out to meet him at the Valley of Shaveh (that *is,* the King's Valley), after his return from the defeat of Chedorlaomer and the kings who *were* with him.

Abram and Melchizedek

¹⁸Then Melchizedek king of Salem brought out bread and wine; he *was* the priest of God Most High. ¹⁹And he blessed him and said:

> "Blessed be Abram of God Most High,
> Possessor of heaven and earth;
> ²⁰ And blessed be God Most High,

13:15 *ᵃLiterally seed,* and so throughout the book *goyim*   14:9 *ᵃHebrew goyim*   14:13 *ᵃHebrew Alon Mamre*   13:18 *ᵃHebrew Alon Mamre*   14:1 *ᵃHebrew*

Who has delivered your enemies into
your hand."

14:18 Melchizedek king of Salem. His name meant
"righteous king," and he was a king-priest over
ancient Jerusalem. The lack of biographical and
genealogical details about this ruler allowed later
revelation to use him as a type of Christ (see Ps. 110:4;
Heb. 7:17,21). His superior status is attested to by
Abram's both accepting a blessing from him and also
giving a tithe to him. This is the first mention in
Scripture of giving a 10-percent offering (v. 20).
Abram's gift was purely voluntary.

And he gave him a tithe of all.

²¹Now the king of Sodom said to Abram,
"Give me the persons, and take the goods
for yourself."

²²But Abram said to the king of Sodom, "I
have raised my hand to the LORD, God
Most High, the Possessor of heaven and
earth, ²³that I *will take* nothing, from a
thread to a sandal strap, and that I will not
take anything that *is* yours, lest you should
say, 'I have made Abram rich'— ²⁴except
only what the young men have eaten, and
the portion of the men who went with me:
Aner, Eshcol, and Mamre; let them take
their portion."

God's Covenant with Abram

15 After these things the word of the
LORD came to Abram in a vision,
saying, "Do not be afraid, Abram. I *am* your
shield, your exceedingly great reward."

²But Abram said, "Lord GOD, what will
You give me, seeing I go childless, and the
heir of my house *is* Eliezer of Damascus?"
³Then Abram said, "Look, You have given
me no offspring; indeed one born in my
house is my heir!"

⁴And behold, the word of the LORD *came*
to him, saying, "This one shall not be your
heir, but one who will come from your own
body shall be your heir." ⁵Then He brought
him outside and said, "Look now toward
heaven, and count the stars if you are able
to number them." And He said to him, "So
shall your descendants be."

⁶And he believed in the LORD, and He accounted it to him for righteousness.

⁷Then He said to him, "I *am* the LORD,
who brought you out of Ur of the Chaldeans, to give you this land to inherit it."

⁸And he said, "Lord GOD, how shall I
know that I will inherit it?"

⁹So He said to him, "Bring Me a three-
year-old heifer, a three-year-old female
goat, a three-year-old ram, a turtledove,
and a young pigeon." ¹⁰Then he brought all
these to Him and cut them in two, down
the middle, and placed each piece opposite
the other; but he did not cut the birds in
two. ¹¹And when the vultures came down
on the carcasses, Abram drove them away.

¹²Now when the sun was going down, a
deep sleep fell upon Abram; and behold,
horror *and* great darkness fell upon him.
¹³Then He said to Abram: "Know certainly
that your descendants will be strangers in a
land *that is* not theirs, and will serve them,
and they will afflict them four hundred
years. ¹⁴And also the nation whom they
serve I will judge; afterward they shall come
out with great possessions. ¹⁵Now as for
you, you shall go to your fathers in peace;
you shall be buried at a good old age. ¹⁶But
in the fourth generation they shall return
here, for the iniquity of the Amorites *is* not
yet complete."

¹⁷And it came to pass, when the sun went
down and it was dark, that behold, there
appeared a smoking oven and a burning
torch that passed between those pieces.
¹⁸On the same day the LORD made a covenant with Abram, saying:

"To your descendants I have given this
land, from the river of Egypt to the great
river, the River Euphrates— ¹⁹the Kenites,
the Kenezzites, the Kadmonites, ²⁰the Hittites, the Perizzites, the Rephaim, ²¹the
Amorites, the Canaanites, the Girgashites,
and the Jebusites."

15:17 smoking oven...burning torch. These objects
symbolized the presence of God, who solemnly
promised to fulfill His promises to Abram by alone
passing between the animal pieces.

Hagar and Ishmael

16 Now Sarai, Abram's wife, had borne
him no *children*. And she had an
Egyptian maidservant whose name was
Hagar. ²So Sarai said to Abram, "See now,
the LORD has restrained me from bearing
children. Please, go in to my maid; perhaps
I shall obtain children by her." And Abram

heeded the voice of Sarai. [3]Then Sarai, Abram's wife, took Hagar her maid, the Egyptian, and gave her to her husband Abram to be his wife, after Abram had dwelt ten years in the land of Canaan. [4]So he went in to Hagar, and she conceived. And when she saw that she had conceived, her mistress became despised in her eyes.

16:3 gave her to her husband. After 10 childless years, Sarai resorted to the ancient custom by which a barren wife could have a child through one of her own maidservants. Abram ignored the divine assurance he had received when he had attempted to appoint an heir (see 15:2-5) and sinfully yielded to Sarai's insistence; thus, Ishmael was born.

[5]Then Sarai said to Abram, "My wrong *be* upon you! I gave my maid into your embrace; and when she saw that she had conceived, I became despised in her eyes. The LORD judge between you and me."

[6]So Abram said to Sarai, "Indeed your maid *is* in your hand; do to her as you please." And when Sarai dealt harshly with her, she fled from her presence.

[7]Now the Angel of the LORD found her by a spring of water in the wilderness, by the spring on the way to Shur. [8]And He said, "Hagar, Sarai's maid, where have you come from, and where are you going?"

She said, "I am fleeing from the presence of my mistress Sarai."

[9]The Angel of the LORD said to her, "Return to your mistress, and submit yourself under her hand." [10]Then the Angel of the LORD said to her, "I will multiply your descendants exceedingly, so that they shall not be counted for multitude." [11]And the Angel of the LORD said to her:

"Behold, you *are* with child,
    And you shall bear a son.
    You shall call his name Ishmael,
    Because the LORD has heard your
        affliction.

16:11 call his name Ishmael. With her son's name meaning "God hears," Hagar the servant could never forget how God had heard her cry of affliction.

[12] He shall be a wild man;
    His hand *shall be* against every man,
    And every man's hand against him.
    And he shall dwell in the presence of
        all his brethren."

[13]Then she called the name of the LORD who spoke to her, You-Are-the-God-Who-Sees; for she said, "Have I also here seen Him who sees me?" [14]Therefore the well was called Beer Lahai Roi;[a] observe, *it is* between Kadesh and Bered.

[15]So Hagar bore Abram a son; and Abram named his son, whom Hagar bore, Ishmael. [16]Abram *was* eighty-six years old when Hagar bore Ishmael to Abram.

The Sign of the Covenant

17 When Abram was ninety-nine years old, the LORD appeared to Abram and said to him, "I *am* Almighty God; walk before Me and be blameless. [2]And I will make My covenant between Me and you, and will multiply you exceedingly." [3]Then Abram fell on his face, and God talked with him, saying: [4]"As for Me, behold, My covenant is with you, and you shall be a father of many nations. [5]No longer shall your name be called Abram, but your name shall be Abraham; for I have made you a father of many nations. [6]I will make you exceedingly fruitful; and I will make nations of you, and kings shall come from you. [7]And I will establish My covenant between Me and you and your descendants after you in their generations, for an everlasting covenant, to be God to you and your descendants after you. [8]Also I give to you and your descendants after you the land in which you are a stranger, all the land of Canaan, as an everlasting possession; and I will be their God."

17:5 your name shall be Abraham. The name meant "father of many nations" and reflected Abraham's new relationship to God as well as his new identity based on God's promise of seed. See Rom. 4:17.

[9]And God said to Abraham: "As for you, you shall keep My covenant, you and your descendants after you throughout their

---

16:14 [a]Literally *Well of the One Who Lives and Sees Me*

generations. ¹⁰This *is* My covenant which you shall keep, between Me and you and your descendants after you: Every male child among you shall be circumcised; ¹¹and you shall be circumcised in the flesh of your foreskins, and it shall be a sign of the covenant between Me and you. ¹²He who is eight days old among you shall be circumcised, every male child in your generations, he who is born in your house or bought with money from any foreigner who is not your descendant. ¹³He who is born in your house and he who is bought with your money must be circumcised, and My covenant shall be in your flesh for an everlasting covenant. ¹⁴And the uncircumcised male child, who is not circumcised in the flesh of his foreskin, that person shall be cut off from his people; he has broken My covenant."

¹⁵Then God said to Abraham, "As for Sarai your wife, you shall not call her name Sarai, but Sarah *shall be* her name. ¹⁶And I will bless her and also give you a son by her; then I will bless her, and she shall be *a mother of* nations; kings of peoples shall be from her."

> **17:15 Sarai...Sarah.** Fittingly, since Sarai ("my princess") would be the ancestress of the promised nations and kings, God changed her name to Sarah ("princess") to take away the limiting personal pronoun "my."

¹⁷Then Abraham fell on his face and laughed, and said in his heart, "Shall *a child* be born to a man who is one hundred years old? And shall Sarah, who is ninety years old, bear *a child?*" ¹⁸And Abraham said to God, "Oh, that Ishmael might live before You!"

¹⁹Then God said: "No, Sarah your wife shall bear you a son, and you shall call his name Isaac; I will establish My covenant with him for an everlasting covenant, *and* with his descendants after him. ²⁰And as for Ishmael, I have heard you. Behold, I have

> **17:19 call his name Isaac.** The name of the promised son meant "he laughs" as an appropriate reminder to Abraham of his initial, faithless response to God's promise.

blessed him, and will make him fruitful, and will multiply him exceedingly. He shall beget twelve princes, and I will make him a great nation. ²¹But My covenant I will establish with Isaac, whom Sarah shall bear to you at this set time next year." ²²Then He finished talking with him, and God went up from Abraham.

²³So Abraham took Ishmael his son, all who were born in his house and all who were bought with his money, every male among the men of Abraham's house, and circumcised the flesh of their foreskins that very same day, as God had said to him. ²⁴Abraham *was* ninety-nine years old when he was circumcised in the flesh of his foreskin. ²⁵And Ishmael his son *was* thirteen years old when he was circumcised in the flesh of his foreskin. ²⁶That very same day Abraham was circumcised, and his son Ishmael; ²⁷and all the men of his house, born in the house or bought with money from a foreigner, were circumcised with him.

The Son of Promise

18 Then the LORD appeared to him by the terebinth trees of Mamre,ᵃ as he was sitting in the tent door in the heat of the day. ²So he lifted his eyes and looked, and behold, three men were standing by him; and when he saw *them,* he ran from the tent door to meet them, and bowed himself to the ground, ³and said, "My Lord, if I have now found favor in Your sight, do not pass on by Your servant. ⁴Please let a little water be brought, and wash your feet, and rest yourselves under the tree. ⁵And I will bring a morsel of bread, that you may refresh your hearts. After that you may pass by, inasmuch as you have come to your servant."

They said, "Do as you have said."

> **18:1 the LORD appeared.** Although Abraham perhaps did not recognize at first that one of his visitors was Yahweh, he humbly greeted and entertained them and properly sent them on their way (v. 16). Later he recognized his sovereign Lord (vv. 27, 30–32).

⁶So Abraham hurried into the tent to Sarah and said, "Quickly, make ready three

measures of fine meal; knead *it* and make cakes." ⁷And Abraham ran to the herd, took a tender and good calf, gave *it* to a young man, and he hastened to prepare it. ⁸So he took butter and milk and the calf which he had prepared, and set *it* before them; and he stood by them under the tree as they ate.

⁹Then they said to him, "Where *is* Sarah your wife?"

So he said, "Here, in the tent."

¹⁰And He said, "I will certainly return to you according to the time of life, and behold, Sarah your wife shall have a son."

(Sarah was listening in the tent door which *was* behind him.) ¹¹Now Abraham and Sarah were old, well advanced in age; *and* Sarah had passed the age of childbearing.ᵃ ¹²Therefore Sarah laughed within herself, saying, "After I have grown old, shall I have pleasure, my lord being old also?"

¹³And the LORD said to Abraham, "Why did Sarah laugh, saying, 'Shall I surely bear *a child*, since I am old?' ¹⁴Is anything too hard for the LORD? At the appointed time I will return to you, according to the time of life, and Sarah shall have a son."

¹⁵But Sarah denied *it*, saying, "I did not laugh," for she was afraid.

And He said, "No, but you did laugh!"

Abraham Intercedes for Sodom

¹⁶Then the men rose from there and looked toward Sodom, and Abraham went with them to send them on the way. ¹⁷And the LORD said, "Shall I hide from Abraham what I am doing, ¹⁸since Abraham shall surely become a great and mighty nation, and all the nations of the earth shall be blessed in him? ¹⁹For I have known him, in order that he may command his children and his household after him, that they keep the way of the LORD, to do righteousness and justice, that the LORD may bring to Abraham what He has spoken to him." ²⁰And the LORD said, "Because the outcry against Sodom and Gomorrah is great, and because their sin is very grave, ²¹I will go down now and see whether they have done altogether according to the outcry against it that has come to Me; and if not, I will know."

²²Then the men turned away from there and went toward Sodom, but Abraham still stood before the LORD. ²³And Abraham came near and said, "Would You also destroy the righteous with the wicked? ²⁴Suppose there were fifty righteous within the city; would You also destroy the place and not spare *it* for the fifty righteous that were in it? ²⁵Far be it from You to do such a thing as this, to slay the righteous with the wicked, so that the righteous should be as the wicked; far be it from You! Shall not the Judge of all the earth do right?"

²⁶So the LORD said, "If I find in Sodom fifty righteous within the city, then I will spare all the place for their sakes."

²⁷Then Abraham answered and said, "Indeed now, I who *am but* dust and ashes have taken it upon myself to speak to the Lord: ²⁸Suppose there were five less than the fifty righteous; would You destroy all of the city for *lack of* five?"

> **18:27 I who *am but* dust and ashes.** Abraham's negotiation was neither intended to anger the Lord nor to be selfish or manipulative but instead showed his humble and compassionate concern for his people and particularly for his nephew Lot, who lived in Sodom.

So He said, "If I find there forty-five, I will not destroy *it*."

²⁹And he spoke to Him yet again and said, "Suppose there should be forty found there?"

So He said, "I will not do *it* for the sake of forty."

³⁰Then he said, "Let not the Lord be angry, and I will speak: Suppose thirty should be found there?"

So He said, "I will not do *it* if I find thirty there."

³¹And he said, "Indeed now, I have taken it upon myself to speak to the Lord: Suppose twenty should be found there?"

So He said, "I will not destroy *it* for the sake of twenty."

³²Then he said, "Let not the Lord be angry, and I will speak but once more: Suppose ten should be found there?"

And He said, "I will not destroy *it* for the sake of ten." ³³So the LORD went His way as

---

18:11 ᵃLiterally *the manner of women had ceased to be with Sarah*

soon as He had finished speaking with Abraham; and Abraham returned to his place.

Sodom's Depravity

19 Now the two angels came to Sodom in the evening, and Lot was sitting in the gate of Sodom. When Lot saw *them*, he rose to meet them, and he bowed himself with his face toward the ground. ²And he said, "Here now, my lords, please turn in to your servant's house and spend the night, and wash your feet; then you may rise early and go on your way."

And they said, "No, but we will spend the night in the open square."

³But he insisted strongly; so they turned in to him and entered his house. Then he made them a feast, and baked unleavened bread, and they ate.

⁴Now before they lay down, the men of the city, the men of Sodom, both old and young, all the people from every quarter, surrounded the house. ⁵And they called to Lot and said to him, "Where are the men who came to you tonight? Bring them out to us that we may know them *carnally*."

> **19:5 know them *carnally*.** The men sought homosexual relations with the visitors. God's attitude toward this vile behavior became clear when He destroyed the city. See Lev. 18:22,29; 20:13; Rom. 1:26; 1 Cor. 6:9; 1 Tim. 1:10 which all prohibit homosexual behavior.

⁶So Lot went out to them through the doorway, shut the door behind him, ⁷and said, "Please, my brethren, do not do so wickedly! ⁸See now, I have two daughters who have not known a man; please, let me bring them out to you, and you may do to them as you wish; only do nothing to these men, since this is the reason they have come under the shadow of my roof." ⁹And they said, "Stand back!" Then they said, "This one came in to stay *here*, and he keeps acting as a judge; now we will deal worse with you than with them." So they pressed hard against the man Lot, and came near to break down the door. ¹⁰But the men reached out their hands and pulled Lot into the house with them, and shut the

door. ¹¹And they struck the men who *were* at the doorway of the house with blindness, both small and great, so that they became weary *trying* to find the door.

Sodom and Gomorrah Destroyed

¹²Then the men said to Lot, "Have you anyone else here? Son-in-law, your sons, your daughters, and whomever you have in the city—take *them* out of this place! ¹³For we will destroy this place, because the outcry against them has grown great before the face of the LORD, and the LORD has sent us to destroy it."

¹⁴So Lot went out and spoke to his sons-in-law, who had married his daughters, and said, "Get up, get out of this place; for the LORD will destroy this city!" But to his sons-in-law he seemed to be joking.

¹⁵When the morning dawned, the angels urged Lot to hurry, saying, "Arise, take your wife and your two daughters who are here, lest you be consumed in the punishment of the city." ¹⁶And while he lingered, the men took hold of his hand, his wife's hand, and the hands of his two daughters, the LORD being merciful to him, and they brought him out and set him outside the city. ¹⁷So it came to pass, when they had brought them outside, that he*ᵃ* said, "Escape for your life! Do not look behind you nor stay anywhere in the plain. Escape to the mountains, lest you be destroyed."

¹⁸Then Lot said to them, "Please, no, my lords! ¹⁹Indeed now, your servant has found favor in your sight, and you have increased your mercy which you have shown me by saving my life; but I cannot escape to the mountains, lest some evil overtake me and I die. ²⁰See now, this city *is* near *enough* to flee to, and it *is* a little one; please let me escape there (*is* it not a little one?) and my soul shall live."

²¹And he said to him, "See, I have favored you concerning this thing also, in that I will not overthrow this city for which you have spoken. ²²Hurry, escape there. For I cannot do anything until you arrive there."

Therefore the name of the city was called Zoar.

²³The sun had risen upon the earth when Lot entered Zoar. ²⁴Then the LORD rained

---

19:17 *ᵃ*Septuagint, Syriac, and Vulgate read *they*.

brimstone and fire on Sodom and Gomorrah, from the LORD out of the heavens. ²⁵So He overthrew those cities, all the plain, all the inhabitants of the cities, and what grew on the ground.

²⁶But his wife looked back behind him, and she became a pillar of salt.

> **19:26 his wife looked back.** Lot's wife was punished for disobeying the angelic warning to flee without a backward glance (v. 17). She became encased in salt and a poignant example of disobedience, just as Sodom and Gomorrah became examples of God's judgment on sin (see Is. 1:9; Rom. 9:29; 2 Pet. 2:5,6).

²⁷And Abraham went early in the morning to the place where he had stood before the LORD. ²⁸Then he looked toward Sodom and Gomorrah, and toward all the land of the plain; and he saw, and behold, the smoke of the land which went up like the smoke of a furnace. ²⁹And it came to pass, when God destroyed the cities of the plain, that God remembered Abraham, and sent Lot out of the midst of the overthrow, when He overthrew the cities in which Lot had dwelt.

The Descendants of Lot

³⁰Then Lot went up out of Zoar and dwelt in the mountains, and his two daughters were with him; for he was afraid to dwell in Zoar. And he and his two daughters dwelt in a cave. ³¹Now the firstborn said to the younger, "Our father *is* old, and *there is* no man on the earth to come in to us as is the custom of all the earth. ³²Come, let us make our father drink wine, and we will lie with him, that we may preserve the lineage of our father." ³³So they made their father drink wine that night. And the first-born went in and lay with her father, and he did not know when she lay down or when she arose.

³⁴It happened on the next day that the firstborn said to the younger, "Indeed I lay with my father last night; let us make him drink wine tonight also, and you go in *and* lie with him, that we may preserve the lineage of our father." ³⁵Then they made their father drink wine that night also. And the younger arose and lay with him, and he did not know when she lay down or when she arose.

³⁶Thus both the daughters of Lot were with child by their father. ³⁷The firstborn bore a son and called his name Moab; he *is* the father of the Moabites to this day. ³⁸And the younger, she also bore a son and called his name Ben-Ammi; he *is* the father of the people of Ammon to this day.

Abraham and Abimelech

20 And Abraham journeyed from there to the South, and dwelt between Kadesh and Shur, and stayed in Gerar. ²Now Abraham said of Sarah his wife, "She *is* my sister." And Abimelech king of Gerar sent and took Sarah.

> **20:2 She *is* my sister.** Twenty-five years earlier, Abraham told the same lie about his wife, forcing him to leave Egypt in disgrace (12:10–20). Again, Abraham reverted to the same ploy.

³But God came to Abimelech in a dream by night, and said to him, "Indeed you *are* a dead man because of the woman whom you have taken, for she *is* a man's wife."

⁴But Abimelech had not come near her; and he said, "Lord, will You slay a righteous nation also? ⁵Did he not say to me, 'She *is* my sister'? And she, even she herself said, 'He *is* my brother.' In the integrity of my heart and innocence of my hands I have done this."

⁶And God said to him in a dream, "Yes, I know that you did this in the integrity of your heart. For I also withheld you from sinning against Me; therefore I did not let you touch her. ⁷Now therefore, restore the man's wife; for he *is* a prophet, and he will pray for you and you shall live. But if you do not restore *her*, know that you shall surely die, you and all who *are* yours."

⁸So Abimelech rose early in the morning, called all his servants, and told all these things in their hearing; and the men were very much afraid. ⁹And Abimelech called Abraham and said to him, "What have you done to us? How have I offended you, that you have brought on me and on my kingdom a great sin? You have done deeds to me that ought not to be done." ¹⁰Then Abimelech said to Abraham, "What did you have in view, that you have done this thing?"

¹¹And Abraham said, "Because I thought, surely the fear of God *is* not in this place; and they will kill me on account of my wife. ¹²But indeed *she is* truly my sister. She *is* the

daughter of my father, but not the daughter of my mother; and she became my wife. ¹³And it came to pass, when God caused me to wander from my father's house, that I said to her, 'This *is* your kindness that you should do for me: in every place, wherever we go, say of me, "He *is* my brother." ' "

¹⁴Then Abimelech took sheep, oxen, and male and female servants, and gave *them* to Abraham; and he restored Sarah his wife to him. ¹⁵And Abimelech said, "See, my land *is* before you; dwell where it pleases you." ¹⁶Then to Sarah he said, "Behold, I have given your brother a thousand *pieces* of silver; indeed this vindicates you[a] before all who *are* with you and before everybody." Thus she was rebuked.

¹⁷So Abraham prayed to God; and God healed Abimelech, his wife, and his female servants. Then they bore *children*; ¹⁸for the LORD had closed up all the wombs of the house of Abimelech because of Sarah, Abraham's wife.

Isaac Is Born

21 And the LORD visited Sarah as He had said, and the LORD did for Sarah as He had spoken. ²For Sarah conceived and bore Abraham a son in his old age, at the set time of which God had spoken to him. ³And Abraham called the name of his son who was born to him—whom Sarah bore to him—Isaac. ⁴Then Abraham circumcised his son Isaac when he was eight days old, as God had commanded him. ⁵Now Abraham was one hundred years old when his son Isaac was born to him. ⁶And Sarah said, "God has made me laugh, *and* all who hear will laugh with me." ⁷She also said, "Who would have said to Abraham that Sarah would nurse children? For I have borne *him* a son in his old age."

> **21:1 the LORD visited Sarah.** Exactly as God had promised, a son was born to the aged couple, and the 25 year suspense ended. Their laughter of derision turned to rejoicing.

Hagar and Ishmael Depart

⁸So the child grew and was weaned. And Abraham made a great feast on the same day that Isaac was weaned.

⁹And Sarah saw the son of Hagar the Egyptian, whom she had borne to Abraham, scoffing. ¹⁰Therefore she said to Abraham, "Cast out this bondwoman and her son; for the son of this bondwoman shall not be heir with my son, *namely* with Isaac." ¹¹And the matter was very displeasing in Abraham's sight because of his son.

¹²But God said to Abraham, "Do not let it be displeasing in your sight because of the lad or because of your bondwoman. Whatever Sarah has said to you, listen to her voice; for in Isaac your seed shall be called. ¹³Yet I will also make a nation of the son of the bondwoman, because he *is* your seed."

¹⁴So Abraham rose early in the morning, and took bread and a skin of water; and putting *it* on her shoulder, he gave *it* and the boy to Hagar, and sent her away. Then she departed and wandered in the Wilderness of Beersheba. ¹⁵And the water in the skin was used up, and she placed the boy under one of the shrubs. ¹⁶Then she went and sat down across from *him* at a distance of about a bowshot; for she said to herself, "Let me not see the death of the boy." So she sat opposite *him*, and lifted her voice and wept.

¹⁷And God heard the voice of the lad. Then the angel of God called to Hagar out of heaven, and said to her, "What ails you, Hagar? Fear not, for God has heard the voice of the lad where he *is*. ¹⁸Arise, lift up the lad and hold him with your hand, for I will make him a great nation."

> **21:17 God heard the voice of the lad.** Desperation turned Ishmael's former scoffing (v. 9) into a cry of anguish, as he feared probable death from thirst (vv. 15,16). God heard his cries, just as He had heard Hagar's cries years before, reminding Hagar of the child's given name ("God hears," see 16:11) and of God's promise made to Abraham about her son (17:20).

¹⁹Then God opened her eyes, and she saw a well of water. And she went and filled the skin with water, and gave the lad a drink. ²⁰So God was with the lad; and he grew and dwelt in the wilderness, and became an archer. ²¹He dwelt in the Wilderness of Paran; and his mother took a wife for him from the land of Egypt.

20:16 [a]Literally *it is a covering of the eyes for you*

A Covenant with Abimelech

²²And it came to pass at that time that Abimelech and Phichol, the commander of his army, spoke to Abraham, saying, "God *is* with you in all that you do. ²³Now therefore, swear to me by God that you will not deal falsely with me, with my offspring, or with my posterity; but that according to the kindness that I have done to you, you will do to me and to the land in which you have dwelt."

²⁴And Abraham said, "I will swear."

²⁵Then Abraham rebuked Abimelech because of a well of water which Abimelech's servants had seized. ²⁶And Abimelech said, "I do not know who has done this thing; you did not tell me, nor had I heard *of it* until today." ²⁷So Abraham took sheep and oxen and gave them to Abimelech, and the two of them made a covenant. ²⁸And Abraham set seven ewe lambs of the flock by themselves.

²⁹Then Abimelech asked Abraham, "What *is the meaning of* these seven ewe lambs which you have set by themselves?"

³⁰And he said, "You will take *these* seven ewe lambs from my hand, that they may be my witness that I have dug this well." ³¹Therefore he called that place Beersheba,ᵃ because the two of them swore an oath there.

³²Thus they made a covenant at Beersheba. So Abimelech rose with Phichol, the commander of his army, and they returned to the land of the Philistines. ³³Then *Abraham* planted a tamarisk tree in Beersheba, and there called on the name of the LORD, the Everlasting God. ³⁴And Abraham stayed in the land of the Philistines many days.

Abraham's Faith Confirmed

22 Now it came to pass after these things that God tested Abraham, and said to him, "Abraham!"

And he said, "Here I am."

²Then He said, "Take now your son, your only *son* Isaac, whom you love, and go to the land of Moriah, and offer him there as a burnt offering on one of the mountains of which I shall tell you."

³So Abraham rose early in the morning and saddled his donkey, and took two of his young men with him, and Isaac his son; and he split the wood for the burnt offering, and arose and went to the place of which God had told him. ⁴Then on the third day Abraham lifted his eyes and saw the place afar off. ⁵And Abraham said to his young men, "Stay here with the donkey; the lad ᵃ and I will go yonder and worship, and we will come back to you."

> **22:5 the lad and I will go...we will come back.** The 3-day journey gave Abraham much time to reflect on God's startling commands to sacrifice his son, who was now over 20 years old. This was a special testing for Abraham, but without wavering or questioning God's purposes, Abraham confidently assured his servants that he and Isaac would return. Hebrews 11:17–19 reveals that he was so confident in the permanence of God's promise that he believed that if Isaac were killed, then God would raise him from the dead or provide a substitute for him.

⁶So Abraham took the wood of the burnt offering and laid *it* on Isaac his son; and he took the fire in his hand, and a knife, and the two of them went together. ⁷But Isaac spoke to Abraham his father and said, "My father!"

And he said, "Here I am, my son."

Then he said, "Look, the fire and the wood, but where *is* the lamb for a burnt offering?"

⁸And Abraham said, "My son, God will provide for Himself the lamb for a burnt offering." So the two of them went together.

⁹Then they came to the place of which God had told him. And Abraham built an altar there and placed the wood in order; and he bound Isaac his son and laid him on the altar, upon the wood. ¹⁰And Abraham stretched out his hand and took the knife to slay his son.

¹¹But the Angel of the LORD called to him from heaven and said, "Abraham, Abraham!"

So he said, "Here I am."

¹²And He said, "Do not lay your hand on the lad, or do anything to him; for now I know that you fear God, since you have not withheld your son, your only *son*, from Me."

¹³Then Abraham lifted his eyes and looked, and there behind *him was* a ram

---

21:31 ᵃLiterally *Well of the Oath* or *Well of the Seven*   22:5 ᵃOr *young man*

caught in a thicket by its horns. So Abraham went and took the ram, and offered it up for a burnt offering instead of his son. [14]And Abraham called the name of the place, The-LORD-Will-Provide;[a] as it is said *to* this day, "In the Mount of the LORD it shall be provided."

> **22:13 instead of his son.** The idea of substitutionary atonement is introduced, which would find its fulfillment in the death of Christ (Is. 53:4–6; John 1:29; 2 Cor. 5:21).

[15]Then the Angel of the LORD called to Abraham a second time out of heaven, [16]and said: "By Myself I have sworn, says the LORD, because you have done this thing, and have not withheld your son, your only *son*— [17]blessing I will bless you, and multiplying I will multiply your descendants as the stars of the heaven and as the sand which *is* on the seashore; and your descendants shall possess the gate of their enemies. [18]In your seed all the nations of the earth shall be blessed, because you have obeyed My voice." [19]So Abraham returned to his young men, and they rose and went together to Beersheba; and Abraham dwelt at Beersheba.

The Family of Nahor
[20]Now it came to pass after these things that it was told Abraham, saying, "Indeed Milcah also has borne children to your brother Nahor: [21]Huz his firstborn, Buz his brother, Kemuel the father of Aram, [22]Chesed, Hazo, Pildash, Jidlaph, and Bethuel." [23]And Bethuel begot Rebekah.[a] These eight Milcah bore to Nahor, Abraham's brother. [24]His concubine, whose name was Reumah, also bore Tebah, Gaham, Thahash, and Maachah.

Sarah's Death and Burial
23 Sarah lived one hundred and twenty-seven years; *these were* the years of the life of Sarah. [2]So Sarah died in Kirjath Arba (that *is*, Hebron) in the land of Canaan, and Abraham came to mourn for Sarah and to weep for her.

[3]Then Abraham stood up from before his

> **23:1,2** Sarah's age—the only woman's age at death recorded in Scripture—suggests both her importance in God's plan and serves as an important reminder that she bore her only son well beyond childbearing age (at 90 years of age, see 17:17), to fulfill God's promise to her and Abraham.

dead, and spoke to the sons of Heth, saying, [4]"I *am* a foreigner and a visitor among you. Give me property for a burial place among you, that I may bury my dead out of my sight."

[5]And the sons of Heth answered Abraham, saying to him, [6]"Hear us, my lord: You *are* a mighty prince among us; bury your dead in the choicest of our burial places. None of us will withhold from you his burial place, that you may bury your dead."

[7]Then Abraham stood up and bowed himself to the people of the land, the sons of Heth. [8]And he spoke with them, saying, "If it is your wish that I bury my dead out of my sight, hear me, and meet with Ephron the son of Zohar for me, [9]that he may give me the cave of Machpelah which he has, which *is* at the end of his field. Let him give it to me at the full price, as property for a burial place among you."

[10]Now Ephron dwelt among the sons of Heth; and Ephron the Hittite answered Abraham in the presence of the sons of Heth, all who entered at the gate of his city, saying, [11]"No, my lord, hear me: I give you the field and the cave that *is* in it; I give it to you in the presence of the sons of my people. I give it to you. Bury your dead!"

[12]Then Abraham bowed himself down before the people of the land; [13]and he spoke to Ephron in the hearing of the people of the land, saying, "If you *will give it,* please hear me. I will give you money for the field; take *it* from me and I will bury my dead there."

[14]And Ephron answered Abraham, saying to him, [15]"My lord, listen to me; the land *is worth* four hundred shekels of silver. What *is* that between you and me? So bury your dead." [16]And Abraham listened to Ephron; and Abraham weighed out the silver for Ephron which he had named in the hearing of the sons of Heth, four hundred shekels of silver, currency of the merchants.

22:14 [a]Hebrew *YHWH Yireh*   22:23 [a]Spelled *Rebecca* in Romans 9:10

¹⁷So the field of Ephron which *was* in Machpelah, which *was* before Mamre, the field and the cave which *was* in it, and all the trees that *were* in the field, which *were* within all the surrounding borders, were deeded ¹⁸to Abraham as a possession in the presence of the sons of Heth, before all who went in at the gate of his city.

¹⁹And after this, Abraham buried Sarah his wife in the cave of the field of Machpelah, before Mamre (that *is*, Hebron) in the land of Canaan. ²⁰So the field and the cave that *is* in it were deeded to Abraham by the sons of Heth as property for a burial place.

A Bride for Isaac

24 Now Abraham was old, well advanced in age; and the LORD had blessed Abraham in all things. ²So Abraham said to the oldest servant of his house, who ruled over all that he had, "Please, put your hand under my thigh, ³and I will make you swear by the LORD, the God of heaven and the God of the earth, that you will not take a wife for my son from the daughters of the Canaanites, among whom I dwell; ⁴but you shall go to my country and to my family, and take a wife for my son Isaac."

24:2 the oldest servant...who ruled. Eliezer, at 85 years of age, had risen to steward, or "chief of staff," a position of substantial authority. If Abraham had died without a son, he would have received all of Abraham's wealth. He loyally served Isaac as well as Abraham, even though Isaac displaced him as heir.

⁵And the servant said to him, "Perhaps the woman will not be willing to follow me to this land. Must I take your son back to the land from which you came?"

⁶But Abraham said to him, "Beware that you do not take my son back there. ⁷The LORD God of heaven, who took me from my father's house and from the land of my family, and who spoke to me and swore to me, saying, 'To your descendants[a] I give this land,' He will send His angel before you, and you shall take a wife for my son from there. ⁸And if the woman is not willing to follow you, then you will be released from this oath; only do not take my son back there." ⁹So the servant put his hand

under the thigh of Abraham his master, and swore to him concerning this matter.

¹⁰Then the servant took ten of his master's camels and departed, for all his master's goods *were in* his hand. And he arose and went to Mesopotamia, to the city of Nahor. ¹¹And he made his camels kneel down outside the city by a well of water at evening time, the time when women go out to draw *water.* ¹²Then he said, "O LORD God of my master Abraham, please give me success this day, and show kindness to my master Abraham. ¹³Behold, *here* I stand by the well of water, and the daughters of the men of the city are coming out to draw water. ¹⁴Now let it be that the young woman to whom I say, 'Please let down your pitcher that I may drink,' and she says, 'Drink, and I will also give your camels a drink'—*let* her *be the one* You have appointed for Your servant Isaac. And by this I will know that You have shown kindness to my master."

24:12–14 The steward's prayer showed not only his trust in God to provide but also the selflessness with which he served Abraham. His patience after prayer, his worship at answered prayer, and his acknowledgment of divine guidance also portrayed his faith.

¹⁵And it happened, before he had finished speaking, that behold, Rebekah, who was born to Bethuel, son of Milcah, the wife of Nahor, Abraham's brother, came out with her pitcher on her shoulder. ¹⁶Now the young woman *was* very beautiful to behold, a virgin; no man had known her. And she went down to the well, filled her pitcher, and came up. ¹⁷And the servant ran to meet her and said, "Please let me drink a little water from your pitcher."

¹⁸So she said, "Drink, my lord." Then she quickly let her pitcher down to her hand, and gave him a drink. ¹⁹And when she had finished giving him a drink, she said, "I will draw *water* for your camels also, until they have finished drinking." ²⁰Then she quickly emptied her pitcher into the trough, ran back to the well to draw *water,* and drew for all his camels. ²¹And the man, wondering at her, remained silent so as to know whether the LORD had made his journey prosperous or not.

24:7 ᵃLiterally *seed*

²²So it was, when the camels had finished drinking, that the man took a golden nose ring weighing half a shekel, and two bracelets for her wrists weighing ten *shekels* of gold, ²³and said, "Whose daughter *are* you? Tell me, please, is there room *in* your father's house for us to lodge?"

²⁴So she said to him, "I *am* the daughter of Bethuel, Milcah's son, whom she bore to Nahor." ²⁵Moreover she said to him, "We have both straw and feed enough, and room to lodge."

²⁶Then the man bowed down his head and worshiped the LORD. ²⁷And he said, "Blessed *be* the LORD God of my master Abraham, who has not forsaken His mercy and His truth toward my master. As for me, being on the way, the LORD led me to the house of my master's brethren." ²⁸So the young woman ran and told her mother's household these things.

²⁹Now Rebekah had a brother whose name *was* Laban, and Laban ran out to the man by the well. ³⁰So it came to pass, when he saw the nose ring, and the bracelets on his sister's wrists, and when he heard the words of his sister Rebekah, saying, "Thus the man spoke to me," that he went to the man. And there he stood by the camels at the well. ³¹And he said, "Come in, O blessed of the LORD! Why do you stand outside? For I have prepared the house, and a place for the camels."

³²Then the man came to the house. And he unloaded the camels, and provided straw and feed for the camels, and water to wash his feet and the feet of the men who *were* with him. ³³*Food* was set before him to eat, but he said, "I will not eat until I have told about my errand."

24:33 I will not eat until. Eliezer focused on his assignment and refused to eat until he could explain his assignment and the Lord's blessings upon his master Abraham and his trip. He tried to immediately conclude his task and return home. This is the portrait of a committed, faithful, and selfless servant!

And he said, "Speak on."

³⁴So he said, "I *am* Abraham's servant. ³⁵The LORD has blessed my master greatly, and he has become great; and He has given him flocks and herds, silver and gold, male and female servants, and camels and don-keys. ³⁶And Sarah my master's wife bore a son to my master when she was old; and to him he has given all that he has. ³⁷Now my master made me swear, saying, 'You shall not take a wife for my son from the daughters of the Canaanites, in whose land I dwell; ³⁸but you shall go to my father's house and to my family, and take a wife for my son.' ³⁹And I said to my master, 'Perhaps the woman will not follow me.' ⁴⁰But he said to me, 'The LORD, before whom I walk, will send His angel with you and prosper your way; and you shall take a wife for my son from my family and from my father's house. ⁴¹You will be clear from this oath when you arrive among my family; for if they will not give *her* to you, then you will be released from my oath.'

⁴²"And this day I came to the well and said, 'O LORD God of my master Abraham, if You will now prosper the way in which I go, ⁴³behold, I stand by the well of water; and it shall come to pass that when the virgin comes out to draw *water*, and I say to her, "Please give me a little water from your pitcher to drink," ⁴⁴and she says to me, "Drink, and I will draw for your camels also,"—*let* her *be* the woman whom the LORD has appointed for my master's son.'

⁴⁵"But before I had finished speaking in my heart, there was Rebekah, coming out with her pitcher on her shoulder; and she went down to the well and drew *water*. And I said to her, 'Please let me drink.' ⁴⁶And she made haste and let her pitcher down from her *shoulder*, and said, 'Drink, and I will give your camels a drink also.' So I drank, and she gave the camels a drink also. ⁴⁷Then I asked her, and said, 'Whose daughter *are* you?' And she said, 'The daughter of Bethuel, Nahor's son, whom Milcah bore to him.' So I put the nose ring on her nose and the bracelets on her wrists. ⁴⁸And I bowed my head and worshiped the LORD, and blessed the LORD God of my master Abraham, who had led me in the way of truth to take the daughter of my master's brother for his son. ⁴⁹Now if you will deal kindly and truly with my master, tell me. And if not, tell me, that I may turn to the right hand or to the left."

⁵⁰Then Laban and Bethuel answered and said, "The thing comes from the LORD; we cannot speak to you either bad or good.

⁵¹Here *is* Rebekah before you; take *her* and go, and let her be your master's son's wife, as the LORD has spoken."

⁵²And it came to pass, when Abraham's servant heard their words, that he worshiped the LORD, *bowing himself* to the earth. ⁵³Then the servant brought out jewelry of silver, jewelry of gold, and clothing, and gave *them* to Rebekah. He also gave precious things to her brother and to her mother.

⁵⁴And he and the men who *were* with him ate and drank and stayed all night. Then they arose in the morning, and he said, "Send me away to my master."

⁵⁵But her brother and her mother said, "Let the young woman stay with us *a few* days, at least ten; after that she may go."

⁵⁶And he said to them, "Do not hinder me, since the LORD has prospered my way; send me away so that I may go to my master."

⁵⁷So they said, "We will call the young woman and ask her personally." ⁵⁸Then they called Rebekah and said to her, "Will you go with this man?"

And she said, "I will go."

24:57,58 Will you go with this man? Commendably, Rebekah showed her confident acceptance of what was providentially coming about in her life by leaving immediately with Eliezer. Her family's blessing for numerous offspring (v. 60) echoed God's promises to Abraham's family.

⁵⁹So they sent away Rebekah their sister and her nurse, and Abraham's servant and his men. ⁶⁰And they blessed Rebekah and said to her:

" Our sister, *may* you *become*
   The mother of thousands of ten
      thousands;
   And may your descendants possess
   The gates of those who hate them."

⁶¹Then Rebekah and her maids arose, and they rode on the camels and followed the man. So the servant took Rebekah and departed.

⁶²Now Isaac came from the way of Beer Lahai Roi, for he dwelt in the South. ⁶³And Isaac went out to meditate in the field in the evening; and he lifted his eyes and looked, and there, the camels *were* coming.

⁶⁴Then Rebekah lifted her eyes, and when she saw Isaac she dismounted from her camel; ⁶⁵for she had said to the servant, "Who *is* this man walking in the field to meet us?"

The servant said, "It *is* my master." So she took a veil and covered herself.

⁶⁶And the servant told Isaac all the things that he had done. ⁶⁷Then Isaac brought her into his mother Sarah's tent; and he took Rebekah and she became his wife, and he loved her. So Isaac was comforted after his mother's *death.*

24:67 his mother Sarah's tent. Isaac thus showed that he accepted her as his wife before he had even seen her beauty. When he did see her, "he loved her."

Abraham and Keturah

25 Abraham again took a wife, and her name *was* Keturah. ²And she bore him Zimran, Jokshan, Medan, Midian, Ishbak, and Shuah. ³Jokshan begot Sheba and Dedan. And the sons of Dedan were Asshurim, Letushim, and Leummim. ⁴And the sons of Midian *were* Ephah, Epher, Hanoch, Abidah, and Eldaah. All these *were* the children of Keturah.

⁵And Abraham gave all that he had to Isaac. ⁶But Abraham gave gifts to the sons of the concubines which Abraham had; and while he was still living he sent them eastward, away from Isaac his son, to the country of the east.

Abraham's Death and Burial

⁷This *is* the sum of the years of Abraham's life which he lived: one hundred and seventy-five years. ⁸Then Abraham breathed his last and died in a good old age, an old man and full *of years*, and was gathered to his people. ⁹And his sons Isaac and Ishmael buried him in the cave of Machpelah, which *is* before Mamre, in the field of Ephron the son of Zohar the Hittite, ¹⁰the field which Abraham purchased from

25:8 gathered to his people. A euphemism for death and an expression of personal continuance beyond death, which involved a reunion with previously departed friends. See Matt. 8:11; Luke 16:22,23.

the sons of Heth. There Abraham was buried, and Sarah his wife. [11]And it came to pass, after the death of Abraham, that God blessed his son Isaac. And Isaac dwelt at Beer Lahai Roi.

The Families of Ishmael and Isaac

[12]Now this *is* the genealogy of Ishmael, Abraham's son, whom Hagar the Egyptian, Sarah's maidservant, bore to Abraham. [13]And these *were* the names of the sons of Ishmael, by their names, according to their generations: The firstborn of Ishmael, Nebajoth; then Kedar, Adbeel, Mibsam, [14]Mishma, Dumah, Massa, [15]Hadar,[a] Tema, Jetur, Naphish, and Kedemah. [16]These *were* the sons of Ishmael and these *were* their names, by their towns and their settlements, twelve princes according to their nations. [17]These *were* the years of the life of Ishmael: one hundred and thirty-seven years; and he breathed his last and died, and was gathered to his people. [18](They dwelt from Havilah as far as Shur, which *is* east of Egypt as you go toward Assyria.) He died in the presence of all his brethren.

[19]This *is* the genealogy of Isaac, Abraham's son. Abraham begot Isaac. [20]Isaac was forty years old when he took Rebekah as wife, the daughter of Bethuel the Syrian of Padan Aram, the sister of Laban the Syrian. [21]Now Isaac pleaded with the LORD for his wife, because she *was* barren; and the LORD granted his plea, and Rebekah his wife conceived. [22]But the children struggled together within her; and she said, "If *all is* well, why *am I like* this?" So she went to inquire of the LORD.

[23]And the LORD said to her:

"Two nations *are* in your womb,
   Two peoples shall be separated from
     your body;

> **25:23 the older shall serve the younger.** This was contrary to the custom in patriarchal times, when the elder son enjoyed the privileges of precedence. At the father's death, he received a double share of the inheritance and became the recognized head of the family. God's sovereign elective purposes do not have to follow custom.

One people shall be stronger than the
   other,
And the older shall serve the
   younger."

[24]So when her days were fulfilled *for her* to give birth, indeed *there were* twins in her womb. [25]And the first came out red. *He was* like a hairy garment all over; so they called his name Esau.[a] [26]Afterward his brother came out, and his hand took hold of Esau's heel; so his name was called Jacob.[a] Isaac *was* sixty years old when she bore them.

[27]So the boys grew. And Esau was a skillful hunter, a man of the field; but Jacob was a mild man, dwelling in tents. [28]And Isaac loved Esau because he ate *of his* game, but Rebekah loved Jacob.

Esau Sells His Birthright

[29]Now Jacob cooked a stew; and Esau came in from the field, and he *was* weary. [30]And Esau said to Jacob, "Please feed me with that same red *stew,* for I *am* weary." Therefore his name was called Edom.[a]

[31]But Jacob said, "Sell me your birthright as of this day."

> **25:31 birthright.** A double portion of the inheritance and the right to be the family chief and priest.

[32]And Esau said, "Look, I *am* about to die; so what *is* this birthright to me?"

[33]Then Jacob said, "Swear to me as of this day."

So he swore to him, and sold his birthright to Jacob. [34]And Jacob gave Esau bread and stew of lentils; then he ate and drank, arose, and went his way. Thus Esau despised *his* birthright.

Isaac and Abimelech

26 There was a famine in the land, besides the first famine that was in the days of Abraham. And Isaac went to Abimelech king of the Philistines, in Gerar. [2]Then the LORD appeared to him and said: "Do not go down to Egypt; live in the land of which I shall tell you. [3]Dwell in this land, and I will be with you and bless you;

25:15 [a]Masoretic Text reads *Hadad.*   25:25 [a]Literally *Hairy*   25:26 [a]Literally *Supplanter*
25:30 [a]Literally *Red*

for to you and your descendants I give all these lands, and I will perform the oath which I swore to Abraham your father. ⁴And I will make your descendants multiply as the stars of heaven; I will give to your descendants all these lands; and in your seed all the nations of the earth shall be blessed; ⁵because Abraham obeyed My voice and kept My charge, My commandments, My statutes, and My laws."

⁶So Isaac dwelt in Gerar. ⁷And the men of the place asked about his wife. And he said, "She *is* my sister"; for he was afraid to say, "*She is* my wife," *because he thought,* "lest the men of the place kill me for Rebekah, because she *is* beautiful to behold." ⁸Now it came to pass, when he had been there a long time, that Abimelech king of the Philistines looked through a window, and saw, and there was Isaac, showing endearment to Rebekah his wife. ⁹Then Abimelech called Isaac and said, "Quite obviously she *is* your wife; so how could you say, 'She *is* my sister'?"

Isaac said to him, "Because I said, 'Lest I die on account of her.'"

¹⁰And Abimelech said, "What *is* this you have done to us? One of the people might soon have lain with your wife, and you would have brought guilt on us." ¹¹So Abimelech charged all *his* people, saying, "He who touches this man or his wife shall surely be put to death."

> **26:2–11** Isaac mixed obedience with deceit. Obeying God's command to dwell in the land yet lying about his wife Rebekah reflected familiar lies told by Abraham (see 12:10–14; 20:1–4).

¹²Then Isaac sowed in that land, and reaped in the same year a hundredfold; and the LORD blessed him. ¹³The man began to prosper, and continued prospering until he became very prosperous; ¹⁴for he had possessions of flocks and possessions of herds and a great number of servants. So the Philistines envied him. ¹⁵Now the Philistines had stopped up all the wells which his father's servants had dug in the days of Abraham his father, and they had filled them with earth. ¹⁶And Abimelech said to Isaac, "Go away from us, for you are much mightier than we."

¹⁷Then Isaac departed from there and pitched his tent in the Valley of Gerar, and dwelt there. ¹⁸And Isaac dug again the wells of water which they had dug in the days of Abraham his father, for the Philistines had stopped them up after the death of Abraham. He called them by the names which his father had called them.

¹⁹Also Isaac's servants dug in the valley, and found a well of running water there. ²⁰But the herdsmen of Gerar quarreled with Isaac's herdsmen, saying, "The water *is* ours." So he called the name of the well Esek,ᵃ because they quarreled with him. ²¹Then they dug another well, and they quarreled over that *one* also. So he called its name Sitnah.ᵃ ²²And he moved from there and dug another well, and they did not quarrel over it. So he called its name Rehoboth,ᵃ because he said, "For now the LORD has made room for us, and we shall be fruitful in the land."

²³Then he went up from there to Beersheba. ²⁴And the LORD appeared to him the same night and said, "I *am* the God of your father Abraham; do not fear, for I *am* with you. I will bless you and multiply your descendants for My servant Abraham's sake." ²⁵So he built an altar there and called on the name of the LORD, and he pitched his tent there; and there Isaac's servants dug a well.

²⁶Then Abimelech came to him from Gerar with Ahuzzath, one of his friends, and Phichol the commander of his army. ²⁷And Isaac said to them, "Why have you come to me, since you hate me and have sent me away from you?"

²⁸But they said, "We have certainly seen that the LORD is with you. So we said, 'Let there now be an oath between us, between you and us; and let us make a covenant with you, ²⁹that you will do us no harm, since we have not touched you, and since we have done nothing to you but good and have sent you away in peace. You *are* now the blessed of the LORD.'"

³⁰So he made them a feast, and they ate and drank. ³¹Then they arose early in the morning and swore an oath with one an-

---

26:20 ᵃLiterally *Quarrel*   26:21 ᵃLiterally *Enmity*   26:22 ᵃLiterally *Spaciousness*

other; and Isaac sent them away, and they departed from him in peace.

³²It came to pass the same day that Isaac's servants came and told him about the well which they had dug, and said to him, "We have found water." ³³So he called it Shebah.ᵃ Therefore the name of the city *is* Beersheba*ᵇ* to this day.

³⁴When Esau was forty years old, he took as wives Judith the daughter of Beeri the Hittite, and Basemath the daughter of Elon the Hittite. ³⁵And they were a grief of mind to Isaac and Rebekah.

26:35 grief of mind. Esau's choice of wives from among the neighboring Hittite women saddened his parents. He deliberately ignored the standard set by Abraham, who sent his servant to choose a wife from his own tribe for his son Issac (see 24:1-3). Abraham's higher motive was to prevent Isaac from marrying a pagan who might lead the people away from the one true God.

Isaac Blesses Jacob

27 Now it came to pass, when Isaac was old and his eyes were so dim that he could not see, that he called Esau his older son and said to him, "My son."

And he answered him, "Here I am."

27:1 At 137 years of age, blind Issac evidently thought he was near death and would not live much longer. He actually did live another 43 years.

²Then he said, "Behold now, I am old. I do not know the day of my death. ³Now therefore, please take your weapons, your quiver and your bow, and go out to the field and hunt game for me. ⁴And make me savory food, such as I love, and bring *it* to me that I may eat, that my soul may bless you before I die."

⁵Now Rebekah was listening when Isaac spoke to Esau his son. And Esau went to the field to hunt game and to bring *it*. ⁶So Rebekah spoke to Jacob her son, saying, "Indeed I heard your father speak to Esau your brother, saying, ⁷'Bring me game and make savory food for me, that I may eat it and bless you in the presence of the LORD before my death.' ⁸Now therefore, my son,

obey my voice according to what I command you. ⁹Go now to the flock and bring me from there two choice kids of the goats, and I will make savory food from them for your father, such as he loves. ¹⁰Then you shall take *it* to your father, that he may eat *it*, and that he may bless you before his death."

¹¹And Jacob said to Rebekah his mother, "Look, Esau my brother *is* a hairy man, and I *am* a smooth-*skinned* man. ¹²Perhaps my father will feel me, and I shall seem to be a deceiver to him; and I shall bring a curse on myself and not a blessing."

¹³But his mother said to him, "*Let* your curse *be* on me, my son; only obey my voice, and go, get *them* for me." ¹⁴And he went and got *them* and brought *them* to his mother, and his mother made savory food, such as his father loved. ¹⁵Then Rebekah took the choice clothes of her elder son Esau, which *were* with her in the house, and put them on Jacob her younger son. ¹⁶And she put the skins of the kids of the goats on his hands and on the smooth part of his neck. ¹⁷Then she gave the savory food and the bread, which she had prepared, into the hand of her son Jacob.

¹⁸So he went to his father and said, "My father."

And he said, "Here I am. Who *are* you, my son?"

¹⁹Jacob said to his father, "I *am* Esau your firstborn; I have done just as you told me; please arise, sit and eat of my game, that your soul may bless me."

²⁰But Isaac said to his son, "How *is it* that you have found *it* so quickly, my son?"

27:20 Because the LORD your God brought *it* to me. Isaac asked a perfectly legitimate question, because hunting took time and Jacob brought goats quickly from the pen. Jacob had an opportunity to confess and stop the deceit, but instead he continued to lie to sustain his previous lies. By the promise of God he would have received the birthright. He didn't need to scheme this deception with his mother, and it carried severe consequences: (1) he never saw his mother again; (2) Esau wanted him dead; (3) his uncle Laban deceived him; (4) his family life was filled with conflict; and (5) he was exiled from his family for years.

26:33 ᵃLiterally *Oath* or *Seven* ᵇLiterally *Well of the Oath* or *Well of the Seven*

And he said, "Because the LORD your God brought *it* to me."

²¹Isaac said to Jacob, "Please come near, that I may feel you, my son, whether you *are* really my son Esau or not." ²²So Jacob went near to Isaac his father, and he felt him and said, "The voice *is* Jacob's voice, but the hands *are* the hands of Esau." ²³And he did not recognize him, because his hands were hairy like his brother Esau's hands; so he blessed him.

²⁴Then he said, "*Are* you really my son Esau?"

He said, "I *am*."

²⁵He said, "Bring *it* near to me, and I will eat of my son's game, so that my soul may bless you." So he brought *it* near to him, and he ate; and he brought him wine, and he drank. ²⁶Then his father Isaac said to him, "Come near now and kiss me, my son." ²⁷And he came near and kissed him; and he smelled the smell of his clothing, and blessed him and said:

"Surely, the smell of my son
    Is like the smell of a field
    Which the LORD has blessed.
28   Therefore may God give you
    Of the dew of heaven,
    Of the fatness of the earth,
    And plenty of grain and wine.
29   Let peoples serve you,
    And nations bow down to you.
    Be master over your brethren,
    And let your mother's sons bow down
        to you.
    Cursed *be* everyone who curses you,
    And blessed *be* those who bless you!"

Esau's Lost Hope

³⁰Now it happened, as soon as Isaac had finished blessing Jacob, and Jacob had scarcely gone out from the presence of Isaac his father, that Esau his brother came in from his hunting. ³¹He also had made savory food, and brought it to his father, and said to his father, "Let my father arise and eat of his son's game, that your soul may bless me."

³²And his father Isaac said to him, "Who *are* you?"

So he said, "I *am* your son, your firstborn, Esau."

³³Then Isaac trembled exceedingly, and said, "Who? Where *is* the one who hunted game and brought *it* to me? I ate all *of it* before you came, and I have blessed him— *and* indeed he shall be blessed."

> **27:33 Isaac trembled exceedingly.** Visibly shocked when the scandal was uncovered by Esau's entrance, the father must have remembered the Lord's words to Rebekah (25:33). He refused to withdraw the blessing and emphatically affirmed its validity that Jacob would be blessed and would be master over his brother. Realization that he had opposed God's will all those years likely made the shock more severe.

³⁴When Esau heard the words of his father, he cried with an exceedingly great and bitter cry, and said to his father, "Bless me—me also, O my father!"

³⁵But he said, "Your brother came with deceit and has taken away your blessing."

³⁶And *Esau* said, "Is he not rightly named Jacob? For he has supplanted me these two times. He took away my birthright, and now look, he has taken away my blessing!" And he said, "Have you not reserved a blessing for me?"

³⁷Then Isaac answered and said to Esau, "Indeed I have made him your master, and all his brethren I have given to him as servants; with grain and wine I have sustained him. What shall I do now for you, my son?"

³⁸And Esau said to his father, "Have you only one blessing, my father? Bless me— me also, O my father!" And Esau lifted up his voice and wept.

³⁹Then Isaac his father answered and said to him:

"Behold, your dwelling shall be of the
        fatness of the earth,
    And of the dew of heaven from
        above.
40   By your sword you shall live,
    And you shall serve your brother;
    And it shall come to pass, when you
        become restless,
    That you shall break his yoke from
        your neck."

Jacob Escapes from Esau

⁴¹So Esau hated Jacob because of the blessing with which his father blessed him, and Esau said in his heart, "The days of

mourning for my father are at hand; then I will kill my brother Jacob."

⁴²And the words of Esau her older son were told to Rebekah. So she sent and called Jacob her younger son, and said to him, "Surely your brother Esau comforts himself concerning you *by intending* to kill you. ⁴³Now therefore, my son, obey my voice: arise, flee to my brother Laban in Haran. ⁴⁴And stay with him a few days, until your brother's fury turns away, ⁴⁵until your brother's anger turns away from you, and he forgets what you have done to him; then I will send and bring you from there. Why should I be bereaved also of you both in one day?"

⁴⁶And Rebekah said to Isaac, "I am weary of my life because of the daughters of Heth; if Jacob takes a wife of the daughters of Heth, like these *who are* the daughters of the land, what good will my life be to me?"

28 Then Isaac called Jacob and blessed him, and charged him, and said to him: "You shall not take a wife from the daughters of Canaan. ²Arise, go to Padan Aram, to the house of Bethuel your mother's father; and take yourself a wife from there of the daughters of Laban your mother's brother.

³   "May God Almighty bless you,
     And make you fruitful and multiply
        you,
     That you may be an assembly of
        peoples;
⁴   And give you the blessing of
        Abraham,
     To you and your descendants with
        you,
     That you may inherit the land
     In which you are a stranger,
     Which God gave to Abraham."

> **28:3,4** This patriarchal blessing revealed a change in Isaac's thinking. He had come to understand that the diving blessings promised to Abraham would go through Jacob, and not Esau, which was a significant reversal of his prior wishes (see 27:27–29).

⁵So Isaac sent Jacob away, and he went to Padan Aram, to Laban the son of Bethuel the Syrian, the brother of Rebekah, the mother of Jacob and Esau.

Esau Marries Mahalath

⁶Esau saw that Isaac had blessed Jacob and sent him away to Padan Aram to take himself a wife from there, *and that* as he blessed him he gave him a charge, saying, "You shall not take a wife from the daughters of Canaan," ⁷and that Jacob had obeyed his father and his mother and had gone to Padan Aram. ⁸Also Esau saw that the daughters of Canaan did not please his father Isaac. ⁹So Esau went to Ishmael and took Mahalath the daughter of Ishmael, Abraham's son, the sister of Nebajoth, to be his wife in addition to the wives he had.

Jacob's Vow at Bethel

¹⁰Now Jacob went out from Beersheba and went toward Haran. ¹¹So he came to a certain place and stayed there all night, because the sun had set. And he took one of the stones of that place and put it at his head, and he lay down in that place to sleep. ¹²Then he dreamed, and behold, a ladder *was* set up on the earth, and its top reached to heaven; and there the angels of God were ascending and descending on it.

> **28:12 a ladder...angels of God were ascending and descending.** This dream was to encourage the lonely traveler that the Lord was personally involved in the affairs of earth, especially as they related to the divine covenant promises to Jacob. God's own appointed angelic messengers ensured the carrying out of His will and plans.

¹³And behold, the LORD stood above it and said: "I *am* the LORD God of Abraham your father and the God of Isaac; the land on which you lie I will give to you and your descendants. ¹⁴Also your descendants shall be as the dust of the earth; you shall spread abroad to the west and the east, to the north and the south; and in you and in your seed all the families of the earth shall be blessed. ¹⁵Behold, I *am* with you and will keep you wherever you go, and will bring you back to this land; for I will not leave you until I have done what I have spoken to you."

¹⁶Then Jacob awoke from his sleep and said, "Surely the LORD is in this place, and I did not know *it*." ¹⁷And he was afraid and said, "How awesome *is* this place! This *is* none other than the house of God, and this *is* the gate of heaven!"

¹⁸Then Jacob rose early in the morning, and took the stone that he had put at his head, set it up as a pillar, and poured oil on top of it. ¹⁹And he called the name of that place Bethel;^a but the name of that city had been Luz previously. ²⁰Then Jacob made a vow, saying, "If God will be with me, and keep me in this way that I am going, and give me bread to eat and clothing to put on, ²¹so that I come back to my father's house in peace, then the LORD shall be my God. ²²And this stone which I have set as a pillar shall be God's house, and of all that You give me I will surely give a tenth to You."

Jacob Meets Rachel

29 So Jacob went on his journey and came to the land of the people of the East. ²And he looked, and saw a well in the field; and behold, there *were* three flocks of sheep lying by it; for out of that well they watered the flocks. A large stone *was* on the well's mouth. ³Now all the flocks would be gathered there; and they would roll the stone from the well's mouth, water the sheep, and put the stone back in its place on the well's mouth.

⁴And Jacob said to them, "My brethren, where *are* you from?"

And they said, "We *are* from Haran."

> **29:1–4** Conveniently meeting at Jacob's destination, these shepherds who knew both Laban and Rachel reflected God's directing hand in Jacob's life, just as He had promised (28:15).

⁵Then he said to them, "Do you know Laban the son of Nahor?"

And they said, "We know him."

⁶So he said to them, "Is he well?"

And they said, "*He is* well. And look, his daughter Rachel is coming with the sheep."

⁷Then he said, "Look, *it is* still high day; *it is* not time for the cattle to be gathered together. Water the sheep, and go and feed *them*."

⁸But they said, "We cannot until all the flocks are gathered together, and they have rolled the stone from the well's mouth; then we water the sheep."

⁹Now while he was still speaking with them, Rachel came with her father's sheep, for she was a shepherdess. ¹⁰And it came to pass, when Jacob saw Rachel the daughter of Laban his mother's brother, and the sheep of Laban his mother's brother, that Jacob went near and rolled the stone from the well's mouth, and watered the flock of Laban his mother's brother. ¹¹Then Jacob kissed Rachel, and lifted up his voice and wept. ¹²And Jacob told Rachel that he *was* her father's relative and that he *was* Rebekah's son. So she ran and told her father.

¹³Then it came to pass, when Laban heard the report about Jacob his sister's son, that he ran to meet him, and embraced him and kissed him, and brought him to his house. So he told Laban all these things. ¹⁴And Laban said to him, "Surely you *are* my bone and my flesh." And he stayed with him for a month.

Jacob Marries Leah and Rachel

¹⁵Then Laban said to Jacob, "Because you *are* my relative, should you therefore serve me for nothing? Tell me, what *should* your wages *be*?" ¹⁶Now Laban had two daughters: the name of the elder *was* Leah, and the name of the younger *was* Rachel. ¹⁷Leah's eyes *were* delicate, but Rachel was beautiful of form and appearance.

> **29:17 eyes *were* delicate.** Probably means that her eyes were a pale color rather than the dark, sparkling eyes most common. Such paleness was considered a blemish.

¹⁸Now Jacob loved Rachel; so he said, "I will serve you seven years for Rachel your younger daughter." ¹⁹And Laban said, "*It is* better that I give her to you than that I should give her to another man. Stay with me." ²⁰So Jacob served seven years for Rachel, and they seemed *only* a few days to him because of the love he had for her.

²¹Then Jacob said to Laban, "Give *me* my wife, for my days are fulfilled, that I may go in to her." ²²And Laban gathered together all the men of the place and made a feast. ²³Now it came to pass in the evening, that

---

28:19 ^aLiterally *House of God*

he took Leah his daughter and brought her to Jacob; and he went in to her. ²⁴And Laban gave his maid Zilpah to his daughter Leah *as* a maid. ²⁵So it came to pass in the morning, that behold, it *was* Leah. And he said to Laban, "What is this you have done to me? Was it not for Rachel that I served you? Why then have you deceived me?"

²⁶And Laban said, "It must not be done so in our country, to give the younger before the firstborn. ²⁷Fulfill her week, and we will give you this one also for the service which you will serve with me still another seven years."

²⁸Then Jacob did so and fulfilled her week. So he gave him his daughter Rachel as wife also. ²⁹And Laban gave his maid Bilhah to his daughter Rachel as a maid. ³⁰Then *Jacob* also went in to Rachel, and he also loved Rachel more than Leah. And he served with Laban still another seven years.

> **29:18–30** His love for Rachel motivated Jacob to work happily during the first seven years in Laban's household, as an adopted son rather than a mere worker. But Jacob the deceiver was about to be deceived. Because of local marriage customs, Laban's greed for more dowry, and Jacob's love for Rachel, Jacob had to work another seven years and now had two wives who jealously competed against each other in childbearing.

The Children of Jacob

³¹When the LORD saw that Leah *was* unloved, He opened her womb; but Rachel *was* barren. ³²So Leah conceived and bore a son, and she called his name Reuben;*ᵃ* for she said, "The LORD has surely looked on my affliction. Now therefore, my husband will love me." ³³Then she conceived again and bore a son, and said, "Because the LORD has heard that I *am* unloved, He has therefore given me this *son* also." And she called his name Simeon.*ᵃ* ³⁴She conceived again and bore a son, and said, "Now this time my husband will become attached to me, because I have borne him three sons." Therefore his name was called Levi.*ᵃ* ³⁵And she conceived again and bore a son, and said, "Now I will praise the LORD." Therefore she called his name Judah.*ᵃ* Then she stopped bearing.

30 Now when Rachel saw that she bore Jacob no children, Rachel envied her sister, and said to Jacob, "Give me children, or else I die!"

²And Jacob's anger was aroused against Rachel, and he said, "*Am* I in the place of God, who has withheld from you the fruit of the womb?"

³So she said, "Here is my maid Bilhah; go in to her, and she will bear *a child* on my knees, that I also may have children by her." ⁴Then she gave him Bilhah her maid as wife, and Jacob went in to her. ⁵And Bilhah conceived and bore Jacob a son. ⁶Then Rachel said, "God has judged my case; and He has also heard my voice and given me a son." Therefore she called his name Dan.*ᵃ* ⁷And Rachel's maid Bilhah conceived again and bore Jacob a second son. ⁸Then Rachel said, "With great wrestlings I have wrestled with my sister, *and* indeed I have prevailed." So she called his name Naphtali.*ᵃ*

⁹When Leah saw that she had stopped bearing, she took Zilpah her maid and gave her to Jacob as wife. ¹⁰And Leah's maid Zilpah bore Jacob a son. ¹¹Then Leah said, "A troop comes!"*ᵃ* So she called his name Gad.*ᵇ* ¹²And Leah's maid Zilpah bore Jacob a second son. ¹³Then Leah said, "I am happy, for the daughters will call me blessed." So she called his name Asher.*ᵃ*

¹⁴Now Reuben went in the days of wheat harvest and found mandrakes in the field, and brought them to his mother Leah. Then Rachel said to Leah, "Please give me *some* of your son's mandrakes."

¹⁵But she said to her, "*Is it* a small matter that you have taken away my husband? Would you take away my son's mandrakes also?"

And Rachel said, "Therefore he will lie with you tonight for your son's mandrakes."

¹⁶When Jacob came out of the field in the evening, Leah went out to meet him and said, "You must come in to me, for I have

---

29:32 *ᵃ*Literally *See, a Son*   29:33 *ᵃ*Literally *Heard*   29:34 *ᵃ*Literally *Attached*   29:35 *ᵃ*Literally *Praise*   30:6 *ᵃ*Literally *Judge*   30:8 *ᵃ*Literally *My Wrestling*   30:11 *ᵃ*Following Qere, Syriac, and Targum; Kethib, Septuagint, and Vulgate read *in fortune.* *ᵇ*Literally *Troop* or *Fortune*   30:13 *ᵃ*Literally *Happy*

surely hired you with my son's mandrakes." And he lay with her that night.

¹⁷And God listened to Leah, and she conceived and bore Jacob a fifth son. ¹⁸Leah said, "God has given me my wages, because I have given my maid to my husband." So she called his name Issachar.ᵃ ¹⁹Then Leah conceived again and bore Jacob a sixth son. ²⁰And Leah said, "God has endowed me *with* a good endowment; now my husband will dwell with me, because I have borne him six sons." So she called his name Zebulun.ᵃ ²¹Afterward she bore a daughter, and called her name Dinah.

> **30:1–21** This competition between the two sisters/ wives became a bitter rivalry, as seen in their using their maids as surrogate mothers, in their bartering for time with the husband, in their desperate prayers to the Lord, and in their accusations and malice toward one another. This intense domestic conflict shows that the evil lay in the system of bigamy itself, which is a violation of God's ordinance (Gen. 2:24), and which cannot yield happiness.

²²Then God remembered Rachel, and God listened to her and opened her womb. ²³And she conceived and bore a son, and said, "God has taken away my reproach." ²⁴So she called his name Joseph,ᵃ and said, "The LORD shall add to me another son."

Jacob's Agreement with Laban

²⁵And it came to pass, when Rachel had borne Joseph, that Jacob said to Laban, "Send me away, that I may go to my own place and to my country. ²⁶Give *me* my wives and my children for whom I have served you, and let me go; for you know my service which I have done for you."

²⁷And Laban said to him, "Please *stay*, if I have found favor in your eyes, *for* I have learned by experience that the LORD has blessed me for your sake." ²⁸Then he said, "Name me your wages, and I will give *it*."

²⁹So *Jacob* said to him, "You know how I have served you and how your livestock has been with me. ³⁰For what you had before I *came was* little, and it has increased to a great amount; the LORD has blessed you since my coming. And now, when shall I also provide for my own house?"

³¹So he said, "What shall I give you?"

And Jacob said, "You shall not give me anything. If you will do this thing for me, I will again feed and keep your flocks: ³²Let me pass through all your flock today, removing from there all the speckled and spotted sheep, and all the brown ones among the lambs, and the spotted and speckled among the goats; and *these* shall be my wages. ³³So my righteousness will answer for me in time to come, when the subject of my wages comes before you: every one that *is* not speckled and spotted among the goats, and brown among the lambs, will be considered stolen, if *it is* with me."

³⁴And Laban said, "Oh, that it were according to your word!" ³⁵So he removed that day the male goats that were speckled and spotted, all the female goats that were speckled and spotted, every one that had *some* white in it, and all the brown ones among the lambs, and gave *them* into the hand of his sons. ³⁶Then he put three days' journey between himself and Jacob, and Jacob fed the rest of Laban's flocks.

> **30:31–36 What shall I give you?** Laban wanted Jacob to stay and asked what it would take to keep him. Jacob wanted nothing except to be in a position for God to bless him. He was willing to stay but not to be further indebted to the scheming, selfish Laban. Jacob offered a plan that would give him as pay any speckled, spotted, striped, or abnormally colored animals born into the flocks. Since most of the animals were solid in color, Laban thought this was a small concession to Jacob. He even separated the abnormally and normally marked animals to prevent mixed breeding. With this plan, Jacob placed himself entirely in God's hands. Only the Lord could determine what animals would be Jacob's.

³⁷Now Jacob took for himself rods of green poplar and of the almond and chestnut trees, peeled white strips in them, and exposed the white which *was* in the rods. ³⁸And the rods which he had peeled, he set before the flocks in the gutters, in the watering troughs where the flocks came to drink, so that they should conceive when they came to drink. ³⁹So the flocks conceived before the rods, and the flocks brought forth streaked, speckled, and spotted. ⁴⁰Then Jacob separated the lambs, and

---

30:18 ᵃLiterally *Wages*   30:20 ᵃLiterally *Dwelling*   30:24 ᵃLiterally *He Will Add*

made the flocks face toward the streaked and all the brown in the flock of Laban; but he put his own flocks by themselves and did not put them with Laban's flock.

⁴¹And it came to pass, whenever the stronger livestock conceived, that Jacob placed the rods before the eyes of the livestock in the gutters, that they might conceive among the rods. ⁴²But when the flocks were feeble, he did not put *them* in; so the feebler were Laban's and the stronger Jacob's. ⁴³Thus the man became exceedingly prosperous, and had large flocks, female and male servants, and camels and donkeys.

30:37–42 rods. Because of Jacob's knowledge about livestock, he knew that uncommonly marked animals had a recessive gene, and he separated them to selectively breed more. He stimulated this process with the use of some methods such as the mandrakes (v. 14). Although they might appear superstitious, most likely Jacob knew that when the bark was peeled, a stimulant was released into the water to increase sexual activity. His plan was successful, and he gave God the credit for the success.

Jacob Flees from Laban

31 Now *Jacob* heard the words of Laban's sons, saying, "Jacob has taken away all that was our father's, and from what was our father's he has acquired all this wealth." ²And Jacob saw the countenance of Laban, and indeed it *was* not *favorable* toward him as before. ³Then the LORD said to Jacob, "Return to the land of your fathers and to your family, and I will be with you."

⁴So Jacob sent and called Rachel and Leah to the field, to his flock, ⁵and said to them, "I see your father's countenance, that it *is* not *favorable* toward me as before; but the God of my father has been with me. ⁶And you know that with all my might I have served your father. ⁷Yet your father has deceived me and changed my wages ten times, but God did not allow him to hurt me. ⁸If he said thus: 'The speckled shall be your wages,' then all the flocks bore speckled. And if he said thus: 'The streaked shall be your wages,' then all the flocks bore streaked. ⁹So God has taken away the livestock of your father and given *them* to me.

¹⁰"And it happened, at the time when the flocks conceived, that I lifted my eyes and saw in a dream, and behold, the rams which leaped upon the flocks *were* streaked, speckled, and gray-spotted. ¹¹Then the Angel of God spoke to me in a dream, saying, 'Jacob.' And I said, 'Here I am.' ¹²And He said, 'Lift your eyes now and see, all the rams which leap on the flocks *are* streaked, speckled, and gray-spotted; for I have seen all that La-

FALSE GODS IN THE OLD TESTAMENT

1. Rachel's household gods (Genesis 31:19)
2. The golden calf at Sinai (Exodus 32)
3. Nanna, the moon god of Ur, worshiped by Abraham before his salvation (Joshua 24:2)
4. Asherah, or Ashtaroth, the chief goddess of Tyre, referred to as the lady of the sea (Judges 6:24–32)
5. Dagon, the chief Philistine agriculture and sea god and father of Baal (Judges 16:23–30; 1 Samuel 5:1–7)
6. Ashtoreth, a Canaanite goddess, another consort of Baal (1 Samuel 7:3,4)
7. Molech, the god of the Ammonites and the most horrible idol in the Scriptures (1 Kings 11:7; 2 Chronicles 28:14; 33:6)
8. The two golden images made by King Jeroboam, set up at the shrines of Dan and Bethel (1 Kings 12:28–31)
9. Baal, the chief deity of Canaan (1 Kings 18:17–40; 2 Kings 10:28; 11:18)
10. Rimmon, the Syrian god of Naaman the leper (2 Kings 5:15–19)
11. Nishroch, the Assyrian god of Sennacherib (2 Kings 19:37)
12. Nebo, the Babylonian god of wisdom and literature (Isaiah 46:1)
13. Merodach, also called Marduk, the chief god of the Babylonian pantheon (Jeremiah 50:2)
14. Tammuz, the husband and brother of Ishtar (Asherah), goddess of fertility (Ezekiel 8:14)
15. The golden image in the plain of Dura (Daniel 2)

ban is doing to you. [13]I *am* the God of Bethel, where you anointed the pillar *and* where you made a vow to Me. Now arise, get out of this land, and return to the land of your family.' "

[14]Then Rachel and Leah answered and said to him, "Is there still any portion or inheritance for us in our father's house? [15]Are we not considered strangers by him? For he has sold us, and also completely consumed our money. [16]For all these riches which God has taken from our father are *really* ours and our children's; now then, whatever God has said to you, do it."

[17]Then Jacob rose and set his sons and his wives on camels. [18]And he carried away all his livestock and all his possessions which he had gained, his acquired livestock which he had gained in Padan Aram, to go to his father Isaac in the land of Canaan. [19]Now Laban had gone to shear his sheep, and Rachel had stolen the household idols that were her father's. [20]And Jacob stole away, unknown to Laban the Syrian, in that he did not tell him that he intended to flee. [21]So he fled with all that he had. He arose and crossed the river, and headed toward the mountains of Gilead.

31:20 stole away. For fear that Laban might forcefully retaliate against him, Jacob slipped away at an appropriate time. With all his entourage, this was not a simple exit.

Laban Pursues Jacob

[22]And Laban was told on the third day that Jacob had fled. [23]Then he took his brethren with him and pursued him for seven days' journey, and he overtook him in the mountains of Gilead. [24]But God had come to Laban the Syrian in a dream by night, and said to him, "Be careful that you speak to Jacob neither good nor bad."

[25]So Laban overtook Jacob. Now Jacob had pitched his tent in the mountains, and Laban with his brethren pitched in the mountains of Gilead. [26]And Laban said to Jacob: "What have you done, that you have stolen away unknown to me, and carried away my daughters like captives *taken* with the sword? [27]Why did you flee away secretly, and steal away from me, and not tell me; for I might

have sent you away with joy and songs, with timbrel and harp? [28]And you did not allow me to kiss my sons and my daughters. Now you have done foolishly in *so* doing. [29]It is in my power to do you harm, but the God of your father spoke to me last night, saying, 'Be careful that you speak to Jacob neither good nor bad.' [30]And now you have surely gone because you greatly long for your father's house, *but* why did you steal my gods?"

[31]Then Jacob answered and said to Laban, "Because I was afraid, for I said, 'Perhaps you would take your daughters from me by force.' [32]With whomever you find your gods, do not let him live. In the presence of our brethren, identify what I have of yours and take *it* with you." For Jacob did not know that Rachel had stolen them.

[33]And Laban went into Jacob's tent, into Leah's tent, and into the two maids' tents, but he did not find *them*. Then he went out of Leah's tent and entered Rachel's tent. [34]Now Rachel had taken the household idols, put them in the camel's saddle, and sat on them. And Laban searched all about the tent but did not find *them*. [35]And she said to her father, "Let it not displease my lord that I cannot rise before you, for the manner of women *is* with me." And he searched but did not find the household idols.

31:35 the manner of women. Rachel claimed she was having her menstrual period.

[36]Then Jacob was angry and rebuked Laban, and Jacob answered and said to Laban: "What *is* my trespass? What *is* my sin, that you have so hotly pursued me? [37]Although you have searched all my things, what part of your household things have you found? Set *it* here before my brethren and your brethren, that they may judge between us both! [38]These twenty years I *have been* with you; your ewes and your female goats have not miscarried their young, and I have not eaten the rams of your flock. [39]That which was torn *by beasts* I did not bring to you; I bore the loss of it. You required it from my hand, *whether* stolen by day or stolen by night. [40]*There* I was! In the day the drought consumed me, and the frost by

night, and my sleep departed from my eyes. ⁴¹Thus I have been in your house twenty years; I served you fourteen years for your two daughters, and six years for your flock, and you have changed my wages ten times. ⁴²Unless the God of my father, the God of Abraham and the Fear of Isaac, had been with me, surely now you would have sent me away empty-handed. God has seen my affliction and the labor of my hands, and rebuked *you* last night."

31:42 Fear of Isaac. Another divine name, signifying Jacob's reverence for the God who caused his father Isaac to revere Him. Also, see "the Fear of his father Isaac" (v. 53).

Laban's Covenant with Jacob

⁴³And Laban answered and said to Jacob, "*These* daughters *are* my daughters, and *these* children *are* my children, and *this* flock *is* my flock; all that you see *is* mine. But what can I do this day to these my daughters or to their children whom they have borne? ⁴⁴Now therefore, come, let us make a covenant, you and I, and let it be a witness between you and me."

⁴⁵So Jacob took a stone and set it up *as* a pillar. ⁴⁶Then Jacob said to his brethren, "Gather stones." And they took stones and made a heap, and they ate there on the heap. ⁴⁷Laban called it Jegar Sahadutha,ᵃ but Jacob called it Galeed.ᵇ ⁴⁸And Laban said, "This heap *is* a witness between you and me this day." Therefore its name was called Galeed, ⁴⁹also Mizpah,ᵃ because he said, "May the LORD watch between you and me when we are absent one from another. ⁵⁰If you afflict my daughters, or if you take *other* wives besides my daughters, *although* no man *is* with us—see, God *is* witness between you and me!"

⁵¹Then Laban said to Jacob, "Here is this heap and here is *this* pillar, which I have placed between you and me. ⁵²This heap *is* a witness, and *this* pillar *is* a witness, that I will not pass beyond this heap to you, and you will not pass beyond this heap and this pillar to me, for harm. ⁵³The God of Abraham, the God of Nahor, and the God of their father judge between us." And Jacob swore by the Fear of his father Isaac. ⁵⁴Then Jacob offered a sacrifice on the mountain, and called his brethren to eat bread. And they ate bread and stayed all night on the mountain. ⁵⁵And early in the morning Laban arose, and kissed his sons and daughters and blessed them. Then Laban departed and returned to his place.

Esau Comes to Meet Jacob

32 So Jacob went on his way, and the angels of God met him. ²When Jacob saw them, he said, "This *is* God's camp." And he called the name of that place Mahanaim.ᵃ

³Then Jacob sent messengers before him to Esau his brother in the land of Seir, the country of Edom. ⁴And he commanded them, saying, "Speak thus to my lord Esau, 'Thus your servant Jacob says: "I have dwelt with Laban and stayed there until now. ⁵I have oxen, donkeys, flocks, and male and female servants; and I have sent to tell my lord, that I may find favor in your sight." ' "

⁶Then the messengers returned to Jacob, saying, "We came to your brother Esau, and he also is coming to meet you, and four hundred men *are* with him." ⁷So Jacob was greatly afraid and distressed; and he divided the people that *were* with him, and the flocks and herds and camels, into two companies. ⁸And he said, "If Esau comes to the one company and attacks it, then the other company which is left will escape."

32:7 greatly afraid and distressed. Jacob had sought reconciliation with Esau, but the report of the envoys confirmed his suspicion that Esau's old threat to kill him had not abated over the years. He expected an attack and prepared by dividing his company of people and animals.

⁹Then Jacob said, "O God of my father Abraham and God of my father Isaac, the LORD who said to me, 'Return to your country and to your family, and I will deal well with you': ¹⁰I am not worthy of the least of all the mercies and of all the truth which You have shown Your servant; for I

31:47 ᵃLiterally, in Aramaic, *Heap of Witness* ᵇLiterally, in Hebrew, *Heap of Witness*
31:49 ᵃLiterally *Watch* 32:2 ᵃLiterally *Double Camp*

crossed over this Jordan with my staff, and now I have become two companies. [11]Deliver me, I pray, from the hand of my brother, from the hand of Esau; for I fear him, lest he come and attack me *and* the mother with the children. [12]For You said, 'I will surely treat you well, and make your descendants as the sand of the sea, which cannot be numbered for multitude.' "

[13]So he lodged there that same night, and took what came to his hand as a present for Esau his brother: [14]two hundred female goats and twenty male goats, two hundred ewes and twenty rams, [15]thirty milk camels with their colts, forty cows and ten bulls, twenty female donkeys and ten foals. [16]Then he delivered *them* to the hand of his servants, every drove by itself, and said to his servants, "Pass over before me, and put some distance between successive droves." [17]And he commanded the first one, saying, "When Esau my brother meets you and asks you, saying, 'To whom do you belong, and where are you going? Whose *are* these in front of you?' [18]then you shall say, 'They *are* your servant Jacob's. It *is* a present sent to my lord Esau; and behold, he also *is* be-

hind us.' " [19]So he commanded the second, the third, and all who followed the droves, saying, "In this manner you shall speak to Esau when you find him; [20]and also say, 'Behold, your servant Jacob *is* behind us.' " For he said, "I will appease him with the present that goes before me, and afterward I will see his face; perhaps he will accept me." [21]So the present went on over before him, but he himself lodged that night in the camp.

Wrestling with God

[22]And he arose that night and took his two wives, his two female servants, and his eleven sons, and crossed over the ford of Jabbok. [23]He took them, sent them over the brook, and sent over what he had. [24]Then Jacob was left alone; and a Man wrestled with him until the breaking of day. [25]Now when He saw that He did not prevail against him, He touched the socket of his hip; and the socket of Jacob's hip was out of joint as He wrestled with him. [26]And He said, "Let Me go, for the day breaks."

But he said, "I will not let You go unless You bless me!"

JACOB RETURNS TO CANAAN

? Exact location questionable

Mediterranean Sea

Sea of Chinnereth

Succoth
Shechem   Mahanaim?
Jabbok R.
Penuel

Bethel
Ai

Ephrath

Hebron   Dead Sea

Beersheba

© 1996 Thomas Nelson, Inc.

32:24 a Man wrestled. That Jacob named the site Peniel, which means "face of God," and the commentary by Hosea (Hos. 12:4) identify this Man with whom Jacob wrestled as the Angel of the Lord, who is also identified as God, a pre-incarnate appearance of the Lord Jesus Christ.

[27]So He said to him, "What *is* your name?"

He said, "Jacob."

[28]And He said, "Your name shall no longer be called Jacob, but Israel;[a] for you have struggled with God and with men, and have prevailed."

32:28 no longer...Jacob, but Israel. Jacob's personal name changed from one meaning "heel-catcher" or "deceiver" to one meaning "God's fighter" or "he struggles with God." **with God and with men.** Emerging victorious from the struggle is an amazing evaluation of what Jacob had accomplished. His life was indeed dominated by struggles: with Esau, with Isaac, with Laban, with his wives, and with God.

32:28 [a]Literally *Prince with God*

²⁹Then Jacob asked, saying, "Tell *me* Your name, I pray."

And He said, "Why *is* it *that* you ask about My name?" And He blessed him there.

³⁰So Jacob called the name of the place Peniel:*a* "For I have seen God face to face, and my life is preserved." ³¹Just as he crossed over Penuel*a* the sun rose on him, and he limped on his hip. ³²Therefore to this day the children of Israel do not eat the muscle that shrank, which *is* on the hip socket, because He touched the socket of Jacob's hip in the muscle that shrank.

Jacob and Esau Meet

33 Now Jacob lifted his eyes and looked, and there, Esau was coming, and with him were four hundred men. So he divided the children among Leah, Rachel, and the two maidservants. ²And he put the maidservants and their children in front, Leah and her children behind, and Rachel and Joseph last. ³Then he crossed over before them and bowed himself to the ground seven times, until he came near to his brother.

> **33:3,4** Jacob approached his brother with fear and deference, as an inferior honored patron, while Esau ran forward with eagerness and joy. "They wept" because after 21 years of troubling separation, old memories and murderous threats were released. Hearts had been changed and brothers reconciled!

⁴But Esau ran to meet him, and embraced him, and fell on his neck and kissed him, and they wept. ⁵And he lifted his eyes and saw the women and children, and said, "Who *are* these with you?"

So he said, "The children whom God has graciously given your servant." ⁶Then the maidservants came near, they and their children, and bowed down. ⁷And Leah also came near with her children, and they bowed down. Afterward Joseph and Rachel came near, and they bowed down.

⁸Then Esau said, "What *do* you *mean by* all this company which I met?"

And he said, "*These are* to find favor in the sight of my lord."

⁹But Esau said, "I have enough, my brother; keep what you have for yourself."

¹⁰And Jacob said, "No, please, if I have now found favor in your sight, then receive my present from my hand, inasmuch as I have seen your face as though I had seen the face of God, and you were pleased with me. ¹¹Please, take my blessing that is brought to you, because God has dealt graciously with me, and because I have enough." So he urged him, and he took *it.*

¹²Then Esau said, "Let us take our journey; let us go, and I will go before you."

¹³But Jacob said to him, "My lord knows that the children *are* weak, and the flocks and herds which are nursing *are* with me. And if the men should drive them hard one day, all the flock will die. ¹⁴Please let my lord go on ahead before his servant. I will lead on slowly at a pace which the livestock that go before me, and the children, are able to endure, until I come to my lord in Seir."

¹⁵And Esau said, "Now let me leave with you *some* of the people who *are* with me."

But he said, "What need is there? Let me find favor in the sight of my lord." ¹⁶So Esau returned that day on his way to Seir. ¹⁷And Jacob journeyed to Succoth, built himself a house, and made booths for his livestock. Therefore the name of the place is called Succoth.*a*

Jacob Comes to Canaan

¹⁸Then Jacob came safely to the city of Shechem, which *is* in the land of Canaan, when he came from Padan Aram; and he pitched his tent before the city. ¹⁹And he bought the parcel of land, where he had pitched his tent, from the children of Hamor, Shechem's father, for one hundred pieces of money. ²⁰Then he erected an altar there and called it El Elohe Israel.*a*

The Dinah Incident

34 Now Dinah the daughter of Leah, whom she had borne to Jacob, went out to see the daughters of the land. ²And when Shechem the son of Hamor the Hivite, prince of the country, saw her, he took

---

32:30 *a*Literally *Face of God*   32:31 *a*Same as *Peniel,* verse 30   33:17 *a*Literally *Booths*
33:20 *a*Literally *God, the God of Israel*

her and lay with her, and violated her. ³His soul was strongly attracted to Dinah the daughter of Jacob, and he loved the young woman and spoke kindly to the young woman. ⁴So Shechem spoke to his father Hamor, saying, "Get me this young woman as a wife."

⁵And Jacob heard that he had defiled Dinah his daughter. Now his sons were with his livestock in the field; so Jacob held his peace until they came. ⁶Then Hamor the father of Shechem went out to Jacob to speak with him. ⁷And the sons of Jacob came in from the field when they heard it; and the men were grieved and very angry, because he had done a disgraceful thing in Israel by lying with Jacob's daughter, a thing which ought not to be done. ⁸But Hamor spoke with them, saying, "The soul of my son Shechem longs for your daughter. Please give her to him as a wife. ⁹And make marriages with us; give your daughters to us, and take our daughters to yourselves. ¹⁰So you shall dwell with us, and the land shall be before you. Dwell and trade in it, and acquire possessions for yourselves in it."

¹¹Then Shechem said to her father and her brothers, "Let me find favor in your eyes, and whatever you say to me I will give. ¹²Ask me ever so much dowry and gift, and I will give according to what you say to me; but give me the young woman as a wife."

¹³But the sons of Jacob answered Shechem and Hamor his father, and spoke deceitfully, because he had defiled Dinah their sister. ¹⁴And they said to them, "We cannot do this thing, to give our sister to one who is uncircumcised, for that would be a reproach to us. ¹⁵But on this condition we will consent to you: If you will become as we are, if every male of you is circumcised, ¹⁶then we will give our daughters to you, and we will take your daughters to us; and we will dwell with you, and we will become one people. ¹⁷But if you will not heed us and be circumcised, then we will take our daughter and be gone."

¹⁸And their words pleased Hamor and Shechem, Hamor's son. ¹⁹So the young man did not delay to do the thing, because he delighted in Jacob's daughter. He was more honorable than all the household of his father.

²⁰And Hamor and Shechem his son came to the gate of their city, and spoke with the men of their city, saying: ²¹"These men are at peace with us. Therefore let them dwell in the land and trade in it. For indeed the land is large enough for them. Let us take their daughters to us as wives, and let us give them our daughters. ²²Only on this condition will the men consent to dwell with us, to be one people: if every male among us is circumcised as they are circumcised. ²³Will not their livestock, their

How are we to interpret the Bible (narratives in Genesis) when the customs of ancient peoples seem so different than our own?

Three tools help us in the task of interpreting events that happened so long ago and so far away: (1) The best interpretive tool in understanding a Bible passage is its immediate context. Surrounding verses will often yield clues to the observant about foreign or unusual details in a particular account. (2) One part of the Bible often explains, expands and comments on another part. An ever-growing familiarity with all of Scripture will equip a student with significant insight into the culture of those who lived the history. (3) Some insight can be gained from ancient sources outside of Scripture, but these only supplement our primary sources in the Bible itself.

Once we are at home in the exotic and unfamiliar contexts of Scripture, we meet people in the Bible pages who are very much like us. These are not aliens, but our ancestors across the ages. Their struggles are ours. Their failures are all to familiar to us. The God who spoke to them still speaks to us.

property, and every animal of theirs *be* ours? Only let us consent to them, and they will dwell with us." [24]And all who went out of the gate of his city heeded Hamor and Shechem his son; every male was circumcised, all who went out of the gate of his city.

[25]Now it came to pass on the third day, when they were in pain, that two of the sons of Jacob, Simeon and Levi, Dinah's brothers, each took his sword and came boldly upon the city and killed all the males. [26]And they killed Hamor and Shechem his son with the edge of the sword, and took Dinah from Shechem's house, and went out. [27]The sons of Jacob came upon the slain, and plundered the city, because their sister had been defiled. [28]They took their sheep, their oxen, and their donkeys, what *was* in the city and what *was* in the field, [29]and all their wealth. All their little ones and their wives they took captive; and they plundered even all that *was* in the houses.

> **34:25–29** The massacre of all the males and the plunder of the whole city far exceeded reasonable, just punishment for the sins of one man. This vengeance far surpassed what the Mosaic law would later legislate (see Deut. 22:28,29).

[30]Then Jacob said to Simeon and Levi, "You have troubled me by making me obnoxious among the inhabitants of the land, among the Canaanites and the Perizzites; and since I *am* few in number, they will gather themselves together against me and kill me. I shall be destroyed, my household and I."

[31]But they said, "Should he treat our sister like a harlot?"

Jacob's Return to Bethel

35 Then God said to Jacob, "Arise, go up to Bethel and dwell there; and make an altar there to God, who appeared to you when you fled from the face of Esau your brother."

[2]And Jacob said to his household and to all who *were* with him, "Put away the foreign gods that *are* among you, purify yourselves, and change your garments. [3]Then let us arise and go up to Bethel; and I will make an altar there to God, who answered me in the day of my distress and has been with me in the way which I have gone." [4]So they gave Jacob all the foreign gods which *were* in their hands, and the earrings which *were* in their ears; and Jacob hid them under the terebinth tree which *was* by Shechem.

[5]And they journeyed, and the terror of God was upon the cities that *were* all around them, and they did not pursue the sons of Jacob. [6]So Jacob came to Luz (that is, Bethel), which *is* in the land of Canaan, he and all the people who *were* with him. [7]And he built an altar there and called the place El Bethel,[a] because there God appeared to him when he fled from the face of his brother.

> **35:5 the terror of God.** A supernaturally induced fear of Israel made the surrounding cities unwilling and powerless to attack Jacob's household, which made Jacob's fear of their retaliation inconsequential (34:30).

[8]Now Deborah, Rebekah's nurse, died, and she was buried below Bethel under the terebinth tree. So the name of it was called Allon Bachuth.[a]

[9]Then God appeared to Jacob again, when he came from Padan Aram, and blessed him. [10]And God said to him, "Your name *is* Jacob; your name shall not be called Jacob anymore, but Israel shall be your name." So He called his name Israel. [11]Also God said to him: "I *am* God Almighty. Be fruitful and multiply; a nation and a company of nations shall proceed from you, and kings shall come from your body. [12]The land which I gave Abraham and Isaac I give to you; and to your descendants after you I give this land." [13]Then God went up from him in the place where He talked with him. [14]So Jacob set up a pillar in the place where He talked with him, a pillar of stone; and he poured a drink offering on it, and he poured oil on it. [15]And Jacob called the name of the place where God spoke with him, Bethel.

Death of Rachel

[16]Then they journeyed from Bethel. And when there was but a little distance to go to Ephrath, Rachel labored *in childbirth*, and

---

35:7 [a]Literally *God of the House of God*   35:8 [a]Literally *Terebinth of Weeping*

she had hard labor. [17]Now it came to pass, when she was in hard labor, that the midwife said to her, "Do not fear; you will have this son also." [18]And so it was, as her soul was departing (for she died), that she called his name Ben-Oni;[a] but his father called him Benjamin.[b] [19]So Rachel died and was buried on the way to Ephrath (that is, Bethlehem). [20]And Jacob set a pillar on her grave, which is the pillar of Rachel's grave to this day.

35:18 Ben-Oni...Benjamin. The dying mother named her newly born son "Son of my sorrow," but the grieving father named him "Son of my right hand," thus assigning him a place of honor in the home. Rachel's prayers at the birth of her firstborn were answered (30:24).

[21]Then Israel journeyed and pitched his tent beyond the tower of Eder. [22]And it happened, when Israel dwelt in that land, that Reuben went and lay with Bilhah his father's concubine; and Israel heard about it.

Jacob's Twelve Sons

Now the sons of Jacob were twelve: [23]the sons of Leah were Reuben, Jacob's firstborn, and Simeon, Levi, Judah, Issachar, and Zebulun; [24]the sons of Rachel were Joseph and Benjamin; [25]the sons of Bilhah, Rachel's maidservant, were Dan and Naphtali; [26]and the sons of Zilpah, Leah's maidservant, were Gad and Asher. These were the sons of Jacob who were born to him in Padan Aram.

Death of Isaac

[27]Then Jacob came to his father Isaac at Mamre, or Kirjath Arba[a] (that is, Hebron), where Abraham and Isaac had dwelt. [28]Now the days of Isaac were one hundred and eighty years. [29]So Isaac breathed his last and died, and was gathered to his people, being old and full of days. And his sons Esau and Jacob buried him.

The Family of Esau

36 Now this is the genealogy of Esau, who is Edom. [2]Esau took his wives from the daughters of Canaan: Adah the daughter of Elon the Hittite; Aholibamah the daughter of Anah, the daughter of Zibeon the Hivite; [3]and Basemath, Ishmael's daughter, sister of Nebajoth. [4]Now Adah bore Eliphaz to Esau, and Basemath bore Reuel. [5]And Aholibamah bore Jeush, Jaalam, and Korah. These were the sons of Esau who were born to him in the land of Canaan.

[6]Then Esau took his wives, his sons, his daughters, and all the persons of his household, his cattle and all his animals, and all his goods which he had gained in the land of Canaan, and went to a country away from the presence of his brother Jacob. [7]For their possessions were too great for them to dwell together, and the land where they were strangers could not support them because of their livestock. [8]So Esau dwelt in Mount Seir. Esau is Edom.

36:7 too great for them to dwell together. Crowded living conditions finally prompted Esau to move permanently to Edom, where he had already established a home (see 32:3; 33:14,16). Because God had promised that Abraham's descendants through Isaac and Jacob would possess the land, it was fitting that God providentially worked out the circumstances to keep Jacob in the land and move Esau out.

[9]And this is the genealogy of Esau the father of the Edomites in Mount Seir. [10]These were the names of Esau's sons: Eliphaz the son of Adah the wife of Esau, and Reuel the son of Basemath the wife of Esau. [11]And the sons of Eliphaz were Teman, Omar, Zepho,[a] Gatam, and Kenaz. [12]Now Timna was the concubine of Eliphaz, Esau's son, and she bore Amalek to Eliphaz. These were the sons of Adah, Esau's wife. [13]These were the sons of Reuel: Nahath, Zerah, Shammah, and Mizzah. These were the sons of Basemath, Esau's wife. [14]These were the sons of Aholibamah, Esau's wife, the daughter of Anah, the daughter of Zibeon. And she bore to Esau: Jeush, Jaalam, and Korah.

The Chiefs of Edom

[15]These were the chiefs of the sons of Esau. The sons of Eliphaz, the firstborn son

---

35:18 [a]Literally Son of My Sorrow [b]Literally Son of the Right Hand   35:27 [a]Literally Town of Arba
36:11 [a]Spelled Zephi in 1 Chronicles 1:36

of Esau, were Chief Teman, Chief Omar, Chief Zepho, Chief Kenaz, ¹⁶Chief Korah,^a Chief Gatam, *and* Chief Amalek. These *were* the chiefs of Eliphaz in the land of Edom. They *were* the sons of Adah.

¹⁷These *were* the sons of Reuel, Esau's son: Chief Nahath, Chief Zerah, Chief Shammah, and Chief Mizzah. These *were* the chiefs of Reuel in the land of Edom. These *were* the sons of Basemath, Esau's wife.

¹⁸And these *were* the sons of Aholibamah, Esau's wife: Chief Jeush, Chief Jaalam, and Chief Korah. These *were* the chiefs *who descended* from Aholibamah, Esau's wife, the daughter of Anah. ¹⁹These *were* the sons of Esau, who is Edom, and these *were* their chiefs.

The Sons of Seir

²⁰These *were* the sons of Seir the Horite who inhabited the land: Lotan, Shobal, Zibeon, Anah, ²¹Dishon, Ezer, and Dishan. These *were* the chiefs of the Horites, the sons of Seir, in the land of Edom.

²²And the sons of Lotan were Hori and Hemam.^a Lotan's sister *was* Timna.

²³These *were* the sons of Shobal: Alvan,^a Manahath, Ebal, Shepho,^b and Onam.

²⁴These *were* the sons of Zibeon: both Ajah and Anah. This *was the* Anah who found the water^a in the wilderness as he pastured the donkeys of his father Zibeon. ²⁵These *were* the children of Anah: Dishon and Aholibamah the daughter of Anah.

²⁶These *were* the sons of Dishon:^a Hemdan,^b Eshban, Ithran, and Cheran. ²⁷These *were* the sons of Ezer: Bilhan, Zaavan, and Akan.^a ²⁸These *were* the sons of Dishan: Uz and Aran.

²⁹These *were* the chiefs of the Horites: Chief Lotan, Chief Shobal, Chief Zibeon, Chief Anah, ³⁰Chief Dishon, Chief Ezer, and Chief Dishan. These *were* the chiefs of the Horites, according to their chiefs in the land of Seir.

The Kings of Edom

³¹Now these *were* the kings who reigned in the land of Edom before any king reigned over the children of Israel: ³²Bela the son of Beor reigned in Edom, and the name of his city *was* Dinhabah. ³³And when Bela died, Jobab the son of Zerah of Bozrah reigned in his place. ³⁴When Jobab died, Husham of the land of the Temanites reigned in his place. ³⁵And when Husham died, Hadad the son of Bedad, who attacked Midian in the field of Moab, reigned in his place. And the name of his city *was* Avith. ³⁶When Hadad died, Samlah of Masrekah reigned in his place. ³⁷And when Samlah died, Saul of Rehoboth-*by*-the-River reigned in his place. ³⁸When Saul died, Baal-Hanan the son of Achbor reigned in his place. ³⁹And when Baal-Hanan the son of Achbor died, Hadar^a reigned in his place; and the name of his city *was* Pau.^b His wife's name *was* Mehetabel, the daughter of Matred, the daughter of Mezahab.

The Chiefs of Esau

⁴⁰And these *were* the names of the chiefs of Esau, according to their families and their places, by their names: Chief Timnah, Chief Alvah,^a Chief Jetheth, ⁴¹Chief Aholibamah, Chief Elah, Chief Pinon, ⁴²Chief Kenaz, Chief Teman, Chief Mibzar, ⁴³Chief Magdiel, and Chief Iram. These *were* the chiefs of Edom, according to their dwelling places in the land of their possession. Esau *was* the father of the Edomites.

Joseph Dreams of Greatness

37 Now Jacob dwelt in the land where his father was a stranger, in the land of Canaan. ²This *is* the history of Jacob.

Joseph, *being* seventeen years old, was feeding the flock with his brothers. And the lad *was* with the sons of Bilhah and the sons of Zilpah, his father's wives; and Joseph brought a bad report of them to his father.

³Now Israel loved Joseph more than all

36:16 ^aSamaritan Pentateuch omits *Chief Korah*.   36:22 ^aSpelled *Homam* in 1 Chronicles 1:39
36:23 ^aSpelled *Alian* in 1 Chronicles 1:40   ^bSpelled *Shephi* in 1 Chronicles 1:40   36:24 ^aFollowing Masoretic Text and Vulgate (*hot springs*); Septuagint reads *Jamin*; Targum reads *mighty men*; Talmud interprets as *mules*.   36:26 ^aHebrew *Dishan*   ^bSpelled *Hamran* in 1 Chronicles 1:41
36:27 ^aSpelled *Jaakan* in 1 Chronicles 1:42   36:39 ^aSpelled *Hadad* in Samaritan Pentateuch, Syriac, and 1 Chronicles 1:50   ^bSpelled *Pai* in 1 Chronicles 1:50   36:40 ^aSpelled *Aliah* in 1 Chronicles 1:51

his children, because he *was* the son of his old age. Also he made him a tunic of *many* colors. ⁴But when his brothers saw that their father loved him more than all his brothers, they hated him and could not speak peaceably to him.

> **37:3 tunic of *many* colors.** This special robe marked the owner as the one whom the father intended to be the future leader of the household, an honor normally given to the firstborn son. Jacob's overt favoritism of Joseph estranged him from his jealous brothers.

⁵Now Joseph had a dream, and he told *it* to his brothers; and they hated him even more. ⁶So he said to them, "Please hear this dream which I have dreamed: ⁷There we were, binding sheaves in the field. Then behold, my sheaf arose and also stood upright; and indeed your sheaves stood all around and bowed down to my sheaf."

⁸And his brothers said to him, "Shall you indeed reign over us? Or shall you indeed have dominion over us?" So they hated him even more for his dreams and for his words.

⁹Then he dreamed still another dream and told it to his brothers, and said, "Look, I have dreamed another dream. And this time, the sun, the moon, and the eleven stars bowed down to me."

¹⁰So he told *it* to his father and his brothers; and his father rebuked him and said to him, "What *is* this dream that you have dreamed? Shall your mother and I and your brothers indeed come to bow down to the earth before you?" ¹¹And his brothers envied him, but his father kept the matter *in mind*.

> **37:5–10** The content of Joseph's dreams aggravated his brothers' hatred toward him, and his father even rebuked him for the second one. The dream symbolism clearly elevated the favored son to ruling status over the brothers.

Joseph Sold by His Brothers

¹²Then his brothers went to feed their father's flock in Shechem. ¹³And Israel said to Joseph, "Are not your brothers feeding *the flock* in Shechem? Come, I will send you to them."

So he said to him, "Here I am."

¹⁴Then he said to him, "Please go and see if it is well with your brothers and well with the flocks, and bring back word to me." So he sent him out of the Valley of Hebron, and he went to Shechem.

¹⁵Now a certain man found him, and there he was, wandering in the field. And the man asked him, saying, "What are you seeking?"

¹⁶So he said, "I am seeking my brothers. Please tell me where they are feeding *their flocks*."

¹⁷And the man said, "They have departed from here, for I heard them say, 'Let us go to Dothan.'" So Joseph went after his brothers and found them in Dothan.

¹⁸Now when they saw him afar off, even before he came near them, they conspired against him to kill him. ¹⁹Then they said to one another, "Look, this dreamer is coming! ²⁰Come therefore, let us now kill him and cast him into some pit; and we shall say, 'Some wild beast has devoured him.' We shall see what will become of his dreams!"

²¹But Reuben heard *it*, and he delivered him out of their hands, and said, "Let us not kill him." ²²And Reuben said to them, "Shed no blood, *but* cast him into this pit which *is* in the wilderness, and do not lay a hand on him"—that he might deliver him

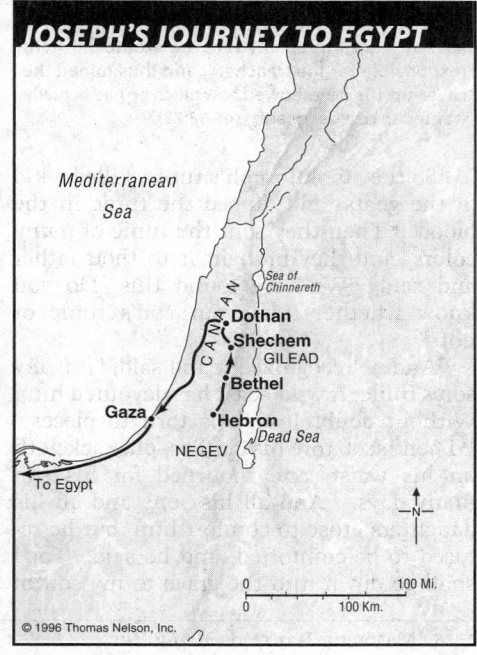

JOSEPH'S JOURNEY TO EGYPT

Mediterranean Sea

Sea of Chinnereth

Dothan
Shechem
GILEAD
Bethel
Gaza
Hebron
Dead Sea
NEGEV
CANAAN
To Egypt

—N—

0   100 Mi.
0   100 Km.

© 1996 Thomas Nelson, Inc.

out of their hands, and bring him back to his father.

23So it came to pass, when Joseph had come to his brothers, that they stripped Joseph *of* his tunic, the tunic of *many* colors that *was* on him. 24Then they took him and cast him into a pit. And the pit *was* empty; *there was* no water in it.

25And they sat down to eat a meal. Then they lifted their eyes and looked, and there was a company of Ishmaelites, coming from Gilead with their camels, bearing spices, balm, and myrrh, on their way to carry *them* down to Egypt. 26So Judah said to his brothers, "What profit *is there* if we kill our brother and conceal his blood? 27Come and let us sell him to the Ishmaelites, and let not our hand be upon him, for he *is* our brother *and* our flesh." And his brothers listened. 28Then Midianite traders passed by; so *the brothers* pulled Joseph up and lifted him out of the pit, and sold him to the Ishmaelites for twenty *shekels* of silver. And they took Joseph to Egypt.

29Then Reuben returned to the pit, and indeed Joseph *was* not in the pit; and he tore his clothes. 30And he returned to his brothers and said, "The lad *is* no *more*; and I, where shall I go?"

> **37:29 Reuben...tore his clothes.** Although he was absent from the actual sale, he would be held responsible for the treachery, and thus joined the cover-up. His grief showed how much he had actually wanted to rescue Joseph (see 42:22).

31So they took Joseph's tunic, killed a kid of the goats, and dipped the tunic in the blood. 32Then they sent the tunic of *many* colors, and they brought *it* to their father and said, "We have found this. Do you know whether it *is* your son's tunic or not?"

33And he recognized it and said, "It is my son's tunic. A wild beast has devoured him. Without doubt Joseph is torn to pieces." 34Then Jacob tore his clothes, put sackcloth on his waist, and mourned for his son many days. 35And all his sons and all his daughters arose to comfort him; but he refused to be comforted, and he said, "For I shall go down into the grave to my son in mourning." Thus his father wept for him.

36Now the Midianites*a* had sold him in Egypt to Potiphar, an officer of Pharaoh *and* captain of the guard.

> **37:36 Potiphar.** He was a prominent court official and high-ranking officer in Egypt, perhaps captain of the royal bodyguard (see 40:3,4).

Judah and Tamar

38It came to pass at that time that Judah departed from his brothers, and visited a certain Adullamite whose name *was* Hirah. 2And Judah saw there a daughter of a certain Canaanite whose name *was* Shua, and he married her and went in to her. 3So she conceived and bore a son, and he called his name Er. 4She conceived again and bore a son, and she called his name Onan. 5And she conceived yet again and bore a son, and called his name Shelah. He was at Chezib when she bore him.

6Then Judah took a wife for Er his firstborn, and her name *was* Tamar. 7But Er, Judah's firstborn, was wicked in the sight of the LORD, and the LORD killed him. 8And Judah said to Onan, "Go in to your brother's wife and marry her, and raise up an heir to your brother." 9But Onan knew that the heir would not be his; and it came to pass, when he went in to his brother's wife, that he emitted on the ground, lest he should give an heir to his brother. 10And the thing which he did displeased the LORD; therefore He killed him also.

> **38:6–10** Judah's two sons were executed by the Lord, one for wickedness and one for rebellious rejection of the duty to marry a relative's widow, which is called a levirate marriage. This was a rather scandalous mark against the line of Judah.

11Then Judah said to Tamar his daughter-in-law, "Remain a widow in your father's house till my son Shelah is grown." For he said, "Lest he also die like his brothers." And Tamar went and dwelt in her father's house.

12Now in the process of time the daughter

37:36 *a*Masoretic Text reads *Medanites*.

of Shua, Judah's wife, died; and Judah was comforted, and went up to his sheepshearers at Timnah, he and his friend Hirah the Adullamite. ¹³And it was told Tamar, saying, "Look, your father-in-law is going up to Timnah to shear his sheep." ¹⁴So she took off her widow's garments, covered *herself* with a veil and wrapped herself, and sat in an open place which *was* on the way to Timnah; for she saw that Shelah was grown, and she was not given to him as a wife. ¹⁵When Judah saw her, he thought she *was* a harlot, because she had covered her face. ¹⁶Then he turned to her by the way, and said, "Please let me come in to you"; for he did not know that she *was* his daughter-in-law.

So she said, "What will you give me, that you may come in to me?"

¹⁷And he said, "I will send a young goat from the flock."

So she said, "Will you give *me* a pledge till you send *it?* "

¹⁸Then he said, "What pledge shall I give you?"

So she said, "Your signet and cord, and your staff that *is* in your hand." Then he gave *them* to her, and went in to her, and she conceived by him. ¹⁹So she arose and went away, and laid aside her veil and put on the garments of her widowhood.

²⁰And Judah sent the young goat by the hand of his friend the Adullamite, to receive *his* pledge from the woman's hand, but he did not find her. ²¹Then he asked the men of that place, saying, "Where is the harlot who *was* openly by the roadside?"

And they said, "There was no harlot in this *place.*"

²²So he returned to Judah and said, "I cannot find her. Also, the men of the place said there was no harlot in this *place.*"

²³Then Judah said, "Let her take *them* for herself, lest we be shamed; for I sent this young goat and you have not found her."

²⁴And it came to pass, about three months after, that Judah was told, saying, "Tamar your daughter-in-law has played the harlot; furthermore she *is* with child by harlotry."

So Judah said, "Bring her out and let her be burned!"

²⁵When she *was* brought out, she sent to her father-in-law, saying, "By the man to whom these belong, I *am* with child." And she said, "Please determine whose these *are*—the signet and cord, and staff."

²⁶So Judah acknowledged *them* and said, "She has been more righteous than I, because I did not give her to Shelah my son." And he never knew her again.

²⁷Now it came to pass, at the time for giving birth, that behold, twins *were* in her womb. ²⁸And so it was, when she was giving birth, that *the one* put out *his* hand; and the midwife took a scarlet *thread* and bound it on his hand, saying, "This one came out first." ²⁹Then it happened, as he drew back his hand, that his brother came out unexpectedly; and she said, "How did you break through? *This* breach *be* upon you!" Therefore his name was called Perez.*ᵃ* ³⁰Afterward his brother came out who had the scarlet *thread* on his hand. And his name was called Zerah.

Joseph a Slave in Egypt

39 Now Joseph had been taken down to Egypt. And Potiphar, an officer of Pharaoh, captain of the guard, an Egyptian, bought him from the Ishmaelites who had taken him down there. ²The Lord was with Joseph, and he was a successful man; and he was in the house of his master the Egyptian. ³And his master saw that the Lord *was* with him and that the Lord made all he did to prosper in his hand. ⁴So Joseph found favor in his sight, and served him. Then he made him overseer of his house, and all *that* he had he put under his authority. ⁵So it was, from the time *that* he had made him overseer of his house and all that he had, that the Lord blessed the Egyptian's house for Joseph's sake; and the blessing of the Lord was on all that he had

39:2 The Lord was with Joseph. Although Joseph was twice a victim of injustice, the Lord never abandoned him. Neither being sold into slavery (37:28) nor being unjustly accused of sexual harassment and imprisoned (vv. 13–18) signaled even a temporary lapse in God's care for His servant Joseph or His people, Israel. Jacob's high position as steward of the whole estate shows how much he was trusted.

38:29 ᵃLiterally *Breach* or *Breakthrough*

in the house and in the field. ⁶Thus he left all that he had in Joseph's hand, and he did not know what he had except for the bread which he ate.

Now Joseph was handsome in form and appearance.

⁷And it came to pass after these things that his master's wife cast longing eyes on Joseph, and she said, "Lie with me."

⁸But he refused and said to his master's wife, "Look, my master does not know what is with me in the house, and he has committed all that he has to my hand. ⁹There is no one greater in this house than I, nor has he kept back anything from me but you, because you are his wife. How then can I do this great wickedness, and sin against God?"

¹⁰So it was, as she spoke to Joseph day by day, that he did not heed her, to lie with her or to be with her.

¹¹But it happened about this time, when Joseph went into the house to do his work, and none of the men of the house was inside, ¹²that she caught him by his garment, saying, "Lie with me." But he left his garment in her hand, and fled and ran outside. ¹³And so it was, when she saw that he had left his garment in her hand and fled outside, ¹⁴that she called to the men of her house and spoke to them, saying, "See, he has brought in to us a Hebrew to mock us. He came in to me to lie with me, and I cried out with a loud voice. ¹⁵And it happened, when he heard that I lifted my voice and cried out, that he left his garment with me, and fled and went outside."

¹⁶So she kept his garment with her until his master came home. ¹⁷Then she spoke to him with words like these, saying, "The Hebrew servant whom you brought to us came in to me to mock me; ¹⁸so it happened, as I lifted my voice and cried out, that he left his garment with me and fled outside."

¹⁹So it was, when his master heard the words which his wife spoke to him, saying, "Your servant did to me after this manner," that his anger was aroused. ²⁰Then Joseph's master took him and put him into the prison, a place where the king's prisoners were confined. And he was there in the prison.

²¹But the LORD was with Joseph and showed him mercy, and He gave him favor in the sight of the keeper of the prison. ²²And the keeper of the prison committed to Joseph's hand all the prisoners who were in the prison; whatever they did there, it was his doing. ²³The keeper of the prison did not look into anything that was under Joseph's authority,^a because the LORD was with him; and whatever he did, the LORD made it prosper.

The Prisoners' Dreams

40 It came to pass after these things that the butler and the baker of the king of Egypt offended their lord, the king of Egypt. ²And Pharaoh was angry with his two officers, the chief butler and the chief baker. ³So he put them in custody in the house of the captain of the guard, in the prison, the place where Joseph was confined. ⁴And the captain of the guard charged Joseph with them, and he served them; so they were in custody for a while.

> **40:2 the chief butler and the chief baker.** The "butler" was the king's cupbearer, who gave him his drinks. The baker cooked his bread. Both had to be trustworthy and beyond the influence of the king's enemies who might wish to poison him.

⁵Then the butler and the baker of the king of Egypt, who were confined in the prison, had a dream, both of them, each man's dream in one night and each man's dream with its own interpretation. ⁶And Joseph came in to them in the morning and looked at them, and saw that they were sad. ⁷So he asked Pharaoh's officers who were with him in the custody of his lord's house, saying, "Why do you look so sad today?"

⁸And they said to him, "We each have had

> **40:8 interpretations belong to God.** Joseph faithfully gave the credit to the Lord. Daniel was the only other Hebrew whom God allowed to interpret revelatory dreams, and he too gave God full praise (Dan. 2:28). Significantly, God chose both men to play an important role for Israel as they stepped forward at the critical moment to interpret the dreams of pagan monarchs and to reveal the future to them.

39:23 ^aLiterally his hand

a dream, and *there is* no interpreter of it."

So Joseph said to them, "Do not interpretations belong to God? Tell *them* to me, please."

⁹Then the chief butler told his dream to Joseph, and said to him, "Behold, in my dream a vine *was* before me, ¹⁰and in the vine *were* three branches; it *was* as though it budded, its blossoms shot forth, and its clusters brought forth ripe grapes. ¹¹Then Pharaoh's cup *was* in my hand; and I took the grapes and pressed them into Pharaoh's cup, and placed the cup in Pharaoh's hand."

¹²And Joseph said to him, "This *is* the interpretation of it: The three branches *are* three days. ¹³Now within three days Pharaoh will lift up your head and restore you to your place, and you will put Pharaoh's cup in his hand according to the former manner, when you were his butler. ¹⁴But remember me when it is well with you, and please show kindness to me; make mention of me to Pharaoh, and get me out of this house. ¹⁵For indeed I was stolen away from the land of the Hebrews; and also I have done nothing here that they should put me into the dungeon."

40:14,15 remember me. A poignant appeal to the butler, whose future alongside the king was secure, to speak in behalf of Joseph for his freedom. The butler quickly forgot Joseph (v. 23) until his memory was prompted at just the right time two years later (41:1,9).

¹⁶When the chief baker saw that the interpretation was good, he said to Joseph, "I also *was* in my dream, and there *were* three white baskets on my head. ¹⁷In the uppermost basket *were* all kinds of baked goods for Pharaoh, and the birds ate them out of the basket on my head."

¹⁸So Joseph answered and said, "This *is* the interpretation of it: The three baskets *are* three days. ¹⁹Within three days Pharaoh will lift off your head from you and hang you on a tree; and the birds will eat your flesh from you."

²⁰Now it came to pass on the third day, *which was* Pharaoh's birthday, that he made a feast for all his servants; and he lifted up the head of the chief butler and of the chief baker among his servants. ²¹Then he

restored the chief butler to his butlership again, and he placed the cup in Pharaoh's hand. ²²But he hanged the chief baker, as Joseph had interpreted to them. ²³Yet the chief butler did not remember Joseph, but forgot him.

Pharaoh's Dreams

41 Then it came to pass, at the end of two full years, that Pharaoh had a dream; and behold, he stood by the river. ²Suddenly there came up out of the river seven cows, fine looking and fat; and they fed in the meadow. ³Then behold, seven other cows came up after them out of the river, ugly and gaunt, and stood by the *other* cows on the bank of the river. ⁴And the ugly and gaunt cows ate up the seven fine looking and fat cows. So Pharaoh awoke. ⁵He slept and dreamed a second time; and suddenly seven heads of grain came up on one stalk, plump and good. ⁶Then behold, seven thin heads, blighted by the east wind, sprang up after them. ⁷And the seven thin heads devoured the seven plump and full heads. So Pharaoh awoke, and indeed, *it was* a dream. ⁸Now it came to pass in the morning that his spirit was troubled, and he sent and called for all the magicians of Egypt and all its wise men. And Pharaoh told them his dreams, but *there was* no one who could interpret them for Pharaoh.

41:8 no one who could interpret. The combined expertise of Pharaoh's full council of advisers and experts could not interpret his two disturbing dreams. Without their knowledge, they set the stage for Joseph's entrance into Egyptian history.

⁹Then the chief butler spoke to Pharaoh, saying: "I remember my faults this day. ¹⁰When Pharaoh was angry with his servants, and put me in custody in the house of the captain of the guard, *both* me and the chief baker, ¹¹we each had a dream in one night, he and I. Each of us dreamed according to the interpretation of his *own* dream. ¹²Now there *was* a young Hebrew man with us there, a servant of the captain of the guard. And we told him, and he interpreted our dreams for us; to each man he interpreted according to his *own* dream. ¹³And it came to pass, just as he interpreted for us,

so it happened. He restored me to my office, and he hanged him."

¹⁴Then Pharaoh sent and called Joseph, and they brought him quickly out of the dungeon; and he shaved, changed his clothing, and came to Pharaoh. ¹⁵And Pharaoh said to Joseph, "I have had a dream, and *there is* no one who can interpret it. But I have heard it said of you *that* you can understand a dream, to interpret it."

¹⁶So Joseph answered Pharaoh, saying, "*It is* not in me; God will give Pharaoh an answer of peace."

41:16 *It is* not in me; God will give. Denying any ability of his own to interpret, Joseph advised Pharaoh at the outset that the answer he desired could only come from God.

¹⁷Then Pharaoh said to Joseph: "Behold, in my dream I stood on the bank of the river. ¹⁸Suddenly seven cows came up out of the river, fine looking and fat; and they fed in the meadow. ¹⁹Then behold, seven other cows came up after them, poor and very ugly and gaunt, such ugliness as I have never seen in all the land of Egypt. ²⁰And the gaunt and ugly cows ate up the first seven, the fat cows. ²¹When they had eaten them up, no one would have known that they had eaten them, for they *were* just as ugly as at the beginning. So I awoke. ²²Also I saw in my dream, and suddenly seven heads came up on one stalk, full and good. ²³Then behold, seven heads, withered, thin, *and* blighted by the east wind, sprang up after them. ²⁴And the thin heads devoured the seven good heads. So I told *this* to the magicians, but *there was* no one who could explain *it* to me."

²⁵Then Joseph said to Pharaoh, "The dreams of Pharaoh *are* one; God has shown Pharaoh what He *is* about to do: ²⁶The seven good cows *are* seven years, and the seven good heads *are* seven years; the dreams *are* one. ²⁷And the seven thin and ugly cows which came up after them *are* seven years, and the seven empty heads blighted by the east wind are seven years of famine. ²⁸This *is* the thing which I have spoken to Pharaoh. God has shown Pharaoh what He *is* about to do. ²⁹Indeed seven years of great plenty will come throughout all the land of Egypt; ³⁰but after them seven years of famine will arise, and all the plenty will be forgotten in the land of Egypt; and the famine will deplete the land. ³¹So the plenty will not be known in the land because of the famine following, for it *will be* very severe. ³²And the dream was repeated to Pharaoh twice because the thing *is* established by God, and God will shortly bring it to pass.

³³"Now therefore, let Pharaoh select a discerning and wise man, and set him over the land of Egypt. ³⁴Let Pharaoh do *this*, and let him appoint officers over the land, to collect one-fifth *of the produce* of the land of Egypt in the seven plentiful years. ³⁵And let them gather all the food of those good years that are coming, and store up grain under the authority of Pharaoh, and let them keep food in the cities. ³⁶Then that food shall be as a reserve for the land for the seven years of famine which shall be in the land of Egypt, that the land may not perish during the famine."

Joseph's Rise to Power

³⁷So the advice was good in the eyes of Pharaoh and in the eyes of all his servants. ³⁸And Pharaoh said to his servants, "Can we find *such a one* as this, a man in whom *is* the Spirit of God?"

³⁹Then Pharaoh said to Joseph, "Inasmuch as God has shown you all this, *there is* no one as discerning and wise as you. ⁴⁰You shall be over my house, and all my people shall be ruled according to your word; only in regard to the throne will I be greater than you." ⁴¹And Pharaoh said to Joseph, "See, I have set you over all the land of Egypt."

41:37–41 To Pharaoh and his officials, only Joseph qualified for the task of implementing this good plan, because they recognized that he spoke truth given by God. Joseph's focus on his Lord took him directly from prison to the palace.

⁴²Then Pharaoh took his signet ring off his hand and put it on Joseph's hand; and he clothed him in garments of fine linen and put a gold chain around his neck. ⁴³And he had him ride in the second chariot which he had; and they cried out before

him, "Bow the knee!" So he set him over all the land of Egypt. ⁴⁴Pharaoh also said to Joseph, "I *am* Pharaoh, and without your consent no man may lift his hand or foot in all the land of Egypt." ⁴⁵And Pharaoh called Joseph's name Zaphnath-Paaneah. And he gave him as a wife Asenath, the daughter of Poti-Pherah priest of On. So Joseph went out over *all* the land of Egypt.

⁴⁶Joseph was thirty years old when he stood before Pharaoh king of Egypt. And Joseph went out from the presence of Pharaoh, and went throughout all the land of Egypt. ⁴⁷Now in the seven plentiful years the ground brought forth abundantly. ⁴⁸So he gathered up all the food of the seven years which were in the land of Egypt, and laid up the food in the cities; he laid up in every city the food of the fields which surrounded them. ⁴⁹Joseph gathered very much grain, as the sand of the sea, until he stopped counting, for *it was* immeasurable.

⁵⁰And to Joseph were born two sons before the years of famine came, whom Asenath, the daughter of Poti-Pherah priest of On, bore to him. ⁵¹Joseph called the name of the firstborn Manasseh:ᵃ "For God has made me forget all my toil and all my father's house." ⁵²And the name of the second he called Ephraim:ᵃ "For God has caused me to be fruitful in the land of my affliction."

⁵³Then the seven years of plenty which were in the land of Egypt ended, ⁵⁴and the seven years of famine began to come, as Joseph had said. The famine was in all lands, but in all the land of Egypt there was bread. ⁵⁵So when all the land of Egypt was famished, the people cried to Pharaoh for bread. Then Pharaoh said to all the Egyptians, "Go to Joseph; whatever he says to you, do." ⁵⁶The famine was over all the face of the earth, and Joseph opened all the storehousesᵃ and sold to the Egyptians. And the famine became severe in the land of Egypt. ⁵⁷So all countries came to Joseph in Egypt to buy *grain,* because the famine was severe in all lands.

Joseph's Brothers Go to Egypt

42 When Jacob saw that there was grain in Egypt, Jacob said to his sons,

"Why do you look at one another?" ²And he said, "Indeed I have heard that there is grain in Egypt; go down to that place and buy for us there, that we may live and not die."

³So Joseph's ten brothers went down to buy grain in Egypt. ⁴But Jacob did not send Joseph's brother Benjamin with his brothers, for he said, "Lest some calamity befall him." ⁵And the sons of Israel went to buy *grain* among those who journeyed, for the famine was in the land of Canaan.

> **42:4 Benjamin.** See 35:16-19. He was the youngest of all twelve sons, the second son of Rachel, Jacob's beloved wife, and his father's favorite since he thought Joseph was dead.

⁶Now Joseph *was* governor over the land; and it was he who sold to all the people of the land. And Joseph's brothers came and bowed down before him with *their* faces to the earth. ⁷Joseph saw his brothers and recognized them, but he acted as a stranger to them and spoke roughly to them. Then he said to them, "Where do you come from?"

And they said, "From the land of Canaan to buy food."

> **42:6 bowed down.** Without their realizing it at the time, Joseph's earlier dreams were fulfilled (37:5–8). It was unlikely that his brothers would recognize him because more than 15 years had passed, he had changed from teenager into mature adult, he had become Egyptian in dress and appearance, he treated them without a hint of familiarity (vv. 7,8), and they thought he was dead (v. 13).

⁸So Joseph recognized his brothers, but they did not recognize him. ⁹Then Joseph remembered the dreams which he had dreamed about them, and said to them, "You *are* spies! You have come to see the nakedness of the land!"

¹⁰And they said to him, "No, my lord, but your servants have come to buy food. ¹¹We *are* all one man's sons; we *are* honest *men;* your servants are not spies."

¹²But he said to them, "No, but you have come to see the nakedness of the land."

¹³And they said, "Your servants *are* twelve brothers, the sons of one man in the

---

41:51 ᵃLiterally *Making Forgetful*   41:52 ᵃLiterally *Fruitfulness*   41:56 ᵃLiterally *all that was in them*

land of Canaan; and in fact, the youngest *is* with our father today, and one *is* no more."

[14]But Joseph said to them, "It *is* as I spoke to you, saying, 'You *are* spies!' [15]In this *manner* you shall be tested: By the life of Pharaoh, you shall not leave this place unless your youngest brother comes here. [16]Send one of you, and let him bring your brother; and you shall be kept in prison, that your words may be tested to see whether *there is* any truth in you; or else, by the life of Pharaoh, surely you *are* spies!" [17]So he put them all together in prison three days.

> **42:15 unless your younger brother comes.** Joseph wanted to find out if they had done the same or a similar thing to his brother Benjamin as they had done to him.

[18]Then Joseph said to them the third day, "Do this and live, *for* I fear God: [19]If you *are* honest *men,* let one of your brothers be confined to your prison house; but you, go and carry grain for the famine of your houses. [20]And bring your youngest brother to me; so your words will be verified, and you shall not die."

And they did so. [21]Then they said to one another, "We *are* truly guilty concerning our brother, for we saw the anguish of his soul when he pleaded with us, and we would not hear; therefore this distress has come upon us."

[22]And Reuben answered them, saying, "Did I not speak to you, saying, 'Do not sin against the boy'; and you would not listen? Therefore behold, his blood is now required of us." [23]But they did not know that Joseph understood *them,* for he spoke to them through an interpreter. [24]And he turned himself away from them and wept. Then he returned to them again, and talked with them. And he took Simeon from them and bound him before their eyes.

> **42:24 took Simeon.** Joseph kept as a hostage not Reuben, the firstborn son, but Simeon, the oldest brother who had willingly participated in the crime against Joseph (37:21–31).

The Brothers Return to Canaan
[25]Then Joseph gave a command to fill their sacks with grain, to restore every

man's money to his sack, and to give them provisions for the journey. Thus he did for them. [26]So they loaded their donkeys with the grain and departed from there. [27]But as one *of them* opened his sack to give his donkey feed at the encampment, he saw his money; and there it was, in the mouth of his sack. [28]So he said to his brothers, "My money has been restored, and there it is, in my sack!" Then their hearts failed *them* and they were afraid, saying to one another, "What *is* this *that* God has done to us?"

[29]Then they went to Jacob their father in the land of Canaan and told him all that had happened to them, saying: [30]"The man *who is* lord of the land spoke roughly to us, and took us for spies of the country. [31]But we said to him, 'We *are* honest *men;* we are not spies. [32]We *are* twelve brothers, sons of our father; one *is* no *more,* and the youngest *is* with our father this day in the land of Canaan.' [33]Then the man, the lord of the country, said to us, 'By this I will know that you *are* honest *men:* Leave one of your brothers *here* with me, take *food for* the famine of your households, and be gone. [34]And bring your youngest brother to me; so I shall know that you *are* not spies, but *that* you *are* honest *men.* I will grant your brother to you, and you may trade in the land.' "

[35]Then it happened as they emptied their sacks, that surprisingly each man's bundle of money *was* in his sack; and when they and their father saw the bundles of money, they were afraid. [36]And Jacob their father said to them, "You have bereaved me: Joseph is no *more,* Simeon is no *more,* and you want to take Benjamin. All these things are against me."

[37]Then Reuben spoke to his father, saying, "Kill my two sons if I do not bring him *back* to you; put him in my hands, and I will bring him back to you."

[38]But he said, "My son shall not go down with you, for his brother is dead, and he is left alone. If any calamity should befall him along the way in which you go, then you would bring down my gray hair with sorrow to the grave."

Joseph's Brothers Return with Benjamin
43 Now the famine *was* severe in the land. [2]And it came to pass, when they had eaten up the grain which they had

brought from Egypt, that their father said to them, "Go back, buy us a little food."

[3]But Judah spoke to him, saying, "The man solemnly warned us, saying, 'You shall not see my face unless your brother *is* with you.' [4]If you send our brother with us, we will go down and buy you food. [5]But if you will not send *him*, we will not go down; for the man said to us, 'You shall not see my face unless your brother *is* with you.' "

[6]And Israel said, "Why did you deal *so* wrongfully with me *as* to tell the man whether you had still *another* brother?"

[7]But they said, "The man asked us pointedly about ourselves and our family, saying, '*Is* your father still alive? Have you *another* brother?' And we told him according to these words. Could we possibly have known that he would say, 'Bring your brother down'?"

[8]Then Judah said to Israel his father, "Send the lad with me, and we will arise and go, that we may live and not die, both we and you *and* also our little ones. [9]I myself will be surety for him; from my hand you shall require him. If I do not bring him *back* to you and set him before you, then let me bear the blame forever. [10]For if we had not lingered, surely by now we would have returned this second time."

43:9 I myself will be surety for him. Although Reuben's offer to guarantee Benjamin's safety had been rejected (42:37,38), Judah's was accepted (v. 11) because of the severity of the famine and the threat that they would all die if they waited much longer (v. 10).

[11]And their father Israel said to them, "If *it must be* so, then do this: Take some of the best fruits of the land in your vessels and carry down a present for the man—a little balm and a little honey, spices and myrrh, pistachio nuts and almonds. [12]Take double money in your hand, and take back in your hand the money that was returned in the mouth of your sacks; perhaps it was an oversight. [13]Take your brother also, and arise, go back to the man. [14]And may God Almighty give you mercy before the man, that he may release your other brother and Benjamin. If I am bereaved, I am bereaved!"

[15]So the men took that present and Benjamin, and they took double money in their hand, and arose and went down to Egypt; and they stood before Joseph. [16]When Joseph saw Benjamin with them, he said to the steward of his house, "Take *these* men to my home, and slaughter an animal and make ready; for *these* men will dine with me at noon." [17]Then the man did as Joseph ordered, and the man brought the men into Joseph's house.

[18]Now the men were afraid because they were brought into Joseph's house; and they said, "*It is* because of the money, which was returned in our sacks the first time, that we are brought in, so that he may make a case against us and seize us, to take us as slaves with our donkeys."

[19]When they drew near to the steward of Joseph's house, they talked with him at the door of the house, [20]and said, "O sir, we indeed came down the first time to buy food; [21]but it happened, when we came to the encampment, that we opened our sacks, and there, *each* man's money *was* in the mouth of his sack, our money in full weight; so we have brought it back in our hand. [22]And we have brought down other money in our hands to buy food. We do not know who put our money in our sacks."

[23]But he said, "Peace *be* with you, do not be afraid. Your God and the God of your father has given you treasure in your sacks; I had your money." Then he brought Simeon out to them.

[24]So the man brought the men into Joseph's house and gave *them* water, and they washed their feet; and he gave their donkeys feed. [25]Then they made the present ready for Joseph's coming at noon, for they heard that they would eat bread there.

[26]And when Joseph came home, they brought him the present which *was* in their hand into the house, and bowed down before him to the earth. [27]Then he asked them about *their* well-being, and said, "*Is* your father well, the old man of whom you spoke? *Is* he still alive?"

43:26 bowed down. Again, Joseph's boyhood dreams (37:5–8) had become reality (see 42:6).

[28]And they answered, "Your servant our father *is* in good health; he *is* still alive."

And they bowed their heads down and prostrated themselves.

²⁹Then he lifted his eyes and saw his brother Benjamin, his mother's son, and said, "*Is* this your younger brother of whom you spoke to me?" And he said, "God be gracious to you, my son." ³⁰Now his heart yearned for his brother; so Joseph made haste and sought *somewhere* to weep. And he went into *his* chamber and wept there. ³¹Then he washed his face and came out; and he restrained himself, and said, "Serve the bread."

³²So they set him a place by himself, and them by themselves, and the Egyptians who ate with him by themselves; because the Egyptians could not eat food with the Hebrews, for that *is* an abomination to the Egyptians. ³³And they sat before him, the firstborn according to his birthright and the youngest according to his youth; and the men looked in astonishment at one another. ³⁴Then he took servings to them from before him, but Benjamin's serving was five times as much as any of theirs. So they drank and were merry with him.

43:34 Benjamin's serving. Joseph first startled them by seating them in their correct birth order, and then he silently tested their attitudes by showing favoritism to Rachel's other son Benjamin. Any long-standing envy, dislike, or hatred could not be easily masked, but none surfaced.

Joseph's Cup

44 And he commanded the steward of his house, saying, "Fill the men's sacks with food, as much as they can carry, and put each man's money in the mouth of his sack. ²Also put my cup, the silver cup, in the mouth of the sack of the youngest, and his grain money." So he did according to the word that Joseph had spoken. ³As soon as the morning dawned, the men were sent away, they and their donkeys. ⁴When they had gone out of the city, *and* were not *yet* far off, Joseph said to his steward, "Get up, follow the men; and when you overtake them, say to them, 'Why have you repaid evil for good? ⁵*Is* not this *the one* from which my lord drinks, and with which he indeed practices divination? You have done evil in so doing.' "

⁶So he overtook them, and he spoke to them these same words. ⁷And they said to him, "Why does my lord say these words? Far be it from us that your servants should do such a thing. ⁸Look, we brought back to you from the land of Canaan the money which we found in the mouth of our sacks. How then could we steal silver or gold from your lord's house? ⁹With whomever of your servants it is found, let him die, and we also will be my lord's slaves."

¹⁰And he said, "Now also *let* it *be* according to your words; he with whom it is found shall be my slave, and you shall be blameless." ¹¹Then each man speedily let down his sack to the ground, and each opened his sack. ¹²So he searched. He began with the oldest and left off with the youngest; and the cup was found in Benjamin's sack. ¹³Then they tore their clothes, and each man loaded his donkey and returned to the city.

44:13 tore their clothes. A well-known, ancient Near Eastern custom of visibly portraying deep pain of heart. They were very upset that Benjamin might become a slave in Egypt. Benjamin appears to have been speechless. They had passed a second test of devotion to Benjamin (the first in v. 34).

¹⁴So Judah and his brothers came to Joseph's house, and he *was* still there; and they fell before him on the ground. ¹⁵And Joseph said to them, "What deed *is* this you have done? Did you not know that such a man as I can certainly practice divination?"

¹⁶Then Judah said, "What shall we say to my lord? What shall we speak? Or how shall we clear ourselves? God has found out the iniquity of your servants; here we are, my lord's slaves, both we and *he* also with whom the cup was found."

¹⁷But he said, "Far be it from me that I should do so; the man in whose hand the cup was found, he shall be my slave. And as for you, go up in peace to your father."

Judah Intercedes for Benjamin

¹⁸Then Judah came near to him and said: "O my lord, please let your servant speak a word in my lord's hearing, and do not let your anger burn against your servant; for you *are* even like Pharaoh. ¹⁹My lord asked his servants, saying, 'Have you a father or a brother?' ²⁰And we said to my lord, 'We

have a father, an old man, and a child of *his* old age; *who is* young; his brother is dead, and he alone is left of his mother's children, and his father loves him.' ²¹Then you said to your servants, 'Bring him down to me, that I may set my eyes on him.' ²²And we said to my lord, 'The lad cannot leave his father, for *if* he should leave his father, *his father* would die.' ²³But you said to your servants, 'Unless your youngest brother comes down with you, you shall see my face no more.'

²⁴"So it was, when we went up to your servant my father, that we told him the words of my lord. ²⁵And our father said, 'Go back *and* buy us a little food.' ²⁶But we said, 'We cannot go down; if our youngest brother is with us, then we will go down; for we may not see the man's face unless our youngest brother *is* with us.' ²⁷Then your servant my father said to us, 'You know that my wife bore me two sons; ²⁸and the one went out from me, and I said, "Surely he is torn to pieces"; and I have not seen him since. ²⁹But if you take this one also from me, and calamity befalls him, you shall bring down my gray hair with sorrow to the grave.'

³⁰"Now therefore, when I come to your servant my father, and the lad *is* not with us, since his life is bound up in the lad's life, ³¹it will happen, when he sees that the lad *is* not *with us*, that he will die. So your servants will bring down the gray hair of your servant our father with sorrow to the grave. ³²For your servant became surety for the lad to my father, saying, 'If I do not bring him *back* to you, then I shall bear the blame before my father forever.' ³³Now therefore, please let your servant remain instead of the lad as a slave to my lord, and let the lad go up with his brothers. ³⁴For how shall I go up to my father if the lad *is* not with me, lest perhaps I see the evil that would come upon my father?"

> **44:18–34** The brothers gave an eloquent and passionate plea for mercy, referring to their aged father's delight in the youngest son (vv. 20,30) and the fatal shock if he were lost. Judah's compassion for Jacob and readiness to substitute himself for Benjamin in slavery finally overwhelmed Joseph. These brothers had changed drastically since they had sold Joseph into slavery.

Joseph Revealed to His Brothers

45 Then Joseph could not restrain himself before all those who stood by him, and he cried out, "Make everyone go out from me!" So no one stood with him while Joseph made himself known to his brothers. ²And he wept aloud, and the Egyptians and the house of Pharaoh heard *it.*

³Then Joseph said to his brothers, "I *am* Joseph; does my father still live?" But his brothers could not answer him, for they were dismayed in his presence. ⁴And Joseph said to his brothers, "Please come near to me." So they came near. Then he said: "I *am* Joseph your brother, whom you sold into Egypt. ⁵But now, do not therefore be grieved or angry with yourselves because you sold me here; for God sent me before you to preserve life. ⁶For these two years the famine *has been* in the land, and *there are* still five years in which *there will be* neither plowing nor harvesting. ⁷And God sent me before you to preserve a posterity for you in the earth, and to save your lives by a great deliverance. ⁸So now *it was* not you *who* sent me here, but God; and He has made me a father to Pharaoh, and lord of all his house, and a ruler throughout all the land of Egypt.

⁹"Hurry and go up to my father, and say to him, 'Thus says your son Joseph: "God has made me lord of all Egypt; come down to me, do not tarry. ¹⁰You shall dwell in the land of Goshen, and you shall be near to me, you and your children, your children's children, your flocks and your herds, and all that you have. ¹¹There I will provide for you, lest you and your household, and all that you have, come to poverty; for *there are* still five years of famine."'

¹²"And behold, your eyes and the eyes of my brother Benjamin see that *it is* my mouth that speaks to you. ¹³So you shall tell my father of all my glory in Egypt, and of all that you have seen; and you shall hurry and bring my father down here."

¹⁴Then he fell on his brother Benjamin's neck and wept, and Benjamin wept on his

> **45:14,15** Their reconciliation had much emotion and clearly showed that Joseph had forgiven them and held no grudges against them, evidencing his spiritual maturity. Twenty-two years had passed since the brothers had sold Joseph into slavery.

neck. [15]Moreover he kissed all his brothers and wept over them, and after that his brothers talked with him.

[16]Now the report of it was heard in Pharaoh's house, saying, "Joseph's brothers have come." So it pleased Pharaoh and his servants well. [17]And Pharaoh said to Joseph, "Say to your brothers, 'Do this: Load your animals and depart; go to the land of Canaan. [18]Bring your father and your households and come to me; I will give you the best of the land of Egypt, and you will eat the fat of the land. [19]Now you are commanded—do this: Take carts out of the land of Egypt for your little ones and your wives; bring your father and come. [20]Also do not be concerned about your goods, for the best of all the land of Egypt is yours.' "

[21]Then the sons of Israel did so; and Joseph gave them carts, according to the command of Pharaoh, and he gave them provisions for the journey. [22]He gave to all of them, to each man, changes of garments; but to Benjamin he gave three hundred pieces of silver and five changes of garments. [23]And he sent to his father these things: ten donkeys loaded with the good things of Egypt, and ten female donkeys loaded with grain, bread, and food for his father for the journey. [24]So he sent his brothers away, and they departed; and he said to them, "See that you do not become troubled along the way."

[25]Then they went up out of Egypt, and came to the land of Canaan to Jacob their father. [26]And they told him, saying, "Joseph is still alive, and he is governor over all the land of Egypt." And Jacob's heart stood still, because he did not believe them. [27]But when they told him all the words which Joseph had said to them, and when he saw the carts which Joseph had sent to carry him, the spirit of Jacob their father revived. [28]Then Israel said, "It is enough. Joseph my son is still alive. I will go and see him before I die."

Jacob's Journey to Egypt

46 So Israel took his journey with all that he had, and came to Beersheba, and offered sacrifices to the God of his father

Isaac. [2]Then God spoke to Israel in the visions of the night, and said, "Jacob, Jacob!"

And he said, "Here I am."

[3]So He said, "I am God, the God of your father; do not fear to go down to Egypt, for I will make of you a great nation there. [4]I will go down with you to Egypt, and I will also surely bring you up again; and Joseph will put his hand on your eyes."

46:2-4 God spoke...in the visions. Jacob felt quite anxious about his departure to Egypt, but the Lord quieted his fears by giving His approval and confirmation that his descendants would return as a nation. The Lord promised Jacob that he would die peacefully in the presence of his beloved son Joseph (see 49:33).

[5]Then Jacob arose from Beersheba; and the sons of Israel carried their father Jacob, their little ones, and their wives, in the carts which Pharaoh had sent to carry him. [6]So they took their livestock and their goods, which they had acquired in the land of Canaan, and went to Egypt, Jacob and all his descendants with him. [7]His sons and his sons' sons, his daughters and his sons' daughters, and all his descendants he brought with him to Egypt.

46:6 went to Egypt. About 1875 B.C. They remained 430 years (Ex. 12:40) until the Exodus in 1445 B.C.

[8]Now these were the names of the children of Israel, Jacob and his sons, who went to Egypt: Reuben was Jacob's firstborn. [9]The sons of Reuben were Hanoch, Pallu, Hezron, and Carmi. [10]The sons of Simeon were Jemuel,[a] Jamin, Ohad, Jachin,[b] Zohar,[c] and Shaul, the son of a Canaanite woman. [11]The sons of Levi were Gershon, Kohath, and Merari. [12]The sons of Judah were Er, Onan, Shelah, Perez, and Zerah (but Er and Onan died in the land of Canaan). The sons of Perez were Hezron and Hamul. [13]The sons of Issachar were Tola, Puvah,[a] Job,[b] and Shimron. [14]The sons of Zebulun were Sered, Elon, and Jahleel. [15]These were the sons of Leah, whom she

---

46:10 [a]Spelled Nemuel in 1 Chronicles 4:24 [b]Called Jarib in 1 Chronicles 4:24 [c]Called Zerah in 1 Chronicles 4:24   46:13 [a]Spelled Puah in 1 Chronicles 7:1 [b]Same as Jashub in Numbers 26:24 and 1 Chronicles 7:1

bore to Jacob in Padan Aram, with his daughter Dinah. All the persons, his sons and his daughters, *were* thirty-three.

¹⁶The sons of Gad *were* Ziphion,*ᵃ* Haggi, Shuni, Ezbon,*ᵇ* Eri, Arodi,*ᶜ* and Areli. ¹⁷The sons of Asher *were* Jimnah, Ishuah, Isui, Beriah, and Serah, their sister. And the sons of Beriah *were* Heber and Malchiel. ¹⁸These *were* the sons of Zilpah, whom Laban gave to Leah his daughter; and these she bore to Jacob: sixteen persons.

¹⁹The sons of Rachel, Jacob's wife, *were* Joseph and Benjamin. ²⁰And to Joseph in the land of Egypt were born Manasseh and Ephraim, whom Asenath, the daughter of Poti-Pherah priest of On, bore to him. ²¹The sons of Benjamin *were* Belah, Becher, Ashbel, Gera, Naaman, Ehi, Rosh, Muppim, Huppim,*ᵃ* and Ard. ²²These *were* the sons of Rachel, who were born to Jacob: fourteen persons in all.

²³The son of Dan *was* Hushim.*ᵃ* ²⁴The sons of Naphtali *were* Jahzeel,*ᵃ* Guni, Jezer, and Shillem.*ᵇ* ²⁵These *were* the sons of Bilhah, whom Laban gave to Rachel his daughter, and she bore these to Jacob: seven persons in all.

²⁶All the persons who went with Jacob to Egypt, who came from his body, besides Jacob's sons' wives, *were* sixty-six persons in all. ²⁷And the sons of Joseph who were born to him in Egypt *were* two persons. All the persons of the house of Jacob who went to Egypt were seventy.

> **46:27 seventy.** Jacob, Joseph, Manasseh, and Ephraim should be added to the sixty-six persons mentioned in v. 26.

Jacob Settles in Goshen

²⁸Then he sent Judah before him to Joseph, to point out before him *the way* to Goshen. And they came to the land of Goshen. ²⁹So Joseph made ready his chariot and went up to Goshen to meet his father Israel; and he presented himself to him, and fell on his neck and wept on his neck a good while.

³⁰And Israel said to Joseph, "Now let me die, since I have seen your face, because you *are* still alive."

³¹Then Joseph said to his brothers and to his father's household, "I will go up and tell Pharaoh, and say to him, 'My brothers and those of my father's house, who *were* in the land of Canaan, have come to me. ³²And the men *are* shepherds, for their occupation has been to feed livestock; and they have brought their flocks, their herds, and all that they have.' ³³So it shall be, when Pharaoh calls you and says, 'What is your occupation?' ³⁴that you shall say, 'Your servants' occupation has been with livestock from our youth even till now, both we *and* also our fathers,' that you may dwell in the land of Goshen; for every shepherd *is* an abomination to the Egyptians."

> **46:31–34** Joseph's instructions about his preparatory interview with Pharaoh were designed to secure a place for his relatives separate from the mainstream Egyptian society. The social stigma against Hebrews (43:32), who were also shepherds (v. 34), helped protect Israel from intermingling and losing their identity in Egypt.

47 Then Joseph went and told Pharaoh, and said, "My father and my brothers, their flocks and their herds and all that they possess, have come from the land of Canaan; and indeed they *are* in the land of Goshen." ²And he took five men from among his brothers and presented them to Pharaoh. ³Then Pharaoh said to his brothers, "What *is* your occupation?"

And they said to Pharaoh, "Your servants *are* shepherds, both we *and* also our fathers." ⁴And they said to Pharaoh, "We have come to dwell in the land, because your servants have no pasture for their flocks, for the famine *is* severe in the land of Canaan. Now therefore, please let your servants dwell in the land of Goshen."

⁵Then Pharaoh spoke to Joseph, saying, "Your father and your brothers have come to you. ⁶The land of Egypt *is* before you. Have your father and brothers dwell in the

---

46:16 *ᵃ*Spelled *Zephon* in Samaritan Pentateuch, Septuagint, and Numbers 26:15 *ᵇ*Called *Ozni* in Numbers 26:16 *ᶜ*Spelled *Arod* in Numbers 26:17 46:21 *ᵃ*Called *Hupham* in Numbers 26:39 46:23 *ᵃ*Called *Shuham* in Numbers 26:42 46:24 *ᵃ*Spelled *Jahziel* in 1 Chronicles 7:13 *ᵇ*Spelled *Shallum* in 1 Chronicles 7:13

best of the land; let them dwell in the land of Goshen. And if you know *any* competent men among them, then make them chief herdsmen over my livestock."

⁷Then Joseph brought in his father Jacob and set him before Pharaoh; and Jacob blessed Pharaoh. ⁸Pharaoh said to Jacob, "How old *are* you?"

⁹And Jacob said to Pharaoh, "The days of the years of my pilgrimage *are* one hundred and thirty years; few and evil have been the days of the years of my life, and they have not attained to the days of the years of the life of my fathers in the days of their pilgrimage." ¹⁰So Jacob blessed Pharaoh, and went out from before Pharaoh.

¹¹And Joseph situated his father and his brothers, and gave them a possession in the land of Egypt, in the best of the land, in the land of Rameses, as Pharaoh had commanded. ¹²Then Joseph provided his father, his brothers, and all his father's household with bread, according to the number in *their* families.

Joseph Deals with the Famine

¹³Now *there was* no bread in all the land; for the famine *was* very severe, so that the land of Egypt and the land of Canaan languished because of the famine. ¹⁴And Joseph gathered up all the money that was found in the land of Egypt and in the land of Canaan, for the grain which they bought; and Joseph brought the money into Pharaoh's house.

¹⁵So when the money failed in the land of Egypt and in the land of Canaan, all the Egyptians came to Joseph and said, "Give us bread, for why should we die in your presence? For the money has failed."

> **47:15 when the money failed.** The severity of the famine finally bankrupted all in Egypt and Canaan. Without money to exchange, a barter system was established, and they exchanged first their livestock and then their land for food.

¹⁶Then Joseph said, "Give your livestock, and I will give you *bread* for your livestock, if the money is gone." ¹⁷So they brought their livestock to Joseph, and Joseph gave

them bread *in exchange* for the horses, the flocks, the cattle of the herds, and for the donkeys. Thus he fed them with bread *in exchange* for all their livestock that year.

¹⁸When that year had ended, they came to him the next year and said to him, "We will not hide from my lord that our money is gone; my lord also has our herds of livestock. There is nothing left in the sight of my lord but our bodies and our lands. ¹⁹Why should we die before your eyes, both we and our land? Buy us and our land for bread, and we and our land will be servants of Pharaoh; give *us* seed, that we may live and not die, that the land may not be desolate."

²⁰Then Joseph bought all the land of Egypt for Pharaoh; for every man of the Egyptians sold his field, because the famine was severe upon them. So the land became Pharaoh's. ²¹And as for the people, he moved them into the cities,ᵃ from *one* end of the borders of Egypt to the *other* end. ²²Only the land of the priests he did not buy; for the priests had rations *allotted to them* by Pharaoh, and they ate their rations which Pharaoh gave them; therefore they did not sell their lands.

²³Then Joseph said to the people, "Indeed I have bought you and your land this day for Pharaoh. Look, *here is* seed for you, and you shall sow the land. ²⁴And it shall come to pass in the harvest that you shall give one-fifth to Pharaoh. Four-fifths shall be your own, as seed for the field and for your food, for those of your households and as food for your little ones."

²⁵So they said, "You have saved our lives; let us find favor in the sight of my lord, and we will be Pharaoh's servants." ²⁶And Joseph made it a law over the land of Egypt to this day, *that* Pharaoh should have one-fifth, except for the land of the priests only, *which* did not become Pharaoh's.

Joseph's Vow to Jacob

²⁷So Israel dwelt in the land of Egypt, in the country of Goshen; and they had possessions there and grew and multiplied exceedingly. ²⁸And Jacob lived in the land of Egypt seventeen years. So the length of Jacob's life was one hundred and forty-

---

47:21 ᵃFollowing Masoretic Text and Targum; Samaritan Pentateuch, Septuagint, and Vulgate read *made the people virtual slaves*.

seven years. ²⁹When the time drew near that Israel must die, he called his son Joseph and said to him, "Now if I have found favor in your sight, please put your hand under my thigh, and deal kindly and truly with me. Please do not bury me in Egypt, ³⁰but let me lie with my fathers; you shall carry me out of Egypt and bury me in their burial place."

And he said, "I will do as you have said."

³¹Then he said, "Swear to me." And he swore to him. So Israel bowed himself on the head of the bed.

Jacob Blesses Joseph's Sons

48 Now it came to pass after these things that Joseph was told, "Indeed your father is sick"; and he took with him his two sons, Manasseh and Ephraim. ²And Jacob was told, "Look, your son Joseph is coming to you"; and Israel strengthened himself and sat up on the bed. ³Then Jacob said to Joseph: "God Almighty appeared to me at Luz in the land of Canaan and blessed me, ⁴and said to me, 'Behold, I will make you fruitful and multiply you, and I will make of you a multitude of people, and give this land to your descendants after you as an everlasting possession.' ⁵And now your two sons, Ephraim and Manasseh, who were born to you in the land of Egypt before I came to you in Egypt, are mine; as Reuben and Simeon, they shall be mine. ⁶Your offspring whom you beget after them shall be yours; they will be called by the name of their brothers in their inheritance. ⁷But as for me, when I came from Padan, Rachel died beside me in the land of Canaan on the way, when there was but a little distance to go to Ephrath; and I buried her there on the way to Ephrath (that is, Bethlehem)."

> **48:3–6** Jacob summarized God's affirmation of the Abrahamic Covenant to himself, and then out of gratitude for Joseph's generosity and preservation of God's people, he formally adopted Joseph's two sons on a par with his own sons in their inheritance. Thus he granted Rachel's two sons (Joseph and Benjamin) three tribal territories in the Land (see v. 16).

⁸Then Israel saw Joseph's sons, and said, "Who are these?"

⁹Joseph said to his father, "They are my sons, whom God has given me in this place."

And he said, "Please bring them to me, and I will bless them." ¹⁰Now the eyes of Israel were dim with age, so that he could not see. Then Joseph brought them near him, and he kissed them and embraced them. ¹¹And Israel said to Joseph, "I had not thought to see your face; but in fact, God has also shown me your offspring!"

¹²So Joseph brought them from beside his knees, and he bowed down with his face to the earth. ¹³And Joseph took them both, Ephraim with his right hand toward Israel's left hand, and Manasseh with his left hand toward Israel's right hand, and brought them near him. ¹⁴Then Israel stretched out his right hand and laid it on Ephraim's head, who was the younger, and his left hand on Manasseh's head, guiding his hands knowingly, for Manasseh was the firstborn. ¹⁵And he blessed Joseph, and said:

> " God, before whom my fathers
>   Abraham and Isaac walked,
>   The God who has fed me all my life
>   long to this day,
> 16   The Angel who has redeemed me
>   from all evil,
>   Bless the lads;
>   Let my name be named upon them,
>   And the name of my fathers Abraham
>   and Isaac;
>   And let them grow into a multitude in
>   the midst of the earth."

> **48:14 guiding his hands knowingly.** By intentionally crossing his hands and placing his right hand on the younger, not on the firstborn, Jacob altered what Joseph had expected. Yet Jacob knew exactly what he was doing. The blessing took on prophetic significance, because Ephraim would become the more influential of the two to the extent that Ephraim would become a substitute name for Israel.

¹⁷Now when Joseph saw that his father laid his right hand on the head of Ephraim, it displeased him; so he took hold of his father's hand to remove it from Ephraim's head to Manasseh's head. ¹⁸And Joseph said to his father, "Not so, my father, for this one is the firstborn; put your right hand on his head."

¹⁹But his father refused and said, "I know, my son, I know. He also shall become a people, and he also shall be great; but truly his younger brother shall be greater than he, and his descendants shall become a multitude of nations."

²⁰So he blessed them that day, saying, "By you Israel will bless, saying, 'May God make you as Ephraim and as Manasseh!'" And thus he set Ephraim before Manasseh.

²¹Then Israel said to Joseph, "Behold, I am dying, but God will be with you and bring you back to the land of your fathers. ²²Moreover I have given to you one portion above your brothers, which I took from the hand of the Amorite with my sword and my bow."

Jacob's Last Words to His Sons

49 And Jacob called his sons and said, "Gather together, that I may tell you what shall befall you in the last days:

2　　"Gather together and hear, you sons of Jacob,
　　And listen to Israel your father.

3　　"Reuben, you are my firstborn,
　　My might and the beginning of my strength,
　　The excellency of dignity and the excellency of power.
4　　Unstable as water, you shall not excel,
　　Because you went up to your father's bed;
　　Then you defiled *it*—
　　He went up to my couch.

> **49:3,4** The seriousness of Reuben's sin (35:22) was not forgotten. Its consequences erased his birthright, and his tribe never received much honor in Israelite history, never producing a single judge, prophet, military leader, or important person.

5　　"Simeon and Levi *are* brothers;
　　Instruments of cruelty *are in* their dwelling place.
6　　Let not my soul enter their council;
　　Let not my honor be united to their assembly;
　　For in their anger they slew a man,
　　And in their self-will they hamstrung an ox.

7　　Cursed *be* their anger, for *it is* fierce;
　　And their wrath, for it is cruel!
　　I will divide them in Jacob
　　And scatter them in Israel.

8　　"Judah, you *are he* whom your brothers shall praise;
　　Your hand *shall be* on the neck of your enemies;
　　Your father's children shall bow down before you.
9　　Judah *is* a lion's whelp;
　　From the prey, my son, you have gone up.
　　He bows down, he lies down as a lion;
　　And as a lion, who shall rouse him?
10　The scepter shall not depart from Judah,
　　Nor a lawgiver from between his feet,
　　Until Shiloh comes;
　　And to Him *shall be* the obedience of the people.
11　Binding his donkey to the vine,
　　And his donkey's colt to the choice vine,
　　He washed his garments in wine,
　　And his clothes in the blood of grapes.
12　His eyes *are* darker than wine,
　　And his teeth whiter than milk.

> **49:8–12** Described as a strong young lion and as a secure old lion, the tribe of Judah was blessed with national prominence and with kingship, including David, Solomon, and their dynasty (640 years later) and especially "the one to whom the scepter belongs," or the Messiah, the one also called the "Lion of the Tribe of Judah" (Rev. 5:5). When the nation marched through the wilderness, Judah led first (Num. 10:14) and had the largest population in Moses' census (see Num. 1:27; 26:22). This imagery (vv. 11,12) describes prosperity so great that people will tie a donkey to a choice vine and let it eat the grapes because there is such abundance. Likely, this is a millennial prophecy.

13　"Zebulun shall dwell by the haven of the sea;
　　He *shall become* a haven for ships,
　　And his border shall adjoin Sidon.

14　"Issachar is a strong donkey,
　　Lying down between two burdens;
15　He saw that rest *was* good,
　　And that the land *was* pleasant;

He bowed his shoulder to bear *a
    burden,*
And became a band of slaves.

16 "Dan shall judge his people
    As one of the tribes of Israel.
17 Dan shall be a serpent by the way,
    A viper by the path,
    That bites the horse's heels
    So that its rider shall fall backward.
18 I have waited for your salvation,
    O LORD!

19 "Gad, a troop shall tramp upon him,
    But he shall triumph at last.

20 "Bread from Asher *shall be* rich,
    And he shall yield royal dainties.

21 "Naphtali *is* a deer let loose;
    He uses beautiful words.

22 "Joseph *is* a fruitful bough,
    A fruitful bough by a well;
    His branches run over the wall.
23 The archers have bitterly grieved him,
    Shot *at him* and hated him.
24 But his bow remained in strength,
    And the arms of his hands were made
        strong
    By the hands of the Mighty *God* of
        Jacob
    (From there *is* the Shepherd, the
        Stone of Israel),
25 By the God of your father who will
        help you,
    And by the Almighty who will bless
        you
    With blessings of heaven above,
    Blessings of the deep that lies
        beneath,
    Blessings of the breasts and of the
        womb.
26 The blessings of your father
    Have excelled the blessings of my
        ancestors,
    Up to the utmost bound of the
        everlasting hills.
    They shall be on the head of Joseph,
    And on the crown of the head of him
        who was separate from his
        brothers.

27 "Benjamin is a ravenous wolf;

In the morning he shall devour the
    prey,
And at night he shall divide the
    spoil."

28All these *are* the twelve tribes of Israel,
and this *is* what their father spoke to them.
And he blessed them; he blessed each one
according to his own blessing.

> **49:1–28** With Judah and Joseph receiving the most
> attention (vv. 8–12,22–26), the father's blessing
> portrayed the future history of each son, seemingly
> based upon their characters up to that time. The
> confusing message of the poetry demands rigorous
> analysis to correlate tribal history with Jacob's last
> word and testament. See Moses' blessing on the
> tribes in Deut. 33.

Jacob's Death and Burial

29Then he charged them and said to
them: "I am to be gathered to my people;
bury me with my fathers in the cave that *is*
in the field of Ephron the Hittite, 30in the
cave that *is* in the field of Machpelah,
which *is* before Mamre in the land of Canaan, which Abraham bought with the field
of Ephron the Hittite as a possession for a
burial place. 31There they buried Abraham
and Sarah his wife, there they buried Isaac
and Rebekah his wife, and there I buried
Leah. 32The field and the cave that *is* there
were purchased from the sons of Heth."
33And when Jacob had finished commanding his sons, he drew his feet up into the
bed and breathed his last, and was gathered
to his people.

ADAM TO ISRAEL'S TWELVE TRIBES

Adam
Cain   Abel   Seth
Lamech   Noah
      Shem   Ham   Japheth
      Terah
Haran   Abraham
Lot   Ishmael   Isaac   Midian
Moab   Ammon   Jacob   Esau
      Twelve Tribes

50

Then Joseph fell on his father's face and wept over him, and kissed him. ²And Joseph commanded his servants the physicians to embalm his father. So the physicians embalmed Israel. ³Forty days were required for him, for such are the days required for those who are embalmed; and the Egyptians mourned for him seventy days.

⁴Now when the days of his mourning were past, Joseph spoke to the household of Pharaoh, saying, "If now I have found favor in your eyes, please speak in the hearing of Pharaoh, saying, ⁵'My father made me swear, saying, "Behold, I am dying; in my grave which I dug for myself in the land of Canaan, there you shall bury me." Now therefore, please let me go up and bury my father, and I will come back.'"

⁶And Pharaoh said, "Go up and bury your father, as he made you swear."

⁷So Joseph went up to bury his father; and with him went up all the servants of Pharaoh, the elders of his house, and all the elders of the land of Egypt, ⁸as well as all the house of Joseph, his brothers, and his father's house. Only their little ones, their flocks, and their herds they left in the land of Goshen. ⁹And there went up with him both chariots and horsemen, and it was a very great gathering.

¹⁰Then they came to the threshing floor of Atad, which *is* beyond the Jordan, and they mourned there with a great and very solemn lamentation. He observed seven days of mourning for his father. ¹¹And when the inhabitants of the land, the Canaanites, saw the mourning at the threshing floor of Atad, they said, "This *is* a deep mourning of the Egyptians." Therefore its name was called Abel Mizraim,ᵃ which *is* beyond the Jordan.

¹²So his sons did for him just as he had commanded them. ¹³For his sons carried him to the land of Canaan, and buried him in the cave of the field of Machpelah, before Mamre, which Abraham bought with the field from Ephron the Hittite as property for a burial place. ¹⁴And after he had buried his father, Joseph returned to Egypt, he and his brothers and all who went up with him to bury his father.

Joseph Reassures His Brothers

¹⁵When Joseph's brothers saw that their father was dead, they said, "Perhaps Joseph

---

50:11 ᵃLiterally *Mourning of Egypt*

JOSEPH—A TYPE OF CHRIST

Joseph	Parallels	Jesus
37:2	A shepherd of his father's sheep	John 10:11,27–29
37:3	His father loved him dearly	Matthew 3:17
37:4	Hated by his brothers	John 7:4,5
37:13,14	Sent by father to brothers	Hebrews 2:11
37:20	Others plotted to harm them	John 11:53
37:23	Robes taken from them	John 19:23,24
37:26	Taken to Egypt	Matthew 2:14,15
37:28	Sold for the price of a slave	Matthew 26:15
39:7	Tempted	Matthew 4:1
39:16–18	Falsely accused	Matthew 26:59,60
39:20	Bound in chains	Matthew 27:2
40:2,3	Placed with two other prisoners, one who was saved and the other lost	Luke 23:32
41:41	Exalted after suffering	Philemon 2:9–11
41:46	Both 30 years old at the beginning of public recognition	Luke 3:23
42:24; 45:2,14,15; 46:29	Both wept	John 11:35
45:1-15	Forgave those who wronged them	Luke 23:34
45:7	Saved their nation	Matthew 1:21
50:20	What men did to hurt them, God turned to good	1 Corinthians 2:7,8

will hate us, and may actually repay us for all the evil which we did to him." ¹⁶So they sent *messengers* to Joseph, saying, "Before your father died he commanded, saying, ¹⁷'Thus you shall say to Joseph: "I beg you, please forgive the trespass of your brothers and their sin; for they did evil to you." ' Now, please, forgive the trespass of the servants of the God of your father." And Joseph wept when they spoke to him.

¹⁸Then his brothers also went and fell down before his face, and they said, "Behold, we *are* your servants."

¹⁹Joseph said to them, "Do not be afraid, for *am* I in the place of God? ²⁰But as for you, you meant evil against me; *but* God meant it for good, in order to bring it about as *it is* this day, to save many people alive. ²¹Now therefore, do not be afraid; I will provide for you and your little ones." And he comforted them and spoke kindly to them.

Death of Joseph

²²So Joseph dwelt in Egypt, he and his father's household. And Joseph lived one hundred and ten years. ²³Joseph saw Eph-

50:20 but God meant it for good. Joseph's wise, theological answer affirmed the genuineness of his forgiveness for his brothers. It has passed down through history as the classic statement of God's sovereignty over the affairs of humanity.

raim's children to the third *generation.* The children of Machir, the son of Manasseh, were also brought up on Joseph's knees.

²⁴And Joseph said to his brethren, "I am dying; but God will surely visit you, and bring you out of this land to the land of which He swore to Abraham, to Isaac, and to Jacob." ²⁵Then Joseph took an oath from the children of Israel, saying, "God will surely visit you, and you shall carry up my bones from here." ²⁶So Joseph died, *being* one hundred and ten years old; and they embalmed him, and he was put in a coffin in Egypt.

50:24 God will surely visit you. Joseph died just as he had lived, firmly trusting God to carry out His promises (see Heb. 11:22). Nearly four centuries later, Moses took Joseph's bones out of Egypt (Ex. 13:19), and Joshua buried them at Shechem (Josh. 24:32).

EXODUS

The descriptive title "Exodus" was given to the second book of Moses by the ancient translators of the Greek Old Testament. Later versions, from the Latin Vulgate to the present translations have simply borrowed the title. In the original Hebrew Bible, the opening words "And (or Now) these are the names," served as the book's title.

AUTHOR AND DATE

Exodus was written by Moses, approximately 1445 to 1405 B.C.

Mosaic authorship of Exodus is unhesitatingly affirmed by Scripture. For example, Moses followed God's instructions when he "wrote all the words of the LORD" (Exodus 24:4). Similar references to Moses as the writer occur elsewhere in the Pentateuch (the first five biblical books).

Old Testament witnesses to Moses' authorship of Exodus: Joshua 1:7,8; 8:31,32; 1 Kings 2:3; 2 Kings 14:6; Nehemiah 13:1; Daniel 9:11–13; Malachi 4:4.

New Testament witnesses to Moses' authorship of Exodus: Mark 7:10; 12:26; Luke 2:22,23; John 7:19; Romans 10:5 all quote or refer to Exodus as part of God's law given through Moses.

Moses wrote this second of his five books during his 40 year tenure as Israel's leader. The events surrounding Israel's departure from Egypt (about 1445 B.C.) place the date of composition in the 15th century B.C.

BACKGROUND AND SETTING

Israel's dramatic exit from Egypt occurred during the Eighteenth Dynasty, a setting of great political and economic strength in Egyptian history. Though born a slave, Moses had entered a culture in rapid expansion and growth. Egypt was a world military, economic, and political super-power. God used the educational and governmental systems of Egypt as well as a wilderness exile in Midian to train Moses. Once ready, Moses represented Israel before powerful Pharaoh Amenhotep II and, then, guided his people on their wilderness journey.

Exodus sketches Moses's early history and records the details of Israel's departure from Egypt. It concludes after the giving of the Law and the construction of the Tabernacle at the foot of Mt. Sinai. At that point, despite the people's terrible sin of idolatry while Moses was on the mountain, God continued to lead Israel to the Promised Land.

The Exodus marked an important transition in God's timing. A time of oppression for Abraham's descendants was concluded as the fulfillment of God's covenant promises to Abraham was drawing closer. These fulfillments included the development of a great nation from a single child and the possession of the Promised Land (Genesis 12:1–3,7). The purpose of Exodus may be summarized thusly: To record the explosion of Jacob's descendants in Egypt, to chronicle their escape, and to document the establishment of a theocratic nation on her way to the Promised Land.

THE **EXODUS MARKED** AN **IMPORTANT TRANSITION** IN **GOD'S TIMING.**

OUTLINE

Israel's Suffering in Egypt

1 Now these *are* the names of the children of Israel who came to Egypt; each man and his household came with Jacob: ²Reuben, Simeon, Levi, and Judah; ³Issachar, Zebulun, and Benjamin; ⁴Dan, Naphtali, Gad, and Asher. ⁵All those who were descendants*[a]* of Jacob were seventy*[b]* persons (for Joseph was in Egypt *already*). ⁶And Joseph died, all his brothers, and all that generation. ⁷But the children of Israel were fruitful and increased abundantly, multiplied and grew exceedingly mighty; and the land was filled with them.

> **1:7** The growth of the nation was phenomenal! It grew from 70 men to 603,000 males, aged 20 or older, thus a total population of roughly 2 million. The promise that Abraham's seed would multiply into a nation had been fulfilled.

⁸Now there arose a new king over Egypt, who did not know Joseph. ⁹And he said to his people, "Look, the people of the children of Israel *are* more and mightier than we; ¹⁰come, let us deal shrewdly with them, lest they multiply, and it happen, in the event of war, that they also join our enemies and fight against us, and *so* go up out of the land." ¹¹Therefore they set taskmasters over them to afflict them with their burdens. And they built for Pharaoh supply cities, Pithom and Raamses. ¹²But the more they afflicted them, the more they multiplied and grew. And they were in dread of the children of Israel. ¹³So the Egyptians made the children of Israel serve with rigor. ¹⁴And they made their lives bitter with hard bondage—in mortar, in brick, and in all manner of service in the field. All their service in which they made them serve *was* with rigor.

¹⁵Then the king of Egypt spoke to the Hebrew midwives, of whom the name of one

> **1:10,11 join our enemies...set taskmasters over them.** The Israelites were considered both a threat to national security and an economic asset. Therefore, slavery was a solution to control the danger while maximizing their usefulness.

was Shiphrah and the name of the other Puah; ¹⁶and he said, "When you do the duties of a midwife for the Hebrew women, and see *them* on the birthstools, if it *is* a son, then you shall kill him; but if it *is* a daughter, then she shall live." ¹⁷But the midwives feared God, and did not do as the king of Egypt commanded them, but saved the male children alive. ¹⁸So the king of Egypt called for the midwives and said to them, "Why have you done this thing, and saved the male children alive?"

¹⁹And the midwives said to Pharaoh, "Because the Hebrew women *are* not like the Egyptian women; for they *are* lively and give birth before the midwives come to them."

²⁰Therefore God dealt well with the midwives, and the people multiplied and grew very mighty. ²¹And so it was, because the midwives feared God, that He provided households for them.

²²So Pharaoh commanded all his people, saying, "Every son who is born*[a]* you shall cast into the river, and every daughter you shall save alive."

Moses Is Born

2 And a man of the house of Levi went and took *as wife* a daughter of Levi. ²So the woman conceived and bore a son. And when she saw that he *was* a beautiful *child*, she hid him three months. ³But when she could no longer hide him, she took an ark of bulrushes for him, daubed it with asphalt and pitch, put the child in it, and laid *it* in the reeds by the river's bank. ⁴And his sister stood afar off, to know what would be done to him.

⁵Then the daughter of Pharaoh came down to bathe at the river. And her maidens walked along the riverside; and when she saw the ark among the reeds, she sent her maid to get it. ⁶And when she opened *it*, she saw the child, and behold, the baby wept. So she had compassion on him, and said, "This is one of the Hebrews' children."

⁷Then his sister said to Pharaoh's daughter, "Shall I go and call a nurse for you from the Hebrew women, that she may nurse the child for you?"

1:5 *[a]*Literally *who came from the loins of* *[b]*Dead Sea Scrolls and Septuagint read *seventy-five* (compare Acts 7:14). 1:22 *[a]*Samaritan Pentateuch, Septuagint, and Targum add *to the Hebrews*.

⁸And Pharaoh's daughter said to her, "Go." So the maiden went and called the child's mother. ⁹Then Pharaoh's daughter said to her, "Take this child away and nurse him for me, and I will give *you* your wages." So the woman took the child and nursed him. ¹⁰And the child grew, and she brought him to Pharaoh's daughter, and he became her son. So she called his name Moses,ᵃ saying, "Because I drew him out of the water."

2:10 became her son. The position of "son" of an Egyptian princess gave Moses special privileges of nobility, such as a formal education. Yet even when he came of age, he did not relinquish his Hebrew identity, for "he refused to be called the son of Pharaoh's daughter" (Heb. 11:24).

Moses Flees to Midian

¹¹Now it came to pass in those days, when Moses was grown, that he went out to his brethren and looked at their burdens. And he saw an Egyptian beating a Hebrew, one of his brethren. ¹²So he looked this way and that way, and when he saw no one, he killed the Egyptian and hid him in the sand. ¹³And when he went out the second day, behold, two Hebrew men were fighting, and he said to the one who did the wrong, "Why are you striking your companion?"

¹⁴Then he said, "Who made you a prince and a judge over us? Do you intend to kill me as you killed the Egyptian?"

So Moses feared and said, "Surely this thing is known!" ¹⁵When Pharaoh heard of this matter, he sought to kill Moses. But Moses fled from the face of Pharaoh and dwelt in the land of Midian; and he sat down by a well.

¹⁶Now the priest of Midian had seven daughters. And they came and drew water, and they filled the troughs to water their father's flock. ¹⁷Then the shepherds came and drove them away; but Moses stood up and helped them, and watered their flock.

¹⁸When they came to Reuel their father, he said, "How *is it that* you have come so soon today?"

¹⁹And they said, "An Egyptian delivered us from the hand of the shepherds, and he also drew enough water for us and watered the flock."

²⁰So he said to his daughters, "And where *is* he? Why *is it that* you have left the man? Call him, that he may eat bread."

²¹Then Moses was content to live with the man, and he gave Zipporah his daughter to Moses. ²²And she bore *him* a son. He called his name Gershom,ᵃ for he said, "I have been a stranger in a foreign land."

²³Now it happened in the process of time that the king of Egypt died. Then the children of Israel groaned because of the bondage, and they cried out; and their cry came up to God because of the bondage. ²⁴So God heard their groaning, and God remembered His covenant with Abraham, with Isaac, and with Jacob. ²⁵And God looked upon the children of Israel, and God acknowledged *them*.

Moses at the Burning Bush

3 Now Moses was tending the flock of Jethro his father-in-law, the priest of Midian. And he led the flock to the back of the desert, and came to Horeb, the mountain of God. ²And the Angel of the LORD appeared to him in a flame of fire from the midst of a bush. So he looked, and behold, the bush was burning with fire, but the bush *was* not consumed. ³Then Moses said, "I will now turn aside and see this great sight, why the bush does not burn."

⁴So when the LORD saw that he turned aside to look, God called to him from the midst of the bush and said, "Moses, Moses!"

MOSES' FLIGHT AND RETURN TO EGPYT

Mediterranean Sea
Heshbon
Beersheba
MOAB
EGYPT
Wilderness of Zin
Raamses
Pithom
GOSHEN
Kadesh Barnea
EDOM
Wilderness of Paran
Ezion Geber
SINAI
MIDIAN
Nile River
Gulf of Suez
(Mt. Sinai) Horeb
0   75 MI.
0   75 Km.
© 1996 Thomas Nelson, Inc.

2:10 ᵃLiterally *Drawn Out*   2:22 ᵃLiterally *Stranger There*

3:2–4 Moses' attention was drawn to a startling sight, that of a burning bush that was not consumed by the fire burning within. No natural explanation is plausible. God was speaking from within the bush, clearly a miraculous event.

And he said, "Here I am."

⁵Then He said, "Do not draw near this place. Take your sandals off your feet, for the place where you stand *is* holy ground." ⁶Moreover He said, "I *am* the God of your father—the God of Abraham, the God of Isaac, and the God of Jacob." And Moses hid his face, for he was afraid to look upon God.

⁷And the LORD said: "I have surely seen the oppression of My people who *are* in Egypt, and have heard their cry because of their taskmasters, for I know their sorrows. ⁸So I have come down to deliver them out of the hand of the Egyptians, and to bring them up from that land to a good and large land, to a land flowing with milk and honey, to the place of the Canaanites and the Hittites and the Amorites and the Perizzites and the Hivites and the Jebusites. ⁹Now therefore, behold, the cry of the children of Israel has come to Me, and I have also seen the oppression with which the Egyptians oppress them. ¹⁰Come now, therefore, and I will send you to Pharaoh that you may bring My people, the children of Israel, out of Egypt."

¹¹But Moses said to God, "Who *am* I that I should go to Pharaoh, and that I should bring the children of Israel out of Egypt?"

¹²So He said, "I will certainly be with you. And this *shall be* a sign to you that I have sent you: When you have brought the people out of Egypt, you shall serve God on this mountain."

¹³Then Moses said to God, "Indeed, *when* I come to the children of Israel and say to them, 'The God of your fathers has sent me to you,' and they say to me, 'What *is* His name?' what shall I say to them?"

¹⁴And God said to Moses, "I AM WHO I AM." And He said, "Thus you shall say to the children of Israel, 'I AM has sent me to you.'" ¹⁵Moreover God said to Moses, "Thus you shall say to the children of Israel: 'The LORD God of your fathers, the God of Abraham, the God of Isaac, and the

God of Jacob, has sent me to you. This *is* My name forever, and this *is* My memorial to all generations.' ¹⁶Go and gather the elders of Israel together, and say to them, 'The LORD God of your fathers, the God of Abraham, of Isaac, and of Jacob, appeared to me, saying, "I have surely visited you and *seen* what is done to you in Egypt; ¹⁷and I have said I will bring you up out of the affliction of Egypt to the land of the Canaanites and the Hittites and the Amorites and the Perizzites and the Hivites and the Jebusites, to a land flowing with milk and honey."' ¹⁸Then they will heed your voice; and you shall come, you and the elders of Israel, to the king of Egypt; and you shall say to him, 'The LORD God of the Hebrews has met with us; and now, please, let us go three days' journey into the wilderness, that we may sacrifice to the LORD our God.' ¹⁹But I am sure that the king of Egypt will not let you go, no, not even by a mighty hand. ²⁰So I will stretch out My hand and strike Egypt with all My wonders which I will do in its midst; and after that he will let you go. ²¹And I will give this people favor in the sight of the Egyptians; and it shall be, when you go, that you shall not go empty-handed. ²²But every woman shall ask of her neighbor, namely, of her who dwells near her house, articles of silver, articles of gold, and clothing; and you shall put *them* on your sons and on your daughters. So you shall plunder the Egyptians."

3:14 I AM WHO I AM. This name that God used for Himself points to His eternal existence. It means "I am the One who is/will be." He is the same God throughout the ages, the same God of the past, the present, and the future! The name *Yahweh* was considered so sacred that it should not be pronounced, and thus the Massoretes inserted the vowels from the name *Adonai* (Master or Lord) into the sacred name, so that the people could call God "Jehovah."

Miraculous Signs for Pharaoh

4 When Moses answered and said, "But suppose they will not believe me or listen to my voice; suppose they say, 'The LORD has not appeared to you.'"

²So the LORD said to him, "What *is* that in your hand?"

He said, "A rod."

³And He said, "Cast it on the ground." So

4:1 Then Moses answered and said. Moses' first objections came from his sense of inadequacy for such a serious mission. He wondered how he, who had been a shepherd for forty years in Midian, could reappear in Egypt after such a long absence. This third objection was an unworthy response, and Moses' conversation with God shifted from reasonable inquiry to objection.

he cast it on the ground, and it became a serpent; and Moses fled from it. ⁴Then the LORD said to Moses, "Reach out your hand and take *it* by the tail" (and he reached out his hand and caught it, and it became a rod in his hand), ⁵"that they may believe that the LORD God of their fathers, the God of Abraham, the God of Isaac, and the God of Jacob, has appeared to you."

⁶Furthermore the LORD said to him, "Now put your hand in your bosom." And he put his hand in his bosom, and when he took it out, behold, his hand *was* leprous, like snow. ⁷And He said, "Put your hand in your bosom again." So he put his hand in his bosom again, and drew it out of his bosom, and behold, it was restored like his *other* flesh. ⁸"Then it will be, if they do not believe you, nor heed the message of the first sign, that they may believe the message of the latter sign. ⁹And it shall be, if they do not believe even these two signs, or listen to your voice, that you shall take water from the river*ᵃ* and pour *it* on the dry *land*. The water which you take from the river will become blood on the dry *land*."

¹⁰Then Moses said to the LORD, "O my Lord, I *am* not eloquent, neither before nor since You have spoken to Your servant; but I *am* slow of speech and slow of tongue."

¹¹So the LORD said to him, "Who has made man's mouth? Or who makes the mute, the deaf, the seeing, or the blind? *Have* not I, the LORD? ¹²Now therefore, go, and I will be with your mouth and teach you what you shall say."

¹³But he said, "O my Lord, please send by the hand of whomever *else* You may send."

¹⁴So the anger of the LORD was kindled against Moses, and He said: "Is not Aaron the Levite your brother? I know that he can speak well. And look, he is also coming out to meet you. When he sees you, he will be glad in his heart. ¹⁵Now you shall speak to him and put the words in his mouth. And I will be with your mouth and with his mouth, and I will teach you what you shall do. ¹⁶So he shall be your spokesman to the people. And he himself shall be as a mouth for you, and you shall be to him as God. ¹⁷And you shall take this rod in your hand, with which you shall do the signs."

4:11,12 Who has made man's mouth? God asked Moses three rhetorical questions to shut the door on any complaints or criticisms about being slow of speech. His follow-up command, "Therefore, go!" and His promise of divine help forbade any further objections.

Moses Goes to Egypt

¹⁸So Moses went and returned to Jethro his father-in-law, and said to him, "Please let me go and return to my brethren who *are* in Egypt, and see whether they are still alive."

And Jethro said to Moses, "Go in peace."

¹⁹Now the LORD said to Moses in Midian, "Go, return to Egypt; for all the men who sought your life are dead." ²⁰Then Moses took his wife and his sons and set them on a donkey, and he returned to the land of Egypt. And Moses took the rod of God in his hand.

²¹And the LORD said to Moses, "When you go back to Egypt, see that you do all those wonders before Pharaoh which I have put in your hand. But I will harden his heart, so that he will not let the people go.

4:21 I will harden his heart. Moses had been told that God was certain of Pharaoh's refusal (3:19). The interplay between God's hardening Pharaoh's heart and Pharaoh's hardening his own heart must be kept in balance. Ten times it is recorded that God hardened Pharaoh's heart (4:21; 7:3; 9:12; 10:1,20,27; 11:10; 14:4,8,17), and ten times it is recorded that the king hardened his own heart (7:13,14,22; 8:15,19,32; 9:7,34,35; 13:15). God has the power to intervene as He chooses, yet He warned Pharaoh that his refusal would bring judgment on him (v. 23). In order to resolve this dilemma of personal responsibility, we must trust in the power, knowledge, and goodness of God.

4:9 *ᵃ*That is, the Nile

²²Then you shall say to Pharaoh, 'Thus says the LORD: "Israel *is* My son, My firstborn. ²³So I say to you, let My son go that he may serve Me. But if you refuse to let him go, indeed I will kill your son, your firstborn." ' "

²⁴And it came to pass on the way, at the encampment, that the LORD met him and sought to kill him. ²⁵Then Zipporah took a sharp stone and cut off the foreskin of her son and cast *it* at *Moses'*[a] feet, and said, "Surely you *are* a husband of blood to me!" ²⁶So He let him go. Then she said, "*You are* a husband of blood!"—because of the circumcision.

> **4:24–26** Zipporah understood that the danger to her husband's life was intimately connected to the family's not bearing the sign of the covenant given to Abraham for all his descendants (Gen. 17:10–14). Her response, "You are a husband of blood to me," suggests her revulsion with the rite of circumcision, which Moses should have performed. The incident emphasizes the importance to God to obey His command to bear the sign of circumcision.

²⁷And the LORD said to Aaron, "Go into the wilderness to meet Moses." So he went and met him on the mountain of God, and kissed him. ²⁸So Moses told Aaron all the words of the LORD who had sent him, and all the signs which He had commanded him. ²⁹Then Moses and Aaron went and gathered together all the elders of the children of Israel. ³⁰And Aaron spoke all the words which the LORD had spoken to Moses. Then he did the signs in the sight of the people. ³¹So the people believed; and when they heard that the LORD had visited the children of Israel and that He had looked on their affliction, then they bowed their heads and worshiped.

First Encounter with Pharaoh

5 Afterward Moses and Aaron went in and told Pharaoh, "Thus says the LORD God of Israel: 'Let My people go, that they may hold a feast to Me in the wilderness.' "

²And Pharaoh said, "Who *is* the LORD, that I should obey His voice to let Israel go? I do not know the LORD, nor will I let Israel go."

> **5:2 Who is the LORD...?** God's command, "Let My people go," began the confrontation between Pharaoh and Moses and Pharaoh and God. Most likely, Pharaoh knew about Israel's God, but his insolent question showed that he rejected God's power to make any demands on him as king.

³So they said, "The God of the Hebrews has met with us. Please, let us go three days' journey into the desert and sacrifice to the LORD our God, lest He fall upon us with pestilence or with the sword."

⁴Then the king of Egypt said to them, "Moses and Aaron, why do you take the people from their work? Get *back* to your labor." ⁵And Pharaoh said, "Look, the people of the land *are* many now, and you make them rest from their labor!"

⁶So the same day Pharaoh commanded the taskmasters of the people and their officers, saying, ⁷"You shall no longer give the people straw to make brick as before. Let them go and gather straw for themselves. ⁸And you shall lay on them the quota of bricks which they made before. You shall not reduce it. For they are idle; therefore they cry out, saying, 'Let us go *and* sacrifice to our God.' ⁹Let more work be laid on the men, that they may labor in it, and let them not regard false words."

¹⁰And the taskmasters of the people and their officers went out and spoke to the people, saying, "Thus says Pharaoh: 'I will not give you straw. ¹¹Go, get yourselves straw where you can find it; yet none of your work will be reduced.' " ¹²So the people were scattered abroad throughout all the land of Egypt to gather stubble instead of straw. ¹³And the taskmasters forced *them* to hurry, saying, "Fulfill your work, *your* daily quota, as when there was straw." ¹⁴Also the officers of the children of Israel, whom Pharaoh's taskmasters had set over them, were beaten *and* were asked, "Why have you not fulfilled your task in making brick both yesterday and today, as before?"

> **5:11 straw.** Straw was a necessary component of bricks, to help bind the clay together. By increasing the Israelites' severe workload, Pharaoh wanted to prove his authority to control the slaves.

4:25 ᵃLiterally *his*

[15]Then the officers of the children of Israel came and cried out to Pharaoh, saying, "Why are you dealing thus with your servants? [16]There is no straw given to your servants, and they say to us, 'Make brick!' And indeed your servants *are* beaten, but the fault *is* in your *own* people."

[17]But he said, "You *are* idle! Idle! Therefore you say, 'Let us go *and* sacrifice to the LORD.' [18]Therefore go now *and* work; for no straw shall be given you, yet you shall deliver the quota of bricks." [19]And the officers of the children of Israel saw *that* they *were* in trouble after it was said, "You shall not reduce *any* bricks from your daily quota."

[20]Then, as they came out from Pharaoh, they met Moses and Aaron who stood there to meet them. [21]And they said to them, "Let the LORD look on you and judge, because you have made us abhorrent in the sight of Pharaoh and in the sight of his servants, to put a sword in their hand to kill us."

Israel's Deliverance Assured

[22]So Moses returned to the LORD and said, "Lord, why have You brought trouble on this people? Why *is* it You have sent me? [23]For since I came to Pharaoh to speak in Your name, he has done evil to this people; neither have You delivered Your people at all."

5:22,23 Moses returned to the LORD. The focus here is that Moses returned immediately to the Lord in prayer. Evidently, Moses had not expected what effect Pharaoh's refusal would have upon his people. So far, the Egyptians resented Israel, and the Israelites resented Moses.

6 Then the LORD said to Moses, "Now you shall see what I will do to Pharaoh. For with a strong hand he will let them go, and with a strong hand he will drive them out of his land."

[2]And God spoke to Moses and said to him: "I *am* the LORD. [3]I appeared to Abraham, to Isaac, and to Jacob, as God Almighty, but *by* My name LORD[a] I was not known to them. [4]I have also established My covenant with them, to give them the land of Canaan, the land of their pilgrimage, in which they were strangers. [5]And I have also

heard the groaning of the children of Israel whom the Egyptians keep in bondage, and I have remembered My covenant. [6]Therefore say to the children of Israel: 'I *am* the LORD; I will bring you out from under the burdens of the Egyptians, I will rescue you from their bondage, and I will redeem you with an outstretched arm and with great judgments. [7]I will take you as My people, and I will be your God. Then you shall know that I *am* the LORD your God who brings you out from under the burdens of the Egyptians. [8]And I will bring you into the land which I swore to give to Abraham, Isaac, and Jacob; and I will give it to you *as* a heritage: I *am* the LORD.' " [9]So Moses spoke thus to the children of Israel; but they did not heed Moses, because of anguish of spirit and cruel bondage.

6:6–8 God instructed Moses to remind Israel of his previous message: of remembering the covenant with Abraham, of His seeing their misery, of His promise to deliver them, of His granting them the land of Canaan, and of His taking them safely there. His repetitive "I will" and his declaration, "I am Yahweh," denoted that His promises would certainly be fulfilled.

[10]And the LORD spoke to Moses, saying, [11]"Go in, tell Pharaoh king of Egypt to let the children of Israel go out of his land." [12]And Moses spoke before the LORD, saying, "The children of Israel have not heeded me. How then shall Pharaoh heed me, for I *am* of uncircumcised lips?" [13]Then the LORD spoke to Moses and Aaron, and gave them a command for the children of Israel and for Pharaoh king of Egypt, to bring the children of Israel out of the land of Egypt.

The Family of Moses and Aaron

[14]These *are* the heads of their fathers' houses: The sons of Reuben, the firstborn of Israel, *were* Hanoch, Pallu, Hezron, and Carmi. These are the families of Reuben. [15]And the sons of Simeon *were* Jemuel,[a] Jamin, Ohad, Jachin, Zohar, and Shaul the son of a Canaanite woman. These *are* the families of Simeon. [16]These *are* the names of the sons of Levi according to their

---

6:3 [a]Hebrew YHWH, traditionally *Jehovah*   6:15 [a]Spelled *Nemuel* in Numbers 26:12

generations: Gershon, Kohath, and Merari. And the years of the life of Levi *were* one hundred and thirty-seven. ¹⁷The sons of Gershon *were* Libni and Shimi according to their families. ¹⁸And the sons of Kohath *were* Amram, Izhar, Hebron, and Uzziel. And the years of the life of Kohath *were* one hundred and thirty-three. ¹⁹The sons of Merari *were* Mahli and Mushi. These *are* the families of Levi according to their generations.

²⁰Now Amram took for himself Jochebed, his father's sister, as wife; and she bore him Aaron and Moses. And the years of the life of Amram *were* one hundred and thirty-seven. ²¹The sons of Izhar *were* Korah, Nepheg, and Zichri. ²²And the sons of Uzziel *were* Mishael, Elzaphan, and Zithri. ²³Aaron took to himself Elisheba, daughter of Amminadab, sister of Nahshon, as wife; and she bore him Nadab, Abihu, Eleazar, and Ithamar. ²⁴And the sons of Korah *were* Assir, Elkanah, and Abiasaph. These *are* the families of the Korahites. ²⁵Eleazar, Aaron's son, took for himself one of the daughters of Putiel as wife; and she bore him Phinehas. These *are* the heads of the fathers' houses of the Levites according to their families.

²⁶These *are the same* Aaron and Moses to whom the LORD said, "Bring out the children of Israel from the land of Egypt according to their armies." ²⁷These *are* the ones who spoke to Pharaoh king of Egypt, to bring out the children of Israel from Egypt. These *are the same* Moses and Aaron.

Aaron Is Moses' Spokesman

²⁸And it came to pass, on the day the LORD spoke to Moses in the land of Egypt, ²⁹that the LORD spoke to Moses, saying, "I *am* the LORD. Speak to Pharaoh king of Egypt all that I say to you."

³⁰But Moses said before the LORD, "Behold, I *am* of uncircumcised lips, and how shall Pharaoh heed me?"

7 So the LORD said to Moses: "See, I have made you *as* God to Pharaoh, and Aaron your brother shall be your prophet. ²You shall speak all that I command you. And Aaron your brother shall tell Pharaoh to send the children of Israel out of his land. ³And I will harden Pharaoh's heart, and multiply My signs and My wonders in the land of Egypt. ⁴But Pharaoh will not heed you, so that I may lay My hand on Egypt and bring My armies *and* My people, the children of Israel, out of the land of Egypt by great judgments. ⁵And the Egyptians shall know that I *am* the LORD, when I stretch out My hand on Egypt and bring out the children of Israel from among them."

> **7:5 know that I am the LORD.** God repeatedly mentions the purpose of the Exodus in His messages to Pharaoh and in His descriptions of what He was doing. Some of the Egyptians did come to revere Yahweh, and in the end, Egypt could not deny God's involvement in Israel's rescue and Egypt's destruction.

⁶Then Moses and Aaron did *so;* just as the LORD commanded them, so they did. ⁷And Moses *was* eighty years old and Aaron eighty-three years old when they spoke to Pharaoh.

Aaron's Miraculous Rod

⁸Then the LORD spoke to Moses and Aaron, saying, ⁹"When Pharaoh speaks to you, saying, 'Show a miracle for yourselves,' then you shall say to Aaron, 'Take your rod and cast *it* before Pharaoh, *and* let it become a serpent.' " ¹⁰So Moses and Aaron went in to Pharaoh, and they did so, just as the LORD commanded. And Aaron cast down his rod before Pharaoh and before his servants, and it became a serpent.

¹¹But Pharaoh also called the wise men and the sorcerers; so the magicians of Egypt, they also did in like manner with their enchantments. ¹²For every man threw down his rod, and they became serpents. But Aaron's rod swallowed up their rods. ¹³And Pharaoh's heart grew hard, and he did not heed them, as the LORD had said.

The First Plague: Waters Become Blood

¹⁴So the LORD said to Moses: "Pharaoh's heart *is* hard; he refuses to let the people go. ¹⁵Go to Pharaoh in the morning, when he goes out to the water, and you shall stand by the river's bank to meet him; and the rod which was turned to a serpent you shall take in your hand. ¹⁶And you shall say to

him, 'The LORD God of the Hebrews has sent me to you, saying, "Let My people go, that they may serve Me in the wilderness"; but indeed, until now you would not hear! [17]Thus says the LORD: "By this you shall know that I *am* the LORD. Behold, I will strike the waters which *are* in the river with the rod that *is* in my hand, and they shall be turned to blood. [18]And the fish that *are* in the river shall die, the river shall stink, and the Egyptians will loathe to drink the water of the river." ' "

7:15 by the river's bank. The first confrontation of the plague cycle was set on the banks of the Nile, the sacred waterway of the land. Hymns of worship were often sung for the agricultural blessings brought by the Nile, the country's single, greatest economic resource. Thus, the Nile was the perfect setting for God to begin humbling the Egyptians and their false gods.

[19]Then the LORD spoke to Moses, "Say to Aaron, 'Take your rod and stretch out your hand over the waters of Egypt, over their streams, over their rivers, over their ponds, and over all their pools of water, that they may become blood. And there shall be blood throughout all the land of Egypt, both in *buckets of* wood and *pitchers of* stone.' " [20]And Moses and Aaron did so, just as the LORD commanded. So he lift-

ed up the rod and struck the waters that *were* in the river, in the sight of Pharaoh and in the sight of his servants. And all the waters that *were* in the river were turned to blood. [21]The fish that *were* in the river died, the river stank, and the Egyptians could not drink the water of the river. So there was blood throughout all the land of Egypt.

[22]Then the magicians of Egypt did so with their enchantments; and Pharaoh's heart grew hard, and he did not heed them, as the LORD had said. [23]And Pharaoh turned and went into his house. Neither was his heart moved by this. [24]So all the Egyptians dug all around the river for water to drink, because they could not drink the water of the river. [25]And seven days passed after the LORD had struck the river.

The Second Plague: Frogs

8 And the LORD spoke to Moses, "Go to Pharaoh and say to him, 'Thus says the LORD: "Let My people go, that they may serve Me. [2]But if you refuse to let *them* go, behold, I will smite all your territory with frogs. [3]So the river shall bring forth frogs abundantly, which shall go up and come into your house, into your bedroom, on your bed, into the houses of your servants, on your people, into your ovens, and into your kneading bowls. [4]And the frogs shall

THE TEN PLAGUES ON EGYPT

The Plague	Egyptian Deity	The Effect
1. Blood (7:20)	Hapi	Pharaoh hardened (7:22)
2. Frogs (8:6)	Heqt	Pharaoh begs relief, promises freedom (8:8), but is hardened (8:15)
3. Lice (8:17)	Hathor, Nut	Pharaoh hardened (8:19)
4. Flies (8:24)	Shu, Isis	Pharaoh bargains (8:28), but is hardened (8:32)
5. Livestock diseased (9:6)	Apis	Pharaoh hardened (9:7)
6. Boils (9:10)	Sekhmet	Pharaoh hardened (9:12)
7. Hail (9:23)	Geb	Pharaoh begs relief (9:27), promises freedom (9:28), but is hardened (9:35)
8. Locusts (10:13)	Serapis	Pharaoh bargains (10:11), begs relief (10:17), but is hardened (10:20)
9. Darkness (10:22)	Ra	Pharaoh bargains (10:24), but is hardened (10:27)
10. Death of firstborn (12:29)		Pharaoh and Egyptians beg Israel to leave Egypt (12:31–33)

come up on you, on your people, and on all your servants." ' "

> **8:2 frogs.** The Egyptians actually considered frogs sacred, thus prohibiting the intentional killing of them. They believed that frogs signified that the gods who controlled the Nile's flooding and receding had once again made the land fertile. The abundance of frogs everywhere brought only frustration and discomfort, rather than the normal signal that the fields were ready for harvest.

⁵Then the LORD spoke to Moses, "Say to Aaron, 'Stretch out your hand with your rod over the streams, over the rivers, and over the ponds, and cause frogs to come up on the land of Egypt.' " ⁶So Aaron stretched out his hand over the waters of Egypt, and the frogs came up and covered the land of Egypt. ⁷And the magicians did so with their enchantments, and brought up frogs on the land of Egypt.

⁸Then Pharaoh called for Moses and Aaron, and said, "Entreat the LORD that He may take away the frogs from me and from my people; and I will let the people go, that they may sacrifice to the LORD."

⁹And Moses said to Pharaoh, "Accept the honor of saying when I shall intercede for you, for your servants, and for your people, to destroy the frogs from you and your houses, *that* they may remain in the river only."

¹⁰So he said, "Tomorrow." And he said, "*Let it be* according to your word, that you may know that *there is* no one like the LORD our God. ¹¹And the frogs shall depart from you, from your houses, from your servants, and from your people. They shall remain in the river only."

¹²Then Moses and Aaron went out from Pharaoh. And Moses cried out to the LORD concerning the frogs which He had brought against Pharaoh. ¹³So the LORD did according to the word of Moses. And the frogs died out of the houses, out of the courtyards, and out of the fields. ¹⁴They gathered them together in heaps, and the land stank. ¹⁵But when Pharaoh saw that there was relief, he hardened his heart and did not heed them, as the LORD had said.

The Third Plague: Lice

¹⁶So the LORD said to Moses, "Say to Aaron, 'Stretch out your rod, and strike the dust of the land, so that it may become lice throughout all the land of Egypt.' " ¹⁷And they did so. For Aaron stretched out his hand with his rod and struck the dust of the earth, and it became lice on man and beast. All the dust of the land became lice throughout all the land of Egypt.

¹⁸Now the magicians so worked with their enchantments to bring forth lice, but they could not. So there were lice on man and beast. ¹⁹Then the magicians said to Pharaoh, "This *is* the finger of God." But Pharaoh's heart grew hard, and he did not heed them, just as the LORD had said.

The Fourth Plague: Flies

²⁰And the LORD said to Moses, "Rise early in the morning and stand before Pharaoh as he comes out to the water. Then say to him, 'Thus says the LORD: "Let My people go, that they may serve Me. ²¹Or else, if you will not let My people go, behold, I will send swarms *of flies* on you and your servants, on your people and into your houses. The houses of the Egyptians shall be full of swarms *of flies*, and also the ground on which they *stand*. ²²And in that day I will set apart the land of Goshen, in which My people dwell, that no swarms *of flies* shall be there, in order that you may know that I *am* the LORD in the midst of the land. ²³I will make a difference* between My people and your people. Tomorrow this sign shall be." ' " ²⁴And the LORD did so. Thick swarms *of flies* came into the house of Pharaoh, *into* his servants' houses, and into all the land of Egypt. The land was corrupted because of the swarms *of flies*.

²⁵Then Pharaoh called for Moses and Aaron, and said, "Go, sacrifice to your God in the land."

> **8:22 set apart the land of Goshen.** For the first time in connection with the plagues, God specifically discriminated between Egypt and Israel—Israel would be untouched! God's protection of His people highlighted God's personal and powerful oversight of His people.

8:23 ªLiterally *set a ransom* (compare Exodus 9:4 and 11:7)

26And Moses said, "It is not right to do so, for we would be sacrificing the abomination of the Egyptians to the LORD our God. If we sacrifice the abomination of the Egyptians before their eyes, then will they not stone us? 27We will go three days' journey into the wilderness and sacrifice to the LORD our God as He will command us."

28So Pharaoh said, "I will let you go, that you may sacrifice to the LORD your God in the wilderness; only you shall not go very far away. Intercede for me."

29Then Moses said, "Indeed I am going out from you, and I will entreat the LORD, that the swarms *of flies* may depart tomorrow from Pharaoh, from his servants, and from his people. But let Pharaoh not deal deceitfully anymore in not letting the people go to sacrifice to the LORD."

30So Moses went out from Pharaoh and entreated the LORD. 31And the LORD did according to the word of Moses; He removed the swarms *of flies* from Pharaoh, from his servants, and from his people. Not one remained. 32But Pharaoh hardened his heart at this time also; neither would he let the people go.

8:31 Not one remained. God's total divine removal of flies demonstrated that God heard Moses' request but still did not persuade Pharaoh. As soon as he was safe from the humiliating effects of the plague, he stubbornly resisted again.

The Fifth Plague: Livestock Diseased

9 Then the LORD said to Moses, "Go in to Pharaoh and tell him, 'Thus says the LORD God of the Hebrews: "Let My people go, that they may serve Me. 2For if you refuse to let *them* go, and still hold them, 3behold, the hand of the LORD will be on your cattle in the field, on the horses, on the donkeys, on the camels, on the oxen, and on the sheep—a very severe pestilence. 4And the LORD will make a difference between the livestock of Israel and the livestock of Egypt. So nothing shall die of all *that* belongs to the children of Israel." ' " 5Then the LORD appointed a set time, saying, "Tomorrow the LORD will do this thing in the land." 6So the LORD did this thing on the next

day, and all the livestock of Egypt died; but of the livestock of the children of Israel, not one died. 7Then Pharaoh sent, and indeed, not even one of the livestock of the Israelites was dead. But the heart of Pharaoh became hard, and he did not let the people go.

The Sixth Plague: Boils

8So the LORD said to Moses and Aaron, "Take for yourselves handfuls of ashes from a furnace, and let Moses scatter it toward the heavens in the sight of Pharaoh. 9And it will become fine dust in all the land of Egypt, and it will cause boils that break out in sores on man and beast throughout all the land of Egypt." 10Then they took ashes from the furnace and stood before Pharaoh, and Moses scattered *them* toward heaven. And *they* caused boils that break out in sores on man and beast. 11And the magicians could not stand before Moses because of the boils, for the boils were on the magicians and on all the Egyptians. 12But the LORD hardened the heart of Pharaoh; and he did not heed them, just as the LORD had spoken to Moses.

9:10 ashes from the furnace. Aaron and Moses took two handfuls of ash from a brick-making furnace, the very kind that the Israelite slaves used to make bricks. Ironically, that which had been such a crucial part of their oppression became the source of a painful health hazard for the oppressors! This was the first plague to target human health.

The Seventh Plague: Hail

13Then the LORD said to Moses, "Rise early in the morning and stand before Pharaoh, and say to him, 'Thus says the LORD God of the Hebrews: "Let My people go, that they may serve Me, 14for at this time I will send all My plagues to your very heart, and on your servants and on your people, that you may know that *there is* none like Me in all the earth. 15Now if I had stretched out My hand and struck you and your people with pestilence, then you would have been cut off from the earth. 16But indeed for this *purpose* I have raised you up, that I may show My power *in* you, and that My name may be declared in all the earth. 17As yet you exalt yourself against My people in that you will not let them go. 18Behold, tomorrow about this time I will cause very

heavy hail to rain down, such as has not been in Egypt since its founding until now. [19]Therefore send now *and* gather your livestock and all that you have in the field, for the hail shall come down on every man and every animal which is found in the field and is not brought home; and they shall die." ' "

9:14–19 Before the seventh plague, God unveiled more of His purpose and plan to Pharaoh: (1) His purpose was that Egypt would recognize Him as the one God, that His power would be demonstrated through them, and that His name and power would be known everywhere. (2) Whatever power Pharaoh had was given to him by God. (3) God had been gracious even in the plagues by not striking the people first. (4) The weather about to be unleashed was unlike anything Egypt had ever seen. (5) Graciously, He instructed them how to protect against severe damage.

[20]He who feared the word of the LORD among the servants of Pharaoh made his servants and his livestock flee to the houses. [21]But he who did not regard the word of the LORD left his servants and his livestock in the field.

[22]Then the LORD said to Moses, "Stretch out your hand toward heaven, that there may be hail in all the land of Egypt—on man, on beast, and on every herb of the field, throughout the land of Egypt." [23]And Moses stretched out his rod toward heaven; and the LORD sent thunder and hail, and fire darted to the ground. And the LORD rained hail on the land of Egypt. [24]So there was hail, and fire mingled with the hail, so very heavy that there was none like it in all the land of Egypt since it became a nation. [25]And the hail struck throughout the whole land of Egypt, all that *was* in the field, both man and beast; and the hail struck every herb of the field and broke every tree of the field. [26]Only in the land of Goshen, where the children of Israel *were*, there was no hail.

[27]And Pharaoh sent and called for Moses and Aaron, and said to them, "I have sinned this time. The LORD *is* righteous, and my people and I *are* wicked. [28]Entreat the LORD, that there may be no *more* mighty thundering and hail, for *it is* enough. I will let you go, and you shall stay no longer."

[29]So Moses said to him, "As soon as I have gone out of the city, I will spread out my hands to the LORD; the thunder will cease, and there will be no more hail, that you may know that the earth *is* the LORD's. [30]But as for you and your servants, I know that you will not yet fear the LORD God." [31]Now the flax and the barley were struck, for the barley *was* in the head and the flax *was* in bud. [32]But the wheat and the spelt were not struck, for they *are* late crops.

[33]So Moses went out of the city from Pharaoh and spread out his hands to the LORD; then the thunder and the hail ceased, and the rain was not poured on the earth. [34]And when Pharaoh saw that the rain, the hail, and the thunder had ceased, he sinned yet more; and he hardened his heart, he and his servants. [35]So the heart of Pharaoh was hard; neither would he let the children of Israel go, as the LORD had spoken by Moses.

The Eighth Plague: Locusts

10 Now the LORD said to Moses, "Go in to Pharaoh; for I have hardened his heart and the hearts of his servants, that I may show these signs of Mine before him, [2]and that you may tell in the hearing of your son and your son's son the mighty things I have done in Egypt, and My signs which I have done among them, that you may know that I *am* the LORD."

[3]So Moses and Aaron came in to Pharaoh and said to him, "Thus says the LORD God of the Hebrews: 'How long will you refuse to humble yourself before Me? Let My people go, that they may serve Me. [4]Or else, if you refuse to let My people go, behold, tomorrow I will bring locusts into your territory. [5]And they shall cover the face of the earth, so that no one will be able to see the earth; and they shall eat the residue of what is left, which remains to you from the hail, and they shall eat every tree which grows up for you out of the field. [6]They shall fill your houses, the houses of all your servants, and the houses of all the Egyptians—which neither your fathers nor your fathers' fathers have seen, since the day that they were on the earth to this day.' " And he turned and went out from Pharaoh.

[7]Then Pharaoh's servants said to him,

"How long shall this man be a snare to us? Let the men go, that they may serve the LORD their God. Do you not yet know that Egypt is destroyed?"

⁸So Moses and Aaron were brought again to Pharaoh, and he said to them, "Go, serve the LORD your God. Who *are* the ones that are going?"

10:8 Who *are* the ones that are going? For the first time, Pharaoh tried to negotiate a deal before the threatened plague struck. He suggested in his question that only the men of Israel needed to go out to worship.

⁹And Moses said, "We will go with our young and our old; with our sons and our daughters, with our flocks and our herds we will go, for we must hold a feast to the LORD."

¹⁰Then he said to them, "The LORD had better be with you when I let you and your little ones go! Beware, for evil is ahead of you. ¹¹Not so! Go now, you *who are* men, and serve the LORD, for that is what you desired." And they were driven out from Pharaoh's presence.

¹²Then the LORD said to Moses, "Stretch out your hand over the land of Egypt for the locusts, that they may come upon the land of Egypt, and eat every herb of the land—all that the hail has left." ¹³So Moses stretched out his rod over the land of Egypt, and the LORD brought an east wind on the land all that day and all *that* night. When it was

morning, the east wind brought the locusts. ¹⁴And the locusts went up over all the land of Egypt and rested on all the territory of Egypt. *They were* very severe; previously there had been no such locusts as they, nor shall there be such after them. ¹⁵For they covered the face of the whole earth, so that the land was darkened; and they ate every herb of the land and all the fruit of the trees which the hail had left. So there remained nothing green on the trees or on the plants of the field throughout all the land of Egypt.

¹⁶Then Pharaoh called for Moses and Aaron in haste, and said, "I have sinned against the LORD your God and against you. ¹⁷Now therefore, please forgive my sin only this once, and entreat the LORD your God, that He may take away from me this death only." ¹⁸So he went out from Pharaoh and entreated the LORD. ¹⁹And the LORD turned a very strong west wind, which took the locusts away and blew them into the Red Sea. There remained not one locust in all the territory of Egypt. ²⁰But the LORD hardened Pharaoh's heart, and he did not let the children of Israel go.

The Ninth Plague: Darkness
²¹Then the LORD said to Moses, "Stretch out your hand toward heaven, that there may be darkness over the land of Egypt, darkness *which* may even be felt." ²²So Moses stretched out his hand toward heaven, and there was thick darkness in all the land of Egypt three days. ²³They did not

Why don't the Egyptian historical records acknowledge the devastation of the plagues, the defeat of the army and Israel's escape that occurred during the Exodus?

The absence of references to Israel in the available Egyptian historical records should come as no surprise. Most of these records exist in the form of official inscriptions in the tombs and monuments of ancient leaders. Such public and lasting memorials were rarely used to record humiliating defeats and disasters. Interestingly, one of the subtle proofs of the truth of Scripture is the way in which it records both the triumphs and the tragedies of God's people. The Bible offers as many examples of failure as it does of faith.

see one another; nor did anyone rise from his place for three days. But all the children of Israel had light in their dwellings.

> **10:24 Go...Let your little ones also go with you.** Pharaoh tried to manipulate the conditions for Israel to go, by forcing them to leave their livestock, which would guarantee that they would return. He had not yet understood that partial obedience to God's command was unacceptable.

²⁴Then Pharaoh called to Moses and said, "Go, serve the LORD; only let your flocks and your herds be kept back. Let your little ones also go with you."

²⁵But Moses said, "You must also give us sacrifices and burnt offerings, that we may sacrifice to the LORD our God. ²⁶Our livestock also shall go with us; not a hoof shall be left behind. For we must take some of them to serve the LORD our God, and even we do not know with what we must serve the LORD until we arrive there."

²⁷But the LORD hardened Pharaoh's heart, and he would not let them go. ²⁸Then Pharaoh said to him, "Get away from me! Take heed to yourself and see my face no more! For in the day you see my face you shall die!"

²⁹So Moses said, "You have spoken well. I will never see your face again."

Death of the Firstborn Announced

11 And the LORD said to Moses, "I will bring one more plague on Pharaoh and on Egypt. Afterward he will let you go from here. When he lets *you* go, he will surely drive you out of here altogether. ²Speak now in the hearing of the people, and let every man ask from his neighbor and every woman from her neighbor, articles of silver and articles of gold." ³And the LORD gave the people favor in the sight of the Egyptians. Moreover the man Moses *was* very great in the land of Egypt, in the sight of Pharaoh's servants and in the sight of the people.

⁴Then Moses said, "Thus says the LORD: 'About midnight I will go out into the midst of Egypt; ⁵and all the firstborn in the land of Egypt shall die, from the firstborn of Pharaoh who sits on his throne, even to the firstborn of the female servant who *is* behind the handmill, and all the firstborn of

the animals. ⁶Then there shall be a great cry throughout all the land of Egypt, such as was not like it *before*, nor shall be like it again. ⁷But against none of the children of Israel shall a dog move its tongue, against man or beast, that you may know that the LORD does make a difference between the Egyptians and Israel.' ⁸And all these your servants shall come down to me and bow down to me, saying, 'Get out, and all the people who follow you!' After that I will go out." Then he went out from Pharaoh in great anger.

> **11:5 the firstborn.** The firstborn held a particularly important position in the family and society. This child was given a double portion of the father's estate and also represented special qualities of life and strength. Pharaoh's firstborn was destined to ascend the throne to be the next king. The intensity of the final plague executed all the firstborn of all classes of the population, including the animals.

⁹But the LORD said to Moses, "Pharaoh will not heed you, so that My wonders may be multiplied in the land of Egypt." ¹⁰So Moses and Aaron did all these wonders before Pharaoh; and the LORD hardened Pharaoh's heart, and he did not let the children of Israel go out of his land.

The Passover Instituted

12 Now the LORD spoke to Moses and Aaron in the land of Egypt, saying, ²"This month *shall be* your beginning of months; it *shall be* the first month of the year to you. ³Speak to all the congregation of Israel, saying: 'On the tenth of this month every man shall take for himself a lamb, according to the house of *his* father, a lamb for a household. ⁴And if the household is too small for the lamb, let him and his neighbor next to his house take *it* according to the number of the persons; according to each man's need you shall make your count for the lamb. ⁵Your lamb shall be without blemish, a male of the first year. You may take *it* from the sheep or from the goats. ⁶Now you shall keep it until the fourteenth day of the same month. Then the whole assembly of the congregation of Israel shall kill it at twilight. ⁷And they shall take *some* of the blood and put *it* on the two doorposts and on the lintel of the

houses where they eat it. [8]Then they shall eat the flesh on that night; roasted in fire, with unleavened bread *and* with bitter *herbs* they shall eat it. [9]Do not eat it raw, nor boiled at all with water, but roasted in fire—its head with its legs and its entrails. [10]You shall let none of it remain until morning, and what remains of it until morning you shall burn with fire. [11]And thus you shall eat it: *with* a belt on your waist, your sandals on your feet, and your staff in your hand. So you shall eat it in haste. It *is* the LORD's Passover.

[12]'For I will pass through the land of Egypt on that night, and will strike all the firstborn in the land of Egypt, both man and beast; and against all the gods of Egypt I will execute judgment: I *am* the LORD. [13]Now the blood shall be a sign for you on the houses where you *are.* And when I see the blood, I will pass over you; and the plague shall not be on you to de-

stroy *you* when I strike the land of Egypt. [14]'So this day shall be to you a memorial; and you shall keep it as a feast to the LORD throughout your generations. You shall keep it as a feast by an everlasting ordinance. [15]Seven days you shall eat unleavened bread. On the first day you shall remove leaven from your houses. For whoever eats leavened bread from the first day until the seventh day, that person shall be cut off from Israel. [16]On the first day *there shall be* a holy convocation, and on the seventh day there shall be a holy convocation for you. No manner of work shall be done on them; but *that* which everyone must eat—that only may be prepared by you. [17]So you shall observe *the Feast of* Unleavened Bread, for on this same day I will have brought your armies out of the land of Egypt. Therefore you shall observe this day throughout your generations as an everlasting ordinance. [18]In the first *month,* on the fourteenth day of the month at evening, you shall eat unleavened bread, until the twenty-first day of the month at evening. [19]For seven days no leaven shall be found in your houses, since whoever eats what is leavened, that same person shall be cut off from the congregation of Israel, whether *he*

12:12 against all the gods. The tenth plague was a judgment against all Egyptian deities. The loss of the firstborn of men and animals had serious theological implications, proving that the pagan deities were powerless to protect the Egyptian people from devastating loss.

CHRONOLOGY OF THE EXODUS

Date	Event	Reference
Fifteenth day, first month, first year	Exodus	Exodus 12
Fifteenth day, second month, first year	Arrival in Wilderness of Sin	Exodus 16:1
Third month, first year	Arrival in Wilderness of Sinai	Exodus 19:1
First day, first month, second year	Erection of Tabernacle	Exodus 40:1,17
	Dedication of Altar	Numbers 7:1
	Consecration of Levites	Numbers 8:1–26
Fourteeneth day, first month, second year	Passover	Numbers 9:5
First day, second month, second year	Census	Numbers 1:1,18
Fourteeneth day, second month, second year	Supplemental Passover	Numbers 9:11
Twentieth day, second month, second year	Departure from Sinai	Numbers 10:11
First month, fortieth year	In Wilderness of Zin	Numbers 20:1,22–29; 33:38
First day, fifth month, fortieth year	Death of Aaron	Numbers 20:22–29; 33:38
First day, eleventh month, fortieth year	Moses' Address	Deuteronomy 1:3

is a stranger or a native of the land. ²⁰You shall eat nothing leavened; in all your dwellings you shall eat unleavened bread.' "

²¹Then Moses called for all the elders of Israel and said to them, "Pick out and take lambs for yourselves according to your families, and kill the Passover *lamb*. ²²And you shall take a bunch of hyssop, dip *it* in the blood that *is* in the basin, and strike the lintel and the two doorposts with the blood that *is* in the basin. And none of you shall go out of the door of his house until morning. ²³For the LORD will pass through to strike the Egyptians; and when He sees the blood on the lintel and on the two doorposts, the LORD will pass over the door and not allow the destroyer to come into your houses to strike *you*. ²⁴And you shall observe this thing as an ordinance for you and your sons forever. ²⁵It will come to pass when you come to the land which the LORD will give you, just as He promised, that you shall keep this service. ²⁶And it shall be,

when your children say to you, 'What do you mean by this service?' ²⁷that you shall say, 'It *is* the Passover sacrifice of the LORD, who passed over the houses of the children of Israel in Egypt when He struck the Egyptians and delivered our households.' " So the people bowed their heads and worshiped. ²⁸Then the children of Israel went away and did *so*; just as the LORD had commanded Moses and Aaron, so they did.

The Tenth Plague: Death of the Firstborn

²⁹And it came to pass at midnight that the LORD struck all the firstborn in the land of Egypt, from the firstborn of Pharaoh who sat on his throne to the firstborn of the captive who *was* in the dungeon, and all the firstborn of livestock. ³⁰So Pharaoh rose in the night, he, all his servants, and all the Egyptians; and there was a great cry in Egypt, for *there was* not a house where *there was* not one dead.

The Exodus

³¹Then he called for Moses and Aaron by night, and said, "Rise, go out from among

> **12:23 the destroyer.** This is most likely the Angel of the Lord (see 2 Sam. 24:16; Is. 37:36).

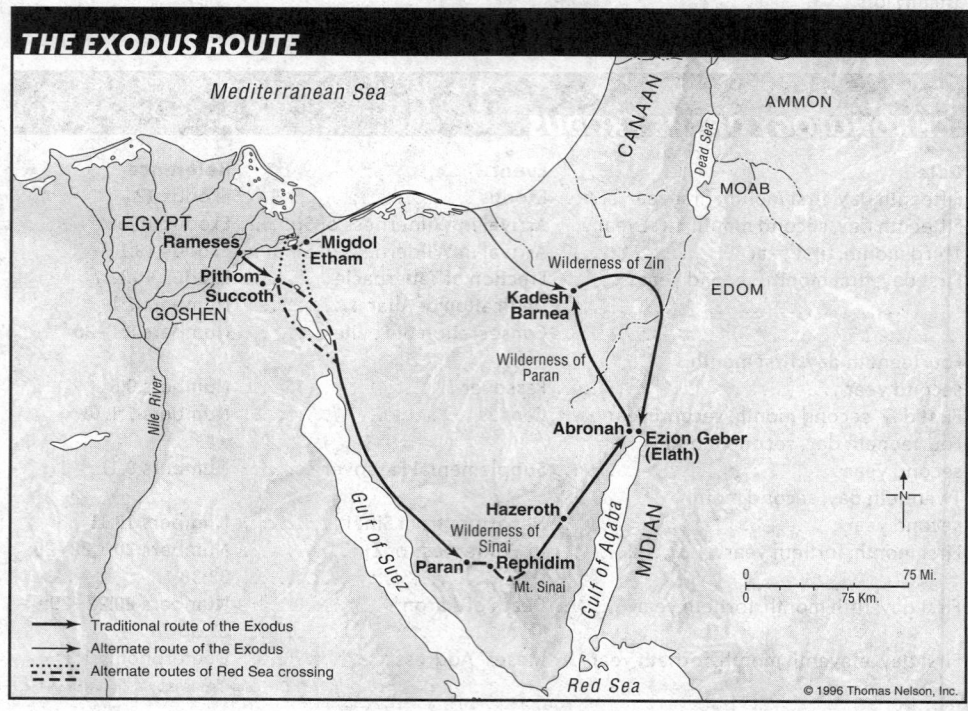

THE EXODUS ROUTE

Mediterranean Sea

CANAAN

AMMON

Dead Sea

MOAB

EGYPT

Rameses

Migdol
Etham

Pithom
Succoth

GOSHEN

Wilderness of Zin

Kadesh
Barnea

EDOM

Wilderness of
Paran

Abronah

Ezion Geber
(Elath)

Nile River

Gulf of Suez

Hazeroth

Wilderness of
Sinai

Paran   Rephidim

Mt. Sinai

Gulf of Aqaba

MIDIAN

0   75 Mi.
0   75 Km.

N

→ Traditional route of the Exodus
→ Alternate route of the Exodus
▪▪▪ Alternate routes of Red Sea crossing

Red Sea

© 1996 Thomas Nelson, Inc.

my people, both you and the children of Israel. And go, serve the LORD as you have said. ³²Also take your flocks and your herds, as you have said, and be gone; and bless me also."

³³And the Egyptians urged the people, that they might send them out of the land in haste. For they said, "We *shall* all *be* dead." ³⁴So the people took their dough before it was leavened, having their kneading bowls bound up in their clothes on their shoulders. ³⁵Now the children of Israel had done according to the word of Moses, and they had asked from the Egyptians articles of silver, articles of gold, and clothing. ³⁶And the LORD had given the people favor in the sight of the Egyptians, so that they granted them *what they requested*. Thus they plundered the Egyptians.

³⁷Then the children of Israel journeyed from Rameses to Succoth, about six hundred thousand men on foot, besides children. ³⁸A mixed multitude went up with them also, and flocks and herds—a great deal of livestock. ³⁹And they baked unleavened cakes of the dough which they had brought out of Egypt; for it was not leavened, because they were driven out of Egypt and could not wait, nor had they prepared provisions for themselves.

⁴⁰Now the sojourn of the children of Israel who lived in Egypt*ᵃ was* four hundred and thirty years. ⁴¹And it came to pass at the end of the four hundred and thirty years—on that very same day—it came to pass that all the armies of the LORD went out from the land of Egypt. ⁴²It *is* a night of solemn observance to the LORD for bringing them out of the land of Egypt. This *is* that night of the LORD, a solemn observance for all the children of Israel throughout their generations.

12:40,41 four hundred and thirty years. God had told Abraham that his descendants would be aliens mistreated in a foreign land for 400 years, using a figure rounded to the nearer hundred (Gen. 15:13).

Passover Regulations

⁴³And the LORD said to Moses and Aaron, "This *is* the ordinance of the Passover: No foreigner shall eat it. ⁴⁴But every man's servant who is bought for money, when you have circumcised him, then he may eat it. ⁴⁵A sojourner and a hired servant shall not eat it. ⁴⁶In one house it shall be eaten; you shall not carry any of the flesh outside the house, nor shall you break one of its bones. ⁴⁷All the congregation of Israel shall keep it. ⁴⁸And when a stranger dwells with you *and wants* to keep the Passover to the LORD, let all his males be circumcised, and then let him come near and keep it; and he shall be as a native of the land. For no uncircumcised person shall eat it. ⁴⁹One law shall be for the native-born and for the stranger who dwells among you."

12:46 break...bones. Christ, the Christian's Passover lamb (1 Cor. 5:7), had no bones broken when He was crucified (John 19:36).

⁵⁰Thus all the children of Israel did; as the LORD commanded Moses and Aaron, so they did. ⁵¹And it came to pass, on that very same day, that the LORD brought the children of Israel out of the land of Egypt according to their armies.

The Firstborn Consecrated

13 Then the LORD spoke to Moses, saying, ²"Consecrate to Me all the firstborn, whatever opens the womb among the children of Israel, *both* of man and beast; it is Mine."

The Feast of Unleavened Bread

³And Moses said to the people: "Remember this day in which you went out of Egypt, out of the house of bondage; for by strength of hand the LORD brought you out of this *place*. No leavened bread shall be eaten. ⁴On this day you are going out, in the month Abib. ⁵And it shall be, when the LORD brings you into the land of the Canaanites and the Hittites and the Amorites and the Hivites and the Jebusites, which He swore to your fathers to give you, a land flowing with milk and honey, that you shall keep this service in this month. ⁶Seven days you shall eat unleavened bread, and on the seventh day *there shall be* a feast to the

---

12:40 ᵃSamaritan Pentateuch and Septuagint read *Egypt and Canaan.*

LORD. [7]Unleavened bread shall be eaten seven days. And no leavened bread shall be seen among you, nor shall leaven be seen among you in all your quarters. [8]And you shall tell your son in that day, saying, 'This is done because of what the LORD did for me when I came up from Egypt.' [9]It shall be as a sign to you on your hand and as a memorial between your eyes, that the LORD's law may be in your mouth; for with a strong hand the LORD has brought you out of Egypt. [10]You shall therefore keep this ordinance in its season from year to year.

> **13:8 for me when I.** This first generation who experienced the Exodus could personally speak of God's care over their firstborn. Later generations could only say, "for us...when we," but the original generation could apply this phrase in a very personal way.

The Law of the Firstborn

[11]"And it shall be, when the LORD brings you into the land of the Canaanites, as He swore to you and your fathers, and gives it to you, [12]that you shall set apart to the LORD all that open the womb, that is, every firstborn that comes from an animal which you have; the males *shall be* the LORD's. [13]But every firstborn of a donkey you shall redeem with a lamb; and if you will not redeem *it*, then you shall break its neck. And all the firstborn of man among your sons you shall redeem. [14]So it shall be, when your son asks you in time to come, saying, 'What *is* this?' that you shall say to him, 'By strength of hand the LORD brought us out of Egypt, out of the house of bondage. [15]And it came to pass, when Pharaoh was stubborn about letting us go, that the LORD killed all the firstborn in the land of Egypt, both the firstborn of man and the firstborn of beast. Therefore I sacrifice to the LORD all males that open the womb, but all the firstborn of my sons I redeem.' [16]It shall be as a sign on your hand and as frontlets between your eyes, for by strength of hand the LORD brought us out of Egypt."

The Wilderness Way

[17]Then it came to pass, when Pharaoh had let the people go, that God did not lead them *by* way of the land of the Philistines, although that *was* near; for God said, "Lest perhaps the people change their minds when they see war, and return to Egypt." [18]So God led the people around *by* way of the wilderness of the Red Sea. And the children of Israel went up in orderly ranks out of the land of Egypt.

[19]And Moses took the bones of Joseph with him, for he had placed the children of Israel under solemn oath, saying, "God will surely visit you, and you shall carry up my bones from here with you."[a]

> **13:19 the bones of Joseph.** Roughly 360 years earlier, Joseph had foreseen the day when God would bring His people out of Egypt to the Promised Land, and certain of God's promise, Joseph asked that his bones be carried there.

[20]So they took their journey from Succoth and camped in Etham at the edge of the wilderness. [21]And the LORD went before them by day in a pillar of cloud to lead the way, and by night in a pillar of fire to give them light, so as to go by day and night. [22]He did not take away the pillar of cloud by day or the pillar of fire by night *from* before the people.

> **13:21 a pillar of cloud...a pillar of fire.** This single column was cloud by day and fire by night and was God's means of leading the people.

The Red Sea Crossing

14 Now the LORD spoke to Moses, saying: [2]"Speak to the children of Israel, that they turn and camp before Pi Hahiroth, between Migdol and the sea, opposite Baal Zephon; you shall camp before it by the sea. [3]For Pharaoh will say of the children of Israel, 'They *are* bewildered by the land; the wilderness has closed them in.' [4]Then I will harden Pharaoh's heart, so that he will pursue them; and I will gain honor over Pharaoh and over all his army, that the Egyptians may know that I *am* the LORD." And they did so.

[5]Now it was told the king of Egypt that the people had fled, and the heart of Pharaoh and his servants was turned against the people; and they said, "Why have we

13:19 [a]Genesis 50:25

done this, that we have let Israel go from serving us?" [6]So he made ready his chariot and took his people with him. [7]Also, he took six hundred choice chariots, and all the chariots of Egypt with captains over every one of them. [8]And the LORD hardened the heart of Pharaoh king of Egypt, and he pursued the children of Israel; and the children of Israel went out with boldness. [9]So the Egyptians pursued them, all the horses *and* chariots of Pharaoh, his horsemen and his army, and overtook them camping by the sea beside Pi Hahiroth, before Baal Zephon.

[10]And when Pharaoh drew near, the children of Israel lifted their eyes, and behold, the Egyptians marched after them. So they were very afraid, and the children of Israel cried out to the LORD. [11]Then they said to Moses, "Because *there were* no graves in Egypt, have you taken us away to die in the wilderness? Why have you so dealt with us, to bring us up out of Egypt? [12]*Is* this not the word that we told you in Egypt, saying, 'Let us alone that we may serve the Egyptians'? For *it would have been* better for us to serve the Egyptians than that we should die in the wilderness."

14:12 serve the Egyptians? The Israelites conveniently forgot the degree of their enslavement, as shown by their "We told you so" attitude.

[13]And Moses said to the people, "Do not be afraid. Stand still, and see the salvation of the LORD, which He will accomplish for you today. For the Egyptians whom you see today, you shall see again no more forever. [14]The LORD will fight for you, and you shall hold your peace."

[15]And the LORD said to Moses, "Why do you cry to Me? Tell the children of Israel to go forward. [16]But lift up your rod, and stretch out your hand over the sea and divide it. And the children of Israel shall go on dry *ground* through the midst of the sea. [17]And I indeed will harden the hearts of the Egyptians, and they shall follow them. So I will gain honor over Pharaoh and over all his army, his chariots, and his horsemen. [18]Then the Egyptians shall know that I *am*

the LORD, when I have gained honor for Myself over Pharaoh, his chariots, and his horsemen."

[19]And the Angel of God, who went before the camp of Israel, moved and went behind them; and the pillar of cloud went from before them and stood behind them. [20]So it came between the camp of the Egyptians and the camp of Israel. Thus it was a cloud and darkness *to the one,* and it gave light by night *to the other,* so that the one did not come near the other all that night.

14:19 stood behind them. The Angel of the Lord, and the pillar of cloud and fire, moved from being advance guard to being rear guard, from leading to protecting.

[21]Then Moses stretched out his hand over the sea; and the LORD caused the sea to go *back* by a strong east wind all that night, and made the sea into dry *land,* and the waters were divided. [22]So the children of Israel went into the midst of the sea on the dry *ground,* and the waters *were* a wall to them on their right hand and on their left. [23]And the Egyptians pursued and went after them into the midst of the sea, all Pharaoh's horses, his chariots, and his horsemen. [24]Now it came to pass, in the morning watch, that the LORD looked down upon the army of the Egyptians through the pillar of fire and cloud, and He troubled the army of the Egyptians. [25]And He took off[a] their chariot wheels, so that they drove them with difficulty; and the Egyptians said, "Let us flee from the face of Israel, for the LORD fights for them against the Egyptians."

14:24,25 the LORD looked down...and He troubled. Not only was the Lord fully aware of exactly what was happening, but He also wreaked havoc among them. Trapped in the valley between the walls of water, the Egyptians acknowledged that the Lord was fighting against them.

[26]Then the LORD said to Moses, "Stretch out your hand over the sea, that the waters

---

14:25 [a]Samaritan Pentateuch, Septuagint, and Syriac read *bound.*

may come back upon the Egyptians, on their chariots, and on their horsemen." 27And Moses stretched out his hand over the sea; and when the morning appeared, the sea returned to its full depth, while the Egyptians were fleeing into it. So the LORD overthrew the Egyptians in the midst of the sea. 28Then the waters returned and covered the chariots, the horsemen, *and* all the army of Pharaoh that came into the sea after them. Not so much as one of them remained. 29But the children of Israel had walked on dry *land* in the midst of the sea, and the waters *were* a wall to them on their right hand and on their left.

30So the LORD saved Israel that day out of the hand of the Egyptians, and Israel saw the Egyptians dead on the seashore. 31Thus Israel saw the great work which the LORD had done in Egypt; so the people feared the LORD, and believed the LORD and His servant Moses.

The Song of Moses

15 Then Moses and the children of Israel sang this song to the LORD, and spoke, saying:

"I will sing to the LORD,
For He has triumphed gloriously!
The horse and its rider
He has thrown into the sea!
2 The LORD *is* my strength and song,
And He has become my salvation;
He *is* my God, and I will praise Him;
My father's God, and I will exalt
Him.
3 The LORD *is* a man of war;
The LORD *is* His name.
4 Pharaoh's chariots and his army He
has cast into the sea;
His chosen captains also are drowned
in the Red Sea.
5 The depths have covered them;
They sank to the bottom like a stone.

6 "Your right hand, O LORD, has become
glorious in power;
Your right hand, O LORD, has dashed
the enemy in pieces.
7 And in the greatness of Your
excellence
You have overthrown those who rose
against You;

You sent forth Your wrath;
It consumed them like stubble.
8 And with the blast of Your nostrils
The waters were gathered together;
The floods stood upright like a heap;
The depths congealed in the heart of
the sea.
9 The enemy said, 'I will pursue,
I will overtake,
I will divide the spoil;
My desire shall be satisfied on them.
I will draw my sword,
My hand shall destroy them.'
10 You blew with Your wind,
The sea covered them;
They sank like lead in the mighty
waters.

11 "Who *is* like You, O LORD, among the
gods?
Who *is* like You, glorious in holiness,
Fearful in praises, doing wonders?
12 You stretched out Your right hand;
The earth swallowed them.
13 You in Your mercy have led forth
The people whom You have
redeemed;
You have guided *them* in Your
strength
To Your holy habitation.

14 "The people will hear *and* be afraid;
Sorrow will take hold of the
inhabitants of Philistia.
15 Then the chiefs of Edom will be
dismayed;
The mighty men of Moab,
Trembling will take hold of them;
All the inhabitants of Canaan will
melt away.
16 Fear and dread will fall on them;
By the greatness of Your arm
They will be *as* still as a stone,
Till Your people pass over, O LORD,
Till the people pass over
Whom You have purchased.
17 You will bring them in and plant
them
In the mountain of Your inheritance,
In the place, O LORD, *which* You
have made
For Your own dwelling,
The sanctuary, O LORD, *which* Your
hands have established.

[18] "The LORD shall reign forever and
     ever."

[19]For the horses of Pharaoh went with his chariots and his horsemen into the sea, and the LORD brought back the waters of the sea upon them. But the children of Israel went on dry *land* in the midst of the sea.

The Song of Miriam

[20]Then Miriam the prophetess, the sister of Aaron, took the timbrel in her hand; and all the women went out after her with timbrels and with dances. [21]And Miriam answered them:

> "Sing to the LORD,
> For He has triumphed gloriously!
> The horse and its rider
> He has thrown into the sea!"

15:20 the prophetess. Miriam was the first woman to be given the honor of the Lord's speaking through her. She apparently played an important role in the rescue events (see Mic. 6:4).

Bitter Waters Made Sweet

[22]So Moses brought Israel from the Red Sea; then they went out into the Wilderness of Shur. And they went three days in the wilderness and found no water. [23]Now when they came to Marah, they could not drink the waters of Marah, for they *were* bitter. Therefore the name of it was called Marah.[a] [24]And the people complained against Moses, saying, "What shall we drink?" [25]So he cried out to the LORD, and the LORD showed him a tree. When he cast *it* into the waters, the waters were made sweet.

There He made a statute and an ordinance for them, and there He tested them, [26]and said, "If you diligently heed the voice of the LORD your God and do what is right in His sight, give ear to His commandments and keep all His statutes, I will put none of the diseases on you which I have brought on the Egyptians. For I *am* the LORD who heals you."

[27]Then they came to Elim, where there *were* twelve wells of water and seventy palm trees; so they camped there by the waters.

15:23 *a*Literally *Bitter*

How are we in the twenty-first century supposed to think about the astonishing miracles that Exodus so matter-of-factly reports—like the burning bush, the plagues, God's presence in the pillar of fire and cloud, parting the Red Sea, and manna, to name a few?

The scientific materialism of many twenty-first century people makes it difficult for them to consider any so-called miracles. If the laws of nature are considered supreme, the existence of a personal Supreme Being above the laws of nature and able to override them becomes inconceivable. Examples of miracles do little to convince someone who is already convinced that miracles are impossible.

Miracles can demonstrate God's existence; they don't prove it. Human beings display an amazing ability to come up with alternative explanations for God's activity in history. The situation is not that twenty-first century people can't believe in miracles; rather, it is that twenty-first century people often won't believe in miracles.

For Christians, the matter is settled by faith. In becoming Christians, we had to believe in the central miracle: God came in the flesh, Jesus Christ, who lived, died and rose from the dead to reign eternally as Lord and Savior. In the light of that miracle, the miracles of Exodus become less a matter for speculation and more a matter of wonder and worship. They are examples of the lengths to which God went to communicate to people. Even twenty-first century Christians are humbled and awestruck by God's amazing power!

Bread from Heaven

16 And they journeyed from Elim, and all the congregation of the children of Israel came to the Wilderness of Sin, which is between Elim and Sinai, on the fifteenth day of the second month after they departed from the land of Egypt. ²Then the whole congregation of the children of Israel complained against Moses and Aaron in the wilderness. ³And the children of Israel said to them, "Oh, that we had died by the hand of the LORD in the land of Egypt, when we sat by the pots of meat *and* when we ate bread to the full! For you have brought us out into this wilderness to kill this whole assembly with hunger."

16:2 the whole congregation...complained. Sadly, what characterized the people as a whole was their negative attitude, short memory of God's miracles, and self-centeredness. The country that had enslaved them suddenly looked good compared to the wilderness.

---

⁴Then the LORD said to Moses, "Behold, I will rain bread from heaven for you. And the people shall go out and gather a certain quota every day, that I may test them, whether they will walk in My law or not. ⁵And it shall be on the sixth day that they shall prepare what they bring in, and it shall be twice as much as they gather daily."

⁶Then Moses and Aaron said to all the children of Israel, "At evening you shall know that the LORD has brought you out of the land of Egypt. ⁷And in the morning you shall see the glory of the LORD; for He hears your complaints against the LORD. But what *are* we, that you complain against us?" ⁸Also Moses said, "*This shall be seen* when the LORD gives you meat to eat in the evening, and in the morning bread to the full; for the LORD hears your complaints which you make against Him. And what *are* we? Your complaints *are* not against us but against the LORD."

⁹Then Moses spoke to Aaron, "Say to all the congregation of the children of Israel, 'Come near before the LORD, for He has heard your complaints.' " ¹⁰Now it came to pass, as Aaron spoke to the whole congregation of the children of Israel, that they looked toward the wilderness, and behold, the glory of the LORD appeared in the cloud.

¹¹And the LORD spoke to Moses, saying, ¹²"I have heard the complaints of the children of Israel. Speak to them, saying, 'At twilight you shall eat meat, and in the morning you shall be filled with bread. And you shall know that I *am* the LORD your God.' "

¹³So it was that quails came up at evening and covered the camp, and in the morning the dew lay all around the camp. ¹⁴And when the layer of dew lifted, there, on the surface of the wilderness, was a small round substance, *as* fine as frost on the ground. ¹⁵So when the children of Israel saw *it*, they said to one another, "What is it?" For they did not know what it *was*.

16:13 quails. These feathered fowl were real birds, and the psalmist describes that God "rained meat" on the people (Ps. 78:27).

And Moses said to them, "This *is* the bread which the LORD has given you to eat. ¹⁶This is the thing which the LORD has commanded: 'Let every man gather it according to each one's need, one omer for each person, *according to the* number of persons; let every man take for *those* who *are* in his tent.' "

¹⁷Then the children of Israel did so and gathered, some more, some less. ¹⁸So when they measured *it* by omers, he who gathered much had nothing left over, and he who gathered little had no lack. Every man had gathered according to each one's need. ¹⁹And Moses said, "Let no one leave any of it till morning." ²⁰Notwithstanding they did not heed Moses. But some of them left part of it until morning, and it bred worms and stank. And Moses was angry with them. ²¹So they gathered it every morning, every man according to his need. And when the sun became hot, it melted.

²²And so it was, on the sixth day, *that* they gathered twice as much bread, two omers for each one. And all the rulers of the congregation came and told Moses. ²³Then he said to them, "This *is what* the LORD has said: 'Tomorrow *is* a Sabbath rest, a holy Sabbath to the LORD. Bake what you will bake *today,* and boil what you will boil; and lay up for yourselves all that remains, to be kept until morning.' " ²⁴So they laid it

up till morning, as Moses commanded; and it did not stink, nor were there any worms in it. [25]Then Moses said, "Eat that today, for today *is* a Sabbath to the LORD; today you will not find it in the field. [26]Six days you shall gather it, but on the seventh day, the Sabbath, there will be none."

[27]Now it happened *that some* of the people went out on the seventh day to gather, but they found none. [28]And the LORD said to Moses, "How long do you refuse to keep My commandments and My laws? [29]See! For the LORD has given you the Sabbath; therefore He gives you on the sixth day bread for two days. Let every man remain in his place; let no man go out of his place on the seventh day." [30]So the people rested on the seventh day.

[31]And the house of Israel called its name Manna.*a* And it *was* like white coriander seed, and the taste of it *was* like wafers *made* with honey.

> **16:31 Manna.** The name "manna" was derived from their question, "What is it?" The psalmist referred to manna as the "bread of heaven" and "angels' food" which rained down after God had opened the windows of heaven (Ps. 78:23–25). No natural explanation can account for the supernatural appearance of the food on the ground every day except the Sabbath for the next 40 years.

[32]Then Moses said, "This *is* the thing which the LORD has commanded: 'Fill an omer with it, to be kept for your generations, that they may see the bread with which I fed you in the wilderness, when I brought you out of the land of Egypt.'" [33]And Moses said to Aaron, "Take a pot and put an omer of manna in it, and lay it up before the LORD, to be kept for your generations." [34]As the LORD commanded Moses, so Aaron laid it up before the Testimony, to be kept. [35]And the children of Israel ate manna forty years, until they came to an inhabited land; they ate manna until they came to the border of the land of Canaan. [36]Now an omer *is* one-tenth of an ephah.

Water from the Rock

17 Then all the congregation of the children of Israel set out on their journey from the Wilderness of Sin, according to the commandment of the LORD, and camped in Rephidim; but *there was* no water for the people to drink. [2]Therefore the people contended with Moses, and said, "Give us water, that we may drink."

So Moses said to them, "Why do you contend with me? Why do you tempt the LORD?"

[3]And the people thirsted there for water, and the people complained against Moses, and said, "Why *is* it you have brought us up out of Egypt, to kill us and our children and our livestock with thirst?"

[4]So Moses cried out to the LORD, saying, "What shall I do with this people? They are almost ready to stone me!"

> **17:4 Moses cried out to the LORD.** The leader turned to God in prayer, whereas the people turned on their leader instead of following his example. Moses' life was characterized by prayer and by turning to God for solutions to problems and crises.

[5]And the LORD said to Moses, "Go on before the people, and take with you some of the elders of Israel. Also take in your hand your rod with which you struck the river, and go. [6]Behold, I will stand before you there on the rock in Horeb; and you shall strike the rock, and water will come out of it, that the people may drink." And Moses did so in the sight of the elders of Israel. [7]So he called the name of the place Massah*a* and Meribah,*b* because of the contention of the children of Israel, and because they tempted the LORD, saying, "Is the LORD among us or not?"

Victory over the Amalekites

[8]Now Amalek came and fought with Israel in Rephidim. [9]And Moses said to Joshua, "Choose us some men and go out, fight with Amalek. Tomorrow I will stand on the top of the hill with the rod of God in

> **17:9 the rod of God.** The staff which Moses held up in his hands was not a magic wand but rather a symbol of God's personal and powerful involvement. Previously, Moses had used it to initiate the miracles of God in Egypt. The raised staff demonstrated their dependence upon God in battle.

16:31 *a*Literally *What?* (compare Exodus 16:15)   17:7 *a*Literally *Tempted*   *b*Literally *Contention*

my hand." [10]So Joshua did as Moses said to him, and fought with Amalek. And Moses, Aaron, and Hur went up to the top of the hill. [11]And so it was, when Moses held up his hand, that Israel prevailed; and when he let down his hand, Amalek prevailed. [12]But Moses' hands *became* heavy; so they took a stone and put *it* under him, and he sat on it. And Aaron and Hur supported his hands, one on one side, and the other on the other side; and his hands were steady until the going down of the sun. [13]So Joshua defeated Amalek and his people with the edge of the sword.

[14]Then the LORD said to Moses, "Write this *for* a memorial in the book and recount *it* in the hearing of Joshua, that I will utterly blot out the remembrance of Amalek from under heaven." [15]And Moses built an altar and called its name, The-LORD-Is-My-Banner;[a] [16]for he said, "Because the LORD has sworn: the LORD *will have* war with Amalek from generation to generation."

Jethro's Advice

18And Jethro, the priest of Midian, Moses' father-in-law, heard of all that God had done for Moses and for Israel His people—that the LORD had brought Israel out of Egypt. [2]Then Jethro, Moses' father-in-law, took Zipporah, Moses' wife, after he had sent her back, [3]with her two sons, of whom the name of one *was* Gershom (for he said, "I have been a stranger in a foreign land")[a] [4]and the name of the other *was* Eliezer[a] (for *he said,* "The God of my father *was* my help, and delivered me from the sword of Pharaoh"); [5]and Jethro, Moses' father-in-law, came with his sons and his wife to Moses in the wilderness, where he was encamped at the mountain of God. [6]Now he had said to Moses, "I, your father-in-law Jethro, am coming to you with your wife and her two sons with her."

[7]So Moses went out to meet his father-in-law, bowed down, and kissed him. And they asked each other about *their* well-being, and they went into the tent. [8]And Moses told his father-in-law all that the LORD had done to Pharaoh and to the Egyptians for Israel's sake, all the hardship that had come upon them on the way, and *how* the LORD had delivered them. [9]Then Jethro rejoiced for all the good which the LORD had done for Israel, whom He had delivered out of the hand of the Egyptians. [10]And Jethro said, "Blessed *be* the LORD, who has delivered you out of the hand of the Egyptians and out of the hand of Pharaoh, *and* who has delivered the people from under the hand of the Egyptians. [11]Now I know that the LORD *is* greater than all the gods; for in the very thing in which they behaved proudly, *He was* above them." [12]Then Jethro, Moses' father-in-law, took[a] a burnt offering and *other* sacrifices *to offer* to God. And Aaron came with all the elders of Israel to eat bread with Moses' father-in-law before God.

18:7–12 Jethro's response of praise showed his belief in Yahweh, proving that the priest of Midian did not worship Midian's gods. He joined Aaron and the elders in worship together (v. 12).

[13]And so it was, on the next day, that Moses sat to judge the people; and the people stood before Moses from morning until evening. [14]So when Moses' father-in-law saw all that he did for the people, he said, "What *is* this thing that you are doing for the people? Why do you alone sit, and all the people stand before you from morning until evening?"

[15]And Moses said to his father-in-law, "Because the people come to me to inquire of God. [16]When they have a difficulty, they come to me, and I judge between one and another; and I make known the statutes of God and His laws."

[17]So Moses' father-in-law said to him, "The thing that you do *is* not good. [18]Both you and these people who *are* with you will surely wear yourselves out. For this thing *is* too much for you; you are not able to perform it by yourself. [19]Listen now to my voice; I will give you counsel, and God will be with you: Stand before God for the people, so that you may bring the difficulties to God. [20]And you shall teach them the statutes and the laws, and show them the way

---

17:15 [a]Hebrew *YHWH Nissi*   18:3 [a]Compare Exodus 2:22   18:4 [a]Literally *My God Is Help*
18:12 [a]Following Masoretic Text and Septuagint; Syriac, Targum, and Vulgate read *offered.*

in which they must walk and the work they must do. ²¹Moreover you shall select from all the people able men, such as fear God, men of truth, hating covetousness; and place *such* over them *to be* rulers of thousands, rulers of hundreds, rulers of fifties, and rulers of tens. ²²And let them judge the people at all times. Then it will be *that* every great matter they shall bring to you, but every small matter they themselves shall judge. So it will be easier for you, for they will bear *the burden* with you. ²³If you do this thing, and God *so* commands you, then you will be able to endure, and all this people will also go to their place in peace."

²⁴So Moses heeded the voice of his father-in-law and did all that he had said. ²⁵And Moses chose able men out of all Israel, and made them heads over the people: rulers of thousands, rulers of hundreds, rulers of fifties, and rulers of tens. ²⁶So they judged the people at all times; the hard cases they brought to Moses, but they judged every small case themselves.

²⁷Then Moses let his father-in-law depart, and he went his way to his own land.

18:13–27 Jethro's practical wisdom was an immense benefit to Moses and Israel and is still praised today for its example of delegation, management, and efficiency.

Israel at Mount Sinai

19 In the third month after the children of Israel had gone out of the land of Egypt, on the same day, they came *to* the Wilderness of Sinai. ²For they had departed from Rephidim, had come *to* the Wilderness of Sinai, and camped in the wilderness. So Israel camped there before the mountain.

³And Moses went up to God, and the LORD called to him from the mountain, saying, "Thus you shall say to the house of Jacob, and tell the children of Israel: ⁴'You have seen what I did to the Egyptians, and *how* I bore you on eagles' wings and brought you to Myself. ⁵Now therefore, if you will indeed obey My voice and keep My covenant, then you shall be a special treasure to Me above all people; for all the earth *is* Mine. ⁶And you shall be to Me a kingdom of priests and a holy nation.' These *are* the

words which you shall speak to the children of Israel."

19:4 bore you on eagles' wings. With an appropriate metaphor, God described the Exodus and the journey to Sinai. Eagles carried their young out of the nests on their wings and taught them to fly, catching them if necessary on their outspread wings.

⁷So Moses came and called for the elders of the people, and laid before them all these words which the LORD commanded him. ⁸Then all the people answered together and said, "All that the LORD has spoken we will do." So Moses brought back the words of the people to the LORD. ⁹And the LORD said to Moses, "Behold, I come to you in the thick cloud, that the people may hear when I speak with you, and believe you forever."

So Moses told the words of the people to the LORD.

¹⁰Then the LORD said to Moses, "Go to the people and consecrate them today and tomorrow, and let them wash their clothes. ¹¹And let them be ready for the third day. For on the third day the LORD will come down upon Mount Sinai in the sight of all the people. ¹²You shall set bounds for the people all around, saying, 'Take heed to yourselves *that* you do *not* go up to the mountain or touch its base. Whoever touches the mountain shall surely be put to death. ¹³Not a hand shall touch him, but he shall surely be stoned or shot *with an arrow*; whether man or beast, he shall not live.' When the trumpet sounds long, they shall come near the mountain."

19:10 consecrate them. The inward preparation for meeting with God was mirrored in the outward actions of maintaining bodily cleanliness.

¹⁴So Moses went down from the mountain to the people and sanctified the people, and they washed their clothes. ¹⁵And he said to the people, "Be ready for the third day; do not come near *your* wives."

¹⁶Then it came to pass on the third day, in the morning, that there were thunderings and lightnings, and a thick cloud on the mountain; and the sound of the trumpet was very loud, so that all the people who *were* in the camp trembled. ¹⁷And

Moses brought the people out of the camp to meet with God, and they stood at the foot of the mountain. ¹⁸Now Mount Sinai *was* completely in smoke, because the LORD descended upon it in fire. Its smoke ascended like the smoke of a furnace, and the whole mountain*a* quaked greatly. ¹⁹And when the blast of the trumpet sounded long and became louder and louder, Moses spoke, and God answered him by voice. ²⁰Then the LORD came down upon Mount Sinai, on the top of the mountain. And the LORD called Moses to the top of the mountain, and Moses went up.

²¹And the LORD said to Moses, "Go down and warn the people, lest they break through to gaze at the LORD, and many of them perish. ²²Also let the priests who come near the LORD consecrate themselves, lest the LORD break out against them."

²³But Moses said to the LORD, "The people cannot come up to Mount Sinai; for You warned us, saying, 'Set bounds around the mountain and consecrate it.' "

²⁴Then the LORD said to him, "Away! Get down and then come up, you and Aaron with you. But do not let the priests and the people break through to come up to the LORD, lest He break out against them." ²⁵So Moses went down to the people and spoke to them.

The Ten Commandments

20 And God spoke all these words, saying:

² "I *am* the LORD your God, who brought you out of the land of Egypt, out of the house of bondage.

³ "You shall have no other gods before Me.

⁴ "You shall not make for yourself a carved image—any likeness *of anything* that *is* in heaven above, or that *is* in the earth beneath, or that *is* in the water under the earth; ⁵you shall not bow down to them nor serve them. For I, the LORD your God, *am* a jealous God, visiting the iniquity of the fathers upon the children to the third and fourth *generations* of those who hate Me, ⁶but showing mercy to thousands, to those who love Me and keep My commandments.

⁷ "You shall not take the name of the LORD your God in vain, for the LORD will not hold *him* guiltless who takes His name in vain.

⁸ "Remember the Sabbath day, to keep it holy. ⁹Six days you shall labor and do all your work, ¹⁰but the seventh day *is* the Sabbath of the LORD your God. *In it* you shall do no work: you, nor your son, nor your daughter, nor your male servant, nor your female servant, nor your cattle, nor your stranger who *is* within your gates. ¹¹For *in* six days the LORD made the heavens and the earth, the sea, and all that *is* in them, and rested the seventh day. Therefore

---

19:18 *a*Septuagint reads *all the people.*

The Ten Commandments: outmoded expectations or divine demands?

People make a serious error when they speak about "breaking the Ten Commandments." History amply displays the fact that people persist in breaking *themselves* on the Ten Commandments. They represent God's absolute and unchanging standard despite any arguments over their interpretation and application.

The title "Ten Commandments" comes from Moses (Exodus 34:28). The emphasis on God Himself speaking and writing these words makes unacceptable any theories of Israel's borrowing legal patterns or concepts from surrounding nations.

The Ten Commandments may be grouped into two broad categories: the vertical—humanity's relationship to God (Exodus 20:2–11); and the horizontal—humanity's relationship to the community (Exodus 20:12–17). By these Ten Commandments, true theology and true worship, the name of God, family honor, life, marriage, property, truth and virtue are well protected.

the LORD blessed the Sabbath day and hallowed it.

12 "Honor your father and your mother, that your days may be long upon the land which the LORD your God is giving you.

13 "You shall not murder.

> **20:13 murder.** God imposed a death sentence on any person who killed another intentionally (see 21:12; Num. 35:17–21). These passages emphasize the sacredness of human life.

14 "You shall not commit adultery.

> **20:14 adultery.** This command protected the sacredness of the marriage relationship and applied to both men and women.

15 "You shall not steal.

16 "You shall not bear false witness against your neighbor.

17 "You shall not covet your neighbor's house; you shall not covet your neighbor's wife, nor his male servant, nor his female servant, nor his ox, nor his donkey, nor anything that is your neighbor's."

> **20:17 covet.** The thoughts and desires of the heart do not escape attention. A strong longing for what belongs to another is wrong. This command proves that all ten commandments apply not only to external acts but also to internal thoughts.

The People Afraid of God's Presence

18 Now all the people witnessed the thunderings, the lightning flashes, the sound of the trumpet, and the mountain smoking; and when the people saw it, they trembled and stood afar off. 19 Then they said to Moses, "You speak with us, and we will hear; but let not God speak with us, lest we die."

20 And Moses said to the people, "Do not fear; for God has come to test you, and that His fear may be before you, so that you may not sin." 21 So the people stood afar off, but Moses drew near the thick darkness where God was.

The Law of the Altar

22 Then the LORD said to Moses, "Thus you shall say to the children of Israel: 'You have seen that I have talked with you from heaven. 23 You shall not make anything to be with Me—gods of silver or gods of gold you shall not make for yourselves. 24 An altar of earth you shall make for Me, and you shall sacrifice on it your burnt offerings and your peace offerings, your sheep and your oxen. In every place where I record My name I will come to you, and I will bless you. 25 And if you make Me an altar of stone, you shall not build it of hewn stone; for if you use your tool on it, you have profaned it. 26 Nor shall you go up by steps to My altar, that your nakedness may not be exposed on it.'

The Law Concerning Servants

21 "Now these are the judgments which you shall set before them: 2 If you buy a Hebrew servant, he shall serve six years; and in the seventh he shall go out free and pay nothing. 3 If he comes in by

THE TEN COMMANDMENTS

Commandment Restatement	Old Testament Statement	Old Testament Death Penalty	New Testament
1st Polytheism	Exodus 20:3	Exodus 22:20; Deuteronomy 6:13–15	Acts 14:15
2nd Graven Images	Exodus 20:4	Deuteronomy 27:15	1 John 5:21
3rd Swearing	Exodus 20:7	Leviticus 24:15,16	James 5:12
4th Sabbath	Exodus 20:8	Numbers 15:32–36	Colossians 2:16 nullifies
5th Obedience to parents	Exodus 20:12	Exodus 21:15–17	Ephesians 6:1
6th Murder	Exodus 20:13	Exodus 21:12	1 John 3:15
7th Adultery	Exodus 20:14	Leviticus 20:10	1 Corinthians 6:9,10
8th Theft	Exodus 20:15	Exodus 21:16	Ephesians 4:28
9th False Witness	Exodus 20:16	Deuteronomy 18:16–21	Colossians 3:9,10
10th Coveting	Exodus 20:17		Ephesians 5:3

himself, he shall go out by himself; if he *comes in* married, then his wife shall go out with him. ⁴If his master has given him a wife, and she has borne him sons or daughters, the wife and her children shall be her master's, and he shall go out by himself. ⁵But if the servant plainly says, 'I love my master, my wife, and my children; I will not go out free,' ⁶then his master shall bring him to the judges. He shall also bring him to the door, or to the doorpost, and his master shall pierce his ear with an awl; and he shall serve him forever.

⁷"And if a man sells his daughter to be a female slave, she shall not go out as the male slaves do. ⁸If she does not please her master, who has betrothed her to himself, then he shall let her be redeemed. He shall have no right to sell her to a foreign people, since he has dealt deceitfully with her. ⁹And if he has betrothed her to his son, he shall deal with her according to the custom of daughters. ¹⁰If he takes another *wife*, he shall not diminish her food, her clothing, and her marriage rights. ¹¹And if he does not do these three for her, then she shall go out free, without *paying* money.

The Law Concerning Violence

¹²"He who strikes a man so that he dies shall surely be put to death. ¹³However, if he did not lie in wait, but God delivered *him* into his hand, then I will appoint for you a place where he may flee.

¹⁴"But if a man acts with premeditation against his neighbor, to kill him by treachery, you shall take him from My altar, that he may die.

¹⁵"And he who strikes his father or his mother shall surely be put to death.

¹⁶"He who kidnaps a man and sells him, or if he is found in his hand, shall surely be put to death.

¹⁷"And he who curses his father or his mother shall surely be put to death.

¹⁸"If men contend with each other, and one strikes the other with a stone or with *his* fist, and he does not die but is confined to *his* bed, ¹⁹if he rises again and walks about outside with his staff, then he who struck *him* shall be acquitted. He shall only pay *for* the loss of his time, and shall provide *for him* to be thoroughly healed.

²⁰"And if a man beats his male or female servant with a rod, so that he dies under his hand, he shall surely be punished. ²¹Notwithstanding, if he remains alive a day or two, he shall not be punished; for he *is* his property.

²²"If men fight, and hurt a woman with child, so that she gives birth prematurely, yet no harm follows, he shall surely be punished accordingly as the woman's husband imposes on him; and he shall pay as the judges *determine*. ²³But if *any* harm follows, then you shall give life for life, ²⁴eye for eye, tooth for tooth, hand for hand, foot for foot, ²⁵burn for burn, wound for wound, stripe for stripe.

> **21:23,24** The principle of retaliation applied if injury did occur to either mother or child. The punishment matched, but did not exceed, the damage done to the victim. These laws protected a pregnant woman and considered a fetus a person, which is significant in today's abortion debate.

²⁶"If a man strikes the eye of his male or female servant, and destroys it, he shall let him go free for the sake of his eye. ²⁷And if he knocks out the tooth of his male or female servant, he shall let him go free for the sake of his tooth.

Animal Control Laws

²⁸"If an ox gores a man or a woman to death, then the ox shall surely be stoned, and its flesh shall not be eaten; but the owner of the ox *shall be* acquitted. ²⁹But if the ox tended to thrust with its horn in times past, and it has been made known to his owner, and he has not kept it confined, so that it has killed a man or a woman, the ox shall be stoned and its owner also shall be put to death. ³⁰If there is imposed on him a sum of money, then he shall pay to redeem his life, whatever is imposed on him. ³¹Whether it has gored a son or gored a daughter, according to this judgment it shall be done to him. ³²If the ox gores a male or female servant, he shall give to their master thirty shekels of silver, and the ox shall be stoned.

³³"And if a man opens a pit, or if a man digs a pit and does not cover it, and an ox or a donkey falls in it, ³⁴the owner of the pit shall make *it* good; he shall give money to their owner, but the dead *animal* shall be his.

³⁵"If one man's ox hurts another's, so that it dies, then they shall sell the live ox and divide the money from it; and the dead ox they shall also divide. ³⁶Or if it was known that the ox tended to thrust in time past, and its owner has not kept it confined, he shall surely pay ox for ox, and the dead animal shall be his own.

Responsibility for Property

22 "If a man steals an ox or a sheep, and slaughters it or sells it, he shall restore five oxen for an ox and four sheep for a sheep. ²If the thief is found breaking in, and he is struck so that he dies, *there shall be* no guilt for his bloodshed. ³If the sun has risen on him, *there shall be* guilt for his bloodshed. He should make full restitution; if he has nothing, then he shall be sold for his theft. ⁴If the theft is certainly found alive in his hand, whether it is an ox or donkey or sheep, he shall restore double.

⁵"If a man causes a field or vineyard to be grazed, and lets loose his animal, and it feeds in another man's field, he shall make restitution from the best of his own field and the best of his own vineyard.

⁶"If fire breaks out and catches in thorns, so that stacked grain, standing grain, or the field is consumed, he who kindled the fire shall surely make restitution.

⁷"If a man delivers to his neighbor money or articles to keep, and it is stolen out of the man's house, if the thief is found, he shall pay double. ⁸If the thief is not found, then the master of the house shall be brought to the judges *to see* whether he has put his hand into his neighbor's goods.

⁹"For any kind of trespass, *whether it* concerns an ox, a donkey, a sheep, or clothing, *or* for any kind of lost thing which *another* claims to be his, the cause of both parties shall come before the judges; *and* whomever the judges condemn shall pay double to his neighbor. ¹⁰If a man delivers to his neighbor a donkey, an ox, a sheep, or any animal to keep, and it dies, is hurt, or driven away, no one seeing *it,* ¹¹*then* an oath of the LORD shall be between them both, that he has not put his hand into his neighbor's goods; and the owner of it shall accept *that,* and he shall not make *it* good. ¹²But if, in fact, it is stolen from him, he shall make restitution to the owner of it.

¹³If it is torn to pieces *by a beast, then* he shall bring it as evidence, *and* he shall not make good what was torn.

¹⁴"And if a man borrows *anything* from his neighbor, and it becomes injured or dies, the owner of it not *being* with it, he shall surely make *it* good. ¹⁵If its owner *was* with it, he shall not make *it* good; if it *was* hired, it came for its hire.

Moral and Ceremonial Principles

¹⁶"If a man entices a virgin who is not betrothed, and lies with her, he shall surely pay the bride-price for her *to be* his wife. ¹⁷If her father utterly refuses to give her to him, he shall pay money according to the bride-price of virgins.

¹⁸"You shall not permit a sorceress to live.

¹⁹"Whoever lies with an animal shall surely be put to death.

²⁰"He who sacrifices to *any* god, except to the LORD only, he shall be utterly destroyed.

²¹"You shall neither mistreat a stranger nor oppress him, for you were strangers in the land of Egypt.

²²"You shall not afflict any widow or fatherless child. ²³If you afflict them in any way, *and* they cry at all to Me, I will surely hear their cry; ²⁴and My wrath will become hot, and I will kill you with the sword; your wives shall be widows, and your children fatherless.

> **22:22 widow or fatherless child.** God reserved His special attention for widows and orphans who often had no one to care for them. He reserved His wrath for those who abused or exploited them.

²⁵"If you lend money to *any of* My people who are poor among you, you shall not be like a moneylender to him; you shall not charge him interest. ²⁶If you ever take your neighbor's garment as a pledge, you shall return it to him before the sun goes down. ²⁷For that *is* his only covering, it *is* his garment for his skin. What will he sleep in? And it will be that when he cries to Me, I will hear, for I *am* gracious.

²⁸"You shall not revile God, nor curse a ruler of your people.

²⁹"You shall not delay *to offer* the first of your ripe produce and your juices. The

firstborn of your sons you shall give to Me. ³⁰Likewise you shall do with your oxen *and* your sheep. It shall be with its mother seven days; on the eighth day you shall give it to Me.

³¹"And you shall be holy men to Me: you shall not eat meat torn *by beasts* in the field; you shall throw it to the dogs.

> **22:31 holy men to Me.** All of these laws and regulations set Israel apart in conduct, not just in name. The special calling as Yahweh's firstborn son, His treasured possession, a kingdom of priests, and a holy nation mandated ethical uprightness.

Justice for All

23 "You shall not circulate a false report. Do not put your hand with the wicked to be an unrighteous witness. ²You shall not follow a crowd to do evil; nor shall you testify in a dispute so as to turn aside after many to pervert *justice*. ³You shall not show partiality to a poor man in his dispute.

⁴"If you meet your enemy's ox or his donkey going astray, you shall surely bring it back to him again. ⁵If you see the donkey of one who hates you lying under its burden, and you would refrain from helping it, you shall surely help him with it.

⁶"You shall not pervert the judgment of your poor in his dispute. ⁷Keep yourself far from a false matter; do not kill the innocent and righteous. For I will not justify the wicked. ⁸And you shall take no bribe, for a bribe blinds the discerning and perverts the words of the righteous.

⁹"Also you shall not oppress a stranger, for you know the heart of a stranger, because you were strangers in the land of Egypt.

The Law of Sabbaths

¹⁰"Six years you shall sow your land and gather in its produce, ¹¹but the seventh *year* you shall let it rest and lie fallow, that the poor of your people may eat; and what they leave, the beasts of the field may eat. In like manner you shall do with your vineyard *and* your olive grove. ¹²Six days you shall do your work, and on the seventh day you shall rest, that your ox and your donkey may rest, and the son of your female servant and the stranger may be refreshed.

¹³"And in all that I have said to you, be circumspect and make no mention of the name of other gods, nor let it be heard from your mouth.

Three Annual Feasts

¹⁴"Three times you shall keep a feast to Me in the year: ¹⁵You shall keep the Feast of Unleavened Bread (you shall eat unleavened bread seven days, as I commanded you, at the time appointed in the month of Abib, for in it you came out of Egypt; none shall appear before Me empty); ¹⁶and the Feast of Harvest, the firstfruits of your labors which you have sown in the field; and the Feast of Ingathering at the end of the year, when you have gathered in *the fruit of* your labors from the field.

¹⁷"Three times in the year all your males shall appear before the Lord GOD.*ᵃ*

> **23:10,11 seventh year.** A sabbatical year of rest after six years of farming benefited both the land and the poor. This pattern of allowing a field to lie fallow appears to have been unique with Israel.

¹⁸"You shall not offer the blood of My sacrifice with leavened bread; nor shall the fat of My sacrifice remain until morning. ¹⁹The first of the firstfruits of your land you shall bring into the house of the LORD your God. You shall not boil a young goat in its mother's milk.

The Angel and the Promises

²⁰"Behold, I send an Angel before you to keep you in the way and to bring you into the place which I have prepared. ²¹Beware of Him and obey His voice; do not provoke Him, for He will not pardon your transgressions; for My name *is* in Him. ²²But if you indeed obey His voice and do all that I speak, then I will be an enemy to your enemies and an adversary to your adversaries. ²³For My Angel will go before you and bring you in to the Amorites and the Hittites and the Perizzites and the Canaanites and the Hivites and the Jebusites; and I will cut them off. ²⁴You shall not bow down to their gods, nor serve them, nor do according to

23:17 *ᵃ*Hebrew *YHWH,* usually translated LORD

their works; but you shall utterly overthrow them and completely break down their *sacred* pillars.

²⁵"So you shall serve the LORD your God, and He will bless your bread and your water. And I will take sickness away from the midst of you. ²⁶No one shall suffer miscarriage or be barren in your land; I will fulfill the number of your days.

> **23:25,26** Proper worship brought with it wonderful rewards, including good harvests, a good water supply, and physical health, such as fertility and safe pregnancies.

²⁷"I will send My fear before you, I will cause confusion among all the people to whom you come, and will make all your enemies turn *their* backs to you. ²⁸And I will send hornets before you, which shall drive out the Hivite, the Canaanite, and the Hittite from before you. ²⁹I will not drive them out from before you in one year, lest the land become desolate and the beasts of the field become too numerous for you. ³⁰Little by little I will drive them out from before you, until you have increased, and you inherit the land. ³¹And I will set your bounds from the Red Sea to the sea, Philistia, and from the desert to the River.ᵃ For I will deliver the inhabitants of the land into your hand, and you shall drive them out before you. ³²You shall make no covenant with them, nor with their gods. ³³They shall not dwell in your land, lest they make you sin against Me. For *if* you serve their gods, it will surely be a snare to you."

Israel Affirms the Covenant

24 Now He said to Moses, "Come up to the LORD, you and Aaron, Nadab and Abihu, and seventy of the elders of Israel, and worship from afar. ²And Moses alone shall come near the LORD, but they shall not come near; nor shall the people go up with him."

³So Moses came and told the people all the words of the LORD and all the judgments. And all the people answered with one voice and said, "All the words which the LORD has said we will do." ⁴And Moses wrote all the words of the LORD. And he

rose early in the morning, and built an altar at the foot of the mountain, and twelve pillars according to the twelve tribes of Israel. ⁵Then he sent young men of the children of Israel, who offered burnt offerings and sacrificed peace offerings of oxen to the LORD. ⁶And Moses took half the blood and put *it* in basins, and half the blood he sprinkled on the altar. ⁷Then he took the Book of the Covenant and read in the hearing of the people. And they said, "All that the LORD has said we will do, and be obedient." ⁸And Moses took the blood, sprinkled *it* on the people, and said, "This is the blood of the covenant which the LORD has made with you according to all these words."

> **24:7 the Book of the Covenant.** On Mt. Sinai, Moses received civil, social, and religious laws, which were then orally presented, written down, and read to the people.

On the Mountain with God

⁹Then Moses went up, also Aaron, Nadab, and Abihu, and seventy of the elders of Israel, ¹⁰and they saw the God of Israel. And *there was* under His feet as it were a paved work of sapphire stone, and it was like the very heavens in *its* clarity. ¹¹But on the nobles of the children of Israel He did not lay His hand. So they saw God, and they ate and drank.

¹²Then the LORD said to Moses, "Come up to Me on the mountain and be there; and I will give you tablets of stone, and the law and commandments which I have written, that you may teach them."

¹³So Moses arose with his assistant Joshua, and Moses went up to the mountain of God. ¹⁴And he said to the elders, "Wait here for us until we come back to you. Indeed, Aaron and Hur *are* with you. If any man has a difficulty, let him go to them." ¹⁵Then Moses went up into the mountain, and a cloud covered the mountain.

¹⁶Now the glory of the LORD rested on Mount Sinai, and the cloud covered it six days. And on the seventh day He called to Moses out of the midst of the cloud. ¹⁷The sight of the glory of the LORD *was* like a consuming fire on the top of the mountain

---

23:31 ᵃHebrew *Nahar*, the Euphrates

in the eyes of the children of Israel. [18]So Moses went into the midst of the cloud and went up into the mountain. And Moses was on the mountain forty days and forty nights.

Offerings for the Sanctuary

25 Then the LORD spoke to Moses, saying: [2]"Speak to the children of Israel, that they bring Me an offering. From everyone who gives it willingly with his heart you shall take My offering. [3]And this *is* the offering which you shall take from them: gold, silver, and bronze; [4]blue, purple, and scarlet *thread,* fine linen, and goats' *hair;* [5]ram skins dyed red, badger skins, and acacia wood; [6]oil for the light, and spices for the anointing oil and for the sweet incense; [7]onyx stones, and stones to be set in the ephod and in the breastplate. [8]And let them make Me a sanctuary, that I may dwell among them. [9]According to all that I show you, *that is,* the pattern of the tabernacle and the pattern of all its furnishings, just so you shall make *it.*

25:8 I may dwell. The tabernacle is a noun derived from the verb "to dwell" and was an appropriate name for the place of God's presence with His people. His presence would be between the cherubim and from there He would meet with Moses.

The Ark of the Testimony

[10]"And they shall make an ark of acacia wood; two and a half cubits *shall be* its length, a cubit and a half its width, and a cubit and a half its height. [11]And you shall overlay it with pure gold, inside and out you shall overlay it, and shall make on it a molding of gold all around. [12]You shall cast four rings of gold for it, and put *them* in its four corners; two rings *shall be* on one side, and two rings on the other side. [13]And you shall make poles *of* acacia wood, and overlay them with gold. [14]You shall put the poles into the rings on the sides of the ark, that the ark may be carried by them. [15]The poles shall be in the rings of the ark; they shall not be taken from it. [16]And you shall put into the ark the Testimony which I will give you.

[17]"You shall make a mercy seat of pure gold; two and a half cubits *shall be* its length and a cubit and a half its width.

[18]And you shall make two cherubim of gold; of hammered work you shall make them at the two ends of the mercy seat. [19]Make one cherub at one end, and the other cherub at the other end; you shall make the cherubim at the two ends of it *of one piece* with the mercy seat. [20]And the cherubim shall stretch out *their* wings above, covering the mercy seat with their wings, and they shall face one another; the faces of the cherubim *shall be* toward the mercy seat. [21]You shall put the mercy seat on top of the ark, and in the ark you shall put the Testimony that I will give you. [22]And there I will meet with you, and I will speak with you from above the mercy seat, from between the two cherubim which *are* on the ark of the Testimony, about everything which I will give you in commandment to the children of Israel.

25:17 mercy seat. The cover of the ark was called the "mercy seat," or the place where atonement took place. Placed between the tablets of law inside the ark and the glory cloud above the ark was the blood-sprinkled cover, showing that blood from the sacrifices separated the broken law from the holy God.

The Table for the Showbread

[23]"You shall also make a table of acacia wood; two cubits *shall be* its length, a cubit its width, and a cubit and a half its height. [24]And you shall overlay it with pure gold, and make a molding of gold all around. [25]You shall make for it a frame of a handbreadth all around, and you shall make a gold molding for the frame all around. [26]And you shall make for it four rings of gold, and put the rings on the four corners that *are* at its four legs. [27]The rings shall be close to the frame, as holders for the poles to bear the table. [28]And you shall make the poles of acacia wood, and overlay them with gold, that the table may be carried with them. [29]You shall make its dishes, its pans, its pitchers, and its bowls for pouring. You shall make them of pure gold. [30]And you shall set the showbread on the table before Me always.

The Gold Lampstand

[31]"You shall also make a lampstand of pure gold; the lampstand shall be of hammered work. Its shaft, its branches, its

bowls, its *ornamental* knobs, and flowers shall be *of one piece.* ³²And six branches shall come out of its sides: three branches of the lampstand out of one side, and three branches of the lampstand out of the other side. ³³Three bowls *shall be* made like almond *blossoms* on one branch, *with* an *ornamental* knob and a flower, and three bowls made like almond *blossoms* on the other branch, *with* an *ornamental* knob and a flower—and so for the six branches that come out of the lampstand. ³⁴On the lampstand itself four bowls *shall be* made like almond *blossoms, each with* its *ornamental* knob and flower. ³⁵And *there shall be* a knob under the *first* two branches of the same, a knob under the *second* two branches of the same, and a knob under the *third* two branches of the same, according to the six branches that extend from the lampstand. ³⁶Their knobs and their branches *shall be of one piece;* all of it *shall be* one hammered piece of pure gold. ³⁷You shall make seven lamps for it, and they shall arrange its lamps so that they give light in front of it. ³⁸And its wick-trimmers and their trays *shall be* of pure gold. ³⁹It shall be made of a talent of pure gold, with all these utensils. ⁴⁰And see to it that you make *them* according to the pattern which was shown you on the mountain.

The Tabernacle

26 "Moreover you shall make the tabernacle *with* ten curtains *of* fine woven linen and blue, purple, and scarlet *thread;* with artistic designs of cherubim you shall weave them. ²The length of each curtain *shall be* twenty-eight cubits, and the width of each curtain four cubits. And every one of the curtains shall have the same measurements. ³Five curtains shall be coupled to one another, and *the other* five curtains *shall be* coupled to one another. ⁴And you shall make loops of blue *yarn* on the edge of the curtain on the selvedge of *one* set, and likewise you shall do on the outer edge of *the other* curtain of the second set. ⁵Fifty loops you shall make in the one curtain, and fifty loops you shall make on the edge of the curtain that *is* on the end of the second set, that the loops may be clasped to one another. ⁶And you shall make fifty clasps of gold, and couple the curtains together with the clasps, so that it may be one tabernacle.

⁷"You shall also make curtains of goats' *hair,* to be a tent over the tabernacle. You shall make eleven curtains. ⁸The length of each curtain *shall be* thirty cubits, and the width of each curtain four cubits; and the eleven curtains shall all have the same measurements. ⁹And you shall couple five curtains by themselves and six curtains by

Why all the specific details about the Tabernacle and what do they mean for us today?

Ever since God dictated the blueprints of the Tabernacle to Moses, people have wondered about the significance of the exact details. Several terms are used to indicate times in the Bible when events, persons or things represent larger ideas: typology and foreshadowing. For example, the sacrifice of the lambs in the Old Testament had not only a limited immediate significance in understanding the cost of forgiveness, but this practice also foreshadowed the eventual sacrifice of the Lamb of God, Jesus, on the cross.

Because at least some parts of the tabernacle hold special significance—the Ark representing God's covenant with His people—students of Scripture have looked for other possible deeper meanings. Ingenuity in linking every item of furniture and every piece of building material to Christ may appear most intriguing, but if New Testament statements and allusions do not support such linkage and typology, students ought to proceed with caution. The beauty and efficiency of the Tabernacle's design present a tribute to God's creative character, but those who look for hidden meaning in every tent peg and covering stitch run the risk of missing the big picture in the details. The New Testament points repeatedly to the awesome fact of God's presence with people as represented in the Tabernacle. Other New Testament lessons (particularly the Book of Hebrews) help identify the intended symbols and deeper meanings.

themselves, and you shall double over the sixth curtain at the forefront of the tent. [10]You shall make fifty loops on the edge of the curtain that is outermost in *one* set, and fifty loops on the edge of the curtain of the second set. [11]And you shall make fifty bronze clasps, put the clasps into the loops, and couple the tent together, that it may be one. [12]The remnant that remains of the curtains of the tent, the half curtain that remains, shall hang over the back of the tabernacle. [13]And a cubit on one side and a cubit on the other side, of what remains of the length of the curtains of the tent, shall hang over the sides of the tabernacle, on this side and on that side, to cover it.

[14]"You shall also make a covering of ram skins dyed red for the tent, and a covering of badger skins above that.

[15]"And for the tabernacle you shall make the boards of acacia wood, standing upright. [16]Ten cubits *shall be* the length of a board, and a cubit and a half *shall be* the width of each board. [17]Two tenons *shall be* in each board for binding one to another.

Thus you shall make for all the boards of the tabernacle. [18]And you shall make the boards for the tabernacle, twenty boards for the south side. [19]You shall make forty sockets of silver under the twenty boards: two sockets under each of the boards for its two tenons. [20]And for the second side of the tabernacle, the north side, *there shall be* twenty boards [21]and their forty sockets of silver: two sockets under each of the boards. [22]For the far side of the tabernacle, westward, you shall make six boards. [23]And you shall also make two boards for the two back corners of the tabernacle. [24]They shall be coupled together at the bottom and they shall be coupled together at the top by one ring. Thus it shall be for both of them. They shall be for the two corners. [25]So there shall be eight boards with their sockets of silver—sixteen sockets—two sockets under each of the boards.

[26]"And you shall make bars of acacia wood: five for the boards on one side of the tabernacle, [27]five bars for the boards on the other side of the tabernacle, and five bars

THE PLAN OF THE TABERNACLE

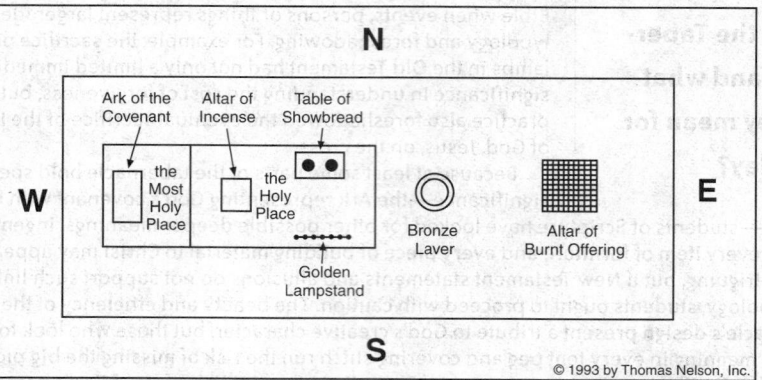

The tabernacle was to provide a place where God might dwell among His people. The term *tabernacle* sometimes refers to the tent, including the Holy Place and the Most Holy Place, which was covered with embroidered curtains. But in other places it refers to the entire complex, including the curtained court in which the tent stood.

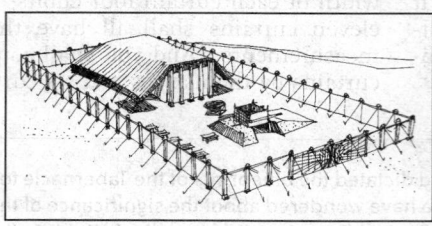

N

| Ark of the Covenant | Altar of Incense | Table of Showbread |

the Most Holy Place — the Holy Place

Golden Lampstand

Bronze Laver — Altar of Burnt Offering

W E

S

© 1993 by Thomas Nelson, Inc.

This illustration shows relative positions of the tabernacle furniture used in Israelite worship. The tabernacle is enlarged for clarity.

for the boards of the side of the tabernacle, for the far side westward. ²⁸The middle bar shall pass through the midst of the boards from end to end. ²⁹You shall overlay the boards with gold, make their rings of gold *as* holders for the bars, and overlay the bars with gold. ³⁰And you shall raise up the tabernacle according to its pattern which you were shown on the mountain.

26:15–29 The frame on which the curtains and outer coverings were draped also received precise instructions. The whole structure was designed to be portable. Throughout the wilderness wanderings, it could be quickly dismantled, readily transported, and rapidly re-erected.

³¹"You shall make a veil woven of blue, purple, and scarlet *thread,* and fine woven linen. It shall be woven with an artistic design of cherubim. ³²You shall hang it upon the four pillars of acacia *wood* overlaid with gold. Their hooks *shall be* gold, upon four sockets of silver. ³³And you shall hang the veil from the clasps. Then you shall bring the ark of the Testimony in there, behind the veil. The veil shall be a divider for you between the holy *place* and the Most Holy. ³⁴You shall put the mercy seat upon the ark of the Testimony in the Most Holy. ³⁵You shall set the table outside the veil, and the lampstand across from the table on the side of the tabernacle toward the south; and you shall put the table on the north side.

³⁶"You shall make a screen for the door of the tabernacle, *woven of* blue, purple, and scarlet *thread,* and fine woven linen, made by a weaver. ³⁷And you shall make for the screen five pillars of acacia *wood,* and overlay them with gold; their hooks *shall be* gold, and you shall cast five sockets of bronze for them.

The Altar of Burnt Offering

27 "You shall make an altar of acacia wood, five cubits long and five cubits wide—the altar shall be square—and

27:1 altar. The largest piece of equipment in the tabernacle, the altar, was placed in the courtyard. It was covered in bronze. Like the other pieces of furniture, it was built to be carried by poles.

its height *shall be* three cubits. ²You shall make its horns on its four corners; its horns shall be of one piece with it. And you shall overlay it with bronze. ³Also you shall make its pans to receive its ashes, and its shovels and its basins and its forks and its firepans; you shall make all its utensils of bronze. ⁴You shall make a grate for it, a network of bronze; and on the network you shall make four bronze rings at its four corners. ⁵You shall put it under the rim of the altar beneath, that the network may be midway up the altar. ⁶And you shall make poles for the altar, poles of acacia wood, and overlay them with bronze. ⁷The poles shall be put in the rings, and the poles shall be on the two sides of the altar to bear it. ⁸You shall make it hollow with boards; as it was shown you on the mountain, so shall they make *it.*

The Court of the Tabernacle

⁹"You shall also make the court of the tabernacle. For the south side *there shall be* hangings for the court *made of* fine woven linen, one hundred cubits long for one side. ¹⁰And its twenty pillars and their twenty sockets *shall be* bronze. The hooks of the pillars and their bands *shall be* silver. ¹¹Likewise along the length of the north side *there shall be* hangings one hundred *cubits* long, with its twenty pillars and their twenty sockets of bronze, and the hooks of the pillars and their bands of silver.

¹²"And along the width of the court on the west side *shall be* hangings of fifty cubits, with their ten pillars and their ten sockets. ¹³The width of the court on the east side *shall be* fifty cubits. ¹⁴The hangings on *one* side *of the gate shall be* fifteen cubits, *with* their three pillars and their three sockets. ¹⁵And on the other side *shall be* hangings of fifteen *cubits, with* their three pillars and their three sockets.

¹⁶"For the gate of the court *there shall be* a screen twenty cubits long, *woven of* blue, purple, and scarlet *thread,* and fine woven linen, made by a weaver. It *shall have* four pillars and four sockets. ¹⁷All the pillars around the court shall have bands of silver; their hooks *shall be* of silver and their sockets of bronze. ¹⁸The length of the court *shall be* one hundred cubits, the width fifty throughout, and the height five cubits,

made of fine woven linen, and its sockets of bronze. ¹⁹All the utensils of the tabernacle for all its service, all its pegs, and all the pegs of the court, *shall be* of bronze.

The Care of the Lampstand

²⁰"And you shall command the children of Israel that they bring you pure oil of pressed olives for the light, to cause the lamp to burn continually. ²¹In the tabernacle of meeting, outside the veil which *is* before the Testimony, Aaron and his sons shall tend it from evening until morning before the LORD. *It shall be* a statute forever to their generations on behalf of the children of Israel.

Garments for the Priesthood

28 "Now take Aaron your brother, and his sons with him, from among the children of Israel, that he may minister to Me as priest, Aaron *and* Aaron's sons: Nadab, Abihu, Eleazar, and Ithamar. ²And you

> **28:1 minister to Me as priest.** Aaron, his descendants, and the tribe of Levi were selected by God to be Israel's priests—they did not appoint themselves to the position. The role of priest was an important, exalted position which included duties that related to worship, sacrifices in the tabernacle, and the nation's covenantal relationship to God.

shall make holy garments for Aaron your brother, for glory and for beauty. ³So you shall speak to all *who are* gifted artisans, whom I have filled with the spirit of wisdom, that they may make Aaron's garments, to consecrate him, that he may minister to Me as priest. ⁴And these *are* the garments which they shall make: a breastplate, an ephod,*ᵃ* a robe, a skillfully woven tunic, a turban, and a sash. So they shall make holy garments for Aaron your brother and his sons, that he may minister to Me as priest.

> **28:3 gifted artisans.** God specially empowered certain men to work skillfully on the construction project.

The Ephod

⁵"They shall take the gold, blue, purple, and scarlet *thread*, and the fine linen, ⁶and they shall make the ephod of gold, blue,

purple, *and* scarlet *thread*, and fine woven linen, artistically worked. ⁷It shall have two shoulder straps joined at its two edges, and so it shall be joined together. ⁸And the intricately woven band of the ephod, which *is* on it, shall be of the same workmanship, *made of* gold, blue, purple, and scarlet *thread*, and fine woven linen.

⁹"Then you shall take two onyx stones and engrave on them the names of the sons of Israel: ¹⁰six of their names on one stone and six names on the other stone, in order of their birth. ¹¹With the work of an engraver in stone, *like* the engravings of a signet, you shall engrave the two stones with the names of the sons of Israel. You shall set them in settings of gold. ¹²And you shall put the two stones on the shoulders of the ephod *as* memorial stones for the sons of Israel. So Aaron shall bear their names before the LORD on his two shoulders as a memorial. ¹³You shall also make settings of gold, ¹⁴and you shall make two chains of pure gold like braided cords, and fasten the braided chains to the settings.

> **28:5–13 ephod.** Whenever Aaron entered the sanctuary, he carried on his shoulders the badge and the engraved stones that represented the twelve tribes.

The Breastplate

¹⁵"You shall make the breastplate of judgment. Artistically woven according to the workmanship of the ephod you shall make it: of gold, blue, purple, and scarlet *thread*, and fine woven linen, you shall make it. ¹⁶It shall be doubled into a square: a span *shall be* its length, and a span *shall be* its width. ¹⁷And you shall put settings of stones in it, four rows of stones: *The first* row *shall be* a sardius, a topaz, and an emerald; *this shall be* the first row; ¹⁸the second row *shall be* a turquoise, a sapphire, and a diamond; ¹⁹the third row, a jacinth, an agate, and an amethyst; ²⁰and the fourth row, a beryl, an onyx, and a jasper. They shall be set in gold settings. ²¹And the stones shall have the names of the sons of Israel, twelve according to their names, *like* the engravings of a signet, each one with its own name; they shall be according to the twelve tribes.

²²"You shall make chains for the breast-

28:4 *ᵃ*That is, an ornamented vest

plate at the end, like braided cords of pure gold. ²³And you shall make two rings of gold for the breastplate, and put the two rings on the two ends of the breastplate. ²⁴Then you shall put the two braided *chains* of gold in the two rings which are on the ends of the breastplate; ²⁵and the *other* two ends of the two braided *chains* you shall fasten to the two settings, and put them on the shoulder straps of the ephod in the front.

²⁶"You shall make two rings of gold, and put them on the two ends of the breast-plate, on the edge of it, which is on the in-ner side of the ephod. ²⁷And two *other* rings of gold you shall make, and put them on the two shoulder straps, underneath the ephod toward its front, right at the seam above the intricately woven band of the ephod. ²⁸They shall bind the breastplate by means of its rings to the rings of the ephod, using a blue cord, so that it is above the in-tricately woven band of the ephod, and so that the breastplate does not come loose from the ephod.

²⁹"So Aaron shall bear the names of the sons of Israel on the breastplate of judg-ment over his heart, when he goes into the holy *place*, as a memorial before the LORD continually. ³⁰And you shall put in the breastplate of judgment the Urim and the Thummim,ᵃ and they shall be over Aaron's heart when he goes in before the LORD. So Aaron shall bear the judgment of the chil-dren of Israel over his heart before the LORD continually.

Other Priestly Garments

³¹"You shall make the robe of the ephod all of blue. ³²There shall be an opening for his head in the middle of it; it shall have a woven binding all around its opening, like the opening in a coat of mail, so that it does not tear. ³³And upon its hem you shall make pomegranates of blue, purple, and scarlet, all around its hem, and bells of gold between them all around: ³⁴a golden bell

---

28:33 bells of gold. The sound of the tinkling bells sewn on the hem of the High Priest's robe signaled to those waiting outside the Holy Place that he was still alive and moving.

---

and a pomegranate, a golden bell and a pomegranate, upon the hem of the robe all around. ³⁵And it shall be upon Aaron when he ministers, and its sound will be heard when he goes into the holy *place* before the LORD and when he comes out, that he may not die.

³⁶"You shall also make a plate of pure gold and engrave on it, *like* the engraving of a signet:

HOLINESS TO THE LORD.

³⁷And you shall put it on a blue cord, that it may be on the turban; it shall be on the front of the turban. ³⁸So it shall be on Aaron's forehead, that Aaron may bear the iniquity of the holy things which the chil-dren of Israel hallow in all their holy gifts; and it shall always be on his forehead, that they may be accepted before the LORD.

³⁹"You shall skillfully weave the tunic of fine linen *thread*, you shall make the tur-ban of fine linen, and you shall make the sash of woven work.

⁴⁰"For Aaron's sons you shall make tu-nics, and you shall make sashes for them. And you shall make hats for them, for glory and beauty. ⁴¹So you shall put them on Aaron your brother and on his sons with him. You shall anoint them, consecrate them, and sanctify them, that they may minister to Me as priests. ⁴²And you shall make for them linen trousers to cover their nakedness; they shall reach from the waist to the thighs. ⁴³They shall be on Aaron and on his sons when they come into the taber-nacle of meeting, or when they come near the altar to minister in the holy *place*, that they do not incur iniquity and die. *It shall be* a statute forever to him and his descen-dants after him.

Aaron and His Sons Consecrated

29 "And this is what you shall do to them to hallow them for minis-tering to Me as priests: Take one young bull and two rams without blemish, ²and un-leavened bread, unleavened cakes mixed with oil, and unleavened wafers anointed with oil (you shall make them of wheat flour). ³You shall put them in one basket

---

28:30 ᵃLiterally *the Lights and the Perfections* (compare Leviticus 8:8)

and bring them in the basket, with the bull and the two rams.

4"And Aaron and his sons you shall bring to the door of the tabernacle of meeting, and you shall wash them with water. 5Then you shall take the garments, put the tunic on Aaron, and the robe of the ephod, the ephod, and the breastplate, and gird him with the intricately woven band of the ephod. 6You shall put the turban on his head, and put the holy crown on the turban. 7And you shall take the anointing oil, pour it on his head, and anoint him. 8Then you shall bring his sons and put tunics on them. 9And you shall gird them with sashes, Aaron and his sons, and put the hats on them. The priesthood shall be theirs for a perpetual statute. So you shall consecrate Aaron and his sons.

10"You shall also have the bull brought before the tabernacle of meeting, and Aaron and his sons shall put their hands on the head of the bull. 11Then you shall kill the bull before the LORD, by the door of the tabernacle of meeting. 12You shall take some of the blood of the bull and put it on the horns of the altar with your finger, and pour all the blood beside the base of the altar. 13And you shall take all the fat that covers the entrails, the fatty lobe attached to the liver, and the two kidneys and the fat that is on them, and burn them on the altar. 14But the flesh of the bull, with its skin and its offal, you shall burn with fire outside the camp. It is a sin offering.

15"You shall also take one ram, and Aaron and his sons shall put their hands on the head of the ram; 16and you shall kill the ram, and you shall take its blood and sprinkle it all around on the altar. 17Then you shall cut the ram in pieces, wash its entrails and its legs, and put them with its pieces and with its head. 18And you shall burn the whole ram on the altar. It is a burnt offering to the LORD; it is a sweet aroma, an offering made by fire to the LORD.

19"You shall also take the other ram, and Aaron and his sons shall put their hands on the head of the ram. 20Then you shall kill the ram, and take some of its blood and put it on the tip of the right ear of Aaron and on the tip of the right ear of his sons, on the thumb of their right hand and on the big toe of their right foot, and sprinkle the blood all around on the altar. 21And you shall take some of the blood that is on the altar, and some of the anointing oil, and sprinkle it on Aaron and on his garments, on his sons and on the garments of his sons with him; and he and his garments shall be hallowed, and his sons and his sons' garments with him.

> **29:19,20** Putting blood on the right ear, hand, and big toe symbolically sanctified the ear to hear the Word of God, the hand to do the work of God, and the foot to walk in the way of God.

22"Also you shall take the fat of the ram, the fat tail, the fat that covers the entrails, the fatty lobe attached to the liver, the two kidneys and the fat on them, the right thigh (for it is a ram of consecration), 23one loaf of bread, one cake made with oil, and one wafer from the basket of the unleavened bread that is before the LORD; 24and you shall put all these in the hands of Aaron and in the hands of his sons, and you shall wave them as a wave offering before the LORD. 25You shall receive them back from their hands and burn them on the altar as a burnt offering, as a sweet aroma before the LORD. It is an offering made by fire to the LORD.

26"Then you shall take the breast of the ram of Aaron's consecration and wave it as a wave offering before the LORD; and it shall be your portion. 27And from the ram of the consecration you shall consecrate the breast of the wave offering which is waved, and the thigh of the heave offering which is raised, of that which is for Aaron and of that which is for his sons. 28It shall be from the children of Israel for Aaron and his sons by a statute forever. For it is a heave offering; it shall be a heave offering from the children of Israel from the sacrifices of their peace offerings, that is, their heave offering to the LORD.

29"And the holy garments of Aaron shall be his sons' after him, to be anointed in them and to be consecrated in them. 30That son who becomes priest in his place shall put them on for seven days, when he enters the tabernacle of meeting to minister in the holy place.

31"And you shall take the ram of the con-

secration and boil its flesh in the holy place. ³²Then Aaron and his sons shall eat the flesh of the ram, and the bread that *is* in the basket, *by* the door of the tabernacle of meeting. ³³They shall eat those things with which the atonement was made, to consecrate *and* to sanctify them; but an outsider shall not eat *them*, because they *are* holy. ³⁴And if any of the flesh of the consecration offerings, or of the bread, remains until the morning, then you shall burn the remainder with fire. It shall not be eaten, because it *is* holy.

³⁵"Thus you shall do to Aaron and his sons, according to all that I have commanded you. Seven days you shall consecrate them. ³⁶And you shall offer a bull every day *as* a sin offering for atonement. You shall cleanse the altar when you make atonement for it, and you shall anoint it to sanctify it. ³⁷Seven days you shall make atonement for the altar and sanctify it. And the altar shall be most holy. Whatever touches the altar must be holy.*ᵃ*

The Daily Offerings

³⁸"Now this *is* what you shall offer on the altar: two lambs of the first year, day by day continually. ³⁹One lamb you shall offer in the morning, and the other lamb you shall offer at twilight. ⁴⁰With the one lamb shall be one-tenth *of an ephah* of flour mixed with one-fourth of a hin of pressed oil, and one-fourth of a hin of wine *as* a drink offering. ⁴¹And the other lamb you shall offer at twilight; and you shall offer with it the grain offering and the drink offering, as in the morning, for a sweet aroma, an offering made by fire to the LORD. ⁴²*This shall be* a continual burnt offering throughout your generations *at* the door of the tabernacle of meeting before the LORD, where I will meet you to speak with you. ⁴³And there I will meet with the children of Israel, and *the tabernacle* shall be sanctified by My glory. ⁴⁴So I will consecrate the tabernacle of meeting and the altar. I will also consecrate both Aaron and his sons to minister to Me as priests. ⁴⁵I will dwell among the children of Israel and will be their God. ⁴⁶And they shall know that I *am* the LORD their God, who brought them up out of the land of

Egypt, that I may dwell among them. I *am* the LORD their God.

> **29:45 I will dwell.** To the new nation of Israel, the promise of God to actually dwell with them was a very important reality. Their God was above all and dwelt in heaven, but he also dwelt in their very midst.

The Altar of Incense

30 "You shall make an altar to burn incense on; you shall make it of acacia wood. ²A cubit *shall be* its length and a cubit its width—it shall be square—and two cubits *shall be* its height. Its horns *shall be* of one piece with it. ³And you shall overlay its top, its sides all around, and its horns with pure gold; and you shall make for it a molding of gold all around. ⁴Two gold rings you shall make for it, under the molding on both its sides. You shall place *them* on its two sides, and they will be holders for the poles with which to bear it. ⁵You shall make the poles of acacia wood, and overlay them with gold. ⁶And you shall put it before the veil that *is* before the ark of the Testimony, before the mercy seat that *is* over the Testimony, where I will meet with you.

⁷"Aaron shall burn on it sweet incense every morning; when he tends the lamps, he shall burn incense on it. ⁸And when Aaron lights the lamps at twilight, he shall burn incense on it, a perpetual incense before the LORD throughout your generations. ⁹You shall not offer strange incense on it, or a burnt offering, or a grain offering; nor shall you pour a drink offering on it. ¹⁰And Aaron shall make atonement upon its horns once a year with the blood of the sin offering of atonement; once a year he shall make atonement upon it throughout your generations. It *is* most holy to the LORD."

The Ransom Money

¹¹Then the LORD spoke to Moses, saying: ¹²"When you take the census of the children of Israel for their number, then every man shall give a ransom for himself to the LORD, when you number them, that there may be no plague among them when *you* number them. ¹³This is what everyone among those who are numbered shall give: half a shekel according to the shekel of the

---

29:37 *ᵃ*Compare Numbers 4:15 and Haggai 2:11–13

sanctuary (a shekel *is* twenty gerahs). The half-shekel *shall be* an offering to the LORD. [14]Everyone included among those who are numbered, from twenty years old and above, shall give an offering to the LORD. [15]The rich shall not give more and the poor shall not give less than half a shekel, when *you* give an offering to the LORD, to make atonement for yourselves. [16]And you shall take the atonement money of the children of Israel, and shall appoint it for the service of the tabernacle of meeting, that it may be a memorial for the children of Israel before the LORD, to make atonement for yourselves."

The Bronze Laver

[17]Then the LORD spoke to Moses, saying: [18]"You shall also make a laver of bronze, with its base also of bronze, for washing. You shall put it between the tabernacle of meeting and the altar. And you shall put water in it, [19]for Aaron and his sons shall wash their hands and their feet in water from it. [20]When they go into the tabernacle of meeting, or when they come near the altar to minister, to burn an offering made by fire to the LORD, they shall wash with water, lest they die. [21]So they shall wash their hands and their feet, lest they die. And it shall be a statute forever to them—to him and his descendants throughout their generations."

> **30:18–21 laver of bronze.** The priests were required to wash their hands and feet before engaging in their duties. Their purification was a serious matter, as shown in the threat of death if they neglected this cleansing.

The Holy Anointing Oil

[22]Moreover the LORD spoke to Moses, saying: [23]"Also take for yourself quality spices—five hundred *shekels* of liquid myrrh, half as much sweet-smelling cinnamon (two hundred and fifty *shekels*), two hundred and fifty *shekels* of sweet-smelling cane, [24]five hundred *shekels* of cassia, according to the shekel of the sanctuary, and a hin of olive oil. [25]And you shall make from these a holy anointing oil, an ointment compounded according to the art of

the perfumer. It shall be a holy anointing oil. [26]With it you shall anoint the tabernacle of meeting and the ark of the Testimony; [27]the table and all its utensils, the lampstand and its utensils, and the altar of incense; [28]the altar of burnt offering with all its utensils, and the laver and its base. [29]You shall consecrate them, that they may be most holy; whatever touches them must be holy.[a] [30]And you shall anoint Aaron and his sons, and consecrate them, that *they* may minister to Me as priests.

[31]"And you shall speak to the children of Israel, saying: 'This shall be a holy anointing oil to Me throughout your generations. [32]It shall not be poured on man's flesh; nor shall you make *any other* like it, according to its composition. It *is* holy, *and* it shall be holy to you. [33]Whoever compounds *any* like it, or whoever puts *any* of it on an outsider, shall be cut off from his people.' "

The Incense

[34]And the LORD said to Moses: "Take sweet spices, stacte and onycha and galbanum, and pure frankincense with *these* sweet spices; there shall be equal amounts of each. [35]You shall make of these an incense, a compound according to the art of the perfumer, salted, pure, *and* holy. [36]And you shall beat *some* of it very fine, and put some of it before the Testimony in the tabernacle of meeting where I will meet with you. It shall be most holy to you. [37]But *as for* the incense which you shall make, you shall not make any for yourselves, according to its composition. It shall be to you holy for the LORD. [38]Whoever makes *any* like it, to smell it, he shall be cut off from his people."

Artisans for Building the Tabernacle

31 Then the LORD spoke to Moses, saying: [2]"See, I have called by name Bezalel the son of Uri, the son of Hur, of the tribe of Judah. [3]And I have filled him with the Spirit of God, in wisdom, in understanding, in knowledge, and in all *manner of* workmanship, [4]to design artistic works, to work in gold, in silver, in bronze, [5]in cutting jewels for setting, in carving wood, and to work in all *manner of* workmanship.

30:29 [a]Compare Numbers 4:15 and Haggai 2:11–13

⁶"And I, indeed I, have appointed with him Aholiab the son of Ahisamach, of the tribe of Dan; and I have put wisdom in the hearts of all the gifted artisans, that they may make all that I have commanded you: ⁷the tabernacle of meeting, the ark of the Testimony and the mercy seat that *is* on it, and all the furniture of the tabernacle— ⁸the table and its utensils, the pure *gold* lampstand with all its utensils, the altar of incense, ⁹the altar of burnt offering with all its utensils, and the laver and its base— ¹⁰the garments of ministry,ᵃ the holy garments for Aaron the priest and the garments of his sons, to minister as priests, ¹¹and the anointing oil and sweet incense for the holy *place*. According to all that I have commanded you they shall do."

The Sabbath Law

¹²And the LORD spoke to Moses, saying, ¹³"Speak also to the children of Israel, saying: 'Surely My Sabbaths you shall keep, for it *is* a sign between Me and you throughout your generations, that *you* may know that I *am* the LORD who sanctifies you. ¹⁴You shall keep the Sabbath, therefore, for *it is* holy to you. Everyone who profanes it shall surely be put to death; for whoever does *any* work on it, that person shall be cut off from among his people. ¹⁵Work shall be done for six days, but the seventh *is* the Sabbath of rest, holy to the LORD. Whoever does *any* work on the Sabbath day, he shall surely be put to death. ¹⁶Therefore the children of Israel shall keep the Sabbath, to observe the Sabbath throughout their generations *as* a perpetual covenant. ¹⁷It *is* a sign between Me and the children of Israel forever; for *in* six days the LORD made the heavens and the earth, and on the seventh day He rested and was refreshed.' "

¹⁸And when He had made an end of speaking with him on Mount Sinai, He gave Moses two tablets of the Testimony, tablets of stone, written with the finger of God.

The Gold Calf

32 Now when the people saw that Moses delayed coming down from the mountain, the people gathered together

to Aaron, and said to him, "Come, make us gods that shall go before us; for *as for* this Moses, the man who brought us up out of the land of Egypt, we do not know what has become of him."

> **32:1 make us gods.** In a time of panic, the Israelites adopted pagan idolatry and asked for gods to lead them forward. What is especially alarming about their sin was how rapidly they forgot God's real-life leading and betrayed His goodness.

²And Aaron said to them, "Break off the golden earrings which *are* in the ears of your wives, your sons, and your daughters, and bring *them* to me." ³So all the people broke off the golden earrings which *were* in their ears, and brought *them* to Aaron. ⁴And he received *the* gold from their hand, and he fashioned it with an engraving tool, and made a molded calf.

Then they said, "This *is* your god, O Israel, that brought you out of the land of Egypt!"

⁵So when Aaron saw *it*, he built an altar before it. And Aaron made a proclamation and said, "Tomorrow *is* a feast to the LORD." ⁶Then they rose early on the next day, offered burnt offerings, and brought peace offerings; and the people sat down to eat and drink, and rose up to play.

⁷And the LORD said to Moses, "Go, get down! For your people whom you brought out of the land of Egypt have corrupted *themselves*. ⁸They have turned aside quickly out of the way which I commanded them. They have made themselves a molded calf, and worshiped it and sacrificed to it, and said, 'This *is* your god, O Israel, that brought you out of the land of Egypt!' " ⁹And the LORD said to Moses, "I have seen this people, and indeed it *is* a stiff-necked people! ¹⁰Now therefore, let Me alone, that My wrath may burn hot against them and I may consume them. And I will make of you a great nation."

> **32:10 make of you a great nation.** God could have consumed all of the people and started His great nation all over again with Moses, just as He had done earlier with Abraham (Gen. 12).

31:10 ᵃOr *woven garments*

¹¹Then Moses pleaded with the LORD his God, and said: "LORD, why does Your wrath burn hot against Your people whom You have brought out of the land of Egypt with great power and with a mighty hand? ¹²Why should the Egyptians speak, and say, 'He brought them out to harm them, to kill them in the mountains, and to consume them from the face of the earth'? Turn from Your fierce wrath, and relent from this harm to Your people. ¹³Remember Abraham, Isaac, and Israel, Your servants, to whom You swore by Your own self, and said to them, 'I will multiply your descendants as the stars of heaven; and all this land that I have spoken of I give to your descendants, and they shall inherit it forever.' "ᵃ ¹⁴So the LORD relented from the harm which He said He would do to His people.

¹⁵And Moses turned and went down from the mountain, and the two tablets of the Testimony were in his hand. The tablets were written on both sides; on the one side and on the other they were written. ¹⁶Now the tablets were the work of God, and the writing was the writing of God engraved on the tablets.

¹⁷And when Joshua heard the noise of the people as they shouted, he said to Moses, "There is a noise of war in the camp."
¹⁸But he said:

> "It is not the noise of the shout of
>   victory,
> Nor the noise of the cry of defeat,
> But the sound of singing I hear."

¹⁹So it was, as soon as he came near the camp, that he saw the calf and the dancing. So Moses' anger became hot, and he cast the tablets out of his hands and broke them at the foot of the mountain. ²⁰Then he took the calf which they had made, burned it in the fire, and ground it to powder; and he scattered it on the water and made the children of Israel drink it. ²¹And Moses said to Aaron, "What did this people do to you that you have brought so great a sin upon them?"

²²So Aaron said, "Do not let the anger of my lord become hot. You know the people, that they are set on evil. ²³For they said to me, 'Make us gods that shall go before us; as for this Moses, the man who brought us out of the land of Egypt, we do not know what has become of him.' ²⁴And I said to them, 'Whoever has any gold, let them break it off.' So they gave it to me, and I cast it into the fire, and this calf came out."

²⁵Now when Moses saw that the people were unrestrained (for Aaron had not restrained them, to their shame among their enemies), ²⁶then Moses stood in the entrance of the camp, and said, "Whoever is on the LORD's side—come to me!" And all the sons of Levi gathered themselves together to him. ²⁷And he said to them, "Thus says the LORD God of Israel: 'Let every man put his sword on his side, and go in and out from entrance to entrance throughout the camp, and let every man kill his brother, every man his companion, and every man his neighbor.' " ²⁸So the sons of Levi did according to the word of Moses. And about three thousand men of the people fell that day. ²⁹Then Moses said, "Consecrate yourselves today to the LORD, that He may bestow on you a blessing this day, for every man has opposed his son and his brother."

32:26 Whoever is on the LORD's side. Only the tribe of Levi responded to the judgment call. They seemed to understand that in the battle between good and evil, neutrality could not exist. The Lord's will was to use the sword to preserve His honor and glory, and they obeyed God to put to death those who continued in idolatry and immorality.

³⁰Now it came to pass on the next day that Moses said to the people, "You have committed a great sin. So now I will go up to the LORD; perhaps I can make atonement for your sin." ³¹Then Moses returned to the LORD and said, "Oh, these people have committed a great sin, and have made for themselves a god of gold! ³²Yet now, if You will forgive their sin—but if not, I pray, blot me out of Your book which You have written."

³³And the LORD said to Moses, "Whoever has sinned against Me, I will blot him out of My book. ³⁴Now therefore, go, lead the people to the place of which I have spoken

to you. Behold, My Angel shall go before you. Nevertheless, in the day when I visit for punishment, I will visit punishment upon them for their sin."

35So the LORD plagued the people because of what they did with the calf which Aaron made.

The Command to Leave Sinai

33 Then the LORD said to Moses, "Depart *and* go up from here, you and the people whom you have brought out of the land of Egypt, to the land of which I swore to Abraham, Isaac, and Jacob, saying, 'To your descendants I will give it.' 2And I will send *My* Angel before you, and I will drive out the Canaanite and the Amorite and the Hittite and the Perizzite and the Hivite and the Jebusite. 3*Go up* to a land flowing with milk and honey; for I will not go up in your midst, lest I consume you on the way, for you *are* a stiff-necked people."

4And when the people heard this bad news, they mourned, and no one put on his ornaments. 5For the LORD had said to Moses, "Say to the children of Israel, 'You *are* a stiff-necked people. I could come up into your midst in one moment and consume you. Now therefore, take off your ornaments, that I may know what to do to you.'" 6So the children of Israel stripped themselves of their ornaments by Mount Horeb.

Moses Meets with the LORD

7Moses took his tent and pitched it outside the camp, far from the camp, and called it the tabernacle of meeting. And it came to pass *that* everyone who sought the LORD went out to the tabernacle of meeting which *was* outside the camp. 8So it was, whenever Moses went out to the tabernacle, *that* all the people rose, and each man stood *at* his tent door and watched Moses until he had gone into the tabernacle. 9And it came to pass, when Moses entered the tabernacle, that the pillar of cloud descended and stood *at* the door of the tabernacle, and *the* LORD talked with Moses. 10All the people saw the pillar of cloud standing *at* the tabernacle door, and all the people rose and worshiped, each man *in* his tent door. 11So the LORD spoke to Moses face to face, as a man speaks to his friend. And he would return to the camp, but his servant Joshua the son of Nun, a young man, did not depart from the tabernacle.

The Promise of God's Presence

12Then Moses said to the LORD, "See, You say to me, 'Bring up this people.' But You have not let me know whom You will send with me. Yet You have said, 'I know you by name, and you have also found grace in My sight.' 13Now therefore, I pray, if I have found grace in Your sight, show me now Your way, that I may know You and that I may find grace in Your sight. And consider that this nation *is* Your people."

14And He said, "My Presence will go *with you,* and I will give you rest."

15Then he said to Him, "If Your Presence does not go *with us,* do not bring us up from here. 16For how then will it be known that Your people and I have found grace in Your sight, except You go with us? So we shall be separate, Your people and I, from all the people who *are* upon the face of the earth."

17So the LORD said to Moses, "I will also do this thing that you have spoken; for you have found grace in My sight, and I know you by name."

18And he said, "Please, show me Your glory."

19Then He said, "I will make all My goodness pass before you, and I will proclaim the name of the LORD before you. I will be gracious to whom I will be gracious, and I will have compassion on whom I will have compassion." 20But He said, "You cannot see My face; for no man shall see Me, and live." 21And the LORD said, "Here is a place by Me, and you shall stand on the rock. 22So it shall be, while My glory passes by, that I

33:7 the tabernacle of meeting. Before the construction of the tabernacle, Moses' tent became the special meeting place for Moses to talk intimately, "face to face" (v. 11), with God. This undoubtedly reminded the people who were watching from afar of the removal of God's immediate presence.

33:18–23 Moses could not see God's face and live, so God protected him as He showed him His nature. Moses saw the blazing light of God's back.

will put you in the cleft of the rock, and will cover you with My hand while I pass by. ²³Then I will take away My hand, and you shall see My back; but My face shall not be seen."

Moses Makes New Tablets

34 And the LORD said to Moses, "Cut two tablets of stone like the first *ones*, and I will write on *these* tablets the words that were on the first tablets which you broke. ²So be ready in the morning, and come up in the morning to Mount Sinai, and present yourself to Me there on the top of the mountain. ³And no man shall come up with you, and let no man be seen throughout all the mountain; let neither flocks nor herds feed before that mountain."

⁴So he cut two tablets of stone like the first *ones*. Then Moses rose early in the morning and went up Mount Sinai, as the LORD had commanded him; and he took in his hand the two tablets of stone. ⁵Now the LORD descended in the cloud and stood with him there, and proclaimed the name of the LORD. ⁶And the LORD passed before him and proclaimed, "The LORD, the LORD God, merciful and gracious, longsuffering, and abounding in goodness and truth, ⁷keeping mercy for thousands, forgiving iniquity and transgression and sin, by no means clearing *the guilty*, visiting the iniquity of the fathers upon the children and the children's children to the third and the fourth generation."

⁸So Moses made haste and bowed his head toward the earth, and worshiped. ⁹Then he said, "If now I have found grace in Your sight, O Lord, let my Lord, I pray, go among us, even though we *are* a stiffnecked people; and pardon our iniquity and our sin, and take us as Your inheritance."

The Covenant Renewed

¹⁰And He said: "Behold, I make a covenant. Before all your people I will do marvels such as have not been done in all the earth, nor in any nation; and all the people among whom you *are* shall see the work of the LORD. For it *is* an awesome thing that I will do with you. ¹¹Observe what I command you this day. Behold, I am driving out

from before you the Amorite and the Canaanite and the Hittite and the Perizzite and the Hivite and the Jebusite. ¹²Take heed to yourself, lest you make a covenant with the inhabitants of the land where you are going, lest it be a snare in your midst. ¹³But you shall destroy their altars, break their *sacred* pillars, and cut down their wooden images ¹⁴(for you shall worship no other god, for the LORD, whose name *is* Jealous, *is* a jealous God), ¹⁵lest you make a covenant with the inhabitants of the land, and they play the harlot with their gods and make sacrifice to their gods, and *one of them* invites you and you eat of his sacrifice, ¹⁶and you take of his daughters for your sons, and his daughters play the harlot with their gods and make your sons play the harlot with their gods.

¹⁷"You shall make no molded gods for yourselves.

34:12–17 God warned His people about how easily they could be ensnared by idolatry if they allowed themselves to intermarry foreigners or to join in their neighbors' festivities. Their future history showed the disaster of disobeying this instruction.

¹⁸"The Feast of Unleavened Bread you shall keep. Seven days you shall eat unleavened bread, as I commanded you, in the appointed time of the month of Abib; for in the month of Abib you came out from Egypt.

¹⁹"All that open the womb *are* Mine, and every male firstborn among your livestock, *whether* ox or sheep. ²⁰But the firstborn of a donkey you shall redeem with a lamb. And if you will not redeem *him*, then you shall break his neck. All the firstborn of your sons you shall redeem.

"And none shall appear before Me empty-handed.

²¹"Six days you shall work, but on the seventh day you shall rest; in plowing time and in harvest you shall rest.

²²"And you shall observe the Feast of Weeks, of the firstfruits of wheat harvest, and the Feast of Ingathering at the year's end.

²³"Three times in the year all your men shall appear before the Lord, the LORD God of Israel. ²⁴For I will cast out the nations before you and enlarge your borders; nei-

ther will any man covet your land when you go up to appear before the LORD your God three times in the year.

²⁵"You shall not offer the blood of My sacrifice with leaven, nor shall the sacrifice of the Feast of the Passover be left until morning.

²⁶"The first of the firstfruits of your land you shall bring to the house of the LORD your God. You shall not boil a young goat in its mother's milk."

²⁷Then the LORD said to Moses, "Write these words, for according to the tenor of these words I have made a covenant with you and with Israel." ²⁸So he was there with the LORD forty days and forty nights; he neither ate bread nor drank water. And He wrote on the tablets the words of the covenant, the Ten Commandments.[a]

The Shining Face of Moses

²⁹Now it was so, when Moses came down from Mount Sinai (and the two tablets of the Testimony *were* in Moses' hand when he came down from the mountain), that Moses did not know that the skin of his face shone while he talked with Him. ³⁰So when Aaron and all the children of Israel saw Moses, behold, the skin of his face shone, and they were afraid to come near him. ³¹Then Moses called to them, and Aaron and all the rulers of the congregation returned to him; and Moses talked with them. ³²Afterward all the children of Israel came near, and he gave them as commandments all that the LORD had spoken with him on Mount Sinai. ³³And when Moses had finished speaking with them, he put a veil on his face. ³⁴But whenever Moses went in before the LORD to speak with Him, he would take the veil off until he came out; and he would come out and speak to the

children of Israel whatever he had been commanded. ³⁵And whenever the children of Israel saw the face of Moses, that the skin of Moses' face shone, then Moses would put the veil on his face again, until he went in to speak with Him.

Sabbath Regulations

35 Then Moses gathered all the congregation of the children of Israel together, and said to them, "These *are* the words which the LORD has commanded *you* to do: ²Work shall be done for six days, but the seventh day shall be a holy day for you, a Sabbath of rest to the LORD. Whoever does any work on it shall be put to death. ³You shall kindle no fire throughout your dwellings on the Sabbath day."

Offerings for the Tabernacle

⁴And Moses spoke to all the congregation of the children of Israel, saying, "This *is* the thing which the LORD commanded, saying: ⁵'Take from among you an offering to the LORD. Whoever *is* of a willing heart, let him bring it as an offering to the LORD: gold, silver, and bronze; ⁶blue, purple, and scarlet *thread*, fine linen, and goats' *hair*; ⁷ram skins dyed red, badger skins, and acacia wood; ⁸oil for the light, and spices for the anointing oil and for the sweet incense; ⁹onyx stones, and stones to be set in the ephod and in the breastplate.

Articles of the Tabernacle

¹⁰'All *who are* gifted artisans among you shall come and make all that the LORD has commanded: ¹¹the tabernacle, its tent, its covering, its clasps, its boards, its bars, its pillars, and its sockets; ¹²the ark and its poles, *with* the mercy seat, and the veil of the covering; ¹³the table and its poles, all its utensils, and the showbread; ¹⁴also the lampstand for the light, its utensils, its lamps, and the oil for the light; ¹⁵the incense altar, its poles, the anointing oil, the sweet incense, and the screen for the door at the entrance of the tabernacle; ¹⁶the altar of burnt offering with its bronze grating, its poles, all its utensils, *and* the laver and its base; ¹⁷the hangings of the court, its pillars, their sockets, and the screen for the gate of

34:29–35 The second time that Moses met with God on the mountain was different from the first. Although both were 40 days and nights in length, during the second absence Moses neither ate nor drank, and his face reflected the radiance of the Lord's presence. Whereas the first visit abruptly ended when the Lord sent Moses back to deal with sin in the camp, after the second visit, the children feared the evidence of God's presence.

34:28 [a]Literally *Ten Words*

the court; [18]the pegs of the tabernacle, the pegs of the court, and their cords; [19]the garments of ministry,[a] for ministering in the holy *place*—the holy garments for Aaron the priest and the garments of his sons, to minister as priests.' "

The Tabernacle Offerings Presented

[20]And all the congregation of the children of Israel departed from the presence of Moses. [21]Then everyone came whose heart was stirred, and everyone whose spirit was willing, *and* they brought the LORD's offering for the work of the tabernacle of meeting, for all its service, and for the holy garments. [22]They came, both men and women, as many as had a willing heart, *and* brought earrings and nose rings, rings and necklaces, all jewelry of gold, that is, every man who *made* an offering of gold to the LORD. [23]And every man, with whom was found blue, purple, and scarlet *thread*, fine linen, goats' *hair*, red skins of rams, and badger skins, brought *them*. [24]Everyone who offered an offering of silver or bronze brought the LORD's offering. And everyone with whom was found acacia wood for any work of the service, brought *it*. [25]All the women *who were* gifted artisans spun yarn with their hands, and brought what they had spun, of blue, purple, *and* scarlet, and fine linen. [26]And all the women whose hearts stirred with wisdom spun yarn of goats' *hair*. [27]The rulers brought onyx stones, and the stones to be set in the ephod and in the breastplate, [28]and spices and oil for the light, for the anointing oil, and for the sweet incense. [29]The children of Israel brought a freewill offering to the LORD, all the men and women whose hearts were willing to bring *material* for all kinds of work which the LORD, by the hand of Moses, had commanded to be done.

The Artisans Called by God

[30]And Moses said to the children of Israel, "See, the LORD has called by name Bezalel the son of Uri, the son of Hur, of the tribe of Judah; [31]and He has filled him with the Spirit of God, in wisdom and understanding, in knowledge and all manner of workmanship, [32]to design artistic works, to work in gold and silver and bronze, [33]in cutting jewels for setting, in carving wood, and to work in all manner of artistic workmanship.

[34]"And He has put in his heart the ability to teach, *in* him and Aholiab the son of Ahisamach, of the tribe of Dan. [35]He has filled them with skill to do all manner of work of the engraver and the designer and the tapestry maker, in blue, purple, and scarlet *thread*, and fine linen, and of the weaver—those who do every work and those who design artistic works.

36 "And Bezalel and Aholiab, and every gifted artisan in whom the LORD has put wisdom and understanding, to know how to do all manner of work for the service of the sanctuary, shall do according to all that the LORD has commanded."

The People Give More than Enough

[2]Then Moses called Bezalel and Aholiab, and every gifted artisan in whose heart the LORD had put wisdom, everyone whose heart was stirred, to come and do the work. [3]And they received from Moses all the offering which the children of Israel had brought for the work of the service of making the sanctuary. So they continued bringing to him freewill offerings every morning. [4]Then all the craftsmen who were doing all the work of the sanctuary came, each from the work he was doing, [5]and they spoke to Moses, saying, "The people bring much more than enough for the service of the work which the LORD commanded *us* to do."

[6]So Moses gave a commandment, and they caused it to be proclaimed throughout the camp, saying, "Let neither man nor woman do any more work for the offering of the sanctuary." And the people were restrained from bringing, [7]for the material they had was sufficient for all the work to be done—indeed too much.

36:2–7 Although the people were stubborn and disobedient at times, they rose to the occasion and voluntarily brought much more than was needed for the building of the tabernacle.

35:19 [a]Or *woven garments*

Building the Tabernacle

⁸Then all the gifted artisans among them who worked on the tabernacle made ten curtains woven of fine linen, and of blue, purple, and scarlet *thread; with* artistic designs of cherubim they made them. ⁹The length of each curtain *was* twenty-eight cubits, and the width of each curtain four cubits; the curtains *were* all the same size. ¹⁰And he coupled five curtains to one another, and *the other* five curtains he coupled to one another. ¹¹He made loops of blue *yarn* on the edge of the curtain on the selvedge of one set; likewise he did on the outer edge of *the other* curtain of the second set. ¹²Fifty loops he made on one curtain, and fifty loops he made on the edge of the curtain on the end of the second set; the loops held one *curtain* to another. ¹³And he made fifty clasps of gold, and coupled the curtains to one another with the clasps, that it might be one tabernacle.

¹⁴He made curtains of goats' *hair* for the tent over the tabernacle; he made eleven curtains. ¹⁵The length of each curtain *was* thirty cubits, and the width of each curtain four cubits; the eleven curtains *were* the same size. ¹⁶He coupled five curtains by themselves and six curtains by themselves. ¹⁷And he made fifty loops on the edge of the curtain that is outermost in one set, and fifty loops he made on the edge of the curtain of the second set. ¹⁸He also made fifty bronze clasps to couple the tent together, that it might be one. ¹⁹Then he made a covering for the tent of ram skins dyed red, and a covering of badger skins above *that.*

²⁰For the tabernacle he made boards of acacia wood, standing upright. ²¹The length of each board *was* ten cubits, and the width of each board a cubit and a half. ²²Each board had two tenons for binding one to another. Thus he made for all the boards of the tabernacle. ²³And he made boards for the tabernacle, twenty boards for the south side. ²⁴Forty sockets of silver he made to go under the twenty boards: two sockets under each of the boards for its two tenons. ²⁵And for the other side of the tabernacle, the north side, he made twenty boards ²⁶and their forty sockets of silver: two sockets under each of the boards. ²⁷For the west side of the tabernacle he made six boards. ²⁸He also made two boards for the two back corners of the tabernacle. ²⁹And they were coupled at the bottom and coupled together at the top by one ring. Thus he made both of them for the two corners. ³⁰So there were eight boards and their sockets—sixteen sockets of silver—two sockets under each of the boards.

³¹And he made bars of acacia wood: five for the boards on one side of the tabernacle, ³²five bars for the boards on the other side of the tabernacle, and five bars for the boards of the tabernacle on the far side westward. ³³And he made the middle bar to pass through the boards from one end to the other. ³⁴He overlaid the boards with gold, made their rings of gold *to be* holders for the bars, and overlaid the bars with gold.

³⁵And he made a veil of blue, purple, and scarlet *thread*, and fine woven linen; it was worked *with* an artistic design of cherubim. ³⁶He made for it four pillars of acacia *wood*, and overlaid them with gold, with their hooks of gold; and he cast four sockets of silver for them. ³⁷He also made a screen for the tabernacle door, of blue, purple, and scarlet *thread*, and fine woven linen, made by a weaver, ³⁸and its five pillars with their hooks. And he overlaid their capitals and their rings with gold, but their five sockets *were* bronze.

Making the Ark of the Testimony

37 Then Bezalel made the ark of acacia wood; two and a half cubits *was* its length, a cubit and a half its width, and a cubit and a half its height. ²He overlaid it with pure gold inside and outside, and made a molding of gold all around it. ³And he cast for it four rings of gold *to be set* in its four corners: two rings on one side, and two rings on the other side of it. ⁴He made poles of acacia wood, and overlaid them with gold. ⁵And he put the poles into the rings at the sides of the ark, to bear the ark. ⁶He also made the mercy seat of pure gold; two and a half cubits *was* its length and a cubit and a half its width. ⁷He made two cherubim of beaten gold; he made them of one piece at the two ends of the mercy seat: ⁸one cherub at one end on this side, and the other cherub at the *other* end on that side. He made the cherubim at the two ends of

one piece with the mercy seat. ⁹The cherubim spread out *their* wings above, *and* covered the mercy seat with their wings. They faced one another; the faces of the cherubim were toward the mercy seat.

Making the Table for the Showbread

¹⁰He made the table of acacia wood; two cubits *was* its length, a cubit its width, and a cubit and a half its height. ¹¹And he overlaid it with pure gold, and made a molding of gold all around it. ¹²Also he made a frame of a handbreadth all around it, and made a molding of gold for the frame all around it. ¹³And he cast for it four rings of gold, and put the rings on the four corners that *were* at its four legs. ¹⁴The rings were close to the frame, as holders for the poles to bear the table. ¹⁵And he made the poles of acacia wood to bear the table, and overlaid them with gold. ¹⁶He made of pure gold the utensils which were on the table: its dishes, its cups, its bowls, and its pitchers for pouring.

Making the Gold Lampstand

¹⁷He also made the lampstand of pure gold; of hammered work he made the lampstand. Its shaft, its branches, its bowls, its *ornamental* knobs, and its flowers were of the same piece. ¹⁸And six branches came out of its sides: three branches of the lampstand out of one side, and three branches of the lampstand out of the other side. ¹⁹There were three bowls made like almond *blossoms* on one branch, with an *ornamental* knob and a flower, and three bowls made like almond *blossoms* on the other branch, with an *ornamental* knob and a flower— and so for the six branches coming out of the lampstand. ²⁰And on the lampstand itself *were* four bowls made like almond *blossoms, each with* its *ornamental* knob and flower. ²¹*There was* a knob under the *first* two branches of the same, a knob under the *second* two branches of the same, and a knob under the *third* two branches of the same, according to the six branches extending from it. ²²Their knobs and their branches were of one piece; all of it *was* one hammered piece of pure gold. ²³And he made its seven lamps, its wick-trimmers, and its trays of pure gold. ²⁴Of a talent of pure gold he made it, with all its utensils.

Making the Altar of Incense

²⁵He made the incense altar of acacia wood. Its length *was* a cubit and its width a cubit—*it was* square—and two cubits *was* its height. Its horns were *of one piece* with it. ²⁶And he overlaid it with pure gold: its top, its sides all around, and its horns. He also made for it a molding of gold all around it. ²⁷He made two rings of gold for it under its molding, by its two corners on both sides, as holders for the poles with which to bear it. ²⁸And he made the poles of acacia wood, and overlaid them with gold.

Making the Anointing Oil and the Incense

²⁹He also made the holy anointing oil and the pure incense of sweet spices, according to the work of the perfumer.

36:8–39:43 The whole report of the work done highlights how carefully the workers carried out the instructions they received.

Making the Altar of Burnt Offering

38He made the altar of burnt offering of acacia wood; five cubits *was* its length and five cubits its width—*it was* square—and its height *was* three cubits. ²He made its horns on its four corners; the horns were *of one piece* with it. And he overlaid it with bronze. ³He made all the utensils for the altar: the pans, the shovels, the basins, the forks, and the firepans; all its utensils he made of bronze. ⁴And he made a grate of bronze network for the altar, under its rim, midway from the bottom. ⁵He cast four rings for the four corners of the bronze grating, *as* holders for the poles. ⁶And he made the poles of acacia wood, and overlaid them with bronze. ⁷Then he put the poles into the rings on the sides of the altar, with which to bear it. He made the altar hollow with boards.

Making the Bronze Laver

⁸He made the laver of bronze and its base of bronze, from the bronze mirrors of the serving women who assembled at the door of the tabernacle of meeting.

Making the Court of the Tabernacle

⁹Then he made the court on the south side; the hangings of the court *were of* fine

woven linen, one hundred cubits long. [10]There *were* twenty pillars for them, with twenty bronze sockets. The hooks of the pillars and their bands *were* silver. [11]On the north side *the hangings were* one hundred cubits *long*, with twenty pillars and their twenty bronze sockets. The hooks of the pillars and their bands *were* silver. [12]And on the west side *there were* hangings of fifty cubits, with ten pillars and their ten sockets. The hooks of the pillars and their bands *were* silver. [13]For the east side *the hangings were* fifty cubits. [14]The hangings of one side *of the gate were* fifteen cubits *long, with* their three pillars and their three sockets, [15]and the same for the other side of the court gate; on this side and that *were* hangings of fifteen cubits, *with* their three pillars and their three sockets. [16]All the hangings of the court all around *were of* fine woven linen. [17]The sockets for the pillars *were* bronze, the hooks of the pillars and their bands *were* silver, and the overlay of their capitals *was* silver; and all the pillars of the court had bands of silver. [18]The screen for the gate of the court *was* woven of blue, purple, and scarlet *thread*, and of fine woven linen. The length *was* twenty cubits, and the height along its width *was* five cubits, corresponding to the hangings of the court. [19]And *there were* four pillars *with* their four sockets of bronze; their hooks *were* silver, and the overlay of their capitals and their bands *was* silver. [20]All the pegs of the tabernacle, and of the court all around, *were* bronze.

Materials of the Tabernacle

[21]This is the inventory of the tabernacle, the tabernacle of the Testimony, which was counted according to the commandment of Moses, for the service of the Levites, by the hand of Ithamar, son of Aaron the priest. [22]Bezalel the son of Uri, the son of Hur, of the tribe of Judah, made all that the LORD had commanded Moses. [23]And with him *was* Aholiab the son of Ahisamach, of the tribe of Dan, an engraver and designer, a weaver of blue, purple, and scarlet *thread*, and of fine linen. [24]All the gold that was used in all the work of the holy *place*, that is, the gold of

the offering, was twenty-nine talents and seven hundred and thirty shekels, according to the shekel of the sanctuary. [25]And the silver from those who were numbered of the congregation *was* one hundred talents and one thousand seven hundred and seventy-five shekels, according to the shekel of the sanctuary: [26]a bekah for each man (*that is*, half a shekel, according to the shekel of the sanctuary), for everyone included in the numbering from twenty years old and above, for six hundred and three thousand, five hundred and fifty *men*. [27]And from the hundred talents of silver were cast the sockets of the sanctuary and the bases of the veil: one hundred sockets from the hundred talents, one talent for each socket. [28]Then from the one thousand seven hundred and seventy-five *shekels* he made hooks for the pillars, overlaid their capitals, and made bands for them.

[29]The offering of bronze *was* seventy talents and two thousand four hundred shekels. [30]And with it he made the sockets for the door of the tabernacle of meeting, the bronze altar, the bronze grating for it, and all the utensils for the altar, [31]the sockets for the court all around, the bases for the court gate, all the pegs for the tabernacle, and all the pegs for the court all around.

Making the Garments of the Priesthood

39 Of the blue, purple, and scarlet *thread* they made garments of ministry,[a] for ministering in the holy *place*, and made the holy garments for Aaron, as the LORD had commanded Moses.

> **39:1 as the LORD had commanded Moses.** This refrain is repeated many times in this section to tell the listener in Israel and the reader today just how carefully God's detailed instructions to Moses were followed. The Israelite artisans took every detail seriously.

Making the Ephod

[2]He made the ephod of gold, blue, purple, and scarlet *thread*, and of fine woven linen. [3]And they beat the gold into thin sheets and cut *it into* threads, to work *it in with* the blue, purple, and scarlet *thread*, and the fine linen, *into* artistic designs. [4]They made shoulder straps for it to couple *it*

39:1 [a]Or *woven garments*

together; it was coupled together at its two edges. ⁵And the intricately woven band of his ephod that *was* on it *was* of the same workmanship, *woven of* gold, blue, purple, and scarlet *thread*, and of fine woven linen, as the LORD had commanded Moses.

⁶And they set onyx stones, enclosed in settings of gold; they were engraved, as signets are engraved, with the names of the sons of Israel. ⁷He put them on the shoulders of the ephod *as* memorial stones for the sons of Israel, as the LORD had commanded Moses.

Making the Breastplate

⁸And he made the breastplate, artistically woven like the workmanship of the ephod, of gold, blue, purple, and scarlet *thread*, and of fine woven linen. ⁹They made the breastplate square by doubling it; a span *was* its length and a span its width when doubled. ¹⁰And they set in it four rows of stones: a row with a sardius, a topaz, and an emerald *was* the first row; ¹¹the second row, a turquoise, a sapphire, and a diamond; ¹²the third row, a jacinth, an agate, and an amethyst; ¹³the fourth row, a beryl, an onyx, and a jasper. *They were* enclosed in settings of gold in their mountings. ¹⁴*There were* twelve stones according to the names of the sons of Israel: according to their names, *engraved like* a signet, each one with its own name according to the twelve tribes. ¹⁵And they made chains for the breastplate at the ends, like braided cords of pure gold. ¹⁶They also made two settings of gold and two gold rings, and put the two rings on the two ends of the breastplate. ¹⁷And they put the two braided *chains* of gold in the two rings on the ends of the breastplate. ¹⁸The two ends of the two braided *chains* they fastened in the two settings, and put them on the shoulder straps of the ephod in the front. ¹⁹And they made two rings of gold and put *them* on the two ends of the breastplate, on the edge of it, which *was* on the inward side of the ephod. ²⁰They made two *other* gold rings and put them on the two shoulder straps, underneath the ephod toward its front, right at the seam above the intricately woven band of the ephod. ²¹And they bound the breastplate by means of its rings to the rings of the ephod with a blue cord, so that

it would be above the intricately woven band of the ephod, and that the breastplate would not come loose from the ephod, as the LORD had commanded Moses.

Making the Other Priestly Garments

²²He made the robe of the ephod of woven work, all of blue. ²³And *there was* an opening in the middle of the robe, like the opening in a coat of mail, *with* a woven binding all around the opening, so that it would not tear. ²⁴They made on the hem of the robe pomegranates of blue, purple, and scarlet, and of fine woven *linen*. ²⁵And they made bells of pure gold, and put the bells between the pomegranates on the hem of the robe all around between the pomegranates: ²⁶a bell and a pomegranate, a bell and a pomegranate, all around the hem of the robe to minister in, as the LORD had commanded Moses.

²⁷They made tunics, artistically woven of fine linen, for Aaron and his sons, ²⁸a turban of fine linen, exquisite hats of fine linen, short trousers of fine woven linen, ²⁹and a sash of fine woven linen with blue, purple, and scarlet *thread*, made by a weaver, as the LORD had commanded Moses.

³⁰Then they made the plate of the holy crown of pure gold, and wrote on it an inscription *like* the engraving of a signet:

HOLINESS TO THE LORD.

³¹And they tied to it a blue cord, to fasten *it* above on the turban, as the LORD had commanded Moses.

The Work Completed

³²Thus all the work of the tabernacle of the tent of meeting was finished. And the children of Israel did according to all that the LORD had commanded Moses; so they did. ³³And they brought the tabernacle to Moses, the tent and all its furnishings: its clasps, its boards, its bars, its pillars, and

39:32 Thus all the work...was finished. Finally the moment arrived when all the individual tasks were completed and the overall product was ready for formal presentation to Israel's leader. **And the children of Israel.** No individual artisan is singled out; rather, the whole nation was recognized for obeying the Lord's instructions.

its sockets; [34]the covering of ram skins dyed red, the covering of badger skins, and the veil of the covering; [35]the ark of the Testimony with its poles, and the mercy seat; [36]the table, all its utensils, and the showbread; [37]the pure *gold* lampstand with its lamps (the lamps set in order), all its utensils, and the oil for light; [38]the gold altar, the anointing oil, and the sweet incense; the screen for the tabernacle door; [39]the bronze altar, its grate of bronze, its poles, and all its utensils; the laver with its base; [40]the hangings of the court, its pillars and its sockets, the screen for the court gate, its cords, and its pegs; all the utensils for the service of the tabernacle, for the tent of meeting; [41]and the garments of ministry,[a] to minister in the holy *place:* the holy garments for Aaron the priest, and his sons' garments, to minister as priests.

[42]According to all that the LORD had commanded Moses, so the children of Israel did all the work. [43]Then Moses looked over all the work, and indeed they had done it; as the LORD had commanded, just so they had done it. And Moses blessed them.

39:43 Then Moses looked over all the work. Fittingly, the one who had been with God on the mount and who had passed on the Lord's instructions to the people was the one who personally inspected the work and confirmed its completion. **And Moses blessed them.** Moses gave his final approval on the product of their earnest, diligent efforts and expressed his desire that good would come to them from their God.

The Tabernacle Erected and Arranged

40 Then the LORD spoke to Moses, saying: [2]"On the first day of the first month you shall set up the tabernacle of the tent of meeting. [3]You shall put in it the ark of the Testimony, and partition off the ark with the veil. [4]You shall bring in the table and arrange the things that are to be set in order on it; and you shall bring in the lampstand and light its lamps. [5]You shall also set the altar of gold for the incense before the ark of the Testimony, and put up the screen for the door of the tabernacle. [6]Then you shall set the altar of the burnt offering before the door of the tabernacle of the tent of meeting. [7]And you shall set the laver between the tabernacle of meeting and the altar, and put water in it. [8]You shall set up the court all around, and hang up the screen at the court gate.

[9]"And you shall take the anointing oil, and anoint the tabernacle and all that *is* in it; and you shall hallow it and all its utensils, and it shall be holy. [10]You shall anoint the altar of the burnt offering and all its utensils, and consecrate the altar. The altar shall be most holy. [11]And you shall anoint the laver and its base, and consecrate it.

[12]"Then you shall bring Aaron and his sons to the door of the tabernacle of meeting and wash them with water. [13]You shall put the holy garments on Aaron, and anoint him and consecrate him, that he may minister to Me as priest. [14]And you shall bring his sons and clothe them with tunics. [15]You shall anoint them, as you anointed their father, that they may minister to Me as priests; for their anointing shall surely be an everlasting priesthood throughout their generations."

[16]Thus Moses did; according to all that the LORD had commanded him, so he did.

[17]And it came to pass in the first month of the second year, on the first *day* of the month, *that* the tabernacle was raised up. [18]So Moses raised up the tabernacle, fastened its sockets, set up its boards, put in its bars, and raised up its pillars. [19]And he spread out the tent over the tabernacle and put the covering of the tent on top of it, as the LORD had commanded Moses. [20]He took the Testimony and put *it* into the ark, inserted the poles through the rings of the ark, and put the mercy seat on top of the ark. [21]And he brought the ark into the tabernacle, hung up the veil of the covering, and partitioned off the ark of the Testimony, as the LORD had commanded Moses.

[22]He put the table in the tabernacle of meeting, on the north side of the tabernacle, outside the veil; [23]and he set the bread in order upon it before the LORD, as the LORD had commanded Moses. [24]He put the lampstand in the tabernacle of meeting, across from the table, on the south side of the tabernacle; [25]and he lit the lamps before the LORD, as the LORD had commanded

---

39:41 [a]Or *woven garments*

Moses. ²⁶He put the gold altar in the tabernacle of meeting in front of the veil; ²⁷and he burned sweet incense on it, as the LORD had commanded Moses. ²⁸He hung up the screen *at* the door of the tabernacle. ²⁹And he put the altar of burnt offering *before* the door of the tabernacle of the tent of meeting, and offered upon it the burnt offering and the grain offering, as the LORD had commanded Moses. ³⁰He set the laver between the tabernacle of meeting and the altar, and put water there for washing; ³¹and Moses, Aaron, and his sons would wash their hands and their feet *with water* from it. ³²Whenever they went into the tabernacle of meeting, and when they came near the altar, they washed, as the LORD had commanded Moses. ³³And he raised up the court all around the tabernacle and the altar, and hung up the screen of the court gate. So Moses finished the work.

The Cloud and the Glory

³⁴Then the cloud covered the tabernacle of meeting, and the glory of the LORD filled the tabernacle. ³⁵And Moses was not able to enter the tabernacle of meeting, because the cloud rested above it, and the glory of the LORD filled the tabernacle. ³⁶Whenever the cloud was taken up from above the tabernacle, the children of Israel would go onward in all their journeys. ³⁷But if the cloud was not taken up, then they did not journey till the day that it was taken up. ³⁸For the cloud of the LORD *was* above the tabernacle by day, and fire was over it by night, in the sight of all the house of Israel, throughout all their journeys.

40:34 the cloud covered...the glory of the LORD filled. When God moved into the tabernacle, He confirmed for Moses and the people that all the work had been obediently and satisfactorily done in His eyes.

LEVITICUS

Ancient scholars translating this book from Hebrew to Greek gave it a descriptive title—"*Leuitikon*"—which means "matters of the Levites." Later translators borrowed the word directly.

AUTHOR AND DATE

Leviticus was written by Moses, approximately 1445 to 1405 B.C.

The concluding verse of this book serves as a signature: "These are the commandments which the LORD commanded Moses for the children of Israel on Mount Sinai" (27:34). From the first verse, the laws and instructions in this book were given by God to Moses for God's people.

The date of Leviticus depends on the events surrounding God's revelation of these instructions. Since the Exodus occurred in 1445 B.C., and the tabernacle was constructed a year later, the timing of Leviticus fits a date of 1444–43 B.C.

BACKGROUND AND SETTING

The Exodus radically changed the way God related to Israel. Until that point in the history of God's people, the following had never occurred: (1) the glory of God had not been visible among the Israelites; (2) a central place of worship, like the tabernacle, had never existed; (3) the yearly calendar had no feasts or sacrifices which required participation; (4) no formal structure of priests or other religious workers had been appointed.

During Israel's departure from Egypt, however, God made His presence visible to them with a pillar of cloud and fire. At Mt. Sinai, Aaron and his family were appointed as priests. The plans for the tabernacle were also revealed and carried out. These developments set the stage for God's instructions about lifestyle, worship and the yearly calendar recorded in Leviticus.

Leviticus records no geographical movement. The people of Israel remained at Mt. Sinai, the place where God came down to give His law (Leviticus 25:1).

Two ideas make up the core of Leviticus: (1) God's holy character; and (2) God's intention to build a holy nation. Humankind's sinfulness, the role of sacrifice, God's presence in the tabernacle, along with God's holiness receive repeated attention in the book.

With a clear, authoritative tone, Leviticus sets forth God's insistence on personal holiness. The following verses offer specific examples: 11:44,45; 19:2; 20:7,26. The underlying motive for the pursuit of personal holiness comes from the holiness of God. God backs up his commands and instructions by repeatedly stating, "I am the LORD" and "I am holy."

HUMANKIND'S SINFULNESS, THE ROLE OF SACRIFICE, GOD'S PRESENCE IN THE TABERNACLE, ALONG WITH GOD'S HOLINESS RECEIVE REPEATED ATTENTION IN THE BOOK.

Leviticus also fills in the picture of the Mosaic Covenant. Details about the consequences of obedience as well as disobedience receive special attention. Later events in Israel's history serve to highlight just how serious God is about His promises and warnings. God's covenant with Israel continues to be part of God's plan for world history.

Leviticus includes specific instructions about five sacrifices and offerings. The external and exact details of these actions symbolizes what God expects to occur in His people. As accusations like Amos 5:21–27 make clear, when worshipers' hearts are not penitent and thankful, God is not pleased with the ritual.

OUTLINE

The Burnt Offering

1 Now the LORD called to Moses, and spoke to him from the tabernacle of meeting, saying, ²"Speak to the children of Israel, and say to them: 'When any one of you brings an offering to the LORD, you shall bring your offering of the livestock—of the herd and of the flock.

³'If his offering *is* a burnt sacrifice of the herd, let him offer a male without blemish; he shall offer it of his own free will at the door of the tabernacle of meeting before the LORD. ⁴Then he shall put his hand on the head of the burnt offering, and it will be accepted on his behalf to make atonement for him. ⁵He shall kill the bull before the LORD; and the priests, Aaron's sons, shall bring the blood and sprinkle the blood all around on the altar that *is by* the door of the tabernacle of meeting. ⁶And he shall skin the burnt offering and cut it into its pieces. ⁷The sons of Aaron the priest shall put fire on the altar, and lay the wood in order on the fire. ⁸Then the priests, Aaron's sons, shall lay the parts, the head, and the fat in order on the wood that *is* on the fire upon the altar; ⁹but he shall wash its entrails and its legs with water. And the priest shall burn all on the altar as a burnt sacrifice, an offering made by fire, a sweet aroma to the LORD.

> **1:4 make atonement.** The word means "cover." The psalmist defines it by saying, "Blessed is he whose transgression is forgiven, whose sin is covered" (Ps. 32:1). The atonement of the OT covered sin temporarily but did not eliminate it entirely. The one-time sacrifice of Jesus Christ fully atoned for sin, thus satisfying God's wrath forever and insuring eternal salvation for all those who put their saving faith in God.

¹⁰'If his offering *is* of the flocks—of the sheep or of the goats—as a burnt sacrifice, he shall bring a male without blemish. ¹¹He shall kill it on the north side of the altar before the LORD; and the priests, Aaron's sons, shall sprinkle its blood all around on the altar. ¹²And he shall cut it into its pieces, with its head and its fat; and the priest shall lay them in order on the wood that *is* on the fire upon the altar; ¹³but he shall wash the entrails and the legs with water. Then the priest shall bring *it* all and burn *it* on the altar; it *is* a burnt sacrifice,

an offering made by fire, a sweet aroma to the LORD.

¹⁴And if the burnt sacrifice of his offering to the LORD *is* of birds, then he shall bring his offering of turtledoves or young pigeons. ¹⁵The priest shall bring it to the altar, wring off its head, and burn *it* on the altar; its blood shall be drained out at the side of the altar. ¹⁶And he shall remove its crop with its feathers and cast it beside the altar on the east side, into the place for ashes. ¹⁷Then he shall split it at its wings, *but* shall not divide *it* completely; and the priest shall burn it on the altar, on the wood that *is* on the fire. It *is* a burnt sacrifice, an offering made by fire, a sweet aroma to the LORD.

> **1:14–17 of birds.** This section describes the sacrifice of birds. God does not ask the poor to bring the same burnt offering as those who are wealthy, because the relative cost to the giver is an important factor. Jesus' parents brought this sacrifice after Christ's birth (see Luke 2:22–24).

The Grain Offering

2 'When anyone offers a grain offering to the LORD, his offering shall be *of* fine flour. And he shall pour oil on it, and put frankincense on it. ²He shall bring it to Aaron's sons, the priests, one of whom shall take from it his handful of fine flour and oil with all the frankincense. And the priest shall burn *it* as a memorial on the altar, an offering made by fire, a sweet aroma to the LORD. ³The rest of the grain offering *shall be* Aaron's and his sons'. *It is* most holy of the offerings to the LORD made by fire.

⁴'And if you bring as an offering a grain offering baked in the oven, *it shall be* unleavened cakes of fine flour mixed with oil, or unleavened wafers anointed with oil. ⁵But if your offering *is* a grain offering *baked* in a pan, *it shall be of* fine flour, unleavened, mixed with oil. ⁶You shall break it in pieces and pour oil on it; it *is* a grain offering.

⁷'If your offering *is* a grain offering *baked* in a covered pan, it shall be made *of* fine flour with oil. ⁸You shall bring the grain offering that is made of these things to the LORD. And when it is presented to the priest, he shall bring it to the altar. ⁹Then the priest shall take from the grain offering a memorial portion, and burn *it* on the al-

tar. *It is* an offering made by fire, a sweet aroma to the LORD. [10]And what is left of the grain offering *shall be* Aaron's and his sons'. *It is* most holy of the offerings to the LORD made by fire.

[11]'No grain offering which you bring to the LORD shall be made with leaven, for you shall burn no leaven nor any honey in any offering to the LORD made by fire. [12]As for the offering of the firstfruits, you shall offer them to the LORD, but they shall not be burned on the altar for a sweet aroma. [13]And every offering of your grain offering you shall season with salt; you shall not allow the salt of the covenant of your God to be lacking from your grain offering. With all your offerings you shall offer salt.

2:13 the salt of the covenant. This was included in all of the offerings in 2:4–10,14–16 since salt symbolized permanence or loyalty to the covenant.

[14]'If you offer a grain offering of your firstfruits to the LORD, you shall offer for the grain offering of your firstfruits green heads of grain roasted on the fire, grain beaten from full heads. [15]And you shall put oil on it, and lay frankincense on it. It *is* a grain offering. [16]Then the priest shall burn the memorial portion: *part* of its beaten grain and *part* of its oil, with all the frankincense, as an offering made by fire to the LORD.

The Peace Offering

3 'When his offering *is* a sacrifice of a peace offering, if he offers *it* of the herd, whether male or female, he shall offer it without blemish before the LORD. [2]And he shall lay his hand on the head of his offering, and kill it *at* the door of the tabernacle of meeting; and Aaron's sons, the priests, shall sprinkle the blood all around on the altar. [3]Then he shall offer from the sacrifice of the peace offering an offering made by fire to the LORD. The fat that covers the entrails and all the fat that *is* on the entrails, [4]the two kidneys and the fat that *is* on them by the flanks, and the fatty lobe *attached* to the liver above the kidneys, he shall remove; [5]and Aaron's sons shall burn it on the altar upon the burnt sacrifice, which *is* on the wood that *is* on the fire, *as* an offering made by fire, a sweet aroma to the LORD.

[6]'If his offering as a sacrifice of a peace offering to the LORD *is* of the flock, *whether* male or female, he shall offer it without blemish. [7]If he offers a lamb as his offering, then he shall offer it before the LORD. [8]And he shall lay his hand on the head of his offering, and kill it before the tabernacle of meeting; and Aaron's sons shall sprinkle its blood all around on the altar.

[9]'Then he shall offer from the sacrifice of the peace offering, as an offering made by fire to the LORD, its fat *and* the whole fat tail which he shall remove close to the backbone. And the fat that covers the entrails and all the fat that *is* on the entrails, [10]the two kidneys and the fat that *is* on them by the flanks, and the fatty lobe *attached* to the liver above the kidneys, he shall remove; [11]and the priest shall burn

CHRIST IN THE LEVITICAL OFFERINGS

Offering	Christ's Provision	Christ's Character
1. Burnt Offering (Leviticus 1:3–17; 6:8–13)	atonement	Christ's sinless nature
2. Grain Offering (Leviticus 2:1–16; 6:14–23)	dedication/ consecration	Christ was wholly devoted to the Father's purposes
3. Peace Offering (Leviticus 3:1–17; 7:11–36)	reconciliation/ fellowship	Christ was at peace with God
4. Sin Offering (Leviticus 4:1–5:13; 6:24–30)	propitiation	Christ's substitutionary death
5. Trespass Offering (Leviticus 5:14–6:7; 7:1–10)	repentance	Christ paid it all for redemption

them on the altar *as* food, an offering made by fire to the LORD.

¹²And if his offering *is* a goat, then he shall offer it before the LORD. ¹³He shall lay his hand on its head and kill it before the tabernacle of meeting; and the sons of Aaron shall sprinkle its blood all around on the altar. ¹⁴Then he shall offer from it his offering, as an offering made by fire to the LORD. The fat that covers the entrails and all the fat that *is* on the entrails, ¹⁵the two kidneys and the fat that *is* on them by the flanks, and the fatty lobe *attached* to the liver above the kidneys, he shall remove; ¹⁶and the priest shall burn them on the altar *as* food, an offering made by fire for a sweet aroma; all the fat *is* the LORD's.

¹⁷'*This shall be* a perpetual statute throughout your generations in all your dwellings: you shall eat neither fat nor blood.' "

The Sin Offering

4 Now the LORD spoke to Moses, saying, ²"Speak to the children of Israel, saying:

'If a person sins unintentionally against any of the commandments of the LORD *in anything* which ought not to be done, and does any of them, ³if the anointed priest sins, bringing guilt on the people, then let him offer to the LORD for his sin which he has sinned a young bull without blemish as a sin offering. ⁴He shall bring the bull to the door of the tabernacle of meeting before the LORD, lay his hand on the bull's head, and kill the bull before the LORD. ⁵Then the anointed priest shall take some of the bull's blood and bring it to the tabernacle of meeting. ⁶The priest shall dip his finger in the blood and sprinkle some of the blood seven

times before the LORD, in front of the veil of the sanctuary. ⁷And the priest shall put some of the blood on the horns of the altar of sweet incense before the LORD, which is in the tabernacle of meeting; and he shall pour the remaining blood of the bull at the base of the altar of the burnt offering, which is at the door of the tabernacle of meeting. ⁸He shall take from it all the fat of the bull as the sin offering. The fat that covers the entrails and all the fat which *is* on the entrails, ⁹the two kidneys and the fat that *is* on them by the flanks, and the fatty lobe *attached* to the liver above the kidneys, he shall remove, ¹⁰as it was taken from the bull of the sacrifice of the peace offering; and the priest shall burn them on the altar of the burnt offering. ¹¹But the bull's hide and all its flesh, with its head and legs, its entrails and offal— ¹²the whole bull he shall carry outside the camp to a clean place, where the ashes are poured out, and burn it on wood with fire; where the ashes are poured out it shall be burned.

¹³'Now if the whole congregation of Israel sins unintentionally, and the thing is hidden from the eyes of the assembly, and they have done *something against* any of the commandments of the LORD *in anything* which should not be done, and are guilty; ¹⁴when the sin which they have committed becomes known, then the assembly shall offer a young bull for the sin, and bring it before the tabernacle of meeting. ¹⁵And the elders of the congregation shall lay their hands on the head of the bull before the LORD. Then the bull shall be killed before the LORD. ¹⁶The anointed priest shall bring some of the bull's blood to the tabernacle of meeting. ¹⁷Then the priest shall dip his finger in the blood and sprinkle *it* seven times before the LORD, in front of the veil. ¹⁸And he shall put *some* of the blood on the horns of the altar which *is* before the LORD, which *is* in the tabernacle of meeting; and he shall pour the remaining blood at the base of the altar of burnt offering, which is at the door of the tabernacle of meeting. ¹⁹He shall take all the fat from it and burn *it* on the altar.

²⁰And he shall do with the bull as he did with the bull as a sin offering; thus he shall do with it. So the priest shall make atonement for them, and it shall be forgiven them. ²¹Then he shall carry the bull outside the camp, and burn it as he burned the first bull. It *is* a sin offering for the assembly.

²²'When a ruler has sinned, and done *something* unintentionally *against* any of the commandments of the LORD his God *in anything* which should not be done, and is guilty, ²³or if his sin which he has committed comes to his knowledge, he shall bring as his offering a kid of the goats, a male without blemish. ²⁴And he shall lay his hand on the head of the goat, and kill it at the place where they kill the burnt offering before the LORD. It *is* a sin offering. ²⁵The priest shall take some of the blood of the sin offering with his finger, put *it* on the horns of the altar of burnt offering, and pour its blood at the base of the altar of burnt offering. ²⁶And he shall burn all its fat on the altar, like the fat of the sacrifice of the peace offering. So the priest shall make atonement for him concerning his sin, and it shall be forgiven him.

²⁷'If anyone of the common people sins unintentionally by doing *something against* any of the commandments of the LORD *in anything* which ought not to be done, and is guilty, ²⁸or if his sin which he has committed comes to his knowledge, then he shall bring as his offering a kid of the goats, a female without blemish, for his sin which

he has committed. ²⁹And he shall lay his hand on the head of the sin offering, and kill the sin offering at the place of the burnt offering. ³⁰Then the priest shall take *some* of its blood with his finger, put *it* on the horns of the altar of burnt offering, and pour all *the remaining* blood at the base of the altar. ³¹He shall remove all its fat, as fat is removed from the sacrifice of the peace offering; and the priest shall burn it on the altar for a sweet aroma to the LORD. So the priest shall make atonement for him, and it shall be forgiven him.

³²'If he brings a lamb as his sin offering, he shall bring a female without blemish. ³³Then he shall lay his hand on the head of the sin offering, and kill it as a sin offering at the place where they kill the burnt offering. ³⁴The priest shall take *some* of the blood of the sin offering with his finger, put *it* on the horns of the altar of burnt offering, and pour all *the remaining* blood at the base of the altar. ³⁵He shall remove all its fat, as the fat of the lamb is removed from the sacrifice of the peace offering. Then the priest shall burn it on the altar, according to the offerings made by fire to the LORD. So the priest shall make atonement for his sin that he has committed, and it shall be forgiven him.

The Trespass Offering

5 'If a person sins in hearing the utterance of an oath, and *is* a witness, whether he has seen or known *of the matter*—if he does not tell *it,* he bears guilt.

OLD TESTAMENT SACRIFICES COMPARED TO CHRIST'S SACRIFICE

Leviticus		Hebrews
1. Old Covenant (temporary)	Hebrews 7:22; 8:6,13; 10:20	1. New Covenant (permanent)
2. Obsolete promises	Hebrews 8:6–13	2. Better promises
3. A shadow	Hebrews 8:5; 9:23,24; 10:1	3. The reality
4. Aaronic priesthood (many)	Hebrews 6:19–7:25	4. Melchizedekian priesthood (one)
5. Sinful priesthood	Hebrews 7:26,27; 9:7	5. Sinless priest
6. Limited-by-death priesthood	Hebrews 7:16,17,23,24	6. Forever priesthood
7. Daily sacrifices	Hebrews 7:27; 9:12,25,26; 10:9,10,12	7. Once-for-all sacrifice
8. Animal sacrifices	Hebrews 9:11–15,26; 10:4–10,19	8. Sacrifice of God's Son
9. Ongoing sacrifices	Hebrews 10:11–14,18	9. Sacrifices no longer needed
10. One year atonement	Hebrews 7:25; 9:12,15; 10:1–4,12	10. Eternal propitiation

²'Or if a person touches any unclean thing, whether *it is* the carcass of an unclean beast, or the carcass of unclean livestock, or the carcass of unclean creeping things, and he is unaware of it, he also shall be unclean and guilty. ³Or if he touches human uncleanness—whatever uncleanness with which a man may be defiled, and he is unaware of it—when he realizes *it*, then he shall be guilty.

⁴'Or if a person swears, speaking thoughtlessly with *his* lips to do evil or to do good, whatever *it is* that a man may pronounce by an oath, and he is unaware of it—when he realizes *it*, then he shall be guilty in any of these *matters*.

⁵And it shall be, when he is guilty in any of these *matters*, that he shall confess that he has sinned in that *thing*; ⁶and he shall bring his trespass offering to the LORD for his sin which he has committed, a female from the flock, a lamb or a kid of the goats as a sin offering. So the priest shall make atonement for him concerning his sin.

> **5:5 he shall confess.** Confession must accompany the sacrifice as the outward expression of a repentant heart. Sacrifice without true faith, repentance, and obedience was hypocrisy.

⁷'If he is not able to bring a lamb, then he shall bring to the LORD, for his trespass which he has committed, two turtledoves or two young pigeons: one as a sin offering and the other as a burnt offering. ⁸And he shall bring them to the priest, who shall offer *that* which *is* for the sin offering first, and wring off its head from its neck, but shall not divide *it* completely. ⁹Then he shall sprinkle *some* of the blood of the sin offering on the side of the altar, and the rest of the blood shall be drained out at the base of the altar. It *is* a sin offering. ¹⁰And he shall offer the second *as* a burnt offering according to the prescribed manner. So the priest shall make atonement on his behalf for his sin which he has committed, and it shall be forgiven him.

¹¹'But if he is not able to bring two turtledoves or two young pigeons, then he who sinned shall bring for his offering one-tenth of an ephah of fine flour as a sin offering. He shall put no oil on it, nor shall he put frankincense on it, for it *is* a sin offering.

¹²Then he shall bring it to the priest, and the priest shall take his handful of it as a memorial portion, and burn *it* on the altar according to the offerings made by fire to the LORD. It *is* a sin offering. ¹³The priest shall make atonement for him, for his sin that he has committed in any of these matters; and it shall be forgiven him. *The rest* shall be the priest's as a grain offering.' "

Offerings with Restitution

¹⁴Then the LORD spoke to Moses, saying: ¹⁵"If a person commits a trespass, and sins unintentionally in regard to the holy things of the LORD, then he shall bring to the LORD as his trespass offering a ram without blemish from the flocks, with your valuation in shekels of silver according to the shekel of the sanctuary, as a trespass offering. ¹⁶And he shall make restitution for the harm that he has done in regard to the holy thing, and shall add one-fifth to it and give it to the priest. So the priest shall make atonement for him with the ram of the trespass offering, and it shall be forgiven him.

¹⁷"If a person sins, and commits any of these things which are forbidden to be done by the commandments of the LORD, though he does not know *it*, yet he is guilty and shall bear his iniquity. ¹⁸And he shall bring to the priest a ram without blemish from the flock, with your valuation, as a trespass offering. So the priest shall make atonement for him regarding his ignorance in which he erred and did not know *it*, and it shall be forgiven him. ¹⁹It is a trespass offering; he has certainly trespassed against the LORD."

> **1:1–6:7** God gave detailed instructions regarding how the people should offer sacrifices to Him. Five sacrifices were described, the first three being voluntary and the last two required: (1) burnt offering; (2) grain offering; (3) peace offering; (4) sin offering; and (5) trespass offering. All of these offerings were forms of worship to God, to express penitent and thankful hearts. Some gave with a true attitude of worship, but for others they were external rituals only.

6 And the LORD spoke to Moses, saying: ²"If a person sins and commits a trespass against the LORD by lying to his neighbor about what was delivered to him for safekeeping, or about a pledge, or about a robbery, or if he has extorted from his

neighbor, [3]or if he has found what was lost and lies concerning it, and swears falsely— in any one of these things that a man may do in which he sins: [4]then it shall be, because he has sinned and is guilty, that he shall restore what he has stolen, or the thing which he has extorted, or what was delivered to him for safekeeping, or the lost thing which he found, [5]or all that about which he has sworn falsely. He shall restore its full value, add one-fifth more to it, *and* give it to whomever it belongs, on the day of his trespass offering. [6]And he shall bring his trespass offering to the LORD, a ram without blemish from the flock, with your valuation, as a trespass offering, to the priest. [7]So the priest shall make atonement for him before the LORD, and he shall be forgiven for any one of these things that he may have done in which he trespasses."

> **6:1–7** All sins are against God, but some are direct and others are indirect, involving people. This list of violations is not exhaustive but gives samples to illustrate the principle.

The Law of the Burnt Offering

[8]Then the LORD spoke to Moses, saying, [9]"Command Aaron and his sons, saying, 'This *is* the law of the burnt offering: The burnt offering *shall be* on the hearth upon the altar all night until morning, and the fire of the altar shall be kept burning on it. [10]And the priest shall put on his linen garment, and his linen trousers he shall put on his body, and take up the ashes of the burnt offering which the fire has consumed on the altar, and he shall put them beside the altar. [11]Then he shall take off his garments, put on other garments, and carry the ashes outside the camp to a clean place. [12]And the fire on the altar shall be kept burning on it; it shall not be put out. And the priest shall burn wood on it every morning, and lay the burnt offering in order on it; and he shall burn on it the fat of the peace offerings. [13]A

> **6:13 always be burning.** The perpetual flame indicated that God was always ready to receive confession and restitution through sacrifice.

fire shall always be burning on the altar; it shall never go out.

The Law of the Grain Offering

[14]'This *is* the law of the grain offering: The sons of Aaron shall offer it on the altar before the LORD. [15]He shall take from it his handful of the fine flour of the grain offering, with its oil, and all the frankincense which *is* on the grain offering, and shall burn *it* on the altar *for* a sweet aroma, as a memorial to the LORD. [16]And the remainder of it Aaron and his sons shall eat; with unleavened bread it shall be eaten in a holy place; in the court of the tabernacle of meeting they shall eat it. [17]It shall not be baked with leaven. I have given it *as* their portion of My offerings made by fire; it *is* most holy, like the sin offering and the trespass offering. [18]All the males among the children of Aaron may eat it. *It shall be* a statute forever in your generations concerning the offerings made by fire to the LORD. Everyone who touches them must be holy.' "[a]

[19]And the LORD spoke to Moses, saying, [20]"This *is* the offering of Aaron and his sons, which they shall offer to the LORD, *beginning* on the day when he is anointed: one-tenth of an ephah of fine flour as a daily grain offering, half of it in the morning and half of it at night. [21]It shall be made in a pan with oil. *When it is* mixed, you shall bring it in. The baked pieces of the grain offering you shall offer *for* a sweet aroma to the LORD. [22]The priest from among his sons, who is anointed in his place, shall offer it. *It is* a statute forever to the LORD. It shall be wholly burned. [23]For every grain offering for the priest shall be wholly burned. It shall not be eaten."

The Law of the Sin Offering

[24]Also the LORD spoke to Moses, saying, [25]"Speak to Aaron and to his sons, saying, 'This *is* the law of the sin offering: In the place where the burnt offering is killed, the sin offering shall be killed before the LORD. It *is* most holy. [26]The priest who offers it for sin shall eat it. In a holy place it shall be eaten, in the court of the tabernacle of meeting. [27]Everyone who touches its flesh

6:18 [a]Compare Numbers 4:15 and Haggai 2:11–13

must be holy.[a] And when its blood is sprinkled on any garment, you shall wash that on which it was sprinkled, in a holy place. [28]But the earthen vessel in which it is boiled shall be broken. And if it is boiled in a bronze pot, it shall be both scoured and rinsed in water. [29]All the males among the priests may eat it. It *is* most holy. [30]But no sin offering from which *any* of the blood is brought into the tabernacle of meeting, to make atonement in the holy *place*,[a] shall be eaten. It shall be burned in the fire.

> **6:26 priest...eat.** The priest who put the offering on the brazen altar could use it for food if the sacrifice was for a ruler or the people.

The Law of the Trespass Offering

7 [1]'Likewise this *is* the law of the trespass offering (it *is* most holy): [2]In the place where they kill the burnt offering they shall kill the trespass offering. And its blood he shall sprinkle all around on the altar. [3]And he shall offer from it all its fat. The fat tail and the fat that covers the entrails, [4]the two kidneys and the fat that *is* on them by the flanks, and the fatty lobe *attached* to the liver above the kidneys, he shall remove; [5]and the priest shall burn them on the altar *as* an offering made by fire to the LORD. It *is* a trespass offering. [6]Every male among the priests may eat it. It shall be eaten in a holy place. It *is* most holy. [7]The trespass offering *is* like the sin offering; *there is* one law for them both: the priest who makes atonement with it shall have *it*. [8]And the priest who offers anyone's burnt offering, that priest shall have for himself the skin of the burnt offering which he has offered. [9]Also every grain offering that is baked in the oven and all that is prepared in the covered pan, or in a pan, shall be the priest's who offers it. [10]Every grain offering, *whether* mixed with oil or dry, shall belong to all the sons of Aaron, to one *as much* as the other.

The Law of Peace Offerings

[11]'This *is* the law of the sacrifice of peace offerings which he shall offer to the LORD: [12]If he offers it for a thanksgiving, then he shall offer, with the sacrifice of thanksgiving, unleavened cakes mixed with oil, unleavened wafers anointed with oil, or cakes of blended flour mixed with oil. [13]Besides the cakes, *as* his offering he shall offer leavened bread with the sacrifice of thanksgiving of his peace offering. [14]And from it he shall offer one cake from each offering *as* a heave offering to the LORD. It shall belong to the priest who sprinkles the blood of the peace offering.

[15]'The flesh of the sacrifice of his peace offering for thanksgiving shall be eaten the same day it is offered. He shall not leave any of it until morning. [16]But if the sacrifice of his offering *is* a vow or a voluntary offering, it shall be eaten the same day that he offers his sacrifice; but on the next day the remainder of it also may be eaten; [17]the remainder of the flesh of the sacrifice on the third day must be burned with fire. [18]And if *any* of the flesh of the sacrifice of his peace offering is eaten at all on the third day, it shall not be accepted, nor shall it be imputed to him; it shall be an abomination *to* him who offers it, and the person who eats of it shall bear guilt.

[19]'The flesh that touches any unclean thing shall not be eaten. It shall be burned with fire. And as for the *clean* flesh, all who are clean may eat of it. [20]But the person who eats the flesh of the sacrifice of the peace offering that *belongs* to the LORD, while he is unclean, that person shall be cut off from his people. [21]Moreover the person who touches any unclean thing, *such as* human uncleanness, *an* unclean animal, or any abominable unclean thing,[a] and who eats the flesh of the sacrifice of the peace offering that *belongs* to the LORD, that person shall be cut off from his people.' "

Fat and Blood May Not Be Eaten

[22]And the LORD spoke to Moses, saying, [23]"Speak to the children of Israel, saying: 'You shall not eat any fat, of ox or sheep or goat. [24]And the fat of an animal that dies *naturally*, and the fat of what is torn by wild beasts, may be used in any other way; but you shall by no means eat it. [25]For whoever

---

6:27 [a]Compare Numbers 4:15 and Haggai 2:11–13   6:30 [a]The Most Holy Place when capitalized
7:21 [a]Following Masoretic Text, Septuagint, and Vulgate; Samaritan Pentateuch, Syriac, and Targum read *swarming thing* (compare 5:2).

eats the fat of the animal of which men offer an offering made by fire to the LORD, the person who eats *it* shall be cut off from his people. ²⁶Moreover you shall not eat any blood in any of your dwellings, *whether* of bird or beast. ²⁷Whoever eats any blood, that person shall be cut off from his people.' "

The Portion of Aaron and His Sons

²⁸Then the LORD spoke to Moses, saying: ²⁹"Speak to the children of Israel, saying: 'He who offers the sacrifice of his peace offering to the LORD shall bring his offering to the LORD from the sacrifice of his peace offering. ³⁰His own hands shall bring the offerings made by fire to the LORD. The fat with the breast he shall bring, that the breast may be waved *as* a wave offering before the LORD. ³¹And the priest shall burn the fat on the altar, but the breast shall be Aaron's and his sons'. ³²Also the right thigh you shall give to the priest *as* a heave offering from the sacrifices of your peace offerings. ³³He among the sons of Aaron, who offers the blood of the peace offering and the fat, shall have the right thigh for *his* part. ³⁴For the breast of the wave offering and the thigh of the heave offering I have taken from the children of Israel, from the sacrifices of their peace offerings, and I have given them to Aaron the priest and to his sons from the children of Israel by a statute forever.' "

> **7:30–32 wave offering...heave offering.** These were symbolic acts indicating the offering was for the Lord. Bread, meat, gold, oil, and grain all served as wave offerings. Heave offerings were more rare. Jewish tradition portrayed wave offerings as presented with a horizontal motion and heave offerings with a vertical motion.

³⁵This *is* the consecrated portion for Aaron and his sons, from the offerings made by fire to the LORD, on the day when *Moses* presented them to minister to the LORD as priests. ³⁶The LORD commanded this to be given to them by the children of Israel, on the day that He anointed them, *by* a statute forever throughout their generations.

³⁷This *is* the law of the burnt offering, the grain offering, the sin offering, the trespass offering, the consecrations, and the sacrifice of the peace offering, ³⁸which the LORD commanded Moses on Mount Sinai, on the day when He commanded the children of Israel to offer their offerings to the LORD in the Wilderness of Sinai.

Aaron and His Sons Consecrated

8 And the LORD spoke to Moses, saying: ²"Take Aaron and his sons with him, and the garments, the anointing oil, a bull as the sin offering, two rams, and a basket of unleavened bread; ³and gather all the congregation together at the door of the tabernacle of meeting."

⁴So Moses did as the LORD commanded him. And the congregation was gathered together at the door of the tabernacle of meeting. ⁵And Moses said to the congregation, "This *is* what the LORD commanded to be done."

⁶Then Moses brought Aaron and his sons and washed them with water. ⁷And he put the tunic on him, girded him with the sash, clothed him with the robe, and put the ephod on him; and he girded him with the intricately woven band of the ephod, and with it tied *the ephod* on him. ⁸Then he put the breastplate on him, and he put the Urim and the Thummim[a] in the breastplate. ⁹And he put the turban on his head. Also on the turban, on its front, he put the golden plate, the holy crown, as the LORD had commanded Moses.

¹⁰Also Moses took the anointing oil, and anointed the tabernacle and all that *was* in it, and consecrated them. ¹¹He sprinkled some of it on the altar seven times, anointed the altar and all its utensils, and the laver and its base, to consecrate them. ¹²And he poured some of the anointing oil on Aaron's head and anointed him, to consecrate him.

¹³Then Moses brought Aaron's sons and

> **8:1–10:20** This section describes the beginning of the priesthood, starting with Aaron. Before this time, the patriarchs and the fathers had offered sacrifices to God, but along with Aaron came the detailed priestly service.

8:8 [a]Literally *the Lights and the Perfections* (compare Exodus 28:30)

put tunics on them, girded them with sashes, and put hats on them, as the LORD had commanded Moses.

¹⁴And he brought the bull for the sin offering. Then Aaron and his sons laid their hands on the head of the bull for the sin offering, ¹⁵and Moses killed *it*. Then he took the blood, and put *some* on the horns of the altar all around with his finger, and purified the altar. And he poured the blood at the base of the altar, and consecrated it, to make atonement for it. ¹⁶Then he took all the fat that *was* on the entrails, the fatty lobe *attached to* the liver, and the two kidneys with their fat, and Moses burned *them* on the altar. ¹⁷But the bull, its hide, its flesh, and its offal, he burned with fire outside the camp, as the LORD had commanded Moses.

¹⁸Then he brought the ram as the burnt offering. And Aaron and his sons laid their hands on the head of the ram, ¹⁹and Moses killed *it*. Then he sprinkled the blood all around on the altar. ²⁰And he cut the ram into pieces; and Moses burned the head, the pieces, and the fat. ²¹Then he washed the entrails and the legs in water. And Moses burned the whole ram on the altar. It *was* a burnt sacrifice for a sweet aroma, an offering made by fire to the LORD, as the LORD had commanded Moses.

²²And he brought the second ram, the ram of consecration. Then Aaron and his sons laid their hands on the head of the ram, ²³and Moses killed *it*. Also he took *some* of its blood and put it on the tip of Aaron's right ear, on the thumb of his right hand, and on the big toe of his right foot. ²⁴Then he brought Aaron's sons. And Moses put *some* of the blood on the tips of their right ears, on the thumbs of their right hands, and on the big toes of their right feet. And Moses sprinkled the blood all around on the altar. ²⁵Then he took the fat and the fat tail, all the fat that *was* on the entrails, the fatty lobe *attached to* the liver, the two kidneys and their fat, and the right thigh; ²⁶and from the basket of unleav-

ened bread that was before the LORD he took one unleavened cake, a cake of bread *anointed with* oil, and one wafer, and put *them* on the fat and on the right thigh; ²⁷and he put all *these* in Aaron's hands and in his sons' hands, and waved them *as a* wave offering before the LORD. ²⁸Then Moses took them from their hands and burned *them* on the altar, on the burnt offering. They *were* consecration offerings for a sweet aroma. That *was* an offering made by fire to the LORD. ²⁹And Moses took the breast and waved it *as* a wave offering before the LORD. It was Moses' part of the ram of consecration, as the LORD had commanded Moses.

³⁰Then Moses took some of the anointing oil and some of the blood which *was* on the altar, and sprinkled *it* on Aaron, on his garments, on his sons, and on the garments of his sons with him; and he consecrated Aaron, his garments, his sons, and the garments of his sons with him.

³¹And Moses said to Aaron and his sons, "Boil the flesh *at* the door of the tabernacle of meeting, and eat it there with the bread that *is* in the basket of consecration offerings, as I commanded, saying, 'Aaron and his sons shall eat it.' ³²What remains of the flesh and of the bread you shall burn with fire. ³³And you shall not go outside the door of the tabernacle of meeting *for* seven days, until the days of your consecration are ended. For seven days he shall consecrate you. ³⁴As he has done this day, *so* the LORD has commanded to do, to make atonement for you. ³⁵Therefore you shall stay *at* the door of the tabernacle of meeting day and night for seven days, and keep the charge of the LORD, so that you may not die; for so I have been commanded." ³⁶So Aaron and his sons did all the things that the LORD had commanded by the hand of Moses.

The Priestly Ministry Begins

9 It came to pass on the eighth day that Moses called Aaron and his sons and the elders of Israel. ²And he said to Aaron, "Take for yourself a young bull as a sin offering and a ram as a burnt offering, without blemish, and offer *them* before the LORD. ³And to the children of Israel you shall speak, saying, 'Take a kid of the goats as a sin offering, and a calf and a lamb, *both*

8:23,24 right ear...right hand...right foot. Aaron and his sons were consecrated to listen to God's holy Word, to carry out His holy assignments, and to live holy lives.

of the first year, without blemish, as a burnt offering, 'also a bull and a ram as peace offerings, to sacrifice before the LORD, and a grain offering mixed with oil; for today the LORD will appear to you.' "

5So they brought what Moses commanded before the tabernacle of meeting. And all the congregation drew near and stood before the LORD. 6Then Moses said, "This is the thing which the LORD commanded you to do, and the glory of the LORD will appear to you." 7And Moses said to Aaron, "Go to the altar, offer your sin offering and your burnt offering, and make atonement for yourself and for the people. Offer the offering of the people, and make atonement for them, as the LORD commanded."

9:4,6 the glory of the LORD. The Bible speaks of the glory of God, the visible appearance of His beauty and perfection appearing as blazing light. His glory appeared to Moses in a burning bush, led the people as a pillar of fire and cloud, and filled the tabernacle. God revealed His righteousness, holiness, truth, wisdom, and grace. His glory was most perfectly expressed through Jesus Christ.

8Aaron therefore went to the altar and killed the calf of the sin offering, which was for himself. 9Then the sons of Aaron brought the blood to him. And he dipped his finger in the blood, put it on the horns of the altar, and poured the blood at the base of the altar. 10But the fat, the kidneys, and the fatty lobe from the liver of the sin offering he burned on the altar, as the LORD had commanded Moses. 11The flesh and the hide he burned with fire outside the camp.

12And he killed the burnt offering; and Aaron's sons presented to him the blood, which he sprinkled all around on the altar. 13Then they presented the burnt offering to him, with its pieces and head, and he burned them on the altar. 14And he washed the entrails and the legs, and burned them with the burnt offering on the altar.

15Then he brought the people's offering, and took the goat, which was the sin offering for the people, and killed it and offered it for sin, like the first one. 16And he brought the burnt offering and offered it according to the prescribed manner. 17Then he brought the grain offering, took a hand-

ful of it, and burned it on the altar, besides the burnt sacrifice of the morning.

18He also killed the bull and the ram as sacrifices of peace offerings, which were for the people. And Aaron's sons presented to him the blood, which he sprinkled all around on the altar, 19and the fat from the bull and the ram—the fatty tail, what covers the entrails and the kidneys, and the fatty lobe attached to the liver; 20and they put the fat on the breasts. Then he burned the fat on the altar; 21but the breasts and the right thigh Aaron waved as a wave offering before the LORD, as Moses had commanded.

22Then Aaron lifted his hand toward the people, blessed them, and came down from offering the sin offering, the burnt offering, and peace offerings. 23And Moses and Aaron went into the tabernacle of meeting, and came out and blessed the people. Then the glory of the LORD appeared to all the people, 24and fire came out from before the LORD and consumed the burnt offering and the fat on the altar. When all the people saw it, they shouted and fell on their faces.

9:24 fire came out...consumed. This fire miraculously signified that God had accepted their offering, and the people shouted for joy and worshiped God.

The Profane Fire of Nadab and Abihu

10 Then Nadab and Abihu, the sons of Aaron, each took his censer and put fire in it, put incense on it, and offered profane fire before the LORD, which He had not commanded them. 2So fire went out from the LORD and devoured them, and they died before the LORD. 3And Moses said to Aaron, "This is what the LORD spoke, saying:

'By those who come near Me
I must be regarded as holy;
And before all the people
I must be glorified.' "

10:1 Nadab and Abihu. The two oldest sons of Aaron. **profane fire.** In some way, they violated God's instructions for offering incense, probably because they were drunk. Their carelessness, irreverence, and lack of consideration for God had to be punished for all priests to see as a warning.

So Aaron held his peace.

[4]Then Moses called Mishael and Elzaphan, the sons of Uzziel the uncle of Aaron, and said to them, "Come near, carry your brethren from before the sanctuary out of the camp." [5]So they went near and carried them by their tunics out of the camp, as Moses had said.

[6]And Moses said to Aaron, and to Eleazar and Ithamar, his sons, "Do not uncover your heads nor tear your clothes, lest you die, and wrath come upon all the people. But let your brethren, the whole house of Israel, bewail the burning which the LORD has kindled. [7]You shall not go out from the door of the tabernacle of meeting, lest you die, for the anointing oil of the LORD is upon you." And they did according to the word of Moses.

Conduct Prescribed for Priests

[8]Then the LORD spoke to Aaron, saying: [9]"Do not drink wine or intoxicating drink, you, nor your sons with you, when you go into the tabernacle of meeting, lest you die. It shall be a statute forever throughout your generations, [10]that you may distinguish between holy and unholy, and between unclean and clean, [11]and that you may teach the children of Israel all the statutes which the LORD has spoken to them by the hand of Moses."

> **10:11 that you may teach the children of Israel.** It was essential that alcohol not hinder the clarity of the priests' minds, since they were to teach God's law to the children of Israel.

[12]And Moses spoke to Aaron, and to Eleazar and Ithamar, his sons who were left: "Take the grain offering that remains of the offerings made by fire to the LORD, and eat it without leaven beside the altar; for it is most holy. [13]You shall eat it in a holy place, because it is your due and your sons' due, of the sacrifices made by fire to the LORD; for so I have been commanded. [14]The breast of the wave offering and the thigh of the heave offering you shall eat in a clean place, you, your sons, and your daughters with you; for they are your due and your sons' due, which are given from the sacrifices of peace offerings of the children of Israel. [15]The thigh of the heave offering and the breast of the wave offering they shall bring with the offerings of fat made by fire, to offer as a wave offering before the LORD. And it shall be yours and your sons' with you, by a statute forever, as the LORD has commanded."

[16]Then Moses made careful inquiry about the goat of the sin offering, and there it was—burned up. And he was angry with Eleazar and Ithamar, the sons of Aaron who were left, saying, [17]"Why have you not eaten the sin offering in a holy place, since it is most holy, and God has given it to you to bear the guilt of the congregation, to make atonement for them before the LORD? [18]See! Its blood was not brought inside the holy place;[a] indeed you should have eaten it in a holy place, as I commanded."

[19]And Aaron said to Moses, "Look, this day they have offered their sin offering and their burnt offering before the LORD, and such things have befallen me! If I had eaten the sin offering today, would it have been accepted in the sight of the LORD?" [20]So when Moses heard that, he was content.

> **10:16–20** The priests were responsible to eat the meat in a sacred feast after the blood was sprinkled on the altar, but they had disobeyed and burned it outside the camp instead. When Moses questioned the two sons, Aaron answered for them, explaining that they had followed the sacrifice instructions except for eating the meat because they were too dejected for a feast after the deaths of his older sons. Moses accepted Aaron's answer.

Foods Permitted and Forbidden

11 Now the LORD spoke to Moses and Aaron, saying to them, [2]"Speak to the children of Israel, saying, 'These are the animals which you may eat among all the animals that are on the earth: [3]Among the animals, whatever divides the hoof, having cloven hooves and chewing the cud—that you may eat. [4]Nevertheless these you shall not eat among those that chew the cud or those that have cloven hooves: the camel, because it chews the cud but does not have cloven hooves, is unclean to you; [5]the rock hyrax, because it chews the cud but does not have cloven hooves, is un-

10:18 [a]The Most Holy Place when capitalized

clean to you; ⁶the hare, because it chews the cud but does not have cloven hooves, *is* unclean to you; ⁷and the swine, though it divides the hoof, having cloven hooves, yet does not chew the cud, *is* unclean to you. ⁸Their flesh you shall not eat, and their carcasses you shall not touch. They *are* unclean to you.

⁹'These you may eat of all that *are* in the water: whatever in the water has fins and scales, whether in the seas or in the rivers—that you may eat. ¹⁰But all in the seas or in the rivers that do not have fins and scales, all that move in the water or any living thing which *is* in the water, they *are* an abomination to you. ¹¹They shall be an abomination to you; you shall not eat their flesh, but you shall regard their carcasses as an abomination. ¹²Whatever in the water does not have fins or scales—that *shall be* an abomination to you.

¹³'And these you shall regard as an abomination among the birds; they shall not be eaten, they *are* an abomination: the eagle, the vulture, the buzzard, ¹⁴the kite, and the falcon after its kind; ¹⁵every raven after its kind, ¹⁶the ostrich, the short-eared owl, the sea gull, and the hawk after its kind; ¹⁷the little owl, the fisher owl, and the screech owl; ¹⁸the white owl, the jackdaw, and the carrion vulture; ¹⁹the stork, the heron after its kind, the hoopoe, and the bat.

²⁰'All flying insects that creep on *all* fours *shall be* an abomination to you. ²¹Yet these you may eat of every flying insect that creeps on *all* fours: those which have jointed legs above their feet with which to leap on the earth. ²²These you may eat: the locust after its kind, the destroying locust after its kind, the cricket after its kind, and the grasshopper after its kind. ²³But all *other* flying insects which have four feet *shall be* an abomination to you.

Unclean Animals

²⁴'By these you shall become unclean; whoever touches the carcass of any of them shall be unclean until evening; ²⁵whoever carries part of the carcass of any of them shall wash his clothes and be unclean until evening: ²⁶*The carcass* of any animal which divides the foot, but is not cloven-hoofed or does not chew the cud, *is* unclean to you. Everyone who touches it shall be unclean.

²⁷And whatever goes on its paws, among all kinds of animals that go on *all* fours, those *are* unclean to you. Whoever touches any such carcass shall be unclean until evening. ²⁸Whoever carries *any such* carcass shall wash his clothes and be unclean until evening. It *is* unclean to you.

11:1–47 After the flood, God granted man permission to eat meat (Gen. 9:1–4), but here He gave the specific rules about the consumption of animals. Israel was to obey God's absolute standard. Such a unique diet was specified (1) so that Israel would find it difficult to eat with the idolatrous people around them and thus would stay separate from them, and (2) for dietary and hygienic benefits.

²⁹'These also *shall be* unclean to you among the creeping things that creep on the earth: the mole, the mouse, and the large lizard after its kind; ³⁰the gecko, the monitor lizard, the sand reptile, the sand lizard, and the chameleon. ³¹These *are* unclean to you among all that creep. Whoever touches them when they are dead shall be unclean until evening. ³²Anything on which *any* of them falls, when they are dead shall be unclean, whether *it is* any item of wood or clothing or skin or sack, whatever item *it is*, in which *any* work is done, it must be put in water. And it shall be unclean until evening; then it shall be clean. ³³Any earthen vessel into which *any* of them falls you shall break; and whatever *is* in it shall be unclean: ³⁴in such a vessel, any edible food upon which water falls becomes unclean, and any drink that may be drunk from it becomes unclean. ³⁵And everything on which *a part* of *any such* carcass falls shall be unclean; *whether it is* an oven or cooking stove, it shall be broken down; *for* they *are* unclean, and shall be unclean to you. ³⁶Nevertheless a spring or a cistern, *in which there is* plenty of water, shall be clean, but whatever touches any such carcass becomes unclean. ³⁷And if a part of *any such* carcass falls on any planting seed which is to be sown, it *remains* clean. ³⁸But if water is put on the seed, and if *a part* of *any such* carcass falls on it, it *becomes* unclean to you.

³⁹'And if any animal which you may eat dies, he who touches its carcass shall be unclean until evening. ⁴⁰He who eats of its

carcass shall wash his clothes and be unclean until evening. He also who carries its carcass shall wash his clothes and be unclean until evening.

⁴¹And every creeping thing that creeps on the earth *shall be* an abomination. It shall not be eaten. ⁴²Whatever crawls on its belly, whatever goes on *all* fours, or whatever has many feet among all creeping things that creep on the earth—these you shall not eat, for they *are* an abomination. ⁴³You shall not make yourselves abominable with any creeping thing that creeps; nor shall you make yourselves unclean with them, lest you be defiled by them. ⁴⁴For I *am* the LORD your God. You shall therefore consecrate yourselves, and you shall be holy; for I *am* holy. Neither shall you defile yourselves with any creeping thing that creeps on the earth. ⁴⁵For I *am* the LORD who brings you up out of the land of Egypt, to be your God. You shall therefore be holy, for I *am* holy.

> **11:44,45 consecrate yourselves...be holy; for I *am* holy.** In all of this, God is teaching His people to live separate from the other nations and to live His way in everything. He is teaching obedience in every seemingly mundane area of life, so as to learn how crucial obedience is. The only motivation given for all these laws is to learn to be holy because God is holy. The theme of holiness is central to Leviticus.

⁴⁶'This *is* the law of the animals and the birds and every living creature that moves in the waters, and of every creature that creeps on the earth, ⁴⁷to distinguish between the unclean and the clean, and between the animal that may be eaten and the animal that may not be eaten.' "

The Ritual After Childbirth

12 Then the LORD spoke to Moses, saying, ²"Speak to the children of Israel, saying: 'If a woman has conceived, and borne a male child, then she shall be unclean seven days; as in the days of her customary impurity she shall be unclean. ³And on the eighth day the flesh of his foreskin shall be circumcised. ⁴She shall then continue in the blood of *her* purification thirty-three days. She shall not touch any hallowed thing, nor come into the sanctu-

ary until the days of her purification are fulfilled.

⁵But if she bears a female child, then she shall be unclean two weeks, as in her customary impurity, and she shall continue in the blood of *her* purification sixty-six days.

> **12:5 two weeks...sixty-six days.** Apparently mothers were unclean twice as long after the birth of a daughter as a son, which reflected the stigma on women for Eve's part in the Fall. This stigma is removed in Christ.

⁶'When the days of her purification are fulfilled, whether for a son or a daughter, she shall bring to the priest a lamb of the first year as a burnt offering, and a young pigeon or a turtledove as a sin offering, to the door of the tabernacle of meeting. ⁷Then he shall offer it before the LORD, and make atonement for her. And she shall be clean from the flow of her blood. This *is* the law for her who has borne a male or a female.

> **12:6 burnt offering...sin offering.** Even on this joyous occasion, the sacrifices were required in order to impress upon the parents the reality that the child had inherited a sin nature. Circumcision involved cutting away the male foreskin, which could carry infections and diseases in its folds. This cleansing was a picture of the deep need for cleansing at the very core of a person.

⁸'And if she is not able to bring a lamb, then she may bring two turtledoves or two young pigeons—one as a burnt offering and the other as a sin offering. So the priest shall make atonement for her, and she will be clean.' "

The Law Concerning Leprosy

13 And the LORD spoke to Moses and Aaron, saying: ²"When a man has on the skin of his body a swelling, a scab, or a bright spot, and it becomes on the skin of his body *like* a leprous*ᵃ* sore, then he shall be brought to Aaron the priest or to one of his sons the priests. ³The priest shall examine the sore on the skin of the body; and if the hair on the sore has turned white, and the sore appears *to be* deeper than the skin

13:2 *ᵃ*Hebrew *saraath,* disfiguring skin diseases, including leprosy, and so in verses 2–46 and 14:1–32

of his body, it *is* a leprous sore. Then the priest shall examine him, and pronounce him unclean. ⁴But if the bright spot *is* white on the skin of his body, and does not appear *to be* deeper than the skin, and its hair has not turned white, then the priest shall isolate *the one who has* the sore seven days. ⁵And the priest shall examine him on the seventh day; and indeed *if* the sore appears to be as it was, *and* the sore has not spread on the skin, then the priest shall isolate him another seven days. ⁶Then the priest shall examine him again on the seventh day; and indeed *if* the sore has faded, *and* the sore has not spread on the skin, then the priest shall pronounce him clean; it *is* only a scab, and he shall wash his clothes and be clean. ⁷But if the scab should at all spread over the skin, after he has been seen by the priest for his cleansing, he shall be seen by the priest again. ⁸And *if* the priest sees that the scab has indeed spread on the skin, then the priest shall pronounce him unclean. It *is* leprosy.

⁹"When the leprous sore is on a person, then he shall be brought to the priest. ¹⁰And the priest shall examine *him*; and indeed *if* the swelling on the skin *is* white, and it has turned the hair white, and *there is* a spot of raw flesh in the swelling, ¹¹it *is* an old leprosy on the skin of his body. The priest shall pronounce him unclean, and shall not isolate him, for he *is* unclean.

¹²"And if leprosy breaks out all over the skin, and the leprosy covers all the skin of *the one who has* the sore, from his head to his foot, wherever the priest looks, ¹³then the priest shall consider; and indeed *if* the leprosy has covered all his body, he shall pronounce *him* clean *who has* the sore. It has all turned white. He *is* clean. ¹⁴But

when raw flesh appears on him, he shall be unclean. ¹⁵And the priest shall examine the raw flesh and pronounce him to be unclean; *for* the raw flesh *is* unclean. It *is* leprosy. ¹⁶Or if the raw flesh changes and turns white again, he shall come to the priest. ¹⁷And the priest shall examine him; and indeed *if* the sore has turned white, then the priest shall pronounce *him* clean *who has* the sore. He *is* clean.

¹⁸"If the body develops a boil in the skin, and it is healed, ¹⁹and in the place of the boil there comes a white swelling or a bright spot, reddish-white, then it shall be shown to the priest; ²⁰and *if*, when the priest sees it, it indeed *appears* deeper than the skin, and its hair has turned white, the priest shall pronounce him unclean. It *is* a leprous sore which has broken out of the boil. ²¹But if the priest examines it, and indeed *there are* no white hairs in it, and it *is* not deeper than the skin, but has faded, then the priest shall isolate him seven days; ²²and if it should at all spread over the skin, then the priest shall pronounce him unclean. It *is* a leprous sore. ²³But if the bright spot stays in one place, *and* has not spread, it *is* the scar of the boil; and the priest shall pronounce him clean.

²⁴"Or if the body receives a burn on its skin by fire, and the raw *flesh* of the burn becomes a bright spot, reddish-white or white, ²⁵then the priest shall examine it; and indeed *if* the hair of the bright spot has turned white, and it appears deeper than the skin, it *is* leprosy broken out in the burn. Therefore the priest shall pronounce him unclean. It *is* a leprous sore. ²⁶But if the priest examines it, and indeed *there are* no white hairs in the bright spot, and it *is* not deeper than the skin, but has faded,

Why did God have so many specific rules for the Israelites?

God's purpose was to create a separate, holy people (Leviticus 11:44,45). Their lives were to reflect His character and contrast with the behavior of their neighbor nations. They were to obey God's rules even when they didn't necessarily understand the reasons.

Looking back over history, we can often see that God had several reasons behind His rules. One of the interesting discoveries about the Levitical rules for cleanliness is that they measure up to recent standards of hygienic living. They represent just the sort of precautions taken by medical personnel today in order to prevent infections and the spread of diseases. God did not ask His people to behave in ways that were at all harmful to them.

then the priest shall isolate him seven days. [27]And the priest shall examine him on the seventh day. If it has at all spread over the skin, then the priest shall pronounce him unclean. It *is* a leprous sore. [28]But if the bright spot stays in one place, *and* has not spread on the skin, but has faded, it *is* a swelling from the burn. The priest shall pronounce him clean, for it *is* the scar from the burn.

[29]"If a man or woman has a sore on the head or the beard, [30]then the priest shall examine the sore; and indeed if it appears deeper than the skin, *and there is* in it thin yellow hair, then the priest shall pronounce him unclean. It *is* a scaly leprosy of the head or beard. [31]But if the priest examines the scaly sore, and indeed it does not appear deeper than the skin, and *there is* no black hair in it, then the priest shall isolate *the one who has* the scale seven days. [32]And on the seventh day the priest shall examine the sore; and indeed *if* the scale has not spread, and there is no yellow hair in it, and the scale does not appear deeper than the skin, [33]he shall shave himself, but the scale he shall not shave. And the priest shall isolate *the one who has* the scale another seven days. [34]On the seventh day the priest shall examine the scale; and indeed *if* the scale has not spread over the skin, and does not appear deeper than the skin, then the priest shall pronounce him clean. He shall wash his clothes and be clean. [35]But if the scale should at all spread over the skin after his cleansing, [36]then the priest shall examine him; and indeed *if* the scale has spread over the skin, the priest need not seek for yellow hair. He *is* unclean. [37]But if the scale appears to be at a standstill, and there is black hair grown up in it, the scale has healed. He *is* clean, and the priest shall pronounce him clean.

[38]"If a man or a woman has bright spots on the skin of the body, *specifically* white bright spots, [39]then the priest shall look; and indeed if the bright spots on the skin of the body *are* dull white, it *is* a white spot *that* grows on the skin. He *is* clean.

[40]"As for the man whose hair has fallen from his head, he *is* bald, *but* he *is* clean. [41]He whose hair has fallen from his fore-head, he *is* bald on the forehead, *but* he *is* clean. [42]And if there is on the bald head or bald forehead a reddish-white sore, it *is* leprosy breaking out on his bald head or his bald forehead. [43]Then the priest shall examine it; and indeed *if* the swelling of the sore *is* reddish-white on his bald head or on his bald forehead, as the appearance of leprosy on the skin of the body, [44]he is a leprous man. He *is* unclean. The priest shall surely pronounce him unclean; his sore *is* on his head.

[45]"Now the leper on whom the sore *is*, his clothes shall be torn and his head bare; and he shall cover his mustache, and cry, 'Unclean! Unclean!' [46]He shall be unclean. All the days he has the sore he shall be unclean. He *is* unclean, and he shall dwell alone; his dwelling *shall be* outside the camp.

The Law Concerning Leprous Garments

[47]"Also, if a garment has a leprous plague[a] in it, *whether it is* a woolen garment or a linen garment, [48]whether *it is* in the warp or woof of linen or wool, whether in leather or in anything made of leather, [49]and if the plague is greenish or reddish in the garment or in the leather, whether in the warp or in the woof, or in anything made of leather, it *is* a leprous plague and shall be shown to the priest. [50]The priest shall examine the plague and isolate *that which has* the plague seven days. [51]And he shall examine the plague on the seventh day. If the plague has spread in the garment, either in the warp or in the woof, in the leather *or* in anything made of leather, the plague *is* an active leprosy. It *is* unclean. [52]He shall therefore burn that garment in which is the plague, whether warp or woof, in wool or in linen, or anything of leather, for it *is* an active leprosy; *the garment* shall be burned in the fire.

[53]"But if the priest examines *it*, and indeed the plague has not spread in the garment, either in the warp or in the woof, or in anything made of leather, [54]then the priest shall command that they wash *the thing* in which *is* the plague; and he shall isolate it another seven days. [55]Then the priest shall examine the plague after it has

13:47   [a]A mold, fungus, or similar infestation, and so in verses 47–59

been washed; and indeed *if* the plague has not changed its color, though the plague has not spread, it *is* unclean, and you shall burn it in the fire; it continues eating away, *whether* the damage *is* outside or inside. [56]If the priest examines *it*, and indeed the plague has faded after washing it, then he shall tear it out of the garment, whether out of the warp or out of the woof, or out of the leather. [57]But if it appears again in the garment, either in the warp or in the woof, or in anything made of leather, it *is* a spreading *plague*; you shall burn with fire that in which is the plague. [58]And if you wash the garment, either warp or woof, or whatever is made of leather, if the plague has disappeared from it, then it shall be washed a second time, and shall be clean.

[59]"This *is* the law of the leprous plague in a garment of wool or linen, either in the warp or woof, or in anything made of leather, to pronounce it clean or to pronounce it unclean."

13:59 to pronounce it clean or...unclean. The primary purpose of these laws was to help the priest determine the presence of contagious skin disease, including those that affect the clothes as well as the person. This also illustrates the devastating infection of sin and how essential cleansing was spiritually.

The Ritual for Cleansing Healed Lepers

14 Then the LORD spoke to Moses, saying, [2]"This shall be the law of the leper for the day of his cleansing: He shall be brought to the priest. [3]And the priest shall go out of the camp, and the priest shall examine *him*; and indeed, *if* the leprosy is healed in the leper, [4]then the priest shall command to take for him who is to be cleansed two living *and* clean birds, cedar wood, scarlet, and hyssop. [5]And the priest shall command that one of the birds be killed in an earthen vessel over running water. [6]As for the living bird, he shall take it, the cedar wood and the scarlet and the hyssop, and dip them and the living bird in the blood of the bird *that was* killed over the running water. [7]And he shall sprinkle it seven times on him who is to be cleansed from the leprosy, and shall pronounce him clean, and shall let the living bird loose in the open field. [8]He who is to be cleansed shall wash his clothes, shave off all his hair,

and wash himself in water, that he may be clean. After that he shall come into the camp, and shall stay outside his tent seven days. [9]But on the seventh day he shall shave all the hair off his head and his beard and his eyebrows—all his hair he shall shave off. He shall wash his clothes and wash his body in water, and he shall be clean.

14:8 outside his tent. The movement was progressive until finally he could enter and dwell in his own tent again. This was a powerful lesson from God on the holiness He desired for those who lived among His people. This has not changed.

[10]"And on the eighth day he shall take two male lambs without blemish, one ewe lamb of the first year without blemish, three-tenths *of an ephah* of fine flour mixed with oil as a grain offering, and one log of oil. [11]Then the priest who makes *him* clean shall present the man who is to be made clean, and those things, before the LORD, *at* the door of the tabernacle of meeting. [12]And the priest shall take one male lamb and offer it as a trespass offering, and the log of oil, and wave them *as* a wave offering before the LORD. [13]Then he shall kill the lamb in the place where he kills the sin offering and the burnt offering, in a holy place; for as the sin offering *is* the priest's, so *is* the trespass offering. It *is* most holy. [14]The priest shall take *some* of the blood of the trespass offering, and the priest shall put *it* on the tip of the right ear of him who is to be cleansed, on the thumb of his right hand, and on the big toe of his right foot. [15]And the priest shall take *some* of the log of oil, and pour *it* into the palm of his own left hand. [16]Then the priest shall dip his right finger in the oil that *is* in his left hand, and shall sprinkle some of the oil with his finger seven times before the LORD. [17]And of the rest of the oil in his hand, the priest shall put *some* on the tip of the right ear of him who is to be cleansed, on the thumb of his right hand, and on the big toe of his right foot, on the blood of the trespass offering. [18]The rest of the oil that *is* in the priest's hand he shall put on the head of him who is to be cleansed. So the priest shall make atonement for him before the LORD.

19"Then the priest shall offer the sin offering, and make atonement for him who is to be cleansed from his uncleanness. Afterward he shall kill the burnt offering. 20And the priest shall offer the burnt offering and the grain offering on the altar. So the priest shall make atonement for him, and he shall be clean.

21"But if he *is* poor and cannot afford it, then he shall take one male lamb *as* a trespass offering to be waved, to make atonement for him, one-tenth *of an ephah* of fine flour mixed with oil as a grain offering, a log of oil, 22and two turtledoves or two young pigeons, such as he is able to afford: one shall be a sin offering and the other a burnt offering. 23He shall bring them to the priest on the eighth day for his cleansing, to the door of the tabernacle of meeting, before the LORD. 24And the priest shall take the lamb of the trespass offering and the log of oil, and the priest shall wave them *as a* wave offering before the LORD. 25Then he shall kill the lamb of the trespass offering, and the priest shall take *some* of the blood of the trespass offering and put *it* on the tip of the right ear of him who is to be cleansed, on the thumb of his right hand, and on the big toe of his right foot. 26And the priest shall pour some of the oil into the palm of his own left hand. 27Then the priest shall sprinkle with his right finger *some* of the oil that *is* in his left hand seven times before the LORD. 28And the priest shall put *some* of the oil that *is* in his hand on the tip of the right ear of him who is to be cleansed, on the thumb of the right hand, and on the big toe of his right foot, on the place of the blood of the trespass offering. 29The rest of the oil that *is* in the priest's hand he shall put on the head of him who is to be cleansed, to make atonement for him before the LORD. 30And he shall offer one of the turtledoves or young pigeons, such as he can afford— 31such as he is able to afford, the one *as* a sin offering and the other *as* a burnt offering, with the grain offering. So the priest shall make atonement for him who is to be cleansed before the LORD. 32This *is* the law *for one* who had a leprous sore, who cannot afford the usual cleansing."

The Law Concerning Leprous Houses

33And the LORD spoke to Moses and Aaron, saying: 34"When you have come into the land of Canaan, which I give you as a possession, and I put the leprous plague*a* in a house in the land of your possession, 35and he who owns the house comes and tells the priest, saying, 'It seems to me that *there is* some plague in the house,' 36then the priest shall command that they empty the house, before the priest goes *into it* to examine the plague, that all that *is* in the house may not be made unclean; and afterward the priest shall go in to examine the house. 37And he shall examine the plague; and indeed *if* the plague *is* on the walls of the house with ingrained streaks, greenish or reddish, which appear to be deep in the wall, 38then the priest shall go out of the house, to the door of the house, and shut up the house seven days. 39And the priest shall come again on the seventh day and look; and indeed *if* the plague has spread on the walls of the house, 40then the priest shall command that they take away the stones in which *is* the plague, and they shall cast them into an unclean place outside the city. 41And he shall cause the house to be scraped inside, all around, and the dust that they scrape off they shall pour out in an unclean place outside the city. 42Then they shall take other stones and put *them* in the place of *those* stones, and he shall take other mortar and plaster the house.

> **14:34 I put the leprous plague.** God's sovereign hand is acknowledged in the diseases that were in Canaan. He always has a purpose for these afflictions. Uniquely, in Israel's case, they tied to object lessons on holiness.

43"Now if the plague comes back and breaks out in the house, after he has taken away the stones, after he has scraped the house, and after it is plastered, 44then the priest shall come and look; and indeed *if* the plague has spread in the house, it *is* an active leprosy in the house. It *is* unclean. 45And he shall break down the house, its stones, its timber, and all the plaster of the house, and he shall carry *them* outside the city to an unclean place. 46Moreover he who

---

14:34 *a*Decomposition by mildew, mold, dry rot, etc., and so in verses 34–53

goes into the house at all while it is shut up shall be unclean until evening. ⁴⁷And he who lies down in the house shall wash his clothes, and he who eats in the house shall wash his clothes.

⁴⁸"But if the priest comes in and examines *it*, and indeed the plague has not spread in the house after the house was plastered, then the priest shall pronounce the house clean, because the plague is healed. ⁴⁹And he shall take, to cleanse the house, two birds, cedar wood, scarlet, and hyssop. ⁵⁰Then he shall kill one of the birds in an earthen vessel over running water; ⁵¹and he shall take the cedar wood, the hyssop, the scarlet, and the living bird, and dip them in the blood of the slain bird and in the running water, and sprinkle the house seven times. ⁵²And he shall cleanse the house with the blood of the bird and the running water and the living bird, with the cedar wood, the hyssop, and the scarlet. ⁵³Then he shall let the living bird loose outside the city in the open field, and make atonement for the house, and it shall be clean.

⁵⁴"This *is* the law for any leprous sore and scale, ⁵⁵for the leprosy of a garment and of a house, ⁵⁶for a swelling and a scab and a bright spot, ⁵⁷to teach when *it is* unclean and when *it is* clean. This *is* the law of leprosy."

14:57 to teach when *it is* unclean and when *it is* clean. The priest needed instructions to identify the diseases and the cleansing required, to teach people the importance of holiness.

The Law Concerning Bodily Discharges

15 And the LORD spoke to Moses and Aaron, saying, ²"Speak to the children of Israel, and say to them: 'When any man has a discharge from his body, his discharge *is* unclean. ³And this shall be his uncleanness in regard to his discharge— whether his body runs with his discharge, or his body is stopped up by his discharge, it *is* his uncleanness. ⁴Every bed is unclean on which he who has the discharge lies, and everything on which he sits shall be unclean. ⁵And whoever touches his bed shall wash his clothes and bathe in water, and be unclean until evening. ⁶He who sits on anything on which he who has the discharge

sat shall wash his clothes and bathe in water, and be unclean until evening. ⁷And he who touches the body of him who has the discharge shall wash his clothes and bathe in water, and be unclean until evening. ⁸If he who has the discharge spits on him who is clean, then he shall wash his clothes and bathe in water, and be unclean until evening. ⁹Any saddle on which he who has the discharge rides shall be unclean. ¹⁰Whoever touches anything that was under him shall be unclean until evening. He who carries *any of* those things shall wash his clothes and bathe in water, and be unclean until evening. ¹¹And whomever the one who has the discharge touches, and has not rinsed his hands in water, he shall wash his clothes and bathe in water, and be unclean until evening. ¹²The vessel of earth that he who has the discharge touches shall be broken, and every vessel of wood shall be rinsed in water.

¹³'And when he who has a discharge is cleansed of his discharge, then he shall count for himself seven days for his cleansing, wash his clothes, and bathe his body in running water; then he shall be clean. ¹⁴On the eighth day he shall take for himself two turtledoves or two young pigeons, and come before the LORD, to the door of the tabernacle of meeting, and give them to the priest. ¹⁵Then the priest shall offer them, the one *as* a sin offering and the other *as* a burnt offering. So the priest shall make atonement for him before the LORD because of his discharge.

¹⁶'If any man has an emission of semen, then he shall wash all his body in water, and be unclean until evening. ¹⁷And any garment and any leather on which there is semen, it shall be washed with water, and be unclean until evening. ¹⁸Also, when a woman lies with a man, and *there is* an emission of semen, they shall bathe in water, and be unclean until evening.

¹⁹'If a woman has a discharge, *and the* discharge from her body is blood, she shall be set apart seven days; and whoever touches her shall be unclean until evening. ²⁰Everything that she lies on during her impurity shall be unclean; also everything that she sits on shall be unclean. ²¹Whoever touches her bed shall wash his clothes and bathe in water, and be unclean until

evening. ²²And whoever touches anything that she sat on shall wash his clothes and bathe in water, and be unclean until evening. ²³If *anything* is on *her* bed or on anything on which she sits, when he touches it, he shall be unclean until evening. ²⁴And if any man lies with her at all, so that her impurity is on him, he shall be unclean seven days; and every bed on which he lies shall be unclean.

²⁵'If a woman has a discharge of blood for many days, other than at the time of her *customary* impurity, or if it runs beyond her *usual time of* impurity, all the days of her unclean discharge shall be as the days of her *customary* impurity. She *shall be* unclean. ²⁶Every bed on which she lies all the days of her discharge shall be to her as the bed of her impurity; and whatever she sits on shall be unclean, as the uncleanness of her impurity. ²⁷Whoever touches those things shall be unclean; he shall wash his clothes and bathe in water, and be unclean until evening.

²⁸'But if she is cleansed of her discharge, then she shall count for herself seven days, and after that she shall be clean. ²⁹And on the eighth day she shall take for herself two turtledoves or two young pigeons, and bring them to the priest, to the door of the tabernacle of meeting. ³⁰Then the priest shall offer the one *as* a sin offering and the other *as* a burnt offering, and the priest shall make atonement for her before the LORD for the discharge of her uncleanness.

³¹'Thus you shall separate the children of Israel from their uncleanness, lest they die in their uncleanness when they defile My tabernacle that *is* among them. ³²This *is* the law for one who has a discharge, and *for him* who emits semen and is unclean thereby, ³³and for her who is indisposed because of her *customary* impurity, and for one who has a discharge, either man or woman, and for him who lies with her who is unclean.' "

> **15:31–33** In all of these instructions, God was showing the Israelites that they must have a profound reverence for holy things. He required them to be completely pure and did not allow them to come before Him when defiled by any uncleanness, whether ceremonial, natural, physical, or spiritual. Since God required personal purity and purity of heart, His rules were neither too stringent nor too minute.

The Day of Atonement

16 Now the LORD spoke to Moses after the death of the two sons of Aaron, when they offered *profane fire* before the LORD, and died; ²and the LORD said to Moses: "Tell Aaron your brother not to come at *just* any time into the Holy *Place* inside the veil, before the mercy seat which *is* on the ark, lest he die; for I will appear in the cloud above the mercy seat.

> **16:2 the mercy seat.** Meaning the "place of atonement," it referred to the throne of God between the cherubim, where God manifested Himself for the purpose of atonement.

³"Thus Aaron shall come into the Holy *Place*: with *the blood of* a young bull as a sin offering, and *of* a ram as a burnt offering. ⁴He shall put the holy linen tunic and the linen trousers on his body; he shall be girded with a linen sash, and with the linen turban he shall be attired. These *are* holy garments. Therefore he shall wash his body in water, and put them on. ⁵And he shall take from the congregation of the children of Israel two kids of the goats as a sin offering, and one ram as a burnt offering.

⁶"Aaron shall offer the bull as a sin offering, which *is* for himself, and make atonement for himself and for his house. ⁷He shall take the two goats and present them before the LORD *at* the door of the tabernacle of meeting. ⁸Then Aaron shall cast lots for the two goats: one lot for the LORD and the other lot for the scapegoat. ⁹And Aaron shall bring the goat on which the LORD's lot fell, and offer it *as* a sin offering. ¹⁰But the goat on which the lot fell to be the scapegoat shall be presented alive before the LORD, to make atonement upon it, *and* to let it go as the scapegoat into the wilderness.

> **16:8 the scapegoat.** This goat symbolized the substitutionary bearing of sin and its total removal, which was later fully accomplished by Jesus Christ.

¹¹"And Aaron shall bring the bull of the sin offering, which is for himself, and make atonement for himself and for his house, and shall kill the bull as the sin offering which *is* for himself. ¹²Then he shall take a censer full of burning coals of fire from the

altar before the LORD, with his hands full of sweet incense beaten fine, and bring *it* inside the veil. [13]And he shall put the incense on the fire before the LORD, that the cloud of incense may cover the mercy seat that *is* on the Testimony, lest he die. [14]He shall take some of the blood of the bull and sprinkle *it* with his finger on the mercy seat on the east *side*; and before the mercy seat he shall sprinkle some of the blood with his finger seven times.

16:12 inside the veil. The veil separated everyone from the holy and consuming presence of God. At the death of Christ, this veil in the temple tore from top to bottom, signifying access into God's presence through Jesus Christ (see Matt. 27:51).

[15]"Then he shall kill the goat of the sin offering, which *is* for the people, bring its blood inside the veil, do with that blood as he did with the blood of the bull, and sprinkle it on the mercy seat and before the mercy seat. [16]So he shall make atonement for the Holy *Place*, because of the uncleanness of the children of Israel, and because of their transgressions, for all their sins; and so he shall do for the tabernacle of meeting which remains among them in the midst of their uncleanness. [17]There shall be no man in the tabernacle of meeting when he goes

in to make atonement in the Holy *Place*, until he comes out, that he may make atonement for himself, for his household, and for all the assembly of Israel. [18]And he shall go out to the altar that *is* before the LORD, and make atonement for it, and shall take some of the blood of the bull and some of the blood of the goat, and put it on the horns of the altar all around. [19]Then he shall sprinkle some of the blood on it with his finger seven times, cleanse it, and consecrate it from the uncleanness of the children of Israel.

[20]"And when he has made an end of atoning for the Holy *Place*, the tabernacle of meeting, and the altar, he shall bring the live goat. [21]Aaron shall lay both his hands on the head of the live goat, confess over it all the iniquities of the children of Israel, and all their transgressions, concerning all their sins, putting them on the head of the goat, and shall send *it* away into the wilderness by the hand of a suitable man. [22]The goat shall bear on itself all their iniquities to an uninhabited land; and he shall release the goat in the wilderness.

[23]"Then Aaron shall come into the tabernacle of meeting, shall take off the linen garments which he put on when he went into the Holy *Place*, and shall leave them there. [24]And he shall wash his body with

What does the term "type of Christ" mean when used to describe someone in the Old Testament?

Certain persons and practices recorded in the Old Testament serve as hints, clues and pre-illustrations of what Jesus Christ would accomplish by his life, death, and resurrection. In most cases, the similarities or parallels are pointed out in the New Testament. The following people are some of those mentioned as representing, in a narrow way, what Christ accomplished perfectly: (1) Adam (Romans 5:14; 1 Corinthians 15:45); (2) Abel (Genesis 4:8,10; Hebrews 12:24); (3) Aaron (Exodus 28:1; Hebrews 5:4,5; 9:7, 24); (4) David (2 Samuel 8:15; Philippians 2:9); (5) Jonah (Jonah 1:17; Matthew 12:40); (6) Melchizedek (Genesis 14:18–20; Hebrews 7:1–17); (7) Moses (Numbers 12:7; Hebrews 3:2); (8) Noah (Genesis 5:29; 2 Corinthians 1:5); (9) Samson (Judges 16:30; Colossians 2:14–15); (10) Solomon (2 Samuel 7:12,13; 1 Peter 2:5).

The following events and practices also prefigure Christ: (1) Ark (Genesis 7:16; 1 Peter 3:20,21); (2) Atonement sacrifices (Leviticus 16:15,16; Hebrews 9:12,24); (3) Brazen serpent (Numbers 21:9; John 3:14,15); (4) Mercy seat (Exodus 25:17–22; Romans 3:25; Hebrews 4:16); (5) Passover lamb (Exodus 12:3–6,46; John 19:36; 1 Corinthians 5:7); (6) Red heifer (Leviticus 3:1; Ephesians 2:14,16); (7) Rock of Horeb (Exodus 17:6; 1 Corinthians 10:4); (8) Scapegoat (Leviticus 16:20–22); (9) Tabernacle (Exodus 40:2,34; Hebrews 9:11; Colossians 2:9); (10) Veil of the tabernacle (Exodus 40:21; Hebrews 10:20).

water in a holy place, put on his garments, come out and offer his burnt offering and the burnt offering of the people, and make atonement for himself and for the people. ²⁵The fat of the sin offering he shall burn on the altar. ²⁶And he who released the goat as the scapegoat shall wash his clothes and bathe his body in water, and afterward he may come into the camp. ²⁷The bull *for* the sin offering and the goat *for* the sin offering, whose blood was brought in to make atonement in the Holy *Place*, shall be carried outside the camp. And they shall burn in the fire their skins, their flesh, and their offal. ²⁸Then he who burns them shall wash his clothes and bathe his body in water, and afterward he may come into the camp.

²⁹"*This* shall be a statute forever for you: In the seventh month, on the tenth *day* of the month, you shall afflict your souls, and do no work at all, *whether* a native of your own country or a stranger who dwells among you. ³⁰For on that day *the priest* shall make atonement for you, to cleanse you, *that* you may be clean from all your sins before the LORD. ³¹It *is* a sabbath of solemn rest for you, and you shall afflict your souls. *It is* a statute forever. ³²And the priest, who is anointed and consecrated to minister as priest in his father's place, shall make atonement, and put on the linen clothes, the holy garments; ³³then he shall make atonement for the Holy Sanctuary,ᵃ and he shall make atonement for the tabernacle of meeting and for the altar, and he shall make atonement for the priests and for all the people of the assembly. ³⁴This shall be an everlasting statute for you, to make atonement for the children of Israel, for all their sins, once a year." And he did as the LORD commanded Moses.

The Sanctity of Blood

17 And the LORD spoke to Moses, saying, ²"Speak to Aaron, to his sons, and to all the children of Israel, and say to them, 'This *is* the thing which the LORD has commanded, saying: ³"Whatever man of the house of Israel who kills an ox or lamb or goat in the camp, or who kills *it* outside the camp, ⁴and does not bring it to the door of the tabernacle of meeting to offer an offering to the LORD before the tabernacle of the LORD, the guilt of bloodshed shall be imputed to that man. He has shed blood; and that man shall be cut off from among his people, ⁵to the end that the children of Israel may bring their sacrifices which they offer in the open field, that they may bring them to the LORD at the door of the tabernacle of meeting, to the priest, and offer them *as* peace offerings to the LORD. ⁶And the priest shall sprinkle the blood on the altar of the LORD *at* the door of the tabernacle of meeting, and burn the fat for a sweet aroma to the LORD. ⁷They shall no more offer their sacrifices to demons, after whom they have played the harlot. This shall be a statute forever for them throughout their generations." '

⁸"Also you shall say to them: 'Whatever man of the house of Israel, or of the strangers who dwell among you, who offers a burnt offering or sacrifice, ⁹and does not bring it to the door of the tabernacle of meeting, to offer it to the LORD, that man shall be cut off from among his people.

¹⁰And whatever man of the house of Israel, or of the strangers who dwell among you, who eats any blood, I will set My face against that person who eats blood, and will cut him off from among his people. ¹¹For the life of the flesh *is* in the blood, and I have given it to you upon the altar to

---

16:1–34 This section describes the Day of Atonement, an annual sacrifice to cover the sins of the nation, both corporately and individually, for those sins that remained unacknowledged and therefore without specific forgiveness. This special, inclusive sacrifice was the holiest of all Israel's festivals and was designed to cover all unforgiven sins.

17:11 life of the flesh *is* in the blood. Because blood carries life-sustaining elements to all parts of the body, it therefore represents the essence of life. Conversely, the shedding of blood represents death. **blood *that* makes atonement.** Shed blood from a substitute atones for, or covers, the sinner, who is then allowed to live.

16:33 ᵃThat is, the Most Holy Place

make atonement for your souls; for it *is* the blood *that* makes atonement for the soul.' [12]Therefore I said to the children of Israel, 'No one among you shall eat blood, nor shall any stranger who dwells among you eat blood.'

[13]"Whatever man of the children of Israel, or of the strangers who dwell among you, who hunts and catches any animal or bird that may be eaten, he shall pour out its blood and cover it with dust; [14]for *it is* the life of all flesh. Its blood sustains its life. Therefore I said to the children of Israel, 'You shall not eat the blood of any flesh, for the life of all flesh is its blood. Whoever eats it shall be cut off.'

[15]"And every person who eats what died *naturally* or what was torn *by beasts,* *whether he is* a native of your own country or a stranger, he shall both wash his clothes and bathe in water, and be unclean until evening. Then he shall be clean. [16]But if he does not wash *them* or bathe his body, then he shall bear his guilt."

Laws of Sexual Morality

18 Then the LORD spoke to Moses, saying, [2]"Speak to the children of Israel, and say to them: 'I am the LORD your God. [3]According to the doings of the land of Egypt, where you dwelt, you shall not do; and according to the doings of the land of Canaan, where I am bringing you, you shall not do; nor shall you walk in their ordinances. [4]You shall observe My judgments and keep My ordinances, to walk in them: I *am* the LORD your God. [5]You shall therefore keep My statutes and My judgments, which if a man does, he shall live by them: I *am* the LORD.

> **18:5 if a man does, he shall live by them.** Special blessing was promised to the Israelites if they were obedient to God's law. This promise can be clearly seen in their history, for the times when they enjoyed pure religion, they were blessed with national prosperity. This promise also relates to spiritual life; although obedience does not save from sin and hell, it does mark those who are saved.

[6]'None of you shall approach anyone who is near of kin to him, to uncover his nakedness: I *am* the LORD. [7]The nakedness of your father or the nakedness of your moth-er you shall not uncover. She *is* your mother; you shall not uncover her nakedness. [8]The nakedness of your father's wife you shall not uncover; it *is* your father's nakedness. [9]The nakedness of your sister, the daughter of your father, or the daughter of your mother, *whether* born at home or elsewhere, their nakedness you shall not uncover. [10]The nakedness of your son's daughter or your daughter's daughter, their nakedness you shall not uncover; for theirs *is* your own nakedness. [11]The nakedness of your father's wife's daughter, begotten by your father—she *is* your sister—you shall not uncover her nakedness. [12]You shall not uncover the nakedness of your father's sister; she *is* near of kin to your father. [13]You shall not uncover the nakedness of your mother's sister, for she *is* near of kin to your mother. [14]You shall not uncover the nakedness of your father's brother. You shall not approach his wife; she *is* your aunt. [15]You shall not uncover the nakedness of your daughter-in-law—she *is* your son's wife—you shall not uncover her nakedness. [16]You shall not uncover the nakedness of your brother's wife; it *is* your brother's nakedness. [17]You shall not uncover the nakedness of a woman and her daughter, nor shall you take her son's daughter or her daughter's daughter, to uncover her nakedness. They *are* near of kin to her. It *is* wickedness. [18]Nor shall you take a woman as a rival to her sister, to uncover her nakedness while the other is alive.

[19]'Also you shall not approach a woman to uncover her nakedness as long as she is in her *customary* impurity. [20]Moreover you shall not lie carnally with your neighbor's wife, to defile yourself with her. [21]And you shall not let any of your descendants pass through *the fire* to Molech, nor shall you profane the name of your God: I *am* the LORD. [22]You shall not lie with a male as with a woman. It *is* an abomination. [23]Nor shall you mate with any animal, to defile yourself with it. Nor shall any woman stand before an animal to mate with it. It *is* perversion.

> **18:22 not lie with a male.** This command outlaws all homosexuality (see 20:13; Rom. 1:27; 1 Cor. 6:9; 1 Tim. 1:10).

²⁴'Do not defile yourselves with any of these things; for by all these the nations are defiled, which I am casting out before you. ²⁵For the land is defiled; therefore I visit the punishment of its iniquity upon it, and the land vomits out its inhabitants. ²⁶You shall therefore keep My statutes and My judgments, and shall not commit *any* of these abominations, *either* any of your own nation or any stranger who dwells among you ²⁷(for all these abominations the men of the land have done, who *were* before you, and thus the land is defiled), ²⁸lest the land vomit you out also when you defile it, as it vomited out the nations that *were* before you. ²⁹For whoever commits any of these abominations, the persons who commit *them* shall be cut off from among their people.

³⁰'Therefore you shall keep My ordinance, so that *you* do not commit *any* of these abominable customs which were committed before you, and that you do not defile yourselves by them: I *am* the LORD your God.' "

Moral and Ceremonial Laws

19 And the LORD spoke to Moses, saying, ²"Speak to all the congregation of the children of Israel, and say to them: 'You shall be holy, for I the LORD your God *am* holy.

> **19:2 I the LORD your God *am* holy.** This statement gives the reason for holy living among God's people and is the central theme in Leviticus. Israel was called to be a holy nation (set apart), and the holy character of God was their model to follow.

³'Every one of you shall revere his mother and his father, and keep My Sabbaths: I *am* the LORD your God.

⁴'Do not turn to idols, nor make for yourselves molded gods: I *am* the LORD your God.

⁵'And if you offer a sacrifice of a peace offering to the LORD, you shall offer it of your own free will. ⁶It shall be eaten the same day you offer *it*, and on the next day. And if any remains until the third day, it shall be burned in the fire. ⁷And if it is eaten at all on the third day, it *is* an abomination. It shall not be accepted. ⁸Therefore *everyone* who eats it shall bear his iniquity, because he has profaned the hallowed *offering* of the

LORD; and that person shall be cut off from his people.

⁹'When you reap the harvest of your land, you shall not wholly reap the corners of your field, nor shall you gather the gleanings of your harvest. ¹⁰And you shall not glean your vineyard, nor shall you gather *every* grape of your vineyard; you shall leave them for the poor and the stranger: I *am* the LORD your God.

¹¹'You shall not steal, nor deal falsely, nor lie to one another. ¹²And you shall not swear by My name falsely, nor shall you profane the name of your God: I *am* the LORD.

¹³'You shall not cheat your neighbor, nor rob *him*. The wages of him who is hired shall not remain with you all night until morning. ¹⁴You shall not curse the deaf, nor put a stumbling block before the blind, but shall fear your God: I *am* the LORD.

¹⁵'You shall do no injustice in judgment. You shall not be partial to the poor, nor honor the person of the mighty. In righteousness you shall judge your neighbor. ¹⁶You shall not go about *as* a talebearer among your people; nor shall you take a stand against the life of your neighbor: I *am* the LORD.

¹⁷'You shall not hate your brother in your heart. You shall surely rebuke your neighbor, and not bear sin because of him. ¹⁸You shall not take vengeance, nor bear any grudge against the children of your people, but you shall love your neighbor as yourself: I *am* the LORD.

¹⁹'You shall keep My statutes. You shall not let your livestock breed with another kind. You shall not sow your field with mixed seed. Nor shall a garment of mixed linen and wool come upon you.

²⁰'Whoever lies carnally with a woman who *is* betrothed to a man as a concubine, and who has not at all been redeemed nor given her freedom, for this there shall be scourging; *but* they shall not be put to death, because she was not free. ²¹And he shall bring his trespass offering to the LORD, to the door of the tabernacle of meeting, a ram as a trespass offering. ²²The priest shall make atonement for him with the ram of the trespass offering before the LORD for his sin which he has committed. And the sin which he has committed shall be forgiven him.

²³'When you come into the land, and have planted all kinds of trees for food, then you shall count their fruit as uncircumcised. Three years it shall be as uncircumcised to you. *It* shall not be eaten. ²⁴But in the fourth year all its fruit shall be holy, a praise to the LORD. ²⁵And in the fifth year you may eat its fruit, that it may yield to you its increase: I *am* the LORD your God.

²⁶'You shall not eat *anything* with the blood, nor shall you practice divination or soothsaying. ²⁷You shall not shave around the sides of your head, nor shall you disfigure the edges of your beard. ²⁸You shall not make any cuttings in your flesh for the dead, nor tattoo any marks on you: I *am* the LORD.

> **19:27,28** The pagan practices described here were associated with idolatry. Making deep gashes on the face, arms, and legs in times of grief was a pagan mark of respect for the dead and an offering to the gods. Tattoos were connected to names of idols and were thus permanent signs of idolatry.

²⁹'Do not prostitute your daughter, to cause her to be a harlot, lest the land fall into harlotry, and the land become full of wickedness.

³⁰'You shall keep My Sabbaths and reverence My sanctuary: I *am* the LORD.

³¹'Give no regard to mediums and familiar spirits; do not seek after them, to be defiled by them: I *am* the LORD your God.

³²'You shall rise before the gray headed and honor the presence of an old man, and fear your God: I *am* the LORD.

³³'And if a stranger dwells with you in your land, you shall not mistreat him. ³⁴The stranger who dwells among you shall be to you as one born among you, and you shall love him as yourself; for you were strangers in the land of Egypt: I *am* the LORD your God.

³⁵'You shall do no injustice in judgment, in measurement of length, weight, or volume. ³⁶You shall have honest scales, honest weights, an honest ephah, and an honest hin: I *am* the LORD your God, who brought you out of the land of Egypt.

³⁷'Therefore you shall observe all My statutes and all My judgments, and perform them: I *am* the LORD.' "

Penalties for Breaking the Law

20 Then the LORD spoke to Moses, saying, ²"Again, you shall say to the children of Israel: 'Whoever of the children of Israel, or of the strangers who dwell in Israel, who gives *any* of his descendants to Molech, he shall surely be put to death. The people of the land shall stone him with stones. ³I will set My face against that man, and will cut him off from his people, because he has given *some* of his descendants to Molech, to defile My sanctuary and profane My holy name. ⁴And if the people of the land should in any way hide their eyes from the man, when he gives *some* of his descendants to Molech, and they do not kill him, ⁵then I will set My face against that man and against his family; and I will cut him off from his people, and all who prostitute themselves with him to commit harlotry with Molech.

> **20:2 gives *any* of his descendants to Molech.** Molech, the Ammonite god of the people surrounding Israel, required human sacrifices, especially child sacrifices.

⁶'And the person who turns to mediums and familiar spirits, to prostitute himself with them, I will set My face against that person and cut him off from his people. ⁷Consecrate yourselves therefore, and be holy, for I *am* the LORD your God. ⁸And you shall keep My statutes, and perform them: I *am* the LORD who sanctifies you.

⁹'For everyone who curses his father or his mother shall surely be put to death. He has cursed his father or his mother. His blood *shall be* upon him.

¹⁰'The man who commits adultery with *another* man's wife, *he* who commits adultery with his neighbor's wife, the adulterer and the adulteress, shall surely be put to death. ¹¹The man who lies with his father's wife has uncovered his father's nakedness; both of them shall surely be put to death. Their blood *shall be* upon them. ¹²If a man lies with his daughter-in-law, both of them shall surely be put to death. They have committed perversion. Their blood *shall be* upon them. ¹³If a man lies with a male as he lies with a woman, both of them have committed an abomination. They shall surely be put to death. Their blood *shall be* upon

them. ¹⁴If a man marries a woman and her mother, it *is* wickedness. They shall be burned with fire, both he and they, that there may be no wickedness among you. ¹⁵If a man mates with an animal, he shall surely be put to death, and you shall kill the animal. ¹⁶If a woman approaches any animal and mates with it, you shall kill the woman and the animal. They shall surely be put to death. Their blood *is* upon them.

¹⁷'If a man takes his sister, his father's daughter or his mother's daughter, and sees her nakedness and she sees his nakedness, it *is* a wicked thing. And they shall be cut off in the sight of their people. He has uncovered his sister's nakedness. He shall bear his guilt. ¹⁸If a man lies with a woman during her sickness and uncovers her nakedness, he has exposed her flow, and she has uncovered the flow of her blood. Both of them shall be cut off from their people.

¹⁹'You shall not uncover the nakedness of your mother's sister nor of your father's sister, for that would uncover his near of kin. They shall bear their guilt. ²⁰If a man lies with his uncle's wife, he has uncovered his uncle's nakedness. They shall bear their sin; they shall die childless. ²¹If a man takes his brother's wife, it *is* an unclean thing. He has uncovered his brother's nakedness. They shall be childless.

²²'You shall therefore keep all My statutes and all My judgments, and perform them, that the land where I am bringing you to dwell may not vomit you out. ²³And you shall not walk in the statutes of the nation which I am casting out before you; for they commit all these things, and therefore I abhor them. ²⁴But I have said to you, "You shall inherit their land, and I will give it to you to possess, a land flowing with milk and honey." I *am* the LORD your God, who has separated you from the peoples. ²⁵You shall therefore distinguish between clean animals and unclean, between unclean birds and clean, and you shall not make yourselves abominable by beast or by bird,

or by any kind of living thing that creeps on the ground, which I have separated from you as unclean. ²⁶And you shall be holy to Me, for I the LORD *am* holy, and have separated you from the peoples, that you should be Mine.

²⁷'A man or a woman who is a medium, or who has familiar spirits, shall surely be put to death; they shall stone them with stones. Their blood *shall be* upon them.' "

Regulations for Conduct of Priests

21 And the LORD said to Moses, "Speak to the priests, the sons of Aaron, and say to them: 'None shall defile himself for the dead among his people, ²except for his relatives who are nearest to him: his mother, his father, his son, his daughter, and his brother; ³also his virgin sister who is near to him, who has had no husband, for her he may defile himself. ⁴*Otherwise* he shall not defile himself, *being* a chief man among his people, to profane himself.

⁵'They shall not make any bald *place* on their heads, nor shall they shave the edges of their beards nor make any cuttings in their flesh. ⁶They shall be holy to their God and not profane the name of their God, for they offer the offerings of the LORD made by fire, *and* the bread of their God; therefore they shall be holy. ⁷They shall not take a wife *who is* a harlot or a defiled woman, nor shall they take a woman divorced from her husband; for *the priest*ᵃ is holy to his God. ⁸Therefore you shall consecrate him, for he offers the bread of your God. He shall be holy to you, for I the LORD, who sanctify you, *am* holy. ⁹The daughter of any priest, if she profanes herself by playing the harlot, she profanes her father. She shall be burned with fire.

21:7,8 A priest was allowed to marry, but only in the purest circumstances. The priests were to be living models of the holy union between God and His people.

¹⁰*He who is* the high priest among his brethren, on whose head the anointing oil was poured and who is consecrated to wear the garments, shall not uncover his head nor tear his clothes; ¹¹nor shall he go near

20:22 may not vomit you out. God warned Israel repeatedly that remaining in the land required obedience to His laws.

21:7 ᵃLiterally *he*

any dead body, nor defile himself for his father or his mother; [12]nor shall he go out of the sanctuary, nor profane the sanctuary of his God; for the consecration of the anointing oil of his God *is* upon him: I *am* the LORD. [13]And he shall take a wife in her virginity. [14]A widow or a divorced woman or a defiled woman *or* a harlot—these he shall not marry; but he shall take a virgin of his own people as wife. [15]Nor shall he profane his posterity among his people, for I the LORD sanctify him.' "

21:10-15 The standards for the High-Priest were the highest and most holy because of his utmost sacred responsibility.

[16]And the LORD spoke to Moses, saying, [17]"Speak to Aaron, saying: 'No man of your descendants in *succeeding* generations, who has *any* defect, may approach to offer the bread of his God. [18]For any man who has a defect shall not approach: a man blind or lame, who has a marred *face* or any *limb* too long, [19]a man who has a broken foot or broken hand, [20]or is a hunchback or a dwarf, or *a man* who has a defect in his eye, or eczema or scab, or is a eunuch. [21]No man of the descendants of Aaron the priest, who has a defect, shall come near to offer the offerings made by fire to the LORD. He has a defect; he shall not come near to offer the bread of his God. [22]He may eat the bread of his God, *both* the most holy and the holy; [23]only he shall not go near the veil or approach the altar, because he has a defect, lest he profane My sanctuaries; for I the LORD sanctify them.' "

[24]And Moses told *it* to Aaron and his sons, and to all the children of Israel.

22 Then the LORD spoke to Moses, saying, [2]"Speak to Aaron and his sons, that they separate themselves from the holy things of the children of Israel, and that they do not profane My holy name *by* what they dedicate to Me: I *am* the LORD. [3]Say to them: 'Whoever of all your descendants throughout your generations, who goes near the holy things which the children of Israel dedicate to the LORD, while he has uncleanness upon him, that person shall be cut off from My presence: I *am* the LORD.

[4]"Whatever man of the descendants of Aaron, who *is* a leper or has a discharge, shall not eat the holy offerings until he is

To what degree can believers today submit to the rules and regulations God gave the people of Israel?

Believers' understanding of the Old Testament must be shaped by Jesus and the New Testament. Jesus talked about this when he said, "Do not think I came to destroy the Law or the Prophets. I did not come to destroy but to fulfill" (Matthew 5:17,18).

In relation to the Old Testament ceremonial law, the Levitical priesthood and the sanctuary, the New Testament records a number of instances of how this fulfillment by Jesus worked itself out in individual understanding and practice (Matthew 27:51; Acts 10:1–16, Colossians 2:16,17; 1 Peter 2:9; Revelation 1:6; 5:10; 20:6). The very institution of the New Covenant in and by Jesus (Matthew 26:28; 2 Corinthians 3:6–18; Hebrews 7–10) places the Old Testament in a new light.

Rather than try to practice the old ceremonies or look for some deeper spiritual significance in them, the focus should be on the holy and divine character of God behind them. This may partly be the reason why explanations that Moses often gave in the prescriptions for cleanness offer greater insight into the mind of God than do the ceremonies themselves. The spiritual principles in which the rituals were rooted are timeless because they reflect the nature of God.

The most profitable study in Leviticus focuses on the truths contained in the understanding of sin, guilt, substitutionary death, and atonement by noting features that are not explained or illustrated elsewhere in Old Testament Scripture. Later Old Testament authors, and especially New Testament writers, build on the basic understanding of these matters provided by Leviticus. The sacrificial features of Leviticus point to their ultimate, one-time fulfillment in the substitutionary death of Jesus Christ (Hebrews 9:11–22).

clean. And whoever touches anything made unclean *by* a corpse, or a man who has had an emission of semen, [5]or whoever touches any creeping thing by which he would be made unclean, or any person by whom he would become unclean, whatever his uncleanness may be— [6]the person who has touched any such thing shall be unclean until evening, and shall not eat the holy *offerings* unless he washes his body with water. [7]And when the sun goes down he shall be clean; and afterward he may eat the holy *offerings*, because it *is* his food. [8]Whatever dies *naturally* or is torn *by beasts* he shall not eat, to defile himself with it: I *am* the LORD.

[9]"They shall therefore keep My ordinance, lest they bear sin for it and die thereby, if they profane it: I the LORD sanctify them.

[10]"No outsider shall eat the holy *offering*; one who dwells with the priest, or a hired servant, shall not eat the holy thing. [11]But if the priest buys a person with his money, he may eat it; and one who is born in his house may eat his food. [12]If the priest's daughter is married to an outsider, she may not eat of the holy offerings. [13]But if the priest's daughter is a widow or divorced, and has no child, and has returned to her father's house as in her youth, she may eat her father's food; but no outsider shall eat it.

[14]And if a man eats the holy *offering* unintentionally, then he shall restore a holy *offering* to the priest, and add one-fifth to it. [15]They shall not profane the holy *offerings* of the children of Israel, which they offer to the LORD, [16]or allow them to bear the guilt of trespass when they eat their holy *offerings*; for I the LORD sanctify them.' "

Offerings Accepted and Not Accepted

[17]And the LORD spoke to Moses, saying, [18]"Speak to Aaron and his sons, and to all the children of Israel, and say to them: 'Whatever man of the house of Israel, or of the strangers in Israel, who offers his sacrifice for any of his vows or for any of his freewill offerings, which they offer to the LORD as a burnt offering— [19]*you shall offer* of your own free will a male without blemish from the cattle, from the sheep, or from the goats. [20]Whatever has a defect, you shall

not offer, for it shall not be acceptable on your behalf. [21]And whoever offers a sacrifice of a peace offering to the LORD, to fulfill *his* vow, or a freewill offering from the cattle or the sheep, it must be perfect to be accepted; there shall be no defect in it. [22]Those *that are* blind or broken or maimed, or have an ulcer or eczema or scabs, you shall not offer to the LORD, nor make an offering by fire of them on the altar to the LORD. [23]Either a bull or a lamb that has any limb too long or too short you may offer *as* a freewill offering, but for a vow it shall not be accepted.

[24]"You shall not offer to the LORD what is bruised or crushed, or torn or cut; nor shall you make *any offering of them* in your land. [25]Nor from a foreigner's hand shall you offer any of these as the bread of your God, because their corruption *is* in them, *and* defects *are* in them. They shall not be accepted on your behalf.' "

[26]And the LORD spoke to Moses, saying: [27]"When a bull or a sheep or a goat is born, it shall be seven days with its mother; and from the eighth day and thereafter it shall be accepted as an offering made by fire to the LORD. [28]*Whether it is* a cow or ewe, do not kill both her and her young on the same day. [29]And when you offer a sacrifice of thanksgiving to the LORD, offer *it* of your own free will. [30]On the same day it shall be eaten; you shall leave none of it until morning: I *am* the LORD.

[31]"Therefore you shall keep My commandments, and perform them: I *am* the LORD. [32]You shall not profane My holy name, but I will be hallowed among the children of Israel. I *am* the LORD who sanctifies you, [33]who brought you out of the land of Egypt, to be your God: I *am* the LORD."

Feasts of the LORD

23 And the LORD spoke to Moses, saying, [2]"Speak to the children of Israel, and say to them: 'The feasts of the LORD,

---

23:2 proclaim *to be* holy convocations. These festivals did not involve gatherings of the whole nation. Only the feasts of (1) Unleavened Bread; (2) Weeks; and (3) Tabernacles required that all males gather in Jerusalem.

which you shall proclaim *to be* holy convocations, these *are* My feasts.

The Sabbath

³'Six days shall work be done, but the seventh day *is* a Sabbath of solemn rest, a holy convocation. You shall do no work *on it;* it *is* the Sabbath of the LORD in all your dwellings.

The Passover and Unleavened Bread

⁴'These *are* the feasts of the LORD, holy convocations which you shall proclaim at their appointed times. ⁵On the fourteenth *day* of the first month at twilight *is* the LORD's Passover. ⁶And on the fifteenth day of the same month *is* the Feast of Unleavened Bread to the LORD; seven days you must eat unleavened bread. ⁷On the first day you shall have a holy convocation; you shall do no customary work on it. ⁸But you shall offer an offering made by fire to the LORD for seven days. The seventh day *shall be* a holy convocation; you shall do no customary work *on it.'* "

The Feast of Firstfruits

⁹And the LORD spoke to Moses, saying, ¹⁰"Speak to the children of Israel, and say to them: 'When you come into the land which I give to you, and reap its harvest, then you shall bring a sheaf of the firstfruits of your harvest to the priest. ¹¹He shall wave the

sheaf before the LORD, to be accepted on your behalf; on the day after the Sabbath the priest shall wave it. ¹²And you shall offer on that day, when you wave the sheaf, a male lamb of the first year, without blemish, as a burnt offering to the LORD. ¹³Its grain offering *shall be* two-tenths *of an ephah* of fine flour mixed with oil, an offering made by fire to the LORD, for a sweet aroma; and its drink offering *shall be* of wine, one-fourth of a hin. ¹⁴You shall eat neither bread nor parched grain nor fresh grain until the same day that you have brought an offering to your God; *it shall be* a statute forever throughout your generations in all your dwellings.

23:9–14 the firstfruits of your harvest. This festival involved presenting to the Lord a sheaf of barley, accompanied by burnt, grain, and drink offerings. Firstfruits symbolized the consecration of the whole harvest to God and was a pledge of the whole harvest to come.

The Feast of Weeks

¹⁵'And you shall count for yourselves from the day after the Sabbath, from the day that you brought the sheaf of the wave offering: seven Sabbaths shall be completed. ¹⁶Count fifty days to the day after the seventh Sabbath; then you shall offer a new grain offering to the LORD. ¹⁷You shall bring from your dwellings two wave *loaves* of

JEWISH FEASTS

Feast of	Month on Jewish Calendar	Day	Corresponding Month	References
Passover	Nisan	14	Mar.-Apr.	Exodus 12:1–14; Matthew 26:17–20
*Unleavened Bread	Nisan	15–21	Mar.-Apr.	Exodus 12:15–20
Firstfruits	Nisan	16	Mar.-Apr.	Leviticus 23:9–14
	or Sivan	6	May-June	Numbers 28:26
*Pentecost (Harvest or Weeks)	Sivan	6 (50 days after barley harvest)	May-June	Deuteronomy 16:9–12; Acts 2:1
Trumpets, Rosh Hashanah	Tishri	1, 2	Sept.-Oct.	Numbers 29:1–6
Day of Atonement, Yom Kippur	Tishri	10	Sept.-Oct.	Leviticus 23:26–32; Hebrews 9:7
*Tabernacles (Booths or Ingathering)	Tishri	15–22	Sept.-Oct.	Nehemiah 8:13–18; John 7:2
Dedication (Lights), Hanukkah	Chislev	25 (8 days)	Nov.-Dec.	John 10:22
Purim (Lots)	Adar	14, 15	Feb.-Mar.	Esther 9:18–32

*The three major feasts for which all males of Israel were required to travel to the temple in Jerusalem (Ex. 23:14–19).

two-tenths *of an ephah*. They shall be of fine flour; they shall be baked with leaven. *They are* the firstfruits to the LORD. [18]And you shall offer with the bread seven lambs of the first year, without blemish, one young bull, and two rams. They shall be *as* a burnt offering to the LORD, with their grain offering and their drink offerings, an offering made by fire for a sweet aroma to the LORD. [19]Then you shall sacrifice one kid of the goats as a sin offering, and two male lambs of the first year as a sacrifice of a peace offering. [20]The priest shall wave them with the bread of the firstfruits *as* a wave offering before the LORD, with the two lambs. They shall be holy to the LORD for the priest. [21]And you shall proclaim on the same day *that* it is a holy convocation to you. You shall do no customary work *on it. It shall be* a statute forever in all your dwellings throughout your generations.

[22]"When you reap the harvest of your land, you shall not wholly reap the corners of your field when you reap, nor shall you gather any gleaning from your harvest. You shall leave them for the poor and for the stranger: I *am* the LORD your God.' "

The Feast of Trumpets

[23]Then the LORD spoke to Moses, saying, [24]"Speak to the children of Israel, saying: 'In the seventh month, on the first *day* of the month, you shall have a sabbath-*rest*, a memorial of blowing of trumpets, a holy convocation. [25]You shall do no customary work *on it*; and you shall offer an offering made by fire to the LORD.' "

The Day of Atonement

[26]And the LORD spoke to Moses, saying: [27]"Also the tenth *day* of this seventh month

shall be the Day of Atonement. It shall be a holy convocation for you; you shall afflict your souls, and offer an offering made by fire to the LORD. [28]And you shall do no work on that same day, for it *is* the Day of Atonement, to make atonement for you before the LORD your God. [29]For any person who is not afflicted *in soul* on that same day shall be cut off from his people. [30]And any person who does any work on that same day, that person I will destroy from among his people. [31]You shall do no manner of work; *it shall be* a statute forever throughout your generations in all your dwellings. [32]It *shall be* to you a sabbath of *solemn* rest, and you shall afflict your souls; on the ninth *day* of the month at evening, from evening to evening, you shall celebrate your sabbath."

> **23:26–32 Day of Atonement.** The annual Day of Atonement provided for the forgiveness and cleansing of sin for the priests, the nation, and the tabernacle.

The Feast of Tabernacles

[33]Then the LORD spoke to Moses, saying, [34]"Speak to the children of Israel, saying: 'The fifteenth day of this seventh month *shall be* the Feast of Tabernacles *for* seven days to the LORD. [35]On the first day *there shall be* a holy convocation. You shall do no customary work *on it*. [36]For seven days you shall offer an offering made by fire to the LORD. On the eighth day you shall have a holy convocation, and you shall offer an offering made by fire to the LORD. It *is* a sacred assembly, *and* you shall do no customary work *on it*.

[37]'These *are* the feasts of the LORD which

CHRIST FULFILLS ISRAEL'S FEASTS

The Feasts (Leviticus 23)	Christ's Fulfillment
Passover (March/April)	Death of Christ (1 Corinthians 5:7)
Unleavened Bread (March/April)	Sinlessness of Christ (1 Corinthians 5:8)
Firstfruits (March/April)	Resurrection of Christ (1 Corinthians 15:23)
Pentecost (May/June)	Outpouring of Spirit of Christ (Acts 1:5; 2:4)
Trumpets (Sept./Oct.)	Israel's Regathering by Christ (Matthew 24:31)
Atonement (Sept./Oct.)	Substitutionary Sacrifice by Christ (Romans 11:26)
Tabernacles (Sept./Oct.)	Rest and Reunion with Christ (Zechariah 14:16–19)

you shall proclaim *to be* holy convocations, to offer an offering made by fire to the LORD, a burnt offering and a grain offering, a sacrifice and drink offerings, everything on its day— [38]besides the Sabbaths of the LORD, besides your gifts, besides all your vows, and besides all your freewill offerings which you give to the LORD.

[39]Also on the fifteenth day of the seventh month, when you have gathered in the fruit of the land, you shall keep the feast of the LORD *for* seven days; on the first day *there shall be* a sabbath-*rest,* and on the eighth day a sabbath-*rest.* [40]And you shall take for yourselves on the first day the fruit of beautiful trees, branches of palm trees, the boughs of leafy trees, and willows of the brook; and you shall rejoice before the LORD your God for seven days. [41]You shall keep it as a feast to the LORD for seven days in the year. *It shall be* a statute forever in your generations. You shall celebrate it in the seventh month. [42]You shall dwell in booths for seven days. All who are native Israelites shall dwell in booths, [43]that your generations may know that I made the children of Israel dwell in booths when I brought them out of the land of Egypt: I *am* the LORD your God.' "

> **23:33–43 Feast of Tabernacles.** This festival commemorated God's deliverance, protection, and provision during the wilderness wanderings. It was also known as the Feast of Booths and Feast of Ingathering. The people lived in booths or huts made from limbs to commemorate their wilderness experience.

[44]So Moses declared to the children of Israel the feasts of the LORD.

Care of the Tabernacle Lamps

24 Then the LORD spoke to Moses, saying: [2]"Command the children of Israel that they bring to you pure oil of pressed olives for the light, to make the lamps burn continually. [3]Outside the veil of the Testimony, in the tabernacle of meeting, Aaron shall be in charge of it from evening until morning before the LORD continually; *it shall be* a statute forever in your generations. [4]He shall be in charge of the lamps on the pure *gold* lampstand before the LORD continually.

The Bread of the Tabernacle

[5]"And you shall take fine flour and bake twelve cakes with it. Two-tenths *of an ephah* shall be in each cake. [6]You shall set them in two rows, six in a row, on the pure *gold* table before the LORD. [7]And you shall put pure frankincense on *each* row, that it may be on the bread for a memorial, an offering made by fire to the LORD. [8]Every Sabbath he shall set it in order before the LORD continually, *being taken* from the children of Israel by an everlasting covenant. [9]And it shall be for Aaron and his sons, and they shall eat it in a holy place; for it *is* most holy to him from the offerings of the LORD made by fire, by a perpetual statute."

The Penalty for Blasphemy

[10]Now the son of an Israelite woman, whose father *was* an Egyptian, went out among the children of Israel; and this Israelite *woman's* son and a man of Israel fought each other in the camp. [11]And the Israelite woman's son blasphemed the name *of the LORD* and cursed; and so they brought him to Moses. (His mother's name *was* Shelomith the daughter of Dibri, of the tribe of Dan.) [12]Then they put him in custody, that the mind of the LORD might be shown to them.

> **24:12 put him in custody.** Israel had no jails but had probably restrained this man in a pit until they could decide his punishment. Punishments were corporal, banishment, or death. After a punishment, the criminal tried to repay those whom he had violated.

[13]And the LORD spoke to Moses, saying, [14]"Take outside the camp him who has cursed; then let all who heard *him* lay their hands on his head, and let all the congregation stone him. [15]"Then you shall speak to the children of Israel, saying: 'Whoever curses his God shall bear his sin. [16]And whoever blasphemes the name of the LORD shall surely be put to death. All the congregation shall certainly stone him, the stranger as well as him who is born in the land. When he blasphemes the name *of the LORD,* he shall be put to death.

[17]'Whoever kills any man shall surely be put to death. [18]Whoever kills an animal shall make it good, animal for animal.

¹⁹'If a man causes disfigurement of his neighbor, as he has done, so shall it be done to him— ²⁰fracture for fracture, eye for eye, tooth for tooth; as he has caused disfigurement of a man, so shall it be done to him. ²¹And whoever kills an animal shall restore it; but whoever kills a man shall be put to death. ²²You shall have the same law for the stranger and for one from your own country; for I *am* the LORD your God.'"

²³Then Moses spoke to the children of Israel; and they took outside the camp him who had cursed, and stoned him with stones. So the children of Israel did as the LORD commanded Moses.

The Sabbath of the Seventh Year

25 And the LORD spoke to Moses on Mount Sinai, saying, ²"Speak to the children of Israel, and say to them: 'When you come into the land which I give you, then the land shall keep a sabbath to the LORD. ³Six years you shall sow your field, and six years you shall prune your vineyard, and gather its fruit; ⁴but in the seventh year there shall be a sabbath of solemn rest for the land, a sabbath to the LORD. You shall neither sow your field nor prune your vineyard. ⁵What grows of its own accord of your harvest you shall not reap, nor gather the grapes of your untended vine, *for* it is a year of rest for the land. ⁶And the sabbath *produce* of the land shall be food for you: for you, your male and female servants, your hired man, and the stranger who dwells with you, ⁷for your livestock and the beasts that *are* in your land—all its produce shall be for food.

25:1–7 This is intended to revitalize the land. The seventh year of rest would invigorate and replenish the nutrients in the soil. Whatever grew naturally was free for anyone to take.

The Year of Jubilee

⁸'And you shall count seven sabbaths of years for yourself, seven times seven years; and the time of the seven sabbaths of years shall be to you forty-nine years. ⁹Then you shall cause the trumpet of the Jubilee to sound on the tenth *day* of the seventh month; on the Day of Atonement you shall make the trumpet to sound throughout all your land. ¹⁰And you shall consecrate the fiftieth year, and proclaim liberty throughout *all* the land to all its inhabitants. It shall be a Jubilee for you; and each of you shall return to his possession, and each of you shall return to his family. ¹¹That fiftieth year shall be a Jubilee to you; in it you shall neither sow nor reap what grows of its own accord, nor gather *the grapes* of your untended vine. ¹²For it *is* the Jubilee; it shall be holy to you; you shall eat its produce from the field.

¹³'In this Year of Jubilee, each of you shall return to his possession. ¹⁴And if you sell anything to your neighbor or buy from your neighbor's hand, you shall not oppress one another. ¹⁵According to the number of years after the Jubilee you shall buy from your neighbor, and according to the number of years of crops he shall sell to you. ¹⁶According to the multitude of years you shall increase its price, and according to the fewer number of years you shall diminish its price; for he sells to you *according* to the number *of the years* of the crops. ¹⁷Therefore you shall not oppress one another, but you shall fear your God; for I *am* the LORD your God.

25:17 you shall not oppress one another. No one should take advantage of or abuse another person, because cruelty violates the very character of God. Penalties for crime were to be swift and exact.

Provisions for the Seventh Year

¹⁸'So you shall observe My statutes and keep My judgments, and perform them; and you will dwell in the land in safety. ¹⁹Then the land will yield its fruit, and you will eat your fill, and dwell there in safety.

²⁰'And if you say, "What shall we eat in the seventh year, since we shall not sow nor gather in our produce?" ²¹Then I will command My blessing on you in the sixth year, and it will bring forth produce enough for three years. ²²And you shall sow in the eighth year, and eat old produce until the ninth year; until its produce comes in, you shall eat *of* the old *harvest*.

Redemption of Property

²³'The land shall not be sold permanently, for the land *is* Mine; for you *are* strangers and sojourners with Me. ²⁴And in

all the land of your possession you shall grant redemption of the land.

> **25:23 the land *is* Mine.** God owns the earth and all that is in it. The people of Israel were only tenants on the land, by the Lord's grace. Therefore, ownership of property was temporary, not permanent.

25'If one of your brethren becomes poor, and has sold *some* of his possession, and if his redeeming relative comes to redeem it, then he may redeem what his brother sold. ²⁶Or if the man has no one to redeem it, but he himself becomes able to redeem it, ²⁷then let him count the years since its sale, and restore the remainder to the man to whom he sold it, that he may return to his possession. ²⁸But if he is not able to have *it* restored to himself, then what was sold shall remain in the hand of him who bought it until the Year of Jubilee; and in the Jubilee it shall be released, and he shall return to his possession.

²⁹'If a man sells a house in a walled city, then he may redeem it within a whole year after it is sold; *within* a full year he may redeem it. ³⁰But if it is not redeemed within the space of a full year, then the house in the walled city shall belong permanently to him who bought it, throughout his generations. It shall not be released in the Jubilee. ³¹However the houses of villages which have no wall around them shall be counted as the fields of the country. They may be redeemed, and they shall be released in the Jubilee. ³²Nevertheless the cities of the Levites, *and* the houses in the cities of their possession, the Levites may redeem at any time. ³³And if a man purchases a house from the Levites, then the house that was sold in the city of his possession shall be released in the Jubilee; for the houses in the cities of the Levites *are* their possession among the children of Israel. ³⁴But the field of the common-land of their cities may not be sold, for it *is* their perpetual possession.

Lending to the Poor

³⁵'If one of your brethren becomes poor, and falls into poverty among you, then you shall help him, like a stranger or a sojourner, that he may live with you. ³⁶Take no usury or interest from him; but fear your God, that your brother may live with you.

³⁷You shall not lend him your money for usury, nor lend him your food at a profit. ³⁸I *am* the LORD your God, who brought you out of the land of Egypt, to give you the land of Canaan *and* to be your God.

The Law Concerning Slavery

³⁹And if *one of* your brethren *who dwells* by you becomes poor, and sells himself to you, you shall not compel him to serve as a slave. ⁴⁰As a hired servant *and* a sojourner he shall be with you, *and* shall serve you until the Year of Jubilee. ⁴¹And *then* he shall depart from you—he and his children with him—and shall return to his own family. He shall return to the possession of his fathers. ⁴²For they *are* My servants, whom I brought out of the land of Egypt; they shall not be sold as slaves. ⁴³You shall not rule over him with rigor, but you shall fear your God. ⁴⁴And as for your male and female slaves whom you may have—from the nations that are around you, from them you may buy male and female slaves. ⁴⁵Moreover you may buy the children of the strangers who dwell among you, and their families who are with you, which they beget in your land; and they shall become your property. ⁴⁶And you may take them as an inheritance for your children after you, to inherit *them as* a possession; they shall be your permanent slaves. But regarding your brethren, the children of Israel, you shall not rule over one another with rigor.

⁴⁷'Now if a sojourner or stranger close to you becomes rich, and *one of* your brethren *who dwells* by him becomes poor, and sells himself to the stranger *or* sojourner close to you, or to a member of the stranger's family, ⁴⁸after he is sold he may be redeemed again. One of his brothers may redeem him; ⁴⁹or his uncle or his uncle's son may redeem him; or *anyone* who is near of kin to him in his family may redeem him; or if he is able he may redeem himself. ⁵⁰Thus he shall reckon with him who bought him: The price of his release shall be according to the number of years, from the year that he was sold to him until the Year of Jubilee; *it shall be* according to the time of a hired servant for him. ⁵¹If *there are* still many years *remaining*, according to them he shall repay the price of his redemption from the money with which he was bought. ⁵²And if

there remain but a few years until the Year of Jubilee, then he shall reckon with him, *and* according to his years he shall repay him the price of his redemption. ⁵³He shall be with him as a yearly hired servant, and he shall not rule with rigor over him in your sight. ⁵⁴And if he is not redeemed in these *years,* then he shall be released in the Year of Jubilee—he and his children with him. ⁵⁵For the children of Israel *are* servants to Me; they *are* My servants whom I brought out of the land of Egypt: I *am* the LORD your God.

25:8–55 The Year of Jubilee was a year of release from indebtedness and bondage. All prisoners and captives were set free, slaves were released, and debtors were absolved. All property reverted to original owners. This plan curbed inflation and gave new opportunities to people who had fallen on hard times.

Promise of Blessing and Retribution

26 'You shall not make idols for yourselves;
neither a carved image nor a *sacred* pillar shall you rear up for yourselves;
nor shall you set up an engraved stone in your land, to bow down to it;
for I *am* the LORD your God.
² You shall keep My Sabbaths and reverence My sanctuary:
I *am* the LORD.

³ 'If you walk in My statutes and keep My commandments, and perform them,
⁴ then I will give you rain in its season, the land shall yield its produce, and the trees of the field shall yield their fruit.
⁵ Your threshing shall last till the time of vintage, and the vintage shall last till the time of sowing;
you shall eat your bread to the full, and dwell in your land safely.
⁶ I will give peace in the land, and you shall lie down, and none will make *you* afraid;
I will rid the land of evil beasts, and the sword will not go through your land.
⁷ You will chase your enemies, and they shall fall by the sword before you.

⁸ Five of you shall chase a hundred, and a hundred of you shall put ten thousand to flight;
your enemies shall fall by the sword before you.

⁹ 'For I will look on you favorably and make you fruitful, multiply you and confirm My covenant with you.
¹⁰ You shall eat the old harvest, and clear out the old because of the new.
¹¹ I will set My tabernacle among you, and My soul shall not abhor you.
¹² I will walk among you and be your God, and you shall be My people.

26:12 your God...My people. This promises an intimate covenant relationship with the God of the universe.

¹³ I *am* the LORD your God, who brought you out of the land of Egypt, that *you* should not be their slaves;
I have broken the bands of your yoke and made you walk upright.

¹⁴ 'But if you do not obey Me, and do not observe all these commandments,
¹⁵ and if you despise My statutes, or if your soul abhors My judgments, so that you do not perform all My commandments, *but* break My covenant,

26:15 break My covenant. To disobey God's commandments was to break this conditional covenant. Unlike the covenant made with Abraham, that guaranteed blessings unconditionally, the blessings of the covenant of Mosaic law were contingent upon obedience.

¹⁶ I also will do this to you:
I will even appoint terror over you, wasting disease and fever which shall consume the eyes and cause sorrow of heart.
And you shall sow your seed in vain, for your enemies shall eat it.
¹⁷ I will set My face against you, and you shall be defeated by your enemies.
Those who hate you shall reign over you, and you shall flee when no one pursues you.

18 'And after all this, if you do not obey Me, then I will punish you seven times more for your sins.

19 I will break the pride of your power; I will make your heavens like iron and your earth like bronze.

20 And your strength shall be spent in vain; for your land shall not yield its produce, nor shall the trees of the land yield their fruit.

21 'Then, if you walk contrary to Me, and are not willing to obey Me, I will bring on you seven times more plagues, according to your sins.

22 I will also send wild beasts among you, which shall rob you of your children, destroy your livestock, and make you few in number; and your highways shall be desolate.

23 'And if by these things you are not reformed by Me, but walk contrary to Me,

24 then I also will walk contrary to you, and I will punish you yet seven times for your sins.

25 And I will bring a sword against you that will execute the vengeance of the covenant; when you are gathered together within your cities I will send pestilence among you; and you shall be delivered into the hand of the enemy.

26 When I have cut off your supply of bread, ten women shall bake your bread in one oven, and they shall bring back your bread by weight, and you shall eat and not be satisfied.

27 'And after all this, if you do not obey Me, but walk contrary to Me,

28 then I also will walk contrary to you in fury; and I, even I, will chastise you seven times for your sins.

29 You shall eat the flesh of your sons, and you shall eat the flesh of your daughters.

30 I will destroy your high places, cut down your incense altars, and cast your carcasses on the lifeless forms of your idols; and My soul shall abhor you.

31 I will lay your cities waste and bring your sanctuaries to desolation, and I will not smell the fragrance of your sweet aromas.

32 I will bring the land to desolation, and your enemies who dwell in it shall be astonished at it.

33 I will scatter you among the nations and draw out a sword after you; your land shall be desolate and your cities waste.

34 Then the land shall enjoy its sabbaths as long as it lies desolate and you *are* in your enemies' land; then the land shall rest and enjoy its sabbaths.

35 As long as *it* lies desolate it shall rest— for the time it did not rest on your sabbaths when you dwelt in it.

26:31–35 All of this was fulfilled in the terrible invasion of the northern kingdom of Israel in 722 B.C. by the Assyrians and the destruction of the southern kingdom of Judah in 605–586 B.C. by the Babylonians. In the case of the kingdom of Judah, it was a 70-year captivity to rest the land for all the Sabbath years that had been violated (see 2 Chr. 36:17–21).

36 'And as for those of you who are left, I will send faintness into their hearts in the lands of their enemies; the sound of a shaken leaf shall cause them to flee; they shall flee as though fleeing from a sword, and they shall fall when no one pursues.

37 They shall stumble over one another, as it were before a sword, when no one pursues; and you shall have no *power* to stand before your enemies.

38 You shall perish among the nations, and the land of your enemies shall eat you up.

39 And those of you who are left shall waste away in their iniquity in your enemies' lands; also in their fathers' iniquities, which are with them, they shall waste away.

40 'But if they confess their iniquity and the iniquity of their fathers, with their unfaithfulness in which they were unfaithful to Me, and that they also have walked contrary to Me,

41 and *that* I also have walked contrary to them and have brought them into the land of their enemies;

if their uncircumcised hearts are humbled, and they accept their guilt—

42 then I will remember My covenant with Jacob, and My covenant with Isaac and My covenant with Abraham I will remember; I will remember the land.

26:40–42 if they confess...I will remember My covenant. God's covenant was rooted in the relationship He had initiated with His people. He will always honor true repentance.

43 The land also shall be left empty by them, and will enjoy its sabbaths while it lies desolate without them; they will accept their guilt, because they despised My judgments and because their soul abhorred My statutes.

44 Yet for all that, when they are in the land of their enemies, I will not cast them away, nor shall I abhor them, to utterly destroy them and break My covenant with them; for I *am* the LORD their God.

45 But for their sake I will remember the covenant of their ancestors, whom I brought out of the land of Egypt in the sight of the nations, that I might be their God: I *am* the LORD.' "

46 These *are* the statutes and judgments and laws which the LORD made between Himself and the children of Israel on Mount Sinai by the hand of Moses.

Redeeming Persons and Property Dedicated to God

27 Now the LORD spoke to Moses, saying, 2"Speak to the children of Israel, and say to them: 'When a man consecrates by a vow certain persons to the LORD, according to your valuation, 3if your valuation is of a male from twenty years old up to sixty years old, then your valuation shall be fifty shekels of silver, according to the shekel of the sanctuary. 4If it *is* a female, then your valuation shall be thirty shekels; 5and if from five years old up to twenty years old, then your valuation for a male shall be twenty shekels, and for a female ten shekels; 6and if from a month old up to five years old, then your valuation for a male shall be five shekels of silver, and for a female your valuation shall be three shekels of silver; 7and if from sixty years old and above, if it *is* a male, then your valuation shall be fifteen shekels, and for a female ten shekels.

8'But if he is too poor to pay your valuation, then he shall present himself before the priest, and the priest shall set a value for him; according to the ability of him who vowed, the priest shall value him.

9'If *it is* an animal that men may bring as an offering to the LORD, all that *anyone* gives to the LORD shall be holy. 10He shall not substitute it or exchange it, good for bad or bad for good; and if he at all exchanges animal for animal, then both it and the one exchanged for it shall be holy. 11If *it is* an unclean animal which they do not offer as a sacrifice to the LORD, then he shall present the animal before the priest; 12and the priest shall set a value for it, whether it is good or bad; as you, the priest, value it, so it shall be. 13But if he *wants* at all *to* redeem it, then he must add one-fifth to your valuation.

14And when a man dedicates his house *to be* holy to the LORD, then the priest shall set a value for it, whether it is good or bad; as the priest values it, so it shall stand. 15If he who dedicated it *wants to* redeem his house, then he must add one-fifth of the money of your valuation to it, and it shall be his.

16'If a man dedicates to the LORD *part* of a field of his possession, then your valuation shall be according to the seed for it. A homer of barley seed *shall be valued* at fifty shekels of silver. 17If he dedicates his field from the Year of Jubilee, according to your valuation it shall stand. 18But if he dedicates his field after the Jubilee, then the priest shall reckon to him the money due according to the years that remain till the

Year of Jubilee, and it shall be deducted from your valuation. ¹⁹And if he who dedicates the field ever wishes to redeem it, then he must add one-fifth of the money of your valuation to it, and it shall belong to him. ²⁰But if he does not want to redeem the field, or if he has sold the field to another man, it shall not be redeemed anymore; ²¹but the field, when it is released in the Jubilee, shall be holy to the LORD, as a devoted field; it shall be the possession of the priest.

²²'And if a man dedicates to the LORD a field which he has bought, which is not the field of his possession, ²³then the priest shall reckon to him the worth of your valuation, up to the Year of Jubilee, and he shall give your valuation on that day *as* a holy *offering* to the LORD. ²⁴In the Year of Jubilee the field shall return to him from whom it was bought, to the one who *owned* the land as a possession. ²⁵And all your valuations shall be according to the shekel of the sanctuary: twenty gerahs to the shekel.

²⁶'But the firstborn of the animals, which should be the LORD's firstborn, no man shall dedicate; whether *it is* an ox or sheep, it *is* the LORD's. ²⁷And if *it is* an unclean animal, then he shall redeem *it* according to your valuation, and shall add one-fifth to it; or if it is not redeemed, then it shall be sold according to your valuation.

²⁸'Nevertheless no devoted *offering* that a man may devote to the LORD of all that he has, *both* man and beast, or the field of his possession, shall be sold or redeemed; every devoted *offering is* most holy to the LORD. ²⁹No person under the ban, who may become doomed to destruction among men, shall be redeemed, *but* shall surely be put to death. ³⁰And all the tithe of the land, *whether* of the seed of the land *or* of the fruit of the tree, *is* the LORD's. It *is* holy to the LORD. ³¹If a man wants at all to redeem *any* of his tithes, he shall add one-fifth to it. ³²And concerning the tithe of the herd or the flock, of whatever passes under the rod, the tenth one shall be holy to the LORD. ³³He shall not inquire whether it is good or bad, nor shall he exchange it; and if he exchanges it at all, then both it and the one exchanged for it shall be holy; it shall not be redeemed.' "

27:30–32 tithe. This general tithe was given to the Levites and is the only mention of tithe or ten percent offering in Leviticus. Along with this offering, two other OT tithes are mentioned, which total about 23 percent annually (see Deut. 14:22,28,29; 26:12).

³⁴These *are* the commandments which the LORD commanded Moses for the children of Israel on Mount Sinai.

NUMBERS

Originally, the Hebrew designation of the fourth book of the Bible was an expression meaning "in the wilderness." The ancient Greek title of this book is *"arithmoi"* which comes to us in the English word "arithmetic." Later, Latin translators gave the book the title *"numeri,"* which English has borrowed as its general word "numbers." The translators were referring to the numberings (census) recorded in the book. In another sense, the book records the 39 years in which God's people were in the wilderness, counting down the time of their punishment.

AUTHOR AND DATE

Numbers was written by Moses, approximately 1405 B.C.

Like the other first five books of the Bible, Numbers is identified as Moses' writing by the rest of Scripture. Numbers itself mentions Moses twice (33:2; 36:13) as the recorder of events and commandments.

Numbers was written in the final year of Moses' life. Biblical sequence requires a completion date for Numbers of shortly before the 11th month of the 40th year after the Exodus since that is the specific date given for Deuteronomy (Deuteronomy 1:3).

Old Testament witnesses to Moses' authorship of Numbers: Joshua 8:31; 2 Kings 14:6; Nehemiah 8:1.

New Testament witnesses to Moses' authorship of Numbers: Mark 12:26; John 7:19.

BACKGROUND AND SETTING

Most of the events in Numbers are set in the wilderness. The people were forced to live as nomads for 40 years, though their actual moves were infrequent. Numbers 33 lists a complete itinerary of their travels. The Israelites broke camp roughly 40 times in 40 years.

The greatest portion of the book describes the events leading up to the first failed journey to the Promised Land as well as the final preparations for the second march almost four decades later. In between, the tragedy of 37 wasted years is emphasized by being largely ignored.

Numbers records the death of one generation and the rise of a new one. With the notable exception of Caleb and Joshua, the adults who participated in the Exodus from Egypt did not live to enter the Promised Land. They hesitated at the very border of Canaan and paid for their rebellion by living out their days in the desert. Their children became the inheritors of the Promised Land.

Three theological themes permeate Numbers. First, since the Lord Himself communicated to Israel through Moses (1:1; 7:89; 12:6–8), the words of Moses had divine authority. Israel's response to Moses mirrored her obedience or disobedience to the Lord. Numbers includes examples of each kind of response to the word of the Lord: obedience (chapters 1–10); disobedience (chapters 11–25); renewed obedience (chapters 26–36). Second, Numbers highlights God's righteous judgments. Repeatedly, Israel's sin aroused the "anger" of the Lord (11:1,10,33; 12:9; 14:18; 25:3,4; 32:10,13,14). Third, Numbers emphasizes the faithfulness of the Lord to keep His promise to give the land of Canaan to the offspring of Abraham (15:2; 26:52–56; 27:12; 33:50–56; 34:1–29).

> ## NUMBERS RECORDS THE DEATH OF ONE GENERATION AND THE RISE OF A NEW ONE.

OUTLINE

I. THE EXPERIENCE OF THE FIRST GENERATION OF ISRAEL IN THE WILDERNESS (1:1–25:18)

    A. The Obedience of Israel toward the Lord (1:1–10:36)

        1. The organization of Israel around the tabernacle of the Lord (1:1–6:27)

        2. The orientation of Israel toward the tabernacle of the Lord (7:1–10:36)

    B. The Disobedience of Israel toward the Lord (11:1–25:18)

        1. The complaining of Israel on the journey (11:1–12:16)

        2. The rebellion of Israel and its leaders at Kadesh (13:1–20:29)

            a. The rebellion of Israel and the consequences (13:1–19:22)

            b. The rebellion of Moses and Aaron and the consequences (20:1–29)

        3. The renewed complaining of Israel on the journey (21:1–22:1)

        4. The blessing of Israel by Balaam (22:2–24:25)

        5. The final rebellion of Israel with Baal of Peor (25:1–18)

II. THE EXPERIENCE OF THE SECOND GENERATION OF ISRAEL IN THE PLAINS OF MOAB:

A RENEWED OBEDIENCE OF ISRAEL TOWARD THE LORD (26:1–36:13)

    A. The Preparations for the Conquest of the Land (26:1–32:42)

    B. The Review of the Journey in the Wilderness (33:1–49)

    C. The Anticipation of the Conquest of the Land (33:50–36:13)

1:1–10:36 The first ten chapters of Numbers record the final preparations that Israel had to make before their conquest of the land of Canaan. In this section, the Lord spoke to Israel through Moses, and Moses and Israel responded in obedience. These ten chapters divide into two parts (1:1–6:27 and 7:1–10:36), and both end with an invocation of the Lord's blessing on Israel.

The First Census of Israel

1 Now the LORD spoke to Moses in the Wilderness of Sinai, in the tabernacle of meeting, on the first *day* of the second month, in the second year after they had come out of the land of Egypt, saying: ²"Take a census of all the congregation of the children of Israel, by their families, by their fathers' houses, according to the number of names, every male individually, ³from twenty years old and above—all who *are able to* go to war in Israel. You and Aaron shall number them by their armies. ⁴And with you there shall be a man from every tribe, each one the head of his father's house.

1:3 go to war. The purpose of this census was to form a roster of fighting men. The book of Numbers includes the preparation to invade the Promised Land (see Gen. 12:1–3).

⁵"These are the names of the men who shall stand with you: from Reuben, Elizur the son of Shedeur; ⁶from Simeon, Shelumiel the son of Zurishaddai; ⁷from Judah, Nahshon the son of Amminadab; ⁸from Issachar, Nethanel the son of Zuar; ⁹from Zebulun, Eliab the son of Helon; ¹⁰from the sons of Joseph: from Ephraim, Elishama the son of Ammihud; from Manasseh, Gamaliel the son of Pedahzur; ¹¹from Benjamin, Abidan the son of Gideoni; ¹²from Dan, Ahiezer the son of Ammishaddai; ¹³from Asher, Pagiel the son of Ocran; ¹⁴from Gad, Eliasaph the son of Deuel;ᵃ ¹⁵from Naphtali, Ahira the son of Enan." ¹⁶These *were* chosen from the congregation, leaders of their fathers' tribes, heads of the divisions in Israel.

¹⁷Then Moses and Aaron took these men who had been mentioned by name, ¹⁸and they assembled all the congregation together on the first *day* of the second month; and they recited their ancestry by families, by their fathers' houses, according to the number of names, from twenty years old and above, each one individually. ¹⁹As the LORD commanded Moses, so he numbered them in the Wilderness of Sinai.

²⁰Now the children of Reuben, Israel's oldest son, their genealogies by their families, by their fathers' house, according to

1:14 ᵃSpelled *Reuel* in 2:14

The size of Israel's population provokes questions about the accuracy of the numbers in Numbers. Were there that many people wandering in the wilderness? How did they survive? How did they manage themselves?

Twice during the wilderness wanderings a census of the people of Israel was taken (Numbers 1:46; 26:51). Each time the resulting total count of fighting men exceeded 600,000. These numbers indicate a population for Israel in the wilderness of around 2.5 million people at any time. Viewed naturally, this total appears too high to sustain in wilderness conditions.

Before concluding that Moses inflated the numbers, several factors must be considered. First, the Lord supernaturally took care of Israel for 40 years (Deuteronomy 8:1–5). Miraculous provision of food was a daily event. Second, God also spelled out sanitary practices that prevented the kind of health crises that might have occurred under those conditions. Third, while Israel wandered in the wilderness for 40 years, they only moved camp about 40 times. Spending about a year in each campsite allowed for some normal life without creating a permanent settlement. This preserved some grazing for the herds while keeping the people's pollution to a manageable amount. Each census was meant to be an accurate accounting of God's people. They ought to be taken at face value.

the number of names, every male individually, from twenty years old and above, all who *were able to* go to war: [21]those who were numbered of the tribe of Reuben *were* forty-six thousand five hundred.

[22]From the children of Simeon, their genealogies by their families, by their fathers' house, of those who were numbered, according to the number of names, every male individually, from twenty years old and above, all who *were able to* go to war: [23]those who were numbered of the tribe of Simeon *were* fifty-nine thousand three hundred.

[24]From the children of Gad, their genealogies by their families, by their fathers' house, according to the number of names, from twenty years old and above, all who *were able to* go to war: [25]those who were numbered of the tribe of Gad *were* forty-five thousand six hundred and fifty.

[26]From the children of Judah, their genealogies by their families, by their fathers' house, according to the number of names, from twenty years old and above, all who *were able to* go to war: [27]those who were numbered of the tribe of Judah *were* seventy-four thousand six hundred.

[28]From the children of Issachar, their genealogies by their families, by their fathers' house, according to the number of names, from twenty years old and above, all who *were able to* go to war: [29]those who were numbered of the tribe of Issachar *were* fifty-four thousand four hundred.

[30]From the children of Zebulun, their genealogies by their families, by their fathers' house, according to the number of names, from twenty years old and above, all who *were able to* go to war: [31]those who were numbered of the tribe of Zebulun *were* fifty-seven thousand four hundred.

[32]From the sons of Joseph, the children of Ephraim, their genealogies by their families, by their fathers' house, according to the number of names, from twenty years old and above, all who *were able to* go to war: [33]those who were numbered of the tribe of Ephraim *were* forty thousand five hundred.

[34]From the children of Manasseh, their genealogies by their families, by their fathers' house, according to the number of names, from twenty years old and above,

all who *were able to* go to war: [35]those who were numbered of the tribe of Manasseh *were* thirty-two thousand two hundred.

[36]From the children of Benjamin, their genealogies by their families, by their fathers' house, according to the number of names, from twenty years old and above, all who *were able to* go to war: [37]those who were numbered of the tribe of Benjamin *were* thirty-five thousand four hundred.

[38]From the children of Dan, their genealogies by their families, by their fathers' house, according to the number of names, from twenty years old and above, all who *were able to* go to war: [39]those who were numbered of the tribe of Dan *were* sixty-two thousand seven hundred.

[40]From the children of Asher, their genealogies by their families, by their fathers' house, according to the number of names, from twenty years old and above, all who *were able to* go to war: [41]those who were numbered of the tribe of Asher *were* forty-one thousand five hundred.

[42]From the children of Naphtali, their genealogies by their families, by their fathers' house, according to the number of names, from twenty years old and above, all who *were able to* go to war: [43]those who were numbered of the tribe of Naphtali *were* fifty-three thousand four hundred.

[44]These are the ones who were numbered, whom Moses and Aaron numbered, with the leaders of Israel, twelve men, each one representing his father's house. [45]So all who were numbered of the children of Israel, by their fathers' houses, from twenty years old and above, all who *were able to* go to war in Israel— [46]all who were numbered were six hundred and three thousand five hundred and fifty.

1:46 six hundred and three thousand five hundred and fifty. Combine this number with the 22,000 Levite males one month old or older (3:39) and the total population count is greater than 2,000,000 Israelites. There is no indication that these numbers are symbolic. This shows that God cared for more than 2,000,000 people in the wilderness during the 40 year period. God's purpose for these numbers is to show His power in behalf of Israel.

[47]But the Levites were not numbered among them by their fathers' tribe; [48]for the

LORD had spoken to Moses, saying: ⁴⁹"Only the tribe of Levi you shall not number, nor take a census of them among the children of Israel; ⁵⁰but you shall appoint the Levites over the tabernacle of the Testimony, over all its furnishings, and over all things that belong to it; they shall carry the tabernacle and all its furnishings; they shall attend to it and camp around the tabernacle. ⁵¹And when the tabernacle is to go forward, the Levites shall take it down; and when the tabernacle is to be set up, the Levites shall set it up. The outsider who comes near shall be put to death. ⁵²The children of Israel shall pitch their tents, everyone by his own camp, everyone by his own standard, according to their armies; ⁵³but the Levites shall camp around the tabernacle of the Testimony, that there may be no wrath on the congregation of the children of Israel; and the Levites shall keep charge of the tabernacle of the Testimony."

1:50 appoint the Levites. The tribe of Levi was not included in the overall census because they were exempt from military service. The Levites served the Lord by carrying and attending to the tabernacle.

⁵⁴Thus the children of Israel did; according to all that the LORD commanded Moses, so they did.

The Tribes and Leaders by Armies

2 And the LORD spoke to Moses and Aaron, saying: ²"Everyone of the children of Israel shall camp by his own standard, beside the emblems of his father's house; they shall camp some distance from the tabernacle of meeting. ³On the east side, toward the rising of the sun, those of the standard of the forces with Judah shall camp according to their armies; and Nahshon the son of Amminadab *shall be* the leader of the children of Judah." ⁴And his army was numbered at seventy-four thousand six hundred.

2:3 On the east side...Judah. Judah occupied the place of honor to the east. Genesis 49:8–12 describes the central role this tribe would play in defeating Israel's enemies, and this was also the tribe through which the Messiah would be born.

⁵"Those who camp next to him *shall be* the tribe of Issachar, and Nethanel the son of Zuar *shall be* the leader of the children of

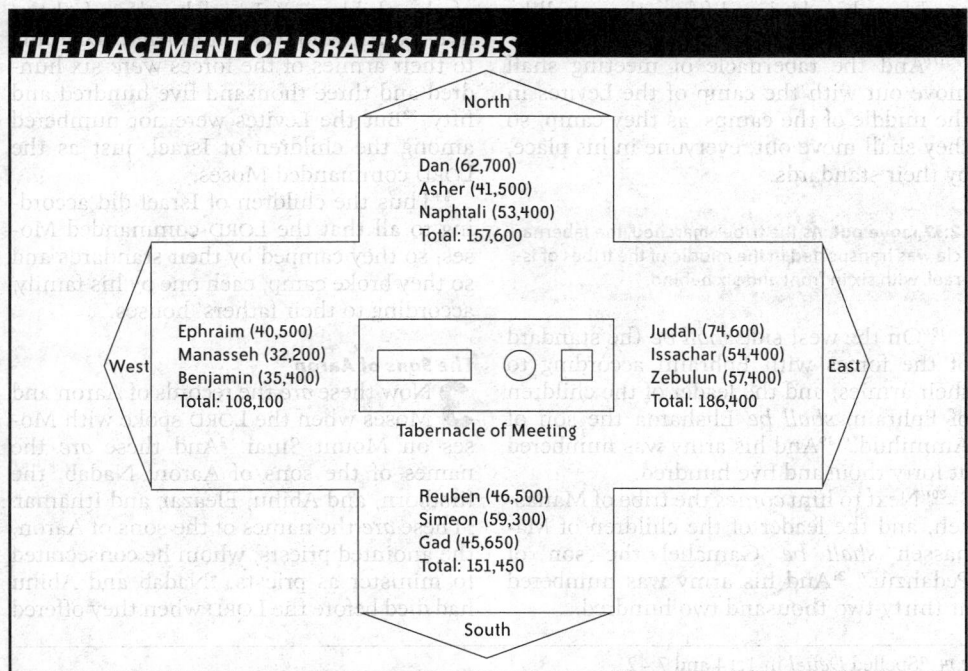

THE PLACEMENT OF ISRAEL'S TRIBES

North

Dan (62,700)
Asher (41,500)
Naphtali (53,400)
Total: 157,600

West

Ephraim (40,500)
Manasseh (32,200)
Benjamin (35,400)
Total: 108,100

Tabernacle of Meeting

Judah (74,600)
Issachar (54,400)
Zebulun (57,400)
Total: 186,400

East

Reuben (46,500)
Simeon (59,300)
Gad (45,650)
Total: 151,450

South

Issachar." [6]And his army was numbered at fifty-four thousand four hundred.

[7]"Then *comes* the tribe of Zebulun, and Eliab the son of Helon *shall be* the leader of the children of Zebulun." [8]And his army was numbered at fifty-seven thousand four hundred. [9]"All who were numbered according to their armies of the forces with Judah, one hundred and eighty-six thousand four hundred—these shall break camp first.

[10]"On the south side *shall be* the standard of the forces with Reuben according to their armies, and the leader of the children of Reuben *shall be* Elizur the son of Shedeur." [11]And his army was numbered at forty-six thousand five hundred.

[12]"Those who camp next to him *shall be* the tribe of Simeon, and the leader of the children of Simeon *shall be* Shelumiel the son of Zurishaddai." [13]And his army was numbered at fifty-nine thousand three hundred.

[14]"Then *comes* the tribe of Gad, and the leader of the children of Gad *shall be* Eliasaph the son of Reuel."[a] [15]And his army was numbered at forty-five thousand six hundred and fifty. [16]"All who were numbered according to their armies of the forces with Reuben, one hundred and fifty-one thousand four hundred and fifty—they shall be the second to break camp.

[17]"And the tabernacle of meeting shall move out with the camp of the Levites in the middle of the camps; as they camp, so they shall move out, everyone in his place, by their standards.

2:17 move out. As the tribes marched, the tabernacle was transported in the middle of the tribes of Israel, with six in front and six behind.

[18]"On the west side *shall be* the standard of the forces with Ephraim according to their armies, and the leader of the children of Ephraim *shall be* Elishama the son of Ammihud." [19]And his army was numbered at forty thousand five hundred.

[20]"Next to him *comes* the tribe of Manasseh, and the leader of the children of Manasseh *shall be* Gamaliel the son of Pedahzur." [21]And his army was numbered at thirty-two thousand two hundred.

[22]"Then *comes* the tribe of Benjamin, and the leader of the children of Benjamin *shall be* Abidan the son of Gideoni." [23]And his army was numbered at thirty-five thousand four hundred. [24]"All who were numbered according to their armies of the forces with Ephraim, one hundred and eight thousand one hundred—they shall be the third to break camp.

[25]"The standard of the forces with Dan *shall be* on the north side according to their armies, and the leader of the children of Dan *shall be* Ahiezer the son of Ammishaddai." [26]And his army was numbered at sixty-two thousand seven hundred.

[27]"Those who camp next to him *shall be* the tribe of Asher, and the leader of the children of Asher *shall be* Pagiel the son of Ocran." [28]And his army was numbered at forty-one thousand five hundred.

[29]"Then *comes* the tribe of Naphtali, and the leader of the children of Naphtali *shall be* Ahira the son of Enan." [30]And his army was numbered at fifty-three thousand four hundred. [31]"All who were numbered of the forces with Dan, one hundred and fifty-seven thousand six hundred—they shall break camp last, with their standards."

[32]These *are* the ones who were numbered of the children of Israel by their fathers' houses. All who were numbered according to their armies of the forces *were* six hundred and three thousand five hundred and fifty. [33]But the Levites were not numbered among the children of Israel, just as the LORD commanded Moses.

[34]Thus the children of Israel did according to all that the LORD commanded Moses; so they camped by their standards and so they broke camp, each one by his family, according to their fathers' houses.

The Sons of Aaron

3 Now these *are* the records of Aaron and Moses when the LORD spoke with Moses on Mount Sinai. [2]And these *are* the names of the sons of Aaron: Nadab, the firstborn, and Abihu, Eleazar, and Ithamar. [3]These *are* the names of the sons of Aaron, the anointed priests, whom he consecrated to minister as priests. [4]Nadab and Abihu had died before the LORD when they offered

2:14 [a]Spelled *Deuel* in 1:14 and 7:42

profane fire before the LORD in the Wilderness of Sinai; and they had no children. So Eleazar and Ithamar ministered as priests in the presence of Aaron their father.

The Levites Serve in the Tabernacle

⁵And the LORD spoke to Moses, saying: ⁶"Bring the tribe of Levi near, and present them before Aaron the priest, that they may serve him. ⁷And they shall attend to his needs and the needs of the whole congregation before the tabernacle of meeting, to do the work of the tabernacle. ⁸Also they shall attend to all the furnishings of the tabernacle of meeting, and to the needs of the children of Israel, to do the work of the tabernacle. ⁹And you shall give the Levites to Aaron and his sons; they *are* given entirely to him*ᵃ* from among the children of Israel. ¹⁰So you shall appoint Aaron and his sons, and they shall attend to their priesthood; but the outsider who comes near shall be put to death."

> **3:6 the tribe of Levi.** The specific task of the Levites was to serve all of Israel by doing the work of the tabernacle, under the leadership of Aaron and his sons. God specifically gave all the priestly duties to the Levites, perhaps partly because of their holy zeal in the golden calf incident (see Ex. 32:29).

¹¹Then the LORD spoke to Moses, saying: ¹²"Now behold, I Myself have taken the Levites from among the children of Israel instead of every firstborn who opens the womb among the children of Israel. Therefore the Levites shall be Mine, ¹³because all the firstborn *are* Mine. On the day that I struck all the firstborn in the land of Egypt, I sanctified to Myself all the firstborn in Israel, both man and beast. They shall be Mine: I *am* the LORD."

Census of the Levites Commanded

¹⁴Then the LORD spoke to Moses in the Wilderness of Sinai, saying: ¹⁵"Number the children of Levi by their fathers' houses, by their families; you shall number every male from a month old and above." ¹⁶So Moses numbered them according to the word of the LORD, as he was commanded.

¹⁷These were the sons of Levi by their names: Gershon, Kohath, and Merari. ¹⁸And these *are* the names of the sons of Gershon by their families: Libni and Shimei. ¹⁹And the sons of Kohath by their families: Amram, Izehar, Hebron, and Uzziel. ²⁰And the sons of Merari by their families: Mahli and Mushi. These *are* the families of the Levites by their fathers' houses.

²¹From Gershon *came* the family of the Libnites and the family of the Shimites; these *were* the families of the Gershonites. ²²Those who were numbered, according to the number of all the males from a month old and above—of those who were numbered *there were* seven thousand five hundred. ²³The families of the Gershonites were to camp behind the tabernacle westward. ²⁴And the leader of the father's house of the Gershonites *was* Eliasaph the son of Lael. ²⁵The duties of the children of Gershon in the tabernacle of meeting *included* the tabernacle, the tent with its covering, the screen for the door of the tabernacle of meeting, ²⁶the screen for the door of the court, the hangings of the court which *are* around the tabernacle and the altar, and their cords, according to all the work relating to them.

²⁷From Kohath *came* the family of the Amramites, the family of the Izharites, the family of the Hebronites, and the family of the Uzzielites; these *were* the families of the Kohathites. ²⁸According to the number of all the males, from a month old and above, *there were* eight thousand six*ᵃ* hundred keeping charge of the sanctuary. ²⁹The families of the children of Kohath were to camp on the south side of the tabernacle. ³⁰And the leader of the fathers' house of the families of the Kohathites *was* Elizaphan the son of Uzziel. ³¹Their duty *included* the ark, the table, the lampstand, the altars, the utensils of the sanctuary with which they ministered, the screen, and all the work relating to them.

³²And Eleazar the son of Aaron the priest *was to be* chief over the leaders of the Levites, *with* oversight of those who kept charge of the sanctuary.

³³From Merari *came* the family of the

3:9 *ᵃ*Samaritan Pentateuch and Septuagint read *Me.*   3:28 *ᵃ*Some manuscripts of the Septuagint read *three.*

Mahlites and the family of the Mushites; these *were* the families of Merari. ³⁴And those who were numbered, according to the number of all the males from a month old and above, *were* six thousand two hundred. ³⁵The leader of the fathers' house of the families of Merari *was* Zuriel the son of Abihail. These *were* to camp on the north side of the tabernacle. ³⁶And the appointed duty of the children of Merari *included* the boards of the tabernacle, its bars, its pillars, its sockets, its utensils, all the work relating to them, ³⁷and the pillars of the court all around, with their sockets, their pegs, and their cords.

³⁸Moreover those who were to camp before the tabernacle on the east, before the tabernacle of meeting, *were* Moses, Aaron, and his sons, keeping charge of the sanctuary, to meet the needs of the children of Israel; but the outsider who came near was to be put to death. ³⁹All who were numbered of the Levites, whom Moses and Aaron numbered at the commandment of the LORD, by their families, all the males from a month old and above, *were* twenty-two thousand.

> **3:38 Moses, Aaron.** Moses and Aaron and his sons were given the place of honor to the east of the tabernacle. They gave overall supervision to the Levites. Eleazar oversaw the Kohathites (who were responsible for the holy objects in the tabernacle), and Ithamar oversaw the Gershonites (who were responsible for the tabernacle coverings) and the Merarites (who were responsible for the wooden framework of the tabernacle).

Levites Dedicated Instead of the Firstborn

⁴⁰Then the LORD said to Moses: "Number all the firstborn males of the children of Israel from a month old and above, and take the number of their names. ⁴¹And you shall take the Levites for Me—I *am* the LORD—instead of all the firstborn among the children of Israel, and the livestock of the Levites instead of all the firstborn among the livestock of the children of Israel." ⁴²So Moses numbered all the firstborn among the children of Israel, as the LORD commanded him. ⁴³And all the firstborn males, according to the number of names from a month old and above, of those who were numbered of them, were twenty-two thousand two hundred and seventy-three.

⁴⁴Then the LORD spoke to Moses, saying: ⁴⁵"Take the Levites instead of all the firstborn among the children of Israel, and the livestock of the Levites instead of their livestock. The Levites shall be Mine: I *am* the LORD. ⁴⁶And for the redemption of the two hundred and seventy-three of the firstborn of the children of Israel, who are more than the number of the Levites, ⁴⁷you shall take five shekels for each one individually; you shall take *them* in the currency of the shekel of the sanctuary, the shekel of twenty gerahs. ⁴⁸And you shall give the money, with which the excess number of them is redeemed, to Aaron and his sons."

⁴⁹So Moses took the redemption money from those who were over and above those who were redeemed by the Levites. ⁵⁰From the firstborn of the children of Israel he took the money, one thousand three hundred and sixty-five *shekels*, according to the shekel of the sanctuary. ⁵¹And Moses gave their redemption money to Aaron and his sons, according to the word of the LORD, as the LORD commanded Moses.

Duties of the Sons of Kohath

4 Then the LORD spoke to Moses and Aaron, saying: ²"Take a census of the sons of Kohath from among the children of Levi, by their families, by their fathers' house, ³from thirty years old and above, even to fifty years old, all who enter the service to do the work in the tabernacle of meeting.

> **4:3 thirty...to fifty.** This second census of the Levites determined who would carry the tabernacle on the upcoming journey to Canaan. Only those between the ages of 30 and 50 were called to the Lord for this task.

⁴"This *is* the service of the sons of Kohath in the tabernacle of meeting, *relating to* the most holy things: ⁵When the camp prepares to journey, Aaron and his sons shall come, and they shall take down the covering veil and cover the ark of the Testimony with it. ⁶Then they shall put on it a covering of badger skins, and spread over *that* a cloth entirely of blue; and they shall insert its poles.

⁷"On the table of showbread they shall spread a blue cloth, and put on it the

dishes, the pans, the bowls, and the pitchers for pouring; and the showbread[a] shall be on it. [8]They shall spread over them a scarlet cloth, and cover the same with a covering of badger skins; and they shall insert its poles. [9]And they shall take a blue cloth and cover the lampstand of the light, with its lamps, its wick-trimmers, its trays, and all its oil vessels, with which they service it. [10]Then they shall put it with all its utensils in a covering of badger skins, and put it on a carrying beam.

[11]"Over the golden altar they shall spread a blue cloth, and cover it with a covering of badger skins; and they shall insert its poles. [12]Then they shall take all the utensils of service with which they minister in the sanctuary, put them in a blue cloth, cover them with a covering of badger skins, and put them on a carrying beam. [13]Also they shall take away the ashes from the altar, and spread a purple cloth over it. [14]They shall put on it all its implements with which they minister there—the firepans, the forks, the shovels, the basins, and all the utensils of the altar—and they shall spread on it a covering of badger skins, and insert its poles. [15]And when Aaron and his sons have finished covering the sanctuary and all the furnishings of the sanctuary, when the camp is set to go, then the sons of Kohath shall come to carry them; but they shall not touch any holy thing, lest they die.

"These are the things in the tabernacle of meeting which the sons of Kohath are to carry.

[16]"The appointed duty of Eleazar the son of Aaron the priest is the oil for the light, the sweet incense, the daily grain offering, the anointing oil, the oversight of all the tabernacle, of all that is in it, with the sanctuary and its furnishings."

[17]Then the LORD spoke to Moses and Aaron, saying: [18]"Do not cut off the tribe of the families of the Kohathites from among

---

4:4–16 Kohath. The Kohathites carried the furnishings of the tabernacle, but only after they had been covered by Aaron and his sons. If the Kohathites touched or saw any of the holy things, they would die.

---

the Levites; [19]but do this in regard to them, that they may live and not die when they approach the most holy things: Aaron and his sons shall go in and appoint each of them to his service and his task. [20]But they shall not go in to watch while the holy things are being covered, lest they die."

Duties of the Sons of Gershon

[21]Then the LORD spoke to Moses, saying: [22]"Also take a census of the sons of Gershon, by their fathers' house, by their families. [23]From thirty years old and above, even to fifty years old, you shall number them, all who enter to perform the service, to do the work in the tabernacle of meeting. [24]This is the service of the families of the Gershonites, in serving and carrying: [25]They shall carry the curtains of the tabernacle and the tabernacle of meeting with its covering, the covering of badger skins that is on it, the screen for the door of the tabernacle of meeting, [26]the screen for the door of the gate of the court, the hangings of the court which are around the tabernacle and altar, and their cords, all the furnishings for their service and all that is made for these things: so shall they serve.

[27]"Aaron and his sons shall assign all the service of the sons of the Gershonites, all their tasks and all their service. And you shall appoint to them all their tasks as their duty. [28]This is the service of the families of the sons of Gershon in the tabernacle of meeting. And their duties shall be under the authority[a] of Ithamar the son of Aaron the priest.

Duties of the Sons of Merari

[29]"As for the sons of Merari, you shall number them by their families and by their fathers' house. [30]From thirty years old and above, even to fifty years old, you shall number them, everyone who enters the service to do the work of the tabernacle of meeting. [31]And this is what they must carry as all their service for the tabernacle of meeting: the boards of the tabernacle, its bars, its pillars, its sockets, [32]and the pillars around the court with their sockets, pegs, and cords, with all their furnishings and all

---

4:7 [a]Literally the continual bread   4:28 [a]Literally hand

their service; and you shall assign *to each man* by name the items he must carry. [33]This *is* the service of the families of the sons of Merari, as all their service for the tabernacle of meeting, under the authority[a] of Ithamar the son of Aaron the priest."

Census of the Levites

[34]And Moses, Aaron, and the leaders of the congregation numbered the sons of the Kohathites by their families and by their fathers' house, [35]from thirty years old and above, even to fifty years old, everyone who entered the service for work in the tabernacle of meeting; [36]and those who were numbered by their families were two thousand seven hundred and fifty. [37]These *were* the ones who were numbered of the families of the Kohathites, all who might serve in the tabernacle of meeting, whom Moses and Aaron numbered according to the commandment of the LORD by the hand of Moses.

[38]And those who were numbered of the sons of Gershon, by their families and by their fathers' house, [39]from thirty years old and above, even to fifty years old, everyone who entered the service for work in the tabernacle of meeting— [40]those who were numbered by their families, by their fathers' house, were two thousand six hundred and thirty. [41]These *are* the ones who were numbered of the families of the sons of Gershon, of all who might serve in the tabernacle of meeting, whom Moses and Aaron numbered according to the commandment of the LORD.

[42]Those of the families of the sons of Merari who were numbered, by their families, by their fathers' house, [43]from thirty years old and above, even to fifty years old, everyone who entered the service for work in the tabernacle of meeting— [44]those who were numbered by their families were three thousand two hundred. [45]These *are* the ones who were numbered of the families of the sons of Merari, whom Moses and Aaron numbered according to the word of the LORD by the hand of Moses.

[46]All who were numbered of the Levites, whom Moses, Aaron, and the leaders of Israel numbered, by their families and by their fathers' houses, [47]from thirty years old and above, even to fifty years old, everyone who came to do the work of service and the work of bearing burdens in the tabernacle of meeting— [48]those who were numbered were eight thousand five hundred and eighty.

[49]According to the commandment of the LORD they were numbered by the hand of Moses, each according to his service and according to his task; thus were they numbered by him, as the LORD commanded Moses.

Ceremonially Unclean Persons Isolated

5 And the LORD spoke to Moses, saying: [2]"Command the children of Israel that they put out of the camp every leper, everyone who has a discharge, and whoever becomes defiled by a corpse. [3]You shall put out both male and female; you shall put them outside the camp, that they may not defile their camps in the midst of which I dwell." [4]And the children of Israel did so, and put them outside the camp; as the LORD spoke to Moses, so the children of Israel did.

> **5:2 corpse.** Physical contact with a dead body. All of these prohibitions had sensible health benefits, and they also illustrated the need for moral cleanliness when approaching the holy presence of God.

Confession and Restitution

[5]Then the LORD spoke to Moses, saying, [6]"Speak to the children of Israel: 'When a man or woman commits any sin that men commit in unfaithfulness against the LORD, and that person is guilty, [7]then he shall confess the sin which he has committed. He shall make restitution for his trespass in full, plus one-fifth of it, and give *it* to the one he has wronged. [8]But if the man has no relative to whom restitution may be made for the wrong, the restitution for the wrong *must go* to the LORD for the priest, in addition to the ram of the atonement with which atonement is made for him. [9]Every offering of all the holy things of the children of Israel, which they bring to the priest, shall be his. [10]And every man's holy things shall be his; whatever any man gives the priest shall be his.' "

Concerning Unfaithful Wives

[11]And the LORD spoke to Moses, saying, [12]"Speak to the children of Israel, and say to them: 'If any man's wife goes astray and behaves unfaithfully toward him, [13]and a man lies with her carnally, and it is hidden from the eyes of her husband, and it is concealed that she has defiled herself, and *there was* no witness against her, nor was she caught— [14]if the spirit of jealousy comes upon him and he becomes jealous of his wife, who has defiled herself; or if the spirit of jealousy comes upon him and he becomes jealous of his wife, although she has not defiled herself— [15]then the man shall bring his wife to the priest. He shall bring the offering required for her, one-tenth of an ephah of barley meal; he shall pour no oil on it and put no frankincense on it, because it *is* a grain offering of jealousy, an offering for remembering, for bringing iniquity to remembrance.

[16]'And the priest shall bring her near, and set her before the LORD. [17]The priest shall take holy water in an earthen vessel, and take some of the dust that is on the floor of the tabernacle and put *it* into the water. [18]Then the priest shall stand the woman before the LORD, uncover the woman's head, and put the offering for remembering in her hands, which *is* the grain offering of jealousy. And the priest shall have in his hand the bitter water that brings a curse. [19]And the priest shall put her under oath, and say to the woman, "If no man has lain with you, and if you have not gone astray to uncleanness *while* under your husband's *authority*, be free from this bitter water that brings a curse. [20]But if you have gone astray *while* under your husband's *authority*, and

if you have defiled yourself and some man other than your husband has lain with you"— [21]then the priest shall put the woman under the oath of the curse, and he shall say to the woman—"the LORD make you a curse and an oath among your people, when the LORD makes your thigh rot and your belly swell; [22]and may this water that causes the curse go into your stomach, and make *your* belly swell and *your* thigh rot."

'Then the woman shall say, "Amen, so be it."

[23]'Then the priest shall write these curses in a book, and he shall scrape *them* off into the bitter water. [24]And he shall make the woman drink the bitter water that brings a curse, and the water that brings the curse shall enter her *to become* bitter. [25]Then the priest shall take the grain offering of jealousy from the woman's hand, shall wave the offering before the LORD, and bring it to the altar; [26]and the priest shall take a handful of the offering, as its memorial portion, burn *it* on the altar, and afterward make the woman drink the water. [27]When he has made her drink the water, then it shall be, if she has defiled herself and behaved unfaithfully toward her husband, that the water that brings a curse will enter her *and become* bitter, and her belly will swell, her thigh will rot, and the woman will become a curse among her people. [28]But if the woman has not defiled herself, and is clean, then she shall be free and may conceive children.

[29]'This *is* the law of jealousy, when a wife, *while* under her husband's *authority*, goes astray and defiles herself, [30]or when the spirit of jealousy comes upon a man, and he becomes jealous of his wife; then he shall stand the woman before the LORD, and the priest shall execute all this law upon her. [31]Then the man shall be free from iniquity, but that woman shall bear her guilt.' "

The Law of the Nazirite

6 Then the LORD spoke to Moses, saying, [2]"Speak to the children of Israel, and say to them: 'When either a man or woman consecrates an offering to take the vow of a Nazirite, to separate himself to the LORD, [3]he shall separate himself from wine and *similar* drink; he shall drink neither vinegar

---

5:18 before the LORD. The woman was brought to a priest at the tabernacle, where she stood in the presence of the Lord, who knew whether she was guilty or innocent. **uncover the woman's head.** This action signifies mourning. If she were proven guilty, she could expect judgment, causing her to mourn. **the bitter water.** The bitter water included dust from the tabernacle floor and the ink used to write the curses. When the woman drank the water, if she was guilty, the water would cause her thigh to rot and her belly to swell. This public, frightening test assaulted the conscience so strongly that it could not fail to show guilt or innocence.

made from wine nor vinegar made from *similar* drink; neither shall he drink any grape juice, nor eat fresh grapes or raisins. [4]All the days of his separation he shall eat nothing that is produced by the grapevine, from seed to skin.

6:2 the vow of a Nazirite. The Nazirite made an extraordinary vow to dedicate himself to the Lord by separating himself from (1) grape products, (2) the cutting of his hair, and (3) contact with a dead body. Like the High-Priest, the Nazirite was holy to the Lord all the days of his vow.

[5]All the days of the vow of his separation no razor shall come upon his head; until the days are fulfilled for which he separated himself to the LORD, he shall be holy. *Then* he shall let the locks of the hair of his head grow. [6]All the days that he separates himself to the LORD he shall not go near a dead body. [7]He shall not make himself unclean even for his father or his mother, for his brother or his sister, when they die, because his separation to God *is* on his head. [8]All the days of his separation he shall be holy to the LORD.

[9]And if anyone dies very suddenly beside him, and he defiles his consecrated head, then he shall shave his head on the day of his cleansing; on the seventh day he shall shave it. [10]Then on the eighth day he shall bring two turtledoves or two young pigeons to the priest, to the door of the tabernacle of meeting; [11]and the priest shall offer one as a sin offering and *the* other as a burnt offering, and make atonement for him, because he sinned in regard to the corpse; and he shall sanctify his head that same day. [12]He shall consecrate to the LORD the days of his separation, and bring a male lamb in its first year as a trespass offering; but the former days shall be lost, because his separation was defiled.

[13]Now this *is* the law of the Nazirite: When the days of his separation are fulfilled, he shall be brought to the door of the tabernacle of meeting. [14]And he shall present his offering to the LORD: one male lamb in its first year without blemish as a burnt offering, one ewe lamb in its first year without blemish as a sin offering, one ram without blemish as a peace offering, [15]a basket of unleavened bread, cakes of fine flour

mixed with oil, unleavened wafers anointed with oil, and their grain offering with their drink offerings.

[16]Then the priest shall bring *them* before the LORD and offer his sin offering and his burnt offering; [17]and he shall offer the ram as a sacrifice of a peace offering to the LORD, with the basket of unleavened bread; the priest shall also offer its grain offering and its drink offering. [18]Then the Nazirite shall shave his consecrated head *at* the door of the tabernacle of meeting, and shall take the hair from his consecrated head and put *it* on the fire which is under the sacrifice of the peace offering.

[19]And the priest shall take the boiled shoulder of the ram, one unleavened cake from the basket, and one unleavened wafer, and put *them* upon the hands of the Nazirite after he has shaved his consecrated *hair,* [20]and the priest shall wave them as a wave offering before the LORD; they *are* holy for the priest, together with the breast of the wave offering and the thigh of the heave offering. After that the Nazirite may drink wine.'

[21]This is the law of the Nazirite who vows to the LORD the offering for his separation, and besides that, whatever else his hand is able to provide; according to the vow which he takes, so he must do according to the law of his separation."

The Priestly Blessing

[22]And the LORD spoke to Moses, saying: [23]"Speak to Aaron and his sons, saying, 'This is the way you shall bless the children of Israel. Say to them:

[24] "The LORD bless you and keep you;

6:24 bless. The Lord blessed His people by shining His face on them in benevolence and by looking at them. **keep.** The results of the Lord's blessing were His preservation of Israel ("keep"), His kindness toward her ("be gracious"), and her total well-being ("peace").

[25]   The LORD make His face shine upon
       you,
       And be gracious to you;
[26]   The LORD lift up His countenance
       upon you,
       And give you peace." '

[27]"So they shall put My name on the children of Israel, and I will bless them."

> **6:27 put My name.** The name of the Lord represented His person and character. The priests called for God to dwell among His people and to meet all their needs.

Offerings of the Leaders

7 Now it came to pass, when Moses had finished setting up the tabernacle, that he anointed it and consecrated it and all its furnishings, and the altar and all its utensils; so he anointed them and consecrated them. [2]Then the leaders of Israel, the heads of their fathers' houses, who *were* the leaders of the tribes and over those who were numbered, made an offering. [3]And they brought their offering before the LORD, six covered carts and twelve oxen, a cart for *every* two of the leaders, and for each one an ox; and they presented them before the tabernacle.

[4]Then the LORD spoke to Moses, saying, [5]"Accept *these* from them, that they may be used in doing the work of the tabernacle of meeting; and you shall give them to the Levites, *to* every man according to his service." [6]So Moses took the carts and the oxen, and gave them to the Levites. [7]Two carts and four oxen he gave to the sons of Gershon, according to their service; [8]and four carts and eight oxen he gave to the sons of Merari, according to their service, under the authority[a] of Ithamar the son of Aaron the priest. [9]But to the sons of Kohath he gave none, because theirs *was* the service of the holy things, *which* they carried on their shoulders.

> **7:6 the carts and the oxen.** The Levites used these to transport the tabernacle. According to v. 9, the sons of Kohath did not receive a cart, because they were to carry the holy things of the tabernacle on their shoulders.

[10]Now the leaders offered the dedication *offering* for the altar when it was anointed; so the leaders offered their offering before the altar. [11]For the LORD said to Moses, "They shall offer their offering, one leader each day, for the dedication of the altar."

[12]And the one who offered his offering on the first day *was* Nahshon the son of Amminadab, from the tribe of Judah. [13]His offering *was* one silver platter, the weight of which *was* one hundred and thirty *shekels,* and one silver bowl of seventy shekels, according to the shekel of the sanctuary, both of them full of fine flour mixed with oil as a grain offering; [14]one gold pan of ten *shekels,* full of incense; [15]one young bull, one ram, and one male lamb in its first year, as a burnt offering; [16]one kid of the goats as a sin offering; [17]and for the sacrifice of peace offerings: two oxen, five rams, five male goats, and five male lambs in their first year. This *was* the offering of Nahshon the son of Amminadab.

[18]On the second day Nethanel the son of Zuar, leader of Issachar, presented *an offering.* [19]*For* his offering he offered one silver platter, the weight of which *was* one hundred and thirty *shekels,* and one silver bowl of seventy shekels, according to the shekel of the sanctuary, both of them full of fine flour mixed with oil as a grain offering; [20]one gold pan of ten *shekels,* full of incense; [21]one young bull, one ram, and one male lamb in its first year, as a burnt offering; [22]one kid of the goats as a sin offering; [23]and as the sacrifice of peace offerings: two oxen, five rams, five male goats, and five male lambs in their first year. This *was* the offering of Nethanel the son of Zuar.

[24]On the third day Eliab the son of Helon, leader of the children of Zebulun, *presented an offering.* [25]His offering *was* one silver platter, the weight of which *was* one hundred and thirty *shekels,* and one silver bowl of seventy shekels, according to the shekel of the sanctuary, both of them full of fine flour mixed with oil as a grain offering; [26]one gold pan of ten *shekels,* full of incense; [27]one young bull, one ram, and one male lamb in its first year, as a burnt offering; [28]one kid of the goats as a sin offering; [29]and for the sacrifice of peace offerings: two oxen, five rams, five male goats, and five male lambs in their first year. This *was* the offering of Eliab the son of Helon.

[30]On the fourth day Elizur the son of Shedeur, leader of the children of Reuben, *presented an offering.* [31]His offering *was*

7:8 [a]Literally *hand*

one silver platter, the weight of which *was* one hundred and thirty *shekels,* and one silver bowl of seventy shekels, according to the shekel of the sanctuary, both of them full of fine flour mixed with oil as a grain offering; [32]one gold pan of ten *shekels,* full of incense; [33]one young bull, one ram, and one male lamb in its first year, as a burnt offering; [34]one kid of the goats as a sin offering; [35]and as the sacrifice of peace offerings: two oxen, five rams, five male goats, and five male lambs in their first year. This *was* the offering of Elizur the son of Shedeur.

[36]On the fifth day Shelumiel the son of Zurishaddai, leader of the children of Simeon, *presented an offering.* [37]His offering *was* one silver platter, the weight of which *was* one hundred and thirty *shekels,* and one silver bowl of seventy shekels, according to the shekel of the sanctuary, both of them full of fine flour mixed with oil as a grain offering; [38]one gold pan of ten *shekels,* full of incense; [39]one young bull, one ram, and one male lamb in its first year, as a burnt offering; [40]one kid of the goats as a sin offering; [41]and as the sacrifice of peace offerings: two oxen, five rams, five male goats, and five male lambs in their first year. This *was* the offering of Shelumiel the son of Zurishaddai.

[42]On the sixth day Eliasaph the son of Deuel,[a] leader of the children of Gad, *presented an offering.* [43]His offering *was* one silver platter, the weight of which *was* one hundred and thirty *shekels,* and one silver bowl of seventy shekels, according to the shekel of the sanctuary, both of them full of fine flour mixed with oil as a grain offering; [44]one gold pan of ten *shekels,* full of incense; [45]one young bull, one ram, and one male lamb in its first year, as a burnt offering; [46]one kid of the goats as a sin offering; [47]and as the sacrifice of peace offerings: two oxen, five rams, five male goats, and five male lambs in their first year. This *was* the offering of Eliasaph the son of Deuel.

[48]On the seventh day Elishama the son of Ammihud, leader of the children of Ephraim, *presented an offering.* [49]His offering *was* one silver platter, the weight of which *was* one hundred and thirty *shekels,* and one silver bowl of seventy shekels, according to the shekel of the sanctuary, both of them full of fine flour mixed with oil as a grain offering; [50]one gold pan of ten *shekels,* full of incense; [51]one young bull, one ram, and one male lamb in its first year, as a burnt offering; [52]one kid of the goats as a sin offering; [53]and as the sacrifice of peace offerings: two oxen, five rams, five male goats, and five male lambs in their first year. This *was* the offering of Elishama the son of Ammihud.

[54]On the eighth day Gamaliel the son of Pedahzur, leader of the children of Manasseh, *presented an offering.* [55]His offering *was* one silver platter, the weight of which *was* one hundred and thirty *shekels,* and one silver bowl of seventy shekels, according to the shekel of the sanctuary, both of them full of fine flour mixed with oil as a grain offering; [56]one gold pan of ten *shekels,* full of incense; [57]one young bull, one ram, and one male lamb in its first year, as a burnt offering; [58]one kid of the goats as a sin offering; [59]and as the sacrifice of peace offerings: two oxen, five rams, five male goats, and five male lambs in their first year. This *was* the offering of Gamaliel the son of Pedahzur.

[60]On the ninth day Abidan the son of Gideoni, leader of the children of Benjamin, *presented an offering.* [61]His offering *was* one silver platter, the weight of which *was* one hundred and thirty *shekels,* and one silver bowl of seventy shekels, according to the shekel of the sanctuary, both of them full of fine flour mixed with oil as a grain offering; [62]one gold pan of ten *shekels,* full of incense; [63]one young bull, one ram, and one male lamb in its first year, as a burnt offering; [64]one kid of the goats as a sin offering; [65]and as the sacrifice of peace offerings: two oxen, five rams, five male goats, and five male lambs in their first year. This *was* the offering of Abidan the son of Gideoni.

[66]On the tenth day Ahiezer the son of Ammishaddai, leader of the children of Dan, *presented an offering.* [67]His offering *was* one silver platter, the weight of which *was* one hundred and thirty *shekels,* and one silver bowl of seventy shekels, according to the shekel of the sanctuary, both of

---

7:42 [a]Spelled *Reuel* in 2:14

them full of fine flour mixed with oil as a grain offering; 68one gold pan of ten *shekels*, full of incense; 69one young bull, one ram, and one male lamb in its first year, as a burnt offering; 70one kid of the goats as a sin offering; 71and as the sacrifice of peace offerings: two oxen, five rams, five male goats, and five male lambs in their first year. This *was* the offering of Ahiezer the son of Ammishaddai.

72On the eleventh day Pagiel the son of Ocran, leader of the children of Asher, *presented an offering.* 73His offering *was* one silver platter, the weight of which *was* one hundred and thirty *shekels*, and one silver bowl of seventy shekels, according to the shekel of the sanctuary, both of them full of fine flour mixed with oil as a grain offering; 74one gold pan of ten *shekels*, full of incense; 75one young bull, one ram, and one male lamb in its first year, as a burnt offering; 76one kid of the goats as a sin offering; 77and as the sacrifice of peace offerings: two oxen, five rams, five male goats, and five male lambs in their first year. This *was* the offering of Pagiel the son of Ocran.

78On the twelfth day Ahira the son of Enan, leader of the children of Naphtali, *presented an offering.* 79His offering *was* one silver platter, the weight of which *was* one hundred and thirty *shekels*, and one silver bowl of seventy shekels, according to the shekel of the sanctuary, both of them full of fine flour mixed with oil as a grain offering; 80one gold pan of ten *shekels*, full of incense; 81one young bull, one ram, and one male lamb in its first year, as a burnt offering; 82one kid of the goats as a sin offering; 83and as the sacrifice of peace offerings: two oxen, five rams, five male goats, and five male lambs in their first year. This *was* the offering of Ahira the son of Enan.

84This *was* the dedication *offering* for the altar from the leaders of Israel, when it was anointed: twelve silver platters, twelve silver bowls, and twelve gold pans. 85Each silver platter *weighed* one hundred and thirty *shekels* and each bowl seventy *shekels*. All the silver of the vessels *weighed* two thousand four hundred *shekels*, according to the shekel of the sanctuary. 86The twelve gold pans full of incense *weighed* ten *shekels* apiece, according to the shekel of the sanctuary; all the gold of the pans *weighed* one

hundred and twenty *shekels*. 87All the oxen for the burnt offering *were* twelve young bulls, the rams twelve, the male lambs in their first year twelve, with their grain offering, and the kids of the goats as a sin offering twelve. 88And all the oxen for the sacrifice of peace offerings were twenty-four bulls, the rams sixty, the male goats sixty, and the lambs in their first year sixty. This *was* the dedication *offering* for the altar after it was anointed.

89Now when Moses went into the tabernacle of meeting to speak with Him, he heard the voice of One speaking to him from above the mercy seat that *was* on the ark of the Testimony, from between the two cherubim; thus He spoke to him.

7:89 He spoke to him. After the tabernacle was completed, the Lord communicated His Word to Moses from the mercy seat in the Holy of Holies.

Arrangement of the Lamps

8 And the LORD spoke to Moses, saying: 2"Speak to Aaron, and say to him, 'When you arrange the lamps, the seven lamps shall give light in front of the lampstand.' " 3And Aaron did so; he arranged the lamps to face toward the front of the lampstand, as the LORD commanded Moses. 4Now this workmanship of the lampstand *was* hammered gold; from its shaft to its flowers it *was* hammered work. According to the pattern which the LORD had shown Moses, so he made the lampstand.

Cleansing and Dedication of the Levites

5Then the LORD spoke to Moses, saying: 6"Take the Levites from among the children of Israel and cleanse them *ceremonially*. 7Thus you shall do to them to cleanse them: Sprinkle water of purification on them, and let them shave all their body, and let them wash their clothes, and *so* make themselves clean. 8Then let them take a young bull with its grain offering of fine flour mixed with oil, and you shall take

8:6 cleanse. In contrast to the priests, who were consecrated, the Levites were cleansed. This cleansing included the sprinkling of water, the shaving of the body, and the washing of clothes. This cleansing of the Levites made them pure so that they could come into contact with the holy objects of the tabernacle.

another young bull as a sin offering. ⁹And you shall bring the Levites before the tabernacle of meeting, and you shall gather together the whole congregation of the children of Israel. ¹⁰So you shall bring the Levites before the LORD, and the children of Israel shall lay their hands on the Levites; ¹¹and Aaron shall offer the Levites before the LORD *like* a wave offering from the children of Israel, that they may perform the work of the LORD. ¹²Then the Levites shall lay their hands on the heads of the young bulls, and you shall offer one as a sin offering and the other as a burnt offering to the LORD, to make atonement for the Levites.

¹³"And you shall stand the Levites before Aaron and his sons, and then offer them *like* a wave offering to the LORD. ¹⁴Thus you shall separate the Levites from among the children of Israel, and the Levites shall be Mine. ¹⁵After that the Levites shall go in to service the tabernacle of meeting. So you shall cleanse them and offer them *like* a wave offering. ¹⁶For they *are* wholly given to Me from among the children of Israel; I have taken them for Myself instead of all who open the womb, the firstborn of all the children of Israel. ¹⁷For all the firstborn among the children of Israel *are* Mine, *both* man and beast; on the day that I struck all the firstborn in the land of Egypt I sanctified them to Myself. ¹⁸I have taken the Levites instead of all the firstborn of the children of Israel. ¹⁹And I have given the Levites as a gift to Aaron and his sons from among the children of Israel, to do the work for the children of Israel in the tabernacle of meeting, and to make atonement for the children of Israel, that there be no plague among the children of Israel when the children of Israel come near the sanctuary."

8:19 a gift to Aaron. God gave the Levites to Aaron and his sons to assist the priests.

²⁰Thus Moses and Aaron and all the congregation of the children of Israel did to the Levites; according to all that the LORD commanded Moses concerning the Levites, so the children of Israel did to them. ²¹And the Levites purified themselves and washed their clothes; then Aaron presented them *like* a wave offering before the LORD, and

Aaron made atonement for them to cleanse them. ²²After that the Levites went in to do their work in the tabernacle of meeting before Aaron and his sons; as the LORD commanded Moses concerning the Levites, so they did to them.

²³Then the LORD spoke to Moses, saying, ²⁴"This *is* what *pertains* to the Levites: From twenty-five years old and above one may enter to perform service in the work of the tabernacle of meeting; ²⁵and at the age of fifty years they must cease performing this work, and shall work no more. ²⁶They may minister with their brethren in the tabernacle of meeting, to attend to needs, but they *themselves* shall do no work. Thus you shall do to the Levites regarding their duties."

The Second Passover

9 Now the LORD spoke to Moses in the Wilderness of Sinai, in the first month of the second year after they had come out of the land of Egypt, saying: ²"Let the children of Israel keep the Passover at its appointed time. ³On the fourteenth day of this month, at twilight, you shall keep it at its appointed time. According to all its rites and ceremonies you shall keep it." ⁴So Moses told the children of Israel that they should keep the Passover. ⁵And they kept the Passover on the fourteenth day of the first month, at twilight, in the Wilderness of Sinai; according to all that the LORD commanded Moses, so the children of Israel did.

⁶Now there were *certain* men who were defiled by a human corpse, so that they could not keep the Passover on that day; and they came before Moses and Aaron that day. ⁷And those men said to him, "We *became* defiled by a human corpse. Why are we kept from presenting the offering of the LORD at its appointed time among the children of Israel?"

⁸And Moses said to them, "Stand still, that I may hear what the LORD will command concerning you."

⁹Then the LORD spoke to Moses, saying, ¹⁰"Speak to the children of Israel, saying: 'If anyone of you or your posterity is unclean because of a corpse, or *is* far away on a journey, he may still keep the LORD's Passover. ¹¹On the fourteenth day of the second

month, at twilight, they may keep it. They shall eat it with unleavened bread and bitter herbs. [12]They shall leave none of it until morning, nor break one of its bones. According to all the ordinances of the Passover they shall keep it. [13]But the man who *is* clean and is not on a journey, and ceases to keep the Passover, that same person shall be cut off from among his people, because he did not bring the offering of the LORD at its appointed time; that man shall bear his sin.

> **9:13 cut off.** If any Israelite did not keep the Passover at the appointed time, and he was not exempt because he was unclean or away from the land, then he was to be "cut off," which implies that he would be killed.

[14]'And if a stranger dwells among you, and would keep the LORD's Passover, he must do so according to the rite of the Passover and according to its ceremony; you shall have one ordinance, both for the stranger and the native of the land.' "

The Cloud and the Fire

[15]Now on the day that the tabernacle was raised up, the cloud covered the tabernacle, the tent of the Testimony; from evening until morning it was above the tabernacle like the appearance of fire. [16]So it was always: the cloud covered it *by day*, and the appearance of fire by night. [17]Whenever the cloud was taken up from above the tabernacle, after that the children of Israel would journey; and in the place where the cloud settled, there the children of Israel would pitch their tents. [18]At the command of the LORD the children of Israel would journey, and at the command of the LORD they would camp; as long as the cloud stayed above the tabernacle they remained encamped. [19]Even when the cloud continued long, many days above the tabernacle, the children of Israel kept the charge of the LORD and did not journey. [20]So it was, when the cloud was above the tabernacle a few days: according to the command of the LORD they would remain encamped, and according to the command of the LORD they would journey. [21]So it was, when the cloud remained only from evening until morning: when the cloud was taken up in the morning, then they would journey; whether by day or by night, whenever the cloud was taken up, they would journey. [22]*Whether it was* two days, a month, or a year that the cloud remained above the tabernacle, the children of Israel would remain encamped and not journey; but when it was taken up, they would journey. [23]At the command of the LORD they remained encamped, and at the command of the LORD they journeyed; they kept the charge of the LORD, at the command of the LORD by the hand of Moses.

> **9:15–23** The cloud was the visible symbol of the Lord's presence. When the cloud moved, it signaled to Israel that they were to follow it on their journey. The cloud by day became a fire that was seen at night (see Lev. 16:2).

Two Silver Trumpets

10And the LORD spoke to Moses, saying: [2]"Make two silver trumpets for yourself; you shall make them of hammered work; you shall use them for calling the congregation and for directing the movement of the camps. [3]When they blow both of them, all the congregation shall gather before you at the door of the tabernacle of meeting. [4]But if they blow *only* one, then the leaders, the heads of the divisions of Israel, shall gather to you. [5]When you sound the advance, the camps that lie on the east side shall then begin their journey. [6]When you sound the advance the second time, then the camps that lie on the south side shall begin their journey; they shall sound the call for them to begin their journeys. [7]And when the assembly is to be gathered together, you shall blow, but not sound the advance. [8]The sons of Aaron, the priests, shall blow the trumpets; and these shall be to you as an ordinance forever throughout your generations.

[9]"When you go to war in your land against the enemy who oppresses you, then you shall sound an alarm with the trumpets, and you will be remembered before the LORD your God, and you will be saved from your enemies. [10]Also in the day of your gladness, in your appointed feasts, and at the beginning of your months, you shall blow the trumpets over your burnt offerings and over the sacrifices of your peace

offerings; and they shall be a memorial for you before your God: I *am* the LORD your God."

10:3–8 The first function of the trumpets was to gather the people to the tabernacle. If both trumpets were blown, all adult males gathered; if only one was blown, then only the leaders came. The second purpose of the trumpets was to signal that the tribes were to set out on their march. The blowing of the horns was to be a perpetual ordinance in Israel, calling the people to worship or to war.

Departure from Sinai

[11]Now it came to pass on the twentieth *day* of the second month, in the second year, that the cloud was taken up from above the tabernacle of the Testimony. [12]And the children of Israel set out from the Wilderness of Sinai on their journeys; then the cloud settled down in the Wilderness of Paran. [13]So they started out for the first time according to the command of the LORD by the hand of Moses.

[14]The standard of the camp of the children of Judah set out first according to their armies; over their army was Nahshon the son of Amminadab. [15]Over the army of the tribe of the children of Issachar *was* Nethanel the son of Zuar. [16]And over the army of the tribe of the children of Zebulun *was* Eliab the son of Helon.

10:14 In accordance with Gen. 49:8–12, the tribe of Judah was given preeminence as the ruling tribe and led the march into the Promised Land.

[17]Then the tabernacle was taken down; and the sons of Gershon and the sons of Merari set out, carrying the tabernacle. [18]And the standard of the camp of Reuben set out according to their armies; over their army *was* Elizur the son of Shedeur. [19]Over the army of the tribe of the children of Simeon *was* Shelumiel the son of Zurishaddai. [20]And over the army of the tribe of the children of Gad *was* Eliasaph the son of Deuel. [21]Then the Kohathites set out, carrying the holy things. (The tabernacle would be prepared for their arrival.) [22]And the standard of the camp of the children of Ephraim set out according to

their armies; over their army *was* Elishama the son of Ammihud. [23]Over the army of the tribe of the children of Manasseh *was* Gamaliel the son of Pedahzur. [24]And over the army of the tribe of the children of Benjamin *was* Abidan the son of Gideoni.

[25]Then the standard of the camp of the children of Dan (the rear guard of all the camps) set out according to their armies; over their army *was* Ahiezer the son of Ammishaddai. [26]Over the army of the tribe of the children of Asher *was* Pagiel the son of Ocran. [27]And over the army of the tribe of the children of Naphtali *was* Ahira the son of Enan.

[28]Thus *was* the order of march of the children of Israel, according to their armies, when they began their journey.

[29]Now Moses said to Hobab the son of Reuel[a] the Midianite, Moses' father-in-law, "We are setting out for the place of which the LORD said, 'I will give it to you.' Come with us, and we will treat you well; for the LORD has promised good things to Israel."

[30]And he said to him, "I will not go, but I will depart to my *own* land and to my relatives."

[31]So *Moses* said, "Please do not leave, inasmuch as you know how we are to camp in the wilderness, and you can be our eyes. [32]And it shall be, if you go with us—indeed it shall be—that whatever good the LORD will do to us, the same we will do to you."

[33]So they departed from the mountain of the LORD on a journey of three days; and the ark of the covenant of the LORD went before them for the three days' journey, to search out a resting place for them. [34]And the cloud of the LORD *was* above them by day when they went out from the camp.

[35]So it was, whenever the ark set out, that Moses said:

"Rise up, O LORD!
Let Your enemies be scattered,
And let those who hate You flee
before You."

[36]And when it rested, he said:

"Return, O LORD,
To the many thousands of Israel."

10:29 [a]Septuagint reads *Raguel* (compare Exodus 2:18).

11:1–25:18 A major change occurs in the attitude of the Israelites, from obedient to complaining (11:1; 16:1–3) and rebellious (14:9; 17:10). Ultimately even Moses and Aaron rebelled (20:10, 24). Israel's disobedience roused the Lord's anger, and He plagued His people (14:37; 16:46–50). Even though God judged that generation, He will still fulfill His promises to Abraham (23:5–24:24).

The People Complain

11 Now *when* the people complained, it displeased the LORD; for the LORD heard *it,* and His anger was aroused. So the fire of the LORD burned among them, and consumed *some* in the outskirts of the camp. ²Then the people cried out to Moses, and when Moses prayed to the LORD, the fire was quenched. ³So he called the name of the place Taberah,*ᵃ* because the fire of the LORD had burned among them.

⁴Now the mixed multitude who were among them yielded to intense craving; so the children of Israel also wept again and said: "Who will give us meat to eat? ⁵We remember the fish which we ate freely in Egypt, the cucumbers, the melons, the leeks, the onions, and the garlic; ⁶but now our whole being *is* dried up; *there is* nothing at all except this manna *before* our eyes!"

⁷Now the manna *was* like coriander seed, and its color like the color of bdellium. ⁸The people went about and gathered *it,* ground *it* on millstones or beat *it* in the mortar, cooked *it* in pans, and made cakes of it; and its taste was like the taste of pastry prepared with oil. ⁹And when the dew fell on the camp in the night, the manna fell on it.

¹⁰Then Moses heard the people weeping throughout their families, everyone at the door of his tent; and the anger of the LORD was greatly aroused; Moses also was displeased. ¹¹So Moses said to the LORD, "Why have You afflicted Your servant? And why have I not found favor in Your sight, that You have laid the burden of all these people on me? ¹²Did I conceive all these people? Did I beget them, that You should say to me, 'Carry them in your bosom, as a guardian carries a nursing child,' to the land which You swore to their fathers? ¹³Where

am I to get meat to give to all these people? For they weep all over me, saying, 'Give us meat, that we may eat.' ¹⁴I am not able to bear all these people alone, because the burden *is* too heavy for me. ¹⁵If You treat me like this, please kill me here and now—if I have found favor in Your sight—and do not let me see my wretchedness!"

11:13,14 Moses confessed to God that he was unable to provide for the people's demand for meat. Their complaining discouraged him so much that he desired death from the Lord's hand. In response to Moses' despair, the Lord gave him 70 men to help him lead.

The Seventy Elders

¹⁶So the LORD said to Moses: "Gather to Me seventy men of the elders of Israel, whom you know to be the elders of the people and officers over them; bring them to the tabernacle of meeting, that they may stand there with you. ¹⁷Then I will come down and talk with you there. I will take of the Spirit that *is* upon you and will put *the same* upon them; and they shall bear the burden of the people with you, that you may not bear *it* yourself alone. ¹⁸Then you shall say to the people, 'Consecrate yourselves for tomorrow, and you shall eat meat; for you have wept in the hearing of the LORD, saying, "Who will give us meat to eat? For *it was* well with us in Egypt." Therefore the LORD will give you meat, and you shall eat. ¹⁹You shall eat, not one day, nor two days, nor five days, nor ten days, nor twenty days, ²⁰but *for* a whole month, until it comes out of your nostrils and becomes loathsome to you, because you have despised the LORD who is among you, and have wept before Him, saying, "Why did we ever come up out of Egypt?" ' "

11:17 the Spirit. This refers to the Spirit of God. The Holy Spirit empowered Moses to lead Israel. In v. 25, the Lord gave the Spirit to the 70 men chosen to aide Moses.

²¹And Moses said, "The people whom I *am* among *are* six hundred thousand men on foot; yet You have said, 'I will give them meat, that they may eat *for* a whole

---

11:3 *ᵃ*Literally *Burning*

month.' ²²Shall flocks and herds be slaughtered for them, to provide enough for them? Or shall all the fish of the sea be gathered together for them, to provide enough for them?"

²³And the LORD said to Moses, "Has the LORD's arm been shortened? Now you shall see whether what I say will happen to you or not."

11:23 Has the LORD's arm been shortened? A figure of speech indicating that the Lord was able to provide meat for the 600,000 men of Israel and their families for one month.

²⁴So Moses went out and told the people the words of the LORD, and he gathered the seventy men of the elders of the people and placed them around the tabernacle. ²⁵Then the LORD came down in the cloud, and spoke to him, and took of the Spirit that *was* upon him, and placed *the same* upon the seventy elders; and it happened, when the Spirit rested upon them, that they prophesied, although they never did *so* again.*

²⁶But two men had remained in the camp: the name of one *was* Eldad, and the name of the other Medad. And the Spirit rested upon them. Now they *were* among those listed, but who had not gone out to the tabernacle; yet they prophesied in the camp. ²⁷And a young man ran and told Moses, and said, "Eldad and Medad are prophesying in the camp."

²⁸So Joshua the son of Nun, Moses' assistant, *one* of his choice men, answered and said, "Moses my lord, forbid them!"

²⁹Then Moses said to him, "Are you zealous for my sake? Oh, that all the LORD's people were prophets *and* that the LORD would put His Spirit upon them!" ³⁰And Moses returned to the camp, he and the elders of Israel.

The LORD Sends Quail

³¹Now a wind went out from the LORD, and it brought quail from the sea and left *them* fluttering near the camp, about a day's journey on this side and about a day's journey on the other side, all around the camp, and about two cubits above the surface of the ground. ³²And the people stayed up all that day, all night, and all the next day, and gathered the quail (he who gathered least gathered ten homers); and they spread *them* out for themselves all around the camp. ³³But while the meat *was* still between their teeth, before it was chewed, the wrath of the LORD was aroused against the people, and the LORD struck the people with a very great plague. ³⁴So he called the name of that place Kibroth Hattaavah,* because there they buried the people who had yielded to craving.

³⁵From Kibroth Hattaavah the people moved to Hazeroth, and camped at Hazeroth.

Dissension of Aaron and Miriam

12 Then Miriam and Aaron spoke against Moses because of the Ethiopian woman whom he had married; for he had married an Ethiopian woman. ²So they said, "Has the LORD indeed spoken only through Moses? Has He not spoken through us also?" And the LORD heard *it.* ³(Now the man Moses *was* very humble, more than all men who *were* on the face of the earth.)

12:2 spoken only through Moses. Aaron and Miriam opposed Moses' leadership and asserted that God had spoken to them in the same way that He had spoken to Moses.

⁴Suddenly the LORD said to Moses, Aaron, and Miriam, "Come out, you three, to the tabernacle of meeting!" So the three came out. ⁵Then the LORD came down in the pillar of cloud and stood *in* the door of the tabernacle, and called Aaron and Miriam. And they both went forward. ⁶Then He said,

"Hear now My words:
If there is a prophet among you,
I, the LORD, make Myself known to him in a vision;
I speak to him in a dream.
⁷   Not so with My servant Moses;
He *is* faithful in all My house.
⁸   I speak with him face to face,
Even plainly, and not in dark sayings;

11:25 *ᵃ*Targum and Vulgate read *did not cease.*   11:34 *ᵃ*Literally *Graves of Craving*

And he sees the form of the LORD.
Why then were you not afraid
To speak against My servant Moses?"

12:7,8 faithful in all My house. Moses loyally performed his role as the covenant mediator between the Lord and Israel. **face to face.** God spoke to Moses plainly, not through visions and dreams. He had the most explicit, intimate encounters with God. **the form of the LORD.** The likeness or representation of the Lord which Moses was privileged to see (see Ex. 33:23).

⁹So the anger of the LORD was aroused against them, and He departed. ¹⁰And when the cloud departed from above the tabernacle, suddenly Miriam *became* leprous, as *white as* snow. Then Aaron turned toward Miriam, and there she was, a leper. ¹¹So Aaron said to Moses, "Oh, my lord! Please do not lay *this* sin on us, in which we have done foolishly and in which we have sinned. ¹²Please do not let her be as one dead, whose flesh is half consumed when he comes out of his mother's womb!"

12:10 leprous. In judgment for Miriam's opposition to Moses, the Lord struck her with leprosy. A public sin required a public response from the Lord.

¹³So Moses cried out to the LORD, saying, "Please heal her, O God, I pray!"
¹⁴Then the LORD said to Moses, "If her father had but spit in her face, would she not be shamed seven days? Let her be shut out of the camp seven days, and afterward she may be received *again*." ¹⁵So Miriam was shut out of the camp seven days, and the people did not journey till Miriam was brought in *again*. ¹⁶And afterward the people moved from Hazeroth and camped in the Wilderness of Paran.

Spies Sent into Canaan

13 And the LORD spoke to Moses, saying, ²"Send men to spy out the land of Canaan, which I am giving to the children of Israel; from each tribe of their fathers you shall send a man, every one a leader among them."
³So Moses sent them from the Wilderness of Paran according to the command of

13:2 spy out the land of Canaan. The spies were called to explore the Promised Land before their conquest. They were sent to find valuable information for Moses, such as the nature of the Land itself and the strengths and weaknesses of the people.

the LORD, all of them men who *were* heads of the children of Israel. ⁴Now these *were* their names: from the tribe of Reuben, Shammua the son of Zaccur; ⁵from the tribe of Simeon, Shaphat the son of Hori; ⁶from the tribe of Judah, Caleb the son of Jephunneh; ⁷from the tribe of Issachar, Igal the son of Joseph; ⁸from the tribe of Ephraim, Hoshea*ᵃ* the son of Nun; ⁹from the tribe of Benjamin, Palti the son of Raphu; ¹⁰from the tribe of Zebulun, Gaddiel the son of Sodi; ¹¹from the tribe of Joseph, *that is,* from the tribe of Manasseh, Gaddi the son of Susi; ¹²from the tribe of Dan, Ammiel the son of Gemalli; ¹³from the tribe of Asher, Sethur the son of Michael; ¹⁴from the tribe of Naphtali, Nahbi the son of Vophsi; ¹⁵from the tribe of Gad, Geuel the son of Machi.
¹⁶These *are* the names of the men whom Moses sent to spy out the land. And Moses called Hoshea*ᵃ* the son of Nun, Joshua.

13:16 Hoshea...Joshua. For unknown reasons, Moses changed the name of Hoshea, meaning "desire for salvation," to Joshua, meaning "the Lord is salvation."

¹⁷Then Moses sent them to spy out the land of Canaan, and said to them, "Go up this *way* into the South, and go up to the mountains, ¹⁸and see what the land is like: whether the people who dwell in it *are* strong or weak, few or many; ¹⁹whether the land they dwell in *is* good or bad; whether the cities they inhabit *are* like camps or strongholds; ²⁰whether the land *is* rich or poor; and whether there are forests there or not. Be of good courage. And bring some of the fruit of the land." Now the time *was* the season of the first ripe grapes.
²¹So they went up and spied out the land from the Wilderness of Zin as far as Rehob, near the entrance of Hamath. ²²And they went up through the South and came to Hebron; Ahiman, Sheshai, and Talmai, the

---

13:8 *ᵃ*Septuagint and Vulgate read *Oshea*. 13:16 *ᵃ*Septuagint and Vulgate read *Oshea*.

descendants of Anak, *were* there. (Now Hebron was built seven years before Zoan in Egypt.) ²³Then they came to the Valley of Eshcol, and there cut down a branch with one cluster of grapes; they carried it between two of them on a pole. *They* also *brought* some of the pomegranates and figs. ²⁴The place was called the Valley of Eshcol,*ᵃ* because of the cluster which the men of Israel cut down there. ²⁵And they returned from spying out the land after forty days.

²⁶Now they departed and came back to Moses and Aaron and all the congregation of the children of Israel in the Wilderness of Paran, at Kadesh; they brought back word to them and to all the congregation, and showed them the fruit of the land. ²⁷Then they told him, and said: "We went to the land where you sent us. It truly flows with milk and honey, and this *is* its fruit. ²⁸Nevertheless the people who dwell in the land *are* strong; the cities *are* fortified *and* very large; moreover we saw the descendants of Anak there. ²⁹The Amalekites dwell in the land of the South; the Hittites, the Jebusites, and the Amorites dwell in the mountains; and the Canaanites dwell by the sea and along the banks of the Jordan."

³⁰Then Caleb quieted the people before Moses, and said, "Let us go up at once and take possession, for we are well able to overcome it."

³¹But the men who had gone up with him said, "We are not able to go up against the people, for they *are* stronger than we." ³²And they gave the children of Israel a bad report of the land which they had spied out, saying, "The land through which we have gone as spies *is* a land that devours its inhabitants, and all the people whom we saw in it *are* men of *great* stature. ³³There we saw the giants*ᵃ* (the descendants of Anak came from the giants); and we were like grasshoppers in our own sight, and so we were in their sight."

13:32 a bad report. The spies reported that the Land was good but that the people were too strong to conquer. The report was evil because it exaggerated the dangers of the Land, made the people afraid, and did not express faith in God to fulfill His promises.

Israel Refuses to Enter Canaan

14 So all the congregation lifted up their voices and cried, and the people wept that night. ²And all the children of Israel complained against Moses and Aaron, and the whole congregation said to them, "If only we had died in the land of Egypt! Or if only we had died in this wilderness! ³Why has the LORD brought us to this land to fall by the sword, that our wives and children should become victims? Would it not be better for us to return to Egypt?" ⁴So they said to one another, "Let us select a leader and return to Egypt."

⁵Then Moses and Aaron fell on their faces before all the assembly of the congregation of the children of Israel.

⁶But Joshua the son of Nun and Caleb the son of Jephunneh, *who were* among those who had spied out the land, tore their clothes; ⁷and they spoke to all the congregation of the children of Israel, saying: "The land we passed through to spy out *is* an exceedingly good land. ⁸If the LORD delights in us, then He will bring us into this land and give it to us, 'a land which flows with milk and honey.'*ᵃ* ⁹Only do not rebel against the LORD, nor fear the people of the land, for they *are* our bread; their protection has departed from them, and the LORD *is* with us. Do not fear them."

14:7–9 Joshua and Caleb reaffirmed their appraisal that the Land was good and that they were confident that the Lord would deliver it and the people into their hands.

¹⁰And all the congregation said to stone them with stones. Now the glory of the LORD appeared in the tabernacle of meeting before all the children of Israel.

Moses Intercedes for the People

¹¹Then the LORD said to Moses: "How long will these people reject Me? And how long will they not believe Me, with all the signs which I have performed among them? ¹²I will strike them with the pestilence and disinherit them, and I will make of you a nation greater and mightier than they."

¹³And Moses said to the LORD: "Then the Egyptians will hear *it,* for by Your might

13:24 *ᵃ*Literally *Cluster*   13:33 *ᵃ*Hebrew *nephilim*   14:8 *ᵃ*Exodus 3:8

You brought these people up from among them, [14]and they will tell *it* to the inhabitants of this land. They have heard that You, LORD, *are* among these people; that You, LORD, are seen face to face and Your cloud stands above them, and You go before them in a pillar of cloud by day and in a pillar of fire by night. [15]Now *if* You kill these people as one man, then the nations which have heard of Your fame will speak, saying, [16]'Because the LORD was not able to bring this people to the land which He swore to give them, therefore He killed them in the wilderness.' [17]And now, I pray, let the power of my Lord be great, just as You have spoken, saying, [18]'The LORD is longsuffering and abundant in mercy, forgiving iniquity and transgression; but He by no means clears *the guilty*, visiting the iniquity of the fathers on the children to the third and fourth *generation*.'*a* [19]Pardon the iniquity of this people, I pray, according to the greatness of Your mercy, just as You have forgiven this people, from Egypt even until now."

[20]Then the LORD said: "I have pardoned, according to your word; [21]but truly, as I live, all the earth shall be filled with the glory of the LORD— [22]because all these men who have seen My glory and the signs which I did in Egypt and in the wilderness, and have put Me to the test now these ten times, and have not heeded My voice, [23]they certainly shall not see the land of which I swore to their fathers, nor shall any of those who rejected Me see it. [24]But My servant Caleb, because he has a different spirit in him and has followed Me fully, I will bring into the land where he went, and his descendants shall inherit it. [25]Now the Amalekites and the Canaanites dwell in the valley; tomorrow turn and move out into the wilderness by the Way of the Red Sea."

Death Sentence on the Rebels

[26]And the LORD spoke to Moses and Aaron, saying, [27]"How long *shall I bear with* this evil congregation who complain against Me? I have heard the complaints which the children of Israel make against Me. [28]Say to them, 'As I live,' says the LORD, 'just as you have spoken in My hearing, so I will do to you: [29]The carcasses of you who have complained against Me shall fall in this wilderness, all of you who were numbered, according to your entire number, from twenty years old and above. [30]Except for Caleb the son of Jephunneh and Joshua the son of Nun, you shall by no means enter the land which I swore I would make you dwell in. [31]But your little ones, whom you said would be victims, I will bring in, and they shall know the land which you have despised. [32]But *as for* you, your carcasses shall fall in this wilderness. [33]And your sons shall be shepherds in the wilderness forty years, and bear the brunt of your infidelity, until your carcasses are consumed in the wilderness. [34]According to the number of the days in which you spied out the land, forty days, for each day you shall bear your guilt one year, *namely* forty years, and you shall know My rejection. [35]I the LORD have spoken this. I will surely do so to all this evil congregation who are gathered together against Me. In this wilderness they shall be consumed, and there they shall die.' "

14:26–35 The Lord granted Israel's wish as their judgment—"if only we had died in this wilderness!" (14:2). The present generation of rebels spent forty years in the wilderness, one year for each day the spies were in Canaan. They would die there, but God would bring their children into the Land.

[36]Now the men whom Moses sent to spy out the land, who returned and made all the congregation complain against him by bringing a bad report of the land, [37]those very men who brought the evil report about the land, died by the plague before the LORD. [38]But Joshua the son of Nun and Caleb the son of Jephunneh remained alive, of the men who went to spy out the land.

A Futile Invasion Attempt

[39]Then Moses told these words to all the children of Israel, and the people mourned greatly. [40]And they rose early in the morning and went up to the top of the mountain, saying, "Here we are, and we will go up to the place which the LORD has promised, for we have sinned!"

14:18 *a*Exodus 34:6,7

[41]And Moses said, "Now why do you transgress the command of the LORD? For this will not succeed. [42]Do not go up, lest you be defeated by your enemies, for the LORD *is* not among you. [43]For the Amalekites and the Canaanites *are* there before you, and you shall fall by the sword; because you have turned away from the LORD, the LORD will not be with you."

[44]But they presumed to go up to the mountaintop. Nevertheless, neither the ark of the covenant of the LORD nor Moses departed from the camp. [45]Then the Amalekites and the Canaanites who dwelt in that mountain came down and attacked them, and drove them back as far as Hormah.

Laws of Grain and Drink Offerings

15 And the LORD spoke to Moses, saying, [2]"Speak to the children of Israel, and say to them: 'When you have come into the land you are to inhabit, which I am giving to you, [3]and you make an offering by fire to the LORD, a burnt offering or a sacrifice, to fulfill a vow or as a freewill offering or in your appointed feasts, to make a sweet aroma to the LORD, from the herd or the flock, [4]then he who presents his offering to the LORD shall bring a grain offering of one-tenth *of an ephah* of fine flour mixed with one-fourth of a hin of oil; [5]and one-fourth of a hin of wine as a drink offering you shall prepare with the burnt offering or the sacrifice, for each lamb. [6]Or for a ram you shall prepare as a grain offering two-tenths *of an ephah* of fine flour mixed with one-third of a hin of oil; [7]and as a drink offering you shall offer one-third of a hin of wine as a sweet aroma to the LORD. [8]And when you prepare a young bull as a burnt offering, or as a sacrifice to fulfill a vow, or as a peace offering to the LORD, [9]then shall be offered with the young bull a grain offering of three-tenths *of an ephah* of fine flour mixed with half a hin of oil; [10]and you shall bring as the drink offering half a hin of wine as an offering made by fire, a sweet aroma to the LORD.

[11]'Thus it shall be done for each young bull, for each ram, or for each lamb or young goat. [12]According to the number that you prepare, so you shall do with everyone according to their number. [13]All who are native-born shall do these things in this manner, in presenting an offering made by fire, a sweet aroma to the LORD. [14]And if a stranger dwells with you, or whoever *is* among you throughout your generations, and would present an offering made by fire, a sweet aroma to the LORD, just as you do, so shall he do. [15]One ordinance *shall be* for you of the assembly and for the stranger who dwells *with you,* an ordinance forever throughout your generations; as you are, so shall the stranger be before the LORD. [16]One law and one custom shall be for you and for the stranger who dwells with you.' "[a]

[17]Again the LORD spoke to Moses, saying, [18]"Speak to the children of Israel, and say to them: 'When you come into the land to which I bring you, [19]then it will be, when you eat of the bread of the land, that you shall offer up a heave offering to the LORD. [20]You shall offer up a cake of the first of your ground meal *as* a heave offering; as a heave offering of the threshing floor, so shall you offer it up. [21]Of the first of your ground meal you shall give to the LORD a heave offering throughout your generations.

> **15:17–21** When the people entered the land of Canaan and began to enjoy its produce, they showed their devotion to the Lord by presenting to Him a cake baked from the first cuttings of the grain.

Laws Concerning Unintentional Sin

[22]'If you sin unintentionally, and do not observe all these commandments which the LORD has spoken to Moses— [23]all that the LORD has commanded you by the hand of Moses, from the day the LORD gave commandment and onward throughout your generations— [24]then it will be, if it is unintentionally committed, without the knowledge of the congregation, that the whole congregation shall offer one young bull as a burnt offering, as a sweet aroma to the LORD, with its grain offering and its drink offering, according to the ordinance, and one kid of the goats as a sin offering. [25]So the priest shall make atonement for the whole congregation of the children of Israel, and it shall be forgiven them, for it

---

15:16 [a]Compare Exodus 12:49

was unintentional; they shall bring their offering, an offering made by fire to the LORD, and their sin offering before the LORD, for their unintended sin. ²⁶It shall be forgiven the whole congregation of the children of Israel and the stranger who dwells among them, because all the people *did it* unintentionally.

²⁷And if a person sins unintentionally, then he shall bring a female goat in its first year as a sin offering. ²⁸So the priest shall make atonement for the person who sins unintentionally, when he sins unintentionally before the LORD, to make atonement for him; and it shall be forgiven him. ²⁹You shall have one law for him who sins unintentionally, *for* him who is native-born among the children of Israel and for the stranger who dwells among them.

Law Concerning Presumptuous Sin

³⁰'But the person who does *anything* presumptuously, *whether he is* native-born or a stranger, that one brings reproach on the LORD, and he shall be cut off from among his people. ³¹Because he has despised the word of the LORD, and has broken His commandment, that person shall be completely cut off; his guilt *shall be* upon him.' "

15:30 does *anything* presumptuously. Sins that were committed knowingly and deliberately were described as blasphemous because they were arrogant insubordination against the Lord. Anyone guilty of presumptuous sin was to be excommunicated from Israel and put to death.

Penalty for Violating the Sabbath

³²Now while the children of Israel were in the wilderness, they found a man gathering sticks on the Sabbath day. ³³And those who found him gathering sticks brought him to Moses and Aaron, and to all the congregation. ³⁴They put him under guard, because it had not been explained what should be done to him.

³⁵Then the LORD said to Moses, "The man must surely be put to death; all the congregation shall stone him with stones outside the camp." ³⁶So, as the LORD commanded Moses, all the congregation brought him outside the camp and stoned him with stones, and he died.

Tassels on Garments

³⁷Again the LORD spoke to Moses, saying, ³⁸"Speak to the children of Israel: Tell them to make tassels on the corners of their garments throughout their generations, and to put a blue thread in the tassels of the corners. ³⁹And you shall have the tassel, that you may look upon it and remember all the commandments of the LORD and do them, and that you *may* not follow the harlotry to which your own heart and your own eyes are inclined, ⁴⁰and that you may remember and do all My commandments, and be holy for your God. ⁴¹I *am* the LORD your God, who brought you out of the land of Egypt, to be your God: I *am* the LORD your God."

16:1–18:32 In 16:1–40, a Levite named Korah allied with other Israelite leaders and organized an opposition to the authority of Aaron and the priests. Angry that only Moses and Aaron had the unique right to represent the people before God, they rebelled. The Lord reaffirmed His choice of Aaron and restated the duties of the priests and Levites.

Rebellion Against Moses and Aaron

16 Now Korah the son of Izhar, the son of Kohath, the son of Levi, with Dathan and Abiram the sons of Eliab, and On the son of Peleth, sons of Reuben, took *men;* ²and they rose up before Moses with some of the children of Israel, two hundred and fifty leaders of the congregation, representatives of the congregation, men of renown. ³They gathered together against Moses and Aaron, and said to them, "*You take* too much upon yourselves, for all the congregation *is* holy, every one of them, and the LORD *is* among them. Why then do you exalt yourselves above the assembly of the LORD?"

⁴So when Moses heard *it,* he fell on his face; ⁵and he spoke to Korah and all his company, saying, "Tomorrow morning the LORD will show who *is* His and *who is* holy, and will cause *him* to come near to Him. That one whom He chooses He will cause to come near to Him. ⁶Do this: Take censers, Korah and all your company; ⁷put fire in them and put incense in them before the LORD tomorrow, and it shall be *that* the man whom the LORD chooses *is* the holy one. *You take* too much upon yourselves, you sons of Levi!"

⁸Then Moses said to Korah, "Hear now, you sons of Levi: ⁹*Is it* a small thing to you that the God of Israel has separated you from the congregation of Israel, to bring you near to Himself, to do the work of the tabernacle of the LORD, and to stand before the congregation to serve them; ¹⁰and that He has brought you near *to Himself*, you and all your brethren, the sons of Levi, with you? And are you seeking the priesthood also? ¹¹Therefore you and all your company *are* gathered together against the LORD. And what *is* Aaron that you complain against him?"

¹²And Moses sent to call Dathan and Abiram the sons of Eliab, but they said, "We will not come up! ¹³*Is it* a small thing that you have brought us up out of a land flowing with milk and honey, to kill us in the wilderness, that you should keep acting like a prince over us? ¹⁴Moreover you have not brought us into a land flowing with milk and honey, nor given us inheritance of fields and vineyards. Will you put out the eyes of these men? We will not come up!"

16:12 Dathan and Abiram. Two men of the tribe of Reuben who blamed Moses for leading Israel out of Egypt without bringing them into the land of Canaan. Because of Moses' perceived failure, they rebelled against him with Korah.

¹⁵Then Moses was very angry, and said to the LORD, "Do not respect their offering. I have not taken one donkey from them, nor have I hurt one of them."

¹⁶And Moses said to Korah, "Tomorrow, you and all your company be present before the LORD—you and they, as well as Aaron. ¹⁷Let each take his censer and put incense in it, and each of you bring his censer before the LORD, two hundred and fifty censers; both you and Aaron, each *with* his censer." ¹⁸So every man took his censer, put fire in it, laid incense on it, and stood at the door of the tabernacle of meeting with Moses and Aaron. ¹⁹And Korah gathered all the congregation against them at the door of the tabernacle of meeting. Then the glory of the LORD appeared to all the congregation.

²⁰And the LORD spoke to Moses and Aaron, saying, ²¹"Separate yourselves from among this congregation, that I may consume them in a moment."

²²Then they fell on their faces, and said, "O God, the God of the spirits of all flesh, shall one man sin, and You be angry with all the congregation?"

²³So the LORD spoke to Moses, saying, ²⁴"Speak to the congregation, saying, 'Get away from the tents of Korah, Dathan, and Abiram.' "

²⁵Then Moses rose and went to Dathan and Abiram, and the elders of Israel followed him. ²⁶And he spoke to the congregation, saying, "Depart now from the tents of these wicked men! Touch nothing of theirs, lest you be consumed in all their sins." ²⁷So they got away from around the tents of Korah, Dathan, and Abiram; and Dathan and Abiram came out and stood at the door of their tents, with their wives, their sons, and their little children.

²⁸And Moses said: "By this you shall know that the LORD has sent me to do all these works, for *I have* not *done them* of my own will. ²⁹If these men die naturally like all men, or if they are visited by the common fate of all men, *then* the LORD has not sent me. ³⁰But if the LORD creates a new thing, and the earth opens its mouth and swallows them up with all that belongs to them, and they go down alive into the pit, then you will understand that these men have rejected the LORD."

³¹Now it came to pass, as he finished speaking all these words, that the ground split apart under them, ³²and the earth opened its mouth and swallowed them up, with their households and all the men with Korah, with all *their* goods. ³³So they and all those with them went down alive into the pit; the earth closed over them, and they perished from among the assembly. ³⁴Then all Israel who *were* around them fled at their cry, for they said, "Lest the earth swallow us up *also!*"

³⁵And a fire came out from the LORD and consumed the two hundred and fifty men who were offering incense.

16:16–35 God judged the men who rebelled against Moses and Aaron by putting them to death.

³⁶Then the LORD spoke to Moses, saying: ³⁷"Tell Eleazar, the son of Aaron the priest, to pick up the censers out of the blaze, for

they are holy, and scatter the fire some distance away. ³⁸The censers of these men who sinned against their own souls, let them be made into hammered plates as a covering for the altar. Because they presented them before the LORD, therefore they are holy; and they shall be a sign to the children of Israel." ³⁹So Eleazar the priest took the bronze censers, which those who were burned up had presented, and they were hammered out as a covering on the altar, ⁴⁰to be a memorial to the children of Israel that no outsider, who is not a descendant of Aaron, should come near to offer incense before the LORD, that he might not become like Korah and his companions, just as the LORD had said to him through Moses.

Complaints of the People

⁴¹On the next day all the congregation of the children of Israel complained against Moses and Aaron, saying, "You have killed the people of the LORD." ⁴²Now it happened, when the congregation had gathered against Moses and Aaron, that they turned toward the tabernacle of meeting; and suddenly the cloud covered it, and the glory of the LORD appeared. ⁴³Then Moses and Aaron came before the tabernacle of meeting.

⁴⁴And the LORD spoke to Moses, saying, ⁴⁵"Get away from among this congregation, that I may consume them in a moment."

And they fell on their faces.

⁴⁶So Moses said to Aaron, "Take a censer and put fire in it from the altar, put incense on it, and take it quickly to the congregation and make atonement for them; for wrath has gone out from the LORD. The plague has begun." ⁴⁷Then Aaron took it as Moses commanded, and ran into the midst of the assembly; and already the plague had begun among the people. So he put in the incense and made atonement for the people. ⁴⁸And he stood between the dead and the living; so the plague was stopped. ⁴⁹Now those who died in the plague were fourteen thousand seven hundred, besides

those who died in the Korah incident. ⁵⁰So Aaron returned to Moses at the door of the tabernacle of meeting, for the plague had stopped.

The Budding of Aaron's Rod

17 And the LORD spoke to Moses, saying: ²"Speak to the children of Israel, and get from them a rod from each father's house, all their leaders according to their fathers' houses—twelve rods. Write each man's name on his rod. ³And you shall write Aaron's name on the rod of Levi. For there shall be one rod for the head of each father's house. ⁴Then you shall place them in the tabernacle of meeting before the Testimony, where I meet with you. ⁵And it shall be that the rod of the man whom I choose will blossom; thus I will rid Myself of the complaints of the children of Israel, which they make against you."

17:4 before the Testimony. The Testimony is the Ten Commandments, which were written on two stone tablets and kept in the ark of the covenant. The phrase "before the Testimony" is synonymous with "before the ark."

⁶So Moses spoke to the children of Israel, and each of their leaders gave him a rod apiece, for each leader according to their fathers' houses, twelve rods; and the rod of Aaron was among their rods. ⁷And Moses placed the rods before the LORD in the tabernacle of witness.

⁸Now it came to pass on the next day that Moses went into the tabernacle of witness, and behold, the rod of Aaron, of the house of Levi, had sprouted and put forth buds, had produced blossoms and yielded ripe almonds. ⁹Then Moses brought out all the rods from before the LORD to all the children of Israel; and they looked, and each man took his rod.

17:8 the rod of Aaron. God had stated that the stick of the man He had chosen would blossom (17:5). Aaron's stick not only blossomed but also yielded ripe almonds. Thus God exceeded the demands of His own test to confirm without doubt that Aaron had been chosen as High Priest.

16:41–50 The Lord's wrath led to more complaining rather than repentance. The children of Israel blamed Moses and Aaron for the deaths of the people killed by the Lord, but only because of Moses and Aaron's intervention did God spare the entire nation from destruction.

¹⁰And the LORD said to Moses, "Bring Aaron's rod back before the Testimony, to

be kept as a sign against the rebels, that you may put their complaints away from Me, lest they die." [11]Thus did Moses; just as the LORD had commanded him, so he did.

[12]So the children of Israel spoke to Moses, saying, "Surely we die, we perish, we all perish! [13]Whoever even comes near the tabernacle of the LORD must die. Shall we all utterly die?"

Duties of Priests and Levites

18Then the LORD said to Aaron: "You and your sons and your father's house with you shall bear the iniquity *related to* the sanctuary, and you and your sons with you shall bear the iniquity *associated with* your priesthood. [2]Also bring with you your brethren of the tribe of Levi, the tribe of your father, that they may be joined with you and serve you while you and your sons *are* with you before the tabernacle of witness. [3]They shall attend to your needs and all the needs of the tabernacle; but they shall not come near the articles of the sanctuary and the altar, lest they die—they and you also. [4]They shall be joined with you and attend to the needs of the tabernacle of meeting, for all the work of the tabernacle; but an outsider shall not come near you. [5]And you shall attend to the duties of the sanctuary and the duties of the altar, that there *may* be no more wrath on the children of Israel. [6]Behold, I Myself have taken your brethren the Levites from among the children of Israel; *they are* a gift to you, given by the LORD, to do the work of the tabernacle of meeting. [7]Therefore you and your sons with you shall attend to your priesthood for everything at the altar and behind the veil; and you shall serve. I give your priesthood *to you* as a gift for service, but the outsider who comes near shall be put to death."

> **18:1 bear the iniquity.** Aaron and his sons were held responsible for any offense against the holiness of the tabernacle or violations of the rules of priesthood.

Offerings for Support of the Priests

[8]And the LORD spoke to Aaron: "Here, I Myself have also given you charge of My heave offerings, all the holy gifts of the children of Israel; I have given them as a portion to you and your sons, as an ordinance forever. [9]This shall be yours of the most holy things *reserved* from the fire: every offering of theirs, every grain offering and every sin offering and every trespass offering which they render to Me, *shall be* most holy for you and your sons. [10]In a most holy *place* you shall eat it; every male shall eat it. It shall be holy to you.

[11]"This also *is* yours: the heave offering of their gift, with all the wave offerings of the children of Israel; I have given them to you, and your sons and daughters with you, as an ordinance forever. Everyone who is clean in your house may eat it.

[12]"All the best of the oil, all the best of the new wine and the grain, their firstfruits which they offer to the LORD, I have given them to you. [13]Whatever first ripe fruit is in their land, which they bring to the LORD, shall be yours. Everyone who is clean in your house may eat it.

[14]"Every devoted thing in Israel shall be yours.

[15]"Everything that first opens the womb of all flesh, which they bring to the LORD, whether man or beast, shall be yours; nevertheless the firstborn of man you shall surely redeem, and the firstborn of unclean animals you shall redeem. [16]And those redeemed of the devoted things you shall redeem when one month old, according to your valuation, for five shekels of silver, according to the shekel of the sanctuary, which *is* twenty gerahs. [17]But the firstborn of a cow, the firstborn of a sheep, or the firstborn of a goat you shall not redeem; they *are* holy. You shall sprinkle their blood on the altar, and burn their fat *as* an offering made by fire for a sweet aroma to the LORD. [18]And their flesh shall be yours, just as the wave breast and the right thigh are yours.

[19]"All the heave offerings of the holy things, which the children of Israel offer to the LORD, I have given to you and your sons

> **18:19 a covenant of salt forever.** Because salt does not burn, it is a metaphor for durability. Just as salt retains its flavor, so the Lord's covenant with the priesthood endured. The Levites received the tithes of the Israelites as their source of income and compensation for their service. Through the offerings, the Lord provided for His priests forever.

and daughters with you as an ordinance forever; it *is* a covenant of salt forever before the LORD with you and your descendants with you."

²⁰Then the LORD said to Aaron: "You shall have no inheritance in their land, nor shall you have any portion among them; I *am* your portion and your inheritance among the children of Israel.

Tithes for Support of the Levites

²¹"Behold, I have given the children of Levi all the tithes in Israel as an inheritance in return for the work which they perform, the work of the tabernacle of meeting. ²²Hereafter the children of Israel shall not come near the tabernacle of meeting, lest they bear sin and die. ²³But the Levites shall perform the work of the tabernacle of meeting, and they shall bear their iniquity; *it shall be* a statute forever, throughout your generations, that among the children of Israel they shall have no inheritance. ²⁴For the tithes of the children of Israel, which they offer up *as* a heave offering to the LORD, I have given to the Levites as an inheritance; therefore I have said to them, 'Among the children of Israel they shall have no inheritance.' "

The Tithe of the Levites

²⁵Then the LORD spoke to Moses, saying, ²⁶"Speak thus to the Levites, and say to them: 'When you take from the children of Israel the tithes which I have given you from them as your inheritance, then you shall offer up a heave offering of it to the LORD, a tenth of the tithe. ²⁷And your heave offering shall be reckoned to you as though *it were* the grain of the threshing floor and as the fullness of the winepress. ²⁸Thus you shall also offer a heave offering to the LORD from all your tithes which you receive from the children of Israel, and you shall give the LORD's heave offering from it to Aaron the priest. ²⁹Of all your gifts you shall offer up every heave offering due to the LORD, from all the best of them, the consecrated part of them.' ³⁰Therefore you shall say to them: 'When you have lifted up the best of it, then *the rest* shall be accounted to the Levites as the produce of the threshing floor and as

the produce of the winepress. ³¹You may eat it in any place, you and your households, for it *is* your reward for your work in the tabernacle of meeting. ³²And you shall bear no sin because of it, when you have lifted up the best of it. But you shall not profane the holy gifts of the children of Israel, lest you die.' "

> **18:25–32** As the Levites themselves received the tithe, they were also required to present a tithe of what they received to the Lord.

Laws of Purification

19 Now the LORD spoke to Moses and Aaron, saying, ²"This *is* the ordinance of the law which the LORD has commanded, saying: 'Speak to the children of Israel, that they bring you a red heifer without blemish, in which there *is* no defect *and* on which a yoke has never come. ³You shall give it to Eleazar the priest, that he may take it outside the camp, and it shall be slaughtered before him; ⁴and Eleazar the priest shall take some of its blood with his finger, and sprinkle some of its blood seven times directly in front of the tabernacle of meeting. ⁵Then the heifer shall be burned in his sight: its hide, its flesh, its blood, and its offal shall be burned. ⁶And the priest shall take cedar wood and hyssop and scarlet, and cast *them* into the midst of the fire burning the heifer. ⁷Then the priest shall wash his clothes, he shall bathe in water, and afterward he shall come into the camp; the priest shall be unclean until evening. ⁸And the one who burns it shall wash his clothes in water, bathe in water, and shall be unclean until evening. ⁹Then a man *who is* clean shall gather up the ashes of the heifer, and store *them* outside the camp in a clean place; and they shall be kept for the congregation of the children of Israel for the water of purification;^a it *is* for purifying from sin. ¹⁰And the one who gathers the ashes of the heifer shall wash his clothes, and be unclean until evening. It shall be a statute forever to the children of Israel and to the stranger who dwells among them.

¹¹'He who touches the dead body of anyone shall be unclean seven days. ¹²He shall purify himself with the water on the third

---

19:9 ^aLiterally *impurity*

day and on the seventh day; *then* he will be clean. But if he does not purify himself on the third day and on the seventh day, he will not be clean. ¹³Whoever touches the body of anyone who has died, and does not purify himself, defiles the tabernacle of the LORD. That person shall be cut off from Israel. He shall be unclean, because the water of purification was not sprinkled on him; his uncleanness *is* still on him.

¹⁴'This *is* the law when a man dies in a tent: All who come into the tent and all who *are* in the tent shall be unclean seven days; ¹⁵and every open vessel, which has no cover fastened on it, *is* unclean. ¹⁶Whoever in the open field touches one who is slain by a sword or who has died, or a bone of a man, or a grave, shall be unclean seven days.

¹⁷'And for an unclean *person* they shall take some of the ashes of the heifer burnt for purification from sin, and running water shall be put on them in a vessel. ¹⁸A clean person shall take hyssop and dip *it* in the water, sprinkle *it* on the tent, on all the vessels, on the persons who were there, or on the one who touched a bone, the slain, the dead, or a grave. ¹⁹The clean *person* shall sprinkle the unclean on the third day and on the seventh day; and on the seventh day he shall purify himself, wash his clothes, and bathe in water; and at evening he shall be clean.

²⁰'But the man who is unclean and does not purify himself, that person shall be cut off from among the assembly, because he has defiled the sanctuary of the LORD. The water of purification has not been sprinkled on him; he *is* unclean. ²¹It shall be a perpetual statute for them. He who sprinkles the water of purification shall wash his clothes; and he who touches the water of purification shall be unclean until evening. ²²Whatever the unclean *person* touches shall be unclean; and the person who touches *it* shall be unclean until evening.' "

19:1–22 Over the period of 38 1/2 years, more than 1.2 million people died in the wilderness because of God's judgment. The Israelites continually came into contact with dead bodies, which led to ceremonial uncleanness. Therefore the Lord provided a means of purification to cleanse the people.

Moses' Error at Kadesh

20 Then the children of Israel, the whole congregation, came into the Wilderness of Zin in the first month, and the people stayed in Kadesh; and Miriam died there and was buried there.

²Now there was no water for the congregation; so they gathered together against Moses and Aaron. ³And the people contended with Moses and spoke, saying: "If only we had died when our brethren died before the LORD! ⁴Why have you brought up the assembly of the LORD into this wilderness, that we and our animals should die here? ⁵And why have you made us come up out of Egypt, to bring us to this evil place? It *is* not a place of grain or figs or vines or pomegranates; nor *is* there any water to drink." ⁶So Moses and Aaron went from the presence of the assembly to the door of the tabernacle of meeting, and they fell on their faces. And the glory of the LORD appeared to them.

20:2 no water. During their 40 years in the wilderness, water was their greatest physical need. The Lord had provided it continually, beginning at Horeb (Ex. 17:1–7). The present lack of water caused them to contend with Moses.

⁷Then the LORD spoke to Moses, saying, ⁸"Take the rod; you and your brother Aaron gather the congregation together. Speak to the rock before their eyes, and it will yield its water; thus you shall bring water for them out of the rock, and give drink to the congregation and their animals." ⁹So Moses took the rod from before the LORD as He commanded him.

¹⁰And Moses and Aaron gathered the assembly together before the rock; and he said to them, "Hear now, you rebels! Must we bring water for you out of this rock?" ¹¹Then Moses lifted his hand and struck the rock twice with his rod; and water came out abundantly, and the congregation and their animals drank.

¹²Then the LORD spoke to Moses and Aaron, "Because you did not believe Me, to hallow Me in the eyes of the children of Israel, therefore you shall not bring this assembly into the land which I have given them."

20:12 you did not believe Me. Although God told Moses to take the rod with him, he was only to speak to the rock for it to yield water. Moses' failure was that he failed to take God at His Word and thus to treat Him as holy before the people. **you shall not bring this assembly into the land.** His punishment for striking the rock was that he would not lead Israel into the Promised Land.

[13]This *was* the water of Meribah,[a] because the children of Israel contended with the LORD, and He was hallowed among them.

Passage Through Edom Refused

[14]Now Moses sent messengers from Kadesh to the king of Edom. "Thus says your brother Israel: 'You know all the hardship that has befallen us, [15]how our fathers went down to Egypt, and we dwelt in Egypt a long time, and the Egyptians afflicted us and our fathers. [16]When we cried out to the LORD, He heard our voice and sent the Angel and brought us up out of Egypt; now here we are in Kadesh, a city on the edge of your border. [17]Please let us pass through your country. We will not pass through fields or vineyards, nor will we drink water from wells; we will go along the King's Highway; we will not turn aside to the right hand or to the left until we have passed through your territory.' "

[18]Then Edom said to him, "You shall not pass through my *land*, lest I come out against you with the sword."

[19]So the children of Israel said to him, "We will go by the Highway, and if I or my livestock drink any of your water, then I will pay for it; let me only pass through on foot, nothing *more*."

[20]Then he said, "You shall not pass through." So Edom came out against them with many men and with a strong hand. [21]Thus Edom refused to give Israel passage through his territory; so Israel turned away from him.

Death of Aaron

[22]Now the children of Israel, the whole congregation, journeyed from Kadesh and came to Mount Hor. [23]And the LORD spoke to Moses and Aaron in Mount Hor by the border of the land of Edom, saying: [24]"Aaron shall be gathered to his people, for he shall not enter the land which I have given to the children of Israel, because you rebelled against My word at the water of Meribah. [25]Take Aaron and Eleazar his son, and bring them up to Mount Hor; [26]and strip Aaron of his garments and put them on Eleazar his son; for Aaron shall be gathered *to his people* and die there." [27]So Moses did just as the LORD commanded, and they went up to Mount Hor in the sight of all the congregation. [28]Moses stripped Aaron of his garments and put them on Eleazar his son; and Aaron died there on the top of the mountain. Then Moses and Eleazar came down from the mountain. [29]Now when all the congregation saw that Aaron was dead, all the house of Israel mourned for Aaron thirty days.

20:20 with many men and with a strong hand. The king of Edom sent out his army to intercept Israel. Since God had forbidden Israel to fight against Edom (Deut. 2:4–6), they turned away from Edom's border.

Canaanites Defeated at Hormah

21 The king of Arad, the Canaanite, who dwelt in the South, heard that Israel was coming on the road to Atharim. Then he fought against Israel and took *some* of them prisoners. [2]So Israel made a vow to the LORD, and said, "If You will indeed deliver this people into my hand, then I will utterly destroy their cities." [3]And the LORD listened to the voice of Israel and delivered up the Canaanites, and they utterly destroyed them and their cities. So the name of that place was called Hormah.[a]

The Bronze Serpent

[4]Then they journeyed from Mount Hor by the Way of the Red Sea, to go around the land of Edom; and the soul of the people became very discouraged on the way. [5]And the people spoke against God and against Moses: "Why have you brought us up out of Egypt to die in the wilderness? For *there is* no food and no

21:5 this worthless bread. The people's impatience caused them to despise the manna.

20:13 [a]Literally *Contention*   21:3 [a]Literally *Utter Destruction*

water, and our soul loathes this worthless bread." [6]So the LORD sent fiery serpents among the people, and they bit the people; and many of the people of Israel died.

[7]Therefore the people came to Moses, and said, "We have sinned, for we have spoken against the LORD and against you; pray to the LORD that He take away the serpents from us." So Moses prayed for the people.

[8]Then the LORD said to Moses, "Make a fiery *serpent*, and set it on a pole; and it shall be that everyone who is bitten, when he looks at it, shall live." [9]So Moses made a bronze serpent, and put it on a pole; and so it was, if a serpent had bitten anyone, when he looked at the bronze serpent, he lived.

From Mount Hor to Moab

[10]Now the children of Israel moved on and camped in Oboth. [11]And they journeyed from Oboth and camped at Ije Abarim, in the wilderness which *is* east of Moab, toward the sunrise. [12]From there they moved and camped in the Valley of Zered. [13]From there they moved and camped on the other side of the Arnon, which *is* in the wilderness that extends from the border of the Amorites; for the Arnon *is* the border of Moab, between Moab and the Amorites. [14]Therefore it is said in the Book of the Wars of the LORD:

> **21:14 the Book of the Wars of the LORD.** Apparently, this was a book of victory songs that was current at the time of Moses, possibly even written by Moses or a contemporary.

"Waheb in Suphah,[a]
The brooks of the Arnon,
[15]   And the slope of the brooks
That reaches to the dwelling of Ar,
And lies on the border of Moab."

[16]From there *they went* to Beer, which *is* the well where the LORD said to Moses, "Gather the people together, and I will give them water." [17]Then Israel sang this song:

"Spring up, O well!
All of you sing to it—
[18]   The well the leaders sank,
Dug by the nation's nobles,
By the lawgiver, with their staves."

And from the wilderness *they went* to Mattanah, [19]from Mattanah to Nahaliel, from Nahaliel to Bamoth, [20]and from Bamoth, *in* the valley that *is* in the country of Moab, to the top of Pisgah which looks down on the wasteland.[a]

King Sihon Defeated

[21]Then Israel sent messengers to Sihon king of the Amorites, saying, [22]"Let me pass through your land. We will not turn aside into fields or vineyards; we will not drink water from wells. We will go by the King's Highway until we have passed through your territory." [23]But Sihon would not allow Israel to pass through his territory. So Sihon gathered all his people together and went out against Israel in the wilderness, and he came to Jahaz and fought against Israel. [24]Then Israel defeated him with the

21:14 [a]Ancient unknown places; Vulgate reads *What He did in the Red Sea.*   21:20 [a]Hebrew *Jeshimon*

Wasn't it idol worship for the Israelites to look at the bronze serpent Moses created in Numbers 21:4–9?

The circumstances leading up to the casting of the bronze serpent were all too familiar. The people were tired and discouraged. They were angry with God and complained to Moses. They were convinced that things couldn't get any worse; but God showed them otherwise. He sent "fiery serpents" among the people and some of the Israelites died. Others suffered excruciating bites.

Realizing their mistake, the people came in repentance to Moses and begged for help. They were not worshiping the bronze serpent but were acting in faith, in obedience to God's and Moses' directions.

edge of the sword, and took possession of his land from the Arnon to the Jabbok, as far as the people of Ammon; for the border of the people of Ammon *was* fortified. [25]So Israel took all these cities, and Israel dwelt in all the cities of the Amorites, in Heshbon and in all its villages. [26]For Heshbon *was* the city of Sihon king of the Amorites, who had fought against the former king of Moab, and had taken all his land from his hand as far as the Arnon. [27]Therefore those who speak in proverbs say:

> "Come to Heshbon, let it be built;
> Let the city of Sihon be repaired.

[28] "For fire went out from Heshbon,
> A flame from the city of Sihon;
> It consumed Ar of Moab,
> The lords of the heights of the Arnon.
[29] Woe to you, Moab!
> You have perished, O people of Chemosh!
> He has given his sons as fugitives,
> And his daughters into captivity,
> To Sihon king of the Amorites.

[30] "But we have shot at them;
> Heshbon has perished as far as Dibon.
> Then we laid waste as far as Nophah,
> Which *reaches* to Medeba."

[31]Thus Israel dwelt in the land of the Amorites. [32]Then Moses sent to spy out Jazer; and they took its villages and drove out the Amorites who *were* there.

King Og Defeated

[33]And they turned and went up by the way to Bashan. So Og king of Bashan went out against them, he and all his people, to battle at Edrei. [34]Then the LORD said to Moses, "Do not fear him, for I have delivered him into your hand, with all his people and his land; and you shall do to him as you did to Sihon king of the Amorites, who dwelt at Heshbon." [35]So they defeated him, his sons, and all his people, until there was no survivor left him; and they took possession of his land.

Balak Sends for Balaam

22 Then the children of Israel moved, and camped in the plains of Moab on the side of the Jordan *across from* Jericho.

[2]Now Balak the son of Zippor saw all that Israel had done to the Amorites. [3]And Moab was exceedingly afraid of the people because they *were* many, and Moab was sick with dread because of the children of Israel. [4]So Moab said to the elders of Midian, "Now this company will lick up everything around us, as an ox licks up the grass of the field." And Balak the son of Zippor *was* king of the Moabites at that time. [5]Then he sent messengers to Balaam the son of Beor at Pethor, which *is* near the River[a] in the land of the sons of his people,[b] to call him, saying: "Look, a people has come from Egypt. See, they cover the face of the earth, and are settling next to me! [6]Therefore please come at once, curse this people for me, for they *are* too mighty for me. Perhaps I shall be able to defeat them and drive them out of the land, for I know that he whom you bless *is* blessed, and he whom you curse is cursed."

> **22:6 curse this people.** Knowing that Israel was too strong for his military, Balak called for the pagan prophet Balaam to come and curse Israel. A curse was a spoken word that was believed to bring misfortune upon the one it was against. Balaam had the reputation for pronouncing curses that actually worked.

[7]So the elders of Moab and the elders of Midian departed with the diviner's fee in their hand, and they came to Balaam and spoke to him the words of Balak. [8]And he said to them, "Lodge here tonight, and I will bring back word to you, as the LORD speaks to me." So the princes of Moab stayed with Balaam.

[9]Then God came to Balaam and said, "Who *are* these men with you?"

[10]So Balaam said to God, "Balak the son of Zippor, king of Moab, has sent to me, *saying,* [11]'Look, a people has come out of Egypt, and they cover the face of the earth. Come now, curse them for me; perhaps I shall be able to overpower them and drive them out.'"

22:5 [a]That is, the Euphrates [b]Or *the people of Amau*

¹²And God said to Balaam, "You shall not go with them; you shall not curse the people, for they *are* blessed."

¹³So Balaam rose in the morning and said to the princes of Balak, "Go back to your land, for the LORD has refused to give me permission to go with you."

¹⁴And the princes of Moab rose and went to Balak, and said, "Balaam refuses to come with us."

¹⁵Then Balak again sent princes, more numerous and more honorable than they. ¹⁶And they came to Balaam and said to him, "Thus says Balak the son of Zippor: 'Please let nothing hinder you from coming to me; ¹⁷for I will certainly honor you greatly, and I will do whatever you say to me. Therefore please come, curse this people for me.' "

¹⁸Then Balaam answered and said to the servants of Balak, "Though Balak were to give me his house full of silver and gold, I could not go beyond the word of the LORD my God, to do less or more. ¹⁹Now therefore, please, you also stay here tonight, that I may know what more the LORD will say to me."

²⁰And God came to Balaam at night and said to him, "If the men come to call you, rise *and* go with them; but only the word which I speak to you—that you shall do." ²¹So Balaam rose in the morning, saddled his donkey, and went with the princes of Moab.

Balaam, the Donkey, and the Angel

²²Then God's anger was aroused because he went, and the Angel of the LORD took His stand in the way as an adversary against him. And he was riding on his donkey, and his two servants *were* with him. ²³Now the donkey saw the Angel of the LORD standing in the way with His drawn sword in His hand, and the donkey turned aside out of the way and went into the field. So Balaam struck the donkey to turn her back onto the road. ²⁴Then the Angel of the

22:22 because he went. Even though God gave Balaam permission to go, He was angry with Balaam because his motive was not right. God confronted Balaam to reaffirm that he could only speak the words God wanted him to speak. **the Angel of the LORD.** The Lord Himself appeared in some form.

LORD stood in a narrow path between the vineyards, *with* a wall on this side and a wall on that side. ²⁵And when the donkey saw the Angel of the LORD, she pushed herself against the wall and crushed Balaam's foot against the wall; so he struck her again. ²⁶Then the Angel of the LORD went further, and stood in a narrow place where there *was* no way to turn either to the right hand or to the left. ²⁷And when the donkey saw the Angel of the LORD, she lay down under Balaam; so Balaam's anger was aroused, and he struck the donkey with his staff.

²⁸Then the LORD opened the mouth of the donkey, and she said to Balaam, "What have I done to you, that you have struck me these three times?"

22:28 the LORD opened the mouth of the donkey. Balaam's donkey could see the Angel of the Lord with his drawn sword. Realizing the danger to herself, the donkey avoided the Angel, thus saving Balaam as well. Miraculously, the donkey spoke to Balaam.

²⁹And Balaam said to the donkey, "Because you have abused me. I wish there were a sword in my hand, for now I would kill you!"

³⁰So the donkey said to Balaam, "*Am* I not your donkey on which you have ridden, ever since *I became* yours, to this day? Was I ever disposed to do this to you?"

And he said, "No."

³¹Then the LORD opened Balaam's eyes, and he saw the Angel of the LORD standing in the way with His drawn sword in His hand; and he bowed his head and fell flat on his face. ³²And the Angel of the LORD said to him, "Why have you struck your donkey these three times? Behold, I have come out to stand against you, because *your* way is perverse before Me. ³³The donkey saw Me and turned aside from Me these three times. If she had not turned aside from Me, surely I would also have killed you by now, and let her live."

³⁴And Balaam said to the Angel of the LORD, "I have sinned, for I did not know You stood in the way against me. Now therefore, if it displeases You, I will turn back."

³⁵Then the Angel of the LORD said to Balaam, "Go with the men, but only the word

that I speak to you, that you shall speak." So Balaam went with the princes of Balak.

³⁶Now when Balak heard that Balaam was coming, he went out to meet him at the city of Moab, which is on the border at the Arnon, the boundary of the territory. ³⁷Then Balak said to Balaam, "Did I not earnestly send to you, calling for you? Why did you not come to me? Am I not able to honor you?"

³⁸And Balaam said to Balak, "Look, I have come to you! Now, have I any power at all to say anything? The word that God puts in my mouth, that I must speak." ³⁹So Balaam went with Balak, and they came to Kirjath Huzoth. ⁴⁰Then Balak offered oxen and sheep, and he sent some to Balaam and to the princes who were with him.

> **22:41–23:12** Balaam's first oracle emphatically stated that Israel could not be cursed, for she was unlike all the other nations of the world. Balaam even wished to share in her blessing.

Balaam's First Prophecy

⁴¹So it was, the next day, that Balak took Balaam and brought him up to the high places of Baal, that from there he might observe the extent of the people.

23 Then Balaam said to Balak, "Build seven altars for me here, and prepare for me here seven bulls and seven rams."

²And Balak did just as Balaam had spoken, and Balak and Balaam offered a bull and a ram on each altar. ³Then Balaam said to Balak, "Stand by your burnt offering, and I will go; perhaps the LORD will come to meet me, and whatever He shows me I will tell you." So he went to a desolate height. ⁴And God met Balaam, and he said to Him,

"I have prepared the seven altars, and I have offered on each altar a bull and a ram."

⁵Then the LORD put a word in Balaam's mouth, and said, "Return to Balak, and thus you shall speak." ⁶So he returned to him, and there he was, standing by his burnt offering, he and all the princes of Moab.

⁷And he took up his oracle and said:

"Balak the king of Moab has brought me from Aram,
From the mountains of the east.
'Come, curse Jacob for me,
And come, denounce Israel!'

8 "How shall I curse whom God has not cursed?
And how shall I denounce whom the LORD has not denounced?
9 For from the top of the rocks I see him,
And from the hills I behold him;
There! A people dwelling alone,
Not reckoning itself among the nations.

10 "Who can count the dustᵃ of Jacob,
Or number one-fourth of Israel?
Let me die the death of the righteous,
And let my end be like his!"

¹¹Then Balak said to Balaam, "What have you done to me? I took you to curse my enemies, and look, you have blessed them bountifully!"

¹²So he answered and said, "Must I not take heed to speak what the LORD has put in my mouth?"

23:10 ᵃOr dust cloud

Why does a pagan and greedy prophet like Balaam receive so much attention in the biblical story?

Balaam, whose story is recorded in Numbers 22:2–24:25, does seem to receive special treatment. Even though Balaam claimed to know the Lord (Numbers 22:18), Scripture consistently refers to him as a false prophet (2 Peter 2:15–16; Jude 11). Apparently, God placed such a priority on the message that the character of the messenger became a secondary consideration. The Lord used Balaam as His mouthpiece to speak the true words He put in his mouth. God had a purpose for Balaam despite the pagan prophet's own plans.

Balaam's Second Prophecy

¹³Then Balak said to him, "Please come with me to another place from which you may see them; you shall see only the outer part of them, and shall not see them all; curse them for me from there." ¹⁴So he brought him to the field of Zophim, to the top of Pisgah, and built seven altars, and offered a bull and a ram on *each* altar.

¹⁵And he said to Balak, "Stand here by your burnt offering while I meet[a] the LORD over there."

¹⁶Then the LORD met Balaam, and put a word in his mouth, and said, "Go back to Balak, and thus you shall speak." ¹⁷So he came to him, and there he was, standing by his burnt offering, and the princes of Moab were with him. And Balak said to him, "What has the LORD spoken?"

¹⁸Then he took up his oracle and said:

"Rise up, Balak, and hear!
Listen to me, son of Zippor!

¹⁹ "God *is* not a man, that He should lie,
Nor a son of man, that He should repent.
Has He said, and will He not do?
Or has He spoken, and will He not make it good?

> **23:19 God is not a man.** In contrast to unreliable men, like Balaam himself, God is reliable and unchanging; therefore, His Words always come to pass.

²⁰ Behold, I have received *a command* to bless;
He has blessed, and I cannot reverse it.

²¹ "He has not observed iniquity in Jacob,
Nor has He seen wickedness in Israel.
The LORD his God *is* with him,
And the shout of a King *is* among them.

²² God brings them out of Egypt;
He has strength like a wild ox.

²³ "For *there is* no sorcery against Jacob,
Nor any divination against Israel.
It now must be said of Jacob

And of Israel, 'Oh, what God has done!'

²⁴ Look, a people rises like a lioness,
And lifts itself up like a lion;
It shall not lie down until it devours the prey,
And drinks the blood of the slain."

²⁵Then Balak said to Balaam, "Neither curse them at all, nor bless them at all!"

²⁶So Balaam answered and said to Balak, "Did I not tell you, saying, 'All that the LORD speaks, that I must do'?"

> **23:13–26** Balaam's second oracle reaffirmed the Lord's determination to bless Israel. He mercifully set her sin aside (23:21), brought her out of Egypt (23:22), and planned to give her victory over all her enemies (23:24).

Balaam's Third Prophecy

²⁷Then Balak said to Balaam, "Please come, I will take you to another place; perhaps it will please God that you may curse them for me from there." ²⁸So Balak took Balaam to the top of Peor, that overlooks the wasteland.[a] ²⁹Then Balaam said to Balak, "Build for me here seven altars, and prepare for me here seven bulls and seven rams." ³⁰And Balak did as Balaam had said, and offered a bull and a ram on *every* altar.

> **23:27–24:14** Balaam's third oracle focused on the ultimate King, the Messiah, who would bring the blessings of the Abrahamic covenant to Israel and to all the world.

24 Now when Balaam saw that it pleased the LORD to bless Israel, he did not go as at other times, to seek to use sorcery, but he set his face toward the wilderness. ²And Balaam raised his eyes, and saw Israel encamped according to their tribes; and the Spirit of God came upon him. ³Then he took up his oracle and said:

"The utterance of Balaam the son of Beor,
The utterance of the man whose eyes are opened,
⁴ The utterance of him who hears the words of God,

23:15 [a]Following Masoretic Text, Targum, and Vulgate; Syriac reads *call*; Septuagint reads *go and ask God.*   23:28 [a]Hebrew *Jeshimon*

Who sees the vision of the Almighty,
Who falls down, with eyes wide open:

5 "How lovely are your tents, O Jacob!
Your dwellings, O Israel!
6 Like valleys that stretch out,
Like gardens by the riverside,
Like aloes planted by the LORD,
Like cedars beside the waters.
7 He shall pour water from his buckets,
And his seed *shall be* in many waters.

"His king shall be higher than Agag,
And his kingdom shall be exalted.

8 "God brings him out of Egypt;
He has strength like a wild ox;
He shall consume the nations, his
enemies;
He shall break their bones
And pierce *them* with his arrows.
9 'He bows down, he lies down as a lion;
And as a lion, who shall rouse him?'ᵃ

"Blessed *is* he who blesses you,
And cursed *is* he who curses you."

¹⁰Then Balak's anger was aroused against Balaam, and he struck his hands together; and Balak said to Balaam, "I called you to curse my enemies, and look, you have bountifully blessed *them* these three times! ¹¹Now therefore, flee to your place. I said I would greatly honor you, but in fact, the LORD has kept you back from honor."

¹²So Balaam said to Balak, "Did I not also speak to your messengers whom you sent to me, saying, ¹³'If Balak were to give me his house full of silver and gold, I could not go beyond the word of the LORD, to do good or bad of my own will. What the LORD says, that I must speak'? ¹⁴And now, indeed, I am going to my people. Come, I will advise you what this people will do to your people in the latter days."

Balaam's Fourth Prophecy

¹⁵So he took up his oracle and said:

"The utterance of Balaam the son of
Beor,

And the utterance of the man whose
eyes are opened;
16 The utterance of him who hears the
words of God,
And has the knowledge of the Most
High,
Who sees the vision of the Almighty,
Who falls down, with eyes wide open:

17 "I see Him, but not now;
I behold Him, but not near;
A Star shall come out of Jacob;
A Scepter shall rise out of Israel,
And batter the brow of Moab,
And destroy all the sons of tumult.ᵃ
18 "And Edom shall be a possession;
Seir also, his enemies, shall be a
possession,
While Israel does valiantly.
19 Out of Jacob One shall have
dominion,
And destroy the remains of the city."

24:15–19 Balaam's fourth oracle predicted the future king of Israel, who will "batter the brow of Moab" and conquer Edom. He will have total dominion.

---

²⁰Then he looked on Amalek, and he took up his oracle and said:

"Amalek *was* first among the nations,
But *shall be* last until he perishes."

²¹Then he looked on the Kenites, and he took up his oracle and said:

"Firm is your dwelling place,
And your nest is set in the rock;
22 Nevertheless Kain shall be burned.
How long until Asshur carries you
away captive?"

²³Then he took up his oracle and said:

"Alas! Who shall live when God does
this?
24 But ships *shall come* from the coasts
of Cyprus,ᵃ

24:9 ᵃGenesis 49:9　24:17 ᵃHebrew *Sheth* (compare Jeremiah 48:45)　24:24 ᵃHebrew *Kittim*

And they shall afflict Asshur and
    afflict Eber,
And so shall *Amalek,*[b] until he
    perishes."

[25]So Balaam rose and departed and returned to his place; Balak also went his
way.

Israel's Harlotry in Moab

25 Now Israel remained in Acacia
Grove,[a] and the people began to
commit harlotry with the women of Moab.
[2]They invited the people to the sacrifices of
their gods, and the people ate and bowed
down to their gods. [3]So Israel was joined to
Baal of Peor, and the anger of the LORD was
aroused against Israel.

[4]Then the LORD said to Moses, "Take all
the leaders of the people and hang the offenders before the LORD, out in the sun,
that the fierce anger of the LORD may turn
away from Israel."

[5]So Moses said to the judges of Israel,
"Every one of you kill his men who were
joined to Baal of Peor."

[6]And indeed, one of the children of Israel
came and presented to his brethren a Midianite woman in the sight of Moses and in
the sight of all the congregation of the children of Israel, who *were* weeping at the
door of the tabernacle of meeting. [7]Now
when Phinehas the son of Eleazar, the son
of Aaron the priest, saw *it,* he rose from
among the congregation and took a javelin
in his hand; [8]and he went after the man of
Israel into the tent and thrust both of them
through, the man of Israel, and the woman
through her body. So the plague was
stopped among the children of Israel. [9]And
those who died in the plague were twenty-
four thousand.

[10]Then the LORD spoke to Moses, saying:
[11]"Phinehas the son of Eleazar, the son of
Aaron the priest, has turned back My wrath
from the children of Israel, because he was
zealous with My zeal among them, so that I
did not consume the children of Israel in
My zeal. [12]Therefore say, 'Behold, I give to
him My covenant of peace; [13]and it shall be
to him and his descendants after him a covenant of an everlasting priesthood, because
he was zealous for his God, and made
atonement for the children of Israel.' "

[14]Now the name of the Israelite who was
killed, who was killed with the Midianite
woman, *was* Zimri the son of Salu, a leader
of a father's house among the Simeonites.
[15]And the name of the Midianite woman
who was killed *was* Cozbi the daughter of
Zur; he *was* head of the people of a father's
house in Midian.

[16]Then the LORD spoke to Moses, saying:
[17]"Harass the Midianites, and attack them;
[18]for they harassed you with their schemes
by which they seduced you in the matter of
Peor and in the matter of Cozbi, the daughter of a leader of Midian, their sister, who
was killed in the day of the plague because
of Peor."

> **25:1–18** Israel's final failure before taking the Prom-
> ised Land. According to 31:16, since Balaam was un-
> able to curse Israel, he told the Moabites and
> Midianites how to provoke the Lord's anger against
> His people.

The Second Census of Israel

26 And it came to pass, after the
plague, that the LORD spoke to Mo-

24:24 [b]*Literally he* or *that one*   **25:1** [a]Hebrew *Shittim*

What are modern readers to do with Balaam's talking donkey? (Numbers 22:22–35)

Several observations come to mind when a question like this is
asked. First, the question assumes that ancient readers had
fewer problems with talking donkeys than modern people do.
This incident was not recorded as a commonplace occurrence
but as something unusual and noteworthy. Second, one can just
as easily wonder why God didn't (or doesn't) use talking animals
more often—we would all probably be better off. Third, why not
recognize God's sense of humor in this account? Fourth, God's
display of patience and persistence in these events ought to provoke in us a sense of humble
worship. Fifth, the incident, unusual as it may be, should be accepted at face value as true.

26:1–36:13 The final major section of Numbers records the renewed obedience of Israel. Most of the commandments in this section related to Israel's life after they entered the Promised Land.

ses and Eleazar the son of Aaron the priest, saying: ²"Take a census of all the congregation of the children of Israel from twenty years old and above, by their fathers' houses, all who are able to go to war in Israel." ³So Moses and Eleazar the priest spoke with them in the plains of Moab by the Jordan, *across from* Jericho, saying: ⁴"*Take a census of the people* from twenty years old and above, just as the LORD commanded Moses and the children of Israel who came out of the land of Egypt."

⁵Reuben *was* the firstborn of Israel. The children of Reuben *were:* of Hanoch, the family of the Hanochites; *of* Pallu, the family of the Palluites; ⁶*of* Hezron, the family of the Hezronites; *of* Carmi, the family of the Carmites. ⁷These *are* the families of the Reubenites: those who were numbered of them were forty-three thousand seven hundred and thirty. ⁸And the son of Pallu *was* Eliab. ⁹The sons of Eliab *were* Nemuel, Dathan, and Abiram. These *are* the Dathan and Abiram, representatives of the congregation, who contended against Moses and Aaron in the company of Korah, when they contended against the LORD; ¹⁰and the earth opened its mouth and swallowed them up together with Korah when that company died, when the fire devoured two hundred and fifty men; and they became a sign. ¹¹Nevertheless the children of Korah did not die.

¹²The sons of Simeon according to their families *were:* of Nemuel,ᵃ the family of the Nemuelites; *of* Jamin, the family of the Jaminites; *of* Jachin,ᵇ the family of the Jachinites; ¹³*of* Zerah,ᵃ the family of the Zarhites; *of* Shaul, the family of the Shaulites. ¹⁴These *are* the families of the Simeonites: twenty-two thousand two hundred.

¹⁵The sons of Gad according to their fam-

ilies *were:* of Zephon,ᵃ the family of the Zephonites; *of* Haggi, the family of the Haggites; *of* Shuni, the family of the Shunites; ¹⁶*of* Ozni,ᵃ the family of the Oznites; *of* Eri, the family of the Erites; ¹⁷*of* Arod,ᵃ the family of the Arodites; *of* Areli, the family of the Arelites. ¹⁸These *are* the families of the sons of Gad according to those who were numbered of them: forty thousand five hundred.

¹⁹The sons of Judah *were* Er and Onan; and Er and Onan died in the land of Canaan. ²⁰And the sons of Judah according to their families were: *of* Shelah, the family of the Shelanites; *of* Perez, the family of the Parzites; *of* Zerah, the family of the Zarhites. ²¹And the sons of Perez were: *of* Hezron, the family of the Hezronites; *of* Hamul, the family of the Hamulites. ²²These *are* the families of Judah according to those who were numbered of them: seventy-six thousand five hundred.

²³The sons of Issachar according to their families *were:* of Tola, the family of the Tolaites; of Puah,ᵃ the family of the Punites;ᵇ ²⁴of Jashub, the family of the Jashubites; of Shimron, the family of the Shimronites. ²⁵These *are* the families of Issachar according to those who were numbered of them: sixty-four thousand three hundred.

²⁶The sons of Zebulun according to their families *were:* of Sered, the family of the Sardites; of Elon, the family of the Elonites; of Jahleel, the family of the Jahleelites. ²⁷These *are* the families of the Zebulunites according to those who were numbered of them: sixty thousand five hundred.

²⁸The sons of Joseph according to their families, by Manasseh and Ephraim, *were:* ²⁹The sons of Manasseh: of Machir, the family of the Machirites; and Machir begot Gilead; of Gilead, the family of the Gileadites. ³⁰These *are* the sons of Gilead: *of* Jeezer,ᵃ the family of the Jeezerites; of Helek, the family of the Helekites; ³¹*of* Asriel, the family of the Asrielites; *of* Shechem,

---

26:12 ᵃSpelled *Jemuel* in Genesis 46:10 and Exodus 6:15 ᵇCalled *Jarib* in 1 Chronicles 4:24
26:13 ᵃCalled *Zohar* in Genesis 46:10 **26:15** ᵃCalled *Ziphion* in Genesis 46:16 **26:16** ᵃCalled *Ezbon* in Genesis 46:16 **26:17** ᵃSpelled *Arodi* in Samaritan Pentateuch, Syriac, and Genesis 46:16
26:23 ᵃHebrew *Puvah* (compare Genesis 46:13 and 1 Chronicles 7:1); Samaritan Pentateuch, Septuagint, Syriac, and Vulgate read *Puah.* ᵇSamaritan Pentateuch, Septuagint, Syriac, and Vulgate read *Puaites.* **26:30** ᵃCalled *Abiezer* in Joshua 17:2

the family of the Shechemites; ³²*of* Shemida, the family of the Shemidaites; *of* Hepher, the family of the Hepherites. ³³Now Zelophehad the son of Hepher had no sons, but daughters; and the names of the daughters of Zelophehad *were* Mahlah, Noah, Hoglah, Milcah, and Tirzah. ³⁴These *are* the families of Manasseh; and those who were numbered of them *were* fifty-two thousand seven hundred.

³⁵These *are* the sons of Ephraim according to their families: of Shuthelah, the family of the Shuthalhites; of Becher,^a the family of the Bachrites; of Tahan, the family of the Tahanites. ³⁶And these *are* the sons of Shuthelah: of Eran, the family of the Eranites. ³⁷These *are* the families of the sons of Ephraim according to those who were numbered of them: thirty-two thousand five hundred.

These *are* the sons of Joseph according to their families.

³⁸The sons of Benjamin according to their families were: of Bela, the family of the Belaites; of Ashbel, the family of the Ashbelites; of Ahiram, the family of the Ahiramites; ³⁹of Shupham,^a the family of the Shuphamites; of Hupham,^b the family of the Huphamites. ⁴⁰And the sons of Bela were Ard^a and Naaman: *of Ard,* the family of the Ardites; of Naaman, the family of the Naamites. ⁴¹These *are* the sons of Benjamin according to their families; and those who were numbered of them *were* forty-five thousand six hundred.

⁴²These *are* the sons of Dan according to their families: of Shuham,^a the family of the Shuhamites. These *are* the families of Dan according to their families. ⁴³All the families of the Shuhamites, according to those who were numbered of them, *were* sixty-four thousand four hundred.

⁴⁴The sons of Asher according to their families *were:* of Jimna, the family of the Jimnites; of Jesui, the family of the Jesuites; of Beriah, the family of the Beriites. ⁴⁵Of the sons of Beriah: of Heber, the family of the Heberites; of Malchiel, the family of the Malchielites. ⁴⁶And the name of the daughter of Asher *was* Serah. ⁴⁷These *are* the families of the sons of Asher according to those who were numbered of them: fifty-three thousand four hundred.

⁴⁸The sons of Naphtali according to their families *were:* of Jahzeel,^a the family of the Jahzeelites; of Guni, the family of the Gunites; ⁴⁹of Jezer, the family of the Jezerites; of Shillem, the family of the Shillemites. ⁵⁰These *are* the families of Naphtali according to their families; and those who were numbered of them *were* forty-five thousand four hundred.

⁵¹These *are* those who were numbered of the children of Israel: six hundred and one thousand seven hundred and thirty.

⁵²Then the LORD spoke to Moses, saying: ⁵³"To these the land shall be divided as an inheritance, according to the number of names. ⁵⁴To a large *tribe* you shall give a larger inheritance, and to a small *tribe* you shall give a smaller inheritance. Each shall be given its inheritance according to those who were numbered of them. ⁵⁵But the land shall be divided by lot; they shall inherit according to the names of the tribes of their fathers. ⁵⁶According to the lot their inheritance shall be divided between the larger and the smaller."

26:52–56 These census numbers would be used to decide the size of each tribe's inheritance in the Land. The exact locations would be determined by lot (see Josh. 13:1–7).

⁵⁷And these *are* those who were numbered of the Levites according to their families: of Gershon, the family of the Gershonites; of Kohath, the family of the Kohathites; of Merari, the family of the Merarites. ⁵⁸These *are* the families of the Levites: the family of the Libnites, the family of the Hebronites, the family of the Mahlites, the family of the Mushites, and the family of the Korathites. And Kohath begot Amram. ⁵⁹The name of Amram's wife *was* Jochebed the daughter of Levi, who was born to Levi in Egypt; and to Amram she bore Aaron and Moses and their sister Miriam. ⁶⁰To Aaron were born Nadab and

---

26:35 ^aCalled *Bered* in 1 Chronicles 7:20   **26:39** ^aMasoretic Text reads *Shephupham,* spelled *Shephuphan* in 1 Chronicles 8:5.   ^bCalled *Huppim* in Genesis 46:21   **26:40** ^aCalled *Addar* in 1 Chronicles 8:3   **26:42** ^aCalled *Hushim* in Genesis 46:23   **26:48** ^aSpelled *Jahziel* in 1 Chronicles 7:13

Abihu, Eleazar and Ithamar. ⁶¹And Nadab and Abihu died when they offered profane fire before the LORD.

⁶²Now those who were numbered of them were twenty-three thousand, every male from a month old and above; for they were not numbered among the other children of Israel, because there was no inheritance given to them among the children of Israel.

⁶³These *are* those who were numbered by Moses and Eleazar the priest, who numbered the children of Israel in the plains of Moab by the Jordan, *across from* Jericho. ⁶⁴But among these there was not a man of those who were numbered by Moses and Aaron the priest when they numbered the children of Israel in the Wilderness of Sinai. ⁶⁵For the LORD had said of them, "They shall surely die in the wilderness." So there was not left a man of them, except Caleb the son of Jephunneh and Joshua the son of Nun.

Inheritance Laws

27 Then came the daughters of Zelophehad the son of Hepher, the son of Gilead, the son of Machir, the son of Manasseh, from the families of Manasseh the son of Joseph; and these *were* the names of his daughters: Mahlah, Noah, Hoglah, Milcah, and Tirzah. ²And they stood before Moses, before Eleazar the priest, and before the leaders and all the congregation, *by* the doorway of the tabernacle of meeting, saying: ³"Our father died in the wilderness; but he was not in the company of those who gathered together against the LORD, in company with Korah, but he died in his own sin; and he had no sons. ⁴Why should the name of our father be removed from among his family because he had no son? Give us a possession among our father's brothers."

⁵So Moses brought their case before the LORD.

⁶And the LORD spoke to Moses, saying: ⁷"The daughters of Zelophehad speak *what is right*; you shall surely give them a possession of inheritance among their father's brothers, and cause the inheritance of their father to pass to them. ⁸And you shall speak to the children of Israel, saying: 'If a man dies and has no son, then you shall

cause his inheritance to pass to his daughter. ⁹If he has no daughter, then you shall give his inheritance to his brothers. ¹⁰If he has no brothers, then you shall give his inheritance to his father's brothers. ¹¹And if his father has no brothers, then you shall give his inheritance to the relative closest to him in his family, and he shall possess it.' " And it shall be to the children of Israel a statute of judgment, just as the LORD commanded Moses.

> **27:1–11** The distribution of land in Canaan posed a problem for the family of Zelophehad since he had no sons. His five daughters boldly asked that they inherit their father's name and his inheritance, and the Lord granted their request. The Lord set the order of inheritance as son, daughter, brother, paternal uncle, and closest relative in the family.

Joshua the Next Leader of Israel

¹²Now the LORD said to Moses: "Go up into this Mount Abarim, and see the land which I have given to the children of Israel. ¹³And when you have seen it, you also shall be gathered to your people, as Aaron your brother was gathered. ¹⁴For in the Wilderness of Zin, during the strife of the congregation, you rebelled against My command to hallow Me at the waters before their eyes." (These *are* the waters of Meribah, at Kadesh in the Wilderness of Zin.)

¹⁵Then Moses spoke to the LORD, saying: ¹⁶"Let the LORD, the God of the spirits of all flesh, set a man over the congregation, ¹⁷who may go out before them and go in before them, who may lead them out and bring them in, that the congregation of the LORD may not be like sheep which have no shepherd."

¹⁸And the LORD said to Moses: "Take Joshua the son of Nun with you, a man in whom *is* the Spirit, and lay your hand on him; ¹⁹set him before Eleazar the priest and before all the congregation, and inaugurate him in their sight. ²⁰And you shall give *some* of your authority to him, that all the

> **27:18 lay your hand on him.** The Lord provided a good leader, who was like a shepherd, to replace Moses, and He empowered him with the Holy Spirit. Moses publicly laid his hands upon Joshua to signify the transfer of leadership from Moses to Joshua.

congregation of the children of Israel may be obedient. 21He shall stand before Eleazar the priest, who shall inquire before the LORD for him by the judgment of the Urim. At his word they shall go out, and at his word they shall come in, he and all the children of Israel with him—all the congregation."

22So Moses did as the LORD commanded him. He took Joshua and set him before Eleazar the priest and before all the congregation. 23And he laid his hands on him and inaugurated him, just as the LORD commanded by the hand of Moses.

Daily Offerings

28 Now the LORD spoke to Moses, saying, 2"Command the children of Israel, and say to them, 'My offering, My food for My offerings made by fire as a sweet aroma to Me, you shall be careful to offer to Me at their appointed time.'

3"And you shall say to them, 'This is the offering made by fire which you shall offer to the LORD: two male lambs in their first year without blemish, day by day, as a regular burnt offering. 4The one lamb you shall offer in the morning, the other lamb you shall offer in the evening, 5and one-tenth of an ephah of fine flour as a grain offering mixed with one-fourth of a hin of pressed oil. 6It is a regular burnt offering which was ordained at Mount Sinai for a sweet aroma, an offering made by fire to the LORD. 7And its drink offering shall be one-fourth of a hin for each lamb; in a holy place you shall pour out the drink to the LORD as an offering. 8The other lamb you shall offer in the evening; as the morning grain offering and its drink offering, you shall offer it as an offering made by fire, a sweet aroma to the LORD.

Sabbath Offerings

9And on the Sabbath day two lambs in their first year, without blemish, and two-tenths of an ephah of fine flour as a grain offering, mixed with oil, with its drink offering— 10this is the burnt offering for every Sabbath, besides the regular burnt offering with its drink offering.

Monthly Offerings

11At the beginnings of your months you shall present a burnt offering to the LORD: two young bulls, one ram, and seven lambs in their first year, without blemish; 12three-tenths of an ephah of fine flour as a grain offering, mixed with oil, for each bull; two-tenths of an ephah of fine flour as a grain offering, mixed with oil, for the one ram; 13and one-tenth of an ephah of fine flour, mixed with oil, as a grain offering for each lamb, as a burnt offering of sweet aroma, an offering made by fire to the LORD. 14Their drink offering shall be half a hin of wine for a bull, one-third of a hin for a ram, and one-fourth of a hin for a lamb; this is the burnt offering for each month throughout the months of the year. 15Also one kid of the goats as a sin offering to the LORD shall be offered, besides the regular burnt offering and its drink offering.

Offerings at Passover

16On the fourteenth day of the first month is the Passover of the LORD. 17And on the fifteenth day of this month is the feast; unleavened bread shall be eaten for seven days. 18On the first day you shall have a holy convocation. You shall do no customary work. 19And you shall present an offering made by fire as a burnt offering to the LORD: two young bulls, one ram, and seven lambs in their first year. Be sure they are without blemish. 20Their grain offering shall be of fine flour mixed with oil: three-tenths of an ephah you shall offer for a bull, and two-tenths for a ram; 21you shall offer one-tenth of an ephah for each of the seven lambs; 22also one goat as a sin offering, to make atonement for you. 23You shall offer these besides the burnt offering of the morning, which is for a regular burnt offering. 24In this manner you shall offer the food of the offering made by fire daily for seven days, as a sweet aroma to the LORD; it shall be offered besides the regular burnt offering and its drink offering. 25And on the seventh day you shall have a holy convocation. You shall do no customary work.

Offerings at the Feast of Weeks

26Also on the day of the firstfruits, when you bring a new grain offering to the LORD at your Feast of Weeks, you shall have a holy convocation. You shall do no customary work. 27You shall present a burnt offering as a sweet aroma to the LORD: two

young bulls, one ram, and seven lambs in their first year, ²⁸with their grain offering of fine flour mixed with oil: three-tenths *of an ephah* for each bull, two-tenths for the one ram, ²⁹and one-tenth for each of the seven lambs; ³⁰*also* one kid of the goats, to make atonement for you. ³¹Be sure they are without blemish. You shall present *them* with their drink offerings, besides the regular burnt offering with its grain offering.

Offerings at the Feast of Trumpets

29 ¹And in the seventh month, on the first *day* of the month, you shall have a holy convocation. You shall do no customary work. For you it is a day of blowing the trumpets. ²You shall offer a burnt offering as a sweet aroma to the LORD: one young bull, one ram, *and* seven lambs in their first year, without blemish. ³Their grain offering *shall be* fine flour mixed with oil: three-tenths *of an ephah* for the bull, two-tenths for the ram, ⁴and one-tenth for each of the seven lambs; ⁵also one kid of the goats *as* a sin offering, to make atonement for you; ⁶besides the burnt offering with its grain offering for the New Moon, the regular burnt offering with its grain offering, and their drink offerings, according to their ordinance, as a sweet aroma, an offering made by fire to the LORD.

Offerings on the Day of Atonement

⁷On the tenth *day* of this seventh month you shall have a holy convocation. You shall afflict your souls; you shall not do any work. ⁸You shall present a burnt offering to the LORD *as* a sweet aroma: one young bull, one ram, *and* seven lambs in their first year. Be sure they are without blemish. ⁹Their grain offering *shall be of* fine flour mixed with oil: three-tenths *of an ephah* for the bull, two-tenths for the one ram, ¹⁰and one-tenth for each of the seven lambs; ¹¹also one kid of the goats *as* a sin offering, besides the sin offering for atonement, the regular burnt offering with its grain offering, and their drink offerings.

Offerings at the Feast of Tabernacles

¹²On the fifteenth day of the seventh month you shall have a holy convocation. You shall do no customary work, and you shall keep a feast to the LORD seven days.

¹³You shall present a burnt offering, an offering made by fire as a sweet aroma to the LORD: thirteen young bulls, two rams, *and* fourteen lambs in their first year. They shall be without blemish. ¹⁴Their grain offering *shall be of* fine flour mixed with oil: three-tenths *of an ephah* for each of the thirteen bulls, two-tenths for each of the two rams, ¹⁵and one-tenth for each of the fourteen lambs; ¹⁶also one kid of the goats *as* a sin offering, besides the regular burnt offering, its grain offering, and its drink offering.

¹⁷On the second day *present* twelve young bulls, two rams, fourteen lambs in their first year without blemish, ¹⁸and their grain offering and their drink offerings for the bulls, for the rams, and for the lambs, by their number, according to the ordinance; ¹⁹also one kid of the goats *as* a sin offering, besides the regular burnt offering with its grain offering, and their drink offerings.

²⁰On the third day *present* eleven bulls, two rams, fourteen lambs in their first year without blemish, ²¹and their grain offering and their drink offerings for the bulls, for the rams, and for the lambs, by their number, according to the ordinance; ²²also one goat *as* a sin offering, besides the regular burnt offering, its grain offering, and its drink offering.

²³On the fourth day *present* ten bulls, two rams, *and* fourteen lambs in their first year, without blemish, ²⁴and their grain offering and their drink offerings for the bulls, for the rams, and for the lambs, by their number, according to the ordinance; ²⁵also one kid of the goats *as* a sin offering, besides the regular burnt offering, its grain offering, and its drink offering.

²⁶On the fifth day *present* nine bulls, two rams, *and* fourteen lambs in their first year without blemish, ²⁷and their grain offering and their drink offerings for the bulls, for the rams, and for the lambs, by their number, according to the ordinance; ²⁸also one goat *as* a sin offering, besides the regular burnt offering, its grain offering, and its drink offering.

²⁹On the sixth day *present* eight bulls, two rams, *and* fourteen lambs in their first year without blemish, ³⁰and their grain offering and their drink offerings for the

bulls, for the rams, and for the lambs, by their number, according to the ordinance; ³¹also one goat *as* a sin offering, besides the regular burnt offering, its grain offering, and its drink offering.

³²'On the seventh day *present* seven bulls, two rams, *and* fourteen lambs in their first year without blemish, ³³and their grain offering and their drink offerings for the bulls, for the rams, and for the lambs, by their number, according to the ordinance; ³⁴also one goat *as* a sin offering, besides the regular burnt offering, its grain offering, and its drink offering.

³⁵'On the eighth day you shall have a sacred assembly. You shall do no customary work. ³⁶You shall present a burnt offering, an offering made by fire as a sweet aroma to the LORD: one bull, one ram, seven lambs in their first year without blemish, ³⁷and their grain offering and their drink offerings for the bull, for the ram, and for the lambs, by their number, according to the ordinance; ³⁸also one goat *as* a sin offering, besides the regular burnt offering, its grain offering, and its drink offering.

³⁹'These you shall present to the LORD at your appointed feasts (besides your vowed offerings and your freewill offerings) as your burnt offerings and your grain offerings, as your drink offerings and your peace offerings.' "

⁴⁰So Moses told the children of Israel everything, just as the LORD commanded Moses.

The Law Concerning Vows

30 Then Moses spoke to the heads of the tribes concerning the children of Israel, saying, "This *is* the thing which the LORD has commanded: ²If a man makes a vow to the LORD, or swears an oath to bind himself by some agreement, he shall not break his word; he shall do according to all that proceeds out of his mouth.

³"Or if a woman makes a vow to the LORD, and binds *herself* by some agreement while in her father's house in her youth, ⁴and her father hears her vow and the agreement by which she has bound herself, and her father holds his peace, then all her vows shall stand, and every agreement with which she has bound herself shall stand. ⁵But if her father overrules her on the day

that he hears, then none of her vows nor her agreements by which she has bound herself shall stand; and the LORD will release her, because her father overruled her.

⁶"If indeed she takes a husband, while bound by her vows or by a rash utterance from her lips by which she bound herself, ⁷and her husband hears *it*, and makes no response to her on the day that he hears, then her vows shall stand, and her agreements by which she bound herself shall stand. ⁸But if her husband overrules her on the day that he hears *it*, he shall make void her vow which she took and what she uttered with her lips, by which she bound herself, and the LORD will release her.

⁹"Also any vow of a widow or a divorced woman, by which she has bound herself, shall stand against her.

¹⁰"If she vowed in her husband's house, or bound herself by an agreement with an oath, ¹¹and her husband heard *it*, and made no response to her *and* did not overrule her, then all her vows shall stand, and every agreement by which she bound herself shall stand. ¹²But if her husband truly made them void on the day he heard *them*, then whatever proceeded from her lips concerning her vows or concerning the agreement binding her, it shall not stand; her husband has made them void, and the LORD will release her. ¹³Every vow and every binding oath to afflict her soul, her husband may confirm it, or her husband may make it void. ¹⁴Now if her husband makes no response whatever to her from day to day, then he confirms all her vows or all the agreements that bind her; he confirms them, because he made no response to her on the day that he heard *them*. ¹⁵But if he does make them void after he has heard *them*, then he shall bear her guilt."

¹⁶These *are* the statutes which the LORD commanded Moses, between a man and his wife, and between a father and his daughter in her youth in her father's house.

> **30:1–16** This chapter clarified the laws regarding vows. The basic principle is restated in v. 2. A man was also responsible for the vows made by women in his household. A father or husband could overrule the vow of a daughter or wife, but if he knew of it and remained silent, then the vow must be accomplished.

Vengeance on the Midianites

31 And the LORD spoke to Moses, saying: [2]"Take vengeance on the Midianites for the children of Israel. Afterward you shall be gathered to your people."

> **31:2 gathered to your people.** A phrase referring to death.

[3]So Moses spoke to the people, saying, "Arm some of yourselves for war, and let them go against the Midianites to take vengeance for the LORD on Midian. [4]A thousand from each tribe of all the tribes of Israel you shall send to the war."

[5]So there were recruited from the divisions of Israel one thousand from *each* tribe, twelve thousand armed for war. [6]Then Moses sent them to the war, one thousand from *each* tribe; he sent them to the war with Phinehas the son of Eleazar the priest, with the holy articles and the signal trumpets in his hand. [7]And they warred against the Midianites, just as the LORD commanded Moses, and they killed all the males. [8]They killed the kings of Midian with *the rest of* those who were killed— Evi, Rekem, Zur, Hur, and Reba, the five kings of Midian. Balaam the son of Beor they also killed with the sword.

[9]And the children of Israel took the women of Midian captive, with their little ones, and took as spoil all their cattle, all their flocks, and all their goods. [10]They also burned with fire all the cities where they dwelt, and all their forts. [11]And they took all the spoil and all the booty—of man and beast.

> **31:1–11** Israel was commanded to take vengeance on Midian because they had corrupted Israel at Peor (25:1–18). All the Midianites, except the virgin women, were to be put to death.

Return from the War

[12]Then they brought the captives, the booty, and the spoil to Moses, to Eleazar the priest, and to the congregation of the children of Israel, to the camp in the plains of Moab by the Jordan, *across from* Jericho. [13]And Moses, Eleazar the priest, and all the leaders of the congregation, went to meet them outside the camp. [14]But Moses was angry with the officers of the army, *with* the captains over thousands and captains over hundreds, who had come from the battle. [15]And Moses said to them: "Have you kept all the women alive? [16]Look, these *women* caused the children of Israel, through the counsel of Balaam, to trespass against the LORD in the incident of Peor, and there was a plague among the congregation of the LORD. [17]Now therefore, kill every male among the little ones, and kill every woman who has known a man intimately. [18]But keep alive for yourselves all the young girls who have not known a man intimately. [19]And as for you, remain outside the camp seven days; whoever has killed any person, and whoever has touched any slain, purify yourselves and your captives on the third day and on the seventh day. [20]Purify every garment, everything made of leather, everything woven of goats' *hair*, and everything made of wood."

[21]Then Eleazar the priest said to the men of war who had gone to the battle, "This *is* the ordinance of the law which the LORD commanded Moses: [22]"Only the gold, the silver, the bronze, the iron, the tin, and the lead, [23]everything that can endure fire, you shall put through the fire, and it shall be clean; and it shall be purified with the water of purification. But all that cannot endure fire you shall put through water. [24]And you shall wash your clothes on the seventh day and be clean, and afterward you may come into the camp."

Division of the Plunder

[25]Now the LORD spoke to Moses, saying: [26]"Count up the plunder that was taken—of man and beast—you and Eleazar the priest and the chief fathers of the congregation; [27]and divide the plunder into two parts, between those who took part in the war, who went out to battle, and all the congregation. [28]And levy a tribute for the LORD on the men of war who went out to battle: one of every five hundred of the persons, the cattle, the donkeys, and the sheep; [29]take *it* from their half, and give *it* to Eleazar the priest as a heave offering to the LORD. [30]And from the children of Israel's half you shall take one of every fifty, drawn from the persons, the cattle, the donkeys, and the sheep, from all the livestock, and give them to the Levites who keep charge of the tabernacle of the

LORD." [31]So Moses and Eleazar the priest did as the LORD commanded Moses.

[32]The booty remaining from the plunder, which the men of war had taken, was six hundred and seventy-five thousand sheep, [33]seventy-two thousand cattle, [34]sixty-one thousand donkeys, [35]and thirty-two thousand persons in all, of women who had not known a man intimately. [36]And the half, the portion for those who had gone out to war, was in number three hundred and thirty-seven thousand five hundred sheep; [37]and the LORD's tribute of the sheep was six hundred and seventy-five. [38]The cattle *were* thirty-six thousand, of which the LORD's tribute *was* seventy-two. [39]The donkeys *were* thirty thousand five hundred, of which the LORD's tribute *was* sixty-one. [40]The persons *were* sixteen thousand, of which the LORD's tribute *was* thirty-two persons. [41]So Moses gave the tribute *which was* the LORD's heave offering to Eleazar the priest, as the LORD commanded Moses.

[42]And from the children of Israel's half, which Moses separated from the men who fought— [43]now the half belonging to the congregation was three hundred and thirty-seven thousand five hundred sheep, [44]thirty-six thousand cattle, [45]thirty thousand five hundred donkeys, [46]and sixteen thousand persons— [47]and from the children of Israel's half Moses took one of every fifty, drawn from man and beast, and gave them to the Levites, who kept charge of the tabernacle of the LORD, as the LORD commanded Moses.

[48]Then the officers who *were* over thousands of the army, the captains of thousands and captains of hundreds, came near to Moses; [49]and they said to Moses, "Your servants have taken a count of the men of war who *are* under our command, and not a man of us is missing. [50]Therefore we have brought an offering for the LORD, what every man found of ornaments of gold: armlets and bracelets and signet rings and earrings and necklaces, to make atonement for ourselves before the LORD." [51]So Moses and Eleazar the priest received the gold from them, all the fashioned ornaments. [52]And all the gold of the offering that they offered to the LORD, from the captains of thousands and captains of hundreds, was sixteen thousand seven hundred and fifty shekels. [53](The men of war had taken spoil, every man for himself.) [54]And Moses and Eleazar the priest received the gold from the captains of thousands and of hundreds, and brought it into the tabernacle of meeting as a memorial for the children of Israel before the LORD.

> **31:25–54** The plunder was divided equally between those who went and fought and those who stayed.

The Tribes Settling East of the Jordan

32 Now the children of Reuben and the children of Gad had a very great multitude of livestock; and when they saw the land of Jazer and the land of Gilead, that indeed the region *was* a place for livestock, [2]the children of Gad and the children of Reuben came and spoke to Moses, to Eleazar the priest, and to the leaders of the congregation, saying, [3]"Ataroth, Dibon, Jazer, Nimrah, Heshbon, Elealeh, Shebam, Nebo, and Beon, [4]the country which the LORD defeated before the congregation of Israel, *is* a land for livestock, and your servants have livestock." [5]Therefore they said, "If we have found favor in your sight, let this land be given to your servants as a possession. Do not take us over the Jordan."

[6]And Moses said to the children of Gad and to the children of Reuben: "Shall your brethren go to war while you sit here? [7]Now why will you discourage the heart of the children of Israel from going over into the land which the LORD has given them? [8]Thus your fathers did when I sent them away from Kadesh Barnea to see the land. [9]For when they went up to the Valley of Eshcol and saw the land, they discouraged the heart of the children of Israel, so that they did not go into the land which the LORD had given them. [10]So the LORD's anger was aroused on that day, and He swore an oath, saying, [11]'Surely none of the men who came up from Egypt, from twenty years old and above, shall see the land of which I swore to Abraham, Isaac, and Jacob, because they have not wholly followed Me, [12]except Caleb the son of Jephunneh, the Kenizzite, and Joshua the son of Nun, for they have wholly followed the LORD.' [13]So the LORD's anger was aroused against Israel, and He made them wander in the wilderness forty years, until all the genera-

tion that had done evil in the sight of the LORD was gone. [14]And look! You have risen in your fathers' place, a brood of sinful men, to increase still more the fierce anger of the LORD against Israel. [15]For if you turn away from following Him, He will once again leave them in the wilderness, and you will destroy all these people."

[16]Then they came near to him and said: "We will build sheepfolds here for our livestock, and cities for our little ones, [17]but we ourselves will be armed, ready *to go* before the children of Israel until we have brought them to their place; and our little ones will dwell in the fortified cities because of the inhabitants of the land. [18]We will not return to our homes until every one of the children of Israel has received his inheritance. [19]For we will not inherit with them on the other side of the Jordan and beyond, because our inheritance has fallen to us on this eastern side of the Jordan."

[20]Then Moses said to them: "If you do this thing, if you arm yourselves before the LORD for the war, [21]and all your armed men cross over the Jordan before the LORD until He has driven out His enemies from before Him, [22]and the land is subdued before the LORD, then afterward you may return and be blameless before the LORD and before Israel; and this land shall be your possession before the LORD. [23]But if you do not do so, then take note, you have sinned against the LORD; and be sure your sin will find you out. [24]Build cities for your little ones and folds for your sheep, and do what has proceeded out of your mouth."

[25]And the children of Gad and the children of Reuben spoke to Moses, saying: "Your servants will do as my lord commands. [26]Our little ones, our wives, our flocks, and all our livestock will be there in the cities of Gilead; [27]but your servants will cross over, every man armed for war, before the LORD to battle, just as my lord says."

[28]So Moses gave command concerning them to Eleazar the priest, to Joshua the son of Nun, and to the chief fathers of the tribes of the children of Israel. [29]And Moses said to them: "If the children of Gad and the children of Reuben cross over the Jordan with you, every man armed for battle

before the LORD, and the land is subdued before you, then you shall give them the land of Gilead as a possession. [30]But if they do not cross over armed with you, they shall have possessions among you in the land of Canaan."

[31]Then the children of Gad and the children of Reuben answered, saying: "As the LORD has said to your servants, so we will do. [32]We will cross over armed before the LORD into the land of Canaan, but the possession of our inheritance *shall remain* with us on this side of the Jordan."

[33]So Moses gave to the children of Gad, to the children of Reuben, and to half the tribe of Manasseh the son of Joseph, the kingdom of Sihon king of the Amorites and the kingdom of Og king of Bashan, the land with its cities within the borders, the cities of the surrounding country. [34]And the children of Gad built Dibon and Ataroth and Aroer, [35]Atroth and Shophan and Jazer and Jogbehah, [36]Beth Nimrah and Beth Haran, fortified cities, and folds for sheep. [37]And the children of Reuben built Heshbon and Elealeh and Kirjathaim, [38]Nebo and Baal Meon (*their* names being changed) and Shibmah; and they gave *other* names to the cities which they built.

[39]And the children of Machir the son of Manasseh went to Gilead and took it, and dispossessed the Amorites who *were* in it. [40]So Moses gave Gilead to Machir the son of Manasseh, and he dwelt in it. [41]Also Jair the son of Manasseh went and took its small towns, and called them Havoth Jair.[a] [42]Then Nobah went and took Kenath and its villages, and he called it Nobah, after his own name.

> **32:1–42** The tribes of Reuben and Gad desired to live in the land they had already conquered, because they possessed much livestock and the land was good for grazing. Moses gave portions of the land to these two tribes and to the half tribe of Manasseh on the condition that they would fully participate in the conquest of Canaan.

Israel's Journey from Egypt Reviewed

33 These *are* the journeys of the children of Israel, who went out of the land of Egypt by their armies under the

---

32:41 [a]Literally *Towns of Jair*

hand of Moses and Aaron. [2]Now Moses wrote down the starting points of their journeys at the command of the LORD. And these *are* their journeys according to their starting points:

[3]They departed from Rameses in the first month, on the fifteenth day of the first month; on the day after the Passover the children of Israel went out with boldness in the sight of all the Egyptians. [4]For the Egyptians were burying all *their* firstborn, whom the LORD had killed among them. Also on their gods the LORD had executed judgments.

[5]Then the children of Israel moved from Rameses and camped at Succoth. [6]They departed from Succoth and camped at Etham, which *is* on the edge of the wilderness. [7]They moved from Etham and turned back to Pi Hahiroth, which *is* east of Baal Zephon; and they camped near Migdol. [8]They departed from before Hahiroth[a] and passed through the midst of the sea into the wilderness, went three days' journey in the Wilderness of Etham, and camped at Marah. [9]They moved from Marah and came to Elim. At Elim *were* twelve springs of water and seventy palm trees; so they camped there.

[10]They moved from Elim and camped by the Red Sea. [11]They moved from the Red Sea and camped in the Wilderness of Sin. [12]They journeyed from the Wilderness of Sin and camped at Dophkah. [13]They departed from Dophkah and camped at Alush. [14]They moved from Alush and camped at Rephidim, where there was no water for the people to drink.

[15]They departed from Rephidim and camped in the Wilderness of Sinai. [16]They moved from the Wilderness of Sinai and camped at Kibroth Hattaavah. [17]They departed from Kibroth Hattaavah and camped at Hazeroth. [18]They departed from Hazeroth and camped at Rithmah. [19]They departed from Rithmah and camped at Rimmon Perez. [20]They departed from Rimmon Perez and camped at Libnah. [21]They moved from Libnah and camped at Rissah. [22]They journeyed from Rissah and camped at Kehelathah. [23]They went from Kehela-

thah and camped at Mount Shepher. [24]They moved from Mount Shepher and camped at Haradah. [25]They moved from Haradah and camped at Makheloth. [26]They moved from Makheloth and camped at Tahath. [27]They departed from Tahath and camped at Terah. [28]They moved from Terah and camped at Mithkah. [29]They went from Mithkah and camped at Hashmonah. [30]They departed from Hashmonah and camped at Moseroth. [31]They departed from Moseroth and camped at Bene Jaakan. [32]They moved from Bene Jaakan and camped at Hor Hagidgad. [33]They went from Hor Hagidgad and camped at Jotbathah. [34]They moved from Jotbathah and camped at Abronah. [35]They departed from Abronah and camped at Ezion Geber. [36]They moved from Ezion Geber and camped in the Wilderness of Zin, which *is* Kadesh. [37]They moved from Kadesh and camped at Mount Hor, on the boundary of the land of Edom.

[38]Then Aaron the priest went up to Mount Hor at the command of the LORD, and died there in the fortieth year after the children of Israel had come out of the land of Egypt, on the first *day* of the fifth month. [39]Aaron *was* one hundred and twenty-three years old when he died on Mount Hor.

[40]Now the king of Arad, the Canaanite, who dwelt in the South in the land of Canaan, heard of the coming of the children of Israel.

[41]So they departed from Mount Hor and camped at Zalmonah. [42]They departed from Zalmonah and camped at Punon. [43]They departed from Punon and camped at Oboth. [44]They departed from Oboth and camped at Ije Abarim, at the border of Moab. [45]They departed from Ijim[a] and camped at Dibon Gad. [46]They moved from Dibon Gad and camped at Almon Diblathaim. [47]They moved from Almon Diblathaim and camped in the mountains of Abarim, before Nebo. [48]They departed from the mountains of Abarim and camped in the plains of Moab by the Jordan, *across from* Jericho. [49]They camped by the Jordan, from Beth Jesimoth as far as the Abel Acacia Grove[a] in the plains of Moab.

33:8 [a]Many Hebrew manuscripts, Samaritan Pentateuch, Syriac, Targum, and Vulgate read *from Pi Hahiroth* (compare verse 7).   33:45 [a]Same as *Ije Abarim*, verse 44   33:49 [a]Hebrew *Abel Shittim*

33:1–49 The Lord commanded Moses to write a list of Israel's encampments between Egypt and the plains of Moab. Significantly, 40 places were mentioned, reflecting the 40 years spent in the wilderness. The same God who led them through the wilderness would also lead them in the conquest of Canaan.

33:50–36:13 The Promised Land had always been Israel's goal from the beginning of Numbers. This last part of the book anticipated their settlement in Canaan.

Instructions for the Conquest of Canaan

⁵⁰Now the LORD spoke to Moses in the plains of Moab by the Jordan, *across from* Jericho, saying, ⁵¹"Speak to the children of Israel, and say to them: 'When you have crossed the Jordan into the land of Canaan, ⁵²then you shall drive out all the inhabitants of the land from before you, destroy all their engraved stones, destroy all their molded images, and demolish all their high places; ⁵³you shall dispossess *the inhabitants of* the land and dwell in it, for I have given you the land to possess. ⁵⁴And you shall divide the land by lot as an inheritance among your families; to the larger you shall give a larger inheritance, and to the smaller you shall give a smaller inheritance; there everyone's *inheritance* shall be whatever falls to him by lot. You shall inherit according to the tribes of your fathers. ⁵⁵But if you do not drive out the inhabitants of the land from before you, then it shall be that those whom you let remain *shall be* irritants in your eyes and thorns in your sides, and they shall harass you in the land where you dwell. ⁵⁶Moreover it shall be *that* I will do to you as I thought to do to them.' "

33:50–56 God commanded that all of the Canaanites were to be put to death and their idols destroyed.

The Appointed Boundaries of Canaan

34 Then the LORD spoke to Moses, saying, ²"Command the children of Israel, and say to them: 'When you come into the land of Canaan, this *is* the land that shall fall to you as an inheritance—the land of Canaan to its boundaries. ³Your southern border shall be from the Wilderness of Zin along the border of Edom; then your southern border shall extend eastward to the end of the Salt Sea; ⁴your border shall turn from the southern side of the Ascent of Akrabbim, continue to Zin, and be on the south of Kadesh Barnea; then it shall go on to Hazar Addar, and continue to Azmon; ⁵the border shall turn from Azmon to the Brook of Egypt, and it shall end at the Sea.

⁶'As for the western border, you shall have the Great Sea for a border; this shall be your western border.

⁷'And this shall be your northern border: From the Great Sea you shall mark out your *border* line to Mount Hor; ⁸from Mount Hor you shall mark out *your border* to the entrance of Hamath; then the direction of the border shall be toward Zedad; ⁹the border shall proceed to Ziphron, and it shall end at Hazar Enan. This shall be your northern border.

¹⁰'You shall mark out your eastern border from Hazar Enan to Shepham; ¹¹the border shall go down from Shepham to Riblah on the east side of Ain; the border shall go down and reach to the eastern side of the Sea of Chinnereth; ¹²the border shall go down along the Jordan, and it shall end at the Salt Sea. This shall be your land with its surrounding boundaries.' "

¹³Then Moses commanded the children of Israel, saying: "This *is* the land which you shall inherit by lot, which the LORD has commanded to give to the nine tribes and to the half-tribe. ¹⁴For the tribe of the children of Reuben according to the house of their fathers, and the tribe of the children of Gad according to the house of their fathers, have received *their inheritance*; and the half-tribe of Manasseh has received its inheritance. ¹⁵The two tribes and the half-tribe have received their inheritance on this side of the Jordan, *across from* Jericho eastward, toward the sunrise."

The Leaders Appointed to Divide the Land

¹⁶And the LORD spoke to Moses, saying, ¹⁷"These *are* the names of the men who shall divide the land among you as an inheritance: Eleazar the priest and Joshua the son of Nun. ¹⁸And you shall take one leader of every tribe to divide the land for the inheritance. ¹⁹These *are* the names of the

men: from the tribe of Judah, Caleb the son of Jephunneh; ²⁰from the tribe of the children of Simeon, Shemuel the son of Ammihud; ²¹from the tribe of Benjamin, Elidad the son of Chislon; ²²a leader from the tribe of the children of Dan, Bukki the son of Jogli; ²³from the sons of Joseph: a leader from the tribe of the children of Manasseh, Hanniel the son of Ephod, ²⁴and a leader from the tribe of the children of Ephraim, Kemuel the son of Shiphtan; ²⁵a leader from the tribe of the children of Zebulun, Elizaphan the son of Parnach; ²⁶a leader from the tribe of the children of Issachar, Paltiel the son of Azzan; ²⁷a leader from the tribe of the children of Asher, Ahihud the son of Shelomi; ²⁸and a leader from the tribe of the children of Naphtali, Pedahel the son of Ammihud."

²⁹These *are* the ones the LORD commanded to divide the inheritance among the children of Israel in the land of Canaan.

Cities for the Levites

35 And the LORD spoke to Moses in the plains of Moab by the Jordan *across from* Jericho, saying: ²"Command the children of Israel that they give the Levites cities to dwell in from the inheritance of their possession, and you shall *also* give the Levites common-land around the cities. ³They shall have the cities to dwell in; and their common-land shall be for their cattle, for their herds, and for all their animals. ⁴The common-land of the cities which you will give the Levites *shall extend* from the wall of the city outward a thousand cubits all around. ⁵And you shall measure outside the city on the east side two thousand cubits, on the south side two thousand cubits, on the west side two thousand cubits, and on the north side two thousand cubits. The city *shall be* in the middle. This shall belong to them as common-land for the cities.

⁶"Now among the cities which you will give to the Levites *you shall appoint* six cities of refuge, to which a manslayer may flee. And to these you shall add forty-two cities. ⁷So all the cities you will give the Levites *shall be* forty-eight; these *you shall give* with their common-land. ⁸And the cities which you will give *shall be* from the possession of the children of Israel; from

the larger *tribe* you shall give many, from the smaller you shall give few. Each shall give some of its cities to the Levites, in proportion to the inheritance that each receives."

Cities of Refuge

⁹Then the LORD spoke to Moses, saying, ¹⁰"Speak to the children of Israel, and say to them: 'When you cross the Jordan into the land of Canaan, ¹¹then you shall appoint cities to be cities of refuge for you, that the manslayer who kills any person accidentally may flee there. ¹²They shall be cities of refuge for you from the avenger, that the manslayer may not die until he stands before the congregation in judgment. ¹³And of the cities which you give, you shall have six cities of refuge. ¹⁴You shall appoint three cities on this side of the Jordan, and three cities you shall appoint in the land of Canaan, *which* will be cities of refuge. ¹⁵These six cities shall be for refuge for the children of Israel, for the stranger, and for the sojourner among them, that anyone who kills a person accidentally may flee there.

¹⁶"But if he strikes him with an iron implement, so that he dies, he *is* a murderer; the murderer shall surely be put to death. ¹⁷And if he strikes him with a stone in the hand, by which one could die, and he does die, he *is* a murderer; the murderer shall surely be put to death. ¹⁸Or *if* he strikes him with a wooden hand weapon, by which one could die, and he does die, he *is* a murderer; the murderer shall surely be put to death. ¹⁹The avenger of blood himself shall put the murderer to death; when he meets him, he shall put him to death. ²⁰If he pushes him out of hatred or, while lying in wait, hurls something at him so that he dies, ²¹or in enmity he strikes him

with his hand so that he dies, the one who struck *him* shall surely be put to death. He *is* a murderer. The avenger of blood shall put the murderer to death when he meets him.

²²'However, if he pushes him suddenly without enmity, or throws anything at him without lying in wait, ²³or uses a stone, by which a man could die, throwing *it* at him without seeing *him*, so that he dies, while he was not his enemy or seeking his harm, ²⁴then the congregation shall judge between the manslayer and the avenger of blood according to these judgments. ²⁵So the congregation shall deliver the manslayer from the hand of the avenger of blood, and the congregation shall return him to the city of refuge where he had fled, and he shall remain there until the death of the high priest who was anointed with the holy oil. ²⁶But if the manslayer at any time goes outside the limits of the city of refuge where he fled, ²⁷and the avenger of blood finds him outside the limits of his city of refuge, and the avenger of blood kills the manslayer, he shall not be guilty of blood, ²⁸because he should have remained in his city of refuge until the death of the high priest. But after the death of the high priest the manslayer may return to the land of his possession.

> **35:24 the congregation shall judge between the manslayer and the avenger.** The congregation decided the motive of the killer, whether it was hostile or accidental. If the killer had evil intent, then he would be turned over to the avenger to be put to death. If hostility could not be proven, then the killer was allowed to remain safely in the city.

²⁹And these *things* shall be a statute of judgment to you throughout your generations in all your dwellings. ³⁰Whoever kills a person, the murderer shall be put to death on the testimony of witnesses; but one witness is not *sufficient* testimony against a person for the death *penalty.* ³¹Moreover you shall take no ransom for the life of a murderer who *is* guilty of death, but he shall surely be put to death. ³²And you shall take no ransom for him who has fled to his city of refuge, that he may return to dwell in the land before the death of the priest. ³³So you shall not pollute the land where you *are;* for blood defiles the land, and no

atonement can be made for the land, for the blood that is shed on it, except by the blood of him who shed it. ³⁴Therefore do not defile the land which you inhabit, in the midst of which I dwell; for I the LORD dwell among the children of Israel.' "

> **35:9–34** Six of the Levitical cities were to be set aside as "cities of refuge" (see Deut. 19:1–13). These were havens of protection for any person who accidentally killed another person.

Marriage of Female Heirs

36 Now the chief fathers of the families of the children of Gilead the son of Machir, the son of Manasseh, of the families of the sons of Joseph, came near and spoke before Moses and before the leaders, the chief fathers of the children of Israel. ²And they said: "The LORD commanded my lord *Moses* to give the land as an inheritance by lot to the children of Israel, and my lord was commanded by the LORD to give the inheritance of our brother Zelophehad to his daughters. ³Now if they are married to any of the sons of the *other* tribes of the children of Israel, then their inheritance will be taken from the inheritance of our fathers, and it will be added to the inheritance of the tribe into which they marry; so it will be taken from the lot of our inheritance. ⁴And when the Jubilee of the children of Israel comes, then their inheritance will be added to the inheritance of the tribe into which they marry; so their inheritance will be taken away from the inheritance of the tribe of our fathers."

⁵Then Moses commanded the children of Israel according to the word of the LORD, saying: "What the tribe of the sons of Joseph speaks is right. ⁶This *is* what the LORD commands concerning the daughters of Zelophehad, saying, 'Let them marry whom they think best, but they may marry only within the family of their father's tribe.' ⁷So the inheritance of the children of Israel shall not change hands from tribe to tribe, for every one of the children of Israel shall keep the inheritance of the tribe of his fathers. ⁸And every daughter who possesses an inheritance in any tribe of the children of Israel shall be the wife of one of the family of her father's tribe, so that the children of Israel each may possess the inheritance

of his fathers. [9]Thus no inheritance shall change hands from *one* tribe to another, but every tribe of the children of Israel shall keep its own inheritance."

[10]Just as the LORD commanded Moses, so did the daughters of Zelophehad; [11]for Mahlah, Tirzah, Hoglah, Milcah, and Noah, the daughters of Zelophehad, were married to the sons of their father's brothers. [12]They were married into the families of the children of Manasseh the son of Joseph, and their inheritance remained in the tribe of their father's family.

36:12 They were married into...Manasseh. The daughters of Zelophehad exemplified obedience to God's commands, and their inheritance was a direct result. They were an example to all of Israel. Obedience was a basic lesson stressed throughout the whole book of Numbers.

[13]These *are* the commandments and the judgments which the LORD commanded the children of Israel by the hand of Moses in the plains of Moab by the Jordan, *across from* Jericho.

DEUTERONOMY

The Hebrew designation of this fifth biblical book simply uses two words that mean "These are the words." Ancient Greek translators based their title on Deuteronomy 17:18 which mentions "a copy of this law." The Greek word actually means *"deutero"*—"second" and *"nomos"*—"law." They were noting the fact that much of Deuteronomy is a review of God's Law by Moses in his final days. Both the later Latin version and our English versions transliterated the Greek expression into "Deuteronomy."

AUTHOR AND DATE

Deuteronomy was written by Moses, approximately 1405 B.C.

Moses has generally been accepted as the author of Deuteronomy in large part because the book itself makes that claim. Both the Old Testament and the New Testament support the claim of Mosaic authorship. While Deuteronomy 32:48–34:12 was added after Moses's death (probably by Joshua), the rest of the book must have originated with Moses shortly before his death in 1405 B.C.

Indications of Mosaic authorship in Deuteronomy: 1:1,5; 31:9,22,24

Old Testament passages supporting Moses as author of Deuteronomy: 1 Kings 2:3; 8:53; 2 Kings 14:6; 18:12

New Testament passages supporting Moses as author of Deuteronomy: Acts 3:22–23; Romans 10:19

BACKGROUND AND SETTING

Like Leviticus, the events in Deuteronomy take place in one location. The people of Israel were camped in their final staging area before invading the Promised Land. Numbers 36:13 identifies the location as "the plains of Moab."

The first thirty chapters of Deuteronomy record Moses' review and commentary on God's Law. The only two other events included are: (1) Moses' official acts of recording the Law in written form and commissioning Joshua as the new leader (31:1–29) and (2) Moses' death after viewing the Promised Land from the distant peak of Mt. Nebo (32:48–52; 34:1–12).

All of the original recipients of Deuteronomy were the generation that had grown up or been born in the wilderness during the forty years since the Exodus from Egypt. Here they stood on the border of the Promised Land, poised to do what their parents had refused to do.

In contrast with Leviticus and its priestly duties, the legal details in Deuteronomy emphasize the responsibilities of the people before God. Moses called the replacement generation of Israel to trust the Lord and be obedient to God's covenant made at Horeb (Sinai). He reminded them of past lessons and warnings from their history—the pattern of God's faithfulness (2:24–3:11; 29:2,7,8) and the people's rebellious tendencies (1:26–46; 9:7–10:11). Moses renewed the challenge for the people to take the land God had promised (1:8; 6:10; 9:5). Moses also looked into the future and predicted Israel's future failures, the painful consequences, and God's continuing faithfulness to His promises (4:25–31; 29:22–30; 31:26–29).

The book of Deuteronomy, along with Psalms and Isaiah, reveals much about the attributes of God. These three books receive the most frequent quoting by the New Testament authors. Among its central themes, Deuteronomy includes the following: the Lord is the only God (4:39; 6:4); God is jealous (4:24); God is faithful (7:9); God is loving (7:13); God is merciful (4:31); God is angered by sin (6:15).

> ## MOSES RENEWED THE CHALLENGE FOR THE PEOPLE TO TAKE THE LAND GOD HAD PROMISED.

Over 250 times, Moses used the phrase, "the Lord your God" when addressing Israel. God claimed Israel for Himself. Israel was called to obey (28:2), to fear (10:12), to love (10:12), and to serve (10:12) God by living according to His commandments (10:12,13). God guaranteed His blessings on the people of Israel as long as they obeyed Him (28:1–14).

Deuteronomy also teaches that obedience and the pursuit of personal holiness must be based on the character of God. Because God is holy, His people are to be holy (7:6–11; 8:6,11,18; 10:12,16,17; 11:13; 13:3,4; 14:1,2).

OUTLINE

The Previous Command to Enter Canaan

1 These *are* the words which Moses spoke to all Israel on this side of the Jordan in the wilderness, in the plain*a* opposite Suph,*b* between Paran, Tophel, Laban, Hazeroth, and Dizahab. ²*It is* eleven days' *journey* from Horeb by way of Mount Seir to Kadesh Barnea. ³Now it came to pass in the fortieth year, in the eleventh month, on the first *day* of the month, *that* Moses spoke to the children of Israel according to all that the LORD had given him as commandments to them, ⁴after he had killed Sihon king of the Amorites, who dwelt in Heshbon, and Og king of Bashan, who dwelt at Ashtaroth in*a* Edrei.

> **1:1 The words which Moses spoke.** Almost the entire book of Deuteronomy consists of speeches given by Moses at the end of his life. According to v. 3, Moses acted upon the authority of God to speak inspired words in accordance with the commandments that God had given.

⁵On this side of the Jordan in the land of Moab, Moses began to explain this law, saying, ⁶"The LORD our God spoke to us in Horeb, saying: 'You have dwelt long enough at this mountain. ⁷Turn and take your journey, and go to the mountains of the Amorites, to all the neighboring *places* in the plain,*a* in the mountains and in the lowland, in the South and on the seacoast, to the land of the Canaanites and to Lebanon, as far as the great river, the River Euphrates. ⁸See, I have set the land before you; go in and possess the land which the LORD swore to your fathers—to Abraham, Isaac, and Jacob—to give to them and their descendants after them.'

> **1:5 explain.** To clarify. The purpose of the book was to make the purpose of the law clear to the people as they entered the Land. It was to be their guide to the law while living in the Land. Deuteronomy does not review the law given at Horeb (Sinai), which is recorded in Exodus, Leviticus, and Numbers but rather gives Israel instructions in how to walk with God and how to fulfill His will in the Land and be blessed.

Tribal Leaders Appointed

⁹"And I spoke to you at that time, saying: 'I alone am not able to bear you. ¹⁰The LORD your God has multiplied you, and here you *are* today, as the stars of heaven in multitude. ¹¹May the LORD God of your fathers make you a thousand times more numerous than you are, and bless you as He has promised you! ¹²How can I alone bear your problems and your burdens and your complaints? ¹³Choose wise, understanding, and knowledgeable men from among your tribes, and I will make them heads over you.' ¹⁴And you answered me and said, 'The thing which you have told *us* to do *is* good.' ¹⁵So I took the heads of your tribes, wise and knowledgeable men, and made them heads over you, leaders of thousands, leaders of hundreds, leaders of fifties, leaders of tens, and officers for your tribes.

¹⁶"Then I commanded your judges at that time, saying, 'Hear *the cases* between your brethren, and judge righteously between a man and his brother or the stranger who is with him. ¹⁷You shall not show partiality in judgment; you shall hear the small as well as the great; you shall not be afraid in any man's presence, for the judgment *is* God's. The case that is too hard for you, bring to me, and I will hear it.' ¹⁸And I commanded you at that time all the things which you should do.

Israel's Refusal to Enter the Land

¹⁹"So we departed from Horeb, and went through all that great and terrible wilderness which you saw on the way to the mountains of the Amorites, as the LORD our God had commanded us. Then we came to Kadesh Barnea. ²⁰And I said to you, 'You have come to the mountains of the Amorites, which the LORD our God is giving us. ²¹Look, the LORD your God has set the land before you; go up *and* possess *it,* as the LORD God of your fathers has spoken to you; do not fear or be discouraged.'

²²"And every one of you came near to me and said, 'Let us send men before us, and let them search out the land for us, and bring back word to us of the way by which

---

1:1 *a*Hebrew *arabah*   *b*One manuscript of the Septuagint, also Targum and Vulgate, read *Red Sea.*
1:4 *a*Septuagint, Syriac, and Vulgate read *and* (compare Joshua 12:4).   1:7 *a*Hebrew *arabah*

we should go up, and of the cities into which we shall come.'

23"The plan pleased me well; so I took twelve of your men, one man from *each* tribe. 24And they departed and went up into the mountains, and came to the Valley of Eshcol, and spied it out. 25They also took *some* of the fruit of the land in their hands and brought *it* down to us; and they brought back word to us, saying, 'It is a good land which the LORD our God is giving us.'

26"Nevertheless you would not go up, but rebelled against the command of the LORD your God; 27and you complained in your tents, and said, 'Because the LORD hates us, He has brought us out of the land of Egypt to deliver us into the hand of the Amorites, to destroy us. 28Where can we go up? Our brethren have discouraged our hearts, saying, "The people *are* greater and taller than we; the cities *are* great and fortified up to heaven; moreover we have seen the sons of the Anakim there." '

29"Then I said to you, 'Do not be terrified, or afraid of them. 30The LORD your God, who goes before you, He will fight for you, according to all He did for you in Egypt before your eyes, 31and in the wilderness where you saw how the LORD your God carried you, as a man carries his son, in all the way that you went until you came to this place.' 32Yet, for all that, you did not believe the LORD your God, 33who went in the way before you to search out a place for you to pitch your tents, to show you the way you should go, in the fire by night and in the cloud by day.

1:33 in the fire...and in the cloud. God used the cloud by day and the fire by night to direct Israel in the wilderness. The Lord who guided Israel through the wandering journey was the same Lord who had already searched out their place in the Land.

The Penalty for Israel's Rebellion

34"And the LORD heard the sound of your words, and was angry, and took an oath, saying, 35'Surely not one of these men of this evil generation shall see that good land of which I swore to give to your fathers, 36except Caleb the son of Jephunneh; he shall see it, and to him and his children I am giving the land on which he walked, be-cause he wholly followed the LORD.' 37The LORD was also angry with me for your sakes, saying, 'Even you shall not go in there. 38Joshua the son of Nun, who stands before you, he shall go in there. Encourage him, for he shall cause Israel to inherit it.

1:37 The LORD was also angry with me. Although Moses' disobedience occurred almost 39 years after Israel's failure at Kadesh (see Num. 20:1–13), Moses included it with Israel's because his disobedience was of the same kind. Moses failed to honor the Word of the Lord, and in rebellion for self glory, disobeyed God's command to speak to the rock and struck it instead. He suffered the same result of God's anger and was not permitted to go into the Land (Num. 20:12).

39'Moreover your little ones and your children, who you say will be victims, who today have no knowledge of good and evil, they shall go in there; to them I will give it, and they shall possess it. 40But *as for* you, turn and take your journey into the wilderness by the Way of the Red Sea.'

41"Then you answered and said to me, 'We have sinned against the LORD; we will go up and fight, just as the LORD our God commanded us.' And when everyone of you had girded on his weapons of war, you were ready to go up into the mountain.

42"And the LORD said to me, 'Tell them, "Do not go up nor fight, for I *am* not among you; lest you be defeated before your enemies." ' 43So I spoke to you; yet you would not listen, but rebelled against the command of the LORD, and presumptuously went up into the mountain. 44And the Amorites who dwelt in that mountain came out against you and chased you as bees do, and drove you back from Seir to Hormah. 45Then you returned and wept before the LORD, but the LORD would not listen to your voice nor give ear to you.

46"So you remained in Kadesh many days, according to the days that you spent *there*.

The Desert Years

2 "Then we turned and journeyed into the wilderness of the Way of the Red Sea, as the LORD spoke to me, and we skirted Mount Seir for many days.

2"And the LORD spoke to me, saying:

³'You have skirted this mountain long enough; turn northward. ⁴And command the people, saying, "You *are about to* pass through the territory of your brethren, the descendants of Esau, who live in Seir; and they will be afraid of you. Therefore watch yourselves carefully. ⁵Do not meddle with them, for I will not give you *any* of their land, no, not so much as one footstep, because I have given Mount Seir to Esau *as a* possession. ⁶You shall buy food from them with money, that you may eat; and you shall also buy water from them with money, that you may drink.

⁷"For the LORD your God has blessed you in all the work of your hand. He knows your trudging through this great wilderness. These forty years the LORD your God *has been* with you; you have lacked nothing." '

⁸"And when we passed beyond our brethren, the descendants of Esau who dwell in Seir, away from the road of the plain, away from Elath and Ezion Geber, we turned and passed by way of the Wilderness of Moab. ⁹Then the LORD said to me, 'Do not harass Moab, nor contend with them in battle, for I will not give you *any* of their land *as* a possession, because I have given Ar to the descendants of Lot *as* a possession.' "

¹⁰(The Emim had dwelt there in times past, a people as great and numerous and tall as the Anakim. ¹¹They were also regarded as giants,ᵃ like the Anakim, but the Moabites call them Emim. ¹²The Horites formerly dwelt in Seir, but the descendants of Esau dispossessed them and destroyed them from before them, and dwelt in their place, just as Israel did to the land of their possession which the LORD gave them.)

¹³" 'Now rise and cross over the Valley of the Zered.' So we crossed over the Valley of the Zered. ¹⁴And the time we took to come from Kadesh Barnea until we crossed over the Valley of the Zered *was* thirty-eight

> **2:13 Zered.** A brook that ran into the Dead Sea from the SE and constituted the southern boundary of Moab. In contrast to the disobedience associated with Kadesh (Num. 20:1–13), the people obeyed and crossed the brook Zered. The people showed a new spirit of obedience.

years, until all the generation of the men of war was consumed from the midst of the camp, just as the LORD had sworn to them. ¹⁵For indeed the hand of the LORD was against them, to destroy them from the midst of the camp until they were consumed.

¹⁶"So it was, when all the men of war had finally perished from among the people, ¹⁷that the LORD spoke to me, saying: ¹⁸'This day you are to cross over at Ar, the boundary of Moab. ¹⁹And *when* you come near the people of Ammon, do not harass them or meddle with them, for I will not give you *any* of the land of the people of Ammon *as* a possession, because I have given it to the descendants of Lot *as* a possession.' "

²⁰(That was also regarded as a land of giants;ᵃ giants formerly dwelt there. But the Ammonites call them Zamzummim, ²¹a people as great and numerous and tall as the Anakim. But the LORD destroyed them before them, and they dispossessed them and dwelt in their place, ²²just as He had done for the descendants of Esau, who dwelt in Seir, when He destroyed the Horites from before them. They dispossessed them and dwelt in their place, even to this day. ²³And the Avim, who dwelt in villages as far as Gaza—the Caphtorim, who came from Caphtor, destroyed them and dwelt in their place.)

²⁴" 'Rise, take your journey, and cross over the River Arnon. Look, I have given into your hand Sihon the Amorite, king of Heshbon, and his land. Begin to possess *it*, and engage him in battle. ²⁵This day I will begin to put the dread and fear of you upon the nations under the whole heaven, who shall hear the report of you, and shall tremble and be in anguish because of you.'

> **2:25 fear of you.** As the conquest began, God put the fear of Israel into the hearts of their enemies.

King Sihon Defeated

²⁶"And I sent messengers from the Wilderness of Kedemoth to Sihon king of Heshbon, with words of peace, saying, ²⁷'Let me pass through your land; I will keep strictly to the road, and I will turn neither to the right nor to the left. ²⁸You shall

2:11 ᵃHebrew *rephaim*   2:20 ᵃHebrew *rephaim*

sell me food for money, that I may eat, and give me water for money, that I may drink; only let me pass through on foot, ²⁹just as the descendants of Esau who dwell in Seir and the Moabites who dwell in Ar did for me, until I cross the Jordan to the land which the LORD our God is giving us.'

³⁰"But Sihon king of Heshbon would not let us pass through, for the LORD your God hardened his spirit and made his heart obstinate, that He might deliver him into your hand, as *it is* this day.

³¹"And the LORD said to me, 'See, I have begun to give Sihon and his land over to you. Begin to possess *it*, that you may inherit his land.' ³²Then Sihon and all his people came out against us to fight at Jahaz. ³³And the LORD our God delivered him over to us; so we defeated him, his sons, and all his people. ³⁴We took all his cities at that time, and we utterly destroyed the men, women, and little ones of every city; we left none remaining. ³⁵We took only the livestock as plunder for ourselves, with the spoil of the cities which we took. ³⁶From Aroer, which *is* on the bank of the River Arnon, and *from* the city that *is* in the ravine, as far as Gilead, there was not one city too strong for us; the LORD our God delivered all to us. ³⁷Only you did not go near the land of the people of Ammon—anywhere along the River Jabbok, or to the cities of the mountains, or wherever the LORD our God had forbidden us.

King Og Defeated

3 "Then we turned and went up the road to Bashan; and Og king of Bashan came out against us, he and all his people, to battle at Edrei. ²And the LORD said to me, 'Do not fear him, for I have delivered him and all his people and his land into your hand; you shall do to him as you did to Sihon king of the Amorites, who dwelt at Heshbon.'

³"So the LORD our God also delivered into our hands Og king of Bashan, with all his people, and we attacked him until he had no survivors remaining. ⁴And we took all his cities at that time; there was not a city which we did not take from them: sixty cities, all the region of Argob, the kingdom of Og in Bashan. ⁵All these cities *were* fortified with high walls, gates, and bars, besides a great many rural towns. ⁶And we utterly destroyed them, as we did to Sihon king of Heshbon, utterly destroying the men, women, and children of every city. ⁷But all the livestock and the spoil of the cities we took as booty for ourselves.

⁸"And at that time we took the land from the hand of the two kings of the Amorites who *were* on this side of the Jordan, from the River Arnon to Mount Hermon ⁹(the Sidonians call Hermon Sirion, and the Amorites call it Senir), ¹⁰all the cities of the plain, all Gilead, and all Bashan, as far as Salcah and Edrei, cities of the kingdom of Og in Bashan.

Is Deuteronomy simply Moses' version of the secular covenants and treaties of his day, or does it represent a unique revelation from God?

The format that Moses used in recording not only the material in Deuteronomy but also the rest of the Pentateuch bears some resemblance to other official documents from a particular time in history. This fact can be used by historians in trying to establish a date for the book. This fact can also be used by those who question God's unique revelation when they claim that Moses must have merely been copying the style of other nations of his time.

The people whom God enlisted to record His revelation did not shed their personalities, education, or style as they wrote for God. Moses had the equivalent of advanced degrees in the best training Egypt had to offer young princes (Acts 7:22). If we think of the Pentateuch as Moses' God-guided journaling during the wilderness wanderings, it will not seem unusual that his writing style bears similarities to the official and political writings of his day. What sets Moses' writings, along with the rest of Scripture, apart is not so much the style but their authoritative and God inspired content.

¹¹"For only Og king of Bashan remained of the remnant of the giants.*a* Indeed his bedstead *was* an iron bedstead. (*Is* it not in Rabbah of the people of Ammon?) Nine cubits *is* its length and four cubits its width, according to the standard cubit.

3:11 an iron bedstead. The bedstead might actually have been a coffin. The size of the bedstead, 13 1/2 by 6 ft., emphasized the immense size of Og, who was a giant, the last of the race of giants called the Rephaim. As God had given Israel victory over Og, so He would give them victory over the giants in the Land.

The Land East of the Jordan Divided

¹²"And this land, *which* we possessed at that time, from Aroer, which *is* by the River Arnon, and half the mountains of Gilead and its cities, I gave to the Reubenites and the Gadites. ¹³The rest of Gilead, and all Bashan, the kingdom of Og, I gave to half the tribe of Manasseh. (All the region of Argob, with all Bashan, was called the land of the giants.*a* ¹⁴Jair the son of Manasseh took all the region of Argob, as far as the border of the Geshurites and the Maachathites, and called Bashan after his own name, Havoth Jair,*a* to this day.)

¹⁵"Also I gave Gilead to Machir. ¹⁶And to the Reubenites and the Gadites I gave from Gilead as far as the River Arnon, the middle of the river as *the* border, as far as the River Jabbok, the border of the people of Ammon; ¹⁷the plain also, with the Jordan as *the* border, from Chinnereth as far as the east side of the Sea of the Arabah (the Salt Sea), below the slopes of Pisgah.

¹⁸"Then I commanded you at that time, saying: 'The LORD your God has given you this land to possess. All you men of valor shall cross over armed before your brethren, the children of Israel. ¹⁹But your wives, your little ones, and your livestock (I know that you have much livestock) shall stay in your cities which I have given you, ²⁰until the LORD has given rest to your brethren as to you, and they also possess the land which the LORD your God is giving them beyond the Jordan. Then each of you may return to his possession which I have given you.'

²¹"And I commanded Joshua at that time, saying, 'Your eyes have seen all that the LORD your God has done to these two kings; so will the LORD do to all the kingdoms through which you pass. ²²You must not fear them, for the LORD your God Himself fights for you.'

3:22 the LORD your God Himself fights for you. Moses commanded Joshua not to be afraid because the Lord Himself would give them the victory (see Josh. 1:9).

Moses Forbidden to Enter the Land

²³"Then I pleaded with the LORD at that time, saying: ²⁴'O Lord GOD, You have begun to show Your servant Your greatness and Your mighty hand; for what god *is there* in heaven or on earth who can do *anything* like Your works and Your mighty *deeds?* ²⁵I pray, let me cross over and see the good land beyond the Jordan, those pleasant mountains, and Lebanon.'

²⁶"But the LORD was angry with me on your account, and would not listen to me. So the LORD said to me: 'Enough of that! Speak no more to Me of this matter. ²⁷Go up to the top of Pisgah, and lift your eyes toward the west, the north, the south, and the east; behold *it* with your eyes, for you shall not cross over this Jordan. ²⁸But command Joshua, and encourage him and strengthen him; for he shall go over before this people, and he shall cause them to inherit the land which you will see.'

²⁹"So we stayed in the valley opposite Beth Peor.

Moses Commands Obedience

4 "Now, O Israel, listen to the statutes and the judgments which I teach you to observe, that you may live, and go in and possess the land which the LORD God of your fathers is giving you. ²You shall not add to the word which I command you, nor

4:2 You shall not add...nor take from. The Word that God had given to Moses at Horeb was complete and sufficient to direct the people. Anything that changed, added to, reduced, or contradicted the Law would not be tolerated (see 12:32).

3:11 *a*Hebrew *rephaim*   3:13 *a*Hebrew *rephaim*   3:14 *a*Literally *Towns of Jair*

take from it, that you may keep the commandments of the LORD your God which I command you. ³Your eyes have seen what the LORD did at Baal Peor; for the LORD your God has destroyed from among you all the men who followed Baal of Peor. ⁴But you who held fast to the LORD your God *are* alive today, every one of you.

⁵"Surely I have taught you statutes and judgments, just as the LORD my God commanded me, that you should act according to *them* in the land which you go to possess. ⁶Therefore be careful to observe *them*; for this *is* your wisdom and your understanding in the sight of the peoples who will hear all these statutes, and say, 'Surely this great nation *is* a wise and understanding people.'

4:6 the peoples. Israel's obedience to God's law would testify to the world that God was near to His people and that His laws were righteous. One purpose of the law was to make Israel morally and spiritually unique among all the nations and to draw those nations to the true and living God. From the beginning, Israel was a witness nation.

⁷"For what great nation *is there* that has God *so* near to it, as the LORD our God *is* to us, for whatever *reason* we may call upon Him? ⁸And what great nation *is there* that has *such* statutes and righteous judgments as are in all this law which I set before you this day? ⁹Only take heed to yourself, and diligently keep yourself, lest you forget the things your eyes have seen, and lest they depart from your heart all the days of your life. And teach them to your children and your grandchildren, ¹⁰*especially concerning* the day you stood before the LORD your God in Horeb, when the LORD said to me, 'Gather the people to Me, and I will let them hear My words, that they may learn to fear

4:6–8 The nations would see three things in Israel. First, the Israelites would be "a wise and understanding people" (v. 6) and know how to apply God's knowledge to discern and judge matters accurately. Second, Israel had "God so near to it" (v. 7), showing that He had established intimacy with them. Third, the other nations would see from Israel's "statutes and righteous judgments" (v. 8) that their law was distinctive, for its source was the Lord, which made it righteous in character.

Me all the days they live on the earth, and *that* they may teach their children.'

¹¹"Then you came near and stood at the foot of the mountain, and the mountain burned with fire to the midst of heaven, with darkness, cloud, and thick darkness. ¹²And the LORD spoke to you out of the midst of the fire. You heard the sound of the words, but saw no form; *you* only *heard* a voice. ¹³So He declared to you His covenant which He commanded you to perform, the Ten Commandments; and He wrote them on two tablets of stone. ¹⁴And the LORD commanded me at that time to teach you statutes and judgments, that you might observe them in the land which you cross over to possess.

Beware of Idolatry

¹⁵"Take careful heed to yourselves, for you saw no form when the LORD spoke to you at Horeb out of the midst of the fire, ¹⁶lest you act corruptly and make for yourselves a carved image in the form of any figure: the likeness of male or female, ¹⁷the likeness of any animal that *is* on the earth or the likeness of any winged bird that flies in the air, ¹⁸the likeness of anything that creeps on the ground or the likeness of any fish that *is* in the water beneath the earth. ¹⁹And *take heed*, lest you lift your eyes to heaven, and *when* you see the sun, the moon, and the stars, all the host of heaven, you feel driven to worship them and serve them, which the LORD your God has given to all the peoples under the whole heaven as a heritage. ²⁰But the LORD has taken you and brought you out of the iron furnace, out of Egypt, to be His people, an inheritance, as you are this day. ²¹Furthermore the LORD was angry with me for your sakes, and swore that I would not cross over the Jordan, and that I would not enter the good land which the LORD your God is giving you as an inheritance. ²²But I must die in this land, I must not cross over the Jordan; but you shall cross over and possess that good land. ²³Take heed to yourselves, lest you forget the covenant of the LORD your God which He made with you, and make for yourselves a carved image in the form of anything which the LORD your God has forbidden you. ²⁴For the LORD your God *is* a consuming fire, a jealous God.

4:24 a jealous God. God is zealous to protect what belongs to Him. He will not allow another to have the honor that is due to Him alone (see Is. 42:8; 48:11).

25"When you beget children and grandchildren and have grown old in the land, and act corruptly and make a carved image in the form of anything, and do evil in the sight of the LORD your God to provoke Him to anger, 26I call heaven and earth to witness against you this day, that you will soon utterly perish from the land which you cross over the Jordan to possess; you will not prolong *your* days in it, but will be utterly destroyed. 27And the LORD will scatter you among the peoples, and you will be left few in number among the nations where the LORD will drive you. 28And there you will serve gods, the work of men's hands, wood and stone, which neither see nor hear nor eat nor smell. 29But from there you will seek the LORD your God, and you will find *Him* if you seek Him with all your heart and with all your soul. 30When you are in distress, and all these things come upon you in the latter days, when you turn to the LORD your God and obey His voice 31(for the LORD your God *is* a merciful God), He will not forsake you nor destroy you, nor forget the covenant of your fathers which He swore to them.

32"For ask now concerning the days that are past, which were before you, since the day that God created man on the earth, and *ask* from one end of heaven to the other, whether *any* great *thing* like this has happened, or *anything* like it has been heard. 33Did *any* people *ever* hear the voice of God speaking out of the midst of the fire, as you have heard, and live? 34Or did God *ever* try to go *and* take for Himself a nation from the midst of *another* nation, by trials, by signs, by wonders, by war, by a mighty hand and an outstretched arm, and by great terrors, according to all that the LORD your God did for you in Egypt before your eyes? 35To you it was shown, that you might know that the LORD Himself *is* God; *there is* none other besides Him. 36Out of heaven He let you hear His voice, that He might instruct you; on earth He showed you His great fire, and you heard His words out of the midst of the fire. 37And because He loved your fathers, therefore He chose their descendants after them; and He brought you out of Egypt with His Presence, with His mighty power, 38driving out from before you nations greater and mightier than you, to bring you in, to give you their land *as* an inheritance, as *it is* this day. 39Therefore know this day, and consider *it* in your heart, that the LORD Himself *is* God in heaven above and on the earth beneath; *there is* no other. 40You shall therefore keep His statutes and His commandments which I command you today, that it may go well with you and with your children after you, and that you may prolong *your* days in the land which the LORD your God is giving you for all time."

4:32–39 since the day that God created man on the earth. In all of human history, no other nation has had the privilege that Israel had of hearing God speak (as He did in giving the law at Mt. Sinai) and of surviving such an awesome experience. Israel was blessed, chosen, and delivered from bondage by mighty, unique miracles. God did all this to reveal to them that He alone is God.

Cities of Refuge East of the Jordan

41Then Moses set apart three cities on this side of the Jordan, toward the rising of the sun, 42that the manslayer might flee there, who kills his neighbor unintentionally, without having hated him in time past, and that by fleeing to one of these cities he might live: 43Bezer in the wilderness on the plateau for the Reubenites, Ramoth in Gilead for the Gadites, and Golan in Bashan for the Manassites.

4:44–26:68 The heart of Deuteronomy is found in this long second speech by Moses. After a brief introduction (4:44–49), Moses explained what the law said concerning their relationship with the Lord in the Land (5:1–26:19), and then he concluded by recounting the blessings or curses which would come upon the nation as a consequence to their obedience or disobedience (27:1–28:68).

Introduction to God's Law

44Now this *is* the law which Moses set before the children of Israel. 45These *are* the testimonies, the statutes, and the judgments which Moses spoke to the children of Israel after they came out of Egypt, 46on

this side of the Jordan, in the valley opposite Beth Peor, in the land of Sihon king of the Amorites, who dwelt at Heshbon, whom Moses and the children of Israel defeated after they came out of Egypt. ⁴⁷And they took possession of his land and the land of Og king of Bashan, two kings of the Amorites, who *were* on this side of the Jordan, toward the rising of the sun, ⁴⁸from Aroer, which *is* on the bank of the River Arnon, even to Mount Sion*ᵃ* (that is, Hermon), ⁴⁹and all the plain on the east side of the Jordan as far as the Sea of the Arabah, below the slopes of Pisgah.

The Ten Commandments Reviewed

5 And Moses called all Israel, and said to them: "Hear, O Israel, the statutes and judgments which I speak in your hearing today, that you may learn them and be careful to observe them. ²The LORD our God made a covenant with us in Horeb. ³The LORD did not make this covenant with our fathers, but with us, those who *are* here today, all of us who *are* alive. ⁴The LORD talked with you face to face on the mountain from the midst of the fire. ⁵I stood between the LORD and you at that time, to declare to you the word of the LORD; for you were afraid because of the fire, and you did not go up the mountain. *He* said:

5:1 Hear, O Israel. The verb "hear" carried the implication to "obey." A hearing that leads to obedience was demanded of all the people.

---

⁶ 'I *am* the LORD your God who brought you out of the land of Egypt, out of the house of bondage.

⁷ 'You shall have no other gods before Me.

⁸ 'You shall not make for yourself a carved image—any likeness *of anything* that *is* in heaven above, or that *is* in the earth beneath, or that *is* in the water under the earth; ⁹you shall not bow down to them nor serve them. For I, the LORD your God, *am* a jealous God, visiting the iniquity of the fathers upon the children to the third and fourth *generations* of those who hate Me, ¹⁰but showing mercy to thousands, to those who love Me and keep My commandments.

¹¹ 'You shall not take the name of the LORD your God in vain, for the LORD will not hold *him* guiltless who takes His name in vain.

¹² 'Observe the Sabbath day, to keep it holy, as the LORD your God commanded you. ¹³Six days you shall labor and do all your work, ¹⁴but the seventh day *is* the Sabbath of the LORD your God. *In it* you shall do no work: you, nor your son, nor your daughter, nor your male servant, nor your female servant, nor your ox, nor your donkey, nor any of your cattle, nor your stranger who *is* within your gates, that your male servant and your female servant may rest as well as you. ¹⁵And remember that you were a slave in the land of Egypt, and the LORD your God brought you out from there by a mighty hand and by an outstretched arm; therefore the LORD your God commanded you to keep the Sabbath day.

¹⁶ 'Honor your father and your mother, as the LORD your God has commanded you, that your days may be long, and that it may be well with you in the land which the LORD your God is giving you.

¹⁷ 'You shall not murder.

¹⁸ 'You shall not commit adultery.

¹⁹ 'You shall not steal.

²⁰ 'You shall not bear false witness against your neighbor.

²¹ 'You shall not covet your neighbor's wife; and you shall not desire your neighbor's house, his field, his male servant, his female servant, his ox, his donkey, or anything that *is* your neighbor's.'

5:6–21 The first five commandments involve relationship with God, and the last five deal with human relationships. Together they compose the foundation of Israel's life before God.

4:48 *ᵃ*Syriac reads *Sirion* (compare 3:9).

22"These words the LORD spoke to all your assembly, in the mountain from the midst of the fire, the cloud, and the thick darkness, with a loud voice; and He added no more. And He wrote them on two tablets of stone and gave them to me.

The People Afraid of God's Presence

23"So it was, when you heard the voice from the midst of the darkness, while the mountain was burning with fire, that you came near to me, all the heads of your tribes and your elders. 24And you said: 'Surely the LORD our God has shown us His glory and His greatness, and we have heard His voice from the midst of the fire. We have seen this day that God speaks with man; yet he *still* lives. 25Now therefore, why should we die? For this great fire will consume us; if we hear the voice of the LORD our God anymore, then we shall die. 26For who *is there* of all flesh who has heard the voice of the living God speaking from the midst of the fire, as we *have*, and lived? 27You go near and hear all that the LORD our God may say, and tell us all that the LORD our God says to you, and we will hear and do *it*.'

> **5:22–27** God's presence at Sinai so frightened the people that they asked Moses to receive the words from God and then communicate those words to them, after which they promised to obey them all.

28"Then the LORD heard the voice of your words when you spoke to me, and the LORD said to me: 'I have heard the voice of the words of this people which they have spoken to you. They are right *in* all that they have spoken. 29Oh, that they had such a heart in them that they would fear Me and always keep all My commandments, that it might be well with them and with their children forever! 30Go and say to them, "Return to your tents." 31But as for you, stand here by Me, and I will speak to you all the commandments, the statutes, and the judgments which you shall teach them, that they may observe *them* in the land which I am giving them to possess.'

32"Therefore you shall be careful to do as the LORD your God has commanded you; you shall not turn aside to the right hand or to the left. 33You shall walk in all the ways which the LORD your God has commanded you, that you may live and *that it may be* well with you, and *that* you may prolong *your* days in the land which you shall possess.

The Greatest Commandment

6 "Now this *is* the commandment, *and these are* the statutes and judgments which the LORD your God has commanded to teach you, that you may observe *them* in the land which you are crossing over to possess, 2that you may fear the LORD your God, to keep all His statutes and His commandments which I command you, you and your son and your grandson, all the days of your life, and that your days may be prolonged. 3Therefore hear, O Israel, and be careful to observe *it*, that it may be well with you, and that you may multiply greatly as the LORD God of your fathers has promised you—'a land flowing with milk and honey.'*a*

4"Hear, O Israel: The LORD our God, the LORD *is* one!*a* 5You shall love the LORD your God with all your heart, with all your soul, and with all your strength.

> **6:4 Hear, O Israel.** Deut. 6:4–9 is known as the *Shema* (Hebrew for "hear") and is the Jewish confession of faith, recited twice daily by the devout. **The LORD...the LORD *is* one.** These words are intended to show the truth of monotheism, that there is only one God. The word used for "one" does not mean "singleness," but "unity." The same word is used in Gen. 2:24 that speaks of the husband and wife as "one flesh." Thus, while this verse clearly affirms monotheism, it does not exclude the concept of the Trinity.

6"And these words which I command you today shall be in your heart. 7You shall teach them diligently to your children, and shall talk of them when you sit in your house, when you walk by the way, when you lie down, and when you rise up. 8You shall bind them as a sign on your hand, and they shall be as frontlets between your eyes. 9You shall write them on the doorposts of your house and on your gates.

6:3 *a*Exodus 3:8   6:4 *a*Or *The LORD is our God, the LORD alone* (that is, the only one)

6:5–9 You shall love the LORD your God. The first essential command is unreserved, wholehearted commitment expressed in love to God. This relationship would be demonstrated in obedience to God's law in daily life (see 11:16-21).

Caution Against Disobedience

10"So it shall be, when the LORD your God brings you into the land of which He swore to your fathers, to Abraham, Isaac, and Jacob, to give you large and beautiful cities which you did not build, 11houses full of all good things, which you did not fill, hewn-out wells which you did not dig, vineyards and olive trees which you did not plant—when you have eaten and are full— 12*then* beware, lest you forget the LORD who brought you out of the land of Egypt, from the house of bondage. 13You shall fear the LORD your God and serve Him, and shall take oaths in His name. 14You shall not go after other gods, the gods of the peoples who *are* all around you 15(for the LORD your God *is* a jealous God among you), lest the anger of the LORD your God be aroused against you and destroy you from the face of the earth.

16"You shall not tempt the LORD your God as you tempted *Him* in Massah. 17You shall diligently keep the commandments of the LORD your God, His testimonies, and His statutes which He has commanded you. 18And you shall do *what is* right and good in the sight of the LORD, that it may be well with you, and that you may go in and possess the good land of which the LORD swore to your fathers, 19to cast out all your enemies from before you, as the LORD has spoken.

20"When your son asks you in time to come, saying, 'What *is the meaning of* the testimonies, the statutes, and the judgments which the LORD our God has commanded you?' 21then you shall say to your son: 'We were slaves of Pharaoh in Egypt, and the LORD brought us out of Egypt with a mighty hand; 22and the LORD showed signs and wonders before our eyes, great and severe, against Egypt, Pharaoh, and all his household. 23Then He brought us out from there, that He might bring us in, to give us the land of which He swore to our

fathers. 24And the LORD commanded us to observe all these statutes, to fear the LORD our God, for our good always, that He might preserve us alive, as *it is* this day. 25Then it will be righteousness for us, if we are careful to observe all these commandments before the LORD our God, as He has commanded us.'

A Chosen People

7 "When the LORD your God brings you into the land which you go to possess, and has cast out many nations before you, the Hittites and the Girgashites and the Amorites and the Canaanites and the Perizzites and the Hivites and the Jebusites, seven nations greater and mightier than you, 2and when the LORD your God delivers them over to you, you shall conquer them *and* utterly destroy them. You shall make no covenant with them nor show mercy to them. 3Nor shall you make marriages with them. You shall not give your daughter to their son, nor take their daughter for your son. 4For they will turn your sons away from following Me, to serve other gods; so the anger of the LORD will be aroused against you and destroy you suddenly. 5But thus you shall deal with them: you shall destroy their altars, and break down their *sacred* pillars, and cut down their wooden images,*a* and burn their carved images with fire.

7:2 utterly destroy them. All the men, women, and children were to be put to death. Even though this command seems extreme, keep in mind that the Canaanites continually hated God and that they constituted a moral cancer that could potentially lead Israel astray to idolatry and immorality.

6"For you *are* a holy people to the LORD your God; the LORD your God has chosen you to be a people for Himself, a special treasure above all the peoples on the face of the earth. 7The LORD did not set His love on you nor choose you because you were more in number than any other people, for you were the least of all peoples; 8but because the LORD loves you, and because He would keep the oath which He swore to your fathers, the LORD has brought you out

7:5 *a*Hebrew *Asherim*, Canaanite deities

with a mighty hand, and redeemed you from the house of bondage, from the hand of Pharaoh king of Egypt.

⁹"Therefore know that the LORD your God, He *is* God, the faithful God who keeps covenant and mercy for a thousand generations with those who love Him and keep His commandments; ¹⁰and He repays those who hate Him to their face, to destroy them. He will not be slack with him who hates Him; He will repay him to his face. ¹¹Therefore you shall keep the commandment, the statutes, and the judgments which I command you today, to observe them.

Blessings of Obedience

¹²"Then it shall come to pass, because you listen to these judgments, and keep and do them, that the LORD your God will keep with you the covenant and the mercy which He swore to your fathers. ¹³And He will love you and bless you and multiply you; He will also bless the fruit of your womb and the fruit of your land, your grain and your new wine and your oil, the increase of your cattle and the offspring of your flock, in the land of which He swore to your fathers to give you. ¹⁴You shall be blessed above all peoples; there shall not be a male or female barren among you or among your livestock. ¹⁵And the LORD will take away from you all sickness, and will afflict you with none of the terrible diseases of Egypt which you have known, but will lay *them* on all those who hate you. ¹⁶Also you shall destroy all the peoples whom the LORD your God delivers over to you; your eye shall have no pity on them; nor shall you serve their gods, for that *will be* a snare to you.

> **7:12 the LORD your God will keep with you the covenant.** If Israel obeyed God, then He would bless them with covenantal mercy. However, if they disobeyed God, then they would forfeit His blessings.

¹⁷"If you should say in your heart, 'These nations are greater than I; how can I dispossess them?'— ¹⁸you shall not be afraid of them, *but* you shall remember well what the LORD your God did to Pharaoh and to all Egypt: ¹⁹the great trials which your eyes saw, the signs and the wonders, the mighty hand and the outstretched arm, by which the LORD your God brought you out. So shall the LORD your God do to all the peoples of whom you are afraid. ²⁰Moreover the LORD your God will send the hornet among them until those who are left, who hide themselves from you, are destroyed. ²¹You shall not be terrified of them; for the LORD your God, the great and awesome God, *is* among you. ²²And the LORD your God will drive out those nations before you little by little; you will be unable to destroy them at once, lest the beasts of the field become *too* numerous for you. ²³But the LORD your God will deliver them over to you, and will inflict defeat upon them until they are destroyed. ²⁴And He will deliver their kings into your hand, and you will destroy their name from under heaven; no one shall be able to stand against you until you have destroyed them. ²⁵You shall burn the carved images of their gods with fire; you shall not covet the silver or gold *that is* on them, nor take *it* for yourselves, lest you be snared by it; for it *is* an abomination to the LORD your God. ²⁶Nor shall you bring an abomination into your house, lest you be doomed to destruction like it. You shall utterly detest it and utterly abhor it, for it *is* an accursed thing.

Remember the LORD Your God

8 "Every commandment which I command you today you must be careful to observe, that you may live and multiply, and go in and possess the land of which the LORD swore to your fathers. ²And you shall remember that the LORD your God led you all the way these forty years in the wilderness, to humble you *and* test you, to know what *was* in your heart, whether you would keep His commandments or not. ³So He humbled you, allowed you to hunger, and fed you with manna which you did not know nor did your fathers know, that He

> **8:2 to know what *was* in your heart.** Israel's 40 years in the wilderness was a time of God's testing so that the collective attitude of the people toward God would be made known. God sustained His hungry people in the wilderness by a new means they had never before seen. Through this miraculous provision, God both humbled the people and tested their obedience.

might make you know that man shall not live by bread alone; but man lives by every *word* that proceeds from the mouth of the LORD. ⁴Your garments did not wear out on you, nor did your foot swell these forty years. ⁵You should know in your heart that as a man chastens his son, *so* the LORD your God chastens you.

⁶"Therefore you shall keep the commandments of the LORD your God, to walk in His ways and to fear Him. ⁷For the LORD your God is bringing you into a good land, a land of brooks of water, of fountains and springs, that flow out of valleys and hills; ⁸a land of wheat and barley, of vines and fig trees and pomegranates, a land of olive oil and honey; ⁹a land in which you will eat bread without scarcity, in which you will lack nothing; a land whose stones *are* iron and out of whose hills you can dig copper. ¹⁰When you have eaten and are full, then you shall bless the LORD your God for the good land which He has given you.

¹¹"Beware that you do not forget the LORD your God by not keeping His commandments, His judgments, and His statutes which I command you today, ¹²lest—*when* you have eaten and are full, and have built beautiful houses and dwell *in them*; ¹³and *when* your herds and your flocks multiply, and your silver and your gold are multiplied, and all that you have is multiplied; ¹⁴when your heart is lifted up, and you forget the LORD your God who brought you out of the land of Egypt, from the house of bondage; ¹⁵who led you through that great and terrible wilderness, *in which were* fiery serpents and scorpions and thirsty land where there was no water; who brought water for you out of the flinty rock; ¹⁶who fed you in the wilderness with manna, which your fathers did not know, that He might humble you and that He might test you, to do you good in the end— ¹⁷then you say in your heart, 'My power and the might of my hand have gained me this wealth.'

¹⁸"And you shall remember the LORD your God, for *it is* He who gives you power to get wealth, that He may establish His covenant which He swore to your fathers, as *it is* this day. ¹⁹Then it shall be, if you by any means forget the LORD your God, and follow other gods, and serve them and worship them, I testify against you this day that you shall surely perish. ²⁰As the nations which the LORD destroys before you, so you shall perish, because you would not be obedient to the voice of the LORD your God.

Israel's Rebellions Reviewed

9 "Hear, O Israel: You *are* to cross over the Jordan today, and go in to dispossess nations greater and mightier than yourself, cities great and fortified up to heaven, ²a people great and tall, the descendants of the Anakim, whom you know, and *of whom* you heard *it said*, 'Who can stand before the descendants of Anak?' ³Therefore understand today that the LORD your God *is* He who goes over before you *as* a consuming fire. He will destroy them and bring them down before you; so you shall drive them out and destroy them quickly, as the LORD has said to you.

⁴"Do not think in your heart, after the LORD your God has cast them out before you, saying, 'Because of my righteousness the LORD has brought me in to possess this land'; but *it is* because of the wickedness of these nations *that* the LORD is driving them out from before you. ⁵*It is* not because of your righteousness or the uprightness of your heart *that* you go in to possess their land, but because of the wickedness of these nations *that* the LORD your God drives them out from before you, and that He may fulfill the word which the LORD swore to your fathers, to Abraham, Isaac, and Jacob. ⁶Therefore understand that the LORD your God is not giving you this good land to possess because of your righteousness, for you *are* a stiff-necked people.

⁷"Remember! Do not forget how you

8:11 do not forget the LORD your God. While in the wilderness, Israel had to depend on God for their basic food and necessities, but in the Promised Land they would have sufficient food. This abundant food could tempt Israel to feel self-sufficient, as if their own strength had produced their wealth, and then they might forget God.

9:6 a stiff-necked people. A figure of speech to describe the stubborn, unbending attitude of Israel. In vv. 7–29, Moses illustrated Israel's rebellious attitude and actions toward the Lord.

provoked the LORD your God to wrath in the wilderness. From the day that you departed from the land of Egypt until you came to this place, you have been rebellious against the LORD. [8]Also in Horeb you provoked the LORD to wrath, so that the LORD was angry *enough* with you to have destroyed you. [9]When I went up into the mountain to receive the tablets of stone, the tablets of the covenant which the LORD made with you, then I stayed on the mountain forty days and forty nights. I neither ate bread nor drank water. [10]Then the LORD delivered to me two tablets of stone written with the finger of God, and on them *were* all the words which the LORD had spoken to you on the mountain from the midst of the fire in the day of the assembly. [11]And it came to pass, at the end of forty days and forty nights, *that* the LORD gave me the two tablets of stone, the tablets of the covenant.

9:10 the finger of God. God Himself had written the Ten Commandments on the two tablets of stone at Mt. Sinai (see Ex. 31:18).

[12]"Then the LORD said to me, 'Arise, go down quickly from here, for your people whom you brought out of Egypt have acted corruptly; they have quickly turned aside from the way which I commanded them; they have made themselves a molded image.'
[13]"Furthermore the LORD spoke to me, saying, 'I have seen this people, and indeed they are a stiff-necked people. [14]Let Me alone, that I may destroy them and blot out their name from under heaven; and I will make of you a nation mightier and greater than they.'
[15]"So I turned and came down from the mountain, and the mountain burned with fire; and the two tablets of the covenant *were* in my two hands. [16]And I looked, and behold, you had sinned against the LORD your God—had made for yourselves a molded calf! You had turned aside quickly from the way which the LORD had commanded you. [17]Then I took the two tablets and threw them out of my two hands and broke them before your eyes. [18]And I fell down before the LORD, as at the first, forty days and forty nights; I neither ate bread

nor drank water, because of all your sin which you committed in doing wickedly in the sight of the LORD, to provoke Him to anger. [19]For I was afraid of the anger and hot displeasure with which the LORD was angry with you, to destroy you. But the LORD listened to me at that time also. [20]And the LORD was very angry with Aaron *and* would have destroyed him; so I prayed for Aaron also at the same time. [21]Then I took your sin, the calf which you had made, and burned it with fire and crushed it *and* ground *it* very small, until it was as fine as dust; and I threw its dust into the brook that descended from the mountain.
[22]"Also at Taberah and Massah and Kibroth Hattaavah you provoked the LORD to wrath. [23]Likewise, when the LORD sent you from Kadesh Barnea, saying, 'Go up and possess the land which I have given you,' then you rebelled against the commandment of the LORD your God, and you did not believe Him nor obey His voice. [24]You have been rebellious against the LORD from the day that I knew you.

9:20 I prayed for Aaron. As the High-Priest, Aaron was held immediately responsible for the sin of the golden calf. Aaron incurred God's wrath, and his life was in danger. Moses interceded on his behalf, and God answered Moses' prayer.

[25]"Thus I prostrated myself before the LORD; forty days and forty nights I kept prostrating myself, because the LORD had said He would destroy you. [26]Therefore I prayed to the LORD, and said: 'O Lord GOD, do not destroy Your people and Your inheritance whom You have redeemed through Your greatness, whom You have brought out of Egypt with a mighty hand. [27]Remember Your servants, Abraham, Isaac, and Jacob; do not look on the stubbornness of this people, or on their wickedness or their sin, [28]lest the land from which You brought us should say, "Because the LORD was not able to bring them to the land which He promised them, and because He hated them, He has brought them out to kill them in the wilderness." [29]Yet they *are* Your people and Your inheritance, whom You brought out by Your mighty power and by Your outstretched arm.'

The Second Pair of Tablets

10 "At that time the LORD said to me, 'Hew for yourself two tablets of stone like the first, and come up to Me on the mountain and make yourself an ark of wood. ²And I will write on the tablets the words that were on the first tablets, which you broke; and you shall put them in the ark.'

³"So I made an ark of acacia wood, hewed two tablets of stone like the first, and went up the mountain, having the two tablets in my hand. ⁴And He wrote on the tablets according to the first writing, the Ten Commandments, which the LORD had spoken to you in the mountain from the midst of the fire in the day of the assembly; and the LORD gave them to me. ⁵Then I turned and came down from the mountain, and put the tablets in the ark which I had made; and there they are, just as the LORD commanded me."

10:1–3 two tablets of stone like the first. God listened to Moses' intercession and dealt mercifully with the Israelites who had broken the covenant. He rewrote the Ten Commandments on the two new tablets that were the same size and material as the first.

⁶(Now the children of Israel journeyed from the wells of Bene Jaakan to Moserah, where Aaron died, and where he was buried; and Eleazar his son ministered as priest in his stead. ⁷From there they journeyed to Gudgodah, and from Gudgodah to Jotbathah, a land of rivers of water. ⁸At that time the LORD separated the tribe of Levi to bear the ark of the covenant of the LORD, to stand before the LORD to minister to Him and to bless in His name, to this day. ⁹Therefore Levi has no portion nor inheritance with his brethren; the LORD is his inheritance, just as the LORD your God promised him.)

¹⁰"As at the first time, I stayed in the mountain forty days and forty nights; the LORD also heard me at that time, and the LORD chose not to destroy you. ¹¹Then the LORD said to me, 'Arise, begin your journey before the people, that they may go in and possess the land which I swore to their fathers to give them.'

10:12,13 what does the LORD your God require of you...? Moses then stated God's five basic requirements for His people: (1) **to fear the LORD your God.** To hold God in awe and submit to Him; (2) **to walk in all His ways.** To live according to God's will; (3) **to love Him.** To choose to set one's affections on the Lord alone; (4) **to serve the Lord your God.** For worship to be the central focus of one's life; (5) **to keep the commandments of the Lord.** To obey the Lord's requirements.

The Essence of the Law

¹²"And now, Israel, what does the LORD your God require of you, but to fear the LORD your God, to walk in all His ways and to love Him, to serve the LORD your God with all your heart and with all your soul, ¹³and to keep the commandments of the LORD and His statutes which I command you today for your good? ¹⁴Indeed heaven and the highest heavens belong to the LORD your God, also the earth with all that is in it. ¹⁵The LORD delighted only in your fathers, to love them; and He chose their descendants after them, you above all peoples, as it is this day. ¹⁶Therefore circumcise the foreskin of your heart, and be stiff-necked no longer. ¹⁷For the LORD your God is God of gods and Lord of lords, the great God, mighty and awesome, who shows no partiality nor takes a bribe. ¹⁸He administers justice for the fatherless and the widow, and loves the stranger, giving him food and clothing. ¹⁹Therefore love the stranger, for you were strangers in the land of Egypt. ²⁰You shall fear the LORD your God; you shall serve Him, and to Him you shall hold fast, and take oaths in His name. ²¹He is your praise, and He is your God, who has done for you these great and awesome things which your eyes have seen. ²²Your fathers went down to Egypt with seventy persons, and now the LORD your God has made you as the stars of heaven in multitude.

10:20 to Him you shall hold fast. The verb means "to stick to," "to cling to," or "to hold onto." As a husband is to be united to his wife (see Gen. 2:24), so Israel was to cling intimately to her God.

Love and Obedience Rewarded

11 "Therefore you shall love the LORD your God, and keep His charge, His

statutes, His judgments, and His commandments always. ²Know today that *I do not speak* with your children, who have not known and who have not seen the chastening of the LORD your God, His greatness and His mighty hand and His outstretched arm— ³His signs and His acts which He did in the midst of Egypt, to Pharaoh king of Egypt, and to all his land; ⁴what He did to the army of Egypt, to their horses and their chariots: how He made the waters of the Red Sea overflow them as they pursued you, and *how* the LORD has destroyed them to this day; ⁵what He did for you in the wilderness until you came to this place; ⁶and what He did to Dathan and Abiram the sons of Eliab, the son of Reuben: how the earth opened its mouth and swallowed them up, their households, their tents, and all the substance that *was* in their possession, in the midst of all Israel— ⁷but your eyes have seen every great act of the LORD which He did.

⁸"Therefore you shall keep every commandment which I command you today, that you may be strong, and go in and possess the land which you cross over to possess, ⁹and that you may prolong *your* days in the land which the LORD swore to give your fathers, to them and their descendants, 'a land flowing with milk and honey.'ᵃ ¹⁰For the land which you go to possess *is* not like the land of Egypt from which you have come, where you sowed your seed and watered *it* by foot, as a vegetable garden; ¹¹but the land which you cross over to possess *is* a land of hills and valleys, which drinks water from the rain of heaven, ¹²a land for which the LORD your God cares; the eyes of the LORD your God *are* always on it, from the beginning of the year to the very end of the year.

¹³And it shall be that if you earnestly

obey My commandments which I command you today, to love the LORD your God and serve Him with all your heart and with all your soul, ¹⁴then Iᵃ will give *you* the rain for your land in its season, the early rain and the latter rain, that you may gather in your grain, your new wine, and your oil. ¹⁵And I will send grass in your fields for your livestock, that you may eat and be filled.' ¹⁶Take heed to yourselves, lest your heart be deceived, and you turn aside and serve other gods and worship them, ¹⁷lest the LORD's anger be aroused against you, and He shut up the heavens so that there be no rain, and the land yield no produce, and you perish quickly from the good land which the LORD is giving you.

¹⁸"Therefore you shall lay up these words of mine in your heart and in your soul, and bind them as a sign on your hand, and they shall be as frontlets between your eyes. ¹⁹You shall teach them to your children, speaking of them when you sit in your house, when you walk by the way, when you lie down, and when you rise up. ²⁰And you shall write them on the doorposts of your house and on your gates, ²¹that your days and the days of your children may be multiplied in the land of which the LORD swore to your fathers to give them, like the days of the heavens above the earth.

²²"For if you carefully keep all these commandments which I command you to do— to love the LORD your God, to walk in all His ways, and to hold fast to Him— ²³then the LORD will drive out all these nations from before you, and you will dispossess greater and mightier nations than yourselves. ²⁴Every place on which the sole of

11:10,11 the land which you go to possess. The land of Canaan was different from Egypt, which depended on the Nile River for its fertility. By contrast, Canaan depended upon the rains that came from heaven for its fertility. Thus God promised to send rain in response to their obedience (see v. 14).

11:24 Every place...your foot treads. In response to Israel's obedience, the Lord promised to give them all of the land they personally walked to the extent of the boundaries He had given. If Israel had obeyed faithfully, her boundaries would have been enlarged to fulfill God's promise to Abraham (see Gen.15:18), but because of her disobedience, they did not receive the whole land. That promise of the complete land will be fulfilled in the future kingdom of the Messiah (see Ezek. 36:8–38).

11:9 ᵃExodus 3:8   11:14 ᵃFollowing Masoretic Text and Targum; Samaritan Pentateuch, Septuagint, and Vulgate read *He*.

your foot treads shall be yours: from the wilderness and Lebanon, from the river, the River Euphrates, even to the Western Sea,[a] shall be your territory. [25]No man shall be able to stand against you; the LORD your God will put the dread of you and the fear of you upon all the land where you tread, just as He has said to you.

[26]"Behold, I set before you today a blessing and a curse: [27]the blessing, if you obey the commandments of the LORD your God which I command you today; [28]and the curse, if you do not obey the commandments of the LORD your God, but turn aside from the way which I command you today, to go after other gods which you have not known. [29]Now it shall be, when the LORD your God has brought you into the land which you go to possess, that you shall put the blessing on Mount Gerizim and the curse on Mount Ebal. [30]*Are* they not on the other side of the Jordan, toward the setting sun, in the land of the Canaanites who dwell in the plain opposite Gilgal, beside the terebinth trees of Moreh? [31]For you will cross over the Jordan and go in to possess the land which the LORD your God is giving you, and you will possess it and dwell in it. [32]And you shall be careful to observe all the statutes and judgments which I set before you today.

11:26–32 As a final, concrete symbol to stress the importance of obedience, Moses instructed the people to perform a ceremony when they entered the land, in which they would read the blessings and the curses of the covenant on Mt. Gerizim and Mt. Ebal (see 27:11–28:68; Josh. 8:30–35).

A Prescribed Place of Worship

12 "These *are* the statutes and judgments which you shall be careful to observe in the land which the LORD God of your fathers is giving you to possess, all the days that you live on the earth. [2]You shall utterly destroy all the places where the nations which you shall dispossess served their gods, on the high mountains and on the hills and under every green tree. [3]And you shall destroy their altars, break their *sacred* pillars, and burn their wooden images with fire; you shall cut down the carved images of their gods and destroy their names from that place. [4]You shall not worship the LORD your God *with* such *things.*

[5]"But you shall seek the place where the LORD your God chooses, out of all your tribes, to put His name for His dwelling place; and there you shall go. [6]There you shall take your burnt offerings, your sacrifices, your tithes, the heave offerings of your hand, your vowed offerings, your freewill offerings, and the firstborn of your herds and flocks. [7]And there you shall eat before the LORD your God, and you shall rejoice in all to which you have put your hand, you and your households, in which the LORD your God has blessed you.

[8]"You shall not at all do as we are doing here today—every man doing whatever *is* right in his own eyes— [9]for as yet you have not come to the rest and the inheritance which the LORD your God is giving you. [10]But *when* you cross over the Jordan and dwell in the land which the LORD your God is giving you to inherit, and He gives you rest from all your enemies round about, so that you dwell in safety, [11]then there will be the place where the LORD your God chooses to make His name abide. There you shall bring all that I command you: your burnt offerings, your sacrifices, your tithes, the heave offerings of your hand, and all your choice offerings which you vow to the LORD. [12]And you shall rejoice before the LORD your God, you and your sons and your daughters, your male and female servants, and the Levite who *is* within your gates, since he has no portion nor inheritance with you. [13]Take heed to yourself that you do not offer your burnt offerings in every place that you see; [14]but in the place which the LORD chooses, in one of your tribes, there you shall offer your burnt offerings, and there you shall do all that I command you.

[15]"However, you may slaughter and eat meat within all your gates, whatever your heart desires, according to the blessing of the LORD your God which He has given you; the unclean and the clean may eat of it, of the gazelle and the deer alike. [16]Only you shall not eat the blood; you shall pour

---

11:24 [a]That is, the Mediterranean

it on the earth like water. [17]You may not eat within your gates the tithe of your grain or your new wine or your oil, of the firstborn of your herd or your flock, of any of your offerings which you vow, of your freewill offerings, or of the heave offering of your hand. [18]But you must eat them before the LORD your God in the place which the LORD your God chooses, you and your son and your daughter, your male servant and your female servant, and the Levite who is within your gates; and you shall rejoice before the LORD your God in all to which you put your hands. [19]Take heed to yourself that you do not forsake the Levite as long as you live in your land.

[20]"When the LORD your God enlarges your border as He has promised you, and you say, 'Let me eat meat,' because you long to eat meat, you may eat as much meat as your heart desires. [21]If the place where the LORD your God chooses to put His name is too far from you, then you may slaughter from your herd and from your flock which the LORD has given you, just as I have commanded you, and you may eat within your gates as much as your heart desires. [22]Just as the gazelle and the deer are eaten, so you may eat them; the unclean and the clean alike may eat them. [23]Only be sure that you do not eat the blood, for the blood is the life; you may not eat the life with the meat. [24]You shall not eat it; you shall pour it on the earth like water. [25]You shall not eat it, that it may go well with you and your children after you, when you do what is right in the sight of the LORD. [26]Only the holy things which you have, and your vowed offerings, you shall take and go to the place which the LORD chooses. [27]And you shall offer your burnt offerings, the meat and the blood, on the altar of the LORD your God; and the blood of your sacrifices shall be poured out on the altar of the LORD your God, and you shall eat the meat. [28]Observe and obey all these words which I command you, that it may go well

with you and your children after you forever, when you do what is good and right in the sight of the LORD your God.

Beware of False Gods

[29]"When the LORD your God cuts off from before you the nations which you go to dispossess, and you displace them and dwell in their land, [30]take heed to yourself that you are not ensnared to follow them, after they are destroyed from before you, and that you do not inquire after their gods, saying, 'How did these nations serve their gods? I also will do likewise.' [31]You shall not worship the LORD your God in that way; for every abomination to the LORD which He hates they have done to their gods; for they burn even their sons and daughters in the fire to their gods.

> **12:31 they burn even their sons and daughters.** One of the detestable practices of Canaanite worship was the burning of their sons and daughters in the fire as sacrifices to their false god Molech (see Lev. 18:21; 20:2–5).

[32]"Whatever I command you, be careful to observe it; you shall not add to it nor take away from it.

Punishment of Apostates

13 "If there arises among you a prophet or a dreamer of dreams, and he gives you a sign or a wonder, [2]and the sign or the wonder comes to pass, of which he spoke to you, saying, 'Let us go after other gods'—which you have not known—'and let us serve them,' [3]you shall not listen to the words of that prophet or that dreamer of dreams, for the LORD your God is testing you to know whether you love the LORD your God with all your heart and with all your soul. [4]You shall walk after the LORD your God and fear Him, and keep His commandments and obey His voice; you shall serve Him and hold fast to Him. [5]But that prophet or that dreamer of dreams shall be

> **12:23 the blood is the life.** The blood symbolized life (see Gen. 9:4–6). By not eating blood, the Israelite showed respect for life and for the Creator of life. Since blood represented life, it was the ransom price, or atonement, for sins, thus making it sacred (see Lev. 16; Heb. 9:12–14).

> **13:3 the LORD your God is testing you.** At times, God allowed false prophets to entice the people to worship other gods. While the temptation was dangerous, by overcoming it they would test and strengthen their love for God and their obedience to His commandments (see 6:5).

put to death, because he has spoken in order to turn *you* away from the LORD your God, who brought you out of the land of Egypt and redeemed you from the house of bondage, to entice you from the way in which the LORD your God commanded you to walk. So you shall put away the evil from your midst.

6"If your brother, the son of your mother, your son or your daughter, the wife of your bosom, or your friend who is as your own soul, secretly entices you, saying, 'Let us go and serve other gods,' which you have not known, neither you nor your fathers, 7of the gods of the people which *are* all around you, near to you or far off from you, from one end of the earth to the *other* end of the earth, 8you shall not consent to him or listen to him, nor shall your eye pity him, nor shall you spare him or conceal him; 9but you shall surely kill him; your hand shall be first against him to put him to death, and afterward the hand of all the people. 10And you shall stone him with stones until he dies, because he sought to entice you

13:10 until he dies. The convicting witness cast the first stone. Even love for family and friends must never take precedence over devotion to God (see Luke 14:26).

away from the LORD your God, who brought you out of the land of Egypt, from the house of bondage. 11So all Israel shall hear and fear, and not again do such wickedness as this among you.

12"If you hear someone in one of your cities, which the LORD your God gives you to dwell in, saying, 13'Corrupt men have gone out from among you and enticed the inhabitants of their city, saying, "Let us go and serve other gods" '—which you have not known— 14then you shall inquire, search out, and ask diligently. And *if it is* indeed true *and* certain *that* such an abomination was committed among you, 15you shall surely strike the inhabitants of that city with the edge of the sword, utterly destroying it, all that is in it and its livestock— with the edge of the sword. 16And you shall gather all its plunder into the middle of the street, and completely burn with fire the city and all its plunder, for the LORD your God. It shall be a heap forever; it shall not be built again. 17So none of the accursed things shall remain in your hand, that the LORD may turn from the fierceness of His anger and show you mercy, have compassion on you and multiply you, just as He swore to your fathers, 18because you have listened to the voice of the LORD your God, to keep all His commandments which I

THE DEATH PENALTY

Crime	Scripture Reference
1. Premeditated Murder	Genesis 9:6; Exodus 21:12–14,22,23
2. Kidnapping	Exodus 21:16; Deuteronomy 24:7
3. Striking or Cursing Parents	Exodus 21:15; Leviticus 20:9; Proverbs 20:20; Matthew 15:4; Mark 7:10
4. Magic and Divination	Exodus 22:18
5. Bestiality	Exodus 22:19; Leviticus 20:15,16
6. Sacrificing to False Gods	Exodus 22:20
7. Profaning the Sabbath	Exodus 35:2; Numbers 15:32–36
8. Offering Human Sacrifice	Leviticus 20:2
9. Adultery	Leviticus 20:10–21; Deuteronomy 22:22
10. Incest	Leviticus 20:11,12,14
11. Homosexuality	Leviticus 20:13
12. Blasphemy	Leviticus 24:11–14,16,23
13. False Prophecy	Deuteronomy 13:1–10
14. Incorrigible Rebelliousness	Deuteronomy 17:12; 21:18–21
15. Fornication	Deuteronomy 22:20,21
16. Rape of Betrothed Virgin	Deuteronomy 22:23–27

command you today, to do *what is* right in the eyes of the LORD your God.

Improper Mourning

14 "You *are* the children of the LORD your God; you shall not cut yourselves nor shave the front of your head for the dead. ²For you *are* a holy people to the LORD your God, and the LORD has chosen you to be a people for Himself, a special treasure above all the peoples who *are* on the face of the earth.

> **14:2 you *are* a holy people to the LORD your God.** Again Moses reminds them of their peculiar relationship with God. Over 250 times, Moses emphasized to Israel, "the Lord *your* God."

Clean and Unclean Meat

³"You shall not eat any detestable thing. ⁴These *are* the animals which you may eat: the ox, the sheep, the goat, ⁵the deer, the gazelle, the roe deer, the wild goat, the mountain goat,ᵃ the antelope, and the mountain sheep. ⁶And you may eat every animal with cloven hooves, having the hoof split into two parts, *and that* chews the cud, among the animals. ⁷Nevertheless, of those that chew the cud or have cloven hooves, you shall not eat, *such as* these: the camel, the hare, and the rock hyrax; for they chew the cud but do not have cloven hooves; they *are* unclean for you. ⁸Also the swine is unclean for you, because it has cloven hooves, yet *does* not *chew* the cud; you shall not eat their flesh or touch their dead carcasses.

⁹"These you may eat of all that *are* in the waters: you may eat all that have fins and scales. ¹⁰And whatever does not have fins and scales you shall not eat; it *is* unclean for you.

¹¹"All clean birds you may eat. ¹²But these you shall not eat: the eagle, the vulture, the buzzard, ¹³the red kite, the falcon, and the kite after their kinds; ¹⁴every raven after its kind; ¹⁵the ostrich, the short-eared owl, the sea gull, and the hawk after their kinds; ¹⁶the little owl, the screech owl, the white owl, ¹⁷the jackdaw, the carrion vulture, the fisher owl, ¹⁸the stork, the heron after its kind, and the hoopoe and the bat.

¹⁹"Also every creeping thing that flies is unclean for you; they shall not be eaten. ²⁰"You may eat all clean birds.

²¹"You shall not eat anything that dies *of itself*; you may give it to the alien who *is* within your gates, that he may eat it, or you may sell it to a foreigner; for you *are* a holy people to the LORD your God.

"You shall not boil a young goat in its mother's milk.

Tithing Principles

²²"You shall truly tithe all the increase of your grain that the field produces year by year. ²³And you shall eat before the LORD your God, in the place where He chooses to make His name abide, the tithe of your grain and your new wine and your oil, of the firstborn of your herds and your flocks, that you may learn to fear the LORD your God always. ²⁴But if the journey is too long for you, so that you are not able to carry *the tithe, or* if the place where the LORD your God chooses to put His name is too far from you, when the LORD your God has blessed you, ²⁵then you shall exchange *it* for money, take the money in your hand, and go to the place which the LORD your God chooses. ²⁶And you shall spend that money for whatever your heart desires: for oxen or sheep, for wine or similar drink, for whatever your heart desires; you shall eat there before the LORD your God, and you shall rejoice, you and your household. ²⁷You shall not forsake the Levite who *is* within your gates, for he has no part nor inheritance with you.

²⁸"At the end of *every* third year you shall bring out the tithe of your produce of that year and store *it* up within your gates. ²⁹And the Levite, because he has no portion nor inheritance with you, and the stranger and the fatherless and the widow who *are* within your gates, may come and eat and be

> **14:28 At the end of *every* third year.** In years 3 and 6 of the 7-year sabbatical cycle, the tithe was stored within the individual cities of the Land rather than taken to the central sanctuary. This tithe was used to feed the Levites, the orphan, the widow, and the stranger (or foreigner) who lived among them (see 26:12; Num. 18:26–32).

14:5 ᵃOr *addax*

satisfied, that the LORD your God may bless you in all the work of your hand which you do.

Debts Canceled Every Seven Years

15 "At the end of *every* seven years you shall grant a release *of debts.* ²And this *is* the form of the release: Every creditor who has lent *anything* to his neighbor shall release *it;* he shall not require *it* of his neighbor or his brother, because it is called the LORD's release. ³Of a foreigner you may require *it;* but you shall give up your claim to what is owed by your brother, ⁴except when there may be no poor among you; for the LORD will greatly bless you in the land which the LORD your God is giving you to possess *as* an inheritance— ⁵only if you carefully obey the voice of the LORD your God, to observe with care all these commandments which I command you today. ⁶For the LORD your God will bless you just as He promised you; you shall lend to many nations, but you shall not borrow; you shall reign over many nations, but they shall not reign over you.

Generosity to the Poor

⁷"If there is among you a poor man of your brethren, within any of the gates in your land which the LORD your God is giving you, you shall not harden your heart nor shut your hand from your poor brother, ⁸but you shall open your hand wide to him and willingly lend him sufficient for his need, whatever he needs. ⁹Beware lest there be a wicked thought in your heart, saying, 'The seventh year, the year of release, is at hand,' and your eye be evil against your poor brother and you give him nothing, and he cry out to the LORD against you, and it become sin among you. ¹⁰You shall surely give to him, and your heart should not be grieved when you give to him, because for this thing the LORD your God will bless you in all your works and in all to which you

> **15:8 willingly lend him sufficient for his need.** The Israelites were to show a warm, generous attitude toward the poor in their community. The poor were given whatever was necessary to meet their needs, with the understanding that such "loans" would never need to be repaid.

put your hand. ¹¹For the poor will never cease from the land; therefore I command you, saying, 'You shall open your hand wide to your brother, to your poor and your needy, in your land.'

The Law Concerning Bondservants

¹²"If your brother, a Hebrew man, or a Hebrew woman, is sold to you and serves you six years, then in the seventh year you shall let him go free from you. ¹³And when you send him away free from you, you shall not let him go away empty-handed; ¹⁴you shall supply him liberally from your flock, from your threshing floor, and from your winepress. *From what* the LORD has blessed you with, you shall give to him. ¹⁵You shall remember that you were a slave in the land of Egypt, and the LORD your God redeemed you; therefore I command you this thing today. ¹⁶And if it happens that he says to you, 'I will not go away from you,' because he loves you and your house, since he prospers with you, ¹⁷then you shall take an awl and thrust *it* through his ear to the door, and he shall be your servant forever. Also to your female servant you shall do likewise. ¹⁸It shall not seem hard to you when you send him away free from you; for he has been worth a double hired servant in serving you six years. Then the LORD your God will bless you in all that you do.

> **15:15 remember.** Since the Israelites had formerly been slaves in Egypt, they were to treat their own slaves as God had treated them.

The Law Concerning Firstborn Animals

¹⁹"All the firstborn males that come from your herd and your flock you shall sanctify to the LORD your God; you shall do no work with the firstborn of your herd, nor shear the firstborn of your flock. ²⁰You and your household shall eat *it* before the LORD your God year by year in the place which the LORD chooses. ²¹But if there is a defect in it, *if it is* lame or blind *or has* any serious defect, you shall not sacrifice it to the LORD your God. ²²You may eat it within your gates; the unclean and the clean *person* alike *may eat it,* as *if it were* a gazelle or a deer. ²³Only you shall not eat its blood; you shall pour it on the ground like water.

The Passover Reviewed

16 "Observe the month of Abib, and keep the Passover to the LORD your God, for in the month of Abib the LORD your God brought you out of Egypt by night. ²Therefore you shall sacrifice the Passover to the LORD your God, from the flock and the herd, in the place where the LORD chooses to put His name. ³You shall eat no leavened bread with it; seven days you shall eat unleavened bread with it, *that is,* the bread of affliction (for you came out of the land of Egypt in haste), that you may remember the day in which you came out of the land of Egypt all the days of your life. ⁴And no leaven shall be seen among you in all your territory for seven days, nor shall *any* of the meat which you sacrifice the first day at twilight remain overnight until morning.

> **16:3 remember.** This was the key word at Passover time as it is for the Lord's Supper today (see Matt. 26:26–30; 1 Cor. 11:23–26).

⁵"You may not sacrifice the Passover within any of your gates which the LORD your God gives you; ⁶but at the place where the LORD your God chooses to make His name abide, there you shall sacrifice the Passover at twilight, at the going down of the sun, at the time you came out of Egypt. ⁷And you shall roast and eat *it* in the place which the LORD your God chooses, and in the morning you shall turn and go to your tents. ⁸Six days you shall eat unleavened bread, and on the seventh day there *shall be* a sacred assembly to the LORD your God. You shall do no work *on it.*

The Feast of Weeks Reviewed

⁹"You shall count seven weeks for yourself; begin to count the seven weeks from *the time* you begin *to put* the sickle to the grain. ¹⁰Then you shall keep the Feast of Weeks to the LORD your God with the tribute of a freewill offering from your hand, which you shall give as the LORD your God blesses you. ¹¹You shall rejoice before the LORD your God, you and your son and your daughter, your male servant and your female servant, the Levite who *is* within your gates, the stranger and the fatherless and the widow who *are* among you, at the place where the LORD your God chooses to make His name abide. ¹²And you shall remember that you were a slave in Egypt, and you shall be careful to observe these statutes.

> **16:10–12 the Feast of Weeks.** Seven weeks later they celebrated this second feast, which was also called the "Feast of Harvest" or the "day of firstfruits" and later came to be known as "Pentecost" (Acts 2:1). This one-day festival of rejoicing came after the grain harvest was finished. Fifty days after the death of Christ at the Passover, the Holy Spirit was poured out on Pentecost, thus giving special meaning to that day for Christians (see Joel 2:28–32; Acts 2:14–18).

The Feast of Tabernacles Reviewed

¹³"You shall observe the Feast of Tabernacles seven days, when you have gathered from your threshing floor and from your winepress. ¹⁴And you shall rejoice in your feast, you and your son and your daughter, your male servant and your female servant and the Levite, the stranger and the fatherless and the widow, who *are* within your gates. ¹⁵Seven days you shall keep a sacred feast to the LORD your God in the place which the LORD chooses, because the LORD your God will bless you in all your produce and in all the work of your hands, so that you surely rejoice.

¹⁶"Three times a year all your males shall appear before the LORD your God in the place which He chooses: at the Feast of Unleavened Bread, at the Feast of Weeks, and at the Feast of Tabernacles; and they shall not appear before the LORD empty-handed. ¹⁷Every man *shall give* as he is able, according to the blessing of the LORD your God which He has given you.

Justice Must Be Administered

¹⁸"You shall appoint judges and officers in all your gates, which the LORD your God gives you, according to your tribes, and they shall judge the people with just judgment. ¹⁹You shall not pervert justice; you shall not show partiality, nor take a bribe, for a bribe blinds the eyes of the wise and twists the words of the righteous. ²⁰You shall follow what is altogether just, that you may live and inherit the land which the LORD your God is giving you.

²¹"You shall not plant for yourself any tree, as a wooden image, near the altar

which you build for yourself to the LORD your God. ²²You shall not set up a sacred pillar, which the LORD your God hates.

17 "You shall not sacrifice to the LORD your God a bull or sheep which has any blemish *or* defect, for that *is* an abomination to the LORD your God.

> **17:1 any...defect.** To bring a defective sacrifice to the Lord was forbidden, for it was an abomination to the Lord. To offer less than the best to God was to despise His name (see Mal. 1:6–8). Offering an imperfect sacrifice was, in effect, a failure to acknowledge God as the One who provides all that is best in life.

²"If there is found among you, within any of your gates which the LORD your God gives you, a man or a woman who has been wicked in the sight of the LORD your God, in transgressing His covenant, ³who has gone and served other gods and worshiped them, either the sun or moon or any of the host of heaven, which I have not commanded, ⁴and it is told you, and you hear *of it,* then you shall inquire diligently. And if *it is* indeed true *and* certain that such an abomination has been committed in Israel, ⁵then you shall bring out to your gates that man or woman who has committed that wicked thing, and shall stone to death that man or woman with stones. ⁶Whoever is deserving of death shall be put to death on the testimony of two or three witnesses; he shall not be put to death on the testimony of one witness. ⁷The hands of the witnesses shall be the first against him to put him to death, and afterward the hands of all the people. So you shall put away the evil from among you.

⁸"If a matter arises which is too hard for you to judge, between degrees of guilt for bloodshed, between one judgment or another, or between one punishment or another, matters of controversy within your gates, then you shall arise and go up to the place which the LORD your God chooses. ⁹And you shall come to the priests, the Levites, and to the judge *there* in those days, and inquire *of them;* they shall pronounce upon you the sentence of judgment. ¹⁰You shall do according to the sentence which they pronounce upon you in that place which the LORD chooses. And you shall be careful to do according to all that they order you. ¹¹According to the sentence of the law in which they instruct you, according to the judgment which they tell you, you shall do; you shall not turn aside *to* the right hand or *to* the left from the sentence which they pronounce upon you. ¹²Now the man who acts presumptuously and will not heed the priest who stands to minister there before the LORD your God, or the judge, that man shall die. So you shall put away the evil from Israel. ¹³And all the people shall hear and fear, and no longer act presumptuously.

Principles Governing Kings

¹⁴"When you come to the land which the LORD your God is giving you, and possess it and dwell in it, and say, 'I will set a king over me like all the nations that *are* around me,' ¹⁵you shall surely set a king over you whom the LORD your God chooses; *one* from among your brethren you shall set as king over you; you may not set a foreigner over you, who *is* not your brother. ¹⁶But he

ISRAEL'S CALENDAR

Month Pre-/Post-Exilic	Of Year Sacred/Civil	Modern Equivalent	Characteristics
Abib/Nisan	1/7	March/April	Latter Rains; Barley Harvest
Ziv/Iyyar	2/8	April/ May	Dry Season Begins
Sivan	3/9	May/ June	Wheat Harvest; Early Figs
Tammuz	4/10	June/ July	Hot Season; Grape Harvest
Ab	5/11	July/ August	Olive Harvest
Elul	8/12	August/ September	Dates, Summer Figs
Ethanim/Tishri	7/1	September/ October	Former Rains; Plowing Time
Bul/Heshvan	8/2	October/ November	Rains; Wheat, Barley Sown
Chislev	9/3	November/ December	Winter Begins

shall not multiply horses for himself, nor cause the people to return to Egypt to multiply horses, for the LORD has said to you, 'You shall not return that way again.' [17]Neither shall he multiply wives for himself, lest his heart turn away; nor shall he greatly multiply silver and gold for himself.

17:16,17 multiply...multiply...multiply. Restrictions were placed on the king: (1) he must not acquire many horses; (2) he must not take multiple wives; and (3) he must not accumulate much silver and gold. The king was not to rely on strength or wealth for his position as king, but he was to look to the Lord. David violated the last two restrictions; Solomon violated all three. His wives introduced idolatry into Jerusalem, which divided the kingdom (see 1 Kin. 11:1–43).

[18]"Also it shall be, when he sits on the throne of his kingdom, that he shall write for himself a copy of this law in a book, from *the one* before the priests, the Levites. [19]And it shall be with him, and he shall read it all the days of his life, that he may learn to fear the LORD his God and be careful to observe all the words of this law and these statutes, [20]that his heart may not be lifted above his brethren, that he may not turn aside from the commandment *to* the right hand or *to* the left, and that he may prolong *his* days in his kingdom, he and his children in the midst of Israel.

17:20 his heart may not be lifted above his brethren. The king was not above God's law, any more than any other Israelite.

The Portion of the Priests and Levites

18 "The priests, the Levites—all the tribe of Levi—shall have no part nor inheritance with Israel; they shall eat the offerings of the LORD made by fire, and His portion. [2]Therefore they shall have no inheritance among their brethren; the LORD is their inheritance, as He said to them.

[3]"And this shall be the priest's due from the people, from those who offer a sacrifice, whether *it is* bull or sheep: they shall give to the priest the shoulder, the cheeks, and the stomach. [4]The firstfruits of your grain and your new wine and your oil, and the first of the fleece of your sheep, you shall give him.

[5]For the LORD your God has chosen him out of all your tribes to stand to minister in the name of the LORD, him and his sons forever.

[6]"So if a Levite comes from any of your gates, from where he dwells among all Israel, and comes with all the desire of his mind to the place which the LORD chooses, [7]then he may serve in the name of the LORD his God as all his brethren the Levites *do*, who stand there before the LORD. [8]They shall have equal portions to eat, besides what comes from the sale of his inheritance.

Avoid Wicked Customs

[9]"When you come into the land which the LORD your God is giving you, you shall not learn to follow the abominations of those nations. [10]There shall not be found among you *anyone* who makes his son or his daughter pass through the fire, *or one* who practices witchcraft, *or* a soothsayer, or one who interprets omens, or a sorcerer, [11]or one who conjures spells, or a medium, or a spiritist, or one who calls up the dead. [12]For all who do these things *are* an abomination to the LORD, and because of these abominations the LORD your God drives them out from before you. [13]You shall be blameless before the LORD your God. [14]For these nations which you will dispossess listened to soothsayers and diviners; but as for you, the LORD your God has not appointed such for you.

18:9-12 the abominations of those nations. Moses gave strict commands not to copy the detestable practices of the Canaanites: (1) the sacrifice of children in the fire, (2) witchcraft, (3) soothsaying, attempting to control the future through power given by evil spirits, (4) interpreting omens, telling the future based on signs, (5) sorcery, inducing magical effects by drugs, (6) casting spells, (7) being a medium, one who supposedly communicates with the dead but actually communicates with demons, (8) being a spiritist, one who connects with the demonic world, (9) calling up the dead. For these nine reasons, the Lord was going to drive the Canaanites out of the land.

A New Prophet Like Moses

[15]"The LORD your God will raise up for you a Prophet like me from your midst, from your brethren. Him you shall hear, [16]according to all you desired of the LORD

your God in Horeb in the day of the assembly, saying, 'Let me not hear again the voice of the LORD my God, nor let me see this great fire anymore, lest I die.'

17"And the LORD said to me: 'What they have spoken is good. 18I will raise up for them a Prophet like you from among their brethren, and will put My words in His mouth, and He shall speak to them all that I command Him. 19And it shall be *that* whoever will not hear My words, which He speaks in My name, I will require *it* of him. 20But the prophet who presumes to speak a word in My name, which I have not commanded him to speak, or who speaks in the name of other gods, that prophet shall die.' 21And if you say in your heart, 'How shall we know the word which the LORD has not spoken?'— 22when a prophet speaks in the name of the LORD, if the thing does not happen or come to pass, that *is* the thing which the LORD has not spoken; the prophet has spoken it presumptuously; you shall not be afraid of him.

18:15-19 a Prophet like me. This refers to the coming Messiah (see Acts 3:22–23; 7:37). Jesus had several other similarities to Moses: (1) He was spared death as a baby (Ex. 2; Matt. 2:13–23); (2) He renounced a royal court (Phil. 2:5–8; Heb. 11:24–27); (3) He had compassion on His people (Num. 27:17; Matt. 9:36); (4) He interceded for the people (Deut. 9:18; Heb. 7:25); (5) He spoke with God face to face (Ex. 34:29,30; 2 Cor. 3:7); and (6) He was the mediator of a covenant (Deut. 29:1; Heb. 8:6,7).

Three Cities of Refuge

19 "When the LORD your God has cut off the nations whose land the LORD your God is giving you, and you dispossess them and dwell in their cities and in their houses, 2you shall separate three cities for yourself in the midst of your land which the LORD your God is giving you to possess. 3You shall prepare roads for yourself, and divide into three parts the territory of your land which the LORD your God is giving you to inherit, that any manslayer may flee there.

4"And this *is* the case of the manslayer who flees there, that he may live: Whoever kills his neighbor unintentionally, not having hated him in time past— 5as when *a man* goes to the woods with his neighbor to cut timber, and his hand swings a stroke with the ax to cut down the tree, and the head slips from the handle and strikes his neighbor so that he dies—he shall flee to one of these cities and live; 6lest the avenger of blood, while his anger is hot, pursue the manslayer and overtake him, because the way is long, and kill him, though he *was* not deserving of death, since he had not hated the victim in time past. 7Therefore I command you, saying, 'You shall separate three cities for yourself.'

8"Now if the LORD your God enlarges your territory, as He swore to your fathers, and gives you the land which He promised to give to your fathers, 9and if you keep all these commandments and do them, which I command you today, to love the LORD your God and to walk always in His ways, then you shall add three more cities for yourself besides these three, 10lest innocent blood be shed in the midst of your land which the LORD your God is giving you *as* an inheritance, and *thus* guilt of bloodshed be upon you.

11"But if anyone hates his neighbor, lies in wait for him, rises against him and strikes him mortally, so that he dies, and he flees to one of these cities, 12then the elders of his city shall send and bring him from there, and deliver him over to the hand of the avenger of blood, that he may die. 13Your eye shall not pity him, but you shall put away *the guilt of* innocent blood from Israel, that it may go well with you.

Property Boundaries

14"You shall not remove your neighbor's landmark, which the men of old have set, in your inheritance which you will inherit in the land that the LORD your God is giving you to possess.

The Law Concerning Witnesses

15"One witness shall not rise against a man concerning any iniquity or any sin that he commits; by the mouth of two or

19:15 by the mouth of two or three witnesses. In order to protect an innocent person from being punished for a false charge, more than one witness was necessary to convict a person of a crime. By requiring more than one witness, the verdict was more accurate and objective.

three witnesses the matter shall be established. ¹⁶If a false witness rises against any man to testify against him of wrongdoing, ¹⁷then both men in the controversy shall stand before the LORD, before the priests and the judges who serve in those days. ¹⁸And the judges shall make careful inquiry, and indeed, *if* the witness *is* a false witness, who has testified falsely against his brother, ¹⁹then you shall do to him as he thought to have done to his brother; so you shall put away the evil from among you. ²⁰And those who remain shall hear and fear, and hereafter they shall not again commit such evil among you. ²¹Your eye shall not pity: life *shall be* for life, eye for eye, tooth for tooth, hand for hand, foot for foot.

Principles Governing Warfare

20 "When you go out to battle against your enemies, and see horses and chariots *and* people more numerous than you, do not be afraid of them; for the LORD your God *is* with you, who brought you up from the land of Egypt. ²So it shall be, when you are on the verge of battle, that the priest shall approach and speak to the people. ³And he shall say to them, 'Hear, O Israel: Today you are on the verge of battle with your enemies. Do not let your heart faint, do not be afraid, and do not tremble or be terrified because of them; ⁴for the LORD your God *is* He who goes with you, to fight for you against your enemies, to save you.'

> **20:1 do not be afraid.** During battle, the Israelites were never to fear an enemy because the outcome of the battle would not be determined by mere military strength. The command not to fear was based on God's power and faithfulness, which had been proven dramatically in Israel's deliverance from Egypt.

⁵"Then the officers shall speak to the people, saying: 'What man *is there* who has built a new house and has not dedicated it? Let him go and return to his house, lest he die in the battle and another man dedicate it. ⁶Also what man *is there* who has planted a vineyard and has not eaten of it? Let him

go and return to his house, lest he die in the battle and another man eat of it. ⁷And what man *is there* who is betrothed to a woman and has not married her? Let him go and return to his house, lest he die in the battle and another man marry her.'

⁸"The officers shall speak further to the people, and say, 'What man *is there who is* fearful and fainthearted? Let him go and return to his house, lest the heart of his brethren faint^a like his heart.' ⁹And so it shall be, when the officers have finished speaking to the people, that they shall make captains of the armies to lead the people.

¹⁰"When you go near a city to fight against it, then proclaim an offer of peace to it. ¹¹And it shall be that if they accept your offer of peace, and open to you, then all the people *who are* found in it shall be placed under tribute to you, and serve you. ¹²Now if *the city* will not make peace with you, but war against you, then you shall besiege it. ¹³And when the LORD your God delivers it into your hands, you shall strike every male in it with the edge of the sword. ¹⁴But the women, the little ones, the livestock, and all that is in the city, all its spoil, you shall plunder for yourself; and you shall eat the enemies' plunder which the LORD your God gives you. ¹⁵Thus you shall do to all the cities *which are* very far from you, which *are* not of the cities of these nations.

¹⁶"But of the cities of these peoples which the LORD your God gives you *as* an inheritance, you shall let nothing that breathes remain alive, ¹⁷but you shall utterly destroy them: the Hittite and the Amorite and the Canaanite and the Perizzite and the Hivite and the Jebusite, just as the LORD your God has commanded you, ¹⁸lest they teach you to do according to all their abominations which they have done for their gods, and you sin against the LORD your God.

> **20:16–18 utterly destroy.** The Canaanite cities were to be totally destroyed. Israel was to spare nothing, in order to destroy the influence toward idolatry (see 7:22–26).

20:8 ^aFollowing Masoretic Text and Targum; Samaritan Pentateuch, Septuagint, Syriac, and Vulgate read *lest he make his brother's heart faint.*

¹⁹"When you besiege a city for a long time, while making war against it to take it, you shall not destroy its trees by wielding an ax against them; if you can eat of them, do not cut them down to use in the siege, for the tree of the field *is* man's *food.* ²⁰Only the trees which you know *are* not trees for food you may destroy and cut down, to build siegeworks against the city that makes war with you, until it is subdued.

The Law Concerning Unsolved Murder

21 "If *anyone* is found slain, lying in the field in the land which the LORD your God is giving you to possess, *and* it is not known who killed him, ²then your elders and your judges shall go out and measure *the distance* from the slain man to the surrounding cities. ³And it shall be *that* the elders of the city nearest to the slain man will take a heifer which has not been worked *and* which has not pulled with a yoke. ⁴The elders of that city shall bring the heifer down to a valley with flowing water, which is neither plowed nor sown, and they shall break the heifer's neck there in the valley. ⁵Then the priests, the sons of Levi, shall come near, for the LORD your God has chosen them to minister to Him and to bless in the name of the LORD; by their word every controversy and every assault shall be *settled.* ⁶And all the elders of that city nearest to the slain *man* shall wash their hands over the heifer whose neck was broken in the valley. ⁷Then they shall answer and say, 'Our hands have not shed this blood, nor have our eyes seen *it.* ⁸Provide atonement, O LORD, for Your people Israel, whom You have redeemed, and do not lay innocent blood to the charge of Your people Israel.' And atonement shall be provided on their behalf for the blood. ⁹So you shall put away the *guilt of* innocent blood from among you when you do *what is* right in the sight of the LORD.

Female Captives

¹⁰"When you go out to war against your enemies, and the LORD your God delivers them into your hand, and you take them captive, ¹¹and you see among the captives a beautiful woman, and desire her and would take her for your wife, ¹²then you shall bring her home to your house, and she shall shave her head and trim her nails. ¹³She shall put off the clothes of her captivity, remain in your house, and mourn her father and her mother a full month; after that you may go in to her and be her husband, and she shall be your wife. ¹⁴And it shall be, if you have no delight in her, then you shall set her free, but you certainly shall not sell her for money; you shall not treat her brutally, because you have humbled her.

21:11–14 a beautiful woman. According to ancient war customs, a female captive became the servant of the victors. In the event that her conqueror wanted to marry her, one month was required to elapse, during which her troubled feelings could settle, she could adjust to her new conditions, and she could grieve the loss of her parents. The usual mourning period for Jews was one month, and the typical signs of Jewish grief were shaving the head, trimming the nails, and removing ornate clothes (on the eve of captivity, ladies wore beautiful clothes to be attractive to their captors). This month tested the strength of the man's affection. If he later divorced her, he could not sell her as a slave, for he had "humbled her" (refers to sexual activity).

Firstborn Inheritance Rights

¹⁵"If a man has two wives, one loved and the other unloved, and they have borne him children, *both* the loved and the unloved, and *if* the firstborn son is of her who is unloved, ¹⁶then it shall be, on the day he bequeaths his possessions to his sons, *that* he must not bestow firstborn status on the son of the loved wife in preference to the son of the unloved, the *true* firstborn. ¹⁷But he shall acknowledge the son of the unloved wife *as* the firstborn by giving him a double portion of all that he has, for he *is* the beginning of his strength; the right of the firstborn *is* his.

The Rebellious Son

¹⁸"If a man has a stubborn and rebellious son who will not obey the voice of his father or the voice of his mother, and *who,* when they have chastened him, will not heed them, ¹⁹then his father and his mother shall take hold of him and bring him out to the elders of his city, to the gate of his city. ²⁰And they shall say to the elders of his city, 'This son of ours is stubborn and rebellious; he will not obey our voice; he is a glutton and a drunkard.' ²¹Then all the men

of his city shall stone him to death with stones; so you shall put away the evil from among you, and all Israel shall hear and fear.

Miscellaneous Laws

22"If a man has committed a sin deserving of death, and he is put to death, and you hang him on a tree, 23his body shall not remain overnight on the tree, but you shall surely bury him that day, so that you do not defile the land which the LORD your God is giving you *as* an inheritance; for he who is hanged *is* accursed of God.

> **22:1–26:19** While loving God was the first duty (see 6:5), loving one's neighbor came next (see Matt. 22:37–40). In this section, the law of loving one's neighbor is applied to domestic and social relationships.

22 "You shall not see your brother's ox or his sheep going astray, and hide yourself from them; you shall certainly bring them back to your brother. 2And if your brother *is* not near you, or if you do not know him, then you shall bring it to your own house, and it shall remain with you until your brother seeks it; then you shall restore it to him. 3You shall do the same with his donkey, and so shall you do with his garment; with any lost thing of your brother's, which he has lost and you have found, you shall do likewise; you must not hide yourself.

4"You shall not see your brother's donkey or his ox fall down along the road, and hide yourself from them; you shall surely help him lift *them* up again.

5"A woman shall not wear anything that pertains to a man, nor shall a man put on a woman's garment, for all who do so *are* an abomination to the LORD your God.

6"If a bird's nest happens to be before you along the way, in any tree or on the ground, with young ones or eggs, with the mother sitting on the young or on the eggs, you shall not take the mother with the young; 7you shall surely let the mother go, and take the young for yourself, that it may be well with you and *that* you may prolong *your* days.

8"When you build a new house, then you shall make a parapet for your roof, that you may not bring guilt of bloodshed on your household if anyone falls from it.

9"You shall not sow your vineyard with different kinds of seed, lest the yield of the seed which you have sown and the fruit of your vineyard be defiled.

10"You shall not plow with an ox and a donkey together.

11"You shall not wear a garment of different sorts, *such as* wool and linen mixed together.

12"You shall make tassels on the four corners of the clothing with which you cover *yourself.*

Laws of Sexual Morality

13"If any man takes a wife, and goes in to her, and detests her, 14and charges her with shameful conduct, and brings a bad name on her, and says, 'I took this woman, and when I came to her I found she *was* not a virgin,' 15then the father and mother of the young woman shall take and bring out *the evidence of* the young woman's virginity to the elders of the city at the gate. 16And the young woman's father shall say to the elders, 'I gave my daughter to this man as wife, and he detests her. 17Now he has charged her with shameful conduct, saying, "I found your daughter *was* not a virgin," and yet these *are the evidences of* my daughter's virginity.' And they shall spread the cloth before the elders of the city. 18Then the elders of that city shall take that man and punish him; 19and they shall fine him one hundred *shekels* of silver and give *them* to the father of the young woman, because he has brought a bad name on a virgin of Israel. And she shall be his wife; he cannot divorce her all his days.

> **22:15 *the evidence of* the young woman's virginity.** This evidence was probably a bloodstained garment or a bed sheet from the wedding night.

20"But if the thing is true, *and evidences of* virginity are not found for the young woman, 21then they shall bring out the young woman to the door of her father's house, and the men of her city shall stone her to death with stones, because she has done a disgraceful thing in Israel, to play the harlot in her father's house. So you shall put away the evil from among you.

22"If a man is found lying with a woman married to a husband, then both of them

shall die—the man that lay with the woman, and the woman; so you shall put away the evil from Israel.

23"If a young woman *who is* a virgin is betrothed to a husband, and a man finds her in the city and lies with her, 24then you shall bring them both out to the gate of that city, and you shall stone them to death with stones, the young woman because she did not cry out in the city, and the man because he humbled his neighbor's wife; so you shall put away the evil from among you.

25"But if a man finds a betrothed young woman in the countryside, and the man forces her and lies with her, then only the man who lay with her shall die. 26But you shall do nothing to the young woman; *there is* in the young woman no sin *deserving* of death, for just as when a man rises against his neighbor and kills him, even so *is* this matter. 27For he found her in the countryside, *and* the betrothed young woman cried out, but *there was* no one to save her.

28"If a man finds a young woman *who is* a virgin, who is not betrothed, and he seizes her and lies with her, and they are found out, 29then the man who lay with her shall give to the young woman's father fifty *shekels* of silver, and she shall be his wife because he has humbled her; he shall not be permitted to divorce her all his days.

30"A man shall not take his father's wife, nor uncover his father's bed.

Those Excluded from the Congregation

23 "He who is emasculated by crushing or mutilation shall not enter the assembly of the LORD.

2"One of illegitimate birth shall not enter the assembly of the LORD; even to the tenth generation none of his *descendants* shall enter the assembly of the LORD.

3"An Ammonite or Moabite shall not enter the assembly of the LORD; even to the tenth generation none of his *descendants* shall enter the assembly of the LORD forever, 4because they did not meet you with bread and water on the road when you came out of Egypt, and because they hired against you Balaam the son of Beor from Pethor of Mesopotamia,*a* to curse you.

5Nevertheless the LORD your God would not listen to Balaam, but the LORD your God turned the curse into a blessing for you, because the LORD your God loves you. 6You shall not seek their peace nor their prosperity all your days forever.

> **23:1 the assembly of the LORD.** This law excluded the emasculated, the illegitimate, and the Ammonites and Moabites from public office and from worshiping the Lord. Most foreigners were allowed to convert to the Jewish faith, but these three groups were not. Eunuchs were forbidden because such willful mutilation (generally done by crushing) violated God's creation of man and was associated with idolatry. The illegitimate were excluded in order to discourage sexual misconduct. Ammonites and Moabites were excluded because of their hostility toward God and Israel. Individuals from all three of these outcast groups are offered grace and acceptance upon personal faith in the true God (see Is. 56:1–8). Ruth is a notable example (Ruth 1:4,16).

7"You shall not abhor an Edomite, for he *is* your brother. You shall not abhor an Egyptian, because you were an alien in his land. 8The children of the third generation born to them may enter the assembly of the LORD.

Cleanliness of the CampSite

9"When the army goes out against your enemies, then keep yourself from every wicked thing. 10If there is any man among you who becomes unclean by some occurrence in the night, then he shall go outside the camp; he shall not come inside the camp. 11But it shall be, when evening comes, that he shall wash with water; and when the sun sets, he may come into the camp. 12"Also you shall have a place outside the camp, where you may go out; 13and you shall have an implement among your equipment, and when you sit down outside, you shall dig with it and turn and cover your refuse. 14For the LORD your God walks in the midst of your camp, to deliver you and give your enemies over to you; therefore your camp shall be holy, that He may see no unclean thing among you, and turn away from you.

23:4 *a*Hebrew *Aram Naharaim*

Miscellaneous Laws

[15]"You shall not give back to his master the slave who has escaped from his master to you. [16]He may dwell with you in your midst, in the place which he chooses within one of your gates, where it seems best to him; you shall not oppress him.

23:15,16 A fugitive slave was not to be turned over to his master. Evidently this was to protect a slave from the Canaanites or other neighboring nations who was driven out by oppression or who escaped with a desire to know God.

[17]"There shall be no *ritual* harlot[a] of the daughters of Israel, or a perverted[b] one of the sons of Israel. [18]You shall not bring the wages of a harlot or the price of a dog to the house of the LORD your God for any vowed offering, for both of these *are* an abomination to the LORD your God.

[19]"You shall not charge interest to your brother—interest on money *or* food *or* anything that is lent out at interest. [20]To a foreigner you may charge interest, but to your brother you shall not charge interest, that the LORD your God may bless you in all to which you set your hand in the land which you are entering to possess.

[21]"When you make a vow to the LORD your God, you shall not delay to pay it; for the LORD your God will surely require it of you, and it would be sin to you. [22]But if you abstain from vowing, it shall not be sin to you. [23]That which has gone from your lips you shall keep and perform, for you voluntarily vowed to the LORD your God what you have promised with your mouth.

[24]"When you come into your neighbor's vineyard, you may eat your fill of grapes at your pleasure, but you shall not put *any* in your container. [25]When you come into your neighbor's standing grain, you may pluck the heads with your hand, but you shall not use a sickle on your neighbor's standing grain.

Law Concerning Divorce

24 "When a man takes a wife and marries her, and it happens that she finds no favor in his eyes because he has found some uncleanness in her, and he writes her a certificate of divorce, puts *it* in her hand, and sends her out of his house, [2]when she has departed from his house, and goes and becomes another man's *wife,* [3]if the latter husband detests her and writes her a certificate of divorce, puts *it* in her hand, and sends her out of his house, or if the latter husband dies who took her as his wife, [4]*then* her former husband who divorced her must not take her back to be his wife after she has been defiled; for that *is* an abomination before the LORD, and you shall not bring sin on the land which the LORD your God is giving you *as* an inheritance.

24:1–4 This passage does not command, commend, condone, or even suggest divorce. Rather, it recognizes that divorce occurs and permits it only on restricted grounds. God hates divorce (Mal. 2:16), He has designed marriage for life, and He allowed divorce only because of hard hearts (Matt. 19:8). The case presented here shows that illegitimate divorce proliferates adultery (see Matt. 5:31,32; 19:4–9).

Miscellaneous Laws

[5]"When a man has taken a new wife, he shall not go out to war or be charged with any business; he shall be free at home one year, and bring happiness to his wife whom he has taken.

[6]"No man shall take the lower or the upper millstone in pledge, for he takes *one's* living in pledge.

[7]"If a man is found kidnapping any of his brethren of the children of Israel, and mistreats him or sells him, then that kidnapper shall die; and you shall put away the evil from among you.

[8]"Take heed in an outbreak of leprosy, that you carefully observe and do according to all that the priests, the Levites, shall teach you; just as I commanded them, *so* you shall be careful to do. [9]Remember what the LORD your God did to Miriam on the way when you came out of Egypt!

[10]"When you lend your brother anything, you shall not go into his house to get his pledge. [11]You shall stand outside, and the man to whom you lend shall bring the

---

23:17 [a]Hebrew *qedeshah*, feminine of *qadesh* (see note b)   [b]Hebrew *qadesh*, that is, one practicing sodomy and prostitution in religious rituals

pledge out to you. ¹²And if the man *is* poor, you shall not keep his pledge overnight. ¹³You shall in any case return the pledge to him again when the sun goes down, that he may sleep in his own garment and bless you; and it shall be righteousness to you before the LORD your God.

24:10–13 his pledge. The pledge was often a cloak, an outer garment given in pledge to guarantee the repayment of a loan. A righteous lender did not forcefully exact repayment and allowed a poor person to keep his cloak overnight to stay warm. Lending to the poor was permitted but only without interest, coercion to repay, or extension of the loan beyond the sabbatical year.

¹⁴"You shall not oppress a hired servant *who is* poor and needy, *whether* one of your brethren or one of the aliens who *is* in your land within your gates. ¹⁵Each day you shall give *him* his wages, and not let the sun go down on it, for he *is* poor and has set his heart on it; lest he cry out against you to the LORD, and it be sin to you.

¹⁶"Fathers shall not be put to death for *their* children, nor shall children be put to death for *their* fathers; a person shall be put to death for his own sin.

¹⁷"You shall not pervert justice due the stranger or the fatherless, nor take a widow's garment as a pledge. ¹⁸But you shall remember that you were a slave in Egypt, and the LORD your God redeemed you from there; therefore I command you to do this thing.

¹⁹"When you reap your harvest in your field, and forget a sheaf in the field, you shall not go back to get it; it shall be for the stranger, the fatherless, and the widow, that the LORD your God may bless you in all the work of your hands. ²⁰When you beat your olive trees, you shall not go over the boughs again; it shall be for the stranger, the fatherless, and the widow. ²¹When you gather the grapes of your vineyard, you shall not glean *it* afterward; it shall be for the stranger, the fatherless, and the widow. ²²And you shall remember that you were a slave in the land

24:19–22 The practice of allowing the needy to glean in the field was grounded in the remembrance of Israel's hard poverty in Egypt.

of Egypt; therefore I command you to do this thing.

25 "If there is a dispute between men, and they come to court, that *the judges* may judge them, and they justify the righteous and condemn the wicked, ²then it shall be, if the wicked man deserves to be beaten, that the judge will cause him to lie down and be beaten in his presence, according to his guilt, with a certain number of blows. ³Forty blows he may give him *and* no more, lest he should exceed this and beat him with many blows above these, and your brother be humiliated in your sight.

⁴"You shall not muzzle an ox while it treads out *the grain.*

Marriage Duty of the Surviving Brother

⁵"If brothers dwell together, and one of them dies and has no son, the widow of the dead man shall not be *married* to a stranger outside *the family*; her husband's brother shall go in to her, take her as his wife, and perform the duty of a husband's brother to her. ⁶And it shall be *that* the firstborn son which she bears will succeed to the name of his dead brother, that his name may not be blotted out of Israel. ⁷But if the man does not want to take his brother's wife, then let his brother's wife go up to the gate to the elders, and say, 'My husband's brother refuses to raise up a name to his brother in Israel; he will not perform the duty of my husband's brother.' ⁸Then the elders of his city shall call him and speak to him. But *if* he stands firm and says, 'I do not want to take her,' ⁹then his brother's wife shall come to him in the presence of the elders, remove his sandal from his foot, spit in his face, and answer and say, 'So shall it be done to the man who will not build up his brother's house.' ¹⁰And his name shall be called in Israel, 'The house of him who had his sandal removed.'

25:5–10 Levirate marriages were arranged so that if a man died childless, then his brother would marry his widow in order to provide an heir. These were not required marriages but were strongly pressured by the elders upon a brother who was single and shared the estate. This act showed fraternal affection and affirmed the high dignity of the individual by preserving the deceased's name.

Miscellaneous Laws

¹¹"If *two* men fight together, and the wife of one draws near to rescue her husband from the hand of the one attacking him, and puts out her hand and seizes him by the genitals, ¹²then you shall cut off her hand; your eye shall not pity *her*.

¹³"You shall not have in your bag differing weights, a heavy and a light. ¹⁴You shall not have in your house differing measures, a large and a small. ¹⁵You shall have a perfect and just weight, a perfect and just measure, that your days may be lengthened in the land which the LORD your God is giving you. ¹⁶For all who do such things, all who behave unrighteously, *are* an abomination to the LORD your God.

Destroy the Amalekites

¹⁷"Remember what Amalek did to you on the way as you were coming out of Egypt, ¹⁸how he met you on the way and attacked your rear ranks, all the stragglers at your rear, when you *were* tired and weary; and he did not fear God. ¹⁹Therefore it shall be, when the LORD your God has given you rest from your enemies all around, in the land which the LORD your God is giving you to possess *as* an inheritance, *that* you will blot out the remembrance of Amalek from under heaven. You shall not forget.

Offerings of Firstfruits and Tithes

26 "And it shall be, when you come into the land which the LORD your God is giving you *as* an inheritance, and you possess it and dwell in it, ²that you shall take some of the first of all the produce of the ground, which you shall bring from your land that the LORD your God is giving you, and put *it* in a basket and go to the place where the LORD your God chooses to make His name abide. ³And you shall go to the one who is priest in those days, and say to him, 'I declare today to the LORD your*ᵃ* God that I have come to the country which the LORD swore to our fathers to give us.'

⁴"Then the priest shall take the basket out of your hand and set it down before the altar of the LORD your God. ⁵And you shall answer and say before the LORD your God: 'My father *was* a Syrian,*ᵃ* about to perish, and he went down to Egypt and dwelt there, few in number; and there he became a nation, great, mighty, and populous. ⁶But the Egyptians mistreated us, afflicted us, and laid hard bondage on us. ⁷Then we cried out to the LORD God of our fathers, and the LORD heard our voice and looked on our affliction and our labor and our oppression. ⁸So the LORD brought us out of Egypt with a mighty hand and with an outstretched arm, with great terror and with signs and wonders. ⁹He has brought us to this place and has given us this land, "a land flowing with milk and honey";*ᵃ* ¹⁰and now, behold, I have brought the firstfruits of the land which you, O LORD, have given me.'

> **26:5 you shall...say before the LORD your God.** The firstfruits offering was accompanied by an elaborate confession of the Lord's faithfulness in preserving Israel. The three essential parts of the visit to the sanctuary were the firstfruits, bowing in worship, and rejoicing in the Lord's goodness.

"Then you shall set it before the LORD your God, and worship before the LORD your God. ¹¹So you shall rejoice in every good *thing* which the LORD your God has given to you and your house, you and the Levite and the stranger who *is* among you.

¹²"When you have finished laying aside all the tithe of your increase in the third year—the year of tithing—and have given *it* to the Levite, the stranger, the fatherless, and the widow, so that they may eat within your gates and be filled, ¹³then you shall say before the LORD your God: 'I have removed the holy *tithe* from *my* house, and also have given them to the Levite, the stranger, the fatherless, and the widow, according to all Your commandments which You have commanded me; I have not transgressed Your commandments, nor have I forgotten *them*. ¹⁴I have not eaten any of it when in

> **26:13,14 you shall say before the LORD your God.** The confession to be made along with the tithe was a statement of obedience and a prayer for God's blessing. The Israelite confessed his continued dependence on God and waited for His blessing.

26:3 *ᵃ*Septuagint reads *my*.   26:5 *ᵃ*Or *Aramean*   26:9 *ᵃ*Exodus 3:8

mourning, nor have I removed *any* of it for an unclean *use*, nor given *any* of it for the dead. I have obeyed the voice of the LORD my God, and have done according to all that You have commanded me. ¹⁵Look down from Your holy habitation, from heaven, and bless Your people Israel and the land which You have given us, just as You swore to our fathers, "a land flowing with milk and honey." '*a*

A Special People of God

¹⁶"This day the LORD your God commands you to observe these statutes and judgments; therefore you shall be careful to observe them with all your heart and with all your soul. ¹⁷Today you have proclaimed the LORD to be your God, and that you will walk in His ways and keep His statutes, His commandments, and His judgments, and that you will obey His voice. ¹⁸Also today the LORD has proclaimed you to be His special people, just as He promised you, that *you* should keep all His commandments, ¹⁹and that He will set you high above all nations which He has made, in praise, in name, and in honor, and that you may be a holy people to the LORD your God, just as He has spoken."

The Law Inscribed on Stones

27 Now Moses, with the elders of Israel, commanded the people, saying: "Keep all the commandments which I command you today. ²And it shall be, on the day when you cross over the Jordan to the land which the LORD your God is giving you, that you shall set up for yourselves large stones, and whitewash them with lime. ³You shall write on them all the words of this law, when you have crossed over, that you may enter the land which the LORD your God is giving you, 'a land flowing with milk and honey,'*a* just as the LORD God of your fathers promised you. ⁴Therefore it shall be, when you have crossed over the Jordan, *that* on Mount Ebal you shall set up these stones, which I command you today, and you shall whitewash them with lime. ⁵And there you shall build an altar to the LORD your God, an altar of stones; you

shall not use an iron *tool* on them. ⁶You shall build with whole stones the altar of the LORD your God, and offer burnt offerings on it to the LORD your God. ⁷You shall offer peace offerings, and shall eat there, and rejoice before the LORD your God. ⁸And you shall write very plainly on the stones all the words of this law."

> **27:5–7 build an altar.** The Israelites were also to build an altar of uncut stones, on which to offer burnt offerings to the Lord. The burnt offerings were completely consumed and represented complete devotion to God; the peace offerings expressed thanks to Him.

⁹Then Moses and the priests, the Levites, spoke to all Israel, saying, "Take heed and listen, O Israel: This day you have become the people of the LORD your God. ¹⁰Therefore you shall obey the voice of the LORD your God, and observe His commandments and His statutes which I command you today."

Curses Pronounced from Mount Ebal

¹¹And Moses commanded the people on the same day, saying, ¹²"These shall stand on Mount Gerizim to bless the people, when you have crossed over the Jordan: Simeon, Levi, Judah, Issachar, Joseph, and Benjamin; ¹³and these shall stand on Mount Ebal to curse: Reuben, Gad, Asher, Zebulun, Dan, and Naphtali.

¹⁴"And the Levites shall speak with a loud voice and say to all the men of Israel: ¹⁵'Cursed *is* the one who makes a carved or molded image, an abomination to the LORD, the work of the hands of the craftsman, and sets *it* up in secret.'

"And all the people shall answer and say, 'Amen!'

¹⁶'Cursed *is* the one who treats his father or his mother with contempt.'

"And all the people shall say, 'Amen!'

¹⁷'Cursed *is* the one who moves his neighbor's landmark.'

"And all the people shall say, 'Amen!'

¹⁸'Cursed *is* the one who makes the blind to wander off the road.'

"And all the people shall say, 'Amen!'

¹⁹'Cursed *is* the one who perverts the

26:15 *a*Exodus 3:8   27:3 *a*Exodus 3:8

justice due the stranger, the fatherless, and widow.'

"And all the people shall say, 'Amen!'

²⁰"Cursed *is* the one who lies with his father's wife, because he has uncovered his father's bed.'

"And all the people shall say, 'Amen!'

²¹"Cursed *is* the one who lies with any kind of animal.'

"And all the people shall say, 'Amen!'

²²"Cursed *is* the one who lies with his sister, the daughter of his father or the daughter of his mother.'

"And all the people shall say, 'Amen!'

²³"Cursed *is* the one who lies with his mother-in-law.'

"And all the people shall say, 'Amen!'

²⁴"Cursed *is* the one who attacks his neighbor secretly.'

"And all the people shall say, 'Amen!'

²⁵"Cursed *is* the one who takes a bribe to slay an innocent person.'

"And all the people shall say, 'Amen!'

²⁶"Cursed *is* the one who does not confirm *all* the words of this law by observing them.'

"And all the people shall say, 'Amen!' "

27:26 does not confirm *all* the words of this law. This final curse covered all other unspecified commandments. God requires our total obedience, but only the Lord Jesus Christ accomplished this (2 Cor. 5:21). **Amen!** The word means "so be it." The people thus indicated their understanding and agreement with the statement that was made, but they soon violated their promise.

Blessings on Obedience

28 "Now it shall come to pass, if you diligently obey the voice of the LORD your God, to observe carefully all His commandments which I command you today, that the LORD your God will set you high above all nations of the earth. ²And all these blessings shall come upon you and overtake you, because you obey the voice of the LORD your God:

³"Blessed *shall* you *be* in the city, and blessed *shall* you *be* in the country.

⁴"Blessed *shall be* the fruit of your body, the produce of your ground and the increase of your herds, the increase of your cattle and the offspring of your flocks.

⁵"Blessed *shall be* your basket and your kneading bowl.

⁶"Blessed *shall* you *be* when you come in, and blessed *shall* you *be* when you go out.

⁷"The LORD will cause your enemies who rise against you to be defeated before your face; they shall come out against you one way and flee before you seven ways.

⁸"The LORD will command the blessing on you in your storehouses and in all to which you set your hand, and He will bless you in the land which the LORD your God is giving you.

⁹"The LORD will establish you as a holy people to Himself, just as He has sworn to you, if you keep the commandments of the LORD your God and walk in His ways. ¹⁰Then all peoples of the earth shall see that you are called by the name of the LORD, and they shall be afraid of you. ¹¹And the LORD will grant you plenty of goods, in the fruit of your body, in the increase of your livestock, and in the produce of your ground, in the land of which the LORD swore to your fathers to give you. ¹²The LORD will open to you His good treasure, the heavens, to give the rain to your land in its season, and to bless all the work of your hand. You shall lend to many nations, but you shall not borrow. ¹³And the LORD will make you the head and not the tail; you shall be above only, and not be beneath, if you heed the commandments of the LORD your God, which I command you today, and are careful to observe *them.* ¹⁴So you shall not turn aside from any of the words which I command you this day, *to* the right or the left, to go after other gods to serve them.

28:10 called by the name of the LORD. Israel's obedience and blessing would cause all the people of the earth to fear them because they were clearly God's chosen people. This was God's intention all along, for Israel to be a witness to the nations of the one true and living God and to draw the Gentiles out of idol worship.

Curses on Disobedience

¹⁵"But it shall come to pass, if you do not obey the voice of the LORD your God, to observe carefully all His commandments and His statutes which I command you today, that all these curses will come upon you and overtake you:

[16]"Cursed *shall* you *be* in the city, and cursed *shall* you *be* in the country.

[17]"Cursed *shall be* your basket and your kneading bowl.

[18]"Cursed *shall be* the fruit of your body and the produce of your land, the increase of your cattle and the offspring of your flocks.

[19]"Cursed *shall* you *be* when you come in, and cursed *shall* you *be* when you go out.

[20]"The LORD will send on you cursing, confusion, and rebuke in all that you set your hand to do, until you are destroyed and until you perish quickly, because of the wickedness of your doings in which you have forsaken Me. [21]The LORD will make the plague cling to you until He has consumed you from the land which you are going to possess. [22]The LORD will strike you with consumption, with fever, with inflammation, with severe burning fever, with the sword, with scorching, and with mildew; they shall pursue you until you perish. [23]And your heavens which *are* over your head shall be bronze, and the earth which is under you *shall be* iron. [24]The LORD will change the rain of your land to powder and dust; from the heaven it shall come down on you until you are destroyed.

> **28:23 bronze...iron.** The heavens would be as bright as bronze, but no rain would fall from them to water the ground. The earth would be as hard as iron, so what little rain did fall would run off and not soak in (see Amos 4:7).

[25]"The LORD will cause you to be defeated before your enemies; you shall go out one way against them and flee seven ways before them; and you shall become troublesome to all the kingdoms of the earth. [26]Your carcasses shall be food for all the birds of the air and the beasts of the earth, and no one shall frighten *them* away. [27]The LORD will strike you with the boils of Egypt, with tumors, with the scab, and with the itch, from which you cannot be healed. [28]The LORD will strike you with madness and blindness and confusion of heart. [29]And you shall grope at noonday, as a blind man gropes in darkness; you shall not prosper in your ways; you shall be only oppressed and plundered continually, and no one shall save *you*.

[30]"You shall betroth a wife, but another man shall lie with her; you shall build a house, but you shall not dwell in it; you shall plant a vineyard, but shall not gather its grapes. [31]Your ox *shall be* slaughtered before your eyes, but you shall not eat of it; your donkey *shall be* violently taken away from before you, and shall not be restored to you; your sheep *shall be* given to your enemies, and you shall have no one to rescue *them*. [32]Your sons and your daughters *shall be* given to another people, and your eyes shall look and fail *with longing* for them all day long; and *there shall be* no strength in your hand. [33]A nation whom you have not known shall eat the fruit of your land and the produce of your labor, and you shall be only oppressed and crushed continually. [34]So you shall be driven mad because of the sight which your eyes see. [35]The LORD will strike you in the knees and on the legs with severe boils which cannot be healed, and from the sole of your foot to the top of your head.

[36]"The LORD will bring you and the king whom you set over you to a nation which neither you nor your fathers have known, and there you shall serve other gods—wood and stone. [37]And you shall become an astonishment, a proverb, and a byword among all nations where the LORD will drive you.

> **28:36 the king whom you set over you.** Although they did not have a king yet, Moses anticipated that they would have one when this curse was enacted. **to a nation which neither you nor your fathers have known.** Israel and their king would be taken captive to a nation that was particularly steeped in idolatry (see 2 Kin. 17:41; Jer. 16:13).

[38]"You shall carry much seed out to the field but gather little in, for the locust shall consume it. [39]You shall plant vineyards and tend *them*, but you shall neither drink *of* the wine nor gather the *grapes*; for the worms shall eat them. [40]You shall have olive trees throughout all your territory, but you shall not anoint *yourself* with the oil; for your olives shall drop off. [41]You shall beget sons and daughters, but they shall not be yours; for they shall go into captivity. [42]Locusts shall consume all your trees and the produce of your land.

43"The alien who *is* among you shall rise higher and higher above you, and you shall come down lower and lower. 44He shall lend to you, but you shall not lend to him; he shall be the head, and you shall be the tail.

45"Moreover all these curses shall come upon you and pursue and overtake you, until you are destroyed, because you did not obey the voice of the LORD your God, to keep His commandments and His statutes which He commanded you. 46And they shall be upon you for a sign and a wonder, and on your descendants forever.

47"Because you did not serve the LORD your God with joy and gladness of heart, for the abundance of everything, 48therefore you shall serve your enemies, whom the LORD will send against you, in hunger, in thirst, in nakedness, and in need of everything; and He will put a yoke of iron on your neck until He has destroyed you. 49The LORD will bring a nation against you from afar, from the end of the earth, *as swift* as the eagle flies, a nation whose language you will not understand, 50a nation of fierce countenance, which does not respect the elderly nor show favor to the young. 51And they shall eat the increase of your livestock and the produce of your land, until you are destroyed; they shall not leave you grain or new wine or oil, *or* the increase of your cattle or the offspring of your flocks, until they have destroyed you.

28:49 a nation...from the end of the earth. God would empower a nation to act as His own instrument of judgment against His ungrateful people. This foreign nation came from a far land, arose quickly, and completely devastated the Land. Assyria fulfilled this first (Is. 5:26; 7:18–20) and Babylon second (Jer. 5:15; Lam. 4:19).

52"They shall besiege you at all your gates until your high and fortified walls, in which you trust, come down throughout all your land; and they shall besiege you at all your gates throughout all your land which the LORD your God has given you. 53You shall eat the fruit of your own body, the flesh of your sons and your daughters whom the LORD your God has given you, in the siege and desperate straits in which your enemy

shall distress you. 54The sensitive and very refined man among you will be hostile toward his brother, toward the wife of his bosom, and toward the rest of his children whom he leaves behind, 55so that he will not give any of them the flesh of his children whom he will eat, because he has nothing left in the siege and desperate straits in which your enemy shall distress you at all your gates. 56The tender and delicate woman among you, who would not venture to set the sole of her foot on the ground because of her delicateness and sensitivity, will refuse*a* to the husband of her bosom, and to her son and her daughter, 57her placenta which comes out from between her feet and her children whom she bears; for she will eat them secretly for lack of everything in the siege and desperate straits in which your enemy shall distress you at all your gates.

58"If you do not carefully observe all the words of this law that are written in this book, that you may fear this glorious and awesome name, THE LORD YOUR GOD, 59then the LORD will bring upon you and your descendants extraordinary plagues—great and prolonged plagues—and serious and prolonged sicknesses. 60Moreover He will bring back on you all the diseases of Egypt, of which you were afraid, and they shall cling to you. 61Also every sickness and every plague, which *is* not written in this Book of the Law, will the LORD bring upon you until you are destroyed. 62You shall be left few in number, whereas you were as the stars of heaven in multitude, because you would not obey the voice of the LORD your God. 63And it shall be, *that* just as the LORD rejoiced over you to do you good and multiply you, so the LORD will rejoice over you to destroy you and bring you to nothing; and you shall be plucked from off the land which you go to possess.

28:58–63 this glorious and awesome name, THE LORD YOUR GOD. Israel's obedience to the law would cause them to fear the Lord, whose name represents His character. Once Israel's disobedience hardened into disregard for the glorious name of God, they would receive the full measure of the divine curses.

28:56 *a*Literally *her eye shall be evil toward*

⁶⁴"Then the LORD will scatter you among all peoples, from one end of the earth to the other, and there you shall serve other gods, which neither you nor your fathers have known—wood and stone. ⁶⁵And among those nations you shall find no rest, nor shall the sole of your foot have a resting place; but there the LORD will give you a trembling heart, failing eyes, and anguish of soul. ⁶⁶Your life shall hang in doubt before you; you shall fear day and night, and have no assurance of life. ⁶⁷In the morning you shall say, 'Oh, that it were evening!' And at evening you shall say, 'Oh, that it were morning!' because of the fear which terrifies your heart, and because of the sight which your eyes see.

⁶⁸"And the LORD will take you back to Egypt in ships, by the way of which I said to you, 'You shall never see it again.' And there you shall be offered for sale to your enemies as male and female slaves, but no one will buy you."

The Covenant Renewed in Moab

29 These *are* the words of the covenant which the LORD commanded Moses to make with the children of Israel in the land of Moab, besides the covenant which He made with them in Horeb.

²Now Moses called all Israel and said to them: "You have seen all that the LORD did before your eyes in the land of Egypt, to Pharaoh and to all his servants and to all his land— ³the great trials which your eyes have seen, the signs, and those great wonders. ⁴Yet the LORD has not given you a heart to perceive and eyes to see and ears to hear, to this *very* day. ⁵And I have led you forty years in the wilderness. Your clothes have not worn out on you, and your sandals have not worn out on your feet. ⁶You have not eaten bread, nor have you drunk wine or *similar* drink, that you may know that I *am* the LORD your God. ⁷And when you

came to this place, Sihon king of Heshbon and Og king of Bashan came out against us to battle, and we conquered them. ⁸We took their land and gave it as an inheritance to the Reubenites, to the Gadites, and to half the tribe of Manasseh. ⁹Therefore keep the words of this covenant, and do them, that you may prosper in all that you do.

¹⁰"All of you stand today before the LORD your God: your leaders and your tribes and your elders and your officers, all the men of Israel, ¹¹your little ones and your wives— also the stranger who *is* in your camp, from the one who cuts your wood to the one who draws your water— ¹²that you may enter into covenant with the LORD your God, and into His oath, which the LORD your God makes with you today, ¹³that He may establish you today as a people for Himself, and *that* He may be God to you, just as He has spoken to you, and just as He has sworn to your fathers, to Abraham, Isaac, and Jacob.

> **29:10,11 All of you stand today before the LORD your God.** Even though all the people were likely standing in organized ranks before Moses, this was not a call to outward order but to inward devotion, to make the covenant a matter of the heart and life.

¹⁴"I make this covenant and this oath, not with you alone, ¹⁵but with *him* who stands here with us today before the LORD our God, as well as with *him* who *is* not here with us today ¹⁶(for you know that we dwelt in the land of Egypt and that we came through the nations which you passed by, ¹⁷and you saw their abominations and their idols which *were* among them—wood and stone and silver and gold); ¹⁸so that there may not be among you man or woman or family or tribe, whose heart turns away today from the LORD our God, to go *and* serve the gods of these nations, and that there may not be among you a root bearing bitterness or wormwood; ¹⁹and so it may not happen, when he hears the words of this curse, that he blesses himself in his heart, saying, 'I shall have peace, even though I follow the dictates*ᵃ* of my heart'—as though the drunkard could be included with the sober.

²⁰"The LORD would not spare him; for

> **29:4 the LORD has not given you...eyes to see.** Despite all they had experienced, Israel was still spiritually blind to the significance of what the Lord had done for them. The Lord had not given them an understanding heart, simply because the people had not penitently sought it (see 2 Chr. 7:14).

29:19 *ᵃOr stubbornness*

then the anger of the LORD and His jealousy would burn against that man, and every curse that is written in this book would settle on him, and the LORD would blot out his name from under heaven. [21]And the LORD would separate him from all the tribes of Israel for adversity, according to all the curses of the covenant that are written in this Book of the Law, [22]so that the coming generation of your children who rise up after you, and the foreigner who comes from a far land, would say, when they see the plagues of that land and the sicknesses which the LORD has laid on it:

[23]'The whole land is brimstone, salt, and burning; it is not sown, nor does it bear, nor does any grass grow there, like the overthrow of Sodom and Gomorrah, Admah, and Zeboiim, which the LORD overthrew in His anger and His wrath.' [24]All nations would say, 'Why has the LORD done so to this land? What does the heat of this great anger mean?' [25]Then people would say: 'Because they have forsaken the covenant of the LORD God of their fathers, which He made with them when He brought them out of the land of Egypt; [26]for they went and served other gods and worshiped them, gods that they did not know and that He had not given to them. [27]Then the anger of the LORD was aroused against this land, to bring on it every curse that is written in this book. [28]And the LORD uprooted them from their land in anger, in wrath, and in great indignation, and cast them into another land, as it is this day.'

[29]"The secret things belong to the LORD our God, but those things which are revealed belong to us and to our children forever, that we may do all the words of this law.

29:29 The secret things...those things which are revealed. That which is revealed included the law with its promises and threats. That which is hidden must be the specific way in which God will carry out His will in the future, which is revealed in His Word and completed in His great work of salvation.

The Blessing of Returning to God

30 "Now it shall come to pass, when all these things come upon you, the blessing and the curse which I have set before you, and you call them to mind among all the nations where the LORD your God drives you, [2]and you return to the LORD your God and obey His voice, according to all that I command you today, you and your children, with all your heart and with all your soul, [3]that the LORD your God will bring you back from captivity, and have compassion on you, and gather you again from all the nations where the LORD your God has scattered you. [4]If any of you are driven out to the farthest parts under heaven, from there the LORD your God will gather you, and from there He will bring you. [5]Then the LORD your God will bring you to the land which your fathers possessed, and you shall possess it. He will prosper you and multiply you more than your fathers. [6]And the LORD your God will circumcise your heart and the heart of your descendants, to love the LORD your God with all your heart and with all your soul, that you may live.

30:6 the LORD...will circumcise your heart. God's work in a person's innermost being is true salvation, granting a new will to obey Him in place of the former spiritual insensitivity and stubbornness. With a new heart, one can love the Lord wholeheartedly, and this is the essential component of the New Covenant (see Jer. 31:31–34).

[7]"Also the LORD your God will put all these curses on your enemies and on those who hate you, who persecuted you. [8]And you will again obey the voice of the LORD and do all His commandments which I command you today. [9]The LORD your God will make you abound in all the work of your hand, in the fruit of your body, in the increase of your livestock, and in the produce of your land for good. For the LORD will again rejoice over you for good as He rejoiced over your fathers, [10]if you obey the voice of the LORD your God, to keep His commandments and His statutes which are written in this Book of the Law, and if you turn to the LORD your God with all your heart and with all your soul.

The Choice of Life or Death

[11]"For this commandment which I command you today is not too mysterious for you, nor is it far off. [12]It is not in heaven, that you should say, 'Who will ascend into

heaven for us and bring it to us, that we may hear it and do it?' [13]Nor *is* it beyond the sea, that you should say, 'Who will go over the sea for us and bring it to us, that we may hear it and do it?' [14]But the word *is* very near you, in your mouth and in your heart, that you may do it.

> **30:11–14** Moses encouraged them to make the right choice: to love God so deeply as to obey Him and thus enjoy salvation and blessings. This simple, yet profound choice was stated in terms that they could easily understand. They knew the truth in their hearts and minds.

[15]"See, I have set before you today life and good, death and evil, [16]in that I command you today to love the LORD your God, to walk in His ways, and to keep His commandments, His statutes, and His judgments, that you may live and multiply; and the LORD your God will bless you in the land which you go to possess. [17]But if your heart turns away so that you do not hear, and are drawn away, and worship other gods and serve them, [18]I announce to you today that you shall surely perish; you shall not prolong *your* days in the land which you cross over the Jordan to go in and possess. [19]I call heaven and earth as witnesses today against you, *that* I have set before you life and death, blessing and cursing; therefore choose life, that both you and your descendants may live; [20]that you may love the LORD your God, that you may obey His voice, and that you may cling to Him, for He *is* your life and the length of your days; and that you may dwell in the land which the LORD swore to your fathers, to Abraham, Isaac, and Jacob, to give them."

Joshua the New Leader of Israel

31 Then Moses went and spoke these words to all Israel. [2]And he said to them: "I *am* one hundred and twenty years old today. I can no longer go out and come in. Also the LORD has said to me, 'You shall not cross over this Jordan.' [3]The LORD your God Himself crosses over before you; He will destroy these nations from before you, and you shall dispossess them. Joshua himself crosses over before you, just as the LORD has said. [4]And the LORD will do to them as He did to Sihon and Og, the kings

of the Amorites and their land, when He destroyed them. [5]The LORD will give them over to you, that you may do to them according to every commandment which I have commanded you. [6]Be strong and of good courage, do not fear nor be afraid of them; for the LORD your God, He *is* the One who goes with you. He will not leave you nor forsake you."

> **31:2 one hundred and twenty years old.** Moses' age at his death. His life is broken down into three parts: 40 years in Egypt (Ex. 2:1–15), 40 years in Midian tending sheep (see Acts 7:30), and 40 years leading Israel out of Egypt and through the wilderness to the Promised Land. **go out and come in.** To do a normal day's work. Moses admitted that he could no longer provide the daily leadership for Israel. Furthermore, God would not allow him to enter the Land over the Jordan because of his sin at the waters of Meribah (see 32:51).

[7]Then Moses called Joshua and said to him in the sight of all Israel, "Be strong and of good courage, for you must go with this people to the land which the LORD has sworn to their fathers to give them, and you shall cause them to inherit it. [8]And the LORD, He *is* the One who goes before you. He will be with you, He will not leave you nor forsake you; do not fear nor be dismayed."

The Law to Be Read Every Seven Years

[9]So Moses wrote this law and delivered it to the priests, the sons of Levi, who bore the ark of the covenant of the LORD, and to all the elders of Israel. [10]And Moses commanded them, saying: "At the end of *every* seven years, at the appointed time in the year of release, at the Feast of Tabernacles, [11]when all Israel comes to appear before the LORD your God in the place which He chooses, you shall read this law before all Israel in their hearing. [12]Gather the people together, men and women and little ones, and the stranger who *is* within your gates, that they may hear and that they may learn to fear the LORD your God and carefully observe all the words of this law, [13]and *that* their children, who have not known it, may hear and learn to fear the LORD your God as long as you live in the land which you cross the Jordan to possess."

Prediction of Israel's Rebellion

[14]Then the LORD said to Moses, "Behold, the days approach when you must die; call Joshua, and present yourselves in the tabernacle of meeting, that I may inaugurate him."

So Moses and Joshua went and presented themselves in the tabernacle of meeting. [15]Now the LORD appeared at the tabernacle in a pillar of cloud, and the pillar of cloud stood above the door of the tabernacle.

[16]And the LORD said to Moses: "Behold, you will rest with your fathers; and this people will rise and play the harlot with the gods of the foreigners of the land, where they go to be among them, and they will forsake Me and break My covenant which I have made with them. [17]Then My anger shall be aroused against them in that day, and I will forsake them, and I will hide My face from them, and they shall be devoured. And many evils and troubles shall befall them, so that they will say in that day, 'Have not these evils come upon us because our God is not among us?' [18]And I will surely hide My face in that day because of all the evil which they have done, in that they have turned to other gods.

[19]"Now therefore, write down this song for yourselves, and teach it to the children of Israel; put it in their mouths, that this song may be a witness for Me against the children of Israel. [20]When I have brought them to the land flowing with milk and honey, of which I swore to their fathers, and they have eaten and filled themselves and grown fat, then they will turn to other gods and serve them; and they will provoke Me and break My covenant. [21]Then it shall be, when many evils and troubles have come upon them, that this song will testify against them as a witness; for it will not be forgotten in the mouths of their descendants, for I know the inclination of their behavior today, even before I have brought

---

31:16–21 they will forsake Me and break My covenant. After Moses' death, the Lord Himself predicts that in spite of His commands, the Israelites would forsake Him by worshiping other gods. When they would forsake God, He would forsake them, resulting in disaster for them at every turn. This is one of the saddest texts in the OT. After all God had done, He knew they would forsake Him.

---

them to the land of which I swore to give them."

[22]Therefore Moses wrote this song the same day, and taught it to the children of Israel. [23]Then He inaugurated Joshua the son of Nun, and said, "Be strong and of good courage; for you shall bring the children of Israel into the land of which I swore to them, and I will be with you."

[24]So it was, when Moses had completed writing the words of this law in a book, when they were finished, [25]that Moses commanded the Levites, who bore the ark of the covenant of the LORD, saying: [26]"Take this Book of the Law, and put it beside the ark of the covenant of the LORD your God, that it may be there as a witness against you; [27]for I know your rebellion and your stiff neck. If today, while I am yet alive with you, you have been rebellious against the LORD, then how much more after my death? [28]Gather to me all the elders of your tribes, and your officers, that I may speak these words in their hearing and call heaven and earth to witness against them. [29]For I know that after my death you will become utterly corrupt, and turn aside from the way which I have commanded you. And evil will befall you in the latter days, because you will do evil in the sight of the LORD, to provoke Him to anger through the work of your hands."

The Song of Moses

[30]Then Moses spoke in the hearing of all the assembly of Israel the words of this song until they were ended:

32

"Give ear, O heavens, and I will speak;
And hear, O earth, the words of my mouth.
[2] Let my teaching drop as the rain,
My speech distill as the dew,
As raindrops on the tender herb,
And as showers on the grass.
[3] For I proclaim the name of the LORD:
Ascribe greatness to our God.
[4] He is the Rock, His work is perfect;
For all His ways are justice,
A God of truth and without injustice;
Righteous and upright is He.

[5] "They have corrupted themselves;

32:4 the Rock. This image of God as a rock illustrates His stability and permanence. It is one of the principle themes in this song, emphasizing the unchanging nature of God in contrast with the fickle nature of the people.

They are not His children,
Because of their blemish:
A perverse and crooked generation.
6 Do you thus deal with the LORD,
O foolish and unwise people?
Is He not your Father, *who* bought you?
Has He not made you and established you?

7 "Remember the days of old,
Consider the years of many generations.
Ask your father, and he will show you;
Your elders, and they will tell you:
8 When the Most High divided their inheritance to the nations,
When He separated the sons of Adam,
He set the boundaries of the peoples
According to the number of the children of Israel.
9 For the LORD's portion *is* His people;
Jacob *is* the place of His inheritance.

10 "He found him in a desert land
And in the wasteland, a howling wilderness;
He encircled him, He instructed him,
He kept him as the apple of His eye.
11 As an eagle stirs up its nest,
Hovers over its young,
Spreading out its wings, taking them up,

32:11 Hovers over its young. The Lord cared for Israel like an eagle caring for its young. As they learned to fly, they were still weak and would start to fall. At that point, an eagle would rescue them by spreading its wings so they could land on them; so the Lord has carried Israel and not let them fall. He has been training them to fly on His wings of love and power.

Carrying them on its wings,
12 So the LORD alone led him,
And *there was* no foreign god with him.

13 "He made him ride in the heights of the earth,
That he might eat the produce of the fields;
He made him draw honey from the rock,
And oil from the flinty rock;
14 Curds from the cattle, and milk of the flock,
With fat of lambs;
And rams of the breed of Bashan, and goats,
With the choicest wheat;
And you drank wine, the blood of the grapes.

15 "But Jeshurun grew fat and kicked;
You grew fat, you grew thick,
You are obese!
Then he forsook God *who* made him,
And scornfully esteemed the Rock of his salvation.
16 They provoked Him to jealousy with foreign *gods;*
With abominations they provoked Him to anger.
17 They sacrificed to demons, not to God,
To gods they did not know,
To new *gods*, new arrivals
That your fathers did not fear.

32:17 demons. (See Lev. 17:7; 2 Chr. 11:15) Demons are those angels who fell from heaven with Satan and who constitute the evil force that fights against God and His holy angels. Idol worship is a form of demon worship—demons impersonate idols and work through the system of false religion tied to the idols.

18 Of the Rock *who* begot you, you are unmindful,
And have forgotten the God who fathered you.

19 "And when the LORD saw *it*, He spurned *them*,
Because of the provocation of His sons and His daughters.
20 And He said: 'I will hide My face from them,
I will see what their end *will be*,
For they *are* a perverse generation,
Children in whom *is* no faith.
21 They have provoked Me to jealousy by *what* is not God;

They have moved Me to anger by
   their foolish idols.
But I will provoke them to jealousy by
   those who are not a nation;
I will move them to anger by a foolish
   nation.

22 For a fire is kindled in My anger,
   And shall burn to the lowest hell;
   It shall consume the earth with her
      increase,
   And set on fire the foundations of the
      mountains.

23 'I will heap disasters on them;
   I will spend My arrows on them.
24 *They shall be* wasted with hunger,
   Devoured by pestilence and bitter
      destruction;
   I will also send against them the teeth
      of beasts,
   With the poison of serpents of the
      dust.
25 The sword shall destroy outside;
   There shall be terror within
   For the young man and virgin,
   The nursing child with the man of
      gray hairs.
26 I would have said, "I will dash them
      in pieces,
   I will make the memory of them to
      cease from among men,"
27 Had I not feared the wrath of the
      enemy,
   Lest their adversaries should
      misunderstand,
   Lest they should say, "Our hand *is*
      high;
   And it is not the LORD who has done
      all this." '

28 "For they *are* a nation void of counsel,
   Nor *is there any* understanding in
      them.
29 Oh, that they were wise, *that* they
      understood this,
   That they would consider their latter
      end!
30 How could one chase a thousand,
   And two put ten thousand to flight,
   Unless their Rock had sold them,
   And the LORD had surrendered them?
31 For their rock *is* not like our Rock,
   Even our enemies themselves *being*
      judges.

32 For their vine *is* of the vine of Sodom
   And of the fields of Gomorrah;
   Their grapes *are* grapes of gall,
   Their clusters *are* bitter.

32:32 the vine of Sodom. Using the metaphor of a vineyard and its grapes and wine, the wickedness of Israel's enemies was described as having its roots in Sodom and Gomorrah, the evil cities destroyed by God (see Gen. 19:1–29).

33 Their wine *is* the poison of serpents,
   And the cruel venom of cobras.
34 '*Is* this not laid up in store with Me,
   Sealed up among My treasures?
35 Vengeance is Mine, and recompense;
   Their foot shall slip in *due* time;
   For the day of their calamity *is* at
      hand,
   And the things to come hasten upon
      them.'

36 "For the LORD will judge His people
   And have compassion on His servants,
   When He sees that *their* power is
      gone,
   And *there is* no one *remaining*, bond
      or free.
37 He will say: 'Where *are* their gods,
   The rock in which they sought
      refuge?
38 Who ate the fat of their sacrifices,
   And drank the wine of their drink
      offering?
   Let them rise and help you,
   And be your refuge.

39 'Now see that I, *even* I, *am* He,
   And *there is* no God besides Me;
   I kill and I make alive;
   I wound and I heal;
   Nor *is there any* who can deliver from
      My hand.
40 For I raise My hand to heaven,
   And say, "*As* I live forever,
41 If I whet My glittering sword,

32:39 I, *even* I, *am* He. In contrast to the worthlessness of false gods, this declaration of the nature of God was presented to show that He is the living God, the only One who can help and protect them. He has the power of life and death, the power to wound and to heal.

And My hand takes hold on
   judgment,
I will render vengeance to My enemies,
And repay those who hate Me.
[42] I will make My arrows drunk with
   blood,
And My sword shall devour flesh,
With the blood of the slain and the
   captives,
From the heads of the leaders of the
   enemy." '

[43] "Rejoice, O Gentiles, *with* His people; *a*
For He will avenge the blood of His
   servants,
And render vengeance to His
   adversaries;
He will provide atonement for His
   land *and* His people."

[44]So Moses came with Joshua*a* the son of
Nun and spoke all the words of this song in
the hearing of the people. [45]Moses finished
speaking all these words to all Israel, [46]and
he said to them: "Set your hearts on all the
words which I testify among you today,
which you shall command your children to
be careful to observe—all the words of this
law. [47]For it *is* not a futile thing for you, because it *is* your life, and by this word you
shall prolong *your* days in the land which
you cross over the Jordan to possess."

32:47 *it is* your life. Moses emphasized that obedience to God's commands was the key to living long
in the Land. He called for this song to be a kind of
national anthem that the leaders should have the
people frequently repeat to motivate them to love
and obey God.

Moses to Die on Mount Nebo

[48]Then the LORD spoke to Moses that
very same day, saying: [49]"Go up this mountain of the Abarim, Mount Nebo, which *is*
in the land of Moab, across from Jericho;
view the land of Canaan, which I give to the
children of Israel as a possession; [50]and die
on the mountain which you ascend, and be
gathered to your people, just as Aaron your
brother died on Mount Hor and was gathered to his people; [51]because you trespassed
against Me among the children of Israel at

the waters of Meribah Kadesh, in the Wilderness of Zin, because you did not hallow
Me in the midst of the children of Israel.
[52]Yet you shall see the land before *you,*
though you shall not go there, into the land
which I am giving to the children of Israel."

Moses' Final Blessing on Israel

33 Now this *is* the blessing with which
Moses the man of God blessed the
children of Israel before his death. [2]And he
said:

"The LORD came from Sinai,
And dawned on them from Seir;
He shone forth from Mount Paran,
And He came with ten thousands of
   saints;
From His right hand
Came a fiery law for them.
[3] Yes, He loves the people;
All His saints *are* in Your hand;
They sit down at Your feet;
Everyone receives Your words.
[4] Moses commanded a law for us,

33:3 He loves the people. The law was given in kindness and love to provide earthly and eternal blessings to those who obey it (see Rom. 13:8–10).

A heritage of the congregation of Jacob.
[5] And He was King in Jeshurun,
When the leaders of the people were
   gathered,
All the tribes of Israel together.

[6] "Let Reuben live, and not die,
Nor let his men be few."

[7]And this he said of Judah:

"Hear, LORD, the voice of Judah,
And bring him to his people;
Let his hands be sufficient for him,
And may You be a help against his
   enemies."

[8]And of Levi he said:

"*Let* Your Thummim and Your Urim
be with Your holy one,

32:43 *a*A Dead Sea Scroll fragment adds *And let all the gods (angels) worship Him* (compare
Septuagint and Hebrews 1:6). **32:44** *a*Hebrew *Hoshea* (compare Numbers 13:8, 16)

Whom You tested at Massah,
And with whom You contended at the
    waters of Meribah,

9 Who says of his father and mother,
'I have not seen them';
Nor did he acknowledge his brothers,
Or know his own children;
For they have observed Your word
And kept Your covenant.

10 They shall teach Jacob Your judgments,
And Israel Your law.
They shall put incense before You,
And a whole burnt sacrifice on Your
    altar.

11 Bless his substance, LORD,
And accept the work of his hands;
Strike the loins of those who rise
    against him,
And of those who hate him, that they
    rise not again."

12 Of Benjamin he said:

"The beloved of the LORD shall dwell
    in safety by Him,
Who shelters him all the day long;
And he shall dwell between His
    shoulders."

13 And of Joseph he said:

"Blessed of the LORD is his land,
With the precious things of heaven,
    with the dew,
And the deep lying beneath,

14 With the precious fruits of the sun,
With the precious produce of the
    months,

15 With the best things of the ancient
    mountains,
With the precious things of the
    everlasting hills,

16 With the precious things of the earth
    and its fullness,
And the favor of Him who dwelt in
    the bush.
Let the blessing come 'on the head of
    Joseph,
And on the crown of the head of him
    who was separate from his
    brothers.'a

17 His glory is like a firstborn bull,

And his horns like the horns of the
    wild ox;
Together with them
He shall push the peoples
To the ends of the earth;
They are the ten thousands of
    Ephraim,
And they are the thousands of
    Manasseh."

33:13–17 Joseph. This included both Ephraim and Manasseh, who would be blessed with material prosperity and military might, to compensate them for the Egyptian slavery of their father Joseph. Ephraim would have greater military success than Manasseh, fulfilling Jacob's blessing of the younger over the older (see Gen. 48:20).

18 And of Zebulun he said:

"Rejoice, Zebulun, in your going out,
And Issachar in your tents!

19 They shall call the peoples to the
    mountain;
There they shall offer sacrifices of
    righteousness;
For they shall partake of the
    abundance of the seas
And of treasures hidden in the sand."

20 And of Gad he said:

"Blessed is he who enlarges Gad;
He dwells as a lion,
And tears the arm and the crown of
    his head.

21 He provided the first part for himself,
Because a lawgiver's portion was
    reserved there.
He came with the heads of the people;
He administered the justice of the
    LORD,
And His judgments with Israel."

22 And of Dan he said:

"Dan is a lion's whelp;
He shall leap from Bashan."

23 And of Naphtali he said:

"O Naphtali, satisfied with favor,

33:16 aGenesis 49:26

And full of the blessing of the LORD,
Possess the west and the south."

[24]And of Asher he said:

"Asher *is* most blessed of sons;
Let him be favored by his brothers,
And let him dip his foot in oil.

[25]   Your sandals *shall be* iron and bronze;
     As your days, *so shall* your strength *be.*

[26]   "*There is* no one like the God of
          Jeshurun,
     Who rides the heavens to help you,
     And in His excellency on the clouds.
[27]   The eternal God *is your* refuge,
     And underneath *are* the everlasting
          arms;
     He will thrust out the enemy from
          before you,
     And will say, 'Destroy!'
[28]   Then Israel shall dwell in safety,
     The fountain of Jacob alone,
     In a land of grain and new wine;
     His heavens shall also drop dew.
[29]   Happy *are* you, O Israel!
     Who *is* like you, a people saved by the
          LORD,
     The shield of your help
     And the sword of your majesty!
     Your enemies shall submit to you,
     And you shall tread down their high
          places."

Moses Dies on Mount Nebo

34 Then Moses went up from the plains of Moab to Mount Nebo, to the top of Pisgah, which is across from Jericho. And the LORD showed him all the land of Gilead as far as Dan, [2]all Naphtali and the land of Ephraim and Manasseh, all the land of Judah as far as the Western Sea,[a] [3]the South, and the plain of the Valley of Jericho, the city of palm trees, as far as Zoar. [4]Then the LORD said to him, "This *is* the land of which I swore to give Abraham, Isaac, and Jacob, saying, 'I will give it to your descendants.' I have caused you to see *it* with your eyes, but you shall not cross over there."

[5]So Moses the servant of the LORD died there in the land of Moab, according to the word of the LORD. [6]And He buried him in a valley in the land of Moab, opposite Beth Peor; but no one knows his grave to this day. [7]Moses *was* one hundred and twenty years old when he died. His eyes were not dim nor his natural vigor diminished. [8]And the children of Israel wept for Moses in the plains of Moab thirty days. So the days of weeping *and* mourning for Moses ended.

[9]Now Joshua the son of Nun was full of the spirit of wisdom, for Moses had laid his hands on him; so the children of Israel heeded him, and did as the LORD had commanded Moses.

[10]But since then there has not arisen in Israel a prophet like Moses, whom the LORD knew face to face, [11]in all the signs and wonders which the LORD sent him to do in the land of Egypt, before Pharaoh, before all his servants, and in all his land, [12]and by all that mighty power and all the great terror which Moses performed in the sight of all Israel.

34:2 [a]That is, the Mediterranean

JOSHUA

Yes, Joshua fought the battle of Jericho when the walls came tumbling down. That famous victory, the first in the conquest of the Promised Land, marks the early days of Joshua's leadership of Israel. After Moses died, Joshua was confirmed as Moses' successor, Israel's leader. Now, with the wilderness and the Jordan River behind them, the people face a hopeful future following Joshua and obeying God.

This book heads the list of twelve historical books in the Old Testament. The meaning of Joshua's name matches the significance of his role. "Joshua" means "Jehovah saves" or "the LORD is salvation" and is an earlier form of the New Testament name "Jesus."

AUTHOR AND DATE

Joshua was written by Joshua, approximately 1405 to 1385 B.C.

Although the book does not name its author, the most probable candidate is Joshua, the key eyewitness to the events recorded (18:9; 24:26). A trusted assistant may have attached such comments as the details of Joshua's death (24:29–33).

Details such as the mention of Rahab still being alive at the time of writing (6:25) indicate an early date for this book. Other internal clues, such as the continuing presence of the Jebusites in Jerusalem (15:63) place the completion date before the reign of David (2 Samuel 5:5–9). The likely writing period is about 1405—1385 B.C.

Born as a slave in Egypt, Joshua trained under Moses, and by God's choice he rose to lead Israel into the Promised Land. The following list represents outstanding features of Joshua's character and life: (1) serving (Exodus 17:10; 24:13); (2) soldiering (Exodus 17:9–13); (3) scouting (Numbers 13:1–14:38); (4) chosen by God (Numbers 27:18–21); (5) led by the Spirit (Numbers 27:18; Deuteronomy 34:9); (6) commissioned by Moses (Numbers 27:18–23; Deuteronomy 31:7,8, 13-15); (7) following the Lord selflessly (Joshua 24:15; Numbers 32:12).

BACKGROUND AND SETTING

When Joshua replaced Moses as leader (Deuteronomy 34), the children of Israel had reached the end of their 40 year wilderness wandering. At that time, Joshua was nearly 90 years old. He eventually died at 110 years of age (24:29), having led Israel in driving out most of the Canaanites and having divided the Land among the 12 tribes.

As the Book of Joshua opens, the nation of Israel is camped on the east side of the Jordan River, awaiting God's instructions. Across the river lived nations so devoted to sinfulness that God would cause the land, so to speak, to "vomit out" these inhabitants (Leviticus 18:25). God would give Israel the Land by conquest, primarily to fulfill the covenant He had made with Abraham and his descendants. Through this invasion, God also would pass judgment on the sinful inhabitants (Genesis 15:16). Some of them had possessed part of the Land since before Abraham's time (Genesis 10:15–19; 12:6; 13:7). Their persistent moral decline and pagan worship led to God's response. They lost their land.

HISTORICAL AND THEOLOGICAL THEMES

In this book, the Promised Land becomes the possession of Israel. God demonstrates His faithfulness by fulfilling His promise to give the land to Abraham's descendants (Genesis 12:7; 15:18–21; 17:8). The word "possess" appears nearly 20 times in the 24 chapters.

Alongside the record of divinely arranged victories lay tragic accounts of sin induced failures and defeats. Israel did not conquer every part of the Land (Joshua 13:1). The Book of Judges describes the sad results from this sin.

> GOD DEMONSTRATES HIS FAITHFULNESS BY FULFILLING HIS PROMISE TO GIVE THE LAND TO ABRAHAM'S DESCENDANTS.

This book features several key themes: (1) Possession of the Land results from God's promise and His help (1:3,6; 5:14–6:2); (2) Knowing and meditating on God's law results in success (1:8); (3) Although Israel conquered the Land as a whole, many local areas remained under pagan control (11:23; 21:45; 22:4).

OUTLINE

God's Commission to Joshua

1 After the death of Moses the servant of the LORD, it came to pass that the LORD spoke to Joshua the son of Nun, Moses' assistant, saying: ²"Moses My servant is dead. Now therefore, arise, go over this Jordan, you and all this people, to the land which I am giving to them—the children of Israel. ³Every place that the sole of your foot will tread upon I have given you, as I said to Moses. ⁴From the wilderness and this Lebanon as far as the great river, the River Euphrates, all the land of the Hittites, and to the Great Sea toward the going down of the sun, shall be your territory. ⁵No man shall *be able to* stand before you all the days of your life; as I was with Moses, *so* I will be with you. I will not leave you nor forsake you. ⁶Be strong and of good courage, for to this people you shall divide as an inheritance the land which I swore to their fathers to give them. ⁷Only be strong and very courageous, that you may observe to do according to all the law which Moses My servant

---

How can we justify the harsh commands of God to utterly destroy cities and peoples in the conquest of the Promised Land with the character of God as revealed in the rest of Scripture?

When Joshua issued orders for the destruction of Jericho, he was echoing God's very clear commands. Passages like Exodus 23:32,33; 34:11–16; Deuteronomy 7:1–5; 20:16–18 make it impossible to soften or avoid the truth that God ordered the destruction of entire populations. Those were not just soldiers killing soldiers—many of the victims were women and children. The challenge for serious and humble Bible students is to face these horrors and the hard lessons they teach without trying to explain them away.

If we do not have a growing awe about the holiness of God and His righteous judgment of sin, our understanding of God's grace and mercy will fade away. Without an acknowledgment that God can and does punish, the possibility of mercy and forgiveness carries little weight. If we do not seek to see the entire scope of God's actions and character, we will tend to gravitate to what we like or don't like and miss the connections. The gaps in our understanding can be partly filled by the following biblical insights.

<u>God warns and waits, sometimes for a very long time.</u> Genesis 15:13–16 explains part of the reason that Abraham's descendants endured slavery in Egypt for over 400 years: " . . . the iniquity of the Amorites is not yet complete." God gave the people of Canaan generations of time. They chose not to repent and, instead, piled up iniquity. In God's time, He carried out the threat in His warning.

<u>Even when judgment has been passed, God does not overlook opportunities for mercy</u>. Abraham discovered that God was willing to spare Sodom and Gomorrah for the sake of ten righteous men. In the end, God removed Lot and obliterated the cities. And Rahab was saved by faith from a city destined for destruction.

<u>The people of Israel's role in applying God's judgment had nothing to do with their own righteousness</u>. But for God's grace, they would easily be in the place of the condemned. "Do not think in your heart, after the LORD your God has cast them out before you, saying, 'Because of my righteousness the LORD has brought me in to possess this land'; but it is because of the wickedness of these nations that the LORD is driving them out from before you" (Deuteronomy 9:4).

<u>God could have used sickness, famine, fire, or flood to clear out the Land, but He chose to use the people of Israel</u>. In terrible natural disasters, everyone suffers. It isn't easy to accept that little children share the fate of their parents. But they do. And they did as Israel carried out God's judgments. Did God unfairly include these children in punishment or do the parents and leaders bear added responsibility for putting the innocent in harm's way by their rejection of God? Some of these issues will have to be settled beyond death. That's when the final judgment happens anyway (Hebrews 9:27).

commanded you; do not turn from it to the right hand or to the left, that you may prosper wherever you go. [8]This Book of the Law shall not depart from your mouth, but you shall meditate in it day and night, that you may observe to do according to all that is written in it. For then you will make your way prosperous, and then you will have good success. [9]Have I not commanded you? Be strong and of good courage; do not be afraid, nor be dismayed, for the LORD your God *is* with you wherever you go."

The Order to Cross the Jordan

[10]Then Joshua commanded the officers of the people, saying, [11]"Pass through the camp and command the people, saying, 'Prepare provisions for yourselves, for within three days you will cross over this Jordan, to go in to possess the land which the LORD your God is giving you to possess.' "

> **1:12 half the tribe of Manasseh.** In Genesis 48, Jacob blessed both the sons of Joseph, Ephraim and Manasseh, so that Joseph actually received a double blessing (see Gen. 48:22). Thus the Land was divided into 12 allotments, since the tribe of Levi was excluded because of their priestly function.

[12]And to the Reubenites, the Gadites, and half the tribe of Manasseh Joshua spoke, saying, [13]"Remember the word which Mo-

ses the servant of the LORD commanded you, saying, 'The LORD your God is giving you rest and is giving you this land.' [14]Your wives, your little ones, and your livestock shall remain in the land which Moses gave you on this side of the Jordan. But you shall pass before your brethren armed, all your mighty men of valor, and help them, [15]until the LORD has given your brethren rest, as He *gave* you, and they also have taken possession of the land which the LORD your God is giving them. Then you shall return to the land of your possession and enjoy it, which Moses the LORD's servant gave you on this side of the Jordan toward the sunrise."

[16]So they answered Joshua, saying, "All that you command us we will do, and wherever you send us we will go. [17]Just as we heeded Moses in all things, so we will heed you. Only the LORD your God be with you, as He was with Moses. [18]Whoever rebels against your command and does not heed your words, in all that you command him, shall be put to death. Only be strong and of good courage."

Rahab Hides the Spies

2 Now Joshua the son of Nun sent out two men from Acacia Grove[a] to spy secretly, saying, "Go, view the land, especially Jericho."

2:1 [a]Hebrew *Shittim*

JOSHUA'S PREPARATION FOR MINISTRY

1.	Exodus 17:9,10,13–14	Joshua led the victorious battle against the Amalekites.
2.	Exodus 24:13	Joshua, the servant of Moses, accompanied the Jewish leader to the mountain of God (see 32:17).
3.	Numbers 11:28	Joshua was the attendant of Moses from his youth.
4.	Numbers 13:16	Moses changed his name from Hosea ("salvation") to Joshua ("the LORD saves").
5.	Numbers 14:6–10,30,38	Joshua, along with Caleb, spied out the land of Canaan with 10 others. Only Joshua and Caleb urged the nation to possess the land and, thus, only they of the 12 actually entered Canaan.
6.	Numbers 27:18	Joshua was indwelt by the Holy Spirit.
7.	Numbers 27:18–23	Joshua was commissioned for spiritual service the first time, to assist Moses.
8.	Numbers 32:12	Joshua followed the Lord fully.
9.	Deuteronomy 31:23	Joshua was commissioned a second time, to replace Moses.
10.	Deuteronomy 34:9	Joshua was filled with the spirit of wisdom.

2:1 house of a harlot. The spies did not have impure purposes but simply sought an inconspicuous place to hide. Rahab's house was a good cover, a house on the city wall from which they could have a quick getaway (v. 15). In His sovereignty, God planned for the salvation of the harlot, a woman at the bottom of the social ladder, because of her faith, just as he saved Abraham, a rich man. Most importantly, by God's grace Rahab was in the Messianic line (Matt. 1:5).

So they went, and came to the house of a harlot named Rahab, and lodged there. ²And it was told the king of Jericho, saying, "Behold, men have come here tonight from the children of Israel to search out the country."

³So the king of Jericho sent to Rahab, saying, "Bring out the men who have come to you, who have entered your house, for they have come to search out all the country."

⁴Then the woman took the two men and hid them. So she said, "Yes, the men came to me, but I did not know where they *were* from. ⁵And it happened as the gate was being shut, when it was dark, that the men went out. Where the men went I do not know; pursue them quickly, for you may overtake them." ⁶(But she had brought them up to the roof and hidden them with the stalks of flax, which she had laid in order on the roof.) ⁷Then the men pursued them by the road to the Jordan, to the fords. And as soon as those who pursued them had gone out, they shut the gate.

2:4,5 Lying is still sin to God (Ex. 20:16), for He cannot lie. God commended her faith (Heb. 11:31), not her lie. He never condones sin. Yet no one is without sin, and He honors true faith with His saving grace.

⁸Now before they lay down, she came up to them on the roof, ⁹and said to the men: "I know that the LORD has given you the land, that the terror of you has fallen on us, and that all the inhabitants of the land are fainthearted because of you. ¹⁰For we have heard how the LORD dried up the water of the Red Sea for you when you came out of Egypt, and what you did to the two kings of the Amorites who *were* on the other side of the Jordan, Sihon and Og, whom you utterly destroyed. ¹¹And as soon as we heard *these things*, our hearts melted; neither did there remain any more courage in anyone

because of you, for the LORD your God, He *is* God in heaven above and on earth beneath. ¹²Now therefore, I beg you, swear to me by the LORD, since I have shown you kindness, that you also will show kindness to my father's house, and give me a true token, ¹³and spare my father, my mother, my brothers, my sisters, and all that they have, and deliver our lives from death."

¹⁴So the men answered her, "Our lives for yours, if none of you tell this business of ours. And it shall be, when the LORD has given us the land, that we will deal kindly and truly with you."

¹⁵Then she let them down by a rope through the window, for her house *was* on the city wall; she dwelt on the wall. ¹⁶And she said to them, "Get to the mountain, lest the pursuers meet you. Hide there three days, until the pursuers have returned. Afterward you may go your way."

¹⁷So the men said to her: "We *will be* blameless of this oath of yours which you have made us swear, ¹⁸unless, *when* we come into the land, you bind this line of scarlet cord in the window through which you let us down, and unless you bring your father, your mother, your brothers, and all your father's household to your own home. ¹⁹So it shall be *that* whoever goes outside the doors of your house into the street, his blood *shall be* on his own head, and we *will be* guiltless. And whoever is with you in the house, his blood *shall be* on our head if a hand is laid on him. ²⁰And if you tell this business of ours, then we will be free from your oath which you made us swear."

2:18 cord. Scarlet is a striking color to mark the house for protection, much more visible than a drab green, brown, or gray. The color was also appropriate for those whose blood (v. 19) was under God's pledge of safety.

²¹Then she said, "According to your words, so *be it*." And she sent them away, and they departed. And she bound the scarlet cord in the window.

²²They departed and went to the mountain, and stayed there three days until the pursuers returned. The pursuers sought *them* all along the way, but did not find *them*. ²³So the two men returned, descended from the mountain, and crossed over;

and they came to Joshua the son of Nun, and told him all that had befallen them. [24]And they said to Joshua, "Truly the LORD has delivered all the land into our hands, for indeed all the inhabitants of the country are fainthearted because of us."

Israel Crosses the Jordan

3 Then Joshua rose early in the morning; and they set out from Acacia Grove[a] and came to the Jordan, he and all the children of Israel, and lodged there before they crossed over. [2]So it was, after three days, that the officers went through the camp; [3]and they commanded the people, saying, "When you see the ark of the covenant of the LORD your God, and the priests, the Levites, bearing it, then you shall set out from your place and go after it. [4]Yet there shall be a space between you and it, about

> **3:3 the ark.** The ark symbolized God's presence leading His people. Customarily, the Kohathites carried the ark (Num. 4:15) but in this unusual case the Levitical priests transported it.

3:1 [a]Hebrew *Shittim*

THE PEOPLES AROUND THE PROMISED LAND

(see Exodus 34:10–17; Deuteronomy 20:17; Joshua 3:10; 9:1; 24:11)

1.	AMALEKITES	The descendants of Amalek, the firstborn of Esau (Genesis 36:12), who dwelt south of Palestine in the Negev.
2.	AMMONITES	The descendants of Ammon, the grandson of Lot by his youngest daughter (Genesis 19:38), who lived east of the Jordan River and north of Moab.
3.	AMORITES	A general term for the inhabitants of the Land, but especially for the descendants of Canaan who inhabited the hill country on both sides of the Jordan.
4.	CANAANITES	Broadly speaking, these are the descendants of Canaan, son of Ham, son of Noah (see Genesis 10:15–18), and included many of the other groups named here.
5.	EDOMITES	The descendants of Esau who settled southeast of Palestine (see Genesis 25:30) in the land of Seir.
6.	GEBALITES	People of the ancient seaport later known as Byblos, about 20 miles north of modern Beirut (Joshua 13:5).
7.	GESHURITES	The inhabitants of Geshur, east of the Jordan and to the south of Syria (Joshua 12:5).
8.	GIBEONITES	The inhabitants of Gibeon and surrounding area (Joshua 9:17).
9.	GIRGASHITES	A tribe descended from Canaan, which was included among the general population of the Land without specific geographical identity.
10.	GIRZITES	An obscure group which lived in the northwest part of the Negev, before they were destroyed by David (1 Samuel 27:8,9).
11.	HITTITES	Immigrants from the Hittite Empire (in the region of Syria) to the central region of the Land (see Genesis 23:10; 2 Samuel 11:3).
12.	HIVITES	Descendants of Canaan who lived in the northern reaches of the Land.
13.	HORITES	Ancient residents of Edom from an unknown origin who were destroyed by Esau's descendants (Deuteronomy 2:22).
14.	JEBUSITES	Descendants of Canaan who dwelt in the hill country around Jerusalem (see Genesis 15:21; Exodus 3:8).
15.	KENITES	A Midianite tribe that originally dwelt in the Gulf of Aqabah region (1 Samuel 27:10).
16.	MOABITES	The descendants of Moab, the grandson of Lot by his eldest daughter (Genesis 19:37), who lived east of the Dead Sea.
17.	PERIZZITES	People included among the general population of the Land who do not trace their lineage to Canaan. Their exact identity is uncertain.

two thousand cubits by measure. Do not come near it, that you may know the way by which you must go, for you have not passed *this* way before."

⁵And Joshua said to the people, "Sanctify yourselves, for tomorrow the LORD will do wonders among you." ⁶Then Joshua spoke to the priests, saying, "Take up the ark of the covenant and cross over before the people."

So they took up the ark of the covenant and went before the people.

⁷And the LORD said to Joshua, "This day I will begin to exalt you in the sight of all Israel, that they may know that, as I was with Moses, *so* I will be with you. ⁸You shall command the priests who bear the ark of the covenant, saying, 'When you have come to the edge of the water of the Jordan, you shall stand in the Jordan.' "

⁹So Joshua said to the children of Israel, "Come here, and hear the words of the LORD your God." ¹⁰And Joshua said, "By this you shall know that the living God *is* among you, and *that* He will without fail drive out from before you the Canaanites and the Hittites and the Hivites and the Perizzites and the Girgashites and the Amorites and the Jebusites: ¹¹Behold, the ark of the covenant of the Lord of all the earth is crossing over before you into the Jordan. ¹²Now therefore, take for yourselves twelve men from the tribes of Israel, one man from every tribe. ¹³And it shall come to pass, as soon as the soles of the feet of the priests who bear the ark of the LORD, the Lord of all the earth, shall rest in the waters of the Jordan, *that* the waters of the Jordan shall be cut off, the waters that come down from upstream, and they shall stand as a heap."

3:10 The Canaanite people who were to be killed were extremely sinful (see Gen. 15:16). As the righteous Judge, God has the right to punish people at any time He deems appropriate for His purposes, as He will at the end (Rev. 20:11–15). The question is not why He chose to destroy these sinners, but why He does not destroy all sinners sooner. Only by grace are we allowed to draw one more breath of life (see Gen. 2:17; Ezek 18:20; Rom. 6:23).

¹⁴So it was, when the people set out from their camp to cross over the Jordan, with the priests bearing the ark of the covenant before the people, ¹⁵and as those who bore the ark came to the Jordan, and the feet of the priests who bore the ark dipped in the edge of the water (for the Jordan overflows all its banks during the whole time of harvest), ¹⁶that the waters which came down from upstream stood *still, and* rose in a heap very far away at Adam, the city that *is* beside Zaretan. So the waters that went down into the Sea of the Arabah, the Salt Sea, failed, *and* were cut off; and the people crossed over opposite Jericho. ¹⁷Then the priests who bore the ark of the covenant of the LORD stood firm on dry ground in the midst of the Jordan; and all Israel crossed over on dry ground, until all the people had crossed completely over the Jordan.

3:16 rose in a heap. God worked a dazzling miracle here. He dammed the waters up at Adam, a city 15 miles north of the crossing, and also in tributary creeks. After all the people had walked to the other side on dry ground, God permitted the waters to flow again. Just as the Exodus had begun with the crossing of the Red Sea on dry ground (see Ex. 14), so it ended with another miraculous crossing.

The Memorial Stones

4 And it came to pass, when all the people had completely crossed over the Jordan, that the LORD spoke to Joshua, saying: ²"Take for yourselves twelve men from the people, one man from every tribe, ³and command them, saying, 'Take for yourselves twelve stones from here, out of the midst of the Jordan, from the place where the priests' feet stood firm. You shall carry them over with you and leave them in the lodging place where you lodge tonight.' "

⁴Then Joshua called the twelve men whom he had appointed from the children of Israel, one man from every tribe; ⁵and Joshua said to them: "Cross over before the ark of the LORD your God into the midst of the Jordan, and each one of you take up a stone on his shoulder, according to the number of the tribes of the children of Israel, ⁶that this may be a sign among you when your children ask in time to come, saying, 'What do these stones *mean* to you?' ⁷Then you shall answer them that the waters of the Jordan were cut off before the ark of the covenant of the LORD; when it

crossed over the Jordan, the waters of the Jordan were cut off. And these stones shall be for a memorial to the children of Israel forever."

⁸And the children of Israel did so, just as Joshua commanded, and took up twelve stones from the midst of the Jordan, as the LORD had spoken to Joshua, according to the number of the tribes of the children of Israel, and carried them over with them to the place where they lodged, and laid them down there. ⁹Then Joshua set up twelve stones in the midst of the Jordan, in the place where the feet of the priests who bore the ark of the covenant stood; and they are there to this day.

4:1–8 The twelve stones chosen from the riverbed became a memorial to God's faithfulness, set up at Gilgal, their first campsite in the invaded land. Joshua also placed twelve stones in the riverbed itself to commemorate the place that God miraculously dried up (vv. 9–11, 21–24).

¹⁰So the priests who bore the ark stood in the midst of the Jordan until everything was finished that the LORD had commanded Joshua to speak to the people, according to all that Moses had commanded Joshua; and the people hurried and crossed over. ¹¹Then it came to pass, when all the people had completely crossed over, that the ark of the LORD and the priests crossed over in the presence of the people. ¹²And the men of Reuben, the men of Gad, and half the tribe of Manasseh crossed over armed before the children of Israel, as Moses had spoken to them. ¹³About forty thousand prepared for war crossed over before the LORD for battle, to the plains of Jericho. ¹⁴On that day the LORD exalted Joshua in the sight of all Israel; and they feared him, as they had feared Moses, all the days of his life.

¹⁵Then the LORD spoke to Joshua, saying, ¹⁶"Command the priests who bear the ark of the Testimony to come up from the Jordan." ¹⁷Joshua therefore commanded the priests, saying, "Come up from the Jordan." ¹⁸And it came to pass, when the priests bore the ark of the covenant of the LORD

had come from the midst of the Jordan, *and* the soles of the priests' feet touched the dry land, that the waters of the Jordan returned to their place and overflowed all its banks as before.

¹⁹Now the people came up from the Jordan on the tenth *day* of the first month, and they camped in Gilgal on the east border of Jericho. ²⁰And those twelve stones which they took out of the Jordan, Joshua set up in Gilgal. ²¹Then he spoke to the children of Israel, saying: "When your children ask their fathers in time to come, saying, 'What *are* these stones?' ²²then you shall let your children know, saying, 'Israel crossed over this Jordan on dry land'; ²³for the LORD your God dried up the waters of the Jordan before you until you had crossed over, as the LORD your God did to the Red Sea, which He dried up before us until we had crossed over, ²⁴that all the peoples of the earth may know the hand of the LORD, that it *is* mighty, that you may fear the LORD your God forever."

The Second Generation Circumcised

5 So it was, when all the kings of the Amorites who *were* on the west side of the Jordan, and all the kings of the Canaanites who *were* by the sea, heard that the LORD had dried up the waters of the Jordan from before the children of Israel until we[a] had crossed over, that their heart melted; and there was no spirit in them any longer because of the children of Israel.

5:1 heard. Reports of God's miraculously drying up the crossing in the Jordan struck fear into the Canaanites. This miracle was even more incredible since He performed it when the Jordan was swollen to flood level (3:15). To the Canaanites, this miracle powerfully proved that God is mighty and enforced their fear from reports about the Red Sea miracle (2:10).

²At that time the LORD said to Joshua, "Make flint knives for yourself, and circumcise the sons of Israel again the second time." ³So Joshua made flint knives for himself, and circumcised the sons of Israel at the hill of the foreskins.[a] ⁴And this *is* the

5:1 [a]Following Kethib; Qere, some Hebrew manuscripts and editions, Septuagint, Syriac, Targum, and Vulgate read *they.* **5:3** [a]Hebrew *Gibeath Haaraloth*

reason why Joshua circumcised them: All the people who came out of Egypt *who were* males, all the men of war, had died in the wilderness on the way, after they had come out of Egypt. ⁵For all the people who came out had been circumcised, but all the people born in the wilderness, on the way as they came out of Egypt, had not been circumcised. ⁶For the children of Israel walked forty years in the wilderness, till all the people *who were* men of war, who came out of Egypt, were consumed, because they did not obey the voice of the LORD—to whom the LORD swore that He would not show them the land which the LORD had sworn to their fathers that He would give us, "a land flowing with milk and honey."ᵃ ⁷Then Joshua circumcised their sons *whom* He raised up in their place; for they were uncircumcised, because they had not been circumcised on the way.

⁸So it was, when they had finished circumcising all the people, that they stayed in their places in the camp till they were healed. ⁹Then the LORD said to Joshua, "This day I have rolled away the reproach of Egypt from you." Therefore the name of the place is called Gilgalᵃ to this day.

¹⁰Now the children of Israel camped in Gilgal, and kept the Passover on the fourteenth day of the month at twilight on the plains of Jericho. ¹¹And they ate of the produce of the land on the day after the Passover, unleavened bread and parched grain, on the very same day. ¹²Then the manna ceased on the day after they had eaten the produce of the land; and the children of Israel no longer had manna, but they ate the food of the land of Canaan that year.

> **5:13–15** The Commander was the Lord Jesus Christ in a pre-incarnate appearance. He came as the Angel (Messenger) of the Lord, as if He were a man (see Gen. 18, one of three "angels"). Joshua fell in reverent worship. The Commander's drawn sword showed that He would give Israel victory over the Canaanites (see 6:2; 1:3).

The Commander of the Army of the LORD

¹³And it came to pass, when Joshua was by Jericho, that he lifted his eyes and looked, and behold, a Man stood opposite him with His sword drawn in His hand. And Joshua went to Him and said to Him, "*Are* You for us or for our adversaries?"

¹⁴So He said, "No, but *as* Commander of the army of the LORD I have now come."

And Joshua fell on his face to the earth and worshiped, and said to Him, "What does my Lord say to His servant?"

¹⁵Then the Commander of the LORD's army said to Joshua, "Take your sandal off your foot, for the place where you stand *is* holy." And Joshua did so.

The Destruction of Jericho

6 Now Jericho was securely shut up because of the children of Israel; none went out, and none came in. ²And the LORD said to Joshua: "See! I have given Jericho into your hand, its king, *and* the mighty men of valor. ³You shall march around the city, all *you* men of war; you shall go all around the city once. This you shall do six days. ⁴And seven priests shall bear seven trumpets of rams' horns before the ark. But the seventh day you shall march around the city seven times, and the priests shall blow the trumpets. ⁵It shall come to pass, when they make a long *blast* with the ram's horn, *and* when you hear the sound of the trumpet, that all the people shall shout with a great shout; then the wall of the city will fall down flat. And the people shall go up every man straight before him."

> **6:1 Jericho.** The city was fortified by a double ring of walls, the outer wall 6 feet thick and the inner 12. Timbers were laid across these to support houses on the walls. Since Jericho was built on a hill, the Israelites had to approach up a steep incline, which was a great disadvantage. An attacking army would typically use a siege of several months to force surrender through starvation.

⁶Then Joshua the son of Nun called the priests and said to them, "Take up the ark of the covenant, and let seven priests bear seven trumpets of rams' horns before the ark of the LORD." ⁷And he said to the people, "Proceed, and march around the city, and let him who is armed advance before the ark of the LORD."

5:6 ᵃExodus 3:8   5:9 ᵃLiterally *Rolling*

[8]So it was, when Joshua had spoken to the people, that the seven priests bearing the seven trumpets of rams' horns before the LORD advanced and blew the trumpets, and the ark of the covenant of the LORD followed them. [9]The armed men went before the priests who blew the trumpets, and the rear guard came after the ark, while *the priests* continued blowing the trumpets. [10]Now Joshua had commanded the people, saying, "You shall not shout or make any noise with your voice, nor shall a word proceed out of your mouth, until the day I say to you, 'Shout!' Then you shall shout." [11]So he had the ark of the LORD circle the city, going around *it* once. Then they came into the camp and lodged in the camp.

[12]And Joshua rose early in the morning, and the priests took up the ark of the LORD. [13]Then seven priests bearing seven trumpets of rams' horns before the ark of the LORD went on continually and blew with the trumpets. And the armed men went before them. But the rear guard came after the ark of the LORD, while *the priests* continued blowing the trumpets. [14]And the second day they marched around the city once and returned to the camp. So they did six days.

[15]But it came to pass on the seventh day that they rose early, about the dawning of the day, and marched around the city seven times in the same manner. On that day only they marched around the city seven times. [16]And the seventh time it happened, when the priests blew the trumpets, that Joshua said to the people: "Shout, for the LORD has given you the city! [17]Now the city shall be doomed by the LORD to destruction, it and all who *are* in it. Only Rahab the harlot shall live, she and all who *are* with her in the house, because she hid the messengers that we sent. [18]And you, by all means abstain from the accursed things, lest you become accursed when you take of the accursed things, and make the camp of Israel a curse, and trouble it. [19]But all the silver and gold, and vessels of bronze and iron, *are* consecrated to the LORD; they shall come into the treasury of the LORD."

[20]So the people shouted when *the priests* blew the trumpets. And it happened when the people heard the sound of the trumpet, and the people shouted with a great shout, that the wall fell down flat. Then the people went up into the city, every man straight before him, and they took the city. [21]And they utterly destroyed all that *was* in the city, both man and woman, young and old, ox and sheep and donkey, with the edge of the sword.

[22]But Joshua had said to the two men

Why did God bless Rahab and give her a unique role in history in spite of her lie?

Rahab's life was not spared because of her lie; it was spared because she put her faith in God. Rahab was given a gracious opportunity to side with God by protecting the two Israelite spies, and she acted within her circumstances. She lied daringly and elaborately. Perhaps her initial response was simply a habit of her profession. From the perspective of the king of Jericho, Rahab would have been guilty of treason, not just lying. She had a new allegiance, and she didn't yet know that the God she now wanted to trust had a rule about lying.

While those around her feared what the God of Israel might do, Rahab feared enough to boldly trust Him as the one true God, " . . . for the LORD your God, He is God in heaven above and on earth beneath" (2:11b). She understood that God wasn't a local or a national god. She knew enough to act.

The spies were impressed and indebted. When Rahab asked them for protection, they recognized their obligation. They were exact in promising to preserve the lives of those in her house, indicated by the scarlet cord from the window.

The radical change that came into Rahab's life when those spies knocked on her door can be seen in several ways. She risked her life to trust God. The book of Ruth also reveals that Rahab married and became the great, great-grandmother of King David and one of the ancestors of Jesus. Centuries later, Rahab was one of the women listed in Hebrews 11 because of her faith.

6:3–21 The bizarre military strategy of marching around Jericho forced the Israelites to take God at His promise and also made the defenders uneasy. Seven is often God's number signifying completeness (see 2 Kin. 5:10,14).

who had spied out the country, "Go into the harlot's house, and from there bring out the woman and all that she has, as you swore to her." ²³And the young men who had been spies went in and brought out Rahab, her father, her mother, her brothers, and all that she had. So they brought out all her relatives and left them outside the camp of Israel. ²⁴But they burned the city and all that *was* in it with fire. Only the silver and gold, and the vessels of bronze and iron, they put into the treasury of the house of the LORD. ²⁵And Joshua spared Rahab the harlot, her father's household, and all that she had. So she dwells in Israel to this day, because she hid the messengers whom Joshua sent to spy out Jericho.

²⁶Then Joshua charged *them* at that time, saying, "Cursed *be* the man before the LORD who rises up and builds this city Jericho; he shall lay its foundation with his firstborn, and with his youngest he shall set up its gates."

²⁷So the LORD was with Joshua, and his fame spread throughout all the country.

Defeat at Ai

7 But the children of Israel committed a trespass regarding the accursed things, for Achan the son of Carmi, the son of Zabdi,ᵃ the son of Zerah, of the tribe of Judah, took of the accursed things; so the anger of the LORD burned against the children of Israel.

²Now Joshua sent men from Jericho to Ai, which *is* beside Beth Aven, on the east side of Bethel, and spoke to them, saying, "Go up and spy out the country." So the men went up and spied out Ai. ³And they returned to Joshua and said to him, "Do not let all the people go up, but let about two or three thousand men go up and attack Ai. Do not weary all the people there, for *the people of Ai are* few." ⁴So about three thousand men went up there from the people, but they fled before the men of Ai.

⁵And the men of Ai struck down about thirty-six men, for they chased them *from* before the gate as far as Shebarim, and struck them down on the descent; therefore the hearts of the people melted and became like water.

⁶Then Joshua tore his clothes, and fell to the earth on his face before the ark of the LORD until evening, he and the elders of Israel; and they put dust on their heads. ⁷And Joshua said, "Alas, Lord GOD, why have You brought this people over the Jordan at all—to deliver us into the hand of the Amorites, to destroy us? Oh, that we had been content, and dwelt on the other side of the Jordan! ⁸O Lord, what shall I say when Israel turns its back before its enemies? ⁹For the Canaanites and all the inhabitants of the land will hear *it*, and surround us, and cut off our name from the earth. Then what will You do for Your great name?"

7:9 what will You do for Your great name? The main issue is the glory and honor of God's name (see Daniel's prayer in Dan. 9:16–19).

The Sin of Achan

¹⁰So the LORD said to Joshua: "Get up! Why do you lie thus on your face? ¹¹Israel has sinned, and they have also transgressed My covenant which I commanded them. For they have even taken some of the accursed things, and have both stolen and deceived; and they have also put *it* among their own stuff. ¹²Therefore the children of Israel could not stand before their enemies, *but* turned *their* backs before their enemies, because they have become doomed to destruction. Neither will I be with you anymore, unless you destroy the accursed from among you. ¹³Get up, sanctify the people, and say, 'Sanctify yourselves for tomorrow, because thus says the LORD God of Israel: "*There is* an accursed thing in your midst, O Israel; you cannot stand before your enemies until you take away the accursed thing from among you." ¹⁴In the morning therefore you shall be brought according to your tribes. And it shall be *that* the tribe which the LORD takes shall come according to families; and the family which the LORD takes shall come by households; and the

household which the LORD takes shall come man by man. [15]Then it shall be *that* he who is taken with the accursed thing shall be burned with fire, he and all that he has, because he has transgressed the covenant of the LORD, and because he has done a disgraceful thing in Israel.' "

[16]So Joshua rose early in the morning and brought Israel by their tribes, and the tribe of Judah was taken. [17]He brought the clan of Judah, and he took the family of the Zarhites; and he brought the family of the Zarhites man by man, and Zabdi was taken. [18]Then he brought his household man by man, and Achan the son of Carmi, the son of Zabdi, the son of Zerah, of the tribe of Judah, was taken.

[19]Now Joshua said to Achan, "My son, I beg you, give glory to the LORD God of Israel, and make confession to Him, and tell me now what you have done; do not hide *it* from me."

[20]And Achan answered Joshua and said, "Indeed I have sinned against the LORD God of Israel, and this is what I have done: [21]When I saw among the spoils a beautiful Babylonian garment, two hundred shekels of silver, and a wedge of gold weighing fifty shekels, I coveted them and took them. And there they are, hidden in the earth in the midst of my tent, with the silver under it."

[22]So Joshua sent messengers, and they ran to the tent; and there it was, hidden in his tent, with the silver under it. [23]And they took them from the midst of the tent, brought them to Joshua and to all the children of Israel, and laid them out before the LORD. [24]Then Joshua, and all Israel with him, took Achan the son of Zerah, the silver, the garment, the wedge of gold, his sons, his daughters, his oxen, his donkeys, his sheep, his tent, and all that he had, and they brought them to the Valley of Achor. [25]And Joshua said, "Why have you troubled

us? The LORD will trouble you this day." So all Israel stoned him with stones; and they burned them with fire after they had stoned them with stones.

[26]Then they raised over him a great heap of stones, still there to this day. So the LORD turned from the fierceness of His anger. Therefore the name of that place has been called the Valley of Achor[a] to this day.

The Fall of Ai

8 Now the LORD said to Joshua: "Do not be afraid, nor be dismayed; take all the people of war with you, and arise, go up to Ai. See, I have given into your hand the king of Ai, his people, his city, and his land. [2]And you shall do to Ai and its king as you did to Jericho and its king. Only its spoil and its cattle you shall take as booty for yourselves. Lay an ambush for the city behind it."

[3]So Joshua arose, and all the people of war, to go up against Ai; and Joshua chose thirty thousand mighty men of valor and sent them away by night. [4]And he commanded them, saying: "Behold, you shall lie in ambush against the city, behind the city. Do not go very far from the city, but all of you be ready. [5]Then I and all the people who *are* with me will approach the city; and it will come about, when they come out against us as at the first, that we shall flee before them. [6]For they will come out after us till we have drawn them from the city, for they will say, '*They are* fleeing before us as at the first.' Therefore we will flee before them. [7]Then you shall rise from the ambush and seize the city, for the LORD your God will deliver it into your hand. [8]And it will be, when you have taken the city, *that* you shall set the city on fire. According to the commandment of the LORD you shall do. See, I have commanded you."

[9]Joshua therefore sent them out; and they went to lie in ambush, and stayed between Bethel and Ai, on the west side of Ai;

7:15,24,25 Achan's family was executed with him because they were co-conspirators in what he did. They helped cover up his guilt and withheld information from others. Similarly, family members died in Korah's rebellion (Num. 16), Haman's fall (Esth. 9:13,14), and after Daniel's escape (Dan. 6:24).

8:7 God will deliver it into your hand. Although Joshua's elite force was far superior to Ai, who had a population of only 12,000, God had caused their defeat because of Achan's disobedience (7:1–5). Yet this time, despite Israel's overwhelming numbers, God was still the sovereign power for this victory (8:7).

7:26 *a*Literally *Trouble*

but Joshua lodged that night among the people. ¹⁰Then Joshua rose up early in the morning and mustered the people, and went up, he and the elders of Israel, before the people to Ai. ¹¹And all the people of war who *were* with him went up and drew near; and they came before the city and camped on the north side of Ai. Now a valley *lay* between them and Ai. ¹²So he took about five thousand men and set them in ambush between Bethel and Ai, on the west side of the city. ¹³And when they had set the people, all the army that *was* on the north of the city, and its rear guard on the west of the city, Joshua went that night into the midst of the valley.

¹⁴Now it happened, when the king of Ai saw *it,* that the men of the city hurried and rose early and went out against Israel to battle, he and all his people, at an appointed place before the plain. But he did not know that *there was* an ambush against him behind the city. ¹⁵And Joshua and all Israel made as if they were beaten before them, and fled by the way of the wilderness. ¹⁶So all the people who *were* in Ai were called together to pursue them. And they pursued Joshua and were drawn away from the city. ¹⁷There was not a man left in Ai or Bethel who did not go out after Israel. So they left the city open and pursued Israel.

¹⁸Then the LORD said to Joshua, "Stretch out the spear that *is* in your hand toward Ai, for I will give it into your hand." And Joshua stretched out the spear that *was* in his hand toward the city. ¹⁹So *those in* ambush arose quickly out of their place; they ran as soon as he had stretched out his hand, and they entered the city and took it, and hurried to set the city on fire. ²⁰And when the men of Ai looked behind them, they saw, and behold, the smoke of the city ascended to heaven. So they had no power to flee this way or that way, and the people who had fled to the wilderness turned back on the pursuers.

²¹Now when Joshua and all Israel saw that the ambush had taken the city and that the smoke of the city ascended, they turned back and struck down the men of Ai. ²²Then the others came out of the city against them; so they were *caught* in the midst of Israel, some on this side and some on that side. And they struck them down, so that they let none of them remain or escape. ²³But the king of Ai they took alive, and brought him to Joshua.

²⁴And it came to pass when Israel had made an end of slaying all the inhabitants of Ai in the field, in the wilderness where they pursued them, and when they all had fallen by the edge of the sword until they were consumed, that all the Israelites returned to Ai and struck it with the edge of the sword. ²⁵So it was *that* all who fell that day, both men and women, *were* twelve thousand—all the people of Ai. ²⁶For Joshua did not draw back his hand, with which he stretched out the spear, until he had utterly destroyed all the inhabitants of Ai. ²⁷Only the livestock and the spoil of that city Israel took as booty for themselves, according to the word of the LORD which He had commanded Joshua. ²⁸So Joshua burned Ai and made it a heap forever, a desolation to this day. ²⁹And the king of Ai he hanged on a tree until evening. And as soon as the sun was down, Joshua commanded that they should take his corpse down from the tree, cast it at the entrance of the gate of the city, and raise over it a great heap of stones *that remains* to this day.

Joshua Renews the Covenant

³⁰Now Joshua built an altar to the LORD God of Israel in Mount Ebal, ³¹as Moses the servant of the LORD had commanded the children of Israel, as it is written in the Book of the Law of Moses: "an altar of whole stones over which no man has wielded an iron *tool.*"*ᵃ* And they offered on it burnt offerings to the LORD, and sacrificed

---

8:18 the spear. Joshua hoisted the javelin as a sign to attack Ai. The raised javelin also signified confidence in God, just as Moses' uplifted rod and arms signified trust in God for victory over Amalek (Ex. 17:8–13).

8:30,31 Thanks is given to God for the victory. The altar was built of uncut stones, to keep worship simple and untainted by man's showmanship (see Ex. 20:24–26).

8:31 *ᵃ*Deuteronomy 27:5,6

peace offerings. [32]And there, in the presence of the children of Israel, he wrote on the stones a copy of the law of Moses, which he had written. [33]Then all Israel, with their elders and officers and judges, stood on either side of the ark before the priests, the Levites, who bore the ark of the covenant of the LORD, the stranger as well as he who was born among them. Half of them *were* in front of Mount Gerizim and half of them in front of Mount Ebal, as Moses the servant of the LORD had commanded before, that they should bless the people of Israel. [34]And afterward he read all the words of the law, the blessings and the cursings, according to all that is written in the Book of the Law. [35]There was not a word of all that Moses had commanded which Joshua did not read before all the assembly of Israel, with the women, the little ones, and the strangers who were living among them.

The Treaty with the Gibeonites

9And it came to pass when all the kings who *were* on this side of the Jordan, in the hills and in the lowland and in all the coasts of the Great Sea toward Lebanon—the Hittite, the Amorite, the Canaanite, the Perizzite, the Hivite, and the Jebusite—heard *about it*, [2]that they gathered together to fight with Joshua and Israel with one accord.

[3]But when the inhabitants of Gibeon heard what Joshua had done to Jericho and Ai, [4]they worked craftily, and went and pretended to be ambassadors. And they took old sacks on their donkeys, old wineskins torn and mended, [5]old and patched sandals on their feet, and old garments on themselves; and all the bread of their provision was dry *and* moldy. [6]And they went to Joshua, to the camp at Gilgal, and said to him and to the men of Israel, "We have come from a far country; now therefore, make a covenant with us."

[7]Then the men of Israel said to the Hivites, "Perhaps you dwell among us; so how can we make a covenant with you?"

[8]But they said to Joshua, "We *are* your servants."

And Joshua said to them, "Who *are* you, and where do you come from?"

[9]So they said to him: "From a very far country your servants have come, because of the name of the LORD your God; for we have heard of His fame, and all that He did in Egypt, [10]and all that He did to the two kings of the Amorites who *were* beyond the Jordan—to Sihon king of Heshbon, and Og king of Bashan, who was at Ashtaroth. [11]Therefore our elders and all the inhabitants of our country spoke to us, saying, 'Take provisions with you for the journey, and go to meet them, and say to them, "We *are* your servants; now therefore, make a covenant with us." ' [12]This bread of ours we took hot *for* our provision from our houses on the day we departed to come to you. But now look, it is dry and moldy. [13]And these wineskins which we filled *were* new, and see, they are torn; and these our garments and our sandals have become old because of the very long journey."

[14]Then the men of Israel took some of their provisions; but they did not ask counsel of the LORD. [15]So Joshua made peace with them, and made a covenant with them to let them live; and the rulers of the congregation swore to them.

9:4–15 The Gibeonite plot to trick Israel worked, and they made peace with the Gibeonites even though God had instructed them to eliminate the people living in cities in the Land. Israel sinned because they were not vigilant in prayer to assure that they acted by God's counsel.

[16]And it happened at the end of three days, after they had made a covenant with them, that they heard that they *were* their neighbors who dwelt near them. [17]Then the children of Israel journeyed and came to their cities on the third day. Now their cities *were* Gibeon, Chephirah, Beeroth, and Kirjath Jearim. [18]But the children of Israel did not attack them, because the rulers of the congregation had sworn to them by the LORD God of Israel. And all the congregation complained against the rulers.

[19]Then all the rulers said to all the congregation, "We have sworn to them by the LORD God of Israel; now therefore, we may not touch them. [20]This we will do to them: We will let them live, lest wrath be upon us because of the oath which we swore to them." [21]And the rulers said to them, "Let them live, but let them be woodcutters and water carriers for all the con-

gregation, as the rulers had promised them."

²²Then Joshua called for them, and he spoke to them, saying, "Why have you deceived us, saying, 'We *are* very far from you,' when you dwell near us? ²³Now therefore, you *are* cursed, and none of you shall be freed from being slaves—woodcutters and water carriers for the house of my God."

9:21–23 Joshua honored the pledge of peace with the Gibeonites but made them woodcutters and water carriers because of their deception. Joshua made Gibeon part of Benjamin's land area (18:25) and a Levite town (21:17). Gibeonites later helped Nehemiah rebuild the walls of Jerusalem (Neh. 3:7).

²⁴So they answered Joshua and said, "Because your servants were clearly told that the LORD your God commanded His servant Moses to give you all the land, and to destroy all the inhabitants of the land from before you; therefore we were very much afraid for our lives because of you, and have done this thing. ²⁵And now, here we are, in your hands; do with us as it seems good and right to do to us." ²⁶So he did to them, and delivered them out of the hand of the children of Israel, so that they did not kill them. ²⁷And that day Joshua made them woodcutters and water carriers for the congregation and for the altar of the LORD, in the place which He would choose, even to this day.

The Sun Stands Still

10 Now it came to pass when Adoni-Zedek king of Jerusalem heard how Joshua had taken Ai and had utterly destroyed it—as he had done to Jericho and its king, so he had done to Ai and its king—and how the inhabitants of Gibeon had made peace with Israel and were among them, ²that they feared greatly, because Gibeon *was* a great city, like one of the royal cities, and because it *was* greater than Ai, and all its men *were* mighty. ³Therefore Adoni-Zedek king of Jerusalem sent to Hoham king of Hebron, Piram king of Jarmuth, Japhia king of Lachish, and Debir king of Eglon, saying, ⁴"Come up to me and help me, that we may attack Gibeon, for it has made peace with Joshua and with the

children of Israel." ⁵Therefore the five kings of the Amorites, the king of Jerusalem, the king of Hebron, the king of Jarmuth, the king of Lachish, *and* the king of Eglon, gathered together and went up, they and all their armies, and camped before Gibeon and made war against it.

⁶And the men of Gibeon sent to Joshua at the camp at Gilgal, saying, "Do not forsake your servants; come up to us quickly, save us and help us, for all the kings of the Amorites who dwell in the mountains have gathered together against us."

⁷So Joshua ascended from Gilgal, he and all the people of war with him, and all the mighty men of valor. ⁸And the LORD said to Joshua, "Do not fear them, for I have delivered them into your hand; not a man of them shall stand before you." ⁹Joshua therefore came upon them suddenly, having marched all night from Gilgal. ¹⁰So the LORD routed them before Israel, killed them with a great slaughter at Gibeon, chased them along the road that goes to Beth Horon, and struck them down as far as Azekah and Makkedah. ¹¹And it happened, as they fled before Israel *and* were on the descent of Beth Horon, that the LORD cast down large hailstones from heaven on them as far as Azekah, and they died. *There were* more who died from the hailstones than the children of Israel killed with the sword.

10:11 The hailstones were miraculous in many ways: God sent them, they were large, they killed more than the sword, they killed only the enemy, they covered a large area, and they fell as the sun stood still.

¹²Then Joshua spoke to the LORD in the day when the LORD delivered up the Amorites before the children of Israel, and he said in the sight of Israel:

"Sun, stand still over Gibeon;
　And Moon, in the Valley of Aijalon."
¹³　So the sun stood still,
　And the moon stopped,
　Till the people had revenge
　Upon their enemies.

Is this not written in the Book of Jasher? So the sun stood still in the midst of heaven, and did not hasten to go *down* for about a

whole day. [14]And there has been no day like that, before it or after it, that the LORD heeded the voice of a man; for the LORD fought for Israel.

10:12–14 sun stood still, And the moon stopped. Although some try to dismiss this miracle with explanations such as an eclipse, a local refraction of the sun's rays, an exaggeration, or lavish poetic description, these ideas question God's power as Creator. This event is best interpreted as an outright miracle in response to Joshua's command to the sun to delay (Heb., "be still, silent, leave off"). Likely the sun moved to keep perfect pace with the battlefield, giving Joshua's troops time to finish the battle (v. 11).

---

[15]Then Joshua returned, and all Israel with him, to the camp at Gilgal.

The Amorite Kings Executed

[16]But these five kings had fled and hidden themselves in a cave at Makkedah. [17]And it was told Joshua, saying, "The five kings have been found hidden in the cave at Makkedah."

[18]So Joshua said, "Roll large stones against the mouth of the cave, and set men by it to guard them. [19]And do not stay *there* yourselves, *but* pursue your enemies, and attack their rear *guard*. Do not allow them to enter their cities, for the LORD your God has delivered them into your hand." [20]Then it happened, while Joshua and the children of Israel made an end of slaying them with a very great slaughter, till they had finished, that those who escaped entered fortified cities. [21]And all the people returned to the camp, to Joshua at Makkedah, in peace. No one moved his tongue against any of the children of Israel.

[22]Then Joshua said, "Open the mouth of the cave, and bring out those five kings to me from the cave." [23]And they did so, and brought out those five kings to him from the cave: the king of Jerusalem, the king of Hebron, the king of Jarmuth, the king of Lachish, *and* the king of Eglon.

10:24 feet on the necks. This gesture symbolized victory and promised assurance of future victories (v. 25).

---

[24]So it was, when they brought out those kings to Joshua, that Joshua called for all the men of Israel, and said to the captains of the men of war who went with him, "Come near, put your feet on the necks of these kings." And they drew near and put their feet on their necks. [25]Then Joshua said to them, "Do not be afraid, nor be dismayed; be strong and of good courage, for thus the LORD will do to all your enemies against whom you fight." [26]And afterward Joshua struck them and killed them, and hanged them on five trees; and they were hanging on the trees until evening. [27]So it was at the time of the going down of the sun *that* Joshua commanded, and they took them down from the trees, cast them into the cave where they had been hidden, and laid large stones against the cave's mouth, *which remain* until this very day.

Conquest of the Southland

[28]On that day Joshua took Makkedah, and struck it and its king with the edge of the sword. He utterly destroyed them[a]—all the people who *were* in it. He let none remain. He also did to the king of Makkedah as he had done to the king of Jericho.

[29]Then Joshua passed from Makkedah, and all Israel with him, to Libnah; and they fought against Libnah. [30]And the LORD also delivered it and its king into the hand of Israel; he struck it and all the people who *were* in it with the edge of the sword. He let none remain in it, but did to its king as he had done to the king of Jericho.

[31]Then Joshua passed from Libnah, and all Israel with him, to Lachish; and they encamped against it and fought against it. [32]And the LORD delivered Lachish into the hand of Israel, who took it on the second day, and struck it and all the people who *were* in it with the edge of the sword, according to all that he had done to Libnah. [33]Then Horam king of Gezer came up to help Lachish; and Joshua struck him and his people, until he left him none remaining.

[34]From Lachish Joshua passed to Eglon, and all Israel with him; and they encamped against it and fought against it. [35]They took

---

10:28 [a]Following Masoretic Text and most authorities; many Hebrew manuscripts, some manuscripts of the Septuagint, and some manuscripts of the Targum read *it*.

it on that day and struck it with the edge of the sword; all the people who *were* in it he utterly destroyed that day, according to all that he had done to Lachish.

³⁶So Joshua went up from Eglon, and all Israel with him, to Hebron; and they fought against it. ³⁷And they took it and struck it with the edge of the sword—its king, all its cities, and all the people who *were* in it; he left none remaining, according to all that he had done to Eglon, but utterly destroyed it and all the people who *were* in it.

³⁸Then Joshua returned, and all Israel with him, to Debir; and they fought against it. ³⁹And he took it and its king and all its cities; they struck them with the edge of the sword and utterly destroyed all the people who *were* in it. He left none remaining; as he had done to Hebron, so he did to Debir and its king, as he had done also to Libnah and its king.

⁴⁰So Joshua conquered all the land: the mountain country and the South* and the lowland and the wilderness slopes, and all their kings; he left none remaining, but utterly destroyed all that breathed, as the LORD God of Israel had commanded. ⁴¹And Joshua conquered them from Kadesh Bar-nea as far as Gaza, and all the country of Goshen, even as far as Gibeon. ⁴²All these kings and their land Joshua took at one time, because the LORD God of Israel fought for Israel. ⁴³Then Joshua returned, and all Israel with him, to the camp at Gilgal.

> **10:42** Tribute belongs to the Lord for all victories, for "in everything give thanks" (1 Thess. 5:18).

The Northern Conquest

11 And it came to pass, when Jabin king of Hazor heard *these things*, that he sent to Jobab king of Madon, to the king of Shimron, to the king of Achshaph, ²and to the kings who *were* from the north, in the mountains, in the plain south of Chinneroth, in the lowland, and in the heights of Dor on the west, ³to the Canaanites in the east and in the west, the Amorite, the Hittite, the Perizzite, the Jebusite in the mountains, and the Hivite below Hermon in the land of Mizpah. ⁴So they went out, they and all their armies with them, *as* many people *as* the sand that *is* on the seashore in multitude, with very many horses and chariots. ⁵And when all these

---

10:40 *Hebrew *Negev,* and so throughout this book

How does God's guarantee of success to Joshua carry over to us?

The Book of Joshua begins with God's commissioning of Israel's new leader. God described Joshua's mission—to go in and possess the Land (1:2–6). God hinged Joshua's success on three key factors: (1) God's own presence (1:5); (2) Joshua's personal strength and courage (1:7, 9); and (3) Joshua's attention to and application of God's Word (1:7,8).

God spelled out this third factor with some detail for it was to be the basis for all of Joshua's actions. God's Word was to be Joshua's constant conversation, continual meditation and unswerving application. The phrase "This Book of the Law shall not depart from your mouth" (1:8) deserves added attention. While a first impression might lead to the conclusion that Joshua was not supposed to talk about the Book of the Law, the direct opposite is the case: he was not supposed to stop talking about it.

Biblical meditation begins with thoughtful, lingering reading of God's Word. It progresses to familiarity and memorization. In order to "meditate in it day and night" (1:8), the Book of the Law would have be *in Joshua*. The purpose has been achieved when meditation leads us to "observe to do according to all that is written in it" (1:8).

"Then," God told Joshua, "you will make your way prosperous, and then you will have good success" (1:8). Joshua found the ultimate measure of prosperity and success—knowing how God wants His people to live and then living that way. God repeatedly assured Joshua of His own presence "wherever you go." What greater measurement of success could there be than to honor the ever-present God with our obedience?

kings had met together, they came and camped together at the waters of Merom to fight against Israel.

[6]But the LORD said to Joshua, "Do not be afraid because of them, for tomorrow about this time I will deliver all of them slain before Israel. You shall hamstring their horses and burn their chariots with fire." [7]So Joshua and all the people of war with him came against them suddenly by the waters of Merom, and they attacked them. [8]And the LORD delivered them into the hand of Israel, who defeated them and chased them to Greater Sidon, to the Brook Misrephoth,[a] and to the Valley of Mizpah eastward; they attacked them until they left none of them remaining. [9]So Joshua did to them as the LORD had told him: he hamstrung their horses and burned their chariots with fire.

[10]Joshua turned back at that time and took Hazor, and struck its king with the sword; for Hazor was formerly the head of all those kingdoms. [11]And they struck all the people who were in it with the edge of the sword, utterly destroying them. There was none left breathing. Then he burned Hazor with fire.

[12]So all the cities of those kings, and all their kings, Joshua took and struck with the edge of the sword. He utterly destroyed them, as Moses the servant of the LORD had commanded. [13]But as for the cities that stood on their mounds,[a] Israel burned none of them, except Hazor only, which Joshua burned. [14]And all the spoil of these cities and the livestock, the children of Israel took as booty for themselves; but they struck every man with the edge of the sword until they had destroyed them, and they left none breathing. [15]As the LORD had commanded Moses his servant, so Moses commanded Joshua, and so Joshua did. He left nothing undone of all that the LORD had commanded Moses.

Summary of Joshua's Conquests

[16]Thus Joshua took all this land: the mountain country, all the South, all the land of Goshen, the lowland, and the Jordan plain[a]—the mountains of Israel and its lowlands, [17]from Mount Halak and the ascent to Seir, even as far as Baal Gad in the Valley of Lebanon below Mount Hermon. He captured all their kings, and struck them down and killed them. [18]Joshua made war a long time with all those kings. [19]There was not a city that made peace with the children of Israel, except the Hivites, the inhabitants of Gibeon. All the others they took in battle. [20]For it was of the LORD to harden their hearts, that they should come against Israel in battle, that He might utterly destroy them, and that they might receive no mercy, but that He might destroy them, as the LORD had commanded Moses.

> **11:20 it was of the LORD to harden their hearts.** God hardened their hearts so that they would fight Israel, thus bringing a judgment of destruction upon them. They willfully rejected God and were as unfit to remain in the Land as vomit spewed out of the mouth (Lev. 18:24,25).

[21]And at that time Joshua came and cut off the Anakim from the mountains: from Hebron, from Debir, from Anab, from all the mountains of Judah, and from all the mountains of Israel; Joshua utterly destroyed them with their cities. [22]None of the Anakim were left in the land of the children of Israel; they remained only in Gaza, in Gath, and in Ashdod.

[23]So Joshua took the whole land, according to all that the LORD had said to Moses; and Joshua gave it as an inheritance to Israel according to their divisions by their tribes. Then the land rested from war.

The Kings Conquered by Moses

12 These are the kings of the land whom the children of Israel defeated, and whose land they possessed on the other side of the Jordan toward the rising of the sun, from the River Arnon to Mount Hermon, and all the eastern Jordan plain: [2]One king was Sihon king of the Amorites, who dwelt in Heshbon and ruled half of Gilead, from Aroer, which is on the bank of the River Arnon, from the middle of that river, even as far as the River Jabbok, which is the border of the Ammonites, [3]and the eastern Jordan plain from the Sea of

---

11:8 [a]Hebrew Misrephoth Maim   11:13 [a]Hebrew tel, a heap of successive city ruins   11:16 [a]Hebrew arabah

13:1,2 very much land. Pockets of land still lay untouched by their former victories. When Joshua allotted land to the tribes, they then bore the responsibility to drive out the lingering Canaanites in obedience to God's command to rid the land of indigenous peoples. Failure to obey is the sad theme in Judges 1.

Chinneroth as far as the Sea of the Arabah (the Salt Sea), the road to Beth Jeshimoth, and southward below the slopes of Pisgah. [4]*The other king was* Og king of Bashan and his territory, *who was* of the remnant of the giants, who dwelt at Ashtaroth and at Edrei, [5]and reigned over Mount Hermon, over Salcah, over all Bashan, as far as the border of the Geshurites and the Maachathites, and over half of Gilead *to* the border of Sihon king of Heshbon.

[6]These Moses the servant of the LORD and the children of Israel had conquered; and Moses the servant of the LORD had given it *as* a possession to the Reubenites, the Gadites, and half the tribe of Manasseh.

The Kings Conquered by Joshua

[7]And these *are* the kings of the country which Joshua and the children of Israel conquered on this side of the Jordan, on the west, from Baal Gad in the Valley of Lebanon as far as Mount Halak and the ascent to Seir, which Joshua gave to the tribes of Israel *as* a possession according to their divisions, [8]in the mountain country, in the lowlands, in the *Jordan* plain, in the slopes, in the wilderness, and in the South—the Hittites, the Amorites, the Canaanites, the Perizzites, the Hivites, and the Jebusites: [9]the king of Jericho, one; the king of Ai, which *is* beside Bethel, one; [10]the king of Jerusalem, one; the king of Hebron, one; [11]the king of Jarmuth, one; the king of Lachish, one; [12]the king of Eglon, one; the king of Gezer, one; [13]the king of Debir, one; the king of Geder, one; [14]the king of Hormah, one; the king of Arad, one; [15]the king of Libnah, one; the king of Adullam, one; [16]the king of Makkedah, one; the king of Bethel, one; [17]the king of Tappuah, one; the king of Hepher, one; [18]the king of Aphek, one; the king of Lasharon, one; [19]the king of Madon,

one; the king of Hazor, one; [20]the king of Shimron Meron, one; the king of Achshaph, one; [21]the king of Taanach, one; the king of Megiddo, one; [22]the king of Kedesh, one; the king of Jokneam in Carmel, one; [23]the king of Dor in the heights of Dor, one; the king of the people of Gilgal, one; [24]the king of Tirzah, one—all the kings, thirty-one.

Remaining Land to Be Conquered

13 Now Joshua was old, advanced in years. And the LORD said to him: "You are old, advanced in years, and there remains very much land yet to be possessed. [2]This is the land that yet remains: all the territory of the Philistines and all *that of* the Geshurites, [3]from Sihor, which *is* east of Egypt, as far as the border of Ekron northward (*which* is counted as Canaanite); the five lords of the Philistines—the Gazites, the Ashdodites, the Ashkelonites, the Gittites, and the Ekronites; also the Avites; [4]from the south, all the land of the Canaanites, and Mearah that belongs to the Sidonians as far as Aphek, to the border of the Amorites; [5]the land of the Gebalites,*a* and all Lebanon, toward the sunrise, from Baal Gad below Mount Hermon as far as the entrance to Hamath; [6]all the inhabitants of the mountains from Lebanon as far as the Brook Misrephoth,*a and* all the Sidonians—them I will drive out from before the children of Israel; only divide it by lot to Israel as an inheritance, as I have commanded you. [7]Now therefore, divide this land as an inheritance to the nine tribes and half the tribe of Manasseh."

The Land Divided East of the Jordan

[8]With the other half-tribe the Reubenites and the Gadites received their inheritance, which Moses had given them, beyond the Jordan eastward, as Moses the servant of the LORD had given them: [9]from Aroer which *is* on the bank of the River Arnon, and the town that *is* in the midst of the ravine, and all the plain of Medeba as far as Dibon; [10]all the cities of Sihon king of the Amorites, who reigned in Heshbon, as far as the border of the children of Ammon; [11]Gilead, and the border of the Geshurites

---

13:5 *a*Or *Giblites*   13:6 *a*Hebrew *Misrephoth Maim*

and Maachathites, all Mount Hermon, and all Bashan as far as Salcah; [12]all the kingdom of Og in Bashan, who reigned in Ashtaroth and Edrei, who remained of the remnant of the giants; for Moses had defeated and cast out these.

[13]Nevertheless the children of Israel did not drive out the Geshurites or the Maachathites, but the Geshurites and the Maachathites dwell among the Israelites until this day.

[14]Only to the tribe of Levi he had given no inheritance; the sacrifices of the LORD God of Israel made by fire *are* their inheritance, as He said to them.

The Land of Reuben

[15]And Moses had given to the tribe of the children of Reuben *an inheritance* according to their families. [16]Their territory was from Aroer, which *is* on the bank of the River Arnon, and the city that *is* in the midst of the ravine, and all the plain by Medeba; [17]Heshbon and all its cities that *are* in the plain: Dibon, Bamoth Baal, Beth Baal Meon, [18]Jahaza, Kedemoth, Mephaath, [19]Kirjathaim, Sibmah, Zereth Shahar on the mountain of the valley, [20]Beth Peor, the slopes of Pisgah, and Beth Jeshimoth— [21]all the cities of the plain and all the kingdom of Sihon king of the Amorites, who reigned in Heshbon, whom Moses had struck with the princes of Midian: Evi, Rekem, Zur, Hur, and Reba, who *were* princes of Sihon dwelling in the country. [22]The children of Israel also killed with the sword Balaam the son of Beor, the soothsayer, among those who were killed by them. [23]And the border of the children of Reuben was the bank of the Jordan. This *was* the inheritance of the children of Reuben according to their families, the cities and their villages.

The Land of Gad

[24]Moses also had given *an inheritance* to the tribe of Gad, to the children of Gad according to their families. [25]Their territory was Jazer, and all the cities of Gilead, and half the land of the Ammonites as far as Aroer, which *is* before Rabbah, [26]and from Heshbon to Ramath Mizpah and Betonim, and from Mahanaim to the border of Debir, [27]and in the valley Beth Haram, Beth Nim-

rah, Succoth, and Zaphon, the rest of the kingdom of Sihon king of Heshbon, with the Jordan as *its* border, as far as the edge of the Sea of Chinnereth, on the other side of the Jordan eastward. [28]This *is* the inheritance of the children of Gad according to their families, the cities and their villages.

Half the Tribe of Manasseh (East)

[29]Moses also had given *an inheritance* to half the tribe of Manasseh; it was for half the tribe of the children of Manasseh according to their families: [30]Their territory was from Mahanaim, all Bashan, all the kingdom of Og king of Bashan, and all the towns of Jair which are in Bashan, sixty cities; [31]half of Gilead, and Ashtaroth and Edrei, cities of the kingdom of Og in Bashan, *were* for the children of Machir the son of Manasseh, for half of the children of Machir according to their families.

[32]These *are the areas* which Moses had distributed as an inheritance in the plains of Moab on the other side of the Jordan, by Jericho eastward. [33]But to the tribe of Levi Moses had given no inheritance; the LORD

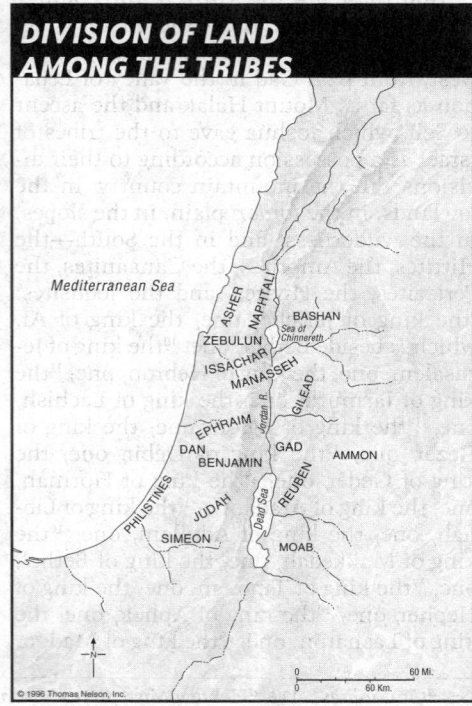

DIVISION OF LAND AMONG THE TRIBES

Mediterranean Sea

ASHER
NAPHTALI
BASHAN
Sea of Chinnereth
ZEBULUN
ISSACHAR
MANASSEH
GILEAD
Jordan R.
EPHRAIM
DAN
BENJAMIN
GAD
AMMON
PHILISTINES
JUDAH
Dead Sea
REUBEN
SIMEON
MOAB

N

0   60 Mi.
0   60 Km.

© 1996 Thomas Nelson, Inc.

God of Israel *was* their inheritance, as He had said to them.

The Land Divided West of the Jordan

14 These *are the areas* which the children of Israel inherited in the land of Canaan, which Eleazar the priest, Joshua the son of Nun, and the heads of the fathers of the tribes of the children of Israel distributed as an inheritance to them. ²Their inheritance *was* by lot, as the LORD had commanded by the hand of Moses, for the nine tribes and the half-tribe. ³For Moses had given the inheritance of the two tribes and the half-tribe on the other side of the Jordan; but to the Levites he had given no inheritance among them. ⁴For the children of Joseph were two tribes: Manasseh and Ephraim. And they gave no part to the Levites in the land, except cities to dwell *in*, with their common-lands for their livestock and their property. ⁵As the LORD had commanded Moses, so the children of Israel did; and they divided the land.

Caleb Inherits Hebron

⁶Then the children of Judah came to Joshua in Gilgal. And Caleb the son of Jephunneh the Kenizzite said to him: "You know the word which the LORD said to Moses the man of God concerning you and me in Kadesh Barnea. ⁷I *was* forty years old when Moses the servant of the LORD sent me from Kadesh Barnea to spy out the land, and I brought back word to him as *it was* in my heart. ⁸Nevertheless my brethren who went up with me made the heart of the people melt, but I wholly followed the LORD my God. ⁹So Moses swore on that day, saying, 'Surely the land where your foot has trodden shall be your inheritance and your children's forever, because you have wholly followed the LORD my God.' ¹⁰And now, behold, the LORD has kept me alive, as He said, these forty-five years, ever since the LORD spoke this word to Moses while Israel wandered in the wilderness; and now, here I am this day, eighty-five years old. ¹¹As yet I *am as* strong this day as on the day that Moses sent me; just as my strength *was* then, so now *is* my strength for war, both for going out and for coming in. ¹²Now therefore, give me this mountain of which the LORD spoke in that day; for you heard

in that day how the Anakim *were* there, and *that* the cities *were* great *and* fortified. It may be that the LORD *will be* with me, and I shall be able to drive them out as the LORD said."

¹³And Joshua blessed him, and gave Hebron to Caleb the son of Jephunneh as an inheritance. ¹⁴Hebron therefore became the inheritance of Caleb the son of Jephunneh the Kenizzite to this day, because he wholly followed the LORD God of Israel. ¹⁵And the name of Hebron formerly was Kirjath Arba (*Arba was* the greatest man among the Anakim).

Then the land had rest from war.

14:12–14 God granted Caleb's request for Hebron because of his faithfulness when he believed that God would give them the Land, as He had promised.

The Land of Judah

15 So *this* was the lot of the tribe of the children of Judah according to their families:

The border of Edom at the Wilderness of Zin southward *was* the extreme southern boundary. ²And their southern border began at the shore of the Salt Sea, from the bay that faces southward. ³Then it went out to the southern side of the Ascent of Akrabbim, passed along to Zin, ascended on the south side of Kadesh Barnea, passed along to Hezron, went up to Adar, and went around to Karkaa. ⁴*From there* it passed toward Azmon and went out to the Brook of Egypt; and the border ended at the sea. This shall be your southern border.

⁵The east border *was* the Salt Sea as far as the mouth of the Jordan.

And the border on the northern quarter *began* at the bay of the sea at the mouth of the Jordan. ⁶The border went up to Beth Hoglah and passed north of Beth Arabah; and the border went up to the stone of Bohan the son of Reuben. ⁷Then the border went up toward Debir from the Valley of Achor, and it turned northward toward Gilgal, which *is* before the Ascent of Adummim, which *is* on the south side of the valley. The border continued toward the waters of En Shemesh and ended at En Rogel. ⁸And the border went up by the Valley of the Son of Hinnom to the southern slope of the Jebusite *city* (which *is* Jerusalem).

The border went up to the top of the mountain that *lies* before the Valley of Hinnom westward, which *is* at the end of the Valley of Rephaim[a] northward. [9]Then the border went around from the top of the hill to the fountain of the water of Nephtoah, and extended to the cities of Mount Ephron. And the border went around to Baalah (which *is* Kirjath Jearim). [10]Then the border turned westward from Baalah to Mount Seir, passed along to the side of Mount Jearim on the north (which *is* Chesalon), went down to Beth Shemesh, and passed on to Timnah. [11]And the border went out to the side of Ekron northward. Then the border went around to Shicron, passed along to Mount Baalah, and extended to Jabneel; and the border ended at the sea.

[12]The west border *was* the coastline of the Great Sea. This *is* the boundary of the children of Judah all around according to their families.

Caleb Occupies Hebron and Debir

[13]Now to Caleb the son of Jephunneh he gave a share among the children of Judah, according to the commandment of the LORD to Joshua, *namely*, Kirjath Arba, which *is* Hebron (*Arba was* the father of Anak). [14]Caleb drove out the three sons of Anak from there: Sheshai, Ahiman, and Talmai, the children of Anak. [15]Then he went up from there to the inhabitants of Debir (formerly the name of Debir *was* Kirjath Sepher).

[16]And Caleb said, "He who attacks Kirjath Sepher and takes it, to him I will give Achsah my daughter as wife." [17]So Othniel the son of Kenaz, the brother of Caleb, took it; and he gave him Achsah his daughter as wife. [18]Now it was so, when she came *to him*, that she persuaded him to ask her father for a field. So she dismounted from *her* donkey, and Caleb said to her, "What do you wish?" [19]She answered, "Give me a blessing; since you have given me land in the South, give me also springs of water." So he gave her the upper springs and the lower springs.

> **15:18,19** Caleb's daughter sought blessing and exercised real faith for it—like father, like daughter.

The Cities of Judah

[20]This *was* the inheritance of the tribe of the children of Judah according to their families:

[21]The cities at the limits of the tribe of the children of Judah, toward the border of Edom in the South, were Kabzeel, Eder, Jagur, [22]Kinah, Dimonah, Adadah, [23]Kedesh, Hazor, Ithnan, [24]Ziph, Telem, Bealoth, [25]Hazor, Hadattah, Kerioth, Hezron (which *is* Hazor), [26]Amam, Shema, Moladah, [27]Hazar Gaddah, Heshmon, Beth Pelet, [28]Hazar Shual, Beersheba, Bizjothjah, [29]Baalah, Ijim, Ezem, [30]Eltolad, Chesil, Hormah, [31]Ziklag, Madmannah, Sansannah, [32]Lebaoth, Shilhim, Ain, and Rimmon: all the cities *are* twenty-nine, with their villages.

[33]In the lowland: Eshtaol, Zorah, Ashnah, [34]Zanoah, En Gannim, Tappuah, Enam, [35]Jarmuth, Adullam, Socoh, Azekah, [36]Sharaim, Adithaim, Gederah, and Gederothaim: fourteen cities with their villages; [37]Zenan, Hadashah, Migdal Gad, [38]Dilean, Mizpah, Joktheel, [39]Lachish, Bozkath, Eglon, [40]Cabbon, Lahmas,[a] Kithlish, [41]Gederoth, Beth Dagon, Naamah, and Makkedah: sixteen cities with their villages; [42]Libnah, Ether, Ashan, [43]Jiphtah, Ashnah, Nezib, [44]Keilah, Achzib, and Mareshah: nine cities with their villages; [45]Ekron, with its towns and villages; [46]from Ekron to the sea, all that *lay* near Ashdod, with their villages; [47]Ashdod with its towns and villages, Gaza with its towns and villages—as far as the Brook of Egypt and the Great Sea with *its* coastline.

[48]And in the mountain country: Shamir, Jattir, Sochoh, [49]Dannah, Kirjath Sannah (which *is* Debir), [50]Anab, Eshtemoh, Anim, [51]Goshen, Holon, and Giloh: eleven cities with their villages; [52]Arab, Dumah, Eshean, [53]Janum, Beth Tappuah, Aphekah, [54]Humtah, Kirjath Arba (which *is* Hebron), and Zior: nine cities with their villages; [55]Maon, Carmel, Ziph, Juttah, [56]Jezreel, Jokdeam, Zanoah, [57]Kain, Gibeah, and Timnah: ten cities with their villages; [58]Halhul, Beth Zur, Gedor, [59]Maarath, Beth Anoth, and Eltekon: six cities with their villages; [60]Kirjath Baal (which *is* Kirjath Jearim) and Rabbah: two cities with their villages.

[61]In the wilderness: Beth Arabah, Mid-

15:8 [a]Literally *Giants*   **15:40** [a]Or *Lahmam*

din, Secacah, ⁶²Nibshan, the City of Salt, and En Gedi: six cities with their villages.

⁶³As for the Jebusites, the inhabitants of Jerusalem, the children of Judah could not drive them out; but the Jebusites dwell with the children of Judah at Jerusalem to this day.

Ephraim and West Manasseh

16 The lot fell to the children of Joseph from the Jordan, by Jericho, to the waters of Jericho on the east, to the wilderness that goes up from Jericho through the mountains to Bethel, ²then went out from Bethel to Luz,ᵃ passed along to the border of the Archites at Ataroth, ³and went down westward to the boundary of the Japhletites, as far as the boundary of Lower Beth Horon to Gezer; and it ended at the sea.

⁴So the children of Joseph, Manasseh and Ephraim, took their inheritance.

> **16:1–4 children of Joseph.** Joseph's territory was double in size, because both his sons, Manasseh and Ephraim, were given inheritances. Joseph's land stretched over a good portion of the central area of the Promised Land.

The Land of Ephraim

⁵The border of the children of Ephraim, according to their families, was *thus:* The border of their inheritance on the east side was Ataroth Addar as far as Upper Beth Horon.

⁶And the border went out toward the sea on the north side of Michmethath; then the border went around eastward to Taanath Shiloh, and passed by it on the east of Janohah. ⁷Then it went down from Janohah to Ataroth and Naarah,ᵃ reached to Jericho, and came out at the Jordan.

⁸The border went out from Tappuah westward to the Brook Kanah, and it ended at the sea. This *was* the inheritance of the tribe of the children of Ephraim according to their families. ⁹The separate cities for the children of Ephraim *were* among the inheritance of the children of Manasseh, all the cities with their villages.

¹⁰And they did not drive out the Canaanites who dwelt in Gezer; but the Canaanites dwell among the Ephraimites to this day and have become forced laborers.

> **16:10** Ephraim ignored God's command to drive out the idolaters and spared the Canaanites in their land. This is the first instance of this disobedience, which became a fatal mistake (see Deut. 20:16).

The Other Half-Tribe of Manasseh (West)

17 There was also a lot for the tribe of Manasseh, for he *was* the firstborn of Joseph: *namely* for Machir the firstborn of Manasseh, the father of Gilead, because he was a man of war; therefore he was given Gilead and Bashan. ²And there was *a lot* for the rest of the children of Manasseh according to their families: for the children of Abiezer,ᵃ the children of Helek, the children of Asriel, the children of Shechem, the children of Hepher, and the children of Shemida; these *were* the male children of Manasseh the son of Joseph according to their families.

³But Zelophehad the son of Hepher, the son of Gilead, the son of Machir, the son of Manasseh, had no sons, but only daughters. And these *are* the names of his daughters: Mahlah, Noah, Hoglah, Milcah, and Tirzah. ⁴And they came near before Eleazar the priest, before Joshua the son of Nun, and before the rulers, saying, "The LORD commanded Moses to give us an inheritance among our brothers." Therefore, according to the commandment of the LORD, he gave them an inheritance among their father's brothers. ⁵Ten shares fell to Manasseh, besides the land of Gilead and Bashan, which *were* on the other side of the Jordan, ⁶because the daughters of Manasseh received an inheritance among his sons; and the rest of Manasseh's sons had the land of Gilead.

> **17:3–6 Zelophehad.** This man had no sons as heirs, so his five daughters received the inheritance. God gave this right to women (Num. 27:1–11).

⁷And the territory of Manasseh was from Asher to Michmethath, that *lies* east of Shechem; and the border went along south

---

16:2 ᵃSeptuagint reads *Bethel* (that is, Luz).   16:7 ᵃOr *Naaran* (compare 1 Chronicles 7:28)
17:2 ᵃCalled *Jeezer* in Numbers 26:30

to the inhabitants of En Tappuah. ⁸Manasseh had the land of Tappuah, but Tappuah on the border of Manasseh *belonged* to the children of Ephraim. ⁹And the border descended to the Brook Kanah, southward to the brook. These cities of Ephraim *are* among the cities of Manasseh. The border of Manasseh *was* on the north side of the brook; and it ended at the sea.

¹⁰Southward *it was* Ephraim's, northward *it was* Manasseh's, and the sea was its border. Manasseh's territory was adjoining Asher on the north and Issachar on the east. ¹¹And in Issachar and in Asher, Manasseh had Beth Shean and its towns, Ibleam and its towns, the inhabitants of Dor and its towns, the inhabitants of En Dor and its towns, the inhabitants of Taanach and its towns, and the inhabitants of Megiddo and its towns—three hilly regions. ¹²Yet the children of Manasseh could not drive out *the inhabitants of* those cities, but the Canaanites were determined to dwell in that land. ¹³And it happened, when the children of Israel grew strong, that they put the Canaanites to forced labor, but did not utterly drive them out.

More Land for Ephraim and Manasseh

¹⁴Then the children of Joseph spoke to Joshua, saying, "Why have you given us *only* one lot and one share to inherit, since we *are* a great people, inasmuch as the LORD has blessed us until now?"

¹⁵So Joshua answered them, "If you *are* a great people, *then* go up to the forest *country* and clear a place for yourself there in the land of the Perizzites and the giants, since the mountains of Ephraim are too confined for you."

¹⁶But the children of Joseph said, "The mountain country is not enough for us; and all the Canaanites who dwell in the land of the valley have chariots of iron, *both those* who *are* of Beth Shean and its

---

17:12-18 children of Manasseh. Men of Manasseh complained that they did not have enough land for their numbers and that the Canaanites were too tough for them to drive out altogether. Joshua gave them extra land in forested hills and assured them that they could drive out the Canaanites because God had promised to be with them, even against chariots (Deut. 20:1).

---

towns and *those* who *are* of the Valley of Jezreel."

¹⁷And Joshua spoke to the house of Joseph—to Ephraim and Manasseh—saying, "You *are* a great people and have great power; you shall not have *only* one lot, ¹⁸but the mountain country shall be yours. Although it *is* wooded, you shall cut it down, and its farthest extent shall be yours; for you shall drive out the Canaanites, though they have iron chariots *and* are strong."

The Remainder of the Land Divided

18 Now the whole congregation of the children of Israel assembled together at Shiloh, and set up the tabernacle of meeting there. And the land was subdued before them. ²But there remained among the children of Israel seven tribes which had not yet received their inheritance.

³Then Joshua said to the children of Israel: "How long will you neglect to go and possess the land which the LORD God of your fathers has given you? ⁴Pick out from among you three men for *each* tribe, and I will send them; they shall rise and go through the land, survey it according to their inheritance, and come *back* to me. ⁵And they shall divide it into seven parts. Judah shall remain in their territory on the south, and the house of Joseph shall remain in their territory on the north. ⁶You shall therefore survey the land in seven parts and bring *the survey* here to me, that I may cast lots for you here before the LORD our God. ⁷But the Levites have no part among you, for the priesthood of the LORD *is* their inheritance. And Gad, Reuben, and half the tribe of Manasseh have received their inheritance beyond the Jordan on the east, which Moses the servant of the LORD gave them."

⁸Then the men arose to go away; and Joshua charged those who went to survey the land, saying, "Go, walk through the land, survey it, and come back to me, that I may cast lots for you here before the LORD in Shiloh." ⁹So the men went, passed through the land, and wrote the survey in a book in seven parts by cities; and they came to Joshua at the camp in Shiloh. ¹⁰Then Joshua cast lots for them in Shiloh before

the LORD, and there Joshua divided the land to the children of Israel according to their divisions.

The Land of Benjamin

¹¹Now the lot of the tribe of the children of Benjamin came up according to their families, and the territory of their lot came out between the children of Judah and the children of Joseph. ¹²Their border on the north side began at the Jordan, and the border went up to the side of Jericho on the north, and went up through the mountains westward; it ended at the Wilderness of Beth Aven. ¹³The border went over from there toward Luz, to the side of Luz (which is Bethel) southward; and the border descended to Ataroth Addar, near the hill that lies on the south side of Lower Beth Horon.

¹⁴Then the border extended around the west side to the south, from the hill that lies before Beth Horon southward; and it ended at Kirjath Baal (which is Kirjath Jearim), a city of the children of Judah. This was the west side.

¹⁵The south side began at the end of Kirjath Jearim, and the border extended on the west and went out to the spring of the waters of Nephtoah. ¹⁶Then the border came down to the end of the mountain that lies before the Valley of the Son of Hinnom, which is in the Valley of the Rephaim[a] on the north, descended to the Valley of Hinnom, to the side of the Jebusite city on the south, and descended to En Rogel. ¹⁷And it went around from the north, went out to En Shemesh, and extended toward Geliloth, which is before the Ascent of Adummim, and descended to the stone of Bohan the son of Reuben. ¹⁸Then it passed along toward the north side of Arabah,[a] and went down to Arabah. ¹⁹And the border passed along to the north side of Beth Hoglah; then the border ended at the north bay at the Salt Sea, at the south end of the

Jordan. This was the southern boundary. ²⁰The Jordan was its border on the east side. This was the inheritance of the children of Benjamin, according to its boundaries all around, according to their families.

²¹Now the cities of the tribe of the children of Benjamin, according to their families, were Jericho, Beth Hoglah, Emek Keziz, ²²Beth Arabah, Zemaraim, Bethel, ²³Avim, Parah, Ophrah, ²⁴Chephar Haammoni, Ophni, and Gaba: twelve cities with their villages; ²⁵Gibeon, Ramah, Beeroth, ²⁶Mizpah, Chephirah, Mozah, ²⁷Rekem, Irpeel, Taralah, ²⁸Zelah, Eleph, Jebus (which is Jerusalem), Gibeath, and Kirjath: fourteen cities with their villages. This was the inheritance of the children of Benjamin according to their families.

Simeon's Inheritance with Judah

19 The second lot came out for Simeon, for the tribe of the children of Simeon according to their families. And their inheritance was within the inheritance of the children of Judah. ²They had in their inheritance Beersheba (Sheba), Moladah, ³Hazar Shual, Balah, Ezem, ⁴Eltolad, Bethul, Hormah, ⁵Ziklag, Beth Marcaboth, Hazar Susah, ⁶Beth Lebaoth, and Sharuhen: thirteen cities and their villages; ⁷Ain, Rimmon, Ether, and Ashan: four cities and their villages; ⁸and all the villages that were all around these cities as far as Baalath Beer, Ramah of the South. This was the inheritance of the tribe of the children of Simeon according to their families.

⁹The inheritance of the children of Simeon was included in the share of the children of Judah, for the share of the children of Judah was too much for them. Therefore the children of Simeon had their inheritance within the inheritance of that people.

The Land of Zebulun

¹⁰The third lot came out for the children of Zebulun according to their families, and the border of their inheritance was as far as Sarid. ¹¹Their border went toward the west

---

18:16 ᵃLiterally Giants   18:18 ᵃOr Beth Arabah (compare 15:6 and 18:22)

and to Maralah, went to Dabbasheth, and extended along the brook that is east of Jokneam. ¹²Then from Sarid it went eastward toward the sunrise along the border of Chisloth Tabor, and went out toward Daberath, bypassing Japhia. ¹³And from there it passed along on the east of Gath Hepher, toward Eth Kazin, and extended to Rimmon, which borders on Neah. ¹⁴Then the border went around it on the north side of Hannathon, and it ended in the Valley of Jiphthah El. ¹⁵Included were Kattath, Nahallal, Shimron, Idalah, and Bethlehem: twelve cities with their villages. ¹⁶This *was* the inheritance of the children of Zebulun according to their families, these cities with their villages.

The Land of Issachar

¹⁷The fourth lot came out to Issachar, for the children of Issachar according to their families. ¹⁸And their territory went to Jezreel, and *included* Chesulloth, Shunem, ¹⁹Haphraim, Shion, Anaharath, ²⁰Rabbith, Kishion, Abez, ²¹Remeth, En Gannim, En Haddah, and Beth Pazzez. ²²And the border reached to Tabor, Shahazimah, and Beth Shemesh; their border ended at the Jordan: sixteen cities with their villages. ²³This *was* the inheritance of the tribe of the children of Issachar according to their families, the cities and their villages.

The Land of Asher

²⁴The fifth lot came out for the tribe of the children of Asher according to their families. ²⁵And their territory included Helkath, Hali, Beten, Achshaph, ²⁶Alammelech, Amad, and Mishal; it reached to Mount Carmel westward, along *the Brook* Shihor Libnath. ²⁷It turned toward the sunrise to Beth Dagon; and it reached to Zebulun and to the Valley of Jiphthah El, then northward beyond Beth Emek and Neiel, bypassing Cabul *which was* on the left, ²⁸including Ebron,ᵃ Rehob, Hammon, and Kanah, as far as Greater Sidon. ²⁹And the border turned to Ramah and to the fortified city of Tyre; then the border turned to Hosah, and ended at the sea by the region of Achzib. ³⁰Also Ummah, Aphek, and Rehob

were included: twenty-two cities with their villages. ³¹This *was* the inheritance of the tribe of the children of Asher according to their families, these cities with their villages.

The Land of Naphtali

³²The sixth lot came out to the children of Naphtali, for the children of Naphtali according to their families. ³³And their border began at Heleph, enclosing the territory from the terebinth tree in Zaanannim, Adami Nekeb, and Jabneel, as far as Lakkum; it ended at the Jordan. ³⁴From Heleph the border extended westward to Aznoth Tabor, and went out from there toward Hukkok; it adjoined Zebulun on the south side and Asher on the west side, and ended at Judah by the Jordan toward the sunrise. ³⁵And the fortified cities *are* Ziddim, Zer, Hammath, Rakkath, Chinnereth, ³⁶Adamah, Ramah, Hazor, ³⁷Kedesh, Edrei, En Hazor, ³⁸Iron, Migdal El, Horem, Beth Anath, and Beth Shemesh: nineteen cities with their villages. ³⁹This *was* the inheritance of the tribe of the children of Naphtali according to their families, the cities and their villages.

19:33 terebinth tree. This was an oak tree, or an oak forest near Kedesh, NW of the waters at Merom. According to Judg. 4:11, this was the site where Jael killed Sisera with a hammer and tent peg.

The Land of Dan

⁴⁰The seventh lot came out for the tribe of the children of Dan according to their families. ⁴¹And the territory of their inheritance was Zorah, Eshtaol, Ir Shemesh, ⁴²Shaalabbin, Aijalon, Jethlah, ⁴³Elon, Timnah, Ekron, ⁴⁴Eltekeh, Gibbethon, Baalath, ⁴⁵Jehud, Bene Berak, Gath Rimmon, ⁴⁶Me Jarkon, and Rakkon, with the region near Joppa. ⁴⁷And the border of the children of Dan went beyond these, because the children of Dan went up to fight against Leshem and took it; and they struck it with the edge of the sword, took possession of it, and dwelt in it. They called Leshem, Dan, after the name of Dan their father. ⁴⁸This *is* the inheritance of the tribe of the children

---

19:28 ᵃFollowing Masoretic Text, Targum, and Vulgate; a few Hebrew manuscripts read *Abdon* (compare 21:30 and 1 Chronicles 6:74).

of Dan according to their families, these cities with their villages.

Joshua's Inheritance

⁴⁹When they had made an end of dividing the land as an inheritance according to their borders, the children of Israel gave an inheritance among them to Joshua the son of Nun. ⁵⁰According to the word of the LORD they gave him the city which he asked for, Timnath Serah in the mountains of Ephraim; and he built the city and dwelt in it.

> **19:49,50** Joshua received a special inheritance from Israel, an area he requested in the hills of his tribe, Ephraim. He built a city, Timnath Serah, and his inheritance fulfilled part of God's promise to him and Caleb (see Num. 14:30).

⁵¹These *were* the inheritances which Eleazar the priest, Joshua the son of Nun, and the heads of the fathers of the tribes of the children of Israel divided as an inheritance by lot in Shiloh before the LORD, at the door of the tabernacle of meeting. So they made an end of dividing the country.

The Cities of Refuge

20 The LORD also spoke to Joshua, saying, ²"Speak to the children of Israel, saying: 'Appoint for yourselves cities of refuge, of which I spoke to you through Moses, ³that the slayer who kills a person accidentally *or* unintentionally may flee there; and they shall be your refuge from the avenger of blood. ⁴And when he flees to one of those cities, and stands at the entrance of the gate of the city, and declares his case in the hearing of the elders of that city, they shall take him into the city as one of them, and give him a place, that he may dwell among them. ⁵Then if the avenger of blood pursues him, they shall not deliver the slayer into his hand, because he struck his neighbor unintentionally, but did not hate him beforehand. ⁶And he shall dwell in that city until he stands before the congregation for judgment, *and* until the death of the one who is high priest in those days. Then the slayer may return and come to his own city and his own house, to the city from which he fled.' "

⁷So they appointed Kedesh in Galilee, in the mountains of Naphtali, Shechem in the mountains of Ephraim, and Kirjath Arba (which *is* Hebron) in the mountains of Judah. ⁸And on the other side of the Jordan, by Jericho eastward, they assigned Bezer in the wilderness on the plain, from the tribe of Reuben, Ramoth in Gilead, from the tribe of Gad, and Golan in Bashan, from the tribe of Manasseh. ⁹These were the cities appointed for all the children of Israel and for the stranger who dwelt among them, that whoever killed a person accidentally might flee there, and not die by the hand of the avenger of blood until he stood before the congregation.

> **20:1–9 cities of refuge.** Moses had designated six cities of refuge, as God had commanded, where a person could flee if he unintentionally killed someone. Three cities lay on each side of the Jordan. A killer could seek protection in these cities from an avenging family member. Authorities would protect him and ensure he received a proper trial. If found innocent, he was guarded in the city until the death of the High-Priest, at which time he could return home. If found guilty, he was punished.

Cities of the Levites

21 Then the heads of the fathers' *houses* of the Levites came near to Eleazar the priest, to Joshua the son of Nun, and to the heads of the fathers' *houses* of the tribes of the children of Israel. ²And they spoke to them at Shiloh in the land of Canaan, saying, "The LORD commanded through Moses to give us cities to dwell in, with their common-lands for our livestock." ³So the children of Israel gave to the Levites from their inheritance, at the commandment of the LORD, these cities and their common-lands:

> **21:3–42 the children of Israel gave to the Levites.** The twelve tribes donated 48 cities for the Levites (including the six cities of refuge) and the surrounding land for their livestock. From these cities, the Levites could minister spiritually to the people nearby. Larger tribes devoted more land, and smaller tribes less. Only the branch of Levites called the Kohathites were priests, and the other branches assisted in roles of worship and labor.

⁴Now the lot came out for the families of the Kohathites. And the children of Aaron the priest, *who were* of the Levites, had

thirteen cities by lot from the tribe of Judah, from the tribe of Simeon, and from the tribe of Benjamin. [5]The rest of the children of Kohath had ten cities by lot from the families of the tribe of Ephraim, from the tribe of Dan, and from the half-tribe of Manasseh.

[6]And the children of Gershon had thirteen cities by lot from the families of the tribe of Issachar, from the tribe of Asher, from the tribe of Naphtali, and from the half-tribe of Manasseh in Bashan.

[7]The children of Merari according to their families had twelve cities from the tribe of Reuben, from the tribe of Gad, and from the tribe of Zebulun.

[8]And the children of Israel gave these cities with their common-lands by lot to the Levites, as the LORD had commanded by the hand of Moses.

[9]So they gave from the tribe of the children of Judah and from the tribe of the children of Simeon these cities which are designated by name, [10]which were for the children of Aaron, one of the families of the Kohathites, *who were* of the children of Levi; for the lot was theirs first. [11]And they gave them Kirjath Arba (*Arba was* the father of Anak), which *is* Hebron, in the mountains of Judah, with the common-land surrounding it. [12]But the fields of the city and its villages they gave to Caleb the son of Jephunneh as his possession.

[13]Thus to the children of Aaron the priest they gave Hebron with its common-land (a city of refuge for the slayer), Libnah with its common-land, [14]Jattir with its common-land, Eshtemoa with its common-land, [15]Holon with its common-land, Debir with its common-land, [16]Ain with its common-land, Juttah with its common-land, and Beth Shemesh with its common-land: nine cities from those two tribes; [17]and from the tribe of Benjamin, Gibeon with its common-land, Geba with its common-land, [18]Anathoth with its common-land, and Almon with its common-land: four cities. [19]All the cities of the children of Aaron, the priests, *were* thirteen cities with their common-lands.

[20]And the families of the children of Kohath, the Levites, the rest of the children of Kohath, even they had the cities of their lot from the tribe of Ephraim. [21]For they gave them Shechem with its common-land in the mountains of Ephraim (a city of refuge for the slayer), Gezer with its common-land, [22]Kibzaim with its common-land, and Beth Horon with its common-land: four cities; [23]and from the tribe of Dan, Eltekeh with its common-land, Gibbethon with its common-land, [24]Aijalon with its common-land, *and* Gath Rimmon with its common-land: four cities; [25]and from the half-tribe of Manasseh, Tanach with its common-land and Gath Rimmon with its common-land: two cities. [26]All the ten cities with their common-lands were for the rest of the families of the children of Kohath.

[27]Also to the children of Gershon, of the families of the Levites, from the *other* half-tribe of Manasseh, *they gave* Golan in Bashan with its common-land (a city of refuge for the slayer), and Be Eshterah with its common-land: two cities; [28]and from the tribe of Issachar, Kishion with its common-land, Daberath with its common-land, [29]Jarmuth with its common-land, *and* En Gannim with its common-land: four cities; [30]and from the tribe of Asher, Mishal with its common-land, Abdon with its common-land, [31]Helkath with its common-land, and Rehob with its common-land: four cities; [32]and from the tribe of Naphtali, Kedesh in Galilee with its common-land (a city of refuge for the slayer), Hammoth Dor with its common-land, and Kartan with its common-land: three cities. [33]All the cities of the Gershonites according to their families *were* thirteen cities with their common-lands.

[34]And to the families of the children of Merari, the rest of the Levites, from the tribe of Zebulun, Jokneam with its common-land, Kartah with its common-land, [35]Dimnah with its common-land, *and* Nahalal with its common-land: four cities; [36]and from the tribe of Reuben, Bezer with its common-land, Jahaz with its common-land, [37]Kedemoth with its common-land, and Mephaath with its common-land: four cities;[a] [38]and from the tribe of Gad, Ramoth

---

21:37 [a]Following Septuagint and Vulgate (compare 1 Chronicles 6:78,79); Masoretic Text, Bomberg, and Targum omit verses 36 and 37.

in Gilead with its common-land (a city of refuge for the slayer), Mahanaim with its common-land, ³⁹Heshbon with its common-land, *and* Jazer with its common-land: four cities in all. ⁴⁰So all the cities for the children of Merari according to their families, the rest of the families of the Levites, were *by* their lot twelve cities.

⁴¹All the cities of the Levites within the possession of the children of Israel *were* forty-eight cities with their common-lands. ⁴²Every one of these cities had its common-land surrounding it; thus *were* all these cities.

The Promise Fulfilled

⁴³So the LORD gave to Israel all the land of which He had sworn to give to their fathers, and they took possession of it and dwelt in it. ⁴⁴The LORD gave them rest all around, according to all that He had sworn to their fathers. And not a man of all their enemies stood against them; the LORD delivered all their enemies into their hand. ⁴⁵Not a word failed of any good thing which the LORD had spoken to the house of Israel. All came to pass.

21:43–45 So the LORD gave to Israel all the land. God fulfilled His covenant promise to give Abraham's people the Land (Gen. 12:7) and kept His Word that He would give them rest (Deut. 12:9,10). The Canaanites were in check but had not been driven out fully, which created problems later. The people failed to exercise their responsibility to possess their land to the fullest degree.

Eastern Tribes Return to Their Lands

22 Then Joshua called the Reubenites, the Gadites, and half the tribe of Manasseh, ²and said to them: "You have kept all that Moses the servant of the LORD commanded you, and have obeyed my voice in all that I commanded you. ³You have not left your brethren these many days, up to this day, but have kept the charge of the commandment of the LORD your God. ⁴And now the LORD your God has given rest to your brethren, as He

22:4 Moses…gave you. Through Moses and Joshua, God gave these tribes permission to settle east of the Jordan (Num. 32:30–33).

promised them; now therefore, return and go to your tents *and* to the land of your possession, which Moses the servant of the LORD gave you on the other side of the Jordan. ⁵But take careful heed to do the commandment and the law which Moses the servant of the LORD commanded you, to love the LORD your God, to walk in all His ways, to keep His commandments, to hold fast to Him, and to serve Him with all your heart and with all your soul." ⁶So Joshua blessed them and sent them away, and they went to their tents.

⁷Now to half the tribe of Manasseh Moses had given a possession in Bashan, but to the *other* half of it Joshua gave *a possession* among their brethren on this side of the Jordan, westward. And indeed, when Joshua sent them away to their tents, he blessed them, ⁸and spoke to them, saying, "Return with much riches to your tents, with very much livestock, with silver, with gold, with bronze, with iron, and with very much clothing. Divide the spoil of your enemies with your brethren."

⁹So the children of Reuben, the children of Gad, and half the tribe of Manasseh returned, and departed from the children of Israel at Shiloh, which *is* in the land of Canaan, to go to the country of Gilead, to the land of their possession, which they had obtained according to the word of the LORD by the hand of Moses.

An Altar by the Jordan

¹⁰And when they came to the region of the Jordan which *is* in the land of Canaan, the children of Reuben, the children of Gad, and half the tribe of Manasseh built an altar there by the Jordan—a great, impressive altar. ¹¹Now the children of Israel heard *someone* say, "Behold, the children of Reuben, the children of Gad, and half the tribe of Manasseh have built an altar on the frontier of the land of Canaan, in the region of the Jordan—on the children of Israel's side." ¹²And when the children of Israel heard *of it*, the whole congregation of the children of Israel gathered together at Shiloh to go to war against them.

¹³Then the children of Israel sent Phinehas the son of Eleazar the priest to the children of Reuben, to the children of Gad, and to half the tribe of Manasseh, into the land

of Gilead, ¹⁴and with him ten rulers, one ruler each from the chief house of every tribe of Israel; and each one *was* the head of the house of his father among the divisions*ᵃ* of Israel. ¹⁵Then they came to the children of Reuben, to the children of Gad, and to half the tribe of Manasseh, to the land of Gilead, and they spoke with them, saying, ¹⁶"Thus says the whole congregation of the LORD: 'What treachery *is* this that you have committed against the God of Israel, to turn away this day from following the LORD, in that you have built for yourselves an altar, that you might rebel this day against the LORD? ¹⁷*Is* the iniquity of Peor not enough for us, from which we are not cleansed till this day, although there was a plague in the congregation of the LORD, ¹⁸but that you must turn away this day from following the LORD? And it shall be, if you rebel today against the LORD, that tomorrow He will be angry with the whole congregation of Israel. ¹⁹Nevertheless, if the land of your possession *is* unclean, *then* cross over to the land of the possession of the LORD, where the LORD's tabernacle stands, and take possession among us; but do not rebel against the LORD, nor rebel against us, by building yourselves an altar besides the altar of the LORD our God. ²⁰Did not Achan the son of Zerah commit a trespass in the accursed thing, and wrath fell on all the congregation of Israel? And that man did not perish alone in his iniquity.' "

²¹Then the children of Reuben, the children of Gad, and half the tribe of Manasseh answered and said to the heads of the divisions*ᵃ* of Israel: ²²"The LORD God of gods, the LORD God of gods, He knows, and let Israel itself know—if *it is* in rebellion, or if in treachery against the LORD, do not save us this day. ²³If we have built ourselves an altar to turn from following the LORD, or if to offer on it burnt offerings or grain offerings, or if to offer peace offerings on it, let the LORD Himself require *an account.* ²⁴But in fact we have done it for fear, for a reason, saying, 'In time to come your descendants may speak to our descendants, saying, "What have you to do with the LORD God of Israel? ²⁵For the LORD has made the Jor-

dan a border between you and us, *you* children of Reuben and children of Gad. You have no part in the LORD." So your descendants would make our descendants cease fearing the LORD.' ²⁶Therefore we said, 'Let us now prepare to build ourselves an altar, not for burnt offering nor for sacrifice, ²⁷but *that* it *may be* a witness between you and us and our generations after us, that we may perform the service of the LORD before Him with our burnt offerings, with our sacrifices, and with our peace offerings; that your descendants may not say to our descendants in time to come, "You have no part in the LORD." ' ²⁸Therefore we said that it will be, when they say *this* to us or to our generations in time to come, that we may say, 'Here is the replica of the altar of the LORD which our fathers made, though not for burnt offerings nor for sacrifices; but it *is* a witness between you and us.' ²⁹Far be it from us that we should rebel against the LORD, and turn from following the LORD this day, to build an altar for burnt offerings, for grain offerings, or for sacrifices, besides the altar of the LORD our God which *is* before His tabernacle."

³⁰Now when Phinehas the priest and the rulers of the congregation, the heads of the divisions*ᵃ* of Israel who *were* with him, heard the words that the children of Reuben, the children of Gad, and the children of Manasseh spoke, it pleased them. ³¹Then Phinehas the son of Eleazar the priest said to the children of Reuben, the children of Gad, and the children of Manasseh, "This day we perceive that the LORD *is* among us, because you have not committed this treachery against the LORD. Now you have delivered the children of Israel out of the hand of the LORD."

³²And Phinehas the son of Eleazar the priest, and the rulers, returned from the children of Reuben and the children of Gad, from the land of Gilead to the land of Canaan, to the children of Israel, and brought back word to them. ³³So the thing pleased the children of Israel, and the children of Israel blessed God; they spoke no more of going against them in battle, to destroy the land where the children of Reuben and Gad dwelt.

22:14 *ᵃ*Literally *thousands*   22:21 *ᵃ*Literally *thousands*   22:30 *ᵃ*Literally *thousands*

³⁴The children of Reuben and the children of Gad*ᵃ* called the altar, *Witness,* "For *it is* a witness between us that the LORD *is* God."

> **22:10–34 an altar...by the Jordan.** The 2½ tribes east of the river built a special altar and aroused the suspicions of the western tribes, who feared they were rebelling against the Shiloh altar that served all the tribes in unity. The men assured them that they intended to follow God, remain unified with Israel, and not be regarded as outsiders. The other Israelites accepted their answer.

Joshua's Farewell Address

23 Now it came to pass, a long time after the LORD had given rest to Israel from all their enemies round about, that Joshua was old, advanced in age. ²And Joshua called for all Israel, for their elders, for their heads, for their judges, and for their officers, and said to them:

"I am old, advanced in age. ³You have seen all that the LORD your God has done to all these nations because of you, for the LORD your God *is* He who has fought for you. ⁴See, I have divided to you by lot these nations that remain, to be an inheritance for your tribes, from the Jordan, with all the nations that I have cut off, as far as the Great Sea westward. ⁵And the LORD your God will expel them from before you and drive them out of your sight. So you shall possess their land, as the LORD your God promised you. ⁶Therefore be very courageous to keep and to do all that is written in the Book of the Law of Moses, lest you turn aside from it to the right hand or to the left, ⁷*and* lest you go among these nations, these who remain among you. You shall not make mention of the name of their gods, nor cause *anyone* to swear *by them;* you shall not serve them nor bow down to them, ⁸but you shall hold fast to the LORD your God, as you have done to this day. ⁹For

> **23:5 the LORD...will expel them.** God was willing to help His people drive out the remaining Canaanites so that they could possess their claims more fully. Such moves needed to be gradual but determined, in obedience to God.

the LORD has driven out from before you great and strong nations; but *as for* you, no one has been able to stand against you to this day. ¹⁰One man of you shall chase a thousand, for the LORD your God *is* He who fights for you, as He promised you. ¹¹Therefore take careful heed to yourselves, that you love the LORD your God. ¹²Or else, if indeed you do go back, and cling to the remnant of these nations—these that remain among you—and make marriages with them, and go in to them and they to you, ¹³know for certain that the LORD your God will no longer drive out these nations from before you. But they shall be snares and traps to you, and scourges on your sides and thorns in your eyes, until you perish from this good land which the LORD your God has given you.

> **23:7,8** The danger of not completely driving out the Canaanites was that Israel might intermingle, intermarry, and drift from God because of their idolatrous influence. The Canaanites became snares to Israel, eventually causing them to lose the Land.

¹⁴"Behold, this day I *am* going the way of all the earth. And you know in all your hearts and in all your souls that not one thing has failed of all the good things which the LORD your God spoke concerning you. All have come to pass for you; not one word of them has failed. ¹⁵Therefore it shall come to pass, that as all the good things have come upon you which the LORD your God promised you, so the LORD will bring upon you all harmful things, until He has destroyed you from this good land which the LORD your God has given you. ¹⁶When you have transgressed the covenant of the LORD your God, which He commanded you, and have gone and served other gods, and bowed down to them, then the anger of the LORD will burn against you, and you shall perish quickly from the good land which He has given you."

The Covenant at Shechem

24 Then Joshua gathered all the tribes of Israel to Shechem and called for the elders of Israel, for their heads, for their judges, and for their officers; and

---

22:34 *ᵃ*Septuagint adds *and half the tribe of Manasseh*

they presented themselves before God. [2]And Joshua said to all the people, "Thus says the LORD God of Israel: 'Your fathers, *including* Terah, the father of Abraham and the father of Nahor, dwelt on the other side of the River[a] in old times; and they served other gods. [3]Then I took your father Abraham from the other side of the River, led him throughout all the land of Canaan, and multiplied his descendants and gave him Isaac. [4]To Isaac I gave Jacob and Esau. To Esau I gave the mountains of Seir to possess, but Jacob and his children went down to Egypt. [5]Also I sent Moses and Aaron, and I plagued Egypt, according to what I did among them. Afterward I brought you out.

[6]'Then I brought your fathers out of Egypt, and you came to the sea; and the Egyptians pursued your fathers with chariots and horsemen to the Red Sea. [7]So they cried out to the LORD; and He put darkness between you and the Egyptians, brought the sea upon them, and covered them. And your eyes saw what I did in Egypt. Then you dwelt in the wilderness a long time. [8]And I brought you into the land of the Amorites, who dwelt on the other side of the Jordan, and they fought with you. But I gave them into your hand, that you might possess their land, and I destroyed them from before you. [9]Then Balak the son of Zippor, king of Moab, arose to make war against Israel, and sent and called Balaam the son of Beor to curse you. [10]But I would not listen to Balaam; therefore he continued to bless you. So I delivered you out of his hand. [11]Then you went over the Jordan and came to Jericho. And the men of Jericho fought against you—*also* the Amorites, the Perizzites, the Canaanites, the Hittites, the Girgashites, the Hivites, and the Jebusites. But I delivered them into your hand. [12]I sent the hornet before you which drove them out from before you, *also* the two kings of the Amorites, *but* not with your sword or with your bow. [13]I have given you a land for which you did not labor, and cities which you did not build, and you dwell in them; you eat of the vineyards and olive groves which you did not plant.'

[14]"Now therefore, fear the LORD, serve Him in sincerity and in truth, and put away the gods which your fathers served on the other side of the River and in Egypt. Serve the LORD! [15]And if it seems evil to you to serve the LORD, choose for yourselves this day whom you will serve, whether the gods which your fathers served that *were* on the other side of the River, or the gods of the Amorites, in whose land you dwell. But as for me and my house, we will serve the LORD."

24:15 choose...this day whom you will serve. Reminiscent of Abraham's leadership in Gen. 18:19, Joshua set a model for Israel to follow, as he led his own family to serve God alone. He called others in Israel to commit themselves to the Lord.

[16]So the people answered and said: "Far be it from us that we should forsake the LORD to serve other gods; [17]for the LORD our God *is* He who brought us and our fathers up out of the land of Egypt, from the house of bondage, who did those great signs in our sight, and preserved us in all the way that we went and among all the people through whom we passed. [18]And the LORD drove out from before us all the people, including the Amorites who dwelt in the land. We also will serve the LORD, for He *is* our God."

[19]But Joshua said to the people, "You cannot serve the LORD, for He *is* a holy God. He *is* a jealous God; He will not forgive your transgressions nor your sins. [20]If you forsake the LORD and serve foreign gods, then He will turn and do you harm and consume you, after He has done you good."

[21]And the people said to Joshua, "No, but we will serve the LORD!"

[22]So Joshua said to the people, "You *are* witnesses against yourselves that you have chosen the LORD for yourselves, to serve Him."

And they said, "*We are* witnesses!"

[23]"Now therefore," *he said,* "put away the foreign gods which *are* among you, and incline your heart to the LORD God of Israel."

[24]And the people said to Joshua, "The LORD our God we will serve, and His voice we will obey!"

[25]So Joshua made a covenant with the people that day, and made for them a statute and an ordinance in Shechem.

24:2 [a]Hebrew *Nahar,* the Euphrates, and so in verses 3, 14, and 15

²⁶Then Joshua wrote these words in the Book of the Law of God. And he took a large stone, and set it up there under the oak that *was* by the sanctuary of the LORD. ²⁷And Joshua said to all the people, "Behold, this stone shall be a witness to us, for it has heard all the words of the LORD which He spoke to us. It shall therefore be a witness to you, lest you deny your God." ²⁸So Joshua let the people depart, each to his own inheritance.

Death of Joshua and Eleazar

²⁹Now it came to pass after these things that Joshua the son of Nun, the servant of the LORD, died, *being* one hundred and ten years old. ³⁰And they buried him within the border of his inheritance at Timnath Serah, which *is* in the mountains of Ephraim, on the north side of Mount Gaash.

³¹Israel served the LORD all the days of Joshua, and all the days of the elders who outlived Joshua, who had known all the works of the LORD which He had done for Israel.

³²The bones of Joseph, which the children of Israel had brought up out of Egypt, they buried at Shechem, in the plot of ground which Jacob had bought from the sons of Hamor the father of Shechem for one hundred pieces of silver, and which had become an inheritance of the children of Joseph.

³³And Eleazar the son of Aaron died. They buried him in a hill *belonging to* Phinehas his son, which was given to him in the mountains of Ephraim.

24:29–33 Three prominent leaders were buried as the conquering generation was passing on: Joshua, Joseph, and the High-Priest Eleazar. The Israelites had carried the bones of Joseph from Egypt (Ex 13:19) as he had made them promise (Gen. 50:25). He wanted his remains buried in the Land promised in the covenant (Gen. 12:7).

JUDGES

The final verse of Judges provides a summary for the book: "In those days there was no king in Israel; everyone did what was right in his own eyes" (21:25). Israel's dependence on God required by their journey in the wilderness and subsequent military campaigns to conquer the land quickly gave way to a complacent independence of settled people. They forgot that they still needed God. He had given them the land, and they could not hold it without Him.

Israel's failure to evict the peoples of the Land as God had commanded led to the results God had predicted (Joshua 1:27–2:4). The Canaanite nations became thorns to Israel, and the land was in constant turmoil. In desperate times, Israel would realize the slide into sinfulness and cry to God for forgiveness and deliverance. At each occasion, God would send unique leaders (judges) to deliver them (Joshua 2:16–19). In Hebrew, the title of this book can also mean "deliverers" or "saviors." Judges records the careers of 12 God-chosen leaders.

AUTHOR AND DATE

Judges was probably written by Samuel, approximately 1043 to 1004 B.C.

Though Judges does not indicate an author, ancient Jewish tradition assigns that task to Samuel. Samuel's life spanned the end of the period of Judges and the early years of the monarchy in Israel. Internal evidence in the book indicates at least a contemporary of Samuel who could summarize the period of history and acknowledge the kings, yet also note that Jerusalem was still under the control of the Jacobites. A comparison of 1:21 with 2 Samuel 5:6,7 leads to the conclusion that this book was recorded between Saul's rise to the throne in 1043 B.C. and David's capture of Jerusalem in 1004 B.C.

BACKGROUND AND SETTING

The Book of Judges represents a tragic sequel to Joshua. In the Book of Joshua, most of the people were obedient to God in conquering the Land. Judges portrays them as disobedient, idolatrous, and often defeated. After touching on the final days of Joshua and his death (1:1–3:6), the book describes seven distinct cycles in Israel's stormy relationship with God. These cycles reveal five basic reasons that lie behind the downward spiral of Israel's moral and spiritual life: (1) disobedience in their failure to drive out the Canaanites from the Land (1:19,21,35); (2) idolatry in adopting local gods and religious practices (2:12); (3) intermarriage with

wicked Canaanites against God's instructions (3:1–6); (4) minimal cooperation with the judges (2:17); (5) turning away from God after the death of each judge (2:19).

The seven cycles also demonstrate the repeated four-step sequence of God's intervention in Israel's life: (1) Israel departs from following God's ways; (2) God faithfully corrects by allowing military defeat and foreign domination; (3) Israel cries out for deliverance; (4) God raises up "judges" who serve as civil or military champions and lead victories over the oppressors.

HISTORICAL AND THEOLOGICAL THEMES

Judges offers a thematic rather than chronological overview of this part of Israel's history. Foremost among the themes are God's power and God's covenant mercy. These are repeatedly demonstrated as He delivers Israel from the consequences of their failures

EVERY PART OF ISRAEL FAILED GOD, BUT GOD WAS FAITHFUL TO ALL OF ISRAEL.

which have resulted from their sinful compromises (2:18,19; 21:25). The seven cycles that follow the people from salvation to sin and back around highlight God's far flung compassion, intervening throughout the Promised Land, as each region suffers its particular time of decay and deliverance. Every part of Israel failed God, but God was faithful to all of Israel. Even in the darkest moments of sin recorded in this book, God continually drew people to Himself, preserving those who would carry His promises into the future.

OUTLINE

The Continuing Conquest of Canaan

1 Now after the death of Joshua it came to pass that the children of Israel asked the LORD, saying, "Who shall be first to go up for us against the Canaanites to fight against them?"

²And the LORD said, "Judah shall go up. Indeed I have delivered the land into his hand."

> **1:2 Judah shall go up.** This tribe received God's first permission to conquest their full territory. God wanted Judah to be the leader among the tribes (Gen. 49:8–12; 1 Chr. 5:1,2) and to set the example for the rest to follow.

³So Judah said to Simeon his brother, "Come up with me to my allotted territory, that we may fight against the Canaanites; and I will likewise go with you to your allotted territory." And Simeon went with him. ⁴Then Judah went up, and the LORD delivered the Canaanites and the Perizzites into their hand; and they killed ten thousand men at Bezek. ⁵And they found Adoni-Bezek in Bezek, and fought against him; and they defeated the Canaanites and the Perizzites. ⁶Then Adoni-Bezek fled, and they pursued him and caught him and cut off his thumbs and big toes. ⁷And Adoni-Bezek said, "Seventy kings with their thumbs and big toes cut off used to gather *scraps* under my table; as I have done, so God has repaid me." Then they brought him to Jerusalem, and there he died.

⁸Now the children of Judah fought against Jerusalem and took it; they struck it with the edge of the sword and set the city on fire. ⁹And afterward the children of Judah went down to fight against the Canaanites who dwelt in the mountains, in the South,ᵃ and in the lowland. ¹⁰Then Judah went against the Canaanites who dwelt in Hebron. (Now the name of Hebron *was* formerly Kirjath Arba.) And they killed Sheshai, Ahiman, and Talmai.

¹¹From there they went against the inhabitants of Debir. (The name of Debir *was* formerly Kirjath Sepher.)

¹²Then Caleb said, "Whoever attacks Kirjath Sepher and takes it, to him I will give my daughter Achsah as wife." ¹³And Othniel the son of Kenaz, Caleb's younger brother, took it; so he gave him his daughter Achsah as wife. ¹⁴Now it happened, when she came *to him*, that she urged himᵃ to ask her father for a field. And she dismounted from *her* donkey, and Caleb said to her, "What do you wish?" ¹⁵So she said to him, "Give me a blessing; since you have given me land in the South, give me also springs of water."

And Caleb gave her the upper springs and the lower springs.

¹⁶Now the children of the Kenite, Moses' father-in-law, went up from the City of Palms with the children of Judah into the Wilderness of Judah, which *lies* in the South *near* Arad; and they went and dwelt among the people. ¹⁷And Judah went with his brother Simeon, and they attacked the Canaanites who inhabited Zephath, and utterly destroyed it. So the name of the city was called Hormah. ¹⁸Also Judah took Gaza with its territory, Ashkelon with its territory, and Ekron with its territory. ¹⁹So the LORD was with Judah. And they drove out the mountaineers, but they could not drive out the inhabitants of the lowland, because they had chariots of iron. ²⁰And they gave Hebron to Caleb, as Moses had said. Then he expelled from there the three sons of Anak. ²¹But the children of Benjamin did not drive out the Jebusites who inhabited Jerusalem; so the Jebusites dwell with the children of Benjamin in Jerusalem to this day.

> **1:19 they could not drive out.** God permitted the enemy to hold out to test His people's obedience. Although Joshua had promised them that they could conquer the lowland (Josh. 17:16,18), they failed to fully trust and obey God to empower them for victory. They compromised for less than what God could give them.

²²And the house of Joseph also went up against Bethel, and the LORD *was* with them. ²³So the house of Joseph sent men to spy out Bethel. (The name of the city *was* formerly Luz.) ²⁴And when the spies saw a man coming out of the city, they said to him, "Please show us the entrance to the city, and we will show you mercy."

1:9 ᵃHebrew *Negev*, and so throughout this book   1:14 ᵃSeptuagint and Vulgate read *he urged her.*

²⁵So he showed them the entrance to the city, and they struck the city with the edge of the sword; but they let the man and all his family go. ²⁶And the man went to the land of the Hittites, built a city, and called its name Luz, which *is* its name to this day.

Incomplete Conquest of the Land

²⁷However, Manasseh did not drive out *the inhabitants of* Beth Shean and its villages, or Taanach and its villages, or the inhabitants of Dor and its villages, or the inhabitants of Ibleam and its villages, or the inhabitants of Megiddo and its villages; for the Canaanites were determined to dwell in that land. ²⁸And it came to pass, when Israel was strong, that they put the Canaanites under tribute, but did not completely drive them out.

²⁹Nor did Ephraim drive out the Canaanites who dwelt in Gezer; so the Canaanites dwelt in Gezer among them.

³⁰Nor did Zebulun drive out the inhabitants of Kitron or the inhabitants of Nahalol; so the Canaanites dwelt among them, and were put under tribute.

³¹Nor did Asher drive out the inhabitants of Acco or the inhabitants of Sidon, or of Ahlab, Achzib, Helbah, Aphik, or Rehob. ³²So the Asherites dwelt among the Canaanites, the inhabitants of the land; for they did not drive them out.

³³Nor did Naphtali drive out the inhabitants of Beth Shemesh or the inhabitants of Beth Anath; but they dwelt among the Canaanites, the inhabitants of the land. Nevertheless the inhabitants of Beth Shemesh and Beth Anath were put under tribute to them.

³⁴And the Amorites forced the children of Dan into the mountains, for they would not allow them to come down to the valley; ³⁵and the Amorites were determined to dwell in Mount Heres, in Aijalon, and in Shaalbim;ᵃ yet when the strength of the house of Joseph became greater, they were put under tribute.

³⁶Now the boundary of the Amorites *was* from the Ascent of Akrabbim, from Sela, and upward.

Israel's Disobedience

2 Then the Angel of the LORD came up from Gilgal to Bochim, and said: "I led you up from Egypt and brought you to the land of which I swore to your fathers; and I said, 'I will never break My covenant with you. ²And you shall make no covenant with the inhabitants of this land; you shall tear down their altars.' But you have not obeyed My voice. Why have you done this? ³Therefore I also said, 'I will not drive them out before you; but they shall be *thorns* in your side,ᵃ and their gods shall be a snare to you.' " ⁴So it was, when the Angel of the LORD spoke these words to all the children of Israel, that the people lifted up their voices and wept.

> **2:1 the Angel of the LORD.** One of three, preincarnate appearances by the Lord Jesus Christ in the book of Judges (see 6:11-18; 13:3-23).

⁵Then they called the name of that place Bochim;ᵃ and they sacrificed there to the LORD. ⁶And when Joshua had dismissed the people, the children of Israel went each to his own inheritance to possess the land.

Death of Joshua

⁷So the people served the LORD all the days of Joshua, and all the days of the elders who outlived Joshua, who had seen all the great works of the LORD which He had done for Israel. ⁸Now Joshua the son of Nun, the servant of the LORD, died *when he was* one hundred and ten years old. ⁹And they buried him within the border of his inheritance at Timnath Heres, in the mountains of Ephraim, on the north side of Mount Gaash. ¹⁰When all that generation had been gathered to their fathers, another generation arose after them who did not

> **2:10 another generation...did not know.** The first people in the Land vividly remembered all of God's miracles and were devoted to faith, duty, and purity. But the new generation was ignorant of their parents' experiences and yielded more easily to corruption. Some of the people did genuinely know the Lord, however.

1:35 ᵃSpelled *Shaalabbin* in Joshua 19:42   2:3 ᵃSeptuagint, Targum, and Vulgate read *enemies to you*.   2:5 ᵃLiterally *Weeping*

know the LORD nor the work which He had done for Israel.

Israel's Unfaithfulness

[11]Then the children of Israel did evil in the sight of the LORD, and served the Baals; [12]and they forsook the LORD God of their fathers, who had brought them out of the land of Egypt; and they followed other gods from *among* the gods of the people who *were* all around them, and they bowed down to them; and they provoked the LORD to anger. [13]They forsook the LORD and served Baal and the Ashtoreths.[a] [14]And the anger of the LORD was hot against Israel. So He delivered them into the hands of plunderers who despoiled them; and He sold them into the hands of their enemies all around, so that they could no longer stand before their enemies. [15]Wherever they went out, the hand of the LORD was against them for calamity, as the LORD had said, and as the LORD had sworn to them. And they were greatly distressed.

[16]Nevertheless, the LORD raised up judges who delivered them out of the hand of those who plundered them. [17]Yet they would not listen to their judges, but they played the harlot with other gods, and bowed down to them. They turned quickly from the way in which their fathers walked, in obeying the commandments of the LORD; they did not do so. [18]And when the LORD raised up judges for them, the LORD was with the judge and delivered them out of the hand of their enemies all the days of the judge; for the LORD was moved to pity by their groaning because of those who oppressed them and harassed them. [19]And it came to pass, when the judge was dead, that they reverted and behaved more corruptly than their fathers, by following other gods, to serve them and bow down to them. They did not cease from their own doings nor from their stubborn way.

> **2:16 the LORD raised up judges.** A "judge" or deliverer is different from a judge in the modern sense. A judge led military expeditions against foes and decided legal matters. They were chosen by God to lead and rescue the people.

[20]Then the anger of the LORD was hot against Israel; and He said, "Because this nation has transgressed My covenant which I commanded their fathers, and has not heeded My voice, [21]I also will no longer drive out before them any of the nations which Joshua left when he died, [22]so that through them I may test Israel, whether they will keep the ways of the LORD, to walk in them as their fathers kept *them,* or not." [23]Therefore the LORD left those nations, without driving them out immediately; nor did He deliver them into the hand of Joshua.

The Nations Remaining in the Land

3 Now these *are* the nations which the LORD left, that He might test Israel by them, *that is,* all who had not known any of the wars in Canaan [2](*this was* only so that the generations of the children of Israel might be taught to know war, at least those who had not formerly known it), [3]namely, five lords of the Philistines, all the Canaanites, the Sidonians, and the Hivites who dwelt in Mount Lebanon, from Mount Baal Hermon to the entrance of Hamath. [4]And they were *left, that He might* test Israel by them, to know whether they would obey the commandments of the LORD, which He had commanded their fathers by the hand of Moses.

[5]Thus the children of Israel dwelt among the Canaanites, the Hittites, the Amorites, the Perizzites, the Hivites, and the Jebusites. [6]And they took their daughters to be their wives, and gave their daughters to their sons; and they served their gods.

> **3:6** The Israelites repeatedly failed God's tests when they were enticed into marriages with Canaanites and into worship of other gods. Eventually God expelled them from the Land, using the Assyrians and Babylonians.

Othniel

[7]So the children of Israel did evil in the sight of the LORD. They forgot the LORD their God, and served the Baals and Asherahs.[a] [8]Therefore the anger of the LORD was hot against Israel, and He sold them into the hand of Cushan-Rishathaim

---

2:13 [a]Canaanite goddesses   3:7 [a]Name or symbol for Canaanite goddesses

THE JUDGES OF ISRAEL

Judge and Tribe	Scripture References	Oppressors	Period of Oppression/Rest
(1) **Othniel** (Judah) Son of Kenaz, younger brother of Caleb	Judges 1:11–15; 3:1–11; Joshua 15:16–19; 1 Chronicles 4:13	Cushan-Rishathaim, king of Mesopotamia	8 years/40 years
(2) **Ehud** (Benjamin) Son of Gera	Judges 3:12–4:1	Eglon, king of Moab; Ammonites; Amalekites	18 years/80 years
(3) **Shamgar** (Perhaps foreign) Son of Anath	Judges 3:31; 5:6	Philistines	Not given/Not given
(4) **Deborah** (Ephraim), **Barak** (Naphtali) Son of Abinoam	Judges 4:1–5:31 Hebrews 11:32	Jabin, king of Canaan; Sisera commander of the army	20 years/40 years
(5) **Gideon** (Manasseh) Son of Joash the Abiezrite. Also called: Jerubbaal (6:32; 7:1); Jerubbesheth (2 Samuel 11:21)	Judges 6:1–8:32 Hebrews 11:32	Midianites; Amalekites; "People of the East"	7 years/40 years
(6) **Abimelech** (Manasseh) Son of Gideon by a concubine	Judges 8:33–9:57; 2 Samuel 11:21	Civil war	Abimelech ruled over Israel 3 years
(7) **Tola** (Issachar) Son of Puah	Judges 10:1, 2		Judged Israel 23 years
(8) **Jair** (Gilead-Manasseh)	Judges 10:3–5		Judged Israel 22 years
(9) **Jephthah** (Gilead-Manasseh) Son of Gilead by a harlot	Judges 10:6–12:7 Hebrews 11:32	Philistines; Ammonites; Civil war with the Ephramites	18 years/ Judged Israel 6 years
(10) **Ibzan** (Judah or Zebulun) (Bethlehem-Zebulun; see Joshua 19:15)	Judges 12:8–10		Judged Israel 7 years
(11) **Elon** (Zebulun)	Judges 12:11,12		Judged Israel 10 years
(12) **Abdon** (Ephraim) Son of Hillel	Judges 12:13–15		Judged Israel 8 years
(13) **Samson** (Dan) Son of Manoah	Judges 13:1–16:31 Hebrews 11:32	Philistines	40 years/ Judged Israel 20 years

king of Mesopotamia; and the children of Israel served Cushan-Rishathaim eight years. ⁹When the children of Israel cried out to the LORD, the LORD raised up a deliverer for the children of Israel, who delivered them: Othniel the son of Kenaz, Caleb's younger brother. ¹⁰The Spirit of the LORD came upon him, and he judged Israel. He went out to war, and the LORD delivered Cushan-Rishathaim king of Mesopotamia into his hand; and his hand prevailed over Cushan-Rishathaim. ¹¹So the land had rest for forty years. Then Othniel the son of Kenaz died.

> **3:10 The Spirit of the LORD came.** The Bible records that certain judges were blessed with the Spirit of the Lord upon them (see 6:34; 11:29; 13:25; 14:6,19; 15:14). This expression signifies God's presence with them, granting them power and wisdom for victory, but it does not guarantee that the judges acted perfectly (see 8:24–27,30; 16:1).

Ehud

¹²And the children of Israel again did evil in the sight of the LORD. So the LORD strengthened Eglon king of Moab against Israel, because they had done evil in the sight of the LORD. ¹³Then he gathered to himself the people of Ammon and Amalek, went and defeated Israel, and took possession of the City of Palms. ¹⁴So the children of Israel served Eglon king of Moab eighteen years.

¹⁵But when the children of Israel cried out to the LORD, the LORD raised up a deliverer for them: Ehud the son of Gera, the Benjamite, a left-handed man. By him the children of Israel sent tribute to Eglon king of Moab. ¹⁶Now Ehud made himself a dagger (it was double-edged and a cubit in length) and fastened it under his clothes on his right thigh. ¹⁷So he brought the tribute to Eglon king of Moab. (Now Eglon *was* a very fat man.) ¹⁸And when he had finished presenting the tribute, he sent away the people who had carried the tribute. ¹⁹But he himself turned back from the stone images that *were* at Gilgal, and said, "I have a secret message for you, O king."

He said, "Keep silence!" And all who attended him went out from him.

²⁰So Ehud came to him (now he was sitting upstairs in his cool private chamber). Then Ehud said, "I have a message from God for you." So he arose from *his* seat. ²¹Then Ehud reached with his left hand, took the dagger from his right thigh, and thrust it into his belly. ²²Even the hilt went in after the blade, and the fat closed over the blade, for he did not draw the dagger out of his belly; and his entrails came out. ²³Then Ehud went out through the porch and shut the doors of the upper room behind him and locked them.

> **3:24 "He is...attending to his needs..."** The king's servants guessed that he was using the bathroom, which would explain the locked door.

²⁴When he had gone out, *Eglon's*ᵃ servants came to look, and *to their* surprise, the doors of the upper room were locked. So they said, "He is probably attending to his needs in the cool chamber." ²⁵So they waited till they were embarrassed, and still he had not opened the doors of the upper room. Therefore they took the key and opened *them*. And there was their master, fallen dead on the floor.

²⁶But Ehud had escaped while they delayed, and passed beyond the stone images and escaped to Seirah. ²⁷And it happened, when he arrived, that he blew the trumpet in the mountains of Ephraim, and the children of Israel went down with him from the mountains; and he led them. ²⁸Then he said to them, "Follow *me*, for the LORD has delivered your enemies the Moabites into your hand." So they went down after him, seized the fords of the Jordan leading to Moab, and did not allow anyone to cross over. ²⁹And at that time they killed about ten thousand men of Moab, all stout men of valor; not a man escaped. ³⁰So Moab was subdued that day under the hand of Israel. And the land had rest for eighty years.

Shamgar

³¹After him was Shamgar the son of Anath, who killed six hundred men of the Philistines with an ox goad; and he also delivered Israel.

3:24 ᵃLiterally *his*

Deborah

4 When Ehud was dead, the children of Israel again did evil in the sight of the LORD. ²So the LORD sold them into the hand of Jabin king of Canaan, who reigned in Hazor. The commander of his army *was* Sisera, who dwelt in Harosheth Hagoyim. ³And the children of Israel cried out to the LORD; for Jabin had nine hundred chariots of iron, and for twenty years he had harshly oppressed the children of Israel.

⁴Now Deborah, a prophetess, the wife of Lapidoth, was judging Israel at that time. ⁵And she would sit under the palm tree of Deborah between Ramah and Bethel in the mountains of Ephraim. And the children of Israel came up to her for judgment. ⁶Then she sent and called for Barak the son of Abinoam from Kedesh in Naphtali, and said to him, "Has not the LORD God of Israel commanded, 'Go and deploy *troops* at Mount Tabor; take with you ten thousand men of the sons of Naphtali and of the sons of Zebulun; ⁷and against you I will deploy Sisera, the commander of Jabin's army, with his chariots and his multitude at the River Kishon; and I will deliver him into your hand'?"

> **4:4 Deborah, a prophetess.** She was an unusual woman with great wisdom and influence, who served as a judge but did not lead the military. God uses women in mighty ways, e.g. Huldah the prophetess (2 Kin. 22:14). Because Barak cowardly refused to lead, God used Deborah instead.

⁸And Barak said to her, "If you will go with me, then I will go; but if you will not go with me, I will not go!"

⁹So she said, "I will surely go with you; nevertheless there will be no glory for you in the journey you are taking, for the LORD will sell Sisera into the hand of a woman." Then Deborah arose and went with Barak to Kedesh. ¹⁰And Barak called Zebulun and Naphtali to Kedesh; he went up with ten thousand men under his command,ᵃ and Deborah went up with him.

¹¹Now Heber the Kenite, of the children of Hobab the father-in-law of Moses, had separated himself from the Kenites and pitched his tent near the terebinth tree at Zaanaim, which *is* beside Kedesh.

¹²And they reported to Sisera that Barak the son of Abinoam had gone up to Mount Tabor. ¹³So Sisera gathered together all his chariots, nine hundred chariots of iron, and all the people who *were* with him, from Harosheth Hagoyim to the River Kishon.

¹⁴Then Deborah said to Barak, "Up! For this *is* the day in which the LORD has delivered Sisera into your hand. Has not the LORD gone out before you?" So Barak went down from Mount Tabor with ten thousand men following him. ¹⁵And the LORD routed Sisera and all *his* chariots and all *his* army with the edge of the sword before Barak; and Sisera alighted from *his* chariot and fled away on foot. ¹⁶But Barak pursued the chariots and the army as far as Harosheth Hagoyim, and all the army of Sisera fell by the edge of the sword; not a man was left.

¹⁷However, Sisera had fled away on foot to the tent of Jael, the wife of Heber the Kenite; for *there was* peace between Jabin king of Hazor and the house of Heber the Kenite. ¹⁸And Jael went out to meet Sisera, and said to him, "Turn aside, my lord, turn

4:10 ᵃLiterally *at his feet*

What can we gain by studying the lives of the Judges of Israel?

God's Word includes a rich panorama of human experience. Despite the superficial transformation of much of the world, the people who inhabit it remain the same. When we study the lives of the Judges we discover ourselves. The shared victories, defeats, mistakes and right choices form a common link across the centuries and turn our attention to the God who was active in their lives. The invitation from the ancients remains silently compelling: If we were to live as boldly for God, surely we would discover each day that same kind of God's immediate presence that was such a part of their experience.

aside to me; do not fear." And when he had turned aside with her into the tent, she covered him with a blanket.

19Then he said to her, "Please give me a little water to drink, for I am thirsty." So she opened a jug of milk, gave him a drink, and covered him. 20And he said to her, "Stand at the door of the tent, and if any man comes and inquires of you, and says, 'Is there any man here?' you shall say, 'No.'"

21Then Jael, Heber's wife, took a tent peg and took a hammer in her hand, and went softly to him and drove the peg into his temple, and it went down into the ground; for he was fast asleep and weary. So he died. 22And then, as Barak pursued Sisera, Jael came out to meet him, and said to him, "Come, I will show you the man whom you seek." And when he went into her *tent*, there lay Sisera, dead with the peg in his temple.

23So on that day God subdued Jabin king of Canaan in the presence of the children of Israel. 24And the hand of the children of Israel grew stronger and stronger against Jabin king of Canaan, until they had destroyed Jabin king of Canaan.

The Song of Deborah

5 Then Deborah and Barak the son of Abinoam sang on that day, saying:

> **5:1 sang on that day.** The song praised God for the victory He gave them in Judg. 4:13–25. Other songs of praise include Moses' (Ex. 15), David's (2 Sam. 23:1–7), and the Lamb's (Rev. 15:3,4).

2   "When leaders lead in Israel,
        When the people willingly offer
            themselves,
        Bless the LORD!

3   "Hear, O kings! Give ear, O princes!
        I, *even* I, will sing to the LORD;
        I will sing praise to the LORD God of
            Israel.

4   "LORD, when You went out from Seir,
        When You marched from the field of
            Edom,
        The earth trembled and the heavens
            poured,

5   The clouds also poured water;
        The mountains gushed before the
            LORD,
        This Sinai, before the LORD God of
            Israel.

6   "In the days of Shamgar, son of
            Anath,
        In the days of Jael,
        The highways were deserted,
        And the travelers walked along the
            byways.

7   Village life ceased, it ceased in Israel,
        Until I, Deborah, arose,
        Arose a mother in Israel.

8   They chose new gods;
        Then *there was* war in the gates;
        Not a shield or spear was seen among
            forty thousand in Israel.

9   My heart *is* with the rulers of Israel
        Who offered themselves willingly with
            the people.
        Bless the LORD!

10 "Speak, you who ride on white
            donkeys,
        Who sit in judges' attire,
        And who walk along the road.

11   Far from the noise of the archers,
            among the watering places,
        There they shall recount the righteous
            acts of the LORD,
        The righteous acts *for* His villagers in
            Israel;
        Then the people of the LORD shall go
            down to the gates.

12 "Awake, awake, Deborah!
        Awake, awake, sing a song!
        Arise, Barak, and lead your captives
            away,
        O son of Abinoam!

13 "Then the survivors came down, the
            people against the nobles;
        The LORD came down for me against
            the mighty.

14   From Ephraim *were* those whose
            roots were in Amalek.
        After you, Benjamin, with your
            peoples,
        From Machir rulers came down,
        And from Zebulun those who bear the
            recruiter's staff.

15 And the princes of Issachar*a* *were*
        with Deborah;
    As Issachar, so *was* Barak
    Sent into the valley under his
        command;*b*
    Among the divisions of Reuben
    There were great resolves of heart.
16 Why did you sit among the
        sheepfolds,
    To hear the pipings for the flocks?
    The divisions of Reuben have great
        searchings of heart.
17 Gilead stayed beyond the Jordan,
    And why did Dan remain on ships?*a*
    Asher continued at the seashore,
    And stayed by his inlets.
18 Zebulun *is* a people *who* jeopardized
        their lives to the point of death,
    Naphtali also, on the heights of the
        battlefield.

19 "The kings came *and* fought,
    Then the kings of Canaan fought
    In Taanach, by the waters of Megiddo;
    They took no spoils of silver.
20 They fought from the heavens;
    The stars from their courses fought
        against Sisera.

5:20 stars...fought. A poetic expression to show that
God used the stars to help Israel. The stars represent
the sky, from which He sent the powerful storm and
flood ("torrent" in v.21) that swept the Syrians from
their chariots. He also hid the stars by clouds so that
the Syrians could not see clearly.

21 The torrent of Kishon swept them
        away,
    That ancient torrent, the torrent of
        Kishon.
    O my soul, march on in strength!
22 Then the horses' hooves pounded,
    The galloping, galloping of his
        steeds.
23 'Curse Meroz,' said the angel*a* of the
        LORD,
    'Curse its inhabitants bitterly,
    Because they did not come to the help
        of the LORD,
    To the help of the LORD against the
        mighty.'

24 "Most blessed among women is Jael,
    The wife of Heber the Kenite;
    Blessed is she among women in tents.
25 He asked for water, she gave milk;
    She brought out cream in a lordly
        bowl.
26 She stretched her hand to the tent
        peg,
    Her right hand to the workmen's
        hammer;
    She pounded Sisera, she pierced his
        head,
    She split and struck through his
        temple.
27 At her feet he sank, he fell, he lay
        still;
    At her feet he sank, he fell;
    Where he sank, there he fell dead.

28 "The mother of Sisera looked through
        the window,
    And cried out through the lattice,
    'Why is his chariot *so* long in coming?
    Why tarries the clatter of his
        chariots?'
29 Her wisest ladies answered her,
    Yes, she answered herself,
30 'Are they not finding and dividing the
        spoil:
    To every man a girl *or* two;
    For Sisera, plunder of dyed garments,
    Plunder of garments embroidered and
        dyed,
    Two pieces of dyed embroidery for the
        neck of the looter?'

31 "Thus let all Your enemies perish,
        O LORD!
    But *let* those who love Him *be* like
        the sun
    When it comes out in full strength."

So the land had rest for forty years.

Midianites Oppress Israel

6 Then the children of Israel did evil in
the sight of the LORD. So the LORD delivered them into the hand of Midian for
seven years, ²and the hand of Midian prevailed against Israel. Because of the Midianites, the children of Israel made for

---

5:15 *a*Following Septuagint, Syriac, Targum, and Vulgate; Masoretic Text reads *And my princes in
Issachar.*   *b*Literally *at his feet*   5:17 *a*Or *at ease*   5:23 *a*Or *Angel*

themselves the dens, the caves, and the strongholds which *are* in the mountains. ³So it was, whenever Israel had sown, Midianites would come up; also Amalekites and the people of the East would come up against them. ⁴Then they would encamp against them and destroy the produce of the earth as far as Gaza, and leave no sustenance for Israel, neither sheep nor ox nor donkey. ⁵For they would come up with their livestock and their tents, coming in as numerous as locusts; both they and their camels were without number; and they would enter the land to destroy it. ⁶So Israel was greatly impoverished because of the Midianites, and the children of Israel cried out to the LORD.

⁷And it came to pass, when the children of Israel cried out to the LORD because of the Midianites, ⁸that the LORD sent a prophet to the children of Israel, who said to them, "Thus says the LORD God of Israel: 'I brought you up from Egypt and brought you out of the house of bondage; ⁹and I delivered you out of the hand of the Egyptians and out of the hand of all who oppressed you, and drove them out before you and gave you their land. ¹⁰Also I said to you, "I *am* the LORD your God; do not fear the gods of the Amorites, in whose land you dwell." But you have not obeyed My voice.' "

Gideon
¹¹Now the Angel of the LORD came and sat under the terebinth tree which *was* in Ophrah, which *belonged* to Joash the Abi-

ezrite, while his son Gideon threshed wheat in the winepress, in order to hide *it* from the Midianites. ¹²And the Angel of the LORD appeared to him, and said to him, "The LORD *is* with you, you mighty man of valor!"

¹³Gideon said to Him, "O my lord,ᵃ if the LORD is with us, why then has all this happened to us? And where *are* all His miracles which our fathers told us about, saying, 'Did not the LORD bring us up from Egypt?' But now the LORD has forsaken us and delivered us into the hands of the Midianites."

¹⁴Then the LORD turned to him and said, "Go in this might of yours, and you shall save Israel from the hand of the Midianites. Have I not sent you?"

¹⁵So he said to Him, "O my Lord,ᵃ how can I save Israel? Indeed my clan *is* the weakest in Manasseh, and I *am* the least in my father's house."

¹⁶And the LORD said to him, "Surely I will be with you, and you shall defeat the Midianites as one man."

¹⁷Then he said to Him, "If now I have found favor in Your sight, then show me a sign that it is You who talk with me. ¹⁸Do not depart from here, I pray, until I come to You and bring out my offering and set *it* before You."

And He said, "I will wait until you come back."

¹⁹So Gideon went in and prepared a young goat, and unleavened bread from an ephah of flour. The meat he put in a basket, and he put the broth in a pot; and he brought *them* out to Him under the terebinth tree and presented *them*. ²⁰The Angel of God said to him, "Take the meat and the unleavened bread and lay *them* on this rock, and pour out the broth." And he did so.

²¹Then the Angel of the LORD put out the end of the staff that *was* in His hand, and touched the meat and the unleavened bread; and fire rose out of the rock and con-

sumed the meat and the unleavened bread. And the Angel of the LORD departed out of his sight.

²²Now Gideon perceived that He *was* the Angel of the LORD. So Gideon said, "Alas, O Lord GOD! For I have seen the Angel of the LORD face to face."

²³Then the LORD said to him, "Peace *be* with you; do not fear, you shall not die." ²⁴So Gideon built an altar there to the LORD, and called it The-LORD-*Is*-Peace.ᵃ To this day it *is* still in Ophrah of the Abiezrites.

²⁵Now it came to pass the same night that the LORD said to him, "Take your father's young bull, the second bull of seven years old, and tear down the altar of Baal that your father has, and cut down the wooden imageᵃ that *is* beside it; ²⁶and build an altar to the LORD your God on top of this rock in the proper arrangement, and take the second bull and offer a burnt sacrifice with the wood of the image which you shall cut down." ²⁷So Gideon took ten men from among his servants and did as the LORD had said to him. But because he feared his father's household and the men of the city too much to do *it* by day, he did *it* by night.

Gideon Destroys the Altar of Baal

²⁸And when the men of the city arose early in the morning, there was the altar of Baal, torn down; and the wooden image that *was* beside it was cut down, and the second bull was being offered on the altar *which had been* built. ²⁹So they said to one another, "Who has done this thing?" And when they had inquired and asked, they said, "Gideon the son of Joash has done this thing." ³⁰Then the men of the city said to Joash, "Bring out your son, that he may die, because he has torn down the altar of Baal, and because he has cut down the wooden image that *was* beside it." ³¹But Joash said to all who stood against him, "Would you plead for Baal? Would you save him? Let the one who would plead for him be put to death by morning! If he *is* a god, let him plead for himself, because his altar has been torn down!" ³²Therefore on that day he called him Jerubbaal,ᵃ saying,

"Let Baal plead against him, because he has torn down his altar."

³³Then all the Midianites and Amalekites, the people of the East, gathered together; and they crossed over and encamped in the Valley of Jezreel. ³⁴But the Spirit of the LORD came upon Gideon; then he blew the trumpet, and the Abiezrites gathered behind him. ³⁵And he sent messengers throughout all Manasseh, who also gathered behind him. He also sent messengers to Asher, Zebulun, and Naphtali; and they came up to meet them.

The Sign of the Fleece

³⁶So Gideon said to God, "If You will save Israel by my hand as You have said— ³⁷look, I shall put a fleece of wool on the threshing floor; if there is dew on the fleece only, and *it is* dry on all the ground, then I shall know that You will save Israel by my hand, as You have said." ³⁸And it was so. When he rose early the next morning and squeezed the fleece together, he wrung the dew out of the fleece, a bowlful of water. ³⁹Then Gideon said to God, "Do not be angry with me, but let me speak just once more: Let me test, I pray, just once more with the fleece; let it now be dry only on the fleece, but on all the ground let there be dew." ⁴⁰And God did so that night. It was dry on the fleece only, but there was dew on all the ground.

> **6:36–40** Gideon showed somewhat weak faith by asking for signs, since God had already promised victory (vv.12,14,16). But his were legitimate requests for confirmation against seemingly impossible odds. God did not reprimand him but compassionately affirmed him and even volunteered another sign in 7:10–15.

Gideon's Valiant Three Hundred

7 Then Jerubbaal (that *is,* Gideon) and all the people who *were* with him rose early and encamped beside the well of Harod, so that the camp of the Midianites was on the north side of them by the hill of Moreh in the valley.

²And the LORD said to Gideon, "The people who *are* with you *are* too many for Me to give the Midianites into their hands, lest

---

6:24 ᵃHebrew *YHWH Shalom*   6:25 ᵃHebrew *Asherah,* a Canaanite goddess   6:32 ᵃLiterally *Let Baal Plead*

Israel claim glory for itself against Me, saying, 'My own hand has saved me.' ³Now therefore, proclaim in the hearing of the people, saying, 'Whoever *is* fearful and afraid, let him turn and depart at once from Mount Gilead.' " And twenty-two thousand of the people returned, and ten thousand remained.

⁴But the LORD said to Gideon, "The people *are* still *too* many; bring them down to the water, and I will test them for you there. Then it will be, *that* of whom I say to you, 'This one shall go with you,' the same shall go with you; and of whomever I say to you, 'This one shall not go with you,' the same shall not go." ⁵So he brought the people down to the water. And the LORD said to Gideon, "Everyone who laps from the water with his tongue, as a dog laps, you shall set apart by himself; likewise everyone who gets down on his knees to drink." ⁶And the number of those who lapped, *putting* their hand to their mouth, was three hundred men; but all the rest of the people got down on their knees to drink water. ⁷Then the LORD said to Gideon, "By the three hundred men who lapped I will save you, and deliver the Midianites into your hand. Let all the *other* people go, every man to his place." ⁸So the people took provisions and their trumpets in their hands. And he sent away all *the rest of* Israel, every man to his tent, and retained those three hundred men. Now the camp of Midian was below him in the valley.

7:5 Everyone who laps. Soldiers who lapped as a dog, scooping water with their hands the way a dog uses its tongue, were chosen, while those who sank to their knees to drink were rejected. This was an arbitrary distinction, saying nothing about their skill as soldiers. Their skill was inconsequential anyway, because the enemy soldiers killed themselves.

⁹It happened on the same night that the LORD said to him, "Arise, go down against the camp, for I have delivered it into your hand. ¹⁰But if you are afraid to go down, go down to the camp with Purah your servant, ¹¹and you shall hear what they say; and afterward your hands shall be strengthened to go down against the camp." Then he went down with Purah his servant to the outpost of the armed men who *were* in the camp. ¹²Now the Midianites and Amalekites, all the people of the East, were lying in the valley as numerous as locusts; and their camels *were* without number, as the sand by the seashore in multitude.

¹³And when Gideon had come, there was a man telling a dream to his companion. He said, "I have had a dream: *To my* surprise, a loaf of barley bread tumbled into the camp of Midian; it came to a tent and struck it so that it fell and overturned, and the tent collapsed."

¹⁴Then his companion answered and said, "This *is* nothing else but the sword of Gideon the son of Joash, a man of Israel! Into his hand God has delivered Midian and the whole camp."

¹⁵And so it was, when Gideon heard the telling of the dream and its interpretation, that he worshiped. He returned to the camp of Israel, and said, "Arise, for the LORD has delivered the camp of Midian into your hand." ¹⁶Then he divided the three hundred men *into* three companies, and he put a trumpet into every man's hand, with empty pitchers, and torches inside the pitchers. ¹⁷And he said to them, "Look at me and do likewise; watch, and when I come to the edge of the camp you shall do as I do: ¹⁸When I blow the trumpet, I and all who *are* with me, then you also blow the trumpets on every side of the whole camp, and say, 'The sword of the LORD and of Gideon!' "

7:16 The concealed trumpets and torches were suddenly displayed in one, startling moment. The impression caused by the blaring noise, terrible shouts, and sudden lights made the army think that each light had a legion behind it, meaning a whole army was attacking them.

¹⁹So Gideon and the hundred men who *were* with him came to the outpost of the camp at the beginning of the middle watch, just as they had posted the watch; and they blew the trumpets and broke the pitchers that *were* in their hands. ²⁰Then the three companies blew the trumpets and broke the pitchers—they held the torches in their left hands and the trumpets in their right hands for blowing—and they cried, "The sword of the LORD and of Gideon!" ²¹And every man stood in his place all around the

camp; and the whole army ran and cried out and fled. ²²When the three hundred blew the trumpets, the LORD set every man's sword against his companion throughout the whole camp; and the army fled to Beth Acacia,ᵃ toward Zererah, as far as the border of Abel Meholah, by Tabbath.

> **7:22 every man's sword against his companion.** Panic followed shock. Every soldier was on his own, and in the darkness, they were unable to distinguish friend from enemy. They killed their own men trying to escape.

²³And the men of Israel gathered together from Naphtali, Asher, and all Manasseh, and pursued the Midianites.

²⁴Then Gideon sent messengers throughout all the mountains of Ephraim, saying, "Come down against the Midianites, and seize from them the watering places as far as Beth Barah and the Jordan." Then all the men of Ephraim gathered together and seized the watering places as far as Beth Barah and the Jordan. ²⁵And they captured two princes of the Midianites, Oreb and Zeeb. They killed Oreb at the rock of Oreb, and Zeeb they killed at the winepress of Zeeb. They pursued Midian and brought the heads of Oreb and Zeeb to Gideon on the other side of the Jordan.

Gideon Subdues the Midianites

8 Now the men of Ephraim said to him, "Why have you done this to us by not calling us when you went to fight with the Midianites?" And they reprimanded him sharply.

²So he said to them, "What have I done now in comparison with you? *Is* not the gleaning *of the grapes* of Ephraim better than the vintage of Abiezer? ³God has delivered into your hands the princes of Midian, Oreb and Zeeb. And what was I able to do in comparison with you?" Then their anger toward him subsided when he said that.

⁴When Gideon came to the Jordan, he and the three hundred men who *were* with him crossed over, exhausted but still in pursuit. ⁵Then he said to the men of Succoth, "Please give loaves of bread to the people who follow me, for they are exhausted, and

I am pursuing Zebah and Zalmunna, kings of Midian."

⁶And the leaders of Succoth said, "*Are* the hands of Zebah and Zalmunna now in your hand, that we should give bread to your army?"

⁷So Gideon said, "For this cause, when the LORD has delivered Zebah and Zalmunna into my hand, then I will tear your flesh with the thorns of the wilderness and with briers!" ⁸Then he went up from there to Penuel and spoke to them in the same way. And the men of Penuel answered him as the men of Succoth had answered. ⁹So he also spoke to the men of Penuel, saying, "When I come back in peace, I will tear down this tower!"

> **8:7 thorns.** Because the men of Succoth would not help their brothers, he disciplined the elders with a cruel, ancient torture: they were dragged under heavy weights over thorns and briers, which painfully tore their bodies.

¹⁰Now Zebah and Zalmunna *were* at Karkor, and their armies with them, about fifteen thousand, all who were left of all the army of the people of the East; for one hundred and twenty thousand men who drew the sword had fallen. ¹¹Then Gideon went up by the road of those who dwell in tents on the east of Nobah and Jogbehah; and he attacked the army while the camp felt secure. ¹²When Zebah and Zalmunna fled, he pursued them; and he took the two kings of Midian, Zebah and Zalmunna, and routed the whole army.

¹³Then Gideon the son of Joash returned from battle, from the Ascent of Heres. ¹⁴And he caught a young man of the men of Succoth and interrogated him; and he wrote down for him the leaders of Succoth and its elders, seventy-seven men. ¹⁵Then he came to the men of Succoth and said, "Here are Zebah and Zalmunna, about whom you ridiculed me, saying, 'Are the hands of Zebah and Zalmunna now in your hand, that we should give bread to your weary men?' " ¹⁶And he took the elders of the city, and thorns of the wilderness and briers, and with them he taught the men of Succoth. ¹⁷Then he tore down

---

7:22 ᵃHebrew *Beth Shittah*

the tower of Penuel and killed the men of the city.

[18]And he said to Zebah and Zalmunna, "What kind of men *were they* whom you killed at Tabor?"

So they answered, "As you *are*, so *were* they; each one resembled the son of a king."

[19]Then he said, "They *were* my brothers, the sons of my mother. *As* the LORD lives, if you had let them live, I would not kill you." [20]And he said to Jether his firstborn, "Rise, kill them!" But the youth would not draw his sword; for he was afraid, because he *was* still a youth.

[21]So Zebah and Zalmunna said, "Rise yourself, and kill us; for as a man *is, so is* his strength." So Gideon arose and killed Zebah and Zalmunna, and took the crescent ornaments that *were* on their camels' necks.

Gideon's Ephod

[22]Then the men of Israel said to Gideon, "Rule over us, both you and your son, and your grandson also; for you have delivered us from the hand of Midian."

[23]But Gideon said to them, "I will not rule over you, nor shall my son rule over you; the LORD shall rule over you." [24]Then Gideon said to them, "I would like to make a request of you, that each of you would give me the earrings from his plunder." For they had golden earrings, because they *were* Ishmaelites.

> **8:22,23 Rule over us.** Israel sinned by asking that Gideon reign as king, but to his credit, the leader declined and insisted that God alone should rule (see Ex. 19:5,6).

[25]So they answered, "We will gladly give *them*." And they spread out a garment, and each man threw into it the earrings from his plunder. [26]Now the weight of the gold earrings that he requested was one thousand seven hundred *shekels* of gold, besides the crescent ornaments, pendants, and purple robes which *were* on the kings of Midian, and besides the chains that *were* around their camels' necks. [27]Then Gideon made it into an ephod and set it up in his city, Ophrah. And all Israel played the harlot with it there. It became a snare to Gideon and to his house.

[28]Thus Midian was subdued before the children of Israel, so that they lifted their heads no more. And the country was quiet for forty years in the days of Gideon.

Death of Gideon

[29]Then Jerubbaal the son of Joash went and dwelt in his own house. [30]Gideon had seventy sons who were his own offspring, for he had many wives. [31]And his concubine who *was* in Shechem also bore him a son, whose name he called Abimelech. [32]Now Gideon the son of Joash died at a good old age, and was buried in the tomb of Joash his father, in Ophrah of the Abiezrites.

> **8:24-31** Gideon had a sad end to his influence. The ephod that he made (vv.24-27), although probably innocently intended to show civil power, became the object of idolatrous worship and led Israel astray. He also fell severely into the sin of polygamy, which was tolerated by many but never approved of by God.

[33]So it was, as soon as Gideon was dead, that the children of Israel again played the harlot with the Baals, and made Baal-Berith their god. [34]Thus the children of Israel did not remember the LORD their God, who had delivered them from the hands of all their enemies on every side; [35]nor did they show kindness to the house of Jerubbaal (Gideon) in accordance with the good he had done for Israel.

Abimelech's Conspiracy

9 Then Abimelech the son of Jerubbaal went to Shechem, to his mother's brothers, and spoke with them and with all the family of the house of his mother's father, saying, [2]"Please speak in the hearing of all the men of Shechem: 'Which is better for you, that all seventy of the sons of Jerubbaal reign over you, or that one reign over you?' Remember that I *am* your own flesh and bone."

[3]And his mother's brothers spoke all these words concerning him in the hearing of all the men of Shechem; and their heart was inclined to follow Abimelech, for they said, "He is our brother." [4]So they gave him seventy *shekels* of silver from the temple of Baal-Berith, with which Abimelech hired worthless and reckless men; and they followed him. [5]Then he went to his father's

house at Ophrah and killed his brothers, the seventy sons of Jerubbaal, on one stone. But Jotham the youngest son of Jerubbaal was left, because he hid himself. 6And all the men of Shechem gathered together, all of Beth Millo, and they went and made Abimelech king beside the terebinth tree at the pillar that *was* in Shechem.

The Parable of the Trees

7Now when they told Jotham, he went and stood on top of Mount Gerizim, and lifted his voice and cried out. And he said to them:

> "Listen to me, you men of Shechem,
> That God may listen to you!

8 "The trees once went forth to anoint a
>   king over them.
> And they said to the olive tree,
> 'Reign over us!'
9 But the olive tree said to them,
> 'Should I cease giving my oil,
> With which they honor God and men,
> And go to sway over trees?'

10 "Then the trees said to the fig tree,
> 'You come *and* reign over us!'
11 But the fig tree said to them,
> 'Should I cease my sweetness and my
>   good fruit,
> And go to sway over trees?'

12 "Then the trees said to the vine,
> 'You come *and* reign over us!'
13 But the vine said to them,
> 'Should I cease my new wine,
> Which cheers *both* God and men,
> And go to sway over trees?'

14 "Then all the trees said to the bramble,
> 'You come *and* reign over us!'

9:14 You come *and* reign over us! In Jotham's parable of trees asking for a king (vv.7–15), the olive, fig, and vine decline. They do not represent specific men but rather heighten the idea that the bramble, or thornbush, is inferior and unsuitable—representing Abimelech (vv.6,16).

15   And the bramble said to the trees,
> 'If in truth you anoint me as king over
>   you,

> *Then* come *and* take shelter in my
>   shade;
> But if not, let fire come out of the
>   bramble
> And devour the cedars of Lebanon!'

16"Now therefore, if you have acted in truth and sincerity in making Abimelech king, and if you have dealt well with Jerubbaal and his house, and have done to him as he deserves—17for my father fought for you, risked his life, and delivered you out of the hand of Midian; 18but you have risen up against my father's house this day, and killed his seventy sons on one stone, and made Abimelech, the son of his female servant, king over the men of Shechem, because he is your brother—19if then you have acted in truth and sincerity with Jerubbaal and with his house this day, *then* rejoice in Abimelech, and let him also rejoice in you. 20But if not, let fire come from Abimelech and devour the men of Shechem and Beth Millo; and let fire come from the men of Shechem and from Beth Millo and devour Abimelech!" 21And Jotham ran away and fled; and he went to Beer and dwelt there, for fear of Abimelech his brother.

Downfall of Abimelech

22After Abimelech had reigned over Israel three years, 23God sent a spirit of ill will between Abimelech and the men of Shechem; and the men of Shechem dealt treacherously with Abimelech, 24that the crime *done* to the seventy sons of Jerubbaal might be settled and their blood be laid on Abimelech their brother, who killed them, and on the men of Shechem, who aided him in the killing of his brothers. 25And the men of Shechem set men in ambush against him on the tops of the mountains, and they robbed all who passed by them along that way; and it was told Abimelech.

9:23 God sent a spirit of ill will. God allowed their jealousy, distrust, and hate to work as punishment for the idolatry and mass murder.

26Now Gaal the son of Ebed came with his brothers and went over to Shechem; and the men of Shechem put their confidence in him. 27So they went out into the fields, and gathered *grapes* from their vine-

yards and trod *them*, and made merry. And they went into the house of their god, and ate and drank, and cursed Abimelech. ²⁸Then Gaal the son of Ebed said, "Who *is* Abimelech, and who *is* Shechem, that we should serve him? *Is he* not the son of Jerubbaal, and *is not* Zebul his officer? Serve the men of Hamor the father of Shechem; but why should we serve him? ²⁹If only this people were under my authority!ᵃ Then I would remove Abimelech." So heᵇ said to Abimelech, "Increase your army and come out!"

> **9:45 sowed it with salt.** To sow the city with salt pollutes the soil and water and symbolizes permanent barrenness (Deut. 29:23). Abimelech's intent was nullified by Jeroboam I, who rebuilt the city as his capital, ca. 930–910 B.C.

³⁰When Zebul, the ruler of the city, heard the words of Gaal the son of Ebed, his anger was aroused. ³¹And he sent messengers to Abimelech secretly, saying, "Take note! Gaal the son of Ebed and his brothers have come to Shechem; and here they are, fortifying the city against you. ³²Now therefore, get up by night, you and the people who *are* with you, and lie in wait in the field. ³³And it shall be, as soon as the sun is up in the morning, *that* you shall rise early and rush upon the city; and *when* he and the people who are with him come out against you, you may then do to them as you find opportunity."

³⁴So Abimelech and all the people who *were* with him rose by night, and lay in wait against Shechem in four companies. ³⁵When Gaal the son of Ebed went out and stood in the entrance to the city gate, Abimelech and the people who *were* with him rose from lying in wait. ³⁶And when Gaal saw the people, he said to Zebul, "Look, people are coming down from the tops of the mountains!"

But Zebul said to him, "You see the shadows of the mountains as *if they were* men."

³⁷So Gaal spoke again and said, "See, people are coming down from the center of the land, and another company is coming from the Diviners'ᵃ Terebinth Tree."

³⁸Then Zebul said to him, "Where indeed *is* your mouth now, with which you said, 'Who is Abimelech, that we should serve him?' *Are* not these the people whom you despised? Go out, if you will, and fight with them now."

³⁹So Gaal went out, leading the men of Shechem, and fought with Abimelech. ⁴⁰And Abimelech chased him, and he fled from him; and many fell wounded, to the *very* entrance of the gate. ⁴¹Then Abimelech dwelt at Arumah, and Zebul drove out Gaal and his brothers, so that they would not dwell in Shechem.

⁴²And it came about on the next day that the people went out into the field, and they told Abimelech. ⁴³So he took his people, divided them into three companies, and lay in wait in the field. And he looked, and there were the people, coming out of the city; and he rose against them and attacked them. ⁴⁴Then Abimelech and the company that *was* with him rushed forward and stood at the entrance of the gate of the city; and the *other* two companies rushed upon all who *were* in the fields and killed them. ⁴⁵So Abimelech fought against the city all that day; he took the city and killed the people who *were* in it; and he demolished the city and sowed it with salt.

⁴⁶Now when all the men of the tower of Shechem had heard *that*, they entered the stronghold of the temple of the god Berith. ⁴⁷And it was told Abimelech that all the men of the tower of Shechem were gathered together. ⁴⁸Then Abimelech went up to Mount Zalmon, he and all the people who *were* with him. And Abimelech took an ax in his hand and cut down a bough from the trees, and took it and laid *it* on his shoulder; then he said to the people who were with him, "What you have seen me do, make haste *and* do as I *have done*." ⁴⁹So each of the people likewise cut down his own bough and followed Abimelech, put *them* against the stronghold, and set the stronghold on fire above them, so that all the people of the tower of Shechem died, about a thousand men and women.

⁵⁰Then Abimelech went to Thebez, and he encamped against Thebez and took it.

9:29 ᵃLiterally *hand*   ᵇFollowing Masoretic Text and Targum; Dead Sea Scrolls read *they*; Septuagint reads *I*.   9:37 ᵃHebrew *Meonenim*

⁵¹But there was a strong tower in the city, and all the men and women—all the people of the city—fled there and shut themselves in; then they went up to the top of the tower. ⁵²So Abimelech came as far as the tower and fought against it; and he drew near the door of the tower to burn it with fire. ⁵³But a certain woman dropped an upper millstone on Abimelech's head and crushed his skull. ⁵⁴Then he called quickly to the young man, his armorbearer, and said to him, "Draw your sword and kill me, lest men say of me, 'A woman killed him.' " So his young man thrust him through, and he died. ⁵⁵And when the men of Israel saw that Abimelech was dead, they departed, every man to his place.

⁵⁶Thus God repaid the wickedness of Abimelech, which he had done to his father by killing his seventy brothers. ⁵⁷And all the evil of the men of Shechem God returned on their own heads, and on them came the curse of Jotham the son of Jerubbaal.

Tola

10 After Abimelech there arose to save Israel Tola the son of Puah, the son of Dodo, a man of Issachar; and he dwelt in Shamir in the mountains of Ephraim. ²He judged Israel twenty-three years; and he died and was buried in Shamir.

Jair

³After him arose Jair, a Gileadite; and he judged Israel twenty-two years. ⁴Now he had thirty sons who rode on thirty donkeys; they also had thirty towns, which are called "Havoth Jair"ᵃ to this day, which are in the land of Gilead. ⁵And Jair died and was buried in Camon.

Israel Oppressed Again

⁶Then the children of Israel again did evil in the sight of the LORD, and served the Baals and the Ashtoreths, the gods of Syria, the gods of Sidon, the gods of Moab, the gods of the people of Ammon, and the gods of the Philistines; and they forsook the LORD and did not serve Him. ⁷So the anger of the LORD was hot against Israel; and He sold them into the hands of the Philistines and into the hands of the people of Ammon. ⁸From that year they harassed and oppressed the children of Israel for eighteen years—all the children of Israel who were on the other side of the Jordan in the land of the Amorites, in Gilead. ⁹Moreover the people of Ammon crossed over the Jordan to fight against Judah also, against Benjamin, and against the house of Ephraim, so that Israel was severely distressed.

¹⁰And the children of Israel cried out to the LORD, saying, "We have sinned against You, because we have both forsaken our God and served the Baals!"

> **10:10 We have sinned.** Their confession was followed by true repentance (see vv.15,16). Genuine repentance acknowledges that God is right and just, thus glorifying Him. They finally cast aside sin to pursue holiness.

¹¹So the LORD said to the children of Israel, "Did I not deliver you from the Egyptians and from the Amorites and from the people of Ammon and from the Philistines? ¹²Also the Sidonians and Amalekites and Maonitesᵃ oppressed you; and you cried out to Me, and I delivered you from their hand. ¹³Yet you have forsaken Me and served other gods. Therefore I will deliver you no more. ¹⁴Go and cry out to the gods which you have chosen; let them deliver you in your time of distress."

¹⁵And the children of Israel said to the LORD, "We have sinned! Do to us whatever seems best to You; only deliver us this day, we pray." ¹⁶So they put away the foreign gods from among them and served the LORD. And His soul could no longer endure the misery of Israel.

¹⁷Then the people of Ammon gathered together and encamped in Gilead. And the children of Israel assembled together and encamped in Mizpah. ¹⁸And the people, the leaders of Gilead, said to one another, "Who is the man who will begin the fight against the people of Ammon? He shall be head over all the inhabitants of Gilead."

10:4 ᵃLiterally Towns of Jair (compare Numbers 32:41 and Deuteronomy 3:14)   10:12 ᵃSome Septuagint manuscripts read Midianites.

Jephthah

11 Now Jephthah the Gileadite was a mighty man of valor, but he *was* the son of a harlot; and Gilead begot Jephthah. ²Gilead's wife bore sons; and when his wife's sons grew up, they drove Jephthah out, and said to him, "You shall have no inheritance in our father's house, for you *are* the son of another woman." ³Then Jephthah fled from his brothers and dwelt in the land of Tob; and worthless men banded together with Jephthah and went out *raiding* with him.

> **11:1 mighty man of valor.** A strong, skilled warrior for battle, such as Gideon (6:12). When they repented, God raised up Jephthah to lead them to freedom from their 18 years of oppression.

⁴It came to pass after a time that the people of Ammon made war against Israel. ⁵And so it was, when the people of Ammon made war against Israel, that the elders of Gilead went to get Jephthah from the land of Tob. ⁶Then they said to Jephthah, "Come and be our commander, that we may fight against the people of Ammon."

⁷So Jephthah said to the elders of Gilead, "Did you not hate me, and expel me from my father's house? Why have you come to me now when you are in distress?"

⁸And the elders of Gilead said to Jephthah, "That is why we have turned again to you now, that you may go with us and fight against the people of Ammon, and be our head over all the inhabitants of Gilead."

⁹So Jephthah said to the elders of Gilead, "If you take me back home to fight against the people of Ammon, and the LORD delivers them to me, shall I be your head?"

¹⁰And the elders of Gilead said to Jephthah, "The LORD will be a witness between us, if we do not do according to your words." ¹¹Then Jephthah went with the elders of Gilead, and the people made him head and commander over them; and Jephthah spoke all his words before the LORD in Mizpah.

¹²Now Jephthah sent messengers to the king of the people of Ammon, saying, "What do you have against me, that you have come to fight against me in my land?"

¹³And the king of the people of Ammon answered the messengers of Jephthah, "Because Israel took away my land when they came up out of Egypt, from the Arnon as far as the Jabbok, and to the Jordan. Now therefore, restore those *lands* peaceably."

> **11:13 Israel took away my land.** The Ammonite ruler claimed rights to the Israelites' land, but Jephthah gave a direct answer: (1) when Israel took the land, it belonged to the Amorites; (2) Israel had been there 300 years; and (3) God had chosen to give them the land, thus entitling them to it.

¹⁴So Jephthah again sent messengers to the king of the people of Ammon, ¹⁵and said to him, "Thus says Jephthah: 'Israel did not take away the land of Moab, nor the land of the people of Ammon; ¹⁶for when Israel came up from Egypt, they walked through the wilderness as far as the Red Sea and came to Kadesh. ¹⁷Then Israel sent messengers to the king of Edom, saying, 'Please let me pass through your land.' But the king of Edom would not heed. And in like manner they sent to the king of Moab, but he would not *consent*. So Israel remained in Kadesh. ¹⁸And they went along through the wilderness and bypassed the land of Edom and the land of Moab, came to the east side of the land of Moab, and encamped on the other side of the Arnon. But they did not enter the border of Moab, for the Arnon *was* the border of Moab. ¹⁹Then Israel sent messengers to Sihon king of the Amorites, king of Heshbon; and Israel said to him, "Please let us pass through your land into our place." ²⁰But Sihon did not trust Israel to pass through his territory. So Sihon gathered all his people together, encamped in Jahaz, and fought against Israel. ²¹And the LORD God of Israel delivered Sihon and all his people into the hand of Israel, and they defeated them. Thus Israel gained possession of all the land of the Amorites, who inhabited that country. ²²They took possession of all the territory of the Amorites, from the Arnon to the Jabbok and from the wilderness to the Jordan.

²³And now the LORD God of Israel has dispossessed the Amorites from before His people Israel; should you then possess it? ²⁴Will you not possess whatever Chemosh your god gives you to possess? So whatever the LORD our God takes possession of be-

fore us, we will possess. ²⁵And now, *are* you any better than Balak the son of Zippor, king of Moab? Did he ever strive against Israel? Did he ever fight against them? ²⁶While Israel dwelt in Heshbon and its villages, in Aroer and its villages, and in all the cities along the banks of the Arnon, for three hundred years, why did you not recover *them* within that time? ²⁷Therefore I have not sinned against you, but you wronged me by fighting against me. May the LORD, the Judge, render judgment this day between the children of Israel and the people of Ammon.' " ²⁸However, the king of the people of Ammon did not heed the words which Jephthah sent him.

Jephthah's Vow and Victory

²⁹Then the Spirit of the LORD came upon Jephthah, and he passed through Gilead and Manasseh, and passed through Mizpah of Gilead; and from Mizpah of Gilead he advanced *toward* the people of Ammon. ³⁰And Jephthah made a vow to the LORD, and said, "If You will indeed deliver the people of Ammon into my hands, ³¹then it will be that whatever comes out of the doors of my house to meet me, when I return in peace from the people of Ammon, shall surely be the LORD's, and I will offer it up as a burnt offering."

> **11:29 the Spirit...came upon Jephthah.** Even though the Lord empowered him for war, that does not mean that all his decisions were right. The rash vow (vv.30,31) is an example.

³²So Jephthah advanced toward the people of Ammon to fight against them, and the LORD delivered them into his hands. ³³And he defeated them from Aroer as far as Minnith—twenty cities—and to Abel Keramim,ᵃ with a very great slaughter. Thus the people of Ammon were subdued before the children of Israel.

Jephthah's Daughter

³⁴When Jephthah came to his house at Mizpah, there was his daughter, coming out to meet him with timbrels and dancing; and she *was his* only child. Besides her he had neither son nor daughter. ³⁵And it came

to pass, when he saw her, that he tore his clothes, and said, "Alas, my daughter! You have brought me very low! You are among those who trouble me! For I have given my word to the LORD, and I cannot go back on it."

> **11:30–35** This was a custom among generals to promise their god something of great value as a reward for victory. His daughter was thus his sacrificial pledge. Jephthah felt great pain in taking the life of his only daughter to satisfy his pious but foolish pledge.

³⁶So she said to him, "My father, *if* you have given your word to the LORD, do to me according to what has gone out of your mouth, because the LORD has avenged you of your enemies, the people of Ammon." ³⁷Then she said to her father, "Let this thing be done for me: let me alone for two months, that I may go and wander on the mountains and bewail my virginity, my friends and I."

³⁸So he said, "Go." And he sent her away *for* two months; and she went with her friends, and bewailed her virginity on the mountains. ³⁹And it was so at the end of two months that she returned to her father, and he carried out his vow with her which he had vowed. She knew no man.

And it became a custom in Israel ⁴⁰*that* the daughters of Israel went four days each year to lament the daughter of Jephthah the Gileadite.

Jephthah's Conflict with Ephraim

12 Then the men of Ephraim gathered together, crossed over toward Zaphon, and said to Jephthah, "Why did you cross over to fight against the people of Ammon, and did not call us to go with you? We will burn your house down on you with fire!"

²And Jephthah said to them, "My people and I were in a great struggle with the people of Ammon; and when I called you, you did not deliver me out of their hands. ³So when I saw that you would not deliver *me*, I took my life in my hands and crossed over against the people of Ammon; and the LORD delivered them into my hand. Why then have you come up to me this day to

---

11:33 ᵃLiterally *Plain of Vineyards*

fight against me?" ⁴Now Jephthah gathered together all the men of Gilead and fought against Ephraim. And the men of Gilead defeated Ephraim, because they said, "You Gileadites *are* fugitives of Ephraim among the Ephraimites *and* among the Manassites." ⁵The Gileadites seized the fords of the Jordan before the Ephraimites *arrived.* And when *any* Ephraimite who escaped said, "Let me cross over," the men of Gilead would say to him, "*Are* you an Ephraimite?" If he said, "No," ⁶then they would say to him, "Then say, 'Shibboleth'!" And he would say, "Sibboleth," for he could not pronounce *it* right. Then they would take him and kill him at the fords of the Jordan. There fell at that time forty-two thousand Ephraimites.

> **12:6 Shibboleth.** The Ephraimites mispronounced this word, using an "s" rather than "sh" sound. Their unique dialect gave them away.

⁷And Jephthah judged Israel six years. Then Jephthah the Gileadite died and was buried among the cities of Gilead.

Ibzan, Elon, and Abdon

⁸After him, Ibzan of Bethlehem judged Israel. ⁹He had thirty sons. And he gave away thirty daughters in marriage, and brought in thirty daughters from elsewhere for his sons. He judged Israel seven years. ¹⁰Then Ibzan died and was buried at Bethlehem.
¹¹After him, Elon the Zebulunite judged Israel. He judged Israel ten years. ¹²And Elon the Zebulunite died and was buried at Aijalon in the country of Zebulun.
¹³After him, Abdon the son of Hillel the Pirathonite judged Israel. ¹⁴He had forty sons and thirty grandsons, who rode on seventy young donkeys. He judged Israel eight years. ¹⁵Then Abdon the son of Hillel the Pirathonite died and was buried in Pirathon in the land of Ephraim, in the mountains of the Amalekites.

The Birth of Samson

13 Again the children of Israel did evil in the sight of the LORD, and the LORD delivered them into the hand of the Philistines for forty years.
²Now there was a certain man from Zorah, of the family of the Danites, whose name *was* Manoah; and his wife *was* barren and had no children. ³And the Angel of the LORD appeared to the woman and said to her, "Indeed now, you are barren and have borne no children, but you shall conceive and bear a son. ⁴Now therefore, please be careful not to drink wine or *similar* drink, and not to eat anything unclean. ⁵For behold, you shall conceive and bear a son. And no razor shall come upon his head, for the child shall be a Nazirite to God from the womb; and he shall begin to deliver Israel out of the hand of the Philistines."

> **13:5 Nazirite.** The word comes from the Heb. "to separate." God gave three restrictions: no wine, no razor cutting the hair, and no touching a dead body and being defiled. Such outward actions indicated an inner dedication to God.

⁶So the woman came and told her husband, saying, "A Man of God came to me, and His countenance *was* like the countenance of the Angel of God, very awesome; but I did not ask Him where He *was* from, and He did not tell me His name. ⁷And He said to me, 'Behold, you shall conceive and bear a son. Now drink no wine or *similar* drink, nor eat anything unclean, for the child shall be a Nazirite to God from the womb to the day of his death.' "
⁸Then Manoah prayed to the LORD, and said, "O my Lord, please let the Man of God whom You sent come to us again and teach us what we shall do for the child who will be born."
⁹And God listened to the voice of Manoah, and the Angel of God came to the woman again as she was sitting in the field; but Manoah her husband *was* not with her. ¹⁰Then the woman ran in haste and told her husband, and said to him, "Look, the Man who came to me the *other* day has just now appeared to me!"
¹¹So Manoah arose and followed his wife. When he came to the Man, he said to Him, "Are You the Man who spoke to this woman?"
And He said, "I *am.*"
¹²Manoah said, "Now let Your words come *to pass!* What will be the boy's rule of life, and his work?"
¹³So the Angel of the LORD said to Manoah, "Of all that I said to the woman let

her be careful. [14]She may not eat anything that comes from the vine, nor may she drink wine or *similar* drink, nor eat anything unclean. All that I commanded her let her observe."

[15]Then Manoah said to the Angel of the LORD, "Please let us detain You, and we will prepare a young goat for You."

[16]And the Angel of the LORD said to Manoah, "Though you detain Me, I will not eat your food. But if you offer a burnt offering, you must offer it to the LORD." (For Manoah did not know He *was* the Angel of the LORD.)

[17]Then Manoah said to the Angel of the LORD, "What *is* Your name, that when Your words come *to pass* we may honor You?"

> **13:17 What *is* Your name?** The secret name again indicates that the Angel is the Lord.

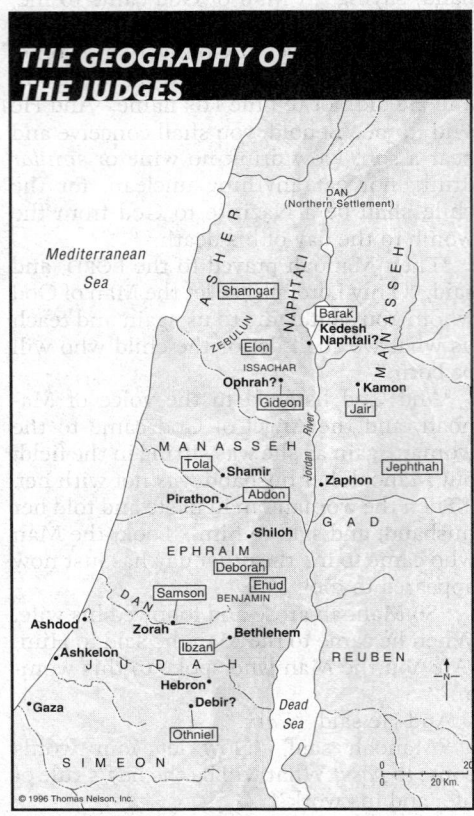

THE GEOGRAPHY OF THE JUDGES

Mediterranean Sea

ASHER
NAPHTALI
ZEBULUN
MANASSEH
ISSACHAR
DAN (Northern Settlement)
Shamgar
Barak
Kedesh Naphtali?
Elon
Ophrah?
Gideon
Kamon
Jair
MANASSEH
Tola
Shamir
Pirathon
Abdon
Zaphon
Jephthah
Jordan River
Shiloh
GAD
EPHRAIM
Deborah
Samson
Ehud
BENJAMIN
DAN
Ashdod
Zorah
Bethlehem
Ashkelon
Ibzan
REUBEN
J U D A H
Hebron
Gaza
Debir?
Dead Sea
Othniel
S I M E O N
Jair

© 1996 Thomas Nelson, Inc.

[18]And the Angel of the LORD said to him, "Why do you ask My name, seeing it *is* wonderful?"

[19]So Manoah took the young goat with the grain offering, and offered it upon the rock to the LORD. And He did a wondrous thing while Manoah and his wife looked on—[20]it happened as the flame went up toward heaven from the altar—the Angel of the LORD ascended in the flame of the altar! When Manoah and his wife saw *this*, they fell on their faces to the ground. [21]When the Angel of the LORD appeared no more to Manoah and his wife, then Manoah knew that He *was* the Angel of the LORD.

[22]And Manoah said to his wife, "We shall surely die, because we have seen God!"

[23]But his wife said to him, "If the LORD had desired to kill us, He would not have accepted a burnt offering and a grain offering from our hands, nor would He have shown us all these *things*, nor would He have told us *such things* as these at this time."

[24]So the woman bore a son and called his name Samson; and the child grew, and the LORD blessed him. [25]And the Spirit of the LORD began to move upon him at Mahaneh Dan[a] between Zorah and Eshtaol.

Samson's Philistine Wife

14 Now Samson went down to Timnah, and saw a woman in Timnah of the daughters of the Philistines. [2]So he went up and told his father and mother, saying, "I have seen a woman in Timnah of the daughters of the Philistines; now therefore, get her for me as a wife."

[3]Then his father and mother said to him, "*Is there* no woman among the daughters of your brethren, or among all my people, that you must go and get a wife from the uncircumcised Philistines?"

> **14:1–4 she pleases me well.** The Philistines were not among the 7 nations of Canaan that Israel was forbidden to marry, but his choice was still very weak. Although Samson sinned, God was able to turn the situation for good by working against the wicked Philistines and helping His people. He destroyed them not with an army but with a single man.

13:25 [a]Literally *Camp of Dan* (compare 18:12)

And Samson said to his father, "Get her for me, for she pleases me well."

⁴But his father and mother did not know that it was of the LORD—that He was seeking an occasion to move against the Philistines. For at that time the Philistines had dominion over Israel.

⁵So Samson went down to Timnah with his father and mother, and came to the vineyards of Timnah.

Now *to his* surprise, a young lion *came* roaring against him. ⁶And the Spirit of the LORD came mightily upon him, and he tore the lion apart as one would have torn apart a young goat, though *he had* nothing in his hand. But he did not tell his father or his mother what he had done.

⁷Then he went down and talked with the woman; and she pleased Samson well. ⁸After some time, when he returned to get her, he turned aside to see the carcass of the lion. And behold, a swarm of bees and honey *were* in the carcass of the lion. ⁹He took some of it in his hands and went along, eating. When he came to his father and mother, he gave *some* to them, and they also ate. But he did not tell them that he had taken the honey out of the carcass of the lion.

¹⁰So his father went down to the woman. And Samson gave a feast there, for young men used to do so. ¹¹And it happened, when they saw him, that they brought thirty companions to be with him.

¹²Then Samson said to them, "Let me pose a riddle to you. If you can correctly solve and explain it to me within the seven days of the feast, then I will give you thirty linen garments and thirty changes of clothing. ¹³But if you cannot explain *it* to me, then you shall give me thirty linen garments and thirty changes of clothing."

And they said to him, "Pose your riddle, that we may hear it."

¹⁴So he said to them:

"Out of the eater came something to
        eat,
And out of the strong came
        something sweet."

Now for three days they could not explain the riddle.

¹⁵But it came to pass on the seventh*ᵃ* day that they said to Samson's wife, "Entice your husband, that he may explain the riddle to us, or else we will burn you and your father's house with fire. Have you invited us in order to take what is ours? *Is that* not *so?*"

¹⁶Then Samson's wife wept on him, and said, "You only hate me! You do not love me! You have posed a riddle to the sons of my people, but you have not explained *it* to me."

And he said to her, "Look, I have not explained *it* to my father or my mother; so should I explain *it* to you?" ¹⁷Now she had wept on him the seven days while their feast lasted. And it happened on the seventh day that he told her, because she pressed him so much. Then she explained the riddle to the sons of her people. ¹⁸So the men of the city said to him on the seventh day before the sun went down:

"What *is* sweeter than honey?
    And what *is* stronger than a lion?"

And he said to them:

"If you had not plowed with my heifer,
    You would not have solved my
        riddle!"

14:16–18 Samson's wife wept. She cheated and manipulated. The men also cheated and pressured her into telling them. They had murder in their hearts (v.15).

¹⁹Then the Spirit of the LORD came upon him mightily, and he went down to Ashkelon and killed thirty of their men, took their apparel, and gave the changes *of clothing* to those who had explained the riddle. So his anger was aroused, and he went back up to his father's house. ²⁰And Samson's wife was *given* to his companion, who had been his best man.

Samson Defeats the Philistines

15 After a while, in the time of wheat harvest, it happened that Samson visited his wife with a young goat. And he said, "Let me go in to my wife, into *her*

14:15 *ᵃ*Following Masoretic Text, Targum, and Vulgate; Septuagint and Syriac read *fourth.*

room." But her father would not permit him to go in.

²Her father said, "I really thought that you thoroughly hated her; therefore I gave her to your companion. *Is* not her younger sister better than she? Please, take her instead."

³And Samson said to them, "This time I shall be blameless regarding the Philistines if I harm them!" ⁴Then Samson went and caught three hundred foxes; and he took torches, turned *the foxes* tail to tail, and put a torch between each pair of tails. ⁵When he had set the torches on fire, he let *the foxes* go into the standing grain of the Philistines, and burned up both the shocks and the standing grain, as well as the vineyards *and* olive groves.

> **15:4 caught three hundred foxes.** The Philistine father treacherously gave his daughter away without reason, and Samson took vengeance. Apparently he caught 300 foxes, tied them in pairs with a slow-burning torch, and sent them down the hills into fields thrashing with fire, igniting all the standing grain. This was a great loss to Philistine farmers.

⁶Then the Philistines said, "Who has done this?"

And they answered, "Samson, the son-in-law of the Timnite, because he has taken his wife and given her to his companion." So the Philistines came up and burned her and her father with fire.

⁷Samson said to them, "Since you would do a thing like this, I will surely take revenge on you, and after that I will cease." ⁸So he attacked them hip and thigh with a great slaughter; then he went down and dwelt in the cleft of the rock of Etam.

⁹Now the Philistines went up, encamped in Judah, and deployed themselves against Lehi. ¹⁰And the men of Judah said, "Why have you come up against us?"

So they answered, "We have come up to arrest Samson, to do to him as he has done to us."

¹¹Then three thousand men of Judah went down to the cleft of the rock of Etam, and said to Samson, "Do you not know that the Philistines rule over us? What *is* this you have done to us?"

And he said to them, "As they did to me, so I have done to them."

¹²But they said to him, "We have come down to arrest you, that we may deliver you into the hand of the Philistines."

Then Samson said to them, "Swear to me that you will not kill me yourselves."

¹³So they spoke to him, saying, "No, but we will tie you securely and deliver you into their hand; but we will surely not kill you." And they bound him with two new ropes and brought him up from the rock.

¹⁴When he came to Lehi, the Philistines came shouting against him. Then the Spirit of the LORD came mightily upon him; and the ropes that *were* on his arms became like flax that is burned with fire, and his bonds broke loose from his hands. ¹⁵He found a fresh jawbone of a donkey, reached out his hand and took it, and killed a thousand men with it. ¹⁶Then Samson said:

> **15:15 killed a thousand men.** God gave Samson miraculous power not only to destroy the Philistines but also to prove to timid Israel that God was with them, despite their lack of trust.

"With the jawbone of a donkey,
  Heaps upon heaps,
  With the jawbone of a donkey
  I have slain a thousand men!"

¹⁷And so it was, when he had finished speaking, that he threw the jawbone from his hand, and called that place Ramath Lehi.ᵃ

¹⁸Then he became very thirsty; so he cried out to the LORD and said, "You have given this great deliverance by the hand of Your servant; and now shall I die of thirst and fall into the hand of the uncircumcised?" ¹⁹So God split the hollow place that *is* in Lehi,ᵃ and water came out, and he drank; and his spirit returned, and he revived. Therefore he called its name En Hakkore,ᵇ which is in Lehi to this day. ²⁰And he judged Israel twenty years in the days of the Philistines.

Samson and Delilah

16 Now Samson went to Gaza and saw a harlot there, and went in to her.

15:17 ᵃLiterally *Jawbone Height*   15:19 ᵃLiterally *Jawbone* (compare verse 14)   ᵇLiterally *Spring of the Caller*

²*When* the Gazites *were told,* "Samson has come here!" they surrounded *the place* and lay in wait for him all night at the gate of the city. They were quiet all night, saying, "In the morning, when it is daylight, we will kill him." ³And Samson lay *low* till midnight; then he arose at midnight, took hold of the doors of the gate of the city and the two gateposts, pulled them up, bar and all, put *them* on his shoulders, and carried them to the top of the hill that faces Hebron.

> **16:4 loved...Delilah.** He had a weakness for women of low character and Philistine loyalty. He sinned continually by going to her daily, allowing himself to be trapped by her deceptions.

⁴Afterward it happened that he loved a woman in the Valley of Sorek, whose name *was* Delilah. ⁵And the lords of the Philistines came up to her and said to her, "Entice him, and find out where his great strength *lies,* and by what *means* we may overpower him, that we may bind him to afflict him; and every one of us will give you eleven hundred *pieces* of silver."

⁶So Delilah said to Samson, "Please tell me where your great strength *lies,* and with what you may be bound to afflict you."

⁷And Samson said to her, "If they bind me with seven fresh bowstrings, not yet dried, then I shall become weak, and be like any *other* man."

⁸So the lords of the Philistines brought up to her seven fresh bowstrings, not yet dried, and she bound him with them. ⁹Now *men were* lying in wait, staying with her in the room. And she said to him, "The Philistines *are* upon you, Samson!" But he broke the bowstrings as a strand of yarn breaks when it touches fire. So the secret of his strength was not known.

¹⁰Then Delilah said to Samson, "Look, you have mocked me and told me lies. Now, please tell me what you may be bound with."

¹¹So he said to her, "If they bind me securely with new ropes that have never been used, then I shall become weak, and be like any *other* man."

¹²Therefore Delilah took new ropes and bound him with them, and said to him, "The Philistines *are* upon you, Samson!" And *men were* lying in wait, staying in the room. But he broke them off his arms like a thread.

¹³Delilah said to Samson, "Until now you have mocked me and told me lies. Tell me what you may be bound with."

And he said to her, "If you weave the seven locks of my head into the web of the loom"—

¹⁴So she wove *it* tightly with the batten of the loom, and said to him, "The Philistines *are* upon you, Samson!" But he awoke from his sleep, and pulled out the batten and the web from the loom.

¹⁵Then she said to him, "How can you say, 'I love you,' when your heart *is* not with me? You have mocked me these three times, and have not told me where your

---

Men like Gideon, Jephthah, and Samson seem to exhibit as many gross failures as they do successes. Why does God make use of leaders with such obvious weaknesses?

One obvious answer to the question is that as long as God chooses to use people at all, He will end up using people with obvious weaknesses. No one escapes that category. The point is that God uses people in His plans in spite of their obvious weaknesses.

Does this mean that the sins of a leader are somehow to be excused? Of course not. In fact, leaders bear a higher level of accountability. Note, for example, the fact that Moses forfeited his opportunity to enter the Promised Land because of an angry outburst (Numbers 20:10; Deuteronomy 3:24–27). Jephthah made a rash vow for which his daughter had to bear the primary consequence (Judges 11:29–40). What probably ought to attract our attention to these servants of God is not so much their weaknesses, or even the great accomplishments that God worked through them, but the fact that they remained faithful to God despite their failures.

great strength *lies.*" ¹⁶And it came to pass, when she pestered him daily with her words and pressed him, *so* that his soul was vexed to death, ¹⁷that he told her all his heart, and said to her, "No razor has ever come upon my head, for I *have been* a Nazirite to God from my mother's womb. If I am shaven, then my strength will leave me, and I shall become weak, and be like any *other* man."

> **16:17 If I am shaven.** His strength came from his unique relationship to God, for he was set apart with a Nazirite pledge. His long hair was only a sign of it. But, when Delilah became more important to him than God, his strength was removed.

¹⁸When Delilah saw that he had told her all his heart, she sent and called for the lords of the Philistines, saying, "Come up once more, for he has told me all his heart." So the lords of the Philistines came up to her and brought the money in their hand. ¹⁹Then she lulled him to sleep on her knees, and called for a man and had him shave off the seven locks of his head. Then she began to torment him,ᵃ and his strength left him. ²⁰And she said, "The Philistines *are* upon you, Samson!" So he awoke from his sleep, and said, "I will go out as before, at other times, and shake myself free!" But he did not know that the LORD had departed from him.

²¹Then the Philistines took him and put out his eyes, and brought him down to Gaza. They bound him with bronze fetters, and he became a grinder in the prison. ²²However, the hair of his head began to grow again after it had been shaven.

Samson Dies with the Philistines

²³Now the lords of the Philistines gathered together to offer a great sacrifice to Dagon their god, and to rejoice. And they said:

> "Our god has delivered into our hands
> Samson our enemy!"

²⁴When the people saw him, they praised their god; for they said:

> "Our god has delivered into our hands
> our enemy,
> The destroyer of our land,
> And the one who multiplied our
> dead."

²⁵So it happened, when their hearts were merry, that they said, "Call for Samson, that he may perform for us." So they called for Samson from the prison, and he performed for them. And they stationed him between the pillars. ²⁶Then Samson said to the lad who held him by the hand, "Let me feel the pillars which support the temple, so that I can lean on them." ²⁷Now the temple was full of men and women. All the lords of the Philistines *were* there—about three thousand men and women on the roof watching while Samson performed.

²⁸Then Samson called to the LORD, saying, "O Lord GOD, remember me, I pray! Strengthen me, I pray, just this once, O God, that I may with one *blow* take vengeance on the Philistines for my two eyes!" ²⁹And Samson took hold of the two middle pillars which supported the temple, and he braced himself against them, one on his right and the other on his left. ³⁰Then Samson said, "Let me die with the Philistines!" And he pushed with *all his* might, and the temple fell on the lords and all the people who *were* in it. So the dead that he killed at his death were more than he had killed in his life.

> **16:29,30** This Philistine temple had roofs that overlooked a courtyard and that were supported by columns. The two central pillars were set close together to give extra support for the roof. God gave Samson his full strength again so that he was able to buckle the columns, collapsing the roof, and killing the Philistines. He died for Israel, not as suicide, but as an act of judgment on his enemies. He was the greatest champion of all Israel and yet a man of passion capable of severe sin. Still, he is listed among the faithful (see Heb. 11:32).

³¹And his brothers and all his father's household came down and took him, and brought *him* up and buried him between Zorah and Eshtaol in the tomb of his father Manoah. He had judged Israel twenty years.

16:19 ᵃFollowing Masoretic Text, Targum, and Vulgate; Septuagint reads *he began to be weak.*

Micah's Idolatry

17 Now there was a man from the mountains of Ephraim, whose name was Micah. ²And he said to his mother, "The eleven hundred *shekels* of silver that were taken from you, and on which you put a curse, even saying it in my ears—here *is* the silver with me; I took it."

And his mother said, "*May you be blessed by the LORD, my son!*" ³So when he had returned the eleven hundred *shekels* of silver to his mother, his mother said, "I had wholly dedicated the silver from my hand to the LORD for my son, to make a carved image and a molded image; now therefore, I will return it to you." ⁴Thus he returned the silver to his mother. Then his mother took two hundred *shekels* of silver and gave them to the silversmith, and he made it into a carved image and a molded image; and they were in the house of Micah.

⁵The man Micah had a shrine, and made an ephod and household idols;*ᵃ* and he consecrated one of his sons, who became his priest. ⁶In those days *there was* no king in Israel; everyone did *what was* right in his own eyes.

> **17:6 everyone did...own eyes.** This description of sinful behavior characterized that time as well as all sinful times. This attitude had surfaced much earlier in Israel's history (see Deut. 12:8; Judg. 21:25).

⁷Now there was a young man from Bethlehem in Judah, of the family of Judah; he *was* a Levite, and was staying there. ⁸The man departed from the city of Bethlehem in Judah to stay wherever he could find *a place*. Then he came to the mountains of Ephraim, to the house of Micah, as he journeyed. ⁹And Micah said to him, "Where do you come from?"

So he said to him, "I *am* a Levite from Bethlehem in Judah, and I am on my way to find *a place* to stay."

¹⁰Micah said to him, "Dwell with me, and be a father and a priest to me, and I will give you ten *shekels* of silver per year, a suit of clothes, and your sustenance." So the Levite went in. ¹¹Then the Levite was content to dwell with the man; and the young man became like one of his sons to him. ¹²So Micah consecrated the Levite, and the young man became his priest, and lived in the house of Micah. ¹³Then Micah said, "Now I know that the LORD will be good to me, since I have a Levite as priest!"

The Danites Adopt Micah's Idolatry

18 In those days *there was* no king in Israel. And in those days the tribe of the Danites was seeking an inheritance for itself to dwell in; for until that day *their* inheritance among the tribes of Israel had not fallen to them. ²So the children of Dan sent five men of their family from their territory, men of valor from Zorah and Eshtaol, to spy out the land and search it. They said to them, "Go, search the land." So they went to the mountains of Ephraim, to the house of Micah, and lodged there. ³While they *were* at the house of Micah, they recognized the voice of the young Levite. They turned aside and said to him, "Who brought you here? What are you doing in this *place*? What do you have here?"

⁴He said to them, "Thus and so Micah did for me. He has hired me, and I have become his priest."

> **18:5 Please inquire of God.** The passage does not say if the Levite really did seek God's counsel before giving reassurance. The Danites should have prayed to seek God's counsel before making this trip instead of consulting a disobedient priest.

⁵So they said to him, "Please inquire of God, that we may know whether the journey on which we go will be prosperous."

⁶And the priest said to them, "Go in peace. The presence of the LORD *be* with you on your way."

⁷So the five men departed and went to Laish. They saw the people who *were* there, how they dwelt safely, in the manner of the Sidonians, quiet and secure. *There were* no rulers in the land who might put *them* to shame for anything. They *were* far from the Sidonians, and they had no ties with anyone.*ᵃ*

⁸Then *the spies* came back to their brethren at Zorah and Eshtaol, and their

---

17:5 *ᵃ*Hebrew *teraphim*   18:7 *ᵃ*Following Masoretic Text, Targum, and Vulgate; Septuagint reads *with Syria*.

brethren said to them, "What *is* your *report?*"

⁹So they said, "Arise, let us go up against them. For we have seen the land, and indeed it *is* very good. *Would* you *do* nothing? Do not hesitate to go, *and* enter to possess the land. ¹⁰When you go, you will come to a secure people and a large land. For God has given it into your hands, a place where *there is* no lack of anything that *is* on the earth."

¹¹And six hundred men of the family of the Danites went from there, from Zorah and Eshtaol, armed with weapons of war. ¹²Then they went up and encamped in Kirjath Jearim in Judah. (Therefore they call that place Mahaneh Dan*ᵃ* to this day. There *it is,* west of Kirjath Jearim.) ¹³And they passed from there to the mountains of Ephraim, and came to the house of Micah.

¹⁴Then the five men who had gone to spy out the country of Laish answered and said to their brethren, "Do you know that there are in these houses an ephod, household idols, a carved image, and a molded image? Now therefore, consider what you should do." ¹⁵So they turned aside there, and came to the house of the young Levite man—to the house of Micah—and greeted him. ¹⁶The six hundred men armed with their weapons of war, who *were* of the children of Dan, stood by the entrance of the gate. ¹⁷Then the five men who had gone to spy out the land went up. Entering there, they took the carved image, the ephod, the household idols, and the molded image. The priest stood at the entrance of the gate with the six hundred men *who were* armed with weapons of war. ¹⁸When these went into Micah's house and took the carved image, the ephod, the household idols, and the molded image, the priest said to them, "What are you doing?" ¹⁹And they said to him, "Be quiet, put your hand over your mouth, and come with us; be a father and a priest to us. *Is it* better for you to be a priest to the household of one man, or that you be a priest to a tribe and a family in Israel?" ²⁰So the priest's heart was glad; and he took the ephod, the household idols, and the carved image, and took his place among the people.

²¹Then they turned and departed, and put the little ones, the livestock, and the goods in front of them. ²²When they were a good way from the house of Micah, the men who *were* in the houses near Micah's house gathered together and overtook the children of Dan. ²³And they called out to the children of Dan. So they turned around and said to Micah, "What ails you, that you have gathered such a company?"

²⁴So he said, "You have taken away my gods which I made, and the priest, and you have gone away. Now what more do I have? How can you say to me, 'What ails you?' "

²⁵And the children of Dan said to him, "Do not let your voice be heard among us, lest angry men fall upon you, and you lose your life, with the lives of your household!" ²⁶Then the children of Dan went their way. And when Micah saw that they *were* too strong for him, he turned and went back to his house.

18:14–26 The Danites sinfully stole Micah's false idols, believing that they would give them power to seize the land. Jonathan, the sinful Levite who had served Micah as priest, then sold out again to be a priest for the Danites, who were not bothered by his defection but actually believed in his spiritual power.

Danites Settle in Laish

²⁷So they took *the things* Micah had made, and the priest who had belonged to him, and went to Laish, to a people quiet and secure; and they struck them with the edge of the sword and burned the city with fire. ²⁸*There was* no deliverer, because it *was* far from Sidon, and they had no ties with anyone. It was in the valley that belongs to Beth Rehob. So they rebuilt the city and dwelt there. ²⁹And they called the name of the city Dan, after the name of Dan their father, who was born to Israel. However, the name of the city formerly *was* Laish.

³⁰Then the children of Dan set up for themselves the carved image; and Jonathan the son of Gershom, the son of Manasseh,*ᵃ* and his sons were priests to the tribe of Dan until the day of the captivity of the land. ³¹So they set up for themselves Micah's carved image which he made, all

18:12 *ᵃ*Literally *Camp of Dan*   18:30 *ᵃ*Septuagint and Vulgate read *Moses.*

the time that the house of God was in Shiloh.

The Levite's Concubine

19 And it came to pass in those days, when *there was* no king in Israel, that there was a certain Levite staying in the remote mountains of Ephraim. He took for himself a concubine from Bethlehem in Judah. ²But his concubine played the harlot against him, and went away from him to her father's house at Bethlehem in Judah, and was there four whole months. ³Then her husband arose and went after her, to speak kindly to her *and* bring her back, having his servant and a couple of donkeys with him. So she brought him into her father's house; and when the father of the young woman saw him, he was glad to meet him. ⁴Now his father-in-law, the young woman's father, detained him; and he stayed with him three days. So they ate and drank and lodged there.

> **19:2 played the harlot.** The law required that she should be killed for her sin, but the priest ignored the Scripture and holiness and instead sought her back. A priest was not allowed to marry a harlot (Lev. 21:14), so his ministry was greatly tainted.

⁵Then it came to pass on the fourth day that they arose early in the morning, and he stood to depart; but the young woman's father said to his son-in-law, "Refresh your heart with a morsel of bread, and afterward go your way." ⁶So they sat down, and the two of them ate and drank together. Then the young woman's father said to the man, "Please be content to stay all night, and let your heart be merry." ⁷And when the man stood to depart, his father-in-law urged him; so he lodged there again. ⁸Then he arose early in the morning on the fifth day to depart, but the young woman's father said, "Please refresh your heart." So they delayed until afternoon; and both of them ate. ⁹And when the man stood to depart—he and his concubine and his servant—his father-in-law, the young woman's father, said to him, "Look, the day is now drawing toward evening; please spend the night. See, the day is coming to an end; lodge here, that your heart may be merry. Tomorrow go your way early, so that you may get home."

¹⁰However, the man was not willing to spend that night; so he rose and departed, and came opposite Jebus (that *is*, Jerusalem). With him were the two saddled donkeys; his concubine *was* also with him. ¹¹They *were* near Jebus, and the day was far spent; and the servant said to his master, "Come, please, and let us turn aside into this city of the Jebusites and lodge in it."

> **19:10 Jebus.** An early title for Jerusalem because of Jebusite control (Judg. 1:21), until David made it his capital (2 Sam. 5:6–9). Another early name for the city was Salem (Gen. 14:18).

¹²But his master said to him, "We will not turn aside here into a city of foreigners, who *are* not of the children of Israel; we will go on to Gibeah." ¹³So he said to his servant, "Come, let us draw near to one of these places, and spend the night in Gibeah or in Ramah." ¹⁴And they passed by and went their way; and the sun went down on them near Gibeah, which belongs to Benjamin. ¹⁵They turned aside there to go in to lodge in Gibeah. And when he went in, he sat down in the open square of the city, for no one would take them into *his* house to spend the night.

¹⁶Just then an old man came in from his work in the field at evening, who also *was* from the mountains of Ephraim; he was staying in Gibeah, whereas the men of the place *were* Benjamites. ¹⁷And when he raised his eyes, he saw the traveler in the open square of the city; and the old man said, "Where are you going, and where do you come from?"

¹⁸So he said to him, "We *are* passing from Bethlehem in Judah toward the remote mountains of Ephraim; I *am* from there. I went to Bethlehem in Judah; *now* I am going to the house of the LORD. But there *is* no one who will take me into his house, ¹⁹although we have both straw and fodder for our donkeys, and bread and wine for myself, for your female servant, and for the young man *who is* with your servant; *there is* no lack of anything."

²⁰And the old man said, "Peace *be* with you! However, *let* all your needs *be* my responsibility; only do not spend the night in

the open square." [21]So he brought him into his house, and gave fodder to the donkeys. And they washed their feet, and ate and drank.

Gibeah's Crime

[22]As they were enjoying themselves, suddenly certain men of the city, perverted men,[a] surrounded the house *and* beat on the door. They spoke to the master of the house, the old man, saying, "Bring out the man who came to your house, that we may know him *carnally!*"

[23]But the man, the master of the house, went out to them and said to them, "No, my brethren! I beg you, do not act so wickedly! Seeing this man has come into my house, do not commit this outrage. [24]Look, *here is* my virgin daughter and *the man's*[a] concubine; let me bring them out now. Humble them, and do with them as you please; but to this man do not do such a vile thing!" [25]But the men would not heed him. So the man took his concubine and brought *her* out to them. And they knew her and abused her all night until morning; and when the day began to break, they let her go.

> **19:24 let me bring them out.** The host and the priest should have done everything in their power to protect the women, even at the risk of their own lives. He disgracefully offered to hand his daughter or the guest concubine over to the men. This is unthinkable, weak cowardice for any man, especially a priest of God.

[26]Then the woman came as the day was dawning, and fell down at the door of the man's house where her master *was*, till it was light. [27]When her master arose in the morning, and opened the doors of the house and went out to go his way, there was his concubine, fallen *at* the door of the house with her hands on the threshold. [28]And he said to her, "Get up and let us be going." But there was no answer. So the man lifted her onto the donkey; and the man got up and went to his place.

[29]When he entered his house he took a knife, laid hold of his concubine, and divided her into twelve pieces, limb by limb,[a]

and sent her throughout all the territory of Israel. [30]And so it was that all who saw it said, "No such deed has been done or seen from the day that the children of Israel came up from the land of Egypt until this day. Consider it, confer, and speak up!"

> **19:29 divided her into twelve pieces.** The Levite's bizarre butchery dividing her body into 12 pieces was a shocking, radical summons to arouse Israelite indignation for vengeance. Apparently he sent a messenger and a message with each part, and the response was universal indignation and horror.

Israel's War with the Benjamites

20 So all the children of Israel came out, from Dan to Beersheba, as well as from the land of Gilead, and the congregation gathered together as one man before the LORD at Mizpah. [2]And the leaders of all the people, all the tribes of Israel, presented themselves in the assembly of the people of God, four hundred thousand foot soldiers who drew the sword. [3](Now the children of Benjamin heard that the children of Israel had gone up to Mizpah.)

Then the children of Israel said, "Tell *us*, how did this wicked deed happen?"

[4]So the Levite, the husband of the woman who was murdered, answered and said, "My concubine and I went into Gibeah, which belongs to Benjamin, to spend the night. [5]And the men of Gibeah rose against me, and surrounded the house at night because of me. They intended to kill me, but instead they ravished my concubine so that she died. [6]So I took hold of my concubine, cut her in pieces, and sent her throughout all the territory of the inheritance of Israel, because they committed lewdness and outrage in Israel. [7]Look! All of you *are* children of Israel; give your advice and counsel here and now!"

[8]So all the people arose as one man, saying, "None *of us* will go to his tent, nor will any turn back to his house; [9]but now this *is* the thing which we will do to Gibeah: *We will go up* against it by lot. [10]We will take ten men out of *every* hundred throughout all the tribes of Israel, a hundred out of *every* thousand, and a thousand out of *every* ten thousand, to make provisions for

---

19:22 [a]Literally *sons of Belial*   19:24 [a]Literally *his*   19:29 [a]Literally *with her bones*

the people, that when they come to Gibeah in Benjamin, they may repay all the vileness that they have done in Israel." [11]So all the men of Israel were gathered against the city, united together as one man.

[12]Then the tribes of Israel sent men through all the tribe of Benjamin, saying, "What *is* this wickedness that has occurred among you? [13]Now therefore, deliver up the men, the perverted men*[a]* who *are* in Gibeah, that we may put them to death and remove the evil from Israel!" But the children of Benjamin would not listen to the voice of their brethren, the children of Israel. [14]Instead, the children of Benjamin gathered together from their cities to Gibeah, to go to battle against the children of Israel. [15]And from their cities at that time the children of Benjamin numbered twenty-six thousand men who drew the sword, besides the inhabitants of Gibeah, who numbered seven hundred select men. [16]Among all this people *were* seven hundred select men *who were* left-handed; every one could sling a stone at a hair's *breadth* and not miss. [17]Now besides Benjamin, the men of Israel numbered four hundred thousand men who drew the sword; all of these *were* men of war.

20:18 to inquire of God. The children of Israel humbly came to seek God's help. The Lord gave His counsel from the location of the ark at Shiloh. The tribe of Judah was responsible to lead in battle since God had chosen a leadership role for that tribe (Gen. 49:8–12; 1 Chr. 5:1,2).

[18]Then the children of Israel arose and went up to the house of God*[a]* to inquire of God. They said, "Which of us shall go up first to battle against the children of Benjamin?"

The LORD said, "Judah first!"

[19]So the children of Israel rose in the morning and encamped against Gibeah. [20]And the men of Israel went out to battle against Benjamin, and the men of Israel put themselves in battle array to fight against them at Gibeah. [21]Then the children of Benjamin came out of Gibeah, and on that day cut down to the ground twenty-two thousand men of the Israelites. [22]And

the people, that is, the men of Israel, encouraged themselves and again formed the battle line at the place where they had put themselves in array on the first day. [23]Then the children of Israel went up and wept before the LORD until evening, and asked counsel of the LORD, saying, "Shall I again draw near for battle against the children of my brother Benjamin?"

And the LORD said, "Go up against him."

[24]So the children of Israel approached the children of Benjamin on the second day. [25]And Benjamin went out against them from Gibeah on the second day, and cut down to the ground eighteen thousand more of the children of Israel; all these drew the sword.

20:22–25 The Lord allowed Israel great defeat and death twice, to shake them to their senses regarding the cost of tolerating sin. They were relying too much on their own skill. Finally they were desperate enough and fasted and offered sacrifices. The Lord then gave victory, similar to that at Ai (Josh. 8).

[26]Then all the children of Israel, that is, all the people, went up and came to the house of God*[a]* and wept. They sat there before the LORD and fasted that day until evening; and they offered burnt offerings and peace offerings before the LORD. [27]So the children of Israel inquired of the LORD (the ark of the covenant of God *was* there in those days, [28]and Phinehas the son of Eleazar, the son of Aaron, stood before it in those days), saying, "Shall I yet again go out to battle against the children of my brother Benjamin, or shall I cease?"

And the LORD said, "Go up, for tomorrow I will deliver them into your hand."

[29]Then Israel set men in ambush all around Gibeah. [30]And the children of Israel went up against the children of Benjamin on the third day, and put themselves in battle array against Gibeah as at the other times. [31]So the children of Benjamin went out against the people, *and* were drawn away from the city. They began to strike down *and* kill some of the people, as at the other times, in the highways (one of which goes up to Bethel and the other to Gibeah) and in the field, about thirty men of Israel.

20:13 *[a]*Literally *sons of Belial*   20:18 *[a]*Or *Bethel*   20:26 *[a]*Or *Bethel*

³²And the children of Benjamin said, "They *are* defeated before us, as at first."

But the children of Israel said, "Let us flee and draw them away from the city to the highways." ³³So all the men of Israel rose from their place and put themselves in battle array at Baal Tamar. Then Israel's men in ambush burst forth from their position in the plain of Geba. ³⁴And ten thousand select men from all Israel came against Gibeah, and the battle was fierce. But *the Benjamites*[a] did not know that disaster *was* upon them. ³⁵The LORD defeated Benjamin before Israel. And the children of Israel destroyed that day twenty-five thousand one hundred Benjamites; all these drew the sword.

³⁶So the children of Benjamin saw that they were defeated. The men of Israel had given ground to the Benjamites, because they relied on the men in ambush whom they had set against Gibeah. ³⁷And the men in ambush quickly rushed upon Gibeah; the men in ambush spread out and struck the whole city with the edge of the sword. ³⁸Now the appointed signal between the men of Israel and the men in ambush was that they would make a great cloud of smoke rise up from the city, ³⁹whereupon the men of Israel would turn in battle. Now Benjamin had begun to strike *and* kill about thirty of the men of Israel. For they said, "Surely they are defeated before us, as *in* the first battle." ⁴⁰But when the cloud began to rise from the city in a column of smoke, the Benjamites looked behind them, and there was the whole city going up *in smoke* to heaven. ⁴¹And when the men of Israel turned back, the men of Benjamin panicked, for they saw that disaster had come upon them. ⁴²Therefore they turned *their backs* before the men of Israel in the direction of the wilderness; but the battle overtook them, and whoever *came* out of the cities they destroyed in their midst. ⁴³They surrounded the Benjamites, chased them, *and* easily trampled them down as far as the front of Gibeah toward the east. ⁴⁴And eighteen thousand men of Benjamin fell; all these *were* men of valor. ⁴⁵Then they[a] turned and fled toward the wilderness to the rock of Rimmon; and

they cut down five thousand of them on the highways. Then they pursued them relentlessly up to Gidom, and killed two thousand of them. ⁴⁶So all who fell of Benjamin that day were twenty-five thousand men who drew the sword; all these *were* men of valor.

⁴⁷But six hundred men turned and fled toward the wilderness to the rock of Rimmon, and they stayed at the rock of Rimmon for four months. ⁴⁸And the men of Israel turned back against the children of Benjamin, and struck them down with the edge of the sword—from *every* city, men and beasts, all who were found. They also set fire to all the cities they came to.

Wives Provided for the Benjamites

21 Now the men of Israel had sworn an oath at Mizpah, saying, "None of us shall give his daughter to Benjamin as a wife." ²Then the people came to the house of God,[a] and remained there before God till evening. They lifted up their voices and wept bitterly, ³and said, "O LORD God of Israel, why has this come to pass in Israel, that today there should be one tribe *missing* in Israel?"

⁴So it was, on the next morning, that the people rose early and built an altar there, and offered burnt offerings and peace offerings. ⁵The children of Israel said, "Who *is there* among all the tribes of Israel who did not come up with the assembly to the LORD?" For they had made a great oath concerning anyone who had not come up to the LORD at Mizpah, saying, "He shall surely be put to death." ⁶And the children of Israel grieved for Benjamin their brother, and said, "One tribe is cut off from Israel today. ⁷What shall we do for wives for those who remain, seeing we have sworn by the LORD that we will not give them our daughters as wives?"

⁸And they said, "What one *is there* from the tribes of Israel who did not come up to Mizpah to the LORD?" And, in fact, no one had come to the camp from Jabesh Gilead to the assembly. ⁹For when the people were counted, indeed, not one of the inhabitants of Jabesh Gilead *was* there. ¹⁰So the congregation sent out there twelve thousand of

---

20:34 [a]Literally *they*   20:45 [a]Septuagint reads *the rest*.   21:2 [a]Or *Bethel*

21:8–16 Jabesh Gilead. The Israelites placed such a premium on tribal unity that they regarded this city's non-participation in battle as worthy of death. The passage does not give God's approval for killing men, women, and children. It is a bizarre action of men motivated by what is right in their own eyes, which is the point that both begins and ends this dark, final section (17:6; 21:25).

their most valiant men, and commanded them, saying, "Go and strike the inhabitants of Jabesh Gilead with the edge of the sword, including the women and children. [11]And this *is* the thing that you shall do: You shall utterly destroy every male, and every woman who has known a man intimately." [12]So they found among the inhabitants of Jabesh Gilead four hundred young virgins who had not known a man intimately; and they brought them to the camp at Shiloh, which is in the land of Canaan.

[13]Then the whole congregation sent *word* to the children of Benjamin who *were* at the rock of Rimmon, and announced peace to them. [14]So Benjamin came back at that time, and they gave them the women whom they had saved alive of the women of Jabesh Gilead; and yet they had not found enough for them.

[15]And the people grieved for Benjamin, because the LORD had made a void in the tribes of Israel.

[16]Then the elders of the congregation said, "What shall we do for wives for those who remain, since the women of Benjamin have been destroyed?" [17]And they said, "*There must be* an inheritance for the survivors of Benjamin, that a tribe may not be destroyed from Israel. [18]However, we cannot give them wives from our daughters, for the children of Israel have sworn an oath, saying, 'Cursed *be* the one who gives a wife to Benjamin.' " [19]Then they said, "In fact, *there is* a yearly feast of the LORD in Shiloh,

which *is* north of Bethel, on the east side of the highway that goes up from Bethel to Shechem, and south of Lebonah."

21:16 wives for those who remain. Recognizing that the other 200 men needed wives, they allowed them to snatch brides on their own at a dance in Shiloh, not believing that this violated their oath of not directly "giving" their daughters.

[20]Therefore they instructed the children of Benjamin, saying, "Go, lie in wait in the vineyards, [21]and watch; and just when the daughters of Shiloh come out to perform their dances, then come out from the vineyards, and every man catch a wife for himself from the daughters of Shiloh; then go to the land of Benjamin. [22]Then it shall be, when their fathers or their brothers come to us to complain, that we will say to them, 'Be kind to them for our sakes, because we did not take a wife for any of them in the war; for *it is* not *as though* you have given the *women* to them at this time, making yourselves guilty of your oath.' "

[23]And the children of Benjamin did so; they took enough wives for their number from those who danced, whom they caught. Then they went and returned to their inheritance, and they rebuilt the cities and dwelt in them. [24]So the children of Israel departed from there at that time, every man to his tribe and family; they went out from there, every man to his inheritance.

[25]In those days *there was* no king in Israel; everyone did *what was* right in his own eyes.

21:25 Judges 17–21 vividly demonstrates how bizarre and deep sin can take hold of people when they throw off God's authority. This was the tragic but appropriate conclusion to this bleak period of Israelite history (see Deut. 12:8).

Even the title of the Book of Ruth includes several noteworthy facts: (1) this book is the only one in the Old Testament named after a non-Jewish person; (2) this book is one of only two books in the Bible named after a woman (Ruth, like Esther, serves as the central character of the story); (3) this book is the only one in the Old Testament named after an ancestor of Jesus.

The name, Ruth, was most likely a shared Hebrew/Moabite term meaning "friendship." As her brief biography demonstrates, Ruth certainly lived up to her name.

AUTHOR AND DATE

Ruth was probably written by Samuel, approximately 1003 to 1010 B.C.

The book offers little help in identifying its author. Ancient Jewish traditions name Samuel. The closing verses mention David, but not Solomon, indicating that the book probably was written near the end of or shortly after Samuel's life (4:17,22). Whomever the author, the effort yielded an enduring work of exquisite storytelling.

BACKGROUND AND SETTING

Only two geographic locations provide the context of the action in Ruth: the city of Bethlehem, just south of Jerusalem and the country of Moab, to the southeast and beyond the Dead Sea. Moab and Israel shared a distant but shameful ancestral relationship. The Moabites were descendants of Abraham's nephew Lot through incest (Genesis 19:37). Tensions were often high between the two nations. The events in Ruth's life apparently occurred during a time of relative peace between the two peoples.

The famine that had driven Elimelech and Naomi to relocate to Moab illustrates a method God would use, in addition to foreign conflicts, to discipline His unruly people (1:1). According to the book, the events occurred during the time of the judges (1:1). No famines are recorded in Judges, but the brief genealogy of David indicates that Ruth probably lived during the judgeship of Jair (Judges 10:3–5).

This book offers an intimate look at the daily life of ordinary people in ancient Israel. It also connects that life with God's marvelous plans for the world. Ruth reminds us that God makes every life significant.

At least seven major theological themes emerge in this book: (1) Ruth the Moabitess illustrates that God's redemptive plan extends beyond the Jews to Gentiles (2:12); (2) Ruth demonstrates that women are co-heirs with men of God's salvation grace (Galatians 3:28); (3) Ruth portrays the virtuous woman of Proverbs 31:10 (3:11); (4) Ruth illustrates God's sovereign and providential care (1:6; 2:3; 4:13); (5) Ruth, along with Tamar (Genesis 38), Rahab (Joshua 2), and Bathsheba (2 Samuel 11,12), contributed to the genealogy of the messianic line (4:17–22; Matthew 1:5); (6) Boaz, as a type of Christ, became Ruth's kinsman-redeemer (4:1–12); (7) the book records David's ancestral right (and therefore Christ's right) to the throne of Israel (4:18–22; Genesis 49:8–12).

> **RUTH REMINDS** US THAT **GOD MAKES** EVERY LIFE **SIGNIFICANT.**

OUTLINE

Elimelech's Family Goes to Moab

1 Now it came to pass, in the days when the judges ruled, that there was a famine in the land. And a certain man of Bethlehem, Judah, went to dwell in the country of Moab, he and his wife and his two sons. ²The name of the man *was* Elimelech, the name of his wife *was* Naomi, and the names of his two sons *were* Mahlon and Chilion—Ephrathites of Bethlehem, Judah. And they went to the country of Moab and remained there. ³Then Elimelech, Naomi's husband, died; and she was left, and her two sons. ⁴Now they took wives of the women of Moab: the name of the one *was* Orpah, and the name of the other Ruth. And they dwelt there about ten years. ⁵Then both Mahlon and Chilion also died; so the woman survived her two sons and her husband.

> **1:2–4 Elimelech.** His name means "my God is king," signifying devout commitment to God. He was likely a prominent man in the community. **Naomi.** Her name means "pleasant." **Mahlon and Chilion.** Their names mean "sick" and "pining" respectively. **Orpah.** Her name means "stubborn." **Ruth.** Her name means "friendship."

Naomi Returns with Ruth

⁶Then she arose with her daughters-in-law that she might return from the country of Moab, for she had heard in the country of Moab that the LORD had visited His people by giving them bread. ⁷Therefore she went out from the place where she was, and her two daughters-in-law with her; and they went on the way to return to the land of Judah. ⁸And Naomi said to her two daughters-in-law, "Go, return each to her mother's house. The LORD deal kindly with you, as you have dealt with the dead and with me. ⁹The LORD grant that you may find rest, each in the house of her husband."

So she kissed them, and they lifted up their voices and wept. ¹⁰And they said to her, "Surely we will return with you to your people."

¹¹But Naomi said, "Turn back, my daughters; why will you go with me? *Are* there still sons in my womb, that they may be your husbands? ¹²Turn back, my daughters, go—for I am too old to have a husband. If I should say I have hope, *if* I should have a husband tonight and should also bear sons, ¹³would you wait for them till they were grown? Would you restrain yourselves from having husbands? No, my daughters; for it grieves me very much for your sakes that the hand of the LORD has gone out against me!"

¹⁴Then they lifted up their voices and wept again; and Orpah kissed her mother-in-law, but Ruth clung to her.

¹⁵And she said, "Look, your sister-in-law has gone back to her people and to her gods; return after your sister-in-law."

¹⁶But Ruth said:

> "Entreat me not to leave you,
> *Or to* turn back from following after you;
> For wherever you go, I will go;
> And wherever you lodge, I will lodge;
> Your people *shall be* my people,
> And your God, my God.

> **1:16 And your God, my God.** Ruth's testimony showed that she had converted from worshiping the Moabite god Chemosh to the true God of Israel.

¹⁷ Where you die, I will die,
And there will I be buried.
The LORD do so to me, and more also,
If *anything but* death parts you and me."

¹⁸When she saw that she was determined to go with her, she stopped speaking to her.

¹⁹Now the two of them went until they came to Bethlehem. And it happened, when they had come to Bethlehem, that all the city was excited because of them; and the women said, *"Is this Naomi?"*

²⁰But she said to them, "Do not call me Naomi;ᵃ call me Mara,ᵇ for the Almighty has dealt very bitterly with me. ²¹I went out full, and the LORD has brought me home again empty. Why do you call me Naomi, since the LORD has testified against me, and the Almighty has afflicted me?"

²²So Naomi returned, and Ruth the Mo-

1:20 ᵃLiterally *Pleasant*   ᵇLiterally *Bitter*

abitess her daughter-in-law with her, who returned from the country of Moab. Now they came to Bethlehem at the beginning of barley harvest.

1:20,21 Naomi...Mara...full...empty. Naomi asked to be renamed "Mara," which means "bitter." Even though she still believed in God, she had lost hope. Very discouraged from her losses, she did not see the possibilities before her: the hope of a good harvest, her faithful daughter-in-law Ruth, and her kinsman Boaz.

Ruth Meets Boaz

2 There was a relative of Naomi's husband, a man of great wealth, of the family of Elimelech. His name *was* Boaz. ²So Ruth the Moabitess said to Naomi, "Please let me go to the field, and glean heads of grain after *him* in whose sight I may find favor."

And she said to her, "Go, my daughter."

2:1 relative...of the family. Boaz may have even been the brother of Elimelech (Naomi's husband) or at least within the same tribe or clan. **a man of great wealth.** Lit. "a man of valor" (see Judg. 6:12; 11:1) who had unusual capacity to obtain and protect his property. **Boaz.** His name means "in him is strength." He had never married or was a widower (see 1 Chr. 2:11,12; Matt. 1:5).

³Then she left, and went and gleaned in the field after the reapers. And she happened to come to the part of the field *belonging* to Boaz, who *was* of the family of Elimelech.

⁴Now behold, Boaz came from Bethlehem, and said to the reapers, "The LORD *be* with you!"

And they answered him, "The LORD bless you!"

⁵Then Boaz said to his servant who was in charge of the reapers, "Whose young woman *is* this?"

⁶So the servant who was in charge of the reapers answered and said, "It *is* the young Moabite woman who came back with Naomi from the country of Moab. ⁷And she said, 'Please let me glean and gather after the reapers among the sheaves.' So she came and has continued from morning until now, though she rested a little in the house."

⁸Then Boaz said to Ruth, "You will listen, my daughter, will you not? Do not go to glean in another field, nor go from here, but stay close by my young women. ⁹*Let* your eyes *be* on the field which they reap, and go after them. Have I not commanded the young men not to touch you? And when you are thirsty, go to the vessels and drink from what the young men have drawn."

¹⁰So she fell on her face, bowed down to the ground, and said to him, "Why have I found favor in your eyes, that you should take notice of me, since I *am* a foreigner?"

¹¹And Boaz answered and said to her, "It has been fully reported to me, all that you have done for your mother-in-law since the death of your husband, and *how* you have left your father and your mother and the land of your birth, and have come to a people whom you did not know before. ¹²The LORD repay your work, and a full reward be given you by the LORD God of Israel, under whose wings you have come for refuge."

2:12 wings...refuge. God is portrayed as a mother bird sheltering the young and fragile with her wings (see Pss. 17:8; 36:7; Ex. 19:4). Boaz blessed Ruth for her new commitment to the Lord. Later, he became God's answer to this prayer (see 3:9).

¹³Then she said, "Let me find favor in your sight, my lord; for you have comforted me, and have spoken kindly to your maidservant, though I am not like one of your maidservants."

¹⁴Now Boaz said to her at mealtime, "Come here, and eat of the bread, and dip your piece of bread in the vinegar." So she sat beside the reapers, and he passed parched *grain* to her; and she ate and was satisfied, and kept some back. ¹⁵And when she rose up to glean, Boaz commanded his young men, saying, "Let her glean even among the sheaves, and do not reproach her. ¹⁶Also let *grain* from the bundles fall purposely for her; leave *it* that she may glean, and do not rebuke her."

¹⁷So she gleaned in the field until evening, and beat out what she had gleaned, and it was about an ephah of barley. ¹⁸Then she took *it* up and went into the city, and her mother-in-law saw what she had gleaned. So she brought out and gave to her what she had kept back after she had been satisfied.

¹⁹And her mother-in-law said to her, "Where have you gleaned today? And where did you work? Blessed be the one who took notice of you."

So she told her mother-in-law with whom she had worked, and said, "The man's name with whom I worked today is Boaz."

²⁰Then Naomi said to her daughter-in-law, "Blessed be he of the LORD, who has not forsaken His kindness to the living and the dead!" And Naomi said to her, "This man is a relation of ours, one of our close relatives."

> **2:20 His kindness.** Without human help, Ruth found Boaz, and then Naomi began to understand God's working. **one of our close relatives.** The great kinsman-redeemer theme of Ruth begins here. A close relative could redeem (1) a family member sold into slavery, (2) land that was sold because of financial hardship, or (3) the family name, by virtue of a levirate marriage. This earthly custom of redemption mirrors Christ's redemption of sinners. At this point, Naomi's darkness has been broken by the dawning of new hope (see Rom. 8:28–39).

²¹Ruth the Moabitess said, "He also said to me, 'You shall stay close by my young men until they have finished all my harvest.' "

²²And Naomi said to Ruth her daughter-in-law, "It is good, my daughter, that you go out with his young women, and that people do not meet you in any other field." ²³So she stayed close by the young women of Boaz, to glean until the end of barley harvest and wheat harvest; and she dwelt with her mother-in-law.

Ruth's Redemption Assured

3 Then Naomi her mother-in-law said to her, "My daughter, shall I not seek security for you, that it may be well with you? ²Now Boaz, whose young women you were with, is he not our relative? In fact, he is winnowing barley tonight at the threshing floor. ³Therefore wash yourself and anoint yourself, put on your best garment and go down to the threshing floor; but do not make yourself known to the man until he has finished eating and drinking. ⁴Then it shall be, when he lies down, that you shall notice the place where he lies; and you shall go in, uncover his feet, and lie down; and he will tell you what you should do."

⁵And she said to her, "All that you say to me I will do."

⁶So she went down to the threshing floor and did according to all that her mother-in-law instructed her. ⁷And after Boaz had eaten and drunk, and his heart was cheerful, he went to lie down at the end of the heap of grain; and she came softly, uncovered his feet, and lay down.

⁸Now it happened at midnight that the man was startled, and turned himself; and there, a woman was lying at his feet. ⁹And he said, "Who are you?"

So she answered, "I am Ruth, your maidservant. Take your maidservant under your wing,ᵃ for you are a close relative."

¹⁰Then he said, "Blessed are you of the LORD, my daughter! For you have shown more kindness at the end than at the beginning, in that you did not go after young men, whether poor or rich. ¹¹And now, my

---

3:9 ᵃOr Spread the corner of your garment over your maidservant

---

What is the "kinsman-redeemer," a prominent part in the story of Ruth?

When Boaz negotiated with another relative about the settlement of Elimelech and Naomi's estate (4:1–12), he referred to a law established by Moses in Deuteronomy 25:5–10. That law set out specific actions to be taken by the surviving family if a married son were to die without a son to inherit or carry on his name. Another (presumably unmarried) man in the family was to marry the widow. The first resulting child would inherit the estate of the man who had died.

Boaz's relative was willing to work out a financial arrangement with Naomi over her estate, but he didn't realize that Ruth was part of the settlement. When Boaz informed the man, he immediately released his right to claim responsibility for the estate. That cleared the way for Boaz and Ruth to marry. The whole exchange conveys a commitment to integrity and honor.

daughter, do not fear. I will do for you all that you request, for all the people of my town know that you *are* a virtuous woman. ¹²Now it is true that I *am* a close relative; however, there is a relative closer than I.

RUTH: THE PROVERBS 31 WIFE

The "virtuous" wife of Proverbs 31:10 is personified by "virtuous" Ruth of whom the same Hebrew word is used (3:11). With amazing parallel, they share at least eight character traits (see below). One wonders (in concert with Jewish tradition) if King Lemuel's mother might not have been Bathsheba who orally passed the family heritage of Ruth's spotless reputation along to David's son Solomon. Lemuel, which means "devoted to God," could have been a family name for Solomon (cf. Jedediah, 2 Sam. 12:25) who then could have penned Proverbs 31:10–31 with Ruth in mind:

1. Devoted to her family (Ruth 1:15–18 // Prov. 31:10–12,23)
2. Delighted in her work (Ruth 2:2 // Prov. 31:13)
3. Diligent in her labor (Ruth 2:7,17,23 // Prov. 31:14–18,19–21,24,27)
4. Dedicated to godly speech (Ruth 2:10,13 // Prov. 13:26)
5. Dependent on God (Ruth 2:12 // Prov. 31:25b,30)
6. Dressed with care (Ruth 3:3 // Prov. 31:22,25a)
7. Discreet with men (Ruth 3:6–13 // Prov. 31:11,12,23)
8. Delivered blessings (Ruth 4:14,15 // Prov. 31:28,29,31)[1]

¹³Stay this night, and in the morning it shall be *that* if he will perform the duty of a close relative for you—good; let him do it. But if he does not want to perform the duty for you, then I will perform the duty for you, *as* the LORD lives! Lie down until morning." ¹⁴So she lay at his feet until morning, and she arose before one could recognize another. Then he said, "Do not let it be known that the woman came to the threshing floor." ¹⁵Also he said, "Bring the shawl that *is* on you and hold it." And when she held it, he measured six *ephahs* of barley, and laid *it* on her. Then she[a] went into the city.

¹⁶When she came to her mother-in-law, she said, "*Is* that you, my daughter?"

Then she told her all that the man had done for her. ¹⁷And she said, "These six *ephahs* of barley he gave me; for he said to me, 'Do not go empty-handed to your mother-in-law.'"

¹⁸Then she said, "Sit still, my daughter, until you know how the matter will turn out; for the man will not rest until he has concluded the matter this day."

Boaz Redeems Ruth

4 Now Boaz went up to the gate and sat down there; and behold, the close relative of whom Boaz had spoken came by. So Boaz said, "Come aside, friend,[a] sit down here." So he came aside and sat down. ²And he took ten men of the elders of the city, and said, "Sit down here." So they sat down. ³Then he said to the close relative, "Naomi, who has come back from the country of Moab, sold the piece of land which *belonged* to our brother Elimelech. ⁴And I thought to inform you, saying, 'Buy *it* back in the presence of the inhabitants and the elders of my people. If you will redeem *it*, redeem *it*; but if you[a] will not redeem *it*, *then* tell me, that I may know; for *there is* no one but you to redeem *it*, and I *am* next after you.'"

And he said, "I will redeem *it.*"

⁵Then Boaz said, "On the day you buy the field from the hand of Naomi, you must

3:15 [a]Many Hebrew manuscripts, Syriac, and Vulgate read *she*; Masoretic Text, Septuagint, and Targum read *he*.   4:1 [a]Hebrew *peloni almoni*; literally *so and so*   4:4 [a]Following many Hebrew manuscripts, Septuagint, Syriac, Targum, and Vulgate; Masoretic Text reads *he*.

also buy *it* from Ruth the Moabitess, the wife of the dead, to perpetuate[a] the name of the dead through his inheritance."

⁶And the close relative said, "I cannot redeem *it* for myself, lest I ruin my own inheritance. You redeem my right of redemption for yourself, for I cannot redeem *it.*"

4:7 took off his sandal. The writer of Ruth explained to his own generation this custom from former generations (Deut 22:5–10). The closer relative legally transferred his right to the property as symbolized by the sandal, most likely belonging to the nearer relative.

⁷Now this *was the custom* in former times in Israel concerning redeeming and exchanging, to confirm anything: one man took off his sandal and gave *it* to the other, and this *was* a confirmation in Israel.

⁸Therefore the close relative said to Boaz, "Buy *it* for yourself." So he took off his sandal. ⁹And Boaz said to the elders and all the people, "You *are* witnesses this day that I have bought all that was Elimelech's, and all that *was* Chilion's and Mahlon's, from the hand of Naomi. ¹⁰Moreover, Ruth the Moabitess, the widow of Mahlon, I have acquired as my wife, to perpetuate the name of the dead through his inheritance, that the name of the dead may not be cut off from among his brethren and from his position at the gate.[a] You *are* witnesses this day."

¹¹And all the people who *were* at the gate, and the elders, said, "*We are* witnesses. The LORD make the woman who is coming to your house like Rachel and Leah, the two who built the house of Israel; and may you prosper in Ephrathah and be famous in Bethlehem. ¹²May your house be like the house of Perez, whom Tamar bore to Judah, because of the offspring which the LORD will give you from this young woman."

Descendants of Boaz and Ruth

¹³So Boaz took Ruth and she became his wife; and when he went in to her, the LORD gave her conception, and she bore a son. ¹⁴Then the women said to Naomi, "Blessed *be* the LORD, who has not left you this day without a close relative; and may his name be famous in Israel! ¹⁵And may he be to you a restorer of life and a nourisher of your old age; for your daughter-in-law, who loves you, who is better to you than seven sons, has borne him." ¹⁶Then Naomi took the child and laid him on her bosom, and became a nurse to him. ¹⁷Also the neighbor women gave him a name, saying, "There is a son born to Naomi." And they called his name Obed. He *is* the father of Jesse, the father of David.

4:17 the neighbor women gave him a name. This is the only instance in the OT of a child being named by someone other than the immediate family. Obed means "servant." **a son born to Naomi.** Ruth vicariously bore the son that restored the family name of Naomi's deceased son Mahlon. **Obed...Jesse...David.** Boaz and Ruth were the great-grandparents of David.

¹⁸Now this *is* the genealogy of Perez: Perez begot Hezron; ¹⁹Hezron begot Ram, and Ram begot Amminadab; ²⁰Amminadab begot Nahshon, and Nahshon begot Salmon;[a] ²¹Salmon begot Boaz, and Boaz begot Obed; ²²Obed begot Jesse, and Jesse begot David.

4:1-22 God's divine plan fully blossomed as Boaz redeemed Naomi's land and Ruth's hand in marriage. Naomi was once empty (1:21) and is now full; Ruth was once widowed and is now married; and most importantly, the Lord had prepared Christ's line through Boaz, Obed, and David, and tying back to Judah (Gen. 49:10) to fulfill the proper messianic lineage.

4:5 [a]Literally *raise up*   4:10 [a]Probably his civic office   4:20 [a]Hebrew *Salmah*

1 & 2 SAMUEL

The tribes that formed the nation of Israel eventually became a kingdom, and these books tell the story. First and Second Samuel continue the history of Israel where Judges ends.

Samuel's life spanned significant changes among the Chosen People. He can be called the last and greatest of the judges (Acts 13:20). Samuel's ministry also made him the first of the prophets (Acts 3:24). He anointed the first two kings of Israel (Saul and David). The two books that now bear his name were originally one scroll, divided for convenience by those who hand copied the record.

AUTHOR AND DATE

Samuel was written approximately 931 B.C. by unknown author(s).

First Chronicles 29:29 seems to support the ancient traditions of Israel in assigning the writing of 1 and 2 Samuel to Samuel himself or to Samuel, Nathan, and Gad. But the verse above actually confirms only the fact that Samuel, Nathan, and Gad were all writers. The writer(s) of 1 Chronicles was simply acknowledging the more detailed sources behind the summary of David's reign. Likewise, written records by Samuel, Nathan, and Gad were probably used in compiling 1 and 2 Samuel. But all three men lived and died during the period covered by the two books. First Samuel 25:1, for example, records Samuel's death. The original human author of 1 and 2 Samuel remains anonymous.

The Books of Samuel contain no conclusive indications about when they were written. Although the history in these books ends while David is still alive, the records include an awareness of the divided kingdom of Israel and Judah, which did not occur until after Solomon, David's successor. Because the literary style of the two Samuel books differs so much from 1 and 2 Kings, scholars often date the former as having been written late in the period of the divided kingdom, shortly before the Babylonian captivity (931–722 B.C.).

BACKGROUND AND SETTING

For the first time in Scripture, the events recorded in 1 and 2 Samuel occurred within the borders of the Promised Land. Familiar places like Jerusalem, Bethlehem, Ramah, and Hebron become Jewish cities. Daily life includes continual warfare and strife with the peoples who resisted displacement when Israel conquered the Promised Land. The people demand a king. Saul and particularly David rule the Land with power. Samuel lives through the times of upheaval and speaks for God to the people and the leaders.

The action in 1 and 2 Samuel begins in about 1105 B.C. with the birth of Samuel (1 Samuel 1:1–28). The account ends with David's final words in about 971 B.C. (2 Samuel 23:1–7). The books cover about 135 years of history. During those eventful years, Israel was transformed from a loosely knit group of tribes guided by "judges" into a united nation under a king. Three men are prominent in 1 and 2 Samuel: Samuel who ministered from 1105 to 1030 B.C.; Saul who reigned as king from 1052 to 1011; David who reigned from 1011 to 971.

HISTORICAL AND THEOLOGICAL THEMES

As 1 Samuel opens, Israel staggers under the weight of several desperate spiritual problems: (1) a corrupt priesthood (2:12–17,22–26); (2) the ark of the covenant falls into enemy hands (4:3–7:2); (3) rampant idolatry (7:3,4); and, (4) dishonest judges (8:2,3). By the time 2 Samuel ends, these conditions have been reversed or corrected. God works primarily through Samuel and David to build up the nation.

During the years recorded by 1 and 2 Samuel, the great empires of the world were in a state of weakness. Neither Egypt on the south nor Babylon and Assyria to the northeast presented much threat to Israel. But smaller nations (the Philistines and the Ammonites) continually carried out hostile operations against the Jews. David eventually subdued these and other enemies (2 Samuel 8:2–14).

> **GOD WORKS** PRIMARILY **THROUGH SAMUEL** AND **DAVID** TO **BUILD UP** THE **NATION.**

Four predominant theological themes can be found throughout 1 and 2 Samuel: (1) God's covenant with David (2 Samuel 7:12–16); (2) the sovereignty of God (1 Samuel 9:17; 16:12,13); (3) the work of the Holy Spirit in Old Testament settings (1 Samuel 10:10; 16:13); and, (4) the personal and national effects of sin (1 Samuel 2:12–17; 6:19; 2 Samuel 12:13,14).

OUTLINE OF 1 SAMUEL

The Family of Elkanah

1 Now there was a certain man of Ramathaim Zophim, of the mountains of Ephraim, and his name *was* Elkanah the son of Jeroham, the son of Elihu,[a] the son of Tohu,[b] the son of Zuph, an Ephraimite. ²And he had two wives: the name of one *was* Hannah, and the name of the other Peninnah. Peninnah had children, but Hannah had no children. ³This man went up from his city yearly to worship and sacrifice to the LORD of hosts in Shiloh. Also the two sons of Eli, Hophni and Phinehas, the priests of the LORD, *were* there. ⁴And whenever the time came for Elkanah to make an offering, he would give portions to Peninnah his wife and to all her sons and daughters. ⁵But to Hannah he would give a double portion, for he loved Hannah, although the LORD had closed her womb. ⁶And her rival also provoked her severely, to make her miserable, because the LORD had closed her womb. ⁷So it was, year by year, when she went up to the house of the LORD, that she provoked her; therefore she wept and did not eat.

> **1:2 two wives.** Although God does not approve of polygamy (Gen. 2:24), it was tolerated in Israel (see Deut. 21:15–17). Elkanah probably married Peninnah because Hannah, his first wife, was barren.

Hannah's Vow

⁸Then Elkanah her husband said to her, "Hannah, why do you weep? Why do you not eat? And why is your heart grieved? *Am* I not better to you than ten sons?"

⁹So Hannah arose after they had finished eating and drinking in Shiloh. Now Eli the priest was sitting on the seat by the doorpost of the tabernacle[a] of the LORD. ¹⁰And she *was* in bitterness of soul, and prayed to the LORD and wept in anguish. ¹¹Then she made a vow and said, "O LORD of hosts, if You will indeed look on the affliction of Your maidservant and remember me, and not forget Your maidservant, but will give Your maidservant a male child, then I will give him to the LORD all the days of his life, and no razor shall come upon his head."

¹²And it happened, as she continued praying before the LORD, that Eli watched her mouth. ¹³Now Hannah spoke in her heart; only her lips moved, but her voice was not heard. Therefore Eli thought she was drunk. ¹⁴So Eli said to her, "How long will you be drunk? Put your wine away from you!"

> **1:13 drunk.** In Israel, people usually prayed out loud. Hannah was praying silently, so Eli assumed she was drunk.

¹⁵But Hannah answered and said, "No, my lord, I *am* a woman of sorrowful spirit. I have drunk neither wine nor intoxicating drink, but have poured out my soul before the LORD. ¹⁶Do not consider your maidservant a wicked woman,[a] for out of the abundance of my complaint and grief I have spoken until now."

¹⁷Then Eli answered and said, "Go in peace, and the God of Israel grant your petition which you have asked of Him."

¹⁸And she said, "Let your maidservant find favor in your sight." So the woman went her way and ate, and her face was no longer *sad.*

Samuel Is Born and Dedicated

¹⁹Then they rose early in the morning and worshiped before the LORD, and returned and came to their house at Ramah. And Elkanah knew Hannah his wife, and the LORD remembered her. ²⁰So it came to pass in the process of time that Hannah conceived and bore a son, and called his name Samuel,[a] *saying,* "Because I have asked for him from the LORD."

²¹Now the man Elkanah and all his house went up to offer to the LORD the yearly sacrifice and his vow. ²²But Hannah did not go up, for she said to her husband, "*Not* until the child is weaned; then I will take him, that he may appear before the LORD and remain there forever."

> **1:22 weaned.** It was the custom in those days for children to be breast fed for two to three years. After this time, Samuel was taken to the tabernacle to serve the Lord for the rest of his life.

1:1 [a]Spelled *Eliel* in 1 Chronicles 6:34   [b]Spelled *Toah* in 1 Chronicles 6:34   1:9 [a]Hebrew *heykal,* palace or temple   1:16 [a]Literally *daughter of Belial*   1:20 [a]Literally *Heard by God*

²³So Elkanah her husband said to her, "Do what seems best to you; wait until you have weaned him. Only let the LORD establish His^a word." Then the woman stayed and nursed her son until she had weaned him.

²⁴Now when she had weaned him, she took him up with her, with three bulls,^a one ephah of flour, and a skin of wine, and brought him to the house of the LORD in Shiloh. And the child *was* young. ²⁵Then they slaughtered a bull, and brought the child to Eli. ²⁶And she said, "O my lord! As your soul lives, my lord, I *am* the woman who stood by you here, praying to the LORD. ²⁷For this child I prayed, and the LORD has granted me my petition which I asked of Him. ²⁸Therefore I also have lent him to the LORD; as long as he lives he shall be lent to the LORD." So they worshiped the LORD there.

Hannah's Prayer

2 And Hannah prayed and said:

"My heart rejoices in the LORD;
My horn^a is exalted in the LORD.
I smile at my enemies,
Because I rejoice in Your salvation.

² "No one is holy like the LORD,
For *there is* none besides You,
Nor *is there* any rock like our God.

³ "Talk no more so very proudly;
Let no arrogance come from your mouth,
For the LORD *is* the God of knowledge;
And by Him actions are weighed.

⁴ "The bows of the mighty men *are* broken,
And those who stumbled are girded with strength.

⁵ *Those who were* full have hired themselves out for bread,
And the hungry have ceased *to hunger.*
Even the barren has borne seven,
And she who has many children has become feeble.

⁶ "The LORD kills and makes alive;
He brings down to the grave and brings up.

⁷ The LORD makes poor and makes rich;
He brings low and lifts up.

⁸ He raises the poor from the dust
And lifts the beggar from the ash heap,
To set *them* among princes
And make them inherit the throne of glory.

"For the pillars of the earth *are* the LORD's,
And He has set the world upon them.

⁹ He will guard the feet of His saints,
But the wicked shall be silent in darkness.

"For by strength no man shall prevail.

¹⁰ The adversaries of the LORD shall be broken in pieces;
From heaven He will thunder against them.
The LORD will judge the ends of the earth.

"He will give strength to His king,
And exalt the horn of His anointed."

2:1–10 Here Hannah prayed joyfully (unlike her bitter prayer in v. 10), proclaiming the Lord as a righteous judge. God had brought down the proud (Peninnah) and exalted the humble (Hannah). This prayer has four sections: (1) Hannah prays to the Lord for His salvation (vv. 1,2); (2) Hannah warned the proud of the Lord's humbling (vv. 3–8d); (3) Hannah affirmed the Lord's faithful care for His people (vv. 8e–9b); and (4) Hannah asked the Lord to judge the world and to bless His anointed king (v. 10d,e). This prayer has many similarities to David's song in 2 Sam. 22:2–51.

¹¹Then Elkanah went to his house at Ramah. But the child ministered to the LORD before Eli the priest.

1:23 ^aFollowing Masoretic Text, Targum, and Vulgate; Dead Sea Scrolls, Septuagint, and Syriac read *your.* 1:24 ^aDead Sea Scrolls, Septuagint, and Syriac read *a three-year-old bull.* 2:1 ^aThat is, strength

The Wicked Sons of Eli

¹²Now the sons of Eli *were* corrupt;ᵃ they did not know the LORD. ¹³And the priests' custom with the people *was that* when any man offered a sacrifice, the priest's servant would come with a three-pronged flesh-hook in his hand while the meat was boiling. ¹⁴Then he would thrust *it* into the pan, or kettle, or caldron, or pot; and the priest would take for himself all that the fleshhook brought up. So they did in Shiloh to all the Israelites who came there. ¹⁵Also, before they burned the fat, the priest's servant would come and say to the man who sacrificed, "Give meat for roasting to the priest, for he will not take boiled meat from you, but raw."

> **2:13–15 the priests' custom.** Eli's sons took for themselves whatever meat a 3-pronged fork would collect from the boiling pot and demanded raw meat, along with the fat. This was against the law, as specified portions of the sacrifices were to be given to the priests (Deut. 18:3), and the fat from the sacrificial animal was to be burned on the altar to the Lord (Lev. 7:31).

¹⁶And *if* the man said to him, "They should really burn the fat first; *then* you may take as *much* as your heart desires," he would then answer him, "*No*, but you must give *it* now; and if not, I will take *it* by force."

¹⁷Therefore the sin of the young men was very great before the LORD, for men abhorred the offering of the LORD.

Samuel's Childhood Ministry

¹⁸But Samuel ministered before the LORD, *even as* a child, wearing a linen ephod. ¹⁹Moreover his mother used to make him a little robe, and bring *it* to him year by year when she came up with her husband to offer the yearly sacrifice. ²⁰And Eli would bless Elkanah and his wife, and say, "The LORD give you descendants from this woman for the loan that was given to the LORD." Then they would go to their own home.

²¹And the LORD visited Hannah, so that she conceived and bore three sons and two daughters. Meanwhile the child Samuel grew before the LORD.

Prophecy Against Eli's Household

²²Now Eli was very old; and he heard everything his sons did to all Israel,ᵃ and how they lay with the women who assembled at the door of the tabernacle of meeting. ²³So he said to them, "Why do you do such things? For I hear of your evil dealings from all the people. ²⁴No, my sons! For *it is* not a good report that I hear. You make the LORD's people transgress. ²⁵If one man sins against another, God will judge him. But if a man sins against the LORD, who will intercede for him?" Nevertheless they did not heed the voice of their father, because the LORD desired to kill them.

> **2:25 God will judge.** Eli explained to his sons that if God judges those who sin against other men, then He will judge those who sin against Him even more. **the LORD desired to kill them.** God had already determined to judge Eli's sons because they persisted in their evil ways and refused to repent.

²⁶And the child Samuel grew in stature, and in favor both with the LORD and men.

²⁷Then a man of God came to Eli and said to him, "Thus says the LORD: 'Did I not clearly reveal Myself to the house of your father when they were in Egypt in Pharaoh's house? ²⁸Did I not choose him out of all the tribes of Israel *to be* My priest, to offer upon My altar, to burn incense, and to wear an ephod before Me? And did I not give to the house of your father all the offerings of the children of Israel made by fire? ²⁹Why do you kick at My sacrifice and My offering which I have commanded *in My* dwelling place, and honor your sons more than Me, to make yourselves fat with the best of all the offerings of Israel My people?' ³⁰Therefore the LORD God of Israel says: 'I

> **2:29 honor.** Eli was unworthy of the Lord's blessing because he had condoned the disobedience of his sons, Hophni and Phinehas. Samuel, in contrast, received God's blessing for his faithfulness and obedience.

2:12 ᵃLiterally *sons of Belial* 2:22 ᵃFollowing Masoretic Text, Targum, and Vulgate; Dead Sea Scrolls and Septuagint omit the rest of this verse.

said indeed *that* your house and the house of your father would walk before Me forever.' But now the LORD says: 'Far be it from Me; for those who honor Me I will honor, and those who despise Me shall be lightly esteemed. ³¹Behold, the days are coming that I will cut off your arm and the arm of your father's house, so that there will not be an old man in your house. ³²And you will see an enemy *in My* dwelling place, *despite* all the good which God does for Israel. And there shall not be an old man in your house forever. ³³But any of your men *whom* I do not cut off from My altar shall consume your eyes and grieve your heart. And all the descendants of your house shall die in the flower of their age. ³⁴Now this *shall be* a sign to you that will come upon your two sons, on Hophni and Phinehas: in one day they shall die, both of them. ³⁵Then I will raise up for Myself a faithful priest *who* shall do according to what *is* in My heart and in My mind. I will build him a sure house, and he shall walk before My anointed forever. ³⁶And it shall come to pass that everyone who is left in your house will come *and* bow down to him for a piece of silver and a morsel of bread, and say, "Please, put me in one of the priestly positions, that I may eat a piece of bread." ' "

2:35 I will raise up for Myself a faithful priest. Some have identified this priest as Samuel, and others, Christ. However, it is better to view the prophecy as fulfilled in the accession of Zadok and his family to the priesthood in the time of Solomon (see 1 Kin. 1:7,8). This reestablished the office of High-Priest in the line of Eleazar and Phinehas (see Num. 25:10–13). **My anointed.** This refers to the messiah who will defeat God's enemies and establish His rule in the Millennium (see v. 10).

Samuel's First Prophecy

3 Now the boy Samuel ministered to the LORD before Eli. And the word of the LORD was rare in those days; *there was* no widespread revelation. ²And it came to pass at that time, while Eli *was* lying down in his place, and when his eyes had begun to grow so dim that he could not see, ³and before the lamp of God went out in the tabernacleᵃ of the LORD where the ark of

God *was*, and while Samuel was lying down, ⁴that the LORD called Samuel. And he answered, "Here I am!" ⁵So he ran to Eli and said, "Here I am, for you called me."

And he said, "I did not call; lie down again." And he went and lay down.

⁶Then the LORD called yet again, "Samuel!"

So Samuel arose and went to Eli, and said, "Here I am, for you called me." He answered, "I did not call, my son; lie down again." ⁷(Now Samuel did not yet know the LORD, nor was the word of the LORD yet revealed to him.)

⁸And the LORD called Samuel again the third time. So he arose and went to Eli, and said, "Here I am, for you did call me."

Then Eli perceived that the LORD had called the boy. ⁹Therefore Eli said to Samuel, "Go, lie down; and it shall be, if He calls you, that you must say, 'Speak, LORD, for Your servant hears.' " So Samuel went and lay down in his place.

¹⁰Now the LORD came and stood and called as at other times, "Samuel! Samuel!"

And Samuel answered, "Speak, for Your servant hears."

¹¹Then the LORD said to Samuel: "Behold, I will do something in Israel at which both ears of everyone who hears it will tingle. ¹²In that day I will perform against Eli all that I have spoken concerning his house, from beginning to end. ¹³For I have told him that I will judge his house forever for the iniquity which he knows, because his sons made themselves vile, and he did not restrain them. ¹⁴And therefore I have sworn to the house of Eli that the iniquity of Eli's house shall not be atoned for by sacrifice or offering forever."

¹⁵So Samuel lay down until morning,ᵃ and opened the doors of the house of the LORD. And Samuel was afraid to tell Eli the vision. ¹⁶Then Eli called Samuel and said, "Samuel, my son!"

He answered, "Here I am."

¹⁷And he said, "What *is* the word that *the* LORD spoke to you? Please do not hide *it* from me. God do so to you, and more also, if you hide anything from me of all the things that He said to you." ¹⁸Then Samuel

---

3:3 ᵃHebrew *heykal*, palace or temple   3:15 ᵃFollowing Masoretic Text, Targum, and Vulgate; Septuagint adds *and he arose in the morning.*

told him everything, and hid nothing from him. And he said, "It *is* the LORD. Let Him do what seems good to Him."

[19]So Samuel grew, and the LORD was with him and let none of his words fall to the ground. [20]And all Israel from Dan to Beersheba knew that Samuel *had been* established as a prophet of the LORD. [21]Then the LORD appeared again in Shiloh. For the LORD revealed Himself to Samuel in Shiloh by the word of the LORD.

3:19 the LORD was with him. The Lord's presence was with Samuel, as it would later be with David (16:18). The Lord's presence made it clear that He had chosen Samuel for His service. **let none of his words fall to the ground.** Everything Samuel said with divine authorization came true, which proved he was a true prophet of God (see Deut. 18:21,22).

4 And the word of Samuel came to all Israel.[a]

The Ark of God Captured

Now Israel went out to battle against the Philistines, and encamped beside Ebenezer; and the Philistines encamped in Aphek. [2]Then the Philistines put themselves in battle array against Israel. And when they joined battle, Israel was defeated by the Philistines, who killed about four thousand men of the army in the field. [3]And when the people had come into the camp, the elders of Israel said, "Why has the LORD defeated us today before the Philistines? Let us bring the ark of the covenant of the LORD from Shiloh to us, that when it comes among us it may save us from the

4:3 Why has the LORD defeated us. The elders knew that the Lord had both fought their battles (2:10) and allowed their defeat. To be defeated meant that God was not "with" them (Num. 14:42). They took their problems into their own hands instead of asking the Lord for direction. **Let us bring the ark.** Israel didn't understand that the ark symbolized the presence and power of the Lord. They thought it was the presence of God Himself and therefore used the ark as a good-luck charm to bring them victory over the Philistines.

hand of our enemies." [4]So the people sent to Shiloh, that they might bring from there the ark of the covenant of the LORD of hosts, who dwells *between* the cherubim. And the two sons of Eli, Hophni and Phinehas, *were* there with the ark of the covenant of God.

[5]And when the ark of the covenant of the LORD came into the camp, all Israel shouted so loudly that the earth shook. [6]Now when the Philistines heard the noise of the shout, they said, "What *does* the sound of this great shout in the camp of the Hebrews *mean?*" Then they understood that the ark of the LORD had come into the camp. [7]So the Philistines were afraid, for they said, "God has come into the camp!" And they said, "Woe to us! For such a thing has never happened before. [8]Woe to us! Who will deliver us from the hand of these mighty gods? These *are* the gods who struck the Egyptians with all the plagues in the wilderness. [9]Be strong and conduct yourselves like men, you Philistines, that you do not become servants of the Hebrews, as they have been to you. Conduct yourselves like men, and fight!"

[10]So the Philistines fought, and Israel was defeated, and every man fled to his tent. There was a very great slaughter, and there fell of Israel thirty thousand foot soldiers. [11]Also the ark of God was captured; and the two sons of Eli, Hophni and Phinehas, died.

4:11 the ark of God was captured. Israel could not manipulate God into giving them victory. They were defeated, and the ark fell into the hands of the Philistines, who also shared Israel's view that possessing the ark meant having control of God. **Hophni and Phinehas, died.** In fulfillment of 2:34 and 3:12, Eli's sons died together.

Death of Eli

[12]Then a man of Benjamin ran from the battle line the same day, and came to Shiloh with his clothes torn and dirt on his head. [13]Now when he came, there was Eli, sitting on a seat by the wayside watching,[a] for his heart trembled for the ark of God.

4:1 [a]Following Masoretic Text and Targum; Septuagint and Vulgate add *And it came to pass in those days that the Philistines gathered themselves together to fight*; Septuagint adds further *against Israel.*
4:13 [a]Following Masoretic Text and Vulgate; Septuagint reads *beside the gate watching the road.*

And when the man came into the city and told *it*, all the city cried out. ¹⁴When Eli heard the noise of the outcry, he said, "What *does* the sound of this tumult *mean?*" And the man came quickly and told Eli. ¹⁵Eli was ninety-eight years old, and his eyes were so dim that he could not see.

¹⁶Then the man said to Eli, "I *am* he who came from the battle. And I fled today from the battle line."

And he said, "What happened, my son?"

¹⁷So the messenger answered and said, "Israel has fled before the Philistines, and there has been a great slaughter among the people. Also your two sons, Hophni and Phinehas, are dead; and the ark of God has been captured."

¹⁸Then it happened, when he made mention of the ark of God, that Eli fell off the seat backward by the side of the gate; and his neck was broken and he died, for the man was old and heavy. And he had judged Israel forty years.

Ichabod

¹⁹Now his daughter-in-law, Phinehas' wife, was with child, *due* to be delivered; and when she heard the news that the ark of God was captured, and that her father-in-law and her husband were dead, she bowed herself and gave birth, for her labor pains came upon her. ²⁰And about the time of her death the women who stood by her said to her, "Do not fear, for you have borne a son." But she did not answer, nor did she regard *it*. ²¹Then she named the child Ichabod,ᵃ saying, "The glory has departed from Israel!" because the ark of God had been captured and because of her father-in-law and her husband. ²²And she said, "The glory has departed from Israel, for the ark of God has been captured."

The Philistines and the Ark

5 Then the Philistines took the ark of God and brought it from Ebenezer to Ashdod. ²When the Philistines took the ark of God, they brought it into the house of Dagonᵃ and set it by Dagon. ³And when the people of Ashdod arose early in the morning, there was Dagon, fallen on its face to the earth before the ark of the LORD. So they took Dagon and set it in its place again. ⁴And when they arose early the next morning, there was Dagon, fallen on its face to the ground before the ark of the LORD. The head of Dagon and both the palms of its hands *were* broken off on the threshold; only Dagon's torsoᵃ was left of it. ⁵Therefore neither the priests of Dagon nor any who come into Dagon's house tread on the threshold of Dagon in Ashdod to this day.

⁶But the hand of the LORD was heavy on the people of Ashdod, and He ravaged them and struck them with tumors,ᵃ *both* Ashdod and its territory. ⁷And when the men of Ashdod saw how *it was*, they said, "The ark of the God of Israel must not remain with us, for His hand is harsh toward us and Dagon our god." ⁸Therefore they sent and gathered to themselves all the lords of the Philistines, and said, "What shall we do with the ark of the God of Israel?"

> **5:4–6 head...hands *were* broken off.** God showed His divine judgment over the false idol, Dagon, by cutting off its head and hands, which was a common sign that the enemy was dead (Judg. 7:25). **the hand of the LORD was heavy.** The Lord was pictured as actively involved in judging the Philistines. The imagery of God's hand is found throughout the ark narrative.

And they answered, "Let the ark of the God of Israel be carried away to Gath." So they carried the ark of the God of Israel away. ⁹So it was, after they had carried it away, that the hand of the LORD was against the city with a very great destruction; and He struck the men of the city, both small and great, and tumors broke out on them.

¹⁰Therefore they sent the ark of God to Ekron. So it was, as the ark of God came to Ekron, that the Ekronites cried out, saying, "They have brought the ark of the God of Israel to us, to kill us and our people!" ¹¹So they sent and gathered together all the

---

4:21 ᵃLiterally *Inglorious*   5:2 ᵃA Philistine idol   5:4 ᵃFollowing Septuagint, Syriac, Targum, and Vulgate; Masoretic Text reads *Dagon*.   5:6 ᵃProbably bubonic plague. Septuagint and Vulgate add here *And in the midst of their land rats sprang up, and there was a great death panic in the city*.

lords of the Philistines, and said, "Send away the ark of the God of Israel, and let it go back to its own place, so that it does not kill us and our people." For there was a deadly destruction throughout all the city; the hand of God was very heavy there. ¹²And the men who did not die were stricken with the tumors, and the cry of the city went up to heaven.

The Ark Returned to Israel

6 Now the ark of the LORD was in the country of the Philistines seven months. ²And the Philistines called for the priests and the diviners, saying, "What shall we do with the ark of the LORD? Tell us how we should send it to its place."

³So they said, "If you send away the ark of the God of Israel, do not send it empty; but by all means return it to Him with a trespass offering. Then you will be healed, and it will be known to you why His hand is not removed from you."

⁴Then they said, "What is the trespass offering which we shall return to Him?"

They answered, "Five golden tumors and five golden rats, according to the number of the lords of the Philistines. For the same plague was on all of you and on your lords. ⁵Therefore you shall make images of your tumors and images of your rats that ravage the land, and you shall give glory to the God of Israel; perhaps He will lighten His hand from you, from your gods, and from your land. ⁶Why then do you harden your hearts as the Egyptians and Pharaoh hardened their hearts? When He did mighty things among them, did they not let the people go, that they might depart? ⁷Now therefore, make a new cart, take two milk cows which have never been yoked, and hitch the cows to the cart; and take their calves home, away from them. ⁸Then take the ark of the LORD and set it on the cart; and put the articles of gold which you are returning to Him as a trespass offering in a

> **6:5 give glory to the God of Israel...He will lighten His hand.** In contrast to the Philistine custom of sympathetic magic for healing, here they sought to find healing from the Lord. The intention behind their offerings to the Lord was to stop their dishonor, confess their sin, and give glory to God, acknowledging that they had offended Him, the supreme Deity.

chest by its side. Then send it away, and let it go. ⁹And watch: if it goes up the road to its own territory, to Beth Shemesh, then He has done us this great evil. But if not, then we shall know that it is not His hand that struck us—it happened to us by chance."

¹⁰Then the men did so; they took two milk cows and hitched them to the cart, and shut up their calves at home. ¹¹And they set the ark of the LORD on the cart, and the chest with the gold rats and the images of their tumors. ¹²Then the cows headed straight for the road to Beth Shemesh, and went along the highway, lowing as they went, and did not turn aside to the right hand or the left. And the lords of the Philistines went after them to the border of Beth Shemesh.

> **6:7–12 never been yoked.** The diviners devised a plan to know without a doubt that the God of Israel was behind all their troubles. They planned to use cows that had "never been yoked," meaning that they were untrained to pull a cart. **take their calves...away from them.** They also planned to use nursing cows that were separated from their calves. If the cows walked away from their calves, which would be unnatural, then it would show that the cause of their judgment was supernatural. **lowing as they went.** The cows moaned as they left their calves, yet they went straight to Beth Shemesh, showing the clear judgment of God.

¹³Now the people of Beth Shemesh were reaping their wheat harvest in the valley; and they lifted their eyes and saw the ark, and rejoiced to see it. ¹⁴Then the cart came into the field of Joshua of Beth Shemesh, and stood there; a large stone was there. So they split the wood of the cart and offered the cows as a burnt offering to the LORD. ¹⁵The Levites took down the ark of the LORD and the chest that was with it, in which were the articles of gold, and put them on the large stone. Then the men of Beth Shemesh offered burnt offerings and made sacrifices the same day to the LORD. ¹⁶So when the five lords of the Philistines had seen it, they returned to Ekron the same day.

¹⁷These are the golden tumors which the Philistines returned as a trespass offering to the LORD: one for Ashdod, one for Gaza, one for Ashkelon, one for Gath, one for Ekron; ¹⁸and the golden rats, according to the

number of all the cities of the Philistines *belonging* to the five lords, *both* fortified cities and country villages, even as far as the large *stone of* Abel on which they set the ark of the LORD, *which stone remains* to this day in the field of Joshua of Beth Shemesh.

¹⁹Then He struck the men of Beth Shemesh, because they had looked into the ark of the LORD. He struck fifty thousand and seventy men*a* of the people, and the people lamented because the LORD had struck the people with a great slaughter.

The Ark at Kirjath Jearim

²⁰And the men of Beth Shemesh said, "Who is able to stand before this holy LORD God? And to whom shall it go up from us?" ²¹So they sent messengers to the inhabitants of Kirjath Jearim, saying, "The Philistines have brought back the ark of the LORD; come down *and* take it up with you."

6:19,20 looked into the ark. Looking into the ark was the sin of presumption, which is unacceptable to God. **Who is able to stand.** No one is able to stand against God's judgment, which is the point of the narrative of the ark. This judgment applied to people outside the covenant as well as those inside the covenant. **to whom shall it go.** The expression was used to indicate that they did not want the ark with them.

7 Then the men of Kirjath Jearim came and took the ark of the LORD, and brought it into the house of Abinadab on the hill, and consecrated Eleazar his son to keep the ark of the LORD.

Samuel Judges Israel

²So it was that the ark remained in Kirjath Jearim a long time; it was there twenty years. And all the house of Israel lamented after the LORD.

³Then Samuel spoke to all the house of Israel, saying, "If you return to the LORD with all your hearts, *then* put away the foreign gods and the Ashtoreths*a* from among you, and prepare your hearts for the LORD, and serve Him only; and He will deliver you from the hand of the Philistines." ⁴So the children of Israel put away the Baals

and the Ashtoreths,*a* and served the LORD only.

⁵And Samuel said, "Gather all Israel to Mizpah, and I will pray to the LORD for you." ⁶So they gathered together at Mizpah, drew water, and poured *it* out before the LORD. And they fasted that day, and said there, "We have sinned against the LORD." And Samuel judged the children of Israel at Mizpah.

7:6 drew water, and poured *it* out before the LORD. Pouring out water before the Lord was a sign of repentance (see 2 Sam. 23:16). **We have sinned against the LORD.** True repentance had taken place as Samuel poured out the water and the people acknowledged their sin. **Samuel judged.** Samuel is introduced as the judge of Israel, both in domestic leadership as well as in war. Samuel took over Eli's judgeship and served as the last judge before the first king (see 1 Sam. 8:50).

⁷Now when the Philistines heard that the children of Israel had gathered together at Mizpah, the lords of the Philistines went up against Israel. And when the children of Israel heard *of it,* they were afraid of the Philistines. ⁸So the children of Israel said to Samuel, "Do not cease to cry out to the LORD our God for us, that He may save us from the hand of the Philistines."

⁹And Samuel took a suckling lamb and offered *it as* a whole burnt offering to the LORD. Then Samuel cried out to the LORD for Israel, and the LORD answered him. ¹⁰Now as Samuel was offering up the burnt offering, the Philistines drew near to battle against Israel. But the LORD thundered with a loud thunder upon the Philistines that day, and so confused them that they were overcome before Israel. ¹¹And the men of Israel went out of Mizpah and pursued the Philistines, and drove them back as far as below Beth Car. ¹²Then Samuel took a stone and set *it* up between Mizpah and Shen, and called its name Ebenezer,*a* saying, "Thus far the LORD has helped us."

¹³So the Philistines were subdued, and they did not come anymore into the territory of Israel. And the hand of the LORD was against the Philistines all the days of Samuel. ¹⁴Then the cities which the Philistines

---

6:19 *a*Or *He struck seventy men of the people and fifty oxen of a man*   7:3 *a*Canaanite goddesses
7:4 *a*Canaanite goddesses   7:12 *a*Literally *Stone of Help*

had taken from Israel were restored to Israel, from Ekron to Gath; and Israel recovered its territory from the hands of the Philistines. Also there was peace between Israel and the Amorites.

¹⁵And Samuel judged Israel all the days of his life. ¹⁶He went from year to year on a circuit to Bethel, Gilgal, and Mizpah, and judged Israel in all those places. ¹⁷But he always returned to Ramah, for his home was there. There he judged Israel, and there he built an altar to the LORD.

Israel Demands a King

8 Now it came to pass when Samuel was old that he made his sons judges over Israel. ²The name of his firstborn was Joel, and the name of his second, Abijah; they were judges in Beersheba. ³But his sons did not walk in his ways; they turned aside after dishonest gain, took bribes, and perverted justice.

⁴Then all the elders of Israel gathered together and came to Samuel at Ramah, ⁵and said to him, "Look, you are old, and your sons do not walk in your ways. Now make us a king to judge us like all the nations."

⁶But the thing displeased Samuel when they said, "Give us a king to judge us." So Samuel prayed to the LORD. ⁷And the LORD said to Samuel, "Heed the voice of the people in all that they say to you; for they have not rejected you, but they have rejected Me, that I should not reign over them. ⁸According to all the works which they have done since the day that I brought them up out of Egypt, even to this day—with which they have forsaken Me and served other gods—so they are doing to you also. ⁹Now therefore, heed their voice. However, you shall solemnly forewarn them, and show them

> **8:9 you shall solemnly forewarn them.** Samuel obeyed the Lord and warned the people that they would live to regret their decision for a king. This king would: (1) draft young men and women for his service (vv. 11–13); (2) tax the people's crops and flocks (vv. 14,15,17a); (3) seize the best of their animals and servants (v. 16); and (4) place limitations on their personal freedom (verse 17b).

the behavior of the king who will reign over them."

¹⁰So Samuel told all the words of the LORD to the people who asked him for a king. ¹¹And he said, "This will be the behavior of the king who will reign over you: He will take your sons and appoint them for his own chariots and to be his horsemen, and some will run before his chariots. ¹²He will appoint captains over his thousands and captains over his fifties, will set some to plow his ground and reap his harvest, and some to make his weapons of war and equipment for his chariots. ¹³He will take your daughters to be perfumers, cooks, and bakers. ¹⁴And he will take the best of your fields, your vineyards, and your olive groves, and give them to his servants. ¹⁵He will take a tenth of your grain and your vintage, and give it to his officers and servants. ¹⁶And he will take your male servants, your female servants, your finest young men,ᵃ and your donkeys, and put them to his work. ¹⁷He will take a tenth of your sheep. And you will be his servants. ¹⁸And you will cry out in that day because of your king whom you have chosen for yourselves, and the LORD will not hear you in that day."

¹⁹Nevertheless the people refused to obey the voice of Samuel; and they said, "No, but we will have a king over us, ²⁰that we also may be like all the nations, and that our king may judge us and go out before us and fight our battles."

²¹And Samuel heard all the words of the people, and he repeated them in the hearing of the LORD. ²²So the LORD said to Samuel, "Heed their voice, and make them a king."

And Samuel said to the men of Israel, "Every man go to his city."

Saul Chosen to Be King

9 There was a man of Benjamin whose name was Kish the son of Abiel, the son of Zeror, the son of Bechorath, the son of Aphiah, a Benjamite, a mighty man of power. ²And he had a choice and handsome son whose name was Saul. There was not a more handsome person than he among the children of Israel. From his shoulders upward he was taller than any of the people.

8:16 ᵃSeptuagint reads cattle.

9:2 a choice and handsome son. External appearance of leaders was important (see 16:18). **Saul.** Saul was the son of Kish, a Benjamite. He was Israel's first king. The Hebrew root for "Saul" means "asked (of God)." God appointed Saul because the people had requested a king (8:10). However, God's choice would have been from the tribe of Judah (see Gen. 49:10).

³Now the donkeys of Kish, Saul's father, were lost. And Kish said to his son Saul, "Please take one of the servants with you, and arise, go and look for the donkeys." ⁴So he passed through the mountains of Ephraim and through the land of Shalisha, but they did not find *them.* Then they passed through the land of Shaalim, and *they were* not *there.* Then he passed through the land of the Benjamites, but they did not find *them.* ⁵When they had come to the land of Zuph, Saul said to his servant who *was* with him, "Come, let us return, lest my father cease *caring* about the donkeys and become worried about us."

⁶And he said to him, "Look now, *there is* in this city a man of God, and *he is* an honorable man; all that he says surely comes to pass. So let us go there; perhaps he can show us the way that we should go."

⁷Then Saul said to his servant, "But look, *if* we go, what shall we bring the man? For the bread in our vessels is all gone, and *there is* no present to bring to the man of God. What do we have?"

⁸And the servant answered Saul again and said, "Look, I have here at hand one-fourth of a shekel of silver. I will give *that* to the man of God, to tell us our way." ⁹(Formerly in Israel, when a man went to inquire of God, he spoke thus: "Come, let us go to the seer"; for *he who is* now *called* a prophet was formerly called a seer.)

¹⁰Then Saul said to his servant, "Well said; come, let us go." So they went to the city where the man of God *was.*

¹¹As they went up the hill to the city, they met some young women going out to draw water, and said to them, "Is the seer here?"

¹²And they answered them and said, "Yes, there he is, just ahead of you. Hurry now; for today he came to this city, because there is a sacrifice of the people today on the high place. ¹³As soon as you come into the city, you will surely find him before he goes up to the high place to eat. For the people will not eat until he comes, because he must bless the sacrifice; afterward those who are invited will eat. Now therefore, go up, for about this time you will find him." ¹⁴So they went up to the city. As they were coming into the city, there was Samuel,

Was the rule of kings part of God's plan all along, or did the people's demand for a king bring about a monarchy as a form of divine discipline?

When Israel entered the Promised Land, they encountered Canaanite city-states that were ruled by kings (Joshua 12:7–14). Later, during the time of the judges, Israel was enslaved and oppressed by nations led by kings (Judges 3:8,12; 4:2; 8:5; 11:12). The book of Judges repeatedly mentions the lack of a king (Judges 17:6; 18:1; 19:1; 21:25). The idea of having a king like the surrounding nations became a powerful temptation. According to Deuteronomy 17:14, however, God knew this would be their desire and He foretold his permission. First Samuel 8:4–20 reveals that their motive actually involved a rejection of God.

In spite of Samuel's dire warnings about the drawbacks of kings, the people offered what they thought were three compelling reasons why they needed a king (1 Samuel 8:20): (1) to be like the other nations; (2) to have a national judge; and (3) to have a war champion. Each of these contradicted God's specific purposes: (1) Israel was to be a holy nation, not like any other; (2) God was their ultimate judge; and (3) God had fought their battles for them—a king would send them to battle. Israel's problem was not about having a king, but rather, it was about replacing God with a human ruler. They exchanged an awesome and powerful Ruler they could not see for one they could see who was utterly capable of failure.

coming out toward them on his way up to the high place.

[15]Now the LORD had told Samuel in his ear the day before Saul came, saying, [16]"Tomorrow about this time I will send you a man from the land of Benjamin, and you shall anoint him commander over My people Israel, that he may save My people from the hand of the Philistines; for I have looked upon My people, because their cry has come to Me."

[17]So when Samuel saw Saul, the LORD said to him, "There he is, the man of whom I spoke to you. This one shall reign over My people." [18]Then Saul drew near to Samuel in the gate, and said, "Please tell me, where *is* the seer's house?"

[19]Samuel answered Saul and said, "I *am* the seer. Go up before me to the high place, for you shall eat with me today; and tomorrow I will let you go and will tell you all that *is* in your heart. [20]But as for your donkeys that were lost three days ago, do not be anxious about them, for they have been found. And on whom *is* all the desire of Israel? *Is it* not on you and on all your father's house?"

[21]And Saul answered and said, "*Am* I not a Benjamite, of the smallest of the tribes of Israel, and my family the least of all the families of the tribe[a] of Benjamin? Why then do you speak like this to me?"

> **9:21 a Benjamite...the least of all the families.** Saul's humility was expressed by his proper assessment of his tribe and of his family.

[22]Now Samuel took Saul and his servant and brought them into the hall, and had them sit in the place of honor among those who were invited; there *were* about thirty persons. [23]And Samuel said to the cook, "Bring the portion which I gave you, of which I said to you, 'Set it apart.' " [24]So the cook took up the thigh with its upper part and set *it* before Saul. And *Samuel* said, "Here it is, what was kept back. *It* was set apart for you. Eat; for until this time it has

been kept for you, since I said I invited the people." So Saul ate with Samuel that day.

[25]When they had come down from the high place into the city, *Samuel* spoke with Saul on the top of the house.[a] [26]They arose early; and it was about the dawning of the day that Samuel called to Saul on the top of the house, saying, "Get up, that I may send you on your way." And Saul arose, and both of them went outside, he and Samuel.

Saul Anointed King

[27]As they were going down to the outskirts of the city, Samuel said to Saul, "Tell the servant to go on ahead of us." And he went on. "But you stand here awhile, that I may announce to you the word of God."

10 Then Samuel took a flask of oil and poured *it* on his head, and kissed him and said: "*Is it* not because the LORD has anointed you commander over His inheritance?[a] [2]When you have departed from me today, you will find two men by Rachel's tomb in the territory of Benjamin at Zelzah; and they will say to you, 'The donkeys which you went to look for have been found. And now your father has ceased caring about the donkeys and is worrying about you, saying, "What shall I do about my son?" ' [3]Then you shall go on forward from there and come to the terebinth tree of Tabor. There three men going up to God at Bethel will meet you, one carrying three young goats, another carrying three loaves of bread, and another carrying a skin of wine. [4]And they will greet you and give you two *loaves* of bread, which you shall receive from their hands. [5]After that you shall come to the hill of God where the

> **10:1 the LORD has anointed you commander.** The Lord appointed Saul as the leader of Israel. This was demonstrated through the anointing by Samuel, which symbolized that Saul was set aside for God's service (see 2:10). **His inheritance.** The inheritance was Israel, the nation uniquely belonging to God (Deut. 4:20).

9:21 [a]Literally *tribes*   9:25 [a]Following Masoretic Text and Targum; Septuagint omits *He spoke with Saul on the top of the house*; Septuagint and Vulgate add *And he prepared a bed for Saul on the top of the house, and he slept.*   10:1 [a]Following Masoretic Text, Targum, and Vulgate; Septuagint reads *His people Israel; and you shall rule the people of the Lord*; Septuagint and Vulgate add *And you shall deliver His people from the hands of their enemies all around them. And this shall be a sign to you, that God has anointed you to be a prince.*

Philistine garrison *is*. And it will happen, when you have come there to the city, that you will meet a group of prophets coming down from the high place with a stringed instrument, a tambourine, a flute, and a harp before them; and they will be prophesying. ⁶Then the Spirit of the LORD will come upon you, and you will prophesy with them and be turned into another man. ⁷And let it be, when these signs come to you, *that* you do as the occasion demands; for God *is* with you. ⁸You shall go down before me to Gilgal; and surely I will come down to you to offer burnt offerings *and* make sacrifices of peace offerings. Seven days you shall wait, till I come to you and show you what you should do."

10:6 the Spirit of the LORD will come upon you. The Holy Spirit would enable Saul to declare the Word of the Lord along with the prophets. **turned into another man.** Saul would be equipped for deeds of valor like Gideon and Jepthah (Judg. 6:34) and have a new heart (see v. 9) as a result of the empowerment of the Holy Spirit.

⁹So it was, when he had turned his back to go from Samuel, that God gave him another heart; and all those signs came to pass that day. ¹⁰When they came there to the hill, there was a group of prophets to meet him; then the Spirit of God came upon him, and he prophesied among them. ¹¹And it happened, when all who knew him formerly saw that he indeed prophesied among the prophets, that the people said to one another, "What *is* this *that* has come upon the son of Kish? *Is* Saul also among the prophets?" ¹²Then a man from there answered and said, "But who *is* their father?" Therefore it became a proverb: "*Is* Saul also among the prophets?" ¹³And when he had finished prophesying, he went to the high place.

¹⁴Then Saul's uncle said to him and his servant, "Where did you go?"

So he said, "To look for the donkeys. When we saw that *they were* nowhere *to be found*, we went to Samuel."

¹⁵And Saul's uncle said, "Tell me, please, what Samuel said to you."

¹⁶So Saul said to his uncle, "He told us plainly that the donkeys had been found." But about the matter of the kingdom, he did not tell him what Samuel had said.

Saul Proclaimed King

¹⁷Then Samuel called the people together to the LORD at Mizpah, ¹⁸and said to the children of Israel, "Thus says the LORD God of Israel: 'I brought up Israel out of Egypt, and delivered you from the hand of

How do 1 and 2 Samuel help us understand the role of the Holy Spirit in the time of the Old Testament?

When Jesus spoke of the Comforter that he and the Father would send, he was announcing a new way in which God would relate to his people (John 14:26–28; 15:26,27; 16:7–15). That gift first arrived at Pentecost (Acts 2:1–13). Although God's Spirit was certainly active in the world before this time, God chose certain self-imposed limits on the role the Holy Spirit played in people's lives.

First and Second Samuel illustrate part of the Holy Spirit's role in the Old Testament. His specific actions are noted in the following passages: 1 Samuel 10:6,10; 11:6; 16:13,14; 19:20,23; 2 Samuel 23:2. These references offer several conclusions regarding the Holy Spirit's ministry; (1) It was an occasional "coming upon" a chosen person for a particular task or statement; (2) The Spirit's ministry was not controlled by the person(s); (3) The expectation of the Spirit's help could be given and withdrawn; and (4) The Holy Spirit inspired certain people to speak or write God's message.

Jesus promised the indwelling presence of the Holy Spirit, not surprise visits. Certainly at times believers might experience a particular empowering by the Holy Spirit for a task, but the picture of the Holy Spirit's ministry changes from the Old Testament idea of an external visitation by God to the New Testament picture of a resident presence by God in the life of a believer.

the Egyptians *and* from the hand of all kingdoms and from those who oppressed you.' [19]But you have today rejected your God, who Himself saved you from all your adversities and your tribulations; and you have said to Him, 'No, set a king over us!' Now therefore, present yourselves before the LORD by your tribes and by your clans."[a]

[20]And when Samuel had caused all the tribes of Israel to come near, the tribe of Benjamin was chosen. [21]When he had caused the tribe of Benjamin to come near by their families, the family of Matri was chosen. And Saul the son of Kish was chosen. But when they sought him, he could not be found. [22]Therefore they inquired of the LORD further, "Has the man come here yet?"

And the LORD answered, "There he is, hidden among the equipment."

[23]So they ran and brought him from there; and when he stood among the people, he was taller than any of the people from his shoulders upward. [24]And Samuel said to all the people, "Do you see him whom the LORD has chosen, that *there is* no one like him among all the people?"

So all the people shouted and said, "Long live the king!"

[25]Then Samuel explained to the people the behavior of royalty, and wrote *it* in a book and laid *it* up before the LORD. And Samuel sent all the people away, every man to his house. [26]And Saul also went home to Gibeah; and valiant *men* went with him, whose hearts God had touched. [27]But some rebels said, "How can this man save us?" So they despised him, and brought him no presents. But he held his peace.

Saul Saves Jabesh Gilead

11 Then Nahash the Ammonite came up and encamped against Jabesh Gilead; and all the men of Jabesh said to Nahash, "Make a covenant with us, and we will serve you."

[2]And Nahash the Ammonite answered them, "On this *condition* I will make *a covenant* with you, that I may put out all your right eyes, and bring reproach on all Israel."

> **11:2 put out all your right eyes.** This was a common punishment of usurpers in the ancient Near East to make them useless in battle.

[3]Then the elders of Jabesh said to him, "Hold off for seven days, that we may send messengers to all the territory of Israel. And then, if *there is* no one to save us, we will come out to you."

[4]So the messengers came to Gibeah of Saul and told the news in the hearing of the people. And all the people lifted up their voices and wept. [5]Now there was Saul, coming behind the herd from the field; and Saul said, "What *troubles* the people, that they weep?" And they told him the words of the men of Jabesh. [6]Then the Spirit of God came upon Saul when he heard this news, and his anger was greatly aroused. [7]So he took a yoke of oxen and cut them in pieces, and sent *them* throughout all the territory of Israel by the hands of messengers, saying, "Whoever does not go out with Saul and Samuel to battle, so it shall be done to his oxen."

And the fear of the LORD fell on the people, and they came out with one consent. [8]When he numbered them in Bezek, the children of Israel were three hundred thousand, and the men of Judah thirty thousand. [9]And they said to the messengers who came, "Thus you shall say to the men of Jabesh Gilead: 'Tomorrow, by *the time* the sun is hot, you shall have help.' " Then the messengers came and reported *it* to the men of Jabesh, and they were glad. [10]Therefore the men of Jabesh said, "Tomorrow we will come out to you, and you may do with us whatever seems good to you."

[11]So it was, on the next day, that Saul put the people in three companies; and they came into the midst of the camp in the morning watch, and killed Ammonites until the heat of the day. And it happened that those who survived were scattered, so that no two of them were left together.

[12]Then the people said to Samuel, "Who is he who said, 'Shall Saul reign over us?' Bring the men, that we may put them to death."

[13]But Saul said, "Not a man shall be put

to death this day, for today the LORD has accomplished salvation in Israel."

¹⁴Then Samuel said to the people, "Come, let us go to Gilgal and renew the kingdom there." ¹⁵So all the people went to Gilgal, and there they made Saul king before the LORD in Gilgal. There they made sacrifices of peace offerings before the LORD, and there Saul and all the men of Israel rejoiced greatly.

Samuel's Address at Saul's Coronation

12 Now Samuel said to all Israel: "Indeed I have heeded your voice in all that you said to me, and have made a king over you. ²And now here is the king, walking before you; and I am old and grayheaded, and look, my sons *are* with you. I have walked before you from my childhood to this day. ³Here I am. Witness against me before the LORD and before His anointed: Whose ox have I taken, or whose donkey have I taken, or whom have I cheated? Whom have I oppressed, or from whose hand have I received *any* bribe with which to blind my eyes? I will restore *it* to you."

⁴And they said, "You have not cheated us or oppressed us, nor have you taken anything from any man's hand."

⁵Then he said to them, "The LORD *is* witness against you, and His anointed *is* witness this day, that you have not found anything in my hand."

And they answered, "*He is* witness."

⁶Then Samuel said to the people, "*It is* the LORD who raised up Moses and Aaron, and who brought your fathers up from the land of Egypt. ⁷Now therefore, stand still, that I may reason with you before the LORD concerning all the righteous acts of the LORD which He did to you and your fathers: ⁸When Jacob had gone into Egypt,^a and your fathers cried out to the LORD, then the

LORD sent Moses and Aaron, who brought your fathers out of Egypt and made them dwell in this place. ⁹And when they forgot the LORD their God, He sold them into the hand of Sisera, commander of the army of Hazor, into the hand of the Philistines, and into the hand of the king of Moab; and they fought against them. ¹⁰Then they cried out to the LORD, and said, 'We have sinned, because we have forsaken the LORD and served the Baals and Ashtoreths;^a but now deliver us from the hand of our enemies, and we will serve You.' ¹¹And the LORD sent Jerubbaal,^a Bedan,^b Jephthah, and Samuel,^c and delivered you out of the hand of your enemies on every side; and you dwelt in safety. ¹²And when you saw that Nahash king of the Ammonites came against you, you said to me, 'No, but a king shall reign over us,' when the LORD your God *was* your king.

¹³"Now therefore, here is the king whom you have chosen *and* whom you have desired. And take note, the LORD has set a king over you. ¹⁴If you fear the LORD and serve Him and obey His voice, and do not rebel against the commandment of the LORD, then both you and the king who reigns over you will continue following the LORD your God. ¹⁵However, if you do not obey the voice of the LORD, but rebel against the commandment of the LORD, then the hand of the LORD will be against you, as *it was* against your fathers.

¹⁶"Now therefore, stand and see this great thing which the LORD will do before your eyes: ¹⁷*Is* today not the wheat harvest? I will call to the LORD, and He will send thunder and rain, that you may perceive and see that your wickedness *is* great, which you have done in the sight of the LORD, in asking a king for yourselves."

¹⁸So Samuel called to the LORD, and the LORD sent thunder and rain that day; and

---

12:8 ^aFollowing Masoretic Text, Targum, and Vulgate; Septuagint adds *and the Egyptians afflicted them*.   12:10 ^aCanaanite goddesses   12:11 ^aSyriac reads *Deborah*; Targum reads *Gideon*. ^bSeptuagint and Syriac read *Barak*; Targum reads *Simson*.   ^cSyriac reads *Simson*.

all the people greatly feared the LORD and Samuel.

¹⁹And all the people said to Samuel, "Pray for your servants to the LORD your God, that we may not die; for we have added to all our sins the evil of asking a king for ourselves."

> **12:19 Pray for your servants.** After seeing the power of God in the thunder and rain, the people responded by recognizing their sinful motives in asking for a king and asked Samuel to pray for them.

²⁰Then Samuel said to the people, "Do not fear. You have done all this wickedness; yet do not turn aside from following the LORD, but serve the LORD with all your heart. ²¹And do not turn aside; for *then you would go* after empty things which cannot profit or deliver, for they *are* nothing. ²²For the LORD will not forsake His people, for His great name's sake, because it has pleased the LORD to make you His people. ²³Moreover, as for me, far be it from me that I should sin against the LORD in ceasing to pray for you; but I will teach you the good and the right way. ²⁴Only fear the LORD, and serve Him in truth with all your heart; for consider what great things He has done for you. ²⁵But if you still do wickedly, you shall be swept away, both you and your king."

Saul's Unlawful Sacrifice

13 Saul reigned one year; and when he had reigned two years over Israel,ᵃ ²Saul chose for himself three thousand *men* of Israel. Two thousand were with Saul in Michmash and in the mountains of Bethel, and a thousand were with Jonathan in Gibeah of Benjamin. The rest of the people he sent away, every man to his tent.

³And Jonathan attacked the garrison of the Philistines that *was* in Geba, and the Philistines heard *of it.* Then Saul blew the trumpet throughout all the land, saying, "Let the Hebrews hear!" ⁴Now all Israel heard it said *that* Saul had attacked a garrison of the Philistines, and *that* Israel had also become an abomination to the Philis-

tines. And the people were called together to Saul at Gilgal.

⁵Then the Philistines gathered together to fight with Israel, thirtyᵃ thousand chariots and six thousand horsemen, and people as the sand which *is* on the seashore in multitude. And they came up and encamped in Michmash, to the east of Beth Aven. ⁶When the men of Israel saw that they were in danger (for the people were distressed), then the people hid in caves, in thickets, in rocks, in holes, and in pits. ⁷And *some of* the Hebrews crossed over the Jordan to the land of Gad and Gilead.

As for Saul, he *was* still in Gilgal, and all the people followed him trembling. ⁸Then he waited seven days, according to the time set by Samuel. But Samuel did not come to Gilgal; and the people were scattered from him. ⁹So Saul said, "Bring a burnt offering and peace offerings here to me." And he offered the burnt offering. ¹⁰Now it happened, as soon as he had finished presenting the burnt offering, that Samuel came; and Saul went out to meet him, that he might greet him.

> **13:9 he offered the burnt offering.** Saul's sin was not specifically that he made a sacrifice (see 2 Sam. 24:25) but that he did not wait for priestly assistance from Samuel (see 10:8). Samuel had wanted the 7 days as a test of Saul's character and obedience to God. Because Saul wished to rule with absolute power in civil and sacred matters, he went ahead with the sacrifice and failed the test.

¹¹And Samuel said, "What have you done?"

Saul said, "When I saw that the people were scattered from me, and *that* you did not come within the days appointed, and *that* the Philistines gathered together at Michmash, ¹²then I said, 'The Philistines will now come down on me at Gilgal, and I have not made supplication to the LORD.' Therefore I felt compelled, and offered a burnt offering."

¹³And Samuel said to Saul, "You have done foolishly. You have not kept the commandment of the LORD your God, which

---

13:1 ᵃThe Hebrew is difficult (compare 2 Samuel 5:4; 2 Kings 14:2; see also 2 Samuel 2:10; Acts 13:21).   13:5 ᵃFollowing Masoretic Text, Septuagint, Targum, and Vulgate; Syriac and some manuscripts of the Septuagint read *three.*

He commanded you. For now the LORD would have established your kingdom over Israel forever. [14]But now your kingdom shall not continue. The LORD has sought for Himself a man after His own heart, and the LORD has commanded him *to be* commander over His people, because you have not kept what the LORD commanded you."

> **13:14 a man after His own heart.** Instead of Saul, God wanted a leader who would be obedient to Him. **commander.** Someone else, namely David, had already been chosen to be God's leader over His people.

[15]Then Samuel arose and went up from Gilgal to Gibeah of Benjamin.*a* And Saul numbered the people present with him, about six hundred men.

No Weapons for the Army

[16]Saul, Jonathan his son, and the people present with them remained in Gibeah of Benjamin. But the Philistines encamped in Michmash. [17]Then raiders came out of the camp of the Philistines in three companies. One company turned onto the road to Ophrah, to the land of Shual, [18]another company turned to the road *to* Beth Horon, and another company turned *to* the road of the border that overlooks the Valley of Zeboim toward the wilderness.

[19]Now there was no blacksmith to be found throughout all the land of Israel, for the Philistines said, "Lest the Hebrews make swords or spears." [20]But all the Israelites would go down to the Philistines to sharpen each man's plowshare, his mattock, his ax, and his sickle; [21]and the charge for a sharpening was a pim*a* for the plowshares, the mattocks, the forks, and the axes, and to set the points of the goads. [22]So it came about, on the day of battle, that there was neither sword nor spear found in the hand of any of the people who *were* with Saul and Jonathan. But they were found with Saul and Jonathan his son.

[23]And the garrison of the Philistines went out to the pass of Michmash.

Jonathan Defeats the Philistines

14 Now it happened one day that Jonathan the son of Saul said to the young man who bore his armor, "Come, let us go over to the Philistines' garrison that *is* on the other side." But he did not tell his father. [2]And Saul was sitting in the outskirts of Gibeah under a pomegranate tree which *is* in Migron. The people who *were* with him *were* about six hundred men. [3]Ahijah the son of Ahitub, Ichabod's brother, the son of Phinehas, the son of Eli, the LORD's priest in Shiloh, was wearing an ephod. But the people did not know that Jonathan had gone.

[4]Between the passes, by which Jonathan sought to go over to the Philistines' garrison, *there was* a sharp rock on one side and a sharp rock on the other side. And the name of one *was* Bozez, and the name of the other Seneh. [5]The front of one faced northward opposite Michmash, and the other southward opposite Gibeah.

[6]Then Jonathan said to the young man who bore his armor, "Come, let us go over to the garrison of these uncircumcised; it may be that the LORD will work for us. For nothing restrains the LORD from saving by many or by few." [7]So his armorbearer said to him, "Do all that is in your heart. Go then; here I am with you, according to your heart."

[8]Then Jonathan said, "Very well, let us cross over to *these* men, and we will show ourselves to them. [9]If they say thus to us, 'Wait until we come to you,' then we will stand still in our place and not go up to them. [10]But if they say thus, 'Come up to us,' then we will go up. For the LORD has delivered them into our hand, and this *will be* a sign to us."

[11]So both of them showed themselves to the garrison of the Philistines. And the Philistines said, "Look, the Hebrews are coming out of the holes where they have hidden." [12]Then the men of the garrison called to Jonathan and his armorbearer, and said, "Come up to us, and we will show you something."

Jonathan said to his armorbearer, "Come

13:15 *a*Following Masoretic Text and Targum; Septuagint and Vulgate add *And the rest of the people went up after Saul to meet the people who fought against them, going from Gilgal to Gibeah in the hill of Benjamin.*   13:21 *a*About two-thirds shekel weight

up after me, for the LORD has delivered them into the hand of Israel." [13]And Jonathan climbed up on his hands and knees with his armorbearer after him; and they fell before Jonathan. And as he came after him, his armorbearer killed them. [14]That first slaughter which Jonathan and his armorbearer made was about twenty men within about half an acre of land.[a]

[15]And there was trembling in the camp, in the field, and among all the people. The garrison and the raiders also trembled; and the earth quaked, so that it was a very great trembling. [16]Now the watchmen of Saul in Gibeah of Benjamin looked, and there was the multitude, melting away; and they went here and there. [17]Then Saul said to the people who were with him, "Now call the roll and see who has gone from us." And when they had called the roll, surprisingly, Jonathan and his armorbearer were not there. [18]And Saul said to Ahijah, "Bring the ark[a] of God here" (for at that time the ark[b] of God was with the children of Israel). [19]Now it happened, while Saul talked to the priest, that the noise which was in the camp of the Philistines continued to increase; so Saul said to the priest, "Withdraw your hand." [20]Then Saul and all the people who were with him assembled, and they went to the battle; and indeed every man's sword was against his neighbor, and there was very great confusion. [21]Moreover the Hebrews who were with the Philistines before that time, who went up with them into the camp from the surrounding country, they also joined the Israelites who were with Saul and Jonathan. [22]Likewise all the men of Israel who had hidden in the mountains of Ephraim, when they heard that the Philistines fled, they also followed hard after them in the battle. [23]So the LORD saved Israel that day, and the battle shifted to Beth Aven.

> **14:15 the earth quaked.** The earthquake shows that God aided Jonathan and his armorbearer in their raid, as it caused the Philistines to panic. God would have done the same for Saul had he chosen to be faithfully patient (see 13:9).

Saul's Rash Oath

[24]And the men of Israel were distressed that day, for Saul had placed the people under oath, saying, "Cursed is the man who eats any food until evening, before I have taken vengeance on my enemies." So none of the people tasted food. [25]Now all the people of the land came to a forest; and there was honey on the ground. [26]And when the people had come into the woods, there was the honey, dripping; but no one put his hand to his mouth, for the people feared the oath. [27]But Jonathan had not heard his father charge the people with the oath; therefore he stretched out the end of the rod that was in his hand and dipped it in a honeycomb, and put his hand to his mouth; and his countenance brightened. [28]Then one of the people said, "Your father strictly charged the people with an oath, saying, 'Cursed is the man who eats food this day.'" And the people were faint.

> **14:24 were distressed.** Saul failed to provide for the physical needs of his men, leaving them weak and fatigued. **Cursed.** Saul's foolish oath pronounced a curse upon anyone tasting food until the battle was over. This happened after Jonathan had left.

[29]But Jonathan said, "My father has troubled the land. Look now, how my countenance has brightened because I tasted a little of this honey. [30]How much better if the people had eaten freely today of the spoil of their enemies which they found! For now would there not have been a much greater slaughter among the Philistines?"

[31]Now they had driven back the Philistines that day from Michmash to Aijalon. So the people were very faint. [32]And the people rushed on the spoil, and took sheep, oxen, and calves, and slaughtered them on the ground; and the people ate them with the blood. [33]Then they told Saul, saying, "Look, the people are sinning against the LORD by eating with the blood!"

So he said, "You have dealt treacherously; roll a large stone to me this day." [34]Then Saul said, "Disperse yourselves among the people, and say to them, 'Bring

---

14:14 [a]Literally *half the area plowed by a yoke* (of oxen in a day)   14:18 [a]Following Masoretic Text, Targum, and Vulgate; Septuagint reads *ephod*.   [b]Following Masoretic Text, Targum, and Vulgate; Septuagint reads *ephod*.

me here every man's ox and every man's sheep, slaughter *them* here, and eat; and do not sin against the LORD by eating with the blood.' " So every one of the people brought his ox with him that night, and slaughtered *it* there. ³⁵Then Saul built an altar to the LORD. This was the first altar that he built to the LORD.

³⁶Now Saul said, "Let us go down after the Philistines by night, and plunder them until the morning light; and let us not leave a man of them."

And they said, "Do whatever seems good to you."

Then the priest said, "Let us draw near to God here."

³⁷So Saul asked counsel of God, "Shall I go down after the Philistines? Will You deliver them into the hand of Israel?" But He did not answer him that day. ³⁸And Saul said, "Come over here, all you chiefs of the people, and know and see what this sin was today. ³⁹For *as* the LORD lives, who saves Israel, though it be in Jonathan my son, he shall surely die." But not a man among all the people answered him. ⁴⁰Then he said to all Israel, "You be on one side, and my son Jonathan and I will be on the other side."

And the people said to Saul, "Do what seems good to you."

> **14:37 Saul asked counsel of God.** At the request of Ahijah, Saul asked God for help regarding his battle plan. **He did not answer him.** Because of the sin that Saul had caused in his army, God would not answer him. This would not be the last time that the Lord would refuse to respond to sinful Saul (see 28:6).

⁴¹Therefore Saul said to the LORD God of Israel, "Give a perfect *lot.*"ᵃ So Saul and Jonathan were taken, but the people escaped. ⁴²And Saul said, "Cast *lots* between my son Jonathan and me." So Jonathan was taken. ⁴³Then Saul said to Jonathan, "Tell me what you have done."

And Jonathan told him, and said, "I only tasted a little honey with the end of the rod that *was* in my hand. So now I must die!"

⁴⁴Saul answered, "God do so and more

also; for you shall surely die, Jonathan."

⁴⁵But the people said to Saul, "Shall Jonathan die, who has accomplished this great deliverance in Israel? Certainly not! As the LORD lives, not one hair of his head shall fall to the ground, for he has worked with God this day." So the people rescued Jonathan, and he did not die.

> **14:44,45 God do so and more also.** Saul, proud and concerned with his own authority and honor, was intent on fulfilling his vow. **worked with God this day.** In contrast to his father the king, Jonathan understood the sufficiency of God for the task and obediently relied on Him for the victory.

⁴⁶Then Saul returned from pursuing the Philistines, and the Philistines went to their own place.

Saul's Continuing Wars

⁴⁷So Saul established his sovereignty over Israel, and fought against all his enemies on every side, against Moab, against the people of Ammon, against Edom, against the kings of Zobah, and against the Philistines. Wherever he turned, he harassed *them.*ᵃ ⁴⁸And he gathered an army and attacked the Amalekites, and delivered Israel from the hands of those who plundered them.

⁴⁹The sons of Saul were Jonathan, Jishui,ᵃ and Malchishua. And the names of his two daughters *were these:* the name of the firstborn Merab, and the name of the younger Michal. ⁵⁰The name of Saul's wife *was* Ahinoam the daughter of Ahimaaz. And the name of the commander of his army *was* Abner the son of Ner, Saul's uncle. ⁵¹Kish *was* the father of Saul, and Ner the father of Abner *was* the son of Abiel.

⁵²Now there was fierce war with the Philistines all the days of Saul. And when Saul saw any strong man or any valiant man, he took him for himself.

Saul Spares King Agag

15 Samuel also said to Saul, "The LORD sent me to anoint you king

---

14:41 ᵃFollowing Masoretic Text and Targum; Septuagint and Vulgate read *Why do You not answer Your servant today? If the injustice is with me or Jonathan my son, O Lord God of Israel, give proof; and if You say it is with Your people Israel, give holiness.*   14:47 ᵃSeptuagint and Vulgate read *prospered.*   14:49 ᵃCalled *Abinadab* in 1 Chronicles 8:33 and 9:39

over His people, over Israel. Now therefore, heed the voice of the words of the LORD. ²Thus says the LORD of hosts: 'I will punish Amalek *for* what he did to Israel, how he ambushed him on the way when he came up from Egypt. ³Now go and attack Amalek, and utterly destroy all that they have, and do not spare them. But kill both man and woman, infant and nursing child, ox and sheep, camel and donkey.' "

⁴So Saul gathered the people together and numbered them in Telaim, two hundred thousand foot soldiers and ten thousand men of Judah. ⁵And Saul came to a city of Amalek, and lay in wait in the valley.

⁶Then Saul said to the Kenites, "Go, depart, get down from among the Amalekites, lest I destroy you with them. For you showed kindness to all the children of Israel when they came up out of Egypt." So the Kenites departed from among the Amalekites. ⁷And Saul attacked the Amalekites, from Havilah all the way to Shur, which is east of Egypt. ⁸He also took Agag king of the Amalekites alive, and utterly destroyed all the people with the edge of the sword. ⁹But Saul and the people spared Agag and the best of the sheep, the oxen, the fatlings, the lambs, and all *that was* good, and were unwilling to utterly destroy them. But everything despised and worthless, that they utterly destroyed.

Saul Rejected as King

¹⁰Now the word of the LORD came to Samuel, saying, ¹¹"I greatly regret that I have set up Saul *as* king, for he has turned back from following Me, and has not performed My commandments." And it grieved Samuel, and he cried out to the LORD all night. ¹²So when Samuel rose early in the morning to meet Saul, it was told Samuel, saying, "Saul went to Carmel, and indeed, he set up a monument for himself; and he has gone on around, passed by, and gone down to Gilgal." ¹³Then Samuel went to Saul, and Saul said to him, "Blessed *are*

15:11 grieved Samuel. Samuel, as priest over his people, was concerned over the poor performance of the king, who was behaving like the kings of other nations (1 Sam. 6:19,20). He was self-centered, self-willed, and disobedient to the things of God.

---

you of the LORD! I have performed the commandment of the LORD."

¹⁴But Samuel said, "What then *is* this bleating of the sheep in my ears, and the lowing of the oxen which I hear?"

¹⁵And Saul said, "They have brought them from the Amalekites; for the people spared the best of the sheep and the oxen, to sacrifice to the LORD your God; and the rest we have utterly destroyed."

¹⁶Then Samuel said to Saul, "Be quiet! And I will tell you what the LORD said to me last night."

And he said to him, "Speak on."

¹⁷So Samuel said, "When you *were* little in your own eyes, *were* you not head of the tribes of Israel? And did not the LORD anoint you king over Israel? ¹⁸Now the LORD sent you on a mission, and said, 'Go, and utterly destroy the sinners, the Amalekites, and fight against them until they are consumed.' ¹⁹Why then did you not obey the voice of the LORD? Why did you swoop down on the spoil, and do evil in the sight of the LORD?"

²⁰And Saul said to Samuel, "But I have obeyed the voice of the LORD, and gone on the mission on which the LORD sent me, and brought back Agag king of Amalek; I have utterly destroyed the Amalekites. ²¹But the people took of the plunder, sheep and oxen, the best of the things which should have been utterly destroyed, to sacrifice to the LORD your God in Gilgal."

²²So Samuel said:

"Has the LORD *as great* delight in
    burnt offerings and sacrifices,
As in obeying the voice of the LORD?
Behold, to obey is better than
    sacrifice,
And to heed than the fat of rams.

15:22 to obey is better than sacrifice. God desires obedience from our hearts rather than from the ritual sacrifice of animals (see Ps. 51:16,17). The sacrificial system was never meant to take the place of living an obedient life, but was rather to be an expression of it (see Hos. 6:6).

---

²³   For rebellion *is as* the sin of
        witchcraft,
    And stubbornness *is as* iniquity and
        idolatry.

Because you have rejected the word of
the LORD,
He also has rejected you from *being*
king."

²⁴Then Saul said to Samuel, "I have
sinned, for I have transgressed the commandment of the LORD and your words,
because I feared the people and obeyed their
voice. ²⁵Now therefore, please pardon my
sin, and return with me, that I may worship the LORD."

²⁶But Samuel said to Saul, "I will not return with you, for you have rejected the
word of the LORD, and the LORD has rejected you from being king over Israel."

²⁷And as Samuel turned around to go
away, *Saul* seized the edge of his robe, and
it tore. ²⁸So Samuel said to him, "The LORD
has torn the kingdom of Israel from you today, and has given it to a neighbor of yours,
who is better than you. ²⁹And also the
Strength of Israel will not lie nor relent. For
He *is* not a man, that He should relent."

³⁰Then he said, "I have sinned; *yet* honor
me now, please, before the elders of my
people and before Israel, and return with
me, that I may worship the LORD your
God." ³¹So Samuel turned back after Saul,
and Saul worshiped the LORD.

³²Then Samuel said, "Bring Agag king of
the Amalekites here to me." So Agag came
to him cautiously.

And Agag said, "Surely the bitterness of
death is past."

³³But Samuel said, "As your sword has
made women childless, so shall your mother be childless among women." And Samuel hacked Agag in pieces before the LORD
in Gilgal.

> **15:33 hacked Agag in pieces.** This was an act of di-
> vine judgment to show God's wrath against sin. Sadly,
> the Israelites did not destroy the wicked Amalekites,
> so later they came back to raid the southern territory,
> taking women and children, including David's fam-
> ily (see 1 Sam. 30).

³⁴Then Samuel went to Ramah, and Saul
went up to his house at Gibeah of Saul.
³⁵And Samuel went no more to see Saul

until the day of his death. Nevertheless
Samuel mourned for Saul, and the LORD
regretted that He had made Saul king over
Israel.

David Anointed King

16 Now the LORD said to Samuel,
"How long will you mourn for Saul,
seeing I have rejected him from reigning
over Israel? Fill your horn with oil, and go; I
am sending you to Jesse the Bethlehemite.
For I have provided Myself a king among
his sons."

²And Samuel said, "How can I go? If Saul
hears *it,* he will kill me."

But the LORD said, "Take a heifer with
you, and say, 'I have come to sacrifice to the
LORD.' ³Then invite Jesse to the sacrifice,
and I will show you what you shall do; you
shall anoint for Me the one I name to you."

⁴So Samuel did what the LORD said, and
went to Bethlehem. And the elders of the
town trembled at his coming, and said, "Do
you come peaceably?"

⁵And he said, "Peaceably; I have come to
sacrifice to the LORD. Sanctify yourselves,
and come with me to the sacrifice." Then
he consecrated Jesse and his sons, and invited them to the sacrifice.

⁶So it was, when they came, that he
looked at Eliab and said, "Surely the LORD's
anointed *is* before Him!"

⁷But the LORD said to Samuel, "Do not
look at his appearance or at his physical
stature, because I have refused him. For *the
LORD does* not *see* as man sees;*ᵃ* for man
looks at the outward appearance, but the
LORD looks at the heart."

> **16:7 his appearance...physical stature.** Samuel
> needed to be reminded that God's anointed was not
> chosen because of physical attributes. This was ini-
> tially hard for Samuel to understand, as he was ac-
> customed to a king whose only positive attributes
> were physical. **the LORD looks at the heart.** The life
> of the man will reflect his heart (see Matt. 12:34,35).
> The Hebrew concept of "heart" includes emotions,
> will, intellect, and desires.

⁸So Jesse called Abinadab, and made him
pass before Samuel. And he said, "Neither
has the LORD chosen this one." ⁹Then Jesse

16:7 *ᵃ*Septuagint reads *For God does not see as man sees;* Targum reads *It is not by the appearance of
a man;* Vulgate reads *Nor do I judge according to the looks of a man.*

made Shammah pass by. And he said, "Neither has the LORD chosen this one." [10]Thus Jesse made seven of his sons pass before Samuel. And Samuel said to Jesse, "The LORD has not chosen these." [11]And Samuel said to Jesse, "Are all the young men here?" Then he said, "There remains yet the youngest, and there he is, keeping the sheep."

And Samuel said to Jesse, "Send and bring him. For we will not sit down[a] till he comes here." [12]So he sent and brought him in. Now he *was* ruddy, with bright eyes, and good-looking. And the LORD said, "Arise, anoint him; for this *is* the one!" [13]Then Samuel took the horn of oil and anointed him in the midst of his brothers; and the Spirit of the LORD came upon David from that day forward. So Samuel arose and went to Ramah.

A Distressing Spirit Troubles Saul

[14]But the Spirit of the LORD departed from Saul, and a distressing spirit from the LORD troubled him. [15]And Saul's servants said to him, "Surely, a distressing spirit from God is troubling you. [16]Let our master now command your servants, *who are* before you, to seek out a man *who is* a skillful player on the harp. And it shall be that he will play it with his hand when the distressing spirit from God is upon you, and you shall be well."

> **16:14 the Spirit of the LORD departed from Saul.** Even though Saul remained on the throne for years to come, he was no longer an effective king without the empowerment of the Holy Spirit (15:28). **a distressing spirit.** God allowed an evil spirit to torment Saul (see Judg. 9:23) for His purpose of establishing David's throne. This demon spirit attacked Saul from the outside, for there is no evidence that the demon indwelt him. **troubled him.** Saul began to experience God's judgment in the form of depression, anger, and delusion, which was aggravated by the evil spirit's attacks. For other occasions in the Bible when God turned people over to evil spirits for judgment or for testing, see Acts 5:1–3; 1Cor. 5:1–7; Job 1:1–2:6.

[17]So Saul said to his servants, "Provide me now a man who can play well, and bring *him* to me."

[18]Then one of the servants answered and said, "Look, I have seen a son of Jesse the Bethlehemite, *who is* skillful in playing, a mighty man of valor, a man of war, prudent in speech, and a handsome person; and the LORD *is* with him."

[19]Therefore Saul sent messengers to Jesse, and said, "Send me your son David, who *is* with the sheep." [20]And Jesse took a donkey *loaded with* bread, a skin of wine, and a young goat, and sent *them* by his son David to Saul. [21]So David came to Saul and stood before him. And he loved him greatly, and he became his armorbearer. [22]Then Saul sent to Jesse, saying, "Please let David stand before me, for he has found favor in my sight." [23]And so it was, whenever the spirit from God was upon Saul, that David would take a harp and play *it* with his hand. Then Saul would become refreshed and well, and the distressing spirit would depart from him.

> **16:21 he loved him greatly.** Saul loved David for his abilities, but later he grew to jealously hate him because he was blessed by the Lord (see 18:29). **his armorbearer.** David was most likely one of many such young men assigned to Saul's barracks.

David and Goliath

17 Now the Philistines gathered their armies together to battle, and were gathered at Sochoh, which *belongs* to Judah; they encamped between Sochoh and Azekah, in Ephes Dammim. [2]And Saul and the men of Israel were gathered together, and they encamped in the Valley of Elah, and drew up in battle array against the Philistines. [3]The Philistines stood on a mountain on one side, and Israel stood on a mountain on the other side, with a valley between them.

[4]And a champion went out from the camp of the Philistines, named Goliath, from Gath, whose height *was* six cubits and a span. [5]*He had* a bronze helmet on his head, and he *was* armed with a coat of mail, and the weight of the coat *was* five thousand shekels of bronze. [6]And *he had* bronze armor on his legs and a bronze javelin between his shoulders. [7]Now the staff of

---

16:11 [a]Following Septuagint and Vulgate; Masoretic Text reads *turn around*; Targum and Syriac read *turn away*.

his spear *was* like a weaver's beam, and his iron spearhead *weighed* six hundred shekels; and a shield-bearer went before him. [8]Then he stood and cried out to the armies of Israel, and said to them, "Why have you come out to line up for battle? *Am* I not a Philistine, and you the servants of Saul? Choose a man for yourselves, and let him come down to me. [9]If he is able to fight with me and kill me, then we will be your servants. But if I prevail against him and kill him, then you shall be our servants and serve us." [10]And the Philistine said, "I defy the armies of Israel this day; give me a man, that we may fight together." [11]When Saul and all Israel heard these words of the Philistine, they were dismayed and greatly afraid.

> **17:11 Saul...dismayed and greatly afraid.** Saul and Israel were greatly concerned with outward appearances (10:23,24; 15:30) and were influenced by the fear of men (12:12; 15:24). It was natural for them to fear Goliath, who stood about 9 feet, 9 inches in height (1 Chr. 11:23).

[12]Now David *was* the son of that Ephrathite of Bethlehem Judah, whose name *was* Jesse, and who had eight sons. And the man was old, advanced *in years,* in the days of Saul. [13]The three oldest sons of Jesse had gone to follow Saul to the battle. The names of his three sons who went to the battle *were* Eliab the firstborn, next to him Abinadab, and the third Shammah. [14]David *was* the youngest. And the three oldest followed Saul. [15]But David occasionally went and returned from Saul to feed his father's sheep at Bethlehem.

[16]And the Philistine drew near and presented himself forty days, morning and evening.

[17]Then Jesse said to his son David, "Take now for your brothers an ephah of this dried *grain* and these ten loaves, and run to your brothers at the camp. [18]And carry these ten cheeses to the captain of *their* thousand, and see how your brothers fare, and bring back news of them." [19]Now Saul and they and all the men of Israel *were* in the Valley of Elah, fighting with the Philistines.

[20]So David rose early in the morning, left the sheep with a keeper, and took *the things* and went as Jesse had commanded him. And he came to the camp as the army was going out to the fight and shouting for the battle. [21]For Israel and the Philistines had drawn up in battle array, army against army. [22]And David left his supplies in the hand of the supply keeper, ran to the army, and came and greeted his brothers. [23]Then as he talked with them, there was the champion, the Philistine of Gath, Goliath by name, coming up from the armies of the Philistines; and he spoke according to the same words. So David heard *them.* [24]And all the men of Israel, when they saw the man, fled from him and were dreadfully afraid. [25]So the men of Israel said, "Have you seen this man who has come up? Surely he has come up to defy Israel; and it shall be *that* the man who kills him the king will enrich with great riches, will give him his daughter, and give his father's house exemption *from taxes* in Israel."

[26]Then David spoke to the men who stood by him, saying, "What shall be done for the man who kills this Philistine and takes away the reproach from Israel? For who *is* this uncircumcised Philistine, that he should defy the armies of the living God?" [27]And the people answered him in this manner, saying, "So shall it be done for the man who kills him."

[28]Now Eliab his oldest brother heard when he spoke to the men; and Eliab's anger was aroused against David, and he said, "Why did you come down here? And with whom have you left those few sheep in the wilderness? I know your pride and the insolence of your heart, for you have come down to see the battle." [29]And David said, "What have I done now? *Is there* not a cause?" [30]Then he turned from him toward another and said the same thing; and these people answered him as the first ones *did.*

[31]Now when the words which David spoke were heard, they reported *them* to Saul; and he sent for him. [32]Then David said to Saul, "Let no man's heart fail because of him; your servant will go and fight with this Philistine." [33]And Saul said to David, "You are not able to go against this Philistine to fight with him; for you *are* a youth, and he a man of war from his youth."

17:33 You are not able. David's faith, like that of Joshua and Caleb, was met with disbelief by Saul. By all outward appearances, Saul was absolutely correct in his assessment, but he failed to consider the Lord's presence in David's life.

³⁴But David said to Saul, "Your servant used to keep his father's sheep, and when a lion or a bear came and took a lamb out of the flock, ³⁵I went out after it and struck it, and delivered *the lamb* from its mouth; and when it arose against me, I caught *it* by its beard, and struck and killed it. ³⁶Your servant has killed both lion and bear; and this uncircumcised Philistine will be like one of them, seeing he has defied the armies of the living God." ³⁷Moreover David said, "The LORD, who delivered me from the paw of the lion and from the paw of the bear, He will deliver me from the hand of this Philistine."

And Saul said to David, "Go, and the LORD be with you!"

³⁸So Saul clothed David with his armor, and he put a bronze helmet on his head; he also clothed him with a coat of mail. ³⁹David fastened his sword to his armor and tried to walk, for he had not tested *them*. And David said to Saul, "I cannot walk with these, for I have not tested *them*." So David took them off.

⁴⁰Then he took his staff in his hand; and he chose for himself five smooth stones from the brook, and put them in a shepherd's bag, in a pouch which he had, and his sling was in his hand. And he drew near to the Philistine. ⁴¹So the Philistine came, and began drawing near to David, and the man who bore the shield *went* before him. ⁴²And when the Philistine looked about and saw David, he disdained him; for he was *only* a youth, ruddy and good-looking. ⁴³So the Philistine said to David, "*Am* I a dog, that you come to me with sticks?" And the Philistine cursed David by his gods. ⁴⁴And the Philistine said to David, "Come to me, and I will give your flesh to the birds of the air and the beasts of the field!"

⁴⁵Then David said to the Philistine, "You come to me with a sword, with a spear, and with a javelin. But I come to you in the name of the LORD of hosts, the God of the armies of Israel, whom you have defied. ⁴⁶This day the LORD will deliver you into my hand, and I will strike you and take your head from you. And this day I will give the carcasses of the camp of the Philistines to the birds of the air and the wild beasts of the earth, that all the earth may know that there is a God in Israel. ⁴⁷Then all this assembly shall know that the LORD does not save with sword and spear; for the battle *is* the LORD's, and He will give you into our hands."

⁴⁸So it was, when the Philistine arose and came and drew near to meet David, that David hurried and ran toward the army to meet the Philistine. ⁴⁹Then David put his hand in his bag and took out a stone; and he slung *it* and struck the Philistine in his forehead, so that the stone sank into his forehead, and he fell on his face to the earth. ⁵⁰So David prevailed over the Philistine with a sling and a stone, and struck the Philistine and killed him. But *there was* no sword in the hand of David. ⁵¹Therefore David ran and stood over the Philistine, took his sword and drew it out of its sheath and killed him, and cut off his head with it.

17:47,48 the battle *is* the LORD's. David fully understood that the Philistines were challenging the Lord by confronting the Lord's people (see Deut. 31:6). **David...ran.** David, without armor or fear, and bold in his faith in God, ran to meet Goliath.

And when the Philistines saw that their champion was dead, they fled. ⁵²Now the men of Israel and Judah arose and shouted, and pursued the Philistines as far as the entrance of the valley*ᵃ* and to the gates of Ekron. And the wounded of the Philistines fell along the road to Shaaraim, even as far as Gath and Ekron. ⁵³Then the children of Israel returned from chasing the Philistines, and they plundered their tents. ⁵⁴And David took the head of the Philistine and brought it to Jerusalem, but he put his armor in his tent.

⁵⁵When Saul saw David going out against the Philistine, he said to Abner, the commander of the army, "Abner, whose son *is* this youth?"

17:52　ᵃFollowing Masoretic Text, Syriac, Targum, and Vulgate; Septuagint reads *Gath*.

And Abner said, "As your soul lives, O king, I do not know."

⁵⁶So the king said, "Inquire whose son this young man *is*."

⁵⁷Then, as David returned from the slaughter of the Philistine, Abner took him and brought him before Saul with the head of the Philistine in his hand. ⁵⁸And Saul said to him, "Whose son *are* you, young man?"

So David answered, "*I am* the son of your servant Jesse the Bethlehemite."

Saul Resents David

18 Now when he had finished speaking to Saul, the soul of Jonathan was knit to the soul of David, and Jonathan loved him as his own soul. ²Saul took him that day, and would not let him go home to his father's house anymore. ³Then Jonathan and David made a covenant, because he loved him as his own soul. ⁴And Jonathan took off the robe that *was* on him and gave it to David, with his armor, even to his sword and his bow and his belt.

> **18:1 Jonathan loved him.** Jonathan loved David with the loyalty and devotion of a covenantal love (18:3). Hiram of Tyre had a similar covenantal love for David (see 2 Sam. 5:11). David's later reign from Jerusalem is marked by loyalty to his covenant with Jonathan (2 Sam. 9:1).

⁵So David went out wherever Saul sent him, *and* behaved wisely. And Saul set him over the men of war, and he was accepted in the sight of all the people and also in the sight of Saul's servants. ⁶Now it had happened as they were coming *home*, when David was returning from the slaughter of the Philistine, that the women had come out of all the cities of Israel, singing and dancing, to meet King Saul, with tambourines, with joy, and with musical instruments. ⁷So the women sang as they danced, and said:

> **18:7 David his ten thousands.** Saul grew to hate this song (see 21:11; 28:5) because it exalted David over him.

"Saul has slain his thousands,
And David his ten thousands."

⁸Then Saul was very angry, and the saying displeased him; and he said, "They have ascribed to David ten thousands, and to me they have ascribed *only* thousands. Now *what* more can he have but the kingdom?" ⁹So Saul eyed David from that day forward.

¹⁰And it happened on the next day that the distressing spirit from God came upon Saul, and he prophesied inside the house. So David played *music* with his hand, as at other times; but *there was* a spear in Saul's hand. ¹¹And Saul cast the spear, for he said, "I will pin David to the wall!" But David escaped his presence twice.

¹²Now Saul was afraid of David, because the LORD was with him, but had departed from Saul. ¹³Therefore Saul removed him from his presence, and made him his captain over a thousand; and he went out and came in before the people. ¹⁴And David behaved wisely in all his ways, and the LORD *was* with him. ¹⁵Therefore, when Saul saw that he behaved very wisely, he was afraid of him. ¹⁶But all Israel and Judah loved David, because he went out and came in before them.

David Marries Michal

¹⁷Then Saul said to David, "Here is my older daughter Merab; I will give her to you as a wife. Only be valiant for me, and fight the LORD's battles." For Saul thought, "Let my hand not be against him, but let the hand of the Philistines be against him."

¹⁸So David said to Saul, "Who *am* I, and what *is* my life *or* my father's family in Israel, that I should be son-in-law to the king?" ¹⁹But it happened at the time when Merab, Saul's daughter, should have been given to David, that she was given to Adriel the Meholathite as a wife.

²⁰Now Michal, Saul's daughter, loved David. And they told Saul, and the thing pleased him. ²¹So Saul said, "I will give her to him, that she may be a snare to him, and that the hand of the Philistines may be against him." Therefore Saul said to David a second time, "You shall be my son-in-law today."

> **18:20 Michal.** Lit. "Who is like God?" Michal sincerely loved David and perhaps was aware, as Jonathan was, of David's right to the throne. Saul offered her to David as a "snare" (v. 21).

²²And Saul commanded his servants, "Communicate with David secretly, and say, 'Look, the king has delight in you, and all his servants love you. Now therefore, become the king's son-in-law.' "

²³So Saul's servants spoke those words in the hearing of David. And David said, "Does it seem to you *a* light *thing* to be a king's son-in-law, seeing I *am* a poor and lightly esteemed man?" ²⁴And the servants of Saul told him, saying, "In this manner David spoke."

²⁵Then Saul said, "Thus you shall say to David: 'The king does not desire any dowry but one hundred foreskins of the Philistines, to take vengeance on the king's enemies.' " But Saul thought to make David fall by the hand of the Philistines. ²⁶So when his servants told David these words, it pleased David well to become the king's son-in-law. Now the days had not expired; ²⁷therefore David arose and went, he and his men, and killed two hundred men of the Philistines. And David brought their foreskins, and they gave them in full count to the king, that he might become the king's son-in-law. Then Saul gave him Michal his daughter as a wife.

²⁸Thus Saul saw and knew that the LORD *was* with David, and *that* Michal, Saul's daughter, loved him; ²⁹and Saul was still more afraid of David. So Saul became David's enemy continually. ³⁰Then the princes of the Philistines went out *to war.* And so it was, whenever they went out, *that* David behaved more wisely than all the servants of Saul, so that his name became highly esteemed.

18:29 Saul became David's enemy. Saul's plans to destroy David failed. Saul asked for 100 Philistine foreskins; David brought him 200. Saul offered Michal to David as a "snare"; Michal loved David as did Saul's own son, Jonathan. As a result, Saul's hatred for David grew.

Saul Persecutes David

19 Now Saul spoke to Jonathan his son and to all his servants, that they should kill David; but Jonathan, Saul's son, delighted greatly in David. ²So Jonathan told David, saying, "My father Saul seeks to kill you. Therefore please be on your guard until morning, and stay in a secret *place* and hide. ³And I will go out and stand beside my father in the field where you *are,* and I will speak with my father about you. Then what I observe, I will tell you."

⁴Thus Jonathan spoke well of David to Saul his father, and said to him, "Let not the king sin against his servant, against David, because he has not sinned against you, and because his works *have been* very good toward you. ⁵For he took his life in his hands and killed the Philistine, and the LORD brought about a great deliverance for all Israel. You saw *it* and rejoiced. Why then will you sin against innocent blood, to kill David without a cause?"

⁶So Saul heeded the voice of Jonathan, and Saul swore, "*As* the LORD lives, he shall not be killed." ⁷Then Jonathan called David, and Jonathan told him all these things. So Jonathan brought David to Saul, and he was in his presence as in times past.

19:6 he shall not be killed. Saul temporarily responded in his heart to Jonathan's reason and conviction, but his response did not last long, as his mental capacity was so unbalanced.

⁸And there was war again; and David went out and fought with the Philistines, and struck them with a mighty blow, and they fled from him.

⁹Now the distressing spirit from the LORD came upon Saul as he sat in his house with his spear in his hand. And David was playing *music* with *his* hand. ¹⁰Then Saul sought to pin David to the wall with the spear, but he slipped away from Saul's presence; and he drove the spear into the wall. So David fled and escaped that night.

¹¹Saul also sent messengers to David's house to watch him and to kill him in the morning. And Michal, David's wife, told him, saying, "If you do not save your life tonight, tomorrow you will be killed." ¹²So Michal let David down through a window. And he went and fled and escaped. ¹³And Michal took an image and laid *it* in the bed, put a cover of goats' *hair* for his head, and covered *it* with clothes. ¹⁴So when Saul sent messengers to take David, she said, "He *is* sick."

¹⁵Then Saul sent the messengers *back* to

see David, saying, "Bring him up to me in the bed, that I may kill him." ¹⁶And when the messengers had come in, there was the image in the bed, with a cover of goats' *hair* for his head. ¹⁷Then Saul said to Michal, "Why have you deceived me like this, and sent my enemy away, so that he has escaped?"

And Michal answered Saul, "He said to me, 'Let me go! Why should I kill you?' "

¹⁸So David fled and escaped, and went to Samuel at Ramah, and told him all that Saul had done to him. And he and Samuel went and stayed in Naioth. ¹⁹Now it was told Saul, saying, "Take note, David *is* at Naioth in Ramah!" ²⁰Then Saul sent messengers to take David. And when they saw the group of prophets prophesying, and Samuel standing *as* leader over them, the Spirit of God came upon the messengers of Saul, and they also prophesied. ²¹And when Saul was told, he sent other messengers, and they prophesied likewise. Then Saul sent messengers again the third time, and they prophesied also. ²²Then he also went to Ramah, and came to the great well that *is* at Sechu. So he asked, and said, "Where *are* Samuel and David?"

And *someone* said, "Indeed *they are* at Naioth in Ramah." ²³So he went there to Naioth in Ramah. Then the Spirit of God was upon him also, and he went on and prophesied until he came to Naioth in Ramah. ²⁴And he also stripped off his clothes and prophesied before Samuel in like manner, and lay down naked all that day and all that night. Therefore they say, "*Is* Saul also among the prophets?"*ᵃ*

> **19:24 stripped off his clothes.** Prompted by the Spirit of God, Saul removed his armor and royal garments (see Jonathan's actions in 18:4), which signified God's rejection of him as king over Israel. **lay down naked.** Without his royal garment, Saul was "naked," and perhaps so overwhelmed by the Spirit of God that he was in a deep sleep. This was one of the most humbling events in Saul's life (see 28:20 and 31:4–6). *Is Saul also among the prophets?* This final comment ties together the Spirit of God's presence at Saul's inauguration (10:10,11) and the final departure of the Spirit at Saul's rejection.

Jonathan's Loyalty to David

20 Then David fled from Naioth in Ramah, and went and said to Jonathan, "What have I done? What *is* my iniquity, and what *is* my sin before your father, that he seeks my life?"

²So Jonathan said to him, "By no means! You shall not die! Indeed, my father will do nothing either great or small without first telling me. And why should my father hide this thing from me? It *is* not *so!*"

> **20:2 my father hide this thing from me.** Jonathan was certain that Saul was not seeking David's life, as he was trusting in his father's oath not to harm David (19:6). He was probably unaware of the most recent attempts on David's life (19:9–24). Jonathan expected to be informed by Saul of any change in his plans.

³Then David took an oath again, and said, "Your father certainly knows that I have found favor in your eyes, and he has said, 'Do not let Jonathan know this, lest he be grieved.' But truly, *as* the LORD lives and *as* your soul lives, *there is* but a step between me and death."

⁴So Jonathan said to David, "Whatever you yourself desire, I will do *it* for you."

⁵And David said to Jonathan, "Indeed tomorrow *is* the New Moon, and I should not fail to sit with the king to eat. But let me go, that I may hide in the field until the third *day* at evening. ⁶If your father misses me at all, then say, 'David earnestly asked *permission* of me that he might run over to Bethlehem, his city, for *there is* a yearly sacrifice there for all the family.' ⁷If he says thus: '*It is* well,' your servant will be safe. But if he is very angry, be sure that evil is determined by him. ⁸Therefore you shall deal kindly with your servant, for you have brought your servant into a covenant of the LORD with you. Nevertheless, if there is iniquity in me, kill me yourself, for why should you bring me to your father?"

⁹But Jonathan said, "Far be it from you! For if I knew certainly that evil was determined by my father to come upon you, then would I not tell you?"

¹⁰Then David said to Jonathan, "Who

---

will tell me, or what *if* your father answers you roughly?"

¹¹And Jonathan said to David, "Come, let us go out into the field." So both of them went out into the field. ¹²Then Jonathan said to David: "The LORD God of Israel *is* witness! When I have sounded out my father sometime tomorrow, *or* the third *day,* and indeed *there is* good toward David, and I do not send to you and tell you, ¹³may the LORD do so and much more to Jonathan. But if it pleases my father *to do* you evil, then I will report it to you and send you away, that you may go in safety. And the LORD be with you as He has been with my father. ¹⁴And you shall not only show me the kindness of the LORD while I still live, that I may not die; ¹⁵but you shall not cut off your kindness from my house forever, no, not when the LORD has cut off every one of the enemies of David from the face of the earth." ¹⁶So Jonathan made *a covenant* with the house of David, *saying,* "Let the LORD require *it* at the hand of David's enemies."

¹⁷Now Jonathan again caused David to vow, because he loved him; for he loved him as he loved his own soul. ¹⁸Then Jonathan said to David, "Tomorrow *is* the New Moon; and you will be missed, because your seat will be empty. ¹⁹And *when* you have stayed three days, go down quickly and come to the place where you hid on the day of the deed; and remain by the stone Ezel. ²⁰Then I will shoot three arrows to the side, as though I shot at a target; ²¹and there I will send a lad, *saying,* 'Go, find the arrows.' If I expressly say to the lad, 'Look, the arrows *are* on this side of you; get them and come'—then, as the LORD lives, *there is* safety for you and no harm. ²²But if I say thus to the young man, 'Look, the arrows *are* beyond you'—go your way, for the LORD has sent you away. ²³And as for the matter

---

20:17 vow. In response to Jonathan's words, David solemnly pledged to fulfill the covenant between himself and Jonathan. **loved him as...his own soul.** Jonathan and David held deep concern and affection toward each other, which is the basis for a covenantal relationship (see Lev. 19:18; Matt. 22:39).

---

which you and I have spoken of, indeed the LORD *be* between you and me forever."

²⁴Then David hid in the field. And when the New Moon had come, the king sat down to eat the feast. ²⁵Now the king sat on his seat, as at other times, on a seat by the wall. And Jonathan arose,ᵃ and Abner sat by Saul's side, but David's place was empty. ²⁶Nevertheless Saul did not say anything that day, for he thought, "Something has happened to him; he *is* unclean, surely he *is* unclean." ²⁷And it happened the next day, the second *day* of the month, that David's place was empty. And Saul said to Jonathan his son, "Why has the son of Jesse not come to eat, either yesterday or today?"

²⁸So Jonathan answered Saul, "David earnestly asked *permission* of me *to go* to Bethlehem. ²⁹And he said, 'Please let me go, for our family has a sacrifice in the city, and my brother has commanded me *to be there.* And now, if I have found favor in your eyes, please let me get away and see my brothers.' Therefore he has not come to the king's table."

³⁰Then Saul's anger was aroused against Jonathan, and he said to him, "You son of a perverse, rebellious *woman!* Do I not know that you have chosen the son of Jesse to your own shame and to the shame of your mother's nakedness? ³¹For as long as the son of Jesse lives on the earth, you shall not be established, nor your kingdom. Now therefore, send and bring him to me, for he shall surely die."

³²And Jonathan answered Saul his father, and said to him, "Why should he be killed? What has he done?" ³³Then Saul cast a spear at him to kill him, by which Jonathan knew that it was determined by his father to kill David.

³⁴So Jonathan arose from the table in fierce anger, and ate no food the second day of the month, for he was grieved for David, because his father had treated him shamefully.

³⁵And so it was, in the morning, that Jonathan went out into the field at the time appointed with David, and a little lad *was* with him. ³⁶Then he said to his lad, "Now run, find the arrows which I shoot." As the

---

20:25 ᵃFollowing Masoretic Text, Syriac, Targum, and Vulgate; Septuagint reads *he sat across from Jonathan.*

lad ran, he shot an arrow beyond him. [37]When the lad had come to the place where the arrow was which Jonathan had shot, Jonathan cried out after the lad and said, "*Is* not the arrow beyond you?" [38]And Jonathan cried out after the lad, "Make haste, hurry, do not delay!" So Jonathan's lad gathered up the arrows and came back to his master. [39]But the lad did not know anything. Only Jonathan and David knew of the matter. [40]Then Jonathan gave his weapons to his lad, and said to him, "Go, carry *them* to the city."

[41]As soon as the lad had gone, David arose from *a place* toward the south, fell on his face to the ground, and bowed down three times. And they kissed one another; and they wept together, but David more so. [42]Then Jonathan said to David, "Go in peace, since we have both sworn in the name of the LORD, saying, 'May the LORD be between you and me, and between your descendants and my descendants, forever.' " So he arose and departed, and Jonathan went into the city.

20:41 bowed down three times. David's bowing down more than once acknowledged Jonathan as the prince and expressed humble affection for him.

David and the Holy Bread

21 Now David came to Nob, to Ahimelech the priest. And Ahimelech was afraid when he met David, and said to him, "Why *are* you alone, and no one is with you?"

[2]So David said to Ahimelech the priest, "The king has ordered me on some business, and said to me, 'Do not let anyone know anything about the business on which I send you, or what I have commanded you.' And I have directed *my* young men to such and such a place. [3]Now therefore, what have you on hand? Give *me* five *loaves of* bread in my hand, or whatever can be found."

[4]And the priest answered David and said, "*There is* no common bread on hand; but there is holy bread, if the young men have at least kept themselves from women."

[5]Then David answered the priest, and said to him, "Truly, women *have been* kept from us about three days since I came out. And the vessels of the young men are holy, and *the bread is* in effect common, even though it was consecrated in the vessel this day."

[6]So the priest gave him holy *bread*; for there was no bread there but the showbread which had been taken from before the LORD, in order to put hot bread *in its place* on the day when it was taken away.

[7]Now a certain man of the servants of Saul *was* there that day, detained before the LORD. And his name *was* Doeg, an Edomite, the chief of the herdsmen who *belonged* to Saul.

[8]And David said to Ahimelech, "Is there not here on hand a spear or a sword? For I have brought neither my sword nor my weapons with me, because the king's business required haste."

[9]So the priest said, "The sword of Goliath the Philistine, whom you killed in the Valley of Elah, there it is, wrapped in a cloth behind the ephod. If you will take that, take *it*. For *there is* no other except that one here."

And David said, "*There is* none like it; give it to me."

David Flees to Gath

[10]Then David arose and fled that day from before Saul, and went to Achish the king of Gath. [11]And the servants of Achish said to him, "*Is* this not David the king of the land? Did they not sing of him to one another in dances, saying:

'Saul has slain his thousands,
    And David his ten thousands'?"[a]

[12]Now David took these words to heart, and was very much afraid of Achish the

---

21:2 The king has ordered me. David, fearing that someone might tell Saul where he was, deceived Ahimelech the priest into thinking that he was on official business for the king. David supposed that it is excusable to lie for the purpose of saving one's life, but what is sinful can never change its immoral character (see Ps. 119:29). David's lying led to the deaths of the priests (22:9–18).

---

king of Gath. ¹³So he changed his behavior before them, pretended madness in their hands, scratched on the doors of the gate, and let his saliva fall down on his beard. ¹⁴Then Achish said to his servants, "Look, you see the man is insane. Why have you brought him to me? ¹⁵Have I need of madmen, that you have brought this *fellow* to play the madman in my presence? Shall this *fellow* come into my house?"

> **21:13 changed his behavior.** David, fearing for his life, pretended to be insane to persuade Achish to send him away. Drooling in one's beard was considered in the East an intolerable indignity, as was spitting in another's beard.

David's Four Hundred Men

22 David therefore departed from there and escaped to the cave of Adullam. So when his brothers and all his father's house heard *it,* they went down there to him. ²And everyone *who was* in distress, everyone who *was* in debt, and everyone *who was* discontented gathered to him. So he became captain over them. And there were about four hundred men with him.

³Then David went from there to Mizpah of Moab; and he said to the king of Moab, "Please let my father and mother come here with you, till I know what God will do for me." ⁴So he brought them before the king of Moab, and they dwelt with him all the time that David was in the stronghold.

⁵Now the prophet Gad said to David, "Do not stay in the stronghold; depart, and go to the land of Judah." So David departed and went into the forest of Hereth.

Saul Murders the Priests

⁶When Saul heard that David and the men who *were* with him had been discovered—now Saul was staying in Gibeah under a tamarisk tree in Ramah, with his spear in his hand, and all his servants standing about him— ⁷then Saul said to his servants who stood about him, "Hear now, you Benjamites! Will the son of Jesse give every one of you fields and vineyards, *and* make you all captains of thousands and captains of hundreds? ⁸All of you have conspired against me, and *there is* no one who reveals to me that my son has made a covenant with the son of Jesse; and *there is* not one of you who is sorry for me or reveals to me that my son has stirred up my servant against me, to lie in wait, as *it is* this day."

⁹Then answered Doeg the Edomite, who was set over the servants of Saul, and said, "I saw the son of Jesse going to Nob, to Ahimelech the son of Ahitub. ¹⁰And he inquired of the LORD for him, gave him provisions, and gave him the sword of Goliath the Philistine."

¹¹So the king sent to call Ahimelech the priest, the son of Ahitub, and all his father's house, the priests who *were* in Nob. And they all came to the king. ¹²And Saul said, "Hear now, son of Ahitub!"

He answered, "Here I am, my lord."

¹³Then Saul said to him, "Why have you conspired against me, you and the son of Jesse, in that you have given him bread and a sword, and have inquired of God for him, that he should rise against me, to lie in wait, as it is this day?"

¹⁴So Ahimelech answered the king and said, "And who among all your servants *is as* faithful as David, who is the king's son-in-law, who goes at your bidding, and is honorable in your house? ¹⁵Did I then begin to inquire of God for him? Far be it from me! Let not the king impute anything to his servant, *or* to any in the house of my father. For your servant knew nothing of all this, little or much."

¹⁶And the king said, "You shall surely die, Ahimelech, you and all your father's house!" ¹⁷Then the king said to the guards who stood about him, "Turn and kill the priests of the LORD, because their hand also *is* with David, and because they knew when he fled and did not tell it to me." But the servants of the king would not lift their hands to strike the priests of the LORD. ¹⁸And the king said to Doeg, "You turn and kill the priests!" So Doeg the Edomite turned and struck the priests, and killed on that day eighty-five men who wore a linen ephod. ¹⁹Also Nob, the city of the priests, he struck with the edge of the sword, both

> **22:17 would not...strike the priests.** Although Saul condemned Ahimelech and the priests to death, his servants knew better than to raise their weapons against the priests of the Lord.

men and women, children and nursing infants, oxen and donkeys and sheep—with the edge of the sword.

20Now one of the sons of Ahimelech the son of Ahitub, named Abiathar, escaped and fled after David. 21And Abiathar told David that Saul had killed the LORD's priests. 22So David said to Abiathar, "I knew that day, when Doeg the Edomite *was* there, that he would surely tell Saul. I have caused *the death* of all the persons of your father's house. 23Stay with me; do not fear. For he who seeks my life seeks your life, but with me you *shall be* safe."

> **22:22 I have caused.** David recognized his responsibility for causing the deaths of the priests' families and animals, acknowledging the consequences of his lie to Ahimelech (see 21:1,2).

David Saves the City of Keilah

23 Then they told David, saying, "Look, the Philistines are fighting against Keilah, and they are robbing the threshing floors."

2Therefore David inquired of the LORD, saying, "Shall I go and attack these Philistines?"

And the LORD said to David, "Go and attack the Philistines, and save Keilah."

3But David's men said to him, "Look, we are afraid here in Judah. How much more then if we go to Keilah against the armies of the Philistines?" 4Then David inquired of the LORD once again.

And the LORD answered him and said, "Arise, go down to Keilah. For I will deliver the Philistines into your hand." 5And David and his men went to Keilah and fought with the Philistines, struck them with a mighty blow, and took away their livestock. So David saved the inhabitants of Keilah.

6Now it happened, when Abiathar the son of Ahimelech fled to David at Keilah, *that* he went down *with* an ephod in his hand.

7And Saul was told that David had gone to Keilah. So Saul said, "God has delivered him into my hand, for he has shut himself in by entering a town that has gates and bars." 8Then Saul called all the people together for war, to go down to Keilah to besiege David and his men.

9When David knew that Saul plotted evil against him, he said to Abiathar the priest, "Bring the ephod here." 10Then David said, "O LORD God of Israel, Your servant has certainly heard that Saul seeks to come to Keilah to destroy the city for my sake. 11Will the men of Keilah deliver me into his hand? Will Saul come down, as Your servant has heard? O LORD God of Israel, I pray, tell Your servant."

And the LORD said, "He will come down."

12Then David said, "Will the men of Keilah deliver me and my men into the hand of Saul?"

And the LORD said, "They will deliver *you.*"

13So David and his men, about six hundred, arose and departed from Keilah and went wherever they could go. Then it was told Saul that David had escaped from Keilah; so he halted the expedition.

David in Wilderness Strongholds

14And David stayed in strongholds in the wilderness, and remained in the mountains in the Wilderness of Ziph. Saul sought him every day, but God did not deliver him into his hand. 15So David saw that Saul had come out to seek his life. And David *was* in the Wilderness of Ziph in a forest.[a] 16Then Jonathan, Saul's son, arose and went to David in the woods and strengthened his hand in God. 17And he said to him, "Do not fear, for the hand of Saul my father shall not find you. You shall be king over Israel, and I shall be next to you. Even my father Saul knows that." 18So the two of them made a covenant before the LORD. And David stayed in the woods, and Jonathan went to his own house.

> **23:16,17 strengthened his hand in God.** Jonathan encouraged David by reminding him of the Lord's concern for him and promise to him, that he would be the next king over Israel, as Saul well knew (see 20:30,31).

19Then the Ziphites came up to Saul at Gibeah, saying, "Is David not hiding with us in strongholds in the woods, in the hill of Hachilah, which *is* on the south of

---

23:15 [a]Or *in Horesh*

Jeshimon? 20Now therefore, O king, come down according to all the desire of your soul to come down; and our part *shall be* to deliver him into the king's hand."

21And Saul said, "Blessed *are* you of the LORD, for you have compassion on me. 22Please go and find out for sure, and see the place where his hideout is, *and* who has seen him there. For I am told he is very crafty. 23See therefore, and take knowledge of all the lurking places where he hides; and come back to me with certainty, and I will go with you. And it shall be, if he is in the land, that I will search for him throughout all the clans*a* of Judah."

24So they arose and went to Ziph before Saul. But David and his men *were* in the Wilderness of Maon, in the plain on the south of Jeshimon. 25When Saul and his men went to seek *him*, they told David. Therefore he went down to the rock, and stayed in the Wilderness of Maon. And when Saul heard *that*, he pursued David in the Wilderness of Maon. 26Then Saul went on one side of the mountain, and David and his men on the other side of the mountain. So David made haste to get away from Saul, for Saul and his men were encircling David and his men to take them.

27But a messenger came to Saul, saying, "Hurry and come, for the Philistines have invaded the land!" 28Therefore Saul returned from pursuing David, and went against the Philistines; so they called that place the Rock of Escape.*a* 29Then David went up from there and dwelt in strongholds at En Gedi.

David Spares Saul

24 Now it happened, when Saul had returned from following the Philistines, that it was told him, saying, "Take note! David *is* in the Wilderness of En Gedi." 2Then Saul took three thousand chosen men from all Israel, and went to seek David and his men on the Rocks of the Wild Goats. 3So he came to the sheepfolds by the road, where there *was* a cave; and Saul went in to attend to his needs. (David and his men were staying in the recesses of the cave.) 4Then the men of David said to him, "This is the day of which the LORD

said to you, 'Behold, I will deliver your enemy into your hand, that you may do to him as it seems good to you.' " And David arose and secretly cut off a corner of Saul's robe. 5Now it happened afterward that David's heart troubled him because he had cut Saul's *robe*. 6And he said to his men, "The LORD forbid that I should do this thing to my master, the LORD's anointed, to stretch out my hand against him, seeing he *is* the anointed of the LORD." 7So David restrained his servants with *these* words, and did not allow them to rise against Saul. And Saul got up from the cave and went on *his* way.

> **24:6 LORD's anointed.** David recognized that the Lord Himself had placed Saul into the kingship, so the judgment and removal of Saul had to be left to the Lord.

8David also arose afterward, went out of the cave, and called out to Saul, saying, "My lord the king!" And when Saul looked behind him, David stooped with his face to the earth, and bowed down. 9And David said to Saul: "Why do you listen to the words of men who say, 'Indeed David seeks your harm'? 10Look, this day your eyes have seen that the LORD delivered you today into my hand in the cave, and *someone* urged *me* to kill you. But *my eye* spared you, and I said, 'I will not stretch out my hand against my lord, for he *is* the LORD's anointed.' 11Moreover, my father, see! Yes, see the corner of your robe in my hand! For in that I cut off the corner of your robe, and did not kill you, know and see that *there is* neither evil nor rebellion in my hand, and I have not sinned against you. Yet you hunt my life to take it. 12Let the LORD judge between you and me, and let the LORD avenge me on you. But my hand shall not be against you. 13As the proverb of the ancients says, 'Wickedness proceeds from the wicked.' But my hand shall not be against you. 14After whom has the king of Israel come out? Whom do you pursue? A dead dog? A flea? 15Therefore let the LORD be judge, and judge between you and me, and see and plead my case, and deliver me out of your hand."

23:23 *a*Literally *thousands*   23:28 *a*Hebrew *Sela Hammahlekoth*

[16]So it was, when David had finished speaking these words to Saul, that Saul said, "*Is* this your voice, my son David?" And Saul lifted up his voice and wept. [17]Then he said to David: "You *are* more righteous than I; for you have rewarded me with good, whereas I have rewarded you with evil. [18]And you have shown this day how you have dealt well with me; for when the LORD delivered me into your hand, you did not kill me. [19]For if a man finds his enemy, will he let him get away safely? Therefore may the LORD reward you with good for what you have done to me this day. [20]And now I know indeed that you shall surely be king, and that the kingdom of Israel shall be established in your hand. [21]Therefore swear now to me by the LORD that you will not cut off my descendants after me, and that you will not destroy my name from my father's house."

24:17 You *are* more righteous than I. Saul was moved with emotion and acknowledged that David was more righteous than he was, which showed that he recognized David's right to the kingship.

[22]So David swore to Saul. And Saul went home, but David and his men went up to the stronghold.

Death of Samuel

25 Then Samuel died; and the Israelites gathered together and lamented for him, and buried him at his home in Ramah. And David arose and went down to the Wilderness of Paran.[a]

David and the Wife of Nabal

[2]Now *there was* a man in Maon whose business *was* in Carmel, and the man *was* very rich. He had three thousand sheep and a thousand goats. And he was shearing his sheep in Carmel. [3]The name of the man *was* Nabal, and the name of his wife Abigail. And *she was* a woman of good understanding and beautiful appearance; but the man *was* harsh and evil in *his* doings. He *was* of the house of Caleb.

[4]When David heard in the wilderness that Nabal was shearing his sheep, [5]David sent ten young men; and David said to the young men, "Go up to Carmel, go to Nabal, and greet him in my name. [6]And thus you shall say to him who lives *in prosperity:* 'Peace *be* to you, peace to your house, and peace to all that you have! [7]Now I have heard that you have shearers. Your shepherds were with us, and we did not hurt them, nor was there anything missing from them all the while they were in Carmel. [8]Ask your young men, and they will tell you. Therefore let *my* young men find favor in your eyes, for we come on a feast day. Please give whatever comes to your hand to your servants and to your son David.' "

[9]So when David's young men came, they spoke to Nabal according to all these words in the name of David, and waited.

[10]Then Nabal answered David's servants, and said, "Who *is* David, and who *is* the son of Jesse? There are many servants nowadays who break away each one from his master. [11]Shall I then take my bread and my water and my meat that I have killed for my shearers, and give *it* to men when I do not know where they *are* from?"

[12]So David's young men turned on their heels and went back; and they came and told him all these words. [13]Then David said to his men, "Every man gird on his sword." So every man girded on his sword, and David also girded on his sword. And about four hundred men went with David, and two hundred stayed with the supplies.

[14]Now one of the young men told Abigail, Nabal's wife, saying, "Look, David sent messengers from the wilderness to greet our master; and he reviled them. [15]But the men *were* very good to us, and we were not hurt, nor did we miss anything as long as we accompanied them, when we were in the fields. [16]They were a wall to us both by night and day, all the time we were with them keeping the sheep. [17]Now therefore, know and consider what you will do, for harm is determined against our master and against all his household. For he *is such* a scoundrel[a] that *one* cannot speak to him."

[18]Then Abigail made haste and took two hundred *loaves* of bread, two skins of wine, five sheep already dressed, five seahs of

---

25:1 [a]Following Masoretic Text, Syriac, Targum, and Vulgate; Septuagint reads *Maon*.
25:17 [a]Literally *son of Belial*

roasted *grain*, one hundred clusters of raisins, and two hundred cakes of figs, and loaded *them* on donkeys. ¹⁹And she said to her servants, "Go on before me; see, I am coming after you." But she did not tell her husband Nabal.

> **25:19 did not tell her husband.** Abigail knew that Nabal would disagree with her actions, but because she knew that God had chosen David (v. 28), she recognized the consequences involved in Nabal's cursing of David. She chose to obey God instead of her husband (see Acts 5:29).

²⁰So it was, *as* she rode on the donkey, that she went down under cover of the hill; and there were David and his men, coming down toward her, and she met them. ²¹Now David had said, "Surely in vain I have protected all that this *fellow* has in the wilderness, so that nothing was missed of all that *belongs* to him. And he has repaid me evil for good. ²²May God do so, and more also, to the enemies of David, if I leave one male of all who *belong* to him by morning light."

²³Now when Abigail saw David, she dismounted quickly from the donkey, fell on her face before David, and bowed down to the ground. ²⁴So she fell at his feet and said: "On me, my lord, *on* me *let* this iniquity *be!* And please let your maidservant speak in your ears, and hear the words of your maidservant. ²⁵Please, let not my lord regard this scoundrel Nabal. For as his name *is,* so *is* he: Nabal*ᵃ is* his name, and folly *is* with him! But I, your maidservant, did not see the young men of my lord whom you sent. ²⁶Now therefore, my lord, *as* the LORD lives and *as* your soul lives, since the LORD has held you back from coming to bloodshed and from avenging yourself with your own hand, now then, let your enemies and those who seek harm for my lord be as Nabal. ²⁷And now this present which your

> **25:28 an enduring house.** Abigail's perceptive insight fit an essential feature of the Davidic Covenant (see 2 Sam. 7:11–16). **fights the battles of the LORD.** David was a man who fought the Lord's battles, unlike Saul (8:20).

maidservant has brought to my lord, let it be given to the young men who follow my lord. ²⁸Please forgive the trespass of your maidservant. For the LORD will certainly make for my lord an enduring house, because my lord fights the battles of the LORD, and evil is not found in you throughout your days. ²⁹Yet a man has risen to pursue you and seek your life, but the life of my lord shall be bound in the bundle of the living with the LORD your God; and the lives of your enemies He shall sling out, *as from* the pocket of a sling. ³⁰And it shall come to pass, when the LORD has done for my lord according to all the good that He has spoken concerning you, and has appointed you ruler over Israel, ³¹that this will be no grief to you, nor offense of heart to my lord, either that you have shed blood without cause, or that my lord has avenged himself. But when the LORD has dealt well with my lord, then remember your maidservant."

³²Then David said to Abigail: "Blessed *is* the LORD God of Israel, who sent you this day to meet me! ³³And blessed *is* your advice and blessed *are* you, because you have kept me this day from coming to bloodshed and from avenging myself with my own hand. ³⁴For indeed, *as* the LORD God of Israel lives, who has kept me back from hurting you, unless you had hurried and come to meet me, surely by morning light no males would have been left to Nabal!" ³⁵So David received from her hand what she had brought him, and said to her, "Go up in peace to your house. See, I have heeded your voice and respected your person."

³⁶Now Abigail went to Nabal, and there he was, holding a feast in his house, like the feast of a king. And Nabal's heart *was* merry within him, for he *was* very drunk; therefore she told him nothing, little or much, until morning light. ³⁷So it was, in the morning, when the wine had gone from Nabal, and his wife had told him these things, that his heart died within him, and

> **25:37,38 heart died...became *like* a stone.** Nabal was intoxicated and apparently suffered a stroke, becoming paralyzed until he died.

he became *like* a stone. [38]Then it happened, *after* about ten days, that the LORD struck Nabal, and he died.

[39]So when David heard that Nabal was dead, he said, "Blessed *be* the LORD, who has pleaded the cause of my reproach from the hand of Nabal, and has kept His servant from evil! For the LORD has returned the wickedness of Nabal on his own head."

And David sent and proposed to Abigail, to take her as his wife. [40]When the servants of David had come to Abigail at Carmel, they spoke to her saying, "David sent us to you, to ask you to become his wife."

[41]Then she arose, bowed her face to the earth, and said, "Here is your maidservant, a servant to wash the feet of the servants of my lord." [42]So Abigail rose in haste and rode on a donkey, attended by five of her maidens; and she followed the messengers of David, and became his wife. [43]David also took Ahinoam of Jezreel, and so both of them were his wives.

[44]But Saul had given Michal his daughter, David's wife, to Palti[a] the son of Laish, who *was* from Gallim.

David Spares Saul a Second Time

26 Now the Ziphites came to Saul at Gibeah, saying, "Is David not hiding in the hill of Hachilah, opposite Jeshimon?" [2]Then Saul arose and went down to the Wilderness of Ziph, having three thousand chosen men of Israel with him, to seek David in the Wilderness of Ziph. [3]And Saul encamped in the hill of Hachilah, which *is* opposite Jeshimon, by the road. But David stayed in the wilderness, and he saw that Saul came after him into the wilderness. [4]David therefore sent out spies, and understood that Saul had indeed come.

[5]So David arose and came to the place where Saul had encamped. And David saw the place where Saul lay, and Abner the son of Ner, the commander of his army. Now Saul lay within the camp, with the people encamped all around him. [6]Then David answered, and said to Ahimelech the Hittite and to Abishai the son of Zeruiah, brother of Joab, saying, "Who will go down with me to Saul in the camp?"

And Abishai said, "I will go down with you."

[7]So David and Abishai came to the people by night; and there Saul lay sleeping within the camp, with his spear stuck in the ground by his head. And Abner and the people lay all around him. [8]Then Abishai said to David, "God has delivered your enemy into your hand this day. Now therefore, please, let me strike him at once with the spear, right to the earth; and I will not *have to strike* him a second time!"

[9]But David said to Abishai, "Do not destroy him; for who can stretch out his hand against the LORD's anointed, and be guiltless?" [10]David said furthermore, "*As* the LORD lives, the LORD shall strike him, or his day shall come to die, or he shall go out to battle and perish. [11]The LORD forbid that I should stretch out my hand against the LORD's anointed. But please, take now the spear and the jug of water that *are* by his head, and let us go." [12]So David took the spear and the jug of water *by* Saul's head, and they got away; and no man saw or knew *it* or awoke. For they *were* all asleep, because a deep sleep from the LORD had fallen on them.

> **26:12 spear and the jug.** Like the corner of Saul's robe (24:4), these were taken as proof that David had Saul's life in his hands (see v. 16). **a deep sleep from the LORD.** As with Adam in Gen. 2:21 and Abraham in Gen. 15:12, the Lord caused Saul to be unaware of what was happening around him.

[13]Now David went over to the other side, and stood on the top of a hill afar off, a great distance *being* between them. [14]And David called out to the people and to Abner the son of Ner, saying, "Do you not answer, Abner?"

Then Abner answered and said, "Who *are* you, calling out to the king?"

[15]So David said to Abner, "*Are* you not a man? And who *is* like you in Israel? Why then have you not guarded your lord the king? For one of the people came in to destroy your lord the king. [16]This thing that you have done *is* not good. *As* the LORD lives, you deserve to die, because you have not guarded your master, the LORD's

anointed. And now see where the king's spear *is*, and the jug of water that *was* by his head."

[17]Then Saul knew David's voice, and said, "*Is* that your voice, my son David?"

David said, "*It is* my voice, my lord, O king." [18]And he said, "Why does my lord thus pursue his servant? For what have I done, or what evil *is* in my hand? [19]Now therefore, please, let my lord the king hear the words of his servant: If the LORD has stirred you up against me, let Him accept an offering. But if *it is* the children of men, *may* they *be* cursed before the LORD, for they have driven me out this day from sharing in the inheritance of the LORD, saying, 'Go, serve other gods.' [20]So now, do not let my blood fall to the earth before the face of the LORD. For the king of Israel has come out to seek a flea, as when one hunts a partridge in the mountains."

26:20 flea...partridge. The flea represents something that was worthless and the partridge something that was impossible to catch. Saul was wasting his time pursuing David.

[21]Then Saul said, "I have sinned. Return, my son David. For I will harm you no more, because my life was precious in your eyes this day. Indeed I have played the fool and erred exceedingly."

[22]And David answered and said, "Here is the king's spear. Let one of the young men come over and get it. [23]May the LORD repay every man *for* his righteousness and his faithfulness; for the LORD delivered you into *my* hand today, but I would not stretch out my hand against the LORD's anointed. [24]And indeed, as your life was valued much this day in my eyes, so let my life be valued much in the eyes of the LORD, and let Him deliver me out of all tribulation."

[25]Then Saul said to David, "*May* you *be* blessed, my son David! You shall both do great things and also still prevail."

So David went on his way, and Saul returned to his place.

David Allied with the Philistines

27 And David said in his heart, "Now I shall perish someday by the hand of Saul. *There is* nothing better for me than that I should speedily escape to the land of the Philistines; and Saul will despair of me, to seek me anymore in any part of Israel. So I shall escape out of his hand." [2]Then David arose and went over with the six hundred men who *were* with him to Achish the son of Maoch, king of Gath. [3]So David dwelt with Achish at Gath, he and his men, each man with his household, *and* David with his two wives, Ahinoam the Jezreelitess, and Abigail the Carmelitess, Nabal's widow. [4]And it was told Saul that David had fled to Gath; so he sought him no more.

28:2 what your servant can do. David was a man of honor and would not fail to help those who had shown him kindness. David had proven himself a successful warrior and assured Achish of his fidelity and ability. **chief guardians.** In light of David's victory over Goliath and his fictitious bad reputation among the Israelites, Achish trusted David's loyalty and ability, for "chief guardian" lit. means "keeper of my head."

[5]Then David said to Achish, "If I have now found favor in your eyes, let them give me a place in some town in the country, that I may dwell there. For why should your servant dwell in the royal city with you?" [6]So Achish gave him Ziklag that day. Therefore Ziklag has belonged to the kings of Judah to this day. [7]Now the time that David dwelt in the country of the Philistines was one full year and four months.

[8]And David and his men went up and raided the Geshurites, the Girzites,[a] and the Amalekites. For those nations were the inhabitants of the land from of old, as you go to Shur, even as far as the land of Egypt. [9]Whenever David attacked the land, he left neither man nor woman alive, but took away the sheep, the oxen, the donkeys, the camels, and the apparel, and returned and came to Achish. [10]Then Achish would say, "Where have you made a raid today?" And David would say, "Against the southern *area* of Judah, or against the southern *area* of the Jerahmeelites, or against the southern *area* of the Kenites." [11]David would save neither man nor woman alive, to bring

---

27:8 [a]Or *Gezrites*

news to Gath, saying, "Lest they should inform on us, saying, 'Thus David did.'" And thus *was* his behavior all the time he dwelt in the country of the Philistines. [12]So Achish believed David, saying, "He has made his people Israel utterly abhor him; therefore he will be my servant forever."

28 Now it happened in those days that the Philistines gathered their armies together for war, to fight with Israel. And Achish said to David, "You assuredly know that you will go out with me to battle, you and your men."

[2]So David said to Achish, "Surely you know what your servant can do."

And Achish said to David, "Therefore I will make you one of my chief guardians forever."

Saul Consults a Medium

[3]Now Samuel had died, and all Israel had lamented for him and buried him in Ramah, in his own city. And Saul had put the mediums and the spiritists out of the land.

[4]Then the Philistines gathered together, and came and encamped at Shunem. So Saul gathered all Israel together, and they encamped at Gilboa. [5]When Saul saw the army of the Philistines, he was afraid, and his heart trembled greatly. [6]And when Saul inquired of the LORD, the LORD did not answer him, either by dreams or by Urim or by the prophets.

[7]Then Saul said to his servants, "Find me a woman who is a medium, that I may go to her and inquire of her."

And his servants said to him, "In fact, *there is* a woman who is a medium at En Dor."

[8]So Saul disguised himself and put on other clothes, and he went, and two men with him; and they came to the woman by night. And he said, "Please conduct a séance for me, and bring up for me the one I shall name to you."

[9]Then the woman said to him, "Look, you know what Saul has done, how he has cut off the mediums and the spiritists from the land. Why then do you lay a snare for my life, to cause me to die?"

[10]And Saul swore to her by the LORD, saying, "As the LORD lives, no punishment shall come upon you for this thing."

[11]Then the woman said, "Whom shall I bring up for you?"

And he said, "Bring up Samuel for me."

[12]When the woman saw Samuel, she cried out with a loud voice. And the woman spoke to Saul, saying, "Why have you deceived me? For you *are* Saul!"

> **28:12 the woman saw Samuel.** Samuel, not an apparition, was evident to the eyes of the medium. God permitted the actual spirit of Samuel to speak (vv. 16–19). Because the medium knew she had no power to raise the dead, she immediately believed that it must have been by the power of God and that her disguised inquirer must be Saul.

[13]And the king said to her, "Do not be afraid. What did you see?"

And the woman said to Saul, "I saw a spirit[a] ascending out of the earth."

> **28:3–13** Saul walked in foolishness again by seeking out a medium he had previously removed from the land. He swore an oath to the medium using the Lord's name, even though he was disobeying God. Saul's curiosity to consult Samuel, who was dead, was satisfied by the medium's willingness to "bring up" Samuel.

[14]So he said to her, "What *is* his form?"

And she said, "An old man is coming up, and he *is* covered with a mantle." And Saul perceived that it *was* Samuel, and he stooped with *his* face to the ground and bowed down.

[15]Now Samuel said to Saul, "Why have you disturbed me by bringing me up?"

And Saul answered, "I am deeply distressed; for the Philistines make war against me, and God has departed from me and does not answer me anymore, neither by prophets nor by dreams. Therefore I have called you, that you may reveal to me what I should do."

[16]Then Samuel said: "So why do you ask me, seeing the LORD has departed from you and has become your enemy? [17]And the LORD has done for Himself[a] as He spoke by me. For the LORD has torn the kingdom out of your hand and given it to your neighbor,

---

28:13 [a]Hebrew *elohim*   28:17 [a]Or *him,* that is, David

David. [18]Because you did not obey the voice of the LORD nor execute His fierce wrath upon Amalek, therefore the LORD has done this thing to you this day. [19]Moreover the LORD will also deliver Israel with you into the hand of the Philistines. And tomorrow you and your sons *will be* with me. The LORD will also deliver the army of Israel into the hand of the Philistines."

[20]Immediately Saul fell full length on the ground, and was dreadfully afraid because of the words of Samuel. And there was no strength in him, for he had eaten no food all day or all night.

[21]And the woman came to Saul and saw that he was severely troubled, and said to him, "Look, your maidservant has obeyed your voice, and I have put my life in my hands and heeded the words which you spoke to me. [22]Now therefore, please, heed also the voice of your maidservant, and let me set a piece of bread before you; and eat, that you may have strength when you go on *your* way."

[23]But he refused and said, "I will not eat."

So his servants, together with the woman, urged him; and he heeded their voice. Then he arose from the ground and sat on the bed. [24]Now the woman had a fatted calf in the house, and she hastened to kill it. And she took flour and kneaded *it*, and baked unleavened bread from it. [25]So she brought *it* before Saul and his servants, and they ate. Then they rose and went away that night.

28:20–25 no strength in him. Saul was already afraid of the Philistines (v. 5) and now was even more afraid by the words of Samuel. His fear deprived him of strength and vigor, which was reinforced by a lack of nourishment. The woman met his physical needs, giving him bread to eat, and he returned to his camp to await his doom (vv. 21–25).

The Philistines Reject David

29 Then the Philistines gathered together all their armies at Aphek, and the Israelites encamped by a fountain which *is* in Jezreel. [2]And the lords of the Philistines passed in review by hundreds and by thousands, but David and his men passed in review at the rear with Achish.

[3]Then the princes of the Philistines said, "What *are* these Hebrews *doing here?*"

And Achish said to the princes of the Philistines, "*Is* this not David, the servant of Saul king of Israel, who has been with me these days, or these years? And to this day I have found no fault in him since he defected *to me.*"

[4]But the princes of the Philistines were angry with him; so the princes of the Philistines said to him, "Make this fellow return, that he may go back to the place which you have appointed for him, and do not let him go down with us to battle, lest in the battle he become our adversary. For with what could he reconcile himself to his master, if not with the heads of these men? [5]*Is* this not David, of whom they sang to one another in dances, saying:

'Saul has slain his thousands,
    And David his ten thousands'?"[a]

29:4 he become our adversary. The Philistine lords were not as willing as Achish to trust David. They realized that he might be feigning loyalty to the Philistines in order to betray them in battle.

[6]Then Achish called David and said to him, "Surely, *as* the LORD lives, you have been upright, and your going out and your coming in with me in the army *is* good in my sight. For to this day I have not found evil in you since the day of your coming to me. Nevertheless the lords do not favor you. [7]Therefore return now, and go in peace, that you may not displease the lords of the Philistines."

[8]So David said to Achish, "But what have I done? And to this day what have you found in your servant as long as I have been with you, that I may not go and fight against the enemies of my lord the king?"

[9]Then Achish answered and said to David, "I know that you *are* as good in my sight as an angel of God; nevertheless the princes of the Philistines have said, 'He shall not go up with us to the battle.' [10]Now therefore, rise early in the morning with your master's servants who have come

---

with you.*a* And as soon as you are up early in the morning and have light, depart."

¹¹So David and his men rose early to depart in the morning, to return to the land of the Philistines. And the Philistines went up to Jezreel.

David's Conflict with the Amalekites

30 Now it happened, when David and his men came to Ziklag, on the third day, that the Amalekites had invaded the South and Ziklag, attacked Ziklag and burned it with fire, ²and had taken captive the women and those who *were* there, from small to great; they did not kill anyone, but carried *them* away and went their way. ³So David and his men came to the city, and there it was, burned with fire; and their wives, their sons, and their daughters had been taken captive. ⁴Then David and the people who *were* with him lifted up their voices and wept, until they had no more power to weep. ⁵And David's two wives, Ahinoam the Jezreelitess, and Abigail the widow of Nabal the Carmelite, had been taken captive. ⁶Now David was greatly distressed, for the people spoke of stoning him, because the soul of all the people was grieved, every man for his sons and his daughters. But David strengthened himself in the LORD his God.

⁷Then David said to Abiathar the priest, Ahimelech's son, "Please bring the ephod here to me." And Abiathar brought the ephod to David. ⁸So David inquired of the LORD, saying, "Shall I pursue this troop? Shall I overtake them?"

And He answered him, "Pursue, for you shall surely overtake *them* and without fail recover *all*."

> **30:7 Abiathar brought the ephod.** David sought out the High-Priest's ephod, a source through which one could make direct inquiry into the will of God. David was desperate to know what God would have him do in the midst of his distress over the treasonous thoughts of his men.

⁹So David went, he and the six hundred men who *were* with him, and came to the Brook Besor, where those stayed who were left behind. ¹⁰But David pursued, he and four hundred men; for two hundred stayed *behind*, who were so weary that they could not cross the Brook Besor.

¹¹Then they found an Egyptian in the field, and brought him to David; and they gave him bread and he ate, and they let him drink water. ¹²And they gave him a piece of a cake of figs and two clusters of raisins. So when he had eaten, his strength came back to him; for he had eaten no bread nor drunk water for three days and three nights. ¹³Then David said to him, "To whom do you *belong*, and where *are* you from?"

And he said, "I *am* a young man from Egypt, servant of an Amalekite; and my master left me behind, because three days ago I fell sick. ¹⁴We made an invasion of the southern *area* of the Cherethites, in the *territory* which *belongs* to Judah, and of the southern *area* of Caleb; and we burned Ziklag with fire."

¹⁵And David said to him, "Can you take me down to this troop?"

So he said, "Swear to me by God that you will neither kill me nor deliver me into the hands of my master, and I will take you down to this troop."

¹⁶And when he had brought him down, there they were, spread out over all the land, eating and drinking and dancing, because of all the great spoil which they had taken from the land of the Philistines and from the land of Judah. ¹⁷Then David attacked them from twilight until the evening of the next day. Not a man of them escaped, except four hundred young men who rode on camels and fled. ¹⁸So David recovered all that the Amalekites had carried away, and David rescued his two wives. ¹⁹And nothing of theirs was lacking, either small or great, sons or daughters, spoil or anything which they had taken from them; David recovered all. ²⁰Then David took all the flocks and herds they had driven before those *other* livestock, and said, "This *is* David's spoil."

²¹Now David came to the two hundred

29:10 *a*Following Masoretic Text, Targum, and Vulgate; Septuagint adds *and go to the place which I have selected for you there; and set no bothersome word in your heart, for you are good before me. And rise on your way.*

men who had been so weary that they could not follow David, whom they also had made to stay at the Brook Besor. So they went out to meet David and to meet the people who *were* with him. And when David came near the people, he greeted them. ²²Then all the wicked and worthless men*a* of those who went with David answered and said, "Because they did not go with us, we will not give them *any* of the spoil that we have recovered, except for every man's wife and children, that they may lead *them* away and depart."

²³But David said, "My brethren, you shall not do so with what the LORD has given us, who has preserved us and delivered into our hand the troop that came against us. ²⁴For who will heed you in this matter? But as his part *is* who goes down to the battle, so *shall* his part *be* who stays by the supplies; they shall share alike." ²⁵So it was, from that day forward; he made it a statute and an ordinance for Israel to this day.

²⁶Now when David came to Ziklag, he sent *some* of the spoil to the elders of Judah, to his friends, saying, "Here is a present for you from the spoil of the enemies of the LORD"—²⁷to *those* who *were* in Bethel, *those* who *were* in Ramoth of the South, *those* who *were* in Jattir, ²⁸*those* who *were* in Aroer, *those* who *were* in Siphmoth, *those* who *were* in Eshtemoa, ²⁹*those* who *were* in Rachal, *those* who *were* in the cities of the Jerahmeelites, *those* who *were* in the cities of the Kenites, ³⁰*those* who *were* in Hormah, *those* who *were* in Chorashan,*a* *those* who *were* in Athach, ³¹*those* who *were* in Hebron, and to all the places where David himself and his men were accustomed to rove.

> **30:26–31** David realized the important role that so many others had played in giving him safety and welfare. David missed no opportunity to reciprocate kindness and generosity, expressing his debt of gratitude for the kindness and support shown him.

The Tragic End of Saul and His Sons

31 Now the Philistines fought against Israel; and the men of Israel fled from before the Philistines, and fell slain on Mount Gilboa. ²Then the Philistines followed hard after Saul and his sons. And the Philistines killed Jonathan, Abinadab, and Malchishua, Saul's sons. ³The battle became fierce against Saul. The archers hit him, and he was severely wounded by the archers.

⁴Then Saul said to his armorbearer, "Draw your sword, and thrust me through with it, lest these uncircumcised men come and thrust me through and abuse me."

> **31:4 abuse.** Saul had succeeded in provoking hatred and resentment from the Philistines since he had been engaged in several battles against them. As the king, Saul had received cruel treatment from the hands of his enemies. **Saul took a sword and fell on it.** Though Saul's suicide is considered by some to be an act of heroism, Saul should have found his strength and courage in God, as David did in 23:16 and 30:6, to fight to the end. Saul's suicide is the ultimate expression of faithlessness toward God.

But his armorbearer would not, for he was greatly afraid. Therefore Saul took a sword and fell on it. ⁵And when his armorbearer saw that Saul was dead, he also fell on his sword, and died with him. ⁶So Saul, his three sons, his armorbearer, and all his men died together that same day.

⁷And when the men of Israel who *were* on the other side of the valley, and *those* who *were* on the other side of the Jordan, saw that the men of Israel had fled and that Saul and his sons were dead, they forsook the cities and fled; and the Philistines came and dwelt in them. ⁸So it happened the next day, when the Philistines came to strip the slain, that they found Saul and his three sons fallen on Mount Gilboa. ⁹And they cut off his head and stripped off his armor, and sent *word* throughout the land of the Philistines, to proclaim *it in* the temple of their idols and among the people. ¹⁰Then they put his armor in the temple of the Ashtoreths, and they fastened his body to the wall of Beth Shan.*a*

¹¹Now when the inhabitants of Jabesh Gilead heard what the Philistines had

---

30:22 *a*Literally *men of Belial*   30:30 *a*Or *Borashan*   31:10 *a*Spelled *Beth Shean* in Joshua 17:11 and elsewhere

done to Saul, ¹²all the valiant men arose and traveled all night, and took the body of Saul and the bodies of his sons from the wall of Beth Shan; and they came to Jabesh and burned them there. ¹³Then they took their bones and buried *them* under the tamarisk tree at Jabesh, and fasted seven days.

31:12,13 bodies...burned. It is thought that the people of Jabesh Gilead burned Saul's body to hide the damage from his head being cut off. **bones buried.** It was disrespectful not to bury the dead. For example, Abraham went to great lengths to bury Sarah (Gen. 23:4–15). **fasted seven days.** Fasting was often associated with mourning in the Hebrew culture and was a sign of respect, seriousness, and grief.

OUTLINE OF 2 SAMUEL

I. THE REIGN OF DAVID AS KING OVER ISRAEL (1:1–20:26)

    A. David's Accession to Kingship over Judah (1:1–3:5)

        1. The deaths of Saul and Jonathan (1:1–27)

        2. David anointed by Judah (2:1–7)

        3. David's victories over the house of Saul (2:8–3:1)

        4. David's wives and sons in Hebron (3:2–5)

    B. David's Accession to Kingship over Israel (3:6–5:16)

        1. The death of Abner and Ishbosheth (3:6–4:12)

        2. David anointed by all Israel (5:1–5)

        3. David's conquest of Jerusalem (5:6–12)

        4. David's wives/sons in Jerusalem (5:13–16)

    C. David's Triumphal Reign (5:17–8:18)

        1. David's victories over the Philistines (5:17–25)

        2. David's spiritual victories (6:1–7:29)

        3. David's victories over the Philistines, Moabites, Arameans, and Edomites (8:1–18)

    D. David's Troubled Reign (9:1–20:26)

        1. David's kindness to Mephibosheth (9:1–13)

        2. David's sins of adultery and murder (10:1–12:31)

        3. David's family troubles (13:1–14:33)

            a. The rape of Tamar (13:1–22)

            b. The murder of Amnon (13:23–39)

            c. The recall and return of Absalom (14:1–33)

        4. The rebellions against David (15:1–20:26)

            a. The rebellion of Absalom (15:1–19:43)

            b. The rebellion of Sheba (20:1–26)

II. EPILOGUE (21:1–24:25)

    A. The Lord's Judgment against Israel (21:1–14)

    B. David's Heroes (21:15–22)

    C. David's Song of Praise (22:1–51)

    D. David's Last Words (23:1–7)

    E. David's Mighty Men (23:8–39)

    F. The Lord's Judgment against David (24:1–25)

The Report of Saul's Death

1 Now it came to pass after the death of Saul, when David had returned from the slaughter of the Amalekites, and David had stayed two days in Ziklag, ²on the third day, behold, it happened that a man came from Saul's camp with his clothes torn and dust on his head. So it was, when he came to David, that he fell to the ground and prostrated himself.

> **1:2 clothes torn and dust on his head.** This was a common cultural sign of anguish over a death (see 15:32).

³And David said to him, "Where have you come from?"

So he said to him, "I have escaped from the camp of Israel."

⁴Then David said to him, "How did the matter go? Please tell me."

And he answered, "The people have fled from the battle, many of the people are fallen and dead, and Saul and Jonathan his son are dead also."

⁵So David said to the young man who told him, "How do you know that Saul and Jonathan his son are dead?"

⁶Then the young man who told him said, "As I happened by chance *to be* on Mount Gilboa, there was Saul, leaning on his spear; and indeed the chariots and horsemen followed hard after him. ⁷Now when he looked behind him, he saw me and called to me. And I answered, 'Here I am.' ⁸And he said to me, 'Who *are* you?' So I answered him, 'I *am* an Amalekite.' ⁹He said to me again, 'Please stand over me and kill me, for anguish has come upon me, but my life still *remains* in me.' ¹⁰So I stood over him and killed him, because I was sure that he could not live after he had fallen. And I took the crown that *was* on his head and the bracelet that *was* on his arm, and have brought them here to my lord."

> **1:10 killed him.** The Amalekite claimed to have killed Saul. However, 1 Sam. 31:3–6 makes it clear that Saul died by falling on his own sword. The Amalekite reached Saul's body before the Philistines and lied about killing him to ingratiate himself with the new king. He brought Saul's crown and bracelet to David, which shows that he was the first to pass by the body of Saul.

¹¹Therefore David took hold of his own clothes and tore them, and *so did* all the men who *were* with him. ¹²And they mourned and wept and fasted until evening for Saul and for Jonathan his son, for the people of the LORD and for the house of Israel, because they had fallen by the sword.

¹³Then David said to the young man who told him, "Where *are* you from?"

And he answered, "I *am* the son of an alien, an Amalekite."

¹⁴So David said to him, "How was it you were not afraid to put forth your hand to destroy the LORD's anointed?" ¹⁵Then David called one of the young men and said, "Go near, *and* execute him!" And he struck him so that he died. ¹⁶So David said to him, "Your blood *is* on your own head, for your own mouth has testified against you, saying, 'I have killed the LORD's anointed.' "

The Song of the Bow

¹⁷Then David lamented with this lamentation over Saul and over Jonathan his son, ¹⁸and he told *them* to teach the children of Judah *the Song of* the Bow; indeed *it is* written in the Book of Jasher:

¹⁹ "The beauty of Israel is slain on your
          high places!
     How the mighty have fallen!
²⁰ Tell *it* not in Gath,
     Proclaim *it* not in the streets of
          Ashkelon—
     Lest the daughters of the Philistines
          rejoice,
     Lest the daughters of the
          uncircumcised triumph.

²¹ "O mountains of Gilboa,
     Let there be no dew nor rain upon
          you,
     Nor fields of offerings.
     For the shield of the mighty is cast
          away there!
     The shield of Saul, not anointed with
          oil.
²² From the blood of the slain,
     From the fat of the mighty,
     The bow of Jonathan did not turn
          back,
     And the sword of Saul did not return
          empty.

23 "Saul and Jonathan *were* beloved and
    pleasant in their lives,
  And in their death they were not
    divided;
  They were swifter than eagles,
  They were stronger than lions.

24 "O daughters of Israel, weep over Saul,
  Who clothed you in scarlet, with
    luxury;
  Who put ornaments of gold on your
    apparel.

25 "How the mighty have fallen in the
    midst of the battle!
  Jonathan *was* slain in your high
    places.
26 I am distressed for you, my brother
    Jonathan;
  You have been very pleasant to me;
  Your love to me was wonderful,
  Surpassing the love of women.

> **1:26 Surpassing the love of women.** The love be-
> tween David and Jonathan was strong, but this does
> not mean that their friendship was superior to the
> bond of love between a man and a woman. They
> shared a noble and loyal commitment of selfless de-
> votion (see 1 Sam. 18:3), which neither had ever felt
> for a woman.

27 "How the mighty have fallen,
  And the weapons of war perished!"

David Anointed King of Judah

2 It happened after this that David inquired of the LORD, saying, "Shall I go
up to any of the cities of Judah?"

And the LORD said to him, "Go up."

David said, "Where shall I go up?"

And He said, "To Hebron."

²So David went up there, and his two
wives also, Ahinoam the Jezreelitess, and
Abigail the widow of Nabal the Carmelite.
³And David brought up the men who *were*
with him, every man with his household.
So they dwelt in the cities of Hebron.
⁴Then the men of Judah came, and there
they anointed David king over the house of
Judah. And they told David, saying, "The
men of Jabesh Gilead *were the ones* who
buried Saul." ⁵So David sent messengers to

the men of Jabesh Gilead, and said to them,
"You *are* blessed of the LORD, for you have
shown this kindness to your lord, to Saul,
and have buried him. ⁶And now may the
LORD show kindness and truth to you. I
also will repay you this kindness, because
you have done this thing. ⁷Now therefore,
let your hands be strengthened, and be valiant; for your master Saul is dead, and also
the house of Judah has anointed me king
over them."

> **2:4 anointed David king.** David had already been
> privately anointed king by Samuel (see 1 Sam. 16:3).
> This anointing recognized his rule in the southern
> area of Judah. Later he would be anointed as king
> over all Israel (see 2 Sam. 5:3).

Ishbosheth Made King of Israel

⁸But Abner the son of Ner, commander of
Saul's army, took Ishbosheth[a] the son of
Saul and brought him over to Mahanaim;
⁹and he made him king over Gilead, over
the Ashurites, over Jezreel, over Ephraim,
over Benjamin, and over all Israel.
¹⁰Ishbosheth, Saul's son, *was* forty years
old when he began to reign over Israel, and
he reigned two years. Only the house of Judah followed David. ¹¹And the time that
David was king in Hebron over the house of
Judah was seven years and six months.

> **2:8 Abner.** Abner was Saul's cousin and the general
> of his army (1 Sam. 14:50,51). He placed Ishbosheth
> on the throne, as he did not recognize David as king.
> This caused tension between Judah and the rest of
> the tribes in Israel. **Ishbosheth.** He was Saul's only
> surviving son and was placed as king over the north-
> ern tribes of Israel and the eastern ones across the
> Jordan. His name means "man of shame."

Israel and Judah at War

¹²Now Abner the son of Ner, and the servants of Ishbosheth the son of Saul, went
out from Mahanaim to Gibeon. ¹³And Joab
the son of Zeruiah, and the servants of David, went out and met them by the pool of
Gibeon. So they sat down, one on one side
of the pool and the other on the other side
of the pool. ¹⁴Then Abner said to Joab, "Let
the young men now arise and compete before us."

2:8 ᵃCalled *Esh-Baal* in 1 Chronicles 8:33 and 9:39

And Joab said, "Let them arise."

¹⁵So they arose and went over by number, twelve from Benjamin, *followers* of Ishbosheth the son of Saul, and twelve from the servants of David. ¹⁶And each one grasped his opponent by the head and *thrust* his sword in his opponent's side; so they fell down together. Therefore that place was called the Field of Sharp Swords,ᵃ which *is* in Gibeon. ¹⁷So there was a very fierce battle that day, and Abner and the men of Israel were beaten before the servants of David.

¹⁸Now the three sons of Zeruiah were there: Joab and Abishai and Asahel. And Asahel *was as* fleet of foot as a wild gazelle. ¹⁹So Asahel pursued Abner, and in going he did not turn to the right hand or to the left from following Abner.

²⁰Then Abner looked behind him and said, "*Are* you Asahel?"

He answered, "I *am*."

²¹And Abner said to him, "Turn aside to your right hand or to your left, and lay hold on one of the young men and take his armor for yourself." But Asahel would not turn aside from following him. ²²So Abner said again to Asahel, "Turn aside from following me. Why should I strike you to the ground? How then could I face your brother Joab?" ²³However, he refused to turn aside. Therefore Abner struck him in the stomach with the blunt end of the spear, so that the spear came out of his back; and he fell down there and died on the spot. So it was *that* as many as came to the place where Asahel fell down and died, stood still.

2:22 How then could I face your brother Joab? Abner wanted to spare Asahel in order to avoid vengeance from Joab or David, but Asahel would not stop his pursuit. Asahel refused to listen to Abner, so Abner was forced to stop Asahel by fatally stabbing him.

²⁴Joab and Abishai also pursued Abner. And the sun was going down when they came to the hill of Ammah, which *is* before Giah by the road to the Wilderness of Gibeon. ²⁵Now the children of Benjamin gathered together behind Abner and became a unit, and took their stand on top of a hill. ²⁶Then Abner called to Joab and said, "Shall the sword devour forever? Do you not know that it will be bitter in the latter end? How long will it be then until you tell the people to return from pursuing their brethren?"

²⁷And Joab said, "*As* God lives, unless you had spoken, surely then by morning all the people would have given up pursuing their brethren." ²⁸So Joab blew a trumpet; and all the people stood still and did not pursue Israel anymore, nor did they fight anymore. ²⁹Then Abner and his men went on all that night through the plain, crossed over the Jordan, and went through all Bithron; and they came to Mahanaim.

³⁰So Joab returned from pursuing Abner. And when he had gathered all the people together, there were missing of David's servants nineteen men and Asahel. ³¹But the servants of David had struck down, of Benjamin and Abner's men, three hundred and sixty men who died. ³²Then they took up Asahel and buried him in his father's tomb, which *was in* Bethlehem. And Joab and his men went all night, and they came to Hebron at daybreak.

3 Now there was a long war between the house of Saul and the house of David. But David grew stronger and stronger, and the house of Saul grew weaker and weaker.

Sons of David

²Sons were born to David in Hebron: His firstborn was Amnon by Ahinoam the Jezreelitess; ³his second, Chileab, by Abigail the widow of Nabal the Carmelite; the third, Absalom the son of Maacah, the daughter of Talmai, king of Geshur; ⁴the fourth, Adonijah the son of Haggith; the fifth, Shephatiah the son of Abital; ⁵and the sixth, Ithream, by David's wife Eglah. These were born to David in Hebron.

Abner Joins Forces with David

⁶Now it was so, while there was war between the house of Saul and the house of David, that Abner was strengthening *his* hold on the house of Saul.

⁷And Saul had a concubine, whose name *was* Rizpah, the daughter of Aiah. So *Ishbosheth* said to Abner, "Why have you gone in to my father's concubine?"

2:16 ᵃHebrew *Helkath Hazzurim*

3:7 Rizpah. Abner took Rizpah, the concubine of Saul, to show the people that he would take the place of Saul as king over Israel. Going in to the king's concubine was a statement of power and rightful claim to the throne (see 16:21,22). Ishbosheth reacted strongly against Abner, and Abner took revenge by taking sides with David (vv. 9,10).

[8]Then Abner became very angry at the words of Ishbosheth, and said, *"Am* I a dog's head that belongs to Judah? Today I show loyalty to the house of Saul your father, to his brothers, and to his friends, and have not delivered you into the hand of David; and you charge me today with a fault concerning this woman? [9]May God do so to Abner, and more also, if I do not do for David as the LORD has sworn to him—[10]to transfer the kingdom from the house of Saul, and set up the throne of David over Israel and over Judah, from Dan to Beersheba." [11]And he could not answer Abner another word, because he feared him.

[12]Then Abner sent messengers on his behalf to David, saying, "Whose *is* the land?" saying *also,* "Make your covenant with me, and indeed my hand *shall be* with you to bring all Israel to you."

[13]And *David* said, "Good, I will make a covenant with you. But one thing I require of you: you shall not see my face unless you first bring Michal, Saul's daughter, when you come to see my face." [14]So David sent messengers to Ishbosheth, Saul's son, saying, "Give *me* my wife Michal, whom I betrothed to myself for a hundred foreskins of the Philistines." [15]And Ishbosheth sent and took her from *her* husband, from Paltiel[a] the son of Laish. [16]Then her husband went along with her to Bahurim, weeping behind her. So Abner said to him, "Go, return!" And he returned.

[17]Now Abner had communicated with the elders of Israel, saying, "In time past

3:13 Michal, Saul's daughter. David requested Michal for two reasons: (1) It would right the wrong Saul had committed by giving Michal, David's first wife who loved him, to another man (1 Sam. 25:44); and (2) it would strengthen David's claim to the throne to have some of Saul's house favorable to his cause.

you were seeking for David *to be* king over you. [18]Now then, do *it!* For the LORD has spoken of David, saying, 'By the hand of My servant David, I[a] will save My people Israel from the hand of the Philistines and the hand of all their enemies.' " [19]And Abner also spoke in the hearing of Benjamin. Then Abner also went to speak in the hearing of David in Hebron all that seemed good to Israel and the whole house of Benjamin.

[20]So Abner and twenty men with him came to David at Hebron. And David made a feast for Abner and the men who *were* with him. [21]Then Abner said to David, "I will arise and go, and gather all Israel to my lord the king, that they may make a covenant with you, and that you may reign over all that your heart desires." So David sent Abner away, and he went in peace.

Joab Murders Abner

[22]At that moment the servants of David and Joab came from a raid and brought much spoil with them. But Abner *was* not with David in Hebron, for he had sent him away, and he had gone in peace. [23]When Joab and all the troops that *were* with him had come, they told Joab, saying, "Abner the son of Ner came to the king, and he sent him away, and he has gone in peace." [24]Then Joab came to the king and said, "What have you done? Look, Abner came to you; why *is* it *that* you sent him away, and he has already gone? [25]Surely you realize that Abner the son of Ner came to deceive you, to know your going out and your coming in, and to know all that you are doing."

[26]And when Joab had gone from David's presence, he sent messengers after Abner, who brought him back from the well of Sirah. But David did not know *it.* [27]Now when Abner had returned to Hebron, Joab took him aside in the gate to speak with

3:27 in the stomach. Abner's death was similar to the death of Joab's brother Asahel, the man whom he had killed (2:23). However, Abner struck Asahel during battle in self-defense, while Joab murdered Abner to avenge Asahel's death.

3:15 [a]Spelled *Palti* in 1 Samuel 25:44　　3:18 [a]Following many Hebrew manuscripts, Septuagint, Syriac, and Targum; Masoretic Text reads *he.*

him privately, and there stabbed him in the stomach, so that he died for the blood of Asahel his brother.

²⁸Afterward, when David heard *it*, he said, "My kingdom and I *are* guiltless before the LORD forever of the blood of Abner the son of Ner. ²⁹Let it rest on the head of Joab and on all his father's house; and let there never fail to be in the house of Joab one who has a discharge or is a leper, who leans on a staff or falls by the sword, or who lacks bread." ³⁰So Joab and Abishai his brother killed Abner, because he had killed their brother Asahel at Gibeon in the battle.

David's Mourning for Abner

³¹Then David said to Joab and to all the people who were with him, "Tear your clothes, gird yourselves with sackcloth, and mourn for Abner." And King David followed the coffin. ³²So they buried Abner in Hebron; and the king lifted up his voice and wept at the grave of Abner, and all the people wept. ³³And the king sang *a lament* over Abner and said:

"Should Abner die as a fool dies?
³⁴ Your hands were not bound
Nor your feet put into fetters;
As a man falls before wicked men, *so* you fell."

Then all the people wept over him again.

³⁵And when all the people came to persuade David to eat food while it was still day, David took an oath, saying, "God do so to me, and more also, if I taste bread or anything else till the sun goes down!" ³⁶Now all the people took note *of it*, and it pleased them, since whatever the king did pleased all the people. ³⁷For all the people and all Israel understood that day that it had not been the king's *intent* to kill Abner the son of Ner. ³⁸Then the king said to his servants, "Do you not know that a prince and a great man has fallen this day in Israel? ³⁹And I *am* weak today, though anointed king; and these men, the sons of Zeruiah, *are* too harsh for me. The LORD shall repay the evildoer according to his wickedness."

3:35–39 David's feelings and conduct in response to Abner's death removed all suspicion of guilt from him and caused the people to favor him as a ruler who would reign more honorably than Abner had (3:17–19).

Ishbosheth Is Murdered

4 When Saul's son[a] heard that Abner had died in Hebron, he lost heart, and all Israel was troubled. ²Now Saul's son *had* two men *who were* captains of troops. The name of one *was* Baanah and the name of the other Rechab, the sons of Rimmon the Beerothite, of the children of Benjamin. (For Beeroth also was *part* of Benjamin, ³because the Beerothites fled to Gittaim and have been sojourners there until this day.)

⁴Jonathan, Saul's son, had a son *who was* lame in *his* feet. He was five years old when the news about Saul and Jonathan came from Jezreel; and his nurse took him up and fled. And it happened, as she made haste to flee, that he fell and became lame. His name *was* Mephibosheth.[a]

⁵Then the sons of Rimmon the Beerothite, Rechab and Baanah, set out and came at about the heat of the day to the house of Ishbosheth, who was lying on his bed at noon. ⁶And they came there, all the way into the house, *as though* to get wheat, and they stabbed him in the stomach. Then Rechab and Baanah his brother escaped. ⁷For when they came into the house, he was lying on his bed in his bedroom; then they struck him and killed him, beheaded him and took his head, and were all night escaping through the plain. ⁸And they brought the head of Ishbosheth to David at Hebron, and said to the king, "Here is the head of Ishbosheth, the son of Saul your enemy, who sought your life; and the LORD has avenged my lord the king this day of Saul and his descendants."

4:8 the LORD has avenged. The murderers of Ishbosheth were surprised when David saw their deed as murder and not as the Lord's vengeance.

⁹But David answered Rechab and Baanah his brother, the sons of Rimmon the Beerothite, and said to them, "*As the LORD lives, who has redeemed my life from all

---

4:1 ᵃThat is, Ishbosheth   4:4 ᵃCalled *Merib-Baal* in 1 Chronicles 8:34 and 9:40

adversity, [10]when someone told me, saying, 'Look, Saul is dead,' thinking to have brought good news, I arrested him and had him executed in Ziklag—the one who *thought* I would give him a reward for *his* news. [11]How much more, when wicked men have killed a righteous person in his own house on his bed? Therefore, shall I not now require his blood at your hand and remove you from the earth?" [12]So David commanded his young men, and they executed them, cut off their hands and feet, and hanged *them* by the pool in Hebron. But they took the head of Ishbosheth and buried *it* in the tomb of Abner in Hebron.

David Reigns over All Israel

5 Then all the tribes of Israel came to David at Hebron and spoke, saying, "Indeed we *are* your bone and your flesh. [2]Also, in time past, when Saul was king over us, you were the one who led Israel out and brought them in; and the LORD said to you, 'You shall shepherd My people Israel, and be ruler over Israel.' " [3]Therefore all the elders of Israel came to the king at Hebron, and King David made a covenant with them at Hebron before the LORD. And they anointed David king over Israel. [4]David *was* thirty years old when he began to reign, *and* he reigned forty years. [5]In Hebron he reigned over Judah seven years and six months, and in Jerusalem he reigned thirty-three years over all Israel and Judah.

> **5:1,2 all the tribes of Israel.** The term "all" is used 3 times (vv. 1,3,5) to emphasize that the kingdom established under King David was a united monarchy. The "elders" of Israel (v. 3), representing the "tribes" (v. 1), came to David to submit to his rule. The Israelites wanted David as king because he was an Israelite brother (see Deut. 17:15), he was Israel's best warrior, and he had been chosen as king by the Lord.

The Conquest of Jerusalem

[6]And the king and his men went to Jerusalem against the Jebusites, the inhabitants of the land, who spoke to David, saying, "You shall not come in here; but the blind and the lame will repel you," thinking, "David cannot come in here." [7]Neverthe-

less David took the stronghold of Zion (that *is*, the City of David).

> **5:7 City of David.** Both Bethlehem, David's birthplace (Luke 2:4), and Jerusalem, David's place of reign, were called by this name.

[8]Now David said on that day, "Whoever climbs up by way of the water shaft and defeats the Jebusites (the lame and the blind, *who are* hated by David's soul), *he shall be chief and captain.*[a] Therefore they say, "The blind and the lame shall not come into the house."

[9]Then David dwelt in the stronghold, and called it the City of David. And David built all around from the Millo[a] and inward. [10]So David went on and became great, and the LORD God of hosts *was* with him.

[11]Then Hiram king of Tyre sent messengers to David, and cedar trees, and carpenters and masons. And they built David a house. [12]So David knew that the LORD had established him as king over Israel, and that He had exalted His kingdom for the sake of His people Israel.

[13]And David took more concubines and wives from Jerusalem, after he had come from Hebron. Also more sons and daughters were born to David. [14]Now these *are* the names of those who were born to him in Jerusalem: Shammua,[a] Shobab, Nathan, Solomon, [15]Ibhar, Elishua,[a] Nepheg, Japhia, [16]Elishama, Eliada, and Eliphelet.

> **5:13 more concubines and wives.** These marriages probably (see 2 Sam. 3:3) reflected David's involvement in foreign treaties and alliances. This cultural institution accounted for some of David's, and many of Solomon's, wives (see 1 Kin. 11:1–3). In each case of polygamy in Scripture, the law of God was violated (see Deut. 17:17), and the consequences were negative.

The Philistines Defeated

[17]Now when the Philistines heard that they had anointed David king over Israel, all the Philistines went up to search for David. And David heard *of it* and went down to the stronghold. [18]The Philistines also went and deployed themselves in the

---

5:8 [a]Compare 1 Chronicles 11:6   5:9 [a]Literally *The Landfill*   5:14 [a]Spelled *Shimea* in 1 Chronicles 3:5   5:15 [a]Spelled *Elishama* in 1 Chronicles 3:6

Valley of Rephaim. ¹⁹So David inquired of the LORD, saying, "Shall I go up against the Philistines? Will You deliver them into my hand?"

And the LORD said to David, "Go up, for I will doubtless deliver the Philistines into your hand."

²⁰So David went to Baal Perazim, and David defeated them there; and he said, "The LORD has broken through my enemies before me, like a breakthrough of water." Therefore he called the name of that place Baal Perazim.ᵃ ²¹And they left their images there, and David and his men carried them away.

²²Then the Philistines went up once again and deployed themselves in the Valley of Rephaim. ²³Therefore David inquired of the LORD, and He said, "You shall not go up; circle around behind them, and come upon them in front of the mulberry trees. ²⁴And it shall be, when you hear the sound of marching in the tops of the mulberry trees, then you shall advance quickly. For then the LORD will go out before you to strike the camp of the Philistines." ²⁵And David did so, as the LORD commanded him; and he drove back the Philistines from Gebaᵃ as far as Gezer.

The Ark Brought to Jerusalem

6 Again David gathered all the choice men of Israel, thirty thousand. ²And David arose and went with all the people who were with him from Baale Judah to bring up from there the ark of God, whose name is called by the Name,ᵃ the LORD of Hosts, who dwells between the cherubim. ³So they set the ark of God on a new cart, and brought it out of the house of Abinadab, which was on the hill; and Uzzah and Ahio, the sons of Abinadab, drove the new cart.ᵃ ⁴And they brought it out of the house of Abinadab, which was on the hill, accompanying the ark of God; and Ahio went before the ark. ⁵Then David and all the house of Israel played music before the LORD on all kinds of instruments of fir wood, on harps, on stringed instruments,

on tambourines, on sistrums, and on cymbals.

⁶And when they came to Nachon's threshing floor, Uzzah put out his hand to the ark of God and took hold of it, for the oxen stumbled. ⁷Then the anger of the LORD was aroused against Uzzah, and God struck him there for his error; and he died there by the ark of God. ⁸And David became angry because of the LORD's outbreak against Uzzah; and he called the name of the place Perez Uzzahᵃ to this day.

> **6:7,8 for his error.** Touching the ark directly violated God's law and resulted in death (see Num. 4:15). This was to preserve the sense of God's holiness and the fear of drawing near to Him without appropriate preparation. **David became angry.** David was probably angry with himself for being careless. He hesitated in taking the ark to Jerusalem, fearing that more death and calamity would come on him or the people (v. 10). He probably waited for God's wrath to subside before moving the ark.

⁹David was afraid of the LORD that day; and he said, "How can the ark of the LORD come to me?" ¹⁰So David would not move the ark of the LORD with him into the City of David; but David took it aside into the house of Obed-Edom the Gittite. ¹¹The ark of the LORD remained in the house of Obed-Edom the Gittite three months. And the LORD blessed Obed-Edom and all his household.

¹²Now it was told King David, saying, "The LORD has blessed the house of Obed-Edom and all that belongs to him, because of the ark of God." So David went and brought up the ark of God from the house of Obed-Edom to the City of David with gladness. ¹³And so it was, when those bearing the ark of the LORD had gone six paces, that he sacrificed oxen and fatted sheep. ¹⁴Then David danced before the LORD with

> **6:14 David danced before the LORD.** The Hebrews had physical expressions of religious joys as they praised God (see Ps. 150:4). **linen ephod.** See 1 Sam. 2:18.

5:20 ᵃLiterally *Master of Breakthroughs*   5:25 ᵃFollowing Masoretic Text, Targum, and Vulgate; Septuagint reads *Gibeon*.   6:2 ᵃSeptuagint, Targum, and Vulgate omit *by the Name*; many Hebrew manuscripts and Syriac read *there*.   6:3 ᵃSeptuagint adds *with the ark*.   6:8 ᵃLiterally *Outburst Against Uzzah*

all *his* might; and David *was* wearing a linen ephod. [15]So David and all the house of Israel brought up the ark of the LORD with shouting and with the sound of the trumpet.

[16]Now as the ark of the LORD came into the City of David, Michal, Saul's daughter, looked through a window and saw King David leaping and whirling before the LORD; and she despised him in her heart. [17]So they brought the ark of the LORD, and set it in its place in the midst of the tabernacle that David had erected for it. Then David offered burnt offerings and peace offerings before the LORD. [18]And when David had finished offering burnt offerings and peace offerings, he blessed the people in the name of the LORD of hosts. [19]Then he distributed among all the people, among the whole multitude of Israel, both the women and the men, to everyone a loaf of bread, a piece *of meat*, and a cake of raisins. So all the people departed, everyone to his house.

[20]Then David returned to bless his household. And Michal the daughter of Saul came out to meet David, and said, "How glorious was the king of Israel today, uncovering himself today in the eyes of the maids of his servants, as one of the base fellows shamelessly uncovers himself!"

[21]So David said to Michal, "*It was* before the LORD, who chose me instead of your father and all his house, to appoint me ruler over the people of the LORD, over Israel. Therefore I will play *music* before the LORD. [22]And I will be even more undignified than this, and will be humble in my own sight. But as for the maidservants of whom you have spoken, by them I will be held in honor."

[23]Therefore Michal the daughter of Saul had no children to the day of her death.

God's Covenant with David

7 Now it came to pass when the king was dwelling in his house, and the LORD had given him rest from all his enemies all around, [2]that the king said to Nathan the prophet, "See now, I dwell in a house of cedar, but the ark of God dwells inside tent curtains."

[3]Then Nathan said to the king, "Go, do all that *is* in your heart, for the LORD *is* with you."

7:5 Would you build a house. The question refers to whether or not David was the one to build the temple. David was not chosen by God to build the temple because he was a blood-shedding warrior (see 1 Chr. 22:8; 28:3).

[4]But it happened that night that the word of the LORD came to Nathan, saying, [5]"Go and tell My servant David, 'Thus says the LORD: "Would you build a house for Me to dwell in? [6]For I have not dwelt in a house since the time that I brought the children of Israel up from Egypt, even to this day, but have moved about in a tent and in a tabernacle. [7]Wherever I have moved about with all the children of Israel, have I ever spoken a word to anyone from the tribes of Israel, whom I commanded to shepherd My people Israel, saying, 'Why have you not built Me a house of cedar?' " ' [8]Now therefore, thus shall you say to My servant David, 'Thus says the LORD of hosts: "I took you from the sheepfold, from following the sheep, to be ruler over My people, over Israel. [9]And I have been with you wherever you have gone, and have cut off all your enemies from before you, and have made you a great name, like the name of the great men who *are* on the earth. [10]Moreover I will appoint a place for My people Israel, and will plant them, that they may dwell in a place of their own and move no more; nor shall the sons of wickedness oppress them anymore, as previously, [11]since the time that I commanded judges *to be* over My people Israel, and have caused you to rest from all your enemies. Also the LORD tells you that He will make you a house.*a*

7:1–17 See 1 Chr. 17:1–15. These verses record the establishment of the Davidic Covenant, God's promise that He would choose a king from the line of David to rule forever (v. 16). This will ultimately be fulfilled through Christ's second coming and His millennial kingdom (see Ezek. 37; Rev. 19). God has made five unconditional covenants in history: (1) Noahic (Gen. 9:8–17); (2) Abrahamic (Gen. 15:12–21); (3) Levitic (Num. 3:1–18); (4) Davidic; and (5) New (Jer. 31:31–34). The last mentioned covenant was accomplished by the death and resurrection of Jesus Christ.

7:11 *a*That is, a royal dynasty

¹²"When your days are fulfilled and you rest with your fathers, I will set up your seed after you, who will come from your body, and I will establish his kingdom. ¹³He shall build a house for My name, and I will establish the throne of his kingdom forever. ¹⁴I will be his Father, and he shall be My son. If he commits iniquity, I will chasten him with the rod of men and with the blows of the sons of men. ¹⁵But My mercy shall not depart from him, as I took *it* from Saul, whom I removed from before you. ¹⁶And your house and your kingdom shall be established forever before you.*ᵃ* Your throne shall be established forever." ' "

> **7:16 your house...your kingdom...Your throne.** Luke 1:32b,33 indicates that these 3 terms are fulfilled in Jesus. **forever.** This word could mean an indeterminately long time or eternity. It does not mean that there cannot be interruptions, but rather that the outcome is guaranteed. Christ's Davidic reign will conclude human history on this side of eternity future.

¹⁷According to all these words and according to all this vision, so Nathan spoke to David.

David's Thanksgiving to God

¹⁸Then King David went in and sat before the LORD; and he said: "Who *am* I, O Lord GOD? And what is my house, that You have brought me this far? ¹⁹And yet this was a small thing in Your sight, O Lord GOD; and You have also spoken of Your servant's house for a great while to come. *Is* this the manner of man, O Lord GOD? ²⁰Now what more can David say to You? For You, Lord GOD, know Your servant. ²¹For Your word's sake, and according to Your own heart, You have done all these great things, to make Your servant know *them*. ²²Therefore You are great, O Lord GOD.*ᵃ* For *there is* none like You, nor *is there any* God besides You, according to all that we have heard with our ears. ²³And who *is* like Your people, like Israel, the one nation on the earth whom God went to redeem for Himself as a people, to make for Himself a name—and to do for Yourself great and awesome deeds for

Your land—before Your people whom You redeemed for Yourself from Egypt, the nations, and their gods? ²⁴For You have made Your people Israel Your very own people forever; and You, LORD, have become their God.

²⁵"Now, O LORD God, the word which You have spoken concerning Your servant and concerning his house, establish *it* forever and do as You have said. ²⁶So let Your name be magnified forever, saying, 'The LORD of hosts *is* the God over Israel.' And let the house of Your servant David be established before You. ²⁷For You, O LORD of hosts, God of Israel, have revealed *this* to Your servant, saying, 'I will build you a house.' Therefore Your servant has found it in his heart to pray this prayer to You.

²⁸"And now, O Lord GOD, You are God, and Your words are true, and You have promised this goodness to Your servant. ²⁹Now therefore, let it please You to bless the house of Your servant, that it may continue before You forever; for You, O Lord GOD, have spoken *it*, and with Your blessing let the house of Your servant be blessed forever."

David's Further Conquests

8 After this it came to pass that David attacked the Philistines and subdued them. And David took Metheg Ammah from the hand of the Philistines.

²Then he defeated Moab. Forcing them down to the ground, he measured them off with a line. With two lines he measured off those to be put to death, and with one full line those to be kept alive. So the Moabites became David's servants, *and* brought tribute.

³David also defeated Hadadezer the son of Rehob, king of Zobah, as he went to recover his territory at the River Euphrates. ⁴David took from him one thousand *chariots*, seven hundred*ᵃ* horsemen, and twenty thousand foot soldiers. Also David hamstrung all the chariot horses, except that he spared *enough* of them for one hundred chariots.

⁵When the Syrians of Damascus came to help Hadadezer king of Zobah, David killed

---

7:16 *ᵃ*Septuagint reads *Me*.   7:22 *ᵃ*Targum and Syriac read *O LORD God*.   8:4 *ᵃ*Or *seven thousand* (compare 1 Chronicles 18:4)

twenty-two thousand of the Syrians. [6]Then David put garrisons in Syria of Damascus; and the Syrians became David's servants, *and* brought tribute. So the LORD preserved David wherever he went. [7]And David took the shields of gold that had belonged to the servants of Hadadezer, and brought them to Jerusalem. [8]Also from Betah[a] and from Berothai, cities of Hadadezer, King David took a large amount of bronze.

[9]When Toi[a] king of Hamath heard that David had defeated all the army of Hadadezer, [10]then Toi sent Joram[a] his son to King David, to greet him and bless him, because he had fought against Hadadezer and defeated him (for Hadadezer had been at war with Toi); and *Joram* brought with him articles of silver, articles of gold, and articles of bronze. [11]King David also dedicated these to the LORD, along with the silver and gold that he had dedicated from all the nations which he had subdued—[12]from Syria,[a] from Moab, from the people of Ammon, from the Philistines, from Amalek, and from the spoil of Hadadezer the son of Rehob, king of Zobah.

[13]And David made *himself* a name when he returned from killing eighteen thousand Syrians[a] in the Valley of Salt. [14]He also put garrisons in Edom; throughout all Edom he put garrisons, and all the Edomites became David's servants. And the LORD preserved David wherever he went.

David's Administration

[15]So David reigned over all Israel; and David administered judgment and justice to all his people. [16]Joab the son of Zeruiah *was* over the army; Jehoshaphat the son of Ahilud *was* recorder; [17]Zadok the son of

Ahitub and Ahimelech the son of Abiathar *were* the priests; Seraiah[a] *was* the scribe; [18]Benaiah the son of Jehoiada *was over* both the Cherethites and the Pelethites; and David's sons were chief ministers.

David's Kindness to Mephibosheth

9 Now David said, "Is there still anyone who is left of the house of Saul, that I may show him kindness for Jonathan's sake?"

> **9:1 show him kindness for Jonathan's sake.** David continued to display loving loyalty toward Jonathan (1 Sam. 20:42) by ministering to the physical needs of his crippled son, Mephibosheth (see 4:4).

[2]And *there was* a servant of the house of Saul whose name *was* Ziba. So when they had called him to David, the king said to him, "*Are* you Ziba?"

He said, "At your service!"

[3]Then the king said, "*Is* there not still someone of the house of Saul, to whom I may show the kindness of God?"

And Ziba said to the king, "There is still a son of Jonathan *who is* lame in *his* feet."

[4]So the king said to him, "Where *is* he?"

And Ziba said to the king, "Indeed he *is* in the house of Machir the son of Ammiel, in Lo Debar."

[5]Then King David sent and brought him out of the house of Machir the son of Ammiel, from Lo Debar.

[6]Now when Mephibosheth the son of Jonathan, the son of Saul, had come to David, he fell on his face and prostrated himself. Then David said, "Mephibosheth?"

And he answered, "Here is your servant!"

[7]So David said to him, "Do not fear, for I will surely show you kindness for Jonathan your father's sake, and will restore to you all the land of Saul your grandfather; and

> **9:1–20:26** These chapters begin with "the house of Saul" (9:1) and end with "Sheba...a Benjamite" (20:1). David is shown to be a failed, but repentant, king. It was only the grace and mercy of the Lord and His irrevocable covenant that kept David from being removed from the kingship, as Saul had been (see 7:15). The emphasis in this section is on the troubles that David brought upon himself by his own sin.

> **9:7 restore...the land of Saul your grandfather.** The estate of Saul was probably quite substantial. **eat bread at my table.** David honored Mephibosheth by bringing him into the royal palace and providing for his daily needs (see 2 Kin. 25:29).

8:8 [a]Spelled *Tibhath* in 1 Chronicles 18:8   8:9 [a]Spelled *Tou* in 1 Chronicles 18:9   8:10 [a]Spelled *Hadoram* in 1 Chronicles 18:10   8:12 [a]Septuagint, Syriac, and some Hebrew manuscripts read *Edom*.   8:13 [a]Septuagint, Syriac, and some Hebrew manuscripts read *Edomites* (compare 1 Chronicles 18:12).   8:17 [a]Spelled *Shavsha* in 1 Chronicles 18:16

you shall eat bread at my table continually."

⁸Then he bowed himself, and said, "What *is* your servant, that you should look upon such a dead dog as I?"

⁹And the king called to Ziba, Saul's servant, and said to him, "I have given to your master's son all that belonged to Saul and to all his house. ¹⁰You therefore, and your sons and your servants, shall work the land for him, and you shall bring in *the harvest*, that your master's son may have food to eat. But Mephibosheth your master's son shall eat bread at my table always." Now Ziba had fifteen sons and twenty servants.

¹¹Then Ziba said to the king, "According to all that my lord the king has commanded his servant, so will your servant do."

"As for Mephibosheth," *said the king,* "he shall eat at my table*ᵃ* like one of the king's sons." ¹²Mephibosheth had a young son whose name *was* Micha. And all who dwelt in the house of Ziba *were* servants of Mephibosheth. ¹³So Mephibosheth dwelt in Jerusalem, for he ate continually at the king's table. And he was lame in both his feet.

The Ammonites and Syrians Defeated

10 It happened after this that the king of the people of Ammon died, and Hanun his son reigned in his place. ²Then David said, "I will show kindness to Hanun the son of Nahash, as his father showed kindness to me."

So David sent by the hand of his servants to comfort him concerning his father. And David's servants came into the land of the people of Ammon. ³And the princes of the people of Ammon said to Hanun their lord, "Do you think that David really honors your father because he has sent comforters to you? Has David not *rather* sent his servants to you to search the city, to spy it out, and to overthrow it?"

⁴Therefore Hanun took David's servants, shaved off half of their beards, cut off their garments in the middle, at their buttocks, and sent them away. ⁵When they told David, he sent to meet them, because the men were greatly ashamed. And the king said, "Wait at Jericho until your beards have grown, and *then* return."

> **10:4 shaved off half of their beards.** Forced shaving was considered an insult and a sign of submission (see Is. 7:20). **cut off their garments...at their buttocks.** Exposure of the buttocks was a shameful practice inflicted on prisoners of war (see Is. 20:4). Perhaps this was partly the concern of Michal in regard to David's dancing in 6:14,20.

⁶When the people of Ammon saw that they had made themselves repulsive to David, the people of Ammon sent and hired the Syrians of Beth Rehob and the Syrians of Zoba, twenty thousand foot soldiers; and from the king of Maacah one thousand men, and from Ish-Tob twelve thousand men. ⁷Now when David heard *of it*, he sent Joab and all the army of the mighty men. ⁸Then the people of Ammon came out and put themselves in battle array at the entrance of the gate. And the Syrians of Zoba, Beth Rehob, Ish-Tob, and Maacah *were* by themselves in the field.

THE KINGDOM OF DAVID

HAMATH

(ZOBAH)

Mediterranean Sea

PHOENICIA

Damascus

Tyre   Dan

Megiddo
Beth Shan
Shechem
Joppa   ISRAEL
        Bethel   Jericho   Rabbah
Ashdod   Jerusalem   (AMMON)
Ashkelon   Gath
Gaza   Hebron   Dead
            Sea
 Raphia   Beersheba
                    (MOAB)
            Zoar

        Bozrah
Kadesh Barnea
        (EDOM)

                    N

Elath

0   60 Mi.
0   60 Km.

© 1996 Thomas Nelson, Inc.

⁹When Joab saw that the battle line was against him before and behind, he chose some of Israel's best and put *them* in battle array against the Syrians. ¹⁰And the rest of the people he put under the command of Abishai his brother, that he might set *them* in battle array against the people of Ammon. ¹¹Then he said, "If the Syrians are too strong for me, then you shall help me; but if the people of Ammon are too strong for you, then I will come and help you. ¹²Be of good courage, and let us be strong for our people and for the cities of our God. And may the LORD do *what is* good in His sight."

¹³So Joab and the people who *were* with him drew near for the battle against the Syrians, and they fled before him. ¹⁴When the people of Ammon saw that the Syrians were fleeing, they also fled before Abishai, and entered the city. So Joab returned from the people of Ammon and went to Jerusalem.

¹⁵When the Syrians saw that they had been defeated by Israel, they gathered together. ¹⁶Then Hadadezer*ᵃ* sent and brought out the Syrians who *were* beyond the River,*ᵇ* and they came to Helam. And Shobach the commander of Hadadezer's army *went* before them. ¹⁷When it was told David, he gathered all Israel, crossed over the Jordan, and came to Helam. And the Syrians set themselves in battle array against David and fought with him. ¹⁸Then the Syrians fled before Israel; and David killed seven hundred charioteers and forty thousand horsemen of the Syrians, and struck Shobach the commander of their army, who died there. ¹⁹And when all the kings *who were* servants to Hadadezer*ᵃ* saw that they were defeated by Israel, they made peace with Israel and served them. So the Syrians were afraid to help the people of Ammon anymore.

David, Bathsheba, and Uriah

11 It happened in the spring of the year, at the time when kings go out *to battle*, that David sent Joab and his servants with him, and all Israel; and they destroyed the people of Ammon and besieged Rabbah. But David remained at Jerusalem.

²Then it happened one evening that David arose from his bed and walked on the roof of the king's house. And from the roof he saw a woman bathing, and the woman *was* very beautiful to behold. ³So David sent and inquired about the woman. And *someone* said, "*Is* this not Bathsheba, the daughter of Eliam, the wife of Uriah the Hittite?" ⁴Then David sent messengers, and took her; and she came to him, and he lay with her, for she was cleansed from her impurity; and she returned to her house. ⁵And the woman conceived; so she sent and told David, and said, "I *am* with child."

11:5 I *am* with child. Bathsheba acknowledged the consequence of her sin. Her sin was punishable by death (Lev. 20:10).

⁶Then David sent to Joab, *saying*, "Send me Uriah the Hittite." And Joab sent Uriah to David. ⁷When Uriah had come to him, David asked how Joab was doing, and how the people were doing, and how the war prospered. ⁸And David said to Uriah, "Go down to your house and wash your feet." So Uriah departed from the king's house, and a gift *of food* from the king followed him. ⁹But Uriah slept at the door of the king's house with all the servants of his lord, and did not go down to his house. ¹⁰So when they told David, saying, "Uriah did not go down to his house," David said to Uriah, "Did you not come from a journey? Why did you not go down to your house?"

11:9 Uriah slept. Wanting to be a loyal example to his soldiers who were still in the field, Uriah did not take advantage of the king's less-than-honorable offer to go home to his wife (v. 11).

¹¹And Uriah said to David, "The ark and Israel and Judah are dwelling in tents, and my lord Joab and the servants of my lord are encamped in the open fields. Shall I then go to my house to eat and drink, and to lie with my wife? *As* you live, and *as* your soul lives, I will not do this thing." ¹²Then David said to Uriah, "Wait here today also, and tomorrow I will let you depart." So Uriah remained in Jerusalem that day and the next. ¹³Now when David called

---

10:16 *ᵃ*Hebrew *Hadarezer*   *ᵇ*That is, the Euphrates   10:19 *ᵃ*Hebrew *Hadarezer*

him, he ate and drank before him; and he made him drunk. And at evening he went out to lie on his bed with the servants of his lord, but he did not go down to his house. [14]In the morning it happened that David wrote a letter to Joab and sent *it* by the hand of Uriah. [15]And he wrote in the letter, saying, "Set Uriah in the forefront of the hottest battle, and retreat from him, that he may be struck down and die." [16]So it was, while Joab besieged the city, that he assigned Uriah to a place where he knew there *were* valiant men. [17]Then the men of the city came out and fought with Joab. And *some* of the people of the servants of David fell; and Uriah the Hittite died also.

> **11:15 he may...die.** Failing twice to cover up his own sin, David panicked and plotted the murder of Uriah. He took advantage of Uriah's loyalty to him and even had Uriah deliver his own death warrant. Thus David engaged in another crime punishable by death (Lev. 24:17).

[18]Then Joab sent and told David all the things concerning the war, [19]and charged the messenger, saying, "When you have finished telling the matters of the war to the king, [20]if it happens that the king's wrath rises, and he says to you: 'Why did you approach so near to the city when you fought? Did you not know that they would shoot from the wall? [21]Who struck Abimelech the son of Jerubbesheth?[a] Was it not a woman who cast a piece of a millstone on him from the wall, so that he died in Thebez? Why did you go near the wall?'—then you shall say, 'Your servant Uriah the Hittite is dead also.' "

[22]So the messenger went, and came and told David all that Joab had sent by him. [23]And the messenger said to David, "Surely the men prevailed against us and came out to us in the field; then we drove them back as far as the entrance of the gate. [24]The archers shot from the wall at your servants; and *some* of the king's servants are dead, and your servant Uriah the Hittite is dead also."

[25]Then David said to the messenger, "Thus you shall say to Joab: 'Do not let this thing displease you, for the sword devours one as well as another. Strengthen your attack against the city, and overthrow it.' So encourage him."

[26]When the wife of Uriah heard that Uriah her husband was dead, she mourned for her husband. [27]And when her mourning was over, David sent and brought her to his house, and she became his wife and bore him a son. But the thing that David had done displeased the LORD.

Nathan's Parable and David's Confession

12 Then the LORD sent Nathan to David. And he came to him, and said to him: "There were two men in one city, one rich and the other poor. [2]The rich *man* had exceedingly many flocks and herds. [3]But the poor *man* had nothing, except one little ewe lamb which he had bought and nourished; and it grew up together with him and with his children. It ate of his own food and drank from his own cup and lay in his bosom; and it was like a daughter to him. [4]And a traveler came to the rich man, who refused to take from his own flock and from his own herd to prepare one for the wayfaring man who had come to him; but he took the poor man's lamb and prepared it for the man who had come to him."

[5]So David's anger was greatly aroused against the man, and he said to Nathan, "*As* the LORD lives, the man who has done this shall surely die! [6]And he shall restore fourfold for the lamb, because he did this thing and because he had no pity."

> **12:5 shall surely die.** The rich man represented David, the poor man, Uriah, and the ewe lamb, Bathsheba. Here, the stealing and slaughtering of the lamb represented the adultery with Bathsheba and the murder of Uriah by David. According to the Mosaic law, both adultery (Lev. 20:10) and murder (Lev. 24:17) required punishment by death. David condemned himself to death with his judgment on the rich man in the parable.

[7]Then Nathan said to David, "You *are* the man! Thus says the LORD God of Israel: 'I anointed you king over Israel, and I delivered you from the hand of Saul. [8]I gave you your master's house and your master's wives into your keeping, and gave you the

---

11:21 [a]Same as *Jerubbaal* (Gideon), Judges 6:32ff

house of Israel and Judah. And if *that had been* too little, I also would have given you much more! ⁹Why have you despised the commandment of the LORD, to do evil in His sight? You have killed Uriah the Hittite with the sword; you have taken his wife *to be* your wife, and have killed him with the sword of the people of Ammon. ¹⁰Now therefore, the sword shall never depart from your house, because you have despised Me, and have taken the wife of Uriah the Hittite to be your wife.' ¹¹Thus says the LORD: 'Behold, I will raise up adversity against you from your own house; and I will take your wives before your eyes and give *them* to your neighbor, and he shall lie with your wives in the sight of this sun. ¹²For you did *it* secretly, but I will do this thing before all Israel, before the sun.' "

¹³So David said to Nathan, "I have sinned against the LORD."

And Nathan said to David, "The LORD also has put away your sin; you shall not die. ¹⁴However, because by this deed you have given great occasion to the enemies of the LORD to blaspheme, the child also *who is* born to you shall surely die." ¹⁵Then Nathan departed to his house.

> **12:13 I have sinned against the LORD.** David did not attempt to justify his sin. His confession was immediate (see Pss. 32, 51). **The LORD also has put away your sin.** The Lord graciously forgave David, but David still experienced the consequences of his sin. **you shall not die.** Although David deserved death for his sin, the Lord graciously removed the death penalty from him. At times in the Old Testament God showed justice by requiring death, and other times He spared a sinner by grace.

The Death of David's Son

And the LORD struck the child that Uriah's wife bore to David, and it became ill. ¹⁶David therefore pleaded with God for the child, and David fasted and went in and lay all night on the ground. ¹⁷So the elders of his house arose *and went* to him, to raise him up from the ground. But he would not, nor did he eat food with them. ¹⁸Then on the seventh day it came to pass that the child died. And the servants of David were afraid to tell him that the child was dead. For they said, "Indeed, while the child was alive, we spoke to him, and he would not heed our voice. How can we tell him that the child is dead? He may do some harm!" ¹⁹When David saw that his servants were whispering, David perceived that the child was dead. Therefore David said to his servants, "Is the child dead?"

And they said, "He is dead."

²⁰So David arose from the ground, washed and anointed himself, and changed his clothes; and he went into the house of the LORD and worshiped. Then he went to his own house; and when he requested, they set food before him, and he ate. ²¹Then his servants said to him, "What *is* this that you have done? You fasted and wept for the child *while he was* alive, but when the child died, you arose and ate food."

²²And he said, "While the child was alive, I fasted and wept; for I said, 'Who can tell *whether* the LORD[a] will be gracious to me, that the child may live?' ²³But now he is dead; why should I fast? Can I bring him back again? I shall go to him, but he shall not return to me."

Solomon Is Born

²⁴Then David comforted Bathsheba his wife, and went in to her and lay with her. So she bore a son, and he[a] called his name Solomon. Now the LORD loved him, ²⁵and He sent *word* by the hand of Nathan the prophet: So he[a] called his name Jedidiah,[b] because of the LORD.

> **12:25 Jedidiah.** "Beloved of the LORD" was Nathan's name for Solomon, who was loved in the sense of being chosen by the Lord to be the successor to David's throne, a remarkable example of God's grace considering the sinful nature of the marriage.

Rabbah Is Captured

²⁶Now Joab fought against Rabbah of the people of Ammon, and took the royal city. ²⁷And Joab sent messengers to David, and said, "I have fought against Rabbah, and I have taken the city's water *supply*. ²⁸Now therefore, gather the rest of the people to-

---

12:22 [a]A few Hebrew manuscripts and Syriac read *God*.   12:24 [a]Following Kethib, Septuagint, and Vulgate; Qere, a few Hebrew manuscripts, Syriac, and Targum read *she*.   12:25 [a]Qere, some Hebrew manuscripts, Syriac, and Targum read *she*.   [b]Literally *Beloved of the LORD*

gether and encamp against the city and take it, lest I take the city and it be called after my name." ²⁹So David gathered all the people together and went to Rabbah, fought against it, and took it. ³⁰Then he took their king's crown from his head. Its weight *was* a talent of gold, with precious stones. And it was *set* on David's head. Also he brought out the spoil of the city in great abundance. ³¹And he brought out the people who *were* in it, and put *them to work* with saws and iron picks and iron axes, and made them cross over to the brick works. So he did to all the cities of the people of Ammon. Then David and all the people returned to Jerusalem.

Amnon and Tamar

13 After this Absalom the son of David had a lovely sister, whose name *was* Tamar; and Amnon the son of David loved her. ²Amnon was so distressed over his sister Tamar that he became sick; for she *was* a virgin. And it was improper for Amnon to do anything to her. ³But Amnon had a friend whose name *was* Jonadab the son of Shimeah, David's brother. Now Jonadab *was* a very crafty man. ⁴And he said to him, "Why *are* you, the king's son, becoming thinner day after day? Will you not tell me?"

Amnon said to him, "I love Tamar, my brother Absalom's sister."

⁵So Jonadab said to him, "Lie down on your bed and pretend to be ill. And when your father comes to see you, say to him, 'Please let my sister Tamar come and give me food, and prepare the food in my sight, that I may see *it* and eat it from her hand.' "
⁶Then Amnon lay down and pretended to be ill; and when the king came to see him, Amnon said to the king, "Please let Tamar my sister come and make a couple of cakes for me in my sight, that I may eat from her hand."

⁷And David sent home to Tamar, saying, "Now go to your brother Amnon's house, and prepare food for him." ⁸So Tamar went to her brother Amnon's house; and he was lying down. Then she took flour and kneaded *it*, made cakes in his sight, and baked the cakes. ⁹And she took the pan and placed *them* out before him, but he refused to eat. Then Amnon said, "Have everyone go out from me." And they all went out

from him. ¹⁰Then Amnon said to Tamar, "Bring the food into the bedroom, that I may eat from your hand." And Tamar took the cakes which she had made, and brought *them* to Amnon her brother in the bedroom. ¹¹Now when she had brought *them* to him to eat, he took hold of her and said to her, "Come, lie with me, my sister."

¹²But she answered him, "No, my brother, do not force me, for no such thing should be done in Israel. Do not do this disgraceful thing! ¹³And I, where could I take my shame? And as for you, you would be like one of the fools in Israel. Now therefore, please speak to the king; for he will not withhold me from you." ¹⁴However, he would not heed her voice; and being stronger than she, he forced her and lay with her.

> **13:12,13 this disgraceful thing.** Tamar appealed to Amnon with 4 reasons why he should not rape her. First, it violated the law of God (see Lev. 18:11). **my shame.** Second, Tamar would be scorned for being defiled. **like one of the fools in Israel.** Third, the people would regard Amnon as a wicked fool for jeopardizing his right to the throne. **the king...will not withhold me from you.** Fourth, Tamar desperately appealed to Amnon to marry her first.

¹⁵Then Amnon hated her exceedingly, so that the hatred with which he hated her *was* greater than the love with which he had loved her. And Amnon said to her, "Arise, be gone!"

¹⁶So she said to him, "No, indeed! This evil of sending me away *is* worse than the other that you did to me."

But he would not listen to her. ¹⁷Then he called his servant who attended him, and said, "Here! Put this *woman* out, away from me, and bolt the door behind her." ¹⁸Now she had on a robe of many colors, for the king's virgin daughters wore such apparel. And his servant put her out and bolted the door behind her.

¹⁹Then Tamar put ashes on her head, and tore her robe of many colors that *was* on her, and laid her hand on her head and went away crying bitterly. ²⁰And Absalom her brother said to her, "Has Amnon your brother been with you? But now hold your peace, my sister. He *is* your brother; do not take this thing to heart." So Tamar remained desolate in her brother Absalom's house.

²¹But when King David heard of all these things, he was very angry. ²²And Absalom spoke to his brother Amnon neither good nor bad. For Absalom hated Amnon, because he had forced his sister Tamar.

Absalom Murders Amnon

²³And it came to pass, after two full years, that Absalom had sheepshearers in Baal Hazor, which *is* near Ephraim; so Absalom invited all the king's sons. ²⁴Then Absalom came to the king and said, "Kindly note, your servant has sheepshearers; please, let the king and his servants go with your servant."

²⁵But the king said to Absalom, "No, my son, let us not all go now, lest we be a burden to you." Then he urged him, but he would not go; and he blessed him.

²⁶Then Absalom said, "If not, please let my brother Amnon go with us."

And the king said to him, "Why should he go with you?" ²⁷But Absalom urged him; so he let Amnon and all the king's sons go with him.

²⁸Now Absalom had commanded his servants, saying, "Watch now, when Amnon's heart is merry with wine, and when I say to you, 'Strike Amnon!' then kill him. Do not be afraid. Have I not commanded you? Be courageous and valiant." ²⁹So the servants of Absalom did to Amnon as Absalom had commanded. Then all the king's sons arose, and each one got on his mule and fled.

³⁰And it came to pass, while they were on the way, that news came to David, saying, "Absalom has killed all the king's sons, and not one of them is left!" ³¹So the king arose and tore his garments and lay on the ground, and all his servants stood by with their clothes torn. ³²Then Jonadab the son of Shimeah, David's brother, answered and said, "Let not my lord suppose they have killed all the young men, the king's sons, for only Amnon is dead. For by the command of Absalom this has been determined from the day that he forced his sister Tamar. ³³Now therefore, let not my lord the king take the thing to his heart, to think that all the king's sons are dead. For only Amnon is dead."

Absalom Flees to Geshur

³⁴Then Absalom fled. And the young man who was keeping watch lifted his eyes and looked, and there, many people were coming from the road on the hillside behind him.ᵃ ³⁵And Jonadab said to the king, "Look, the king's sons are coming; as your servant said, so it is." ³⁶So it was, as soon as he had finished speaking, that the king's sons indeed came, and they lifted up their voice and wept. Also the king and all his servants wept very bitterly.

³⁷But Absalom fled and went to Talmai the son of Ammihud, king of Geshur. And *David* mourned for his son every day. ³⁸So Absalom fled and went to Geshur, and was there three years. ³⁹And King Davidᵃ longed to go toᵇ Absalom. For he had been comforted concerning Amnon, because he was dead.

Absalom Returns to Jerusalem

14 So Joab the son of Zeruiah perceived that the king's heart *was* concerned about Absalom. ²And Joab sent to Tekoa and brought from there a wise woman, and said to her, "Please pretend to be a mourner, and put on mourning apparel; do not anoint yourself with oil, but act like a woman who has been mourning a long

---

13:34 ᵃSeptuagint adds *And the watchman went and told the king, and said, "I see men from the way of Horonaim, from the regions of the mountains."* 13:39 ᵃFollowing Masoretic Text, Syriac, and Vulgate; Septuagint reads *the spirit of the king;* Targum reads *the soul of King David.* ᵇFollowing Masoretic Text and Targum; Septuagint and Vulgate read *ceased to pursue after.*

time for the dead. ³Go to the king and speak to him in this manner." So Joab put the words in her mouth.

⁴And when the woman of Tekoa spoke[a] to the king, she fell on her face to the ground and prostrated herself, and said, "Help, O king!"

⁵Then the king said to her, "What troubles you?"

And she answered, "Indeed I *am* a widow, my husband is dead. ⁶Now your maidservant had two sons; and the two fought with each other in the field, and *there was* no one to part them, but the one struck the other and killed him. ⁷And now the whole family has risen up against your maidservant, and they said, 'Deliver him who struck his brother, that we may execute him for the life of his brother whom he killed; and we will destroy the heir also.' So they would extinguish my ember that is left, and leave to my husband *neither* name nor remnant on the earth."

⁸Then the king said to the woman, "Go to your house, and I will give orders concerning you."

⁹And the woman of Tekoa said to the king, "My lord, O king, *let* the iniquity *be* on me and on my father's house, and the king and his throne *be* guiltless."

¹⁰So the king said, "Whoever says *anything* to you, bring him to me, and he shall not touch you anymore."

¹¹Then she said, "Please let the king remember the LORD your God, and do not permit the avenger of blood to destroy anymore, lest they destroy my son."

And he said, "*As* the LORD lives, not one hair of your son shall fall to the ground."

¹²Therefore the woman said, "Please, let your maidservant speak *another* word to my lord the king."

And he said, "Say on."

¹³So the woman said: "Why then have you schemed such a thing against the people of God? For the king speaks this thing

as one who is guilty, *in that* the king does not bring his banished one home again. ¹⁴For we will surely die and *become* like water spilled on the ground, which cannot be gathered up again. Yet God does not take away a life; but He devises means, so that His banished ones are not expelled from Him. ¹⁵Now therefore, I have come to speak of this thing to my lord the king because the people have made me afraid. And your maidservant said, 'I will now speak to the king; it may be that the king will perform the request of his maidservant. ¹⁶For the king will hear and deliver his maidservant from the hand of the man *who would* destroy me and my son together from the inheritance of God.' ¹⁷Your maidservant said, 'The word of my lord the king will now be comforting; for as the angel of God, so *is* my lord the king in discerning good and evil. And may the LORD your God be with you.' "

¹⁸Then the king answered and said to the woman, "Please do not hide from me anything that I ask you."

And the woman said, "Please, let my lord the king speak."

¹⁹So the king said, "*Is* the hand of Joab with you in all this?" And the woman answered and said, "*As* you live, my lord the king, no one can turn to the right hand or to the left from anything that my lord the king has spoken. For your servant Joab commanded me, and he put all these words in the mouth of your maidservant. ²⁰To bring about this change of affairs your servant Joab has done this thing; but my lord *is* wise, according to the wisdom of the angel of God, to know everything that *is* in the earth."

²¹And the king said to Joab, "All right, I have granted this thing. Go therefore, bring back the young man Absalom."

²²Then Joab fell to the ground on his face and bowed himself, and thanked the king. And Joab said, "Today your servant knows that I have found favor in your sight, my lord, O king, in that the king has fulfilled the request of his servant." ²³So Joab arose and went to Geshur, and brought Absalom to Jerusalem. ²⁴And the king said, "Let him return to his own house, but do not let him

14:13 against the people of God. The woman claimed that by allowing Absalom to remain in exile, David had jeopardized the future welfare of Israel. If he would be so generous to a son and a family he did not know, would he not forgive his own son?

14:4 [a]Many Hebrew manuscripts, Septuagint, Syriac, and Vulgate read *came*.

see my face." So Absalom returned to his own house, but did not see the king's face.

David Forgives Absalom

25Now in all Israel there was no one who was praised as much as Absalom for his good looks. From the sole of his foot to the crown of his head there was no blemish in him. 26And when he cut the hair of his head—at the end of every year he cut *it* because it was heavy on him—when he cut it, he weighed the hair of his head at two hundred shekels according to the king's standard. 27To Absalom were born three sons, and one daughter whose name *was* Tamar. She was a woman of beautiful appearance.

14:25 his good looks. Absalom looked like a king, just as Saul had (1 Sam. 9:1,2). His popularity came from his appearance.

28And Absalom dwelt two full years in Jerusalem, but did not see the king's face. 29Therefore Absalom sent for Joab, to send him to the king, but he would not come to him. And when he sent again the second time, he would not come. 30So he said to his servants, "See, Joab's field is near mine, and he has barley there; go and set it on fire." And Absalom's servants set the field on fire.

14:28 two full years. David stayed away from Absalom in order to lead his son through a time of repentance and restoration. Rather than producing repentance, however, Absalom's non-access to the royal court frustrated him so that he sent for Joab to intercede (v. 29).

31Then Joab arose and came to Absalom's house, and said to him, "Why have your servants set my field on fire?"

32And Absalom answered Joab, "Look, I sent to you, saying, 'Come here, so that I may send you to the king, to say, "Why have I come from Geshur? *It would be* better for me *to be* there still." ' Now therefore, let me see the king's face; but if there is iniquity in me, let him execute me."

33So Joab went to the king and told him. And when he had called for Absalom, he came to the king and bowed himself on his face to the ground before the king. Then the king kissed Absalom.

Absalom's Treason

15 After this it happened that Absalom provided himself with chariots and horses, and fifty men to run before him. 2Now Absalom would rise early and stand beside the way to the gate. *So* it was, whenever anyone who had a lawsuit came to the king for a decision, that Absalom would call to him and say, "What city *are* you from?" And he would say, "Your servant *is* from such and such a tribe of Israel." 3Then Absalom would say to him, "Look, your case *is* good and right; but *there is* no deputy of the king to hear you." 4Moreover Absalom would say, "Oh, that I were made judge in the land, and everyone who has any suit or cause would come to me; then I would give him justice." 5And *so* it was, whenever anyone came near to bow down to him, that he would put out his hand and take him and kiss him. 6In this manner Absalom acted toward all Israel who came to the king for judgment. So Absalom stole the hearts of the men of Israel.

15:1–6 stole the hearts. King David was busy with other matters, such as war, leaving many matters unresolved. This caused feelings of resentment among the people. Absalom used the situation to undermine his father and positioned himself outside the city gates to win the people's favor with his warm, seemingly innocent cordiality.

7Now it came to pass after forty[a] years that Absalom said to the king, "Please, let me go to Hebron and pay the vow which I made to the LORD. 8For your servant took a vow while I dwelt at Geshur in Syria, saying, 'If the LORD indeed brings me back to Jerusalem, then I will serve the LORD.' "

9And the king said to him, "Go in peace." So he arose and went to Hebron.

10Then Absalom sent spies throughout all the tribes of Israel, saying, "As soon as you hear the sound of the trumpet, then you shall say, 'Absalom reigns in Hebron!' " 11And with Absalom went two hundred men invited from Jerusalem, and they went along innocently and did not know any-

---

15:7 [a]Septuagint manuscripts, Syriac, and Josephus read *four*.

thing. [12]Then Absalom sent for Ahithophel the Gilonite, David's counselor, from his city—from Giloh—while he offered sacrifices. And the conspiracy grew strong, for the people with Absalom continually increased in number.

> **15:10–12** Absalom conspired against David by taking some of the leading men to create the impression that the King was sharing his kingdom in his old age. This was all a disguise so that Absalom could freely plan his revolution. His cleverness and his father's carelessness allowed him to do it (see 1 Kin. 1:6).

David Escapes from Jerusalem

[13]Now a messenger came to David, saying, "The hearts of the men of Israel are with Absalom."

[14]So David said to all his servants who *were* with him at Jerusalem, "Arise, and let us flee, or we shall not escape from Absalom. Make haste to depart, lest he overtake us suddenly and bring disaster upon us, and strike the city with the edge of the sword."

[15]And the king's servants said to the king, "We *are* your servants, *ready to do* whatever my lord the king commands." [16]Then the king went out with all his household after him. But the king left ten women, concubines, to keep the house. [17]And the king went out with all the people after him, and stopped at the outskirts. [18]Then all his servants passed before him; and all the Cherethites, all the Pelethites, and all the Gittites, six hundred men who had followed him from Gath, passed before the king.

[19]Then the king said to Ittai the Gittite, "Why are you also going with us? Return and remain with the king. For you *are* a foreigner and also an exile from your own place. [20]In fact, you came *only* yesterday. Should I make you wander up and down with us today, since I go I know not where? Return, and take your brethren back. Mercy and truth *be* with you."

[21]But Ittai answered the king and said, "*As* the LORD lives, and *as* my lord the king lives, surely in whatever place my lord the king shall be, whether in death or life, even there also your servant will be."

[22]So David said to Ittai, "Go, and cross over." Then Ittai the Gittite and all his men and all the little ones who *were* with him crossed over. [23]And all the country wept with a loud voice, and all the people crossed over. The king himself also crossed over the Brook Kidron, and all the people crossed over toward the way of the wilderness.

[24]There was Zadok also, and all the Levites with him, bearing the ark of the covenant of God. And they set down the ark of God, and Abiathar went up until all the people had finished crossing over from the city. [25]Then the king said to Zadok, "Carry the ark of God back into the city. If I find favor in the eyes of the LORD, He will bring me back and show me *both* it and His dwelling place. [26]But if He says thus: 'I have no delight in you,' here I am, let Him do to me as seems good to Him." [27]The king also said to Zadok the priest, "*Are* you *not* a seer? Return to the city in peace, and your two sons with you, Ahimaaz your son, and Jonathan the son of Abiathar. [28]See, I will wait in the plains of the wilderness until word comes from you to inform me." [29]Therefore Zadok and Abiathar carried the ark of God back to Jerusalem. And they remained there.

[30]So David went up by the Ascent of the *Mount of* Olives, and wept as he went up; and he had his head covered and went barefoot. And all the people who *were* with him covered their heads and went up, weeping as they went up. [31]Then *someone* told David, saying, "Ahithophel *is* among the conspirators with Absalom." And David said, "O LORD, I pray, turn the counsel of Ahithophel into foolishness!"

[32]Now it happened when David had come to the top *of the mountain*, where he worshiped God—there was Hushai the Archite coming to meet him with his robe torn and dust on his head. [33]David said to him, "If you go on with me, then you will become a burden to me. [34]But if you return to the city, and say to Absalom, 'I will be your servant, O king; *as* I *was* your father's servant previously, so I *will* now also *be* your servant,' then you may defeat the counsel of Ahithophel for me. [35]And *do* you not *have* Zadok and Abiathar the priests with you there? Therefore it will be *that* whatever you hear from the king's house, you shall tell to Zadok and Abiathar the priests. [36]Indeed *they have* there with them their two sons,

Ahimaaz, Zadok's *son*, and Jonathan, Abiathar's *son;* and by them you shall send me everything you hear."

37So Hushai, David's friend, went into the city. And Absalom came into Jerusalem.

Mephibosheth's Servant

16 When David was a little past the top of *the mountain*, there was Ziba the servant of Mephibosheth, who met him with a couple of saddled donkeys, and on them two hundred *loaves* of bread, one hundred clusters of raisins, one hundred summer fruits, and a skin of wine. 2And the king said to Ziba, "What do you mean to do with these?"

So Ziba said, "The donkeys *are* for the king's household to ride on, the bread and summer fruit for the young men to eat, and the wine for those who are faint in the wilderness to drink."

3Then the king said, "And where *is* your master's son?"

And Ziba said to the king, "Indeed he is staying in Jerusalem, for he said, 'Today the house of Israel will restore the kingdom of my father to me.' "

16:3 restore the kingdom of my father. Ziba tried to commend himself in the eyes of David by bringing gifts and accusing his master of disloyalty to the king and participation in Absalom's conspiracy. He wanted the house of Saul to re-take the throne so that he would be king. This was a false accusation (see 19:24,25), but David believed the story and made a severe decision that inflicted injury on a true friend, Mephibosheth.

4So the king said to Ziba, "Here, all that *belongs* to Mephibosheth *is* yours."

And Ziba said, "I humbly bow before you, *that* I may find favor in your sight, my lord, O king!"

Shimei Curses David

5Now when King David came to Bahurim, there was a man from the family of the house of Saul, whose name *was* Shimei the son of Gera, coming from there. He came out, cursing continuously as he came. 6And

If we accept the scholarly view that the surviving ancient manuscripts of 1 and 2 Samuel were relatively poorly preserved, what should be our attitude toward these books as part of God's Word?

Given the challenges involved in hand-copying and preserving scrolls, it is a wonder that we have the ancient documents that we do have. Our attitude ought to lean more towards amazement that we have such few discrepancies rather than over the ones that puzzle and challenge us.

Many of the discoveries in the science of analyzing ancient manuscripts involve the typical errors that commonly appear when handwritten documents are copied. For example, when two lines of text end with the same word or words, the eye of the copyist tends to skip the second line, deleting it completely. Careful comparisons between manuscripts and reconstruction of the text often reveal these simple errors.

In the case of 1 and 2 Samuel we have two ancient text families: (1) the Masoretic text, in the Hebrew language and (2) the LXX (Septuagint) text in Greek that was translated by Jewish scholars in about 100 B.C. Comparing the two, it is clear that the two differ in more places with the Samuel books than with other Old Testament books. There are frequent disagreements between the texts when it comes to numbers. In settling these discrepancies, the age and language of the Masoretic text is generally considered a closer version of the original manuscript unless grammar and context indicate a copying error.

A central fact to remember when thinking about the possibility of textual errors in the Scriptures we have is the following: The central doctrines of the Christian faith are never based on a single verse of Scripture, nor do they rely on a disputed section of Scripture. God's plan of salvation and the main outline of Christian teaching can be found throughout Scripture.

he threw stones at David and at all the servants of King David. And all the people and all the mighty men *were* on his right hand and on his left. [7]Also Shimei said thus when he cursed: "Come out! Come out! You bloodthirsty man, you rogue! [8]The LORD has brought upon you all the blood of the house of Saul, in whose place you have reigned; and the LORD has delivered the kingdom into the hand of Absalom your son. So now you *are caught* in your own evil, because you are a bloodthirsty man!"

[9]Then Abishai the son of Zeruiah said to the king, "Why should this dead dog curse my lord the king? Please, let me go over and take off his head!"

[10]But the king said, "What have I to do with you, you sons of Zeruiah? So let him curse, because the LORD has said to him, 'Curse David.' Who then shall say, 'Why have you done so?'"

[11]And David said to Abishai and all his servants, "See how my son who came from my own body seeks my life. How much more now *may this* Benjamite? Let him alone, and let him curse; for so the LORD has ordered him. [12]It may be that the LORD will look on my affliction,[a] and that the LORD will repay me with good for his cursing this day." [13]And as David and his men went along the road, Shimei went along the hillside opposite him and cursed as he went, threw stones at him and kicked up dust. [14]Now the king and all the people who *were* with him became weary; so they refreshed themselves there.

16:10–14 David's patience and restraint on this occasion were different than his violent reaction to the slanderous words of Nabal (1 Sam. 25:2ff). On that occasion he was eager to kill the man before Abigail calmed him. This time, he was a broken, repentant man, and he knew that Shimei's accusations were true, even though his cursing and actions were uncalled for.

The Advice of Ahithophel

[15]Meanwhile Absalom and all the people, the men of Israel, came to Jerusalem; and Ahithophel *was* with him. [16]And so it was, when Hushai the Archite, David's friend, came to Absalom, that Hushai said to Absalom, "*Long* live the king! *Long* live the king!"

[17]So Absalom said to Hushai, "*Is* this your loyalty to your friend? Why did you not go with your friend?"

[18]And Hushai said to Absalom, "No, but whom the LORD and this people and all the men of Israel choose, his I will be, and with him I will remain. [19]"Furthermore, whom should I serve? *Should I* not *serve* in the presence of his son? As I have served in your father's presence, so will I be in your presence."

[20]Then Absalom said to Ahithophel, "Give advice as to what we should do."

[21]And Ahithophel said to Absalom, "Go in to your father's concubines, whom he has left to keep the house; and all Israel will hear that you are abhorred by your father. Then the hands of all who are with you will be strong." [22]So they pitched a tent for Absalom on the top of the house, and Absalom went in to his father's concubines in the sight of all Israel.

16:21,22 your father's concubines. David had left 10 concubines in Jerusalem to take care of the palace (15:16). Ahithophel advised Absalom to have sexual relations with David's concubines in order to claim his right to his father's throne. A tent was set up for this scandalous event on the roof of the palace, in the most public place (see 11:2). This fulfilled the judgment announced by Nathan in 12:11,12.

[23]Now the advice of Ahithophel, which he gave in those days, *was* as if one had inquired at the oracle of God. So *was* all the advice of Ahithophel both with David and with Absalom.

17 Moreover Ahithophel said to Absalom, "Now let me choose twelve thousand men, and I will arise and pursue David tonight. [2]I will come upon him while he *is* weary and weak, and make him afraid. And all the people who *are* with him will flee, and I will strike only the king. [3]Then I will bring back all the people to you. When all return except the man whom you seek, all the people will be at peace." [4]And the saying pleased Absalom and all the elders of Israel.

16:12 [a]Following Kethib, Septuagint, Syriac, and Vulgate; Qere reads *my eyes;* Targum reads *tears of my eyes.*

The Advice of Hushai

[5] Then Absalom said, "Now call Hushai the Archite also, and let us hear what he says too." [6] And when Hushai came to Absalom, Absalom spoke to him, saying, "Ahithophel has spoken in this manner. Shall we do as he says? If not, speak up."

[7] So Hushai said to Absalom: "The advice that Ahithophel has given is not good at this time. [8] For," said Hushai, "you know your father and his men, that they *are* mighty men, and they *are* enraged in their minds, like a bear robbed of her cubs in the field; and your father *is* a man of war, and will not camp with the people. [9] Surely by now he is hidden in some pit, or in some *other* place. And it will be, when some of them are overthrown at the first, that whoever hears *it* will say, 'There is a slaughter among the people who follow Absalom.' [10] And even he *who is* valiant, whose heart *is* like the heart of a lion, will melt completely. For all Israel knows that your father *is* a mighty man, and *those* who *are* with him *are* valiant men. [11] Therefore I advise that all Israel be fully gathered to you, from Dan to Beersheba, like the sand that *is* by the sea for multitude, and that you go to battle in person. [12] So we will come upon him in some place where he may be found, and we will fall on him as the dew falls on the ground. And of him and all the men who *are* with him there shall not be left so much as one. [13] Moreover, if he has withdrawn into a city, then all Israel shall bring ropes to that city; and we will pull it into the river, until there is not one small stone found there."

> **17:7–13** The Lord used Hushai's counsel to control the situation so that David had time to prepare for war. The plan called for an army larger than 12,000 (v. 1) so that Absalom would not lose, and it stated that the king should lead the army into battle, which appealed to Absalom's arrogance.

[14] So Absalom and all the men of Israel said, "The advice of Hushai the Archite *is* better than the advice of Ahithophel." For the LORD had purposed to defeat the good advice of Ahithophel, to the intent that the LORD might bring disaster on Absalom.

Hushai Warns David to Escape

[15] Then Hushai said to Zadok and Abiathar the priests, "Thus and so Ahithophel advised Absalom and the elders of Israel, and thus and so I have advised. [16] Now therefore, send quickly and tell David, saying, 'Do not spend this night in the plains of the wilderness, but speedily cross over, lest the king and all the people who *are* with him be swallowed up.' " [17] Now Jonathan and Ahimaaz stayed at En Rogel, for they dared not be seen coming into the city; so a female servant would come and tell them, and they would go and tell King David. [18] Nevertheless a lad saw them, and told Absalom. But both of them went away quickly and came to a man's house in Bahurim, who had a well in his court; and they went down into it. [19] Then the woman took and spread a covering over the well's mouth, and spread ground grain on it; and the thing was not known. [20] And when Absalom's servants came to the woman at the house, they said, "Where *are* Ahimaaz and Jonathan?"

So the woman said to them, "They have gone over the water brook."

And when they had searched and could not find *them*, they returned to Jerusalem. [21] Now it came to pass, after they had departed, that they came up out of the well and went and told King David, and said to David, "Arise and cross over the water quickly. For thus has Ahithophel advised against you." [22] So David and all the people who *were* with him arose and crossed over the Jordan. By morning light not one of them was left who had not gone over the Jordan.

[23] Now when Ahithophel saw that his advice was not followed, he saddled a donkey, and arose and went home to his house, to his city. Then he put his household in order, and hanged himself, and died; and he was buried in his father's tomb.

[24] Then David went to Mahanaim. And Absalom crossed over the Jordan, he and all the men of Israel with him. [25] And Absalom made Amasa captain of the army instead of Joab. This Amasa *was* the son of a man whose name *was* Jithra,[a] an Israelite,[b] who

---

17:25 [a] Spelled *Jether* in 1 Chronicles 2:17 and elsewhere   [b] Following Masoretic Text, some manuscripts of the Septuagint, and Targum; some manuscripts of the Septuagint read *Ishmaelite* (compare 1 Chronicles 2:17); Vulgate reads *of Jezrael.*

had gone in to Abigail the daughter of Nahash, sister of Zeruiah, Joab's mother. ²⁶So Israel and Absalom encamped in the land of Gilead.

²⁷Now it happened, when David had come to Mahanaim, that Shobi the son of Nahash from Rabbah of the people of Ammon, Machir the son of Ammiel from Lo Debar, and Barzillai the Gileadite from Rogelim, ²⁸brought beds and basins, earthen vessels and wheat, barley and flour, parched *grain* and beans, lentils and parched *seeds,* ²⁹honey and curds, sheep and cheese of the herd, for David and the people who *were* with him to eat. For they said, "The people are hungry and weary and thirsty in the wilderness."

Absalom's Defeat and Death

18 And David numbered the people who *were* with him, and set captains of thousands and captains of hundreds over them. ²Then David sent out one third of the people under the hand of Joab, one third under the hand of Abishai the son of Zeruiah, Joab's brother, and one third under the hand of Ittai the Gittite. And the king said to the people, "I also will surely go out with you myself."

³But the people answered, "You shall not go out! For if we flee away, they will not care about us; nor if half of us die, will they care about us. But *you are* worth ten thousand of us now. For you are now more help to us in the city."

> **18:3 You shall not go out.** David desired to lead his men into battle. However, the people recognized that the death of David would mean sure defeat, and Absalom would then be king. So David was persuaded to remain at Mahanaim.

⁴Then the king said to them, "Whatever seems best to you I will do." So the king stood beside the gate, and all the people went out by hundreds and by thousands. ⁵Now the king had commanded Joab, Abishai, and Ittai, saying, "*Deal* gently for my sake with the young man Absalom." And all the people heard when the king gave all the captains orders concerning Absalom.

⁶So the people went out into the field of battle against Israel. And the battle was in the woods of Ephraim. ⁷The people of Israel were overthrown there before the servants of David, and a great slaughter of twenty thousand took place there that day. ⁸For the battle there was scattered over the face of the whole countryside, and the woods devoured more people that day than the sword devoured.

⁹Then Absalom met the servants of David. Absalom rode on a mule. The mule went under the thick boughs of a great terebinth tree, and his head caught in the terebinth; so he was left hanging between heaven and earth. And the mule which *was* under him went on. ¹⁰Now a certain man saw *it* and told Joab, and said, "I just saw Absalom hanging in a terebinth tree!"

¹¹So Joab said to the man who told him, "You just saw *him!* And why did you not strike him there to the ground? I would have given you ten *shekels* of silver and a belt."

¹²But the man said to Joab, "Though I were to receive a thousand *shekels* of silver in my hand, I would not raise my hand against the king's son. For in our hearing the king commanded you and Abishai and Ittai, saying, 'Beware lest anyone *touch* the young man Absalom!'*ᵃ* ¹³Otherwise I would have dealt falsely against my own life. For there is nothing hidden from the king, and you yourself would have set yourself against *me.*"

¹⁴Then Joab said, "I cannot linger with you." And he took three spears in his hand and thrust them through Absalom's heart, while he was *still* alive in the midst of the terebinth tree. ¹⁵And ten young men who bore Joab's armor surrounded Absalom, and struck and killed him.

¹⁶So Joab blew the trumpet, and the people returned from pursuing Israel. For Joab held back the people. ¹⁷And they took

> **18:17 a very large heap of stones.** Absalom was buried in a deep pit, covered with stones. This could have been symbolic of stoning, which was the legal penalty due to a rebel son (Deut. 21:20). A heap of stones often showed that the one buried was a criminal or enemy (Josh. 7:26; 8:29).

18:12 *ᵃ*The ancient versions read '*Protect the young man Absalom for me!*'

Absalom and cast him into a large pit in the woods, and laid a very large heap of stones over him. Then all Israel fled, everyone to his tent.

¹⁸Now Absalom in his lifetime had taken and set up a pillar for himself, which *is* in the King's Valley. For he said, "I have no son to keep my name in remembrance." He called the pillar after his own name. And to this day it is called Absalom's Monument.

David Hears of Absalom's Death

¹⁹Then Ahimaaz the son of Zadok said, "Let me run now and take the news to the king, how the LORD has avenged him of his enemies."

²⁰And Joab said to him, "You shall not take the news this day, for you shall take the news another day. But today you shall take no news, because the king's son is dead." ²¹Then Joab said to the Cushite, "Go, tell the king what you have seen." So the Cushite bowed himself to Joab and ran.

²²And Ahimaaz the son of Zadok said again to Joab, "But whatever happens, please let me also run after the Cushite."

So Joab said, "Why will you run, my son, since you have no news ready?"

²³"But whatever happens," *he said*, "let me run."

So he said to him, "Run." Then Ahimaaz ran by way of the plain, and outran the Cushite.

²⁴Now David was sitting between the two gates. And the watchman went up to the roof over the gate, to the wall, lifted his eyes and looked, and there was a man, running alone. ²⁵Then the watchman cried out and told the king. And the king said, "If he *is* alone, *there is* news in his mouth." And he came rapidly and drew near.

²⁶Then the watchman saw *another* man running, and the watchman called to the gatekeeper and said, "There is *another* man, running alone!"

And the king said, "He also brings news."

²⁷So the watchman said, "I think the running of the first is like the running of Ahimaaz the son of Zadok."

And the king said, "He *is* a good man, and comes with good news."

²⁸So Ahimaaz called out and said to the king, "All is well!" Then he bowed down with his face to the earth before the king,

and said, "Blessed *be* the LORD your God, who has delivered up the men who raised their hand against my lord the king!"

²⁹The king said, "Is the young man Absalom safe?"

Ahimaaz answered, "When Joab sent the king's servant and *me* your servant, I saw a great tumult, but I did not know what *it was about.*"

³⁰And the king said, "Turn aside *and* stand here." So he turned aside and stood still.

³¹Just then the Cushite came, and the Cushite said, "There is good news, my lord the king! For the LORD has avenged you this day of all those who rose against you."

³²And the king said to the Cushite, "Is the young man Absalom safe?"

So the Cushite answered, "May the enemies of my lord the king, and all who rise against you to do harm, be like *that* young man!"

David's Mourning for Absalom

³³Then the king was deeply moved, and went up to the chamber over the gate, and wept. And as he went, he said thus: "O my son Absalom—my son, my son Absalom—if only I had died in your place! O Absalom my son, my son!"

18:33 my son. David lamented the death of his son, Absalom (see 19:5), in spite of all the harm that Absalom had caused. David mourned his personal loss in a melancholy way that seems to be consistent with his weakness as a father.

19 And Joab was told, "Behold, the king is weeping and mourning for Absalom." ²So the victory that day was *turned* into mourning for all the people. For the people heard it said that day, "The king is grieved for his son." ³And the people stole back into the city that day, as people who are ashamed steal away when they flee in battle. ⁴But the king covered his face, and the king cried out with a loud voice, "O my son Absalom! O Absalom, my son, my son!"

⁵Then Joab came into the house to the king, and said, "Today you have disgraced all your servants who today have saved your life, the lives of your sons and daughters, the lives of your wives and the lives of

19:5 disgraced all your servants. Joab sternly rebuked David for being so absorbed in his personal loss that he failed to appreciate the victory his men had won for him.

your concubines, [6]in that you love your enemies and hate your friends. For you have declared today that you regard neither princes nor servants; for today I perceive that if Absalom had lived and all of us had died today, then it would have pleased you well. [7]Now therefore, arise, go out and speak comfort to your servants. For I swear by the LORD, if you do not go out, not one will stay with you this night. And that will be worse for you than all the evil that has befallen you from your youth until now." [8]Then the king arose and sat in the gate. And they told all the people, saying, "There is the king, sitting in the gate." So all the people came before the king.

For everyone of Israel had fled to his tent.

David Returns to Jerusalem

[9]Now all the people were in a dispute throughout all the tribes of Israel, saying, "The king saved us from the hand of our enemies, he delivered us from the hand of the Philistines, and now he has fled from the land because of Absalom. [10]But Absalom, whom we anointed over us, has died in battle. Now therefore, why do you say nothing about bringing back the king?"

[11]So King David sent to Zadok and Abiathar the priests, saying, "Speak to the elders of Judah, saying, 'Why are you the last to bring the king back to his house, since the words of all Israel have come to the king, to his *very* house? [12]You *are* my brethren, you *are* my bone and my flesh. Why then are you the last to bring back the king?' [13]And say to Amasa, '*Are* you not my bone and my flesh? God do so to me, and more also, if you are not commander of the army before me continually in place of

19:13 commander of the army...in place of Joab. David appointed Amasa as commander of his army, hoping to secure the allegiance of those who had followed Amasa when he led Absalom's forces. This appointment persuaded the tribe of Judah to support David's return to the kingship (v. 14) and caused Joab to resent Amasa for taking his place (see 20:8–10).

Joab.' " [14]So he swayed the hearts of all the men of Judah, just as *the heart of* one man, so that they sent *this word* to the king: "Return, you and all your servants!"

[15]Then the king returned and came to the Jordan. And Judah came to Gilgal, to go to meet the king, to escort the king across the Jordan. [16]And Shimei the son of Gera, a Benjamite, who *was* from Bahurim, hurried and came down with the men of Judah to meet King David. [17]*There were* a thousand men of Benjamin with him, and Ziba the servant of the house of Saul, and his fifteen sons and his twenty servants with him; and they went over the Jordan before the king. [18]Then a ferryboat went across to carry over the king's household, and to do what he thought good.

David's Mercy to Shimei

Now Shimei the son of Gera fell down before the king when he had crossed the Jordan. [19]Then he said to the king, "Do not let my lord impute iniquity to me, or remember what wrong your servant did on the day that my lord the king left Jerusalem, that the king should take *it* to heart. [20]For I, your servant, know that I have sinned. Therefore here I am, the first to come today of all the house of Joseph to go down to meet my lord the king."

[21]But Abishai the son of Zeruiah answered and said, "Shall not Shimei be put to death for this, because he cursed the LORD's anointed?"

[22]And David said, "What have I to do with you, you sons of Zeruiah, that you should be adversaries to me today? Shall any man be put to death today in Israel? For do I not know that today I *am* king over Israel?" [23]Therefore the king said to Shimei, "You shall not die." And the king swore to him.

David and Mephibosheth Meet

[24]Now Mephibosheth the son of Saul came down to meet the king. And he had not cared for his feet, nor trimmed his mustache, nor washed his clothes, from the day the king departed until the day he returned in peace. [25]So it was, when he had come to Jerusalem to meet the king, that the king said to him, "Why did you not go with me, Mephibosheth?"

²⁶And he answered, "My lord, O king, my servant deceived me. For your servant said, 'I will saddle a donkey for myself, that I may ride on it and go to the king,' because your servant *is* lame. ²⁷And he has slandered your servant to my lord the king, but my lord the king *is* like the angel of God. Therefore do *what is* good in your eyes. ²⁸For all my father's house were but dead men before my lord the king. Yet you set your servant among those who eat at your own table. Therefore what right have I still to cry out anymore to the king?"

²⁹So the king said to him, "Why do you speak anymore of your matters? I have said, 'You and Ziba divide the land.' "

19:29 divide the land. David had given the estate of Saul to Mephibosheth to be farmed under him by Ziba (9:9,10). When David was deceived, he gave it all to Ziba (16:4). Now David decided to divide the estate between Mephibosheth and Ziba, because he was unsure if Mephibosheth spoke the truth. Mephibosheth unselfishly suggested that the disloyal Ziba take it all, as it was enough for him that David returned.

³⁰Then Mephibosheth said to the king, "Rather, let him take it all, inasmuch as my lord the king has come back in peace to his own house."

David's Kindness to Barzillai

³¹And Barzillai the Gileadite came down from Rogelim and went across the Jordan with the king, to escort him across the Jordan. ³²Now Barzillai was a very aged man, eighty years old. And he had provided the king with supplies while he stayed at Mahanaim, for he *was* a very rich man. ³³And the king said to Barzillai, "Come across with me, and I will provide for you while you are with me in Jerusalem."

³⁴But Barzillai said to the king, "How long have I to live, that I should go up with the king to Jerusalem? ³⁵I *am* today eighty years old. Can I discern between the good and bad? Can your servant taste what I eat or what I drink? Can I hear any longer the voice of singing men and singing women? Why then should your servant be a further burden to my lord the king? ³⁶Your servant will go a little way across the Jordan with

the king. And why should the king repay me *with* such a reward? ³⁷Please let your servant turn back again, that I may die in my own city, near the grave of my father and mother. But here is your servant Chimham; let him cross over with my lord the king, and do for him what seems good to you."

³⁸And the king answered, "Chimham shall cross over with me, and I will do for him what seems good to you. Now whatever you request of me, I will do for you." ³⁹Then all the people went over the Jordan. And when the king had crossed over, the king kissed Barzillai and blessed him, and he returned to his own place.

The Quarrel About the King

⁴⁰Now the king went on to Gilgal, and Chimham*ᵃ* went on with him. And all the people of Judah escorted the king, and also half the people of Israel. ⁴¹Just then all the men of Israel came to the king, and said to the king, "Why have our brethren, the men of Judah, stolen you away and brought the king, his household, and all David's men with him across the Jordan?"

⁴²So all the men of Judah answered the men of Israel, "Because the king *is* a close relative of ours. Why then are you angry over this matter? Have we ever eaten at the king's *expense?* Or has he given us any gift?"

⁴³And the men of Israel answered the men of Judah, and said, "We have ten shares in the king; therefore we also have more *right* to David than you. Why then do you despise us—were we not the first to advise bringing back our king?"

Yet the words of the men of Judah were fiercer than the words of the men of Israel.

19:43 ten shares. This is a problem of jealousy. The men of Israel told the men of Judah that they had a greater right to David, since there were 10 northern tribes in contrast to the one tribe of Judah. **you despise us.** This hostility between Israel and Judah led to the rebellion of Sheba (20:1–22) and eventually to the division of the united kingdom (1 Kin. 12:1–24).

The Rebellion of Sheba

20 And there happened to be there a rebel,*ᵃ* whose name *was* Sheba the

son of Bichri, a Benjamite. And he blew a trumpet, and said:

> "We have no share in David,
> Nor do we have inheritance in the son
>   of Jesse;
> Every man to his tents, O Israel!"

²So every man of Israel deserted David, *and* followed Sheba the son of Bichri. But the men of Judah, from the Jordan as far as Jerusalem, remained loyal to their king.

³Now David came to his house at Jerusalem. And the king took the ten women, his concubines whom he had left to keep the house, and put them in seclusion and supported them, but did not go in to them. So they were shut up to the day of their death, living in widowhood.

⁴And the king said to Amasa, "Assemble the men of Judah for me within three days, and be present here yourself." ⁵So Amasa went to assemble *the men of* Judah. But he delayed longer than the set time which David had appointed him. ⁶And David said to Abishai, "Now Sheba the son of Bichri will do us more harm than Absalom. Take your lord's servants and pursue him, lest he find for himself fortified cities, and escape us." ⁷So Joab's men, with the Cherethites, the Pelethites, and all the mighty men, went out after him. And they went out of Jerusalem to pursue Sheba the son of Bichri. ⁸When they *were* at the large stone which *is* in Gibeon, Amasa came before them. Now Joab was dressed in battle armor; on it was a belt *with* a sword fastened in its sheath at his hips; and as he was going forward, it fell out. ⁹Then Joab said to Amasa, "*Are* you in health, my brother?" And Joab took Amasa by the beard with his right hand to kiss him. ¹⁰But Amasa did not notice the sword that *was* in Joab's hand. And he struck him with it in the stomach, and his entrails poured out on the ground; and he did not *strike* him again. Thus he died.

Then Joab and Abishai his brother pursued Sheba the son of Bichri. ¹¹Meanwhile one of Joab's men stood near Amasa, and said, "Whoever favors Joab and whoever *is* for David—follow Joab!" ¹²But Amasa wallowed in *his* blood in the middle of the highway. And when the man saw that all the people stood still, he moved Amasa from the highway to the field and threw a garment over him, when he saw that everyone who came upon him halted. ¹³When he was removed from the highway, all the people went on after Joab to pursue Sheba the son of Bichri.

> **20:11 one of Joab's men.** The troops reinstated Joab as commander of David's army. Joab had much influence over the army; even though he murdered David's chosen commander right before their eyes they still unanimously followed him as their leader in pursuit of Sheba.

¹⁴And he went through all the tribes of Israel to Abel and Beth Maachah and all the Berites. So they were gathered together and also went after *Sheba.ᵃ* ¹⁵Then they came and besieged him in Abel of Beth Maachah; and they cast up a siege mound against the city, and it stood by the rampart. And all the people who *were* with Joab battered the wall to throw it down.

¹⁶Then a wise woman cried out from the city, "Hear, hear! Please say to Joab, 'Come nearby, that I may speak with you.' " ¹⁷When he had come near to her, the woman said, "*Are* you Joab?"

He answered, "I *am*."

Then she said to him, "Hear the words of your maidservant."

And he answered, "I am listening."

¹⁸So she spoke, saying, "They used to talk in former times, saying, 'They shall surely seek *guidance* at Abel,' and so they would end *disputes.* ¹⁹I *am among the* peaceable *and* faithful in Israel. You seek to destroy a city and a mother in Israel. Why would you swallow up the inheritance of the LORD?"

²⁰And Joab answered and said, "Far be it, far be it from me, that I should swallow up or destroy! ²¹That *is* not so. But a man from the mountains of Ephraim, Sheba the son of Bichri by name, has raised his hand against the king, against David. Deliver him only, and I will depart from the city."

So the woman said to Joab, "Watch, his head will be thrown to you over the wall." ²²Then the woman in her wisdom went to

all the people. And they cut off the head of Sheba the son of Bichri, and threw *it* out to Joab. Then he blew a trumpet, and they withdrew from the city, every man to his tent. So Joab returned to the king at Jerusalem.

David's Government Officers

²³And Joab *was* over all the army of Israel; Benaiah the son of Jehoiada *was* over the Cherethites and the Pelethites; ²⁴Adoram *was* in charge of revenue; Jehoshaphat the son of Ahilud *was* recorder; ²⁵Sheva *was* scribe; Zadok and Abiathar *were* the priests; ²⁶and Ira the Jairite was a chief minister under David.

David Avenges the Gibeonites

21 Now there was a famine in the days of David for three years, year after year; and David inquired of the LORD. And the LORD answered, "*It is* because of Saul and *his* bloodthirsty house, because he killed the Gibeonites." ²So the king called the Gibeonites and spoke to them. Now the Gibeonites *were* not of the children of Israel, but of the remnant of the Amorites; the children of Israel had sworn protection to them, but Saul had sought to kill them in his zeal for the children of Israel and Judah.

> **21:1,2 Saul and *his* bloodthirsty house.** The famine was a result of Saul's sin of killing the Gibeonites. Saul sought to obey God by ridding the land of the heathen, but he sinned by breaking a covenant that had been made 400 years before between Joshua and the Gibeonites, who were in the land when Israel took possession of it. Although they had deceived Joshua into making the covenant, it was still a covenant (see Josh. 9:3–27), and required by God to be kept (see Josh. 9:20).

³Therefore David said to the Gibeonites, "What shall I do for you? And with what shall I make atonement, that you may bless the inheritance of the LORD?"

⁴And the Gibeonites said to him, "We will have no silver or gold from Saul or from his house, nor shall you kill any man in Israel for us."

So he said, "Whatever you say, I will do for you."

⁵Then they answered the king, "As for the man who consumed us and plotted against us, *that* we should be destroyed from remaining in any of the territories of Israel, ⁶let seven men of his descendants be delivered to us, and we will hang them before the LORD in Gibeah of Saul, *whom* the LORD chose."

And the king said, "I will give *them*."

⁷But the king spared Mephibosheth the son of Jonathan, the son of Saul, because of the LORD's oath that *was* between them, between David and Jonathan the son of Saul. ⁸So the king took Armoni and Mephibosheth, the two sons of Rizpah the daughter of Aiah, whom she bore to Saul, and the five sons of Michal*ᵃ* the daughter of Saul, whom she brought up for Adriel the son of Barzillai the Meholathite; ⁹and he delivered them into the hands of the Gibeonites, and they hanged them on the hill before the LORD. So they fell, *all* seven together, and were put to death in the days of harvest, in the first *days*, in the beginning of barley harvest.

> **21:7 the LORD's oath...between David and Jonathan.** Mephibosheth, the son of Jonathan, was spared because of the covenant between David and Jonathan (1 Sam. 20:14,15) and also between David and Saul.

¹⁰Now Rizpah the daughter of Aiah took sackcloth and spread it for herself on the rock, from the beginning of harvest until the late rains poured on them from heaven. And she did not allow the birds of the air to rest on them by day nor the beasts of the field by night.

> **21:10 sackcloth...spread.** Rizpah put up a tent nearby to keep watch over the bodies, to scare away birds and animals. It was considered a disgrace for dead bodies to become food for the birds and animals (see. Deut. 28:26). **the late rains.** This was an unseasonably late spring or early summer shower that ended the drought.

¹¹And David was told what Rizpah the daughter of Aiah, the concubine of Saul, had done. ¹²Then David went and took the bones of Saul, and the bones of Jonathan

---

21:8 *ᵃ*Or *Merab* (compare 1 Samuel 18:19 and 25:44; 2 Samuel 3:14 and 6:23)

his son, from the men of Jabesh Gilead who had stolen them from the street of Beth Shan,[a] where the Philistines had hung them up, after the Philistines had struck down Saul in Gilboa. [13]So he brought up the bones of Saul and the bones of Jonathan his son from there; and they gathered the bones of those who had been hanged. [14]They buried the bones of Saul and Jonathan his son in the country of Benjamin in Zelah, in the tomb of Kish his father. So they performed all that the king commanded. And after that God heeded the prayer for the land.

Philistine Giants Destroyed

[15]When the Philistines were at war again with Israel, David and his servants with him went down and fought against the Philistines; and David grew faint. [16]Then Ishbi-Benob, who *was* one of the sons of the giant, the weight of whose bronze spear *was* three hundred *shekels*, who was bearing a new *sword*, thought he could kill David. [17]But Abishai the son of Zeruiah came to his aid, and struck the Philistine and killed him. Then the men of David swore to him, saying, "You shall go out no more with us to battle, lest you quench the lamp of Israel."

[18]Now it happened afterward that there was again a battle with the Philistines at Gob. Then Sibbechai the Hushathite killed Saph,[a] who *was* one of the sons of the giant. [19]Again there was war at Gob with the Philistines, where Elhanan the son of Jaare-Oregim[a] the Bethlehemite killed *the brother of* Goliath the Gittite, the shaft of whose spear *was* like a weaver's beam. [20]Yet again there was war at Gath, where there was a man of *great* stature, who had six fingers on each hand and six toes on each foot, twenty-four in number; and he also was born to the giant. [21]So when he defied Israel, Jonathan the son of Shimea,[a] David's brother, killed him. [22]These four were born to the giant in Gath, and fell by the hand of David and by the hand of his servants.

Praise for God's Deliverance

22 Then David spoke to the LORD the words of this song, on the day when the LORD had delivered him from the hand of all his enemies, and from the hand of Saul. [2]And he said:[a]

> **22:1 all his enemies.** See 7:1,9,11. David composed this song toward the end of his life, when the Lord had given him a peaceful kingdom and the Davidic Covenant, which promised the Messianic seed.

"The LORD *is* my rock and my fortress
  and my deliverer;
3 The God of my strength, in whom I
  will trust;
My shield and the horn of my
  salvation,
My stronghold and my refuge;
My Savior, You save me from
  violence.
4 I will call upon the LORD, *who is
  worthy* to be praised;
So shall I be saved from my enemies.

5 "When the waves of death surrounded
  me,
The floods of ungodliness made me
  afraid.
6 The sorrows of Sheol surrounded me;
The snares of death confronted me.
7 In my distress I called upon the
  LORD,
And cried out to my God;
He heard my voice from His temple,
And my cry *entered* His ears.

8 "Then the earth shook and trembled;
The foundations of heaven[a] quaked
  and were shaken,
Because He was angry.
9 Smoke went up from His nostrils,
And devouring fire from His mouth;
Coals were kindled by it.
10 He bowed the heavens also, and came
  down
With darkness under His feet.
11 He rode upon a cherub, and flew;

21:12 [a]Spelled *Beth Shean* in Joshua 17:11 and elsewhere   21:18 [a]Spelled *Sippai* in 1 Chronicles 20:4   21:19 [a]Spelled *Jair* in 1 Chronicles 20:5   21:21 [a]Spelled *Shammah* in 1 Samuel 16:9 and elsewhere   22:2 [a]Compare Psalm 18   22:8 [a]Following Masoretic Text, Septuagint, and Targum; Syriac and Vulgate read *hills* (compare Psalm 18:7).

And He was seen[a] upon the wings of
the wind.

12 He made darkness canopies around
Him,
Dark waters *and* thick clouds of the
skies.

13 From the brightness before Him
Coals of fire were kindled.

14 "The LORD thundered from heaven,
And the Most High uttered His voice.

15 He sent out arrows and scattered
them;
Lightning bolts, and He vanquished
them.

16 Then the channels of the sea were
seen,
The foundations of the world were
uncovered,
At the rebuke of the LORD,
At the blast of the breath of His
nostrils.

17 "He sent from above, He took me,
He drew me out of many waters.

18 He delivered me from my strong
enemy,
From those who hated me;
For they were too strong for me.

19 They confronted me in the day of my
calamity,
But the LORD was my support.

20 He also brought me out into a broad
place;
He delivered me because He delighted
in me.

21 "The LORD rewarded me according to
my righteousness;
According to the cleanness of my
hands
He has recompensed me.

22 For I have kept the ways of the LORD,
And have not wickedly departed from
my God.

23 For all His judgments *were* before me;

And *as for* His statutes, I did not
depart from them.

24 I was also blameless before Him,
And I kept myself from my iniquity.

25 Therefore the LORD has recompensed
me according to my righteousness,
According to my cleanness in His
eyes.[a]

22:21–25 David did not claim to be righteous or
sinless. Rather, he was considered righteous by faith
because he believed God and desired to please Him.
Because of this, he was blameless when compared to
his enemies.

26 "With the merciful You will show
Yourself merciful;
With a blameless man You will show
Yourself blameless;

27 With the pure You will show Yourself
pure;
And with the devious You will show
Yourself shrewd.

28 You will save the humble people;
But Your eyes *are* on the haughty, *that*
You may bring *them* down.

29 "For You *are* my lamp, O LORD;
The LORD shall enlighten my
darkness.

30 For by You I can run against a troop;
By my God I can leap over a wall.

31 *As for* God, His way *is* perfect;
The word of the LORD *is* proven;
He *is* a shield to all who trust in Him.

32 "For who *is* God, except the LORD?
And who *is* a rock, except our God?

33 God *is* my strength *and* power,[a]
And He makes my[b] way perfect.

34 He makes my[a] feet like the *feet* of
deer,
And sets me on my high places.

35 He teaches my hands to make war,
So that my arms can bend a bow of
bronze.

22:11 [a]Following Masoretic Text and Septuagint; many Hebrew manuscripts, Syriac, and Vulgate read
He flew (compare Psalm 18:10); Targum reads *He spoke with power*.   22:25 [a]Septuagint, Syriac, and
Vulgate read *the cleanness of my hands in His sight* (compare Psalm 18:24); Targum reads *my
cleanness before His word*.   22:33 [a]Dead Sea Scrolls, Septuagint, Syriac, and Vulgate read *It is God
who arms me with strength* (compare Psalm 18:32); Targum reads *It is God who sustains me with
strength*.   [b]Following Qere, Septuagint, Syriac, Targum, and Vulgate (compare Psalm 18:32); Kethib
reads *His*.   22:34 [a]Following Qere, Septuagint, Syriac, Targum, and Vulgate (compare Psalm 18:33);
Kethib reads *His*.

And come frightened[a] from their hideouts.

22:1–51 David's song of praise here is almost identical to Ps. 18. Together with Hannah's prayer, David's song forms the framework for the books of Samuel. The song focuses on the Lord's deliverance of David from his enemies: how the Lord delivered him (vv. 5–20), why the Lord delivered him (vv. 21–28), and to what extent the Lord delivered him (vv. 29–46). The song concludes with David's resolve to praise the Lord, even among the Gentiles (vv. 47–51).

47 "The LORD lives!
   Blessed *be* my Rock!
   Let God be exalted,
   The Rock of my salvation!
48 *It is* God who avenges me,
   And subdues the peoples under me;
49 He delivers me from my enemies.
   You also lift me up above those who
      rise against me;
   You have delivered me from the
      violent man.
50 Therefore I will give thanks to You, O
      LORD, among the Gentiles,
   And sing praises to Your name.

51 *"He is* the tower of salvation to His
      king,
   And shows mercy to His anointed,
   To David and his descendants
      forevermore."

22:51 His king…His anointed. These terms refer to the promised "seed," the Messiah (see 7:12). David's deliverance and triumph foreshadow that of the coming Messiah. At the end of David's life he looked forward in hope to the fulfillment of God's promises in the coming of a future "king," the "anointed one."

36 "You have also given me the shield of
      Your salvation;
   Your gentleness has made me
      great.
37 You enlarged my path under me;
   So my feet did not slip.

38 "I have pursued my enemies and
      destroyed them;
   Neither did I turn back again till they
      were destroyed.
39 And I have destroyed them and
      wounded them,
   So that they could not rise;
   They have fallen under my feet.
40 For You have armed me with strength
      for the battle;
   You have subdued under me those
      who rose against me.
41 You have also given me the necks of
      my enemies,
   So that I destroyed those who hated
      me.
42 They looked, but *there was* none to
      save;
   Even to the LORD, but He did not
      answer them.
43 Then I beat them as fine as the dust
      of the earth;
   I trod them like dirt in the streets,
   And I spread them out.

44 "You have also delivered me from the
      strivings of my people;
   You have kept me as the head of the
      nations.
   A people I have not known shall serve
      me.
45 The foreigners submit to me;
   As soon as they hear, they obey me.
46 The foreigners fade away,

David's Last Words

23 Now these *are* the last words of David.

   Thus says David the son of Jesse;
   Thus says the man raised up on high,
   The anointed of the God of Jacob,
   And the sweet psalmist of Israel:

2 "The Spirit of the LORD spoke by me,
   And His word *was* on my tongue.
3 The God of Israel said,
   The Rock of Israel spoke to me:
   'He who rules over men *must be* just,
   Ruling in the fear of God.
4 And *he shall be* like the light of the
      morning *when* the sun rises,
   A morning without clouds,
   Like the tender grass *springing* out of
      the earth,
   By clear shining after rain.'

22:46 [a]Following Septuagint, Targum, and Vulgate (compare Psalm 18:45); Masoretic Text reads *gird themselves*.

5   "Although my house *is* not so with
      God,
      Yet He has made with me an
        everlasting covenant ,
      Ordered in all *things* and secure.
      For *this is* all my salvation and all *my*
        desire;
      Will He not make *it* increase?

23:5 my house *is* not so with God. David's house had not always ruled over God's people with righteousness. None of the kings of David's line met God's standard of righteous obedience. **everlasting covenant.** The Lord's promise in 7:12–16 is referred to here as a "covenant." Although David and his household had failed, David believed that the Lord would not fail. He would fulfill His promise of hope in the coming of the anointed one, who would establish a kingdom of righteousness and peace forever.

6   But *the sons* of rebellion *shall* all *be*
      as thorns thrust away,
      Because they cannot be taken with
        hands.
7   But the man *who* touches them
      Must be armed with iron and the
        shaft of a spear,
      And they shall be utterly burned with
        fire in *their* place."

David's Mighty Men

8 These *are* the names of the mighty men whom David had: Josheb-Basshebeth[a] the Tachmonite, chief among the captains.[b] He was called Adino the Eznite, because he had killed eight hundred men at one time. 9 And after him *was* Eleazar the son of Dodo,[a] the Ahohite, *one* of the three mighty men with David when they defied the Philistines *who* were gathered there for battle, and the men of Israel had retreated. 10 He arose and attacked the Philistines until his hand was weary, and his hand stuck to the sword. The LORD brought about a great victory that day; and the people returned after him only to plunder. 11 And after him *was* Shammah the son of Agee the Hararite. The Philistines had gathered together into a troop where there was a piece of ground full of lentils. So the people fled from the Philistines. 12 But he stationed himself in the middle of the field, defended it, and killed the Philistines. So the LORD brought about a great victory.

13 Then three of the thirty chief men went down at harvest time and came to David at the cave of Adullam. And the troop of Philistines encamped in the Valley of Rephaim. 14 David *was* then in the stronghold, and the garrison of the Philistines *was* then *in* Bethlehem. 15 And David said with longing, "Oh, that someone would give me a drink of the water from the well of Bethlehem, which *is* by the gate!" 16 So the three mighty men broke through the camp of the Philistines, drew water from the well of Bethlehem that *was* by the gate, and took it and brought *it* to David. Nevertheless he would not drink it, but poured it out to the LORD. 17 And he said, "Far be it from me, O LORD, that I should do this! Is *this not* the blood of the men who went in *jeopardy of* their lives?" Therefore he would not drink it.

23:16 poured it out to the LORD. Because David's men brought him water from Bethlehem's well at the risk of their own lives, he considered it as "blood" and refused to drink it. Instead, he poured it on the ground as a sacrifice to the Lord (see Gen. 35:14).

These things were done by the three mighty men. 18 Now Abishai the brother of Joab, the son of Zeruiah, was chief of *another* three.[a] He lifted his spear against three hundred *men*, killed *them*, and won a name among *these* three. 19 Was he not the most honored of three? Therefore he became their captain. However, he did not attain to the *first* three. 20 Benaiah *was* the son of Jehoiada, the son of a valiant man from Kabzeel, who had done many deeds. He had killed two lionlike heroes of Moab. He also had gone down and killed a lion in the midst of a pit on a snowy day. 21 And he killed an Egyptian, a spectacular man. The Egyptian *had* a spear in his hand; so he went down to him with a staff, wrested the spear out of

---

23:8 [a]Literally *One Who Sits in the Seat* (compare 1 Chronicles 11:11) [b]Following Masoretic Text and Targum; Septuagint and Vulgate read *the three.*   23:9 [a]Spelled *Dodai* in 1 Chronicles 27:4
23:18 [a]Following Masoretic Text, Septuagint, and Vulgate; some Hebrew manuscripts and Syriac read *thirty*; Targum reads *the mighty men.*

the Egyptian's hand, and killed him with his own spear. [22]These *things* Benaiah the son of Jehoiada did, and won a name among three mighty men. [23]He was more honored than the thirty, but he did not attain to the *first* three. And David appointed him over his guard.

[24]Asahel the brother of Joab *was* one of the thirty; Elhanan the son of Dodo of Bethlehem, [25]Shammah the Harodite, Elika the Harodite, [26]Helez the Paltite, Ira the son of Ikkesh the Tekoite, [27]Abiezer the Anathothite, Mebunnai the Hushathite, [28]Zalmon the Ahohite, Maharai the Netophathite, [29]Heleb the son of Baanah (the Netophathite), Ittai the son of Ribai from Gibeah of the children of Benjamin, [30]Benaiah a Pirathonite, Hiddai from the brooks of Gaash, [31]Abi-Albon the Arbathite, Azmaveth the Barhumite, [32]Eliahba the Shaalbonite (of the sons of Jashen), Jonathan, [33]Shammah the Hararite, Ahiam the son of Sharar the Hararite, [34]Eliphelet the son of Ahasbai, the son of the Maachathite, Eliam the son of Ahithophel the Gilonite, [35]Hezrai[a] the Carmelite, Paarai the Arbite, [36]Igal the son of Nathan of Zobah, Bani the Gadite, [37]Zelek the Ammonite, Naharai the Beerothite (armorbearer of Joab the son of Zeruiah), [38]Ira the Ithrite, Gareb the Ithrite, [39]*and* Uriah the Hittite: thirty-seven in all.

David's Census of Israel and Judah

24 Again the anger of the LORD was aroused against Israel, and He moved David against them to say, "Go, number Israel and Judah."

[2]So the king said to Joab the commander of the army who *was* with him, "Now go throughout all the tribes of Israel, from Dan to Beersheba, and count the people, that I may know the number of the people."

[3]And Joab said to the king, "Now may the LORD your God add to the people a hundred times more than there are, and may the eyes of my lord the king see *it*. But why does my lord the king desire this thing?" [4]Nevertheless the king's word prevailed against Joab and against the captains of the army. Therefore Joab and the captains of the army went out from the presence of the king to count the people of Israel.

[5]And they crossed over the Jordan and camped in Aroer, on the right side of the town which *is* in the midst of the ravine of Gad, and toward Jazer. [6]Then they came to Gilead and to the land of Tahtim Hodshi; they came to Dan Jaan and around to Sidon; [7]and they came to the stronghold of Tyre and to all the cities of the Hivites and the Canaanites. Then they went out to South Judah *as far as* Beersheba. [8]So when they had gone through all the land, they came to Jerusalem at the end of nine months and twenty days. [9]Then Joab gave the sum of the number of the people to the king. And there were in Israel eight hundred thousand valiant men who drew the sword, and the men of Judah were five hundred thousand men.

The Judgment on David's Sin

[10]And David's heart condemned him after he had numbered the people. So David said to the LORD, "I have sinned greatly in what I have done; but now, I pray, O LORD, take away the iniquity of Your servant, for I have done very foolishly."

24:1 against Israel. The census was a punishment on Israel from the Lord for some unspecified sins. **He moved David.** Satan encouraged David to take this census, and the Lord used Satan to accomplish His will. **number Israel and Judah.** The census was used for military purposes (see v. 9) and had been done in the past (Num. 1:1,2; 26:1–4) Yet this census did not have the sanction of the Lord and proceeded from wrong motives. David may have wanted to glory in the size of his army or to take more territory than what the Lord had granted him. He shifted his trust from God to his army (this is a constant theme in the Psalms; see 20:7).

24:10 sinned greatly...done very foolishly. David recognized his rebellion against God. He had relied on numerical strength instead of on the Lord, who is able to deliver using many or few (see 1 Sam. 14:6).

[11]Now when David arose in the morning, the word of the LORD came to the prophet Gad, David's seer, saying, [12]"Go and tell David, 'Thus says the LORD: "I offer you three *things*; choose one of them for yourself, that I may do *it* to you." ' " [13]So Gad came to

David and told him; and he said to him, "Shall seven[a] years of famine come to you in your land? Or shall you flee three months before your enemies, while they pursue you? Or shall there be three days' plague in your land? Now consider and see what answer I should take back to Him who sent me."

[14] And David said to Gad, "I am in great distress. Please let us fall into the hand of the LORD, for His mercies *are* great; but do not let me fall into the hand of man."

[15] So the LORD sent a plague upon Israel from the morning till the appointed time. From Dan to Beersheba seventy thousand men of the people died. [16] And when the angel[a] stretched out His hand over Jerusalem to destroy it, the LORD relented from the destruction, and said to the angel who was destroying the people, "It is enough; now restrain your hand." And the angel of the LORD was by the threshing floor of Araunah[b] the Jebusite.

[17] Then David spoke to the LORD when he saw the angel who was striking the people, and said, "Surely I have sinned, and I have done wickedly; but these sheep, what have they done? Let Your hand, I pray, be against me and against my father's house."

> **24:17 Let Your hand...be against me.** David asked for judgment on himself and his own family, for he did not want his people to suffer further destruction (see Ex. 32:32).

The Altar on the Threshing Floor

[18] And Gad came that day to David and said to him, "Go up, erect an altar to the LORD on the threshing floor of Araunah the Jebusite." [19] So David, according to the word of Gad, went up as the LORD commanded. [20] Now Araunah looked, and saw the king and his servants coming toward him. So Araunah went out and bowed before the king with his face to the ground.

[21] Then Araunah said, "Why has my lord the king come to his servant?"

And David said, "To buy the threshing floor from you, to build an altar to the LORD, that the plague may be withdrawn from the people."

[22] Now Araunah said to David, "Let my lord the king take and offer up whatever *seems* good to him. Look, *here are* oxen for burnt sacrifice, and threshing implements and the yokes of the oxen for wood. [23] All these, O king, Araunah has given to the king."

And Araunah said to the king, "May the LORD your God accept you."

[24] Then the king said to Araunah, "No, but I will surely buy *it* from you for a price; nor will I offer burnt offerings to the LORD my God with that which costs me nothing." So David bought the threshing floor and the oxen for fifty shekels of silver. [25] And David built there an altar to the LORD, and offered burnt offerings and peace offerings. So the LORD heeded the prayers for the land, and the plague was withdrawn from Israel.

> **24:24 costs me nothing.** Sacrifice is an essential part of worship and service to God (see Mal.1:6–10).

24:13 [a] Following Masoretic Text, Syriac, Targum, and Vulgate; Septuagint reads *three* (compare 1 Chronicles 21:12).　24:16 [a] Or *Angel* [b] Spelled *Ornan* in 1 Chronicles 21:15

1 & 2 KINGS

Kings come in many shapes and sizes. Their character varies widely. Some lead successfully while others fail miserably. Some build, only to be replaced by those who destroy. Some fight, some surrender, and some do practically nothing at all. Some kings leave a legacy of good; others a legacy of evil. At their best or worst, however, monarchs demonstrate one overwhelming truth: kings simply cannot replace God.

Like 1 and 2 Samuel, 1 and 2 Kings were originally a single scroll. Unlike the Samuel books, Kings was divided with little consideration for the contents. The break comes in the middle of Elijah's ministry. Together, the books present a powerful case for the failure of human leadership when it turns away from God.

AUTHOR AND DATE

Kings was written by an unknown author, approximately 561 to 538 B.C.

Though Jewish tradition has suggested Jeremiah as the likely author of 1 and 2 Kings, the books themselves raise some objections. For example, 2 Kings 25:27–30 records events that took place in Babylon in 561 B.C. Jeremiah never went to Babylon, but to Egypt (Jeremiah 43:1–7). The central role of God's prophets in these books does indicate, however, that the author was probably from among the prophets—someone whose name we would recognize, or one of the many nameless prophets who served God among the people.

Events mentioned or absent in 1 and 2 Kings help indicate a date for the writing—between 561 and 538 B.C. The first of these dates locates the final event described in 2 Kings. The second (538 B.C.) dates the release from exile in Babylon and would likely have been mentioned if the book(s) had been recorded after that date.

First and Second Kings clearly identify some of the sources used by the author in compiling the history: (1) "the book of the acts of Solomon" (1 Kings 11:41); (2) "the chronicles of the kings of Israel" (1 Kings 14:19; 16:5,14,20,27; 2 Kings 1:18; 15:11,15,21,26,31); (3) "the chronicles of the kings of Judah" (1 Kings 15:7,23; 2 Kings 15:6,36; 21:17,25). Further, Isaiah 36:1–39:8 provided information used in 2 Kings 18:9–20:19, and Jeremiah 52:31–34 seems to have been the source for 2 Kings 25:27–29. Nevertheless, the final work was written by a divinely inspired author, probably living in Babylon during the Exile.

BACKGROUND AND SETTING

Two streams of thought run through 1 and 2 Kings: (1) the accounts of eyewitnesses to events, and (2) the commentary on those events by the final author. The

first accurately conveys history; the second accurately interprets history. Using reliable sources, Kings traces the histories of two sets of kings and two nations of disobedient people, Israel and Judah, both of whom grew indifferent to God's law and God's prophets. That indifference led them to humiliation, defeat, and crushing captivity.

The author, exiled in Babylon, produced a book that went beyond a compilation of historical records. He also interpreted the lessons from Israel's history for his fellow exiles. He pointed out clearly that their present condition was a direct consequence of God's judgment over long established patterns of disobedience (1 Kings 9:3–9).

The book also records God's efforts to confront and warn the people along the way, using the prophets as his spokesmen. The prophets fearlessly foretold the eventual results of national sin, which would culminate in exile. Always, the prophets also held out the offer of God's mercy whenever the people would humble themselves.

HISTORICAL AND THEOLOGICAL THEMES

With the exception of Saul and David, the first two occupants of the throne of the people of Israel, Kings chronicles the monarchy in Israel and Judah from unity under Solomon to division, moral decay, and defeat under the remaining kings. The narration skips back and forth chronologically between the two kingdoms.

The author followed a set plan in recording each reign: (a) introduction; then (b) narration. The introductions include seven components: (1) the king's name and his relation to his predecessor; (2) the king's date of accession corresponding to the reign of his contemporary in the other kingdom; (3) the king's age on coming to the throne (for the kings of Judah only); (4) the king's length of reign; (5) the king's place of reign; (6) the king's mother's name (for the kings of Judah only); and (7) a spiritual appraisal of the king's reign.

> ALTHOUGH **DAVID'S DESCENDANTS** REPEATEDLY **PROVED** TO BE **CORRUPT**, GOD **KEPT FAITH** WITH THAT **FAMILY.**

The narratives of each reign vary widely but include the following details: (1) a citation of sources; (2) additional historical notes; (3) notice of death; (4) notice of burial; (5) the name of the king's successor; and (6) an occasional postscript (1 Kings 15:32; 2 Kings 10:36).

Three theological themes receive special attention in Kings. First, God's judgment on Judah and Israel was a consequence of their disobedience to His law (2 Kings 17:7–23). Second, the warnings and promises of God's prophets came true literally and exactly (1 Kings 13:2–3; 2 Kings 23:16). Third, the Lord remembered His promise to David (1 Kings 11:12–13; 2 Kings 8:19). Although David's descendants repeatedly proved to be corrupt, God kept faith with that family. The line was kept alive and so was the hope based on the "seed" of the promised Savior who would eventually come through David's lineage (2 Samuel 7:12–16; 2 Kings 25:27–30). God remains faithful and His Word proves trustworthy.

OUTLINE OF 1 KINGS

I. THE UNITED KINGDOM: THE REIGN OF SOLOMON (1 KINGS 1:1–11:43)
    A. The Rise of Solomon (1:1–2:46)
    B. The Beginning of Solomon's Wisdom and Wealth (3:1–4:34)
    C. The Preparations for the Building of the Temple (5:1–18)
    D. The Building of the Temple and Solomon's House (6:1–9:9)
    E. The Further Building Projects of Solomon (9:10–28)
    F. The Culmination of Solomon's Wisdom and Wealth (10:1–29)
    G. The Decline of Solomon (11:1–43)

II. THE DIVIDED KINGDOM: THE KINGS OF ISRAEL AND JUDAH (12:1–22:53)
    A. The Rise of Idolatry: Jeroboam of Israel/Rehoboam of Judah (12:1–14:31)
    B. Kings of Judah/Israel (15:1–16:22)
    C. The Dynasty of Omri and Its Influence: The Rise and Fall of Baal Worship in Israel and Judah (16:23–22:53)
        1. The introduction of Baal worship (16:23–34)
        2. Elijah and the opposition to Baal worship (17:1–22:53)

THE KINGS OF ISRAEL AND JUDAH

King	Scripture

United Kingdom

Saul . . . . 1 Samuel 9:1–31:13; 1 Chronicles 10:1–14
David . . . . 2 Samuel; 1Kings 1:1–2:9; 1 Chronicles 11:1–29:30
Solomon . . . . 1 Kings 2:10–11:43; 2 Chronicles 1:1–9:31

Northern Kingdom (Israel)

Jeroboam I . . . . 1 Kings 12:25–14:20
Nadab . . . . 1 Kings 15:25–31
Baasha . . . . 1 Kings 15:32–16:7
Elah . . . . 1 Kings 16:8–14
Zimri . . . . 1 Kings 16:15–20
Tibni . . . . 1 Kings 16:21,22
Omri . . . . 1 Kings 16:21–28
Ahab . . . . 1 Kings 16:29–22:40
Ahaziah . . . . 1 Kings 22:51–53; 2 Kings 1:1–18
Jehoram (Joram) . . . . 2 Kings 2:1–8:15
Jehu . . . . 2 Kings 9:1–10:36
Jehoahaz . . . . 2 Kings 13:1–9
Jehoash (Joash) . . . . 2 Kings 13:10–25
Jeroboam II . . . . 2 Kings 14:23–29
Zechariah . . . . 2 Kings 15:8–12
Shallum . . . . 2 Kings 15:13–15
Menahem . . . . 2 Kings 15:16–22
Pekahiah . . . . 2 Kings 15:23–26
Pekah . . . . 2 Kings 15:27–31
Hoshea . . . . 2 Kings 17:1–41

Southern Kingdom (Judah)

Rehoboam . . . . 1 Kings 12:1–14:31; 2 Chronicles 10:1–12:16
Abijam (Abijah) . . . . 1 Kings 15:1–8; 2 Chronicles 13:1–22
Asa . . . . 1 Kings 15:9–24; 2 Chronicles 14:1–16:14
Jehoshaphat . . . . 1 Kings 22:41–50; 2 Chronicles 17:1–20:37
Joram (Jehoram) . . . . 2 Kings 8:16–24; 2 Chronicles 21:1–20
Ahaziah . . . . 2 Kings 8:25–29; 2 Chronicles 22:1–9
Athaliah (queen) . . . . 2 Kings 11:1–16; 2 Chronicles 22:10–23:21
Joash (Jehoash) . . . . 2 Kings 11:17–12:21; 2 Chronicles 23:1–24:27
Amaziah . . . . 2K ings 14:1–22; 2 Chronicles 25:1–28
Uzziah (Azariah) . . . . 2 Kings 15:1–7; 2 Chronicles 26:1–23
Jotham . . . . 2 Kings 15:32–38; 2 Chronicles 27:1–9
Ahaz . . . . 2 Kings 16:1–20; 2 Chronicles 28:1–27
Hezekiah . . . . 2 Kings 18:1–20:21; 2 Chronicles 29:1–32:33
Manasseh . . . . 2 Kings 21:1–18; 2 Chronicles 33:1–20
Amon . . . . 2 Kings 21:19–26; 2 Chronicles 33:21–25
Josiah . . . . 2 Kings 22:1–23:30; 2 Chronicles 34:1–35:27
Jehoahaz . . . . 2 Kings 23:31–33; 2 Chronicles 36:1–4
Jehoiakim . . . . 2 Kings 23:34–24:7; 2 Chronicles 36:5–8
Jehoiachin . . . . 2 Kings 24:8–16; 2 Chronicles 36:9,10
Zedekiah . . . . 2 Kings 24:18–25:21; 2 Chronicles 36:11–21

Adonijah Presumes to Be King

1 Now King David was old, advanced in years; and they put covers on him, but he could not get warm. ²Therefore his servants said to him, "Let a young woman, a virgin, be sought for our lord the king, and let her stand before the king, and let her care for him; and let her lie in your bosom, that our lord the king may be warm." ³So they sought for a lovely young woman throughout all the territory of Israel, and found Abishag the Shunammite, and brought her to the king. ⁴The young woman *was* very lovely; and she cared for the king, and served him; but the king did not know her.

> **1:2 the king may be warm.** In his old age, King David had circulatory problems that made it difficult to keep warm. The royal staff suggested that a young virgin nurse watch over him and warm him with her body heat at night. This was a legitimate medical custom of that day.

⁵Then Adonijah the son of Haggith exalted himself, saying, "I will be king"; and he prepared for himself chariots and horsemen, and fifty men to run before him. ⁶(And his father had not rebuked him at any time by saying, "Why have you done so?" He *was* also very good-looking. *His mother* had borne him after Absalom.) ⁷Then he conferred with Joab the son of Zeruiah and with Abiathar the priest, and they followed and helped Adonijah. ⁸But Zadok the priest, Benaiah the son of Jehoiada, Nathan the prophet, Shimei, Rei, and the mighty men who *belonged* to David were not with Adonijah.

⁹And Adonijah sacrificed sheep and oxen and fattened cattle by the stone of Zoheleth, which *is* by En Rogel; he also invited all his brothers, the king's sons, and all the men of Judah, the king's servants. ¹⁰But he did not invite Nathan the prophet, Benaiah, the mighty men, or Solomon his brother.

¹¹So Nathan spoke to Bathsheba the mother of Solomon, saying, "Have you not heard that Adonijah the son of Haggith has become king, and David our lord does not know *it*? ¹²Come, please, let me now give you advice, that you may save your own life and the life of your son Solomon. ¹³Go immediately to King David and say to him, 'Did you not, my lord, O king, swear to your maidservant, saying, "Assuredly your son Solomon shall reign after me, and he shall sit on my throne"? Why then has Adonijah become king?' ¹⁴Then, while you are still talking there with the king, I also will come in after you and confirm your words."

> **1:13 Did you not...swear.** This oath was given privately by David, perhaps to both Nathan and Bathsheba. Solomon's choice by the Lord was implicit in his name Jedediah, meaning, "loved by the LORD" (2 Sam. 12:24,25) and explicit in David's declaration to Solomon (1 Chr. 22:6–13).

¹⁵So Bathsheba went into the chamber to the king. (Now the king was very old, and Abishag the Shunammite was serving the king.) ¹⁶And Bathsheba bowed and did homage to the king. Then the king said, "What is your wish?"

¹⁷Then she said to him, "My lord, you swore by the LORD your God to your maidservant, *saying*, 'Assuredly Solomon your son shall reign after me, and he shall sit on my throne.' ¹⁸So now, look! Adonijah has become king; and now, my lord the king, you do not know about *it*. ¹⁹He has sacrificed oxen and fattened cattle and sheep in abundance, and has invited all the sons of the king, Abiathar the priest, and Joab the commander of the army; but Solomon your servant he has not invited. ²⁰And as for you, my lord, O king, the eyes of all Israel *are* on you, that you should tell them who will sit on the throne of my lord the king after him. ²¹Otherwise it will happen, when my lord the king rests with his fathers, that I and my son Solomon will be counted as offenders."

²²And just then, while she was still talking with the king, Nathan the prophet also came in. ²³So they told the king, saying, "Here is Nathan the prophet." And when he came in before the king, he bowed down before the king with his face to the ground. ²⁴And Nathan said, "My lord, O king, have you said, 'Adonijah shall reign after me, and he shall sit on my throne'? ²⁵For he has gone down today, and has sacrificed oxen and fattened cattle and sheep in abundance, and has invited all the king's sons, and the commanders of the army, and Abi-

athar the priest; and look! They are eating and drinking before him; and they say, 'Long live King Adonijah!' ²⁶But he has not invited me—me your servant—nor Zadok the priest, nor Benaiah the son of Jehoiada, nor your servant Solomon. ²⁷Has this thing been done by my lord the king, and you have not told your servant who should sit on the throne of my lord the king after him?"

David Proclaims Solomon King

²⁸Then King David answered and said, "Call Bathsheba to me." So she came into the king's presence and stood before the king. ²⁹And the king took an oath and said, "As the LORD lives, who has redeemed my life from every distress, ³⁰just as I swore to you by the LORD God of Israel, saying, 'Assuredly Solomon your son shall be king after me, and he shall sit on my throne in my place,' so I certainly will do this day."

³¹Then Bathsheba bowed with her face to the earth, and paid homage to the king, and said, "Let my lord King David live forever!"

³²And King David said, "Call to me Zadok the priest, Nathan the prophet, and Benaiah the son of Jehoiada." So they came before the king. ³³The king also said to them, "Take with you the servants of your lord, and have Solomon my son ride on my own mule, and take him down to Gihon. ³⁴There let Zadok the priest and Nathan the prophet anoint him king over Israel; and blow the horn, and say, 'Long live King Solomon!' ³⁵Then you shall come up after him, and he shall come and sit on my throne, and he shall be king in my place. For I have appointed him to be ruler over Israel and Judah."

> **1:33 my own mule.** By riding David's royal mule, Solomon was shown to be David's chosen successor.

³⁶Benaiah the son of Jehoiada answered the king and said, "Amen! May the LORD God of my lord the king say so too. ³⁷As the LORD has been with my lord the king, even so may He be with Solomon, and make his throne greater than the throne of my lord King David."

³⁸So Zadok the priest, Nathan the prophet, Benaiah the son of Jehoiada, the Cherethites, and the Pelethites went down and had

Solomon ride on King David's mule, and took him to Gihon. ³⁹Then Zadok the priest took a horn of oil from the tabernacle and anointed Solomon. And they blew the horn, and all the people said, "Long live King Solomon!" ⁴⁰And all the people went up after him; and the people played the flutes and rejoiced with great joy, so that the earth seemed to split with their sound.

> **1:39 tabernacle.** This was the tent that David set up in Jerusalem to house the ark of the covenant, not the tabernacle of Moses (see 3:4; 2 Sam. 6:17).

⁴¹Now Adonijah and all the guests who were with him heard it as they finished eating. And when Joab heard the sound of the horn, he said, "Why is the city in such a noisy uproar?" ⁴²While he was still speaking, there came Jonathan, the son of Abiathar the priest. And Adonijah said to him, "Come in, for you are a prominent man, and bring good news."

⁴³Then Jonathan answered and said to Adonijah, "No! Our lord King David has made Solomon king. ⁴⁴The king has sent with him Zadok the priest, Nathan the prophet, Benaiah the son of Jehoiada, the Cherethites, and the Pelethites; and they have made him ride on the king's mule. ⁴⁵So Zadok the priest and Nathan the prophet have anointed him king at Gihon; and they have gone up from there rejoicing, so that the city is in an uproar. This is the noise that you have heard. ⁴⁶Also Solomon sits on the throne of the kingdom. ⁴⁷And moreover the king's servants have gone to bless our lord King David, saying, 'May God make the name of Solomon better than your name, and may He make his throne greater than your throne.' Then the king bowed himself on the bed. ⁴⁸Also the king said thus, 'Blessed be the LORD God of Israel, who has given one to sit on my throne this day, while my eyes see it!' "

⁴⁹So all the guests who were with Adonijah were afraid, and arose, and each one went his way.

⁵⁰Now Adonijah was afraid of Solomon; so he arose, and went and took hold of the horns of the altar. ⁵¹And it was told Solomon, saying, "Indeed Adonijah is afraid of King Solomon; for look, he has taken hold

of the horns of the altar, saying, 'Let King Solomon swear to me today that he will not put his servant to death with the sword.' "

1:50 horns of the altar. The "horns" were corner projections on the altar of burnt offering where priests smeared the blood of the sacrifices (Ex. 27:2; 29:12). Adonijah sought God's protection by taking hold of the horns (see 2:28; Ex. 21:13,14)

⁵²Then Solomon said, "If he proves himself a worthy man, not one hair of him shall fall to the earth; but if wickedness is found in him, he shall die." ⁵³So King Solomon sent them to bring him down from the altar. And he came and fell down before King Solomon; and Solomon said to him, "Go to your house."

David's Instructions to Solomon

2 Now the days of David drew near that he should die, and he charged Solomon his son, saying: ²"I go the way of all the earth; be strong, therefore, and prove yourself a man. ³And keep the charge of the LORD your God: to walk in His ways, to keep His statutes, His commandments, His judgments, and His testimonies, as it is written in the Law of Moses, that you may prosper in all that you do and wherever you turn; ⁴that the LORD may fulfill His word which He spoke concerning me, saying, 'If your sons take heed to their way, to walk before Me in truth with all their heart and with all their soul,' He said, 'you shall not lack a man on the throne of Israel.'

2:2 the way of all the earth. This was an expression for death (Josh. 23:14). **be strong...prove yourself a man.** This was an expression of encouragement (Deut. 31:7,23; Josh. 1:6,7,9,18) with which David sought to prepare Solomon for the difficult tasks and battles in his future.

⁵"Moreover you know also what Joab the son of Zeruiah did to me, *and* what he did to the two commanders of the armies of Israel, to Abner the son of Ner and Amasa the son of Jether, whom he killed. And he shed the blood of war in peacetime, and put the blood of war on his belt that *was* around his waist, and on his sandals that *were* on his feet. ⁶Therefore do according to your wisdom, and do not let his gray hair go

down to the grave in peace. ⁷"But show kindness to the sons of Barzillai the Gileadite, and let them be among those who eat at your table, for so they came to me when I fled from Absalom your brother. ⁸"And see, *you have* with you Shimei the son of Gera, a Benjamite from Bahurim, who cursed me with a malicious curse in the day when I went to Mahanaim. But he came down to meet me at the Jordan, and I swore to him by the LORD, saying, 'I will not put you to death with the sword.' ⁹Now therefore, do not hold him guiltless, for you *are* a wise man and know what you ought to do to him; but bring his gray hair down to the grave with blood."

Death of David

¹⁰So David rested with his fathers, and was buried in the City of David. ¹¹The period that David reigned over Israel *was* forty years; seven years he reigned in Hebron, and in Jerusalem he reigned thirty-three years. ¹²Then Solomon sat on the throne of his father David; and his kingdom was firmly established.

2:12 firmly established. Solomon's succession was blessed by the Lord's approval, and he experienced, unchallenged authority, prosperity, and renown (v. 46).

Solomon Executes Adonijah

¹³Now Adonijah the son of Haggith came to Bathsheba the mother of Solomon. So she said, "Do you come peaceably?"

And he said, "Peaceably." ¹⁴Moreover he said, "I have something *to say* to you."

And she said, "Say it."

¹⁵Then he said, "You know that the kingdom was mine, and all Israel had set their expectations on me, that I should reign. However, the kingdom has been turned over, and has become my brother's; for it was his from the LORD. ¹⁶Now I ask one petition of you; do not deny me."

And she said to him, "Say it."

¹⁷Then he said, "Please speak to King Solomon, for he will not refuse you, that he may give me Abishag the Shunammite as wife."

¹⁸So Bathsheba said, "Very well, I will speak for you to the king."

¹⁹Bathsheba therefore went to King Solomon, to speak to him for Adonijah. And the king rose up to meet her and bowed down to her, and sat down on his throne and had a throne set for the king's mother; so she sat at his right hand. ²⁰Then she said, "I desire one small petition of you; do not refuse me."

And the king said to her, "Ask it, my mother, for I will not refuse you."

²¹So she said, "Let Abishag the Shunammite be given to Adonijah your brother as wife."

²²And King Solomon answered and said to his mother, "Now why do you ask Abishag the Shunammite for Adonijah? Ask for him the kingdom also—for he *is* my older brother—for him, and for Abiathar the priest, and for Joab the son of Zeruiah." ²³Then King Solomon swore by the LORD, saying, "May God do so to me, and more also, if Adonijah has not spoken this word against his own life! ²⁴Now therefore, *as the* LORD lives, who has confirmed me and set me on the throne of David my father, and who has established a house*ᵃ* for me, as He promised, Adonijah shall be put to death today!"

> **2:17–22 give me Abishag.** Possession of the royal harem was a sign of kingship (see 2 Sam. 3:8). Adonijah's request for Abishag was an attempt to support his claim to the kingship and perhaps generate a revolt to usurp the throne. **Ask for...the kingdom also.** Solomon recognized Adonijah's disloyal request as an attempt to usurp the throne, and he pronounced a legal death sentence on Adonijah (vv. 23,24).

²⁵So King Solomon sent by the hand of Benaiah the son of Jehoiada; and he struck him down, and he died.

Abiathar Exiled, Joab Executed

²⁶And to Abiathar the priest the king said, "Go to Anathoth, to your own fields, for you *are* deserving of death; but I will not put you to death at this time, because you carried the ark of the Lord GOD before my father David, and because you were afflicted every time my father was afflicted." ²⁷So Solomon removed Abiathar from being priest to the LORD, that he might fulfill the word of the LORD which He spoke concerning the house of Eli at Shiloh.

²⁸Then news came to Joab, for Joab had defected to Adonijah, though he had not defected to Absalom. So Joab fled to the tabernacle of the LORD, and took hold of the horns of the altar. ²⁹And King Solomon was told, "Joab has fled to the tabernacle of the LORD; there *he is,* by the altar." Then Solomon sent Benaiah the son of Jehoiada, saying, "Go, strike him down." ³⁰So Benaiah went to the tabernacle of the LORD, and said to him, "Thus says the king, 'Come out!' "

And he said, "No, but I will die here." And Benaiah brought back word to the king, saying, "Thus said Joab, and thus he answered me."

³¹Then the king said to him, "Do as he has said, and strike him down and bury him, that you may take away from me and from the house of my father the innocent blood which Joab shed. ³²So the LORD will return his blood on his head, because he struck down two men more righteous and better than he, and killed them with the sword—Abner the son of Ner, the commander of the army of Israel, and Amasa the son of Jether, the commander of the army of Judah—though my father David did not know *it.* ³³Their blood shall therefore return upon the head of Joab and upon the head of his descendants forever. But upon David and his descendants, upon his house and his throne, there shall be peace forever from the LORD."

> **2:31 strike him down.** Like Adonijah (1:50), Joab sought protection at the altar (2:28). Protection at the altar only applied to accidental crimes, not to murder (Ex. 21:14), so Solomon ordered Benaiah to kill Joab, as David had advised (2:6).

³⁴So Benaiah the son of Jehoiada went up and struck and killed him; and he was buried in his own house in the wilderness. ³⁵The king put Benaiah the son of Jehoiada in his place over the army, and the king put Zadok the priest in the place of Abiathar.

Shimei Executed

³⁶Then the king sent and called for Shimei, and said to him, "Build yourself a house in

---

2:24 *ᵃ*That is, a royal dynasty

Jerusalem and dwell there, and do not go out from there anywhere. ³⁷For it shall be, on the day you go out and cross the Brook Kidron, know for certain you shall surely die; your blood shall be on your own head."

³⁸And Shimei said to the king, "The saying *is* good. As my lord the king has said, so your servant will do." So Shimei dwelt in Jerusalem many days.

³⁹Now it happened at the end of three years, that two slaves of Shimei ran away to Achish the son of Maachah, king of Gath. And they told Shimei, saying, "Look, your slaves *are* in Gath!" ⁴⁰So Shimei arose, saddled his donkey, and went to Achish at Gath to seek his slaves. And Shimei went and brought his slaves from Gath. ⁴¹And Solomon was told that Shimei had gone from Jerusalem to Gath and had come back. ⁴²Then the king sent and called for Shimei, and said to him, "Did I not make you swear by the LORD, and warn you, saying, 'Know for certain that on the day you go out and travel anywhere, you shall surely die'? And you said to me, 'The word I have heard *is* good.' ⁴³Why then have you not kept the oath of the LORD and the commandment that I gave you?" ⁴⁴The king said moreover to Shimei, "You know, as your heart acknowledges, all the wickedness that you did to my father David; therefore the LORD will return your wickedness on your own head. ⁴⁵But King Solomon *shall be* blessed, and the throne of David shall be established before the LORD forever."

⁴⁶So the king commanded Benaiah the son of Jehoiada; and he went out and struck him down, and he died. Thus the kingdom was established in the hand of Solomon.

Solomon Requests Wisdom

3 Now Solomon made a treaty with Pharaoh king of Egypt, and married Pharaoh's daughter; then he brought her to the City of David until he had finished building his own house, and the house of the LORD, and the wall all around Jerusalem. ²Meanwhile the people sacrificed at the high places, because there was no house built for the name of the LORD until those days. ³And Solomon loved the LORD, walking in the statutes of his father David, except that he sacrificed and burned incense at the high places.

⁴Now the king went to Gibeon to sacrifice there, for that *was* the great high place: Solomon offered a thousand burnt offerings on that altar. ⁵At Gibeon the LORD appeared to Solomon in a dream by night; and God said, "Ask! What shall I give you?"

3:5 dream. God often gave revelation in dreams (Gen. 26:24; Dan. 2:7). This dream was unique in that it was a two-way conversation between the Lord and Solomon.

⁶And Solomon said: "You have shown great mercy to Your servant David my father, because he walked before You in truth, in righteousness, and in uprightness of heart with You; You have continued this great kindness for him, and You have given him a son to sit on his throne, as *it is* this day. ⁷Now, O LORD my God, You have made Your servant king instead of my father David, but I *am* a little child; I do not know *how* to go out or come in. ⁸And Your servant *is* in the midst of Your people whom You have chosen, a great people, too numerous to be numbered or counted. ⁹Therefore give to Your servant an understanding heart to judge Your people, that I may discern between good and evil. For who is able to judge this great people of Yours?"

¹⁰The speech pleased the LORD, that Solomon had asked this thing. ¹¹Then God said to him: "Because you have asked this thing, and have not asked long life for yourself, nor have asked riches for yourself, nor have asked the life of your enemies, but have asked for yourself understanding to discern justice, ¹²behold, I have done according to your words; see, I have given you a wise and understanding heart, so that there has not been anyone like you before you, nor shall any like you arise after you. ¹³And I have also given you what you have not asked: both riches and honor, so that there shall not be anyone like you among the kings all your days. ¹⁴So if you walk in

3:9,10 an understanding heart. Solomon desired "a listening heart" to govern God's people with wisdom. **pleased the LORD.** The Lord was delighted that Solomon had not asked for personal benefits such as long life, wealth, or the death of his enemies.

My ways, to keep My statutes and My commandments, as your father David walked, then I will lengthen your days."

¹⁵Then Solomon awoke; and indeed it had been a dream. And he came to Jerusalem and stood before the ark of the covenant of the LORD, offered up burnt offerings, offered peace offerings, and made a feast for all his servants.

Solomon's Wise Judgment

¹⁶Now two women *who were* harlots came to the king, and stood before him. ¹⁷And one woman said, "O my lord, this woman and I dwell in the same house; and I gave birth while she *was* in the house. ¹⁸Then it happened, the third day after I had given birth, that this woman also gave birth. And we *were* together; no one *was* with us in the house, except the two of us in the house. ¹⁹And this woman's son died in the night, because she lay on him. ²⁰So she arose in the middle of the night and took my son from my side, while your maidservant slept, and laid him in her bosom, and laid her dead child in my bosom. ²¹And when I rose in the morning to nurse my son, there he was, dead. But when I had examined him in the morning, indeed, he was not my son whom I had borne."

²²Then the other woman said, "No! But the living one *is* my son, and the dead one *is* your son."

And the first woman said, "No! But the dead one *is* your son, and the living one *is* my son."

Thus they spoke before the king.

²³And the king said, "The one says, 'This *is* my son, who lives, and your son *is* the dead one'; and the other says, 'No! But your son *is* the dead one, and my son *is* the living one.' " ²⁴Then the king said, "Bring me a sword." So they brought a sword before the king. ²⁵And the king said, "Divide the living child in two, and give half to one, and half to the other."

²⁶Then the woman whose son *was* living spoke to the king, for she yearned with compassion for her son; and she said, "O my lord, give her the living child, and by no means kill him!"

But the other said, "Let him be neither mine nor yours, *but* divide *him.*"

²⁷So the king answered and said, "Give the first woman the living child, and by no means kill him; she *is* his mother."

²⁸And all Israel heard of the judgment which the king had rendered; and they feared the king, for they saw that the wisdom of God *was* in him to administer justice.

Solomon's Administration

4 So King Solomon was king over all Israel. ²And these *were* his officials: Azariah the son of Zadok, the priest; ³Elihoreph and Ahijah, the sons of Shisha, scribes; Jehoshaphat the son of Ahilud, the recorder; ⁴Benaiah the son of Jehoiada, over the army; Zadok and Abiathar, the priests; ⁵Azariah the son of Nathan, over the officers; Zabud the son of Nathan, a priest *and* the king's friend; ⁶Ahishar, over the household; and Adoniram the son of Abda, over the labor force.

⁷And Solomon had twelve governors over all Israel, who provided food for the king and his household; each one made provision for one month of the year. ⁸These *are* their names: Ben-Hur,ᵃ in the mountains of Ephraim; ⁹Ben-Deker,ᵃ in Makaz, Shaalbim, Beth Shemesh, and Elon Beth Hanan; ¹⁰Ben-Hesed,ᵃ in Arubboth; to him *belonged* Sochoh and all the land of Hepher; ¹¹Ben-Abinadab,ᵃ *in* all the regions of Dor; he had Taphath the daughter of Solomon as wife; ¹²Baana the son of Ahilud, *in* Taanach, Megiddo, and all Beth Shean, which *is* beside Zaretan below Jezreel, from Beth Shean to Abel Meholah, as far as the other side of Jokneam; ¹³Ben-Geber,ᵃ in Ramoth

---

3:25 half...half. In ordering his servants to cut the child in two, Solomon knew the real mother would object (see Ex. 21:35).

4:7 twelve governors. Solomon divided the land into 12 geographical districts, each supervised by a governor. Each month a different governor collected provisions in his district to supply the king and his staff.

4:8 ᵃLiterally *Son of Hur*   **4:9** ᵃLiterally *Son of Deker*   **4:10** ᵃLiterally *Son of Hesed*   **4:11** ᵃLiterally *Son of Abinadab*   **4:13** ᵃLiterally *Son of Geber*

Gilead; to him *belonged* the towns of Jair the son of Manasseh, in Gilead; to him *also belonged* the region of Argob in Bashan— sixty large cities with walls and bronze gate-bars; ¹⁴Ahinadab the son of Iddo, *in* Mahanaim; ¹⁵Ahimaaz, in Naphtali; he also took Basemath the daughter of Solomon as wife; ¹⁶Baanah the son of Hushai, in Asher and Aloth; ¹⁷Jehoshaphat the son of Paruah, in Issachar; ¹⁸Shimei the son of Elah, in Benjamin; ¹⁹Geber the son of Uri, in the land of Gilead, *in* the country of Sihon king of the Amorites, and of Og king of Bashan. *He was* the only governor who *was* in the land.

Prosperity and Wisdom of Solomon's Reign

²⁰Judah and Israel *were* as numerous as the sand by the sea in multitude, eating and drinking and rejoicing. ²¹So Solomon reigned over all kingdoms from the River*ᵃ to* the land of the Philistines, as far as the border of Egypt. *They* brought tribute and served Solomon all the days of his life.

> **4:20 numerous as the sand by the sea.** This is an allusion to the Lord's promise to Abraham in Gen. 22:17. The early years of Solomon's reign were characterized by population growth, peace, and prosperity. This was a foreshadowing of the blessings that would prevail in Israel when the Abrahamic Covenant would be fulfilled.

²²Now Solomon's provision for one day was thirty kors of fine flour, sixty kors of meal, ²³ten fatted oxen, twenty oxen from the pastures, and one hundred sheep, besides deer, gazelles, roebucks, and fatted fowl. ²⁴For he had dominion over all *the region* on this side of the River*ᵃ* from Tiphsah even to Gaza, namely over all the kings on this side of the River; and he had peace on every side all around him. ²⁵And Judah and Israel dwelt safely, each man under his vine and his fig tree, from Dan as far as Beersheba, all the days of Solomon. ²⁶Solomon had forty*ᵃ* thousand stalls of horses for his chariots, and twelve thousand horsemen. ²⁷And these governors,

each man in his month, provided food for King Solomon and for all who came to King Solomon's table. There was no lack in their supply. ²⁸They also brought barley and straw to the proper place, for the horses and steeds, each man according to his charge.

²⁹And God gave Solomon wisdom and exceedingly great understanding, and largeness of heart like the sand on the seashore. ³⁰Thus Solomon's wisdom excelled the wisdom of all the men of the East and all the wisdom of Egypt. ³¹For he was wiser than all men—than Ethan the Ezrahite, and Heman, Chalcol, and Darda, the sons of Mahol; and his fame was in all the surrounding nations. ³²He spoke three thousand proverbs, and his songs were one thousand and five. ³³Also he spoke of trees, from the cedar tree of Lebanon even to the hyssop that springs out of the wall; he spoke also of animals, of birds, of creeping things, and of fish. ³⁴And men of all nations, from all the kings of the earth who had heard of his wisdom, came to hear the wisdom of Solomon.

> **4:30 the East...Egypt.** The men to the east of Israel in Mesopotamia and Arabia (see Job 1:3) and in Egypt were known for their wisdom. Egypt was known for its learning, science, and culture. Solomon's wisdom was superior to all (v. 31).

Solomon Prepares to Build the Temple

5 Now Hiram king of Tyre sent his servants to Solomon, because he heard that they had anointed him king in place of his father, for Hiram had always loved David. ²Then Solomon sent to Hiram, saying:

3   You know how my father David could not build a house for the name of the LORD his God because of the wars which were fought against him on every side, until the LORD put *his* foes*ᵃ* under the soles of his feet.

4   But now the LORD my God has given me rest on every side; *there is* neither adversary nor evil occurrence.

5   And behold, I propose to build a house for the name of the LORD my

---

4:21 *ᵃ*That is, the Euphrates   **4:24** *ᵃ*That is, the Euphrates   **4:26** *ᵃ*Following Masoretic Text and most other authorities; some manuscripts of the Septuagint read *four* (compare 2 Chronicles 9:25).
5:3 *ᵃ*Literally *them*

God, as the LORD spoke to my father David, saying, "Your son, whom I will set on your throne in your place, he shall build the house for My name."
⁶ Now therefore, command that they cut down cedars for me from Lebanon; and my servants will be with your servants, and I will pay you wages for your servants according to whatever you say. For you know *there is* none among us who has skill to cut timber like the Sidonians.

⁷So it was, when Hiram heard the words of Solomon, that he rejoiced greatly and said,

Blessed *be* the LORD this day, for He has given David a wise son over this great people!

5:7 Blessed *be* the LORD. Hiram may have been a worshiper of God, but he may have only acknowledged Jehovah as God of the Hebrews (see 2 Chr. 2:16). **a wise son.** Hiram recognized Solomon's wisdom in seeking to honor his father David's desires.

⁸Then Hiram sent to Solomon, saying:

I have considered *the message* which you sent me, *and* I will do all you desire concerning the cedar and cypress logs.
⁹ My servants shall bring *them* down from Lebanon to the sea; I will float them in rafts by sea to the place you indicate to me, and will have them broken apart there; then you can take *them* away. And you shall fulfill my desire by giving food for my household.

¹⁰Then Hiram gave Solomon cedar and cypress logs *according to* all his desire. ¹¹And Solomon gave Hiram twenty thousand kors of wheat *as* food for his household, and twenty*ᵃ* kors of pressed oil. Thus Solomon gave to Hiram year by year.

¹²So the LORD gave Solomon wisdom, as He had promised him; and there was peace between Hiram and Solomon, and the two of them made a treaty together.
¹³Then King Solomon raised up a labor force out of all Israel; and the labor force was thirty thousand men. ¹⁴And he sent them to Lebanon, ten thousand a month in shifts: they were one month in Lebanon *and* two months at home; Adoniram *was* in charge of the labor force. ¹⁵Solomon had seventy thousand who carried burdens, and eighty thousand who quarried *stone* in the mountains, ¹⁶besides three thousand three hundred*ᵃ* from the chiefs of Solomon's deputies, who supervised the people who labored in the work. ¹⁷And the king commanded them to quarry large stones, costly stones, *and* hewn stones, to lay the foundation of the temple.*ᵃ* ¹⁸So Solomon's builders, Hiram's builders, and the Gebalites quarried *them*; and they prepared timber and stones to build the temple.

Solomon Builds the Temple

6 And it came to pass in the four hundred and eightieth*ᵃ* year after the children of Israel had come out of the land of Egypt, in the fourth year of Solomon's reign over Israel, in the month of Ziv, which *is* the second month, that he began to build the house of the LORD. ²Now the house which King Solomon built for the LORD, its length *was* sixty cubits, its width twenty, and its height thirty cubits. ³The vestibule in front of the sanctuary*ᵃ* of the house *was* twenty cubits long across the width of the house, *and* the width of *the vestibule*ᵇ extended

6:2 cubits. Normally the cubit was about 18 inches. This would make the temple 90 feet long, 30 feet wide, and 45 feet high. However, 2 Chr. 3:3 may indicate that the cubit used in constructing the temple was 21 inches. With this measurement, the temple would have been 105 feet long, 35 feet wide, and 52 and a half feet high. The dimensions of the temple seem to be double those of the tabernacle (see Ex. 26:15–30).

5:11 *ᵃ*Following Masoretic Text, Targum, and Vulgate; Septuagint and Syriac read *twenty thousand*. 5:16 *ᵃ*Following Masoretic Text, Targum, and Vulgate; Septuagint reads *three thousand six hundred*. 5:17 *ᵃ*Literally *house,* and so frequently throughout this book   6:1 *ᵃ*Following Masoretic Text, Targum, and Vulgate; Septuagint reads *fortieth*.   6:3 *ᵃ*Hebrew *heykal;* here the main room of the temple, elsewhere called the holy place (compare Exodus 26:33 and Ezekiel 41:1)   *ᵇ*Literally *it*

ten cubits from the front of the house. ⁴And he made for the house windows with beveled frames.

⁵Against the wall of the temple he built chambers all around, *against* the walls of the temple, all around the sanctuary and the inner sanctuary.*ᵃ* Thus he made side chambers all around it. ⁶The lowest chamber *was* five cubits wide, the middle *was* six cubits wide, and the third *was* seven cubits wide; for he made narrow ledges around the outside of the temple, so that *the support beams* would not be fastened into the walls of the temple. ⁷And the temple, when it was being built, was built with stone finished at the quarry, so that no hammer or chisel *or* any iron tool was heard in the temple while it was being built. ⁸The doorway for the middle story*ᵃ was* on the right side of the temple. They went up by stairs to the mid-

dle *story*, and from the middle to the third.

⁹So he built the temple and finished it, and he paneled the temple with beams and boards of cedar. ¹⁰And he built side chambers against the entire temple, each five cubits high; they were attached to the temple with cedar beams.

¹¹Then the word of the LORD came to Solomon, saying: ¹²"Concerning this temple

> **6:11–13** The Lord spoke to Solomon during the construction of the temple, probably through a prophet. Solomon was reminded that he must obey the Lord's commands in order for God to fulfill His Word to David (see 2:3,4; 3:14). God's words, "I will dwell among the children of Israel," in v. 13 implied that Solomon's temple was to succeed the tabernacle. The Lord forewarned Solomon and Israel that only their obedience to Him would assure His presence in the temple.

6:5 *ᵃ*Hebrew *debir;* here the inner room of the temple, elsewhere called the Most Holy Place (compare verse 16)   6:8 *ᵃ*Following Masoretic Text and Vulgate; Septuagint reads *upper story;* Targum reads *ground story.*

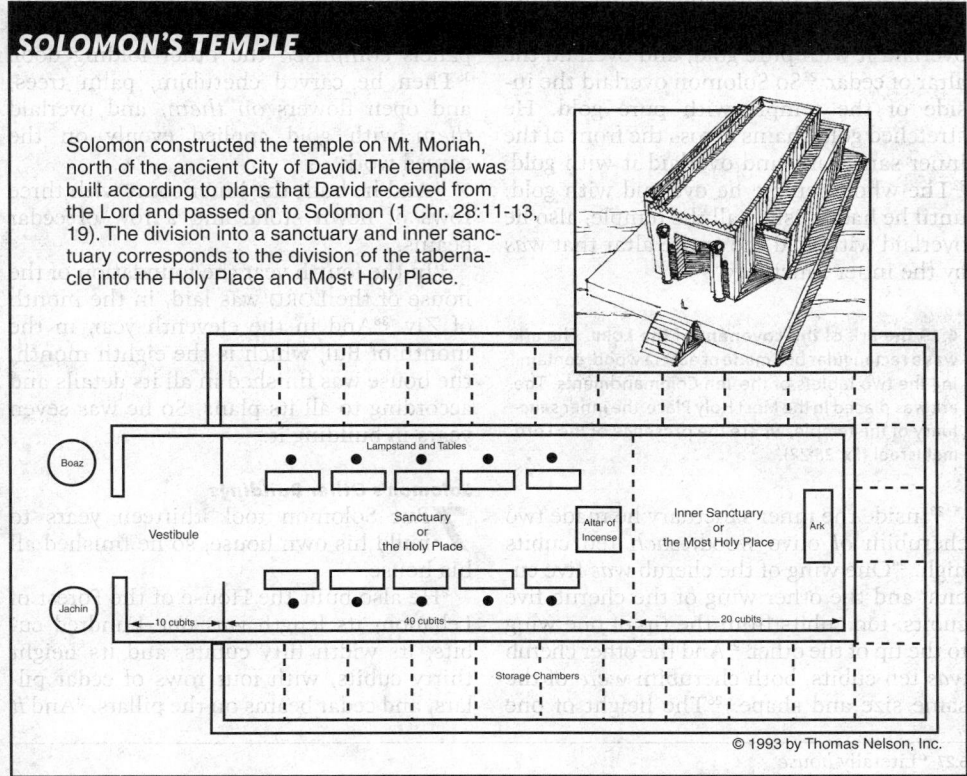

SOLOMON'S TEMPLE

Solomon constructed the temple on Mt. Moriah, north of the ancient City of David. The temple was built according to plans that David received from the Lord and passed on to Solomon (1 Chr. 28:11-13, 19). The division into a sanctuary and inner sanctuary corresponds to the division of the tabernacle into the Holy Place and Most Holy Place.

which you are building, if you walk in My statutes, execute My judgments, keep all My commandments, and walk in them, then I will perform My word with you, which I spoke to your father David. ¹³And I will dwell among the children of Israel, and will not forsake My people Israel."

¹⁴So Solomon built the temple and finished it. ¹⁵And he built the inside walls of the temple with cedar boards; from the floor of the temple to the ceiling he paneled the inside with wood; and he covered the floor of the temple with planks of cypress. ¹⁶Then he built the twenty-cubit room at the rear of the temple, from floor to ceiling, with cedar boards; he built *it* inside as the inner sanctuary, as the Most Holy *Place.* ¹⁷And in front of it the temple sanctuary was forty cubits *long.* ¹⁸The inside of the temple was cedar, carved with ornamental buds and open flowers. All *was* cedar; there was no stone *to be* seen.

¹⁹And he prepared the inner sanctuary inside the temple, to set the ark of the covenant of the LORD there. ²⁰The inner sanctuary *was* twenty cubits long, twenty cubits wide, and twenty cubits high. He overlaid it with pure gold, and overlaid the altar of cedar. ²¹So Solomon overlaid the inside of the temple with pure gold. He stretched gold chains across the front of the inner sanctuary, and overlaid it with gold. ²²The whole temple he overlaid with gold, until he had finished all the temple; also he overlaid with gold the entire altar that *was* by the inner sanctuary.

6:19 the ark of the covenant of the LORD. The ark was a rectangular box made of acacia wood, containing the two tablets of the Ten Commandments. The ark was placed in the Most Holy Place, the inner sanctuary of the temple, where the presence of the Lord met Israel (Ex. 25:22).

²³Inside the inner sanctuary he made two cherubim *of* olive wood, *each* ten cubits high. ²⁴One wing of the cherub *was* five cubits, and the other wing of the cherub five cubits: ten cubits from the tip of one wing to the tip of the other. ²⁵And the other cherub *was* ten cubits; both cherubim *were* of the same size and shape. ²⁶The height of one cherub *was* ten cubits, and so *was* the other cherub. ²⁷Then he set the cherubim inside the inner room;[a] and they stretched out the wings of the cherubim so that the wing of the one touched *one* wall, and the wing of the other cherub touched the other wall. And their wings touched each other in the middle of the room. ²⁸Also he overlaid the cherubim with gold.

²⁹Then he carved all the walls of the temple all around, both the inner and outer *sanctuaries,* with carved figures of cherubim, palm trees, and open flowers. ³⁰And the floor of the temple he overlaid with gold, both the inner and outer *sanctuaries.*

³¹For the entrance of the inner sanctuary he made doors *of* olive wood; the lintel *and* doorposts *were* one-fifth *of the wall.* ³²The two doors *were of* olive wood; and he carved on them figures of cherubim, palm trees, and open flowers, and overlaid *them* with gold; and he spread gold on the cherubim and on the palm trees. ³³So for the door of the sanctuary he also made doorposts *of* olive wood, one-fourth *of the wall.* ³⁴And the two doors *were of* cypress wood; two panels *comprised* one folding door, and two panels *comprised* the other folding door. ³⁵Then he carved cherubim, palm trees, and open flowers *on them,* and overlaid *them* with gold applied evenly on the carved work.

³⁶And he built the inner court with three rows of hewn stone and a row of cedar beams.

³⁷In the fourth year the foundation of the house of the LORD was laid, in the month of Ziv. ³⁸And in the eleventh year, in the month of Bul, which is the eighth month, the house was finished in all its details and according to all its plans. So he was seven years in building it.

Solomon's Other Buildings

7But Solomon took thirteen years to build his own house; so he finished all his house.

²He also built the House of the Forest of Lebanon; its length *was* one hundred cubits, its width fifty cubits, and its height thirty cubits, with four rows of cedar pillars, and cedar beams on the pillars. ³And *it*

6:27 ᵃLiterally *house*

7:1 thirteen years. After building the house for the Lord, Solomon built his own house, which took almost twice as long to build as the temple. It probably took longer because it had less preparation and urgency. Together, the temple and Solomon's house took 20 years to complete (see 9:10).

was paneled with cedar above the beams that *were* on forty-five pillars, fifteen *to* a row. ⁴*There were* windows *with beveled frames in* three rows, and window *was* opposite window *in* three tiers. ⁵And all the doorways and doorposts *had* rectangular frames; and window *was* opposite window *in* three tiers.

⁶He also made the Hall of Pillars: its length *was* fifty cubits, and its width thirty cubits; and in front of them *was* a portico with pillars, and a canopy *was* in front of them.

⁷Then he made a hall for the throne, the Hall of Judgment, where he might judge; and *it was* paneled with cedar from floor to ceiling.*ᵃ*

⁸And the house where he dwelt *had* another court inside the hall, of like workmanship. Solomon also made a house like this hall for Pharaoh's daughter, whom he had taken *as wife.*

⁹All these *were of* costly stones cut to size, trimmed with saws, inside and out, from the foundation to the eaves, and also on the outside to the great court. ¹⁰The foundation *was of* costly stones, large stones, some ten cubits and some eight cubits. ¹¹And above *were* costly stones, hewn to size, and cedar wood. ¹²The great court *was* enclosed with three rows of hewn stones and a row of cedar beams. So were the inner court of the house of the LORD and the vestibule of the temple.

7:9–12 A fortune was spent on building the palace, which was adjacent to the temple. The palace contained the king's home, the courtyard in the middle, and the house of the women on the other side.

Hiram the Craftsman

¹³Now King Solomon sent and brought Huram*ᵃ* from Tyre. ¹⁴He *was* the son of a widow from the tribe of Naphtali, and his father *was* a man of Tyre, a bronze worker; he was filled with wisdom and understanding and skill in working with all kinds of bronze work. So he came to King Solomon and did all his work.

The Bronze Pillars for the Temple

¹⁵And he cast two pillars of bronze, each one eighteen cubits high, and a line of twelve cubits measured the circumference of each. ¹⁶Then he made two capitals *of* cast bronze, to set on the tops of the pillars. The height of one capital *was* five cubits, and the height of the other capital *was* five cubits. ¹⁷*He made* a lattice network, with wreaths of chainwork, for the capitals which *were* on top of the pillars: seven chains for one capital and seven for the other capital. ¹⁸So he made the pillars, and two rows of pomegranates above the network all around to cover the capitals that *were* on top; and thus he did for the other capital.

¹⁹The capitals which *were* on top of the pillars in the hall *were* in the shape of lilies, four cubits. ²⁰The capitals on the two pillars also *had pomegranates* above, by the convex surface which *was* next to the network; and there *were* two hundred such pomegranates in rows on each of the capitals all around.

²¹Then he set up the pillars by the vestibule of the temple; he set up the pillar on the right and called its name Jachin, and he set up the pillar on the left and called its name Boaz. ²²The tops of the pillars were in the shape of lilies. So the work of the pillars was finished.

The Sea and the Oxen

²³And he made the Sea of cast bronze, ten cubits from one brim to the other; *it was* completely round. Its height *was* five cubits, and a line of thirty cubits measured its circumference.

7:23 the Sea. A huge, circular, bronze basin that held approximately 12,000 gallons of water. The Sea stood in the courtyard on the temple's southeast side and provided water for the priests to wash themselves and their sacrifices and to fill the 10 movable basins (vv. 38,39).

7:7 *ᵃ*Literally *floor,* that is, of the upper level   7:13 *ᵃ*Hebrew *Hiram* (compare 2 Chronicles 2:13,14)

²⁴Below its brim *were* ornamental buds encircling it all around, ten to a cubit, all the way around the Sea. The ornamental buds *were* cast in two rows when it was cast. ²⁵It stood on twelve oxen: three looking toward the north, three looking toward the west, three looking toward the south, and three looking toward the east; the Sea *was set* upon them, and all their back parts *pointed* inward. ²⁶It *was* a handbreadth thick; and its brim was shaped like the brim of a cup, *like* a lily blossom. It contained two thousand*ᵃ* baths.

The Carts and the Lavers

²⁷He also made ten carts of bronze; four cubits *was* the length of each cart, four cubits its width, and three cubits its height. ²⁸And this *was* the design of the carts: They had panels, and the panels *were* between frames; ²⁹on the panels that *were* between the frames *were* lions, oxen, and cherubim. And on the frames *was* a pedestal on top. Below the lions and oxen *were* wreaths of plaited work. ³⁰Every cart had four bronze wheels and axles of bronze, and its four feet had supports. Under the laver *were* supports of cast *bronze* beside each wreath. ³¹Its opening inside the crown at the top *was* one cubit in diameter; and the opening *was* round, shaped *like* a pedestal, one and a half cubits in outside diameter; and also on the opening *were* engravings, but the panels were square, not round. ³²Under the panels *were* the four wheels, and the axles of the wheels *were joined* to the cart. The height of a wheel *was* one and a half cubits. ³³The workmanship of the wheels *was* like the workmanship of a chariot wheel; their axle pins, their rims, their spokes, and their hubs *were* all of cast *bronze.* ³⁴And *there were* four supports at the four corners of each cart; its supports *were* part of the cart itself. ³⁵On the top of the cart, at the height of half a cubit, *it was* perfectly round. And on the top of the cart, its flanges and its panels *were* of the same casting. ³⁶On the plates of its flanges and on its panels he engraved cherubim, lions, and palm trees, wherever there was a clear space on each, with wreaths all around. ³⁷Thus he made the ten carts. All of them were of the same mold, one measure, *and* one shape.

³⁸Then he made ten lavers of bronze; each laver contained forty baths, *and* each laver *was* four cubits. On each of the ten carts *was* a laver. ³⁹And he put five carts on the right side of the house, and five on the left side of the house. He set the Sea on the right side of the house, toward the southeast.

> **7:38 lavers.** Huram made 10 bronze basins as water containers for the stands. Each basin measured 6 feet across and held approximately 240 gallons of water.

Furnishings of the Temple

⁴⁰Huram*ᵃ* made the lavers and the shovels and the bowls. So Huram finished doing all the work that he was to do for King Solomon *for* the house of the LORD: ⁴¹the two pillars, the *two* bowl-shaped capitals that *were* on top of the two pillars; the two networks covering the two bowl-shaped capitals which *were* on top of the pillars; ⁴²four hundred pomegranates for the two networks (two rows of pomegranates for each network, to cover the two bowl-shaped capitals that *were* on top of the pillars); ⁴³the ten carts, and ten lavers on the carts; ⁴⁴one Sea, and twelve oxen under the Sea; ⁴⁵the pots, the shovels, and the bowls.

All these articles which Huram*ᵃ* made for King Solomon *for* the house of the LORD *were of* burnished bronze. ⁴⁶In the plain of Jordan the king had them cast in clay molds, between Succoth and Zaretan. ⁴⁷And Solomon did not weigh all the articles, because *there were* so many; the weight of the bronze was not determined.

⁴⁸Thus Solomon had all the furnishings made for the house of the LORD: the altar of gold, and the table of gold on which *was* the showbread; ⁴⁹the lampstands of pure gold, five on the right *side* and five on the left in front of the inner sanctuary, with the flowers and the lamps and the wick-trimmers of gold; ⁵⁰the basins, the trimmers, the bowls, the ladles, and the censers of pure gold; and the hinges of gold, *both* for the doors of the inner room (the Most Holy *Place*) *and* for the doors of the main hall of the temple.

7:26 *ᵃ*Or *three thousand* (compare 2 Chronicles 4:5)   7:40 *ᵃ*Hebrew *Hiram* (compare 2 Chronicles 2:13,14)   7:45 *ᵃ*Hebrew *Hiram* (compare 2 Chronicles 2:13,14)

⁵¹So all the work that King Solomon had done for the house of the LORD was finished; and Solomon brought in the things which his father David had dedicated: the silver and the gold and the furnishings. He put them in the treasuries of the house of the LORD.

The Ark Brought into the Temple

8 Now Solomon assembled the elders of Israel and all the heads of the tribes, the chief fathers of the children of Israel, to King Solomon in Jerusalem, that they might bring up the ark of the covenant of the LORD from the City of David, which *is* Zion. ²Therefore all the men of Israel assembled with King Solomon at the feast in the month of Ethanim, which *is* the seventh month. ³So all the elders of Israel came, and the priests took up the ark. ⁴Then they brought up the ark of the LORD, the tabernacle of meeting, and all the holy furnishings that *were* in the tabernacle. The priests and the Levites brought them up. ⁵Also King Solomon, and all the congregation of Israel who were assembled with him, *were* with him before the ark, sacrificing sheep and oxen that could not be counted or numbered for multitude. ⁶Then the priests brought in the ark of the covenant of the LORD to its place, into the inner sanctuary of the temple, to the Most Holy *Place*, under the wings of the cherubim. ⁷For the cherubim spread *their* two wings over the place of the ark, and the cherubim overshadowed the ark and its poles. ⁸The poles extended so that the ends of the poles could be seen from the holy *place*, in front of the inner sanctuary; but they could not be seen from outside. And they are there to this day. ⁹Nothing *was* in the ark except the two tablets of stone which Moses put there at Horeb, when the LORD made *a covenant*

8:2 seventh month. Solomon finished building the temple in the eighth month of the previous year (6:38). The detail of the temple showed the magnificence of God's glory. Solomon scheduled the dedication of the temple in the seventh month during the Feast of Tabernacles and during a Jubilee year, when he knew there would be a general assembly of the people in Jerusalem.

with the children of Israel, when they came out of the land of Egypt.

¹⁰And it came to pass, when the priests came out of the holy *place*, that the cloud filled the house of the LORD, ¹¹so that the priests could not continue ministering because of the cloud; for the glory of the LORD filled the house of the LORD.

¹²Then Solomon spoke:

8:10 the cloud. The cloud was "the glory of the LORD" and was a symbol of God's presence. It signaled the Lord's approval of the new temple. A similar manifestation took place when the tabernacle was dedicated (Ex. 40:34,35).

" The LORD said He would dwell in the
      dark cloud.
¹³   I have surely built You an exalted
         house,
      And a place for You to dwell in
         forever."

Solomon's Speech at Completion of the Work

¹⁴Then the king turned around and blessed the whole assembly of Israel, while all the assembly of Israel was standing. ¹⁵And he said: "Blessed *be* the LORD God of Israel, who spoke with His mouth to my father David, and with His hand has fulfilled *it*, saying, ¹⁶'Since the day that I brought My people Israel out of Egypt, I have chosen no city from any tribe of Israel *in which* to build a house, that My name might be there; but I chose David to be over My people Israel.' ¹⁷Now it was in the heart of my father David to build a temple*ᵃ* for the name of the LORD God of Israel. ¹⁸But the LORD said to my father David, 'Whereas it was in your heart to build a temple for My name, you did well that it was in your heart. ¹⁹Nevertheless you shall not build the temple, but your son who will come from your body, he shall build the temple for My name.' ²⁰So the LORD has fulfilled His word which He spoke; and I have filled the position of my father David, and sit on the throne of Israel, as the LORD promised; and I have built a temple for the name of the LORD God of Israel. ²¹And there I have made a place for the ark, in which *is* the covenant of the LORD which

---

8:17 *ᵃ*Literally *house*, and so in verses 18–20

He made with our fathers, when He brought them out of the land of Egypt."

> **8:14–21** After addressing the Lord, Solomon spoke to the Israelites gathered at the temple. He told the story of 2 Sam. 7:12–16, claiming that he fulfilled God's promise to David because he built the temple. Solomon's claim was premature, though, because the Lord later appeared to him and declared that he must be obedient in order for his throne to be established (9:4–9). Solomon would later become disobedient (11:6,9,10).

Solomon's Prayer of Dedication

²²Then Solomon stood before the altar of the LORD in the presence of all the assembly of Israel, and spread out his hands toward heaven; ²³and he said: "LORD God of Israel, *there is* no God in heaven above or on earth below like You, who keep *Your* covenant and mercy with Your servants who walk before You with all their hearts. ²⁴You have kept what You promised Your servant David my father; You have both spoken with Your mouth and fulfilled *it* with Your hand, as *it is* this day. ²⁵Therefore, LORD God of Israel, now keep what You promised Your servant David my father, saying, 'You shall not fail to have a man sit before Me on the throne of Israel, only if your sons take heed to their way, that they walk before Me as you have walked before Me.' ²⁶And now I pray, O God of Israel, let Your word come true, which You have spoken to Your servant David my father.

²⁷"But will God indeed dwell on the earth? Behold, heaven and the heaven of heavens cannot contain You. How much less this temple which I have built! ²⁸Yet regard the prayer of Your servant and his supplication, O LORD my God, and listen to the cry and the prayer which Your servant is praying before You today: ²⁹that Your eyes may be open toward this temple night and day, toward the place of which You said, 'My name shall be there,' that You may hear the prayer which Your servant makes toward this place. ³⁰And may You hear the supplication of Your servant and of Your

> **8:27 heaven...cannot contain You.** Even though the Lord had chosen to dwell among His people in the cloud at the temple, nothing in all creation could contain Him.

people Israel, when they pray toward this place. Hear in heaven Your dwelling place; and when You hear, forgive.

³¹"When anyone sins against his neighbor, and is forced to take an oath, and comes *and* takes an oath before Your altar in this temple, ³²then hear in heaven, and act, and judge Your servants, condemning the wicked, bringing his way on his head, and justifying the righteous by giving him according to his righteousness.

³³"When Your people Israel are defeated before an enemy because they have sinned against You, and when they turn back to You and confess Your name, and pray and make supplication to You in this temple, ³⁴then hear in heaven, and forgive the sin of Your people Israel, and bring them back to the land which You gave to their fathers.

³⁵"When the heavens are shut up and there is no rain because they have sinned against You, when they pray toward this place and confess Your name, and turn from their sin because You afflict them, ³⁶then hear in heaven, and forgive the sin of Your servants, Your people Israel, that You may teach them the good way in which they should walk; and send rain on Your land which You have given to Your people as an inheritance.

³⁷"When there is famine in the land, pestilence *or* blight *or* mildew, locusts *or* grasshoppers; when their enemy besieges them in the land of their cities; whatever plague or whatever sickness *there is*; ³⁸whatever prayer, whatever supplication is made by anyone, *or* by all Your people Israel, when each one knows the plague of his own heart, and spreads out his hands toward this temple: ³⁹then hear in heaven Your dwelling place, and forgive, and act, and give to everyone according to all his ways, whose heart You know (for You alone know the hearts of all the sons of men), ⁴⁰that they may fear You all the days that they live in the land which You gave to our fathers.

⁴¹"Moreover, concerning a foreigner, who *is* not of Your people Israel, but has come from a far country for Your name's sake ⁴²(for they will hear of Your great name and Your strong hand and Your outstretched arm), when he comes and prays toward this temple, ⁴³hear in heaven Your dwelling place, and do according to all for which the

foreigner calls to You, that all peoples of the earth may know Your name and fear You, as *do* Your people Israel, and that they may know that this temple which I have built is called by Your name.

44"When Your people go out to battle against their enemy, wherever You send them, and when they pray to the LORD toward the city which You have chosen and the temple which I have built for Your name, 45then hear in heaven their prayer and their supplication, and maintain their cause.

46"When they sin against You (for *there is* no one who does not sin), and You become angry with them and deliver them to the enemy, and they take them captive to the land of the enemy, far or near; 47yet when they come to themselves in the land where they were carried captive, and repent, and make supplication to You in the land of those who took them captive, saying, 'We have sinned and done wrong, we have committed wickedness'; 48and *when* they return to You with all their heart and with all their soul in the land of their enemies who led them away captive, and pray to You toward their land which You gave to their fathers, the city which You have chosen and the temple which I have built for Your name: 49then hear in heaven Your dwelling place their prayer and their supplication, and maintain their cause, 50and forgive Your people who have sinned against You, and all their transgressions which they have transgressed against You; and grant them compassion before those who took them captive, that they may have compassion on them 51(for they *are* Your people and Your inheritance, whom You brought out of Egypt, out of the iron furnace), 52that Your eyes may be open to the supplication of Your servant and the supplication of Your people Israel, to listen to them whenever they call to You. 53For You separated them

from among all the peoples of the earth *to be* Your inheritance, as You spoke by Your servant Moses, when You brought our fathers out of Egypt, O Lord GOD."

Solomon Blesses the Assembly

54And so it was, when Solomon had finished praying all this prayer and supplication to the LORD, that he arose from before the altar of the LORD, from kneeling on his knees with his hands spread up to heaven. 55Then he stood and blessed all the assembly of Israel with a loud voice, saying: 56"Blessed *be* the LORD, who has given rest to His people Israel, according to all that He promised. There has not failed one word of all His good promise, which He promised through His servant Moses. 57May the LORD our God be with us, as He was with our fathers. May He not leave us nor forsake us, 58that He may incline our hearts to Himself, to walk in all His ways, and to keep His commandments and His statutes and His judgments, which He commanded our fathers. 59And may these words of mine, with which I have made supplication before the LORD, be near the LORD our God day and night, that He may maintain the cause of His servant and the cause of His people Israel, as each day may require, 60that all the peoples of the earth may know that the LORD *is* God; *there is* no other. 61Let your heart therefore be loyal to the LORD our God, to walk in His statutes and keep His commandments, as at this day."

Solomon Dedicates the Temple

62Then the king and all Israel with him offered sacrifices before the LORD. 63And Solomon offered a sacrifice of peace offerings, which he offered to the LORD, twenty-two thousand bulls and one hundred and twenty thousand sheep. So the king and all the children of Israel dedicated the house of the LORD. 64On the same day the king consecrated the middle of the court that *was* in front of the house of the LORD; for there he offered burnt offerings, grain offerings, and the fat of the peace offerings, because the bronze altar that *was* before the LORD *was* too small to receive the burnt offerings, the grain offerings, and the fat of the peace offerings.

8:22–53. At the altar of burnt offering, Solomon prayed to the Lord. He affirmed that no god could compare to Israel's God. He asked the Lord for His continued presence and protection, and he listed 7 common Israelite prayers that would require the Lord's response (see Deut. 28:15–68). Solomon prayed for judgment, forgiveness, mercy, victory, and restoration.

⁶⁵At that time Solomon held a feast, and all Israel with him, a great assembly from the entrance of Hamath to the Brook of Egypt, before the LORD our God, seven days and seven *more* days—fourteen days. ⁶⁶On the eighth day he sent the people away; and they blessed the king, and went to their tents joyful and glad of heart for all the good that the LORD had done for His servant David, and for Israel His people.

God's Second Appearance to Solomon

9 And it came to pass, when Solomon had finished building the house of the LORD and the king's house, and all Solomon's desire which he wanted to do, ²that the LORD appeared to Solomon the second time, as He had appeared to him at Gibeon. ³And the LORD said to him: "I have heard your prayer and your supplication that you have made before Me; I have consecrated this house which you have built to put My name there forever, and My eyes and My heart will be there perpetually. ⁴Now if you walk before Me as your father David walked, in integrity of heart and in uprightness, to do according to all that I have commanded you, *and* if you keep My statutes and My judgments, ⁵then I will establish the throne of your kingdom over Israel forever, as I promised David your father, saying, 'You shall not fail to have a man on the throne of Israel.' ⁶*But* if you or your sons at all turn from following Me, and do not keep My commandments *and* My statutes which I have set before you, but go and serve other gods and worship them, ⁷then I will cut off Israel from the land which I have given them; and this house which I have consecrated for My name I will cast out of My sight. Israel will be a proverb and a byword among all peoples. ⁸And *as for* this house, *which* is exalted, everyone who passes by it will be astonished and will hiss, and say, 'Why has the LORD done thus to this land and to this house?' ⁹Then they will answer, 'Because they forsook the LORD their God, who brought their fathers out of the land of Egypt, and have embraced other gods, and worshiped them and served them; therefore the LORD has brought all this calamity on them.' "

Solomon and Hiram Exchange Gifts

¹⁰Now it happened at the end of twenty years, when Solomon had built the two houses, the house of the LORD and the king's house ¹¹(Hiram the king of Tyre had supplied Solomon with cedar and cypress and gold, as much as he desired), *that* King Solomon then gave Hiram twenty cities in the land of Galilee. ¹²Then Hiram went from Tyre to see the cities which Solomon had given him, but they did not please him. ¹³So he said, "What *kind of* cities *are* these which you have given me, my brother?" And he called them the land of Cabul,ᵃ as they are to this day. ¹⁴Then Hiram sent the king one hundred and twenty talents of gold.

Solomon's Additional Achievements

¹⁵And this *is* the reason for the labor force which King Solomon raised: to build the house of the LORD, his own house, the Millo,ᵃ the wall of Jerusalem, Hazor, Megiddo, and Gezer. ¹⁶(Pharaoh king of Egypt had gone up and taken Gezer and burned it with fire, had killed the Canaanites who dwelt in the city, and had given it *as* a dowry to his daughter, Solomon's wife.) ¹⁷And Solomon built Gezer, Lower Beth Horon, ¹⁸Baalath, and Tadmor in the wilderness, in the land *of Judah*, ¹⁹all the storage cities that Solomon had, cities for his chariots and cities for his cavalry, and

9:3 consecrated. The Lord made the temple holy by His presence in the cloud (see 8:10). **forever.** God would not dwell in the actual temple building forever, for it was destroyed by the Babylonians less than 400 years later (see vv. 7–9). Jerusalem and the temple mount will be His earthly throne as long as the earth remains (see Is. 2:1–4). **eyes...heart.** These symbolized the Lord's constant attention toward and deep affection for Israel. He promised them access to His presence and answers to their prayers.

9:19 storage cities. These cities were meant to store food (2 Chr. 17:12). **cities for his chariots.** Solomon built military outposts for his chariots and horses. These cities were located along key roads throughout the nation in order to defend the kingdom.

whatever Solomon desired to build in Jerusalem, in Lebanon, and in all the land of his dominion.

²⁰All the people *who were* left of the Amorites, Hittites, Perizzites, Hivites, and Jebusites, who *were* not of the children of Israel—²¹that is, their descendants who were left in the land after them, whom the children of Israel had not been able to destroy completely—from these Solomon raised forced labor, as it is to this day. ²²But of the children of Israel Solomon made no forced laborers, because they *were* men of war and his servants: his officers, his captains, commanders of his chariots, and his cavalry.

²³Others *were* chiefs of the officials who *were* over Solomon's work: five hundred and fifty, who ruled over the people who did the work.

²⁴But Pharaoh's daughter came up from the City of David to her house which *Solomonᵃ* had built for her. Then he built the Millo.

²⁵Now three times a year Solomon offered burnt offerings and peace offerings on the altar which he had built for the LORD, and he burned incense with them *on the altar* that *was* before the LORD. So he finished the temple.

²⁶King Solomon also built a fleet of ships at Ezion Geber, which *is* near Elathᵃ on the shore of the Red Sea, in the land of Edom. ²⁷Then Hiram sent his servants with the fleet, seamen who knew the sea, to work with the servants of Solomon. ²⁸And they went to Ophir, and acquired four hundred and twenty talents of gold from there, and brought *it* to King Solomon.

> **9:25 Solomon offered.** Solomon stopped sacrificing to God at the high places once the temple had been built (see 3:2–4). He kept Israel's 3 great annual feasts at the temple in Jerusalem: Unleavened Bread, Pentecost, and Tabernacles (Deut. 16:1–17).

The Queen of Sheba's Praise of Solomon

10 Now when the queen of Sheba heard of the fame of Solomon concerning the name of the LORD, she came to test him

> **10:1 concerning the name of the LORD.** The queen's motive for visiting was to verify Solomon's reputation for wisdom and devotion to the Lord. **hard questions.** These were riddles that confused the hearer (see Judg. 14:12).

with hard questions. ²She came to Jerusalem with a very great retinue, with camels that bore spices, very much gold, and precious stones; and when she came to Solomon, she spoke with him about all that was in her heart. ³So Solomon answered all her questions; there was nothing so difficult for the king that he could not explain *it* to her. ⁴And when the queen of Sheba had seen all the wisdom of Solomon, the house that he had built, ⁵the food on his table, the seating of his servants, the service of his waiters and their apparel, his cupbearers, and his entryway by which he went up to the house of the LORD, there was no more spirit in her. ⁶Then she said to the king: "It was a true report which I heard in my own land about your words and your wisdom. ⁷However I did not believe the words until I came and saw with my own eyes; and indeed the half was not told me. Your wisdom and prosperity exceed the fame of which I heard. ⁸Happy *are* your men and happy *are* these your servants, who stand continually before you *and* hear your wisdom! ⁹Blessed be the LORD your God, who delighted in you, setting you on the throne of Israel! Because the LORD has loved Israel forever, therefore He made you king, to do justice and righteousness."

> **10:9 the LORD your God.** The queen credited Solomon's wisdom to the God of Israel, yet she made no confession that Solomon's God had become her God. There is no record that she made any offerings to God at the temple.

¹⁰Then she gave the king one hundred and twenty talents of gold, spices in great quantity, and precious stones. There never again came such abundance of spices as the queen of Sheba gave to King Solomon. ¹¹Also, the ships of Hiram, which brought gold from Ophir, brought great *quantities* of almugᵃ wood and precious stones from

---

9:24 ᵃLiterally *he* (compare 2 Chronicles 8:11)   9:26 ᵃHebrew *Eloth* (compare 2 Kings 14:22)
10:11 ᵃOr *algum* (compare 2 Chronicles 9:10,11)

Ophir. [12]And the king made steps of the almug wood for the house of the LORD and for the king's house, also harps and stringed instruments for singers. There never again came such almug wood, nor has the like been seen to this day.

[13]Now King Solomon gave the queen of Sheba all she desired, whatever she asked, besides what Solomon had given her according to the royal generosity. So she turned and went to her own country, she and her servants.

Solomon's Great Wealth

[14]The weight of gold that came to Solomon yearly was six hundred and sixty-six talents of gold, [15]besides *that* from the traveling merchants, from the income of traders, from all the kings of Arabia, and from the governors of the country.

[16]And King Solomon made two hundred large shields *of* hammered gold; six hundred *shekels* of gold went into each shield. [17]He also *made* three hundred shields *of* hammered gold; three minas of gold went into each shield. The king put them in the House of the Forest of Lebanon.

[18]Moreover the king made a great throne of ivory, and overlaid it with pure gold. [19]The throne had six steps, and the top of the throne *was* round at the back; *there were* armrests on either side of the place of the seat, and two lions stood beside the armrests. [20]Twelve lions stood there, one on each side of the six steps; nothing like *this* had been made for any *other* kingdom.

[21]All King Solomon's drinking vessels *were* gold, and all the vessels of the House of the Forest of Lebanon *were* pure gold. Not *one was* silver, for this was accounted as nothing in the days of Solomon. [22]For the king had merchant ships[a] at sea with the fleet of Hiram. Once every three years the merchant ships came bringing gold, silver, ivory, apes, and monkeys.[b] [23]So King Solomon surpassed all the kings of the earth in riches and wisdom.

[24]Now all the earth sought the presence of Solomon to hear his wisdom, which God had put in his heart. [25]Each man brought his present: articles of silver and gold, garments, armor, spices, horses, and mules, at a set rate year by year.

[26]And Solomon gathered chariots and horsemen; he had one thousand four hundred chariots and twelve thousand horsemen, whom he stationed[a] in the chariot cities and with the king at Jerusalem. [27]The king made silver *as common* in Jerusalem as stones, and he made cedar trees as abundant as the sycamores which *are* in the lowland.

[28]Also Solomon had horses imported from Egypt and Keveh; the king's merchants bought them in Keveh at the *current* price. [29]Now a chariot that was imported from Egypt cost six hundred *shekels* of silver, and a horse one hundred and fifty; and thus, through their agents,[a] they exported *them* to all the kings of the Hittites and the kings of Syria.

Solomon's Heart Turns from the LORD

11 But King Solomon loved many foreign women, as well as the daughter of Pharaoh: women of the Moabites, Ammonites, Edomites, Sidonians, *and* Hittites— [2]from the nations of whom the LORD had said to the children of Israel, "You shall not intermarry with them, nor they with you. Surely they will turn away your hearts after their gods." Solomon clung to these in love. [3]And he had seven hundred wives, princesses, and three hundred concubines; and his wives turned away his heart. [4]For it was so, when Solomon was old, that his wives turned his heart after other gods; and his heart was not loyal to the LORD his God, as *was* the heart of his father David. [5]For Solomon went after Ashtoreth the goddess of the Sidonians, and after Milcom the abomination of the Ammonites. [6]Solomon did evil in the sight of the LORD, and did not fully follow the LORD, as *did* his father David. [7]Then Solomon built a high place for Chemosh the abomination of Moab, on the hill that *is* east of Jerusalem, and for Molech the abomination of the people of Ammon. [8]And he did likewise for all his foreign

---

10:22 [a]Literally *ships of Tarshish*, deep-sea vessels [b]Or *peacocks* 10:26 [a]Following Septuagint, Syriac, Targum, and Vulgate (compare 2 Chronicles 9:25); Masoretic Text reads *led*. 10:29 [a]Literally *by their hands*

11:1–6 loved many foreign women. Many of Solomon's marriages were arranged as foreign treaties. Multiple wives also signified wealth and importance. Deut. 17:17 prohibited having many royal wives because it would turn the king's heart away from the Lord, which it did to Solomon. He did not measure up to the high standard set by his father David, who although he sinned, yet repented from his sin (Pss. 32, 51) and did not allow sin to continue as the pattern of his life.

wives, who burned incense and sacrificed to their gods.

⁹So the LORD became angry with Solomon, because his heart had turned from the LORD God of Israel, who had appeared to him twice, ¹⁰and had commanded him concerning this thing, that he should not go after other gods; but he did not keep what the LORD had commanded. ¹¹Therefore the LORD said to Solomon, "Because you have done this, and have not kept My covenant and My statutes, which I have commanded you, I will surely tear the kingdom away from you and give it to your servant. ¹²Nevertheless I will not do it in your days, for the sake of your father David; I will tear it out of the hand of your son. ¹³However I will not tear away the whole kingdom; I will give one tribe to your son for the sake of My servant David, and for the sake of Jerusalem which I have chosen."

11:13 one tribe. Judah was the one tribe that remained loyal to the Davidic dynasty (see 12:20). **for the sake of Jerusalem.** The Lord chose Jerusalem as the place where His name would dwell forever (9:3). Jerusalem and the temple remained so the divine promise could stand.

Adversaries of Solomon

¹⁴Now the LORD raised up an adversary against Solomon, Hadad the Edomite; he *was* a descendant of the king in Edom. ¹⁵For it happened, when David was in Edom, and Joab the commander of the army had gone up to bury the slain, after he had killed every male in Edom ¹⁶(because for six months Joab remained there with all Israel, until he had cut down every male in Edom), ¹⁷that Hadad fled to go to Egypt, he and certain Edomites of his father's servants with him. Hadad *was* still a little child. ¹⁸Then

they arose from Midian and came to Paran; and they took men with them from Paran and came to Egypt, to Pharaoh king of Egypt, who gave him a house, apportioned food for him, and gave him land. ¹⁹And Hadad found great favor in the sight of Pharaoh, so that he gave him as wife the sister of his own wife, that is, the sister of Queen Tahpenes. ²⁰Then the sister of Tahpenes bore him Genubath his son, whom Tahpenes weaned in Pharaoh's house. And Genubath was in Pharaoh's household among the sons of Pharaoh.

²¹So when Hadad heard in Egypt that David rested with his fathers, and that Joab the commander of the army was dead, Hadad said to Pharaoh, "Let me depart, that I may go to my own country."

²²Then Pharaoh said to him, "But what have you lacked with me, that suddenly you seek to go to your own country?"

So he answered, "Nothing, but do let me go anyway."

²³And God raised up *another* adversary against him, Rezon the son of Eliadah, who had fled from his lord, Hadadezer king of Zobah. ²⁴So he gathered men to him and became captain over a band *of raiders,* when David killed those *of Zobah.* And they went to Damascus and dwelt there, and reigned in Damascus. ²⁵He was an adversary of Israel all the days of Solomon (besides the trouble that Hadad *caused*); and he abhorred Israel, and reigned over Syria.

Jeroboam's Rebellion

²⁶Then Solomon's servant, Jeroboam the son of Nebat, an Ephraimite from Zereda, whose mother's name *was* Zeruah, a widow, also rebelled against the king.

11:26 Jeroboam the son of Nebat. Jeroboam was an internal adversary from the town of Ephraim, the leading tribe of Israel's northern 10 tribes. Solomon appointed him leader over the building works around Jerusalem. Because of his talent and energy, Jeroboam was favored by the people.

²⁷And this *is* what caused him to rebel against the king: Solomon had built the Millo *and* repaired the damages to the City of David his father. ²⁸The man Jeroboam *was* a mighty man of valor; and Solomon,

seeing that the young man was industrious, made him the officer over all the labor force of the house of Joseph.

²⁹Now it happened at that time, when Jeroboam went out of Jerusalem, that the prophet Ahijah the Shilonite met him on the way; and he had clothed himself with a new garment, and the two *were* alone in the field. ³⁰Then Ahijah took hold of the new garment that *was* on him, and tore it *into* twelve pieces. ³¹And he said to Jeroboam, "Take for yourself ten pieces, for thus says the LORD, the God of Israel: 'Behold, I will tear the kingdom out of the hand of Solomon and will give ten tribes to you ³²(but he shall have one tribe for the sake of My servant David, and for the sake of Jerusalem, the city which I have chosen out of all the tribes of Israel), ³³because they have*ᵃ* forsaken Me, and worshiped Ashtoreth the goddess of the Sidonians, Chemosh the god of the Moabites, and Milcom the god of the people of Ammon, and have not walked in My ways to do *what is* right in My eyes and *keep* My statutes and My judgments, as *did* his father David. ³⁴However I will not take the whole kingdom out of his hand, because I have made him ruler all the days of his life for the sake of My servant David, whom I chose because he kept My commandments and My statutes. ³⁵But I will take the kingdom out of his son's hand and give it to you—ten tribes. ³⁶And to his son I will give one tribe, that My servant David may always have a lamp before Me in Jerusalem, the city which I have chosen for Myself, to put My name there. ³⁷So I will take you, and you shall reign over all your heart desires, and you shall be king over Israel. ³⁸Then it shall be, if you heed all that I command you, walk in My ways, and do *what is* right in My sight, to keep My statutes and My commandments, as My servant David did, then I will be with you and build for you an enduring house, as I built for David, and will give Israel to you. ³⁹And

> **11:38 if you heed all that I command you.** The Lord promised an enduring dynasty over the 10 northern tribes of Israel to Jeroboam if he obeyed His law (2:3,4; 3:14).

I will afflict the descendants of David because of this, but not forever.' "

⁴⁰Solomon therefore sought to kill Jeroboam. But Jeroboam arose and fled to Egypt, to Shishak king of Egypt, and was in Egypt until the death of Solomon.

Death of Solomon

⁴¹Now the rest of the acts of Solomon, all that he did, and his wisdom, *are* they not written in the book of the acts of Solomon? ⁴²And the period that Solomon reigned in Jerusalem over all Israel *was* forty years. ⁴³Then Solomon rested with his fathers, and was buried in the City of David his father. And Rehoboam his son reigned in his place.

The Revolt Against Rehoboam

12 And Rehoboam went to Shechem, for all Israel had gone to Shechem to make him king. ²So it happened, when Jeroboam the son of Nebat heard *it* (he was still in Egypt, for he had fled from the presence of King Solomon and had been dwelling in Egypt), ³that they sent and called him. Then Jeroboam and the whole assembly of Israel came and spoke to Rehoboam, saying, ⁴"Your father made our yoke heavy; now therefore, lighten the burdensome service of your father, and his heavy yoke which he put on us, and we will serve you."

⁵So he said to them, "Depart *for* three days, then come back to me." And the people departed.

⁶Then King Rehoboam consulted the elders who stood before his father Solomon while he still lived, and he said, "How do you advise *me* to answer these people?"

⁷And they spoke to him, saying, "If you will be a servant to these people today, and serve them, and answer them, and speak good words to them, then they will be your servants forever."

⁸But he rejected the advice which the elders had given him, and consulted the young men who had grown up with him, who stood before him. ⁹And he said to them, "What advice do you give? How should we answer this people who have spoken to me, saying, 'Lighten the yoke which your father put on us'?"

11:33 *ᵃ*Following Masoretic Text and Targum; Septuagint, Syriac, and Vulgate read *he has*.

[10]Then the young men who had grown up with him spoke to him, saying, "Thus you should speak to this people who have spoken to you, saying, 'Your father made our yoke heavy, but you make *it* lighter on us'— thus you shall say to them: 'My little *finger* shall be thicker than my father's waist! [11]And now, whereas my father put a heavy yoke on you, I will add to your yoke; my father chastised you with whips, but I will chastise you with scourges!' "*a*

12:6–10 the elders. The elders were older, experienced counselors and administrators who served Solomon. They counseled Rehoboam to give concessions to the 10 tribes. **the young men.** These men (about 40 years of age) advised Rehoboam to be harsher on the 10 tribes than Solomon had been.

[12]So Jeroboam and all the people came to Rehoboam the third day, as the king had directed, saying, "Come back to me the third day." [13]Then the king answered the people roughly, and rejected the advice which the elders had given him; [14]and he spoke to them according to the advice of the young men, saying, "My father made your yoke heavy, but I will add to your yoke; my father chastised you with whips, but I will chastise you with scourges!"*a* [15]So the king did not listen to the people; for the turn *of events* was from the LORD, that He might fulfill His word, which the LORD had spoken by Ahijah the Shilonite to Jeroboam the son of Nebat.

[16]Now when all Israel saw that the king did not listen to them, the people answered the king, saying:

"What share have we in David?
  We have no inheritance in the son of
    Jesse.
  To your tents, O Israel!
  Now, see to your own house,
    O David!"

So Israel departed to their tents. [17]But Rehoboam reigned over the children of Israel who dwelt in the cities of Judah.

[18]Then King Rehoboam sent Adoram, who *was* in charge of the revenue; but all Israel stoned him with stones, and he died.

Therefore King Rehoboam mounted his chariot in haste to flee to Jerusalem. [19]So Israel has been in rebellion against the house of David to this day.

[20]Now it came to pass when all Israel heard that Jeroboam had come back, they sent for him and called him to the congregation, and made him king over all Israel. There was none who followed the house of David, but the tribe of Judah only.

[21]And when Rehoboam came to Jerusalem, he assembled all the house of Judah with the tribe of Benjamin, one hundred and eighty thousand chosen *men* who were warriors, to fight against the house of Israel, that he might restore the kingdom to Rehoboam the son of Solomon. [22]But the word of God came to Shemaiah the man of God, saying, [23]"Speak to Rehoboam the son of Solomon, king of Judah, to all the house of Judah and Benjamin, and to the rest of

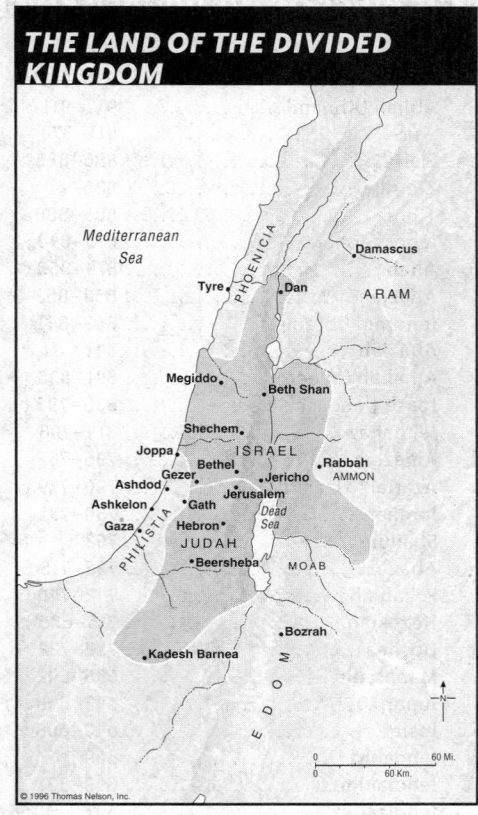

THE LAND OF THE DIVIDED KINGDOM

© 1996 Thomas Nelson, Inc.

the people, saying, [24'] Thus says the LORD: "You shall not go up nor fight against your brethren the children of Israel. Let every man return to his house, for this thing is from Me." '" Therefore they obeyed the word of the LORD, and turned back, according to the word of the LORD.

> **12:20-24** The kingdom was divided. Israel (the 10 northern tribes) had its own king. The tribe of Benjamin had split loyalty and land during this time. Only the tribe of Judah remained loyal to the house of David.

Jeroboam's Gold Calves

[25]Then Jeroboam built Shechem in the mountains of Ephraim, and dwelt there. Also he went out from there and built Penuel. [26]And Jeroboam said in his heart, "Now the kingdom may return to the house of David: [27]If these people go up to offer sacrifices in the house of the LORD at Jerusalem, then the heart of this people will turn back to their lord, Rehoboam king of Judah, and they will kill me and go back to Rehoboam king of Judah."

[28]Therefore the king asked advice, made two calves of gold, and said to the people, "It is too much for you to go up to Jerusalem. Here are your gods, O Israel, which brought you up from the land of Egypt!" [29]And he set up one in Bethel, and the other he put in Dan. [30]Now this thing became a sin, for the people went *to worship* before the one as far as Dan. [31]He made shrines[a] on the high places, and made priests from

12:31 [a]Literally *a house*

THE KINGS OF THE DIVIDED KINGDOM

Judah	B.C.	Israel	B.C.
Rehoboam	931–913	Jeroboam I	931–910
Abijah (Abijam)	913–911	Nadab	910–909
Asa	911–870	Baasha	909–886
Elah	886–885		
Zimri	885		
Tibni	885–880		
Jehoshaphat	873–848	Omri	885–874
Ahab	874–853		
Ahaziah	853–852		
Jehoram (Joram)	853–841	Joram (Jehoram)	852–841
Ahaziah	841	Jehu	841–814
Athaliah (queen)	841–835		
Joash (Jehoash)	835–796		
Jehoahaz	814–798		
Amaziah	796–767	Jehoash (Joash)	798–782
Azariah (Uzziah)	790–739	Jeroboam II	793–753
Jotham	750–731	Zechariah	753
Shallum	752		
Ahaz	735–715	Menahem	752–742
Pekahiah	742–740		
Hezekiah	715–686	Pekah	752–732
Hoshea	732–722		
Manasseh	695–642		
Amon	642–640		
Josiah	640–609		
Jehoahaz	609		
Jehoiakim	609–597		
Jehoiachin	597		
Zedekiah	597–586		

every class of people, who were not of the sons of Levi.

³²Jeroboam ordained a feast on the fifteenth day of the eighth month, like the feast that *was* in Judah, and offered sacrifices on the altar. So he did at Bethel, sacrificing to the calves that he had made. And at Bethel he installed the priests of the high places which he had made. ³³So he made offerings on the altar which he had made at Bethel on the fifteenth day of the eighth month, in the month which he had devised in his own heart. And he ordained a feast for the children of Israel, and offered sacrifices on the altar and burned incense.

12:32 ordained a feast. Jeroboam created his religious festival in order to compete with the Feast of the Tabernacles, which took place in the temple in Jerusalem.

The Message of the Man of God

13 And behold, a man of God went from Judah to Bethel by the word of the LORD, and Jeroboam stood by the altar to burn incense. ²Then he cried out against the altar by the word of the LORD, and said, "O altar, altar! Thus says the LORD: 'Behold, a child, Josiah by name, shall be born to the house of David; and on you he shall sacrifice the priests of the high places who burn incense on you, and men's bones shall be burned on you.' " ³And he gave a sign the same day, saying, "This *is* the sign which the LORD has spoken: Surely the altar shall split apart, and the ashes on it shall be poured out."

⁴So it came to pass when King Jeroboam heard the saying of the man of God, who cried out against the altar in Bethel, that he stretched out his hand from the altar, saying, "Arrest him!" Then his hand, which he stretched out toward him, withered, so that he could not pull it back to himself. ⁵The altar also was split apart, and the ashes poured out from the altar, according to the sign which the man of God had given by the word of the LORD. ⁶Then the king answered and said to the man of God, "Please entreat the favor of the LORD your God, and pray for me, that my hand may be restored to me."

So the man of God entreated the LORD, and the king's hand was restored to him, and became as before. ⁷Then the king said to the man of God, "Come home with me and refresh yourself, and I will give you a reward."

⁸But the man of God said to the king, "If you were to give me half your house, I would not go in with you; nor would I eat bread nor drink water in this place. ⁹For so it was commanded me by the word of the LORD, saying, 'You shall not eat bread, nor drink water, nor return by the same way you came.' " ¹⁰So he went another way and did not return by the way he came to Bethel.

13:9 commanded me by the word of the LORD. The prophet was commanded not to receive any hospitality at Bethel, and he was told not to take the same route home, so as not to be recognized. His conduct represented the Lord's rejection of Israel's false worship.

Death of the Man of God

¹¹Now an old prophet dwelt in Bethel, and his sons came and told him all the works that the man of God had done that day in Bethel; they also told their father the words which he had spoken to the king. ¹²And their father said to them, "Which way did he go?" For his sons had seen*a* which way the man of God went who came from Judah. ¹³Then he said to his sons, "Saddle the donkey for me." So they saddled the donkey for him; and he rode on it, ¹⁴and went after the man of God, and found him sitting under an oak. Then he said to him, "*Are* you the man of God who came from Judah?"

And he said, "I *am*."

¹⁵Then he said to him, "Come home with me and eat bread."

¹⁶And he said, "I cannot return with you nor go in with you; neither can I eat bread nor drink water with you in this place. ¹⁷For I have been told by the word of the LORD, 'You shall not eat bread nor drink water there, nor return by going the way you came.' "

¹⁸He said to him, "I too *am* a prophet as you *are*, and an angel spoke to me by the word of the LORD, saying, 'Bring him back

---

13:12 *a*Septuagint, Syriac, Targum, and Vulgate read *showed him*.

with you to your house, that he may eat bread and drink water.' " (He was lying to him.)

> **13:18 He was lying to him.** The old prophet may have deceived the man of God because his own sons were worshipers or priests at Bethel, and he wanted to gain favor with the king by claiming the man of God to be a false prophet. The man of God should have been suspicious of the old prophet and sought God's reasoning for this change in His commands.

¹⁹So he went back with him, and ate bread in his house, and drank water.

²⁰Now it happened, as they sat at the table, that the word of the LORD came to the prophet who had brought him back; ²¹and he cried out to the man of God who came from Judah, saying, "Thus says the LORD: 'Because you have disobeyed the word of the LORD, and have not kept the commandment which the LORD your God commanded you, ²²but you came back, ate bread, and drank water in the place of which *the LORD* said to you, "Eat no bread and drink no water," your corpse shall not come to the tomb of your fathers.' "

²³So it was, after he had eaten bread and after he had drunk, that he saddled the donkey for him, the prophet whom he had brought back. ²⁴When he was gone, a lion met him on the road and killed him. And his corpse was thrown on the road, and the donkey stood by it. The lion also stood by the corpse. ²⁵And there, men passed by and saw the corpse thrown on the road, and the lion standing by the corpse. Then they went and told *it* in the city where the old prophet dwelt.

> **13:24 lion...donkey.** The donkey did not run, and the lion did not attack the donkey or disturb the man's body. These animals both acted unnaturally according to God's will, unlike the disobedient prophet.

²⁶Now when the prophet who had brought him back from the way heard *it,* he said, "It *is* the man of God who was disobedient to the word of the LORD. Therefore the LORD has delivered him to the lion, which has torn him and killed him, according to the word of the LORD which He

spoke to him." ²⁷And he spoke to his sons, saying, "Saddle the donkey for me." So they saddled *it.* ²⁸Then he went and found his corpse thrown on the road, and the donkey and the lion standing by the corpse. The lion had not eaten the corpse nor torn the donkey. ²⁹And the prophet took up the corpse of the man of God, laid it on the donkey, and brought it back. So the old prophet came to the city to mourn, and to bury him. ³⁰Then he laid the corpse in his own tomb; and they mourned over him, *saying,* "Alas, my brother!" ³¹So it was, after he had buried him, that he spoke to his sons, saying, "When I am dead, then bury me in the tomb where the man of God *is* buried; lay my bones beside his bones. ³²For the saying which he cried out by the word of the LORD against the altar in Bethel, and against all the shrines*ᵃ* on the high places which *are* in the cities of Samaria, will surely come to pass."

³³After this event Jeroboam did not turn from his evil way, but again he made priests from every class of people for the high places; whoever wished, he consecrated him, and he became *one* of the priests of the high places. ³⁴And this thing was the sin of the house of Jeroboam, so as to exterminate and destroy *it* from the face of the earth.

Judgment on the House of Jeroboam

14 At that time Abijah the son of Jeroboam became sick. ²And Jeroboam said to his wife, "Please arise, and disguise yourself, that they may not recognize you as the wife of Jeroboam, and go to Shiloh. Indeed, Ahijah the prophet *is* there, who told me that *I would be* king over this people. ³Also take with you ten loaves, *some* cakes, and a jar of honey, and go to him; he will tell you what will become of the child." ⁴And Jeroboam's wife did so; she arose and went to Shiloh, and came to the house of Ahijah. But Ahijah could not see, for his eyes were glazed by reason of his age.

⁵Now the LORD had said to Ahijah, "Here is the wife of Jeroboam, coming to ask you something about her son, for he *is* sick. Thus and thus you shall say to her; for it will be, when she comes in, that she will pretend *to be* another *woman.*"

13:32 *ᵃ*Literally *houses*

⁶And so it was, when Ahijah heard the sound of her footsteps as she came through the door, he said, "Come in, wife of Jeroboam. Why do you pretend *to be* another *person?* For I *have been* sent to you *with* bad *news.* ⁷Go, tell Jeroboam, 'Thus says the LORD God of Israel: "Because I exalted you from among the people, and made you ruler over My people Israel, ⁸and tore the kingdom away from the house of David, and gave it to you; and *yet* you have not been as My servant David, who kept My commandments and who followed Me with all his heart, to do only *what was* right in My eyes; ⁹but you have done more evil than all who were before you, for you have gone and made for yourself other gods and molded images to provoke Me to anger, and have cast Me behind your back—¹⁰therefore behold! I will bring disaster on the house of Jeroboam, and will cut off from Jeroboam every male in Israel, bond and free; I will take away the remnant of the house of Jeroboam, as one takes away refuse until it is all gone. ¹¹The dogs shall eat whoever belongs to Jeroboam and dies in the city, and the birds of the air shall eat whoever dies in the field; for the LORD has spoken!" ' ¹²Arise therefore, go to your own house. When your feet enter the city, the child shall die. ¹³And all Israel shall mourn for him and bury him, for he is the only one of Jeroboam who shall come to the grave, because in him there is found something good toward the LORD God of Israel in the house of Jeroboam.

14:9 more evil. Jeroboam's wickedness was greater than that of Saul and Solomon. He created a system of pagan worship for the northern kingdom (see 16:25,30).

¹⁴"Moreover the LORD will raise up for Himself a king over Israel who shall cut off the house of Jeroboam; this is the day. What? Even now! ¹⁵For the LORD will strike Israel, as a reed is shaken in the water. He will uproot Israel from this good land which He gave to their fathers, and will scatter them beyond the River,*ᵃ* because they have made their wooden images,*ᵇ* provoking the LORD to anger. ¹⁶And He will give Israel up because of the sins of Jeroboam, who sinned and who made Israel sin."

¹⁷Then Jeroboam's wife arose and departed, and came to Tirzah. When she came to the threshold of the house, the child died. ¹⁸And they buried him; and all Israel mourned for him, according to the word of the LORD which He spoke through His servant Ahijah the prophet.

Death of Jeroboam

¹⁹Now the rest of the acts of Jeroboam, how he made war and how he reigned, indeed they *are* written in the book of the chronicles of the kings of Israel. ²⁰The period that Jeroboam reigned *was* twenty-two years. So he rested with his fathers. Then Nadab his son reigned in his place.

Rehoboam Reigns in Judah

²¹And Rehoboam the son of Solomon reigned in Judah. Rehoboam *was* forty-one years old when he became king. He reigned seventeen years in Jerusalem, the city which the LORD had chosen out of all the tribes of Israel, to put His name there. His mother's name *was* Naamah, an Ammonitess. ²²Now Judah did evil in the sight of the LORD, and they provoked Him to jealousy with their sins which they committed, more than all that their fathers had done. ²³For they also built for themselves high places, *sacred* pillars, and wooden images on every high hill and under every green tree. ²⁴And there were also perverted persons*ᵃ* in the land. They did according to all the abominations of the nations which the LORD had cast out before the children of Israel.

²⁵It happened in the fifth year of King Rehoboam *that* Shishak king of Egypt came up against Jerusalem. ²⁶And he took away the treasures of the house of the LORD and the treasures of the king's house; he took

14:22–24 Judah provoked the Lord to jealous anger because of the extent of her evil (v. 22). Idolatrous practice and sacred prostitution to promote fertility were everywhere (vv. 23,24).

14:15 *ᵃ*That is, the Euphrates   *ᵇ*Hebrew *Asherim,* Canaanite deities   14:24 *ᵃ*Hebrew *qadesh,* that is, one practicing sodomy and prostitution in religious rituals

away everything. He also took away all the gold shields which Solomon had made. [27]Then King Rehoboam made bronze shields in their place, and committed *them* to the hands of the captains of the guard, who guarded the doorway of the king's house. [28]And whenever the king entered the house of the LORD, the guards carried them, then brought them back into the guardroom.

[29]Now the rest of the acts of Rehoboam, and all that he did, *are* they not written in the book of the chronicles of the kings of Judah? [30]And there was war between Rehoboam and Jeroboam all *their* days. [31]So Rehoboam rested with his fathers, and was buried with his fathers in the City of David. His mother's name *was* Naamah, an Ammonitess. Then Abijam[a] his son reigned in his place.

Abijam Reigns in Judah

15 In the eighteenth year of King Jeroboam the son of Nebat, Abijam became king over Judah. [2]He reigned three years in Jerusalem. His mother's name *was* Maachah the granddaughter of Abishalom. [3]And he walked in all the sins of his father, which he had done before him; his heart was not loyal to the LORD his God, as was the heart of his father David. [4]Nevertheless for David's sake the LORD his God gave him a lamp in Jerusalem, by setting up his son after him and by establishing Jerusalem; [5]because David did *what was* right in the eyes of the LORD, and had not turned aside from anything that He commanded him all the days of his life, except in the matter of Uriah the Hittite. [6]And there was war between Rehoboam[a] and Jeroboam all the days of his life. [7]Now the rest of the acts of Abijam, and all that he did, *are* they not written in the book of the chronicles of the kings of Judah? And there was war between Abijam and Jeroboam.

> **15:5 *what was* right in the eyes of the LORD.** This phrase is frequently used to describe the kings of Judah, to show that what they did or did not do was generally acceptable to God (see verse 11).

[8]So Abijam rested with his fathers, and they buried him in the City of David. Then Asa his son reigned in his place.

Asa Reigns in Judah

[9]In the twentieth year of Jeroboam king of Israel, Asa became king over Judah. [10]And he reigned forty-one years in Jerusalem. His grandmother's name *was* Maachah the granddaughter of Abishalom. [11]Asa did *what was* right in the eyes of the LORD, as *did* his father David. [12]And he banished the perverted persons[a] from the land, and removed all the idols that his fathers had made. [13]Also he removed Maachah his grandmother from *being* queen mother, because she had made an obscene image of Asherah.[a] And Asa cut down her obscene image and burned *it* by the Brook Kidron. [14]But the high places were not removed. Nevertheless Asa's heart was loyal to the LORD all his days. [15]He also brought into the house of the LORD the things which his father had dedicated, and the things which he himself had dedicated: silver and gold and utensils.

> **15:11–15 Asa.** He was the first of the good kings of Judah. He removed the "sacred" prostitutes, rid the land of all the idols, removed the corrupt queen mother and burned the idol she had made, and placed "holy things" back in the temple (v. 15). Asa never engaged in idolatry, but he failed by tolerating "the high place."

[16]Now there was war between Asa and Baasha king of Israel all their days. [17]And Baasha king of Israel came up against Judah, and built Ramah, that he might let none go out or come in to Asa king of Judah. [18]Then Asa took all the silver and gold *that was* left in the treasuries of the house of the LORD and the treasuries of the king's house, and delivered them into the hand of his servants. And King Asa sent them to Ben-Hadad the son of Tabrimmon, the son of Hezion, king of Syria, who dwelt in Damascus, saying, [19]*Let there be* a treaty between you and me, as there was between my father and your father. See, I have

---

14:31 [a]Spelled *Abijah* in 2 Chronicles 12:16ff   15:6 [a]Following Masoretic Text, Septuagint, Targum, and Vulgate; some Hebrew manuscripts and Syriac read *Abijam*.   15:12 [a]Hebrew *qedeshim*, that is, those practicing sodomy and prostitution in religious rituals   15:13 [a]A Canaanite goddess

sent you a present of silver and gold. Come and break your treaty with Baasha king of Israel, so that he will withdraw from me."

²⁰So Ben-Hadad heeded King Asa, and sent the captains of his armies against the cities of Israel. He attacked Ijon, Dan, Abel Beth Maachah, and all Chinneroth, with all the land of Naphtali. ²¹Now it happened, when Baasha heard *it*, that he stopped building Ramah, and remained in Tirzah.

²²Then King Asa made a proclamation throughout all Judah; none *was* exempted. And they took away the stones and timber of Ramah, which Baasha had used for building; and with them King Asa built Geba of Benjamin, and Mizpah.

²³The rest of all the acts of Asa, all his might, all that he did, and the cities which he built, *are* they not written in the book of the chronicles of the kings of Judah? But in the time of his old age he was diseased in his feet. ²⁴So Asa rested with his fathers, and was buried with his fathers in the City of David his father. Then Jehoshaphat his son reigned in his place.

Nadab Reigns in Israel

²⁵Now Nadab the son of Jeroboam became king over Israel in the second year of Asa king of Judah, and he reigned over Israel two years. ²⁶And he did evil in the sight of the LORD, and walked in the way of his father, and in his sin by which he had made Israel sin.

²⁷Then Baasha the son of Ahijah, of the house of Issachar, conspired against him. And Baasha killed him at Gibbethon, which *belonged* to the Philistines, while Nadab and all Israel laid siege to Gibbethon. ²⁸Baasha killed him in the third year of Asa king of Judah, and reigned in his place. ²⁹And it was so, when he became king, *that* he killed all the house of Jeroboam. He did not leave to Jeroboam anyone that breathed, until he had destroyed him,

15:29 he killed all the house of Jeroboam. Ahijah had prophesied against Jeroboam, stating that all the males in Jeroboam's family would be killed (see 14:9–11). Baasha, the northern king, killed all of Jeroboam's family, including the women and children, which exceeded the prophecy.

according to the word of the LORD which He had spoken by His servant Ahijah the Shilonite, ³⁰because of the sins of Jeroboam, which he had sinned and by which he had made Israel sin, because of his provocation with which he had provoked the LORD God of Israel to anger.

³¹Now the rest of the acts of Nadab, and all that he did, *are* they not written in the book of the chronicles of the kings of Israel? ³²And there was war between Asa and Baasha king of Israel all their days.

Baasha Reigns in Israel

³³In the third year of Asa king of Judah, Baasha the son of Ahijah became king over all Israel in Tirzah, and *reigned* twenty-four years. ³⁴He did evil in the sight of the LORD, and walked in the way of Jeroboam, and in his sin by which he had made Israel sin.

16 Then the word of the LORD came to Jehu the son of Hanani, against Baasha, saying: ²"Inasmuch as I lifted you out of the dust and made you ruler over My people Israel, and you have walked in the way of Jeroboam, and have made My people Israel sin, to provoke Me to anger with their sins, ³surely I will take away the posterity of Baasha and the posterity of his house, and I will make your house like the house of Jeroboam the son of Nebat. ⁴The dogs shall eat whoever belongs to Baasha and dies in the city, and the birds of the air shall eat whoever dies in the fields."

16:1 Jehu the son of Hanani. Hanani may have been the prophet who warned King Asa (2 Chr. 16:7–9). Jehu delivered the Lord's message of judgment to the king of Israel. The Lord used His prophets in the book of Kings to confront the sin of Israel's kings.

⁵Now the rest of the acts of Baasha, what he did, and his might, *are* they not written in the book of the chronicles of the kings of Israel? ⁶So Baasha rested with his fathers and was buried in Tirzah. Then Elah his son reigned in his place.

⁷And also the word of the LORD came by the prophet Jehu the son of Hanani against Baasha and his house, because of all the evil that he did in the sight of the LORD in provoking Him to anger with the work of

his hands, in being like the house of Jeroboam, and because he killed them.

Elah Reigns in Israel

⁸In the twenty-sixth year of Asa king of Judah, Elah the son of Baasha became king over Israel, *and reigned* two years in Tirzah. ⁹Now his servant Zimri, commander of half *his* chariots, conspired against him as he was in Tirzah drinking himself drunk in the house of Arza, steward of *his* house in Tirzah. ¹⁰And Zimri went in and struck him and killed him in the twenty-seventh year of Asa king of Judah, and reigned in his place.

¹¹Then it came to pass, when he began to reign, as soon as he was seated on his throne, *that* he killed all the household of Baasha; he did not leave him one male, neither of his relatives nor of his friends. ¹²Thus Zimri destroyed all the household of Baasha, according to the word of the LORD, which He spoke against Baasha by Jehu the prophet, ¹³for all the sins of Baasha and the sins of Elah his son, by which they had sinned and by which they had made Israel sin, in provoking the LORD God of Israel to anger with their idols.

¹⁴Now the rest of the acts of Elah, and all that he did, *are* they not written in the book of the chronicles of the kings of Israel?

Zimri Reigns in Israel

¹⁵In the twenty-seventh year of Asa king of Judah, Zimri had reigned in Tirzah seven days. And the people *were* encamped against Gibbethon, which *belonged* to the Philistines. ¹⁶Now the people *who were* encamped heard it said, "Zimri has conspired and also has killed the king." So all Israel made Omri, the commander of the army, king over Israel that day in the camp. ¹⁷Then Omri and all Israel with him went up from Gibbethon, and they besieged Tirzah. ¹⁸And it happened, when Zimri saw that the city was taken, that he went into the citadel of the king's house and burned the king's house down upon himself with fire, and died, ¹⁹because of the sins which he had committed in doing evil in the sight

---

16:15 seven days. Zimri's reign (885 B.C.) was the shortest of any king of Israel.

---

of the LORD, in walking in the way of Jeroboam, and in his sin which he had committed to make Israel sin.

²⁰Now the rest of the acts of Zimri, and the treason he committed, *are* they not written in the book of the chronicles of the kings of Israel?

Omri Reigns in Israel

²¹Then the people of Israel were divided into two parts: half of the people followed Tibni the son of Ginath, to make him king, and half followed Omri. ²²But the people who followed Omri prevailed over the people who followed Tibni the son of Ginath. So Tibni died and Omri reigned. ²³In the thirty-first year of Asa king of Judah, Omri became king over Israel, *and reigned* twelve years. Six years he reigned in Tirzah. ²⁴And he bought the hill of Samaria from Shemer for two talents of silver; then he built on the hill, and called the name of the city which he built, Samaria, after the name of Shemer, owner of the hill. ²⁵Omri did evil in the eyes of the LORD, and did worse than all who *were* before him. ²⁶For he walked in all the ways of Jeroboam the son of Nebat, and in his sin by which he had made Israel sin, provoking the LORD God of Israel to anger with their idols.

²⁷Now the rest of the acts of Omri which he did, and the might that he showed, *are* they not written in the book of the chronicles of the kings of Israel?

²⁸So Omri rested with his fathers and was buried in Samaria. Then Ahab his son reigned in his place.

Ahab Reigns in Israel

²⁹In the thirty-eighth year of Asa king of Judah, Ahab the son of Omri became king over Israel; and Ahab the son of Omri reigned over Israel in Samaria twenty-two years. ³⁰Now Ahab the son of Omri did evil in the sight of the LORD, more than all who *were* before him. ³¹And it came to pass, as though it had been a trivial thing for him to walk in the sins of Jeroboam the son of Nebat, that he took as wife Jezebel the daughter of Ethbaal, king of the Sidonians; and he went and served Baal and worshiped him. ³²Then he set up an altar for Baal in the temple of Baal, which he had built in Samaria. ³³And Ahab made a wooden

image.ᵃ Ahab did more to provoke the LORD God of Israel to anger than all the kings of Israel who were before him. ³⁴In his days Hiel of Bethel built Jericho. He laid its foundation with Abiram his firstborn, and with his youngest *son* Segub he set up its gates, according to the word of the LORD, which He had spoken through Joshua the son of Nun.ᵃ

> **16:31,32 Jezebel.** She was the wretched wife of Ahab who symbolized the evil of false religion (see Rev. 2:20). **Baal.** Baal means "lord, husband, owner." He was the predominant god in the Canaanite religion, the storm god who provided rain for the fertility of the land. The worship of Baal was widespread in Israel even before Ahab (Judg. 2:11; 1 Sam. 12:10). Ahab built a temple for Baal in Samaria (see 2 Kin. 3:2).

Elijah Proclaims a Drought

17 And Elijah the Tishbite, of the inhabitants of Gilead, said to Ahab, "*As* the LORD God of Israel lives, before whom I stand, there shall not be dew nor rain these years, except at my word."

> **17:1 Elijah.** His name means "the LORD is God." He was sent by God to confront Baalism and to declare to Israel that the Lord was God. **not be dew nor rain.** God threatened to withhold these if His people served other gods (Lev. 26:18,19). Elijah prayed for a drought (see James 5:17), and God answered. The drought lasted 3 years and 6 months and proved that Baal was impotent before the Lord.

²Then the word of the LORD came to him, saying, ³"Get away from here and turn eastward, and hide by the Brook Cherith, which flows into the Jordan. ⁴And it will be *that* you shall drink from the brook, and I have commanded the ravens to feed you there."

⁵So he went and did according to the word of the LORD, for he went and stayed by the Brook Cherith, which flows into the Jordan. ⁶The ravens brought him bread and meat in the morning, and bread and meat in the evening; and he drank from the brook. ⁷And it happened after a while that the brook dried up, because there had been no rain in the land.

Elijah and the Widow

⁸Then the word of the LORD came to him, saying, ⁹"Arise, go to Zarephath, which *belongs* to Sidon, and dwell there. See, I have commanded a widow there to provide for you." ¹⁰So he arose and went to Zarephath. And when he came to the gate of the city, indeed a widow *was* there gathering sticks. And he called to her and said, "Please bring me a little water in a cup, that I may drink." ¹¹And as she was going to get *it*, he called to her and said, "Please bring me a morsel of bread in your hand."

¹²So she said, "As the LORD your God lives, I do not have bread, only a handful of flour in a bin, and a little oil in a jar; and see, I *am* gathering a couple of sticks that I may go in and prepare it for myself and my son, that we may eat it, and die."

¹³And Elijah said to her, "Do not fear; go *and* do as you have said, but make me a small cake from it first, and bring *it* to me; and afterward make *some* for yourself and your son. ¹⁴For thus says the LORD God of Israel: 'The bin of flour shall not be used up, nor shall the jar of oil run dry, until the day the LORD sends rain on the earth.' "

¹⁵So she went away and did according to the word of Elijah; and she and he and her household ate for *many* days. ¹⁶The bin of flour was not used up, nor did the jar of oil run dry, according to the word of the LORD which He spoke by Elijah.

Elijah Revives the Widow's Son

¹⁷Now it happened after these things *that* the son of the woman who owned the house became sick. And his sickness was so serious that there was no breath left in him. ¹⁸So she said to Elijah, "What have I to do with you, O man of God? Have you come to me to bring my sin to remembrance, and to kill my son?"

¹⁹And he said to her, "Give me your son." So he took him out of her arms and carried him to the upper room where he was staying, and laid him on his own bed. ²⁰Then he cried out to the LORD and said, "O LORD my God, have You also brought tragedy on the widow with whom I lodge, by killing her son?" ²¹And he stretched himself out on

---

16:33 ᵃHebrew *Asherah*, a Canaanite goddess   16:34 ᵃCompare Joshua 6:26

the child three times, and cried out to the LORD and said, "O LORD my God, I pray, let this child's soul come back to him." ²²Then the LORD heard the voice of Elijah; and the soul of the child came back to him, and he revived.

²³And Elijah took the child and brought him down from the upper room into the house, and gave him to his mother. And Elijah said, "See, your son lives!"

²⁴Then the woman said to Elijah, "Now by this I know that you *are* a man of God, *and* that the word of the LORD in your mouth *is* the truth."

Elijah's Message to Ahab

18 And it came to pass *after* many days that the word of the LORD came to Elijah, in the third year, saying, "Go, present yourself to Ahab, and I will send rain on the earth."

²So Elijah went to present himself to Ahab; and *there was* a severe famine in Samaria. ³And Ahab had called Obadiah, who *was* in charge of *his* house. (Now Obadiah feared the LORD greatly. ⁴For so it was, while Jezebel massacred the prophets of the LORD, that Obadiah had taken one hundred prophets and hidden them, fifty to a cave, and had fed them with bread and water.) ⁵And Ahab had said to Obadiah, "Go into the land to all the springs of water and to all the brooks; perhaps we may find grass to keep the horses and mules alive, so that we will not have to kill any livestock." ⁶So they divided the land between them to explore

it; Ahab went one way by himself, and Obadiah went another way by himself.

⁷Now as Obadiah was on his way, suddenly Elijah met him; and he recognized him, and fell on his face, and said, "*Is that* you, my lord Elijah?"

⁸And he answered him, "*It is* I. Go, tell your master, 'Elijah *is here.'* "

⁹So he said, "How have I sinned, that you are delivering your servant into the hand of Ahab, to kill me? ¹⁰*As* the LORD your God lives, there is no nation or kingdom where my master has not sent someone to hunt for you; and when they said, '*He is* not *here,*' he took an oath from the kingdom or nation that they could not find you. ¹¹And now you say, 'Go, tell your master, "Elijah *is here*"'! ¹²And it shall come to pass, *as soon as* I am gone from you, that the Spirit of the LORD will carry you to a place I do not know; so when I go and tell Ahab, and he cannot find you, he will kill me. But I your servant have feared the LORD from my youth. ¹³Was it not reported to my lord what I did when Jezebel killed the prophets of the LORD, how I hid one hundred men of the LORD's prophets, fifty to a cave, and fed them with bread and water? ¹⁴And now you say, 'Go, tell your master, "Elijah *is here.*"' He will kill me!"

¹⁵Then Elijah said, "*As* the LORD of hosts lives, before whom I stand, I will surely present myself to him today."

18:2 famine. The famine was to allow Ahab time to repent, as he was the cause of this national judgment. If he repented, rain would come.

18:12 the Spirit of the LORD will carry you. Obadiah was to tell Ahab that Elijah was present to speak with him, but he was afraid because Ahab was seeking after Elijah. Obadiah was also afraid that the Holy Spirit would carry Elijah away again and that Ahab would kill him if he gave a false report of Elijah's presence.

RESUSCITATIONS FROM THE DEAD

1. Widow of Zarephath's son, raised by Elijah		1 Kings 17:22
2. Shunammite woman's son, raised by Elisha		2 Kings 4:34,35
3. Man raised when he came into contact with the bones of Elisha		2 Kings 13:20,21
4. Widow of Nain's son, raised by Jesus		Luke 7:14,15
5. Jairus' daughter, raised by Jesus		Luke 8:52–56
6. Lazarus of Bethany, brother of Mary and Martha, raised by Jesus		John 11
7. Dorcas, raised by Peter		Acts 9:40
8. Eutychus, raised by Paul		Acts 20:9–12

¹⁶So Obadiah went to meet Ahab, and told him; and Ahab went to meet Elijah.

¹⁷Then it happened, when Ahab saw Elijah, that Ahab said to him, "*Is that* you, O troubler of Israel?"

¹⁸And he answered, "I have not troubled Israel, but you and your father's house *have*, in that you have forsaken the commandments of the LORD and have followed the Baals. ¹⁹Now therefore, send *and* gather all Israel to me on Mount Carmel, the four hundred and fifty prophets of Baal, and the four hundred prophets of Asherah,ᵃ who eat at Jezebel's table."

Elijah's Mount Carmel Victory

²⁰So Ahab sent for all the children of Israel, and gathered the prophets together on Mount Carmel. ²¹And Elijah came to all the people, and said, "How long will you falter between two opinions? If the LORD *is* God, follow Him; but if Baal, follow him." But the people answered him not a word. ²²Then Elijah said to the people, "I alone am left a prophet of the LORD; but Baal's prophets *are* four hundred and fifty men. ²³Therefore let them give us two bulls; and let them choose one bull for themselves, cut it in pieces, and lay *it* on the wood, but put no fire *under it*; and I will prepare the other bull, and lay *it* on the wood, but put no fire *under it.* ²⁴Then you call on the name of your gods, and I will call on the name of the LORD; and the God who answers by fire, He is God."

18:21 falter between two opinions. Israel had not completely rejected the Lord. Instead, they sought to combine the worship of God with the worship of Baal. Elijah told Israel that they must choose who was God and then serve Him wholeheartedly.

So all the people answered and said, "It is well spoken."

²⁵Now Elijah said to the prophets of Baal, "Choose one bull for yourselves and prepare *it* first, for you *are* many; and call on the name of your god, but put no fire *under it.*"

²⁶So they took the bull which was given them, and they prepared *it*, and called on the name of Baal from morning even till noon, saying, "O Baal, hear us!" But *there was* no voice; no one answered. Then they leaped about the altar which they had made.

²⁷And so it was, at noon, that Elijah mocked them and said, "Cry aloud, for he *is* a god; either he is meditating, or he is busy, or he is on a journey, *or* perhaps he is sleeping and must be awakened." ²⁸So they cried aloud, and cut themselves, as was their custom, with knives and lances, until the blood gushed out on them. ²⁹And when midday was past, they prophesied until the *time* of the offering of the *evening* sacrifice. But *there was* no voice; no one answered, no one paid attention.

18:29 no...no...no. This 3-fold declaration emphasized the lack of response on the part of Baal. Baal's silence indicated his impotence and non-existence (Jer. 10:5).

³⁰Then Elijah said to all the people, "Come near to me." So all the people came near to him. And he repaired the altar of the LORD *that was* broken down. ³¹And Elijah took twelve stones, according to the number of the tribes of the sons of Jacob, to whom the word of the LORD had come, saying, "Israel shall be your name."ᵃ ³²Then with the stones he built an altar in the name of the LORD; and he made a trench around the altar large enough to hold two seahs of seed. ³³And he put the wood in order, cut the bull in pieces, and laid *it* on the wood, and said, "Fill four waterpots with water, and pour *it* on the burnt sacrifice and on the wood." ³⁴Then he said, "Do *it* a second time," and they did *it* a second time; and he said, "Do *it* a third time," and they did *it* a third time. ³⁵So the water ran all around the altar; and he also filled the trench with water.

³⁶And it came to pass, at *the time of* the offering of the *evening* sacrifice, that Elijah the prophet came near and said, "LORD God of Abraham, Isaac, and Israel, let it be known this day that You *are* God in Israel and I *am* Your servant, and *that* I have done all these things at Your word. ³⁷Hear me, O LORD, hear me, that this people may know that You *are* the LORD God, and *that* You

---

18:19 ᵃA Canaanite goddess   18:31 ᵃGenesis 32:28

have turned their hearts back *to You* again."

³⁸Then the fire of the LORD fell and consumed the burnt sacrifice, and the wood and the stones and the dust, and it licked up the water that *was* in the trench. ³⁹Now when all the people saw *it*, they fell on their faces; and they said, "The LORD, He *is* God! The LORD, He *is* God!"

⁴⁰And Elijah said to them, "Seize the prophets of Baal! Do not let one of them escape!" So they seized them; and Elijah brought them down to the Brook Kishon and executed them there.

The Drought Ends

⁴¹Then Elijah said to Ahab, "Go up, eat and drink; for *there is* the sound of abundance of rain." ⁴²So Ahab went up to eat and drink. And Elijah went up to the top of Carmel; then he bowed down on the ground, and put his face between his knees, ⁴³and said to his servant, "Go up now, look toward the sea."

So he went up and looked, and said, "*There is* nothing." And seven times he said, "Go again."

⁴⁴Then it came to pass the seventh *time,* that he said, "There is a cloud, as small as a man's hand, rising out of the sea!" So he said, "Go up, say to Ahab, 'Prepare *your* chariot, and go down before the rain stops you.' "

⁴⁵Now it happened in the meantime that the sky became black with clouds and wind, and there was a heavy rain. So Ahab rode away and went to Jezreel. ⁴⁶Then the hand of the LORD came upon Elijah; and he girded up his loins and ran ahead of Ahab to the entrance of Jezreel.

18:46 ran ahead. It was the custom for kings to have runners before their chariots. Elijah was loyal to Ahab by running the 15 to 25 miles from Mount Carmel to Jezreel ahead of his chariot.

Elijah Escapes from Jezebel

19 And Ahab told Jezebel all that Elijah had done, also how he had executed all the prophets with the sword. ²Then Jezebel sent a messenger to Elijah, saying, "So let the gods do *to me,* and more also, if I do not make your life as the life of one of them

by tomorrow about this time." ³And when he saw *that,* he arose and ran for his life, and went to Beersheba, which *belongs* to Judah, and left his servant there.

⁴But he himself went a day's journey into the wilderness, and came and sat down under a broom tree. And he prayed that he might die, and said, "It is enough! Now, LORD, take my life, for I *am* no better than my fathers!"

19:4 take my life. Israelites believed that suicide was an affront to the Lord and never an option. Elijah asked the Lord for death (see Jon. 4:3,8) because he felt the situation was hopeless.

⁵Then as he lay and slept under a broom tree, suddenly an angel^a touched him, and said to him, "Arise *and* eat." ⁶Then he looked, and there by his head *was* a cake baked on coals, and a jar of water. So he ate and drank, and lay down again. ⁷And the angel^a of the LORD came back the second time, and touched him, and said, "Arise *and* eat, because the journey *is* too great for you." ⁸So he arose, and ate and drank; and he went in the strength of that food forty days and forty nights as far as Horeb, the mountain of God.

⁹And there he went into a cave, and spent the night in that place; and behold, the word of the LORD *came* to him, and He said to him, "What are you doing here, Elijah?"

¹⁰So he said, "I have been very zealous for the LORD God of hosts; for the children of Israel have forsaken Your covenant, torn down Your altars, and killed Your prophets with the sword. I alone am left; and they seek to take my life."

God's Revelation to Elijah

¹¹Then He said, "Go out, and stand on the mountain before the LORD." And behold, the LORD passed by, and a great and strong wind tore into the mountains and

19:11 the LORD passed by. Wind, earthquakes, and fire announced the arrival of the Lord (see Ex. 19:16–19; Ps. 18:7–15). The Lord revealed Himself to Elijah in the form of a faint, whispering voice. Elijah learned that God was quietly doing His work in Israel.

broke the rocks in pieces before the LORD, *but* the LORD *was* not in the wind; and after the wind an earthquake, *but* the LORD *was* not in the earthquake; [12]and after the earthquake a fire, *but* the LORD *was* not in the fire; and after the fire a still small voice.

[13]So it was, when Elijah heard *it*, that he wrapped his face in his mantle and went out and stood in the entrance of the cave. Suddenly a voice *came* to him, and said, "What are you doing here, Elijah?"

[14]And he said, "I have been very zealous for the LORD God of hosts; because the children of Israel have forsaken Your covenant, torn down Your altars, and killed Your prophets with the sword. I alone am left; and they seek to take my life."

[15]Then the LORD said to him: "Go, return on your way to the Wilderness of Damascus; and when you arrive, anoint Hazael *as* king over Syria. [16]Also you shall anoint Jehu the son of Nimshi *as* king over Israel. And Elisha the son of Shaphat of Abel Meholah you shall anoint *as* prophet in your place. [17]It shall be *that* whoever escapes the sword of Hazael, Jehu will kill; and whoever escapes the sword of Jehu, Elisha will kill. [18]Yet I have reserved seven thousand in Israel, all whose knees have not bowed to Baal, and every mouth that has not kissed him."

Elisha Follows Elijah

[19]So he departed from there, and found Elisha the son of Shaphat, who *was* plowing *with* twelve yoke *of oxen* before him, and he was with the twelfth. Then Elijah passed by him and threw his mantle on him. [20]And he left the oxen and ran after Elijah, and said, "Please let me kiss my father and my mother, and *then* I will follow you."

And he said to him, "Go back again, for what have I done to you?"

[21]So *Elisha* turned back from him, and took a yoke of oxen and slaughtered them and boiled their flesh, using the oxen's

19:21 slaughtered. The slaughter of the oxen was a farewell feast for family and friends, indicating that Elisha was making a decisive break. He followed Elijah and became his servant, just as Joshua had been Moses' aide. Just as Elijah resembled Moses, so Elisha also resembled Joshua.

equipment, and gave it to the people, and they ate. Then he arose and followed Elijah, and became his servant.

Ahab Defeats the Syrians

20 Now Ben-Hadad the king of Syria gathered all his forces together; thirty-two kings *were* with him, with horses and chariots. And he went up and besieged Samaria, and made war against it. [2]Then he sent messengers into the city to Ahab king of Israel, and said to him, "Thus says Ben-Hadad: [3]'Your silver and your gold *are* mine; your loveliest wives and children are mine.'"

[4]And the king of Israel answered and said, "My lord, O king, just as you say, I and all that I have *are* yours."

[5]Then the messengers came back and said, "Thus speaks Ben-Hadad, saying, 'Indeed I have sent to you, saying, "You shall deliver to me your silver and your gold, your wives and your children"; [6]but I will send my servants to you tomorrow about this time, and they shall search your house and the houses of your servants. And it shall be, *that* whatever is pleasant in your eyes, they will put *it* in their hands and take *it*.'"

[7]So the king of Israel called all the elders of the land, and said, "Notice, please, and see how this *man* seeks trouble; for he sent to me for my wives, my children, my silver, and my gold; and I did not deny him."

[8]And all the elders and all the people said to him, "Do not listen or consent."

[9]Therefore he said to the messengers of Ben-Hadad, "Tell my lord the king, 'All that you sent for to your servant the first time I will do, but this thing I cannot do.'" And the messengers departed and brought back word to him.

[10]Then Ben-Hadad sent to him and said, "The gods do so to me, and more also, if enough dust is left of Samaria for a handful for each of the people who follow me."

[11]So the king of Israel answered and said, "Tell *him*, 'Let not the one who puts on *his* armor boast like the one who takes *it off*.'"

[12]And it happened when *Ben-Hadad* heard this message, as he and the kings *were* drinking at the command post, that he said to his servants, "Get ready." And they got ready to attack the city.

[13]Suddenly a prophet approached Ahab king of Israel, saying, "Thus says the LORD: 'Have you seen all this great multitude? Behold, I will deliver it into your hand today, and you shall know that I *am* the LORD.' "

20:13 I will deliver it into your hand today. The Lord assured Israel of His help before the battles (Josh. 6:2,16; 8:1). The victory would show Ahab that the Lord was the mighty God He claimed to be. Even though the people and king of Israel had dishonored God, He would not abandon them.

[14]So Ahab said, "By whom?"

And he said, "Thus says the LORD: 'By the young leaders of the provinces.' "

Then he said, "Who will set the battle in order?"

And he answered, "You."

[15]Then he mustered the young leaders of the provinces, and there were two hundred and thirty-two; and after them he mustered all the people, all the children of Israel— seven thousand.

[16]So they went out at noon. Meanwhile Ben-Hadad and the thirty-two kings helping him were getting drunk at the command post. [17]The young leaders of the provinces went out first. And Ben-Hadad sent out *a patrol,* and they told him, saying, "Men are coming out of Samaria!" [18]So he said, "If they have come out for peace, take them alive; and if they have come out for war, take them alive."

[19]Then these young leaders of the provinces went out of the city with the army which followed them. [20]And each one killed his man; so the Syrians fled, and Israel pursued them; and Ben-Hadad the king of Syria escaped on a horse with the cavalry. [21]Then the king of Israel went out and attacked the horses and chariots, and killed the Syrians with a great slaughter.

20:17–21 The battle strategy was to send out the young leaders who could approach the Syrians without causing any alarm. Then, at a given signal, they would initiate a charge, joined by Ahab's main striking force, to catch the drunken Syrians off guard and confuse them. The victory was granted so that Ahab and his people would know that God was sovereign.

[22]And the prophet came to the king of Israel and said to him, "Go, strengthen yourself; take note, and see what you should do, for in the spring of the year the king of Syria will come up against you."

The Syrians Again Defeated

[23]Then the servants of the king of Syria said to him, "Their gods *are* gods of the hills. Therefore they were stronger than we; but if we fight against them in the plain, surely we will be stronger than they. [24]So do this thing: Dismiss the kings, each from his position, and put captains in their places; [25]and you shall muster an army like the army that you have lost, horse for horse and chariot for chariot. Then we will fight against them in the plain; surely we will be stronger than they."

And he listened to their voice and did so.

[26]So it was, in the spring of the year, that Ben-Hadad mustered the Syrians and went up to Aphek to fight against Israel. [27]And the children of Israel were mustered and given provisions, and they went against them. Now the children of Israel encamped before them like two little flocks of goats, while the Syrians filled the countryside.

[28]Then a man of God came and spoke to the king of Israel, and said, "Thus says the LORD: 'Because the Syrians have said, "The LORD *is* God of the hills, but He *is* not God of the valleys," therefore I will deliver all this great multitude into your hand, and you shall know that I *am* the LORD.' " [29]And they encamped opposite each other for seven days. So it was that on the seventh day the battle was joined; and the children of Israel killed one hundred thousand foot soldiers *of* the Syrians in one day. [30]But the rest fled to Aphek, into the city; then a wall fell on twenty-seven thousand of the men *who were* left.

And Ben-Hadad fled and went into the city, into an inner chamber.

Ahab's Treaty with Ben-Hadad

[31]Then his servants said to him, "Look now, we have heard that the kings of the house of Israel *are* merciful kings. Please, let us put sackcloth around our waists and ropes around our heads, and go out to the king of Israel; perhaps he will spare your life." [32]So they wore sackcloth around their waists and *put* ropes around their heads, and came to the king of Israel and said,

"Your servant Ben-Hadad says, 'Please let me live.' "

And he said, "*Is* he still alive? He *is* my brother."

³³Now the men were watching closely to see whether *any sign of mercy would come* from him; and they quickly grasped *at this word* and said, "Your brother Ben-Hadad."

So he said, "Go, bring him." Then Ben-Hadad came out to him; and he had him come up into the chariot.

³⁴So *Ben-Hadad* said to him, "The cities which my father took from your father I will restore; and you may set up market-places for yourself in Damascus, as my father did in Samaria."

Then *Ahab said*, "I will send you away with this treaty." So he made a treaty with him and sent him away.

Ahab Condemned

³⁵Now a certain man of the sons of the prophets said to his neighbor by the word of the LORD, "Strike me, please." And the man refused to strike him. ³⁶Then he said to him, "Because you have not obeyed the voice of the LORD, surely, as soon as you depart from me, a lion shall kill you." And as soon as he left him, a lion found him and killed him.

> **20:35,36** The prophet needed to be wounded, as if in battle, in order to carry out the drama. The refusal to wound him was wrong, as it was withholding aid to a prophet of God in the discharge of his duty. It was punished as a warning to others (see 13:2–24).

³⁷And he found another man, and said, "Strike me, please." So the man struck him, inflicting a wound. ³⁸Then the prophet departed and waited for the king by the road, and disguised himself with a bandage over his eyes. ³⁹Now as the king passed by, he cried out to the king and said, "Your servant went out into the midst of the battle; and there, a man came over and brought a man to me, and said, 'Guard this man; if by any means he is missing, your life shall be for his life, or else you shall pay a talent of silver.' ⁴⁰While your servant was busy here and there, he was gone."

Then the king of Israel said to him, "So *shall* your judgment *be*; you yourself have decided *it*."

⁴¹And he hastened to take the bandage away from his eyes; and the king of Israel recognized him as one of the prophets. ⁴²Then he said to him, "Thus says the LORD: 'Because you have let slip out of *your* hand a man whom I appointed to utter destruction, therefore your life shall go for his life, and your people for his people.' "

⁴³So the king of Israel went to his house sullen and displeased, and came to Samaria.

> **20:39–43** Just as a soldier pays dearly for losing a prisoner in war, Ahab must pay for letting Ben-Hadad, the idolatrous enemy of God, live. This illustration was designed to trap Ahab into announcing the punishment for his own crime (see 2 Sam. 12:1–12).

Naboth Is Murdered for His Vineyard

21 And it came to pass after these things *that* Naboth the Jezreelite had a vineyard which *was* in Jezreel, next to the palace of Ahab king of Samaria. ²So Ahab spoke to Naboth, saying, "Give me your vineyard, that I may have it for a vegetable garden, because it *is* near, next to my house; and for it I will give you a vineyard better than it. *Or*, if it seems good to you, I will give you its worth in money."

³But Naboth said to Ahab, "The LORD forbid that I should give the inheritance of my fathers to you!"

> **21:3 The LORD forbid.** Out of loyalty to God, Naboth declined Ahab's offer because trading or selling his property would be against the law (see 1 Sam. 24:6). This was because the vineyard was his ancestral property, and God had forbidden Israelites to permanently surrender ownership of family lands (Lev. 25:23–28).

⁴So Ahab went into his house sullen and displeased because of the word which Naboth the Jezreelite had spoken to him; for he had said, "I will not give you the inheritance of my fathers." And he lay down on his bed, and turned away his face, and would eat no food. ⁵But Jezebel his wife came to him, and said to him, "Why is your spirit so sullen that you eat no food?"

⁶He said to her, "Because I spoke to Naboth the Jezreelite, and said to him, 'Give me your vineyard for money; or else, if it pleases you, I will give you *another* vine-

yard for it.' And he answered, 'I will not give you my vineyard.' "

⁷Then Jezebel his wife said to him, "You now exercise authority over Israel! Arise, eat food, and let your heart be cheerful; I will give you the vineyard of Naboth the Jezreelite."

⁸And she wrote letters in Ahab's name, sealed *them* with his seal, and sent the letters to the elders and the nobles who *were* dwelling in the city with Naboth. ⁹She wrote in the letters, saying,

Proclaim a fast, and seat Naboth with high honor among the people; ¹⁰and seat two men, scoundrels, before him to bear witness against him, saying, You have blasphemed God and the king. *Then* take him out, and stone him, that he may die.

¹¹So the men of his city, the elders and nobles who were inhabitants of his city, did as Jezebel had sent to them, as it *was* written in the letters which she had sent to them. ¹²They proclaimed a fast, and seated Naboth with high honor among the people. ¹³And two men, scoundrels, came in and sat before him; and the scoundrels witnessed against him, against Naboth, in the presence of the people, saying, "Naboth has blasphemed God and the king!" Then they took him outside the city and stoned him with stones, so that he died. ¹⁴Then they sent to Jezebel, saying, "Naboth has been stoned and is dead."

¹⁵And it came to pass, when Jezebel heard that Naboth had been stoned and was dead, that Jezebel said to Ahab, "Arise, take possession of the vineyard of Naboth the Jezreelite, which he refused to give you for money; for Naboth is not alive, but dead." ¹⁶So it was, when Ahab heard that Naboth was dead, that Ahab got up and went down to take possession of the vineyard of Naboth the Jezreelite.

The LORD Condemns Ahab

¹⁷Then the word of the LORD came to Elijah the Tishbite, saying, ¹⁸"Arise, go down to meet Ahab king of Israel, who *lives* in

Samaria. There *he is*, in the vineyard of Naboth, where he has gone down to take possession of it. ¹⁹You shall speak to him, saying, 'Thus says the LORD: "Have you murdered and also taken possession?" ' And you shall speak to him, saying, 'Thus says the LORD: "In the place where dogs licked the blood of Naboth, dogs shall lick your blood, even yours." ' "

²⁰So Ahab said to Elijah, "Have you found me, O my enemy?"

And he answered, "I have found *you,* because you have sold yourself to do evil in the sight of the LORD: ²¹'Behold, I will bring calamity on you. I will take away your posterity, and will cut off from Ahab every male in Israel, both bond and free. ²²I will make your house like the house of Jeroboam the son of Nebat, and like the house of Baasha the son of Ahijah, because of the provocation with which you have provoked *Me* to anger, and made Israel sin.' ²³And concerning Jezebel the LORD also spoke, saying, 'The dogs shall eat Jezebel by the wallᵃ of Jezreel.' ²⁴The dogs shall eat whoever belongs to Ahab and dies in the city, and the birds of the air shall eat whoever dies in the field."

21:23 concerning Jezebel. Jezebel was singled out for judgment because she had encouraged Ahab in promoting Baalism. Elijah's prophecy concerning her was fulfilled in 2 Kin. 9:10,30–37.

²⁵But there was no one like Ahab who sold himself to do wickedness in the sight of the LORD, because Jezebel his wife stirred him up. ²⁶And he behaved very abominably in following idols, according to all *that* the Amorites had done, whom the LORD had cast out before the children of Israel.

²⁷So it was, when Ahab heard those words, that he tore his clothes and put sackcloth on his body, and fasted and lay in sackcloth, and went about mourning. ²⁸And the word of the LORD came to Elijah the Tishbite, saying, ²⁹"See how Ahab has humbled himself before Me? Because he has humbled himself before Me, I will not bring the calamity in his days. In the

21:23 ᵃFollowing Masoretic Text and Septuagint; some Hebrew manuscripts, Syriac, Targum, and Vulgate read *plot of ground* (compare 2 Kings 9:36).

days of his son I will bring the calamity on his house."

Micaiah Warns Ahab

22 Now three years passed without war between Syria and Israel. ²Then it came to pass, in the third year, that Jehoshaphat the king of Judah went down to *visit* the king of Israel.

³And the king of Israel said to his servants, "Do you know that Ramoth in Gilead *is* ours, but we hesitate to take it out of the hand of the king of Syria?" ⁴So he said to Jehoshaphat, "Will you go with me to fight at Ramoth Gilead?"

Jehoshaphat said to the king of Israel, "I *am* as you *are*, my people as your people, my horses as your horses." ⁵Also Jehoshaphat said to the king of Israel, "Please inquire for the word of the LORD today."

⁶Then the king of Israel gathered the prophets together, about four hundred men, and said to them, "Shall I go against Ramoth Gilead to fight, or shall I refrain?"

So they said, "Go up, for the Lord will deliver *it* into the hand of the king."

⁷And Jehoshaphat said, "*Is there* not still a prophet of the LORD here, that we may inquire of Him?"ᵃ

> **22:6,7 prophets.** The 400 prophets of Ahab were not of the Lord. They worshiped in the golden-calf center at Bethel, and their words were designed to please Ahab. They did not use the covenant name for Israel's God, "LORD." Jehoshaphat recognized that they were not true prophets and wished to hear from a true prophet.

⁸So the king of Israel said to Jehoshaphat, "*There is* still one man, Micaiah the son of Imlah, by whom we may inquire of the LORD; but I hate him, because he does not prophesy good concerning me, but evil."

And Jehoshaphat said, "Let not the king say such things!"

⁹Then the king of Israel called an officer and said, "Bring Micaiah the son of Imlah quickly!"

¹⁰The king of Israel and Jehoshaphat the king of Judah, having put on *their* robes, sat each on his throne, at a threshing floor at the entrance of the gate of Samaria; and all the prophets prophesied before them. ¹¹Now Zedekiah the son of Chenaanah had made horns of iron for himself; and he said, "Thus says the LORD: 'With these you shall gore the Syrians until they are destroyed.'"

¹²And all the prophets prophesied so, saying, "Go up to Ramoth Gilead and prosper, for the LORD will deliver *it* into the king's hand."

¹³Then the messenger who had gone to call Micaiah spoke to him, saying, "Now listen, the words of the prophets with one accord encourage the king. Please, let your word be like the word of one of them, and speak encouragement."

¹⁴And Micaiah said, "*As* the LORD lives, whatever the LORD says to me, that I will speak."

¹⁵Then he came to the king; and the king said to him, "Micaiah, shall we go to war against Ramoth Gilead, or shall we refrain?"

And he answered him, "Go and prosper, for the LORD will deliver *it* into the hand of the king!"

¹⁶So the king said to him, "How many times shall I make you swear that you tell me nothing but the truth in the name of the LORD?"

¹⁷Then he said, "I saw all Israel scattered on the mountains, as sheep that have no shepherd. And the LORD said, 'These have no master. Let each return to his house in peace.'"

> **22:17 sheep that have no shepherd.** The king as a shepherd and his people as the sheep was a familiar image (Num. 27:16,17). Micaiah's point was that Israel's shepherd, King Ahab, would be killed and his army scattered.

¹⁸And the king of Israel said to Jehoshaphat, "Did I not tell you he would not prophesy good concerning me, but evil?"

¹⁹Then *Micaiah* said, "Therefore hear the word of the LORD: I saw the LORD sitting on His throne, and all the host of heaven standing by, on His right hand and on His left. ²⁰And the LORD said, 'Who will persuade Ahab to go up, that he may fall at Ramoth Gilead?' So one spoke in this manner, and another spoke in that manner.

22:7 ᵃOr *him*

²¹Then a spirit came forward and stood before the LORD, and said, 'I will persuade him.' ²²The LORD said to him, 'In what way?' So he said, 'I will go out and be a lying spirit in the mouth of all his prophets.' And the LORD said, 'You shall persuade *him,* and also prevail. Go out and do so.' ²³Therefore look! The LORD has put a lying spirit in the mouth of all these prophets of yours, and the LORD has declared disaster against you."

²⁴Now Zedekiah the son of Chenaanah went near and struck Micaiah on the cheek, and said, "Which way did the spirit from the LORD go from me to speak to you?"

²⁵And Micaiah said, "Indeed, you shall see on that day when you go into an inner chamber to hide!"

²⁶So the king of Israel said, "Take Micaiah, and return him to Amon the governor of the city and to Joash the king's son; ²⁷and say, 'Thus says the king: "Put this *fellow* in prison, and feed him with bread of affliction and water of affliction, until I come in peace." ' "

²⁸But Micaiah said, "If you ever return in peace, the LORD has not spoken by me." And he said, "Take heed, all you people!"

> **22:28 If you ever return.** Micaiah declared that if Ahab lived to return from the battle, then he had uttered a false prophecy (Deut. 18:21).

Ahab Dies in Battle

²⁹So the king of Israel and Jehoshaphat the king of Judah went up to Ramoth Gilead. ³⁰And the king of Israel said to Jehoshaphat, "I will disguise myself and go into battle; but you put on your robes." So the king of Israel disguised himself and went into battle.

³¹Now the king of Syria had commanded the thirty-two captains of his chariots, saying, "Fight with no one small or great, but only with the king of Israel." ³²So it was, when the captains of the chariots saw Jehoshaphat, that they said, "Surely it *is* the

> **22:32 Jehoshaphat cried out.** This was a prayer for the Lord's deliverance (2 Chr. 18:31). Jehoshaphat's cry showed the Syrians that he was not Ahab.

king of Israel!" Therefore they turned aside to fight against him, and Jehoshaphat cried out. ³³And it happened, when the captains of the chariots saw that it *was* not the king of Israel, that they turned back from pursuing him. ³⁴Now a *certain* man drew a bow at random, and struck the king of Israel between the joints of his armor. So he said to the driver of his chariot, "Turn around and take me out of the battle, for I am wounded."

³⁵The battle increased that day; and the king was propped up in his chariot, facing the Syrians, and died at evening. The blood ran out from the wound onto the floor of the chariot. ³⁶Then, as the sun was going down, a shout went throughout the army, saying, "Every man to his city, and every man to his own country!"

³⁷So the king died, and was brought to Samaria. And they buried the king in Samaria. ³⁸Then *someone* washed the chariot at a pool in Samaria, and the dogs licked up his blood while the harlots bathed,ᵃ according to the word of the LORD which He had spoken.

³⁹Now the rest of the acts of Ahab, and all that he did, the ivory house which he built and all the cities that he built, *are* they not written in the book of the chronicles of the kings of Israel? ⁴⁰So Ahab rested with his fathers. Then Ahaziah his son reigned in his place.

Jehoshaphat Reigns in Judah

⁴¹Jehoshaphat the son of Asa had become king over Judah in the fourth year of Ahab king of Israel. ⁴²Jehoshaphat *was* thirty-five years old when he became king, and he reigned twenty-five years in Jerusalem. His mother's name *was* Azubah the daughter of Shilhi. ⁴³And he walked in all the ways of his father Asa. He did not turn aside from them, doing *what was* right in the eyes of the LORD. Nevertheless the high places were not taken away, *for* the people offered

> **22:43 doing *what was* right.** Jehoshaphat faithfully did what pleased the Lord, as his father Asa had. But like his father, he failed to close down the high places.

22:38 ᵃSyriac and Targum read *they washed his armor.*

sacrifices and burned incense on the high places. ⁴⁴Also Jehoshaphat made peace with the king of Israel.

⁴⁵Now the rest of the acts of Jehoshaphat, the might that he showed, and how he made war, *are* they not written in the book of the chronicles of the kings of Judah? ⁴⁶And the rest of the perverted persons,*ᵃ* who remained in the days of his father Asa, he banished from the land. ⁴⁷*There was* then no king in Edom, only a deputy of the king.

⁴⁸Jehoshaphat made merchant ships*ᵃ* to go to Ophir for gold; but they never sailed, for the ships were wrecked at Ezion Geber. ⁴⁹Then Ahaziah the son of Ahab said to Jehoshaphat, "Let my servants go with your servants in the ships." But Jehoshaphat would not.

⁵⁰And Jehoshaphat rested with his fathers, and was buried with his fathers in the City of David his father. Then Jehoram his son reigned in his place.

Ahaziah Reigns in Israel

⁵¹Ahaziah the son of Ahab became king over Israel in Samaria in the seventeenth year of Jehoshaphat king of Judah, and reigned two years over Israel. ⁵²He did evil in the sight of the LORD, and walked in the way of his father and in the way of his mother and in the way of Jeroboam the son of Nebat, who had made Israel sin; ⁵³for he served Baal and worshiped him, and provoked the LORD God of Israel to anger, according to all that his father had done.

22:46 *ᵃ*Hebrew *qadesh,* that is, one practicing sodomy and prostitution in religious rituals   22:48 *ᵃ*Or *ships of Tarshish*

OUTLINE OF 2 KINGS

God Judges Ahaziah

1 Moab rebelled against Israel after the death of Ahab.

[2]Now Ahaziah fell through the lattice of his upper room in Samaria, and was injured; so he sent messengers and said to them, "Go, inquire of Baal-Zebub, the god of Ekron, whether I shall recover from this injury." [3]But the angel[a] of the LORD said to Elijah the Tishbite, "Arise, go up to meet the messengers of the king of Samaria, and say to them, '*Is it* because *there is* no God in Israel *that* you are going to inquire of Baal-Zebub, the god of Ekron?' [4]Now therefore, thus says the LORD: 'You shall not come down from the bed to which you have gone up, but you shall surely die.'" So Elijah departed.

[5]And when the messengers returned to him, he said to them, "Why have you come back?"

> **1:4 you shall surely die.** Because Ahaziah had consulted a false god, God punished him by not healing his injuries. God showed him mercy by not killing him (see Ex. 22:20).

[6]So they said to him, "A man came up to meet us, and said to us, 'Go, return to the king who sent you, and say to him, "Thus says the LORD: '*Is it* because *there is* no God in Israel *that* you are sending to inquire of Baal-Zebub, the god of Ekron? Therefore you shall not come down from the bed to which you have gone up, but you shall surely die.'"'"

[7]Then he said to them, "What kind of man *was it* who came up to meet you and told you these words?"

[8]So they answered him, "A hairy man wearing a leather belt around his waist."

And he said, "It *is* Elijah the Tishbite."

[9]Then the king sent to him a captain of fifty with his fifty men. So he went up to him; and there he was, sitting on the top of a hill. And he spoke to him: "Man of God, the king has said, 'Come down!'"

[10]So Elijah answered and said to the captain of fifty, "If I *am* a man of God, then let fire come down from heaven and consume you and your fifty men." And fire came down from heaven and consumed him and

his fifty. [11]Then he sent to him another captain of fifty with his fifty men.

And he answered and said to him: "Man of God, thus has the king said, 'Come down quickly!'"

[12]So Elijah answered and said to them, "If I *am* a man of God, let fire come down from heaven and consume you and your fifty men." And the fire of God came down from heaven and consumed him and his fifty.

> **1:10–12 fire came down from heaven.** This proved that Elijah was the Lord's prophet and deserved respect. It also indicated that Elijah was like Moses, who was also validated as the Lord's prophet by fire from heaven (Num. 16:35).

[13]Again, he sent a third captain of fifty with his fifty men. And the third captain of fifty went up, and came and fell on his knees before Elijah, and pleaded with him, and said to him: "Man of God, please let my life and the life of these fifty servants of yours be precious in your sight. [14]Look, fire has come down from heaven and burned up the first two captains of fifties with their fifties. But let my life now be precious in your sight."

[15]And the angel[a] of the LORD said to Elijah, "Go down with him; do not be afraid of him." So he arose and went down with him to the king. [16]Then he said to him, "Thus says the LORD: 'Because you have sent messengers to inquire of Baal-Zebub, the god of Ekron, *is it* because *there is* no God in Israel to inquire of His word? Therefore you shall not come down from the bed to which you have gone up, but you shall surely die.'"

[17]So *Ahaziah* died according to the word of the LORD which Elijah had spoken. Because he had no son, Jehoram[a] became king in his place, in the second year of Jehoram the son of Jehoshaphat, king of Judah.

[18]Now the rest of the acts of Ahaziah which he did, *are* they not written in the book of the chronicles of the kings of Israel?

Elijah Ascends to Heaven

2 And it came to pass, when the LORD was about to take up Elijah into heaven by a whirlwind, that Elijah went with

---

1:3 [a]Or *Angel*   1:15 [a]Or *Angel*   1:17 [a]The son of Ahab king of Israel (compare 3:1)

Elisha from Gilgal. ²Then Elijah said to Elisha, "Stay here, please, for the LORD has sent me on to Bethel."

But Elisha said, "*As* the LORD lives, and *as* your soul lives, I will not leave you!" So they went down to Bethel.

³Now the sons of the prophets who *were* at Bethel came out to Elisha, and said to him, "Do you know that the LORD will take away your master from over you today?"

And he said, "Yes, I know; keep silent!"

2:3 take away. The same term was used when Enoch was taken into heaven (Gen. 5:24). The question by the sons of the prophets implied that the Lord had revealed Elijah's departure to them in advance. **from over you.** Students traditionally sat at their master's feet, who taught and supervised them from an elevated platform. Elisha would soon take a master's position among the prophets.

---

⁴Then Elijah said to him, "Elisha, stay here, please, for the LORD has sent me on to Jericho."

But he said, "*As* the LORD lives, and *as* your soul lives, I will not leave you!" So they came to Jericho.

⁵Now the sons of the prophets who *were* at Jericho came to Elisha and said to him, "Do you know that the LORD will take away your master from over you today?"

So he answered, "Yes, I know; keep silent!"

⁶Then Elijah said to him, "Stay here, please, for the LORD has sent me on to the Jordan."

But he said, "*As* the LORD lives, and *as* your soul lives, I will not leave you!" So the two of them went on. ⁷And fifty men of the sons of the prophets went and stood facing *them* at a distance, while the two of them stood by the Jordan. ⁸Now Elijah took his mantle, rolled *it* up, and struck the water; and it was divided this way and that, so that the two of them crossed over on dry ground.

⁹And so it was, when they had crossed

2:9 a double portion. It was customary for the firstborn son to inherit a double share of his father's possessions along with the right of succession (Deut. 21:17). Elisha's request was to succeed Elijah in the prophetic office and to receive the spiritual power necessary for the position.

---

over, that Elijah said to Elisha, "Ask! What may I do for you, before I am taken away from you?"

Elisha said, "Please let a double portion of your spirit be upon me."

¹⁰So he said, "You have asked a hard thing. *Nevertheless,* if you see me *when I am* taken from you, it shall be so for you; but if not, it shall not be *so.*" ¹¹Then it happened, as they continued on and talked, that suddenly a chariot of fire *appeared* with horses of fire, and separated the two of them; and Elijah went up by a whirlwind into heaven.

¹²And Elisha saw *it,* and he cried out, "My father, my father, the chariot of Israel and its horsemen!" So he saw him no more. And he took hold of his own clothes and tore them into two pieces. ¹³He also took up the mantle of Elijah that had fallen from him, and went back and stood by the bank of the Jordan. ¹⁴Then he took the mantle of Elijah that had fallen from him, and struck the water, and said, "Where *is* the LORD God of Elijah?" And when he also had struck the water, it was divided this way and that; and Elisha crossed over.

¹⁵Now when the sons of the prophets who *were* from Jericho saw him, they said, "The spirit of Elijah rests on Elisha." And they came to meet him, and bowed to the ground before him. ¹⁶Then they said to him, "Look now, there are fifty strong men with your servants. Please let them go and search for your master, lest perhaps the Spirit of the LORD has taken him up and cast him upon some mountain or into some valley."

And he said, "You shall not send anyone."

¹⁷But when they urged him till he was ashamed, he said, "Send *them!*" Therefore they sent fifty men, and they searched for three days but did not find him. ¹⁸And when they came back to him, for he had stayed in Jericho, he said to them, "Did I not say to you, 'Do not go'?"

Elisha Performs Miracles

¹⁹Then the men of the city said to Elisha, "Please notice, the situation of this city *is* pleasant, as my lord sees; but the water *is* bad, and the ground barren."

²⁰And he said, "Bring me a new bowl, and

put salt in it." So they brought *it* to him. ²¹Then he went out to the source of the water, and cast in the salt there, and said, "Thus says the LORD: 'I have healed this water; from it there shall be no more death or barrenness.' " ²²So the water remains healed to this day, according to the word of Elisha which he spoke.

²³Then he went up from there to Bethel; and as he was going up the road, some youths came from the city and mocked him, and said to him, "Go up, you baldhead! Go up, you baldhead!"

2:23 youths. These were not children, but infidels and idolatrous young men in their teens and twenties. **baldhead.** Baldness was regarded as a disgrace (see Is. 3:17,24). Elisha may not have been bald but just called bald as a mockery. The youths taunted and insulted the Lord's prophet, telling him to "go up" as Elijah had.

²⁴So he turned around and looked at them, and pronounced a curse on them in the name of the LORD. And two female bears came out of the woods and mauled forty-two of the youths.

²⁵Then he went from there to Mount Carmel, and from there he returned to Samaria.

Moab Rebels Against Israel

3 Now Jehoram the son of Ahab became king over Israel at Samaria in the eighteenth year of Jehoshaphat king of Judah, and reigned twelve years. ²And he did evil in the sight of the LORD, but not like his father and mother; for he put away the *sacred* pillar of Baal that his father had made. ³Nevertheless he persisted in the sins of Jeroboam the son of Nebat, who had made Israel sin; he did not depart from them.

⁴Now Mesha king of Moab was a sheepbreeder, and he regularly paid the king of Israel one hundred thousand lambs and the wool of one hundred thousand rams. ⁵But it happened, when Ahab died, that the king of Moab rebelled against the king of Israel.

⁶So King Jehoram went out of Samaria at that time and mustered all Israel. ⁷Then he went and sent to Jehoshaphat king of Judah, saying, "The king of Moab has rebelled against me. Will you go with me to fight against Moab?"

And he said, "I will go up; I *am* as you

are, my people as your people, my horses as your horses." ⁸Then he said, "Which way shall we go up?"

And he answered, "By way of the Wilderness of Edom."

⁹So the king of Israel went with the king of Judah and the king of Edom, and they marched on that roundabout route seven days; and there was no water for the army, nor for the animals that followed them. ¹⁰And the king of Israel said, "Alas! For the LORD has called these three kings together to deliver them into the hand of Moab."

¹¹But Jehoshaphat said, "*Is there* no prophet of the LORD here, that we may inquire of the LORD by him?"

So one of the servants of the king of Israel answered and said, "Elisha the son of Shaphat *is* here, who poured water on the hands of Elijah."

3:11 poured water on the hands. This probably refers to the custom of washing one's hands before and after every meal. Elisha is recognized as having served Elijah, and also as a servant of the Lord (verse 12).

¹²And Jehoshaphat said, "The word of the LORD is with him." So the king of Israel and Jehoshaphat and the king of Edom went down to him.

¹³Then Elisha said to the king of Israel, "What have I to do with you? Go to the prophets of your father and the prophets of your mother."

But the king of Israel said to him, "No, for the LORD has called these three kings *together* to deliver them into the hand of Moab."

¹⁴And Elisha said, "*As* the LORD of hosts lives, before whom I stand, surely were it not that I regard the presence of Jehoshaphat king of Judah, I would not look at you, nor see you. ¹⁵But now bring me a musician."

Then it happened, when the musician played, that the hand of the LORD came upon him. ¹⁶And he said, "Thus says the LORD: 'Make this valley full of ditches.' ¹⁷For thus says the LORD: 'You shall not see wind, nor shall you see rain; yet that valley shall be filled with water, so that you, your cattle, and your animals may drink.' ¹⁸And this is a simple matter in the sight of the LORD; He will also deliver the Moabites into your hand. ¹⁹Also you shall attack

every fortified city and every choice city, and shall cut down every good tree, and stop up every spring of water, and ruin every good piece of land with stones."

²⁰Now it happened in the morning, when the grain offering was offered, that suddenly water came by way of Edom, and the land was filled with water.

²¹And when all the Moabites heard that the kings had come up to fight against them, all who were able to bear arms and older were gathered; and they stood at the border. ²²Then they rose up early in the morning, and the sun was shining on the water; and the Moabites saw the water on the other side *as* red as blood. ²³And they said, "This is blood; the kings have surely struck swords and have killed one another; now therefore, Moab, to the spoil!"

²⁴So when they came to the camp of Israel, Israel rose up and attacked the Moabites, so that they fled before them; and they entered *their* land, killing the Moabites. ²⁵Then they destroyed the cities, and each man threw a stone on every good piece of land and filled it; and they stopped up all the springs of water and cut down all the good trees. But they left the stones of Kir Haraseth *intact.* However the slingers surrounded and attacked it.

²⁶And when the king of Moab saw that the battle was too fierce for him, he took with him seven hundred men who drew swords, to break through to the king of Edom, but they could not. ²⁷Then he took his eldest son who would have reigned in his place, and offered him *as* a burnt offering upon the wall; and there was great indignation against Israel. So they departed from him and returned to *their* own land.

Elisha and the Widow's Oil

4 A certain woman of the wives of the sons of the prophets cried out to Elisha, saying, "Your servant my husband is dead,

and you know that your servant feared the LORD. And the creditor is coming to take my two sons to be his slaves."

²So Elisha said to her, "What shall I do for you? Tell me, what do you have in the house?" And she said, "Your maidservant has nothing in the house but a jar of oil."

³Then he said, "Go, borrow vessels from everywhere, from all your neighbors—empty vessels; do not gather just a few. ⁴And when you have come in, you shall shut the door behind you and your sons; then pour it into all those vessels, and set aside the full ones."

> **4:4 shut the door behind you.** The provision was private because the widow's need was private. Elisha's absence showed that the miracle happened only by God's power.

⁵So she went from him and shut the door behind her and her sons, who brought *the vessels* to her; and she poured *it* out. ⁶Now it came to pass, when the vessels were full, that she said to her son, "Bring me another vessel."

And he said to her, "*There is* not another vessel." So the oil ceased. ⁷Then she came and told the man of God. And he said, "Go, sell the oil and pay your debt; and you *and* your sons live on the rest."

Elisha Raises the Shunammite's Son

⁸Now it happened one day that Elisha went to Shunem, where there *was* a notable woman, and she persuaded him to eat some food. So it was, as often as he passed by, he would turn in there to eat some food. ⁹And she said to her husband, "Look now, I know that this *is* a holy man of God, who passes by us regularly. ¹⁰Please, let us make a small upper room on the wall; and let us put a bed for him there, and a table and a chair and a lampstand; so it will be, whenever he comes to us, he can turn in there."

¹¹And it happened one day that he came there, and he turned in to the upper room and lay down there. ¹²Then he said to Gehazi his servant, "Call this Shunammite woman." When he had called her, she stood before him. ¹³And he said to him, "Say now to her, 'Look, you have been concerned for us with all this care. What *can I* do for you? Do you want me to speak on your behalf to

> **3:27 his eldest son...offered him.** Desperately trying to have the Moabites delivered from defeat, Mesha sacrificed his oldest son to his idol god, Chemosh. **great indignation against Israel.** The king's sacrifice probably inspired the Moabites to hate Israel more and to fight even harder. Israel may have believed that Chemosh was helping the Moabites because of their increased fierceness.

the king or to the commander of the army?' "

She answered, "I dwell among my own people."

¹⁴So he said, "What then *is* to be done for her?"

And Gehazi answered, "Actually, she has no son, and her husband is old."

¹⁵So he said, "Call her." When he had called her, she stood in the doorway. ¹⁶Then he said, "About this time next year you shall embrace a son."

And she said, "No, my lord. Man of God, do not lie to your maidservant!"

¹⁷But the woman conceived, and bore a son when the appointed time had come, of which Elisha had told her.

¹⁸And the child grew. Now it happened one day that he went out to his father, to the reapers. ¹⁹And he said to his father, "My head, my head!"

So he said to a servant, "Carry him to his mother." ²⁰When he had taken him and brought him to his mother, he sat on her knees till noon, and *then* died. ²¹And she went up and laid him on the bed of the man of God, shut *the door* upon him, and went out. ²²Then she called to her husband, and said, "Please send me one of the young men and one of the donkeys, that I may run to the man of God and come back."

²³So he said, "Why are you going to him today? *It is* neither the New Moon nor the Sabbath."

And she said, "*It is* well." ²⁴Then she saddled a donkey, and said to her servant, "Drive, and go forward; do not slacken the pace for me unless I tell you." ²⁵And so she departed, and went to the man of God at Mount Carmel.

4:23 neither the New Moon nor the Sabbath. The first day of the month and the seventh day of the week were both days of special religious observances and rest from work (Num. 28:9–15). Only on these days would a person visit a prophet. She may have concealed the boy's death from her husband because she believed that the prophet might miraculously heal the boy.

So it was, when the man of God saw her afar off, that he said to his servant Gehazi, "Look, the Shunammite woman! ²⁶Please run now to meet her, and say to her, 'Is it well with you? Is it well with your husband? Is it well with the child?' "

And she answered, "It is well." ²⁷Now when she came to the man of God at the hill, she caught him by the feet, but Gehazi came near to push her away. But the man of God said, "Let her alone; for her soul *is* in deep distress, and the LORD has hidden *it* from me, and has not told me."

²⁸So she said, "Did I ask a son of my lord? Did I not say, 'Do not deceive me'?"

²⁹Then he said to Gehazi, "Get yourself ready, and take my staff in your hand, and be on your way. If you meet anyone, do not greet him; and if anyone greets you, do not answer him; but lay my staff on the face of the child."

³⁰And the mother of the child said, "*As* the LORD lives, and *as* your soul lives, I will not leave you." So he arose and followed her. ³¹Now Gehazi went on ahead of them, and laid the staff on the face of the child; but *there was* neither voice nor hearing. Therefore he went back to meet him, and told him, saying, "The child has not awakened."

³²When Elisha came into the house, there was the child, lying dead on his bed. ³³He went in therefore, shut the door behind the two of them, and prayed to the LORD. ³⁴And he went up and lay on the child, and put his mouth on his mouth, his eyes on his eyes, and his hands on his hands; and he stretched himself out on the child, and the flesh of the child became warm. ³⁵He returned and walked back and forth in the house, and again went up and stretched himself out on him; then the child sneezed seven times, and the child opened his eyes. ³⁶And he called Gehazi and said, "Call this Shunammite woman." So he called her. And when she came in to him, he said, "Pick up your son." ³⁷So she went in, fell at his feet, and bowed to the ground; then she picked up her son and went out.

4:34 stretched himself out on the child. Like Elijah, Elisha demonstrated power over death by raising the child from the dead.

Elisha Purifies the Pot of Stew

³⁸And Elisha returned to Gilgal, and *there was* a famine in the land. Now the sons of the prophets *were* sitting before him; and he said to his servant, "Put on the

large pot, and boil stew for the sons of the prophets." ³⁹So one went out into the field to gather herbs, and found a wild vine, and gathered from it a lapful of wild gourds, and came and sliced *them* into the pot of stew, though they did not know *what they were.* ⁴⁰Then they served it to the men to eat. Now it happened, as they were eating the stew, that they cried out and said, "Man of God, *there is* death in the pot!" And they could not eat *it.*

⁴¹So he said, "Then bring some flour." And he put *it* into the pot, and said, "Serve *it* to the people, that they may eat." And there was nothing harmful in the pot.

Elisha Feeds One Hundred Men

⁴²Then a man came from Baal Shalisha, and brought the man of God bread of the firstfruits, twenty loaves of barley bread, and newly ripened grain in his knapsack. And he said, "Give *it* to the people, that they may eat."

⁴³But his servant said, "What? Shall I set this before one hundred men?"

He said again, "Give it to the people, that they may eat; for thus says the LORD: 'They shall eat and have *some* left over.' " ⁴⁴So he set *it* before them; and they ate and had *some* left over, according to the word of the LORD.

> **4:43,44** Multiplying the loaves in obedience to the Word of the Lord through His prophet foreshadowed the ministry of Jesus (see Matt. 14:16–20).

Naaman's Leprosy Healed

5 Now Naaman, commander of the army of the king of Syria, was a great and honorable man in the eyes of his master, because by him the LORD had given victory to Syria. He was also a mighty man of valor, *but* a leper. ²And the Syrians had gone out on raids, and had brought back captive a young girl from the land of Israel. She waited on Naaman's wife. ³Then she said to her mistress, "If only my master *were* with the prophet who *is* in Samaria! For he would heal him of his leprosy." ⁴And *Naaman* went in and told his master, saying, "Thus and thus said the girl who *is* from the land of Israel."

⁵Then the king of Syria said, "Go now, and I will send a letter to the king of Israel."

So he departed and took with him ten talents of silver, six thousand *shekels* of gold, and ten changes of clothing. ⁶Then he brought the letter to the king of Israel, which said,

> Now be advised, when this letter comes to you, that I have sent Naaman my servant to you, that you may heal him of his leprosy.

⁷And it happened, when the king of Israel read the letter, that he tore his clothes and said, "*Am* I God, to kill and make alive, that this man sends a man to me to heal him of his leprosy? Therefore please consider, and see how he seeks a quarrel with me."

⁸So it was, when Elisha the man of God heard that the king of Israel had torn his clothes, that he sent to the king, saying, "Why have you torn your clothes? Please let him come to me, and he shall know that there is a prophet in Israel."

⁹Then Naaman went with his horses and chariot, and he stood at the door of Elisha's house. ¹⁰And Elisha sent a messenger to him, saying, "Go and wash in the Jordan seven times, and your flesh shall be restored to you, and *you shall* be clean." ¹¹But Naaman became furious, and went away and said, "Indeed, I said to myself, 'He will surely come out *to me,* and stand and call on the name of the LORD his God, and wave his hand over the place, and heal the leprosy.' ¹²*Are* not the Abanah[a] and the Pharpar, the rivers of Damascus, better than all the waters of Israel? Could I not wash in them and be clean?" So he turned and went away in a rage. ¹³And his servants came near and spoke to him, and said, "My father, *if* the prophet had told you *to do* something great, would you not have done *it?* How much more then, when he says to

> **5:11 surely come out *to me.*** Naaman expected a personal cleansing ceremony from Elisha because of who he was and what he had done. When Elisha only sent a messenger with instructions for healing, Naaman became angry.

5:12 [a]Following Kethib, Septuagint, and Vulgate; Qere, Syriac, and Targum read *Amanah.*

you, 'Wash, and be clean'?" [14]So he went down and dipped seven times in the Jordan, according to the saying of the man of God; and his flesh was restored like the flesh of a little child, and he was clean.

[15]And he returned to the man of God, he and all his aides, and came and stood before him; and he said, "Indeed, now I know that *there is* no God in all the earth, except in Israel; now therefore, please take a gift from your servant."

[16]But he said, "*As* the LORD lives, before whom I stand, I will receive nothing." And he urged him to take *it*, but he refused.

[17]So Naaman said, "Then, if not, please let your servant be given two mule-loads of earth; for your servant will no longer offer either burnt offering or sacrifice to other gods, but to the LORD. [18]Yet in this thing may the LORD pardon your servant: when my master goes into the temple of Rimmon to worship there, and he leans on my hand, and I bow down in the temple of Rimmon—when I bow down in the temple of Rimmon, may the LORD please pardon your servant in this thing."

5:17 two mule-loads of earth. It was customary to only worship a god on the soil of the nation in which he was bound. For this reason Naaman wanted soil from Israel so he could make burnt offerings to the Lord back in Damascus. This request showed how he had changed.

[19]Then he said to him, "Go in peace." So he departed from him a short distance.

Gehazi's Greed

[20]But Gehazi, the servant of Elisha the man of God, said, "Look, my master has spared Naaman this Syrian, while not receiving from his hands what he brought; but *as* the LORD lives, I will run after him and take something from him." [21]So Gehazi pursued Naaman. When Naaman saw *him* running after him, he got down from the chariot to meet him, and said, "*Is* all well?"

[22]And he said, "All *is* well. My master has sent me, saying, 'Indeed, just now two young men of the sons of the prophets have come to me from the mountains of Ephraim. Please give them a talent of silver and two changes of garments.'"

[23]So Naaman said, "Please, take two talents." And he urged him, and bound two talents of silver in two bags, with two changes of garments, and handed *them* to two of his servants; and they carried *them* on ahead of him. [24]When he came to the citadel, he took *them* from their hand, and stored *them* away in the house; then he let the men go, and they departed. [25]Now he went in and stood before his master. Elisha said to him, "Where *did you go*, Gehazi?"

And he said, "Your servant did not go anywhere."

[26]Then he said to him, "Did not my heart go *with you* when the man turned back from his chariot to meet you? *Is it* time to receive money and to receive clothing, olive groves and vineyards, sheep and oxen, male and female servants? [27]Therefore the leprosy of Naaman shall cling to you and your descendants forever." And he went out from his presence leprous, *as white* as snow.

5:27 leprosy...shall cling to you. Gehazi's greed tarnished the integrity of the prophetic office, and made him no better than a false prophet in the people's thinking. This act showed that he did not believe God would provide. As a result, he and his descendants were punished with a skin disease forever.

The Floating Ax Head

6 And the sons of the prophets said to Elisha, "See now, the place where we dwell with you is too small for us. [2]Please, let us go to the Jordan, and let every man take a beam from there, and let us make there a place where we may dwell."

So he answered, "Go."

[3]Then one said, "Please consent to go with your servants."

And he answered, "I will go." [4]So he went with them. And when they came to the Jordan, they cut down trees. [5]But as one was cutting down a tree, the iron *ax head* fell into the water; and he cried out and said, "Alas, master! For it was borrowed."

[6]So the man of God said, "Where did it fall?" And he showed him the place. So he cut off a stick, and threw *it* in there; and he made the iron float. [7]Therefore he said, "Pick *it* up for yourself." So he reached out his hand and took it.

The Blinded Syrians Captured

[8]Now the king of Syria was making war against Israel; and he consulted with his

servants, saying, "My camp *will be* in such and such a place." [9]And the man of God sent to the king of Israel, saying, "Beware that you do not pass this place, for the Syrians are coming down there." [10]Then the king of Israel sent *someone* to the place of which the man of God had told him. Thus he warned him, and he was watchful there, not just once or twice.

[11]Therefore the heart of the king of Syria was greatly troubled by this thing; and he called his servants and said to them, "Will you not show me which of us *is* for the king of Israel?"

[12]And one of his servants said, "None, my lord, O king; but Elisha, the prophet who *is* in Israel, tells the king of Israel the words that you speak in your bedroom."

[13]So he said, "Go and see where he *is*, that I may send and get him."

And it was told him, saying, "Surely *he is* in Dothan."

[14]Therefore he sent horses and chariots and a great army there, and they came by night and surrounded the city. [15]And when the servant of the man of God arose early and went out, there was an army, surrounding the city with horses and chariots. And his servant said to him, "Alas, my master! What shall we do?"

[16]So he answered, "Do not fear, for those who *are* with us *are* more than those who *are* with them." [17]And Elisha prayed, and said, "LORD, I pray, open his eyes that he may see." Then the LORD opened the eyes of the young man, and he saw. And behold, the mountain *was* full of horses and chariots of fire all around Elisha. [18]So when *the Syrians* came down to him, Elisha prayed to the LORD, and said, "Strike this people, I pray, with blindness." And He struck them with blindness according to the word of Elisha.

> **6:17 open his eyes.** Elisha asked the Lord to help his servant see the heavenly host. God responded by allowing him to see the spiritual world where God's heavenly armies were waiting to battle the Syrians (see Gen. 32:1,2).

[19]Now Elisha said to them, "This *is* not the way, nor *is* this the city. Follow me, and I will bring you to the man whom you seek." But he led them to Samaria.

[20]So it was, when they had come to Samaria, that Elisha said, "LORD, open the eyes of these *men*, that they may see." And the LORD opened their eyes, and they saw; and there *they were*, inside Samaria!

[21]Now when the king of Israel saw them, he said to Elisha, "My father, shall I kill *them*? Shall I kill *them*?"

[22]But he answered, "You shall not kill *them*. Would you kill those whom you have taken captive with your sword and your bow? Set food and water before them, that they may eat and drink and go to their master." [23]Then he prepared a great feast for them; and after they ate and drank, he sent them away and they went to their master. So the bands of Syrian *raiders* came no more into the land of Israel.

> **6:23 a great feast.** In that culture, a common meal could signify the making of a covenant between two parties (Lev. 7:15–18).

Syria Besieges Samaria in Famine

[24]And it happened after this that Ben-Hadad king of Syria gathered all his army, and went up and besieged Samaria. [25]And there was a great famine in Samaria; and indeed they besieged it until a donkey's head was *sold* for eighty *shekels* of silver, and one-fourth of a kab of dove droppings for five *shekels* of silver.

[26]Then, as the king of Israel was passing by on the wall, a woman cried out to him, saying, "Help, my lord, O king!"

[27]And he said, "If the LORD does not help you, where can I find help for you? From the threshing floor or from the winepress?" [28]Then the king said to her, "What is troubling you?"

And she answered, "This woman said to me, 'Give your son, that we may eat him today, and we will eat my son tomorrow.' [29]So we boiled my son, and ate him. And I said to her on the next day, 'Give your son, that we may eat him'; but she has hidden her son."

[30]Now it happened, when the king heard the words of the woman, that he tore his clothes; and as he passed by on the wall, the people looked, and there underneath *he had* sackcloth on his body. [31]Then he said, "God do so to me and more also, if the head

of Elisha the son of Shaphat remains on him today!"

³²But Elisha was sitting in his house, and the elders were sitting with him. And *the king* sent a man ahead of him, but before the messenger came to him, he said to the elders, "Do you see how this son of a murderer has sent someone to take away my head? Look, when the messenger comes, shut the door, and hold him fast at the door. *Is* not the sound of his master's feet behind him?" ³³And while he was still talking with them, there was the messenger, coming down to him; and then *the king* said, "Surely this calamity *is* from the LORD; why should I wait for the LORD any longer?"

7 Then Elisha said, "Hear the word of the LORD. Thus says the LORD: 'Tomorrow about this time a seah of fine flour *shall be sold* for a shekel, and two seahs of barley for a shekel, at the gate of Samaria.' "

²So an officer on whose hand the king leaned answered the man of God and said, "Look, *if* the LORD would make windows in heaven, could this thing be?"

And he said, "In fact, you shall see *it* with your eyes, but you shall not eat of it."

The Syrians Flee

³Now there were four leprous men at the entrance of the gate; and they said to one another, "Why are we sitting here until we die? ⁴If we say, 'We will enter the city,' the famine *is* in the city, and we shall die there. And if we sit here, we die also. Now therefore, come, let us surrender to the army of the Syrians. If they keep us alive, we shall live; and if they kill us, we shall only die." ⁵And they rose at twilight to go to the camp of the Syrians; and when they had come to the outskirts of the Syrian camp, to their surprise no one *was* there. ⁶For the LORD had caused the army of the Syrians to hear the noise of chariots and the noise of horses—the noise of a great army; so they said to one another, "Look, the king of Israel has hired against us the kings of the Hittites and the kings of the Egyptians to attack us!" ⁷Therefore they arose and fled at twilight, and left the camp intact—their tents, their horses, and their donkeys—and they fled for their lives. ⁸And when these lepers came to the outskirts of the camp, they went into one tent and ate and drank, and carried from it silver and gold and clothing, and went and hid *them;* then they came back and entered another tent, and carried *some* from there *also,* and went and hid *it.*

⁹Then they said to one another, "We are not doing right. This day *is* a day of good news, and we remain silent. If we wait until morning light, some punishment will come upon us. Now therefore, come, let us go and tell the king's household." ¹⁰So they went and called to the gatekeepers of the city, and told them, saying, "We went to the Syrian camp, and surprisingly no one *was* there, not a human sound—only horses and donkeys tied, and the tents intact." ¹¹And the gatekeepers called out, and they told *it* to the king's household inside.

¹²So the king arose in the night and said to his servants, "Let me now tell you what the Syrians have done to us. They know that we *are* hungry; therefore they have gone out of the camp to hide themselves in the field, saying, 'When they come out of the city, we shall catch them alive, and get into the city.' "

¹³And one of his servants answered and said, "Please, let several *men* take five of the remaining horses which are left in the city. Look, they *may either become* like all the multitude of Israel that are left in it; or indeed, *I say,* they *may become* like all the multitude of Israel left from those who are

consumed; so let us send them and see." 14Therefore they took two chariots with horses; and the king sent them in the direction of the Syrian army, saying, "Go and see." 15And they went after them to the Jordan; and indeed all the road *was* full of garments and weapons which the Syrians had thrown away in their haste. So the messengers returned and told the king. 16Then the people went out and plundered the tents of the Syrians. So a seah of fine flour was *sold* for a shekel, and two seahs of barley for a shekel, according to the word of the LORD.

17Now the king had appointed the officer on whose hand he leaned to have charge of the gate. But the people trampled him in the gate, and he died, just as the man of God had said, who spoke when the king came down to him. 18So it happened just as the man of God had spoken to the king, saying, "Two seahs of barley for a shekel, and a seah of fine flour for a shekel, shall be *sold* tomorrow about this time in the gate of Samaria."

19Then that officer had answered the man of God, and said, "Now look, *if* the LORD would make windows in heaven, could such a thing be?"

And he had said, "In fact, you shall see *it* with your eyes, but you shall not eat of it." 20And so it happened to him, for the people trampled him in the gate, and he died.

The King Restores the Shunammite's Land

8 Then Elisha spoke to the woman whose son he had restored to life, saying, "Arise and go, you and your household, and stay wherever you can; for the LORD has called for a famine, and furthermore, it will come upon the land for seven years." 2So the woman arose and did according to the saying of the man of God, and she went with her household and dwelt in the land of the Philistines seven years.

> **8:3 an appeal to the king.** The Shunammite woman did this to support her ownership claim. Providentially, she arrived just in time to hear Gehazi's story of how Elisha had raised her son from the dead (v. 5).

3It came to pass, at the end of seven years, that the woman returned from the land of the Philistines; and she went to make an appeal to the king for her house and for her land. 4Then the king talked with Gehazi, the servant of the man of God, saying, "Tell me, please, all the great things Elisha has done." 5Now it happened, as he was telling the king how he had restored the dead to life, that there was the woman whose son he had restored to life, appealing to the king for her house and for her land. And Gehazi said, "My lord, O king, this *is* the woman, and this *is* her son whom Elisha restored to life." 6And when the king asked the woman, she told him.

So the king appointed a certain officer for her, saying, "Restore all that *was* hers, and all the proceeds of the field from the day that she left the land until now."

Death of Ben-Hadad

7Then Elisha went to Damascus, and Ben-Hadad king of Syria was sick; and it was told him, saying, "The man of God has come here." 8And the king said to Hazael, "Take a present in your hand, and go to meet the man of God, and inquire of the LORD by him, saying, 'Shall I recover from this disease?'" 9So Hazael went to meet him and took a present with him, of every good thing of Damascus, forty camel-loads; and he came and stood before him, and said, "Your son Ben-Hadad king of Syria has sent me to you, saying, 'Shall I recover from this disease?'"

10And Elisha said to him, "Go, say to him, 'You shall certainly recover.' However the LORD has shown me that he will really die." 11Then he set his countenance in a stare until he was ashamed; and the man of God wept. 12And Hazael said, "Why is my lord weeping?"

> **8:11 he was ashamed.** Elisha stared at Hazael because God told him what Hazael would do, including the murder of Ben-Hadad (v. 15). Surmising that Elisha knew of his plans, he became embarrassed.

He answered, "Because I know the evil that you will do to the children of Israel: Their strongholds you will set on fire, and their young men you will kill with the sword; and you will dash their children, and rip open their women with child."

13So Hazael said, "But what *is* your ser-

vant—a dog, that he should do this gross thing?"

And Elisha answered, "The LORD has shown me that you *will become* king over Syria."

¹⁴Then he departed from Elisha, and came to his master, who said to him, "What did Elisha say to you?" And he answered, "He told me you would surely recover." ¹⁵But it happened on the next day that he took a thick cloth and dipped *it* in water, and spread *it* over his face so that he died; and Hazael reigned in his place.

Jehoram Reigns in Judah

¹⁶Now in the fifth year of Joram the son of Ahab, king of Israel, Jehoshaphat *having been* king of Judah, Jehoram the son of Jehoshaphat began to reign as king of Judah. ¹⁷He was thirty-two years old when he became king, and he reigned eight years in Jerusalem. ¹⁸And he walked in the way of the kings of Israel, just as the house of Ahab had done, for the daughter of Ahab was his wife; and he did evil in the sight of the LORD. ¹⁹Yet the LORD would not destroy Judah, for the sake of his servant David, as He promised him to give a lamp to him *and* his sons forever.

> **8:18 as the house of Ahab.** Jehoram made Baal worship the official religion in Judah, as Ahab had in Israel (1 Kin. 16:31–33). **the daughter of Ahab.** Jehoram was married to Athalia, daughter of Ahab and Jezebel (verse 26). Athalia encouraged Jehoram to do evil before the Lord just as Jezebel had to Ahab (1 Kin. 21:25).

²⁰In his days Edom revolted against Judah's authority, and made a king over themselves. ²¹So Joram*ᵃ* went to Zair, and all his chariots with him. Then he rose by night and attacked the Edomites who had surrounded him and the captains of the chariots; and the troops fled to their tents. ²²Thus Edom has been in revolt against Judah's authority to this day. And Libnah revolted at that time.

²³Now the rest of the acts of Joram, and all that he did, *are* they not written in the book of the chronicles of the kings of Judah? ²⁴So Joram rested with his fathers, and

was buried with his fathers in the City of David. Then Ahaziah his son reigned in his place.

Ahaziah Reigns in Judah

²⁵In the twelfth year of Joram the son of Ahab, king of Israel, Ahaziah the son of Jehoram, king of Judah, began to reign. ²⁶Ahaziah *was* twenty-two years old when he became king, and he reigned one year in Jerusalem. His mother's name *was* Athaliah the granddaughter of Omri, king of Israel. ²⁷And he walked in the way of the house of Ahab, and did evil in the sight of the LORD, like the house of Ahab, for he *was* the son-in-law of the house of Ahab.

²⁸Now he went with Joram the son of Ahab to war against Hazael king of Syria at Ramoth Gilead; and the Syrians wounded Joram. ²⁹Then King Joram went back to Jezreel to recover from the wounds which the Syrians had inflicted on him at Ramah, when he fought against Hazael king of Syria. And Ahaziah the son of Jehoram, king of Judah, went down to see Joram the son of Ahab in Jezreel, because he was sick.

Jehu Anointed King of Israel

9 And Elisha the prophet called one of the sons of the prophets, and said to him, "Get yourself ready, take this flask of oil in your hand, and go to Ramoth Gilead. ²Now when you arrive at that place, look there for Jehu the son of Jehoshaphat, the son of Nimshi, and go in and make him rise up from among his associates, and take him to an inner room. ³Then take the flask of oil, and pour *it* on his head, and say, 'Thus says the LORD: "I have anointed you king over Israel."' Then open the door and flee, and do not delay."

> **9:2 Jehu.** The Lord had told Elijah that Jehu would become Israel's king and kill those who worshiped Baal. The fulfillment of this prophecy is recorded from 9:1–10:31. **inner room.** This was a private room where a young prophet, commissioned by Elisha, anointed Jehu. The anointing was to take place in secret, without Elisha, so Jehoram would not suspect that a coup was coming.

⁴So the young man, the servant of the prophet, went to Ramoth Gilead. ⁵And

when he arrived, there *were* the captains of the army sitting; and he said, "I have a message for you, Commander."

Jehu said, "For which *one* of us?"

And he said, "For you, Commander." 6Then he arose and went into the house. And he poured the oil on his head, and said to him, "Thus says the LORD God of Israel: 'I have anointed you king over the people of the LORD, over Israel. 7You shall strike down the house of Ahab your master, that I may avenge the blood of My servants the prophets, and the blood of all the servants of the LORD, at the hand of Jezebel. 8For the whole house of Ahab shall perish; and I will cut off from Ahab all the males in Israel, both bond and free. 9So I will make the house of Ahab like the house of Jeroboam the son of Nebat, and like the house of Baasha the son of Ahijah. 10The dogs shall eat Jezebel on the plot *of ground* at Jezreel, and *there shall be* none to bury *her.*' " And he opened the door and fled.

> **9:10 dogs shall eat.** Dogs were scavengers in the East and would devour the corpse of Jezebel. **Jezreel.** This was formerly where Naboth had his vineyard (1 Kin. 21:1–16). **none to bury her.** In Israel, it was a disgrace not to be buried.

11Then Jehu came out to the servants of his master, and *one* said to him, "*Is* all well? Why did this madman come to you?"

And he said to them, "You know the man and his babble."

12And they said, "A lie! Tell us now."

So he said, "Thus and thus he spoke to me, saying, 'Thus says the LORD: "I have anointed you king over Israel." ' "

13Then each man hastened to take his garment and put *it* under him on the top of the steps; and they blew trumpets, saying, "Jehu is king!"

Joram of Israel Killed

14So Jehu the son of Jehoshaphat, the son of Nimshi, conspired against Joram. (Now Joram had been defending Ramoth Gilead, he and all Israel, against Hazael king of Syria. 15But King Joram had returned to Jezreel to recover from the wounds which the Syrians had inflicted on him when he fought with Hazael king of Syria.) And Jehu said, "If you are so minded, let no one leave *or* escape from the city to go and tell *it* in Jezreel." 16So Jehu rode in a chariot and went to Jezreel, for Joram was laid up there; and Ahaziah king of Judah had come down to see Joram.

17Now a watchman stood on the tower in Jezreel, and he saw the company of Jehu as he came, and said, "I see a company of men."

And Joram said, "Get a horseman and send him to meet them, and let him say, '*Is it* peace?' "

18So the horseman went to meet him, and said, "Thus says the king: '*Is it* peace?' "

And Jehu said, "What have you to do with peace? Turn around and follow me."

So the watchman reported, saying, "The messenger went to them, but is not coming back."

19Then he sent out a second horseman who came to them, and said, "Thus says the king: '*Is it* peace?' "

And Jehu answered, "What have you to do with peace? Turn around and follow me."

20So the watchman reported, saying, "He went up to them and is not coming back; and the driving *is* like the driving of Jehu the son of Nimshi, for he drives furiously!"

21Then Joram said, "Make ready." And his chariot was made ready. Then Joram king of Israel and Ahaziah king of Judah went out, each in his chariot; and they went out to meet Jehu, and met him on the property of Naboth the Jezreelite. 22Now it happened, when Joram saw Jehu, that he said, "*Is it* peace, Jehu?"

So he answered, "What peace, as long as the harlotries of your mother Jezebel and her witchcraft *are so* many?"

> **9:22 What peace.** Joram was unsure of Jehu's rebellious plans and wanted to know if Jehu had come in peace. Jehu replied that there could be no peace in Israel because of Jezebel's idolatrous influence. Idolatry had lured Israel into demonic practices.

23Then Joram turned around and fled, and said to Ahaziah, "Treachery, Ahaziah!" 24Now Jehu drew his bow with full strength and shot Jehoram between his arms; and the arrow came out at his heart, and he

sank down in his chariot. ²⁵Then *Jehu* said to Bidkar his captain, "Pick *him* up, *and* throw him into the tract of the field of Naboth the Jezreelite; for remember, when you and I were riding together behind Ahab his father, that the LORD laid this burden upon him: ²⁶'Surely I saw yesterday the blood of Naboth and the blood of his sons,' says the LORD, 'and I will repay you in this plot,' says the LORD. Now therefore, take *and* throw him on the plot *of ground*, according to the word of the LORD."

Ahaziah of Judah Killed

²⁷But when Ahaziah king of Judah saw *this*, he fled by the road to Beth Haggan.*ᵃ* So Jehu pursued him, and said, "Shoot him also in the chariot." *And they shot him* at the Ascent of Gur, which is by Ibleam. Then he fled to Megiddo, and died there. ²⁸And his servants carried him in the chariot to Jerusalem, and buried him in his tomb with his fathers in the City of David. ²⁹In the eleventh year of Joram the son of Ahab, Ahaziah had become king over Judah.

Jezebel's Violent Death

³⁰Now when Jehu had come to Jezreel, Jezebel heard *of it*; and she put paint on her eyes and adorned her head, and looked through a window. ³¹Then, as Jehu entered at the gate, she said, "*Is it* peace, Zimri, murderer of your master?"

³²And he looked up at the window, and said, "Who *is* on my side? Who?" So two *or* three eunuchs looked out at him. ³³Then he said, "Throw her down." So they threw her down, and *some* of her blood spattered on the wall and on the horses; and he trampled her underfoot. ³⁴And when he had gone in, he ate and drank. Then he said, "Go now, see to this accursed *woman*, and bury her, for she was a king's daughter." ³⁵So they went to bury her, but they found no more of her than the skull and the feet and the palms of *her* hands. ³⁶Therefore they came back and told him. And he said, "This *is* the word of the LORD, which He spoke by His servant Elijah the Tishbite, saying, 'On the plot *of ground* at Jezreel dogs shall eat

the flesh of Jezebel;*ᵃ* ³⁷and the corpse of Jezebel shall be as refuse on the surface of the field, in the plot at Jezreel, so that they shall not say, "Here *lies* Jezebel." ' "

Ahab's Seventy Sons Killed

10 Now Ahab had seventy sons in Samaria. And Jehu wrote and sent letters to Samaria, to the rulers of Jezreel,*ᵃ* to the elders, and to those who reared Ahab's *sons*, saying:

> **10:1 seventy sons.** These were all of the male descendants of Ahab. These living relatives could avenge the person responsible for the death of their family member (see Num. 35:12), so Jehu's life was in danger while Ahab's male descendants were alive.

² Now as soon as this letter comes to you, since your master's sons *are* with you, and you have chariots and horses, a fortified city also, and weapons, ³choose the best qualified of your master's sons, set *him* on his father's throne, and fight for your master's house.

⁴But they were exceedingly afraid, and said, "Look, two kings could not stand up to him; how then can we stand?" ⁵And he who *was* in charge of the house, and he who *was* in charge of the city, the elders also, and those who reared *the sons*, sent to Jehu, saying, "We *are* your servants, we will do all you tell us; but we will not make anyone king. Do *what is* good in your sight." ⁶Then he wrote a second letter to them, saying:

> If you *are* for me and will obey my voice, take the heads of the men, your master's sons, and come to me at Jezreel by this time tomorrow.

Now the king's sons, seventy persons, *were* with the great men of the city, *who* were rearing them. ⁷So it was, when the letter came to them, that they took the king's sons and slaughtered seventy persons, put their heads in baskets and sent *them* to him at Jezreel. ⁸Then a messenger came and told him,

---

9:27 *ᵃ*Literally *The Garden House*   9:36 *ᵃ*1 Kings 21:23   10:1 *ᵃ*Following Masoretic Text, Syriac, and Targum; Septuagint reads *Samaria*; Vulgate reads *city*.

saying, "They have brought the heads of the king's sons."

And he said, "Lay them in two heaps at the entrance of the gate until morning."

⁹So it was, in the morning, that he went out and stood, and said to all the people, "You *are* righteous. Indeed I conspired against my master and killed him; but who killed all these? ¹⁰Know now that nothing shall fall to the earth of the word of the LORD which the LORD spoke concerning the house of Ahab; for the LORD has done what He spoke by His servant Elijah." ¹¹So Jehu killed all who remained of the house of Ahab in Jezreel, and all his great men and his close acquaintances and his priests, until he left him none remaining.

> **10:11 Jehu killed all.** Jehu disobeyed God's instructions by executing all of Ahab's officials, therefore bringing future judgment upon his house (see Hos. 1:4).

Ahaziah's Forty-two Brothers Killed

¹²And he arose and departed and went to Samaria. On the way, at Beth Eked*ᵃ* of the Shepherds, ¹³Jehu met with the brothers of Ahaziah king of Judah, and said, "Who *are* you?"

So they answered, "We *are* the brothers of Ahaziah; we have come down to greet the sons of the king and the sons of the queen mother."

¹⁴And he said, "Take them alive!" So they took them alive, and killed them at the well of Beth Eked, forty-two men; and he left none of them.

The Rest of Ahab's Family Killed

¹⁵Now when he departed from there, he met Jehonadab the son of Rechab, *coming* to meet him; and he greeted him and said to him, "Is your heart right, as my heart *is* toward your heart?"

And Jehonadab answered, "It is."

Jehu said, "If it is, give *me* your hand." So he gave *him* his hand, and he took him up to him into the chariot. ¹⁶Then he said, "Come with me, and see my zeal for the LORD." So they had him ride in his chariot. ¹⁷And when he came to Samaria, he killed all who remained to Ahab in Samaria, till

he had destroyed them, according to the word of the LORD which He spoke to Elijah.

Worshipers of Baal Killed

¹⁸Then Jehu gathered all the people together, and said to them, "Ahab served Baal a little, Jehu will serve him much. ¹⁹Now therefore, call to me all the prophets of Baal, all his servants, and all his priests. Let no one be missing, for I have a great sacrifice for Baal. Whoever is missing shall not live." But Jehu acted deceptively, with the intent of destroying the worshipers of Baal. ²⁰And Jehu said, "Proclaim a solemn assembly for Baal." So they proclaimed *it.* ²¹Then Jehu sent throughout all Israel; and all the worshipers of Baal came, so that there was not a man left who did not come. So they came into the temple*ᵃ* of Baal, and the temple of Baal was full from one end to the other. ²²And he said to the one in charge of the wardrobe, "Bring out vestments for all the worshipers of Baal." So he brought out vestments for them. ²³Then Jehu and Jehonadab the son of Rechab went into the temple of Baal, and said to the worshipers of Baal, "Search and see that no servants of the LORD are here with you, but only the worshipers of Baal." ²⁴So they went in to offer sacrifices and burnt offerings. Now Jehu had appointed for himself eighty men on the outside, and had said, "*If any of the men whom I have brought into your hands escapes, whoever lets him escape, it shall be* his life for the life of the other."

> **10:21 temple of Baal.** This was the idolatrous place of worship Ahab built in Samaria (1 Kin. 16:32). Because of the influence of Elijah and Elisha and the decline of Baal worship under Joram, far fewer people attended the temple of Baal.

²⁵Now it happened, as soon as he had made an end of offering the burnt offering, that Jehu said to the guard and to the captains, "Go in *and* kill them; let no one come out!" And they killed them with the edge of the sword; then the guards and the officers threw *them* out, and went into the inner room of the temple of Baal. ²⁶And they brought the *sacred* pillars out of the temple of Baal and burned them. ²⁷Then

---

10:12 *ᵃOr The Shearing House*   10:21 *ᵃLiterally house,* and so elsewhere in this chapter

they broke down the *sacred* pillar of Baal, and tore down the temple of Baal and made it a refuse dump to this day. ²⁸Thus Jehu destroyed Baal from Israel.

²⁹However Jehu did not turn away from the sins of Jeroboam the son of Nebat, who had made Israel sin, *that is*, from the golden calves that *were* at Bethel and Dan. ³⁰And the LORD said to Jehu, "Because you have done well in doing *what is* right in My sight, *and* have done to the house of Ahab all that *was* in My heart, your sons shall sit on the throne of Israel to the fourth *generation*." ³¹But Jehu took no heed to walk in the law of the LORD God of Israel with all his heart; for he did not depart from the sins of Jeroboam, who had made Israel sin.

Death of Jehu

³²In those days the LORD began to cut off *parts* of Israel; and Hazael conquered them in all the territory of Israel ³³from the Jordan eastward: all the land of Gilead—Gad, Reuben, and Manasseh—from Aroer, which *is* by the River Arnon, including Gilead and Bashan.

³⁴Now the rest of the acts of Jehu, all that he did, and all his might, *are* they not written in the book of the chronicles of the kings of Israel? ³⁵So Jehu rested with his fathers, and they buried him in Samaria. Then Jehoahaz his son reigned in his place. ³⁶And the period that Jehu reigned over Israel in Samaria *was* twenty-eight years.

Athaliah Reigns in Judah

11 When Athaliah the mother of Ahaziah saw that her son was dead, she arose and destroyed all the royal heirs. ²But Jehosheba, the daughter of King Joram, sister of Ahaziah, took Joash the son of Ahaziah, and stole him away from

---

11:1 Athalia. She was the granddaughter of Omri (8:26) and the daughter of Ahab and Jezebel. After the death of her son Ahaziah, she intensely sought to rule (9:27), and she wanted Baal worship to be the official religion of Judah. She ruled for six years. **destroyed all the royal heirs.** Since Jehoram's brothers (2 Chr. 21:4) and Ahaziah's brothers and relatives were already dead (10:12–14), only Athalia's grandchildren had to be killed to destroy David's royal line.

---

among the king's sons *who were* being murdered; and they hid him and his nurse in the bedroom, from Athaliah, so that he was not killed. ³So he was hidden with her in the house of the LORD for six years, while Athaliah reigned over the land.

Joash Crowned King of Judah

⁴In the seventh year Jehoiada sent and brought the captains of hundreds—of the bodyguards and the escorts—and brought them into the house of the LORD to him. And he made a covenant with them and took an oath from them in the house of the LORD, and showed them the king's son. ⁵Then he commanded them, saying, "This *is* what you shall do: One-third of you who come on duty on the Sabbath shall be keeping watch over the king's house, ⁶one-third *shall be* at the gate of Sur, and one-third at the gate behind the escorts. You shall keep the watch of the house, lest it be broken down. ⁷The two contingents of you who go off duty on the Sabbath shall keep the watch of the house of the LORD for the king. ⁸But you shall surround the king on all sides, every man with his weapons in his hand; and whoever comes within range, let him be put to death. You are to be with the king as he goes out and as he comes in."

⁹So the captains of the hundreds did according to all that Jehoiada the priest commanded. Each of them took his men who were to be on duty on the Sabbath, with those who were going off duty on the Sabbath, and came to Jehoiada the priest. ¹⁰And the priest gave the captains of hundreds the spears and shields which *had belonged* to King David, that were in the temple of the LORD. ¹¹Then the escorts stood, every man with his weapons in his hand, all around the king, from the right side of the temple to the left side of the temple, by the altar and the house. ¹²And he brought out the king's son, put the crown on him, and *gave him* the Testimony;ᵃ they made him king and anointed him, and they clapped their hands and said, "Long live the king!"

Death of Athaliah

¹³Now when Athaliah heard the noise of the escorts *and* the people, she came to the

---

11:12 ᵃThat is, the Law (compare Exodus 25:16,21 and Deuteronomy 31:9)

> **11:12 the Testimony.** This was a copy of the law (Ps. 119:88), which was to be kept with the king in order to guide him (see Deut. 17:18–20). **anointed.** This is an example of how a prophet or priest traditionally anoints kings (1 Sam. 10:1).

people *in* the temple of the LORD. ¹⁴When she looked, there was the king standing by a pillar according to custom; and the leaders and the trumpeters were by the king. All the people of the land were rejoicing and blowing trumpets. So Athaliah tore her clothes and cried out, "Treason! Treason!"

¹⁵And Jehoiada the priest commanded the captains of the hundreds, the officers of the army, and said to them, "Take her outside under guard, and slay with the sword whoever follows her." For the priest had said, "Do not let her be killed in the house of the LORD." ¹⁶So they seized her; and she went by way of the horses' entrance *into* the king's house, and there she was killed.

¹⁷Then Jehoiada made a covenant between the LORD, the king, and the people, that they should be the LORD's people, and *also* between the king and the people. ¹⁸And all the people of the land went to the temple of Baal, and tore it down. They thoroughly broke in pieces its altars and images, and killed Mattan the priest of Baal before the altars. And the priest appointed officers over the house of the LORD. ¹⁹Then he took the captains of hundreds, the bodyguards, the escorts, and all the people of the land; and they brought the king down from the house of the LORD, and went by way of the gate of the escorts to the king's house. Then he sat on the throne of the kings. ²⁰So all the people of the land rejoiced; and the city was quiet, for they had slain Athaliah with the sword *in* the king's house. ²¹Jehoash *was* seven years old when he became king.

> **11:17 a covenant.** Renewing these agreements was appropriate because of the disruption caused by Athalia. A similar ceremony took place during the reign of Josiah (23:1–3).

Jehoash Repairs the Temple

12 In the seventh year of Jehu, Jehoash*ᵃ* became king, and he reigned forty years in Jerusalem. His mother's name *was* Zibiah of Beersheba. ²Jehoash did *what was* right in the sight of the LORD all the days in which Jehoiada the priest instructed him. ³But the high places were not taken away; the people still sacrificed and burned incense on the high places.

> **12:2 all the days...Jehoiada...instructed him.** Joash did what pleased the Lord while Jehoiada was alive but turned away from God once Jehoiada died.

⁴And Jehoash said to the priests, "All the money of the dedicated gifts that are brought into the house of the LORD—each man's census money, each man's assessment money*ᵃ*—and all the money that a man purposes in his heart to bring into the house of the LORD, ⁵let the priests take *it* themselves, each from his constituency; and let them repair the damages of the temple, wherever any dilapidation is found."

⁶Now it was so, by the twenty-third year of King Jehoash, *that* the priests had not repaired the damages of the temple. ⁷So King Jehoash called Jehoiada the priest and the *other* priests, and said to them, "Why have you not repaired the damages of the temple? Now therefore, do not take *more* money from your constituency, but deliver it for repairing the damages of the temple." ⁸And the priests agreed that they would neither receive *more* money from the people, nor repair the damages of the temple.

⁹Then Jehoiada the priest took a chest, bored a hole in its lid, and set it beside the altar, on the right side as one comes into the house of the LORD; and the priests who kept the door put there all the money brought into the house of the LORD. ¹⁰So it was, whenever they saw that *there was* much money in the chest, that the king's scribe and the high priest came up and put it in bags, and counted the money that was found in the house of the LORD. ¹¹Then they gave the money, which had been apportioned, into the hands of those who did the work, who had the oversight of the house of the LORD; and they paid it out to the carpenters and builders who worked on the house of the LORD, ¹²and to masons and stonecutters, and for buying timber and

---

12:1 *ᵃ*Spelled *Joash* in 11:2ff   12:4 *ᵃ*Compare Leviticus 27:2ff

hewn stone, to repair the damage of the house of the LORD, and for all that was paid out to repair the temple. [13]However there were not made for the house of the LORD basins of silver, trimmers, sprinkling-bowls, trumpets, any articles of gold or articles of silver, from the money brought into the house of the LORD. [14]But they gave that to the workmen, and they repaired the house of the LORD with it. [15]Moreover they did not require an account from the men into whose hand they delivered the money to be paid to workmen, for they dealt faithfully. [16]The money from the trespass offerings and the money from the sin offerings was not brought into the house of the LORD. It belonged to the priests.

> **12:16 money from the trespass offerings and...sin offerings.** This money was different from that mentioned in verse 4 and was not used to repair the temple but was kept for the priests (see Lev. 4:1–6:7). The priests' income was not affected by the temple repairs (Lev. 7:7).

Hazael Threatens Jerusalem

[17]Hazael king of Syria went up and fought against Gath, and took it; then Hazael set his face to go up to Jerusalem. [18]And Jehoash king of Judah took all the sacred things that his fathers, Jehoshaphat and Jehoram and Ahaziah, kings of Judah, had dedicated, and his own sacred things, and all the gold found in the treasuries of the house of the LORD and in the king's house, and sent *them* to Hazael king of Syria. Then he went away from Jerusalem.

Death of Joash

[19]Now the rest of the acts of Joash,[a] and all that he did, *are* they not written in the book of the chronicles of the kings of Judah? [20]And his servants arose and formed a conspiracy, and killed Joash in the house of the Millo,[a] which goes down to Silla. [21]For Jozachar[a] the son of Shimeath and Jehozabad the son of Shomer,[b] his servants, struck him. So he died, and they buried him with his fathers in the City of David. Then Amaziah his son reigned in his place.

Jehoahaz Reigns in Israel

13 In the twenty-third year of Joash[a] the son of Ahaziah, king of Judah, Jehoahaz the son of Jehu became king over Israel in Samaria, *and reigned* seventeen years. [2]And he did evil in the sight of the LORD, and followed the sins of Jeroboam the son of Nebat, who had made Israel sin. He did not depart from them.

[3]Then the anger of the LORD was aroused against Israel, and He delivered them into the hand of Hazael king of Syria, and into the hand of Ben-Hadad the son of Hazael, all *their* days. [4]So Jehoahaz pleaded with the LORD, and the LORD listened to him; for He saw the oppression of Israel, because the king of Syria oppressed them. [5]Then the LORD gave Israel a deliverer, so that they escaped from under the hand of the Syrians; and the children of Israel dwelt in their tents as before. [6]Nevertheless they did not depart from the sins of the house of Jeroboam, who had made Israel sin, *but* walked in them; and the wooden image[a] also remained in Samaria. [7]For He left of the army of Jehoahaz only fifty horsemen, ten chariots, and ten thousand foot soldiers; for the king of Syria had destroyed them and made them like the dust at threshing.

> **13:5 a deliverer.** This deliverer could have been Adad-Nirari III, the Assyrian king, who helped the Israelites by attacking the Syrians. He might have been Elisha, who commissioned Joash to defeat the Syrians. Or he could have been Jeroboam II, who extended Israel's boundaries back into Syrian territory.

[8]Now the rest of the acts of Jehoahaz, all that he did, and his might, *are* they not written in the book of the chronicles of the kings of Israel? [9]So Jehoahaz rested with his fathers, and they buried him in Samaria. Then Joash his son reigned in his place.

Jehoash Reigns in Israel

[10]In the thirty-seventh year of Joash king of Judah, Jehoash[a] the son of Jehoahaz became king over Israel in Samaria, *and reigned* sixteen years. [11]And he did evil in

---

12:19 [a]Spelled *Jehoash* in 12:1ff   12:20 [a]Literally *The Landfill*   12:21 [a]Called *Zabad* in 2 Chronicles 24:26   [b]Called *Shimrith* in 2 Chronicles 24:26   13:1 [a]Spelled *Jehoash* in 12:1ff   13:6 [a]Hebrew *Asherah*, a Canaanite goddess   13:10 [a]Spelled *Joash* in verse 9

the sight of the LORD. He did not depart from all the sins of Jeroboam the son of Nebat, who made Israel sin, *but* walked in them.

¹²Now the rest of the acts of Joash, all that he did, and his might with which he fought against Amaziah king of Judah, *are* they not written in the book of the chronicles of the kings of Israel? ¹³So Joash rested with his fathers. Then Jeroboam sat on his throne. And Joash was buried in Samaria with the kings of Israel.

Death of Elisha

¹⁴Elisha had become sick with the illness of which he would die. Then Joash the king of Israel came down to him, and wept over his face, and said, "O my father, my father, the chariots of Israel and their horsemen!"

13:14 Elisha. The first reference to Elisha the prophet since 9:1. Nothing was recorded for over 40 years of his life. He was probably 70 years old when these final things of his life occurred. **my father.** Jehoash used this term out of humble respect for the prophet who had provided valuable counsel for him. **the chariots of Israel and their horsemen.** This metaphor showed that it was the Lord, through Elisha, who was responsible for Israel's military success.

¹⁵And Elisha said to him, "Take a bow and some arrows." So he took himself a bow and some arrows. ¹⁶Then he said to the king of Israel, "Put your hand on the bow." So he put his hand *on it*, and Elisha put his hands on the king's hands. ¹⁷And he said, "Open the east window"; and he opened *it.* Then Elisha said, "Shoot"; and he shot. And he said, "The arrow of the LORD's deliverance and the arrow of deliverance from Syria; for you must strike the Syrians at Aphek till you have destroyed *them.*" ¹⁸Then he said, "Take the arrows"; so he took *them.* And he said to the king of Israel, "Strike the ground"; so he struck three times, and stopped. ¹⁹And the man of God was angry with him, and said, "You should have struck five or six times; then you would have struck Syria till you had destroyed *it!* But now you will strike Syria *only* three times."

²⁰Then Elisha died, and they buried him. And the *raiding* bands from Moab invaded the land in the spring of the year. ²¹So it was, as they were burying a man, that suddenly they spied a band *of raiders;* and they put the man in the tomb of Elisha; and when the man was let down and touched the bones of Elisha, he revived and stood on his feet.

13:21 he revived. A dead man came to life after touching Elisha's bones, therefore showing that God used Elisha even after his death. God's promise to Jehoash through Elisha would be fulfilled after the prophet's death (see verses 19,22–25).

Israel Recaptures Cities from Syria

²²And Hazael king of Syria oppressed Israel all the days of Jehoahaz. ²³But the LORD was gracious to them, had compassion on them, and regarded them, because of His covenant with Abraham, Isaac, and Jacob, and would not yet destroy them or cast them from His presence.

²⁴Now Hazael king of Syria died. Then Ben-Hadad his son reigned in his place. ²⁵And Jehoash*ᵃ* the son of Jehoahaz recaptured from the hand of Ben-Hadad, the son of Hazael, the cities which he had taken out of the hand of Jehoahaz his father by war. Three times Joash defeated him and recaptured the cities of Israel.

Amaziah Reigns in Judah

14 In the second year of Joash the son of Jehoahaz, king of Israel, Amaziah the son of Joash, king of Judah, became king. ²He was twenty-five years old when he became king, and he reigned twenty-nine years in Jerusalem. His mother's name was Jehoaddan of Jerusalem. ³And he did *what was* right in the sight of the LORD, yet not like his father David; he did everything as his father Joash had done. ⁴However the high places were not taken away, and the people still sacrificed and burned incense on the high places.

⁵Now it happened, as soon as the kingdom was established in his hand, that he executed his servants who had murdered his father the king. ⁶But the children of the murderers he did not execute; according to what is written in the Book of the Law of Moses, in which the LORD commanded,

13:25 *ᵃ*Spelled *Joash* in verses 12–14, 25

saying, "Fathers shall not be put to death for their children, nor shall children be put to death for their fathers; but a person shall be put to death for his own sin."[a]

[7]He killed ten thousand Edomites in the Valley of Salt, and took Sela by war, and called its name Joktheel to this day.

[8]Then Amaziah sent messengers to Jehoash[a] the son of Jehoahaz, the son of Jehu, king of Israel, saying, "Come, let us face one another in battle." [9]And Jehoash king of Israel sent to Amaziah king of Judah, saying, "The thistle that was in Lebanon sent to the cedar that was in Lebanon, saying, 'Give your daughter to my son as wife'; and a wild beast that was in Lebanon passed by and trampled the thistle. [10]You have indeed defeated Edom, and your heart has lifted you up. Glory in that, and stay at home; for why should you meddle with trouble so that you fall—you and Judah with you?"

> **14:9 thistle...cedar.** This parable (see Judg. 9:8–15) illustrates how the thistle (Amaziah) sought to be equal with the majestic cedar (Jehoash) but was crushed by a wild animal. Jehoash counseled Amaziah not to go to war with Israel since he would be crushed.

[11]But Amaziah would not heed. Therefore Jehoash king of Israel went out; so he and Amaziah king of Judah faced one another at Beth Shemesh, which belongs to Judah. [12]And Judah was defeated by Israel, and every man fled to his tent. [13]Then Jehoash king of Israel captured Amaziah king of Judah, the son of Jehoash, the son of Ahaziah, at Beth Shemesh; and he went to Jerusalem, and broke down the wall of Jerusalem from the Gate of Ephraim to the Corner Gate—four hundred cubits. [14]And he took all the gold and silver, all the articles that were found in the house of the LORD and in the treasuries of the king's house, and hostages, and returned to Samaria.

[15]Now the rest of the acts of Jehoash which he did—his might, and how he fought with Amaziah king of Judah—are they not written in the book of the chronicles of the kings of Israel? [16]So Jehoash rested with his fathers, and was buried in Samaria with the kings of Israel. Then Jeroboam his son reigned in his place.

[17]Amaziah the son of Joash, king of Judah, lived fifteen years after the death of Jehoash the son of Jehoahaz, king of Israel. [18]Now the rest of the acts of Amaziah, are they not written in the book of the chronicles of the kings of Judah? [19]And they formed a conspiracy against him in Jerusalem, and he fled to Lachish; but they sent after him to Lachish and killed him there. [20]Then they brought him on horses, and he was buried at Jerusalem with his fathers in the City of David.

> **14:18 the acts of Amaziah.** Because of his apostasy (2 Chr. 25:27), his war with Israel, the ruinous condition of Jerusalem, the robbery of the temple, and the loss of hostages, he lost the respect of the people, who ended up killing him.

[21]And all the people of Judah took Azariah,[a] who was sixteen years old, and made him king instead of his father Amaziah. [22]He built Elath and restored it to Judah, after the king rested with his fathers.

Jeroboam II Reigns in Israel

[23]In the fifteenth year of Amaziah the son of Joash, king of Judah, Jeroboam the son of Joash, king of Israel, became king in Samaria, and reigned forty-one years. [24]And he did evil in the sight of the LORD; he did not depart from all the sins of Jeroboam the son of Nebat, who had made Israel sin. [25]He restored the territory of Israel from the entrance of Hamath to the Sea of the Arabah, according to the word of the LORD God of Israel, which He had spoken through His servant Jonah the son of Amittai, the prophet who was from Gath Hepher. [26]For the LORD saw that the affliction of Israel was very bitter; and whether bond or free, there was no helper for Israel. [27]And the LORD did not say that He would blot out the name of Israel from under heaven; but He saved them by the hand of Jeroboam the son of Joash.

[28]Now the rest of the acts of Jeroboam,

14:6 [a]Deuteronomy 24:16　　14:8 [a]Spelled Joash in 13:12ff and 2 Chronicles 25:17ff　　14:21 [a]Called Uzziah in 2 Chronicles 26:1ff, Isaiah 6:1, and elsewhere

and all that he did—his might, how he made war, and how he recaptured for Israel, from Damascus and Hamath, *what had belonged* to Judah—*are* they not written in the book of the chronicles of the kings of Israel? ²⁹So Jeroboam rested with his fathers, the kings of Israel. Then Zechariah his son reigned in his place.

> **14:25,26** Jonah's prophecy is explained here. The Lord witnessed the heavy affliction suffered by Israel, who had no help available. He did not say that He would annihilate Israel, so He had compassion and used Jeroboam II's reign to rescue His suffering people. The books of Hosea and Amos show that Israel did not respond to God's grace with repentance.

Azariah Reigns in Judah

15 In the twenty-seventh year of Jeroboam king of Israel, Azariah the son of Amaziah, king of Judah, became king. ²He was sixteen years old when he became king, and he reigned fifty-two years in Jerusalem. His mother's name *was* Jecholiah of Jerusalem. ³And he did *what was* right in the sight of the LORD, according to all that his father Amaziah had done, ⁴except that the high places were not removed; the people still sacrificed and burned incense on the high places. ⁵Then the LORD struck the king, so that he was a leper until the day of his death; so he dwelt in an isolated house. And Jotham the king's son *was* over the *royal* house, judging the people of the land.

> **15:5 isolated house.** Lit. "in a house of freedom." Azariah was relieved of his royal responsibilities while Jotham, his son, served as co-regent until Azariah's death.

⁶Now the rest of the acts of Azariah, and all that he did, *are* they not written in the book of the chronicles of the kings of Judah? ⁷So Azariah rested with his fathers, and they buried him with his fathers in the City of David. Then Jotham his son reigned in his place.

Zechariah Reigns in Israel

⁸In the thirty-eighth year of Azariah king of Judah, Zechariah the son of Jeroboam reigned over Israel in Samaria six months.

⁹And he did evil in the sight of the LORD, as his fathers had done; he did not depart from the sins of Jeroboam the son of Nebat, who had made Israel sin. ¹⁰Then Shallum the son of Jabesh conspired against him, and struck and killed him in front of the people; and he reigned in his place.

¹¹Now the rest of the acts of Zechariah, indeed they *are* written in the book of the chronicles of the kings of Israel. ¹²This *was* the word of the LORD which He spoke to Jehu, saying, "Your sons shall sit on the throne of Israel to the fourth *generation.*"ᵃ And so it was.

Shallum Reigns in Israel

¹³Shallum the son of Jabesh became king in the thirty-ninth year of Uzziahᵃ king of Judah; and he reigned a full month in Samaria. ¹⁴For Menahem the son of Gadi went up from Tirzah, came to Samaria, and struck Shallum the son of Jabesh in Samaria and killed him; and he reigned in his place.

¹⁵Now the rest of the acts of Shallum, and the conspiracy which he led, indeed they *are* written in the book of the chronicles of the kings of Israel. ¹⁶Then from Tirzah, Menahem attacked Tiphsah, all who *were* there, and its territory. Because they did not surrender, therefore he attacked *it*. All the women there who were with child he ripped open.

Menahem Reigns in Israel

¹⁷In the thirty-ninth year of Azariah king of Judah, Menahem the son of Gadi be-

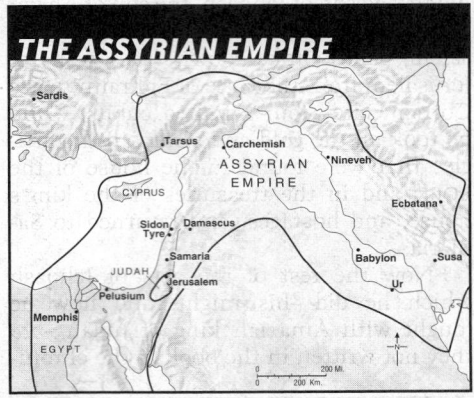

THE ASSYRIAN EMPIRE

15:12 ᵃ2 Kings 10:30   15:13 ᵃCalled *Azariah* in 14:21ff and 15:1ff

came king over Israel, *and reigned* ten years in Samaria. [18]And he did evil in the sight of the LORD; he did not depart all his days from the sins of Jeroboam the son of Nebat, who had made Israel sin. [19]Pul[a] king of Assyria came against the land; and Menahem gave Pul a thousand talents of silver, that his hand might be with him to strengthen the kingdom under his control. [20]And Menahem exacted the money from Israel, from all the very wealthy, from each man fifty shekels of silver, to give to the king of Assyria. So the king of Assyria turned back, and did not stay there in the land.

[21]Now the rest of the acts of Menahem, and all that he did, *are* they not written in the book of the chronicles of the kings of Israel? [22]So Menahem rested with his fathers. Then Pekahiah his son reigned in his place.

Pekahiah Reigns in Israel

[23]In the fiftieth year of Azariah king of Judah, Pekahiah the son of Menahem became king over Israel in Samaria, *and reigned* two years. [24]And he did evil in the sight of the LORD; he did not depart from the sins of Jeroboam the son of Nebat, who had made Israel sin. [25]Then Pekah the son of Remaliah, an officer of his, conspired against him and killed him in Samaria, in the citadel of the king's house, along with Argob and Arieh; and with him were fifty men of Gilead. He killed him and reigned in his place.

[26]Now the rest of the acts of Pekahiah, and all that he did, indeed they *are* written in the book of the chronicles of the kings of Israel.

Pekah Reigns in Israel

[27]In the fifty-second year of Azariah king of Judah, Pekah the son of Remaliah became king over Israel in Samaria, *and reigned* twenty years. [28]And he did evil in the sight of the LORD; he did not depart from the sins of Jeroboam the son of Nebat,

who had made Israel sin. [29]In the days of Pekah king of Israel, Tiglath-Pileser king of Assyria came and took Ijon, Abel Beth Maachah, Janoah, Kedesh, Hazor, Gilead, and Galilee, all the land of Naphtali; and he carried them captive to Assyria. [30]Then Hoshea the son of Elah led a conspiracy against Pekah the son of Remaliah, and struck and killed him; so he reigned in his place in the twentieth year of Jotham the son of Uzziah.

[31]Now the rest of the acts of Pekah, and all that he did, indeed they *are* written in the book of the chronicles of the kings of Israel.

Jotham Reigns in Judah

[32]In the second year of Pekah the son of Remaliah, king of Israel, Jotham the son of Uzziah, king of Judah, began to reign. [33]He was twenty-five years old when he became king, and he reigned sixteen years in Jerusalem. His mother's name *was* Jerusha[a] the daughter of Zadok. [34]And he did *what was* right in the sight of the LORD; he did according to all that his father Uzziah had done. [35]However the high places were not removed; the people still sacrificed and burned incense on the high places. He built the Upper Gate of the house of the LORD.

[36]Now the rest of the acts of Jotham, and all that he did, *are* they not written in the book of the chronicles of the kings of Judah? [37]In those days the LORD began to send Rezin king of Syria and Pekah the son of Remaliah against Judah. [38]So Jotham rested with his fathers, and was buried with his fathers in the City of David his father. Then Ahaz his son reigned in his place.

Ahaz Reigns in Judah

16 In the seventeenth year of Pekah the son of Remaliah, Ahaz the son of Jotham, king of Judah, began to reign. [2]Ahaz *was* twenty years old when he became king, and he reigned sixteen years in Jerusalem; and he did not do *what was* right in the sight of the LORD his God, as his father David *had done.* [3]But he walked in the way of the kings of Israel; indeed he made his son pass through the fire, according to the abominations of the nations whom the

---

15:19 [a]That is, Tiglath-Pileser III (compare verse 29)   15:33 [a]Spelled *Jerushah* in 2 Chronicles 27:1

LORD had cast out from before the children of Israel. ⁴And he sacrificed and burned incense on the high places, on the hills, and under every green tree.

> **16:4 the high places.** Immoral Canaanite practices were performed in the high places (see Hos. 4:13). Although other kings tolerated the high places, Ahaz was the first king in David's line since King Solomon who actually worshiped there.

⁵Then Rezin king of Syria and Pekah the son of Remaliah, king of Israel, came up to Jerusalem to *make* war; and they besieged Ahaz but could not overcome *him*. ⁶At that time Rezin king of Syria captured Elath for Syria, and drove the men of Judah from Elath. Then the Edomites*ᵃ* went to Elath, and dwell there to this day.

⁷So Ahaz sent messengers to Tiglath-Pileser king of Assyria, saying, "I *am* your servant and your son. Come up and save me from the hand of the king of Syria and from the hand of the king of Israel, who rise up against me." ⁸And Ahaz took the silver and gold that was found in the house of the LORD, and in the treasuries of the king's house, and sent *it as* a present to the king of Assyria. ⁹So the king of Assyria heeded him; for the king of Assyria went up against Damascus and took it, carried *its people* captive to Kir, and killed Rezin.

¹⁰Now King Ahaz went to Damascus to meet Tiglath-Pileser king of Assyria, and saw an altar that *was* at Damascus; and King Ahaz sent to Urijah the priest the design of the altar and its pattern, according to all its workmanship. ¹¹Then Urijah the priest built an altar according to all that King Ahaz had sent from Damascus. So Urijah the priest made *it* before King Ahaz came back from Damascus. ¹²And when the king came back from Damascus, the king saw the altar; and the king approached the altar and made offerings on it. ¹³So he

> **16:10 the altar.** Ahaz changed the temple altar to look like the one from Damascus that he liked better, because he worshiped the Assyrian god to whom the altar was built. Ahaz sinned against God, for God had given exact instructions for how the altar should be built (Ex. 25:40).

burned his burnt offering and his grain offering; and he poured his drink offering and sprinkled the blood of his peace offerings on the altar. ¹⁴He also brought the bronze altar which *was* before the LORD, from the front of the temple—from between the *new* altar and the house of the LORD—and put it on the north side of the *new* altar. ¹⁵Then King Ahaz commanded Urijah the priest, saying, "On the great *new* altar burn the morning burnt offering, the evening grain offering, the king's burnt sacrifice, and his grain offering, with the burnt offering of all the people of the land, their grain offering, and their drink offerings; and sprinkle on it all the blood of the burnt offering and all the blood of the sacrifice. And the bronze altar shall be for me to inquire *by*." ¹⁶Thus did Urijah the priest, according to all that King Ahaz commanded.

¹⁷And King Ahaz cut off the panels of the carts, and removed the lavers from them; and he took down the Sea from the bronze oxen that *were* under it, and put it on a pavement of stones. ¹⁸Also he removed the Sabbath pavilion which they had built in the temple, and he removed the king's outer entrance from the house of the LORD, on account of the king of Assyria.

¹⁹Now the rest of the acts of Ahaz which he did, *are* they not written in the book of the chronicles of the kings of Judah? ²⁰So Ahaz rested with his fathers, and was buried with his fathers in the City of David. Then Hezekiah his son reigned in his place.

Hoshea Reigns in Israel

17 In the twelfth year of Ahaz king of Judah, Hoshea the son of Elah became king of Israel in Samaria, *and he reigned* nine years. ²And he did evil in the sight of the LORD, but not as the kings of Israel who were before him. ³Shalmaneser king of Assyria came up against him; and Hoshea became his vassal, and paid him

> **17:2 he did evil.** Though characterized as evil, Hoshea was an improvement on the kings of Israel before him, since it is not written that he promoted the religious practices of Jeroboam I. This was not enough to divert Israel's inevitable doom, however.

16:6 *ᵃ*Some ancient authorities read *Syrians.*

tribute money. ⁴And the king of Assyria uncovered a conspiracy by Hoshea; for he had sent messengers to So, king of Egypt, and brought no tribute to the king of Assyria, as *he had done* year by year. Therefore the king of Assyria shut him up, and bound him in prison.

Israel Carried Captive to Assyria

⁵Now the king of Assyria went throughout all the land, and went up to Samaria and besieged it for three years. ⁶In the ninth year of Hoshea, the king of Assyria took Samaria and carried Israel away to Assyria, and placed them in Halah and by the Habor, the River of Gozan, and in the cities of the Medes.

⁷For so it was that the children of Israel had sinned against the LORD their God, who had brought them up out of the land of Egypt, from under the hand of Pharaoh king of Egypt; and they had feared other gods, ⁸and had walked in the statutes of the nations whom the LORD had cast out from before the children of Israel, and of the kings of Israel, which they had made. ⁹Also the children of Israel secretly did against the LORD their God things that *were* not right, and they built for themselves high places in all their cities, from watchtower to fortified city. ¹⁰They set up for themselves *sacred* pillars and wooden images*ᵃ* on every high hill and under every green tree. ¹¹There they burned incense on all the high places, like the nations whom the LORD had carried away before them; and they did wicked things to provoke the LORD to anger, ¹²for they served idols, of which the LORD had said to them, "You shall not do this thing."

> **17:7 feared other gods.** The primary reason for Israel's exile was the worship of other gods. In fearing these Canaanite gods, Israel obeyed their laws, which led to the results recorded in verses 9–12,16,17.

¹³Yet the LORD testified against Israel and against Judah, by all of His prophets, every seer, saying, "Turn from your evil ways, and keep My commandments *and* My statutes, according to all the law which I commanded your fathers, and which I sent to you by My servants the prophets." ¹⁴Nevertheless they would not hear, but stiffened their necks, like the necks of their fathers, who did not believe in the LORD their God. ¹⁵And they rejected His statutes and His covenant that He had made with their fathers, and His testimonies which He had testified against them; they followed idols, became idolaters, and *went* after the nations who *were* all around them, *concerning* whom the LORD had charged them that they should not do like them. ¹⁶So they left all the commandments of the LORD their God, made for themselves a molded image *and* two calves, made a wooden image and worshiped all the host of heaven, and served Baal. ¹⁷And they caused their sons and daughters to pass through the fire, practiced witchcraft and soothsaying, and sold themselves to do evil in the sight of the LORD, to provoke Him to anger. ¹⁸Therefore the LORD was very angry with Israel, and removed them from His sight; there was none left but the tribe of Judah alone.

> **17:17 pass through the fire...witchcraft and soothsaying.** Isaiah prophesied the devastation these practices would produce (Is. 8:19–22).

¹⁹Also Judah did not keep the commandments of the LORD their God, but walked in the statutes of Israel which they made. ²⁰And the LORD rejected all the descendants of Israel, afflicted them, and delivered them into the hand of plunderers, until He had cast them from His sight. ²¹For He tore Israel from the house of David, and they made Jeroboam the son of Nebat king. Then Jeroboam drove Israel from following the LORD, and made them commit a great sin. ²²For the children of Israel walked in all the sins of Jeroboam which he did; they did not depart from them, ²³until the LORD removed Israel out of His sight, as He had said by all His servants the prophets. So Israel was carried away from their own land to Assyria, *as it is* to this day.

Assyria Resettles Samaria

²⁴Then the king of Assyria brought *people* from Babylon, Cuthah, Ava, Hamath,

---

17:10 *ᵃ*Hebrew *Asherim*, Canaanite deities

and from Sepharvaim, and placed *them* in the cities of Samaria instead of the children of Israel; and they took possession of Samaria and dwelt in its cities. ²⁵And it was so, at the beginning of their dwelling there, *that* they did not fear the LORD; therefore the LORD sent lions among them, which killed *some* of them. ²⁶So they spoke to the king of Assyria, saying, "The nations whom you have removed and placed in the cities of Samaria do not know the rituals of the God of the land; therefore He has sent lions among them, and indeed, they are killing them because they do not know the rituals of the God of the land." ²⁷Then the king of Assyria commanded, saying, "Send there one of the priests whom you brought from there; let him go and dwell there, and let him teach them the rituals of the God of the land." ²⁸Then one of the priests whom they had carried away from Samaria came and dwelt in Bethel, and taught them how they should fear the LORD.

> **17:25,26 lions among them.** Lions were occasionally used by God as instruments of punishment (see 1 Kin. 13:24). **the rituals of the God.** The newcomers believed the lions to be a punishment from the God of Israel, a deity whom they believed required placating. They appealed to Sargon II to help them know how to appease God.

²⁹However every nation continued to make gods of its own, and put *them* in the shrines on the high places which the Samaritans had made, *every* nation in the cities where they dwelt. ³⁰The men of Babylon made Succoth Benoth, the men of Cuth made Nergal, the men of Hamath made Ashima, ³¹and the Avites made Nibhaz and Tartak; and the Sepharvites burned their children in fire to Adrammelech and Anammelech, the gods of Sepharvaim. ³²So they feared the LORD, and from every class they appointed for themselves priests of the high places, who sacrificed for them in the shrines of the high places. ³³They feared the LORD, yet served their own gods—according to the rituals of the nations from among whom they were carried away.

³⁴To this day they continue practicing the former rituals; they do not fear the LORD,

nor do they follow their statutes or their ordinances, or the law and commandment which the LORD had commanded the children of Jacob, whom He named Israel, ³⁵with whom the LORD had made a covenant and charged them, saying: "You shall not fear other gods, nor bow down to them nor serve them nor sacrifice to them; ³⁶but the LORD, who brought you up from the land of Egypt with great power and an outstretched arm, Him you shall fear, Him you shall worship, and to Him you shall offer sacrifice. ³⁷And the statutes, the ordinances, the law, and the commandment which He wrote for you, you shall be careful to observe forever; you shall not fear other gods. ³⁸And the covenant that I have made with you, you shall not forget, nor shall you fear other gods. ³⁹But the LORD your God you shall fear; and He will deliver you from the hand of all your enemies." ⁴⁰However they did not obey, but they followed their former rituals. ⁴¹So these nations feared the LORD, yet served their carved images; also their children and their children's children have continued doing as their fathers did, even to this day.

> **16:1—17:41** This narrative focuses on Assyria's defeat of Israel. The reasons why Israel is punished are given in 17:7–23. A primary reason was the sinful religion originally established by Jeroboam I and followed subsequently by every king in Israel. Since Ahaz of Judah followed suit, Judah would later be punished.

Hezekiah Reigns in Judah

18 Now it came to pass in the third year of Hoshea the son of Elah, king of Israel, *that* Hezekiah the son of Ahaz, king of Judah, began to reign. ²He was twenty-five years old when he became king, and he reigned twenty-nine years in Jerusalem. His mother's name *was* Abi[a] the daughter of Zechariah. ³And he did *what was* right in the sight of the LORD, according to all that his father David had done.

⁴He removed the high places and broke the *sacred* pillars, cut down the wooden image[a] and broke in pieces the bronze serpent that Moses had made; for until those

---

18:2 [a]Called *Abijah* in 2 Chronicles 29:1ff　　18:4 [a]Hebrew *Asherah*, a Canaanite goddess

18:1–25:21 With the fall of Samaria, Israel's northern kingdom came to an end (17:5,6). This last major section of the book covers the southern kingdom of Judah between 722 B.C. and its captivity and destruction in 586 B.C. The focus is on two good kings, Hezekiah and Josiah. Judah's eventual exile was due to the previous apostasy led by Ahaz and Manasseh.

days the children of Israel burned incense to it, and called it Nehushtan.*b* 5He trusted in the LORD God of Israel, so that after him was none like him among all the kings of Judah, nor who were before him. 6For he held fast to the LORD; he did not depart from following Him, but kept His commandments, which the LORD had commanded Moses. 7The LORD was with him; he prospered wherever he went. And he rebelled against the king of Assyria and did not serve him. 8He subdued the Philistines, as far as Gaza and its territory, from watchtower to fortified city.

18:7 He rebelled against...Assyria. Before Hezekiah became king, his father, Ahaz, had submitted to Assyria. Hezekiah courageously broke that relationship with Assyria by asserting Judah's independence (see Deut. 7:2).

9Now it came to pass in the fourth year of King Hezekiah, which *was* the seventh year of Hoshea the son of Elah, king of Israel, *that* Shalmaneser king of Assyria came up against Samaria and besieged it. 10And at the end of three years they took it. In the sixth year of Hezekiah, that *is,* the ninth year of Hoshea king of Israel, Samaria was taken. 11Then the king of Assyria carried Israel away captive to Assyria, and put them in Halah and by the Habor, the River of Gozan, and in the cities of the Medes, 12because they did not obey the voice of the LORD their God, but transgressed His covenant *and* all that Moses the servant of the LORD had commanded; and they would neither hear nor do *them.*

13And in the fourteenth year of King Hezekiah, Sennacherib king of Assyria came up against all the fortified cities of Judah and took them. 14Then Hezekiah king of Judah sent to the king of Assyria at Lachish, saying, "I have done wrong; turn away from me; whatever you impose on me I will pay." And the king of Assyria assessed Hezekiah king of Judah three hundred talents of silver and thirty talents of gold. 15So Hezekiah gave *him* all the silver that was found in the house of the LORD and in the treasuries of the king's house. 16At that time Hezekiah stripped *the gold from* the doors of the temple of the LORD, and *from* the pillars which Hezekiah king of Judah had overlaid, and gave it to the king of Assyria.

18:14–16 Hezekiah admitted his error in rebelling and sought to rectify the situation by paying whatever the Assyrian king demanded. In total, Sennacherib asked for about 11 tons of silver and one ton of gold.

Sennacherib Boasts Against the LORD

17Then the king of Assyria sent *the* Tartan,*a* the Rabsaris,*b* and the Rabshakeh*c* from Lachish, with a great army against Jerusalem, to King Hezekiah. And they went up and came to Jerusalem. When they had come up, they went and stood by the aqueduct from the upper pool, which *was* on the highway to the Fuller's Field. 18And when they had called to the king, Eliakim the son of Hilkiah, who *was* over the household, Shebna the scribe, and Joah the son of Asaph, the recorder, came out to them. 19Then *the* Rabshakeh said to them, "Say now to Hezekiah, 'Thus says the great king, the king of Assyria: "What confidence *is* this in which you trust? 20You speak of *having* plans and power for war; but *they are* mere words. And in whom do you trust, that you rebel against me? 21Now look! You are trusting in the staff of this broken reed, Egypt, on which if a man leans, it will go into his hand and pierce it. So *is* Pharaoh king of Egypt to all who trust in him. 22But if you say to me, 'We trust in the LORD our God,' *is* it not He whose high places and whose altars Hezekiah has taken away, and said to Judah and Jerusalem, 'You shall worship before this altar in Jerusalem'?" ' 23Now therefore, I urge you, give a pledge to my master the king of Assyria, and I will

---

18:2 *b*Literally *Bronze Thing*   18:17 *a*A title, probably *Commander in Chief*   *b*A title, probably *Chief Officer*   *c*A title, probably *Chief of Staff* or *Governor*

give you two thousand horses—if you are able on your part to put riders on them! ²⁴How then will you repel one captain of the least of my master's servants, and put your trust in Egypt for chariots and horsemen? ²⁵Have I now come up without the LORD against this place to destroy it? The LORD said to me, 'Go up against this land, and destroy it.' "

²⁶Then Eliakim the son of Hilkiah, Shebna, and Joah said to *the* Rabshakeh, "Please speak to your servants in Aramaic, for we understand *it;* and do not speak to us in Hebrew*ᵃ* in the hearing of the people who *are* on the wall."

²⁷But *the* Rabshakeh said to them, "Has my master sent me to your master and to you to speak these words, and not to the men who sit on the wall, who will eat and drink their own waste with you?"

²⁸Then *the* Rabshakeh stood and called out with a loud voice in Hebrew, and spoke, saying, "Hear the word of the great king, the king of Assyria! ²⁹Thus says the king: 'Do not let Hezekiah deceive you, for he shall not be able to deliver you from his hand; ³⁰nor let Hezekiah make you trust in the LORD, saying, "The LORD will surely deliver us; this city shall not be given into the hand of the king of Assyria." ' ³¹Do not listen to Hezekiah; for thus says the king of Assyria: 'Make *peace* with me by a present and come out to me; and every one of you eat from his own vine and every one from his own fig tree, and every one of you drink the waters of his own cistern; ³²until I come and take you away to a land like your own land, a land of grain and new wine, a land of bread and vineyards, a land of olive groves and honey, that you may live and not die. But do not listen to Hezekiah, lest he persuade you, saying, "The LORD will deliver us." ³³Has any of the gods of the nations at all delivered its land from the hand of the king of Assyria? ³⁴Where *are* the gods

of Hamath and Arpad? Where *are* the gods of Sepharvaim and Hena and Ivah? Indeed, have they delivered Samaria from my hand? ³⁵Who among all the gods of the lands have delivered their countries from my hand, that the LORD should deliver Jerusalem from my hand?' "

³⁶But the people held their peace and answered him not a word; for the king's commandment was, "Do not answer him." ³⁷Then Eliakim the son of Hilkiah, who *was* over the household, Shebna the scribe, and Joah the son of Asaph, the recorder, came to Hezekiah with *their* clothes torn, and told him the words of *the* Rabshakeh.

Isaiah Assures Deliverance

19 And so it was, when King Hezekiah heard *it,* that he tore his clothes, covered himself with sackcloth, and went into the house of the LORD. ²Then he sent Eliakim, who *was* over the household, Shebna the scribe, and the elders of the priests, covered with sackcloth, to Isaiah the prophet, the son of Amoz. ³And they said to him, "Thus says Hezekiah: 'This day *is* a day of trouble, and rebuke, and blasphemy; for the children have come to birth, but *there is* no strength to bring them forth. ⁴It may be that the LORD your God will hear all the words of *the* Rabshakeh, whom his master the king of Assyria has sent to reproach the living God, and will rebuke the words which the LORD your God has heard. Therefore lift up *your* prayer for the remnant that is left.' "

> **19:1 tore...sackcloth.** A symbol that showed Hezekiah's grief, repentance, and contrition. The king led the nation in repentance.

⁵So the servants of King Hezekiah came to Isaiah. ⁶And Isaiah said to them, "Thus you shall say to your master, 'Thus says the LORD: "Do not be afraid of the words which you have heard, with which the

> **18:28–32** The Rabshakeh spoke Hebrew in an attempt to get the people to abandon Hezekiah and to surrender to the king of Assyria, to give tribute to him, and to be willing to go into a rich and rewarding exile.

> **19:6 Do not be afraid.** Sennacherib had blasphemed the Lord by equating Him with other gods. The Lord would ensure that the Assyrian king witnessed His superiority over all other so-called gods.

18:26 *ᵃ*Literally *Judean*

servants of the king of Assyria have blasphemed Me. ⁷Surely I will send a spirit upon him, and he shall hear a rumor and return to his own land; and I will cause him to fall by the sword in his own land." ' "

Sennacherib's Threat and Hezekiah's Prayer

⁸Then *the* Rabshakeh returned and found the king of Assyria warring against Libnah, for he heard that he had departed from Lachish. ⁹And the king heard concerning Tirhakah king of Ethiopia, "Look, he has come out to make war with you." So he again sent messengers to Hezekiah, saying, ¹⁰"Thus you shall speak to Hezekiah king of Judah, saying: 'Do not let your God in whom you trust deceive you, saying, "Jerusalem shall not be given into the hand of the king of Assyria." ¹¹Look! You have heard what the kings of Assyria have done to all lands by utterly destroying them; and shall you be delivered? ¹²Have the gods of the nations delivered those whom my fathers have destroyed, Gozan and Haran and Rezeph, and the people of Eden who *were* in Telassar? ¹³Where *is* the king of Hamath, the king of Arpad, and the king of the city of Sepharvaim, Hena, and Ivah?' "

¹⁴And Hezekiah received the letter from the hand of the messengers, and read it; and Hezekiah went up to the house of the LORD, and spread it before the LORD. ¹⁵Then Hezekiah prayed before the LORD, and said: "O LORD God of Israel, *the One* who dwells *between* the cherubim, You are God, You alone, of all the kingdoms of the earth. You have made heaven and earth. ¹⁶Incline Your ear, O LORD, and hear; open Your eyes, O LORD, and see; and hear the words of Sennacherib, which he has sent to reproach the living God. ¹⁷Truly, LORD, the kings of Assyria have laid waste the nations and their lands, ¹⁸and have cast their gods into the fire; for they *were* not gods, but the work of men's hands—wood and stone. Therefore they destroyed them. ¹⁹Now therefore, O LORD our God, I pray, save us

> **19:14 house of the LORD.** Hezekiah went directly before the Lord, in contrast to Ahaz, who when in a similar crisis, refused to even ask a sign from the Lord (Is. 7:11,12).

from his hand, that all the kingdoms of the earth may know that You *are* the LORD God, You alone."

The Word of the LORD Concerning Sennacherib

²⁰Then Isaiah the son of Amoz sent to Hezekiah, saying, "Thus says the LORD God of Israel: 'Because you have prayed to Me against Sennacherib king of Assyria, I have heard.' ²¹This *is* the word which the LORD has spoken concerning him:

'The virgin, the daughter of Zion,
  Has despised you, laughed you to
    scorn;
  The daughter of Jerusalem
  Has shaken *her* head behind your
    back!

22 'Whom have you reproached and
      blasphemed?
  Against whom have you raised *your*
      voice,
  And lifted up your eyes on high?
  Against the Holy *One* of Israel.
23 By your messengers you have
      reproached the Lord,
  And said: "By the multitude of my
      chariots
  I have come up to the height of the
      mountains,
  To the limits of Lebanon;
  I will cut down its tall cedars
  And its choice cypress trees;
  I will enter the extremity of its
      borders,
  To its fruitful forest.
24 I have dug and drunk strange water,
  And with the soles of my feet I have
      dried up
  All the brooks of defense."

25 'Did you not hear long ago
  How I made it,
  From ancient times that I formed it?
  Now I have brought it to pass,
  That you should be
  For crushing fortified cities *into* heaps
      of ruins.
26 Therefore their inhabitants had little
      power;
  They were dismayed and confounded;
  They were *as* the grass of the field
  And the green herb,

As the grass on the housetops
And *grain* blighted before it is
    grown.

27 'But I know your dwelling place,
    Your going out and your coming in,
    And your rage against Me.
28 Because your rage against Me and
        your tumult
    Have come up to My ears,
    Therefore I will put My hook in your
        nose
    And My bridle in your lips,
    And I will turn you back
    By the way which you came.

29 'This *shall be* a sign to you:

    You shall eat this year such as grows
        of itself,
    And in the second year what springs
        from the same;
    Also in the third year sow and reap,
    Plant vineyards and eat the fruit of
        them.
30   And the remnant who have escaped of
        the house of Judah
    Shall again take root downward,
    And bear fruit upward.
31   For out of Jerusalem shall go a
        remnant,
    And those who escape from Mount
        Zion.
    The zeal of the LORD of hosts[a] will do
        this.'

32 "Therefore thus says the LORD concerning the king of Assyria:

    'He shall not come into this city,
    Nor shoot an arrow there,
    Nor come before it with shield,
    Nor build a siege mound against it.
33   By the way that he came,
    By the same shall he return;
    And he shall not come into this
        city,'
    Says the LORD.
34   'For I will defend this city, to save it
    For My own sake and for My servant
        David's sake.' "

> **19:34 For My own sake.** Sennacherib challenged the Lord's faithfulness (verse 10), therefore putting God's faithfulness on the line before the Assyrians (see Ezek. 36:22,23).

Sennacherib's Defeat and Death

35 And it came to pass on a certain night that the angel[a] of the LORD went out, and killed in the camp of the Assyrians one hundred and eighty-five thousand; and when *people* arose early in the morning, there were the corpses—all dead. 36So Sennacherib king of Assyria departed and went away, returned *home*, and remained at Nineveh. 37Now it came to pass, as he was worshiping in the temple of Nisroch his god, that his sons Adrammelech and Sharezer struck him down with the sword; and they escaped into the land of Ararat. Then Esarhaddon his son reigned in his place.

Hezekiah's Life Extended

20 In those days Hezekiah was sick and near death. And Isaiah the prophet, the son of Amoz, went to him and said to him, "Thus says the LORD: 'Set your house in order, for you shall die, and not live.' " 2Then he turned his face toward the wall, and prayed to the LORD, saying, 3"Remember now, O LORD, I pray, how I have walked before You in truth and with a loyal heart, and have done *what was* good in Your sight." And Hezekiah wept bitterly.

> **20:1–3 Set your house in order.** Instructions to Hezekiah to finalize his will for his family (see 2 Sam. 17:23). **you shall die, and not live.** Though God had apparently made up His mind, Hezekiah knew God would hear his appeal (see Ex. 32:7–14). **prayed... wept bitterly.** Hezekiah reminded God of his piety and devotion to God but did not ask to be healed. He may have wept because he thought that his death would give Sennacherib reason to boast, or because his son, Manasseh, was too young to be king.

4 And it happened, before Isaiah had gone out into the middle court, that the word of the LORD came to him, saying, 5"Return and tell Hezekiah the leader of My people,

---

19:31 [a]Following many Hebrew manuscripts and ancient versions (compare Isaiah 37:32); Masoretic Text omits *of hosts*.   19:35 [a]Or *Angel*

'Thus says the LORD, the God of David your father: "I have heard your prayer, I have seen your tears; surely I will heal you. On the third day you shall go up to the house of the LORD. ⁶And I will add to your days fifteen years. I will deliver you and this city from the hand of the king of Assyria; and I will defend this city for My own sake, and for the sake of My servant David." ' "

⁷Then Isaiah said, "Take a lump of figs." So they took and laid *it* on the boil, and he recovered.

⁸And Hezekiah said to Isaiah, "What *is* the sign that the LORD will heal me, and that I shall go up to the house of the LORD the third day?"

⁹Then Isaiah said, "This *is* the sign to you from the LORD, that the LORD will do the thing which He has spoken: *shall* the shadow go forward ten degrees or go backward ten degrees?"

¹⁰And Hezekiah answered, "It is an easy thing for the shadow to go down ten degrees; no, but let the shadow go backward ten degrees."

¹¹So Isaiah the prophet cried out to the LORD, and He brought the shadow ten degrees backward, by which it had gone down on the sundial of Ahaz.

The Babylonian Envoys

¹²At that time Berodach-Baladan*ᵃ* the son of Baladan, king of Babylon, sent letters and a present to Hezekiah, for he heard that Hezekiah had been sick. ¹³And Hezeki-

ah was attentive to them, and showed them all the house of his treasures—the silver and gold, the spices and precious ointment, and all*ᵃ* his armory—all that was found among his treasures. There was nothing in his house or in all his dominion that Hezekiah did not show them.

¹⁴Then Isaiah the prophet went to King Hezekiah, and said to him, "What did these men say, and from where did they come to you?"

So Hezekiah said, "They came from a far country, from Babylon."

¹⁵And he said, "What have they seen in your house?"

So Hezekiah answered, "They have seen all that *is* in my house; there is nothing among my treasures that I have not shown them."

¹⁶Then Isaiah said to Hezekiah, "Hear the word of the LORD: ¹⁷'Behold, the days are coming when all that *is* in your house, and what your fathers have accumulated until this day, shall be carried to Babylon; nothing shall be left,' says the LORD. ¹⁸'And they shall take away some of your sons who will descend from you, whom you will beget; and they shall be eunuchs in the palace of the king of Babylon.' "

¹⁹So Hezekiah said to Isaiah, "The word of the LORD which you have spoken *is* good!" For he said, "Will there not be peace and truth at least in my days?"

20:19 word of the LORD...good. A surprising response to the negative prophesy of vv. 16–18. Hezekiah recognized Isaiah as God's messenger and acknowledged God's goodness in that He did not destroy Jerusalem during Hezekiah's life. **peace and truth...in my days.** Possibly a selfish reaction, though perhaps he was looking for some hope in the gloomy fate of his descendants.

Death of Hezekiah

²⁰Now the rest of the acts of Hezekiah— all his might, and how he made a pool and a tunnel and brought water into the city— *are* they not written in the book of the chronicles of the kings of Judah? ²¹So Hezekiah rested with his fathers. Then Manasseh his son reigned in his place.

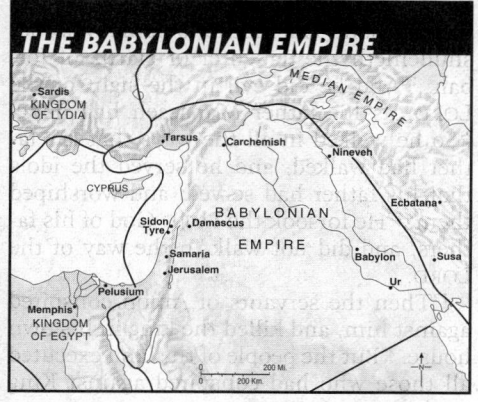

THE BABYLONIAN EMPIRE

Sardis
KINGDOM OF LYDIA
MEDIAN EMPIRE
Tarsus
Carchemish
Nineveh
CYPRUS
Ecbatana
Sidon
Tyre
Damascus
BABYLONIAN
EMPIRE
Babylon
Susa
Samaria
Jerusalem
Ur
Pelusium
Memphis
KINGDOM OF EGYPT
200 Mi.
200 Km.

20:12 *ᵃ*Spelled *Merodach-Baladan* in Isaiah 39:1 20:13 *ᵃ*Following many Hebrew manuscripts, Syriac, and Targum; Masoretic Text omits *all*.

Manasseh Reigns in Judah

21 Manasseh *was* twelve years old when he became king, and he reigned fifty-five years in Jerusalem. His mother's name *was* Hephzibah. ²And he did evil in the sight of the LORD, according to the abominations of the nations whom the LORD had cast out before the children of Israel. ³For he rebuilt the high places which Hezekiah his father had destroyed; he raised up altars for Baal, and made a wooden image,*ª* as Ahab king of Israel had done; and he worshiped all the host of heaven*ᵇ* and served them. ⁴He also built altars in the house of the LORD, of which the LORD had said, "In Jerusalem I will put My name." ⁵And he built altars for all the host of heaven in the two courts of the house of the LORD. ⁶Also he made his son pass through the fire, practiced soothsaying, used witchcraft, and consulted spiritists and mediums. He did much evil in the sight of the LORD, to provoke *Him* to anger. ⁷He even set a carved image of Asherah*ª* that he had made, in the house of which the LORD had said to David and to Solomon his son, "In this house and in Jerusalem, which I have chosen out of all the tribes of Israel, I will put My name forever; ⁸and I will not make the feet of Israel wander anymore from the land which I gave their fathers—only if they are careful to do according to all that I have commanded them, and according to all the law that My servant Moses commanded them." ⁹But they paid no attention, and Manasseh seduced them to do more evil than the nations whom the LORD had destroyed before the children of Israel.

¹⁰And the LORD spoke by His servants the prophets, saying, ¹¹"Because Manasseh king of Judah has done these abominations (he has acted more wickedly than all the Amorites who *were* before him, and has also made Judah sin with his idols), ¹²therefore thus says the LORD God of Israel: 'Behold, *I* am bringing *such* calamity upon Jerusalem and Judah, that whoever hears of it, both his ears will tingle. ¹³And I will stretch over Jerusalem the measuring line of Samaria and the plummet of the house of Ahab; I will wipe Jerusalem as *one* wipes a dish, wiping *it* and turning *it* upside down. ¹⁴So I will forsake the remnant of My inheritance and deliver them into the hand of their enemies; and they shall become victims of plunder to all their enemies, ¹⁵be-

> **21:13 the plummet.** These weighted lines were dropped from walls to see if they were structurally straight (see Is. 28:17). If not, they were torn down. The Lord measured Jerusalem by His Word and determined that Jerusalem would have the same fate as Samaria (Israel). **wipe Jerusalem.** As one would wipe food off a plate, God would wipe Jerusalem off the earth.

cause they have done evil in My sight, and have provoked Me to anger since the day their fathers came out of Egypt, even to this day.' "

¹⁶Moreover Manasseh shed very much innocent blood, till he had filled Jerusalem from one end to another, besides his sin by which he made Judah sin, in doing evil in the sight of the LORD.

¹⁷Now the rest of the acts of Manasseh—all that he did, and the sin that he committed—*are* they not written in the book of the chronicles of the kings of Judah? ¹⁸So Manasseh rested with his fathers, and was buried in the garden of his own house, in the garden of Uzza. Then his son Amon reigned in his place.

Amon's Reign and Death

¹⁹Amon *was* twenty-two years old when he became king, and he reigned two years in Jerusalem. His mother's name *was* Meshullemeth the daughter of Haruz of Jotbah. ²⁰And he did evil in the sight of the LORD, as his father Manasseh had done. ²¹So he walked in all the ways that his father had walked; and he served the idols that his father had served, and worshiped them. ²²He forsook the LORD God of his fathers, and did not walk in the way of LORD.

²³Then the servants of Amon conspired against him, and killed the king in his own house. ²⁴But the people of the land executed all those who had conspired against King

---

21:3 *ª*Hebrew *Asherah*, a Canaanite goddess   *ᵇ*The gods of the Assyrians   21:7 *ª*A Canaanite goddess

Amon. Then the people of the land made his son Josiah king in his place.

> **21:24 the people of the land.** Probably a group of Judah's national leaders who killed the assassins of Amon and made his son, Josiah, king in order to maintain David's dynasty (see 2 Kin. 11:14–18).

25Now the rest of the acts of Amon which he did, *are* they not written in the book of the chronicles of the kings of Judah? 26And he was buried in his tomb in the garden of Uzza. Then Josiah his son reigned in his place.

Josiah Reigns in Judah

22 Josiah *was* eight years old when he became king, and he reigned thirty-one years in Jerusalem. His mother's name *was* Jedidah the daughter of Adaiah of Bozkath. 2And he did *what was* right in the sight of the LORD, and walked in all the ways of his father David; he did not turn aside to the right hand or to the left.

Hilkiah Finds the Book of the Law

3Now it came to pass, in the eighteenth year of King Josiah, *that* the king sent Shaphan the scribe, the son of Azaliah, the son of Meshullam, to the house of the LORD, saying: 4"Go up to Hilkiah the high priest, that he may count the money which has been brought into the house of the LORD, which the doorkeepers have gathered from the people. 5And let them deliver it into the hand of those doing the work, who are the overseers in the house of the LORD; let them give it to those who *are* in the house of the LORD doing the work, to repair the damages of the house—6to carpenters and builders and masons—and to buy timber and hewn stone to repair the house. 7However there need be no accounting made with them of the money delivered into their hand, because they deal faithfully."

8Then Hilkiah the high priest said to Shaphan the scribe, "I have found the Book of the Law in the house of the LORD." And Hilkiah gave the book to Shaphan, and he read it. 9So Shaphan the scribe went to the king, bringing the king word, saying, "Your servants have gathered the money that was found in the house, and have delivered it into the hand of those who do the work, who oversee the house of the LORD." 10Then Shaphan the scribe showed the king, saying, "Hilkiah the priest has given me a book." And Shaphan read it before the king.

> **22:8 the Book of the Law.** A scroll containing the Torah (the Pentateuch). Though Manasseh may have destroyed all unhidden copies, they could have found the official copy that was laid beside the ark of the covenant in the Most Holy Place (Deut. 31:25,26). The ark may have been moved by Ahaz, Manasseh, or Amon (see 2 Chr. 35:3) and discovered during repair work.

11Now it happened, when the king heard the words of the Book of the Law, that he tore his clothes. 12Then the king commanded Hilkiah the priest, Ahikam the son of Shaphan, Achbor*a* the son of Michaiah, Shaphan the scribe, and Asaiah a servant of the king, saying, 13"Go, inquire of the LORD for me, for the people and for all Judah, concerning the words of this book that has been found; for great *is* the wrath of the LORD that is aroused against us, because our fathers have not obeyed the words of this book, to do according to all that is written concerning us."

14So Hilkiah the priest, Ahikam, Achbor, Shaphan, and Asaiah went to Huldah the prophetess, the wife of Shallum the son of Tikvah, the son of Harhas, keeper of the wardrobe. (She dwelt in Jerusalem in the Second Quarter.) And they spoke with her. 15Then she said to them, "Thus says the LORD God of Israel, 'Tell the man who sent you to Me, 16"Thus says the LORD: 'Behold, I will bring calamity on this place and on its inhabitants—all the words of the book which the king of Judah has read—17because they have forsaken Me and burned incense to other gods, that they might provoke Me to anger with all the works of their hands. Therefore My wrath shall be aroused against this place and shall not be quenched.' " ' 18But as for the king of Judah, who sent you to inquire of the LORD, in this manner you shall speak to him, 'Thus says the LORD God of Israel: "*Concerning* the

---

22:12 *a*Abdon the son of Micah in 2 Chronicles 34:20

words which you have heard—[19]because your heart was tender, and you humbled yourself before the LORD when you heard what I spoke against this place and against its inhabitants, that they would become a desolation and a curse, and you tore your clothes and wept before Me, I also have heard *you*," says the LORD. [20]Surely, therefore, I will gather you to your fathers, and you shall be gathered to your grave in peace; and your eyes shall not see all the calamity which I will bring on this place." ' " So they brought back word to the king.

22:15–20 Through Josiah's messengers, Huldah gave God's message to Josiah that God would judge Jerusalem because of her idolatry and that Josiah would die "in peace," escaping the horrors in store for Jerusalem. This second promise was in response to Josiah's tenderness and humility upon hearing of Jerusalem's destruction from the scroll.

Josiah Restores True Worship

23 Now the king sent them to gather all the elders of Judah and Jerusalem to him. [2]The king went up to the house of the LORD with all the men of Judah, and with him all the inhabitants of Jerusalem— the priests and the prophets and all the people, both small and great. And he read in their hearing all the words of the Book of the Covenant which had been found in the house of the LORD.

[3]Then the king stood by a pillar and made a covenant before the LORD, to follow the LORD and to keep His commandments and His testimonies and His statutes, with all *his* heart and all *his* soul, to perform the words of this covenant that were written in this book. And all the people took a stand for the covenant. [4]And the king commanded Hilkiah the high priest, the priests of the second order, and the doorkeepers, to bring out of the temple of the LORD all the arti-

23:3 a covenant...this covenant. Josiah made a public, binding agreement to be obedient to all that was commanded in the Book of the Covenant. In turn, the people made the same commitment.

cles that were made for Baal, for Asherah,[a] and for all the host of heaven;[b] and he burned them outside Jerusalem in the fields of Kidron, and carried their ashes to Bethel. [5]Then he removed the idolatrous priests whom the kings of Judah had ordained to burn incense on the high places in the cities of Judah and in the places all around Jerusalem, and those who burned incense to Baal, to the sun, to the moon, to the constellations, and to all the host of heaven. [6]And he brought out the wooden image[a] from the house of the LORD, to the Brook Kidron outside Jerusalem, burned it at the Brook Kidron and ground *it* to ashes, and threw its ashes on the graves of the common people. [7]Then he tore down the *ritual* booths of the perverted persons[a] that *were* in the house of the LORD, where the women wove hangings for the wooden image. [8]And he brought all the priests from the cities of Judah, and defiled the high places where the priests had burned incense, from Geba to Beersheba; also he broke down the high places at the gates which *were* at the entrance of the Gate of Joshua the governor of the city, which *were* to the left of the city gate. [9]Nevertheless the priests of the high places did not come up to the altar of the LORD in Jerusalem, but they ate unleavened bread among their brethren.

[10]And he defiled Topheth, which *is* in the Valley of the Son[a] of Hinnom, that no man might make his son or his daughter pass through the fire to Molech. [11]Then he removed the horses that the kings of Judah had dedicated to the sun, at the entrance to the house of the LORD, by the chamber of Nathan-Melech, the officer who *was* in the court; and he burned the chariots of the sun with fire. [12]The altars that *were* on the roof, the upper chamber of Ahaz, which the kings of Judah had made, and the altars

23:10 Topheth. Meaning "a drum," and possibly called this because of the drums beaten to drown out the cries of the children sacrificed in this area of the Valley of Hinnom (see Is. 30:33).

23:4 [a]A Canaanite goddess [b]The gods of the Assyrians **23:6** [a]Hebrew *Asherah*, a Canaanite goddess **23:7** [a]Hebrew *qedeshim*, that is, those practicing sodomy and prostitution in religious rituals **23:10** [a]Kethib reads *Sons*.

which Manasseh had made in the two courts of the house of the LORD, the king broke down and pulverized there, and threw their dust into the Brook Kidron. [13]Then the king defiled the high places that *were* east of Jerusalem, which *were* on the south of the Mount of Corruption, which Solomon king of Israel had built for Ashtoreth the abomination of the Sidonians, for Chemosh the abomination of the Moabites, and for Milcom the abomination of the people of Ammon. [14]And he broke in pieces the *sacred* pillars and cut down the wooden images, and filled their places with the bones of men.

[15]Moreover the altar that *was* at Bethel, *and* the high place which Jeroboam the son of Nebat, who made Israel sin, had made, both that altar and the high place he broke down; and he burned the high place *and* crushed *it* to powder, and burned the wooden image. [16]As Josiah turned, he saw the tombs that *were* there on the mountain. And he sent and took the bones out of the tombs and burned *them* on the altar, and defiled it according to the word of the LORD which the man of God proclaimed, who proclaimed these words. [17]Then he said, "What gravestone *is* this that I see?"

23:15,16 the altar...at Bethel. Josiah reduced the altar that Jeroboam I had built to dust and ashes (see 1 Kin. 12:28–33). **tombs.** Josiah had the bones of (most likely) idolatrous priests removed from their tombs and burned on the altar at Bethel to defile it. This was a fulfillment of a prophecy given approximately 300 years earlier (1 Kin. 13:2).

So the men of the city told him, "*It is* the tomb of the man of God who came from Judah and proclaimed these things which you have done against the altar of Bethel." [18]And he said, "Let him alone; let no one move his bones." So they let his bones alone, with the bones of the prophet who came from Samaria.

[19]Now Josiah also took away all the shrines of the high places that *were* in the cities of Samaria, which the kings of Israel had made to provoke the LORD[a] to anger; and he did to them according to all the deeds he had done in Bethel. [20]He executed all the priests of the high places who *were* there, on the altars, and burned men's bones on them; and he returned to Jerusalem.

[21]Then the king commanded all the people, saying, "Keep the Passover to the LORD your God, as *it is* written in this Book of the Covenant." [22]Such a Passover surely had never been held since the days of the judges who judged Israel, nor in all the days of the kings of Israel and the kings of Judah. [23]But in the eighteenth year of King Josiah this Passover was held before the LORD in Jerusalem. [24]Moreover Josiah put away those who consulted mediums and spiritists, the household gods and idols, all the abominations that were seen in the land of Judah and in Jerusalem, that he might perform the words of the law which were written in the book that Hilkiah the priest found in the house of the LORD. [25]Now before him there was no king like him, who turned to the LORD with all his heart, with all his soul, and with all his might, according to all the Law of Moses; nor after him did *any* arise like him.

23:25 no king like him. No king in David's line, including David, more closely resembled the royal ideal given in Deut. 17:14–20 than Josiah (see Matt. 22:37), despite his having many wives (see verses 31,36). Yet, he could not deter the wrath of God incited by Manasseh's sin (vv. 26,27).

Impending Judgment on Judah

[26]Nevertheless the LORD did not turn from the fierceness of His great wrath, with which His anger was aroused against Judah, because of all the provocations with which Manasseh had provoked Him. [27]And the LORD said, "I will also remove Judah from My sight, as I have removed Israel, and will cast off this city Jerusalem which I have chosen, and the house of which I said, 'My name shall be there.' "[a]

Josiah Dies in Battle

[28]Now the rest of the acts of Josiah, and all that he did, *are* they not written in the book of the chronicles of the kings of

---

23:19 [a]Following Septuagint, Syriac, and Vulgate; Masoretic Text and Targum omit *the* LORD.
23:27 [a]1 Kings 8:29

Judah? ²⁹In his days Pharaoh Necho king of Egypt went to the aid of the king of Assyria, to the River Euphrates; and King Josiah went against him. And *Pharaoh Necho* killed him at Megiddo when he confronted him. ³⁰Then his servants moved his body in a chariot from Megiddo, brought him to Jerusalem, and buried him in his own tomb. And the people of the land took Jehoahaz the son of Josiah, anointed him, and made him king in his father's place.

The Reign and Captivity of Jehoahaz

³¹Jehoahaz *was* twenty-three years old when he became king, and he reigned three months in Jerusalem. His mother's name *was* Hamutal the daughter of Jeremiah of Libnah. ³²And he did evil in the sight of the LORD, according to all that his fathers had done. ³³Now Pharaoh Necho put him in prison at Riblah in the land of Hamath, that he might not reign in Jerusalem; and he imposed on the land a tribute of one hundred talents of silver and a talent of gold. ³⁴Then Pharaoh Necho made Eliakim the son of Josiah king in place of his father Josiah, and changed his name to Jehoiakim. And *Pharaoh* took Jehoahaz and went to Egypt, and he*ᵃ* died there.

23:34 Eliakim...Jehoiakim. Necho changed Eliakim's name, meaning "God has established," to Jehoiakim, meaning "the LORD has established," in order to demonstrate that he was the lord that controlled Judah. The giving of a name was a sign of authority.

Jehoiakim Reigns in Judah

³⁵So Jehoiakim gave the silver and gold to Pharaoh; but he taxed the land to give money according to the command of Pharaoh; he exacted the silver and gold from the people of the land, from every one according to his assessment, to give *it* to Pharaoh Necho. ³⁶Jehoiakim *was* twenty-five years old when he became king, and he reigned eleven years in Jerusalem. His mother's name *was* Zebudah the daughter of Pedaiah of Rumah. ³⁷And he did evil in the sight of the LORD, according to all that his fathers had done.

Judah Overrun by Enemies

24 In his days Nebuchadnezzar king of Babylon came up, and Jehoiakim became his vassal *for* three years. Then he turned and rebelled against him. ²And the LORD sent against him *raiding* bands of Chaldeans, bands of Syrians, bands of Moabites, and bands of the people of Ammon; He sent them against Judah to destroy it, according to the word of the LORD which He had spoken by His servants the prophets. ³Surely at the commandment of the LORD *this* came upon Judah, to remove *them* from His sight because of the sins of Manasseh, according to all that he had done, ⁴and also because of the innocent blood that he had shed; for he had filled Jerusalem with innocent blood, which the LORD would not pardon.

⁵Now the rest of the acts of Jehoiakim, and all that he did, *are* they not written in the book of the chronicles of the kings of Judah? ⁶So Jehoiakim rested with his fathers. Then Jehoiachin his son reigned in his place.

⁷And the king of Egypt did not come out of his land anymore, for the king of Babylon had taken all that belonged to the king of Egypt from the Brook of Egypt to the River Euphrates.

The Reign and Captivity of Jehoiachin

⁸Jehoiachin *was* eighteen years old when he became king, and he reigned in Jerusalem three months. His mother's name *was* Nehushta the daughter of Elnathan of Jerusalem. ⁹And he did evil in the sight of the LORD, according to all that his father had done.

24:8 eighteen. This reading is preferred over the "eight" of 2 Chr. 36:9. **three months.** Nebuchadnezzar again invaded Judah in the spring of 597 B.C., but was not able to enter Jerusalem before Jehoiakim died and was succeeded by his son, Jehoiachin.

¹⁰At that time the servants of Nebuchadnezzar king of Babylon came up against Jerusalem, and the city was besieged. ¹¹And Nebuchadnezzar king of Babylon came against the city, as his servants were besieg-

---

23:34 *ᵃ*That is, Jehoahaz

ing it. ¹²Then Jehoiachin king of Judah, his mother, his servants, his princes, and his officers went out to the king of Babylon; and the king of Babylon, in the eighth year of his reign, took him prisoner.

The Captivity of Jerusalem

¹³And he carried out from there all the treasures of the house of the LORD and the treasures of the king's house, and he cut in pieces all the articles of gold which Solomon king of Israel had made in the temple of the LORD, as the LORD had said. ¹⁴Also he carried into captivity all Jerusalem: all the captains and all the mighty men of valor, ten thousand captives, and all the craftsmen and smiths. None remained except the poorest people of the land. ¹⁵And he carried Jehoiachin captive to Babylon. The king's mother, the king's wives, his officers, and the mighty of the land he carried into captivity from Jerusalem to Babylon. ¹⁶All the valiant men, seven thousand, and craftsmen and smiths, one thousand, all who were strong and fit for war, these

24:14–16 In 597 B.C., Nebuchadnezzar took 10,000 captives, most of whom were leaders, back to Babylon. The prophet Ezekiel was part of this deportation. Only the lower class remained because the Babylonians took the strong and the leaders, elevating those left behind to leadership positions to earn their loyalty. Those taken to Babylon were allowed to work and live in mainstream society, which made it possible for the Jews to remain together. This made it possible for them to return, as Ezra records.

the king of Babylon brought captive to Babylon.

Zedekiah Reigns in Judah

¹⁷Then the king of Babylon made Mattaniah, *Jehoiachin's*ᵃ uncle, king in his place, and changed his name to Zedekiah.

¹⁸Zedekiah *was* twenty-one years old when he became king, and he reigned eleven years in Jerusalem. His mother's name *was* Hamutal the daughter of Jeremiah of Libnah. ¹⁹He also did evil in the sight of the LORD, according to all that Jehoiakim had done. ²⁰For because of the anger of the LORD *this* happened in Jerusalem and Judah, that He finally cast them out from His presence. Then Zedekiah rebelled against the king of Babylon.

The Fall and Captivity of Judah

25 Now it came to pass in the ninth year of his reign, in the tenth month, on the tenth *day* of the month, *that* Nebuchadnezzar king of Babylon and all his army came against Jerusalem and encamped against it; and they built a siege wall against it all around. ²So the city was besieged until the eleventh year of King Zedekiah. ³By the ninth *day* of the *fourth* month the famine had become so severe in

25:1 ninth year. Responding to Zedekiah's rebellion (24:20), Nebuchadnezzar's army besieged Jerusalem in the ninth year of Zedekiah's reign. The "siege wall" was comprised of either wood towers higher than the city walls or a dirt rampart encircling the city.

24:17 ᵃLiterally *his*

How are the six books—1 and 2 Samuel, 1 and 2 Kings, and 1 and 2 Chronicles—related to one another in recording the history of the Kingdom of Israel?

First and 2 Samuel and 1 and 2 Kings provide a chronological account of the Kingdom of Israel in its original and divided state. First and 2 Chronicles serve as a special review of the line of David (the kings of Judah).

Those who add up the numbers given for the lengths of reign in these books are sometimes surprised that the math produces inconsistencies. Extrabiblical sources also provide some dating that creates problems when correlated with the text. Two important factors help explain the apparent inconsistencies in these records: (1) A number of cases had co-regencies (fathers and sons sharing the throne) in which each king's years were listed without accounting for the overlap; (2) Neither the calendars nor the official reckoning of years was always the same in both kingdoms.

the city that there was no food for the people of the land.

⁴Then the city wall was broken through, and all the men of war *fled* at night by way of the gate between two walls, which was by the king's garden, even though the Chaldeans *were* still encamped all around against the city. And *the king*ᵃ went by way of the plain.*ᵇ* ⁵But the army of the Chaldeans pursued the king, and they overtook him in the plains of Jericho. All his army was scattered from him. ⁶So they took the king and brought him up to the king of Babylon at Riblah, and they pronounced judgment on him. ⁷Then they killed the sons of Zedekiah before his eyes, put out the eyes of Zedekiah, bound him with bronze fetters, and took him to Babylon.

⁸And in the fifth month, on the seventh *day* of the month (which *was* the nineteenth year of King Nebuchadnezzar king of Babylon), Nebuzaradan the captain of the guard, a servant of the king of Babylon, came to Jerusalem. ⁹He burned the house of the LORD and the king's house; all the houses of Jerusalem, that is, all the houses of the great, he burned with fire. ¹⁰And all the army of the Chaldeans who *were with* the captain of the guard broke down the walls of Jerusalem all around.

¹¹Then Nebuzaradan the captain of the guard carried away captive the rest of the people *who* remained in the city and the defectors who had deserted to the king of Babylon, with the rest of the multitude. ¹²But the captain of the guard left *some* of the poor of the land as vinedressers and farmers. ¹³The bronze pillars that *were* in the house of the LORD, and the carts and the bronze Sea that *were* in the house of the LORD, the Chaldeans broke in pieces, and carried their bronze to Babylon. ¹⁴They also took away the pots, the shovels, the trimmers, the spoons, and all the bronze utensils with which the priests ministered. ¹⁵The firepans and the basins, the things of solid gold and solid silver, the captain of the guard took away. ¹⁶The two pillars, one Sea, and the carts, which Solomon had made for the house of the LORD, the bronze of all these articles was beyond measure. ¹⁷The height of one pillar *was* eighteen cubits,

and the capital on it *was* of bronze. The height of the capital was three cubits, and the network and pomegranates all around the capital were all of bronze. The second pillar was the same, with a network.

25:8–21 The destruction of Jerusalem by the Babylonians was done in an orderly fashion: Jerusalem's most important buildings were burned, the outer walls were torn down, the remaining Judeans were forced into exile in Babylon, the precious metals in the temple were taken, and Jerusalem's remaining leaders were executed, thus ensuring no future rebellions.

¹⁸And the captain of the guard took Seraiah the chief priest, Zephaniah the second priest, and the three doorkeepers. ¹⁹He also took out of the city an officer who had charge of the men of war, five men of the king's close associates who were found in the city, the chief recruiting officer of the army, who mustered the people of the land, and sixty men of the people of the land *who were* found in the city. ²⁰So Nebuzaradan, captain of the guard, took these and brought them to the king of Babylon at Riblah. ²¹Then the king of Babylon struck them and put them to death at Riblah in the land of Hamath. Thus Judah was carried away captive from its own land.

25:21 Judah...carried away captive. Exile was the ultimate curse brought upon Judah for disobeying the Mosaic Covenant (see Lev. 26:33). Jeremiah's sorrow over the destruction of Jerusalem is recorded in Lamentations.

Gedaliah Made Governor of Judah

²²Then he made Gedaliah the son of Ahikam, the son of Shaphan, governor over the people who remained in the land of Judah, whom Nebuchadnezzar king of Babylon had left. ²³Now when all the captains of the armies, they and *their* men, heard that the king of Babylon had made Gedaliah governor, they came to Gedaliah at Mizpah—Ishmael the son of Nethaniah, Johanan the son of Careah, Seraiah the son of Tanhumeth the Netophathite, and Jaazaniahᵃ the son of a Maachathite, they and their men. ²⁴And Gedaliah took an oath before them

and their men, and said to them, "Do not be afraid of the servants of the Chaldeans. Dwell in the land and serve the king of Babylon, and it shall be well with you."

²⁵But it happened in the seventh month that Ishmael the son of Nethaniah, the son of Elishama, of the royal family, came with ten men and struck and killed Gedaliah, the Jews, as well as the Chaldeans who were with him at Mizpah. ²⁶And all the people, small and great, and the captains of the armies, arose and went to Egypt; for they were afraid of the Chaldeans.

Jehoiachin Released from Prison

²⁷Now it came to pass in the thirty-seventh year of the captivity of Jehoiachin king of Judah, in the twelfth month, on the twenty-seventh *day* of the month, *that* Evil-Merodach*ᵃ* king of Babylon, in the year that he began to reign, released Jehoiachin king of Judah from prison. ²⁸He spoke kindly to him, and gave him a more prominent seat than those of the kings who *were* with him in Babylon. ²⁹So Jehoiachin changed from his prison garments, and he ate bread regularly before the king all the days of his life. ³⁰And as for his provisions, *there was* a regular ration given him by the king, a portion for each day, all the days of his life.

25:28–30 spoke kindly to him. These words to the surviving representative of the line of David served as a concluding reminder of God's good Word to David. Because David's line survived the exile, there was still hope that God's promise to send a seed who would build the temple and establish God's eternal kingdom would be fulfilled (see 2 Sam. 7:12–16). Second Kings opens with faithful Elijah carried up to heaven and closes with unfaithful Israel and Judah carried away to pagan lands.

25:27 *ᵃ*Literally *Man of Marduk*

1 & 2 CHRONICLES

Before video cameras and tape recorders, there were chroniclers. Somewhere in the corner of every throne room sat people whose duty was to record the events of the day. The two-part book of Chronicles provides a summary of history back to the beginning—a review that includes material from Genesis to 2 Kings. The original Hebrew title for this book meant "The Annals of the Days." It became two books around 200 B.C. when the Septuagint translators divided the original long scroll. First and Second Chronicles are among the few Old Testament books not directly quoted in the New Testament.

AUTHOR AND DATE

Chronicles was possibly written by Ezra, approximately 450 to 430 B.C.

First and Second Chronicles contain no specific indications of authorship. Ancient traditions favor Ezra the priest (Ezra 7:6), who lived in the time period and was known as a scribe. These records were most likely written between 450 and 430 B.C. The genealogical record in 1 Chronicles 1–9 suggests a date after 450 B.C.

BACKGROUND AND SETTING

Chronicles provides a large scale perspective for a people during a time of chaotic change. After seventy years of captivity in Babylon, Jews were returning to Israel. This occurred in three phases: (1) Zerubbabel's group around 538 B.C. (Ezra 1–6); (2) Ezra's group around 458 B.C. (Ezra 7–10); and (3)Nehemiah's group around 445 B.C. (Nehemiah 1–13). The exiles needed to see God's hand in the history of their nation so that they could cope with the set-backs and difficulties of the time in which they lived.

To put it mildly, the exiles' future looked bleak compared to their majestic past, particularly the glory years of David and Solomon. The return to the Promised Land could be described as bittersweet—bitter because their present poverty brought hurtful memories about what was forfeited by God's judgment on their ancestor's sin, and sweet because at least they were back in the Land God had given Abraham 17 centuries earlier (Genesis 12:1–3).

The chronicler's selective genealogy and history of Israel, stretching from Adam (1 Chronicles 1:1) to the return from Babylon (2 Chronicles 26:23), was intended to remind the Jews of God's promises and intentions regarding: (1) the land; (2) their identity as a nation; (3) the Davidic royal line; (4) the Levitical priesthood; (5) the Temple; and (6) true worship. God made it clear that none of those

had been abolished or erased by the Babylonian captivity. By summarizing the Jews' unique spiritual heritage, Chronicles encouraged readers to remain faithful to God in difficult times.

Chronicles provides an excellent example of the ways in which history and theology are inextricably linked in Scripture. God's divine purposes for Israel have been and will be played out on the stage of world history. The human side of the covenant between God and human beings may prove weak, faithless, sinful, but God will remain true to His promises.

> **CHRONICLES PROVIDES AN EXCELLENT EXAMPLE OF THE WAYS IN WHICH HISTORY AND THEOLOGY ARE INEXTRICABLY LINKED IN SCRIPTURE.**

Two basic theological principles illustrated in these books echo throughout the Old Testament: (1) obedience brings God's blessing; and (2) disobedience brings God's judgment. In Chronicles, when a king obeyed and trusted the Lord, God blessed and protected. But when a king disobeyed and put his trust in something or someone other than the Lord, God withdrew His blessing and protection. Three basic failures by the kings of Judah brought God's wrath: (1) personal sin; (2) false worship/idolatry; or (3) trust in a human being rather than God.

OUTLINE OF 1 CHRONICLES

I. SELECTIVE GENEALOGY (1:1–9:34)
- A. Adam to Just Before David (1:1–2:55)
- B. David to the Captivity (3:1–24)
- C. The Twelve Tribes (4:1–9:2)
- D. Jerusalem Dwellers (9:3–34)

II. DAVID'S ASCENT (9:35–12:40)
- A. Saul's Heritage and Death (9:35–10:14)
- B. David's Anointing (11:1–3)
- C. Jerusalem's Conquest (11:4–9)
- D. David's Men (11:10–12:40)

III. DAVID'S REIGN (13:1–29:30)
- A. The Ark of the Covenant (13:1–16:43)
- B. The Davidic Covenant (17:1–27)
- C. Selected Military History (18:1–21:30)
- D. Temple-Building Preparations (22:1–29:20)
- E. Transition to Solomon (29:21–30)

1:1–9:44 This is the genealogy from Adam to Noah (Gen. 1–6), from Noah's son, Shem, to Abraham (Gen. 7–11), from Abraham to Jacob (Gen. 12–25), from Jacob to the 12 tribes (Gen. 25–50), and from the 12 tribes to those who had returned to Jerusalem after the 70-year captivity (Ex. 1:1–2 Chr. 36:23).

The Family of Adam—Seth to Abraham

1 Adam, Seth, Enosh, ²Cainan,*ª* Mahalalel, Jared, ³Enoch, Methuselah, Lamech, ⁴Noah,*ª* Shem, Ham, and Japheth.

⁵The sons of Japheth *were* Gomer, Magog, Madai, Javan, Tubal, Meshech, and Tiras. ⁶The sons of Gomer *were* Ashkenaz, Diphath,*ª* and Togarmah. ⁷The sons of Javan *were* Elishah, Tarshishah,*ª* Kittim, and Rodanim.*ᵇ*

⁸The sons of Ham *were* Cush, Mizraim, Put, and Canaan. ⁹The sons of Cush *were* Seba, Havilah, Sabta,*ª* Raama,*ᵇ* and Sabtecha. The sons of Raama *were* Sheba and Dedan. ¹⁰Cush begot Nimrod; he began to be a mighty one on the earth. ¹¹Mizraim begot Ludim, Anamim, Lehabim, Naphtuhim, ¹²Pathrusim, Casluhim (from whom came the Philistines and the Caphtorim). ¹³Canaan begot Sidon, his firstborn, and Heth; ¹⁴the Jebusite, the Amorite, and the Girgashite; ¹⁵the Hivite, the Arkite, and the Sinite; ¹⁶the Arvadite, the Zemarite, and the Hamathite.

¹⁷The sons of Shem *were* Elam, Asshur, Arphaxad, Lud, Aram, Uz, Hul, Gether, and Meshech.*ª* ¹⁸Arphaxad begot Shelah, and Shelah begot Eber. ¹⁹To Eber were born two sons: the name of one *was* Peleg,*ª* for in his days the earth was divided; and his brother's name *was* Joktan. ²⁰Joktan begot Almodad, Sheleph, Hazarmaveth, Jerah, ²¹Hadoram, Uzal, Diklah, ²²Ebal,*ª* Abimael, Sheba, ²³Ophir, Havilah, and Jobab. All these *were* the sons of Joktan.

1:19 days...divided. Peleg, which means "divided," lived when God scattered the human race because of Babel (see Gen. 11:1–9).

²⁴Shem, Arphaxad, Shelah, ²⁵Eber, Peleg, Reu, ²⁶Serug, Nahor, Terah, ²⁷and Abram, who *is* Abraham. ²⁸The sons of Abraham *were* Isaac and Ishmael.

The Family of Ishmael

²⁹These *are* their genealogies: The firstborn of Ishmael *was* Nebajoth; then Kedar, Adbeel, Mibsam, ³⁰Mishma, Dumah, Massa, Hadad,*ª* Tema, ³¹Jetur, Naphish, and Kedemah. These *were* the sons of Ishmael.

1:28–31 The 12 sons of Ishmael developed the 12 tribes that settled the northern desert of Arabia and became Arab peoples.

The Family of Keturah

³²Now the sons born to Keturah, Abraham's concubine, *were* Zimran, Jokshan, Medan, Midian, Ishbak, and Shuah. The sons of Jokshan *were* Sheba and Dedan. ³³The sons of Midian *were* Ephah, Epher, Hanoch, Abida, and Eldaah. All these were the children of Keturah.

The Family of Isaac

³⁴And Abraham begot Isaac. The sons of Isaac *were* Esau and Israel. ³⁵The sons of Esau *were* Eliphaz, Reuel, Jeush, Jaalam, and Korah. ³⁶And the sons of Eliphaz *were* Teman, Omar, Zephi,*ª* Gatam, *and* Kenaz; and *by* Timna,*ᵇ* Amalek. ³⁷The sons of Reuel *were* Nahath, Zerah, Shammah, and Mizzah.

The Family of Seir

³⁸The sons of Seir *were* Lotan, Shobal, Zibeon, Anah, Dishon, Ezer, and Dishan. ³⁹And the sons of Lotan *were* Hori and Homam; Lotan's sister *was* Timna. ⁴⁰The sons of Shobal *were* Alian,*ª* Manahath, Ebal, Shephi,*ᵇ* and Onam. The sons of Zibeon *were* Ajah and Anah. ⁴¹The son of Anah *was* Dishon. The sons of Dishon *were* Hamran,*ª* Eshban, Ithran, and Cheran. ⁴²The sons of Ezer *were* Bilhan, Zaavan,

and Jaakan.*ᵃ* The sons of Dishan *were* Uz and Aran.

The Kings of Edom

⁴³Now these *were* the kings who reigned in the land of Edom before a king reigned over the children of Israel: Bela the son of Beor, and the name of his city was Dinhabah. ⁴⁴And when Bela died, Jobab the son of Zerah of Bozrah reigned in his place. ⁴⁵When Jobab died, Husham of the land of the Temanites reigned in his place. ⁴⁶And when Husham died, Hadad the son of Bedad, who attacked Midian in the field of Moab, reigned in his place. The name of his city *was* Avith. ⁴⁷When Hadad died, Samlah of Masrekah reigned in his place. ⁴⁸And when Samlah died, Saul of Rehoboth-by-the-River reigned in his place. ⁴⁹When Saul died, Baal-Hanan the son of Achbor reigned in his place. ⁵⁰And when Baal-Hanan died, Hadad*ᵃ* reigned in his place; and the name of his city was Pai.*ᵇ* His wife's name was Mehetabel the daughter of Matred, the daughter of Mezahab. ⁵¹Hadad died also. And the chiefs of Edom were Chief Timnah, Chief Aliah,*ᵃ* Chief Jetheth, ⁵²Chief Aholibamah, Chief Elah, Chief Pinon, ⁵³Chief Kenaz, Chief Teman, Chief Mibzar, ⁵⁴Chief Magdiel, and Chief Iram. These *were* the chiefs of Edom.

The Family of Israel

2 These *were* the sons of Israel: Reuben, Simeon, Levi, Judah, Issachar, Zebulun, ²Dan, Joseph, Benjamin, Naphtali, Gad, and Asher.

From Judah to David

³The sons of Judah *were* Er, Onan, and Shelah. *These* three were born to him by the daughter of Shua, the Canaanitess. Er, the firstborn of Judah, was wicked in the sight of the LORD; so He killed him. ⁴And Tamar, his daughter-in-law, bore him Perez and Zerah. All the sons of Judah *were* five. ⁵The sons of Perez *were* Hezron and Hamul. ⁶The sons of Zerah *were* Zimri, Ethan, Heman, Calcol, and Dara—five of them in all.

⁷The son of Carmi *was* Achar,*ᵃ* the troubler of Israel, who transgressed in the accursed thing.

> **2:7 Achar.** Achar, also referred to as Achan (Joshua 7:1–26), disobeyed the Lord by stealing goods from the fallen Jericho.

⁸The son of Ethan *was* Azariah.

⁹Also the sons of Hezron who were born to him *were* Jerahmeel, Ram, and Chelubai.*ᵃ* ¹⁰Ram begot Amminadab, and Amminadab begot Nahshon, leader of the children of Judah; ¹¹Nahshon begot Salma,*ᵃ* and Salma begot Boaz; ¹²Boaz begot Obed, and Obed begot Jesse; ¹³Jesse begot Eliab his firstborn, Abinadab the second, Shimea*ᵃ* the third, ¹⁴Nethanel the fourth, Raddai the fifth, ¹⁵Ozem the sixth, *and* David the seventh.

¹⁶Now their sisters *were* Zeruiah and Abigail. And the sons of Zeruiah *were* Abishai, Joab, and Asahel—three. ¹⁷Abigail bore Amasa; and the father of Amasa *was* Jether the Ishmaelite.*ᵃ*

The Family of Hezron

¹⁸Caleb the son of Hezron had children by Azubah, *his* wife, and by Jerioth. Now these were her sons: Jesher, Shobab, and Ardon. ¹⁹When Azubah died, Caleb took Ephrath*ᵃ* as his wife, who bore him Hur. ²⁰And Hur begot Uri, and Uri begot Bezalel.

²¹Now afterward Hezron went in to the daughter of Machir the father of Gilead, whom he married when he *was* sixty years old; and she bore him Segub. ²²Segub begot Jair, who had twenty-three cities in the land of Gilead. ²³(Geshur and Syria took from them the towns of Jair, with Kenath and its towns—sixty towns.) All these *belonged to* the sons of Machir the father of Gilead. ²⁴After Hezron died in Caleb Ephrathah, Hezron's wife Abijah bore him Ashhur the father of Tekoa.

1:42 *ᵃ*Spelled *Akan* in Genesis 36:27   1:50 *ᵃ*Spelled *Hadar* in Genesis 36:39   *ᵇ*Spelled *Pau* in Genesis 36:39   1:51 *ᵃ*Spelled *Alvah* in Genesis 36:40   2:7 *ᵃ*Spelled *Achan* in Joshua 7:1 and elsewhere   2:9 *ᵃ*Spelled *Caleb* in 2:18, 42   2:11 *ᵃ*Spelled *Salmon* in Ruth 4:21 and Luke 3:32   2:13 *ᵃ*Spelled *Shammah* in 1 Samuel 16:9 and elsewhere   2:17 *ᵃ*Compare 2 Samuel 17:25   2:19 *ᵃ*Spelled *Ephrathah* elsewhere

The Family of Jerahmeel

²⁵The sons of Jerahmeel, the firstborn of Hezron, *were* Ram, the firstborn, and Bunah, Oren, Ozem, *and* Ahijah. ²⁶Jerahmeel had another wife, whose name was Atarah; she was the mother of Onam. ²⁷The sons of Ram, the firstborn of Jerahmeel, were Maaz, Jamin, and Eker. ²⁸The sons of Onam were Shammai and Jada. The sons of Shammai *were* Nadab and Abishur. ²⁹And the name of the wife of Abishur *was* Abihail, and she bore him Ahban and Molid. ³⁰The sons of Nadab *were* Seled and Appaim; Seled died without children. ³¹The son of Appaim *was* Ishi, the son of Ishi *was* Sheshan, and Sheshan's son *was* Ahlai. ³²The sons of Jada, the brother of Shammai, *were* Jether and Jonathan; Jether died without children. ³³The sons of Jonathan *were* Peleth and Zaza. These were the sons of Jerahmeel.

³⁴Now Sheshan had no sons, only daughters. And Sheshan had an Egyptian servant whose name *was* Jarha. ³⁵Sheshan gave his daughter to Jarha his servant as wife, and she bore him Attai. ³⁶Attai begot Nathan, and Nathan begot Zabad; ³⁷Zabad begot Ephlal, and Ephlal begot Obed; ³⁸Obed begot Jehu, and Jehu begot Azariah; ³⁹Azariah begot Helez, and Helez begot Eleasah; ⁴⁰Eleasah begot Sismai, and Sismai begot Shallum; ⁴¹Shallum begot Jekamiah, and Jekamiah begot Elishama.

The Family of Caleb

⁴²The descendants of Caleb the brother of Jerahmeel *were* Mesha, his firstborn, who was the father of Ziph, and the sons of Mareshah the father of Hebron. ⁴³The sons of Hebron *were* Korah, Tappuah, Rekem, and Shema. ⁴⁴Shema begot Raham the father of Jorkoam, and Rekem begot Shammai. ⁴⁵And the son of Shammai *was* Maon, and Maon *was* the father of Beth Zur.

⁴⁶Ephah, Caleb's concubine, bore Haran, Moza, and Gazez; and Haran begot Gazez. ⁴⁷And the sons of Jahdai *were* Regem, Jotham, Geshan, Pelet, Ephah, and Shaaph.

⁴⁸Maachah, Caleb's concubine, bore Sheber and Tirhanah. ⁴⁹She also bore Shaaph the father of Madmannah, Sheva the father of Machbenah and the father of Gibea. And the daughter of Caleb *was* Achsah.

⁵⁰These were the descendants of Caleb: The sons of Hur, the firstborn of Ephrathah, *were* Shobal the father of Kirjath Jearim, ⁵¹Salma the father of Bethlehem, *and* Hareph the father of Beth Gader.

⁵²And Shobal the father of Kirjath Jearim had descendants: Haroeh, *and* half of the *families* of Manuhoth.ᵃ ⁵³The families of Kirjath Jearim *were* the Ithrites, the Puthites, the Shumathites, and the Mishraites. From these came the Zorathites and the Eshtaolites.

⁵⁴The sons of Salma *were* Bethlehem, the Netophathites, Atroth Beth Joab, half of the Manahethites, and the Zorites.

⁵⁵And the families of the scribes who dwelt at Jabez *were* the Tirathites, the Shimeathites, *and* the Suchathites. These *were* the Kenites who came from Hammath, the father of the house of Rechab.

2:52 ᵃSame as *the Manahethites*, verse 54

A SHORT HARMONY OF SAMUEL, KINGS, AND CHRONICLES

1. Selected Genealogies	———	1 Chronicles 1–9
2. Samuel's Judgeship	1 Samuel 1–8	———
3. Saul's Reign	1 Samuel 9–31	1 Chronicles 10
4. David's Reign	2 Samuel 1–24	1 Chronicles 11–29
5. Solomon's Reign	1 Kings 1–11	2 Chronicles 1–9
6. Divided Kingdom Pt. 1 (to the Assyrian exile)	1 Kings 12–2 Kings 17	2 Chronicles 10–27
7. Divided Kingdom Pt. 2 (to the Babylonian exile)	2 Kings 18–25	2 Chronicles 28–36:21
8. Return from Babylon	———	2 Chronicles 36:22,23

The Family of David

3 Now these were the sons of David who were born to him in Hebron: The firstborn *was* Amnon, by Ahinoam the Jezreelitess; the second, Daniel,[a] by Abigail the Carmelitess; ²the third, Absalom the son of Maacah, the daughter of Talmai, king of Geshur; the fourth, Adonijah the son of Haggith; ³the fifth, Shephatiah, by Abital; the sixth, Ithream, by his wife Eglah.

3:1 David. These genealogies affirm the line of Christ from Adam (Luke 3:38) through Abraham and David (Matt. 1:1).

⁴*These* six were born to him in Hebron. There he reigned seven years and six months, and in Jerusalem he reigned thirty-three years. ⁵And these were born to him in Jerusalem: Shimea,[a] Shobab, Nathan, and Solomon—four by Bathshua[b] the daughter of Ammiel.[c] ⁶Also *there* were Ibhar, Elishama,[a] Eliphelet,[b] ⁷Nogah, Nepheg, Japhia, ⁸Elishama, Eliada,[a] and Eliphelet—nine *in all.* ⁹*These were* all the sons of David, besides the sons of the concubines, and Tamar their sister.

The Family of Solomon

¹⁰Solomon's son *was* Rehoboam; Abijah[a] *was* his son, Asa his son, Jehoshaphat his son, ¹¹Joram[a] his son, Ahaziah his son, Joash[b] his son, ¹²Amaziah his son, Azariah[a] his son, Jotham his son, ¹³Ahaz his son, Hezekiah his son, Manasseh his son, ¹⁴Amon his son, *and* Josiah his son. ¹⁵The sons of Josiah *were* Johanan the firstborn, the second Jehoiakim, the third Zedekiah, and the fourth Shallum.[a] ¹⁶The sons of Jehoiakim *were* Jeconiah his son *and* Zedekiah[a] his son.

The Family of Jeconiah

¹⁷And the sons of Jeconiah[a] *were* Assir,[b] Shealtiel his son, ¹⁸*and* Malchiram, Peda-

3:16 Jeconiah. God enforced the curse given by Jeremiah (Jer. 22:30) that Jeconiah would never have royal descendants in his line. Even though Jeconiah was in the messianic line, Christ was not a physical child of that line because of his virgin birth. Thus, Jesus had the right of kingship through the lineage of his earthly father Joseph, a descendant in the royal line of David. But his mother Mary was in David's line through his son Nathan, not Solomon (see Luke 3:31).

iah, Shenazzar, Jecamiah, Hoshama, and Nedabiah. ¹⁹The sons of Pedaiah *were* Zerubbabel and Shimei. The sons of Zerubbabel *were* Meshullam, Hananiah, Shelomith their sister, ²⁰and Hashubah, Ohel, Berechiah, Hasadiah, and Jushab-Hesed—five *in all.*

²¹The sons of Hananiah *were* Pelatiah and Jeshaiah, the sons of Rephaiah, the sons of Arnan, the sons of Obadiah, and the sons of Shechaniah. ²²The son of Shechaniah was Shemaiah. The sons of Shemaiah *were* Hattush, Igal, Bariah, Neariah, and Shaphat—six *in all.* ²³The sons of Neariah *were* Elioenai, Hezekiah, and Azrikam—three *in all.* ²⁴The sons of Elioenai *were* Hodaviah, Eliashib, Pelaiah, Akkub, Johanan, Delaiah, and Anani—seven *in all.*

The Family of Judah

4 The sons of Judah *were* Perez, Hezron, Carmi, Hur, and Shobal. ²And Reaiah the son of Shobal begot Jahath, and Jahath begot Ahumai and Lahad. These *were* the families of the Zorathites. ³These *were* the sons *of the father* of Etam: Jezreel, Ishma, and Idbash; and the name of their sister *was* Hazelelponi; ⁴and Penuel *was* the father of Gedor, and Ezer *was the* father of Hushah.

These *were* the sons of Hur, the firstborn of Ephrathah the father of Bethlehem.

⁵And Ashhur the father of Tekoa had two wives, Helah and Naarah. ⁶Naarah bore him Ahuzzam, Hepher, Temeni, and Haahashtari. These *were* the sons of Naarah.

3:1 ᵃCalled *Chileab* in 2 Samuel 3:3   3:5 ᵃSpelled *Shammua* in 14:4 and 2 Samuel 5:14   ᵇSpelled *Bathsheba* in 2 Samuel 11:3   ᶜCalled *Eliam* in 2 Samuel 11:3   3:6 ᵃSpelled *Elishua* in 14:5 and 2 Samuel 5:15   ᵇSpelled *Elpelet* in 14:5   3:8 ᵃSpelled *Beeliada* in 14:7   3:10 ᵃSpelled *Abijam* in 1 Kings 15:1   3:11 ᵃSpelled *Jehoram* in 2 Kings 1:17 and 8:16   ᵇSpelled *Jehoash* in 2 Kings 12:1   3:12 ᵃCalled *Uzziah* in Isaiah 6:1   3:15 ᵃCalled *Jehoahaz* in 2 Kings 23:31   3:16 ᵃCompare 2 Kings 24:17   3:17 ᵃAlso called *Coniah* in Jeremiah 22:24 and *Jehoiachin* in 2 Kings 24:8   ᵇOr *Jeconiah the captive were*

⁷The sons of Helah *were* Zereth, Zohar, and Ethnan; ⁸and Koz begot Anub, Zobebah, and the families of Aharhel the son of Harum.

⁹Now Jabez was more honorable than his brothers, and his mother called his name Jabez,*ᵃ* saying, "Because I bore *him* in pain." ¹⁰And Jabez called on the God of Israel saying, "Oh, that You would bless me indeed, and enlarge my territory, that Your hand would be with me, and that You would keep *me* from evil, that I may not cause pain!" So God granted him what he requested.

¹¹Chelub the brother of Shuhah begot Mehir, who *was* the father of Eshton. ¹²And Eshton begot Beth-Rapha, Paseah, and Tehinnah the father of Ir-Nahash. These *were* the men of Rechah.

¹³The sons of Kenaz *were* Othniel and Seraiah. The sons of Othniel *were* Hathath,*ᵃ* ¹⁴and Meonothai *who* begot Ophrah. Seraiah begot Joab the father of Ge Harashim,*ᵃ* for they were craftsmen. ¹⁵The sons of Caleb the son of Jephunneh *were* Iru, Elah, and Naam. The son of Elah *was* Kenaz. ¹⁶The sons of Jehallelel *were* Ziph, Ziphah, Tiria, and Asarel. ¹⁷The sons of Ezrah *were* Jether, Mered, Epher, and Jalon. And *Mered's wifeᵃ* bore Miriam, Shammai, and Ishbah the father of Eshtemoa. ¹⁸(His wife Jehudijahᵃ bore Jered the father of Gedor, Heber the father of Sochoh, and Jekuthiel the father of Zanoah.) And these were the sons of Bithiah the daughter of Pharaoh, whom Mered took.

¹⁹The sons of Hodiah's wife, the sister of Naham, *were* the fathers of Keilah the Garmite and of Eshtemoa the Maachathite. ²⁰And the sons of Shimon *were* Amnon, Rinnah, Ben-Hanan, and Tilon. And the sons of Ishi *were* Zoheth and Ben-Zoheth.

²¹The sons of Shelah the son of Judah *were* Er the father of Lecah, Laadah the father of Mareshah, and the families of the house of the linen workers of the house of Ashbea; ²²also Jokim, the men of Chozeba, and Joash; Saraph, who ruled in Moab, and Jashubi-Lehem. Now the records are an-

cient. ²³These *were* the potters and those who dwell at Netaimᵃ and Gederah;ᵇ there they dwelt with the king for his work.

The Family of Simeon

²⁴The sons of Simeon *were* Nemuel, Jamin, Jarib,*ᵃ* Zerah,*ᵇ and* Shaul, ²⁵Shallum his son, Mibsam his son, and Mishma his son. ²⁶And the sons of Mishma *were* Hamuel his son, Zacchur his son, and Shimei his son. ²⁷Shimei had sixteen sons and six daughters; but his brothers did not have many children, nor did any of their families multiply as much as the children of Judah.

²⁸They dwelt at Beersheba, Moladah, Hazar Shual, ²⁹Bilhah, Ezem, Tolad, ³⁰Bethuel, Hormah, Ziklag, ³¹Beth Marcaboth, Hazar Susim, Beth Biri, and at Shaaraim. These *were* their cities until the reign of David. ³²And their villages *were* Etam, Ain, Rimmon, Tochen, and Ashan—five cities— ³³and all the villages that *were* around these cities as far as Baal.*ᵃ* These *were* their dwelling places, and they maintained their genealogy: ³⁴Meshobab, Jamlech, and Joshah the son of Amaziah; ³⁵Joel, and Jehu the son of Joshibiah, the son of Seraiah, the son of Asiel; ³⁶Elioenai, Jaakobah, Jeshohaiah, Asaiah, Adiel, Jesimiel, and Benaiah; ³⁷Ziza the son of Shiphi, the son of Allon, the son of Jedaiah, the son of Shimri, the son of Shemaiah— ³⁸these mentioned by name *were* leaders in their families, and their father's house increased greatly.

³⁹So they went to the entrance of Gedor, as far as the east side of the valley, to seek pasture for their flocks. ⁴⁰And they found rich, good pasture, and the land *was* broad, quiet, and peaceful; for some Hamites formerly lived there.

⁴¹These recorded by name came in the days of Hezekiah king of Judah; and they attacked their tents and the Meunites who were found there, and utterly destroyed them, as it is to this day. So they dwelt in their place, because *there was* pasture for their flocks there. ⁴²Now *some* of them, five hundred men of the sons of Simeon, went

---

4:9 *ᵃLiterally He Will Cause Pain*   4:13 *ᵃSeptuagint and Vulgate add and Meonothai.*   4:14 *ᵃLiterally Valley of Craftsmen*   4:17 *ᵃLiterally she*   4:18 *ᵃOr His Judean wife*   4:23 *ᵃLiterally Plants*   *ᵇLiterally Hedges*   4:24 *ᵃCalled Jachin in Genesis 46:10*   *ᵇCalled Zohar in Genesis 46:10*   4:33 *ᵃOr Baalath Beer* (compare Joshua 19:8)

to Mount Seir, having as their captains Pel-atiah, Neariah, Rephaiah, and Uzziel, the sons of Ishi. [43]And they defeated the rest of the Amalekites who had escaped. They have dwelt there to this day.

The Family of Reuben

5 Now the sons of Reuben the firstborn of Israel—he *was* indeed the firstborn, but because he defiled his father's bed, his birthright was given to the sons of Joseph, the son of Israel, so that the genealogy is not listed according to the birthright; [2]yet Judah prevailed over his brothers, and from him *came* a ruler, although the birthright was Joseph's— [3]the sons of Reuben the firstborn of Israel were Hanoch, Pallu, Hezron, and Carmi.

> **5:2 Judah prevailed.** As a result of Jacob's blessing (Gen. 49:10), the king of Israel was to come from Judah, fulfilling the Davidic Covenant (see 2 Sam. 7).

[4]The sons of Joel *were* Shemaiah his son, Gog his son, Shimei his son, [5]Micah his son, Reaiah his son, Baal his son, [6]and Beerah his son, whom Tiglath-Pileser[a] king of Assyria carried into captivity. He *was* leader of the Reubenites. [7]And his brethren by their families, when the genealogy of their generations was registered: the chief, Jeiel, and Zechariah, [8]and Bela the son of Azaz, the son of Shema, the son of Joel, who dwelt in Aroer, as far as Nebo and Baal Meon. [9]Eastward they settled as far as the entrance of the wilderness this side of the River Euphrates, because their cattle had multiplied in the land of Gilead. [10]Now in the days of Saul they made war with the Hagrites, who fell by their hand; and they dwelt in their tents throughout the entire *area* east of Gilead.

The Family of Gad

[11]And the children of Gad dwelt next to them in the land of Bashan as far as Salcah: [12]Joel *was* the chief, Shapham the next, then Jaanai and Shaphat in Bashan, [13]and their brethren of their father's house: Michael, Meshullam, Sheba, Jorai, Jachan, Zia, and Eber—seven *in all*. [14]These *were* the children of Abihail the son of Huri, the son of Jaroah, the son of Gilead, the son of Michael, the son of Jeshishai, the son of Jahdo, the son of Buz; [15]Ahi the son of Abdiel, the son of Guni, *was* chief of their father's house. [16]And *the Gadites* dwelt in Gilead, in Bashan and in its villages, and in all the common-lands of Sharon within their borders. [17]All these were registered by genealogies in the days of Jotham king of Judah, and in the days of Jeroboam king of Israel.

[18]The sons of Reuben, the Gadites, and half the tribe of Manasseh *had* forty-four thousand seven hundred and sixty valiant men, men able to bear shield and sword, to shoot with the bow, and skillful in war, who went to war. [19]They made war with the Hagrites, Jetur, Naphish, and Nodab. [20]And they were helped against them, and the Hagrites were delivered into their hand, and all who *were* with them, for they cried out to God in the battle. He heeded their prayer, because they put their trust in Him. [21]Then they took away their livestock—fifty thousand of their camels, two hundred and fifty thousand of their sheep, and two thousand of their donkeys—also one hundred thousand of their men; [22]for many fell dead, because the war *was* God's. And they dwelt in their place until the captivity.

The Family of Manasseh (East)

[23]So the children of the half-tribe of Manasseh dwelt in the land. Their *numbers* increased from Bashan to Baal Hermon, that is, to Senir, or Mount Hermon. [24]These *were* the heads of their fathers' houses: Epher, Ishi, Eliel, Azriel, Jeremiah, Hodaviah, and Jahdiel. They were mighty men of valor, famous men, *and* heads of their fathers' houses. [25]And they were unfaithful to the God of their fathers, and played the harlot after the gods of the peoples of the land, whom God had destroyed before them. [26]So the God of Israel stirred up the spirit of Pul king of Assyria, that is, Tiglath-Pileser[a] king of Assyria. He carried the Reubenites, the Gadites, and the half-tribe of Manasseh into captivity. He took them to Halah, Habor, Hara, and the river of Gozan to this day.

5:6 [a]Hebrew *Tilgath-Pilneser*   5:26 [a]Hebrew *Tilgath-Pilneser*

The Family of Levi

6 The sons of Levi were Gershon, Kohath, and Merari. ²The sons of Kohath were Amram, Izhar, Hebron, and Uzziel. ³The children of Amram were Aaron, Moses, and Miriam. And the sons of Aaron were Nadab, Abihu, Eleazar, and Ithamar. ⁴Eleazar begot Phinehas, and Phinehas begot Abishua; ⁵Abishua begot Bukki, and Bukki begot Uzzi; ⁶Uzzi begot Zerahiah, and Zerahiah begot Meraioth; ⁷Meraioth begot Amariah, and Amariah begot Ahitub; ⁸Ahitub begot Zadok, and Zadok begot Ahimaaz; ⁹Ahimaaz begot Azariah, and Azariah begot Johanan; ¹⁰Johanan begot Azariah (it was he who ministered as priest in the temple that Solomon built in Jerusalem); ¹¹Azariah begot Amariah, and Amariah begot Ahitub; ¹²Ahitub begot Zadok, and Zadok begot Shallum; ¹³Shallum begot Hilkiah, and Hilkiah begot Azariah; ¹⁴Azariah begot Seraiah, and Seraiah begot Jehozadak. ¹⁵Jehozadak went into captivity when the LORD carried Judah and Jerusalem into captivity by the hand of Nebuchadnezzar.

6:1–15 This section lists the lineage of the High-Priests, including Levi, Aaron, Eleazar and Phinehas, with whom God made a covenant for a perpetual priesthood (Num. 25:11–13).

¹⁶The sons of Levi were Gershon,ᵃ Kohath, and Merari. ¹⁷These are the names of the sons of Gershon: Libni and Shimei. ¹⁸The sons of Kohath were Amram, Izhar, Hebron, and Uzziel. ¹⁹The sons of Merari were Mahli and Mushi. Now these are the families of the Levites according to their fathers: ²⁰Of Gershon were Libni his son, Jahath his son, Zimmah his son, ²¹Joah his son, Iddo his son, Zerah his son, and Jeatherai his son. ²²The sons of Kohath were Amminadab his son, Korah his son, Assir his son, ²³Elkanah his son, Ebiasaph his son, Assir his son, ²⁴Tahath his son, Uriel his son, Uzziah his son, and Shaul his son. ²⁵The sons of Elkanah were Amasai and Ahimoth. ²⁶As for Elkanah,ᵃ the sons of Elkanah were Zophaiᵇ his son, Nahathᶜ his son, ²⁷Eliabᵃ his son, Jeroham his son, and Elkanah his son. ²⁸The sons of Samuel were Joelᵃ the firstborn, and Abijah the second.ᵇ ²⁹The sons of Merari were Mahli, Libni his son, Shimei his son, Uzzah his son, ³⁰Shimea his son, Haggiah his son, and Asaiah his son.

6:28 Samuel's name in the line of Levi validates his acceptance into the priesthood (see 1 Sam. 1:24–28).

Musicians in the House of the LORD

³¹Now these are the men whom David appointed over the service of song in the house of the LORD, after the ark came to rest. ³²They were ministering with music before the dwelling place of the tabernacle of meeting, until Solomon had built the house of the LORD in Jerusalem, and they served in their office according to their order.

³³And these are the ones who ministered with their sons: Of the sons of the Kohathites were Heman the singer, the son of Joel, the son of Samuel, ³⁴the son of Elkanah, the son of Jeroham, the son of Eliel,ᵃ the son of Toah,ᵇ ³⁵the son of Zuph, the son of Elkanah, the son of Mahath, the son of Amasai, ³⁶the son of Elkanah, the son of Joel, the son of Azariah, the son of Zephaniah, ³⁷the son of Tahath, the son of Assir, the son of Ebiasaph, the son of Korah, ³⁸the son of Izhar, the son of Kohath, the son of Levi, the son of Israel. ³⁹And his brother Asaph, who stood at his right hand, was Asaph the son of Berachiah, the son of Shimea, ⁴⁰the son of Michael, the son of Baaseiah, the son of Malchijah, ⁴¹the son of Ethni, the son of Zerah, the son of Adaiah, ⁴²the son of Ethan, the son of Zimmah, the son of Shimei, ⁴³the son of Jahath, the son of Gershon, the son of Levi.

⁴⁴Their brethren, the sons of Merari, on the left hand, were Ethan the son of Kishi, the son of Abdi, the son of Malluch, ⁴⁵the son of Hashabiah, the son of Amaziah, the son of Hilkiah, ⁴⁶the son of Amzi, the son of Bani, the son of Shamer, ⁴⁷the son of Mahli, the son of Mushi, the son of Merari, the son of Levi.

6:16 ᵃHebrew Gershom (alternate spelling of Gershon, as in verses 1,17,20,43,62, and 71)
6:26 ᵃCompare verse 35   ᵇSpelled Zuph in verse 35 and 1 Samuel 1:1   ᶜCompare verse 34
6:27 ᵃCompare verse 34   6:28 ᵃFollowing Septuagint, Syriac, and Arabic (compare verse 33 and 1 Samuel 8:2)   ᵇHebrew Vasheni   6:34 ᵃSpelled Elihu in 1 Samuel 1:1   ᵇSpelled Tohu in 1 Samuel 1:1

⁴⁸And their brethren, the Levites, *were* appointed to every kind of service of the tabernacle of the house of God.

6:31–48 The Levitical musicians are listed as they related to the following people: (1) Kohath and Heman; (2) Gershon and Asaph; and (3) Merari and Ethan.

The Family of Aaron

⁴⁹But Aaron and his sons offered sacrifices on the altar of burnt offering and on the altar of incense, for all the work of the Most Holy *Place*, and to make atonement for Israel, according to all that Moses the servant of God had commanded. ⁵⁰Now these *are* the sons of Aaron: Eleazar his son, Phinehas his son, Abishua his son, ⁵¹Bukki his son, Uzzi his son, Zerahiah his son, ⁵²Meraioth his son, Amariah his son, Ahitub his son, ⁵³Zadok his son, *and* Ahimaaz his son.

Dwelling Places of the Levites

⁵⁴Now these *are* their dwelling places throughout their settlements in their territory, for they were *given* by lot to the sons of Aaron, of the family of the Kohathites: ⁵⁵They gave them Hebron in the land of Judah, with its surrounding common-lands. ⁵⁶But the fields of the city and its villages they gave to Caleb the son of Jephunneh. ⁵⁷And to the sons of Aaron they gave *one of* the cities of refuge, Hebron; also Libnah with its common-lands, Jattir, Eshtemoa with its common-lands, ⁵⁸Hilen*ᵃ* with its common-lands, Debir with its common-lands, ⁵⁹Ashan*ᵃ* with its common-lands, and Beth Shemesh with its common-lands. ⁶⁰And from the tribe of Benjamin: Geba with its common-lands, Alemeth*ᵃ* with its common-lands, and Anathoth with its common-lands. All their cities among their families *were* thirteen.

⁶¹To the rest of the family of the tribe of the Kohathites *they gave* by lot ten cities from half the tribe of Manasseh. ⁶²And to the sons of Gershon, throughout their families, *they gave* thirteen cities from the tribe of Issachar, from the tribe of Asher, from the tribe of Naphtali, and from the tribe of Manasseh in Bashan. ⁶³To the sons of Merari, throughout their families, *they gave* twelve cities from the tribe of Reuben, from the tribe of Gad, and from the tribe of Zebulun. ⁶⁴So the children of Israel gave *these* cities with their common-lands to the Levites. ⁶⁵And they gave by lot from the tribe of the children of Judah, from the tribe of the children of Simeon, and from the tribe of the children of Benjamin these cities which are called by *their* names.

⁶⁶Now some of the families of the sons of Kohath *were given* cities as their territory from the tribe of Ephraim. ⁶⁷And they gave them *one of* the cities of refuge, Shechem with its common-lands, in the mountains of Ephraim, also Gezer with its common-lands, ⁶⁸Jokmeam with its common-lands, Beth Horon with its common-lands, ⁶⁹Aijalon with its common-lands, and Gath Rimmon with its common-lands. ⁷⁰And from the half-tribe of Manasseh: Aner with its common-lands and Bileam with its common-lands, for the rest of the family of the sons of Kohath.

⁷¹From the family of the half-tribe of Manasseh the sons of Gershon *were given* Golan in Bashan with its common-lands and Ashtaroth with its common-lands. ⁷²And from the tribe of Issachar: Kedesh with its common-lands, Daberath with its common-lands, ⁷³Ramoth with its common-lands, and Anem with its common-lands. ⁷⁴And from the tribe of Asher: Mashal with its common-lands, Abdon with its common-lands, ⁷⁵Hukok with its common-lands, and Rehob with its common-lands. ⁷⁶And from the tribe of Naphtali: Kedesh in Galilee with its common-lands, Hammon with its common-lands, and Kirjathaim with its common-lands.

⁷⁷From the tribe of Zebulun the rest of the children of Merari *were given* Rimmon*ᵃ* with its common-lands and Tabor with its common-lands. ⁷⁸And on the other side of the Jordan, across from Jericho, on the east side of the Jordan, *they were given* from the tribe of Reuben: Bezer in the wilderness with its common-lands, Jahzah with its common-lands, ⁷⁹Kedemoth with

---

6:58 *ᵃ*Spelled *Holon* in Joshua 21:15   6:59 *ᵃ*Spelled *Ain* in Joshua 21:16   6:60 *ᵃ*Spelled *Almon* in Joshua 21:18   6:77 *ᵃ*Hebrew *Rimmono*, alternate spelling of *Rimmon*; see 4:32

its common-lands, and Mephaath with its common-lands. ⁸⁰And from the tribe of Gad: Ramoth in Gilead with its common-lands, Mahanaim with its common-lands, ⁸¹Heshbon with its common-lands, and Jazer with its common-lands.

> **6:54–81** This section reviews the 48 cities that were given to the Levites instead of a section of land (see Num. 35:1–8; Josh. 21:1–42). God clearly intended for the Jewish nation to have a priesthood and to live in the land first given to Abraham (see Gen. 12:1–3).

The Family of Issachar

7 The sons of Issachar *were* Tola, Puah,*ᵃ* Jashub, and Shimron—four *in all*. ²The sons of Tola *were* Uzzi, Rephaiah, Jeriel, Jahmai, Jibsam, and Shemuel, heads of their father's house. *The sons* of Tola *were* mighty men of valor in their generations; their number in the days of David *was* twenty-two thousand six hundred. ³The son of Uzzi *was* Izrahiah, and the sons of Izrahiah *were* Michael, Obadiah, Joel, and Ishiah. All five of them *were* chief men. ⁴And with them, by their generations, according to their fathers' houses, *were* thirty-six thousand troops ready for war; for they had many wives and sons.

⁵Now their brethren among all the families of Issachar *were* mighty men of valor, listed by their genealogies, eighty-seven thousand in all.

The Family of Benjamin

⁶*The sons* of Benjamin *were* Bela, Becher, and Jediael—three *in all*. ⁷The sons of Bela *were* Ezbon, Uzzi, Uzziel, Jerimoth, and Iri—five *in all*. They *were* heads of *their* fathers' houses, and they were listed by their genealogies, twenty-two thousand and thirty-four mighty men of valor.

⁸The sons of Becher *were* Zemirah, Joash, Eliezer, Elioenai, Omri, Jerimoth, Abijah, Anathoth, and Alemeth. All these *are* the sons of Becher. ⁹And they were recorded by genealogy according to their generations, heads of their fathers' houses, twenty thousand two hundred mighty men of valor.

¹⁰The son of Jediael *was* Bilhan, and the sons of Bilhan *were* Jeush, Benjamin, Ehud, Chenaanah, Zethan, Tharshish, and Ahishahar. ¹¹All these sons of Jediael *were* heads of their fathers' houses; *there were* seventeen thousand two hundred mighty men of valor fit to go out for war *and* battle. ¹²Shuppim and Huppim*ᵃ were* the sons of Ir, *and* Hushim *was* the son of Aher.

The Family of Naphtali

¹³The sons of Naphtali *were* Jahziel,*ᵃ* Guni, Jezer, and Shallum,*ᵇ* the sons of Bilhah.

The Family of Manasseh (West)

¹⁴The descendants of Manasseh: his Syrian concubine bore him Machir the father of Gilead, the father of Asriel.*ᵃ* ¹⁵Machir took as his wife *the sister* of Huppim and Shuppim,*ᵃ* whose name *was* Maachah. The name of *Gilead's* grandson*ᵇ was* Zelophehad,*ᶜ* but Zelophehad begot only daughters. ¹⁶(Maachah the wife of Machir bore a son, and she called his name Peresh. The name of his brother *was* Sheresh, and his sons *were* Ulam and Rakem. ¹⁷The son of Ulam *was* Bedan.) These *were* the descendants of Gilead the son of Machir, the son of Manasseh.

¹⁸His sister Hammoleketh bore Ishhod, Abiezer, and Mahlah.

¹⁹And the sons of Shemida were Ahian, Shechem, Likhi, and Aniam.

The Family of Ephraim

²⁰The sons of Ephraim *were* Shuthelah, Bered his son, Tahath his son, Eladah his son, Tahath his son, ²¹Zabad his son, Shuthelah his son, and Ezer and Elead. The men of Gath who were born in *that* land killed *them* because they came down to take away their cattle. ²²Then Ephraim their father mourned many days, and his brethren came to comfort him.

²³And when he went in to his wife, she conceived and bore a son; and he called his name Beriah,*ᵃ* because tragedy had come

---

7:1 *ᵃ*Spelled *Puvah* in Genesis 46:13   7:12 *ᵃ*Called *Hupham* in Numbers 26:39   7:13 *ᵃ*Spelled *Jahzeel* in Genesis 46:24   *ᵇ*Spelled *Shillem* in Genesis 46:24   7:14 *ᵃ*The son of Gilead (compare Numbers 26:30,31)   7:15 *ᵃ*Compare verse 12   *ᵇ*Literally *the second*   *ᶜ*Compare Numbers 26:30–33   7:23 *ᵃ*Literally *In Tragedy*

upon his house. [24]Now his daughter *was* Sheerah, who built Lower and Upper Beth Horon and Uzzen Sheerah; [25]and Rephah *was* his son, *as well* as Resheph, and Telah his son, Tahan his son, [26]Laadan his son, Ammihud his son, Elishama his son, [27]Nun[a] his son, and Joshua his son.

[28]Now their possessions and dwelling places *were* Bethel and its towns: to the east Naaran, to the west Gezer and its towns, and Shechem and its towns, as far as Ayyah[a] and its towns; [29]and by the borders of the children of Manasseh *were* Beth Shean and its towns, Taanach and its towns, Megiddo and its towns, Dor and its towns. In these dwelt the children of Joseph, the son of Israel.

The Family of Asher

[30]The sons of Asher *were* Imnah, Ishvah, Ishvi, Beriah, and their sister Serah. [31]The sons of Beriah *were* Heber and Malchiel, who was the father of Birzaith.[a] [32]And Heber begot Japhlet, Shomer,[a] Hotham,[b] and their sister Shua. [33]The sons of Japhlet *were* Pasach, Bimhal, and Ashvath. These *were* the children of Japhlet. [34]The sons of Shemer *were* Ahi, Rohgah, Jehubbah, and Aram. [35]And the sons of his brother Helem *were* Zophah, Imna, Shelesh, and Amal. [36]The sons of Zophah *were* Suah, Harnepher, Shual, Beri, Imrah, [37]Bezer, Hod, Shamma, Shilshah, Jithran,[a] and Beera. [38]The sons of Jether *were* Jephunneh, Pispah, and Ara. [39]The sons of Ulla *were* Arah, Haniel, and Rizia.

[40]All these *were* the children of Asher, heads of *their* fathers' houses, choice men, mighty men of valor, chief leaders. And they were recorded by genealogies among the army fit for battle; their number *was* twenty-six thousand.

The Family Tree of King Saul of Benjamin

8 Now Benjamin begot Bela his firstborn, Ashbel the second, Aharah[a] the third, [2]Nohah the fourth, and Rapha the fifth. [3]The sons of Bela *were* Addar,[a] Gera, Abihud, [4]Abishua, Naaman, Ahoah, [5]Gera, Shephuphan, and Huram.

8:1–40 The tribe of Benjamin had an important relationship with Judah in the southern kingdom. These two tribes, taken in captivity together, and the Levites made up the returning remnant in 538 B.C.

[6]These *are* the sons of Ehud, who were the heads of the fathers' *houses* of the inhabitants of Geba, and who forced them to move to Manahath: [7]Naaman, Ahijah, and Gera who forced them to move. He begot Uzza and Ahihud.

[8]Also Shaharaim had children in the country of Moab, after he had sent away Hushim and Baara his wives. [9]By Hodesh his wife he begot Jobab, Zibia, Mesha, Malcam, [10]Jeuz, Sachiah, and Mirmah. These *were* his sons, heads of their fathers' *houses*.

[11]And by Hushim he begot Abitub and Elpaal. [12]The sons of Elpaal *were* Eber, Misham, and Shemed, who built Ono and Lod with its towns; [13]and Beriah and Shema, who *were* heads of their fathers' *houses* of the inhabitants of Aijalon, who drove out the inhabitants of Gath. [14]Ahio, Shashak, Jeremoth, [15]Zebadiah, Arad, Eder, [16]Michael, Ispah, and Joha *were* the sons of Beriah. [17]Zebadiah, Meshullam, Hizki, Heber, [18]Ishmerai, Jizliah, and Jobab *were* the sons of Elpaal. [19]Jakim, Zichri, Zabdi, [20]Elienai, Zillethai, Eliel, [21]Adaiah, Beraiah, and Shimrath *were* the sons of Shimei. [22]Ishpan, Eber, Eliel, [23]Abdon, Zichri, Hanan, [24]Hananiah, Elam, Antothijah, [25]Iphdeiah, and Penuel *were* the sons of Shashak. [26]Shamsherai, Shehariah, Athaliah, [27]Jaareshiah, Elijah, and Zichri *were* the sons of Jeroham.

[28]These *were* heads of the fathers' *houses* by their generations, chief men. These dwelt in Jerusalem.

[29]Now the father of Gibeon, whose wife's name *was* Maacah, dwelt at Gibeon. [30]And his firstborn son *was* Abdon, then Zur, Kish, Baal, Nadab, [31]Gedor, Ahio, Zecher, [32]and Mikloth, *who* begot Shimeah.[a] They

---

7:27 [a]Hebrew *Non*   7:28 [a]Many Hebrew manuscripts, Bomberg, Septuagint, Targum, and Vulgate read *Gazza*.   7:31 [a]Or *Birzavith* or *Birzoth*   7:32 [a]Spelled *Shemer* in verse 34   [b]Spelled *Helem* in verse 35   7:37 [a]Spelled *Jether* in verse 38   8:1 [a]Spelled *Ahiram* in Numbers 26:38   8:3 [a]Called *Ard* in Numbers 26:40   8:32 [a]Spelled *Shimeam* in 9:38

also dwelt alongside their relatives in Jerusalem, with their brethren. [33]Ner[a] begot Kish, Kish begot Saul, and Saul begot Jonathan, Malchishua, Abinadab,[b] and Esh-Baal.[c] [34]The son of Jonathan *was* Merib-Baal,[a] and Merib-Baal begot Micah. [35]The sons of Micah *were* Pithon, Melech, Tarea, and Ahaz. [36]And Ahaz begot Jehoaddah;[a] Jehoaddah begot Alemeth, Azmaveth, and Zimri; and Zimri begot Moza. [37]Moza begot Binea, Raphah[a] his son, Eleasah his son, *and* Azel his son.

[38]Azel had six sons whose names *were* these: Azrikam, Bocheru, Ishmael, Sheariah, Obadiah, and Hanan. All these *were* the sons of Azel. [39]And the sons of Eshek his brother *were* Ulam his firstborn,

Jeush the second, and Eliphelet the third.

[40]The sons of Ulam were mighty men of valor—archers. *They* had many sons and grandsons, one hundred and fifty *in all*. These *were* all sons of Benjamin.

9 So all Israel was recorded by genealogies, and indeed, they *were* inscribed in the book of the kings of Israel. But Judah was carried away captive to Babylon because of their unfaithfulness. [2]And the first inhabitants who *dwelt* in their possessions

---

9:1 all Israel. Many from the 10 tribes of the northern kingdom of Israel migrated south after the division in 931 B.C. Therefore Judah, the southern kingdom, had people from all tribes, "all Israel."

8:33 [a]Also the son of Gibeon (compare 9:36,39) [b]Called *Jishui* in 1 Samuel 14:49 [c]Called *Ishbosheth* in 2 Samuel 2:8 and elsewhere 8:34 [a]Called *Mephibosheth* in 2 Samuel 4:4 8:36 [a]Spelled *Jarah* in 9:42 8:37 [a]Spelled *Rephaiah* in 9:43

THE CHRONICLES' SOURCES

The inspiration of Scripture (2 Timothy 3:16) was sometimes accomplished through direct revelation from God without a human writer, e.g., the Mosaic law. At other times, God used human sources, as mentioned in Luke 1:1–4. Such was the experience of the chronicler as evidenced by the many contributing sources. Whether the material came through direct revelation or by existing resources, God's inspiration through the Holy Spirit prevented the original human authors of Scripture from any error (2 Peter 1:19–21). Although relatively few scribal errors have been made in copying Scripture, they can be identified and corrected. Thus, the original, inerrant content of the Bible has been preserved.

1. Book of the Kings of Israel/Judah (1 Chronicles 9:1; 2 Chronicles 16:11; 20:34; 25:26; 27:7; 28:26; 32:32; 35:27; 36:8)
2. The Chronicles of David (1 Chronicles 27:24)
3. Book of Samuel (1 Chronicles 29:29)
4. Book of Nathan (1 Chronicles 29:29; 2 Chronicles 9:29)
5. Book of Gad (1 Chronicles 29:29)
6. Prophecy of Ahijah the Shilonite (2 Chronicles 9:29)
7. Visions of Iddo (2 Chronicles 9:29)
8. Records of Shemaiah (2 Chronicles 12:15)
9. Records of Iddo (2 Chronicles 12:15)
10. Annals of Iddo (2 Chronicles 13:22)
11. Annals of Jehu (2 Chronicles 20:34)
12. Commentary on the Book of the Kings (2 Chronicles 24:27)
13. Acts of Uzziah by Isaiah (2 Chronicles 26:22)
14. Letters/Message of Sennacherib (2 Chronicles 32:10–17)
15. Vision of Isaiah (2 Chronicles 32:32)
16. Words of the Seers (2 Chronicles 33:18)
17. Sayings of Hozai (2 Chronicles 33:19)
18. Written instructions of David and Solomon (2 Chronicles 35:4)
19. The Laments (2 Chronicles 35:25)

in their cities *were* Israelites, priests, Levites, and the Nethinim.

Dwellers in Jerusalem

³Now in Jerusalem the children of Judah dwelt, and some of the children of Benjamin, and of the children of Ephraim and Manasseh: ⁴Uthai the son of Ammihud, the son of Omri, the son of Imri, the son of Bani, of the descendants of Perez, the son of Judah. ⁵Of the Shilonites: Asaiah the firstborn and his sons. ⁶Of the sons of Zerah: Jeuel, and their brethren—six hundred and ninety. ⁷Of the sons of Benjamin: Sallu the son of Meshullam, the son of Hodaviah, the son of Hassenuah; ⁸Ibneiah the son of Jeroham; Elah the son of Uzzi, the son of Michri; Meshullam the son of Shephatiah, the son of Reuel, the son of Ibnijah; ⁹and their brethren, according to their generations—nine hundred and fifty-six. All these men *were* heads of a father's *house* in their fathers' houses.

The Priests at Jerusalem

¹⁰Of the priests: Jedaiah, Jehoiarib, and Jachin; ¹¹Azariah the son of Hilkiah, the son of Meshullam, the son of Zadok, the son of Meraioth, the son of Ahitub, the officer over the house of God; ¹²Adaiah the son of Jeroham, the son of Pashur, the son of Malchijah; Maasai the son of Adiel, the son of Jahzerah, the son of Meshullam, the son of Meshillemith, the son of Immer; ¹³and their brethren, heads of their fathers' houses—one thousand seven hundred and sixty. *They were* very able men for the work of the service of the house of God.

The Levites at Jerusalem

¹⁴Of the Levites: Shemaiah the son of Hasshub, the son of Azrikam, the son of Hashabiah, of the sons of Merari; ¹⁵Bakbakkar, Heresh, Galal, and Mattaniah the son of Micah, the son of Zichri, the son of Asaph; ¹⁶Obadiah the son of Shemaiah, the son of Galal, the son of Jeduthun; and Berechiah the son of Asa, the son of Elkanah, who lived in the villages of the Netophathites.

The Levite Gatekeepers

¹⁷And the gatekeepers *were* Shallum, Akkub, Talmon, Ahiman, and their brethren. Shallum *was* the chief. ¹⁸Until then *they had been* gatekeepers for the camps of the children of Levi at the King's Gate on the east.

¹⁹Shallum the son of Kore, the son of Ebiasaph, the son of Korah, and his brethren, from his father's house, the Korahites, *were* in charge of the work of the service, gatekeepers of the tabernacle. Their fathers had been keepers of the entrance to the camp of the LORD. ²⁰And Phinehas the son of Eleazar had been the officer over them in time past; the LORD *was* with him. ²¹Zechariah the son of Meshelemiah *was* keeper of the door of the tabernacle of meeting.

²²All those chosen as gatekeepers *were* two hundred and twelve. They were recorded by their genealogy, in their villages. David and Samuel the seer had appointed them to their trusted office. ²³So they and their children *were* in charge of the gates of the house of the LORD, the house of the tabernacle, by assignment. ²⁴The gatekeepers were assigned to the four directions: the east, west, north, and south. ²⁵And their brethren in their villages *had* to come with them from time to time for seven days. ²⁶For in this trusted office *were* four chief gatekeepers; they were Levites. And they had charge over the chambers and treasuries of the house of God. ²⁷And they lodged *all* around the house of God because they *had* the responsibility, and they *were* in charge of opening *it* every morning.

Other Levite Responsibilities

²⁸Now *some* of them were in charge of the serving vessels, for they brought them in and took them out by count. ²⁹*Some* of them *were* appointed over the furnishings and over all the implements of the sanctuary, and over the fine flour and the wine and the oil and the incense and the spices. ³⁰And *some* of the sons of the priests made the ointment of the spices.

³¹Mattithiah of the Levites, the firstborn of Shallum the Korahite, had the trusted office over the things that were baked in the pans. ³²And some of their brethren of the sons of the Kohathites *were* in charge of preparing the showbread for every Sabbath.

³³These are the singers, heads of the fathers' *houses* of the Levites, *who lodged* in the chambers, *and were* free *from other du-*

ties; for they were employed in *that* work day and night. ³⁴These heads of the fathers' *houses* of the Levites *were* heads throughout their generations. They dwelt at Jerusalem.

The Family of King Saul

³⁵Jeiel the father of Gibeon, whose wife's name *was* Maacah, dwelt at Gibeon. ³⁶His firstborn son *was* Abdon, then Zur, Kish, Baal, Ner, Nadab, ³⁷Gedor, Ahio, Zechariah,ª and Mikloth. ³⁸And Mikloth begot Shimeam.ª They also dwelt alongside their relatives in Jerusalem, with their brethren. ³⁹Ner begot Kish, Kish begot Saul, and Saul begot Jonathan, Malchishua, Abinadab, and Esh-Baal. ⁴⁰The son of Jonathan *was* Merib-Baal, and Merib-Baal begot Micah. ⁴¹The sons of Micah *were* Pithon, Melech, Tahrea,ª and Ahaz.ᵇ ⁴²And Ahaz begot Jarah;ª Jarah begot Alemeth, Azmaveth, and Zimri; and Zimri begot Moza; ⁴³Moza begot Binea, Rephaiahª his son, Eleasah his son, and Azel his son.

⁴⁴And Azel had six sons whose names *were* these: Azrikam, Bocheru, Ishmael, Sheariah, Obadiah, and Hanan; these *were* the sons of Azel.

9:35–44 This section records Saul's lineage as a transition to the kingship of David.

Tragic End of Saul and His Sons

10 Now the Philistines fought against Israel; and the men of Israel fled from before the Philistines, and fell slain on Mount Gilboa. ²Then the Philistines followed hard after Saul and his sons. And the Philistines killed Jonathan, Abinadab, and Malchishua, Saul's sons. ³The battle became fierce against Saul. The archers hit him, and he was wounded by the archers. ⁴Then Saul said to his armorbearer, "Draw your sword, and thrust me through with it, lest these uncircumcised men come and abuse me." But his armorbearer would not, for he was greatly afraid. Therefore Saul took a sword and fell on it. ⁵And when his armorbearer saw that Saul was dead, he also fell on his sword and died. ⁶So Saul and

his three sons died, and all his house died together. ⁷And when all the men of Israel who *were* in the valley saw that they had fled and that Saul and his sons were dead, they forsook their cities and fled; then the Philistines came and dwelt in them.

⁸So it happened the next day, when the Philistines came to strip the slain, that they found Saul and his sons fallen on Mount Gilboa. ⁹And they stripped him and took his head and his armor, and sent word *throughout* the land of the Philistines to proclaim the news *in the temple* of their idols and among the people. ¹⁰Then they put his armor in the temple of their gods, and fastened his head in the temple of Dagon.

¹¹And when all Jabesh Gilead heard all that the Philistines had done to Saul, ¹²all the valiant men arose and took the body of Saul and the bodies of his sons; and they brought them to Jabesh, and buried their bones under the tamarisk tree at Jabesh, and fasted seven days.

¹³So Saul died for his unfaithfulness which he had committed against the LORD, because he did not keep the word of the LORD, and also because he consulted a medium for guidance. ¹⁴But *he* did not inquire of the LORD; therefore He killed him, and turned the kingdom over to David the son of Jesse.

10:14 He killed him. Though Saul killed himself, it was God's judgment on him for consulting a medium, an act punishable by death (see Deut. 17:1–6).

David Made King over All Israel

11 Then all Israel came together to David at Hebron, saying, "Indeed we *are* your bone and your flesh. ²Also, in time past, even when Saul was king, you *were* the one who led Israel out and brought them in; and the LORD your God said to you, 'You shall shepherd My people Israel, and be ruler over My people Israel.'" ³Therefore all the elders of Israel came to the king at Hebron, and David made a covenant with them at Hebron before the LORD. And they anointed David king over

---

9:37 ªCalled *Zecher* in 8:31   **9:38** ªSpelled *Shimeah* in 8:32   **9:41** ªSpelled *Tarea* in 8:35   ᵇFollowing Arabic, Syriac, Targum, and Vulgate (compare 8:35); Masoretic Text and Septuagint omit *and Ahaz*.
9:42 ªSpelled *Jehoaddah* in 8:36   **9:43** ªSpelled *Raphah* in 8:37

Israel, according to the word of the LORD by Samuel.

The City of David

⁴And David and all Israel went to Jerusalem, which is Jebus, where the Jebusites *were*, the inhabitants of the land. ⁵But the inhabitants of Jebus said to David, "You shall not come in here!" Nevertheless David took the stronghold of Zion (that is, the City of David). ⁶Now David said, "Whoever attacks the Jebusites first shall be chief and captain." And Joab the son of Zeruiah went up first, and became chief. ⁷Then David dwelt in the stronghold; therefore they called it the City of David. ⁸And he built the city around it, from the Millo*ᵃ* to the surrounding area. Joab repaired the rest of the city. ⁹So David went on and became great, and the LORD of hosts *was* with him.

> **11:1–29:30** This section recounts the reign of David. It emphasizes the placement of the ark in Jerusalem and the preparations to build the temple.

The Mighty Men of David

¹⁰Now these *were* the heads of the mighty men whom David had, who strengthened themselves with him in his kingdom, with all Israel, to make him king, according to the word of the LORD concerning Israel.

¹¹And this *is* the number of the mighty men whom David had: Jashobeam the son of a Hachmonite, chief of the captains;*ᵃ* he had lifted up his spear against three hundred, killed *by him* at one time.

¹²After him *was* Eleazar the son of Dodo, the Ahohite, who *was one* of the three mighty men. ¹³He was with David at Pasdammim. Now there the Philistines were gathered for battle, and there was a piece of ground full of barley. So the people fled from the Philistines. ¹⁴But they stationed themselves in the middle of *that* field, defended it, and killed the Philistines. So the LORD brought about a great victory.

¹⁵Now three of the thirty chief men went down to the rock to David, into the cave of Adullam; and the army of the Philistines encamped in the Valley of Rephaim. ¹⁶David *was* then in the stronghold, and the garrison of the Philistines *was* then in Bethlehem. ¹⁷And David said with longing, "Oh, that someone would give me a drink of water from the well of Bethlehem, which is by the gate!" ¹⁸So the three broke through the camp of the Philistines, drew water from the well of Bethlehem that *was* by the gate, and took *it* and brought *it* to David. Nevertheless David would not drink it, but poured it out to the LORD. ¹⁹And he said, "Far be it from me, O my God, that I should do this! Shall I drink the blood of these men *who have put* their lives *in jeopardy?* For at the risk of their lives they brought it." Therefore he would not drink it. These things were done by the three mighty men.

²⁰Abishai the brother of Joab was chief of *another* three.*ᵃ* He had lifted up his spear against three hundred *men*, killed *them*, and won a name among *these* three. ²¹Of the three he was more honored than the other two men. Therefore he became their captain. However he did not attain to the *first* three.

²²Benaiah was the son of Jehoiada, the son of a valiant man from Kabzeel, who had done many deeds. He had killed two lionlike heroes of Moab. He also had gone down and killed a lion in the midst of a pit on a snowy day. ²³And he killed an Egyptian, a man of *great* height, five cubits tall. In the Egyptian's hand *there was* a spear like a weaver's beam; and he went down to him with a staff, wrested the spear out of the Egyptian's hand, and killed him with his own spear. ²⁴These *things* Benaiah the son of Jehoiada did, and won a name among three mighty men. ²⁵Indeed he was more honored than the thirty, but he did not attain to the *first* three. And David appointed him over his guard.

²⁶Also the mighty warriors *were* Asahel the brother of Joab, Elhanan the son of Dodo of Bethlehem, ²⁷Shammoth the Harorite,*ᵃ* Helez the Pelonite,*ᵇ* ²⁸Ira the son of Ikkesh the Tekoite, Abiezer the Anathothite, ²⁹Sibbechai the Hushathite, Ilai the Ahohite, ³⁰Maharai the Netophathite,

---

11:8 *ᵃ*Literally *The Landfill*   11:11 *ᵃ*Following Qere; Kethib, Septuagint, and Vulgate read *the thirty* (compare 2 Samuel 23:8).   11:20 *ᵃ*Following Masoretic Text, Septuagint, and Vulgate; Syriac reads *thirty*.   11:27 *ᵃ*Spelled *Harodite* in 2 Samuel 23:25   *ᵇ*Called *Paltite* in 2 Samuel 23:26

Heled*a* the son of Baanah the Netopha-thite, [31]Ithai*a* the son of Ribai of Gibeah, of the sons of Benjamin, Benaiah the Pira-thonite, [32]Hurai*a* of the brooks of Gaash, Abiel*b* the Arbathite, [33]Azmaveth the Baha-rumite,*a* Eliahba the Shaalbonite, [34]the sons of Hashem the Gizonite, Jonathan the son of Shageh the Hararite, [35]Ahiam the son of Sacar the Hararite, Eliphal the son of Ur, [36]Hepher the Mecherathite, Ahijah the Pelonite, [37]Hezro the Carmelite, Naarai the son of Ezbai, [38]Joel the brother of Nathan, Mibhar the son of Hagri, [39]Zelek the Am-monite, Naharai the Berothite*a* (the armorbearer of Joab the son of Zeruiah), [40]Ira the Ithrite, Gareb the Ithrite, [41]Uriah the Hittite, Zabad the son of Ahlai, [42]Adina the son of Shiza the Reubenite (a chief of the Reubenites) and thirty with him, [43]Ha-nan the son of Maachah, Joshaphat the Mithnite, [44]Uzzia the Ashterathite, Shama and Jeiel the sons of Hotham the Aroerite, [45]Jediael the son of Shimri, and Joha his brother, the Tizite, [46]Eliel the Mahavite, Jer-ibai and Joshaviah the sons of Elnaam, Ith-mah the Moabite, [47]Eliel, Obed, and Jaasiel the Mezobaite.

The Growth of David's Army

12 Now these *were* the men who came to David at Ziklag while he was still a fugitive from Saul the son of Kish; and they *were* among the mighty men, helpers in the war, [2]armed with bows, using both the right hand and the left in *hurling* stones and *shooting* arrows with the bow. *They were* of Benjamin, Saul's brethren.

> **12:1 Ziklag.** This territory was located in the South near the Edomite border. During the reign of Saul, when he was pursuing David, the Philistines made David a ruler over Ziklag (see 1 Sam. 27:6,7).

[3]The chief *was* Ahiezer, then Joash, the sons of Shemaah the Gibeathite; Jeziel and Pelet the sons of Azmaveth; Berachah, and Jehu the Anathothite; [4]Ishmaiah the Gibe-onite, a mighty man among the thirty, and over the thirty; Jeremiah, Jahaziel, Joha-nan, and Jozabad the Gederathite; [5]Eluzai, Jerimoth, Bealiah, Shemariah, and Shepha-tiah the Haruphite; [6]Elkanah, Jisshiah, Az-arel, Joezer, and Jashobeam, the Korahites; [7]and Joelah and Zebadiah the sons of Jero-ham of Gedor.

[8]*Some* Gadites joined David at the stronghold in the wilderness, mighty men of valor, men trained for battle, who could handle shield and spear, whose faces *were like* the faces of lions, and *were* as swift as gazelles on the mountains: [9]Ezer the first, Obadiah the second, Eliab the third, [10]Mishmannah the fourth, Jeremiah the fifth, [11]Attai the sixth, Eliel the seventh, [12]Johanan the eighth, Elzabad the ninth, [13]Jeremiah the tenth, and Machbanai the eleventh. [14]These *were* from the sons of Gad, captains of the army; the least was over a hundred, and the greatest was over a thousand. [15]These *are* the ones who crossed the Jordan in the first month, when it had overflowed all its banks; and they put to flight all *those* in the valleys, to the east and to the west.

[16]Then some of the sons of Benjamin and Judah came to David at the stronghold. [17]And David went out to meet them, and answered and said to them, "If you have come peaceably to me to help me, my heart will be united with you; but if to betray me to my enemies, since *there is* no wrong in my hands, may the God of our fathers look and bring judgment." [18]Then the Spirit came upon Amasai, chief of the captains, *and he said:*

"*We are* yours, O David;
We *are* on your side, O son of Jesse!
Peace, peace to you,
And peace to your helpers!
For your God helps you."

So David received them, and made them captains of the troop.

> **12:18 the Spirit.** Amasai was temporarily empow-ered by the Holy Spirit to assure David that he had God's blessing and the loyalty of the Benjamites and Judahites.

11:30 *a*Spelled *Heleb* in 2 Samuel 23:29 and *Heldai* in 1 Chronicles 27:15   11:31 *a*Spelled *Ittai* in 2 Samuel 23:29   11:32 *a*Spelled *Hiddai* in 2 Samuel 23:30   *b*Spelled *Abi-Albon* in 2 Samuel 23:31   11:33 *a*Spelled *Barhumite* in 2 Samuel 23:31   11:39 *a*Spelled *Beerothite* in 2 Samuel 23:37

[19]And *some* from Manasseh defected to David when he was going with the Philistines to battle against Saul; but they did not help them, for the lords of the Philistines sent him away by agreement, saying, "He may defect to his master Saul *and endanger our heads.*" [20]When he went to Ziklag, those of Manasseh who defected to him were Adnah, Jozabad, Jediael, Michael, Jozabad, Elihu, and Zillethai, captains of the thousands who *were* from Manasseh. [21]And they helped David against the bands *of raiders,* for they *were* all mighty men of valor, and they were captains in the army. [22]For at *that* time they came to David day by day to help him, until *it was* a great army, like the army of God.

David's Army at Hebron

[23]Now these *were* the numbers of the divisions *that were* equipped for war, *and* came to David at Hebron to turn *over* the kingdom of Saul to him, according to the word of the LORD: [24]of the sons of Judah bearing shield and spear, six thousand eight hundred armed for war; [25]of the sons of Simeon, mighty men of valor fit for war, seven thousand one hundred; [26]of the sons of Levi four thousand six hundred; [27]Jehoiada, the leader of the Aaronites, and with him three thousand seven hundred; [28]Zadok, a young man, a valiant warrior, and from his father's house twenty-two captains; [29]of the sons of Benjamin, relatives of Saul, three thousand (until then the greatest part of them had remained loyal to the house of Saul); [30]of the sons of Ephraim twenty thousand eight hundred, mighty men of valor, famous men throughout their father's house; [31]of the half-tribe of Manasseh eighteen thousand, who were designated by name to come and make David king; [32]of the sons of Issachar who had understanding of the times, to know what Israel ought to do, their chiefs were two hundred; and all their brethren were at their command; [33]of Zebulun there were fifty thousand who went out to battle, expert in war with all weapons of war, stouthearted men who could keep ranks; [34]of Naphtali one thousand captains, and with them thirty-seven thousand with shield and spear; [35]of the Danites who could keep battle formation, twenty-eight thousand six hundred; [36]of Asher, those who could go out to war, able to keep battle formation, forty thousand; [37]of the Reubenites and the Gadites and the half-tribe of Manasseh, from the other side of the Jordan, one hundred and twenty thousand armed for battle with every *kind* of weapon of war.

[38]All these men of war, who could keep ranks, came to Hebron with a loyal heart, to make David king over all Israel; and all the rest of Israel *were* of one mind to make David king. [39]And they were there with David three days, eating and drinking, for their brethren had prepared for them. [40]Moreover those who were near to them, from as far away as Issachar and Zebulun and Naphtali, were bringing food on donkeys and camels, on mules and oxen—provisions of flour and cakes of figs and cakes of raisins, wine and oil and oxen and sheep abundantly, for *there was* joy in Israel.

The Ark Brought from Kirjath Jearim

13 Then David consulted with the captains of thousands and hundreds, *and* with every leader. [2]And David said to all the assembly of Israel, "If *it seems* good to you, and if it is of the LORD our God, let us send out to our brethren everywhere *who are* left in all the land of Israel, and with them to the priests and Levites *who are* in their cities *and* their common-lands, that they may gather together to us; [3]and let us bring the ark of our God back to us, for we have not inquired at it since the days of Saul." [4]Then all the assembly said that they would do so, for the thing was right in the eyes of all the people.

> **13:3 the ark of our God.** The ark had been stolen and profaned by the Philistines (1 Sam. 5,6). After it was returned, Saul did not seek God's instruction for it and only once sought after it (see 1 Sam. 14:18).

[5]So David gathered all Israel together, from Shihor in Egypt to as far as the entrance of Hamath, to bring the ark of God from Kirjath Jearim. [6]And David and all Israel went up to Baalah,[a] to Kirjath Jearim, which belonged to Judah, to bring up from

13:6 [a]Called *Baale Judah* in 2 Samuel 6:2

there the ark of God the LORD, who dwells *between* the cherubim, where *His* name is proclaimed. [7]So they carried the ark of God on a new cart from the house of Abinadab, and Uzza and Ahio drove the cart. [8]Then David and all Israel played *music* before God with all *their* might, with singing, on harps, on stringed instruments, on tambourines, on cymbals, and with trumpets.

[9]And when they came to Chidon's[a] threshing floor, Uzza put out his hand to hold the ark, for the oxen stumbled. [10]Then the anger of the LORD was aroused against Uzza, and He struck him because he put his hand to the ark; and he died there before God. [11]And David became angry because of the LORD's outbreak against Uzza; therefore that place is called Perez Uzza[a] to this day. [12]David was afraid of God that day, saying, "How can I bring the ark of God to me?"

[13]So David would not move the ark with him into the City of David, but took it aside into the house of Obed-Edom the Gittite. [14]The ark of God remained with the family of Obed-Edom in his house three months. And the LORD blessed the house of Obed-Edom and all that he had.

David Established at Jerusalem

14 Now Hiram king of Tyre sent messengers to David, and cedar trees, with masons and carpenters, to build him a house. [2]So David knew that the LORD had established him as king over Israel, for his kingdom was highly exalted for the sake of His people Israel.

[3]Then David took more wives in Jerusalem, and David begot more sons and daughters. [4]And these are the names of his children whom he had in Jerusalem: Shammua,[a] Shobab, Nathan, Solomon, [5]Ibhar, Elishua,[a] Elpelet,[b] [6]Nogah, Nepheg, Japhia, [7]Elishama, Beeliada,[a] and Eliphelet.

The Philistines Defeated

[8]Now when the Philistines heard that David had been anointed king over all Israel, all the Philistines went up to search for David. And David heard *of it* and went out

against them. [9]Then the Philistines went and made a raid on the Valley of Rephaim. [10]And David inquired of God, saying, "Shall I go up against the Philistines? Will You deliver them into my hand?"

The LORD said to him, "Go up, for I will deliver them into your hand."

[11]So they went up to Baal Perazim, and David defeated them there. Then David said, "God has broken through my enemies by my hand like a breakthrough of water." Therefore they called the name of that place Baal Perazim.[a] [12]And when they left their gods there, David gave a commandment, and they were burned with fire.

[13]Then the Philistines once again made a raid on the valley. [14]Therefore David inquired again of God, and God said to him, "You shall not go up after them; circle around them, and come upon them in front of the mulberry trees. [15]And it shall be, when you hear a sound of marching in the tops of the mulberry trees, then you shall go out to battle, for God has gone out before you to strike the camp of the Philistines." [16]So David did as God commanded him, and they drove back the army of the Philistines from Gibeon as far as Gezer. [17]Then the fame of David went out into all lands, and the LORD brought the fear of him upon all nations.

> **14:8–17** The Philistines planned to kill David, but God gave him victory over them (unlike Saul), declaring His support of Israel's new king.

The Ark Brought to Jerusalem

15 *David* built houses for himself in the City of David; and he prepared a place for it the ark of God, and pitched a tent for it. [2]Then David said, "No one may carry the ark of God but the Levites, for the LORD has chosen them to carry the ark of God and to minister before Him forever." [3]And

> **15:2 carry the ark.** After 3 months, David followed the Mosaic directions for moving the ark (see Num. 4:1–49). These directions had been violated when the ark was moved from Kirjath-Jearim to Obed-Edom, costing Uzza his life (see 13:6–11).

13:9 [a]Called *Nachon* in 2 Samuel 6:6   13:11 [a]Literally *Outburst Against Uzza*   14:4 [a]Spelled *Shimea* in 3:5   14:5 [a]Spelled *Elishama* in 3:6   [b]Spelled *Eliphelet* in 3:6   14:7 [a]Spelled *Eliada* in 3:8   14:11 [a]Literally *Master of Breakthroughs*

David gathered all Israel together at Jerusalem, to bring up the ark of the LORD to its place, which he had prepared for it. ⁴Then David assembled the children of Aaron and the Levites: ⁵of the sons of Kohath, Uriel the chief, and one hundred and twenty of his brethren; ⁶of the sons of Merari, Asaiah the chief, and two hundred and twenty of his brethren; ⁷of the sons of Gershom, Joel the chief, and one hundred and thirty of his brethren; ⁸of the sons of Elizaphan, Shemaiah the chief, and two hundred of his brethren; ⁹of the sons of Hebron, Eliel the chief, and eighty of his brethren; ¹⁰of the sons of Uzziel, Amminadab the chief, and one hundred and twelve of his brethren.

¹¹And David called for Zadok and Abiathar the priests, and for the Levites: for Uriel, Asaiah, Joel, Shemaiah, Eliel, and Amminadab. ¹²He said to them, "You *are* the heads of the fathers' *houses* of the Levites; sanctify yourselves, you and your brethren, that you may bring up the ark of the LORD God of Israel to *the place* I have prepared for it. ¹³For because you *did* not *do it* the first *time*, the LORD our God broke out against us, because we did not consult Him about the proper order."

> **15:13 broke out.** God's anger "broke out" when the ark had been improperly handled and transported by Uzza (2 Sam. 6:6–8).

¹⁴So the priests and the Levites sanctified themselves to bring up the ark of the LORD God of Israel. ¹⁵And the children of the Levites bore the ark of God on their shoulders, by its poles, as Moses had commanded according to the word of the LORD.

¹⁶Then David spoke to the leaders of the Levites to appoint their brethren *to be* the singers accompanied by instruments of music, stringed instruments, harps, and cymbals, by raising the voice with resounding joy. ¹⁷So the Levites appointed Heman the son of Joel; and of his brethren, Asaph the son of Berechiah; and of their brethren, the sons of Merari, Ethan the son of Kushaiah; ¹⁸and with them their brethren of the second *rank:* Zechariah, Ben,[a] Jaaziel, Shemiramoth, Jehiel, Unni, Eliab, Benaiah, Maaseiah, Mattithiah, Elipheleh, Mikne-

iah, Obed-Edom, and Jeiel, the gatekeepers; ¹⁹the singers, Heman, Asaph, and Ethan, *were* to sound the cymbals of bronze; ²⁰Zechariah, Aziel, Shemiramoth, Jehiel, Unni, Eliab, Maaseiah, and Benaiah, with strings according to Alamoth; ²¹Mattithiah, Elipheleh, Mikneiah, Obed-Edom, Jeiel, and Azaziah, to direct with harps on the Sheminith; ²²Chenaniah, leader of the Levites, was instructor *in charge of* the music, because he *was* skillful; ²³Berechiah and Elkanah *were* doorkeepers for the ark; ²⁴Shebaniah, Joshaphat, Nethanel, Amasai, Zechariah, Benaiah, and Eliezer, the priests, were to blow the trumpets before the ark of God; and Obed-Edom and Jehiah, doorkeepers for the ark.

²⁵So David, the elders of Israel, and the captains over thousands went to bring up the ark of the covenant of the LORD from the house of Obed-Edom with joy. ²⁶And so it was, when God helped the Levites who bore the ark of the covenant of the LORD, that they offered seven bulls and seven rams. ²⁷David was clothed with a robe of fine linen, as were all the Levites who bore the ark, the singers, and Chenaniah the music master *with* the singers. David also wore a linen ephod. ²⁸Thus all Israel brought up the ark of the covenant of the LORD with shouting and with the sound of the horn, with trumpets and with cymbals, making music with stringed instruments and harps.

²⁹And it happened, *as* the ark of the covenant of the LORD came to the City of David, that Michal, Saul's daughter, looked through a window and saw King David whirling and playing music; and she despised him in her heart.

The Ark Placed in the Tabernacle

16 So they brought the ark of God, and set it in the midst of the tabernacle that David had erected for it. Then they offered burnt offerings and peace offerings before God. ²And when David had finished offering the burnt offerings and the peace offerings, he blessed the people in the name of the LORD. ³Then he distributed to everyone of Israel, both man and woman, to everyone a loaf of bread, a piece *of meat,* and a cake of raisins.

15:18 ᵃFollowing Masoretic Text and Vulgate; Septuagint omits *Ben.*

⁴And he appointed some of the Levites to minister before the ark of the LORD, to commemorate, to thank, and to praise the LORD God of Israel: ⁵Asaph the chief, and next to him Zechariah, *then* Jeiel, Shemiramoth, Jehiel, Mattithiah, Eliab, Benaiah, and Obed-Edom: Jeiel with stringed instruments and harps, but Asaph made music with cymbals; ⁶Benaiah and Jahaziel the priests regularly *blew* the trumpets before the ark of the covenant of God.

16:4–6 Levites...minister. The Levites began their duties as soon as the ark was placed into its tent.

David's Song of Thanksgiving

⁷On that day David first delivered *this psalm* into the hand of Asaph and his brethren, to thank the LORD:

⁸　Oh, give thanks to the LORD!
　　Call upon His name;
　　Make known His deeds among the
　　　peoples!
⁹　Sing to Him, sing psalms to Him;
　　Talk of all His wondrous works!
¹⁰　Glory in His holy name;
　　Let the hearts of those rejoice who
　　　seek the LORD!
¹¹　Seek the LORD and His strength;
　　Seek His face evermore!
¹²　Remember His marvelous works
　　　which He has done,
　　His wonders, and the judgments of
　　　His mouth,
¹³　O seed of Israel His servant,
　　You children of Jacob, His chosen
　　　ones!

¹⁴　He *is* the LORD our God;
　　His judgments *are* in all the earth.
¹⁵　Remember His covenant forever,
　　The word which He commanded, for
　　　a thousand generations,
¹⁶　*The covenant which* He made with
　　　Abraham,
　　And His oath to Isaac,
¹⁷　And confirmed it to Jacob for a
　　　statute,
　　To Israel *for* an everlasting covenant,
¹⁸　Saying, "To you I will give the land of
　　　Canaan

　　As the allotment of your
　　　inheritance,"
¹⁹　When you were few in number,
　　Indeed very few, and strangers in it.

²⁰　When they went from one nation to
　　　another,
　　And from *one* kingdom to another
　　　people,
²¹　He permitted no man to do them
　　　wrong;
　　Yes, He rebuked kings for their sakes,
²²　*Saying,* "Do not touch My anointed
　　　ones,
　　And do My prophets no harm." ᵃ

²³　Sing to the LORD, all the earth;
　　Proclaim the good news of His
　　　salvation from day to day.
²⁴　Declare His glory among the nations,
　　His wonders among all peoples.
²⁵　For the LORD *is* great and greatly to be
　　　praised;
　　He *is* also to be feared above all gods.
²⁶　For all the gods of the peoples *are*
　　　idols,
　　But the LORD made the heavens.
²⁷　Honor and majesty *are* before Him;
　　Strength and gladness are in His
　　　place.

²⁸　Give to the LORD, O families of the
　　　peoples,
　　Give to the LORD glory and strength.
²⁹　Give to the LORD the glory *due* His
　　　name;
　　Bring an offering, and come before
　　　Him.
　　Oh, worship the LORD in the beauty
　　　of holiness!
³⁰　Tremble before Him, all the earth.
　　The world also is firmly established,
　　It shall not be moved.

³¹　Let the heavens rejoice, and let the
　　　earth be glad;
　　And let them say among the nations,
　　　"The LORD reigns."
³²　Let the sea roar, and all its fullness;
　　Let the field rejoice, and all that *is* in
　　　it.

16:22 ᵃCompare verses 8–22 with Psalm 105:1–15

33 Then the trees of the woods shall
      rejoice before the LORD,
   For He is coming to judge the earth.*a*

34 Oh, give thanks to the LORD, for *He is*
      good!
   For His mercy *endures* forever.*a*

35 And say, "Save us, O God of our
      salvation;
   Gather us together, and deliver us
      from the Gentiles,
   To give thanks to Your holy name,
   To triumph in Your praise."

36 Blessed *be* the LORD God of Israel
   From everlasting to everlasting!*a*

And all the people said, "Amen!" and
praised the LORD.

Regular Worship Maintained

37So he left Asaph and his brothers there
before the ark of the covenant of the LORD
to minister before the ark regularly, as every
day's work required; 38and Obed-Edom
with his sixty-eight brethren, including
Obed-Edom the son of Jeduthun, and Hosah, *to be* gatekeepers; 39and Zadok the
priest and his brethren the priests, before
the tabernacle of the LORD at the high place
that *was* at Gibeon, 40to offer burnt offerings to the LORD on the altar of burnt offering regularly morning and evening, and *to
do* according to all that is written in the
Law of the LORD which He commanded Israel; 41and with them Heman and Jeduthun
and the rest who were chosen, who were
designated by name, to give thanks to the
LORD, because His mercy *endures* forever;
42and with them Heman and Jeduthun, to
sound aloud with trumpets and cymbals
and the musical instruments of God. Now
the sons of Jeduthun *were* gatekeepers.

16:37–42 regularly...every day's work. The ministry was established with regular completion of duties.

43Then all the people departed, every
man to his house; and David returned to
bless his house.

God's Covenant with David

17 Now it came to pass, when David
      was dwelling in his house, that Da-
vid said to Nathan the prophet, "See now, I
dwell in a house of cedar, but the ark of the
covenant of the LORD *is* under tent curtains."

2Then Nathan said to David, "Do all that
is in your heart, for God *is* with you."

3But it happened that night that the word
of God came to Nathan, saying, 4"Go and
tell My servant David, 'Thus says the
LORD: "You shall not build Me a house to
dwell in. 5For I have not dwelt in a house
since the time that I brought up Israel, even
to this day, but have gone from tent to tent,
and from *one* tabernacle *to another.* 6Wher-
ever I have moved about with all Israel,
have I ever spoken a word to any of the
judges of Israel, whom I commanded to
shepherd My people, saying, 'Why have
you not built Me a house of cedar?' " ' 7Now
therefore, thus shall you say to My servant
David, 'Thus says the LORD of hosts: "I
took you from the sheepfold, from following the sheep, to be ruler over My people
Israel. 8And I have been with you wherever
you have gone, and have cut off all your enemies from before you, and have made you
a name like the name of the great men who
are on the earth. 9Moreover I will appoint a
place for My people Israel, and will plant
them, that they may dwell in a place of
their own and move no more; nor shall
the sons of wickedness oppress them anymore, as previously, 10since the time that
I commanded judges *to be* over My people
Israel. Also I will subdue all your enemies. Furthermore I tell you that the LORD
will build you a house.*a* 11And it shall be,
when your days are fulfilled, when you
must go *to be* with your fathers, that I
will set up your seed after you, who will
be of your sons; and I will establish his
kingdom. 12He shall build Me a house,
and I will establish his throne forever. 13I
will be his Father, and he shall be My son;
and I will not take My mercy away from
him, as I took *it* from *him* who was before
you. 14And I will establish him in My
house and in My kingdom forever; and

16:33 *a*Compare verses 23–33 with Psalm 96:1–13   16:34 *a*Compare verse 34 with Psalm 106:1
16:36 *a*Compare verses 35, 36 with Psalm 106:47,48   17:10 *a*That is, a royal dynasty

his throne shall be established forever." ' "

¹⁵According to all these words and according to all this vision, so Nathan spoke to David.

¹⁶Then King David went in and sat before the LORD; and he said: "Who *am* I, O LORD God? And what is my house, that You have brought me this far? ¹⁷And *yet* this was a small thing in Your sight, O God; and You have *also* spoken of Your servant's house for a great while to come, and have regarded me according to the rank of a man of high degree, O LORD God. ¹⁸What more can David *say* to You for the honor of Your servant? For You know Your servant. ¹⁹O LORD, for Your servant's sake, and according to Your own heart, You have done all this greatness, in making known all these great things. ²⁰O LORD, *there is* none like You, nor *is there any* God besides You, according to all that we have heard with our ears. ²¹And who *is* like Your people Israel, the one nation on the earth whom God went to redeem for Himself *as* a people—to make for Yourself a name by great and awesome deeds, by driving out nations from before Your people whom You redeemed from Egypt? ²²For You have made Your people Israel Your very own people forever; and You, LORD, have become their God.

²³"And now, O LORD, the word which You have spoken concerning Your servant and concerning his house, *let it* be established forever, and do as You have said. ²⁴So let it be established, that Your name may be magnified forever, saying, 'The LORD of hosts, the God of Israel, *is* Israel's God.' And let the house of Your servant David be established before You. ²⁵For You, O my God, have revealed to Your servant that You will build him a house. Therefore Your servant has found it *in his heart* to pray before You. ²⁶And now, LORD, You are God, and have promised this goodness to Your servant. ²⁷Now You have been pleased to bless the house of Your servant, that it may continue before You forever; for You have blessed it, O LORD, and *it shall be* blessed forever."

18:1–21:30 This section recounts David's military exploits (see 2 Sam. 8:1–12).

David's Further Conquests

18 After this it came to pass that David attacked the Philistines, subdued them, and took Gath and its towns from the hand of the Philistines. ²Then he defeated Moab, and the Moabites became David's servants, *and* brought tribute.

³And David defeated Hadadezer[a] king of Zobah *as far as* Hamath, as he went to establish his power by the River Euphrates. ⁴David took from him one thousand chariots, seven thousand[a] horsemen, and twenty thousand foot soldiers. Also David hamstrung all the chariot *horses,* except that he spared enough of them for one hundred chariots.

⁵When the Syrians of Damascus came to help Hadadezer king of Zobah, David killed twenty-two thousand of the Syrians. ⁶Then David put *garrisons* in Syria of Damascus; and the Syrians became David's servants, *and* brought tribute. So the LORD preserved David wherever he went. ⁷And David took the shields of gold that were on the servants of Hadadezer, and brought them to Jerusalem. ⁸Also from Tibhath[a] and from Chun, cities of Hadadezer, David brought a large amount of bronze, with which Solomon made the bronze Sea, the pillars, and the articles of bronze.

⁹Now when Tou[a] king of Hamath heard that David had defeated all the army of Hadadezer king of Zobah, ¹⁰he sent Hadoram[a] his son to King David, to greet him and bless him, because he had fought against Hadadezer and defeated him (for Hadadezer had been at war with Tou); and *Hadoram brought with him* all kinds of articles of gold, silver, and bronze. ¹¹King David also dedicated these to the LORD, along with the silver and gold that he had brought from all *these* nations—from Edom, from Moab, from the people of Ammon, from the Philistines, and from Amalek.

¹²Moreover Abishai the son of Zeruiah killed eighteen thousand Edomites[a] in the

---

18:3 *ª*Hebrew *Hadarezer,* and so throughout chapters 18 and 19   18:4 *ª*Or *seven hundred* (compare 2 Samuel 8:4)   18:8 *ª*Spelled *Betah* in 2 Samuel 8:8   18:9 *ª*Spelled *Toi* in 2 Samuel 8:9,10   18:10 *ª*Spelled *Joram* in 2 Samuel 8:10   18:12 *ª*Or *Syrians* (compare 2 Samuel 8:13)

Valley of Salt. ¹³He also put garrisons in Edom, and all the Edomites became David's servants. And the LORD preserved David wherever he went.

David's Administration

¹⁴So David reigned over all Israel, and administered judgment and justice to all his people. ¹⁵Joab the son of Zeruiah *was* over the army; Jehoshaphat the son of Ahilud *was* recorder; ¹⁶Zadok the son of Ahitub and Abimelech the son of Abiathar *were* the priests; Shavsha*ᵃ was* the scribe; ¹⁷Benaiah the son of Jehoiada *was* over the Cherethites and the Pelethites; and David's sons *were* chief ministers at the king's side.

The Ammonites and Syrians Defeated

19 It happened after this that Nahash the king of the people of Ammon died, and his son reigned in his place. ²Then David said, "I will show kindness to Hanun the son of Nahash, because his father showed kindness to me." So David sent messengers to comfort him concerning his father. And David's servants came to Hanun in the land of the people of Ammon to comfort him.

³And the princes of the people of Ammon said to Hanun, "Do you think that David really honors your father because he has sent comforters to you? Did his servants not come to you to search and to overthrow and to spy out the land?"

⁴Therefore Hanun took David's servants, shaved them, and cut off their garments in the middle, at their buttocks, and sent them away. ⁵Then *some* went and told Da-

---

THE DAVIDIC COVENANT IN CHRONICLES

1. 1 Chr. 17:7–27	God to Nathan to David
2. 1 Chr. 22:6–16	David to Solomon
3. 1 Chr. 28:6,7	David to Solomon
4. 2 Chr. 6:8,9,16,17	Solomon to the nation
5. 2 Chr. 7:17,18	God to Solomon
6. 2 Chr. 13:4,5	Abijah to Jeroboam
7. 2 Chr. 21:7	Chronicle's commentary

---

vid about the men; and he sent to meet them, because the men were greatly ashamed. And the king said, "Wait at Jericho until your beards have grown, and *then* return."

⁶When the people of Ammon saw that they had made themselves repulsive to David, Hanun and the people of Ammon sent a thousand talents of silver to hire for themselves chariots and horsemen from Mesopotamia,*ᵃ* from Syrian Maacah, and from Zobah.*ᵇ* ⁷So they hired for themselves thirty-two thousand chariots, with the king of Maacah and his people, who came and encamped before Medeba. Also the people of Ammon gathered together from their cities, and came to battle.

⁸Now when David heard *of it,* he sent Joab and all the army of the mighty men. ⁹Then the people of Ammon came out and put themselves in battle array before the gate of the city, and the kings who had come *were* by themselves in the field.

¹⁰When Joab saw that the battle line was against him before and behind, he chose some of Israel's best, and put *them* in battle array against the Syrians. ¹¹And the rest of the people he put under the command of Abishai his brother, and they set *themselves* in battle array against the people of Ammon. ¹²Then he said, "If the Syrians are too strong for me, then you shall help me; but if the people of Ammon are too strong for you, then I will help you. ¹³Be of good courage, and let us be strong for our people and for the cities of our God. And may the LORD do *what is* good in His sight."

¹⁴So Joab and the people who *were* with him drew near for the battle against the Syrians, and they fled before him. ¹⁵When the people of Ammon saw that the Syrians were fleeing, they also fled before Abishai his brother, and entered the city. So Joab went to Jerusalem.

¹⁶Now when the Syrians saw that they had been defeated by Israel, they sent messengers and brought the Syrians who were beyond the River,*ᵃ* and Shophach*ᵇ* the commander of Hadadezer's army *went* before them. ¹⁷When it was told David, he gathered all Israel, crossed over the Jordan and

---

18:16 *ᵃ*Spelled *Seraiah* in 2 Samuel 8:17   19:6 *ᵃ*Hebrew *Aram Naharaim*   *ᵇ*Spelled *Zoba* in 2 Samuel 10:6   19:16 *ᵃ*That is, the Euphrates   *ᵇ*Spelled *Shobach* in 2 Samuel 10:16

came upon them, and set up in battle array against them. So when David had set up in *battle* array against the Syrians, they fought with him. [18]Then the Syrians fled before Israel; and David killed seven thousand[a] charioteers and forty thousand foot soldiers[b] of the Syrians, and killed Shophach the commander of the army. [19]And when the servants of Hadadezer saw that they were defeated by Israel, they made peace with David and became his servants. So the Syrians were not willing to help the people of Ammon anymore.

Rabbah Is Conquered

20 It happened in the spring of the year, at the time kings go out *to battle*, that Joab led out the armed forces and ravaged the country of the people of Ammon, and came and besieged Rabbah. But David stayed at Jerusalem. And Joab defeated Rabbah and overthrew it. [2]Then David took their king's crown from his head, and found it to weigh a talent of gold, and *there were* precious stones in it. And it was set on David's head. Also he brought out the spoil of the city in great abundance. [3]And he brought out the people who *were* in it, and put *them* to work[a] with saws, with iron picks, and with axes. So David did to all the cities of the people of Ammon. Then David and all the people returned *to* Jerusalem.

20:1–3 The chronicler did not mention David's sins of adultery, murder, or the revolt of his son, Absalom. These were most likely omitted because the book was written to focus on God's permanent interest in His people, not the darkness of David's kingdom.

Philistine Giants Destroyed

[4]Now it happened afterward that war broke out at Gezer with the Philistines, at which time Sibbechai the Hushathite killed Sippai,[a] *who was one* of the sons of the giant. And they were subdued. [5]Again there was war with the Philistines, and Elhanan the son of Jair[a] killed Lahmi the brother of Goliath the Gittite, the shaft of whose spear *was* like a weaver's beam. [6]Yet again there was war at Gath, where

there was a man of *great* stature, with twenty-four fingers and toes, six *on each hand* and six *on each foot*; and he also was born to the giant. [7]So when he defied Israel, Jonathan the son of Shimea,[a] David's brother, killed him.

[8]These were born to the giant in Gath, and they fell by the hand of David and by the hand of his servants.

The Census of Israel and Judah

21 Now Satan stood up against Israel, and moved David to number Israel. [2]So David said to Joab and to the leaders of the people, "Go, number Israel from Beersheba to Dan, and bring the number of them to me that I may know *it*."

21:1 Satan...moved. It was God who "moved" David (2 Sam. 24:1), yet we must understand that God uses Satan to achieve His purpose: He uses Satan to judge sinners (Mark 4:15), refine saints (Job 1:8–2:10), discipline those in the church (1 Cor. 5:1–5), and to purify obedient believers (2 Cor. 12:7–10). God allowed Satan to tempt David, but it was David who chose to sin. **number Israel.** David's purpose for the census was to gratify his pride in the great strength of his army. He angered God by taking credit for his victories instead of trusting in God.

[3]And Joab answered, "May the LORD make His people a hundred times more than they are. But, my lord the king, *are* they not all my lord's servants? Why then does my lord require this thing? Why should he be a cause of guilt in Israel?"

[4]Nevertheless the king's word prevailed against Joab. Therefore Joab departed and went throughout all Israel and came to Jerusalem. [5]Then Joab gave the sum of the number of the people to David. All Israel *had* one million one hundred thousand men who drew the sword, and Judah *had* four hundred and seventy thousand men who drew the sword. [6]But he did not count Levi and Benjamin among them, for the king's word was abominable to Joab.

[7]And God was displeased with this thing; therefore He struck Israel. [8]So David said to God, "I have sinned greatly, because I have

---

> **21:7 He struck Israel.** God's wrath was experienced by the entire kingdom as a result of David's sin.

done this thing; but now, I pray, take away the iniquity of Your servant, for I have done very foolishly."

⁹Then the LORD spoke to Gad, David's seer, saying, ¹⁰"Go and tell David, saying, 'Thus says the LORD: "I offer you three *things*; choose one of them for yourself, that I may do *it* to you." ' "

¹¹So Gad came to David and said to him, "Thus says the LORD: 'Choose for yourself, ¹²either three*ᵃ* years of famine, or three months to be defeated by your foes with the sword of your enemies overtaking *you*, or else for three days the sword of the LORD— the plague in the land, with the angel*ᵇ* of the LORD destroying throughout all the territory of Israel.' Now consider what answer I should take back to Him who sent me."

¹³And David said to Gad, "I am in great distress. Please let me fall into the hand of the LORD, for His mercies *are* very great; but do not let me fall into the hand of man."

¹⁴So the LORD sent a plague upon Israel, and seventy thousand men of Israel fell. ¹⁵And God sent an angel to Jerusalem to destroy it. As he*ᵃ* was destroying, the LORD looked and relented of the disaster, and said to the angel who was destroying, "It is enough; now restrain your*ᵇ* hand." And the angel of the LORD stood by the threshing floor of Ornan*ᶜ* the Jebusite.

> **21:16** The angel of the Lord was the executioner poised to destroy Jerusalem, whose destruction was halted because David and the leaders repented, as indicated by their "sackcloth" and falling "on their faces."

¹⁶Then David lifted his eyes and saw the angel of the LORD standing between earth and heaven, having in his hand a drawn sword stretched out over Jerusalem. So David and the elders, clothed in sackcloth, fell on their faces. ¹⁷And David said to God, "Was it not I who commanded the people to be numbered? I am the one who has sinned and done evil indeed; but these sheep, what have they done? Let Your hand, I pray, O LORD my God, be against me and my father's house, but not against Your people that they should be plagued."

¹⁸Therefore, the angel of the LORD commanded Gad to say to David that David should go and erect an altar to the LORD on the threshing floor of Ornan the Jebusite. ¹⁹So David went up at the word of Gad, which he had spoken in the name of the LORD. ²⁰Now Ornan turned and saw the angel; and his four sons *who were* with him hid themselves, but Ornan continued threshing wheat. ²¹So David came to Ornan, and Ornan looked and saw David. And he went out from the threshing floor, and bowed before David with *his* face to the ground. ²²Then David said to Ornan, "Grant me the place of *this* threshing floor, that I may build an altar on it to the LORD. You shall grant it to me at the full price, that the plague may be withdrawn from the people."

²³But Ornan said to David, "Take *it* to yourself, and let my lord the king do *what is* good in his eyes. Look, I *also* give *you* the oxen for burnt offerings, the threshing implements for wood, and the wheat for the grain offering; I give *it* all."

²⁴Then King David said to Ornan, "No, but I will surely buy *it* for the full price, for I will not take what is yours for the LORD, nor offer burnt offerings with *that which* costs *me* nothing." ²⁵So David gave Ornan six hundred shekels of gold by weight for the place. ²⁶And David built there an altar to the LORD, and offered burnt offerings and peace offerings, and called on the LORD; and He answered him from heaven by fire on the altar of burnt offering. ²⁷So the LORD commanded the angel, and he returned his sword to its sheath.

²⁸At that time, when David saw that the LORD had answered him on the threshing floor of Ornan the Jebusite, he sacrificed there. ²⁹For the tabernacle of the LORD and the altar of the burnt offering, which Moses had made in the wilderness, *were* at that

---

21:12 *ᵃ*Or *seven* (compare 2 Samuel 24:13)   *ᵇ*Or *Angel*, and so elsewhere in this chapter
21:15 *ᵃ*Or *He*   *ᵇ*Or *Your*   *ᶜ*Spelled *Araunah* in 2 Samuel 24:16

time at the high place in Gibeon. ³⁰But David could not go before it to inquire of God, for he was afraid of the sword of the angel of the LORD.

> **21:30 the sword.** David continued to offer sacrifices at the threshing floor because the Lord had appeared to him there (2 Chr. 3:1). He feared going to Gibeon, the center of worship, because of a menacing angel.

David Prepares to Build the Temple

22 Then David said, "This is the house of the LORD God, and this is the altar of burnt offering for Israel." ²So David commanded to gather the aliens who *were* in the land of Israel; and he appointed masons to cut hewn stones to build the house of God. ³And David prepared iron in abundance for the nails of the doors of the gates and for the joints, and bronze in abundance beyond measure, ⁴and cedar trees in abundance; for the Sidonians and those from Tyre brought much cedar wood to David.

⁵Now David said, "Solomon my son *is* young and inexperienced, and the house to be built for the LORD *must be* exceedingly magnificent, famous and glorious throughout all countries. I will now make preparation for it." So David made abundant preparations before his death.

> **22:5 young.** Solomon was at this time between 20 and 30 years of age. The challenge of building such a great building required an experienced leader.

⁶Then he called for his son Solomon, and charged him to build a house for the LORD God of Israel. ⁷And David said to Solomon: "My son, as for me, it was in my mind to build a house to the name of the LORD my God; ⁸but the word of the LORD came to me, saying, 'You have shed much blood and have made great wars; you shall not build a house for My name, because you have shed much blood on the earth in My sight. ⁹Behold, a son shall be born to you, who shall be a man of rest; and I will give him rest from all his enemies all around. His name shall be Solomon,^a for I will give peace and quietness to Israel in his days. ¹⁰He shall build a house for My name, and he shall be My son, and I *will be* his Father; and I will

establish the throne of his kingdom over Israel forever.' ¹¹Now, my son, may the LORD be with you; and may you prosper, and build the house of the LORD your God, as He has said to you. ¹²Only may the LORD give you wisdom and understanding, and give you charge concerning Israel, that you may keep the law of the LORD your God. ¹³Then you will prosper, if you take care to fulfill the statutes and judgments with which the LORD charged Moses concerning Israel. Be strong and of good courage; do not fear nor be dismayed. ¹⁴Indeed I have taken much trouble to prepare for the house of the LORD one hundred thousand talents of gold and one million talents of silver, and bronze and iron beyond measure, for it is so abundant. I have prepared timber and stone also, and you may add to them. ¹⁵Moreover *there are* workmen with you in abundance: woodsmen and stonecutters, and all types of skillful men for every kind of work. ¹⁶Of gold and silver and bronze and iron *there is* no limit. Arise and begin working, and the LORD be with you."

¹⁷David also commanded all the leaders of Israel to help Solomon his son, *saying*, ¹⁸"*Is* not the LORD your God with you? And has He *not* given you rest on every side? For He has given the inhabitants of the land into my hand, and the land is subdued before the LORD and before His people. ¹⁹Now set your heart and your soul to seek the LORD your God. Therefore arise and build the sanctuary of the LORD God, to bring the ark of the covenant of the LORD and the holy articles of God into the house that is to be built for the name of the LORD."

> **22:17–19** David enlisted his leaders to help Solomon, who was young and inexperienced, to undertake the massive project of building the temple. He knew they would be loyal to Solomon and carry out David's last wishes. The Lord eventually made Solomon the wisest man on earth (see 1 Kin. 3:3–14).

The Divisions of the Levites

23 So when David was old and full of days, he made his son Solomon king over Israel.

²And he gathered together all the leaders of Israel, with the priests and the Levites.

22:9 ^aLiterally *Peaceful*

³Now the Levites were numbered from the age of thirty years and above; and the number of individual males was thirty-eight thousand. ⁴Of these, twenty-four thousand *were* to look after the work of the house of the LORD, six thousand *were* officers and judges, ⁵four thousand *were* gatekeepers, and four thousand praised the LORD with *musical* instruments, "which I made," *said David*, "for giving praise."

⁶Also David separated them into divisions among the sons of Levi: Gershon, Kohath, and Merari.

⁷Of the Gershonites: Laadan*ᵃ* and Shimei. ⁸The sons of Laadan: the first Jehiel, then Zetham and Joel—three *in all*. ⁹The sons of Shimei: Shelomith, Haziel, and Haran—three *in all*. These were the heads of the fathers' *houses* of Laadan. ¹⁰And the sons of Shimei: Jahath, Zina,*ᵃ* Jeush, and Beriah. These *were* the four sons of Shimei. ¹¹Jahath was the first and Zizah the second. But Jeush and Beriah did not have many sons; therefore they were assigned as one father's house.

¹²The sons of Kohath: Amram, Izhar, Hebron, and Uzziel—four *in all*. ¹³The sons of Amram: Aaron and Moses; and Aaron was set apart, he and his sons forever, that he should sanctify the most holy things, to burn incense before the LORD, to minister to Him, and to give the blessing in His name forever. ¹⁴Now the sons of Moses the man of God were reckoned to the tribe of Levi. ¹⁵The sons of Moses *were* Gershon*ᵃ* and Eliezer. ¹⁶Of the sons of Gershon, Shebuel*ᵃ was* the first. ¹⁷Of the descendants of Eliezer, Rehabiah was the first. And Eliezer had no other sons, but the sons of Rehabiah were very many. ¹⁸Of the sons of Izhar, Shelomith *was* the first. ¹⁹Of the sons of Hebron, Jeriah *was* the first, Amariah the second, Jahaziel the third, and Jekameam the fourth. ²⁰Of the sons of Uzziel, Michah *was* the first and Jesshiah the second.

²¹The sons of Merari *were* Mahli and

23:7 *ᵃ*Spelled *Libni* in Exodus 6:17   23:10 *ᵃ*Septuagint and Vulgate read *Zizah* (compare verse 11). 23:15 *ᵃ*Hebrew *Gershom* (compare 6:16)   23:16 *ᵃ*Spelled *Shubael* in 24:20

TEMPLE DUTIES

Administrative Duties	Supervisors	1 Chronicles 23:4,5
	Baliffs	1 Chronicles 23:4,5
	Judges	1 Chronicles 23:4,5
	Public administrators	1 Chronicles 26:29,30
Ministerial Duties	Priests	1 Chronicles 24:1,2
	Prophets	1 Chronicles 25:1
	Assistants for sacrifices	1 Chronicles 23:29–31
	Assistants for purification ceremonies	1 Chronicles 23:27,28
Service Duties	Bakers of the Bread of the Presence	1 Chronicles 23:29
	Those who checked the weights and measures	1 Chronicles 23:29
	Custodians	1 Chronicles 23:28
Financial Duties	Those who cared for the treasury	1 Chronicles 26:20
	Those who cared for dedicated items	1 Chronicles 26:26–28
Artistic Duties	Musicians	1 Chronicles 25:6
	Singers	1 Chronicles 25:7
Protective Duties	Temple guards	1 Chronicles 23:5
	Guards for the gates and storehouses	1 Chronicles 26:12–18
Individual Assignments	Recording secretary	1 Chronicles 24:6
	Chaplain to the king	1 Chronicles 25:4
	Private prophet to the king	1 Chronicles 25:2
	Captain of the guard	1 Chronicles 26:1
	Chief officer of the treasury	1 Chronicles 26:23,24

Mushi. The sons of Mahli *were* Eleazar and Kish. ²²And Eleazar died, and had no sons, but only daughters; and their brethren, the sons of Kish, took them *as wives.* ²³The sons of Mushi *were* Mahli, Eder, and Jeremoth—three *in all.*

²⁴These *were* the sons of Levi by their fathers' houses—the heads of the fathers' *houses* as they were counted individually by the number of their names, who did the work for the service of the house of the LORD, from the age of twenty years and above.

23:1–27:34 David divided the tasks of the new temple between Levites, priests, singers, gatekeepers, administrators, the army, and the leaders. The original readers of Chronicles were Jews returning from Babylonian exile to rebuild the destroyed temple. This reminded them of what their fathers' sin forfeited, and how inferior their new temple was to Solomon's.

²⁵For David said, "The LORD God of Israel has given rest to His people, that they may dwell in Jerusalem forever"; ²⁶and also to the Levites, "They shall no longer carry the tabernacle, or any of the articles for its service." ²⁷For by the last words of David the Levites *were* numbered from twenty years old and above; ²⁸because their duty *was* to help the sons of Aaron in the service of the house of the LORD, in the courts and in the chambers, in the purifying of all holy things and the work of the service of the house of God, ²⁹both with the showbread and the fine flour for the grain offering, with the unleavened cakes and *what is baked in* the pan, with what is mixed and with all kinds of measures and sizes; ³⁰to stand every morning to thank and praise the LORD, and likewise at evening; ³¹and at every presentation of a burnt offering to the LORD on the Sabbaths and on the New Moons and on the set feasts, by number according to the ordinance governing them, regularly before the LORD; ³²and that they should attend to the needs of the tabernacle of meeting, the needs of the holy *place,* and the needs of the sons of Aaron their brethren in the work of the house of the LORD.

The Divisions of the Priests

24 Now *these are* the divisions of the sons of Aaron. The sons of Aaron *were* Nadab, Abihu, Eleazar, and Ithamar. ²And Nadab and Abihu died before their father, and had no children; therefore Eleazar and Ithamar ministered as priests. ³Then David with Zadok of the sons of Eleazar, and Ahimelech of the sons of Ithamar, divided them according to the schedule of their service.

⁴There were more leaders found of the sons of Eleazar than of the sons of Ithamar, and *thus* they were divided. Among the sons of Eleazar *were* sixteen heads of *their* fathers' houses, and eight heads of their fathers' houses among the sons of Ithamar. ⁵Thus they were divided by lot, one group as another, for there were officials of the sanctuary and officials *of the house* of God, from the sons of Eleazar and from the sons of Ithamar. ⁶And the scribe, Shemaiah the son of Nethanel, *one of* the Levites, wrote them down before the king, the leaders, Zadok the priest, Ahimelech the son of Abiathar, and the heads of the fathers' *houses* of the priests and Levites, one father's house taken for Eleazar and *one* for Ithamar.

24:5 divided by lot. This method of discerning God's will was used to sort out all the duties in order to avoid pride or jealousy (see v. 31; Prov. 16:33).

⁷Now the first lot fell to Jehoiarib, the second to Jedaiah, ⁸the third to Harim, the fourth to Seorim, ⁹the fifth to Malchijah, the sixth to Mijamin, ¹⁰the seventh to Hakkoz, the eighth to Abijah, ¹¹the ninth to Jeshua, the tenth to Shecaniah, ¹²the eleventh to Eliashib, the twelfth to Jakim, ¹³the thirteenth to Huppah, the fourteenth to Jeshebeab, ¹⁴the fifteenth to Bilgah, the sixteenth to Immer, ¹⁵the seventeenth to Hezir, the eighteenth to Happizzez,ᵃ ¹⁶the nineteenth to Pethahiah, the twentieth to Jehezekel,ᵃ ¹⁷the twenty-first to Jachin, the twenty-second to Gamul, ¹⁸the twenty-third to Delaiah, the twenty-fourth to Maaziah.

¹⁹This *was* the schedule of their service

24:15 ᵃSeptuagint and Vulgate read *Aphses.* **24:16** ᵃMasoretic Text reads *Jehezkel.*

for coming into the house of the LORD according to their ordinance by the hand of Aaron their father, as the LORD God of Israel had commanded him.

> **24:4–19** The priesthood duties were divided into 24 divisions, 16 of Eleazar and 8 of Ithamar. Eleazar's family had twice as many divisions because he had received the birthright, more descendants, and more leadership ability. The divisions of priests served for either two-week periods annually or a one-month period every two years (see 27:1–15). The rest of the time they ministered to the people in their own hometowns. These divisions extended into the time of Christ (see Luke 1:5–9).

Other Levites

²⁰And the rest of the sons of Levi: of the sons of Amram, Shubael;ᵃ of the sons of Shubael, Jehdeiah. ²¹Concerning Rehabiah, of the sons of Rehabiah, the first *was* Isshiah. ²²Of the Izharites, Shelomoth;ᵃ of the sons of Shelomoth, Jahath. ²³Of the sons *of Hebron,*ᵃ Jeriah *was the first,*ᵇ Amariah the second, Jahaziel the third, *and* Jekameam the fourth. ²⁴*Of* the sons of Uzziel, Michah; of the sons of Michah, Shamir. ²⁵The brother of Michah, Isshiah; of the sons of Isshiah, Zechariah. ²⁶The sons of Merari *were* Mahli and Mushi; the son of Jaaziah, Beno. ²⁷The sons of Merari by Jaaziah *were* Beno, Shoham, Zaccur, and Ibri. ²⁸Of Mahli: Eleazar, who had no sons. ²⁹Of Kish: the son of Kish, Jerahmeel.

³⁰Also the sons of Mushi *were* Mahli, Eder, and Jerimoth. These *were* the sons of the Levites according to their fathers' houses.

³¹These also cast lots just as their brothers the sons of Aaron did, in the presence of King David, Zadok, Ahimelech, and the heads of the fathers' *houses* of the priests and Levites. The chief fathers *did* just as their younger brethren.

> **25:1–31** David established music as a central feature in the worship of God.

The Musicians

25 Moreover David and the captains of the army separated for the service *some* of the sons of Asaph, of Heman, and of Jeduthun, who *should* prophesy with harps, stringed instruments, and cymbals. And the number of the skilled men performing their service was: ²Of the sons of Asaph: Zaccur, Joseph, Nethaniah, and Asharelah;ᵃ the sons of Asaph *were* under the direction of Asaph, who prophesied according to the order of the king. ³Of Jeduthun, the sons of Jeduthun: Gedaliah, Zeri,ᵃ Jeshaiah, Shimei, Hashabiah, and Mattithiah, six,ᵇ under the direction of their father Jeduthun, who prophesied with a harp to give thanks and to praise the LORD. ⁴Of Heman, the sons of Heman: Bukkiah, Mattaniah, Uzziel,ᵃ Shebuel,ᵇ Jerimoth,ᶜ Hananiah, Hanani, Eliathah, Giddalti, Romamti-Ezer, Joshbekashah, Mallothi, Hothir, *and* Mahazioth. ⁵All these *were* the sons of Heman the king's seer in the words of God, to exalt his horn.ᵃ For God gave Heman fourteen sons and three daughters.

> **25:1 prophesy.** Prophesying is not necessarily predicting the future or speaking direct revelation. It is proclaiming truth to people (see 1 Cor. 14:3), and music is a way to proclaim this truth through the lyrics. David and the leaders selected those most capable of leading the people to worship God through their music.

⁶All these *were* under the direction of their father for the music *in* the house of the LORD, with cymbals, stringed instruments, and harps, for the service of the house of God. Asaph, Jeduthun, and Heman *were* under the authority of the king. ⁷So the number of them, with their brethren who were instructed in the songs of the LORD, all who were skillful, *was* two hundred and eighty-eight. ⁸And they cast lots for their duty, the

---

24:20 ᵃSpelled *Shebuel* in 23:16   24:22 ᵃSpelled *Shelomith* in 23:18   24:23 ᵃSupplied from 23:19 (following some Hebrew manuscripts and Septuagint manuscripts)   ᵇSupplied from 23:19 (following some Hebrew manuscripts and Septuagint manuscripts)   25:2 ᵃSpelled *Jesharelah* in verse 14   25:3 ᵃSpelled *Jizri* in verse 11   ᵇ*Shimei,* appearing in one Hebrew and several Septuagint manuscripts, completes the total of six sons (compare verse 17).   25:4 ᵃSpelled *Azarel* in verse 18   ᵇSpelled *Shubael* in verse 20   ᶜSpelled *Jeremoth* in verse 22   25:5 ᵃThat is, to increase his power or influence

small as well as the great, the teacher with the student.

⁹Now the first lot for Asaph came out for Joseph; the second for Gedaliah, him with his brethren and sons, twelve; ¹⁰the third for Zaccur, his sons and his brethren, twelve; ¹¹the fourth for Jizri,ᵃ his sons and his brethren, twelve; ¹²the fifth for Nethaniah, his sons and his brethren, twelve; ¹³the sixth for Bukkiah, his sons and his brethren, twelve; ¹⁴the seventh for Jesharelah,ᵃ his sons and his brethren, twelve; ¹⁵the eighth for Jeshaiah, his sons and his brethren, twelve; ¹⁶the ninth for Mattaniah, his sons and his brethren, twelve; ¹⁷the tenth for Shimei, his sons and his brethren, twelve; ¹⁸the eleventh for Azarel,ᵃ his sons and his brethren, twelve; ¹⁹the twelfth for Hashabiah, his sons and his brethren, twelve; ²⁰the thirteenth for Shubael,ᵃ his sons and his brethren, twelve; ²¹the fourteenth for Mattithiah, his sons and his brethren, twelve; ²²the fifteenth for Jeremoth,ᵃ his sons and his brethren, twelve; ²³the sixteenth for Hananiah, his sons and his brethren, twelve; ²⁴the seventeenth for Joshbekashah, his sons and his brethren, twelve; ²⁵the eighteenth for Hanani, his sons and his brethren, twelve; ²⁶the nineteenth for Mallothi, his sons and his brethren, twelve; ²⁷the twentieth for Eliathah, his sons and his brethren, twelve; ²⁸the twenty-first for Hothir, his sons and his brethren, twelve; ²⁹the twenty-second for Giddalti, his sons and his brethren, twelve; ³⁰the twenty-third for Mahazioth, his sons and his brethren, twelve; ³¹the twenty-fourth for Romamti-Ezer, his sons and his brethren, twelve.

The Gatekeepers

26 Concerning the divisions of the gatekeepers: of the Korahites, Meshelemiah the son of Kore, of the sons of Asaph. ²And the sons of Meshelemiah *were* Zechariah the firstborn, Jediael the second, Zebadiah the third, Jathniel the fourth, ³Elam the fifth, Jehohanan the sixth, Eliehoenai the seventh.

⁴Moreover the sons of Obed-Edom *were* Shemaiah the firstborn, Jehozabad the sec-

ond, Joah the third, Sacar the fourth, Nethanel the fifth, ⁵Ammiel the sixth, Issachar the seventh, Peulthai the eighth; for God blessed him.

⁶Also to Shemaiah his son were sons born who governed their fathers' houses, because they *were* men of great ability. ⁷The sons of Shemaiah *were* Othni, Raphael, Obed, and Elzabad, whose brothers Elihu and Semachiah *were* able men.

⁸All these *were* of the sons of Obed-Edom, they and their sons and their brethren, able men with strength for the work: sixty-two of Obed-Edom.

⁹And Meshelemiah had sons and brethren, eighteen able men.

¹⁰Also Hosah, of the children of Merari, had sons: Shimri the first (for *though* he was not the firstborn, his father made him the first), ¹¹Hilkiah the second, Tebaliah the third, Zechariah the fourth; all the sons and brethren of Hosah *were* thirteen.

¹²Among these *were* the divisions of the gatekeepers, among the chief men, *having* duties just like their brethren, to serve in the house of the LORD. ¹³And they cast lots for each gate, the small as well as the great, according to their father's house. ¹⁴The lot for the East *Gate* fell to Shelemiah. Then they cast lots *for* his son Zechariah, a wise counselor, and his lot came out for the North Gate; ¹⁵to Obed-Edom the South Gate, and to his sons the storehouse.ᵃ ¹⁶To Shuppim and Hosah *the lot came out* for the West Gate, with the Shallecheth Gate on the ascending highway—watchman opposite watchman. ¹⁷On the east were *six* Levites, on the north four each day, on the south four each day, and for the storehouseᵃ two by two. ¹⁸As for the Parbarᵃ on the west, *there were* four on the highway *and* two at the Parbar. ¹⁹These were the divisions of the gatekeepers among the sons of Korah and among the sons of Merari.

The Treasuries and Other Duties

²⁰Of the Levites, Ahijah *was* over the treasuries of the house of God and over the treasuries of the dedicated things. ²¹The sons of Laadan, the descendants of the

---

Gershonites of Laadan, heads of their fathers' *houses*, of Laadan the Gershonite: Jehieli. ²²The sons of Jehieli, Zetham and Joel his brother, *were* over the treasuries of the house of the LORD. ²³Of the Amramites, the Izharites, the Hebronites, and the Uzzielites: ²⁴Shebuel the son of Gershom, the son of Moses, *was* overseer of the treasuries. ²⁵And his brethren by Eliezer *were* Rehabiah his son, Jeshaiah his son, Joram his son, Zichri his son, and Shelomith his son.

²⁶This Shelomith and his brethren *were* over all the treasuries of the dedicated things which King David and the heads of fathers' *houses*, the captains over thousands and hundreds, and the captains of the army, had dedicated. ²⁷Some of the spoils won in battles they dedicated to maintain the house of the LORD. ²⁸And all that Samuel the seer, Saul the son of Kish, Abner the son of Ner, and Joab the son of Zeruiah had dedicated, every dedicated *thing*, was under the hand of Shelomith and his brethren.

²⁹Of the Izharites, Chenaniah and his sons *performed* duties as officials and judges over Israel outside Jerusalem.

³⁰Of the Hebronites, Hashabiah and his brethren, one thousand seven hundred able men, had the oversight of Israel on the west side of the Jordan for all the business of the LORD, and in the service of the king. ³¹Among the Hebronites, Jerijah *was* head of the Hebronites according to his genealogy of the fathers. In the fortieth year of the reign of David they were sought, and there were found among them capable men at Jazer of Gilead. ³²And his brethren *were* two thousand seven hundred able men, heads of fathers' *houses*, whom King David made officials over the Reubenites, the Gadites, and the half-tribe of Manasseh, for every matter pertaining to God and the affairs of the king.

The Military Divisions

27 And the children of Israel, according to their number, the heads of fathers' *houses*, the captains of thousands and hundreds and their officers, served the king in every matter of the *military* divisions. *These divisions* came in and went out month by month throughout all the months of the year, each division *having* twenty-four thousand.

²Over the first division for the first month *was* Jashobeam the son of Zabdiel, and in his division *were* twenty-four thousand; ³*he was* of the children of Perez, and the chief of all the captains of the army for the first month. ⁴Over the division of the second month *was* Dodai*ᵃ* an Ahohite, and of his division Mikloth also *was* the leader; in his division *were* twenty-four thousand. ⁵The third captain of the army for the third month *was* Benaiah, the son of Jehoiada the priest, who was chief; in his division *were* twenty-four thousand. ⁶This was the Benaiah *who was* mighty *among* the thirty, and was over the thirty; in his division *was* Ammizabad his son. ⁷The fourth *captain* for the fourth month *was* Asahel the brother of Joab, and Zebadiah his son after him; in his division *were* twenty-four thousand. ⁸The fifth *captain* for the fifth month *was* Shamhuth*ᵃ* the Izrahite; in his division *were* twenty-four thousand. ⁹The sixth *captain* for the sixth month *was* Ira the son of Ikkesh the Tekoite; in his division *were* twenty-four thousand. ¹⁰The seventh *captain* for the seventh month *was* Helez the Pelonite, of the children of Ephraim; in his division *were* twenty-four thousand. ¹¹The eighth *captain* for the eighth month *was* Sibbechai the Hushathite, of the Zarhites; in his division *were* twenty-four thousand. ¹²The ninth *captain* for the ninth month *was* Abiezer the Anathothite, of the Benjamites; in his division *were* twenty-four thousand. ¹³The tenth *captain* for the tenth month *was* Maharai the Netophathite, of the Zarhites; in his division *were* twenty-four thousand. ¹⁴The eleventh *captain* for the eleventh month *was* Benaiah the Pirathonite, of the children of Ephraim; in his division *were* twenty-four thousand. ¹⁵The

27:4 *ᵃ*Hebrew *Dodai*, usually spelled *Dodo* (compare 2 Samuel 23:9)   27:8 *ᵃ*Spelled *Shammoth* in 11:27 and *Shammah* in 2 Samuel 23:11

twelfth *captain* for the twelfth month *was* Heldai[a] the Netophathite, of Othniel; in his division *were* twenty-four thousand.

Leaders of Tribes

¹⁶Furthermore, over the tribes of Israel: the officer over the Reubenites *was* Eliezer the son of Zichri; over the Simeonites, Shephatiah the son of Maachah; ¹⁷*over* the Levites, Hashabiah the son of Kemuel; over the Aaronites, Zadok; ¹⁸*over* Judah, Elihu, *one* of David's brothers; *over* Issachar, Omri the son of Michael; ¹⁹*over* Zebulun, Ishmaiah the son of Obadiah; *over* Naphtali, Jerimoth the son of Azriel; ²⁰*over* the children of Ephraim, Hoshea the son of Azaziah; *over* the half-tribe of Manasseh, Joel the son of Pedaiah; ²¹*over* the half-*tribe* of Manasseh in Gilead, Iddo the son of Zechariah; *over* Benjamin, Jaasiel the son of Abner; ²²*over* Dan, Azarel the son of Jeroham. These *were* the leaders of the tribes of Israel.

²³But David did not take the number of those twenty years old and under, because the LORD had said He would multiply Israel like the stars of the heavens. ²⁴Joab the son of Zeruiah began a census, but he did not finish, for wrath came upon Israel because of this census; nor was the number recorded in the account of the chronicles of King David.

Other State Officials

²⁵And Azmaveth the son of Adiel *was* over the king's treasuries; and Jehonathan the son of Uzziah was over the storehouses in the field, in the cities, in the villages, and in the fortresses. ²⁶Ezri the son of Chelub was over those who did the work of the field for tilling the ground. ²⁷And Shimei the Ramathite *was* over the vineyards, and Zabdi the Shiphmite was over the produce of the vineyards for the supply of wine. ²⁸Baal-Hanan the Gederite was over the olive trees and the sycamore trees that *were* in the lowlands, and Joash *was* over the store of oil. ²⁹And Shitrai the Sharonite *was* over the herds that fed in Sharon, and Shaphat the son of Adlai was over the herds *that were* in the valleys. ³⁰Obil the Ishmaelite *was* over the camels, Jehdeiah the Merono-

thite *was* over the donkeys, ³¹and Jaziz the Hagrite *was* over the flocks. All these *were* the officials over King David's property.

³²Also Jehonathan, David's uncle, *was* a counselor, a wise man, and a scribe; and Jehiel the son of Hachmoni *was* with the king's sons. ³³Ahithophel *was* the king's counselor, and Hushai the Archite *was* the king's companion. ³⁴After Ahithophel *was* Jehoiada the son of Benaiah, then Abiathar. And the general of the king's army *was* Joab.

> **27:23,24** During his census (see 1 Chr. 21:1–30), David did not try to number all the Israelites because there were too many. He never finished the census, for he was interrupted by guilt and judgment. No records were kept of this census because it was too painful.

Solomon Instructed to Build the Temple

28 Now David assembled at Jerusalem all the leaders of Israel: the officers of the tribes and the captains of the divisions who served the king, the captains over thousands and captains over hundreds, and the stewards over all the substance and possessions of the king and of his sons, with the officials, the valiant men, and all the mighty men of valor.

²Then King David rose to his feet and said, "Hear me, my brethren and my people: I *had* it in my heart to build a house of rest for the ark of the covenant of the LORD, and for the footstool of our God, and had made preparations to build it. ³But God said to me, 'You shall not build a house for My name, because you *have been* a man of war and have shed blood.' ⁴However the LORD God of Israel chose me above all the house of my father to be king over Israel forever, for He has chosen Judah *to be* the ruler. And of the house of Judah, the house of my father, and among the sons of my father, He was pleased with me to make *me* king over all Israel. ⁵And of all my sons (for the LORD has given me many sons) He has chosen my son Solomon to sit on the throne of the kingdom of the LORD over Israel. ⁶Now He said to me, 'It is your son Solomon *who* shall build My house and My courts; for I have chosen him *to be* My son,

and I will be his Father. [7]Moreover I will establish his kingdom forever, if he is steadfast to observe My commandments and My judgments, as it is this day.' [8]Now therefore, in the sight of all Israel, the assembly of the LORD, and in the hearing of our God, be careful to seek out all the commandments of the LORD your God, that you may possess this good land, and leave *it* as an inheritance for your children after you forever.

> **28:2–8** For the people's sake, David testified to the Davidic Covenant originally given to him by God in 2 Sam. 7. He made it clear that God had chosen Solomon (see 2 Sam. 12:24,25) just as the coming Christ will be God's chosen Son to ultimately fulfill the covenant.

[9]"As for you, my son Solomon, know the God of your father, and serve Him with a loyal heart and with a willing mind; for the LORD searches all hearts and understands all the intent of the thoughts. If you seek Him, He will be found by you; but if you forsake Him, He will cast you off forever. [10]Consider now, for the LORD has chosen you to build a house for the sanctuary; be strong, and do it."

[11]Then David gave his son Solomon the plans for the vestibule, its houses, its treasuries, its upper chambers, its inner chambers, and the place of the mercy seat; [12]and the plans for all that he had by the Spirit, of the courts of the house of the LORD, of all the chambers all around, of the treasuries of the house of God, and of the treasuries for the dedicated things; [13]also for the division of the priests and the Levites, for all the work of the service of the house of the LORD, and for all the articles of service in the house of the LORD. [14]*He gave* gold by weight for *things* of gold, for all articles used in every kind of service; also *silver* for all articles of silver by weight, for all articles used in every kind of service; [15]the weight for the lampstands of gold, and their lamps of gold, by weight for each lampstand and its lamps; for the lampstands of silver by weight, for the lampstand and its lamps, according to the use of each lampstand. [16]And by weight *he gave* gold for the tables of the showbread, for each table, and silver for the tables of silver; [17]also pure gold for the forks, the basins, the pitchers of pure gold, and the golden bowls—*he gave gold* by weight for every bowl; and for the silver bowls, *silver* by weight for every bowl; [18]and refined gold by weight for the altar of incense, and for the construction of the chariot, that is, the gold cherubim that spread *their wings* and overshadowed the ark of the covenant of the LORD. [19]"All *this*," said *David*, "the LORD made me understand in writing, by *His* hand upon me, all the works of these plans."

[20]And David said to his son Solomon, "Be strong and of good courage, and do *it*; do not fear nor be dismayed, for the LORD God—my God—*will be* with you. He will not leave you nor forsake you, until you have finished all the work for the service of the house of the LORD. [21]*Here are* the divisions of the priests and the Levites for all the service of the house of God; and every willing craftsman *will be* with you for all manner of workmanship, for every kind of service; also the leaders and all the people *will be* completely at your command."

> **28:9–21** David speaks to Solomon regarding spiritual devotion, architectural execution, divine intervention, and human participation.

Offerings for Building the Temple

29 Furthermore King David said to all the assembly: "My son Solomon, whom alone God has chosen, *is* young and inexperienced; and the work *is* great, because the temple[a] *is* not for man but for the LORD God. [2]Now for the house of my God I have prepared with all my might: gold for *things to be made of* gold, silver for *things of* silver, bronze for *things of* bronze, iron for *things of* iron, wood for *things of* wood, onyx stones, *stones* to be set, glistening stones of various colors, all kinds of precious stones, and marble slabs in abundance. [3]Moreover, because I have set my affection on the house of my God, I have given to the house of my God, over and above all that I have prepared for the holy house, my own special treasure of gold and silver: [4]three thousand talents of gold, of

---

29:1 [a]Literally *palace*

the gold of Ophir, and seven thousand talents of refined silver, to overlay the walls of the houses; ⁵the gold for *things of* gold and the silver for *things of* silver, and for all kinds of work *to be done* by the hands of craftsmen. Who *then* is willing to consecrate himself this day to the LORD?"

> **29:1–5** David called for consecrated giving to the project (see 28:1) based on the example of his own generosity. He gave an almost immeasurable personal fortune to the temple building.

⁶Then the leaders of the fathers' *houses,* leaders of the tribes of Israel, the captains of thousands and of hundreds, with the officers over the king's work, offered willingly. ⁷They gave for the work of the house of God five thousand talents and ten thousand darics of gold, ten thousand talents of silver, eighteen thousand talents of bronze, and one hundred thousand talents of iron. ⁸And whoever had *precious* stones gave *them* to the treasury of the house of the LORD, into the hand of Jehiel*ᵃ* the Gershonite. ⁹Then the people rejoiced, for they had offered willingly, because with a loyal heart they had offered willingly to the LORD; and King David also rejoiced greatly.

> **29:6–9 willingly.** At this time, tithes were required by law to be paid. Giving willingly, however, is the voluntary giving from the heart to the Lord. The New Testament never demands a tithe to be given to God, but requires that taxes be paid to one's government (see Luke 6:38; Rom. 13:6,7). Biblical giving involves paying taxes and giving to God the gift we bring willingly.

David's Praise to God

¹⁰Therefore David blessed the LORD before all the assembly; and David said:

"Blessed are You, LORD God of Israel,
    our Father, forever and ever.
¹¹ Yours, O LORD, *is* the greatness,
    The power and the glory,
    The victory and the majesty;
    For all *that is* in heaven and in earth
      is Yours;
    Yours *is* the kingdom, O LORD,
    And You are exalted as head over all.

¹² Both riches and honor *come* from
      You,
    And You reign over all.
    In Your hand *is* power and might;
    In Your hand *it is* to make great
    And to give strength to all.

¹³ "Now therefore, our God,
    We thank You
    And praise Your glorious name.
¹⁴ But who *am* I, and who *are* my
      people,
    That we should be able to offer so
      willingly as this?
    For all things *come* from You,
    And of Your own we have given You.
¹⁵ For we *are* aliens and pilgrims before
      You,
    As *were* all our fathers;
    Our days on earth *are* as a shadow,
    And without hope.

> **29:10–15** David responds to the people's willing sacrifices of wealth and praise by offering a prayer of thanksgiving to the Lord. He acknowledges that all things belong to and come from God, and he gives God the credit for the people's generosity.

¹⁶"O LORD our God, all this abundance that we have prepared to build You a house for Your holy name is from Your hand, and *is* all Your own. ¹⁷I know also, my God, that You test the heart and have pleasure in uprightness. As for me, in the uprightness of my heart I have willingly offered all these *things;* and now with joy I have seen Your people, who are present here to offer willingly to You. ¹⁸O LORD God of Abraham, Isaac, and Israel, our fathers, keep this forever in the intent of the thoughts of the heart of Your people, and fix their heart toward You. ¹⁹And give my son Solomon a loyal heart to keep Your commandments and Your testimonies and Your statutes, to do all *these things,* and to build the temple*ᵃ* for which I have made provision."

> **29:17 test the heart.** Opportunities to give to God are tests of character of a believer's devotion to Him. David acknowledges that the attitude of one's heart is more important that the amount of offering one gives.

29:8 *ᵃ*Possibly the same as *Jehieli* (compare 26:21,22)   **29:19** *ᵃ*Literally *palace*

[20]Then David said to all the assembly, "Now bless the LORD your God." So all the assembly blessed the LORD God of their fathers, and bowed their heads and prostrated themselves before the LORD and the king.

Solomon Anointed King

[21]And they made sacrifices to the LORD and offered burnt offerings to the LORD on the next day: a thousand bulls, a thousand rams, a thousand lambs, with their drink offerings, and sacrifices in abundance for all Israel. [22]So they ate and drank before the LORD with great gladness on that day. And they made Solomon the son of David king the second time, and anointed *him* before the LORD *to be* the leader, and Zadok *to be* priest. [23]Then Solomon sat on the throne of the LORD as king instead of David his father, and prospered; and all Israel obeyed him. [24]All the leaders and the mighty men, and also all the sons of King David, submitted themselves to King Solomon. [25]So the LORD exalted Solomon exceedingly in the sight of all Israel, and bestowed on him *such* royal majesty as had not been on any king before him in Israel.

The Close of David's Reign

[26]Thus David the son of Jesse reigned over all Israel. [27]And the period that he reigned over Israel *was* forty years; seven years he reigned in Hebron, and thirty-three *years* he reigned in Jerusalem. [28]So he died in a good old age, full of days and riches and honor; and Solomon his son reigned in his place. [29]Now the acts of King David, first and last, indeed they *are* written in the book of Samuel the seer, in the book of Nathan the prophet, and in the book of Gad the seer, [30]with all his reign and his might, and the events that happened to him, to Israel, and to all the kingdoms of the lands.

OUTLINE OF 2 CHRONICLES

1:1–9:31 This section continues from 1 Chr. and covers the rule of Solomon (about 971–931 B.C.). The major theme is the building of the temple in Jerusalem in order to centralize and unify Israel in the worship of God.

Solomon Requests Wisdom

1 Now Solomon the son of David was strengthened in his kingdom, and the LORD his God *was* with him and exalted him exceedingly.

²And Solomon spoke to all Israel, to the captains of thousands and of hundreds, to the judges, and to every leader in all Israel, the heads of the fathers' *houses.* ³Then Solomon, and all the assembly with him, went to the high place that *was* at Gibeon; for the tabernacle of meeting with God was there, which Moses the servant of the LORD had made in the wilderness. ⁴But David had brought up the ark of God from Kirjath Jearim to *the place* David had prepared for it, for he had pitched a tent for it at Jerusalem. ⁵Now the bronze altar that Bezalel the son of Uri, the son of Hur, had made, he put*ᵃ* before the tabernacle of the LORD; Solomon and the assembly sought Him *there.* ⁶And Solomon went up there to the bronze altar before the LORD, which *was* at the tabernacle of meeting, and offered a thousand burnt offerings on it.

1:3 Gibeon. The tabernacle remained at Gibeon, and the ark stayed in Jerusalem while the temple was being built. **tabernacle.** This tent, built in the days of Moses, was where God met with His people (see Ex. 25:22). It was the center of worship until the temple was built.

⁷On that night God appeared to Solomon, and said to him, "Ask! What shall I give you?"

⁸And Solomon said to God: "You have shown great mercy to David my father, and have made me king in his place. ⁹Now, O LORD God, let Your promise to David my father be established, for You have made me king over a people like the dust of the earth in multitude. ¹⁰Now give me wisdom and knowledge, that I may go out and come in before this people; for who can judge this great people of Yours?"

¹¹Then God said to Solomon: "Because this was in your heart, and you have not asked riches or wealth or honor or the life of your enemies, nor have you asked long life—but have asked wisdom and knowledge for yourself, that you may judge My people over whom I have made you king— ¹²wisdom and knowledge *are* granted to you; and I will give you riches and wealth and honor, such as none of the kings have had who *were* before you, nor shall any after you have the like."

Solomon's Military and Economic Power

¹³So Solomon came to Jerusalem from the high place that *was* at Gibeon, from before the tabernacle of meeting, and reigned over Israel. ¹⁴And Solomon gathered chariots and horsemen; he had one thousand four hundred chariots and twelve thousand horsemen, whom he stationed in the chariot cities and with the king in Jerusalem. ¹⁵Also the king made silver and gold as common in Jerusalem as stones, and he made cedars as abundant as the sycamores which *are* in the lowland. ¹⁶And Solomon had horses imported from Egypt and Keveh; the king's merchants bought them in Keveh at the *current* price. ¹⁷They also acquired and imported from Egypt a chariot for six hundred *shekels* of silver, and a horse for one hundred and fifty; thus, through their agents,*ᵃ* they exported them to all the kings of the Hittites and the kings of Syria.

1:10 Solomon agreed with his father on his need for wisdom, and he asked God for it (see 1 Chr. 22:5; 1 Kin. 3:3–15).

Solomon Prepares to Build the Temple

2 Then Solomon determined to build a temple for the name of the LORD, and a royal house for himself. ²Solomon selected seventy thousand men to bear burdens, eighty thousand to quarry *stone* in the mountains, and three thousand six hundred to oversee them.

³Then Solomon sent to Hiram*ᵃ* king of Tyre, saying:

1:5 *ᵃ*Some authorities read *it was there.*   1:17 *ᵃ*Literally *by their hands*   2:3 *ᵃ*Hebrew *Huram* (compare 1 Kings 5:1)

As you have dealt with David my father, and sent him cedars to build himself a house to dwell in, *so deal with me.* ⁴Behold, I am building a temple for the name of the LORD my God, to dedicate *it* to Him, to burn before Him sweet incense, for the continual showbread, for the burnt offerings morning and evening, on the Sabbaths, on the New Moons, and on the set feasts of the LORD our God. This *is an ordinance* forever to Israel.

⁵ And the temple which I build *will be* great, for our God is greater than all gods. ⁶But who is able to build Him a temple, since heaven and the heaven of heavens cannot contain Him? Who *am* I then, that I should build Him a temple, except to burn sacrifice before Him?

⁷ Therefore send me at once a man skillful to work in gold and silver, in bronze and iron, in purple and crimson and blue, who has skill to engrave with the skillful men who are with me in Judah and Jerusalem, whom David my father provided. ⁸Also send me cedar and cypress and algum logs from Lebanon, for I know that your servants have skill to cut timber in Lebanon; and indeed my servants *will be* with your servants, ⁹to prepare timber for me in abundance, for the temple which I am about to build *shall be* great and wonderful.

¹⁰ And indeed I will give to your servants, the woodsmen who cut timber, twenty thousand kors of ground wheat, twenty thousand kors of barley, twenty thousand baths of wine, and twenty thousand baths of oil.

¹¹Then Hiram king of Tyre answered in writing, which he sent to Solomon:

Because the LORD loves His people, He has made you king over them.

¹²Hiram*ᵃ* also said:

Blessed *be* the LORD God of Israel, who made heaven and earth, for He has given King David a wise son, endowed with prudence and understanding, who will build a temple for the LORD and a royal house for himself!

> **2:12 God...who made heaven and earth.** This was the common identification of the true God when pagans spoke of or were told of Him (see 2 Chr. 36:23; Ezra 1:2).

¹³ And now I have sent a skillful man, endowed with understanding, Huram*ᵃ* my master*ᵇ* *craftsman* ¹⁴(the son of a woman of the daughters of Dan, and his father was a man of Tyre), skilled to work in gold and silver, bronze and iron, stone and wood, purple and blue, fine linen and crimson, and to make any engraving and to accomplish any plan which may be given to him, with your skillful men and with the skillful men of my lord David your father.

¹⁵ Now therefore, the wheat, the barley, the oil, and the wine which my lord has spoken of, let him send to his servants. ¹⁶And we will cut wood from Lebanon, as much as you need; we will bring it to you in rafts by sea to Joppa, and you will carry it up to Jerusalem.

¹⁷Then Solomon numbered all the aliens who *were* in the land of Israel, after the census in which David his father had numbered them; and there were found to be one hundred and fifty-three thousand six hundred. ¹⁸And he made seventy thousand of them bearers of burdens, eighty thousand stonecutters in the mountain, and three thousand six hundred overseers to make the people work.

Solomon Builds the Temple

3 Now Solomon began to build the house of the LORD at Jerusalem on Mount

---

2:12 *ᵃ*Hebrew *Huram* (compare 1 Kings 5:1)   2:13 *ᵃ*Spelled *Hiram* in 1 Kings 7:13   *ᵇ*Literally *father* (compare 1 Kings 7:13,14)

Moriah, where *the LORD*^a had appeared to his father David, at the place that David had prepared on the threshing floor of Ornan^b the Jebusite. ²And he began to build on the second *day* of the second month in the fourth year of his reign.

³This is the foundation which Solomon laid for building the house of God: The length *was* sixty cubits (by cubits according to the former measure) and the width twenty cubits. ⁴And the vestibule that *was* in front *of the sanctuary*^a was twenty cubits long across the width of the house, and the height *was* one hundred and^b twenty. He overlaid the inside with pure gold. ⁵The larger room^a he paneled with cypress which he overlaid with fine gold, and he carved palm trees and chainwork on it. ⁶And he decorated the house with precious stones for beauty, and the gold *was* gold from Parvaim. ⁷He also overlaid the house—the beams and doorposts, its walls and doors—with gold; and he carved cherubim on the walls.

⁸And he made the Most Holy Place. Its length was according to the width of the house, twenty cubits, and its width twenty cubits. He overlaid it with six hundred talents of fine gold. ⁹The weight of the nails *was* fifty shekels of gold; and he overlaid the upper area with gold. ¹⁰In the Most Holy Place he made two cherubim, fashioned by carving, and overlaid them with gold. ¹¹The wings of the cherubim *were* twenty cubits in *overall* length: one wing *of the one cherub was* five cubits, touching the wall of the room, and the other wing *was* five cubits, touching the wing of the other cherub; ¹²*one* wing of the other cherub *was* five cubits, touching the wall of the room, and the other wing *also was* five cubits, touching the wing of the other cherub. ¹³The wings of these cherubim spanned twenty cubits overall. They stood on their feet, and they faced inward. ¹⁴And he made the veil of blue, purple, crimson, and fine linen, and wove cherubim into it.

> **3:14 veil.** This is the veil of the tabernacle (see Ex. 26:31–35) that separated the Holy Place from the Most Holy Place, which was entered only once a year by the High Priest on the Day of Atonement (see Lev. 16). At Christ's death, the veil in Herod's temple was torn in two (Matt. 27:51), and believers were given full access to God through Jesus, the Mediator and once-for-all sacrifice (Heb. 3:14–16).

¹⁵Also he made in front of the temple^a two pillars thirty-five^b cubits high, and the capital that *was* on the top of each of *them* was five cubits. ¹⁶He made wreaths of chainwork, as in the inner sanctuary, and put *them* on top of the pillars; and he made one hundred pomegranates, and put *them* on the wreaths of chainwork. ¹⁷Then he set up the pillars before the temple, one on the right hand and the other on the left; he called the name of the one on the right hand Jachin, and the name of the one on the left Boaz.

Furnishings of the Temple

4 Moreover he made a bronze altar: twenty cubits *was* its length, twenty cubits its width, and ten cubits its height.

> **4:1 bronze altar.** This is the main altar on which sacrifices were offered (see Ezek. 43:13–17). The altar was 30 feet by 30 feet by 15 feet high (if the 18-inch cubit was used rather than the 21-inch royal cubit).

²Then he made the Sea of cast *bronze*, ten cubits from one brim to the other; *it was* completely round. Its height *was* five cubits, and a line of thirty cubits measured its circumference. ³And under it *was* the likeness of oxen encircling it all around, ten to a cubit, all the way around the Sea. The oxen *were* cast in two rows, when it was cast. ⁴It stood on twelve oxen: three looking toward the north, three looking toward the west, three looking toward the south, and three looking toward the east; the Sea *was set* upon them, and all their back parts *pointed* inward. ⁵It *was* a handbreadth thick;

3:1 ^aLiterally *He,* following Masoretic Text and Vulgate; Septuagint reads *the* LORD; Targum reads *the Angel of the* LORD.   ^bSpelled *Araunah* in 2 Samuel 24:16ff   **3:4** ^aThe main room of the temple; elsewhere called the holy place (compare 1 Kings 6:3)   ^bFollowing Masoretic Text, Septuagint, and Vulgate; Arabic, some manuscripts of the Septuagint, and Syriac omit *one hundred and.*   **3:5** ^aLiterally *house*   **3:15** ^aLiterally *house*   ^bOr *eighteen* (compare 1 Kings 7:15; 2 Kings 25:17; and Jeremiah 52:21)

and its brim was shaped like the brim of a cup, *like* a lily blossom. It contained three thousand*[a]* baths.

⁶He also made ten lavers, and put five on the right side and five on the left, to wash in them; such things as they offered for the burnt offering they would wash in them, but the Sea *was* for the priests to wash in. ⁷And he made ten lampstands of gold according to their design, and set *them* in the temple, five on the right side and five on the left. ⁸He also made ten tables, and placed *them* in the temple, five on the right side and five on the left. And he made one hundred bowls of gold.

⁹Furthermore he made the court of the priests, and the great court and doors for the court; and he overlaid these doors with bronze. ¹⁰He set the Sea on the right side, toward the southeast.

¹¹Then Huram made the pots and the shovels and the bowls. So Huram finished doing the work that he was to do for King Solomon for the house of God: ¹²the two pillars and the bowl-shaped capitals *that were* on top of the two pillars; the two networks covering the two bowl-shaped capitals which *were* on top of the pillars; ¹³four hundred pomegranates for the two networks (two rows of pomegranates for each network, to cover the two bowl-shaped capitals that *were* on the pillars); ¹⁴he also made carts and the lavers on the carts; ¹⁵one Sea and twelve oxen under it; ¹⁶also the pots, the shovels, the forks—and all their articles Huram his master*[a]* craftsman made of burnished bronze for King Solomon for the house of the LORD.

¹⁷In the plain of Jordan the king had them cast in clay molds, between Succoth and Zeredah.*[a]* ¹⁸And Solomon had all these articles made in such great abundance that the weight of the bronze was not determined.

¹⁹Thus Solomon had all the furnishings made for the house of God: the altar of gold and the tables on which *was* the showbread; ²⁰the lampstands with their lamps of pure gold, to burn in the prescribed manner in front of the inner sanctuary; ²¹with the flowers and the lamps and the wick-trimmers of gold, of purest gold;

²²the trimmers, the bowls, the ladles, and the censers of pure gold. As for the entry of the sanctuary, its inner doors to the Most Holy *Place*, and the doors of the main hall of the temple, *were* gold.

5 So all the work that Solomon had done for the house of the LORD was finished; and Solomon brought in the things which his father David had dedicated: the silver and the gold and all the furnishings. And he put *them* in the treasuries of the house of God.

> **5:1** The temple took 7 years and 6 months to build and was completed in Solomon's 11th year (959 B.C.) and dedicated 11 months later, to coincide with the Feast of Tabernacles. The temple was emphasized in the Old Testament because it was the center of worship, a place of prayer, and the symbol of God's presence, forgiveness, and grace. It prepared the people for Jesus.

The Ark Brought into the Temple

²Now Solomon assembled the elders of Israel and all the heads of the tribes, the chief fathers of the children of Israel, in Jerusalem, that they might bring the ark of the covenant of the LORD up from the City of David, which *is* Zion. ³Therefore all the men of Israel assembled with the king at the feast, which *was* in the seventh month. ⁴So all the elders of Israel came, and the Levites took up the ark. ⁵Then they brought up the ark, the tabernacle of meeting, and all the holy furnishings that *were* in the tabernacle. The priests and the Levites brought them up. ⁶Also King Solomon, and all the congregation of Israel who were assembled with him before the ark, were sacrificing sheep and oxen that could not be counted or numbered for multitude. ⁷Then the priests brought in the ark of the covenant of the LORD to its place, into the inner sanctuary of the temple,*[a]* to the Most Holy *Place*, under the wings of the cherubim. ⁸For the cherubim spread *their* wings over the place of the ark, and the cherubim overshadowed the ark and its poles. ⁹The poles extended so that the ends of the poles of the ark could be seen from *the holy place*, in front of the inner sanctuary; but

---

4:5 *[a]*Or *two thousand* (compare 1 Kings 7:26)　4:16 *[a]*Literally *father*　4:17 *[a]*Spelled *Zaretan* in 1 Kings 7:46　5:7 *[a]*Literally *house*

they could not be seen from outside. And they are there to this day. [10]Nothing was in the ark except the two tablets which Moses put *there* at Horeb, when the LORD made *a covenant* with the children of Israel, when they had come out of Egypt.

[11]And it came to pass when the priests came out of the *Most* Holy *Place* (for all the priests who *were* present had sanctified themselves, without keeping to their divisions), [12]and the Levites *who were* the singers, all those of Asaph and Heman and Jeduthun, with their sons and their brethren, stood at the east end of the altar, clothed in white linen, having cymbals, stringed instruments and harps, and with them one hundred and twenty priests sounding with trumpets— [13]indeed it came to pass, when the trumpeters and singers *were* as one, to make one sound to be heard in praising and thanking the LORD, and when they lifted up their voice with the trumpets and cymbals and instruments of music, and praised the LORD, *saying:*

"*For He is* good,
  For His mercy *endures* forever,"[a]

that the house, the house of the LORD, was filled with a cloud, [14]so that the priests could not continue ministering because of the cloud; for the glory of the LORD filled the house of God.

6 Then Solomon spoke:

  "The LORD said He would dwell in the dark cloud.
[2] I have surely built You an exalted house,
  And a place for You to dwell in forever."

Solomon's Speech upon Completion of the Work

[3]Then the king turned around and blessed the whole assembly of Israel, while all the assembly of Israel was standing. [4]And he said: "Blessed *be* the LORD God of Israel, who has fulfilled with His hands *what* He spoke with His mouth to my father David, saying, [5]'Since the day that I brought My people out of the land of Egypt,

I have chosen no city from any tribe of Israel *in which* to build a house, that My name might be there, nor did I choose any man to be a ruler over My people Israel. [6]Yet I have chosen Jerusalem, that My name may be there, and I have chosen David to be over My people Israel.' [7]Now it was in the heart of my father David to build a temple[a] for the name of the LORD God of Israel. [8]But the LORD said to my father David, 'Whereas it was in your heart to build a temple for My name, you did well in that it was in your heart. [9]Nevertheless you shall not build the temple, but your son who will come from your body, he shall build the temple for My name.' [10]So the LORD has fulfilled His word which He spoke, and I have filled the position of my father David, and sit on the throne of Israel, as the LORD promised; and I have built the temple for the name of the LORD God of Israel. [11]And there I have put the ark, in which *is* the covenant of the LORD which He made with the children of Israel."

Solomon's Prayer of Dedication

[12]Then *Solomon*[a] stood before the altar of the LORD in the presence of all the assembly of Israel, and spread out his hands [13](for Solomon had made a bronze platform five cubits long, five cubits wide, and three cubits high, and had set it in the midst of the court; and he stood on it, knelt down on his knees before all the assembly of Israel, and spread out his hands toward heaven); [14]and he said: "LORD God of Israel, *there is* no God in heaven or on earth like You, who keep *Your* covenant and mercy with Your servants who walk before You with all their hearts. [15]You have kept what You promised Your servant David my father; You have both spoken with Your mouth and fulfilled *it* with Your hand, as *it is* this day. [16]Therefore, LORD God of Israel, now keep what You promised Your servant David my father, saying, 'You shall not fail to have a man sit before Me on the throne of Israel,

6:13 knelt. Solomon acknowledged God's sovereignty, an unusually humbling act for a king.

5:13 [a]Compare Psalm 106:1   6:7 [a]Literally *house*, and so in verses 8–10   6:12 [a]Literally *he* (compare 1 Kings 8:22)

only if your sons take heed to their way, that they walk in My law as you have walked before Me.' [17]And now, O LORD God of Israel, let Your word come true, which You have spoken to Your servant David.

[18]"But will God indeed dwell with men on the earth? Behold, heaven and the heaven of heavens cannot contain You. How much less this temple[a] which I have built! [19]Yet regard the prayer of Your servant and his supplication, O LORD my God, and listen to the cry and the prayer which Your servant is praying before You: [20]that Your eyes may be open toward this temple day and night, toward the place where *You* said *You would* put Your name, that You may hear the prayer which Your servant makes toward this place. [21]And may You hear the supplications of Your servant and of Your people Israel, when they pray toward this place. Hear from heaven Your dwelling place, and when You hear, forgive.

[22]"If anyone sins against his neighbor, and is forced to take an oath, and comes *and* takes an oath before Your altar in this temple, [23]then hear from heaven, and act, and judge Your servants, bringing retribution on the wicked by bringing his way on his own head, and justifying the righteous by giving him according to his righteousness.

[24]"Or if Your people Israel are defeated before an enemy because they have sinned against You, and return and confess Your name, and pray and make supplication before You in this temple, [25]then hear from heaven and forgive the sin of Your people Israel, and bring them back to the land which You gave to them and their fathers.

[26]"When the heavens are shut up and there is no rain because they have sinned against You, when they pray toward this place and confess Your name, and turn from their sin because You afflict them, [27]then hear *in* heaven, and forgive the sin of Your servants, Your people Israel, that You may teach them the good way in which they should walk; and send rain on Your land which You have given to Your people as an inheritance.

[28]"When there is famine in the land, pestilence or blight or mildew, locusts or grasshoppers; when their enemies besiege them in the land of their cities; whatever plague or whatever sickness *there is*; [29]whatever prayer, whatever supplication is *made* by anyone, or by all Your people Israel, when each one knows his own burden and his own grief, and spreads out his hands to this temple: [30]then hear from heaven Your dwelling place, and forgive, and give to everyone according to all his ways, whose heart You know (for You alone know the hearts of the sons of men), [31]that they may fear You, to walk in Your ways as long as they live in the land which You gave to our fathers.

[32]"Moreover, concerning a foreigner, who is not of Your people Israel, but has come from a far country for the sake of Your great name and Your mighty hand and Your outstretched arm, when they come and pray in this temple; [33]then hear from heaven Your dwelling place, and do according to all for which the foreigner calls to You, that all peoples of the earth may know Your name and fear You, as *do* Your people Israel, and that they may know that this temple which I have built is called by Your name.

[34]"When Your people go out to battle against their enemies, wherever You send them, and when they pray to You toward this city which You have chosen and the temple which I have built for Your name, [35]then hear from heaven their prayer and their supplication, and maintain their cause.

[36]"When they sin against You (for *there is* no one who does not sin), and You become angry with them and deliver them to the enemy, and they take them captive to a land far or near; [37]*yet* when they come to themselves in the land where they were carried captive, and repent, and make supplication to You in the land of their captivity, saying, 'We have sinned, we have done wrong, and have committed wickedness'; [38]and *when* they return to You with all their heart and with all their soul in the land of their captivity, where they have been carried captive, and pray toward their land which You gave to their fathers, the city which You have chosen, and toward the temple which I have built for Your name:

6:18 [a]Literally *house*

³⁹then hear from heaven Your dwelling place their prayer and their supplications, and maintain their cause, and forgive Your people who have sinned against You. ⁴⁰Now, my God, I pray, let Your eyes be open and *let* Your ears *be* attentive to the prayer *made* in this place.

⁴¹ "Now therefore,
   Arise, O LORD God, to Your resting
      place,
   You and the ark of Your strength.
   Let Your priests, O LORD God, be
      clothed with salvation,
   And let Your saints rejoice in
      goodness.

⁴² "O LORD God, do not turn away the
      face of Your Anointed;
   Remember the mercies of Your
      servant David."ᵃ

Solomon Dedicates the Temple

7 When Solomon had finished praying, fire came down from heaven and consumed the burnt offering and the sacrifices; and the glory of the LORD filled the temple.ᵃ ²And the priests could not enter the house of the LORD, because the glory of the LORD had filled the LORD's house. ³When all the children of Israel saw how the fire came down, and the glory of the LORD on the temple, they bowed their faces to the ground on the pavement, and worshiped and praised the LORD, *saying:*

   "For *He is* good,
   For His mercy *endures* forever."ᵃ

7:1–3 fire came down. This was the genuine dedication, because only God can truly sanctify. This also occurred when the tabernacle was dedicated (Lev. 9:23,24).

⁴Then the king and all the people offered sacrifices before the LORD. ⁵King Solomon offered a sacrifice of twenty-two thousand bulls and one hundred and twenty thousand sheep. So the king and all the people dedicated the house of God. ⁶And the priests attended to their services; the Le-

vites also with instruments of the music of the LORD, which King David had made to praise the LORD, saying, "For His mercy *endures* forever,"ᵃ whenever David offered praise by their ministry. The priests sounded trumpets opposite them, while all Israel stood.

⁷Furthermore Solomon consecrated the middle of the court that *was* in front of the house of the LORD; for there he offered burnt offerings and the fat of the peace offerings, because the bronze altar which Solomon had made was not able to receive the burnt offerings, the grain offerings, and the fat.

⁸At that time Solomon kept the feast seven days, and all Israel with him, a very great assembly from the entrance of Hamath to the Brook of Egypt.ᵃ ⁹And on the eighth day they held a sacred assembly, for they observed the dedication of the altar seven days, and the feast seven days. ¹⁰On the twenty-third day of the seventh month he sent the people away to their tents, joyful and glad of heart for the good that the LORD had done for David, for Solomon, and for His people Israel. ¹¹Thus Solomon finished the house of the LORD and the king's house; and Solomon successfully accomplished all that came into his heart to make in the house of the LORD and in his own house.

God's Second Appearance to Solomon

¹²Then the LORD appeared to Solomon by night, and said to him: "I have heard your prayer, and have chosen this place for Myself as a house of sacrifice. ¹³When I shut up heaven and there is no rain, or command the locusts to devour the land, or send pestilence among My people, ¹⁴if My people who are called by My name will humble themselves, and pray and seek My face, and turn from their wicked ways, then I will hear from heaven, and will forgive their sin and heal their land. ¹⁵Now My eyes will be open and My ears attentive to prayer *made* in this place. ¹⁶For now I have chosen and sanctified this house, that My name may be there forever; and My eyes and My heart will be there perpetually. ¹⁷As for you, if you

6:42 ᵃCompare Psalm 132:8–10   7:1 ᵃLiterally *house*   7:3 ᵃCompare Psalm 106:1   7:6 ᵃCompare Psalm 106:1   7:8 ᵃThat is, the Shihor (compare 1 Chronicles 13:5)

7:13–16 This section features humility, prayer, longing for God, and repentance as the condition for forgiveness of Israel's sin (1 Kin. 9:3).

walk before Me as your father David walked, and do according to all that I have commanded you, and if you keep My statutes and My judgments, [18]then I will establish the throne of your kingdom, as I covenanted with David your father, saying, 'You shall not fail *to have* a man as ruler in Israel.'

7:17,18 if...then. If Israel was obedient, then the kingdom would be established and would have "a man as ruler." Their disobedience, the destruction of their kingdom, and their dispersion were legendary. When Israel is saved, then their King Messiah will set up this glorious kingdom (see Rom 11:25–27; Rev. 20:1).

[19]"But if you turn away and forsake My statutes and My commandments which I have set before you, and go and serve other gods, and worship them, [20]then I will uproot them from My land which I have given them; and this house which I have sanctified for My name I will cast out of My sight, and will make it a proverb and a byword among all peoples.

[21]"And *as for* this house, which is exalted, everyone who passes by it will be astonished and say, 'Why has the LORD done thus to this land and this house?' [22]Then they will answer, 'Because they forsook the LORD God of their fathers, who brought them out of the land of Egypt, and embraced other gods, and worshiped them and served them; therefore He has brought all this calamity on them.' "

Solomon's Additional Achievements

8 It came to pass at the end of twenty years, when Solomon had built the house of the LORD and his own house, [2]that the cities which Hiram[a] had given to Solomon, Solomon built them; and he settled the children of Israel there. [3]And Solomon went to Hamath Zobah and seized it. [4]He also built Tadmor in the wilderness, and all the storage cities which he built in Ha-

math. [5]He built Upper Beth Horon and Lower Beth Horon, fortified cities *with* walls, gates, and bars, [6]also Baalath and all the storage cities that Solomon had, and all the chariot cities and the cities of the cavalry, and all that Solomon desired to build in Jerusalem, in Lebanon, and in all the land of his dominion.

8:3–6 Solomon was building storage places for his commercial enterprises and fortifying his borders to secure his kingdom from invasion.

[7]All the people *who were* left of the Hittites, Amorites, Perizzites, Hivites, and Jebusites, who *were* not of Israel— [8]that is, their descendants who were left in the land after them, whom the children of Israel did not destroy—from these Solomon raised forced labor, as it is to this day. [9]But Solomon did not make the children of Israel servants for his work. Some *were* men of war, captains of his officers, captains of his chariots, and his cavalry. [10]And others *were* chiefs of the officials of King Solomon: two hundred and fifty, who ruled over the people.

[11]Now Solomon brought the daughter of Pharaoh up from the City of David to the house he had built for her, for he said, "My wife shall not dwell in the house of David king of Israel, because *the places* to which the ark of the LORD has come are holy."

8:11 the daughter of Pharaoh. Solomon had married her and brought her to Jerusalem (see 1 Kin. 9:24). Until the palace was built, Solomon lived in David's palace but would not let her live there. She was a heathen, and the ark of God had once been in David's house. Solomon knew that his marriage to this pagan did not please God (Deut. 7:3,4). His pagan wives later caused tragic consequences (1 Kin. 11:1–11).

[12]Then Solomon offered burnt offerings to the LORD on the altar of the LORD which he had built before the vestibule, [13]according to the daily rate, offering according to the commandment of Moses, for the Sabbaths, the New Moons, and the three appointed yearly feasts—the Feast of Unleavened Bread, the Feast of Weeks, and the Feast of Tabernacles. [14]And, according to the

8:2 [a]Hebrew *Huram* (compare 2 Chronicles 2:3)

order of David his father, he appointed the divisions of the priests for their service, the Levites for their duties (to praise and serve before the priests) as the duty of each day required, and the gatekeepers by their divisions at each gate; for so David the man of God had commanded. ¹⁵They did not depart from the command of the king to the priests and Levites concerning any matter or concerning the treasuries.

¹⁶Now all the work of Solomon was well-ordered from*a* the day of the foundation of the house of the LORD until it was finished. So the house of the LORD was completed.

¹⁷Then Solomon went to Ezion Geber and Elath*a* on the seacoast, in the land of Edom. ¹⁸And Hiram sent him ships by the hand of his servants, and servants who knew the sea. They went with the servants of Solomon to Ophir, and acquired four hundred and fifty talents of gold from there, and brought it to King Solomon.

The Queen of Sheba's Praise of Solomon

9 Now when the queen of Sheba heard of the fame of Solomon, she came to Jerusalem to test Solomon with hard questions, *having* a very great retinue, camels that bore spices, gold in abundance, and precious stones; and when she came to Solomon, she spoke with him about all that was in her heart. ²So Solomon answered all her questions; there was nothing so difficult for Solomon that he could not explain it to her. ³And when the queen of Sheba had seen the wisdom of Solomon, the house that he had built, ⁴the food on his table, the seating of his servants, the service of his waiters and their apparel, his cupbearers and their apparel, and his entryway by which he went up to the house of the LORD, there was no more spirit in her.

⁵Then she said to the king: "*It was* a true report which I heard in my own land about your words and your wisdom. ⁶However I did not believe their words until I came and saw with my own eyes; and indeed the half of the greatness of your wisdom was not told me. You exceed the fame of which I heard. ⁷Happy *are* your men and happy *are*

these your servants, who stand continually before you and hear your wisdom! ⁸Blessed be the LORD your God, who delighted in you, setting you on His throne *to be* king for the LORD your God! Because your God has loved Israel, to establish them forever, therefore He made you king over them, to do justice and righteousness."

9:8 His throne. The queen of Sheba does not mention that Solomon sat on God's throne in 1 Kin. 10:9. God's blessing on Solomon and on Israel was to last as long as he followed the Lord as David had (2 Chr. 7:17–21).

⁹And she gave the king one hundred and twenty talents of gold, spices in great abundance, and precious stones; there never were any spices such as those the queen of Sheba gave to King Solomon.

¹⁰Also, the servants of Hiram and the servants of Solomon, who brought gold from Ophir, brought algum*a* wood and precious stones. ¹¹And the king made walkways *of* the algum*a* wood for the house of the LORD and for the king's house, also harps and stringed instruments for singers; and there were none such *as these* seen before in the land of Judah.

¹²Now King Solomon gave to the queen of Sheba all she desired, whatever she asked, *much more* than she had brought to the king. So she turned and went to her own country, she and her servants.

Solomon's Great Wealth

¹³The weight of gold that came to Solomon yearly was six hundred and sixty-six talents of gold, ¹⁴besides *what* the traveling merchants and traders brought. And all the kings of Arabia and governors of the country brought gold and silver to Solomon. ¹⁵And King Solomon made two hundred large shields of hammered gold; six hundred *shekels* of hammered gold went into each shield. ¹⁶*He* also *made* three hundred shields of hammered gold; three hundred *shekels*a of gold went into each shield. The king put them in the House of the Forest of Lebanon.

8:16 *a*Following Septuagint, Syriac, and Vulgate; Masoretic Text reads *as far as.* 8:17 *a*Hebrew *Eloth* (compare 2 Kings 14:22) 9:10 *a*Or *almug* (compare 1 Kings 10:11, 12) 9:11 *a*Or *almug* (compare 1 Kings 10:11, 12) 9:16 *a*Or *three minas* (compare 1 Kings 10:17)

¹⁷Moreover the king made a great throne of ivory, and overlaid it with pure gold. ¹⁸The throne *had* six steps, with a footstool of gold, *which were* fastened to the throne; there were armrests on either side of the place of the seat, and two lions stood beside the armrests. ¹⁹Twelve lions stood there, one on each side of the six steps; nothing like *this* had been made for any *other* kingdom.

²⁰All King Solomon's drinking vessels *were* gold, and all the vessels of the House of the Forest of Lebanon *were* pure gold. Not *one was* silver, for this was accounted as nothing in the days of Solomon. ²¹For the king's ships went to Tarshish with the servants of Hiram.*ᵃ* Once every three years the merchant ships*ᵇ* came, bringing gold, silver, ivory, apes, and monkeys.*ᶜ*

²²So King Solomon surpassed all the kings of the earth in riches and wisdom. ²³And all the kings of the earth sought the presence of Solomon to hear his wisdom, which God had put in his heart. ²⁴Each man brought his present: articles of silver and gold, garments, armor, spices, horses, and mules, at a set rate year by year.

²⁵Solomon had four thousand stalls for horses and chariots, and twelve thousand horsemen whom he stationed in the chariot cities and with the king at Jerusalem.

²⁶So he reigned over all the kings from the River*ᵃ* to the land of the Philistines, as far as the border of Egypt. ²⁷The king made silver *as common* in Jerusalem as stones, and he made cedar trees as abundant as the sycamores which *are* in the lowland. ²⁸And they brought horses to Solomon from Egypt and from all lands.

Death of Solomon

²⁹Now the rest of the acts of Solomon, first and last, *are* they not written in the book of Nathan the prophet, in the prophecy of Ahijah the Shilonite, and in the visions of Iddo the seer concerning Jeroboam the son of Nebat? ³⁰Solomon reigned in Jerusalem over all Israel forty years. ³¹Then Solomon rested with his fathers, and was buried in the City of David his father. And Rehoboam his son reigned in his place.

9:29 Solomon's deeds were written in "the book of the acts of Solomon" (1 Kin. 11:41). Later in his life, Solomon turned away from God, and, due to the influence of his wives, he led the nation into idolatry. This split the kingdom, leading to their defeat and dispersion. The Chronicles do not record this but rather focus on encouraging the Jews returning from Babylon.

9:21 *ᵃ*Hebrew *Huram* (compare 1 Kings 10:22)   *ᵇ*Literally *ships of Tarshish,* deep-sea vessels   *ᶜ*Or *peacocks*   9:26 *ᵃ*That is, the Euphrates

---

Does the use of outside sources affect the claim of inerrancy for Scripture? Were these other documents also inspired Scripture?

First and Second Chronicles repeatedly quote other sources. Ezra includes many direct quotes from Persian documents. Other Scriptures include extrabiblical references. The answer to this question must reflect, not the isolated cases of outside texts, but the numerous places the Bible quotes foreign decrees, pagan leaders, and other secular texts.

The fact that an extrabiblical source is quoted in Scripture does not endorse that entire source as inspired. Biblical content is truth. Biblical content remains true even when quoted outside the Bible. Some items of truth originally recorded outside Scripture that were available to those God inspired to write the Bible were used in Scripture.

These extrabiblical factors have the added effect of reminding us that God's Word was given in real historical situations—lived out and written out by people under God's guidance. These quotes emphasize the Scripture's relationship with reality. God's Word reveals the real God: ultimate reality.

The Revolt Against Rehoboam

10 And Rehoboam went to Shechem, for all Israel had gone to Shechem to make him king. [2]So it happened, when Jeroboam the son of Nebat heard *it* (he was in Egypt, where he had fled from the presence of King Solomon), that Jeroboam returned from Egypt. [3]Then they sent for him and called him. And Jeroboam and all Israel came and spoke to Rehoboam, saying, [4]"Your father made our yoke heavy; now therefore, lighten the burdensome service of your father and his heavy yoke which he put on us, and we will serve you."

[5]So he said to them, "Come back to me after three days." And the people departed.

[6]Then King Rehoboam consulted the elders who stood before his father Solomon while he still lived, saying, "How do you advise *me* to answer these people?"

[7]And they spoke to him, saying, "If you are kind to these people, and please them, and speak good words to them, they will be your servants forever."

[8]But he rejected the advice which the elders had given him, and consulted the young men who had grown up with him, who stood before him. [9]And he said to them, "What advice do you give? How should we answer this people who have spoken to me, saying, 'Lighten the yoke which your father put on us'?"

[10]Then the young men who had grown up with him spoke to him, saying, "Thus you should speak to the people who have spoken to you, saying, 'Your father made our yoke heavy, but you make *it* lighter on us'— thus you shall say to them: 'My little *finger* shall be thicker than my father's waist! [11]And now, whereas my father put a heavy yoke on you, I will add to your yoke; my father chastised you with whips, but I *will chastise you* with scourges!' "[a]

[12]So Jeroboam and all the people came to Rehoboam on the third day, as the king had directed, saying, "Come back to me the third day." [13]Then the king answered them roughly. King Rehoboam rejected the advice of the elders, [14]and he spoke to them according to the advice of the young men, saying, "My father[a] made your yoke heavy, but I will add to it; my father chastised you with whips, but I *will chastise you* with scourges!"[b] [15]So the king did not listen to the people; for the turn *of events* was from God, that the LORD might fulfill His word, which He had spoken by the hand of Ahijah the Shilonite to Jeroboam the son of Nebat.

[16]Now when all Israel *saw* that the king did not listen to them, the people answered the king, saying:

> "What share have we in David?
> *We have* no inheritance in the son of Jesse.
> Every man to your tents, O Israel!
> Now see to your own house,
> O David!"

So all Israel departed to their tents. [17]But Rehoboam reigned over the children of Israel who dwelt in the cities of Judah.

[18]Then King Rehoboam sent Hadoram, who *was* in charge of revenue; but the children of Israel stoned him with stones, and he died. Therefore King Rehoboam mounted *his* chariot in haste to flee to Jerusalem. [19]So Israel has been in rebellion against the house of David to this day.

10:16–19 This is the beginning of the divided kingdom. Israel included the 10 tribes who followed Jeroboam. The tribes of Benjamin and Judah accepted Rehoboam's rule and were called Judah. At times, Benjamin did not remain loyal to David's line.

11 Now when Rehoboam came to Jerusalem, he assembled from the house of Judah and Benjamin one hundred and eighty thousand chosen *men* who were warriors, to fight against Israel, that he might restore the kingdom to Rehoboam. [2]But the word of the LORD came to Shemaiah the man of God, saying, [3]"Speak to Rehoboam the son of Solomon, king of Judah, and to all Israel in Judah and Benjamin, saying, [4]'Thus says the LORD: "You shall not go up or fight against your brethren! Let every man return to his house, for this thing is from Me." ' " Therefore they obeyed the words of the LORD, and turned back from attacking Jeroboam.

10:11 [a]Literally *scorpions*   10:14 [a]Following many Hebrew manuscripts, Septuagint, Syriac, and Vulgate (compare verse 10 and 1 Kings 12:14); Masoretic Text reads *I*.   [b]Literally *scorpions*

10:1–11:4 Rehoboam followed foolish advice from novices rather than from wise men. This resulted in the division of Israel. He tried to unite the people by force, but God would not allow it (11:1–4).

Rehoboam Fortifies the Cities

⁵So Rehoboam dwelt in Jerusalem, and built cities for defense in Judah. ⁶And he built Bethlehem, Etam, Tekoa, ⁷Beth Zur, Sochoh, Adullam, ⁸Gath, Mareshah, Ziph, ⁹Adoraim, Lachish, Azekah, ¹⁰Zorah, Aijalon, and Hebron, which are in Judah and Benjamin, fortified cities. ¹¹And he fortified the strongholds, and put captains in them, and stores of food, oil, and wine. ¹²Also in every city *he put* shields and spears, and made them very strong, having Judah and Benjamin on his side.

Priests and Levites Move to Judah

¹³And from all their territories the priests and the Levites who *were* in all Israel took their stand with him. ¹⁴For the Levites left their common-lands and their possessions and came to Judah and Jerusalem, for Jeroboam and his sons had rejected them from serving as priests to the LORD. ¹⁵Then he appointed for himself priests for the high places, for the demons, and the calf idols which he had made. ¹⁶And after *the Levites left,*ᵃ those from all the tribes of Israel, such as set their heart to seek the LORD God of Israel, came to Jerusalem to sacrifice to the LORD God of their fathers. ¹⁷So they strengthened the kingdom of Judah, and made Rehoboam the son of Solomon strong for three years, because they walked in the way of David and Solomon for three years.

The Family of Rehoboam

¹⁸Then Rehoboam took for himself as wife Mahalath the daughter of Jerimoth the son of David, *and of* Abihail the daughter of Eliah the son of Jesse. ¹⁹And she bore him children: Jeush, Shamariah, and Zaham. ²⁰After her he took Maachah the granddaughterᵃ of Absalom; and she bore him Abijah, Attai, Ziza, and Shelomith. ²¹Now Rehoboam loved Maachah the granddaughter of Absalom more than all his wives and his concubines; for he took eigh-

teen wives and sixty concubines, and begot twenty-eight sons and sixty daughters. ²²And Rehoboam appointed Abijah the son of Maachah as chief, *to be* leader among his brothers; for he *intended* to make him king. ²³He dealt wisely, and dispersed some of his sons throughout all the territories of Judah and Benjamin, to every fortified city; and he gave them provisions in abundance. He also sought many wives *for them.*

Egypt Attacks Judah

12 Now it came to pass, when Rehoboam had established the kingdom and had strengthened himself, that he forsook the law of the LORD, and all Israel along with him. ²And it happened in the fifth year of King Rehoboam *that* Shishak king of Egypt came up against Jerusalem, because they had transgressed against the LORD, ³with twelve hundred chariots, sixty thousand horsemen, and people without number who came with him out of Egypt— the Lubim and the Sukkiim and the Ethiopians. ⁴And he took the fortified cities of Judah and came to Jerusalem.

⁵Then Shemaiah the prophet came to Rehoboam and the leaders of Judah, who were gathered together in Jerusalem because of Shishak, and said to them, "Thus says the LORD: 'You have forsaken Me, and therefore I also have left you in the hand of Shishak.' "

⁶So the leaders of Israel and the king humbled themselves; and they said, "The LORD *is* righteous."

⁷Now when the LORD saw that they humbled themselves, the word of the LORD came to Shemaiah, saying, "They have humbled themselves; *therefore* I will not destroy them, but I will grant them some deliverance. My wrath shall not be poured out on Jerusalem by the hand of Shishak. ⁸Nevertheless they will be his servants, that they may distinguish My service from the service of the kingdoms of the nations."

⁹So Shishak king of Egypt came up against Jerusalem, and took away the treasures of the house of the LORD and the treasures of the king's house; he took everything. He also carried away the gold

---

11:16 ᵃLiterally *after them*   11:20 ᵃLiterally *daughter,* but in the broader sense of granddaughter (compare 2 Chronicles 13:2)

shields which Solomon had made. [10]Then King Rehoboam made bronze shields in their place, and committed *them* to the hands of the captains of the guard, who guarded the doorway of the king's house. [11]And whenever the king entered the house of the LORD, the guard would go and bring them out; then they would take them back into the guardroom. [12]When he humbled himself, the wrath of the LORD turned from him, so as not to destroy *him* completely; and things also went well in Judah.

The End of Rehoboam's Reign

[13]Thus King Rehoboam strengthened himself in Jerusalem and reigned. Now Rehoboam *was* forty-one years old when he became king; and he reigned seventeen years in Jerusalem, the city which the LORD had chosen out of all the tribes of Israel, to put His name there. His mother's name *was* Naamah, an Ammonitess. [14]And he did evil, because he did not prepare his heart to seek the LORD.

[15]The acts of Rehoboam, first and last, *are* they not written in the book of Shemaiah the prophet, and of Iddo the seer concerning genealogies? And *there were* wars between Rehoboam and Jeroboam all their days. [16]So Rehoboam rested with his fathers, and was buried in the City of David. Then Abijah[a] his son reigned in his place.

Abijah Reigns in Judah

13 In the eighteenth year of King Jeroboam, Abijah became king over Judah. [2]He reigned three years in Jerusalem. His mother's name *was* Michaiah[a] the daughter of Uriel of Gibeah.

And there was war between Abijah and Jeroboam. [3]Abijah set the battle in order with an army of valiant warriors, four hundred thousand choice men. Jeroboam also drew up in battle formation against him with eight hundred thousand choice men, mighty men of valor.

[4]Then Abijah stood on Mount Zemaraim, which *is* in the mountains of Ephraim, and said, "Hear me, Jeroboam and all Is-

rael: [5]Should you not know that the LORD God of Israel gave the dominion over Israel to David forever, to him and his sons, by a covenant of salt? [6]Yet Jeroboam the son of Nebat, the servant of Solomon the son of David, rose up and rebelled against his lord. [7]Then worthless rogues gathered to him, and strengthened themselves against Rehoboam the son of Solomon, when Rehoboam was young and inexperienced and could not withstand them. [8]And now you think to withstand the kingdom of the LORD, which is in the hand of the sons of David; and you *are* a great multitude, and with you are the gold calves which Jeroboam made for you as gods. [9]Have you not cast out the priests of the LORD, the sons of Aaron, and the Levites, and made for yourselves priests, like the peoples of *other* lands, so that whoever comes to consecrate himself with a young bull and seven rams may be a priest of *things that are* not gods? [10]But as for us, the LORD *is* our God, and we have not forsaken Him; and the priests who minister to the LORD *are* the sons of Aaron, and the Levites *attend* to *their* duties. [11]And they burn to the LORD every morning and every evening burnt sacrifices and sweet incense; *they* also *set* the showbread *in order on* the pure *gold* table, and the lampstand of gold with its lamps to burn every evening; for we keep the command of the LORD our God, but you have forsaken Him. [12]Now look, God Himself is with us as *our* head, and His priests with sounding trumpets to sound the alarm against you. O children of Israel, do not fight against the LORD God of your fathers, for you shall not prosper!"

[13]But Jeroboam caused an ambush to go around behind them; so they were in front of Judah, and the ambush *was* behind them. [14]And when Judah looked around, to their surprise the battle line *was* at both

---

12:16 *a*Spelled *Abijam* in 1 Kings 14:31   13:2 *a*Spelled *Maachah* in 11:20,21 and 1 Kings 15:2

front and rear; and they cried out to the LORD, and the priests sounded the trumpets. [15]Then the men of Judah gave a shout; and as the men of Judah shouted, it happened that God struck Jeroboam and all Israel before Abijah and Judah. [16]And the children of Israel fled before Judah, and God delivered them into their hand. [17]Then Abijah and his people struck them with a great slaughter; so five hundred thousand choice men of Israel fell slain. [18]Thus the children of Israel were subdued at that time; and the children of Judah prevailed, because they relied on the LORD God of their fathers.

[19]And Abijah pursued Jeroboam and took cities from him: Bethel with its villages, Jeshanah with its villages, and Ephrain[a] with its villages. [20]So Jeroboam did not recover strength again in the days of Abijah; and the LORD struck him, and he died.

[21]But Abijah grew mighty, married fourteen wives, and begot twenty-two sons and sixteen daughters. [22]Now the rest of the acts of Abijah, his ways, and his sayings are written in the annals of the prophet Iddo.

14 So Abijah rested with his fathers, and they buried him in the City of David. Then Asa his son reigned in his place. In his days the land was quiet for ten years.

Asa Reigns in Judah

[2]Asa did what was good and right in the eyes of the LORD his God, [3]for he removed the altars of the foreign gods and the high places, and broke down the sacred pillars and cut down the wooden images. [4]He commanded Judah to seek the LORD God of their fathers, and to observe the law and the commandment. [5]He also removed the high places and the incense altars from all the cities of Judah, and the kingdom was quiet under him. [6]And he built fortified cities in Judah, for the land had rest; he had no war in those years, because the LORD had given him rest. [7]Therefore he said to

Judah, "Let us build these cities and make walls around them, and towers, gates, and bars, while the land is yet before us, because we have sought the LORD our God; we have sought Him, and He has given us rest on every side." So they built and prospered. [8]And Asa had an army of three hundred thousand from Judah who carried shields and spears, and from Benjamin two hundred and eighty thousand men who carried shields and drew bows; all these were mighty men of valor.

[9]Then Zerah the Ethiopian came out against them with an army of a million men and three hundred chariots, and he came to Mareshah. [10]So Asa went out against him, and they set the troops in battle array in the Valley of Zephathah at Mareshah. [11]And Asa cried out to the LORD his God, and said, "LORD, it is nothing for You to help, whether with many or with those who have no power; help us, O LORD our God, for we rest on You, and in Your name we go against this multitude. O LORD, You are our God; do not let man prevail against You!"

[12]So the LORD struck the Ethiopians before Asa and Judah, and the Ethiopians fled. [13]And Asa and the people who were with him pursued them to Gerar. So the Ethiopians were overthrown, and they could not recover, for they were broken before the LORD and His army. And they carried away very much spoil. [14]Then they defeated all the cities around Gerar, for the fear of the LORD came upon them; and they plundered all the cities, for there was exceedingly much spoil in them. [15]They also attacked the livestock enclosures, and carried off sheep and camels in abundance, and returned to Jerusalem.

The Reforms of Asa

15 Now the Spirit of God came upon Azariah the son of Oded. [2]And he

---

14:1,2 Times of peace were used for strengthening. Asa honored God while building the kingdom, as David had done (1 Kin. 15:11).

15:1 Spirit of God. The Holy Spirit often enabled servants of God to speak or act uniquely for Him in the Old Testament. **Azariah.** He was a prophet who met Asa as he returned from the victory and spoke to him before his army.

---

went out to meet Asa, and said to him: "Hear me, Asa, and all Judah and Benjamin. The LORD *is* with you while you are with Him. If you seek Him, He will be found by you; but if you forsake Him, He will forsake you. ³For a long time Israel *has been* without the true God, without a teaching priest, and without law; ⁴but when in their trouble they turned to the LORD God of Israel, and sought Him, He was found by them. ⁵And in those times *there was* no peace to the one who went out, nor to the one who came in, but great turmoil *was* on all the inhabitants of the lands. ⁶So nation was destroyed by nation, and city by city, for God troubled them with every adversity. ⁷But you, be strong and do not let your hands be weak, for your work shall be rewarded!"

⁸And when Asa heard these words and the prophecy of Oded*ᵃ* the prophet, he took courage, and removed the abominable idols from all the land of Judah and Benjamin and from the cities which he had taken in the mountains of Ephraim; and he restored the altar of the LORD that *was* before the vestibule of the LORD. ⁹Then he gathered all Judah and Benjamin, and those who dwelt with them from Ephraim, Manasseh, and Simeon, for they came over to him in great numbers from Israel when they saw that the LORD his God was with him.

¹⁰So they gathered together at Jerusalem in the third month, in the fifteenth year of the reign of Asa. ¹¹And they offered to the LORD at that time seven hundred bulls and seven thousand sheep from the spoil they had brought. ¹²Then they entered into a covenant to seek the LORD God of their fathers with all their heart and with all their soul; ¹³and whoever would not seek the LORD God of Israel was to be put to death, whether small or great, whether man or woman. ¹⁴Then they took an oath before

the LORD with a loud voice, with shouting and trumpets and rams' horns. ¹⁵And all Judah rejoiced at the oath, for they had sworn with all their heart and sought Him with all their soul; and He was found by them, and the LORD gave them rest all around.

¹⁶Also he removed Maachah, the mother of Asa the king, from *being* queen mother, because she had made an obscene image of Asherah;*ᵃ* and Asa cut down her obscene image, then crushed and burned *it* by the Brook Kidron. ¹⁷But the high places were not removed from Israel. Nevertheless the heart of Asa was loyal all his days. ¹⁸He also brought into the house of God the things that his father had dedicated and that he himself had dedicated: silver and gold and utensils. ¹⁹And there was no war until the thirty-fifth year of the reign of Asa.

Asa's Treaty with Syria

16 In the thirty-sixth year of the reign of Asa, Baasha king of Israel came up against Judah and built Ramah, that he might let none go out or come in to Asa king of Judah. ²Then Asa brought silver and gold from the treasuries of the house of the LORD and of the king's house, and sent to Ben-Hadad king of Syria, who dwelt in Damascus, saying, ³"*Let there be* a treaty between you and me, as there was between my father and your father. See, I have sent you silver and gold; come, break your treaty with Baasha king of Israel, so that he will withdraw from me."

⁴So Ben-Hadad heeded King Asa, and sent the captains of his armies against the cities of Israel. They attacked Ijon, Dan, Abel Maim, and all the storage cities of Naphtali. ⁵Now it happened, when Baasha heard *it*, that he stopped building Ramah and ceased his work. ⁶Then King Asa took all Judah, and they carried away the stones and timber of Ramah, which Baasha had used for building; and with them he built Geba and Mizpah.

Hanani's Message to Asa

⁷And at that time Hanani the seer came to Asa king of Judah, and said to him: "Be-

---

15:11–15 The worshipers renewed their promise to obey (see Ex. 24:1) and to enforce the laws that made idolatry punishable by death (see Deut. 17:2–5). They sacrificed animals taken in spoil from the Ethiopians to offer up their promise.

15:8 *ᵃ*Following Masoretic Text and Septuagint; Syriac and Vulgate read *Azariah the son of Oded* (compare verse 1).   15:16 *ᵃ*A Canaanite deity

cause you have relied on the king of Syria, and have not relied on the LORD your God, therefore the army of the king of Syria has escaped from your hand. [8]Were the Ethiopians and the Lubim not a huge army with very many chariots and horsemen? Yet, because you relied on the LORD, He delivered them into your hand. [9]For the eyes of the LORD run to and fro throughout the whole earth, to show Himself strong on behalf of *those* whose heart *is* loyal to Him. In this you have done foolishly; therefore from now on you shall have wars." [10]Then Asa was angry with the seer, and put him in prison, for *he was* enraged at him because of this. And Asa oppressed *some* of the people at that time.

> **16:7 Hanani.** God used this prophet to rebuke Asa for his wicked use of temple treasures to purchase power and for his trust in a pagan king instead of the Lord. **army of the king of Syria has escaped.** Because of his sin, Asa was not given victory over Israel or Syria. A victory over Syria could have been even greater than one over the Ethiopians, depriving Syria of successful future attacks on Judah.

Illness and Death of Asa

[11]Note that the acts of Asa, first and last, are indeed written in the book of the kings of Judah and Israel. [12]And in the thirty-ninth year of his reign, Asa became diseased in his feet, and his malady was severe; yet in his disease he did not seek the LORD, but the physicians.

> **16:10–12** During Asa's last 6 years, he demonstrated ungodly behavior by being angry at truth, oppressing God's prophet and His people, and seeking man instead of God.

[13]So Asa rested with his fathers; he died in the forty-first year of his reign. [14]They buried him in his own tomb, which he had made for himself in the City of David; and they laid him in the bed which was filled with spices and various ingredients prepared in a mixture of ointments. They made a very great burning for him.

Jehoshaphat Reigns in Judah

17 Then Jehoshaphat his son reigned in his place, and strengthened himself against Israel. [2]And he placed troops in all the fortified cities of Judah, and set garrisons in the land of Judah and in the cities of Ephraim which Asa his father had taken. [3]Now the LORD was with Jehoshaphat, because he walked in the former ways of his father David; he did not seek the Baals, [4]but sought the God[a] of his father, and walked in His commandments and not according to the acts of Israel. [5]Therefore the LORD established the kingdom in his hand; and all Judah gave presents to Jehoshaphat, and he had riches and honor in abundance. [6]And his heart took delight in the ways of the LORD; moreover he removed the high places and wooden images from Judah.

[7]Also in the third year of his reign he sent his leaders, Ben-Hail, Obadiah, Zechariah, Nethanel, and Michaiah, to teach in the cities of Judah. [8]And with them *he sent* Levites: Shemaiah, Nethaniah, Zebadiah, Asahel, Shemiramoth, Jehonathan, Adonijah, Tobijah, and Tobadonijah—the Levites; and with them Elishama and Jehoram, the priests. [9]So they taught in Judah, and *had* the Book of the Law of the LORD with them; they went throughout all the cities of Judah and taught the people.

[10]And the fear of the LORD fell on all the kingdoms of the lands that *were* around Judah, so that they did not make war against Jehoshaphat. [11]Also *some* of the Philistines brought Jehoshaphat presents and silver as tribute; and the Arabians brought him flocks, seven thousand seven hundred rams and seven thousand seven hundred male goats.

> **17:3–11** Jehoshaphat obeyed the Lord, removed false worship from the land, and sent out teachers who taught the people the law of the Lord. This spiritual strategy brought God's blessing and protection.

[12]So Jehoshaphat became increasingly powerful, and he built fortresses and storage cities in Judah. [13]He had much property in the cities of Judah; and the men of war, mighty men of valor, *were* in Jerusalem. [14]These *are* their numbers, according to their fathers' houses. Of Judah, the captains of thousands: Adnah the captain, and with him three hundred thousand mighty

---

17:4 [a]Septuagint reads LORD God.

men of valor; ¹⁵and next to him *was* Jehohanan the captain, and with him two hundred and eighty thousand; ¹⁶and next to him *was* Amasiah the son of Zichri, who willingly offered himself to the LORD, and with him two hundred thousand mighty men of valor. ¹⁷Of Benjamin: Eliada a mighty man of valor, and with him two hundred thousand men armed with bow and shield; ¹⁸and next to him *was* Jehozabad, and with him one hundred and eighty thousand prepared for war. ¹⁹These served the king, besides those the king put in the fortified cities throughout all Judah.

Micaiah Warns Ahab

18 Jehoshaphat had riches and honor in abundance; and by marriage he allied himself with Ahab. ²After some years he went down to *visit* Ahab in Samaria; and Ahab killed sheep and oxen in abundance for him and the people who were with him, and persuaded him to go up *with him* to Ramoth Gilead. ³So Ahab king of Israel said to Jehoshaphat king of Judah, "Will you go with me *against* Ramoth Gilead?"

And he answered him, "I *am* as you *are*, and my people as your people; *we will be* with you in the war."

⁴Also Jehoshaphat said to the king of Israel, "Please inquire for the word of the LORD today."

⁵Then the king of Israel gathered the prophets together, four hundred men, and said to them, "Shall we go to war against Ramoth Gilead, or shall I refrain?"

So they said, "Go up, for God will deliver it into the king's hand."

> **18:5** Evil kings had false prophets who told them what they wanted to hear (see Is. 30:10,11; Jer. 14:13–16). The true prophet spoke God's Word and was arrested for speaking the unfavorable truth.

⁶But Jehoshaphat said, "*Is there* not still a prophet of the LORD here, that we may inquire of Him?"^a

⁷So the king of Israel said to Jehoshaphat, "*There is* still one man by whom we may inquire of the LORD; but I hate him, because he never prophesies good concerning me, but always evil. He *is* Micaiah the son of Imla."

And Jehoshaphat said, "Let not the king say such things!"

⁸Then the king of Israel called one *of his* officers and said, "Bring Micaiah the son of Imla quickly!"

⁹The king of Israel and Jehoshaphat king of Judah, clothed in *their* robes, sat each on his throne; and they sat at a threshing floor at the entrance of the gate of Samaria; and all the prophets prophesied before them. ¹⁰Now Zedekiah the son of Chenaanah had made horns of iron for himself; and he said, "Thus says the LORD: 'With these you shall gore the Syrians until they are destroyed.' "

¹¹And all the prophets prophesied so, saying, "Go up to Ramoth Gilead and prosper, for the LORD will deliver *it* into the king's hand."

¹²Then the messenger who had gone to call Micaiah spoke to him, saying, "Now listen, the words of the prophets with one accord encourage the king. Therefore please let your word be like *the word of* one of them, and speak encouragement."

¹³And Micaiah said, "*As* the LORD lives, whatever my God says, that I will speak."

¹⁴Then he came to the king; and the king said to him, "Micaiah, shall we go to war against Ramoth Gilead, or shall I refrain?"

And he said, "Go and prosper, and they shall be delivered into your hand!"

¹⁵So the king said to him, "How many times shall I make you swear that you tell me nothing but the truth in the name of the LORD?"

¹⁶Then he said, "I saw all Israel scattered on the mountains, as sheep that have no shepherd. And the LORD said, 'These have no master. Let each return to his house in peace.' "

¹⁷And the king of Israel said to Jehoshaphat, "Did I not tell you he would not prophesy good concerning me, but evil?"

¹⁸Then *Micaiah* said, "Therefore hear the word of the LORD: I saw the LORD sitting on His throne, and all the host of heaven standing on His right hand and His left. ¹⁹And the LORD said, 'Who will persuade Ahab king of Israel to go up, that he may fall at Ramoth Gilead?' So one spoke in this

18:6 ^aOr *him*

manner, and another spoke in that manner. ²⁰Then a spirit came forward and stood before the LORD, and said, 'I will persuade him.' The LORD said to him, 'In what way?' ²¹So he said, 'I will go out and be a lying spirit in the mouth of all his prophets.' And *the* LORD said, 'You shall persuade *him* and also prevail; go out and do so.' ²²Therefore look! The LORD has put a lying spirit in the mouth of these prophets of yours, and the LORD has declared disaster against you."

²³Then Zedekiah the son of Chenaanah went near and struck Micaiah on the cheek, and said, "Which way did the spirit from the LORD go from me to speak to you?"

²⁴And Micaiah said, "Indeed you shall see on that day when you go into an inner chamber to hide!"

²⁵Then the king of Israel said, "Take Micaiah, and return him to Amon the governor of the city and to Joash the king's son; ²⁶and say, 'Thus says the king: "Put this *fellow* in prison, and feed him with bread of affliction and water of affliction, until I return in peace." ' "

²⁷But Micaiah said, "If you ever return in peace, the LORD has not spoken by me." And he said, "Take heed, all you people!"

Ahab Dies in Battle

²⁸So the king of Israel and Jehoshaphat the king of Judah went up to Ramoth Gilead. ²⁹And the king of Israel said to Jehoshaphat, "I will disguise myself and go into battle; but you put on your robes." So the king of Israel disguised himself, and they went into battle.

³⁰Now the king of Syria had commanded the captains of the chariots who *were* with him, saying, "Fight with no one small or great, but only with the king of Israel." ³¹So it was, when the captains of the chariots saw Jehoshaphat, that they said, "It *is* the king of Israel!" Therefore they surrounded him to attack; but Jehoshaphat cried out, and the LORD helped him, and God diverted them from him. ³²For so it was, when the captains of the chariots saw that it was not the king of Israel, that they turned back from pursuing him. ³³Now a certain man drew a bow at random, and struck the king of Israel between the joints

of his armor. So he said to the driver of his chariot, "Turn around and take me out of the battle, for I am wounded." ³⁴The battle increased that day, and the king of Israel propped *himself* up in *his* chariot facing the Syrians until evening; and about the time of sunset he died.

> **18:1–34** Jehoshaphat relied on other kings and sought alliances with them (see 2 Chr. 20:35–37). He arranged for his son to marry Athaliah, the daughter of the wicked king Ahab of Israel, which angered God. After Jehoshaphat died, Athaliah became queen, seized the throne, and killed almost all of David's descendants. She brought wicked idols of Israel into Judah, leading to the nation's destruction and captivity in Babylon.

19 Then Jehoshaphat the king of Judah returned safely to his house in Jerusalem. ²And Jehu the son of Hanani the seer went out to meet him, and said to King Jehoshaphat, "Should you help the wicked and love those who hate the LORD? Therefore the wrath of the LORD *is* upon you. ³Nevertheless good things are found in you, in that you have removed the wooden images from the land, and have prepared your heart to seek God."

> **19:1–3** Jehoshaphat faced possible death that was diverted by God. The prophet rebuked him for his alliance with God's enemy, Ahab (1 Kin. 22:2). God displayed mercy on Jehoshaphat, along with His wrath, because of the king's concern for the true worship of God.

The Reforms of Jehoshaphat

⁴So Jehoshaphat dwelt at Jerusalem; and he went out again among the people from Beersheba to the mountains of Ephraim, and brought them back to the LORD God of their fathers. ⁵Then he set judges in the land throughout all the fortified cities of Judah, city by city, ⁶and said to the judges, "Take heed to what you are doing, for you do not judge for man but for the LORD, who *is* with you in the judgment. ⁷Now therefore, let the fear of the LORD be upon you; take care and do *it*, for *there is* no iniquity with the LORD our God, no partiality, nor taking of bribes."

⁸Moreover in Jerusalem, for the judgment of the LORD and for controversies,

Jehoshaphat appointed some of the Levites and priests, and some of the chief fathers of Israel, when they returned to Jerusalem.*ª* ⁹And he commanded them, saying, "Thus you shall act in the fear of the LORD, faithfully and with a loyal heart: ¹⁰Whatever case comes to you from your brethren who dwell in their cities, whether of bloodshed or offenses against law or commandment, against statutes or ordinances, you shall warn them, lest they trespass against the LORD and wrath come upon you and your brethren. Do this, and you will not be guilty. ¹¹And take notice: Amariah the chief priest *is* over you in all matters of the LORD; and Zebadiah the son of Ishmael, the ruler of the house of Judah, for all the king's matters; also the Levites *will be* officials before you. Behave courageously, and the LORD will be with the good."

Ammon, Moab, and Mount Seir Defeated

20 It happened after this *that* the people of Moab with the people of Ammon, and *others* with them besides the Ammonites,*ª* came to battle against Jehoshaphat. ²Then some came and told Jehoshaphat, saying, "A great multitude is coming against you from beyond the sea, from Syria;*ª* and they are in Hazazon Tamar" (which *is* En Gedi). ³And Jehoshaphat feared, and set himself to seek the LORD, and proclaimed a fast throughout all Judah. ⁴So Judah gathered together to ask *help* from the LORD; and from all the cities of Judah they came to seek the LORD.

⁵Then Jehoshaphat stood in the assembly of Judah and Jerusalem, in the house of the LORD, before the new court, ⁶and said: "O LORD God of our fathers, *are* You not God in heaven, and do You *not* rule over all the kingdoms of the nations, and in Your hand *is there not* power and might, so that no one is able to withstand You? ⁷*Are* You not our God, *who* drove out the inhabitants of this land before Your people Israel, and gave it to the descendants of Abraham Your friend forever? ⁸And they dwell in it, and have built You a sanctuary in it for Your name, saying, ⁹'If disaster comes upon us—

sword, judgment, pestilence, or famine—we will stand before this temple and in Your presence (for Your name *is* in this temple), and cry out to You in our affliction, and You will hear and save.' ¹⁰And now, here are the people of Ammon, Moab, and Mount Seir— whom You would not let Israel invade when they came out of the land of Egypt, but they turned from them and did not destroy them— ¹¹here they are, rewarding us by coming to throw us out of Your possession which You have given us to inherit. ¹²O our God, will You not judge them? For we have no power against this great multitude that is coming against us; nor do we know what to do, but our eyes *are* upon You."

> **20:5–12** Jehoshaphat stood praying for the nation in the redecorated center court. He appealed to the promises, glory, and reputation of God that were at stake because He was identified with Judah. Jehoshaphat acknowledged God's sovereignty, His covenant, His presence, His goodness, His possession, and their reliance on Him.

¹³Now all Judah, with their little ones, their wives, and their children, stood before the LORD.

¹⁴Then the Spirit of the LORD came upon Jahaziel the son of Zechariah, the son of Benaiah, the son of Jeiel, the son of Mattaniah, a Levite of the sons of Asaph, in the midst of the assembly. ¹⁵And he said, "Listen, all you of Judah and you inhabitants of Jerusalem, and you, King Jehoshaphat! Thus says the LORD to you: 'Do not be afraid nor dismayed because of this great multitude, for the battle *is* not yours, but God's. ¹⁶Tomorrow go down against them. They will surely come up by the Ascent of Ziz, and you will find them at the end of the brook before the Wilderness of Jeruel. ¹⁷You will not *need* to fight in this *battle*. Position yourselves, stand still and see the salvation of the LORD, who is with you, O Judah and Jerusalem!' Do not fear or be dismayed; tomorrow go out against them, for the LORD *is* with you."

¹⁸And Jehoshaphat bowed his head with *his* face to the ground, and all Judah and

19:8 *ª*Septuagint and Vulgate read *for the inhabitants of Jerusalem.* **20:1** *ª*Following Masoretic Text and Vulgate; Septuagint reads *Meunites* (compare 26:7). **20:2** *ª*Following Masoretic Text, Septuagint, and Vulgate; some Hebrew manuscripts and Old Latin read *Edom.*

the inhabitants of Jerusalem bowed before the LORD, worshiping the LORD. ¹⁹Then the Levites of the children of the Kohathites and of the children of the Korahites stood up to praise the LORD God of Israel with voices loud and high.

²⁰So they rose early in the morning and went out into the Wilderness of Tekoa; and as they went out, Jehoshaphat stood and said, "Hear me, O Judah and you inhabitants of Jerusalem: Believe in the LORD your God, and you shall be established; believe His prophets, and you shall prosper." ²¹And when he had consulted with the people, he appointed those who should sing to the LORD, and who should praise the beauty of holiness, as they went out before the army and were saying:

"Praise the LORD,
  For His mercy *endures* forever."ᵃ

> **20:18–21** Here was the praise of faith. They were confident in God's promise of victory and praised Him before the battle was won. Their trust was so great that the choir marched in front of the army, singing psalms.

²²Now when they began to sing and to praise, the LORD set ambushes against the people of Ammon, Moab, and Mount Seir, who had come against Judah; and they were defeated. ²³For the people of Ammon and Moab stood up against the inhabitants of Mount Seir to utterly kill and destroy *them*. And when they had made an end of the inhabitants of Seir, they helped to destroy one another.

²⁴So when Judah came to a place overlooking the wilderness, they looked toward the multitude; and there *were* their dead bodies, fallen on the earth. No one had escaped.

²⁵When Jehoshaphat and his people came to take away their spoil, they found among them an abundance of valuables on the dead bodies,ᵃ and precious jewelry, which they stripped off for themselves, more than they could carry away; and they were three days gathering the spoil because there was so much. ²⁶And on the fourth day they assembled in the Valley of Berachah, for there they blessed the LORD; therefore the name of that place was called The Valley of Berachahᵃ until this day. ²⁷Then they returned, every man of Judah and Jerusalem, with Jehoshaphat in front of them, to go back to Jerusalem with joy, for the LORD had made them rejoice over their enemies. ²⁸So they came to Jerusalem, with stringed instruments and harps and trumpets, to the house of the LORD. ²⁹And the fear of God was on all the kingdoms of *those* countries when they heard that the LORD had fought against the enemies of Israel. ³⁰Then the realm of Jehoshaphat was quiet, for his God gave him rest all around.

The End of Jehoshaphat's Reign

³¹So Jehoshaphat was king over Judah. *He was* thirty-five years old when he became king, and he reigned twenty-five years in Jerusalem. His mother's name *was* Azubah the daughter of Shilhi. ³²And he walked in the way of his father Asa, and did not turn aside from it, doing *what was* right in the sight of the LORD. ³³Nevertheless the high places were not taken away, for as yet the people had not directed their hearts to the God of their fathers.

³⁴Now the rest of the acts of Jehoshaphat, first and last, indeed they *are* written in the book of Jehu the son of Hanani, which *is* mentioned in the book of the kings of Israel.

³⁵After this Jehoshaphat king of Judah allied himself with Ahaziah king of Israel, who acted very wickedly. ³⁶And he allied himself with him to make ships to go to Tarshish, and they made the ships in Ezion Geber. ³⁷But Eliezer the son of Dodavah of Mareshah prophesied against Jehoshaphat, saying, "Because you have allied yourself with Ahaziah, the LORD has destroyed your works." Then the ships were wrecked, so that they were not able to go to Tarshish.

Jehoram Reigns in Judah

21 And Jehoshaphat rested with his fathers, and was buried with his fathers in the City of David. Then Jehoram

---

20:21 ᵃCompare Psalm 106:1   20:25 ᵃA few Hebrew manuscripts, Old Latin, and Vulgate read *garments*; Septuagint reads *armor.*   20:26 ᵃLiterally *Blessing*

his son reigned in his place. [2]He had brothers, the sons of Jehoshaphat: Azariah, Jehiel, Zechariah, Azaryahu, Michael, and Shephatiah; all these *were* the sons of Jehoshaphat king of Israel. [3]Their father gave them great gifts of silver and gold and precious things, with fortified cities in Judah; but he gave the kingdom to Jehoram, because he *was* the firstborn.

[4]Now when Jehoram was established over the kingdom of his father, he strengthened himself and killed all his brothers with the sword, and also *others* of the princes of Israel.

[5]Jehoram *was* thirty-two years old when he became king, and he reigned eight years in Jerusalem. [6]And he walked in the way of the kings of Israel, just as the house of Ahab had done, for he had the daughter of Ahab as a wife; and he did evil in the sight of the LORD. [7]Yet the LORD would not destroy the house of David, because of the covenant that He had made with David, and since He had promised to give a lamp to him and to his sons forever.

> **21:2–5** When the co-regency with his father ended at his father's death, Jehoram killed all who might have threatened his throne.

[8]In his days Edom revolted against Judah's authority, and made a king over themselves. [9]So Jehoram went out with his officers, and all his chariots with him. And he rose by night and attacked the Edomites who had surrounded him and the captains of the chariots. [10]Thus Edom has been in revolt against Judah's authority to this day. At that time Libnah revolted against his rule, because he had forsaken the LORD God of his fathers. [11]Moreover he made high places in the mountains of Judah, and caused the inhabitants of Jerusalem to commit harlotry, and led Judah astray.

> **21:11 led Judah astray.** Jehoram had not learned from Solomon's sinful example. He was influenced by his marriage to Ahab's daughter and by the alliance, just as his father had been (2 Chr. 18:1). His wicked wife, Athaliah, later became ruler over Judah and tried to wipe out David's royal line (2 Chr. 22:10).

[12]And a letter came to him from Elijah the prophet, saying,

Thus says the LORD God of your father David:

Because you have not walked in the ways of Jehoshaphat your father, or in the ways of Asa king of Judah, [13]but have walked in the way of the kings of Israel, and have made Judah and the inhabitants of Jerusalem to play the harlot like the harlotry of the house of Ahab, and also have killed your brothers, those of your father's household, *who were* better than yourself, [14]behold, the LORD will strike your people with a serious affliction—your children, your wives, and all your possessions; [15]and you *will become* very sick with a disease of your intestines, until your intestines come out by reason of the sickness, day by day.

[16]Moreover the LORD stirred up against Jehoram the spirit of the Philistines and the Arabians who *were* near the Ethiopians. [17]And they came up into Judah and invaded it, and carried away all the possessions that were found in the king's house, and also his sons and his wives, so that there was not a son left to him except Jehoahaz,[a] the youngest of his sons.

[18]After all this the LORD struck him in his intestines with an incurable disease. [19]Then it happened in the course of time, after the end of two years, that his intestines came out because of his sickness; so he died in severe pain. And his people made no burning for him, like the burning for his fathers.

[20]He was thirty-two years old when he became king. He reigned in Jerusalem eight years and, to no one's sorrow, departed. However they buried him in the City of David, but not in the tombs of the kings.

Ahaziah Reigns in Judah

22 Then the inhabitants of Jerusalem made Ahaziah his youngest son king in his place, for the raiders who came with the Arabians into the camp had killed

---

21:17 [a]Elsewhere called *Ahaziah* (compare 2 Chronicles 22:1)

all the older *sons*. So Ahaziah the son of Jehoram, king of Judah, reigned. [2]Ahaziah *was* forty-two[a] years old when he became king, and he reigned one year in Jerusalem. His mother's name *was* Athaliah the granddaughter of Omri. [3]He also walked in the ways of the house of Ahab, for his mother advised him to do wickedly. [4]Therefore he did evil in the sight of the LORD, like the house of Ahab; for they were his counselors after the death of his father, to his destruction. [5]He also followed their advice, and went with Jehoram[a] the son of Ahab king of Israel to war against Hazael king of Syria at Ramoth Gilead; and the Syrians wounded Joram. [6]Then he returned to Jezreel to recover from the wounds which he had received at Ramah, when he fought against Hazael king of Syria. And Azariah[a] the son of Jehoram, king of Judah, went down to see Jehoram the son of Ahab in Jezreel, because he was sick.

> **22:3 his mother advised him...wickedly.** Athaliah and the rest of Ahab's house taught him wickedness and led him to moral corruption, idolatry, and folly in going to war with the Syrians.

[7]His going to Joram was God's occasion for Ahaziah's downfall; for when he arrived, he went out with Jehoram against Jehu the son of Nimshi, whom the LORD had anointed to cut off the house of Ahab. [8]And it happened, when Jehu was executing judgment on the house of Ahab, and found the princes of Judah and the sons of Ahaziah's brothers who served Ahaziah, that he killed them. [9]Then he searched for Ahaziah; and they caught him (he was hiding in Samaria), and brought him to Jehu. When they had killed him, they buried him, "because," they said, "he is the son of Jehoshaphat, who sought the LORD with all his heart."

So the house of Ahaziah had no one to assume power over the kingdom.

Athaliah Reigns in Judah

[10]Now when Athaliah the mother of Ahaziah saw that her son was dead, she arose

and destroyed all the royal heirs of the house of Judah. [11]But Jehoshabeath,[a] the daughter of the king, took Joash the son of Ahaziah, and stole him away from among the king's sons who were being murdered, and put him and his nurse in a bedroom. So Jehoshabeath, the daughter of King Jehoram, the wife of Jehoiada the priest (for she was the sister of Ahaziah), hid him from Athaliah so that she did not kill him. [12]And he was hidden with them in the house of God for six years, while Athaliah reigned over the land.

Joash Crowned King of Judah

23 In the seventh year Jehoiada strengthened himself, *and made a* covenant with the captains of hundreds: Azariah the son of Jeroham, Ishmael the son of Jehohanan, Azariah the son of Obed, Maaseiah the son of Adaiah, and Elishaphat the son of Zichri. [2]And they went throughout Judah and gathered the Levites from all the cities of Judah, and the chief fathers of Israel, and they came to Jerusalem.

[3]Then all the assembly made a covenant with the king in the house of God. And he said to them, "Behold, the king's son shall reign, as the LORD has said of the sons of David. [4]This *is* what you shall do: One-third of you entering on the Sabbath, of the priests and the Levites, *shall be* keeping watch over the doors; [5]one-third *shall be* at the king's house; and one-third at the Gate of the Foundation. All the people *shall be* in the courts of the house of the LORD. [6]But let no one come into the house of the LORD except the priests and those of the Levites who serve. They may go in, for they *are* holy; but all the people shall keep the watch of the LORD. [7]And the Levites shall

> **23:3 as the LORD...said.** This is one of the most dramatic moments in messianic history. Joash was the only offspring of David left. If he had died, there would have been no heir to the Davidic throne, meaning the destruction of the line of the Messiah. God protected Joash (2 Chr. 22:10–12) and eliminated Athaliah (1 Chr. 23:12–21).

22:2 [a]Or *twenty-two* (compare 2 Kings 8:26)   22:5 [a]Also spelled *Joram* (compare verses 5 and 7; 2 Kings 8:28; and elsewhere)   22:6 [a]Some Hebrew manuscripts, Septuagint, Syriac, Vulgate, and 2 Kings 8:29 read *Ahaziah*.   22:11 [a]Spelled *Jehosheba* in 2 Kings 11:2

surround the king on all sides, every man with his weapons in his hand; and whoever comes into the house, let him be put to death. You are to be with the king when he comes in and when he goes out."

⁸So the Levites and all Judah did according to all that Jehoiada the priest commanded. And each man took his men who were to be on duty on the Sabbath, with those who were going *off duty* on the Sabbath; for Jehoiada the priest had not dismissed the divisions. ⁹And Jehoiada the priest gave to the captains of hundreds the spears and the large and small shields which *had belonged* to King David, that *were* in the temple of God. ¹⁰Then he set all the people, every man with his weapon in his hand, from the right side of the temple to the left side of the temple, along by the altar and by the temple, all around the king. ¹¹And they brought out the king's son, put the crown on him, *gave him* the Testimony,ᵃ and made him king. Then Jehoiada and his sons anointed him, and said, "*Long* live the king!"

> **23:11 Testimony.** The term usually refers to a copy of the law (see Deut. 17:18).

Death of Athaliah

¹²Now when Athaliah heard the noise of the people running and praising the king, she came to the people *in* the temple of the LORD. ¹³*When* she looked, there was the king standing by his pillar at the entrance; and the leaders and the trumpeters *were* by the king. All the people of the land were rejoicing and blowing trumpets, also the singers with musical instruments, and those who led in praise. So Athaliah tore her clothes and said, "Treason! Treason!"

¹⁴And Jehoiada the priest brought out the captains of hundreds who were set over the army, and said to them, "Take her outside under guard, and slay with the sword whoever follows her." For the priest had said, "Do not kill her in the house of the LORD."

¹⁵So they seized her; and she went by way of the entrance of the Horse Gate *into* the king's house, and they killed her there.

¹⁶Then Jehoiada made a covenant between himself, the people, and the king, that they should be the LORD's people. ¹⁷And all the people went to the templeᵃ of Baal, and tore it down. They broke in pieces its altars and images, and killed Mattan the priest of Baal before the altars. ¹⁸Also Jehoiada appointed the oversight of the house of the LORD to the hand of the priests, the Levites, whom David had assigned in the house of the LORD, to offer the burnt offerings of the LORD, as *it is* written in the Law of Moses, with rejoicing and with singing, *as it was established* by David. ¹⁹And he set the gatekeepers at the gates of the house of the LORD, so that no one *who was* in any way unclean should enter.

²⁰Then he took the captains of hundreds, the nobles, the governors of the people, and all the people of the land, and brought the king down from the house of the LORD; and they went through the Upper Gate to the king's house, and set the king on the throne of the kingdom. ²¹So all the people of the land rejoiced; and the city was quiet, for they had slain Athaliah with the sword.

Joash Repairs the Temple

24 Joash *was* seven years old when he became king, and he reigned forty years in Jerusalem. His mother's name *was* Zibiah of Beersheba. ²Joash did *what was* right in the sight of the LORD all the days of Jehoiada the priest. ³And Jehoiada took two wives for him, and he had sons and daughters.

> **24:1–27** The reign of Joash (about 835-796 B.C.). The prophet Joel probably prophesied during his reign, and his prophecy gives much helpful background to this time.

⁴Now it happened after this *that* Joash set his heart on repairing the house of the LORD. ⁵Then he gathered the priests and the Levites, and said to them, "Go out to the cities of Judah, and gather from all Israel money to repair the house of your God from year to year, and see that you do it quickly."

However the Levites did not do it quickly. ⁶So the king called Jehoiada the chief *priest*, and said to him, "Why have you not re-

---

23:11 ᵃThat is, the Law (compare Exodus 25:16,21; 31:18) 23:17 ᵃLiterally *house*

quired the Levites to bring in from Judah and from Jerusalem the collection, *according to the commandment* of Moses the servant of the LORD and of the assembly of Israel, for the tabernacle of witness?" [7]For the sons of Athaliah, that wicked woman, had broken into the house of God, and had also presented all the dedicated things of the house of the LORD to the Baals.

[8]Then at the king's command they made a chest, and set it outside at the gate of the house of the LORD. [9]And they made a proclamation throughout Judah and Jerusalem to bring to the LORD the collection *that* Moses the servant of God *had imposed* on Israel in the wilderness. [10]Then all the leaders and all the people rejoiced, brought their contributions, and put *them* into the chest until all had given. [11]So it was, at that time, when the chest was brought to the king's official by the hand of the Levites, and when they saw that *there was* much money, that the king's scribe and the high priest's officer came and emptied the chest, and took it and returned it to its place. Thus they did day by day, and gathered money in abundance.

[12]The king and Jehoiada gave it to those who did the work of the service of the house of the LORD; and they hired masons and carpenters to repair the house of the LORD, and also those who worked in iron and bronze to restore the house of the LORD. [13]So the workmen labored, and the work was completed by them; they restored the house of God to its original condition and reinforced it. [14]When they had finished, they brought the rest of the money before the king and Jehoiada; they made from it articles for the house of the LORD, articles for serving and offering, spoons and vessels of gold and silver. And they offered burnt offerings in the house of the LORD continually all the days of Jehoiada.

Apostasy of Joash

[15]But Jehoiada grew old and was full of days, and he died; *he was* one hundred and thirty years old when he died. [16]And they buried him in the City of David among the kings, because he had done good in Israel, both toward God and His house.

24:15,16 Jehoiada. He was the High-Priest of Athaliah's and Joash's reigns (see 2 Chr. 23:1–24:16). He led the fight against idols, permitted the coup against Athaliah, and granted the throne to Joash to bring about the revival.

[17]Now after the death of Jehoiada the leaders of Judah came and bowed down to the king. And the king listened to them. [18]Therefore they left the house of the LORD God of their fathers, and served wooden images and idols; and wrath came upon Judah and Jerusalem because of their trespass. [19]Yet He sent prophets to them, to bring them back to the LORD; and they testified against them, but they would not listen.

24:18b,19 God judged Judah for her evil, yet by His mercy sent prophets to preach the truth of repentance.

[20]Then the Spirit of God came upon Zechariah the son of Jehoiada the priest, who stood above the people, and said to them, "Thus says God: 'Why do you transgress the commandments of the LORD, so that you cannot prosper? Because you have forsaken the LORD, He also has forsaken you.' " [21]So they conspired against him, and at the command of the king they stoned him with stones in the court of the house of the LORD. [22]Thus Joash the king did not remember the kindness which Jehoiada his father had done to him, but killed his son; and as he died, he said, "The LORD look on *it*, and repay!"

Death of Joash

[23]So it happened in the spring of the year *that* the army of Syria came up against him; and they came to Judah and Jerusalem, and destroyed all the leaders of the people from among the people, and sent all their spoil to the king of Damascus. [24]For the army of the Syrians came with a small company of men; but the LORD delivered a very great army into their hand, because they had forsaken the LORD God of their fathers. So they executed judgment against Joash. [25]And when they had withdrawn from him (for they left him severely wounded), his own servants conspired against him because of the blood of the sons[a] of Jehoiada

---

24:25 [a]Septuagint and Vulgate read *son* (compare verses 20–22).

the priest, and killed him on his bed. So he died. And they buried him in the City of David, but they did not bury him in the tombs of the kings.

> **24:24 small company.** As the Lord had previously given victory to Judah's smaller army because of her faithfulness (2 Chr. 13:2–20), He gave Judah defeat at the hands of a lesser force because of her wickedness.

[26]These are the ones who conspired against him: Zabad[a] the son of Shimeath the Ammonitess, and Jehozabad the son of Shimrith[b] the Moabitess. [27]Now *concerning* his sons, and the many oracles about him, and the repairing of the house of God, indeed they *are* written in the annals of the book of the kings. Then Amaziah his son reigned in his place.

Amaziah Reigns in Judah

25 Amaziah *was* twenty-five years old *when* he became king, and he reigned twenty-nine years in Jerusalem. His mother's name *was* Jehoaddan of Jerusalem. [2]And he did *what was* right in the sight of the LORD, but not with a loyal heart.

[3]Now it happened, as soon as the kingdom was established for him, that he executed his servants who had murdered his father the king. [4]However he did not execute their children, but *did* as *it is* written in the Law in the Book of Moses, where the LORD commanded, saying, "The fathers shall not be put to death for their children, nor shall the children be put to death for their fathers; but a person shall die for his own sin."[a]

The War Against Edom

[5]Moreover Amaziah gathered Judah together and set over them captains of thousands and captains of hundreds, according to *their* fathers' houses, throughout all Judah and Benjamin; and he numbered them from twenty years old and above, and found them to be three hundred thousand choice *men, able* to go to war, who could handle spear and shield. [6]He also hired one hundred thousand mighty men of valor from Israel for one hundred talents of silver. [7]But a man of God came to him, saying, "O king, do not let the army of Israel go with you, for the LORD *is* not with Israel—*not with* any of the children of Ephraim. [8]But if you go, be gone! Be strong in battle! *Even so,* God shall make you fall before the enemy; for God has power to help and to overthrow."

> **25:7 man of God.** This term is used about 70 times in the Old Testament and refers to one who spoke for God. Amaziah was warned not to make idolatrous Israel his ally because the Lord was not with Ephraim.

[9]Then Amaziah said to the man of God, "But what *shall we* do about the hundred talents which I have given to the troops of Israel?"

And the man of God answered, "The LORD is able to give you much more than this." [10]So Amaziah discharged the troops that had come to him from Ephraim, to go back home. Therefore their anger was greatly aroused against Judah, and they returned home in great anger.

[11]Then Amaziah strengthened himself, and leading his people, he went to the Valley of Salt and killed ten thousand of the people of Seir. [12]Also the children of Judah took captive ten thousand alive, brought them to the top of the rock, and cast them down from the top of the rock, so that they all were dashed in pieces.

[13]But as for the soldiers of the army which Amaziah had discharged, so that they would not go with him to battle, they raided the cities of Judah from Samaria to Beth Horon, killed three thousand in them, and took much spoil.

[14]Now it was so, after Amaziah came from the slaughter of the Edomites, that he brought the gods of the people of Seir, set them up *to be* his gods, and bowed down before them and burned incense to them. [15]Therefore the anger of the LORD was aroused against Ama-ziah, and He sent him a prophet who said to him, "Why have you sought the gods of the people, which could not rescue their own people from your hand?"

24:26 [a]Or *Jozachar* (compare 2 Kings 12:21)   [b]Or *Shomer* (compare 2 Kings 12:21)
25:4 [a]Deuteronomy 24:16

[16]So it was, as he talked with him, that *the king* said to him, "Have we made you the king's counselor? Cease! Why should you be killed?"

Then the prophet ceased, and said, "I know that God has determined to destroy you, because you have done this and have not heeded my advice."

> **25:14–16** Amaziah embraced the false gods of the people whom he had defeated. He was seduced by the wicked pleasures of idolatry and thought it would help him in assuring no further threat from Edom. Instead, it brought destruction on him.

Israel Defeats Judah

[17]Now Amaziah king of Judah asked advice and sent to Joash[a] the son of Jehoahaz, the son of Jehu, king of Israel, saying, "Come, let us face one another *in battle.*"

[18]And Joash king of Israel sent to Amaziah king of Judah, saying, "The thistle that *was* in Lebanon sent to the cedar that was in Lebanon, saying, 'Give your daughter to my son as wife'; and a wild beast that *was* in Lebanon passed by and trampled the thistle. [19]Indeed you say that you have defeated the Edomites, and your heart is lifted up to boast. Stay at home now; why should you meddle with trouble, that you should fall—you and Judah with you?"

[20]But Amaziah would not heed, for it *came* from God, that He might give them into the hand *of their enemies,* because they sought the gods of Edom. [21]So Joash king of Israel went out; and he and Amaziah king of Judah faced one another at Beth Shemesh, which *belongs* to Judah. [22]And Judah was defeated by Israel, and every man fled to his tent. [23]Then Joash the king of Israel captured Amaziah king of Judah, the son of Joash, the son of Jehoahaz, at Beth Shemesh; and he brought him to Jerusalem, and broke down the wall of Jerusalem from the Gate of Ephraim to the Corner Gate—four hundred cubits. [24]And *he took* all the gold and silver, all the articles that were found in the house of God with Obed-Edom, the treasures of the king's house, and hostages, and returned to Samaria.

Death of Amaziah

[25]Amaziah the son of Joash, king of Judah, lived fifteen years after the death of Joash the son of Jehoahaz, king of Israel. [26]Now the rest of the acts of Amaziah, from first to last, indeed *are* they not written in the book of the kings of Judah and Israel? [27]After the time that Amaziah turned away from following the LORD, they made a conspiracy against him in Jerusalem, and he fled to Lachish; but they sent after him to Lachish and killed him there. [28]Then they brought him on horses and buried him with his fathers in the City of Judah.

Uzziah Reigns in Judah

26 Now all the people of Judah took Uzziah,[a] who *was* sixteen years old, and made him king instead of his father Amaziah. [2]He built Elath[a] and restored it to Judah, after the king rested with his fathers.

[3]Uzziah *was* sixteen years old when he became king, and he reigned fifty-two years in Jerusalem. His mother's name was Jecholiah of Jerusalem. [4]And he did *what was* right in the sight of the LORD, according to all that his father Amaziah had done. [5]He sought God in the days of Zechariah, who had understanding in the visions[a] of God; and as long as he sought the LORD, God made him prosper.

[6]Now he went out and made war against the Philistines, and broke down the wall of Gath, the wall of Jabneh, and the wall of Ashdod; and he built cities *around* Ashdod and among the Philistines. [7]God helped him against the Philistines, against the Arabians who lived in Gur Baal, and against the Meunites. [8]Also the Ammonites brought tribute to Uzziah. His fame spread as far as the entrance of Egypt, for he became exceedingly strong.

[9]And Uzziah built towers in Jerusalem at the Corner Gate, at the Valley Gate, and at the corner buttress of the wall; then he fortified them. [10]Also he built towers in the desert. He dug many wells, for he had much livestock, both in the lowlands and in the plains; *he also had* farmers and vinedressers in the mountains and in Carmel, for he loved the soil.

25:17 [a]Spelled *Jehoash* in 2 Kings 14:8ff   26:1 [a]Called *Azariah* in 2 Kings 14:21ff   26:2 [a]Hebrew *Eloth*   26:5 [a]Several Hebrew manuscripts, Septuagint, Syriac, Targum, and Arabic read *fear.*

[11]Moreover Uzziah had an army of fighting men who went out to war by companies, according to the number on their roll as prepared by Jeiel the scribe and Maaseiah the officer, under the hand of Hananiah, *one* of the king's captains. [12]The total number of chief officers[a] of the mighty men of valor *was* two thousand six hundred. [13]And under their authority *was* an army of three hundred and seven thousand five hundred, that made war with mighty power, to help the king against the enemy. [14]Then Uzziah prepared for them, for the entire army, shields, spears, helmets, body armor, bows, and slings *to cast* stones. [15]And he made devices in Jerusalem, invented by skillful men, to be on the towers and the corners, to shoot arrows and large stones. So his fame spread far and wide, for he was marvelously helped till he became strong.

The Penalty for Uzziah's Pride

[16]But when he was strong his heart was lifted up, to *his* destruction, for he transgressed against the LORD his God by entering the temple of the LORD to burn incense on the altar of incense. [17]So Azariah the priest went in after him, and with him were eighty priests of the LORD—valiant men. [18]And they withstood King Uzziah, and said to him, "*It* is not for you, Uzziah, to burn incense to the LORD, but for the priests, the sons of Aaron, who are consecrated to burn incense. Get out of the sanctuary, for you have trespassed! You *shall have* no honor from the LORD God." [19]Then Uzziah became furious; and he *had* a censer in his hand to burn incense. And while he was angry with the priests, leprosy broke out on his forehead, before the priests in the house of the LORD, beside the incense altar. [20]And Azariah the chief priest and all the priests looked at him, and there, on his forehead, he *was* leprous; so

26:19,20 God judged Uzziah for refusing to heed the law, but He mercifully did not kill him. With leprosy, Uzziah had to submit to the priests in a new way according to the laws of leprosy (see Lev. 13,14) and endured isolation from the temple for the rest of his life.

they thrust him out of that place. Indeed he also hurried to get out, because the LORD had struck him.

[21]King Uzziah was a leper until the day of his death. He dwelt in an isolated house, because he was a leper; for he was cut off from the house of the LORD. Then Jotham his son *was* over the king's house, judging the people of the land.

[22]Now the rest of the acts of Uzziah, from first to last, the prophet Isaiah the son of Amoz wrote. [23]So Uzziah rested with his fathers, and they buried him with his fathers in the field of burial which *belonged* to the kings, for they said, "He is a leper." Then Jotham his son reigned in his place.

Jotham Reigns in Judah

27 Jotham *was* twenty-five years old when he became king, and he reigned sixteen years in Jerusalem. His mother's name *was* Jerushah[a] the daughter of Zadok. [2]And he did *what was* right in the sight of the LORD, according to all that his father Uzziah had done (although he did not enter the temple of the LORD). But still the people acted corruptly.

[3]He built the Upper Gate of the house of the LORD, and he built extensively on the wall of Ophel. [4]Moreover he built cities in the mountains of Judah, and in the forests he built fortresses and towers. [5]He also fought with the king of the Ammonites and defeated them. And the people of Ammon gave him in that year one hundred talents of silver, ten thousand kors of wheat, and ten thousand of barley. The people of Ammon paid this to him in the second and third years also. [6]So Jotham became mighty, because he prepared his ways before the LORD his God.

27:6 Ahaz failed in not removing the idolatrous high places and stopping idol worship by the people (see 2 Kin. 15:35).

[7]Now the rest of the acts of Jotham, and all his wars and his ways, indeed they *are* written in the book of the kings of Israel and Judah. [8]He was twenty-five years old when he became king, and he reigned sixteen years in Jerusalem. [9]So Jotham rested

---

26:12 *a*Literally *chief fathers*   27:1 *a*Spelled *Jerusha* in 2 Kings 15:33

with his fathers, and they buried him in the City of David. Then Ahaz his son reigned in his place.

Ahaz Reigns in Judah

28 Ahaz *was* twenty years old when he became king, and he reigned sixteen years in Jerusalem; and he did not do *what was* right in the sight of the LORD, as his father David *had done.* ²For he walked in the ways of the kings of Israel, and made molded images for the Baals. ³He burned incense in the Valley of the Son of Hinnom, and burned his children in the fire, according to the abominations of the nations whom the LORD had cast out before the children of Israel. ⁴And he sacrificed and burned incense on the high places, on the hills, and under every green tree.

Syria and Israel Defeat Judah

⁵Therefore the LORD his God delivered him into the hand of the king of Syria. They defeated him, and carried away a great multitude of them as captives, and brought *them* to Damascus. Then he was also delivered into the hand of the king of Israel, who defeated him with a great slaughter. ⁶For Pekah the son of Remaliah killed one hundred and twenty thousand in Judah in one day, all valiant men, because they had forsaken the LORD God of their fathers. ⁷Zichri, a mighty man of Ephraim, killed Maaseiah the king's son, Azrikam the officer over the house, and Elkanah *who was* second to the king. ⁸And the children of Israel carried away captive of their brethren two hundred thousand women, sons, and daughters; and they also took away much spoil from them, and brought the spoil to Samaria.

> **28:5b–8** Ahaz received God's wrath for his disobedience. Both Syria and Israel defeated his army, as they had done in Jotham's day (2 Kin. 15:37). This was a continuation of the same campaign against Judah that had begun earlier.

Israel Returns the Captives

⁹But a prophet of the LORD was there, whose name *was* Oded; and he went out before the army that came to Samaria, and said to them: "Look, because the LORD God of your fathers was angry with Judah, He has delivered them into your hand; but you have killed them in a rage *that* reaches up to heaven. ¹⁰And now you propose to force the children of Judah and Jerusalem to be your male and female slaves; *but are* you not also guilty before the LORD your God? ¹¹Now hear me, therefore, and return the captives, whom you have taken captive from your brethren, for the fierce wrath of the LORD *is* upon you."

¹²Then some of the heads of the children of Ephraim, Azariah the son of Johanan, Berechiah the son of Meshillemoth, Jehizkiah the son of Shallum, and Amasa the son of Hadlai, stood up against those who came from the war, ¹³and said to them, "You shall not bring the captives here, for we *already* have offended the LORD. You intend to add to our sins and to our guilt; for our guilt is great, and *there is* fierce wrath against Israel." ¹⁴So the armed men left the captives and the spoil before the leaders and all the assembly. ¹⁵Then the men who were designated by name rose up and took the captives, and from the spoil they clothed all who were naked among them, dressed them and gave them sandals, gave them food and drink, and anointed them; and they let all the feeble ones ride on donkeys. So they brought them to their brethren at Jericho, the city of palm trees. Then they returned to Samaria.

Assyria Refuses to Help Judah

¹⁶At the same time King Ahaz sent to the kings*ᵃ* of Assyria to help him. ¹⁷For again the Edomites had come, attacked Judah, and carried away captives. ¹⁸The Philistines also had invaded the cities of the lowland and of the South of Judah, and had taken Beth Shemesh, Aijalon, Gederoth, Sochoh with its villages, Timnah with its villages, and Gimzo with its villages; and they dwelt there. ¹⁹For the LORD brought Judah low because of Ahaz king of Israel, for he had encouraged moral decline in Judah and had been continually unfaithful to the LORD. ²⁰Also Tiglath-Pileser*ᵃ* king of Assyria came to him and distressed him, and did not assist him. ²¹For Ahaz took part *of the*

28:16 *ᵃ*Septuagint, Syriac, and Vulgate read *king* (compare verse 20).   28:20 *ᵃ*Hebrew *Tilgath-Pilneser*

treasures from the house of the LORD, from the house of the king, and from the leaders, and he gave *it* to the king of Assyria; but he did not help him.

Apostasy and Death of Ahaz

²²Now in the time of his distress King Ahaz became increasingly unfaithful to the LORD. This *is that* King Ahaz. ²³For he sacrificed to the gods of Damascus which had defeated him, saying, "Because the gods of the kings of Syria help them, I will sacrifice to them that they may help me." But they were the ruin of him and of all Israel. ²⁴So Ahaz gathered the articles of the house of God, cut in pieces the articles of the house of God, shut up the doors of the house of the LORD, and made for himself altars in every corner of Jerusalem. ²⁵And in every single city of Judah he made high places to burn incense to other gods, and provoked to anger the LORD God of his fathers.

²⁶Now the rest of his acts and all his ways, from first to last, indeed they *are* written in the book of the kings of Judah and Israel. ²⁷So Ahaz rested with his fathers, and they buried him in the city, in Jerusalem; but they did not bring him into the tombs of the kings of Israel. Then Hezekiah his son reigned in his place.

> **29:1–32:33** This is the reign of Hezekiah (about 715-686 B.C.). Hezekiah's trust in the Lord had not been equaled by any king before or after him (2 Kin. 18:5). Isaiah, Hosea, and Micah prophesied during his reign.

Hezekiah Reigns in Judah

29 Hezekiah became king *when he was* twenty-five years old, and he reigned twenty-nine years in Jerusalem. His mother's name *was* Abijah[a] the daughter of Zechariah. ²And he did *what was* right in the sight of the LORD, according to all that his father David had done.

Hezekiah Cleanses the Temple

³In the first year of his reign, in the first month, he opened the doors of the house of the LORD and repaired them. ⁴Then he brought in the priests and the Levites, and gathered them in the East Square, ⁵and said

> **29:3 first year...first month.** Hezekiah made it his priority to bring revival to Judah by reversing the policy of his father, repairing the temple, and returning proper temple worship as God had prescribed in His Word. Hezekiah knew such a revival would turn God's wrath away from Judah.

to them: "Hear me, Levites! Now sanctify yourselves, sanctify the house of the LORD God of your fathers, and carry out the rubbish from the holy *place*. ⁶For our fathers have trespassed and done evil in the eyes of the LORD our God; they have forsaken Him, have turned their faces away from the dwelling place of the LORD, and turned *their* backs *on Him*. ⁷They have also shut up the doors of the vestibule, put out the lamps, and have not burned incense or offered burnt offerings in the holy *place* to the God of Israel. ⁸Therefore the wrath of the LORD fell upon Judah and Jerusalem, and He has given them up to trouble, to desolation, and to jeering, as you see with your eyes. ⁹For indeed, because of this our fathers have fallen by the sword; and our sons, our daughters, and our wives *are* in captivity.

¹⁰"Now *it is* in my heart to make a covenant with the LORD God of Israel, that His fierce wrath may turn away from us. ¹¹My sons, do not be negligent now, for the LORD has chosen you to stand before Him, to serve Him, and that you should minister to Him and burn incense."

¹²Then these Levites arose: Mahath the son of Amasai and Joel the son of Azariah, of the sons of the Kohathites; of the sons of Merari, Kish the son of Abdi and Azariah the son of Jehallelel; of the Gershonites, Joah the son of Zimmah and Eden the son of Joah; ¹³of the sons of Elizaphan, Shimri and Jeiel; of the sons of Asaph, Zechariah and Mattaniah; ¹⁴of the sons of Heman, Jehiel and Shimei; and of the sons of Jeduthun, Shemaiah and Uzziel.

¹⁵And they gathered their brethren, sanctified themselves, and went according to the commandment of the king, at the words of the LORD, to cleanse the house of the LORD. ¹⁶Then the priests went into the inner part of the house of the LORD to cleanse *it*, and brought out all the debris

---

29:1 [a]Spelled *Abi* in 2 Kings 18:2

that they found in the temple of the LORD to the court of the house of the LORD. And the Levites took *it* out and carried *it* to the Brook Kidron.

¹⁷Now they began to sanctify on the first *day* of the first month, and on the eighth day of the month they came to the vestibule of the LORD. So they sanctified the house of the LORD in eight days, and on the sixteenth day of the first month they finished.

¹⁸Then they went in to King Hezekiah and said, "We have cleansed all the house of the LORD, the altar of burnt offerings with all its articles, and the table of the showbread with all its articles. ¹⁹Moreover all the articles which King Ahaz in his reign had cast aside in his transgression we have prepared and sanctified; and there they *are*, before the altar of the LORD."

29:15–19 to cleanse. Beginning with the outer courts and then working their way in, they cleansed the temple for 8 days. Since the Levites were not allowed within the walls of the holy places, the priests had to carry out all the debris to be carted off, which took more than 8 days.

Hezekiah Restores Temple Worship

²⁰Then King Hezekiah rose early, gathered the rulers of the city, and went up to the house of the LORD. ²¹And they brought seven bulls, seven rams, seven lambs, and seven male goats for a sin offering for the kingdom, for the sanctuary, and for Judah. Then he commanded the priests, the sons of Aaron, to offer *them* on the altar of the LORD. ²²So they killed the bulls, and the priests received the blood and sprinkled *it* on the altar. Likewise they killed the rams and sprinkled the blood on the altar. They also killed the lambs and sprinkled the blood on the altar. ²³Then they brought out the male goats *for* the sin offering before the king and the assembly, and they laid their hands on them. ²⁴And the priests killed them; and they presented their blood on the altar as a sin offering to make an atonement for all Israel, for the king commanded *that* the burnt offering and the sin offering *be made* for all Israel.

²⁵And he stationed the Levites in the house of the LORD with cymbals, with stringed instruments, and with harps, according to the commandment of David, of Gad the king's seer, and of Nathan the prophet; for thus *was* the commandment of the LORD by his prophets. ²⁶The Levites stood with the instruments of David, and the priests with the trumpets. ²⁷Then Hezekiah commanded *them* to offer the burnt offering on the altar. And when the burnt offering began, the song of the LORD *also* began, with the trumpets and with the instruments of David king of Israel. ²⁸So all the assembly worshiped, the singers sang, and the trumpeters sounded; all *this continued* until the burnt offering was finished. ²⁹And when they had finished offering, the king and all who were present with him bowed and worshiped. ³⁰Moreover King Hezekiah and the leaders commanded the Levites to sing praise to the LORD with the words of David and of Asaph the seer. So they sang praises with gladness, and they bowed their heads and worshiped.

³¹Then Hezekiah answered and said, "Now *that* you have consecrated yourselves to the LORD, come near, and bring sacrifices and thank offerings into the house of the LORD." So the assembly brought in sacrifices and thank offerings, and as many as were of a willing heart *brought* burnt offerings. ³²And the number of the burnt offerings which the assembly brought was seventy bulls, one hundred rams, *and* two hundred lambs; all these *were* for a burnt offering to the LORD. ³³The consecrated things *were* six hundred bulls and three thousand sheep. ³⁴But the priests were too few, so that they could not skin all the burnt offerings; therefore their brethren the Levites helped them until the work was ended and until the *other* priests had sanctified themselves, for the Levites were more diligent in sanctifying themselves than the priests. ³⁵Also the burnt offerings *were* in abundance, with the fat of the peace offerings and *with* the drink offerings for *every* burnt offering.

So the service of the house of the LORD was set in order. ³⁶Then Hezekiah and all the people rejoiced that God had prepared

29:20–36 Hezekiah restored true temple worship as practiced in the time of David and Solomon, which produced great joy (v. 36).

the people, since the events took place so suddenly.

Hezekiah Keeps the Passover

30 And Hezekiah sent to all Israel and Judah, and also wrote letters to Ephraim and Manasseh, that they should come to the house of the LORD at Jerusalem, to keep the Passover to the LORD God of Israel. [2]For the king and his leaders and all the assembly in Jerusalem had agreed to keep the Passover in the second month. [3]For they could not keep it at the regular time,[a] because a sufficient number of priests had not consecrated themselves, nor had the people gathered together at Jerusalem. [4]And the matter pleased the king and all the assembly. [5]So they resolved to make a proclamation throughout all Israel, from Beersheba to Dan, that they should come to keep the Passover to the LORD God of Israel at Jerusalem, since they had not done it for a long time in the prescribed manner.

[6]Then the runners went throughout all Israel and Judah with the letters from the king and his leaders, and spoke according to the command of the king: "Children of Israel, return to the LORD God of Abraham, Isaac, and Israel; then He will return to the remnant of you who have escaped from the hand of the kings of Assyria. [7]And do not be like your fathers and your brethren, who trespassed against the LORD God of their fathers, so that He gave them up to desolation, as you see. [8]Now do not be stiff-necked, as your fathers were, but yield yourselves to the LORD; and enter His sanctuary, which He has sanctified forever, and serve the LORD your God, that the fierceness of His wrath may turn away from you. [9]For if you return to the LORD, your brethren and your children will be treated with compassion by those who lead them cap-

tive, so that they may come back to this land; for the LORD your God is gracious and merciful, and will not turn His face from you if you return to Him."

30:8 stiff-necked. This term basically means, "Don't be obstinate." See Acts 7:51–53 for Stephen's use of these words.

[10]So the runners passed from city to city through the country of Ephraim and Manasseh, as far as Zebulun; but they laughed at them and mocked them. [11]Nevertheless some from Asher, Manasseh, and Zebulun humbled themselves and came to Jerusalem. [12]Also the hand of God was on Judah to give them singleness of heart to obey the command of the king and the leaders, at the word of the LORD.

[13]Now many people, a very great assembly, gathered at Jerusalem to keep the Feast of Unleavened Bread in the second month. [14]They arose and took away the altars that were in Jerusalem, and they took away all the incense altars and cast them into the Brook Kidron. [15]Then they slaughtered the Passover lambs on the fourteenth day of the second month. The priests and the Levites were ashamed, and sanctified themselves, and brought the burnt offerings to the house of the LORD. [16]They stood in their place according to their custom, according to the Law of Moses the man of God; the priests sprinkled the blood received from the hand of the Levites. [17]For there were many in the assembly who had not sanctified themselves; therefore the Levites had charge of the slaughter of the Passover lambs for everyone who was not clean, to sanctify them to the LORD. [18]For a multitude of the people, many from Ephraim, Manasseh, Issachar, and Zebulun, had not cleansed themselves, yet they ate the Passover contrary to what was written. But Hezekiah prayed for them, saying, "May the good LORD provide atonement for everyone

30:1–27 Hezekiah restored the Feast of Unleavened Bread and the Passover (Ex. 12:1–20), which celebrated God's forgiveness and redemption of His people. It had not been properly or regularly observed since the division of the kingdom 215 years earlier. The Passover would later be revived again by Josiah (2 Chr. 35:1–9) and Zerubbabel (Ezra 6:19–22).

30:18–20 The attitude of the heart was to prevail over their outward activity (1 Sam. 15:22). Hezekiah reminded them that God forgives even the most heinous sins, which He did (v. 20).

30:3 [a]That is, the first month (compare Leviticus 23:5); literally at that time

[19]*who* prepares his heart to seek God, the LORD God of his fathers, though *he is* not *cleansed* according to the purification of the sanctuary." [20]And the LORD listened to Hezekiah and healed the people.

[21]So the children of Israel who were present at Jerusalem kept the Feast of Unleavened Bread seven days with great gladness; and the Levites and the priests praised the LORD day by day, *singing* to the LORD, accompanied by loud instruments. [22]And Hezekiah gave encouragement to all the Levites who taught the good knowledge of the LORD; and they ate throughout the feast seven days, offering peace offerings and making confession to the LORD God of their fathers.

[23]Then the whole assembly agreed to keep *the feast* another seven days, and they kept it *another* seven days with gladness. [24]For Hezekiah king of Judah gave to the assembly a thousand bulls and seven thousand sheep, and the leaders gave to the assembly a thousand bulls and ten thousand sheep; and a great number of priests sanctified themselves. [25]The whole assembly of Judah rejoiced, also the priests and Levites, all the assembly that came from Israel, the sojourners who came from the land of Israel, and those who dwelt in Judah. [26]So there was great joy in Jerusalem, for since the time of Solomon the son of David, king of Israel, *there had* been nothing like this in Jerusalem. [27]Then the priests, the Levites, arose and blessed the people, and their voice was heard; and their prayer came *up* to His holy dwelling place, to heaven.

The Reforms of Hezekiah

31 Now when all this was finished, all Israel who were present went out to the cities of Judah and broke the sacred pillars in pieces, cut down the wooden images,

31:1 Judah, Benjamin, Ephraim, and Manasseh. The first two referred to the southern kingdom, and the last two to the northern kingdom. They carried the conviction of the revived Passover back to their homes to "utterly destroy" all the idolatry, restoring the worship of God. The people returned home with hope of divine blessing and a future of peace and prosperity.

and threw down the high places and the altars—from all Judah, Benjamin, Ephraim, and Manasseh—until they had utterly destroyed them all. Then all the children of Israel returned to their own cities, every man to his possession.

[2]And Hezekiah appointed the divisions of the priests and the Levites according to their divisions, each man according to his service, the priests and Levites for burnt offerings and peace offerings, to serve, to give thanks, and to praise in the gates of the camp[a] of the LORD. [3]The king also *appointed* a portion of his possessions for the burnt offerings: for the morning and evening burnt offerings, the burnt offerings for the Sabbaths and the New Moons and the set feasts, as *it is* written in the Law of the LORD.

[4]Moreover he commanded the people who dwelt in Jerusalem to contribute support for the priests and the Levites, that they might devote themselves to the Law of the LORD.

[5]As soon as the commandment was circulated, the children of Israel brought in abundance the firstfruits of grain and wine, oil and honey, and of all the produce of the field; and they brought in abundantly the tithe of everything. [6]And the children of Israel and Judah, who dwelt in the cities of Judah, brought the tithe of oxen and sheep; also the tithe of holy things which were consecrated to the LORD their God they laid in heaps.

31:6 tithe. The people were to give the tenth (tithe) to supply the needs of the Levites (Lev. 27:30–33; Num. 18:21,24). Deut. 12:6,7 called for a second tithe, the festival tithe, to support the national festivals at the temple in Jerusalem. A third tithe was required every 3 years for the poor (Deut. 14:28,29). This totaled a 23 percent annual tax. Mal. 3:8 says they were robbing God if they did not give the tithe.

[7]In the third month they began laying them in heaps, and they finished in the seventh month. [8]And when Hezekiah and the leaders came and saw the heaps, they blessed the LORD and His people Israel. [9]Then Hezekiah questioned the priests and the Levites concerning the heaps. [10]And Azariah the chief priest, from the house of

31:2 *a*That is, the temple

Zadok, answered him and said, "Since *the people* began to bring the offerings into the house of the LORD, we have had enough to eat and have plenty left, for the LORD has blessed His people; and what is left *is* this great abundance."

[11]Now Hezekiah commanded *them* to prepare rooms in the house of the LORD, and they prepared them. [12]Then they faithfully brought in the offerings, the tithes, and the dedicated things; Cononiah the Levite had charge of them, and Shimei his brother *was* the next. [13]Jehiel, Azaziah, Nahath, Asahel, Jerimoth, Jozabad, Eliel, Ismachiah, Mahath, and Benaiah *were* overseers under the hand of Cononiah and Shimei his brother, at the commandment of Hezekiah the king and Azariah the ruler of the house of God. [14]Kore the son of Imnah the Levite, the keeper of the East Gate, *was* over the freewill offerings to God, to distribute the offerings of the LORD and the most holy things. [15]And under him *were* Eden, Miniamin, Jeshua, Shemaiah, Amariah, and Shecaniah, *his* faithful assistants in the cities of the priests, to distribute allotments to their brethren by divisions, to the great as well as the small.

31:11 rooms. These were stone houses and cellars, built to replace old ones, where the Levites stored the tithes.

[16]Besides those males from three years old and up who were written in the genealogy, they distributed to everyone who entered the house of the LORD his daily portion for the work of his service, by his division, [17]and to the priests who were written in the genealogy according to their father's house, and to the Levites from twenty years old and up according to their work, by their divisions, [18]and to all who were written in the genealogy—their little ones and their wives, their sons and daughters, the whole company of them—for in their faithfulness they sanctified themselves in holiness.

[19]Also for the sons of Aaron the priests, who were in the fields of the common-lands of their cities, in every single city,

there were men who were designated by name to distribute portions to all the males among the priests and to all who were listed by genealogies among the Levites.

31:19 common-lands. Refers to the 48 Levitical cities. The tithes/taxes collected from the people were used for the festivals at the temple and also for the regular daily support of the priests living and leading the people of the land.

[20]Thus Hezekiah did throughout all Judah, and he did what *was* good and right and true before the LORD his God. [21]And in every work that he began in the service of the house of God, in the law and in the commandment, to seek his God, he did *it* with all his heart. So he prospered.

Sennacherib Boasts Against the Lord

32 After these deeds of faithfulness, Sennacherib king of Assyria came and entered Judah; he encamped against the fortified cities, thinking to win them over to himself. [2]And when Hezekiah saw that Sennacherib had come, and that his purpose was to make war against Jerusalem, [3]he consulted with his leaders and commanders[a] to stop the water from the springs which *were* outside the city; and they helped him. [4]Thus many people gathered together who stopped all the springs and the brook that ran through the land, saying, "Why should the kings[a] of Assyria come and find much water?" [5]And he strengthened himself, built up all the wall that was broken, raised *it* up to the towers, and *built* another wall outside; also he repaired the Millo[a] *in* the City of David, and made weapons and shields in abundance. [6]Then he set military captains over the people, gathered them together to him in the open square of the city gate, and gave them encouragement, saying, [7]"Be strong and courageous; do not be afraid nor dismayed before the king of Assyria, nor before all the multitude that *is* with him; for *there are* more with us than with him. [8]With him *is* an arm of flesh; but with us *is* the LORD our God, to help us and to fight

---

32:3 [a]Literally *mighty men*   32:4 [a]Following Masoretic Text and Vulgate; Arabic, Septuagint, and Syriac read *king*.   32:5 [a]Literally *The Landfill*

our battles." And the people were strengthened by the words of Hezekiah king of Judah.

> **32:1–23** Hezekiah wanted to reassert Judah's independence, and he refused to pay the tribute that his father had bound him to pay to the Assyrian king. In response, Sennacherib retaliated, and Hezekiah fortified the city and trusted God, who delivered them.

⁹After this Sennacherib king of Assyria sent his servants to Jerusalem (but he and all the forces with him *laid siege* against Lachish), to Hezekiah king of Judah, and to all Judah who *were* in Jerusalem, saying, ¹⁰"Thus says Sennacherib king of Assyria: 'In what do you trust, that you remain under siege in Jerusalem? ¹¹Does not Hezekiah persuade you to give yourselves over to die by famine and by thirst, saying, "The LORD our God will deliver us from the hand of the king of Assyria"? ¹²Has not the same Hezekiah taken away His high places and His altars, and commanded Judah and Jerusalem, saying, "You shall worship before one altar and burn incense on it"? ¹³Do you not know what I and my fathers have done to all the peoples of *other* lands? Were the gods of the nations of those lands in any way able to deliver their lands out of my hand? ¹⁴Who *was there* among all the gods of those nations that my fathers utterly destroyed that could deliver his people from my hand, that your God should be able to deliver you from my hand? ¹⁵Now therefore, do not let Hezekiah deceive you or persuade you like this, and do not believe him; for no god of any nation or kingdom was able to deliver his people from my hand or the hand of my fathers. How much less will your God deliver you from my hand?' "

¹⁶Furthermore, his servants spoke against the LORD God and against His servant Hezekiah. ¹⁷He also wrote letters to revile the LORD God of Israel, and to speak against Him, saying, "As the gods of the nations of *other* lands have not delivered their people from my hand, so the God of Hezekiah will not deliver His people from my hand." ¹⁸Then they called out with a loud voice in Hebrew*ᵃ* to the people of Jerusalem who

were on the wall, to frighten them and trouble them, that they might take the city. ¹⁹And they spoke against the God of Jerusalem, as against the gods of the people of the earth—the work of men's hands.

Sennacherib's Defeat and Death

²⁰Now because of this King Hezekiah and the prophet Isaiah, the son of Amoz, prayed and cried out to heaven. ²¹Then the LORD sent an angel who cut down every mighty man of valor, leader, and captain in the camp of the king of Assyria. So he returned shamefaced to his own land. And when he had gone into the temple of his god, some of his own offspring struck him down with the sword there. ²²Thus the LORD saved Hezekiah and the inhabitants of Jerusalem from the hand of Sennacherib the king of Assyria, and from the hand of all *others*, and guided them*ᵃ* on every side. ²³And many brought gifts to the LORD at Jerusalem, and presents to Hezekiah king of Judah, so that he was exalted in the sight of all nations thereafter.

> **32:1–23** The Assyrian king Sennacherib came because Hezekiah, determined to recover the independence of his nation, refused to pay the tribute his father had bound him to pay to Assyria. Sennacherib retaliated. Hezekiah fortified the city and trusted God, who delivered them and was glorified.

Hezekiah Humbles Himself

²⁴In those days Hezekiah was sick and near death, and he prayed to the LORD; and He spoke to him and gave him a sign. ²⁵But Hezekiah did not repay according to the favor *shown* him, for his heart was lifted up; therefore wrath was looming over him and over Judah and Jerusalem. ²⁶Then Hezekiah humbled himself for the pride of his heart, he and the inhabitants of Jerusalem, so that the wrath of the LORD did not come upon them in the days of Hezekiah.

Hezekiah's Wealth and Honor

²⁷Hezekiah had very great riches and honor. And he made himself treasuries for silver, for gold, for precious stones, for spices, for shields, and for all kinds of desirable items; ²⁸storehouses for the harvest of

---

32:18 *ᵃ*Literally *Judean*   32:22 *ᵃ*Septuagint reads *gave them rest;* Vulgate reads *gave them treasures.*

grain, wine, and oil; and stalls for all kinds of livestock, and folds for flocks.[a] [29]Moreover he provided cities for himself, and possessions of flocks and herds in abundance; for God had given him very much property. [30]This same Hezekiah also stopped the water outlet of Upper Gihon, and brought the water by tunnel[a] to the west side of the City of David. Hezekiah prospered in all his works.

[31]However, *regarding* the ambassadors of the princes of Babylon, whom they sent to him to inquire about the wonder that was *done* in the land, God withdrew from him, in order to test him, that He might know all *that was* in his heart.

> **32:31 Babylon.** This empire was gradually gaining power as Assyria declined due to internal strife and weak kings. Assyria was crushed in 612 B.C. and Babylon, under Nebuchadnezzar, became the world ruler (see 2 Kin. 20:14).

Death of Hezekiah

[32]Now the rest of the acts of Hezekiah, and his goodness, indeed they *are* written in the vision of Isaiah the prophet, the son of Amoz, *and* in the book of the kings of Judah and Israel. [33]So Hezekiah rested with his fathers, and they buried him in the upper tombs of the sons of David; and all Judah and the inhabitants of Jerusalem honored him at his death. Then Manasseh his son reigned in his place.

Manasseh Reigns in Judah

33 Manasseh *was* twelve years old when he became king, and he reigned fifty-five years in Jerusalem. [2]But he did evil in the sight of the LORD, according to the abominations of the nations whom the LORD had cast out before the children of Israel. [3]For he rebuilt the high places which Hezekiah his father had broken down; he raised up altars for the Baals, and made wooden images; and he worshiped all the host of heaven[a] and served them. [4]He also built altars in the house of the LORD, of which the LORD had said, "In Jerusalem shall My name be forever." [5]And

> **33:6 Hinnom.** This was a valley to the south and east of the temple where children were burned to death under the worship of Molech (Ps. 106:37). This was forbidden (Lev. 18:21), yet this horrible practice took place in Israel from the time of Ahaz.

he built altars for all the host of heaven in the two courts of the house of the LORD. [6]Also he caused his sons to pass through the fire in the Valley of the Son of Hinnom; he practiced soothsaying, used witchcraft and sorcery, and consulted mediums and spiritists. He did much evil in the sight of the LORD, to provoke Him to anger. [7]He even set a carved image, the idol which he had made, in the house of God, of which God had said to David and to Solomon his son, "In this house and in Jerusalem, which I have chosen out of all the tribes of Israel, I will put My name forever; [8]and I will not again remove the foot of Israel from the land which I have appointed for your fathers—only if they are careful to do all that I have commanded them, according to the whole law and the statutes and the ordinances by the hand of Moses." [9]So Manasseh seduced Judah and the inhabitants of Jerusalem to do more evil than the nations whom the LORD had destroyed before the children of Israel.

Manasseh Restored After Repentance

[10]And the LORD spoke to Manasseh and his people, but they would not listen. [11]Therefore the LORD brought upon them the captains of the army of the king of Assyria, who took Manasseh with hooks,[a] bound him with bronze *fetters*, and carried him off to Babylon. [12]Now when he was in affliction, he implored the LORD his God, and humbled himself greatly before the God of his fathers, [13]and prayed to Him; and He received his entreaty, heard his supplication, and brought him back to Jerusalem into his kingdom. Then Manasseh knew that the LORD *was* God.

[14]After this he built a wall outside the City of David on the west side of Gihon, in the valley, as far as the entrance of the Fish Gate; and *it* enclosed Ophel, and he raised

---

32:28 [a]Following Septuagint and Vulgate; Arabic and Syriac omit *folds for flocks*; Masoretic Text reads *flocks for sheepfolds*.   32:30 [a]Literally *brought it straight* (compare 2 Kings 20:20)   33:3 [a]The gods of the Assyrians   33:11 [a]That is, nose hooks (compare 2 Kings 19:28)

it to a very great height. Then he put military captains in all the fortified cities of Judah. [15]He took away the foreign gods and the idol from the house of the LORD, and all the altars that he had built in the mount of the house of the LORD and in Jerusalem; and he cast *them* out of the city. [16]He also repaired the altar of the LORD, sacrificed peace offerings and thank offerings on it, and commanded Judah to serve the LORD God of Israel. [17]Nevertheless the people still sacrificed on the high places, *but* only to the LORD their God.

33:12,13 Manasseh. He was a king who worshiped idols, murdered his children, and desecrated the temple. God graciously forgave him when he repented and sought to reverse the effect of his life. God had commanded the people to offer sacrifices only in certain places (Deut. 12:13,14) to keep them from corrupting the prescribed forms and to protect them from pagan influence. Disobedience to God in this matter contributed to the decline under the next king, Amon, whose corruption had to be eliminated by his successor, Josiah.

Death of Manasseh

[18]Now the rest of the acts of Manasseh, his prayer to his God, and the words of the seers who spoke to him in the name of the LORD God of Israel, indeed they *are written* in the book[a] of the kings of Israel. [19]Also his prayer and *how God* received his entreaty, and all his sin and trespass, and the sites where he built high places and set up wooden images and carved images, before he was humbled, indeed they *are* written among the sayings of Hozai.[a] [20]So Manasseh rested with his fathers, and they buried him in his own house. Then his son Amon reigned in his place.

Amon's Reign and Death

[21]Amon *was* twenty-two years old when he became king, and he reigned two years in Jerusalem. [22]But he did evil in the sight of the LORD, as his father Manasseh had done; for Amon sacrificed to all the carved images which his father Manasseh had made, and served them. [23]And he did not humble himself before the LORD, as his father Manasseh had humbled him-

self; but Amon trespassed more and more. [24]Then his servants conspired against him, and killed him in his own house. [25]But the people of the land executed all those who had conspired against King Amon. Then the people of the land made his son Josiah king in his place.

Josiah Reigns in Judah

34 Josiah *was* eight years old when he became king, and he reigned thirty-one years in Jerusalem. [2]And he did *what was* right in the sight of the LORD, and walked in the ways of his father David; he did *not* turn aside to the right hand or to the left.

34:1,2 At the age of 16, Josiah began to cultivate a love for God that continued to grow. By the age of 20 he went into action to purge his nation.

[3]For in the eighth year of his reign, while he was still young, he began to seek the God of his father David; and in the twelfth year he began to purge Judah and Jerusalem of the high places, the wooden images, the carved images, and the molded images. [4]They broke down the altars of the Baals in his presence, and the incense altars which *were* above them he cut down; and the wooden images, the carved images, and the molded images he broke in pieces, and made dust of them and scattered *it* on the graves of those who had sacrificed to them. [5]He also burned the bones of the priests on their altars, and cleansed Judah and Jerusalem. [6]And *so he did* in the cities of Manasseh, Ephraim, and Simeon, as far as Naphtali and all around, with axes.[a] [7]When he had broken down the altars and the wooden images, had beaten the carved images into powder, and cut down all the incense altars throughout all the land of Israel, he returned to Jerusalem.

Hilkiah Finds the Book of the Law

[8]In the eighteenth year of his reign, when he had purged the land and the temple,[a] he sent Shaphan the son of Azaliah, Maaseiah the governor of the city, and Joah the son of Joahaz the recorder, to repair the house of

---

33:18 [a]Literally *words*   33:19 [a]Septuagint reads *the seers.*   34:6 [a]Literally *swords*   34:8 [a]Literally *house*

34:8 repair the house of the LORD. During the 55-year reign of King Manasseh (33:1) and the two-year reign of Amon (33:21), Hezekiah's work on the temple restoration came undone, which called for another extensive enterprise to "repair and restore" (vv. 9–13).

the LORD his God. ⁹When they came to Hilkiah the high priest, they delivered the money that was brought into the house of God, which the Levites who kept the doors had gathered from the hand of Manasseh and Ephraim, from all the remnant of Israel, from all Judah and Benjamin, and *which* they had brought back to Jerusalem. ¹⁰Then they put *it* in the hand of the foremen who had the oversight of the house of the LORD; and they gave it to the workmen who worked in the house of the LORD, to repair and restore the house. ¹¹They gave *it* to the craftsmen and builders to buy hewn stone and timber for beams, and to floor the houses which the kings of Judah had destroyed. ¹²And the men did the work faithfully. Their overseers *were* Jahath and Obadiah the Levites, of the sons of Merari, and Zechariah and Meshullam, of the sons of the Kohathites, to supervise. *Others of* the Levites, all of whom were skillful with instruments of music, ¹³*were* over the burden bearers and *were* overseers of all who did work in any kind of service. And *some* of the Levites *were* scribes, officers, and gatekeepers.

¹⁴Now when they brought out the money that was brought into the house of the LORD, Hilkiah the priest found the Book of the Law of the LORD *given* by Moses. ¹⁵Then Hilkiah answered and said to Shaphan the scribe, "I have found the Book of the Law in the house of the LORD." And Hilkiah gave the book to Shaphan. ¹⁶So Shaphan carried the book to the king, bringing the king word, saying, "All that was committed to your servants they are doing. ¹⁷And they have gathered the money that was found in the house of the LORD, and have delivered it into the hand of the overseers and the workmen." ¹⁸Then Shaphan the scribe told the king, saying, "Hil-

kiah the priest has given me a book." And Shaphan read it before the king.

¹⁹Thus it happened, when the king heard the words of the Law, that he tore his clothes. ²⁰Then the king commanded Hilkiah, Ahikam the son of Shaphan, Abdon*ᵃ* the son of Micah, Shaphan the scribe, and Asaiah a servant of the king, saying, ²¹"Go, inquire of the LORD for me, and for those who are left in Israel and Judah, concerning the words of the book that is found; for great *is* the wrath of the LORD that is poured out on us, because our fathers have not kept the word of the LORD, to do according to all that is written in this book."

²²So Hilkiah and those the king *had appointed* went to Huldah the prophetess, the wife of Shallum the son of Tokhath,*ᵃ* the son of Hasrah,*ᵇ* keeper of the wardrobe. (She dwelt in Jerusalem in the Second Quarter.) And they spoke to her to that *effect.*

²³Then she answered them, "Thus says the LORD God of Israel, 'Tell the man who sent you to Me, ²⁴"Thus says the LORD: 'Behold, I will bring calamity on this place and on its inhabitants, all the curses that are written in the book which they have read before the king of Judah, ²⁵because they have forsaken Me and burned incense to other gods, that they might provoke Me to anger with all the works of their hands. Therefore My wrath will be poured out on this place, and not be quenched.' " ' ²⁶But as for the king of Judah, who sent you to inquire of the LORD, in this manner you shall speak to him, 'Thus says the LORD God of Israel: "*Concerning* the words which you have heard— ²⁷because your heart was tender, and you humbled yourself before God when you heard His words against this place and against its inhabitants, and you humbled yourself before Me, and you tore your clothes and wept before Me, I also have heard *you*," says the LORD. ²⁸"Surely I will gather you to your fathers, and you shall be gathered to your grave in peace; and your eyes shall not see all the calamity which I will bring on this place and its inhabitants." ' " So they brought back word to the king.

34:20 *ᵃAchbor the son of Michaiah* in 2 Kings 22:12   34:22 *ᵃ*Spelled *Tikvah* in 2 Kings 22:14   *ᵇ*Spelled *Harhas* in 2 Kings 22:14

Josiah Restores True Worship

²⁹Then the king sent and gathered all the elders of Judah and Jerusalem. ³⁰The king went up to the house of the LORD, with all the men of Judah and the inhabitants of Jerusalem—the priests and the Levites, and all the people, great and small. And he read in their hearing all the words of the Book of the Covenant which had been found in the house of the LORD. ³¹Then the king stood in his place and made a covenant before the LORD, to follow the LORD, and to keep His commandments and His testimonies and His statutes with all his heart and all his soul, to perform the words of the covenant that were written in this book. ³²And he made all who were present in Jerusalem and Benjamin take a stand. So the inhabitants of Jerusalem did according to the covenant of God, the God of their fathers. ³³Thus Josiah removed all the abominations from all the country that *belonged* to the children of Israel, and made all who were present in Israel diligently serve the LORD their God. All his days they did not depart from following the LORD God of their fathers.

> **34:33 All his days.** Josiah had a life-long influence due to his godly life and devotion to God and His Word, which began when he was a young man. His strength held the nation together serving the Lord.

Josiah Keeps the Passover

35 Now Josiah kept a Passover to the LORD in Jerusalem, and they slaughtered the Passover *lambs* on the fourteenth *day* of the first month. ²And he set the priests in their duties and encouraged them for the service of the house of the LORD. ³Then he said to the Levites who taught all Israel, who were holy to the LORD: "Put the holy ark in the house which Solomon the

> **35:3 the holy ark.** The ark of the covenant was probably moved from the Most Holy Place by Manasseh, who set a carved image in its place. During the tabernacle days, the law required the ark to be moved by putting poles through the rings on the sides and being carried by the Levites. They could not touch it (see Ex. 25:14). Uzza died for touching the ark while improperly transporting it on a cart (1 Chr. 13:6–10). The ark no longer needed to be transported now that it had a permanent place in the temple.

son of David, king of Israel, built. *It shall* no longer *be* a burden on *your* shoulders. Now serve the LORD your God and His people Israel. ⁴Prepare *yourselves* according to your fathers' houses, according to your divisions, following the written instruction of David king of Israel and the written instruction of Solomon his son. ⁵And stand in the holy *place* according to the divisions of the fathers' houses of your brethren the *lay* people, and *according to* the division of the father's house of the Levites. ⁶So slaughter the Passover *offerings*, consecrate yourselves, and prepare *them* for your brethren, that *they* may do according to the word of the LORD by the hand of Moses."

⁷Then Josiah gave the *lay* people lambs and young goats from the flock, all for Passover *offerings* for all who were present, to the number of thirty thousand, as well as three thousand cattle; these *were* from the king's possessions. ⁸And his leaders gave willingly to the people, to the priests, and to the Levites. Hilkiah, Zechariah, and Jehiel, rulers of the house of God, gave to the priests for the Passover *offerings* two thousand six hundred *from the flock*, and three hundred cattle. ⁹Also Conaniah, his brothers Shemaiah and Nethanel, and Hashabiah and Jeiel and Jozabad, chief of the Levites, gave to the Levites for Passover *offerings* five thousand *from the flock* and five hundred cattle.

¹⁰So the service was prepared, and the priests stood in their places, and the Levites in their divisions, according to the king's command. ¹¹And they slaughtered the Passover *offerings*; and the priests sprinkled *the blood* with their hands, while the Levites skinned *the animals.* ¹²Then they removed the burnt offerings that *they* might give them to the divisions of the fathers' houses of the *lay* people, to offer to the LORD, as *it is* written in the Book of Moses. And so *they did* with the cattle. ¹³Also they roasted the Passover *offerings* with fire according to the ordinance; but the *other* holy *offerings* they boiled in pots, in caldrons, and in pans, and divided *them* quickly among all the *lay* people. ¹⁴Then afterward they prepared portions for themselves and for the priests, because the priests, the sons of Aaron, *were busy* in offering burnt offerings and fat until night; therefore the Levites

prepared portions for themselves and for the priests, the sons of Aaron. ¹⁵And the singers, the sons of Asaph, *were* in their places, according to the command of David, Asaph, Heman, and Jeduthun the king's seer. Also the gatekeepers were at each gate; they did not have to leave their position, because their brethren the Levites prepared portions for them.

¹⁶So all the service of the LORD was prepared the same day, to keep the Passover and to offer burnt offerings on the altar of the LORD, according to the command of King Josiah. ¹⁷And the children of Israel who were present kept the Passover at that time, and the Feast of Unleavened Bread for seven days. ¹⁸There had been no Passover kept in Israel like that since the days of Samuel the prophet; and none of the kings of Israel had kept such a Passover as Josiah kept, with the priests and the Levites, all Judah and Israel who were present, and the inhabitants of Jerusalem. ¹⁹In the eighteenth year of the reign of Josiah this Passover was kept.

Josiah Dies in Battle

²⁰After all this, when Josiah had prepared the temple, Necho king of Egypt came up to fight against Carchemish by the Euphrates; and Josiah went out against him. ²¹But he sent messengers to him, saying, "What have I to do with you, king of Judah? *I have* not *come* against you this day, but against the house with which I have war; for God commanded me to make haste. Refrain *from meddling with* God, who *is* with me, lest He destroy you." ²²Nevertheless Josiah would not turn his face from him, but disguised himself so that he might fight with him, and did not heed the words of Necho from the mouth of God. So he came to fight in the Valley of Megiddo.

²³And the archers shot King Josiah; and

> **35:21 God commanded me.** Josiah did not believe that Necho spoke the Word of God. There is no reason to assume his death was punishment for refusing to believe. He probably thought Necho was lying and, once victorious with Assyria over Babylon, they would later assault Israel together.

the king said to his servants, "Take me away, for I am severely wounded." ²⁴His servants therefore took him out of that chariot and put him in the second chariot that he had, and they brought him to Jerusalem. So he died, and was buried in *one of* the tombs of his fathers. And all Judah and Jerusalem mourned for Josiah.

²⁵Jeremiah also lamented for Josiah. And to this day all the singing men and the singing women speak of Josiah in their lamentations. They made it a custom in Israel; and indeed they *are* written in the Laments.

²⁶Now the rest of the acts of Josiah and his goodness, according to *what was* written in the Law of the LORD, ²⁷and his deeds from first to last, indeed they *are* written in the book of the kings of Israel and Judah.

The Reign and Captivity of Jehoahaz

36 Then the people of the land took Jehoahaz the son of Josiah, and made him king in his father's place in Jerusalem. ²Jehoahaz^a *was* twenty-three years old when he became king, and he reigned three months in Jerusalem. ³Now the king of Egypt deposed him at Jerusalem; and he imposed on the land a tribute of one hundred talents of silver and a talent of gold. ⁴Then the king of Egypt made *Jehoahaz's*^a brother Eliakim king over Judah and Jerusalem, and changed his name to Jehoiakim. And Necho took Jehoahaz^b his brother and carried him off to Egypt.

The Reign and Captivity of Jehoiakim

⁵Jehoiakim *was* twenty-five years old when he became king, and he reigned eleven years in Jerusalem. And he did evil in the sight of the LORD his God. ⁶Nebuchadnezzar king of Babylon came up against him, and bound him in bronze *fetters* to carry him off to Babylon. ⁷Nebuchadnezzar also carried off *some* of the articles from the house of the LORD to Babylon, and put them in his temple at Babylon. ⁸Now the rest of the acts of Jehoiakim, the abominations which he did, and what was found against him, indeed they *are* written in the book of the kings of Israel and Judah. Then Jehoiachin his son reigned in his place.

36:2 ^aMasoretic Text reads *Joahaz*.   36:4 ^aLiterally *his*   ^bMasoretic Text reads *Joahaz*.

The Reign and Captivity of Jehoiachin

[9]Jehoiachin *was* eight[a] years old when he became king, and he reigned in Jerusalem three months and ten days. And he did evil in the sight of the LORD. [10]At the turn of the year King Nebuchadnezzar summoned *him* and took him to Babylon, with the costly articles from the house of the LORD, and made Zedekiah, *Jehoiakim's*[a] brother, king over Judah and Jerusalem.

> **36:9 eight years old.** Eighteen years old is actually preferable, as recorded in 2 Kin. 24:8, because of the full development of his wickedness. See Ezekiel's description of him in Ezek. 19:5–9.

Zedekiah Reigns in Judah

[11]Zedekiah *was* twenty-one years old when he became king, and he reigned eleven years in Jerusalem. [12]He did evil in the sight of the LORD his God, *and* did not humble himself before Jeremiah the prophet, *who spoke* from the mouth of the LORD. [13]And he also rebelled against King Nebuchadnezzar, who had made him swear *an oath* by God; but he stiffened his neck and hardened his heart against turning to the LORD God of Israel. [14]Moreover all the leaders of the priests and the people transgressed more and more, *according* to all the abominations of the nations, and defiled the house of the LORD which He had consecrated in Jerusalem.

The Fall of Jerusalem

[15]And the LORD God of their fathers sent *warnings* to them by His messengers, rising up early and sending *them*, because He had compassion on His people and on His dwelling place. [16]But they mocked the messengers of God, despised His words, and scoffed at His prophets, until the wrath of the LORD arose against His people, till *there was* no remedy. [17]Therefore He brought against them the king of the Chaldeans, who killed their young men with the sword in the house of their sanctuary, and had no compassion on young man or virgin, on the aged or the weak; He gave *them* all into his hand. [18]And all the articles from the house of God, great and small, the treasures of the house of the LORD, and the treasures of the king and of his leaders, all *these* he took to Babylon. [19]Then they burned the house of God, broke down the wall of Jerusalem, burned all its palaces with fire, and destroyed all its precious possessions. [20]And those who escaped from the sword he carried away to Babylon, where they became servants to him and his sons until the rule of the kingdom of Persia, [21]to fulfill the word of the LORD by the mouth of Jeremiah, until the land had enjoyed her Sabbaths. As long as she lay desolate she kept Sabbath, to fulfill seventy years.

> **36:11–21** This is the reign of Zedekiah (597–586 B.C.). Jeremiah prophesied during this reign and wrote Lamentations to mourn the destruction of Jerusalem and the temple in 586 B.C. Ezekiel received his commission during this reign (Ezek. 1:1) and prophesied from 592 B.C. until his death in 560 B.C.

The Proclamation of Cyrus

[22]Now in the first year of Cyrus king of Persia, that the word of the LORD by the mouth of Jeremiah might be fulfilled, the LORD stirred up the spirit of Cyrus king of Persia, so that he made a proclamation throughout all his kingdom, and also *put it* in writing, saying,

[23]   Thus says Cyrus king of Persia:
    All the kingdoms of the earth the
    LORD God of heaven has given me.
    And He has commanded me to build
    Him a house at Jerusalem which is in
    Judah. Who *is* among you of all His
    people? May the LORD his God *be*
    with him, and let him go up!

> **36:22,23** The chronicler ended with hope because the 70 years had ended (see Dan. 9:1,2) and Abraham's offspring were returning to the Land to rebuild the temple.

36:9 [a]Some Hebrew manuscripts, Septuagint, Syriac, and 2 Kings 24:8 read *eighteen*.
36:10 [a]Literally *his* (compare 2 Kings 24:17)

EZRA

Some people set out to be obedient to God and turn out to be heroes. Ezra was such a man. His name represents the historical significance of the times in which he lived. It means in Hebrew "Jehovah helps," and constantly reminds the reader that God was acting behind the scenes to return His people to the Promised Land.

AUTHOR AND DATE

Ezra was possibly written by Ezra, approximately 457 to 444 B.C.

Although Ezra's name does not occur until the seventh chapter of the book that bears his name, he has long been considered the most likely author of both Ezra and Nehemiah. One strong internal clue about authorship has to do with writing perspective. Once his own departure for Jerusalem becomes part of the record (7:28), Ezra switches from writing in the third person to writing in the first. If he did write 1 and 2 Chronicles, the continued narrative in Ezra makes perfect sense. Ezra begins with the ongoing chronicle of God's people in exile. Babylon had just been defeated by Persia, the new world power. Ezra's own participation in that history allowed him a natural point at which to make the chronicle autobiographical.

Ezra's scribal duties allowed him access to the various administrative documents quoted in Ezra and Nehemiah. He took advantage of special privileges he had in the royal archives of the Persian Empire. These passages are direct quotes from official Persian records: 1:2–4; 4:9–22; 5:7–17; 6:3–12. Other passages reveal Ezra as a devoted student and a strong and godly leader: 7:10; Nehemiah 8:1–9; 12:36. Ancient tradition also indicates that Ezra had a key role in the formation of the Old Testament Scriptures as the recognized canon of God's written revelation.

Ezra led the second Jewish group's return from Persia around 458 B.C. The book was probably completed sometime in the next decades (457–444 B.C.).

BACKGROUND AND SETTING

Events in the life of the people of Israel must always be seen in the light of God's plan for them. He chose them in their ancestor Abraham. He gave them a Land. He brought Israel out of the slave markets of Egypt in the Exodus. Hundreds of years later, still before Ezra, God warned His people that if they chose to break their covenant with Him, He would again allow other nations to take them into slavery (Jeremiah 2:14–25). God's repeated warnings were persistently ignored.

Immorality and idolatry were the national pastimes. God was faithful and followed through on His warnings.

In 722 B.C. the Assyrians defeated and deported the 10 northern tribes and scattered them all over their empire. Several centuries later, in 605–586 B.C., God allowed the Babylonians to destroy and depopulate Jerusalem. God chastened what was left of His people with 70 years of exile in Babylon. In 539 B.C., Cyrus the Persian overthrew Babylon. A year later, as recorded by Ezra, Cyrus permitted the return of Jews to Jerusalem.

The Jews were originally deported in three waves (605 B.C., 597 B.C., and 586 B.C.). Their return followed the same pattern over a 9-decade span. Zerubbabel led the first group home in 538 B.C. Ezra followed with the second group in 458 B.C. Then Nehemiah led the third group in 445 B.C. Jerusalem and the Temple were eventually rebuilt, but, like the nation itself, only shadows of their former glory.

HISTORICAL AND THEOLOGICAL THEMES

The Jew's return from the Babylonian captivity included many parallels with the Exodus from Egypt. The following examples stand out: (1) like the provision of the tabernacle for worship, the returning exiles rebuilt the temple and the city walls; (2) like the original giving of the Law, the exiles under Zerubbabel, Ezra, and Nehemiah re-affirmed God's law; (3) like the opposition faced during the original journey to the Promised Land, the returning exiles were harassed by local enemies; and (4) the newly freed exiles faced the same temptation to intermarry with non-Jews and began another round of disobedience and idolatry. These and other parallels with Exodus must have given the faithful among the exiles reason to believe God was offering them a new start.

> THE **BOOK** OF **EZRA STANDS** AS AN **EXAMPLE** OF **GOD'S PLANS** TO **REDEEM** THE **WORLD THROUGH HIS** CONTINUING **COVENANT** OF **GRACE** WITH **ISRAEL.**

Ezra's use of foreign documents illustrates the point that God works within the scene of world history. Kingly decrees merely reflect God's overriding will. The book of Ezra stands as an example of God's plans to redeem the world through His continuing covenant of grace with Israel.

Another theological theme prominent in Ezra highlights the role of local opposition. The consequences of long-past failures to obey God continue to haunt the descendants of the disobedient. God's people would not be able to live in the Land unchallenged. But the Lord, through the preaching of Haggai and Zechariah, rekindled the spirit of the people and their leaders to build. Their message was, " . . . be strong. . . . and work; for I *am* with you" (4:24–5:2; Haggai 2:4). God remained committed in spite of opposition. Reconstruction resumed (520 B.C.) and the temple was soon finished, dedicated, and back in service to God (516 B.C.).

OUTLINE

End of the Babylonian Captivity

1 Now in the first year of Cyrus king of Persia, that the word of the LORD by the mouth of Jeremiah might be fulfilled, the LORD stirred up the spirit of Cyrus king of Persia, so that he made a proclamation throughout all his kingdom, and also *put it* in writing, saying,

> **1:1 first year.** About 538 B.C. **Cyrus king of Persia.** About 550–530 B.C. The historian Josephus records an account of the day when Daniel read Isaiah's prophecy to Cyrus (Is. 44:28), and in response he was moved to declare the proclamation of 1:2–4 (538 B.C.). **by the mouth of Jeremiah.** Jeremiah had prophesied the return of the exiles after a 70-year captivity in Babylon (Jer. 25:11). This was part of the covenant made to Abraham (Gen. 12:1–3). **made a proclamation.** This was the most common form of public communication, given by the king to a herald, who would go the city gate and deliver the proclamation to the people. **put it in writing.** Proclamations were often written down for record keeping.

2 Thus says Cyrus king of Persia:
All the kingdoms of the earth the
LORD God of heaven has given me.
And He has commanded me to build
Him a house at Jerusalem which *is* in
Judah. ³Who *is* among you of all His
people? May his God be with him,
and let him go up to Jerusalem which
is in Judah, and build the house of the
LORD God of Israel (He *is* God),
which *is* in Jerusalem. ⁴And whoever
is left in any place where he dwells,
let the men of his place help him with
silver and gold, with goods and
livestock, besides the freewill offerings
for the house of God which *is* in
Jerusalem.

⁵Then the heads of the fathers' *houses* of Judah and Benjamin, and the priests and the Levites, with all whose spirits God had moved, arose to go up and build the house of the LORD which *is* in Jerusalem. ⁶And all those who *were* around them encouraged them with articles of silver and gold, with goods and livestock, and with precious

> **1:5 whose spirits God had moved.** Ezra's and Nehemiah's messages were that God works in perfect timing with His plan. The 70 years of captivity were complete, so God stirred up Cyrus to make the decree and had His people build up Jerusalem and the temple.

things, besides all *that* was willingly offered.

⁷King Cyrus also brought out the articles of the house of the LORD, which Nebuchadnezzar had taken from Jerusalem and put in the temple of his gods; ⁸and Cyrus king of Persia brought them out by the hand of Mithredath the treasurer, and counted them out to Sheshbazzar the prince of Judah. ⁹This *is* the number of them: thirty gold platters, one thousand silver platters, twenty-nine knives, ¹⁰thirty gold basins, four hundred and ten silver basins of a similar *kind, and* one thousand other articles. ¹¹All the articles of gold and silver *were* five thousand four hundred. All *these* Sheshbazzar took with the captives who were brought from Babylon to Jerusalem.

The Captives Who Returned to Jerusalem

2 Now[a] these *are* the people of the province who came back from the captivity, of those who had been carried away, whom Nebuchadnezzar the king of Babylon had

2:1 [a]Compare this chapter with Nehemiah 7:6–73.

POST-EXILIC RETURNS TO JERUSALEM

Sequence	Date	Scripture	Jewish Leader	Persian Ruler
First	538 B.C.	Ezra 1–6	Zerubbabel, Joshua	Cyrus
Second	458 B.C.	Ezra 7–10	Ezra	Artaxerxes
Third	445 B.C.	Nehemiah 1–13	Nehemiah	Artaxerxes[1]

[1]John F. MacArthur, Jr., *The MacArthur Study Bible*, (Dallas: Word Publishing) 1997.

carried away to Babylon, and who returned to Jerusalem and Judah, everyone to his *own* city.

²*Those* who came with Zerubbabel *were* Jeshua, Nehemiah, Seraiah, Reelaiah, Mordecai, Bilshan, Mispar,*ᵃ* Bigvai, Rehum,*ᵇ* *and* Baanah. The number of the men of the people of Israel: ³the people of Parosh, two thousand one hundred and seventy-two; ⁴the people of Shephatiah, three hundred and seventy-two; ⁵the people of Arah, seven hundred and seventy-five; ⁶the people of Pahath-Moab, of the people of Jeshua *and* Joab, two thousand eight hundred and

> **2:2 Zerubbabel.** His name means "offspring of Babylon," indicating his place of birth. He was the rightful leader of Judah, of the line of David through Jehoiakin (see 1 Chr. 3:17). He did not serve as king because of the curse on Jehoiakin's line (see Jer. 22:24–30), but he was still in the messianic line because the curse was bypassed through a levirate marriage of his mother to Pedaiah (1 Chr. 3:19). The curse was later bypassed for Christ by way of the virgin birth.

twelve; ⁷the people of Elam, one thousand two hundred and fifty-four; ⁸the people of Zattu, nine hundred and forty-five; ⁹the people of Zaccai, seven hundred and sixty; ¹⁰the people of Bani,*ᵃ* six hundred and forty-two; ¹¹the people of Bebai, six hundred and twenty-three; ¹²the people of Azgad, one thousand two hundred and twenty-two; ¹³the people of Adonikam, six hundred and sixty-six; ¹⁴the people of Bigvai, two thousand and fifty-six; ¹⁵the people of Adin, four hundred and fifty-four; ¹⁶the people of Ater of Hezekiah, ninety-eight; ¹⁷the people of Bezai, three hundred and twenty-three; ¹⁸the people of Jorah,*ᵃ* one hundred and twelve; ¹⁹the people of Hashum, two hundred and twenty-three; ²⁰the people of Gibbar,*ᵃ* ninety-five; ²¹the people of Bethlehem, one hundred and twenty-three; ²²the men of Netophah, fifty-six; ²³the men of Anathoth, one hundred and twenty-eight; ²⁴the people of Azmaveth,*ᵃ* forty-two; ²⁵the people of Kirjath Arim,*ᵃ* Chephirah, and

Beeroth, seven hundred and forty-three; ²⁶the people of Ramah and Geba, six hundred and twenty-one; ²⁷the men of Michmas, one hundred and twenty-two; ²⁸the men of Bethel and Ai, two hundred and twenty-three; ²⁹the people of Nebo, fifty-two; ³⁰the people of Magbish, one hundred and fifty-six; ³¹the people of the other Elam, one thousand two hundred and fifty-four; ³²the people of Harim, three hundred and twenty; ³³the people of Lod, Hadid, and Ono, seven hundred and twenty-five; ³⁴the people of Jericho, three hundred and forty-five; ³⁵the people of Senaah, three thousand six hundred and thirty.

³⁶The priests: the sons of Jedaiah, of the house of Jeshua, nine hundred and seventy-three; ³⁷the sons of Immer, one thousand and fifty-two; ³⁸the sons of Pashhur, one thousand two hundred and forty-seven; ³⁹the sons of Harim, one thousand and seventeen.

⁴⁰The Levites: the sons of Jeshua and Kadmiel, of the sons of Hodaviah,*ᵃ* seventy-four.

⁴¹The singers: the sons of Asaph, one hundred and twenty-eight.

⁴²The sons of the gatekeepers: the sons of Shallum, the sons of Ater, the sons of Talmon, the sons of Akkub, the sons of Hatita, and the sons of Shobai, one hundred and thirty-nine *in* all.

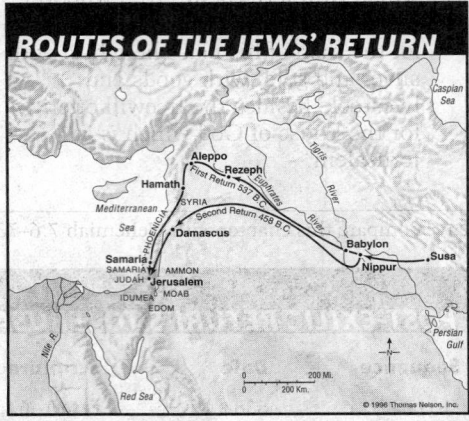

ROUTES OF THE JEWS' RETURN

2:2 *ᵃ*Spelled *Mispereth* in Nehemiah 7:7　*ᵇ*Spelled *Nehum* in Nehemiah 7:7　2:10 *ᵃ*Spelled *Binnui* in Nehemiah 7:15　2:18 *ᵃ*Called *Hariph* in Nehemiah 7:24　2:20 *ᵃ*Called *Gibeon* in Nehemiah 7:25　2:24 *ᵃ*Called *Beth Azmaveth* in Nehemiah 7:28　2:25 *ᵃ*Called *Kirjath Jearim* in Nehemiah 7:29　2:40 *ᵃ*Spelled *Hodevah* in Nehemiah 7:43

[43]The Nethinim: the sons of Ziha, the sons of Hasupha, the sons of Tabbaoth, [44]the sons of Keros, the sons of Siaha,[a] the sons of Padon, [45]the sons of Lebanah, the sons of Hagabah, the sons of Akkub, [46]the sons of Hagab, the sons of Shalmai, the sons of Hanan, [47]the sons of Giddel, the sons of Gahar, the sons of Reaiah, [48]the sons of Rezin, the sons of Nekoda, the sons of Gazzam, [49]the sons of Uzza, the sons of Paseah, the sons of Besai, [50]the sons of Asnah, the sons of Meunim, the sons of Nephusim,[a] [51]the sons of Bakbuk, the sons of Hakupha, the sons of Harhur, [52]the sons of Bazluth,[a] the sons of Mehida, the sons of Harsha, [53]the sons of Barkos, the sons of Sisera, the sons of Tamah, [54]the sons of Neziah, and the sons of Hatipha.

2:43–54 Nethinim. These were temple servants, descendants of the Gibeonites, who performed duties at the temple.

[55]The sons of Solomon's servants: the sons of Sotai, the sons of Sophereth, the sons of Peruda,[a] [56]the sons of Jaala, the sons of Darkon, the sons of Giddel, [57]the sons of Shephatiah, the sons of Hattil, the sons of Pochereth of Zebaim, and the sons of Ami.[a] [58]All the Nethinim and the children of Solomon's servants were three hundred and ninety-two.

[59]And these *were* the ones who came up from Tel Melah, Tel Harsha, Cherub, Addan,[a] and Immer; but they could not identify their father's house or their genealogy,[b] whether they *were* of Israel: [60]the sons of Delaiah, the sons of Tobiah, and the sons of Nekoda, six hundred and fifty-two; [61]and of the sons of the priests: the sons of Habaiah, the sons of Koz,[a] and the sons of Barzillai, who took a wife of the daughters of Barzillai the Gileadite, and was called by their name. [62]These sought their listing *among* those who were registered by genealogy, but they were not found; therefore they *were excluded* from the priesthood as defiled. [63]And the governor[a] said to them that they should not eat of the most holy things till a priest could consult with the Urim and Thummim.

[64]The whole assembly together *was* forty-

2:44 [a]Spelled *Sia* in Nehemiah 7:47   2:50 [a]Spelled *Nephishesim* in Nehemiah 7:52   2:52 [a]Spelled *Bazlith* in Nehemiah 7:54   2:55 [a]Spelled *Perida* in Nehemiah 7:57   2:57 [a]Spelled *Amon* in Nehemiah 7:59   2:59 [a]Spelled *Addon* in Nehemiah 7:61   [b]Literally *seed*   2:61 [a]Or *Hakkoz*   2:63 [a]Hebrew *Tirshatha*

What parts of the Old Testament and what people were active in the events surrounding the return of the Jews from exile?

Five historical books (1 and 2 Chronicles, Ezra, Nehemiah, and Esther) come from or cover events after the exile. Three prophetic books (Haggai, Zechariah, and Malachi) come from the same period. The term "post-Exilic" is often used to describe these books and people.

First and Second Chronicles provide a summary of history viewed from the final days of the exile. Ezra and Nehemiah journal the thrilling and trying days of the return to Judah and the rebuilding of the nation. Haggai and Zechariah were prophets active during the time recorded in Ezra 4–6 when the Temple was under reconstruction. Malachi wrote and prophesied during Nehemiah's revisit to Persia (Nehemiah 13:6).

Although part of the purpose of these books confirms God's continued covenant with the house of David and the unbroken kingly line, the emphasis shifts from royalty to other servants of God. A scribe, a cupbearer, and prophets become God's central agents. Even Esther, although a queen, had to rely on God rather than her position and power to accomplish God's role for her in preserving the Jews in Persia.

All of this sets the stage for the mixed expectations that surrounded the birth of Jesus, the fulfillment of God's covenant with David, God's personal involvement in the history of salvation.

2:63 Urim and Thummim. These objects, kept in the breastplate of the High-Priest, were used to determine God's will.

two thousand three hundred *and* sixty, ⁶⁵besides their male and female servants, of whom *there were* seven thousand three hundred and thirty-seven; and they had two hundred men and women singers. ⁶⁶Their horses *were* seven hundred and thirty-six, their mules two hundred and forty-five, ⁶⁷their camels four hundred and thirty-five, and *their* donkeys six thousand seven hundred and twenty.

⁶⁸*Some* of the heads of the fathers' *houses*, when they came to the house of the LORD which *is* in Jerusalem, offered freely for the house of God, to erect it in its place: ⁶⁹According to their ability, they gave to the treasury for the work sixty-one thousand gold drachmas, five thousand minas of silver, and one hundred priestly garments.

⁷⁰So the priests and the Levites, *some* of the people, the singers, the gatekeepers, and the Nethinim, dwelt in their cities, and all Israel in their cities.

Worship Restored at Jerusalem

3 And when the seventh month had come, and the children of Israel *were* in the cities, the people gathered together as one man to Jerusalem. ²Then Jeshua the son of Jozadak*ᵃ* and his brethren the priests, and Zerubbabel the son of Shealtiel and his brethren, arose and built the altar of the God of Israel, to offer burnt offerings on it, as *it is* written in the Law of Moses the man of God. ³Though fear *had come* upon them because of the people of those countries, they set the altar on its bases; and they offered burnt offerings on it to the LORD, *both* the morning and evening burnt

3:1 After taking care of their homes in and around Jerusalem, the Israelites built the altar of burnt offering in time for the Feasts of Trumpets, Atonement, and Tabernacles, which they had not celebrated for 70 years. This occurred in the seventh month. They obeyed God's Word (Lev. 23:24–44).

offerings. ⁴They also kept the Feast of Tabernacles, as *it is* written, and *offered* the daily burnt offerings in the number required by ordinance for each day. ⁵Afterwards *they offered* the regular burnt offering, and *those* for New Moons and for all the appointed feasts of the LORD that were consecrated, and *those* of everyone who willingly offered a freewill offering to the LORD. ⁶From the first day of the seventh month they began to offer burnt offerings to the LORD, although the foundation of the temple of the LORD had not been laid. ⁷They also gave money to the masons and the carpenters, and food, drink, and oil to the people of Sidon and Tyre to bring cedar logs from Lebanon to the sea, to Joppa, according to the permission which they had from Cyrus king of Persia.

Restoration of the Temple Begins

⁸Now in the second month of the second year of their coming to the house of God at Jerusalem, Zerubbabel the son of Shealtiel, Jeshua the son of Jozadak,*ᵃ* and the rest of their brethren the priests and the Levites, and all those who had come out of the captivity to Jerusalem, began *work* and appointed the Levites from twenty years old and above to oversee the work of the house of the LORD. ⁹Then Jeshua *with* his sons and brothers, Kadmiel *with* his sons, and the sons of Judah,*ᵃ* arose as one to oversee those working on the house of God: the sons of Henadad *with* their sons and their brethren the Levites.

¹⁰When the builders laid the foundation of the temple of the LORD, the priests stood*ᵃ* in their apparel with trumpets, and the Levites, the sons of Asaph, with cymbals, to praise the LORD, according to the ordinance of David king of Israel. ¹¹And they sang responsively, praising and giving thanks to the LORD:

"For *He is* good,
  For His mercy *endures* forever toward Israel."*ᵃ*

Then all the people shouted with a great shout, when they praised the LORD, be-

---

3:2 *ᵃ*Spelled *Jehozadak* in 1 Chronicles 6:14   3:8 *ᵃ*Spelled *Jehozadak* in 1 Chronicles 6:14
3:9 *ᵃ*Or *Hodaviah* (compare 2:40)   3:10 *ᵃ*Following Septuagint, Syriac, and Vulgate; Masoretic Text reads *they stationed the priests.*   3:11 *ᵃ*Compare Psalm 136:1

cause the foundation of the house of the LORD was laid.

¹²But many of the priests and Levites and heads of the fathers' *houses,* old men who had seen the first temple, wept with a loud voice when the foundation of this temple was laid before their eyes. Yet many shouted aloud for joy, ¹³so that the people could not discern the noise of the shout of joy from the noise of the weeping of the people, for the people shouted with a loud shout, and the sound was heard afar off.

3:12 the first temple. This was the temple built by Solomon (see 1 Kin. 5–7). **wept with a loud voice.** The older men (60 or older) wept, knowing that this second temple could not compare with the splendor of the first temple, which was destroyed 50 years earlier. The second temple was smaller and less beautiful, it had no great riches, the ark was gone, and the presence of God did not reside in it (see Hag. 2:1–4).

Resistance to Rebuilding the Temple

4 Now when the adversaries of Judah and Benjamin heard that the descendants of the captivity were building the temple of the LORD God of Israel, ²they came to Zerubbabel and the heads of the fathers' *houses,* and said to them, "Let us build with you, for we seek your God as you *do;* and we have sacrificed to Him since the days of Esarhaddon king of Assyria, who brought us here." ³But Zerubbabel and Jeshua and the rest of the heads of the fathers' *houses* of Israel said to them, "You may do nothing with us to build a house for our God; but we alone will build to the LORD God of Israel, as King Cyrus the king of Persia has commanded us." ⁴Then the people of the land tried to discourage the people of Judah. They troubled them in building, ⁵and hired counselors against them to frustrate their purpose all the days of Cyrus king of Persia, even until the reign of Darius king of Persia.

4:3 we alone. They wanted to avoid idolatry since it was the main reason for Judah's exile to Babylon. They still had spiritual problems (Ezra 9,10), but they rejected any mixed religion.

Rebuilding of Jerusalem Opposed

⁶In the reign of Ahasuerus, in the beginning of his reign, they wrote an accusation against the inhabitants of Judah and Jerusalem.

⁷In the days of Artaxerxes also, Bishlam, Mithredath, Tabel, and the rest of their companions wrote to Artaxerxes king of Persia; and the letter *was* written in Aramaic script, and translated into the Aramaic language. ⁸Rehum*ᵃ* the commander and Shimshai the scribe wrote a letter against Jerusalem to King Artaxerxes in this fashion:

⁹   From*ᵃ* Rehum the commander, Shimshai the scribe, and the rest of their companions—*representatives* of the Dinaites, the Apharsathchites, the Tarpelites, the people of Persia and Erech and Babylon and Shushan,*ᵇ* the Dehavites, the Elamites, ¹⁰and the rest of the nations whom the great and noble Osnapper took captive and settled in the cities of Samaria and the remainder beyond the River*ᵃ*—and so forth.*ᵇ*

¹¹(This *is* a copy of the letter that they sent him)

To King Artaxerxes from your servants, the men *of the region* beyond the River, and so forth:*ᵃ*

¹²   Let it be known to the king that the Jews who came up from you have come to us at Jerusalem, and are building the rebellious and evil city, and are finishing *its* walls and repairing the foundations. ¹³Let it now be known to the king that, if this city is built and the walls completed, they will not pay tax, tribute, or custom,

---

4:12 Jews. This name was used after the Captivity because those who returned were mainly of Judah. Most of the people of the 10 northern tribes had dispersed, and the largest number of those who returned came from the two southern tribes.

4:8 *ᵃ*The original language of Ezra 4:8 through 6:18 is Aramaic.   4:9 *ᵃ*Literally *Then*   *ᵇ*Or *Susa*
4:10 *ᵃ*That is, the Euphrates   *ᵇ*Literally *and now*   4:11 *ᵃ*Literally *and now*

and the king's treasury will be diminished. ¹⁴Now because we receive support from the palace, it was not proper for us to see the king's dishonor; therefore we have sent and informed the king, ¹⁵that search may be made in the book of the records of your fathers. And you will find in the book of the records and know that this city *is* a rebellious city, harmful to kings and provinces, and that they have incited sedition within the city in former times, for which cause this city was destroyed.

¹⁶ We inform the king that if this city is rebuilt and its walls are completed, the result will be that you will have no dominion beyond the River.

¹⁷The king sent an answer:

To Rehum the commander, *to* Shimshai the scribe, *to* the rest of their companions who dwell in Samaria, and *to* the remainder beyond the River:

Peace, and so forth.ᵃ

¹⁸ The letter which you sent to us has been clearly read before me. ¹⁹And I gave the command, and a search has been made, and it was found that this city in former times has revolted against kings, and rebellion and sedition have been fostered in it. ²⁰There have also been mighty kings over Jerusalem, who have ruled over all *the region* beyond the River; and tax, tribute, and custom were paid to them. ²¹Now give the command to make these men cease, that this city may not be built until the command is given by me.

4:21 Now give the command. The efforts of 50,000 were called to a halt by the king's decree. This decree would not lose its authority until the king established a new decree.

²²Take heed now that you do not fail to do this. Why should damage increase to the hurt of the kings?

²³Now when the copy of King Artaxerxes' letter *was* read before Rehum, Shimshai the scribe, and their companions, they went up in haste to Jerusalem against the Jews, and by force of arms made them cease. ²⁴Thus the work of the house of God which *is* at Jerusalem ceased, and it was discontinued until the second year of the reign of Darius king of Persia.

Restoration of the Temple Resumed

5 Then the prophet Haggai and Zechariah the son of Iddo, prophets, prophesied to the Jews who *were* in Judah and Jerusalem, in the name of the God of Israel, *who was* over them. ²So Zerubbabel the son of Shealtiel and Jeshua the son of Jozadakᵃ rose up and began to build the house of God which *is* in Jerusalem; and the prophets of God *were* with them, helping them.

5:1 Haggai and Zechariah. Part of the message of the book of Haggai is addressed to Zerubbabel, the political leader, and Joshua, the religious leader, telling them to work on the temple because God was with them (Hag. 2:4). Both Haggai and Zechariah promised national prosperity to the Jews if they returned to building the temple. As a result, the people returned to building the temple after a 16-year hiatus.

³At the same time Tattenai the governor of *the region* beyond the Riverᵃ and Shethar-Boznai and their companions came to them and spoke thus to them: "Who has commanded you to build this temple and finish this wall?" ⁴Then, accordingly, we told them the names of the men who were constructing this building. ⁵But the eye of their God was upon the elders of the Jews, so that they could not make them cease till a report could go to Darius. Then a written answer was returned concerning this *matter.* ⁶This is a copy of the letter that Tattenai sent:

The governor of *the region* beyond the River, and Shethar-Boznai, and his

---

4:17 ᵃLiterally *and now*   5:2 ᵃSpelled *Jehozadak* in 1 Chronicles 6:14   5:3 ᵃThat is, the Euphrates

companions, the Persians who *were in the region* beyond the River, to Darius the king.

[7](They sent a letter to him, in which was written thus)

To Darius the king:

All peace.

[8] Let it be known to the king that we went into the province of Judea, to the temple of the great God, which is being built with heavy stones, and timber is being laid in the walls; and this work goes on diligently and prospers in their hands.

[9] Then we asked those elders, *and* spoke thus to them: "Who commanded you to build this temple and to finish these walls?" [10]We also asked them their names to inform you, that we might write the names of the men who *were* chief among them.

[11] And thus they returned us an answer, saying: "We are the servants of the God of heaven and earth, and we are rebuilding the temple that was built many years ago, which a great king of Israel built and completed. [12]But because our fathers provoked the God of heaven to wrath, He gave them into the hand of Nebuchadnezzar king of Babylon, the Chaldean, *who* destroyed this temple and carried the people away to Babylon. [13]However, in the first year of Cyrus king of Babylon, King Cyrus issued a decree to build this house of God. [14]Also, the gold and silver articles of the house of

5:12 gave them into the hand of Nebuchadnezzar. The expression is used when a king relinquishes some of his authority to a lower administrative official, while keeping him completely under his command. Here God satisfied His wrath by relinquishing authority to Nebuchadnezzar, the greatest king of the Near East, while still administrating as a sovereign Lord.

God, which Nebuchadnezzar had taken from the temple that *was* in Jerusalem and carried into the temple of Babylon—those King Cyrus took from the temple of Babylon, and they were given to one named Sheshbazzar, whom he had made governor. [15]And he said to him, 'Take these articles; go, carry them to the temple *site* that *is* in Jerusalem, and let the house of God be rebuilt on its former site.' [16]Then the same Sheshbazzar came *and* laid the foundation of the house of God which *is* in Jerusalem; but from that time even until now it has been under construction, and it is not finished."

[17] Now therefore, if *it seems* good to the king, let a search be made in the king's treasure house, which *is* there in Babylon, whether it is *so* that a decree was issued by King Cyrus to build this house of God at Jerusalem, and let the king send us his pleasure concerning this *matter*.

The Decree of Darius

6 Then King Darius issued a decree, and a search was made in the archives,[a] where the treasures were stored in Babylon. [2]And at Achmetha,[a] in the palace that *is* in the province of Media, a scroll was found, and in it a record *was* written thus:

[3] In the first year of King Cyrus, King Cyrus issued a decree *concerning* the house of God at Jerusalem: "Let the house be rebuilt, the place where they offered sacrifices; and let the foundations of it be firmly laid, its height sixty cubits *and* its width sixty cubits, [4]with three rows of heavy stones and one row of new timber. Let the expenses be paid from the king's treasury. [5]Also let the gold and silver articles of the house of God, which Nebuchadnezzar took from the temple which *is* in Jerusalem and brought to Babylon, be restored and taken back to the temple which *is* in Jerusalem, *each* to its

---

6:1 [a]Literally *house of the scrolls*   6:2 [a]Probably *Ecbatana*, the ancient capital of Media

place; and deposit *them* in the house of God"—

6   Now *therefore,* Tattenai, governor of *the region* beyond the River, and Shethar-Boznai, and your companions the Persians who *are* beyond the River, keep yourselves far from there. ⁷Let the work of this house of God alone; let the governor of the Jews and the elders of the Jews build this house of God on its site.

8   Moreover I issue a decree *as to* what you shall do for the elders of these Jews, for the building of this house of God: Let the cost be paid at the king's expense from taxes *on the region* beyond the River; this is to be given immediately to these men, so that they are not hindered. ⁹And whatever they need—young bulls, rams, and lambs for the burnt offerings of the God of heaven, wheat, salt, wine, and oil, according to the request of the priests who *are* in Jerusalem—let it be given them day by day without fail, ¹⁰that they may offer sacrifices of sweet aroma to the God of heaven, and pray for the life of the king and his sons.

6:6–10 Because He favored the Jews, God did not allow the officials to interfere with the building project. The officials had to help finance the project by giving the Jews portions of taxes collected for the Persian king. The Jews could draw from the provincial treasury.

11   Also I issue a decree that whoever alters this edict, let a timber be pulled from his house and erected, and let him be hanged on it; and let his house be made a refuse heap because of this. ¹²And may the God who causes His name to dwell there destroy any king or people who put their hand to alter it, or to destroy this house of God which is in Jerusalem. I Darius issue a decree; let it be done diligently.

The Temple Completed and Dedicated

¹³Then Tattenai, governor of *the region* beyond the River, Shethar-Boznai, and their companions diligently did according to what King Darius had sent. ¹⁴So the elders of the Jews built, and they prospered through the prophesying of Haggai the prophet and Zechariah the son of Iddo. And they built and finished *it,* according to the commandment of the God of Israel, and according to the command of Cyrus, Darius, and Artaxerxes king of Persia. ¹⁵Now the temple was finished on the third day of the month of Adar, which was in the sixth year of the reign of King Darius. ¹⁶Then the children of Israel, the priests and the Levites and the rest of the descendants of the captivity, celebrated the dedication of this house of God with joy. ¹⁷And they offered sacrifices at the dedication of this house of God, one hundred bulls, two hundred rams, four hundred lambs, and as a sin offering for all Israel twelve male goats, according to the number of the tribes of Israel. ¹⁸They assigned the priests to their divisions and the Levites to their divisions, over the service of God in Jerusalem, as it is written in the Book of Moses.

The Passover Celebrated

¹⁹And the descendants of the captivity kept the Passover on the fourteenth *day* of the first month. ²⁰For the priests and the Levites had purified themselves; all of them *were ritually* clean. And they slaughtered the Passover *lambs* for all the descendants of the captivity, for their brethren the priests, and for themselves. ²¹Then the children of Israel who had returned from the captivity ate together with all who had separated themselves from the filth of the nations of the land in order to seek the LORD God of Israel. ²²And they kept the Feast of Unleavened Bread seven days with joy; for the LORD made them joyful, and turned the heart of the king of Assyria toward them, to strengthen their hands in the work of the house of God, the God of Israel.

6:22 turned the heart of the king of Assyria toward them. God encouraged the people by turning the heart of the king to allow them to complete the rebuilding of the temple. The title "King of Assyria" was given to every king who succeeded the great Neo-Assyrian Empire.

The Arrival of Ezra

7 Now after these things, in the reign of Artaxerxes king of Persia, Ezra the son of Seraiah, the son of Azariah, the son of Hilkiah, ²the son of Shallum, the son of Zadok, the son of Ahitub, ³the son of Amariah, the son of Azariah, the son of Meraioth, ⁴the son of Zerahiah, the son of Uzzi, the son of Bukki, ⁵the son of Abishua, the son of Phinehas, the son of Eleazar, the son of Aaron the chief priest— ⁶this Ezra came up from Babylon; and he *was* a skilled scribe in the Law of Moses, which the LORD God of Israel had given. The king granted him all his request, according to the hand of the LORD his God upon him. ⁷*Some* of the children of Israel, the priests, the Levites, the singers, the gatekeepers, and the Nethinim came up to Jerusalem in the seventh year of King Artaxerxes. ⁸And Ezra came to Jerusalem in the fifth month, which *was* in the seventh year of the king. ⁹On the first *day* of the first month he began *his* journey from Babylon, and on the first *day* of the fifth month he came to Jerusalem, according to the good hand of his God upon him. ¹⁰For Ezra had prepared his heart to seek the Law of the LORD, and to do *it*, and to teach statutes and ordinances in Israel.

> **7:6 a skilled scribe.** The leaders of the nation had to interpret the law, which was difficult because so much had changed in the 1,000 years since the law was first given. Ezra, the scribe, knew the law and could write it from memory.

The Letter of Artaxerxes to Ezra

¹¹This *is* a copy of the letter that King Artaxerxes gave Ezra the priest, the scribe, expert in the words of the commandments of the LORD, and of His statutes to Israel:

¹² Artaxerxes,ᵃ king of kings,

To Ezra the priest, a scribe of the Law of the God of heaven:

Perfect *peace*, and so forth.ᵇ

¹³ I issue a decree that all those of the people of Israel and the priests and Levites in my realm, who volunteer to go up to Jerusalem, may go with you. ¹⁴And whereas you are being sent by the king and his seven counselors to inquire concerning Judah and Jerusalem, with regard to the Law of your God which *is* in your hand; ¹⁵and *whereas you are* to carry the silver and gold which the king and his counselors have freely offered to the God of Israel, whose dwelling *is* in Jerusalem; ¹⁶and *whereas* all the silver and gold that you may find in all the province of Babylon, along with the freewill offering of the people and the priests, *are to be* freely offered for the house of their God in Jerusalem— ¹⁷now therefore, be careful to buy with this money bulls, rams, and lambs, with their grain offerings and their drink offerings, and offer them on the altar of the house of your God in Jerusalem.

¹⁸ And whatever seems good to you and your brethren to do with the rest of the silver and the gold, do it according to the will of your God. ¹⁹Also the articles that are given to you for the service of the house of your God, deliver in full before the God of Jerusalem. ²⁰And whatever more may be needed for the house of your God, which you may have occasion to provide, pay *for it* from the king's treasury.

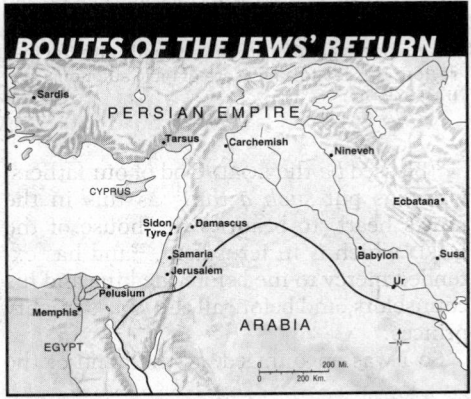

ROUTES OF THE JEWS' RETURN

Sardis • PERSIAN EMPIRE • Tarsus • Carchemish • Nineveh • CYPRUS • Sidon • Tyre • Damascus • Ecbatana • Samaria • Jerusalem • Babylon • Susa • Ur • Pelusium • Memphis • ARABIA • EGYPT

200 Mi.
200 Km.

7:12 ᵃThe original language of Ezra 7:12–26 is Aramaic. ᵇLiterally *and now*

21 And I, *even* I, Artaxerxes the king, issue a decree to all the treasurers who *are in the region* beyond the River, that whatever Ezra the priest, the scribe of the Law of the God of heaven, may require of you, let it be done diligently, 22up to one hundred talents of silver, one hundred kors of wheat, one hundred baths of wine, one hundred baths of oil, and salt without prescribed limit. 23Whatever is commanded by the God of heaven, let it diligently be done for the house of the God of heaven. For why should there be wrath against the realm of the king and his sons?

24 Also we inform you that it shall not be lawful to impose tax, tribute, or custom *on* any of the priests, Levites, singers, gatekeepers, Nethinim, or servants of this house of God. 25And you, Ezra, according to your God-given wisdom, set magistrates and judges who may judge all the people who *are in the region* beyond the River, all such as know the laws of your God; and teach those who do not know *them.* 26Whoever will not observe the law of your God and the law of the king, let judgment be executed speedily on him, whether *it be* death, or banishment, or confiscation of goods, or imprisonment.

7:25 And you, Ezra. The letter with the decree was written to Ezra. The king trusted him and granted him permission to appoint magistrates and judges for the region. This led to a measure of local autonomy for the Jews.

27Blessed *be* the LORD God of our fathers, who has put *such a thing* as this in the king's heart, to beautify the house of the LORD which *is* in Jerusalem, 28and has extended mercy to me before the king and his counselors, and before all the king's mighty princes.

So I was encouraged, as the hand of the

LORD my God *was* upon me; and I gathered leading men of Israel to go up with me.

Heads of Families Who Returned with Ezra

8 These *are* the heads of their fathers' houses, and *this is* the genealogy of those who went up with me from Babylon, in the reign of King Artaxerxes: 2of the sons of Phinehas, Gershom; of the sons of Ithamar, Daniel; of the sons of David, Hattush; 3of the sons of Shecaniah, of the sons of Parosh, Zechariah; and registered with him *were* one hundred and fifty males; 4of the sons of Pahath-Moab, Eliehoenai the son of Zerahiah, and with him two hundred males; 5of the sons of Shechaniah,*a* Ben-Jahaziel, and with him three hundred males; 6of the sons of Adin, Ebed the son of Jonathan, and with him fifty males; 7of the sons of Elam, Jeshaiah the son of Athaliah, and with him seventy males; 8of the sons of Shephatiah, Zebadiah the son of Michael, and with him eighty males; 9of the sons of Joab, Obadiah the son of Jehiel, and with him two hundred and eighteen males; 10of the sons of Shelomith,*a* Ben-Josiphiah, and with him one hundred and sixty males; 11of the sons of Bebai, Zechariah the son of Bebai, and with him twenty-eight males; 12of the sons of Azgad, Johanan the son of Hakkatan, and with him one hundred and ten males; 13of the last sons of Adonikam, whose names *are* these—Eliphelet, Jeiel, and Shemaiah—and with them sixty males; 14also of the sons of Bigvai, Uthai and Zabbud, and with them seventy males.

8:1–14 from Babylon. This list includes the people who lived in the surrounding area. The total number of men counted is 1,496 plus the men mentioned by name, plus the women and children, which brings the total population to 7–8,000. Conflicts arose between those exiles who stayed in Babylon and those who returned at different times, for the different groups grew comfortable with their respective lifestyles.

Servants for the Temple

15Now I gathered them by the river that flows to Ahava, and we camped there three days. And I looked among the people and

---

8:5 *a*Following Masoretic Text and Vulgate; Septuagint reads *the sons of Zatho, Shechaniah.*
8:10 *a*Following Masoretic Text and Vulgate; Septuagint reads *the sons of Banni, Shelomith.*

the priests, and found none of the sons of Levi there. [16]Then I sent for Eliezer, Ariel, Shemaiah, Elnathan, Jarib, Elnathan, Nathan, Zechariah, and Meshullam, leaders; also for Joiarib and Elnathan, men of understanding. [17]And I gave them a command for Iddo the chief man at the place Casiphia, and I told them what they should say to Iddo *and* his brethren[a] the Nethinim at the place Casiphia—that they should bring us servants for the house of our God. [18]Then, by the good hand of our God upon us, they brought us a man of understanding, of the sons of Mahli the son of Levi, the son of Israel, namely Sherebiah, with his sons and brothers, eighteen men; [19]and Hashabiah, and with him Jeshaiah of the sons of Merari, his brothers and their sons, twenty men; [20]also of the Nethinim, whom David and the leaders had appointed for the service of the Levites, two hundred and twenty Nethinim. All of them were designated by name.

Fasting and Prayer for Protection

[21]Then I proclaimed a fast there at the river of Ahava, that we might humble ourselves before our God, to seek from Him the right way for us and our little ones and all our possessions. [22]For I was ashamed to request of the king an escort of soldiers and horsemen to help us against the enemy on the road, because we had spoken to the king, saying, "The hand of our God *is* upon all those for good who seek Him, but His power and His wrath *are* against all those who forsake Him." [23]So we fasted and entreated our God for this, and He answered our prayer.

> **8:21–23 I proclaimed a fast.** Ezra and the people would soon begin the long, dangerous journey. It was common to travel in caravans to ensure safety, as there were many thieves on the roads. Ezra and the people fasted to ask for God's protection, as they did not want to confuse the king regarding their trust in God for safety. God honored their prayer and protected them.

Gifts for the Temple

[24]And I separated twelve of the leaders of the priests—Sherebiah, Hashabiah, and ten of their brethren with them— [25]and weighed out to them the silver, the gold, and the articles, the offering for the house of our God which the king and his counselors and his princes, and all Israel *who were* present, had offered. [26]I weighed into their hand six hundred and fifty talents of silver, silver articles *weighing* one hundred talents, one hundred talents of gold, [27]twenty gold basins *worth* a thousand drachmas, and two vessels of fine polished bronze, precious as gold. [28]And I said to them, "You *are* holy to the LORD; the articles *are* holy also; and the silver and the gold *are* a freewill offering to the LORD God of your fathers. [29]Watch and keep *them* until you weigh *them* before the leaders of the priests and the Levites and heads of the fathers' *houses* of Israel in Jerusalem, *in* the chambers of the house of the LORD." [30]So the priests and the Levites received the silver and the gold and the articles by weight, to bring *them* to Jerusalem to the house of our God.

The Return to Jerusalem

[31]Then we departed from the river of Ahava on the twelfth *day* of the first month, to go to Jerusalem. And the hand of our God was upon us, and He delivered us from the hand of the enemy and from ambush along the road. [32]So we came to Jerusalem, and stayed there three days.

[33]Now on the fourth day the silver and the gold and the articles were weighed in the house of our God by the hand of Meremoth the son of Uriah the priest, and with him *was* Eleazar the son of Phinehas; with them *were* the Levites, Jozabad the son of Jeshua and Noadiah the son of Binnui, [34]with the number *and* weight of everything. All the weight was written down at that time.

[35]The children of those who had been carried away captive, who had come from the captivity, offered burnt offerings to the God of Israel: twelve bulls for all Israel, ninety-six rams, seventy-seven lambs, and twelve male goats *as* a sin offering. All *this was* a burnt offering to the LORD.

[36]And they delivered the king's orders to the king's satraps and the governors *in the region* beyond the River. So they gave support to the people and the house of God.

8:17 [a]Following Vulgate; Masoretic Text reads *to Iddo his brother*; Septuagint reads *to their brethren*.

Intermarriage with Pagans

9 When these things were done, the leaders came to me, saying, "The people of Israel and the priests and the Levites have not separated themselves from the peoples of the lands, with respect to the abominations of the Canaanites, the Hittites, the Perizzites, the Jebusites, the Ammonites, the Moabites, the Egyptians, and the Amorites. ²For they have taken some of their daughters *as wives* for themselves and their sons, so that the holy seed is mixed with the peoples of *those* lands. Indeed, the hand of the leaders and rulers has been foremost in this trespass." ³So when I heard this thing, I tore my garment and my robe, and plucked out some of the hair of my

9:1 abominations. Israel had been warned not to make covenants with nations that would result in intermarriages and eventually to the worship of foreign gods (Ex. 34:10–17). This was to keep the people pure. When Ezra found out that they were intermarrying again, he called for immediate repentance.

head and beard, and sat down astonished. ⁴Then everyone who trembled at the words of the God of Israel assembled to me, because of the transgression of those who had been carried away captive, and I sat astonished until the evening sacrifice.

9:4 trembled at the words. There were those who saw intermarriage as a sin and feared the Lord's judgment on them again (see Is. 66:2,5). They joined Ezra before the evening sacrifice, where the people prayed and confessed their sin while Ezra fasted, lamented, and prayed to lead the people to repentance.

⁵At the evening sacrifice I arose from my fasting; and having torn my garment and my robe, I fell on my knees and spread out my hands to the LORD my God. ⁶And I said: "O my God, I am too ashamed and humiliated to lift up my face to You, my God; for our iniquities have risen higher than *our* heads, and our guilt has grown up to the heavens. ⁷Since the days of our fathers to

How does Ezra's handling of the intermarriage and divorce situation fit into the overall pattern of Biblical teaching on these important matters?

Ezra 9,10 record a critical time in the re-establishment of the Jewish people in their homeland. In the years before Ezra arrived from Persia, many of the returned Jewish men intermarried with pagan women from the area. This practice reflects no circumstances like we find in the marriages of Rahab or Ruth, Gentiles who became believers in God. The pagan background of these women was not taken into account by their husbands. Ezra received this news as part of the report when he reached Jerusalem.

For Ezra, this was almost the worst possible news. Intermarriage with pagans had historically been a key in the repeated downfalls of the nation. These marriages were an act of disobedience. Ezra was overwhelmed with shame and distress over the situation (Ezra 9:3,4). His grief was open and convicting.

Eventually, the people themselves confessed their error and decided that those who had married pagan women would have to "put away" (divorce) these wives.

God had not changed his mind about divorce. Malachi, who lived in this time period, declared that God hates divorce (Malachi 2:16).

Several important notes can be made about this passage in Ezra. It does not establish a norm about divorce. It is also easy to overlook the fact that while the solution of divorce was a group decision, each of these marriages was examined individually. Presumably, cases in which the women had become believers were treated differently than cases in which the women involved saw questions of faith as violation of the marriage agreement.

In the humility of the guilty and the care in confronting these issues, a great deal of God's mercy comes through. A strict interpretation of the law could have led to the stoning death of all involved. The eagerness to set things right opened the doorway for a solution, even though in some of the cases it involved the grief and sadness of divorce.

this day we *have been* very guilty, and for our iniquities we, our kings, *and* our priests have been delivered into the hand of the kings of the lands, to the sword, to captivity, to plunder, and to humiliation, as *it is* this day. ⁸And now for a little while grace has been *shown* from the LORD our God, to leave us a remnant to escape, and to give us a peg in His holy place, that our God may enlighten our eyes and give us a measure of revival in our bondage. ⁹For we *were* slaves. Yet our God did not forsake us in our bondage; but He extended mercy to us in the sight of the kings of Persia, to revive us, to repair the house of our God, to rebuild its ruins, and to give us a wall in Judah and Jerusalem. ¹⁰And now, O our God, what shall we say after this? For we have forsaken Your commandments, ¹¹which You commanded by Your servants the prophets, saying, 'The land which you are entering to possess is an unclean land, with the uncleanness of the peoples of the lands, with their abominations which have filled it from one end to another with their impurity. ¹²Now therefore, do not give your daughters as wives for their sons, nor take their daughters to your sons; and never seek their peace or prosperity, that you may be strong and eat the good of the land, and leave *it* as an inheritance to your children forever.' ¹³And after all that has come upon us for our evil deeds and for our great guilt, since You our God have punished us less than our iniquities *deserve*, and have given us *such* deliverance as this, ¹⁴should we again break Your commandments, and join in marriage with the people *committing* these abominations? Would You not be angry with us until You had consumed *us*, so that *there would be* no remnant or survivor? ¹⁵O LORD God of Israel, You *are* righteous, for we are left as a remnant, as *it is* this day. Here we *are* before You, in our guilt, though no one can stand before You because of this!"

Confession of Improper Marriages

10 Now while Ezra was praying, and while he was confessing, weeping, and bowing down before the house of God, a very large assembly of men, women, and children gathered to him from Israel; for the people wept very bitterly. ²And

10:1 praying...confessing, weeping, and bowing down. Ezra's contrite spirit before the people was evident, and they joined him. This demonstrated the seriousness of their sin and the genuineness of their repentance.

Shechaniah the son of Jehiel, *one* of the sons of Elam, spoke up and said to Ezra, "We have trespassed against our God, and have taken pagan wives from the peoples of the land; yet now there is hope in Israel in spite of this. ³Now therefore, let us make a covenant with our God to put away all these wives and those who have been born to them, according to the advice of my master and of those who tremble at the commandment of our God; and let it be done according to the law. ⁴Arise, for *this* matter *is* your *responsibility*. We also *are* with you. Be of good courage, and do *it*."

10:4 your *responsibility*. Ezra, as the chief spiritual leader with divine authority, had the human responsibility to deal with divorces for many (see vv. 18–44).

⁵Then Ezra arose, and made the leaders of the priests, the Levites, and all Israel swear an oath that they would do according to this word. So they swore an oath. ⁶Then Ezra rose up from before the house of God, and went into the chamber of Jehohanan the son of Eliashib; and *when* he came there, he ate no bread and drank no water, for he mourned because of the guilt of those from the captivity.

⁷And they issued a proclamation throughout Judah and Jerusalem to all the descendants of the captivity, that they must gather at Jerusalem, ⁸and that whoever would not come within three days, according to the instructions of the leaders and elders, all his property would be confiscated, and he himself would be separated from the assembly of those from the captivity.

⁹So all the men of Judah and Benjamin gathered at Jerusalem within three days. It *was* the ninth month, on the twentieth of the month; and all the people sat in the open square of the house of God, trembling because of *this* matter and because of heavy rain. ¹⁰Then Ezra the priest stood up and

said to them, "You have transgressed and have taken pagan wives, adding to the guilt of Israel. [11]Now therefore, make confession to the LORD God of your fathers, and do His will; separate yourselves from the peoples of the land, and from the pagan wives."

> **10:11 confession...separate.** The two essential elements of repentance are agreeing with God and taking righteous action to separate from sin.

[12]Then all the assembly answered and said with a loud voice, "Yes! As you have said, so we must do. [13]But *there are* many people; *it is* the season for heavy rain, and we are not able to stand outside. Nor *is this* the work of one or two days, for *there are* many of us who have transgressed in this matter. [14]Please, let the leaders of our entire assembly stand; and let all those in our cities who have taken pagan wives come at appointed times, together with the elders and judges of their cities, until the fierce wrath of our God is turned away from us in this matter." [15]Only Jonathan the son of Asahel and Jahaziah the son of Tikvah opposed this, and Meshullam and Shabbethai the Levite gave them support.

[16]Then the descendants of the captivity did so. And Ezra the priest, *with* certain heads of the fathers' *households*, were set apart by the fathers' *households*, each of them by name; and they sat down on the first day of the tenth month to examine the matter. [17]By the first day of the first month they finished *questioning* all the men who had taken pagan wives.

Pagan Wives Put Away

[18]And among the sons of the priests who had taken pagan wives *the following* were found of the sons of Jeshua the son of Jozadak,[a] and his brothers: Maaseiah, Eliezer, Jarib, and Gedaliah. [19]And they gave their promise that they would put away their wives; and *being* guilty, *they* presented a ram of the flock as their trespass offering.

[20]Also of the sons of Immer: Hanani and Zebadiah; [21]of the sons of Harim: Maaseiah, Elijah, Shemaiah, Jehiel, and Uzziah; [22]of the sons of Pashhur: Elioenai, Maaseiah, Ishmael, Nethanel, Jozabad, and Elasah.

[23]Also of the Levites: Jozabad, Shimei, Kelaiah (the same *is* Kelita), Pethahiah, Judah, and Eliezer.

[24]Also of the singers: Eliashib; and of the gatekeepers: Shallum, Telem, and Uri.

[25]And others of Israel: of the sons of Parosh: Ramiah, Jeziah, Malchiah, Mijamin, Eleazar, Malchijah, and Benaiah; [26]of the sons of Elam: Mattaniah, Zechariah, Jehiel, Abdi, Jeremoth, and Eliah; [27]of the sons of Zattu: Elioenai, Eliashib, Mattaniah, Jeremoth, Zabad, and Aziza; [28]of the sons of Bebai: Jehohanan, Hananiah, Zabbai, *and* Athlai; [29]of the sons of Bani: Meshullam, Malluch, Adaiah, Jashub, Sheal, *and* Ramoth;[a] [30]of the sons of Pahath-Moab: Adna, Chelal, Benaiah, Maaseiah, Mattaniah, Bezalel, Binnui, and Manasseh; [31]*of* the sons of Harim: Eliezer, Ishijah, Malchijah, Shemaiah, Shimeon, [32]Benjamin, Malluch, *and* Shemariah; [33]of the sons of Hashum: Mattenai, Mattattah, Zabad, Eliphelet, Jeremai, Manasseh, *and* Shimei; [34]of the sons of Bani: Maadai, Amram, Uel, [35]Benaiah, Bedeiah, Cheluh,[a] [36]Vaniah, Meremoth, Eliashib, [37]Mattaniah, Mattenai, Jaasai,[a] [38]Bani, Binnui, Shimei, [39]Shelemiah, Nathan, Adaiah, [40]Machnadebai, Shashai, Sharai, [41]Azarel, Shelemiah, Shemariah, [42]Shallum, Amariah, *and* Joseph; [43]of the sons of Nebo: Jeiel, Mattithiah, Zabad, Zebina, Jaddai,[a] Joel, *and* Benaiah.

[44]All these had taken pagan wives, and *some* of them had wives *by whom* they had children.

> **10:44** Provision was made for the divorced wives and their children.

10:18 [a]Spelled *Jehozadak* in 1 Chronicles 6:14   10:29 [a]Or *Jeremoth*   10:35 [a]Or *Cheluhi*, or *Cheluhu*   10:37 [a]Or *Jaasu*   10:43 [a]Or *Jaddu*

NEHEMIAH

God puts His servants in unlikely places and gets surprising results. Nehemiah was a king's cup-bearer in Persia. His name only appears in this book, though Nehemiah certainly fits the descriptions of various people in the Hall of Faith listed in Hebrews 11. God worked through Nehemiah as a key participant in the re-establishment of the Jewish nation in the Promised Land after the exile. Nehemiah's character provides a powerful case study in leadership, integrity, and faith.

AUTHOR AND DATE

Nehemiah was probably written by Ezra, approximately 424 to 400 B.C.

Much of this book was drawn from Nehemiah's personal diaries. But although these reports were written in the first person (1:1–7:5; 12:27–43; 13:4–31), both Jewish and Christian traditions have long identified Ezra as the author. Three clues can be cited to back up Ezra's authorship: (1) the two books Ezra and Nehemiah were originally one book (indicated in the Greek Septuagint and the Latin Vulgate); (2) the recurring phrase "hand of the Lord" in both books points to a single author; and (3) the sources used (official Persian documents) probably included Nehemiah's reports which were available to Ezra.

The events in Nehemiah can be dated as early as 446 B.C., the 20th year of the Persian king Artaxerxes (464–423 B.C.). Details from both of Nehemiah's terms as governor of Jerusalem help narrow the most likely date of composition to sometime between 424 and 400 B.C.

BACKGROUND AND SETTING

The book of Nehemiah grows out of a background of pain and glory. The opening scenes occur in Persia. A new chapter in God's dealings with His people begins. Recent history has included the final carrying out of God's promised judgment, with the Land first invaded by the Assyrians, leading to the deportation and loss of the 10 northern tribes. Later the Babylonians sacked, destroyed and nearly depopulated Jerusalem, deporting the best of Judah to Babylon. God chastened His people with 70 years of captivity in Babylon (Jeremiah 25:11).

The ensuing years saw the rise of the Persian Empire. King Cyrus eventually set into motion the events leading to the Jews' return to Jerusalem. Ezra, Esther, Daniel, Nehemiah, and Malachi provide the details for these years in the history of God's faithfulness. The last two books share the distinction of being the final records in the Old Testament.

By the close of Nehemiah, God has allowed His people to re-establish a foot-

hold in the Promised Land. God remains committed to His promises in spite of the fickle nature of His human partners. A 400-year silence will follow these events. When God's revelation again takes written form, God will also have taken on flesh and visited the planet.

HISTORICAL AND THEOLOGICAL THEMES

Central among the historical themes of Nehemiah is the lesson that God remains sovereign and acts on the stage of world history. He is not a local or tribal god but proves to be the God of the universe, the author of history.

The importance and effectiveness of God's Word provides a major theological theme. Spiritual revival came in response to Ezra's reading of "the book of the Law of Moses" (8:1). Decisions and judgments that will govern the course of the nation are rooted in the written Word (8:13; 10:29,34,36).

A second major theme, the obedience of Nehemiah, permeates this book. Nehemiah's confidence and cooperation with God reverses even the wicked plans of the enemies. Nehemiah personally admits that his leadership decisions were not based on his own abilities but on God's guidance. Nehemiah left revenge up to God—"My God, remember Tobiah and Sanballat" (6:14). He also gave God credit for success—"my God put it into my heart" (7:5).

> **GOD IS NOT A LOCAL OR TRIBAL GOD BUT PROVES TO BE THE GOD OF THE UNIVERSE, THE AUTHOR OF HISTORY.**

A third theological theme can be found in the way Nehemiah indicates the positive results that came from the fierce opposition the people faced. They were driven to their knees in dependence on God. The results were dramatic. In spite of opposition from without and heartbreaking corruption and dissension from within, Judah completed the walls of Jerusalem in only 52 days (6:15). There also followed a sweeping revival under Ezra and a glorious celebration of the Feast of Tabernacles (8:14) affirming God's role in the re-establishment of His people in the Land.

OUTLINE

Nehemiah Prays for His People

1 The words of Nehemiah the son of Hachaliah.

It came to pass in the month of Chislev, *in* the twentieth year, as I was in Shushan*ᵃ* the citadel, ²that Hanani one of my brethren came with men from Judah; and I asked them concerning the Jews who had escaped, who had survived the captivity, and concerning Jerusalem. ³And they said to me, "The survivors who are left from the captivity in the province *are* there in great distress and reproach. The wall of Jerusalem *is* also broken down, and its gates *are* burned with fire."

⁴So it was, when I heard these words, that I sat down and wept, and mourned *for many* days; I was fasting and praying before the God of heaven.

> **1:4 sat down and wept, and mourned *for many* days.** Nehemiah was neither a prophet nor a priest. He was a royal cupbearer, whose name means "Jehovah comforts." He knew of Jerusalem's significance to God and was greatly distressed by the state of Jerusalem, knowing it did not bring glory to God.

⁵And I said: "I pray, LORD God of heaven, O great and awesome God, *You* who keep *Your* covenant and mercy with those who love You*ᵃ* and observe Your*ᵇ* command-

> **1:5–11 keep *Your* covenant and mercy with those who love You.** After 70 years of captivity, God kept His promise to restore His people to the Promised Land. The promise seemed to be failing, and Nehemiah prayed to God, asking Him to fulfill His pledges to His people. This prayer represents one of Scripture's most moving confessions and intercessions before God.

ments, ⁶please let Your ear be attentive and Your eyes open, that You may hear the prayer of Your servant which I pray before You now, day and night, for the children of Israel Your servants, and confess the sins of the children of Israel which we have sinned against You. Both my father's house and I have sinned. ⁷We have acted very corruptly against You, and have not kept the commandments, the statutes, nor the ordinances which You commanded Your servant Moses. ⁸Remember, I pray, the word that You commanded Your servant Moses, saying, 'If you are unfaithful, I will scatter you among the nations;*ᵃ* ⁹but *if* you return to Me, and keep My commandments and do them, though some of you were cast out to the farthest part of the heavens, *yet* I will gather them from there, and bring them to the place which I have chosen as a dwelling for My name.'*ᵃ* ¹⁰Now these *are* Your servants and Your people, whom You

---

1:1 *ᵃ*Or *Susa*   1:5 *ᵃ*Literally *Him* *ᵇ*Literally *His*   1:8 *ᵃ*Leviticus 26:33   1:9 *ᵃ*Deuteronomy 30:2–5

TIME LINE OF NEHEMIAH

Reference	Date	Event
1:1,4	Nov./Dec. ..... 446 B.C. (Kislev)	Nehemiah hears of problems and prays.
2:1,5	Mar./Apr. ..... 445 B.C. (Nisan)	Nehemiah is dispatched to Jerusalem.
3:1; 6:15	July/Aug. ...... 445 B.C. (Ab)	Nehemiah starts the wall.
6:15	Aug./Sept. ... 445 B.C. (Elul)	Nehemiah completes the wall.
7:73b	Sept./Oct. ..... 445 B.C. (Tishri)	Day of Trumpets celebrated (implied).
8:13–15	Sept./Oct. ..... 445 B.C. (Tishri)	Feast of Tabernacles celebrated.
9:1	Sept./Oct. ..... 445 B.C. (Tishri)	Time of confession.
12:27	Sept./Oct. ..... 445 B.C.(Tishri)	Wall dedicated.
13:6	.... 445–433 B.C.	Nehemiah's first term as governor (Nehemiah 1–12).
13:6	.... 433–424 B.C. (?)	Nehemiah returns to Persia.
No ref.	.... 433–? B.C.	Malachi prophesies in Jerusalem during Nehemiah's absence.
13:1,4,7	.... 424–? B.C.	Nehemiah returns and serves a second term as governor (Nehemiah 13).

have redeemed by Your great power, and by Your strong hand. ¹¹O Lord, I pray, please let Your ear be attentive to the prayer of Your servant, and to the prayer of Your servants who desire to fear Your name; and let Your servant prosper this day, I pray, and grant him mercy in the sight of this man."

For I was the king's cupbearer.

> **1:11 the king's cupbearer.** The cupbearer had the advantage of petitioning the king since he escorted him at meals, risking his life by testing all the king's beverages. The king owed the cupbearer his life, and the two developed a strong relationship. God used this relationship between a Gentile and a Jew to deliver His people.

Nehemiah Sent to Judah

2 And it came to pass in the month of Nisan, in the twentieth year of King Artaxerxes, *when* wine *was* before him, that I took the wine and gave it to the king. Now I had never been sad in his presence before. ²Therefore the king said to me, "Why *is* your face sad, since you *are* not sick? This *is* nothing but sorrow of heart."

> **2:1,2 Now I had never been sad.** It was dangerous to express sadness in the presence of the king. The king wanted his subjects to be happy, since it reflected on his administrative capabilities. **dreadfully afraid.** Nehemiah feared that either his countenance, his explanation, or his request would anger the king and thus lead to his death (see Esth. 4:11).

So I became dreadfully afraid, ³and said to the king, "May the king live forever! Why should my face not be sad, when the city, the place of my fathers' tombs, *lies* waste, and its gates are burned with fire?"

⁴Then the king said to me, "What do you request?"

So I prayed to the God of heaven. ⁵And I said to the king, "If it pleases the king, and if your servant has found favor in your sight, I ask that you send me to Judah, to the city of my fathers' tombs, that I may rebuild it."

⁶Then the king said to me (the queen also sitting beside him), "How long will your journey be? And when will you return?" So it pleased the king to send me; and I set him a time.

⁷Furthermore I said to the king, "If it pleases the king, let letters be given to me for the governors *of the region* beyond the River,*ᵃ* that they must permit me to pass through till I come to Judah, ⁸and a letter to Asaph the keeper of the king's forest, that he must give me timber to make beams for the gates of the citadel which *pertains* to the temple,*ᵃ* for the city wall, and for the house that I will occupy." And the king granted *them* to me according to the good hand of my God upon me.

⁹Then I went to the governors *in the region* beyond the River, and gave them the king's letters. Now the king had sent captains of the army and horsemen with me. ¹⁰When Sanballat the Horonite and Tobiah the Ammonite official*ᵃ* heard *of it,* they were deeply disturbed that a man had come to seek the well-being of the children of Israel.

Nehemiah Views the Wall of Jerusalem

¹¹So I came to Jerusalem and was there three days. ¹²Then I arose in the night, I and a few men with me; I told no one what my God had put in my heart to do at Jerusalem; nor was there any animal with me, except the one on which I rode. ¹³And I went out by night through the Valley Gate to the Serpent Well and the Refuse Gate, and viewed the walls of Jerusalem which were broken down and its gates which were burned with fire. ¹⁴Then I went on to the Fountain Gate and to the King's Pool, but *there was* no room for the animal under me to pass. ¹⁵So I went up in the night by the valley, and viewed the wall; then I turned back and entered by the Valley Gate, and so returned. ¹⁶And the officials did not know where I had gone or what I had done; I had

> **2:11–16** Nehemiah spent 3 days deciding which course to follow before telling anyone of his plan. Then he secretly viewed the terrain and surveyed the southern end of the city, observing its broken and burnt walls and gates.

2:7 *ᵃ*That is, the Euphrates, and so elsewhere in this book   2:8 *ᵃ*Literally *house*   2:10 *ᵃ*Literally *servant,* and so elsewhere in this book

not yet told the Jews, the priests, the nobles, the officials, or the others who did the work.

[17]Then I said to them, "You see the distress that we *are* in, how Jerusalem *lies* waste, and its gates are burned with fire. Come and let us build the wall of Jerusalem, that we may no longer be a reproach." [18]And I told them of the hand of my God which had been good upon me, and also of the king's words that he had spoken to me.

So they said, "Let us rise up and build." Then they set their hands to *this* good *work*.

[19]But when Sanballat the Horonite, Tobiah the Ammonite official, and Geshem the Arab heard *of it*, they laughed at us and despised us, and said, "What *is* this thing that you are doing? Will you rebel against the king?"

[20]So I answered them, and said to them, "The God of heaven Himself will prosper us; therefore we His servants will arise and build, but you have no heritage or right or memorial in Jerusalem."

Rebuilding the Wall

3 Then Eliashib the high priest rose up with his brethren the priests and built the Sheep Gate; they consecrated it and hung its doors. They built as far as the Tower of the Hundred,[a] *and* consecrated it, then as far as the Tower of Hananel. [2]Next to *Eliashib*[a] the men of Jericho built. And next to them Zaccur the son of Imri built.

> **3:1 Tower of the Hundred...Tower of Hananel.** This northern section of Jerusalem opened up to the central Benjamin plateau where enemy forces could attack most easily from the north. The remaining perimeter of the city was protected by a valley.

[3]Also the sons of Hassenaah built the Fish Gate; they laid its beams and hung its doors with its bolts and bars. [4]And next to them Meremoth the son of Urijah, the son of Koz,[a] made repairs. Next to them Meshullam the son of Berechiah, the son of Meshezabel, made repairs. Next to them Zadok the son of Baana made repairs. [5]Next to them the Tekoites made repairs;

3:1 [a]Hebrew *Hammeah,* also at 12:39   3:2 [a]Literally *On his hand*   3:4 [a]Or *Hakkoz*

What leadership qualities does Nehemiah illustrate by his life?

Like many biblical leaders, Nehemiah demonstrated an understanding of God's call over his life. Whether as cupbearer to a king or as the rebuilder of Jerusalem, Nehemiah pursued his goals with commitment, careful planning, strategic delegation, creative problem solving, focus on the task at hand, and a continual reliance on God, particularly regarding areas beyond his control. Each of the leadership qualities above can be illustrated from Nehemiah's successful completion of the effort to rebuild the walls of Jerusalem.

First, Nehemiah demonstrated his commitment by his interest and his deep concern over the condition of his fellow Jews in Judah. Next, Nehemiah prayed and planned. He claimed God's promise to bring His people back to the Promised Land, but he didn't assume that he would be part of God's action. He declared himself available (1:11; 2:5).

Even when he arrived in Jerusalem, Nehemiah personally inspected the need before he revealed his plans. Then he enlisted the help of the local leadership. He challenged them to take responsibility for the common good. He placed before them a very specific goal—to rebuild the wall. Workers were assigned to work on the wall where it ran closest to their own homes. That way they could see the benefit in having the protective barrier near where they lived.

As the work sped forward, Nehemiah did not allow himself to be distracted by attacks of various kings or tricks from enemies. He took threats seriously enough to arm the people but not so seriously that the work came to a halt. At every turn, we find Nehemiah conferring in prayer with God, placing every decision before the ultimate Decider. Nehemiah succeeded because he never lost sight of the true reasons for the work and the source of power with which to do the work.

but their nobles did not put their shoulders[a] to the work of their Lord.

3:5 nobles did not put their shoulders to the work of their Lord. One explanation, beyond just the laziness of the rich, is that these nobles had been pledged to Tobiah for personal gain.

[6]Moreover Jehoiada the son of Paseah and Meshullam the son of Besodeiah repaired the Old Gate; they laid its beams and hung its doors, with its bolts and bars.

[7]And next to them Melatiah the Gibeonite, Jadon the Meronothite, the men of Gibeon and Mizpah, repaired the residence[a] of the governor *of the region* beyond the River. [8]Next to him Uzziel the son of Harhaiah, one of the goldsmiths, made repairs. Also next to him Hananiah, one[a] of the perfumers, made repairs; and they fortified Jerusalem as far as the Broad Wall. [9]And next to them Rephaiah the son of Hur, leader of half the district of Jerusalem, made repairs. [10]Next to them Jedaiah the son of

3:5 [a]Literally *necks*   3:7 [a]Literally *throne*   3:8 [a]Literally *the son*

JERUSALEM IN NEHEMIAH'S DAY

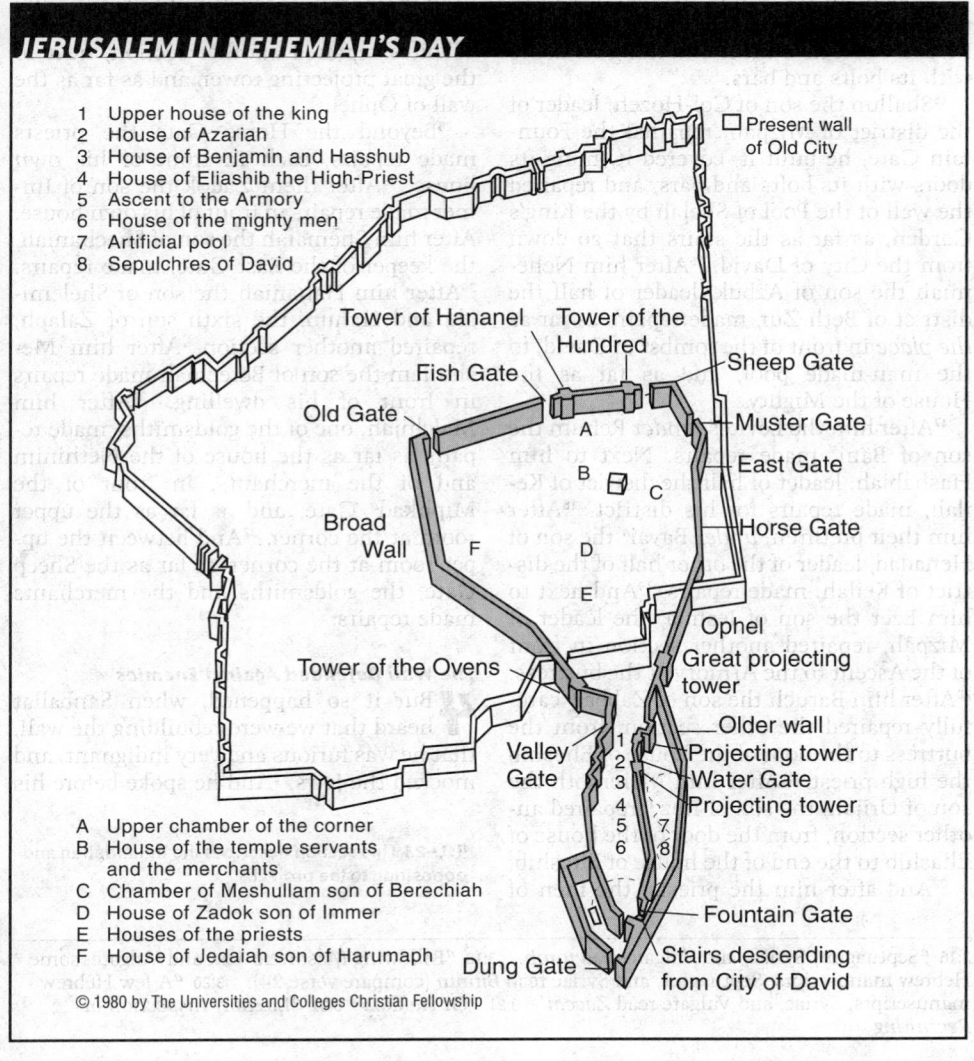

1 Upper house of the king
2 House of Azariah
3 House of Benjamin and Hasshub
4 House of Eliashib the High-Priest
5 Ascent to the Armory
6 House of the mighty men
7 Artificial pool
8 Sepulchres of David

☐ Present wall of Old City

Tower of Hananel
Tower of the Hundred
Fish Gate
Old Gate
Sheep Gate
Muster Gate
East Gate
Broad Wall
Horse Gate
Tower of the Ovens
Ophel
Great projecting tower
Older wall
Valley Gate
Projecting tower
Water Gate
Projecting tower
Fountain Gate
Dung Gate
Stairs descending from City of David

A Upper chamber of the corner
B House of the temple servants and the merchants
C Chamber of Meshullam son of Berechiah
D House of Zadok son of Immer
E Houses of the priests
F House of Jedaiah son of Harumaph

Harumaph made repairs in front of his house. And next to him Hattush the son of Hashabniah made repairs.

¹¹Malchijah the son of Harim and Hashub the son of Pahath-Moab repaired another section, as well as the Tower of the Ovens. ¹²And next to him was Shallum the son of Hallohesh, leader of half the district of Jerusalem; he and his daughters made repairs.

¹³Hanun and the inhabitants of Zanoah repaired the Valley Gate. They built it, hung its doors with its bolts and bars, and *repaired* a thousand cubits of the wall as far as the Refuse Gate.

¹⁴Malchijah the son of Rechab, leader of the district of Beth Haccerem, repaired the Refuse Gate; he built it and hung its doors with its bolts and bars.

¹⁵Shallun the son of Col-Hozeh, leader of the district of Mizpah, repaired the Fountain Gate; he built it, covered it, hung its doors with its bolts and bars, and repaired the wall of the Pool of Shelah by the King's Garden, as far as the stairs that go down from the City of David. ¹⁶After him Nehemiah the son of Azbuk, leader of half the district of Beth Zur, made repairs as far as *the place* in front of the tombs*ᵃ* of David, to the man-made pool, and as far as the House of the Mighty.

¹⁷After him the Levites, *under* Rehum the son of Bani, made repairs. Next to him Hashabiah, leader of half the district of Keilah, made repairs for his district. ¹⁸After him their brethren, *under* Bavai*ᵃ* the son of Henadad, leader of the *other* half of the district of Keilah, made repairs. ¹⁹And next to him Ezer the son of Jeshua, the leader of Mizpah, repaired another section in front of the Ascent to the Armory at the buttress. ²⁰After him Baruch the son of Zabbai*ᵃ* carefully repaired the other section, from the buttress to the door of the house of Eliashib the high priest. ²¹After him Meremoth the son of Urijah, the son of Koz,*ᵃ* repaired another section, from the door of the house of Eliashib to the end of the house of Eliashib.

²²And after him the priests, the men of the plain, made repairs. ²³After him Benjamin and Hasshub made repairs opposite their house. After them Azariah the son of Maaseiah, the son of Ananiah, made repairs by his house. ²⁴After him Binnui the son of Henadad repaired another section, from the house of Azariah to the buttress, even as far as the corner. ²⁵Palal the son of Uzai *made repairs* opposite the buttress, and on the tower which projects from the king's upper house that *was* by the court of the prison. After him Pedaiah the son of Parosh *made repairs.*

²⁶Moreover the Nethinim who dwelt in Ophel *made repairs* as far as *the place* in front of the Water Gate toward the east, and on the projecting tower. ²⁷After them the Tekoites repaired another section, next to the great projecting tower, and as far as the wall of Ophel.

²⁸Beyond the Horse Gate the priests made repairs, each in front of his *own* house. ²⁹After them Zadok the son of Immer made repairs in front of his *own* house. After him Shemaiah the son of Shechaniah, the keeper of the East Gate, made repairs. ³⁰After him Hananiah the son of Shelemiah, and Hanun, the sixth son of Zalaph, repaired another section. After him Meshullam the son of Berechiah made repairs in front of his dwelling. ³¹After him Malchijah, one of the goldsmiths, made repairs as far as the house of the Nethinim and of the merchants, in front of the Miphkad*ᵃ* Gate, and as far as the upper room at the corner. ³²And between the upper room at the corner, as far as the Sheep Gate, the goldsmiths and the merchants made repairs.

The Wall Defended Against Enemies

4 But it so happened, when Sanballat heard that we were rebuilding the wall, that he was furious and very indignant, and mocked the Jews. ²And he spoke before his

---

4:1–23 This section describes the intimidation and opposition to the project.

3:16 *ᵃ*Septuagint, Syriac, and Vulgate read *tomb*.   3:18 *ᵃ*Following Masoretic Text and Vulgate; some Hebrew manuscripts, Septuagint, and Syriac read *Binnui* (compare verse 24).   3:20 *ᵃ*A few Hebrew manuscripts, Syriac, and Vulgate read *Zaccai*.   3:21 *ᵃ*Or *Hakkoz*   3:31 *ᵃ*Literally *Inspection* or *Recruiting*

brethren and the army of Samaria, and said, "What are these feeble Jews doing? Will they fortify themselves? Will they offer sacrifices? Will they complete it in a day? Will they revive the stones from the heaps of rubbish—*stones* that are burned?"

³Now Tobiah the Ammonite *was* beside him, and he said, "Whatever they build, if even a fox goes up *on it*, he will break down their stone wall."

⁴Hear, O our God, for we are despised; turn their reproach on their own heads, and give them as plunder to a land of captivity! ⁵Do not cover their iniquity, and do not let their sin be blotted out from before You; for they have provoked *You* to anger before the builders.

⁶So we built the wall, and the entire wall was joined together up to half its *height*, for the people had a mind to work.

⁷Now it happened, when Sanballat, Tobiah, the Arabs, the Ammonites, and the Ashdodites heard that the walls of Jerusalem were being restored and the gaps were beginning to be closed, that they became very angry, ⁸and all of them conspired together to come *and* attack Jerusalem and create confusion. ⁹Nevertheless we made our prayer to our God, and because of them we set a watch against them day and night.

¹⁰Then Judah said, "The strength of the laborers is failing, and *there is* so much rubbish that we are not able to build the wall."

¹¹And our adversaries said, "They will neither know nor see anything, till we come into their midst and kill them and cause the work to cease."

¹²So it was, when the Jews who dwelt near them came, that they told us ten times, "From whatever place you turn, *they will be* upon us."

¹³Therefore I positioned *men* behind the lower parts of the wall, at the openings; and I set the people according to their families, with their swords, their spears, and their bows. ¹⁴And I looked, and arose and said to the nobles, to the leaders, and to the rest of the people, "Do not be afraid of them. Remember the Lord, great and awesome, and fight for your brethren, your sons, your daughters, your wives, and your houses."

¹⁵And it happened, when our enemies heard that it was known to us, and *that* God had brought their plot to nothing, that all of us returned to the wall, everyone to his work. ¹⁶So it was, from that time on, *that* half of my servants worked at construction, while the other half held the spears, the shields, the bows, and *wore* armor; and the leaders *were* behind all the house of Judah. ¹⁷Those who built on the wall, and those who carried burdens, loaded themselves so that with one hand they worked at construction, and with the other held a weapon. ¹⁸Every one of the builders had his sword girded at his side as he built. And the one who sounded the trumpet *was* beside me.

4:13–18a positioned *men*. Nehemiah and the others were given word that Sanballat had mustered the army of Samaria. God allowed the Jews to know of the strategy so they would report it to Judah's leaders. They carried weapons as they worked in case of attack. Nehemiah and those he led gave God the glory for their victories and construction successes.

SEVEN ATTEMPTS TO STOP NEHEMIAH'S WORK

1. 2:19   Sanballat, Tobiah, and Geshem mocked Nehemiah.
2. 4:1–3   Sanballat and Tobiah mocked Nehemiah.
3. 4:7–23   The enemy threatened a military attack.
4. 6:1–4   Sanballat and Geshem attempted to lure Nehemiah outside of Jerusalem to Ono.
5. 6:5–9   Sanballat threatened Nehemiah with false charges.
6. 6:10–14   Shemaiah, Noadiah, and others were paid to prophesy falsely and discredit Nehemiah.
7. 6:17–19   Tobiah had spies in Jerusalem and wrote Nehemiah letters in order to frighten him.

¹⁹Then I said to the nobles, the rulers, and the rest of the people, "The work *is* great and extensive, and we are separated far from one another on the wall. ²⁰Wherever you hear the sound of the trumpet, rally to us there. Our God will fight for us."

²¹So we labored in the work, and half of *the men*[a] held the spears from daybreak until the stars appeared. ²²At the same time I also said to the people, "Let each man and his servant stay at night in Jerusalem, that they may be our guard by night and a working party by day." ²³So neither I, my brethren, my servants, nor the men of the guard who followed me took off our clothes, *except* that everyone took them off for washing.

Nehemiah Deals with Oppression

5 And there was a great outcry of the people and their wives against their Jewish brethren. ²For there were those who said, "We, our sons, and our daughters *are* many; therefore let us get grain, that we may eat and live."

> **5:1–5 Jewish brethren.** This could refer to the nobles who would not work and who had alliances with the enemies. They exploited the people, forcing them to sell their homes and children. By law, the children could be released through the remission of debts which occurred every 7 years. But the people were poor and could not "buy back" the enslaved children. They had to borrow to pay their taxes, and they were exhausted from hard labor and from the constant harassment of enemies.

³There were also *some* who said, "We have mortgaged our lands and vineyards and houses, that we might buy grain because of the famine."

⁴There were also those who said, "We have borrowed money for the king's tax *on* our lands and vineyards. ⁵Yet now our flesh *is* as the flesh of our brethren, our children as their children; and indeed we are forcing our sons and our daughters to be slaves, and *some* of our daughters have been brought into slavery. *It is* not in our power to *redeem them*, for other men have our lands and vineyards."

⁶And I became very angry when I heard their outcry and these words. ⁷After serious thought, I rebuked the nobles and rulers, and said to them, "Each of you is exacting usury from his brother." So I called a great assembly against them. ⁸And I said to them, "According to our ability we have redeemed our Jewish brethren who were sold to the nations. Now indeed, will you even sell your brethren? Or should they be sold to us?"

> **5:7 exacting usury.** Usury refers to either normal or excessive interest. The Jews were forbidden to take interest from their brothers when loaning anything. If the person was destitute, they should generously consider it a gift (see Lev. 25:36,37; Ps. 15:5). Interest could, however, be taken from foreigners, and interest loans were known to exceed 50 percent in ancient nations. This usury took advantage of people's desperation and was impossible to repay, reducing the debtors to permanent slavery.

Then they were silenced and found nothing *to say.* ⁹Then I said, "What you are doing *is* not good. Should you not walk in the fear of our God because of the reproach of the nations, our enemies? ¹⁰I also, *with* my brethren and my servants, am lending them money and grain. Please, let us stop this usury! ¹¹Restore now to them, even this day, their lands, their vineyards, their olive groves, and their houses, also a hundredth of the money and the grain, the new wine and the oil, that you have charged them."

¹²So they said, "We will restore *it*, and will require nothing from them; we will do as you say."

Then I called the priests, and required an oath from them that they would do according to this promise. ¹³Then I shook out the fold of my garment[a] and said, "So may God shake out each man from his house, and from his property, who does not perform this promise. Even thus may he be shaken out and emptied."

And all the assembly said, "Amen!" and praised the LORD. Then the people did according to this promise.

The Generosity of Nehemiah

¹⁴Moreover, from the time that I was appointed to be their governor in the land of Judah, from the twentieth year until the

---

4:21 [a]Literally *them*   5:13 [a]Literally *my lap*

thirty-second year of King Artaxerxes, twelve years, neither I nor my brothers ate the governor's provisions. ¹⁵But the former governors who *were* before me laid burdens on the people, and took from them bread and wine, besides forty shekels of silver. Yes, even their servants bore rule over the people, but I did not do so, because of the fear of God. ¹⁶Indeed, I also continued the work on this wall, and we*^a* did not buy any land. All my servants *were* gathered there for the work.

¹⁷And at my table *were* one hundred and fifty Jews and rulers, besides those who came to us from the nations around us. ¹⁸Now *that* which was prepared daily *was* one ox *and* six choice sheep. Also fowl were prepared for me, and once every ten days an abundance of all kinds of wine. Yet in spite of this I did not demand the governor's provisions, because the bondage was heavy on this people.

¹⁹Remember me, my God, for good, *according to* all that I have done for this people.

Conspiracy Against Nehemiah

6 Now it happened when Sanballat, Tobiah, Geshem the Arab, and the rest of our enemies heard that I had rebuilt the wall, and *that* there were no breaks left in it (though at that time I had not hung the doors in the gates), ²that Sanballat and Geshem sent to me, saying, "Come, let us meet together among the villages in the plain of Ono." But they thought to do me harm.

³So I sent messengers to them, saying, "I *am* doing a great work, so that I cannot come down. Why should the work cease while I leave it and go down to you?" ⁴But they sent me this message four times, and I answered them in the same manner.

⁵Then Sanballat sent his servant to me as before, the fifth time, with an open letter in his hand. ⁶In it *was* written:

It is reported among the nations, and Geshem*^a* says, *that* you and the Jews plan to rebel; therefore, according to these rumors, you are rebuilding the

wall, that you may be their king. ⁷And you have also appointed prophets to proclaim concerning you at Jerusalem, saying, "*There is* a king in Judah!" Now these matters will be reported to the king. So come, therefore, and let us consult together.

6:6 It is reported among the nations. The letter suggested that Nehemiah's intent to revolt was known and that the king of Persia would find out if Nehemiah did not come to the requested conference. **you and the Jews plan to rebel.** This information would have brought Persian troops against the Jews had it been true. Judah had a reputation for breaking its allegiances with overlord kings, but this time it was not the case.

⁸Then I sent to him, saying, "No such things as you say are being done, but you invent them in your own heart."

⁹For they all *were trying to* make us afraid, saying, "Their hands will be weakened in the work, and it will not be done." Now therefore, *O God*, strengthen my hands.

¹⁰Afterward I came to the house of Shemaiah the son of Delaiah, the son of Mehetabel, who *was* a secret informer; and he said, "Let us meet together in the house of God, within the temple, and let us close the doors of the temple, for they are coming to kill you; indeed, at night they will come to kill you."

6:10 secret informer. Nehemiah's enemies decided to hire a false prophet, Shemaiah, to lure him into the Holy Place in the temple for refuge from a murder plot. Shemaiah was the son of a priest, and a friend of Nehemiah. This plan would give Nehemiah's enemies grounds to raise an evil report on him, as it would be a desecration of the house of God if Nehemiah, who was not a priest, were to enter the Holy Place. It would cause the people to question his courage.

¹¹And I said, "Should such a man as I flee? And who *is there* such as I who would go into the temple to save his life? I will not go in!" ¹²Then I perceived that God had not sent him at all, but that he pronounced *this* prophecy against me because Tobiah and Sanballat had hired him. ¹³For this reason

---

5:16 *^a*Following Masoretic Text; Septuagint, Syriac, and Vulgate read *I.*   6:6 *^a*Hebrew *Gashmu*

he *was* hired, that I should be afraid and act that way and sin, so *that* they might have *cause* for an evil report, that they might reproach me.

¹⁴My God, remember Tobiah and Sanballat, according to these their works, and the prophetess Noadiah and the rest of the prophets who would have made me afraid.

The Wall Completed

¹⁵So the wall was finished on the twenty-fifth *day* of Elul, in fifty-two days. ¹⁶And it happened, when all our enemies heard *of it*, and all the nations around us saw *these things*, that they were very disheartened in their own eyes; for they perceived that this work was done by our God.

> **6:16 this work was done by our God.** Nehemiah's enemies concluded that God works through faithful people.

¹⁷Also in those days the nobles of Judah sent many letters to Tobiah, and *the letters of* Tobiah came to them. ¹⁸For many in Judah were pledged to him, because he was the son-in-law of Shechaniah the son of Arah, and his son Jehohanan had married the daughter of Meshullam the son of Berechiah. ¹⁹Also they reported his good deeds before me, and reported my words to him. Tobiah sent letters to frighten me.

7 Then it was, when the wall was built and I had hung the doors, when the gatekeepers, the singers, and the Levites had been appointed, ²that I gave the charge of Jerusalem to my brother Hanani, and Hananiah the leader of the citadel, for he *was* a faithful man and feared God more than many. ³And I said to them, "Do not let the gates of Jerusalem be opened until the sun is hot; and while they stand *guard*, let them shut and bar the doors; and appoint guards from

> **7:3** City gates were opened at sunrise and closed at sunset. Nehemiah recommended that this not be done because of the hostility of the enemies. He advised that the gates be kept shut until late in the morning and that they be guarded by sentinels at watch stations and in front of vulnerable homes.

among the inhabitants of Jerusalem, one at his watch station and another in front of his own house."

The Captives Who Returned to Jerusalem

⁴Now the city *was* large and spacious, but the people in it *were* few, and the houses *were* not rebuilt. ⁵Then my God put it into my heart to gather the nobles, the rulers, and the people, that they might be registered by genealogy. And I found a register of the genealogy of those who had come up in the first *return*, and found written in it:

6   These*ª* *are* the people of the province who came back from the captivity, of those who had been carried away, whom Nebuchadnezzar the king of Babylon had carried away, and who returned to Jerusalem and Judah, everyone to his city.

7   Those who came with Zerubbabel *were* Jeshua, Nehemiah, Azariah, Raamiah, Nahamani, Mordecai, Bilshan, Mispereth,*ª* Bigvai, Nehum, and Baanah.

The number of the men of the people of Israel: ⁸the sons of Parosh, two thousand one hundred and seventy-two;
⁹the sons of Shephatiah, three hundred and seventy-two;
¹⁰the sons of Arah, six hundred and fifty-two;
¹¹the sons of Pahath-Moab, of the sons of Jeshua and Joab, two thousand eight hundred and eighteen;
¹²the sons of Elam, one thousand two hundred and fifty-four;
¹³the sons of Zattu, eight hundred and forty-five;
¹⁴the sons of Zaccai, seven hundred and sixty;
¹⁵the sons of Binnui,*ª* six hundred and forty-eight;
¹⁶the sons of Bebai, six hundred and twenty-eight;
¹⁷the sons of Azgad, two thousand three hundred and twenty-two;

7:6 *ª*Compare verses 6–72 with Ezra 2:1–70   7:7 *ª*Spelled *Mispar* in Ezra 2:2   7:15 *ª*Spelled *Bani* in Ezra 2:10

¹⁸the sons of Adonikam, six hundred and sixty-seven;

¹⁹the sons of Bigvai, two thousand and sixty-seven;

²⁰the sons of Adin, six hundred and fifty-five;

²¹the sons of Ater of Hezekiah, ninety-eight;

²²the sons of Hashum, three hundred and twenty-eight;

²³the sons of Bezai, three hundred and twenty-four;

²⁴the sons of Hariph,*a* one hundred and twelve;

²⁵the sons of Gibeon,*a* ninety-five;

²⁶the men of Bethlehem and Netophah, one hundred and eighty-eight;

²⁷the men of Anathoth, one hundred and twenty-eight;

²⁸the men of Beth Azmaveth,*a* forty-two;

²⁹the men of Kirjath Jearim, Chephirah, and Beeroth, seven hundred and forty-three;

³⁰the men of Ramah and Geba, six hundred and twenty-one;

³¹the men of Michmas, one hundred and twenty-two;

³²the men of Bethel and Ai, one hundred and twenty-three;

³³the men of the other Nebo, fifty-two;

³⁴the sons of the other Elam, one thousand two hundred and fifty-four;

³⁵the sons of Harim, three hundred and twenty;

³⁶the sons of Jericho, three hundred and forty-five;

³⁷the sons of Lod, Hadid, and Ono, seven hundred and twenty-one;

³⁸the sons of Senaah, three thousand nine hundred and thirty.

39 The priests: the sons of Jedaiah, of the house of Jeshua, nine hundred and seventy-three;

⁴⁰the sons of Immer, one thousand and fifty-two;

⁴¹the sons of Pashhur, one thousand two hundred and forty-seven;

⁴²the sons of Harim, one thousand and seventeen.

43 The Levites: the sons of Jeshua, of Kadmiel, *and* of the sons of Hodevah,*a* seventy-four.

44 The singers: the sons of Asaph, one hundred and forty-eight.

45 The gatekeepers: the sons of Shallum, the sons of Ater, the sons of Talmon, the sons of Akkub, the sons of Hatita, the sons of Shobai, one hundred and thirty-eight.

7:24 *a*Called *Jorah* in Ezra 2:18   7:25 *a*Called *Gibbar* in Ezra 2:20   7:28 *a*Called *Azmaveth* in Ezra 2:24   7:43 *a*Spelled *Hodaviah* in Ezra 2:40

How does Nehemiah fit into the time line of world history?

It is unclear how Nehemiah became King Artaxerxes' cupbearer, but the fact that Esther was the king's stepmother may have inclined the king to consider a Jew for such a trusted position. When Nehemiah carried out his mission to rebuild the walls of Jerusalem, the Persian Empire had been dominant for almost 100 years. King Cyrus' decree of repatriation given back in 539 B.C. had instigated a group of Jews to return to Israel under Zerubbabel. Their desperate state almost a century later spurred Nehemiah into action.

Ancient Egyptian documents (Elephantine papyri) dated around the 5th century B.C. independently confirm part of Nehemiah's account. Sanballat the governor of Samaria (2:19), Jehohanan (6:18; 12:23) and Nehemiah himself receive mention.

The events recorded in Nehemiah, along with Malachi's prophecies, make up the final inspired writings of the Old Testament. God chose to then remain silent for 400 years. That silence ended with the announcements of John the Baptist's and Jesus' births.

46 The Nethinim: the sons of Ziha,
the sons of Hasupha,
the sons of Tabbaoth,
47 the sons of Keros,
the sons of Sia,[a]
the sons of Padon,
48 the sons of Lebana,[a]
the sons of Hagaba,[b]
the sons of Salmai,[c]
49 the sons of Hanan,
the sons of Giddel,
the sons of Gahar,
50 the sons of Reaiah,
the sons of Rezin,
the sons of Nekoda,
51 the sons of Gazzam,
the sons of Uzza,
the sons of Paseah,
52 the sons of Besai,
the sons of Meunim,
the sons of Nephishesim,[a]
53 the sons of Bakbuk,
the sons of Hakupha,
the sons of Harhur,
54 the sons of Bazlith,[a]
the sons of Mehida,
the sons of Harsha,
55 the sons of Barkos,
the sons of Sisera,
the sons of Tamah,
56 the sons of Neziah,
and the sons of Hatipha.

57 The sons of Solomon's servants: the
sons of Sotai,
the sons of Sophereth,
the sons of Perida,[a]
58 the sons of Jaala,
the sons of Darkon,
the sons of Giddel,
59 the sons of Shephatiah,
the sons of Hattil,
the sons of Pochereth of Zebaim,
and the children of Amon.[a]
60 All the Nethinim, and the sons of
Solomon's servants, were three
hundred and ninety-two.

61 And these were the ones who came
up from Tel Melah, Tel Harsha,
Cherub, Addon,[a] and Immer, but they
could not identify their father's house
nor their lineage, whether they were
of Israel: 62 the sons of Delaiah,
the sons of Tobiah,
the sons of Nekoda, six hundred and
forty-two;
63 and of the priests: the sons of
Habaiah,
the sons of Koz,[a]
the sons of Barzillai, who took a wife
of the daughters of Barzillai the
Gileadite, and was called by their
name.
64 These sought their listing among
those who were registered by
genealogy, but it was not found;
therefore they were excluded from the
priesthood as defiled. 65 And the
governor[a] said to them that they
should not eat of the most holy things
till a priest could consult with the
Urim and Thummim.

> **7:65 consult with the Urim and Thummim.** This
> was one of the methods used to discern the will of
> God.

66 Altogether the whole assembly was
forty-two thousand three hundred and
sixty, 67 besides their male and female
servants, of whom there were seven
thousand three hundred and thirty-
seven; and they had two hundred and
forty-five men and women singers.
68 Their horses were seven hundred
and thirty-six, their mules two
hundred and forty-five, 69 their camels
four hundred and thirty-five, and
donkeys six thousand seven hundred
and twenty.

70 And some of the heads of the fathers'
houses gave to the work. The
governor[a] gave to the treasury one
thousand gold drachmas, fifty basins,
and five hundred and thirty priestly
garments. 71 Some of the heads of the

7:47 [a]Spelled Siaha in Ezra 2:44   7:48 [a]Masoretic Text reads Lebanah.   [b]Masoretic Text reads
Hogabah.   [c]Or Shalmai, or Shamlai   7:52 [a]Spelled Nephusim in Ezra 2:50   7:54 [a]Spelled Bazluth in
Ezra 2:52   7:57 [a]Spelled Peruda in Ezra 2:55   7:59 [a]Spelled Ami in Ezra 2:57   7:61 [a]Spelled Addan
in Ezra 2:59   7:63 [a]Or Hakkoz   7:65 [a]Hebrew Tirshatha   7:70 [a]Hebrew Tirshatha

fathers' *houses* gave to the treasury of the work twenty thousand gold drachmas, and two thousand two hundred silver minas. [72]And that which the rest of the people gave *was* twenty thousand gold drachmas, two thousand silver minas, and sixty-seven priestly garments.

[73]So the priests, the Levites, the gatekeepers, the singers, *some* of the people, the Nethinim, and all Israel dwelt in their cities.

Ezra Reads the Law

When the seventh month came, the children of Israel *were* in their cities.

8 Now all the people gathered together as one man in the open square that *was* in front of the Water Gate; and they told Ezra the scribe to bring the Book of the Law of Moses, which the LORD had commanded Israel. [2]So Ezra the priest brought the Law before the assembly of men and women and all who *could* hear with understanding on the first day of the seventh month. [3]Then he read from it in the open square that *was* in front of the Water Gate from morning until midday, before the men and women and those who could understand; and the ears of all the people *were attentive* to the Book of the Law.

8:1,2 the Book...the Law. Ezra brought the Law of the Lord that he desired to study, practice and teach to the people per their request (see Ezra 7:10). Such a reading of the Law, then on a scroll, was required every 7 years at the Feast of Tabernacles (see Deut. 31:10–13). Throughout the entire reading the people stood out of respect, as if God were there Himself. It had been neglected during the Babylonian captivity.

[4]So Ezra the scribe stood on a platform of wood which they had made for the purpose; and beside him, at his right hand, stood Mattithiah, Shema, Anaiah, Urijah, Hilkiah, and Maaseiah; and at his left hand Pedaiah, Mishael, Malchijah, Hashum, Hashbadana, Zechariah, *and* Meshullam. [5]And Ezra opened the book in the sight of all the people, for he was *standing* above all the people; and when he opened it, all the

people stood up. [6]And Ezra blessed the LORD, the great God.

Then all the people answered, "Amen, Amen!" while lifting up their hands. And they bowed their heads and worshiped the LORD with *their* faces to the ground.

[7]Also Jeshua, Bani, Sherebiah, Jamin, Akkub, Shabbethai, Hodijah, Maaseiah, Kelita, Azariah, Jozabad, Hanan, Pelaiah, and the Levites, helped the people to understand the Law; and the people *stood* in their place. [8]So they read distinctly from the book, in the Law of God; and they gave the sense, and helped *them* to understand the reading.

[9]And Nehemiah, who *was* the governor,[a] Ezra the priest *and* scribe, and the Levites who taught the people said to all the people, "This day *is* holy to the LORD your God; do not mourn nor weep." For all the people wept, when they heard the words of the Law.

8:9 wept, when they heard the words of the Law. Hearing the Law convicted them of their violations, causing them to weep from grief (v. 11) and the punishment of captivity brought on by their sin.

[10]Then he said to them, "Go your way, eat the fat, drink the sweet, and send portions to those for whom nothing is prepared; for *this* day *is* holy to our Lord. Do not sorrow, for the joy of the LORD is your strength." [11]So the Levites quieted all the people, saying, "Be still, for the day *is* holy; do not be grieved." [12]And all the people went their way to eat and drink, to send portions and rejoice greatly, because they understood the words that were declared to them.

The Feast of Tabernacles

[13]Now on the second day the heads of the fathers' *houses* of all the people, with the priests and Levites, were gathered to Ezra the scribe, in order to understand the words of the Law. [14]And they found written in the Law, which the LORD had commanded by Moses, that the children of Israel should dwell in booths during the feast of the seventh month, [15]and that they should announce and proclaim in all their cities and

in Jerusalem, saying, "Go out to the mountain, and bring olive branches, branches of oil trees, myrtle branches, palm branches, and branches of leafy trees, to make booths, as *it is* written."

¹⁶Then the people went out and brought *them* and made themselves booths, each one on the roof of his house, or in their courtyards or the courts of the house of God, and in the open square of the Water Gate and in the open square of the Gate of Ephraim. ¹⁷So the whole assembly of those who had returned from the captivity made booths and sat under the booths; for since the days of Joshua the son of Nun until that day the children of Israel had not done so. And there was very great gladness. ¹⁸Also day by day, from the first day until the last day, he read from the Book of the Law of God. And they kept the feast seven days; and on the eighth day *there was* a sacred assembly, according to the *prescribed* manner.

The People Confess Their Sins

9 Now on the twenty-fourth day of this month the children of Israel were assembled with fasting, in sackcloth, and with dust on their heads.*ᵃ* ²Then those of Israelite lineage separated themselves from all foreigners; and they stood and confessed their sins and the iniquities of their fathers. ³And they stood up in their place and read from the Book of the Law of the LORD their God *for one*-fourth of the day; and *for another* fourth they confessed and worshiped the LORD their God.

> **9:2 separated themselves from all foreigners.** This call to divorce all heathen wives was necessary since the previous call, prompted by Ezra 13 years ago, was only partially successful. A complete divorce from heathen wives was successful.

⁴Then Jeshua, Bani, Kadmiel, Shebaniah, Bunni, Sherebiah, Bani, *and* Chenani stood on the stairs of the Levites and cried out with a loud voice to the LORD their God. ⁵And the Levites, Jeshua, Kadmiel, Bani, Hashabniah, Sherebiah, Hodijah, Shebaniah, *and* Pethahiah, said:

" Stand up *and* bless the LORD your God
Forever and ever!

" Blessed be Your glorious name,
Which is exalted above all blessing and praise!
6   You alone *are* the LORD;
You have made heaven,
The heaven of heavens, with all their host,
The earth and everything on it,
The seas and all that is in them,
And You preserve them all.
The host of heaven worships You.

7   " You *are* the LORD God,
Who chose Abram,
And brought him out of Ur of the Chaldeans,
And gave him the name Abraham;
8   You found his heart faithful before You,
And made a covenant with him
To give the land of the Canaanites,
The Hittites, the Amorites,
The Perizzites, the Jebusites,
And the Girgashites—
To give *it* to his descendants.
You have performed Your words,
For You *are* righteous.

> **9:8 a covenant with him to give the land.** This was a covenant of salvation, but also involved the Promised Land. Since God had returned them from the land from captivity, they emphasized that portion of the covenant.

9   " You saw the affliction of our fathers in Egypt,
And heard their cry by the Red Sea.
10   You showed signs and wonders against Pharaoh,
Against all his servants,
And against all the people of his land.
For You knew that they acted proudly against them.
So You made a name for Yourself, as *it is* this day.
11   And You divided the sea before them,
So that they went through the midst of the sea on the dry land;

9:1 *ᵃ*Literally *earth on them*

And their persecutors You threw into
   the deep,
As a stone into the mighty waters.
12 Moreover You led them by day with a
   cloudy pillar,
And by night with a pillar of fire,
To give them light on the road
Which they should travel.
13 "You came down also on Mount Sinai,
And spoke with them from heaven,
And gave them just ordinances and
   true laws,
Good statutes and commandments.
14 You made known to them Your holy
   Sabbath,
And commanded them precepts,
   statutes and laws,
By the hand of Moses Your servant.
15 You gave them bread from heaven for
   their hunger,
And brought them water out of the
   rock for their thirst,
And told them to go in to possess the
   land
Which You had sworn to give them.
16 "But they and our fathers acted
   proudly,
Hardened their necks,
And did not heed Your
   commandments.
17 They refused to obey,
And they were not mindful of Your
   wonders
That You did among them.
But they hardened their necks,
And in their rebellion*a*
They appointed a leader
To return to their bondage.
But You *are* God,
Ready to pardon,
Gracious and merciful,
Slow to anger,

> **9:17 They appointed a leader.** The Hebrew of this
> statement is essentially the same as Num. 14:4, which
> records the people's discontent with God's plan and
> Moses' leadership.

Abundant in kindness,
And did not forsake them.
18 "Even when they made a molded calf
   for themselves,
And said, 'This *is* your god
That brought you up out of Egypt,'
And worked great provocations,
19 Yet in Your manifold mercies
You did not forsake them in the
   wilderness.
The pillar of the cloud did not depart
   from them by day,
To lead them on the road;
Nor the pillar of fire by night,
To show them light,
And the way they should go.
20 You also gave Your good Spirit to
   instruct them,
And did not withhold Your manna
   from their mouth,
And gave them water for their thirst.
21 Forty years You sustained them in the
   wilderness;
They lacked nothing;
Their clothes did not wear out*a*
And their feet did not swell.
22 "Moreover You gave them kingdoms
   and nations,
And divided them into districts.*a*
So they took possession of the land of
   Sihon,
The land of*b* the king of Heshbon,
And the land of Og king of Bashan.

> **9:22 gave them kingdoms and nations.** Canaan was
> made of several politically semi-autonomous groups
> that were loosely connected under the weakened
> Egyptian authority. It was divided into tribal districts,
> thus establishing Israel's portion of the Land.

23 You also multiplied their children as
   the stars of heaven,
And brought them into the land
Which You had told their fathers
To go in and possess.
24 So the people went in
And possessed the land;

9:17 *a*Following Masoretic Text and Vulgate; Septuagint reads *in Egypt*.   9:21 *a*Compare
Deuteronomy 29:5   9:22 *a*Literally *corners*   *b*Following Masoretic Text and Vulgate; Septuagint
omits *The land of*.

You subdued before them the
inhabitants of the land,
The Canaanites,
And gave them into their hands,
With their kings
And the people of the land,
That they might do with them as they
wished.
25 And they took strong cities and a rich
land,
And possessed houses full of all goods,
Cisterns *already* dug, vineyards, olive
groves,
And fruit trees in abundance.
So they ate and were filled and grew
fat,
And delighted themselves in Your
great goodness.

26 "Nevertheless they were disobedient
And rebelled against You,
Cast Your law behind their backs
And killed Your prophets, who
testified against them
To turn them to Yourself;
And they worked great provocations.
27 Therefore You delivered them into the
hand of their enemies,
Who oppressed them;
And in the time of their trouble,
When they cried to You,
You heard from heaven;
And according to Your abundant
mercies
You gave them deliverers who saved
them
From the hand of their enemies.

28 "But after they had rest,
They again did evil before You.
Therefore You left them in the hand
of their enemies,
So that they had dominion over them;
Yet when they returned and cried out
to You,
You heard from heaven;
And many times You delivered them
according to Your mercies,
29 And testified against them,
That You might bring them back to
Your law.
Yet they acted proudly,

And did not heed Your
commandments,
But sinned against Your judgments,
'Which if a man does, he shall live by
them.'[a]
And they shrugged their shoulders,
Stiffened their necks,
And would not hear.
30 Yet for many years You had patience
with them,
And testified against them by Your
Spirit in Your prophets.
Yet they would not listen;
Therefore You gave them into the
hand of the peoples of the lands.
31 Nevertheless in Your great mercy
You did not utterly consume them nor
forsake them;
For You *are* God, gracious and
merciful.

32 "Now therefore, our God,
The great, the mighty, and awesome
God,
Who keeps covenant and mercy:
Do not let all the trouble seem small
before You
That has come upon us,
Our kings and our princes,
Our priests and our prophets,
Our fathers and on all Your people,
From the days of the kings of Assyria
until this day.
33 However You *are* just in all that has
befallen us;
For You have dealt faithfully,
But we have done wickedly.
34 Neither our kings nor our princes,
Our priests nor our fathers,
Have kept Your law,
Nor heeded Your commandments and
Your testimonies,
With which You testified against
them.
35 For they have not served You in their
kingdom,
Or in the many good *things* that You
gave them,
Or in the large and rich land which
You set before them;
Nor did they turn from their wicked
works.

9:29 [a]Leviticus 18:5

³⁶ "Here we *are,* servants today!
And the land that You gave to our
     fathers,
To eat its fruit and its bounty,
Here we *are,* servants in it!

³⁷ And it yields much increase to the
     kings
You have set over us,
Because of our sins;
Also they have dominion over our
     bodies and our cattle
At their pleasure;
And we *are* in great distress.

³⁸ "And because of all this,
We make a sure *covenant* and write
     it;
Our leaders, our Levites, *and* our
     priests seal *it."*

> **9:38 We make a sure *covenant* and write *it*.** A cov-
> enant was a formalized relationship with commit-
> ments to loyalty. In this case, the nation initiated a
> covenant with God.

The People Who Sealed the Covenant

10 Now those who placed *their* seal on
the document were:

Nehemiah the governor, the son of
Hacaliah, and Zedekiah, ²Seraiah,
Azariah, Jeremiah, ³Pashhur,
Amariah, Malchijah, ⁴Hattush,
Shebaniah, Malluch, ⁵Harim,
Meremoth, Obadiah, ⁶Daniel,
Ginnethon, Baruch, ⁷Meshullam,
Abijah, Mijamin, ⁸Maaziah, Bilgai,
and Shemaiah. These were the
priests.

     ⁹The Levites: Jeshua the son of
Azaniah, Binnui of the sons of
Henadad, *and* Kadmiel.
     ¹⁰Their brethren: Shebaniah,
Hodijah, Kelita, Pelaiah, Hanan,
¹¹Micha, Rehob, Hashabiah, ¹²Zaccur,
Sherebiah, Shebaniah, ¹³Hodijah,
Bani, *and* Beninu.
     ¹⁴The leaders of the people: Parosh,
Pahath-Moab, Elam, Zattu, Bani,
¹⁵Bunni, Azgad, Bebai, ¹⁶Adonijah,
Bigvai, Adin, ¹⁷Ater, Hezekiah, Azzur,
¹⁸Hodijah, Hashum, Bezai, ¹⁹Hariph,
Anathoth, Nebai, ²⁰Magpiash,
Meshullam, Hezir, ²¹Meshezabel,

Zadok, Jaddua, ²²Pelatiah, Hanan,
Anaiah, ²³Hoshea, Hananiah,
Hasshub, ²⁴Hallohesh, Pilha, Shobek,
²⁵Rehum, Hashabnah, Maaseiah,
²⁶Ahijah, Hanan, Anan, ²⁷Malluch,
Harim, *and* Baanah.

The Covenant That Was Sealed

²⁸Now the rest of the people—the priests,
the Levites, the gatekeepers, the singers,
the Nethinim, and all those who had separated themselves from the peoples of the
lands to the Law of God, their wives, their
sons, and their daughters, everyone who
had knowledge and understanding—²⁹these
joined with their brethren, their nobles,
and entered into a curse and an oath to
walk in God's Law, which was given by
Moses the servant of God, and to observe
and do all the commandments of the LORD
our Lord, and His ordinances and His statutes: ³⁰We would not give our daughters as
wives to the peoples of the land, nor take
their daughters for our sons; ³¹*if* the peoples
of the land brought wares or any grain to
sell on the Sabbath day, we would not buy it
from them on the Sabbath, or on a holy
day; and we would forego the seventh
year's *produce* and the exacting of every
debt.

> **10:28 who had separated themselves.** These are
> those who had followed the demand of Ezra and
> Nehemiah to divorce heathen spouses, as well as
> those who had been left in the Land but had not
> joined with any heathen. Israel's unfaithfulness to
> the covenant prior to captivity was largely due to for-
> bidden intermarriage.

³²Also we made ordinances for ourselves,
to exact from ourselves yearly one-third of a
shekel for the service of the house of our
God: ³³for the showbread, for the regular
grain offering, for the regular burnt offering
of the Sabbaths, the New Moons, and the
set feasts; for the holy things, for the sin
offerings to make atonement for Israel, and
all the work of the house of our God. ³⁴We
cast lots among the priests, the Levites, and
the people, for *bringing* the wood offering
into the house of our God, according to our
fathers' houses, at the appointed times year
by year, to burn on the altar of the LORD our
God as *it is* written in the Law.

³⁵And *we made ordinances* to bring the firstfruits of our ground and the firstfruits of all fruit of all trees, year by year, to the house of the LORD; ³⁶to bring the firstborn of our sons and our cattle, as *it is* written in the Law, and the firstborn of our herds and our flocks, to the house of our God, to the priests who minister in the house of our God; ³⁷to bring the firstfruits of our dough, our offerings, the fruit from all kinds of trees, *the* new wine and oil, to the priests, to the storerooms of the house of our God; and to bring the tithes of our land to the Levites, for the Levites should receive the tithes in all our farming communities. ³⁸And the priest, the descendant of Aaron, shall be with the Levites when the Levites receive tithes; and the Levites shall bring up a tenth of the tithes to the house of our God, to the rooms of the storehouse.

> **10:35–37 firstfruits...firstborn...firstborn.** These laws required firstfruits of the ground (see Ex. 23:19), of the trees (see Lev. 19:24), the firstborn sons redeemed by the estimated price of the priest (see Num.18:15), and the firstborn of the herds and flocks (see Ex. 13:12). These were used to support the priests and Levites. The Levites gave ten percent of theirs to the priests (see Num. 18:26).

³⁹For the children of Israel and the children of Levi shall bring the offering of the grain, of the new wine and the oil, to the storerooms where the articles of the sanctuary *are, where* the priests who minister and the gatekeepers and the singers *are;* and we will not neglect the house of our God.

The People Dwelling in Jerusalem

11 Now the leaders of the people dwelt at Jerusalem; the rest of the people cast lots to bring one out of ten to dwell in Jerusalem, the holy city, and nine-tenths *were to dwell* in *other* cities. ²And the peo-

> **11:1 cast lots.** God honored this method of making decisions (Prov. 16:33). Nehemiah redistributed the population, placing one out of every 10 Jews in Jerusalem and the other 9 in the Land to reestablish their family heritage.

ple blessed all the men who willingly offered themselves to dwell at Jerusalem.

³These *are* the heads of the province who dwelt in Jerusalem. (But in the cities of Judah everyone dwelt in his own possession in their cities—Israelites, priests, Levites, Nethinim, and descendants of Solomon's servants.) ⁴Also in Jerusalem dwelt *some* of the children of Judah and of the children of Benjamin.

The children of Judah: Athaiah the son of Uzziah, the son of Zechariah, the son of Amariah, the son of Shephatiah, the son of Mahalalel, of the children of Perez; ⁵and Maaseiah the son of Baruch, the son of Col-Hozeh, the son of Hazaiah, the son of Adaiah, the son of Joiarib, the son of Zechariah, the son of Shiloni. ⁶All the sons of Perez who dwelt at Jerusalem *were* four hundred and sixty-eight valiant men.

⁷And these are the sons of Benjamin: Sallu the son of Meshullam, the son of Joed, the son of Pedaiah, the son of Kolaiah, the son of Maaseiah, the son of Ithiel, the son of Jeshaiah; ⁸and after him Gabbai *and* Sallai, nine hundred and twenty-eight. ⁹Joel the son of Zichri *was* their overseer, and Judah the son of Senuah^a *was* second over the city.

¹⁰Of the priests: Jedaiah the son of Joiarib, and Jachin; ¹¹Seraiah the son of Hilkiah, the son of Meshullam, the son of Zadok, the son of Meraioth, the son of Ahitub, *was* the leader of the house of God. ¹²Their brethren who did the work of the house *were* eight hundred and twenty-two; and Adaiah the son of Jeroham, the son of Pelaliah, the son of Amzi, the son of Zechariah, the son of Pashhur, the son of Malchijah, ¹³and his brethren, heads of the fathers' *houses, were* two hundred and forty-two; and Amashai the son of Azarel, the son of Ahzai, the son of Meshillemoth, the son of Immer, ¹⁴and their brethren, mighty men of valor, *were* one hundred and twenty-eight. Their overseer *was* Zabdiel the son of *one of* the great men.^a

¹⁵Also of the Levites: Shemaiah the son of Hasshub, the son of Azrikam, the son of Hashabiah, the son of Bunni; ¹⁶Shabbethai and Jozabad, of the heads of the Levites, *had* the oversight of the business outside of

the house of God; ¹⁷Mattaniah the son of Micha,^a the son of Zabdi, the son of Asaph, the leader who began the thanksgiving with prayer; Bakbukiah, the second among his brethren; and Abda the son of Shammua, the son of Galal, the son of Jeduthun. ¹⁸All the Levites in the holy city were two hundred and eighty-four.

¹⁹Moreover the gatekeepers, Akkub, Talmon, and their brethren who kept the gates, were one hundred and seventy-two.

²⁰And the rest of Israel, of the priests and Levites, were in all the cities of Judah, everyone in his inheritance. ²¹But the Nethinim dwelt in Ophel. And Ziha and Gishpa were over the Nethinim.

²²Also the overseer of the Levites at Jerusalem was Uzzi the son of Bani, the son of Hashabiah, the son of Mattaniah, the son of Micha, of the sons of Asaph, the singers in charge of the service of the house of God. ²³For it was the king's command concerning them that a certain portion should be for the singers, a quota day by day. ²⁴Pethahiah the son of Meshezabel, of the children of Zerah the son of Judah, was the king's deputy^a in all matters concerning the people.

The People Dwelling Outside Jerusalem

²⁵And as for the villages with their fields, some of the children of Judah dwelt in Kirjath Arba and its villages, Dibon and its villages, Jekabzeel and its villages; ²⁶in Jeshua, Moladah, Beth Pelet, ²⁷Hazar Shual, and Beersheba and its villages; ²⁸in Ziklag and Meconah and its villages; ²⁹in En Rimmon, Zorah, Jarmuth, ³⁰Zanoah, Adullam, and their villages; in Lachish and its fields; in Azekah and its villages. They dwelt from Beersheba to the Valley of Hinnom.

³¹Also the children of Benjamin from Geba dwelt in Michmash, Aija, and Bethel, and their villages; ³²in Anathoth, Nob, Ananiah; ³³in Hazor, Ramah, Gittaim; ³⁴in Hadid, Zeboim, Neballat; ³⁵in Lod, Ono, and the Valley of Craftsmen. ³⁶Some of the Judean divisions of Levites were in Benjamin.

The Priests and Levites

12 Now these are the priests and the Levites who came up with Zerubbabel the son of Shealtiel, and Jeshua: Seraiah, Jeremiah, Ezra, ²Amariah, Malluch, Hattush, ³Shechaniah, Rehum, Meremoth, ⁴Iddo, Ginnethoi,^a Abijah, ⁵Mijamin, Maadiah, Bilgah, ⁶Shemaiah, Joiarib, Jedaiah, ⁷Sallu, Amok, Hilkiah, and Jedaiah.

These were the heads of the priests and their brethren in the days of Jeshua.

12:1–26 Originally there were 24 courses of priests, each one serving in the temple for a period of either two weeks per year or for one month biannually (see 1 Chr. 24:1–20). Only 22 are mentioned here. Two may have been omitted because their families had become extinct. Some of the key priests and Levites from the time of Zerubbabel were Jeshua, Joiakim, and Eliashib.

⁸Moreover the Levites were Jeshua, Binnui, Kadmiel, Sherebiah, Judah, and Mattaniah who led the thanksgiving psalms, he and his brethren. ⁹Also Bakbukiah and Unni, their brethren, stood across from them in their duties.

¹⁰Jeshua begot Joiakim, Joiakim begot Eliashib, Eliashib begot Joiada, ¹¹Joiada begot Jonathan, and Jonathan begot Jaddua.

¹²Now in the days of Joiakim, the priests, the heads of the fathers' houses were: of Seraiah, Meraiah; of Jeremiah, Hananiah; ¹³of Ezra, Meshullam; of Amariah, Jehohanan; ¹⁴of Melichu,^a Jonathan; of Shebaniah,^b Joseph; ¹⁵of Harim,^a Adna; of Meraioth,^b Helkai; ¹⁶of Iddo, Zechariah; of Ginnethon, Meshullam; ¹⁷of Abijah, Zichri; the son of Minjamin;^a of Moadiah,^b Piltai; ¹⁸of Bilgah, Shammua; of Shemaiah, Jehonathan; ¹⁹of Joiarib, Mattenai; of Jedaiah, Uzzi; ²⁰of Sallai,^a Kallai; of Amok, Eber; ²¹of Hilkiah, Hashabiah; and of Jedaiah, Nethanel.

²²During the reign of Darius the Persian, a record was also kept of the Levites and priests who had been heads of their fathers' houses in the days of Eliashib, Joiada, Johanan, and Jaddua. ²³The sons of Levi, the

---

11:17 ^aOr Michah   11:24 ^aLiterally at the king's hand   12:4 ^aOr Ginnethon (compare verse 16)   12:14 ^aOr Malluch (compare verse 2)   ^bOr Shechaniah (compare verse 3)   12:15 ^aOr Rehum (compare verse 3)   ^bOr Meremoth (compare verse 3)   12:17 ^aOr Mijamin (compare verse 5)   ^bOr Maadiah (compare verse 5)   12:20 ^aOr Sallu (compare verse 7)

heads of the fathers' *houses* until the days of Johanan the son of Eliashib, *were* written in the book of the chronicles.

²⁴And the heads of the Levites *were* Hashabiah, Sherebiah, and Jeshua the son of Kadmiel, with their brothers across from them, to praise *and* give thanks, group alternating with group, according to the command of David the man of God. ²⁵Mattaniah, Bakbukiah, Obadiah, Meshullam, Talmon, and Akkub *were* gatekeepers keeping the watch at the storerooms of the gates. ²⁶These *lived* in the days of Joiakim the son of Jeshua, the son of Jozadak,ᵃ and in the days of Nehemiah the governor, and of Ezra the priest, the scribe.

Nehemiah Dedicates the Wall

²⁷Now at the dedication of the wall of Jerusalem they sought out the Levites in all their places, to bring them to Jerusalem to celebrate the dedication with gladness, both with thanksgivings and singing, *with* cymbals and stringed instruments and harps. ²⁸And the sons of the singers gathered together from the countryside around Jerusalem, from the villages of the Netophathites, ²⁹from the house of Gilgal, and from the fields of Geba and Azmaveth; for the singers had built themselves villages all around Jerusalem. ³⁰Then the priests and Levites purified themselves, and purified the people, the gates, and the wall.

³¹So I brought the leaders of Judah up on the wall, and appointed two large thanksgiving choirs. *One* went to the right hand on the wall toward the Refuse Gate. ³²After them went Hoshaiah and half of the leaders of Judah, ³³and Azariah, Ezra, Meshullam, ³⁴Judah, Benjamin, Shemaiah, Jeremiah, ³⁵and some of the priests' sons with trumpets—Zechariah the son of Jonathan, the son of Shemaiah, the son of Mattaniah, the son of Michaiah, the son of Zaccur, the son of Asaph, ³⁶and his brethren, Shemaiah, Azarel, Milalai, Gilalai, Maai, Nethanel, Judah, *and* Hanani, with the musical instruments of David the man of God. And Ezra the scribe *went* before them. ³⁷By the Fountain Gate, in front of them, they went up the stairs of the City of David, on the stairway of the wall, beyond the house of David, as far as the Water Gate eastward.

³⁸The other thanksgiving choir went the opposite *way*, and I *was* behind them with half of the people on the wall, going past the Tower of the Ovens as far as the Broad Wall, ³⁹and above the Gate of Ephraim, above the Old Gate, above the Fish Gate, the Tower of Hananel, the Tower of the Hundred, as far as the Sheep Gate; and they stopped by the Gate of the Prison.

⁴⁰So the two thanksgiving choirs stood in the house of God, likewise I and the half of the rulers with me; ⁴¹and the priests, Eliakim, Maaseiah, Minjamin,ᵃ Michaiah, Elioenai, Zechariah, *and* Hananiah, with trumpets; ⁴²also Maaseiah, Shemaiah, Eleazar, Uzzi, Jehohanan, Malchijah, Elam, and Ezer. The singers sang loudly with Jezrahiah the director.

⁴³Also that day they offered great sacrifices, and rejoiced, for God had made them rejoice with great joy; the women and the children also rejoiced, so that the joy of Jerusalem was heard afar off.

> **12:27–43 the dedication of the wall.** The rebuilt walls were dedicated with music of thanksgiving, in the same manner as the dedications of the rebuilt temple several decades earlier and the temple in Solomon's day (2 Chr. 5–7).

Temple Responsibilities

⁴⁴And at the same time some were appointed over the rooms of the storehouse for the offerings, the firstfruits, and the tithes, to gather into them from the fields of the cities the portions specified by the Law for the priests and Levites; for Judah rejoiced over the priests and Levites who ministered. ⁴⁵Both the singers and the gatekeepers kept the charge of their God and the charge of the purification, according to the command of David *and* Solomon his son. ⁴⁶For in the days of David and Asaph of old *there were* chiefs of the singers, and songs of praise and thanksgiving to God. ⁴⁷In the days of Zerubbabel and in the days of Nehemiah all Israel gave the portions for the singers and the gatekeepers, a portion for each day. They also consecrated *holy*

12:26 ᵃSpelled *Jehozadak* in 1 Chronicles 6:14   12:41 ᵃOr *Mijamin* (compare verse 5)

things for the Levites, and the Levites consecrated *them* for the children of Aaron.

Principles of Separation

13 On that day they read from the Book of Moses in the hearing of the people, and in it was found written that no Ammonite or Moabite should ever come into the assembly of God, ²because they had not met the children of Israel with bread and water, but hired Balaam against them to curse them. However, our God turned the curse into a blessing. ³So it was, when they had heard the Law, that they separated all the mixed multitude from Israel.

The Reforms of Nehemiah

⁴Now before this, Eliashib the priest, having authority over the storerooms of the house of our God, *was* allied with Tobiah. ⁵And he had prepared for him a large room, where previously they had stored the grain offerings, the frankincense, the articles, the tithes of grain, the new wine and oil, which were commanded *to be given* to the Levites and singers and gatekeepers, and the offerings for the priests. ⁶But during all this I was not in Jerusalem, for in the thirty-second year of Artaxerxes king of Babylon I had returned to the king. Then after certain days I obtained leave from the king, ⁷and I came to Jerusalem and discovered the evil that Eliashib had done for Tobiah, in preparing a room for him in the courts of the house of God. ⁸And it grieved me bitterly; therefore I threw all the household goods of Tobiah out of the room. ⁹Then I commanded them to cleanse the rooms; and I brought back into them the articles of the house of God, with the grain offering and the frankincense.

¹⁰I also realized that the portions for the Levites had not been given *them*; for each of the Levites and the singers who did the work had gone back to his field. ¹¹So I contended with the rulers, and said, "Why is the house of God forsaken?" And I gathered them together and set them in their place. ¹²Then all Judah brought the tithe of the grain and the new wine and the oil to the storehouse. ¹³And I appointed as treasurers over the storehouse Shelemiah the priest and Zadok the scribe, and of the Levites, Pedaiah; and next to them *was* Hanan the son of Zaccur, the son of Mattaniah; for they were considered faithful, and their task *was* to distribute to their brethren.

¹⁴Remember me, O my God, concerning this, and do not wipe out my good deeds that I have done for the house of my God, and for its services!

¹⁵In those days I saw *people* in Judah treading wine presses on the Sabbath, and bringing in sheaves, and loading donkeys with wine, grapes, figs, and all *kinds of* burdens, which they brought into Jerusalem on the Sabbath day. And I warned *them* about the day on which they were selling provisions. ¹⁶Men of Tyre dwelt there also, who brought in fish and all kinds of goods, and sold *them* on the Sabbath to the children of Judah, and in Jerusalem.

¹⁷Then I contended with the nobles of Judah, and said to them, "What evil thing *is* this that you do, by which you profane the Sabbath day? ¹⁸Did not your fathers do thus, and did not our God bring all this disaster on us and on this city? Yet you bring added wrath on Israel by profaning the Sabbath."

¹⁹So it was, at the gates of Jerusalem, as it began to be dark before the Sabbath, that I commanded the gates to be shut, and charged that they must not be opened till after the Sabbath. Then I posted *some* of my servants at the gates, *so that* no burdens would be brought in on the Sabbath day. ²⁰Now the merchants and sellers of all kinds of wares lodged outside Jerusalem once or twice. ²¹Then I warned them, and said to them, "Why do you spend the night around the wall? If you do *so* again, I will lay hands on

you!" From that time on they came no *more* on the Sabbath. [22]And I commanded the Levites that they should cleanse themselves, and that they should go and guard the gates, to sanctify the Sabbath day.

Remember me, O my God, *concerning* this also, and spare me according to the greatness of Your mercy!

[23]In those days I also saw Jews *who* had married women of Ashdod, Ammon, *and* Moab. [24]And half of their children spoke the language of Ashdod, and could not speak the language of Judah, but spoke according to the language of one or the other people.

> **13:23–29** The priests and the people had married pagans, which violated the Mosaic Law (see Ex. 34:15), the earlier reforms of Ezra (see Ezra 9,10), and their own covenant. Malachi spoke out against this sin (Mal. 2:10–16).

[25]So I contended with them and cursed them, struck some of them and pulled out their hair, and made them swear by God, *saying,* "You shall not give your daughters as wives to their sons, nor take their daughters for your sons or yourselves. [26]Did not Solomon king of Israel sin by these things? Yet among many nations there was no king like him, who was beloved of his God; and God made him king over all Israel. Nevertheless pagan women caused even him to sin. [27]Should we then hear of your doing all this great evil, transgressing against our God by marrying pagan women?"

[28]And *one* of the sons of Joiada, the son of Eliashib the high priest, *was* a son-in-law of Sanballat the Horonite; therefore I drove him from me.

[29]Remember them, O my God, because they have defiled the priesthood and the covenant of the priesthood and the Levites.

[30]Thus I cleansed them of everything pagan. I also assigned duties to the priests and the Levites, each to his service, [31]and *to bringing* the wood offering and the firstfruits at appointed times.

Remember me, O my God, for good!

> **13:31 Remember me.** Nehemiah prayed this for the third time, desiring God's blessing on his obedient efforts.

ESTHER

Two Old Testament books bear the names of women—Ruth, the foreigner who became a believer, and Esther, the Jewish girl who became a Persian queen. Among Jewish people, Esther is remembered by her Hebrew name, "Hadassah" (2:7), which means "myrtle." Her life became a channel through which God continued His protection of the Chosen People from the murderous plans of an enemy.

AUTHOR AND DATE

Esther was written by an unknown author, before 331 B.C.

Although Mordecai (Esther's cousin), Ezra, and Nehemiah have all been suggested, the author remains anonymous. Whoever penned Esther reveals a detailed knowledge of Persian customs, etiquette, and history. He or she was no stranger to the palace in Shushan (1:5–7). Intimate knowledge of the Hebrew calendar and customs shapes the story. The account also exhibits a strong sense of Jewish nationalism. The writer may well have been a Persian Jew who had returned to Israel.

Because neither king Ahasuerus' assassination around 465 B.C. nor the fall of the Persian Empire receive any mention in Esther, the book was most likely written well before 331 B.C., the date of the Greek conquest. Esther occupies the final position among the Old Testament historical books.

BACKGROUND AND SETTING

During the time of Esther, the Persian Empire ruled the world (539–331 B.C.). Esther's husband Ahasuerus reigned from 486 to 465 B.C. The events in this book occurred between 483 and 473 B.C.

Against the backdrop of Jewish history, Esther fits during the time span between the first return of the Jews to Jerusalem under Zerubbabel around 538 B.C. (Ezra 1–6) and the second return led by Ezra around 458 B.C. (Ezra 7–10). The danger from which Esther rescued her people must have provided an added incentive for many of the Jews to return to Israel.

Like Exodus, Esther chronicles how vigorously foreign powers tried to eliminate the Jewish race as well as how powerfully God preserved His people. God continually honored His covenant promises to Abraham (Genesis 12:1–3; 17:1–8). Esther also documents the origin of a new annual festival among the Jews, called Purim. It is held during the twelfth month (February-March). The festival celebrates God's deliverance through Esther.

Along with Ruth, Song of Solomon, Ecclesiastes, and Lamentations, Esther completes the Hebrew Old Testament section called the Megilloth. Rabbis would read these books in the synagogue during five special occasions each year. Esther's story was reserved for Purim.

Neither God's name nor His presence receive direct mention in Esther. This has led to questions regarding the book's legitimacy as Scripture. But recognition of Esther's authenticity and divine inspiration can be traced back to the earliest gathering of the Old Testament books.

Although the conflict between Haman and Mordecai seems merely personal, it has long and deep historical roots. As descendants of the Amalekites and Jews respectively, Haman and Mordecai represented ancient enemies. Major clashes between these nations occurred during the Exodus from Egypt (Exodus 17:8–16) and during the reign of Saul in Israel (1 Samuel 15:2–33). Haman's murderous hatred against the Jews finally sealed the fate of his own people. Back in Exodus 17:14, God had ordered the extinguishing of the Amalekite race. That order was finally carried out in self-defense under Esther.

The book also presents a case study of the deadly strategic struggle between God's people in this world and Satan, their arch-enemy. The outlook on any day may be desperate, but God will always turn the tables on evil. These specific events form a thrilling chapter in the story of God's plan of salvation. That plan and conflict eventually lead to the cross of Jesus Christ, where death appears momentarily to win, yet is then defeated by the resurrection.

> THE **OUTLOOK** ON **ANY DAY** MAY BE **DESPERATE,** BUT **GOD** WILL **ALWAYS TURN** THE **TABLES** ON **EVIL.**

OUTLINE

The King Dethrones Queen Vashti

1 Now it came to pass in the days of Ahasuerus[a] (this *was* the Ahasuerus who reigned over one hundred and twenty-seven provinces, from India to Ethiopia), [2]in those days when King Ahasuerus sat on the throne of his kingdom, which *was* in Shushan[a] the citadel, [3]*that* in the third year of his reign he made a feast for all his officials and servants—the powers of Persia and Media, the nobles, and the princes of the provinces *being* before him—[4]when he showed the riches of his glorious kingdom and the splendor of his excellent majesty for many days, one hundred and eighty days *in all.*

[5]And when these days were completed, the king made a feast lasting seven days for all the people who were present in Shushan the citadel, from great to small, in the court of the garden of the king's palace. [6]*There were* white and blue linen *curtains* fastened with cords of fine linen and purple on silver rods and marble pillars; *and the* couches *were* of gold and silver on a *mosaic* pavement of alabaster, turquoise, and white and black marble. [7]And they served drinks in golden vessels, each vessel being different from the other, with royal wine in abundance, according to the generosity of the king. [8]In accordance with the law, the drinking was not compulsory; for so the king had ordered all the officers of his household, that they should do according to each man's pleasure.

[9]Queen Vashti also made a feast for the women *in* the royal palace which *belonged* to King Ahasuerus.

[10]On the seventh day, when the heart of the king was merry with wine, he commanded Mehuman, Biztha, Harbona, Bigtha, Abagtha, Zethar, and Carcas, seven eunuchs who served in the presence of King Ahasuerus, [11]to bring Queen Vashti before the king, *wearing* her royal crown, in order to show her beauty to the people and the officials, for she *was* beautiful to behold. [12]But Queen Vashti refused to come at the king's command *brought* by *his* eunuchs; therefore the king was furious, and his anger burned within him.

> **1:12 Vashti refused.** Her reasons may have been that her appearance may have involved inappropriate behavior before drunken men or that she was still pregnant with Artaxerxes.

[13]Then the king said to the wise men who understood the times (for this *was* the king's manner toward all who knew law and justice, [14]those closest to him *being* Carshena, Shethar, Admatha, Tarshish, Meres, Marsena, and Memucan, the seven princes of Persia and Media, who had access to the king's presence, *and* who ranked highest in the kingdom): [15]"What *shall we* do to

---

1:1 [a]Generally identified with Xerxes I (485–464 B.C.)   1:2 [a]Or *Susa,* and so throughout this book

---

Why isn't God directly mentioned in Esther?

The question naturally arises when reading the book. Even the usual clues about God's presence seem absent. No one refers to the Law of God, sacrifices, worship, or prayer. God does not appear to receive public or private recognition for the preservation of the Jews. When it comes to God, Esther seems strangely silent.

In fact, the silence is so obvious that it becomes an argument. Esther challenges the tendency to demand that God prove His power and presence. Must God be apparent? All too quickly we expect God to demonstrate in unmistakable ways His identity. Yet God has repeatedly resisted human ultimatums. God reveals Himself for His own purposes, not human requirements.

Throughout history, God has more readily operated behind the scenes than in plain sight. The Scriptures are filled with unusual circumstances in which God worked obviously. But Esther comes close to revealing God's standard procedure. God's fingerprints are all over Esther's story. His superficial absence points to a deeper presence. God chose to be subtle, but He was there. The events in Esther give us a model for hope when God works in less than obvious ways in our lives.

Queen Vashti, according to law, because she did not obey the command of King Ahasuerus *brought to her* by the eunuchs?"

¹⁶And Memucan answered before the king and the princes: "Queen Vashti has not only wronged the king, but also all the princes, and all the people who *are* in all the provinces of King Ahasuerus. ¹⁷For the queen's behavior will become known to all women, so that they will despise their husbands in their eyes, when they report, 'King Ahasuerus commanded Queen Vashti to be brought in before him, but she did not come.' ¹⁸This very day the *noble* ladies of Persia and Media will say to all the king's officials that they have heard of the behavior of the queen. Thus *there will be* excessive contempt and wrath. ¹⁹If it pleases the king, let a royal decree go out from him, and let it be recorded in the laws of the Persians and the Medes, so that it will not be altered, that Vashti shall come no more before King Ahasuerus; and let the king give her royal position to another who is better than she. ²⁰When the king's decree which he will make is proclaimed throughout all his empire (for it is great), all wives will honor their husbands, both great and small."

> **1:19 will not be altered.** The irrevocable nature of Persian Law (see Dan. 6:8,12,15) significantly influenced the conclusion of the book of Esther (8:8)

²¹And the reply pleased the king and the princes, and the king did according to the word of Memucan. ²²Then he sent letters to all the king's provinces, to each province in its own script, and to every people in their own language, that each man should be master in his own house, and speak in the language of his own people.

Esther Becomes Queen

2 After these things, when the wrath of King Ahasuerus subsided, he remembered Vashti, what she had done, and what had been decreed against her. ²Then the king's servants who attended him said: "Let beautiful young virgins be sought for the king; ³and let the king appoint officers in all the provinces of his kingdom, that they may gather all the beautiful young virgins to Shushan the citadel, into the women's quarters, under the custody of Hegai[a] the king's eunuch, custodian of the women. And let beauty preparations be given *them*. ⁴Then let the young woman who pleases the king be queen instead of Vashti."

This thing pleased the king, and he did so.

> **2:1 he remembered Vashti.** Because the king could not legally restore Vashti, the counselors proposed a better plan.

⁵In Shushan the citadel there was a certain Jew whose name *was* Mordecai the son of Jair, the son of Shimei, the son of Kish, a Benjamite. ⁶*Kish*[a] had been carried away from Jerusalem with the captives who had been captured with Jeconiah[b] king of

---

2:3 [a]Hebrew *Hege*   2:6 [a]Literally *Who*   [b]Same as *Jehoiachin*, 2 Kings 24:6 and elsewhere

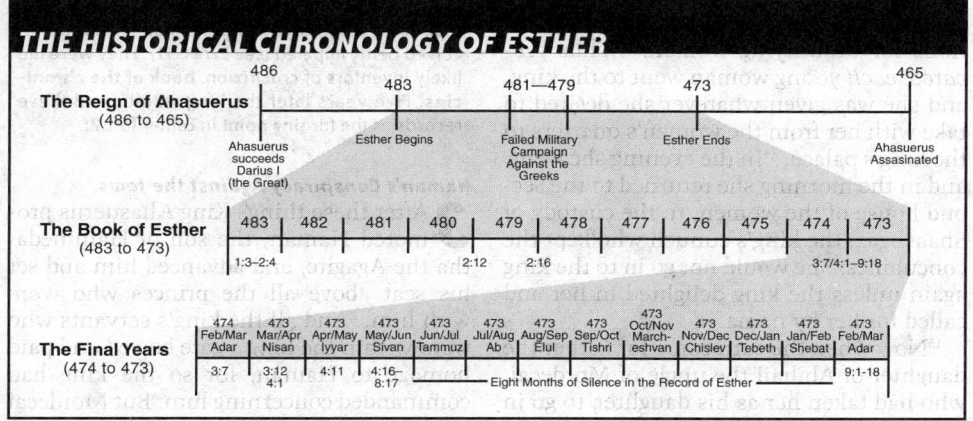

THE HISTORICAL CHRONOLOGY OF ESTHER

The Reign of Ahasuerus (486 to 465)	486		483		481—479			473			465
	Ahasuerus succeeds Darius I (the Great)		Esther Begins		Failed Military Campaign Against the Greeks			Esther Ends			Ahasuerus Assasinated

The Book of Esther (483 to 473)	483	482	481	480	479	478	477	476	475	474	473
	1:3–2:4				2:12	2:16				3:7/4:1–9:18	

The Final Years (474 to 473)	474 Feb/Mar Adar	473 Mar/Apr Nisan	473 Apr/May Iyyar	473 May/Jun Sivan	473 Jun/Jul Tammuz	473 Jul/Aug Ab	473 Aug/Sep Elul	473 Sep/Oct Tishri	473 Oct/Nov March-eshvan	473 Nov/Dec Chislev	473 Dec/Jan Tebeth	473 Jan/Feb Shebat	473 Feb/Mar Adar
	3:7	3:12 4:1	4:11	4:16– 8:17			Eight Months of Silence in the Record of Esther						9:1-18

Judah, whom Nebuchadnezzar the king of Babylon had carried away. [7]And *Mordecai* had brought up Hadassah, that *is,* Esther, his uncle's daughter, for she had neither father nor mother. The young woman *was* lovely and beautiful. When her father and mother died, Mordecai took her as his own daughter.

[8]So it was, when the king's command and decree were heard, and when many young women were gathered at Shushan the citadel, *under* the custody of Hegai, that Esther also was taken to the king's palace, into the care of Hegai the custodian of the women. [9]Now the young woman pleased him, and she obtained his favor; so he readily gave beauty preparations to her, besides her allowance. Then seven choice maidservants were provided for her from the king's palace, and he moved her and her maidservants to the best *place* in the house of the women.

[10]Esther had not revealed her people or family, for Mordecai had charged her not to reveal *it.* [11]And every day Mordecai paced in front of the court of the women's quarters, to learn of Esther's welfare and what was happening to her.

2:10 not to reveal *it*. This was possibly done because of the threatening letter in Ezra 4:6 or because of anti-Semitic feelings of Haman and others.

[12]Each young woman's turn came to go in to King Ahasuerus after she had completed twelve months' preparation, according to the regulations for the women, for thus were the days of their preparation apportioned: six months with oil of myrrh, and six months with perfumes and preparations for beautifying women. [13]Thus *prepared, each* young woman went to the king, and she was given whatever she desired to take with her from the women's quarters to the king's palace. [14]In the evening she went, and in the morning she returned to the second house of the women, to the custody of Shaashgaz, the king's eunuch who kept the concubines. She would not go in to the king again unless the king delighted in her and called for her by name.

[15]Now when the turn came for Esther the daughter of Abihail the uncle of Mordecai, who had taken her as his daughter, to go in to the king, she requested nothing but what Hegai the king's eunuch, the custodian of the women, advised. And Esther obtained favor in the sight of all who saw her. [16]So Esther was taken to King Ahasuerus, into his royal palace, in the tenth month, which *is* the month of Tebeth, in the seventh year of his reign. [17]The king loved Esther more than all the *other* women, and she obtained grace and favor in his sight more than all the virgins; so he set the royal crown upon her head and made her queen instead of Vashti. [18]Then the king made a great feast, the Feast of Esther, for all his officials and servants; and he proclaimed a holiday in the provinces and gave gifts according to the generosity of a king.

Mordecai Discovers a Plot

[19]When virgins were gathered together a second time, Mordecai sat within the king's gate. [20]*Now* Esther had not revealed her family and her people, just as Mordecai had charged her, for Esther obeyed the command of Mordecai as when she was brought up by him.

[21]In those days, while Mordecai sat within the king's gate, two of the king's eunuchs, Bigthan and Teresh, doorkeepers, became furious and sought to lay hands on King Ahasuerus. [22]So the matter became known to Mordecai, who told Queen Esther, and Esther informed the king in Mordecai's name. [23]And when an inquiry was made into the matter, it was confirmed, and both were hanged on a gallows; and it was written in the book of the chronicles in the presence of the king.

2:23 hanged on a gallows. Persian execution involved being impaled (see Ezra 6:11). They were the likely inventors of crucifixion. **book of the chronicles.** Five years later the king would read these records as the turning point in Esther (6:1,2).

Haman's Conspiracy Against the Jews

3 After these things King Ahasuerus promoted Haman, the son of Hammedatha the Agagite, and advanced him and set his seat above all the princes who *were* with him. [2]And all the king's servants who *were* within the king's gate bowed and paid homage to Haman, for so the king had commanded concerning him. But Mordecai

would not bow or pay homage. ³Then the king's servants who *were* within the king's gate said to Mordecai, "Why do you transgress the king's command?" ⁴Now it happened, when they spoke to him daily and he would not listen to them, that they told *it* to Haman, to see whether Mordecai's words would stand; for *Mordecai* had told them that he *was* a Jew. ⁵When Haman saw that Mordecai did not bow or pay him homage, Haman was filled with wrath. ⁶But he disdained to lay hands on Mordecai alone, for they had told him of the people of Mordecai. Instead, Haman sought to destroy all the Jews who *were* throughout the whole kingdom of Ahasuerus—the people of Mordecai.

3:4 he was a Jew. He was probably reluctant to reveal his ethnic background because of Haman's attempted genocide and the apparent anti-Semitism in Shushan.

⁷In the first month, which is the month of Nisan, in the twelfth year of King Ahasuerus, they cast Pur (that *is*, the lot), before Haman to determine the day and the month,*ᵃ* until it fell on the twelfth month,*ᵇ* which *is* the month of Adar.

⁸Then Haman said to King Ahasuerus, "There is a certain people scattered and dispersed among the people in all the provinces of your kingdom; their laws *are* different from all *other* people's, and they do not keep the king's laws. Therefore it *is* not fitting for the king to let them remain. ⁹If it pleases the king, let *a decree* be written that they be destroyed, and I will pay ten thousand talents of silver into the hands of those who do the work, to bring *it* into the king's treasuries."

¹⁰So the king took his signet ring from his hand and gave it to Haman, the son of Hammedatha the Agagite, the enemy of the Jews. ¹¹And the king said to Haman, "The money and the people *are* given to you, to do with them as seems good to you."

¹²Then the king's scribes were called on the thirteenth day of the first month, and *a decree* was written according to all that

Haman commanded—to the king's satraps, to the governors who *were* over each province, to the officials of all people, to every province according to its script, and to every people in their language. In the name of King Ahasuerus it was written, and sealed with the king's signet ring. ¹³And the letters were sent by couriers into all the king's provinces, to destroy, to kill, and to annihilate all the Jews, both young and old, little children and women, in one day, on the thirteenth *day* of the twelfth *month,* which *is* the month of Adar, and to plunder their possessions.*ᵃ* ¹⁴A copy of the document was to be issued as law in every province, being published for all people, that they should be ready for that day. ¹⁵The couriers went out, hastened by the king's command; and the decree was proclaimed in Shushan the citadel. So the king and Haman sat down to drink, but the city of Shushan was perplexed.

3:12 sealed...king's signet ring. This would serve as his signature. The date has been calculated to be Apr. 7, 474 B.C.

Esther Agrees to Help the Jews

4 When Mordecai learned all that had happened, he tore his clothes and put on sackcloth and ashes, and went out into the midst of the city. He cried out with a loud and bitter cry. ²He went as far as the front of the king's gate, for no one *might* enter the king's gate clothed with sackcloth. ³And in every province where the king's command and decree arrived, *there was* great mourning among the Jews, with fasting, weeping, and wailing; and many lay in sackcloth and ashes.

⁴So Esther's maids and eunuchs came and told her, and the queen was deeply distressed. Then she sent garments to clothe Mordecai and take his sackcloth away from him, but he would not accept *them.* ⁵Then Esther called Hathach, *one* of the king's eunuchs whom he had appointed to attend her, and she gave him a command concerning Mordecai, to learn what and why this *was.* ⁶So Hathach went out to Mordecai in

---

3:7 *ᵃ*Septuagint adds *to destroy the people of Mordecai in one day;* Vulgate adds *the nation of the Jews should be destroyed.* *ᵇ*Following Masoretic Text and Vulgate; Septuagint reads *and the lot fell on the fourteenth of the month.*   **3:13** *ᵃ*Septuagint adds the text of the letter here.

the city square that *was* in front of the king's gate. [7]And Mordecai told him all that had happened to him, and the sum of money that Haman had promised to pay into the king's treasuries to destroy the Jews. [8]He also gave him a copy of the written decree for their destruction, which was given at Shushan, that he might show it to Esther and explain it to her, and that he might command her to go in to the king to make supplication to him and plead before him for her people. [9]So Hathach returned and told Esther the words of Mordecai.

[10]Then Esther spoke to Hathach, and gave him a command for Mordecai: [11]"All the king's servants and the people of the king's provinces know that any man or woman who goes into the inner court to the king, who has not been called, *he has* but one law: put *all* to death, except the one to whom the king holds out the golden scepter, that he may live. Yet I myself have not been called to go in to the king these thirty days." [12]So they told Mordecai Esther's words.

4:11 golden scepter. This was done to protect the king from assassins. The king would extend it (a sign of authority) for those he knew or welcomed (see 5:2). **these thirty days.** Esther may have feared that she had lost the king's favor because she had not been recently summoned.

[13]And Mordecai told *them* to answer Esther: "Do not think in your heart that you will escape in the king's palace any more than all the other Jews. [14]For if you remain completely silent at this time, relief and deliverance will arise for the Jews from another place, but you and your father's house will perish. Yet who knows whether you have come to the kingdom for *such a time as this?*"

[15]Then Esther told *them* to reply to Mordecai: [16]"Go, gather all the Jews who are present in Shushan, and fast for me; neither eat nor drink for three days, night or day. My maids and I will fast likewise. And so I will go to the king, which *is* against the law; and if I perish, I perish!"

[17]So Mordecai went his way and did according to all that Esther commanded him.[a]

Esther's Banquet

5 Now it happened on the third day that Esther put on *her* royal *robes* and stood in the inner court of the king's palace, across from the king's house, while the king sat on his royal throne in the royal house, facing the entrance of the house.[a] [2]So it was, when the king saw Queen Esther standing in the court, *that* she found favor in his sight, and the king held out to Esther the golden scepter that *was* in his hand. Then Esther went near and touched the top of the scepter.

[3]And the king said to her, "What do you wish, Queen Esther? What *is* your request? It shall be given to you—up to half the kingdom!"

[4]So Esther answered, "If it pleases the king, let the king and Haman come today to the banquet that I have prepared for him."

[5]Then the king said, "Bring Haman quickly, that he may do as Esther has said." So the king and Haman went to the banquet that Esther had prepared.

[6]At the banquet of wine the king said to Esther, "What *is* your petition? It shall be granted you. What *is* your request, up to half the kingdom? It shall be done!"

5:3,6 up to half the kingdom. A royal figure of speech not to be taken literally (see Mark 6:22,23).

[7]Then Esther answered and said, "My petition and request *is this:* [8]If I have found favor in the sight of the king, and if it pleases the king to grant my petition and fulfill my request, then let the king and Haman come to the banquet which I will prepare for them, and tomorrow I will do as the king has said."

Haman's Plot Against Mordecai

[9]So Haman went out that day joyful and with a glad heart; but when Haman saw Mordecai in the king's gate, and that he did not stand or tremble before him, he was filled with indignation against Mordecai.

4:17 [a]Septuagint adds a prayer of Mordecai here. 5:1 [a]Septuagint adds many extra details in verses 1 and 2.

¹⁰Nevertheless Haman restrained himself and went home, and he sent and called for his friends and his wife Zeresh. ¹¹Then Haman told them of his great riches, the multitude of his children, everything in which the king had promoted him, and how he had advanced him above the officials and servants of the king.

¹²Moreover Haman said, "Besides, Queen Esther invited no one but me to come in with the king to the banquet that she prepared; and tomorrow I am again invited by her, along with the king. ¹³Yet all this avails me nothing, so long as I see Mordecai the Jew sitting at the king's gate."

¹⁴Then his wife Zeresh and all his friends said to him, "Let a gallows be made, fifty cubits high, and in the morning suggest to the king that Mordecai be hanged on it; then go merrily with the king to the banquet."

And the thing pleased Haman; so he had the gallows made.

The King Honors Mordecai

6 That night the king could not sleep. So one was commanded to bring the book of the records of the chronicles; and they were read before the king. ²And it was found written that Mordecai had told of Bigthana and Teresh, two of the king's eunuchs, the doorkeepers who had sought to lay hands on King Ahasuerus. ³Then the king said, "What honor or dignity has been bestowed on Mordecai for this?"

And the king's servants who attended him said, "Nothing has been done for him."

⁴So the king said, "Who *is* in the court?" Now Haman had *just* entered the outer court of the king's palace to suggest that the king hang Mordecai on the gallows that he had prepared for him.

⁵The king's servants said to him, "Haman is there, standing in the court."

And the king said, "Let him come in."

⁶So Haman came in, and the king asked him, "What shall be done for the man whom the king delights to honor?"

6:4,6,7 Who *is* in the court? The plot thickened when Haman entered at the wrong time and for the wrong reason. Haman unknowingly prescribed how the king was to honor Mordecai.

Now Haman thought in his heart, "Whom would the king delight to honor more than me?" ⁷And Haman answered the king, "*For* the man whom the king delights to honor, ⁸let a royal robe be brought which the king has worn, and a horse on which the king has ridden, which has a royal crest placed on its head. ⁹Then let this robe and horse be delivered to the hand of one of the king's most noble princes, that he may array the man whom the king delights to honor. Then parade him on horseback through the city square, and proclaim before him: 'Thus shall it be done to the man whom the king delights to honor!' "

¹⁰Then the king said to Haman, "Hurry, take the robe and the horse, as you have suggested, and do so for Mordecai the Jew who sits within the king's gate! Leave nothing undone of all that you have spoken."

¹¹So Haman took the robe and the horse, arrayed Mordecai and led him on horseback through the city square, and proclaimed before him, "Thus shall it be done to the man whom the king delights to honor!"

¹²Afterward Mordecai went back to the king's gate. But Haman hurried to his house, mourning and with his head covered. ¹³When Haman told his wife Zeresh and all his friends everything that had happened to him, his wise men and his wife Zeresh said to him, "If Mordecai, before whom you have begun to fall, is of Jewish descent, you will not prevail against him but will surely fall before him."

¹⁴While they *were* still talking with him, the king's eunuchs came, and hastened to bring Haman to the banquet which Esther had prepared.

Haman Hanged Instead of Mordecai

7 So the king and Haman went to dine with Queen Esther. ²And on the second day, at the banquet of wine, the king again said to Esther, "What *is* your petition, Queen Esther? It shall be granted you. And what *is* your request, up to half the kingdom? It shall be done!"

³Then Queen Esther answered and said, "If I have found favor in your sight, O king, and if it pleases the king, let my life be given me at my petition, and my people at my request. ⁴For we have been sold, my

people and I, to be destroyed, to be killed, and to be annihilated. Had we been sold as male and female slaves, I would have held my tongue, although the enemy could never compensate for the king's loss."

[5]So King Ahasuerus answered and said to Queen Esther, "Who is he, and where is he, who would dare presume in his heart to do such a thing?"

[6]And Esther said, "The adversary and enemy *is* this wicked Haman!"

So Haman was terrified before the king and queen.

[7]Then the king arose in his wrath from the banquet of wine *and went* into the palace garden; but Haman stood before Queen Esther, pleading for his life, for he saw that evil was determined against him by the king. [8]When the king returned from the palace garden to the place of the banquet of wine, Haman had fallen across the couch where Esther *was.* Then the king said, "Will he also assault the queen while I *am* in the house?"

As the word left the king's mouth, they covered Haman's face. [9]Now Harbonah, one of the eunuchs, said to the king, "Look! The gallows, fifty cubits high, which Haman made for Mordecai, who spoke good

on the king's behalf, is standing at the house of Haman."

Then the king said, "Hang him on it!"

7:9 Harbonah...Look! The prepared place for Mordecai's execution towered above the city, and it became obvious that Haman would actually die there. **Mordecai, who spoke good.** The third capital offense was charged against him. He manipulated the king into planning to kill the queen's people, he appeared as if he were trying to seduce the queen, and he planned to kill a man whom the king had just honored for loyalty to the kingdom.

[10]So they hanged Haman on the gallows that he had prepared for Mordecai. Then the king's wrath subsided.

Esther Saves the Jews

8 On that day King Ahasuerus gave Queen Esther the house of Haman, the enemy of the Jews. And Mordecai came before the king, for Esther had told how he *was related* to her. [2]So the king took off his signet ring, which he had taken from Haman, and gave it to Mordecai; and Esther appointed Mordecai over the house of Haman.

[3]Now Esther spoke again to the king, fell down at his feet, and implored him with

---

Why do Esther and Mordecai appear so secular in their lifestyles?

In contrast to their near contemporaries Ezra, Nehemiah, and Daniel, the central people in Esther seem worldly. The lack of references to God is most obvious in Esther and Mordecai's conversations. Are these all subtle indications that Esther and Mordecai were people whose faith had little or no effect on their daily lives?

The book of Esther does not settle this question. There are several important factors, however, that might hold us back from jumping to conclusions about Esther and Mordecai. Primary among these is the fact that the book has a limited scope. Only a few key events are recorded. Few if any details of the inner life of either main character are revealed. Yet the integrity of their actions ought to incline us toward giving them the benefit of the doubt when it comes to faith (4:13–16).

Here are a few other considerations regarding this question: (1) While Mordecai's caution about announcing his and Esther's heritage publicly might be questioned, it must also be pointed out that others were also cautious about this same matter (Nehemiah 2:1–8 makes no mention of God in his conversation with Artaxerxes); (2) Public events such as Passover had fallen out of practice during the captivity, meaning that there were fewer occasions in which faith was practiced in the open (this doesn't mean however that the Jews were not a marked people, since they could be identified for the purpose of Haman's law); (3) When it was appropriate, Esther did openly identify her Jewish heritage (7:3,4). These considerations do not remove the charge that Esther and Mordecai seem less devoted to God than, for example, Daniel. But the fact that God did work out His purposes in their lives comes through clearly in the book.

tears to counteract the evil of Haman the Agagite, and the scheme which he had devised against the Jews. ⁴And the king held out the golden scepter toward Esther. So Esther arose and stood before the king, ⁵and said, "If it pleases the king, and if I have found favor in his sight and the thing *seems* right to the king and I am pleasing in his eyes, let it be written to revoke the letters devised by Haman, the son of Hammedatha the Agagite, which he wrote to annihilate the Jews who *are* in all the king's provinces. ⁶For how can I endure to see the evil that will come to my people? Or how can I endure to see the destruction of my countrymen?"

8:5 to revoke. The inflexible nature of the king's edicts made this impossible (1:19), however a counter-decree was possible (see 8:8,11,12).

⁷Then King Ahasuerus said to Queen Esther and Mordecai the Jew, "Indeed, I have given Esther the house of Haman, and they have hanged him on the gallows because he *tried to* lay his hand on the Jews. ⁸You yourselves write *a decree* concerning the Jews, as you please, in the king's name, and seal *it* with the king's signet ring; for whatever is written in the king's name and sealed with the king's signet ring no one can revoke."

⁹So the king's scribes were called at that time, in the third month, which *is* the month of Sivan, on the twenty-third *day;* and it was written, according to all that Mordecai commanded, to the Jews, the satraps, the governors, and the princes of the provinces from India to Ethiopia, one hundred and twenty-seven provinces *in all,* to every province in its own script, to every people in their own language, and to the Jews in their own script and language. ¹⁰And he wrote in the name of King Ahasuerus, sealed *it* with the king's signet ring, and sent letters by couriers on horseback, riding on royal horses bred from swift steeds.ᵃ

¹¹By these letters the king permitted the Jews who *were* in every city to gather together and protect their lives—to destroy, kill, and annihilate all the forces of any

people or province that would assault them, *both* little children and women, and to plunder their possessions, ¹²on one day in all the provinces of King Ahasuerus, on the thirteenth *day* of the twelfth month, which *is* the month of Adar.ᵃ ¹³A copy of the document was to be issued as a decree in every province and published for all people, so that the Jews would be ready on that day to avenge themselves on their enemies. ¹⁴The couriers who rode on royal horses went out, hastened and pressed on by the king's command. And the decree was issued in Shushan the citadel.

¹⁵So Mordecai went out from the presence of the king in royal apparel of blue and white, with a great crown of gold and a garment of fine linen and purple; and the city of Shushan rejoiced and was glad. ¹⁶The Jews had light and gladness, joy and honor. ¹⁷And in every province and city, wherever the king's command and decree came, the Jews had joy and gladness, a feast and a holiday. Then many of the people of the land became Jews, because fear of the Jews fell upon them.

The Jews Destroy Their Tormentors

9 Now in the twelfth month, that *is,* the month of Adar, on the thirteenth day, *the time* came for the king's command and his decree to be executed. On the day that the enemies of the Jews had hoped to overpower them, the opposite occurred, in that the Jews themselves overpowered those who hated them. ²The Jews gathered together in their cities throughout all the provinces of King Ahasuerus to lay hands on those who sought their harm. And no one could withstand them, because fear of them fell upon all people. ³And all the officials of the provinces, the satraps, the governors, and all those doing the king's work, helped the Jews, because the fear of Mordecai fell upon them. ⁴For Mordecai *was* great in the king's palace, and his fame spread throughout all the provinces; for this man Mordecai became increasingly prominent. ⁵Thus the Jews defeated all their enemies with the stroke of the sword, with slaughter and destruction, and did what they pleased with those who hated them.

8:10 ᵃLiterally *sons of the swift horses*   8:12 ᵃSeptuagint adds the text of the letter here.

⁶And in Shushan the citadel the Jews killed and destroyed five hundred men. ⁷Also Parshandatha, Dalphon, Aspatha, ⁸Poratha, Adalia, Aridatha, ⁹Parmashta, Arisai, Aridai, and Vajezatha—¹⁰the ten sons of Haman the son of Hammedatha, the enemy of the Jews—they killed; but they did not lay a hand on the plunder.

¹¹On that day the number of those who were killed in Shushan the citadel was brought to the king. ¹²And the king said to Queen Esther, "The Jews have killed and destroyed five hundred men in Shushan the citadel, and the ten sons of Haman. What have they done in the rest of the king's provinces? Now what *is* your petition? It shall be granted to you. Or what *is* your further request? It shall be done."

9:12 further request? This pagan king aided God's decree to annihilate the Amalekites (Ex. 17:14) by allowing a second day of killing to eliminate the Jewish enemies.

¹³Then Esther said, "If it pleases the king, let it be granted to the Jews who *are* in Shushan to do again tomorrow according to today's decree, and let Haman's ten sons be hanged on the gallows."

¹⁴So the king commanded this to be done; the decree was issued in Shushan, and they hanged Haman's ten sons.

¹⁵And the Jews who *were* in Shushan gathered together again on the fourteenth day of the month of Adar and killed three hundred men at Shushan; but they did not lay a hand on the plunder.

¹⁶The remainder of the Jews in the king's provinces gathered together and protected their lives, had rest from their enemies, and killed seventy-five thousand of their enemies; but they did not lay a hand on the plunder. ¹⁷This *was* on the thirteenth day of the month of Adar. And on the fourteenth of *the month*ᵃ they rested and made it a day of feasting and gladness.

The Feast of Purim

¹⁸But the Jews who *were* at Shushan assembled together on the thirteenth *day,* as well as on the fourteenth; and on the fifteenth of *the month*ᵃ they rested, and made it a day of feasting and gladness. ¹⁹Therefore the Jews of the villages who dwelt in the unwalled towns celebrated the fourteenth day of the month of Adar *with* gladness and feasting, as a holiday, and for sending presents to one another.

²⁰And Mordecai wrote these things and sent letters to all the Jews, near and far, who *were* in all the provinces of King Ahasuerus, ²¹to establish among them that they should celebrate yearly the fourteenth and fifteenth days of the month of Adar, ²²as the days on which the Jews had rest from their enemies, as the month which was turned from sorrow to joy for them, and from mourning to a holiday; that they should make them days of feasting and joy, of sending presents to one another and gifts to the poor. ²³So the Jews accepted the custom which they had begun, as Mordecai had written to them, ²⁴because Haman, the son of Hammedatha the Agagite, the enemy of all the Jews, had plotted against the Jews to annihilate them, and had cast Pur (that *is,* the lot), to consume them and destroy them; ²⁵but when *Esther*ᵃ came before the king, he commanded by letter that this*ᵇ* wicked plot which *Haman* had devised against the Jews should return on his own head, and that he and his sons should be hanged on the gallows.

²⁶So they called these days Purim, after the name Pur. Therefore, because of all the words of this letter, what they had seen concerning this matter, and what had happened to them, ²⁷the Jews established and imposed it upon themselves and their descendants and all who would join them, that without fail they should celebrate these two days every year, according to the written *instructions* and according to the *prescribed* time, ²⁸that these days *should be* remembered and kept throughout every generation, every family, every province, and every city, that these days of Purim should not fail *to be observed* among the Jews, and *that* the memory of

9:26 Purim. This was the first and last biblically revealed, non-Mosaic festival that had perpetual significance.

9:17 ᵃLiterally *it*   9:18 ᵃLiterally *it*   9:25 ᵃLiterally *she* or *it*   ᵇLiterally *his*

them should not perish among their descendants.

[29]Then Queen Esther, the daughter of Abihail, with Mordecai the Jew, wrote with full authority to confirm this second letter about Purim. [30]And *Mordecai* sent letters to all the Jews, to the one hundred and twenty-seven provinces of the kingdom of Ahasuerus, *with* words of peace and truth, [31]to confirm these days of Purim at their *appointed* time, as Mordecai the Jew and Queen Esther had prescribed for them, and as they had decreed for themselves and their descendants concerning matters of their fasting and lamenting. [32]So the decree of Esther confirmed these matters of Purim, and it was written in the book.

9:32 written in the book. This could either be the chronicle spoken of in 10:3 or another archival document, but it does not mean that Esther wrote this book.

Mordecai's Advancement

10 And King Ahasuerus imposed tribute on the land and *on* the islands of the sea. [2]Now all the acts of his power and his might, and the account of the greatness of Mordecai, to which the king advanced him, *are* they not written in the book of the chronicles of the kings of Media and Persia? [3]For Mordecai the Jew *was* second to King Ahasuerus, and was great among the Jews and well received by the multitude of his brethren, seeking the good of his people and speaking peace to all his countrymen.[a]

10:3 Mordecai...*was* second. He became an important Jewish leader like Joseph (Gen. 41:37–45) and Daniel (Dan. 2:46–49). **speaking peace.** Ahasuerus was assassinated less than 10 years later (about 465 B.C.). There are no further details regarding Esther or Mordecai. What Mordecai did for Israel in less than a decade, Jesus, the Prince of Peace (Is. 9:6,7), will do eternally.

JOB

Times change, but people throughout history remain the same. Their deepest questions echo through the centuries. For example, the questions that Job asked thousands of years ago probably crossed your mind in the past week. The book of Job records the biography of a person who was severely tested. Through Job's experience readers also learn a great deal about the character of God. New Testament writers quoted Job twice (Romans 11:35; 1 Corinthians 3:19), and both Ezekiel (14:14, 20) and James (5:11) referred to Job as a historical figure.

AUTHOR AND DATE

Job was written by an unknown author, possibly before 1445 B.C. (it may be the oldest book in the Bible).

Few internal or external clues point to a specific author for this book. Moses and Solomon have been suggested, but with little support. The ancient Jewish tradition of Mosaic authorship is based on the proximity of Moses' lengthy stay in Midian which was a neighbor of Uz, Job's homeland (1:1). Others simply conclude that the mind-stretching and faith-challenging content of Job certainly fits with Solomon's quest for wisdom. These are educated guesses, not verifiable conclusions.

The Book of Job was probably recorded long after the events occurred. Job's life-span of almost 200 years fits better in the period of the patriarchs—Job and Abraham lived about the same number of years (42:16; Genesis 25:7). Other clues about the antiquity of Job's story can be found in these details: (1) the central social unit was the patriarchal family; (2) the Chaldeans who murdered Job's servants (1:17) were still nomads but are remembered in history as city dwellers; (3) Job's wealth is reported in livestock rather than gold and silver (1:3; 42:12); (4) Job functioned in a priestly role within his family (1:4–5); and (5)there is no mention of central Old Testament themes, such as God's covenant with Abraham, the nation of Israel, the Exodus, or the Law of Moses. At the same time, Job seemed to know about Adam (31:33) as well as the Flood (12:15). These cultural and historical features found in the book place Job's life in the time period following Babel (Genesis 11:1–9) yet before or around the time of Abraham (Genesis 11:27ff).

BACKGROUND AND SETTING

The divine inspiration of this book becomes clear in the early scene that occurs in heaven (1:6–2:10). The reader learns that Job suffered because God was contest-

ing with Satan. Since neither Job nor his friends were aware of the big picture, their attempts to explain the suffering relied on ignorance and misunderstanding. Job finally rested in nothing but faith in God's goodness and the hope of God's redemption. God's vindication of Job's trust is the central message of the book. The reader must consider the possibility that trust in God sometimes goes beyond rational or theological explanations of pain and suffering.

HISTORICAL AND THEOLOGICAL THEMES

Although this book clearly presents Job as an historical figure, the story is timeless. Job's life and his sufferings present significant questions for the faith of believers in all ages. The enduring lesson of this book shocks people with the challenge to trust God despite God's refusal to answer every question or to explain everything that happens in life.

GOD'S PEOPLE DO SUFFER. BAD THINGS HAPPEN ALL THE TIME TO GOOD PEOPLE.

Among the theological themes in Job, two stand out as major: (1) the struggle in the spiritual realm between God and rebellious creatures led by Satan—a struggle with consequences in human life; and (2) the awesome character of God which is to be trusted farther than it can be understood. An exploration of these themes as they are presented throughout the book will lead readers to the following conclusions illustrated by Job's experience:

• There are heavenly events about which believers know nothing, yet these events affect their lives.

• Even the best efforts to explain many of life's issues can be useless.

• God's people do suffer. Bad things happen all the time to good people, so one cannot judge a person's spirituality by either their painful circumstances or their successes.

• Even though God seems far away, perseverance in faith is a most noble virtue because God is good and will prove Himself trustworthy to those who leave their lives in His hands.

• The believer in the midst of suffering should not abandon God but should draw near to Him, so that out of that fellowship can come comfort even if an explanation or understanding never does.

• Suffering may be intense but will ultimately end for the righteous, and God will bless abundantly.

OUTLINE

I. **THE DILEMMA (1:1–2:13)**
 A. Introduction (1:1–5)
 B. Divine Debates with Satan (1:6–2:10)
 C. Arrival of Friends (2:11–13)

II. **THE DEBATES (3:1–37:24)**
 A. The First Cycle (3:1–14:22)
  1. Job's first speech expresses despair (3:1–26)
  2. Eliphaz's first speech kindly protests and urges humility and repentance (4:1–5:27)
  3. Job's reply to Eliphaz expresses anguish and questions the trials, asking for sympathy in his pain (6:1–7:21)
  4. Bildad's first speech accuses Job of impugning God (8:1–22)
  5. Job's response to Bildad admits he is not perfect but may protest what seems unfair (9:1–10:22)
  6. Zophar's first speech tells Job to get right with God (11:1–20)
  7. Job's response to Zophar tells his friends they are wrong and only God knows and will, hopefully, speak to him (12:1–14:22)
 B. The Second Cycle (15:1–21:34)
  1. Eliphaz's second speech accuses Job of presumption and disregarding the wisdom of the ancients (15:1–35)
  2. Job's response to Eliphaz appeals to God against his unjust accusers (16:1–17:16)
  3. Bildad's second speech tells Job he is suffering just what he deserves (18:1–21)
  4. Job's response to Bildad cries out to God for pity (19:1–29)
  5. Zophar's second speech accuses Job of rejecting God by questioning His justice (20:1–29)
  6. Job's response to Zophar says he is out of touch with reality (21:1–34)
 C. The Third Cycle (22:1–26:14)
  1. Eliphaz's third speech denounces Job's criticism of God's justice (22:1–30)
  2. Job's response to Eliphaz is that God knows he is

without guilt; yet in God's providence and refining purpose He permits temporary success for the wicked (23:1–24:25)

3. Bildad's third speech scoffs at Job's direct appeal to God (25:1–6)

4. Job's response to Bildad is that God is indeed perfectly wise and absolutely sovereign but not simplistic as they thought (26:1–14)

D. The Final Defense of Job (27:1–31:40)

1. Job's first monologue affirms his righteousness and that humans can't discover God's wisdom (27:1–28:28)

2. Job's second monologue remembers his past, describes his present, defends his innocence, and asks for God to defend him (29:1–31:40)

E. The Speeches of Elihu (32:1–37:24)

1. Elihu enters into the debate to break the impasse (32:1–22)

2. Elihu charges Job with presumption in criticizing God, not recognizing that God may have a loving purpose, even in allowing Job to suffer (33:1–33)

3. Elihu declares that Job has impugned God's integrity by claiming that it does not pay to lead a godly life (34:1–37)

4. Elihu urges Job to wait patiently for the Lord (35:1–16)

5. Elihu states that he believes God is disciplining Job (36:1–21)

6. Elihu argues that human observers can hardly expect to understand adequately God's dealings in administering justice and mercy (36:22–37:24)

III. THE DELIVERANCE (38:1–42:17)

A. God Interrogates Job (38:1–41:34)

1. God's first response to Job (38:1–40:2)

2. Job's answer to God (40:3–5)

3. God's second response to Job (40:6–41:34)

B. Job Confesses and Worships and is Vindicated (42:1–17)

1. Job passes judgment on himself (42:1–6)

2. God rebukes Eliphaz, Bildad, and Zophar (42:7–9)

3. God restores Job's family, wealth, and long life (42:10–17)

Job and His Family in Uz

1 There was a man in the land of Uz, whose name *was* Job; and that man was blameless and upright, and one who feared God and shunned evil. ²And seven sons and three daughters were born to him. ³Also, his possessions were seven thousand sheep, three thousand camels, five hundred yoke of oxen, five hundred female donkeys, and a very large household, so that this man was the greatest of all the people of the East.

> **1:1–2:13 Job.** He is the central figure of the story. He is a good, rich, well-known family man with 7 sons and 3 daughters. **blameless...upright...feared God...shunned evil.** Though he was not perfect, Job lived a God-honoring, integrity-filled life, and apparently trusted God for redemption.

⁴And his sons would go and feast *in their* houses, each on his *appointed* day, and would send and invite their three sisters to eat and drink with them. ⁵So it was, when the days of feasting had run their course, that Job would send and sanctify them, and he would rise early in the morning and offer burnt offerings *according to* the number of them all. For Job said, "It may be that my sons have sinned and cursed[a] God in their hearts." Thus Job did regularly.

Satan Attacks Job's Character

⁶Now there was a day when the sons of God came to present themselves before the LORD, and Satan[a] also came among them. ⁷And the LORD said to Satan, "From where do you come?"

> **1:6 sons of God.** In this setting God sits in the midst of His heavenly court when the angelic host (see Ps. 29:1), with Satan present, give their ministry report. **Satan.** Given his previous success with Adam (Gen. 3:6–12,17–19), he thought that Job would easily turn against God as well. Satan is known as the accuser of the righteous (Rev. 12:10), though his efforts are still unsuccessful (Rom. 8:31–39).

So Satan answered the LORD and said, "From going to and fro on the earth, and from walking back and forth on it."

⁸Then the LORD said to Satan, "Have you considered My servant Job, that *there is* none like him on the earth, a blameless and upright man, one who fears God and shuns evil?"

⁹So Satan answered the LORD and said, "Does Job fear God for nothing? ¹⁰Have You not made a hedge around him, around his household, and around all that he has on every side? You have blessed the work of his hands, and his possessions have increased in the land. ¹¹But now, stretch out Your hand and touch all that he has, and he will surely curse You to Your face!"

> **1:9–11** Satan's goal was to prove that saving faith could be broken if one suffered enough. He used this same tactic with Jesus (see Matt. 4), Peter (see Luke 22:31), and Paul (see 2 Cor. 12:7). Many Old Testament passages describe God's promise to sustain His children (see Ps. 37:23).

¹²And the LORD said to Satan, "Behold, all that he has *is* in your power; only do not lay a hand on his *person*."

So Satan went out from the presence of the LORD.

Job Loses His Property and Children

¹³Now there was a day when his sons and daughters *were* eating and drinking wine in their oldest brother's house; ¹⁴and a messenger came to Job and said, "The oxen were plowing and the donkeys feeding beside them, ¹⁵when the Sabeans[a] raided *them* and took them away—indeed they

BIOGRAPHICAL SKETCH OF JOB

1. A spiritually mature man (1:1, 8; 2:3)
2. Father of many children (1:2; 42:13)
3. Owner of many herds (1:3; 42:12)
4. A wealthy and influential man (1:3b)
5. A priest to his family (1:5)
6. A loving, wise husband (2:9)
7. A man of prominence in community affairs (29:7–11)
8. A man of benevolence (29:12–17; 31:32)
9. A wise leader (29:21–24)
10. Grower of crops (31:38–40)

1:5 *a*Literally *blessed*, but used here in the evil sense, and so in verse 11 and 2:5, 9   1:6 *a*Literally *the Adversary*, and so throughout this book   1:15 *a*Literally *Sheba* (compare 6:19)

have killed the servants with the edge of the sword; and I alone have escaped to tell you!"

¹⁶While he *was* still speaking, another also came and said, "The fire of God fell from heaven and burned up the sheep and the servants, and consumed them; and I alone have escaped to tell you!"

¹⁷While he *was* still speaking, another also came and said, "The Chaldeans formed three bands, raided the camels and took them away, yes, and killed the servants with the edge of the sword; and I alone have escaped to tell you!"

¹⁸While he *was* still speaking, another also came and said, "Your sons and daughters *were* eating and drinking wine in their oldest brother's house, ¹⁹and suddenly a great wind came from across*ᵃ* the wilderness and struck the four corners of the house, and it fell on the young people, and they are dead; and I alone have escaped to tell you!"

²⁰Then Job arose, tore his robe, and shaved his head; and he fell to the ground and worshiped. ²¹And he said:

> "Naked I came from my mother's
>   womb,
> And naked shall I return there.
> The LORD gave, and the LORD has
>   taken away;
> Blessed be the name of the LORD."

> **1:20,21 worshiped.** Not until Job heard that his children died did he show major grief (see Gen. 37:34). He worshiped God instead of cursing Him, disproving Satan's accusation.

²²In all this Job did not sin nor charge God with wrong.

Satan Attacks Job's Health

2 Again there was a day when the sons of God came to present themselves before the LORD, and Satan came also among them to present himself before the LORD. ²And the LORD said to Satan, "From where do you come?"

Satan answered the LORD and said, "From going to and fro on the earth, and from walking back and forth on it."

³Then the LORD said to Satan, "Have you considered My servant Job, that *there is* none like him on the earth, a blameless and upright man, one who fears God and shuns evil? And still he holds fast to his integrity, although you incited Me against him, to destroy him without cause."

> **2:3 he holds fast to his integrity.** God affirms Job's victory after the first attack. **without cause.** God implies that Satan is the guilty party, not Job. Job's friends, however, accuse him of wrongdoing. Job's suffering had divine purposes.

⁴So Satan answered the LORD and said, "Skin for skin! Yes, all that a man has he will give for his life. ⁵But stretch out Your hand now, and touch his bone and his flesh, and he will surely curse You to Your face!"

⁶And the LORD said to Satan, "Behold, he *is* in your hand, but spare his life."

⁷So Satan went out from the presence of the LORD, and struck Job with painful boils from the sole of his foot to the crown of his head. ⁸And he took for himself a potsherd with which to scrape himself while he sat in the midst of the ashes.

⁹Then his wife said to him, "Do you still hold fast to your integrity? Curse God and die!"

¹⁰But he said to her, "You speak as one of the foolish women speaks. Shall we indeed accept good from God, and shall we not accept adversity?" In all this Job did not sin with his lips.

Job's Three Friends

¹¹Now when Job's three friends heard of all this adversity that had come upon him, each one came from his own place—Eliphaz the Temanite, Bildad the Shuhite, and Zophar the Naamathite. For they had made an appointment together to come and mourn with him, and to comfort him. ¹²And when they raised their eyes from afar, and did not recognize him, they lifted their voices and wept; and each one tore his robe

> **2:11–13** In this scene Job's friends grieve with and comfort him in the traditional manner.

1:19 ᵃSeptuagint omits *across.*

and sprinkled dust on his head toward heaven. ¹³So they sat down with him on the ground seven days and seven nights, and no one spoke a word to him, for they saw that *his* grief was very great.

Job Deplores His Birth

3 After this Job opened his mouth and cursed the day of his *birth*. ²And Job spoke, and said:

³ "May the day perish on which I was born,
   And the night *in which* it was said,
   'A male child is conceived.'
⁴ May that day be darkness;
   May God above not seek it,
   Nor the light shine upon it.
⁵ May darkness and the shadow of death claim it;
   May a cloud settle on it;
   May the blackness of the day terrify it.
⁶ *As for* that night, may darkness seize it;
   May it not rejoice*ᵃ* among the days of the year,
   May it not come into the number of the months.
⁷ Oh, may that night be barren!
   May no joyful shout come into it!
⁸ May those curse it who curse the day,
   Those who are ready to arouse Leviathan.

⁹ May the stars of its morning be dark;
   May it look for light, but *have* none,
   And not see the dawning of the day;
¹⁰ Because it did not shut up the doors of my *mother's* womb,
   Nor hide sorrow from my eyes.

¹¹ "Why did I not die at birth?
   Why did I *not* perish when I came from the womb?
¹² Why did the knees receive me?
   Or why the breasts, that I should nurse?
¹³ For now I would have lain still and been quiet,
   I would have been asleep;
   Then I would have been at rest
¹⁴ With kings and counselors of the earth,
   Who built ruins for themselves,
¹⁵ Or with princes who had gold,
   Who filled their houses *with* silver;
¹⁶ Or *why* was I not hidden like a stillborn child,
   Like infants who never saw light?
¹⁷ There the wicked cease *from* troubling,
   And there the weary are at rest.
¹⁸ *There* the prisoners rest together;
   They do not hear the voice of the oppressor.
¹⁹ The small and great are there,
   And the servant *is* free from his master.

3:6 *ᵃ*Septuagint, Syriac, Targum, and Vulgate read *be joined*.

What kind of relationship does Satan have with God in the Book of Job?

Satan may be God's sworn enemy, but they are not equals. Satan is a creature; God is the Creator. Satan was an angel unwilling to serve in his exalted role, and he rebelled against God.

The continual conflict between Satan and God is illustrated when Satan states that righteous people remain faithful to God only because of what they get. They trust in God only as long as God is nice to them. Satan challenged God's claims of Job's righteousness by calling it untested, if not questionable. Apparently Satan was convinced that he could destroy Job's faith in God by inflicting suffering on him.

Satan suffered another defeat as God demonstrated through Job's life that saving faith can't be destroyed no matter how much trouble the believer suffers or how incomprehensible and undeserved the suffering seems.

After failing to destroy Job, Satan disappears from the story. He remains God's defeated enemy, still raging against God's inevitable triumph.

20 "Why is light given to him who is in
     misery,
   And life to the bitter of soul,
21 Who long for death, but it does not
     come,
   And search for it more than hidden
     treasures;
22 Who rejoice exceedingly,
   And are glad when they can find the
     grave?
23 *Why is light given* to a man whose
     way is hidden,
   And whom God has hedged in?
24 For my sighing comes before I eat,*a*
   And my groanings pour out like
     water.
25 For the thing I greatly feared has
     come upon me,
   And what I dreaded has happened to
     me.
26 I am not at ease, nor am I quiet;
   I have no rest, for trouble comes."

> **3:11–26** Job finally comes to the point where he wishes death upon himself. There is no hint at suicide, given that he still trusts God to be sovereign; however, he does consider how death would be an improvement upon his current situation.

Eliphaz: Job Has Sinned

4 Then Eliphaz the Temanite answered
     and said:

2 "*If* one attempts a word with you, will
     you become weary?
   But who can withhold himself from
     speaking?
3 Surely you have instructed many,
   And you have strengthened weak
     hands.

4 Your words have upheld him who was
     stumbling,
   And you have strengthened the feeble
     knees;
5 But now it comes upon you, and you
     are weary;
   It touches you, and you are troubled.
6 *Is* not your reverence your confidence?
   And the integrity of your ways your
     hope?

7 "Remember now, who *ever* perished
     being innocent?
   Or where were the upright *ever* cut
     off?

> **4:7 who *ever* perished being innocent?** Eliphaz recognized Job's integrity and reverence. He believed that Job would not die because of heinous sin, but something he did must have incited God's wrath. His understanding of the moral order was too simplistic; suffering does not equate with punishment for sin (see Ex. 4:11).

8 Even as I have seen,
   Those who plow iniquity
   And sow trouble reap the same.
9 By the blast of God they perish,
   And by the breath of His anger they
     are consumed.
10 The roaring of the lion,
   The voice of the fierce lion,
   And the teeth of the young lions are
     broken.
11 The old lion perishes for lack of prey,
   And the cubs of the lioness are
     scattered.

12 "Now a word was secretly brought to
     me,
   And my ear received a whisper of it.
13 In disquieting thoughts from the
     visions of the night,
   When deep sleep falls on men,
14 Fear came upon me, and trembling,
   Which made all my bones shake.
15 Then a spirit passed before my face;
   The hair on my body stood up.
16 It stood still,
   But I could not discern its
     appearance.
   A form *was* before my eyes;

3:24 *a*Literally *my bread*

There was silence;
Then I heard a voice *saying:*

17 'Can a mortal be more righteous than
God?
Can a man be more pure than his
Maker?

4:17 Eliphaz concluded that Job suffered because he was not holy or righteous enough.

18 If He puts no trust in His servants,
If He charges His angels with error,
19 How much more those who dwell in
houses of clay,
Whose foundation is in the dust,
Who are crushed before a moth?
20 They are broken in pieces from
morning till evening;
They perish forever, with no one
regarding.
21 Does not their own excellence go
away?
They die, even without wisdom.'

Eliphaz: Job Is Chastened by God

5 "Call out now;
Is there anyone who will answer you?
And to which of the holy ones will
you turn?
2 For wrath kills a foolish man,
And envy slays a simple one.
3 I have seen the foolish taking root,
But suddenly I cursed his dwelling
place.
4 His sons are far from safety,
They are crushed in the gate,
And *there is* no deliverer.
5 Because the hungry eat up his harvest,
Taking it even from the thorns,[a]
And a snare snatches their substance.[b]
6 For affliction does not come from the
dust,
Nor does trouble spring from the
ground;
7 Yet man is born to trouble,
As the sparks fly upward.

8 "But as for me, I would seek God,
And to God I would commit my
cause—

9 Who does great things, and
unsearchable,
Marvelous things without number.
10 He gives rain on the earth,
And sends waters on the fields.
11 He sets on high those who are lowly,
And those who mourn are lifted to
safety.
12 He frustrates the devices of the crafty,
So that their hands cannot carry out
their plans.
13 He catches the wise in their own
craftiness,
And the counsel of the cunning
comes quickly upon them.
14 They meet with darkness in the
daytime,
And grope at noontime as in the night.
15 But He saves the needy from the
sword,
From the mouth of the mighty,
And from their hand.
16 So the poor have hope,
And injustice shuts her mouth.

17 "Behold, happy *is* the man whom God
corrects;
Therefore do not despise the
chastening of the Almighty.

5:17 happy *is* the man whom God corrects. Eliphaz attempted to cheer Job up by saying that it is a good thing when God cares enough about a person to correct him.

18 For He bruises, but He binds up;
He wounds, but His hands make
whole.
19 He shall deliver you in six troubles,
Yes, in seven no evil shall touch you.
20 In famine He shall redeem you from
death,
And in war from the power of the
sword.
21 You shall be hidden from the scourge
of the tongue,
And you shall not be afraid of
destruction when it comes.
22 You shall laugh at destruction and
famine,

5:5 [a]Septuagint reads *They shall not be taken from evil men;* Vulgate reads *And the armed man shall take him by violence.* [b]Septuagint reads *The might shall draw them off;* Vulgate reads *And the thirsty shall drink up their riches.*

And you shall not be afraid of the
    beasts of the earth.

23 For you shall have a covenant with
    the stones of the field,
And the beasts of the field shall be at
    peace with you.

24 You shall know that your tent *is* in
    peace;
You shall visit your dwelling and find
    nothing amiss.

25 You shall also know that your
    descendants *shall be* many,
And your offspring like the grass of
    the earth.

26 You shall come to the grave at a full
    age,
As a sheaf of grain ripens in its
    season.

27 Behold, this we have searched out;
It *is* true.
Hear it, and know for yourself."

Job: My Complaint Is Just

6 Then Job answered and said:

2 "Oh, that my grief were fully weighed,
And my calamity laid with it on the
    scales!

3 For then it would be heavier than the
    sand of the sea—
Therefore my words have been rash.

4 For the arrows of the Almighty *are*
    within me;
My spirit drinks in their poison;
The terrors of God are arrayed against
    me.

5 Does the wild donkey bray when it
    has grass,
Or does the ox low over its fodder?

6 Can flavorless food be eaten without
    salt?
Or is there *any* taste in the white of
    an egg?

7 My soul refuses to touch them;
They *are* as loathsome food to me.

6:1–7:21 This records Job's response to Eliphaz, who had just bombarded him with insensitive and ignorant words.

8 "Oh, that I might have my request,
That God would grant *me* the thing
    that I long for!

9 That it would please God to crush me,

That He would loose His hand and
    cut me off!

10 Then I would still have comfort;
Though in anguish I would exult,
He will not spare;
For I have not concealed the words of
    the Holy One.

11 "What strength do I have, that I should
    hope?
And what *is* my end, that I should
    prolong my life?

12 *Is* my strength the strength of stones?
Or is my flesh bronze?

13 *Is* my help not within me?
And is success driven from me?

14 "To him who is afflicted, kindness
    should be shown by his friend,
Even though he forsakes the fear of
    the Almighty.

15 My brothers have dealt deceitfully like
    a brook,
Like the streams of the brooks that
    pass away,

16 Which are dark because of the ice,
And into which the snow vanishes.

17 When it is warm, they cease to flow;
When it is hot, they vanish from their
    place.

18 The paths of their way turn aside,
They go nowhere and perish.

19 The caravans of Tema look,
The travelers of Sheba hope for them.

20 They are disappointed because they
    were confident;
They come there and are confused.

21 For now you are nothing,
You see terror and are afraid.

22 Did I ever say, 'Bring *something* to
    me'?
Or, 'Offer a bribe for me from your
    wealth'?

23 Or, 'Deliver me from the enemy's
    hand'?
Or, 'Redeem me from the hand of
    oppressors'?

6:15–23 Job essentially tells his friends that their counsel is of no help to him.

24 "Teach me, and I will hold my tongue;
Cause me to understand wherein I
    have erred.

25 How forceful are right words!
   But what does your arguing prove?
26 Do you intend to rebuke *my* words,
   And the speeches of a desperate one,
     which are as wind?
27 Yes, you overwhelm the fatherless,
   And you undermine your friend.
28 Now therefore, be pleased to look at
     me;
   For I would never lie to your face.
29 Yield now, let there be no injustice!
   Yes, concede, my righteousness still
     stands!
30 Is there injustice on my tongue?
   Cannot my taste discern the unsavory?

Job: My Suffering Is Comfortless

7 "*Is there* not a time of hard service
     for man on earth?
   Are not his days also like the days of a
     hired man?
2 Like a servant who earnestly desires
     the shade,
   And like a hired man who eagerly
     looks for his wages,
3 So I have been allotted months of
     futility,
   And wearisome nights have been
     appointed to me.

JOB'S LIVING DEATH

1. Painful boils from head to toe (2:7,13;
   30:17)
2. Severe itching/irritation (2:7,8)
3. Great grief (2:13)
4. Lost appetite (3:24; 6:6,7)
5. Agonizing discomfort (3:24)
6. Insomnia (7:4)
7. Worm and dust infested flesh (7:5)
8. Continual oozing of boils (7:5)
9. Hallucinations (7:14)
10. Decaying skin (13:28)
11. Shriveled up (16:8; 17:7; 19:20)
12. Severe halitosis (19:17)
13. Teeth fell out (19:20)
14. Relentless pain (30:17)
15. Skin turned black (30:30)
16. Raging fever (30:30)
17. Dramatic weight loss (33:21)

4 When I lie down, I say, 'When shall I
     arise,
   And the night be ended?'
   For I have had my fill of tossing till
     dawn.
5 My flesh is caked with worms and
     dust,
   My skin is cracked and breaks out
     afresh.

6 "My days are swifter than a weaver's
     shuttle,
   And are spent without hope.
7 Oh, remember that my life *is* a breath!
   My eye will never again see good.
8 The eye of him who sees me will see
     me no *more*;
   While your *eyes* are upon me, I shall
     no longer *be*.
9 *As* the cloud disappears and vanishes
     away,
   So he who goes down to the grave
     does not come up.
10 He shall never return to his house,
   Nor shall his place know him
     anymore.

> **7:1–10 a time of hard service.** In this passage, Job attempts to reconcile in his own mind what God is doing.

11 "Therefore I will not restrain my
     mouth;
   I will speak in the anguish of my
     spirit;
   I will complain in the bitterness of
     my soul.
12 *Am* I a sea, or a sea serpent,
   That You set a guard over me?
13 When I say, 'My bed will comfort me,
   My couch will ease my complaint,'
14 Then You scare me with dreams
   And terrify me with visions,
15 So that my soul chooses strangling
   And death rather than my body.*a*
16 I loathe *my life*;
   I would not live forever.
   Let me alone,
   For my days *are but* a breath.

17 "What *is* man, that You should exalt
     him,

7:15 *a*Literally *my bones*

That You should set Your heart on
   him,
18 That You should visit him every
   morning,
   And test him every moment?
19 How long?
   Will You not look away from me,
   And let me alone till I swallow my
   saliva?
20 Have I sinned?
   What have I done to You, O watcher
   of men?
   Why have You set me as Your target,
   So that I am a burden to myself?*a*
21 Why then do You not pardon my
   transgression,
   And take away my iniquity?
   For now I will lie down in the dust,
   And You will seek me diligently,
   But I *will* no longer *be.*"

Bildad: Job Should Repent

8 Then Bildad the Shuhite answered and
said:

2 "How long will you speak these *things,*
   And the words of your mouth *be like*
   a strong wind?
3 Does God subvert judgment?
   Or does the Almighty pervert justice?
4 If your sons have sinned against
   Him,
   He has cast them away for their
   transgression.
5 If you would earnestly seek God
   And make your supplication to the
   Almighty,
6 If you *were* pure and upright,
   Surely now He would awake for you,
   And prosper your rightful dwelling
   place.
7 Though your beginning was small,
   Yet your latter end would increase
   abundantly.

8:2–7 Bildad, sure that Job should repent of his sin,
accused him of unjustly defending his innocence.
Believing that something was wrong with Job's relationship with God—sin—he encouraged Job to repent so that he would once again be blessed.

8 "For inquire, please, of the former age,
   And consider the things discovered by
   their fathers;
9 For we *were born* yesterday, and know
   nothing,
   Because our days on earth *are* a
   shadow.
10 Will they not teach you and tell you,
   And utter words from their heart?

11 "Can the papyrus grow up without a
   marsh?
   Can the reeds flourish without water?
12 While it *is* yet green *and* not cut
   down,
   It withers before any *other* plant.
13 So *are* the paths of all who forget God;
   And the hope of the hypocrite shall
   perish,
14 Whose confidence shall be cut off,
   And whose trust *is* a spider's web.
15 He leans on his house, but it does not
   stand.
   He holds it fast, but it does not endure.
16 He grows green in the sun,
   And his branches spread out in his
   garden.
17 His roots wrap around the rock heap,
   And look for a place in the stones.
18 If he is destroyed from his place,
   Then *it* will deny him, *saying,* 'I have
   not seen you.'

19 "Behold, this is the joy of His way,
   And out of the earth others will grow.

8:11–19 Bildad used the illustration of nature for his
cause and effect argument in order to reasonably
connect suffering with sin. He failed to consider that
God may work in different ways.

20 Behold, God will not cast away the
   blameless,
   Nor will He uphold the evildoers.
21 He will yet fill your mouth with
   laughing,
   And your lips with rejoicing.
22 Those who hate you will be clothed
   with shame,
   And the dwelling place of the wicked
   will come to nothing."*a*

7:20 *a*Following Masoretic Text, Targum, and Vulgate; Septuagint and Jewish tradition read *to You.*
8:22 *a*Literally *will not be*

Job: There Is No Mediator

9 Then Job answered and said:

2 "Truly I know *it is* so,
But how can a man be righteous
before God?
3 If one wished to contend with Him,
He could not answer Him one time
out of a thousand.
4 *God is* wise in heart and mighty in
strength.
Who has hardened *himself* against
Him and prospered?
5 He removes the mountains, and they
do not know
When He overturns them in His
anger;
6 He shakes the earth out of its place,
And its pillars tremble;
7 He commands the sun, and it does
not rise;
He seals off the stars;
8 He alone spreads out the heavens,
And treads on the waves of the sea;
9 He made the Bear, Orion, and the
Pleiades,
And the chambers of the south;
10 He does great things past finding out,
Yes, wonders without number.
11 If He goes by me, I do not see *Him*;
If He moves past, I do not perceive
Him;
12 If He takes away, who can hinder
Him?
Who can say to Him, 'What are You
doing?'
13 God will not withdraw His anger,
The allies of the proud[a] lie prostrate
beneath Him.

9:1–10:22 Job, in despair, responds to Bildad and
finally admits that God is holy, wise and strong. Job
wonders if God is fair and why He would not make
Himself known to him earlier. He believes that if God
is not fair then all is hopeless.

14 "How then can I answer Him,
And choose my words *to reason* with
Him?
15 For though I were righteous, I could
not answer Him;
I would beg mercy of my Judge.

16 If I called and He answered me,
I would not believe that He was
listening to my voice.
17 For He crushes me with a tempest,
And multiplies my wounds without
cause.
18 He will not allow me to catch my
breath,
But fills me with bitterness.
19 If *it is a matter* of strength, indeed *He
is* strong;
And if of justice, who will appoint my
day *in court?*
20 Though I were righteous, my own
mouth would condemn me;
Though I *were* blameless, it would
prove me perverse.
21 "I am blameless, yet I do not know
myself;
I despise my life.
22 It *is* all one *thing;*
Therefore I say, 'He destroys the
blameless and the wicked.'
23 If the scourge slays suddenly,
He laughs at the plight of the
innocent.
24 The earth is given into the hand of
the wicked.
He covers the faces of its judges.
If it is not *He,* who else could it be?

9:24 covers the faces of its judges. Here Job accuses God of being unfair and of making it so that
earthly judges also rule unjustly. God eventually responds to these charges (see chaps. 38–41).

25 "Now my days are swifter than a
runner;
They flee away, they see no good.
26 They pass by like swift ships,
Like an eagle swooping on its prey.
27 If I say, 'I will forget my complaint,
I will put off my sad face and wear a
smile,'
28 I am afraid of all my sufferings;
I know that You will not hold me
innocent.
29 *If* I am condemned,
Why then do I labor in vain?
30 If I wash myself with snow water,
And cleanse my hands with soap,

9:13 [a]Hebrew *rahab*

31 Yet You will plunge me into the pit,
And my own clothes will abhor me.

32 "For *He is* not a man, as I *am,*
That I may answer Him,
And that we should go to court
together.

33 Nor is there any mediator between us,
Who may lay his hand on us both.

34 Let Him take His rod away from me,
And do not let dread of Him terrify
me.

35 *Then* I would speak and not fear Him,
But it is not so with me.

Job: I Would Plead with God

10 "My soul loathes my life;
I will give free course to my
complaint,
I will speak in the bitterness of my
soul.

2 I will say to God, 'Do not condemn
me;
Show me why You contend with me.

> **10:2 condemn me.** Job explains that he would ask
> God not to make him suffer physically. He also wants
> to ask Him why all of this has happened to him.

3 *Does it* seem good to You that You
should oppress,
That You should despise the work of
Your hands,
And smile on the counsel of the
wicked?

4 Do You have eyes of flesh?
Or do You see as man sees?

5 *Are* Your days like the days of a
mortal man?
Are Your years like the days of a
mighty man,

6 That You should seek for my iniquity
And search out my sin,

7 Although You know that I am not
wicked,
And *there is* no one who can deliver
from Your hand?

8 'Your hands have made me and
fashioned me,
An intricate unity;
Yet You would destroy me.

9 Remember, I pray, that You have
made me like clay.

And will You turn me into dust
again?

10 Did You not pour me out like milk,
And curdle me like cheese,

11 Clothe me with skin and flesh,
And knit me together with bones and
sinews?

12 You have granted me life and favor,
And Your care has preserved my
spirit.

13 'And these *things* You have hidden in
Your heart;
I know that this *was* with You:

14 If I sin, then You mark me,
And will not acquit me of my iniquity.

15 If I am wicked, woe to me;
Even *if* I am righteous, I cannot lift up
my head.
I am full of disgrace;
See my misery!

16 If *my head* is exalted,
You hunt me like a fierce lion,
And again You show Yourself
awesome against me.

17 You renew Your witnesses against me,
And increase Your indignation toward
me;
Changes and war are *ever* with me.

18 'Why then have You brought me out of
the womb?
Oh, that I had perished and no eye
had seen me!

19 I would have been as though I had not
been.
I would have been carried from the
womb to the grave.

20 Are not my days few?
Cease! Leave me alone, that I may
take a little comfort,

21 Before I go *to the place from which* I
shall not return,
To the land of darkness and the
shadow of death,

22 A land as dark as darkness *itself,*
As the shadow of death, without any
order,
Where even the light *is* like
darkness.' "

Zophar Urges Job to Repent

11 Then Zophar the Naamathite answered and said:

2 "Should not the multitude of words be
      answered?
   And should a man full of talk be
      vindicated?
3 Should your empty talk make men
      hold their peace?
   And when you mock, should no one
      rebuke you?
4 For you have said,
   'My doctrine *is* pure,
   And I am clean in your eyes.'

> **11:4 clean in your eyes.** Job did not claim to be perfect; he still sinned (7:21). He stated that he had not committed a great transgression or maintained an attitude of unrepentance. This infuriated Zophar.

5 But oh, that God would speak,
   And open His lips against you,
6 That He would show you the secrets
      of wisdom!
   For *they would* double *your*
      prudence.
   Know therefore that God exacts from
      you
   Less than your iniquity *deserves.*

7 "Can you search out the deep things of
      God?
   Can you find out the limits of the
      Almighty?
8 *They are* higher than heaven— what
      can you do?
   Deeper than Sheol— what can you
      know?
9 Their measure *is* longer than the
      earth
   And broader than the sea.

10 "If He passes by, imprisons, and
      gathers *to judgment,*
   Then who can hinder Him?
11 For He knows deceitful men;
   He sees wickedness also.
   Will He not then consider *it?*
12 For an empty-headed man will be wise,
   When a wild donkey's colt is born a
      man.

13 "If you would prepare your heart,
   And stretch out your hands toward
      Him;

14 If iniquity *were* in your hand, *and you*
      put it far away,
   And would not let wickedness dwell
      in your tents;

> **11:13,14** Zophar wanted Job to devote his heart to God, plead for forgiveness, repent from his sin, and allow no sin to enter his household. By doing these things Job would be blessed. Zophar believed that these are qualities of a godly life. However, he failed to consider the unpredictable—and seemingly unfair—nature of how God works.

15 Then surely you could lift up your
      face without spot;
   Yes, you could be steadfast, and not
      fear;
16 Because you would forget *your* misery,
   And remember *it* as waters *that have*
      passed away,
17 And *your* life would be brighter than
      noonday.
   Though you were dark, you would be
      like the morning.
18 And you would be secure, because
      there is hope;
   Yes, you would dig *around you, and*
      take your rest in safety.
19 You would also lie down, and no one
      would make *you* afraid;
   Yes, many would court your favor.
20 But the eyes of the wicked will fail,
   And they shall not escape,
   And their hope—loss of life!"

Job Answers His Critics

12 Then Job answered and said:

2 "No doubt you *are* the people,
   And wisdom will die with you!
3 But I have understanding as well as
      you;
   I *am* not inferior to you.
   Indeed, who does not *know* such
      things as these?

4 "I am one mocked by his friends,
   Who called on God, and He answered
      him,
   The just and blameless *who is*
      ridiculed.
5 A lamp[a] is despised in the thought of
      one who is at ease;

12:5 [a]Or *disaster*

It is made ready for those whose feet
slip.

6 The tents of robbers prosper,
And those who provoke God are
secure—
In what God provides by His hand.

12:6 God provides. Job contended that the arguments of his friends did not hold up since God also allowed the wicked to prosper.

7 "But now ask the beasts, and they will
teach you;
And the birds of the air, and they will
tell you;
8 Or speak to the earth, and it will
teach you;
And the fish of the sea will explain to
you.
9 Who among all these does not know
That the hand of the LORD has done
this,
10 In whose hand *is* the life of every
living thing,
And the breath of all mankind?
11 Does not the ear test words
And the mouth taste its food?
12 Wisdom *is* with aged men,
And with length of days,
understanding.

13 "With Him *are* wisdom and strength,
He has counsel and understanding.
14 If He breaks *a thing* down, it cannot
be rebuilt;
If He imprisons a man, there can be
no release.
15 If He withholds the waters, they dry
up;
If He sends them out, they
overwhelm the earth.
16 With Him *are* strength and prudence.
The deceived and the deceiver *are*
His.
17 He leads counselors away plundered,
And makes fools of the judges.
18 He loosens the bonds of kings,
And binds their waist with a belt.
19 He leads princes*ᵃ* away plundered,
And overthrows the mighty.
20 He deprives the trusted ones of
speech,

And takes away the discernment of
the elders.
21 He pours contempt on princes,
And disarms the mighty.
22 He uncovers deep things out of
darkness,
And brings the shadow of death to
light.
23 He makes nations great, and destroys
them;
He enlarges nations, and guides them.
24 He takes away the understanding*ᵃ* of
the chiefs of the people of the
earth,
And makes them wander in a pathless
wilderness.
25 They grope in the dark without light,
And He makes them stagger like a
drunken *man.*

13 "Behold, my eye has seen all *this,*
My ear has heard and understood
it.
2 What you know, I also know;
I *am* not inferior to you.
3 But I would speak to the Almighty,
And I desire to reason with God.

12:13–13:3 This section provides a vivid description of God's wisdom, power and sovereignty. Job affirms God's power throughout every aspect of life. Despite this, Job was not comforted and wanted to take his case before God instead of arguing with his friends.

4 But you forgers of lies,
You *are* all worthless physicians.
5 Oh, that you would be silent,
And it would be your wisdom!
6 Now hear my reasoning,
And heed the pleadings of my lips.
7 Will you speak wickedly for God,
And talk deceitfully for Him?
8 Will you show partiality for Him?
Will you contend for God?
9 Will it be well when He searches you
out?
Or can you mock Him as one mocks
a man?
10 He will surely rebuke you
If you secretly show partiality.
11 Will not His excellence make you
afraid,

And the dread of Him fall upon you?

12 Your platitudes *are* proverbs of ashes,
Your defenses are defenses of clay.

13 "Hold your peace with me, and let me
　　speak,
Then let come on me what *may!*

14 Why do I take my flesh in my teeth,
And put my life in my hands?

15 Though He slay me, yet will I trust
　　Him.
Even so, I will defend my own ways
　　before Him.

> **13:15 Though He slay me, yet will I trust Him.** Job
> continued his stance of innocence and claimed that
> he would still trust God despite everything. This re-
> futed his friends' belief that Job just wanted to avoid
> looking bad by admitting something heinous.

16 He also *shall* be my salvation,
For a hypocrite could not come before
　　Him.

17 Listen carefully to my speech,
And to my declaration with your ears.

18 See now, I have prepared *my* case,
I know that I shall be vindicated.

19 Who *is* he *who* will contend with me?
If now I hold my tongue, I perish.

Job's Despondent Prayer

20 "Only two *things* do not do to me,
Then I will not hide myself from You:

21 Withdraw Your hand far from me,
And let not the dread of You make me
　　afraid.

22 Then call, and I will answer;
Or let me speak, then You respond to
　　me.

23 How many *are* my iniquities and
　　sins?
Make me know my transgression and
　　my sin.

24 Why do You hide Your face,
And regard me as Your enemy?

25 Will You frighten a leaf driven to and
　　fro?
And will You pursue dry stubble?

26 For You write bitter things against me,
And make me inherit the iniquities of
　　my youth.

27 You put my feet in the stocks,

And watch closely all my paths.
You set a limit*ᵃ* for the soles of my
　　feet.

28 "*Man*ᵃ decays like a rotten thing,
Like a garment that is moth-eaten.

14 "Man *who is* born of woman
Is of few days and full of trouble.

2 He comes forth like a flower and fades
　　away;
He flees like a shadow and does not
　　continue.

3 And do You open Your eyes on such a
　　one,
And bring me*ᵃ* to judgment with
　　Yourself?

4 Who can bring a clean *thing* out of an
　　unclean?
No one!

5 Since his days *are* determined,
The number of his months *is* with
　　You;
You have appointed his limits, so that
　　he cannot pass.

6 Look away from him that he may
　　rest,
Till like a hired man he finishes his
　　day.

7 "For there is hope for a tree,
If it is cut down, that it will sprout
　　again,
And that its tender shoots will not
　　cease.

8 Though its root may grow old in the
　　earth,
And its stump may die in the ground,

9 *Yet* at the scent of water it will bud
And bring forth branches like a plant.

10 But man dies and is laid away;
Indeed he breathes his last
And where *is* he?

11 *As* water disappears from the sea,
And a river becomes parched and
　　dries up,

> **14:1–12** Job accepted God's sovereignty but chal-
> lenged the meaningfulness of life. He asked for a
> decrease in the pain and judgment and an increase
> in the grace and rest.

13:27 ᵃLiterally *inscribe a print*　　13:28 ᵃLiterally *He*　　14:3 ᵃSeptuagint, Syriac, and Vulgate read *him.*

12 So man lies down and does not rise.
   Till the heavens *are* no more,
   They will not awake
   Nor be roused from their sleep.

13 "Oh, that You would hide me in the
      grave,
   That You would conceal me until
      Your wrath is past,
   That You would appoint me a set
      time, and remember me!

14 If a man dies, shall he live *again*?
   All the days of my hard service I will
      wait,
   Till my change comes.

15 You shall call, and I will answer You;
   You shall desire the work of Your
      hands.

16 For now You number my steps,
   But do not watch over my sin.

17 My transgression *is* sealed up in a bag,
   And You cover[a] my iniquity.

18 "But *as* a mountain falls *and* crumbles
      away,
   And *as* a rock is moved from its place;

19 *As* water wears away stones,
   And as torrents wash away the soil of
      the earth;
   So You destroy the hope of man.

20 You prevail forever against him, and
      he passes on;
   You change his countenance and send
      him away.

21 His sons come to honor, and he does
      not know *it*;
   They are brought low, and he does not
      perceive *it*.

22 But his flesh will be in pain over it,
   And his soul will mourn over it."

Eliphaz Accuses Job of Folly

15 Then Eliphaz the Temanite an-
      swered and said:

2 "Should a wise man answer with
      empty knowledge,
   And fill himself with the east wind?

3 Should he reason with unprofitable
      talk,
   Or by speeches with which he can do
      no good?

4 Yes, you cast off fear,
   And restrain prayer before God.

5 For your iniquity teaches your mouth,
   And you choose the tongue of the
      crafty.

6 Your own mouth condemns you, and
      not I;
   Yes, your own lips testify against you.

> **15:1–6** Eliphaz accuses Job of sinfully complaining
> to God, of speaking empty words, of lacking godly
> fear, and of foregoing righteous prayer.

7 "*Are* you the first man *who* was born?
   Or were you made before the hills?

8 Have you heard the counsel of God?
   Do you limit wisdom to yourself?

9 What do you know that we do not
      know?
   What do you understand that *is* not in
      us?

10 Both the gray-haired and the aged *are*
      among us,
   Much older than your father.

11 *Are* the consolations of God too small
      for you,
   And the word *spoken* gently[a] with
      you?

12 Why does your heart carry you away,
   And what do your eyes wink at,

13 That you turn your spirit against
      God,
   And let *such* words go out of your
      mouth?

14 "What *is* man, that he could be pure?
   And *he who is* born of a woman, that
      he could be righteous?

15 If *God* puts no trust in His saints,
   And the heavens are not pure in His
      sight,

16 How much less man, *who is*
      abominable and filthy,
   Who drinks iniquity like water!

17 "I will tell you, hear me;
   What I have seen I will declare,

18 What wise men have told,
   Not hiding *anything received* from
      their fathers,

19 To whom alone the land was given,
   And no alien passed among them:

14:17 [a]Literally *plaster over*   15:11 [a]Septuagint reads *a secret thing.*

20 The wicked man writhes with pain all
    his days,
And the number of years is hidden
    from the oppressor.
21 Dreadful sounds *are* in his ears;
In prosperity the destroyer comes
    upon him.
22 He does not believe that he will
    return from darkness,
For a sword is waiting for him.
23 He wanders about for bread, *saying,*
    'Where *is it?*'
He knows that a day of darkness is
    ready at his hand.
24 Trouble and anguish make him
    afraid;
They overpower him, like a king
    ready for battle.
25 For he stretches out his hand against
    God,
And acts defiantly against the
    Almighty,
26 Running stubbornly against Him
With his strong, embossed shield.

27 "Though he has covered his face with
    his fatness,
And made *his* waist heavy with fat,
28 He dwells in desolate cities,
In houses which no one inhabits,
Which are destined to become ruins.
29 He will not be rich,
Nor will his wealth continue,
Nor will his possessions overspread
    the earth.
30 He will not depart from darkness;
The flame will dry out his
    branches,
And by the breath of His mouth he
    will go away.
31 Let him not trust in futile *things,*
    deceiving himself,
For futility will be his reward.
32 It will be accomplished before his
    time,
And his branch will not be green.
33 He will shake off his unripe grape like
    a vine,
And cast off his blossom like an olive
    tree.
34 For the company of hypocrites *will be*
    barren,
And fire will consume the tents of
    bribery.

35 They conceive trouble and bring forth
    futility;
Their womb prepares deceit."

15:17–35 Eliphaz continues to argue that Job's sin and hypocrisy bring God's judgment, and he parallels Job with the wicked.

Job Reproaches His Pitiless Friends

16 Then Job answered and said:

2 "I have heard many such things;
Miserable comforters *are* you all!
3 Shall words of wind have an end?
Or what provokes you that you
    answer?
4 I also could speak as you *do,*
If your soul were in my soul's place.
I could heap up words against you,
And shake my head at you;
5 *But* I would strengthen you with my
    mouth,
And the comfort of my lips would
    relieve *your grief.*

16:2–5 Miserable comforters *are* you all! The original attempt of Job's friends to comfort him failed when they repeatedly (and wrongly) accused him of sin and unrepentance. Job would not have done the same if the tables were turned.

6 "Though I speak, my grief is not
    relieved;
And *if* I remain silent, how am I
    eased?
7 But now He has worn me out;
You have made desolate all my
    company.
8 You have shriveled me up,
And it is a witness *against me;*
My leanness rises up against me
And bears witness to my face.
9 He tears *me* in His wrath, and hates
    me;
He gnashes at me with His teeth;
My adversary sharpens His gaze on
    me.
10 They gape at me with their mouth,
They strike me reproachfully on the
    cheek,
They gather together against me.
11 God has delivered me to the ungodly,
And turned me over to the hands of
    the wicked.

¹² I was at ease, but He has shattered me;
He also has taken *me* by my neck,
	and shaken me to pieces;
He has set me up for His target,
¹³ His archers surround me.
He pierces my heart^a and does not
	pity;
He pours out my gall on the ground.
¹⁴ He breaks me with wound upon
	wound;
He runs at me like a warrior.^a

¹⁵ "I have sewn sackcloth over my skin,
And laid my head^a in the dust.
¹⁶ My face is flushed from weeping,
And on my eyelids *is* the shadow of
	death;
¹⁷ Although no violence *is* in my hands,
And my prayer *is* pure.

¹⁸ "O earth, do not cover my blood,
And let my cry have no *resting* place!
¹⁹ Surely even now my witness *is* in
	heaven,
And my evidence *is* on high.
²⁰ My friends scorn me;
My eyes pour out *tears* to God.
²¹ Oh, that one might plead for a man
	with God,

16:15–20 Job could not turn to anyone but God, and
even He was silent.

As a man *pleads* for his neighbor!
²² For when a few years are finished,
I shall go the way of no return.

Job Prays for Relief

17 "My spirit is broken,
	My days are extinguished,
The grave *is ready* for me.
² *Are* not mockers with me?
And does not my eye dwell on their
	provocation?

³ "Now put down a pledge for me with
	Yourself.
Who *is* he *who* will shake hands with
	me?
⁴ For You have hidden their heart from
	understanding;

Therefore You will not exalt *them*.
⁵ He who speaks flattery to *his* friends,
Even the eyes of his children will fail.

⁶ "But He has made me a byword of the
	people,
And I have become one in whose face
	men spit.
⁷ My eye has also grown dim because of
	sorrow,
And all my members *are* like
	shadows.
⁸ Upright *men* are astonished at this,
And the innocent stirs himself up
	against the hypocrite.
⁹ Yet the righteous will hold to his
	way,
And he who has clean hands will be
	stronger and stronger.

17:9 Yet the righteous will hold to his way. Those
who suffer, including Job, must remain righteous
because, as Job knew, suffering produces strength
(2 Cor. 12:7–10).

¹⁰ "But please, come back again, all of
	you,^a
For I shall not find *one* wise *man*
	among you.
¹¹ My days are past,
My purposes are broken off,
Even the thoughts of my heart.
¹² They change the night into day;
'The light *is* near,' *they say*, in the face
	of darkness.
¹³ If I wait *for* the grave *as* my house,
If I make my bed in the darkness,
¹⁴ If I say to corruption, 'You *are* my
	father,'
And to the worm, 'You *are* my mother
	and my sister,'
¹⁵ Where then *is* my hope?
As for my hope, who can see it?
¹⁶ *Will* they go down to the gates of
	Sheol?
Shall *we have* rest together in the
	dust?"

Bildad: The Wicked Are Punished

18 Then Bildad the Shuhite answered
	and said:

16:13 ^aLiterally *kidneys*   16:14 ^aVulgate reads *giant*.   16:15 ^aLiterally *horn*   17:10 ^aFollowing some
Hebrew manuscripts, Septuagint, Syriac, and Vulgate; Masoretic Text and Targum read *all of them*.

2 "How long *till* you put an end to
      words?
   Gain understanding, and afterward
      we will speak.
3 Why are we counted as beasts,
   And regarded as stupid in your sight?
4 You who tear yourself in anger,
   Shall the earth be forsaken for you?
   Or shall the rock be removed from its
      place?

5 "The light of the wicked indeed goes
      out,
   And the flame of his fire does not
      shine.
6 The light is dark in his tent,
   And his lamp beside him is put out.
7 The steps of his strength are
      shortened,
   And his own counsel casts him down.
8 For he is cast into a net by his own
      feet,
   And he walks into a snare.
9 The net takes *him* by the heel,
   And a snare lays hold of him.
10 A noose *is* hidden for him on the
      ground,
   And a trap for him in the road.
11 Terrors frighten him on every side,
   And drive him to his feet.
12 His strength is starved,
   And destruction *is* ready at his side.
13 It devours patches of his skin;
   The firstborn of death devours his
      limbs.
14 He is uprooted from the shelter of his
      tent,
   And they parade him before the king
      of terrors.
15 They dwell in his tent *who are* none
      of his;
   Brimstone is scattered on his
      dwelling.
16 His roots are dried out below,
   And his branch withers above.
17 The memory of him perishes from
      the earth,
   And he has no name among the
      renowned.*ª*
18 He is driven from light into darkness,
   And chased out of the world.

19 He has neither son nor posterity
      among his people,
   Nor any remaining in his dwellings.
20 Those in the west are astonished at
      his day,
   As those in the east are frightened.
21 Surely such *are* the dwellings of the
      wicked,
   And this *is* the place *of him who* does
      not know God."

18:1–21 Bildad told Job to stop complaining and to be reasonable; he recounted another story about how the wicked suffer judgment.

Job Trusts in His Redeemer

19 Then Job answered and said:

2 "How long will you torment my soul,
   And break me in pieces with words?
3 These ten times you have reproached
      me;
   You are not ashamed *that* you have
      wronged me.*ª*
4 And if indeed I have erred,
   My error remains with me.
5 If indeed you exalt *yourselves* against
      me,
   And plead my disgrace against me,
6 Know then that God has wronged me,
   And has surrounded me with His net.

19:5–7 Job felt that if God sent him friends like Bildad, he did not need enemies.

7 "If I cry out concerning wrong, I am
      not heard.
   If I cry aloud, *there is* no justice.
8 He has fenced up my way, so that I
      cannot pass;
   And He has set darkness in my paths.
9 He has stripped me of my glory,
   And taken the crown *from* my head.
10 He breaks me down on every side,
   And I am gone;
   My hope He has uprooted like a tree.
11 He has also kindled His wrath against
      me,
   And He counts me as *one of* His
      enemies.

18:17 *ª*Literally *before the outside,* meaning distinguished, famous   19:3 *ª*A Jewish tradition reads *make yourselves strange to me.*

12 His troops come together
And build up their road against me;
They encamp all around my tent.

13 "He has removed my brothers far from
me,
And my acquaintances are completely
estranged from me.

14 My relatives have failed,
And my close friends have forgotten
me.

15 Those who dwell in my house, and
my maidservants,
Count me as a stranger;
I am an alien in their sight.

16 I call my servant, but he gives no
answer;
I beg him with my mouth.

17 My breath is offensive to my wife,
And I am repulsive to the children of
my own body.

18 Even young children despise me;
I arise, and they speak against me.

19 All my close friends abhor me,
And those whom I love have turned
against me.

20 My bone clings to my skin and to my
flesh,
And I have escaped by the skin of my
teeth.

21 "Have pity on me, have pity on me,
O you my friends,
For the hand of God has struck me!

22 Why do you persecute me as God does,
And are not satisfied with my flesh?

23 "Oh, that my words were written!
Oh, that they were inscribed in a
book!

24 That they were engraved on a rock
With an iron pen and lead, forever!

25 For I know that my Redeemer lives,
And He shall stand at last on the
earth;

26 And after my skin is destroyed, this I
know,
That in my flesh I shall see God,

27 Whom I shall see for myself,
And my eyes shall behold, and not
another.
How my heart yearns within me!

28 If you should say, 'How shall we
persecute him?'—

Since the root of the matter is found
in me,

29 Be afraid of the sword for yourselves;
For wrath brings the punishment of
the sword,
That you may know there is a
judgment."

19:23–29 Job declared God as his Redeemer in his darkest hour. He deeply desired for his life story to be recorded so that all would know that he did not sin as he was accused. He knew he would be redeemed at the final judgment.

Zophar's Sermon on the Wicked Man

20 Then Zophar the Naamathite answered and said:

2 "Therefore my anxious thoughts make
me answer,
Because of the turmoil within me.

3 I have heard the rebuke that
reproaches me,
And the spirit of my understanding
causes me to answer.

4 "Do you not know this of old,
Since man was placed on earth,

5 That the triumphing of the wicked is
short,
And the joy of the hypocrite is but for
a moment?

6 Though his haughtiness mounts up
to the heavens,
And his head reaches to the clouds,

7 Yet he will perish forever like his own
refuse;
Those who have seen him will say,
'Where is he?'

8 He will fly away like a dream, and not
be found;
Yes, he will be chased away like a
vision of the night.

9 The eye that saw him will see him no
more,
Nor will his place behold him
anymore.

10 His children will seek the favor of the
poor,
And his hands will restore his wealth.

11 His bones are full of his youthful
vigor,
But it will lie down with him in the
dust.

12 "Though evil is sweet in his mouth,
And he hides it under his tongue,
13 *Though* he spares it and does not
forsaken it,
But still keeps it in his mouth,
14 *Yet* his food in his stomach turns
sour;
It becomes cobra venom within him.
15 He swallows down riches
And vomits them up again;
God casts them out of his belly.
16 He will suck the poison of cobras;
The viper's tongue will slay him.
17 He will not see the streams,
The rivers flowing with honey and
cream.
18 He will restore that for which he
labored,
And will not swallow *it* down;
From the proceeds of business
He will get no enjoyment.
19 For he has oppressed *and* forsaken the
poor,
He has violently seized a house which
he did not build.

20 "Because he knows no quietness in his
heart,ᵃ
He will not save anything he desires.
21 Nothing is left for him to eat;
Therefore his well-being will not last.
22 In his self-sufficiency he will be in
distress;
Every hand of misery will come
against him.

20:12–22 Zophar implied that Job had no joy in his
life because of the sin in his heart.

23 *When* he is about to fill his stomach,
God will cast on him the fury of His
wrath,
And will rain *it* on him while he is
eating.
24 He will flee from the iron weapon;
A bronze bow will pierce him
through.
25 It is drawn, and comes out of the
body;
Yes, the glittering *point comes* out of
his gall.
Terrors *come* upon him;

26 Total darkness *is* reserved for his
treasures.
An unfanned fire will consume him;
It shall go ill with him who is left in
his tent.
27 The heavens will reveal his iniquity,
And the earth will rise up against
him.
28 The increase of his house will depart,
And his goods will flow away in the
day of His wrath.
29 This *is* the portion from God for a
wicked man,
The heritage appointed to him by
God."

Job's Discourse on the Wicked

21 Then Job answered and said:

2 "Listen carefully to my speech,
And let this be your consolation.
3 Bear with me that I may speak,
And after I have spoken, keep
mocking.

4 "As for me, *is* my complaint against
man?
And if *it were,* why should I not be
impatient?
5 Look at me and be astonished;
Put *your* hand over *your* mouth.
6 Even when I remember I am terrified,
And trembling takes hold of my flesh.
7 Why do the wicked live *and* become
old,
Yes, become mighty in power?
8 Their descendants are established
with them in their sight,
And their offspring before their eyes.
9 Their houses *are* safe from fear,
Neither *is* the rod of God upon them.
10 Their bull breeds without failure;
Their cow calves without miscarriage.
11 They send forth their little ones like a
flock,
And their children dance.
12 They sing to the tambourine and
harp,
And rejoice to the sound of the flute.
13 They spend their days in wealth,
And in a moment go down to the
grave.ᵃ

20:20 ᵃLiterally *belly*   21:13 ᵃOr *Sheol*

14 Yet they say to God, 'Depart from
      us,
   For we do not desire the knowledge of
      Your ways.
15 Who *is* the Almighty, that we should
      serve Him?
   And what profit do we have if we pray
      to Him?'
16 Indeed their prosperity *is* not in their
      hand;
   The counsel of the wicked is far from
      me.

17 "How often is the lamp of the wicked
      put out?
   How often does their destruction
      come upon them,
   The sorrows *God* distributes in His
      anger?
18 They are like straw before the wind,
   And like chaff that a storm carries
      away.
19 *They say,* 'God lays up one's*ᵃ* iniquity
      for his children';
   Let Him recompense him, that he
      may know *it.*

20 Let his eyes see his destruction,
   And let him drink of the wrath of the
      Almighty.
21 For what does he care about his
      household after him,
   When the number of his months is
      cut in half?

22 "Can *anyone* teach God knowledge,
   Since He judges those on high?

> **21:17–22** Job contends against his friends' senti-
> ments and suggests that his friends are guilty of tell-
> ing God how He should deal with people.

23 One dies in his full strength,
   Being wholly at ease and secure;
24 His pails*ᵃ* are full of milk,
   And the marrow of his bones is
      moist.
25 Another man dies in the bitterness of
      his soul,
   Never having eaten with pleasure.
26 They lie down alike in the dust,
   And worms cover them.

21:19 *ᵃ*Literally *his*   21:24 *ᵃ*Septuagint and Vulgate read *bowels;* Syriac reads *sides;* Targum reads *breasts.*

Why do righteous and innocent people suffer?

Of course no human being is truly righteous or innocent. The Bible clearly states that all have sinned (Romans 3:23). And all sinners deserve to be punished, eternally. That's what makes God's grace so amazing!

In understanding that truth, however, it must be admitted that on a relative human scale, righteous and innocent people exist. That is, some people are more moral and virtuous than others and some are more innocent. Consider, for example, a person who strives to live out the Golden Rule, or another who gives generously to the poor. And certainly most consider small children to have a naive innocence. So this question could be rephrased: "Why do little children and people who live exemplary lives suffer?"

This question reveals the assumption that there is a direct connection between righteousness and innocence on the one hand and pain-free living on the other. There may be a connection, but it is not direct. Indeed, sin eventually does lead to suffering, but suffering is not an infallible indicator of sin. Job's friends could not see beyond this point. For them, a person's suffering was *always* an effect whose only cause could be that person's sin.

The righteous and the innocent do indeed suffer for a variety of reasons: (1) Sometimes righteous actions in a sinful world involve suffering—as when a righteous person sacrifices his or her life for another; (2) Sometimes the sins of others involve the righteous in suffering—a child may be deeply hurt as a result of his or her parent's actions; (3) The righteous and innocent are not exempt from the painful situations which arise in life, in an imperfect and sinful world—like toothaches and smashed fingers; and (4) People sometimes suffer for no specific reason that can be clarified. Job is a perfect illustration of this last experience.

27 "Look, I know your thoughts,
And the schemes *with which* you
would wrong me.
28 For you say,
'Where *is* the house of the prince?
And where *is* the tent,[a]
The dwelling place of the wicked?'
29 Have you not asked those who travel
the road?
And do you not know their signs?
30 For the wicked are reserved for the
day of doom;
They shall be brought out on the day
of wrath.
31 Who condemns his way to his face?
And who repays him *for what* he has
done?
32 Yet he shall be brought to the grave,
And a vigil kept over the tomb.
33 The clods of the valley shall be sweet
to him;
Everyone shall follow him,
As countless *have gone* before him.
34 How then can you comfort me with
empty words,
Since falsehood remains in your
answers?"

> **21:1–34** Job again refutes the cause-and-effect rela-
> tionship of sin and suffering and shows that the wick-
> ed also prosper. By implication, the righteous could
> also suffer. This presents problems for his friends'
> convictions.

Eliphaz Accuses Job of Wickedness

22 Then Eliphaz the Temanite answered and said:

2 "Can a man be profitable to God,
Though he who is wise may be
profitable to himself?
3 *Is it* any pleasure to the Almighty that
you are righteous?
Or *is it* gain *to Him* that you make
your ways blameless?

4 "Is it because of your fear of Him that
He corrects you,
And enters into judgment with you?
5 *Is* not your wickedness great,
And your iniquity without end?

6 For you have taken pledges from your
brother for no reason,
And stripped the naked of their
clothing.
7 You have not given the weary water to
drink,
And you have withheld bread from
the hungry.
8 But the mighty man possessed the
land,
And the honorable man dwelt in it.
9 You have sent widows away empty,
And the strength of the fatherless was
crushed.
10 Therefore snares *are* all around you,
And sudden fear troubles you,
11 Or darkness *so that* you cannot see;
And an abundance of water covers
you.

12 "Is not God in the height of heaven?
And see the highest stars, how lofty
they are!
13 And you say, 'What does God know?
Can He judge through the deep
darkness?
14 Thick clouds cover Him, so that He
cannot see,
And He walks above the circle of
heaven.'
15 Will you keep to the old way
Which wicked men have trod,
16 Who were cut down before their time,
Whose foundations were swept away
by a flood?
17 They said to God, 'Depart from us!
What can the Almighty do to them?'[a]
18 Yet He filled their houses with good
things;
But the counsel of the wicked is far
from me.

19 "The righteous see *it* and are glad,
And the innocent laugh at them:
20 'Surely our adversaries[a] are cut down,
And the fire consumes their
remnant.'

21 "Now acquaint yourself with Him, and
be at peace;
Thereby good will come to you.

21:28 [a]Vulgate omits *the tent*.   22:17 [a]Septuagint and Syriac read *us*.   22:20 [a]Septuagint reads
substance.

22 Receive, please, instruction from His
    mouth,
    And lay up His words in your heart.
23 If you return to the Almighty, you will
    be built up;
    You will remove iniquity far from
    your tents.
24 Then you will lay your gold in the
    dust,
    And the *gold* of Ophir among the
    stones of the brooks.
25 Yes, the Almighty will be your gold[a]
    And your precious silver;
26 For then you will have your delight in
    the Almighty,
    And lift up your face to God.
27 You will make your prayer to Him,
    He will hear you,
    And you will pay your vows.
28 You will also declare a thing,
    And it will be established for you;
    So light will shine on your ways.
29 When they cast *you* down, and you
    say, 'Exaltation *will come!'*
    Then He will save the humble *person.*
30 He will *even* deliver one who is not
    innocent;
    Yes, he will be delivered by the purity
    of your hands."

22:1–30 Eliphaz's final words are biting and full of
frustration. He does not believe that God is directly
concerned with insignificant Job, his complaints, or
his claims to righteousness. He blames Job's great
sins against humanity for his suffering.

Job Proclaims God's Righteous Judgments

23 Then Job answered and said:

2 "Even today my complaint is bitter;
    My[a] hand is listless because of my
    groaning.
3 Oh, that I knew where I might find
    Him,
    That I might come to His seat!
4 I would present *my* case before Him,
    And fill my mouth with arguments.
5 I would know the words *which* He
    would answer me,
    And understand what He would say
    to me.

6 Would He contend with me in His
    great power?
    No! But He would take *note* of me.
7 There the upright could reason with
    Him,
    And I would be delivered forever from
    my Judge.
8 "Look, I go forward, but He is not
    there,
    And backward, but I cannot perceive
    Him;
9 When He works on the left hand, I
    cannot behold *Him;*
    When He turns to the right hand, I
    cannot see *Him.*
10 But He knows the way that I take;
    When He has tested me, I shall come
    forth as gold.
11 My foot has held fast to His steps;
    I have kept His way and not turned
    aside.
12 I have not departed from the
    commandment of His lips;
    I have treasured the words of His
    mouth
    More than my necessary *food.*
13 "But He *is* unique, and who can make
    Him change?
    And *whatever* His soul desires, *that*
    He does.
14 For He performs *what is* appointed for
    me,
    And many such *things are* with Him.

23:14 He performs *what is* appointed for me. Job
repeatedly resigned himself to God's sovereignty,
despite times of doubt. Even though he did not understand, Job trusted God.

15 Therefore I am terrified at His
    presence;
    When I consider *this,* I am afraid of
    Him.
16 For God made my heart weak,
    And the Almighty terrifies me;
17 Because I was not cut off from the
    presence of darkness,
    And He did *not* hide deep darkness
    from my face.

22:25 [a]The ancient versions suggest *defense;* Hebrew reads *gold* as in verse 24.   23:2 [a]Following
Masoretic Text, Targum, and Vulgate; Septuagint and Syriac read *His.*

Job Complains of Violence on the Earth

24 "*Since* times are not hidden from the Almighty,
Why do those who know Him see not His days?

2 "*Some* remove landmarks;
They seize flocks violently and feed *on them*;

3 They drive away the donkey of the fatherless;
They take the widow's ox as a pledge.

4 They push the needy off the road;
All the poor of the land are forced to hide.

5 Indeed, *like* wild donkeys in the desert,
They go out to their work, searching for food.
The wilderness *yields* food for them *and* for *their* children.

6 They gather their fodder in the field
And glean in the vineyard of the wicked.

7 They spend the night naked, without clothing,
And have no covering in the cold.

24:7 spend the night. Outer garments were commonly taken as a pledge for money owed. The OT did not allow them to be held overnight for the sake of the owner's health.

8 They are wet with the showers of the mountains,
And huddle around the rock for want of shelter.

9 "*Some* snatch the fatherless from the breast,
And take a pledge from the poor.

10 They cause *the poor* to go naked, without clothing;
And they take away the sheaves from the hungry.

11 They press out oil within their walls,
And tread winepresses, yet suffer thirst.

12 The dying groan in the city,
And the souls of the wounded cry out;
Yet God does not charge *them* with wrong.

13 "There are those who rebel against the light;
They do not know its ways
Nor abide in its paths.

14 The murderer rises with the light;
He kills the poor and needy;
And in the night he is like a thief.

15 The eye of the adulterer waits for the twilight,
Saying, 'No eye will see me';
And he disguises *his* face.

16 In the dark they break into houses
Which they marked for themselves in the daytime;
They do not know the light.

17 For the morning is the same to them as the shadow of death;
If *someone* recognizes *them*,
They are in the terrors of the shadow of death.

18 "They *should be* swift on the face of the waters,
Their portion *should be* cursed in the earth,
So that no *one would* turn into the way of their vineyards.

19 As drought and heat consume the snow waters,
So the grave*ᵃ* consumes *those who* have sinned.

20 The womb *should* forget him,
The worm *should* feed sweetly on him;
He *should* be remembered no more,
And wickedness *should* be broken like a tree.

21 For he preys on the barren *who* do not bear,
And does no good for the widow.

22 "But *God* draws the mighty away with His power;
He rises up, but no *man* is sure of life.

23 He gives them security, and they rely *on it*;
Yet His eyes *are* on their ways.

24 They are exalted for a little while,
Then they are gone.
They are brought low;

They are taken out of the way like all
    others;
They dry out like the heads of grain.

25 "Now if *it is* not *so*, who will prove me
    a liar,
And make my speech worth
    nothing?"

> **23:1–24:25** Job's reply to Eliphaz was that he yearned for fellowship with God so he could again know His love and discover the meaning for his suffering.

Bildad: How Can Man Be Righteous?

25 Then Bildad the Shuhite answered and said:

2 "Dominion and fear *belong* to Him;
He makes peace in His high places.
3 Is there any number to His armies?
Upon whom does His light not rise?
4 How then can man be righteous
    before God?
Or how can he be pure *who is* born of
    a woman?
5 If even the moon does not shine,
And the stars are not pure in His
    sight,
6 How much less man, *who is* a
    maggot,
And a son of man, *who is* a worm?"

> **25:1–6** In the last speech by one of the friends, Bildad contended that God is exalted and humans are sinful.

Job: Man's Frailty and God's Majesty

26 But Job answered and said:

2 "How have you helped *him who is*
    without power?
How have you saved the arm *that has*
    no strength?
3 How have you counseled *one who has*
    no wisdom?
And *how* have you declared sound
    advice to many?
4 To whom have you uttered words?
And whose spirit came from you?

5 "The dead tremble,
Those under the waters and those
    inhabiting them.

6 Sheol *is* naked before Him,
And Destruction has no covering.
7 He stretches out the north over empty
    space;
He hangs the earth on nothing.
8 He binds up the water in His thick
    clouds,
Yet the clouds are not broken under
    it.
9 He covers the face of *His* throne,
And spreads His cloud over it.
10 He drew a circular horizon on the face
    of the waters,
At the boundary of light and
    darkness.

> **26:7,10 hangs the earth on nothing.** This is a scientifically accurate statement from an ancient perspective and points to Scripture's divine authorship. **a circular horizon.** This is also a scientifically accurate claim made when most thought the world was flat.

11 The pillars of heaven tremble,
And are astonished at His rebuke.
12 He stirs up the sea with His power,
And by His understanding He breaks
    up the storm.
13 By His Spirit He adorned the heavens;
His hand pierced the fleeing serpent.
14 Indeed these *are* the mere edges of
    His ways,
And how small a whisper we hear of
    Him!
But the thunder of His power who can
    understand?"

Job Maintains His Integrity

27 Moreover Job continued his discourse, and said:

2 "*As* God lives, *who* has taken away my
    justice,
And the Almighty, *who* has made my
    soul bitter,
3 As long as my breath *is* in me,
And the breath of God in my nostrils,
4 My lips will not speak wickedness,
Nor my tongue utter deceit.
5 Far be it from me
That I should say you are right;
Till I die I will not put away my
    integrity from me.
6 My righteousness I hold fast, and will
    not let it go;

My heart shall not reproach *me* as
long as I live.

7 "May my enemy be like the wicked,
And he who rises up against me like
the unrighteous.
8 For what is the hope of the hypocrite,
Though he may gain *much*,
If God takes away his life?
9 Will God hear his cry
When trouble comes upon him?
10 Will he delight himself in the
Almighty?
Will he always call on God?

11 "I will teach you about the hand of
God;
What *is* with the Almighty I will not
conceal.

27:11 I will teach you about the hand of God. Job
and his friends disagreed about how God judges sin,
since Job concluded that suffering is not necessarily
a result of sin. His comments here introduce his
thoughts on wisdom.

12 Surely all of you have seen *it*;
Why then do you behave with
complete nonsense?

13 "This is the portion of a wicked man
with God,
And the heritage of oppressors,
received from the Almighty:
14 If his children are multiplied, *it is* for
the sword;
And his offspring shall not be
satisfied with bread.
15 Those who survive him shall be
buried in death,
And their*a* widows shall not weep,
16 Though he heaps up silver like dust,
And piles up clothing like clay—
17 He may pile *it* up, but the just will
wear *it*,
And the innocent will divide the silver.
18 He builds his house like a moth,*a*
Like a booth *which* a watchman
makes.

19 The rich man will lie down,
But not be gathered *up;a*
He opens his eyes,
And he *is* no more.
20 Terrors overtake him like a flood;
A tempest steals him away in the
night.
21 The east wind carries him away, and
he is gone;
It sweeps him out of his place.
22 It hurls against him and does not
spare;
He flees desperately from its power.
23 *Men* shall clap their hands at him,
And shall hiss him out of his place.

Job's Discourse on Wisdom

28 "Surely there is a mine for silver,
And a place *where* gold is
refined.
2 Iron is taken from the earth,
And copper *is* smelted *from* ore.
3 *Man* puts an end to darkness,
And searches every recess
For ore in the darkness and the
shadow of death.
4 He breaks open a shaft away from
people;
In places forgotten by feet
They hang far away from men;
They swing to and fro.
5 *As for* the earth, from it comes bread,
But underneath it is turned up as by
fire;
6 Its stones *are* the source of sapphires,
And it contains gold dust.
7 *That* path no bird knows,
Nor has the falcon's eye seen it.
8 The proud lions*a* have not trodden it,
Nor has the fierce lion passed over it.
9 He puts his hand on the flint;
He overturns the mountains at the
roots.
10 He cuts out channels in the rocks,
And his eye sees every precious thing.
11 He dams up the streams from
trickling;
What is hidden he brings forth to
light.

27:15 *a*Literally *his*   27:18 *a*Following Masoretic Text and Vulgate; Septuagint and Syriac read *spider*
(compare 8:14); Targum reads *decay*.   27:19 *a*Following Masoretic Text and Targum; Septuagint and
Syriac read *But* shall not add (that is, do it again); Vulgate reads *But take away nothing*.
28:8 *a*Literally *sons of pride*, figurative of the great lions

¹² "But where can wisdom be found?
And where *is* the place of
understanding?
¹³ Man does not know its value,
Nor is it found in the land of the
living.
¹⁴ The deep says, '*It is* not in me';
And the sea says, '*It is* not with me.'
¹⁵ It cannot be purchased for gold,
Nor can silver be weighed *for* its price.
¹⁶ It cannot be valued in the gold of
Ophir,
In precious onyx or sapphire.
¹⁷ Neither gold nor crystal can equal it,
Nor can it be exchanged for jewelry of
fine gold.
¹⁸ No mention shall be made of coral or
quartz,
For the price of wisdom *is* above
rubies.
¹⁹ The topaz of Ethiopia cannot equal it,
Nor can it be valued in pure gold.

²⁰ "From where then does wisdom come?
And where *is* the place of
understanding?
²¹ It is hidden from the eyes of all living,
And concealed from the birds of the
air.
²² Destruction and Death say,
'We have heard a report about it with
our ears.'
²³ God understands its way,
And He knows its place.

> **28:23 God understands its way, and He knows its place.** After all of their arguments, Job concludes that the wisdom required to understand his suffering is not accessible to man.

²⁴ For He looks to the ends of the earth,
And sees under the whole heavens,
²⁵ To establish a weight for the wind,
And apportion the waters by measure.
²⁶ When He made a law for the rain,
And a path for the thunderbolt,
²⁷ Then He saw *wisdom*ᵃ and declared
it;
He prepared it, indeed, He searched it
out.
²⁸ And to man He said,

'Behold, the fear of the Lord, that *is*
wisdom,
And to depart from evil *is*
understanding.' "

> **28:1–28** Job's conviction about the cause of suffering did not explain his case since he was righteous. He challenged his friends to consider that God's wisdom may be beyond their comprehension. We can only know the wisdom of God that He reveals to us.

Job's Summary Defense

29 Job further continued his discourse, and said:

² "Oh, that I were as *in* months past,
As *in* the days *when* God watched
over me;
³ When His lamp shone upon my
head,
And when by His light I walked
through darkness;
⁴ Just as I was in the days of my prime,
When the friendly counsel of God *was*
over my tent;
⁵ When the Almighty *was* yet with me,
When my children *were* around me;
⁶ When my steps were bathed with
cream,ᵃ
And the rock poured out rivers of oil
for me!

⁷ "When I went out to the gate by the
city,
When I took my seat in the open
square,
⁸ The young men saw me and hid,
And the aged arose *and* stood;
⁹ The princes refrained from talking,
And put *their* hand on their mouth;
¹⁰ The voice of nobles was hushed,
And their tongue stuck to the roof of
their mouth.
¹¹ When the ear heard, then it blessed
me,
And when the eye saw, then it
approved me;
¹² Because I delivered the poor who cried
out,
The fatherless and *the one who* had
no helper.

28:27 ᵃLiterally *it*　**29:6** ᵃMasoretic Text reads *wrath*; ancient versions and some Hebrew manuscripts read *cream* (compare 20:17).

13 The blessing of a perishing *man* came
upon me,
And I caused the widow's heart to
sing for joy.

14 I put on righteousness, and it clothed
me;
My justice *was* like a robe and a
turban.
15 I *was* eyes to the blind,
And I *was* feet to the lame.
16 I *was* a father to the poor,
And I searched out the case *that* I did
not know.
17 I broke the fangs of the wicked,
And plucked the victim from his
teeth.

18 "Then I said, 'I shall die in my nest,
And multiply *my* days as the sand.
19 My root *is* spread out to the waters,
And the dew lies all night on my
branch.
20 My glory *is* fresh within me,
And my bow is renewed in my hand.'

21 "*Men* listened to me and waited,
And kept silence for my counsel.
22 After my words they did not speak
again,
And my speech settled on them *as*
dew.
23 They waited for me *as* for the rain,
And they opened their mouth wide *as*
for the spring rain.
24 *If* I mocked at them, they did not
believe *it*,
And the light of my countenance they
did not cast down.
25 I chose the way for them, and sat as
chief;

So I dwelt as a king in the army,
As one *who* comforts mourners.

30 "But now they mock at me, *men*
younger than I,
Whose fathers I disdained to put with
the dogs of my flock.
2 Indeed, what *profit* is the strength of
their hands to me?
Their vigor has perished.
3 *They are* gaunt from want and
famine,
Fleeing late to the wilderness,
desolate and waste,
4 Who pluck mallow by the bushes,
And broom tree roots *for* their food.
5 They were driven out from among
men,
They shouted at them as *at* a thief.
6 *They had* to live in the clefts of the
valleys,
In caves of the earth and the rocks.
7 Among the bushes they brayed,
Under the nettles they nestled.
8 *They were* sons of fools,
Yes, sons of vile men;
They were scourged from the land.

9 "And now I am their taunting song;
Yes, I am their byword.
10 They abhor me, they keep far from
me;
They do not hesitate to spit in my
face.
11 Because He has loosed my*ᵃ* bowstring
and afflicted me,
They have cast off restraint before
me.
12 At *my* right *hand* the rabble arises;
They push away my feet,
And they raise against me their ways
of destruction.
13 They break up my path,
They promote my calamity;
They have no helper.
14 They come as broad breakers;
Under the ruinous storm they roll
along.
15 Terrors are turned upon me;
They pursue my honor as the wind,
And my prosperity has passed like a
cloud.

30:11 *ᵃ*Following Masoretic Text, Syriac, and Targum; Septuagint and Vulgate read *His.*

16 "And now my soul is poured out
    because of my *plight*;
    The days of affliction take hold of me.
17 My bones are pierced in me at night,
    And my gnawing pains take no rest.
18 By great force my garment is
    disfigured;
    It binds me about as the collar of my
    coat.
19 He has cast me into the mire,
    And I have become like dust and
    ashes.

20 "I cry out to You, but You do not
    answer me;
    I stand up, and You regard me.

30:20 God's silence was the cruelest part of Job's
suffering.

21 *But* You have become cruel to me;
    With the strength of Your hand You
    oppose me.
22 You lift me up to the wind and cause
    me to ride *on it*;
    You spoil my success.
23 For I know *that* You will bring me *to*
    death,
    And *to* the house appointed for all
    living.

24 "Surely He would not stretch out *His*
    hand against a heap of ruins,
    If they cry out when He destroys *it*.
25 Have I not wept for him who was in
    trouble?
    Has *not* my soul grieved for the poor?
26 But when I looked for good, evil came
    to me;
    And when I waited for light, then
    came darkness.
27 My heart is in turmoil and cannot
    rest;
    Days of affliction confront me.
28 I go about mourning, but not in the
    sun;
    I stand up in the assembly *and* cry
    out for help.
29 I am a brother of jackals,
    And a companion of ostriches.
30 My skin grows black and falls from
    me;
    My bones burn with fever.
31 My harp is *turned* to mourning,

And my flute to the voice of those
    who weep.

31 "I have made a covenant with my
    eyes;
    Why then should I look upon a young
    woman?
2 For what *is* the allotment of God from
    above,
    And the inheritance of the Almighty
    from on high?
3 *Is* it not destruction for the wicked,
    And disaster for the workers of
    iniquity?
4 Does He not see my ways,
    And count all my steps?

5 "If I have walked with falsehood,
    Or if my foot has hastened to deceit,
6 Let me be weighed on honest scales,
    That God may know my integrity.
7 If my step has turned from the way,
    Or my heart walked after my eyes,
    Or if any spot adheres to my hands,
8 *Then* let me sow, and another eat;
    Yes, let my harvest be rooted out.

9 "If my heart has been enticed by a
    woman,
    Or *if* I have lurked at my neighbor's
    door,
10 *Then* let my wife grind for another,
    And let others bow down over her.
11 For that *would be* wickedness;
    Yes, it *would be* iniquity *deserving of*
    judgment.
12 For that *would be* a fire *that*
    consumes to destruction,
    And would root out all my increase.

13 "If I have despised the cause of my
    male or female servant
    When they complained against me,
14 What then shall I do when God rises
    up?
    When He punishes, how shall I
    answer Him?
15 Did not He who made me in the
    womb make them?
    Did not the same One fashion us in
    the womb?

16 "If I have kept the poor from *their*
    desire,

Or caused the eyes of the widow to
fail,

17 Or eaten my morsel by myself,
So that the fatherless could not eat of
it

18 (But from my youth I reared him as a
father,
And from my mother's womb I
guided *the widow*[a]);

19 If I have seen anyone perish for lack
of clothing,
Or any poor *man* without covering;

20 If his heart[a] has not blessed me,
And *if* he was *not* warmed with the
fleece of my sheep;

21 If I have raised my hand against the
fatherless,
When I saw I had help in the gate;

22 *Then* let my arm fall from my
shoulder,
Let my arm be torn from the socket.

23 For destruction *from* God *is* a terror
to me,
And because of His magnificence I
cannot endure.

24 "If I have made gold my hope,
Or said to fine gold, *'You are* my
confidence';

25 If I have rejoiced because my wealth
was great,
And because my hand had gained
much;

26 If I have observed the sun[a] when it
shines,
Or the moon moving *in* brightness,

27 So that my heart has been secretly
enticed,
And my mouth has kissed my hand;

28 This also *would be* an iniquity
deserving of judgment,
For I would have denied God *who is*
above.

31:1–40 Job began to insist upon his innocence and
demanded justice. In those days an oath taken before
a king or deity connoted innocence. The "if...then"
statements are the language of an oath, and Job
pleaded for his innocence to be recognized. His answers give no evidence of sinful patterns.

29 "If I have rejoiced at the destruction of
him who hated me,
Or lifted myself up when evil found
him

30 (Indeed I have not allowed my mouth
to sin
By asking for a curse on his soul);

31 If the men of my tent have not said,
'Who is there that has not been
satisfied with his meat?'

32 (*But* no sojourner had to lodge in the
street,
For I have opened my doors to the
traveler[a]);

33 If I have covered my transgressions as
Adam,
By hiding my iniquity in my bosom,

34 Because I feared the great multitude,
And dreaded the contempt of families,
So that I kept silence
And did not go out of the door—

35 Oh, that I had one to hear me!
Here is my mark.
Oh, that the Almighty would answer
me,
That my Prosecutor had written a
book!

31:35 my Prosecutor had written a book. Job
wished that God, the perfect Prosecutor, had recorded His divine plan in a book so that his suffering
could be explained. He would then be cleared of his
friends' charges.

36 Surely I would carry it on my shoulder,
And bind it on me *like* a crown;

37 I would declare to Him the number of
my steps;
Like a prince I would approach Him.

38 "If my land cries out against me,
And its furrows weep together;

39 If I have eaten its fruit[a] without
money,
Or caused its owners to lose their
lives;

40 *Then* let thistles grow instead of
wheat,
And weeds instead of barley."

The words of Job are ended.

31:18 [a]Literally *her* (compare verse 16)   31:20 [a]Literally *loins*   31:26 [a]Literally *light*   31:32 [a]Following
Septuagint, Syriac, Targum, and Vulgate; Masoretic Text reads *road*.   31:39 [a]Literally *its strength*

Elihu Contradicts Job's Friends

32 So these three men ceased answering Job, because he *was* righteous in his own eyes. ²Then the wrath of Elihu, the son of Barachel the Buzite, of the family of Ram, was aroused against Job; his wrath was aroused because he justified himself rather than God. ³Also against his three friends his wrath was aroused, because they had found no answer, and *yet* had condemned Job.

⁴Now because they *were* years older than he, Elihu had waited to speak to Job.ᵃ ⁵When Elihu saw that *there was* no answer in the mouth of these three men, his wrath was aroused.

> **32:1–37:24** The younger Elihu, a new speaker who had been there with the others, had some of his own thoughts for Job. Though his approach is full of anger and arrogance, it is fresh. Unfortunately, it is not helpful.

⁶So Elihu, the son of Barachel the Buzite, answered and said:

"I *am* young in years, and you *are* very old;
Therefore I was afraid,
And dared not declare my opinion to you.
⁷ I said, 'Ageᵃ should speak,
And multitude of years should teach wisdom.'
⁸ But *there is* a spirit in man,
And the breath of the Almighty gives him understanding.

> **32:6–8** Though Elihu refers to this as an "opinion," he claims that his words are divinely inspired (see 33:6,33).

⁹ Great menᵃ are not *always* wise,
Nor do the aged *always* understand justice.
¹⁰ "Therefore I say, 'Listen to me,
I also will declare my opinion.'
¹¹ Indeed I waited for your words,

I listened to your reasonings, while
you searched out what to say.
¹² I paid close attention to you;
And surely not one of you convinced Job,
Or answered his words—
¹³ Lest you say,
'We have found wisdom';
God will vanquish him, not man.
¹⁴ Now he has not directed *his* words against me;
So I will not answer him with your words.

¹⁵ "They are dismayed and answer no more;
Words escape them.
¹⁶ And I have waited, because they did not speak,
Because they stood still *and* answered no more.
¹⁷ I also will answer my part,
I too will declare my opinion.
¹⁸ For I am full of words;
The spirit within me compels me.
¹⁹ Indeed my belly *is* like wine *that* has no vent;
It is ready to burst like new wineskins.
²⁰ I will speak, that I may find relief;
I must open my lips and answer.
²¹ Let me not, I pray, show partiality to anyone;
Nor let me flatter any man.
²² For I do not know how to flatter,
Else my Maker would soon take me away.

Elihu Contradicts Job

33 "But please, Job, hear my speech,
And listen to all my words.
² Now, I open my mouth;
My tongue speaks in my mouth.
³ My words *come* from my upright heart;
My lips utter pure knowledge.
⁴ The Spirit of God has made me,
And the breath of the Almighty gives me life.
⁵ If you can answer me,
Set *your words* in order before me;

32:4 ᵃVulgate reads *till Job had spoken.*   **32:7** ᵃLiterally *Days,* that is, years   **32:9** ᵃOr *Men of many years*

Take your stand.

6 Truly I *am* as your spokesman[a] before God;
I also have been formed out of clay.
7 Surely no fear of me will terrify you,
Nor will my hand be heavy on you.

8 "Surely you have spoken in my hearing,
And I have heard the sound of *your* words, *saying,*
9 'I *am* pure, without transgression;
I *am* innocent, and *there is* no iniquity in me.
10 Yet He finds occasions against me,
He counts me as His enemy;
11 He puts my feet in the stocks,
He watches all my paths.'

12 "Look, *in* this you are not righteous.
I will answer you,
For God is greater than man.
13 Why do you contend with Him?
For He does not give an accounting of any of His words.

> **33:13** Elihu reminded Job that God did not have to reveal His will or defend Himself to anyone.

14 For God may speak in one way, or in another,
Yet man does not perceive it.
15 In a dream, in a vision of the night,
When deep sleep falls upon men,
While slumbering on their beds,
16 Then He opens the ears of men,
And seals their instruction.
17 In order to turn man *from his* deed,
And conceal pride from man,
18 He keeps back his soul from the Pit,
And his life from perishing by the sword.

19 "*Man* is also chastened with pain on his bed,
And with strong *pain* in many of his bones,
20 So that his life abhors bread,
And his soul succulent food.
21 His flesh wastes away from sight,
And his bones stick out *which once* were not seen.

22 Yes, his soul draws near the Pit,
And his life to the executioners.

23 "If there is a messenger for him,
A mediator, one among a thousand,
To show man His uprightness,
24 Then He is gracious to him, and says,
'Deliver him from going down to the Pit;
I have found a ransom';
25 His flesh shall be young like a child's,
He shall return to the days of his youth.
26 He shall pray to God, and He will delight in him,
He shall see His face with joy,
For He restores to man His righteousness.
27 Then he looks at men and says,
'I have sinned, and perverted *what was* right,
And it did not profit me.'
28 He will redeem his[a] soul from going down to the Pit,
And his[b] life shall see the light.

29 "Behold, God works all these *things,*
Twice, *in fact,* three *times* with a man,
30 To bring back his soul from the Pit,
That he may be enlightened with the light of life.

31 "Give ear, Job, listen to me;
Hold your peace, and I will speak.
32 If you have anything to say, answer me;
Speak, for I desire to justify you.

> **33:32 I desire to justify you.** Elihu desired for Job to be cleared of his friends' charges and allowed Job to discuss with him in a conversation.

33 If not, listen to me;
Hold your peace, and I will teach you wisdom."

Elihu Proclaims God's Justice

34 Elihu further answered and said:

2 "Hear my words, you wise *men;*
Give ear to me, you who have knowledge.

33:6 [a]Literally *as your mouth*   33:28 [a]Or *my* (Kethib)   [b]Or *my* (Kethib)

3   For the ear tests words
    As the palate tastes food.
4   Let us choose justice for ourselves;
    Let us know among ourselves what is
        good.

5   "For Job has said, 'I am righteous,
    But God has taken away my justice;
6   Should I lie concerning my right?
    My wound is incurable, though I am
        without transgression.'
7   What man is like Job,
    Who drinks scorn like water,
8   Who goes in company with the
        workers of iniquity,
    And walks with wicked men?
9   For he has said, 'It profits a man
        nothing
    That he should delight in God.'

34:9 For he has said. Elihu falsely attributed words
to Job that he did not say.

10 "Therefore listen to me, you men of
        understanding:
    Far be it from God to do wickedness,
    And from the Almighty to commit
        iniquity.
11 For He repays man according to his
        work,
    And makes man to find a reward
        according to his way.
12 Surely God will never do wickedly,
    Nor will the Almighty pervert justice.
13 Who gave Him charge over the earth?
    Or who appointed Him over the
        whole world?
14 If He should set His heart on it,
    If He should gather to Himself His
        Spirit and His breath,
15 All flesh would perish together,
    And man would return to dust.

16 "If you have understanding, hear this;
    Listen to the sound of my words:
17 Should one who hates justice govern?
    Will you condemn Him who is most
        just?
18 Is it fitting to say to a king, 'You are
        worthless,'
    And to nobles, 'You are wicked'?
19 Yet He is not partial to princes,
    Nor does He regard the rich more
        than the poor;

    For they are all the work of His
        hands.
20 In a moment they die, in the middle
        of the night;
    The people are shaken and pass
        away;
    The mighty are taken away without a
        hand.

21 "For His eyes are on the ways of man,
    And He sees all his steps.
22 There is no darkness nor shadow of
        death
    Where the workers of iniquity may
        hide themselves.
23 For He need not further consider a
        man,
    That he should go before God in
        judgment.
24 He breaks in pieces mighty men
        without inquiry,
    And sets others in their place.
25 Therefore He knows their works;
    He overthrows them in the night,
    And they are crushed.
26 He strikes them as wicked men
    In the open sight of others,
27 Because they turned back from
        Him,
    And would not consider any of His
        ways,
28 So that they caused the cry of the
        poor to come to Him;
    For He hears the cry of the afflicted.
29 When He gives quietness, who then
        can make trouble?
    And when He hides His face, who
        then can see Him,
    Whether it is against a nation or a
        man alone?—
30 That the hypocrite should not reign,
    Lest the people be ensnared.

31 "For has anyone said to God,
    'I have borne chastening;
    I will offend no more;
32 Teach me what I do not see;
    If I have done iniquity, I will do no
        more'?
33 Should He repay it according to your
        terms,
    Just because you disavow it?
    You must choose, and not I;
    Therefore speak what you know.

34 "Men of understanding say to me,
Wise men who listen to me:

35 'Job speaks without knowledge,
His words *are* without wisdom.'

36 Oh, that Job were tried to the utmost,
Because *his* answers *are like* those of
wicked men!

37 For he adds rebellion to his sin;
He claps *his hands* among us,
And multiplies his words against God."

Elihu Condemns Self-Righteousness

35 Moreover Elihu answered and said:

2 "Do you think this is right?
Do you say,
'My righteousness is more than
God's'?

3 For you say,
'What advantage will it be to You?
What profit shall I have, more than *if*
I had sinned?'

4 "I will answer you,
And your companions with you.

5 Look to the heavens and see;
And behold the clouds—
They are higher than you.

6 If you sin, what do you accomplish
against Him?
Or, *if* your transgressions are
multiplied, what do you do to
Him?

7 If you are righteous, what do you give
Him?
Or what does He receive from your
hand?

8 Your wickedness affects a man such
as you,
And your righteousness a son of man.

9 "Because of the multitude of
oppressions they cry out;
They cry out for help because of the
arm of the mighty.

10 But no one says, 'Where *is* God my
Maker,
Who gives songs in the night,

11 Who teaches us more than the beasts
of the earth,
And makes us wiser than the birds of
heaven?'

12 There they cry out, but He does not
answer,

Because of the pride of evil men.

13 Surely God will not listen to empty
talk,
Nor will the Almighty regard it.

14 Although you say you do not see
Him,
Yet justice *is* before Him, and you
must wait for Him.

15 And now, because He has not
punished in His anger,
Nor taken much notice of folly,

16 Therefore Job opens his mouth in
vain;
He multiplies words without
knowledge."

Elihu Proclaims God's Goodness

36 Elihu also proceeded and said:

2 "Bear with me a little, and I will show
you
That *there are* yet words to speak on
God's behalf.

3 I will fetch my knowledge from afar;
I will ascribe righteousness to my
Maker.

4 For truly my words *are* not false;
One who is perfect in knowledge *is*
with you.

5 "Behold, God *is* mighty, but despises
no one;
He is mighty in strength of
understanding.

6 He does not preserve the life of the
wicked,
But gives justice to the oppressed.

7 He does not withdraw His eyes from
the righteous;
But *they are* on the throne with kings,
For He has seated them forever,
And they are exalted.

8 And if *they are* bound in fetters,
Held in the cords of affliction,

9 Then He tells them their work and
their transgressions—
That they have acted defiantly.

10 He also opens their ear to instruction,
And commands that they turn from
iniquity.

11 If they obey and serve *Him,*
They shall spend their days in
prosperity,
And their years in pleasures.

12 But if they do not obey,
They shall perish by the sword,
And they shall die without
knowledge.*

13 "But the hypocrites in heart store up
wrath;
They do not cry for help when He
binds them.

14 They die in youth,
And their life *ends* among the
perverted persons.*

15 He delivers the poor in their
affliction,
And opens their ears in oppression.

16 "Indeed He would have brought you
out of dire distress,
Into a broad place where *there is* no
restraint;
And what is set on your table *would
be* full of richness.

17 But you are filled with the judgment
due the wicked;
Judgment and justice take hold *of you.*

18 Because *there is* wrath, *beware* lest
He take you away with *one* blow;

For a large ransom would not help
you avoid *it.*

19 Will your riches,
Or all the mighty forces,
Keep you from distress?

20 Do not desire the night,
When people are cut off in their place.

21 Take heed, do not turn to iniquity,
For you have chosen this rather than
affliction.

22 "Behold, God is exalted by His power;
Who teaches like Him?

23 Who has assigned Him His way,
Or who has said, 'You have done
wrong'?

Elihu Proclaims God's Majesty

24 "Remember to magnify His work,
Of which men have sung.

25 Everyone has seen it;
Man looks on *it* from afar.

26 "Behold, God *is* great, and we do not
know *Him;*
Nor can the number of His years *be*
discovered.

36:12 *Masoretic Text reads *as one without knowledge.* · 36:14 *Hebrew *qedeshim,* that is, those
practicing sodomy and prostitution in religious rituals

What kind of relationship did Job have with God?

Job's biography begins with a four part description of his character: "blameless and upright, and one who feared God and shunned evil" (1:1). He prayed for his children and was concerned about their relationship with God (1:5). He was successful and wealthy—the stereotype of a blessed man. In fact, God adds his own glowing approval of Job, using the same traits that open the book (1:8).

Faced with the sudden, crushing loss of everything—children, servants, herds—Job's initial response was to grieve and recognize God's sovereignty. "'The LORD gave, and the LORD has taken away; Blessed be the name of the LORD.' In all this Job did not sin nor charge God with wrong" (1:21b,22).

Under the harsh judgments of his friends, Job eventually struggled to understand why God seemed unwilling to settle matters. Once God did speak, at least part of Job's problem becomes clear—he confused a relationship with God with familiarity with God. The Lord did not rebuke Job's faith or sincerity; instead, God questioned Job's insistence on an answer for his difficulties. By allowing Job to hear just a little of the extent of his ignorance, God showed Job that there was a great deal of knowledge he would never understand. As a creature, Job simply had no right to demand an answer from his Creator. Job's final words are filled with humility and repentance: "I have heard of You by the hearing of the ear, but now my eye sees You. Therefore I abhor myself, and repent in dust and ashes" (42:5,6).

Job spent his last days enjoying the same kind of relationship he had earlier with God. He prayed for his friends and raised another family of godly children. He lived a full life.

27 For He draws up drops of water,
Which distill as rain from the mist,
28 Which the clouds drop down
And pour abundantly on man.
29 Indeed, can *anyone* understand the
spreading of clouds,
The thunder from His canopy?
30 Look, He scatters His light upon it,
And covers the depths of the sea.
31 For by these He judges the peoples;
He gives food in abundance.
32 He covers *His* hands with lightning,
And commands it to strike.
33 His thunder declares it,
The cattle also, concerning the rising
storm.

37 "At this also my heart trembles,
And leaps from its place.
2 Hear attentively the thunder of His
voice,
And the rumbling *that* comes from
His mouth.
3 He sends it forth under the whole
heaven,
His lightning to the ends of the earth.
4 After it a voice roars;
He thunders with His majestic
voice,
And He does not restrain them when
His voice is heard.
5 God thunders marvelously with His
voice;
He does great things which we cannot
comprehend.
6 For He says to the snow, 'Fall *on* the
earth';
Likewise to the gentle rain and the
heavy rain of His strength.
7 He seals the hand of every man,
That all men may know His work.
8 The beasts go into dens,
And remain in their lairs.
9 From the chamber *of the south* comes
the whirlwind,
And cold from the scattering winds *of
the north.*
10 By the breath of God ice is given,
And the broad waters are frozen.
11 Also with moisture He saturates the
thick clouds;
He scatters His bright clouds.

12 And they swirl about, being turned by
His guidance,
That they may do whatever He
commands them
On the face of the whole earth.[a]
13 He causes it to come,
Whether for correction,
Or for His land,
Or for mercy.

14 "Listen to this, O Job;
Stand still and consider the wondrous
works of God.
15 Do you know when God dispatches
them,
And causes the light of His cloud to
shine?
16 Do you know how the clouds are
balanced,
Those wondrous works of Him who is
perfect in knowledge?
17 Why *are* your garments hot,
When He quiets the earth by the
south *wind?*
18 With Him, have you spread out the
skies,
Strong as a cast metal mirror?

19 "Teach us what we should say to Him,
For we can prepare nothing because of
the darkness.
20 Should He be told that I *wish to* speak?
If a man were to speak, surely he
would be swallowed up.

> **37:19,20** Elihu argues that since man cannot explain God's power, he is not in position to question Him either. To do so is unwise and could bring judgment.

21 Even now *men* cannot look at the
light *when it is* bright in the skies,
When the wind has passed and
cleared them.
22 He comes from the north *as* golden
splendor;
With God *is* awesome majesty.
23 *As for* the Almighty, we cannot find
Him;
He is excellent in power,
In judgment and abundant justice;
He does not oppress.
24 Therefore men fear Him;

37:12 [a]Literally *the world of the earth*

He shows no partiality to any *who are* wise of heart."

The LORD Reveals His Omnipotence to Job

38 Then the LORD answered Job out of the whirlwind, and said:

> **38:1 out of the whirlwind.** God finally breaks His silence and addresses some of Job's previous statements about Him. Although God later declares Job innocent of his charges, He first provides Job with a correct understanding of Himself.

2 "Who *is* this who darkens counsel
    By words without knowledge?
3 Now prepare yourself like a man;
    I will question you, and you shall
        answer Me.

4 "Where were you when I laid the
        foundations of the earth?
    Tell *Me*, if you have understanding.
5 Who determined its measurements?
    Surely you know!
    Or who stretched the line upon it?
6 To what were its foundations
        fastened?
    Or who laid its cornerstone,
7 When the morning stars sang together,
    And all the sons of God shouted for
        joy?

8 "Or *who* shut in the sea with doors,
    When it burst forth *and* issued from
        the womb;
9 When I made the clouds its garment,
    And thick darkness its swaddling
        band;
10 When I fixed My limit for it,
    And set bars and doors;
11 When I said,
    'This far you may come, but no farther,
    And here your proud waves must
        stop!'

12 "Have you commanded the morning
        since your days *began*,
    And caused the dawn to know its
        place,
13 That it might take hold of the ends of
        the earth,
    And the wicked be shaken out of it?
14 It takes on form like clay *under* a seal,
    And stands out like a garment.

> **38:14 clay *under* a seal.** Documents written on clay tablets were signed with personally engraved seals where the bearer wrote his name. This was to symbolize the earth's spinning on its axis, just as the seal is rolled over the clay. Only God could reveal this phenomenon of nature.

15 From the wicked their light is
        withheld,
    And the upraised arm is broken.

16 "Have you entered the springs of the
        sea?
    Or have you walked in search of the
        depths?
17 Have the gates of death been revealed
        to you?
    Or have you seen the doors of the
        shadow of death?
18 Have you comprehended the breadth
        of the earth?
    Tell *Me*, if you know all this.

19 "Where *is* the way *to* the dwelling of
        light?
    And darkness, where *is* its place,
20 That you may take it to its territory,
    That you may know the paths *to* its
        home?
21 Do you know *it*, because you were
        born then,
    Or *because* the number of your days
        is great?

22 "Have you entered the treasury of snow,
    Or have you seen the treasury of hail,
23 Which I have reserved for the time of
        trouble,
    For the day of battle and war?
24 By what way is light diffused,
    Or the east wind scattered over the
        earth?

25 "Who has divided a channel for the
        overflowing *water*,
    Or a path for the thunderbolt,
26 To cause it to rain on a land *where
        there is* no one,
    A wilderness in which *there is* no man;
27 To satisfy the desolate waste,
    And cause to spring forth the growth
        of tender grass?
28 Has the rain a father?
    Or who has begotten the drops of dew?

29 From whose womb comes the ice?
And the frost of heaven, who gives it
birth?
30 The waters harden like stone,
And the surface of the deep is frozen.

31 "Can you bind the cluster of the
Pleiades,
Or loose the belt of Orion?
32 Can you bring out Mazzaroth*a* in its
season?
Or can you guide the Great Bear with
its cubs?
33 Do you know the ordinances of the
heavens?
Can you set their dominion over the
earth?

34 "Can you lift up your voice to the
clouds,
That an abundance of water may
cover you?
35 Can you send out lightnings, that
they may go,
And say to you, 'Here we *are!*'?
36 Who has put wisdom in the mind?*a*

38:36 wisdom…understanding. This is a key point.
The same God who created and sustains the universe
is the same God who is in control over man's suffering.

Or who has given understanding to
the heart?
37 Who can number the clouds by
wisdom?
Or who can pour out the bottles of
heaven,
38 When the dust hardens in clumps,
And the clods cling together?

39 "Can you hunt the prey for the lion,
Or satisfy the appetite of the young
lions,
40 When they crouch in *their* dens,
Or lurk in their lairs to lie in wait?
41 Who provides food for the raven,
When its young ones cry to God,
And wander about for lack of food?

39 "Do you know the time when the
wild mountain goats bear
young?
Or can you mark when the deer gives
birth?
2 Can you number the months *that*
they fulfill?
Or do you know the time when they
bear young?
3 They bow down,
They bring forth their young,
They deliver their offspring.*a*
4 Their young ones are healthy,

38:32 *a*Literally *Constellations*   38:36 *a*Literally *inward parts*   39:3 *a*Literally *pangs*, figurative of
offspring

Why doesn't God answer all of Job's (and our) questions?

This question assumes that if God answered all our questions,
it would be easier to believe. This is not true. Trust goes beyond
answers. Sometimes, questions become a way to avoid trust.

Take for example a little girl invited to jump off the stairs
into her father's waiting hands. She asks, "Will you catch me,
Daddy?" He answers, "Yes, I will!" She may jump or she may
proceed to ask endless versions of her first question. If she
does jump, it will be more because of whom she knows her
father to be than because of his answer to one of her questions. The fact that she jumps does
not mean that she has run out of fears or questions; it means that her trust is *greater* than her
fears or questions.

In the end, we must trust God more than our capacity to understand God's ways. The
lesson from Job's experience does not forbid us from asking questions. Often these questions will lead us to the reasons for our suffering. But Job's experience also warns us that we
may not be able to understand all our suffering all the time, or even any of it some of the
time.

God doesn't answer all of our questions because we are simply unable to understand
many of his answers.

They grow strong with grain;
They depart and do not return to
    them.

5 "Who set the wild donkey free?
Who loosed the bonds of the onager,
6 Whose home I have made the
    wilderness,
And the barren land his dwelling?
7 He scorns the tumult of the city;
He does not heed the shouts of the
    driver.
8 The range of the mountains *is* his
    pasture,
And he searches after every green
    thing.

9 "Will the wild ox be willing to serve
    you?
Will he bed by your manger?
10 Can you bind the wild ox in the
    furrow with ropes?
Or will he plow the valleys behind
    you?
11 Will you trust him because his
    strength *is* great?
Or will you leave your labor to him?
12 Will you trust him to bring home
    your grain,
And gather it to your threshing floor?

13 "The wings of the ostrich wave
    proudly,
But are her wings and pinions *like the*
    kindly stork's?
14 For she leaves her eggs on the ground,
And warms them in the dust;
15 She forgets that a foot may crush
    them,
Or that a wild beast may break them.
16 She treats her young harshly, as
    though *they were* not hers;
Her labor is in vain, without concern,
17 Because God deprived her of wisdom,
And did not endow her with
    understanding.
18 When she lifts herself on high,
She scorns the horse and its rider.

19 "Have you given the horse strength?
Have you clothed his neck with
    thunder?[a]

20 Can you frighten him like a locust?
His majestic snorting strikes terror.
21 He paws in the valley, and rejoices in
    his strength;
He gallops into the clash of arms.
22 He mocks at fear, and is not
    frightened;
Nor does he turn back from the
    sword.
23 The quiver rattles against him,
The glittering spear and javelin.
24 He devours the distance with
    fierceness and rage;
Nor does he come to a halt because
    the trumpet *has* sounded.
25 At *the blast of* the trumpet he says,
    'Aha!'
He smells the battle from afar,
The thunder of captains and
    shouting.

26 "Does the hawk fly by your wisdom,
And spread its wings toward the
    south?
27 Does the eagle mount up at your
    command,
And make its nest on high?
28 On the rock it dwells and resides,
On the crag of the rock and the
    stronghold.
29 From there it spies out the prey;
Its eyes observe from afar.
30 Its young ones suck up blood;
And where the slain *are*, there it *is*."

40 Moreover the LORD answered Job, and said:

2 "Shall the one who contends with the
    Almighty correct *Him?*
He who rebukes God, let him answer
    it."

40:2 God's questioning was rhetorical. He did not intend for Job to answer but for him to admit his weakness and inability to comprehend the wisdom of God. Job needed to know that God's sovereign control is enough.

Job's Response to God
3 Then Job answered the LORD and said:

39:19 [a]Or *a mane*

4 "Behold, I am vile;
    What shall I answer You?
    I lay my hand over my mouth.
5 Once I have spoken, but I will not
        answer;
    Yes, twice, but I will proceed no
        further."

God's Challenge to Job

6 Then the LORD answered Job out of the whirlwind, and said:

7 "Now prepare yourself like a man;
    I will question you, and you shall
        answer Me:

8 "Would you indeed annul My
        judgment?
    Would you condemn Me that you
        may be justified?
9 Have you an arm like God?
    Or can you thunder with a voice like
        His?
10 Then adorn yourself *with* majesty and
        splendor,
    And array yourself with glory and
        beauty.
11 Disperse the rage of your wrath;
    Look on everyone *who is* proud, and
        humble him.
12 Look on everyone *who is* proud, *and*
        bring him low;
    Tread down the wicked in their place.
13 Hide them in the dust together,
    Bind their faces in hidden *darkness*.
14 Then I will also confess to you
    That your own right hand can save
        you.

40:6–41:34 God's second line of questioning is similar to the first, except that He focuses on two ferocious and feared animals—Behemoth and Leviathan. Only God can control these creatures, not man.

15 "Look now at the behemoth,[a] which I
        made *along* with you;
    He eats grass like an ox.
16 See now, his strength *is* in his hips,
    And his power *is* in his stomach
        muscles.
17 He moves his tail like a cedar;

The sinews of his thighs are tightly
    knit.
18 His bones *are like* beams of bronze,
    His ribs like bars of iron.
19 He *is* the first of the ways of God;
    Only He who made him can bring
        near His sword.
20 Surely the mountains yield food for
        him,
    And all the beasts of the field play
        there.
21 He lies under the lotus trees,
    In a covert of reeds and marsh.
22 The lotus trees cover him *with* their
        shade;
    The willows by the brook surround
        him.
23 Indeed the river may rage,
    Yet he is not disturbed;
    He is confident, though the Jordan
        gushes into his mouth,
24 *Though* he takes it in his eyes,
    Or one pierces *his* nose with a snare.

41 "Can you draw out Leviathan[a] with
        a hook,
    Or *snare* his tongue with a line *which*
        you lower?

41:1 Leviathan. Every mention of this creature (see Ps. 74:14) describes it as a large and powerful beast of the sea. Different opinions portray it to be a crocodile, a killer whale, a Great White Shark, or a dinosaur.

2 Can you put a reed through his nose,
    Or pierce his jaw with a hook?
3 Will he make many supplications to
        you?
    Will he speak softly to you?
4 Will he make a covenant with you?
    Will you take him as a servant
        forever?
5 Will you play with him as *with* a bird,
    Or will you leash him for your
        maidens?
6 Will *your* companions make a
        banquet[a] of him?
    Will they apportion him among the
        merchants?
7 Can you fill his skin with harpoons,

40:15 [a]A large animal, exact identity unknown   41:1 [a]A large sea creature, exact identity unknown
41:6 [a]Or *bargain over him*

Or his head with fishing spears?
8 Lay your hand on him;
Remember the battle—
Never do it again!
9 Indeed, *any* hope of *overcoming* him
is false;
Shall *one not* be overwhelmed at the
sight of him?
10 No one *is so* fierce that he would dare
stir him up.
Who then is able to stand against Me?

> **41:10 Who then is able to stand against Me?** This past section points to this question. If Job could not stand a chance against the creatures, then he had no business questioning the God who made them.

11 Who has preceded Me, that I should
pay *him*?
Everything under heaven is Mine.

12 "I will not conceal*ᵃ* his limbs,
His mighty power, or his graceful
proportions.
13 Who can remove his outer coat?
Who can approach *him* with a double
bridle?
14 Who can open the doors of his face,
With his terrible teeth all around?
15 *His* rows of scales are *his* pride,
Shut up tightly *as with* a seal;
16 One is so near another
That no air can come between them;
17 They are joined one to another,
They stick together and cannot be
parted.
18 His sneezings flash forth light,
And his eyes *are* like the eyelids of the
morning.
19 Out of his mouth go burning lights;
Sparks of fire shoot out.
20 Smoke goes out of his nostrils,
As *from* a boiling pot and burning
rushes.
21 His breath kindles coals,
And a flame goes out of his mouth.
22 Strength dwells in his neck,
And sorrow dances before him.
23 The folds of his flesh are joined
together;
They are firm on him and cannot be
moved.

24 His heart is as hard as stone,
Even as hard as the lower *millstone*.
25 When he raises himself up, the
mighty are afraid;
Because of his crashings they are
beside*ᵃ* themselves.
26 *Though* the sword reaches him, it
cannot avail;
Nor does spear, dart, or javelin.
27 He regards iron as straw,
And bronze as rotten wood.
28 The arrow cannot make him flee;
Slingstones become like stubble to
him.
29 Darts are regarded as straw;
He laughs at the threat of javelins.
30 His undersides *are* like sharp
potsherds;
He spreads pointed *marks* in the
mire.
31 He makes the deep boil like a pot;
He makes the sea like a pot of
ointment.
32 He leaves a shining wake behind him;
One would think the deep had white
hair.
33 On earth there is nothing like him,
Which is made without fear.
34 He beholds every high *thing*;
He *is* king over all the children of
pride."

Job's Repentance and Restoration

42 Then Job answered the LORD and
said:
2 "I know that You can do everything,
And that no purpose *of Yours* can be
withheld from You.
3 *You asked,* 'Who *is* this who hides
counsel without knowledge?'
Therefore I have uttered what I did
not understand,
Things too wonderful for me, which I
did not know.

> **42:1–6** Job finally confessed. Even though he did not understand why everything happened, he repented for questioning God's wisdom. God's greatness moved him to humility, stripped of everything. Satan's and Job's accusers were all wrong in their convictions. Job was also wrong in his thoughts about God's ways.

41:12 *ᵃ*Literally *keep silent about*   41:25 *ᵃ*Or *purify themselves*

⁴   Listen, please, and let me speak;
      You said, 'I will question you, and you
         shall answer Me.'

⁵   "I have heard of You by the hearing of
         the ear,
      But now my eye sees You.
⁶   Therefore I abhor *myself,*
      And repent in dust and ashes."

⁷And so it was, after the LORD had spoken these words to Job, that the LORD said to Eliphaz the Temanite, "My wrath is aroused against you and your two friends, for you have not spoken of Me *what is* right, as My servant Job *has.* ⁸Now therefore, take for yourselves seven bulls and seven rams, go to My servant Job, and offer up for yourselves a burnt offering; and My servant Job shall pray for you. For I will accept him, lest I deal with you *according to your* folly; because you have not spoken of Me *what is* right, as My servant Job *has.*"

> **42:7,8 you have not spoken of Me *what is* right.** God was pleased that Job refuted the friends' arguments, and they were rebuked for their misrepresentation of God.

⁹So Eliphaz the Temanite and Bildad the Shuhite *and* Zophar the Naamathite went and did as the LORD commanded them; for the LORD had accepted Job. ¹⁰And the LORD restored Job's losses^a when he prayed for his friends. Indeed the LORD gave Job twice as much as he had before. ¹¹Then all his brothers, all his sisters, and all those who had been his acquaintances before, came to him and ate food with him in his house; and they consoled him and comforted him for all the adversity that the LORD had brought upon him. Each one gave him a piece of silver and each a ring of gold.

¹²Now the LORD blessed the latter *days* of Job more than his beginning; for he had fourteen thousand sheep, six thousand camels, one thousand yoke of oxen, and one thousand female donkeys. ¹³He also had seven sons and three daughters. ¹⁴And he called the name of the first Jemimah, the name of the second Keziah, and the name of the third Keren-Happuch. ¹⁵In all the land were found no women *so* beautiful as the daughters of Job; and their father gave them an inheritance among their brothers.

> **42:13 seven sons...three daughters.** The animals are given in twice the amount originally owned by Job, but his children were in the same amount. This is because he had 7 sons and 3 daughters already waiting for him in the presence of God.

¹⁶After this Job lived one hundred and forty years, and saw his children and grandchildren *for* four generations. ¹⁷So Job died, old and full of days.

> **42:17 So Job died, old and full of days.** The life of Job comes full-circle—prosperous and blessed by God. God's servants are still learning from this account of Job's life how to trust in the God of the universe for what they cannot understand.

42:10 ^aLiterally *Job's captivity,* that is, what was captured from Job

PSALMS

A person reading through the Bible knows from the first lines of Psalms that he or she has entered into a new and wonderful part of Scripture. It is poetry written for and about God. Psalms explores the full range of human experience and emotion. People meet God in the Psalms, and they discover a lot about themselves as well.

This collection originated as Israel's ancient, God-breathed hymnbook. The Hebrews called the book "Praises." As it defined the proper spirit and content of worship throughout Scripture, Psalms continues to influence and guide the worship of the church today.

AUTHOR AND DATE

Psalms was written by several authors, approximately 1410 to 500 B.C.

Although the word inspired is often used to describe poetry, that word is used in a special way to describe the Psalms and the rest of Scripture. The Bible claims to be "inspired by God" (2 Timothy 3:16). The content, truth, and reliability of Scripture rest on this claim. God employed many writers to compose His Word, but He remained the author. The uniqueness of the writers can be seen in their style, experiences, and subjects, but God edited the final content.

Among the writers of Psalms, at least 7 individuals or groups can be identified: (1) King David wrote at least 75 of the 150 Psalms; (2) the sons of Korah are credited with 10; (3) Asaph contributed 12; (4) Solomon, (5) Moses, (6) Heman, and (7) Ethan all wrote at least one Psalm each. The writers of 48 Psalms are best listed as anonymous.

If the earliest of the Psalms was Moses' Psalm 90 (approximately 1410 B.C.) and the latest Psalm was the anonymous post-exile Psalm 126 (approximately 500 B.C.), the various compositions in the book span a time of 900 years in Jewish history.

BACKGROUND AND SETTING

The Psalms were first compiled during the early days of Israel's extended worship training in the wilderness. The original spontaneous or prepared responses to God that make up many of the Psalms were recorded and reused. Even the intense individual meditations—for example, Psalm 23—were incorporated as expressions of universal truths about God.

The Psalms are a product as well as a record of the acts of God in creation and history, particularly the history of Israel. They are the accumulated memories and

reflections of a people in relationship with God. The Psalms express and teach the proper praise and worship of God.

HISTORICAL AND THEOLOGICAL THEMES

The recurring theme throughout Psalms involves the exploration of real living in a real world. This exploration includes two dimensions that operate simultaneously: (1) a horizontal or temporal reality, and (2) a vertical or transcendent reality. This translates in various Psalms as expressions of deep pain, doubt, and anger with circumstances in the earthly dimension that are balanced by testimonies and challenges from those who have learned that the people of God are to live joyfully and dependently on the Person and promises that represent the heavenly, eternal dimension. Life's cycles of troubles and triumphs provide occasions for expressing a full range of human complaints, questions, confidence, prayers and praise to Israel's sovereign Lord.

Because of their broad theme, the Psalms touch on a equally broad array of theological lessons. These are expressed in practical, daily realities. For example, the sinfulness of humanity is documented, not only through the behavior patterns of the wicked but also through the stumblings of believers. The sovereignty of God is everywhere recognized but not at the expense of genuine human responsibility. A Psalm may begin

> **"THE SOVEREIGNTY OF GOD IS EVERYWHERE RECOGNIZED BUT NOT AT THE EXPENSE OF GENUINE HUMAN RESPONSIBILITY."**

with a jarring description of life out of control yet move toward a renewed understanding of God's divine will and timetable being worked out in the events and situations of human experience. In Psalms, God's sovereignty is not determined by how much humans control or understand.

OUTLINE

This outline simply follows the ancient Hebrew way of organizing the Psalms.

Book One: Psalms 1–41

PSALM 1

The Way of the Righteous and the End of the Ungodly

1 Blessed *is* the man
　Who walks not in the counsel of the
　　ungodly,
　　Nor stands in the path of sinners,
　　Nor sits in the seat of the scornful;

> **1:1 Blessed.** This refers to deep joy and contentment in God for an individual, and to redemptive favor for a community (see Deut. 27:11–28:6). **walks not...Nor stands...Nor sits.** The "beatitude" man (see Matt. 5:3–11) is first described as one who does not associate with those who exemplify the lure of sin.

2 But his delight *is* in the law of the
　　LORD,
　　And in His law he meditates day
　　　and night.
3 He shall be like a tree
　　Planted by the rivers of water,
　That brings forth its fruit in its
　　season,
　　Whose leaf also shall not wither;
　And whatever he does shall prosper.

4 The ungodly *are* not so,
　But *are* like the chaff which the wind
　　drives away.
5 Therefore the ungodly shall not stand
　　in the judgment,
　Nor sinners in the congregation of the
　　righteous.

6 For the LORD knows the way of the
　　righteous,
　But the way of the ungodly shall
　　perish.

> **1:6 the LORD knows.** This refers to God's personal intimacy and involvement with His righteous ones (see 2 Tim. 2:19). **the way of.** The repetition of this phrase reflects "path" imagery, symbolizing one's total course of life. These two courses arrive at the ways of life and death (see Deut. 30:19). **shall perish.** One day the wicked person's way will end in ruin; a new, righteous order is coming.

TYPES OF PSALMS

Type	Psalms	Act of Worship
Individual and Communal Lament	3–7; 12; 13; 22; 25–28; 35; 38–40; 42–44; 51; 54–57; 59–61; 63; 64; 69–71; 74; 79; 80; 83; 85; 86; 88; 90; 102; 109; 120; 123; 130; 140–143	Express need for God's deliverance
Thanksgiving	8; 18; 19; 29; 30; 32–34; 36; 40; 41; 66; 103–106; 111; 113; 116; 117; 124; 129; 135; 136; 138; 139; 146–148; 150	Make aware of God's blessings; Express thanks
Enthronement	47; 93; 96–99	Describe God's sovereign rule
Pilgrimage	43; 46; 48; 76; 84; 87; 120–134	Establish a mood of worship
Royal	2; 18; 20; 21; 45; 72; 89; 101; 110; 132; 144	Portray Christ the Sovereign Ruler
Wisdom	1; 37; 119	Instruct as to God's will
Imprecatory	7; 35; 40; 55; 58; 59; 69; 79; 109; 137; 139; 144	Invoke God's wrath and judgment against His enemies

PSALM 2

The Messiah's Triumph and Kingdom

1 Why do the nations rage,
   And the people plot a vain thing?
2 The kings of the earth set themselves,
   And the rulers take counsel together,
   Against the LORD and against His
   Anointed, *saying,*
3 "Let us break Their bonds in pieces
   And cast away Their cords from us."

4 He who sits in the heavens shall
   laugh;
   The LORD shall hold them in
   derision.
5 Then He shall speak to them in His
   wrath,
   And distress them in His deep
   displeasure:
6 "Yet I have set My King
   On My holy hill of Zion."

7 "I will declare the decree:
   The LORD has said to Me,
   'You *are* My Son,
   Today I have begotten You.

2:7 You *are* My Son. Second Sam. 7:8–16 is the only Old Testament reference to the Father/Son relationship in the Trinity, a relationship seen throughout the New Testament. **Today I have begotten You.** This expresses the privileges of relationship, with its prophetic application to the Son, the Messiah. This verse is quoted in the New Testament in reference to the birth of Jesus (Heb. 1:5,6) and to His resurrection (Acts 13:33,34) as the ultimate fulfillments of the verse.

8 Ask of Me, and I will give *You*
   The nations *for* Your inheritance,
   And the ends of the earth *for* Your
   possession.
9 You shall break[a] them with a rod of
   iron;
   You shall dash them to pieces like a
   potter's vessel.' "

10 Now therefore, be wise, O kings;
   Be instructed, you judges of the earth.
11 Serve the LORD with fear,

   And rejoice with trembling.
12 Kiss the Son,[a] lest He[b] be angry,
   And you perish *in* the way,
   When His wrath is kindled but a
   little.
   Blessed *are* all those who put their
   trust in Him.

2:12 Kiss the Son. This symbolic act indicates allegiance and submission (see 1 Sam. 10:1). This word for "Son" is not the Hebrew word for "son" that is used in v. 7. Rather, it is the Aramaic counterpart for the word (see Dan. 7:13), which addresses the command to "nations" (v. 1). **perish *in* the way.** These words pick up the major burden of Ps. 1.

PSALM 3

The LORD Helps His Troubled People

A Psalm of David when he fled from
Absalom his son.

1 LORD, how they have increased who
   trouble me!
   Many *are* they who rise up against
   me.
2 Many *are* they who say of me,
   "*There is* no help for him in God."
                                      Selah

3 But You, O LORD, *are* a shield for me,
   My glory and the One who lifts up my
   head.
4 I cried to the LORD with my voice,
   And He heard me from His holy hill.
                                      Selah

5 I lay down and slept;
   I awoke, for the LORD sustained me.
6 I will not be afraid of ten thousands of
   people
   Who have set *themselves* against me
   all around.

7 Arise, O LORD;
   Save me, O my God!
   For You have struck all my enemies
   on the cheekbone;
   You have broken the teeth of the
   ungodly.

2:9 [a]Following Masoretic Text and Targum; Septuagint, Syriac, and Vulgate read *rule* (compare Revelation 2:27).   2:12 [a]Septuagint and Vulgate read *Embrace discipline;* Targum reads *Receive instruction.*   [b]Septuagint reads *the LORD.*

8   Salvation *belongs* to the LORD.
Your blessing *is* upon Your people.
                Selah

PSALM 4

The Safety of the Faithful

*To the Chief Musician. With stringed
instruments. A Psalm of David.*

1   Hear me when I call, O God of my
       righteousness!
You have relieved me in *my* distress;
Have mercy on me, and hear my
       prayer.

> **4:1 O God of my righteousness.** The ultimate basis
> for divine intervention is God's righteousness, not
> the psalmist's (see Jer. 23:6). **distress.** This word de-
> scribes the psalmist in painful situations. When he
> says, "you have relieved me," he conveys the picture
> that God has provided space for him.

2   How long, O you sons of men,
Will you turn my glory to shame?

How long will you love
       worthlessness
And seek falsehood?   Selah
3   But know that the LORD has set
       apart[a] for Himself him who is
       godly;
The LORD will hear when I call to
       Him.

4   Be angry, and do not sin.
Meditate within your heart on your
       bed, and be still.   Selah
5   Offer the sacrifices of
       righteousness,
And put your trust in the LORD.

6   *There are* many who say,
"Who will show us *any* good?"
LORD, lift up the light of Your
       countenance upon us.
7   You have put gladness in my heart,
More than in the season that their
       grain and wine increased.
8   I will both lie down in peace, and
       sleep;
For You alone, O LORD, make me
       dwell in safety.

4:3 [a]Many Hebrew manuscripts, Septuagint, Targum, and Vulgate read *made wonderful*.

HISTORICAL BACKGROUND TO PSALMS BY DAVID

Psalm	Historical Background	OT Text
Psalm 3	when David fled from Absalom his son	2 Samuel 15:13–17
Psalm 7	concerning the words of Cush a Benjamite	2 Samuel 16:5; 19:16
Psalm 18	the day the Lord delivered David from his enemies/Saul	2 Samuel 22:1–51
Psalm 30	at the dedication of the house of David	2 Samuel 5:11,12; 6:17
Psalm 34	when David pretended madness before Abimelech	1 Samuel 21:10–15
Psalm 51	when Nathan confronted David over sin with Bathsheba	2 Samuel 12:1–14
Psalm 52	when Doeg the Edomite warned Saul about David	1 Samuel 22:9,10
Psalm 54	when the Ziphites warned Saul about David	1 Samuel 23:19
Psalm 56	when the Philistines captured David in Gath	1 Samuel 21:10,11
Psalm 57	when David fled from Saul into the cave	1 Samuel 22:1; 24:3
Psalm 59	when Saul sent men to watch the house in order to kill David	1 Samuel 19:11
Psalm 60	when David fought against Mesopotamia and Syria	2 Samuel 8:3,13
Psalm 63	when David was in the wilderness of Judea	1 Samuel 23:14; or 2 Samuel 15:23–28
Psalm 142	when David was in a cave	1 Samuel 22:1; 24:3

PSALM 5

A Prayer for Guidance

To the Chief Musician. With flutes.[a]
A Psalm of David.

1 Give ear to my words, O LORD,
  Consider my meditation.
2 Give heed to the voice of my cry,
  My King and my God,
  For to You I will pray.

5:2 My King and my God. David was the anointed king on earth, but he fully understood that the ultimate King of all Israel, and of the whole earth, is God.

3 My voice You shall hear in the
    morning, O LORD;
  In the morning I will direct *it* to You,
  And I will look up.

4 For You *are* not a God who takes
    pleasure in wickedness,
  Nor shall evil dwell with You.
5 The boastful shall not stand in Your
    sight;
  You hate all workers of iniquity.
6 You shall destroy those who speak
    falsehood;
  The LORD abhors the bloodthirsty
    and deceitful man.

7 But as for me, I will come into Your
    house in the multitude of Your
    mercy;
  In fear of You I will worship toward
    Your holy temple.
8 Lead me, O LORD, in Your
    righteousness because of my
    enemies;
  Make Your way straight before my
    face.

9 For *there is* no faithfulness in their
    mouth;
  Their inward part *is* destruction;
  Their throat *is* an open tomb;
  They flatter with their tongue.
10 Pronounce them guilty, O God!
  Let them fall by their own counsels;

Cast them out in the multitude of
    their transgressions,
  For they have rebelled against You.

11 But let all those rejoice who put their
    trust in You;
  Let them ever shout for joy, because
    You defend them;
  Let those also who love Your name
  Be joyful in You.
12 For You, O LORD, will bless the
    righteous;
  With favor You will surround him as
    with a shield.

PSALM 6

A Prayer of Faith in Time of Distress

To the Chief Musician. With stringed
instruments. On an eight-stringed harp.[a]
A Psalm of David.

1 O LORD, do not rebuke me in Your
    anger,
  Nor chasten me in Your hot
    displeasure.
2 Have mercy on me, O LORD, for I *am*
    weak;
  O LORD, heal me, for my bones are
    troubled.
3 My soul also is greatly troubled;
  But You, O LORD—how long?

4 Return, O LORD, deliver me!
  Oh, save me for Your mercies' sake!

6:4 deliver me!...for Your mercies' sake. This introduces a new synonym for salvation, connoting an action of drawing off or out. He desires the Lord to graciously liberate him (see Job 36:15).

5 For in death *there is* no remembrance
    of You;
  In the grave who will give You
    thanks?

6 I am weary with my groaning;
  All night I make my bed swim;
  I drench my couch with my tears.
7 My eye wastes away because of grief;

5:title *a*Hebrew *nehiloth*   6:title *a*Hebrew *sheminith*

It grows old because of all my
enemies.

8 Depart from me, all you workers of
iniquity;
For the LORD has heard the voice of
my weeping.
9 The LORD has heard my supplication;
The LORD will receive my prayer.
10 Let all my enemies be ashamed and
greatly troubled;
Let them turn back *and* be ashamed
suddenly.

6:1–10 David's circumstances seem hopeless, and
he is sleepless. The early Christian church regarded
this psalm as the first among the "penitential psalms"
(see Pss. 32;38). David's cries, coming from the depths
of his personal pit of persecution, indicate a radical
change in his frame of mind as he addresses both
God and his enemies.

PSALM 7

Prayer and Praise for Deliverance from Enemies

*A Meditation[a] of David, which he sang
to the LORD concerning the words
of Cush, a Benjamite.*

1 O LORD my God, in You I put my
trust;
Save me from all those who persecute
me;
And deliver me,
2 Lest they tear me like a lion,
Rending *me* in pieces, while *there is*
none to deliver.

3 O LORD my God, if I have done this:
If there is iniquity in my hands,
4 If I have repaid evil to him who was
at peace with me,
Or have plundered my enemy without
cause,
5 Let the enemy pursue me and
overtake *me*;
Yes, let him trample my life to the
earth,
And lay my honor in the dust.   Selah

6 Arise, O LORD, in Your anger;
Lift Yourself up because of the rage of
my enemies;
Rise up for me[a] *to* the judgment You
have commanded!
7 So the congregation of the peoples
shall surround You;
For their sakes, therefore, return on
high.
8 The LORD shall judge the peoples;
Judge me, O LORD, according to my
righteousness,
And according to my integrity within
me.

9 Oh, let the wickedness of the wicked
come to an end,
But establish the just;
For the righteous God tests the hearts
and minds.

7:1–17 David pleas for divine vindication in light of
the oppressor's allegations and actions. His confidence in the Divine Judge is the backbone of Ps. 7
(see Gen. 18:25). David's anxiety turns to assurance
through 3 stages in this psalm: he begs the attention
of the Divine Judge, argues his case before Him, and
finally waits patiently for the verdict.

10 My defense *is* of God,
Who saves the upright in heart.

11 God *is* a just judge,
And God is angry *with the wicked*
every day.
12 If he does not turn back,
He will sharpen His sword;
He bends His bow and makes it
ready.
13 He also prepares for Himself
instruments of death;
He makes His arrows into fiery
shafts.

14 Behold, *the wicked* brings forth
iniquity;
Yes, he conceives trouble and brings
forth falsehood.
15 He made a pit and dug it out,

7:title [a]Hebrew *Shiggaion*   **7:6** [a]Following Masoretic Text, Targum, and Vulgate; Septuagint
reads O LORD my God.

And has fallen into the ditch *which*
    he made.
16 His trouble shall return upon his own
    head,
    And his violent dealing shall come
    down on his own crown.

17 I will praise the LORD according to
    His righteousness,
    And will sing praise to the name of
    the LORD Most High.

PSALM 8

The Glory of the LORD in Creation

To the Chief Musician. On the instrument
of Gath.[a] A Psalm of David.

1 O LORD, our Lord,
    How excellent *is* Your name in all the
    earth,
    Who have set Your glory above the
    heavens!

8:1 LORD...Lord. The first "LORD" refers to God's specially revealed name Yahweh (Ex. 3:14), and the second emphasizes His sovereignty. **Your name.** The name of God refers to the revealed Person of God, encompassing all of His attributes.

2 Out of the mouth of babes and
    nursing infants
    You have ordained strength,
    Because of Your enemies,
    That You may silence the enemy and
    the avenger.

3 When I consider Your heavens, the
    work of Your fingers,
    The moon and the stars, which You
    have ordained,
4 What is man that You are mindful of
    him,
    And the son of man that You visit
    him?
5 For You have made him a little lower
    than the angels,[a]
    And You have crowned him with glory
    and honor.

6 You have made him to have dominion
    over the works of Your hands;
    You have put all *things* under his feet,
7 All sheep and oxen—
    Even the beasts of the field,
8 The birds of the air,
    And the fish of the sea
    That pass through the paths of the
    seas.

9 O LORD, our Lord,
    How excellent *is* Your name in all the
    earth!

PSALM 9

Prayer and Thanksgiving for the LORD'S Righteous Judgments

To the Chief Musician. To the tune
of "Death of the Son."[a]
A Psalm of David.

1 I will praise *You*, O LORD, with my
    whole heart;
    I will tell of all Your marvelous works.

9:1 Your marvelous works. This refers to God's extraordinary interventions on behalf of His people throughout history (see the Exodus events).

2 I will be glad and rejoice in You;
    I will sing praise to Your name,
      O Most High.

3 When my enemies turn back,
    They shall fall and perish at Your
    presence.
4 For You have maintained my right
    and my cause;
    You sat on the throne judging in
    righteousness.
5 You have rebuked the nations,
    You have destroyed the wicked;
    You have blotted out their name
    forever and ever.

6 O enemy, destructions are finished
    forever!
    And you have destroyed cities;

8:title [a]Hebrew *Al Gittith*   8:5 [a]Hebrew *Elohim, God;* Septuagint, Syriac, Targum, and Jewish tradition translate as *angels.*   9:title [a]Hebrew *Muth Labben*

Even their memory has perished.

7   But the LORD shall endure forever;
    He has prepared His throne for
        judgment.
8   He shall judge the world in
        righteousness,
    And He shall administer judgment for
        the peoples in uprightness.

9   The LORD also will be a refuge for the
        oppressed,
    A refuge in times of trouble.
10 And those who know Your name will
        put their trust in You;
    For You, LORD, have not forsaken
        those who seek You.

11 Sing praises to the LORD, who dwells
        in Zion!
    Declare His deeds among the people.
12 When He avenges blood, He
        remembers them;
    He does not forget the cry of the
        humble.

13 Have mercy on me, O LORD!
    Consider my trouble from those who
        hate me,
    You who lift me up from the gates of
        death,
14 That I may tell of all Your praise
    In the gates of the daughter of Zion.
    I will rejoice in Your salvation.

15 The nations have sunk down in the
        pit which they made;
    In the net which they hid, their own
        foot is caught.
16 The LORD is known by the judgment
        He executes;
    The wicked is snared in the work of
        his own hands.
                Meditation.*   Selah

17 The wicked shall be turned into hell,
    And all the nations that forget God.
18 For the needy shall not always be
        forgotten;
    The expectation of the poor shall not
        perish forever.

19 Arise, O LORD,

Do not let man prevail;
Let the nations be judged in Your
    sight.
20 Put them in fear, O LORD,
    That the nations may know
        themselves to be but men.   Selah

10:1–18 This psalm begins in despair; injustice is rampant, and God seems disinterested. The psalmist slowly turns around from walking more by sight than faith as his focus shifts from empirical observations to theological truths. It is not easy for him, for he is surrounded by atheists. Ps. 10 exemplifies how true believers seem to live with discouragement and encouragement at the same time.

PSALM 10

A Song of Confidence in God's Triumph over Evil

1   Why do You stand afar off, O LORD?
    Why do You hide in times of trouble?
2   The wicked in his pride persecutes the
        poor;
    Let them be caught in the plots which
        they have devised.

3   For the wicked boasts of his heart's
        desire;
    He blesses the greedy and renounces
        the LORD.
4   The wicked in his proud countenance
        does not seek God;
    God is in none of his thoughts.
5   His ways are always prospering;
    Your judgments are far above, out of
        his sight;
    As for all his enemies, he sneers at
        them.

10:5 His ways are always prospering. God seems to reward the ruthless. The psalmist's question insinuates, "Has God also abandoned His own standards for retribution and reward?" (see Job 20:2; Jer. 12:1).

6   He has said in his heart, "I shall not
        be moved;
    I shall never be in adversity."

7   His mouth is full of cursing and
deceit and oppression;
Under his tongue *is* trouble and
iniquity.

8   He sits in the lurking places of the
villages;
In the secret places he murders the
innocent;
His eyes are secretly fixed on the
helpless.

9   He lies in wait secretly, as a lion in
his den;
He lies in wait to catch the poor;
He catches the poor when he draws
him into his net.

10   So he crouches, he lies low,
That the helpless may fall by his
strength.

11   He has said in his heart,
"God has forgotten;
He hides His face;
He will never see."

12   Arise, O LORD!
O God, lift up Your hand!
Do not forget the humble.

13   Why do the wicked renounce God?
He has said in his heart,
"You will not require *an account.*"

14   But You have seen, for You observe
trouble and grief,
To repay *it* by Your hand.
The helpless commits himself to You;
You are the helper of the fatherless.

15   Break the arm of the wicked and the
evil *man;*
Seek out his wickedness *until* You
find none.

16   The LORD *is* King forever and ever;
The nations have perished out of His
land.

17   LORD, You have heard the desire of
the humble;
You will prepare their heart;
You will cause Your ear to hear,

18   To do justice to the fatherless and the
oppressed,
That the man of the earth may
oppress no more.

PSALM 11

Faith in the LORD's Righteousness

To the Chief Musician. A Psalm of David.

1   In the LORD I put my trust;
How can you say to my soul,
"Flee *as* a bird to your mountain"?

2   For look! The wicked bend *their* bow,
They make ready their arrow on the
string,
That they may shoot secretly at the
upright in heart.

3   If the foundations are destroyed,
What can the righteous do?

4   The LORD *is* in His holy temple,
The LORD's throne *is* in heaven;
His eyes behold,
His eyelids test the sons of men.

5   The LORD tests the righteous,
But the wicked and the one who loves
violence His soul hates.

6   Upon the wicked He will rain coals;
Fire and brimstone and a burning
wind
Shall be the portion of their cup.

7   For the LORD *is* righteous,
He loves righteousness;
His countenance beholds the
upright.[a]

11:1–7 Here David is peaceful, while his counselors panic. Because of David's attitude, this psalm is considered a psalm of confidence (Pss. 4;16). The union of the king and the people is apparent, as the phrases shift from being singular to plural. This psalm reveals that, although David heard the different voices of flight and faith, he made up his mind to trust only in the Lord.

PSALM 12

Man's Treachery and God's Constancy

To the Chief Musician. On an eight-stringed harp.[a] A Psalm of David.

1   Help, LORD, for the godly man ceases!
For the faithful disappear from among
the sons of men.

11:7 *[a]Or The upright beholds His countenance*   12:title *[a]Hebrew sheminith*

2   They speak idly everyone with his
      neighbor;
    With flattering lips *and* a double heart
      they speak.

3   May the LORD cut off all flattering
      lips,
    And the tongue that speaks proud
      things,
4   Who have said,
    "With our tongue we will prevail;
    Our lips *are* our own;
    Who *is* lord over us?"

5   "For the oppression of the poor, for the
      sighing of the needy,
    Now I will arise," says the LORD;
    "I will set *him* in the safety for which
      he yearns."

12:1–8 Men's words hurt, but the Lord's words heal.
These thoughts preoccupy David in this Psalm, which
begins and ends with the reality of the reign of the
wicked. These verses contain subtle repetitions and
bold contrasts. Here David provides a model for
passing a spiritual hearing test: genuine disciples
will listen and properly respond to two opposite
kinds of speech, depraved and divine.

6   The words of the LORD *are* pure
      words,
    Like silver tried in a furnace of earth,
    Purified seven times.
7   You shall keep them, O LORD,
    You shall preserve them from this
      generation forever.
8   The wicked prowl on every side,
    When vileness is exalted among the
      sons of men.

PSALM 13

Trust in the Salvation of the LORD

To the Chief Musician. A Psalm of David.

1   How long, O LORD? Will You forget
      me forever?
    How long will You hide Your face
      from me?
2   How long shall I take counsel in my
      soul,
    Having sorrow in my heart daily?

    How long will my enemy be exalted
      over me?

13:1,2 These lines reintroduce the triangle of the
psalmist, his God, and his enemies. This 3-way relationship produces perplexity and pain. In view of
God's apparent absence, the psalmist seems left to
his own resources, which are insufficient in facing
his enemies.

3   Consider *and* hear me, O LORD my
      God;
    Enlighten my eyes,
    Lest I sleep the *sleep of* death;
4   Lest my enemy say,
    "I have prevailed against him";
    Lest those who trouble me rejoice
      when I am moved.

5   But I have trusted in Your mercy;
    My heart shall rejoice in Your
      salvation.
6   I will sing to the LORD,
    Because He has dealt bountifully with
      me.

PSALM 14

Folly of the Godless, and God's Final Triumph

To the Chief Musician. A Psalm of David.

1   The fool has said in his heart,
    "*There is* no God."
    They are corrupt,
    They have done abominable works,
    There is none who does good.

14:1 The fool. In the Bible, this designation carries
moral, rather than intellectual, meaning (Is. 32:6).

2   The LORD looks down from heaven
      upon the children of men,
    To see if there are any who
      understand, who seek God.
3   They have all turned aside,
    They have together become corrupt;
    There is none who does good,
    No, not one.

4   Have all the workers of iniquity no
      knowledge,

Who eat up my people *as* they eat
bread,
And do not call on the LORD?

5 There they are in great fear,
For God *is* with the generation of the
righteous.
6 You shame the counsel of the poor,
But the LORD *is* his refuge.

7 Oh, that the salvation of Israel *would
come* out of Zion!
When the LORD brings back the
captivity of His people,
Let Jacob rejoice *and* Israel be glad.

PSALM 15

The Character of Those Who May Dwell
with the LORD

A Psalm of David.

1 LORD, who may abide in Your
tabernacle?
Who may dwell in Your holy hill?

2 He who walks uprightly,
And works righteousness,
And speaks the truth in his
heart;
3 He *who* does not backbite with his
tongue,
Nor does evil to his neighbor,
Nor does he take up a reproach
against his friend;
4 In whose eyes a vile person is
despised,
But he honors those who fear the
LORD;
He *who* swears to his own hurt and
does not change;
5 He *who* does not put out his money
at usury,
Nor does he take a bribe against
the innocent.

He who does these *things* shall never
be moved.

PSALM 16

The Hope of the Faithful, and the
Messiah's Victory

A Michtam of David.

1 Preserve me, O God, for in You I put
my trust.

2 *O my soul,* you have said to the
LORD,
"You *are* my Lord,
My goodness is nothing apart from
You."
3 As for the saints who *are* on the
earth,
"They are the excellent ones, in whom
is all my delight."

4 Their sorrows shall be multiplied who
hasten *after* another *god;*
Their drink offerings of blood I will
not offer,
Nor take up their names on my lips.

5 O LORD, *You are* the portion of my
inheritance and my cup;
You maintain my lot.
6 The lines have fallen to me in
pleasant *places;*
Yes, I have a good inheritance.

7 I will bless the LORD who has given
me counsel;
My heart also instructs me in the
night seasons.
8 I have set the LORD always before
me;
Because *He is* at my right hand I shall
not be moved.

9 Therefore my heart is glad, and my
glory rejoices;
My flesh also will rest in hope.
10 For You will not leave my soul in
Sheol,
Nor will You allow Your Holy One to
see corruption.

15:5 usury. Interest rates ran as high as 50 percent, but God's law put strict regulations on borrowing and lending (see Deut. 23:19,20).

16:10 These words expressed the confidence of the lesser David but were applied to the resurrection of the Greater David, Jesus Christ (see Peter's words in Acts 2:25–28 and Paul's in Acts 13:35).

11 You will show me the path of life;
   In Your presence *is* fullness of joy;
   At Your right hand *are* pleasures
      forevermore.

17:1–15 This "prayer" contains as many as 17 petitions, many paralleling with Ps. 16. It is a prayer for protection and contains themes and phrases from the Exodus narrative (see Ex. 15). David shifts his focus to his enemies and then back to himself. He seeks justice and appeals for help to deal with response and recognition, rescue and relief, and retribution and rest.

PSALM 17

Prayer with Confidence in Final Salvation

A Prayer of David.

1 Hear a just cause, O LORD,
   Attend to my cry;
   Give ear to my prayer *which is* not
      from deceitful lips.
2 Let my vindication come from Your
      presence;
   Let Your eyes look on the things that
      are upright.

3 You have tested my heart;
   You have visited *me* in the night;
   You have tried me and have found
      nothing;
   I have purposed that my mouth shall
      not transgress.
4 Concerning the works of men,
   By the word of Your lips,
   I have kept away from the paths of
      the destroyer.
5 Uphold my steps in Your paths,
   That my footsteps may not slip.

6 I have called upon You, for You will
      hear me, O God;
   Incline Your ear to me, *and* hear my
      speech.
7 Show Your marvelous lovingkindness
      by Your right hand,
   O You who save those who trust *in You*
   From those who rise up *against them.*
8 Keep me as the apple of Your eye;

17:8 the apple of Your eye. This expression means the pupil of the human eye. As a person protects his eye, so God protects His people.

MESSIANIC PROPHECIES IN THE PSALMS

Prophecy	Psalm	Fulfillment
1. God will announce Christ to be His Son	2:7	Matthew 3:17; Acts 13:33; Hebrews 1:5
2. All things will be put under Christ's feet	8:6	1 Corinthians 15:27; Hebrews 2:8
3. Christ will be resurrected from the grave	16:10	Mark 16:6,7; Acts 13:35
4. God will forsake Christ in His moment of agony	22:1	Matthew 27:46; Mark 15:34
5. Christ will be scorned and ridiculed	22:7,8	Matthew 27:39–43; Luke 23:35
6. Christ's hands and feet will be pierced	22:16	John 20:25,27; Acts 2:23
7. Others will gamble for Christ's clothes	22:18	Matthew 27:35,36
8. Not one of Christ's bones will be broken	34:20	John 19:32,33,36
9. Christ will be hated unjustly	35:19	John 15:25
10. Christ will come to do God's will	40:7,8	Hebrews 10:7
11. Christ will be betrayed by a friend	41:9	John 13:18
12. Christ's throne will be eternal	45:6	Hebrews 1:8
13. Christ will ascend to heaven	68:18	Ephesians 4:8
14. Zeal for God's temple will consume Christ	69:9	John 2:17
15. Christ will be given vinegar and gall	69:21	Matthew 27:34; John 19:28–30
16. Christ's betrayer will be replaced	109:8	Acts 1:20
17. Christ's enemies will bow down to Him	110:1	Acts 2:34,35
18. Christ will be a priest like Melchizedek	110:4	Hebrews 5:6; 6:20; 7:17
19. Christ will be the chief cornerstone	118:22	Matthew 21:42; Acts 4:11
20. Christ will come in the name of the Lord	118:26	Matthew 21:9

Hide me under the shadow of Your
    wings,
9 From the wicked who oppress me,
    From my deadly enemies who
    surround me.

10 They have closed up their fat *hearts;*
    With their mouths they speak
    proudly.
11 They have now surrounded us in our
    steps;
    They have set their eyes, crouching
    down to the earth,
12 As a lion is eager to tear his prey,
    And like a young lion lurking in
    secret places.

13 Arise, O LORD,
    Confront him, cast him down;
    Deliver my life from the wicked with
    Your sword,
14 With Your hand from men, O LORD,
    From men of the world *who have*
    their portion in *this* life,
    And whose belly You fill with Your
    hidden treasure.
    They are satisfied with children,
    And leave the rest of their *possession*
    for their babes.

15 As for me, I will see Your face in
    righteousness;
    I shall be satisfied when I awake in
    Your likeness.

PSALM 18

God the Sovereign Savior

To the Chief Musician. A Psalm of David
the servant of the LORD, who spoke to
the LORD the words of this song on the day
that the LORD delivered him from the hand
of all his enemies and from the hand
of Saul. And he said:

1 I will love You, O LORD, my strength.
2 The LORD is my rock and my fortress
    and my deliverer;
    My God, my strength, in whom I will
    trust;

> **18:1 love.** This word for love does not bear covenant meaning (Deut. 7:8), but it is a rare verb that describes tender intimacy. David's choice of words intended to express very strong devotion, like Peter's in John 21:15–17.

    My shield and the horn of my
    salvation, my stronghold.
3 I will call upon the LORD, *who is*
    worthy to be praised;
    So shall I be saved from my enemies.

4 The pangs of death surrounded me,
    And the floods of ungodliness made
    me afraid.
5 The sorrows of Sheol surrounded me;
    The snares of death confronted me.
6 In my distress I called upon the
    LORD,
    And cried out to my God;
    He heard my voice from His temple,
    And my cry came before Him, *even* to
    His ears.

7 Then the earth shook and trembled;
    The foundations of the hills also
    quaked and were shaken,
    Because He was angry.
8 Smoke went up from His nostrils,
    And devouring fire from His mouth;
    Coals were kindled by it.
9 He bowed the heavens also, and came
    down
    With darkness under His feet.
10 And He rode upon a cherub, and flew;
    He flew upon the wings of the wind.
11 He made darkness His secret place;
    His canopy around Him *was* dark
    waters
    And thick clouds of the skies.
12 From the brightness before Him,
    His thick clouds passed with
    hailstones and coals of fire.

13 The LORD thundered from heaven,
    And the Most High uttered His voice,
    Hailstones and coals of fire.[a]
14 He sent out His arrows and scattered
    the foe,
    Lightnings in abundance, and He
    vanquished them.

18:13 [a]Following Masoretic Text, Targum, and Vulgate; a few Hebrew manuscripts and Septuagint omit *Hailstones and coals of fire.*

15 Then the channels of the sea were
       seen,
   The foundations of the world were
       uncovered
   At Your rebuke, O LORD,
   At the blast of the breath of Your
       nostrils.

16 He sent from above, He took me;
   He drew me out of many waters.
17 He delivered me from my strong
       enemy,
   From those who hated me,
   For they were too strong for me.
18 They confronted me in the day of my
       calamity,
   But the LORD was my support.
19 He also brought me out into a broad
       place;
   He delivered me because He delighted
       in me.

20 The LORD rewarded me according to
       my righteousness;
   According to the cleanness of my
       hands
   He has recompensed me.
21 For I have kept the ways of the LORD,
   And have not wickedly departed from
       my God.
22 For all His judgments were before me,
   And I did not put away His statutes
       from me.
23 I was also blameless before Him,
   And I kept myself from my iniquity.
24 Therefore the LORD has recompensed
       me according to my righteousness,
   According to the cleanness of my
       hands in His sight.

25 With the merciful You will show
       Yourself merciful;
   With a blameless man You will show
       Yourself blameless;
26 With the pure You will show Yourself
       pure;
   And with the devious You will show
       Yourself shrewd.
27 For You will save the humble people,
   But will bring down haughty looks.

28 For You will light my lamp;
   The LORD my God will enlighten my
       darkness.

29 For by You I can run against a troop,
   By my God I can leap over a wall.
30 As for God, His way is perfect;
   The word of the LORD is proven;
   He is a shield to all who trust in Him.

18:1–50 This is an individual psalm of thanksgiving. Its poetry and themes resemble ancient testimonies to God's great historical deliverance (see Ex. 15; Judg. 5). David praises God by describing the stages of his life, ethical integrity, and the atmosphere of leadership.

31 For who is God, except the LORD?
   And who is a rock, except our God?
32 It is God who arms me with strength,
   And makes my way perfect.
33 He makes my feet like the feet of deer,
   And sets me on my high places.
34 He teaches my hands to make war,
   So that my arms can bend a bow of
       bronze.

35 You have also given me the shield of
       Your salvation;
   Your right hand has held me up,
   Your gentleness has made me great.
36 You enlarged my path under me,
   So my feet did not slip.

37 I have pursued my enemies and
       overtaken them;
   Neither did I turn back again till they
       were destroyed.
38 I have wounded them,
   So that they could not rise;
   They have fallen under my feet.
39 For You have armed me with strength
       for the battle;
   You have subdued under me those
       who rose up against me.
40 You have also given me the necks of
       my enemies,
   So that I destroyed those who hated me.
41 They cried out, but there was none to
       save;
   Even to the LORD, but He did not
       answer them.
42 Then I beat them as fine as the dust
       before the wind;
   I cast them out like dirt in the streets.

43 You have delivered me from the
       strivings of the people;

You have made me the head of the
nations;
A people I have not known shall serve
me.

44 As soon as they hear of me they obey
me;
The foreigners submit to me.

45 The foreigners fade away,
And come frightened from their
hideouts.

46 The LORD lives!
Blessed *be* my Rock!
Let the God of my salvation be
exalted.

47 *It is* God who avenges me,
And subdues the peoples under me;

48 He delivers me from my enemies.
You also lift me up above those who
rise against me;
You have delivered me from the
violent man.

49 Therefore I will give thanks to You,
O LORD, among the Gentiles,
And sing praises to Your name.

50 Great deliverance He gives to His
king,
And shows mercy to His anointed,
To David and his descendants
forevermore.

PSALM 19

The Perfect Revelation of the LORD

To the Chief Musician. A Psalm of David.

1 The heavens declare the glory of
God;
And the firmament shows His
handiwork.

2 Day unto day utters speech,
And night unto night reveals
knowledge.

3 *There is* no speech nor language
Where their voice is not heard.

4 Their line*a* has gone out through all
the earth,
And their words to the end of the
world.

In them He has set a tabernacle for
the sun,

5 Which *is* like a bridegroom coming
out of his chamber,
And rejoices like a strong man to run
its race.

6 Its rising *is* from one end of heaven,
And its circuit to the other end;
And there is nothing hidden from its
heat.

19:1–6 The testimony of God through the universe
is clear, but humanity persistently resists it. General
revelation cannot convert sinners, but it does make
them accountable (see Rom. 1:18). Salvation comes
ultimately through special revelation, as the Word of
God is understood through His Spirit.

7 The law of the LORD *is* perfect,
converting the soul;
The testimony of the LORD *is* sure,
making wise the simple;

8 The statutes of the LORD *are* right,
rejoicing the heart;
The commandment of the LORD *is*
pure, enlightening the eyes;

9 The fear of the LORD *is* clean,
enduring forever;
The judgments of the LORD *are* true
and righteous altogether.

10 More to be desired *are they* than gold,
Yea, than much fine gold;
Sweeter also than honey and the
honeycomb.

11 Moreover by them Your servant is
warned,
And in keeping them *there is* great
reward.

12 Who can understand *his* errors?
Cleanse me from secret *faults.*

13 Keep back Your servant also from
presumptuous *sins;*
Let them not have dominion over me.
Then I shall be blameless,

19:12,13 The psalmist concerns himself with unintentional sins and high-handed infractions (see Lev.
4:1). David, by God's grace and provisions, deals with
his sins and does not deny them. This reflects the
attitude of a maturing disciple.

19:4 *a*Septuagint, Syriac, and Vulgate read *sound;* Targum reads *business.*

And I shall be innocent of great
  transgression.

14 Let the words of my mouth and the
  meditation of my heart
  Be acceptable in Your sight,
  O LORD, my strength and my
  Redeemer.

PSALM 20

The Assurance of God's Saving Work

To the Chief Musician. A Psalm of David.

1 May the LORD answer you in the day
  of trouble;
  May the name of the God of Jacob
  defend you;
2 May He send you help from the
  sanctuary,
  And strengthen you out of Zion;
3 May He remember all your offerings,
  And accept your burnt sacrifice.
                                Selah

20:2 from the sanctuary...out of Zion. These refer to the location of the ark of God, which symbolized His presence. David recaptured and placed it in the tabernacle on Mount Zion. The people hoped that the Lord would uphold, support, and sustain the king-general with His extending, powerful presence throughout the military campaign.

4 May He grant you according to your
  heart's *desire,*
  And fulfill all your purpose.
5 We will rejoice in your salvation,
  And in the name of our God we will
  set up *our* banners!
  May the LORD fulfill all your
  petitions.

6 Now I know that the LORD saves His
  anointed;
  He will answer him from His holy
  heaven
  With the saving strength of His right
  hand.

7 Some *trust* in chariots, and some in
  horses;

But we will remember the name of
  the LORD our God.
8 They have bowed down and fallen;
  But we have risen and stand upright.

9 Save, LORD!
  May the King answer us when we call.

PSALM 21

Joy in the Salvation of the LORD

To the Chief Musician. A Psalm of David.

1 The king shall have joy in Your
  strength, O LORD;
  And in Your salvation how greatly
  shall he rejoice!
2 You have given him his heart's
  desire,
  And have not withheld the request of
  his lips.   Selah

3 For You meet him with the blessings
  of goodness;
  You set a crown of pure gold upon his
  head.
4 He asked life from You, *and* You gave
  it to him—
  Length of days forever and ever.
5 His glory *is* great in Your salvation;
  Honor and majesty You have placed
  upon him.
6 For You have made him most blessed
  forever;
  You have made him exceedingly glad
  with Your presence.
7 For the king trusts in the LORD,
  And through the mercy of the Most
  High he shall not be moved.

21:7 For the king. The king's dependent trust in God shows his responsibility to receive God's blessings. But the sovereign grace of God provides the ultimate basis so that one is not moved or shaken (see Ps. 15:5).

8 Your hand will find all Your enemies;
  Your right hand will find those who
  hate You.
9 You shall make them as a fiery oven
  in the time of Your anger;

The LORD shall swallow them up in
His wrath,
And the fire shall devour them.
10 Their offspring You shall destroy from
the earth,
And their descendants from among
the sons of men.
11 For they intended evil against You;
They devised a plot *which* they are
not able *to perform.*
12 Therefore You will make them turn
their back;
You will make ready *Your arrows* on
Your string toward their faces.

13 Be exalted, O LORD, in Your own
strength!
We will sing and praise Your power.

PSALM 22

The Suffering, Praise, and Posterity
of the Messiah

*To the Chief Musician. Set to "The Deer
of the Dawn."*[a] *A Psalm of David.*

1 My God, My God, why have You
forsaken Me?
Why are You so far from helping Me,
And from the words of My groaning?
2 O My God, I cry in the daytime, but
You do not hear;
And in the night season, and am not
silent.

22:1 My God, My God, why have You forsaken Me?
The repeated noun of direct address to God reflects
a small amount of personal hope in a seemingly
hopeless situation. "Forsaken" expresses the personal abandonment felt by David and supremely
experienced by Christ on the cross (Matt. 27:46).

3 But You *are* holy,
Enthroned in the praises of Israel.
4 Our fathers trusted in You;
They trusted, and You delivered
them.
5 They cried to You, and were delivered;
They trusted in You, and were not
ashamed.

6 But I *am* a worm, and no man;
A reproach of men, and despised by
the people.
7 All those who see Me ridicule Me;
They shoot out the lip, they shake the
head, *saying,*
8 "He trusted[a] in the LORD, let Him
rescue Him;
Let Him deliver Him, since He
delights in Him!"

9 But You *are* He who took Me out of
the womb;
You made Me trust *while* on My
mother's breasts.
10 I was cast upon You from birth.
From My mother's womb
You *have been* My God.
11 Be not far from Me,
For trouble *is* near;
For *there is* none to help.

12 Many bulls have surrounded Me;
Strong *bulls* of Bashan have encircled
Me.
13 They gape at Me *with* their mouths,
Like a raging and roaring lion.

14 I am poured out like water,
And all My bones are out of joint;

IMAGES OF GOD IN THE PSALMS

Images of God as	Reference in Psalms
Shield	3:3; 28:7; 119:114
Rock	18:2; 42:9; 95:1
King	5:2; 44:4; 74:12
Shepherd	23:1; 80:1
Judge	7:11
Refuge	46:1; 62:7
Fortress	31:3; 71:3
Avenger	26:1
Creator	8:1,6
Deliverer	37:39,40
Healer	30:2
Protector	5:11
Provider	78:23–29
Redeemer	107:2

©2001 by Thomas Nelson, Inc.

22:title *ª*Hebrew *Aijeleth Hashahar*   22:8 *ª*Septuagint, Syriac, and Vulgate read *hoped;* Targum reads
praised.

My heart is like wax;
It has melted within Me.
15 My strength is dried up like a
potsherd,
And My tongue clings to My jaws;
You have brought Me to the dust of
death.

16 For dogs have surrounded Me;
The congregation of the wicked has
enclosed Me.
They pierced[a] My hands and My feet;
17 I can count all My bones.
They look *and* stare at Me.
18 They divide My garments among
them,
And for My clothing they cast lots.

> **22:16–18 They pierced My hands and My feet.** The Hebrew text reads "like a lion," describing the viciousness of enemies. This messianic prophecy refers to crucifixion.
>
> **They divide...they cast.** All 4 Gospel writers appeal to this imagery in describing Christ's crucifixion (Matt. 27:35; Mark 15:24; Luke 23:34; John 19:24).

19 But You, O LORD, do not be far from
Me;
O My Strength, hasten to help Me!
20 Deliver Me from the sword,
My precious *life* from the power of the
dog.
21 Save Me from the lion's mouth
And from the horns of the wild oxen!

You have answered Me.

22 I will declare Your name to My
brethren;
In the midst of the assembly I will
praise You.
23 You who fear the LORD, praise Him!
All you descendants of Jacob, glorify
Him,
And fear Him, all you offspring of
Israel!
24 For He has not despised nor abhorred
the affliction of the afflicted;

Nor has He hidden His face from
Him;
But when He cried to Him, He heard.

25 My praise *shall be* of You in the great
assembly;
I will pay My vows before those who
fear Him.
26 The poor shall eat and be satisfied;
Those who seek Him will praise the
LORD.
Let your heart live forever!

27 All the ends of the world
Shall remember and turn to the
LORD,
And all the families of the nations
Shall worship before You.[a]
28 For the kingdom *is* the LORD's,
And He rules over the nations.

29 All the prosperous of the earth
Shall eat and worship;
All those who go down to the dust
Shall bow before Him,
Even he who cannot keep himself
alive.
30 A posterity shall serve Him.
It will be recounted of the Lord to the
next generation,
31 They will come and declare His
righteousness to a people who will
be born,
That He has done *this*.

PSALM 23

The LORD the Shepherd of His People

A Psalm of David.

1 The LORD *is* my shepherd;
I shall not want.
2 He makes me to lie down in green
pastures;
He leads me beside the still waters.
3 He restores my soul;

22:16 [a]Following some Hebrew manuscripts, Septuagint, Syriac, Vulgate; Masoretic Text reads *Like a lion*. 22:27 [a]Following Masoretic Text, Septuagint, and Targum; Arabic, Syriac, and Vulgate read *Him*.

He leads me in the paths of
righteousness
For His name's sake.

4 Yea, though I walk through the valley
of the shadow of death,
I will fear no evil;
For You *are* with me;
Your rod and Your staff, they comfort
me.

> **23:4 the valley of the shadow of death.** This de-
> scribes a perilously threatening environment (see
> Job 10:21). **Your rod and Your staff.** The rod and staff
> were perceived as instruments of comfort, protec-
> tion, and direction.

5 You prepare a table before me in the
presence of my enemies;
You anoint my head with oil;
My cup runs over.
6 Surely goodness and mercy shall
follow me
All the days of my life;

> **23:1–6** David testifies to God's faithfulness through-
> out his life. This hymn of confidence pictures the
> Lord as the Shepherd-King-Host. David uses com-
> mon, ancient Near Eastern imagery to unveil his per-
> sonal relationship with the Lord.

And I will dwell[a] in the house of the
Lord
Forever.

PSALM 24

The King of Glory and His Kingdom

A Psalm of David.

1 The earth *is* the Lord's, and all its
fullness,
The world and those who dwell
therein.
2 For He has founded it upon the seas,
And established it upon the waters.

3 Who may ascend into the hill of the
Lord?
Or who may stand in His holy place?
4 He who has clean hands and a pure
heart,
Who has not lifted up his soul to an
idol,
Nor sworn deceitfully.
5 He shall receive blessing from the
Lord,
And righteousness from the God of
his salvation.
6 This *is* Jacob, the generation of those
who seek Him,
Who seek Your face.   Selah

23:6 [a]Following Septuagint, Syriac, Targum, and Vulgate; Masoretic Text reads *return*.

Why are there so many uncomfortable expressions in the Psalms, sometimes right in the middle of favorite chapters—for example, Psalms 23 and 139?

Because the Psalms genuinely reflect real life, we should expect that they will be uncomfortable in the same places that life is uncomfortable. According to the best-known Psalm 23, life isn't just about green pastures and still waters; it also includes death and enemies. The psalmists were convinced they knew the only true God. When someone was picking on them or their people, they would at times cry out for very specific judgment to be applied by God on their enemies. An amazing fact about the Psalms is their unblushing record of these cries to God that, if we are honest, echo some of our deepest hidden complaints before God.

In David's case, the role that he filled as the king and representative of God's people often blurs with his individual self-awareness. At times it is difficult to tell whether he is speaking for himself alone or for the people as a whole. This explains some of the vehemence behind the curse-pronouncing psalms. They unabashedly invoke God's righteous wrath and judgment against His enemies.

7 Lift up your heads, O you gates!
And be lifted up, you everlasting doors!
And the King of glory shall come in.

8 Who is this King of glory?
The LORD strong and mighty,
The LORD mighty in battle.

9 Lift up your heads, O you gates!
Lift up, you everlasting doors!
And the King of glory shall come in.

10 Who is this King of glory?
The LORD of hosts,
He is the King of glory.   Selah

PSALM 25

A Plea for Deliverance and Forgiveness

A Psalm of David.

1 To You, O LORD, I lift up my soul.
2 O my God, I trust in You;
Let me not be ashamed;
Let not my enemies triumph over me.
3 Indeed, let no one who waits on You
be ashamed;
Let those be ashamed who deal
treacherously without cause.

4 Show me Your ways, O LORD;
Teach me Your paths.
5 Lead me in Your truth and teach me,
For You are the God of my salvation;
On You I wait all the day.

6 Remember, O LORD, Your tender
mercies and Your
lovingkindnesses,
For they are from of old.
7 Do not remember the sins of my
youth, nor my transgressions;
According to Your mercy remember
me,
For Your goodness' sake, O LORD.

8 Good and upright is the LORD;
Therefore He teaches sinners in the
way.

25:6,7 Remember...do not remember...remember.
The psalmist reminds God about His gracious covenant promises and provisions, all of which are
grounded upon His goodness' sake.

9 The humble He guides in justice,
And the humble He teaches His way.
10 All the paths of the LORD are mercy
and truth,
To such as keep His covenant and His
testimonies.
11 For Your name's sake, O LORD,
Pardon my iniquity, for it is great.

12 Who is the man that fears the LORD?
Him shall He[a] teach in the way He[b]
chooses.
13 He himself shall dwell in prosperity,
And his descendants shall inherit the
earth.
14 The secret of the LORD is with those
who fear Him,
And He will show them His covenant.
15 My eyes are ever toward the LORD,
For He shall pluck my feet out of the
net.

16 Turn Yourself to me, and have mercy
on me,
For I am desolate and afflicted.
17 The troubles of my heart have
enlarged;
Bring me out of my distresses!
18 Look on my affliction and my pain,
And forgive all my sins.
19 Consider my enemies, for they are
many;
And they hate me with cruel hatred.
20 Keep my soul, and deliver me;
Let me not be ashamed, for I put my
trust in You.
21 Let integrity and uprightness preserve
me,
For I wait for You.

22 Redeem Israel, O God,
Out of all their troubles!

PSALM 26

A Prayer for Divine Scrutiny and Redemption

A Psalm of David.

1 Vindicate me, O LORD,
For I have walked in my integrity.
I have also trusted in the LORD;

25:12 [a]Or he [b]Or he

I shall not slip.

2 Examine me, O LORD, and prove me;
Try my mind and my heart.

3 For Your lovingkindness *is* before my
eyes,
And I have walked in Your truth.

4 I have not sat with idolatrous
mortals,
Nor will I go in with hypocrites.

5 I have hated the assembly of
evildoers,
And will not sit with the wicked.

> **26:1 Vindicate me.** Lit. "Judge me!" The psalmist desires freedom from a false accusation under the protection of the covenant stipulations (see Ps. 7:8). **my integrity.** He claims innocence within the context of ungrounded charges (see Prov. 10:9).

6 I will wash my hands in innocence;
So I will go about Your altar, O LORD,

7 That I may proclaim with the voice of
thanksgiving,
And tell of all Your wondrous works.

8 LORD, I have loved the habitation of
Your house,
And the place where Your glory
dwells.

9 Do not gather my soul with sinners,
Nor my life with bloodthirsty men,

10 In whose hands *is* a sinister scheme,
And whose right hand is full of bribes.

11 But as for me, I will walk in my
integrity;
Redeem me and be merciful to me.

12 My foot stands in an even place;
In the congregations I will bless the
LORD.

PSALM 27

An Exuberant Declaration of Faith

A Psalm of David.

1 The LORD *is* my light and my
salvation;
Whom shall I fear?
The LORD *is* the strength of my life;
Of whom shall I be afraid?

2 When the wicked came against me

To eat up my flesh,
My enemies and foes,
They stumbled and fell.

3 Though an army may encamp against
me,
My heart shall not fear;
Though war may rise against me,
In this I *will be* confident.

4 One *thing* I have desired of the LORD,
That will I seek:
That I may dwell in the house of the
LORD
All the days of my life,
To behold the beauty of the LORD,
And to inquire in His temple.

5 For in the time of trouble
He shall hide me in His pavilion;
In the secret place of His tabernacle
He shall hide me;
He shall set me high upon a rock.

> **27:4 One *thing*.** The primary issue in David's life was to live in God's presence and by His purpose (see Ps. 15:1).

6 And now my head shall be lifted up
above my enemies all around me;
Therefore I will offer sacrifices of joy
in His tabernacle;
I will sing, yes, I will sing praises to
the LORD.

7 Hear, O LORD, *when* I cry with my
voice!
Have mercy also upon me, and
answer me.

8 *When You said*, "Seek My face,"
My heart said to You, "Your face,
LORD, I will seek."

9 Do not hide Your face from me;
Do not turn Your servant away in
anger;
You have been my help;
Do not leave me nor forsake me,
O God of my salvation.

> **27:8,9 "Seek My face,"...Your face...Your face.** God's "face" indicates His personal presence or being (Ps. 24:6). Seeking His face is a primary characteristic of believers who desire fellowship with God (see Deut. 4:29).

10 When my father and my mother
         forsake me,
      Then the LORD will take care of me.

11 Teach me Your way, O LORD,
      And lead me in a smooth path,
         because of my enemies.
12 Do not deliver me to the will of my
         adversaries;
      For false witnesses have risen against
         me,
      And such as breathe out violence.
13 *I would have lost heart,* unless I had
         believed
      That I would see the goodness of the
         LORD
      In the land of the living.

14 Wait on the LORD;
      Be of good courage,
      And He shall strengthen your heart;
      Wait, I say, on the LORD!

PSALM 28

Rejoicing in Answered Prayer

A Psalm of David.

1   To You I will cry, O LORD my Rock:
      Do not be silent to me,
      Lest, if You *are* silent to me,
      I become like those who go down to
         the pit.
2   Hear the voice of my supplications
      When I cry to You,
      When I lift up my hands toward Your
         holy sanctuary.

3   Do not take me away with the wicked
      And with the workers of iniquity,
      Who speak peace to their neighbors,
      But evil *is* in their hearts.
4   Give them according to their deeds,
      And according to the wickedness of
         their endeavors;
      Give them according to the work of
         their hands;
      Render to them what they deserve.

5   Because they do not regard the works
         of the LORD,
      Nor the operation of His hands,
      He shall destroy them
      And not build them up.

> **28:1–9** David shifts from lamentation and prayer to
> thanksgiving. He shows confidence in crisis, and in
> doing so, magnifies the justice of God.

6   Blessed *be* the LORD,
      Because He has heard the voice of my
         supplications!
7   The LORD *is* my strength and my
         shield;
      My heart trusted in Him, and I am
         helped;
      Therefore my heart greatly rejoices,
      And with my song I will praise Him.

8   The LORD *is* their strength,[a]
      And He *is* the saving refuge of His
         anointed.
9   Save Your people,
      And bless Your inheritance;
      Shepherd them also,
      And bear them up forever.

PSALM 29

Praise to God in His Holiness and Majesty

A Psalm of David.

1   Give unto the LORD, O you mighty
         ones,
      Give unto the LORD glory and
         strength.
2   Give unto the LORD the glory due to
         His name;
      Worship the LORD in the beauty of
         holiness.

3   The voice of the LORD *is* over the
         waters;
      The God of glory thunders;
      The LORD *is* over many waters.
4   The voice of the LORD *is* powerful;

28:8 [a]Following Masoretic Text and Targum; Septuagint, Syriac, and Vulgate read *the strength of His people.*

The voice of the LORD *is* full of
   majesty.

5   The voice of the LORD breaks the
      cedars,
   Yes, the LORD splinters the cedars of
      Lebanon.
6   He makes them also skip like a calf,
   Lebanon and Sirion like a young wild
      ox.
7   The voice of the LORD divides the
      flames of fire.

8   The voice of the LORD shakes the
      wilderness;
   The LORD shakes the Wilderness of
      Kadesh.
9   The voice of the LORD makes the deer
      give birth,
   And strips the forests bare;
   And in His temple everyone says,
      "Glory!"

29:3–9 This dramatic manifestation of God establishes His supremacy as the only true God in comparison to the gods of Israel's pagan neighbors.

10   The LORD sat *enthroned* at the Flood,
   And the LORD sits as King forever.
11   The LORD will give strength to His
      people;
   The LORD will bless His people with
      peace.

PSALM 30

The Blessedness of Answered Prayer

*A Psalm. A Song at the dedication
   of the house of David.*

1   I will extol You, O LORD, for You have
      lifted me up,
   And have not let my foes rejoice over
      me.
2   O LORD my God, I cried out to You,
   And You healed me.
3   O LORD, You brought my soul up
      from the grave;

You have kept me alive, that I should
   not go down to the pit.[a]

30:2,3 You healed me. God alone is the unique
healer (see Ex. 15:26). David extols God for bringing
him back from a near-death experience.

4   Sing praise to the LORD, you saints of
      His,
   And give thanks at the remembrance
      of His holy name.[a]
5   For His anger *is but for* a moment,
   His favor *is for* life;
   Weeping may endure for a night,
   But joy *comes* in the morning.

6   Now in my prosperity I said,
   "I shall never be moved."
7   LORD, by Your favor You have made
      my mountain stand strong;
   You hid Your face, *and* I was troubled.

8   I cried out to You, O LORD;
   And to the LORD I made supplication:
9   "What profit *is there* in my blood,
   When I go down to the pit?
   Will the dust praise You?
   Will it declare Your truth?
10   Hear, O LORD, and have mercy on
      me;
   LORD, be my helper!"

11   You have turned for me my mourning
      into dancing;
   You have put off my sackcloth and
      clothed me with gladness,
12   To the end that *my* glory may sing
      praise to You and not be silent.
   O LORD my God, I will give thanks to
      You forever.

PSALM 31

The LORD a Fortress in Adversity

To the Chief Musician. A Psalm of David.

1   In You, O LORD, I put my trust;
   Let me never be ashamed;

30:3 [a]Following Qere and Targum; Kethib, Septuagint, Syriac, and Vulgate read *from those who
descend to the pit.*   30:4 [a]Or *His holiness*

Deliver me in Your righteousness.
2 Bow down Your ear to me,
Deliver me speedily;
Be my rock of refuge,
A fortress of defense to save me.

3 For You *are* my rock and my fortress;
Therefore, for Your name's sake,
Lead me and guide me.
4 Pull me out of the net which they
have secretly laid for me,
For You *are* my strength.
5 Into Your hand I commit my spirit;
You have redeemed me, O LORD God
of truth.

31:5 Into Your hand. This applies to both the lesser David and the Greater David (Jesus, the Messiah; see Luke 23:46). This metaphor depicts trust in God's power and control.

6 I have hated those who regard useless
idols;
But I trust in the LORD.
7 I will be glad and rejoice in Your
mercy,
For You have considered my trouble;
You have known my soul in
adversities,
8 And have not shut me up into the
hand of the enemy;
You have set my feet in a wide place.

9 Have mercy on me, O LORD, for I am
in trouble;
My eye wastes away with grief,
Yes, my soul and my body!
10 For my life is spent with grief,
And my years with sighing;
My strength fails because of my
iniquity,
And my bones waste away.
11 I am a reproach among all my
enemies,
But especially among my neighbors,
And *am* repulsive to my
acquaintances;
Those who see me outside flee from
me.
12 I am forgotten like a dead man, out of
mind;
I am like a broken vessel.
13 For I hear the slander of many;

Fear *is* on every side;
While they take counsel together
against me,
They scheme to take away my life.

14 But as for me, I trust in You, O LORD;
I say, "You *are* my God."
15 My times *are* in Your hand;
Deliver me from the hand of my
enemies,
And from those who persecute me.
16 Make Your face shine upon Your
servant;
Save me for Your mercies' sake.
17 Do not let me be ashamed, O LORD,
for I have called upon You;
Let the wicked be ashamed;
Let them be silent in the grave.
18 Let the lying lips be put to silence,
Which speak insolent things proudly
and contemptuously against the
righteous.

19 Oh, how great *is* Your goodness,
Which You have laid up for those who
fear You,
Which You have prepared for those
who trust in You
In the presence of the sons of men!
20 You shall hide them in the secret
place of Your presence
From the plots of man;
You shall keep them secretly in a
pavilion
From the strife of tongues.

21 Blessed *be* the LORD,
For He has shown me His marvelous
kindness in a strong city!
22 For I said in my haste,
"I am cut off from before Your eyes";
Nevertheless You heard the voice of
my supplications
When I cried out to You.

23 Oh, love the LORD, all you His saints!
For the LORD preserves the faithful,
And fully repays the proud person.

31:23 love the LORD. Biblical love includes a response and obedience (see Deut. 6:4,5). The assurance of both reward and retribution is a biblical truth (see Deut. 7:9,10).

24 Be of good courage,
And He shall strengthen your heart,
All you who hope in the LORD.

PSALM 32

The Joy of Forgiveness

A Psalm of David. A Contemplation.[a]

1 Blessed *is he whose* transgression *is*
forgiven,
Whose sin *is* covered.
2 Blessed *is* the man to whom the LORD
does not impute iniquity,
And in whose spirit *there is* no deceit.

3 When I kept silent, my bones grew
old
Through my groaning all the day
long.
4 For day and night Your hand was
heavy upon me;
My vitality was turned into the
drought of summer.   Selah
5 I acknowledged my sin to You,
And my iniquity I have not hidden.
I said, "I will confess my
transgressions to the LORD,"
And You forgave the iniquity of my
sin.   Selah

6 For this cause everyone who is godly
shall pray to You
In a time when You may be found;
Surely in a flood of great waters
They shall not come near him.
7 You *are* my hiding place;
You shall preserve me from trouble;
You shall surround me with songs of
deliverance.   Selah

8 I will instruct you and teach you in
the way you should go;
I will guide you with My eye.
9 Do not be like the horse *or* like the
mule,
Which have no understanding,
Which must be harnessed with bit
and bridle,
Else they will not come near you.

10 Many sorrows *shall be* to the wicked;
But he who trusts in the LORD, mercy
shall surround him.
11 Be glad in the LORD and rejoice, you
righteous;
And shout for joy, all *you* upright in
heart!

32:1–11 This is one of the seven penitential psalms
and deals with sin, confession, and forgiveness.

PSALM 33

The Sovereignty of the LORD in Creation and History

1 Rejoice in the LORD, O you righteous!
For praise from the upright is
beautiful.
2 Praise the LORD with the harp;
Make melody to Him with an
instrument of ten strings.
3 Sing to Him a new song;
Play skillfully with a shout of joy.

4 For the word of the LORD *is* right,
And all His work *is done* in truth.
5 He loves righteousness and justice;
The earth is full of the goodness of
the LORD.

6 By the word of the LORD the heavens
were made,
And all the host of them by the breath
of His mouth.
7 He gathers the waters of the sea
together as a heap;[a]
He lays up the deep in storehouses.

8 Let all the earth fear the LORD;
Let all the inhabitants of the world
stand in awe of Him.
9 For He spoke, and it was *done*;
He commanded, and it stood fast.

10 The LORD brings the counsel of the
nations to nothing;
He makes the plans of the peoples of
no effect.
11 The counsel of the LORD stands
forever,

32:title *a*Hebrew *Maschil*   33:7 *a*Septuagint, Targum, and Vulgate read *in a vessel.*

The plans of His heart to all
generations.

¹² Blessed *is* the nation whose God *is*
the LORD,
The people He has chosen as His own
inheritance.

¹³ The LORD looks from heaven;
He sees all the sons of men.
¹⁴ From the place of His dwelling He
looks
On all the inhabitants of the earth;
¹⁵ He fashions their hearts individually;
He considers all their works.

33:15 He fashions their hearts. This is the potter's word (see Gen. 2:7). For the significance of this statement, see Is. 29:15,16.

¹⁶ No king *is* saved by the multitude of
an army;
A mighty man is not delivered by
great strength.
¹⁷ A horse *is* a vain hope for safety;
Neither shall it deliver *any* by its
great strength.
¹⁸ Behold, the eye of the LORD *is* on
those who fear Him,
On those who hope in His mercy,
¹⁹ To deliver their soul from death,
And to keep them alive in famine.

²⁰ Our soul waits for the LORD;
He *is* our help and our shield.
²¹ For our heart shall rejoice in Him,
Because we have trusted in His holy
name.
²² Let Your mercy, O LORD, be upon us,
Just as we hope in You.

PSALM 34

The Happiness of Those Who Trust in God

*A Psalm of David when he pretended
madness before Abimelech, who drove
him away, and he departed.*

¹ I will bless the LORD at all times;

His praise *shall* continually *be* in my
mouth.
² My soul shall make its boast in the
LORD;
The humble shall hear *of it* and be
glad.
³ Oh, magnify the LORD with me,
And let us exalt His name together.

⁴ I sought the LORD, and He heard me,
And delivered me from all my fears.
⁵ They looked to Him and were
radiant,
And their faces were not ashamed.
⁶ This poor man cried out, and the
LORD heard *him*,
And saved him out of all his troubles.
⁷ The angel*ᵃ* of the LORD encamps all
around those who fear Him,
And delivers them.

34:7 The angel of the LORD. This is a special manifestation of Yahweh, possibly a pre-incarnate appearance of Jesus Christ, at strategic historical points (see Gen. 16:7).

⁸ Oh, taste and see that the LORD *is*
good;
Blessed *is* the man *who* trusts in
Him!
⁹ Oh, fear the LORD, you His saints!
There is no want to those who fear
Him.
¹⁰ The young lions lack and suffer
hunger;
But those who seek the LORD shall
not lack any good *thing*.

¹¹ Come, you children, listen to me;
I will teach you the fear of the LORD.
¹² Who *is* the man *who* desires life,
And loves *many* days, that he may see
good?
¹³ Keep your tongue from evil,
And your lips from speaking deceit.
¹⁴ Depart from evil and do good;
Seek peace and pursue it.

¹⁵ The eyes of the LORD *are* on the
righteous,
And His ears *are open* to their cry.

34:7 *ᵃ*Or *Angel*

16 The face of the LORD *is* against those
   who do evil,
To cut off the remembrance of them
   from the earth.
17 *The righteous* cry out, and the LORD
   hears,
And delivers them out of all their
   troubles.
18 The LORD *is* near to those who have a
   broken heart,
And saves such as have a contrite
   spirit.

34:18 broken heart...contrite spirit. These graphic idioms describe dependent disciples (see Ps. 51:17; Is. 57:15).

19 Many *are* the afflictions of the
   righteous,
But the LORD delivers him out of
   them all.
20 He guards all his bones;
Not one of them is broken.
21 Evil shall slay the wicked,
And those who hate the righteous
   shall be condemned.
22 The LORD redeems the soul of His
   servants,
And none of those who trust in Him
   shall be condemned.

PSALM 35

The LORD the Avenger of His People

A Psalm of David.

1 Plead *my cause,* O LORD, with those
   who strive with me;
Fight against those who fight against
   me.
2 Take hold of shield and buckler,
And stand up for my help.
3 Also draw out the spear,
And stop those who pursue me.
Say to my soul,
"I *am* your salvation."

4 Let those be put to shame and
   brought to dishonor

Who seek after my life;
Let those be turned back and brought
   to confusion
Who plot my hurt.
5 Let them be like chaff before the
   wind,
And let the angel[a] of the LORD chase
   them.
6 Let their way be dark and slippery,
And let the angel of the LORD pursue
   them.
7 For without cause they have hidden
   their net for me *in* a pit,
Which they have dug without cause
   for my life.
8 Let destruction come upon him
   unexpectedly,
And let his net that he has hidden
   catch himself;
Into that very destruction let him
   fall.

35:1–28 David laments that he has been accused and is about to be attacked by a foreign power with whom he had previously entered into a covenant. He presents his "case" before the Divine Judge, moving from complaining about the situation, to prayer, and finally to praise when the Lord justly intervenes.

9 And my soul shall be joyful in the
   LORD;
It shall rejoice in His salvation.
10 All my bones shall say,
"LORD, who *is* like You,
Delivering the poor from him who is
   too strong for him,
Yes, the poor and the needy from him
   who plunders him?"
11 Fierce witnesses rise up;
They ask me *things* that I do not
   know.
12 They reward me evil for good,
To the sorrow of my soul.
13 But as for me, when they were sick,
My clothing *was* sackcloth;
I humbled myself with fasting;
And my prayer would return to my
   own heart.
14 I paced about as though *he were* my
   friend *or* brother;

I bowed down heavily, as one who
  mourns *for his* mother.

15 But in my adversity they rejoiced
  And gathered together;
  Attackers gathered against me,
  And I did not know *it*;
  They tore *at me* and did not cease;
16 With ungodly mockers at feasts
  They gnashed at me with their
    teeth.

17 Lord, how long will You look on?
  Rescue me from their destructions,
  My precious *life* from the lions.
18 I will give You thanks in the great
    assembly;
  I will praise You among many people.

19 Let them not rejoice over me who are
    wrongfully my enemies;
  Nor let them wink with the eye who
    hate me without a cause.
20 For they do not speak peace,
  But they devise deceitful matters
  Against *the* quiet ones in the land.
21 They also opened their mouth wide
    against me,
  And said, "Aha, aha!
  Our eyes have seen *it*."

22 *This* You have seen, O LORD;
  Do not keep silence.
  O Lord, do not be far from me.
23 Stir up Yourself, and awake to my
    vindication,
  To my cause, my God and my Lord.
24 Vindicate me, O LORD my God,
    according to Your righteousness;
  And let them not rejoice over me.
25 Let them not say in their hearts, "Ah,
    so we would have it!"
  Let them not say, "We have swallowed
    him up."

> **35:21,22 Our eyes have seen *it*. *This* you have seen, O LORD.** David knew that God would vindicate him based on true evidence. The Lord had seen perfectly what the enemy allegedly saw.

26 Let them be ashamed and brought to
    mutual confusion
  Who rejoice at my hurt;

Let them be clothed with shame and
    dishonor
  Who exalt themselves against me.

27 Let them shout for joy and be glad,
  Who favor my righteous cause;
  And let them say continually,
  "Let the LORD be magnified,
  Who has pleasure in the prosperity of
    His servant."
28 And my tongue shall speak of Your
    righteousness
  And of Your praise all the day long.

PSALM 36

Man's Wickedness and God's Perfections

*To the Chief Musician. A Psalm of David
  the servant of the LORD.*

1 An oracle within my heart concerning
    the transgression of the wicked:
  There is no fear of God before his
    eyes.
2 For he flatters himself in his own
    eyes,
  When he finds out his iniquity *and*
    when he hates.
3 The words of his mouth *are*
    wickedness and deceit;
  He has ceased to be wise *and* to do
    good.
4 He devises wickedness on his bed;
  He sets himself in a way *that is* not
    good;
  He does not abhor evil.

> **36:1 no fear.** The word here means "dread" or "terror" (see Deut. 2:25), the opposite of the attitude that characterizes true disciples.

5 Your mercy, O LORD, *is* in the
    heavens;
  Your faithfulness *reaches* to the
    clouds.
6 Your righteousness *is* like the great
    mountains;
  Your judgments *are* a great deep;
  O LORD, You preserve man and beast.

7 How precious *is* Your lovingkindness,
    O God!

Therefore the children of men put
    their trust under the shadow of
    Your wings.
8 They are abundantly satisfied with
    the fullness of Your house,
    And You give them drink from the
    river of Your pleasures.
9 For with You *is* the fountain of life;
    In Your light we see light.

36:7 the shadow of Your wings. This refers to the protective care of a parent bird for its young (Deut. 32:11), although some may say it refers to the wings of the cherubim over the ark.

10 Oh, continue Your lovingkindness to
    those who know You,
    And Your righteousness to the upright
    in heart.
11 Let not the foot of pride come against
    me,
    And let not the hand of the wicked
    drive me away.
12 There the workers of iniquity have
    fallen;
    They have been cast down and are
    not able to rise.

PSALM 37

The Heritage of the Righteous and the Calamity of the Wicked

A Psalm of David.

1 Do not fret because of evildoers,
    Nor be envious of the workers of
    iniquity.
2 For they shall soon be cut down like
    the grass,
    And wither as the green herb.

3 Trust in the LORD, and do good;
    Dwell in the land, and feed on His
    faithfulness.
4 Delight yourself also in the LORD,
    And He shall give you the desires of
    your heart.

5 Commit your way to the LORD,
    Trust also in Him,
    And He shall bring *it* to pass.

6 He shall bring forth your
    righteousness as the light,
    And your justice as the noonday.

7 Rest in the LORD, and wait patiently
    for Him;
    Do not fret because of him who
    prospers in his way,
    Because of the man who brings
    wicked schemes to pass.
8 Cease from anger, and forsake wrath;
    Do not fret—*it* only *causes* harm.

9 For evildoers shall be cut off;
    But those who wait on the LORD,
    They shall inherit the earth.
10 For yet a little while and the wicked
    shall be no *more;*
    Indeed, you will look carefully for his
    place,
    But it *shall be* no *more.*
11 But the meek shall inherit the earth,
    And shall delight themselves in the
    abundance of peace.

12 The wicked plots against the just,
    And gnashes at him with his teeth.
13 The Lord laughs at him,
    For He sees that his day is coming.
14 The wicked have drawn the sword
    And have bent their bow,
    To cast down the poor and needy,
    To slay those who are of upright
    conduct.
15 Their sword shall enter their own
    heart,
    And their bows shall be broken.

16 A little that a righteous man has
    Is better than the riches of many
    wicked.
17 For the arms of the wicked shall be
    broken,
    But the LORD upholds the righteous.

37:17 the arms of the wicked shall be broken. Their arms shall be shattered for grabbing and getting wealth (see Job 38:15).

18 The LORD knows the days of the
    upright,
    And their inheritance shall be
    forever.

19 They shall not be ashamed in the evil
time,
And in the days of famine they shall
be satisfied.

20 But the wicked shall perish;
And the enemies of the LORD,
Like the splendor of the meadows,
shall vanish.
Into smoke they shall vanish away.

21 The wicked borrows and does not
repay,
But the righteous shows mercy and
gives.

22 For *those* blessed by Him shall inherit
the earth,
But *those* cursed by Him shall be cut
off.

23 The steps of a *good* man are ordered
by the LORD,
And He delights in his way.

24 Though he fall, he shall not be utterly
cast down;
For the LORD upholds *him with* His
hand.

25 I have been young, and *now* am old;
Yet I have not seen the righteous
forsaken,
Nor his descendants begging bread.

26 *He is* ever merciful, and lends;
And his descendants *are* blessed.

27 Depart from evil, and do good;
And dwell forevermore.

28 For the LORD loves justice,
And does not forsake His saints;
They are preserved forever,
But the descendants of the wicked
shall be cut off.

29 The righteous shall inherit the land,
And dwell in it forever.

30 The mouth of the righteous speaks
wisdom,
And his tongue talks of justice.

31 The law of his God *is* in his heart;
None of his steps shall slide.

32 The wicked watches the righteous,
And seeks to slay him.

> **37:31 The law of his God *is* in his heart.** This speaks of God's internalized instruction (see Deut. 6:6; Ps. 40:8).

33 The LORD will not leave him in his
hand,
Nor condemn him when he is judged.

34 Wait on the LORD,
And keep His way,
And He shall exalt you to inherit the
land;
When the wicked are cut off, you shall
see *it*.

35 I have seen the wicked in great power,
And spreading himself like a native
green tree.

36 Yet he passed away,[a] and behold, he
was no *more*;
Indeed I sought him, but he could not
be found.

37 Mark the blameless *man*, and observe
the upright;
For the future of *that* man *is* peace.

38 But the transgressors shall be
destroyed together;
The future of the wicked shall be cut
off.

39 But the salvation of the righteous *is*
from the LORD;
He is their strength in the time of
trouble.

40 And the LORD shall help them and
deliver them;
He shall deliver them from the
wicked,
And save them,
Because they trust in Him.

PSALM 38

Prayer in Time of Chastening

*A Psalm of David. To bring
to remembrance.*

1 O LORD, do not rebuke me in Your
wrath,

37:36 [a]Following Masoretic Text, Septuagint, and Targum; Syriac and Vulgate read *I passed by.*

Nor chasten me in Your hot
   displeasure!
2 For Your arrows pierce me deeply,
   And Your hand presses me down.

3 *There is* no soundness in my flesh
   Because of Your anger,
   Nor *any* health in my bones
   Because of my sin.
4 For my iniquities have gone over my
   head;
   Like a heavy burden they are too
   heavy for me.
5 My wounds are foul *and* festering
   Because of my foolishness.

6 I am troubled, I am bowed down
   greatly;
   I go mourning all the day long.
7 For my loins are full of inflammation,
   And *there is* no soundness in my
   flesh.
8 I am feeble and severely broken;
   I groan because of the turmoil of my
   heart.

9 Lord, all my desire *is* before You;
   And my sighing is not hidden from
   You.
10 My heart pants, my strength fails
   me;
   As for the light of my eyes, it also has
   gone from me.

11 My loved ones and my friends stand
   aloof from my plague,
   And my relatives stand afar off.
12 Those also who seek my life lay
   snares *for me;*
   Those who seek my hurt speak of
   destruction,
   And plan deception all the day long.

13 But I, like a deaf *man,* do not hear;
   And *I am* like a mute *who* does not
   open his mouth.
14 Thus I am like a man who does not
   hear,
   And in whose mouth *is* no response.

15 For in You, O LORD, I hope;
   You will hear, O Lord my God.
16 For I said, "*Hear me,* lest they rejoice
   over me,

Lest, when my foot slips, they exalt
   themselves against me."

17 For I *am* ready to fall,
   And my sorrow *is* continually before
   me.
18 For I will declare my iniquity;
   I will be in anguish over my sin.
19 But my enemies *are* vigorous, *and*
   they are strong;
   And those who hate me wrongfully
   have multiplied.
20 Those also who render evil for good,
   They are my adversaries, because I
   follow *what is* good.

21 Do not forsake me, O LORD;
   O my God, be not far from me!
22 Make haste to help me,
   O Lord, my salvation!

PSALM 39

Prayer for Wisdom and Forgiveness

To the Chief Musician. To Jeduthun.
A Psalm of David.

1 I said, "I will guard my ways,
   Lest I sin with my tongue;
   I will restrain my mouth with a
   muzzle,
   While the wicked are before me."
2 I was mute with silence,
   I held my peace *even* from good;
   And my sorrow was stirred up.
3 My heart was hot within me;
   While I was musing, the fire burned.
   Then I spoke with my tongue:

4 "LORD, make me to know my end,
   And what *is* the measure of my days,
   That I may know how frail I *am.*
5 Indeed, You have made my days *as*
   handbreadths,
   And my age *is* as nothing before You;

39:5 handbreadths. He measures the length of his life with the smallest popular measuring unit of ancient times (1 Kin. 7:26). **and my age *is* as nothing before You.** Comparing man's age to God's age (see Ps. 90:2). **vapor.** This word in Hebrew also means "vanity" and occurs 31 times in Ecclesiastes.

Certainly every man at his best state
    is but vapor.   Selah

6 Surely every man walks about like a
    shadow;
Surely they busy themselves in vain;
He heaps up *riches*,
And does not know who will gather
    them.

7 "And now, Lord, what do I wait for?
My hope *is* in You.

8 Deliver me from all my
    transgressions;
Do not make me the reproach of the
    foolish.

9 I was mute, I did not open my mouth,
Because it was You who did *it*.

10 Remove Your plague from me;
I am consumed by the blow of Your
    hand.

11 When with rebukes You correct man
    for iniquity,
You make his beauty melt away like a
    moth;
Surely every man *is* vapor.   Selah

39:1–13 This lament compares with Job 7 and with much of Ecclesiastes. It carries on the here-today, gone-tomorrow emphasis (see Ps. 37) with an application to *all* men, especially the psalmist. David breaks his silence here with requests and reflections about the brevity and burdens of life.

12 "Hear my prayer, O LORD,
And give ear to my cry;
Do not be silent at my tears;
For I *am* a stranger with You,
A sojourner, as all my fathers *were*.

13 Remove Your gaze from me, that I
    may regain strength,
Before I go away and am no more."

PSALM 40

Faith Persevering in Trial

To the Chief Musician. A Psalm of David.

1 I waited patiently for the LORD;
And He inclined to me,
And heard my cry.

2 He also brought me up out of a
    horrible pit,

Out of the miry clay,
And set my feet upon a rock,
And established my steps.

3 He has put a new song in my
    mouth—
Praise to our God;
Many will see *it* and fear,
And will trust in the LORD.

40:2 a horrible pit…the miry clay. The imagery describes his past hopeless and helpless situation (see Ps. 69:2,14). By His grace, God lifted him from a place of no footing and gave him sure footing.

4 Blessed *is* that man who makes the
    LORD his trust,
And does not respect the proud, nor
    such as turn aside to lies.

5 Many, O LORD my God, *are* Your
    wonderful works
Which You have done;
And Your thoughts toward us
Cannot be recounted to You in order;
If I would declare and speak *of them*,
They are more than can be
    numbered.

6 Sacrifice and offering You did not
    desire;
My ears You have opened.
Burnt offering and sin offering You
    did not require.

7 Then I said, "Behold, I come;
In the scroll of the book *it is* written
    of me.

8 I delight to do Your will, O my
    God,
And Your law *is* within my heart."

40:6 Sacrifice and offering You did not desire. Sacrifices must be offered with the right attitude of the heart. **My ears You have opened.** Lit. "ears" or "two ears You have dug for me." This pictures obedience and dedication.

9 I have proclaimed the good news of
    righteousness
In the great assembly;
Indeed, I do not restrain my lips,
O LORD, You Yourself know.

10 I have not hidden Your righteousness
    within my heart;

I have declared Your faithfulness and
    Your salvation;
I have not concealed Your
    lovingkindness and Your truth
From the great assembly.

11 Do not withhold Your tender mercies
    from me, O LORD;
Let Your lovingkindness and Your
    truth continually preserve me.

12 For innumerable evils have
    surrounded me;
My iniquities have overtaken me, so
    that I am not able to look up;
They are more than the hairs of my
    head;
Therefore my heart fails me.

13 Be pleased, O LORD, to deliver me;
O LORD, make haste to help me!

14 Let them be ashamed and brought to
    mutual confusion
Who seek to destroy my life;
Let them be driven backward and
    brought to dishonor
Who wish me evil.

15 Let them be confounded because of
    their shame,
Who say to me, "Aha, aha!"

16 Let all those who seek You rejoice and
    be glad in You;
Let such as love Your salvation say
    continually,
"The LORD be magnified!"

17 But I *am* poor and needy;
Yet the LORD thinks upon me.
You *are* my help and my deliverer;
Do not delay, O my God.

PSALM 41

The Blessing and Suffering of the Godly

To the Chief Musician. A Psalm of David.

1 Blessed *is* he who considers the poor;
The LORD will deliver him in time of
    trouble.

2 The LORD will preserve him and keep
    him alive,
And he will be blessed on the earth;
You will not deliver him to the will of
    his enemies.

3 The LORD will strengthen him on his
    bed of illness;
You will sustain him on his sickbed.

41:3 You will sustain him on his sickbed. This pictures God as a Physician dispensing His tender,
loving care.

4 I said, "LORD, be merciful to me;
Heal my soul, for I have sinned
    against You."

5 My enemies speak evil of me:
"When will he die, and his name
    perish?"

6 And if he comes to see *me,* he speaks
    lies;
His heart gathers iniquity to itself;
When he goes out, he tells *it.*

7 All who hate me whisper together
    against me;
Against me they devise my hurt.

8 "An evil disease," *they say,* "clings to
    him.
And *now* that he lies down, he will
    rise up no more."

9 Even my own familiar friend in whom
    I trusted,
Who ate my bread,
Has lifted up *his* heel against me.

10 But You, O LORD, be merciful to me,
    and raise me up,
That I may repay them.

11 By this I know that You are well
    pleased with me,
Because my enemy does not triumph
    over me.

12 As for me, You uphold me in my
    integrity,
And set me before Your face forever.

13 Blessed *be* the LORD God of Israel
From everlasting to everlasting!
Amen and Amen.

41:1–13 This general psalm applies to anyone in
distress. The most painful and specific factor addressed here is the insult that is added to the
psalmist's injury (see Ps. 6:38). David speaks of God's
tender, loving care in critical moments of life and
focuses on confidence, prayer, and lament.

Book Two: Psalms 42–72

PSALM 42

Yearning for God in the Midst of Distresses

To the Chief Musician. A Contemplation[a]
of the sons of Korah.

1   As the deer pants for the water
     brooks,
   So pants my soul for You, O God.

2   My soul thirsts for God, for the living
     God.
   When shall I come and appear before
     God?[a]

3   My tears have been my food day and
     night,
   While they continually say to me,
   "Where *is* your God?"

4   When I remember these *things*,
   I pour out my soul within me.
   For I used to go with the multitude;
   I went with them to the house of
     God,
   With the voice of joy and praise,
   With a multitude that kept a pilgrim
     feast.

> **42:2–4 My soul thirsts for God.** He desires the water of God (see Ps. 36:8,9). **When I remember these things, I pour out my soul.** These are attempts to unburden oneself from intolerable pain, grief, and agony, the "pouring out of one's soul" (see 1 Sam. 1:15). Such language is also found in Jeremiah's Lamentations.

5   Why are you cast down, O my soul?
   And *why* are you disquieted within
     me?
   Hope in God, for I shall yet praise
     Him
   For the help of His countenance.[a]

6   O my God,[a] my soul is cast down
     within me;

   Therefore I will remember You from
     the land of the Jordan,
   And from the heights of Hermon,
   From the Hill Mizar.

7   Deep calls unto deep at the noise of
     Your waterfalls;
   All Your waves and billows have gone
     over me.

8   The LORD will command His
     lovingkindness in the daytime,
   And in the night His song *shall be*
     with me—
   A prayer to the God of my life.

9   I will say to God my Rock,
   "Why have You forgotten me?
   Why do I go mourning because of the
     oppression of the enemy?"

10   *As* with a breaking of my bones,
   My enemies reproach me,
   While they say to me all day long,
   "Where *is* your God?"

11   Why are you cast down, O my soul?
   And why are you disquieted within
     me?
   Hope in God;
   For I shall yet praise Him,
   The help of my countenance and my
     God.

PSALM 43

Prayer to God in Time of Trouble

1   Vindicate me, O God,
   And plead my cause against an
     ungodly nation;
   Oh, deliver me from the deceitful and
     unjust man!

2   For You *are* the God of my strength;
   Why do You cast me off?
   Why do I go mourning because of the
     oppression of the enemy?

3   Oh, send out Your light and Your
     truth!
   Let them lead me;

42:title [a]Hebrew *Maschil*   42:2 [a]Following Masoretic Text and Vulgate; some Hebrew manuscripts, Septuagint, Syriac, and Targum read *I see the face of God.*   42:5 [a]Following Masoretic Text and Targum; a few Hebrew manuscripts, Septuagint, Syriac, and Vulgate read *The help of my countenance, my God.*   42:6 [a]Following Masoretic Text and Targum; a few Hebrew manuscripts, Septuagint, Syriac, and Vulgate put *my God* at the end of verse 5.

Let them bring me to Your holy hill
And to Your tabernacle.
4 Then I will go to the altar of God,
To God my exceeding joy;
And on the harp I will praise You,
O God, my God.

43:3 Your light and Your truth! Let them lead me; Let them bring me. The psalmist desires these bold personifications of divine guidance to bring him successfully to Israel's designated place of worship.

5 Why are you cast down, O my soul?
And why are you disquieted within me?
Hope in God;
For I shall yet praise Him,
The help of my countenance and my God.

PSALM 44

Redemption Remembered in Present Dishonor

*To the Chief Musician. A Contemplation[a]
of the sons of Korah.*

1 We have heard with our ears, O God,
Our fathers have told us,
The deeds You did in their days,
In days of old:
2 You drove out the nations with Your hand,
But them You planted;
You afflicted the peoples, and cast them out.
3 For they did not gain possession of the land by their own sword,
Nor did their own arm save them;
But it was Your right hand, Your arm, and the light of Your countenance,
Because You favored them.

4 You are my King, O God;[a]
Command[b] victories for Jacob.
5 Through You we will push down our enemies;
Through Your name we will trample those who rise up against us.

6 For I will not trust in my bow,
Nor shall my sword save me.
7 But You have saved us from our enemies,
And have put to shame those who hated us.
8 In God we boast all day long,
And praise Your name forever.   Selah

44:1–26 This national lament follows a great defeat in battle. The speakers in this psalm shift between first person plural and first person singular. This may indicate that the psalm was originally sung antiphonally, alternating between the beaten king and his defeated nation. The prayers are offered in unison as the climax.

9 But You have cast *us* off and put us to shame,
And You do not go out with our armies.
10 You make us turn back from the enemy,
And those who hate us have taken spoil for themselves.
11 You have given us up like sheep *intended* for food,
And have scattered us among the nations.
12 You sell Your people for *next to* nothing,
And are not enriched by selling them.

13 You make us a reproach to our neighbors,
A scorn and a derision to those all around us.
14 You make us a byword among the nations,
A shaking of the head among the peoples.
15 My dishonor *is* continually before me,
And the shame of my face has covered me,
16 Because of the voice of him who reproaches and reviles,
Because of the enemy and the avenger.

44:title [a]Hebrew *Maschil*   **44:4** [a]Following Masoretic Text and Targum; Septuagint and Vulgate read *and my God.*   [b]Following Masoretic Text and Targum; Septuagint, Syriac, and Vulgate read *Who commands.*

¹⁷ All this has come upon us;
But we have not forgotten You,
Nor have we dealt falsely with Your
covenant.

¹⁸ Our heart has not turned back,
Nor have our steps departed from
Your way;

¹⁹ But You have severely broken us in
the place of jackals,
And covered us with the shadow of
death.

²⁰ If we had forgotten the name of our
God,
Or stretched out our hands to a
foreign god,

²¹ Would not God search this out?
For He knows the secrets of the heart.

²² Yet for Your sake we are killed all day
long;
We are accounted as sheep for the
slaughter.

²³ Awake! Why do You sleep, O Lord?
Arise! Do not cast *us* off forever.

²⁴ Why do You hide Your face,
And forget our affliction and our
oppression?

²⁵ For our soul is bowed down to the
dust;
Our body clings to the ground.

²⁶ Arise for our help,
And redeem us for Your mercies' sake.

45:Title Two new notations are found, "Set to The Lilies" and "A Song of Love." The first most likely had to do with the tune used in accompaniment with its words. The second notation refers to content and indicates this psalm was a royal wedding composition.

PSALM 45

The Glories of the Messiah and His Bride

To the Chief Musician. Set to "The Lilies."[a]
A Contemplation[b] *of the sons of Korah.*
A Song of Love.

¹ My heart is overflowing with a good
theme;

I recite my composition concerning
the King;
My tongue *is* the pen of a ready
writer.

² You are fairer than the sons of men;
Grace is poured upon Your lips;
Therefore God has blessed You
forever.

³ Gird Your sword upon *Your* thigh,
O Mighty One,
With Your glory and Your majesty.

⁴ And in Your majesty ride prosperously
because of truth, humility, *and*
righteousness;
And Your right hand shall teach You
awesome things.

⁵ Your arrows *are* sharp in the heart of
the King's enemies;
The peoples fall under You.

⁶ Your throne, O God, *is* forever and
ever;
A scepter of righteousness *is* the
scepter of Your kingdom.

⁷ You love righteousness and hate
wickedness;
Therefore God, Your God, has
anointed You
With the oil of gladness more than
Your companions.

⁸ All Your garments are scented with
myrrh and aloes *and* cassia,
Out of the ivory palaces, by which
they have made You glad.

⁹ Kings' daughters *are* among Your
honorable women;
At Your right hand stands the queen
in gold from Ophir.

¹⁰ Listen, O daughter,
Consider and incline your ear;
Forget your own people also, and your
father's house;

¹¹ So the King will greatly desire your
beauty;
Because He *is* your Lord, worship
Him.

¹² And the daughter of Tyre *will come*
with a gift;
The rich among the people will seek
your favor.

45:title ^aHebrew *Shoshannim*   ^bHebrew *Maschil*

13 The royal daughter *is* all glorious
  within *the palace*;
  Her clothing *is* woven with gold.
14 She shall be brought to the King in
  robes of many colors;
  The virgins, her companions who
  follow her, shall be brought to
  You.
15 With gladness and rejoicing they shall
  be brought;
  They shall enter the King's palace.

16 Instead of Your fathers shall be Your
  sons,
  Whom You shall make princes in all
  the earth.
17 I will make Your name to be
  remembered in all generations;
  Therefore the people shall praise You
  forever and ever.

PSALM 46

**God the Refuge of His People and
Conqueror of the Nations**

*To the Chief Musician. A Psalm of the sons
of Korah. A Song for Alamoth.*

1 God *is* our refuge and strength,
  A very present help in trouble.
2 Therefore we will not fear,
  Even though the earth be removed,
  And though the mountains be carried
  into the midst of the sea;
3 *Though* its waters roar *and* be
  troubled,
  Though the mountains shake with its
  swelling.   Selah

46:2 Even though the earth be removed. This alludes to earthquakes. The "earth" and "mountains"
are regarded as symbols of stability, and they terrify
people when they "dance." But even when the most
stable becomes unstable, they should not fear, for
they trust in God's stability.

4 *There is* a river whose streams shall
  make glad the city of God,
  The holy *place* of the tabernacle of
  the Most High.

5 God *is* in the midst of her, she shall
  not be moved;
  God shall help her, just at the break
  of dawn.
6 The nations raged, the kingdoms were
  moved;
  He uttered His voice, the earth
  melted.

46:4 *There is* a river whose streams. These words
about refreshing waters contrast with those about
the threatening torrents of v. 3. The garden of paradise concept is often mentioned in ancient Near Eastern literature. **the city of God.** These words in their
present setting refer to Jerusalem, God's chosen
earthly residence (see Ps. 48:1,2).

7 The LORD of hosts *is* with us;
  The God of Jacob *is* our refuge.
              Selah

8 Come, behold the works of the
  LORD,
  Who has made desolations in the
  earth.
9 He makes wars cease to the end of the
  earth;
  He breaks the bow and cuts the spear
  in two;
  He burns the chariot in the fire.

10 Be still, and know that I *am* God;
  I will be exalted among the nations,
  I will be exalted in the earth!

46:10 Be still, and know that I *am* God. This twin
command to be calm and to recognize His sovereignty
is probably given both as a comfort to His nation and
also as a warning to all other nations.

11 The LORD of hosts *is* with us;
  The God of Jacob *is* our refuge.
              Selah

46:1–11 Psalm 46 was the scriptural catalyst for
Martin Luther's great hymn, "A Mighty Fortress Is Our
God." It launches a trilogy of psalms of triumph. This
psalm is grouped among the "songs of Zion." The
psalm recognizes God's provision of protection and
stability for His people who face threats from nature
and the nations.

PSALM 47

Praise to God, the Ruler of the Earth

*To the Chief Musician. A Psalm
of the sons of Korah.*

1 Oh, clap your hands, all you peoples!
Shout to God with the voice of
triumph!
2 For the LORD Most High *is* awesome;
He is a great King over all the earth.
3 He will subdue the peoples under us,
And the nations under our feet.
4 He will choose our inheritance for us,
The excellence of Jacob whom He
loves.   Selah

5 God has gone up with a shout,
The LORD with the sound of a
trumpet.
6 Sing praises to God, sing praises!
Sing praises to our King, sing praises!
7 For God *is* the King of all the earth;
Sing praises with understanding.

8 God reigns over the nations;
God sits on His holy throne.
9 The princes of the people have
gathered together,
The people of the God of Abraham.
For the shields of the earth *belong* to
God;
He is greatly exalted.

PSALM 48

The Glory of God in Zion

A Song. A Psalm of the sons of Korah.

1 Great *is* the LORD, and greatly to be
praised
In the city of our God,
In His holy mountain.
2 Beautiful in elevation,
The joy of the whole earth,
Is Mount Zion *on* the sides of the
north,
The city of the great King.
3 God *is* in her palaces;
He is known as her refuge.

4 For behold, the kings assembled,
They passed by together.
5 They saw *it, and* so they marveled;
They were troubled, they hastened
away.
6 Fear took hold of them there,
And pain, as of a woman in birth pangs,
7 *As when* You break the ships of
Tarshish
With an east wind.

8 As we have heard,
So we have seen
In the city of the LORD of hosts,
In the city of our God:
God will establish it forever.   Selah

9 We have thought, O God, on Your
lovingkindness,
In the midst of Your temple.
10 According to Your name, O God,
So *is* Your praise to the ends of the
earth;
Your right hand is full of righteousness.
11 Let Mount Zion rejoice,
Let the daughters of Judah be glad,
Because of Your judgments.

12 Walk about Zion,
And go all around her.
Count her towers;
13 Mark well her bulwarks;
Consider her palaces;
That you may tell *it* to the generation
following.
14 For this *is* God,
Our God forever and ever;
He will be our guide
Even to death.[a]

PSALM 49

The Confidence of the Foolish

*To the Chief Musician. A Psalm
of the sons of Korah.*

1 Hear this, all peoples;
Give ear, all inhabitants of the world,
2 Both low and high,
Rich and poor together.
3 My mouth shall speak wisdom,

48:14 [a]Following Masoretic Text and Syriac; Septuagint and Vulgate read *Forever*.

And the meditation of my heart *shall
give* understanding.
⁴ I will incline my ear to a proverb;
I will disclose my dark saying on the
harp.

⁵ Why should I fear in the days of evil,
When the iniquity at my heels
surrounds me?
⁶ Those who trust in their wealth
And boast in the multitude of their
riches,
⁷ None *of them* can by any means
redeem *his* brother,
Nor give to God a ransom for him—
⁸ For the redemption of their souls *is*
costly,
And it shall cease forever—
⁹ That he should continue to live
eternally,
And not see the Pit.

49:7–9 None of *them* can. No one can escape death (Heb. 9:27). This passage refers to the second death, which is hell (see Rev. 20:11–15). Jesus Christ's death on the cross is the only ransom that saves (see Matt. 20:28).

¹⁰ For he sees wise men die;
Likewise the fool and the senseless
person perish,
And leave their wealth to others.
¹¹ Their inner thought *is that* their
houses *will last* forever,ᵃ
Their dwelling places to all
generations;
They call *their* lands after their own
names.
¹² Nevertheless man, *though* in honor,
does not remain;ᵃ
He is like the beasts *that* perish.

¹³ This is the way of those who *are*
foolish,
And of their posterity who approve
their sayings.   Selah
¹⁴ Like sheep they are laid in the grave;
Death shall feed on them;
The upright shall have dominion over
them in the morning;

And their beauty shall be consumed
in the grave, far from their
dwelling.
¹⁵ But God will redeem my soul from
the power of the grave,
For He shall receive me.   Selah

49:1–20 Psalm 49 addresses death, warning the rich and famous and comforting the poor. In places it sounds much like portions of Job, Proverbs, and Ecclesiastes. It falls into the category of a didactic or wisdom poem, for it contains practical lessons. See similar New Testament messages in Luke 12 (parable of the rich fool) and Luke 16 (parable of the rich man and Lazarus).

¹⁶ Do not be afraid when one becomes
rich,
When the glory of his house is
increased;
¹⁷ For when he dies he shall carry
nothing away;
His glory shall not descend after him.
¹⁸ Though while he lives he blesses
himself
(For *men* will praise you when you do
well for yourself),
¹⁹ He shall go to the generation of his
fathers;
They shall never see light.
²⁰ A man *who is* in honor, yet does not
understand,
Is like the beasts *that* perish.

50:Title This is the first psalm entitled "a psalm of Asaph" (see Pss. 73–83). "Asaph" may stand for the longer expression "the sons of Asaph." Each of these psalms should be examined to understand what the relationship between that psalm and "Asaph" might be, whether "Asaph" composed the psalm, handed it down, or sung it. Many older commentators believe that Ps. 50 was authored by the original "Asaph."

PSALM 50

God the Righteous Judge

A Psalm of Asaph.

¹ The Mighty One, God the LORD,
Has spoken and called the earth

49:11 ᵃSeptuagint, Syriac, Targum, and Vulgate read *Their graves shall be their houses forever.*
49:12 ᵃFollowing Masoretic Text and Targum; Septuagint, Syriac, and Vulgate read *understand* (compare verse 20).

From the rising of the sun to its going
    down.
2 Out of Zion, the perfection of beauty,
    God will shine forth.
3 Our God shall come, and shall not
    keep silent;
    A fire shall devour before Him,
    And it shall be very tempestuous all
    around Him.

4 He shall call to the heavens from
    above,
    And to the earth, that He may judge
    His people:
5 "Gather My saints together to Me,
    Those who have made a covenant
    with Me by sacrifice."
6 Let the heavens declare His
    righteousness,
    For God Himself *is* Judge.   Selah

7 "Hear, O My people, and I will speak,
    O Israel, and I will testify against you;
    I *am* God, your God!
8 I will not rebuke you for your
    sacrifices
    Or your burnt offerings,
    Which are continually before Me.
9 I will not take a bull from your house,
    Nor goats out of your folds.
10 For every beast of the forest *is* Mine,
    And the cattle on a thousand hills.
11 I know all the birds of the mountains,
    And the wild beasts of the field *are*
    Mine.

50:8 I will not rebuke you for your sacrifices. The Divine Judge condemns the people for their attitude toward sacrifice, not for the act of sacrificing (see 1 Sam. 15:22). Thanksgiving is the sacrifice that always pleases Him (v. 14).

ANOINTING OF THE HOLY SPIRIT IN THE OLD TESTAMENT

Old Testament Israel had mediators who stood between God and His people. To empower the OT mediators, the Holy Spirit gave special administrative ability to carry out the management of the nation and military skills which enabled them to defeat the theocracy's enemies. The Lord first anointed Moses with this ministry of the Spirit, and then in a truly dramatic scene, took some of this ministry of the Spirit and shared it with the 70 elders. Thus they were enabled to help Moses administer Israel (Num. 11:17–25).

Also Joshua (Deut. 34:9), the judges (Judg. 3:10; 6:34), and the kings of united Israel and the southern kingdom were anointed with this special ministry of the Spirit. When the Spirit of the Lord came upon King Saul, for example, he was in effect given "another heart" (1 Sam. 10:6–10). This does not mean that he was regenerated at this point in his life, but that he was given skills to be a king. Later the theocratic anointing was taken from Saul and given to David (1 Sam. 16:1–14). Saul, from that time on, became a totally incapable leader.

King David no doubt had this special ministry of the Spirit in mind in his prayer of repentance in Psalm 51. He was not afraid of losing his salvation when he prayed, "do not take your Holy Spirit from me" (Ps. 51:11), but rather was concerned that God would remove this spiritual wisdom and administrative skill from him. David had earlier seen such the tragedy in the life of Saul when that king of Israel lost the anointing of the Holy Spirit. David was thus pleading with God not to remove His hand of guidance.

King Solomon also perceived his youthful inabilities at the beginning of his reign and requested God to give him special wisdom in administering Israel. God was greatly pleased with this request and granted an extra measure to the young man (1 Kin. 3:7–12,28; 4:29–34). Although the OT is silent in this regard about the kings who succeeded Solomon, the theocratic anointing of the Spirit likely came on all of the descendants of David in connection with the Davidic Covenant.

When the theocracy went out of existence as Judah was carried away into captivity, and the last Davidic king was disempowered, the theocratic anointing was no longer given (Ezek. 8–11). The kings of the northern tribes, on the other hand, being essentially apostate and not in the Davidic line, never had the benefit of this special ministry of the Spirit.

12 "If I were hungry, I would not tell you;
For the world *is* Mine, and all its
    fullness.
13 Will I eat the flesh of bulls,
Or drink the blood of goats?
14 Offer to God thanksgiving,
And pay your vows to the Most High.
15 Call upon Me in the day of trouble;
I will deliver you, and you shall glorify
    Me."

16 But to the wicked God says:
 "What *right* have you to declare My
    statutes,
Or take My covenant in your mouth,
17 Seeing you hate instruction
And cast My words behind you?
18 When you saw a thief, you consented[a]
    with him,
And have been a partaker with
    adulterers.
19 You give your mouth to evil,
And your tongue frames deceit.
20 You sit *and* speak against your
    brother;
You slander your own mother's son.
21 These *things* you have done, and I
    kept silent;
You thought that I was altogether like
    you;
But I will rebuke you,
And set *them* in order before your eyes.

22 "Now consider this, you who forget
    God,
Lest I tear *you* in pieces,
And *there be* none to deliver:
23 Whoever offers praise glorifies Me;
And to him who orders *his* conduct
    aright
I will show the salvation of God."

PSALM 51

A Prayer of Repentance

*To the Chief Musician. A Psalm of David
when Nathan the prophet went to him,
  after he had gone in to Bathsheba.*

1 Have mercy upon me, O God,
According to Your lovingkindness;

According to the multitude of Your
    tender mercies,
Blot out my transgressions.
2 Wash me thoroughly from my
    iniquity,
And cleanse me from my sin.

3 For I acknowledge my transgressions,
And my sin *is* always before me.
4 Against You, You only, have I sinned,
And done *this* evil in Your sight—
That You may be found just when
    You speak,[a]
And blameless when You judge.

51:4 Against You, You only. David realized that even
though he had wronged Bathsheba and Uriah, his
ultimate sin was against God and His holy law (see
2 Sam. 1:27).

5 Behold, I was brought forth in
    iniquity,
And in sin my mother conceived me.
6 Behold, You desire truth in the inward
    parts,
And in the hidden *part* You will make
    me to know wisdom.

7 Purge me with hyssop, and I shall be
    clean;
Wash me, and I shall be whiter than
    snow.
8 Make me hear joy and gladness,
That the bones You have broken may
    rejoice.
9 Hide Your face from my sins,
And blot out all my iniquities.

10 Create in me a clean heart, O God,
And renew a steadfast spirit within
    me.
11 Do not cast me away from Your
    presence,
And do not take Your Holy Spirit from
    me.

51:11 Your Holy Spirit from me. This refers to the
special anointing of the Holy Spirit on the chosen
Israelite kings.

50:18 [a]Septuagint, Syriac, Targum, and Vulgate read *ran*.   51:4 [a]Septuagint, Targum, and Vulgate read
in Your words.

12 Restore to me the joy of Your
     salvation,
And uphold me *by Your* generous
     Spirit.
13 *Then* I will teach transgressors Your
     ways,
And sinners shall be converted to You.

14 Deliver me from the guilt of
     bloodshed, O God,
The God of my salvation,
And my tongue shall sing aloud of
     Your righteousness.
15 O Lord, open my lips,
And my mouth shall show forth Your
     praise.
16 For You do not desire sacrifice, or else
     I would give *it*;
You do not delight in burnt offering.
17 The sacrifices of God *are* a broken
     spirit,
A broken and a contrite heart—
These, O God, You will not despise.

18 Do good in Your good pleasure to Zion;
Build the walls of Jerusalem.
19 Then You shall be pleased with the
     sacrifices of righteousness,
With burnt offering and whole burnt
     offering;
Then they shall offer bulls on Your
     altar.

51:1–19 David wrote this psalm of repentance and forgiveness after he had an affair with Bathsheba and had her husband Uriah killed (2 Sam. 11,12). It is one of the 7 penitential psalms. David recognized how horrendous his sin was, accepted the blame, and begged for God's forgiveness.

PSALM 52

The End of the Wicked and the Peace of the Godly

*To the Chief Musician. A Contemplation[a]
of David when Doeg the Edomite went and
told Saul, and said to him, "David has
gone to the house of Ahimelech."*

1 Why do you boast in evil, O mighty
     man?

54:1 by Your name. In the ancient world, a person's name essentially represented the person himself. Here, God's name includes His covenant protection. **vindicate.** David asks God to execute justice for him, as in a court trial when a defendant is declared "not guilty."

     The goodness of God *endures*
     continually.
2 Your tongue devises destruction,
Like a sharp razor, working
     deceitfully.
3 You love evil more than good,
Lying rather than speaking
     righteousness.   Selah
4 You love all devouring words,
You deceitful tongue.

5 God shall likewise destroy you
     forever;
He shall take you away, and pluck you
     out of *your* dwelling place,
And uproot you from the land of the
     living.   Selah
6 The righteous also shall see and fear,
And shall laugh at him, *saying,*
7 "Here is the man *who* did not make
     God his strength,
But trusted in the abundance of his
     riches,
And strengthened himself in his
     wickedness."

8 But I *am* like a green olive tree in the
     house of God;
I trust in the mercy of God forever
     and ever.
9 I will praise You forever,
Because You have done *it*;
And in the presence of Your saints
I will wait on Your name, for *it is*
     good.

PSALM 53

Folly of the Godless, and the Restoration of Israel

*To the Chief Musician. Set to "Mahalath."
A Contemplation[a] of David.*

1 The fool has said in his heart,

"*There is* no God."
They are corrupt, and have done
abominable iniquity;
There is none who does good.

2 God looks down from heaven upon
the children of men,
To see if there are *any* who
understand, who seek God.

3 Every one of them has turned aside;
They have together become corrupt;
There is none who does good,
No, not one.

4 Have the workers of iniquity no
knowledge,
Who eat up my people *as* they eat
bread,
And do not call upon God?

5 There they are in great fear
Where no fear was,
For God has scattered the bones of
him who encamps against you;
You have put *them* to shame,
Because God has despised them.

6 Oh, that the salvation of Israel would
come out of Zion!
When God brings back the captivity
of His people,
Let Jacob rejoice *and* Israel be glad.

PSALM 54

Answered Prayer for Deliverance from Adversaries

To the Chief Musician. With stringed
instruments.[a] *A Contemplation*[b] *of David*
when the Ziphites went and said to Saul,
"Is David not hiding with us?"

1 Save me, O God, by Your name,
And vindicate me by Your strength.
2 Hear my prayer, O God;
Give ear to the words of my mouth.
3 For strangers have risen up against
me,
And oppressors have sought after my
life;
They have not set God before them.
Selah

4 Behold, God *is* my helper;
The Lord *is* with those who uphold
my life.
5 He will repay my enemies for their
evil.
Cut them off in Your truth.

6 I will freely sacrifice to You;
I will praise Your name, O LORD, for
it is good.
7 For He has delivered me out of all
trouble;
And my eye has seen *its desire* upon
my enemies.

PSALM 55

Trust in God Concerning the Treachery of Friends

To the Chief Musician. With stringed
instruments.[a] *A Contemplation*[b] *of David.*

1 Give ear to my prayer, O God,
And do not hide Yourself from my
supplication.
2 Attend to me, and hear me;
I am restless in my complaint, and
moan noisily,
3 Because of the voice of the enemy,
Because of the oppression of the
wicked;
For they bring down trouble upon me,
And in wrath they hate me.

4 My heart is severely pained within
me,
And the terrors of death have fallen
upon me.
5 Fearfulness and trembling have come
upon me,
And horror has overwhelmed me.
6 So I said, "Oh, that I had wings like a
dove!
I would fly away and be at rest.
7 Indeed, I would wander far off,
And remain in the wilderness.   Selah
8 I would hasten my escape
From the windy storm *and* tempest."

9 Destroy, O Lord, *and* divide their
tongues,

54:title [a]Hebrew *neginoth*   [b]Hebrew *Maschil*   55:title [a]Hebrew *neginoth*   [b]Hebrew *Maschil*

55:1–23 David laments his betrayal by a formerly close friend. This could have been the betrayal of Absalom or Ahithophel (see 2 Sam. 5–18). The psalm alternates between prayers for his enemy's ruin and praises for God's blessings. Though despairing, David expresses ultimate confidence in God.

For I have seen violence and strife in
 the city.
10 Day and night they go around it on its
 walls;
 Iniquity and trouble *are* also in the
 midst of it.
11 Destruction *is* in its midst;
 Oppression and deceit do not depart
 from its streets.

12 For *it is* not an enemy *who* reproaches
 me;
 Then I could bear *it.*
 Nor *is it* one *who* hates me who has
 exalted *himself* against me;
 Then I could hide from him.
13 But *it was* you, a man my equal,
 My companion and my acquaintance.
14 We took sweet counsel together,
 And walked to the house of God in
 the throng.

15 Let death seize them;
 Let them go down alive into hell,
 For wickedness *is* in their dwellings
 and among them.

55:15 go down alive into hell. Since God had done this once with the enemies of Moses (Num. 16:30), David asks Him to perform the same judgment on his enemies.

16 As for me, I will call upon God,
 And the LORD shall save me.
17 Evening and morning and at noon
 I will pray, and cry aloud,
 And He shall hear my voice.
18 He has redeemed my soul in peace
 from the battle *that was* against
 me,
 For there were many against me.
19 God will hear, and afflict them,
 Even He who abides from of old.
 Selah

Because they do not change,
Therefore they do not fear God.
20 He has put forth his hands against
 those who were at peace with him;
 He has broken his covenant.
21 *The words* of his mouth were
 smoother than butter,
 But war *was* in his heart;
 His words were softer than oil,
 Yet they *were* drawn swords.

22 Cast your burden on the LORD,
 And He shall sustain you;
 He shall never permit the righteous to
 be moved.

23 But You, O God, shall bring them
 down to the pit of destruction;
 Bloodthirsty and deceitful men shall
 not live out half their days;
 But I will trust in You.

PSALM 56

Prayer for Relief from Tormentors

*To the Chief Musician. Set to "The Silent
 Dove in Distant Lands."[a] A Michtam
 of David when the Philistines
 captured him in Gath.*

1 Be merciful to me, O God, for man
 would swallow me up;
 Fighting all day he oppresses me.
2 My enemies would hound *me* all day,
 For *there are* many who fight against
 me, O Most High.

3 Whenever I am afraid,
 I will trust in You.
4 In God (I will praise His word),
 In God I have put my trust;
 I will not fear.
 What can flesh do to me?

5 All day they twist my words;
 All their thoughts *are* against me for
 evil.
6 They gather together,
 They hide, they mark my steps,
 When they lie in wait for my life.

56:title [a]Hebrew *Jonath Elem Rechokim*

7   Shall they escape by iniquity?
    In anger cast down the peoples,
        O God!

56:1–13 David wrote this psalm when he was endangered by the Philistines (1 Sam. 21:10–15). He expresses confidence in the Lord, which is what believers should do in terrifying experiences. David's natural reaction was panic, but he showed how a believer can replace terror with trust in God.

8   You number my wanderings;
    Put my tears into Your bottle;
    Are they not in Your book?
9   When I cry out *to You,*
    Then my enemies will turn back;
    This I know, because God *is* for me.
10 In God (I will praise *His* word),
    In the LORD (I will praise *His* word),
11 In God I have put my trust;
    I will not be afraid.
    What can man do to me?

12 Vows *made* to You *are binding* upon
        me, O God;
    I will render praises to You,
13 For You have delivered my soul from
        death.
    Have You not *kept* my feet from
        falling,
    That I may walk before God
    In the light of the living?

PSALM 57

Prayer for Safety from Enemies

*To the Chief Musician. Set to "Do Not
Destroy." [a] A Michtam of David when
he fled from Saul into the cave.*

1   Be merciful to me, O God, be merciful
        to me!

57:1 the shadow of Your wings. God cares for His own as a mother bird protects her young. Symbolically, this may refer to the cherubim wings on the ark of the covenant where God was present (see Ex. 37:1–16). **I will make my refuge.** During calamity, only a relationship with God calms the soul.

For my soul trusts in You;
And in the shadow of Your wings I
    will make my refuge,
Until *these* calamities have passed
    by.
2   I will cry out to God Most High,
    To God who performs *all things* for
        me.
3   He shall send from heaven and save
        me;
    He reproaches the one who would
        swallow me up.   Selah
    God shall send forth His mercy and
        His truth.

4   My soul *is* among lions;
    I lie *among* the sons of men
    Who are set on fire,
    Whose teeth *are* spears and arrows,
    And their tongue a sharp sword.
5   Be exalted, O God, above the
        heavens;
    Let Your glory *be* above all the earth.

6   They have prepared a net for my
        steps;
    My soul is bowed down;
    They have dug a pit before me;
    Into the midst of it they *themselves*
        have fallen.   Selah

7   My heart is steadfast, O God, my
        heart is steadfast;
    I will sing and give praise.
8   Awake, my glory!
    Awake, lute and harp!
    I will awaken the dawn.

9   I will praise You, O Lord, among the
        peoples;
    I will sing to You among the
        nations.
10 For Your mercy reaches unto the
        heavens,
    And Your truth unto the clouds.

11 Be exalted, O God, above the
        heavens;
    Let Your glory *be* above all the earth.

57:title *a*Hebrew *Al Tashcheth*

PSALM 58

The Just Judgment of the Wicked

*To the Chief Musician. Set to
"Do Not Destroy."[a]
A Michtam of David.*

1   Do you indeed speak righteousness,
      you silent ones?
    Do you judge uprightly, you sons of
      men?
2   No, in heart you work wickedness;
    You weigh out the violence of your
      hands in the earth.

3   The wicked are estranged from the
      womb;
    They go astray as soon as they are
      born, speaking lies.
4   Their poison *is* like the poison of a
      serpent;
    They are like the deaf cobra *that* stops
      its ear,
5   Which will not heed the voice of
      charmers,
    Charming ever so skillfully.

58:3 as soon as they are born. All people are born
totally depraved. Without being made new creatures
in Christ by God's power, they are prevented by their
wicked nature from pleasing God (see Ps. 51:5).

6   Break their teeth in their mouth,
      O God!
    Break out the fangs of the young
      lions, O LORD!
7   Let them flow away as waters *which*
      run continually;
    When he bends *his* bow,
    Let his arrows be as if cut in pieces.
8   *Let them be* like a snail which melts
      away as it goes,
    Like a stillborn child of a woman,
      that they may not see the sun.

9   Before your pots can feel *the burning*
      thorns,
    He shall take them away as with a
      whirlwind,
    As in His living and burning wrath.

10 The righteous shall rejoice when he
      sees the vengeance;
    He shall wash his feet in the blood of
      the wicked,
11 So that men will say,
    "Surely *there is* a reward for the
      righteous;
    Surely He is God who judges in the
      earth."

PSALM 59

The Assured Judgment of the Wicked

*To the Chief Musician. Set to "Do Not
Destroy."[a] A Michtam of David when
Saul sent men, and they watched
the house in order to kill him.*

1   Deliver me from my enemies,
      O my God;
    Defend me from those who rise up
      against me.
2   Deliver me from the workers of
      iniquity,
    And save me from bloodthirsty men.

3   For look, they lie in wait for my life;
    The mighty gather against me,
    Not *for* my transgression nor *for* my
      sin, O LORD.
4   They run and prepare themselves
      through no fault *of mine.*

    Awake to help me, and behold!
5   You therefore, O LORD God of hosts,
      the God of Israel,
    Awake to punish all the nations;
    Do not be merciful to any wicked
      transgressors.   Selah

6   At evening they return,
    They growl like a dog,
    And go all around the city.
7   Indeed, they belch with their mouth;
    Swords *are* in their lips;
    For *they say,* "Who hears?"

8   But You, O LORD, shall laugh at
      them;
    You shall have all the nations in
      derision.

58:title *a*Hebrew *Al Tashcheth*   59:title *a*Hebrew *Al Tashcheth*

9   I will wait for You, O You his
      Strength;[a]
      For God *is* my defense.
10   My God of mercy[a] shall come to meet
      me;
      God shall let me see *my desire* on my
      enemies.

11   Do not slay them, lest my people
      forget;
      Scatter them by Your power,
      And bring them down,
      O Lord our shield.
12   *For* the sin of their mouth *and* the
      words of their lips,
      Let them even be taken in their pride,
      And for the cursing and lying *which*
      they speak.
13   Consume *them* in wrath, consume
      them,
      That they *may* not *be*;
      And let them know that God rules in
      Jacob
      To the ends of the earth.   Selah

14   And at evening they return,
      They growl like a dog,
      And go all around the city.
15   They wander up and down for food,
      And howl[a] if they are not satisfied.

16   But I will sing of Your power;
      Yes, I will sing aloud of Your mercy in
      the morning;
      For You have been my defense
      And refuge in the day of my trouble.
17   To You, O my Strength, I will sing
      praises;
      For God *is* my defense,
      My God of mercy.

PSALM 60

Urgent Prayer for the Restored Favor of God

*To the Chief Musician. Set to "Lily of
the Testimony."[a] A Michtam of David.*

*For teaching. When he fought against
Mesopotamia and Syria of Zobah, and
Joab returned and killed twelve thousand
Edomites in the Valley of Salt.*

1   O God, You have cast us off;
      You have broken us down;
      You have been displeased;
      Oh, restore us again!
2   You have made the earth tremble;
      You have broken it;
      Heal its breaches, for it is shaking.
3   You have shown Your people hard
      things;
      You have made us drink the wine of
      confusion.

4   You have given a banner to those who
      fear You,
      That it may be displayed because of
      the truth.   Selah
5   That Your beloved may be delivered,
      Save *with* Your right hand, and hear
      me.

6   God has spoken in His holiness:
   "I will rejoice;
      I will divide Shechem
      And measure out the Valley of
      Succoth.
7   Gilead *is* Mine, and Manasseh *is*
      Mine;
      Ephraim also *is* the helmet for My
      head;
      Judah *is* My lawgiver.
8   Moab *is* My washpot;
      Over Edom I will cast My shoe;
      Philistia, shout in triumph because of
      Me."

60:1–12 This is a national lament written after the unexpected military setback in 2 Sam. 8:13 and 1 Chr. 18:12. While David and his army fought in the north, one of Israel's other neighboring enemies, Edom, successfully attacked the southern part of Judah. David prevailed in victory, but the psalm expresses the shock and confusion of the people when they felt God had abandoned them in this tragedy.

59:9 [a]Following Masoretic Text and Syriac; some Hebrew manuscripts, Septuagint, Targum, and Vulgate read *my Strength*.   59:10 [a]Following Qere; some Hebrew manuscripts, Septuagint, and Vulgate read *My God, His mercy*; Kethib, some Hebrew manuscripts and Targum read *O God, my mercy*; Syriac reads *O God, Your mercy*.   59:15 [a]Following Septuagint and Vulgate; Masoretic Text, Syriac, and Targum read *spend the night*.   60:title [a]Hebrew *Shushan Eduth*

9 Who will bring me *to* the strong city?
Who will lead me to Edom?
10 *Is it* not You, O God, *who* cast us off?
And You, O God, *who* did not go out
with our armies?
11 Give us help from trouble,
For the help of man *is* useless.
12 Through God we will do valiantly,
For *it is* He *who* shall tread down our
enemies.*a*

8 So I will sing praise to Your name
forever,
That I may daily perform my vows.

> **61:1–8** David may have written this psalm when his son, Absalom, temporarily drove him away from his throne in Israel (2 Sam. 15–18). The psalm refers to God's covenants with Israel. David demonstrates a godly response to overwhelming and depressing circumstances.

PSALM 61

Assurance of God's Eternal Protection

*To the Chief Musician. On a stringed
instrument.*a *A Psalm of David.*

1 Hear my cry, O God;
Attend to my prayer.
2 From the end of the earth I will cry to
You,
When my heart is overwhelmed;
Lead me to the rock that is higher
than I.

> **61:2 From the end of the earth.** David shares his feelings of discouragement and exhaustion from being away from his homeland. He also hints at feelings of estrangement from God. **my heart is overwhelmed.** David's hope and courage were failing. **the rock that is higher.** David expresses his disregard of personal autonomy and his reliance on God as his refuge.

3 For You have been a shelter for me,
A strong tower from the enemy.
4 I will abide in Your tabernacle forever;
I will trust in the shelter of Your
wings.   Selah

5 For You, O God, have heard my
vows;
You have given *me* the heritage of
those who fear Your name.
6 You will prolong the king's life,
His years as many generations.
7 He shall abide before God forever.
Oh, prepare mercy and truth, *which*
may preserve him!

PSALM 62

A Calm Resolve to Wait for the Salvation of God

*To the Chief Musician. To Jeduthun.
A Psalm of David.*

1 Truly my soul silently *waits* for God;
From Him *comes* my salvation.
2 He only *is* my rock and my salvation;
He is my defense;
I shall not be greatly moved.

3 How long will you attack a man?
You shall be slain, all of you,
Like a leaning wall and a tottering
fence.
4 They only consult to cast *him* down
from his high position;
They delight in lies;
They bless with their mouth,
But they curse inwardly.   Selah

5 My soul, wait silently for God alone,
For my expectation *is* from Him.
6 He only *is* my rock and my salvation;
He is my defense;
I shall not be moved.
7 In God *is* my salvation and my glory;
The rock of my strength,
And my refuge, *is* in God.

8 Trust in Him at all times, you people;
Pour out your heart before Him;
God *is* a refuge for us.   Selah

9 Surely men of low degree *are* a vapor,
Men of high degree *are* a lie;
If they are weighed on the scales,

60:12 *a*Compare verses 5–12 with 108:6–13   61:title *a*Hebrew *neginah*

They *are* altogether *lighter* than vapor.
10 Do not trust in oppression,
Nor vainly hope in robbery;
If riches increase,
Do not set *your* heart *on them*.

11 God has spoken once,
Twice I have heard this:
That power *belongs* to God.
12 Also to You, O Lord, *belongs* mercy;
For You render to each one according
to his work.

63:1–11 David expresses his intense love for his Lord. He wrote the psalm while he was in the Judean wilderness, either during his flight from Saul (1 Sam. 23) or, more likely, from Absalom (2 Sam. 15). He writes about seeking God's presence, remembering His power, and anticipating His judgment.

PSALM 63

Joy in the Fellowship of God

*A Psalm of David when he was
in the wilderness of Judah.*

1 O God, You *are* my God;
Early will I seek You;
My soul thirsts for You;
My flesh longs for You
In a dry and thirsty land
Where there is no water.
2 So I have looked for You in the
sanctuary,
To see Your power and Your glory.

63:1 Early will I seek You. This refers more to eagerness to be with the Lord in every situation than a certain time of day. **My soul thirsts.** David longs for God's presence like a wanderer in a desert longs for water. **In a dry and thirsty land.** David writes this while hiding in the wilderness of Judea, longing to be back worshiping in Jerusalem.

3 Because Your lovingkindness *is* better
than life,
My lips shall praise You.
4 Thus I will bless You while I live;
I will lift up my hands in Your name.
5 My soul shall be satisfied as with
marrow and fatness,

And my mouth shall praise You with
joyful lips.

6 When I remember You on my bed,
I meditate on You in the *night*
watches.
7 Because You have been my help,
Therefore in the shadow of Your
wings I will rejoice.
8 My soul follows close behind You;
Your right hand upholds me.

9 But those *who* seek my life, to destroy
it,
Shall go into the lower parts of the
earth.
10 They shall fall by the sword;
They shall be a portion for jackals.

11 But the king shall rejoice in God;
Everyone who swears by Him shall
glory;
But the mouth of those who speak
lies shall be stopped.

PSALM 64

Oppressed by the Wicked but Rejoicing in the LORD

To the Chief Musician. A Psalm of David.

1 Hear my voice, O God, in my
meditation;
Preserve my life from fear of the
enemy.
2 Hide me from the secret plots of the
wicked,
From the rebellion of the workers of
iniquity,
3 Who sharpen their tongue like a sword,
And bend *their bows to shoot* their
arrows—bitter words,
4 That they may shoot in secret at the
blameless;
Suddenly they shoot at him and do
not fear.

5 They encourage themselves *in* an evil
matter;
They talk of laying snares secretly;
They say, "Who will see them?"
6 They devise iniquities:
"We have perfected a shrewd scheme."

Both the inward thought and the
    heart of man are deep.

64:6 inward though...heart...deep. The evil intent
of the unrighteous flows from inward depravity.

7 But God shall shoot at them *with* an
    arrow;
    Suddenly they shall be wounded.
8 So He will make them stumble over
    their own tongue;
    All who see them shall flee away.
9 All men shall fear,
    And shall declare the work of God;
    For they shall wisely consider His
    doing.

10 The righteous shall be glad in the
    LORD, and trust in Him.
    And all the upright in heart shall
    glory.

PSALM 65

Praise to God for His Salvation and Providence

*To the Chief Musician. A Psalm
of David. A Song.*

1 Praise is awaiting You, O God, in
    Zion;
    And to You the vow shall be
    performed.
2 O You who hear prayer,
    To You all flesh will come.
3 Iniquities prevail against me;
    As for our transgressions,
    You will provide atonement for them.

65:3 atonement. This word, found 3 times in Psalms,
means to cover over sin and its effects. In the Old
Testament, atonement was symbolized by sacrificial
ritual (see Ex. 30:10), though actual forgiveness of
sin was ultimately based on the death of Christ (see
Heb. 9).

4 Blessed *is the man* You choose,
    And cause to approach *You,*
    That he may dwell in Your courts.
    We shall be satisfied with the
    goodness of Your house,
    Of Your holy temple.

5 *By* awesome deeds in righteousness
    You will answer us,
    O God of our salvation,
    You who are the confidence of all the
    ends of the earth,
    And of the far-off seas;
6 Who established the mountains by
    His strength,
    Being clothed with power;
7 You who still the noise of the seas,
    The noise of their waves,
    And the tumult of the peoples.
8 They also who dwell in the farthest
    parts are afraid of Your signs;
    You make the outgoings of the
    morning and evening rejoice.

9 You visit the earth and water it,
    You greatly enrich it;
    The river of God is full of water;
    You provide their grain,
    For so You have prepared it.
10 You water its ridges abundantly,
    You settle its furrows;
    You make it soft with showers,
    You bless its growth.

11 You crown the year with Your
    goodness,
    And Your paths drip *with* abundance.
12 They drop *on* the pastures of the
    wilderness,
    And the little hills rejoice on every
    side.
13 The pastures are clothed with flocks;
    The valleys also are covered with
    grain;
    They shout for joy, they also sing.

PSALM 66

Praise to God for His Awesome Works

*To the Chief Musician. A Song.
A Psalm.*

1 Make a joyful shout to God, all the
    earth!
2 Sing out the honor of His name;
    Make His praise glorious.
3 Say to God,
    "How awesome are Your works!
    Through the greatness of Your power

Your enemies shall submit themselves
to You.

4 All the earth shall worship You
And sing praises to You;
They shall sing praises *to* Your
name."   Selah

5 Come and see the works of God;
He is awesome *in His* doing toward
the sons of men.

6 He turned the sea into dry *land;*
They went through the river on foot.
There we will rejoice in Him.

7 He rules by His power forever;
His eyes observe the nations;
Do not let the rebellious exalt
themselves.   Selah

8 Oh, bless our God, you peoples!
And make the voice of His praise to
be heard,

9 Who keeps our soul among the
living,
And does not allow our feet to be
moved.

10 For You, O God, have tested us;
You have refined us as silver is
refined.

11 You brought us into the net;
You laid affliction on our backs.

12 You have caused men to ride over our
heads;
We went through fire and through
water;
But You brought us out to rich
fulfillment.

66:1–20 This joyful psalm begins with group praise
and then focuses on the individual's worship. The
psalmist rehearses some of the major miracles in
Israel's history and testifies that God has always
been faithful in the midst of troubles.

13 I will go into Your house with burnt
offerings;
I will pay You my vows,

14 Which my lips have uttered
And my mouth has spoken when I
was in trouble.

15 I will offer You burnt sacrifices of fat
animals,

With the sweet aroma of rams;
I will offer bulls with goats.   Selah

16 Come *and* hear, all you who fear
God,
And I will declare what He has done
for my soul.

17 I cried to Him with my mouth,
And He was extolled with my tongue.

18 If I regard iniquity in my heart,
The Lord will not hear.

19 *But* certainly God has heard *me;*
He has attended to the voice of my
prayer.

20 Blessed *be* God,
Who has not turned away my prayer,
Nor His mercy from me!

PSALM 67

An Invocation and a Doxology

*To the Chief Musician. On stringed
instruments.[a] A Psalm. A Song.*

1 God be merciful to us and bless us,
And cause His face to shine upon us,
Selah

2 That Your way may be known on
earth,
Your salvation among all nations.

3 Let the peoples praise You, O God;
Let all the peoples praise You.

4 Oh, let the nations be glad and sing
for joy!
For You shall judge the people
righteously,
And govern the nations on earth.
Selah

5 Let the peoples praise You, O God;
Let all the peoples praise You.

6 *Then* the earth shall yield her
increase;
God, our own God, shall bless us.

7 God shall bless us,
And all the ends of the earth shall
fear Him.

67:title *a*Hebrew *neginoth*

PSALM 68

The Glory of God in His Goodness to Israel

*To the Chief Musician. A Psalm
of David. A Song.*

1 Let God arise,
Let His enemies be scattered;
Let those also who hate Him flee
before Him.
2 As smoke is driven away,
So drive *them* away;
As wax melts before the fire,
So let the wicked perish at the
presence of God.
3 But let the righteous be glad;
Let them rejoice before God;
Yes, let them rejoice exceedingly.

4 Sing to God, sing praises to His
name;
Extol Him who rides on the clouds,[a]
By His name YAH,
And rejoice before Him.

5 A father of the fatherless, a defender
of widows,
Is God in His holy habitation.
6 God sets the solitary in families;
He brings out those who are bound
into prosperity;
But the rebellious dwell in a dry *land.*

68:6 solitary in families. God cares for those who
have lost families, especially the orphans and widows (see Ex. 22:22–24). **brings out...bound.** This
refers to God's liberating prisoners of war.

7 O God, when You went out before
Your people,
When You marched through the
wilderness,   Selah
8 The earth shook;
The heavens also dropped *rain* at the
presence of God;
Sinai itself *was moved* at the presence
of God, the God of Israel.
9 You, O God, sent a plentiful rain,
Whereby You confirmed Your
inheritance,

When it was weary.
10 Your congregation dwelt in it;
You, O God, provided from Your
goodness for the poor.

11 The Lord gave the word;
Great *was* the company of those who
proclaimed *it:*
12 "Kings of armies flee, they flee,
And she who remains at home divides
the spoil.
13 Though you lie down among the
sheepfolds,
You will be like the wings of a dove
covered with silver,
And her feathers with yellow gold."
14 When the Almighty scattered kings in
it,
It was *white* as snow in Zalmon.

15 A mountain of God *is* the mountain
of Bashan;
A mountain *of many* peaks *is* the
mountain of Bashan.
16 Why do you fume with envy, you
mountains of *many* peaks?
This is the mountain *which* God
desires to dwell in;
Yes, the LORD will dwell *in it* forever.

17 The chariots of God *are* twenty
thousand,
Even thousands of thousands;
The Lord is among them *as in* Sinai,
in the Holy *Place.*
18 You have ascended on high,
You have led captivity captive;
You have received gifts among men,
Even *from* the rebellious,
That the LORD God might dwell
there.

68:17 Sinai, in the Holy Place. God's presence had
been with the armies in the same way it had been on
Mount Sinai at the giving of the law (see Ex. 19).

19 Blessed *be* the Lord,
Who daily loads us *with benefits,*
The God of our salvation!   Selah
20 Our God *is* the God of salvation;
And to GOD the Lord *belong* escapes
from death.

68:4 [a]Masoretic Text reads *deserts;* Targum reads *heavens* (compare verse 34 and Isaiah 19:1).

21 But God will wound the head of His
       enemies,
    The hairy scalp of the one who still
       goes on in his trespasses.
22 The Lord said, "I will bring back from
       Bashan,
    I will bring *them* back from the
       depths of the sea,
23 That your foot may crush *them*[a] in
       blood,
    And the tongues of your dogs *may
       have* their portion from *your*
       enemies."

24 They have seen Your procession,
       O God,
    The procession of my God, my King,
       into the sanctuary.
25 The singers went before, the players
       on instruments *followed* after;
    Among *them were* the maidens
       playing timbrels.
26 Bless God in the congregations,
    The Lord, from the fountain of Israel.
27 There *is* little Benjamin, their leader,
    The princes of Judah *and* their
       company,
    The princes of Zebulun *and* the
       princes of Naphtali.

68:1–35 This psalm includes prayer, praise, thanksgiving, historical reminder, and imprecation. It expresses a pride in Jehovah God for His care over His
people and His majesty in the universe. David may
have written this during the restoration of the ark of
the covenant to Jerusalem (see 2 Sam. 6:12–15).

28 Your God has commanded[a] your
       strength;
    Strengthen, O God, what You have
       done for us.
29 Because of Your temple at Jerusalem,
    Kings will bring presents to You.
30 Rebuke the beasts of the reeds,
    The herd of bulls with the calves of
       the peoples,
    Till everyone submits himself with
       pieces of silver.
    Scatter the peoples *who* delight in
       war.
31 Envoys will come out of Egypt;

Ethiopia will quickly stretch out her
    hands to God.

32 Sing to God, you kingdoms of the
       earth;
    Oh, sing praises to the Lord,   Selah
33 To Him who rides on the heaven of
       heavens, *which were* of old!
    Indeed, He sends out His voice, a
       mighty voice.
34 Ascribe strength to God;
    His excellence *is* over Israel,
    And His strength *is* in the clouds.
35 O God, *You are* more awesome than
       Your holy places.
    The God of Israel *is* He who gives
       strength and power to *His* people.

Blessed *be* God!

PSALM 69

An Urgent Plea for Help in Trouble

To the Chief Musician. Set to "The Lilies."[a]
              A Psalm of David.

1   Save me, O God!
    For the waters have come up to *my*
       neck.
2   I sink in deep mire,
    Where *there is* no standing;
    I have come into deep waters,
    Where the floods overflow me.
3   I am weary with my crying;
    My throat is dry;
    My eyes fail while I wait for my God.

4   Those who hate me without a cause
    Are more than the hairs of my head;
    They are mighty who would destroy
       me,
    Being my enemies wrongfully;
    Though I have stolen nothing,
    I *still* must restore *it.*

5   O God, You know my foolishness;
    And my sins are not hidden from You.
6   Let not those who wait for You,
       O Lord GOD of hosts, be ashamed
       because of me;

68:23 [a]Septuagint, Syriac, Targum, and Vulgate read *you may dip your foot.*   68:28 [a]Septuagint,
Syriac, Targum, and Vulgate read *Command, O God.*   69:title [a]Hebrew *Shoshannim*

Let not those who seek You be
    confounded because of me, O God
    of Israel.
7 Because for Your sake I have borne
    reproach;
    Shame has covered my face.
8 I have become a stranger to my
    brothers,
    And an alien to my mother's
    children;
9 Because zeal for Your house has eaten
    me up,
    And the reproaches of those who
    reproach You have fallen on me.
10 When I wept *and chastened* my soul
    with fasting,
    That became my reproach.
11 I also made sackcloth my garment;
    I became a byword to them.
12 Those who sit in the gate speak
    against me,
    And I *am* the song of the drunkards.

69:9 has eaten me up. The psalmist brought hatred and hostility on himself by insisting that the behavior of the people measure up to their outward claim of devotion to God. Because he loved God so deeply, he felt pain whenever God was dishonored.

13 But as for me, my prayer *is* to You,
    O LORD, *in* the acceptable time;
    O God, in the multitude of Your
    mercy,
    Hear me in the truth of Your
    salvation.
14 Deliver me out of the mire,
    And let me not sink;
    Let me be delivered from those who
    hate me,
    And out of the deep waters.
15 Let not the floodwater overflow me,
    Nor let the deep swallow me up;
    And let not the pit shut its mouth on
    me.

16 Hear me, O LORD, for Your
    lovingkindness *is* good;
    Turn to me according to the
    multitude of Your tender mercies.
17 And do not hide Your face from Your
    servant,
    For I am in trouble;
    Hear me speedily.

18 Draw near to my soul, *and* redeem it;
    Deliver me because of my enemies.
19 You know my reproach, my shame,
    and my dishonor;
    My adversaries *are* all before You.
20 Reproach has broken my heart,
    And I am full of heaviness;
    I looked *for someone* to take pity, but
    there was none;
    And for comforters, but I found none.
21 They also gave me gall for my food,
    And for my thirst they gave me
    vinegar to drink.

69:21 gall...vinegar. Gall was a poisonous herb and serves as a metaphor for betrayal. Friends, who should provide sustenance to the psalmist, had turned against him. Gall in vinegar was actually offered to Christ while He was on the cross (Matt. 27:34).

22 Let their table become a snare before
    them,
    And their well-being a trap.
23 Let their eyes be darkened, so that
    they do not see;
    And make their loins shake
    continually.
24 Pour out Your indignation upon them,
    And let Your wrathful anger take hold
    of them.
25 Let their dwelling place be desolate;
    Let no one live in their tents.
26 For they persecute the *ones* You have
    struck,
    And talk of the grief of those You have
    wounded.
27 Add iniquity to their iniquity,
    And let them not come into Your
    righteousness.
28 Let them be blotted out of the book of
    the living,
    And not be written with the
    righteous.

29 But I *am* poor and sorrowful;
    Let Your salvation, O God, set me up
    on high.
30 I will praise the name of God with a
    song,
    And will magnify Him with
    thanksgiving.

31 *This* also shall please the LORD better
   than an ox *or* bull,
   Which has horns and hooves.
32 The humble shall see *this and* be glad;
   And you who seek God, your hearts
   shall live.
33 For the LORD hears the poor,
   And does not despise His prisoners.

> **69:31 horns and hooves.** This implies a grown ani-
> mal, one that would be especially valuable.

34 Let heaven and earth praise Him,
   The seas and everything that moves
   in them.
35 For God will save Zion
   And build the cities of Judah,
   That they may dwell there and
   possess it.
36 Also, the descendants of His servants
   shall inherit it,
   And those who love His name shall
   dwell in it.

PSALM 70

Prayer for Relief from Adversaries

To the Chief Musician. A Psalm of David.
To bring to remembrance.

1 *Make haste,* O God, to deliver me!
   Make haste to help me, O LORD!

> **70:1–5** This prayer for deliverance from one's
> enemies is nearly identical to Ps. 40:13–17, but it
> substitutes "God" for "LORD."

2 Let them be ashamed and confounded
   Who seek my life;
   Let them be turned back[a] and
   confused
   Who desire my hurt.
3 Let them be turned back because of
   their shame,
   Who say, "Aha, aha!"

4 Let all those who seek You rejoice and
   be glad in You;

And let those who love Your salvation
   say continually,
   "Let God be magnified!"

5 But I *am* poor and needy;
   Make haste to me, O God!
   You *are* my help and my deliverer;
   O LORD, do not delay.

PSALM 71

God the Rock of Salvation

1 In You, O LORD, I put my trust;
   Let me never be put to shame.
2 Deliver me in Your righteousness, and
   cause me to escape;
   Incline Your ear to me, and save me.
3 Be my strong refuge,
   To which I may resort continually;
   You have given the commandment to
   save me,
   For You *are* my rock and my fortress.

4 Deliver me, O my God, out of the
   hand of the wicked,
   Out of the hand of the unrighteous
   and cruel man.
5 For You are my hope, O Lord GOD;
   You are my trust from my youth.
6 By You I have been upheld from birth;
   You are He who took me out of my
   mother's womb.
   My praise *shall be* continually of You.

7 I have become as a wonder to many,
   But You *are* my strong refuge.
8 Let my mouth be filled *with* Your
   praise
   And with Your glory all the day.

9 Do not cast me off in the time of old
   age;
   Do not forsake me when my strength
   fails.
10 For my enemies speak against me;
   And those who lie in wait for my life
   take counsel together,
11 Saying, "God has forsaken him;
   Pursue and take him, for *there is*
   none to deliver *him*."

70:2 [a]Following Masoretic Text, Septuagint, Targum, and Vulgate; some Hebrew manuscripts and
Syriac read *be appalled* (compare 40:15).

71:1–24 At a time in his life when he thinks he should be exempt from certain kinds of troubles (old age), the psalmist finds himself personally attacked. His enemies conclude that God abandoned him, but the psalmist is confident in God's faithfulness.

12 O God, do not be far from me;
O my God, make haste to help me!
13 Let them be confounded *and*
consumed
Who are adversaries of my life;
Let them be covered *with* reproach
and dishonor
Who seek my hurt.

14 But I will hope continually,
And will praise You yet more and
more.
15 My mouth shall tell of Your
righteousness
And Your salvation all the day,
For I do not know *their* limits.
16 I will go in the strength of the Lord
GOD;
I will make mention of Your
righteousness, of Yours only.

17 O God, You have taught me from my
youth;
And to this *day* I declare Your
wondrous works.
18 Now also when *I am* old and
grayheaded,
O God, do not forsake me,
Until I declare Your strength to *this*
generation,
Your power to everyone *who* is to
come.

19 Also Your righteousness, O God, *is*
very high,
You who have done great things;
O God, who *is* like You?
20 *You,* who have shown me great and
severe troubles,
Shall revive me again,
And bring me up again from the
depths of the earth.
21 You shall increase my greatness,
And comfort me on every side.

22 Also with the lute I will praise You—
And Your faithfulness, O my God!
To You I will sing with the harp,
O Holy One of Israel.
23 My lips shall greatly rejoice when I
sing to You,
And my soul, which You have
redeemed.
24 My tongue also shall talk of Your
righteousness all the day long;
For they are confounded,
For they are brought to shame
Who seek my hurt.

PSALM 72

Glory and Universality of the Messiah's Reign

A Psalm of Solomon.

1 Give the king Your judgments,
O God,
And Your righteousness to the king's
Son.
2 He will judge Your people with
righteousness,
And Your poor with justice.
3 The mountains will bring peace to the
people,
And the little hills, by righteousness.
4 He will bring justice to the poor of the
people;
He will save the children of the needy,
And will break in pieces the
oppressor.

5 They shall fear You[a]
As long as the sun and moon endure,
Throughout all generations.
6 He shall come down like rain upon
the grass before mowing,
Like showers *that* water the earth.
7 In His days the righteous shall
flourish,
And abundance of peace,
Until the moon is no more.

8 He shall have dominion also from sea
to sea,
And from the River to the ends of the
earth.

72:5 [a]Following Masoretic Text and Targum; Septuagint and Vulgate read *They shall continue.*

9 Those who dwell in the wilderness
　　will bow before Him,
And His enemies will lick the dust.
10 The kings of Tarshish and of the isles
Will bring presents;
The kings of Sheba and Seba
Will offer gifts.
11 Yes, all kings shall fall down before
　　Him;
All nations shall serve Him.

12 For He will deliver the needy when he
　　cries,
The poor also, and *him* who has no
　　helper.
13 He will spare the poor and needy,
And will save the souls of the needy.
14 He will redeem their life from
　　oppression and violence;
And precious shall be their blood in
　　His sight.

72:1–20 This Coronation Psalm is dedicated to the prosperity of Solomon at the beginning of his reign (1 Kin. 2). It has messianic inferences, as it describes a reign when God, the king, nature, all classes of society, and foreign nations will all live together in harmony.

15 And He shall live;
And the gold of Sheba will be given to
　　Him;
Prayer also will be made for Him
　　continually,
And daily He shall be praised.

16 There will be an abundance of grain
　　in the earth,
On the top of the mountains;
Its fruit shall wave like Lebanon;
And *those* of the city shall flourish
　　like grass of the earth.

17 His name shall endure forever;
His name shall continue as long as
　　the sun.
And *men* shall be blessed in Him;
All nations shall call Him blessed.

18 Blessed *be* the LORD God, the God of
　　Israel,

Who only does wondrous things!
19 And blessed *be* His glorious name
　　forever!
And let the whole earth be filled *with*
　　His glory.
Amen and Amen.

20 The prayers of David the son of Jesse
　　are ended.

73:Title. Asaph. Asaph was a Levite who led one of the temple choirs (1 Chr. 15:19). His name is identified with Pss. 73–83 and also Ps. 50. Either he wrote these psalms, his choir sang them, or later choirs in the tradition of Asaph sang them.

Book Three: Psalms 73–89

PSALM 73

The Tragedy of the Wicked, and the Blessedness of Trust in God

A Psalm of Asaph.

1 Truly God *is* good to Israel,
To such as are pure in heart.
2 But as for me, my feet had almost
　　stumbled;
My steps had nearly slipped.
3 For I *was* envious of the boastful,
When I saw the prosperity of the
　　wicked.

4 For *there are* no pangs in their death,
But their strength *is* firm.
5 They *are* not in trouble *as other* men,
Nor are they plagued like *other* men.
6 Therefore pride serves as their
　　necklace;
Violence covers them *like* a garment.
7 Their eyes bulge[a] with abundance;
They have more than heart could
　　wish.
8 They scoff and speak wickedly
　　concerning oppression;
They speak loftily.
9 They set their mouth against the
　　heavens,
And their tongue walks through the
　　earth.

73:7 [a]Targum reads *face bulges*; Septuagint, Syriac, and Vulgate read *iniquity bulges*.

10 Therefore his people return here,
And waters of a full *cup* are drained
by them.
11 And they say, "How does God know?
And is there knowledge in the Most
High?"
12 Behold, these *are* the ungodly,
Who are always at ease;
They increase *in* riches.
13 Surely I have cleansed my heart *in*
vain,
And washed my hands in innocence.
14 For all day long I have been plagued,
And chastened every morning.

15 If I had said, "I will speak thus,"
Behold, I would have been untrue to
the generation of Your children.
16 When I thought *how* to understand
this,
It *was* too painful for me—
17 Until I went into the sanctuary of
God;
Then I understood their end.

18 Surely You set them in slippery
places;
You cast them down to destruction.
19 Oh, how they are *brought* to
desolation, as in a moment!
They are utterly consumed with
terrors.
20 As a dream when *one* awakes,
So, Lord, when You awake,
You shall despise their image.

21 Thus my heart was grieved,
And I was vexed in my mind.
22 I *was* so foolish and ignorant;
I was *like* a beast before You.
23 Nevertheless I *am* continually with
You;
You hold *me* by my right hand.

73:1–28 This psalm illustrates the results of allowing self-pity to bury one's faith in God. The psalmist grew depressed as he contrasted the prosperity of the wicked with the difficulties of living a righteous life, but his attitude changed as he perceived that the sovereign, holy God controls all of life. He concluded that it is the wicked, not the righteous, who have blundered.

24 You will guide me with Your counsel,
And afterward receive me *to* glory.
25 Whom have I in heaven *but You?*
And *there is* none upon earth *that* I
desire besides You.
26 My flesh and my heart fail;
But God *is* the strength of my heart
and my portion forever.

27 For indeed, those who are far from
You shall perish;
You have destroyed all those who
desert You for harlotry.
28 But *it is* good for me to draw near to
God;
I have put my trust in the Lord GOD,
That I may declare all Your works.

PSALM 74

A Plea for Relief from Oppressors

A Contemplation[a] of Asaph.

1 O God, why have You cast *us* off
forever?
Why does Your anger smoke against
the sheep of Your pasture?
2 Remember Your congregation, *which*
You have purchased of old,
The tribe of Your inheritance, *which*
You have redeemed—
This Mount Zion where You have
dwelt.
3 Lift up Your feet to the perpetual
desolations.
The enemy has damaged everything
in the sanctuary.
4 Your enemies roar in the midst of
Your meeting place;
They set up their banners *for* signs.
5 They seem like men who lift up
Axes among the thick trees.
6 And now they break down its carved
work, all at once,
With axes and hammers.
7 They have set fire to Your sanctuary;
They have defiled the dwelling place
of Your name to the ground.
8 They said in their hearts,
"Let us destroy them altogether."

74:title *a*Hebrew *Maschil*

They have burned up all the meeting
places of God in the land.

9 We do not see our signs;
There is no longer any prophet;
Nor *is there* any among us who
knows how long.

10 O God, how long will the adversary
reproach?
Will the enemy blaspheme Your name
forever?

11 Why do You withdraw Your hand,
even Your right hand?
Take it out of Your bosom and destroy
them.

12 For God *is* my King from of old,
Working salvation in the midst of the
earth.

13 You divided the sea by Your strength;
You broke the heads of the sea
serpents in the waters.

14 You broke the heads of Leviathan in
pieces,
And gave him *as* food to the people
inhabiting the wilderness.

15 You broke open the fountain and the
flood;
You dried up mighty rivers.

16 The day *is* Yours, the night also *is*
Yours;
You have prepared the light and the
sun.

17 You have set all the borders of the
earth;
You have made summer and winter.

> **74:1–23** The psalmist expresses the agony of his
> people after Israel's enemies destroyed the temple
> (see 2 Kin. 25), when it seemed that God had aban-
> doned them. In his prayer, the psalmist reminds God
> of His bond with Israel and His past supernatural
> protection, and he begs God to save His covenant
> nation now (see Ps. 137).

18 Remember this, *that* the enemy has
reproached, O LORD,
And *that* a foolish people has
blasphemed Your name.

19 Oh, do not deliver the life of Your
turtledove to the wild beast!
Do not forget the life of Your poor
forever.

20 Have respect to the covenant;
For the dark places of the earth are
full of the haunts of cruelty.

21 Oh, do not let the oppressed return
ashamed!
Let the poor and needy praise Your
name.

22 Arise, O God, plead Your own cause;
Remember how the foolish man
reproaches You daily.

23 Do not forget the voice of Your
enemies;
The tumult of those who rise up
against You increases continually.

PSALM 75

Thanksgiving for God's Righteous Judgment

*To the Chief Musician. Set to "Do Not
Destroy."*[a] *A Psalm of Asaph. A Song.*

1 We give thanks to You, O God, we
give thanks!
For Your wondrous works declare *that*
Your name is near.

2 "When I choose the proper time,
I will judge uprightly.

3 The earth and all its inhabitants are
dissolved;
I set up its pillars firmly.   Selah

4 "I said to the boastful, 'Do not deal
boastfully,'
And to the wicked, 'Do not lift up the
horn.

5 Do not lift up your horn on high;
Do *not* speak with a stiff neck.' "

> **75:4 Do not lift up the horn.** The horn symbolized
> an animal's or human's strength and majesty (see
> Deut. 33:17). Lifting up the horn described a stubborn
> animal that would resist the yoke by holding its head
> up high. The phrase means insolence or rebellion.

6 For exaltation *comes* neither from the
east
Nor from the west nor from the
south.

75:title [a]Hebrew *Al Tashcheth*

7 But God *is* the Judge:
He puts down one,
And exalts another.

8 For in the hand of the LORD *there is* a
    cup,
And the wine is red;
It is fully mixed, and He pours it out;
Surely its dregs shall all the wicked of
    the earth
Drain *and* drink down.

9 But I will declare forever,
I will sing praises to the God of
    Jacob.

10 "All the horns of the wicked I will also
    cut off,
But the horns of the righteous shall
    be exalted."

75:1–10 God never loses control of the universe. He gives stability to earthly life, and He will judge the wicked. The psalm revolves around the following metaphors: pillars of the earth, horns, and God's cup of wrath.

PSALM 76

The Majesty of God in Judgment

*To the Chief Musician. On stringed
instruments.[a] A Psalm of Asaph. A Song.*

1 In Judah God *is* known;
His name *is* great in Israel.
2 In Salem[a] also is His tabernacle,
And His dwelling place in Zion.
3 There He broke the arrows of the
    bow,
The shield and sword of battle.   Selah

4 You *are* more glorious and excellent
Than the mountains of prey.
5 The stouthearted were plundered;
They have sunk into their sleep;
And none of the mighty men have
    found the use of their hands.
6 At Your rebuke, O God of Jacob,
Both the chariot and horse were cast
    into a dead sleep.

7 You, Yourself, *are* to be feared;
And who may stand in Your presence
When once You are angry?
8 You caused judgment to be heard
    from heaven;
The earth feared and was still,
9 When God arose to judgment,
To deliver all the oppressed of the
    earth.   Selah

10 Surely the wrath of man shall praise
    You;
With the remainder of wrath You
    shall gird Yourself.

11 Make vows to the LORD your God,
    and pay *them*;
Let all who are around Him bring
    presents to Him who ought to be
    feared.
12 He shall cut off the spirit of princes;
He is awesome to the kings of the
    earth.

PSALM 77

The Consoling Memory of God's Redemptive Works

*To the Chief Musician. To Jeduthun.
A Psalm of Asaph.*

1 I cried out to God with my voice—
To God with my voice;
And He gave ear to me.
2 In the day of my trouble I sought the
    Lord;
My hand was stretched out in the
    night without ceasing;
My soul refused to be comforted.
3 I remembered God, and was troubled;
I complained, and my spirit was
    overwhelmed.   Selah

4 You hold my eyelids *open*;
I am so troubled that I cannot speak.
5 I have considered the days of old,
The years of ancient times.
6 I call to remembrance my song in the
    night;
I meditate within my heart,

76:title [a]Hebrew *neginoth*   76:2 [a]That is, Jerusalem

And my spirit makes diligent search.

7 Will the Lord cast off forever?
And will He be favorable no more?
8 Has His mercy ceased forever?
Has *His* promise failed forevermore?
9 Has God forgotten to be gracious?
Has He in anger shut up His tender
mercies?   Selah

77:1–20 At the beginning, the depressed psalmist complained bitterly when he thought about God. His mood changed as he focused on God's goodness and past acts of deliverance. His lament changed into a hymn of praise.

10 And I said, "This *is* my anguish;
But I will remember the years of the
right hand of the Most High."
11 I will remember the works of the
LORD;
Surely I will remember Your wonders
of old.
12 I will also meditate on all Your work,
And talk of Your deeds.
13 Your way, O God, *is* in the sanctuary;
Who *is* so great a God as *our* God?
14 You *are* the God who does wonders;
You have declared Your strength
among the peoples.
15 You have with *Your* arm redeemed
Your people,
The sons of Jacob and Joseph.   Selah

16 The waters saw You, O God;
The waters saw You, they were
afraid;
The depths also trembled.
17 The clouds poured out water;
The skies sent out a sound;
Your arrows also flashed about.
18 The voice of Your thunder *was* in the
whirlwind;
The lightnings lit up the world;
The earth trembled and shook.
19 Your way *was* in the sea,
Your path in the great waters,
And Your footsteps were not known.
20 You led Your people like a flock
By the hand of Moses and Aaron.

PSALM 78

God's Kindness to Rebellious Israel

A Contemplation[a] of Asaph.

1 Give ear, O my people, *to* my law;
Incline your ears to the words of my
mouth.
2 I will open my mouth in a parable;
I will utter dark sayings of old,
3 Which we have heard and known,
And our fathers have told us.
4 We will not hide *them* from their
children,
Telling to the generation to come the
praises of the LORD,
And His strength and His wonderful
works that He has done.

5 For He established a testimony in
Jacob,
And appointed a law in Israel,
Which He commanded our fathers,
That they should make them known
to their children;
6 That the generation to come might
know *them*,
The children *who* would be born,
That they may arise and declare *them*
to their children,
7 That they may set their hope in God,
And not forget the works of God,
But keep His commandments;
8 And may not be like their fathers,
A stubborn and rebellious generation,
A generation *that* did not set its heart
aright,
And whose spirit was not faithful to
God.

9 The children of Ephraim, *being* armed
and carrying bows,
Turned back in the day of battle.
10 They did not keep the covenant of God;
They refused to walk in His law,
11 And forgot His works
And His wonders that He had shown
them.

12 Marvelous things He did in the sight
of their fathers,

In the land of Egypt, *in* the field of
    Zoan.
13 He divided the sea and caused them
    to pass through;
    And He made the waters stand up
    like a heap.
14 In the daytime also He led them with
    the cloud,
    And all the night with a light of fire.
15 He split the rocks in the wilderness,
    And gave *them* drink in abundance
    like the depths.
16 He also brought streams out of the
    rock,
    And caused waters to run down like
    rivers.

78:13 waters stand up like a heap. This describes
the parting of the Red Sea at the beginning of the
Exodus, which allowed Israel to escape from
the Egyptians. The Old Testament saints regard this
as the most spectacular miracle of their history (see
Ex. 14).

17 But they sinned even more against
    Him
    By rebelling against the Most High in
    the wilderness.
18 And they tested God in their heart
    By asking for the food of their fancy.
19 Yes, they spoke against God:
    They said, "Can God prepare a table
    in the wilderness?
20 Behold, He struck the rock,
    So that the waters gushed out,
    And the streams overflowed.
    Can He give bread also?
    Can He provide meat for His people?"

21 Therefore the LORD heard *this* and
    was furious;
    So a fire was kindled against Jacob,
    And anger also came up against
    Israel,
22 Because they did not believe in God,
    And did not trust in His salvation.
23 Yet He had commanded the clouds
    above,
    And opened the doors of heaven,
24 Had rained down manna on them to
    eat,
    And given them of the bread of
    heaven.

25 Men ate angels' food;
    He sent them food to the full.
26 He caused an east wind to blow in the
    heavens;
    And by His power He brought in the
    south wind.
27 He also rained meat on them like the
    dust,
    Feathered fowl like the sand of the
    seas;
28 And He let *them* fall in the midst of
    their camp,
    All around their dwellings.
29 So they ate and were well filled,
    For He gave them their own desire.
30 They were not deprived of their
    craving;
    But while their food *was* still in their
    mouths,
31 The wrath of God came against
    them,
    And slew the stoutest of them,
    And struck down the choice *men* of
    Israel.

78:27 rained meat. This describes the quail that
dropped into Israel's camp in the wilderness (Num.
11:31–35).

32 In spite of this they still sinned,
    And did not believe in His wondrous
    works.
33 Therefore their days He consumed in
    futility,
    And their years in fear.
34 When He slew them, then they
    sought Him;
    And they returned and sought
    earnestly for God.
35 Then they remembered that God *was*
    their rock,
    And the Most High God their
    Redeemer.
36 Nevertheless they flattered Him with
    their mouth,
    And they lied to Him with their
    tongue;
37 For their heart was not steadfast with
    Him,
    Nor were they faithful in His
    covenant.

38 But He, *being* full of compassion,
forgave *their* iniquity,
And did not destroy *them*.
Yes, many a time He turned His anger
away,
And did not stir up all His wrath;

39 For He remembered that they *were*
but flesh,
A breath that passes away and does
not come again.

40 How often they provoked Him in the
wilderness,
And grieved Him in the desert!

41 Yes, again and again they tempted
God,
And limited the Holy One of Israel.

42 They did not remember His power:
The day when He redeemed them
from the enemy,

43 When He worked His signs in Egypt,
And His wonders in the field of
Zoan;

44 Turned their rivers into blood,
And their streams, that they could
not drink.

45 He sent swarms of flies among them,
which devoured them,
And frogs, which destroyed them.

46 He also gave their crops to the
caterpillar,
And their labor to the locust.

47 He destroyed their vines with hail,
And their sycamore trees with frost.

48 He also gave up their cattle to the
hail,
And their flocks to fiery lightning.

49 He cast on them the fierceness of His
anger,
Wrath, indignation, and trouble,
By sending angels of destruction
among them.

50 He made a path for His anger;
He did not spare their soul from
death,
But gave their life over to the plague,

51 And destroyed all the firstborn in
Egypt,
The first of *their* strength in the tents
of Ham.

52 But He made His own people go forth
like sheep,
And guided them in the wilderness
like a flock;

53 And He led them on safely, so that
they did not fear;
But the sea overwhelmed their
enemies.

54 And He brought them to His holy
border,
This mountain *which* His right hand
had acquired.

55 He also drove out the nations before
them,
Allotted them an inheritance by
survey,
And made the tribes of Israel dwell in
their tents.

78:1–72 This didactic psalm was written to teach children how gracious God had been in the past in spite of their ancestors' rebellion and ingratitude. If the children learned from their nation's history, hopefully they would "not be like their father." The psalmist focused on the history of the Exodus.

56 Yet they tested and provoked the Most
High God,
And did not keep His testimonies,

57 But turned back and acted
unfaithfully like their fathers;
They were turned aside like a
deceitful bow.

58 For they provoked Him to anger with
their high places,
And moved Him to jealousy with
their carved images.

59 When God heard *this*, He was
furious,
And greatly abhorred Israel,

60 So that He forsook the tabernacle of
Shiloh,
The tent He had placed among men,

61 And delivered His strength into
captivity,
And His glory into the enemy's hand.

62 He also gave His people over to the
sword,
And was furious with His inheritance.

63 The fire consumed their young men,
And their maidens were not given in
marriage.

64 Their priests fell by the sword,
And their widows made no
lamentation.

65 Then the Lord awoke as *from* sleep,

Like a mighty man who shouts
  because of wine.
66 And He beat back His enemies;
  He put them to a perpetual reproach.

67 Moreover He rejected the tent of
  Joseph,
  And did not choose the tribe of
  Ephraim,
68 But chose the tribe of Judah,
  Mount Zion which He loved.
69 And He built His sanctuary like the
  heights,
  Like the earth which He has
  established forever.
70 He also chose David His servant,
  And took him from the sheepfolds;
71 From following the ewes that had
  young He brought him,
  To shepherd Jacob His people,
  And Israel His inheritance.
72 So he shepherded them according to
  the integrity of his heart,
  And guided them by the skillfulness
  of his hands.

78:68 the tribe of Judah. God chose Judah instead of a prestigious tribe because David and his descendants came from Judah, and Mount Zion, the central location of worship, was located in Judah.

PSALM 79

A Dirge and a Prayer for Israel, Destroyed by Enemies

A Psalm of Asaph.

1 O God, the nations have come into
  Your inheritance;
  Your holy temple they have defiled;
  They have laid Jerusalem in heaps.
2 The dead bodies of Your servants
  They have given *as* food for the birds
  of the heavens,
  The flesh of Your saints to the beasts
  of the earth.
3 Their blood they have shed like water
  all around Jerusalem,
  And *there was* no one to bury *them.*
4 We have become a reproach to our
  neighbors,
  A scorn and derision to those who are
  around us.

5 How long, LORD?
  Will You be angry forever?
  Will Your jealousy burn like fire?
6 Pour out Your wrath on the nations
  that do not know You,
  And on the kingdoms that do not call
  on Your name.
7 For they have devoured Jacob,
  And laid waste his dwelling place.

8 Oh, do not remember former
  iniquities against us!
  Let Your tender mercies come speedily
  to meet us,
  For we have been brought very low.
9 Help us, O God of our salvation,
  For the glory of Your name;
  And deliver us, and provide
  atonement for our sins,
  For Your name's sake!
10 Why should the nations say,
  "Where *is* their God?"
  Let there be known among the
  nations in our sight
  The avenging of the blood of Your
  servants *which has been* shed.

79:10 "Where is their God?" The heathen mocked Israel's God by saying that the destruction of the nation implied a nonexistent God.

11 Let the groaning of the prisoner come
  before You;
  According to the greatness of Your
  power
  Preserve those who are appointed to
  die;
12 And return to our neighbors sevenfold
  into their bosom
  Their reproach with which they have
  reproached You, O Lord.

13 So we, Your people and sheep of Your
  pasture,
  Will give You thanks forever;

79:1–13 The psalmist laments Nebuchadnezzar's destruction of the temple in 586 B.C. (see Ps. 74). He prays for the nation's spiritual needs, curses their enemies, and praises God's anticipated actions. This psalm helps the believer express his anguish in a situation where God does not seem present.

We will show forth Your praise to all
  generations.

PSALM 80

Prayer for Israel's Restoration

To the Chief Musician. Set to "The Lilies."[a]
A Testimony[b] of Asaph. A Psalm.

1 Give ear, O Shepherd of Israel,
  You who lead Joseph like a flock;
  You who dwell *between* the
    cherubim, shine forth!
2 Before Ephraim, Benjamin, and
    Manasseh,
  Stir up Your strength,
  And come *and* save us!

3 Restore us, O God;
  Cause Your face to shine,
  And we shall be saved!

4 O LORD God of hosts,
  How long will You be angry
  Against the prayer of Your people?
5 You have fed them with the bread of
    tears,
  And given them tears to drink in great
    measure.
6 You have made us a strife to our
    neighbors,
  And our enemies laugh among
    themselves.

7 Restore us, O God of hosts;
  Cause Your face to shine,
  And we shall be saved!

8 You have brought a vine out of Egypt;
  You have cast out the nations, and
    planted it.
9 You prepared *room* for it,
  And caused it to take deep root,
  And it filled the land.
10 The hills were covered with its
    shadow,

80:8 vine out of Egypt. The vine is a metaphor for
Israel, whom God delivered out of Egypt and nur-
tured into a powerful nation (see Is. 5:1–7).

And the mighty cedars with its
    boughs.
11 She sent out her boughs to the Sea,[a]
  And her branches to the River.[b]

12 Why have You broken down her
    hedges,
  So that all who pass by the way pluck
    her *fruit?*
13 The boar out of the woods uproots it,
  And the wild beast of the field
    devours it.

14 Return, we beseech You, O God of
    hosts;
  Look down from heaven and see,
  And visit this vine
15 And the vineyard which Your right
    hand has planted,
  And the branch *that* You made strong
    for Yourself.
16 *It is* burned with fire, *it is* cut down;
  They perish at the rebuke of Your
    countenance.
17 Let Your hand be upon the man of
    Your right hand,
  Upon the son of man *whom* You
    made strong for Yourself.
18 Then we will not turn back from You;
  Revive us, and we will call upon Your
    name.

80:17 son of man. This phrase refers to Israel. It
could also allude to the Davidic dynasty and even to
the Messiah, as He is frequently given that title in the
New Testament.

19 Restore us, O LORD God of hosts;
  Cause Your face to shine,
  And we shall be saved!

PSALM 81

An Appeal for Israel's Repentance

To the Chief Musician. On an instrument
of Gath.[a] A Psalm of Asaph.

1 Sing aloud to God our strength;
  Make a joyful shout to the God of
    Jacob.

80:title [a]Hebrew *Shoshannim*   [b]Hebrew *Eduth*   80:11 [a]That is, the Mediterranean   [b]That is, the
Euphrates   81:title [a]Hebrew *Al Gittith*

2　Raise a song and strike the timbrel,
　　The pleasant harp with the lute.

3　Blow the trumpet at the time of the
　　　New Moon,
　　At the full moon, on our solemn feast
　　　day.
4　For this *is* a statute for Israel,
　　A law of the God of Jacob.
5　This He established in Joseph *as* a
　　　testimony,
　　When He went throughout the land of
　　　Egypt,
　　Where I heard a language I did not
　　　understand.

6　"I removed his shoulder from the
　　　burden;
　　His hands were freed from the
　　　baskets.
7　You called in trouble, and I delivered
　　　you;
　　I answered you in the secret place of
　　　thunder;
　　I tested you at the waters of Meribah.
　　　　　　　　　　　　　　　　　Selah

8　"Hear, O My people, and I will
　　　admonish you!
　　O Israel, if you will listen to Me!
9　There shall be no foreign god among
　　　you;
　　Nor shall you worship any foreign
　　　god.
10　I *am* the LORD your God,
　　Who brought you out of the land of
　　　Egypt;
　　Open your mouth wide, and I will
　　　fill it.

11　"But My people would not heed My
　　　voice,
　　And Israel would *have* none of Me.
12　So I gave them over to their own
　　　stubborn heart,
　　To walk in their own counsels.

13　"Oh, that My people would listen to
　　　Me,
　　That Israel would walk in My ways!
14　I would soon subdue their enemies,

And turn My hand against their
　　adversaries.
15　The haters of the LORD would pretend
　　　submission to Him,
　　But their fate would endure forever.
16　He would have fed them also with the
　　　finest of wheat;
　　And with honey from the rock I
　　　would have satisfied you."

PSALM 82

A Plea for Justice

A Psalm of Asaph.

1　God stands in the congregation of the
　　　mighty;
　　He judges among the gods.[a]
2　How long will you judge unjustly,
　　And show partiality to the wicked?
　　　　　　　　　　　　　　　　Selah
3　Defend the poor and fatherless;
　　Do justice to the afflicted and needy.
4　Deliver the poor and needy;
　　Free *them* from the hand of the
　　　wicked.

82:1 congregation of the mighty. The scene opens after God called all the world leaders together. **among the gods.** This could refer to demons or false pagan gods. Many believe that these "gods" are human leaders, such as judges, kings, legislators, and presidents (see Ex. 22:8,9). God, the Great Judge, presides over these lesser judges.

5　They do not know, nor do they
　　　understand;
　　They walk about in darkness;
　　All the foundations of the earth are
　　　unstable.

6　I said, "You *are* gods,[a]
　　And all of you *are* children of the
　　　Most High.
7　But you shall die like men,
　　And fall like one of the princes."

8　Arise, O God, judge the earth;
　　For You shall inherit all nations.

82:1 [a]Hebrew *elohim, mighty ones;* that is, the judges　82:6 [a]Hebrew *elohim, mighty ones;* that is, the judges

82:6 **I said.** It is God who sets up kings and judges (Ps. 2:6). He invests authority in human leaders for the stability of the universe (see Rom. 13:1–7). **"You are gods."** In John 10:34, Jesus uses a play on words, calling the human leaders "gods" and the Messiah "God." **children of the Most High.** Created by God for noble life.

PSALM 83

Prayer to Frustrate Conspiracy Against Israel

A Song. A Psalm of Asaph.

1 Do not keep silent, O God!
  Do not hold Your peace,
  And do not be still, O God!
2 For behold, Your enemies make a
    tumult;
  And those who hate You have lifted
    up their head.
3 They have taken crafty counsel
    against Your people,
  And consulted together against Your
    sheltered ones.
4 They have said, "Come, and let us cut
    them off from *being* a nation,
  That the name of Israel may be
    remembered no more."

5 For they have consulted together with
    one consent;
  They form a confederacy against You:
6 The tents of Edom and the
    Ishmaelites;
  Moab and the Hagrites;
7 Gebal, Ammon, and Amalek;
  Philistia with the inhabitants of Tyre;
8 Assyria also has joined with them;
  They have helped the children of Lot.
    Selah

9 Deal with them as *with* Midian,
  As *with* Sisera,
  As *with* Jabin at the Brook Kishon,
10 Who perished at En Dor,
  Who became *as* refuse on the earth.
11 Make their nobles like Oreb and like
    Zeeb,
  Yes, all their princes like Zebah and
    Zalmunna,
12 Who said, "Let us take for ourselves

The pastures of God for a
    possession."

13 O my God, make them like the
    whirling dust,
  Like the chaff before the wind!
14 As the fire burns the woods,
  And as the flame sets the mountains
    on fire,
15 So pursue them with Your tempest,
  And frighten them with Your storm.
16 Fill their faces with shame,
  That they may seek Your name,
    O LORD.
17 Let them be confounded and
    dismayed forever;
  Yes, let them be put to shame and
    perish,
18 That they may know that You, whose
    name alone *is* the LORD,
  Are the Most High over all the earth.

83:18 **know...Most High.** The purpose for the curses against the hostile nations was so that they may know and glorify God. **whose name alone *is* the LORD.** "Alone" should precede "*are*" in the next phrase. The Gentile nations need to know that the God of the Bible is the only God.

PSALM 84

The Blessedness of Dwelling in the House of God

To the Chief Musician. On an instrument of Gath.[a] A Psalm of the sons of Korah.

1 How lovely *is* Your tabernacle,
  O LORD of hosts!
2 My soul longs, yes, even faints
  For the courts of the LORD;
  My heart and my flesh cry out for the
    living God.

3 Even the sparrow has found a home,
  And the swallow a nest for herself,
  Where she may lay her young—
  Even Your altars, O LORD of hosts,
  My King and my God.
4 Blessed *are* those who dwell in Your
    house;
  They will still be praising You.   Selah

84:title [a]Hebrew *Al Gittith*

5　Blessed *is* the man whose strength *is*
　　　in You,
　　Whose heart *is* set on pilgrimage.
6　*As they* pass through the Valley of
　　　Baca,
　　They make it a spring;
　　The rain also covers it with pools.
7　They go from strength to strength;
　　Each one appears before God in
　　　Zion.[a]

84:7 strength to strength. Anticipation of joyous worship of God in Jerusalem overcame the pilgrims' natural weariness in their difficult journey.

8　O LORD God of hosts, hear my prayer;
　　Give ear, O God of Jacob! 　　Selah
9　O God, behold our shield,
　　And look upon the face of Your
　　　anointed.

10　For a day in Your courts *is* better than
　　　a thousand.
　　I would rather be a doorkeeper in the
　　　house of my God
　　Than dwell in the tents of
　　　wickedness.
11　For the LORD God *is* a sun and shield;
　　The LORD will give grace and glory;
　　No good *thing* will He withhold
　　From those who walk uprightly.

12　O LORD of hosts,
　　Blessed *is* the man who trusts in You!

PSALM 85

Prayer that the LORD Will Restore Favor to the Land

*To the Chief Musician. A Psalm
of the sons of Korah.*

1　LORD, You have been favorable to
　　　Your land;
　　You have brought back the captivity of
　　　Jacob.
2　You have forgiven the iniquity of Your
　　　people;
　　You have covered all their sin. 　　Selah
3　You have taken away all Your wrath;

　　You have turned from the fierceness
　　　of Your anger.

4　Restore us, O God of our salvation,
　　And cause Your anger toward us to
　　　cease.
5　Will You be angry with us forever?
　　Will You prolong Your anger to all
　　　generations?
6　Will You not revive us again,
　　That Your people may rejoice in You?
7　Show us Your mercy, LORD,
　　And grant us Your salvation.

8　I will hear what God the LORD will
　　　speak,
　　For He will speak peace
　　To His people and to His saints;
　　But let them not turn back to folly.
9　Surely His salvation *is* near to those
　　　who fear Him,
　　That glory may dwell in our land.

85:9 salvation...who fear Him. Only those who renounce their sin and trust in God will participate in the blessings of salvation and the future kingdom (see John 3:3–5). **glory may dwell in our land.** God withdrew His glory, which signified His presence, due to the apostasy of the nation before the Babylonian Exile (see Ezek. 8–11). The return of His glory in the future millennial temple is foretold in Ezek. 43:1–4 (see Ps. 26:8).

10　Mercy and truth have met together;
　　Righteousness and peace have kissed.
11　Truth shall spring out of the earth,
　　And righteousness shall look down
　　　from heaven.
12　Yes, the LORD will give *what is* good;
　　And our land will yield its increase.
13　Righteousness will go before Him,

85:1–13 The psalmist pledges that God will again demonstrate His covenant love to Israel, just as He had been merciful in the past. Although He is angry presently, He will restore Israel in the future (see Deut. 30), because He is faithful to His promises. This psalm may express the feelings of the Jews returning from exile. They were grateful for restoration of their land but were disappointed in the condition of it (see Ezra 3:12,13).

84:7 [a]Septuagint, Syriac, and Vulgate read *The God of gods shall be seen.*

And shall make His footsteps *our* pathway.

PSALM 86

Prayer for Mercy, with Meditation on the Excellencies of the LORD

A Prayer of David.

1 Bow down Your ear, O LORD, hear me;
For I *am* poor and needy.
2 Preserve my life, for I *am* holy;
You are my God;
Save Your servant who trusts in You!
3 Be merciful to me, O Lord,
For I cry to You all day long.
4 Rejoice the soul of Your servant,
For to You, O Lord, I lift up my soul.
5 For You, Lord, *are* good, and ready to forgive,
And abundant in mercy to all those who call upon You.

6 Give ear, O LORD, to my prayer;
And attend to the voice of my supplications.
7 In the day of my trouble I will call upon You,
For You will answer me.

8 Among the gods *there is* none like You, O Lord;
Nor *are there any works* like Your works.
9 All nations whom You have made
Shall come and worship before You, O Lord,
And shall glorify Your name.
10 For You *are* great, and do wondrous things;
You alone *are* God.

11 Teach me Your way, O LORD;
I will walk in Your truth;
Unite my heart to fear Your name.
12 I will praise You, O Lord my God, with all my heart,
And I will glorify Your name forevermore.
13 For great *is* Your mercy toward me,
And You have delivered my soul from the depths of Sheol.

14 O God, the proud have risen against me,
And a mob of violent *men* have sought my life,
And have not set You before them.
15 But You, O Lord, *are* a God full of compassion, and gracious,
Longsuffering and abundant in mercy and truth.

16 Oh, turn to me, and have mercy on me!
Give Your strength to Your servant,
And save the son of Your maidservant.
17 Show me a sign for good,
That those who hate me may see *it* and be ashamed,
Because You, LORD, have helped me and comforted me.

PSALM 87

The Glories of the City of God

A Psalm of the sons of Korah. A Song.

1 His foundation *is* in the holy mountains.
2 The LORD loves the gates of Zion
More than all the dwellings of Jacob.
3 Glorious things are spoken of you,
O city of God!   Selah

87:2 gates of Zion. Zion is a spiritual description of Jerusalem, the center of worship. The gates represent the place where the worshiper could enter into a relationship with God. **More than all the dwellings of Jacob.** The other cities were not chosen by God to be the place of His special dwelling.

4 "I will make mention of Rahab and Babylon to those who know Me;
Behold, O Philistia and Tyre, with Ethiopia:
'This *one* was born there.' "
5 And of Zion it will be said,
"This *one* and that *one* were born in her;
And the Most High Himself shall establish her."
6 The LORD will record,

When He registers the peoples:
"This *one* was born there."   Selah

7   Both the singers and the players on
       instruments *say,*
    "All my springs *are* in you."

> **87:7 "All my springs *are* in you."** "Springs" is a
> metaphor for the source of joyful blessings. Eternal
> salvation through the death and resurrection of Jesus
> Christ is rooted in Jerusalem. The prophets also tell
> of a literal fountain, flowing from the temple in Jeru-
> salem, which will water the surrounding land (see
> Joel 3:18).

PSALM 88

A Prayer for Help in Despondency

*A Song. A Psalm of the sons of Korah. To
the Chief Musician. Set to "Mahalath
Leannoth." A Contemplation[a]
of Heman the Ezrahite.*

1   O LORD, God of my salvation,
    I have cried out day and night before
       You.
2   Let my prayer come before You;
    Incline Your ear to my cry.

3   For my soul is full of troubles,
    And my life draws near to the grave.
4   I am counted with those who go down
       to the pit;
    I am like a man *who has* no strength,
5   Adrift among the dead,
    Like the slain who lie in the grave,
    Whom You remember no more,
    And who are cut off from Your hand.

> **88:4 go down to the pit.** "Pit" refers to the grave, a
> place of destruction.

6   You have laid me in the lowest pit,
    In darkness, in the depths.
7   Your wrath lies heavy upon me,
    And You have afflicted *me* with all
       Your waves.   Selah
8   You have put away my acquaintances
       far from me;

You have made me an abomination to
    them;
I am shut up, and I cannot get out;
9   My eye wastes away because of
       affliction.

LORD, I have called daily upon You;
I have stretched out my hands to You.
10 Will You work wonders for the dead?
    Shall the dead arise *and* praise You?
                             Selah
11 Shall Your lovingkindness be declared
       in the grave?
    Or Your faithfulness in the place of
       destruction?
12 Shall Your wonders be known in the
       dark?
    And Your righteousness in the land of
       forgetfulness?

13 But to You I have cried out, O LORD,
    And in the morning my prayer comes
       before You.
14 LORD, why do You cast off my soul?
    Why do You hide Your face from me?
15 *I have been* afflicted and ready to die
       from *my* youth;
    I suffer Your terrors;
    I am distraught.
16 Your fierce wrath has gone over me;
    Your terrors have cut me off.
17 They came around me all day long
       like water;
    They engulfed me altogether.
18 Loved one and friend You have put far
       from me,
    And my acquaintances into darkness.

PSALM 89

Remembering the Covenant with David,
and Sorrow for Lost Blessings

A Contemplation[a] of Ethan the Ezrahite.

1   I will sing of the mercies of the LORD
       forever;
    With my mouth will I make known
       Your faithfulness to all
       generations.
2   For I have said, "Mercy shall be built
       up forever;

88:title [a]Hebrew *Maschil*   89:title [a]Hebrew *Maschil*

Your faithfulness You shall establish
  in the very heavens."

3 "I have made a covenant with My
    chosen,
  I have sworn to My servant David:
4 'Your seed I will establish forever,
  And build up your throne to all
    generations.' "   Selah

89:4 seed...forever...throne. The covenant with
David guaranteed that the rightful heir to the throne
would always be a descendant of David (see 2 Sam.
7:13). The genealogies of Jesus qualify Him for the
throne (see Matt. 1:1–17).

5 And the heavens will praise Your
    wonders, O LORD;
  Your faithfulness also in the assembly
    of the saints.
6 For who in the heavens can be
    compared to the LORD?
  Who among the sons of the mighty
    can be likened to the LORD?
7 God is greatly to be feared in the
    assembly of the saints,
  And to be held in reverence by all
    those around Him.
8 O LORD God of hosts,
  Who *is* mighty like You, O LORD?
  Your faithfulness also surrounds You.
9 You rule the raging of the sea;
  When its waves rise, You still them.
10 You have broken Rahab in pieces, as
    one who is slain;
  You have scattered Your enemies with
    Your mighty arm.

11 The heavens *are* Yours, the earth also
    is Yours;
  The world and all its fullness, You
    have founded them.
12 The north and the south, You have
    created them;
  Tabor and Hermon rejoice in Your
    name.
13 You have a mighty arm;
  Strong is Your hand, *and* high is Your
    right hand.
14 Righteousness and justice *are* the
    foundation of Your throne;

Mercy and truth go before Your face.
15 Blessed *are* the people who know the
    joyful sound!
  They walk, O LORD, in the light of
    Your countenance.
16 In Your name they rejoice all day long,
  And in Your righteousness they are
    exalted.
17 For You *are* the glory of their
    strength,
  And in Your favor our horn is exalted.
18 For our shield *belongs* to the LORD,
  And our king to the Holy One of
    Israel.

19 Then You spoke in a vision to Your
    holy one,[a]
  And said: "I have given help to *one*
    who is mighty;
  I have exalted one chosen from the
    people.
20 I have found My servant David;
  With My holy oil I have anointed
    him,
21 With whom My hand shall be
    established;
  Also My arm shall strengthen him.
22 The enemy shall not outwit him,
  Nor the son of wickedness afflict him.
23 I will beat down his foes before his
    face,
  And plague those who hate him.

89:19 Your holy one. The "holy one" was the prophet,
Nathan, whom the Lord used to tell David about His
covenant with David (2 Sam. 7:4).

24 "But My faithfulness and My mercy
    shall be with him,
  And in My name his horn shall be
    exalted.
25 Also I will set his hand over the sea,
  And his right hand over the rivers.
26 He shall cry to Me, 'You *are* my
    Father,
  My God, and the rock of my
    salvation.'
27 Also I will make him *My* firstborn,
  The highest of the kings of the earth.
28 My mercy I will keep for him forever,

89:19 [a]Following many Hebrew manuscripts; Masoretic Text, Septuagint, Targum, and Vulgate read
holy ones.

89:27 My firstborn. The firstborn son was given honor and double the inheritance (Gen. 27). A person could be elevated to the level of a firstborn by a royal grant (see Ps. 2:7). Though not actually the first, Israel was considered the first among nations (Ex. 4:22). Ephraim the younger was treated as the firstborn (Gen. 48:13–20), and David was the firstborn among kings. In the same way, Christ is called the firstborn (Col. 1:15) and is given preeminence over all creation.

And My covenant shall stand firm
   with him.
29 His seed also I will make *to endure*
   forever,
And his throne as the days of heaven.

30 "If his sons forsake My law
   And do not walk in My judgments,
31 If they break My statutes
   And do not keep My commandments,
32 Then I will punish their transgression
   with the rod,
And their iniquity with stripes.
33 Nevertheless My lovingkindness I will
   not utterly take from him,
Nor allow My faithfulness to fail.
34 My covenant I will not break,
   Nor alter the word that has gone out
   of My lips.
35 Once I have sworn by My holiness;
   I will not lie to David:
36 His seed shall endure forever,
   And his throne as the sun before Me;
37 It shall be established forever like the
   moon,
Even *like* the faithful witness in the
   sky."   Selah

38 But You have cast off and abhorred,
   You have been furious with Your
   anointed.
39 You have renounced the covenant of
   Your servant;
You have profaned his crown *by*
   casting it to the ground.
40 You have broken down all his hedges;
   You have brought his strongholds to
   ruin.
41 All who pass by the way plunder
   him;
He is a reproach to his neighbors.

42 You have exalted the right hand of his
   adversaries;
You have made all his enemies
   rejoice.
43 You have also turned back the edge of
   his sword,
And have not sustained him in the
   battle.
44 You have made his glory cease,
   And cast his throne down to the
   ground.
45 The days of his youth You have
   shortened;
You have covered him with shame.   Selah

46 How long, LORD?
   Will You hide Yourself forever?
Will Your wrath burn like fire?
47 Remember how short my time is;
   For what futility have You created all
   the children of men?
48 What man can live and not see death?
   Can he deliver his life from the power
   of the grave?   Selah

49 Lord, where *are* Your former
   lovingkindnesses,
Which You swore to David in Your
   truth?
50 Remember, Lord, the reproach of Your
   servants—
How I bear in my bosom *the reproach*
   of all the many peoples,
51 With which Your enemies have
   reproached, O LORD,
With which they have reproached the
   footsteps of Your anointed.

52 Blessed *be* the LORD forevermore!
   Amen and Amen.

Book Four: Psalms 90–106

PSALM 90

The Eternity of God, and Man's Frailty

A Prayer of Moses the man of God.

1 Lord, You have been our dwelling
   place*ᵃ* in all generations.

90:1 *ᵃ*Septuagint, Targum, and Vulgate read *refuge.*

90:Title. Moses the man of God. Moses was unique in that the Lord knew him "face to face" (Deut. 34:10–12). "Man of God" (Deut. 33:1) is used over 70 times in the Old Testament and refers to one who spoke for God. It is used to describe Timothy in the New Testament (1 Tim. 6:11).

90:1–17 The purpose of this prayer is to ask God for mercy on frail humans living in a sin-cursed universe. Moses reflects on God's eternality, expresses his thoughts about the sorrows and brevity of life, and concludes with a plea for God to enable His people to live a significant life. The psalm was composed as the older generation of Israelites who had left Egypt were dying in the wilderness (Num. 14).

2   Before the mountains were brought
      forth,
  Or ever You had formed the earth and
      the world,
  Even from everlasting to everlasting,
      You *are* God.

3   You turn man to destruction,
  And say, "Return, O children of
      men."
4   For a thousand years in Your sight
  Are like yesterday when it is past,
  And *like* a watch in the night.
5   You carry them away *like* a flood;
  They are like a sleep.
  In the morning they are like grass
      which grows up:
6   In the morning it flourishes and
      grows up;
  In the evening it is cut down and
      withers.

7   For we have been consumed by Your
      anger,
  And by Your wrath we are terrified.
8   You have set our iniquities before
      You,
  Our secret *sins* in the light of Your
      countenance.
9   For all our days have passed away in
      Your wrath;
  We finish our years like a sigh.
10   The days of our lives *are* seventy
      years;
  And if by reason of strength *they are*
      eighty years,
  Yet their boast *is* only labor and
      sorrow;
  For it is soon cut off, and we fly away.
11   Who knows the power of Your anger?
  For as the fear of You, *so is* Your
      wrath.
12   So teach *us* to number our days,
  That we may gain a heart of wisdom.

13   Return, O LORD!
  How long?

  And have compassion on Your
      servants.
14   Oh, satisfy us early with Your mercy,
  That we may rejoice and be glad all
      our days!
15   Make us glad according to the days *in*
      which You have afflicted us,
  The years *in which* we have seen
      evil.
16   Let Your work appear to Your
      servants,
  And Your glory to their children.
17   And let the beauty of the LORD our
      God be upon us,
  And establish the work of our hands
      for us;
  Yes, establish the work of our hands.

90:17 the beauty of the LORD. The Lord's beauty implies His delight, approval, and favor. **establish the work of our hands.** One's life can have value by God's mercy and grace (see 1 Cor. 15:58).

PSALM 91

Safety of Abiding in the Presence of God

1   He who dwells in the secret place of
      the Most High
  Shall abide under the shadow of the
      Almighty.
2   I will say of the LORD, "*He is* my
      refuge and my fortress;
  My God, in Him I will trust."

91:1 secret place of the Most High. This is an intimate place of divine protection. Using "Most High" to describe God emphasizes that no threat can ever overpower Him. **shadow of the Almighty.** In a land where the sun could be dangerous and oppressive, a "shadow" was understood as a metaphor for care and protection.

³ Surely He shall deliver you from the
   snare of the fowler*
And from the perilous pestilence.
⁴ He shall cover you with His feathers,
   And under His wings you shall take
   refuge;
His truth *shall be your* shield and
   buckler.
⁵ You shall not be afraid of the terror by
   night,
Nor of the arrow *that* flies by day,
⁶ *Nor* of the pestilence *that* walks in
   darkness,
Nor of the destruction *that* lays waste
   at noonday.

⁷ A thousand may fall at your side,
   And ten thousand at your right
   hand;
But it shall not come near you.
⁸ Only with your eyes shall you look,
   And see the reward of the wicked.

⁹ Because you have made the LORD,
   who is my refuge,
Even the Most High, your dwelling
   place,
¹⁰ No evil shall befall you,
   Nor shall any plague come near your
   dwelling;
¹¹ For He shall give His angels charge
   over you,
To keep you in all your ways.
¹² In *their* hands they shall bear you up,
   Lest you dash your foot against a
   stone.
¹³ You shall tread upon the lion and the
   cobra,
The young lion and the serpent you
   shall trample underfoot.

¹⁴ "Because he has set his love upon Me,
   therefore I will deliver him;
I will set him on high, because he has
   known My name.
¹⁵ He shall call upon Me, and I will
   answer him;
I *will be* with him in trouble;
I will deliver him and honor him.
¹⁶ With long life I will satisfy him,
   And show him My salvation."

PSALM 92

**Praise to the LORD for His Love
and Faithfulness**

A Psalm. A Song for the Sabbath day.

¹ *It is* good to give thanks to the LORD,
   And to sing praises to Your name,
   O Most High;
² To declare Your lovingkindness in the
   morning,
And Your faithfulness every night,
³ On an instrument of ten strings,
   On the lute,
And on the harp,
   With harmonious sound.
⁴ For You, LORD, have made me glad
   through Your work;
I will triumph in the works of Your
   hands.

⁵ O LORD, how great are Your works!
   Your thoughts are very deep.
⁶ A senseless man does not know,
   Nor does a fool understand this.
⁷ When the wicked spring up like grass,
   And when all the workers of iniquity
   flourish,
It is that they may be destroyed
   forever.

⁸ But You, LORD, *are* on high
   forevermore.
⁹ For behold, Your enemies, O LORD,
   For behold, Your enemies shall perish;
All the workers of iniquity shall be
   scattered.

¹⁰ But my horn You have exalted like a
   wild ox;
I have been anointed with fresh oil.
¹¹ My eye also has seen *my desire* on my
   enemies;
My ears hear *my desire* on the wicked
Who rise up against me.

¹² The righteous shall flourish like a
   palm tree,
He shall grow like a cedar in Lebanon.
¹³ Those who are planted in the house
   of the LORD

91:3 *a*That is, one who catches birds in a trap or snare

Shall flourish in the courts of our God.
14 They shall still bear fruit in old age;
They shall be fresh and flourishing,
15 To declare that the LORD is upright;
He is my rock, and *there is* no unrighteousness in Him.

PSALM 93

The Eternal Reign of the LORD

1 The LORD reigns, He is clothed with majesty;
The LORD is clothed,
He has girded Himself with strength.
Surely the world is established, so that it cannot be moved.
2 Your throne *is* established from of old;
You *are* from everlasting.

3 The floods have lifted up, O LORD,
The floods have lifted up their voice;
The floods lift up their waves.
4 The LORD on high *is* mightier
Than the noise of many waters,
Than the mighty waves of the sea.

5 Your testimonies are very sure;
Holiness adorns Your house,
O LORD, forever.

PSALM 94

God the Refuge of the Righteous

1 O LORD God, to whom vengeance belongs—
O God, to whom vengeance belongs,
shine forth!
2 Rise up, O Judge of the earth;
Render punishment to the proud.

3 LORD, how long will the wicked,
How long will the wicked triumph?

4 They utter speech, *and* speak insolent things;
All the workers of iniquity boast in themselves.
5 They break in pieces Your people, O LORD,
And afflict Your heritage.
6 They slay the widow and the stranger,
And murder the fatherless.
7 Yet they say, "The LORD does not see,
Nor does the God of Jacob understand."

8 Understand, you senseless among the people;
And *you* fools, when will you be wise?
9 He who planted the ear, shall He not hear?
He who formed the eye, shall He not see?
10 He who instructs the nations, shall He not correct,
He who teaches man knowledge?
11 The LORD knows the thoughts of man,
That they *are* futile.

12 Blessed *is* the man whom You instruct, O LORD,
And teach out of Your law,
13 That You may give him rest from the days of adversity,
Until the pit is dug for the wicked.
14 For the LORD will not cast off His people,
Nor will He forsake His inheritance.
15 But judgment will return to righteousness,
And all the upright in heart will follow it.

16 Who will rise up for me against the evildoers?

Who will stand up for me against the
workers of iniquity?

17 Unless the LORD *had been* my help,
My soul would soon have settled in
silence.

18 If I say, "My foot slips,"
Your mercy, O LORD, will hold me up.

19 In the multitude of my anxieties
within me,
Your comforts delight my soul.

20 Shall the throne of iniquity, which
devises evil by law,
Have fellowship with You?

21 They gather together against the life
of the righteous,
And condemn innocent blood.

22 But the LORD has been my defense,
And my God the rock of my refuge.

23 He has brought on them their own
iniquity,
And shall cut them off in their own
wickedness;
The LORD our God shall cut them off.

PSALM 95

A Call to Worship and Obedience

1 Oh come, let us sing to the LORD!
Let us shout joyfully to the Rock of
our salvation.

2 Let us come before His presence with
thanksgiving;
Let us shout joyfully to Him with
psalms.

3 For the LORD *is* the great God,
And the great King above all gods.

4 In His hand *are* the deep places of the
earth;
The heights of the hills *are* His also.

5 The sea *is* His, for He made it;
And His hands formed the dry *land.*

6 Oh come, let us worship and bow
down;
Let us kneel before the LORD our
Maker.

7 For He *is* our God,
And we *are* the people of His pasture,
And the sheep of His hand.

Today, if you will hear His voice:

8 "Do not harden your hearts, as in the
rebellion,*a*
As *in* the day of trial*b* in the
wilderness,

9 When your fathers tested Me;
They tried Me, though they saw My
work.

10 For forty years I was grieved with *that*
generation,
And said, 'It *is* a people who go astray
in their hearts,
And they do not know My ways.'

11 So I swore in My wrath,
'They shall not enter My rest.' "

> **95:8 the rebellion.** This refers to Meribah (trans-
> lated "rebellion"), the place in the wilderness where
> the Israelites rebelled against the Lord. Their com-
> plaint about lack of water demonstrated their lack of
> faith (Ex. 17:1–17).

PSALM 96

A Song of Praise to God Coming in Judgment

1 Oh, sing to the LORD a new song!
Sing to the LORD, all the earth.

2 Sing to the LORD, bless His name;
Proclaim the good news of His
salvation from day to day.

3 Declare His glory among the nations,
His wonders among all peoples.

4 For the LORD *is* great and greatly to be
praised;
He *is* to be feared above all gods.

5 For all the gods of the peoples *are*
idols,
But the LORD made the heavens.

6 Honor and majesty *are* before Him;
Strength and beauty *are* in His
sanctuary.

7 Give to the LORD, O families of the
peoples,
Give to the LORD glory and strength.

8 Give to the LORD the glory *due* His
name;
Bring an offering, and come into His
courts.

95:8 *a*Or *Meribah*   *b*Or *Massah*

9 Oh, worship the LORD in the beauty
of holiness!
Tremble before Him, all the earth.

10 Say among the nations, "The LORD
reigns;
The world also is firmly established,
It shall not be moved;
He shall judge the peoples righteously."

11 Let the heavens rejoice, and let the
earth be glad;
Let the sea roar, and all its fullness;
12 Let the field be joyful, and all that *is*
in it.
Then all the trees of the woods will
rejoice before the LORD.
13 For He is coming, for He is coming to
judge the earth.
He shall judge the world with
righteousness,
And the peoples with His truth.

96:13 He is coming. The Lord's reign described in
this Psalm is not the present universal kingdom (Ps.
93), but one that will be established when Christ returns to earth.

PSALM 97

A Song of Praise to the Sovereign LORD

1 The LORD reigns;
Let the earth rejoice;
Let the multitude of isles be glad!

2 Clouds and darkness surround Him;
Righteousness and justice *are* the
foundation of His throne.
3 A fire goes before Him,
And burns up His enemies round
about.
4 His lightnings light the world;
The earth sees and trembles.
5 The mountains melt like wax at the
presence of the LORD,
At the presence of the Lord of the
whole earth.
6 The heavens declare His
righteousness,
And all the peoples see His glory.

7 Let all be put to shame who serve
carved images,
Who boast of idols.
Worship Him, all *you* gods.
8 Zion hears and is glad,
And the daughters of Judah rejoice
Because of Your judgments, O LORD.
9 For You, LORD, *are* most high above
all the earth;
You are exalted far above all gods.

97:8 Because of Your judgments. The righteous
judgments of Christ on the peoples of the world will
bring joy and well-being to the messianic kingdom
(see Ps. 48:11).

10 You who love the LORD, hate evil!
He preserves the souls of His saints;
He delivers them out of the hand of
the wicked.
11 Light is sown for the righteous,
And gladness for the upright in heart.
12 Rejoice in the LORD, you righteous,
And give thanks at the remembrance
of His holy name.*a*

PSALM 98

A Song of Praise to the LORD for His
Salvation and Judgment

A Psalm.

1 Oh, sing to the LORD a new song!
For He has done marvelous things;
His right hand and His holy arm have
gained Him the victory.
2 The LORD has made known His
salvation;
His righteousness He has revealed in
the sight of the nations.

98:1 right hand...holy arm. These symbolize power.
the victory. The Lord is often pictured in the Old Testament as a divine warrior (Ex. 15:2,3). According to
the prophets, Christ will begin His millennial reign
after His victory over the nations of the world, which
will gather against Israel in the end times (see Zech.
14:1–15).

97:12 *a*Or *His holiness*

3 He has remembered His mercy and
His faithfulness to the house of
Israel;
All the ends of the earth have seen
the salvation of our God.

4 Shout joyfully to the LORD, all the
earth;
Break forth in song, rejoice, and sing
praises.

5 Sing to the LORD with the harp,
With the harp and the sound of a
psalm,

6 With trumpets and the sound of a
horn;
Shout joyfully before the LORD, the
King.

7 Let the sea roar, and all its fullness,
The world and those who dwell in it;

8 Let the rivers clap *their* hands;
Let the hills be joyful together before
the LORD,

9 For He is coming to judge the earth.
With righteousness He shall judge the
world,
And the peoples with equity.

PSALM 99

Praise to the LORD for His Holiness

1 The LORD reigns;
Let the peoples tremble!
He dwells *between* the cherubim;
Let the earth be moved!

2 The LORD *is* great in Zion,
And He *is* high above all the peoples.

3 Let them praise Your great and
awesome name—
He *is* holy.

4 The King's strength also loves
justice;
You have established equity;
You have executed justice and
righteousness in Jacob.

5 Exalt the LORD our God,
And worship at His footstool—
He *is* holy.

6 Moses and Aaron were among His
priests,
And Samuel was among those who
called upon His name;
They called upon the LORD, and He
answered them.

7 He spoke to them in the cloudy pillar;
They kept His testimonies and the
ordinance He gave them.

8 You answered them, O LORD our
God;
You were to them God-Who-Forgives,
Though You took vengeance on their
deeds.

9 Exalt the LORD our God,
And worship at His holy hill;
For the LORD our God *is* holy.

> **99:1–9** The psalmist encourages praise to the King
> for His holiness, which separates God from all other
> creatures and things. The psalmist exults in the truth
> that such a holy God has had an intimate saving re-
> lationship with Israel throughout her history.

PSALM 100

A Song of Praise for the LORD's Faithfulness to His People

A Psalm of Thanksgiving.

1 Make a joyful shout to the LORD, all
you lands!

2 Serve the LORD with gladness;
Come before His presence with
singing.

3 Know that the LORD, He *is* God;
It is He *who* has made us, and not we
ourselves;[a]

> **100:3 Know.** To be completely assured of the truth.
> **the LORD, He *is* God.** Israel's covenant God, Jehovah,
> is the only true God. **made us.** God made and blessed
> Israel as a nation. **His people...His pasture.** The
> shepherd image suggests God's intimate care (see
> Luke 15:3–6). This whole psalm is a benediction to
> the series of psalms that are occupied with the Lord's
> kingdom rule (Pss. 93;95–100).

100:3 [a]Following Kethib, Septuagint, and Vulgate; Qere, many Hebrew manuscripts, and Targum read
we are His.

We are His people and the sheep of
   His pasture.
4 Enter into His gates with
   thanksgiving,
  And into His courts with praise.
  Be thankful to Him, *and* bless His
   name.
5 For the LORD *is* good;
  His mercy *is* everlasting,
  And His truth *endures* to all
   generations.

PSALM 101

Promised Faithfulness to the LORD

A Psalm of David.

1 I will sing of mercy and justice;
  To You, O LORD, I will sing praises.
2 I will behave wisely in a perfect way.
  Oh, when will You come to me?
  I will walk within my house with a
   perfect heart.

101:2 when will You come to me? David expresses
his personal need for God's immanent involvement
in his earthly kingship. **my house.** The king begins
with his personal life and then looks beyond to his
kingdom.

3 I will set nothing wicked before my
   eyes;
  I hate the work of those who fall
   away;
  It shall not cling to me.
4 A perverse heart shall depart from
   me;
  I will not know wickedness.
5 Whoever secretly slanders his
   neighbor,
  Him I will destroy;
  The one who has a haughty look and
   a proud heart,
  Him I will not endure.
6 My eyes *shall be* on the faithful of the
   land,
  That they may dwell with me;
  He who walks in a perfect way,

He shall serve me.
7 He who works deceit shall not dwell
   within my house;
  He who tells lies shall not continue in
   my presence.
8 Early I will destroy all the wicked of
   the land,
  That I may cut off all the evildoers
   from the city of the LORD.

PSALM 102

The LORD's Eternal Love

*A Prayer of the afflicted, when he is
overwhelmed and pours out his
complaint before the LORD.*

1 Hear my prayer, O LORD,
  And let my cry come to You.
2 Do not hide Your face from me in the
   day of my trouble;
  Incline Your ear to me;
  In the day that I call, answer me
   speedily.
3 For my days are consumed like
   smoke,
  And my bones are burned like a
   hearth.
4 My heart is stricken and withered like
   grass,
  So that I forget to eat my bread.
5 Because of the sound of my groaning
  My bones cling to my skin.
6 I am like a pelican of the wilderness;
  I am like an owl of the desert.
7 I lie awake,
  And am like a sparrow alone on the
   housetop.
8 My enemies reproach me all day long;
  Those who deride me swear an oath
   against me.
9 For I have eaten ashes like bread,
  And mingled my drink with weeping,
10 Because of Your indignation and Your
   wrath;
  For You have lifted me up and cast me
   away.
11 My days *are* like a shadow that
   lengthens,
  And I wither away like grass.

12 But You, O LORD, shall endure
        forever,
    And the remembrance of Your name
        to all generations.
13 You will arise *and* have mercy on
        Zion;
    For the time to favor her,
    Yes, the set time, has come.
14 For Your servants take pleasure in her
        stones,
    And show favor to her dust.
15 So the nations shall fear the name of
        the LORD,
    And all the kings of the earth Your
        glory.
16 For the LORD shall build up Zion;
    He shall appear in His glory.
17 He shall regard the prayer of the
        destitute,
    And shall not despise their prayer.

18 This will be written for the generation
        to come,
    That a people yet to be created may
        praise the LORD.
19 For He looked down from the height
        of His sanctuary;
    From heaven the LORD viewed the
        earth,
20 To hear the groaning of the prisoner,
    To release those appointed to death,
21 To declare the name of the LORD in
        Zion,
    And His praise in Jerusalem,
22 When the peoples are gathered
        together,
    And the kingdoms, to serve the LORD.

23 He weakened my strength in the way;
    He shortened my days.
24 I said, "O my God,
    Do not take me away in the midst of
        my days;
    Your years *are* throughout all
        generations.
25 Of old You laid the foundation of the
        earth,
    And the heavens *are* the work of Your
        hands.
26 They will perish, but You will endure;
    Yes, they will all grow old like a
        garment;
    Like a cloak You will change them,
    And they will be changed.

27 But You *are* the same,
    And Your years will have no end.
28 The children of Your servants will
        continue,
    And their descendants will be
        established before You."

102:25–27 This passage clearly affirms the eternality and deity of Christ, who is superior to the angels (Heb. 1:10–12). He is eternal, while the angels had a beginning. He created, but they were created. The unchangeable God will outlast His creation, even into the new creation (see Mal. 3:6).

PSALM 103

Praise for the LORD's Mercies

A Psalm of David.

1 Bless the LORD, O my soul;
    And all that is within me, *bless* His
        holy name!
2 Bless the LORD, O my soul,
    And forget not all His benefits:
3 Who forgives all your iniquities,
    Who heals all your diseases,
4 Who redeems your life from
        destruction,
    Who crowns you with lovingkindness
        and tender mercies,
5 Who satisfies your mouth with good
        things,
    So that your youth is renewed like the
        eagle's.

103:3 diseases. This is not a promise, but rather a testimony which should be understood in the light of Deut. 32:39.

6 The LORD executes righteousness
    And justice for all who are
        oppressed.
7 He made known His ways to Moses,
    His acts to the children of Israel.
8 The LORD *is* merciful and gracious,
    Slow to anger, and abounding in
        mercy.
9 He will not always strive *with us,*
    Nor will He keep *His anger* forever.
10 He has not dealt with us according to
        our sins,

Nor punished us according to our
    iniquities.

11 For as the heavens are high above the
    earth,
So great is His mercy toward those
    who fear Him;

12 As far as the east is from the west,
So far has He removed our
    transgressions from us.

13 As a father pities *his* children,
So the LORD pities those who fear
    Him.

14 For He knows our frame;
He remembers that we *are* dust.

103:14 dust. As Adam was created of dust (Gen. 2:7), so mankind decomposes into dust at death (Gen. 3:19).

15 *As for* man, his days *are* like grass;
As a flower of the field, so he
    flourishes.

16 For the wind passes over it, and it is
    gone,
And its place remembers it no more.*a*

17 But the mercy of the LORD *is* from
    everlasting to everlasting
On those who fear Him,
And His righteousness to children's
    children,

18 To such as keep His covenant,
And to those who remember His
    commandments to do them.

19 The LORD has established His throne
    in heaven,
And His kingdom rules over all.

20 Bless the LORD, you His angels,
Who excel in strength, who do His
    word,
Heeding the voice of His word.

21 Bless the LORD, all *you* His hosts,
You ministers of His, who do His
    pleasure.

22 Bless the LORD, all His works,
In all places of His dominion.

Bless the LORD, O my soul!

PSALM 104

Praise to the Sovereign LORD for His Creation and Providence

1 Bless the LORD, O my soul!

O LORD my God, You are very great:
You are clothed with honor and
    majesty,

2 Who cover *Yourself* with light as *with*
    a garment,
Who stretch out the heavens like a
    curtain.

3 He lays the beams of His upper
    chambers in the waters,
Who makes the clouds His chariot,
Who walks on the wings of the wind,

4 Who makes His angels spirits,
His ministers a flame of fire.

5 *You who* laid the foundations of the
    earth,
So *that* it should not be moved
    forever,

6 You covered it with the deep as *with* a
    garment;
The waters stood above the
    mountains.

7 At Your rebuke they fled;
At the voice of Your thunder they
    hastened away.

8 They went up over the mountains;
They went down into the valleys,
To the place which You founded for
    them.

9 You have set a boundary that they
    may not pass over,
That they may not return to cover the
    earth.

10 He sends the springs into the valleys;
They flow among the hills.

11 They give drink to every beast of the
    field;
The wild donkeys quench their thirst.

12 By them the birds of the heavens have
    their home;
They sing among the branches.

13 He waters the hills from His upper
    chambers;

103:16 *a*Compare Job 7:10

The earth is satisfied with the fruit of
Your works.

14 He causes the grass to grow for the
cattle,
And vegetation for the service of man,
That he may bring forth food from
the earth,
15 And wine *that* makes glad the heart of
man,
Oil to make *his* face shine,
And bread *which* strengthens man's
heart.
16 The trees of the LORD are full *of sap*,
The cedars of Lebanon which He
planted,
17 Where the birds make their nests;
The stork has her home in the fir
trees.
18 The high hills *are* for the wild goats;
The cliffs are a refuge for the rock
badgers.*a*

19 He appointed the moon for seasons;
The sun knows its going down.
20 You make darkness, and it is night,
In which all the beasts of the forest
creep about.
21 The young lions roar after their prey,
And seek their food from God.
22 *When* the sun rises, they gather
together
And lie down in their dens.
23 Man goes out to his work
And to his labor until the evening.

24 O LORD, how manifold are Your
works!
In wisdom You have made them all.
The earth is full of Your
possessions—
25 This great and wide sea,
In which *are* innumerable teeming
things,
Living things both small and great.
26 There the ships sail about;

104:26 Leviathan. Leviathan refers to some mighty
creature, such as a sea monster or dinosaur, which
can overwhelm man, but who is no match for God
(see Job 3:8).

There is that Leviathan
Which You have made to play there.

27 These all wait for You,
That You may give *them* their food in
due season.
28 *What* You give them they gather in;
You open Your hand, they are filled
with good.
29 You hide Your face, they are troubled;
You take away their breath, they die
and return to their dust.
30 You send forth Your Spirit, they are
created;
And You renew the face of the earth.

31 May the glory of the LORD endure
forever;
May the LORD rejoice in His works.
32 He looks on the earth, and it
trembles;
He touches the hills, and they smoke.

33 I will sing to the LORD as long as I
live;
I will sing praise to my God while I
have my being.
34 May my meditation be sweet to Him;
I will be glad in the LORD.
35 May sinners be consumed from the
earth,
And the wicked be no more.

Bless the LORD, O my soul!
Praise the LORD!

104:1–35 The flow of the psalm loosely follows the
order of creation as first reported in Gen. 1:1–31
but closes with an allusion to the end time events recorded in Rev. 20–22.

PSALM 105

The Eternal Faithfulness of the LORD

1 Oh, give thanks to the LORD!
Call upon His name;
Make known His deeds among the
peoples!
2 Sing to Him, sing psalms to Him;
Talk of all His wondrous works!
3 Glory in His holy name;

104:18 *a*Or *rock hyrax* (compare Leviticus 11:5)

Let the hearts of those rejoice who
    seek the LORD!
4 Seek the LORD and His strength;
    Seek His face evermore!
5 Remember His marvelous works
    which He has done,
    His wonders, and the judgments of
    His mouth,
6 O seed of Abraham His servant,
    You children of Jacob, His chosen
    ones!

7 He *is* the LORD our God;
    His judgments *are* in all the earth.
8 He remembers His covenant forever,
    The word *which* He commanded, for
    a thousand generations,
9 *The covenant* which He made with
    Abraham,
    And His oath to Isaac,
10 And confirmed it to Jacob for a
    statute,
    To Israel *as* an everlasting covenant,
11 Saying, "To you I will give the land of
    Canaan
    As the allotment of your inheritance,"
12 When they were few in number,
    Indeed very few, and strangers in it.

105:10 an everlasting covenant. Five OT covenants
are spoken of as "everlasting": the Noahic Covenant
(Gen. 9:16), the Abrahamic Covenant (Gen. 17:1,13),
the Priestly Covenant (Lev. 24:8), the Davidic Covenant (2 Sam. 23:5), and the New Covenant (Jer.
32:40). "Everlasting" indicates from the time of the
covenant into eternity.

13 When they went from one nation to
    another,
    From *one* kingdom to another people,
14 He permitted no one to do them
    wrong;
    Yes, He rebuked kings for their sakes,
15 *Saying,* "Do not touch My anointed
    ones,
    And do My prophets no harm."

16 Moreover He called for a famine in
    the land;
    He destroyed all the provision of
    bread.
17 He sent a man before them—
    Joseph—*who* was sold as a slave.

18 They hurt his feet with fetters,
    He was laid in irons.
19 Until the time that his word came to
    pass,
    The word of the LORD tested him.
20 The king sent and released him,
    The ruler of the people let him go
    free.
21 He made him lord of his house,
    And ruler of all his possessions,
22 To bind his princes at his pleasure,
    And teach his elders wisdom.

23 Israel also came into Egypt,
    And Jacob dwelt in the land of Ham.
24 He increased His people greatly,
    And made them stronger than their
    enemies.
25 He turned their heart to hate His
    people,
    To deal craftily with His servants.

105:1–45 The Psalm looks at Israel's history first
from God's perspective and then from Israel's. It may
have originated by a command of David to Asaph, for
the occasion when the ark of the covenant was first
brought to Jerusalem (2 Sam. 6:12–19).

26 He sent Moses His servant,
    And Aaron whom He had chosen.
27 They performed His signs among
    them,
    And wonders in the land of Ham.
28 He sent darkness, and made *it* dark;
    And they did not rebel against His
    word.
29 He turned their waters into blood,
    And killed their fish.
30 Their land abounded with frogs,
    Even in the chambers of their kings.
31 He spoke, and there came swarms of
    flies,
    And lice in all their territory.
32 He gave them hail for rain,
    And flaming fire in their land.
33 He struck their vines also, and their
    fig trees,
    And splintered the trees of their
    territory.
34 He spoke, and locusts came,
    Young locusts without number,
35 And ate up all the vegetation in their
    land,

And devoured the fruit of their
    ground.

36 He also destroyed all the firstborn in
    their land,
    The first of all their strength.

37 He also brought them out with silver
    and gold,
    And *there was* none feeble among His
    tribes.

38 Egypt was glad when they departed,
    For the fear of them had fallen upon
    them.

39 He spread a cloud for a covering,
    And fire to give light in the night.

40 *The people* asked, and He brought
    quail,
    And satisfied them with the bread of
    heaven.

41 He opened the rock, and water gushed
    out;
    It ran in the dry places *like* a river.

42 For He remembered His holy promise,
    And Abraham His servant.

43 He brought out His people with joy,
    His chosen ones with gladness.

44 He gave them the lands of the
    Gentiles,
    And they inherited the labor of the
    nations,

45 That they might observe His statutes
    And keep His laws.

Praise the LORD!

> **105:42–45** The psalmist concludes with a summary that alludes to Joshua's leading the nation back into the Land, which was first promised to Abraham (Josh. 1–12) and then distributed to the 12 tribes of Israel (Josh. 13–24). God delivered what He promised.

PSALM 106

Joy in Forgiveness of Israel's Sins

1 Praise the LORD!

Oh, give thanks to the LORD, for *He is*
    good!
For His mercy *endures* forever.

2 Who can utter the mighty acts of the
    LORD?
Who can declare all His praise?

3 Blessed *are* those who keep justice,
    And he who does*ª* righteousness at all
    times!

4 Remember me, O LORD, with the
    favor *You have toward* Your
    people.
Oh, visit me with Your salvation,

5 That I may see the benefit of Your
    chosen ones,
That I may rejoice in the gladness of
    Your nation,
That I may glory with Your
    inheritance.

6 We have sinned with our fathers,
We have committed iniquity,
We have done wickedly.

7 Our fathers in Egypt did not
    understand Your wonders;
They did not remember the multitude
    of Your mercies,
But rebelled by the sea—the Red Sea.

8 Nevertheless He saved them for His
    name's sake,
That He might make His mighty
    power known.

9 He rebuked the Red Sea also, and it
    dried up;
So He led them through the depths,
As through the wilderness.

10 He saved them from the hand of him
    who hated *them*,
And redeemed them from the hand of
    the enemy.

11 The waters covered their enemies;
There was not one of them left.

12 Then they believed His words;
They sang His praise.

> **106:8 His name's sake.** God glory's and reputation provide the highest motive for His actions. This phrase appears in 6 other places in the Psalms (see Pss. 23:3; 25:11; 31:3; 79:9; 109:21; 143:11).

13 They soon forgot His works;
They did not wait for His counsel,

106:3 *ª*Septuagint, Syriac, Targum, and Vulgate read *those who do.*

14 But lusted exceedingly in the
    wilderness,
    And tested God in the desert.
15 And He gave them their request,
    But sent leanness into their soul.

16 When they envied Moses in the camp,
    And Aaron the saint of the LORD,
17 The earth opened up and swallowed
    Dathan,
    And covered the faction of Abiram.
18 A fire was kindled in their company;
    The flame burned up the wicked.

106:16–19 Korah, who is not named here, led the rebellion that is recounted (see Num. 16:1–35). As judgment, God sent fire that killed 250 men (see Num. 16:35). **Horeb.** Another name for Mount Sinai (see Ex. 19:11). This special place, called "the mountain of God" (see Ex. 3:1), is where Moses received the commandments of God (Deut. 1:6).

19 They made a calf in Horeb,
    And worshiped the molded image.
20 Thus they changed their glory
    Into the image of an ox that eats
    grass.
21 They forgot God their Savior,
    Who had done great things in Egypt,
22 Wondrous works in the land of Ham,
    Awesome things by the Red Sea.
23 Therefore He said that He would
    destroy them,
    Had not Moses His chosen one stood
    before Him in the breach,
    To turn away His wrath, lest He
    destroy *them.*

24 Then they despised the pleasant land;
    They did not believe His word,
25 But complained in their tents,
    And did not heed the voice of the
    LORD.
26 Therefore He raised His hand *in an*
    oath against them,
    To overthrow them in the wilderness,
27 To overthrow their descendants
    among the nations,
    And to scatter them in the lands.

28 They joined themselves also to Baal
    of Peor,
    And ate sacrifices made to the dead.
29 Thus they provoked *Him* to anger
    with their deeds,
    And the plague broke out among
    them.
30 Then Phinehas stood up and
    intervened,
    And the plague was stopped.
31 And that was accounted to him for
    righteousness
    To all generations forevermore.

106:28–31 This deals with Israel's encounter with the prophet Balaam, who tried to curse Israel on behalf of Balak, King of Moab. God prevented him from cursing Israel. (see Num. 22–24). Balaam failed and advised Balak to entice Israel with immorality and idolatry (see Num. 31:16). Israel sinned, God judged (Num. 25:1–13), and Balaam was later slain by Israel (see Josh. 13:22).

32 They angered *Him* also at the waters
    of strife,[a]
    So that it went ill with Moses on
    account of them;
33 Because they rebelled against His
    Spirit,
    So that he spoke rashly with his lips.

34 They did not destroy the peoples,
    Concerning whom the LORD had
    commanded them,
35 But they mingled with the Gentiles
    And learned their works;
36 They served their idols,
    Which became a snare to them.
37 They even sacrificed their sons
    And their daughters to demons,
38 And shed innocent blood,
    The blood of their sons and
    daughters,
    Whom they sacrificed to the idols of
    Canaan;
    And the land was polluted with blood.
39 Thus they were defiled by their own
    works,
    And played the harlot by their own
    deeds.

106:39 their own works...deeds. God held Israel directly responsible for their sin without excuse.

106:32 [a]Or *Meribah*

40 Therefore the wrath of the LORD was
kindled against His people,
So that He abhorred His own
inheritance.
41 And He gave them into the hand of
the Gentiles,
And those who hated them ruled over
them.
42 Their enemies also oppressed them,
And they were brought into
subjection under their hand.
43 Many times He delivered them;
But they rebelled in their counsel,
And were brought low for their
iniquity.
44 Nevertheless He regarded their
affliction,
When He heard their cry;
45 And for their sake He remembered
His covenant,
And relented according to the
multitude of His mercies.
46 He also made them to be pitied
By all those who carried them away
captive.

47 Save us, O LORD our God,
And gather us from among the
Gentiles,
To give thanks to Your holy name,
To triumph in Your praise.

48 Blessed be the LORD God of Israel
From everlasting to everlasting!
And let all the people say, "Amen!"

Praise the LORD!

Book Five: Psalms 107–150

PSALM 107

Thanksgiving to the LORD for His Great Works of Deliverance

1 Oh, give thanks to the LORD, for He is
good!
For His mercy endures forever.
2 Let the redeemed of the LORD say so,
Whom He has redeemed from the
hand of the enemy,
3 And gathered out of the lands,
From the east and from the west,
From the north and from the south.
4 They wandered in the wilderness in a
desolate way;
They found no city to dwell in.
5 Hungry and thirsty,
Their soul fainted in them.
6 Then they cried out to the LORD in
their trouble,
And He delivered them out of their
distresses.
7 And He led them forth by the right
way,
That they might go to a city for a
dwelling place.
8 Oh, that men would give thanks to
the LORD for His goodness,
And for His wonderful works to the
children of men!
9 For He satisfies the longing soul,
And fills the hungry soul with
goodness.

107:4–9 Here the psalmist may be remembering Israel, ungrateful and faithless, wandering in the desert after the miraculous Exodus (Num. 14–Josh. 2).

10 Those who sat in darkness and in the
shadow of death,
Bound in affliction and irons—
11 Because they rebelled against the
words of God,
And despised the counsel of the Most
High,
12 Therefore He brought down their
heart with labor;
They fell down, and there was none
to help.
13 Then they cried out to the LORD in
their trouble,
And He saved them out of their
distresses.
14 He brought them out of darkness and
the shadow of death,
And broke their chains in pieces.
15 Oh, that men would give thanks to
the LORD for His goodness,
And for His wonderful works to the
children of men!

16 For He has broken the gates of
   bronze,
   And cut the bars of iron in two.

17 Fools, because of their transgression,
   And because of their iniquities, were
   afflicted.
18 Their soul abhorred all manner of
   food,
   And they drew near to the gates of
   death.
19 Then they cried out to the LORD in
   their trouble,
   And He saved them out of their
   distresses.
20 He sent His word and healed them,
   And delivered *them* from their
   destructions.
21 Oh, that *men* would give thanks to
   the LORD *for* His goodness,
   And *for* His wonderful works to the
   children of men!
22 Let them sacrifice the sacrifices of
   thanksgiving,
   And declare His works with rejoicing.

23 Those who go down to the sea in
   ships,
   Who do business on great waters,
24 They see the works of the LORD,
   And His wonders in the deep.
25 For He commands and raises the
   stormy wind,
   Which lifts up the waves of the sea.
26 They mount up to the heavens,
   They go down again to the depths;
   Their soul melts because of trouble.
27 They reel to and fro, and stagger like a
   drunken man,
   And are at their wits' end.
28 Then they cry out to the LORD in
   their trouble,
   And He brings them out of their
   distresses.
29 He calms the storm,
   So that its waves are still.
30 Then they are glad because they are
   quiet;
   So He guides them to their desired
   haven.
31 Oh, that *men* would give thanks to
   the LORD *for* His goodness,
   And *for* His wonderful works to the
   children of men!

32 Let them exalt Him also in the
   assembly of the people,
   And praise Him in the company of
   the elders.

107:4–32 Four situations led to the end of sin in the nation of Israel: wandering in the wilderness, languishing in prison, enduring sickness, and tossing on a stormy sea. Each situation was patterned on four specific events: man's predicament, man's petition, God's pardon, and man's praise.

33 He turns rivers into a wilderness,
   And the watersprings into dry ground;
34 A fruitful land into barrenness,
   For the wickedness of those who dwell
   in it.
35 He turns a wilderness into pools of
   water,
   And dry land into watersprings.
36 There He makes the hungry dwell,
   That they may establish a city for a
   dwelling place,
37 And sow fields and plant vineyards,
   That they may yield a fruitful
   harvest.
38 He also blesses them, and they
   multiply greatly;
   And He does not let their cattle
   decrease.

39 When they are diminished and
   brought low
   Through oppression, affliction and
   sorrow,
40 He pours contempt on princes,
   And causes them to wander in the
   wilderness *where there is* no way;
41 Yet He sets the poor on high, far from
   affliction,
   And makes *their* families like a flock.
42 The righteous see *it* and rejoice,
   And all iniquity stops its mouth.

107:39,40 This refers to either the Assyrian Exile (2 Kin. 17:4–6) or the Babylonian Captivity (2 Kin. 24:14,15).

43 Whoever *is* wise will observe these
   things,
   And they will understand the
   lovingkindness of the LORD.

PSALM 108

Assurance of God's Victory over Enemies

A Song. A Psalm of David.

1 O God, my heart is steadfast;
    I will sing and give praise, even with
        my glory.
2 Awake, lute and harp!
    I will awaken the dawn.
3 I will praise You, O LORD, among the
        peoples,
    And I will sing praises to You among
        the nations.
4 For Your mercy *is* great above the
        heavens,
    And Your truth *reaches* to the
        clouds.

5 Be exalted, O God, above the
        heavens,
    And Your glory above all the earth;
6 That Your beloved may be delivered,
    Save *with* Your right hand, and hear
        me.

7 God has spoken in His holiness:
    "I will rejoice;
    I will divide Shechem
    And measure out the Valley of
        Succoth.
8 Gilead *is* Mine; Manasseh *is* Mine;
    Ephraim also *is* the helmet for My
        head;
    Judah *is* My lawgiver.
9 Moab *is* My washpot;
    Over Edom I will cast My shoe;
    Over Philistia I will triumph."

10 Who will bring me *into* the strong
        city?
    Who will lead me to Edom?
11 *Is it* not You, O God, *who* cast us off?
    And You, O God, *who* did not go out
        with our armies?
12 Give us help from trouble,
    For the help of man is useless.
13 Through God we will do valiantly,
    For *it is* He *who* shall tread down our
        enemies.[a]

PSALM 109

Plea for Judgment of False Accusers

To the Chief Musician. A Psalm of David.

1 Do not keep silent,
    O God of my praise!
2 For the mouth of the wicked and the
        mouth of the deceitful
    Have opened against me;
    They have spoken against me with a
        lying tongue.
3 They have also surrounded me with
        words of hatred,
    And fought against me without a
        cause.
4 In return for my love they are my
        accusers,
    But I *give myself to* prayer.
5 Thus they have rewarded me evil for
        good,
    And hatred for my love.

6 Set a wicked man over him,
    And let an accuser[a] stand at his right
        hand.
7 When he is judged, let him be found
        guilty,
    And let his prayer become sin.
8 Let his days be few,
    And let another take his office.
9 Let his children be fatherless,
    And his wife a widow.
10 Let his children continually be
        vagabonds, and beg;
    Let them seek *their bread*[a] also from
        their desolate places.
11 Let the creditor seize all that he has,
    And let strangers plunder his labor.
12 Let there be none to extend mercy to
        him,
    Nor let there be any to favor his
        fatherless children.
13 Let his posterity be cut off,
    And in the generation following let
        their name be blotted out.

> **109:8** The Apostle Peter cited this verse as justification for replacing Judas, the betrayer, with another apostle (see Acts. 1:20).

108:13 [a]Compare verses 6–13 with 60:5–12   109:6 [a]Hebrew *satan*   109:10 [a]Following Masoretic Text and Targum; Septuagint and Vulgate read *be cast out*.

¹⁴ Let the iniquity of his fathers be
     remembered before the LORD,
   And let not the sin of his mother be
     blotted out.
¹⁵ Let them be continually before the
     LORD,
   That He may cut off the memory of
     them from the earth;
¹⁶ Because he did not remember to show
     mercy,
   But persecuted the poor and needy
     man,
   That he might even slay the broken in
     heart.
¹⁷ As he loved cursing, so let it come to
     him;
   As he did not delight in blessing, so
     let it be far from him.
¹⁸ As he clothed himself with cursing as
     with his garment,
   So let it enter his body like water,
   And like oil into his bones.
¹⁹ Let it be to him like the garment
     which covers him,
   And for a belt with which he girds
     himself continually.
²⁰ *Let* this *be* the LORD's reward to my
     accusers,
   And to those who speak evil against
     my person.

²¹ But You, O GOD the Lord,
   Deal with me for Your name's sake;
   Because Your mercy *is* good, deliver me.
²² For I *am* poor and needy,
   And my heart is wounded within me.
²³ I am gone like a shadow when it
     lengthens;
   I am shaken off like a locust.
²⁴ My knees are weak through fasting,
   And my flesh is feeble from lack of
     fatness.
²⁵ I also have become a reproach to them;
   When they look at me, they shake
     their heads.

²⁶ Help me, O LORD my God!
   Oh, save me according to Your mercy,
²⁷ That they may know that this *is* Your
     hand—
   That You, LORD, have done it!
²⁸ Let them curse, but You bless;
   When they arise, let them be
     ashamed,

But let Your servant rejoice.
²⁹ Let my accusers be clothed with
     shame,
   And let them cover themselves with
     their own disgrace as with a
     mantle.

³⁰ I will greatly praise the LORD with my
     mouth;
   Yes, I will praise Him among the
     multitude.
³¹ For He shall stand at the right hand of
     the poor,
   To save *him* from those who condemn
     him.

PSALM 110

Announcement of the Messiah's Reign

A Psalm of David.

¹ The LORD said to my Lord,
 "Sit at My right hand,
   Till I make Your enemies Your
     footstool."
² The LORD shall send the rod of Your
     strength out of Zion.
   Rule in the midst of Your enemies!

110:1 my Lord. Jesus is the divine/human King of Israel. His humanity descended from David (2 Sam. 7:12), and His deity is shown in the Gospels. Jesus argues that only God could have been Lord to King David (Matt. 22:44). **Your enemies Your footstool.** This implies absolute victory, with one's enemy underfoot (see Ps 8:6,7). It anticipates Jesus' second coming (see Rev. 19:11–21) as a conquering King (see Heb. 10:13).

³ Your people *shall be* volunteers
   In the day of Your power;
   In the beauties of holiness, from the
     womb of the morning,
   You have the dew of Your youth.
⁴ The LORD has sworn
   And will not relent,

110:4 You *are* a priest. This describes the first time in Israel when a king served also as High-Priest. **the order of Melchizedek.** Melchizedek means "king of righteousness." He served as the human priest/king of Salem (Gen. 14:17–20). This provides a picture of the order of Christ's priesthood (see Heb. 5:6,7).

"You *are* a priest forever
According to the order of
   Melchizedek."

5 The Lord *is* at Your right hand;
He shall execute kings in the day of
   His wrath.
6 He shall judge among the nations,
He shall fill *the places* with dead
   bodies,
He shall execute the heads of many
   countries.

110:1–7 Jesus Christ is presented as a holy King and as a royal High-Priest, something that no human king of Israel ever experienced. Christ is now the resurrected Savior in heaven, and in the future He will reign as King on earth. We may associate this messianic psalm with God's declaration of the Davidic Covenant in 2 Sam. 7:4–17.

7 He shall drink of the brook by the
   wayside;
Therefore He shall lift up the head.

111:1–10 Psalms 111 and 112 are alike. Both are acrostics with 22 lines corresponding with 22 letters of the Hebrew alphabet, and both begin with "Praise the LORD!" This psalm exalts the works of God. The author(s) and occasion(s) are unknown.

PSALM 111

Praise to God for His Faithfulness and Justice

1 Praise the LORD!

I will praise the LORD with *my* whole
   heart,
In the assembly of the upright and *in*
   the congregation.

CHRIST IN THE PSALMS (LUKE 24:44)

Psalms	NT Quote	Significance
2:1–12	Acts 4:25,26; 13:33; Hebrews 1:5; 5:5	Incarnation, Crucifixion, Resurrection
8:3–8	1 Corinthians 15:27,28; Ephesians 1:22; Hebrews 2:5–10	Creation
16:8–11	Acts 2:24–31; 13:35–37	Death, Resurrection
22:1–31	Matthew 27:35–46; John 19:23,24; Hebrews 2:12; 5:5	Incarnation, Crucifixion, Resurrection
40:6–8	Hebrews 10:5–9	Incarnation
41:9	John 13:18,21	Betrayal
45:6,7	Hebrews 1:8,9	Deity
68:18	Ephesians 4:8	Ascension, Enthronement
69:20,21,25	Matthew 27:34,48; Acts 1:15–20	Betrayal, Crucifixion
72:6–17	———	Millennial Kingship
78:1,2,15	Matthew 13:35; 1 Corinthians 10:4	Theophany, Earthly teaching ministry
89:3–37	Acts 2:30	Millennial Kingship
102:25–27	Hebrews 1:10–12	Creation, Eternality
109:6–19	Acts 1:15–20	Betrayal
110:1–7	Matthew 22:43–45; Acts 2:33–35; Hebrews 1:13; 5:10; 6:20; 7:24	Deity, Ascension, Heavenly Priesthood, Millennial Kingship
118:22,23	Matthew 21:42; Mark 12:10,11; Luke 20:17; Acts 4:8–12; 1 Peter 2:7	Rejection as Savior
132:12–18	Acts 2:30	Millennial Kingship

2 The works of the LORD *are* great,
Studied by all who have pleasure in
them.
3 His work *is* honorable and glorious,
And His righteousness endures
forever.
4 He has made His wonderful works to
be remembered;
The LORD *is* gracious and full of
compassion.
5 He has given food to those who fear
Him;
He will ever be mindful of His
covenant.
6 He has declared to His people the
power of His works,
In giving them the heritage of the
nations.

7 The works of His hands *are* verity
and justice;
All His precepts *are* sure.
8 They stand fast forever and ever,
And are done in truth and
uprightness.
9 He has sent redemption to His
people;
He has commanded His covenant
forever:
Holy and awesome *is* His name.

10 The fear of the LORD *is* the beginning
of wisdom;
A good understanding have all those
who do *His commandments.*
His praise endures forever.

PSALM 112

The Blessed State of the Righteous

1 Praise the LORD!

Blessed *is* the man *who* fears the
LORD,
Who delights greatly in His
commandments.

2 His descendants will be mighty on
earth;
The generation of the upright will be
blessed.
3 Wealth and riches *will be* in his
house,

And his righteousness endures
forever.
4 Unto the upright there arises light in
the darkness;
He is gracious, and full of
compassion, and righteous.
5 A good man deals graciously and
lends;
He will guide his affairs with
discretion.
6 Surely he will never be shaken;
The righteous will be in everlasting
remembrance.
7 He will not be afraid of evil tidings;
His heart is steadfast, trusting in the
LORD.
8 His heart *is* established;
He will not be afraid,
Until he sees *his desire* upon his
enemies.
9 He has dispersed abroad,
He has given to the poor;
His righteousness endures forever;
His horn will be exalted with honor.
10 The wicked will see *it* and be grieved;
He will gnash his teeth and melt
away;
The desire of the wicked shall perish.

PSALM 113

The Majesty and Condescension of God

1 Praise the LORD!

Praise, O servants of the LORD,
Praise the name of the LORD!
2 Blessed be the name of the LORD
From this time forth and
forevermore!
3 From the rising of the sun to its going
down
The LORD's name *is* to be praised.

113:1 servants. This refers to the redeemed, all of
whom should serve God with obedience. **the name.**
The name of God represents all of His attributes.

4 The LORD *is* high above all nations,
His glory above the heavens.
5 Who *is* like the LORD our God,
Who dwells on high,

6   Who humbles Himself to behold
    The things that are in the heavens
        and in the earth?

7   He raises the poor out of the dust,
    And lifts the needy out of the ash
        heap,
8   That He may seat *him* with
        princes—
    With the princes of His people.
9   He grants the barren woman a
        home,
    Like a joyful mother of children.

    Praise the LORD!

113:7–9 the poor. This is borrowed from Hannah's song in 1 Sam. 2:8. God is responsible for both the rich and the poor, yet He shows compassion on the poor and needy. Christ came to save those who are poor in spirit (see Is. 61:2; Prov. 22:2; Ps. 72:12). **the barren woman.** Sarah (Gen. 21:2), Rebekah (Gen. 25:21), and Rachel (Gen. 30:23) are significant since the Abrahamic Covenant depended on them to be mothers.

PSALM 114

The Power of God in His Deliverance of Israel

1   When Israel went out of Egypt,
    The house of Jacob from a people of
        strange language,
2   Judah became His sanctuary,
    And Israel His dominion.

3   The sea saw *it* and fled;
    Jordan turned back.
4   The mountains skipped like rams,
    The little hills like lambs.
5   What ails you, O sea, that you fled?
    O Jordan, *that* you turned back?
6   O mountains, *that* you skipped like
        rams?
    O little hills, like lambs?

7   Tremble, O earth, at the presence of
        the Lord,
    At the presence of the God of Jacob,
8   Who turned the rock *into* a pool of
        water,
    The flint into a fountain of waters.

PSALM 115

The Futility of Idols and the Trustworthiness of God

1   Not unto us, O LORD, not unto us,
    But to Your name give glory,
    Because of Your mercy,
    Because of Your truth.
2   Why should the Gentiles say,
    "So where *is* their God?"

3   But our God *is* in heaven;
    He does whatever He pleases.
4   Their idols *are* silver and gold,
    The work of men's hands.
5   They have mouths, but they do not
        speak;
    Eyes they have, but they do not see;
6   They have ears, but they do not hear;
    Noses they have, but they do not
        smell;
7   They have hands, but they do not
        handle;
    Feet they have, but they do not walk;
    Nor do they mutter through their
        throat.
8   Those who make them are like them;
    So is everyone who trusts in them.

9   O Israel, trust in the LORD;
    He *is* their help and their shield.
10 O house of Aaron, trust in the LORD;
    He *is* their help and their shield.
11 You who fear the LORD, trust in the
        LORD;
    He *is* their help and their shield.

12 The LORD has been mindful of *us*;
    He will bless us;
    He will bless the house of Israel;
    He will bless the house of Aaron.
13 He will bless those who fear the
        LORD,
    Both small and great.

14 May the LORD give you increase more
        and more,
    You and your children.
15 *May* you *be* blessed by the LORD,
    Who made heaven and earth.

16 The heaven, *even* the heavens, *are*
        the LORD's;

But the earth He has given to the
children of men.
17 The dead do not praise the LORD,
Nor any who go down into silence.
18 But we will bless the LORD
From this time forth and forevermore.

Praise the LORD!

PSALM 116

Thanksgiving for Deliverance from Death

1 I love the LORD, because He has heard
My voice and my supplications.
2 Because He has inclined His ear to
me,
Therefore I will call upon Him as long
as I live.

3 The pains of death surrounded me,
And the pangs of Sheol laid hold of
me;
I found trouble and sorrow.
4 Then I called upon the name of the
LORD:
"O LORD, I implore You, deliver my
soul!"

116:3 Sheol. This is another term for grave/death.

5 Gracious is the LORD, and righteous;
Yes, our God is merciful.
6 The LORD preserves the simple;
I was brought low, and He saved me.
7 Return to your rest, O my soul,
For the LORD has dealt bountifully
with you.

8 For You have delivered my soul from
death,
My eyes from tears,
And my feet from falling.
9 I will walk before the LORD
In the land of the living.
10 I believed, therefore I spoke,
"I am greatly afflicted."
11 I said in my haste,
"All men are liars."

12 What shall I render to the LORD
For all His benefits toward me?
13 I will take up the cup of salvation,

116:13 the cup of salvation. This is the only time in the OT where this exact phrase is used. It could refer to the cup in Pss. 16:5 and 23:5, which represents the redeemed life provided by God.

And call upon the name of the LORD.
14 I will pay my vows to the LORD
Now in the presence of all His people.

15 Precious in the sight of the LORD
Is the death of His saints.

16 O LORD, truly I am Your servant;
I am Your servant, the son of Your
maidservant;
You have loosed my bonds.
17 I will offer to You the sacrifice of
thanksgiving,
And will call upon the name of the
LORD.

18 I will pay my vows to the LORD
Now in the presence of all His people,
19 In the courts of the LORD's house,
In the midst of you, O Jerusalem.

Praise the LORD!

116:1–19 The psalmist thanks the Lord for saving him from death. The occasion and author are unknown, although the language used by Jonah in his prayer from the fish's stomach is similar. This appears to deal with physical death, but it could also refer to spiritual death.

PSALM 117

Let All Peoples Praise the LORD

1 Praise the LORD, all you Gentiles!
Laud Him, all you peoples!
2 For His merciful kindness is great
toward us,
And the truth of the LORD endures
forever.

Praise the LORD!

117:1,2 The seal of redemptive truth is found in this psalm. It is the shortest psalm, the shortest chapter in the Bible, and it is the middle chapter of the Bible. The psalm looks back to God's intent for Adam and Eve in Eden (Gen. 1,2), and it looks ahead to the ultimate fulfillment in the new heaven and earth (Rev. 21,22).

PSALM 118

Praise to God for His Everlasting Mercy

1 Oh, give thanks to the LORD, for *He is*
    good!
  For His mercy *endures* forever.

2 Let Israel now say,
  "His mercy *endures* forever."
3 Let the house of Aaron now say,
  "His mercy *endures* forever."
4 Let those who fear the LORD now say,
  "His mercy *endures* forever."

5 I called on the LORD in distress;
  The LORD answered me *and set me* in
    a broad place.
6 The LORD *is* on my side;
  I will not fear.
  What can man do to me?
7 The LORD is for me among those who
    help me;
  Therefore I shall see *my desire* on
    those who hate me.
8 *It is* better to trust in the LORD
  Than to put confidence in man.
9 *It is* better to trust in the LORD
  Than to put confidence in princes.

10 All nations surrounded me,
  But in the name of the LORD I will
    destroy them.
11 They surrounded me,
  Yes, they surrounded me;
  But in the name of the LORD I will
    destroy them.
12 They surrounded me like bees;
  They were quenched like a fire of
    thorns;
  For in the name of the LORD I will
    destroy them.
13 You pushed me violently, that I might
    fall,
  But the LORD helped me.
14 The LORD *is* my strength and song,
  And He has become my salvation.[a]

15 The voice of rejoicing and salvation
  Is in the tents of the righteous;
  The right hand of the LORD does
    valiantly.
16 The right hand of the LORD is
    exalted;
  The right hand of the LORD does
    valiantly.
17 I shall not die, but live,
  And declare the works of the LORD.
18 The LORD has chastened me severely,
  But He has not given me over to
    death.

19 Open to me the gates of
    righteousness;
  I will go through them,
  And I will praise the LORD.
20 This is the gate of the LORD,
  Through which the righteous shall
    enter.
21 I will praise You,
  For You have answered me,
  And have become my salvation.

22 The stone *which* the builders
    rejected
  Has become the chief cornerstone.
23 This was the LORD's doing;
  It *is* marvelous in our eyes.
24 This *is* the day the LORD has made;
  We will rejoice and be glad in it.

118:22 stone...builders rejected...chief cornerstone. Peter identified the chief cornerstone as Christ (Acts 4:11). Matt. 21:42 likens the rejected son of the vineyard owner to the rejected stone, which became the chief cornerstone (Christ). The experience of Moses, as a type of Christ, pictured Christ's rejection. Moses (stone) was rejected by the Jews (builders) as their God sent the deliverer (chief cornerstone).

25 Save now, I pray, O LORD;
  O LORD, I pray, send now prosperity.
26 Blessed *is* he who comes in the name
    of the LORD!
  We have blessed you from the house
    of the LORD.
27 God *is* the LORD,
  And He has given us light;
  Bind the sacrifice with cords to the
    horns of the altar.
28 You *are* my God, and I will praise You;
  You are my God, I will exalt You.

118:14 [a]Compare Exodus 15:2

118:22–26 This psalm, along with Ps. 110, is intensely messianic and is the most quoted in the NT. If Moses is the author, then the NT writers use a perfect analogy in connecting this passage to Christ. Moses said that God would raise up another prophet like himself (Deut. 18:15). Peter identified this other prophet as Jesus (see Acts 3:11–26). Moses, then, is a biblically recognized type of Christ.

29 Oh, give thanks to the LORD, for *He is* good!
For His mercy *endures* forever.

PSALM 119

Meditations on the Excellencies of the Word of God

א ALEPH
1 Blessed *are* the undefiled in the way,
Who walk in the law of the LORD!
2 Blessed *are* those who keep His testimonies,
Who seek Him with the whole heart!
3 They also do no iniquity;
They walk in His ways.
4 You have commanded *us*
To keep Your precepts diligently.
5 Oh, that my ways were directed
To keep Your statutes!
6 Then I would not be ashamed,
When I look into all Your commandments.
7 I will praise You with uprightness of heart,
When I learn Your righteous judgments.
8 I will keep Your statutes;
Oh, do not forsake me utterly!

119:2 the whole heart. "Heart" refers to intellect, volition, and emotion. Complete commitment, or "whole heart" appears 6 times.

ב BETH
9 How can a young man cleanse his way?
By taking heed according to Your word.
10 With my whole heart I have sought You;
Oh, let me not wander from Your commandments!

11 Your word I have hidden in my heart,
That I might not sin against You.
12 Blessed *are* You, O LORD!
Teach me Your statutes.
13 With my lips I have declared
All the judgments of Your mouth.
14 I have rejoiced in the way of Your testimonies,
As *much as* in all riches.
15 I will meditate on Your precepts,
And contemplate Your ways.
16 I will delight myself in Your statutes;
I will not forget Your word.

ג GIMEL
17 Deal bountifully with Your servant,
That I may live and keep Your word.
18 Open my eyes, that I may see
Wondrous things from Your law.
19 I *am* a stranger in the earth;
Do not hide Your commandments from me.
20 My soul breaks with longing
For Your judgments at all times.
21 You rebuke the proud—the cursed,
Who stray from Your commandments.
22 Remove from me reproach and contempt,
For I have kept Your testimonies.
23 Princes also sit *and* speak against me,
But Your servant meditates on Your statutes.
24 Your testimonies also *are* my delight
And my counselors.

119:1–176 Psalm 119, the longest psalm and chapter in the Bible, exalts God's Word in the form of an acrostic containing 22 sections, each with 8 lines. Scriptural themes occur in each line, including law, testimonies, precepts, statutes, commandments, judgments, word, and ordinances. From before sunrise to beyond sunset, the Word of God dominated the psalmist's life.

ד DALETH
25 My soul clings to the dust;
Revive me according to Your word.
26 I have declared my ways, and You answered me;
Teach me Your statutes.
27 Make me understand the way of Your precepts;

So shall I meditate on Your wonderful
    works.
28 My soul melts from heaviness;
    Strengthen me according to Your
    word.
29 Remove from me the way of lying,
    And grant me Your law graciously.
30 I have chosen the way of truth;
    Your judgments I have laid *before me.*
31 I cling to Your testimonies;
    O Lord, do not put me to shame!
32 I will run the course of Your
    commandments,
    For You shall enlarge my heart.

ה HE

33 Teach me, O Lord, the way of Your
    statutes,
    And I shall keep it *to* the end.
34 Give me understanding, and I shall
    keep Your law;
    Indeed, I shall observe it with *my*
    whole heart.
35 Make me walk in the path of Your
    commandments,
    For I delight in it.
36 Incline my heart to Your testimonies,
    And not to covetousness.
37 Turn away my eyes from looking at
    worthless things,
    And revive me in Your way.[a]
38 Establish Your word to Your servant,
    Who *is devoted* to fearing You.
39 Turn away my reproach which I
    dread,
    For Your judgments *are* good.
40 Behold, I long for Your precepts;
    Revive me in Your righteousness.

119:39 good. The very attributes of God become the characteristics of Scripture. Scripture is trustworthy, true, faithful, unchangeable, eternal, and pure.

ו WAW

41 Let Your mercies come also to me,
    O Lord—
    Your salvation according to Your
    word.
42 So shall I have an answer for him who
    reproaches me,
    For I trust in Your word.
43 And take not the word of truth utterly
    out of my mouth,
    For I have hoped in Your ordinances.
44 So shall I keep Your law continually,
    Forever and ever.
45 And I will walk at liberty,
    For I seek Your precepts.
46 I will speak of Your testimonies also
    before kings,
    And will not be ashamed.
47 And I will delight myself in Your
    commandments,
    Which I love.
48 My hands also I will lift up to Your
    commandments,
    Which I love,
    And I will meditate on Your statutes.

ז ZAYIN

49 Remember the word to Your servant,
    Upon which You have caused me to
    hope.
50 This *is* my comfort in my affliction,
    For Your word has given me life.
51 The proud have me in great derision,

119:37 [a]Following Masoretic Text, Septuagint, and Vulgate; Targum reads *Your words.*

What are the different kinds of Psalms?

The Psalms cover the full breadth of human experience. Some express in general terms while others express in very specific terms the shifting events of life. There's a Psalm for almost any kind of day.

One way to categorize the Psalms groups them by five general types:

1. Wisdom Psalms—instructions for wise living (1; 37; 119)
2. Lamentation Psalms—meditations on the pangs of life (3; 17; 120)
3. Penitential Psalms—meditations on the pangs of sin (51)
4. Kingship Psalms—meditations on God's sovereign rule (2; 21; 144)
5. Thanksgiving Psalms—praise and worship offered to God (19; 32; 111)

Yet I do not turn aside from Your law.
52 I remembered Your judgments of old,
O LORD,
And have comforted myself.
53 Indignation has taken hold of me
Because of the wicked, who forsake
Your law.
54 Your statutes have been my songs
In the house of my pilgrimage.
55 I remember Your name in the night,
O LORD,
And I keep Your law.
56 This has become mine,
Because I kept Your precepts.

ח   HETH
57 *You are* my portion, O LORD;
I have said that I would keep Your
words.
58 I entreated Your favor with *my* whole
heart;
Be merciful to me according to Your
word.
59 I thought about my ways,
And turned my feet to Your
testimonies.
60 I made haste, and did not delay
To keep Your commandments.
61 The cords of the wicked have bound
me,
But I have not forgotten Your law.
62 At midnight I will rise to give thanks
to You,
Because of Your righteous judgments.
63 I *am* a companion of all who fear You,
And of those who keep Your precepts.
64 The earth, O LORD, is full of Your
mercy;
Teach me Your statutes.

ט   TETH
65 You have dealt well with Your servant,
O LORD, according to Your word.
66 Teach me good judgment and
knowledge,
For I believe Your commandments.
67 Before I was afflicted I went astray,
But now I keep Your word.
68 You *are* good, and do good;
Teach me Your statutes.
69 The proud have forged a lie against
me,
But I will keep Your precepts with *my*
whole heart.

70 Their heart is as fat as grease,
But I delight in Your law.
71 *It is* good for me that I have been
afflicted,
That I may learn Your statutes.
72 The law of Your mouth *is* better to
me
Than thousands of *coins of* gold and
silver.

י   YOD
73 Your hands have made me and
fashioned me;
Give me understanding, that I may
learn Your commandments.
74 Those who fear You will be glad when
they see me,
Because I have hoped in Your word.
75 I know, O LORD, that Your judgments
are right,
And *that* in faithfulness You have
afflicted me.
76 Let, I pray, Your merciful kindness be
for my comfort,
According to Your word to Your
servant.
77 Let Your tender mercies come to me,
that I may live;
For Your law *is* my delight.
78 Let the proud be ashamed,
For they treated me wrongfully with
falsehood;
But I will meditate on Your precepts.
79 Let those who fear You turn to me,
Those who know Your testimonies.
80 Let my heart be blameless regarding
Your statutes,
That I may not be ashamed.

כ   KAPH
81 My soul faints for Your salvation,
But I hope in Your word.
82 My eyes fail *from searching* Your
word,
Saying, "When will You comfort me?"
83 For I have become like a wineskin in
smoke,
Yet I do not forget Your statutes.
84 How many *are* the days of Your
servant?
When will You execute judgment on
those who persecute me?
85 The proud have dug pits for me,
Which *is* not according to Your law.

86 All Your commandments *are* faithful;
They persecute me wrongfully;
Help me!

87 They almost made an end of me on
earth,
But I did not forsake Your precepts.

88 Revive me according to Your
lovingkindness,
So that I may keep the testimony of
Your mouth.

ל LAMED

89 Forever, O Lord,
Your word is settled in heaven.

90 Your faithfulness *endures* to all
generations;
You established the earth, and it
abides.

91 They continue this day according to
Your ordinances,
For all *are* Your servants.

92 Unless Your law *had been* my delight,
I would then have perished in my
affliction.

93 I will never forget Your precepts,
For by them You have given me life.

94 I *am* Yours, save me;
For I have sought Your precepts.

95 The wicked wait for me to destroy
me,
But I will consider Your testimonies.

96 I have seen the consummation of all
perfection,
But Your commandment *is*
exceedingly broad.

> **119:89 Forever...settle in heaven.** God's Word will
> not change and is always spiritually relevant.

מ MEM

97 Oh, how I love Your law!
It *is* my meditation all the day.

98 You, through Your commandments,
make me wiser than my enemies;
For they *are* ever with me.

99 I have more understanding than all
my teachers,
For Your testimonies *are* my
meditation.

100 I understand more than the ancients,
Because I keep Your precepts.

101 I have restrained my feet from every
evil way,
That I may keep Your word.

102 I have not departed from Your
judgments,
For You Yourself have taught me.

103 How sweet are Your words to my
taste,
Sweeter than honey to my mouth!

104 Through Your precepts I get
understanding;
Therefore I hate every false way.

נ NUN

105 Your word *is* a lamp to my feet
And a light to my path.

106 I have sworn and confirmed
That I will keep Your righteous
judgments.

107 I am afflicted very much;
Revive me, O Lord, according to Your
word.

108 Accept, I pray, the freewill offerings of
my mouth, O Lord,
And teach me Your judgments.

109 My life *is* continually in my hand,
Yet I do not forget Your law.

110 The wicked have laid a snare for me,
Yet I have not strayed from Your
precepts.

111 Your testimonies I have taken as a
heritage forever,
For they *are* the rejoicing of my heart.

112 I have inclined my heart to perform
Your statutes
Forever, to the very end.

> **119:105 lamp...light.** God's Word provides illumina-
> tion to walk without stumbling.

ס SAMEK

113 I hate the double-minded,
But I love Your law.

114 You *are* my hiding place and my
shield;
I hope in Your word.

115 Depart from me, you evildoers,
For I will keep the commandments of
my God!

116 Uphold me according to Your word,
that I may live;

And do not let me be ashamed of my
hope.
117 Hold me up, and I shall be safe,
And I shall observe Your statutes
continually.
118 You reject all those who stray from
Your statutes,
For their deceit *is* falsehood.
119 You put away all the wicked of the
earth *like* dross;
Therefore I love Your testimonies.
120 My flesh trembles for fear of You,
And I am afraid of Your judgments.

ע AYIN
121 I have done justice and righteousness;
Do not leave me to my oppressors.
122 Be surety for Your servant for good;
Do not let the proud oppress me.
123 My eyes fail *from seeking* Your
salvation
And Your righteous word.
124 Deal with Your servant according to
Your mercy,
And teach me Your statutes.
125 I *am* Your servant;
Give me understanding,
That I may know Your testimonies.
126 *It is* time for *You* to act, O LORD,
For they have regarded Your law as
void.
127 Therefore I love Your commandments
More than gold, yes, than fine gold!
128 Therefore all *Your* precepts
concerning all *things*
I consider *to be* right;
I hate every false way.

פ PE
129 Your testimonies are wonderful;
Therefore my soul keeps them.
130 The entrance of Your words gives
light;
It gives understanding to the simple.
131 I opened my mouth and panted,
For I longed for Your commandments.
132 Look upon me and be merciful to me,
As Your custom *is* toward those who
love Your name.
133 Direct my steps by Your word,
And let no iniquity have dominion
over me.
134 Redeem me from the oppression of
man,

That I may keep Your precepts.
135 Make Your face shine upon Your
servant,
And teach me Your statutes.
136 Rivers of water run down from my
eyes,
Because *men* do not keep Your law.

צ TSADDE
137 Righteous *are* You, O LORD,
And upright *are* Your judgments.
138 Your testimonies, *which* You have
commanded,
Are righteous and very faithful.
139 My zeal has consumed me,
Because my enemies have forgotten
Your words.
140 Your word *is* very pure;
Therefore Your servant loves it.
141 I *am* small and despised,
Yet I do not forget Your precepts.
142 Your righteousness *is* an everlasting
righteousness,
And Your law *is* truth.
143 Trouble and anguish have overtaken
me,
Yet Your commandments *are* my
delights.
144 The righteousness of Your
testimonies *is* everlasting;
Give me understanding, and I shall
live.

> **119:140 very pure.** Like silver refined 7 times (see
> Ps. 12:6), the Word is without impurity. It is inerrant
> in all it teaches.

ק QOPH
145 I cry out with *my* whole heart;
Hear me, O LORD!
I will keep Your statutes.
146 I cry out to You;
Save me, and I will keep Your
testimonies.
147 I rise before the dawning of the
morning,
And cry for help;
I hope in Your word.
148 My eyes are awake through the *night*
watches,
That I may meditate on Your word.
149 Hear my voice according to Your
lovingkindness;

O Lord, revive me according to Your
  justice.
150 They draw near who follow after
  wickedness;
  They are far from Your law.
151 You *are* near, O Lord,
  And all Your commandments *are*
  truth.
152 Concerning Your testimonies,
  I have known of old that You have
  founded them forever.

ר RESH
153 Consider my affliction and deliver
  me,
  For I do not forget Your law.
154 Plead my cause and redeem me;
  Revive me according to Your word.
155 Salvation *is* far from the wicked,
  For they do not seek Your statutes.
156 Great *are* Your tender mercies,
  O Lord;
  Revive me according to Your
  judgments.
157 Many *are* my persecutors and my
  enemies,
  Yet I do not turn from Your
  testimonies.
158 I see the treacherous, and am
  disgusted,
  Because they do not keep Your word.
159 Consider how I love Your precepts;
  Revive me, O Lord, according to Your
  lovingkindness.
160 The entirety of Your word *is* truth,
  And every one of Your righteous
  judgments *endures* forever.

ש SHIN
161 Princes persecute me without a cause,
  But my heart stands in awe of Your
  word.
162 I rejoice at Your word
  As one who finds great treasure.
163 I hate and abhor lying,
  But I love Your law.
164 Seven times a day I praise You,
  Because of Your righteous judgments.
165 Great peace have those who love Your
  law,
  And nothing causes them to stumble.
166 Lord, I hope for Your salvation,
  And I do Your commandments.
167 My soul keeps Your testimonies,

And I love them exceedingly.
168 I keep Your precepts and Your
  testimonies,
  For all my ways *are* before You.

ת TAU
169 Let my cry come before You, O Lord;
  Give me understanding according to
  Your word.
170 Let my supplication come before You;
  Deliver me according to Your word.
171 My lips shall utter praise,
  For You teach me Your statutes.
172 My tongue shall speak of Your word,
  For all Your commandments *are*
  righteousness.
173 Let Your hand become my help,
  For I have chosen Your precepts.
174 I long for Your salvation, O Lord,
  And Your law *is* my delight.
175 Let my soul live, and it shall praise
  You;
  And let Your judgments help me.
176 I have gone astray like a lost sheep;
  Seek Your servant,
  For I do not forget Your
  commandments.

119:176 I have gone astray. In spite of all that he has affirmed regarding Scripture's power in his life, the psalmist confesses that sin is still present in his life (see Rom. 7:15–25). Any decrease of sin in his life should be attributed to the suppression of unrighteousness by the working of God's Word.

PSALM 120

Plea for Relief from Bitter Foes

A Song of Ascents.

1 In my distress I cried to the Lord,
  And He heard me.
2 Deliver my soul, O Lord, from lying
  lips
  And from a deceitful tongue.

3 What shall be given to you,
  Or what shall be done to you,
  You false tongue?
4 Sharp arrows of the warrior,
  With coals of the broom tree!

5 Woe is me, that I dwell in Meshech,

120:4 Sharp arrows...coals. Lies and false accusations are like the pain inflicted in battle by arrows and the pain of being burned with charcoal made from the wood of a broom tree (a desert bush that grows 10 to 15 feet high).

That I dwell among the tents of Kedar!
6 My soul has dwelt too long
With one who hates peace.
7 I *am for* peace;
But when I speak, they *are* for war.

PSALM 121

God the Help of Those Who Seek Him

A Song of Ascents.

1 I will lift up my eyes to the hills—
From whence comes my help?
2 My help *comes* from the LORD,
Who made heaven and earth.

3 He will not allow your foot to be
moved;
He who keeps you will not slumber.
4 Behold, He who keeps Israel
Shall neither slumber nor sleep.

5 The LORD *is* your keeper;
The LORD *is* your shade at your right
hand.
6 The sun shall not strike you by day,
Nor the moon by night.

7 The LORD shall preserve you from all
evil;
He shall preserve your soul.
8 The LORD shall preserve your going
out and your coming in
From this time forth, and even
forevermore.

121:1–8 The author and circumstances are unknown. The psalm gives assurance that God gives help and protection to Israel and to individual believers.

PSALM 122

The Joy of Going to the House of the LORD

A Song of Ascents. Of David.

1 I was glad when they said to me,
"Let us go into the house of the LORD."

2 Our feet have been standing
Within your gates, O Jerusalem!

3 Jerusalem is built
As a city that is compact together,
4 Where the tribes go up,
The tribes of the LORD,
To the Testimony of Israel,
To give thanks to the name of the
LORD.
5 For thrones are set there for
judgment,
The thrones of the house of David.

122:1–9 David rejoiced over Jerusalem because he defeated the Jebusites (see 2 Sam. 5) and brought the ark and the tabernacle to their permanent place (see 2 Sam. 6). David's prayer for peace in Jerusalem was temporarily answered in Solomon's reign (see 1 Kin. 4:24,25), but will not be fully experienced until the Prince of Peace (Is. 9:6) comes to rule permanently (Zech. 14:9,11).

6 Pray for the peace of Jerusalem:
"May they prosper who love you.
7 Peace be within your walls,
Prosperity within your palaces."
8 For the sake of my brethren and
companions,
I will now say, "Peace *be* within you."
9 Because of the house of the LORD our
God
I will seek your good.

122:6–9 The prayer is for Jerusalem, whose name means "city of peace," where the God of peace resides (Is. 9:6). Ironically, it has been the city most fought over throughout history. History has proven that bad times had to come (Pss. 79;137) before the best of times (Rev. 21,22).

PSALM 123

Prayer for Relief from Contempt

A Song of Ascents.

1 Unto You I lift up my eyes,
O You who dwell in the heavens.
2 Behold, as the eyes of servants *look* to
the hand of their masters,
As the eyes of a maid to the hand of
her mistress,

So our eyes *look* to the LORD our God,
Until He has mercy on us.

3 Have mercy on us, O LORD, have
     mercy on us!
For we are exceedingly filled with
     contempt.
4 Our soul is exceedingly filled
With the scorn of those who are at
     ease,
With the contempt of the proud.

PSALM 124

The LORD the Defense of His People

A Song of Ascents. Of David.

1 "If it had not been the LORD who was
     on our side,"
Let Israel now say—
2 "If it had not been the LORD who was
     on our side,
When men rose up against us,
3 Then they would have swallowed us
     alive,
When their wrath was kindled against
     us;
4 Then the waters would have
     overwhelmed us,
The stream would have gone over our
     soul;
5 Then the swollen waters
Would have gone over our soul."

6 Blessed *be* the LORD,
Who has not given us *as* prey to their
     teeth.
7 Our soul has escaped as a bird from
     the snare of the fowlers;*a*
The snare is broken, and we have
     escaped.
8 Our help *is* in the name of the LORD,
Who made heaven and earth.

PSALM 125

The LORD the Strength of His People

A Song of Ascents.

1 Those who trust in the LORD
Are like Mount Zion,

Which cannot be moved, *but* abides
     forever.
2 As the mountains surround
     Jerusalem,
So the LORD surrounds His people
From this time forth and forever.

3 For the scepter of wickedness shall
     not rest
On the land allotted to the righteous,
Lest the righteous reach out their
     hands to iniquity.

4 Do good, O LORD, to *those who are*
     good,
And to *those who are* upright in their
     hearts.

5 As for such as turn aside to their
     crooked ways,
The LORD shall lead them away
With the workers of iniquity.

Peace *be* upon Israel!

PSALM 126

A Joyful Return to Zion

A Song of Ascents.

1 When the LORD brought back the
     captivity of Zion,
We were like those who dream.
2 Then our mouth was filled with
     laughter,
And our tongue with singing.
Then they said among the nations,
"The LORD has done great things for
     them."

126:1–6 Ps. 126 most likely points to one of the 3 returns from the Babylonian Captivity: a return under Zerubbabel in Ezra 1–6 (about 538 B.C.), a return under Ezra in Ezra 7–10 (about 458 B.C.), and a return under Nehemiah in Neh. 1,2 (about 445 B.C.). The occasion for the psalm could be when the foundation for the second temple had been laid (see Ezra 3:8–10) or when the Feast of Tabernacles was reinstated (see Neh. 8:13,14).

124:7 *a*That is, persons who catch birds in a trap or snare

³ The LORD has done great things for
   us,
   And we are glad.

⁴ Bring back our captivity, O LORD,
   As the streams in the South.

⁵ Those who sow in tears
   Shall reap in joy.
⁶ He who continually goes forth
   weeping,
   Bearing seed for sowing,
   Shall doubtless come again with
   rejoicing,
   Bringing his sheaves *with him*.

126:5,6 sow...reap. By sowing tears of repentance
over sin, the nation reaped the harvest of a joyful
return to the land of Israel.

PSALM 127

Laboring and Prospering with the LORD

A Song of Ascents. Of Solomon.

¹ Unless the LORD builds the house,
   They labor in vain who build it;
   Unless the LORD guards the city,
   The watchman stays awake in vain.
² *It is* vain for you to rise up early,
   To sit up late,
   To eat the bread of sorrows;
   For so He gives His beloved sleep.

127:1,2 God's sovereignty is seen in the building of
a house, in the protection of a city, and in earning a
living. In all three circumstances, the sovereign intention of God is more crucial to the outcome than man's
efforts. Without God, man's endeavor is in vain (see
Eccl. 1:2).

³ Behold, children *are* a heritage from
   the LORD,
   The fruit of the womb *is* a reward.
⁴ Like arrows in the hand of a warrior,
   So *are* the children of one's youth.
⁵ Happy *is* the man who has his quiver
   full of them;
   They shall not be ashamed,
   But shall speak with their enemies in
   the gate.

PSALM 128

Blessings of Those Who Fear the LORD

A Song of Ascents.

¹ Blessed *is* every one who fears the
   LORD,
   Who walks in His ways.

² When you eat the labor of your hands,
   You *shall be* happy, and *it shall be*
   well with you.
³ Your wife *shall be* like a fruitful vine
   In the very heart of your house,
   Your children like olive plants
   All around your table.
⁴ Behold, thus shall the man be blessed
   Who fears the LORD.

⁵ The LORD bless you out of Zion,
   And may you see the good of
   Jerusalem
   All the days of your life.
⁶ Yes, may you see your children's
   children.

   Peace *be* upon Israel!

PSALM 129

Song of Victory over Zion's Enemies

A Song of Ascents.

¹ "Many a time they have afflicted me
   from my youth,"
   Let Israel now say—
² "Many a time they have afflicted me
   from my youth;
   Yet they have not prevailed against
   me.
³ The plowers plowed on my back;
   They made their furrows long."
⁴ The LORD *is* righteous;
   He has cut in pieces the cords of the
   wicked.

⁵ Let all those who hate Zion
   Be put to shame and turned back.
⁶ Let them be as the grass *on the*
   housetops,
   Which withers before it grows up,
⁷ With which the reaper does not fill
   his hand,

Nor he who binds sheaves, his arms.
8 Neither let those who pass by them
    say,
"The blessing of the LORD *be* upon
    you;
We bless you in the name of the
    LORD!"

PSALM 130

Waiting for the Redemption of the LORD

A Song of Ascents.

1 Out of the depths I have cried to You,
    O LORD;
2 Lord, hear my voice!
Let Your ears be attentive
To the voice of my supplications.

3 If You, LORD, should mark iniquities,
    O Lord, who could stand?
4 But *there is* forgiveness with You,
That You may be feared.

5 I wait for the LORD, my soul waits,
And in His word I do hope.
6 My soul *waits* for the Lord
More than those who watch for the
    morning—
Yes, more than those who watch for
    the morning.

> **130:5 in His word I do hope.** The psalmist expresses a certain hope since God's Word cannot fail (see Matt. 5:18).

7 O Israel, hope in the LORD;
For with the LORD *there is* mercy,
And with Him *is* abundant
    redemption.
8 And He shall redeem Israel
From all his iniquities.

PSALM 131

Simple Trust in the LORD

A Song of Ascents. Of David.

1 LORD, my heart is not haughty,
Nor my eyes lofty.

Neither do I concern myself with
    great matters,
Nor with things too profound for me.

2 Surely I have calmed and quieted my
    soul,
Like a weaned child with his mother;
Like a weaned child *is* my soul within
    me.

> **131:2 Like a weaned child.** David had been trained to trust God to supply his needs just as a weaned child trusts his mother.

3 O Israel, hope in the LORD
From this time forth and forever.

PSALM 132

The Eternal Dwelling of God in Zion

A Song of Ascents.

1 LORD, remember David
And all his afflictions;
2 How he swore to the LORD,
And vowed to the Mighty One of
    Jacob:
3 "Surely I will not go into the chamber
    of my house,
Or go up to the comfort of my bed;
4 I will not give sleep to my eyes
Or slumber to my eyelids,
5 Until I find a place for the LORD,
A dwelling place for the Mighty One
    of Jacob."

6 Behold, we heard of it in Ephrathah;
We found it in the fields of the
    woods.*a*
7 Let us go into His tabernacle;
Let us worship at His footstool.
8 Arise, O LORD, to Your resting place,
You and the ark of Your strength.
9 Let Your priests be clothed with
    righteousness,
And let Your saints shout for joy.

> **132:7 His footstool.** God's throne is in heaven (see Is. 66:1), and His footstool is on earth (see Ps. 99:5), figuratively speaking. To worship at the ark of the covenant on earth would be at God's footstool.

132:6 *a*Hebrew *Jaar*

10 For Your servant David's sake,
Do not turn away the face of Your
Anointed.

11 The LORD has sworn *in* truth to
David;
He will not turn from it:
"I will set upon your throne the fruit of
your body.

12 If your sons will keep My covenant
And My testimony which I shall
teach them,
Their sons also shall sit upon your
throne forevermore."

13 For the LORD has chosen Zion;
He has desired *it* for His dwelling
place:

14 "This *is* My resting place forever;
Here I will dwell, for I have desired it.

15 I will abundantly bless her provision;
I will satisfy her poor with bread.

16 I will also clothe her priests with
salvation,
And her saints shall shout aloud for
joy.

17 There I will make the horn of David
grow;
I will prepare a lamp for My
Anointed.

18 His enemies I will clothe with shame,
But upon Himself His crown shall
flourish."

132:13–18 The psalmist looks forward to the day
when Jesus Christ, the son of David and of Abraham
(Matt. 1:1), will be installed by God on David's throne
in the city of God, to rule and bring peace on earth,
especially to Israel (see Pss. 2;89;110).

PSALM 133

Blessed Unity of the People of God

A Song of Ascents. Of David.

1 Behold, how good and how pleasant *it is*
For brethren to dwell together in
unity!

2 *It is* like the precious oil upon the
head,

Running down on the beard,
The beard of Aaron,
Running down on the edge of his
garments.

3 *It is* like the dew of Hermon,
Descending upon the mountains of
Zion;
For there the LORD commanded the
blessing—
Life forevermore.

PSALM 134

Praising the LORD in His House at Night

A Song of Ascents.

1 Behold, bless the LORD,
All *you* servants of the LORD,
Who by night stand in the house of
the LORD!

2 Lift up your hands *in* the sanctuary,
And bless the LORD.

3 The LORD who made heaven and
earth
Bless you from Zion!

PSALM 135

Praise to God in Creation and Redemption

1 Praise the LORD!

Praise the name of the LORD;
Praise *Him,* O you servants of the
LORD!

2 You who stand in the house of the
LORD,
In the courts of the house of our God,

3 Praise the LORD, for the LORD *is* good;
Sing praises to His name, for *it is*
pleasant.

4 For the LORD has chosen Jacob for
Himself,
Israel for His special treasure.

5 For I know that the LORD *is* great,
And our Lord *is* above all gods.

6 Whatever the LORD pleases He does,
In heaven and in earth,
In the seas and in all deep places.

7 He causes the vapors to ascend from
the ends of the earth;
He makes lightning for the rain;

He brings the wind out of His
    treasuries.

8 He destroyed the firstborn of Egypt,
    Both of man and beast.
9 He sent signs and wonders into the
    midst of you, O Egypt,
    Upon Pharaoh and all his servants.
10 He defeated many nations
    And slew mighty kings—
11 Sihon king of the Amorites,
    Og king of Bashan,
    And all the kingdoms of Canaan—
12 And gave their land *as* a heritage,
    A heritage to Israel His people.

13 Your name, O LORD, *endures* forever,
    Your fame, O LORD, throughout all
    generations.
14 For the LORD will judge His people,
    And He will have compassion on His
    servants.

15 The idols of the nations *are* silver and
    gold,
    The work of men's hands.
16 They have mouths, but they do not
    speak;
    Eyes they have, but they do not see;
17 They have ears, but they do not hear;
    Nor is there *any* breath in their
    mouths.
18 Those who make them are like them;
    So is everyone who trusts in them.

19 Bless the LORD, O house of Israel!
    Bless the LORD, O house of Aaron!
20 Bless the LORD, O house of Levi!
    You who fear the LORD, bless the LORD!
21 Blessed be the LORD out of Zion,
    Who dwells in Jerusalem!

Praise the LORD!

135:19–20 The categories of Israel, Aaron, Levi, and those who fear the Lord refer to Israel as a whole, the priesthood (Aaron and Levi), and the true believers.

PSALM 136

Thanksgiving to God for His Enduring Mercy

1 Oh, give thanks to the LORD, for *He is*
    good!

    For His mercy *endures* forever.
2 Oh, give thanks to the God of gods!
    For His mercy *endures* forever.
3 Oh, give thanks to the Lord of lords!
    For His mercy *endures* forever:

4 To Him who alone does great
    wonders,
    For His mercy *endures* forever;
5 To Him who by wisdom made the
    heavens,
    For His mercy *endures* forever;
6 To Him who laid out the earth above
    the waters,
    For His mercy *endures* forever;
7 To Him who made great lights,
    For His mercy *endures* forever—
8 The sun to rule by day,
    For His mercy *endures* forever;
9 The moon and stars to rule by night,
    For His mercy *endures* forever.

136:1–26 Ps. 136 uses the antiphonal refrain "For His mercy *endures* forever" after each stanza, perhaps spoken by the people in responsive worship. The author and occasion are unknown.

10 To Him who struck Egypt in their
    firstborn,
    For His mercy *endures* forever;
11 And brought out Israel from among
    them,
    For His mercy *endures* forever;
12 With a strong hand, and with an
    outstretched arm,
    For His mercy *endures* forever;
13 To Him who divided the Red Sea in
    two,
    For His mercy *endures* forever;
14 And made Israel pass through the
    midst of it,
    For His mercy *endures* forever;
15 But overthrew Pharaoh and his army
    in the Red Sea,
    For His mercy *endures* forever;
16 To Him who led His people through
    the wilderness,
    For His mercy *endures* forever;
17 To Him who struck down great kings,
    For His mercy *endures* forever;
18 And slew famous kings,
    For His mercy *endures* forever—
19 Sihon king of the Amorites,

²⁰ For His mercy *endures* forever;
And Og king of Bashan,
For His mercy *endures* forever—

²¹ And gave their land as a heritage,
For His mercy *endures* forever;

²² A heritage to Israel His servant,
For His mercy *endures* forever.

²³ Who remembered us in our lowly
state,
For His mercy *endures* forever;

²⁴ And rescued us from our enemies,
For His mercy *endures* forever;

²⁵ Who gives food to all flesh,
For His mercy *endures* forever.

²⁶ Oh, give thanks to the God of heaven!
For His mercy *endures* forever.

PSALM 137

Longing for Zion in a Foreign Land

¹ By the rivers of Babylon,
There we sat down, yea, we wept
When we remembered Zion.

² We hung our harps
Upon the willows in the midst of it.

³ For there those who carried us away
captive asked of us a song,
And those who plundered us
requested mirth,
Saying, "Sing us *one* of the songs of
Zion!"

> **137:1 the rivers of Babylon.** These are the Tigris and
> Euphrates Rivers. **we wept.** After the exile, the Isra-
> elites wept with sorrow during the rebuilding of the
> temple (see Ezra 3:12). **Zion.** Zion is the dwelling
> place of God on earth (Ps. 9:11) and was destroyed by
> the Babylonians (2 Chr. 36:19).

⁴ How shall we sing the LORD's song
In a foreign land?

⁵ If I forget you, O Jerusalem,
Let my right hand forget *its skill!*

⁶ If I do not remember you,
Let my tongue cling to the roof of my
mouth—
If I do not exalt Jerusalem
Above my chief joy.

⁷ Remember, O LORD, against the sons
of Edom

The day of Jerusalem,
Who said, "Raze *it,* raze *it,*
To its very foundation!"

⁸ O daughter of Babylon, who are to be
destroyed,
Happy the one who repays you as you
have served us!

⁹ Happy the one who takes and dashes
Your little ones against the rock!

PSALM 138

The LORD's Goodness to the Faithful

A Psalm of David.

¹ I will praise You with my whole heart;
Before the gods I will sing praises to
You.

² I will worship toward Your holy
temple,
And praise Your name
For Your lovingkindness and Your
truth;
For You have magnified Your word
above all Your name.

³ In the day when I cried out, You
answered me,
And made me bold *with* strength in
my soul.

⁴ All the kings of the earth shall praise
You, O LORD,
When they hear the words of Your
mouth.

⁵ Yes, they shall sing of the ways of the
LORD,
For great *is* the glory of the LORD.

⁶ Though the LORD *is* on high,
Yet He regards the lowly;
But the proud He knows from afar.

⁷ Though I walk in the midst of
trouble, You will revive me;
You will stretch out Your hand
Against the wrath of my enemies,
And Your right hand will save me.

⁸ The LORD will perfect *that which*
concerns me;
Your mercy, O LORD, *endures* forever;
Do not forsake the works of Your
hands.

PSALM 139

God's Perfect Knowledge of Man

For the Chief Musician. A Psalm of David.

1 O LORD, You have searched me and
       known *me.*
2 You know my sitting down and my
       rising up;
    You understand my thought afar off.
3 You comprehend my path and my
       lying down,
    And are acquainted with all my ways.
4 For *there is* not a word on my tongue,
    But behold, O LORD, You know it
       altogether.
5 You have hedged me behind and
       before,
    And laid Your hand upon me.
6 *Such* knowledge *is* too wonderful for
       me;
    It is high, I cannot *attain* it.

7 Where can I go from Your Spirit?
    Or where can I flee from Your
       presence?
8 If I ascend into heaven, You *are* there;
    If I make my bed in hell, behold, You
       are there.
9 *If* I take the wings of the morning,
    And dwell in the uttermost parts of
       the sea,
10 Even there Your hand shall lead me,
    And Your right hand shall hold me.
11 If I say, "Surely the darkness shall
       fall*[a]* on me,"
    Even the night shall be light about
       me;
12 Indeed, the darkness shall not hide
       from You,
    But the night shines as the day;
    The darkness and the light *are* both
       alike *to* You.

13 For You formed my inward parts;
    You covered me in my mother's
       womb.
14 I will praise You, for I am fearfully
       and wonderfully made;*[a]*

> **139:13 formed...covered.** God, the Divine Designer
> of pregnancy, providentially watches over the devel-
> opment of the child while yet in the mother's womb.

    Marvelous are Your works,
    And *that* my soul knows very well.
15 My frame was not hidden from You,
    When I was made in secret,
    And skillfully wrought in the lowest
       parts of the earth.
16 Your eyes saw my substance, being yet
       unformed.
    And in Your book they all were
       written,
    The days fashioned for me,
    When *as yet there were* none of them.

17 How precious also are Your thoughts
       to me, O God!
    How great is the sum of them!
18 *If* I should count them, they would be
       more in number than the sand;
    When I awake, I am still with You.

19 Oh, that You would slay the wicked,
       O God!
    Depart from me, therefore, you
       bloodthirsty men.
20 For they speak against You wickedly;
    Your enemies take *Your name* in
       vain.*[a]*
21 Do I not hate them, O LORD, who
       hate You?
    And do I not loathe those who rise up
       against You?
22 I hate them with perfect hatred;
    I count them my enemies.

23 Search me, O God, and know my
       heart;
    Try me, and know my anxieties;
24 And see if *there is any* wicked way in
       me,
    And lead me in the way everlasting.

> **139:1–24** David expresses his awe that God knew
> every detail about him. He might have remembered
> the Lords' words, "...the LORD looks at the heart"
> (1 Sam. 16:7). The occasion of this psalm is unknown.

139:11 *[a]*Vulgate and Symmachus read *cover.*   139:14 *[a]*Following Masoretic Text and Targum;
Septuagint, Syriac, and Vulgate read *You are fearfully wonderful.*   139:20 *[a]*Septuagint and Vulgate
read *They take your cities in vain.*

PSALM 140

Prayer for Deliverance from Evil Men

To the Chief Musician. A Psalm of David.

1 Deliver me, O LORD, from evil men;
  Preserve me from violent men,
2 Who plan evil things in *their* hearts;
  They continually gather together *for*
    war.
3 They sharpen their tongues like a
    serpent;
  The poison of asps *is* under their lips.
                                    Selah

> **140:3 asps.** This is a type of snake (see Rom. 3:13), which signifies cunning and venom.

4 Keep me, O LORD, from the hands of
    the wicked;
  Preserve me from violent men,
  Who have purposed to make my steps
    stumble.
5 The proud have hidden a snare for
    me, and cords;
  They have spread a net by the
    wayside;
  They have set traps for me.   Selah
6 I said to the LORD: "You *are* my God;
  Hear the voice of my supplications,
    O LORD.
7 O GOD the Lord, the strength of my
    salvation,
  You have covered my head in the day
    of battle.
8 Do not grant, O LORD, the desires of
    the wicked;
  Do not further his *wicked* scheme,
  Lest they be exalted.   Selah

9 "*As for* the head of those who surround
    me,
  Let the evil of their lips cover them;
10 Let burning coals fall upon them;
  Let them be cast into the fire,
  Into deep pits, that they rise not up
    again.
11 Let not a slanderer be established in
    the earth;
  Let evil hunt the violent man to
    overthrow *him.*"

12 I know that the LORD will maintain
  The cause of the afflicted,
  And justice for the poor.
13 Surely the righteous shall give thanks
    to Your name;
  The upright shall dwell in Your
    presence.

PSALM 141

Prayer for Safekeeping from Wickedness

A Psalm of David.

1 LORD, I cry out to You;
  Make haste to me!
  Give ear to my voice when I cry out to
    You.
2 Let my prayer be set before You *as*
    incense,
  The lifting up of my hands *as* the
    evening sacrifice.

> **141:2 incense...evening sacrifice.** David wanted his prayers and requests for God's help to be as disciplined and regular as the offering of incense and burnt offerings in the tabernacle (see Ps. 68:31; Ex. 30:7,8; Ex. 29:38,39).

3 Set a guard, O LORD, over my mouth;
  Keep watch over the door of my lips.
4 Do not incline my heart to any evil
    thing,
  To practice wicked works
  With men who work iniquity;
  And do not let me eat of their
    delicacies.

5 Let the righteous strike me;
  It shall be a kindness.
  And let him rebuke me;
  It shall be as excellent oil;
  Let my head not refuse it.

  For still my prayer *is* against the deeds
    of the wicked.
6 Their judges are overthrown by the
    sides of the cliff,
  And they hear my words, for they are
    sweet.
7 Our bones are scattered at the mouth
    of the grave,
  As when one plows and breaks up the
    earth.

8 But my eyes *are* upon You, O G OD the
Lord;
In You I take refuge;
Do not leave my soul destitute.
9 Keep me from the snares they have
laid for me,
And from the traps of the workers of
iniquity.
10 Let the wicked fall into their own
nets,
While I escape safely.

PSALM 142

A Plea for Relief from Persecutors

*A Contemplation[a] of David. A Prayer
when he was in the cave.*

1 I cry out to the L ORD with my voice;
With my voice to the L ORD I make
my supplication.
2 I pour out my complaint before Him;
I declare before Him my trouble.

3 When my spirit was overwhelmed
within me,
Then You knew my path.
In the way in which I walk
They have secretly set a snare for me.
4 Look on *my* right hand and see,
For *there is* no one who acknowledges
me;
Refuge has failed me;
No one cares for my soul.

142:1–7 David recounted his desperate days hiding
in the cave of Adullam (1 Sam. 22:1) while Saul sought
to kill him (1 Sam. 18–24). David seems hopeless
without God's intervention. Psalm 91 provides the
solution.

5 I cried out to You, O L ORD:
I said, "You *are* my refuge,
My portion in the land of the living.
6 Attend to my cry,
For I am brought very low;
Deliver me from my persecutors,
For they are stronger than I.
7 Bring my soul out of prison,
That I may praise Your name;
The righteous shall surround me,

For You shall deal bountifully with
me."

PSALM 143

**An Earnest Appeal for Guidance
and Deliverance**

A Psalm of David.

1 Hear my prayer, O L ORD,
Give ear to my supplications!
In Your faithfulness answer me,
And in Your righteousness.
2 Do not enter into judgment with Your
servant,
For in Your sight no one living is
righteous.

143:2 no one living is righteous. David admits his
own unrighteousness and realizes that if he is to be
delivered for righteousness' sake, it will be because
of God's righteousness, not his own.

3 For the enemy has persecuted my
soul;
He has crushed my life to the ground;
He has made me dwell in darkness,
Like those who have long been dead.
4 Therefore my spirit is overwhelmed
within me;
My heart within me is distressed.

5 I remember the days of old;
I meditate on all Your works;
I muse on the work of Your hands.
6 I spread out my hands to You;
My soul *longs* for You like a thirsty
land.   Selah

7 Answer me speedily, O L ORD;
My spirit fails!
Do not hide Your face from me,
Lest I be like those who go down into
the pit.
8 Cause me to hear Your
lovingkindness in the morning,
For in You do I trust;
Cause me to know the way in which I
should walk,
For I lift up my soul to You.

142:title *a*Hebrew *Maschil*

9 Deliver me, O LORD, from my
   enemies;
   In You I take shelter.[a]
10 Teach me to do Your will,
   For You *are* my God;
   Your Spirit *is* good.
   Lead me in the land of uprightness.

11 Revive me, O LORD, for Your name's
   sake!
   For Your righteousness' sake bring my
   soul out of trouble.
12 In Your mercy cut off my enemies,
   And destroy all those who afflict my
   soul;
   For I *am* Your servant.

PSALM 144

A Song to the LORD Who Preserves and Prospers His People

A Psalm of David.

1 Blessed *be* the LORD my Rock,
   Who trains my hands for war,
   And my fingers for battle—
2 My lovingkindness and my fortress,
   My high tower and my deliverer,
   My shield and *the One* in whom I
   take refuge,
   Who subdues my people[a] under me.

> **144:1 my Rock.** David's solid and unshakable foun-
> dation is God (see Ps. 19:14). **trains my hands for
> war.** David lived in the days of Israel's theocracy,
> where God empowered the king to subdue His ene-
> mies.

3 LORD, what *is* man, that You take
   knowledge of him?
   Or the son of man, that You are
   mindful of him?
4 Man is like a breath;
   His days *are* like a passing shadow.

5 Bow down Your heavens, O LORD,
   and come down;
   Touch the mountains, and they shall
   smoke.

6 Flash forth lightning and scatter
   them;
   Shoot out Your arrows and destroy
   them.
7 Stretch out Your hand from above;
   Rescue me and deliver me out of great
   waters,
   From the hand of foreigners,
8 Whose mouth speaks lying words,
   And whose right hand *is* a right hand
   of falsehood.

9 I will sing a new song to You, O God;
   On a harp of ten strings I will sing
   praises to You,
10 *The One* who gives salvation to kings,
   Who delivers David His servant
   From the deadly sword.

11 Rescue me and deliver me from the
   hand of foreigners,
   Whose mouth speaks lying words,
   And whose right hand *is* a right hand
   of falsehood—
12 That our sons *may be* as plants
   grown up in their youth;
   That our daughters *may be* as pillars,
   Sculptured in palace style;
13 *That* our barns *may be* full,
   Supplying all kinds of produce;
   That our sheep may bring forth
   thousands
   And ten thousands in our fields;
14 *That* our oxen *may be* well laden;
   That there be no breaking in or going
   out;
   That there be no outcry in our streets.
15 Happy *are* the people who are in such
   a state;
   Happy *are* the people whose God *is*
   the LORD!

PSALM 145

A Song of God's Majesty and Love

A Praise of David.

1 I will extol You, my God, O King;
   And I will bless Your name forever
   and ever.

143:9 [a]Septuagint and Vulgate read *To You I flee.*   144:2 [a]Following Masoretic Text, Septuagint, and
Vulgate; Syriac and Targum read *the peoples* (compare 18:47).

2   Every day I will bless You,
And I will praise Your name forever
and ever.
3   Great *is* the LORD, and greatly to be
praised;
And His greatness *is* unsearchable.

4   One generation shall praise Your
works to another,
And shall declare Your mighty acts.
5   I*a* will meditate on the glorious
splendor of Your majesty,
And on Your wondrous works.*b*
6   *Men* shall speak of the might of Your
awesome acts,
And I will declare Your greatness.
7   They shall utter the memory of Your
great goodness,
And shall sing of Your righteousness.

8   The LORD *is* gracious and full of
compassion,
Slow to anger and great in mercy.
9   The LORD *is* good to all,
And His tender mercies *are* over all
His works.

10   All Your works shall praise You,
O LORD,
And Your saints shall bless You.
11   They shall speak of the glory of Your
kingdom,
And talk of Your power,
12   To make known to the sons of men
His mighty acts,
And the glorious majesty of His
kingdom.
13   Your kingdom *is* an everlasting
kingdom,
And Your dominion *endures*
throughout all generations.*a*

14   The LORD upholds all who fall,
And raises up all *who are* bowed
down.
15   The eyes of all look expectantly to
You,
And You give them their food in due
season.

16   You open Your hand
And satisfy the desire of every living
thing.

145:14–16 God's grace to all of humanity is emphasized (see Matt. 5:45).

17   The LORD *is* righteous in all His
ways,
Gracious in all His works.
18   The LORD *is* near to all who call upon
Him,
To all who call upon Him in truth.
19   He will fulfill the desire of those who
fear Him;
He also will hear their cry and save
them.
20   The LORD preserves all who love
Him,
But all the wicked He will destroy.
21   My mouth shall speak the praise of
the LORD,
And all flesh shall bless His holy
name
Forever and ever.

145:1–21 This concludes David's 75 psalms. Here
David extols and celebrates the King of Eternity for
who He is, what He has done, and what He has promised. This psalm, rich in content, is an acrostic with
22 letters of the Hebrew alphabet. It begins the cre-
scendo of praise that completes the Psalter and might
be called "The Final Hallel" (Pss. 145–150).

PSALM 146

The Happiness of Those Whose
Help Is the LORD

1   Praise the LORD!

Praise the LORD, O my soul!
2   While I live I will praise the LORD;
I will sing praises to my God while I
have my being.

3   Do not put your trust in princes,
Nor in a son of man, in whom *there is*
no help.

145:5 *a*Following Masoretic Text and Targum; Dead Sea Scrolls, Septuagint, Syriac, and Vulgate read
They. *b*Literally *on the words of Your wondrous works* 145:13 *a*Following Masoretic Text and
Targum; Dead Sea Scrolls, Septuagint, Syriac, and Vulgate add *The LORD is faithful in all His words,
And holy in all His works.*

⁴ His spirit departs, he returns to his
earth;
In that very day his plans perish.

⁵ Happy *is he* who *has* the God of Jacob
for his help,
Whose hope *is* in the LORD his God,

⁶ Who made heaven and earth,
The sea, and all that *is* in them;
Who keeps truth forever,

⁷ Who executes justice for the
oppressed,
Who gives food to the hungry.
The LORD gives freedom to the
prisoners.

⁸ The LORD opens *the eyes of* the blind;
The LORD raises those who are bowed
down;
The LORD loves the righteous.

⁹ The LORD watches over the strangers;
He relieves the fatherless and widow;
But the way of the wicked He turns
upside down.

¹⁰ The LORD shall reign forever—
Your God, O Zion, to all generations.

Praise the LORD!

146:1–10 From here to the end of the Psalter, each psalm begins and ends with, "Praise the LORD" (Pss. 146–150). Neither the composer nor the occasion is known.

PSALM 147

Praise to God for His Word and Providence

¹ Praise the LORD!
For *it is* good to sing praises to our
God;
For *it is* pleasant, *and* praise is
beautiful.

² The LORD builds up Jerusalem;
He gathers together the outcasts of
Israel.

³ He heals the brokenhearted
And binds up their wounds.

⁴ He counts the number of the stars;
He calls them all by name.

⁵ Great *is* our Lord, and mighty in
power;
His understanding *is* infinite.

⁶ The LORD lifts up the humble;
He casts the wicked down to the
ground.

⁷ Sing to the LORD with thanksgiving;
Sing praises on the harp to our God,

⁸ Who covers the heavens with clouds,
Who prepares rain for the earth,
Who makes grass to grow on the
mountains.

⁹ He gives to the beast its food,
And to the young ravens that cry.

¹⁰ He does not delight in the strength of
the horse;
He takes no pleasure in the legs of a
man.

¹¹ The LORD takes pleasure in those
who fear Him,
In those who hope in His mercy.

¹² Praise the LORD, O Jerusalem!
Praise your God, O Zion!

¹³ For He has strengthened the bars of
your gates;
He has blessed your children within
you.

¹⁴ He makes peace *in* your borders,
And fills you with the finest wheat.

¹⁵ He sends out His command *to the*
earth;
His word runs very swiftly.

¹⁶ He gives snow like wool;
He scatters the frost like ashes;

¹⁷ He casts out His hail like morsels;
Who can stand before His cold?

¹⁸ He sends out His word and melts
them;
He causes His wind to blow, *and the*
waters flow.

¹⁹ He declares His word to Jacob,
His statutes and His judgments to
Israel.

²⁰ He has not dealt thus with any
nation;
And *as for His* judgments, they have
not known them.

Praise the LORD!

147:19,20 The psalmist acknowledges God's unique election of Israel from among all nations (see Gen. 12:1–3).

PSALM 148

Praise to the LORD from Creation

1   Praise the LORD!

    Praise the LORD from the heavens;
    Praise Him in the heights!
2   Praise Him, all His angels;
    Praise Him, all His hosts!
3   Praise Him, sun and moon;
    Praise Him, all you stars of light!
4   Praise Him, you heavens of heavens,
    And you waters above the heavens!

5   Let them praise the name of the
        LORD,
    For He commanded and they were
        created.
6   He also established them forever and
        ever;
    He made a decree which shall not
        pass away.

7   Praise the LORD from the earth,
    You great sea creatures and all the
        depths;
8   Fire and hail, snow and clouds;
    Stormy wind, fulfilling His word;
9   Mountains and all hills;
    Fruitful trees and all cedars;
10 Beasts and all cattle;
    Creeping things and flying fowl;
11 Kings of the earth and all peoples;
    Princes and all judges of the earth;
12 Both young men and maidens;
    Old men and children.

13 Let them praise the name of the
        LORD,
    For His name alone is exalted;
    His glory is above the earth and
        heaven.

148:14 the horn. This refers to the strength and prosperity of the nation, which became the cause of praise for Israel. This suggests that Israel enjoyed better times than in the past. **A people near to Him.** This also means "My chosen people" (Is. 43:20) and "His special treasure" (Ps. 135:4).

14 And He has exalted the horn of His
        people,
    The praise of all His saints—
    Of the children of Israel,
    A people near to Him.

    Praise the LORD!

PSALM 149

Praise to God for His Salvation and Judgment

1   Praise the LORD!

    Sing to the LORD a new song,
    And His praise in the assembly of
        saints.

2   Let Israel rejoice in their Maker;
    Let the children of Zion be joyful in
        their King.
3   Let them praise His name with the
        dance;
    Let them sing praises to Him with the
        timbrel and harp.
4   For the LORD takes pleasure in His
        people;
    He will beautify the humble with
        salvation.

5   Let the saints be joyful in glory;
    Let them sing aloud on their beds.
6   Let the high praises of God be in their
        mouth,
    And a two-edged sword in their hand,
7   To execute vengeance on the nations,
    And punishments on the peoples;
8   To bind their kings with chains,
    And their nobles with fetters of iron;
9   To execute on them the written
        judgment—
    This honor have all His saints.

    Praise the LORD!

PSALM 150

Let All Things Praise the LORD

1   Praise the LORD!

    Praise God in His sanctuary;
    Praise Him in His mighty firmament!
2   Praise Him for His mighty acts;

Praise Him according to His excellent greatness!

150:2 God deserves praise for what He has done and for who He is.

3　Praise Him with the sound of the trumpet;
Praise Him with the lute and harp!
4　Praise Him with the timbrel and dance;
Praise Him with stringed instruments and flutes!

5　Praise Him with loud cymbals;
Praise Him with clashing cymbals!

6　Let everything that has breath praise the LORD.

Praise the LORD!

150:1–6 This psalm concludes the Psalter and the Final Hallel (Pss. 145–150) by raising, and then answering, some strategic questions about praise. It deals with the place of praise, the purpose of praise, the proper means of praise, and the people who praise. The author and occasion are unknown.

MANY REASONS TO PRAISE THE LORD!

His works .... "I will praise You, O Lord, with my whole heart; I will tell of all Your marvelous works." (Psalm 9:1)

His power .... "Be exalted, O Lord, in Your own strength! We will sing and praise Your power." (Psalm 21:13)

His care .... "The poor shall eat and be satisfied; those who seek Him will praise the Lord. Let your heart live forever!" (Psalm 22:26)

His help .... "The Lord is my strength and my shield; my heart trusted in Him, and I am helped; therefore my heart greatly rejoices, and with my song I will praise Him." (Psalm 28:7)

His presence .... "Why are you cast down, O my soul? And why are you disquieted within me? Hope in God, for I shall yet praise Him for the help of His countenance." (Psalm 42:5)

His goodness .... "I will freely sacrifice to You; I will praise Your name, O Lord, for it is good." (Psalm 54:6)

His love .... "Because Your lovingkindness is better than life, my lips shall praise You." (Psalm 63:3)

His creation .... "Let heaven and earth praise Him, the seas and everything that moves in them." (Psalm 69:34)

His holiness .... "Let them praise Your great and awesome name—He is holy." (Psalm 99:3)

His mercy .... "Praise the Lord! Oh, give thanks to the Lord, for He is good! For His mercy endures forever." (Psalm 106:1)

His salvation .... "I will praise You, for You have answered me, and have become my salvation." (Psalm 118:21)

His statutes .... "My lips shall utter praise, for You teach me Your statutes." (Psalm 119:171)

His truth .... "I will worship toward Your holy temple, and praise Your name for Your lovingkindness and Your truth; for You have magnified Your word above all Your name." (Psalm 138:2)

His glory .... "Let them praise the name of the Lord, for His name alone is exalted; His glory is above the earth and heaven." (Psalm 148:13)

PROVERBS

The Bible declares that Solomon composed over 3,000 proverbs (1 Kings 4:32; Ecclesiastes 12:9). The Proverbs of Solomon contains a collection of 513 of the king's sayings. These are joined by selections from other wise people.

Proverbs are simple, moral statements or illustrations that highlight and teach fundamental truths and tendencies in life. They originated as insights drawn from common objects and daily events. The word "proverb" means "to be like." Many of the sayings are in fact comparisons between a vivid image and a vivid desire or consequence. For example, "Like one who takes away a garment in cold weather, And like vinegar on soda, Is one who sings songs to a heavy heart" (25:20).

AUTHOR AND DATE

Proverbs was created and compiled by Solomon and several other authors, approximately 71 to 86 B.C.

Proverbs provides a sample of the kind of wisdom that made Solomon famous. He set the standard for wisdom among his people. Perhaps that is why this collection has traditionally been named after Solomon even though he was not the source of the entire book. In fact, the final compilation of these sayings did not occur until the time of Hezekiah, long after Solomon's reign. Two others sages, Agur and Lemuel, are also specifically mentioned as contributors to Proverbs.

BACKGROUND AND SETTING

The contents of Proverbs reflect a three-fold self-identity: (1) general wisdom literature; (2) insights from the royal court; and (3) instructions offered in the mentoring relationship of a father and mother with their children. In each case, the purpose of the proverbs is to focus attention on godly living.

Wisdom literature describes the part of the Old Testament that supplements the Law (Genesis—Deuteronomy), the History (Joshua—Esther), and the Prophets (Isaiah—Malachi). This category includes: Job, Psalms, Proverbs, Ecclesiastes, and Song of Solomon. In Proverbs, Solomon the Sage gives insight into the "knotty" issues of life (1:6). Though it is practical, Proverbs is not superficial or external because it contains moral and ethical elements stressing upright living that flows out of a right relationship with God. Proverbs contains the principles and applications of Scripture that the godly characters of the Bible illustrate throughout their lives.

Solomon came to the throne with great promise, privilege, and opportunity. God granted his request for understanding (1 Kings 3:9–12; 1 Chronicles 1:10,11). His wisdom exceeded that of his peers (1 Kings 4:29). Despite Solomon's advantage in knowledge, however, he failed in practice. His example to Rehoboam was, unfortunately, a more effective teacher than his fatherly counsel. Like his father, Rehoboam also turned from the wisdom he was given.

Proverbs contains a gold mine of biblical theology, expressing the great themes of Scripture in practical terms and directions. These pithy sayings confront human ethical choices, calling into question how men and women think, live, and manage their daily lives. The standard is always divine truth. Proverbs calls people to live as their Creator originally intended them to live.

Proverbs relies heavily on the cause and effect principle that governs much of life. The recurring promise of Proverbs is that the wise generally live longer (9:11), prosper (2:20–22), experience joy (3:13–18), and are blessed by the goodness of God (12:21). Conversely, fools suffer shame (3:35) and death (10:21). While patterns of living are contrasted in the proverbs, their intent is not to reduce life to mechanical basics. They point to general truths that will be demonstrated throughout life, even if sometimes the complications of a situation and the fallenness of

> ## PROVERBS CALLS PEOPLE TO LIVE AS THEIR CREATOR ORIGINALLY INTENDED THEM TO LIVE.

the world will make a proverb seem too clear-cut. For example, "Treasures of wickedness profit nothing, but righteousness delivers from death" (10:2). Seen from the worldly perspective, the wicked seem, far too often, to profit, while the righteous are killed. The ultimate application of this proverb, however, expresses the way that God eventually settles all accounts. Other writings in the Scriptures, including Psalms and Job, help balance the direct truths of Proverbs by reminding us that we cannot always tell how God is working out his sovereignty and faithfulness in the world.

OUTLINE

The Beginning of Knowledge

1 The proverbs of Solomon the son of David, king of Israel:

1:1 proverbs. The proverbs are short, pithy sayings that express timeless truth and wisdom. They cause the reader to reflect and to apply the principles to life situations. Proverbs contains poetry, prose, and commands to obey. **Solomon.** King Solomon sought and received wisdom and knowledge from the Lord (2 Chr. 1:7–12), which led him to wealth, honor, and fame.

2 To know wisdom and instruction,
To perceive the words of
understanding,
3 To receive the instruction of wisdom,
Justice, judgment, and equity;
4 To give prudence to the simple,
To the young man knowledge and
discretion—
5 A wise *man* will hear and increase
learning,
And a man of understanding will
attain wise counsel,
6 To understand a proverb and an
enigma,
The words of the wise and their
riddles.

1:2–6 The purpose of the book is to produce wisdom, instruction, and discernment. To the Hebrew mind, wisdom was not only knowledge but also the skill of living a godly life as God intended man to live (see Deut. 4:5–8). Instruction referred to discipline of the moral nature. It is understanding that matures into spiritual discernment.

7 The fear of the LORD *is* the beginning
of knowledge,
But fools despise wisdom and
instruction.

Shun Evil Counsel

8 My son, hear the instruction of your
father,
And do not forsake the law of your
mother;
9 For they *will be* a graceful ornament
on your head,
And chains about your neck.

10 My son, if sinners entice you,
Do not consent.

1:10 sinners. This term describes unbelievers for whom sin is continual and who continue to persuade even believers to sin with them. The sins of murder and robbery are used as illustrations of such folly.

11 If they say, "Come with us,
Let us lie in wait to *shed* blood;
Let us lurk secretly for the innocent
without cause;
12 Let us swallow them alive like Sheol,*a*
And whole, like those who go down to
the Pit;
13 We shall find all *kinds* of precious
possessions,
We shall fill our houses with spoil;
14 Cast in your lot among us,
Let us all have one purse"—
15 My son, do not walk in the way with
them,
Keep your foot from their path;
16 For their feet run to evil,
And they make haste to shed blood.
17 Surely, in vain the net is spread
In the sight of any bird;
18 But they lie in wait for their *own*
blood,
They lurk secretly for their *own* lives.
19 So *are* the ways of everyone who is
greedy for gain;
It takes away the life of its owners.

The Call of Wisdom

20 Wisdom calls aloud outside;
She raises her voice in the open
squares.
21 She cries out in the chief concourses,*a*
At the openings of the gates in the
city
She speaks her words:
22 "How long, you simple ones, will you
love simplicity?

1:22 How long. Three classes of people need wisdom: (1) the simple, who are ignorant; (2) scorners or mockers, who commit more serious, determined acts; and (3) fools or obstinate unbelievers, who will not listen to the truth. Proverbs directs its wisdom primarily at the first group.

1:12 *a*Or *the grave*   1:21 *a*Septuagint, Syriac, and Targum read *top of the walls*; Vulgate reads *the head of multitudes*.

For scorners delight in their scorning,
And fools hate knowledge.

23 Turn at my rebuke;
Surely I will pour out my spirit on
you;
I will make my words known to you.

24 Because I have called and you refused,
I have stretched out my hand and no
one regarded,

25 Because you disdained all my counsel,
And would have none of my rebuke,

26 I also will laugh at your calamity;
I will mock when your terror comes,

27 When your terror comes like a storm,
And your destruction comes like a
whirlwind,
When distress and anguish come
upon you.

1:20–33 Here wisdom is personified and speaks in the first person, emphasizing the serious consequences that come to those who reject it (see 3:14–18).

28 "Then they will call on me, but I will
not answer;
They will seek me diligently, but they
will not find me.

29 Because they hated knowledge
And did not choose the fear of the
LORD,

30 They would have none of my counsel
And despised my every rebuke.

31 Therefore they shall eat the fruit of
their own way,
And be filled to the full with their
own fancies.

32 For the turning away of the simple
will slay them,
And the complacency of fools will
destroy them;

33 But whoever listens to me will dwell
safely,
And will be secure, without fear of
evil."

The Value of Wisdom

2 My son, if you receive my words,
And treasure my commands within
you,

2 So that you incline your ear to
wisdom,
And apply your heart to
understanding;

3 Yes, if you cry out for discernment,

2:1 my words. Solomon made God's law his own by faith, obedience, and teaching. The wisdom of God's words is available to those who understand its value. Appropriating wisdom begins when one values it above all else.

And lift up your voice for
understanding,

4 If you seek her as silver,
And search for her as for hidden
treasures;

5 Then you will understand the fear of
the LORD,
And find the knowledge of God.

6 For the LORD gives wisdom;
From His mouth come knowledge
and understanding;

7 He stores up sound wisdom for the
upright;
He is a shield to those who walk
uprightly;

8 He guards the paths of justice,
And preserves the way of His saints.

9 Then you will understand
righteousness and justice,
Equity and every good path.

10 When wisdom enters your heart,
And knowledge is pleasant to your
soul,

11 Discretion will preserve you;
Understanding will keep you,

12 To deliver you from the way of evil,
From the man who speaks perverse
things,

13 From those who leave the paths of
uprightness
To walk in the ways of darkness;

14 Who rejoice in doing evil,
And delight in the perversity of the
wicked;

15 Whose ways are crooked,
And who are devious in their paths;

16 To deliver you from the immoral
woman,
From the seductress who flatters with
her words,

17 Who forsakes the companion of her
youth,
And forgets the covenant of her God.

18 For her house leads down to death,
And her paths to the dead;

19 None who go to her return,
Nor do they regain the paths of life—

20 So you may walk in the way of
     goodness,
   And keep *to* the paths of
     righteousness.
21 For the upright will dwell in the land,
   And the blameless will remain in it;
22 But the wicked will be cut off from
     the earth,
   And the unfaithful will be uprooted
     from it.

Guidance for the Young

3 My son, do not forget my law,
   But let your heart keep my commands;
2 For length of days and long life
   And peace they will add to you.

3 Let not mercy and truth forsake you;
   Bind them around your neck,
   Write them on the tablet of your
     heart,

> **3:3 neck...heart.** God's mercy (the Hebrew word for lovingkindness and loyal love) and truth are to become part of us outwardly, in our behavior, and inwardly, as the subject of our meditation (see Deut. 6:4–9). Such inward and outward mercy and truth are evidence of New Covenant salvation (see Jer. 31:33,34).

4 *And* so find favor and high esteem
   In the sight of God and man.

5 Trust in the LORD with all your heart,
   And lean not on your own
     understanding;
6 In all your ways acknowledge Him,
   And He shall direct*ᵃ* your paths.

7 Do not be wise in your own eyes;
   Fear the LORD and depart from evil.
8 It will be health to your flesh,*ᵃ*
   And strength*ᵇ* to your bones.

9 Honor the LORD with your
     possessions,
   And with the firstfruits of all your
     increase;
10 So your barns will be filled with
     plenty,
   And your vats will overflow with new
     wine.

11 My son, do not despise the chastening
     of the LORD,
   Nor detest His correction;
12 For whom the LORD loves He
     corrects,
   Just as a father the son *in whom* he
     delights.

13 Happy *is* the man *who* finds wisdom,
   And the man *who* gains
     understanding;
14 For her proceeds *are* better than the
     profits of silver,
   And her gain than fine gold.
15 She *is* more precious than rubies,
   And all the things you may desire
     cannot compare with her.
16 Length of days *is* in her right hand,
   In her left hand riches and honor.
17 Her ways *are* ways of pleasantness,
   And all her paths *are* peace.
18 She *is* a tree of life to those who take
     hold of her,
   And happy *are all* who retain her.

> **3:1–35** Here the writer commends the study of truth to all people. The contrast between the outcomes of the wise and the wicked enforce this study of truth.

19 The LORD by wisdom founded the
     earth;
   By understanding He established the
     heavens;
20 By His knowledge the depths were
     broken up,
   And clouds drop down the dew.

21 My son, let them not depart from
     your eyes—
   Keep sound wisdom and discretion;
22 So they will be life to your soul
   And grace to your neck.
23 Then you will walk safely in your
     way,
   And your foot will not stumble.
24 When you lie down, you will not be
     afraid;
   Yes, you will lie down and your sleep
     will be sweet.
25 Do not be afraid of sudden terror,

3:6 *ᵃOr make smooth or straight*   **3:8** *ᵃLiterally navel, figurative of the body* *ᵇLiterally drink or refreshment*

Nor of trouble from the wicked when
   it comes;
26 For the LORD will be your confidence,
   And will keep your foot from being
   caught.

27 Do not withhold good from those to
   whom it is due,
   When it is in the power of your hand
   to do *so.*
28 Do not say to your neighbor,
   "Go, and come back,
   And tomorrow I will give *it,*"
   When *you have* it with you.
29 Do not devise evil against your
   neighbor,
   For he dwells by you for safety's sake.
30 Do not strive with a man without
   cause,
   If he has done you no harm.

31 Do not envy the oppressor,
   And choose none of his ways;
32 For the perverse *person is* an
   abomination to the LORD,

3:32 abomination. This is an important theme in Proverbs. An abomination is an attitude or act that is incompatible with God's nature and intolerable to Him, leading to His anger and judgment. **secret counsel.** God discloses Himself and His truth to the upright (see Ps. 25:14).

But His secret counsel *is* with the
   upright.
33 The curse of the LORD *is* on the house
   of the wicked,
   But He blesses the home of the just.
34 Surely He scorns the scornful,
   But gives grace to the humble.
35 The wise shall inherit glory,
   But shame shall be the legacy of fools.

Security in Wisdom

4 Hear, *my* children, the instruction of
   a father,
   And give attention to know
   understanding;
2 For I give you good doctrine:
   Do not forsake my law.
3 When I was my father's son,
   Tender and the only one in the sight
   of my mother,
4 He also taught me, and said to me:
   "Let your heart retain my words;
   Keep my commands, and live.
5 Get wisdom! Get understanding!
   Do not forget, nor turn away from the
   words of my mouth.
6 Do not forsake her, and she will
   preserve you;
   Love her, and she will keep you.
7 Wisdom *is* the principal thing;
   Therefore get wisdom.
   And in all your getting, get
   understanding.

Some of the Proverbs seem unclear or even contradictory. How can we study and apply them if we don't understand them?

More often than not, those Proverbs that at first seem unclear or contradictory turn out, instead, to be elusive and deep. Proverbs sometimes do state obvious truths. Their meaning is crystal clear: "A foolish son is a grief to his father, and bitterness to her who bore him" (17:25). But many proverbs require thoughtful meditation: "The lot is cast into the lap, but its every decision is from the Lord" (16:33) or "There is a way that seems right to a man, but its end is the way of death" (16:25). The fact that we may have to search the rest of Scripture or work at thinking ought to make Proverbs dearer to us. If God has chosen this unusual approach to help us grow, why would we hesitate to give our full attention to Proverbs?

Given the context that surrounds Proverbs—the rest of God's Word—a student's failure to grasp a proverb ought not to lead to the conclusion that there's something wrong with this book. A better conclusion would be that the student doesn't know enough yet or hasn't paid enough attention. A wise person puts an elusive proverb on hold for further understanding rather than rejecting it as useless. God's further lessons in that person's life may well cast a new light on parts of the Bible that have been difficult to interpret.

8 Exalt her, and she will promote you;
  She will bring you honor, when you
    embrace her.
9 She will place on your head an
    ornament of grace;
  A crown of glory she will deliver to
    you."

10 Hear, my son, and receive my sayings,
   And the years of your life will be
     many.
11 I have taught you in the way of
     wisdom;
   I have led you in right paths.
12 When you walk, your steps will not be
     hindered,
   And when you run, you will not
     stumble.
13 Take firm hold of instruction, do not
     let go;
   Keep her, for she *is* your life.

14 Do not enter the path of the wicked,
   And do not walk in the way of evil.
15 Avoid it, do not travel on it;
   Turn away from it and pass on.
16 For they do not sleep unless they have
     done evil;
   And their sleep is taken away unless
     they make *someone* fall.
17 For they eat the bread of wickedness,
   And drink the wine of violence.

18 But the path of the just *is* like the
     shining sun,*a*
   That shines ever brighter unto the
     perfect day.
19 The way of the wicked *is* like
     darkness;
   They do not know what makes them
     stumble.

20 My son, give attention to my words;
   Incline your ear to my sayings.
21 Do not let them depart from your
     eyes;
   Keep them in the midst of your heart;
22 For they *are* life to those who find
     them,
   And health to all their flesh.
23 Keep your heart with all diligence,
   For out of it *spring* the issues of life.

> **4:21–23 heart.** The "heart" commonly refers to the mind, the center of thinking and reason, but it also includes emotions, the will, and the whole inner being. The heart is the place of wisdom, and it is the source of whatever affects speech, sight, and conduct.

24 Put away from you a deceitful mouth,
   And put perverse lips far from you.
25 Let your eyes look straight ahead,
   And your eyelids look right before
     you.
26 Ponder the path of your feet,
   And let all your ways be established.
27 Do not turn to the right or the left;
   Remove your foot from evil.

The Peril of Adultery

5 My son, pay attention to my wisdom;
  Lend your ear to my understanding,
2 That you may preserve discretion,
  And your lips may keep knowledge.
3 For the lips of an immoral woman
    drip honey,
  And her mouth *is* smoother than oil;
4 But in the end she is bitter as
    wormwood,
  Sharp as a two-edged sword.
5 Her feet go down to death,
  Her steps lay hold of hell.*a*
6 Lest you ponder *her* path of life—
  Her ways are unstable;
  You do not know *them.*

7 Therefore hear me now, *my* children,
  And do not depart from the words of
    my mouth.
8 Remove your way far from her,
  And do not go near the door of her
    house,
9 Lest you give your honor to others,
  And your years to the cruel *one;*
10 Lest aliens be filled with your
     wealth,
   And your labors *go* to the house of a
     foreigner;
11 And you mourn at last,
   When your flesh and your body are
     consumed,
12 And say:
  "How I have hated instruction,
   And my heart despised correction!

4:18 *a*Literally *light*   5:5 *a*Or *Sheol*

13 I have not obeyed the voice of my
   teachers,
   Nor inclined my ear to those who
   instructed me!
14 I was on the verge of total ruin,
   In the midst of the assembly and
   congregation."

15 Drink water from your own cistern,
   And running water from your own
   well.
16 Should your fountains be dispersed
   abroad,
   Streams of water in the streets?
17 Let them be only your own,
   And not for strangers with you.

5:16,17 fountains...streams. This pictures the
wastefulness of sexual promiscuity and refers to the
male procreation capacity: the foolish are as fountains scattering precious water. The result of this sin
is called "streams of waters in the streets," a graphic
description of illegitimate street children. Solomon
says, "let them be only your own" and not the children of immoral strangers.

18 Let your fountain be blessed,
   And rejoice with the wife of your
   youth.
19 As a loving deer and a graceful doe,
   Let her breasts satisfy you at all
   times;
   And always be enraptured with her
   love.

5:19 graceful doe. The doe has graceful beauty in
her face and form and is often used in biblical poetry
to describe the beauty of a woman. **breasts.** This is
imagery of affection (see Song 1:13).

20 For why should you, my son, be
   enraptured by an immoral woman,
   And be embraced in the arms of a
   seductress?
21 For the ways of man are before the
   eyes of the LORD,
   And He ponders all his paths.
22 His own iniquities entrap the wicked
   man,
   And he is caught in the cords of his
   sin.

23 He shall die for lack of instruction,
   And in the greatness of his folly he
   shall go astray.

Dangerous Promises

6 My son, if you become surety for your
   friend,
   If you have shaken hands in pledge
   for a stranger,
2 You are snared by the words of your
   mouth;
   You are taken by the words of your
   mouth.
3 So do this, my son, and deliver
   yourself;
   For you have come into the hand of
   your friend:
   Go and humble yourself;
   Plead with your friend.
4 Give no sleep to your eyes,
   Nor slumber to your eyelids.
5 Deliver yourself like a gazelle from
   the hand of the hunter,
   And like a bird from the hand of the
   fowler.[a]

The Folly of Indolence
6 Go to the ant, you sluggard!
   Consider her ways and be wise,

6:6 ant...sluggard. The ant exemplifies diligence,
planning, and industriousness and serves as a rebuke to a sluggard. Folly sends a lazy man to learn
from an ant (see 10:4,26).

7 Which, having no captain,
   Overseer or ruler,
8 Provides her supplies in the summer,
   And gathers her food in the harvest.
9 How long will you slumber,
   O sluggard?
   When will you rise from your sleep?
10 A little sleep, a little slumber,
   A little folding of the hands to
   sleep—
11 So shall your poverty come on you
   like a prowler,
   And your need like an armed man.

The Wicked Man
12 A worthless person, a wicked man,
   Walks with a perverse mouth;

6:5 [a]That is, one who catches birds in a trap or snare

13 He winks with his eyes,
   He shuffles his feet,
   He points with his fingers;
14 Perversity *is* in his heart,
   He devises evil continually,
   He sows discord.
15 Therefore his calamity shall come
      suddenly;
   Suddenly he shall be broken without
      remedy.

16 These six *things* the LORD hates,
   Yes, seven *are* an abomination to
      Him:
17 A proud look,
   A lying tongue,
   Hands that shed innocent blood,
18 A heart that devises wicked plans,
   Feet that are swift in running to
      evil,
19 A false witness *who* speaks lies,
   And one who sows discord among
      brethren.

> **6:16–19 six...seven.** The sequence of these numbers was used to represent totality and to arrest attention (see Job 5:19). The 7 detestable sins provide a profound glimpse into the sinfulness of man.

6:22 *a* Literally *it*

Beware of Adultery

20 My son, keep your father's command,
   And do not forsake the law of your
      mother.
21 Bind them continually upon your
      heart;
   Tie them around your neck.
22 When you roam, they*a* will lead you;
   When you sleep, they will keep you;
   And *when* you awake, they will speak
      with you.
23 For the commandment *is* a lamp,
   And the law a light;
   Reproofs of instruction *are* the way of
      life,
24 To keep you from the evil woman,
   From the flattering tongue of a
      seductress.
25 Do not lust after her beauty in your
      heart,
   Nor let her allure you with her
      eyelids.

> **6:25 lust.** Sexual sin is rooted in lust (see Ex. 20:17; Matt. 5:28). This initial attraction must be consistently rejected (James 1:14,15).

26 For by means of a harlot
   A man is reduced to a crust of bread;

SYMBOLS FOR THE BIBLE

Symbol	Reality	Texts
1. Jesus Christ	Personification of the Word	John 1:1; Revelation 19:13
2. Valuable Metals	Incalculable worth	Psalm 12:6 (silver)
		Psalms 19:10; 119:27 (gold)
3. Seed	Source of new life	Matthew 13:10–23; James 1:18; 1 Peter 1:23
4. Water	Cleansing from sin	Ephesians 5:25–27; Revelation 21:6; 22:17
5. Mirror	Self-examination	James 1:22–25
6. Food	Nourishment to the soul	1 Corinthians 3:3; 1 Peter 2:1–3 (milk)
		Deuteronomy 8:3; Matthew 4:4 (bread)
		1 Corinthians 3:3; Hebrews 5:12–14 (meat)
		Psalm 19:10 (honey)
7. Clothing	A life dressed in truth	Titus 2:10; 1 Peter 3:5
8. Lamp	Light for direction	Psalm 119:105; Proverbs 6:23; 2 Peter 1:19
9. Sword	Spiritual weapon	Ephesians 6:17 (outwardly)
		Hebrews 4:12 (inwardly)
10. Plumb line	Benchmark of spiritual reality	Amos 7:8
11. Hammer	Powerful judgment	Jeremiah 23:29
12. Fire	Painful judgment	Jeremiah 5:14; 20:9; 23:29

And an adulteress[a] will prey upon his
    precious life.

27 Can a man take fire to his bosom,
    And his clothes not be burned?

28 Can one walk on hot coals,
    And his feet not be seared?

29 So *is* he who goes in to his neighbor's
    wife;
    Whoever touches her shall not be
    innocent.

30 *People* do not despise a thief
    If he steals to satisfy himself when he
    is starving.

31 Yet *when* he is found, he must restore
    sevenfold;
    He may have to give up all the
    substance of his house.

32 Whoever commits adultery with a
    woman lacks understanding;
    He *who* does so destroys his own
    soul.

33 Wounds and dishonor he will get,
    And his reproach will not be wiped
    away.

34 For jealousy *is* a husband's fury;
    Therefore he will not spare in the day
    of vengeance.

35 He will accept no recompense,
    Nor will he be appeased though you
    give many gifts.

7 My son, keep my words,
    And treasure my commands within
    you.

2 Keep my commands and live,
    And my law as the apple of your eye.

3 Bind them on your fingers;
    Write them on the tablet of your
    heart.

4 Say to wisdom, "You *are* my sister,"
    And call understanding *your* nearest
    kin,

5 That they may keep you from the
    immoral woman,
    From the seductress *who* flatters with
    her words.

The Crafty Harlot

6 For at the window of my house
    I looked through my lattice,

7 And saw among the simple,

I perceived among the youths,
A young man devoid of
    understanding,

8 Passing along the street near her
    corner;
    And he took the path to her house

9 In the twilight, in the evening,
    In the black and dark night.

10 And there a woman met him,
    With the attire of a harlot, and a
    crafty heart.

11 She *was* loud and rebellious,
    Her feet would not stay at home.

12 At times *she was* outside, at times in
    the open square,
    Lurking at every corner.

13 So she caught him and kissed him;
    With an impudent face she said to him:

14 "*I have* peace offerings with me;
    Today I have paid my vows.

> **7:14 peace offerings.** According to the law of peace
> offerings (Lev. 7:11–18), the meat left over after the
> sacrifice was to be eaten before the end of the day.
> Thus, the woman appears very religious when she
> invited the man to join her, because she had just re-
> turned from making her offering.

15 So I came out to meet you,
    Diligently to seek your face,
    And I have found you.

16 I have spread my bed with tapestry,
    Colored coverings of Egyptian linen.

17 I have perfumed my bed
    With myrrh, aloes, and cinnamon.

18 Come, let us take our fill of love until
    morning;
    Let us delight ourselves with love.

> **7:18 fill of love.** Adultery is not true love but mere
> physical gratification.

19 For my husband *is* not at home;
    He has gone on a long journey;

20 He has taken a bag of money with
    him,
    And will come home on the appointed
    day."

21 With her enticing speech she caused
    him to yield,

6:26 [a]Literally *a man's wife*, that is, of another

With her flattering lips she seduced him.

22 Immediately he went after her, as an ox goes to the slaughter,
Or as a fool to the correction of the stocks,[a]

23 Till an arrow struck his liver.
As a bird hastens to the snare,
He did not know it *would cost* his life.

24 Now therefore, listen to me, *my* children;
Pay attention to the words of my mouth:

25 Do not let your heart turn aside to her ways,
Do not stray into her paths;

26 For she has cast down many wounded,
And all who were slain by her were strong *men.*

7:26 It is not just the weak men who fall; strong men also fall when they do not flee temptation.

27 Her house *is* the way to hell,[a]
Descending to the chambers of death.

The Excellence of Wisdom

8 Does not wisdom cry out,
And understanding lift up her voice?

2 She takes her stand on the top of the high hill,
Beside the way, where the paths meet.

3 She cries out by the gates, at the entry of the city,
At the entrance of the doors:

4 "To you, O men, I call,
And my voice *is* to the sons of men.

5 O you simple ones, understand prudence,
And you fools, be of an understanding heart.

6 Listen, for I will speak of excellent things,
And from the opening of my lips *will come* right things;

7 For my mouth will speak truth;
Wickedness *is* an abomination to my lips.

8 All the words of my mouth *are* with righteousness;
Nothing crooked or perverse *is* in them.

9 They *are* all plain to him who understands,
And right to those who find knowledge.

10 Receive my instruction, and not silver,
And knowledge rather than choice gold;

11 For wisdom *is* better than rubies,
And all the things one may desire cannot be compared with her.

12 "I, wisdom, dwell with prudence,
And find out knowledge *and* discretion.

13 The fear of the LORD *is* to hate evil;
Pride and arrogance and the evil way
And the perverse mouth I hate.

14 Counsel *is* mine, and sound wisdom;
I *am* understanding, I have strength.

15 By me kings reign,
And rulers decree justice.

16 By me princes rule, and nobles,
All the judges of the earth.[a]

17 I love those who love me,
And those who seek me diligently will find me.

18 Riches and honor *are* with me,
Enduring riches and righteousness.

19 My fruit *is* better than gold, yes, than fine gold,
And my revenue than choice silver.

20 I traverse the way of righteousness,
In the midst of the paths of justice,

21 That I may cause those who love me to inherit wealth,
That I may fill their treasuries.

22 "The LORD possessed me at the beginning of His way,
Before His works of old.

23 I have been established from everlasting,
From the beginning, before there was ever an earth.

24 When *there were* no depths I was brought forth,

7:22 [a]Septuagint, Syriac, and Targum read *as a dog to bonds*; Vulgate reads *as a lamb . . . to bonds.*
7:27 [a]Or *Sheol* 8:16 [a]Masoretic Text, Syriac, Targum, and Vulgate read *righteousness*; Septuagint, Bomberg, and some manuscripts and editions read *earth.*

When *there were* no fountains
abounding with water.
25 Before the mountains were settled,
Before the hills, I was brought forth;
26 While as yet He had not made the
earth or the fields,
Or the primal dust of the world.
27 When He prepared the heavens, I *was*
there,
When He drew a circle on the face of
the deep,
28 When He established the clouds
above,
When He strengthened the fountains
of the deep,
29 When He assigned to the sea its limit,
So that the waters would not
transgress His command,
When He marked out the foundations
of the earth,
30 Then I was beside Him *as* a master
craftsman;[a]
And I was daily *His* delight,
Rejoicing always before Him,
31 Rejoicing in His inhabited world,
And my delight *was* with the sons of
men.

8:22–31 The LORD possessed me. Personified wisdom claims credit for everything that God created. Christ used His eternal wisdom in creation (John 1:1–3).

32 "Now therefore, listen to me, *my*
children,
For blessed *are those who* keep my
ways.
33 Hear instruction and be wise,
And do not disdain *it.*
34 Blessed is the man who listens to me,
Watching daily at my gates,
Waiting at the posts of my doors.
35 For whoever finds me finds life,
And obtains favor from the LORD;
36 But he who sins against me wrongs
his own soul;
All those who hate me love death."

The Way of Wisdom

9 Wisdom has built her house,
She has hewn out her seven pillars;
2 She has slaughtered her meat,
She has mixed her wine,

9:2 mixed her wine. Wine was diluted with water (as much as 1 part wine to 8 parts water) to reduce its power to intoxicate. It was also mixed with spices for flavor (Song 8:2). Unmixed wine was called strong drink (see Lev. 10:9).

She has also furnished her table.
3 She has sent out her maidens,
She cries out from the highest places
of the city,
4 "Whoever *is* simple, let him turn in
here!"
As for him who lacks understanding,
she says to him,
5 "Come, eat of my bread
And drink of the wine I have mixed.
6 Forsake foolishness and live,
And go in the way of understanding.

7 "He who corrects a scoffer gets shame
for himself,
And he who rebukes a wicked *man*
only harms himself.
8 Do not correct a scoffer, lest he hate
you;
Rebuke a wise *man,* and he will love
you.
9 Give *instruction* to a wise *man,* and
he will be still wiser;
Teach a just *man,* and he will increase
in learning.
10 "The fear of the LORD *is* the beginning
of wisdom,
And the knowledge of the Holy One
is understanding.
11 For by me your days will be
multiplied,
And years of life will be added to you.
12 If you are wise, you are wise for
yourself,
And *if* you scoff, you will bear *it*
alone."

The Way of Folly
13 A foolish woman is clamorous;
She is simple, and knows nothing.
14 For she sits at the door of her house,
On a seat *by* the highest places of the
city,
15 To call to those who pass by,
Who go straight on their way:

8:30 [a]A Jewish tradition reads *one brought up.*

16 "Whoever *is* simple, let him turn in
    here";
    And *as for* him who lacks
      understanding, she says to him,
17 "Stolen water is sweet,
    And bread *eaten* in secret is
      pleasant."
18 But he does not know that the dead
    are there,
    That her guests *are* in the depths of
      hell.*ᵃ*

Wise Sayings of Solomon

10 The proverbs of Solomon:

    A wise son makes a glad father,
    But a foolish son *is* the grief of his
      mother.

> **10:1–22:16** These are Solomon's 375 individual proverbs. They are in no significant order, grouped occasionally by subject, often without a given context, and based on Solomon's knowledge of the Law and the Prophets. He uses two-line proverbs (the parallel), which are contrasts, in chaps. 10–15, and he uses similarities or comparisons in chaps. 16–22.

2 Treasures of wickedness profit
    nothing,
    But righteousness delivers from
      death.
3 The LORD will not allow the righteous
    soul to famish,
    But He casts away the desire of the
      wicked.

4 He who has a slack hand becomes
    poor,
    But the hand of the diligent makes
      rich.
5 He who gathers in summer *is* a wise
    son;
    He who sleeps in harvest *is* a son
      who causes shame.

6 Blessings *are* on the head of the
    righteous,
    But violence covers the mouth of the
      wicked.
7 The memory of the righteous *is*
    blessed,
    But the name of the wicked will rot.

8 The wise in heart will receive
    commands,
    But a prating fool will fall.

9 He who walks with integrity walks
    securely,
    But he who perverts his ways will
      become known.

> **10:9** Those who live with integrity, living what they believe, do not live in fear of someone discovering evil in their lives, while the perverse person will not be able to hide it (see 11:3).

10 He who winks with the eye causes
    trouble,
    But a prating fool will fall.

11 The mouth of the righteous *is* a well
    of life,
    But violence covers the mouth of the
      wicked.

12 Hatred stirs up strife,
    But love covers all sins.

13 Wisdom is found on the lips of him
    who has understanding,
    But a rod *is* for the back of him who is
      devoid of understanding.

14 Wise *people* store up knowledge,
    But the mouth of the foolish *is* near
      destruction.

15 The rich man's wealth *is* his strong
    city;
    The destruction of the poor *is* their
      poverty.

> **10:15 rich man's...poor.** The rich man thinks he has his walled city for protection (see 18:11), but the poor man knows he has nothing. Both should trust God as their only protection (see Ps. 20:7).

16 The labor of the righteous *leads* to life,
    The wages of the wicked to sin.

17 He who keeps instruction *is in* the
    way of life,
    But he who refuses correction goes
      astray.

9:18 *ᵃ*Or *Sheol*

18 Whoever hides hatred *has* lying lips,
And whoever spreads slander *is* a fool.

19 In the multitude of words sin is not lacking,
But he who restrains his lips *is* wise.

20 The tongue of the righteous *is* choice silver;
The heart of the wicked *is worth* little.

21 The lips of the righteous feed many,
But fools die for lack of wisdom.*a*

22 The blessing of the LORD makes *one* rich,
And He adds no sorrow with it.

23 To do evil *is* like sport to a fool,
But a man of understanding has wisdom.

24 The fear of the wicked will come upon him,
And the desire of the righteous will be granted.

25 When the whirlwind passes by, the wicked *is* no *more*,
But the righteous *has* an everlasting foundation.

26 As vinegar to the teeth and smoke to the eyes,
So *is* the lazy *man* to those who send him.

27 The fear of the LORD prolongs days,
But the years of the wicked will be shortened.

28 The hope of the righteous *will be* gladness,
But the expectation of the wicked will perish.

29 The way of the LORD *is* strength for the upright,
But destruction *will come* to the workers of iniquity.

30 The righteous will never be removed,
But the wicked will not inhabit the earth.

31 The mouth of the righteous brings forth wisdom,

But the perverse tongue will be cut out.

32 The lips of the righteous know what is acceptable,
But the mouth of the wicked *what is* perverse.

11 Dishonest scales *are* an abomination to the LORD,
But a just weight *is* His delight.

2 When pride comes, then comes shame;
But with the humble *is* wisdom.

11:2 pride. The root of pride means "to boil" or "to run over," suggesting an arrogant attitude or behavior. It is used of ordinary men, kings, false prophets, and murderers (see Deut. 17:12,13; Neh. 9:10; Deut. 18:20; Ex. 21:14). **the humble.** This rare word, found in Mic. 6:8, is used to describe a spirit that is directed toward God (see 15:33).

3 The integrity of the upright will guide them,
But the perversity of the unfaithful will destroy them.

4 Riches do not profit in the day of wrath,
But righteousness delivers from death.

5 The righteousness of the blameless will direct*a* his way aright,
But the wicked will fall by his own wickedness.

6 The righteousness of the upright will deliver them,
But the unfaithful will be caught by *their* lust.

7 When a wicked man dies, *his* expectation will perish,
And the hope of the unjust perishes.

8 The righteous is delivered from trouble,
And it comes to the wicked instead.

9 The hypocrite with *his* mouth destroys his neighbor,
But through knowledge the righteous will be delivered.

10 When it goes well with the righteous, the city rejoices;

10:21 *a*Literally *heart*   11:5 *a*Or *make smooth* or *straight*

And when the wicked perish, *there is* jubilation.

11 By the blessing of the upright the city is exalted,
But it is overthrown by the mouth of the wicked.

12 He who is devoid of wisdom despises his neighbor,
But a man of understanding holds his peace.

13 A talebearer reveals secrets,
But he who is of a faithful spirit conceals a matter.

14 Where *there is* no counsel, the people fall;
But in the multitude of counselors *there is* safety.

15 He who is surety for a stranger will suffer,
But one who hates being surety is secure.

16 A gracious woman retains honor,
But ruthless *men* retain riches.

17 The merciful man does good for his own soul,
But *he who is* cruel troubles his own flesh.

18 The wicked *man* does deceptive work,
But he who sows righteousness *will have* a sure reward.

19 As righteousness *leads* to life,
So he who pursues evil *pursues it* to his own death.

20 Those who are of a perverse heart *are* an abomination to the LORD,
But *the* blameless in their ways *are* His delight.

21 *Though they* join forces,[a] the wicked will not go unpunished;

11:21 Though they join forces. The combined power of the wicked cannot free them from judgment, but the unaided children of the righteous find deliverance because of their relationship with God.

But the posterity of the righteous will be delivered.

22 *As* a ring of gold in a swine's snout,
So is a lovely woman who lacks discretion.

23 The desire of the righteous *is* only good,
But the expectation of the wicked *is* wrath.

24 There is *one* who scatters, yet increases more;
And there is *one* who withholds more than is right,
But it *leads* to poverty.

25 The generous soul will be made rich,
And he who waters will also be watered himself.

26 The people will curse him who withholds grain,
But blessing *will be* on the head of him who sells *it*.

11:24–26 scatters, yet increases. Generosity, by God's blessing, secures increase, while stinginess leads to poverty. The one who gives receives far more in return (Ps. 112:9).

27 He who earnestly seeks good finds favor,
But trouble will come to him who seeks *evil*.

28 He who trusts in his riches will fall,
But the righteous will flourish like foliage.

29 He who troubles his own house will inherit the wind,
And the fool *will be* servant to the wise of heart.

30 The fruit of the righteous *is a* tree of life,
And he who wins souls *is* wise.

31 If the righteous will be recompensed on the earth,
How much more the ungodly and the sinner.

11:21 [a]Literally *hand to hand*

12 Whoever loves instruction loves
knowledge,
But he who hates correction *is* stupid.

2 A good *man* obtains favor from the
LORD,
But a man of wicked intentions He
will condemn.

3 A man is not established by
wickedness,
But the root of the righteous cannot
be moved.

4 An excellent[a] wife *is* the crown of her
husband,
But she who causes shame *is* like
rottenness in his bones.

12:4 rottenness in his bones. This speaks of suffering that is like a painful and incurable condition.

5 The thoughts of the righteous *are*
right,
But the counsels of the wicked *are*
deceitful.

6 The words of the wicked *are,* "Lie in
wait for blood,"
But the mouth of the upright will
deliver them.

7 The wicked are overthrown and *are*
no more,
But the house of the righteous will
stand.

8 A man will be commended according
to his wisdom,
But he who is of a perverse heart will
be despised.

9 Better *is the* one who is slighted but
has a servant,
Than he who honors himself but
lacks bread.

10 A righteous *man* regards the life of his
animal,
But the tender mercies of the wicked
are cruel.

11 He who tills his land will be satisfied
with bread,
But he who follows frivolity *is* devoid
of understanding.[a]

12 The wicked covet the catch of evil *men,*
But the root of the righteous yields
fruit.

13 The wicked is ensnared by the
transgression of *his* lips,
But the righteous will come through
trouble.

14 A man will be satisfied with good by
the fruit of *his* mouth,
And the recompense of a man's hands
will be rendered to him.

15 The way of a fool *is* right in his own
eyes,
But he who heeds counsel *is* wise.

12:4 [a]Literally *A wife of valor*   12:11 [a]Literally *heart*

What are some general, time-tested principles that will help rightly interpret Proverbs?

One of the most common characteristics of Proverbs is the use of parallelism—placing truths side by side so that the second statement expands, completes, defines, and emphasizes the first. Sometimes a logical conclusion is reached; at other times, a logical contrast is demonstrated.

The following tools will assist a student in gaining greater confidence as he or she interprets these Proverbs: (1) deter-mine what facts, principles, or circumstances make up the parallel ideas in that proverb—what two central concepts or persons are being compared or contrasted; (2) identify the figures of speech and rephrase the thought without those figures—for example, restate the idea behind "put a knife to your throat" (23:1–3); (3) summarize the lesson or principle of the proverb in a few words; (4) describe the behavior that is being taught or encouraged; and (5) think of examples from elsewhere in Scripture that illustrate the truth of that proverb.

16 A fool's wrath is known at once,
But a prudent *man* covers shame.

17 He *who* speaks truth declares
righteousness,
But a false witness, deceit.

18 There is one who speaks like the
piercings of a sword,
But the tongue of the wise *promotes*
health.

19 The truthful lip shall be established
forever,
But a lying tongue *is* but for a
moment.

20 Deceit is in the heart of those who
devise evil,
But counselors of peace have joy.

21 No grave trouble will overtake the
righteous,
But the wicked shall be filled with
evil.

22 Lying lips *are* an abomination to the
LORD,
But those who deal truthfully *are* His
delight.

23 A prudent man conceals knowledge,
But the heart of fools proclaims
foolishness.

24 The hand of the diligent will rule,
But the lazy *man* will be put to forced
labor.

25 Anxiety in the heart of man causes
depression,
But a good word makes it glad.

26 The righteous should choose his
friends carefully,
For the way of the wicked leads them
astray.

27 The lazy *man* does not roast what he
took in hunting,
But diligence *is* man's precious
possession.

28 In the way of righteousness *is* life,
And in *its* pathway *there is* no death.

13 A wise son *heeds* his father's
instruction,
But a scoffer does not listen to rebuke.

2 A man shall eat well by the fruit of
his mouth,
But the soul of the unfaithful feeds on
violence.

3 He who guards his mouth preserves
his life,
But he who opens wide his lips shall
have destruction.

4 The soul of a lazy *man* desires, and
has nothing;
But the soul of the diligent shall be
made rich.

5 A righteous *man* hates lying,
But a wicked *man* is loathsome and
comes to shame.

6 Righteousness guards *him whose* way
is blameless,
But wickedness overthrows the sinner.

7 There is one who makes himself rich,
yet *has* nothing;
And one who makes himself poor, yet
has great riches.

13:7 makes himself rich...makes himself poor. One
pretends to be rich while the other pretends to be
poor, which shows the weaknesses of both. In contrast, men should be honest and unpretentious (see
2 Cor. 6:10).

8 The ransom of a man's life *is* his
riches,
But the poor does not hear rebuke.

9 The light of the righteous rejoices,
But the lamp of the wicked will be put
out.

10 By pride comes nothing but strife,
But with the well-advised *is* wisdom.

11 Wealth *gained by* dishonesty will be
diminished,
But he who gathers by labor will
increase.

12 Hope deferred makes the heart sick,
But *when* the desire comes, *it is* a
tree of life.

13 He who despises the word will be
destroyed,

But he who fears the commandment
will be rewarded.

14 The law of the wise *is* a fountain of
life,
To turn *one* away from the snares of
death.

15 Good understanding gains favor,
But the way of the unfaithful *is* hard.

16 Every prudent *man* acts with
knowledge,
But a fool lays open *his* folly.

17 A wicked messenger falls into trouble,
But a faithful ambassador *brings*
health.

18 Poverty and shame *will come* to him
who disdains correction,
But he who regards a rebuke will be
honored.

19 A desire accomplished is sweet to the
soul,
But *it is* an abomination to fools to
depart from evil.

20 He who walks with wise *men* will be
wise,
But the companion of fools will be
destroyed.

13:20 walks...companion. This speaks of the power
of association to shape character (see 22:24; Ps. 1).

21 Evil pursues sinners,
But to the righteous, good shall be
repaid.

22 A good *man* leaves an inheritance to
his children's children,
But the wealth of the sinner is stored
up for the righteous.

23 Much food *is in* the fallow *ground* of
the poor,
And for lack of justice there is waste.[a]

24 He who spares his rod hates his son,
But he who loves him disciplines him
promptly.

13:24 rod...disciplines...promptly. Children need
parental discipline along with love. The hope is that
the use of the "divine ordinance" of the rod will produce godly virtue in children and joy in parents. This
discipline must come from the right motivation (Heb.
12:5–11) with appropriate severity (Eph. 6:4). One
who loves his children, but withholds corporal punishment, will produce the same kind of child as one
who hates his child.

25 The righteous eats to the satisfying of
his soul,
But the stomach of the wicked shall
be in want.

14 The wise woman builds her house,
But the foolish pulls it down with
her hands.

2 He who walks in his uprightness fears
the LORD,
But *he who is* perverse in his ways
despises Him.

3 In the mouth of a fool *is* a rod of
pride,
But the lips of the wise will preserve
them.

4 Where no oxen *are,* the trough *is*
clean;
But much increase *comes* by the
strength of an ox.

5 A faithful witness does not lie,
But a false witness will utter lies.

6 A scoffer seeks wisdom and does not
find it,
But knowledge *is* easy to him who
understands.

7 Go from the presence of a foolish
man,
When you do not perceive *in him* the
lips of knowledge.

8 The wisdom of the prudent *is* to
understand his way,
But the folly of fools *is* deceit.

9 Fools mock at sin,
But among the upright *there is*
favor.

13:23 [a]Literally *what is swept away*

10 The heart knows its own bitterness,
And a stranger does not share its joy.

11 The house of the wicked will be
overthrown,
But the tent of the upright will
flourish.

12 There is a way *that seems* right to a
man,
But its end *is* the way of death.

13 Even in laughter the heart may
sorrow,
And the end of mirth *may be* grief.

14 The backslider in heart will be filled
with his own ways,
But a good man *will be satisfied* from
above.*a*

14:14 backslider in heart. This term is used to describe those who are backsliders: the fool, the wicked, and the disobedient. The backslider is contrasted with the godly, wise person.

15 The simple believes every word,
But the prudent considers well his
steps.

16 A wise *man* fears and departs from
evil,
But a fool rages and is self-confident.

17 A quick-tempered *man* acts foolishly,
And a man of wicked intentions is
hated.

18 The simple inherit folly,
But the prudent are crowned with
knowledge.

19 The evil will bow before the good,
And the wicked at the gates of the
righteous.

20 The poor *man* is hated even by his
own neighbor,
But the rich *has* many friends.

21 He who despises his neighbor sins;
But he who has mercy on the poor,
happy *is* he.

22 Do they not go astray who devise evil?
But mercy and truth *belong* to those
who devise good.

23 In all labor there is profit,
But idle chatter*a* *leads* only to
poverty.

24 The crown of the wise is their riches,
But the foolishness of fools *is* folly.

25 A true witness delivers souls,
But a deceitful *witness* speaks lies.

26 In the fear of the LORD *there is* strong
confidence,
And His children will have a place of
refuge.

27 The fear of the LORD *is* a fountain of
life,
To turn *one* away from the snares of
death.

28 In a multitude of people *is* a king's
honor,
But in the lack of people *is* the
downfall of a prince.

29 *He who is* slow to wrath has great
understanding,
But *he who is* impulsive*a* exalts folly.

30 A sound heart *is* life to the body,
But envy *is* rottenness to the bones.

31 He who oppresses the poor reproaches
his Maker,
But he who honors Him has mercy on
the needy.

14:31 oppresses the poor...Maker. It offends the Creator when we neglect the poor, who are part of His creation (see 14:21).

32 The wicked is banished in his
wickedness,
But the righteous has a refuge in his
death.

33 Wisdom rests in the heart of him who
has understanding,
But *what is* in the heart of fools is
made known.

34 Righteousness exalts a nation,
But sin *is* a reproach to *any* people.

14:14 *a*Literally *from above himself*   14:23 *a*Literally *talk of the lips*   14:29 *a*Literally *short of spirit*

35   The king's favor *is* toward a wise
          servant,
      But his wrath *is against* him who
          causes shame.

15 A soft answer turns away wrath,
         But a harsh word stirs up anger.
2   The tongue of the wise uses
          knowledge rightly,
      But the mouth of fools pours forth
          foolishness.

3   The eyes of the LORD *are* in every
          place,
      Keeping watch on the evil and the
          good.

4   A wholesome tongue *is* a tree of life,
      But perverseness in it breaks the
          spirit.

5   A fool despises his father's
          instruction,
      But he who receives correction is
          prudent.

6   *In* the house of the righteous *there is*
          much treasure,
      But in the revenue of the wicked is
          trouble.

7   The lips of the wise disperse
          knowledge,
      But the heart of the fool *does* not *do* so.

8   The sacrifice of the wicked *is* an
          abomination to the LORD,
      But the prayer of the upright *is* His
          delight.

15:8 External acts of worship, although they follow
biblical guidelines, are repulsive to God if the heart
of the worshiper is wicked (see Is. 1:12–15).

9   The way of the wicked *is* an
          abomination to the LORD,
      But He loves him who follows
          righteousness.

10   Harsh discipline *is* for him who
          forsakes the way,
      And he who hates correction will die.

11   Hell[a] and Destruction[b] *are* before the
          LORD;
      So how much more the hearts of the
          sons of men.

12   A scoffer does not love one who
          corrects him,
      Nor will he go to the wise.

13   A merry heart makes a cheerful
          countenance,
      But by sorrow of the heart the spirit is
          broken.

14   The heart of him who has
          understanding seeks
          knowledge,
      But the mouth of fools feeds on
          foolishness.

15   All the days of the afflicted *are* evil,
      But he who is of a merry heart *has* a
          continual feast.

16   Better *is* a little with the fear of the
          LORD,
      Than great treasure with trouble.

17   Better *is* a dinner of herbs[a] where love
          is,
      Than a fatted calf with hatred.

18   A wrathful man stirs up strife,
      But *he who is* slow to anger allays
          contention.

19   The way of the lazy *man is* like a
          hedge of thorns,
      But the way of the upright *is* a
          highway.

20   A wise son makes a father glad,
      But a foolish man despises his
          mother.

21   Folly *is* joy *to him who is* destitute of
          discernment,
      But a man of understanding walks
          uprightly.

22   Without counsel, plans go awry,
      But in the multitude of counselors
          they are established.

15:11 [a]Or *Sheol*   [b]Hebrew *Abaddon*   15:17 [a]Or *vegetables*

23 A man has joy by the answer of his
   mouth,
   And a word *spoken* in due season,
   how good *it is!*

24 The way of life *winds* upward for the
   wise,
   That he may turn away from hell[a]
   below.

25 The LORD will destroy the house of
   the proud,
   But He will establish the boundary of
   the widow.

15:25 God will intervene when evil men try to take
the property of widows (see 22:28). Widows who
have God's help possess a more permanent dwelling
place than the prosperous and self-reliant sinners.

26 The thoughts of the wicked *are* an
   abomination to the LORD,
   But *the words* of the pure *are*
   pleasant.

27 He who is greedy for gain troubles his
   own house,
   But he who hates bribes will live.

28 The heart of the righteous studies
   how to answer,
   But the mouth of the wicked pours
   forth evil.

29 The LORD *is* far from the wicked,
   But He hears the prayer of the
   righteous.

30 The light of the eyes rejoices the
   heart,
   And a good report makes the bones
   healthy.[a]

31 The ear that hears the rebukes of life
   Will abide among the wise.

32 He who disdains instruction despises
   his own soul,
   But he who heeds rebuke gets
   understanding.

33 The fear of the LORD *is* the
   instruction of wisdom,
   And before honor *is* humility.

16 The preparations of the heart
   belong to man,
   But the answer of the tongue *is* from
   the LORD.

16:1 preparations...answer. Human responsibility
is always subject to God's absolute sovereignty (see
3:6).

2 All the ways of a man *are* pure in his
   own eyes,
   But the LORD weighs the spirits.

3 Commit your works to the LORD,
   And your thoughts will be
   established.

4 The LORD has made all for Himself,
   Yes, even the wicked for the day of
   doom.

5 Everyone proud in heart *is* an
   abomination to the LORD;
   Though they join forces,[a] none will go
   unpunished.

6 In mercy and truth
   Atonement is provided for iniquity;
   And by the fear of the LORD *one*
   departs from evil.

7 When a man's ways please the LORD,
   He makes even his enemies to be at
   peace with him.

8 Better *is* a little with righteousness,
   Than vast revenues without justice.

9 A man's heart plans his way,
   But the LORD directs his steps.

10 Divination *is* on the lips of the king;
   His mouth must not transgress in
   judgment.

11 Honest weights and scales *are* the
   LORD's;
   All the weights in the bag *are* His
   work.

12 *It is* an abomination for kings to
   commit wickedness,
   For a throne is established by
   righteousness.

15:24 [a]Or *Sheol*   15:30 [a]Literally *fat*   16:5 [a]Literally *hand to hand*

13 Righteous lips *are* the delight of kings,
And they love him who speaks *what
is* right.
14 As messengers of death *is* the king's
wrath,
But a wise man will appease it.
15 In the light of the king's face *is* life,
And his favor *is* like a cloud of the
latter rain.

16:15 cloud of the latter rain. The late spring rain,
which matured the crop, fell before the harvest (see
2 Sam. 23:3,4). It compares with the king's power to
encourage his subjects.

16 How much better to get wisdom than
gold!
And to get understanding is to be
chosen rather than silver.

17 The highway of the upright *is* to
depart from evil;
He who keeps his way preserves his
soul.

18 Pride *goes* before destruction,
And a haughty spirit before a fall.
19 Better *to be* of a humble spirit with
the lowly,
Than to divide the spoil with the proud.

20 He who heeds the word wisely will
find good,
And whoever trusts in the LORD,
happy *is* he.

21 The wise in heart will be called
prudent,
And sweetness of the lips increases
learning.

22 Understanding *is* a wellspring of life
to him who has it.
But the correction of fools *is* folly.

23 The heart of the wise teaches his
mouth,
And adds learning to his lips.

24 Pleasant words *are like* a honeycomb,
Sweetness to the soul and health to
the bones.

25 There is a way *that seems* right to a
man,
But its end *is* the way of death.

26 The person who labors, labors for
himself,
For his *hungry* mouth drives him *on*.

27 An ungodly man digs up evil,
And *it is* on his lips like a burning
fire.

16:28 sows. The same root word is used for the release of flaming foxes in the grain fields of the Philistines (Judg. 15:4). **whisperer.** A whisperer is a
slanderer or gossip.

28 A perverse man sows strife,
And a whisperer separates the best of
friends.
29 A violent man entices his neighbor,
And leads him in a way *that is* not
good.
30 He winks his eye to devise perverse
things;
He purses his lips *and* brings about
evil.

31 The silver-haired head *is* a crown of
glory,
If it is found in the way of
righteousness.

32 *He who is* slow to anger *is* better than
the mighty,
And he who rules his spirit than he
who takes a city.

33 The lot is cast into the lap,
But its every decision *is* from the
LORD.

17 Better *is* a dry morsel with
quietness,
Than a house full of feasting*a* *with*
strife.

2 A wise servant will rule over a son
who causes shame,
And will share an inheritance among
the brothers.

17:1 *a*Or *sacrificial meals*

3   The refining pot *is* for silver and the
furnace for gold,
But the LORD tests the hearts.

4   An evildoer gives heed to false lips;
A liar listens eagerly to a spiteful
tongue.

5   He who mocks the poor reproaches
his Maker;
He who is glad at calamity will not go
unpunished.

6   Children's children *are* the crown of
old men,
And the glory of children *is* their father.

7   Excellent speech is not becoming to a
fool,
Much less lying lips to a prince.

8   A present *is* a precious stone in the
eyes of its possessor;
Wherever he turns, he prospers.

9   He who covers a transgression seeks
love,
But he who repeats a matter separates
friends.

10   Rebuke is more effective for a wise
man
Than a hundred blows on a fool.

11   An evil *man* seeks only rebellion;
Therefore a cruel messenger will be
sent against him.

12   Let a man meet a bear robbed of her
cubs,
Rather than a fool in his folly.

13   Whoever rewards evil for good,
Evil will not depart from his house.

14   The beginning of strife *is like*
releasing water;
Therefore stop contention before a
quarrel starts.

15   He who justifies the wicked, and he
who condemns the just,

Both of them alike *are* an
abomination to the LORD.

16   Why *is there* in the hand of a fool the
purchase price of wisdom,
Since *he has* no heart *for it?*

17   A friend loves at all times,
And a brother is born for adversity.

18   A man devoid of understanding
shakes hands in a pledge,
And becomes surety for his friend.

19   He who loves transgression loves
strife,
And he who exalts his gate seeks
destruction.

17:19 exalts his gate. This describes a proud man
who flaunts his wealth with a huge house with a large
front door. Pride invites death (see Jer. 22:13–19).

20   He who has a deceitful heart finds no
good,
And he who has a perverse tongue
falls into evil.

21   He who begets a scoffer *does so* to his
sorrow,
And the father of a fool has no joy.

22   A merry heart does good, *like*
medicine,[a]
But a broken spirit dries the bones.

23   A wicked *man* accepts a bribe behind
the back[a]
To pervert the ways of justice.

24   Wisdom *is* in the sight of him who
has understanding,
But the eyes of a fool *are* on the ends
of the earth.

25   A foolish son *is* a grief to his father,
And bitterness to her who bore
him.

26   Also, to punish the righteous *is* not
good,

17:22 [a]Or *makes medicine even better*   17:23 [a]Literally *from the bosom*

Nor to strike princes for *their* uprightness.

27 He who has knowledge spares his
words,
And a man of understanding is of a
calm spirit.
28 Even a fool is counted wise when he
holds his peace;
When he shuts his lips, *he is
considered* perceptive.

18 A man who isolates himself seeks
his own desire;
He rages against all wise judgment.

2 A fool has no delight in
understanding,
But in expressing his own heart.

3 When the wicked comes, contempt
comes also;
And with dishonor *comes* reproach.

4 The words of a man's mouth *are* deep
waters;
The wellspring of wisdom *is* a flowing
brook.

5 *It is* not good to show partiality to the
wicked,
Or to overthrow the righteous in
judgment.

6 A fool's lips enter into contention,
And his mouth calls for blows.
7 A fool's mouth *is* his destruction,
And his lips *are* the snare of his
soul.
8 The words of a talebearer *are* like
tasty trifles,*ᵃ*
And they go down into the inmost
body.

9 He who is slothful in his work
Is a brother to him who is a great
destroyer.

10 The name of the Lord *is* a strong
tower;
The righteous run to it and are safe.

11 The rich man's wealth *is* his strong
city,
And like a high wall in his own
esteem.

12 Before destruction the heart of a man
is haughty,
And before honor *is* humility.

13 He who answers a matter before he
hears *it*,
It *is* folly and shame to him.

14 The spirit of a man will sustain him
in sickness,
But who can bear a broken spirit?

15 The heart of the prudent acquires
knowledge,
And the ear of the wise seeks
knowledge.

16 A man's gift makes room for him,
And brings him before great men.

17 The first *one* to plead his cause *seems*
right,
Until his neighbor comes and
examines him.

18 Casting lots causes contentions to
cease,
And keeps the mighty apart.

19 A brother offended *is harder to win*
than a strong city,
And contentions *are* like the bars of a
castle.

20 A man's stomach shall be satisfied
from the fruit of his mouth;
From the produce of his lips he shall
be filled.

18:8 *ᵃ*A Jewish tradition reads *wounds*.

21 Death and life *are* in the power of the
   tongue,
   And those who love it will eat its
   fruit.

22 *He who* finds a wife finds a good
   thing,
   And obtains favor from the LORD.

23 The poor *man* uses entreaties,
   But the rich answers roughly.

24 A man *who has* friends must himself
   be friendly,*a*
   But there is a friend *who* sticks closer
   than a brother.

> **18:24 must himself be friendly.** The person who
> makes friends too easily and indiscriminately does
> so to his own destruction. In contrast, a friend cho-
> sen wisely is more loyal than a brother. **friend.** The
> word means "one who loves" and was used to de-
> scribe Abraham, God's friend (see 2 Chr. 20:7).

19 Better *is* the poor who walks in his
      integrity
   Than *one who is* perverse in his lips,
   and is a fool.

2 Also it is not good *for* a soul *to be*
   without knowledge,
   And he sins who hastens with *his*
   feet.

3 The foolishness of a man twists his
   way,
   And his heart frets against the LORD.

4 Wealth makes many friends,
   But the poor is separated from his
   friend.

5 A false witness will not go
   unpunished,
   And *he who* speaks lies will not
   escape.

6 Many entreat the favor of the nobility,
   And every man *is* a friend to one who
   gives gifts.

7 All the brothers of the poor hate him;

How much more do his friends go far
from him!
He may pursue *them with* words, *yet*
they abandon *him*.

8 He who gets wisdom loves his own
   soul;
   He who keeps understanding will find
   good.

9 A false witness will not go
   unpunished,
   And *he who* speaks lies shall perish.

10 Luxury is not fitting for a fool,
   Much less for a servant to rule over
   princes.

11 The discretion of a man makes him
   slow to anger,
   And his glory *is* to overlook a
   transgression.

12 The king's wrath *is* like the roaring of
   a lion,
   But his favor *is* like dew on the grass.

13 A foolish son *is* the ruin of his father,
   And the contentions of a wife *are* a
   continual dripping.

> **19:13 continual dripping.** An obstinate, argumenta-
> tive woman is like an unrelenting leak: one has to run
> from it or go mad. An ungodly son and an irritating
> wife devastate a man.

14 Houses and riches *are* an inheritance
   from fathers,
   But a prudent wife *is* from the LORD.

15 Laziness casts *one* into a deep sleep,
   And an idle person will suffer hunger.

16 He who keeps the commandment
   keeps his soul,
   But he who is careless*a* of his ways
   will die.

17 He who has pity on the poor lends to
   the LORD,

18:24 *a*Following Greek manuscripts, Syriac, Targum, and Vulgate; Masoretic Text reads *may come to ruin*.   19:16 *a*Literally *despises*, figurative of recklessness or carelessness

And He will pay back what he has
given.

18 Chasten your son while there is hope,
And do not set your heart on his
destruction.*a*

19 *A man of* great wrath will suffer
punishment;
For if you rescue *him,* you will have to
do it again.

20 Listen to counsel and receive
instruction,
That you may be wise in your latter
days.

21 There are many plans in a man's
heart,
Nevertheless the LORD's counsel—
that will stand.

22 What is desired in a man is kindness,
And a poor man is better than a
liar.

23 The fear of the LORD *leads* to life,
And *he who has it* will abide in
satisfaction;
He will not be visited with evil.

24 A lazy *man* buries his hand in the
bowl,*a*
And will not so much as bring it to
his mouth again.

25 Strike a scoffer, and the simple will
become wary;
Rebuke one who has understanding,
and he will discern knowledge.

26 He who mistreats *his* father *and*
chases away *his* mother
Is a son who causes shame and brings
reproach.

27 Cease listening to instruction, my
son,
And you will stray from the words of
knowledge.

28 A disreputable witness scorns
justice,
And the mouth of the wicked devours
iniquity.

29 Judgments are prepared for
scoffers,
And beatings for the backs of fools.

20 Wine *is* a mocker,
Strong drink *is* a brawler,
And whoever is led astray by it is not
wise.

20:1 Wine...strong drink. Wine was grape juice
mixed with water, but strong drink was unmixed. The
use of these beverages is not condemned, but being
intoxicated always is (Is. 28:7). Rulers were not to
drink, for their judgment should not be clouded
nor their behavior less than exemplary.
mocker...brawler. A "mocker" is also a "scoffer." A
brawler is violent, loud, and uncontrolled. Both describe a drunkard.

2 The wrath*a* of a king *is* like the
roaring of a lion;
Whoever provokes him to anger sins
against his own life.

3 *It is* honorable for a man to stop
striving,
Since any fool can start a quarrel.

4 The lazy *man* will not plow because
of winter;
He will beg during harvest and *have*
nothing.

5 Counsel in the heart of man *is like*
deep water,
But a man of understanding will draw
it out.

6 Most men will proclaim each his own
goodness,
But who can find a faithful man?

7 The righteous *man* walks in his
integrity;
His children *are* blessed after him.

19:18 *a*Literally *to put him to death;* a Jewish tradition reads *on his crying.*   19:24 *a*Septuagint and
Syriac read *bosom;* Targum and Vulgate read *armpit.*   20:2 *a*Literally *fear* or *terror* which is produced
by the king's wrath

8 A king who sits on the throne of judgment
Scatters all evil with his eyes.

9 Who can say, "I have made my heart clean,
I am pure from my sin"?

10 Diverse weights *and* diverse measures,
They *are* both alike, an abomination to the LORD.

11 Even a child is known by his deeds,
Whether what he does *is* pure and right.

12 The hearing ear and the seeing eye,
The LORD has made them both.

13 Do not love sleep, lest you come to poverty;
Open your eyes, *and* you will be satisfied with bread.

14 "*It is* good for nothing,"*a* cries the buyer;
But when he has gone his way, then he boasts.

15 There is gold and a multitude of rubies,
But the lips of knowledge *are* a precious jewel.

16 Take the garment of one who is surety *for* a stranger,
And hold it as a pledge *when it* is for a seductress.

> **20:16** Garments were a common security for a loan, but they always had to be returned by sundown (Ex. 22:26,27). "Seductress" is a "foreigner." Anyone who took on the responsibility for the debt of a stranger or an immoral woman would most likely never be paid back, so he could not pay his creditor unless his own garment was given as security.

17 Bread gained by deceit *is* sweet to a man,
But afterward his mouth will be filled with gravel.

18 Plans are established by counsel;
By wise counsel wage war.

19 He who goes about *as* a talebearer reveals secrets;
Therefore do not associate with one who flatters with his lips.

20 Whoever curses his father or his mother,
His lamp will be put out in deep darkness.

21 An inheritance gained hastily at the beginning
Will not be blessed at the end.

22 Do not say, "I will recompense evil";
Wait for the LORD, and He will save you.

23 Diverse weights *are* an abomination to the LORD,
And dishonest scales *are* not good.

24 A man's steps *are* of the LORD;
How then can a man understand his own way?

25 *It is* a snare for a man to devote rashly *something as* holy,
And afterward to reconsider *his* vows.

> **20:25 to devote rashly.** To promise something to God as an offering was irreversible and serious (see Ecc. 5:4–6).

26 A wise king sifts out the wicked,
And brings the threshing wheel over them.

27 The spirit of a man *is* the lamp of the LORD,
Searching all the inner depths of his heart.*a*

28 Mercy and truth preserve the king,
And by lovingkindness he upholds his throne.

29 The glory of young men *is* their strength,

20:14 *a*Literally *evil, evil*   20:27 *a*Literally *the rooms of the belly*

And the splendor of old men *is* their
gray head.

30 Blows that hurt cleanse away evil,
As *do* stripes the inner depths of the
heart.[a]

21 The king's heart *is* in the hand of
the LORD,
Like the rivers of water; He turns it
wherever He wishes.

2 Every way of a man *is* right in his own
eyes,
But the LORD weighs the hearts.

3 To do righteousness and justice
Is more acceptable to the LORD than
sacrifice.

4 A haughty look, a proud heart,
And the plowing[a] of the wicked *are* sin.

5 The plans of the diligent *lead* surely
to plenty,
But *those of* everyone *who is* hasty,
surely to poverty.

6 Getting treasures by a lying tongue
Is the fleeting fantasy of those who
seek death.[a]

7 The violence of the wicked will
destroy them,[a]
Because they refuse to do justice.

8 The way of a guilty man *is* perverse;[a]
But *as for* the pure, his work *is* right.

9 Better to dwell in a corner of a
housetop,
Than in a house shared with a
contentious woman.

21:9 corner of a housetop. Roofs were open like
patios (see Deut. 22:8), and a small enclosure in the
corner of a flat roof was a very inconvenient place to
live.

10 The soul of the wicked desires evil;
His neighbor finds no favor in his
eyes.

11 When the scoffer is punished, the
simple is made wise;
But when the wise is instructed, he
receives knowledge.

12 The righteous *God* wisely considers
the house of the wicked,
Overthrowing the wicked for *their*
wickedness.

13 Whoever shuts his ears to the cry of
the poor
Will also cry himself and not be
heard.

14 A gift in secret pacifies anger,
And a bribe behind the back,[a] strong
wrath.

15 *It is* a joy for the just to do justice,
But destruction *will come* to the
workers of iniquity.

16 A man who wanders from the way of
understanding
Will rest in the assembly of the
dead.

17 He who loves pleasure *will be* a poor
man;
He who loves wine and oil will not be
rich.

18 The wicked *shall be* a ransom for the
righteous,
And the unfaithful for the upright.

21:18 By suffering the very thing they had devised for
the righteous, the wicked became their substitute in
judgment.

19 Better to dwell in the wilderness,
Than with a contentious and angry
woman.

20:30 [a]Literally *the rooms of the belly*   21:4 [a]Or *lamp*   21:6 [a]Septuagint reads *Pursue vanity on the
snares of death*; Vulgate reads *Is vain and foolish, and shall stumble on the snares of death*; Targum
reads *They shall be destroyed, and they shall fall who seek death.*   21:7 [a]Literally *drag them away*
21:8 [a]Or *The way of a man is perverse and strange*   21:14 [a]Literally *in the bosom*

20 *There is* desirable treasure,
And oil in the dwelling of the wise,
But a foolish man squanders it.

21 He who follows righteousness and
    mercy
Finds life, righteousness and honor.

22 A wise *man* scales the city of the
    mighty,
And brings down the trusted
    stronghold.

23 Whoever guards his mouth and
    tongue
Keeps his soul from troubles.

24 A proud *and* haughty *man*—"Scoffer"
    is his name;
He acts with arrogant pride.

25 The desire of the lazy *man* kills him,
For his hands refuse to labor.

26 He covets greedily all day long,
But the righteous gives and does not
    spare.

27 The sacrifice of the wicked *is* an
    abomination;
How much more *when* he brings it
    with wicked intent!

28 A false witness shall perish,
But the man who hears *him* will
    speak endlessly.

29 A wicked man hardens his face,
But *as for* the upright, he establishes[a]
    his way.

30 *There is* no wisdom or understanding
Or counsel against the LORD.

31 The horse *is* prepared for the day of
    battle,
But deliverance *is* of the LORD.

21:31 prepared...deliverance. This condemns the
reliance on preparation for victory, as reliance
should be on the Lord (see Ezra 8:22).

22 A *good* name is to be chosen
    rather than great riches,
Loving favor rather than silver and
    gold.

2 The rich and the poor have this in
    common,
The LORD *is* the maker of them all.

3 A prudent *man* foresees evil and hides
    himself,
But the simple pass on and are
    punished.

4 By humility *and* the fear of the LORD
Are riches and honor and life.

5 Thorns *and* snares *are* in the way of
    the perverse;
He who guards his soul will be far
    from them.

6 Train up a child in the way he should
    go,
And when he is old he will not depart
    from it.

22:6 way he should go. The only right way is God's
way. Early training secures lifelong habits, so parents
must teach God's Word and consistently enforce it
with loving discipline during the child's upbringing
(see Deut. 4:9; Josh. 24:15).

7 The rich rules over the poor,
And the borrower *is* servant to the
    lender.

8 He who sows iniquity will reap
    sorrow,
And the rod of his anger will fail.

9 He who has a generous eye will be
    blessed,
For he gives of his bread to the poor.

10 Cast out the scoffer, and contention
    will leave;
Yes, strife and reproach will cease.

11 He who loves purity of heart
And has grace on his lips,
The king *will be* his friend.

21:29 [a]Qere and Septuagint read *understands.*

12 The eyes of the LORD preserve
knowledge,
But He overthrows the words of the
faithless.

13 The lazy *man* says, *"There is* a lion
outside!
I shall be slain in the streets!"

14 The mouth of an immoral woman *is* a
deep pit;
He who is abhorred by the LORD will
fall there.

15 Foolishness *is* bound up in the heart
of a child;
The rod of correction will drive it far
from him.

16 He who oppresses the poor to increase
his *riches,*
And he who gives to the rich, *will*
surely *come* to poverty.

> **22:17–24:34** Solomon compiled these 77 proverbs, which were spoken by godly men prior to his reign. The section begins with an introduction, followed by a collection of proverbs in random order with one, two, or three verses each. This is followed by two collections of additional proverbs, which continue with the wisdom themes of this book.

Sayings of the Wise

17 Incline your ear and hear the words of
the wise,
And apply your heart to my
knowledge;

18 For *it is* a pleasant thing if you keep
them within you;
Let them all be fixed upon your lips,

19 So that your trust may be in the LORD;
I have instructed you today, even you.

20 Have I not written to you excellent
things
Of counsels and knowledge,

21 That I may make you know the
certainty of the words of truth,
That you may answer words of truth
To those who send to you?

22 Do not rob the poor because he *is* poor,
Nor oppress the afflicted at the gate;

> **22:22 gate.** The gate was the place where civic and legal issues were settled, so beggars sat at the gate to catch the attention of the many people who passed by there. The "afflicted" sat there to beg or seek justice or mercy. They were to be fairly treated.

23 For the LORD will plead their cause,
And plunder the soul of those who
plunder them.

24 Make no friendship with an angry
man,
And with a furious man do not go,

25 Lest you learn his ways
And set a snare for your soul.

26 Do not be one of those who shakes
hands in a pledge,
One of those who is surety for debts;

27 If you have nothing *with which* to pay,
Why should he take away your bed
from under you?

28 Do not remove the ancient landmark
Which your fathers have set.

29 Do you see a man *who* excels in his
work?
He will stand before kings;
He will not stand before unknown
men.

23 When you sit down to eat with a
ruler,
Consider carefully what *is* before you;
2 And put a knife to your throat
If you *are* a man given to appetite.
3 Do not desire his delicacies,
For they *are* deceptive food.

4 Do not overwork to be rich;
Because of your own understanding,
cease!
5 Will you set your eyes on that which
is not?
For *riches* certainly make themselves
wings;
They fly away like an eagle *toward*
heaven.

6 Do not eat the bread of a miser,[a]
Nor desire his delicacies;

23:6 [a]Literally *one who has an evil eye*

7 For as he thinks in his heart, so *is* he.
"Eat and drink!" he says to you,
But his heart is not with you.

8 The morsel you have eaten, you will
vomit up,
And waste your pleasant words.

9 Do not speak in the hearing of a fool,
For he will despise the wisdom of
your words.

10 Do not remove the ancient
landmark,
Nor enter the fields of the fatherless;

11 For their Redeemer *is* mighty;
He will plead their cause against
you.

23:11 Redeemer. A near kinsman would rescue the one who had fallen upon hard times (see Lev. 25:25) or would avenge the murder of a relative (Num. 35:19). "Redeemer" is applied to God as the Savior of His people (see Gen. 48:16) since the helpless had no voice.

12 Apply your heart to instruction,
And your ears to words of
knowledge.

13 Do not withhold correction from a
child,
For *if* you beat him with a rod, he will
not die.

14 You shall beat him with a rod,
And deliver his soul from hell.[a]

15 My son, if your heart is wise,
My heart will rejoice—indeed, I
myself;

16 Yes, my inmost being will rejoice
When your lips speak right things.

17 Do not let your heart envy sinners,
But *be zealous* for the fear of the
LORD all the day;

18 For surely there is a hereafter,
And your hope will not be cut off.

19 Hear, my son, and be wise;
And guide your heart in the way.

20 Do not mix with winebibbers,
Or with gluttonous eaters of meat;

21 For the drunkard and the glutton will
come to poverty,
And drowsiness will clothe *a man*
with rags.

22 Listen to your father who begot you,
And do not despise your mother when
she is old.

23 Buy the truth, and do not sell *it,*
Also wisdom and instruction and
understanding.

23:23 Buy the truth. Truth must be obtained at all costs (see Matt. 13:44–46) and never relinquished at any price (see Dan. 1:8).

24 The father of the righteous will
greatly rejoice,
And he who begets a wise *child* will
delight in him.

25 Let your father and your mother be
glad,
And let her who bore you rejoice.

26 My son, give me your heart,
And let your eyes observe my ways.

27 For a harlot *is* a deep pit,
And a seductress *is* a narrow well.

28 She also lies in wait as *for* a victim,
And increases the unfaithful among
men.

29 Who has woe?
Who has sorrow?
Who has contentions?
Who has complaints?
Who has wounds without cause?
Who has redness of eyes?

30 Those who linger long at the wine,
Those who go in search of mixed
wine.

31 Do not look on the wine when it is red,
When it sparkles in the cup,
When it swirls around smoothly;

32 At the last it bites like a serpent,
And stings like a viper.

33 Your eyes will see strange things,
And your heart will utter perverse
things.

34 Yes, you will be like one who lies
down in the midst of the sea,

23:14 [a]Or *Sheol*

Or like one who lies at the top of the
    mast, *saying:*
35 "They have struck me, *but* I was not
    hurt;
They have beaten me, but I did not
    feel *it.*
When shall I awake, that I may seek
    another *drink?* "

23:29–35 This passage uses a riddle to warn against
drunkenness. Following the riddle's answer come
exhortations and descriptions of the drunkard's de-
lirious thoughts.

24 Do not be envious of evil men,
    Nor desire to be with them;
2   For their heart devises violence,
    And their lips talk of troublemaking.

3   Through wisdom a house is built,
    And by understanding it is
      established;
4   By knowledge the rooms are filled
    With all precious and pleasant riches.

5   A wise man *is* strong,
    Yes, a man of knowledge increases
      strength;
6   For by wise counsel you will wage
    your own war,
    And in a multitude of counselors
    there is safety.

7   Wisdom *is* too lofty for a fool;
    He does not open his mouth in the
      gate.

8   He who plots to do evil
    Will be called a schemer.
9   The devising of foolishness *is* sin,
    And the scoffer *is* an abomination to
      men.

10   *If* you faint in the day of adversity,
    Your strength *is* small.

11   Deliver *those who* are drawn toward
    death,
    And hold back *those* stumbling to the
      slaughter.
12   If you say, "Surely we did not know
    this,"
    Does not He who weighs the hearts
      consider *it?*

He who keeps your soul, does He *not*
    know *it?*
And will He *not* render to *each* man
    according to his deeds?

24:12 He who weighs the hearts. God knows the
truth about the motives of the heart and the excuses
for failing to do what is right (see James 4:17).

13   My son, eat honey because *it is* good,
    And the honeycomb *which is* sweet to
      your taste;
14   So *shall* the knowledge of wisdom *be*
    to your soul;
    If you have found *it,* there is a
      prospect,
    And your hope will not be cut off.

15   Do not lie in wait, O wicked *man,*
    against the dwelling of the
      righteous;
    Do not plunder his resting place;
16   For a righteous *man* may fall seven
    times
    And rise again,
    But the wicked shall fall by calamity.

17   Do not rejoice when your enemy falls,
    And do not let your heart be glad
    when he stumbles;
18   Lest the LORD see *it,* and it displease
    Him,
    And He turn away His wrath from
      him.

19   Do not fret because of evildoers,
    Nor be envious of the wicked;
20   For there will be no prospect for the
    evil *man;*
    The lamp of the wicked will be put
      out.

21   My son, fear the LORD and the king;
    Do not associate with those given to
      change;
22   For their calamity will rise suddenly,
    And who knows the ruin those two
    can bring?

Further Sayings of the Wise

23 These *things* also *belong* to the wise:

    It is not good to show partiality in
    judgment.

24 He who says to the wicked, "You *are*
   righteous,"
   Him the people will curse;
   Nations will abhor him.
25 But those who rebuke *the wicked* will
   have delight,
   And a good blessing will come upon
   them.

26 He who gives a right answer kisses
   the lips.

24:26 kisses the lips. A just and righteous response
is as desirable as this intimate expression of friendship.

27 Prepare your outside work,
   Make it fit for yourself in the field;
   And afterward build your house.

28 Do not be a witness against your
   neighbor without cause,
   For would you deceive[a] with your
   lips?
29 Do not say, "I will do to him just as
   he has done to me;
   I will render to the man according to
   his work."

30 I went by the field of the lazy *man,*
   And by the vineyard of the man
   devoid of understanding;
31 And there it was, all overgrown with
   thorns;
   Its surface was covered with nettles;
   Its stone wall was broken down.
32 When I saw *it,* I considered *it* well;
   I looked on *it and* received
   instruction:
33 A little sleep, a little slumber,
   A little folding of the hands to rest;
34 So shall your poverty come *like* a
   prowler,
   And your need like an armed man.

Further Wise Sayings of Solomon

25 These also *are* proverbs of Solomon
   which the men of Hezekiah king of
Judah copied:

2 *It is* the glory of God to conceal a
   matter,

25:1 Hezekiah...copied. This collection of 137 proverbs, spoken by Solomon, was most likely copied into
a collection 200 years later during the reign of Hezekiah (about 715-686 B.C.). Hezekiah desired to bring
revival to Judah (2 Chr. 29:30), so he elevated the forgotten wisdom of David and Solomon (see 2 Chr.
29:31).

   But the glory of kings *is* to search out
      a matter.

3 *As* the heavens for height and the
      earth for depth,
   So the heart of kings *is* unsearchable.

4 Take away the dross from silver,
   And it will go to the silversmith *for*
      jewelry.
5 Take away the wicked from before the
      king,
   And his throne will be established in
      righteousness.

6 Do not exalt yourself in the presence
      of the king,
   And do not stand in the place of the
      great;
7 For *it is* better that he say to you,
   "Come up here,"
   Than that you should be put lower in
      the presence of the prince,
   Whom your eyes have seen.

8 Do not go hastily to court;
   For what will you do in the end,
   When your neighbor has put you to
      shame?
9 Debate your case with your neighbor,
   And do not disclose the secret to
      another;
10 Lest he who hears *it* expose your
      shame,
   And your reputation be ruined.

25:8–10 go hastily to court. When conflict arises,
the man with a contentious spirit is quick to go to
court. He is better off talking it over with his neighbor rather than exposing himself to public shame in
court, where everything will be told.

11 A word fitly spoken *is like* apples of
      gold

24:28 [a]Septuagint and Vulgate read *Do not deceive.*

In settings of silver.
12 *Like* an earring of gold and an
ornament of fine gold
Is a wise rebuker to an obedient ear.

13 Like the cold of snow in time of
harvest
Is a faithful messenger to those who
send him,
For he refreshes the soul of his masters.

14 Whoever falsely boasts of giving
Is like clouds and wind without rain.

15 By long forbearance a ruler is
persuaded,
And a gentle tongue breaks a bone.

16 Have you found honey?
Eat only as much as you need,
Lest you be filled with it and vomit.

17 Seldom set foot in your neighbor's
house,
Lest he become weary of you and hate
you.

18 A man who bears false witness
against his neighbor
Is like a club, a sword, and a sharp
arrow.

19 Confidence in an unfaithful *man* in
time of trouble
Is like a bad tooth and a foot out of
joint.

20 *Like* one who takes away a garment in
cold weather,
And like vinegar on soda,
Is one who sings songs to a heavy
heart.

21 If your enemy is hungry, give him
bread to eat;
And if he is thirsty, give him water to
drink;

22 For *so* you will heap coals of fire on
his head,
And the LORD will reward you.

23 The north wind brings forth rain,
And a backbiting tongue an angry
countenance.

24 *It is* better to dwell in a corner of a
housetop,
Than in a house shared with a
contentious woman.

25 *As* cold water to a weary soul,
So *is* good news from a far country.

26 A righteous *man* who falters before
the wicked
Is like a murky spring and a polluted
well.

27 *It is* not good to eat much honey;
So to seek one's own glory *is not*
glory.

28 Whoever *has* no rule over his own
spirit
Is like a city broken down, without
walls.

26 As snow in summer and rain in
harvest,
So honor is not fitting for a fool.

2 Like a flitting sparrow, like a flying
swallow,
So a curse without cause shall not
alight.

3 A whip for the horse,
A bridle for the donkey,
And a rod for the fool's back.

4 Do not answer a fool according to his
folly,
Lest you also be like him.

5 Answer a fool according to his folly,
Lest he be wise in his own eyes.

26:4, 5 answer a fool. These verses teach the appropriate way to answer a fool (an unbeliever who rejects truth). If someone answers by agreeing with his ideas and presuppositions, then he will think he is right. Instead, he should be rebuked and shown the truth so he can see his foolishness.

6 He who sends a message by the hand
of a fool
Cuts off *his own* feet *and* drinks
violence.

7 *Like* the legs of the lame that hang
limp
Is a proverb in the mouth of fools.

8   Like one who binds a stone in a sling
     Is he who gives honor to a fool.
9   *Like* a thorn *that* goes into the hand
     of a drunkard
     Is a proverb in the mouth of fools.
10   The great *God* who formed
     everything
     Gives the fool *his* hire and the
     transgressor *his* wages.*a*
11   As a dog returns to his own vomit,
     So a fool repeats his folly.
12   Do you see a man wise in his own
     eyes?
     There is more hope for a fool than for
     him.

13   The lazy *man* says, "*There is* a lion in
     the road!
     A fierce lion *is* in the streets!"
14   *As* a door turns on its hinges,
     So *does* the lazy *man* on his bed.
15   The lazy *man* buries his hand in the
     bowl;*a*
     It wearies him to bring it back to his
     mouth.
16   The lazy *man is* wiser in his own eyes
     Than seven men who can answer
     sensibly.

17   He who passes by *and* meddles in a
     quarrel not his own
     Is like one who takes a dog by the ears.

18   Like a madman who throws
     firebrands, arrows, and death,
19   *Is* the man *who* deceives his neighbor,
     And says, "I was only joking!"

20   Where *there is* no wood, the fire goes
     out;
     And where *there is* no talebearer,
     strife ceases.
21   *As* charcoal *is* to burning coals, and
     wood to fire,
     So *is* a contentious man to kindle
     strife.
22   The words of a talebearer *are* like
     tasty trifles,
     And they go down into the inmost
     body.

23   Fervent lips with a wicked heart
     Are like earthenware covered with
     silver dross.
24   He who hates, disguises *it* with his
     lips,

26:10 *a*The Hebrew is difficult; ancient and modern translators differ greatly.   26:15 *a*Compare 19:24

Many of the Proverbs appear to impose absolutes on life situations that prove to be unclear. How do the Proverbs apply to specific life decisions and experiences?

Proverbs are divine guidelines and wise observations that teach underlying principles of life (24:3,4). They are not inflexible laws or absolute promises. This is because they are applied in life situations that are rarely clear-cut or uncomplicated by other conditions. The consequences of a fool's behavior as described in Proverbs apply to the complete fool. Most people are only occasionally foolish and therefore experience the occasional consequences of foolish behavior. It becomes apparent that the proverbs usually do have exceptions due to the uncertainty of life and the unpredictable behavior of fallen people.

The marvelous challenge and principle expressed in 3:5,6 puts a heavy emphasis on trusting the Lord with "all your heart" and "in all your ways acknowledge Him." Even partly practicing the conditions of those phrases represents a major challenge. Because of God's grace, we don't have to perfectly carry out the conditions in order to experience the truth that "He shall direct your paths."

God does not guarantee uniform outcome or application for each proverb. By studying them and applying them, a believer is allowed to contemplate God's mind, character, attributes, works, and blessings. In Jesus Christ are hidden all the treasures of wisdom and knowledge which are only partly expressed in Proverbs (Colossians 2:3).

And lays up deceit within himself;

25 When he speaks kindly, do not believe him,
For *there are* seven abominations in his heart;

26 *Though his* hatred is covered by deceit,
His wickedness will be revealed before the assembly.

27 Whoever digs a pit will fall into it,
And he who rolls a stone will have it roll back on him.

28 A lying tongue hates *those who are* crushed by it,
And a flattering mouth works ruin.

27 Do not boast about tomorrow,
For you do not know what a day may bring forth.

2 Let another man praise you, and not your own mouth;
A stranger, and not your own lips.

3 A stone *is* heavy and sand *is* weighty,
But a fool's wrath *is* heavier than both of them.

4 Wrath *is* cruel and anger a torrent,
But who *is* able to stand before jealousy?

5 Open rebuke *is* better
Than love carefully concealed.

6 Faithful *are* the wounds of a friend,
But the kisses of an enemy *are* deceitful.

7 A satisfied soul loathes the honeycomb,
But to a hungry soul every bitter thing *is* sweet.

27:7 The luxury and indolence of wealth make the best things tasteless, while the hard-working person who hungers finds every bitter thing sweet. This applies not only to food, but also to things in general, which mean so much more to those who have little.

8 Like a bird that wanders from its nest
Is a man who wanders from his place.

9 Ointment and perfume delight the heart,
And the sweetness of a man's friend *gives delight* by hearty counsel.

10 Do not forsake your own friend or your father's friend,
Nor go to your brother's house in the day of your calamity;
Better *is* a neighbor nearby than a brother far away.

11 My son, be wise, and make my heart glad,
That I may answer him who reproaches me.

12 A prudent *man* foresees evil *and* hides himself;
The simple pass on *and* are punished.

13 Take the garment of him who is surety for a stranger,
And hold it in pledge *when* he is surety for a seductress.

14 He who blesses his friend with a loud voice, rising early in the morning,
It will be counted a curse to him.

15 A continual dripping on a very rainy day
And a contentious woman are alike;

16 Whoever restrains her restrains the wind,
And grasps oil with his right hand.

17 *As* iron sharpens iron,
So a man sharpens the countenance of his friend.

27:17 iron sharpens iron. Through theological discussion and encouragement, friends can sharpen each other's characters and minds, which will show through the joy in one's face.

18 Whoever keeps the fig tree will eat its fruit;
So he who waits on his master will be honored.

19 As in water face *reflects* face,
So a man's heart *reveals* the man.

20 Hell[a] and Destruction[b] are never
   full;
   So the eyes of man are never satisfied.

21 The refining pot *is* for silver and the
   furnace for gold,
   And a man *is valued* by what others
   say of him.

22 Though you grind a fool in a mortar
   with a pestle along with crushed
   grain,
   Yet his foolishness will not depart
   from him.

23 Be diligent to know the state of your
   flocks,
   And attend to your herds;

24 For riches *are* not forever,
   Nor does a crown *endure* to all
   generations.

25 *When* the hay is removed, and the
   tender grass shows itself,
   And the herbs of the mountains are
   gathered in,

26 The lambs *will provide* your
   clothing,
   And the goats the price of a field;

27 *You shall have* enough goats' milk for
   your food,
   For the food of your household,
   And the nourishment of your
   maidservants.

28 The wicked flee when no one
   pursues,
   But the righteous are bold as a lion.

2 Because of the transgression of a land,
   many *are* its princes;
   But by a man of understanding *and*
   knowledge
   Right will be prolonged.

3 A poor man who oppresses the poor
   Is like a driving rain which leaves no
   food.

4 Those who forsake the law praise the
   wicked,
   But such as keep the law contend
   with them.

5 Evil men do not understand justice,
   But those who seek the LORD
   understand all.

6 Better *is* the poor who walks in his
   integrity
   Than one perverse *in his* ways,
   though he *be* rich.

7 Whoever keeps the law *is* a discerning
   son,
   But a companion of gluttons shames
   his father.

8 One who increases his possessions by
   usury and extortion
   Gathers it for him who will pity the
   poor.

28:8 usury and extortion. The law forbids charging
interest to fellow Jews (see Deut. 23:19,20), but this
was often violated (see Neh. 5:7,11). **Gathers it for
him.** God shows justice by giving that dishonest
wealth to someone who treats the poor fairly.

9 One who turns away his ear from
   hearing the law,
   Even his prayer *is* an abomination.

10 Whoever causes the upright to go
   astray in an evil way,
   He himself will fall into his own pit;
   But the blameless will inherit good.

11 The rich man *is* wise in his own eyes,
   But the poor who has understanding
   searches him out.

28:11 rich man *is* wise in his own eyes. The poor
man is contrasted with the rich man, who is deceived
by his self-confidence. It is not always the rich who
are unrighteous or the poor who are wise, but this
occurs more often because of the blinding nature of
wealth (see Matt. 19:23,24).

12 When the righteous rejoice, *there is*
   great glory;
   But when the wicked arise, men hide
   themselves.

13 He who covers his sins will not
   prosper,

But whoever confesses and forsakes
them will have mercy.

14 Happy *is* the man who is always
reverent,
But he who hardens his heart will fall
into calamity.

15 *Like* a roaring lion and a charging
bear
Is a wicked ruler over poor people.

16 A ruler who lacks understanding *is* a
great oppressor,
But he who hates covetousness will
prolong *his* days.

17 A man burdened with bloodshed will
flee into a pit;
Let no one help him.

18 Whoever walks blamelessly will be
saved,
But *he who is* perverse *in his* ways
will suddenly fall.

19 He who tills his land will have plenty
of bread,
But he who follows frivolity will have
poverty enough!

20 A faithful man will abound with
blessings,
But he who hastens to be rich will not
go unpunished.

21 To show partiality *is* not good,
Because for a piece of bread a man
will transgress.

22 A man with an evil eye hastens after
riches,
And does not consider that poverty
will come upon him.

23 He who rebukes a man will find more
favor afterward
Than he who flatters with the tongue.

24 Whoever robs his father or his
mother,
And says, "It *is* no transgression,"
The same *is* companion to a
destroyer.

25 He who is of a proud heart stirs up
strife,
But he who trusts in the LORD will be
prospered.

26 He who trusts in his own heart is a
fool,
But whoever walks wisely will be
delivered.

27 He who gives to the poor will not
lack,
But he who hides his eyes will have
many curses.

28 When the wicked arise, men hide
themselves;
But when they perish, the righteous
increase.

29 He who is often rebuked, *and*
hardens *his* neck,
Will suddenly be destroyed, and that
without remedy.

2 When the righteous are in authority,
the people rejoice;
But when a wicked *man* rules, the
people groan.

3 Whoever loves wisdom makes his
father rejoice,
But a companion of harlots wastes *his*
wealth.

4 The king establishes the land by
justice,
But he who receives bribes overthrows
it.

5 A man who flatters his neighbor
Spreads a net for his feet.

6 By transgression an evil man is
snared,
But the righteous sings and rejoices.

7 The righteous considers the cause of
the poor,
But the wicked does not understand
such knowledge.

8 Scoffers set a city aflame,
But wise *men* turn away wrath.

9   *If* a wise man contends with a foolish
      man,
      Whether *the fool* rages or laughs,
      there is no peace.

10 The bloodthirsty hate the blameless,
      But the upright seek his well-being.[a]

11 A fool vents all his feelings,[a]
      But a wise *man* holds them back.

12 If a ruler pays attention to lies,
      All his servants *become* wicked.

13 The poor *man* and the oppressor have
      this in common:
      The LORD gives light to the eyes of
      both.

> **29:13 gives light to the eyes.** This phrase means "to sustain life." God gives life to both the poor and the rich oppressor, and He holds each responsible for His truth.

14 The king who judges the poor with
      truth,
      His throne will be established
      forever.

15 The rod and rebuke give wisdom,
      But a child left *to himself* brings
      shame to his mother.

16 When the wicked are multiplied,
      transgression increases;
      But the righteous will see their fall.

17 Correct your son, and he will give you
      rest;
      Yes, he will give delight to your soul.

18 Where *there is* no revelation,[a] the
      people cast off restraint;
      But happy *is* he who keeps the law.

> **29:18 no revelation.** The lack of the Word (1 Sam. 3:1) and the lack of hearing the Word (Amos 8:11,12) lead to lawless rebellion (see Ex. 32:25). The proverb contrasts this with the joy and glory of a lawful society (Mal. 4:4).

19 A servant will not be corrected by
      mere words;
      For though he understands, he will
      not respond.

20 Do you see a man hasty in his words?
      There is more hope for a fool than for
      him.

21 He who pampers his servant from
      childhood
      Will have him as a son in the end.

22 An angry man stirs up strife,
      And a furious man abounds in
      transgression.

23 A man's pride will bring him low,
      But the humble in spirit will retain
      honor.

24 Whoever is a partner with a thief
      hates his own life;
      He swears to tell the truth,[a] but
      reveals nothing.

25 The fear of man brings a snare,
      But whoever trusts in the LORD shall
      be safe.

26 Many seek the ruler's favor,
      But justice for man *comes* from the
      LORD.

27 An unjust man *is* an abomination to
      the righteous,
      And *he who is* upright in the way *is*
      an abomination to the wicked.

The Wisdom of Agur

30 The words of Agur the son of Jakeh,
his utterance. This man declared to
Ithiel—to Ithiel and Ucal:

> **30:1–33 The words of Agur.** Agur was most likely a student of wisdom at the time of Solomon (see 1 Kin. 4:30,31). His proverbs reflect his humility, a deep hatred for arrogance, and a keen theological mind.

2   Surely I *am* more stupid than *any*
        man,

29:10 [a]Literally *soul*   29:11 [a]Literally *spirit*   29:18 [a]Or *prophetic vision*   29:24 [a]Literally *hears the adjuration*

And do not have the understanding of
a man.

3 I neither learned wisdom
Nor have knowledge of the Holy One.

4 Who has ascended into heaven, or
descended?
Who has gathered the wind in His
fists?
Who has bound the waters in a
garment?
Who has established all the ends of
the earth?
What *is* His name, and what *is* His
Son's name,
If you know?

5 Every word of God *is* pure;
He *is* a shield to those who put their
trust in Him.

6 Do not add to His words,
Lest He rebuke you, and you be found
a liar.

7 Two *things* I request of You
(Deprive me not before I die):

8 Remove falsehood and lies far from
me;
Give me neither poverty nor riches—
Feed me with the food allotted to me;

9 Lest I be full and deny *You*,
And say, "Who *is* the LORD?"
Or lest I be poor and steal,
And profane the name of my God.

10 Do not malign a servant to his
master,
Lest he curse you, and you be found
guilty.

11 *There is* a generation *that* curses its
father,
And does not bless its mother.

12 *There is* a generation *that is* pure in
its own eyes,
Yet is not washed from its filthiness.

13 *There is* a generation—oh, how lofty
are their eyes!
And their eyelids are lifted up.

14 *There is* a generation whose teeth *are*
like swords,
And whose fangs *are like* knives,

To devour the poor from off the earth,
And the needy from *among* men.

15 The leech has two daughters—
Give *and* Give!

There are three *things that* are never
satisfied,
Four never say, "Enough!":

16 The grave,[a]
The barren womb,
The earth *that* is not satisfied with
water—
And the fire never says, "Enough!"

17 The eye *that* mocks *his* father,
And scorns obedience to *his* mother,
The ravens of the valley will pick it
out,
And the young eagles will eat it.

18 There are three *things which* are too
wonderful for me,
Yes, four *which* I do not understand:

19 The way of an eagle in the air,
The way of a serpent on a rock,
The way of a ship in the midst of the
sea,
And the way of a man with a virgin.

20 This *is* the way of an adulterous
woman:
She eats and wipes her mouth,
And says, "I have done no
wickedness."

30:18–20 Hypocrisy is illustrated by four natural
analogies of concealment: an eagle leaving no trail in
the air, a snake leaving no trail on the rock, a ship
leaving no trail in the sea, and a man leaving no mark
after sleeping with a virgin. These concealed actions
are similar to how the adulterous woman hides the
evidences of her shame while professing innocence.

21 For three *things* the earth is
perturbed,
Yes, for four it cannot bear up:

22 For a servant when he reigns,
A fool when he is filled with food,

23 A hateful *woman* when she is married,
And a maidservant who succeeds her
mistress.

30:16 *a*Or *Sheol*

24 There are four *things which* are little
　　on the earth,
　　But they *are* exceedingly wise:
25 The ants *are* a people not strong,
　　Yet they prepare their food in the
　　　summer;
26 The rock badgers[a] are a feeble folk,
　　Yet they make their homes in the
　　　crags;
27 The locusts have no king,
　　Yet they all advance in ranks;
28 The spider[a] skillfully grasps with its
　　hands,
　　And it is in kings' palaces.

30:24–28 four *things which* are little. These verses
show four creatures that survive by natural instinct.
The wisdom in these verses reflects on the wise Creator and His creation (see Ps. 8:3–9). Labor, diligence,
organization, planning, and resourcefulness are better than strength, which implies that wisdom is superior to might.

29 There are three *things which* are
　　majestic in pace,
　　Yes, four *which* are stately in walk:
30 A lion, *which is* mighty among
　　beasts
　　And does not turn away from any;
31 A greyhound,[a]
　　A male goat also,
　　And a king *whose* troops *are* with
　　　him.[b]

32 If you have been foolish in exalting
　　yourself,
　　Or if you have devised evil, *put your*
　　hand on *your* mouth.
33 For *as* the churning of milk produces
　　butter,
　　And wringing the nose produces
　　blood,
　　So the forcing of wrath produces
　　strife.

The Words of King Lemuel's Mother

31 The words of King Lemuel, the utterance which his mother taught
him:

31:1–31 This concluding chapter contains poems
about a wise king (31:2–9) and an excellent wife
(31:10–31). They are the teachings of a godly mother
to King Lemuel, whom ancient Jewish tradition identified as King Solomon, but who is otherwise unknown.

2 What, my son?
　　And what, son of my womb?
　　And what, son of my vows?
3 Do not give your strength to women,
　　Nor your ways to that which destroys
　　　kings.

4 *It is* not for kings, O Lemuel,
　　It is not for kings to drink wine,
　　Nor for princes intoxicating drink;
5 Lest they drink and forget the law,
　　And pervert the justice of all the
　　afflicted.
6 Give strong drink to him who is
　　perishing,
　　And wine to those who are bitter of
　　heart.
7 Let him drink and forget his poverty,
　　And remember his misery no more.

8 Open your mouth for the speechless,
　　In the cause of all *who are* appointed
　　to die.[a]
9 Open your mouth, judge righteously,
　　And plead the cause of the poor and
　　needy.

31:2–9 The godly king is told that his reign should be
characterized by holiness, sobriety, and compassion. He is warned against vices to which kings are
susceptible such as immorality, overindulgence,
unrighteous rule, and indifference to those in need.

The Virtuous Wife

10 Who[a] can find a virtuous[b] wife?
　　For her worth *is* far above rubies.
11 The heart of her husband safely trusts
　　her;
　　So he will have no lack of gain.
12 She does him good and not evil
　　All the days of her life.
13 She seeks wool and flax,

30:26 [a]Or *hyraxes*　**30:28** [a]Or *lizard*　**30:31** [a]Exact identity unknown　[b]A Jewish tradition reads *a
king against whom there is no uprising.*　**31:8** [a]Literally *sons of passing away*　**31:10** [a]Verses 10
through 31 are an alphabetic acrostic in Hebrew (compare Psalm 119).　[b]Literally *a wife of valor,* in
the sense of all forms of excellence

And willingly works with her hands.
14 She is like the merchant ships,
She brings her food from afar.
15 She also rises while it is yet night,
And provides food for her household,
And a portion for her maidservants.
16 She considers a field and buys it;
From her profits she plants a
vineyard.
17 She girds herself with strength,
And strengthens her arms.
18 She perceives that her merchandise *is*
good,
And her lamp does not go out by
night.
19 She stretches out her hands to the
distaff,
And her hand holds the spindle.
20 She extends her hand to the poor,
Yes, she reaches out her hands to the
needy.
21 She is not afraid of snow for her
household,
For all her household *is* clothed with
scarlet.
22 She makes tapestry for herself;
Her clothing *is* fine linen and purple.
23 Her husband is known in the gates,
When he sits among the elders of the
land.

31:23 known in the gates. This woman made a significant contribution to her husband's position in the
community and to his success by providing domestic comfort for him. A man's good reputation begins
in his home with the virtue of his wife.

24 She makes linen garments and sells
them,
And supplies sashes for the
merchants.

25 Strength and honor *are* her clothing;
She shall rejoice in time to come.
26 She opens her mouth with wisdom,
And on her tongue *is* the law of
kindness.
27 She watches over the ways of her
household,
And does not eat the bread of
idleness.
28 Her children rise up and call her
blessed;
Her husband *also,* and he praises
her:
29 "Many daughters have done well,
But you excel them all."
30 Charm *is* deceitful and beauty *is*
passing,
But a woman *who* fears the LORD, she
shall be praised.

31:30 Charm...beauty. True holiness and virtue command permanent respect and affection, far more
than charm and beauty of face and form (see 1 Tim.
2:9,10). **a woman *who* fears the LORD.** Proverbs ends
where it began, with a reference to the fear of the
Lord.

31   Give her of the fruit of her hands,
And let her own works praise her in
the gates.

31:10–31 This poem offers a beautiful description of
an excellent wife as described by a wife and mother
(v. 1). The excellent woman's character is marked by
spiritual and practical wisdom and moral virtues.
Although this poem comes from a different setting
and time, the timeless principles apply to every family. They are the prayer of every mother for the future
wife of her son. The 22 verses begin with the 22 letters of the Hebrew alphabet.

ECCLESIASTES

What makes life meaningful? Will enough friends, success, achievement, money, or recognition lead to happiness? King Solomon had the chance to test all the theories of what brings meaning to life. He took full advantage of his opportunity! In the end he declared them all "vanity." The book of Ecclesiastes serves as Solomon's journal of his failed experiment with life in the fast lane. He discovered everything that offers to make life full turns out to make life empty. His final conclusion points to the only source of true meaning: "Fear God and keep His commandments, for this is man's all" (Ecclesiastes 12:13).

AUTHOR AND DATE

Ecclesiastes was written by Solomon, no later than 931 B.C.

The numerous autobiographical notes in this book point to Solomon as the author. Among the most obvious are: (1) the royal titles fit Solomon ("son of David, king in Jerusalem"—1:1, and "king over Israel in Jerusalem"—1:12); (2) the author's moral odyssey parallels what is known of Solomon's life (1 Kings 2–11); and (3) the role of one who "taught the people knowledge" and wrote "many proverbs" (12:9) corresponds with Solomon's profile.

This book was written to young people by an experienced elder. The dispassionate wisdom that makes up Proverbs is illustrated in Ecclesiastes by an intimate, painful, first-hand wisdom learned in the hard school of life. Solomon warned his readers to avoid walking through life on the path of human wisdom. He pointed, instead, to the revealed wisdom of God (12:9–14) as the true answer to life's meaning.

The time of writing fits best around 931 B.C. as Solomon was nearing the end of his reign.

BACKGROUND AND SETTING

Ecclesiastes presents itself as an eyewitness account of a misdirected quest: "I set my heart to seek and search out by wisdom concerning all that is done under heaven" (1:13). Solomon decided to test intuitive wisdom by direct experiments. The risks of disillusionment, despair, and death that Solomon faithfully reported make his experiment a warning to those who would insist on copying Solomon's behavior rather than learning from his mistakes.

David recognized his son's wisdom (1 Kings 2:6,9) even before God deepened Solomon's capacity. After Solomon received a "wise and understanding heart" from

the Lord (1 Kings 3:7–12), he became known for rendering insightful decisions (1 Kings 3:16–28). His reputation for wisdom attracted "all the kings of the earth" to his courts (1 Kings 4:34). Solomon's impressive outpouring of songs, proverbs, and opinions set the stage for his personal engagement in the events of Ecclesiastes. Solomon found himself in a position to try anything and everything. He decided to do just that.

HISTORICAL AND THEOLOGICAL THEMES

As is true of most biblical wisdom literature, little historical narrative occurs in this book, only a few incidental references to Solomon's personal pilgrimage. The kingly sage studied life with high expectations but instead found persistent short-comings. He acknowledged the ongoing effects of the original curse (see Genesis 3:14–19). Despite Solomon's advantages and opportunities, Ecclesiastes describes in painful detail how he squandered God's blessings, living for his own personal pleasure rather than for God's glory. Solomon's warnings to later generations have the same ring of truth found in Paul's counsel to the Corinthians (1 Corinthians 1:18–21; 2:13–16). Honest confessions of failure often provide priceless guidance to those who pay attention.

HONEST CONFESSIONS OF FAILURE OFTEN PROVIDE PRICELESS GUIDANCE TO THOSE WHO PAY ATTENTION.

The key word "vanity" in Ecclesiastes expresses the futile attempt to be satisfied apart from God. The term is used 37 times to describe the illusion of finding meaning within the limits of this life. All earthly goals and ambitions when pursued as ends in themselves produce only emptiness. Solomon did his best to disprove that truth, but he failed.

One of the recurring themes in Ecclesiastes is the value of work—"What profit has a man from all his labor . . . ?"(1:3; 2:24; 3:9). The temptation to despair over apparent purposelessness was as real to Solomon as the lure of achievement and pleasure. Despite Solomon's abilities, the inner workings of God's creation and the personal providence of God in his own life remained a troubling mystery to him. But the reality of judgment for all, despite many unknowns, remained a certainty. Solomon concluded that in the light of God's inevitable judgment, the only fulfilled life is one lived in proper recognition of God and service to Him. Based on this understanding, even work, then, can be appreciated within its limitations. It is not the *source* but an outlet for meaningful living. Any other kind of life is frustrating and pointless—vanity.

Ecclesiastes is applicable to all who will listen and benefit, not so much from Solomon's experience but from the principles he learned as a result. The book answers some of life's most challenging questions, particularly when Solomon reports conclusions contrary to his own expectations. This honesty has led some to unwisely view Ecclesiastes as a book of skepticism. Thoughtful reading reveals that despite his amazingly rash behavior and thinking, Solomon never let go of his faith in God (12:13,14).

OUTLINE

The Vanity of Life

1 The words of the Preacher, the son of David, king in Jerusalem.

2 "Vanity[a] of vanities," says the Preacher;
"Vanity of vanities, all *is* vanity."

> **1:3 profit.** Solomon frequently refers to the gain from labor (see 3:9). Compared to the fleeting moments of life and little gain from work, efforts that achieve God's eternal purposes are much more fulfilling. **labor.** This refers to all of man's activity in life. **under the sun.** This phrase describes daily life.

3 What profit has a man from all his labor
    In which he toils under the sun?
4 *One* generation passes away, and
        another generation comes;
    But the earth abides forever.
5 The sun also rises, and the sun goes
        down,
    And hastens to the place where it
        arose.
6 The wind goes toward the south,

And turns around to the north;
The wind whirls about continually,
And comes again on its circuit.
7 All the rivers run into the sea,
    Yet the sea *is* not full;
    To the place from which the rivers
        come,
    There they return again.
8 All things *are* full of labor;
    Man cannot express *it*.
    The eye is not satisfied with
        seeing,
    Nor the ear filled with hearing.

9 That which has been *is* what will be,
    That which *is* done is what will be
        done,
    And *there is* nothing new under the
        sun.
10 Is there anything of which it may be
        said,
    "See, this *is* new"?
    It has already been in ancient times
        before us.
11 *There is* no remembrance of former
        things,

1:2 [a]Or *Absurdity, Frustration, Futility, Nonsense;* and so throughout this book

---

How does the author's declaration that "all is vanity" relate to the message of the Book of Ecclesiastes?

By stating one of his conclusions in the opening lines, the author of Ecclesiastes challenges readers to pay attention. The word translated "vanity" is used in at least three ways throughout the book. In each case, the term refers to the nature and value of human activity "under the sun":

1. "Vanity" refers to the "fleeting" nature of human accomplishments that James later described as vapor-like (James 4:14).

2. "Vanity" can mean "futile" or "meaningless," which points to the cursed condition of the universe and the debilitating effects it has on human earthly experience.

3. "Vanity" can represent "incomprehensible" or "enigmatic," which gives consideration to life's unanswerable questions. Solomon found that the word applied to his entire experiment.

While the context in each of the 37 appearances of "vanity" helps determine the particular meaning Solomon had in mind, his most frequent usage conveyed the idea of "incomprehensible" or "unknowable." He was expressing the human limits when faced with the mysteries of God's purposes. Solomon's final conclusion to "fear God and keep his commandments" (12:13,14) represents more than the book's summary; it states the only hope of the good life and the only reasonable response of faith and obedience to the sovereign God. God precisely superintends all activities under the sun, each in its time according to His perfect plan, while He discloses only as much as His perfect wisdom dictates. All people remain accountable. Those who refuse to take God and His Word seriously are doomed to lives of the severest vanity.

Nor will there be any remembrance of
things that are to come
By *those* who will come after.

The Grief of Wisdom

[12]I, the Preacher, was king over Israel in Jerusalem. [13]And I set my heart to seek and search out by wisdom concerning all that is done under heaven; this burdensome task God has given to the sons of man, by which they may be exercised. [14]I have seen all the works that are done under the sun; and indeed, all *is* vanity and grasping for the wind.

[15] *What is* crooked cannot be made
         straight,
      And what is lacking cannot be
         numbered.

[16]I communed with my heart, saying, "Look, I have attained greatness, and have gained more wisdom than all who were be-

---

THE "VANITIES" OF
(ECCLESIASTES 1:2; 12:8)

1. Human wisdom	2:14–16
2. Human effort	2:18–23
3. Human achievement	2:26
4. Human life	3:18–22
5. Human rivalry	4:4
6. Human selfish sacrifice	4:7,8
7. Human power	4:16
8. Human greed	5:10
9. Human accumulation	6:1–12
10. Human religion	8:10–14

---

fore me in Jerusalem. My heart has understood great wisdom and knowledge." [17]And I set my heart to know wisdom and to know madness and folly. I perceived that this also is grasping for the wind.

[18] For in much wisdom *is* much grief,
      And he who increases knowledge
         increases sorrow.

The Vanity of Pleasure

2 I said in my heart, "Come now, I will test you with mirth; therefore enjoy pleasure"; but surely, this also *was* vanity. [2]I said of laughter—"Madness!"; and of mirth, "What does it accomplish?" [3]I searched in my heart *how* to gratify my flesh with wine, while guiding my heart with wisdom, and how to lay hold on folly, till I might see what *was* good for the sons of men to do under heaven all the days of their lives.

[4]I made my works great, I built myself houses, and planted myself vineyards. [5]I made myself gardens and orchards, and I planted all *kinds* of fruit trees in them. [6]I made myself water pools from which to water the growing trees of the grove. [7]I acquired male and female servants, and had servants born in my house. Yes, I had greater possessions of herds and flocks than all who were in Jerusalem before me. [8]I also gathered for myself silver and gold and the special treasures of kings and of the provinces. I acquired male and female singers, the delights of the sons of men, *and* musical instruments[a] of all kinds.

[9]So I became great and excelled more than all who were before me in Jerusalem. Also my wisdom remained with me.

[10] Whatever my eyes desired I did not
         keep from them.
      I did not withhold my heart from any
         pleasure,
      For my heart rejoiced in all my labor;
      And this was my reward from all my
         labor.
[11] Then I looked on all the works that
         my hands had done
      And on the labor in which I had
         toiled;

2:8 [a]Exact meaning unknown

And indeed all *was* vanity and
   grasping for the wind.
There was no profit under the sun.

> **2:1–11** Pleasure is not necessarily evil, but it has its shortcomings, as does human wisdom. Solomon reflected upon his tragic experiences in attempting to draw satisfaction purely from pleasure.

The End of the Wise and the Fool

12   Then I turned myself to consider
     wisdom and madness and folly;
   For what *can* the man *do* who
     succeeds the king?—
   Only what he has already done.
13   Then I saw that wisdom excels folly
   As light excels darkness.
14   The wise man's eyes *are* in his head,
   But the fool walks in darkness.
   Yet I myself perceived
   That the same event happens to them
     all.

> **2:14 fool walks in darkness.** The fool is not mentally deficient; he is morally bankrupt. He is capable of learning wisdom, but he refuses to know, fear, and obey God.

15   So I said in my heart,
  "As it happens to the fool,
  It also happens to me,
  And why was I then more wise?"
  Then I said in my heart,
  "This also *is* vanity."
16   For *there is* no more remembrance of
     the wise than of the fool forever,
  Since all that now *is* will be forgotten
     in the days to come.
  And how does a wise *man* die?
  As the fool!

17 Therefore I hated life because the work that was done under the sun *was* distressing to me, for all *is* vanity and grasping for the wind. 18 Then I hated all my labor in which I had toiled under the sun, because I must leave it to the man who will come after me. 19 And who knows whether he will be wise or a fool? Yet he will rule over all my labor in which I toiled and in which I have shown

myself wise under the sun. This also *is* vanity. 20 Therefore I turned my heart and despaired of all the labor in which I had toiled under the sun. 21 For there is a man whose labor *is* with wisdom, knowledge, and skill; yet he must leave his heritage to a man who has not labored for it. This also *is* vanity and a great evil. 22 For what has man for all his labor, and for the striving of his heart with which he has toiled under the sun? 23 For all his days *are* sorrowful, and his work burdensome; even in the night his heart takes no rest. This also is vanity.

24 Nothing *is* better for a man *than* that he should eat and drink, and *that* his soul should enjoy good in his labor. This also, I saw, was from the hand of God. 25 For who can eat, or who can have enjoyment, more than I?[a] 26 For *God* gives wisdom and knowledge and joy to a man who *is* good in His sight; but to the sinner He gives the work of gathering and collecting, that he may give to *him who is* good before God. This also *is* vanity and grasping for the wind.

> **2:24 enjoy good in his labor.** In accepting everything as a gift from his Creator, man is able to see "good" in all his work, even in a cursed world (see 3:13).

Everything Has Its Time

3 To everything *there is* a season,
  A time for every purpose under
     heaven:

2   A time to be born,
   And a time to die;
  A time to plant,
   And a time to pluck *what is*
     planted;
3   A time to kill,
   And a time to heal;
  A time to break down,
   And a time to build up;
4   A time to weep,
   And a time to laugh;
  A time to mourn,
   And a time to dance;
5   A time to cast away stones,
   And a time to gather stones;

2:25 [a]Following Masoretic Text, Targum, and Vulgate; some Hebrew manuscripts, Septuagint, and Syriac read *without Him*.

A time to embrace,
And a time to refrain from
embracing;
6 A time to gain,
And a time to lose;
A time to keep,
And a time to throw away;
7 A time to tear,
And a time to sew;
A time to keep silence,
And a time to speak;
8 A time to love,
And a time to hate;
A time of war,
And a time of peace.

The God-Given Task

9What profit has the worker from that in which he labors? 10I have seen the God-given task with which the sons of men are to be occupied. 11He has made everything beautiful in its time. Also He has put eternity in their hearts, except that no one can

---

3:11 everything. This refers to every activity that has an end. **beautiful.** The phrase means fitting or appropriate (see Gen. 1:31). Activity should not be meaningless, even in a cursed world. Its futility lies in man and his failure to trust the wisdom of God. **put eternity in their hearts.** God made men for His eternal purpose, and nothing since the Fall can bring complete satisfaction.

---

find out the work that God does from beginning to end.
12I know that nothing is better for them than to rejoice, and to do good in their lives, 13and also that every man should eat and drink and enjoy the good of all his labor—it is the gift of God.

14 I know that whatever God does,
It shall be forever.
Nothing can be added to it,
And nothing taken from it.
God does it, that men should fear
before Him.
15 That which is has already been,
And what is to be has already
been;
And God requires an account of what
is past.

Injustice Seems to Prevail

16Moreover I saw under the sun:

In the place of judgment,
Wickedness was there;
And in the place of righteousness,
Iniquity was there.

17I said in my heart,

"God shall judge the righteous and the
wicked,

SOLOMON REFLECTS ON GENESIS

*Toward the end of his life, the penitent King Solomon pondered life
in the wake of the Fall and the outworking of man's sin.
Solomon drew the following conclusions, possibly from his own study of Genesis:*

1. God created the heavens and earth with laws of design and regularity (Ecclesiastes 1:2–7; 3:1–8; cf. Genesis 1:1–31; 8:22).
2. Man is created from dust and returns to dust (Ecclesiastes 3:20; 12:7; cf. Genesis 2:7; 3:19).
3. God placed in man His life-giving breath (Ecclesiastes 12:7; cf. Genesis 2:7).
4. As God ordained it, marriage is one of life's most enjoyable blessings (Ecclesiastes 9:9; cf. Genesis 2:18–25).
5. Divine judgment results from the Fall (Ecclesiastes 3:14–22; 11:9; 12:14; cf. Genesis 2:17; 3:1–19).
6. The effect of the curse on creation is "vanity," i.e., futility (Ecclesiastes 1:5–8; cf. Genesis 3:17–19).
7. Labor after the Fall is difficult and yields little profit (Ecclesiastes 1:3, 13; 2:3; 3:9–11; cf. Genesis 3:17–19).
8. Death overcomes all creatures after the Fall (Ecclesiastes 8:8; 9:4,5; cf. Genesis 2:17; 3:19).
9. After the Fall, man's heart is desperately wicked (Ecclesiastes 7:20; 7:29; 8:11; 9:3; cf. Genesis 3:22; 6:5; 8:21).
10. God withholds certain knowledge and wisdom from man for His wise, but unspoken, reasons (Ecclesiastes 6:12; 8:17; cf. Genesis 3:22).

For *there is* a time there for every purpose and for every work."

[18]I said in my heart, "Concerning the condition of the sons of men, God tests them, that they may see that they themselves are *like* animals." [19]For what happens to the sons of men also happens to animals; one thing befalls them: as one dies, so dies the other. Surely, they all have one breath; man has no advantage over animals, for all *is* vanity. [20]All go to one place: all are from the dust, and all return to dust. [21]Who knows the spirit of the sons of men, which goes upward, and the spirit of the animal, which goes down to the earth?[a] [22]So I perceived that nothing *is* better than that a man should rejoice in his own works, for that *is* his heritage. For who can bring him to see what will happen after him?

4 Then I returned and considered all the oppression that is done under the sun:

And look! The tears of the oppressed,
But they have no comforter—
On the side of their oppressors *there is* power,
But they have no comforter.
[2] Therefore I praised the dead who were already dead,
More than the living who are still alive.
[3] Yet, better than both *is he* who has never existed,
Who has not seen the evil work that is done under the sun.

The Vanity of Selfish Toil

[4]"Again, I saw that for all toil and every skillful work a man is envied by his neighbor. This also *is* vanity and grasping for the wind.

[5]
The fool folds his hands
And consumes his own flesh.

[6]
Better a handful *with* quietness
Than both hands full, *together with* toil and grasping for the wind.

[7]Then I returned, and I saw vanity under the sun:

[8]
There is one alone, without companion:
He has neither son nor brother.
Yet *there is* no end to all his labors,
Nor is his eye satisfied with riches.
But he never asks,
"For whom do I toil and deprive myself of good?"
This also *is* vanity and a grave misfortune.

The Value of a Friend

[9]
Two *are* better than one,
Because they have a good reward for their labor.
[10] For if they fall, one will lift up his companion.
But woe to him *who is* alone when he falls,
For *he has* no one to help him up.
[11] Again, if two lie down together, they will keep warm;
But how can one be warm *alone?*
[12] Though one may be overpowered by another, two can withstand him.
And a threefold cord is not quickly broken.

Popularity Passes Away

[13] Better a poor and wise youth

3:21 [a]Septuagint, Syriac, Targum, and Vulgate read *Who knows whether the spirit . . . goes upward, and whether . . . goes downward to the earth?*

Than an old and foolish king who will
    be admonished no more.
14 For he comes out of prison to be king,
    Although he was born poor in his
    kingdom.
15 I saw all the living who walk under
    the sun;
    They were with the second youth who
    stands in his place.
16 *There was* no end of all the people
    over whom he was made king;
    Yet those who come afterward will not
    rejoice in him.
    Surely this also *is* vanity and grasping
    for the wind.

Fear God, Keep Your Vows

5 Walk prudently when you go to the
house of God; and draw near to hear
rather than to give the sacrifice of fools, for
they do not know that they do evil.

2 Do not be rash with your mouth,
    And let not your heart utter anything
    hastily before God.
    For God *is* in heaven, and you on
    earth;
    Therefore let your words be few.
3 For a dream comes through much
    activity,
    And a fool's voice *is known* by *his*
    many words.

4 When you make a vow to God, do not
    delay to pay it;
    For *He has* no pleasure in fools.
    Pay what you have vowed—
5 Better not to vow than to vow and not
    pay.

6 Do not let your mouth cause your flesh to
sin; nor say before the messenger *of God*
that it *was* an error. Why should God be
angry at your excuse[a] and destroy the work
of your hands? 7 For in the multitude of
dreams and many words *there is* also vanity. But fear God.

The Vanity of Gain and Honor

8 If you see the oppression of the poor, and
the violent perversion of justice and righteousness in a province, do not marvel at

the matter; for high official watches over
high official, and higher officials are over
them.
9 Moreover the profit of the land is for all;
even the king is served from the field.

10 He who loves silver will not be
    satisfied with silver;
    Nor he who loves abundance, with
    increase.
    This also *is* vanity.

11 When goods increase,
    They increase who eat them;
    So what profit have the owners
    Except to see *them* with their eyes?

12 The sleep of a laboring man *is* sweet,
    Whether he eats little or much;
    But the abundance of the rich will not
    permit him to sleep.

13 There is a severe evil *which* I have
    seen under the sun:
    Riches kept for their owner to his
    hurt.
14 But those riches perish through
    misfortune;
    When he begets a son, *there is*
    nothing in his hand.
15 As he came from his mother's womb,
    naked shall he return,
    To go as he came;
    And he shall take nothing from his
    labor
    Which he may carry away in his
    hand.

16 And this also *is* a severe evil—
    Just exactly as he came, so shall he
    go.
    And what profit has he who has
    labored for the wind?
17 All his days he also eats in
    darkness,
    And *he has* much sorrow and
    sickness and anger.

5:12–17 Earthly treasures produce anxiety, pain, and fear. They disappear through bad business and are left at death.

5:6 [a]Literally *voice*

[18]Here is what I have seen: *It is* good and fitting *for one* to eat and drink, and to enjoy the good of all his labor in which he toils under the sun all the days of his life which God gives him; for it *is* his heritage. [19]As for every man to whom God has given riches and wealth, and given him power to eat of it, to receive his heritage and rejoice in his labor—this *is* the gift of God. [20]For he will not dwell unduly on the days of his life, because God keeps *him* busy with the joy of his heart.

6 There is an evil which I have seen under the sun, and it *is* common among men: [2]A man to whom God has given riches and wealth and honor, so that he lacks nothing for himself of all he desires; yet God does not give him power to eat of it, but a foreigner consumes it. This *is* vanity, and it *is* an evil affliction.

> **6:2 God does not give him power to eat.** The Lord gives and takes away for His own purposes. His blessings cannot be taken for granted, but they should be enjoyed with thankfulness while they are available.

[3]If a man begets a hundred *children* and lives many years, so that the days of his years are many, but his soul is not satisfied with goodness, or indeed he has no burial, I say *that* a stillborn child *is* better than he— [4]for it comes in vanity and departs in darkness, and its name is covered with darkness. [5]Though it has not seen the sun or known *anything*, this has more rest than that man, [6]even if he lives a thousand years twice—but has not seen goodness. Do not all go to one place?

7   All the labor of man *is* for his mouth,
And yet the soul is not satisfied.
8   For what more has the wise *man* than
the fool?
What does the poor man have,
Who knows *how* to walk before the
living?
9   Better *is* the sight of the eyes than the
wandering of desire.
This also *is* vanity and grasping for
the wind.

10   Whatever one is, he has been named
already,

For it is known that he *is* man;
And he cannot contend with Him
who is mightier than he.
11   Since there are many things that
increase vanity,
How *is* man the better?

[12]For who knows what *is* good for man in life, all the days of his vain life which he passes like a shadow? Who can tell a man what will happen after him under the sun?

The Value of Practical Wisdom

7 A good name *is* better than precious
ointment,
And the day of death than the day of
one's birth;
2   Better to go to the house of mourning
Than to go to the house of feasting,
For that *is* the end of all men;
And the living will take *it* to heart.
3   Sorrow *is* better than laughter,
For by a sad countenance the heart is
made better.
4   The heart of the wise *is* in the house
of mourning,
But the heart of fools *is* in the house
of mirth.
5   *It is* better to hear the rebuke of the
wise
Than for a man to hear the song of
fools.
6   For like the crackling of thorns under
a pot,
So *is* the laughter of the fool.
This also is vanity.

> **7:2–6** This section emphasizes that more is learned from adversity than from pleasure. Wisdom is developed during life's trials, though Solomon wishes that were not the case when he writes, "this is also vanity" (v. 6).

7   Surely oppression destroys a wise
man's reason,
And a bribe debases the heart.
8   The end of a thing *is* better than its
beginning;
The patient in spirit *is* better than the
proud in spirit.
9   Do not hasten in your spirit to be
angry,

For anger rests in the bosom of fools.
10 Do not say,
"Why were the former days better than
these?"
For you do not inquire wisely
concerning this.

11 Wisdom *is* good with an
inheritance,
And profitable to those who see the
sun.
12 For wisdom *is* a defense *as* money *is* a
defense,
But the excellence of knowledge *is*
that wisdom gives life to those who
have it.

13 Consider the work of God;
For who can make straight what He
has made crooked?
14 In the day of prosperity be joyful,
But in the day of adversity consider:
Surely God has appointed the one as
well as the other,
So that man can find out nothing *that*
will come after him.

7:14 prosperity...adversity. God ordains both kinds of days, and He withholds knowledge of the future.

15 I have seen everything in my days of
vanity:

There is a just *man* who perishes in
his righteousness,
And there is a wicked *man* who
prolongs *life* in his wickedness.

16 Do not be overly righteous,
Nor be overly wise:
Why should you destroy yourself?
17 Do not be overly wicked,
Nor be foolish:
Why should you die before your
time?
18 *It is* good that you grasp this,
And also not remove your hand from
the other;
For he who fears God will escape
them all.

19 Wisdom strengthens the wise
More than ten rulers of the city.

20 For *there is* not a just man on earth
who does good
And does not sin.

21 Also do not take to heart everything
people say,
Lest you hear your servant cursing
you.
22 For many times, also, your own heart
has known
That even you have cursed others.

7:21,22 people say. We should not keep strict accounts of offensive words spoken against us, as we ourselves need forgiveness for saying many offensive words.

23 All this I have proved by wisdom.
I said, "I will be wise";
But it *was* far from me.
24 As for that which is far off and
exceedingly deep,
Who can find it out?
25 I applied my heart to know,
To search and seek out wisdom and
the reason *of things*,
To know the wickedness of folly,
Even of foolishness *and* madness.
26 And I find more bitter than death
The woman whose heart *is* snares and
nets,
Whose hands *are* fetters.
He who pleases God shall escape from
her,
But the sinner shall be trapped by her.
27 "Here is what I have found," says the
Preacher,
"*Adding* one thing to the other to find
out the reason,
28 Which my soul still seeks but I
cannot find:
One man among a thousand I have
found,
But a woman among all these I have
not found.
29 Truly, this only I have found:
That God made man upright,
But they have sought out many
schemes."

8 Who *is* like a wise *man?*
And who knows the interpretation of
a thing?

A man's wisdom makes his face
  shine,
And the sternness of his face is
  changed.

Obey Authorities for God's Sake

[2]I *say*, "Keep the king's commandment for the sake of your oath to God. [3]Do not be hasty to go from his presence. Do not take your stand for an evil thing, for he does whatever pleases him."

4 Where the word of a king *is, there is*
    power;
  And who may say to him, "What are
    you doing?"
5 He who keeps his command will
    experience nothing harmful;
  And a wise man's heart discerns both
    time and judgment,
6 Because for every matter there is a
    time and judgment,
  Though the misery of man increases
    greatly.
7 For he does not know what will
    happen;
  So who can tell him when it will
    occur?
8 No one has power over the spirit to
    retain the spirit,
  And no one has power in the day of
    death.
  There is no release from that war,
  And wickedness will not deliver those
    who are given to it.

> **8:8 spirit.** "Wind" may be a better translation for the word "spirit." Death is as precarious and uncontrollable as the wind.

[9]All this I have seen, and applied my heart to every work that is done under the sun: *There is* a time in which one man rules over another to his own hurt.

Death Comes to All

[10]Then I saw the wicked buried, who had come and gone from the place of holiness, and they were forgotten[a] in the city where they had so done. This also *is* vanity. [11]Because the sentence against an evil work is not executed speedily, therefore the heart of the sons of men is fully set in them to do evil. [12]Though a sinner does evil a hundred *times,* and his *days* are prolonged, yet I surely know that it will be well with those who fear God, who fear before Him. [13]But it will not be well with the wicked; nor will he prolong *his* days, *which are* as a shadow, because he does not fear before God.

[14]There is a vanity which occurs on earth, that there are just *men* to whom it happens according to the work of the wicked; again, there are wicked *men* to whom it happens according to the work of the righteous. I said that this also *is* vanity.

[15]So I commended enjoyment, because a man has nothing better under the sun than to eat, drink, and be merry; for this will remain with him in his labor *all* the days of his life which God gives him under the sun.

> **8:15 enjoyment.** Solomon does not commend unbridled indulgence in sin, which Jesus describes in His account of the man whose barns were full (see Luke 12:19). That man may have justified his sin by quoting this passage by Solomon, but Solomon's focus here is on enjoying life in spite of the injustice that surrounded him.

[16]When I applied my heart to know wisdom and to see the business that is done on earth, even though one sees no sleep day or night, [17]then I saw all the work of God, that a man cannot find out the work that is done under the sun. For though a man labors to discover *it,* yet he will not find *it;* moreover, though a wise *man* attempts to know *it,* he will not be able to find *it.*

9 For I considered all this in my heart, so that I could declare it all: that the righteous and the wise and their works *are* in the hand of God. People know neither love nor hatred *by* anything *they see* before them. [2]All things *come* alike to all:

> **9:1 in the hand of God.** God will be fair in His judgment of the righteous and the wicked, because He remembers both in perfect detail.

One event *happens* to the righteous
  and the wicked;

8:10 [a]Some Hebrew manuscripts, Septuagint, and Vulgate read *praised.*

To the good,[a] the clean, and the
    unclean;
To him who sacrifices and him who
    does not sacrifice.
As is the good, so *is* the sinner;
He who takes an oath as *he* who fears
    an oath.

³This *is* an evil in all that is done under the
sun: that one thing *happens* to all. Truly the
hearts of the sons of men are full of evil; madness *is* in their hearts while they live, and after that *they go* to the dead. ⁴But for him
who is joined to all the living there is hope,
for a living dog is better than a dead lion.

5   For the living know that they will die;
    But the dead know nothing,
    And they have no more reward,
    For the memory of them is forgotten.
6   Also their love, their hatred, and their
      envy have now perished;
    Nevermore will they have a share
    In anything done under the sun.

7   Go, eat your bread with joy,
    And drink your wine with a merry
      heart;
    For God has already accepted your
      works.
8   Let your garments always be white,
    And let your head lack no oil.

⁹Live joyfully with the wife whom you
love all the days of your vain life which He
has given you under the sun, all your days
of vanity; for that *is* your portion in life, and
in the labor which you perform under the
sun.
¹⁰Whatever your hand finds to do, do *it*
with your might; for *there is* no work or device or knowledge or wisdom in the grave
where you are going.
¹¹I returned and saw under the sun that—

    The race *is* not to the swift,
    Nor the battle to the strong,
    Nor bread to the wise,
    Nor riches to men of understanding,
    Nor favor to men of skill;
    But time and chance happen to them
      all.
12   For man also does not know his time:
    Like fish taken in a cruel net,
    Like birds caught in a snare,
    So the sons of men *are* snared in an
      evil time,
    When it falls suddenly upon them.

Wisdom Superior to Folly

¹³This wisdom I have also seen under the
sun, and it *seemed* great to me: ¹⁴*There was*
a little city with few men in it; and a great
king came against it, besieged it, and built
great snares[a] around it. ¹⁵Now there was

9:2 [a]Septuagint, Syriac, and Vulgate read *good and bad*.   9:14 [a]Septuagint, Syriac, and Vulgate read
bulwarks.

**When the writer
of Ecclesiastes
encourages his
readers to "enjoy
life," does he
have any condi-
tions or cautions
in mind?**

Solomon balanced his enjoyment theme with repeated
reminders of divine judgment. Even the best moments in life
ought not to cut a person off from awareness of God as Provider
to whom all will give an account. Solomon declared that the
possibility of enjoyment was based on faith (Ecc. 2:24–26).
    Part of Ecclesiastes reports the king's experiment in trying to
enjoy life without regard for the fear of God's judgment.
Solomon discovered that such an effort was in vain. In the end,
he came to grasp the importance of obedience.
    The tragic results of Solomon's personal experience,
coupled with the insight of extraordinary wisdom, make
Ecclesiastes a book from which all believers can receive
warnings and lessons in their faith (2:1–26). This book
demonstrates that a person who sees each day of existence,
labor, and basic provision as a gift from God, and accepts
whatever God gives, will actually live an abundant life. However, anyone who seeks to be
satisfied apart from God will live with futility regardless of personal successes.

found in it a poor wise man, and he by his wisdom delivered the city. Yet no one remembered that same poor man.

¹⁶Then I said:

"Wisdom *is* better than strength.
Nevertheless the poor man's wisdom
   is despised,
And his words are not heard.
¹⁷ Words of the wise, *spoken* quietly,
   should be heard
Rather than the shout of a ruler of
   fools.
¹⁸ Wisdom *is* better than weapons of
   war;
But one sinner destroys much good."

10 Dead flies putrefy^a the perfumer's
   ointment,
And cause it to give off a foul odor;
So does a little folly to one respected
   for wisdom *and* honor.
² A wise man's heart *is* at his right
   hand,
But a fool's heart at his left.
³ Even when a fool walks along the way,
He lacks wisdom,
And he shows everyone *that* he *is* a
   fool.

10:3 walks. A person who lacks wisdom will manifest that in daily conduct.

⁴ If the spirit of the ruler rises against
   you,
Do not leave your post;
For conciliation pacifies great
   offenses.

⁵ There is an evil I have seen under the
   sun,
As an error proceeding from the ruler:
⁶ Folly is set in great dignity,
While the rich sit in a lowly place.
⁷ I have seen servants on horses,
While princes walk on the ground like
   servants.

⁸ He who digs a pit will fall into it,
And whoever breaks through a wall
   will be bitten by a serpent.

⁹ He who quarries stones may be hurt
   by them,
And he who splits wood may be
   endangered by it.
¹⁰ If the ax is dull,
And one does not sharpen the edge,
Then he must use more strength;
But wisdom brings success.

10:10 wisdom brings success. Wisdom eases the efforts of life. Even though many experiences do not turn out as hoped, wise living usually produces a good outcome. Solomon concludes this in his testing of wisdom.

¹¹ A serpent may bite when *it is* not
   charmed;
The babbler is no different.
¹² The words of a wise man's mouth *are*
   gracious,
But the lips of a fool shall swallow
   him up;
¹³ The words of his mouth begin with
   foolishness,
And the end of his talk *is* raving
   madness.
¹⁴ A fool also multiplies words.
No man knows what is to be;
Who can tell him what will be after
   him?
¹⁵ The labor of fools wearies them,
For they do not even know how to go
   to the city!

¹⁶ Woe to you, O land, when your king
   is a child,
And your princes feast in the
   morning!
¹⁷ Blessed *are* you, O land, when your
   king *is* the son of nobles,
And your princes feast at the proper
   time—
For strength and not for
   drunkenness!
¹⁸ Because of laziness the building
   decays,
And through idleness of hands the
   house leaks.
¹⁹ A feast is made for laughter,
And wine makes merry;
But money answers everything.

10:1 ^aTargum and Vulgate omit *putrefy*.

20 Do not curse the king, even in your
      thought;
   Do not curse the rich, even in your
      bedroom;
   For a bird of the air may carry your
      voice,
   And a bird in flight may tell the
      matter.

The Value of Diligence

11 Cast your bread upon the waters,
      For you will find it after many days.
2 Give a serving to seven, and also to
      eight,
   For you do not know what evil will be
      on the earth.

> **11:1,2 Cast your bread.** Take a wise step forward in
> life, like a farmer who throws his seed on the wet
> ground and waits for it to grow (see Is. 32:20). **Give.**
> Be generous while there is plenty, and make friends
> while time remains, because we never know when
> we might need the favor returned.

3 If the clouds are full of rain,
   They empty *themselves* upon the
      earth;
   And if a tree falls to the south or the
      north,
   In the place where the tree falls, there
      it shall lie.
4 He who observes the wind will not sow,
   And he who regards the clouds will
      not reap.

5 As you do not know what *is* the way
      of the wind,[a]
   Or how the bones *grow* in the womb
      of her who is with child,
   So you do not know the works of God
      who makes everything.
6 In the morning sow your seed,
   And in the evening do not withhold
      your hand;
   For you do not know which will
      prosper,
   Either this or that,
   Or whether both alike *will be* good.

7 Truly the light is sweet,
   And *it is* pleasant for the eyes to
      behold the sun;

> **11:7–12:8** The primary issues of this book are death,
> enjoyment, and judgment. Death is imminent, and
> with it comes retribution. Enjoyment and judgment
> require man's deepest commitment. One does not
> win out over the other. With too much pleasure, judg-
> ment stands as a threatening force; with too much
> judgment, enjoyment suffers. These issues are re-
> solved in our relationship to God.

8 But if a man lives many years
   And rejoices in them all,
   Yet let him remember the days of
      darkness,
   For they will be many.
   All that is coming *is* vanity.

Seek God in Early Life

9 Rejoice, O young man, in your youth,
   And let your heart cheer you in the
      days of your youth;
   Walk in the ways of your heart,
   And in the sight of your eyes;
   But know that for all these
   God will bring you into judgment.
10 Therefore remove sorrow from your
      heart,
   And put away evil from your flesh,
   For childhood and youth *are* vanity.

12 Remember now your Creator in the
      days of your youth,
   Before the difficult days come,
   And the years draw near when you say,
   "I have no pleasure in them":

> **12:1 Remember...your Creator...difficult days.** You
> are God's property, so serve Him from the start of
> your years, not the end of your years when service
> is limited.

2 While the sun and the light,
   The moon and the stars,
   Are not darkened,
   And the clouds do not return after the
      rain;
3 In the day when the keepers of the
      house tremble,
   And the strong men bow down;
   When the grinders cease because they
      are few,
   And those that look through the
      windows grow dim;

11:5 [a]Or *spirit*

4   When the doors are shut in the streets,
    And the sound of grinding is low;
    When one rises up at the sound of a
        bird,
    And all the daughters of music are
        brought low.
5   Also they are afraid of height,
    And of terrors in the way;
    When the almond tree blossoms,
    The grasshopper is a burden,
    And desire fails.
    For man goes to his eternal home,
    And the mourners go about the streets.

6   *Remember your Creator* before the
        silver cord is loosed,[a]
    Or the golden bowl is broken,
    Or the pitcher shattered at the
        fountain,
    Or the wheel broken at the well.
7   Then the dust will return to the earth
        as it was,
    And the spirit will return to God who
        gave it.

8   "Vanity of vanities," says the Preacher,
    "All *is* vanity."

The Whole Duty of Man

9And moreover, because the Preacher was wise, he still taught the people knowledge; yes, he pondered and sought out *and* set in order many proverbs. 10The Preacher sought to find acceptable words; and *what was* written *was* upright—words of truth. 11The words of the wise are like goads, and the words of scholars[a] are like well-driven nails, given by one Shepherd. 12And further, my son, be admonished by these. Of making many books *there is* no end, and much study *is* wearisome to the flesh.

13Let us hear the conclusion of the whole matter:

    Fear God and keep His
        commandments,
    For this is man's all.
14 For God will bring every work into
        judgment,
    Including every secret thing,
    Whether good or evil.

12:13,14 Fear God. Solomon's final focus is on one's relationship to God. Life's pleasures and uncertainties seemed irrelevant to him as he approached death. The finality of retribution gives meaning to life for Solomon, for God will judge every man's actions. Unbelievers will stand at the Great White Throne for judgment (see Rev. 20:11–15), and believers will stand before Christ at the Bema judgment (see 1 Cor. 3:10–15).

12:6 [a]Following Qere and Targum; Kethib reads *removed*; Septuagint and Vulgate read *broken*.
12:11 [a]Literally *masters of the assemblies*

SONG OF SOLOMON

The oldest songs are love songs. Among the most intimate ever written are these lyrics authored by Solomon and named after him. The ancient Hebrew versions of this book entitle it "Song of Songs." Based on the biblical record that Solomon composed 1,005 songs (1 Kings 4:32), the title indicates that this was his best.

AUTHOR AND DATE

Song of Solomon was written by Solomon, shortly after 971 B.C.

Solomon included his own name seven times in the book (1:1,5; 3:7,9,11; 8:11,12). His unequaled reputation as a thinker, writer, and composer point favorably toward the king as the original author. The style of this book also indicates a single, highly creative mind, composing an example of Wisdom literature as complex and delightful as the relationship about which it was written.

The nature of the Song allows it to be dated almost any time in Solomon's 40-year long reign (971–931 B.C.). The youthfulness of the lovers in this book indicates that the events recorded, if not the writing itself, occurred earlier rather than later in Solomon's reign.

BACKGROUND AND SETTING

Two people dominate this true-life, dramatic love song. Solomon the king takes on the role of "the beloved." The identity of the Shulamite maiden (6:13) remains obscure. Her name may indicate her hometown as Shunem, in Galilee. Although some suggest she was the daughter of Pharaoh mentioned in 1 Kings 3:1, the Song itself provides no confirmation. Others have suggested the woman in this song is Abishag, the Shunammite maiden who cared for the aging King David (1 Kings 1:1–4,15), but with very little evidence. We are left with an unknown maiden from Shunem who was Solomon's first wife (9:9). The relationship immortalized in the Song knows nothing of the sin into which Solomon fell when he added 699 other wives and 300 concubines to his household (1 Kings 11:3).

Various small groups fill the supporting roles in this love story. "The daughters of Jerusalem" (1:5), Solomon's friends (3:6–11), and the Shulamite's brothers (8:8,9) each supply an outside perspective for the couple.

The setting includes rural and urban scenes. Part of the story takes place in the hill country north of Jerusalem, where the Shulamite lived (6:13). They may have met while Solomon carried out duties as a vine-grower and shepherd (2:4–7).

The events of the wedding and the early married life of the couple occur in Jerusalem (Song of Solomon 3:6–7:13).

HISTORICAL AND THEOLOGICAL THEMES

Song of Solomon takes its place along with Ruth, Esther, Ecclesiastes, and Lamentations in the Hebrew scriptures as the "Megilloth, or "five scrolls." The Jews traditionally read the Song at Passover, calling it "the Holy of Holies." Surprisingly,

SOLOMON'S ANCIENT **LOVE SONG EXALTS** THE **PURITY** AND **PASSION** OF **MARITAL ROMANTIC AFFECTION.**

God is not mentioned explicitly except possibly in 8:6. No formal theological themes emerge from this book. Song of Solomon receives no direct mention in the New Testament.

Solomon's ancient love song exalts the purity and passion of marital romantic affection. It strongly contradicts the two distorted extremes of ascetic abstinence and lustful perversion outside of marriage. The Song positively illustrates other portions of Scripture that portray God's plan for marriage, including the beauty and sanctity of sexual intimacy between husband and wife. Among these parallel passages are the following: Genesis 2:24; Psalm 45; Proverbs 5:15–23; 1 Corinthians 7:1–5; 13:1–8; Ephesians 5:18–33; Colossians 3:18,19; Hebrews 13:4; 1 Peter 3:1–7.

OUTLINE

1

The song of songs, which *is* Solomon's.

The Banquet

> **1:2–3:5** In this first of 3 major sections to the Song, 32 out of 39 verses are spoken by the Shulamite, who remembers past events and anticipates the arrival of the king to take her to Jerusalem for their wedding. There are brief interludes by her beloved and the daughters of Jerusalem.

THE SHULAMITE[a]

2 Let him kiss me with the kisses of his
      mouth—
   For your[b] love *is* better than wine.
3 Because of the fragrance of your good
      ointments,
   Your name *is* ointment poured forth;
   Therefore the virgins love you.
4 Draw me away!

THE DAUGHTERS OF JERUSALEM

   We will run after you.[a]

THE SHULAMITE

   The king has brought me into his
      chambers.

THE DAUGHTERS OF JERUSALEM

   We will be glad and rejoice in you.[b]

   We will remember your[c] love more
      than wine.

THE SHULAMITE

   Rightly do they love you.[d]

5 I *am* dark, but lovely,
   O daughters of Jerusalem,
   Like the tents of Kedar,
   Like the curtains of Solomon.
6 Do not look upon me, because I *am*
      dark,

> **1:5,6 I am dark.** The Shulamite was concerned that the sun had marred her complexion from working outdoors.

Because the sun has tanned me.
   My mother's sons were angry with
      me;
   They made me the keeper of the
      vineyards,
   But my own vineyard I have not kept.

(TO HER BELOVED)

7 Tell me, O you whom I love,
   Where you feed *your flock,*
   Where you make *it* rest at noon.
   For why should I be as one who veils
      herself[a]
   By the flocks of your companions?

THE BELOVED

8 If you do not know, O fairest among
      women,
   Follow in the footsteps of the flock,
   And feed your little goats
   Beside the shepherds' tents.
9 I have compared you, my love,
   To my filly among Pharaoh's chariots.
10 Your cheeks are lovely with
      ornaments,
   Your neck with chains *of gold.*

THE DAUGHTERS OF JERUSALEM

11 We will make you[a] ornaments of gold
   With studs of silver.

THE SHULAMITE

12 While the king *is* at his table,
   My spikenard sends forth its
      fragrance.
13 A bundle of myrrh *is* my beloved to
      me,
   That lies all night between my
      breasts.
14 My beloved *is* to me a cluster of
      henna *blooms*
   In the vineyards of En Gedi.

THE BELOVED

15 Behold, you *are* fair, my love!
   Behold, you *are* fair!
   You *have* dove's eyes.

1:2 [a]A Palestinian young woman (compare 6:13). The speaker and audience are identified according to the number, gender, and person of the Hebrew words. Occasionally the identity is not certain.   [b]Masculine singular, that is, the Beloved   1:4 [a]Masculine singular, that is, the Beloved   [b]Feminine singular, that is, the Shulamite   1:7 [a]Septuagint, Syriac, and Vulgate read *wanders.*   1:11 [a]Feminine singular, that is, the Shulamite   [c]Masculine singular, that is, the Beloved   [d]Masculine singular, that is, the Beloved

THE SHULAMITE

16 Behold, you *are* handsome, my beloved!
Yes, pleasant!
Also our bed *is* green.

17 The beams of our houses *are* cedar,
And our rafters of fir.

2 I *am* the rose of Sharon,
And the lily of the valleys.

THE BELOVED

2 Like a lily among thorns,
So is my love among the daughters.

THE SHULAMITE

3 Like an apple tree among the trees of
the woods,
So *is* my beloved among the sons.
I sat down in his shade with great
delight,
And his fruit *was* sweet to my taste.

THE SHULAMITE TO THE DAUGHTERS OF JERUSALEM

4 He brought me to the banqueting
house,
And his banner over me *was* love.

5 Sustain me with cakes of raisins,
Refresh me with apples,
For I *am* lovesick.

6 His left hand *is* under my head,
And his right hand embraces me.

7 I charge you, O daughters of Jerusalem,
By the gazelles or by the does of the
field,
Do not stir up nor awaken love
Until it pleases.

2:7 I charge you. This refrain, which is repeated before and after the wedding, expresses the Shulamite's commitment to a chaste life before and during her marriage. She asks the daughters of Jerusalem to hold her accountable.

The Beloved's Request

THE SHULAMITE

8 The voice of my beloved!
Behold, he comes
Leaping upon the mountains,
Skipping upon the hills.

9 My beloved is like a gazelle or a young
stag.

Behold, he stands behind our wall;
He is looking through the windows,
Gazing through the lattice.

10 My beloved spoke, and said to me:
"Rise up, my love, my fair one,
And come away.

11 For lo, the winter is past,
The rain is over *and* gone.

12 The flowers appear on the earth;
The time of singing has come,
And the voice of the turtledove
Is heard in our land.

13 The fig tree puts forth her green figs,
And the vines *with* the tender grapes
Give a good smell.
Rise up, my love, my fair one,
And come away!

14 "O my dove, in the clefts of the rock,
In the secret *places* of the cliff,
Let me see your face,
Let me hear your voice;
For your voice *is* sweet,
And your face *is* lovely."

HER BROTHERS

15 Catch us the foxes,
The little foxes that spoil the vines,
For our vines *have* tender grapes.

THE SHULAMITE

16 My beloved *is* mine, and I *am* his.
He feeds *his flock* among the lilies.

2:16 My beloved *is* mine, and I *am* his. This expresses the sanctity of a monogamous relationship that is built on mutual love (see 6:3).

(TO HER BELOVED)

17 Until the day breaks
And the shadows flee away,
Turn, my beloved,
And be like a gazelle
Or a young stag
Upon the mountains of Bether.*[a]*

A Troubled Night

THE SHULAMITE

3 By night on my bed I sought the one I
love;

2:17 *[a]* Literally *Separation*

I sought him, but I did not find him.
2 "I will rise now," *I said*,
"And go about the city;
In the streets and in the squares
I will seek the one I love."
I sought him, but I did not find him.
3 The watchmen who go about the city
found me;
I said,
"Have you seen the one I love?"

4 Scarcely had I passed by them,
When I found the one I love.
I held him and would not let him go,
Until I had brought him to the house
of my mother,
And into the chamber of her who
conceived me.

5 I charge you, O daughters of
Jerusalem,
By the gazelles or by the does of the
field,
Do not stir up nor awaken love
Until it pleases.

> **3:5** She knows that the intensity of her love for Solomon cannot be experienced until the wedding, so she asks the daughters of Jerusalem to keep her accountable to sexual purity. Up to this point, her desire for Solomon has been expressed in veiled ways. The following expressions are explicit and open, which are completely appropriate for a married couple (see 4:1).

The Coming of Solomon

THE SHULAMITE

6 Who *is* this coming out of the
wilderness
Like pillars of smoke,
Perfumed with myrrh and
frankincense,
With all the merchant's fragrant
powders?
7 Behold, it *is* Solomon's couch,
With sixty valiant men around it,
Of the valiant of Israel.
8 They all hold swords,
Being expert in war.
Every man *has* his sword on his thigh
Because of fear in the night.

9 Of the wood of Lebanon
Solomon the King
Made himself a palanquin:*a*
10 He made its pillars *of* silver,
Its support *of* gold,
Its seat *of* purple,
Its interior paved *with* love
By the daughters of Jerusalem.
11 Go forth, O daughters of Zion,
And see King Solomon with the
crown
With which his mother crowned him
On the day of his wedding,
The day of the gladness of his heart.

THE BELOVED

4 Behold, you *are* fair, my love!
Behold, you *are* fair!
You *have* dove's eyes behind your
veil.
Your hair *is* like a flock of goats,
Going down from Mount Gilead.
2 Your teeth *are* like a flock of shorn
sheep
Which have come up from the
washing,
Every one of which bears twins,
And none *is* barren among them.
3 Your lips *are* like a strand of scarlet,
And your mouth is lovely.
Your temples behind your veil
Are like a piece of pomegranate.
4 Your neck *is* like the tower of David,
Built for an armory,
On which hang a thousand bucklers,
All shields of mighty men.
5 Your two breasts *are* like two fawns,
Twins of a gazelle,
Which feed among the lilies.

6 Until the day breaks
And the shadows flee away,
I will go my way to the mountain of
myrrh
And to the hill of frankincense.

> **3:6–5:1** This second major section describes the king coming for his bride, their return to Jerusalem, the wedding, and the consummation of their union. Solomon does the majority of the speaking here (15 of 23 verses).

3:9 *a*A portable enclosed chair

7 You *are* all fair, my love,
And *there is* no spot in you.
8 Come with me from Lebanon, *my*
 spouse,
With me from Lebanon.
Look from the top of Amana,
From the top of Senir and Hermon,
From the lions' dens,
From the mountains of the leopards.

9 You have ravished my heart,
My sister, *my* spouse;
You have ravished my heart
With one *look* of your eyes,
With one *link* of your necklace.
10 How fair is your love,
My sister, *my* spouse!
How much better than wine is your
 love,
And the scent of your perfumes
Than all spices!
11 Your lips, O *my* spouse,
Drip as the honeycomb;
Honey and milk *are* under your
 tongue;
And the fragrance of your garments
Is like the fragrance of Lebanon.

12 A garden enclosed
Is my sister, *my* spouse,
A spring shut up,
A fountain sealed.
13 Your plants *are* an orchard of
 pomegranates
With pleasant fruits,
Fragrant henna with spikenard,
14 Spikenard and saffron,
Calamus and cinnamon,
With all trees of frankincense,
Myrrh and aloes,
With all the chief spices—
15 A fountain of gardens,
A well of living waters,
And streams from Lebanon.

THE SHULAMITE
16 Awake, O north *wind,*
And come, O south!

> **4:16** The Shulamite portrays herself as an open garden, whereas before she was closed (4:12). She describes herself as "his garden," signifying voluntary sexual surrender (1 Cor. 7:3–5).

Blow upon my garden,
Th*at* its spices may flow out.
Let my beloved come to his garden
And eat its pleasant fruits.

THE BELOVED
5 I have come to my garden, my sister,
 my spouse;
I have gathered my myrrh with my
 spice;
I have eaten my honeycomb with my
 honey;
I have drunk my wine with my milk.

> **5:1 I have.** While the guests feasted, the couple consummated their marriage (see Gen. 29:23), and Solomon announced the blessing (see Gen. 2:25). **Eat, O friends!** Given the intimate and private nature of sexual union, it seems that only God would have spoken those words (see Prov. 5:21). This is the divine affirmation of sexual love between husband and wife as holy and beautiful.

(TO HIS FRIENDS)
Eat, O friends!
Drink, yes, drink deeply,
O beloved ones!

The Shulamite's Troubled Evening

THE SHULAMITE
2 I sleep, but my heart is awake;
It is the voice of my beloved!
He knocks, *saying,*
"Open for me, my sister, my love,
My dove, my perfect one;
For my head is covered with dew,
My locks with the drops of the night."

3 I have taken off my robe;
How can I put it on *again!*
I have washed my feet;
How can I defile them?
4 My beloved put his hand
By the latch *of the door,*
And my heart yearned for him.
5 I arose to open for my beloved,
And my hands dripped *with* myrrh,
My fingers with liquid myrrh,
On the handles of the lock.
6 I opened for my beloved,
But my beloved had turned away *and*
 was gone.

My heart leaped up when he spoke.
I sought him, but I could not find him;
I called him, but he gave me no
    answer.
7 The watchmen who went about the
    city found me.
They struck me, they wounded me;
The keepers of the walls
Took my veil away from me.
8 I charge you, O daughters of
    Jerusalem,
If you find my beloved,
That you tell him I *am* lovesick!

THE DAUGHTERS OF JERUSALEM

9 What *is* your beloved
More than *another* beloved,
O fairest among women?
What *is* your beloved
More than *another* beloved,
That you so charge us?

THE SHULAMITE

10 My beloved *is* white and ruddy,
Chief among ten thousand.
11 His head *is like* the finest gold;
His locks *are* wavy,
And black as a raven.
12 His eyes *are* like doves
By the rivers of waters,
Washed with milk,
And fitly set.
13 His cheeks *are* like a bed of spices,
Banks of scented herbs.
His lips *are* lilies,
Dripping liquid myrrh.

14 His hands *are* rods of gold
Set with beryl.
His body *is* carved ivory
Inlaid *with* sapphires.
15 His legs *are* pillars of marble
Set on bases of fine gold.
His countenance *is* like Lebanon,
Excellent as the cedars.
16 His mouth *is* most sweet,
Yes, he *is* altogether lovely.
This *is* my beloved,

5:2–8:14 This third major section features the couple's first argument and reconciliation. Inevitable discord comes to all marriages. The "little foxes" (problems) of 2:15 have visited the home in this section.

And this *is* my friend,
O daughters of Jerusalem!

THE DAUGHTERS OF JERUSALEM

6 Where has your beloved gone,
O fairest among women?
Where has your beloved turned
    aside,
That we may seek him with you?

THE SHULAMITE

2 My beloved has gone to his garden,
To the beds of spices,
To feed *his flock* in the gardens,
And to gather lilies.
3 I *am* my beloved's,
And my beloved *is* mine.
He feeds *his flock* among the lilies.

Praise of the Shulamite's Beauty

THE BELOVED

4 O my love, you *are as* beautiful as
    Tirzah,
Lovely as Jerusalem,
Awesome as *an army* with banners!

6:4 Lovely as Jerusalem. The nation's capital city was known as "the perfection of beauty, the joy of the whole earth" (see Ps. 48:1,2).

5 Turn your eyes away from me,
For they have overcome me.
Your hair *is* like a flock of goats
Going down from Gilead.
6 Your teeth *are* like a flock of sheep
Which have come up from the
    washing;
Every one bears twins,
And none *is* barren among them.
7 Like a piece of pomegranate
Are your temples behind your veil.

8 There are sixty queens
And eighty concubines,
And virgins without number.
9 My dove, my perfect one,
Is the only one,
The only one of her mother,
The favorite of the one who bore her.
The daughters saw her
And called her blessed,
The queens and the concubines,
And they praised her.

10 Who is she who looks forth as the
      morning,
   Fair as the moon,
   Clear as the sun,
   Awesome as *an army* with banners?

THE SHULAMITE
11 I went down to the garden of nuts
   To see the verdure of the valley,
   To see whether the vine had budded
   And the pomegranates had bloomed.
12 Before I was even aware,
   My soul had made me
   As the chariots of my noble people.*a*

> **6:11,12** Solomon acknowledges that when he left home hastily he returned to agricultural and military matters.

THE BELOVED AND HIS FRIENDS
13 Return, return, O Shulamite;
   Return, return, that we may look
      upon you!

THE SHULAMITE
   What would you see in the Shulamite—
   As it were, the dance of the two
      camps?*a*

Expressions of Praise

THE BELOVED
7 How beautiful are your feet in sandals,
   O prince's daughter!

The curves of your thighs *are* like
   jewels,
The work of the hands of a skillful
   workman.
2 Your navel *is* a rounded goblet;
   It lacks no blended beverage.
   Your waist *is* a heap of wheat
   Set about with lilies.
3 Your two breasts *are* like two fawns,
   Twins of a gazelle.
4 Your neck *is* like an ivory tower,
   Your eyes *like* the pools in Heshbon
   By the gate of Bath Rabbim.
   Your nose *is* like the tower of Lebanon
   Which looks toward Damascus.
5 Your head *crowns* you like *Mount*
      Carmel,
   And the hair of your head *is* like
      purple;
   A king *is* held captive by *your* tresses.

> **7:1 O prince's daughter.** The Shulamite appeared by beauty and dress to be of royal lineage, although she really came from a humble background.

6 How fair and how pleasant you are,
   O love, with your delights!
7 This stature of yours is like a palm
      tree,
   And your breasts *like* its clusters.
8 I said, "I will go up to the palm tree,
   I will take hold of its branches."
   Let now your breasts be like clusters
      of the vine,

6:12 *a*Hebrew *Ammi Nadib*   6:13 *a*Hebrew *Mahanaim*

LOCAL COLOR IN THE SONG OF SOLOMON

7:4	"the pools in Heshbon"	water reservoirs in the Moabite city of Heshbon near modern Amman
7:4	"the gate of Bath Rabbim"	possibly a gate name in Heshbon
7:4	"the tower of Lebanon"	most likely refers to the white color of the mountain rather than its elevation of 10,000 feet
7:4	"Damascus"	the capital city of Syria to the east of the Lebanon mountains
7:5	"Mount Carmel"	a prominent wooded mountain in northern Israel
7:13	"mandrakes"	a pungently fragrant herb considered to be an aphrodisiac (see Genesis 30:14)
8:11	"Baal Hamon"	an unknown location in the hill country north of Jerusalem

The fragrance of your breath like
    apples,
9 And the roof of your mouth like the
    best wine.

THE SHULAMITE

The *wine* goes *down* smoothly for my
    beloved,
Moving gently the lips of sleepers.[a]
10 I *am* my beloved's,
    And his desire *is* toward me.

11 Come, my beloved,
    Let us go forth to the field;
    Let us lodge in the villages.
12 Let us get up early to the vineyards;
    Let us see if the vine has budded,
    Whether the grape blossoms are open,
    And the pomegranates are in bloom.
    There I will give you my love.
13 The mandrakes give off a fragrance,
    And at our gates *are* pleasant *fruits*,
    All manner, new and old,

Which I have laid up for you, my
    beloved.

8 Oh, that you were like my brother,
Who nursed at my mother's breasts!
If I should find you outside,
I would kiss you;
I would not be despised.
2 I would lead you *and* bring you
Into the house of my mother,
She *who* used to instruct me.
I would cause you to drink of spiced
    wine,
Of the juice of my pomegranate.

(TO THE DAUGHTERS OF JERUSALEM)

3 His left hand *is* under my head,
    And his right hand embraces me.
4 I charge you, O daughters of
    Jerusalem,
    Do not stir up nor awaken love
    Until it pleases.

7:9 [a]Septuagint, Syriac, and Vulgate read *lips and teeth*.

Q **What about interpretations of Song of Solomon that allegorize all the expressions to mean, not person-to-person love, but God's love for Israel or Christ's love for the church?**

A Allegorical interpretations of this book tend to be strained. Denying the human and historical setting of this Song reveals more discomfort with the subject matter than insight into the nature of Scripture. The idealistic and allegorical language that lovers use might lead one to assume the freedom to allegorize the entire experience, but the lovers themselves would strongly object. The practice of allegorizing the book comes from outside theological and philosophical frameworks, not the content of the book itself.

One form of interpretation similar to allegorizing takes a "typological" approach. It begins by admitting the historical validity of the story. But it also insists that the idealized language of the lovers can ultimately only accurately describe the kind of love that Christ has demonstrated toward his church.

A more satisfying way to approach Solomon's Song takes the story at face value, interprets it in a normal historical sense, and understands the idealized use of poetic language to depict reality. This interpretation affirms Solomon's account of three phases in his relationship with the Shulamite:

1. his early day of courtship
2. the early days of his first marriage
3. the maturing of the royal couple through the good and bad days of married life.

The Song of Solomon expands on the ancient marriage instructions of Genesis 2:24 by providing shameless and spiritual music for a lifetime of marital harmony. The book serves as God's demonstration of His intentions for the romance and loveliness of marriage, the most precious of human relations and "the grace of life" (1 Peter 3:7).

Love Renewed in Lebanon

A RELATIVE

5   Who *is* this coming up from the
        wilderness,
      Leaning upon her beloved?

      I awakened you under the apple tree.
      There your mother brought you forth;
      There she *who* bore you brought *you*
        forth.

> **8:5b I awakened you.** This is better understood as
> being spoken by Solomon. The Shulamite's dream in
> 3:4 has now been realized in their marriage. **mother.**
> This is the sixth reference to the Shulamite's mother.
> Solomon's mother, Bathsheba, is mentioned only
> once (see 3:11).

THE SHULAMITE TO HER BELOVED

6   Set me as a seal upon your heart,
      As a seal upon your arm;
      For love *is as* strong as death,
      Jealousy *as* cruel as the grave;[a]
      Its flames *are* flames of fire,
      A most vehement[b] flame.

7   Many waters cannot quench love,
      Nor can the floods drown it.
      If a man would give for love
      All the wealth of his house,
      It would be utterly despised.

THE SHULAMITE'S BROTHERS

8   We have a little sister,
      And she has no breasts.

> **8:8,9** The bride's brothers reminded everyone that
> they kept their sister pure before marriage (see Gen.
> 24:50–60). The same standard of purity is taught in
> the New Testament (see 1 Thess. 4:1–8). **wall...door.**
> The wall represents sexual purity; the door portrays
> an openness to immorality.

      What shall we do for our sister
      In the day when she is spoken for?
9   If she *is* a wall,
      We will build upon her
      A battlement of silver;
      And if she *is* a door,
      We will enclose her
      With boards of cedar.

THE SHULAMITE

10 I *am* a wall,
      And my breasts like towers;
      Then I became in his eyes
      As one who found peace.

11 Solomon had a vineyard at Baal
        Hamon;
      He leased the vineyard to keepers;
      Everyone was to bring for its fruit
      A thousand silver coins.

(TO SOLOMON)

12 My own vineyard *is* before me.
      You, O Solomon, *may have* a
        thousand,
      And those who tend its fruit two
        hundred.

THE BELOVED

13 You who dwell in the gardens,
      The companions listen for your
        voice—
      Let me hear it!

> **8:13 The companions.** These could be Solomon's
> shepherd companions, the daughters of Jerusalem,
> or those who escorted the bride to Jerusalem.

THE SHULAMITE

14 Make haste, my beloved,
      And be like a gazelle
      Or a young stag
      On the mountains of spices.

8:6 [a]Or *Sheol*   [b]Literally *A flame of Yah* (a poetic form of *YHWH, the* LORD)

ISAIAH

The Old Testament prophet most often quoted in the New Testament is Isaiah. His thoughts are echoed 65 times and his name is mentioned on at least 20 occasions. "Isaiah," which means "The Lord is salvation," shares roots with the names Joshua, Elisha, and Jesus.

AUTHOR AND DATE

Isaiah was written by Isaiah, approximately 700–681 B.C.

Isaiah, the son of Amoz, prophesied in and around Jerusalem during the reigns of four kings of Judah: Uzziah, Jotham, Ahaz, and Hezekiah. The prophet probably grew up in a prominent family, which explains his easy access to the higher levels of Jewish society, including the kings (7:3). When called by God to prophesy, Isaiah responded readily, though he was told from the beginning that his ministry would be one of fruitless warning and exhortation (6:9–13). Isaiah's marriage produced two sons who bore symbolic names: "Shear-jashub" ("a remnant shall return," 7:3) and "Maher-shalal-hash-baz" ("hasting to the spoil, hurrying to the prey," 8:3). Those names were living versions of God's coming punishment and God's promised faithfulness to His people.

Isaiah was a contemporary of fellow prophets Hosea and Micah. His writing style has no rival in its versatility of expression, brilliance of imagery, and richness of vocabulary. The book that bears Isaiah's name was probably not written all at once, but it is dated before 681 B.C. because the author was able to give an account of Sennacherib's death (37:38), the last major historical event included by the prophet.

BACKGROUND AND SETTING
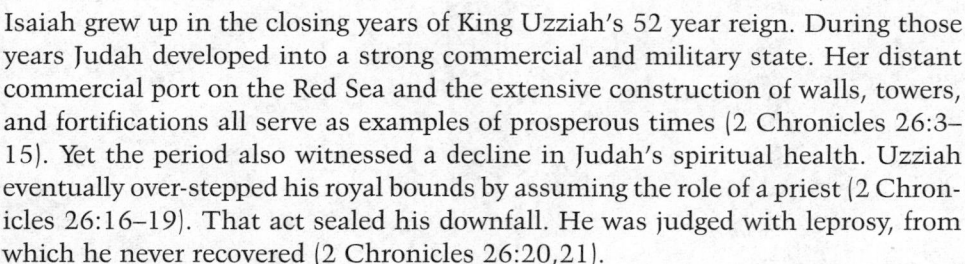

Isaiah grew up in the closing years of King Uzziah's 52 year reign. During those years Judah developed into a strong commercial and military state. Her distant commercial port on the Red Sea and the extensive construction of walls, towers, and fortifications all serve as examples of prosperous times (2 Chronicles 26:3–15). Yet the period also witnessed a decline in Judah's spiritual health. Uzziah eventually over-stepped his royal bounds by assuming the role of a priest (2 Chronicles 26:16–19). That act sealed his downfall. He was judged with leprosy, from which he never recovered (2 Chronicles 26:20,21).

The spiritual decline begun under Uzziah continued during the reigns of his son Jotham and his grandson Ahaz. Second Kings 15:34 describes Jotham's

passive preservation of the spiritual legacy that had been part of Uzziah's reign. Ahaz, however, actively rejected God's ways (2 Kings 16:2–4). The depth of his idolatry included child sacrifice. Meanwhile, the nation was becoming increasingly weak and under the influence of other nations.

By the time Hezekiah came to the throne, the Assyrian empire was a threat held at bay only through the payment of crushing tribute. Hezekiah realized that a spiritual reformation was a priority (2 Kings 18:4,22). Isaiah served as a valuable counselor to Hezekiah. When Assyria did invade Judah, Isaiah's influence caused Hezekiah to trust in God's protection. The nation gained a divine reprieve.

HISTORICAL AND THEOLOGICAL THEMES

Isaiah prophesied throughout the desperate times described above. He condemned the empty ritualism of his day (1:10–15). He confronted the idolatry into which so many of the people had fallen (40:18–20). And he foresaw the coming Babylonian captivity of Judah because of the people's persistent abandonment of the Lord (39:6,7).

The exact fulfillment of some of his prophesies during his lifetime confirmed Isaiah's credentials as God's prophet. Sennacherib's effort to take Jerusalem failed, just as Isaiah had said it would (37:6,7,36–38). The Lord healed Hezekiah's critical illness, as Isaiah had predicted (38:5; 2 Kings 20:7). Isaiah identified Cyrus by name as Judah's deliverer from Babylon long before that king of Persia

> THE **EXACT FULFILLMENT** OF SOME OF HIS **PROPHESIES** DURING **HIS** LIFETIME **CONFIRMED ISAIAH'S CREDENTIALS** AS **GOD'S PROPHET.**

appeared on the scene (44:28; 45:1). Fulfillment of his prophecies about Christ's incarnation (7:14) have further vindicated Isaiah's unique role. This pattern of accuracy offers assurance that Isaiah's prophecies of Christ's second coming will also see literal fulfillment.

OUTLINE

III. SALVATION (40:1–66:24)

A. Deliverance from Captivity (40:1–48:22)
  1. Comfort to the Babylonian exiles (40:1–31)
  2. The end of Israel's misery (41:1–48:22)

B. Sufferings of the Servant of the Lord (49:1–57:21)
  1. The Servant's mission (49:1–52:12)
  2. Redemption by the Suffering Servant (52:13–53:12)
  3. Results of the Suffering Servant's redemption (54:1–57:21)

C. Future Glory of God's People (58:1–66:24)
  1. Two kinds of religion (58:1–14)
  2. Plea to Israel to forsake their sins (59:1–19)
  3. Future blessedness of Zion (59:20–61:11)
  4. Nearing of Zion's deliverance (62:1–63:6)
  5. Prayer for national deliverance (63:7–64:12)
  6. The Lord's answer to Israel's supplication (65:1–66:24)

1 The vision of Isaiah the son of Amoz, which he saw concerning Judah and Jerusalem in the days of Uzziah, Jotham, Ahaz, *and* Hezekiah, kings of Judah.

> **1:2–9** In this courtroom scene, the Lord is the plaintiff, and the nation of Israel is the defendant. The people chose to disobey God instead of responding to His care and provision for them.

The Wickedness of Judah

2 Hear, O heavens, and give ear,
O earth!
For the LORD has spoken:
"I have nourished and brought up children,
And they have rebelled against Me;
3 The ox knows its owner
And the donkey its master's crib;
But Israel does not know,
My people do not consider."

4 Alas, sinful nation,
A people laden with iniquity,
A brood of evildoers,
Children who are corrupters!
They have forsaken the LORD,
They have provoked to anger
The Holy One of Israel,
They have turned away backward.

> **1:4 The Holy One of Israel.** Isaiah uses this special title for God 25 times. He also uses "Holy One" four times and "Holy One of Jacob" one time. In many contexts, the name contrasts the holiness of God with the sinfulness of Israel.

5 Why should you be stricken again?
You will revolt more and more.
The whole head is sick,
And the whole heart faints.
6 From the sole of the foot even to the head,
There is no soundness in it,
But wounds and bruises and putrefying sores;
They have not been closed or bound up,
Or soothed with ointment.

7 Your country *is* desolate,
Your cities *are* burned with fire;
Strangers devour your land in your presence;

And *it is* desolate, as overthrown by strangers.
8 So the daughter of Zion is left as a booth in a vineyard,
As a hut in a garden of cucumbers,
As a besieged city.
9 Unless the LORD of hosts
Had left to us a very small remnant,
We would have become like Sodom,
We would have been made like Gomorrah.

> **1:9 LORD of hosts.** This title (used 60 times in Isaiah) pictures God as a mighty warrior. **remnant.** This term designated the faithful Israelites (see Rom. 9:29). This remnant will be among the returning Israelites when the Messiah returns to earth (see Hos. 1:10,11). **Sodom...Gomorrah.** God destroyed them because of their sinfulness (Gen. 18:20), and they became an example of God's judgment against any people.

10 Hear the word of the LORD,
You rulers of Sodom;
Give ear to the law of our God,
You people of Gomorrah:
11 "To what purpose *is* the multitude of your sacrifices to Me?"
Says the LORD.
"I have had enough of burnt offerings of rams
And the fat of fed cattle.
I do not delight in the blood of bulls,
Or of lambs or goats.

12 "When you come to appear before Me,
Who has required this from your hand,
To trample My courts?
13 Bring no more futile sacrifices;
Incense is an abomination to Me.
The New Moons, the Sabbaths, and the calling of assemblies—
I cannot endure iniquity and the sacred meeting.
14 Your New Moons and your appointed feasts
My soul hates;

> **1:14 My soul hates.** God hates hypocritical religion, robbery for burnt offering (61:8), serving other gods (Jer. 44:4), harboring evil against a neighbor, love for a false oath (Zech. 8:16), divorce (Mal. 2:16), and those who love violence (Ps. 11:5).

They are a trouble to Me,
I am weary of bearing *them*.
15 When you spread out your hands,
I will hide My eyes from you;
Even though you make many
     prayers,
I will not hear.
Your hands are full of blood.

16 "Wash yourselves, make yourselves
     clean;
Put away the evil of your doings from
     before My eyes.
Cease to do evil,
17 Learn to do good;
Seek justice,
Rebuke the oppressor;[a]
Defend the fatherless,
Plead for the widow.

18 "Come now, and let us reason
     together,"
Says the LORD,
"Though your sins are like scarlet,
They shall be as white as snow;
Though they are red like crimson,
They shall be as wool.

1:18 scarlet...crimson. These colors speak of the guilt of those whose hands were "full of blood," alluding to extreme iniquity and perversity (see Ezek. 9:9,10). **white as snow...as wool.** These portray what is clean, the blood-guilt having been removed (see Ps. 51:7). Isaiah emphasizes that forgiveness comes through repentance.

---

19 If you are willing and obedient,
You shall eat the good of the land;
20 But if you refuse and rebel,
You shall be devoured by the
     sword";
For the mouth of the LORD has
     spoken.

1:21 harlot. Spiritual harlotry illustrates the idolatry of God's people (see Jer. 2:20). Here Jerusalem's unfaithfulness included murder and general corruption. **justice; righteousness.** As Isaiah prophesied, ethical depravity had replaced the city's former values.

The Degenerate City

21 How the faithful city has become a
     harlot!
It was full of justice;
Righteousness lodged in it,
But now murderers.
22 Your silver has become dross,
Your wine mixed with water.
23 Your princes *are* rebellious,
And companions of thieves;
Everyone loves bribes,
And follows after rewards.
They do not defend the fatherless,
Nor does the cause of the widow
     come before them.

24 Therefore the Lord says,
The LORD of hosts, the Mighty One
     of Israel,
"Ah, I will rid Myself of My
     adversaries,
And take vengeance on My enemies.
25 I will turn My hand against you,
And thoroughly purge away your
     dross,
And take away all your alloy.
26 I will restore your judges as at the
     first,
And your counselors as at the
     beginning.
Afterward you shall be called the city
     of righteousness, the faithful city."

27 Zion shall be redeemed with justice,
And her penitents with
     righteousness.
28 The destruction of transgressors and
     of sinners *shall be* together,
And those who forsake the LORD shall
     be consumed.
29 For they[a] shall be ashamed of the
     terebinth trees
Which you have desired;
And you shall be embarrassed because
     of the gardens
Which you have chosen.
30 For you shall be as a terebinth whose
     leaf fades,
And as a garden that has no water.
31 The strong shall be as tinder,
And the work of it as a spark;

1:17 [a]Some ancient versions read *the oppressed*.   1:29 [a]Following Masoretic Text, Septuagint, and Vulgate; some Hebrew manuscripts and Targum read *you*.

Both will burn together,
And no one shall quench *them*.

The Future House of God

2 The word that Isaiah the son of Amoz
saw concerning Judah and Jerusalem.

2   Now it shall come to pass in the latter
    days
    That the mountain of the LORD's
        house
    Shall be established on the top of the
        mountains,
    And shall be exalted above the hills;
    And all nations shall flow to it.

2:2 in the latter days. The "latter" (last) days is a time
designation looking forward to the messianic era
(Ezek. 38:16). The New Testament applied this to the
period beginning with the first advent of Jesus (Acts
2:17). The Old Testament applied this to the Messiah's
return to establish His earthly kingdom (Rev. 20:1–
10). **the mountain of the LORD's house.** This is Mount
Zion, the location of the temple in Jerusalem (see
2 Chr. 33:15; Mic. 4:1).

---

3   Many people shall come and say,
    "Come, and let us go up to the
        mountain of the LORD,
    To the house of the God of Jacob;
    He will teach us His ways,
    And we shall walk in His paths."
    For out of Zion shall go forth the law,
    And the word of the LORD from
        Jerusalem.
4   He shall judge between the nations,
    And rebuke many people;
    They shall beat their swords into
        plowshares,
    And their spears into pruning hooks;
    Nation shall not lift up sword against
        nation,
    Neither shall they learn war
        anymore.

The Day of the LORD

5   O house of Jacob, come and let us
        walk
    In the light of the LORD.

6   For You have forsaken Your people,
        the house of Jacob,
    Because they are filled with eastern
        ways;

They *are* soothsayers like the
    Philistines,
And they are pleased with the
    children of foreigners.
7   Their land is also full of silver and
        gold,
    And there is no end to their treasures;
    Their land is also full of horses,
    And there is no end to their chariots.
8   Their land is also full of idols;
    They worship the work of their own
        hands,
    That which their own fingers have
        made.
9   People bow down,
    And each man humbles himself;
    Therefore do not forgive them.

10 Enter into the rock, and hide in the
        dust,
    From the terror of the LORD
    And the glory of His majesty.
11 The lofty looks of man shall be
        humbled,
    The haughtiness of men shall be
        bowed down,
    And the LORD alone shall be exalted
        in that day.

12 For the day of the LORD of hosts
    Shall come upon everything proud
        and lofty,
    Upon everything lifted up—
    And it shall be brought low—

2:12 the day of the LORD. This expresses the time of
God's extreme wrath and can refer to a near future
judgment (Ezek. 13:5) or a far future judgment (Zech.
14:1). Two judgments remain to be fulfilled: at the end
of Daniel's 70th week through providential means
(see Joel 3:14) and at the end of the Millennium at the
hand of God (see 2 Pet. 3:10). Isaiah looks to the far
fulfillment at the end of the time of Jacob's trouble
(Jer. 30:7).

---

13 Upon all the cedars of Lebanon *that
        are* high and lifted up,
    And upon all the oaks of Bashan;
14 Upon all the high mountains,
    And upon all the hills *that are* lifted
        up;
15 Upon every high tower,
    And upon every fortified wall;
16 Upon all the ships of Tarshish,

And upon all the beautiful sloops.

17 The loftiness of man shall be bowed
down,
And the haughtiness of men shall be
brought low;
The LORD alone will be exalted in
that day,

18 But the idols He shall utterly abolish.

19 They shall go into the holes of the
rocks,
And into the caves of the earth,
From the terror of the LORD
And the glory of His majesty,
When He arises to shake the earth
mightily.

20 In that day a man will cast away his
idols of silver
And his idols of gold,
Which they made, *each* for himself to
worship,
To the moles and bats,

21 To go into the clefts of the rocks,
And into the crags of the rugged rocks,
From the terror of the LORD
And the glory of His majesty,
When He arises to shake the earth
mightily.

> **2:22 Sever yourselves.** Isaiah calls the people to stop depending on others and to trust only in God, who alone is worthy.

22 Sever yourselves from such a man,
Whose breath *is* in his nostrils;
For of what account is he?

Judgment on Judah and Jerusalem

3 For behold, the Lord, the LORD of
hosts,
Takes away from Jerusalem and from
Judah
The stock and the store,
The whole supply of bread and the
whole supply of water;

2 The mighty man and the man of war,
The judge and the prophet,
And the diviner and the elder;

3 The captain of fifty and the honorable
man,

The counselor and the skillful artisan,
And the expert enchanter.

4 "I will give children *to be* their princes,
And babes shall rule over them.

5 The people will be oppressed,
Every one by another and every one
by his neighbor;
The child will be insolent toward the
elder,
And the base toward the honorable."

6 When a man takes hold of his
brother
In the house of his father, *saying,*
"You have clothing;
You be our ruler,
And *let* these ruins *be* under your
power,"[a]

7 In that day he will protest, saying,
"I cannot cure *your* ills,
For in my house *is* neither food nor
clothing;
Do not make me a ruler of the
people."

8 For Jerusalem stumbled,
And Judah is fallen,
Because their tongue and their
doings
Are against the LORD,
To provoke the eyes of His glory.

> **3:8 Jerusalem...Judah.** The fall of Jerusalem in 586 B.C. was only a partial fulfillment of this prophecy. The final fulfillment will occur just prior to Christ's second coming. **against the LORD.** Zion's problems stem from rebellion against God. The people sinned and made no effort to conceal it.

9 The look on their countenance
witnesses against them,
And they declare their sin as Sodom;
They do not hide *it.*
Woe to their soul!
For they have brought evil upon
themselves.

10 "Say to the righteous that *it shall be*
well *with them,*
For they shall eat the fruit of their
doings.

3:6 [a]Literally *hand*

11 Woe to the wicked! *It shall be* ill *with him*,
For the reward of his hands shall be given him.
12 *As for* My people, children *are* their oppressors,
And women rule over them.
O My people! Those who lead you cause *you* to err,
And destroy the way of your paths."

Oppression and Luxury Condemned

13 The LORD stands up to plead,
And stands to judge the people.
14 The LORD will enter into judgment
With the elders of His people
And His princes:
"For you have eaten up the vineyard;
The plunder of the poor *is* in your houses.
15 What do you mean by crushing My people
And grinding the faces of the poor?"
Says the Lord GOD of hosts.

16 Moreover the LORD says:

"Because the daughters of Zion are haughty,
And walk with outstretched necks
And wanton eyes,
Walking and mincing *as* they go,
Making a jingling with their feet,

> **3:16 daughters of Zion.** When women cultivate beauty for beauty's sake, they reflect moral decay and detract from the glory of God. Rather than emphasizing outward appearance, they should cultivate the beauty of the inner person (1 Tim. 2:9,10).

17 Therefore the Lord will strike with a scab
The crown of the head of the daughters of Zion,
And the LORD will uncover their secret parts."

18 In that day the Lord will take away the finery:
The jingling anklets, the scarves, and the crescents;
19 The pendants, the bracelets, and the veils;

20 The headdresses, the leg ornaments, and the headbands;
The perfume boxes, the charms,
21 and the rings;
The nose jewels,
22 the festal apparel, and the mantles;
The outer garments, the purses,
23 and the mirrors;
The fine linen, the turbans, and the robes.

24 And so it shall be:

Instead of a sweet smell there will be a stench;
Instead of a sash, a rope;
Instead of well-set hair, baldness;
Instead of a rich robe, a girding of sackcloth;
And branding instead of beauty.
25 Your men shall fall by the sword,
And your mighty in the war.

26 Her gates shall lament and mourn,
And she *being* desolate shall sit on the ground.

4 And in that day seven women shall take hold of one man, saying,
"We will eat our own food and wear our own apparel;
Only let us be called by your name,
To take away our reproach."

The Renewal of Zion

2 In that day the Branch of the LORD shall be beautiful and glorious;
And the fruit of the earth *shall be* excellent and appealing
For those of Israel who have escaped.

> **4:2 Branch.** This messianic title refers to growth (2 Sam. 23:5). The life of the Branch will bear spiritual fruit (see John 15:4,5).

3 And it shall come to pass that *he who is* left in Zion and remains in Jerusalem will be called holy—everyone who is recorded among the living in Jerusalem. 4 When the Lord has washed away the filth of the daughters of Zion, and purged the blood of Jerusalem from her midst, by the spirit of judgment and by the spirit of burning, 5 then the LORD will create above every

dwelling place of Mount Zion, and above her assemblies, a cloud and smoke by day and the shining of a flaming fire by night. For over all the glory there *will be* a covering. ⁶And there will be a tabernacle for shade in the daytime from the heat, for a place of refuge, and for a shelter from storm and rain.

God's Disappointing Vineyard

5 Now let me sing to my Well-beloved
A song of my Beloved regarding His
vineyard:

My Well-beloved has a vineyard
On a very fruitful hill.
² He dug it up and cleared out its
stones,
And planted it with the choicest vine.
He built a tower in its midst,
And also made a winepress in it;
So He expected *it* to bring forth *good*
grapes,
But it brought forth wild grapes.

³ "And now, O inhabitants of Jerusalem
and men of Judah,
Judge, please, between Me and My
vineyard.
⁴ What more could have been done to
My vineyard
That I have not done in it?
Why then, when I expected *it* to bring
forth *good* grapes,
Did it bring forth wild grapes?
⁵ And now, please let Me tell you what
I will do to My vineyard:
I will take away its hedge, and it shall
be burned;
And break down its wall, and it shall
be trampled down.
⁶ I will lay it waste;
It shall not be pruned or dug,
But there shall come up briers and
thorns.
I will also command the clouds
That they rain no rain on it."

⁷ For the vineyard of the LORD of hosts
is the house of Israel,
And the men of Judah are His
pleasant plant.
He looked for justice, but behold,
oppression;

For righteousness, but behold, a cry
for help.

Impending Judgment on Excesses

⁸ Woe to those who join house to
house;
They add field to field,
Till *there is* no place
Where they may dwell alone in the
midst of the land!
⁹ In my hearing the LORD of hosts *said,*
"Truly, many houses shall be desolate,
Great and beautiful ones, without
inhabitant.
¹⁰ For ten acres of vineyard shall yield
one bath,
And a homer of seed shall yield one
ephah."

5:10 one bath...one ephah. God judged the greedy rich by greatly reducing the productivity of their land. One bath was roughly equivalent to 6 gallons. About one-half bushel would be produced from about 6 bushels of planted seed. These amounts indicate famine conditions.

¹¹ Woe to those who rise early in the
morning,
That they may follow intoxicating
drink;
Who continue until night, *till* wine
inflames them!
¹² The harp and the strings,
The tambourine and flute,
And wine are in their feasts;
But they do not regard the work of the
LORD,
Nor consider the operation of His
hands.

¹³ Therefore my people have gone into
captivity,
Because *they have* no knowledge;
Their honorable men *are* famished,
And their multitude dried up with
thirst.
¹⁴ Therefore Sheol has enlarged itself

5:14 Sheol. Here this term pictures death as a great monster with wide-open jaws, ready to receive its victims. This would be the fate of those who perish in the captivity that God will send to judge the people's sinfulness.

And opened its mouth beyond
measure;
Their glory and their multitude and
their pomp,
And he who is jubilant, shall descend
into it.
15 People shall be brought down,
Each man shall be humbled,
And the eyes of the lofty shall be
humbled.
16 But the LORD of hosts shall be exalted
in judgment,
And God who is holy shall be
hallowed in righteousness.
17 Then the lambs shall feed in their
pasture,
And in the waste places of the fat
ones strangers shall eat.

18 Woe to those who draw iniquity with
cords of vanity,
And sin as if with a cart rope;
19 That say, "Let Him make speed *and*
hasten His work,
That we may see *it;*
And let the counsel of the Holy One
of Israel draw near and come,
That we may know *it.*"

20 Woe to those who call evil good, and
good evil;
Who put darkness for light, and light
for darkness;
Who put bitter for sweet, and sweet
for bitter!
21 Woe to *those who are* wise in their
own eyes,
And prudent in their own sight!
22 Woe to men mighty at drinking
wine,
Woe to men valiant for mixing
intoxicating drink,
23 Who justify the wicked for a bribe,
And take away justice from the
righteous man!

24 Therefore, as the fire devours the
stubble,
And the flame consumes the chaff,
So their root will be as rottenness,
And their blossom will ascend like
dust;

Because they have rejected the law of
the LORD of hosts,
And despised the word of the Holy
One of Israel.
25 Therefore the anger of the LORD is
aroused against His people;
He has stretched out His hand
against them
And stricken them,
And the hills trembled.
Their carcasses *were* as refuse in the
midst of the streets.

For all this His anger is not turned
away,
But His hand *is* stretched out still.
26 He will lift up a banner to the nations
from afar,
And will whistle to them from the
end of the earth;
Surely they shall come with speed,
swiftly.

5:26 nations from afar. God would bring Assyria
and Babylon against Israel. Assyria conquered the
northern kingdom in 722 B.C., and Babylon invaded
Jerusalem and destroyed the temple in 586 B.C.

27 No one will be weary or stumble
among them;
No one will slumber or sleep;
Nor will the belt on their loins be
loosed,
Nor the strap of their sandals be
broken;
28 Whose arrows *are* sharp,
And all their bows bent;
Their horses' hooves will seem like
flint,
And their wheels like a whirlwind.
29 Their roaring *will be* like a lion,
They will roar like young lions;
Yes, they will roar
And lay hold of the prey;
They will carry *it* away safely,
And no one will deliver.
30 In that day they will roar against
them
Like the roaring of the sea.
And if *one* looks to the land,
Behold, darkness *and* sorrow;
And the light is darkened by the
clouds.

Isaiah Called to Be a Prophet

6 In the year that King Uzziah died, I saw the Lord sitting on a throne, high and lifted up, and the train of His *robe* filled the temple. ²Above it stood seraphim; each one had six wings: with two he covered his face, with two he covered his feet, and with two he flew. ³And one cried to another and said:

> "Holy, holy, holy *is* the LORD of hosts;
> The whole earth *is* full of His glory!"

> **6:1 King Uzziah died.** Uzziah reigned for 52 years and died of leprosy in 739 B.C. (see 2 Chr. 26:16–23). Isaiah began prophesying in that year. In this verse he describes how he was called to prophesy. **I saw.** Unconscious of the outside world, Isaiah saw with his inner eye what God revealed to him (see Rev. 4:1–11). **temple.** This refers to the throne of God as the heavenly temple (Rev. 4:1–6).

⁴And the posts of the door were shaken by the voice of him who cried out, and the house was filled with smoke.

⁵So I said:

> "Woe *is* me, for I am undone!
> Because I *am* a man of unclean lips,
> And I dwell in the midst of a people
>   of unclean lips;
> For my eyes have seen the King,
> The LORD of hosts."

⁶Then one of the seraphim flew to me, having in his hand a live coal *which* he had taken with the tongs from the altar. ⁷And he touched my mouth *with it,* and said:

> "Behold, this has touched your lips;
> Your iniquity is taken away,
> And your sin purged."

⁸Also I heard the voice of the Lord, saying:

> "Whom shall I send,
> And who will go for Us?"

Then I said, "Here *am* I! Send me."
⁹And He said, "Go, and tell this people:

> 'Keep on hearing, but do not
>   understand;
> Keep on seeing, but do not perceive.'

10   "Make the heart of this people dull,
> And their ears heavy,
> And shut their eyes;
> Lest they see with their eyes,
> And hear with their ears,
> And understand with their heart,
> And return and be healed."

> **6:9,10 do not understand...do not perceive.** God used Isaiah's message to hide the truth from the unreceptive people, as He would do later with Jesus' parables (Matt. 13:14,15; Mark 4:12).

¹¹Then I said, "Lord, how long?"
And He answered:

> "Until the cities are laid waste and
>   without inhabitant,
> The houses are without a man,
> The land is utterly desolate,

12   The LORD has removed men far
>   away,
> And the forsaken places *are* many in
>   the midst of the land.

13   But yet a tenth *will be* in it,
> And will return and be for
>   consuming,
> As a terebinth tree or as an oak,
> Whose stump *remains* when it is cut
>   down.
> So the holy seed *shall be* its stump."

Isaiah Sent to King Ahaz

7 Now it came to pass in the days of Ahaz the son of Jotham, the son of Uzziah, king of Judah, *that* Rezin king of Syria and Pekah the son of Remaliah, king of Israel, went up to Jerusalem to *make* war against it, but could not prevail against it. ²And it was told to the house of David, saying, "Syria's forces are deployed in Ephraim." So his heart and the heart of his people were moved as the trees of the woods are moved with the wind.

> **7:1,2** Syria and Israel (the northern 10 tribes) unsuccessfully tried to invade Judah, which caused the Assyrian king's forces to be a continual threat to Judah. During Ahaz's reign, this threat caused great fear for the king and the people.

³Then the LORD said to Isaiah, "Go out

Reference	Fulfilled Literally	Fulfilled Typically
7:14	The virgin birth of Christ (Matthew 1:23)	
8:14,15		A stone of stumbling and a rock of offense (Romans 9:33; 1 Peter 2:8)
8:17		Christ's hope and trust in God (Hebrews 2:13a)
8:18		The Son of God and the sons of God (Hebrews 2:13b)
9:1,2		The arrival of Jesus in the area of Zebulun and Naphtali (Matthew 4:12–16)
9:6a	The birth of Immanuel (Matthew 1:23; Luke 1:31–33; 2:7,11)	
11:1	Revival of the Davidic dynasty (Matthew 1:6,16; Acts 13:23; Revelation 5:5; 22:16)	
12:3		Water from the wells of salvation (John 4:10,14)
25:8		The swallowing up of death (1 Corinthians 15:54)
28:11		The gift of tongues as an authenticating sign of God's messengers (1 Corinthians 14:21,22)
28:16	Incarnation of Jesus Christ (Matthew 21:42)	
29:18; 35:5		Jesus' healing of the physically deaf and blind (Matthew 11:5)
40:3–5	Preaching of John the Baptist (Matthew 3:3; Mark 1:3; Luke 3:4–6; John 1:23)	
42:1a,2,3	Christ at His baptism (Matthew 3:16,17) and transfiguration (Matthew 17:5) and His general demeanor throughout His first advent	
42:6		Christ extended the benefits of the New Covenant to the church (Hebrews 8:6,10–12)
42:7		Jesus healed physical blindness and provided liberty for the spiritual captives (Matthew 11:5; Luke 4:18)
42:7		Jesus removed spiritual darkness at His first coming (Matthew 4:16)
50:6	Jesus beaten and spat upon (Matthew 26:67; 27:26,30; Mark 14:65; 15:19; Luke 22:63; John 18:22)	
50:7	Jesus resolutely setting His face to go to Jerusalem (Luke 9:51)	
53:1	Israel failed to recognize her Messiah (John 12:38)	
53:4		Jesus healed sick people as a symbol of His bearing of sin (Matthew 8:16,17)
53:7,8	Philip identifies Jesus as the one about whom the prophet wrote (Acts 8:32,33)	
53:7	Jesus remained silent at all phases of His trial (Matthew 26:63; 27:12–14; Mark 14:61; 15:5; Luke 23:9; John 19:9; 1 Peter 2:23)	
53:7	Jesus was the Lamb of God who takes away the sin of the world (John 1:29; 1 Peter 1:18,19; Revelation 5:6)	
53:9	Jesus was completely innocent of all charges against Him (1 Peter 2:22)	
53:11	Jesus saw the need to be crucified between two criminals (Luke 22:37)	
54:13		Jesus saw those who came to Him at His first advent as taught by God (John 6:45)
55:3	Christ's resurrection was prerequisite to His some day occupying David's throne on earth (Acts 13:34)	
61:1,2a		Jesus saw His first-advent ministry as a spiritual counterpart of His second-advent deliverance of Israel (Luke 4:18,19)
62:11	Jesus fulfilled the call to the daughter of Zion in His triumphal entry (Matthew 21:5)	

now to meet Ahaz, you and Shear-Jashub[a] your son, at the end of the aqueduct from the upper pool, on the highway to the Fuller's Field, [4]and say to him: 'Take heed, and be quiet; do not fear or be fainthearted for these two stubs of smoking firebrands, for the fierce anger of Rezin and Syria, and the son of Remaliah. [5]Because Syria, Ephraim, and the son of Remaliah have plotted evil against you, saying, [6]"Let us go up against Judah and trouble it, and let us make a gap in its wall for ourselves, and set a king over them, the son of Tabel"—[7]thus says the Lord GOD:

> "It shall not stand,
> Nor shall it come to pass.
> [8] For the head of Syria is Damascus,
> And the head of Damascus is Rezin.
> Within sixty-five years Ephraim will
> be broken,
> So that it will not be a people.
> [9] The head of Ephraim is Samaria,
> And the head of Samaria is
> Remaliah's son.
> If you will not believe,
> Surely you shall not be
> established." ' "

The Immanuel Prophecy

[10]Moreover the LORD spoke again to Ahaz, saying, [11]"Ask a sign for yourself from the LORD your God; ask it either in the depth or in the height above." [12]But Ahaz said, "I will not ask, nor will I test the LORD!" [13]Then he said, "Hear now, O house of David! Is it a small thing for you to weary men, but will you weary my God also? [14]Therefore the Lord Himself will give you a sign: Behold, the virgin shall conceive and bear a Son, and shall call His name Immanuel.[a] [15]Curds and honey He shall

7:14 sign. Ahaz refused to choose a sign, so the Lord chose His own sign, which would occur after Ahaz's lifetime. **the virgin.** This refers to the birth of the Messiah (Matt. 1:23). The Hebrew word "virgin" refers to an unmarried woman (Gen. 24:43), so the birth of Isaiah's son could not have fulfilled the prophecy (see Gen. 3:25). **Immanuel.** This title, meaning "God with us," refers to Jesus (see Matt. 1:23).

eat, that He may know to refuse the evil and choose the good. [16]For before the Child shall know to refuse the evil and choose the good, the land that you dread will be forsaken by both her kings. [17]The LORD will bring the king of Assyria upon you and your people and your father's house—days that have not come since the day that Ephraim departed from Judah."

> [18] And it shall come to pass in that day
> That the LORD will whistle for the fly
> That is in the farthest part of the
> rivers of Egypt,
> And for the bee that is in the land of
> Assyria.

7:18 fly...bee. Egypt was full of flies, and Assyria was known for beekeeping. The insects represented these nations' armies that God would use to defeat Judah and take the people into exile.

> [19] They will come, and all of them will
> rest
> In the desolate valleys and in the
> clefts of the rocks,
> And on all thorns and in all pastures.
>
> [20] In the same day the Lord will shave
> with a hired razor,
> With those from beyond the River,[a]
> with the king of Assyria,
> The head and the hair of the legs,
> And will also remove the beard.
>
> [21] It shall be in that day
> That a man will keep alive a young
> cow and two sheep;
> [22] So it shall be, from the abundance of
> milk they give,
> That he will eat curds;
> For curds and honey everyone will eat
> who is left in the land.
>
> [23] It shall happen in that day,
> That wherever there could be a
> thousand vines
> Worth a thousand shekels of silver,
> It will be for briers and thorns.
> [24] With arrows and bows men will come
> there,

7:3 [a]Literally A Remnant Shall Return   7:14 [a]Literally God-With-Us   7:20 [a]That is, the Euphrates

Because all the land will become
 briers and thorns.

25 And to any hill which could be dug
  with the hoe,
 You will not go there for fear of briers
  and thorns;
 But it will become a range for oxen
 And a place for sheep to roam.

Assyria Will Invade the Land

8 Moreover the LORD said to me, "Take a
large scroll, and write on it with a
man's pen concerning Maher-Shalal-Hash-
Baz.[a] 2And I will take for Myself faithful
witnesses to record, Uriah the priest and
Zechariah the son of Jeberechiah."

3Then I went to the prophetess, and she
conceived and bore a son. Then the LORD
said to me, "Call his name Maher-Shalal-
Hash-Baz; 4for before the child shall have
knowledge to cry 'My father' and 'My
mother,' the riches of Damascus and the
spoil of Samaria will be taken away before
the king of Assyria."

> **8:3 prophetess.** Isaiah's wife was called a prophet-
> ess because her son was prophetic to the Assyrian
> conquest.

5The LORD also spoke to me again, saying:

6 "Inasmuch as these people refused
 The waters of Shiloah that flow
  softly,
 And rejoice in Rezin and in
  Remaliah's son;
7 Now therefore, behold, the Lord
  brings up over them
 The waters of the River,[a] strong and
  mighty—
 The king of Assyria and all his glory;
 He will go up over all his channels
 And go over all his banks.
8 He will pass through Judah,
 He will overflow and pass over,
 He will reach up to the neck;
 And the stretching out of his wings
 Will fill the breadth of Your land,
  O Immanuel.[a]

9 "Be shattered, O you peoples, and be
  broken in pieces!
 Give ear, all you from far countries.
 Gird yourselves, but be broken in
  pieces;
 Gird yourselves, but be broken in
  pieces.

> **8:9 be broken in pieces.** The prophet reminded As-
> syria and the other nations that they were only in-
> struments for the Lord's use and would eventually
> come to nothing.

10 Take counsel together, but it will
   come to nothing;
 Speak the word, but it will not stand,
 For God is with us."[a]

Fear God, Heed His Word

11For the LORD spoke thus to me with a
strong hand, and instructed me that I
should not walk in the way of this people,
saying:

12 "Do not say, 'A conspiracy,'
  Concerning all that this people call a
   conspiracy,
  Nor be afraid of their threats, nor be
   troubled.
13 The LORD of hosts, Him you shall
   hallow;
  Let Him be your fear,
  And let Him be your dread.
14 He will be as a sanctuary,
  But a stone of stumbling and a rock of
   offense
  To both the houses of Israel,
  As a trap and a snare to the
   inhabitants of Jerusalem.
15 And many among them shall stumble;
  They shall fall and be broken,
  Be snared and taken."

16 Bind up the testimony,
  Seal the law among my disciples.
17 And I will wait on the LORD,
  Who hides His face from the house of
   Jacob;
  And I will hope in Him.
18 Here am I and the children whom the
  LORD has given me!

8:1 [a]Literally *Speed the Spoil, Hasten the Booty*   8:7 [a]That is, the Euphrates   8:8 [a]Literally *God-
With-Us*   8:10 [a]Hebrew *Immanuel*

We are for signs and wonders in
   Israel
From the LORD of hosts,
Who dwells in Mount Zion.

¹⁹And when they say to you, "Seek those
who are mediums and wizards, who whisper and mutter," should not a people seek
their God? *Should they seek* the dead on
behalf of the living? ²⁰To the law and to the
testimony! If they do not speak according
to this word, *it is* because *there is* no light
in them.

> **8:19** *seek* **the dead.** The people were using spiritu-
> alists to communicate with the dead (as King Saul had
> done in 1 Sam. 28:8–10), which was forbidden by law
> (Lev. 19:26).

²¹They will pass through it hard-pressed
and hungry; and it shall happen, when they
are hungry, that they will be enraged and
curse their king and their God, and look
upward. ²²Then they will look to the earth,
and see trouble and darkness, gloom of anguish; and *they will be* driven into darkness.

The Government of the Promised Son

9 Nevertheless the gloom *will* not *be*
   upon her who *is* distressed,
As when at first He lightly esteemed
The land of Zebulun and the land of
   Naphtali,
And afterward more heavily oppressed
   her,
By the way of the sea, beyond the
   Jordan,
In Galilee of the Gentiles.
²   The people who walked in darkness
Have seen a great light;
Those who dwelt in the land of the
   shadow of death,
Upon them a light has shined.

³   You have multiplied the nation
And increased its joy;ᵃ
They rejoice before You
According to the joy of harvest,
As *men* rejoice when they divide the
   spoil.

⁴   For You have broken the yoke of his
   burden
And the staff of his shoulder,
The rod of his oppressor,
As in the day of Midian.
⁵   For every warrior's sandal from the
   noisy battle,
And garments rolled in blood,
Will be used for burning *and* fuel of
   fire.

⁶   For unto us a Child is born,
Unto us a Son is given;
And the government will be upon His
   shoulder.
And His name will be called
Wonderful, Counselor, Mighty God,
Everlasting Father, Prince of Peace.

> **9:6 Child...Son.** Immanuel, the child to be born to the
> virgin, will be the Son of David, with rights to the
> Davidic throne (see Matt. 1:21). **government.** He will
> rule the nations (Rev. 2:27). **Wonderful, Counselor.**
> This King will reign with supernatural wisdom, un-
> like Ahaz (2 Sam. 16:23). **Mighty God.** The Messiah
> will be a powerful warrior (see Deut. 10:17). **Everlast-
> ing Father.** He will be a Father to His people, caring
> for them and disciplining them (Ps. 68:5,6). **Prince of
> Peace.** His government will bring peace to the na-
> tions (Mic. 4:3).

⁷   Of the increase of *His* government
   and peace
There will be no end,
Upon the throne of David and over
   His kingdom,
To order it and establish it with
   judgment and justice
From that time forward, even forever.
The zeal of the Lord of hosts will
   perform this.

The Punishment of Samaria

⁸   The Lord sent a word against Jacob,
And it has fallen on Israel.
⁹   All the people will know—
Ephraim and the inhabitant of
   Samaria—
Who say in pride and arrogance of
   heart:
¹⁰ "The bricks have fallen down,
But we will rebuild with hewn stones;

9:3 ᵃFollowing Qere and Targum; Kethib and Vulgate read *not increased joy;* Septuagint reads *Most of
the people You brought down in Your joy.*

The sycamores are cut down,
But we will replace *them* with
   cedars."
11 Therefore the LORD shall set up
The adversaries of Rezin against him,
And spur his enemies on,
12 The Syrians before and the Philistines
   behind;
And they shall devour Israel with an
   open mouth.

For all this His anger is not turned
   away,
But His hand *is* stretched out still.

13 For the people do not turn to Him
   who strikes them,
Nor do they seek the LORD of hosts.
14 Therefore the LORD will cut off head
   and tail from Israel,
Palm branch and bulrush in one day.
15 The elder and honorable, he *is* the
   head;
The prophet who teaches lies, he *is*
   the tail.
16 For the leaders of this people cause
   them to err,
And *those who are* led by them are
   destroyed.
17 Therefore the Lord will have no joy in
   their young men,
Nor have mercy on their fatherless
   and widows;
For everyone *is* a hypocrite and an
   evildoer,
And every mouth speaks folly.

For all this His anger is not turned
   away,
But His hand *is* stretched out still.

18 For wickedness burns as the fire;
It shall devour the briers and thorns,
And kindle in the thickets of the
   forest;
They shall mount up *like* rising
   smoke.
19 Through the wrath of the LORD of
   hosts
The land is burned up,
And the people shall be as fuel for the
   fire;
No man shall spare his brother.
20 And he shall snatch on the right hand

And be hungry;
He shall devour on the left hand
And not be satisfied;
Every man shall eat the flesh of his
   own arm.
21 Manasseh *shall devour* Ephraim, and
   Ephraim Manasseh;
Together they *shall be* against Judah.

For all this His anger is not turned
   away,
But His hand *is* stretched out still.

9:21 Manasseh...Ephraim...Judah. Descendants of Manasseh and Ephraim (Joseph's sons) had been in a civil war (see Judg. 12:4), but they united in their opposition to Judah.

10

"Woe to those who decree
   unrighteous decrees,
Who write misfortune,
Which they have prescribed
2 To rob the needy of justice,
And to take what is right from the
   poor of My people,
That widows may be their prey,
And *that* they may rob the fatherless.
3 What will you do in the day of
   punishment,
And in the desolation *which* will
   come from afar?
To whom will you flee for help?
And where will you leave your glory?
4 Without Me they shall bow down
   among the prisoners,
And they shall fall among the slain."

For all this His anger is not turned
   away,
But His hand *is* stretched out still.

Arrogant Assyria Also Judged
5 "Woe to Assyria, the rod of My anger
And the staff in whose hand is My
   indignation.
6 I will send him against an ungodly
   nation,
And against the people of My wrath
I will give him charge,
To seize the spoil, to take the prey,
And to tread them down like the mire
   of the streets.
7 Yet he does not mean so,
Nor does his heart think so;

But *it is* in his heart to destroy,
And cut off not a few nations.

10:5,7 rod of My anger. God used Assyria to judge Israel and Judah, as He later did with Babylon against Judah (Hab. 1:6). **he does not mean so.** Assyria did not know she was being used by God and instead thought her conquests were of her own strength.

8 For he says,
   '*Are* not my princes altogether kings?
9 *Is* not Calno like Carchemish?
   Is not Hamath like Arpad?
   Is not Samaria like Damascus?
10 As my hand has found the kingdoms
      of the idols,
   Whose carved images excelled those
      of Jerusalem and Samaria,
11 As I have done to Samaria and her
      idols,
   Shall I not do also to Jerusalem and
      her idols?' "

12Therefore it shall come to pass, when the Lord has performed all His work on Mount Zion and on Jerusalem, *that He will say,* "I will punish the fruit of the arrogant heart of the king of Assyria, and the glory of his haughty looks."

13For he says:

"By the strength of my hand I have
      done *it,*
   And by my wisdom, for I am prudent;
   Also I have removed the boundaries
      of the people,
   And have robbed their treasuries;
   So I have put down the inhabitants
      like a valiant *man.*
14 My hand has found like a nest the
      riches of the people,
   And as one gathers eggs *that are* left,
   I have gathered all the earth;
   And there was no one who moved *his*
      wing,
   Nor opened *his* mouth with even a
      peep."

15 Shall the ax boast itself against him
      who chops with it?
   Or shall the saw exalt itself against
      him who saws with it?

As if a rod could wield *itself* against
      those who lift it up,
   Or as if a staff could lift up, *as if it
      were* not wood!
16 Therefore the Lord, the Lord[a] of
      hosts,
   Will send leanness among his fat ones;
   And under his glory
   He will kindle a burning
   Like the burning of a fire.
17 So the Light of Israel will be for a fire,
   And his Holy One for a flame;
   It will burn and devour
   His thorns and his briers in one day.
18 And it will consume the glory of his
      forest and of his fruitful field,
   Both soul and body;
   And they will be as when a sick man
      wastes away.
19 Then the rest of the trees of his forest
   Will be so few in number
   That a child may write them.

The Returning Remnant of Israel
20 And it shall come to pass in that day
   That the remnant of Israel,
   And such as have escaped of the
      house of Jacob,
   Will never again depend on him who
      defeated them,
   But will depend on the LORD, the
      Holy One of Israel, in truth.

10:20 the remnant of Israel. Only a small number remained obedient to God's law, and God preserved them. He will never forsake the Abrahamic Covenant (see Mic. 2:12).

21 The remnant will return, the remnant
      of Jacob,
   To the Mighty God.
22 For though your people, O Israel, be
      as the sand of the sea,
   A remnant of them will return;
   The destruction decreed shall
      overflow with righteousness.
23 For the Lord GOD of hosts
   Will make a determined end
   In the midst of all the land.

24Therefore thus says the Lord GOD of hosts: "O My people, who dwell in Zion, do

---

10:16 *a*Following Bomberg; Masoretic Text and Dead Sea Scrolls read YHWH (the LORD).

not be afraid of the Assyrian. He shall strike you with a rod and lift up his staff against you, in the manner of Egypt. ²⁵For yet a very little while and the indignation will cease, as will My anger in their destruction." ²⁶And the LORD of hosts will stir up a scourge for him like the slaughter of Midian at the rock of Oreb; *as* His rod was on the sea, so will He lift it up in the manner of Egypt.

> **10:26 Midian...Egypt.** Isaiah told of Gideon's victory over the Midianites (Judg. 7:25) and the slaughter of the Egyptians who pursued the Israelites through the Red Sea (Ex. 14:16,26,27) to illustrate God's future deliverance of Israel.

²⁷ It shall come to pass in that day
     That his burden will be taken away
        from your shoulder,
     And his yoke from your neck,
     And the yoke will be destroyed
        because of the anointing oil.
²⁸ He has come to Aiath,
     He has passed Migron;
     At Michmash he has attended to his
        equipment.
²⁹ They have gone along the ridge,
     They have taken up lodging at Geba.
     Ramah is afraid,
     Gibeah of Saul has fled.
³⁰ Lift up your voice,
     O daughter of Gallim!
     Cause it to be heard as far as Laish—
     O poor Anathoth!^a
³¹ Madmenah has fled,
     The inhabitants of Gebim seek
        refuge.
³² As yet he will remain at Nob that
        day;
     He will shake his fist at the mount of
        the daughter of Zion,
     The hill of Jerusalem.

³³ Behold, the Lord,
     The LORD of hosts,
     Will lop off the bough with terror;
     Those of high stature *will be* hewn
        down,
     And the haughty will be humbled.

³⁴ He will cut down the thickets of the
        forest with iron,
     And Lebanon will fall by the Mighty
        One.

The Reign of Jesse's Offspring

11 There shall come forth a Rod from
        the stem of Jesse,
     And a Branch shall grow out of his
        roots.

> **11:1 stem...roots.** The Davidic dynasty seemed to be destroyed with the Babylonian captivity of 586 B.C. But life remained in the stump and roots of the Davidic line, manifesting itself in the Rod and Branch. **Jesse.** Jesse was David's father, through whose line the messianic king would come (Ruth 4:22). **Branch.** This is a title for Messiah.

² The Spirit of the LORD shall rest upon
        Him,
     The Spirit of wisdom and
        understanding,
     The Spirit of counsel and might,
     The Spirit of knowledge and of the
        fear of the LORD.
³ His delight *is* in the fear of the LORD,
     And He shall not judge by the sight of
        His eyes,
     Nor decide by the hearing of His ears;
⁴ But with righteousness He shall judge
        the poor,
     And decide with equity for the meek
        of the earth;
     He shall strike the earth with the rod
        of His mouth,
     And with the breath of His lips He
        shall slay the wicked.
⁵ Righteousness shall be the belt of His
        loins,
     And faithfulness the belt of His waist.

⁶ "The wolf also shall dwell with the
        lamb,
     The leopard shall lie down with the
        young goat,
     The calf and the young lion and the
        fatling together;
     And a little child shall lead them.
⁷ The cow and the bear shall graze;

10:30 ^aFollowing Masoretic Text, Targum, and Vulgate; Septuagint and Syriac read *Listen to her, O Anathoth.*

Their young ones shall lie down
  together;
And the lion shall eat straw like the
  ox.
8 The nursing child shall play by the
  cobra's hole,
And the weaned child shall put his
  hand in the viper's den.
9 They shall not hurt nor destroy in all
  My holy mountain,
For the earth shall be full of the
  knowledge of the LORD
As the waters cover the sea.

11:9 full of the knowledge of the LORD. Everyone
will know the Lord when He returns to fulfill His New
Covenant with Israel (Jer. 31:34).

10 "And in that day there shall be a Root
  of Jesse,
Who shall stand as a banner to the
  people;
For the Gentiles shall seek Him,
And His resting place shall be
  glorious."

11 It shall come to pass in that day
That the Lord shall set His hand
  again the second time
To recover the remnant of His people
  who are left,
From Assyria and Egypt,
From Pathros and Cush,
From Elam and Shinar,
From Hamath and the islands of the
  sea.

12 He will set up a banner for the
  nations,
And will assemble the outcasts of
  Israel,
And gather together the dispersed of
  Judah
From the four corners of the earth.
13 Also the envy of Ephraim shall
  depart,
And the adversaries of Judah shall be
  cut off;
Ephraim shall not envy Judah,
And Judah shall not harass Ephraim.

14 But they shall fly down upon the
  shoulder of the Philistines toward
  the west;
Together they shall plunder the people
  of the East;
They shall lay their hand on Edom
  and Moab;
And the people of Ammon shall obey
  them.
15 The LORD will utterly destroy[a] the
  tongue of the Sea of Egypt;
With His mighty wind He will shake
  His fist over the River,[b]
And strike it in the seven streams,
And make *men* cross over dryshod.
16 There will be a highway for the
  remnant of His people
Who will be left from Assyria,
As it was for Israel
In the day that he came up from the
  land of Egypt.

A Hymn of Praise

12 And in that day you will say:

"O LORD, I will praise You;
  Though You were angry with me,
  Your anger is turned away, and You
  comfort me.
2 Behold, God *is* my salvation,
  I will trust and not be afraid;
'For YAH, the LORD, *is* my strength
  and song;
  He also has become my salvation.' "[a]

3 Therefore with joy you will draw
  water
From the wells of salvation.

4And in that day you will say:

"Praise the LORD, call upon His name;
  Declare His deeds among the
  peoples,
  Make mention that His name is
  exalted.
5 Sing to the LORD,
  For He has done excellent things;
  This *is* known in all the earth.
6 Cry out and shout, O inhabitant of
  Zion,

11:15 [a]Following Masoretic Text and Vulgate; Septuagint, Syriac, and Targum read *dry up.*   [b]That is,
the Euphrates   12:2 [a]Exodus 15:2

For great *is* the Holy One of Israel in
    your midst!"

13:1–14:27 Verses 13:1–14:24 deal with Babylon and
vv. 25–27 with Assyria. Babylon was not yet a world
power, but Isaiah foresaw a time when she would
overthrow Assyria and become an international
force.

Proclamation Against Babylon

13 The burden against Babylon which
Isaiah the son of Amoz saw.

2   "Lift up a banner on the high
     mountain,
    Raise your voice to them;
    Wave your hand, that they may enter
     the gates of the nobles.
3   I have commanded My sanctified
    ones;

I have also called My mighty ones for
    My anger—
Those who rejoice in My exaltation."

4   The noise of a multitude in the
    mountains,
    Like that of many people!
    A tumultuous noise of the
     kingdoms of nations gathered
     together!
    The LORD of hosts musters
    The army for battle.
5   They come from a far country,
    From the end of heaven—
    The LORD and His weapons of
     indignation,
    To destroy the whole land.

6   Wail, for the day of the LORD *is* at
    hand!

GOD'S JUDGMENT ON THE NATIONS

	Obadiah	Amos	Isaiah	Jeremiah	Habakkuk	Ezekiel
Ammon		1:13–15 Judgment		49:1–6 Judgment; Restoration		25:1–7 Judgment
Babylon			13:1–14:23 Judgment	50,51 Judgment	2:6–17 Judgment	
Damascus		1:3–5 Judgment	17:1–3 Judgment; Remnant	49:23–27 Judgment		
Edom	Judgment	1:11,12 Judgment	21:11,12 Judgment	49:7–22 Judgment		25:12–14 Judgment
Egypt			19 Judgment	46:1–26 Judgment		29–32 Judgment
Moab		2:1–3 Judgment	15,16 Judgment; Remnant	48 Judgment; Restoration		25:8–11 Judgment
Philistia		1:6–8 Judgment	14:29–32 Judgment	47 Judgment; Remnant		25:15–17 Judgment
Tyre		1:9,10 Judgment	23 Judgment; Restoration			26–28 Judgment

It will come as destruction from the
Almighty.
7 Therefore all hands will be limp,
Every man's heart will melt,
8 And they will be afraid.
Pangs and sorrows will take hold of
them;
They will be in pain as a woman in
childbirth;
They will be amazed at one another;
Their faces *will be like* flames.

> **13:8 in pain as a woman in childbirth.** This usual-
> ly described the sufferings of the Israelites before the
> Lord delivered them (Jer. 4:31), but here it describes
> the misery of Babylon.

9 Behold, the day of the LORD comes,
Cruel, with both wrath and fierce
anger,
To lay the land desolate;
And He will destroy its sinners from
it.
10 For the stars of heaven and their
constellations
Will not give their light;
The sun will be darkened in its going
forth,
And the moon will not cause its light
to shine.
11 "I will punish the world for *its* evil,
And the wicked for their iniquity;
I will halt the arrogance of the proud,
And will lay low the haughtiness of
the terrible.
12 I will make a mortal more rare than
fine gold,
A man more than the golden wedge of
Ophir.

> **13:12 more rare.** Human mortality will be very high,
> but God will spare a faithful remnant.

13 Therefore I will shake the heavens,
And the earth will move out of her
place,
In the wrath of the LORD of hosts
And in the day of His fierce anger.
14 It shall be as the hunted gazelle,
And as a sheep that no man takes up;
Every man will turn to his own
people,

And everyone will flee to his own land.
15 Everyone who is found will be thrust
through,
And everyone who is captured will fall
by the sword.
16 Their children also will be dashed to
pieces before their eyes;
Their houses will be plundered
And their wives ravished.
17 "Behold, I will stir up the Medes
against them,
Who will not regard silver;
And *as for* gold, they will not delight
in it.
18 Also *their* bows will dash the young
men to pieces,
And they will have no pity on the
fruit of the womb;
Their eye will not spare children.
19 And Babylon, the glory of kingdoms,
The beauty of the Chaldeans' pride,
Will be as when God overthrew
Sodom and Gomorrah.
20 It will never be inhabited,
Nor will it be settled from generation
to generation;
Nor will the Arabian pitch tents
there,
Nor will the shepherds make their
sheepfolds there.
21 But wild beasts of the desert will lie
there,
And their houses will be full of owls;
Ostriches will dwell there,
And wild goats will caper there.
22 The hyenas will howl in their
citadels,
And jackals in their pleasant palaces.
Her time *is* near to come,
And her days will not be prolonged."

Mercy on Jacob

14 For the LORD will have mercy on
Jacob, and will still choose Israel,
and settle them in their own land. The
strangers will be joined with them, and
they will cling to the house of Jacob. ²Then
people will take them and bring them to
their place, and the house of Israel will possess them for servants and maids in the
land of the LORD; they will take them captive whose captives they were, and rule over
their oppressors.

Fall of the King of Babylon

³It shall come to pass in the day the LORD gives you rest from your sorrow, and from your fear and the hard bondage in which you were made to serve, ⁴that you will take up this proverb against the king of Babylon, and say:

> "How the oppressor has ceased,
> The golden[a] city ceased!

14:1–3 Isaiah describes the final Babylon at the end of the tribulation. He describes the millennial kingdom after the judgment of the final Babylon. The destruction of the future Babylon is connected to the deliverance of Israel from bondage. Babylon must perish so that the Lord may exalt His people.

⁵   The LORD has broken the staff of the
          wicked,
        The scepter of the rulers;
⁶   He who struck the people in wrath
          with a continual stroke,
        He who ruled the nations in anger,
        Is persecuted *and* no one hinders.
⁷   The whole earth is at rest *and* quiet;
        They break forth into singing.
⁸   Indeed the cypress trees rejoice over
          you,
        And the cedars of Lebanon,
        Saying, 'Since you were cut down,
        No woodsman has come up against us.'

⁹   "Hell from beneath is excited about
          you,
        To meet *you* at your coming;
        It stirs up the dead for you,
        All the chief ones of the earth;
        It has raised up from their thrones
        All the kings of the nations.
¹⁰   They all shall speak and say to you:
        'Have you also become as weak as we?
        Have you become like us?
¹¹   Your pomp is brought down to Sheol,
        And the sound of your stringed
          instruments;
        The maggot is spread under you,
        And worms cover you.'

The Fall of Lucifer

¹²   "How you are fallen from heaven,
        O Lucifer,[a] son of the morning!

How you are cut down to the ground,
        You who weakened the nations!
¹³   For you have said in your heart:
        'I will ascend into heaven,
        I will exalt my throne above the stars
          of God;
        I will also sit on the mount of the
          congregation
        On the farthest sides of the north;

14:12 heaven. This scene describes the pride of the king and Satan energizing him. **Lucifer, son of the morning.** Lucifer means "shining one" or "morning star." The stars represented gods battling among themselves for places of preeminence.

¹⁴   I will ascend above the heights of the
          clouds,
        I will be like the Most High.'
¹⁵   Yet you shall be brought down to
          Sheol,
        To the lowest depths of the Pit.

¹⁶   "Those who see you will gaze at you,
        And consider you, *saying:*
        'Is this the man who made the earth
          tremble,
        Who shook kingdoms,
¹⁷   Who made the world as a wilderness
        And destroyed its cities,
        Who did not open the house of his
          prisoners?'

¹⁸   "All the kings of the nations,
        All of them, sleep in glory,
        Everyone in his own house;

14:18 All the kings...sleep in glory. All the kings, except the king of Babylon, were given honorable burials.

¹⁹   But you are cast out of your grave
        Like an abominable branch,
        Like the garment of those who are
          slain,
        Thrust through with a sword,
        Who go down to the stones of the pit,
        Like a corpse trodden underfoot.
²⁰   You will not be joined with them in
          burial,
        Because you have destroyed your land
        And slain your people.

14:4 [a]Or *insolent*   14:12 [a]Literally *Day Star*

The brood of evildoers shall never be
    named.
21 Prepare slaughter for his children
    Because of the iniquity of their
        fathers,
    Lest they rise up and possess the
        land,
    And fill the face of the world with
        cities."

Babylon Destroyed

22 "For I will rise up against them," says
        the LORD of hosts,
    "And cut off from Babylon the name
        and remnant,
    And offspring and posterity," says the
        LORD.

14:22 cut off. According to the Lord's promise in vv.
22,23, Israel will have a remnant, but Babylon will not.

---

23 "I will also make it a possession for the
        porcupine,
    And marshes of muddy water;
    I will sweep it with the broom of
        destruction," says the LORD of
        hosts.

Assyria Destroyed

24 The LORD of hosts has sworn,
        saying,
    "Surely, as I have thought, so it shall
        come to pass,
    And as I have purposed, *so* it shall
        stand:
25 That I will break the Assyrian in My
        land,
    And on My mountains tread him
        underfoot.
    Then his yoke shall be removed from
        them,
    And his burden removed from their
        shoulders.
26 This *is* the purpose that is purposed
        against the whole earth,
    And this *is* the hand that is stretched
        out over all the nations.
27 For the LORD of hosts has purposed,
    And who will annul *it?*
    His hand *is* stretched out,
    And who will turn it back?"

Philistia Destroyed

28 This is the burden which came in the
year that King Ahaz died.

29 "Do not rejoice, all you of Philistia,
    Because the rod that struck you is
        broken;
    For out of the serpent's roots will
        come forth a viper,
    And its offspring *will be* a fiery flying
        serpent.
30 The firstborn of the poor will feed,
    And the needy will lie down in safety;
    I will kill your roots with famine,
    And it will slay your remnant.
31 Wail, O gate! Cry, O city!
    All you of Philistia *are* dissolved;
    For smoke will come from the north,
    And no one *will be* alone in his
        appointed times."

32 What will they answer the messengers
        of the nation?
    That the LORD has founded Zion,
    And the poor of His people shall take
        refuge in it.

Proclamation Against Moab

15 The burden against Moab.

    Because in the night Ar of Moab is
        laid waste
    And destroyed,
    Because in the night Kir of Moab is
        laid waste
    And destroyed,
2   He has gone up to the temple[a] and
        Dibon,
    To the high places to weep.
    Moab will wail over Nebo and over
        Medeba;
    On all their heads *will be* baldness,

15:2 Dibon. Moab chose the temple of the Moabite
god, Chemosh, as the place of weeping because
Chemosh had failed to deliver the nation.
Nebo...Medeba. Nebo is the mountain at the N end
of the Dead Sea where God showed Moses the
Promised Land (Deut. 34:1). Medeba is 5 miles SE of
Nebo. **baldness...every beard.** Shaving heads and
beards was a sign of disgrace and humiliation (Lev.
21:5).

15:2 ªHebrew *bayith,* literally *house*

And every beard cut off.
3 In their streets they will clothe
    themselves with sackcloth;
On the tops of their houses
And in their streets
Everyone will wail, weeping bitterly.
4 Heshbon and Elealeh will cry out,
Their voice shall be heard as far as
    Jahaz;
Therefore the armed soldiers*a* of
    Moab will cry out;
His life will be burdensome to him.

5 "My heart will cry out for Moab;
His fugitives *shall flee* to Zoar,
Like a three-year-old heifer.*a*
For by the Ascent of Luhith
They will go up with weeping;
For in the way of Horonaim
They will raise up a cry of
    destruction.
6 For the waters of Nimrim will be
    desolate,
For the green grass has withered
    away;
The grass fails, there is nothing green.
7 Therefore the abundance they have
    gained,
And what they have laid up,
They will carry away to the Brook of
    the Willows.
8 For the cry has gone all around the
    borders of Moab,
Its wailing to Eglaim
And its wailing to Beer Elim.
9 For the waters of Dimon*a* will be full
    of blood;
Because I will bring more upon
    Dimon,*b*
Lions upon him who escapes from
    Moab,
And on the remnant of the land."

> **15:9 Dimon.** This may be another spelling of "Dibon," a religious center of heathendom in Moab. **Lions.** Escaping the invading armies would only lead to new dangers from the beasts of the wilderness.

Moab Destroyed

16 Send the lamb to the ruler of the
    land,
From Sela to the wilderness,
To the mount of the daughter of Zion.
2 For it shall be as a wandering bird
    thrown out of the nest;
So shall be the daughters of Moab at
    the fords of the Arnon.

3 "Take counsel, execute judgment;
Make your shadow like the night in
    the middle of the day;
Hide the outcasts,
Do not betray him who escapes.
4 Let My outcasts dwell with you,
    O Moab;
Be a shelter to them from the face of
    the spoiler.
For the extortioner is at an end,
Devastation ceases,
The oppressors are consumed out of
    the land.
5 In mercy the throne will be
    established;
And One will sit on it in truth, in the
    tabernacle of David,
Judging and seeking justice and
    hastening righteousness."

6 We have heard of the pride of Moab—
He is very proud—
Of his haughtiness and his pride and
    his wrath;
But his lies *shall* not *be* so.
7 Therefore Moab shall wail for Moab;
Everyone shall wail.
For the foundations of Kir Hareseth
    you shall mourn;
Surely *they are* stricken.

8 For the fields of Heshbon languish,
And the vine of Sibmah;
The lords of the nations have broken
    down its choice plants,
Which have reached to Jazer
And wandered through the
    wilderness.
Her branches are stretched out,

They are gone over the sea.

9 Therefore I will bewail the vine of
   Sibmah,
   With the weeping of Jazer;
   I will drench you with my tears,
   O Heshbon and Elealeh;
   For battle cries have fallen
   Over your summer fruits and your
      harvest.

16:9 I will bewail. Isaiah, reflecting God's emotion, was greatly distressed over the destruction of so rich an agricultural resource.

10 Gladness is taken away,
   And joy from the plentiful field;
   In the vineyards there will be no
      singing,
   Nor will there be shouting;
   No treaders will tread out wine in the
      presses;
   I have made their shouting cease.
11 Therefore my heart shall resound like
      a harp for Moab,
   And my inner being for Kir Heres.
12 And it shall come to pass,
   When it is seen that Moab is weary
      on the high place,
   That he will come to his sanctuary to
      pray;
   But he will not prevail.

13This *is* the word which the LORD has spoken concerning Moab since that time. 14But now the LORD has spoken, saying, "Within three years, as the years of a hired man, the glory of Moab will be despised with all that great multitude, and the remnant *will be* very small *and* feeble."

Proclamation Against Syria and Israel

17 The burden against Damascus.

   "Behold, Damascus will cease from
      being a city,
   And it will be a ruinous heap.
2 The cities of Aroer *are* forsaken;[a]
   They will be for flocks
   Which lie down, and no one will
      make *them* afraid.

3 The fortress also will cease from
      Ephraim,
   The kingdom from Damascus,
   And the remnant of Syria;
   They will be as the glory of the
      children of Israel,"
   Says the LORD of hosts.

17:3 Ephraim. These northern 10 tribes, also known as "Israel," joined with Syria, forming an alliance to fight the Assyrians. Many of Ephraim's cities were destroyed. **remnant of Syria.** After the Assyrian onslaught, Syria was to have a remnant, but not a kingdom.

4 " In that day it shall come to pass
   That the glory of Jacob will wane,
   And the fatness of his flesh grow
      lean.
5 It shall be as when the harvester
      gathers the grain,
   And reaps the heads with his
      arm;
   It shall be as he who gathers heads of
      grain
   In the Valley of Rephaim.
6 Yet gleaning grapes will be left in it,
   Like the shaking of an olive tree,
   Two *or* three olives at the top of the
      uppermost bough,
   Four *or* five in its most fruitful
      branches,"
   Says the LORD God of Israel.

7 In that day a man will look to his
      Maker,
   And his eyes will have respect for the
      Holy One of Israel.
8 He will not look to the altars,

17:7 look to his Maker. In the future, Ephraim's remnant will experience judgment for not depending on the Lord. Then they will repent.

   The work of his hands;
   He will not respect what his fingers
      have made,
   Nor the wooden images[a] nor the
      incense altars.

17:2 [a]Following Masoretic Text and Vulgate; Septuagint reads *It shall be forsaken forever*; Targum reads *Its cities shall be forsaken and desolate.*   17:8 [a]Hebrew *Asherim*, Canaanite deities

9   In that day his strong cities will be as
       a forsaken bough[a]
    And an uppermost branch,[b]
    Which they left because of the
       children of Israel;
    And there will be desolation.

10 Because you have forgotten the God
       of your salvation,
    And have not been mindful of the
       Rock of your stronghold,
    Therefore you will plant pleasant
       plants
    And set out foreign seedlings;
11 In the day you will make your plant to
       grow,
    And in the morning you will make
       your seed to flourish;
    But the harvest *will be* a heap of
       ruins
    In the day of grief and desperate
       sorrow.

12 Woe to the multitude of many people
    Who make a noise like the roar of the
       seas,
    And to the rushing of nations
    That make a rushing like the rushing
       of mighty waters!
13 The nations will rush like the rushing
       of many waters;
    But *God* will rebuke them and they
       will flee far away,
    And be chased like the chaff of the
       mountains before the wind,
    Like a rolling thing before the
       whirlwind.
14 Then behold, at eventide, trouble!
    And before the morning, he *is* no
       more.
    This *is* the portion of those who
       plunder us,
    And the lot of those who rob us.

Proclamation Against Ethiopia

18 Woe to the land shadowed with
       buzzing wings,
    Which *is* beyond the rivers of
       Ethiopia,
2   Which sends ambassadors by sea,

Even in vessels of reed on the waters,
    saying,
"Go, swift messengers, to a nation tall
    and smooth *of skin*,
To a people terrible from their
    beginning onward,
A nation powerful and treading down,
Whose land the rivers divide."

3   All inhabitants of the world and
       dwellers on the earth:
    When he lifts up a banner on the
       mountains, you see *it*;
    And when he blows a trumpet, you
       hear *it*.
4   For so the LORD said to me,
    "I will take My rest,
    And I will look from My dwelling
       place
    Like clear heat in sunshine,
    Like a cloud of dew in the heat of
       harvest."

18:4 I will take My rest. The Lord will wait patiently
until the appropriate time to intervene in human affairs, when sunshine and dew have built to the opportune climax.

5   For before the harvest, when the bud
       is perfect
    And the sour grape is ripening in the
       flower,
    He will both cut off the sprigs with
       pruning hooks
    And take away *and* cut down the
       branches.
6   They will be left together for the
       mountain birds of prey
    And for the beasts of the earth;
    The birds of prey will summer on
       them,
    And all the beasts of the earth will
       winter on them.

7   In that time a present will be brought
       to the LORD of hosts
    From[a] a people tall and smooth *of
       skin*,
    And from a people terrible from their
       beginning onward,

17:9 [a]Septuagint reads *Hivites*; Targum reads *laid waste*; Vulgate reads *as the plows*.   [b]Septuagint
reads *Amorites*; Targum reads *in ruins*; Vulgate reads *corn*.   18:7 [a]Following Dead Sea Scrolls,
Septuagint, and Vulgate; Masoretic Text omits *From*; Targum reads *To*.

A nation powerful and treading down,
Whose land the rivers divide—
To the place of the name of the LORD
of hosts,
To Mount Zion.

Proclamation Against Egypt

19 The burden against Egypt.

Behold, the LORD rides on a swift
cloud,
And will come into Egypt;
The idols of Egypt will totter at His
presence,
And the heart of Egypt will melt in its
midst.

> **19:1 rides on a swift cloud.** Clouds are vehicles for
> the Lord's coming to execute judgment (see Pss.
> 18:10,11; Dan. 7:13).

2   "I will set Egyptians against Egyptians;
Everyone will fight against his brother,
And everyone against his neighbor,
City against city, kingdom against
kingdom.
3   The spirit of Egypt will fail in its
midst;
I will destroy their counsel,
And they will consult the idols and
the charmers,
The mediums and the sorcerers.
4   And the Egyptians I will give
Into the hand of a cruel master,
And a fierce king will rule over them,"
Says the Lord, the LORD of hosts.

5   The waters will fail from the sea,
And the river will be wasted and dried
up.
6   The rivers will turn foul;
The brooks of defense will be emptied
and dried up;
The reeds and rushes will wither.
7   The papyrus reeds by the River,[a] by
the mouth of the River,
And everything sown by the River,
Will wither, be driven away, and be no
more.
8   The fishermen also will mourn;
All those will lament who cast hooks
into the River,

And they will languish who spread
nets on the waters.
9   Moreover those who work in fine flax
And those who weave fine fabric will
be ashamed;
10 And its foundations will be broken.
All who make wages *will be* troubled
of soul.

> **19:10 foundations.** God would remove the "pillars"
> on which the working class depended. This could
> refer to the economic structure of the society or the
> upper class that organized the businesses of the
> land.

11 Surely the princes of Zoan *are* fools;
Pharaoh's wise counselors give foolish
counsel.
How do you say to Pharaoh, "I *am* the
son of the wise,
The son of ancient kings?"
12 Where *are* they?
Where *are* your wise men?
Let them tell you now,
And let them know what the LORD of
hosts has purposed against Egypt.
13 The princes of Zoan have become
fools;
The princes of Noph[a] are deceived;
They have also deluded Egypt,
Those who are the mainstay of its
tribes.
14 The LORD has mingled a perverse
spirit in her midst;
And they have caused Egypt to err in
all her work,
As a drunken man staggers in his
vomit.
15 Neither will there be *any* work for
Egypt,
Which the head or tail,
Palm branch or bulrush, may do.[a]

16In that day Egypt will be like women,
and will be afraid and fear because of the
waving of the hand of the LORD of hosts,
which He waves over it. 17And the land of
Judah will be a terror to Egypt; everyone
who makes mention of it will be afraid in
himself, because of the counsel of the
LORD of hosts which He has determined
against it.

19:7 [a]That is, the Nile   19:13 [a]That is, ancient Memphis   19:15 [a]Compare Isaiah 9:14–16

Egypt, Assyria, and Israel Blessed

¹⁸In that day five cities in the land of Egypt will speak the language of Canaan and swear by the LORD of hosts; one will be called the City of Destruction.^a

¹⁹In that day there will be an altar to the LORD in the midst of the land of Egypt, and a pillar to the LORD at its border. ²⁰And it will be for a sign and for a witness to the LORD of hosts in the land of Egypt; for they will cry to the LORD because of the oppressors, and He will send them a Savior and a Mighty One, and He will deliver them. ²¹Then the LORD will be known to Egypt, and the Egyptians will know the LORD in that day, and will make sacrifice and offering; yes, they will make a vow to the LORD and perform *it.* ²²And the LORD will strike Egypt, He will strike and heal *it;* they will return to the LORD, and He will be entreated by them and heal them.

19:18 five cities. The chances of even one Egyptian city turning to the Lord were remote, but five will turn to Him. **language of Canaan.** Egypt is to fear Judah, speak her language, and convert to her form of worship. **swear by the LORD of hosts.** Egypt will dramatically turn to God. **City of Destruction.** This was probably Heliopolis, the "City of the Sun," the home of the Egyptian sun-god (see Jer. 43:12,13).

---

²³In that day there will be a highway from Egypt to Assyria, and the Assyrian will come into Egypt and the Egyptian into Assyria, and the Egyptians will serve with the Assyrians.

19:23 a highway from Egypt to Assyria. Egypt and Assyria are to reach a lasting peace with each other during "that day" of Christ's reign (27:13).

---

²⁴In that day Israel will be one of three with Egypt and Assyria—a blessing in the midst of the land, ²⁵whom the LORD of hosts shall bless, saying, "Blessed *is* Egypt My people, and Assyria the work of My hands, and Israel My inheritance."

The Sign Against Egypt and Ethiopia

20 In the year that Tartan^a came to Ashdod, when Sargon the king of Assyria sent him, and he fought against Ashdod and took it, ²at the same time the LORD spoke by Isaiah the son of Amoz, saying, "Go, and remove the sackcloth from your body, and take your sandals off your feet." And he did so, walking naked and barefoot.

³Then the LORD said, "Just as My servant Isaiah has walked naked and barefoot three years *for* a sign and a wonder against Egypt and Ethiopia, ⁴so shall the king of Assyria lead away the Egyptians as prisoners and the Ethiopians as captives, young and old, naked and barefoot, with their buttocks uncovered, to the shame of Egypt. ⁵Then they shall be afraid and ashamed of Ethiopia their expectation and Egypt their glory. ⁶And the inhabitant of this territory will say in that day, 'Surely such *is* our expectation, wherever we flee for help to be delivered from the king of Assyria; and how shall we escape?'"

The Fall of Babylon Proclaimed

21 The burden against the Wilderness of the Sea.

As whirlwinds in the South pass
 through,
So it comes from the desert, from a
 terrible land.

2 A distressing vision is declared to me;
The treacherous dealer deals
 treacherously,
And the plunderer plunders.
Go up, O Elam!
Besiege, O Media!
All its sighing I have made to cease.

3 Therefore my loins are filled with
 pain;
Pangs have taken hold of me, like the
 pangs of a woman in labor.
I was distressed when *I* heard *it;*
I was dismayed when *I* saw *it.*

4 My heart wavered, fearfulness
 frightened me;
The night for which I longed He
 turned into fear for me.

5 Prepare the table,
Set a watchman in the tower,

---

^{19:18} ^aSome Hebrew manuscripts, Arabic, Dead Sea Scrolls, Targum, and Vulgate read *Sun;* Septuagint reads *Asedek* (literally *Righteousness*). ^{20:1} ^aOr *the Commander in Chief*

Eat and drink.
Arise, you princes,
Anoint the shield!

6　For thus has the Lord said to me:
"Go, set a watchman,
Let him declare what he sees."
7　And he saw a chariot *with* a pair of
horsemen,
A chariot of donkeys, *and* a chariot of
camels,
And he listened earnestly with great
care.
8　Then he cried, "A lion,*a* my Lord!
I stand continually on the watchtower
in the daytime;
I have sat at my post every night.
9　And look, here comes a chariot of
men *with* a pair of horsemen!"
Then he answered and said,
"Babylon is fallen, is fallen!
And all the carved images of her
gods
He has broken to the ground."

10　Oh, my threshing and the grain of my
floor!
That which I have heard from the
LORD of hosts,
The God of Israel,
I have declared to you.

21:10 my threshing and the grain of my floor! The violent threshing of grain represents Babylon's oppression of Israel, and the resultant grain was Israel's deliverance by God. This phrase brought hope to Israel.

Proclamation Against Edom
11The burden against Dumah.

He calls to me out of Seir,
"Watchman, what of the night?
Watchman, what of the night?"
12　The watchman said,
"The morning comes, and also the
night.
If you will inquire, inquire;
Return! Come back!"

Proclamation Against Arabia
13The burden against Arabia.

In the forest in Arabia you will lodge,
O you traveling companies of
Dedanites.
14　O inhabitants of the land of Tema,
Bring water to him who is thirsty;
With their bread they met him who
fled.
15　For they fled from the swords, from
the drawn sword,
From the bent bow, and from the
distress of war.

16For thus the LORD has said to me:
"Within a year, according to the year of a
hired man, all the glory of Kedar will fail;
17and the remainder of the number of archers, the mighty men of the people of Kedar, will be diminished; for the LORD God of Israel has spoken *it*."

Proclamation Against Jerusalem
22 The burden against the Valley of
Vision.

What ails you now, that you have all
gone up to the housetops,

22:1 Valley of Vision. This referred to Israel, since God often revealed Himself to Jerusalem in visions. The Israelites lacked vision, as they were oblivious to the destruction that awaited them. **What ails you...?** The prophet reproached the people for celebrating with wild parties when they should have been repenting of their sins. He anticipated destruction similar to Jerusalem's fall to the Babylonians in 586 B.C.

2　You who are full of noise,
A tumultuous city, a joyous city?
Your slain *men are* not slain with the
sword,
Nor dead in battle.
3　All your rulers have fled together;
They are captured by the archers.
All who are found in you are bound
together;
They have fled from afar.
4　Therefore I said, "Look away from me,
I will weep bitterly;
Do not labor to comfort me
Because of the plundering of the
daughter of my people."

21:8 *a*Dead Sea Scrolls read *Then the observer cried.*

5 For *it is* a day of trouble and treading
   down and perplexity
By the Lord GOD of hosts
In the Valley of Vision—
Breaking down the walls
And of crying to the mountain.
6 Elam bore the quiver
With chariots of men *and* horsemen,
And Kir uncovered the shield.
7 It shall come to pass *that* your
   choicest valleys
Shall be full of chariots,
And the horsemen shall set
   themselves in array at the gate.

8 He removed the protection of Judah.
You looked in that day to the armor of
   the House of the Forest;
9 You also saw the damage to the city of
   David,
That it was great;
And you gathered together the waters
   of the lower pool.
10 You numbered the houses of
   Jerusalem,
And the houses you broke down
To fortify the wall.

22:10 fortify the wall. Hezekiah trusted God while
he rebuilt the damaged wall (2 Chr. 32:5). His faith is
contrasted with that of the people whom Isaiah addresses.

11 You also made a reservoir between the
   two walls
For the water of the old pool.
But you did not look to its Maker,
Nor did you have respect for Him
   who fashioned it long ago.
12 And in that day the Lord GOD of
   hosts
Called for weeping and for mourning,
For baldness and for girding with
   sackcloth.
13 But instead, joy and gladness,
Slaying oxen and killing sheep,
Eating meat and drinking wine:
"Let us eat and drink, for tomorrow we
   die!"

14 Then it was revealed in my hearing by
   the LORD of hosts,
"Surely for this iniquity there will be
   no atonement for you,
Even to your death," says the Lord
   GOD of hosts.

The Judgment on Shebna
15 Thus says the Lord GOD of hosts:

"Go, proceed to this steward,
   To Shebna, who *is* over the house, *and*
      say:

22:15 Shebna, who *is* over the house. This man
(possibly Egyptian) was second in authority only to
the king. Other Old Testament passages refer to him
as a scribe (2 Kin. 18:37), the position to which he was
reduced, as prophesied by Isaiah.

16 'What have you here, and whom have
   you here,
That you have hewn a sepulcher here,
As he who hews himself a sepulcher
   on high,
Who carves a tomb for himself in a
   rock?
17 Indeed, the LORD will throw you away
   violently,
O mighty man,
And will surely seize you.
18 He will surely turn violently and toss
   you like a ball
Into a large country;
There you shall die, and there your
   glorious chariots
Shall be the shame of your master's
   house.
19 So I will drive you out of your office,
And from your position he will pull
   you down.*a*

20 'Then it shall be in that day,
That I will call My servant Eliakim
   the son of Hilkiah;
21 I will clothe him with your robe
And strengthen him with your belt;
I will commit your responsibility into
   his hand.
He shall be a father to the inhabitants
   of Jerusalem

22:19 *a*Septuagint omits *he will pull you down*; Syriac, Targum, and Vulgate read *I will pull you
down*.

And to the house of Judah.
22 The key of the house of David
   I will lay on his shoulder;
   So he shall open, and no one shall
      shut;
   And he shall shut, and no one shall
      open.

23 I will fasten him *as* a peg in a secure
      place,
   And he will become a glorious throne
      to his father's house.

24 'They will hang on him all the glory of
his father's house, the offspring and the
posterity, all vessels of small quantity, from
the cups to all the pitchers. 25 In that day,'
says the LORD of hosts, 'the peg that is fastened
in the secure place will be removed
and be cut down and fall, and the burden
that *was* on it will be cut off; for the LORD
has spoken.' "

Proclamation Against Tyre

23 The burden against Tyre.

Wail, you ships of Tarshish!
For it is laid waste,
So that there is no house, no harbor;
From the land of Cyprus*a* it is
   revealed to them.

2 Be still, you inhabitants of the
      coastland,
   You merchants of Sidon,
   Whom those who cross the sea have
      filled.*a*
3 And on great waters the grain of
      Shihor,
   The harvest of the River,*a* *is* her
      revenue;
   And she is a marketplace for the
      nations.

4 Be ashamed, O Sidon;
   For the sea has spoken,
   The strength of the sea, saying,
   "I do not labor, nor bring forth
      children;
   Neither do I rear young men,
   Nor bring up virgins."

5 When the report *reaches* Egypt,
   They also will be in agony at the
      report of Tyre.
6 Cross over to Tarshish;
   Wail, you inhabitants of the
      coastland!
7 *Is* this your joyous *city,*
   Whose antiquity *is* from ancient days,
   Whose feet carried her far off to
      dwell?
8 Who has taken this counsel against
      Tyre, the crowning *city,*
   Whose merchants *are* princes,
   Whose traders *are* the honorable of
      the earth?
9 The LORD of hosts has purposed it,
   To bring to dishonor the pride of all
      glory,
   To bring into contempt all the
      honorable of the earth.

10 Overflow through your land like the
      River,*a*
   O daughter of Tarshish;
   There is no more strength.
11 He stretched out His hand over the
      sea,
   He shook the kingdoms;
   The LORD has given a commandment
      against Canaan
   To destroy its strongholds.

23:1 *a*Hebrew *Kittim,* western lands, especially Cyprus 23:2 *a*Following Masoretic Text and Vulgate; Septuagint and Targum read *Passing over the water;* Dead Sea Scrolls read *Your messengers passing over the sea.* 23:3 *a*That is, the Nile 23:10 *a*That is, the Nile

12 And He said, "You will rejoice no
     more,
   O you oppressed virgin daughter of
     Sidon.
   Arise, cross over to Cyprus;
   There also you will have no rest."

13 Behold, the land of the Chaldeans,
   This people *which* was not;
   Assyria founded it for wild beasts of
     the desert.
   They set up its towers,
   They raised up its palaces,
   And brought it to ruin.

14 Wail, you ships of Tarshish!
   For your strength is laid waste.

15Now it shall come to pass in that day
that Tyre will be forgotten seventy years,
according to the days of one king. At the
end of seventy years it will happen to Tyre
as *in* the song of the harlot:

16 "Take a harp, go about the city,
    You forgotten harlot;
    Make sweet melody, sing many songs,
    That you may be remembered."

17And it shall be, at the end of seventy
years, that the LORD will deal with Tyre.
She will return to her hire, and commit fornication with all the kingdoms of the world
on the face of the earth. 18Her gain and her
pay will be set apart for the LORD; it will not
be treasured nor laid up, for her gain will be
for those who dwell before the LORD, to eat
sufficiently, and for fine clothing.

Impending Judgment on the Earth

24 Behold, the LORD makes the earth
       empty and makes it waste,
   Distorts its surface
   And scatters abroad its inhabitants.
2 And it shall be:
   As with the people, so with the
     priest;
   As with the servant, so with his
     master;
   As with the maid, so with her
     mistress;
   As with the buyer, so with the seller;
   As with the lender, so with the
     borrower;

   As with the creditor, so with the
     debtor.
3 The land shall be entirely emptied
     and utterly plundered,
   For the LORD has spoken this word.

4 The earth mourns *and* fades away,
   The world languishes *and* fades away;
   The haughty people of the earth
     languish.

24:4 haughty people. The prophet again emphasized that pride was the reason for God's judgment
(see 23:9).

5 The earth is also defiled under its
     inhabitants,
   Because they have transgressed the
     laws,
   Changed the ordinance,
   Broken the everlasting covenant.
6 Therefore the curse has devoured the
     earth,
   And those who dwell in it are
     desolate.
   Therefore the inhabitants of the earth
     are burned,
   And few men *are* left.

7 The new wine fails, the vine
     languishes,
   All the merry-hearted sigh.
8 The mirth of the tambourine ceases,
   The noise of the jubilant ends,
   The joy of the harp ceases.
9 They shall not drink wine with a
     song;
   Strong drink is bitter to those who
     drink it.
10 The city of confusion is broken down;
   Every house is shut up, so that none
     may go in.
11 *There is* a cry for wine in the streets,
   All joy is darkened,
   The mirth of the land is gone.
12 In the city desolation is left,
   And the gate is stricken with
     destruction.
13 When it shall be thus in the midst of
     the land among the people,
   It shall be like the shaking of an olive
     tree,
   Like the gleaning of grapes when the
     vintage is done.

14 They shall lift up their voice, they
      shall sing;
   For the majesty of the LORD
   They shall cry aloud from the sea.
15 Therefore glorify the LORD in the
      dawning light,
   The name of the LORD God of Israel
      in the coastlands of the sea.
16 From the ends of the earth we have
      heard songs:
   "Glory to the righteous!"
   But I said, "I am ruined, ruined!
   Woe to me!
   The treacherous dealers have dealt
      treacherously,
   Indeed, the treacherous dealers have
      dealt very treacherously."

24:16 Glory to the righteous! "Righteous" refers to
God. **But I.** Because Isaiah pondered the grief and
corruption in the world before God's final victory, he
was able to celebrate God's glory in his present time.

17 Fear and the pit and the snare
   Are upon you, O inhabitant of the
      earth.
18 And it shall be
   That he who flees from the noise of
      the fear
   Shall fall into the pit,
   And he who comes up from the midst
      of the pit
   Shall be caught in the snare;
   For the windows from on high are
      open,
   And the foundations of the earth are
      shaken.

19 The earth is violently broken,
   The earth is split open,
   The earth is shaken exceedingly.
20 The earth shall reel to and fro like a
      drunkard,
   And shall totter like a hut;
   Its transgression shall be heavy upon
      it,
   And it will fall, and not rise again.

24:20 drunkard...hut. These comparisons of a staggering drunkard and a flimsy lean-to hut describe the
ultimate collapse of the presumably strong planet
earth.

21 It shall come to pass in that day
   That the LORD will punish on high
      the host of exalted ones,
   And on the earth the kings of the
      earth.
22 They will be gathered together,
   As prisoners are gathered in the pit,
   And will be shut up in the prison;
   After many days they will be punished.
23 Then the moon will be disgraced
   And the sun ashamed;
   For the LORD of hosts will reign
   On Mount Zion and in Jerusalem
   And before His elders, gloriously.

Praise to God

25 O LORD, You *are* my God.
   I will exalt You,
   I will praise Your name;
   For You have done wonderful *things*;
   Your counsels of old *are* faithfulness
      and truth.
2 For You have made a city a ruin,
   A fortified city a ruin,
   A palace of foreigners to be a city no
      more;
   It will never be rebuilt.
3 Therefore the strong people will
      glorify You;
   The city of the terrible nations will
      fear You.
4 For You have been a strength to the
      poor,
   A strength to the needy in his distress,
   A refuge from the storm,
   A shade from the heat;
   For the blast of the terrible ones *is* as
      a storm *against* the wall.
5 You will reduce the noise of aliens,
   As heat in a dry place;
   As heat in the shadow of a cloud,
   The song of the terrible ones will be
      diminished.

6 And in this mountain
   The LORD of hosts will make for all
      people
   A feast of choice pieces,
   A feast of wines on the lees,
   Of fat things full of marrow,
   Of well-refined wines on the lees.
7 And He will destroy on this mountain
   The surface of the covering cast over
      all people,

And the veil that is spread over all
    nations.
8   He will swallow up death forever,
    And the Lord GOD will wipe away
        tears from all faces;
    The rebuke of His people
    He will take away from all the earth;
    For the LORD has spoken.

25:8 swallow up death. God will swallow up death, which itself swallows up humans (Prov. 1:12; see 1 Cor. 15:54). wipe away tears. God will remove the sorrow of death. Revelation describes the bliss of the redeemed in heaven (7:17) and the ideal conditions of the New Jerusalem (21:4). rebuke...He will take away. Israel will be the head of the nations instead of the tail (Deut. 28:13).

9   And it will be said in that day:
    "Behold, this is our God;
    We have waited for Him, and He will
        save us.
    This is the LORD;
    We have waited for Him;
    We will be glad and rejoice in His
        salvation."

10 For on this mountain the hand of the
        LORD will rest,
    And Moab shall be trampled down
        under Him,
    As straw is trampled down for the
        refuse heap.
11 And He will spread out His hands in
        their midst
    As a swimmer reaches out to swim,
    And He will bring down their pride
    Together with the trickery of their
        hands.
12 The fortress of the high fort of your
        walls
    He will bring down, lay low,
    And bring to the ground, down to the
        dust.

A Song of Salvation
26 In that day this song will be sung in
    the land of Judah:

    "We have a strong city;
    God will appoint salvation for walls
        and bulwarks.

2   Open the gates,
    That the righteous nation which
        keeps the truth may enter in.
3   You will keep him in perfect peace,
    Whose mind is stayed on You,
    Because he trusts in You.

26:3 perfect peace...trusts in You. Trusting in the Lord brings a peace that the wicked can never know. This trust prevents being double-minded (James 1:6–8) and serving two masters (Matt. 6:24).

4   Trust in the LORD forever,
    For in YAH, the LORD, is everlasting
        strength.[a]
5   For He brings down those who dwell
        on high,
    The lofty city;
    He lays it low,
    He lays it low to the ground,
    He brings it down to the dust.
6   The foot shall tread it down—
    The feet of the poor
    And the steps of the needy."

7   The way of the just is uprightness;
    O Most Upright,
    You weigh the path of the just.
8   Yes, in the way of Your judgments,
    O LORD, we have waited for You;
    The desire of our soul is for Your
        name
    And for the remembrance of You.
9   With my soul I have desired You in
        the night,
    Yes, by my spirit within me I will seek
        You early;
    For when Your judgments are in the
        earth,
    The inhabitants of the world will
        learn righteousness.

26:9 in the night...early. The pious long for God at all times. judgments...learn righteousness. God's punishment leads sinners to repentance.

10 Let grace be shown to the wicked,
    Yet he will not learn righteousness;
    In the land of uprightness he will deal
        unjustly,
    And will not behold the majesty of
        the LORD.

26:4 [a]Or Rock of Ages

¹¹ LORD, *when* Your hand is lifted up,
    they will not see.
But they will see and be ashamed
For *their* envy of people;
Yes, the fire of Your enemies shall
    devour them.

¹² LORD, You will establish peace for us,
For You have also done all our works
    in us.
¹³ O LORD our God, masters besides You
Have had dominion over us;
But by You only we make mention of
    Your name.
¹⁴ *They are* dead, they will not live;
They are deceased, they will not rise.
Therefore You have punished and
    destroyed them,
And made all their memory to perish.
¹⁵ You have increased the nation,
    O LORD,
You have increased the nation;
You are glorified;
You have expanded all the borders of
    the land.

¹⁶ LORD, in trouble they have visited
    You,
They poured out a prayer *when* Your
    chastening *was* upon them.
¹⁷ As a woman with child
Is in pain and cries out in her pangs,
When she draws near the time of her
    delivery,
So have we been in Your sight, O LORD.
¹⁸ We have been with child, we have
    been in pain;
We have, as it were, brought forth
    wind;
We have not accomplished any
    deliverance in the earth,
Nor have the inhabitants of the world
    fallen.

¹⁹ Your dead shall live;
Together with my dead body[a] they
    shall arise.
Awake and sing, you who dwell in
    dust;

For your dew *is like* the dew of herbs,
And the earth shall cast out the dead.

Take Refuge from the Coming Judgment
²⁰ Come, my people, enter your
    chambers,
And shut your doors behind you;
Hide yourself, as it were, for a little
    moment,
Until the indignation is past.

26:20 for a little moment. Israel's final restoration was not immediately at hand. She needed to continue praying for restoration until God's wrath had passed.

²¹ For behold, the LORD comes out of
    His place
To punish the inhabitants of the earth
    for their iniquity;
The earth will also disclose her blood,
And will no more cover her slain.

27 In that day the LORD with His
    severe sword, great and strong,
Will punish Leviathan the fleeing
    serpent,
Leviathan that twisted serpent;
And He will slay the reptile that *is* in
    the sea.

The Restoration of Israel
² In that day sing to her,
    "A vineyard of red wine![a]
³ I, the LORD, keep it,
I water it every moment;
Lest any hurt it,
I keep it night and day.
⁴ Fury *is* not in Me.
Who would set briers *and* thorns
Against Me in battle?
I would go through them,
I would burn them together.
⁵ Or let him take hold of My strength,
That he may make peace with Me;
And he shall make peace with Me."

⁶ Those who come He shall cause to
    take root in Jacob;

26:19 [a]Following Masoretic Text and Vulgate; Syriac and Targum read *their dead bodies*; Septuagint reads *those in the tombs.*   27:2 [a]Following Masoretic Text (Kittel's *Biblia Hebraica*), Bomberg, and Vulgate; Masoretic Text (*Biblia Hebraica Stuttgartensia*), some Hebrew manuscripts, and Septuagint read *delight*; Targum reads *choice vineyard.*

Israel shall blossom and bud,
And fill the face of the world with
fruit.

7 Has He struck Israel as He struck
those who struck him?
Or has He been slain according to the
slaughter of those who were slain
by Him?

> **27:7 struck Israel as He struck.** God had compassion on Israel but not on the nations He used to punish Israel.

8 In measure, by sending it away,
You contended with it.
He removes *it* by His rough wind
In the day of the east wind.
9 Therefore by this the iniquity of Jacob
will be covered;
And this *is* all the fruit of taking away
his sin:
When he makes all the stones of the
altar
Like chalkstones that are beaten to
dust,
Wooden images[a] and incense altars
shall not stand.

10 Yet the fortified city *will be* desolate,
The habitation forsaken and left like a
wilderness;
There the calf will feed, and there it
will lie down
And consume its branches.
11 When its boughs are withered, they
will be broken off;
The women come *and* set them on
fire.
For it *is* a people of no
understanding;
Therefore He who made them will
not have mercy on them,
And He who formed them will show
them no favor.

12 And it shall come to pass in that day
That the LORD will thresh,
From the channel of the River[a] to the
Brook of Egypt;
And you will be gathered one by one,
O you children of Israel.

13 So it shall be in that day:
The great trumpet will be blown;
They will come, who are about to
perish in the land of Assyria,
And they who are outcasts in the land
of Egypt,
And shall worship the LORD in the
holy mount at Jerusalem.

Woe to Ephraim and Jerusalem

28 Woe to the crown of pride, to the
drunkards of Ephraim,
Whose glorious beauty *is* a fading
flower
Which *is* at the head of the verdant
valleys,
To those who are overcome with
wine!

> **28:1 Woe.** This implies impending disaster. **crown.** The walls of Samaria were the "crown" of a beautiful hill overlooking a lush valley leading toward the Mediterranean coast. **Ephraim.** The northern kingdom of Israel had fallen to the Assyrians. This was a lesson for Jerusalem regarding forming foreign alliances. **overcome with wine.** Licentious living prevailed in Ephraim before her fall (Amos 4:1,6).

2 Behold, the Lord has a mighty and
strong one,
Like a tempest of hail and a
destroying storm,
Like a flood of mighty waters
overflowing,
Who will bring *them* down to the
earth with *His* hand.
3 The crown of pride, the drunkards of
Ephraim,
Will be trampled underfoot;
4 And the glorious beauty is a fading
flower
Which *is* at the head of the verdant
valley,
Like the first fruit before the summer,
Which an observer sees;
He eats it up while it is still in his
hand.

5 In that day the LORD of hosts will be
For a crown of glory and a diadem of
beauty
To the remnant of His people,

27:9 [a]Hebrew *Asherim,* Canaanite deities   27:12 [a]That is, the Euphrates

6   For a spirit of justice to him who sits
      in judgment,
    And for strength to those who turn
      back the battle at the gate.

7   But they also have erred through
      wine,
    And through intoxicating drink are
      out of the way;
    The priest and the prophet have erred
      through intoxicating drink,
    They are swallowed up by wine,
    They are out of the way through
      intoxicating drink;
    They err in vision, they stumble *in*
      judgment.

8   For all tables are full of vomit *and*
      filth;
    No place *is clean.*

9   "Whom will he teach knowledge?
    And whom will he make to
      understand the message?
    Those *just* weaned from milk?
    Those *just* drawn from the breasts?

10   For precept *must be* upon precept,
      precept upon precept,
    Line upon line, line upon line,
    Here a little, there a little."

28:10 precept upon precept...there a little. The drunkard ridicules the prophet's corrective advice in this imitation of a young child's babbling. The Hebrew monosyllables are *Sav lasav, sav lasav, Kav lakav, kav lakav, Ze'er sham, ze'er sham.*

11   For with stammering lips and another
      tongue
    He will speak to this people,

12   To whom He said, "This *is* the rest
      with which
    You may cause the weary to rest,"
    And, "This *is* the refreshing";
    Yet they would not hear.

13   But the word of the LORD was to
      them,
    "Precept upon precept, precept upon
      precept,
    Line upon line, line upon line,
    Here a little, there a little,"
    That they might go and fall backward,
      and be broken
    And snared and caught.

14   Therefore hear the word of the LORD,
      you scornful men,
    Who rule this people who *are* in
      Jerusalem,

15   Because you have said, "We have
      made a covenant with death,
    And with Sheol we are in agreement.
    When the overflowing scourge passes
      through,
    It will not come to us,
    For we have made lies our refuge,
    And under falsehood we have hidden
      ourselves."

28:15 covenant with death. Scornful leaders in Jerusalem made an agreement with Egypt to help defend themselves against the Assyrians. **overflowing scourge.** The people used images of an overflowing river and a whip to brag about their invincibility to foreign invasion. **lies...falsehood.** Jerusalem's leaders took refuge in deceit and falsehood, yielding to convenience for the sake of security.

A Cornerstone in Zion

16 Therefore thus says the Lord GOD:

    "Behold, I lay in Zion a stone for a
      foundation,
    A tried stone, a precious cornerstone,
      a sure foundation;
    Whoever believes will not act hastily.

17   Also I will make justice the
      measuring line,
    And righteousness the plummet;
    The hail will sweep away the refuge of
      lies,
    And the waters will overflow the
      hiding place.

18   Your covenant with death will be
      annulled,
    And your agreement with Sheol will
      not stand;
    When the overflowing scourge passes
      through,
    Then you will be trampled down by it.

19   As often as it goes out it will take you;
    For morning by morning it will pass
      over,
    And by day and by night;
    It will be a terror just to understand
      the report."

20   For the bed is too short to stretch out
      on,

And the covering so narrow that one
cannot wrap himself *in it.*
21 For the LORD will rise up as *at* Mount
Perazim,
He will be angry as in the Valley of
Gibeon—
That He may do His work, His
awesome work,
And bring to pass His act, His
unusual act.
22 Now therefore, do not be mockers,
Lest your bonds be made strong;
For I have heard from the Lord GOD
of hosts,
A destruction determined even upon
the whole earth.

Listen to the Teaching of God
23 Give ear and hear my voice,
Listen and hear my speech.

> **28:23 Give ear.** The parable of a farmer illustrates
> the lessons of judgment threats in vv. 18–22. As the
> farmer performs his tasks in the right season, so God
> performs His tasks: now mercy, then judgment; pun-
> ishing sooner, then later. He did not intend to destroy
> His people, no more than a farmer threshes and
> plows to destroy his crop.

24 Does the plowman keep plowing all
day to sow?
Does he keep turning his soil and
breaking the clods?
25 When he has leveled its surface,
Does he not sow the black cummin
And scatter the cummin,
Plant the wheat in rows,
The barley in the appointed place,
And the spelt in its place?
26 For He instructs him in right judgment,
His God teaches him.

27 For the black cummin is not threshed
with a threshing sledge,
Nor is a cartwheel rolled over the
cummin;
But the black cummin is beaten out
with a stick,
And the cummin with a rod.
28 Bread *flour* must be ground;
Therefore he does not thresh it
forever,

Break *it with* his cartwheel,
Or crush *it with* his horsemen.
29 This also comes from the LORD of
hosts,
Who is wonderful in counsel *and*
excellent in guidance.

Woe to Jerusalem
29 "Woe to Ariel,[a] to Ariel, the city
where David dwelt!
Add year to year;
Let feasts come around.

> **29:1 Ariel.** This word means "lion of God," referring
> to the city's strength, and perhaps "hearth of God,"
> which was the place where the altar of God always
> burns. This is also a name for Jerusalem (vv. 7,8). The
> chapter deals with the invasion of Jerusalem be-
> cause of her unbelief. *where* **David dwelt.** David
> named Jerusalem "the city of David" (2 Sam. 5:7,9).
> **feasts.** Jerusalem's religious ceremonies were mean-
> ingless to God.

2 Yet I will distress Ariel;
There shall be heaviness and sorrow,
And it shall be to Me as Ariel.
3 I will encamp against you all around,
I will lay siege against you with a
mound,
And I will raise siegeworks against
you.
4 You shall be brought down,
You shall speak out of the ground;
Your speech shall be low, out of the
dust;
Your voice shall be like a medium's,
out of the ground;
And your speech shall whisper out of
the dust.

5 "Moreover the multitude of your foes
Shall be like fine dust,
And the multitude of the terrible ones
Like chaff that passes away;
Yes, it shall be in an instant,
suddenly.
6 You will be punished by the LORD of
hosts
With thunder and earthquake and
great noise,
With storm and tempest
And the flame of devouring fire.

29:1 [a]That is, Jerusalem

7 The multitude of all the nations who
  fight against Ariel,
  Even all who fight against her and her
  fortress,
  And distress her,
  Shall be as a dream of a night vision.

8 It shall even be as when a hungry
  man dreams,
  And look—he eats;
  But he awakes, and his soul is still
  empty;
  Or as when a thirsty man dreams,
  And look—he drinks;
  But he awakes, and indeed *he is* faint,
  And his soul still craves:
  So the multitude of all the nations
  shall be,
  Who fight against Mount Zion."

The Blindness of Disobedience

9 Pause and wonder!
  Blind yourselves and be blind!
  They are drunk, but not with wine;
  They stagger, but not with
  intoxicating drink.

10 For the LORD has poured out on you
   The spirit of deep sleep,
   And has closed your eyes, namely, the
   prophets;
   And He has covered your heads,
   namely, the seers.

11The whole vision has become to you
like the words of a book that is sealed,
which *men* deliver to one who is literate,
saying, "Read this, please."
  And he says, "I cannot, for it *is* sealed."
12Then the book is delivered to one who
is illiterate, saying, "Read this, please."
  And he says, "I am not literate."

29:11,12 one who is literate. Those with the ability
to read could no longer do so because they had surrendered their spiritual sensitivity (see Matt. 13:10–
17). **one who is illiterate.** The uneducated did not
know the contents of the book because the book was
sealed, and he could not read it even if it were not. It
is deplorable when no one is capable of receiving
God's revelation.

13Therefore the Lord said:

"Inasmuch as these people draw near
  with their mouths
And honor Me with their lips,
But have removed their hearts far
  from Me,
And their fear toward Me is taught by
  the commandment of men,

14 Therefore, behold, I will again do a
   marvelous work
   Among this people,
   A marvelous work and a wonder;
   For the wisdom of their wise *men*
   shall perish,
   And the understanding of their
   prudent *men* shall be hidden."

15 Woe to those who seek deep to hide
   their counsel far from the LORD,
   And their works are in the dark;
   They say, "Who sees us?" and, "Who
   knows us?"

16 Surely you have things turned
   around!
   Shall the potter be esteemed as the
   clay;
   For shall the thing made say of him
   who made it,
   "He did not make me"?
   Or shall the thing formed say of him
   who formed it,
   "He has no understanding"?

Future Recovery of Wisdom

17 *Is* it not yet a very little while
   Till Lebanon shall be turned into a
   fruitful field,
   And the fruitful field be esteemed as a
   forest?

18 In that day the deaf shall hear the
   words of the book,
   And the eyes of the blind shall see out
   of obscurity and out of darkness.

29:18 deaf shall hear...blind shall see. The spiritual
blindness of Israel will no longer exist. Jesus applied
this to His ministry of physical healing (Matt. 11:5).

19 The humble also shall increase *their*
   joy in the LORD,
   And the poor among men shall rejoice
   In the Holy One of Israel.

20 For the terrible one is brought to
   nothing,
   The scornful one is consumed,
   And all who watch for iniquity are cut
   off—

21   Who make a man an offender by a
            word,
        And lay a snare for him who reproves
            in the gate,
        And turn aside the just by empty
            words.

²²Therefore thus says the LORD, who redeemed Abraham, concerning the house of
Jacob:

        "Jacob shall not now be ashamed,
            Nor shall his face now grow pale;

29:22 redeemed Abraham. God delivered Abraham
from his pagan background when He brought him to
Canaan (Josh. 24:2,3). Paul elaborates on this in Rom.
4:1–22. **not now be ashamed.** Israel had suffered
disgrace, but the Messiah is to change that in the end
time.

23   But when he sees his children,
        The work of My hands, in his midst,
        They will hallow My name,
        And hallow the Holy One of Jacob,
        And fear the God of Israel.
24   These also who erred in spirit will
            come to understanding,
        And those who complained will learn
            doctrine."

Futile Confidence in Egypt

30

        "Woe to the rebellious children,"
            says the LORD,
        "Who take counsel, but not of Me,
        And who devise plans, but not of My
            Spirit,
        That they may add sin to sin;

30:1 not of Me...not of My Spirit. Hezekiah's advisers urged him to return to the Egyptians, not to God,
for help against the Assyrians. Isaiah denounced this
reliance on Egypt, as God had forbidden such alliances.

2   Who walk to go down to Egypt,
        And have not asked My advice,
        To strengthen themselves in the
            strength of Pharaoh,
        And to trust in the shadow of Egypt!
3   Therefore the strength of Pharaoh
        Shall be your shame,

        And trust in the shadow of Egypt
        Shall be *your* humiliation.
4   For his princes were at Zoan,
        And his ambassadors came to Hanes.
5   They were all ashamed of a people
            who could not benefit them,
        Or be help or benefit,
        But a shame and also a reproach."

⁶The burden against the beasts of the
South.

        Through a land of trouble and
            anguish,
        From which *came* the lioness and
            lion,
        The viper and fiery flying serpent,
        They will carry their riches on the
            backs of young donkeys,
        And their treasures on the humps of
            camels,
        To a people *who* shall not profit;
7   For the Egyptians shall help in vain
            and to no purpose.
        Therefore I have called her
        Rahab-Hem-Shebeth.*ᵃ*

A Rebellious People

8   Now go, write it before them on a
            tablet,
        And note it on a scroll,
        That it may be for time to come,
        Forever and ever:
9   That this *is* a rebellious people,
        Lying children,
        Children *who* will not hear the law of
            the LORD;
10   Who say to the seers, "Do not see,"
        And to the prophets, "Do not
            prophesy to us right things;
        Speak to us smooth things, prophesy
            deceits.
11   Get out of the way,
        Turn aside from the path,
        Cause the Holy One of Israel
        To cease from before us."

¹²Therefore thus says the Holy One of Israel:

        "Because you despise this word,
            And trust in oppression and perversity,

30:7 ᵃLiterally *Rahab Sits Idle*

And rely on them,

13 Therefore this iniquity shall be to you
Like a breach ready to fall,
A bulge in a high wall,
Whose breaking comes suddenly, in
an instant.

14 And He shall break it like the
breaking of the potter's vessel,
Which is broken in pieces;
He shall not spare.
So there shall not be found among its
fragments
A shard to take fire from the hearth,
Or to take water from the cistern."

15 For thus says the Lord GOD, the Holy
One of Israel:

"In returning and rest you shall be
saved;
In quietness and confidence shall be
your strength."
But you would not,

> **30:15 rest...confidence.** The Israelite rebels refused to rest and confide in the Lord.

16 And you said, "No, for we will flee on
horses"—
Therefore you shall flee!
And, "We will ride on swift *horses*"—
Therefore those who pursue you shall
be swift!

17 One thousand *shall flee* at the threat
of one,
At the threat of five you shall flee,
Till you are left as a pole on top of a
mountain
And as a banner on a hill.

God Will Be Gracious
18 Therefore the LORD will wait, that He
may be gracious to you;
And therefore He will be exalted, that
He may have mercy on you.
For the LORD *is* a God of justice;
Blessed *are* all those who wait for
Him.

19 For the people shall dwell in Zion at
Jerusalem;
You shall weep no more.

He will be very gracious to you at the
sound of your cry;
When He hears it, He will answer
you.

20 And *though* the Lord gives you
The bread of adversity and the water
of affliction,
Yet your teachers will not be moved
into a corner anymore,
But your eyes shall see your teachers.

21 Your ears shall hear a word behind
you, saying,
"This *is* the way, walk in it,"
Whenever you turn to the right hand
Or whenever you turn to the left.

> **30:20,21 eyes shall see.** After their period of judgment because of disobedience, God will cause Israel to heed His prophets' message. **a word behind you.** In contrast to their former callousness, the teachers and their pupils will be sensitive to the Lord's prophets.

22 You will also defile the covering of
your images of silver,
And the ornament of your molded
images of gold.
You will throw them away as an
unclean thing;
You will say to them, "Get away!"

23 Then He will give the rain for your
seed
With which you sow the ground,
And bread of the increase of the
earth;
It will be fat and plentiful.
In that day your cattle will feed
In large pastures.

24 Likewise the oxen and the young
donkeys that work the ground
Will eat cured fodder,
Which has been winnowed with the
shovel and fan.

25 There will be on every high mountain
And on every high hill
Rivers *and* streams of waters,
In the day of the great slaughter,
When the towers fall.

26 Moreover the light of the moon will
be as the light of the sun,
And the light of the sun will be
sevenfold,
As the light of seven days,

In the day that the LORD binds up the
bruise of His people
And heals the stroke of their wound.

Judgment on Assyria

27 Behold, the name of the LORD comes
from afar,
Burning *with* His anger,
And *His* burden *is* heavy;
His lips are full of indignation,
And His tongue like a devouring fire.
28 His breath is like an overflowing
stream,
Which reaches up to the neck,
To sift the nations with the sieve of
futility;
And *there shall be* a bridle in the jaws
of the people,
Causing *them* to err.

29 You shall have a song
As in the night *when* a holy festival is
kept,
And gladness of heart as when one
goes with a flute,
To come into the mountain of the
LORD,
To the Mighty One of Israel.

> **30:29 song...holy festival.** While God's judgment
> devastated the Assyrians, the people of Jerusalem
> celebrated one of their feasts, perhaps a Passover.

30 The LORD will cause His glorious
voice to be heard,
And show the descent of His arm,
With the indignation of *His* anger
And the flame of a devouring fire,
With scattering, tempest, and
hailstones.
31 For through the voice of the LORD
Assyria will be beaten down,
As He strikes with the rod.
32 And *in* every place where the staff of
punishment passes,
Which the LORD lays on him,
It will be with tambourines and
harps;
And in battles of brandishing He will
fight with it.
33 For Tophet *was* established of old,
Yes, for the king it is prepared.
He has made *it* deep and large;
Its pyre *is* fire with much wood;

The breath of the LORD, like a stream
of brimstone,
Kindles it.

The Folly of Not Trusting God

31 Woe to those who go down to Egypt
for help,
And rely on horses,
Who trust in chariots because *they
are* many,
And in horsemen because they are
very strong,
But who do not look to the Holy One
of Israel,
Nor seek the LORD!
2 Yet He also *is* wise and will bring
disaster,
And will not call back His words,
But will arise against the house of
evildoers,
And against the help of those who
work iniquity.
3 Now the Egyptians *are* men, and not
God;
And their horses are flesh, and not
spirit.
When the LORD stretches out His
hand,
Both he who helps will fall,
And he who is helped will fall down;
They all will perish together.

> **31:3 flesh...spirit.** Hezekiah, for example, wisely
> chose to rely on the Lord, not on the arm of flesh
> (2 Chr. 32:8).

God Will Deliver Jerusalem

4 For thus the LORD has spoken to me:

"As a lion roars,
And a young lion over his prey
(When a multitude of shepherds is
summoned against him,
He will not be afraid of their voice
Nor be disturbed by their noise),
So the LORD of hosts will come down
To fight for Mount Zion and for its
hill.
5 Like birds flying about,
So will the LORD of hosts defend
Jerusalem.
Defending, He will also deliver *it*;
Passing over, He will preserve *it*."

⁶Return *to Him* against whom the children of Israel have deeply revolted. ⁷For in that day every man shall throw away his idols of silver and his idols of gold—sin, which your own hands have made for yourselves.

8   "Then Assyria shall fall by a sword not of man,
And a sword not of mankind shall devour him.
But he shall flee from the sword,
And his young men shall become forced labor.
9   He shall cross over to his stronghold for fear,
And his princes shall be afraid of the banner,"
Says the LORD,
Whose fire *is* in Zion
And whose furnace *is* in Jerusalem.

31:9 fire *is* in Zion...furnace *is* in Jerusalem. In Isaiah's near and distant future, Jerusalem would be God's headquarters for bringing judgment on foreign nations. God is the fire, waiting for all the enemies who attack Jerusalem.

A Reign of Righteousness

32 Behold, a king will reign in righteousness,
And princes will rule with justice.
2   A man will be as a hiding place from the wind,
And a cover from the tempest,
As rivers of water in a dry place,
As the shadow of a great rock in a weary land.
3   The eyes of those who see will not be dim,
And the ears of those who hear will listen.
4   Also the heart of the rash will understand knowledge,
And the tongue of the stammerers will be ready to speak plainly.

5   The foolish person will no longer be called generous,
Nor the miser said *to be* bountiful;
6   For the foolish person will speak foolishness,
And his heart will work iniquity:
To practice ungodliness,

To utter error against the LORD,
To keep the hungry unsatisfied,
And he will cause the drink of the thirsty to fail.
7   Also the schemes of the schemer *are* evil;
He devises wicked plans
To destroy the poor with lying words,
Even when the needy speaks justice.
8   But a generous man devises generous things,
And by generosity he shall stand.

32:6–8 foolish person...generous man. A fool is unwilling to care for the needy, but a generous person depends on God and provides for the poor. These qualities will be evident to all in the age to come.

Consequences of Complacency

9   Rise up, you women who are at ease,
Hear my voice;
You complacent daughters,
Give ear to my speech.
10   In a year and *some* days
You will be troubled, you complacent women;
For the vintage will fail,
The gathering will not come.
11   Tremble, you *women* who are at ease;
Be troubled, you complacent ones;
Strip yourselves, make yourselves bare,
And gird *sackcloth* on *your* waists.

12   People shall mourn upon their breasts
For the pleasant fields, for the fruitful vine.

32:11,12 Tremble...mourn. Present satisfaction with the status quo shortly changed to an entirely different set of emotions.

13   On the land of my people will come up thorns *and* briers,
Yes, on all the happy homes *in* the joyous city;
14   Because the palaces will be forsaken,
The bustling city will be deserted.
The forts and towers will become lairs forever,
A joy of wild donkeys, a pasture of flocks—

15 Until the Spirit is poured upon us
from on high,
And the wilderness becomes a fruitful
field,
And the fruitful field is counted as a
forest.

The Peace of God's Reign

16 Then justice will dwell in the
wilderness,
And righteousness remain in the
fruitful field.
17 The work of righteousness will be
peace,
And the effect of righteousness,
quietness and assurance forever.
18 My people will dwell in a peaceful
habitation,
In secure dwellings, and in quiet
resting places,
19 Though hail comes down on the
forest,
And the city is brought low in
humiliation.

20 Blessed *are* you who sow beside all
waters,
Who send out freely the feet of the ox
and the donkey.

A Prayer in Deep Distress

33 Woe to you who plunder, though
you *have* not *been* plundered;
And you who deal treacherously,
though they have not dealt
treacherously with you!
When you cease plundering,
You will be plundered;
When you make an end of dealing
treacherously,
They will deal treacherously with
you.

2 O LORD, be gracious to us;
We have waited for You.
Be their*a* arm every morning,
Our salvation also in the time of
trouble.
3 At the noise of the tumult the people
shall flee;

When You lift Yourself up, the nations
shall be scattered;
4 And Your plunder shall be gathered
Like the gathering of the caterpillar;
As the running to and fro of locusts,
He shall run upon them.

5 The LORD is exalted, for He dwells on
high;
He has filled Zion with justice and
righteousness.
6 Wisdom and knowledge will be the
stability of your times,
And the strength of salvation;
The fear of the LORD *is* His treasure.

7 Surely their valiant ones shall cry
outside,
The ambassadors of peace shall weep
bitterly.
8 The highways lie waste,
The traveling man ceases.
He has broken the covenant,
He has despised the cities,*a*
He regards no man.
9 The earth mourns *and* languishes,
Lebanon is shamed *and* shriveled;
Sharon is like a wilderness,
And Bashan and Carmel shake off
their fruits.

> **33:7–9** Jerusalem's situation was hopeless in
> Isaiah's present time. In 701 B.C. the Assyrian army
> surrounded the city, ready to attack.

Impending Judgment on Zion

10 "Now I will rise," says the LORD;
"Now I will be exalted,
Now I will lift Myself up.
11 You shall conceive chaff,
You shall bring forth stubble;
Your breath, *as* fire, shall devour you.
12 And the people shall be *like* the
burnings of lime;
Like thorns cut up they shall be
burned in the fire.
13 Hear, you *who are* afar off, what I
have done;
And you *who are* near, acknowledge
My might."

33:2 *a*Septuagint omits *their*; Syriac, Targum, and Vulgate read *our.*   33:8 *a*Following Masoretic Text
and Vulgate; Dead Sea Scrolls read *witnesses*; Septuagint omits *cities*; Targum reads *They have been
removed from their cities.*

14 The sinners in Zion are afraid;
   Fearfulness has seized the hypocrites:
   "Who among us shall dwell with the
      devouring fire?
   Who among us shall dwell with
      everlasting burnings?"
15 He who walks righteously and speaks
      uprightly,
   He who despises the gain of
      oppressions,
   Who gestures with his hands, refusing
      bribes,
   Who stops his ears from hearing of
      bloodshed,
   And shuts his eyes from seeing evil:
16 He will dwell on high;
   His place of defense *will be* the
      fortress of rocks;
   Bread will be given him,
   His water *will be* sure.

The Land of the Majestic King

17 Your eyes will see the King in His
      beauty;
   They will see the land that is very far
      off.

33:17 King in His beauty. The prophecy moves from
Hezekiah, in his sackcloth, to the Messiah, in His
beauty. Seeing Him in glory is a reward for the righteous. The wonderful, near-future deliverance from
Sennacherib anticipates a more distant wonder,
when the Messiah will sit on His throne.

18 Your heart will meditate on terror:
   "Where *is* the scribe?
   Where *is* he who weighs?
   Where *is* he who counts the
      towers?"
19 You will not see a fierce people,
   A people of obscure speech, beyond
      perception,
   Of a stammering tongue *that you*
      cannot understand.

20 Look upon Zion, the city of our
      appointed feasts;
   Your eyes will see Jerusalem, a quiet
      home,
   A tabernacle *that* will not be taken
      down;
   Not one of its stakes will ever be
      removed,
   Nor will any of its cords be broken.

21 But there the majestic LORD *will be*
      for us
   A place of broad rivers *and* streams,
   In which no galley with oars will sail,
   Nor majestic ships pass by.
22 (For the LORD *is* our Judge,
   The LORD *is* our Lawgiver,
   The LORD *is* our King;
   He will save us);
23 Your tackle is loosed,
   They could not strengthen their mast,
   They could not spread the sail.

   Then the prey of great plunder is
      divided;
   The lame take the prey.
24 And the inhabitant will not say, "I am
      sick";
   The people who dwell in it *will be*
      forgiven *their* iniquity.

33:24 not say, "I am sick"...forgiven *their* iniquity.
When Christ returns to rule, Jerusalem will be free of
physical and spiritual problems.

Judgment on the Nations

34 Come near, you nations, to hear;
   And heed, you people!
   Let the earth hear, and all that is in it,
   The world and all things that come
      forth from it.
2 For the indignation of the LORD *is*
      against all nations,
   And *His* fury against all their armies;
   He has utterly destroyed them,
   He has given them over to the
      slaughter.
3 Also their slain shall be thrown out;
   Their stench shall rise from their
      corpses,
   And the mountains shall be melted
      with their blood.
4 All the host of heaven shall be
      dissolved,
   And the heavens shall be rolled up
      like a scroll;
   All their host shall fall down
   As the leaf falls from the vine,
   And as *fruit* falling from a fig tree.

5 "For My sword shall be bathed in
      heaven;
   Indeed it shall come down on Edom,

And on the people of My curse, for
     judgment.
6   The sword of the LORD is filled with
     blood,
   It is made overflowing with fatness,
   With the blood of lambs and goats,
   With the fat of the kidneys of rams.
   For the LORD has a sacrifice in
     Bozrah,
   And a great slaughter in the land of
     Edom.
7   The wild oxen shall come down with
     them,
   And the young bulls with the mighty
     bulls;
   Their land shall be soaked with
     blood,
   And their dust saturated with fatness."

8   For *it is* the day of the LORD's
     vengeance,
   The year of recompense for the cause
     of Zion.
9   Its streams shall be turned into pitch,
   And its dust into brimstone;
   Its land shall become burning pitch.
10 It shall not be quenched night or day;
   Its smoke shall ascend forever.
   From generation to generation it shall
     lie waste;
   No one shall pass through it forever
     and ever.
11 But the pelican and the porcupine
     shall possess it,
   Also the owl and the raven shall dwell
     in it.
   And He shall stretch out over it
   The line of confusion and the stones
     of emptiness.
12 They shall call its nobles to the
     kingdom,
   But none *shall be* there, and all its
     princes shall be nothing.

13 And thorns shall come up in its
     palaces,
   Nettles and brambles in its fortresses;
   It shall be a habitation of jackals,

A courtyard for ostriches.
14 The wild beasts of the desert shall
     also meet with the jackals,
   And the wild goat shall bleat to its
     companion;
   Also the night creature shall rest
     there,
   And find for herself a place of rest.
15 There the arrow snake shall make her
     nest and lay *eggs*
   And hatch, and gather *them* under
     her shadow;
   There also shall the hawks be
     gathered,
   Every one with her mate.

16 "Search from the book of the LORD,
     and read:
   Not one of these shall fail;
   Not one shall lack her mate.
   For My mouth has commanded it,
     and His Spirit has gathered them.
17 He has cast the lot for them,
   And His hand has divided it among
     them with a measuring line.
   They shall possess it forever;
   From generation to generation they
     shall dwell in it."

The Future Glory of Zion

35 The wilderness and the wasteland
     shall be glad for them,
   And the desert shall rejoice and
     blossom as the rose;
2   It shall blossom abundantly and
     rejoice,
   Even with joy and singing.
   The glory of Lebanon shall be given to
     it,
   The excellence of Carmel and Sharon.
   They shall see the glory of the LORD,
   The excellency of our God.

3   Strengthen the weak hands,
   And make firm the feeble knees.
4   Say to those *who are* fearful-hearted,
   "Be strong, do not fear!
   Behold, your God will come *with*
     vengeance,

With the recompense of God;
He will come and save you."

5　　Then the eyes of the blind shall be
　　　opened,
　　And the ears of the deaf shall be
　　　unstopped.
6　　Then the lame shall leap like a deer,
　　And the tongue of the dumb sing.
　　For waters shall burst forth in the
　　　wilderness,
　　And streams in the desert.
7　　The parched ground shall become a
　　　pool,
　　And the thirsty land springs of water;
　　In the habitation of jackals, where
　　　each lay,
　　There shall be grass with reeds and
　　　rushes.

8　　A highway shall be there, and a road,
　　And it shall be called the Highway of
　　　Holiness.
　　The unclean shall not pass over it,
　　But it *shall be* for others.
　　Whoever walks the road, although a
　　　fool,
　　Shall not go astray.

35:8 Highway of Holiness. This is the way (called the "way of the LORD" in 40:3) that will lead the redeemed back to Jerusalem, to the throne of the Messiah, with Christ Himself as the leader.

9　　No lion shall be there,
　　Nor shall *any* ravenous beast go up on
　　　it;
　　It shall not be found there.
　　But the redeemed shall walk *there,*
10　　And the ransomed of the LORD shall
　　　return,
　　And come to Zion with singing,
　　With everlasting joy on their heads.
　　They shall obtain joy and gladness,
　　And sorrow and sighing shall flee away.

Sennacherib Boasts Against the LORD

36 Now it came to pass in the fourteenth year of King Hezekiah *that* Sennacherib king of Assyria came up against all the fortified cities of Judah and took them. ²Then the king of Assyria sent the Rabshakeh*ᵃ* with a great army from Lachish to King Hezekiah at Jerusalem. And he stood by the aqueduct from the upper pool, on the highway to the Fuller's Field. ³And Eliakim the son of Hilkiah, who was over the household, Shebna the scribe, and Joah the son of Asaph, the recorder, came out to him.

⁴Then *the* Rabshakeh said to them, "Say now to Hezekiah, 'Thus says the great king, the king of Assyria: "What confidence is this in which you trust? ⁵I say you speak of having plans and power for war; but *they are* mere words. Now in whom do you trust, that you rebel against me? ⁶Look! You are trusting in the staff of this broken reed, Egypt, on which if a man leans, it will go into his hand and pierce it. So *is* Pharaoh king of Egypt to all who trust in him. ⁷"But if you say to me, 'We trust in the LORD our God,' *is it* not He whose high places and whose altars Hezekiah has taken away, and said to Judah and Jerusalem, 'You shall worship before this altar'?" ' ⁸Now therefore, I urge you, give a pledge to my master the king of Assyria, and I will give you two thousand horses—if you are able on your part to put riders on them! ⁹How then will you repel one captain of the least of my master's servants, and put your trust in Egypt for chariots and horsemen? ¹⁰Have I now come up without the LORD against this land to destroy it? The LORD said to me, 'Go up against this land, and destroy it.' "

¹¹Then Eliakim, Shebna, and Joah said to *the* Rabshakeh, "Please speak to your servants in Aramaic, for we understand *it;* and do not speak to us in Hebrew*ᵃ* in the hearing of the people who *are* on the wall."

36:11 Aramaic...Hebrew. Hezekiah's representatives asked Rabshekah to speak Aramaic instead of Hebrew, so the people would not understand his words and be terrified. They were alarmed by the suggestion that the Lord was on the Assyrian side.

¹²But *the* Rabshakeh said, "Has my master sent me to your master and to you to speak these words, and not to the men who sit on the wall, who will eat and drink their own waste with you?"

36:2 *ᵃ*A title, probably *Chief of Staff* or *Governor*　36:11 *ᵃ*Literally *Judean*

¹³Then *the* Rabshakeh stood and called out with a loud voice in Hebrew, and said, "Hear the words of the great king, the king of Assyria! ¹⁴Thus says the king: 'Do not let Hezekiah deceive you, for he will not be able to deliver you; ¹⁵nor let Hezekiah make you trust in the LORD, saying, "The LORD will surely deliver us; this city will not be given into the hand of the king of Assyria." ' ¹⁶Do not listen to Hezekiah; for thus says the king of Assyria: 'Make *peace* with me *by a* present and come out to me; and every one of you eat from his own vine and every one from his own fig tree, and every one of you drink the waters of his own cistern; ¹⁷until I come and take you away to a land like your own land, a land of grain and new wine, a land of bread and vineyards. ¹⁸*Beware* lest Hezekiah persuade you, saying, "The LORD will deliver us." Has any one of the gods of the nations delivered its land from the hand of the king of Assyria? ¹⁹Where *are* the gods of Hamath and Arpad? Where *are* the gods of Sepharvaim? Indeed, have they delivered Samaria from my hand? ²⁰Who among all the gods of these lands have delivered their countries from my hand, that the LORD should deliver Jerusalem from my hand?' "

> **36:16 Make...present.** This means "make a blessing with me." The official asked the people to make a covenant with Assyria by surrendering.

²¹But they held their peace and answered him not a word; for the king's commandment was, "Do not answer him." ²²Then Eliakim the son of Hilkiah, who *was* over the household, Shebna the scribe, and Joah the son of Asaph, the recorder, came to Hezekiah with *their* clothes torn, and told him the words of *the* Rabshakeh.

Isaiah Assures Deliverance

37 And so it was, when King Hezekiah heard *it,* that he tore his clothes, covered himself with sackcloth, and went into the house of the LORD. ²Then he sent Eliakim, who *was* over the household, Shebna the scribe, and the elders of the priests, covered with sackcloth, to Isaiah the prophet, the son of Amoz. ³And they said to him, "Thus says Hezekiah: 'This day *is* a day of trouble and rebuke and blas-

phemy; for the children have come to birth, but *there is* no strength to bring them forth. ⁴It may be that the LORD your God will hear the words of *the* Rabshakeh, whom his master the king of Assyria has sent to reproach the living God, and will rebuke the words which the LORD your God has heard. Therefore lift up *your* prayer for the remnant that is left.' "

> **37:3,4 come to birth...no strength.** Helpless to deliver Jerusalem, Hezekiah compared his dilemma to a mother unable to deliver her child in labor. **reproach the living God.** Hezekiah heard that Rabshakeh belittled the Lord by equating Him with other gods. He points out the difference between the living God and the gods who are lifeless and helpless. **remnant that is left.** Only Jerusalem remained unconquered, and Hezekiah asked Isaiah to pray for the city.

⁵So the servants of King Hezekiah came to Isaiah. ⁶And Isaiah said to them, "Thus you shall say to your master, 'Thus says the LORD: "Do not be afraid of the words which you have heard, with which the servants of the king of Assyria have blasphemed Me. ⁷Surely I will send a spirit upon him, and he shall hear a rumor and return to his own land; and I will cause him to fall by the sword in his own land." ' "

Sennacherib's Threat and Hezekiah's Prayer

⁸Then *the* Rabshakeh returned, and found the king of Assyria warring against Libnah, for he heard that he had departed from Lachish. ⁹And the king heard concerning Tirhakah king of Ethiopia, "He has come out to make war with you." So when he heard *it,* he sent messengers to Hezekiah, saying, ¹⁰"Thus you shall speak to Hezekiah king of Judah, saying: 'Do not let your God in whom you trust deceive you, saying, "Jerusalem shall not be given into the hand of the king of Assyria." ¹¹Look! You have heard what the kings of Assyria have done to all lands by utterly destroying them; and shall you be delivered? ¹²Have the gods of the nations delivered those whom my fathers have destroyed, Gozan and Haran and Rezeph, and the people of Eden who *were* in Telassar? ¹³Where *is* the king of Hamath, the king of Arpad, and the king of the city of Sepharvaim, Hena, and Ivah?' "

¹⁴And Hezekiah received the letter from the hand of the messengers, and read it; and Hezekiah went up to the house of the LORD, and spread it before the LORD. ¹⁵Then Hezekiah prayed to the LORD, saying: ¹⁶"O LORD of hosts, God of Israel, *the One* who dwells *between* the cherubim, You *are* God, You alone, of all the kingdoms of the earth. You have made heaven and earth. ¹⁷Incline Your ear, O LORD, and hear; open Your eyes, O LORD, and see; and hear all the words of Sennacherib, which he has sent to reproach the living God. ¹⁸Truly, LORD, the kings of Assyria have laid waste all the nations and their lands, ¹⁹and have cast their gods into the fire; for they *were* not gods, but the work of men's hands— wood and stone. Therefore they destroyed them. ²⁰Now therefore, O LORD our God, save us from his hand, that all the kingdoms of the earth may know that You *are* the LORD, You alone."

37:16 *the One* who dwells...heaven and earth. Hezekiah pleaded to God, not because of Judah's worthiness to be delivered, but because He is the sovereign Creator.

The Word of the LORD Concerning Sennacherib

²¹Then Isaiah the son of Amoz sent to Hezekiah, saying, "Thus says the LORD God of Israel, 'Because you have prayed to Me against Sennacherib king of Assyria, ²²this *is* the word which the LORD has spoken concerning him:

"The virgin, the daughter of Zion,
Has despised you, laughed you to scorn;
The daughter of Jerusalem
Has shaken *her* head behind your back!

²³ "Whom have you reproached and blasphemed?
Against whom have you raised *your* voice,
And lifted up your eyes on high?
Against the Holy One of Israel.

²⁴ By your servants you have reproached the Lord,
And said, 'By the multitude of my chariots
I have come up to the height of the mountains,

To the limits of Lebanon;
I will cut down its tall cedars
And its choice cypress trees;
I will enter its farthest height,
To its fruitful forest.

²⁵ I have dug and drunk water,
And with the soles of my feet I have dried up
All the brooks of defense.'

²⁶ "Did you not hear long ago
How I made it,
From ancient times that I formed it?
Now I have brought it to pass,
That you should be
For crushing fortified cities *into* heaps of ruins.

²⁷ Therefore their inhabitants *had* little power;
They were dismayed and confounded;
They were *as* the grass of the field
And the green herb,
As the grass on the housetops
And grain blighted before it is grown.

²⁸ "But I know your dwelling place,
Your going out and your coming in,
And your rage against Me.

²⁹ Because your rage against Me and your tumult
Have come up to My ears,
Therefore I will put My hook in your nose
And My bridle in your lips,
And I will turn you back
By the way which you came." '

³⁰"This *shall be* a sign to you:

You shall eat this year such as grows of itself,
And the second year what springs from the same;
Also in the third year sow and reap,
Plant vineyards and eat the fruit of them.

³¹ And the remnant who have escaped of the house of Judah
Shall again take root downward,
And bear fruit upward.

³² For out of Jerusalem shall go a remnant,
And those who escape from Mount Zion.

The zeal of the LORD of hosts will do this.

33"Therefore thus says the LORD concerning the king of Assyria:

'He shall not come into this city,
Nor shoot an arrow there,
Nor come before it with shield,
Nor build a siege mound against it.
34 By the way that he came,
By the same shall he return;
And he shall not come into this city,'
Says the LORD.
35 'For I will defend this city, to save it
For My own sake and for My servant
David's sake.' "

Sennacherib's Defeat and Death

36Then the angel[a] of the LORD went out, and killed in the camp of the Assyrians one hundred and eighty-five thousand; and when *people* arose early in the morning, there were the corpses—all dead. 37So Sennacherib king of Assyria departed and went away, returned *home*, and remained at Nineveh. 38Now it came to pass, as he was worshiping in the house of Nisroch his god, that his sons Adrammelech and Sharezer struck him down with the sword; and they escaped into the land of Ararat. Then Esarhaddon his son reigned in his place.

37:35,36 For My own sake. Sennacherib challenged the Lord's faithfulness to His word, so the faithfulness of God was at stake in this contest with the Assyrians (see Ezek. 36:22). **for My servant David's sake.** God promised to preserve David's line on his throne (2 Sam. 7:16). **the angel of the LORD.** This is the only time Isaiah uses this frequent OT title. **killed.** Secular records mention the massive slaughter of Assyrian troops without noting the supernatural nature of it (see Ex. 12:12,29).

Hezekiah's Life Extended

38 In those days Hezekiah was sick and near death. And Isaiah the prophet, the son of Amoz, went to him and said to him, "Thus says the LORD: 'Set your house in order, for you shall die and not live.' "
2Then Hezekiah turned his face toward the wall, and prayed to the LORD, 3and said,

38:1 In those days...sick. Hezekiah became sick before the Assyrians attacked Jerusalem. **Set your house in order.** Hezekiah was instructed to make his final will known to his family (see 2 Sam. 17:23). **you shall die and not live.** This prediction sounded final, but Hezekiah knew God would listen to his appeal (see Ex. 32:7–14).

"Remember now, O LORD, I pray, how I have walked before You in truth and with a loyal heart, and have done *what is* good in Your sight." And Hezekiah wept bitterly.
4And the word of the LORD came to Isaiah, saying, 5"Go and tell Hezekiah, 'Thus says the LORD, the God of David your father: "I have heard your prayer, I have seen your tears; surely I will add to your days fifteen years. 6I will deliver you and this city from the hand of the king of Assyria, and I will defend this city." ' 7And this *is* the sign to you from the LORD, that the LORD will do this thing which He has spoken: 8Behold, I will bring the shadow on the sundial, which has gone down with the sun on the sundial of Ahaz, ten degrees backward." So the sun returned ten degrees on the dial by which it had gone down.

38:7,8 sign...ten degrees backward. This is the first biblical mention of any means of marking time. Hezekiah requested this sign to confirm the Lord's promise of healing (2 Kin. 20:8–10).

9This is the writing of Hezekiah king of Judah, when he had been sick and had recovered from his sickness:

10 I said,
"In the prime of my life
I shall go to the gates of Sheol;
I am deprived of the remainder of my years."
11 I said,
"I shall not see YAH,
The LORD[a] in the land of the living;
I shall observe man no more among the inhabitants of the world.[b]
12 My life span is gone,
Taken from me like a shepherd's tent;
I have cut off my life like a weaver.
He cuts me off from the loom;

37:36 [a]Or *Angel* 38:11 [a]Hebrew YAH, YAH [b]Following some Hebrew manuscripts; Masoretic Text and Vulgate read *rest*; Septuagint omits *among the inhabitants of the world*; Targum reads *land*.

From day until night You make an
end of me.

13 I have considered until morning—
Like a lion,
So He breaks all my bones;
From day until night You make an
end of me.

14 Like a crane *or* a swallow, so I
chattered;
I mourned like a dove;
My eyes fail *from looking* upward.
O LORD,[a] I am oppressed;
Undertake for me!

15 "What shall I say?
He has both spoken to me,[a]
And He Himself has done *it*.
I shall walk carefully all my years
In the bitterness of my soul.

16 O Lord, by these *things men* live;
And in all these *things is* the life of
my spirit;
So You will restore me and make me
live.

17 Indeed *it was* for *my own* peace
That I had great bitterness;
But You have lovingly *delivered* my
soul from the pit of corruption,
For You have cast all my sins behind
Your back.

18 For Sheol cannot thank You,
Death cannot praise You;
Those who go down to the pit cannot
hope for Your truth.

19 The living, the living man, he shall
praise You,
As I *do* this day;
The father shall make known Your
truth to the children.

20 "The LORD *was ready* to save me;
Therefore we will sing my songs with
stringed instruments
All the days of our life, in the house
of the LORD."

21 Now Isaiah had said, "Let them take a
lump of figs, and apply *it* as a poultice on
the boil, and he shall recover."
22 And Hezekiah had said, "What *is* the
sign that I shall go up to the house of the
LORD?"

> **36:1–39:8** These 4 chapters are almost the same as 2 Kin. 18:13–20:19 (see 2 Chr. 32:1–23). Isaiah added this to clarify references to Assyria. Isaiah probably wrote this section, since he wrote the acts of Hezekiah (2 Chr. 32:32). Isaiah's record was added to 2 Kings by the author of that record. These chapters close the first division of Isaiah's prophecy.

The Babylonian Envoys

39 At that time Merodach-Baladan[a] the son of Baladan, king of Babylon, sent letters and a present to Hezekiah, for he heard that he had been sick and had recovered. 2 And Hezekiah was pleased with them, and showed them the house of his treasures—the silver and gold, the spices and precious ointment, and all his armory—all that was found among his treasures. There was nothing in his house or in all his dominion that Hezekiah did not show them.

3 Then Isaiah the prophet went to King Hezekiah, and said to him, "What did these men say, and from where did they come to you?"

So Hezekiah said, "They came to me from a far country, from Babylon."

4 And he said, "What have they seen in your house?"

So Hezekiah answered, "They have seen all that *is* in my house; there is nothing among my treasures that I have not shown them."

5 Then Isaiah said to Hezekiah, "Hear the word of the LORD of hosts: 6 "Behold, the days are coming when all that *is* in your house, and what your fathers have accumulated until this day, shall be carried to Babylon; nothing shall be left,' says the LORD.

> **39:6 nothing shall be left.** Hezekiah tried to impress his visitors by showing all the wealth he could contribute in an alliance against the Assyrians. This sin of parading his wealth backfired, though it was only a symptom of the reason for the captivity. The major cause was the corrupt leadership of Manasseh, Hezekiah's son (2 Kin. 21:11–15).

38:14 [a]Following Bomberg; Masoretic Text and Dead Sea Scrolls read *Lord.* 38:15 [a]Following Masoretic Text and Vulgate; Dead Sea Scrolls and Targum read *And shall I say to Him;* Septuagint omits first half of this verse. 39:1 [a]Spelled *Berodach-Baladan* in 2 Kings 20:12

⁷"And they shall take away *some* of your sons who will descend from you, whom you will beget; and they shall be eunuchs in the palace of the king of Babylon.' "

⁸So Hezekiah said to Isaiah, "The word of the LORD which you have spoken *is* good!" For he said, "At least there will be peace and truth in my days."

God's People Are Comforted

40 "Comfort, yes, comfort My people!"
Says your God.
2 "Speak comfort to Jerusalem, and cry out to her,
That her warfare is ended,
That her iniquity is pardoned;
For she has received from the LORD's hand
Double for all her sins."

> **40:1–66:24** The previous prophecies addressed Judah during Isaiah's ministry (739 B.C.–ca. 686 B.C.). These next prophecies address Judah as if the prophesied Babylonian captivity were a present reality, though the captivity did not begin until 605–586 B.C. The words " 'There is no peace,' says the LORD, 'for the wicked' " signal the divisions of this section into three parts: chaps. 40–48, chaps. 49–57, and chaps. 58–66.

3 The voice of one crying in the wilderness:
"Prepare the way of the LORD;
Make straight in the desert*ᵃ*
A highway for our God.
4 Every valley shall be exalted
And every mountain and hill brought low;
The crooked places shall be made straight
And the rough places smooth;
5 The glory of the LORD shall be revealed,
And all flesh shall see *it* together;
For the mouth of the LORD has spoken."

6 The voice said, "Cry out!"
And he*ᵃ* said, "What shall I cry?"

"All flesh *is* grass,
And all its loveliness *is* like the flower of the field.
7 The grass withers, the flower fades,
Because the breath of the LORD blows upon it;
Surely the people *are* grass.
8 The grass withers, the flower fades,
But the word of our God stands forever."

> **40:6–8 All flesh...flower fades.** Isaiah described humanity as passing away like plants under the hot breath of the withering east wind. James used this illustration to teach the folly of trusting in material wealth (James 1:10,11). Peter used it to describe the passing nature of everything related to humanity (1 Pet. 1:24,25).

9 O Zion,
You who bring good tidings,
Get up into the high mountain;
O Jerusalem,
You who bring good tidings,
Lift up your voice with strength,
Lift *it* up, be not afraid;
Say to the cities of Judah, "Behold your God!"
10 Behold, the Lord GOD shall come with a strong *hand,*
And His arm shall rule for Him;
Behold, His reward *is* with Him,
And His work before Him.
11 He will feed His flock like a shepherd;
He will gather the lambs with His arm,
And carry *them* in His bosom,
And gently lead those who are with young.

12 Who has measured the waters*ᵃ* in the hollow of His hand,
Measured heaven with a span
And calculated the dust of the earth in a measure?
Weighed the mountains in scales
And the hills in a balance?

40:3 *ᵃ*Following Masoretic Text, Targum, and Vulgate; Septuagint omits *in the desert.*
40:6 *ᵃ*Following Masoretic Text and Targum; Dead Sea Scrolls, Septuagint, and Vulgate read *I.*
40:12 *ᵃ*Following Masoretic Text, Septuagint, and Vulgate; Dead Sea Scrolls read *waters of the sea;* Targum reads *waters of the world.*

13 Who has directed the Spirit of the
LORD,
Or *as* His counselor has taught Him?
14 With whom did He take counsel, and
who instructed Him,
And taught Him in the path of
justice?
Who taught Him knowledge,
And showed Him the way of
understanding?

40:13,14 directed the Spirit of the LORD. Isaiah is
pointing to God's wisdom. Paul alluded to this verse
when dealing with the Jews and Gentiles (Rom 11:34)
and with the spiritual believer (1 Cor. 2:16).

15 Behold, the nations *are* as a drop in a
bucket,
And are counted as the small dust on
the scales;
Look, He lifts up the isles as a very
little thing.
16 And Lebanon *is* not sufficient to burn,
Nor its beasts sufficient for a burnt
offering.
17 All nations before Him *are* as
nothing,
And they are counted by Him less
than nothing and worthless.

18 To whom then will you liken God?
Or what likeness will you compare to
Him?
19 The workman molds an image,
The goldsmith overspreads it with
gold,
And the silversmith casts silver
chains.
20 Whoever *is* too impoverished for *such*
a contribution
Chooses a tree *that* will not rot;
He seeks for himself a skillful
workman
To prepare a carved image *that* will
not totter.

21 Have you not known?
Have you not heard?
Has it not been told you from the
beginning?
Have you not understood from the
foundations of the earth?
22 *It is* He who sits above the circle of
the earth,

And its inhabitants *are* like
grasshoppers,
Who stretches out the heavens like a
curtain,
And spreads them out like a tent to
dwell in.
23 He brings the princes to nothing;
He makes the judges of the earth
useless.

24 Scarcely shall they be planted,
Scarcely shall they be sown,
Scarcely shall their stock take root in
the earth,
When He will also blow on them,
And they will wither,
And the whirlwind will take them
away like stubble.

25 "To whom then will you liken Me,
Or *to whom* shall I be equal?" says
the Holy One.
26 Lift up your eyes on high,
And see who has created these *things*,
Who brings out their host by number;
He calls them all by name,
By the greatness of His might
And the strength of *His* power;
Not one is missing.

27 Why do you say, O Jacob,
And speak, O Israel:
"My way is hidden from the LORD,
And my just claim is passed over by
my God"?
28 Have you not known?
Have you not heard?
The everlasting God, the LORD,
The Creator of the ends of the earth,
Neither faints nor is weary.
His understanding is unsearchable.

40:28 Neither faints nor is weary. God is not weak
or fatigued when acting on behalf of His people or
caring for them. Though even the young and strong
become tired and fall, the Ancient of Days never
does. **unsearchable.** Humans are unable to comprehend God's wisdom in how He chooses to fulfill His
promises to deliver Israel. Paul saw this truth in God's
plan for the final restoration of Israel (Rom. 11:33).

29 He gives power to the weak,
And to *those who have* no might He
increases strength.

³⁰ Even the youths shall faint and be
weary,
And the young men shall utterly fall,
³¹ But those who wait on the LORD
Shall renew *their* strength;
They shall mount up with wings like
eagles,
They shall run and not be weary,
They shall walk and not faint.

Israel Assured of God's Help

41 "Keep silence before Me,
O coastlands,
And let the people renew *their*
strength!
Let them come near, then let them
speak;
Let us come near together for
judgment.

² "Who raised up one from the east?
Who in righteousness called him to
His feet?
Who gave the nations before him,
And made *him* rule over kings?
Who gave *them* as the dust *to* his
sword,
As driven stubble to his bow?
³ Who pursued them, *and* passed safely
By the way *that* he had not gone with
his feet?
⁴ Who has performed and done *it*,
Calling the generations from the
beginning?
'I, the LORD, am the first;
And with the last I *am* He.' "

41:4 first...last. God existed before history and will
exist after it (see Rev. 1:17). **I am He.** This title, "I am,"
originally comes from God's self-revelation to Moses
in Ex. 3:14. It is a messianic title that describes the
deity of Jesus (Mark 13:6).

⁵ The coastlands saw *it* and feared,
The ends of the earth were afraid;
They drew near and came.
⁶ Everyone helped his neighbor,
And said to his brother,
"Be of good courage!"
⁷ So the craftsman encouraged the
goldsmith;
He who smooths *with* the hammer
inspired him who strikes the anvil,
Saying, "It *is* ready for the soldering";

Then he fastened it with pegs,
That it might not totter.

⁸ "But you, Israel, *are* My servant,
Jacob whom I have chosen,
The descendants of Abraham My
friend.

41:8 Israel...My servant. The faithful of Israel were
deemed as the corporate servant of the Lord, in contrast to the rest of the nations. **Abraham My friend.**
"Friend" is a higher designation than "servant" (John
15:14) and speaks of a greater faithfulness.

⁹ *You* whom I have taken from the ends
of the earth,
And called from its farthest regions,
And said to you,
'You *are* My servant,
I have chosen you and have not cast
you away:
¹⁰ Fear not, for I *am* with you;
Be not dismayed, for I *am* your God.
I will strengthen you,
Yes, I will help you,
I will uphold you with My righteous
right hand.'

¹¹ "Behold, all those who were incensed
against you
Shall be ashamed and disgraced;
They shall be as nothing,
And those who strive with you shall
perish.
¹² You shall seek them and not find
them—
Those who contended with you.
Those who war against you
Shall be as nothing,
As a nonexistent thing.
¹³ For I, the LORD your God, will hold
your right hand,
Saying to you, 'Fear not, I will help
you.'

¹⁴ "Fear not, you worm Jacob,
You men of Israel!
I will help you," says the LORD
And your Redeemer, the Holy One of
Israel.
¹⁵ "Behold, I will make you into a new
threshing sledge with sharp teeth;
You shall thresh the mountains and
beat *them* small,

41:14 worm. This refers to the contempt of Israel by the ungodly nations. The same term refers to the Messiah on the cross (Ps. 22:6). **Redeemer, the Holy One of Israel.** "Redeemer" (Hebrew) refers to a relative who has the responsibility to buy back what another relative has lost. As the Lord purchased His people from the bondage of Egypt by the blood of the Passover Lamb, He will later purchase them by the blood of Jesus Christ when they turn to Him in faith (see Zech. 12:10–13:1).

And make the hills like chaff.
16 You shall winnow them, the wind
    shall carry them away,
And the whirlwind shall scatter them;
You shall rejoice in the LORD,
And glory in the Holy One of Israel.

17 "The poor and needy seek water, but
    there is none,
Their tongues fail for thirst.
I, the LORD, will hear them;
I, the God of Israel, will not forsake
    them.
18 I will open rivers in desolate heights,
And fountains in the midst of the
    valleys;
I will make the wilderness a pool of
    water,
And the dry land springs of water.
19 I will plant in the wilderness the
    cedar and the acacia tree,
The myrtle and the oil tree;
I will set in the desert the cypress tree
    and the pine
And the box tree together,
20 That they may see and know,
And consider and understand
    together,
That the hand of the LORD has done
    this,
And the Holy One of Israel has
    created it.

The Futility of Idols
21 "Present your case," says the LORD.
"Bring forth your strong *reasons,*" says
    the King of Jacob.
22 "Let them bring forth and show us
    what will happen;
Let them show the former things,
    what they *were,*

That we may consider them,
And know the latter end of them;
Or declare to us things to come.
23 Show the things that are to come
    hereafter,
That we may know that you *are* gods;
Yes, do good or do evil,
That we may be dismayed and see *it*
    together.
24 Indeed you *are* nothing,
And your work *is* nothing;
He who chooses you *is* an
    abomination.

25 "I have raised up one from the north,
And he shall come;
From the rising of the sun he shall
    call on My name;
And he shall come against princes as
    though mortar,
As the potter treads clay.
26 Who has declared from the beginning,
    that we may know?
And former times, that we may say,
    'He is *righteous*'?
Surely *there is* no one who shows,
Surely *there is* no one who declares,
Surely *there is* no one who hears your
    words.
27 The first time *I said* to Zion,
'Look, there they are!'
And I will give to Jerusalem one who
    brings good tidings.
28 For I looked, and *there was* no man;
I looked among them, but *there was*
    no counselor,
Who, when I asked of them, could
    answer a word.
29 Indeed they *are* all worthless;[a]
Their works *are* nothing;
Their molded images *are* wind and
    confusion.

The Servant of the LORD
42 "Behold! My Servant whom I
    uphold,
My Elect One *in whom* My soul
    delights!
I have put My Spirit upon Him;
He will bring forth justice to the
    Gentiles.

41:29 [a]Following Masoretic Text and Vulgate; Dead Sea Scrolls, Syriac, and Targum read *nothing;* Septuagint omits the first line.

42:1 My Servant. This personal Servant of the Lord is His chosen Messiah (Luke 9:35), in whom God delights and puts His Spirit (Matt. 3:16,17). **justice to the Gentiles.** At His second coming, Christ will rule with justice. The millennial kingdom will be experienced by all nations of the world, even though the Messiah will reign on David's throne in Jerusalem, and Israel will be the glorious people.

2   He will not cry out, nor raise *His*
          voice,
       Nor cause His voice to be heard in the
          street.
3   A bruised reed He will not break,
       And smoking flax He will not quench;
       He will bring forth justice for truth.
4   He will not fail nor be discouraged,
       Till He has established justice in the
          earth;
       And the coastlands shall wait for His
          law."

5   Thus says God the LORD,
       Who created the heavens and
          stretched them out,
       Who spread forth the earth and that
          which comes from it,
       Who gives breath to the people on it,
       And spirit to those who walk on it:

42:5 Thus says God the LORD, who created...walk on it. God spoke directly to the Messiah, identified as "You." God's role as Creator of the universe is the basis of certainty for the fulfilling of His will by His Servant, the Messiah.

6   "I, the LORD, have called You in
          righteousness,
       And will hold Your hand;
       I will keep You and give You as a
          covenant to the people,
       As a light to the Gentiles,
7   To open blind eyes,
       To bring out prisoners from the
          prison,
       Those who sit in darkness from the
          prison house.
8   I *am* the LORD, that *is* My name;
       And My glory I will not give to
          another,
       Nor My praise to carved images.
9   Behold, the former things have come
          to pass,
       And new things I declare;

Before they spring forth I tell you of
          them."

Praise to the LORD

10   Sing to the LORD a new song,
       And His praise from the ends of the
          earth,
       You who go down to the sea, and all
          that is in it,
       You coastlands and you inhabitants of
          them!
11   Let the wilderness and its cities lift up
          their voice,
       The villages *that* Kedar inhabits.
       Let the inhabitants of Sela sing,
       Let them shout from the top of the
          mountains.
12   Let them give glory to the LORD,
       And declare His praise in the
          coastlands.
13   The LORD shall go forth like a mighty
          man;
       He shall stir up *His* zeal like a man of
          war.
       He shall cry out, yes, shout aloud;
       He shall prevail against His enemies.

Promise of the LORD's Help

14   "I have held My peace a long time,
       I have been still and restrained
          Myself.
       Now I will cry like a woman in labor,
       I will pant and gasp at once.

42:14 held My peace...been still and restrained Myself. God remained silent from the beginning of creation until it was time for Him to intervene in human affairs. He has not been indifferent to the wickedness in the world, but He will send His Servant in the "fullness of the time" (Gal. 4:4).

15   I will lay waste the mountains and
          hills,
       And dry up all their vegetation;
       I will make the rivers coastlands,
       And I will dry up the pools.
16   I will bring the blind by a way they
          did not know;
       I will lead them in paths they have
          not known.
       I will make darkness light before
          them,
       And crooked places straight.
       These things I will do for them,

And not forsake them.

17 They shall be turned back,
They shall be greatly ashamed,
Who trust in carved images,
Who say to the molded images,
'You *are* our gods.'

18 "Hear, you deaf;
And look, you blind, that you may
see.
19 Who *is* blind but My servant,
Or deaf as My messenger *whom* I
send?
Who *is* blind as *he who is* perfect,
And blind as the LORD's servant?
20 Seeing many things, but you do not
observe;
Opening the ears, but he does not
hear."

Israel's Obstinate Disobedience
21 The LORD is well pleased for His
righteousness' sake;
He will exalt the law and make *it*
honorable.
22 But this *is* a people robbed and
plundered;
All of them are snared in holes,
And they are hidden in prison houses;
They are for prey, and no one
delivers;
For plunder, and no one says,
"Restore!"

23 Who among you will give ear to this?
Who will listen and hear for the time
to come?
24 Who gave Jacob for plunder, and Israel
to the robbers?
Was it not the LORD,
He against whom we have sinned?
For they would not walk in His ways,
Nor were they obedient to His law.
25 Therefore He has poured on him the
fury of His anger
And the strength of battle;
It has set him on fire all around,

42:25 the fury of His anger. Judah fell to Babylon in 586 B.C. because of their disobedience to God, not because of the strength of Babylon. **set him on fire.** Nebuchadnezzar, king of Babylon, burned Jerusalem when he conquered the city (2 Kin. 25:8,9).

Yet he did not know;
And it burned him,
Yet he did not take *it* to heart.

The Redeemer of Israel
43 But now, thus says the LORD, who
created you, O Jacob,
And He who formed you, O Israel:
"Fear not, for I have redeemed you;
I have called *you* by your name;
You *are* Mine.
2 When you pass through the waters, I
will be with you;
And through the rivers, they shall not
overflow you.
When you walk through the fire, you
shall not be burned,
Nor shall the flame scorch you.
3 For I *am* the LORD your God,
The Holy One of Israel, your Savior;
I gave Egypt for your ransom,
Ethiopia and Seba in your place.

43:3 Your Savior. God is a temporal and eternal Savior (see Titus 4:10). He delivered Israel from Egypt and will deliver her from Babylon and all future exiles. He will bring her to spiritual salvation.

4 Since you were precious in My sight,
You have been honored,
And I have loved you;
Therefore I will give men for you,
And people for your life.
5 Fear not, for I *am* with you;
I will bring your descendants from the
east,
And gather you from the west;
6 I will say to the north, 'Give them
up!'
And to the south, 'Do not keep them
back!'
Bring My sons from afar,
And My daughters from the ends of
the earth—
7 Everyone who is called by My name,
Whom I have created for My glory;
I have formed him, yes, I have made
him."

8 Bring out the blind people who have
eyes,
And the deaf who have ears.
9 Let all the nations be gathered
together,

And let the people be assembled.
Who among them can declare this,
And show us former things?
Let them bring out their witnesses,
   that they may be justified;
Or let them hear and say, "*It is* truth."
10 "You *are* My witnesses," says the
   LORD,
"And My servant whom I have chosen,
That you may know and believe Me,
And understand that I *am* He.
Before Me there was no God formed,
Nor shall there be after Me.
11 I, *even* I, *am* the LORD,
And besides Me *there is* no savior.
12 I have declared and saved,
I have proclaimed,
And *there was* no foreign *god* among
   you;
Therefore you *are* My witnesses,"
Says the LORD, "that I *am* God.
13 Indeed before the day *was,* I *am* He;
And *there is* no one who can deliver
   out of My hand;
I work, and who will reverse it?"

43:13 before the day *was.* God existed before the
first day of creation and exists throughout all periods
of history. **no one...My hand.** God's actions are irreversible and can never end in frustration.

14 Thus says the LORD, your Redeemer,
The Holy One of Israel:
"For your sake I will send to Babylon,
And bring them all down as
   fugitives—
The Chaldeans, who rejoice in their
   ships.
15 I *am* the LORD, your Holy One,
The Creator of Israel, your King."

16 Thus says the LORD, who makes a
   way in the sea
And a path through the mighty
   waters,
17 Who brings forth the chariot and
   horse,
The army and the power
(They shall lie down together, they
   shall not rise;
They are extinguished, they are
   quenched like a wick):
18 "Do not remember the former things,

Nor consider the things of old.
19 Behold, I will do a new thing,
Now it shall spring forth;
Shall you not know it?
I will even make a road in the
   wilderness
And rivers in the desert.
20 The beast of the field will honor Me,
The jackals and the ostriches,
Because I give waters in the
   wilderness
And rivers in the desert,
To give drink to My people, My
   chosen.
21 This people I have formed for Myself;
They shall declare My praise.

Pleading with Unfaithful Israel
22 "But you have not called upon Me,
   O Jacob;
And you have been weary of Me,
   O Israel.
23 You have not brought Me the sheep
   for your burnt offerings,
Nor have you honored Me with your
   sacrifices.
I have not caused you to serve with
   grain offerings,
Nor wearied you with incense.
24 You have bought Me no sweet cane
   with money,
Nor have you satisfied Me with the
   fat of your sacrifices;
But you have burdened Me with your
   sins,
You have wearied Me with your
   iniquities.
25 "I, *even* I, *am* He who blots out your
   transgressions for My own sake;
And I will not remember your sins.

43:25 I, *even* I...not remember your sins. The Lord
forgave the sins of Israel despite her unworthiness.
He can forgive their sins and grant righteousness
without compromising His holiness, which He would
accomplish through the work of His Servant. Israel
will always be God's chosen people.

26 Put Me in remembrance;
Let us contend together;
State your *case,* that you may be
   acquitted.
27 Your first father sinned,

And your mediators have transgressed
    against Me.
28 Therefore I will profane the princes of
    the sanctuary;
I will give Jacob to the curse,
And Israel to reproaches.

God's Blessing on Israel

44 "Yet hear me now, O Jacob My
    servant,
And Israel whom I have chosen.
2 Thus says the LORD who made you
And formed you from the womb, *who*
    will help you:
'Fear not, O Jacob My servant;
And you, Jeshurun, whom I have
    chosen.
3 For I will pour water on him who is
    thirsty,
And floods on the dry ground;
I will pour My Spirit on your
    descendants,
And My blessing on your offspring;
4 They will spring up among the grass
Like willows by the watercourses.'
5 One will say, 'I *am* the LORD's';
Another will call *himself* by the name
    of Jacob;
Another will write *with* his hand,
    'The LORD's,'
And name *himself* by the name of
    Israel.

There Is No Other God

6 "Thus says the LORD, the King of
    Israel,
And his Redeemer, the LORD of hosts:
'I *am* the First and I *am* the Last;
Besides Me *there is* no God.

44:6 King...Redeemer...LORD of hosts...First...Last.
The Lord identified Himself as Israel's King, Redeemer, Champion in battle, and Eternal One. Jesus called Himself the First and the Last (see Rev. 1:17). **Besides Me...no God.** God challenged the false gods by His exclusive claim to deity.

7 And who can proclaim as I do?
Then let him declare it and set it in
    order for Me,
Since I appointed the ancient people.
And the things that are coming and
    shall come,
Let them show these to them.

8 Do not fear, nor be afraid;
Have I not told you from that time,
    and declared *it?*
You *are* My witnesses.
Is there a God besides Me?
Indeed *there is* no other Rock;
I know not one.'"

Idolatry Is Foolishness

9 Those who make an image, all of
    them *are* useless,
And their precious things shall not
    profit;
They *are* their own witnesses;
They neither see nor know, that they
    may be ashamed.
10 Who would form a god or mold an
    image
That profits him nothing?
11 Surely all his companions would be
    ashamed;
And the workmen, they *are* mere
    men.
Let them all be gathered together,
Let them stand up;
Yet they shall fear,
They shall be ashamed together.

12 The blacksmith with the tongs works
    one in the coals,
Fashions it with hammers,
And works it with the strength of his
    arms.
Even so, he is hungry, and his
    strength fails;
He drinks no water and is faint.

13 The craftsman stretches out *his* rule,
He marks one out with chalk;
He fashions it with a plane,
He marks it out with the compass,
And makes it like the figure of a man,
According to the beauty of a man,
    that it may remain in the house.
14 He cuts down cedars for himself,
And takes the cypress and the oak;
He secures *it* for himself among the
    trees of the forest.
He plants a pine, and the rain
    nourishes *it.*

15 Then it shall be for a man to burn,
For he will take some of it and warm
    himself;

Yes, he kindles *it* and bakes bread;
Indeed he makes a god and worships
  it;
He makes it a carved image, and falls
  down to it.
16 He burns half of it in the fire;
With this half he eats meat;
He roasts a roast, and is satisfied.
He even warms *himself* and says,
"Ah! I am warm,
I have seen the fire."
17 And the rest of it he makes into a god,
His carved image.
He falls down before it and worships
  it,
Prays to it and says,
"Deliver me, for you *are* my god!"

18 They do not know nor understand;
For He has shut their eyes, so that
  they cannot see,
And their hearts, so that they cannot
  understand.
19 And no one considers in his heart,
Nor *is there* knowledge nor
  understanding to say,
"I have burned half of it in the fire,
Yes, I have also baked bread on its
  coals;
I have roasted meat and eaten *it;*
And shall I make the rest of it an
  abomination?
Shall I fall down before a block of
  wood?"

44:12–19 Human idol-makers used all their energy
only to produce an idol that looked like a man (Deut.
4:15–18), but the idol could not renew their strength.
Yet, they who wait on the Lord will renew their
strength (40:28–31). The idol-makers foolishly worshiped the same piece of wood that they used to
build a fire.

20 He feeds on ashes;
A deceived heart has turned him aside;
And he cannot deliver his soul,
Nor say, "*Is there* not a lie in my right
  hand?"

Israel Is Not Forgotten
21 "Remember these, O Jacob,
And Israel, for you *are* My servant;
I have formed you, you *are* My
  servant;

O Israel, you will not be forgotten by
  Me!
22 I have blotted out, like a thick cloud,
  your transgressions,
And like a cloud, your sins.
Return to Me, for I have redeemed
  you."

44:22 blotted out...your sins. As a person is unable
to see what is ahead because of a "thick cloud," so
God had blotted out Israel's sins that were written in
His book (see Rev. 20:12). **Return to Me.** For those
who turn from sin and return to God there is redemption because of Christ's death on the cross. The Lord
calls His people to repent so they may receive the
promised redemption (see Neh. 1:9).

23 Sing, O heavens, for the LORD has
  done *it!*
Shout, you lower parts of the earth;
Break forth into singing, you
  mountains,
O forest, and every tree in it!
For the LORD has redeemed Jacob,
And glorified Himself in Israel.

Judah Will Be Restored
24 Thus says the LORD, your Redeemer,
And He who formed you from the
  womb:
"I *am* the LORD, who makes all *things,*
Who stretches out the heavens all
  alone,
Who spreads abroad the earth by
  Myself;
25 Who frustrates the signs of the
  babblers,
And drives diviners mad;
Who turns wise men backward,
And makes their knowledge
  foolishness;
26 Who confirms the word of His
  servant,
And performs the counsel of His
  messengers;
Who says to Jerusalem, 'You shall be
  inhabited,'
To the cities of Judah, 'You shall be
  built,'
And I will raise up her waste places;
27 Who says to the deep, 'Be dry!
And I will dry up your rivers';
28 Who says of Cyrus, '*He is* My
  shepherd,

And he shall perform all My pleasure,
Saying to Jerusalem, "You shall be
    built,"
And to the temple, "Your foundation
    shall be laid." '

> **44:28 Cyrus...My shepherd.** The prophecy, given a century and a half before Cyrus lived and became king of Persia, said that God would use Cyrus to gather the faithful remnant of Israel back to the Land. This illustrated how the Lord's Servant would ultimately gather together the sheep of Israel (Mic. 5:4). **Jerusalem...the temple.** In 538 B.C. Cyrus declared the rebuilding of the temple, which was completed in 516 B.C. (Ezra 1:1,2; 6:15), thus fulfilling Isaiah's prophecy.

Cyrus, God's Instrument

45 " Thus says the LORD to His
anointed,
To Cyrus, whose right hand I have
    held—
To subdue nations before him
And loose the armor of kings,
To open before him the double doors,
So that the gates will not be shut:
2 'I will go before you
And make the crooked places*a*
    straight;
I will break in pieces the gates of
    bronze
And cut the bars of iron.
3 I will give you the treasures of
    darkness
And hidden riches of secret places,
That you may know that I, the LORD,
Who call *you* by your name,
Am the God of Israel.
4 For Jacob My servant's sake,
And Israel My elect,
I have even called you by your name;
I have named you, though you have
    not known Me.
5 I *am* the LORD, and *there is* no other;
There is no God besides Me.
I will gird you, though you have not
    known Me,
6 That they may know from the rising
    of the sun to its setting
That *there is* none besides Me.
I *am* the LORD, and *there is* no other;

7 I form the light and create darkness,
I make peace and create calamity;
I, the LORD, do all these *things.*'

8 " Rain down, you heavens, from above,
And let the skies pour down
    righteousness;
Let the earth open, let them bring
    forth salvation,
And let righteousness spring up
    together.
I, the LORD, have created it.

9 " Woe to him who strives with his
    Maker!
Let the potsherd *strive* with the
    potsherds of the earth!
Shall the clay say to him who forms
    it, 'What are you making?'
Or shall your handiwork *say,* 'He has
    no hands'?
10 Woe to him who says to *his* father,
'What are you begetting?'
Or to the woman, 'What have you
    brought forth?' "

> **45:9,10 Woe...Woe.** The illustrations of the potter and the clay and the parent and child show how it is absurd to contend with God over His plans for the future. The Jews were questioning God about their captivity and restoration by a pagan king as well as God's plan to redeem Gentiles as well as Jews (see Rom. 9:20–24).

11   Thus says the LORD,
The Holy One of Israel, and his
    Maker:
" Ask Me of things to come concerning
    My sons;
And concerning the work of My
    hands, you command Me.
12 I have made the earth,
And created man on it.
I—My hands—stretched out the
    heavens,
And all their host I have commanded.
13 I have raised him up in
    righteousness,
And I will direct all his ways;
He shall build My city
And let My exiles go free,

45:2 *a*Dead Sea Scrolls and Septuagint read *mountains;* Targum reads *I will trample down the walls;* Vulgate reads *I will humble the great ones of the earth.*

Not for price nor reward,"
Says the LORD of hosts.

The LORD, the Only Savior

¹⁴Thus says the LORD:

"The labor of Egypt and merchandise
of Cush
And of the Sabeans, men of stature,
Shall come over to you, and they shall
be yours;
They shall walk behind you,
They shall come over in chains;
And they shall bow down to you.
They will make supplication to you,
saying, 'Surely God *is* in you,
And *there is* no other;
There is no other God.'"

¹⁵ Truly You *are* God, who hide Yourself,
O God of Israel, the Savior!
¹⁶ They shall be ashamed
And also disgraced, all of them;
They shall go in confusion together,
Who are makers of idols.
¹⁷ *But* Israel shall be saved by the LORD
With an everlasting salvation;
You shall not be ashamed or disgraced
Forever and ever.

45:16,17 Israel shall be saved. Makers of idols are
disillusioned by the failure of their gods to deliver,
but Israel is to find eternal salvation in the Lord (Rom.
11:25–27).

¹⁸ For thus says the LORD,
Who created the heavens,
Who is God,
Who formed the earth and made it,
Who has established it,
Who did not create it in vain,
Who formed it to be inhabited:
"I *am* the LORD, and *there is* no other.
¹⁹ I have not spoken in secret,
In a dark place of the earth;
I did not say to the seed of Jacob,
'Seek Me in vain';
I, the LORD, speak righteousness,
I declare things that are right.

²⁰ "Assemble yourselves and come;
Draw near together,
You *who have* escaped from the
nations.

They have no knowledge,
Who carry the wood of their carved
image,
And pray to a god *that* cannot save.
²¹ Tell and bring forth *your case;*
Yes, let them take counsel together.
Who has declared this from ancient
time?
Who has told it from that time?
Have not I, the LORD?
And *there is* no other God besides
Me,
A just God and a Savior;
There is none besides Me.

²² "Look to Me, and be saved,
All you ends of the earth!
For I *am* God, and *there is* no other.
²³ I have sworn by Myself;
The word has gone out of My mouth
in righteousness,
And shall not return,
That to Me every knee shall bow,
Every tongue shall take an oath.

45:23 every knee shall bow. All nations will worship God in the kingdom age. This verse applies to
believers' accountability to God when He evaluates
their works (Rom. 14:11). Paul relates these words to
the coming universal knowledge that "Jesus Christ *is*
Lord, to the glory of God the Father" (Phil. 2:10,11).

²⁴ He shall say,
'Surely in the LORD I have
righteousness and strength.
To Him *men* shall come,
And all shall be ashamed
Who are incensed against Him.
²⁵ In the LORD all the descendants of
Israel
Shall be justified, and shall glory.'"

Dead Idols and the Living God

46 Bel bows down, Nebo stoops;
Their idols were on the beasts and
on the cattle.
Your carriages *were* heavily loaded,
A burden to the weary *beast.*
² They stoop, they bow down
together;
They could not deliver the burden,
But have themselves gone into
captivity.

3 "Listen to Me, O house of Jacob,
  And all the remnant of the house of
    Israel,
  Who have been upheld *by Me* from
    birth,
  Who have been carried from the
    womb:
4 Even to *your* old age, I *am* He,
  And *even* to gray hairs I will carry
    you!
  I have made, and I will bear;
  Even I will carry, and will deliver *you.*

5 "To whom will you liken Me, and
    make *Me* equal
  And compare Me, that we should be
    alike?
6 They lavish gold out of the bag,
  And weigh silver on the scales;
  They hire a goldsmith, and he makes
    it a god;
  They prostrate themselves, yes, they
    worship.
7 They bear it on the shoulder, they
    carry it
  And set it in its place, and it stands;
  From its place it shall not move.
  Though *one* cries out to it, yet it
    cannot answer
  Nor save him out of his trouble.

8 "Remember this, and show yourselves
    men;
  Recall to mind, O you transgressors.
9 Remember the former things of old,
  For I *am* God, and *there is* no other;
  I *am* God, and *there is* none like Me,

46:9 Remember the former things of old. Readers are to recall the fulfilled prophecies of the past, miraculous deliverances, and providential blessings. All of these prove that He alone is God.

10 Declaring the end from the
    beginning,
   And from ancient times *things* that
     are not *yet* done,
   Saying, 'My counsel shall stand,
   And I will do all My pleasure,'
11 Calling a bird of prey from the east,
   The man who executes My counsel,
     from a far country.
   Indeed I have spoken *it;*
   I will also bring it to pass.

I have purposed *it;*
I will also do it.

12 "Listen to Me, you stubborn-hearted,
   Who *are* far from righteousness:
13 I bring My righteousness near, it shall
     not be far off;
   My salvation shall not linger.
   And I will place salvation in Zion,
   For Israel My glory.

The Humiliation of Babylon

47 "Come down and sit in the dust,
    O virgin daughter of Babylon;
  Sit on the ground without a throne,
  O daughter of the Chaldeans!
  For you shall no more be called
  Tender and delicate.
2 Take the millstones and grind meal.
  Remove your veil,
  Take off the skirt,
  Uncover the thigh,
  Pass through the rivers.
3 Your nakedness shall be uncovered,
  Yes, your shame will be seen;
  I will take vengeance,
  And I will not arbitrate with a man."

47:1–3 O virgin daughter of Babylon. Babylon is compared to a virgin, as she had never before been captured. Here, Babylon is humiliated: her throne was taken by Persian power. She is depicted as a slave woman forced to exchange her royal garments for working clothes and wade through water to serve. In the East, such duties belonged to women of low rank, which described Babylon's degradation.

4 As *for* our Redeemer, the LORD of
    hosts *is* His name,
  The Holy One of Israel.

5 "Sit in silence, and go into darkness,
    O daughter of the Chaldeans;
  For you shall no longer be called
  The Lady of Kingdoms.
6 I was angry with My people;
  I have profaned My inheritance,

47:6 showed them no mercy. Though God was using Babylon to punish Israel, Babylon's cruel oppression of the captives was cause for the kingdom's overthrow (see Jer. 50:17).

And given them into your hand.
You showed them no mercy;
On the elderly you laid your yoke very
heavily.

7 And you said, 'I shall be a lady
forever,'
So that you did not take these *things*
to heart,
Nor remember the latter end of them.

8 "Therefore hear this now, *you who are*
given to pleasures,
Who dwell securely,
Who say in your heart, 'I *am*, and
there is no one else besides me;
I shall not sit *as* a widow,
Nor shall I know the loss of children';

9 But these two *things* shall come to
you
In a moment, in one day:
The loss of children, and widowhood.
They shall come upon you in their
fullness
Because of the multitude of your
sorceries,
For the great abundance of your
enchantments.

47:9 In a moment, in one day. Babylon decayed suddenly and unexpectedly when Cyrus and the Persian army entered the city (see Dan. 5:28,30). **loss of children, and widowhood.** Babylon lost inhabitants who were killed or taken captive under Cyrus. This prophecy was fulfilled again when Babylon revolted against Darius. Each man chose one woman from his family and strangled the rest to save provisions. Darius impaled 3,000 Babylonians.

10 "For you have trusted in your
wickedness;
You have said, 'No one sees me';
Your wisdom and your knowledge
have warped you;
And you have said in your heart,
'I *am*, and *there is* no one else besides
me.'

11 Therefore evil shall come upon you;
You shall not know from where it
arises.
And trouble shall fall upon you;
You will not be able to put it off.
And desolation shall come upon you
suddenly,
Which you shall not know.

12 "Stand now with your enchantments
And the multitude of your sorceries,
In which you have labored from your
youth—
Perhaps you will be able to profit,
Perhaps you will prevail.

13 You are wearied in the multitude of
your counsels;
Let now the astrologers, the stargazers,
And the monthly prognosticators
Stand up and save you
From what shall come upon you.

14 Behold, they shall be as stubble,
The fire shall burn them;
They shall not deliver themselves
From the power of the flame;
It shall not *be* a coal to be warmed by,
Nor a fire to sit before!

47:14 They shall not deliver themselves. The astrologers were helpless to save themselves or the Babylonians who depended on them. The divine fire came to consume them, not to warn them.

15 Thus shall they be to you
With whom you have labored,
Your merchants from your youth;
They shall wander each one to his
quarter.
No one shall save you.

Israel Refined for God's Glory

48 "Hear this, O house of Jacob,
Who are called by the name of
Israel,
And have come forth from the
wellsprings of Judah;
Who swear by the name of the LORD,
And make mention of the God of
Israel,
But not in truth or in righteousness;

2 For they call themselves after the holy
city,
And lean on the God of Israel;
The LORD of hosts *is* His name:

3 "I have declared the former things
from the beginning;
They went forth from My mouth, and
I caused them to hear it.
Suddenly I did *them*, and they came
to pass.

4 Because I knew that you *were*
obstinate,

And your neck *was* an iron sinew,
And your brow bronze,
5 Even from the beginning I have
    declared *it* to you;
Before it came to pass I proclaimed *it*
    to you,
Lest you should say, 'My idol has
    done them,
And my carved image and my molded
    image
Have commanded them.'

6 "You have heard;
See all this.
And will you not declare *it?*
I have made you hear new things
    from this time,
Even hidden things, and you did not
    know them.
7 They are created now and not from
    the beginning;
And before this day you have not
    heard them,
Lest you should say, 'Of course I knew
    them.'
8 Surely you did not hear,
Surely you did not know;
Surely from long ago your ear was not
    opened.
For I knew that you would deal very
    treacherously,
And were called a transgressor from
    the womb.

9 "For My name's sake I will defer My
    anger,
And *for* My praise I will restrain it
    from you,
So that I do not cut you off.
10 Behold, I have refined you, but not as
    silver;
I have tested you in the furnace of
    affliction.
11 For My own sake, for My own sake, I
    will do *it;*
For how should *My name* be profaned?
And I will not give My glory to
    another.

God's Ancient Plan to Redeem Israel

12 "Listen to Me, O Jacob,
And Israel, My called:

I *am* He, I *am* the First,
I *am* also the Last.
13 Indeed My hand has laid the
    foundation of the earth,
And My right hand has stretched out
    the heavens;
When I call to them,
They stand up together.

14 "All of you, assemble yourselves, and
    hear!
Who among them has declared these
    things?
The LORD loves him;
He shall do His pleasure on Babylon,
And His arm *shall be against* the
    Chaldeans.
15 I, *even* I, have spoken;
Yes, I have called him,
I have brought him, and his way will
    prosper.

> 48:14,15 him; He...His arm...him...him...his way.
> The pronouns refer to Jesus Christ, whom the Lord
> will anoint to defeat the final Babylon and to bring
> Israel to her land and kingdom at His second coming.

16 "Come near to Me, hear this:
I have not spoken in secret from the
    beginning;
From the time that it was, I *was*
    there.
And now the Lord GOD and His Spirit
Have[a] sent Me."

17 Thus says the LORD, your Redeemer,
The Holy One of Israel:
"I *am* the LORD your God,
Who teaches you to profit,
Who leads you by the way you should
    go.
18 Oh, that you had heeded My
    commandments!
Then your peace would have been like
    a river,
And your righteousness like the waves
    of the sea.
19 Your descendants also would have
    been like the sand,
And the offspring of your body like
    the grains of sand;

48:16 [a]The Hebrew verb is singular.

His name would not have been cut off
Nor destroyed from before Me."

> **48:19 like the sand...like the grains of sand.** God's promise to Abraham to multiply his descendants (Gen. 22:17) had not yet been finally fulfilled because of Israel's disobedience. Israel was taken captive by Babylon, was dispersed before 1948 A.D., and will suffer greatly in the time of Jacob's trouble (see Jer. 30:7). However, God will fulfill His promise.

20 Go forth from Babylon!
Flee from the Chaldeans!
With a voice of singing,
Declare, proclaim this,
Utter it to the end of the earth;
Say, "The LORD has redeemed
His servant Jacob!"
21 And they did not thirst
When He led them through the deserts;
He caused the waters to flow from the
rock for them;
He also split the rock, and the waters
gushed out.

22 *"There is* no peace," says the LORD,
"for the wicked."

The Servant, the Light to the Gentiles

49 "Listen, O coastlands, to Me,
And take heed, you peoples from
afar!
The LORD has called Me from the
womb;
From the matrix of My mother He
has made mention of My name.
2 And He has made My mouth like a
sharp sword;

> **49:1 from the womb; From the matrix of My mother.** The whole world will recognize that the Messiah/Servant will be a human being, born of a virgin woman, and that He will be a distinct individual, in contrast to the nation of Israel, which has also been called the "Lord's servant" (41:8,9).

In the shadow of His hand He has
hidden Me,
And made Me a polished shaft;
In His quiver He has hidden Me."

3 "And He said to me,
'You *are* My servant, O Israel,

In whom I will be glorified.'
4 Then I said, 'I have labored in vain,
I have spent my strength for nothing
and in vain;
Yet surely my just reward *is* with the
LORD,
And my work with my God.' "

5 "And now the LORD says,
Who formed Me from the womb *to be*
His Servant,
To bring Jacob back to Him,
So that Israel is gathered to Him[a]
(For I shall be glorious in the eyes of
the LORD,
And My God shall be My strength),
6 Indeed He says,
'It is too small a thing that You should
be My Servant
To raise up the tribes of Jacob,
And to restore the preserved ones of
Israel;
I will also give You as a light to the
Gentiles,
That You should be My salvation to
the ends of the earth.' "

> **49:6 raise up the tribes of Jacob...My salvation to the ends of the earth.** The Servant's goal is to save and restore Israel as well as the Gentiles. Israel's mission was to bring the nations to God. Paul applied this to his ministry to the Gentiles on his first missionary journey (Acts 13:47).

7 Thus says the LORD,
The Redeemer of Israel, their Holy
One,
To Him whom man despises,
To Him whom the nation abhors,
To the Servant of rulers:
"Kings shall see and arise,
Princes also shall worship,
Because of the LORD who is faithful,
The Holy One of Israel;
And He has chosen You."

8 Thus says the LORD:

"In an acceptable time I have heard
You,
And in the day of salvation I have
helped You;

49:5 [a]Qere, Dead Sea Scrolls, and Septuagint read *is gathered to Him;* Kethib reads *is not gathered.*

I will preserve You and give You
As a covenant to the people,
To restore the earth,
To cause them to inherit the desolate
heritages;

9 That You may say to the prisoners,
'Go forth,'
To those who *are* in darkness, 'Show
yourselves.'

"They shall feed along the roads,
And their pastures *shall be* on all
desolate heights.
10 They shall neither hunger nor
thirst,
Neither heat nor sun shall strike
them;
For He who has mercy on them will
lead them,

49:9,10 prisoners...darkness...feed...pastures. After the Messiah returns, Israel's condition will change from captivity and oppression to contentment and prosperity, like a protected, well-fed flock of sheep. John reveals that this condition is a foretaste of heaven (see Rev. 7:16,17).

Even by the springs of water He will
guide them.
11 I will make each of My mountains a
road,
And My highways shall be elevated.

12 Surely these shall come from afar;
Look! Those from the north and the
west,
And these from the land of Sinim."

13 Sing, O heavens!
Be joyful, O earth!
And break out in singing,
O mountains!
For the LORD has comforted His
people,
And will have mercy on His afflicted.

God Will Remember Zion

14 But Zion said, "The LORD has
forsaken me,
And my Lord has forgotten me."

15 "Can a woman forget her nursing child,
And not have compassion on the son
of her womb?
Surely they may forget,
Yet I will not forget you.
16 See, I have inscribed you on the
palms *of My hands*;
Your walls *are* continually before Me.
17 Your sons[a] shall make haste;
Your destroyers and those who laid
you waste
Shall go away from you.
18 Lift up your eyes, look around and
see;

49:17 [a]Dead Sea Scrolls, Septuagint, Targum, and Vulgate read *builders*.

Q **Does Isaiah indicate God's permanent abandonment of the Chosen People, or does God reveal through Isaiah an ongoing plan for them?**

A The long view that Isaiah's prophecies provide supports the future role of Israel in God's plan. God, according to Isaiah, may arrange for harsh punishment of His people, but He has not replaced ethnic Israel with an alleged "new Israel." Isaiah has too much to say about God's faithfulness to Israel. He would not utterly reject the people whom He has created and chosen (Isaiah 43:1). The nation is on the palms of His hands, and Jerusalem's walls are ever before His eyes (Isaiah 49:16). God is bound by His own Word to fulfill the promises He has made to bring them back to Him and bless them in that future day (Isaiah 55:10–12).

The imagery in the New Testament confirms Isaiah's views. Passages like Romans 11 certainly picture Gentiles being grafted into the tree of God's salvation plan, but the message does not imply complete replacement. God does not forget those who belong to Him.

All these gather together *and* come to
you.
As I live," says the LORD,
"You shall surely clothe yourselves
with them all as an ornament,
And bind them *on you* as a bride *does.*

19 "For your waste and desolate places,
And the land of your destruction,
Will even now be too small for the
inhabitants;
And those who swallowed you up will
be far away.
20 The children you will have,
After you have lost the others,
Will say again in your ears,
'The place *is* too small for me;
Give me a place where I may dwell.'
21 Then you will say in your heart,
'Who has begotten these for me,
Since I have lost my children and am
desolate,
A captive, and wandering to and fro?
And who has brought these up?
There I was, left alone;
But these, where *were* they?' "

22 Thus says the Lord GOD:

"Behold, I will lift My hand in an oath
to the nations,
And set up My standard for the
peoples;
They shall bring your sons in *their*
arms,
And your daughters shall be carried
on *their* shoulders;

**49:22 nations...shall bring your sons...And your
daughters.** The nations of the world will assist the
remnant of Israel to their land. Gentiles who believed
in Jesus Christ will enter the kingdom. Nations and
leaders that had oppressed Israel will humble themselves before the redeemed of God's covenant, and
Israel will not be disappointed in waiting on the Lord.

---

23 Kings shall be your foster fathers,
And their queens your nursing
mothers;
They shall bow down to you with
their faces to the earth,

And lick up the dust of your feet.
Then you will know that I *am* the
LORD,
For they shall not be ashamed who
wait for Me."

24 Shall the prey be taken from the
mighty,
Or the captives of the righteous[a] be
delivered?

25 But thus says the LORD:

"Even the captives of the mighty shall
be taken away,
And the prey of the terrible be
delivered;
For I will contend with him who
contends with you,
And I will save your children.
26 I will feed those who oppress you with
their own flesh,
And they shall be drunk with their
own blood as with sweet wine.
All flesh shall know
That I, the LORD, *am* your Savior,
And your Redeemer, the Mighty One
of Jacob."

The Servant, Israel's Hope

50 Thus says the LORD:

"Where *is* the certificate of your
mother's divorce,
Whom I have put away?
Or which of My creditors *is it* to
whom I have sold you?
For your iniquities you have sold
yourselves,
And for your transgressions your
mother has been put away.

**50:1 certificate of your mother's divorce...My cred-
itors.** God gave the non-Davidic northern kingdom a
certificate of divorce, but the unconditional promises
of the Davidic Covenant (2 Sam. 7) prevented such a
divorce for Judah, although there would be a time of
separation because of her sinfulness.

---

2 Why, when I came, *was there* no
man?

49:24 [a]Following Masoretic Text and Targum; Dead Sea Scrolls, Syriac, and Vulgate read *the mighty;*
Septuagint reads *unjustly.*

Why, when I called, *was there* none to
answer?
Is My hand shortened at all that it
cannot redeem?
Or have I no power to deliver?
Indeed with My rebuke I dry up the
sea,
I make the rivers a wilderness;
Their fish stink because *there is* no
water,
And die of thirst.

3 I clothe the heavens with blackness,
And I make sackcloth their covering."

4 "The Lord GOD has given Me
The tongue of the learned,
That I should know how to speak
A word in season to *him who is*
weary.
He awakens Me morning by morning,
He awakens My ear
To hear as the learned.

5 The Lord GOD has opened My ear;
And I was not rebellious,
Nor did I turn away.

6 I gave My back to those who struck
Me,
And My cheeks to those who plucked
out the beard;
I did not hide My face from shame
and spitting.

7 "For the Lord GOD will help Me;
Therefore I will not be disgraced;
Therefore I have set My face like a
flint,
And I know that I will not be
ashamed.

50:7 set My face like a flint. Jesus was so confident in God's help that He was determined to face any hardship (see Ezek. 3:8,9), and He set His face to Jerusalem to be crucified (Luke 9:51).

8 *He is* near who justifies Me;
Who will contend with Me?
Let us stand together.
Who *is* My adversary?
Let him come near Me.

9 Surely the Lord GOD will help Me;
Who *is* he *who* will condemn Me?
Indeed they will all grow old like a
garment;
The moth will eat them up.

10 "Who among you fears the LORD?
Who obeys the voice of His Servant?
Who walks in darkness
And has no light?
Let him trust in the name of the
LORD
And rely upon his God.

11 Look, all you who kindle a fire,
Who encircle *yourselves* with
sparks:
Walk in the light of your fire and in
the sparks you have kindled—
This you shall have from My hand:
You shall lie down in torment.

The LORD Comforts Zion

51 "Listen to Me, you who follow after
righteousness,
You who seek the LORD:
Look to the rock *from which* you were
hewn,
And to the hole of the pit *from which*
you were dug.

2 Look to Abraham your father,
And to Sarah *who* bore you;
For I called him alone,
And blessed him and increased him."

51:1,2 The prophet assured the nation of deliverance by pointing to God's past covenant with Abraham (Gen. 12:13). Abraham was one person, but God multiplied his descendants as He had promised (Gen. 13:16).

3 For the LORD will comfort Zion,
He will comfort all her waste places;
He will make her wilderness like
Eden,
And her desert like the garden of the
LORD;
Joy and gladness will be found in it,
Thanksgiving and the voice of
melody.

4 "Listen to Me, My people;
And give ear to Me, O My nation:
For law will proceed from Me,
And I will make My justice rest
As a light of the peoples.

5 My righteousness *is* near,
My salvation has gone forth,
And My arms will judge the peoples;
The coastlands will wait upon Me,
And on My arm they will trust.

6 Lift up your eyes to the heavens,
And look on the earth beneath.
For the heavens will vanish away like
    smoke,
The earth will grow old like a
    garment,
And those who dwell in it will die in
    like manner;
But My salvation will be forever,
And My righteousness will not be
    abolished.

51:6 heavens will vanish...earth will grow old. This begins during the time of tribulation and sets the stage, along with earthly judgments on land, sea, and fresh water, for a renewed earth during the millennium (see Rev. 6:12–14). The destruction of the present universe (2 Pet.3:10–13) occurs at the end of Christ's millennial reign on earth, when a new heaven and new earth will be formed (2 Pet. 3:10).

7 "Listen to Me, you who know
    righteousness,
You people in whose heart *is* My law:
Do not fear the reproach of men,
Nor be afraid of their insults.
8 For the moth will eat them up like a
    garment,
And the worm will eat them like
    wool;
But My righteousness will be forever,
And My salvation from generation to
    generation."

9 Awake, awake, put on strength,
O arm of the LORD!
Awake as in the ancient days,
In the generations of old.
Are You not *the arm* that cut Rahab
    apart,
And wounded the serpent?
10 *Are* You not *the One* who dried up the
    sea,
The waters of the great deep;
That made the depths of the sea a
    road
For the redeemed to cross over?
11 So the ransomed of the LORD shall
    return,
And come to Zion with singing,
With everlasting joy on their heads.
They shall obtain joy and gladness;
Sorrow and sighing shall flee away.

12 "I, *even* I, *am* He who comforts you.
Who *are* you that you should be afraid
Of a man *who* will die,
And of the son of a man *who* will be
    made like grass?
13 And you forget the LORD your Maker,
Who stretched out the heavens
And laid the foundations of the earth;
You have feared continually every day
Because of the fury of the oppressor,
When *he has* prepared to destroy.
And where *is* the fury of the
    oppressor?
14 The captive exile hastens, that he
    may be loosed,
That he should not die in the pit,
And that his bread should not fail.
15 But I *am* the LORD your God,
Who divided the sea whose waves
    roared—
The LORD of hosts *is* His name.
16 And I have put My words in your
    mouth;
I have covered you with the shadow of
    My hand,
That I may plant the heavens,
Lay the foundations of the earth,
And say to Zion, 'You *are* My
    people.' "

God's Fury Removed

17 Awake, awake!
Stand up, O Jerusalem,
You who have drunk at the hand of
    the LORD
The cup of His fury;
You have drunk the dregs of the cup
    of trembling,
And drained *it* out.
18 *There is* no one to guide her
Among all the sons she has brought
    forth;
Nor *is there any* who takes her by the
    hand
Among all the sons she has brought
    up.
19 These two *things* have come to you;
Who will be sorry for you?—
Desolation and destruction, famine
    and sword—
By whom will I comfort you?
20 Your sons have fainted,
They lie at the head of all the streets,
Like an antelope in a net;

They are full of the fury of the LORD,
The rebuke of your God.

21 Therefore please hear this, you
afflicted,
And drunk but not with wine.
22 Thus says your Lord,
The LORD and your God,
Who pleads the cause of His people:
"See, I have taken out of your hand
The cup of trembling,
The dregs of the cup of My fury;
You shall no longer drink it.

51:21,22 drunk but not with wine. Jerusalem became drunk by the cup of God's wrath (63:6), but her cup will be removed before all the wrath is consumed. Israel's oppressors, however, will drink the full cup of wrath (Rev. 18:6; Jer. 25:15).

---

23 But I will put it into the hand of those
who afflict you,
Who have said to you,*a*
'Lie down, that we may walk over
you.'
And you have laid your body like the
ground,
And as the street, for those who walk
over."

God Redeems Jerusalem

52 Awake, awake!
Put on your strength, O Zion;
Put on your beautiful garments,
O Jerusalem, the holy city!
For the uncircumcised and the
unclean
Shall no longer come to you.
2 Shake yourself from the dust, arise;
Sit down, O Jerusalem!
Loose yourself from the bonds of your
neck,
O captive daughter of Zion!

³For thus says the LORD:

"You have sold yourselves for nothing,
And you shall be redeemed without
money."

⁴For thus says the Lord GOD:

"My people went down at first
Into Egypt to dwell there;
Then the Assyrian oppressed them
without cause.
5 Now therefore, what have I here,"
says the LORD,
"That My people are taken away for
nothing?
Those who rule over them
Make them wail,"*a* says the LORD,
"And My name *is* blasphemed
continually every day.

52:5 My name *is* blasphemed. Foreign rulers despised the God of Israel while His people were in bondage. God delivered Israel, not because of their goodness, but to prove that He was truthful, faithful, and powerful (Ezek. 20:9,14). Paul cited the blasphemy against Israel's God that resulted from the hypocrisy of the first-century Jews who did not live what they taught others (Rom. 2:24).

---

6 Therefore My people shall know My
name;
Therefore *they shall know* in that day
That I *am* He who speaks:
'Behold, *it is* I.' "

7 How beautiful upon the mountains
Are the feet of him who brings good
news,
Who proclaims peace,
Who brings glad tidings of good
things,
Who proclaims salvation,
Who says to Zion,
"Your God reigns!"
8 Your watchmen shall lift up *their*
voices,
With their voices they shall sing
together;
For they shall see eye to eye
When the LORD brings back Zion.
9 Break forth into joy, sing together,
You waste places of Jerusalem!
For the LORD has comforted His
people,
He has redeemed Jerusalem.
10 The LORD has made bare His holy
arm
In the eyes of all the nations;

51:23 *a*Literally *your soul*   52:5 *a*Dead Sea Scrolls read *Mock*; Septuagint reads *Marvel and wail*;
Targum reads *Boast themselves*; Vulgate reads *Treat them unjustly*.

And all the ends of the earth shall see
The salvation of our God.

11 Depart! Depart! Go out from there,
Touch no unclean *thing*;
Go out from the midst of her,
Be clean,
You who bear the vessels of the LORD.
12 For you shall not go out with haste,
Nor go by flight;
For the LORD will go before you,
And the God of Israel *will be* your
rear guard.

The Sin-Bearing Servant

13 Behold, My Servant shall deal
prudently;
He shall be exalted and extolled and
be very high.
14 Just as many were astonished at you,
So His visage was marred more than
any man,
And His form more than the sons of
men;

> **52:14 His visage was marred.** The people looked at the awful appearance of the Servant with astonishment, as He suffered cruelty to the point that He no longer looked human (Ps. 22:6; Matt. 26:27).

15 So shall He sprinkle*a* many nations.
Kings shall shut their mouths at Him;
For what had not been told them they
shall see,
And what they had not heard they
shall consider.

53 Who has believed our report?
And to whom has the arm of the
LORD been revealed?
2 For He shall grow up before Him as a
tender plant,
And as a root out of dry ground.
He has no form or comeliness;
And when we see Him,
There is no beauty that we should
desire Him.
3 He is despised and rejected by men,
A Man of sorrows and acquainted
with grief.
And we hid, as it were, *our* faces from
Him;

> **53:3 despised...rejected...despised.** The prophet foresees the hatred and rejection by mankind toward the Messiah, who suffered external abuse as well as internal grief over the lack of response from those He came to save (Matt. 23:37). **we hid...we did not esteem.** The prophet speaks of his unbelieving nation's aversion to a crucified Messiah and their lack of respect for Him.

He was despised, and we did not
esteem Him.

4 Surely He has borne our griefs
And carried our sorrows;
Yet we esteemed Him stricken,
Smitten by God, and afflicted.
5 But He *was* wounded for our
transgressions,
He was bruised for our iniquities;
The chastisement for our peace *was*
upon Him,
And by His stripes we are healed.
6 All we like sheep have gone astray;
We have turned, every one, to his own
way;
And the LORD has laid on Him the
iniquity of us all.

7 He was oppressed and He was
afflicted,
Yet He opened not His mouth;
He was led as a lamb to the slaughter,
And as a sheep before its shearers is
silent,
So He opened not His mouth.
8 He was taken from prison and from
judgment,
And who will declare His generation?
For He was cut off from the land of
the living;
For the transgressions of My people
He was stricken.
9 And they*a* made His grave with the
wicked—
But with the rich at His death,
Because He had done no violence,
Nor *was any* deceit in His mouth.

10 Yet it pleased the LORD to bruise Him;
He has put *Him* to grief.
When You make His soul an offering
for sin,

52:15 *a*Or *startle*   53:9 *a*Literally *he* or *He*

53:9 with the wicked...with the rich. The Jews wanted a disgraceful burial, along with the thieves, for the Servant, as He suffered a disgraceful death (see John 19:31). Instead, He was buried with "the rich" in an honorable burial through the donated tomb of rich Joseph of Arimathea (Matt. 27:57–60). **no violence, Nor...deceit.** The innocent Servant's execution was undeserved (see 1 Pet. 2:22).

He shall see *His* seed, He shall
   prolong *His* days,
And the pleasure of the LORD shall
   prosper in His hand.
11 He shall see the labor of His soul,[a]
   and be satisfied.
By His knowledge My righteous
   Servant shall justify many,
For He shall bear their iniquities.
12 Therefore I will divide Him a portion
   with the great,
And He shall divide the spoil with the
   strong,
Because He poured out His soul unto
   death,
And He was numbered with the
   transgressors,
And He bore the sin of many,
And made intercession for the
   transgressors.

A Perpetual Covenant of Peace

54 "Sing, O barren,
   You *who* have not borne!
Break forth into singing, and cry
   aloud,
You *who* have not labored with child!
For more *are* the children of the
   desolate
Than the children of the married
   woman," says the LORD.
2 "Enlarge the place of your tent,
And let them stretch out the curtains
   of your dwellings;
Do not spare;
Lengthen your cords,
And strengthen your stakes.

54:2 Enlarge...stretch out...Lengthen. The prophet commanded barren Israel to prepare for the day when she would need a larger dwelling place, due to her numerous inhabitants.

3 For you shall expand to the right and
   to the left,
And your descendants will inherit the
   nations,
And make the desolate cities
   inhabited.

4 "Do not fear, for you will not be
   ashamed;
Neither be disgraced, for you will not
   be put to shame;
For you will forget the shame of your
   youth,
And will not remember the reproach
   of your widowhood anymore.
5 For your Maker *is* your husband,
The LORD of hosts *is* His name;
And your Redeemer *is* the Holy One
   of Israel;
He is called the God of the whole
   earth.
6 For the LORD has called you
Like a woman forsaken and grieved in
   spirit,
Like a youthful wife when you were
   refused,"
Says your God.
7 "For a mere moment I have forsaken
   you,
But with great mercies I will gather
   you.
8 With a little wrath I hid My face from
   you for a moment;
But with everlasting kindness I will
   have mercy on you,"
Says the LORD, your Redeemer.

9 "For this *is* like the waters of Noah to
   Me;
For as I have sworn
That the waters of Noah would no
   longer cover the earth,
So have I sworn
That I would not be angry with you,
   nor rebuke you.
10 For the mountains shall depart
And the hills be removed,
But My kindness shall not depart
   from you,
Nor shall My covenant of peace be
   removed,"

53:11 [a]Following Masoretic Text, Targum, and Vulgate; Dead Sea Scrolls and Septuagint read *From the labor of His soul He shall see light.*

Says the LORD, who has mercy on
you.

11 "O you afflicted one,
   Tossed with tempest, *and* not
      comforted,
   Behold, I will lay your stones with
      colorful gems,
   And lay your foundations with
      sapphires.
12 I will make your pinnacles of rubies,
   Your gates of crystal,
   And all your walls of precious stones.
13 All your children *shall be* taught by
      the LORD,
   And great *shall be* the peace of your
      children.
14 In righteousness you shall be
      established;
   You shall be far from oppression, for
      you shall not fear;
   And from terror, for it shall not come
      near you.
15 Indeed they shall surely assemble, *but*
      not because of Me.
   Whoever assembles against you shall
      fall for your sake.
16 "Behold, I have created the blacksmith
   Who blows the coals in the fire,
   Who brings forth an instrument for
      his work;
   And I have created the spoiler to
      destroy.
17 No weapon formed against you shall
      prosper,
   And every tongue *which* rises against
      you in judgment
   You shall condemn.

This *is* the heritage of the servants of
   the LORD,
And their righteousness *is* from Me,"
Says the LORD.

An Invitation to Abundant Life

55 "Ho! Everyone who thirsts,
      Come to the waters;
   And you who have no money,
   Come, buy and eat.
   Yes, come, buy wine and milk
   Without money and without price.
2 Why do you spend money for *what is*
      not bread,
   And your wages for *what* does not
      satisfy?
   Listen carefully to Me, and eat *what
      is* good,
   And let your soul delight itself in
      abundance.
3 Incline your ear, and come to Me.
   Hear, and your soul shall live;
   And I will make an everlasting
      covenant with you—
   The sure mercies of David.
4 Indeed I have given him *as* a witness
      to the people,
   A leader and commander for the
      people.
5 Surely you shall call a nation you do
      not know,
   And nations *who* do not know you
      shall run to you,
   Because of the LORD your God,
   And the Holy One of Israel;
   For He has glorified you."

6 Seek the LORD while He may be
      found,
   Call upon Him while He is near.
7 Let the wicked forsake his way,
   And the unrighteous man his
      thoughts;
   Let him return to the LORD,

And He will have mercy on him;
And to our God,
For He will abundantly pardon.

8 "For My thoughts *are* not your
    thoughts,
Nor *are* your ways My ways," says the
    LORD.
9 "For *as* the heavens are higher than the
    earth,
So are My ways higher than your
    ways,
And My thoughts than your thoughts.

10 "For as the rain comes down, and the
    snow from heaven,
And do not return there,
But water the earth,
And make it bring forth and bud,
That it may give seed to the sower
And bread to the eater,
11 So shall My word be that goes forth
    from My mouth;
It shall not return to Me void,
But it shall accomplish what I please,
And it shall prosper *in the thing* for
    which I sent it.

12 "For you shall go out with joy,
And be led out with peace;
The mountains and the hills
Shall break forth into singing before
    you,
And all the trees of the field shall clap
    their hands.
13 Instead of the thorn shall come up
    the cypress tree,
And instead of the brier shall come up
    the myrtle tree;
And it shall be to the LORD for a
    name,
For an everlasting sign *that* shall not
    be cut off."

Salvation for the Gentiles

56 Thus says the LORD:

"Keep justice, and do righteousness,
For My salvation *is* about to come,
And My righteousness to be revealed.
2 Blessed *is* the man *who* does this,

And the son of man *who* lays hold on
    it;
Who keeps from defiling the Sabbath,
And keeps his hand from doing any
    evil."

56:2 keeps from defiling the Sabbath. Observing the Sabbath, which was established after the deliverance from Egypt (Ex. 20:8–11), was a sign of fulfilling the Mosaic Covenant (Ex. 31:13–17).

3   Do not let the son of the foreigner
Who has joined himself to the LORD
Speak, saying,
"The LORD has utterly separated me
    from His people";
Nor let the eunuch say,
"Here I am, a dry tree."
4   For thus says the LORD:
"To the eunuchs who keep My
    Sabbaths,
And choose what pleases Me,
And hold fast My covenant,
5   Even to them I will give in My house
And within My walls a place and a
    name
Better than that of sons and
    daughters;
I will give them*ᵃ* an everlasting name
That shall not be cut off.

6   "Also the sons of the foreigner
Who join themselves to the LORD, to
    serve Him,
And to love the name of the LORD, to
    be His servants—
Everyone who keeps from defiling the
    Sabbath,
And holds fast My covenant—
7   Even them I will bring to My holy
    mountain,
And make them joyful in My house of
    prayer.
Their burnt offerings and their
    sacrifices
Will be accepted on My altar;
For My house shall be called a house
    of prayer for all nations."
8   The Lord GOD, who gathers the
    outcasts of Israel, says,

56:5 *ᵃ*Literally *him*

"Yet I will gather to him
Others besides those who are gathered
to him."

Israel's Irresponsible Leaders

9 All you beasts of the field, come to
devour,
All you beasts in the forest.

10 His watchmen *are* blind,
They are all ignorant;
They *are* all dumb dogs,
They cannot bark;
Sleeping, lying down, loving to
slumber.

11 Yes, *they are* greedy dogs
Which never have enough.
And they *are* shepherds
Who cannot understand;
They all look to their own way,
Every one for his own gain,
From his *own* territory.

12 "Come," *one says,* "I will bring wine,
And we will fill ourselves with
intoxicating drink;
Tomorrow will be as today,
And much more abundant."

Israel's Futile Idolatry

57 The righteous perishes,
And no man takes *it* to heart;
Merciful men *are* taken away,
While no one considers
That the righteous is taken away from
evil.

2 He shall enter into peace;
They shall rest in their beds,
Each one walking *in* his uprightness.

3 "But come here,
You sons of the sorceress,
You offspring of the adulterer and the
harlot!

4 Whom do you ridicule?
Against whom do you make a wide
mouth
And stick out the tongue?
Are you not children of transgression,
Offspring of falsehood,

5 Inflaming yourselves with gods under
every green tree,
Slaying the children in the valleys,
Under the clefts of the rocks?

6 Among the smooth *stones* of the
stream
Is your portion;
They, they, *are* your lot!
Even to them you have poured a drink
offering,
You have offered a grain offering.
Should I receive comfort in these?

7 "On a lofty and high mountain
You have set your bed;
Even there you went up
To offer sacrifice.

8 Also behind the doors and their posts
You have set up your remembrance;
For you have uncovered yourself *to
those other* than Me,
And have gone up to them;
You have enlarged your bed
And made *a* covenant with them;
You have loved their bed,
Where you saw *their* nudity.[a]

9 You went to the king with ointment,
And increased your perfumes;
You sent your messengers far off,
And *even* descended to Sheol.

10 You are wearied in the length of your
way;
Yet you did not say, 'There is no
hope.'
You have found the life of your hand;
Therefore you were not grieved.

11 "And of whom have you been afraid, or
feared,
That you have lied
And not remembered Me,
Nor taken *it* to your heart?
Is it not because I have held My peace
from of old
That you do not fear Me?

12 I will declare your righteousness

57:8 [a]Literally *hand*, a euphemism

And your works,
For they will not profit you.

13 When you cry out,
Let your collection *of idols* deliver
     you.
But the wind will carry them all away,
A breath will take *them*.
But he who puts his trust in Me shall
     possess the land,
And shall inherit My holy mountain."

Healing for the Backslider

14 And one shall say,
"Heap it up! Heap it up!
Prepare the way,
Take the stumbling block out of the
     way of My people."

15 For thus says the High and Lofty One
Who inhabits eternity, whose name *is*
     Holy:
"I dwell in the high and holy *place*,
With him *who* has a contrite and
     humble spirit,
To revive the spirit of the humble,
And to revive the heart of the contrite
     ones.

16 For I will not contend forever,
Nor will I always be angry;
For the spirit would fail before Me,
And the souls *which* I have made.

17 For the iniquity of his covetousness
I was angry and struck him;
I hid and was angry,
And he went on backsliding in the
     way of his heart.

18 I have seen his ways, and will heal
     him;
I will also lead him,

And restore comforts to him
And to his mourners.

> **57:15,18 revive the spirit...revive the heart.** The Lord sends revival to the humble and contrite. After all the years of Israel's sin, backsliding, and punishment, God's grace will provide spiritual healing and restoration for her.

19 "I create the fruit of the lips:
Peace, peace to *him who is* far off and
     to *him who is* near,"
Says the LORD,
"And I will heal him."

20 But the wicked *are* like the troubled
     sea,
When it cannot rest,
Whose waters cast up mire and dirt.

21 "*There is* no peace,"
Says my God, "for the wicked."

Fasting that Pleases God

58 "Cry aloud, spare not;
Lift up your voice like a trumpet;
Tell My people their transgression,
And the house of Jacob their sins.

2 Yet they seek Me daily,
And delight to know My ways,
As a nation that did righteousness,
And did not forsake the ordinance of
     their God.
They ask of Me the ordinances of
     justice;
They take delight in approaching
     God.

3 'Why have we fasted,' *they say,* 'and
     You have not seen?

In what ways are Isaiah's prophecies still open to fulfillment, and how?

The literal fulfillment of many of Isaiah's prophecies makes up part of the ancient historical record. Manuscripts like the complete copy of Isaiah found among the Dead Sea scrolls were already well worn when the events of Jesus' life were taking place. The trustworthiness of Isaiah's prophetic statements about the intervening events points strongly toward his accuracy about the future. To argue that those yet unfulfilled can only be non-literally fulfilled is biblically and historically shortsighted. God's Word remains steadfast. The case for proposing that the church receives some of the promises made originally to Israel rests on shaky ground. The kingdom promised to David still belongs to Israel, not the church. The future exaltation of Jerusalem will be on earth, not in heaven. Christ will reign personally on this earth as we know it, as well as in the new heavens and the new earth (Revelation 22:1,3).

Why have we afflicted our souls, and
    You take no notice?'

"In fact, in the day of your fast you
    find pleasure,
And exploit all your laborers.
4 Indeed you fast for strife and debate,
    And to strike with the fist of
      wickedness.
You will not fast as *you do* this day,
To make your voice heard on high.
5 Is it a fast that I have chosen,
    A day for a man to afflict his soul?
Is it to bow down his head like a
    bulrush,
    And to spread out sackcloth and
      ashes?
Would you call this a fast,
    And an acceptable day to the LORD?

6 "*Is* this not the fast that I have chosen:
    To loose the bonds of wickedness,
    To undo the heavy burdens,
    To let the oppressed go free,
    And that you break every yoke?
7 *Is it* not to share your bread with the
    hungry,
    And that you bring to your house the
      poor who are cast out;
When you see the naked, that you
    cover him,
    And not hide yourself from your own
      flesh?

58:3–7 Why. God did not recognize the people's half-hearted fasting, and they complained. Their hypocritical fasting led to contention, quarreling, and pretense, and kept them from genuinely praying to God. True fasting involved penitence and humility, repentance from sin, feeding the hungry, and acting humanely toward the needy.

---

8 Then your light shall break forth like
    the morning,
Your healing shall spring forth
    speedily,
And your righteousness shall go
    before you;
The glory of the LORD shall be your
    rear guard.
9 Then you shall call, and the LORD
    will answer;
You shall cry, and He will say, 'Here I
    am.'

"If you take away the yoke from your
    midst,
The pointing of the finger, and
    speaking wickedness,

58:9 Here I am. The Lord will respond to the prayers of His people when they are converted and give evidence of a repentant heart (vv. 9,10). Israel will truly repent at the time of Christ's return.

---

10 *If* you extend your soul to the hungry
    And satisfy the afflicted soul,
Then your light shall dawn in the
    darkness,
    And your darkness shall *be* as the
      noonday.
11 The LORD will guide you continually,
    And satisfy your soul in drought,
    And strengthen your bones;
You shall be like a watered garden,
    And like a spring of water, whose
      waters do not fail.
12 Those from among you
    Shall build the old waste places;
You shall raise up the foundations of
    many generations;
    And you shall be called the Repairer
      of the Breach,
The Restorer of Streets to Dwell In.

13 "If you turn away your foot from the
    Sabbath,
From doing your pleasure on My holy
    day,
    And call the Sabbath a delight,
The holy *day* of the LORD honorable,
And shall honor Him, not doing your
    own ways,
Nor finding your own pleasure,
    Nor speaking *your own* words,
14 Then you shall delight yourself in the
    LORD;
And I will cause you to ride on the
    high hills of the earth,
And feed you with the heritage of
    Jacob your father.
The mouth of the LORD has spoken."

Separated from God

59 Behold, the LORD's hand is not
    shortened,
    That it cannot save;
Nor His ear heavy,
    That it cannot hear.

2   But your iniquities have separated you
        from your God;
     And your sins have hidden *His* face
        from you,
     So that He will not hear.
3   For your hands are defiled with blood,
     And your fingers with iniquity;
     Your lips have spoken lies,
     Your tongue has muttered perversity.

4   No one calls for justice,
     Nor does *any* plead for truth.
     They trust in empty words and speak
        lies;
     They conceive evil and bring forth
        iniquity.
5   They hatch vipers' eggs and weave the
        spider's web;
     He who eats of their eggs dies,
     And *from* that which is crushed a
        viper breaks out.

6   Their webs will not become garments,
     Nor will they cover themselves with
        their works;
     Their works *are* works of iniquity,
     And the act of violence *is* in their
        hands.
7   Their feet run to evil,
     And they make haste to shed
        innocent blood;
     Their thoughts *are* thoughts of
        iniquity;
     Wasting and destruction *are* in their
        paths.
8   The way of peace they have not
        known,
     And *there is* no justice in their ways;
     They have made themselves crooked
        paths;
     Whoever takes that way shall not
        know peace.

59:7,8 Their feet...shall not know peace. Isaiah focused on the national depravity of Israel that stood
in the way of God's deliverance. What was true of sinful Israel is indicative of the depravity of all mankind
(Rom. 3:15–17).

Sin Confessed
9   Therefore justice is far from us,
     Nor does righteousness overtake us;
     We look for light, but there is
        darkness!

     For brightness, *but* we walk in
        blackness!
10   We grope for the wall like the blind,
     And we grope as if *we had* no eyes;
     We stumble at noonday as at twilight;
     We are as dead *men* in desolate places.
11   We all growl like bears,
     And moan sadly like doves;
     We look for justice, but *there is* none;
     For salvation, *but* it is far from us.
12   For our transgressions are multiplied
        before You,
     And our sins testify against us;
     For our transgressions *are* with us,
     And *as for* our iniquities, we know
        them:
13   In transgressing and lying against the
        LORD,
     And departing from our God,
     Speaking oppression and revolt,
     Conceiving and uttering from the
        heart words of falsehood.
14   Justice is turned back,
     And righteousness stands afar off;
     For truth is fallen in the street,
     And equity cannot enter.

59:12–14 transgressions...sins. Israel's sins remained an obstacle to God's deliverance. They performed religious rituals with impure motives, which
kept them from God (Matt. 12:34). The presence of sin
eliminates righteousness.

15   So truth fails,
     And he *who* departs from evil makes
        himself a prey.

The Redeemer of Zion
     Then the LORD saw *it*, and it
        displeased Him
     That *there was* no justice.
16   He saw that *there was* no man,
     And wondered that *there was* no
        intercessor;
     Therefore His own arm brought
        salvation for Him;
     And His own righteousness, it
        sustained Him.
17   For He put on righteousness as a
        breastplate,
     And a helmet of salvation on His
        head;
     He put on the garments of vengeance
        for clothing,

59:17 righteousness as a breastplate...helmet of salvation. The Lord armed Himself for the deliverance of His people and for taking vengeance on His enemies. Paul used this terminology to describe a believer's spiritual preparation for warding off Satan's attacks (Eph. 6:14,17).

60:3 Gentiles shall come. Jerusalem's light will attract other nations seeking relief from darkness. Believing Jews and Gentiles will enter the earthly kingdom after the Day of the Lord. During the 1,000 years, nations will be populated by unbelievers, but the glory and power of the King in Jerusalem will draw those Gentiles to His light.

And was clad with zeal as a cloak.

18 According to *their* deeds, accordingly
      He will repay,
   Fury to His adversaries,
   Recompense to His enemies;
   The coastlands He will fully repay.

19 So shall they fear
   The name of the LORD from the west,
   And His glory from the rising of the
      sun;
   When the enemy comes in like a
      flood,
   The Spirit of the LORD will lift up a
      standard against him.

20 "The Redeemer will come to Zion,
   And to those who turn from
      transgression in Jacob,"
   Says the LORD.

21 "As for Me," says the LORD, "this *is* My covenant with them: My Spirit who *is* upon you, and My words which I have put in your mouth, shall not depart from your mouth, nor from the mouth of your descendants, nor from the mouth of your descendants' descendants," says the LORD, "from this time and forevermore."

The Gentiles Bless Zion

60 Arise, shine;
      For your light has come!
   And the glory of the LORD is risen
      upon you.

2 For behold, the darkness shall cover
      the earth,
   And deep darkness the people;
   But the LORD will arise over you,
   And His glory will be seen upon you.

3 The Gentiles shall come to your light,
   And kings to the brightness of your
      rising.

4 "Lift up your eyes all around, and see:
   They all gather together, they come to
      you;
   Your sons shall come from afar,

And your daughters shall be nursed at
   your side.

5 Then you shall see and become
      radiant,
   And your heart shall swell with joy;
   Because the abundance of the sea
      shall be turned to you,
   The wealth of the Gentiles shall come
      to you.

6 The multitude of camels shall cover
      your *land,*
   The dromedaries of Midian and
      Ephah;
   All those from Sheba shall come;
   They shall bring gold and incense,
   And they shall proclaim the praises of
      the LORD.

7 All the flocks of Kedar shall be
      gathered together to you,
   The rams of Nebaioth shall minister
      to you;
   They shall ascend with acceptance on
      My altar,
   And I will glorify the house of My
      glory.

8 "Who *are* these *who* fly like a cloud,
   And like doves to their roosts?

9 Surely the coastlands shall wait for
      Me;
   And the ships of Tarshish *will come*
      first,
   To bring your sons from afar,
   Their silver and their gold with them,
   To the name of the LORD your God,
   And to the Holy One of Israel,
   Because He has glorified you.

10 "The sons of foreigners shall build up
      your walls,
   And their kings shall minister to you;
   For in My wrath I struck you,
   But in My favor I have had mercy on
      you.

11 Therefore your gates shall be open
      continually;

They shall not be shut day or night,
That *men* may bring to you the
   wealth of the Gentiles,
And their kings in procession.
12 For the nation and kingdom which
   will not serve you shall perish,
And *those* nations shall be utterly
   ruined.

13 "The glory of Lebanon shall come to
   you,
The cypress, the pine, and the box
   tree together,
To beautify the place of My
   sanctuary;
And I will make the place of My feet
   glorious.
14 Also the sons of those who afflicted
   you
Shall come bowing to you,
And all those who despised you shall
   fall prostrate at the soles of your
   feet;
And they shall call you The City of
   the LORD,
Zion of the Holy One of Israel.

15 "Whereas you have been forsaken and
   hated,
So that no one went through *you,*
I will make you an eternal excellence,
A joy of many generations.
16 You shall drink the milk of the
   Gentiles,
And milk the breast of kings;
You shall know that I, the LORD, *am*
   your Savior
And your Redeemer, the Mighty One
   of Jacob.

60:16 milk...milk. As a mother feeds her infant, so Gentiles and kings will provide wealth and power to Zion. The city, as well as "all flesh" (49:26), will recognize the Lord as her Savior and Redeemer, "the Mighty One of Jacob."

17 "Instead of bronze I will bring gold,
Instead of iron I will bring silver,
Instead of wood, bronze,
And instead of stones, iron.
I will also make your officers peace,
And your magistrates righteousness.
18 Violence shall no longer be heard in
   your land,

Neither wasting nor destruction
   within your borders;
But you shall call your walls
   Salvation,
And your gates Praise.

God the Glory of His People

19 "The sun shall no longer be your light
   by day,
Nor for brightness shall the moon
   give light to you;
But the LORD will be to you an
   everlasting light,
And your God your glory.
20 Your sun shall no longer go down,
Nor shall your moon withdraw itself;
For the LORD will be your everlasting
   light,
And the days of your mourning shall
   be ended.
21 Also your people *shall* all *be*
   righteous;
They shall inherit the land forever,
The branch of My planting,
The work of My hands,
That I may be glorified.
22 A little one shall become a thousand,
And a small one a strong nation.
I, the LORD, will hasten it in its
   time."

The Good News of Salvation

61 "The Spirit of the Lord GOD *is*
   upon Me,
Because the LORD has anointed Me
To preach good tidings to the poor;
He has sent Me to heal the
   brokenhearted,
To proclaim liberty to the captives,
And the opening of the prison to
   those who are bound;
2 To proclaim the acceptable year of the
   LORD,
And the day of vengeance of our God;
To comfort all who mourn,

61:1,2a The Spirit...acceptable year of the LORD. The Servant of the Lord will be the ultimate Preacher and Redeemer of Israel. Jesus refers to His ministry of providing salvation to the spiritually oppressed as the initial fulfillment of this promise (Luke 4:18,19,21). The promise will be ultimately fulfilled in the end time, even though many Jews have been saved from the time of Christ until now (see Zech. 12:10–13).

³ To console those who mourn in Zion,
To give them beauty for ashes,
The oil of joy for mourning,
The garment of praise for the spirit of
   heaviness;
That they may be called trees of
   righteousness,
The planting of the LORD, that He
   may be glorified."

⁴ And they shall rebuild the old ruins,
They shall raise up the former
   desolations,
And they shall repair the ruined cities,
The desolations of many generations.
⁵ Strangers shall stand and feed your
   flocks,
And the sons of the foreigner
Shall be your plowmen and your
   vinedressers.
⁶ But you shall be named the priests of
   the LORD,
They shall call you the servants of our
   God.
You shall eat the riches of the
   Gentiles,
And in their glory you shall boast.
⁷ Instead of your shame *you shall have*
   double *honor,*
And *instead of* confusion they shall
   rejoice in their portion.
Therefore in their land they shall
   possess double;
Everlasting joy shall be theirs.

⁸ "For I, the LORD, love justice;
I hate robbery for burnt offering;
I will direct their work in truth,
And will make with them an
   everlasting covenant.
⁹ Their descendants shall be known
   among the Gentiles,
And their offspring among the people.
All who see them shall acknowledge
   them,
That they *are* the posterity *whom* the
   LORD has blessed."

¹⁰ I will greatly rejoice in the LORD,
My soul shall be joyful in my God;
For He has clothed me with the
   garments of salvation,

He has covered me with the robe of
   righteousness,
As a bridegroom decks *himself* with
   ornaments,
And as a bride adorns *herself* with her
   jewels.

61:10 clothed me...covered me. When a sinner recognizes that he cannot achieve righteousness by works, repents, and calls on the mercy of God, the Lord covers him with His own righteousness by grace. This is the heart of the New Covenant.

¹¹ For as the earth brings forth its bud,
As the garden causes the things that
   are sown in it to spring forth,
So the Lord GOD will cause
   righteousness and praise to spring
   forth before all the nations.

Assurance of Zion's Salvation

62 For Zion's sake I will not hold My
   peace,
And for Jerusalem's sake I will not
   rest,
Until her righteousness goes forth as
   brightness,
And her salvation as a lamp *that*
   burns.
² The Gentiles shall see your
   righteousness,
And all kings your glory.
You shall be called by a new name,
Which the mouth of the LORD will
   name.
³ You shall also be a crown of glory
In the hand of the LORD,
And a royal diadem
In the hand of your God.
⁴ You shall no longer be termed
   Forsaken,
Nor shall your land any more be
   termed Desolate;
But you shall be called Hephzibah,^a
   and your land Beulah;^b
For the LORD delights in you,
And your land shall be married.
⁵ For *as* a young man marries a virgin,
So shall your sons marry you;
And *as* the bridegroom rejoices over
   the bride,
So shall your God rejoice over you.

---

^{62:4} ^aLiterally *My Delight Is in Her* ^bLiterally *Married*

62:5 sons marry you. "Marry" refers to occupying and possessing the city.

6   I have set watchmen on your walls,
        O Jerusalem;
    They shall never hold their peace day
        or night.
    You who make mention of the LORD,
        do not keep silent,
7   And give Him no rest till He
        establishes
    And till He makes Jerusalem a praise
        in the earth.

8   The LORD has sworn by His right
        hand
    And by the arm of His strength:
    "Surely I will no longer give your grain
    As food for your enemies;
    And the sons of the foreigner shall
        not drink your new wine,
    For which you have labored.
9   But those who have gathered it shall
        eat it,
    And praise the LORD;
    Those who have brought it together
        shall drink it in My holy courts."

10 Go through,
    Go through the gates!
    Prepare the way for the people;
    Build up,
    Build up the highway!
    Take out the stones,
    Lift up a banner for the peoples!

11 Indeed the LORD has proclaimed
    To the end of the world:
    "Say to the daughter of Zion,
    'Surely your salvation is coming;
    Behold, His reward is with Him,
    And His work before Him.' "
12 And they shall call them The Holy
        People,
    The Redeemed of the LORD;
    And you shall be called Sought Out,
    A City Not Forsaken.

The LORD in Judgment and Salvation

63 Who is this who comes from Edom,
    With dyed garments from Bozrah,
    This One who is glorious in His
        apparel,
    Traveling in the greatness of His
        strength?—

    "I who speak in righteousness, mighty
        to save."

2   Why is Your apparel red,
    And Your garments like one who
        treads in the winepress?

3   "I have trodden the winepress alone,
    And from the peoples no one was
        with Me.
    For I have trodden them in My anger,
    And trampled them in My fury;
    Their blood is sprinkled upon My
        garments,
    And I have stained all My robes.

63:3 anger...fury...blood. The splattered grape juice staining the Savior's clothing is the "blood" of those He destroyed in judgment. John alludes to vv. 1–3 in describing the second coming of Christ, the Warrior-King (Rev. 19:13,15).

4   For the day of vengeance is in My
        heart,
    And the year of My redeemed has
        come.
5   I looked, but there was no one to
        help,
    And I wondered
    That there was no one to uphold;
    Therefore My own arm brought
        salvation for Me;
    And My own fury, it sustained Me.
6   I have trodden down the peoples in
        My anger,
    Made them drunk in My fury,
    And brought down their strength to
        the earth."

God's Mercy Remembered

7   I will mention the lovingkindnesses of
        the LORD
    And the praises of the LORD,
    According to all that the LORD has
        bestowed on us,
    And the great goodness toward the
        house of Israel,
    Which He has bestowed on them
        according to His mercies,
    According to the multitude of His
        lovingkindnesses.

8 For He said, "Surely they *are* My people,
Children *who* will not lie."
So He became their Savior.

9 In all their affliction He was afflicted,
And the Angel of His Presence saved them;
In His love and in His pity He redeemed them;
And He bore them and carried them
All the days of old.

10 But they rebelled and grieved His Holy Spirit;
So He turned Himself against them as an enemy,
And He fought against them.

63:9,10 Angel of His Presence. The Lord is the Angel who delivered Israel from Egypt (Ex. 14:19). He is sometimes called the Angel of the Lord. He was close enough to His people that He felt their afflictions as if they were His own. **rebelled and grieved His Holy Spirit.** Israel continually turned her back on God in spite of His love toward her (Num. 20:10). The Holy Spirit is a Person, since only a person can be grieved.

11 Then he remembered the days of old,
Moses *and* his people, *saying:*
"Where *is* He who brought them up out of the sea
With the shepherd of His flock?
Where *is* He who put His Holy Spirit within them,

12 Who led *them* by the right hand of Moses,
With His glorious arm,
Dividing the water before them
To make for Himself an everlasting name,

13 Who led them through the deep,
As a horse in the wilderness,
That they might not stumble?"

14 As a beast goes down into the valley,
And the Spirit of the LORD causes him to rest,
So You lead Your people,
To make Yourself a glorious name.

A Prayer of Penitence

15 Look down from heaven,
And see from Your habitation, holy and glorious.

Where *are* Your zeal and Your strength,
The yearning of Your heart and Your mercies toward me?
Are they restrained?

16 Doubtless You *are* our Father,
Though Abraham was ignorant of us,
And Israel does not acknowledge us.
You, O LORD, *are* our Father;
Our Redeemer from Everlasting *is* Your name.

63:16 Abraham...Israel. The Jews had sinned by resting in the privilege of their descent from Abraham and Jacob (see Matt. 3:9), but they finally renounce that to trust God alone as Father.

17 O LORD, why have You made us stray from Your ways,
And hardened our heart from Your fear?
Return for Your servants' sake,
The tribes of Your inheritance.

18 Your holy people have possessed *it* but a little while;
Our adversaries have trodden down Your sanctuary.

19 We have become *like* those of old,
over whom You never ruled,
Those who were never called by Your name.

64 Oh, that You would rend the heavens!
That You would come down!
That the mountains might shake at Your presence—

2 As fire burns brushwood,
As fire causes water to boil—
To make Your name known to Your adversaries,
That the nations may tremble at Your presence!

64:1,2 rend the heavens...shake at Your presence. Israel pleaded that God would execute vengeance on her enemies (see Ps. 18:7–9), manifesting judgment as He had done at Mount Sinai (Ex. 19:18). God's name is to receive glory through His redemption of Israel and to be recognized because of His judgment against her enemies (Ps. 99:1).

3 When You did awesome things *for which* we did not look,

You came down,
The mountains shook at Your
presence.

4 For since the beginning of the world
Men have not heard nor perceived by
the ear,
Nor has the eye seen any God besides
You,
Who acts for the one who waits for
Him.

5 You meet him who rejoices and does
righteousness,
Who remembers You in Your ways.
You are indeed angry, for we have
sinned—
In these ways we continue;
And we need to be saved.

6 But we are all like an unclean *thing*,
And all our righteousnesses *are* like
filthy rags;
We all fade as a leaf,
And our iniquities, like the wind,
Have taken us away.

7 And *there is* no one who calls on Your
name,
Who stirs himself up to take hold of
You;
For You have hidden Your face from
us,
And have consumed us because of our
iniquities.

8 But now, O LORD,
You *are* our Father;
We *are* the clay, and You our potter;
And all we *are* the work of Your hand.

9 Do not be furious, O LORD,
Nor remember iniquity forever;
Indeed, please look—we all *are* Your
people!

> **64:7–9 no one who calls.** Seeking and calling on the
> Lord (55:6,7) cannot occur without the conviction of
> the sinful heart by the Holy Spirit. This prayer recog-
> nizes God as a potter in control of the clay and pleads
> for Him to end His fury and memory of sin.

10 Your holy cities are a wilderness,
Zion is a wilderness,
Jerusalem a desolation.
11 Our holy and beautiful temple,
Where our fathers praised You,
Is burned up with fire;

And all our pleasant things are laid
waste.
12 Will You restrain Yourself because of
these *things*, O LORD?
Will You hold Your peace, and afflict
us very severely?

The Righteousness of God's Judgment

65 "I was sought by *those who* did not
ask *for Me*;
I was found by *those who* did not seek
Me.
I said, 'Here I am, here I am,'
To a nation *that* was not called by My
name.

2 I have stretched out My hands all day
long to a rebellious people,
Who walk in a way *that is* not good,
According to their own thoughts;
3 A people who provoke Me to anger
continually to My face;
Who sacrifice in gardens,
And burn incense on altars of brick;
4 Who sit among the graves,
And spend the night in the tombs;
Who eat swine's flesh,
And the broth of abominable things is
in their vessels;
5 Who say, 'Keep to yourself,
Do not come near me,
For I am holier than you!'
These *are* smoke in My nostrils,
A fire that burns all the day.

6 "Behold, *it is* written before Me:
I will not keep silence, but will
repay—
Even repay into their bosom—
7 Your iniquities and the iniquities of
your fathers together,"
Says the LORD,
"Who have burned incense on the
mountains
And blasphemed Me on the hills;
Therefore I will measure their former
work into their bosom."

8 Thus says the LORD:

"As the new wine is found in the
cluster,
And *one* says, 'Do not destroy it,
For a blessing *is* in it,'
So will I do for My servants' sake,

ISAIAH'S DESCRIPTION OF ISRAEL'S FUTURE KINGDOM

Description	Isaiah passages
1. The Lord will restore the faithful remnant of Israel to the Land to inhabit the kingdom at its beginning.	1:9,25–27; 3:10; 4:3; 6:13; 8:10; 9:1; 10:20,22,25,27; 11:11,12,16; 14:1,2; 14:22,26; 26:1–4; 27:12; 28:5; 35:9; 37:4,31,32; 40:2,3; 41:9; 43:5,6; 46:3,4; 49:5,8; 49:12,22; 51:11; 54:7–10; 55:12; 57:13,18; 60:4,9; 61:1–4,7; 65:8–10; 66:8,9,19
2. As the Lord defeats Israel's enemies, He will provide protection for His people.	4:5,6; 9:1,4; 12:1–6; 13:4; 14:2; 21:9; 26:4,5; 27:1–4; 30:30,31; 32:2; 33:16,22; 35:4; 49:8,9; 49:17,18; 52:6; 54:9,10; 55:10,11; 58:12; 60:10,12,18; 62:9; 66:16
3. In her kingdom, Israel will enjoy great prosperity of many kinds.	26:15,19; 27:2,13; 29:18–20; 22:22,23; 30:20; 32:3; 32:15–20; 33:6,24; 35:3,5,6,8–10; 40:11; 42:6,7,16; 43:5,6,8,10,21; 44:5,14; 46:13; 48:6; 49:10; 52:9; 54:2,3; 55:1,12; 58:9,14; 60:5,16,21; 61:4,6–10; 62:5; 65:13–15,18,24; 66:21,22
4. The city of Jerusalem will rise to world preeminence in the kingdom.	2:2–4; 18:7; 25:6; 40:5,9; 49:19–21; 60:1–5,13–15, 17; 62:3,4
5. Israel will be the center of world attention in the kingdom.	23:18; 54:1–3; 55:5; 56:6–8; 60:5–9; 66:18–21
6. Israel's mission in the kingdom will be to glorify the Lord.	60:21; 61:3
7. Gentiles in the kingdom will receive blessing through the channel of faithful Israel.	11:10; 19:18,24,25; 42:6; 45:22,23; 49:6; 51:5; 56:3,6–8; 60:3,7,8; 61:5; 66:19
8. Worldwide peace will prevail in the kingdom under the rule of the Prince of Peace.	2:4; 9:5,6; 11:10; 19:23; 26:12; 32:18; 54:14; 57:19; 66:12
9. Moral and spiritual conditions in the kingdom will reach their highest plane since the Fall of Adam.	27:6; 28:6,17; 32:16; 42:7; 44:3; 45:8; 51:4; 61:11; 65:21,22
10. Governmental leadership in the kingdom will be superlative with the Messiah heading it up.	9:6,7; 11:2,3; 16:5; 24:23; 25:3; 32:1; 32:5; 33:22; 42:1,4; 43:15; 52:13; 53:12; 55:3–5
11. Humans will enjoy long life in the kingdom.	65:20,22
12. Knowledge of the Lord will be universal in the kingdom.	11:9; 19:21; 33:13; 40:5; 41:20; 45:6,14; 49:26; 52:10,13,15; 54:13; 66:23
13. The world of nature will enjoy a great renewal in the kingdom.	12:3; 30:23–26; 32:15; 35:1–4,6,7; 41:18,19; 43:19,20; 44:3,23; 55:1,2,13; 58:10,11
14. "Wild" animals will be tame in the kingdom.	11:6–9; 35:9; 65:25
15. Sorrow and mourning will not exist in the kingdom.	25:8; 60:20
16. An eternal kingdom, as a part of God's new creation, will follow the millennial kingdom.	24:23; 51:6; 51:16; 54:11,12; 60:11,19; 65:17
17. The King will judge overt sin in the kingdom.	66:24

That I may not destroy them all.

9 I will bring forth descendants from
    Jacob,
And from Judah an heir of My
    mountains;
My elect shall inherit it,
And My servants shall dwell there.

10 Sharon shall be a fold of flocks,
And the Valley of Achor a place for
    herds to lie down,
For My people who have sought Me.

11 "But you *are* those who forsake the
    LORD,
Who forget My holy mountain,
Who prepare a table for Gad,*a*
And who furnish a drink offering for
    Meni.*b*

12 Therefore I will number you for the
    sword,
And you shall all bow down to the
    slaughter;
Because, when I called, you did not
    answer;
When I spoke, you did not hear,
But did evil before My eyes,
And chose *that* in which I do not
    delight."

13 Therefore thus says the Lord GOD:

"Behold, My servants shall eat,
But you shall be hungry;
Behold, My servants shall drink,
But you shall be thirsty;
Behold, My servants shall rejoice,
But you shall be ashamed;

14 Behold, My servants shall sing for joy
    of heart,
But you shall cry for sorrow of heart,
And wail for grief of spirit.

15 You shall leave your name as a curse
    to My chosen;
For the Lord GOD will slay you,
And call His servants by another
    name;

16 So that he who blesses himself in the
    earth
Shall bless himself in the God of
    truth;
And he who swears in the earth
Shall swear by the God of truth;

Because the former troubles are
    forgotten,
And because they are hidden from My
    eyes.

65:16 God of truth. This means "God of Amen" and refers to the True God, who will fulfill His promises to Israel and vindicate Himself in the eyes of all people. In the kingdom of the Messiah, all blessing and swearing will be by the True God, as only the redeemed remnant will be left, and all idols will be vanquished and forgotten.

The Glorious New Creation

17 "For behold, I create new heavens and
    a new earth;
And the former shall not be
    remembered or come to mind.

18 But be glad and rejoice forever in what
    I create;
For behold, I create Jerusalem *as* a
    rejoicing,
And her people a joy.

19 I will rejoice in Jerusalem,
And joy in My people;
The voice of weeping shall no longer
    be heard in her,
Nor the voice of crying.

20 "No more shall an infant from there
    live but a few days,
Nor an old man who has not fulfilled
    his days;
For the child shall die one hundred
    years old,
But the sinner *being* one hundred
    years old shall be accursed.

65:20 No more shall an infant...Nor an old man. Long life will prevail in the millennial kingdom. Death will occur, but not as early as in the time of Isaiah. **sinner...accursed.** During the millennial phase, a sinful person may die at age 100, which will be considered a premature death, as a punishment for sin. The curse will be reversed in the Millennium, but it will not be removed until the eternal state (Rev. 22:3).

21 They shall build houses and inhabit
    them;
They shall plant vineyards and eat
    their fruit.

22 They shall not build and another
    inhabit;

65:11 *a*Literally *Troop* or *Fortune,* a pagan deity   *b*Literally *Number* or *Destiny,* a pagan deity

They shall not plant and another eat;
For as the days of a tree, *so shall be*
the days of My people,
And My elect shall long enjoy the
work of their hands.
23 They shall not labor in vain,
Nor bring forth children for trouble;
For they *shall be* the descendants of
the blessed of the LORD,
And their offspring with them.
24 "It shall come to pass
That before they call, I will answer;
And while they are still speaking, I
will hear.
25 The wolf and the lamb shall feed
together,
The lion shall eat straw like the ox,
And dust *shall be* the serpent's food.
They shall not hurt nor destroy in all
My holy mountain,"
Says the LORD.

True Worship and False

66 Thus says the LORD:

"Heaven *is* My throne,
And earth *is* My footstool.
Where *is* the house that you will build
Me?
And where *is* the place of My rest?
2 For all those *things* My hand has made,
And all those *things* exist,"
Says the LORD.
"But on this *one* will I look:
On *him who is* poor and of a contrite
spirit,
And who trembles at My word.

> **66:1,2** God is not looking to dwell in a temple of stone, but He desires to dwell in a tender and broken heart that is not concerned with the externalities of religion (see Matt. 5:3–9). God desires the heart of a person who takes His word seriously (see John 14:23).

3 "He who kills a bull *is as if* he slays a
man;
He who sacrifices a lamb, *as if* he
breaks a dog's neck;
He who offers a grain offering, *as if he
offers* swine's blood;
He who burns incense, *as if* he blesses
an idol.

Just as they have chosen their own
ways,
And their soul delights in their
abominations,
4 So will I choose their delusions,
And bring their fears on them;
Because, when I called, no one
answered,
When I spoke they did not hear;
But they did evil before My eyes,
And chose *that* in which I do not
delight."

The LORD Vindicates Zion

5 Hear the word of the LORD,
You who tremble at His word:
"Your brethren who hated you,
Who cast you out for My name's sake,
said,
'Let the LORD be glorified,
That we may see your joy.'
But they shall be ashamed."

6 The sound of noise from the city!
A voice from the temple!
The voice of the LORD,
Who fully repays His enemies!

7 "Before she was in labor, she gave
birth;
Before her pain came,
She delivered a male child.
8 Who has heard such a thing?
Who has seen such things?
Shall the earth be made to give birth
in one day?
Or shall a nation be born at once?
For as soon as Zion was in labor,
She gave birth to her children.
9 Shall I bring to the time of birth, and
not cause delivery?" says the
LORD.
"Shall I who cause delivery shut up *the
womb?*" says your God.

> **66:7–9** Israel's suffering will end with a delivery, as birth can come only after labor pains have occurred (see Jer. 30:6,7). The Lord will not allow the remnant to suffer agony without bringing them to the kingdom.

10 "Rejoice with Jerusalem,
And be glad with her, all you who love
her;

Rejoice for joy with her, all you who
mourn for her;
11 That you may feed and be satisfied
With the consolation of her bosom,
That you may drink deeply and be
delighted
With the abundance of her glory."

12For thus says the LORD:

"Behold, I will extend peace to her like
a river,
And the glory of the Gentiles like a
flowing stream.
Then you shall feed;
On *her* sides shall you be carried,
And be dandled on *her* knees.
13 As one whom his mother comforts,
So I will comfort you;
And you shall be comforted in
Jerusalem."

The Reign and Indignation of God
14 When you see *this*, your heart shall
rejoice,
And your bones shall flourish like
grass;
The hand of the LORD shall be known
to His servants,
And *His* indignation to His enemies.
15 For behold, the LORD will come with
fire
And with His chariots, like a
whirlwind,
To render His anger with fury,
And His rebuke with flames of fire.
16 For by fire and by His sword
The LORD will judge all flesh;
And the slain of the LORD shall be
many.

17 "Those who sanctify themselves and
purify themselves,
To go to the gardens
After an *idol* in the midst,
Eating swine's flesh and the
abomination and the mouse,
Shall be consumed together," says the
LORD.

18"For I *know* their works and their
thoughts. It shall be that I will gather all

nations and tongues; and they shall come
and see My glory. 19I will set a sign among
them; and those among them who escape I
will send to the nations: *to* Tarshish and
Pul[a] and Lud, who draw the bow, and Tubal
and Javan, *to* the coastlands afar off who
have not heard My fame nor seen My glory.
And they shall declare My glory among the
Gentiles. 20Then they shall bring all your
brethren for an offering to the LORD out of
all nations, on horses and in chariots and
in litters, on mules and on camels, to My
holy mountain Jerusalem," says the LORD,
"as the children of Israel bring an offering
in a clean vessel into the house of the
LORD. 21And I will also take some of them
for priests *and* Levites," says the LORD.

66:17 sanctify themselves and purify themselves.
Sanctification and purification for the purposes of
idol worship will bring God's judgment.

22 "For as the new heavens and the new
earth
Which I will make shall remain before
Me," says the LORD,
"So shall your descendants and your
name remain.
23 And it shall come to pass
That from one New Moon to
another,
And from one Sabbath to another,
All flesh shall come to worship before
Me," says the LORD.

24 "And they shall go forth and look
Upon the corpses of the men
Who have transgressed against Me.
For their worm does not die,
And their fire is not quenched.
They shall be an abhorrence to all
flesh."

66:24 worm does not die...fire is not quenched.
The corpses of those enduring everlasting torment
will serve to remind everyone of the terrible consequences of rebellion against God. Jesus referred to
the Valley of Hinnom (Gehenna), where a continually burning trash-heap pictured the never-ending
pain of the lost (Mark 9:47,48).

66:19 aFollowing Masoretic Text and Targum; Septuagint reads *Put* (compare Jeremiah 46:9).

JEREMIAH

Anyone serious about knowing what life was like for a prophet must read Jeremiah's writing. His books are autobiographical in more intimate ways than in any other prophet. He not only includes the details of his ministry and the responses he received, but he also recounts the difficulties he faced and the rejection and anger he felt. Jeremiah's name means "Jehovah throws," a term used to refer to laying a foundation. It can also mean "Jehovah establishes, appoints, or sends."

AUTHOR AND DATE

Jeremiah was written by Jeremiah during his ministry, approximately 627 to 570 B.C.

Jeremiah served two vocations during his lifetime: priest and prophet. His hometown was the small village of Anathoth (1:1). He never married. God instructed him to use his celibacy as an object lesson about the hopelessness of days to come for Judah (16:1–4). Jeremiah's life was so filled with sorrow and conflict that he has long been known as the "weeping prophet" (9:1; 13:17; 14:17). His prophecies about the impending judgments coming in the form of invading Babylonians earned him threats, a death penalty trial, punishment in stocks, public humiliation, and imprisonment in a pit. For a time he lived as a fugitive from king Jehoiakim.

During his ministry, Jeremiah was assisted by Baruch, a faithful scribe to whom the prophet dictated his messages. Baruch also copied and safeguarded Jeremiah's writings (36:4,32; 45:1). He served as Jeremiah's secretary and publisher.

The dates of Jeremiah's ministry span five decades. He began to prophesy in king Josiah's 13th year, or approximately 627 B.C. (1:2). Jeremiah continued his work beyond the fall of Jerusalem to Babylon in 586 B.C. (chapters 39,40, and 52). After Jerusalem's destruction, Jeremiah was forced to accompany a group fleeing to Egypt (chapters 43 and 44) where he continued to prophesy (44:30).

Events recorded in the final chapter lend some weight to an ancient Jewish tradition that Jeremiah was still alive during the Babylonian invasion of Egypt in 568/67 B.C. and was then taken captive to Babylon. If he was an eyewitness to the release of Judah's king Jehoiachin, imprisoned in Babylon since 597 B.C., then Jeremiah lived to the ripe old age of between 85 and 90 years (52:31–34).

BACKGROUND AND SETTING

Second Kings 22–25 and 2 Chronicles 34–36 describe the background details of Jeremiah's times. His messages paint word pictures of: (1) his people's sin; (2) the

invader God would send; (3) the rigors of siege; and (4) the horrors of destruction. For 40 years Jeremiah faithfully preached an unwelcome message of impending judgment. During that time, five different kings reigned in Judah: Josiah (640–609 B.C.), Jehoahaz (609 B.C.), Jehoiakim (609–598 B.C.), Jehoiachin (598–597 B.C.), and Zedekiah (597–586 B.C.).

Flagrant idol worship was the primary symptom of the desperate spiritual condition of Judah in Jeremiah's day. Even the horrific practice of child sacrifice, introduced by king Ahaz almost 100 years earlier and temporarily halted under king Hezekiah was again part of the religious life of Judah. King Josiah's reforms reached their apex in 622 B.C. with the abolishment of the worst of these practices, but the deadly cancer of sin simply hid in a temporary remission and flourished again after the shallow revival. Jeremiah's messages aimed at many of the ongoing symptoms of moral and spiritual disease: religious insincerity, dishonesty, adultery, injustice, tyranny against the helpless, and slander. Jeremiah's writing did little more than document the headlong rush of his people toward judgment.

Momentous events on the world stage occurred in Jeremiah's day. Assyria saw its power wane. By 612 B.C., Assyria's seemingly invincible capital, Nineveh, was destroyed. The rising Babylonian empire under Nabopolassar (625–605 B.C.) established its military dominance with victories over Assyria (612 B.C.), Egypt (609–605 B.C.), and Israel (605 B.C.–Daniel 1; 597 B.C.–2 Kings 24:10–16; and 586 B.C.–Jeremiah 39,40,52).

Jeremiah was rarely a single voice of prophecy. His ministry followed the ringing warnings of Joel and Micah. Jeremiah's early contemporaries were Habakkuk and Zephaniah. In Jeremiah's later years, Ezekiel and Daniel also ministered for God to His scattered people.

HISTORICAL AND THEOLOGICAL THEMES

The central theme in Jeremiah concerns God's judgment upon Judah (chapters 1–29). Alongside the somber warnings lie promises of eventual restoration in the future messianic kingdom (23:3–8; 30–33). Contrasted with Isaiah's many chapters about the future glory of Israel (Isaiah 40–66), however, Jeremiah devoted far less space to that subject. Since God's judgment was imminent, Jeremiah concentrated on the current problems as he labored to turn the nation back from the point of no return.

> JEREMIAH'S LIFE, HIS CALLING, AND HIS EXPERIENCES ALL COMBINE TO GIVE A PICTURE OF GOD'S PLANNING AND PURPOSE TO CARRY OUT HIS WILL.

A secondary theme highlights God's willingness to spare and bless the nation only if the people repent. This frequent emphasis receives its most graphic illustration in the potter's shop (18:1–11). The caring yet sovereign relationship between God and His people is further illustrated in the relationship between God and His prophet. Jeremiah's life, his calling, and his experiences all combine to give a picture of God's planning and purpose to carry out His will in persons and in nations (1:5–19; 15:19–21).

Other noteworthy themes in Jeremiah include: (1) God's longing for Israel to be tender toward Him, as in the days of first love (2:1–3); (2) Jeremiah's servant tears, as the "weeping prophet" (9:1; 14:17); (3) the close, intimate relationship God had with Israel and that He yearned to keep (13:11); (4) suffering, as in Jeremiah's trials (11:18–23; 20:1–18) and in God's sufficiency in all trouble (20:11–13); (5) the vital role that God's Word can play in life (15:16); (6) the place of faith in expecting restoration from the God for whom nothing is too difficult (32:17, 27); and (7) prayer for the fulfillment of God's will by God's action in restoring Israel to its land (33:3,6–18).

OUTLINE

1 The words of Jeremiah the son of Hilkiah, of the priests who *were* in Anathoth in the land of Benjamin, ²to whom the word of the LORD came in the days of Josiah the son of Amon, king of Judah, in the thirteenth year of his reign. ³It came also in the days of Jehoiakim the son of Josiah, king of Judah, until the end of the eleventh year of Zedekiah the son of Josiah, king of Judah, until the carrying away of Jerusalem captive in the fifth month.

> **1:2 in the days of.** Jeremiah's ministry spanned at least 5 decades. If he was 20–25 years old in 626 B.C., when Josiah was the king of Judah, then he was 60–65 in 586 B.C. when Jerusalem fell (chap. 39), and 85–90 if alive during the time of 52:31–34.

The Prophet Is Called

⁴Then the word of the LORD came to me, saying:

5   "Before I formed you in the womb I
          knew you;
     Before you were born I sanctified you;
     I ordained you a prophet to the
          nations."

⁶Then said I:

"Ah, Lord GOD!
     Behold, I cannot speak, for I *am* a
          youth."

⁷But the LORD said to me:

"Do not say, 'I *am* a youth,'
     For you shall go to all to whom I send
          you,
     And whatever I command you, you
          shall speak.
8   Do not be afraid of their faces,
     For I *am* with you to deliver you,"
          says the LORD.

⁹Then the LORD put forth His hand and touched my mouth, and the LORD said to me:

"Behold, I have put My words in your
          mouth.
10   See, I have this day set you over the
          nations and over the kingdoms,
     To root out and to pull down,

To destroy and to throw down,
     To build and to plant."

> **1:10 set you over.** Jeremiah's message had divine authority since God spoke through him.

¹¹Moreover the word of the LORD came to me, saying, "Jeremiah, what do you see?"

And I said, "I see a branch of an almond tree."

¹²Then the LORD said to me, "You have seen well, for I am ready to perform My word."

¹³And the word of the LORD came to me the second time, saying, "What do you see?"

And I said, "I see a boiling pot, and it is facing away from the north."

¹⁴Then the LORD said to me:

"Out of the north calamity shall break
          forth

ILLUSTRATIONS OF GOD'S JUDGMENT

An Almond Branch (1:11,12)
A Boiling Caldron (1:13–16)
Lions (2:15; 4:7; 5:6; 50:17)
A Scorching Storm Wind (4:11,12; 18:17; 23:19; 25:32)
Wolf (5:6)
Leopard (5:6)
Stripping Away Judah's Branches (5:10)
Fire (5:14)
Making This House (Worship Center) like Shiloh (7:14)
Serpents, Adders (8:17)
Destroying Olive Branches (11:16,17)
Uprooting (12:17)
Linen Sash Made Worthless (13:1–11)
Bottles Filled with Wine and Dashed Against One Another (13:12–14)
A Potter's Jar Shattered (19:10,11; cf. 22:28)
A Hammer [God's Word] Crushing a Rock (23:29)
A Cup of Wrath (25:15)
Zion Plowed as a Field (26:18)
Wearing Yokes of Wood and Iron (27:2; 28:13)
A Hammer [Babylon] (50:23)
A Mountain of Destruction [Babylon] (51:25)

On all the inhabitants of the land.
15 For behold, I am calling
All the families of the kingdoms of
the north," says the LORD;
"They shall come and each one set his
throne
At the entrance of the gates of
Jerusalem,
Against all its walls all around,
And against all the cities of Judah.
16 I will utter My judgments
Against them concerning all their
wickedness,
Because they have forsaken Me,
Burned incense to other gods,
And worshiped the works of their own
hands.

17 "Therefore prepare yourself and arise,
And speak to them all that I
command you.
Do not be dismayed before their
faces,
Lest I dismay you before them.
18 For behold, I have made you this day
A fortified city and an iron pillar,
And bronze walls against the whole
land—
Against the kings of Judah,
Against its princes,
Against its priests,
And against the people of the land.
19 They will fight against you,
But they shall not prevail against you.
For I *am* with you," says the LORD,
"to deliver you."

God's Case Against Israel

2 Moreover the word of the LORD came to
me, saying, 2"Go and cry in the hearing
of Jerusalem, saying, 'Thus says the LORD:

"I remember you,
The kindness of your youth,
The love of your betrothal,
When you went after Me in the
wilderness,
In a land not sown.
3 Israel *was* holiness to the LORD,
The firstfruits of His increase.
All that devour him will offend;

Disaster will come upon them," says
the LORD.' "

> **2:1–3 Jerusalem...Israel.** Jeremiah reminded Israel
> of God's sensitive care for them during their early
> history (v. 21). After centuries, many were forsaking
> God (vv. 5,31), practicing idolatry (vv. 11,27,28), and
> living without true salvation.

4"Hear the word of the LORD, O house of
Jacob and all the families of the house of
Israel. 5Thus says the LORD:

"What injustice have your fathers
found in Me,
That they have gone far from Me,
Have followed idols,
And have become idolaters?
6 Neither did they say, 'Where *is* the
LORD,
Who brought us up out of the land of
Egypt,
Who led us through the wilderness,
Through a land of deserts and pits,
Through a land of drought and the
shadow of death,
Through a land that no one crossed
And where no one dwelt?'
7 I brought you into a bountiful country,
To eat its fruit and its goodness.
But when you entered, you defiled My
land
And made My heritage an
abomination.
8 The priests did not say, 'Where *is* the
LORD?'
And those who handle the law did not
know Me;
The rulers also transgressed against
Me;
The prophets prophesied by Baal,
And walked after *things that* do not
profit.

9 "Therefore I will yet bring charges
against you," says the LORD,
"And against your children's children I
will bring charges.
10 For pass beyond the coasts of Cyprus*a*
and see,
Send to Kedar*b* and consider diligently,

2:10 *a*Hebrew *Kittim*, western lands, especially Cyprus   *b*In the northern Arabian desert,
representative of the eastern cultures

And see if there has been such *a thing.*

11 Has a nation changed *its* gods,
Which *are* not gods?
But My people have changed their Glory
For *what* does not profit.

12 Be astonished, O heavens, at this,
And be horribly afraid;
Be very desolate," says the LORD.

13 "For My people have committed two evils:
They have forsaken Me, the fountain of living waters,
And hewn themselves cisterns—broken cisterns that can hold no water.

14 "*Is* Israel a servant?
Is he a homeborn *slave?*
Why is he plundered?

15 The young lions roared at him, *and* growled;
They made his land waste;
His cities are burned, without inhabitant.

16 Also the people of Noph*ᵃ* and Tahpanhes

2:16 Noph...Tahpanhes. These two cities represent the entire country of Egypt.

Have broken the crown of your head.

17 Have you not brought this on yourself,

MAJOR TRIALS OF JEREMIAH

1. Trial By Death Threats (11:18–23)
2. Trial By Isolation (15:15–21)
3. Trial By Stocks (19:14–20:18)
4. Trial By Arrest (26:7–24)
5. Trial By Challenge (28:10–16)
6. Trial By Destruction (36:1–32)
7. Trial By Violence and Imprisonment (37:15)
8. Trial By Starvation (38:1–6)
9. Trial By Chains (40:1)
10. Trial By Rejection (42:1–43:4)

In that you have forsaken the LORD your God
When He led you in the way?

18 And now why take the road to Egypt,
To drink the waters of Sihor?
Or why take the road to Assyria,
To drink the waters of the River?*ᵃ*

19 Your own wickedness will correct you,
And your backslidings will rebuke you.
Know therefore and see that *it is* an evil and bitter *thing*
That you have forsaken the LORD your God,
And the fear of Me *is* not in you,"
Says the Lord GOD of hosts.

20 "For of old I have broken your yoke *and* burst your bonds;
And you said, 'I will not transgress,'
When on every high hill and under every green tree
You lay down, playing the harlot.

21 Yet I had planted you a noble vine, a seed of highest quality.
How then have you turned before Me
Into the degenerate plant of an alien vine?

22 For though you wash yourself with lye, and use much soap,
Yet your iniquity is marked before Me," says the Lord GOD.

23 "How can you say, 'I am not polluted,
I have not gone after the Baals'?
See your way in the valley;
Know what you have done:
You are a swift dromedary breaking loose in her ways,

2:23 the Baals. This refers to all false deities. **dromedary.** Israel's chasing after idols is likened to the animal instincts of a female camel and a wild donkey seeking to mate.

24 A wild donkey used to the wilderness,
That sniffs at the wind in her desire;
In her time of mating, who can turn her away?
All those who seek her will not weary themselves;
In her month they will find her.

2:16 *ᵃ*That is, Memphis in ancient Egypt   2:18 *ᵃ*That is, the Euphrates

²⁵ Withhold your foot from being
  unshod, and your throat from
  thirst.
 But you said, 'There is no hope.
 No! For I have loved aliens, and after
  them I will go.'

²⁶ "As the thief is ashamed when he is
  found out,
 So is the house of Israel ashamed;
 They and their kings and their
  princes, and their priests and their
  prophets,
²⁷ Saying to a tree, 'You *are* my father,'
 And to a stone, 'You gave birth to me.'
 For they have turned *their* back to
  Me, and not *their* face.
 But in the time of their trouble
 They will say, 'Arise and save us.'
²⁸ But where *are* your gods that you have
  made for yourselves?
 Let them arise,
 If they can save you in the time of
  your trouble;
 For *according to* the number of your
  cities
 Are your gods, O Judah.

²⁹ "Why will you plead with Me?
 You all have transgressed against Me,"
  says the LORD.
³⁰ "In vain I have chastened your
  children;
 They received no correction.
 Your sword has devoured your
  prophets
 Like a destroying lion.

³¹ "O generation, see the word of the
  LORD!
 Have I been a wilderness to Israel,
 Or a land of darkness?
 Why do My people say, 'We are lords;
 We will come no more to You'?
³² Can a virgin forget her ornaments,
 Or a bride her attire?
 Yet My people have forgotten Me days
  without number.

³³ "Why do you beautify your way to seek
  love?
 Therefore you have also taught
 The wicked women your ways.
³⁴ Also on your skirts is found

 The blood of the lives of the poor
  innocents.
 I have not found it by secret search,
 But plainly on all these things.
³⁵ Yet you say, 'Because I am innocent,
 Surely His anger shall turn from me.'
 Behold, I will plead My case against
  you,
 Because you say, 'I have not sinned.'
³⁶ Why do you gad about so much to
  change your way?
 Also you shall be ashamed of Egypt as
  you were ashamed of Assyria.
³⁷ Indeed you will go forth from him
 With your hands on your head;
 For the LORD has rejected your
  trusted allies,
 And you will not prosper by them.

Israel Is Shameless

3 "They say, 'If a man divorces his wife,
 And she goes from him
 And becomes another man's,
 May he return to her again?'
 Would not that land be greatly
  polluted?
 But you have played the harlot with
  many lovers;
 Yet return to Me," says the LORD.

3:1 If a man divorces. A man was not to take his ex-wife back again after divorcing her (Deut. 24:4), for this would be a scandal and would defile them. Israel was compared to a woman who has many lovers (2:18,25) and idols (2:23–25). The Lord would receive Israel back as His wife if she would repent (3:12–14).

² "Lift up your eyes to the desolate
  heights and see:
 Where have you not lain *with men?*
 By the road you have sat for them
 Like an Arabian in the wilderness;
 And you have polluted the land
 With your harlotries and your
  wickedness.
³ Therefore the showers have been
  withheld,
 And there has been no latter rain.
 You have had a harlot's forehead;
 You refuse to be ashamed.
⁴ Will you not from this time cry to
  Me,
 'My Father, You *are* the guide of my
  youth?

⁵   Will He remain angry forever?
        Will He keep it to the end?'
        Behold, you have spoken and done
            evil things,
        As you were able."

A Call to Repentance

⁶The LORD said also to me in the days of Josiah the king: "Have you seen what backsliding Israel has done? She has gone up on every high mountain and under every green tree, and there played the harlot. ⁷And I said, after she had done all these *things,* 'Return to Me.' But she did not return. And her treacherous sister Judah saw it. ⁸Then I saw that for all the causes for which backsliding Israel had committed adultery, I had put her away and given her a certificate of divorce; yet her treacherous sister Judah did not fear, but went and played the harlot also. ⁹So it came to pass, through her casual harlotry, that she defiled the land and committed adultery with stones and trees. ¹⁰And yet for all this her treacherous sister Judah has not turned to Me with her whole heart, but in pretense," says the LORD.

¹¹Then the LORD said to me, "Backsliding Israel has shown herself more righteous than treacherous Judah. ¹²Go and proclaim these words toward the north, and say:

        'Return, backsliding Israel,' says the
            LORD;
        'I will not cause My anger to fall on
            you.
        For I *am* merciful,' says the LORD;
        'I will not remain angry forever.
¹³   Only acknowledge your iniquity,
        That you have transgressed against
            the LORD your God,
        And have scattered your charms
        To alien deities under every green
            tree,
        And you have not obeyed My voice,'
            says the LORD.

¹⁴"Return, O backsliding children," says the LORD; "for I am married to you. I will take you, one from a city and two from a

3:14 I am married to you. God viewed His relationship with Israel as a marriage. He pleaded with Judah to repent from her wicked ways and to return to Him.

family, and I will bring you to Zion. ¹⁵And I will give you shepherds according to My heart, who will feed you with knowledge and understanding.

¹⁶"Then it shall come to pass, when you are multiplied and increased in the land in those days," says the LORD, "that they will say no more, 'The ark of the covenant of the LORD.' It shall not come to mind, nor shall they remember it, nor shall they visit *it,* nor shall it be made anymore.

¹⁷"At that time Jerusalem shall be called The Throne of the LORD, and all the nations shall be gathered to it, to the name of the LORD, to Jerusalem. No more shall they follow the dictates of their evil hearts.

¹⁸"In those days the house of Judah shall walk with the house of Israel, and they shall come together out of the land of the north to the land that I have given as an inheritance to your fathers.

¹⁹"But I said:

        'How can I put you among the
            children
        And give you a pleasant land,
        A beautiful heritage of the hosts of
            nations?'

"And I said:

        'You shall call Me, "My Father,"
        And not turn away from Me.'

3:20 O...Israel. Since the northern kingdom of Israel had been completely dispersed (722 B.C.), Jeremiah at times referred to just Judah as Israel (3:20–23).

²⁰   Surely, *as* a wife treacherously departs
            from her husband,
        So have you dealt treacherously with
            Me,
        O house of Israel," says the LORD.

²¹   A voice was heard on the desolate
            heights,
        Weeping *and* supplications of the
            children of Israel.
        For they have perverted their way;
        They have forgotten the LORD their
            God.

²²   "Return, you backsliding children,
        And I will heal your backslidings."

"Indeed we do come to You,
For You are the LORD our God.
23 Truly, in vain *is salvation hoped for*
from the hills,
And from the multitude of
mountains;
Truly, in the LORD our God
Is the salvation of Israel.
24 For shame has devoured
The labor of our fathers from our
youth—
Their flocks and their herds,
Their sons and their daughters.
25 We lie down in our shame,
And our reproach covers us.
For we have sinned against the LORD
our God,
We and our fathers,
From our youth even to this day,
And have not obeyed the voice of the
LORD our God."

4 "If you will return, O Israel," says the
LORD,
"Return to Me;
And if you will put away your
abominations out of My sight,
Then you shall not be moved.
2 And you shall swear, 'The LORD
lives,'
In truth, in judgment, and in
righteousness;
The nations shall bless themselves in
Him,
And in Him they shall glory."

3 For thus says the LORD to the men of
Judah and Jerusalem:

"Break up your fallow ground,
And do not sow among thorns.
4 Circumcise yourselves to the LORD,
And take away the foreskins of your
hearts,
You men of Judah and inhabitants of
Jerusalem,
Lest My fury come forth like fire,

And burn so that no one can quench
it,
Because of the evil of your doings."

An Imminent Invasion

5 Declare in Judah and proclaim in Jerusalem, and say:

"Blow the trumpet in the land;
Cry, 'Gather together,'
And say, 'Assemble yourselves,
And let us go into the fortified cities.'
6 Set up the standard toward Zion.
Take refuge! Do not delay!
For I will bring disaster from the
north,
And great destruction."

7 The lion has come up from his
thicket,
And the destroyer of nations is on his
way.
He has gone forth from his place
To make your land desolate.
Your cities will be laid waste,
Without inhabitant.
8 For this, clothe yourself with
sackcloth,
Lament and wail.
For the fierce anger of the LORD
Has not turned back from us.

9 "And it shall come to pass in that day,"
says the LORD,
"*That* the heart of the king shall
perish,
And the heart of the princes;
The priests shall be astonished,
And the prophets shall wonder."

10 Then I said, "Ah, Lord GOD!
Surely You have greatly deceived this
people and Jerusalem,
Saying, 'You shall have peace,'
Whereas the sword reaches to the
heart."

4:4 Circumcise. This physical surgery prevented any diseases from being passed from a husband to his wife. This preserved Israel physically and also symbolized the need to be spiritually cleansed from sin's deadly disease. God called for Israel to change her heart so that she would obey Him.

4:10 deceived. Jeremiah was terrified at these words of judgment. Sometimes God seems responsible for something, when He merely permits it to happen. This is what occurred when false prophets preached peace, therefore deluding sinful Israel (see 6:14). When God sees how people insist on their delusions, He allows it to happen.

11 At that time it will be said
   To this people and to Jerusalem,
   "A dry wind of the desolate heights
   blows in the wilderness
   Toward the daughter of My people—
   Not to fan or to cleanse—
12 A wind too strong for these will come
   for Me;
   Now I will also speak judgment
   against them."

13 "Behold, he shall come up like clouds,
   And his chariots like a whirlwind.
   His horses are swifter than eagles.
   Woe to us, for we are plundered!"

14 O Jerusalem, wash your heart from
   wickedness,
   That you may be saved.
   How long shall your evil thoughts
   lodge within you?
15 For a voice declares from Dan
   And proclaims affliction from Mount
   Ephraim:
16 "Make mention to the nations,
   Yes, proclaim against Jerusalem,
   That watchers come from a far
   country
   And raise their voice against the cities
   of Judah.
17 Like keepers of a field they are against
   her all around,
   Because she has been rebellious
   against Me," says the LORD.
18 "Your ways and your doings
   Have procured these *things* for you.
   This *is* your wickedness,
   Because it is bitter,
   Because it reaches to your heart."

Sorrow for the Doomed Nation

19 O my soul, my soul!
   I am pained in my very heart!
   My heart makes a noise in me;
   I cannot hold my peace,
   Because you have heard, O my soul,
   The sound of the trumpet,
   The alarm of war.
20 Destruction upon destruction is cried,
   For the whole land is plundered.
   Suddenly my tents are plundered,
   And my curtains in a moment.
21 How long will I see the standard,
   And hear the sound of the trumpet?

22 "For My people *are* foolish,
   They have not known Me.
   They *are* silly children,
   And they have no understanding.
   They *are* wise to do evil,
   But to do good they have no
   knowledge."

4:22 wise to do evil. Israel knew how to do evil, but they were not familiar with how to be righteous. Paul borrowed from this idea and encouraged the church in Rome to be wise to do good and unlearned in doing evil (Rom. 16:19).

23 I beheld the earth, and indeed *it was*
   without form, and void;
   And the heavens, they *had* no light.
24 I beheld the mountains, and indeed
   they trembled,
   And all the hills moved back and
   forth.
25 I beheld, and indeed *there was* no
   man,
   And all the birds of the heavens had
   fled.
26 I beheld, and indeed the fruitful land
   was a wilderness,
   And all its cities were broken down
   At the presence of the LORD,
   By His fierce anger.

27 For thus says the LORD:

   "The whole land shall be desolate;
   Yet I will not make a full end.
28 For this shall the earth mourn,
   And the heavens above be black,
   Because I have spoken.
   I have purposed and will not relent,
   Nor will I turn back from it.
29 The whole city shall flee from the
   noise of the horsemen and
   bowmen.
   They shall go into thickets and climb
   up on the rocks.
   Every city *shall be* forsaken,
   And not a man shall dwell in it.

30 "And *when* you *are* plundered,
   What will you do?
   Though you clothe yourself with
   crimson,
   Though you adorn *yourself* with
   ornaments of gold,

Though you enlarge your eyes with
    paint,
In vain you will make yourself fair;
Your lovers will despise you;
They will seek your life.

31 "For I have heard a voice as of a
    woman in labor,
The anguish as of her who brings
    forth her first child,
The voice of the daughter of Zion
    bewailing herself,
She spreads her hands, *saying,*
'Woe *is* me now, for my soul is weary
Because of murderers!'

The Justice of God's Judgment

5 "Run to and fro through the streets of
    Jerusalem;
See now and know;
And seek in her open places
If you can find a man,
If there is *anyone* who executes
    judgment,
Who seeks the truth,
And I will pardon her.
2 Though they say, '*As* the LORD lives,'
Surely they swear falsely."

3 O LORD, *are* not Your eyes on the
    truth?
You have stricken them,
But they have not grieved;
You have consumed them,
But they have refused to receive
    correction.
They have made their faces harder
    than rock;
They have refused to return.

4 Therefore I said, "Surely these *are*
    poor.
They are foolish;
For they do not know the way of the
    LORD,
The judgment of their God.
5 I will go to the great men and speak
    to them,
For they have known the way of the
    LORD,
The judgment of their God."

But these have altogether broken the
    yoke

And burst the bonds.
6 Therefore a lion from the forest shall
    slay them,
A wolf of the deserts shall destroy
    them;
A leopard will watch over their cities.
Everyone who goes out from there
    shall be torn in pieces,
Because their transgressions are
    many;
Their backslidings have increased.

5:6 lion. The lion, the wolf, and the leopard all tear and eat their victims without discretion, therefore making them good analogies of vicious judgment on the poor (v. 4) and rich (v. 5).

7 "How shall I pardon you for this?
Your children have forsaken Me
And sworn by *those that are* not gods.
When I had fed them to the full,
Then they committed adultery
And assembled themselves by troops
    in the harlots' houses.
8 They were *like* well-fed lusty stallions;
Every one neighed after his neighbor's
    wife.
9 Shall I not punish *them* for these
    things?" says the LORD.
"And shall I not avenge Myself on such
    a nation as this?

10 "Go up on her walls and destroy,
But do not make a complete end.
Take away her branches,
For they *are* not the LORD's.

5:10 not the LORD's. Because the people did not genuinely know the Lord and had forsaken Him for other gods, they were fit to be destroyed, like dead branches on the vine.

11 For the house of Israel and the house
    of Judah
Have dealt very treacherously with
    Me," says the LORD.

12 They have lied about the LORD,
And said, "*It is* not He.
Neither will evil come upon us,
Nor shall we see sword or famine.
13 And the prophets become wind,
For the word *is* not in them.
Thus shall it be done to them."

¹⁴Therefore thus says the LORD God of hosts:

"Because you speak this word,
Behold, I will make My words in your mouth fire,
And this people wood,
And it shall devour them.
15 Behold, I will bring a nation against you from afar,
O house of Israel," says the LORD.
"It *is* a mighty nation,
It *is* an ancient nation,
A nation whose language you do not know,
Nor can you understand what they say.
16 Their quiver *is* like an open tomb;
They *are* all mighty men.
17 And they shall eat up your harvest and your bread,
Which your sons and daughters should eat.
They shall eat up your flocks and your herds;
They shall eat up your vines and your fig trees;
They shall destroy your fortified cities,
In which you trust, with the sword.

¹⁸"Nevertheless in those days," says the LORD, "I will not make a complete end of you. ¹⁹And it will be when you say, 'Why does the LORD our God do all these *things* to us?' then you shall answer them, 'Just as you have forsaken Me and served foreign gods in your land, so you shall serve aliens in a land *that is* not yours.'

20 "Declare this in the house of Jacob
And proclaim it in Judah, saying,
21 'Hear this now, O foolish people,
Without understanding,
Who have eyes and see not,
And who have ears and hear not:
22 Do you not fear Me?' says the LORD.
'Will you not tremble at My presence,
Who have placed the sand as the bound of the sea,
By a perpetual decree, that it cannot pass beyond it?
And though its waves toss to and fro,
Yet they cannot prevail;

Though they roar, yet they cannot pass over it.'

5:22 sand...of the sea. God's grace and existence are witnessed in nature, such as in the seashore that prevents flooding, the rain, and the season for harvest. These unappreciated gifts will be taken away if the nation does not turn back to Him (v. 25).

23 But this people has a defiant and rebellious heart;
They have revolted and departed.
24 They do not say in their heart,
"Let us now fear the LORD our God,
Who gives rain, both the former and the latter, in its season.
He reserves for us the appointed weeks of the harvest."
25 Your iniquities have turned these *things* away,
And your sins have withheld good from you.
26 'For among My people are found wicked *men;*
They lie in wait as one who sets snares;
They set a trap;
They catch men.
27 As a cage is full of birds,
So their houses *are* full of deceit.
Therefore they have become great and grown rich.
28 They have grown fat, they are sleek;
Yes, they surpass the deeds of the wicked;
They do not plead the cause,
The cause of the fatherless;
Yet they prosper,
And the right of the needy they do not defend.
29 Shall I not punish *them* for these *things?*' says the LORD.
'Shall I not avenge Myself on such a nation as this?'

30 "An astonishing and horrible thing
Has been committed in the land:
31 The prophets prophesy falsely,
And the priests rule by their *own* power;
And My people love *to have it* so.
But what will you do in the end?

Impending Destruction from the North

6 "O you children of Benjamin,
Gather yourselves to flee from the
midst of Jerusalem!
Blow the trumpet in Tekoa,
And set up a signal-fire in Beth
Haccerem;
For disaster appears out of the north,
And great destruction.
2   I have likened the daughter of Zion
To a lovely and delicate woman.
3   The shepherds with their flocks shall
come to her.
They shall pitch *their* tents against
her all around.
Each one shall pasture in his own
place."

4   "Prepare war against her;
Arise, and let us go up at noon.
Woe to us, for the day goes away,
For the shadows of the evening are
lengthening.
5   Arise, and let us go by night,
And let us destroy her palaces."

6For thus has the LORD of hosts said:

"Cut down trees,
And build a mound against
Jerusalem.
This *is* the city to be punished.
She *is* full of oppression in her midst.
7   As a fountain wells up with water,
So she wells up with her wickedness.
Violence and plundering are heard in
her.
Before Me continually *are* grief and
wounds.
8   Be instructed, O Jerusalem,
Lest My soul depart from you;
Lest I make you desolate,
A land not inhabited."

9Thus says the LORD of hosts:

"They shall thoroughly glean as a vine
the remnant of Israel;

> **6:9 thoroughly glean.** It was customary for food to
> be left in the field after harvest for the poor to eat
> (Lev. 19:9,10). The Babylonians would leave no one
> after their "harvest" of Judah.

As a grape-gatherer, put your hand
back into the branches."

10   To whom shall I speak and give
warning,
That they may hear?
Indeed their ear *is* uncircumcised,
And they cannot give heed.
Behold, the word of the LORD is a
reproach to them;
They have no delight in it.
11   Therefore I am full of the fury of the
LORD.
I am weary of holding *it* in.
"I will pour it out on the children
outside,
And on the assembly of young men
together;
For even the husband shall be taken
with the wife,
The aged with *him who is* full of
days.
12   And their houses shall be turned over
to others,
Fields and wives together;
For I will stretch out My hand
Against the inhabitants of the land,"
says the LORD.
13   "Because from the least of them even
to the greatest of them,
Everyone *is* given to covetousness;
And from the prophet even to the
priest,
Everyone deals falsely.
14   They have also healed the hurt of My
people slightly,
Saying, 'Peace, peace!'
When *there is* no peace.

> **6:14 'Peace, peace!'** This was the false promise
> given by the false priests and prophets that gave
> brief comfort to the people. It did not address the real
> issue, though, which was the need to repent of sin
> and seek spiritual healing from its effects (v. 15).

15   Were they ashamed when they had
committed abomination?
No! They were not at all ashamed;
Nor did they know how to blush.
Therefore they shall fall among those
who fall;
At the time I punish them,
They shall be cast down," says the
LORD.

¹⁶Thus says the LORD:

"Stand in the ways and see,
And ask for the old paths, where the
    good way *is*,
And walk in it;
Then you will find rest for your souls.
But they said, 'We will not walk *in it*.'

¹⁷ Also, I set watchmen over you,
    saying,
'Listen to the sound of the trumpet!'
But they said, 'We will not listen.'

¹⁸ Therefore hear, you nations,
And know, O congregation, what *is*
    among them.

¹⁹ Hear, O earth!
Behold, I will certainly bring calamity
    on this people—
The fruit of their thoughts,
Because they have not heeded My
    words
Nor My law, but rejected it.

²⁰ For what purpose to Me
Comes frankincense from Sheba,
And sweet cane from a far country?
Your burnt offerings *are* not
    acceptable,
Nor your sacrifices sweet to Me."

²¹Therefore thus says the LORD:

"Behold, I will lay stumbling blocks
    before this people,
And the fathers and the sons together
    shall fall on them.
The neighbor and his friend shall
    perish."

²²Thus says the LORD:

"Behold, a people comes from the
    north country,
And a great nation will be raised from
    the farthest parts of the earth.

²³ They will lay hold on bow and spear;
They *are* cruel and have no mercy;
Their voice roars like the sea;
And they ride on horses,
As men of war set in array against
    you, O daughter of Zion."

²⁴ We have heard the report of it;
Our hands grow feeble.
Anguish has taken hold of us,

Pain as of a woman in labor.

²⁵ Do not go out into the field,
Nor walk by the way.
Because of the sword of the enemy,
Fear *is* on every side.

²⁶ O daughter of my people,
Dress in sackcloth
And roll about in ashes!
Make mourning *as for* an only son,
    most bitter lamentation;
For the plunderer will suddenly come
    upon us.

²⁷ "I have set you *as* an assayer *and* a
    fortress among My people,
That you may know and test their
    way.

²⁸ They *are* all stubborn rebels, walking
    as slanderers.
They are bronze and iron,
They *are* all corrupters;

²⁹ The bellows blow fiercely,
The lead is consumed by the fire;
The smelter refines in vain,
For the wicked are not drawn off.

³⁰ *People* will call them rejected silver,
Because the LORD has rejected them."

6:27–30 I have set you. Jeremiah was set up by God to test the people's obedience, like someone who tests metals. The people were not found to be pure, as silver, but impure, as bronze, iron, lead, and even impure silver.

Trusting in Lying Words

7The word that came to Jeremiah from the LORD, saying, ²"Stand in the gate of the LORD's house, and proclaim there this word, and say, 'Hear the word of the LORD, all *you of* Judah who enter in at these gates to worship the LORD!' " ³Thus says the LORD of hosts, the God of Israel: "Amend your ways and your doings, and I will cause you to dwell in this place. ⁴Do not trust in these lying words, saying, 'The temple of the LORD, the temple of the LORD, the temple of the LORD *are* these.'

⁵"For if you thoroughly amend your ways and your doings, if you thoroughly execute judgment between a man and his neighbor, ⁶if you do not oppress the stranger, the fatherless, and the widow, and do not shed innocent blood in this place, or walk after other gods to your hurt, ⁷then I will cause

you to dwell in this place, in the land that I gave to your fathers forever and ever.

8"Behold, you trust in lying words that cannot profit. 9Will you steal, murder, commit adultery, swear falsely, burn incense to Baal, and walk after other gods whom you do not know, 10and *then* come and stand before Me in this house which is called by My name, and say, 'We are delivered to do all these abominations'? 11Has this house, which is called by My name, become a den of thieves in your eyes? Behold, I, even I, have seen *it*," says the LORD.

12"But go now to My place which *was* in Shiloh, where I set My name at the first, and see what I did to it because of the wickedness of My people Israel. 13And now, because you have done all these works," says the LORD, "and I spoke to you, rising up early and speaking, but you did not hear, and I called you, but you did not answer, 14therefore I will do to the house which is called by My name, in which you trust, and to this place which I gave to you and your fathers, as I have done to Shiloh. 15And I will cast you out of My sight, as I have cast out all your brethren—the whole posterity of Ephraim.

7:15 as I have cast out...Ephraim. Because Ephraim was the leading tribe of Israel, it represents the entire northern kingdom (see 2 Kin. 17:23). The southern kingdom would be cast out just as the northern kingdom was exiled into Assyria in 722 B.C.

16"Therefore do not pray for this people, nor lift up a cry or prayer for them, nor make intercession to Me; for I will not hear you. 17Do you not see what they do in the cities of Judah and in the streets of Jerusalem? 18The children gather wood, the fathers kindle the fire, and the women knead dough, to make cakes for the queen of heaven; and *they* pour out drink offerings to other gods, that they may provoke Me to anger. 19Do they provoke Me to anger?" says the LORD. "*Do they* not *provoke* themselves, to the shame of their own faces?"

20Therefore thus says the Lord GOD: "Behold, My anger and My fury will be poured out on this place—on man and on beast, on the trees of the field and on the fruit of the ground. And it will burn and not be quenched."

21Thus says the LORD of hosts, the God of Israel: "Add your burnt offerings to your sacrifices and eat meat. 22For I did not speak to your fathers, or command them in the day that I brought them out of the land of Egypt, concerning burnt offerings or sacrifices. 23But this is what I commanded them, saying, 'Obey My voice, and I will be your God, and you shall be My people. And walk in all the ways that I have commanded you, that it may be well with you.' 24Yet they did not obey or incline their ear, but followed the counsels *and* the dictates of their evil hearts, and went backward and not forward. 25Since the day that your fa-

How can one explain God's forbidding prayer for the Jews (Jeremiah 7:16) and saying that even Moses and Samuel's intervention would not prevent judgment (Jeremiah 15:1)?

General questions about God's willingness or unwillingness to hear someone's prayer must be answered with reference to specific passages. God's direction to Jeremiah not to pray for the people flows from the people's determined attitude of rejection towards God. Jeremiah 7:16 begins with "therefore" and indicates that what follows expresses God's conclusion. The people have no interest in the prayers of Jeremiah, so they are as useless as if God did not hear them.

Later, in Jeremiah 15:1, God describes the desperate sinful condition of His people by stating that even prayers by Moses and Samuel would not stop the consequences that were on the horizon. The spiritual error that God exposes in this passage has to do with the temptation to offer the "right prayer" as a substitute for genuine repentance. The idea that an empty religious ceremony can satisfy the righteous indignation of a holy God was not just an ancient error. Now, as then, God allows people to experience the full results of their behavior as a final opportunity for correction and repentance.

thers came out of the land of Egypt until this day, I have even sent to you all My servants the prophets, daily rising up early and sending *them*. ²⁶Yet they did not obey Me or incline their ear, but stiffened their neck. They did worse than their fathers.

²⁷"Therefore you shall speak all these words to them, but they will not obey you. You shall also call to them, but they will not answer you.

Judgment on Obscene Religion

²⁸"So you shall say to them, 'This *is* a nation that does not obey the voice of the LORD their God nor receive correction. Truth has perished and has been cut off from their mouth. ²⁹Cut off your hair and cast *it* away, and take up a lamentation on the desolate heights; for the LORD has rejected and forsaken the generation of His wrath.' ³⁰For the children of Judah have done evil in My sight," says the LORD. "They have set their abominations in the house which is called by My name, to pollute it. ³¹And they have built the high places of Tophet, which *is* in the Valley of the Son of Hinnom, to burn their sons and their daughters in the fire, which I did not command, nor did it come into My heart.

> **7:31 burn their sons.** Israel offered their sons to Molech, the fire god, as sacrifices, despite the fact that God explicitly forbade this (see Lev. 18:21). They incorrectly believed that this sacrifice would bring reward from Molech.

³²"Therefore behold, the days are coming," says the LORD, "when it will no more be called Tophet, or the Valley of the Son of Hinnom, but the Valley of Slaughter; for they will bury in Tophet until there is no room. ³³The corpses of this people will be food for the birds of the heaven and for the beasts of the earth. And no one will frighten *them away*. ³⁴Then I will cause to cease from the cities of Judah and from the streets of Jerusalem the voice of mirth and the voice of gladness, the voice of the bridegroom and the voice of the bride. For the land shall be desolate.

8 "At that time," says the LORD, "they shall bring out the bones of the kings of Judah, and the bones of its princes, and the bones of the priests, and the bones of the prophets, and the bones of the inhabitants of Jerusalem, out of their graves. ²They shall spread them before the sun and the moon and all the host of heaven, which they have loved and which they have served and after which they have walked, which they have sought and which they have worshiped. They shall not be gathered nor buried; they shall be like refuse on the face of the earth. ³Then death shall be chosen rather than life by all the residue of those who remain of this evil family, who remain in all the places where I have driven them," says the LORD of hosts.

> **8:1 bring out the bones.** Conquerors pillaged the tombs of the Jews and scattered the bones of the rich and honored in order to humiliate them and display the superiority of foreign gods.

The Peril of False Teaching

⁴"Moreover you shall say to them, 'Thus says the LORD:

"Will they fall and not rise?
Will one turn away and not return?
⁵ Why has this people slidden back,
Jerusalem, in a perpetual backsliding?
They hold fast to deceit,
They refuse to return.
⁶ I listened and heard,
But they do not speak aright.
No man repented of his wickedness,
Saying, 'What have I done?'
Everyone turned to his own course,
As the horse rushes into the battle.

⁷ "Even the stork in the heavens
Knows her appointed times;
And the turtledove, the swift, and the
swallow
Observe the time of their coming.
But My people do not know the
judgment of the LORD.

⁸ "How can you say, 'We *are* wise,
And the law of the LORD *is* with us'?
Look, the false pen of the scribe
certainly works falsehood.
⁹ The wise men are ashamed,
They are dismayed and taken.
Behold, they have rejected the word of
the LORD;

So what wisdom do they have?

10 Therefore I will give their wives to
    others,
And their fields to those who will
    inherit *them;*
Because from the least even to the
    greatest
Everyone is given to covetousness;
From the prophet even to the priest
Everyone deals falsely.

11 For they have healed the hurt of the
    daughter of My people slightly,
Saying, 'Peace, peace!'
When *there is* no peace.

12 Were they ashamed when they had
    committed abomination?
No! They were not at all ashamed,
Nor did they know how to blush.
Therefore they shall fall among those
    who fall;
In the time of their punishment
They shall be cast down," says the
    LORD.

13 "I will surely consume them," says the
    LORD.
"No grapes *shall be* on the vine,
Nor figs on the fig tree,
And the leaf shall fade;
And *the things* I have given them
    shall pass away from them." ' "

14 "Why do we sit still?
Assemble yourselves,
And let us enter the fortified cities,
And let us be silent there.
For the LORD our God has put us to
    silence
And given us water of gall to drink,
Because we have sinned against the
    LORD.

15 "*We* looked for peace, but no good
    came;
And for a time of health, and there
    was trouble!

16 The snorting of His horses was heard
    from Dan.
The whole land trembled at the
    sound of the neighing of His strong
    ones;
For they have come and devoured the
    land and all that is in it,
The city and those who dwell in it."

17 "For behold, I will send serpents
    among you,
Vipers which cannot be charmed,
And they shall bite you," says the
    LORD.

The Prophet Mourns for the People

18 I would comfort myself in sorrow;
My heart *is* faint in me.

19 Listen! The voice,
The cry of the daughter of my people
From a far country:
"*Is* not the LORD in Zion?
Is not her King in her?"

"Why have they provoked Me to anger
With their carved images—
With foreign idols?"

8:19 far country. This predicts how the Jews will cry out once they are taken into exile in Babylon. They will wonder why God has allowed this to happen to His land and His people.

20 "The harvest is past,
The summer is ended,
And we are not saved!"

21 For the hurt of the daughter of my
    people I am hurt.
I am mourning;
Astonishment has taken hold of me.

22 *Is there* no balm in Gilead,
Is there no physician there?
Why then is there no recovery
For the health of the daughter of my
    people?

9 Oh, that my head were waters,
And my eyes a fountain of tears,
That I might weep day and night
For the slain of the daughter of my
    people!

2 Oh, that I had in the wilderness
. A lodging place for travelers;
That I might leave my people,
And go from them!
For they *are* all adulterers,
An assembly of treacherous men.

3 "And *like* their bow they have bent
    their tongues *for* lies.
They are not valiant for the truth on
    the earth.

For they proceed from evil to evil,
And they do not know Me," says the
LORD.

4 "Everyone take heed to his neighbor,
And do not trust any brother;
For every brother will utterly
supplant,
And every neighbor will walk with
slanderers.
5 Everyone will deceive his neighbor,
And will not speak the truth;
They have taught their tongue to
speak lies;
They weary themselves to commit
iniquity.
6 Your dwelling place *is* in the midst of
deceit;
Through deceit they refuse to know
Me," says the LORD.

7 Therefore thus says the LORD of hosts:

"Behold, I will refine them and try
them;
For how shall I deal with the daughter
of My people?
8 Their tongue *is* an arrow shot out;
It speaks deceit;
One speaks peaceably to his neighbor
with his mouth,
But in his heart he lies in wait.
9 Shall I not punish them for these
things?" says the LORD.
"Shall I not avenge Myself on such a
nation as this?"

10 I will take up a weeping and wailing
for the mountains,
And for the dwelling places of the
wilderness a lamentation,
Because they are burned up,
So that no one can pass through;
Nor can *men* hear the voice of the
cattle.
Both the birds of the heavens and the
beasts have fled;
They are gone.

11 "I will make Jerusalem a heap of ruins,
a den of jackals.
I will make the cities of Judah
desolate, without an inhabitant."

12 Who *is* the wise man who may understand this? And *who is he* to whom the
mouth of the LORD has spoken, that he
may declare it? Why does the land perish
and burn up like a wilderness, so that no
one can pass through?
13 And the LORD said, "Because they have
forsaken My law which I set before them,
and have not obeyed My voice, nor walked
according to it, 14 but they have walked according to the dictates of their own hearts
and after the Baals, which their fathers
taught them," 15 therefore thus says the
LORD of hosts, the God of Israel: "Behold, I
will feed them, this people, with wormwood, and give them water of gall to drink.
16 I will scatter them also among the Gentiles, whom neither they nor their fathers
have known. And I will send a sword after
them until I have consumed them."

> **9:15 wormwood.** The suffering of Israel is compared
> to the bitterness of this herb. Their food would be bit-
> ter, and their water would be like gall, a poisonous
> herb.

The People Mourn in Judgment
17 Thus says the LORD of hosts:

"Consider and call for the mourning
women,
That they may come;
And send for skillful wailing women,
That they may come.
18 Let them make haste
And take up a wailing for us,
That our eyes may run with tears,
And our eyelids gush with water.
19 For a voice of wailing is heard from
Zion:
'How we are plundered!
We are greatly ashamed,
Because we have forsaken the land,
Because we have been cast out of our
dwellings.' "

20 Yet hear the word of the LORD,
O women,
And let your ear receive the word of
His mouth;
Teach your daughters wailing,
And everyone her neighbor a
lamentation.
21 For death has come through our
windows,

Has entered our palaces,
To kill off the children—*no longer to
be* outside!
And the young men—*no longer* on the
streets!

22 Speak, "Thus says the LORD:

'Even the carcasses of men shall fall as
refuse on the open field,
Like cuttings after the harvester,
And no one shall gather *them*.' "

23 Thus says the LORD:

"Let not the wise *man* glory in his
wisdom,
Let not the mighty *man* glory in his
might,
Nor let the rich *man* glory in his
riches;
24 But let him who glories glory in this,
That he understands and knows Me,
That I *am* the LORD, exercising
lovingkindness, judgment, and
righteousness in the earth.
For in these I delight," says the LORD.

> **9:24 understands and knows Me.** Only a true un-
> derstanding and knowledge of God would save the
> nation. Paul refers to this passage twice (1 Cor. 1:31;
> 2 Cor. 10:17).

25 "Behold, the days are coming," says the
LORD, "that I will punish all *who are*
circumcised with the uncircumcised—
26 Egypt, Judah, Edom, the people of Ammon, Moab, and all *who are* in the farthest
corners, who dwell in the wilderness. For
all *these* nations *are* uncircumcised, and all
the house of Israel *are* uncircumcised in the
heart."

Idols and the True God

10 Hear the word which the LORD
speaks to you, O house of Israel.
2 Thus says the LORD:

"Do not learn the way of the Gentiles;
Do not be dismayed at the signs of
heaven,
For the Gentiles are dismayed at
them.

3 For the customs of the peoples *are*
futile;
For *one* cuts a tree from the forest,
The work of the hands of the
workman, with the ax.
4 They decorate it with silver and gold;
They fasten it with nails and
hammers
So that it will not topple.
5 They *are* upright, like a palm tree,
And they cannot speak;
They must be carried,
Because they cannot go *by
themselves*.
Do not be afraid of them,
For they cannot do evil,
Nor can they do any good."

6 Inasmuch as *there is* none like You,
O LORD
(You *are* great, and Your name *is* great
in might),
7 Who would not fear You, O King of
the nations?
For this is Your rightful due.
For among all the wise *men* of the
nations,
And in all their kingdoms,
There is none like You.

> **10:7 King.** Only God is eternal (see Ps. 47), sovereign,
> completely in control (see vv. 12,16), and trustworthy.
> Idols, on the other hand, are manmade (v. 9) and will
> be destroyed (v. 15).

8 But they are altogether dull-hearted
and foolish;
A wooden idol *is* a worthless doctrine.
9 Silver is beaten into plates;
It is brought from Tarshish,
And gold from Uphaz,
The work of the craftsman
And of the hands of the metalsmith;
Blue and purple *are* their clothing;
They *are* all the work of skillful *men*.
10 But the LORD *is* the true God;
He *is* the living God and the
everlasting King.
At His wrath the earth will tremble,
And the nations will not be able to
endure His indignation.

11 Thus you shall say to them: "The gods
that have not made the heavens and the

earth shall perish from the earth and from under these heavens."

12 He has made the earth by His power,
He has established the world by His wisdom,
And has stretched out the heavens at His discretion.
13 When He utters His voice,
There is a multitude of waters in the heavens:
"And He causes the vapors to ascend from the ends of the earth.
He makes lightning for the rain,
He brings the wind out of His treasuries."[a]

14 Everyone is dull-hearted, without knowledge;
Every metalsmith is put to shame by an image;
For his molded image is falsehood,
And there is no breath in them.
15 They are futile, a work of errors;
In the time of their punishment they shall perish.
16 The Portion of Jacob is not like them,
For He is the Maker of all things,
And Israel is the tribe of His inheritance;
The LORD of hosts is His name.

The Coming Captivity of Judah

17 Gather up your wares from the land,
O inhabitant of the fortress!

18 For thus says the LORD:

"Behold, I will throw out at this time
The inhabitants of the land,
And will distress them,
That they may find it so."

19 Woe is me for my hurt!
My wound is severe.
But I say, "Truly this is an infirmity,
And I must bear it."
20 My tent is plundered,
And all my cords are broken;
My children have gone from me,
And they are no more.

There is no one to pitch my tent anymore,
Or set up my curtains.

10:20 My tent is plundered. Jeremiah used language that the Israelites would use when being invaded. He prophesied that they would cry out over the loss of their homes and the slaying of their children.

21 For the shepherds have become dull-hearted,
And have not sought the LORD;
Therefore they shall not prosper,
And all their flocks shall be scattered.
22 Behold, the noise of the report has come,
And a great commotion out of the north country,
To make the cities of Judah desolate, a den of jackals.

23 O LORD, I know the way of man is not in himself;
It is not in man who walks to direct his own steps.
24 O LORD, correct me, but with justice;
Not in Your anger, lest You bring me to nothing.
25 Pour out Your fury on the Gentiles,
who do not know You,
And on the families who do not call on Your name;
For they have eaten up Jacob,
Devoured him and consumed him,
And made his dwelling place desolate.

10:24,25 Jeremiah identified himself with the people and understood that the nation must be punished, though he prayed for mercy and moderation. He also prayed for God's wrath to be poured out on the nations that influenced the Jews to follow after idols.

The Broken Covenant

11 The word that came to Jeremiah from the LORD, saying, 2"Hear the words of this covenant, and speak to the men of Judah and to the inhabitants of Jerusalem; 3and say to them, 'Thus says the LORD God of Israel: "Cursed is the man who does not obey the words of this covenant

10:13 [a]Psalm 135:7

4which I commanded your fathers in the day I brought them out of the land of Egypt, from the iron furnace, saying, 'Obey My voice, and do according to all that I command you; so shall you be My people, and I will be your God,' 5that I may establish the oath which I have sworn to your fathers, to give them 'a land flowing with milk and honey,'ᵃ as *it is* this day." ' "

And I answered and said, "So be it, LORD."

6Then the LORD said to me, "Proclaim all these words in the cities of Judah and in the streets of Jerusalem, saying: 'Hear the words of this covenant and do them. 7For I earnestly exhorted your fathers in the day I brought them up out of the land of Egypt, until this day, rising early and exhorting, saying, "Obey My voice." 8Yet they did not obey or incline their ear, but everyone followed the dictates of his evil heart; therefore I will bring upon them all the words of this covenant, which I commanded *them* to do, but *which* they have not done.' "

9And the LORD said to me, "A conspiracy has been found among the men of Judah and among the inhabitants of Jerusalem. 10They have turned back to the iniquities of their forefathers who refused to hear My words, and they have gone after other gods to serve them; the house of Israel and the house of Judah have broken My covenant which I made with their fathers."

11Therefore thus says the LORD: "Behold, I will surely bring calamity on them which they will not be able to escape; and though they cry out to Me, I will not listen to them. 12Then the cities of Judah and the inhabitants of Jerusalem will go and cry out to the gods to whom they offer incense, but they will not save them at all in the time of their trouble. 13For *according to* the number of your cities were your gods, O Judah; and *according to* the number of the streets of Jerusalem you have set up altars to *that* shameful thing, altars to burn incense to Baal.

14"So do not pray for this people, or lift up a cry or prayer for them; for I will not hear *them* in the time that they cry out to Me because of their trouble.

15 "What has My beloved to do in My house,
Having done lewd deeds with many?
And the holy flesh has passed from you.
When you do evil, then you rejoice.

11:15 My beloved. God expresses His sensitive love for Israel as a nation (see 2:2). It does not imply that every individual is saved (see 5:10a). **lewd deeds.** These were acts that defiled the practices of temple worship and violated the first 3 commandments (see Ex. 20:27). **holy flesh.** Through sin, they corrupted the animal sacrifices (see 7:10).

16   The LORD called your name,
Green Olive Tree, Lovely *and* of Good Fruit.
With the noise of a great tumult He has kindled fire on it,
And its branches are broken.

17"For the LORD of hosts, who planted you, has pronounced doom against you for the evil of the house of Israel and of the house of Judah, which they have done against themselves to provoke Me to anger in offering incense to Baal."

Jeremiah's Life Threatened

18Now the LORD gave me knowledge *of it*, and I know *it*; for You showed me their doings. 19But I *was* like a docile lamb brought to the slaughter; and I did not know that they had devised schemes against me, *saying*, "Let us destroy the tree with its fruit, and let us cut him off from the land of the living, that his name may be remembered no more."

20   But, O LORD of hosts,
You who judge righteously,
Testing the mind and the heart,
Let me see Your vengeance on them,
For to You I have revealed my cause.

21"Therefore thus says the LORD concerning the men of Anathoth who seek your life, saying, 'Do not prophesy in the name of the LORD, lest you die by our hand'— 22therefore thus says the LORD of hosts: 'Behold, I will punish them. The

11:5 ᵃExodus 3:8

young men shall die by the sword, their sons and their daughters shall die by famine; ²³and there shall be no remnant of them, for I will bring catastrophe on the men of Anathoth, *even* the year of their punishment.' "

Jeremiah's Question

12 Righteous *are* You, O LORD, when I plead with You;
Yet let me talk with You about *Your* judgments.
Why does the way of the wicked prosper?
Why are those happy who deal so treacherously?

² You have planted them, yes, they have taken root;
They grow, yes, they bear fruit.
You *are* near in their mouth
But far from their mind.

³ But You, O LORD, know me;
You have seen me,
And You have tested my heart toward You.
Pull them out like sheep for the slaughter,
And prepare them for the day of slaughter.

⁴ How long will the land mourn,
And the herbs of every field wither?
The beasts and birds are consumed,
For the wickedness of those who dwell there,
Because they said, "He will not see our final end."

The LORD Answers Jeremiah

⁵ "If you have run with the footmen, and they have wearied you,
Then how can you contend with horses?
And *if* in the land of peace,
In which you trusted, *they wearied you,*
Then how will you do in the floodplain*ᵃ* of the Jordan?

⁶ For even your brothers, the house of your father,
Even they have dealt treacherously with you;

Yes, they have called a multitude after you.
Do not believe them,
Even though they speak smooth words to you.

> **12:6 even your brothers.** Jeremiah met antagonism not only from fellow townsmen (see 11:18–23), but also from his own family! He then separated from them (v. 7).

⁷ "I have forsaken My house, I have left My heritage;
I have given the dearly beloved of My soul into the hand of her enemies.

⁸ My heritage is to Me like a lion in the forest;
It cries out against Me;
Therefore I have hated it.

⁹ My heritage *is* to Me *like* a speckled vulture;
The vultures all around *are* against her.
Come, assemble all the beasts of the field,
Bring them to devour!

¹⁰ "Many rulers*ᵃ* have destroyed My vineyard,
They have trodden My portion underfoot;
They have made My pleasant portion a desolate wilderness.

¹¹ They have made it desolate;
Desolate, it mourns to Me;
The whole land is made desolate,
Because no one takes *it* to heart.

¹² The plunderers have come
On all the desolate heights in the wilderness,
For the sword of the LORD shall devour
From *one* end of the land to the *other* end of the land;
No flesh shall have peace.

¹³ They have sown wheat but reaped thorns;

> **12:12 sword of the LORD.** God's strength can be for defending (see 47:6) or, in this case, condemning. The Babylonians were God's sword doing His will.

12:5 *ᵃ*Or *thicket*   12:10 *ᵃ*Literally *shepherds* or *pastors*

They have put themselves to pain *but*
　　do not profit.
But be ashamed of your harvest
Because of the fierce anger of the
　　LORD."

[14]Thus says the LORD: "Against all My evil neighbors who touch the inheritance which I have caused My people Israel to inherit—behold, I will pluck them out of their land and pluck out the house of Judah from among them. [15]Then it shall be, after I have plucked them out, that I will return and have compassion on them and bring them back, everyone to his heritage and everyone to his land. [16]And it shall be, if they will learn carefully the ways of My people, to swear by My name, 'As the LORD lives,' as they taught My people to swear by Baal, then they shall be established in the midst of My people. [17]But if they do not obey, I will utterly pluck up and destroy that nation," says the LORD.

Symbol of the Linen Sash

13Thus the LORD said to me: "Go and get yourself a linen sash, and put it around your waist, but do not put it in water." [2]So I got a sash according to the word of the LORD, and put *it* around my waist.

> **13:1 a linen sash.** This is one of the many signs Jeremiah used to illustrate God's message. The sash was tied around his waste to depict the intimate covenant between God and Israel. **do not put it in water.** The sash, not having been washed, was rotted and good for nothing after it had been buried for a time. This symbolized the uselessness of Israel to God while they remained unclean from sin.

[3]And the word of the LORD came to me the second time, saying, [4]"Take the sash that you acquired, which *is* around your waist, and arise, go to the Euphrates,[a] and hide it there in a hole in the rock." [5]So I went and hid it by the Euphrates, as the LORD commanded me.

[6]Now it came to pass after many days that the LORD said to me, "Arise, go to the Euphrates, and take from there the sash which I commanded you to hide there."

[7]Then I went to the Euphrates and dug, and I took the sash from the place where I had hidden it; and there was the sash, ruined. It was profitable for nothing.

[8]Then the word of the LORD came to me, saying, [9]"Thus says the LORD: 'In this manner I will ruin the pride of Judah and the great pride of Jerusalem. [10]This evil people, who refuse to hear My words, who follow the dictates of their hearts, and walk after other gods to serve them and worship them, shall be just like this sash which is profitable for nothing. [11]For as the sash clings to the waist of a man, so I have caused the whole house of Israel and the whole house of Judah to cling to Me,' says the LORD, 'that they may become My people, for renown, for praise, and for glory; but they would not hear.'

Symbol of the Wine Bottles

[12]"Therefore you shall speak to them this word: 'Thus says the LORD God of Israel: "Every bottle shall be filled with wine." '

"And they will say to you, 'Do we not certainly know that every bottle will be filled with wine?'

[13]"Then you shall say to them, 'Thus says the LORD: "Behold, I will fill all the inhabitants of this land—even the kings who sit on David's throne, the priests, the prophets, and all the inhabitants of Jerusalem—with drunkenness! [14]And I will dash them one against another, even the fathers and the sons together," says the LORD. "I will not pity nor spare nor have mercy, but will destroy them." ' "

Pride Precedes Captivity

[15]　Hear and give ear:
　　Do not be proud,
　　For the LORD has spoken.
[16]　Give glory to the LORD your God
　　Before He causes darkness,
　　And before your feet stumble
　　On the dark mountains,
　　And while you are looking for light,
　　He turns it into the shadow of death
　　And makes *it* dense darkness.
[17]　But if you will not hear it,
　　My soul will weep in secret for *your*
　　pride;

My eyes will weep bitterly
And run down with tears,
Because the LORD's flock has been
  taken captive.

18 Say to the king and to the queen
     mother,
   "Humble yourselves;
   Sit down,
   For your rule shall collapse, the crown
     of your glory."

> **13:18 king...queen mother.** This refers to Jehoia-chin and Nehushta (about 597 B.C.; see 22:24–26). Since the king was only 18 years old, the queen held the real power.

19 The cities of the South shall be shut
     up,
   And no one shall open *them*;
   Judah shall be carried away captive,
     all of it;
   It shall be wholly carried away
     captive.

20 Lift up your eyes and see
   Those who come from the north.
   Where *is* the flock *that* was given to
     you,
   Your beautiful sheep?
21 What will you say when He punishes
     you?
   For you have taught them
   To be chieftains, to be head over you.
   Will not pangs seize you,
   Like a woman in labor?
22 And if you say in your heart,
   "Why have these things come upon
     me?"
   For the greatness of your iniquity
   Your skirts have been uncovered,
   Your heels made bare.

23 Can the Ethiopian change his skin or
     the leopard its spots?
   Then may you also do good who are
     accustomed to do evil.

24 "Therefore I will scatter them like
     stubble
   That passes away by the wind of the
     wilderness.
25 This is your lot,
   The portion of your measures from
     Me," says the LORD,
   "Because you have forgotten Me
   And trusted in falsehood.
26 Therefore I will uncover your skirts
     over your face,
   That your shame may appear.
27 I have seen your adulteries
   And your *lustful* neighings,
   The lewdness of your harlotry,
   Your abominations on the hills in the
     fields.
   Woe to you, O Jerusalem!
   Will you still not be made clean?"

Sword, Famine, and Pestilence

14 The word of the LORD that came to
Jeremiah concerning the droughts.

2 "Judah mourns,
   And her gates languish;
   They mourn for the land,
   And the cry of Jerusalem has gone up.

> **14:2 gates languish.** The "gates" were the place of public affairs, which were empty or filled with mourners during drought and consequent famine.

3 Their nobles have sent their lads for
     water;
   They went to the cisterns *and* found
     no water.
   They returned with their vessels
     empty;
   They were ashamed and confounded
   And covered their heads.
4 Because the ground is parched,
   For there was no rain in the land,
   The plowmen were ashamed;
   They covered their heads.
5 Yes, the deer also gave birth in the
     field,
   But left because there was no grass.

6　And the wild donkeys stood in the
　　　desolate heights;
　　They sniffed at the wind like jackals;
　　Their eyes failed because *there was*
　　　no grass."

7　O LORD, though our iniquities testify
　　　against us,
　　Do it for Your name's sake;
　　For our backslidings are many,
　　We have sinned against You.
8　O the Hope of Israel, his Savior in
　　　time of trouble,
　　Why should You be like a stranger in
　　　the land,
　　And like a traveler *who* turns aside to
　　　tarry for a night?
9　Why should You be like a man
　　　astonished,
　　Like a mighty one *who* cannot save?
　　Yet You, O LORD, *are* in our midst,
　　And we are called by Your name;
　　Do not leave us!

14:7–9 our backslidings. Jeremiah confesses Judah's guilt but reminds God that His reputation is tied to what happens to His people. He asks that He not be indifferent as a foreigner or an overnight visitor.

¹⁰Thus says the LORD to this people:

　" Thus they have loved to wander;
　　They have not restrained their feet.
　　Therefore the LORD does not accept
　　　them;
　　He will remember their iniquity now,
　　And punish their sins."

¹¹Then the LORD said to me, "Do not pray for this people, for *their* good. ¹²When they fast, I will not hear their cry; and when they offer burnt offering and grain offering, I will not accept them. But I will consume them by the sword, by the famine, and by the pestilence."

¹³Then I said, "Ah, Lord GOD! Behold, the prophets say to them, 'You shall not see the sword, nor shall you have famine, but I will give you assured peace in this place.' "

¹⁴And the LORD said to me, "The prophets prophesy lies in My name. I have not sent them, commanded them, nor spoken to them; they prophesy to you a false vision, divination, a worthless thing, and the deceit of their heart. ¹⁵Therefore thus says the LORD concerning the prophets who prophesy in My name, whom I did not send, and who say, 'Sword and famine shall not be in this land'—'By sword and famine those prophets shall be consumed! ¹⁶And the people to whom they prophesy shall be cast out in the streets of Jerusalem because of the famine and the sword; they will have no one to bury them—them nor their wives, their sons nor their daughters—for I will pour their wickedness on them.'

¹⁷"Therefore you shall say this word to them:

　'Let my eyes flow with tears night and
　　　day,
　　And let them not cease;
　　For the virgin daughter of my people
　　Has been broken with a mighty
　　　stroke, with a very severe blow.
18　If I go out to the field,
　　Then behold, those slain with the
　　　sword!
　　And if I enter the city,
　　Then behold, those sick from
　　　famine!
　　Yes, both prophet and priest go about
　　　in a land they do not know.' "

The People Plead for Mercy
19　Have You utterly rejected Judah?
　　Has Your soul loathed Zion?
　　Why have You stricken us so that
　　　there is no healing for us?
　　We looked for peace, but *there was* no
　　　good;
　　And for the time of healing, and there
　　　was trouble.
20　We acknowledge, O LORD, our
　　　wickedness
　　And the iniquity of our fathers,
　　For we have sinned against You.
21　Do not abhor *us,* for Your name's
　　　sake;
　　Do not disgrace the throne of Your
　　　glory.
　　Remember, do not break Your
　　　covenant with us.
22　Are there any among the idols of the
　　　nations that can cause rain?
　　Or can the heavens give showers?
　　Are You not He, O LORD our God?

Therefore we will wait for You,
Since You have made all these.

The LORD Will Not Relent

15 Then the LORD said to me, "*Even*
if Moses and Samuel stood before
Me, My mind *would* not *be* favorable toward this people. Cast *them* out of My
sight, and let them go forth. ²And it shall
be, if they say to you, 'Where should we
go?' then you shall tell them, 'Thus says
the LORD:

"Such as *are* for death, to death;
And such as *are* for the sword, to the
    sword;
And such as *are* for the famine, to the
    famine;
And such as *are* for the captivity, to
    the captivity." '

³"And I will appoint over them four forms
of destruction," says the LORD: "the sword
to slay, the dogs to drag, the birds of the
heavens and the beasts of the earth to devour and destroy. ⁴I will hand them over to
trouble, to all kingdoms of the earth, because of Manasseh the son of Hezekiah,
king of Judah, for what he did in Jerusalem.

⁵ "For who will have pity on you,
       O Jerusalem?
    Or who will bemoan you?
    Or who will turn aside to ask how
       you are doing?
⁶   You have forsaken Me," says the
       LORD,
    "You have gone backward.
    Therefore I will stretch out My hand
       against you and destroy you;
    I am weary of relenting!
⁷   And I will winnow them with a
       winnowing fan in the gates of the
       land;
    I will bereave *them* of children;
    I will destroy My people,
    Since they do not return from their
       ways.
⁸   Their widows will be increased to Me
       more than the sand of the seas;
    I will bring against them,

Against the mother of the young
    men,
A plunderer at noonday;
I will cause anguish and terror to fall
    on them suddenly.
⁹ "She languishes who has borne seven;
    She has breathed her last;
    Her sun has gone down
    While *it was* yet day;
    She has been ashamed and
       confounded.
    And the remnant of them I will
       deliver to the sword
    Before their enemies," says the LORD.

> **15:1–9** It was ineffective at this point to intercede for
> an unrepentant nation. King Manasseh's sin was
> chief among their sin (see 2 Kin. 21:1–18).

Jeremiah's Dejection
¹⁰   Woe is me, my mother,
    That you have borne me,
    A man of strife and a man of
       contention to the whole earth!
    I have neither lent for interest,
    Nor have men lent to me for interest.
    Every one of them curses me.

¹¹The LORD said:

"Surely it will be well with your
    remnant;
Surely I will cause the enemy to
    intercede with you
In the time of adversity and in the
    time of affliction.
¹²   Can anyone break iron,
    The northern iron and the bronze?
¹³   Your wealth and your treasures
    I will give as plunder without price,
    Because of all your sins,
    Throughout your territories.
¹⁴   And I will make *you* cross over with*ᵃ*
    your enemies

> **15:11–14** The Lord promised protection for the obe-
> dient remnant in Judah in the midst of judgment (see
> Mal. 3:16,17). The Babylonians allowed some to stay in
> the land, and Jeremiah was treated kindly (40:1–6).

15:14 *ᵃ*Following Masoretic Text and Vulgate; Septuagint, Syriac, and Targum read *cause you to serve*
(compare 17:4).

Into a land *which* you do not know;
For a fire is kindled in My anger,
Which shall burn upon you."

15 O LORD, You know;
    Remember me and visit me,
    And take vengeance for me on my
        persecutors.
    In Your enduring patience, do not
        take me away.
    Know that for Your sake I have
        suffered rebuke.
16 Your words were found, and I ate
        them,
    And Your word was to me the joy and
        rejoicing of my heart;
    For I am called by Your name,
    O LORD God of hosts.
17 I did not sit in the assembly of the
        mockers,
    Nor did I rejoice;
    I sat alone because of Your hand,
    For You have filled me with
        indignation.
18 Why is my pain perpetual
    And my wound incurable,
    Which refuses to be healed?
    Will You surely be to me like an
        unreliable stream,
    As waters *that* fail?

The LORD Reassures Jeremiah

19Therefore thus says the LORD:

    "If you return,
    Then I will bring you back;
    You shall stand before Me;
    If you take out the precious from the
        vile,
    You shall be as My mouth.
    Let them return to you,
    But you must not return to them.

> **15:19** The Lord reprimanded Jeremiah for his self-pity and impatience. Only his repentance would enable him to be God's mouthpiece again. As a man who was set up to examine the hearts of others, he needed first to examine himself (see Moses, in Ex. 4:22–26).

20 And I will make you to this people a
        fortified bronze wall;
    And they will fight against you,
    But they shall not prevail against you;
    For I *am* with you to save you

And deliver you," says the LORD.
21 "I will deliver you from the hand of the
        wicked,
    And I will redeem you from the grip
        of the terrible."

Jeremiah's Lifestyle and Message

16 The word of the LORD also came to me, saying, 2"You shall not take a wife, nor shall you have sons or daughters in this place." 3For thus says the LORD concerning the sons and daughters who are born in this place, and concerning their mothers who bore them and their fathers who begot them in this land: 4"They shall die gruesome deaths; they shall not be lamented nor shall they be buried, *but* they shall be like refuse on the face of the earth. They shall be consumed by the sword and by famine, and their corpses shall be meat for the birds of heaven and for the beasts of the earth."

5For thus says the LORD: "Do not enter the house of mourning, nor go to lament or bemoan them; for I have taken away My peace from this people," says the LORD, "lovingkindness and mercies. 6Both the great and the small shall die in this land. They shall not be buried; neither shall men lament for them, cut themselves, nor make themselves bald for them. 7Nor shall *men* break *bread* in mourning for them, to comfort them for the dead; nor shall *men* give them the cup of consolation to drink for their father or their mother. 8Also you shall not go into the house of feasting to sit with them, to eat and drink."

9For thus says the LORD of hosts, the God of Israel: "Behold, I will cause to cease from this place, before your eyes and in your days, the voice of mirth and the voice of gladness, the voice of the bridegroom and the voice of the bride.

10"And it shall be, when you show this people all these words, and they say to you, 'Why has the LORD pronounced all this great disaster against us? Or what *is* our iniquity? Or what *is* our sin that we have committed against the LORD our God?' 11then you shall say to them, 'Because your fathers have forsaken Me,' says the LORD; 'they have walked after other gods and have served them and worshiped them, and have forsaken Me and not kept My law. 12And

you have done worse than your fathers, for behold, each one follows the dictates of his own evil heart, so that no one listens to Me. ¹³Therefore I will cast you out of this land into a land that you do not know, neither you nor your fathers; and there you shall serve other gods day and night, where I will not show you favor.'

> **16:15 all the lands.** This extensive reference will be fully realized only in the final gathering into the Messiah's earthly kingdom.

God Will Restore Israel

¹⁴"Therefore behold, the days are coming," says the LORD, "that it shall no more be said, 'The LORD lives who brought up the children of Israel from the land of Egypt,' ¹⁵but, 'The LORD lives who brought up the children of Israel from the land of the north and from all the lands where He had driven them.' For I will bring them back into their land which I gave to their fathers.

¹⁶"Behold, I will send for many fishermen," says the LORD, "and they shall fish them; and afterward I will send for many hunters, and they shall hunt them from every mountain and every hill, and out of the holes of the rocks. ¹⁷For My eyes *are* on all their ways; they are not hidden from My face, nor is their iniquity hidden from My eyes. ¹⁸And first I will repay double for their iniquity and their sin, because they have defiled My land; they have filled My inheritance with the carcasses of their detestable and abominable idols."

¹⁹ O LORD, my strength and my fortress,
My refuge in the day of affliction,
The Gentiles shall come to You
From the ends of the earth and say,
"Surely our fathers have inherited lies,
Worthlessness and unprofitable
things."
²⁰ Will a man make gods for himself,
Which *are* not gods?

²¹ "Therefore behold, I will this once
cause them to know,
I will cause them to know
My hand and My might;

And they shall know that My name *is* the LORD.

Judah's Sin and Punishment

17 "The sin of Judah *is* written with a pen of iron;
With the point of a diamond *it is* engraved
On the tablet of their heart,
And on the horns of your altars,

> **17:1 The sin of Judah.** Further reasons for the judgment include idolatry, relying on the flesh, and dishonesty in amassing wealth. **pen of iron.** This tool was used to engrave the names of idols on the horns of their altars. The picture drawn here is that Judah's sin was permanent, etched into them as if in stone.

² While their children remember
Their altars and their wooden
images^a
By the green trees on the high hills.
³ O My mountain in the field,
I will give as plunder your wealth, all
your treasures,
And your high places of sin within all
your borders.
⁴ And you, even yourself,
Shall let go of your heritage which I
gave you;
And I will cause you to serve your
enemies
In the land which you do not know;
For you have kindled a fire in My
anger *which* shall burn forever."

⁵Thus says the LORD:

"Cursed *is* the man who trusts in
man
And makes flesh his strength,
Whose heart departs from the LORD.
⁶ For he shall be like a shrub in the
desert,
And shall not see when good comes,
But shall inhabit the parched places
in the wilderness,
In a salt land *which is* not inhabited.

⁷ "Blessed *is* the man who trusts in the
LORD,
And whose hope is the LORD.

17:2 ^aHebrew *Asherim,* Canaanite deities

8 For he shall be like a tree planted by
      the waters,
   Which spreads out its roots by the
      river,
   And will not fear[a] when heat comes;
   But its leaf will be green,
   And will not be anxious in the year of
      drought,
   Nor will cease from yielding fruit.

9 "The heart *is* deceitful above all *things*,
   And desperately wicked;
   Who can know it?
10 I, the LORD, search the heart,
   I test the mind,
   Even to give every man according to
      his ways,
   According to the fruit of his doings.

> **17:10 I...search the heart.** God renders final judg-
> ment on every man, whether sinful (vv. 1–4), barren
> (vv. 5,6), or blessed (vv. 7,8).

11 "*As* a partridge that broods but does
      not hatch,
   So is he who gets riches, but not by
      right;
   It will leave him in the midst of his
      days,
   And at his end he will be a fool."

12 A glorious high throne from the
      beginning
   Is the place of our sanctuary.
13 O LORD, the hope of Israel,
   All who forsake You shall be
      ashamed.

   "Those who depart from Me
   Shall be written in the earth,
   Because they have forsaken the LORD,
   The fountain of living waters."

Jeremiah Prays for Deliverance

14 Heal me, O LORD, and I shall be
      healed;
   Save me, and I shall be saved,
   For You *are* my praise.
15 Indeed they say to me,
   "Where *is* the word of the LORD?
   Let it come now!"

16 As for me, I have not hurried away
      from *being* a shepherd *who* follows
      You,
   Nor have I desired the woeful day;
   You know what came out of my lips;
   It was right there before You.
17 Do not be a terror to me;
   You *are* my hope in the day of doom.
18 Let them be ashamed who persecute
      me,
   But do not let me be put to shame;
   Let them be dismayed,
   But do not let me be dismayed.
   Bring on them the day of doom,
   And destroy them with double
      destruction!

Hallow the Sabbath Day

19Thus the LORD said to me: "Go and
stand in the gate of the children of the people, by which the kings of Judah come in
and by which they go out, and in all the
gates of Jerusalem; 20and say to them, 'Hear
the word of the LORD, you kings of Judah,
and all Judah, and all the inhabitants of Jerusalem, who enter by these gates. 21Thus
says the LORD: "Take heed to yourselves,
and bear no burden on the Sabbath day, nor
bring *it* in by the gates of Jerusalem; 22nor
carry a burden out of your houses on the
Sabbath day, nor do any work, but hallow
the Sabbath day, as I commanded your
fathers. 23But they did not obey nor incline
their ear, but made their neck stiff, that
they might not hear nor receive instruction.

24"And it shall be, if you heed Me carefully," says the LORD, "to bring no burden
through the gates of this city on the Sabbath day, but hallow the Sabbath day, to do
no work in it, 25then shall enter the gates of
this city kings and princes sitting on the
throne of David, riding in chariots and on
horses, they and their princes, accompa-

> **17:21–24 Sabbath day.** Israel had ignored both the
> required Sabbath day and the year of Sabbath for the
> land (Lev. 25:1–7). The 70-year captivity correlated
> to the 940 years from Saul to the captivity, which in-
> cluded 70 neglected Sabbath years. When the Jews
> were restored from captivity, special emphasis was
> placed on Sabbath faithfulness (see Neh. 13:19).

17:8 ᵃQere and Targum read *see*.

nied by the men of Judah and the inhabitants of Jerusalem; and this city shall remain forever. ²⁶And they shall come from the cities of Judah and from the places around Jerusalem, from the land of Benjamin and from the lowland, from the mountains and from the South, bringing burnt offerings and sacrifices, grain offerings and incense, bringing sacrifices of praise to the house of the LORD.

²⁷"But if you will not heed Me to hallow the Sabbath day, such as not carrying a burden when entering the gates of Jerusalem on the Sabbath day, then I will kindle a fire in its gates, and it shall devour the palaces of Jerusalem, and it shall not be quenched." ' "

The Potter and the Clay

18 The word which came to Jeremiah from the LORD, saying: ²"Arise and go down to the potter's house, and there I will cause you to hear My words." ³Then I went down to the potter's house, and there he was, making something at the wheel. ⁴And the vessel that he made of clay was marred in the hand of the potter; so he made it again into another vessel, as it seemed good to the potter to make.

⁵Then the word of the LORD came to me, saying: ⁶"O house of Israel, can I not do with you as this potter?" says the LORD. "Look, as the clay *is* in the potter's hand, so *are* you in My hand, O house of Israel! ⁷The instant I speak concerning a nation and concerning a kingdom, to pluck up, to pull down, and to destroy *it*, ⁸if that nation against whom I have spoken turns from its evil, I will relent of the disaster that I thought to bring upon it. ⁹And the instant I speak concerning a nation and concerning a kingdom, to build and to plant *it*, ¹⁰if it does evil in My sight so that it does not obey My voice, then I will relent concerning the good with which I said I would benefit it.

> **18:2–6 potter's house.** Just as the potter shaped a vessel to illustrate a message, Jeremiah used a vessel for his own illustration (19:1ff). The potter's reshaping of the misshapen vessel into a useful one depicted how God would reshape Judah into a "good vessel" if she repented.

¹¹"Now therefore, speak to the men of Judah and to the inhabitants of Jerusalem, saying, 'Thus says the LORD: "Behold, I am fashioning a disaster and devising a plan against you. Return now every one from his evil way, and make your ways and your doings good." ' "

God's Warning Rejected

¹²And they said, "That is hopeless! So we will walk according to our own plans, and we will every one obey the dictates of his evil heart."

> **18:12 That is hopeless!** Israel finally admitted their spiritual condition. Jeremiah's threats had no impact since they had hardened themselves to God, and they now openly professed this without repentance. Jeremiah was not to pray for Israel (7:16) because their hardened hearts were set against changing.

¹³Therefore thus says the LORD:

" Ask now among the Gentiles,
  Who has heard such things?
  The virgin of Israel has done a very
    horrible thing.
¹⁴ Will *a man* leave the snow water of
    Lebanon,
  Which comes from the rock of the
    field?
  Will the cold flowing waters be
    forsaken for strange waters?

¹⁵ " Because My people have forgotten Me,
  They have burned incense to
    worthless idols.
  And they have caused themselves to
    stumble in their ways,
  From the ancient paths,
  To walk in pathways and not on a
    highway,
¹⁶ To make their land desolate *and a*
    perpetual hissing;
  Everyone who passes by it will be
    astonished
  And shake his head.
¹⁷ I will scatter them as with an east
    wind before the enemy;
  I will show them*ᵃ* the back and not
    the face
  In the day of their calamity."

18:17 *ᵃ*Following Septuagint, Syriac, Targum, and Vulgate; Masoretic Text reads *look them in*.

Jeremiah Persecuted

¹⁸Then they said, "Come and let us devise plans against Jeremiah; for the law shall not perish from the priest, nor counsel from the wise, nor the word from the prophet. Come and let us attack him with the tongue, and let us not give heed to any of his words."

¹⁹   Give heed to me, O LORD,
And listen to the voice of those who
     contend with me!
²⁰   Shall evil be repaid for good?
For they have dug a pit for my life.
Remember that I stood before You
To speak good for them,
To turn away Your wrath from them.
²¹   Therefore deliver up their children to
     the famine,
And pour out their *blood*
By the force of the sword;
Let their wives *become* widows
And bereaved of their children.
Let their men be put to death,
Their young men *be* slain
By the sword in battle.
²²   Let a cry be heard from their houses,
When You bring a troop suddenly
     upon them;
For they have dug a pit to take me,
And hidden snares for my feet.
²³   Yet, LORD, You know all their counsel
Which is against me, to slay *me*.
Provide no atonement for their
     iniquity,
Nor blot out their sin from Your sight;
But let them be overthrown before
     You.
Deal *thus* with them
In the time of Your anger.

The Sign of the Broken Flask

19 Thus says the LORD: "Go and get a potter's earthen flask, and *take* some of the elders of the people and some of the elders of the priests. ²And go out to the Valley of the Son of Hinnom, which *is*

> **19:1 elders of the people...the priests.** They were chosen to be credible witnesses of the symbolic action with the earthen flask, so that no one could plead ignorance of the prophesy. The 72 elders who composed the Sanhedrin were partly from the priests and the other tribes.

by the entry of the Potsherd Gate; and proclaim there the words that I will tell you, ³and say, 'Hear the word of the LORD, O kings of Judah and inhabitants of Jerusalem. Thus says the LORD of hosts, the God of Israel: "Behold, I will bring such a catastrophe on this place, that whoever hears of it, his ears will tingle.

⁴"Because they have forsaken Me and made this an alien place, because they have burned incense in it to other gods whom neither they, their fathers, nor the kings of Judah have known, and have filled this place with the blood of the innocents ⁵(they have also built the high places of Baal, to burn their sons with fire *for* burnt offerings to Baal, which I did not command or speak, nor did it come into My mind), ⁶therefore behold, the days are coming," says the LORD, "that this place shall no more be called Tophet or the Valley of the Son of Hinnom, but the Valley of Slaughter. ⁷And I will make void the counsel of Judah and Jerusalem in this place, and I will cause them to fall by the sword before their enemies and by the hands of those who seek their lives; their corpses I will give as meat for the birds of the heaven and for the beasts of the earth. ⁸I will make this city desolate and a hissing; everyone who passes by it will be astonished and hiss because of all its plagues. ⁹And I will cause them to eat the flesh of their sons and the flesh of their daughters, and everyone shall eat the flesh of his friend in the siege and in the desperation with which their enemies and those who seek their lives shall drive them to despair." '

¹⁰"Then you shall break the flask in the sight of the men who go with you, ¹¹and say to them, 'Thus says the LORD of hosts: "Even so I will break this people and this city, as *one* breaks a potter's vessel, which cannot be made whole again; and they shall bury *them* in Tophet till *there is* no place to bury. ¹²Thus I will do to this place," says the LORD, "and to its inhabitants, and make this city like Tophet. ¹³And the houses of Jerusalem and the houses of the kings of Judah shall be defiled like the place of Tophet, because of all the houses on whose roofs they have burned incense to all the host of heaven, and poured out drink offerings to other gods." ' "

¹⁴"Then Jeremiah came from Tophet, where the LORD had sent him to prophesy; and he stood in the court of the Lord's house and said to all the people, ¹⁵"Thus says the LORD of hosts, the God of Israel: 'Behold, I will bring on this city and on all her towns all the doom that I have pronounced against it, because they have stiffened their necks that they might not hear My words.' "

The Word of God to Pashhur

20 Now Pashhur the son of Immer, the priest who *was* also chief governor in the house of the LORD, heard that Jeremiah prophesied these things. ²Then Pashhur struck Jeremiah the prophet, and put him in the stocks that *were* in the high gate of Benjamin, which *was* by the house of the LORD.

> **20:2 struck Jeremiah.** Pashhur, or one of his men, gave Jeremiah 40 lashes (see Deut. 25:3). **put him in the stocks.** His neck, feet and hands were fastened in small holes causing bodily distortion and excruciating pain. **high gate.** This was the northern gate of the upper temple court.

³And it happened on the next day that Pashhur brought Jeremiah out of the stocks. Then Jeremiah said to him, "The LORD has not called your name Pashhur, but Magor-Missabib.ᵃ ⁴For thus says the LORD: 'Behold, I will make you a terror to yourself and to all your friends; and they shall fall by the sword of their enemies, and your eyes shall see *it*. I will give all Judah into the hand of the king of Babylon, and he shall carry them captive to Babylon and slay them with the sword. ⁵Moreover I will deliver all the wealth of this city, all its produce, and all its precious things; all the treasures of the kings of Judah I will give into the hand of their enemies, who will plunder them, seize them, and carry them to Babylon. ⁶And you, Pashhur, and all who dwell in your house, shall go into captivity. You shall go to Babylon, and there you shall die, and be buried there, you and all your friends, to whom you have prophesied lies.' "

Jeremiah's Unpopular Ministry

7   O LORD, You induced me, and I was
          persuaded;
     You are stronger than I, and have
          prevailed.
     I am in derision daily;
     Everyone mocks me.
8   For when I spoke, I cried out;
     I shouted, "Violence and plunder!"
     Because the word of the LORD was
          made to me
     A reproach and a derision daily.
9   Then I said, "I will not make mention
          of Him,
     Nor speak anymore in His name."
     But *His word* was in my heart like a
          burning fire
     Shut up in my bones;
     I was weary of holding *it* back,
     And I could not.
10   For I heard many mocking:
   "Fear on every side!"
   "Report," *they say*, "and we will report
          it!"
     All my acquaintances watched for my
          stumbling, *saying*,
   "Perhaps he can be induced;
     Then we will prevail against him,
     And we will take our revenge on him."

11   But the LORD *is* with me as a mighty,
          awesome One.
     Therefore my persecutors will
          stumble, and will not prevail.
     They will be greatly ashamed, for they
          will not prosper.
     Their everlasting confusion will never
          be forgotten.
12   But, O LORD of hosts,
     You who test the righteous,
     And see the mind and heart,
     Let me see Your vengeance on them;
     For I have pleaded my cause before
          You.

13   Sing to the LORD! Praise the LORD!
     For He has delivered the life of the
          poor
     From the hand of evildoers.

14   Cursed *be* the day in which I was
          born!

20:3 ᵃLiterally *Fear on Every Side*

Let the day not be blessed in which
   my mother bore me!
15 Let the man *be* cursed
   Who brought news to my father,
      saying,
   "A male child has been born to you!"
   Making him very glad.
16 And let that man be like the cities
   Which the LORD overthrew, and did
      not relent;
   Let him hear the cry in the morning
   And the shouting at noon,

> **20:16 the cities Which the LORD overthrew.** This re-
> fers to Sodom and Gomorrah (Gen. 19:25).

17 Because he did not kill me from the
      womb,
   That my mother might have been my
      grave,
   And her womb always enlarged *with
      me.*
18 Why did I come forth from the womb
      to see labor and sorrow,
   That my days should be consumed
      with shame?

Jerusalem's Doom Is Sealed

21 The word which came to Jeremiah
from the LORD when King Zedekiah
sent to him Pashhur the son of Melchiah,
and Zephaniah the son of Maaseiah, the
priest, saying, [2]"Please inquire of the LORD
for us, for Nebuchadnezzar[a] king of Babylon makes war against us. Perhaps the
LORD will deal with us according to all His
wonderful works, that *the king* may go
away from us."

[3]Then Jeremiah said to them, "Thus you
shall say to Zedekiah, [4]'Thus says the
LORD God of Israel: "Behold, I will turn
back the weapons of war that *are* in your
hands, with which you fight against the
king of Babylon and the Chaldeans[a] who
besiege you outside the walls; and I will assemble them in the midst of this city. [5]I
Myself will fight against you with an outstretched hand and with a strong arm, even
in anger and fury and great wrath. [6]I will
strike the inhabitants of this city, both man
and beast; they shall die of a great pestilence. [7]And afterward," says the LORD, "I

will deliver Zedekiah king of Judah, his servants and the people, and such as are left in
this city from the pestilence and the sword
and the famine, into the hand of Nebuchadnezzar king of Babylon, into the hand
of their enemies, and into the hand of those
who seek their life; and he shall strike them
with the edge of the sword. He shall not
spare them, or have pity or mercy." '

[8]"Now you shall say to this people, 'Thus
says the LORD: "Behold, I set before you the
way of life and the way of death. [9]He who
remains in this city shall die by the sword,
by famine, and by pestilence; but he who
goes out and defects to the Chaldeans who
besiege you, he shall live, and his life shall
be as a prize to him. [10]For I have set My face
against this city for adversity and not for
good," says the LORD. "It shall be given into
the hand of the king of Babylon, and he
shall burn it with fire." '

> **21:8,9 life and...death.** Since a persistent lack of re-
> pentance had led to the conquest, Jeremiah urged
> the Jews to submit and surrender to the attacker so
> that they would be taken captive instead of killed.

Message to the House of David

[11]"And concerning the house of the king
of Judah, *say,* 'Hear the word of the LORD,
[12]O house of David! Thus says the LORD:

   "Execute judgment in the morning;
   And deliver *him who is* plundered
   Out of the hand of the oppressor,
   Lest My fury go forth like fire
   And burn so that no one can quench
      it,
   Because of the evil of your doings.

13 "Behold, I *am* against you,
   O inhabitant of the valley,
   And rock of the plain," says the LORD,
   "Who say, 'Who shall come down
      against us?
   Or who shall enter our dwellings?'
14 But I will punish you according to the
      fruit of your doings," says the
      LORD;
   "I will kindle a fire in its forest,
   And it shall devour all things around
      it." ' "

21:2 [a]Hebrew *Nebuchadrezzar,* and so elsewhere   21:4 [a]Or *Babylonians*

22 Thus says the LORD: "Go down to the house of the king of Judah, and there speak this word, ²and say, 'Hear the word of the LORD, O king of Judah, you who sit on the throne of David, you and your servants and your people who enter these gates! ³Thus says the LORD: "Execute judgment and righteousness, and deliver the plundered out of the hand of the oppressor. Do no wrong and do no violence to the stranger, the fatherless, or the widow, nor shed innocent blood in this place. ⁴For if you indeed do this thing, then shall enter the gates of this house, riding on horses and in chariots, accompanied by servants and people, kings who sit on the throne of David. ⁵But if you will not hear these words, I swear by Myself," says the LORD, "that this house shall become a desolation." ' "

⁶For thus says the LORD to the house of the king of Judah:

"You *are* Gilead to Me,
The head of Lebanon;
Yet I surely will make you a
  wilderness,
Cities *which* are not inhabited.
⁷   I will prepare destroyers against you,
Everyone with his weapons;
They shall cut down your choice
  cedars
And cast *them* into the fire.

⁸And many nations will pass by this city; and everyone will say to his neighbor, 'Why has the LORD done so to this great city?' ⁹Then they will answer, 'Because they have forsaken the covenant of the LORD their God, and worshiped other gods and served them.' "

¹⁰   Weep not for the dead, nor bemoan
  him;
Weep bitterly for him who goes away,

22:10 the dead. This probably referred to Josiah, who had died before the destruction (2 Kin. 22:20). When Josiah died, and on each anniversary of his death, there was open public weeping in which Jeremiah participated in order to honor the king (2 Chr. 35:24,25).

For he shall return no more,
Nor see his native country.

Message to the Sons of Josiah

¹¹For thus says the LORD concerning Shallum*ᵃ* the son of Josiah, king of Judah, who reigned instead of Josiah his father, who went from this place: "He shall not return here anymore, ¹²but he shall die in the place where they have led him captive, and shall see this land no more.

¹³   "Woe to him who builds his house by
  unrighteousness
And his chambers by injustice,
Who uses his neighbor's service
  without wages
And gives him nothing for his work,
¹⁴   Who says, 'I will build myself a wide
  house with spacious chambers,
And cut out windows for it,
Paneling *it* with cedar
And painting *it* with vermilion.'
¹⁵   "Shall you reign because you enclose
  yourself in cedar?
Did not your father eat and drink,
And do justice and righteousness?
Then *it was* well with him.
¹⁶   He judged the cause of the poor and
  needy;
Then *it was* well.
Was not this knowing Me?" says the
  LORD.
¹⁷   "Yet your eyes and your heart *are* for
  nothing but your covetousness,
For shedding innocent blood,
And practicing oppression and
  violence."

¹⁸Therefore thus says the LORD concerning Jehoiakim the son of Josiah, king of Judah:

"They shall not lament for him,
Saying, 'Alas, my brother!' or 'Alas, my
  sister!'
They shall not lament for him,
Saying, 'Alas, master!' or 'Alas, his
  glory!'
¹⁹   He shall be buried with the burial of a
  donkey,

22:11 *ᵃ*Also called *Jehoahaz*

Dragged and cast out beyond the gates
of Jerusalem.

22:18,19 Jehoiakim. He was a wicked king who
wrongly taxed the people (2 Kin. 23:35) and made
them build his elaborate palace without pay, violating God's law in Lev. 19:13 and Deut. 24:14,15. He was
killed in Babylon's second siege, and his corpse was
dishonored by being left on the ground for scaven-
gers to devour.

20 "Go up to Lebanon, and cry out,
     And lift up your voice in Bashan;
     Cry from Abarim,
     For all your lovers are destroyed.
21   I spoke to you in your prosperity,
     But you said, 'I will not hear.'
     This *has been* your manner from your
          youth,
     That you did not obey My voice.
22   The wind shall eat up all your rulers,
     And your lovers shall go into
          captivity;
     Surely then you will be ashamed and
          humiliated
     For all your wickedness.
23   O inhabitant of Lebanon,
     Making your nest in the cedars,
     How gracious will you be when pangs
          come upon you,
     Like the pain of a woman in labor?

Message to Coniah

24"As I live," says the LORD, "though
Coniah[a] the son of Jehoiakim, king of Judah, were the signet on My right hand, yet I
would pluck you off; 25and I will give you
into the hand of those who seek your life,
and into the hand *of those* whose face you
fear—the hand of Nebuchadnezzar king of
Babylon and the hand of the Chaldeans.
26So I will cast you out, and your mother
who bore you, into another country where
you were not born; and there you shall die.
27But to the land to which they desire to return, there they shall not return.

28 "Is this man Coniah a despised,
          broken idol—
     A vessel in which *is* no pleasure?
     Why are they cast out, he and his
          descendants,

And cast into a land which they do
     not know?
29   O earth, earth, earth,
     Hear the word of the LORD!
30   Thus says the LORD:
     'Write this man down as childless,
     A man *who* shall not prosper in his
          days;
     For none of his descendants shall
          prosper,
     Sitting on the throne of David,
     And ruling anymore in Judah.' "

The Branch of Righteousness

23 "Woe to the shepherds who destroy and scatter the sheep of My
pasture!" says the LORD. 2Therefore thus
says the LORD God of Israel against the
shepherds who feed My people: "You have
scattered My flock, driven them away, and
not attended to them. Behold, I will attend
to you for the evil of your doings," says the
LORD. 3"But I will gather the remnant of
My flock out of all countries where I have
driven them, and bring them back to their
folds; and they shall be fruitful and increase. 4I will set up shepherds over them
who will feed them; and they shall fear no
more, nor be dismayed, nor shall they be
lacking," says the LORD.

23:1,2 Woe to the shepherds. These were the false
leaders who failed to do their duty to assure the
people's welfare. This group included the kings
(chap. 22) and other civil heads, along with prophets
and priests (v. 11). They were contrasted with the
nation's future shepherds (v. 4).

5 "Behold, *the* days are coming," says
          the LORD,
    "That I will raise to David a Branch of
          righteousness;
     A King shall reign and prosper,
     And execute judgment and
          righteousness in the earth.
6   In His days Judah will be saved,
     And Israel will dwell safely;
     Now this *is* His name by which He
          will be called:

     THE LORD OUR RIGHTEOUSNESS.[a]

22:24 [a]Also called *Jeconiah* and *Jehoiachin*   23:6 [a]Hebrew *YHWH Tsidkenu*

23:6 THE LORD OUR RIGHTEOUSNESS. Righteousness is stressed three times in vv. 5,6. The Messiah's shepherding is contrasted with that of the false shepherds (vv. 1,2,11,14). Through Him, Judah and Israel will be reunited (see Ezek. 37:15–23).

7"Therefore, behold, *the* days are coming," says the LORD, "that they shall no longer say, 'As the LORD lives who brought up the children of Israel from the land of Egypt,' 8but, 'As the LORD lives who brought up and led the descendants of the house of Israel from the north country and from all the countries where I had driven them.' And they shall dwell in their own land."

False Prophets and Empty Oracles

9   My heart within me is broken
        Because of the prophets;
        All my bones shake.
        I am like a drunken man,
        And like a man whom wine has
            overcome,
        Because of the LORD,
        And because of His holy words.
10   For the land is full of adulterers;
        For because of a curse the land
            mourns.
        The pleasant places of the wilderness
            are dried up.
        Their course of life is evil,
        And their might *is* not right.

11   "For both prophet and priest are
            profane;
        Yes, in My house I have found their
            wickedness," says the LORD.
12   "Therefore their way shall be to them
        Like slippery *ways*;
        In the darkness they shall be driven on
        And fall in them;
        For I will bring disaster on them,
        The year of their punishment," says
            the LORD.
13   "And I have seen folly in the prophets
            of Samaria:
        They prophesied by Baal
        And caused My people Israel to err.
14   Also I have seen a horrible thing in
            the prophets of Jerusalem:
        They commit adultery and walk in
            lies;
        They also strengthen the hands of
            evildoers,

So that no one turns back from his
            wickedness.
        All of them are like Sodom to Me,
        And her inhabitants like Gomorrah.

15"Therefore thus says the LORD of hosts concerning the prophets:

        'Behold, I will feed them with
            wormwood,
        And make them drink the water of
            gall;
        For from the prophets of Jerusalem
        Profaneness has gone out into all the
            land.' "

16Thus says the LORD of hosts:

        "Do not listen to the words of the
            prophets who prophesy to you.
        They make you worthless;
        They speak a vision of their own
            heart,
        Not from the mouth of the LORD.
17   They continually say to those who
            despise Me,
        'The LORD has said, "You shall have
            peace" ';
        And *to* everyone who walks according
            to the dictates of his own heart,
            they say,
        'No evil shall come upon you.' "

18   For who has stood in the counsel of
            the LORD,
        And has perceived and heard His
            word?
        Who has marked His word and heard
            it?
19   Behold, a whirlwind of the LORD has
            gone forth in fury—
        A violent whirlwind!
        It will fall violently on the head of the
            wicked.
20   The anger of the LORD will not turn
            back
        Until He has executed and performed
            the thoughts of His heart.
        In the latter days you will understand
            it perfectly.

23:20 latter days. Israel did not understand then, but they will when God's final judgment comes.

21 "I have not sent these prophets, yet
        they ran.
    I have not spoken to them, yet they
        prophesied.
22 But if they had stood in My counsel,
    And had caused My people to hear
        My words,
    Then they would have turned them
        from their evil way
    And from the evil of their doings.

23 "Am I a God near at hand," says the
        LORD,
    "And not a God afar off?
24 Can anyone hide himself in secret
        places,
    So I shall not see him?" says the
        LORD;
    "Do I not fill heaven and earth?" says
        the LORD.

25"I have heard what the prophets have
said who prophesy lies in My name, saying,
'I have dreamed, I have dreamed!' 26How
long will *this* be in the heart of the prophets
who prophesy lies? Indeed *they are* prophets of the deceit of their own heart, 27who
try to make My people forget My name by
their dreams which everyone tells his
neighbor, as their fathers forgot My name
for Baal.

28 "The prophet who has a dream, let
        him tell a dream;
    And he who has My word, let him
        speak My word faithfully.
    What *is* the chaff to the wheat?" says
        the LORD.
29 "Is not My word like a fire?" says the
        LORD,
    "And like a hammer *that* breaks the
        rock in pieces?

30"Therefore behold, I *am* against the
prophets," says the LORD, "who steal My
words every one from his neighbor. 31Be-
hold, I *am* against the prophets," says the
LORD, "who use their tongues and say, 'He
says.' 32Behold, I *am* against those who
prophesy false dreams," says the LORD,
"and tell them, and cause My people to err
by their lies and by their recklessness. Yet I

did not send them or command them;
therefore they shall not profit this people at
all," says the LORD.

33"So when these people or the prophet or
the priest ask you, saying, 'What is the oracle of the LORD?' you shall then say to
them, 'What oracle?'ᵃ I will even forsake
you," says the LORD. 34"And *as for* the
prophet and the priest and the people who
say, 'The oracle of the LORD!' I will even
punish that man and his house. 35Thus every one of you shall say to his neighbor, and
every one to his brother, 'What has the
LORD answered?' and, 'What has the LORD
spoken?' 36And the oracle of the LORD you
shall mention no more. For every man's
word will be his oracle, for you have perverted the words of the living God, the
LORD of hosts, our God. 37Thus you shall
say to the prophet, 'What has the LORD answered you?' and, 'What has the LORD spoken?' 38But since you say, 'The oracle of the
LORD!' therefore thus says the LORD: 'Because you say this word, "The oracle of the
LORD!" and I have sent to you, saying, "Do
not say, 'The oracle of the LORD!' " 39there-
fore behold, I, even I, will utterly forget you
and forsake you, and the city that I gave
you and your fathers, and *will cast you* out
of My presence. 40And I will bring an everlasting reproach upon you, and a perpetual
shame, which shall not be forgotten.' "

23:33 the oracle of the LORD...What oracle? The
people mockingly asked for Jeremiah to give them
his latest prophecy. God's answer through Jeremiah
was that the people would be forsaken—that judgment was coming.

The Sign of Two Baskets of Figs
24 The LORD showed me, and there
were two baskets of figs set before
the temple of the LORD, after Nebuchadnezzar king of Babylon had carried away
captive Jeconiah the son of Jehoiakim, king
of Judah, and the princes of Judah with the
craftsmen and smiths, from Jerusalem, and
had brought them to Babylon. 2One basket
had very good figs, like the figs *that are* first
ripe; and the other basket *had* very bad figs
which could not be eaten, they were so bad.

23:33 ᵃSeptuagint, Targum, and Vulgate read *You are the burden.*

³Then the LORD said to me, "What do you see, Jeremiah?"

And I said, "Figs, the good figs, very good; and the bad, very bad, which cannot be eaten, they are so bad."

⁴Again the word of the LORD came to me, saying, ⁵"Thus says the LORD, the God of Israel: 'Like these good figs, so will I acknowledge those who are carried away captive from Judah, whom I have sent out of this place for *their own* good, into the land of the Chaldeans. ⁶For I will set My eyes on them for good, and I will bring them back to this land; I will build them and not pull *them* down, and I will plant them and not pluck *them* up. ⁷Then I will give them a heart to know Me, that I *am* the LORD; and they shall be My people, and I will be their God, for they shall return to Me with their whole heart.

> **24:5 Like these good figs.** The object lesson was meant to show that the Judeans in Babylon would be treated well and not killed. They would have privileges as colonists and not be held as captives.

⁸'And as the bad figs which cannot be eaten, they are so bad'—surely thus says the LORD—'so will I give up Zedekiah the king of Judah, his princes, the residue of Jerusalem who remain in this land, and those who dwell in the land of Egypt. ⁹I will deliver them to trouble into all the kingdoms of the earth, for *their* harm, *to be* a reproach and a byword, a taunt and a curse, in all places where I shall drive them. ¹⁰And I will send the sword, the famine, and the pestilence among them, till they are consumed from the land that I gave to them and their fathers.'"

Seventy Years of Desolation

25 The word that came to Jeremiah concerning all the people of Judah, in the fourth year of Jehoiakim the son of Josiah, king of Judah (which *was* the first year of Nebuchadnezzar king of Babylon), ²which Jeremiah the prophet spoke to all the people of Judah and to all the inhabitants of Jerusalem, saying: ³"From the thirteenth year of Josiah the son of Amon, king of Judah, even to this day, this *is* the twenty-third year in which the word of the LORD has come to me; and I have spoken to you,

rising early and speaking, but you have not listened. ⁴And the LORD has sent to you all His servants the prophets, rising early and sending *them*, but you have not listened nor inclined your ear to hear. ⁵They said, 'Repent now everyone of his evil way and his evil doings, and dwell in the land that the LORD has given to you and your fathers forever and ever. ⁶Do not go after other gods to serve them and worship them, and do not provoke Me to anger with the works of your hands; and I will not harm you.' ⁷Yet you have not listened to Me," says the LORD, "that you might provoke Me to anger with the works of your hands to your own hurt.

⁸"Therefore thus says the LORD of hosts: 'Because you have not heard My words, ⁹behold, I will send and take all the families of the north,' says the LORD, 'and Nebuchadnezzar the king of Babylon, My servant, and will bring them against this land, against its inhabitants, and against these nations all around, and will utterly destroy them, and make them an astonishment, a hissing, and perpetual desolations. ¹⁰Moreover I will take from them the voice of mirth and the voice of gladness, the voice of the bridegroom and the voice of the bride, the sound of the millstones and the light of the lamp. ¹¹And this whole land shall be a desolation *and* an astonishment, and these nations shall serve the king of Babylon seventy years.

> **25:11 seventy years.** This is the first specific statement on the length of the exile (see 29:10). It began in the fourth year of Jehoiakim's reign (605/04 B.C.) and ended with Cyrus' decree to return the Jews to their land (536/35 B.C.).

¹²'Then it will come to pass, when seventy years are completed, *that* I will punish the king of Babylon and that nation, the land of the Chaldeans, for their iniquity,' says the LORD; 'and I will make it a perpetual desolation. ¹³So I will bring on that land all My words which I have pronounced against it, all that is written in this book, which Jeremiah has prophesied concerning all the nations. ¹⁴(For many nations and great kings shall be served by them also; and I will repay them according to their deeds and according to the works of their own hands.)'"

Judgment on the Nations

¹⁵For thus says the LORD God of Israel to me: "Take this wine cup of fury from My hand, and cause all the nations, to whom I send you, to drink it. ¹⁶And they will drink and stagger and go mad because of the sword that I will send among them."

¹⁷Then I took the cup from the LORD's hand, and made all the nations drink, to whom the LORD had sent me: ¹⁸Jerusalem and the cities of Judah, its kings and its princes, to make them a desolation, an astonishment, a hissing, and a curse, as *it is* this day; ¹⁹Pharaoh king of Egypt, his servants, his princes, and all his people; ²⁰all the mixed multitude, all the kings of the land of Uz, all the kings of the land of the Philistines (namely, Ashkelon, Gaza, Ekron, and the remnant of Ashdod); ²¹Edom, Moab, and the people of Ammon; ²²all the kings of Tyre, all the kings of Sidon, and the kings of the coastlands which *are* across the sea; ²³Dedan, Tema, Buz, and all *who are* in the farthest corners; ²⁴all the kings of Arabia and all the kings of the mixed multitude who dwell in the desert; ²⁵all the kings of Zimri, all the kings of Elam, and all the kings of the Medes; ²⁶all the kings of the north, far and near, one with another; and all the kingdoms of the world which *are* on the face of the earth. Also the king of Sheshach*ᵃ* shall drink after them.

25:17 made all the nations drink. In this vision Jeremiah acted as if representatives from all these nations were present so that he could make them drink in the message of wrath (v. 27) and understand that there was no escape (vv. 28,29).

---

²⁷"Therefore you shall say to them, 'Thus says the LORD of hosts, the God of Israel: "Drink, be drunk, and vomit! Fall and rise no more, because of the sword which I will send among you." ' ²⁸And it shall be, if they refuse to take the cup from your hand to drink, then you shall say to them, 'Thus says the LORD of hosts: "You shall certainly drink! ²⁹For behold, I begin to bring calamity on the city which is called by My name, and should you be utterly unpunished? You shall not be unpunished, for I will call for a sword on all the inhabitants of the earth," says the LORD of hosts.'

³⁰"Therefore prophesy against them all these words, and say to them:

'The LORD will roar from on high,
And utter His voice from His holy
    habitation;
He will roar mightily against His fold.
He will give a shout, as those who
    tread *the grapes*,
Against all the inhabitants of the
    earth.
³¹ A noise will come to the ends of the
    earth—
For the LORD has a controversy with
    the nations;
He will plead His case with all flesh.
He will give those *who are* wicked to
    the sword,' says the LORD."

³²Thus says the LORD of hosts:

"Behold, disaster shall go forth
From nation to nation,
And a great whirlwind shall be raised
    up
From the farthest parts of the earth.

³³"And at that day the slain of the LORD shall be from *one* end of the earth even to the *other* end of the earth. They shall not be lamented, or gathered, or buried; they shall become refuse on the ground.

³⁴ "Wail, shepherds, and cry!
Roll about *in the ashes*,
You leaders of the flock!
For the days of your slaughter and
    your dispersions are fulfilled;
You shall fall like a precious vessel.
³⁵ And the shepherds will have no way
    to flee,
Nor the leaders of the flock to
    escape.
³⁶ A voice of the cry of the shepherds,
And a wailing of the leaders to the
    flock *will be heard*.
For the LORD has plundered their
    pasture,
³⁷ And the peaceful dwellings are cut
    down

25:26 *ᵃ*A code word for Babylon (compare 51:41)

Because of the fierce anger of the
    LORD.
38   He has left His lair like the lion;
    For their land is desolate
    Because of the fierceness of the
        Oppressor,
    And because of His fierce anger."

Jeremiah Saved from Death

26 In the beginning of the reign of Jehoiakim the son of Josiah, king of
Judah, this word came from the LORD, saying, ²"Thus says the LORD: 'Stand in the
court of the LORD's house, and speak to all
the cities of Judah, which come to worship
in the LORD's house, all the words that I
command you to speak to them. Do not diminish a word. ³Perhaps everyone will listen and turn from his evil way, that I may
relent concerning the calamity which I purpose to bring on them because of the evil of
their doings.' ⁴And you shall say to them,
'Thus says the LORD: "If you will not listen
to Me, to walk in My law which I have set
before you, ⁵to heed the words of My servants the prophets whom I sent to you,
both rising up early and sending *them* (but
you have not heeded), ⁶then I will make
this house like Shiloh, and will make this
city a curse to all the nations of the
earth." ' "

⁷So the priests and the prophets and all
the people heard Jeremiah speaking these
words in the house of the LORD. ⁸Now it
happened, when Jeremiah had made an end
of speaking all that the LORD had commanded *him* to speak to all the people, that
the priests and the prophets and all the
people seized him, saying, "You will surely
die! ⁹Why have you prophesied in the name
of the LORD, saying, 'This house shall be
like Shiloh, and this city shall be desolate,
without an inhabitant'?" And all the people
were gathered against Jeremiah in the
house of the LORD.

¹⁰When the princes of Judah heard these
things, they came up from the king's house
to the house of the LORD and sat down in
the entry of the New Gate of the LORD's
house. ¹¹And the priests and the prophets
spoke to the princes and all the people, saying, "This man deserves to die! For he has
prophesied against this city, as you have
heard with your ears."

¹²Then Jeremiah spoke to all the princes
and all the people, saying: "The LORD sent
me to prophesy against this house and
against this city with all the words that you
have heard. ¹³Now therefore, amend your
ways and your doings, and obey the voice of
the LORD your God; then the LORD will relent concerning the doom that He has pronounced against you. ¹⁴As for me, here I
am, in your hand; do with me as seems
good and proper to you. ¹⁵But know for certain that if you put me to death, you will
surely bring innocent blood on yourselves,
on this city, and on its inhabitants; for truly
the LORD has sent me to you to speak all
these words in your hearing."

26:12 Jeremiah spoke. He defended himself from
potential killers without compromising. With spiritual courage and a willingness to die, Jeremiah warned
the crowd that God would hold the guilty accountable (v. 15).

¹⁶So the princes and all the people said to
the priests and the prophets, "This man
does not deserve to die. For he has spoken
to us in the name of the LORD our God."

¹⁷Then certain of the elders of the land
rose up and spoke to all the assembly of the
people, saying: ¹⁸"Micah of Moresheth
prophesied in the days of Hezekiah king of
Judah, and spoke to all the people of Judah,
saying, 'Thus says the LORD of hosts:

"Zion shall be plowed *like* a field,
    Jerusalem shall become heaps of
        ruins,
    And the mountain of the temple*ᵃ*
    Like the bare hills of the forest." '*ᵇ*

¹⁹Did Hezekiah king of Judah and all Judah
ever put him to death? Did he not fear the
LORD and seek the LORD's favor? And the

26:17–19 elders...spoke. These spokesmen cited
Micah (see Mic. 3:12), who prophesied the destruction of Jerusalem and the temple. They reasoned that
since Micah was not killed, God held back His judgment. Therefore, the people decided to let Jeremiah
live so that God would have the same heart.

26:18 *ᵃ*Literally *house* *ᵇ*Compare Micah 3:12

LORD relented concerning the doom which He had pronounced against them. But we are doing great evil against ourselves."

20Now there was also a man who prophesied in the name of the LORD, Urijah the son of Shemaiah of Kirjath Jearim, who prophesied against this city and against this land according to all the words of Jeremiah. 21And when Jehoiakim the king, with all his mighty men and all the princes, heard his words, the king sought to put him to death; but when Urijah heard *it*, he was afraid and fled, and went to Egypt. 22Then Jehoiakim the king sent men to Egypt: Elnathan the son of Achbor, and *other* men *who went* with him to Egypt. 23And they brought Urijah from Egypt and brought him to Jehoiakim the king, who killed him with the sword and cast his dead body into the graves of the common people.

24Nevertheless the hand of Ahikam the son of Shaphan was with Jeremiah, so that they should not give him into the hand of the people to put him to death.

Symbol of the Bonds and Yokes

27 In the beginning of the reign of Jehoiakim*a* the son of Josiah, king of Judah, this word came to Jeremiah from the LORD, saying,*b* 2"Thus says the LORD to me: 'Make for yourselves bonds and yokes, and put them on your neck, 3and send them to the king of Edom, the king of Moab, the king of the Ammonites, the king of Tyre, and the king of Sidon, by the hand of the messengers who come to Jerusalem to Zedekiah king of Judah. 4And command them to say to their masters, "Thus says the LORD of hosts, the God of Israel—thus you shall say to your masters: 5'I have made the earth, the man and the beast that *are* on the ground, by My great power and by My outstretched arm, and have given it to whom it seemed proper to Me. 6And now I have given all these lands into the hand of Nebuchadnezzar the king of Babylon, My servant; and the beasts of the field I have also given him to serve him. 7So all nations shall serve him and his son and his son's son, until the time of his land comes; and then many nations and great kings shall make him serve them. 8And it shall be, *that* the nation and kingdom which will not serve Nebuchadnezzar the king of Babylon, and which will not put its neck under the yoke of the king of Babylon, that nation I will punish,' says the LORD, 'with the sword, the famine, and the pestilence, until I have consumed them by his hand. 9Therefore do not listen to your prophets, your diviners, your dreamers, your soothsayers, or your sorcerers, who speak to you, saying, "You shall not serve the king of Babylon." 10For they prophesy a lie to you, to remove you far from your land; and I will drive you out, and you will perish. 11But the nations that bring their necks under the yoke of the king of Babylon and serve him, I will let them remain in their own land,' says the LORD, 'and they shall till it and dwell in it.' " ' "

12I also spoke to Zedekiah king of Judah according to all these words, saying, "Bring your necks under the yoke of the king of Babylon, and serve him and his people, and live! 13Why will you die, you and your people, by the sword, by the famine, and by the pestilence, as the LORD has spoken against the nation that will not serve the king of Babylon? 14Therefore do not listen to the words of the prophets who speak to you, saying, 'You shall not serve the king of Babylon,' for they prophesy a lie to you; 15for I have not sent them," says the LORD, "yet they prophesy a lie in My name, that I may drive you out, and that you may perish, you and the prophets who prophesy to you."

16Also I spoke to the priests and to all this people, saying, "Thus says the LORD: 'Do not listen to the words of your prophets who prophesy to you, saying, "Behold, the vessels of the LORD's house will now shortly be brought back from Babylon"; for they prophesy a lie to you. 17Do not listen to them; serve the king of Babylon, and live! Why should this city be laid waste? 18But if

27:2 Make...bonds and yokes. The yoke around Jeremiah's neck symbolized Judah's captivity (v. 12), which would then be experienced by 6 other kings at the hand of Babylon (see Jer. 28: 10–12).

27:1 *a*Following Masoretic Text, Targum, and Vulgate; some Hebrew manuscripts, Arabic, and Syriac read *Zedekiah* (compare 27:3,12; 28:1).   *b*Septuagint omits verse 1.

they *are* prophets, and if the word of the LORD is with them, let them now make intercession to the LORD of hosts, that the vessels which are left in the house of the LORD, *in* the house of the king of Judah, and at Jerusalem, do not go to Babylon.'

¹⁹"For thus says the LORD of hosts concerning the pillars, concerning the Sea, concerning the carts, and concerning the remainder of the vessels that remain in this city, ²⁰which Nebuchadnezzar king of Babylon did not take, when he carried away captive Jeconiah the son of Jehoiakim, king of Judah, from Jerusalem to Babylon, and all the nobles of Judah and Jerusalem— ²¹yes, thus says the LORD of hosts, the God of Israel, concerning the vessels that remain in the house of the LORD, and in the house of the king of Judah and of Jerusalem: ²²'They shall be carried to Babylon, and there they shall be until the day that I visit them,' says the LORD. 'Then I will bring them up and restore them to this place.' "

> **27:21,22 vessels.** Jeremiah revealed that Judah's temple vessels taken to Babylon (see 2 Kin. 24:13) would be restored to the temple. Ezra also speaks of this (Ezra 5:13–15).

Hananiah's Falsehood and Doom

28 And it happened in the same year, at the beginning of the reign of Zedekiah king of Judah, in the fourth year *and* in the fifth month, *that* Hananiah the son of Azur the prophet, who *was* from Gibeon, spoke to me in the house of the LORD in the presence of the priests and of all the people, saying, ²"Thus speaks the LORD of hosts, the God of Israel, saying: 'I have broken the yoke of the king of Babylon. ³Within two full years I will bring back to this place all the vessels of the LORD's house, that Nebuchadnezzar king of Babylon took away from this place and carried to Babylon. ⁴And I will bring back to this place Jeconiah the son of Jehoiakim, king of Judah, with all the captives of Judah who went to Babylon,' says the LORD, 'for I will break the yoke of the king of Babylon.' "

⁵Then the prophet Jeremiah spoke to the prophet Hananiah in the presence of the priests and in the presence of all the people who stood in the house of the LORD, ⁶and

the prophet Jeremiah said, "Amen! The LORD do so; the LORD perform your words which you have prophesied, to bring back the vessels of the LORD's house and all who were carried away captive, from Babylon to this place. ⁷Nevertheless hear now this word that I speak in your hearing and in the hearing of all the people: ⁸The prophets who have been before me and before you of old prophesied against many countries and great kingdoms—of war and disaster and pestilence. ⁹As for the prophet who prophesies of peace, when the word of the prophet comes to pass, the prophet will be known *as* one whom the LORD has truly sent."

¹⁰Then Hananiah the prophet took the yoke off the prophet Jeremiah's neck and broke it. ¹¹And Hananiah spoke in the presence of all the people, saying, "Thus says the LORD: 'Even so I will break the yoke of Nebuchadnezzar king of Babylon from the neck of all nations within the space of two full years.' " And the prophet Jeremiah went his way.

¹²Now the word of the LORD came to Jeremiah, after Hananiah the prophet had broken the yoke from the neck of the prophet Jeremiah, saying, ¹³"Go and tell Hananiah, saying, 'Thus says the LORD: "You have broken the yokes of wood, but you have made in their place yokes of iron." ¹⁴For thus says the LORD of hosts, the God of Israel: "I have put a yoke of iron on the neck of all these nations, that they may serve Nebuchadnezzar king of Babylon; and they shall serve him. I have given him the beasts of the field also." ' "

> **28:13 Go and tell Hananiah.** Jeremiah apparently left the meeting, and later God sent him back to confront the liar. He likely wore yokes of iron to replace the wooden ones and to illustrate his message.

¹⁵Then the prophet Jeremiah said to Hananiah the prophet, "Hear now, Hananiah, the LORD has not sent you, but you make this people trust in a lie. ¹⁶Therefore thus says the LORD: 'Behold, I will cast you from the face of the earth. This year you shall die, because you have taught rebellion against the LORD.' "

¹⁷So Hananiah the prophet died the same year in the seventh month.

Jeremiah's Letter to the Captives

29 Now these *are* the words of the letter that Jeremiah the prophet sent from Jerusalem to the remainder of the elders who were carried away captive—to the priests, the prophets, and all the people whom Nebuchadnezzar had carried away captive from Jerusalem to Babylon. ²(This happened after Jeconiah the king, the queen mother, the eunuchs, the princes of Judah and Jerusalem, the craftsmen, and the smiths had departed from Jerusalem.) ³*The letter was sent* by the hand of Elasah the son of Shaphan, and Gemariah the son of Hilkiah, whom Zedekiah king of Judah sent to Babylon, to Nebuchadnezzar king of Babylon, saying,

4   Thus says the LORD of hosts, the God of Israel, to all who were carried away captive, whom I have caused to be carried away from Jerusalem to Babylon:

5   Build houses and dwell *in them*; plant gardens and eat their fruit. ⁶Take wives and beget sons and daughters; and take wives for your sons and give your daughters to husbands, so that they may bear sons and daughters—that you may be increased there, and not diminished. ⁷And seek the peace of the city where I have caused you to be carried away captive, and pray to the LORD for it; for in its peace you will have peace. ⁸For thus says the LORD of hosts, the God of Israel: Do not let your prophets and your diviners who are in your midst deceive you, nor listen to your dreams which you cause to be dreamed. ⁹For they prophesy falsely to you in My name; I have not sent them, says the LORD.

10   For thus says the LORD: After seventy years are completed at Babylon, I will visit you and perform My good word

29:4–10 Jeremiah advised the Israelites in Babylon to live as if they would be there for a long time (70 years). They were also to pray for the city since their own well being rested on its fate.

toward you, and cause you to return to this place. ¹¹For I know the thoughts that I think toward you, says the LORD, thoughts of peace and not of evil, to give you a future and a hope. ¹²Then you will call upon Me and go and pray to Me, and I will listen to you. ¹³And you will seek Me and find *Me*, when you search for Me with all your heart. ¹⁴I will be found by you, says the LORD, and I will bring you back from your captivity; I will gather you from all the nations and from all the places where I have driven you, says the LORD, and I will bring you to the place from which I cause you to be carried away captive.

29:14 I will be found by you. The Lord would answer their prayer by returning them to their land. The fulfillment of this promise would take place in the days of Ezra and Nehemiah. The Second Advent of the Messiah would be the ultimate fulfillment (see Dan. 2:35).

15   Because you have said, "The LORD has raised up prophets for us in Babylon"— ¹⁶therefore thus says the LORD concerning the king who sits on the throne of David, concerning all the people who dwell in this city, and concerning your brethren who have not gone out with you into captivity— ¹⁷thus says the LORD of hosts: Behold, I will send on them the sword, the famine, and the pestilence, and will make them like rotten figs that cannot be eaten, they are so bad. ¹⁸And I will pursue them with the sword, with famine, and with pestilence; and I will deliver them to trouble among all the kingdoms of the earth—to be a curse, an astonishment, a hissing, and a reproach among all the nations where I have driven them, ¹⁹because they have not heeded My words, says the LORD, which I sent to them by My servants the prophets, rising up early and sending *them*; neither would you heed, says the LORD. ²⁰Therefore hear the word of the LORD, all you of the captivity, whom I have sent from Jerusalem to Babylon.

21 Thus says the LORD of hosts, the God of Israel, concerning Ahab the son of Kolaiah, and Zedekiah the son of Maaseiah, who prophesy a lie to you in My name: Behold, I will deliver them into the hand of Nebuchadnezzar king of Babylon, and he shall slay them before your eyes. 22And because of them a curse shall be taken up by all the captivity of Judah who *are* in Babylon, saying, "The LORD make you like Zedekiah and Ahab, whom the king of Babylon roasted in the fire"; 23because they have done disgraceful things in Israel, have committed adultery with their neighbors' wives, and have spoken lying words in My name, which I have not commanded them. Indeed I know, and *am* a witness, says the LORD.

24 You shall also speak to Shemaiah the Nehelamite, saying, 25Thus speaks the LORD of hosts, the God of Israel, saying: You have sent letters in your name to all the people who *are* at Jerusalem, to Zephaniah the son of Maaseiah the priest, and to all the priests, saying, 26"The LORD has made you priest instead of Jehoiada the priest, so that there should be officers *in* the house of the LORD over every man *who* is demented and considers himself a prophet, that you should put him in prison and in the stocks. 27Now therefore, why have you not rebuked Jeremiah of Anathoth who makes himself a prophet to you? 28For he has sent to us *in* Babylon, saying, 'This *captivity is* long; build houses and dwell *in them,* and plant gardens and eat their fruit.' "

29 Now Zephaniah the priest read this letter in the hearing of Jeremiah the prophet. 30Then the word of the LORD came to Jeremiah, saying: 31Send to all those in captivity, saying, Thus says the LORD concerning Shemaiah the Nehelamite: Because Shemaiah has prophesied to you, and I have not sent him, and he has caused you to trust in a lie— 32therefore thus says the

LORD: Behold, I will punish Shemaiah the Nehelamite and his family: he shall not have anyone to dwell among this people, nor shall he see the good that I will do for My people, says the LORD, because he has taught rebellion against the LORD.

Restoration of Israel and Judah

30 The word that came to Jeremiah from the LORD, saying, 2"Thus speaks the LORD God of Israel, saying: 'Write in a book for yourself all the words that I have spoken to you. 3For behold, the days are coming,' says the LORD, 'that I will bring back from captivity My people Israel and Judah,' says the LORD. 'And I will cause them to return to the land that I gave to their fathers, and they shall possess it.' "

30:3 I will bring back. This verse summarizes chapters 30–33. God envisioned a time when Israel would be restored to their land (see 29:10), never to be removed again.

4Now these *are* the words that the LORD spoke concerning Israel and Judah.

5"For thus says the LORD:

'We have heard a voice of trembling,
  Of fear, and not of peace.
6 Ask now, and see,
  Whether a man is ever in labor with
    child?
  So why do I see every man *with* his
    hands on his loins
  Like a woman in labor,
  And all faces turned pale?
7 Alas! For that day *is* great,
  So that none *is* like it;
  And it *is* the time of Jacob's trouble,
  But he shall be saved out of it.

8 'For it shall come to pass in that day,'
  Says the LORD of hosts,
  'That I will break his yoke from your
    neck,
  And will burst your bonds;
  Foreigners shall no more enslave them.
9 But they shall serve the LORD their
    God,
  And David their king,
  Whom I will raise up for them.

30:9 David their king. This verse ultimately refers to the Messiah (2 Sam. 7:16) who would fulfill this promise and would be the hope of Israel (Is. 9:7). No king of David's seed has held the scepter since the captivity. Zerubbabel, of David's line, never claimed the title of king (see Hag. 2:2).

10 "Therefore do not fear, O My servant
        Jacob,' says the LORD,
   'Nor be dismayed, O Israel;
   For behold, I will save you from afar,
   And your seed from the land of their
        captivity.
   Jacob shall return, have rest and be
        quiet,
   And no one shall make *him* afraid.
11 For I *am* with you,' says the LORD, 'to
        save you;
   Though I make a full end of all
        nations where I have scattered
        you,
   Yet I will not make a complete end of
        you.
   But I will correct you in justice,
   And will not let you go altogether
        unpunished.'

12 "For thus says the LORD:

   'Your affliction *is* incurable,
   Your wound *is* severe.
13 *There is* no one to plead your cause,
   That you may be bound up;
   You have no healing medicines.
14 All your lovers have forgotten you;
   They do not seek you;
   For I have wounded you with the
        wound of an enemy,
   With the chastisement of a cruel one,
   For the multitude of your iniquities,
   Because your sins have increased.
15 Why do you cry about your affliction?
   Your sorrow *is* incurable.
   Because of the multitude of your
        iniquities,
   Because your sins have increased,
   I have done these things to you.

16 'Therefore all those who devour you
        shall be devoured;
   And all your adversaries, every one of
        them, shall go into captivity;
   Those who plunder you shall become
        plunder,

And all who prey upon you I will
     make a prey.
17 For I will restore health to you
   And heal you of your wounds,' says
        the LORD,
   'Because they called you an outcast
        saying:
   "This *is* Zion;
   No one seeks her." '

18 "Thus says the LORD:

   'Behold, I will bring back the captivity
        of Jacob's tents,
   And have mercy on his dwelling
        places;
   The city shall be built upon its own
        mound,
   And the palace shall remain according
        to its own plan.
19 Then out of them shall proceed
        thanksgiving
   And the voice of those who make
        merry;
   I will multiply them, and they shall
        not diminish;
   I will also glorify them, and they shall
        not be small.
20 Their children also shall be as before,
   And their congregation shall be
        established before Me;
   And I will punish all who oppress
        them.
21 Their nobles shall be from among
        them,
   And their governor shall come from
        their midst;
   Then I will cause him to draw near,
   And he shall approach Me;
   For who *is* this who pledged his
        heart to approach Me?' says the
        LORD.
22 'You shall be My people,
   And I will be your God.' "

23 Behold, the whirlwind of the LORD
   Goes forth with fury,
   A continuing whirlwind;
   It will fall violently on the head of the
        wicked.
24 The fierce anger of the LORD will not
        return until He has done it,
   And until He has performed the
        intents of His heart.

30:16–24 These absolute and extensive promises have yet to be fulfilled in history. The reign of Christ, the greater David, will take place in the millennial kingdom in the "latter days."

In the latter days you will consider it.

The Remnant of Israel Saved

31 "At the same time," says the LORD, "I will be the God of all the families of Israel, and they shall be My people."
² Thus says the LORD:

"The people who survived the sword
    Found grace in the wilderness—
    Israel, when I went to give him rest."

³   The LORD has appeared of old to me,
        saying:
"Yes, I have loved you with an
        everlasting love;
    Therefore with lovingkindness I have
        drawn you.
⁴   Again I will build you, and you shall
        be rebuilt,
    O virgin of Israel!
    You shall again be adorned with your
        tambourines,
    And shall go forth in the dances of
        those who rejoice.

⁵   You shall yet plant vines on the
        mountains of Samaria;
    The planters shall plant and eat *them*
        as ordinary food.
⁶   For there shall be a day
    When the watchmen will cry on
        Mount Ephraim,
    'Arise, and let us go up *to* Zion,
    To the LORD our God.' "

⁷ For thus says the LORD:

"Sing with gladness for Jacob,
    And shout among the chief of the
        nations;
    Proclaim, give praise, and say,
    'O LORD, save Your people,
    The remnant of Israel!'
⁸   Behold, I will bring them from the
        north country,
    And gather them from the ends of the
        earth,
    Among them the blind and the
        lame,
    The woman with child
    And the one who labors with child,
        together;
    A great throng shall return there.
⁹   They shall come with weeping,
    And with supplications I will lead
        them.

What is the New Covenant?

In Jeremiah 31:31–34 God announced the coming establishment of a New Covenant with His people. This covenant will be different than the one "I made with their fathers in the day that I took them by the hand to lead them out of the land of Egypt, My covenant which they broke" (verse 32).

What is this New Covenant?

"I will put My law in their minds, and write it on their hearts; and I will be their God, and they shall be My people" (verse 33).

The fulfillment of this New Covenant was to individuals as well as to Israel as a nation (verse 36; Romans 11:16–27). Among the final external indicators of this covenant are (1) a reestablishment of the people in their land (verses 38–40 and chapters 30–33) and (2) a time of ultimate difficulty (30:7).

In principle, this covenant, also announced by Jesus (Luke 22:20), began to be exercised on behalf of both Jewish and Gentile believers in the church era (1 Corinthians 11:25; Hebrews 8:7–13; 9:15; 10:14–17; 12:24; 13:20). The idea of a Jewish remnant that appears so often in the Old Testament prophecies, the New Testament identifies as the "remnant according to the election of grace" (Romans 11:5). The New Covenant will be finalized for the people of Israel in the last days, including the regathering to their ancient land, Palestine (chapters 30–33). The streams of the Abrahamic, Davidic, and New Covenants will eventually flow as one in the millennial kingdom ruled by the Messiah.

I will cause them to walk by the rivers
    of waters,
In a straight way in which they shall
    not stumble;
For I am a Father to Israel,
And Ephraim *is* My firstborn.

10 "Hear the word of the LORD,
    O nations,
And declare *it* in the isles afar off, and
    say,
'He who scattered Israel will gather
    him,
And keep him as a shepherd *does* his
    flock.'
11   For the LORD has redeemed Jacob,
And ransomed him from the hand of
    one stronger than he.
12   Therefore they shall come and sing in
    the height of Zion,
Streaming to the goodness of the
    LORD—
For wheat and new wine and oil,
For the young of the flock and the
    herd;
Their souls shall be like a well-
    watered garden,
And they shall sorrow no more at all.

13 "Then shall the virgin rejoice in the
    dance,
And the young men and the old,
    together;
For I will turn their mourning to joy,
Will comfort them,
And make them rejoice rather than
    sorrow.
14   I will satiate the soul of the priests
    with abundance,
And My people shall be satisfied with
    My goodness, says the LORD."

Mercy on Ephraim

15 Thus says the LORD:

"A voice was heard in Ramah,
Lamentation *and* bitter weeping,
Rachel weeping for her children,

Refusing to be comforted for her
    children,
Because they *are* no more."

16 Thus says the LORD:

"Refrain your voice from weeping,
    And your eyes from tears;
For your work shall be rewarded, says
    the LORD,
And they shall come back from the
    land of the enemy.
17   There is hope in your future, says the
    LORD,
That *your* children shall come back to
    their own border.

18 "I have surely heard Ephraim
    bemoaning himself:
'You have chastised me, and I was
    chastised,
Like an untrained bull;
Restore me, and I will return,
For You *are* the LORD my God.
19   Surely, after my turning, I repented;
And after I was instructed, I struck
    myself on the thigh;
I was ashamed, yes, even humiliated,
Because I bore the reproach of my
    youth.'
20   *Is* Ephraim My dear son?
Is he a pleasant child?
For though I spoke against him,
I earnestly remember him still;
Therefore My heart yearns for him;
I will surely have mercy on him, says
    the LORD.

21 "Set up signposts,
Make landmarks;
Set your heart toward the highway,
The way in *which* you went.
Turn back, O virgin of Israel,
Turn back to these your cities.
22   How long will you gad about,
O you backsliding daughter?

31:15 A voice...in Ramah. This reference to a mother weeping over the death of her children during the Babylonian attack provides a sharp contrast to the days of restoration and joy that will be realized when the Messiah reigns.

31:22 A woman shall encompass a man. The exact meaning of this verse is unclear. It may be referring to the formerly virgin Israel (v. 21), who is now a disgraced, divorced wife (3:8). She will one day embrace her former husband, the Lord, and He will receive her back, fully forgiving her.

For the LORD has created a new thing
  in the earth—
A woman shall encompass a man."

Future Prosperity of Judah

23Thus says the LORD of hosts, the God
of Israel: "They shall again use this speech
in the land of Judah and in its cities, when I
bring back their captivity: 'The LORD bless
you, O home of justice, *and* mountain of
holiness!' 24And there shall dwell in Judah
itself, and in all its cities together, farmers
and those going out with flocks. 25For I have
satiated the weary soul, and I have replen-
ished every sorrowful soul."

26After this I awoke and looked around,
and my sleep was sweet to me.

27"Behold, the days are coming, says the
LORD, that I will sow the house of Israel
and the house of Judah with the seed of
man and the seed of beast. 28And it shall
come to pass, *that* as I have watched over
them to pluck up, to break down, to throw
down, to destroy, and to afflict, so I will
watch over them to build and to plant, says
the LORD. 29In those days they shall say no
more:

  'The fathers have eaten sour grapes,
  And the children's teeth are set on
    edge.'

30But every one shall die for his own iniquity; every man who eats the sour grapes, his
teeth shall be set on edge.

A New Covenant

31"Behold, the days are coming, says the
LORD, when I will make a new covenant
with the house of Israel and with the house
of Judah— 32not according to the covenant
that I made with their fathers in the day
that I took them by the hand to lead them
out of the land of Egypt, My covenant
which they broke, though I was a husband
to them,*a* says the LORD. 33But this *is* the
covenant that I will make with the house of
Israel after those days, says the LORD: I will
put My law in their minds, and write it on
their hearts; and I will be their God, and
they shall be My people. 34No more shall

every man teach his neighbor, and every
man his brother, saying, 'Know the LORD,'
for they all shall know Me, from the least of
them to the greatest of them, says the
LORD. For I will forgive their iniquity, and
their sin I will remember no more."

> **31:31–34 a new covenant.** In contrast to the Mosa-
> ic covenant, which Israel failed to keep, God prom-
> ised a New Covenant where those who know Him
> would participate in the blessing of salvation. In the
> last days, the Abrahamic, Davidic, and New Cov-
> enants will find their union in the kingdom of the
> Messiah.

35   Thus says the LORD,
      Who gives the sun for a light by day,
      The ordinances of the moon and the
        stars for a light by night,
      Who disturbs the sea,
      And its waves roar
      (The LORD of hosts *is* His name):

36   "If those ordinances depart
      From before Me, says the LORD,
      Then the seed of Israel shall also
        cease
      From being a nation before Me
        forever."

37Thus says the LORD:

      "If heaven above can be measured,
      And the foundations of the earth
        searched out beneath,
      I will also cast off all the seed of Israel
      For all that they have done, says the
        LORD.

38"Behold, the days are coming, says the
LORD, that the city shall be built for the
LORD from the Tower of Hananel to the
Corner Gate. 39The surveyor's line shall
again extend straight forward over the hill
Gareb; then it shall turn toward Goath.
40And the whole valley of the dead bodies
and of the ashes, and all the fields as far as
the Brook Kidron, to the corner of the
Horse Gate toward the east, *shall be* holy to
the LORD. It shall not be plucked up or
thrown down anymore forever."

31:32 *a*Following Masoretic Text, Targum, and Vulgate; Septuagint and Syriac read *and I turned away
from them.*

Jeremiah Buys a Field

32 The word that came to Jeremiah from the LORD in the tenth year of Zedekiah king of Judah, which was the eighteenth year of Nebuchadnezzar. ²For then the king of Babylon's army besieged Jerusalem, and Jeremiah the prophet was shut up in the court of the prison, which *was in* the king of Judah's house. ³For Zedekiah king of Judah had shut him up, saying, "Why do you prophesy and say, 'Thus says the LORD: "Behold, I will give this city into the hand of the king of Babylon, and he shall take it; ⁴and Zedekiah king of Judah shall not escape from the hand of the Chaldeans, but shall surely be delivered into the hand of the king of Babylon, and shall speak with him face to face,ᵃ and see him eye to eye; ⁵then he shall lead Zedekiah to Babylon, and there he shall be until I visit him," says the LORD; "though you fight with the Chaldeans, you shall not succeed" '?"

> **32:2–5 shut up in...prison.** Judah's final king put Jeremiah into prison for preaching treason against the nation and the king. The king preferred to hear positive talk that boosted the people's morale.

⁶And Jeremiah said, "The word of the LORD came to me, saying, ⁷'Behold, Hanamel the son of Shallum your uncle will come to you, saying, "Buy my field which *is* in Anathoth, for the right of redemption *is* yours to buy *it*." ' ⁸Then Hanamel my uncle's son came to me in the court of the prison according to the word of the LORD, and said to me, 'Please buy my field that *is* in Anathoth, which *is* in the country of Benjamin; for the right of inheritance *is* yours, and the redemption yours; buy *it* for yourself.' Then I knew that this was the word of the LORD. ⁹So I bought the field from Hanamel, the son of my uncle who

> **32:8 the right of inheritance.** A man facing hardship could sell property to raise money. The closest blood relative had the right to redeem it until the Jubilee year. If a stranger had taken it due to unpaid debt, then that relative could buy it back as a family possession (Lev. 25:25). Levite land could be sold only to a Levite (Lev. 25:32–34), such as Jeremiah.

was in Anathoth, and weighed *out to* him the money—seventeen shekels of silver. ¹⁰And I signed the deed and sealed *it*, took witnesses, and weighed the money on the scales. ¹¹So I took the purchase deed, *both* that which was sealed *according* to the law and custom, and that which was open; ¹²and I gave the purchase deed to Baruch the son of Neriah, son of Mahseiah, in the presence of Hanamel my uncle's *son,* and in the presence of the witnesses who signed the purchase deed, before all the Jews who sat in the court of the prison.

¹³"Then I charged Baruch before them, saying, ¹⁴'Thus says the LORD of hosts, the God of Israel: "Take these deeds, both this purchase deed which is sealed and this deed which is open, and put them in an earthen vessel, that they may last many days." ¹⁵For thus says the LORD of hosts, the God of Israel: "Houses and fields and vineyards shall be possessed again in this land." '

Jeremiah Prays for Understanding

¹⁶"Now when I had delivered the purchase deed to Baruch the son of Neriah, I prayed to the LORD, saying: ¹⁷'Ah, Lord GOD! Behold, You have made the heavens and the earth by Your great power and outstretched arm. There is nothing too hard for You. ¹⁸*You* show lovingkindness to thousands, and repay the iniquity of the fathers into the bosom of their children after them—the Great, the Mighty God, whose name *is* the LORD of hosts. ¹⁹*You are* great in counsel and mighty in work, for Your eyes *are* open to all the ways of the sons of men, to give everyone according to his ways and according to the fruit of his doings. ²⁰You have set signs and wonders in the land of Egypt, to this day, and in Israel and among *other* men; and You have made Yourself a name, as it is this day. ²¹You have brought Your people Israel out of the land of Egypt with signs and wonders, with a strong hand and an outstretched arm, and with great terror; ²²You have given them this land, of which You swore to their fathers to give them—"a land flowing with milk and honey."ᵃ ²³And they came in and took possession of it, but they have not obeyed Your voice or walked in Your law.

They have done nothing of all that You commanded them to do; therefore You have caused all this calamity to come upon them.

²⁴"Look, the siege mounds! They have come to the city to take it; and the city has been given into the hand of the Chaldeans who fight against it, because of the sword and famine and pestilence. What You have spoken has happened; there You see *it!* ²⁵And You have said to me, O Lord GOD, "Buy the field for money, and take witnesses"!—yet the city has been given into the hand of the Chaldeans.' "

32:16–25 Jeremiah wondered why God had him redeem the field when God could have exercised His sovereign power to do it Himself.

God's Assurance of the People's Return

²⁶Then the word of the LORD came to Jeremiah, saying, ²⁷"Behold, I *am* the LORD, the God of all flesh. Is there anything too hard for Me? ²⁸Therefore thus says the LORD: 'Behold, I will give this city into the hand of the Chaldeans, into the hand of Nebuchadnezzar king of Babylon, and he shall take it. ²⁹And the Chaldeans who fight against this city shall come and set fire to this city and burn it, with the houses on whose roofs they have offered incense to Baal and poured out drink offerings to other gods, to provoke Me to anger; ³⁰because the children of Israel and the children of Judah have done only evil before Me from their youth. For the children of Israel have provoked Me only to anger with the work of their hands,' says the LORD. ³¹'For this city has been to Me *a provocation of* My anger and My fury from the day that they built it, even to this day; so I will remove it from before My face ³²because of all the evil of the children of Israel and the children of Judah, which they have done to provoke Me to anger—they, their kings, their princes, their priests, their prophets, the men of Judah, and the inhabitants of Jerusalem. ³³And they have turned to Me the back, and not the face; though I taught them, rising up early and teaching *them*, yet they have not listened to receive instruction. ³⁴But they set their abominations in the house which is called by My name, to defile it. ³⁵And they built the high places of Baal which *are* in the Valley of the Son of Hinnom, to cause their sons and their daughters to pass through *the fire* to Molech, which I did not command them, nor did it come into My mind that they should do this abomination, to cause Judah to sin.'

³⁶"Now therefore, thus says the LORD, the God of Israel, concerning this city of which you say, 'It shall be delivered into the hand of the king of Babylon by the sword, by the famine, and by the pestilence: ³⁷Behold, I will gather them out of all countries where I have driven them in My anger, in My fury, and in great wrath; I will bring them back to this place, and I will cause them to dwell safely. ³⁸They shall be My people, and I will be their God; ³⁹then I will give them one heart and one way, that they may fear Me forever, for the good of them and their children after them. ⁴⁰And I will make an everlasting covenant with them, that I will not turn away from doing them good; but I will put My fear in their hearts so that they will not depart from Me. ⁴¹Yes, I will rejoice over them to do them good, and I will assuredly plant them in this land, with all My heart and with all My soul.'

⁴²"For thus says the LORD: 'Just as I have brought all this great calamity on this people, so I will bring on them all the good that I have promised them. ⁴³And fields will be bought in this land of which you say, "It *is* desolate, without man or beast; it has been given into the hand of the Chaldeans." ⁴⁴Men will buy fields for money, sign deeds and seal *them*, and take witnesses, in the land of Benjamin, in the places around Jerusalem, in the cities of Judah, in the cities of the mountains, in the cities of the lowland, and in the cities of the South; for I will cause their captives to return,' says the LORD."

Excellence of the Restored Nation

33 Moreover the word of the LORD came to Jeremiah a second time, while he was still shut up in the court of the prison, saying, ²"Thus says the LORD who made it, the LORD who formed it to establish it (the LORD *is* His name): ³'Call to Me, and I will answer you, and show you great and mighty things, which you do not know.'

⁴"For thus says the LORD, the God of

33:3 Call...I will answer. God invited Jeremiah to pray for the fulfillment of His promises. His answer to Jeremiah's prayer is stated in vv. 4–6.

Israel, concerning the houses of this city and the houses of the kings of Judah, which have been pulled down to fortify[a] against the siege mounds and the sword: 5'They come to fight with the Chaldeans, but only to fill their places[a] with the dead bodies of men whom I will slay in My anger and My fury, all for whose wickedness I have hidden My face from this city. 6Behold, I will bring it health and healing; I will heal them and reveal to them the abundance of peace and truth. 7And I will cause the captives of Judah and the captives of Israel to return, and will rebuild those places as at the first. 8I will cleanse them from all their iniquity by which they have sinned against Me, and I will pardon all their iniquities by which they have sinned and by which they have transgressed against Me. 9Then it shall be to Me a name of joy, a praise, and an honor before all nations of the earth, who shall hear all the good that I do to them; they shall fear and tremble for all the goodness and all the prosperity that I provide for it.'

10"Thus says the LORD: 'Again there shall be heard in this place—of which you say, "It is desolate, without man and without beast"—in the cities of Judah, in the streets of Jerusalem that are desolate, without man and without inhabitant and without beast, 11the voice of joy and the voice of gladness, the voice of the bridegroom and the voice of the bride, the voice of those who will say:

"Praise the LORD of hosts,
For the LORD is good,
For His mercy endures forever"—

and of those who will bring the sacrifice of praise into the house of the LORD. For I will cause the captives of the land to return as at the first,' says the LORD.

12"Thus says the LORD of hosts: 'In this place which is desolate, without man and without beast, and in all its cities, there shall again be a dwelling place of shepherds causing their flocks to lie down. 13In the cit-

ies of the mountains, in the cities of the lowland, in the cities of the South, in the land of Benjamin, in the places around Jerusalem, and in the cities of Judah, the flocks shall again pass under the hands of him who counts them,' says the LORD.

14"Behold, the days are coming,' says the LORD, 'that I will perform that good thing which I have promised to the house of Israel and to the house of Judah:

15   'In those days and at that time
I will cause to grow up to David
A Branch of righteousness;
He shall execute judgment and
righteousness in the earth.
16   In those days Judah will be saved,
And Jerusalem will dwell safely.
And this is the name by which she
will be called:

THE LORD OUR RIGHTEOUSNESS.'[a]

17"For thus says the LORD: 'David shall never lack a man to sit on the throne of the house of Israel; 18nor shall the priests, the Levites, lack a man to offer burnt offerings before Me, to kindle grain offerings, and to sacrifice continually.' "

The Permanence of God's Covenant

19And the word of the LORD came to Jeremiah, saying, 20"Thus says the LORD: 'If you can break My covenant with the day and My covenant with the night, so that there will not be day and night in their season, 21then My covenant may also be broken with David My servant, so that he shall not have a son to reign on his throne, and with the Levites, the priests, My ministers. 22As the host of heaven cannot be numbered, nor the sand of the sea measured, so will I multiply the descendants of David My servant and the Levites who minister to Me.' "

23Moreover the word of the LORD came to Jeremiah, saying, 24"Have you not consid-

33:17–22 God promised to fulfill the Davidic (2 Sam. 17) and Priestly/Levitical (Num. 25:10–13) Covenants without exception. The promise was as certain as the appearance of night and day and the incalculable number of stars or grains of sand (see 31:35–37).

33:4 [a]Compare Isaiah 22:10   33:5 [a]Compare 2 Kings 23:14   33:16 [a]Compare 23:5,6

ered what these people have spoken, saying, 'The two families which the LORD has
chosen, He has also cast them off'? Thus
they have despised My people, as if they
should no more be a nation before them.
²⁵"Thus says the LORD: 'If My covenant *is*
not with day and night, *and if* I have not appointed the ordinances of heaven and earth,
²⁶then I will cast away the descendants of
Jacob and David My servant, *so that* I will
not take *any* of his descendants *to be* rulers
over the descendants of Abraham, Isaac,
and Jacob. For I will cause their captives to
return, and will have mercy on them.'"

Zedekiah Warned by God

34 The word which came to Jeremiah
from the LORD, when Nebuchad-
nezzar king of Babylon and all his army, all
the kingdoms of the earth under his dominion, and all the people, fought against Jerusalem and all its cities, saying, ²"Thus says
the LORD, the God of Israel: 'Go and speak
to Zedekiah king of Judah and tell him,
"Thus says the LORD: 'Behold, I will give
this city into the hand of the king of Babylon, and he shall burn it with fire. ³And you
shall not escape from his hand, but shall
surely be taken and delivered into his hand;
your eyes shall see the eyes of the king of
Babylon, he shall speak with you face to
face,ᵃ and you shall go to Babylon.' " ' ⁴Yet
hear the word of the LORD, O Zedekiah
king of Judah! Thus says the LORD concerning you: 'You shall not die by the
sword. ⁵You shall die in peace; as in the ceremonies of your fathers, the former kings
who were before you, so they shall burn incense for you and lament for you, *saying,*
"Alas, lord!" For I have pronounced the
word, says the LORD.' "

⁶Then Jeremiah the prophet spoke all
these words to Zedekiah king of Judah in
Jerusalem, ⁷when the king of Babylon's
army fought against Jerusalem and all the
cities of Judah that were left, against Lachish and Azekah; for *only* these fortified
cities remained of the cities of Judah.

Treacherous Treatment of Slaves

⁸*This is* the word that came to Jeremiah
from the LORD, after King Zedekiah had
made a covenant with all the people who
were at Jerusalem to proclaim liberty to
them: ⁹that every man should set free his
male and female slave—a Hebrew man or
woman—that no one should keep a Jewish
brother in bondage. ¹⁰Now when all the
princes and all the people, who had entered
into the covenant, heard that everyone
should set free his male and female slaves,
that no one should keep them in bondage
anymore, they obeyed and let *them* go.
¹¹But afterward they changed their minds
and made the male and female slaves return, whom they had set free, and brought
them into subjection as male and female
slaves.

34:11 they changed their minds. Former slave masters ignored their agreement and recalled the slaves.
Some suggest that this happened when the Egyptian
army approached and the Babylonian forces withdrew temporarily (37:5,11), causing the inhabitants to
think that the danger was past.

¹²Therefore the word of the LORD came to
Jeremiah from the LORD, saying, ¹³"Thus
says the LORD, the God of Israel: 'I made a
covenant with your fathers in the day that I
brought them out of the land of Egypt, out
of the house of bondage, saying, ¹⁴"At the
end of seven years let every man set free his
Hebrew brother, who has been sold to him;
and when he has served you six years, you
shall let him go free from you." But your
fathers did not obey Me nor incline their
ear. ¹⁵Then you recently turned and did
what was right in My sight—every man
proclaiming liberty to his neighbor; and
you made a covenant before Me in the
house which is called by My name. ¹⁶Then
you turned around and profaned My name,
and every one of you brought back his male
and female slaves, whom he had set at liberty, at their pleasure, and brought them
back into subjection, to be your male and
female slaves.'

¹⁷"Therefore thus says the LORD: 'You
have not obeyed Me in proclaiming liberty,
every one to his brother and every one to
his neighbor. Behold, I proclaim liberty to
you,' says the LORD—'to the sword, to pestilence, and to famine! And I will deliver

you to trouble among all the kingdoms of the earth. ¹⁸And I will give the men who have transgressed My covenant, who have not performed the words of the covenant which they made before Me, when they cut the calf in two and passed between the parts of it— ¹⁹the princes of Judah, the princes of Jerusalem, the eunuchs, the priests, and all the people of the land who passed between the parts of the calf— ²⁰I will give them into the hand of their enemies and into the hand of those who seek their life. Their dead bodies shall be for meat for the birds of the heaven and the beasts of the earth. ²¹And I will give Zedekiah king of Judah and his princes into the hand of their enemies, into the hand of those who seek their life, and into the hand of the king of Babylon's army which has gone back from you. ²²Behold, I will command,' says the LORD, 'and cause them to return to this city. They will fight against it and take it and burn it with fire; and I will make the cities of Judah a desolation without inhabitant.' "

34:18,21 cut the calf in two. God will give the guilty over to death before the conqueror since they denied the covenant made official by blood. This custom consisted of two parties walking between the halves of animals that they had cut in two. This symbolized that each party would uphold their end of the agreement under penalty of having their own blood shed.

The Obedient Rechabites

35 The word which came to Jeremiah from the LORD in the days of Jehoiakim the son of Josiah, king of Judah, saying, ²"Go to the house of the Rechabites, speak to them, and bring them into the house of the LORD, into one of the chambers, and give them wine to drink."

³Then I took Jaazaniah the son of Jeremiah, the son of Habazziniah, his brothers and all his sons, and the whole house of the Rechabites, ⁴and I brought them into the house of the LORD, into the chamber of the sons of Hanan the son of Igdaliah, a man of God, which *was* by the chamber of the princes, above the chamber of Maaseiah the son of Shallum, the keeper of the door. ⁵Then I set before the sons of the house of the Rechabites bowls full of wine, and cups; and I said to them, "Drink wine."

⁶But they said, "We will drink no wine, for Jonadab the son of Rechab, our father, commanded us, saying, 'You shall drink no wine, you nor your sons, forever. ⁷You shall not build a house, sow seed, plant a vineyard, nor have *any of these*; but all your days you shall dwell in tents, that you may live many days in the land where you are sojourners.' ⁸Thus we have obeyed the voice of Jonadab the son of Rechab, our father, in all that he charged us, to drink no wine all our days, we, our wives, our sons, or our daughters, ⁹nor to build ourselves houses to dwell in; nor do we have vineyard, field, or seed. ¹⁰But we have dwelt in tents, and have obeyed and done according to all that Jonadab our father commanded us. ¹¹But it came to pass, when Nebuchadnezzar king of Babylon came up into the land, that we said, 'Come, let us go to Jerusalem for fear of the army of the Chaldeans and for fear of the army of the Syrians.' So we dwell at Jerusalem."

35:8 obeyed. The sons' steadfast obedience is commended here, not the father's commands about nomadic life. Their obedience was complete and unreserved, whereas Israel disobeyed.

¹²Then came the word of the LORD to Jeremiah, saying, ¹³"Thus says the LORD of hosts, the God of Israel: 'Go and tell the men of Judah and the inhabitants of Jerusalem, "Will you not receive instruction to obey My words?" says the LORD. ¹⁴"The words of Jonadab the son of Rechab, which he commanded his sons, not to drink wine, are performed; for to this day they drink none, and obey their father's commandment. But although I have spoken to you, rising early and speaking, you did not obey Me. ¹⁵I have also sent to you all My servants the prophets, rising up early and sending *them*, saying, 'Turn now everyone from his evil way, amend your doings, and do not go after other gods to serve them; then you will dwell in the land which I have given you and your fathers.' But you have not inclined your ear, nor obeyed Me. ¹⁶Surely the sons of Jonadab the son of Rechab have performed the commandment of their father, which he commanded them, but this people has not obeyed Me." '

¹⁷"Therefore thus says the LORD God of

hosts, the God of Israel: 'Behold, I will bring on Judah and on all the inhabitants of Jerusalem all the doom that I have pronounced against them; because I have spoken to them but they have not heard, and I have called to them but they have not answered.' "

¹⁸And Jeremiah said to the house of the Rechabites, "Thus says the LORD of hosts, the God of Israel: 'Because you have obeyed the commandment of Jonadab your father, and kept all his precepts and done according to all that he commanded you, ¹⁹therefore thus says the LORD of hosts, the God of Israel: "Jonadab the son of Rechab shall not lack a man to stand before Me forever." ' "

The Scroll Read in the Temple

36 Now it came to pass in the fourth year of Jehoiakim the son of Josiah, king of Judah, *that* this word came to Jeremiah from the LORD, saying: ²"Take a scroll of a book and write on it all the words that I have spoken to you against Israel, against Judah, and against all the nations, from the day I spoke to you, from the days of Josiah even to this day. ³It may be that the house of Judah will hear all the adversities which I purpose to bring upon them, that everyone may turn from his evil way, that I may forgive their iniquity and their sin."

⁴Then Jeremiah called Baruch the son of Neriah; and Baruch wrote on a scroll of a book, at the instruction of Jeremiah,*a* all the words of the LORD which He had spoken to him. ⁵And Jeremiah commanded Baruch, saying, "I *am* confined, I cannot go into the house of the LORD. ⁶You go, therefore, and read from the scroll which you have written at my instruction,*a* the words of the LORD, in the hearing of the people in the LORD's house on the day of fasting. And you shall also read them in the hearing of all Judah who come from their cities. ⁷It may be that they will present their supplication before the LORD, and everyone will turn from his evil way. For great *is* the anger and the fury that the LORD has pronounced against this people." ⁸And Baruch the son of Neriah did according to all that Jeremiah the prophet commanded him, reading from the book the words of the LORD in the LORD's house.

⁹Now it came to pass in the fifth year of Jehoiakim the son of Josiah, king of Judah, in the ninth month, *that* they proclaimed a fast before the LORD to all the people in Jerusalem, and to all the people who came from the cities of Judah to Jerusalem. ¹⁰Then Baruch read from the book the words of Jeremiah in the house of the LORD, in the chamber of Gemariah the son of Shaphan the scribe, in the upper court at the entry of the New Gate of the LORD's house, in the hearing of all the people.

> **36:9 fifth year.** This was the next year (604 B.C.) after that of v. 1, which may suggest that it took some part of a year to repeat and record the long series of messages given up to that point (see v. 18). **ninth month.** This was either November or December (see vv. 22,23).

The Scroll Read in the Palace

¹¹When Michaiah the son of Gemariah, the son of Shaphan, heard all the words of the LORD from the book, ¹²he then went down to the king's house, into the scribe's chamber; and there all the princes were sitting—Elishama the scribe, Delaiah the son of Shemaiah, Elnathan the son of Achbor, Gemariah the son of Shaphan, Zedekiah the son of Hananiah, and all the princes. ¹³Then Michaiah declared to them all the words that he had heard when Baruch read the book in the hearing of the people. ¹⁴Therefore all the princes sent Jehudi the son of Nethaniah, the son of Shelemiah, the son of Cushi, to Baruch, saying, "Take in your hand the scroll from which you have read in the hearing of the people, and come." So Baruch the son of Neriah took the scroll in his hand and came to them. ¹⁵And they said to him, "Sit down now, and read it in our hearing." So Baruch read *it* in their hearing.

¹⁶Now it happened, when they had heard

> **36:4 Baruch wrote.** Jeremiah's recording secretary (see 32:12) wrote the prophet's messages (see 45:1), and penned them a second time after the first scroll was burned (see 36:32). He also read the messages in the temple (v. 10) and in the palace (v. 15).

36:4 *a*Literally *from Jeremiah's mouth*   36:6 *a*Literally *from my mouth*

all the words, that they looked in fear from one to another, and said to Baruch, "We will surely tell the king of all these words." [17]And they asked Baruch, saying, "Tell us now, how did you write all these words—at his instruction?"[a]

[18]So Baruch answered them, "He proclaimed with his mouth all these words to me, and I wrote *them* with ink in the book."

[19]Then the princes said to Baruch, "Go and hide, you and Jeremiah; and let no one know where you are."

The King Destroys Jeremiah's Scroll

[20]And they went to the king, into the court; but they stored the scroll in the chamber of Elishama the scribe, and told all the words in the hearing of the king. [21]So the king sent Jehudi to bring the scroll, and he took it from Elishama the scribe's chamber. And Jehudi read it in the hearing of the king and in the hearing of all the princes who stood beside the king. [22]Now the king was sitting in the winter house in the ninth month, with *a fire* burning on the hearth before him. [23]And it happened, when Jehudi had read three or four columns, *that the king* cut it with the scribe's knife and cast *it* into the fire that *was* on the hearth, until all the scroll was consumed in the fire that *was* on the hearth. [24]Yet they were not afraid, nor did they tear their garments, the king nor any of his servants who heard all these words. [25]Nevertheless Elnathan, Delaiah, and Gemariah implored the king not to burn the scroll; but he would not listen to them. [26]And the king commanded Jerahmeel the king's[a] son, Seraiah the son of Azriel, and Shelemiah the son of Abdeel, to seize Baruch the scribe and Jeremiah the prophet, but the LORD hid them.

36:23 cut it. Jehoiakim rejected the message of the Scriptures so much that he cut up the scroll and threw the sections in the fire as it was read.

Jeremiah Rewrites the Scroll

[27]Now after the king had burned the scroll with the words which Baruch had written at the instruction of Jeremiah,[a] the word of the LORD came to Jeremiah, saying: [28]"Take yet another scroll, and write on it all the former words that were in the first scroll which Jehoiakim the king of Judah has burned. [29]And you shall say to Jehoiakim king of Judah, 'Thus says the LORD: "You have burned this scroll, saying, 'Why have you written in it that the king of Babylon will certainly come and destroy this land, and cause man and beast to cease from here?'" [30]Therefore thus says the LORD concerning Jehoiakim king of Judah: "He shall have no one to sit on the throne of David, and his dead body shall be cast out to the heat of the day and the frost of the night. [31]I will punish him, his family, and his servants for their iniquity; and I will bring on them, on the inhabitants of Jerusalem, and on the men of Judah all the doom that I have pronounced against them; but they did not heed."'"

[32]Then Jeremiah took another scroll and gave it to Baruch the scribe, the son of Neriah, who wrote on it at the instruction of Jeremiah[a] all the words of the book which Jehoiakim king of Judah had burned in the fire. And besides, there were added to them many similar words.

Zedekiah's Vain Hope

37 Now King Zedekiah the son of Josiah reigned instead of Coniah the son of Jehoiakim, whom Nebuchadnezzar king of Babylon made king in the land of Judah. [2]But neither he nor his servants nor the people of the land gave heed to the words of the LORD which He spoke by the prophet Jeremiah.

[3]And Zedekiah the king sent Jehucal the son of Shelemiah, and Zephaniah the son of Maaseiah, the priest, to the prophet Jeremiah, saying, "Pray now to the LORD our God for us." [4]Now Jeremiah was coming and going among the people, for they had not *yet* put him in prison. [5]Then Pharaoh's army came up from Egypt; and when the Chaldeans who were besieging Jerusalem heard news of them, they departed from Jerusalem.

[6]Then the word of the LORD came to the prophet Jeremiah, saying, [7]"Thus says the

---

36:17 [a]Literally *with his mouth*   36:26 [a]Hebrew *Hammelech*   36:27 [a]Literally *from Jeremiah's mouth*   36:32 [a]Literally *from Jeremiah's mouth*

LORD, the God of Israel, 'Thus you shall say to the king of Judah, who sent you to Me to inquire of Me: "Behold, Pharaoh's army which has come up to help you will return to Egypt, to their own land. [8]And the Chaldeans shall come back and fight against this city, and take it and burn it with fire." ' [9]Thus says the LORD: 'Do not deceive yourselves, saying, "The Chaldeans will surely depart from us," for they will not depart. [10]For though you had defeated the whole army of the Chaldeans who fight against you, and there remained *only* wounded men among them, they would rise up, every man in his tent, and burn the city with fire.' "

Jeremiah Imprisoned

[11]And it happened, when the army of the Chaldeans left *the siege* of Jerusalem for fear of Pharaoh's army, [12]that Jeremiah went out of Jerusalem to go into the land of Benjamin to claim his property there among the people. [13]And when he was in the Gate of Benjamin, a captain of the guard *was* there whose name *was* Irijah the son of Shelemiah, the son of Hananiah; and he seized Jeremiah the prophet, saying, "You are defecting to the Chaldeans!"

[14]Then Jeremiah said, "False! I am not defecting to the Chaldeans." But he did not listen to him.

So Irijah seized Jeremiah and brought him to the princes. [15]Therefore the princes were angry with Jeremiah, and they struck him and put him in prison in the house of Jonathan the scribe. For they had made that the prison.

[16]When Jeremiah entered the dungeon and the cells, and Jeremiah had remained there many days, [17]then Zedekiah the king sent and took him *out*. The king asked him secretly in his house, and said, "Is there *any* word from the LORD?"

And Jeremiah said, "There is." Then he said, "You shall be delivered into the hand of the king of Babylon!"

[18]Moreover Jeremiah said to King Zedekiah, "What offense have I committed against you, against your servants, or against this people, that you have put me in prison? [19]Where now *are* your prophets

who prophesied to you, saying, 'The king of Babylon will not come against you or against this land?' [20]Therefore please hear now, O my lord the king. Please, let my petition be accepted before you, and do not make me return to the house of Jonathan the scribe, lest I die there."

[21]Then Zedekiah the king commanded that they should commit Jeremiah to the court of the prison, and that they should give him daily a piece of bread from the bakers' street, until all the bread in the city was gone. Thus Jeremiah remained in the court of the prison.

37:21 bread. The king showed a measure of kindness to Jeremiah by returning him to the "court of the prison" (see 32:2), promising him bread as long as it lasted in the siege (see 38:9). Jerusalem was taken soon after the food was gone (38:28).

Jeremiah in the Dungeon

38 Now Shephatiah the son of Mattan, Gedaliah the son of Pashhur, Jucal[a] the son of Shelemiah, and Pashhur the son of Malchiah heard the words that Jeremiah had spoken to all the people, saying, [2]"Thus says the LORD: 'He who remains in this city shall die by the sword, by famine, and by pestilence; but he who goes over to the Chaldeans shall live; his life shall be as a prize to him, and he shall live.'[a] [3]Thus says the LORD: 'This city shall surely be given into the hand of the king of Babylon's army, which shall take it.' "

[4]Therefore the princes said to the king, "Please, let this man be put to death, for thus he weakens the hands of the men of war who remain in this city, and the hands of all the people, by speaking such words to them. For this man does not seek the welfare of this people, but their harm."

38:4 he weakens the hands. The princes thought that Jeremiah's urging Judah to submit to Babylon undermined the people's morale and will. His proclamation that Babylon was victorious made him appear to be a traitor to Judah.

[5]Then Zedekiah the king said, "Look, he *is* in your hand. For the king can *do* nothing against you." [6]So they took Jeremiah and

---

38:1 [a]Same as *Jehucal* (compare 37:3)   38:2 [a]Compare 21:9

cast him into the dungeon of Malchiah the king's*a* son, which *was* in the court of the prison, and they let Jeremiah down with ropes. And in the dungeon *there was* no water, but mire. So Jeremiah sank in the mire.

⁷Now Ebed-Melech the Ethiopian, one of the eunuchs, who was in the king's house, heard that they had put Jeremiah in the dungeon. When the king was sitting at the Gate of Benjamin, ⁸Ebed-Melech went out of the king's house and spoke to the king, saying: ⁹"My lord the king, these men have done evil in all that they have done to Jeremiah the prophet, whom they have cast into the dungeon, and he is likely to die from hunger in the place where he is. For *there is* no more bread in the city." ¹⁰Then the king commanded Ebed-Melech the Ethiopian, saying, "Take from here thirty men with you, and lift Jeremiah the prophet out of the dungeon before he dies." ¹¹So Ebed-Melech took the men with him and went into the house of the king under the treasury, and took from there old clothes and old rags, and let them down by ropes into the dungeon to Jeremiah. ¹²Then Ebed-Melech the Ethiopian said to Jeremiah, "Please put these old clothes and rags under your armpits, under the ropes." And Jeremiah did so. ¹³So they pulled Jeremiah up with ropes and lifted him out of the dungeon. And Jeremiah remained in the court of the prison.

Zedekiah's Fears and Jeremiah's Advice

¹⁴Then Zedekiah the king sent and had Jeremiah the prophet brought to him at the third entrance of the house of the LORD. And the king said to Jeremiah, "I will ask you something. Hide nothing from me."

¹⁵Jeremiah said to Zedekiah, "If I declare *it* to you, will you not surely put me to death? And if I give you advice, you will not listen to me."

¹⁶So Zedekiah the king swore secretly to Jeremiah, saying, "*As* the LORD lives, who made our very souls, I will not put you to death, nor will I give you into the hand of these men who seek your life."

¹⁷Then Jeremiah said to Zedekiah, "Thus says the LORD, the God of hosts, the God of Israel: 'If you surely surrender to the king of Babylon's princes, then your soul shall live; this city shall not be burned with fire, and you and your house shall live. ¹⁸But if you do not surrender to the king of Babylon's princes, then this city shall be given into the hand of the Chaldeans; they shall burn it with fire, and you shall not escape from their hand.' "

¹⁹And Zedekiah the king said to Jeremiah, "I am afraid of the Jews who have defected to the Chaldeans, lest they deliver me into their hand, and they abuse me."

²⁰But Jeremiah said, "They shall not deliver *you*. Please, obey the voice of the LORD which I speak to you. So it shall be well with you, and your soul shall live. ²¹But if you refuse to surrender, this *is* the word that the LORD has shown me: ²²'Now behold, all the women who are left in the king of Judah's house *shall be* surrendered to the king of Babylon's princes, and those *women* shall say:

> "Your close friends have set upon you
> And prevailed against you;
> Your feet have sunk in the mire,
> *And* they have turned away again."

²³'So they shall surrender all your wives and children to the Chaldeans. You shall not escape from their hand, but shall be taken by the hand of the king of Babylon. And you shall cause this city to be burned with fire.' "

38:14–23 I will ask you. This is one of several times that Zedekiah rejected God's Word after asking to hear it. His refusal to accept God's Word meant calamity for Jerusalem, his own capture, and tragedy for his family and others in his palace.

²⁴Then Zedekiah said to Jeremiah, "Let no one know of these words, and you shall not die. ²⁵But if the princes hear that I have talked with you, and they come to you and say to you, 'Declare to us now what you have said to the king, and also what the king said to you; do not hide *it* from us, and we will not put you to death,' ²⁶then you shall say to them, 'I presented my request before the king, that he would not make

---

38:6 *a*Hebrew *Hammelech*

me return to Jonathan's house to die there.'"

27Then all the princes came to Jeremiah and asked him. And he told them according to all these words that the king had commanded. So they stopped speaking with him, for the conversation had not been heard. 28Now Jeremiah remained in the court of the prison until the day that Jerusalem was taken. And he was *there* when Jerusalem was taken.

The Fall of Jerusalem

39 In the ninth year of Zedekiah king of Judah, in the tenth month, Nebuchadnezzar king of Babylon and all his army came against Jerusalem, and besieged it. 2In the eleventh year of Zedekiah, in the fourth month, on the ninth *day* of the month, the city was penetrated.

3Then all the princes of the king of Babylon came in and sat in the Middle Gate: Nergal-Sharezer, Samgar-Nebo, Sarsechim, Rabsaris,*a* Nergal-Sarezer, Rabmag,*b* with the rest of the princes of the king of Babylon.

4So it was, when Zedekiah the king of Judah and all the men of war saw them, that they fled and went out of the city by night, by way of the king's garden, by the gate between the two walls. And he went out by way of the plain.*a* 5But the Chaldean army pursued them and overtook Zedekiah in the plains of Jericho. And when they had captured him, they brought him up to Nebuchadnezzar king of Babylon, to Riblah in the land of Hamath, where he pronounced judgment on him. 6Then the king of Babylon killed the sons of Zedekiah before his eyes in Riblah; the king of Babylon also killed all the nobles of Judah. 7Moreover he put out Zedekiah's eyes, and bound him with bronze fetters to carry him off to Babylon. 8And the Chaldeans burned the king's house and the houses of the people with fire, and broke down the walls of Jerusalem. 9Then Nebuzaradan the captain of the guard carried away captive to Babylon the remnant of the people who remained in the city and those who defected to him, with the rest of the people who remained. 10But

Nebuzaradan the captain of the guard left in the land of Judah the poor people, who had nothing, and gave them vineyards and fields at the same time.

Jeremiah Goes Free

11Now Nebuchadnezzar king of Babylon gave charge concerning Jeremiah to Nebuzaradan the captain of the guard, saying, 12"Take him and look after him, and do him no harm; but do to him just as he says to you." 13So Nebuzaradan the captain of the guard sent Nebushasban, Rabsaris, Nergal-Sharezer, Rabmag, and all the king of Babylon's chief officers; 14then they sent *someone* to take Jeremiah from the court of the prison, and committed him to Gedaliah the son of Ahikam, the son of Shaphan, that he should take him home. So he dwelt among the people.

> **39:14 take Jeremiah from the court.** This is a general summary of the account of Jeremiah's captivity and release (40:1–5). "Gedaliah" was a former supporter of Jeremiah (26:24) and chief among the defectors loyal to Nebuchadnezzar. He was made governor (40:5) over the remnant left in the land.

15Meanwhile the word of the LORD had come to Jeremiah while he was shut up in the court of the prison, saying, 16"Go and speak to Ebed-Melech the Ethiopian, saying, 'Thus says the LORD of hosts, the God of Israel: "Behold, I will bring My words upon this city for adversity and not for good, and they shall be *performed* in that day before you. 17But I will deliver you in that day," says the LORD, "and you shall not be given into the hand of the men of whom you *are* afraid. 18For I will surely deliver you, and you shall not fall by the sword; but your life shall be as a prize to you, because you have put your trust in Me," says the LORD.'"

Jeremiah with Gedaliah the Governor

40 The word that came to Jeremiah from the LORD after Nebuzaradan the captain of the guard had let him go from Ramah, when he had taken him bound in chains among all who were carried away

---

39:3 *a*A title, probably *Chief Officer*; also verse 13   *b*A title, probably *Troop Commander*; also verse 13   39:4 *a*Or *the Arabah*, that is, the Jordan Valley

captive from Jerusalem and Judah, who were carried away captive to Babylon.

²And the captain of the guard took Jeremiah and said to him: "The LORD your God has pronounced this doom on this place. ³Now the LORD has brought *it*, and has done just as He said. Because you *people* have sinned against the LORD, and not obeyed His voice, therefore this thing has come upon you. ⁴And now look, I free you this day from the chains that *were* on your hand. If it seems good to you to come with me to Babylon, come, and I will look after you. But if it seems wrong for you to come with me to Babylon, remain here. See, all the land *is* before you; wherever it seems good and convenient for you to go, go there."

40:2,3 The pagan captain understood the judgment of God better than the leaders of Judah.

⁵Now while Jeremiah had not yet gone back, *Nebuzaradan said*, "Go back to Gedaliah the son of Ahikam, the son of Shaphan, whom the king of Babylon has made governor over the cities of Judah, and dwell with him among the people. Or go wherever it seems convenient for you to go." So the captain of the guard gave him rations and a gift and let him go. ⁶Then Jeremiah went to Gedaliah the son of Ahikam, to Mizpah, and dwelt with him among the people who were left in the land.

⁷And when all the captains of the armies who *were* in the fields, they and their men, heard that the king of Babylon had made Gedaliah the son of Ahikam governor in the land, and had committed to him men, women, children, and the poorest of the land who had not been carried away captive to Babylon, ⁸then they came to Gedaliah at Mizpah—Ishmael the son of Nethaniah, Johanan and Jonathan the sons of Kareah, Seraiah the son of Tanhumeth, the sons of Ephai the Netophathite, and Jezaniah*ᵃ* the son of a Maachathite, they and their men. ⁹And Gedaliah the son of Ahikam, the son of Shaphan, took an oath before them and their men, saying, "Do not be afraid to serve the Chaldeans. Dwell in the land and serve the king of Babylon, and it shall be

well with you. ¹⁰As for me, I will indeed dwell at Mizpah and serve the Chaldeans who come to us. But you, gather wine and summer fruit and oil, put *them* in your vessels, and dwell in your cities that you have taken." ¹¹Likewise, when all the Jews who *were* in Moab, among the Ammonites, in Edom, and who *were* in all the countries, heard that the king of Babylon had left a remnant of Judah, and that he had set over them Gedaliah the son of Ahikam, the son of Shaphan, ¹²then all the Jews returned out of all places where they had been driven, and came to the land of Judah, to Gedaliah at Mizpah, and gathered wine and summer fruit in abundance.

40:9–12 God had lessened the severity of the judgment by allowing a remnant to prosper.

¹³Moreover Johanan the son of Kareah and all the captains of the forces that *were* in the fields came to Gedaliah at Mizpah, ¹⁴and said to him, "Do you certainly know that Baalis the king of the Ammonites has sent Ishmael the son of Nethaniah to murder you?" But Gedaliah the son of Ahikam did not believe them.

¹⁵Then Johanan the son of Kareah spoke secretly to Gedaliah in Mizpah, saying, "Let me go, please, and I will kill Ishmael the son of Nethaniah, and no one will know *it*. Why should he murder you, so that all the Jews who are gathered to you would be scattered, and the remnant in Judah perish?"

¹⁶But Gedaliah the son of Ahikam said to Johanan the son of Kareah, "You shall not do this thing, for you speak falsely concerning Ishmael."

Insurrection Against Gedaliah

41 Now it came to pass in the seventh month *that* Ishmael the son of Nethaniah, the son of Elishama, of the royal family and of the officers of the king, came with ten men to Gedaliah the son of Ahikam, at Mizpah. And there they ate bread together in Mizpah. ²Then Ishmael the son of Nethaniah, and the ten men who were with him, arose and struck Gedaliah the son of Ahikam, the son of Shaphan,

---

40:8 *ᵃ*Spelled *Jaazaniah* in 2 Kings 25:23

with the sword, and killed him whom the king of Babylon had made governor over the land. ³Ishmael also struck down all the Jews who were with him, *that is*, with Gedaliah at Mizpah, and the Chaldeans who were found there, the men of war.

⁴And it happened, on the second day after he had killed Gedaliah, when as yet no one knew *it*, ⁵that certain men came from Shechem, from Shiloh, and from Samaria, eighty men with their beards shaved and their clothes torn, having cut themselves, with offerings and incense in their hand, to bring *them* to the house of the LORD. ⁶Now Ishmael the son of Nethaniah went out from Mizpah to meet them, weeping as he went along; and it happened as he met them that he said to them, "Come to Gedaliah the son of Ahikam!" ⁷So it was, when they came into the midst of the city, that Ishmael the son of Nethaniah killed them *and cast them* into the midst of a pit, he and the men who were with him. ⁸But ten men were found among them who said to Ishmael, "Do not kill us, for we have treasures of wheat, barley, oil, and honey in the field." So he desisted and did not kill them among their brethren. ⁹Now the pit into which Ishmael had cast all the dead bodies of the men whom he had slain, because of Gedaliah, *was* the same one Asa the king had made for fear of Baasha king of Israel. Ishmael the son of Nethaniah filled it with *the* slain. ¹⁰Then Ishmael carried away captive all the rest of the people who *were* in Mizpah, the king's daughters and all the people who remained in Mizpah, whom Nebuzaradan the captain of the guard had committed to Gedaliah the son of Ahikam. And Ishmael the son of Nethaniah carried them away captive and departed to go over to the Ammonites.

> **41:5 eighty men.** Most likely, these men came mourning over the destruction of Jerusalem. Ishmael did a lot of damage with only 10 men. They may have added to their number to accomplish what they did in v. 10.

¹¹But when Johanan the son of Kareah and all the captains of the forces that *were* with him heard of all the evil that Ishmael the son of Nethaniah had done, ¹²they took all the men and went to fight with Ishmael the son of Nethaniah; and they found him by the great pool that *is* in Gibeon. ¹³So it was, when all the people who *were* with Ishmael saw Johanan the son of Kareah, and all the captains of the forces who *were* with him, that they were glad. ¹⁴Then all the people whom Ishmael had carried away captive from Mizpah turned around and came back, and went to Johanan the son of Kareah. ¹⁵But Ishmael the son of Nethaniah escaped from Johanan with eight men and went to the Ammonites.

¹⁶Then Johanan the son of Kareah, and all the captains of the forces that were with him, took from Mizpah all the rest of the people whom he had recovered from Ishmael the son of Nethaniah after he had murdered Gedaliah the son of Ahikam— the mighty men of war and the women and the children and the eunuchs, whom he had brought back from Gibeon. ¹⁷And they departed and dwelt in the habitation of Chimham, which is near Bethlehem, as they went on their way to Egypt, ¹⁸because of the Chaldeans; for they were afraid of them, because Ishmael the son of Nethaniah had murdered Gedaliah the son of Ahikam, whom the king of Babylon had made governor in the land.

The Flight to Egypt Forbidden

42 Now all the captains of the forces, Johanan the son of Kareah, Jezaniah the son of Hoshaiah, and all the people, from the least to the greatest, came near ²and said to Jeremiah the prophet, "Please, let our petition be acceptable to you, and pray for us to the LORD your God, for all this remnant (since we are left *but* a few of many, as you can see), ³that the LORD your God may show us the way in which we should walk and the thing we should do."

⁴Then Jeremiah the prophet said to them, "I have heard. Indeed, I will pray to the LORD your God according to your words, and it shall be, *that* whatever the LORD answers you, I will declare *it* to you. I will keep nothing back from you."

⁵So they said to Jeremiah, "Let the LORD be a true and faithful witness between us, if we do not do according to everything which the LORD your God sends us by you. ⁶Whether *it is* pleasing or displeasing, we will obey the voice of the LORD our God to

whom we send you, that it may be well with us when we obey the voice of the LORD our God."

7And it happened after ten days that the word of the LORD came to Jeremiah. 8Then he called Johanan the son of Kareah, all the captains of the forces which *were* with him, and all the people from the least even to the greatest, 9and said to them, "Thus says the LORD, the God of Israel, to whom you sent me to present your petition before Him: 10'If you will still remain in this land, then I will build you and not pull *you* down, and I will plant you and not pluck *you* up. For I relent concerning the disaster that I have brought upon you. 11Do not be afraid of the king of Babylon, of whom you are afraid; do not be afraid of him,' says the LORD, 'for I *am* with you, to save you and deliver you from his hand. 12And I will show you mercy, that he may have mercy on you and cause you to return to your own land.'

13"But if you say, 'We will not dwell in

> **42:10 I relent.** By this God meant that He was satisfied with the punishment He inflicted on them as long as they did not add any new offenses.

this land,' disobeying the voice of the LORD your God, 14saying, 'No, but we will go to the land of Egypt where we shall see no war, nor hear the sound of the trumpet, nor be hungry for bread, and there we will dwell'— 15Then hear now the word of the LORD, O remnant of Judah! Thus says the LORD of hosts, the God of Israel: 'If you wholly set your faces to enter Egypt, and go to dwell there, 16then it shall be *that* the sword which you feared shall overtake you there in the land of Egypt; the famine of which you were afraid shall follow close after you there *in* Egypt; and there you shall die. 17So shall it be with all the men who set their faces to go to Egypt to dwell there. They shall die by the sword, by famine, and by pestilence. And none of them shall remain or escape from the disaster that I will bring upon them.'

18"For thus says the LORD of hosts, the God of Israel: 'As My anger and My fury have been poured out on the inhabitants of Jerusalem, so will My fury be poured out on you when you enter Egypt. And you shall be an oath, an astonishment, a curse, and a reproach; and you shall see this place no more.'

19"The LORD has said concerning you, O remnant of Judah, 'Do not go to Egypt!' Know certainly that I have admonished you this day. 20For you were hypocrites in your hearts when you sent me to the LORD your God, saying, 'Pray for us to the LORD our God, and according to all that the LORD your God says, so declare to us and we will do *it*.' 21And I have this day declared *it* to you, but you have not obeyed the voice of the LORD your God, or anything which He has sent you by me. 22Now therefore, know certainly that you shall die by the sword, by famine, and by pestilence in the place where you desire to go to dwell."

Jeremiah Taken to Egypt

43 Now it happened, when Jeremiah had stopped speaking to all the people all the words of the LORD their God, for which the LORD their God had sent him to them, all these words, 2that Azariah the son of Hoshaiah, Johanan the son of Kareah, and all the proud men spoke, saying to Jeremiah, "You speak falsely! The LORD our God has not sent you to say, 'Do not go to Egypt to dwell there.' 3But Baruch the son of Neriah has set you against us, to deliver us into the hand of the Chaldeans, that they may put us to death or carry us away captive to Babylon." 4So Johanan the son of Kareah, all the captains of the forces, and all the people would not obey the voice of the LORD, to remain in the land of Judah. 5But Johanan the son of Kareah and all the captains of the forces took all the remnant of Judah who had returned to dwell in the land of Judah, from all nations where they had been driven— 6men, women, children, the king's daughters, and every person whom Nebuzaradan the captain of the guard had left with Gedaliah the son of Ahikam, the son of Shaphan, and Jeremiah the prophet and Baruch the son of Neriah.

> **43:1–7 when Jeremiah...stopped speaking.** The disobedient leaders accused Jeremiah of deceit and forced him and the remnant to go to Egypt. They did this despite the fact that his prophesies about Babylon came to pass. God, therefore, excluded the leaders from His protection and judged them for their disobedience.

7So they went to the land of Egypt, for they did not obey the voice of the LORD. And they went as far as Tahpanhes.

8Then the word of the LORD came to Jeremiah in Tahpanhes, saying, 9"Take large stones in your hand, and hide them in the sight of the men of Judah, in the clay in the brick courtyard which *is* at the entrance to Pharaoh's house in Tahpanhes; 10and say to them, 'Thus says the LORD of hosts, the God of Israel: "Behold, I will send and bring Nebuchadnezzar the king of Babylon, My servant, and will set his throne above these stones that I have hidden. And he will spread his royal pavilion over them. 11When he comes, he shall strike the land of Egypt *and deliver* to death *those appointed* for death, and to captivity *those appointed* for captivity, and to the sword *those appointed* for the sword. 12I*a* will kindle a fire in the houses of the gods of Egypt, and he shall burn them and carry them away captive. And he shall array himself with the land of Egypt, as a shepherd puts on his garment, and he shall go out from there in peace. 13He shall also break the *sacred* pillars of Beth Shemesh*a* that *are* in the land of Egypt; and the houses of the gods of the Egyptians he shall burn with fire." ' "

43:9–13 Take large stones. The stones placed in the brick pavement in the courtyard entrance of the Pharaoh's house signaled the place where the king of Babylon would bring destruction on Egypt and establish his throne. This was fulfilled during the invasion around 568/67 B.C.

Israelites Will Be Punished in Egypt

44 The word that came to Jeremiah concerning all the Jews who dwell in the land of Egypt, who dwell at Migdol, at Tahpanhes, at Noph,*a* and in the country of Pathros, saying, 2"Thus says the LORD of hosts, the God of Israel: 'You have seen all the calamity that I have brought on Jerusalem and on all the cities of Judah; and behold, this day they *are* a desolation, and no one dwells in them, 3because of their wickedness which they have committed to provoke Me to anger, in that they went to burn incense *and* to serve other gods whom they did not know, they nor you nor your fathers. 4However I have sent to you all My servants the prophets, rising early and sending *them,* saying, "Oh, do not do this abominable thing that I hate!" 5But they did not listen or incline their ear to turn from their wickedness, to burn no incense to other gods. 6So My fury and My anger were poured out and kindled in the cities of Judah and in the streets of Jerusalem; and they are wasted *and* desolate, as it is this day.'

7"Now therefore, thus says the LORD, the God of hosts, the God of Israel: 'Why do you commit *this* great evil against yourselves, to cut off from you man and woman, child and infant, out of Judah, leaving none to remain, 8in that you provoke Me to wrath with the works of your hands, burning incense to other gods in the land of Egypt where you have gone to dwell, that you may cut yourselves off and be a curse and a reproach among all the nations of the earth? 9Have you forgotten the wickedness of your fathers, the wickedness of the kings of Judah, the wickedness of their wives, your own wickedness, and the wickedness of your wives, which they committed in the land of Judah and in the streets of Jerusalem? 10They have not been humbled, to this day, nor have they feared; they have not walked in My law or in My statutes that I set before you and your fathers.'

11"Therefore thus says the LORD of hosts, the God of Israel: 'Behold, I will set My face against you for catastrophe and for cutting off all Judah. 12And I will take the remnant of Judah who have set their faces to go into the land of Egypt to dwell there, and they shall all be consumed *and* fall in the land of Egypt. They shall be consumed by the sword *and* by famine. They shall die, from the least to the greatest, by the sword and by famine; and they shall be an oath, an astonishment, a curse and a reproach! 13For I will punish those who dwell in the land of Egypt, as I have punished Jerusalem, by the sword, by famine, and by pestilence, 14so that none of the remnant of Judah who

---

43:12 *a*Following Masoretic Text and Targum; Septuagint, Syriac, and Vulgate read *He.*
43:13 *a*Literally *House of the Sun,* ancient On; later called Heliopolis   44:1 *a*That is, ancient Memphis

have gone into the land of Egypt to dwell there shall escape or survive, lest they return to the land of Judah, to which they desire to return and dwell. For none shall return except those who escape.' "

15Then all the men who knew that their wives had burned incense to other gods, with all the women who stood by, a great multitude, and all the people who dwelt in the land of Egypt, in Pathros, answered Jeremiah, saying: 16"As for the word that you have spoken to us in the name of the LORD, we will not listen to you! 17But we will certainly do whatever has gone out of our own mouth, to burn incense to the queen of heaven and pour out drink offerings to her, as we have done, we and our fathers, our kings and our princes, in the cities of Judah and in the streets of Jerusalem. For then we had plenty of food, were well-off, and saw no trouble. 18But since we stopped burning incense to the queen of heaven and pouring out drink offerings to her, we have lacked everything and have been consumed by the sword and by famine."

19The women also said, "And when we burned incense to the queen of heaven and poured out drink offerings to her, did we make cakes for her, to worship her, and pour out drink offerings to her without our husbands' permission?"

44:17–19 queen of heaven. This is a title Roman Catholicism wrongly attributes to Mary, the mother of Jesus, in a blending of Christianity and paganism. The Jews, in their twisted thinking, credit the idol with the prosperity of Judah before their captivity. They still mocked God's goodness.

20Then Jeremiah spoke to all the people—the men, the women, and all the people who had given him that answer—saying: 21"The incense that you burned in the cities of Judah and in the streets of Jerusalem, you and your fathers, your kings and your princes, and the people of the land, did not the LORD remember them, and did it not come into His mind? 22So the LORD could no longer bear it, because of the evil of your doings and because of the abominations which you committed. Therefore your land is a desolation, an astonishment, a curse, and without an inhabitant, as it is this day. 23Because you have burned incense and because you have sinned against the LORD, and have not obeyed the voice of the LORD or walked in His law, in His statutes or in His testimonies, therefore this calamity has happened to you, as at this day."

24Moreover Jeremiah said to all the people and to all the women, "Hear the word of the LORD, all Judah who are in the land of Egypt! 25Thus says the LORD of hosts, the God of Israel, saying: 'You and your wives have spoken with your mouths and fulfilled with your hands, saying, "We will surely keep our vows that we have made, to burn incense to the queen of heaven and pour out drink offerings to her." You will surely keep your vows and perform your vows!' 26Therefore hear the word of the LORD, all Judah who dwell in the land of Egypt: 'Behold, I have sworn by My great name,' says the LORD, 'that My name shall no more be named in the mouth of any man of Judah in all the land of Egypt, saying, "The Lord GOD lives." 27Behold, I will watch over them for adversity and not for good. And all the men of Judah who are in the land of Egypt shall be consumed by the sword and by famine, until there is an end to them. 28Yet a small number who escape the sword shall return from the land of Egypt to the land of Judah; and all the remnant of Judah, who have gone to the land of Egypt to dwell there, shall know whose words will stand, Mine or theirs. 29And this shall be a sign to you,' says the LORD, 'that I will punish you in this place, that you may know that My words will surely stand against you for adversity.'

30"Thus says the LORD: 'Behold, I will give Pharaoh Hophra king of Egypt into the hand of his enemies and into the hand of those who seek his life, as I gave Zedekiah king of Judah into the hand of Nebuchadnezzar king of Babylon, his enemy who sought his life.' "

Assurance to Baruch

45 The word that Jeremiah the prophet spoke to Baruch the son of Neriah, when he had written these words in a book at the instruction of Jeremiah,a in the

---

45:1 aLiterally from Jeremiah's mouth

fourth year of Jehoiakim the son of Josiah, king of Judah, saying, ²"Thus says the LORD, the God of Israel, to you, O Baruch: ³'You said, "Woe is me now! For the LORD has added grief to my sorrow. I fainted in my sighing, and I find no rest." '

> **45:3 Woe is me now!** Baruch became anxious when his plans for a prosperous future crumbled. He may have also been pressured by others' questioning God's part in this calamity. Jeremiah spoke to encourage him (v. 2).

⁴"Thus you shall say to him, 'Thus says the LORD: "Behold, what I have built I will break down, and what I have planted I will pluck up, that is, this whole land. ⁵And do you seek great things for yourself? Do not seek them; for behold, I will bring adversity on all flesh," says the LORD. "But I will give your life to you as a prize in all places, wherever you go." ' "

Judgment on Egypt

46 The word of the LORD which came to Jeremiah the prophet against the nations. ²Against Egypt.

Concerning the army of Pharaoh Necho, king of Egypt, which was by the River Euphrates in Carchemish, and which Nebuchadnezzar king of Babylon defeated in the fourth year of Jehoiakim the son of Josiah, king of Judah:

> **46:1 against the nations.** Jeremiah had already proclaimed that all nations at some time are to experience God's wrath (25:15–26). In chaps. 46–51 God predicted the doom of certain nations. Jeremiah's prophecies were collected and arranged by nation, not by chronology.

³ "Order the buckler and shield,
    And draw near to battle!
⁴ Harness the horses,
    And mount up, you horsemen!
    Stand forth with your helmets,
    Polish the spears,
    Put on the armor!
⁵ Why have I seen them dismayed and
        turned back?
    Their mighty ones are beaten down;
    They have speedily fled,
    And did not look back,
    For fear was all around," says the LORD.

⁶ "Do not let the swift flee away,
    Nor the mighty man escape;
    They will stumble and fall
    Toward the north, by the River
        Euphrates.

⁷ "Who is this coming up like a flood,
    Whose waters move like the rivers?
⁸ Egypt rises up like a flood,
    And its waters move like the rivers;
    And he says, 'I will go up and cover
        the earth,
    I will destroy the city and its
        inhabitants.'
⁹ Come up, O horses, and rage,
    O chariots!
    And let the mighty men come forth:
    The Ethiopians and the Libyans who
        handle the shield,
    And the Lydians who handle and
        bend the bow.

> **46:10 the day of the Lord GOD.** While this phrase often refers to God's judgment in the last days (such as in Joel 1:15), it also may refer to a historical day. In this case it points to the Egyptian defeat (see Lam. 2:2).

¹⁰ For this is the day of the Lord GOD of
        hosts,
    A day of vengeance,
    That He may avenge Himself on His
        adversaries.
    The sword shall devour;
    It shall be satiated and made drunk
        with their blood;
    For the Lord GOD of hosts has a
        sacrifice
    In the north country by the River
        Euphrates.

¹¹ "Go up to Gilead and take balm,
    O virgin, the daughter of Egypt;
    In vain you will use many medicines;
    You shall not be cured.
¹² The nations have heard of your
        shame,
    And your cry has filled the land;
    For the mighty man has stumbled
        against the mighty;
    They both have fallen together."

Babylonia Will Strike Egypt

¹³The word that the LORD spoke to Jeremiah the prophet, how Nebuchadnezzar

king of Babylon would come *and* strike the land of Egypt.

14 "Declare in Egypt, and proclaim in Migdol;
Proclaim in Noph[a] and in Tahpanhes;
Say, 'Stand fast and prepare yourselves,
For the sword devours all around you.'
15 Why are your valiant *men* swept away?
They did not stand
Because the LORD drove them away.
16 He made many fall;
Yes, one fell upon another.
And they said, 'Arise!
Let us go back to our own people
And to the land of our nativity
From the oppressing sword.'
17 They cried there,
'Pharaoh, king of Egypt, *is but* a noise.
He has passed by the appointed time!'

18 "*As* I live," says the King,
Whose name *is* the LORD of hosts,
"Surely as Tabor *is* among the mountains
And as Carmel by the sea, *so* he shall come.
19 O you daughter dwelling in Egypt,
Prepare yourself to go into captivity!
For Noph[a] shall be waste and desolate, without inhabitant.

20 "Egypt *is* a very pretty heifer,
But destruction comes, it comes from the north.
21 Also her mercenaries are in her midst like fat bulls,
For they also are turned back,
They have fled away together.
They did not stand,
For the day of their calamity had come upon them,
The time of their punishment.
22 Her noise shall go like a serpent,
For they shall march with an army
And come against her with axes,
Like those who chop wood.
23 "They shall cut down her forest," says the LORD,
"Though it cannot be searched,

Because they *are* innumerable,
And more numerous than grasshoppers.
24 The daughter of Egypt shall be ashamed;
She shall be delivered into the hand
Of the people of the north."

25The LORD of hosts, the God of Israel, says: "Behold, I will bring punishment on Amon[a] of No,[b] and Pharaoh and Egypt, with their gods and their kings—Pharaoh and those who trust in him. 26And I will deliver them into the hand of those who seek their lives, into the hand of Nebuchadnezzar king of Babylon and the hand of his servants. Afterward it shall be inhabited as in the days of old," says the LORD.

God Will Preserve Israel

27 "But do not fear, O My servant Jacob,
And do not be dismayed, O Israel!
For behold, I will save you from afar,
And your offspring from the land of their captivity;
Jacob shall return, have rest and be at ease;
No one shall make *him* afraid.
28 Do not fear, O Jacob My servant," says the LORD,
"For I *am* with you;
For I will make a complete end of all the nations
To which I have driven you,
But I will not make a complete end of you.
I will rightly correct you,
For I will not leave you wholly unpunished."

46:27,28 do not fear...Jacob. Though Israel had been scattered to the nations, the nations would still receive judgment, and Israel would be restored as one nation. Israel will never be destroyed, regardless of what judgment befalls them (see Rom. 11:1,2).

Judgment on Philistia

47 The word of the LORD that came to Jeremiah the prophet against the Philistines, before Pharaoh attacked Gaza. 2Thus says the LORD:

46:14 [a]That is, ancient Memphis   46:19 [a]That is, ancient Memphis   46:25 [a]A sun god   [b]That is, ancient Thebes

"Behold, waters rise out of the north,
And shall be an overflowing flood;
They shall overflow the land and all
that is in it,
The city and those who dwell within;
Then the men shall cry,
And all the inhabitants of the land
shall wail.
3   At the noise of the stamping hooves
of his strong horses,
At the rushing of his chariots,
At the rumbling of his wheels,
The fathers will not look back for
their children,
Lacking courage,
4   Because of the day that comes to
plunder all the Philistines,
To cut off from Tyre and Sidon every
helper who remains;
For the LORD shall plunder the
Philistines,
The remnant of the country of Caphtor.
5   Baldness has come upon Gaza,
Ashkelon is cut off
With the remnant of their valley.
How long will you cut yourself?

6   "O you sword of the LORD,
How long until you are quiet?
Put yourself up into your scabbard,
Rest and be still!
7   How can it be quiet,
Seeing the LORD has given it a charge
Against Ashkelon and against the
seashore?
There He has appointed it."

Judgment on Moab

48 Against Moab.
Thus says the LORD of hosts, the
God of Israel:

"Woe to Nebo!
For it is plundered,
Kirjathaim is shamed *and* taken;
The high stronghold*ᵃ* is shamed and
dismayed—
2   No more praise of Moab.
In Heshbon they have devised evil
against her:

'Come, and let us cut her off as a
nation.'
You also shall be cut down,
O Madmen!*ᵃ*
The sword shall pursue you;
3   A voice of crying *shall be* from
Horonaim:
'Plundering and great destruction!'

4   "Moab is destroyed;
Her little ones have caused a cry to be
heard;*ᵃ*
5   For in the Ascent of Luhith they
ascend with continual weeping;
For in the descent of Horonaim the
enemies have heard a cry of
destruction.

6   "Flee, save your lives!
And be like the juniper*ᵃ* in the
wilderness.
7   For because you have trusted in your
works and your treasures,
You also shall be taken.
And Chemosh shall go forth into
captivity,
His priests and his princes together.

48:7 Chemosh. He was the leading god of Moab (see
Num. 21:29).

8   And the plunderer shall come against
every city;
No one shall escape.
The valley also shall perish,
And the plain shall be destroyed,
As the LORD has spoken.

9   "Give wings to Moab,
That she may flee and get away;
For her cities shall be desolate,
Without any to dwell in them.
10   Cursed *is* he who does the work of the
LORD deceitfully,
And cursed *is* he who keeps back his
sword from blood.

11   "Moab has been at ease from his*ᵃ*
youth;
He has settled on his dregs,

48:1 *ᵃ*Hebrew *Misgab*   48:2 *ᵃ*A city of Moab   48:4 *ᵃ*Following Masoretic Text, Targum, and Vulgate;
Septuagint reads *Proclaim it in Zoar.*   48:6 *ᵃ*Or *Aroer*, a city of Moab   48:11 *ᵃ*The Hebrew uses
masculine and feminine pronouns interchangeably in this chapter.

And has not been emptied from vessel
to vessel,
Nor has he gone into captivity.
Therefore his taste remained in him,
And his scent has not changed.

12 "Therefore behold, the days are
coming," says the LORD,
"That I shall send him wine-workers
Who will tip him over
And empty his vessels
And break the bottles.

48:11,12 In the production of sweet wine, the juice was left in a wineskin until the sediment (dregs) settled to the bottom. This process was done until all the dregs were removed. Moab was not taken through suffering after suffering so that her "dregs" would be removed. Therefore, the nation settled into the thick bitterness of its own sin.

13   Moab shall be ashamed of Chemosh,
As the house of Israel was ashamed of
Bethel, their confidence.

14 "How can you say, 'We *are* mighty
And strong men for the war'?
15   Moab is plundered and gone up *from*
her cities;
Her chosen young men have gone
down to the slaughter," says the
King,
Whose name *is* the LORD of hosts.

16 "The calamity of Moab *is* near at hand,
And his affliction comes quickly.
17   Bemoan him, all you who are around
him;
And all you who know his name,
Say, 'How the strong staff is broken,
The beautiful rod!'

18 "O daughter inhabiting Dibon,
Come down from *your* glory,
And sit in thirst;
For the plunderer of Moab has come
against you,
He has destroyed your strongholds.
19   O inhabitant of Aroer,
Stand by the way and watch;
Ask him who flees
And her who escapes;

Say, 'What has happened?'
20   Moab is shamed, for he is broken
down.
Wail and cry!
Tell it in Arnon, that Moab is
plundered.

21 "And judgment has come on the plain
country:
On Holon and Jahzah and Mephaath,
22   On Dibon and Nebo and Beth
Diblathaim,
23   On Kirjathaim and Beth Gamul and
Beth Meon,
24   On Kerioth and Bozrah,
On all the cities of the land of Moab,
Far or near.
25   The horn of Moab is cut off,
And his arm is broken," says the LORD.

48:25 horn...is cut off. The horn of an animal was a symbol of military power in the Old Testament. Moab was to be de-horned.

26 "Make him drunk,
Because he exalted *himself* against the
LORD.
Moab shall wallow in his vomit,
And he shall also be in derision.
27   For was not Israel a derision to you?
Was he found among thieves?
For whenever you speak of him,
You shake *your head in scorn.*
28   You who dwell in Moab,
Leave the cities and dwell in the rock,
And be like the dove *which* makes her
nest
In the sides of the cave's mouth.

29 "We have heard the pride of Moab
(He *is* exceedingly proud),
Of his loftiness and arrogance and
pride,
And of the haughtiness of his heart."
30 "I know his wrath," says the LORD,
"But it *is* not right;
His lies have made nothing right.
31   Therefore I will wail for Moab,
And I will cry out for all Moab;
I*a* will mourn for the men of Kir Heres.

48:31 *a*Following Dead Sea Scrolls, Septuagint, and Vulgate; Masoretic Text reads *He.*

32   O vine of Sibmah! I will weep for you
          with the weeping of Jazer.
      Your plants have gone over the sea,
      They reach to the sea of Jazer.
      The plunderer has fallen on your
          summer fruit and your vintage.
33   Joy and gladness are taken
      From the plentiful field
      And from the land of Moab;
      I have caused wine to fail from the
          winepresses;
      No one will tread with joyous
          shouting—
      Not joyous shouting!

34   "From the cry of Heshbon to Elealeh
          and to Jahaz
      They have uttered their voice,
      From Zoar to Horonaim,
      Like a three-year-old heifer;*a*
      For the waters of Nimrim also shall
          be desolate.

35   "Moreover," says the LORD,
      "I will cause to cease in Moab
          The one who offers *sacrifices* in the
              high places
          And burns incense to his gods.
36   Therefore My heart shall wail like
          flutes for Moab,
      And like flutes My heart shall wail
      For the men of Kir Heres.
      Therefore the riches they have
          acquired have perished.

37   "For every head *shall be* bald, and
          every beard clipped;
      On all the hands *shall be* cuts, and on
          the loins sackcloth—
38   A general lamentation
      On all the housetops of Moab,
      And in its streets;
      For I have broken Moab like a vessel
          in which *is* no pleasure," says the
          LORD.
39   "They shall wail:
      'How she is broken down!
      How Moab has turned her back with
          shame!'
      So Moab shall be a derision
      And a dismay to all those about
          her."

40   For thus says the LORD:

      "Behold, one shall fly like an eagle,
      And spread his wings over Moab.
41   Kerioth is taken,
      And the strongholds are surprised;
      The mighty men's hearts in Moab on
          that day shall be
      Like the heart of a woman in birth
          pangs.
42   And Moab shall be destroyed as a
          people,
      Because he exalted *himself* against the
          LORD.
43   Fear and the pit and the snare *shall be*
          upon you,
      O inhabitant of Moab," says the LORD.
44   "He who flees from the fear shall fall
          into the pit,
      And he who gets out of the pit shall
          be caught in the snare.
      For upon Moab, upon it I will bring
      The year of their punishment," says
          the LORD.

45   "Those who fled stood under the
          shadow of Heshbon
      Because of exhaustion.
      But a fire shall come out of Heshbon,
      A flame from the midst of Sihon,
      And shall devour the brow of Moab,
      The crown of the head of the sons of
          tumult.
46   Woe to you, O Moab!
      The people of Chemosh perish;
      For your sons have been taken captive,
      And your daughters captive.

47   "Yet I will bring back the captives of
          Moab
      In the latter days," says the LORD.

Thus far *is* the judgment of Moab.

Judgment on Ammon

49 Against the Ammonites.
      Thus says the LORD:

> **48:47 I will bring back.** God will allow a remnant of
> Moab to return to the land, through her descendants
> in the messianic era ("the latter days").

48:34 *a*Or *The Third Eglath,* an unknown city (compare Isaiah 15:5)

"Has Israel no sons?
Has he no heir?
Why *then* does Milcom[a] inherit Gad,
And his people dwell in its cities?

2   Therefore behold, the days are
coming," says the LORD,
"That I will cause to be heard an alarm
of war
In Rabbah of the Ammonites;
It shall be a desolate mound,
And her villages shall be burned with
fire.
Then Israel shall take possession of
his inheritance," says the LORD.

> **49:2 an alarm of war.** Nebuchadnezzar defeated Ammon in the fifth year after the destruction of Jerusalem (about 582/81 B.C.).

3   "Wail, O Heshbon, for Ai is
plundered!
Cry, you daughters of Rabbah,
Gird yourselves with sackcloth!
Lament and run to and fro by the
walls;
For Milcom shall go into captivity
With his priests and his princes
together.

4   Why do you boast in the valleys,
Your flowing valley, O backsliding
daughter?
Who trusted in her treasures, *saying*,
'Who will come against me?'

5   Behold, I will bring fear upon you,"
Says the Lord GOD of hosts,
"From all those who are around you;
You shall be driven out, everyone
headlong,
And no one will gather those who
wander off.

6   But afterward I will bring back
The captives of the people of
Ammon," says the LORD.

> **49:6 I will bring back.** God promised that captives would have a chance to return like Moab did. This was partially fulfilled under Cyrus, but will ultimately be realized in the coming messianic kingdom (see 48:47).

Judgment on Edom

7Against Edom.
Thus says the LORD of hosts:

"*Is* wisdom no more in Teman?
Has counsel perished from the
prudent?
Has their wisdom vanished?

8   Flee, turn back, dwell in the depths,
O inhabitants of Dedan!
For I will bring the calamity of Esau
upon him,
The time *that* I will punish him.

9   If grape-gatherers came to you,
Would they not leave *some* gleaning
grapes?
If thieves by night,
Would they not destroy until they
have enough?

10   But I have made Esau bare;
I have uncovered his secret places,[a]
And he shall not be able to hide
himself.
His descendants are plundered,
His brethren and his neighbors,
And he *is* no more.

11   Leave your fatherless children,
I will preserve *them* alive;
And let your widows trust in Me."

12For thus says the LORD: "Behold, those whose judgment *was* not to drink of the cup have assuredly drunk. And *are* you the one who will altogether go unpunished? You shall not go unpunished, but you shall surely drink *of it.* 13For I have sworn by Myself," says the LORD, "that Bozrah shall become a desolation, a reproach, a waste, and a curse. And all its cities shall be perpetual wastes."

14   I have heard a message from the
LORD,
And an ambassador has been sent to
the nations:
"Gather together, come against her,
And rise up to battle!

15   "For indeed, I will make you small
among nations,
Despised among men.

49:1 [a]Hebrew *Malcam*, literally *their king*, a god of the Ammonites; also called *Molech* (compare verse 3)   49:10 [a]Compare Obadiah 5,6

16 Your fierceness has deceived you,
    The pride of your heart,
    O you who dwell in the clefts of the
        rock,
    Who hold the height of the hill!
    Though you make your nest as high
        as the eagle,
    I will bring you down from there,"
        says the LORD.[a]

17 "Edom also shall be an astonishment;
    Everyone who goes by it will be
        astonished
    And will hiss at all its plagues.

49:16,17 Edom was situated in high and rugged
mountains, thus convincing the city that it was invincible. Their ruin would be irreversible.

18 As in the overthrow of Sodom and
        Gomorrah
    And their neighbors," says the LORD,
    "No one shall remain there,
    Nor shall a son of man dwell in it.

19 "Behold, he shall come up like a lion
        from the floodplain[a] of the Jordan
    Against the dwelling place of the
        strong;
    But I will suddenly make him run
        away from her.
    And who is a chosen man that I may
        appoint over her?
    For who is like Me?
    Who will arraign Me?
    And who is that shepherd
    Who will withstand Me?"

20 Therefore hear the counsel of the
        LORD that He has taken against
        Edom,
    And His purposes that He has
        proposed against the inhabitants of
        Teman:
    Surely the least of the flock shall draw
        them out;
    Surely He shall make their dwelling
        places desolate with them.

21 The earth shakes at the noise of their
        fall;
    At the cry its noise is heard at the Red
        Sea.

22 Behold, He shall come up and fly like
        the eagle,
    And spread His wings over Bozrah;
    The heart of the mighty men of Edom
        in that day shall be
    Like the heart of a woman in birth
        pangs.

Judgment on Damascus
23 Against Damascus.

    "Hamath and Arpad are shamed,
    For they have heard bad news.
    They are fainthearted;
    There is trouble on the sea;
    It cannot be quiet.
24 Damascus has grown feeble;
    She turns to flee,
    And fear has seized her.
    Anguish and sorrows have taken her
        like a woman in labor.
25 Why is the city of praise not deserted,
        the city of My joy?
26 Therefore her young men shall fall in
        her streets,
    And all the men of war shall be cut
        off in that day," says the LORD of
        hosts.
27 "I will kindle a fire in the wall of
        Damascus,
    And it shall consume the palaces of
        Ben-Hadad."[a]

49:27 palaces of Ben-Hadad. Many evils were devised against Israel in this palace, which was why it
was overthrown. "Ben-Hadad" was a common name
among Syrian kings, meaning Son of Hadad, an idol.
This is not a reference to the Ben-Hadad of 2 Kin. 13:3.

Judgment on Kedar and Hazor
28 Against Kedar and against the kingdoms of Hazor, which Nebuchadnezzar
king of Babylon shall strike.
    Thus says the LORD:

    "Arise, go up to Kedar,
    And devastate the men of the East!
29 Their tents and their flocks they shall
        take away.
    They shall take for themselves their
        curtains,
    All their vessels and their camels;

49:16 [a]Compare Obadiah 3,4   49:19 [a]Or thicket   49:27 [a]Compare Amos 1:4

And they shall cry out to them,
'Fear *is* on every side!'

30 "Flee, get far away! Dwell in the
    depths,
    O inhabitants of Hazor!" says the
    LORD.
"For Nebuchadnezzar king of Babylon
    has taken counsel against you,
And has conceived a plan against you.

31 "Arise, go up to the wealthy nation
    that dwells securely," says the
    LORD,
"Which has neither gates nor bars,
    Dwelling alone.
32 Their camels shall be for booty,
    And the multitude of their cattle for
    plunder.
I will scatter to all winds those in the
    farthest corners,
And I will bring their calamity from
    all its sides," says the LORD.
33 "Hazor shall be a dwelling for jackals,
    a desolation forever;
No one shall reside there,
    Nor son of man dwell in it."

Judgment on Elam

34The word of the LORD that came to Jeremiah the prophet against Elam, in the beginning of the reign of Zedekiah king of Judah, saying, 35"Thus says the LORD of hosts:

'Behold, I will break the bow of Elam,
    The foremost of their might.
36 Against Elam I will bring the four
    winds
From the four quarters of heaven,
And scatter them toward all those
    winds;
There shall be no nations where the
    outcasts of Elam will not go.
37 For I will cause Elam to be dismayed
    before their enemies
And before those who seek their life.
I will bring disaster upon them,
    My fierce anger,' says the LORD;
'And I will send the sword after them
    Until I have consumed them.
38 I will set My throne in Elam,

And will destroy from there the king
    and the princes,' says the LORD.

> **49:34–39 against Elam.** Babylon fulfilled this prophesy in 596 B.C. Cyrus of Persia later conquered Elam and incorporated the people into the Persian forces. These forces conquered Babylon in 539 B.C.

39 "But it shall come to pass in the latter
    days:
I will bring back the captives of Elam,'
    says the LORD."

Judgment on Babylon and Babylonia

50 The word that the LORD spoke against Babylon *and* against the land of the Chaldeans by Jeremiah the prophet.

2 "Declare among the nations,
    Proclaim, and set up a standard;
    Proclaim—do not conceal *it*—
    Say, 'Babylon is taken, Bel is shamed.
    Merodach*a* is broken in pieces;
    Her idols are humiliated,
    Her images are broken in pieces.'

> **50:2 idols.** Jeremiah discredits Babylon's idols by calling them, in the Hebrew, "dung pellets."

3 For out of the north a nation comes
    up against her,
Which shall make her land desolate,
And no one shall dwell therein.
They shall move, they shall depart,
Both man and beast.

4 "In those days and in that time," says
    the LORD,
"The children of Israel shall come,
They and the children of Judah
    together;
With continual weeping they shall
    come,
And seek the LORD their God.
5 They shall ask the way to Zion,
With their faces toward it, *saying*,
'Come and let us join ourselves to the
    LORD
In a perpetual covenant
That will not be forgotten.'

50:2 *a*A Babylonian god; sometimes spelled *Marduk*

6 "My people have been lost sheep.
Their shepherds have led them
astray;
They have turned them away *on the*
mountains.
They have gone from mountain to
hill;
They have forgotten their resting
place.
7 All who found them have devoured
them;
And their adversaries said, 'We have
not offended,
Because they have sinned against the
LORD, the habitation of justice,
The LORD, the hope of their fathers.'

8 "Move from the midst of Babylon,
Go out of the land of the Chaldeans;
And be like the rams before the
flocks.
9 For behold, I will raise and cause to
come up against Babylon
An assembly of great nations from the
north country,
And they shall array themselves
against her;
From there she shall be captured.
Their arrows *shall be* like *those* of an
expert warrior;[a]
None shall return in vain.
10 And Chaldea shall become plunder;
All who plunder her shall be
satisfied," says the LORD.

50:4–10 children of Israel shall come. Jeremiah
predicted the return of Israel and Judah to both Jerusalem and to the Lord (vv. 17–20) when they had
the opportunity to escape Babylon's doom.

11 "Because you were glad, because you
rejoiced,
You destroyers of My heritage,
Because you have grown fat like a
heifer threshing grain,
And you bellow like bulls,
12 Your mother shall be deeply ashamed;
She who bore you shall be ashamed.
Behold, the least of the nations *shall
be* a wilderness,
A dry land and a desert.

13 Because of the wrath of the LORD
She shall not be inhabited,
But she shall be wholly desolate.
Everyone who goes by Babylon shall
be horrified
And hiss at all her plagues.

14 "Put yourselves in array against
Babylon all around,
All you who bend the bow;
Shoot at her, spare no arrows,
For she has sinned against the LORD.
15 Shout against her all around;
She has given her hand,
Her foundations have fallen,
Her walls are thrown down;
For it *is* the vengeance of the LORD.
Take vengeance on her.
As she has done, so do to her.
16 Cut off the sower from Babylon,
And him who handles the sickle at
harvest time.
For fear of the oppressing sword
Everyone shall turn to his own
people,
And everyone shall flee to his own
land.

17 "Israel *is* like scattered sheep;
The lions have driven *him* away.
First the king of Assyria devoured him;
Now at last this Nebuchadnezzar king
of Babylon has broken his bones."

18 Therefore thus says the LORD of hosts,
the God of Israel:

"Behold, I will punish the king of
Babylon and his land,
As I have punished the king of
Assyria.
19 But I will bring back Israel to his
home,
And he shall feed on Carmel and
Bashan;
His soul shall be satisfied on Mount
Ephraim and Gilead.
20 In those days and in that time," says
the LORD,
"The iniquity of Israel shall be sought,
but *there shall be* none;

50:9 [a]Following some Hebrew manuscripts, Septuagint, and Syriac; Masoretic Text, Targum, and
Vulgate read *a warrior who makes childless.*

And the sins of Judah, but they shall
not be found;
For I will pardon those whom I
preserve.

50:17–20 This passage condenses Israel's history
into her suffering and judgment, the judgment on
those who afflicted her, her return to peace, and the
pardon of her iniquity under the Messiah.

21 "Go up against the land of Merathaim,
against it,
And against the inhabitants of
Pekod.
Waste and utterly destroy them," says
the LORD,
"And do according to all that I have
commanded you.
22 A sound of battle *is* in the land,
And of great destruction.
23 How the hammer of the whole earth
has been cut apart and broken!
How Babylon has become a desolation
among the nations!
I have laid a snare for you;
24 You have indeed been trapped,
O Babylon,
And you were not aware;
You have been found and also caught,
Because you have contended against
the LORD.
25 The LORD has opened His armory,
And has brought out the weapons of
His indignation;
For this *is* the work of the Lord GOD
of hosts
In the land of the Chaldeans.
26 Come against her from the farthest
border;
Open her storehouses;
Cast her up as heaps of ruins,
And destroy her utterly;
Let nothing of her be left.
27 Slay all her bulls,
Let them go down to the slaughter.
Woe to them!
For their day has come, the time of
their punishment.
28 The voice of those who flee and
escape from the land of Babylon

Declares in Zion the vengeance of the
LORD our God,
The vengeance of His temple.

50:28 vengeance of His temple. This refers to the
burning of the temple in the destruction of Jerusalem
(see 51:11).

29 "Call together the archers against
Babylon.
All you who bend the bow, encamp
against it all around;
Let none of them escape.*a*
Repay her according to her work;
According to all she has done, do to
her;
For she has been proud against the
LORD,
Against the Holy One of Israel.
30 Therefore her young men shall fall in
the streets,
And all her men of war shall be cut
off in that day," says the LORD.
31 "Behold, I *am* against you,
O most haughty one!" says the Lord
GOD of hosts;
"For your day has come,
The time *that* I will punish you.*a*
32 The most proud shall stumble and
fall,
And no one will raise him up;
I will kindle a fire in his cities,
And it will devour all around him."

33 Thus says the LORD of hosts:

"The children of Israel *were* oppressed,
Along with the children of Judah;
All who took them captive have held
them fast;
They have refused to let them go.
34 Their Redeemer *is* strong;
The LORD of hosts *is* His name.

50:34 Redeemer. The OT concept of kinsmen-re-
deemer included the protection of a relative's person
and property, the avenging of a relative's person, the
purchase of alienated property, and even the marriage of his widow (see Lev. 25:25).

50:29 *a*Qere, some Hebrew manuscripts, Septuagint, and Targum add *to her.* 50:31 *a*Following
Masoretic Text and Targum; Septuagint and Vulgate read *The time of your punishment.*

He will thoroughly plead their case,
That He may give rest to the land,
And disquiet the inhabitants of
　　Babylon.

35 "A sword *is* against the Chaldeans,"
　　says the LORD,
"Against the inhabitants of Babylon,
And against her princes and her wise
　　men.
36 A sword *is* against the soothsayers,
　　and they will be fools.
A sword *is* against her mighty men,
　　and they will be dismayed.
37 A sword *is* against their horses,
Against their chariots,
And against all the mixed peoples
　　who *are* in her midst;
And they will become like women.
A sword *is* against her treasures, and
　　they will be robbed.
38 A drought[a] *is* against her waters, and
　　they will be dried up.
For it *is* the land of carved images,
And they are insane with *their* idols.

39 "Therefore the wild desert beasts shall
　　dwell *there* with the jackals,
And the ostriches shall dwell in it.
It shall be inhabited no more forever,
Nor shall it be dwelt in from
　　generation to generation.
40 As God overthrew Sodom and
　　Gomorrah
And their neighbors," says the LORD,
"So no one shall reside there,
Nor son of man dwell in it.

> **50:40 As God overthrew Sodom.** What befell Sodom was sudden and total destruction, not like the Media Persia takeover, but like the future devastation of the final Babylon (see Gen. 19; Rev. 17,18).

41 "Behold, a people shall come from the
　　north,
And a great nation and many kings
Shall be raised up from the ends of
　　the earth.
42 They shall hold the bow and the
　　lance;

They *are* cruel and shall not show
　　mercy.
Their voice shall roar like the sea;
They shall ride on horses,
Set in array, like a man for the battle,
Against you, O daughter of Babylon.

43 "The king of Babylon has heard the
　　report about them,
And his hands grow feeble;
Anguish has taken hold of him,
Pangs as of a woman in childbirth.

44 "Behold, he shall come up like a lion
　　from the floodplain[a] of the Jordan
Against the dwelling place of the
　　strong;
But I will make them suddenly run
　　away from her.
And who *is* a chosen *man that* I may
　　appoint over her?
For who *is* like Me?
Who will arraign Me?
And who *is* that shepherd
Who will withstand Me?"

45 Therefore hear the counsel of the
　　LORD that He has taken against
　　Babylon,
And His purposes that He has
　　proposed against the land of the
　　Chaldeans:
Surely the least of the flock shall draw
　　them out;
Surely He will make their dwelling
　　place desolate with them.
46 At the noise of the taking of Babylon
The earth trembles,
And the cry is heard among the
　　nations.

The Utter Destruction of Babylon

51 Thus says the LORD:

"Behold, I will raise up against Babylon,
Against those who dwell in Leb
　　Kamai,[a]
A destroying wind.
2 And I will send winnowers to
　　Babylon,

50:38 [a]Following Masoretic Text, Targum, and Vulgate; Syriac reads *sword*; Septuagint omits *A drought is.* 50:44 [a]Or *thicket* 51:1 [a]A code word for Chaldea (Babylonia); may be translated *The Midst of Those Who Rise Up Against Me*

Who shall winnow her and empty her
   land.
For in the day of doom
They shall be against her all around.
3 Against *her* let the archer bend his
   bow,
And lift himself up against *her* in his
   armor.
Do not spare her young men;
Utterly destroy all her army.
4 Thus the slain shall fall in the land of
   the Chaldeans,
And *those* thrust through in her
   streets.
5 For Israel is not forsaken, nor Judah,
By his God, the LORD of hosts,
Though their land was filled with sin
   against the Holy One of Israel."

6 Flee from the midst of Babylon,
And every one save his life!
Do not be cut off in her iniquity,
For this *is* the time of the LORD's
   vengeance;
He shall recompense her.
7 Babylon *was* a golden cup in the
   LORD's hand,
That made all the earth drunk.
The nations drank her wine;
Therefore the nations are deranged.
8 Babylon has suddenly fallen and been
   destroyed.
Wail for her!
Take balm for her pain;
Perhaps she may be healed.

51:8 suddenly fallen. The focus was first on
Babylon's fall in one night in 539 B.C. (Dan. 5:30). Another view considers the final and sudden destruction
of Babylon near the Second Advent (Rev. 18).

9 We would have healed Babylon,
But she is not healed.
Forsake her, and let us go everyone to
   his own country;
For her judgment reaches to heaven
   and is lifted up to the skies.
10 The LORD has revealed our
   righteousness.
Come and let us declare in Zion the
   work of the LORD our God.

11 Make the arrows bright!
Gather the shields!
The LORD has raised up the spirit of
   the kings of the Medes.
For His plan *is* against Babylon to
   destroy it,
Because it *is* the vengeance of the
   LORD,
The vengeance for His temple.
12 Set up the standard on the walls of
   Babylon;
Make the guard strong,
Set up the watchmen,
Prepare the ambushes.
For the LORD has both devised and
   done
What He spoke against the
   inhabitants of Babylon.
13 O you who dwell by many waters,
Abundant in treasures,
Your end has come,
The measure of your covetousness.
14 The LORD of hosts has sworn by
   Himself:
"Surely I will fill you with men, as
   with locusts,
And they shall lift up a shout against
   you."

15 He has made the earth by His power;
He has established the world by His
   wisdom,
And stretched out the heaven by His
   understanding.
16 When He utters *His* voice—
There is a multitude of waters in the
   heavens:
"He causes the vapors to ascend from
   the ends of the earth;
He makes lightnings for the rain;
He brings the wind out of His
   treasuries."[a]

17 Everyone is dull-hearted, without
   knowledge;
Every metalsmith is put to shame by
   the carved image;
For his molded image *is* falsehood,
And *there is* no breath in them.
18 They *are* futile, a work of errors;
In the time of their punishment they
   shall perish.

51:16 [a]Psalm 135:7

19   The Portion of Jacob *is* not like them,
     For He *is* the Maker of all things;
     And *Israel is* the tribe of His
        inheritance.
     The LORD of hosts *is* His name.

20   "You *are* My battle-ax *and* weapons of
        war:
     For with you I will break the nation in
        pieces;
     With you I will destroy kingdoms;

21   With you I will break in pieces the
        horse and its rider;
     With you I will break in pieces the
        chariot and its rider;

22   With you also I will break in pieces
        man and woman;
     With you I will break in pieces old
        and young;
     With you I will break in pieces the
        young man and the maiden;

23   With you also I will break in pieces
        the shepherd and his flock;
     With you I will break in pieces the
        farmer and his yoke of oxen;
     And with you I will break in pieces
        governors and rulers.

51:20–23 You *are* My battle-ax. Cyrus of Persia was God's war club. The phrase "with you" hits with the force of a hammer 10 times in this passage.

24   "And I will repay Babylon
     And all the inhabitants of Chaldea
     For all the evil they have done
     In Zion in your sight," says the LORD.

25   "Behold, I *am* against you,
       O destroying mountain,
     Who destroys all the earth," says the
       LORD.
     "And I will stretch out My hand
       against you,
     Roll you down from the rocks,
     And make you a burnt mountain.

51:25 destroying mountain. Though Babylon was geographically located on a plain, this phrase was meant as a portrayal of Babylon's looming greatness and powerful military exploits (see 50:23).

26   They shall not take from you a stone
       for a corner

     Nor a stone for a foundation,
     But you shall be desolate forever,"
       says the LORD.

27   Set up a banner in the land,
     Blow the trumpet among the nations!
     Prepare the nations against her,
     Call the kingdoms together against
       her:
     Ararat, Minni, and Ashkenaz.
     Appoint a general against her;
     Cause the horses to come up like the
       bristling locusts.

28   Prepare against her the nations,
     With the kings of the Medes,
     Its governors and all its rulers,
     All the land of his dominion.

29   And the land will tremble and sorrow;
     For every purpose of the LORD shall
       be performed against Babylon,
     To make the land of Babylon a
       desolation without inhabitant.

30   The mighty men of Babylon have
       ceased fighting,
     They have remained in their
       strongholds;
     Their might has failed,
     They became *like* women;
     They have burned her dwelling
       places,
     The bars of her *gate* are broken.

31   One runner will run to meet another,
     And one messenger to meet another,
     To show the king of Babylon that his
       city is taken on *all* sides;

32   The passages are blocked,
     The reeds they have burned with fire,
     And the men of war are terrified.

51:32 The method of capturing the city was to block off the Euphrates River and dry up the river bed under the city wall so that they could walk right in. The "fire" was a successful attempt to frighten the people.

33 For thus says the LORD of hosts, the God of Israel:

     "The daughter of Babylon *is* like a
       threshing floor
     When it is time to thresh her;
     Yet a little while
     And the time of her harvest will
       come."

34 "Nebuchadnezzar the king of Babylon
   Has devoured me, he has crushed me;
   He has made me an empty vessel,
   He has swallowed me up like a
      monster;
   He has filled his stomach with my
      delicacies,
   He has spit me out.
35 Let the violence *done* to me and my
      flesh *be* upon Babylon,"
   The inhabitant of Zion will say;
   "And my blood *be* upon the
      inhabitants of Chaldea!"
   Jerusalem will say.

36 Therefore thus says the LORD:

   "Behold, I will plead your case and take
      vengeance for you.
   I will dry up her sea and make her
      springs dry.
37 Babylon shall become a heap,
   A dwelling place for jackals,
   An astonishment and a hissing,
   Without an inhabitant.
38 They shall roar together like lions,
   They shall growl like lions' whelps.
39 In their excitement I will prepare
      their feasts;
   I will make them drunk,
   That they may rejoice,
   And sleep a perpetual sleep
   And not awake," says the LORD.
40 "I will bring them down
   Like lambs to the slaughter,
   Like rams with male goats.

41 "Oh, how Sheshach[a] is taken!
   Oh, how the praise of the whole earth
      is seized!
   How Babylon has become desolate
      among the nations!
42 The sea has come up over Babylon;
   She is covered with the multitude of
      its waves.
43 Her cities are a desolation,
   A dry land and a wilderness,
   A land where no one dwells,
   Through which no son of man passes.
44 I will punish Bel in Babylon,
   And I will bring out of his mouth
      what he has swallowed;

And the nations shall not stream to
   him anymore.
Yes, the wall of Babylon shall fall.

45 "My people, go out of the midst of her!
   And let everyone deliver himself from
      the fierce anger of the LORD.
46 And lest your heart faint,
   And you fear for the rumor that *will
      be* heard in the land
   (A rumor will come *one* year,
   And after that, in *another* year
   A rumor *will come,*
   And violence in the land,
   Ruler against ruler),
47 Therefore behold, the days are coming
   That I will bring judgment on the
      carved images of Babylon;
   Her whole land shall be ashamed,
   And all her slain shall fall in her
      midst.
48 Then the heavens and the earth and
      all that *is* in them
   Shall sing joyously over Babylon;
   For the plunderers shall come to her
      from the north," says the LORD.

49 As Babylon *has caused* the slain of
      Israel to fall,
   So at Babylon the slain of all the earth
      shall fall.
50 You who have escaped the sword,
   Get away! Do not stand still!
   Remember the LORD afar off,
   And let Jerusalem come to your mind.

51 We are ashamed because we have
      heard reproach.
   Shame has covered our faces,
   For strangers have come into the
      sanctuaries of the LORD's house.

52 "Therefore behold, the days are
      coming," says the LORD,
   "That I will bring judgment on her
      carved images,
   And throughout all her land the
      wounded shall groan.
53 Though Babylon were to mount up to
      heaven,
   And though she were to fortify the
      height of her strength,

51:41 [a]A code word for Babylon (compare Jeremiah 25:26)

Yet from Me plunderers would come
    to her," says the LORD.

54 The sound of a cry *comes* from
    Babylon,
    And great destruction from the land
      of the Chaldeans,
55 Because the LORD is plundering
    Babylon
    And silencing her loud voice,
    Though her waves roar like great
      waters,
    And the noise of their voice is uttered,
56 Because the plunderer comes against
    her, against Babylon,
    And her mighty men are taken.
    Every one of their bows is broken;
    For the LORD *is* the God of
      recompense,
    He will surely repay.

57 "And I will make drunk
    Her princes and wise men,
    Her governors, her deputies, and her
      mighty men.
    And they shall sleep a perpetual sleep
    And not awake," says the King,
    Whose name *is* the LORD of hosts.

58 Thus says the LORD of hosts:

    "The broad walls of Babylon shall be
      utterly broken,
    And her high gates shall be burned
      with fire;
    The people will labor in vain,
    And the nations, because of the fire;
    And they shall be weary."

51:58 labor in vain. People from many nations enslaved in Babylon had built the wall for nothing.

Jeremiah's Command to Seraiah

59 The word which Jeremiah the prophet commanded Seraiah the son of Neriah, the son of Mahseiah, when he went with Zedekiah the king of Judah to Babylon in the fourth year of his reign. And Seraiah *was* the quartermaster. 60 So Jeremiah wrote in a book all the evil that would come upon Babylon, all these words that are written against Babylon. 61 And Jeremiah said to Seraiah, "When you arrive in Babylon and see it, and read all these words, 62 then you shall say, 'O LORD, You have spoken against this place to cut it off, so that none shall remain in it, neither man nor beast, but it shall be desolate forever.' 63 Now it shall be, when you have finished reading this book, *that* you shall tie a stone to it and throw it out into the Euphrates. 64 Then you shall say, 'Thus Babylon shall sink and not rise from the catastrophe that I will bring upon her. And they shall be weary.' "

Thus far *are* the words of Jeremiah.

52:1–34 This chapter is almost identical to 2 Kin. 24:18–25:30 and is a historical supplement detailing Jerusalem's fall. The purpose is to show how accurate Jeremiah's prophesies were concerning Jerusalem and Judah. This event is so crucial that the Old Testament records it four times (see 39:1–14; 2 Kin. 25; 2 Chr. 36:11–21).

The Fall of Jerusalem Reviewed

52 Zedekiah *was* twenty-one years old when he became king, and he reigned eleven years in Jerusalem. His mother's name *was* Hamutal the daughter of Jeremiah of Libnah. 2 He also did evil in the sight of the LORD, according to all that Jehoiakim had done. 3 For because of the anger of the LORD *this* happened in Jerusalem and Judah, till He finally cast them out from His presence. Then Zedekiah rebelled against the king of Babylon.

4 Now it came to pass in the ninth year of his reign, in the tenth month, on the tenth *day* of the month, *that* Nebuchadnezzar king of Babylon and all his army came against Jerusalem and encamped against it; and *they* built a siege wall against it all around. 5 So the city was besieged until the eleventh year of King Zedekiah. 6 By the fourth month, on the ninth day of the month, the famine had become so severe in the city that there was no food for the people of the land. 7 Then the city wall was broken through, and all the men of war fled and went out of the city at night by way of the gate between the two walls, which *was* by the king's garden, even though the Chaldeans *were* near the city all around. And they went by way of the plain.[a]

52:7 [a] Or *the Arabah*, that is, the Jordan Valley

[8]But the army of the Chaldeans pursued the king, and they overtook Zedekiah in the plains of Jericho. All his army was scattered from him. [9]So they took the king and brought him up to the king of Babylon at Riblah in the land of Hamath, and he pronounced judgment on him. [10]Then the king of Babylon killed the sons of Zedekiah before his eyes. And he killed all the princes of Judah in Riblah. [11]He also put out the eyes of Zedekiah; and the king of Babylon bound him in bronze fetters, took him to Babylon, and put him in prison till the day of his death.

The Temple and City Plundered and Burned

[12]Now in the fifth month, on the tenth day of the month (which *was* the nineteenth year of King Nebuchadnezzar king of Babylon), Nebuzaradan, the captain of the guard, *who* served the king of Babylon, came to Jerusalem. [13]He burned the house of the LORD and the king's house; all the houses of Jerusalem, that is, all the houses of the great, he burned with fire. [14]And all the army of the Chaldeans who *were* with the captain of the guard broke down all the walls of Jerusalem all around. [15]Then Nebuzaradan the captain of the guard carried away captive *some* of the poor people, the rest of the people who remained in the city, the defectors who had deserted to the king of Babylon, and the rest of the craftsmen. [16]But Nebuzaradan the captain of the guard left *some* of the poor of the land as vinedressers and farmers.

[17]The bronze pillars that *were* in the house of the LORD, and the carts and the bronze Sea that *were* in the house of the LORD, the Chaldeans broke in pieces, and carried all their bronze to Babylon. [18]They also took away the pots, the shovels, the trimmers, the bowls, the spoons, and all the bronze utensils with which the priests ministered. [19]The basins, the firepans, the bowls, the pots, the lampstands, the spoons, and the cups, whatever *was* solid gold and whatever *was* solid silver, the captain of the guard took away. [20]The two pillars, one Sea, the twelve bronze bulls which *were* under *it, and* the carts, which King Solomon had made for the house of the LORD—the bronze of all these articles was beyond measure. [21]Now *concerning* the pillars: the height of one pillar *was* eighteen cubits, a measuring line of twelve cubits could measure its circumference, and its thickness *was* four fingers; *it was* hollow. [22]A capital of bronze *was* on it; and the height of one capital *was* five cubits, with a network and pomegranates all around the capital, all of bronze. The second pillar, with pomegranates was the same. [23]There were ninety-six pomegranates on the sides; all the pomegranates, all around on the network, *were* one hundred.

The People Taken Captive to Babylonia

[24]The captain of the guard took Seraiah the chief priest, Zephaniah the second priest, and the three doorkeepers. [25]He also took out of the city an officer who had charge of the men of war, seven men of the king's close associates who were found in the city, the principal scribe of the army who mustered the people of the land, and sixty men of the people of the land who were found in the midst of the city. [26]And Nebuzaradan the captain of the guard took these and brought them to the king of Babylon at Riblah. [27]Then the king of Babylon struck them and put them to death at Riblah in the land of Hamath. Thus Judah was carried away captive from its own land.

> **52:24–27** Some Judean leaders were executed by Babylon as an act of power, an act of resentment for Judah's 18 months of resistance (see 52:4–6), and an act of intimidation to prevent future plots.

[28]These *are* the people whom Nebuchadnezzar carried away captive: in the seventh year, three thousand and twenty-three Jews; [29]in the eighteenth year of Nebuchadnezzar he carried away captive from Jerusalem eight hundred and thirty-two persons; [30]in the twenty-third year of Nebuchadnezzar, Nebuzaradan the captain of the guard carried away captive of the Jews seven hundred and forty-five persons. All the persons *were* four thousand six hundred.

> **52:18,19 They also took.** The conquerors took articles from Solomon's temple back to Babylon. First Kin. 6–8 describes these articles. Later, Belshazzar used some of these articles for his immoral banquet as he wrongly attributed his victory to his gods (Dan. 5).

Jehoiachin Released from Prison

³¹Now it came to pass in the thirty-seventh year of the captivity of Jehoiachin king of Judah, in the twelfth month, on the twenty-fifth *day* of the month, *that* Evil-Merodach[a] king of Babylon, in the first *year* of his reign, lifted up the head of Jehoiachin king of Judah and brought him out of prison. ³²And he spoke kindly to him and gave him a more prominent seat than those of the kings who *were* with him in Babylon. ³³So Jehoiachin changed from his prison garments, and he ate bread regularly before the king all the days of his life. ³⁴And as for his provisions, there was a regular ration given him by the king of Babylon, a portion for each day until the day of his death, all the days of his life.

> **52:31–34 captivity of Jehoiachin.** He appears here in 561 B.C. after being a captive since 597 B.C. Though he was detained, the king was released to enjoy previously denied privileges. The Lord did not forget the line of David during the exile.

52:31 *a*Or *Awil-Marduk*

LAMENTATIONS

Sometimes life just makes you want to scream. It can be a shout of victory, a cry of defeat, or a moan of agony, but it expresses the deepest emotions of our souls. Jeremiah lived life with passion. He was seldom passive and often angry. No other book in the Old Testament contains the kind of raw grief that gives this book its name—Lamentations. By allowing us into his pain and sorrow, Jeremiah teaches believers how to deal with suffering.

AUTHOR AND DATE

Lamentations was written by Jeremiah, approximately 586 B.C.

The author of Lamentations is not named within the book, but internal and external indicators point to Jeremiah. The early translation of the Old Testament from Hebrew to Greek, the Septuagint (LXX), introduces Lamentations with a note about Jeremiah's weeping. Other references to Jeremiah himself (Jeremiah 7:29; 2 Chronicles 35:25) highlight his tendency to lament over events around him. The language he used closely matches the vocabulary and style of Jeremiah's longer prophetic book.

Jeremiah wrote Lamentations as an anguished eyewitness account of the shameful destruction of Jerusalem. Likely, Jeremiah saw the destruction of the walls, towers, homes, palace, and temple. He wrote with the painful scenes fresh on his mind.

BACKGROUND AND SETTING

Eight hundred years before the fall of Jerusalem, Joshua predicted the tragedy (Joshua 23:15,16). Jeremiah had invested 40 years in warning his people of coming judgment. Both he and his message had been rejected. Still, when the predicted calamities fell on the disbelieving people, Jeremiah responded with sorrow and compassion. He took no pleasure in the exact confirmation of his prophecies.

Jeremiah recorded his predictions about the fall of Jerusalem in the first 29 chapters of the book that bears his name. In Lamentations, Jeremiah provided the details of the bitter suffering and heartbreak that he and others felt over Jerusalem's devastation. The defeat and destruction of Jerusalem represented a critical moment in the story of God's dealings with Israel and the world. The facts of the tragedy are recorded in four separate Old Testament passages: 2 Kings 25; Jeremiah 39:1–11; 52; and 2 Chronicles 36:11–21.

Jeremiah's deep sadness was directed at both the depth of Judah's sin and the severity of God's judgment. This dual central theme can be traced through the book (1:5,8,18,20; 3:42; 4:6,13,22; 5:16). A second theme that Jeremiah offers among his laments expresses the hope found in God's compassion (3:22–24,31–33). Though the book deals with disgrace, it recognizes God's great faithfulness (3:22–25), and closes on a note of grace as Jeremiah turns from lamentation to consolation (5:19–22).

A third theme that emerges from Lamentations focuses on God's ultimate sovereignty as judge. The shameless and persistent sinfulness of the people created such an offense to God's holiness that God rightfully brought about the destructive consequences. Although a political power (Babylon) carried out the punishment on Judah, God passed the sentence. Throughout Lamentations, only the Lord is identified as the One who dealt with Judah's sins.

Behind all the suffering in Lamentations lies a fourth theme: God's faithfulness. In spite of the hopeless circumstances, Jeremiah continued to cry out to God. Much of the book appears in the mode of prayer. At one moment, Jeremiah's mind

THE WAILING PROPHET NEVER FORGOT THAT THE GOD HE SERVED WAS FAITHFUL.

can only think of confession of sin and anguish over God's distance (1:11,18; 3:8). The next moment, Jeremiah cries out to God for relief as well as retribution on the enemies of Judah (3:55–66). Even while recognizing God's just judgment, Jeremiah could still call for mercy. The wailing prophet never forgot that the God he served was faithful (3:23).

SECOND KINGS, JEREMIAH, AND LAMENTATIONS COMPARED

	2 Kings 25 (See also 2 Chronicles 36:11–21)	Jeremiah	Lamentations
1. The siege of Jerusalem	1,2	39:1–3; 52:4,5	2:20–22; 3:5,7
2. The famine in the city	3	37:21; 52:6	1:11,19; 2:11,12; 2:19,20; 4:4,5,9,10; 5:9,10
3. The flight of the army and the king	4–7	39:4–7; 52:8–11	1:3,6; 2:2; 4:19,20
4. The burning of the palace, temple, and city	8,9	39:8; 52:13	2:3–5; 4:11; 5:18
5. The breaching of the city walls	10	33:4,5; 52:7	2:7–9
6. The exile of the populace	11,12	28:3,4,14; 39:9,10	1:1,4,5,18; 2:9,14; 3:2,19; 4:22; 5:2
7. The looting of the temple	13–15	51:51	1:10; 2:6,7
8. The execution of the leaders	18–21	39:6	1:15; 2:2,20
9. The vassal status of Judah	22–25	40:9	1:1; 5:8,9
10. The collapse of the expected foreign help	24:7	27:1–11; 37:5–10	4:17; 5:6

OUTLINE

Jerusalem in Affliction

1 How lonely sits the city
   That was full of people!
   How like a widow is she,
   Who *was* great among the nations!
   The princess among the provinces
   Has become a slave!

2   She weeps bitterly in the night,
   Her tears *are* on her cheeks;
   Among all her lovers
   She has none to comfort *her.*
   All her friends have dealt
     treacherously with her;
   They have become her enemies.

3   Judah has gone into captivity,
   Under affliction and hard servitude;
   She dwells among the nations,
   She finds no rest;
   All her persecutors overtake her in
     dire straits.

4   The roads to Zion mourn
   Because no one comes to the set
     feasts.
   All her gates are desolate;
   Her priests sigh,
   Her virgins are afflicted,
   And she *is* in bitterness.

5   Her adversaries have become the
     master,
   Her enemies prosper;
   For the LORD has afflicted her
   Because of the multitude of her
     transgressions.
   Her children have gone into captivity
     before the enemy.

6   And from the daughter of Zion
   All her splendor has departed.
   Her princes have become like deer
   That find no pasture,
   That flee without strength
   Before the pursuer.

7   In the days of her affliction and
     roaming,
   Jerusalem remembers all her pleasant
     things
   That she had in the days of old.
   When her people fell into the hand of
     the enemy,
   With no one to help her,
   The adversaries saw her
   And mocked at her downfall.*ᵃ*

8   Jerusalem has sinned gravely,
   Therefore she has become vile.*ᵃ*
   All who honored her despise her

1:1–22 How lonely sits the city. Jerusalem was lonely. The people were mourning, forsaken by formerly friendly nations, in captivity, uprooted from their land, and their temple was violated. Their sins had brought this judgment from God.

1:8 become vile. This most likely refers to the wretched state of continued sin and its ruinous consequences. Jerusalem's condition was despised, shameful, and naked in contrast to her former splendor (v. 6b).

1:7 *ᵃ*Vulgate reads *her Sabbaths.*   1:8 *ᵃ*Septuagint and Vulgate read *moved* or *removed.*

How does the promise of Christ appear in a book like Lamentations?

Jeremiah serves as one of the strong foreshadowing personalities of Jesus in the Old Testament. Jeremiah's tears over Jerusalem (3:48,49) compare closely with Jesus' weeping over the same city (Matthew 23:37–39; Luke 19:41–44). Jeremiah's grief prepares believers to think about God as the righteous judge who can execute punishment while at the same time experiencing grief over the suffering of His people. Isaiah described the principle with this statement: "In all their affliction, He (God) was afflicted" (Isaiah 63:9).

Jeremiah's tears also serve as a reminder of the utter hopelessness of a person without God. Tears point to God's promise to one day remove every cause for tears, and then the tears themselves (Isaiah 25:8; Revelation 7:17; 21:4) when sin shall be no more.

Because they have seen her nakedness;
Yes, she sighs and turns away.

9   Her uncleanness *is* in her skirts;
She did not consider her destiny;
Therefore her collapse was awesome;
She had no comforter.
"O L ORD, behold my affliction,
For *the* enemy is exalted!"

10   The adversary has spread his hand
Over all her pleasant things;
For she has seen the nations enter her
sanctuary,
Those whom You commanded
Not to enter Your assembly.

11   All her people sigh,
They seek bread;
They have given their valuables for
food to restore life.
"See, O L ORD, and consider,
For I am scorned."

12   "*Is it* nothing to you, all you who pass
by?
Behold and see
If there is any sorrow like my sorrow,
Which has been brought on me,
Which the L ORD has inflicted
In the day of His fierce anger.

13   "From above He has sent fire into my
bones,
And it overpowered them;
He has spread a net for my feet
And turned me back;
He has made me desolate
And faint all the day.

14   "The yoke of my transgressions was
bound;*a*
They were woven together by His
hands,
And thrust upon my neck.
He made my strength fail;
The Lord delivered me into the hands
of *those whom* I am not able to
withstand.

15   "The Lord has trampled underfoot all
my mighty *men* in my midst;

He has called an assembly against me
To crush my young men;
The Lord trampled *as* in a winepress
The virgin daughter of Judah.

1:15 in a winepress. This speaks of forcing blood to
burst forth like grape juice from crushed grapes.
Comparable language is used to describe God's final
wrath in Rev. 14:20 and 19:15.

16   "For these *things* I weep;
My eye, my eye overflows with
water;
Because the comforter, who should
restore my life,
Is far from me.
My children are desolate
Because the enemy prevailed."

17   Zion spreads out her hands,
But no one comforts her;
The L ORD has commanded
concerning Jacob
That those around him *become* his
adversaries;
Jerusalem has become an unclean
thing among them.

18   "The L ORD is righteous,
For I rebelled against His
commandment.
Hear now, all peoples,
And behold my sorrow;
My virgins and my young men
Have gone into captivity.

19   "I called for my lovers,
But they deceived me;
My priests and my elders
Breathed their last in the city,
While they sought food
To restore their life.

20   "See, O L ORD, that I *am* in distress;
My soul is troubled;
My heart is overturned within me,
For I have been very rebellious.
Outside the sword bereaves,
At home *it is* like death.

21   "They have heard that I sigh,
But no one comforts me.

1:14 *a*Following Masoretic Text and Targum; Septuagint, Syriac, and Vulgate read *watched over.*

All my enemies have heard of my
    trouble;
They are glad that You have done *it.*
Bring on the day You have
    announced,
That they may become like me.

22 "Let all their wickedness come before
    You,
And do to them as You have done to
    me
For all my transgressions;
For my sighs *are* many,
And my heart *is* faint."

God's Anger with Jerusalem

2 How the Lord has covered the
    daughter of Zion
With a cloud in His anger!
He cast down from heaven to the
    earth
The beauty of Israel,
And did not remember His footstool
In the day of His anger.

> **2:1 How the Lord has.** Much of Lam. 2 depicts God's judgment in vivid portrayals. He covered the Judeans with a cloud, withdrew His hand of protection, bent His bow, and stretched out a surveyor's line. **The beauty of Israel.** This probably refers to Mount Zion and the temple (see Ps. 48:2; Is. 60:13). **His footstool.** This is the ark of the covenant (1 Chr. 28:2; Ps. 99:5).

2 The Lord has swallowed up and has
    not pitied
All the dwelling places of Jacob.
He has thrown down in His wrath
The strongholds of the daughter of
    Judah;
He has brought *them* down to the
    ground;
He has profaned the kingdom and its
    princes.

3 He has cut off in fierce anger
Every horn of Israel;
He has drawn back His right hand
From before the enemy.
He has blazed against Jacob like a
    flaming fire
Devouring all around.

4 Standing like an enemy, He has bent
    His bow;
With His right hand, like an
    adversary,
He has slain all *who were* pleasing to
    His eye;
On the tent of the daughter of Zion,
He has poured out His fury like fire.

5 The Lord was like an enemy.
He has swallowed up Israel,
He has swallowed up all her palaces;
He has destroyed her strongholds,
And has increased mourning and
    lamentation
In the daughter of Judah.

6 He has done violence to His
    tabernacle,
As if it were a garden;
He has destroyed His place of
    assembly;
The LORD has caused
The appointed feasts and Sabbaths to
    be forgotten in Zion.
In His burning indignation He has
    spurned the king and the priest.

7 The Lord has spurned His altar,
He has abandoned His sanctuary;
He has given up the walls of her
    palaces
Into the hand of the enemy.
They have made a noise in the house
    of the LORD
As on the day of a set feast.

Q What appears to be God's purpose in including a book like Lamentations in the Bible?

A The Book of Lamentations presents an implied warning to every reader. Through Jeremiah's words, we see consequences from within. The sorrow and sadness that flow from judgment offer a deterrent. If God did not hesitate to judge His beloved people (Deuteronomy 32:10), what will He do to the nations and peoples of the world who reject His Word?

8   The LORD has purposed to destroy
    The wall of the daughter of Zion.
    He has stretched out a line;
    He has not withdrawn His hand from
        destroying;
    Therefore He has caused the rampart
        and wall to lament;
    They languished together.

9   Her gates have sunk into the ground;
    He has destroyed and broken her bars.
    Her king and her princes *are* among
        the nations;
    The Law *is* no *more,*
    And her prophets find no vision from
        the LORD.

10 The elders of the daughter of Zion
    Sit on the ground *and* keep silence;
    They throw dust on their heads
    And gird themselves with sackcloth.
    The virgins of Jerusalem
    Bow their heads to the ground.

11 My eyes fail with tears,
    My heart is troubled;
    My bile is poured on the ground
    Because of the destruction of the
        daughter of my people,
    Because the children and the infants
    Faint in the streets of the city.

2:6–11 Sin brings tragedy to everyone and everything. Here, tragedy comes to the temple, the feasts
and Sabbaths, leaders, the Lord's altar and holy
places, the city walls, the law, and children.

12 They say to their mothers,
    "Where *is* grain and wine?"
    As they swoon like the wounded
    In the streets of the city,
    As their life is poured out
    In their mothers' bosom.

13 How shall I console you?
    To what shall I liken you,
    O daughter of Jerusalem?
    What shall I compare with you, that I
        may comfort you,
    O virgin daughter of Zion?
    For your ruin *is* spread wide as the
        sea;
    Who can heal you?

14 Your prophets have seen for you
    False and deceptive visions;
    They have not uncovered your
        iniquity,
    To bring back your captives,
    But have envisioned for you false
        prophecies and delusions.

15 All who pass by clap *their* hands at
        you;
    They hiss and shake their heads
    At the daughter of Jerusalem:
    "*Is* this the city that is called
    'The perfection of beauty,
    The joy of the whole earth'?"

16 All your enemies have opened their
        mouth against you;
    They hiss and gnash *their* teeth.
    They say, "We have swallowed *her*
        up!
    Surely this *is* the day we have waited
        for;
    We have found *it,* we have seen *it!*"

17 The LORD has done what He
        purposed;
    He has fulfilled His word
    Which He commanded in days of old.
    He has thrown down and has not
        pitied,
    And He has caused an enemy to
        rejoice over you;
    He has exalted the horn of your
        adversaries.

2:17 He has fulfilled His word. This verse is the fo-
cal point of the chapter (see Jer. 51:12). The enemy
that gloats in vv. 15,16 should recognize that the destruction was God's work.

18 Their heart cried out to the Lord,
    "O wall of the daughter of Zion,
    Let tears run down like a river day
        and night;
    Give yourself no relief;
    Give your eyes no rest.

19 "Arise, cry out in the night,
    At the beginning of the watches;
    Pour out your heart like water before
        the face of the Lord.
    Lift your hands toward Him

For the life of your young children,
Who faint from hunger at the head of
every street."

20 "See, O LORD, and consider!
To whom have You done this?
Should the women eat their
offspring,
The children they have cuddled?[a]
Should the priest and prophet be slain
In the sanctuary of the Lord?

2:20 See, O LORD, and consider! The chapter closes
by placing the issue before God. **women eat their
offspring.** Hunger became so desperate in the 18-
month siege that women resorted to eating their children (see Lev. 26:29; Deut. 28:53).

21 "Young and old lie
On the ground in the streets;
My virgins and my young men
Have fallen by the sword;
You have slain *them* in the day of
Your anger,
You have slaughtered *and* not pitied.

22 "You have invited as to a feast day
The terrors that surround me.
In the day of the LORD's anger
There was no refugee or survivor.
Those whom I have borne and
brought up
My enemies have destroyed."

The Prophet's Anguish and Hope

3 I *am* the man *who* has seen affliction
by the rod of His wrath.
2 He has led me and made *me* walk
In darkness and not *in* light.
3 Surely He has turned His hand
against me
Time and time again throughout the
day.

4 He has aged my flesh and my skin,
And broken my bones.
5 He has besieged me
And surrounded *me* with bitterness
and woe.
6 He has set me in dark places
Like the dead of long ago.

7 He has hedged me in so that I cannot
get out;
He has made my chain heavy.
8 Even when I cry and shout,
He shuts out my prayer.

3:8 He shuts out my prayer. God did not respond to
Jeremiah's prayers because of Israel's perpetual sin
without repentance (Jer. 19:15). Jeremiah knew that
God's righteousness to judge that sin must take place
(Jer. 7:16), but he still prayed, wept, and longed to see
repentance.

9 He has blocked my ways with hewn
stone;
He has made my paths crooked.
10 He *has been* to me a bear lying in
wait,
Like a lion in ambush.
11 He has turned aside my ways and
torn me in pieces;
He has made me desolate.
12 He has bent His bow
And set me up as a target for the
arrow.
13 He has caused the arrows of His
quiver
To pierce my loins.[a]
14 I have become the ridicule of all my
people—
Their taunting song all the day.
15 He has filled me with bitterness,
He has made me drink wormwood.
16 He has also broken my teeth with
gravel,
And covered me with ashes.
17 You have moved my soul far from
peace;
I have forgotten prosperity.
18 And I said, "My strength and my
hope
Have perished from the LORD."

19 Remember my affliction and roaming,
The wormwood and the gall.
20 My soul still remembers
And sinks within me.
21 This I recall to my mind,
Therefore I have hope.

2:20 [a]Vulgate reads *a span long.*   3:13 [a]Literally *kidneys*

22   *Through* the LORD's mercies we are
not consumed,
Because His compassions fail not.

3:22 mercies. This Hebrew word, used about 250
times in the Old Testament, refers to God's gracious
love. This term encompasses love, grace, mercy,
goodness, forgiveness, truth, compassion, and faithfulness.

---

23   *They are* new every morning;
Great *is* Your faithfulness.
24   "The LORD *is* my portion," says my
soul,
"Therefore I hope in Him!"

25   The LORD *is* good to those who wait
for Him,
To the soul *who* seeks Him.
26   *It is* good that *one* should hope and
wait quietly
For the salvation of the LORD.
27   *It is* good for a man to bear
The yoke in his youth.

28   Let him sit alone and keep silent,
Because *God* has laid *it* on him;
29   Let him put his mouth in the dust—
There may yet be hope.
30   Let him give *his* cheek to the one who
strikes him,
And be full of reproach.

31   For the Lord will not cast off forever.
32   Though He causes grief,
Yet He will show compassion
According to the multitude of His
mercies.
33   For He does not afflict willingly,
Nor grieve the children of men.

34   To crush under one's feet
All the prisoners of the earth,

OTHER LAMENTS

Job 3:3–26; 7:1–21; 10:1–22
Psalms (over 40) e.g. Psalms 3;120
Jeremiah 15:15–18; 17:14–18; 18:19–23
Ezekiel 19:1–14; 27:1–36; 32:1–21

---

35   To turn aside the justice *due* a man
Before the face of the Most High,
36   Or subvert a man in his cause—
The Lord does not approve.

37   Who *is* he *who* speaks and it comes to
pass,
When the Lord has not commanded
it?
38   *Is it* not from the mouth of the Most
High
That woe and well-being proceed?
39   Why should a living man complain,
A man for the punishment of his sins?

40   Let us search out and examine our
ways,
And turn back to the LORD;
41   Let us lift our hearts and hands
To God in heaven.
42   We have transgressed and rebelled;
You have not pardoned.

43   You have covered *Yourself* with anger
And pursued us;
You have slain *and* not pitied.
44   You have covered Yourself with a
cloud,
That prayer should not pass through.
45   You have made us an offscouring and
refuse
In the midst of the peoples.

46   All our enemies
Have opened their mouths against us.
47   Fear and a snare have come upon us,
Desolation and destruction.
48   My eyes overflow with rivers of water
For the destruction of the daughter of
my people.

49   My eyes flow and do not cease,
Without interruption,
50   Till the LORD from heaven
Looks down and sees.
51   My eyes bring suffering to my soul
Because of all the daughters of my
city.

52   My enemies without cause
Hunted me down like a bird.
53   They silenced[a] my life in the pit

3:53 [a]Septuagint reads *put to death.*

And threw stones at me.
54 The waters flowed over my head;
I said, "I am cut off!"
55 I called on Your name, O LORD,
From the lowest pit.
56 You have heard my voice:
"Do not hide Your ear
From my sighing, from my cry for
help."
57 You drew near on the day I called on
You,
And said, "Do not fear!"

58 O Lord, You have pleaded the case for
my soul;
You have redeemed my life.
59 O LORD, You have seen *how* I am
wronged;
Judge my case.
60 You have seen all their vengeance,
All their schemes against me.

61 You have heard their reproach,
O LORD,
All their schemes against me,
62 The lips of my enemies

> **3:52–63 My enemies.** Here Jeremiah describes persecution similar to when his enemies at the palace had cast him into the cistern (Jer. 38:4–6). God answered his prayer and redeemed him by sending Ebed-melech to rescue him (see Jer. 38:7–13). Jeremiah pleads with God to judge those enemies.

3:65 ᵃA Jewish tradition reads *sorrow of.*

And their whispering against me all
the day.
63 Look at their sitting down and their
rising up;
I *am* their taunting song.

64 Repay them, O LORD,
According to the work of their hands.
65 Give them a veiledᵃ heart;
Your curse *be* upon them!
66 In Your anger,
Pursue and destroy them
From under the heavens of the LORD.

The Degradation of Zion

4 How the gold has become dim!
How changed the fine gold!
The stones of the sanctuary are
scattered
At the head of every street.

> **4:1 gold has become dim.** The gold adornment of the temple, looted by the conquerors, lost its luster with a coating of dust from where they scattered the remains.

2 The precious sons of Zion,
Valuable as fine gold,
How they are regarded as clay pots,
The work of the hands of the potter!

3 Even the jackals present their breasts
To nurse their young;
But the daughter of my people *is* cruel,
Like ostriches in the wilderness.

What lessons can we find in Jeremiah's bold call for judgment on the enemies of Judah (1:21,22; 3:64–66) and his report that God has shut out his prayers (3:8)?

The prayers of the prophets and psalmists often sound harsh to us. The boldness of their expressions remind us that it is often a good thing that God has not promised to answer our prayers as we have prayed them. We may express our real desires and real emotions in prayer, but we would be foolish to think that God would limit Himself to our perceptions. Jeremiah's call for retribution was partially answered in the fall of Babylon (Isaiah 46–47; Jeremiah 50–51; Daniel 5). God will exercise justice in His time. All accounts will be settled ultimately at the Great White Throne (Revelation 20:11–15).

Jeremiah's description of his prayer life offers a vivid picture of how he felt rather than what God was actually doing. God's non-response to Jeremiah's prayers was not because Jeremiah was guilty of personal sin; rather, it was due to Israel's perpetual sin without repentance. Jeremiah knew that, yet he prayed, wept, and longed to see repentance from his people.

4   The tongue of the infant clings
    To the roof of its mouth for thirst;
    The young children ask for bread,
    But no one breaks *it* for them.

5   Those who ate delicacies
    Are desolate in the streets;
    Those who were brought up in scarlet
    Embrace ash heaps.

6   The punishment of the iniquity of the
        daughter of my people
    Is greater than the punishment of the
        sin of Sodom,
    Which was overthrown in a moment,
    With no hand to help her!

4:6 the sin of Sodom. Sodom was swiftly punished for the sin of homosexuality. Jerusalem's punishment was greater, as her suffering was prolonged.

7   Her Nazirites*a* were brighter than
        snow
    And whiter than milk;
    They were more ruddy in body than
        rubies,
    Like sapphire in their appearance.

8   *Now* their appearance is blacker than
        soot;
    They go unrecognized in the streets;
    Their skin clings to their bones,
    It has become as dry as wood.

9   *Those* slain by the sword are better off
    Than *those* who die of hunger;
    For these pine away,
    Stricken *for lack* of the fruits of the
        field.

10 The hands of the compassionate
        women
    Have cooked their own children;
    They became food for them
    In the destruction of the daughter of
        my people.

11 The LORD has fulfilled His fury,
    He has poured out His fierce anger.
    He kindled a fire in Zion,
    And it has devoured its foundations.

12 The kings of the earth,
    And all inhabitants of the world,
    Would not have believed
    That the adversary and the enemy
    Could enter the gates of Jerusalem—

13 Because of the sins of her prophets
    And the iniquities of her priests,
    Who shed in her midst
    The blood of the just.

14 They wandered blind in the streets;
    They have defiled themselves with
        blood,
    So that no one would touch their
        garments.

15 They cried out to them,
    "Go away, unclean!
    Go away, go away,
    Do not touch us!"
    When they fled and wandered,
    Those among the nations said,
    "They shall no longer dwell *here*."

16 The face*a* of the LORD scattered them;
    He no longer regards them.
    The people do not respect the priests
    Nor show favor to the elders.

17 Still our eyes failed us,
    Watching vainly for our help;
    In our watching we watched
    For a nation *that* could not save *us*.

BEYOND LAMENTATIONS

Hope of Restoration

1. Isaiah 35:1–10
2. Jeremiah 30:1–31:40
3. Ezekiel 37:1–28
4. Hosea 3:5; 14:1–9
5. Joel 3:18–21
6. Amos 9:11–15
7. Micah 7:14–20
8. Zephaniah 3:14–20
9. Zechariah 14:1–11
10. Malachi 4:1–6

4:7 *a*Or *nobles*   4:16 *a*Targum reads *anger.*

18 They tracked our steps
So that we could not walk in our
streets.
Our end was near;
Our days were over,
For our end had come.

19 Our pursuers were swifter
Than the eagles of the heavens.
They pursued us on the mountains
And lay in wait for us in the
wilderness.

20 The breath of our nostrils, the
anointed of the LORD,
Was caught in their pits,
Of whom we said, "Under his shadow
We shall live among the nations."

21 Rejoice and be glad, O daughter of
Edom,
You who dwell in the land of Uz!
The cup shall also pass over to you
And you shall become drunk and
make yourself naked.

22 *The punishment of* your iniquity is
accomplished,
O daughter of Zion;
He will no longer send you into
captivity.
He will punish your iniquity,
O daughter of Edom;
He will uncover your sins!

A Prayer for Restoration

5 Remember, O LORD, what has come
upon us;
Look, and behold our reproach!

5:1 Remember, O LORD. Jeremiah prayed for mercy
on his people. He remembered the nation's wounds
and woes, recalled woes of specific groups, showed
why God judged, and interceded for the renewal of
Israel (see Mic. 7:18–20).

2 Our inheritance has been turned over
to aliens,
And our houses to foreigners.
3 We have become orphans and waifs,
Our mothers *are* like widows.

4 We pay for the water we drink,
And our wood comes at a price.
5 *They* pursue at our heels;[a]
We labor *and* have no rest.
6 We have given our hand *to* the
Egyptians
And the Assyrians, to be satisfied
with bread.

5:6 the Egyptians...the Assyrians. The Jews expressed trust in men for protection and goods by
making unholy alliances (see Jer. 2:18,36).

7 Our fathers sinned *and are* no more,
But we bear their iniquities.
8 Servants rule over us;
There is none to deliver *us* from their
hand.
9 We get our bread *at the risk* of our
lives,
Because of the sword in the
wilderness.
10 Our skin is hot as an oven,
Because of the fever of famine.
11 They ravished the women in Zion,
The maidens in the cities of Judah.
12 Princes were hung up by their hands,
And elders were not respected.
13 Young men ground at the millstones;
Boys staggered under *loads of* wood.
14 The elders have ceased *gathering at*
the gate,
And the young men from their music.

15 The joy of our heart has ceased;
Our dance has turned into mourning.
16 The crown has fallen *from* our head.
Woe to us, for we have sinned!

5:16 The crown has fallen. Israel lost its line of
kings, as the Davidic monarchy was temporarily over.
It will not resume until Christ returns as King (Jer.
23:5–8; Ezek. 37:24–28).

17 Because of this our heart is faint;
Because of these *things* our eyes grow
dim;
18 Because of Mount Zion which is
desolate,
With foxes walking about on it.

5:5 [a]Literally *necks*

19 You, O LORD, remain forever;
　　Your throne from generation to
　　　generation.
20 Why do You forget us forever,
　　And forsake us for so long a time?
21 Turn us back to You, O LORD, and we
　　　will be restored;
　　Renew our days as of old,

5:21 Turn us back to You. God must initiate and enable any return to Him (see Ps. 80:3,7). **Renew our days.** The intercessions of vv. 19–22 will be fulfilled in the New Covenant restoration of Israel (see Jer. 30–33).

22 Unless You have utterly rejected us,
　　And are very angry with us!

EZEKIEL

Ezekiel stands like a lonely pillar in the center of the Bible. Neither the author nor his book are mentioned anywhere else in Scripture. His name means "strengthened by God." The location and the loneliness that surrounded his ministry required the truth of his name. Ezekiel used vivid and memorable visions, prophecies, parables, signs, and symbols to proclaim and dramatize the message of God to His exiled people. Those who listened to Ezekiel were also strengthened by God.

AUTHOR AND DATE

Ezekiel was written by Ezekiel during his ministry, approximately 593 to 570 B.C.

Like his contemporary Daniel, Ezekiel was born in Judah but died in Babylon. He was exiled from Judah in 597 B.C. There he waited with his fellow exiles during the final years of Jerusalem. Five years after his captivity, Ezekiel received God's call to be a prophet to the exiles. His ministry lasted 22 years. This book that bears his name was probably written throughout his years as a prophet. The last prophecy with a date (29:17) was delivered in 571/70 B.C., so the book was completed sometime after that date.

BACKGROUND AND SETTING

The Babylonian Empire ruled the world during Ezekiel's lifetime. After defeating the other world powers, (Assyria 612–605 B.C. and Egypt 605 B.C.), Nebuchadnezzar turned his attention toward lesser kingdoms. The defeat of Judah and the destruction of Jerusalem came in three stages. The first occurred in 605 B.C. when the Babylonians besieged Jerusalem and deported a large group of captives, including Daniel, to Babylon. In 598 B.C. Nebuchadnezzar again besieged Jerusalem. The defeat of the city led to a deportation of 10,000 more captives, including Ezekiel, in 597 B.C. A decade later, the Babylonians again invaded Judah and completely destroyed Jerusalem. The last group of survivors was shipped to Babylon in 586 B.C.

The background of Ezekiel's ministry includes religious, domestic, and prophetic factors. Born during King Josiah's reign, Ezekiel experienced the real but short-lived effects of the spiritual revival that swept the land. Josiah's death in 609 B.C. set the stage for Judah to plunge headlong into a final abyss of sin. The last years (609 B.C.–586 B.C.) saw four kings rise and fall in Judah (Jehoahaz, Jehoiakim, Jehoiachin, and Zedekiah). Ezekiel witnessed the tragedy of superficial religion.

Once in Babylon, life went on for Ezekiel and the other captives more as

immigrants than as prisoners of war. They were allowed to farm tracts of land, and they experienced other favorable conditions. Ezekiel owned his own home (3:24; 20:1). There were strong domestic temptations to minimize the tragedy of the loss of the Promised Land.

On the prophetic front, Ezekiel witnessed the work of false prophets who assured the people that God would never allow Jerusalem to fall completely and that they would soon be returned to Judah. They said this despite abundant prophetic evidence to the contrary. Ezekiel's first prophecies confronted the people's false hopes. Jerusalem would be destroyed, and their exile would be long. Ezekiel received word in 586 B.C. that Jerusalem had indeed fallen. His message then changed to offer hope beyond the exile, when Israel would be restored to her homeland, and the final blessings of the messianic kingdom would follow.

HISTORICAL AND THEOLOGICAL THEMES

Ezekiel includes numerous historical references to Israel's and Judah's persistent disobedience, despite God's kindness. These are described in vivid imagery and graphic language (23:1–27). The prophet provides various factual reasons that lead up to God's judgment over His people.

The "glory of the Lord" expresses Ezekiel's central theological theme (1:28; 3:12,23; 10:4,18; 11:23; 43:4,5; 44:4) and refers to God's holiness and sovereignty. Ezekiel describes frequent contrasts between the brightness of God's character and the dark backdrop of Judah's sins. He highlights the expectation of God's glorious triumph promised by God so that all may "know that I am the LORD."

EZEKIEL DESCRIBES FREQUENT CONTRASTS BETWEEN THE BRIGHTNESS OF GOD'S CHARACTER AND THE DARK BACKDROP OF JUDAH'S SINS.

This divine monogram, by which God signs and authenticates His acts, appears more than 60 times in the book.

Ezekiel used some memorable imagery when illustrating spiritual principles. Examples include the prophet eating a scroll (chapter 2); the faces of four angels representing aspects of creation over which God rules (1:10); a "barbershop" scene (5:1–4); graffiti on temple walls reminding readers of what God really wants in His dwelling place—holiness and not ugliness (8:10); and sprinkled hot coals depicting judgment (10:2,7).

Ezekiel's prophecies also include these themes: (1) God's angels carry out His program behind the scenes (1:5–25; 10:1–22); (2) God holds each individual accountable for pursuing righteousness (18:3–32); (3) Israel and other nations gravitate toward sin (2:3–7; 8:9,10; 25–32); (4) God's wrath necessarily follows to deal with sin (7:1–8; 15:8); and (5) God maintains His gracious pledge to Abraham (Genesis 12:1–3) by preserving a remnant of Israelites and restoring them to the land of the covenant.

OUTLINE

Ezekiel's Vision of God

1 Now it came to pass in the thirtieth year, in the fourth *month*, on the fifth *day* of the month, as I *was* among the captives by the River Chebar, *that* the heavens were opened and I saw visions[a] of God. [2]On the fifth *day* of the month, which *was* in the fifth year of King Jehoiachin's captivity, [3]the word of the LORD came expressly to Ezekiel the priest, the son of Buzi, in the land of the Chaldeans[a] by the River Chebar; and the hand of the LORD was upon him there.

> **1:4 whirlwind...fire.** Judgment on Judah came from Babylon in 588–586 B.C. (Jer. 39,40). Its terror is depicted by a fiery whirlwind symbolizing God's judgments and the golden brightness signifying dazzling glory.

[4]Then I looked, and behold, a whirlwind was coming out of the north, a great cloud with raging fire engulfing itself; and brightness *was* all around it and radiating out of its midst like the color of amber, out of the midst of the fire. [5]Also from within it *came* the likeness of four living creatures. And this *was* their appearance: they had the likeness of a man. [6]Each one had four faces, and each one had four wings. [7]Their legs *were* straight, and the soles of their feet *were* like the soles of calves' feet. They sparkled like the color of burnished bronze. [8]The hands of a man *were* under their wings on their four sides; and each of the four had faces and wings. [9]Their wings touched one another. *The creatures* did not turn when they went, but each one went straight forward.

[10]As for the likeness of their faces, *each* had the face of a man; each of the four had the face of a lion on the right side, each of the four had the face of an ox on the left side, and each of the four had the face of an eagle. [11]Thus *were* their faces. Their wings stretched upward; two *wings* of each one touched one another, and two covered their bodies. [12]And each one went straight forward; they went wherever the spirit wanted to go, and they did not turn when they went.

> **1:10 faces.** These symbols identify the angels as intelligent ("man"), powerful ("lion"), servile ("ox"), and swift ("eagle").

[13]As for the likeness of the living creatures, their appearance *was* like burning coals of fire, like the appearance of torches going back and forth among the living creatures. The fire was bright, and out of the fire went lightning. [14]And the living creatures ran back and forth, in appearance like a flash of lightning.

1:1 [a]Following Masoretic Text, Septuagint, and Vulgate; Syriac and Targum read *a vision*. 1:3 [a]Or *Babylonians*, and so elsewhere in this book

DATES IN EZEKIEL

Event/Verse	Year	Month/Day	Date	Year
1. Call (1:2)	5	4/5	July 31	593
2. Temple tour (8:1)	6	6/5	September 17	592
3. Elders' visit (20:1)	7	5/10	August 17	591
4. Siege begins (24:1)	9	10/10	January 15	588
5. Against Tyre (26:1)	11	?/1	?	587/586
6. Against Egypt (29:1)	10	10/12	January 7	587
7. Against Tyre, Egypt (29:17)	27	1/1	April 26	571
8. Against Pharaoh (30:20)	11	1/7	April 29	587
9. Against Pharaoh (31:1)	11	3/1	June 21	587
10. Lament for Pharaoh (32:1)	12	12/1	March 3	585
11. Pharaoh to Sheol (32:17)	12	?/15	?	586/585
12. Refugee report on Fall of Jerusalem (33:21)	12	10/5	January 8	585
13. Vision of Future Temple Begins (40:1)	25	1/10	April 28	573

¹⁵Now as I looked at the living creatures, behold, a wheel *was* on the earth beside each living creature with its four faces. ¹⁶The appearance of the wheels and their workings *was* like the color of beryl, and all four had the same likeness. The appearance of their workings *was*, as it were, a wheel in the middle of a wheel. ¹⁷When they moved, they went toward any one of four directions; they did not turn aside when they went. ¹⁸As for their rims, they were so high they were awesome; and their rims *were* full of eyes, all around the four of them. ¹⁹When the living creatures went, the wheels went beside them; and when the living creatures were lifted up from the earth, the wheels were lifted up. ²⁰Wherever the spirit wanted to go, they went, *because* there the spirit went; and the wheels were lifted together with them, for the spirit of the living creatures[a] *was* in the wheels. ²¹When those went, *these* went; when those stood, *these* stood; and when those were lifted up from the earth, the wheels were lifted up together with them, for the spirit of the living creatures[a] *was* in the wheels.

> **1:16,18 wheel in the middle of a wheel.** This represents the enormous energy of the complicated revolutions of God's massive judgment machinery bringing about His purposes with unfailing certainty. **eyes.** These may represent God's omniscience. He gave knowledge to His angelic servants so they could judge correctly. God does nothing by blind impulse.

²²The likeness of the firmament above the heads of the living creatures[a] *was* like the color of an awesome crystal, stretched out over their heads. ²³And under the firmament their wings *spread out* straight, one toward another. Each one had two which covered one side, and each one had two which covered the other side of the body. ²⁴When they went, I heard the noise of their wings, like the noise of many waters, like the voice of the Almighty, a tumult like the noise of an army; and when they stood still, they let down their wings. ²⁵A voice came from above the firmament that *was* over their heads; whenever they stood, they let down their wings.

²⁶And above the firmament over their heads *was* the likeness of a throne, in appearance like a sapphire stone; on the likeness of the throne *was* a likeness with the appearance of a man high above it. ²⁷Also from the appearance of His waist and upward I saw, as it were, the color of amber with the appearance of fire all around within it; and from the appearance of His waist and downward I saw, as it were, the appearance of fire with brightness all around. ²⁸Like the appearance of a rainbow in a cloud on a rainy day, so *was* the appearance of the brightness all around it. This *was* the appearance of the likeness of the glory of the LORD.

Ezekiel Sent to Rebellious Israel

So when I saw *it*, I fell on my face, and I heard a voice of One speaking.

2 And He said to me, "Son of man, stand on your feet, and I will speak to you." ²Then the Spirit entered me when He spoke to me, and set me on my feet; and I heard Him who spoke to me. ³And He said to me: "Son of man, I am sending you to the children of Israel, to a rebellious nation that has rebelled against Me; they and their fathers have transgressed against Me to this very day. ⁴For *they are* impudent and stubborn children. I am sending you to them, and you shall say to them, 'Thus says the Lord GOD.' ⁵As for them, whether they hear or whether they refuse—for they *are* a rebellious house—yet they will know that a prophet has been among them.

> **2:1 Son of man.** Ezekiel uses this term over 90 times to indicate his humanness.

⁶"And you, son of man, do not be afraid of them nor be afraid of their words, though briers and thorns *are* with you and you dwell among scorpions; do not be afraid of their words or dismayed by their looks, though they *are* a rebellious house. ⁷You shall speak My words to them, whether

---

1:20 [a]Literally *living creature*; Septuagint and Vulgate read *spirit of life*; Targum reads *creatures*.
1:21 [a]Literally *living creature*; Septuagint and Vulgate read *spirit of life*; Targum reads *creatures*.
1:22 [a]Following Septuagint, Targum, and Vulgate; Masoretic Text reads *living creature*.

they hear or whether they refuse, for they *are* rebellious. [8]But you, son of man, hear what I say to you. Do not be rebellious like that rebellious house; open your mouth and eat what I give you."

2:8 open your mouth and eat. Ezekiel was to obey the command, not literally by eating a scroll, but in a spiritual sense by receiving God's message so that it became an inward passion (see Jer. 15:16).

[9]Now when I looked, there was a hand stretched out to me; and behold, a scroll of a book *was* in it. [10]Then He spread it before me; and *there was* writing on the inside and on the outside, and written on it *were* lamentations and mourning and woe.

3 Moreover He said to me, "Son of man, eat what you find; eat this scroll, and go, speak to the house of Israel." [2]So I opened my mouth, and He caused me to eat that scroll.

[3]And He said to me, "Son of man, feed your belly, and fill your stomach with this scroll that I give you." So I ate, and it was in my mouth like honey in sweetness.

[4]Then He said to me: "Son of man, go to the house of Israel and speak with My words to them. [5]For you *are* not sent to a people of unfamiliar speech and of hard language, *but* to the house of Israel, [6]not to many people of unfamiliar speech and of hard language, whose words you cannot understand. Surely, had I sent you to them, they would have listened to you. [7]But the house of Israel will not listen to you, because they will not listen to Me; for all the house of Israel *are* impudent and hardhearted. [8]Behold, I have made your face strong against their faces, and your forehead strong against their foreheads. [9]Like adamant stone, harder than flint, I have made your forehead; do not be afraid of them, nor be dismayed at their looks, though they *are* a rebellious house."

3:9 rebellious. The Jews were not more responsive to God after the exile and the affliction they endured. Instead, they were hardened by their sufferings. God gave Ezekiel a "hardness" to surpass the people and sustain his ministry as a prophet to the exiles.

[10]Moreover He said to me: "Son of man, receive into your heart all My words that I speak to you, and hear with your ears. [11]And go, get to the captives, to the children of your people, and speak to them and tell them, 'Thus says the Lord GOD,' whether they hear, or whether they refuse."

[12]Then the Spirit lifted me up, and I heard behind me a great thunderous voice: "Blessed *is* the glory of the LORD from His place!" [13]I also *heard* the noise of the wings of the living creatures that touched one another, and the noise of the wheels beside them, and a great thunderous noise. [14]So the Spirit lifted me up and took me away, and I went in bitterness, in the heat of my spirit; but the hand of the LORD was strong upon me. [15]Then I came to the captives at Tel Abib, who dwelt by the River Chebar; and I sat where they sat, and remained there astonished among them seven days.

Ezekiel Is a Watchman

[16]Now it came to pass at the end of seven days that the word of the LORD came to me, saying, [17]"Son of man, I have made you a watchman for the house of Israel; therefore hear a word from My mouth, and give them warning from Me: [18]When I say to the wicked, 'You shall surely die,' and you give him no warning, nor speak to warn the wicked from his wicked way, to save his life, that same wicked *man* shall die in his iniquity; but his blood I will require at your hand. [19]Yet, if you warn the wicked, and he does not turn from his wickedness, nor from his wicked way, he shall die in his iniquity; but you have delivered your soul.

[20]"Again, when a righteous *man* turns from his righteousness and commits iniquity, and I lay a stumbling block before him, he shall die; because you did not give him warning, he shall die in his sin, and his righteousness which he has done shall not be remembered; but his blood I will require

3:18,20 his blood I will require. Each sinner is responsible for his own sin. However, the prophet who does not proclaim the warning message to someone becomes a murderer in a sense when God takes that person's life. The responsibility of the prophet is serious (see James 3:1), and he becomes responsible for that person's death (Gen. 9:5). Preachers today will suffer consequences, such as divine chastening or loss of eternal reward (see 1 Cor. 4:1–5), for neglecting their responsibilities (see Heb. 13:17).

at your hand. ²¹Nevertheless if you warn the righteous *man* that the righteous should not sin, and he does not sin, he shall surely live because he took warning; also you will have delivered your soul."

²²Then the hand of the LORD was upon me there, and He said to me, "Arise, go out into the plain, and there I shall talk with you."

²³So I arose and went out into the plain, and behold, the glory of the LORD stood there, like the glory which I saw by the River Chebar; and I fell on my face. ²⁴Then the Spirit entered me and set me on my feet, and spoke with me and said to me: "Go, shut yourself inside your house. ²⁵And you, O son of man, surely they will put ropes on you and bind you with them, so that you cannot go out among them. ²⁶I will make your tongue cling to the roof of your mouth, so that you shall be mute and not be one to rebuke them, for they *are* a rebellious house. ²⁷But when I speak with you, I will open your mouth, and you shall say to them, 'Thus says the Lord GOD.' He who hears, let him hear; and he who refuses, let him refuse; for they *are* a rebellious house.

3:26,27 you shall be mute. Ezekiel was to act out God's message rather than speak. God occasionally opened his mouth so he could speak. The end of this intermittent dumbness came at the same time Ezekiel received a refugee's report of Jerusalem's fall (24:25–27). Ezekiel also spoke with regard to judgments on other nations (chapters 25–32).

The Siege of Jerusalem Portrayed

4 "You also, son of man, take a clay tablet and lay it before you, and portray on it a city, Jerusalem. ²Lay siege against it, build a siege wall against it, and heap up a mound against it; set camps against it also, and place battering rams against it all around. ³Moreover take for yourself an iron plate, and set it *as* an iron wall between you and the city. Set your face against it, and it shall be besieged, and you shall lay siege against it. This *will be* a sign to the house of Israel.

4:1–3 portray...Jerusalem. Ezekiel used soft tile to create a miniature city layout of Jerusalem with walls and siege objects in order to illustrate Babylon's final coming siege of Jerusalem (588–586 B.C.).

⁴"Lie also on your left side, and lay the iniquity of the house of Israel upon it. *According* to the number of the days that you lie on it, you shall bear their iniquity. ⁵For I have laid on you the years of their iniquity, according to the number of the days, three hundred and ninety days; so you shall bear the iniquity of the house of Israel. ⁶And when you have completed them, lie again on your right side; then you shall bear the iniquity of the house of Judah forty days. I have laid on you a day for each year.

⁷"Therefore you shall set your face toward the siege of Jerusalem; your arm *shall be* uncovered, and you shall prophesy against it. ⁸And surely I will restrain you so that you cannot turn from one side to

EZEKIEL'S SIGN EXPERIENCES

(see Ezekiel 24:24,27)
1. Ezekiel was housebound, tied up, and mute (3:23–27).
2. Ezekiel used a clay tablet and an iron plate as illustrations in his preaching (4:1–3).
3. Ezekiel had to lie on his left side for 390 days and his right side for 40 days (4:4–8).
4. Ezekiel had to eat in an unclean manner (4:9–17).
5. Ezekiel had to shave his head and beard (5:1–4).
6. Ezekiel had to pack his bags and dig through the wall of Jerusalem (12:1–14).
7. Ezekiel had to eat his bread with quaking and drink water with trembling (12:17–20).
8. Ezekiel brandished a sharp sword and struck his hands together (21:8–17).
9. Ezekiel portrayed Israel in the smelting furnace (22:17–22).
10. Ezekiel had to cook a pot of stew (24:1–14).
11. Ezekiel could not mourn at the death of his wife (24:15–24).
12. Ezekiel was mute for a season (24:25–27).
13. Ezekiel put two sticks together and they became one (37:15–28).

another till you have ended the days of your siege.

9"Also take for yourself wheat, barley, beans, lentils, millet, and spelt; put them into one vessel, and make bread of them for yourself. *During* the number of days that you lie on your side, three hundred and ninety days, you shall eat it. 10And your food which you eat *shall be* by weight, twenty shekels a day; from time to time you shall eat it. 11You shall also drink water by measure, one-sixth of a hin; from time to time you shall drink. 12And you shall eat it *as* barley cakes; and bake it using fuel of human waste in their sight."

13Then the LORD said, "So shall the children of Israel eat their defiled bread among the Gentiles, where I will drive them."

14So I said, "Ah, Lord GOD! Indeed I have never defiled myself from my youth till now; I have never eaten what died of itself or was torn by beasts, nor has abominable flesh ever come into my mouth."

15Then He said to me, "See, I am giving you cow dung instead of human waste, and you shall prepare your bread over it."

16Moreover He said to me, "Son of man, surely I will cut off the supply of bread in Jerusalem; they shall eat bread by weight and with anxiety, and shall drink water by measure and with dread, 17that they may lack bread and water, and be dismayed with one another, and waste away because of their iniquity.

A Sword Against Jerusalem

5 "And you, son of man, take a sharp sword, take it as a barber's razor, and pass *it* over your head and your beard; then take scales to weigh and divide the hair. 2You shall burn with fire one-third in the midst of the city, when the days of the siege are finished; then you shall take one-third and strike around *it* with the sword; and one-third you shall scatter in the wind: I will draw out a sword after them. 3You shall also take a small number of them and bind them in the edge of your *garment.* 4Then take some of them again and throw them into the midst of the fire, and burn them in the fire. From there a fire will go out into all the house of Israel.

When reading Ezekiel, it is sometimes difficult to decide whether the language he uses is descriptive of a literal event or symbolic of an idea or principle. Can we use some examples in Ezekiel to demonstrate the difference?

Ezekiel's life offered his audience a sequence of experiences and actions that became teachable moments. Some of these were scenes in visions that held special significance. For example, the first three chapters of the book report extended visions in which the prophet saw a whirlwind, heavenly creatures, and an edible scroll; he also received his call to the prophetic ministry.

In addition, Ezekiel carried out certain unusual or highly symbolic actions that were intended to picture a message or convey a warning. In 4:1–3, the prophet was directed to carve on a clay tablet and then use an iron plate as a sign about the danger facing Jerusalem. Other acted-out sermons followed: symbolic sleeping postures (4:4–8), siege bread-making and baking (4:9–17), and hair-cutting and burning (5:1–4). God instructed Ezekiel to respond even to the tragedies in his life in such a way that a message was communicated to the people. The prophet learned of his wife's impending death but was told by God that his loss would provide an important lesson the people needed to hear. Just as Ezekiel was not allowed to mourn, the people would not be allowed to mourn when they finally faced the "death" of Jerusalem. "'Thus Ezekiel is a sign to you; according to all that he has done you shall do; and when this comes, you shall know that I am the Lord GOD'" (Ezekiel 24:24).

The unique nature of Ezekiel's approach creates a striking contrast between the clarity of his message and the willful rejection of that message by the people. His ministry removed every excuse.

5:1–4 a barber's razor. Shaving his hair illustrated the severe humiliation that would befall Jerusalem at the hand of the Babylonians. Some were punished by fire, others died by the enemy's sword, and some were dispersed and pursued by death. A small part of Ezekiel's hair clung to his garment, depicting a remnant that would remain, some of whom would be subject to further calamity (see Jer. 41–44).

⁵"Thus says the Lord GOD: 'This *is* Jerusalem; I have set her in the midst of the nations and the countries all around her. ⁶She has rebelled against My judgments by doing wickedness more than the nations, and against My statutes more than the countries that *are* all around her; for they have refused My judgments, and they have not walked in My statutes.' ⁷Therefore thus says the Lord GOD: 'Because you have multiplied *disobedience* more than the nations that *are* all around you, have not walked in My statutes nor kept My judgments, nor even done*ᵃ* according to the judgments of the nations that *are* all around you'— ⁸therefore thus says the Lord GOD: 'Indeed I, even I, *am* against you and will execute judgments in your midst in the sight of the nations. ⁹And I will do among you what I have never done, and the like of which I will never do again, because of all your abominations. ¹⁰Therefore fathers shall eat *their* sons in your midst, and sons shall eat their fathers; and I will execute judgments among you, and all of you who remain I will scatter to all the winds.

¹¹'Therefore, *as* I live,' says the Lord GOD, 'surely, because you have defiled My sanctuary with all your detestable things and with all your abominations, therefore I will also diminish *you*; My eye will not spare, nor will I have any pity. ¹²One-third of you shall die of the pestilence, and be consumed with famine in your midst; and

5:11 *as* I live. This oath, found 14 times in this book, pledges the very existence of God for the fulfillment of the prophecy. The people's greatest sin was defiling the sanctuary, showing the height of their wickedness.

one-third shall fall by the sword all around you; and I will scatter another third to all the winds, and I will draw out a sword after them.

¹³'Thus shall My anger be spent, and I will cause My fury to rest upon them, and I will be avenged; and they shall know that I, the LORD, have spoken *it* in My zeal, when I have spent My fury upon them. ¹⁴Moreover I will make you a waste and a reproach among the nations that *are* all around you, in the sight of all who pass by.

¹⁵'So it*ᵃ* shall be a reproach, a taunt, a lesson, and an astonishment to the nations that *are* all around you, when I execute judgments among you in anger and in fury and in furious rebukes. I, the LORD, have spoken. ¹⁶When I send against them the terrible arrows of famine which shall be for destruction, which I will send to destroy you, I will increase the famine upon you and cut off your supply of bread. ¹⁷So I will send against you famine and wild beasts, and they will bereave you. Pestilence and blood shall pass through you, and I will bring the sword against you. I, the LORD, have spoken.' "

Judgment on Idolatrous Israel

6 Now the word of the LORD came to me, saying: ²"Son of man, set your face toward the mountains of Israel, and prophesy against them, ³and say, 'O mountains of Israel, hear the word of the Lord GOD! Thus says the Lord GOD to the mountains, to the hills, to the ravines, and to the valleys: "Indeed I, *even* I, will bring a sword against you, and I will destroy your high places. ⁴Then your altars shall be desolate, your incense altars shall be broken, and I will cast down your slain *men* before your idols. ⁵And I will lay the corpses of the children of Israel before their idols, and I will scatter your bones all around your altars. ⁶In all your dwelling places the cities shall be laid waste, and the high places shall be desolate, so that your altars may be laid waste and made desolate, your idols may be broken and made to cease, your incense altars may be cut down, and your works may be

---

5:7 *ᵃ*Following Masoretic Text, Septuagint, Targum, and Vulgate; many Hebrew manuscripts and Syriac read *but have done* (compare 11:12).   5:15 *ᵃ*Septuagint, Syriac, Targum, and Vulgate read *you.*

abolished. ⁷The slain shall fall in your midst, and you shall know that I *am* the LORD.

> **6:7 you shall know that I *am* the LORD.** The essential reason for judgment is the violation of the character of God. This phrase occurs more than 60 times in the book of Ezekiel. It is also repeatedly acknowledged in Lev. 18–26, where the motive for all obedience to God's law is the fact that He is the Lord God.

⁸"Yet I will leave a remnant, so that you may have *some* who escape the sword among the nations, when you are scattered through the countries. ⁹Then those of you who escape will remember Me among the nations where they are carried captive, because I was crushed by their adulterous heart which has departed from Me, and by their eyes which play the harlot after their idols; they will loathe themselves for the evils which they committed in all their abominations. ¹⁰And they shall know that I *am* the LORD; I have not said in vain that I would bring this calamity upon them."

¹¹'Thus says the Lord GOD: "Pound your fists and stamp your feet, and say, 'Alas, for all the evil abominations of the house of Israel! For they shall fall by the sword, by famine, and by pestilence. ¹²He who is far off shall die by the pestilence, he who is near shall fall by the sword, and he who remains and is besieged shall die by the famine. Thus will I spend My fury upon them. ¹³Then you shall know that I *am* the LORD, when their slain are among their idols all around their altars, on every high hill, on all the mountaintops, under every green tree, and under every thick oak, wherever they offered sweet incense to all their idols. ¹⁴So I will stretch out My hand against them and make the land desolate, yes, more desolate than the wilderness toward Diblah, in all their dwelling places. Then they shall know that I *am* the LORD.' " ' "

Judgment on Israel Is Near

7 Moreover the word of the LORD came to me, saying, ²"And you, son of man, thus says the Lord GOD to the land of Israel:

'An end! The end has come upon the four corners of the land.

³   Now the end *has come* upon you,
And I will send My anger against you;
I will judge you according to your
     ways,
And I will repay you for all your
     abominations.
⁴   My eye will not spare you,
Nor will I have pity;
But I will repay your ways,
And your abominations will be in
     your midst;
Then you shall know that I *am* the
     LORD!'

⁵"Thus says the Lord GOD:

'A disaster, a singular disaster;
Behold, it has come!
⁶   An end has come,
The end has come;
It has dawned for you;
Behold, it has come!
⁷   Doom has come to you, you who
     dwell in the land;
The time has come,
A day of trouble *is* near,
And not of rejoicing in the
     mountains.
⁸   Now upon you I will soon pour out
     My fury,
And spend My anger upon you;
I will judge you according to your
     ways,
And I will repay you for all your
     abominations.

⁹   'My eye will not spare,
Nor will I have pity;
I will repay you according to your
     ways,
And your abominations will be in
     your midst.
Then you shall know that I *am* the
     LORD who strikes.

¹⁰   'Behold, the day!
Behold, it has come!
Doom has gone out;

> **7:10 rod has blossomed.** Violence had grown up into a rod of wickedness (v. 11), which likely refers to Nebuchadnezzar, the instrument of God's vengeance (see Is. 10:5).

The rod has blossomed,
Pride has budded.
11 Violence has risen up into a rod of
    wickedness;
None of them *shall remain*,
None of their multitude,
None of them;
Nor *shall there be* wailing for them.
12 The time has come,
The day draws near.

'Let not the buyer rejoice,
Nor the seller mourn,
For wrath *is* on their whole multitude.
13 For the seller shall not return to what
    has been sold,
Though he may still be alive;
For the vision concerns the whole
    multitude,
And it shall not turn back;
No one will strengthen himself
Who lives in iniquity.

14 'They have blown the trumpet and
    made everyone ready,
But no one goes to battle;
For My wrath *is* on all their multitude.
15 The sword *is* outside,
And the pestilence and famine within.
Whoever *is* in the field
Will die by the sword;
And whoever *is* in the city,
Famine and pestilence will devour
    him.
16 'Those who survive will escape and be
    on the mountains
Like doves of the valleys,
All of them mourning,
Each for his iniquity.
17 Every hand will be feeble,
And every knee will be *as* weak *as*
    water.
18 They will also be girded with
    sackcloth;
Horror will cover them;
Shame *will be* on every face,
Baldness on all their heads.
19 'They will throw their silver into the
    streets,
And their gold will be like refuse;
Their silver and their gold will not be
    able to deliver them

In the day of the wrath of the LORD;
They will not satisfy their souls,
Nor fill their stomachs,
Because it became their stumbling
    block of iniquity.

20 'As for the beauty of his ornaments,
He set it in majesty;
But they made from it
The images of their abominations—
Their detestable things;
Therefore I have made it
Like refuse to them.
21 I will give it as plunder
Into the hands of strangers,
And to the wicked of the earth as
    spoil;
And they shall defile it.
22 I will turn My face from them,
And they will defile My secret place;
For robbers shall enter it and defile it.

7:17–22 This section describes the mourning of the helpless and frightened people. They recognized they had trusted in useless things. Their wealth provided nothing. Their silver, gold, and ornaments were as useless as the idols they made with them.

23 'Make a chain,
For the land is filled with crimes of
    blood,
And the city is full of violence.
24 Therefore I will bring the worst of the
    Gentiles,
And they will possess their houses;
I will cause the pomp of the strong to
    cease,
And their holy places shall be defiled.
25 Destruction comes;
They will seek peace, but *there shall
    be* none.
26 Disaster will come upon disaster,
And rumor will be upon rumor.
Then they will seek a vision from a
    prophet;
But the law will perish from the
    priest,
And counsel from the elders.
27 'The king will mourn,
The prince will be clothed with
    desolation,
And the hands of the common people
    will tremble.

I will do to them according to their
　way;
And according to what they deserve I
　will judge them;
Then they shall know that I *am* the
　LORD!' "

Abominations in the Temple

8 And it came to pass in the sixth year, in
the sixth *month*, on the fifth *day* of the
month, as I sat in my house with the elders
of Judah sitting before me, that the hand of
the Lord GOD fell upon me there. ²Then I
looked, and there was a likeness, like the
appearance of fire—from the appearance of
His waist and downward, fire; and from
His waist and upward, like the appearance
of brightness, like the color of amber. ³He
stretched out the form of a hand, and took
me by a lock of my hair; and the Spirit lifted
me up between earth and heaven, and
brought me in visions of God to Jerusalem,
to the door of the north gate of the inner
court, where the seat of the image of jealousy *was,* which provokes to jealousy. ⁴And
behold, the glory of the God of Israel *was*
there, like the vision that I saw in the plain.

> **8:3 in visions of God.** Ezekiel 8–11 deals with details
> from Ezekiel's visions, which described Israel's cur-
> rent condition. He traveled to Jerusalem and Babylon
> in spirit only, not physically. After God finished the
> visions, Ezekiel told his home audience what he had
> seen. **the seat...image of jealousy.** God represents
> to Ezekiel the image of an idol (see Deut. 4:16) in the
> entrance to the inner court of the temple. It provoked
> the Lord to jealousy (5:13; 16:38).

⁵Then He said to me, "Son of man, lift
your eyes now toward the north." So I lifted
my eyes toward the north, and there, north
of the altar gate, was this image of jealousy
in the entrance.
⁶Furthermore He said to me, "Son of
man, do you see what they are doing, the
great abominations that the house of Israel
commits here, to make Me go far away
from My sanctuary? Now turn again, you
will see greater abominations." ⁷So He
brought me to the door of the court; and
when I looked, there was a hole in the wall.
⁸Then He said to me, "Son of man, dig into
the wall"; and when I dug into the wall,
there was a door.

⁹And He said to me, "Go in, and see the
wicked abominations which they are doing
there." ¹⁰So I went in and saw, and there—
every sort of creeping thing, abominable
beasts, and all the idols of the house of Israel, portrayed all around on the walls.
¹¹And there stood before them seventy men
of the elders of the house of Israel, and in
their midst stood Jaazaniah the son of Shaphan. Each man had a censer in his hand,
and a thick cloud of incense went up.
¹²Then He said to me, "Son of man, have
you seen what the elders of the house of Israel do in the dark, every man in the room
of his idols? For they say, 'The LORD does
not see us, the LORD has forsaken the
land.' "

¹³And He said to me, "Turn again, *and*
you will see greater abominations that they
are doing." ¹⁴So He brought me to the door
of the north gate of the LORD's house; and
to my dismay, women were sitting there
weeping for Tammuz.
¹⁵Then He said to me, "Have you seen
this, O son of man? Turn again, you will see
greater abominations than these." ¹⁶So He
brought me into the inner court of the
LORD's house; and there, at the door of the
temple of the LORD, between the porch and
the altar, *were* about twenty-five men with
their backs toward the temple of the LORD
and their faces toward the east, and they
were worshiping the sun toward the east.
¹⁷And He said to me, "Have you seen
this, O son of man? Is it a trivial thing to
the house of Judah to commit the abominations which they commit here? For they
have filled the land with violence; then they
have returned to provoke Me to anger. Indeed they put the branch to their nose.
¹⁸Therefore I also will act in fury. My eye
will not spare nor will I have pity; and
though they cry in My ears with a loud
voice, I will not hear them."

The Wicked Are Slain

9 Then He called out in my hearing with
a loud voice, saying, "Let those who
have charge over the city draw near, each
with a deadly weapon in his hand." ²And
suddenly six men came from the direction
of the upper gate, which faces north, each
with his battle-ax in his hand. One man
among them *was* clothed with linen and

had a writer's inkhorn at his side. They went in and stood beside the bronze altar.

³Now the glory of the God of Israel had gone up from the cherub, where it had been, to the threshold of the temple.ᵃ And He called to the man clothed with linen, who *had* the writer's inkhorn at his side; ⁴and the LORD said to him, "Go through the midst of the city, through the midst of Jerusalem, and put a mark on the foreheads of the men who sigh and cry over all the abominations that are done within it."

9:4 a mark on the foreheads. God's departure removed all protection and gave the people over to destruction. Because of this, it was necessary for the angelic scribe (Angel of the Lord) to mark the righteous who had been faithful to Him. Those left unmarked were subject to death in Babylon's siege. The mark signified God's elect, identified personally by the pre-incarnate Christ (see Ex. 12:7).

⁵To the others He said in my hearing, "Go after him through the city and kill; do not let your eye spare, nor have any pity. ⁶Utterly slay old *and* young men, maidens and little children and women; but do not come near anyone on whom *is* the mark; and begin at My sanctuary." So they began with the elders who *were* before the temple. ⁷Then He said to them, "Defile the temple, and fill the courts with the slain. Go out!" And they went out and killed in the city.

⁸So it was, that while they were killing them, I was left *alone*; and I fell on my face and cried out, and said, "Ah, Lord GOD! Will You destroy all the remnant of Israel in pouring out Your fury on Jerusalem?"

⁹Then He said to me, "The iniquity of the house of Israel and Judah *is* exceedingly great, and the land is full of bloodshed, and the city full of perversity; for they say, 'The LORD has forsaken the land, and the LORD does not see!' ¹⁰And as for Me also, My eye will neither spare, nor will I have pity, *but* I will recompense their deeds on their own head."

¹¹Just then, the man clothed with linen, who *had* the inkhorn at his side, reported back and said, "I have done as You commanded me."

The Glory Departs from the Temple

10 And I looked, and there in the firmament that was above the head of the cherubim, there appeared something like a sapphire stone, having the appearance of the likeness of a throne. ²Then He spoke to the man clothed with linen, and said, "Go in among the wheels, under the cherub, fill your hands with coals of fire from among the cherubim, and scatter *them* over the city." And he went in as I watched.

10:2 fill...with coals. The marking angel was to reach into the war machine and fill his hands with fiery coals in the presence of the angels of chapter 1. The coals represent the fires of judgment that God's angels are to "scatter" on Jerusalem. Coals were used for purification of the prophet in Is. 6, but here they were used to destroy the wicked (see Heb. 12:29). Fire did destroy Jerusalem in 586 B.C.

³Now the cherubim were standing on the south side of the templeᵃ when the man went in, and the cloud filled the inner court. ⁴Then the glory of the LORD went up from the cherub, *and paused* over the threshold of temple; and the house was filled with the cloud, and the court was full of the brightness of the LORD's glory. ⁵And the sound of the wings of the cherubim was heard *even* in the outer court, like the voice of Almighty God when He speaks.

⁶Then it happened, when He commanded the man clothed in linen, saying, "Take fire from among the wheels, from among the cherubim," that he went in and stood beside the wheels. ⁷And the cherub stretched out his hand from among the cherubim to the fire that *was* among the cherubim, and took *some of it* and put *it* into the hands of the *man* clothed with linen, who took *it* and went out. ⁸The cherubim appeared to have the form of a man's hand under their wings.

⁹And when I looked, there were four wheels by the cherubim, one wheel by one cherub and another wheel by each other cherub; the wheels appeared *to have* the color of a beryl stone. ¹⁰*As for* their appearance, all four looked alike—as it were, a wheel in the middle of a wheel. ¹¹When

---

9:3 ᵃLiterally *house*   10:3 ᵃLiterally *house*, also in verses 4 and 18

they went, they went toward *any of* their four directions; they did not turn aside when they went, but followed in the direction the head was facing. They did not turn aside when they went. ¹²And their whole body, with their back, their hands, their wings, and the wheels that the four had, *were* full of eyes all around. ¹³As for the wheels, they were called in my hearing, "Wheel."

¹⁴Each one had four faces: the first face *was* the face of a cherub, the second face the face of a man, the third the face of a lion, and the fourth the face of an eagle. ¹⁵And the cherubim were lifted up. This *was* the living creature I saw by the River Chebar. ¹⁶When the cherubim went, the wheels went beside them; and when the cherubim lifted their wings to mount up from the earth, the same wheels also did not turn from beside them. ¹⁷When *the cherubim*ᵃ stood still, *the wheels* stood still, and when *one*ᵇ was lifted up, *the other*ᶜ lifted itself up, for the spirit of the living creature *was* in them.

10:9–17 wheels by the cherubim. Four wheels on the chariot mingled with the 4 angels (see 1:15–21), each wheel with a different angel. It looked as if one wheel blended with another. Their appearance was unified, and their action was in unison. The angels had bodies like men, and the wheels were full of eyes, signifying that they could see both the sinners and their fitting judgment. The color beryl was a sparkling yellow or gold.

¹⁸Then the glory of the LORD departed from the threshold of the temple and stood over the cherubim. ¹⁹And the cherubim lifted their wings and mounted up from the earth in my sight. When they went out, the wheels *were* beside them; and they stood at the door of the east gate of the LORD's house, and the glory of the God of Israel *was* above them.

²⁰This *is* the living creature I saw under the God of Israel by the River Chebar, and I knew they *were* cherubim. ²¹Each one had four faces and each one four wings, and the likeness of the hands of a man *was* under their wings. ²²And the likeness of their faces *was* the same *as* the faces which I had seen by the River Chebar, their appearance and their persons. They each went straight forward.

Judgment on Wicked Counselors

11 Then the Spirit lifted me up and brought me to the East Gate of the LORD's house, which faces eastward; and there at the door of the gate were twenty-five men, among whom I saw Jaazaniah the son of Azzur, and Pelatiah the son of Benaiah, princes of the people. ²And He said to me: "Son of man, these *are* the men who devise iniquity and give wicked counsel in this city, ³who say, 'The time is not near to build houses; this *city is* the caldron, and we *are* the meat.' ⁴Therefore prophesy against them, prophesy, O son of man!"

11:1 twenty-five men. In a vision from God, Ezekiel was taken in spirit to the temple, where the glory of God had left in 10:19. He saw the "twenty-five men," who represented the influential leaders (not priests) who gave fatal advice to the people. These wicked leaders were part of God's reason for the judgment.

⁵Then the Spirit of the LORD fell upon me, and said to me, "Speak! 'Thus says the LORD: "Thus you have said, O house of Israel; for I know the things that come into your mind. ⁶You have multiplied your slain in this city, and you have filled its streets with the slain." ⁷Therefore thus says the Lord GOD: "Your slain whom you have laid in its midst, they *are* the meat, and this *city is* the caldron; but I shall bring you out of the midst of it. ⁸You have feared the sword; and I will bring a sword upon you," says the Lord GOD. ⁹"And I will bring you out of its midst, and deliver you into the hands of strangers, and execute judgments on you. ¹⁰You shall fall by the sword. I will judge you at the border of Israel. Then you shall know that I *am* the LORD. ¹¹This *city* shall not be your caldron, nor shall you be the meat in its midst. I will judge you at the border of Israel. ¹²And you shall know that I *am* the LORD; for you have not walked in My statutes nor executed My judgments, but have done according to the customs of the Gentiles which *are* all around you." ' "

¹³Now it happened, while I was prophesying, that Pelatiah the son of Benaiah died.

10:17 ᵃLiterally *they*   ᵇLiterally *they*   ᶜLiterally *they*

Then I fell on my face and cried with a loud voice, and said, "Ah, Lord GOD! Will You make a complete end of the remnant of Israel?"

God Will Restore Israel

[14] Again the word of the LORD came to me, saying, [15] "Son of man, your brethren, your relatives, your countrymen, and all the house of Israel in its entirety, *are* those about whom the inhabitants of Jerusalem have said, 'Get far away from the LORD; this land has been given to us as a possession.' [16] Therefore say, 'Thus says the Lord GOD: "Although I have cast them far off among the Gentiles, and although I have scattered them among the countries, yet I shall be a little sanctuary for them in the countries where they have gone." ' [17] Therefore say, 'Thus says the Lord GOD: "I will gather you from the peoples, assemble you from the countries where you have been scattered, and I will give you the land of Israel." ' [18] And they will go there, and they will take away all its detestable things and all its abominations from there. [19] Then I will give you one heart, and I will put a new spirit within them,[a] and take the stony heart out of their flesh, and give them a heart of flesh, [20] that they may walk in My statutes and keep My judgments and do them; and they shall be My people, and I will be their God. [21] But *as for those* whose hearts follow the desire for their detestable things and their abominations, I will recompense their deeds on their own heads," says the Lord GOD.

> **11:16 little sanctuary.** This means "for a little while." God was to protect and provide for those who had been scattered during the 70 years until they were restored. The exiles may have cast off the Jews, but God had not (Is. 8:14). This is also true for the future restoration of the Jews (vv. 17,18).

[22] So the cherubim lifted up their wings, with the wheels beside them, and the glory of the God of Israel *was* high above them. [23] And the glory of the LORD went up from the midst of the city and stood on the mountain, which *is* on the east side of the city.

[24] Then the Spirit took me up and brought me in a vision by the Spirit of God into Chaldea,[a] to those in captivity. And the vision that I had seen went up from me. [25] So I spoke to those in captivity of all the things the LORD had shown me.

Judah's Captivity Portrayed

12 Now the word of the LORD came to me, saying: [2] "Son of man, you dwell in the midst of a rebellious house, which has eyes to see but does not see, and ears to hear but does not hear; for they *are* a rebellious house.

[3] "Therefore, son of man, prepare your belongings for captivity, and go into captivity by day in their sight. You shall go from your place into captivity to another place in their sight. It may be that they will consider, though they *are* a rebellious house. [4] By day you shall bring out your belongings in their sight, as though going into captivity; and at evening you shall go in their sight, like those who go into captivity. [5] Dig through the wall in their sight, and carry your belongings out through it. [6] In their sight you shall bear *them* on *your* shoulders *and* carry *them* out at twilight; you shall cover your face, so that you cannot see the ground, for I have made you a sign to the house of Israel."

> **12:3 prepare...for captivity.** The prophet called for carrying baggage into exile that contained only the bare necessities. His countrymen carried such baggage when they went into captivity or sought to escape during Babylon's siege of Jerusalem. Some attempting to escape were caught as in a net, like King Zedekiah who was overtaken, blinded, and forced into exile (2 Kin. 24:18–25:7).

[7] So I did as I was commanded. I brought out my belongings by day, as though going into captivity, and at evening I dug through the wall with my hand. I brought *them* out at twilight, *and* I bore *them* on *my* shoulder in their sight.

[8] And in the morning the word of the LORD came to me, saying, [9] "Son of man, has not the house of Israel, the rebellious house, said to you, 'What are you doing?' [10] Say to them, 'Thus says the Lord GOD:

11:19 [a]Literally *you*   11:24 [a]Or *Babylon*, and so elsewhere in this book

"This burden *concerns* the prince in Jerusalem and all the house of Israel who are among them." ' ¹¹Say, 'I *am* a sign to you. As I have done, so shall it be done to them; they shall be carried away into captivity.' ¹²And the prince who *is* among them shall bear *his belongings* on *his* shoulder at twilight and go out. They shall dig through the wall to carry *them* out through it. He shall cover his face, so that he cannot see the ground with *his* eyes. ¹³I will also spread My net over him, and he shall be caught in My snare. I will bring him to Babylon, *to* the land of the Chaldeans; yet he shall not see it, though he shall die there. ¹⁴I will scatter to every wind all who *are* around him to help him, and all his troops; and I will draw out the sword after them.

¹⁵"Then they shall know that I *am* the LORD, when I scatter them among the nations and disperse them throughout the countries. ¹⁶But I will spare a few of their men from the sword, from famine, and from pestilence, that they may declare all their abominations among the Gentiles wherever they go. Then they shall know that I *am* the LORD."

Judgment Not Postponed

¹⁷Moreover the word of the LORD came to me, saying, ¹⁸"Son of man, eat your bread with quaking, and drink your water with trembling and anxiety. ¹⁹And say to the people of the land, 'Thus says the Lord GOD to the inhabitants of Jerusalem *and* to the land of Israel: "They shall eat their bread with anxiety, and drink their water with dread, so that her land may be emptied of all who are in it, because of the violence of all those who dwell in it. ²⁰Then the cities that are inhabited shall be laid waste, and the land shall become desolate; and you shall know that I *am* the LORD." ' "

²¹And the word of the LORD came to me, saying, ²²"Son of man, what *is* this proverb *that* you *people* have about the land of Israel, which says, 'The days are prolonged, and every vision fails'? ²³Tell them therefore, 'Thus says the Lord GOD: "I will lay this proverb to rest, and they shall no more use it as a proverb in Israel." But say to them, "The days are at hand, and the fulfillment of every vision. ²⁴For no more shall there be any false vision or flattering divi-

nation within the house of Israel. ²⁵For I *am* the LORD. I speak, and the word which I speak will come to pass; it will no more be postponed; for in your days, O rebellious house, I will say the word and perform it," says the Lord GOD.' "

²⁶Again the word of the LORD came to me, saying, ²⁷"Son of man, look, the house of Israel is saying, 'The vision that he sees *is* for many days *from now,* and he prophesies of times far off.' ²⁸Therefore say to them, 'Thus says the Lord GOD: "None of My words will be postponed any more, but the word which I speak will be done," says the Lord GOD.' "

Woe to Foolish Prophets

13 And the word of the LORD came to me, saying, ²"Son of man, prophesy against the prophets of Israel who prophesy, and say to those who prophesy out of their own heart, 'Hear the word of the LORD!' "

³Thus says the Lord GOD: "Woe to the foolish prophets, who follow their own spirit and have seen nothing! ⁴O Israel, your prophets are like foxes in the deserts. ⁵You have not gone up into the gaps to build a wall for the house of Israel to stand in battle on the day of the LORD. ⁶They have envisioned futility and false divination, saying, 'Thus says the LORD!' But the LORD has not sent them; yet they hope that the word may be confirmed. ⁷Have you not seen a futile vision, and have you not spoken false divination? You say, 'The LORD says,' but I have not spoken."

⁸Therefore thus says the Lord GOD: "Because you have spoken nonsense and envisioned lies, therefore I *am* indeed against you," says the Lord GOD. ⁹"My hand will be against the prophets who envision futility and who divine lies; they shall not be in the assembly of My people, nor be written in the record of the house of Israel, nor shall they enter into the land of Israel. Then you shall know that I *am* the Lord GOD.

¹⁰"Because, indeed, because they have seduced My people, saying, 'Peace!' when *there is* no peace—and one builds a wall, and they plaster it with untempered *mortar*— ¹¹say to those who plaster *it* with untempered *mortar,* that it will fall. There will be flooding rain, and you, O great hail-

stones, shall fall; and a stormy wind shall tear *it* down. ¹²Surely, when the wall has fallen, will it not be said to you, 'Where *is* the mortar with which you plastered *it?*' "

13:10,11 builds a wall. False prophets had lulled the people into false security. Their "peace" promises created a whitewashed "wall" that looked good, yet the people continued in sin. This "wall" was doomed to collapse when God would bring His storm, which signified the invaders' assault.

¹³Therefore thus says the Lord GOD: "I will cause a stormy wind to break forth in My fury; and there shall be a flooding rain in My anger, and great hailstones in fury to consume *it*. ¹⁴So I will break down the wall you have plastered with untempered *mortar*, and bring it down to the ground, so that its foundation will be uncovered; it will fall, and you shall be consumed in the midst of it. Then you shall know that I *am* the LORD.

¹⁵"Thus will I accomplish My wrath on the wall and on those who have plastered it with untempered *mortar*; and I will say to you, 'The wall *is* no *more*, nor those who plastered it, ¹⁶*that is*, the prophets of Israel who prophesy concerning Jerusalem, and who see visions of peace for her when *there is* no peace,' " says the Lord GOD.

¹⁷"Likewise, son of man, set your face against the daughters of your people, who prophesy out of their own heart; prophesy against them, ¹⁸and say, 'Thus says the Lord GOD: "Woe to the *women* who sew *magic* charms on their sleeves*ᵃ* and make veils for the heads of people of every height to hunt souls! Will you hunt the souls of My people, and keep yourselves alive? ¹⁹And will you profane Me among My people for handfuls of barley and for pieces of bread, killing people who should not die, and keeping people alive who should not live, by your lying to My people who listen to lies?"

²⁰'Therefore thus says the Lord GOD: "Behold, I *am* against your *magic* charms by which you hunt souls there like birds. I will tear them from your arms, and let the souls go, the souls you hunt like birds. ²¹I

will also tear off your veils and deliver My people out of your hand, and they shall no longer be as prey in your hand. Then you shall know that I *am* the LORD.

²²"Because with lies you have made the heart of the righteous sad, whom I have not made sad; and you have strengthened the hands of the wicked, so that he does not turn from his wicked way to save his life. ²³Therefore you shall no longer envision futility nor practice divination; for I will deliver My people out of your hand, and you shall know that I *am* the LORD." ' "

13:17–23 This is the only Old Testament text where false prophetesses are mentioned, although women were rebuked by Isaiah (3:16–4:1) and Amos (4:1–3). Sorcery was practiced mainly by women. Jezebel is called a false prophetess in Rev. 2:20.

Idolatry Will Be Punished

14 Now some of the elders of Israel came to me and sat before me. ²And the word of the LORD came to me, saying, ³"Son of man, these men have set up their idols in their hearts, and put before them that which causes them to stumble into iniquity. Should I let Myself be inquired of at all by them?

14:1–3 elders...came. God revealed to the prophet that these leaders came insincerely seeking God's counsel (see Ps. 66:18). Ezekiel accused them of pursuing evil and defying God's will. False prophets of chapter 13 were thriving as civil leaders and their people set a welcoming climate for deception.

⁴"Therefore speak to them, and say to them, 'Thus says the Lord GOD: "Everyone of the house of Israel who sets up his idols in his heart, and puts before him what causes him to stumble into iniquity, and then comes to the prophet, I the LORD will answer him who comes, according to the multitude of his idols, ⁵that I may seize the house of Israel by their heart, because they are all estranged from Me by their idols." '

⁶"Therefore say to the house of Israel, 'Thus says the Lord GOD: "Repent, turn away from your idols, and turn your faces away from all your abominations. ⁷For

---

13:18 ᵃLiterally *over all the joints of My hands*; Vulgate reads *under every elbow*; Septuagint and Targum read *on all elbows of the hands*.

anyone of the house of Israel, or of the strangers who dwell in Israel, who separates himself from Me and sets up his idols in his heart and puts before him what causes him to stumble into iniquity, then comes to a prophet to inquire of him concerning Me, I the LORD will answer him by Myself. ⁸I will set My face against that man and make him a sign and a proverb, and I will cut him off from the midst of My people. Then you shall know that I *am* the LORD.

⁹"And if the prophet is induced to speak anything, I the LORD have induced that prophet, and I will stretch out My hand against him and destroy him from among My people Israel. ¹⁰And they shall bear their iniquity; the punishment of the prophet shall be the same as the punishment of the one who inquired, ¹¹that the house of Israel may no longer stray from Me, nor be profaned anymore with all their transgressions, but that they may be My people and I may be their God," says the Lord GOD.' "

Judgment on Persistent Unfaithfulness

¹²The word of the LORD came again to me, saying: ¹³"Son of man, when a land sins against Me by persistent unfaithfulness, I will stretch out My hand against it; I will cut off its supply of bread, send famine on it, and cut off man and beast from it. ¹⁴Even *if* these three men, Noah, Daniel, and Job, were in it, they would deliver *only* themselves by their righteousness," says the Lord GOD.

¹⁵"If I cause wild beasts to pass through the land, and they empty it, and make it so desolate that no man may pass through because of the beasts, ¹⁶*even though* these three men *were* in it, *as* I live," says the Lord GOD, "they would deliver neither sons nor daughters; only they would be delivered, and the land would be desolate.

¹⁷"Or *if* I bring a sword on that land, and say, 'Sword, go through the land,' and I cut off man and beast from it, ¹⁸even *though* these three men *were* in it, *as* I live," says the Lord GOD, "they would deliver neither sons nor daughters, but only they themselves would be delivered.

¹⁹"Or *if* I send a pestilence into that land and pour out My fury on it in blood, and

cut off from it man and beast, ²⁰even *though* Noah, Daniel, and Job *were* in it, *as* I live," says the Lord GOD, "they would deliver neither son nor daughter; they would deliver *only* themselves by their righteousness."

²¹For thus says the Lord GOD: "How much more it shall be when I send My four severe judgments on Jerusalem—the sword and famine and wild beasts and pestilence—to cut off man and beast from it? ²²Yet behold, there shall be left in it a remnant who will be brought out, *both* sons and daughters; surely they will come out to you, and you will see their ways and their doings. Then you will be comforted concerning the disaster that I have brought upon Jerusalem, all that I have brought upon it. ²³And they will comfort you, when you see their ways and their doings; and you shall know that I have done nothing without cause that I have done in it," says the Lord GOD.

14:14–20 Noah, Daniel, and Job. Similar to Jeremiah 7:16 and 15:1–4, in which God tells Jeremiah that even Moses and Samuel, well-known for their power in intercessory prayer, could not deliver Jerusalem and the people. The 3 Old Testament heroes mentioned here interceded powerfully on others' behalf (see Gen. 6:18; Job 42:7–10; Dan. 1,2), but they could not deliver anyone but themselves if they prayed earnestly. Even the presence and prayers of the godly could not stop the impending judgment.

The Outcast Vine

15 Then the word of the LORD came to me, saying: ²"Son of man, how is the wood of the vine *better* than any other wood, the vine branch which is among the trees of the forest? ³Is wood taken from it to make any object? Or can *men* make a peg from it to hang any vessel on? ⁴Instead, it is thrown into the fire for fuel; the fire devours both ends of it, and its middle is burned. Is it useful for *any* work? ⁵Indeed, when it was whole, no object could be made from it. How much less will it be useful for

15:1–3 Then the word...came. Israel, often symbolized by a vine (Gen. 49:22; Jer. 2:21) had become useless. She failed to bear fruit, as God had set her apart to do. Other trees can be used for construction of things, but a fruitless vine had no value. In every age God's people have their value in their fruitfulness.

any work when the fire has devoured it, and it is burned?

⁶"Therefore thus says the Lord GOD: 'Like the wood of the vine among the trees of the forest, which I have given to the fire for fuel, so I will give up the inhabitants of Jerusalem; ⁷and I will set My face against them. They will go out from *one* fire, but *another* fire shall devour them. Then you shall know that I *am* the LORD, when I set My face against them. ⁸Thus I will make the land desolate, because they have persisted in unfaithfulness,' says the Lord GOD."

God's Love for Jerusalem

16 Again the word of the LORD came to me, saying, ²"Son of man, cause Jerusalem to know her abominations, ³and say, 'Thus says the Lord GOD to Jerusalem: "Your birth and your nativity *are* from the land of Canaan; your father *was* an Amorite and your mother a Hittite. ⁴*As for* your nativity, on the day you were born your navel cord was not cut, nor were you washed in water to cleanse *you*; you were not rubbed with salt nor wrapped in swaddling cloths. ⁵No eye pitied you, to do any of these things for you, to have compassion on you; but you were thrown out into the open field, when you yourself were loathed on the day you were born.

⁶"And when I passed by you and saw you struggling in your own blood, I said to you in your blood, 'Live!' Yes, I said to you in your blood, 'Live!' ⁷I made you thrive like a plant in the field; and you grew, matured, and became very beautiful. *Your* breasts were formed, your hair grew, but you *were* naked and bare.

⁸"When I passed by you again and looked upon you, indeed your time *was* the time of love; so I spread My wing over you and covered your nakedness. Yes, I swore an oath to you and entered into a covenant with you, and you became Mine," says the Lord GOD.

16:8 the time of love. This refers to the marriageable state. Spreading His "wing" was a marriage custom (see Ruth 3:9) and indicates that God entered into a covenant with the young nation at Mount Sinai (see Ex. 19:5–8). Making a covenant signifies marriage, a symbol of God's relationship with Israel (see Jer. 2:2,3).

⁹"Then I washed you in water; yes, I thoroughly washed off your blood, and I anointed you with oil. ¹⁰I clothed you in embroidered cloth and gave you sandals of badger skin; I clothed you with fine linen and covered you with silk. ¹¹I adorned you with ornaments, put bracelets on your wrists, and a chain on your neck. ¹²And I put a jewel in your nose, earrings in your ears, and a beautiful crown on your head. ¹³Thus you were adorned with gold and silver, and your clothing *was of* fine linen, silk, and embroidered cloth. You ate *pastry of* fine flour, honey, and oil. You were exceedingly beautiful, and succeeded to royalty. ¹⁴Your fame went out among the nations because of your beauty, for it *was* perfect through My splendor which I had bestowed on you," says the Lord GOD.

16:14 My splendor. The nation was a trophy of God's grace (see Deut. 7:6–8). God's presence and glory gave Jerusalem her beauty and prominence.

Jerusalem's Harlotry

¹⁵"But you trusted in your own beauty, played the harlot because of your fame, and poured out your harlotry on everyone passing by who *would have* it. ¹⁶You took some of your garments and adorned multicolored high places for yourself, and played the harlot on them. *Such* things should not happen, nor be. ¹⁷You have also taken your beautiful jewelry from My gold and My silver, which I had given you, and made for yourself male images and played the harlot with them. ¹⁸You took your embroidered garments and covered them, and you set My oil and My incense before them. ¹⁹Also My food which I gave you—the pastry of fine flour, oil, and honey *which* I fed you—you set it before them as sweet incense; and *so* it was," says the Lord GOD.

²⁰"Moreover you took your sons and your daughters, whom you bore to Me, and these you sacrificed to them to be devoured. *Were* your *acts* of harlotry a small matter, ²¹that you have slain My children and offered them up to them by causing them to pass through *the fire?* ²²And in all your abominations and acts of harlotry you did not remember the days of your youth, when you were naked and bare, struggling in your blood.

23"Then it was so, after all your wickedness—'Woe, woe to you!' says the Lord GOD— 24that you also built for yourself a shrine, and made a high place for yourself in every street. 25You built your high places at the head of every road, and made your beauty to be abhorred. You offered yourself to everyone who passed by, and multiplied your acts of harlotry. 26You also committed harlotry with the Egyptians, your very fleshly neighbors, and increased your acts of harlotry to provoke Me to anger.

27"Behold, therefore, I stretched out My hand against you, diminished your allotment, and gave you up to the will of those who hate you, the daughters of the Philistines, who were ashamed of your lewd behavior. 28You also played the harlot with the Assyrians, because you were insatiable; indeed you played the harlot with them and still were not satisfied. 29Moreover you multiplied your acts of harlotry as far as the land of the trader, Chaldea; and even then you were not satisfied.

16:27 ashamed. The wickedness and evil of the Jews scandalized even pagan Philistines.

30"How degenerate is your heart!" says the Lord GOD, "seeing you do all these *things*, the deeds of a brazen harlot.

Jerusalem's Adultery

31"You erected your shrine at the head of every road, and built your high place in every street. Yet you were not like a harlot, because you scorned payment. 32*You are* an adulterous wife, *who* takes strangers instead of her husband. 33Men make payment to all harlots, but you made your payments to all your lovers, and hired them to come to you from all around for your harlotry. 34You are the opposite of *other* women in your harlotry, because no one solicited you to be a harlot. In that you gave payment but no payment was given you, therefore you are the opposite."

Jerusalem's Lovers Will Abuse Her

35'Now then, O harlot, hear the word of the LORD! 36Thus says the Lord GOD: "Because your filthiness was poured out and your nakedness uncovered in your harlotry with your lovers, and with all your abominable idols, and because of the blood of your children which you gave to them, 37surely, therefore, I will gather all your lovers with whom you took pleasure, all those you loved, *and* all those you hated; I will gather them from all around against you and will uncover your nakedness to them, that they may see all your nakedness. 38And I will judge you as women who break wedlock or shed blood are judged; I will bring blood upon you in fury and jealousy. 39I will also give you into their hand, and they shall throw down your shrines and break down your high places. They shall also strip you of your clothes, take your beautiful jewelry, and leave you naked and bare.

40"They shall also bring up an assembly against you, and they shall stone you with stones and thrust you through with their swords. 41They shall burn your houses with fire, and execute judgments on you in the sight of many women; and I will make you cease playing the harlot, and you shall no longer hire lovers. 42So I will lay to rest My fury toward you, and My jealousy shall depart from you. I will be quiet, and be angry no more. 43Because you did not remember the days of your youth, but agitated Me*a* with all these *things*, surely I will also recompense your deeds on *your own* head," says the Lord GOD. "And you shall not commit lewdness in addition to all your abominations.

16:35–40 I...will uncover your nakedness. Public exposure and stoning of prostitutes to make them a shameful spectacle were well-known customs in ancient Israel.

More Wicked than Samaria and Sodom

44"Indeed everyone who quotes proverbs will use *this* proverb against you: 'Like mother, like daughter!' 45You *are* your mother's daughter, loathing husband and children; and you *are* the sister of your sisters, who loathed their husbands and children; your mother *was* a Hittite and your father an Amorite.

16:43 *a*Following Septuagint, Syriac, Targum, and Vulgate; Masoretic Text reads *were agitated with Me.*

⁴⁶"Your elder sister *is* Samaria, who dwells with her daughters to the north of you; and your younger sister, who dwells to the south of you, *is* Sodom and her daughters. ⁴⁷You did not walk in their ways nor act according to their abominations; but, as *if that were* too little, you became more corrupt than they in all your ways.

⁴⁸"*As* I live," says the Lord GOD, "neither your sister Sodom nor her daughters have done as you and your daughters have done. ⁴⁹Look, this was the iniquity of your sister Sodom: She and her daughter had pride, fullness of food, and abundance of idleness; neither did she strengthen the hand of the poor and needy. ⁵⁰And they were haughty and committed abomination before Me; therefore I took them away as I saw *fit.*ᵃ

⁵¹"Samaria did not commit half of your sins; but you have multiplied your abominations more than they, and have justified your sisters by all the abominations which you have done. ⁵²You who judged your sisters, bear your own shame also, because the sins which you committed were more abominable than theirs; they are more righteous than you. Yes, be disgraced also, and bear your own shame, because you justified your sisters.

⁵³"When I bring back their captives, the captives of Sodom and her daughters, and the captives of Samaria and her daughters, then *I will also bring back* the captives of your captivity among them, ⁵⁴that you may bear your own shame and be disgraced by all that you did when you comforted them. ⁵⁵When your sisters, Sodom and her daughters, return to their former state, and Samaria and her daughters return to their former state, then you and your daughters will return to your former state. ⁵⁶For your sister Sodom was not a byword in your mouth in the days of your pride, ⁵⁷before your wickedness was uncovered. It was like the time of the reproach of the daughters of Syriaᵃ and all *those* around her, and of the daughters of the Philistines, who despise you everywhere. ⁵⁸You have paid for your lewdness and your abominations," says the LORD. ⁵⁹For thus says the Lord GOD: "I will deal with you as you have done, who despised the oath by breaking the covenant.

An Everlasting Covenant

⁶⁰"Nevertheless I will remember My covenant with you in the days of your youth, and I will establish an everlasting covenant with you. ⁶¹Then you will remember your ways and be ashamed, when you receive your older and your younger sisters; for I will give them to you for daughters, but not because of My covenant with you. ⁶²And I will establish My covenant with you. Then you shall know that I *am* the LORD, ⁶³that you may remember and be ashamed, and never open your mouth anymore because of your shame, when I provide you an atonement for all you have done," says the Lord GOD.' "

> **16:60 I will remember My covenant.** God demonstrates His grace through covenants with His people. **an everlasting covenant.** This is the unconditional, saving, and everlasting New Covenant (see Is. 59:21), by which Israel will know that God is the Lord. The basis of God's grace will not be the Mosaic Covenant, which the Jews could never fulfill (see Ex. 24:1).

The Eagles and the Vine

17 And the word of the LORD came to me, saying, ²"Son of man, pose a riddle, and speak a parable to the house of Israel, ³and say, 'Thus says the Lord GOD:

"A great eagle with large wings and
     long pinions,
Full of feathers of various colors,
Came to Lebanon
And took from the cedar the highest
     branch.
⁴ He cropped off its topmost young twig
And carried it to a land of trade;
He set it in a city of merchants.
⁵ Then he took some of the seed of the
     land
And planted it in a fertile field;
He placed *it* by abundant waters
And set it like a willow tree.
⁶ And it grew and became a spreading
     vine of low stature;

16:50 ᵃVulgate reads *you saw*; Septuagint reads *he saw*; Targum reads *as was revealed to Me*.
16:57 ᵃFollowing Masoretic Text, Septuagint, Targum, and Vulgate; many Hebrew manuscripts and Syriac read *Edom*.

Its branches turned toward him,
But its roots were under it.
So it became a vine,
Brought forth branches,
And put forth shoots.

7   "But there was another*a* great eagle
          with large wings and many
          feathers;
      And behold, this vine bent its roots
          toward him,
      And stretched its branches toward him,
      From the garden terrace where it had
          been planted,
      That he might water it.
8   It was planted in good soil by many
          waters,
      To bring forth branches, bear fruit,
      And become a majestic vine." '

9 "Say, 'Thus says the Lord GOD:

      "Will it thrive?
      Will he not pull up its roots,
      Cut off its fruit,
      And leave it to wither?
      All of its spring leaves will wither,
      And no great power or many people
      Will be needed to pluck it up by its
          roots.
10   Behold, *it is* planted,
      Will it thrive?
      Will it not utterly wither when the
          east wind touches it?
      It will wither in the garden terrace
          where it grew." ' "

11 Moreover the word of the LORD came to me, saying, 12 "Say now to the rebellious house: 'Do you not know what these *things* mean?' Tell *them,* 'Indeed the king of Babylon went to Jerusalem and took its king and princes, and led them with him to Babylon. 13 And he took the king's offspring, made a covenant with him, and put him under oath. He also took away the mighty of the land, 14 that the kingdom might be brought low and not lift itself up, *but* that by keeping his covenant it might stand. 15 But he rebelled against him by sending his ambassadors to Egypt, that they might give him horses and many people. Will he prosper? Will he who does such *things* escape? Can he break a covenant and still be delivered?

16 *As* I live,' says the Lord GOD, 'surely in the place *where* the king *dwells* who made him king, whose oath he despised and whose covenant he broke—with him in the midst of Babylon he shall die. 17 Nor will Pharaoh with *his* mighty army and great company do anything in the war, when they heap up a siege mound and build a wall to cut off many persons. 18 Since he despised the oath by breaking the covenant, and in fact gave his hand and still did all these *things,* he shall not escape.' "

19 Therefore thus says the Lord GOD: "*As* I live, surely My oath which he despised, and My covenant which he broke, I will recompense on his own head. 20 I will spread My net over him, and he shall be taken in My snare. I will bring him to Babylon and try him there for the treason which he committed against Me. 21 All his fugitives*a* with all his troops shall fall by the sword, and those who remain shall be scattered to every wind; and you shall know that I, the LORD, have spoken."

Israel Exalted at Last

22 Thus says the Lord GOD: "I will take also *one* of the highest branches of the high cedar and set *it* out. I will crop off from the topmost of its young twigs a tender one, and will plant *it* on a high and prominent mountain. 23 On the mountain height of Israel I will plant it; and it will bring forth boughs, and bear fruit, and be a majestic cedar. Under it will dwell birds of every

---

17:7 *a* Following Septuagint, Syriac, and Vulgate; Masoretic Text and Targum read *one.*
17:21 *a* Following Masoretic Text and Vulgate; many Hebrew manuscripts and Syriac read *choice men;* Targum reads *mighty men;* Septuagint omits *All his fugitives.*

sort; in the shadow of its branches they will dwell. [24]And all the trees of the field shall know that I, the LORD, have brought down the high tree and exalted the low tree, dried up the green tree and made the dry tree flourish; I, the LORD, have spoken and have done *it*."

17:22,23 *one* of the highest branches. This messianic prophecy stated that the Messiah will come from the royal line of David ("the high cedar"; see Dan. 2:35,44,45). He will be a "high branch" reigning in the height of success (see Jer. 23:5). He will be "a tender one" growing into a "majestic cedar." All nations will be blessed and Israel will be restored under His rule.

A False Proverb Refuted

18 The word of the LORD came to me again, saying, [2]"What do you mean when you use this proverb concerning the land of Israel, saying:

'The fathers have eaten sour grapes,
    And the children's teeth are set on
        edge'?

[3]"*As* I live," says the Lord GOD, "you shall no longer use this proverb in Israel.

[4]   "Behold, all souls are Mine;
    The soul of the father
        As well as the soul of the son is
            Mine;
    The soul who sins shall die.
[5]   But if a man is just
    And does what is lawful and right;
[6]   If he has not eaten on the mountains,
    Nor lifted up his eyes to the idols of
        the house of Israel,
    Nor defiled his neighbor's wife,
    Nor approached a woman during her
        impurity;
[7]   If he has not oppressed anyone,
    But has restored to the debtor his
        pledge;
    Has robbed no one by violence,
    But has given his bread to the hungry
    And covered the naked with clothing;
[8]   If he has not exacted usury
    Nor taken any increase,
    But has withdrawn his hand from
        iniquity

And executed true judgment between
        man and man;
[9]   *If* he has walked in My statutes
    And kept My judgments faithfully—
    He *is* just;
    He shall surely live!"
    Says the Lord GOD.

18:9 He shall surely live! The just die and live eternally, and the unjust shall perish physically and eternally (John 5:28,29; Rev. 20:11–15). The just will live no matter what the character of his parents or children (see Ex. 20:5).

---

[10]   "If he begets a son *who is* a robber
    Or a shedder of blood,
    Who does any of these *things*
[11]   And does none of those *duties*,
    But has eaten on the mountains
    Or defiled his neighbor's wife;
[12]   If he has oppressed the poor and
        needy,
    Robbed by violence,
    Not restored the pledge,
    Lifted his eyes to the idols,
    Or committed abomination;
[13]   If he has exacted usury
    Or taken increase—
    Shall he then live?
    He shall not live!
    If he has done any of these
        abominations,
    He shall surely die;
    His blood shall be upon him.

[14]   "*If*, however, he begets a son
    Who sees all the sins which his father
        has done,
    And considers but does not do
        likewise;
[15]   Who has not eaten on the mountains,
    Nor lifted his eyes to the idols of the
        house of Israel,
    Nor defiled his neighbor's wife;
[16]   Has not oppressed anyone,
    Nor withheld a pledge,
    Nor robbed by violence,
    But has given his bread to the hungry
    And covered the naked with clothing;
[17]   *Who* has withdrawn his hand from
        the poor[a]
    And not received usury or increase,

18:17 [a]Following Masoretic Text, Targum, and Vulgate; Septuagint reads *iniquity* (compare verse 8).

But has executed My judgments
And walked in My statutes—
He shall not die for the iniquity of his
   father;
He shall surely live!

18   "*As for* his father,
Because he cruelly oppressed,
Robbed his brother by violence,
And did what *is* not good among his
   people,
Behold, he shall die for his iniquity.

Turn and Live

19"Yet you say, 'Why should the son not bear the guilt of the father?' Because the son has done what is lawful and right, and has kept all My statutes and observed them, he shall surely live. 20The soul who sins shall die. The son shall not bear the guilt of the father, nor the father bear the guilt of the son. The righteousness of the righteous shall be upon himself, and the wickedness of the wicked shall be upon himself. 21"But if a wicked man turns from all his sins which he has committed, keeps all My statutes, and does what is lawful and right, he shall surely live; he shall not die. 22None of the transgressions which he has committed shall be remembered against him; because of the righteousness which he has done, he shall live. 23Do I have any pleasure at all that the wicked should die?" says the Lord GOD, "*and* not that he should turn from his ways and live?

24"But when a righteous man turns away from his righteousness and commits iniquity, and does according to all the abominations that the wicked *man* does, shall he live? All the righteousness which he has done shall not be remembered; because of the unfaithfulness of which he is guilty and the sin which he has committed, because of them he shall die. 25"Yet you say, 'The way of the Lord is not fair.' Hear now, O house of Israel, is it not My way which is fair, and your ways which are not fair? 26When a righteous *man* turns away from his righteousness, commits iniquity, and dies in it, it is because of the iniquity which he has done that he dies. 27Again, when a wicked *man* turns away from the wickedness which he committed, and does what is lawful and right, he pre-

serves himself alive. 28Because he considers and turns away from all the transgressions which he committed, he shall surely live; he shall not die. 29Yet the house of Israel says, 'The way of the Lord is not fair.' O house of Israel, is it not My ways which are fair, and your ways which are not fair?

30"Therefore I will judge you, O house of Israel, every one according to his ways," says the Lord GOD. "Repent, and turn from all your transgressions, so that iniquity will not be your ruin. 31Cast away from you all the transgressions which you have committed, and get yourselves a new heart and a new spirit. For why should you die, O house of Israel? 32For I have no pleasure in the death of one who dies," says the Lord GOD. "Therefore turn and live!"

18:32 I have no pleasure. The death of His saints is precious to God (Ps. 116:15). He has no pleasure when a person dies without repentance. God is sovereign in salvation, but man is responsible for his own sin. **turn and live.** This was a call to repent and avoid physical and eternal death (see Ps. 23:6). Ezekiel preached repentance and God's offer of mercy.

Israel Degraded

19 "Moreover take up a lamentation for the princes of Israel, 2and say:

'What *is* your mother? A lioness:
      She lay down among the lions;
      Among the young lions she nourished
         her cubs.
3   She brought up one of her cubs,
      And he became a young lion;
      He learned to catch prey,
      And he devoured men.
4   The nations also heard of him;
      He was trapped in their pit,
      And they brought him with chains to
         the land of Egypt.

5   'When she saw that she waited, *that*
         her hope was lost,
      She took another of her cubs *and*
         made him a young lion.
6   He roved among the lions,
      And became a young lion;
      He learned to catch prey;
      He devoured men.

7   He knew their desolate places,*a*
    And laid waste their cities;
    The land with its fullness was
      desolated
    By the noise of his roaring.
8   Then the nations set against him
      from the provinces on every side,
    And spread their net over him;
    He was trapped in their pit.
9   They put him in a cage with chains,
    And brought him to the king of
      Babylon;
    They brought him in nets,
    That his voice should no longer be
      heard on the mountains of Israel.

> **19:3–9 one of her cubs.** This refers to Jehoahaz, who ruled in 609 B.C. and was deposed by Egypt's Pharaoh Necho after reigning only 3 months (2 Kin. 23:32–34). **another of her cubs.** This refers to Jehoiachin, who was unjust and oppressive during his 3-month reign. He was carried to Babylon in a cage in 597 B.C. (2 Kin. 24:6–15), where he was held captive for 37 years and released at age 55. God used Egypt and Babylon to judge these wicked kings.

10   'Your mother *was* like a vine in your
      bloodline,*a*
    Planted by the waters,
    Fruitful and full of branches
    Because of many waters.
11   She had strong branches for scepters
      of rulers.
    She towered in stature above the thick
      branches,
    And was seen in her height amid the
      dense foliage.
12   But she was plucked up in fury,
    She was cast down to the ground,
    And the east wind dried her fruit.
    Her strong branches were broken and
      withered;
    The fire consumed them.
13   And now she *is* planted in the
      wilderness,
    In a dry and thirsty land.
14   Fire has come out from a rod of her
      branches
    And devoured her fruit,

    So that she has no strong branch—a
      scepter for ruling.' "

This *is* a lamentation, and has become a lamentation.

> **19:14 a rod.** King Zedekiah was blamed for the burning of Jerusalem because of his treachery (see Jer. 38:20–23). The house of David ended in shame, and Israel has had no king from David's line for nearly 2,600 years. When the Messiah came, they rejected Him as King, preferring Caesar. The Messiah still became their Savior and will return as their King.

The Rebellions of Israel

20 It came to pass in the seventh year, in the fifth *month*, on the tenth *day* of the month, *that* certain of the elders of Israel came to inquire of the LORD, and sat before me. ²Then the word of the LORD came to me, saying, ³"Son of man, speak to the elders of Israel, and say to them, 'Thus says the Lord GOD: "Have you come to inquire of Me? *As* I live," says the Lord GOD, "I will not be inquired of by you." ' "Will you judge them, son of man, will you judge *them?* Then make known to them the abominations of their fathers.

⁵"Say to them, 'Thus says the Lord GOD: "On the day when I chose Israel and raised My hand in an oath to the descendants of the house of Jacob, and made Myself known to them in the land of Egypt, I raised My hand in an oath to them, saying, 'I *am* the LORD your God.' ⁶On that day I raised My hand in an oath to them, to bring them out of the land of Egypt into a land that I had searched out for them, 'flowing with milk and honey,'*a* the glory of all lands. ⁷Then I said to them, 'Each of you, throw away the abominations which are before his eyes, and do not defile yourselves with the idols of Egypt. I *am* the LORD your God.' ⁸But they rebelled against Me and would not obey Me. They did not all cast away the abominations which were before their eyes, nor did they forsake the idols of Egypt. Then I said, 'I will pour out My fury on them and fulfill My anger against them

---

19:7 *a*Septuagint reads *He stood in insolence;* Targum reads *He destroyed its palaces;* Vulgate reads *He learned to make widows.*   19:10 *a*Literally *blood,* following Masoretic Text, Syriac, and Vulgate; Septuagint reads *like a flower on a pomegranate tree;* Targum reads *in your likeness.*
20:6 *a*Exodus 3:8

in the midst of the land of Egypt.' ⁹But I acted for My name's sake, that it should not be profaned before the Gentiles among whom they *were*, in whose sight I had made Myself known to them, to bring them out of the land of Egypt.

¹⁰"Therefore I made them go out of the land of Egypt and brought them into the wilderness. ¹¹And I gave them My statutes and showed them My judgments, 'which, *if* a man does, he shall live by them.'ᵃ ¹²Moreover I also gave them My Sabbaths, to be a sign between them and Me, that they might know that I *am* the LORD who sanctifies them. ¹³Yet the house of Israel rebelled against Me in the wilderness; they did not walk in My statutes; they despised My judgments, 'which, *if* a man does, he shall live by them';ᵃ and they greatly defiled My Sabbaths. Then I said I would pour out My fury on them in the wilderness, to consume them. ¹⁴But I acted for My name's sake, that it should not be profaned before the Gentiles, in whose sight I had brought them out. ¹⁵So I also raised My hand in an oath to them in the wilderness, that I would not bring them into the land which I had given *them*, 'flowing with milk and honey,'ᵃ the glory of all lands; ¹⁶because they despised My judgments and did not walk in My statutes, but profaned My Sabbaths; for their heart went after their idols. ¹⁷Nevertheless My eye spared them from destruction. I did not make an end of them in the wilderness.

¹⁸"But I said to their children in the wilderness, 'Do not walk in the statutes of your fathers, nor observe their judgments, nor defile yourselves with their idols. ¹⁹I *am* the LORD your God: Walk in My statutes, keep My judgments, and do them; ²⁰hallow My Sabbaths, and they will be a sign between Me and you, that you may know that I *am* the LORD your God.'

²¹"Notwithstanding, the children rebelled against Me; they did not walk in My statutes, and were not careful to observe My judgments, 'which, *if* a man does, he shall live by them';ᵃ but they profaned My Sabbaths. Then I said I would pour out My fury on them and fulfill My anger against

them in the wilderness. ²²Nevertheless I withdrew My hand and acted for My name's sake, that it should not be profaned in the sight of the Gentiles, in whose sight I had brought them out. ²³Also I raised My hand in an oath to those in the wilderness, that I would scatter them among the Gentiles and disperse them throughout the countries, ²⁴because they had not executed My judgments, but had despised My statutes, profaned My Sabbaths, and their eyes were fixed on their fathers' idols.

²⁵"Therefore I also gave them up to statutes *that were* not good, and judgments by which they could not live; ²⁶and I pronounced them unclean because of their ritual gifts, in that they caused all their firstborn to pass through *the fire*, that I might make them desolate and that they might know that I am the LORD."'

> **20:25,26 I...gave them up.** God allowed the Jews to live in sin (see v. 32; Ps. 81:11,12). The story of the Jews, and all mankind, is one long history of rebellion.

²⁷"Therefore, son of man, speak to the house of Israel, and say to them, 'Thus says the Lord GOD: "In this too your fathers have blasphemed Me, by being unfaithful to Me. ²⁸When I brought them into the land *concerning* which I had raised My hand in an oath to give them, and they saw all the high hills and all the thick trees, there they offered their sacrifices and provoked Me with their offerings. There they also sent up their sweet aroma and poured out their drink offerings. ²⁹Then I said to them, 'What *is* this high place to which you go?' So its name is called Bamahᵃ to this day."' ³⁰Therefore say to the house of Israel, 'Thus says the Lord GOD: "Are you defiling yourselves in the manner of your fathers, and committing harlotry according to their abominations? ³¹For when you offer your gifts and make your sons pass through the fire, you defile yourselves with all your idols, even to this day. So shall I be inquired of by you, O house of Israel? *As* I live," says the Lord GOD, "I will not be inquired of by you. ³²What you have in your mind shall

---

20:11 ᵃLeviticus 18:5   20:13 ᵃLeviticus 18:5   20:15 ᵃExodus 3:8   20:21 ᵃLeviticus 18:5
20:29 ᵃLiterally *High Place*

never be, when you say, 'We will be like the Gentiles, like the families in other countries, serving wood and stone.'

God Will Restore Israel

³³"As I live," says the Lord GOD, "surely with a mighty hand, with an outstretched arm, and with fury poured out, I will rule over you. ³⁴I will bring you out from the peoples and gather you out of the countries where you are scattered, with a mighty hand, with an outstretched arm, and with fury poured out. ³⁵And I will bring you into the wilderness of the peoples, and there I will plead My case with you face to face. ³⁶Just as I pleaded My case with your fathers in the wilderness of the land of Egypt, so I will plead My case with you," says the Lord GOD.

³⁷"I will make you pass under the rod, and I will bring you into the bond of the covenant; ³⁸I will purge the rebels from among you, and those who transgress against Me; I will bring them out of the country where they dwell, but they shall not enter the land of Israel. Then you will know that I am the LORD.

> **20:37 pass under the rod.** God was Israel's Great Shepherd (34:11–13). He brings His sheep home to their fold (see Jer. 33:13), has them file in, separating the sheep from the goats (see Matt. 25), and has them pass under His shepherd's rod to be noted and checked for injury. He will bring them into the New Covenant by giving them His Spirit (36:24–27). This is Israel's final salvation (Rom. 11:26–33).

³⁹"As for you, O house of Israel," thus says the Lord GOD: "Go, serve every one of you his idols—and hereafter—if you will not obey Me; but profane My holy name no more with your gifts and your idols. ⁴⁰For on My holy mountain, on the mountain height of Israel," says the Lord GOD, "there all the house of Israel, all of them in the land, shall serve Me; there I will accept them, and there I will require your offerings and the firstfruits of your sacrifices, together with all your holy things. ⁴¹I will accept you as a sweet aroma when I bring you out from the peoples and gather you out of the countries where you have been scattered;

and I will be hallowed in you before the Gentiles. ⁴²Then you shall know that I am the LORD, when I bring you into the land of Israel, into the country for which I raised My hand in an oath to give to your fathers. ⁴³And there you shall remember your ways and all your doings with which you were defiled; and you shall loathe yourselves in your own sight because of all the evils that you have committed. ⁴⁴Then you shall know that I am the LORD, when I have dealt with you for My name's sake, not according to your wicked ways nor according to your corrupt doings, O house of Israel," says the Lord GOD.' "

> **20:40–42 all...in the land.** When the Israelites gather in the Messiah's earthly kingdom, they will return to the same land from which they were scattered (Palestine). This was the land given to their fathers (Gen. 12:7). They will "all" be there, repentant and saved (Rom. 11:26,27), serving the Lord and worshiping Him together (see Is. 11:13).

Fire in the Forest

⁴⁵Furthermore the word of the LORD came to me, saying, ⁴⁶"Son of man, set your face toward the south; preach against the south and prophesy against the forest land, the South,ᵃ ⁴⁷and say to the forest of the South, 'Hear the word of the LORD! Thus says the Lord GOD: "Behold, I will kindle a fire in you, and it shall devour every green tree and every dry tree in you; the blazing flame shall not be quenched, and all faces from the south to the north shall be scorched by it. ⁴⁸All flesh shall see that I, the LORD, have kindled it; it shall not be quenched." ' "

⁴⁹Then I said, "Ah, Lord GOD! They say of me, 'Does he not speak parables?' "

Babylon, the Sword of God

21 And the word of the LORD came to me, saying, ²"Son of man, set your face toward Jerusalem, preach against the holy places, and prophesy against the land of Israel; ³and say to the land of Israel, 'Thus says the LORD: "Behold, I am against you, and I will draw My sword out of its sheath and cut off both righteous and wicked from you. ⁴Because I will cut off both righ-

teous and wicked from you, therefore My sword shall go out of its sheath against all flesh from south *to* north, ⁵that all flesh may know that I, the LORD, have drawn My sword out of its sheath; it shall not return anymore." ' ⁶Sigh therefore, son of man, with a breaking heart, and sigh with bitterness before their eyes. ⁷And it shall be when they say to you, 'Why are you sighing?' that you shall answer, 'Because of the news; when it comes, every heart will melt, all hands will be feeble, every spirit will faint, and all knees will be weak *as* water. Behold, it is coming and shall be brought to pass,' says the Lord GOD."

> **21:1–7 the word...came.** God's judgment on Israel is depicted in terms of a man unsheathing his sword for deadly thrusts. God is the swordsman, and Babylon is His sword. The historical background for this prophecy is Nebuchadnezzar's campaign in 588 B.C. to quell revolts in Judah, Tyre, and Ammon.

⁸Again the word of the LORD came to me, saying, ⁹"Son of man, prophesy and say, 'Thus says the LORD!' Say:

'A sword, a sword is sharpened
And also polished!
¹⁰ Sharpened to make a dreadful slaughter,
Polished to flash like lightning!
Should we then make mirth?
It despises the scepter of My son,
As it does all wood.
¹¹ And He has given it to be polished,

That it may be handled;
This sword is sharpened, and it is polished
To be given into the hand of the slayer.'

¹² "Cry and wail, son of man;
For it will be against My people,
Against all the princes of Israel.
Terrors including the sword will be against My people;
Therefore strike *your* thigh.
¹³ "Because *it is* a testing,
And what if *the sword* despises even the scepter?
The scepter shall be no *more*,"

says the Lord GOD.

¹⁴ "You therefore, son of man, prophesy,
And strike *your* hands together.
The third time let the sword do double *damage*.
It *is* the sword *that* slays,
The sword that slays the great *men*,
That enters their private chambers.
¹⁵ I have set the point of the sword against all their gates,
That the heart may melt and many may stumble.
Ah! *It is* made bright;
It is grasped for slaughter:
¹⁶ "Swords at the ready!
Thrust right!

Q: Is there a contradiction between 18:1–20, in which individual responsibility for sin is emphasized, and 21:1–7, in which God applies judgment to both the "righteous and wicked" (v. 4)?

A: The specific subject of these two passages is quite different. The first deals with the personal consequences and responsibilities that are part of each person's life. No amount of blaming others or offering excuses can remove a person's accountability before God. The second passage deals with the corporate consequences of living in a fallen world. When God chose to use Babylon as a weapon of punishment, He did so fully aware that some people who honored Him would suffer and die as a result. A person's connection with a society means that the good and evil that may fall on that society may fall on members who have not directly contributed to the cause.

The principles in 18:1–20 prevail in the end because they describe the way in which God will eventually settle moral accounts. Each person will be held responsible for his or her own life. Only those "in Christ" can face that event with hope.

Set your blade!
Thrust left—
Wherever your edge is ordered!

[17] "I also will beat My fists together,
And I will cause My fury to rest;
I, the LORD, have spoken."

[18]The word of the LORD came to me again, saying: [19]"And son of man, appoint for yourself two ways for the sword of the king of Babylon to go; both of them shall go from the same land. Make a sign; put it at the head of the road to the city. [20]Appoint a road for the sword to go to Rabbah of the Ammonites, and to Judah, into fortified Jerusalem. [21]For the king of Babylon stands at the parting of the road, at the fork of the two roads, to use divination: he shakes the arrows, he consults the images, he looks at the liver. [22]In his right hand is the divination for Jerusalem: to set up battering rams, to call for a slaughter, to lift the voice with shouting, to set battering rams against the gates, to heap up a siege mound, and to build a wall. [23]And it will be to them like a false divination in the eyes of those who have sworn oaths with them; but he will bring their iniquity to remembrance, that they may be taken.

21:21 the king...stands...to use divination. Divination seeks guidance from superstitious devices. Babylon's leader shook arrows, let them fall, and read a conclusion from the pattern. He looked at Teraphim (idols), and he examined an animal liver. God controlled this superstition to achieve His will in attacking Jerusalem and Judah. Later, Nebuchadnezzar attacked Rabbah in Ammon E of the Jordan (vv. 28–32).

[24]"Therefore thus says the Lord GOD: 'Because you have made your iniquity to be remembered, in that your transgressions are uncovered, so that in all your doings your sins appear—because you have come to remembrance, you shall be taken in hand.
[25]'Now to you, O profane, wicked prince of Israel, whose day has come, whose iniquity shall end, [26]thus says the Lord GOD:

"Remove the turban, and take off the
crown;
Nothing shall remain the same.

Exalt the humble, and humble the
exalted.
[27] Overthrown, overthrown,
I will make it overthrown!
It shall be no longer,
Until He comes whose right it is,
And I will give it to Him." '

21:27 Until He comes. "Overthrown" is mentioned 3 times here, signifying the severe instability that Israel was to experience. Israel would not have a king until the Messiah comes, when God will give the kingship to Him (see Jer. 23:5–8), the greater "David" (Ezek. 37:24). He has the "right" to the priestly and royal offices (see Heb. 5–7).

A Sword Against the Ammonites

[28]"And you, son of man, prophesy and say, 'Thus says the Lord GOD concerning the Ammonites and concerning their reproach,' and say:

'A sword, a sword is drawn,
Polished for slaughter,
For consuming, for flashing—
[29] While they see false visions for you,
While they divine a lie to you,
To bring you on the necks of the
wicked, the slain
Whose day has come,
Whose iniquity shall end.

[30] 'Return it to its sheath.
I will judge you
In the place where you were created,
In the land of your nativity.
[31] I will pour out My indignation on
you;
I will blow against you with the fire of
My wrath,
And deliver you into the hands of
brutal men who are skillful to
destroy.
[32] You shall be fuel for the fire;
Your blood shall be in the midst of the
land.
You shall not be remembered,
For I the LORD have spoken.' "

Sins of Jerusalem

22 Moreover the word of the LORD came to me, saying, [2]"Now, son of man, will you judge, will you judge the bloody city? Yes, show her all her abominations!

³Then say, 'Thus says the Lord GOD: "The city sheds blood in her own midst, that her time may come; and she makes idols within herself to defile herself. ⁴You have become guilty by the blood which you have shed, and have defiled yourself with the idols which you have made. You have caused your days to draw near, and have come to *the end of* your years; therefore I have made you a reproach to the nations, and a mockery to all countries. ⁵*Those* near and *those* far from you will mock you as infamous *and* full of tumult.

⁶"Look, the princes of Israel: each one has used his power to shed blood in you. ⁷In you they have made light of father and mother; in your midst they have oppressed the stranger; in you they have mistreated the fatherless and the widow. ⁸You have despised My holy things and profaned My Sabbaths. ⁹In you are men who slander to cause bloodshed; in you are those who eat on the mountains; in your midst they commit lewdness. ¹⁰In you men uncover their fathers' nakedness; in you they violate women who are set apart during their impurity. ¹¹One commits abomination with his neighbor's wife; another lewdly defiles his daughter-in-law; and another in you violates his sister, his father's daughter. ¹²In you they take bribes to shed blood; you take usury and increase; you have made profit from your neighbors by extortion, and have forgotten Me," says the Lord GOD.

¹³"Behold, therefore, I beat My fists at the dishonest profit which you have made, and at the bloodshed which has been in your midst. ¹⁴Can your heart endure, or can your hands remain strong, in the days when I shall deal with you? I, the LORD, have spoken, and will do *it*. ¹⁵I will scatter you among the nations, disperse you throughout the countries, and remove your filthiness completely from you. ¹⁶You shall defile yourself in the sight of the nations; then you shall know that I *am* the LORD." ' "

Israel in the Furnace

¹⁷The word of the LORD came to me, saying, ¹⁸"Son of man, the house of Israel has become dross to Me; they *are* all bronze, tin, iron, and lead, in the midst of a furnace; they have become dross from silver. ¹⁹Therefore thus says the Lord GOD: 'Because you have all become dross, therefore behold, I will gather you into the midst of Jerusalem. ²⁰*As men* gather silver, bronze, iron, lead, and tin into the midst of a furnace, to blow fire on it, to melt *it*; so I will gather *you* in My anger and in My fury, and I will leave *you* there and melt you. ²¹Yes, I will gather you and blow on you with the fire of My wrath, and you shall be melted in its midst. ²²As silver is melted in the midst of a furnace, so shall you be melted in its midst; then you shall know that I, the LORD, have poured out My fury on you.' "

Israel's Wicked Leaders

²³And the word of the LORD came to me, saying, ²⁴"Son of man, say to her: 'You *are* a land that is not cleansed[a] or rained on in the day of indignation.' ²⁵The conspiracy of her prophets[a] in her midst is like a roaring lion tearing the prey; they have devoured people; they have taken treasure and precious things; they have made many widows in her midst. ²⁶Her priests have violated My law and profaned My holy things; they have not distinguished between the holy and unholy, nor have they made known *the difference* between the unclean and the clean; and they have hidden their eyes from My Sabbaths, so that I am profaned among them. ²⁷Her princes in her midst *are* like wolves tearing the prey, to shed blood, to destroy people, and to get dishonest gain. ²⁸Her prophets plastered them with untempered *mortar*, seeing false visions, and divining lies for them, saying, 'Thus says the Lord GOD,' when the LORD had not spoken. ²⁹The people of the land have used oppressions, committed robbery, and mistreated the poor and needy; and they wrongfully oppress the stranger. ³⁰So I sought for a man among them who would make a wall, and stand in the gap before Me on behalf of the land, that I should not destroy it; but I found no one. ³¹Therefore I have poured out My indignation on them; I have consumed them with the fire of My wrath; and I have recompensed their

---

22:24 ᵃFollowing Masoretic Text, Syriac, and Vulgate; Septuagint reads *showered upon.*
22:25 ᵃFollowing Masoretic Text and Vulgate; Septuagint reads *princes;* Targum reads *scribes.*

deeds on their own heads," says the Lord GOD.

Two Harlot Sisters

23 The word of the LORD came again to me, saying:

2 "Son of man, there were two women,
    The daughters of one mother.
3   They committed harlotry in Egypt,
    They committed harlotry in their
        youth;
    Their breasts were there embraced,
    Their virgin bosom was there pressed.
4   Their names: Oholah[a] the elder and
        Oholibah[b] her sister;
    They were Mine,
    And they bore sons and daughters.
    As for their names,
    Samaria *is* Oholah, and Jerusalem *is*
        Oholibah.

The Older Sister, Samaria

5 "Oholah played the harlot even though
        she was Mine;
    And she lusted for her lovers, the
        neighboring Assyrians,
6   *Who were* clothed in purple,
    Captains and rulers,
    All of them desirable young men,
    Horsemen riding on horses.
7   Thus she committed her harlotry
        with them,

All of them choice men of Assyria;
    And with all for whom she lusted,
    With all their idols, she defiled
        herself.
8   She has never given up her harlotry
        brought from Egypt,
    For in her youth they had lain with
        her,
    Pressed her virgin bosom,
    And poured out their immorality
        upon her.

9 "Therefore I have delivered her
    Into the hand of her lovers,
    Into the hand of the Assyrians,
    For whom she lusted.
10 They uncovered her nakedness,
    Took away her sons and daughters,
    And slew her with the sword;
    She became a byword among women,
    For they had executed judgment on
        her.

The Younger Sister, Jerusalem

11"Now although her sister Oholibah saw *this*, she became more corrupt in her lust than she, and in her harlotry more corrupt than her sister's harlotry.

12 "She lusted for the neighboring
        Assyrians,
    Captains and rulers,
    Clothed most gorgeously,
    Horsemen riding on horses,
    All of them desirable young men.
13 Then I saw that she was defiled;
    Both *took* the same way.
14 But she increased her harlotry;
    She looked at men portrayed on the
        wall,
    Images of Chaldeans portrayed in
        vermilion,
15 Girded with belts around their
        waists,
    Flowing turbans on their heads,
    All of them looking like captains,

23:4 [a]Literally *Her Own Tabernacle*　[b]Literally *My Tabernacle Is in Her*

In the manner of the Babylonians of
    Chaldea,
The land of their nativity.

16 As soon as her eyes saw them,
    She lusted for them
And sent messengers to them in
    Chaldea.

17 "Then the Babylonians came to her,
    into the bed of love,
And they defiled her with their
    immorality;
So she was defiled by them, and
    alienated herself from them.

18 She revealed her harlotry and
    uncovered her nakedness.
Then I alienated Myself from her,
As I had alienated Myself from her
    sister.

19 "Yet she multiplied her harlotry
In calling to remembrance the days of
    her youth,
When she had played the harlot in the
    land of Egypt.

20 For she lusted for her paramours,
Whose flesh *is like* the flesh of
    donkeys,
And whose issue *is like* the issue of
    horses.

21 Thus you called to remembrance the
    lewdness of your youth,
When the Egyptians pressed your
    bosom
Because of your youthful breasts.

Judgment on Jerusalem

22 "Therefore, Oholibah, thus says the
Lord GOD:

'Behold, I will stir up your lovers
    against you,
From whom you have alienated
    yourself,
And I will bring them against you
    from every side:

23 The Babylonians,
All the Chaldeans,
Pekod, Shoa, Koa,
All the Assyrians with them,
All of them desirable young men,
Governors and rulers,
Captains and men of renown,
All of them riding on horses.

24 And they shall come against you
With chariots, wagons, and war-
    horses,
With a horde of people.
They shall array against you
Buckler, shield, and helmet all
    around.

'I will delegate judgment to them,
And they shall judge you according to
    their judgments.

25 I will set My jealousy against you,
And they shall deal furiously with
    you;
They shall remove your nose and
    your ears,
And your remnant shall fall by the
    sword;
They shall take your sons and your
    daughters,
And your remnant shall be devoured
    by fire.

23:25 remove your nose...your ears. Babylonians practiced facial dismemberment, an ancient punishment for an adulteress in Egypt, Chaldea, and elsewhere.

26 They shall also strip you of your
    clothes
And take away your beautiful jewelry.

27 'Thus I will make you cease your
    lewdness and your harlotry
Brought from the land of Egypt,
So that you will not lift your eyes to
    them,
Nor remember Egypt anymore.'

28 "For thus says the Lord GOD: 'Surely I will deliver you into the hand of those you hate, into the hand *of those* from whom you alienated yourself. 29 They will deal hatefully with you, take away all you have worked for, and leave you naked and bare. The nakedness of your harlotry shall be uncovered, both your lewdness and your harlotry. 30 I will do these *things* to you because you have gone as a harlot after the Gentiles, because you have become defiled by their idols. 31 You have walked in the way of your sister; therefore I will put her cup in your hand.'

32 "Thus says the Lord GOD:

'You shall drink of your sister's cup,
    The deep and wide one;
    You shall be laughed to scorn
    And held in derision;
    It contains much.
33   You will be filled with drunkenness
        and sorrow,
    The cup of horror and desolation,
    The cup of your sister Samaria.
34   You shall drink and drain it,
    You shall break its shards,
    And tear at your own breasts;
    For I have spoken,'
    Says the Lord GOD.

23:32–34 drink of your sister's cup. Judah was to experience the "cup" of God's judgment as Samaria had in 722 B.C. (see 23:46–49). Often the idea of "drinking a cup" symbolizes receiving God's wrath (see Ps. 75:8; Is. 51:17–22).

35"Therefore thus says the Lord GOD:

'Because you have forgotten Me and
    cast Me behind your back,
    Therefore you shall bear the *penalty*
    Of your lewdness and your harlotry.' "

Both Sisters Judged

36The LORD also said to me: "Son of man, will you judge Oholah and Oholibah? Then declare to them their abominations. 37For they have committed adultery, and blood *is* on their hands. They have committed adultery with their idols, and even sacrificed their sons whom they bore to Me, passing them through *the fire*, to devour *them*. 38Moreover they have done this to Me: They have defiled My sanctuary on the same day and profaned My Sabbaths. 39For after they had slain their children for their idols, on the same day they came into My sanctuary to profane it; and indeed thus they have done in the midst of My house.

40"Furthermore you sent for men to come from afar, to whom a messenger *was* sent; and there they came. And you washed yourself for them, painted your eyes, and adorned yourself with ornaments. 41You sat on a stately couch, with a table prepared before it, on which you had set My incense and My oil. 42The sound of a carefree multitude *was* with her, and Sabeans *were* brought from the wilderness with men of the common sort, who put bracelets on their wrists and beautiful crowns on their heads. 43Then I said concerning *her who had grown* old in adulteries, 'Will they commit harlotry with her now, and she *with them?*' 44Yet they went in to her, as men go in to a woman who plays the harlot; thus they went in to Oholah and Oholibah, the lewd women. 45But righteous men will judge them after the manner of adulteresses, and after the manner of women who shed blood, because they *are* adulteresses, and blood *is* on their hands.

46"For thus says the Lord GOD: 'Bring up an assembly against them, give them up to trouble and plunder. 47The assembly shall stone them with stones and execute them with their swords; they shall slay their sons and their daughters, and burn their houses with fire. 48Thus I will cause lewdness to cease from the land, that all women may be taught not to practice your lewdness. 49They shall repay you for your lewdness, and you shall pay for your idolatrous sins. Then you shall know that I *am* the Lord GOD.' "

Symbol of the Cooking Pot

24 Again, in the ninth year, in the tenth month, on the tenth *day* of the month, the word of the LORD came to me, saying, 2"Son of man, write down the name of the day, this very day—the king of Babylon started his siege against Jerusalem this very day. 3And utter a parable to the rebellious house, and say to them, 'Thus says the Lord GOD:

"Put on a pot, set *it* on,
    And also pour water into it.
4   Gather pieces *of meat* in it,
    Every good piece,
    The thigh and the shoulder.
    Fill *it* with choice cuts;
5   Take the choice of the flock.
    Also pile *fuel* bones under it,
    Make it boil well,
    And let the cuts simmer in it."

6'Therefore thus says the Lord GOD:

"Woe to the bloody city,
    To the pot whose scum *is* in it,
    And whose scum is not gone from it!

Bring it out piece by piece,
On which no lot has fallen.
⁷ For her blood is in her midst;
She set it on top of a rock;
She did not pour it on the ground,
To cover it with dust.

24:7 her blood. The city's blood, symbolizing sin, was exposed on top of a rock. When blood was not covered with dust, the law was violated (Lev. 17:13). God's vengeance would come by Babylon's army.

⁸ That it may raise up fury and take
     vengeance,
I have set her blood on top of a rock,
That it may not be covered."

⁹ʻTherefore thus says the Lord GOD:

"Woe to the bloody city!
I too will make the pyre great.
¹⁰ Heap on the wood,
Kindle the fire;
Cook the meat well,
Mix in the spices,
And let the cuts be burned up.

¹¹ "Then set the pot empty on the coals,
That it may become hot and its
     bronze may burn,
That its filthiness may be melted in it,
That its scum may be consumed.
¹² She has grown weary with lies,
And her great scum has not gone
     from her.
Let her scum *be* in the fire!
¹³ In your filthiness *is* lewdness.
Because I have cleansed you, and you
     were not cleansed,
You will not be cleansed of your
     filthiness anymore,
Till I have caused My fury to rest
     upon you.
¹⁴ I, the LORD, have spoken *it;*
It shall come to pass, and I will do *it;*
I will not hold back,
Nor will I spare,
Nor will I relent;
According to your ways
And according to your deeds
They[a] will judge you,"
Says the Lord GOD.' "

The Prophet's Wife Dies

¹⁵Also the word of the LORD came to me, saying, ¹⁶"Son of man, behold, I take away from you the desire of your eyes with one stroke; yet you shall neither mourn nor weep, nor shall your tears run down. ¹⁷Sigh in silence, make no mourning for the dead; bind your turban on your head, and put your sandals on your feet; do not cover *your* lips, and do not eat man's bread *of sorrow.*"

¹⁸So I spoke to the people in the morning, and at evening my wife died; and the next morning I did as I was commanded.

¹⁹And the people said to me, "Will you not tell us what these *things signify* to us, that you behave so?"

24:16–27 Ezekiel's wife died as a sign to Israel. Just as Ezekiel was not to mourn her death, so Israel was not to mourn the death of her families. Ezekiel was obedient to God, even though his wife had been precious to him. He became a heartbreaking sign to his people.

²⁰Then I answered them, "The word of the LORD came to me, saying, ²¹"Speak to the house of Israel, "Thus says the Lord GOD: 'Behold, I will profane My sanctuary, your arrogant boast, the desire of your eyes, the delight of your soul; and your sons and daughters whom you left behind shall fall by the sword. ²²And you shall do as I have done; you shall not cover *your* lips nor eat man's bread *of sorrow.* ²³Your turbans shall be on your heads and your sandals on your feet; you shall neither mourn nor weep, but you shall pine away in your iniquities and mourn with one another. ²⁴Thus Ezekiel is a sign to you; according to all that he has done you shall do; and when this comes, you shall know that I *am* the Lord GOD.' "

²⁵ʻAnd you, son of man—*will it* not *be* in the day when I take from them their stronghold, their joy and their glory, the desire of their eyes, and that on which they set their minds, their sons and their daughters: ²⁶on that day one who escapes will come to you to let *you* hear *it* with *your* ears; ²⁷on that day your mouth will be opened to him who has escaped; you shall speak and no longer be mute. Thus you will be a sign to them, and they shall know that I *am* the LORD.' "

24:14 ᵃSeptuagint, Syriac, Targum, and Vulgate read *I.*

Proclamation Against Ammon

25 The word of the LORD came to me, saying, ²"Son of man, set your face against the Ammonites, and prophesy against them. ³Say to the Ammonites, 'Hear the word of the Lord GOD! Thus says the Lord GOD: "Because you said, 'Aha!' against My sanctuary when it was profaned, and against the land of Israel when it was desolate, and against the house of Judah when they went into captivity, ⁴indeed, therefore, I will deliver you as a possession to the men of the East, and they shall set their encampments among you and make their dwellings among you; they shall eat your fruit, and they shall drink your milk. ⁵And I will make Rabbah a stable for camels and Ammon a resting place for flocks. Then you shall know that I *am* the LORD."

> **25:1 The word of the LORD came.** Ezekiel 25:1–32:32 proclaims judgment on seven other nations, four of which are singled out in this chapter for vindictive jealousy and hatred toward Israel. These nations assumed that when Israel was exiled, their God was also defeated. God shows impartiality to all sinners here and gives the prophet judgments to proclaim on Gentiles.

⁶'For thus says the Lord GOD: "Because you clapped *your* hands, stamped your feet, and rejoiced in heart with all your disdain for the land of Israel, ⁷indeed, therefore, I will stretch out My hand against you, and give you as plunder to the nations; I will cut you off from the peoples, and I will cause you to perish from the countries; I will destroy you, and you shall know that I *am* the LORD."

Proclamation Against Moab

⁸'Thus says the Lord GOD: "Because Moab and Seir say, 'Look! The house of Judah *is* like all the nations,' ⁹therefore, behold, I will clear the territory of Moab of cities, of the cities on its frontier, the glory of the country, Beth Jeshimoth, Baal Meon, and Kirjathaim. ¹⁰To the men of the East I will give it as a possession, together with the Ammonites, that the Ammonites may not be remembered among the nations. ¹¹And I will execute judgments upon Moab, and they shall know that I *am* the LORD."

Proclamation Against Edom

¹²'Thus says the Lord GOD: "Because of what Edom did against the house of Judah by taking vengeance, and has greatly offended by avenging itself on them," ¹³therefore thus says the Lord GOD: "I will also stretch out My hand against Edom, cut off man and beast from it, and make it desolate from Teman; Dedan shall fall by the sword. ¹⁴I will lay My vengeance on Edom by the hand of My people Israel, that they may do in Edom according to My anger and according to My fury; and they shall know My vengeance," says the Lord GOD.

> **25:8–11 Moab and Seir.** The origin of these people is given in Gen. 19:37,38. They lived S of the Arnon River along the lower region of the Dead Sea (see Is. 15,16). The Babylonians destroyed cities there in 582/81 B.C. They were judged because they gloated over Israel's fall and accused Israel of not having a privileged position before God. Both Ammonites and Moabites were absorbed into the Arabian peoples.

Proclamation Against Philistia

¹⁵'Thus says the Lord GOD: "Because the Philistines dealt vengefully and took vengeance with a spiteful heart, to destroy because of the old hatred," ¹⁶therefore thus says the Lord GOD: "I will stretch out My hand against the Philistines, and I will cut off the Cherethites and destroy the remnant of the seacoast. ¹⁷I will execute great vengeance on them with furious rebukes; and they shall know that I *am* the LORD, when I lay My vengeance upon them." ' "

> **25:15–17 the Philistines.** They were judged for their hatred and vengefulness against Israel, which dated as far back as Judg. 13–16. They constantly harassed and oppressed Israel until David broke their power during Saul's reign (1 Sam. 17). They repeatedly rose up and were subdued by Israel. Nebuchadnezzar invaded their land (Jer. 47).

Proclamation Against Tyre

26 And it came to pass in the eleventh year, on the first *day* of the month, *that* the word of the LORD came to me, saying, ²"Son of man, because Tyre has said against Jerusalem, 'Aha! She is broken who *was* the gateway of the peoples; now she is turned over to me; I shall be filled; she is laid waste.'

³"Therefore thus says the Lord GOD: 'Behold, I *am* against you, O Tyre, and will cause many nations to come up against you, as the sea causes its waves to come up. ⁴And they shall destroy the walls of Tyre and break down her towers; I will also scrape her dust from her, and make her like the top of a rock. ⁵It shall be *a place for* spreading nets in the midst of the sea, for I have spoken,' says the Lord GOD; 'it shall become plunder for the nations. ⁶Also her daughter *villages* which *are* in the fields shall be slain by the sword. Then they shall know that I am the LORD.'

> **26:3,4 I *am* against you, O Tyre.** This ancient Phoenician city had great influence during the reigns of David and Solomon. Later, Tyrians sold Jews into slavery (see Joel 3:4–8), for which God judged the city with waves of invaders. Babylon besieged Tyre from 585–573 B.C. Many Tyrians escaped to an island fortress. Alexander's Grecian army attacked in 332 B.C. They piled the rubble from the city into the sea to build a half-mile causeway to the island and attacked by land and by sea. The predictions in chapters 26–28 have been fulfilled with amazing literal accuracy.

⁷"For thus says the Lord GOD: 'Behold, I will bring against Tyre from the north Nebuchadnezzar*ᵃ* king of Babylon, king of kings, with horses, with chariots, and with horsemen, and an army with many people. ⁸He will slay with the sword your daughter *villages* in the fields; he will heap up a siege mound against you, build a wall against you, and raise a defense against you. ⁹He will direct his battering rams against your walls, and with his axes he will break down your towers. ¹⁰Because of the abundance of his horses, their dust will cover you; your walls will shake at the noise of the horsemen, the wagons, and the chariots, when he enters your gates, as men enter a city that has been breached. ¹¹With the hooves of his horses he will trample all your streets; he will slay your people by the sword, and your strong pillars will fall to the ground. ¹²They will plunder your riches and pillage your merchandise; they will break down your walls and destroy your pleasant houses; they will lay your stones, your timber, and your soil in the midst of the water. ¹³I will put an end to the sound of

your songs, and the sound of your harps shall be heard no more. ¹⁴I will make you like the top of a rock; you shall be *a place for* spreading nets, and you shall never be rebuilt, for I the LORD have spoken,' says the Lord GOD.

> **26:7–14** Verses 8–14 describe the siege and devastation by Babylon's King Nebuchadnezzar. He was called "king of kings" (v. 7) because he had many rulers subject to him. God had given him universal rule (see Dan. 2:37).

¹⁵"Thus says the Lord GOD to Tyre: 'Will the coastlands not shake at the sound of your fall, when the wounded cry, when slaughter is made in the midst of you? ¹⁶Then all the princes of the sea will come down from their thrones, lay aside their robes, and take off their embroidered garments; they will clothe themselves with trembling; they will sit on the ground, tremble *every* moment, and be astonished at you. ¹⁷And they will take up a lamentation for you, and say to you:

> "How you have perished,
>   O one inhabited by seafaring men,
>   O renowned city,
> Who was strong at sea,
> She and her inhabitants,
> Who caused their terror *to be* on all
>   her inhabitants!
¹⁸ Now the coastlands tremble on the
>   day of your fall;
> Yes, the coastlands by the sea are
>   troubled at your departure." '

> **26:15–18** A center of commerce could not be destroyed without affecting the nearby nations. The nations around the Mediterranean would consider Tyre's fall a calamity. Rulers would descend from their thrones and disrobe, as was the custom of mourning.

¹⁹"For thus says the Lord GOD: 'When I make you a desolate city, like cities that are not inhabited, when I bring the deep upon you, and great waters cover you, ²⁰then I will bring you down with those who descend into the Pit, to the people of old, and I will make you dwell in the lowest part of

---

26:7 *ᵃ*Hebrew *Nebuchadrezzar,* and so elsewhere in this book

the earth, in places desolate from antiquity, with those who go down to the Pit, so that you may never be inhabited; and I shall establish glory in the land of the living. ²¹I will make you a terror, and you *shall be* no *more;* though you are sought for, you will never be found again,' says the Lord GOD."

Lamentation for Tyre

27 The word of the LORD came again to me, saying, ²"Now, son of man, take up a lamentation for Tyre, ³and say to Tyre, 'You who are situated at the entrance of the sea, merchant of the peoples on many coastlands, thus says the Lord GOD:

> "O Tyre, you have said,
> 'I *am* perfect in beauty.'
>
> ⁴ Your borders *are* in the midst of the seas.
>   Your builders have perfected your beauty.
> ⁵ They made all *your* planks of fir trees from Senir;
>   They took a cedar from Lebanon to make you a mast.
> ⁶ *Of* oaks from Bashan they made your oars;
>   The company of Ashurites have inlaid your planks
>   *With* ivory from the coasts of Cyprus.^a
> ⁷ Fine embroidered linen from Egypt was what you spread for your sail;
>   Blue and purple from the coasts of Elishah was what covered you.
>
> ⁸ "Inhabitants of Sidon and Arvad were your oarsmen;
>   Your wise men, O Tyre, were in you;
>   They became your pilots.
> ⁹ Elders of Gebal and its wise men Were in you to caulk your seams;
>   All the ships of the sea And their oarsmen were in you To market your merchandise.
>
> ¹⁰ "Those from Persia, Lydia,^a and Libya^b Were in your army as men of war;
>   They hung shield and helmet in you;
>   They gave splendor to you.
> ¹¹ Men of Arvad with your army *were* on your walls *all* around,

And the men of Gammad were in your towers;
They hung their shields on your walls *all* around;
They made your beauty perfect.

> **27:1–11 a lamentation for Tyre.** This chapter is a lamentation, describing Tyre as a great trade ship destroyed on the high seas. The proper names indicate the participants in commerce with Tyre.

¹²"Tarshish *was* your merchant because of your many luxury goods. They gave you silver, iron, tin, and lead for your goods. ¹³Javan, Tubal, and Meshech *were* your traders. They bartered human lives and vessels of bronze for your merchandise. ¹⁴Those from the house of Togarmah traded for your wares with horses, steeds, and mules. ¹⁵The men of Dedan *were* your traders; many isles *were* the market of your hand. They brought you ivory tusks and ebony as payment. ¹⁶Syria *was* your merchant because of the abundance of goods you made. They gave you for your wares emeralds, purple, embroidery, fine linen, corals, and rubies. ¹⁷Judah and the land of Israel *were* your traders. They traded for your merchandise wheat of Minnith, millet, honey, oil, and balm. ¹⁸Damascus *was* your merchant because of the abundance of goods you made, because of your many luxury items, with the wine of Helbon and with white wool. ¹⁹Dan and Javan paid for your wares, traversing back and forth. Wrought iron, cassia, and cane were among your merchandise. ²⁰Dedan *was* your merchant in saddlecloths for riding. ²¹Arabia and all the princes of Kedar *were* your regular merchants. They traded with you in lambs, rams, and goats. ²²The merchants of Sheba and Raamah *were* your merchants. They traded for your wares the choicest spices, all kinds of precious stones, and gold. ²³Haran, Canneh, Eden, the merchants of Sheba, Assyria, *and* Chilmad *were* your merchants. ²⁴These *were* your merchants in choice items—in purple clothes, in embroidered garments, in chests of multicolored apparel, in sturdy woven cords, which were in your marketplace.

27:6 ^aHebrew *Kittim,* western lands, especially Cyprus   27:10 ^aHebrew *Lud*   ^bHebrew *Put*

25 " The ships of Tarshish were carriers of
     your merchandise.
     You were filled and very glorious in
       the midst of the seas.
26   Your oarsmen brought you into many
       waters,
     But the east wind broke you in the
       midst of the seas.

27 " Your riches, wares, and merchandise,
     Your mariners and pilots,
     Your caulkers and merchandisers,
     All your men of war who *are* in you,
     And the entire company which *is* in
       your midst,
     Will fall into the midst of the seas on
       the day of your ruin.
28   The common-land will shake at the
       sound of the cry of your pilots.

29 " All who handle the oar,
     The mariners,
     All the pilots of the sea
     Will come down from their ships *and*
       stand on the shore.
30   They will make their voice heard
       because of you;
     They will cry bitterly and cast dust on
       their heads;
     They will roll about in ashes;
31   They will shave themselves
       completely bald because of you,
     Gird themselves with sackcloth,
     And weep for you
     With bitterness of heart *and* bitter
       wailing.
32   In their wailing for you
     They will take up a lamentation,
     And lament for you:
     'What *city is* like Tyre,
     Destroyed in the midst of the sea?

33   'When your wares went out by sea,
     You satisfied many people;
     You enriched the kings of the earth
     With your many luxury goods and
       your merchandise.
34   But you are broken by the seas in the
       depths of the waters;
     Your merchandise and the entire
       company will fall in your midst.
35   All the inhabitants of the isles will be
       astonished at you;
     Their kings will be greatly afraid,

     And *their* countenance will be
       troubled.
36   The merchants among the peoples
       will hiss at you;
     You will become a horror, and *be* no
       more forever.' " ' "

Proclamation Against the King of Tyre

28 The word of the LORD came to me
again, saying, ² "Son of man, say to
the prince of Tyre, 'Thus says the Lord
GOD:

" Because your heart *is* lifted up,
     And you say, 'I *am* a god,
     I sit *in* the seat of gods,
     In the midst of the seas,'
     Yet you *are* a man, and not a god,
     Though you set your heart as the
       heart of a god,

28:2 I am a god. Many ancient kings claimed to be
gods and acted as if they were. When this king
claimed to be a god, he displayed the same proud
attitude as the serpent who promised Adam and Eve
they could be like God (Gen. 3:5).

3   (Behold, you *are* wiser than Daniel!
     There is no secret that can be hidden
       from you!
4   With your wisdom and your
       understanding
     You have gained riches for yourself,
     And gathered gold and silver into your
       treasuries;
5   By your great wisdom in trade you
       have increased your riches,
     And your heart is lifted up because of
       your riches),"

⁶ 'Therefore thus says the Lord GOD:

" Because you have set your heart as
       the heart of a god,
7   Behold, therefore, I will bring
       strangers against you,
     The most terrible of the nations;
     And they shall draw their swords
       against the beauty of your
       wisdom,
     And defile your splendor.
8   They shall throw you down into the
       Pit,

And you shall die the death of the
    slain
In the midst of the seas.

9 "Will you still say before him who
    slays you,
  'I *am* a god'?
But you *shall be* a man, and not a god,
In the hand of him who slays you.
10 You shall die the death of the
    uncircumcised
By the hand of aliens;
For I have spoken," says the Lord
    GOD.' "

Lamentation for the King of Tyre

11Moreover the word of the LORD came to
me, saying, 12"Son of man, take up a lamentation for the king of Tyre, and say to him,
'Thus says the Lord GOD:

> **28:12 the seal of perfection.** The Lord led Ezekiel to
> address the king as the one to be judged, though the
> power behind him was Satan. This phrase describes
> Satan as perfect in angelic beauty before he rebelled
> against God. It can also be used to describe Tyre's
> high status of trade in the ancient world. **Full of wis-
> dom.** This referred to Satan's wisdom as an angel and
> Tyre's skill in trade (see 27:8,9).

  "You *were* the seal of perfection,
  Full of wisdom and perfect in beauty.
13 You were in Eden, the garden of God;
  Every precious stone *was* your
    covering:
  The sardius, topaz, and diamond,
  Beryl, onyx, and jasper,
  Sapphire, turquoise, and emerald with
    gold.
  The workmanship of your timbrels
    and pipes
  Was prepared for you on the day you
    were created.

14 "You *were* the anointed cherub who
    covers;
  I established you;
  You were on the holy mountain of
    God;
  You walked back and forth in the
    midst of fiery stones.
15 You *were* perfect in your ways from
    the day you were created,
  Till iniquity was found in you.

16 "By the abundance of your trading
  You became filled with violence
    within,
  And you sinned;
  Therefore I cast you as a profane
    thing
  Out of the mountain of God;
  And I destroyed you, O covering
    cherub,
  From the midst of the fiery stones.

17 "Your heart was lifted up because of
    your beauty;
  You corrupted your wisdom for the
    sake of your splendor;
  I cast you to the ground,
  I laid you before kings,
  That they might gaze at you.

18 "You defiled your sanctuaries
  By the multitude of your iniquities,
  By the iniquity of your trading;
  Therefore I brought fire from your
    midst;
  It devoured you,
  And I turned you to ashes upon the
    earth
  In the sight of all who saw you.
19 All who knew you among the peoples
    are astonished at you;
  You have become a horror,
  And *shall be* no more forever." ' "

Proclamation Against Sidon

20Then the word of the LORD came to me,
saying, 21"Son of man, set your face toward
Sidon, and prophesy against her, 22and say,
'Thus says the Lord GOD:

  "Behold, I *am* against you, O Sidon;
  I will be glorified in your midst;
  And they shall know that I *am* the
    LORD,
  When I execute judgments in her and
    am hallowed in her.

> **28:21 Sidon.** This seaport is 23 miles north of Tyre
> in Phoenicia. The corrupting influence of this place
> began in the time of the judges (Judg. 10:6). It was the
> headquarters for Baal worship.

23 For I will send pestilence upon her,
  And blood in her streets;

The wounded shall be judged in her
    midst
By the sword against her on every
    side;
Then they shall know that I *am* the
    LORD.

24"And there shall no longer be a pricking brier or a painful thorn for the house of Israel from among all *who are* around them, who despise them. Then they shall know that I *am* the Lord GOD."

Israel's Future Blessing

25'Thus says the Lord GOD: "When I have gathered the house of Israel from the peoples among whom they are scattered, and am hallowed in them in the sight of the Gentiles, then they will dwell in their own land which I gave to My servant Jacob. 26And they will dwell safely there, build houses, and plant vineyards; yes, they will dwell securely, when I execute judgments on all those around them who despise them. Then they shall know that I *am* the LORD their God." ' "

Proclamation Against Egypt

29 In the tenth year, in the tenth *month*, on the twelfth *day* of the month, the word of the LORD came to me, saying, 2"Son of man, set your face against Pharaoh king of Egypt, and prophesy against him, and against all Egypt. 3Speak, and say, 'Thus says the Lord GOD:

"Behold, I *am* against you,
    O Pharaoh king of Egypt,
O great monster who lies in the midst
    of his rivers,
Who has said, 'My River*ᵃ* *is* my own;
    I have made *it* for myself.'
4   But I will put hooks in your jaws,

> **29:3 great monster.** As crocodiles were worshiped by the Egyptians and lived in their rivers, this was most likely the monster used to describe the king. "Rahab" is a general term used for a monster, which often symbolized Egypt.

And cause the fish of your rivers to
    stick to your scales;
I will bring you up out of the midst of
    your rivers,
And all the fish in your rivers will
    stick to your scales.
5 I will leave you in the wilderness,
    You and all the fish of your rivers;
You shall fall on the open field;
You shall not be picked up or
    gathered.*ᵃ*
I have given you as food
To the beasts of the field
And to the birds of the heavens.

6 "Then all the inhabitants of Egypt
    Shall know that I *am* the LORD,
Because they have been a staff of reed
    to the house of Israel.
7 When they took hold of you with the
    hand,
You broke and tore all their
    shoulders;*ᵃ*
When they leaned on you,
You broke and made all their backs
    quiver."

8'Therefore thus says the Lord GOD: "Surely I will bring a sword upon you and cut off from you man and beast. 9And the land of Egypt shall become desolate and waste; then they will know that I *am* the LORD, because he said, 'The River *is* mine, and I have made *it*.' 10Indeed, therefore, I *am* against you and against your rivers, and I will make the land of Egypt utterly waste and desolate, from Migdol*ᵃ to* Syene, as far as the border of Ethiopia. 11Neither foot of man shall pass through it nor foot of beast pass through it, and it shall be uninhabited forty years. 12I will make the land of Egypt desolate in the midst of the countries *that are* desolate; and among the cities *that are* laid waste, her cities shall be desolate forty years; and I will scatter the Egyptians among the nations and disperse them throughout the countries."

13'Yet, thus says the Lord GOD: "At the end of forty years I will gather the Egyptians from the peoples among whom they were

---

29:3 *ᵃ*That is, the Nile   29:5 *ᵃ*Following Masoretic Text, Septuagint, and Vulgate; some Hebrew manuscripts and Targum read *buried.*   29:7 *ᵃ*Following Masoretic Text and Vulgate; Septuagint and Syriac read *hand.*   29:10 *ᵃ*Or *tower*

scattered. ¹⁴I will bring back the captives of Egypt and cause them to return to the land of Pathros, to the land of their origin, and there they shall be a lowly kingdom. ¹⁵It shall be the lowliest of kingdoms; it shall never again exalt itself above the nations, for I will diminish them so that they will not rule over the nations anymore. ¹⁶No longer shall it be the confidence of the house of Israel, but will remind them of *their* iniquity when they turned to follow them. Then they shall know that I *am* the Lord GOD.' "

Babylonia Will Plunder Egypt

¹⁷And it came to pass in the twenty-seventh year, in the first *month*, on the first *day* of the month, *that* the word of the LORD came to me, saying, ¹⁸"Son of man, Nebuchadnezzar king of Babylon caused his army to labor strenuously against Tyre; every head *was* made bald, and every shoulder rubbed raw; yet neither he nor his army received wages from Tyre, for the labor which they expended on it. ¹⁹Therefore thus says the Lord GOD: 'Surely I will give the land of Egypt to Nebuchadnezzar king of Babylon; he shall take away her wealth, carry off her spoil, and remove her pillage; and that will be the wages for his army. ²⁰I have given him the land of Egypt *for* his labor, because they worked for Me,' says the Lord GOD.

> **29:18 labor...against Tyre.** Nebuchadnezzar besieged Tyre (about 585–573 B.C.) for 13 years before subduing the city (see Ezek. 26:1–28:19). Tyrians retreated to an island fortress in the sea and survived, not giving Babylon full satisfaction in spoils ("wages") equal to the many years of attacking the city.

²¹In that day I will cause the horn of the house of Israel to spring forth, and I will open your mouth to speak in their midst. Then they shall know that I *am* the LORD.' "

Egypt and Her Allies Will Fall

30 The word of the LORD came to me again, saying, ²"Son of man, prophesy and say, 'Thus says the Lord GOD:

> **29:21 I will cause the horn...to spring forth.** An animal's horn symbolized power (see 1 Sam. 2:1). God restored Israel's power and authority. Other nations subdued her later, but she will be blessed in messianic times. **I will open your mouth.** Ezekiel's muteness had ceased in 586/85 B.C. when Jerusalem fell (see 33:21,22). This probably refers to the day when his writings would be understood because of their fulfillment.

"Wail, 'Woe to the day!'

³For the day *is* near,
Even the day of the LORD *is* near;
It will be a day of clouds, the time of the Gentiles.

⁴The sword shall come upon Egypt,
And great anguish shall be in Ethiopia,
When the slain fall in Egypt,
And they take away her wealth,
And her foundations are broken down.

⁵"Ethiopia, Libya,^a Lydia,^b all the mingled people, Chub, and the men of the lands who are allied, shall fall with them by the sword."

⁶Thus says the LORD:

"Those who uphold Egypt shall fall,
And the pride of her power shall come down.
From Migdol *to* Syene
Those within her shall fall by the sword,"
Says the Lord GOD.

⁷"They shall be desolate in the midst of the desolate countries,
And her cities shall be in the midst of the cities *that are* laid waste.

⁸Then they will know that I *am* the LORD,
When I have set a fire in Egypt
And all her helpers are destroyed.

⁹On that day messengers shall go forth from Me in ships
To make the careless Ethiopians afraid,
And great anguish shall come upon them,
As on the day of Egypt;
For indeed it is coming!"

10'Thus says the Lord GOD:

"I will also make a multitude of Egypt
    to cease
By the hand of Nebuchadnezzar king
    of Babylon.
11   He and his people with him, the most
        terrible of the nations,
    Shall be brought to destroy the
        land;
    They shall draw their swords against
        Egypt,
    And fill the land with the slain.
12   I will make the rivers dry,
    And sell the land into the hand of the
        wicked;
    I will make the land waste, and all
        that is in it,
    By the hand of aliens.
    I, the LORD, have spoken."

13'Thus says the Lord GOD:

"I will also destroy the idols,
    And cause the images to cease from
        Noph;*a*
    There shall no longer be princes from
        the land of Egypt;
    I will put fear in the land of Egypt.
14   I will make Pathros desolate,
    Set fire to Zoan,
    And execute judgments in No.*a*
15   I will pour My fury on Sin,*a* the
        strength of Egypt;
    I will cut off the multitude of No,
16   And set a fire in Egypt;
    Sin shall have great pain,
    No shall be split open,
    And Noph *shall be in* distress daily.
17   The young men of Aven*a* and Pi
        Beseth shall fall by the sword,
    And these *cities* shall go into
        captivity.
18   At Tehaphnehes*a* the day shall also be
        darkened,*b*
    When I break the yokes of Egypt
        there.
    And her arrogant strength shall cease
        in her;

As for her, a cloud shall cover her,
And her daughters shall go into
    captivity.
19   Thus I will execute judgments on
        Egypt,
    Then they shall know that I *am* the
        LORD.' ' "

Proclamation Against Pharaoh

20And it came to pass in the eleventh
year, in the first *month*, on the seventh *day*
of the month, *that* the word of the LORD
came to me, saying, 21"Son of man, I have
broken the arm of Pharaoh king of Egypt;
and see, it has not been bandaged for healing, nor a splint put on to bind it, to make it
strong enough to hold a sword. 22Therefore
thus says the Lord GOD: 'Surely I *am*
against Pharaoh king of Egypt, and will
break his arms, both the strong one and the
one that was broken; and I will make the
sword fall out of his hand. 23I will scatter
the Egyptians among the nations, and disperse them throughout the countries. 24I
will strengthen the arms of the king of Babylon and put My sword in his hand; but I
will break Pharaoh's arms, and he will
groan before him with the groanings of a
mortally wounded *man*. 25Thus I will
strengthen the arms of the king of Babylon,
but the arms of Pharaoh shall fall down;
they shall know that I *am* the LORD, when I
put My sword into the hand of the king of
Babylon and he stretches it out against the
land of Egypt. 26I will scatter the Egyptians
among the nations and disperse them
throughout the countries. Then they shall
know that I *am* the LORD.' "

30:21 I have broken the arm. This describes God's
act of taking power from Egypt through Nebuchadnezzar, resulting in defeat and dispersion (vv. 23,26).

Egypt Cut Down Like a Great Tree

31 Now it came to pass in the eleventh year, in the third *month*, on the
first *day* of the month, *that* the word of the
LORD came to me, saying, 2"Son of man,

30:13 *a*That is, ancient Memphis   30:14 *a*That is, ancient Thebes   30:15 *a*That is, ancient Pelusium
30:17 *a*That is, ancient On (Heliopolis)   30:18 *a*Spelled *Tahpanhes* in Jeremiah 43:7 and elsewhere
*b*Following many Hebrew manuscripts, Bomberg, Septuagint, Syriac, Targum, and Vulgate; Masoretic
Text reads *refrained*.

say to Pharaoh king of Egypt and to his multitude:

'Whom are you like in your greatness?
3   Indeed Assyria *was* a cedar in Lebanon,
     With fine branches that shaded the forest,
     And of high stature;
     And its top was among the thick boughs.
4   The waters made it grow;
     Underground waters gave it height,
     With their rivers running around the place where it was planted,
     And sent out rivulets to all the trees of the field.

5   'Therefore its height was exalted above all the trees of the field;
     Its boughs were multiplied,
     And its branches became long because of the abundance of water,
     As it sent them out.
6   All the birds of the heavens made their nests in its boughs;
     Under its branches all the beasts of the field brought forth their young;
     And in its shadow all great nations made their home.

7   'Thus it was beautiful in greatness and in the length of its branches,
     Because its roots reached to abundant waters.
8   The cedars in the garden of God could not hide it;
     The fir trees were not like its boughs,
     And the chestnut*a* trees were not like its branches;
     No tree in the garden of God was like it in beauty.
9   I made it beautiful with a multitude of branches,
     So that all the trees of Eden envied it,
     That *were* in the garden of God.'

31:8,9 garden of God...trees of Eden. Since Assyria was in the area of the Garden of Eden (Gen. 13:10), Ezekiel used the ultimate of gardens as a reference by which to describe tree-like Assyria.

10"Therefore thus says the Lord GOD: 'Because you have increased in height, and it set its top among the thick boughs, and its heart was lifted up in its height, 11therefore I will deliver it into the hand of the mighty one of the nations, and he shall surely deal with it; I have driven it out for its wickedness. 12And aliens, the most terrible of the nations, have cut it down and left it; its branches have fallen on the mountains and in all the valleys; its boughs lie broken by all the rivers of the land; and all the peoples of the earth have gone from under its shadow and left it.

13   'On its ruin will remain all the birds of the heavens,
      And all the beasts of the field will come to its branches—

14"So that no trees by the waters may ever again exalt themselves for their height, nor set their tops among the thick boughs, that no tree which drinks water may ever be high enough to reach up to them.

'For they have all been delivered to death,
To the depths of the earth,
Among the children of men who go down to the Pit.'

15"Thus says the Lord GOD: 'In the day when it went down to hell, I caused mourning. I covered the deep because of it. I restrained its rivers, and the great waters were held back. I caused Lebanon to mourn for it, and all the trees of the field wilted because of it. 16I made the nations shake at the sound of its fall, when I cast it down to hell together with those who descend into the Pit; and all the trees of Eden, the choice and best of Lebanon, all that drink water, were comforted in the depths of the earth. 17They also went down to hell with it, with those *slain* by the sword; and *those who were* its *strong* arm dwelt in its shadows among the nations.

18'To which of the trees in Eden will you then be likened in glory and greatness? Yet you shall be brought down with the trees of Eden to the depths of the earth; you shall

---

31:8 *a*Hebrew *armon*

lie in the midst of the uncircumcised, with *those* slain by the sword. This *is* Pharaoh and all his multitude,' says the Lord GOD."

31:2–18 Whom are you like...? Egypt is compared to a huge tree that dominates a forest and to a king/nation that dominates the world (see Dan. 4:1–12). Just as a strong tree like Assyria fell (about 609 B.C.), so will Egypt (about 568 B.C.). If the Egyptians feel proud and invincible, let them remember how the powerful Assyria had fallen.

Lamentation for Pharaoh and Egypt

32 And it came to pass in the twelfth year, in the twelfth *month*, on the first *day* of the month, *that* the word of the LORD came to me, saying, ²"Son of man, take up a lamentation for Pharaoh king of Egypt, and say to him:

'You are like a young lion among the
    nations,
And you *are* like a monster in the
    seas,
Bursting forth in your rivers,
Troubling the waters with your feet,
And fouling their rivers.'

³"Thus says the Lord GOD:

'I will therefore spread My net over you
    with a company of many people,
And they will draw you up in My net.
⁴ Then I will leave you on the land;
    I will cast you out on the open fields,
    And cause to settle on you all the
      birds of the heavens.
    And with you I will fill the beasts of
      the whole earth.
⁵ I will lay your flesh on the
    mountains,
    And fill the valleys with your carcass.
⁶ 'I will also water the land with the
    flow of your blood,
    Even to the mountains;
    And the riverbeds will be full of you.
⁷ When *I* put out your light,
    I will cover the heavens, and make its
      stars dark;
    I will cover the sun with a cloud,
    And the moon shall not give her light.
⁸ All the bright lights of the heavens I
    will make dark over you,

And bring darkness upon your land,'
Says the Lord GOD.

32:7,8 light. This most likely refers to Pharaoh, whose life and power are extinguished, and his leaders and people who are plunged into darkness.

⁹'I will also trouble the hearts of many peoples, when I bring your destruction among the nations, into the countries which you have not known. ¹⁰Yes, I will make many peoples astonished at you, and their kings shall be horribly afraid of you when I brandish My sword before them; and they shall tremble *every* moment, every man for his own life, in the day of your fall.'

¹¹"For thus says the Lord GOD: 'The sword of the king of Babylon shall come upon you. ¹²By the swords of the mighty warriors, all of them the most terrible of the nations, I will cause your multitude to fall.

'They shall plunder the pomp of
    Egypt,
    And all its multitude shall be
      destroyed.
¹³ Also I will destroy all its animals
    From beside its great waters;
    The foot of man shall muddy them
      no more,
    Nor shall the hooves of animals
      muddy them.
¹⁴ Then I will make their waters clear,
    And make their rivers run like oil,'
    Says the Lord GOD.
¹⁵ 'When I make the land of Egypt
    desolate,
    And the country is destitute of all
      that once filled it,
    When I strike all who dwell in it,
    Then they shall know that I *am* the
      LORD.

¹⁶ 'This *is* the lamentation
    With which they shall lament her;
    The daughters of the nations shall
      lament her;
    They shall lament for her, for Egypt,
    And for all her multitude,'
    Says the Lord GOD."

Egypt and Others Consigned to the Pit

¹⁷It came to pass also in the twelfth year, on the fifteenth *day* of the month, *that* the word of the LORD came to me, saying:

¹⁸ "Son of man, wail over the multitude
     of Egypt,
And cast them down to the depths of
     the earth,
Her and the daughters of the famous
     nations,
With those who go down to the Pit:
¹⁹ 'Whom do you surpass in beauty?
Go down, be placed with the
     uncircumcised.'

²⁰ "They shall fall in the midst of *those*
     slain by the sword;
She is delivered to the sword,
Drawing her and all her multitudes.
²¹ The strong among the mighty
Shall speak to him out of the midst of
     hell
With those who help him:
'They have gone down,
They lie with the uncircumcised,
     slain by the sword.'

²² "Assyria *is* there, and all her company,
With their graves all around her,
All of them slain, fallen by the sword.

32:22 Assyria *is* there. The slain of Assyria, Elam, Meshech, Tubal, and Edom are pictured in the afterlife. Although mighty for a time on earth, the fallen, defeated people become equals in death, all conquered by God and condemned to hell.

---

²³   Her graves are set in the recesses of
     the Pit,
And her company is all around her
     grave,
All of them slain, fallen by the sword,
Who caused terror in the land of the
     living.

²⁴ "There *is* Elam and all her multitude,
All around her grave,
All of them slain, fallen by the sword,
Who have gone down uncircumcised
     to the lower parts of the earth,
Who caused their terror in the land of
     the living;

Now they bear their shame with those
     who go down to the Pit.
²⁵ They have set her bed in the midst of
     the slain,
With all her multitude,
With her graves all around it,
All of them uncircumcised, slain by
     the sword;
Though their terror was caused
In the land of the living,
Yet they bear their shame
With those who go down to the Pit;
It was put in the midst of the slain.

²⁶ "There *are* Meshech and Tubal and all
     their multitudes,
With all their graves around it,
All of them uncircumcised, slain by
     the sword,
Though they caused their terror in
     the land of the living.
²⁷ They do not lie with the mighty
Who are fallen of the uncircumcised,
Who have gone down to hell with
     their weapons of war;
They have laid their swords under
     their heads,
But their iniquities will be on their
     bones,
Because of the terror of the mighty in
     the land of the living.
²⁸ Yes, you shall be broken in the midst
     of the uncircumcised,
And lie with *those* slain by the
     sword.

²⁹ "There *is* Edom,
Her kings and all her princes,
Who despite their might
Are laid beside *those* slain by the
     sword;
They shall lie with the
     uncircumcised,
And with those who go down to the
     Pit.
³⁰ There *are* the princes of the north,
All of them, and all the Sidonians,
Who have gone down with the slain
In shame at the terror which they
     caused by their might;
They lie uncircumcised with *those*
     slain by the sword,
And bear their shame with those who
     go down to the Pit.

31 "Pharaoh will see them
   And be comforted over all his
      multitude,
   Pharaoh and all his army,
   Slain by the sword,"
   Says the Lord GOD.

32 "For I have caused My terror in the
      land of the living;
   And he shall be placed in the midst of
      the uncircumcised
   With *those* slain by the sword,
   Pharaoh and all his multitude,"
   Says the Lord GOD.

33:1–33 Again the word...came. This chapter is a transition between God's judgments against Jerusalem and the nations and Israel's bright future when she is restored to her land. It provides God's instructions for national repentance and prefaces the prophecies of comfort and salvation that follow (chapters 34–39).

The Watchman and His Message

33 Again the word of the LORD came to me, saying, 2"Son of man, speak to the children of your people, and say to them: 'When I bring the sword upon a land, and the people of the land take a man from their territory and make him their watchman, 3when he sees the sword coming upon the land, if he blows the trumpet and warns the people, 4then whoever hears the sound of the trumpet and does not take warning, if the sword comes and takes him away, his blood shall be on his *own* head. 5He heard the sound of the trumpet, but did not take warning; his blood shall be upon himself. But he who takes warning will save his life. 6But if the watchman sees the sword coming and does not blow the trumpet, and the people are not warned, and the sword comes and takes *any* person from among them, he is taken away in his iniquity; but his blood I will require at the watchman's hand.'

33:2–9 watchman. Jeremiah and Ezekiel were spiritual watchmen; they warned the people that God would bring a sword upon them, giving them the opportunity to prepare and be safe. This analogy draws from the custom of stationing guards on the city wall to watch for danger and sound the trumpet warning.

7"So you, son of man: I have made you a watchman for the house of Israel; therefore you shall hear a word from My mouth and warn them for Me. 8When I say to the wicked, 'O wicked *man*, you shall surely die!' and you do not speak to warn the wicked from his way, that wicked *man* shall die in his iniquity; but his blood I will require at your hand. 9Nevertheless if you warn the wicked to turn from his way, and he does not turn from his way, he shall die in his iniquity; but you have delivered your soul.

33:8,9 his blood I will require. A prophet who sounded the warning of repentance for sin was not to be judged. The unfaithful one who failed to deliver the message was held accountable and chastened by God.

10"Therefore you, O son of man, say to the house of Israel: 'Thus you say, "If our transgressions and our sins *lie* upon us, and we pine away in them, how can we then live?" ' 11Say to them: 'As I live,' says the Lord GOD, 'I have no pleasure in the death of the wicked, but that the wicked turn from his way and live. Turn, turn from your evil ways! For why should you die, O house of Israel?'

The Fairness of God's Judgment

12"Therefore you, O son of man, say to the children of your people: 'The righteousness of the righteous man shall not deliver him in the day of his transgression; as for the wickedness of the wicked, he shall not fall because of it in the day that he turns from his wickedness; nor shall the righteous be able to live because of *his* righteousness in the day that he sins.' 13When I say to the righteous *that* he shall surely live, but he trusts in his own righteousness and commits iniquity, none of his righteous works shall be remembered; but because of the iniquity that he has committed, he shall die. 14Again, when I say to the wicked, 'You shall surely die,' if he turns from his sin and does what is lawful and right, 15if the wicked restores the pledge, gives back what he has stolen, and walks in the statutes of life without committing iniquity, he shall surely live; he shall not die. 16None of his sins which he has committed shall be remem-

bered against him; he has done what is lawful and right; he shall surely live.

[17]"Yet the children of your people say, 'The way of the LORD is not fair.' But it is their way which is not fair! [18]When the righteous turns from his righteousness and commits iniquity, he shall die because of it. [19]But when the wicked turns from his wickedness and does what is lawful and right, he shall live because of it. [20]Yet you say, 'The way of the LORD is not fair.' O house of Israel, I will judge every one of you according to his own ways."

33:2–20 speak to...your people. Ezekiel was to prepare the exiles' minds to look on the awful calamity in Jerusalem as a just act by God. The people did not heed the warning. Ezekiel had been forbidden to speak to his people (24:26,27) until Jerusalem was captured. Meanwhile, he had spoken to the foreign nations (chapters 25–32).

The Fall of Jerusalem

[21]And it came to pass in the twelfth year of our captivity, in the tenth *month*, on the fifth *day* of the month, *that* one who had escaped from Jerusalem came to me and said, "The city has been captured!"

[22]Now the hand of the LORD had been upon me the evening before the man came who had escaped. And He had opened my mouth; so when he came to me in the morning, my mouth was opened, and I was no longer mute.

The Cause of Judah's Ruin

[23]Then the word of the LORD came to me, saying: [24]"Son of man, they who inhabit those ruins in the land of Israel are saying, 'Abraham was only one, and he inherited the land. But we *are* many; the land has been given to us as a possession.'

[25]"Therefore say to them, 'Thus says the Lord GOD: "You eat *meat* with blood, you lift up your eyes toward your idols, and shed blood. Should you then possess the land? [26]You rely on your sword, you commit abominations, and you defile one another's wives. Should you then possess the land?" '

[27]"Say thus to them, 'Thus says the Lord GOD: "*As* I live, surely those who *are* in the ruins shall fall by the sword, and the one who *is* in the open field I will give to the beasts to be devoured, and those who *are* in

the strongholds and caves shall die of the pestilence. [28]For I will make the land most desolate, her arrogant strength shall cease, and the mountains of Israel shall be so desolate that no one will pass through. [29]Then they shall know that I *am* the LORD, when I have made the land most desolate because of all their abominations which they have committed." '

Hearing and Not Doing

[30]"As for you, son of man, the children of your people are talking about you beside the walls and in the doors of the houses; and they speak to one another, everyone saying to his brother, 'Please come and hear what the word is that comes from the LORD.' [31]So they come to you as people do, they sit before you *as* My people, and they hear your words, but they do not do them; for with their mouth they show much love, *but* their hearts pursue their *own* gain. [32]Indeed you *are* to them as a very lovely song of one who has a pleasant voice and can play well on an instrument; for they hear your words, but they do not do them. [33]And when this comes to pass—surely it will come—then they will know that a prophet has been among them."

33:30–33 The exiles had no intention of obeying the prophet's messages. They listened but did not apply his words. Through bitter experience, they finally recognized that he had spoken the truth of God.

Irresponsible Shepherds

34 And the word of the LORD came to me, saying, [2]"Son of man, prophesy against the shepherds of Israel, prophesy and say to them, 'Thus says the Lord GOD to the shepherds: "Woe to the shepherds of Israel who feed themselves! Should not the shepherds feed the flocks? [3]You eat the fat and clothe yourselves with the wool; you slaughter the fatlings, *but* you do not feed the flock. [4]The weak you have not strengthened, nor have you healed those who were

34:2 prophesy against the shepherds. The reference was to kings, priests, and prophets before the exile. They were like false shepherds, fleecing the flock for personal gain instead of feeding and leading righteously. This stands in contrast to the Lord as Shepherd (see Ps. 23; Is. 40:11).

sick, nor bound up the broken, nor brought back what was driven away, nor sought what was lost; but with force and cruelty you have ruled them. ⁵So they were scattered because *there was* no shepherd; and they became food for all the beasts of the field when they were scattered. ⁶My sheep wandered through all the mountains, and on every high hill; yes, My flock was scattered over the whole face of the earth, and no one was seeking or searching *for them.*"

⁷'Therefore, you shepherds, hear the word of the LORD: ⁸"*As* I live," says the Lord GOD, "surely because My flock became a prey, and My flock became food for every beast of the field, because *there was* no shepherd, nor did My shepherds search for My flock, but the shepherds fed themselves and did not feed My flock"— ⁹therefore, O shepherds, hear the word of the LORD! ¹⁰Thus says the Lord GOD: "Behold, I *am* against the shepherds, and I will require My flock at their hand; I will cause them to cease feeding the sheep, and the shepherds shall feed themselves no more; for I will deliver My flock from their mouths, that they may no longer be food for them."

God, the True Shepherd

¹¹'For thus says the Lord GOD: "Indeed I Myself will search for My sheep and seek them out. ¹²As a shepherd seeks out his flock on the day he is among his scattered sheep, so will I seek out My sheep and deliver them from all the places where they were scattered on a cloudy and dark day. ¹³And I will bring them out from the peoples and gather them from the countries, and will bring them to their own land; I will feed them on the mountains of Israel, in the valleys and in all the inhabited places of the country. ¹⁴I will feed them in good pasture, and their fold shall be on the high mountains of Israel. There they shall lie down in a good fold and feed in rich pasture on the mountains of Israel. ¹⁵I will feed My flock, and I will make them lie down," says the Lord GOD. ¹⁶"I will seek what was lost and bring back what was driven away, bind up the broken and strengthen what was sick; but I will destroy the fat and the strong, and feed them in judgment."

¹⁷'And *as for* you, O My flock, thus says the Lord GOD: "Behold, I shall judge between sheep and sheep, between rams and goats. ¹⁸*Is it* too little for you to have eaten up the good pasture, that you must tread down with your feet the residue of your pasture—and to have drunk of the clear waters, that you must foul the residue with your feet? ¹⁹And *as for* My flock, they eat what you have trampled with your feet, and they drink what you have fouled with your feet."

²⁰'Therefore thus says the Lord GOD to them: "Behold, I Myself will judge between the fat and the lean sheep. ²¹Because you have pushed with side and shoulder, butted all the weak ones with your horns, and scattered them abroad, ²²therefore I will save My flock, and they shall no longer be a prey; and I will judge between sheep and sheep. ²³I will establish one shepherd over them, and he shall feed them—My servant David. He shall feed them and be their shepherd. ²⁴And I, the LORD, will be their God, and My servant David a prince among them; I, the LORD, have spoken.

34:23 one shepherd...David. This refers to the Messiah, who will be Israel's ultimate King over the millennial kingdom (Jer. 30:9). The Lord in v. 24 is God the Father.

²⁵"I will make a covenant of peace with them, and cause wild beasts to cease from the land; and they will dwell safely in the wilderness and sleep in the woods. ²⁶I will make them and the places all around My hill a blessing; and I will cause showers to come down in their season; there shall be showers of blessing. ²⁷Then the trees of the field shall yield their fruit, and the earth shall yield her increase. They shall be safe in their land; and they shall know that I *am* the LORD, when I have broken the bands of their yoke and delivered them from the hand of those who enslaved them. ²⁸And they shall no longer be a prey for the nations, nor shall beasts of the land devour them; but they shall dwell safely, and no one shall make *them* afraid. ²⁹I will raise up for them a garden of renown, and they shall no longer be consumed with hunger in the land, nor bear the shame of the Gentiles anymore. ³⁰Thus they shall know that I, the LORD their God, *am* with them, and

they, the house of Israel, *are* My people,"
says the Lord GOD.' "

³¹"You are My flock, the flock of My pasture; you *are* men, *and* I *am* your God,"
says the Lord GOD.

Judgment on Mount Seir

35 Moreover the word of the LORD came to me, saying, ²"Son of man, set your face against Mount Seir and prophesy against it, ³and say to it, 'Thus says the Lord GOD:

"Behold, O Mount Seir, I *am* against
     you;
I will stretch out My hand against
     you,
And make you most desolate;
⁴   I shall lay your cities waste,
And you shall be desolate.
Then you shall know that I *am* the
     LORD.

⁵"Because you have had an ancient hatred, and have shed *the blood of* the children of Israel by the power of the sword at the time of their calamity, *when* their iniquity *came to an* end, ⁶therefore, *as* I live," says the Lord GOD, "I will prepare you for blood, and blood shall pursue you; since you have not hated blood, therefore blood shall pursue you. ⁷Thus I will make Mount Seir most desolate, and cut off from it the one who leaves and the one who returns. ⁸And I will fill its mountains with the slain; on your hills and in your valleys and in all your ravines those who are slain by the sword shall fall. ⁹I will make you perpetually desolate, and your cities shall be uninhabited; then you shall know that I *am* the LORD.

¹⁰"Because you have said, 'These two nations and these two countries shall be mine, and we will possess them,' although the LORD was there, ¹¹therefore, *as* I live," says the Lord GOD, "I will do according to your anger and according to the envy which you showed in your hatred against them; and I will make Myself known among them when I judge you. ¹²Then you shall know that I *am* the LORD. I have heard all your blasphemies which you have spoken against the mountains of Israel, saying, 'They are desolate; they are given to us to

consume.' ¹³Thus with your mouth you have boasted against Me and multiplied your words against Me; I have heard *them.*"

¹⁴"Thus says the Lord GOD: "The whole earth will rejoice when I make you desolate. ¹⁵As you rejoiced because the inheritance of the house of Israel was desolate, so I will do to you; you shall be desolate, O Mount Seir, as well as all of Edom—all of it! Then they shall know that I *am* the LORD." '

> **35:15 As you rejoiced.** This final reason for doom was Edom's joy over Israel's calamity. **they shall know.** Edom's judgment would reveal God's glory and would show "the whole earth" that God is the Lord. Sinners learn this only through their own destruction (see Heb. 10:31).

Blessing on Israel

36 "And you, son of man, prophesy to the mountains of Israel, and say, 'O mountains of Israel, hear the word of the LORD! ²Thus says the Lord GOD: "Because the enemy has said of you, 'Aha! The ancient heights have become our possession,' " ' ³therefore prophesy, and say, 'Thus says the Lord GOD: "Because they made *you* desolate and swallowed you up on every side, so that you became the possession of the rest of the nations, and you are taken up by the lips of talkers and slandered by the people"— ⁴therefore, O mountains of Israel, hear the word of the Lord GOD! Thus says the Lord GOD to the mountains, the hills, the rivers, the valleys, the desolate wastes, and the cities that have been forsaken, which became plunder and mockery to the rest of the nations all around— ⁵therefore thus says the Lord GOD: "Surely I have spoken in My burning jealousy against the rest of the nations and against all Edom, who gave My land to themselves as a possession, with wholehearted joy *and* spiteful minds, in order to plunder its open country." '

⁶"Therefore prophesy concerning the land of Israel, and say to the mountains, the hills, the rivers, and the valleys, 'Thus says the Lord GOD: "Behold, I have spoken in My jealousy and My fury, because you have borne the shame of the nations." ⁷Therefore thus says the Lord GOD: "I have raised My hand in an oath that surely the

nations that *are* around you shall bear their own shame. ⁸But you, O mountains of Israel, you shall shoot forth your branches and yield your fruit to My people Israel, for they are about to come. ⁹For indeed I *am* for you, and I will turn to you, and you shall be tilled and sown. ¹⁰I will multiply men upon you, all the house of Israel, all of it; and the cities shall be inhabited and the ruins rebuilt. ¹¹I will multiply upon you man and beast; and they shall increase and bear young; I will make you inhabited as in former times, and do better *for you* than at your beginnings. Then you shall know that I *am* the LORD. ¹²Yes, I will cause men to walk on you, My people Israel; they shall take possession of you, and you shall be their inheritance; no more shall you bereave them *of children.*"

¹³Thus says the Lord GOD: "Because they say to you, 'You devour men and bereave your nation *of children,*' ¹⁴therefore you shall devour men no more, nor bereave your nation anymore," says the Lord GOD. ¹⁵Nor will I let you hear the taunts of the nations anymore, nor bear the reproach of the peoples anymore, nor shall you cause your nation to stumble anymore," says the Lord GOD.'"

The Renewal of Israel

¹⁶Moreover the word of the LORD came to me, saying: ¹⁷"Son of man, when the house of Israel dwelt in their own land, they defiled it by their own ways and deeds; to Me their way was like the uncleanness of a woman in her customary impurity. ¹⁸Therefore I poured out My fury on them for the blood they had shed on the land, and for their idols *with which* they had defiled it. ¹⁹So I scattered them among the nations, and they were dispersed throughout the countries; I judged them according to their ways and their deeds. ²⁰When they came to the nations, wherever they went, they profaned My holy name—when they said of them, 'These *are* the people of the LORD, *and* yet they have gone out of His land.' ²¹But I had concern for My holy name, which the house of Israel had profaned among the nations wherever they went.

²²"Therefore say to the house of Israel, 'Thus says the Lord GOD: "I do not do *this*

36:25–27 I will cleanse you. Along with the physical reality of returning to the Land, God promised spiritual renewal to Israel. He promised cleansing from sin, a new heart of the New Covenant (see Jer. 31:31–34), a new spirit inclined to worship Him, and His Spirit to dwell in them. This has not happened because Israel has not trusted Jesus Christ as Messiah and Savior, but she will before the kingdom of the Messiah (see Zech. 12–14).

for your sake, O house of Israel, but for My holy name's sake, which you have profaned among the nations wherever you went. ²³And I will sanctify My great name, which has been profaned among the nations, which you have profaned in their midst; and the nations shall know that I *am* the LORD," says the Lord GOD, "when I am hallowed in you before their eyes. ²⁴For I will take you from among the nations, gather you out of all countries, and bring you into your own land. ²⁵Then I will sprinkle clean water on you, and you shall be clean; I will cleanse you from all your filthiness and from all your idols. ²⁶I will give you a new heart and put a new spirit within you; I will take the heart of stone out of your flesh and give you a heart of flesh. ²⁷I will put My Spirit within you and cause you to walk in My statutes, and you will keep My judgments and do *them.* ²⁸Then you shall dwell in the land that I gave to your fathers; you shall be My people, and I will be your God. ²⁹I will deliver you from all your uncleannesses. I will call for the grain and multiply it, and bring no famine upon you. ³⁰And I will multiply the fruit of your trees and the increase of your fields, so that you need never again bear the reproach of famine among the nations. ³¹Then you will remember your evil ways and your deeds that *were* not good; and you will loathe yourselves in your own sight, for your iniquities and your abominations. ³²Not for your sake do I do *this,*" says the Lord GOD, "let it be

36:25–31 This section is among the most glorious in all Scripture on the subject of Israel's restoration to the Lord and national salvation. This salvation is described as a cleansing that will wash away sin. This washing was symbolized in the Mosaic rites of purification (see Num. 19:17–19). Paul wrote of this washing in Eph. 5:26 and Titus 3:5. Jesus alluded to this promise in John 3:5.

known to you. Be ashamed and confounded for your own ways, O house of Israel!"

33"Thus says the Lord GOD: "On the day that I cleanse you from all your iniquities, I will also enable *you* to dwell in the cities, and the ruins shall be rebuilt. 34The desolate land shall be tilled instead of lying desolate in the sight of all who pass by. 35So they will say, 'This land that was desolate has become like the garden of Eden; and the wasted, desolate, and ruined cities *are now* fortified *and* inhabited.' 36Then the nations which are left all around you shall know that I, the LORD, have rebuilt the ruined places *and* planted what was desolate. I, the LORD, have spoken *it*, and I will do *it*."

37"Thus says the Lord GOD: "I will also let the house of Israel inquire of Me to do this for them: I will increase their men like a flock. 38Like a flock *offered as* holy *sacrifices*, like the flock at Jerusalem on its feast days, so shall the ruined cities be filled with flocks of men. Then they shall know that I *am* the LORD." ' "

> **36:37 inquire of Me to do this.** God will allow the Israelites to return, but He will give them the privilege of praying for it to happen. This prophecy was to stir up the people's prayers.

The Dry Bones Live

37 The hand of the LORD came upon me and brought me out in the Spirit of the LORD, and set me down in the midst of the valley; and it *was* full of bones. 2Then He caused me to pass by them all around, and behold, *there were* very many in the open valley; and indeed *they were* very dry. 3And He said to me, "Son of man, can these bones live?"

So I answered, "O Lord GOD, You know."

> **37:3 "...can these bones live?"** The dry bones represent Israel as dead in their dispersion and waiting for national resurrection. The people knew about the doctrine of individual resurrection; otherwise this prophecy would have had no meaning (see 1 Kin. 17; Is. 25:8).

4Again He said to me, "Prophesy to these bones, and say to them, 'O dry bones, hear the word of the LORD! 5Thus says the Lord GOD to these bones: "Surely I will cause breath to enter into you, and you shall live.

6I will put sinews on you and bring flesh upon you, cover you with skin and put breath in you; and you shall live. Then you shall know that I *am* the LORD." ' "

7So I prophesied as I was commanded; and as I prophesied, there was a noise, and suddenly a rattling; and the bones came together, bone to bone. 8Indeed, as I looked, the sinews and the flesh came upon them, and the skin covered them over; but *there was* no breath in them.

9Also He said to me, "Prophesy to the breath, prophesy, son of man, and say to the breath, 'Thus says the Lord GOD: "Come from the four winds, O breath, and breathe on these slain, that they may live." ' " 10So I prophesied as He commanded me, and breath came into them, and they lived, and stood upon their feet, an exceedingly great army.

11Then He said to me, "Son of man, these bones are the whole house of Israel. They indeed say, 'Our bones are dry, our hope is lost, and we ourselves are cut off!' 12Therefore prophesy and say to them, 'Thus says the Lord GOD: "Behold, O My people, I will open your graves and cause you to come up from your graves, and bring you into the land of Israel. 13Then you shall know that I *am* the LORD, when I have opened your graves, O My people, and brought you up from your graves. 14I will put My Spirit in you, and you shall live, and I will place you in your own land. Then you shall know that I, the LORD, have spoken *it* and performed *it*," says the LORD.' "

One Kingdom, One King

15Again the word of the LORD came to me, saying, 16"As for you, son of man, take a stick for yourself and write on it: 'For Judah and for the children of Israel, his companions.' Then take another stick and write on it, 'For Joseph, the stick of Ephraim, and *for* all the house of Israel, his companions.' 17Then join them one to another for yourself into one stick, and they will become one in your hand.

18"And when the children of your people speak to you, saying, 'Will you not show us what you *mean* by these?'— 19say to them, 'Thus says the Lord GOD: "Surely I will take the stick of Joseph, which *is* in the hand of Ephraim, and the tribes of Israel,

his companions; and I will join them with it, with the stick of Judah, and make them one stick, and they will be one in My hand." ' ²⁰And the sticks on which you write will be in your hand before their eyes.

²¹"Then say to them, 'Thus says the Lord GOD: "Surely I will take the children of Israel from among the nations, wherever they have gone, and will gather them from every side and bring them into their own land; ²²and I will make them one nation in the land, on the mountains of Israel; and one king shall be king over them all; they shall no longer be two nations, nor shall they ever be divided into two kingdoms again. ²³They shall not defile themselves anymore with their idols, nor with their detestable things, nor with any of their transgressions; but I will deliver them from all their dwelling places in which they have sinned, and will cleanse them. Then they shall be My people, and I will be their God.

37:15–23 After the vision, Ezekiel was given an object lesson, which the people observed. He united two sticks together to illustrate that God will return the Israelites to their land and, for the first time since 931 B.C. (1 Kin. 11:26–40), restore union between Israel and Judah in the messianic reign (see Is. 11:12,13).

²⁴"David My servant *shall be* king over them, and they shall all have one shepherd; they shall also walk in My judgments and observe My statutes, and do them. ²⁵Then they shall dwell in the land that I have given to Jacob My servant, where your fathers dwelt; and they shall dwell there, they, their children, and their children's children, forever; and My servant David *shall be* their prince forever. ²⁶Moreover I will make a covenant of peace with them,

37:26 covenant of peace. This is the New Covenant. Israel has not yet been in a state of perpetual peace; this will occur in the future kingdom of the Messiah, who is the "Prince of Peace" (Is. 9:6). **My sanctuary.** God will have a sanctuary in the midst of His people and will dwell with them (see Zech. 6:12,13). God has desired to dwell with man on earth since before the time of Moses (Gen. 17:7,8).

and it shall be an everlasting covenant with them; I will establish them and multiply them, and I will set My sanctuary in their midst forevermore. ²⁷My tabernacle also shall be with them; indeed I will be their God, and they shall be My people. ²⁸The nations also will know that I, the LORD, sanctify Israel, when My sanctuary is in their midst forevermore." ' "

Gog and Allies Attack Israel

38 Now the word of the LORD came to me, saying, ²"Son of man, set your face against Gog, of the land of Magog, the prince of Rosh,ᵃ Meshech, and Tubal, and prophesy against him, ³and say, 'Thus says the Lord GOD: "Behold, I *am* against you, O Gog, the prince of Rosh, Meshech, and Tubal. ⁴I will turn you around, put hooks into your jaws, and lead you out, with all your army, horses, and horsemen, all splendidly clothed, a great company *with* bucklers and shields, all of them handling swords. ⁵Persia, Ethiopia,ᵃ and Libyaᵇ are with them, all of them *with* shield and helmet; ⁶Gomer and all its troops; the house of Togarmah *from* the far north and all its troops—many people *are* with you.

38:2 against Gog. This proper noun is a general title for an enemy of God's people and likely means "high" or "supreme one" (see Num. 24:7). It refers to a person, a "prince," from the land of Magog, who is the final Antichrist. Gog and Magog are used again symbolically in the final world uprising against Jerusalem, its people, and the Messiah (Jer. 20:8–10). This last attack will occur at the end of the 1,000 year kingdom and will come from sinners from around the world.

⁷"Prepare yourself and be ready, you and all your companies that are gathered about you; and be a guard for them. ⁸After many days you will be visited. In the latter years you will come into the land of those brought back from the sword *and* gathered from many people on the mountains of Israel, which had long been desolate; they were brought out of the nations, and now all of them dwell safely. ⁹You will ascend, coming like a storm, covering the land like a cloud, you and all your troops and many peoples with you."

38:2 ᵃTargum, Vulgate, and Aquila read *chief prince of* (also verse 3).   38:5 ᵃHebrew *Cush*
ᵇHebrew *Put*

38:8 In the latter years. The invader will make a final bid on the Land during Israel's restoration (Ezek. 34–39). **brought back from the sword.** Referring to Israelites who have been returned to their land, after the sword had killed or scattered many of their people. **gathered.** Referring to God's final restoration of Israelites to their land (Is. 11:12). **dwell safely.** Referring to Israel's blessed estate after God has brought them back to their land (Jer. 32:37; Zech. 14:11).

[10]'Thus says the Lord GOD: "On that day it shall come to pass *that* thoughts will arise in your mind, and you will make an evil plan: [11]You will say, 'I will go up against a land of unwalled villages; I will go to a peaceful people, who dwell safely, all of them dwelling without walls, and having neither bars nor gates'— [12]to take plunder and to take booty, to stretch out your hand against the waste places *that are again* inhabited, and against a people gathered from the nations, who have acquired livestock and goods, who dwell in the midst of the land. [13]Sheba, Dedan, the merchants of Tarshish, and all their young lions will say to you, 'Have you come to take plunder? Have you gathered your army to take booty, to carry away silver and gold, to take away livestock and goods, to take great plunder?' " '

[14]"Therefore, son of man, prophesy and say to Gog, 'Thus says the Lord GOD: "On that day when My people Israel dwell safely, will you not know it? [15]Then you will come from your place out of the far north, you and many peoples with you, all of them riding on horses, a great company and a mighty army. [16]You will come up against My people Israel like a cloud, to cover the land. It will be in the latter days that I will bring you against My land, so that the nations may know Me, when I am hallowed in you, O Gog, before their eyes." [17]Thus says the Lord GOD: "Are *you* he of whom I have spoken in former days by My servants the prophets of Israel, who prophesied for years in those days that I would bring you against them?

Judgment on Gog

[18]"And it will come to pass at the same time, when Gog comes against the land of Israel," says the Lord GOD, "*that* My fury will show in My face. [19]For in My jealousy *and* in the fire of My wrath I have spoken: 'Surely in that day there shall be a great earthquake in the land of Israel, [20]so that the fish of the sea, the birds of the heavens, the beasts of the field, all creeping things that creep on the earth, and all men who *are* on the face of the earth shall shake at My presence. The mountains shall be thrown down, the steep places shall fall, and every wall shall fall to the ground.' [21]I will call for a sword against Gog throughout all My mountains," says the Lord GOD. "Every man's sword will be against his brother. [22]And I will bring him to judgment with pestilence and bloodshed; I will rain down on him, on his troops, and on the many peoples who *are* with him, flooding rain, great hailstones, fire, and brimstone. [23]Thus I will magnify Myself and sanctify Myself, and I will be known in the eyes of many nations. Then they shall know that I *am* the LORD." '

38:18–23 My fury will show. God will bring a great earthquake to Israel, demonstrating His anger against the attempts by the Antichrist to annihilate Israel. Panic will seize the invading soldiers, who will use their weapons against one another (see 2 Chr. 20:22,23). God will further destroy them by disease, rain, large hailstones, fire, and brimstone (see Rev. 6:12–17).

Gog's Armies Destroyed

39 "And you, son of man, prophesy against Gog, and say, 'Thus says the Lord GOD: "Behold, I *am* against you, O Gog, the prince of Rosh,[a] Meshech, and Tubal; [2]and I will turn you around and lead you on, bringing you up from the far north, and bring you against the mountains of Israel. [3]Then I will knock the bow out of your left hand, and cause the arrows to fall out of your right hand. [4]You shall fall upon the mountains of Israel, you and all your troops and the peoples who *are* with you; I will give you to birds of prey of every sort and *to* the beasts of the field to be devoured. [5]You shall fall on the open field; for I have spoken," says the Lord GOD. [6]"And I will send fire on Magog and on those who live

---

39:1 [a]Targum, Vulgate and Aquila read *chief prince of.*

in security in the coastlands. Then they shall know that I *am* the LORD. ⁷So I will make My holy name known in the midst of My people Israel, and I will not *let them* profane My holy name anymore. Then the nations shall know that *I am* the LORD, the Holy One in Israel. ⁸Surely it is coming, and it shall be done," says the Lord GOD. "This *is* the day of which I have spoken.

⁹"Then those who dwell in the cities of Israel will go out and set on fire and burn the weapons, both the shields and bucklers, the bows and arrows, the javelins and spears; and they will make fires with them for seven years. ¹⁰They will not take wood from the field nor cut down *any* from the forests, because they will make fires with the weapons; and they will plunder those who plundered them, and pillage those who pillaged them," says the Lord GOD.

The Burial of Gog

¹¹"It will come to pass in that day *that* I will give Gog a burial place there in Israel, the valley of those who pass by east of the sea; and it will obstruct travelers, because there they will bury Gog and all his multitude. Therefore they will call *it* the Valley of Hamon Gog.ᵃ ¹²For seven months the house of Israel will be burying them, in order to cleanse the land. ¹³Indeed all the people of the land will be burying, and they will gain renown for it on the day that I am glorified," says the Lord GOD. ¹⁴"They will set apart men regularly employed, with the help of a search party,ᵃ to pass through the land and bury those bodies remaining on the ground, in order to cleanse it. At the end of seven months they will make a search. ¹⁵The search party will pass through the land; and when *anyone* sees a man's bone, he shall set up a marker by it, till the buriers have buried it in the Valley of Hamon Gog. ¹⁶*The* name of *the* city *will* also *be* Hamonah. Thus they shall cleanse the land."

A Triumphant Festival

¹⁷"And as for you, son of man, thus says the Lord GOD, 'Speak to every sort of bird and to every beast of the field:

"Assemble yourselves and come;
Gather together from all sides to My sacrificial meal
Which I am sacrificing for you,
A great sacrificial meal on the mountains of Israel,
That you may eat flesh and drink blood.
18 You shall eat the flesh of the mighty,
Drink the blood of the princes of the earth,
Of rams and lambs,
Of goats and bulls,
All of them fatlings of Bashan.
19 You shall eat fat till you are full,
And drink blood till you are drunk,
At My sacrificial meal
Which I am sacrificing for you.
20 You shall be filled at My table
With horses and riders,
With mighty men
And with all the men of war," says the Lord GOD.

39:17–20 Speak to...bird and...beast. God summons carrion birds and carnivorous animals to consume the fallen flesh, as described in Rev. 19:21.

Israel Restored to the Land

²¹"I will set My glory among the nations; all the nations shall see My judgment which I have executed, and My hand which I have laid on them. ²²So the house of Israel shall know that I *am* the LORD their God from that day forward. ²³The Gentiles shall know that the house of Israel went into captivity for their iniquity; because they were unfaithful to Me, therefore I hid My face from them. I gave them into the hand of their enemies, and they all fell by the sword. ²⁴According to their uncleanness and according to their transgressions I have dealt with them, and hidden My face from them."

²⁵"Therefore thus says the Lord GOD:

39:21–29 I will set My glory. God vanquished Israel's foes so that His enemies and Israel will see His glory and will know that He is the Lord. This is Israel's salvation spoken of in Zech. 12:10–13:9 and Rom. 11:25–27.

39:11 ᵃLiterally *The Multitude of Gog*   39:14 ᵃLiterally *those who pass through*

'Now I will bring back the captives of Jacob, and have mercy on the whole house of Israel; and I will be jealous for My holy name— [26]after they have borne their shame, and all their unfaithfulness in which they were unfaithful to Me, when they dwelt safely in their own land and no one made them afraid. [27]When I have brought them back from the peoples and gathered them out of their enemies' lands, and I am hallowed in them in the sight of many nations, [28]then they shall know that I am the LORD their God, who sent them into captivity among the nations, but also brought them back to their land, and left none of them captive any longer. [29]And I will not hide My face from them anymore; for I shall have poured out My Spirit on the house of Israel,' says the Lord GOD."

> **40:1–48:35** This section on Christ's millennial reign gives more detail to the 1,000 year kingdom than all other Old Testament prophecies combined. These chapters form the climax of Ezekiel's prophecy and Israel's restoration. They include the new temple (40:1–43:12), the new worship (43:13–46:24), and the new apportionment of the Land (47:1–48:35).

A New City, a New Temple

40 In the twenty-fifth year of our captivity, at the beginning of the year, on the tenth day of the month, in the fourteenth year after the city was captured, on the very same day the hand of the LORD was upon me; and He took me there. [2]In the visions of God He took me into the land of Israel and set me on a very high mountain; on it toward the south was something like the structure of a city. [3]He took me there, and behold, there was a man whose appearance was like the appearance of bronze. He had a line of flax and a measuring rod in his hand, and he stood in the gateway.

[4]And the man said to me, "Son of man, look with your eyes and hear with your ears, and fix your mind on everything I show you; for you were brought here so that I might show them to you. Declare to the house of Israel everything you see." [5]Now there was a wall all around the outside of the temple.[a] In the man's hand was

a measuring rod six cubits long, each being a cubit and a handbreadth; and he measured the width of the wall structure, one rod; and the height, one rod.

> **40:4 Declare...everything you see.** Chapters 40–48 describe the millennial conditions under which Israel will live and worship after the Messiah comes and destroys the ungodly (Rev. 19:11). Believing Gentiles will also live in the kingdom as sheep of the Great Shepherd (see Matt. 25:31–46), while all unbelievers will be destroyed. God instructed Ezekiel to write down all the details.

The Eastern Gateway of the Temple

[6]Then he went to the gateway which faced east; and he went up its stairs and measured the threshold of the gateway, which was one rod wide, and the other threshold was one rod wide. [7]Each gate chamber was one rod long and one rod wide; between the gate chambers was a space of five cubits; and the threshold of the gateway by the vestibule of the inside gate was one rod. [8]He also measured the vestibule of the inside gate, one rod. [9]Then he measured the vestibule of the gateway, eight cubits; and the gateposts, two cubits. The vestibule of the gate was on the inside. [10]In the eastern gateway were three gate chambers on one side and three on the other; the three were all the same size; also the gateposts were of the same size on this side and that side.

[11]He measured the width of the entrance to the gateway, ten cubits; and the length of the gate, thirteen cubits. [12]There was a space in front of the gate chambers, one cubit on this side and one cubit on that side; the gate chambers were six cubits on this side and six cubits on that side. [13]Then he measured the gateway from the roof of one gate chamber to the roof of the other; the width was twenty-five cubits, as door faces door. [14]He measured the gateposts, sixty cubits high, and the court all around the gateway extended to the gatepost. [15]From the front of the entrance gate to the front of the vestibule of the inner gate was fifty cubits. [16]There were beveled window frames in the gate chambers and in their intervening archways on the inside of the

---

40:5 [a]Literally house, and so elsewhere in this book

gateway all around, and likewise in the vestibules. *There were* windows all around on the inside. And on each gatepost *were* palm trees.

The Outer Court

¹⁷Then he brought me into the outer court; and *there were* chambers and a pavement made all around the court; thirty chambers faced the pavement. ¹⁸The pavement was by the side of the gateways, corresponding to the length of the gateways; *this was* the lower pavement. ¹⁹Then he measured the width from the front of the lower gateway to the front of the inner court exterior, one hundred cubits toward the east and the north.

The Northern Gateway

²⁰On the outer court was also a gateway facing north, and he measured its length and its width. ²¹Its gate chambers, three on this side and three on that side, its gateposts and its archways, had the same measurements as the first gate; its length *was* fifty cubits and its width twenty-five cubits. ²²Its windows and those of its archways, and also its palm trees, *had* the same measurements as the gateway facing east; it was ascended by seven steps, and its archway *was* in front of it. ²³A gate of the inner court was opposite the northern gateway, just as the eastern *gateway*; and he measured from gateway to gateway, one hundred cubits.

The Southern Gateway

²⁴After that he brought me toward the south, and there a gateway was facing south; and he measured its gateposts and

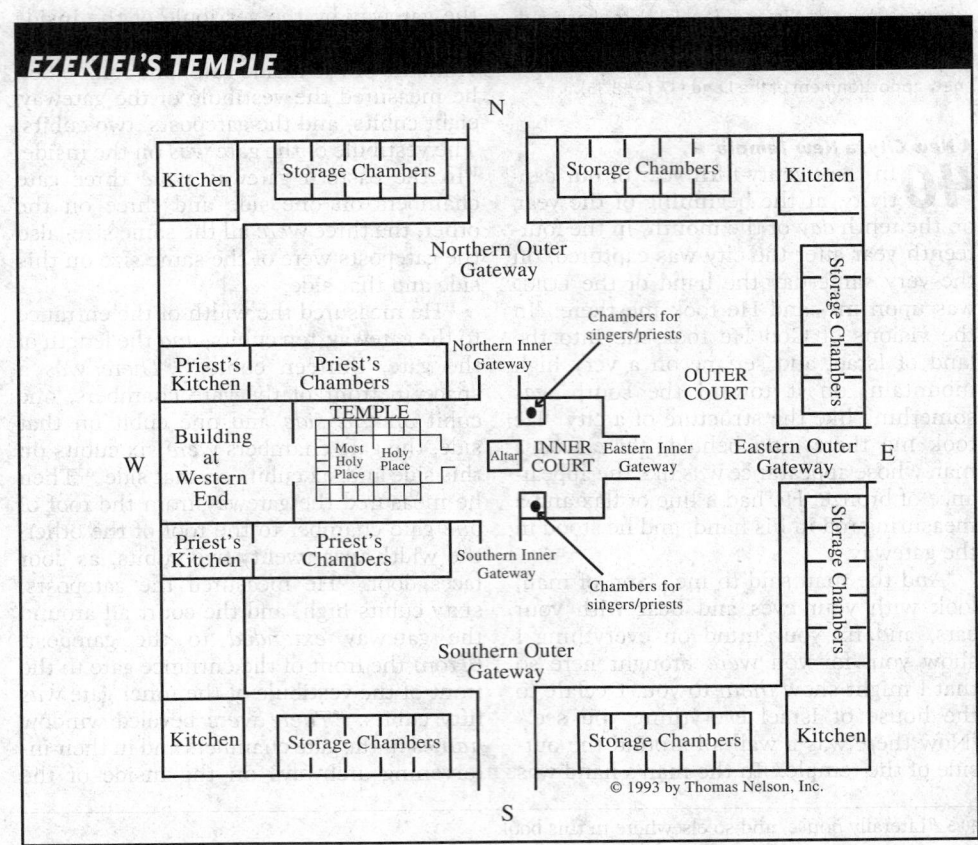

EZEKIEL'S TEMPLE

© 1993 by Thomas Nelson, Inc.

archways according to these same measurements. ²⁵There were windows in it and in its archways all around like those windows; its length was fifty cubits and its width twenty-five cubits. ²⁶Seven steps led up to it, and its archway was in front of them; and it had palm trees on its gateposts, one on this side and one on that side. ²⁷There was also a gateway on the inner court, facing south; and he measured from gateway to gateway toward the south, one hundred cubits.

Gateways of the Inner Court

²⁸Then he brought me to the inner court through the southern gateway; he measured the southern gateway according to these same measurements. ²⁹Also its gate chambers, its gateposts, and its archways were according to these same measurements; there were windows in it and in its archways all around; it was fifty cubits long and twenty-five cubits wide. ³⁰There were archways all around, twenty-five cubits long and five cubits wide. ³¹Its archways faced the outer court, palm trees were on its gateposts, and going up to it were eight steps.

³²And he brought me into the inner court facing east; he measured the gateway according to these same measurements. ³³Also its gate chambers, its gateposts, and its archways were according to these same measurements; and there were windows in it and in its archways all around; it was fifty cubits long and twenty-five cubits wide. ³⁴Its archways faced the outer court, and palm trees were on its gateposts on this side and on that side; and going up to it were eight steps.

³⁵Then he brought me to the north gateway and measured it according to these same measurements—³⁶also its gate chambers, its gateposts, and its archways. It had windows all around; its length was fifty cubits and its width twenty-five cubits. ³⁷Its gateposts faced the outer court, palm trees were on its gateposts on this side and on that side, and going up to it were eight steps.

Where Sacrifices Were Prepared

³⁸There was a chamber and its entrance by the gateposts of the gateway, where they washed the burnt offering. ³⁹In the vestibule of the gateway were two tables on this side and two tables on that side, on which to slay the burnt offering, the sin offering, and the trespass offering. ⁴⁰At the outer side of the vestibule, as one goes up to the entrance of the northern gateway, were two tables; and on the other side of the vestibule of the gateway were two tables. ⁴¹Four tables were on this side and four tables on that side, by the side of the gateway, eight tables on which they slaughtered the sacrifices. ⁴²There were also four tables of hewn stone for the burnt offering, one cubit and a half long, one cubit and a half wide, and one cubit high; on these they laid the instruments with which they slaughtered the burnt offering and the sacrifice. ⁴³Inside were hooks, a handbreadth wide, fastened all around; and the flesh of the sacrifices was on the tables.

40:38–47 This section raises the question of sacrifices in the millennial kingdom. Sacrifices will exist but will continue to be redemptively ineffective as in Old Testament times. No sacrifice, before or after Christ, saves. They only point to Him as the one true Lamb who takes away sin. The Lord's Supper is a memorial that looks back to Calvary and in no way diminishes the cross. Israel rejected their Messiah, but when they have received Him and are in His kingdom, they will have a memorial of sacrifices that point to Him.

Chambers for Singers and Priests

⁴⁴Outside the inner gate were the chambers for the singers in the inner court, one facing south at the side of the northern gateway, and the other facing north at the side of the southern gateway. ⁴⁵Then he said to me, "This chamber which faces south is for the priests who have charge of the temple. ⁴⁶The chamber which faces north is for the priests who have charge of the altar; these are the sons of Zadok, from the sons of Levi, who come near the LORD to minister to Him."

40:46 sons of Zadok. This Levitical family descended from Levi, Aaron, Eleazar, and Phinehas (1 Chr. 6:3–8). Because of God's covenant with Phinehas (Num. 25:10–13), Eli's unfaithfulness (1 Sam. 1,2), and Zadok's faithfulness to David and Solomon (1 Kin. 1:32–40), Zadok's sons serve as priests in the millennial temple.

Dimensions of the Inner Court and Vestibule

⁴⁷And he measured the court, one hundred cubits long and one hundred cubits wide, foursquare. The altar *was* in front of the temple. ⁴⁸Then he brought me to the vestibule of the temple and measured the doorposts of the vestibule, five cubits on this side and five cubits on that side; and the width of the gateway was three cubits on this side and three cubits on that side. ⁴⁹The length of the vestibule *was* twenty cubits, and the width eleven cubits; and by the steps which led up to it *there were* pillars by the doorposts, one on this side and another on that side.

Dimensions of the Sanctuary

41 Then he brought me into the sanctuary*ᵃ* and measured the doorposts, six cubits wide on one side and six cubits wide on the other side—the width of the tabernacle. ²The width of the entryway *was* ten cubits, and the side walls of the entrance *were* five cubits on this side and five cubits on the other side; and he measured its length, forty cubits, and its width, twenty cubits.

³Also he went inside and measured the doorposts, two cubits; and the entrance, six cubits *high;* and the width of the entrance, seven cubits. ⁴He measured the length, twenty cubits; and the width, twenty cu-

> **41:4 the Most Holy *Place.*** This is the Holy of Holies, which the High-Priest entered annually on the Day of Atonement (see Lev. 16). These dimensions are identical to Solomon's (1 Kin. 6:20) and twice those of the tabernacle in the wilderness.

41:1 *ᵃ*Hebrew *heykal,* here the main room of the temple, sometimes called the *holy place* (compare Exodus 26:33)

bits, beyond the sanctuary; and he said to me, "This *is* the Most Holy *Place."*

The Side Chambers on the Wall

⁵Next, he measured the wall of the temple, six cubits. The width of each side chamber all around the temple *was* four cubits on every side. ⁶The side chambers *were* in three stories, one above the other, thirty chambers in each story; they rested on ledges which *were* for the side chambers all around, that they might be supported, but not fastened to the wall of the temple. ⁷As one went up from story to story, the side chambers became wider all around, because their supporting ledges in the wall of the temple ascended like steps; therefore the width of the structure increased as one went up *from* the lowest *story* to the highest by way of the middle one. ⁸I also saw an elevation all around the temple; it was the foundation of the side chambers, a full rod, *that is,* six cubits *high.* ⁹The thickness of the outer wall of the side chambers *was* five cubits, and so also the remaining terrace by the place of the side chambers of the temple. ¹⁰And between *it and* the *wall* chambers was a width of twenty cubits all around the temple on every side. ¹¹The doors of the side chambers opened on the terrace, one door toward the north and another toward the south; and the width of the terrace *was* five cubits all around.

The Building at the Western End

¹²The building that faced the separating courtyard at its western end *was* seventy

MILLENNIAL SACRIFICES

Levitical	Millennial*
1. Burnt—Leviticus 1:3–17	1. Burnt—Ezekiel 40:39
2. Grain—Leviticus 2:1–16	2. Grain—Ezekiel 45:15
3. Peace—Leviticus 3:1–17	3. Peace—Ezekiel 45:15
4. Sin—Leviticus 4:1–35	4. Sin—Ezekiel 40:39
5. Trespass—Leviticus 5:1–6:7	5. Trespass—Ezekiel 40:39
6. Drink—Leviticus 23:13,37	6. Drink—Ezekiel 45:17

* Isaiah 56:7, 66:20–23; Jeremiah 33:18 further confirm the burnt and grain offerings.

cubits wide; the wall of the building *was* five cubits thick all around, and its length ninety cubits.

Dimensions and Design of the Temple Area

[13]So he measured the temple, one hundred cubits long; and the separating courtyard with the building and its walls *was* one hundred cubits long; [14]also the width of the eastern face of the temple, including the separating courtyard, *was* one hundred cubits. [15]He measured the length of the building behind it, facing the separating courtyard, with its galleries on the one side and on the other side, one hundred cubits, as well as the inner temple and the porches of the court, [16]their doorposts and the beveled window frames. And the galleries all around their three stories opposite the threshold were paneled with wood from the ground to the windows—the windows were covered— [17]from the space above the door, even to the inner room,[a] as well as outside, and on every wall all around, inside and outside, by measure.

[18]And *it was* made with cherubim and palm trees, a palm tree between cherub and cherub. *Each* cherub had two faces, [19]so that the face of a man *was* toward a palm tree on one side, and the face of a young lion toward a palm tree on the other side; thus *it was* made throughout the temple all around. [20]From the floor to the space above the door, and on the wall of the sanctuary, cherubim and palm trees *were* carved.

41:18 cherubim and palm trees. Figures of angels with palm trees between them (possibly to depict life and fruitfulness of God's servants) were on the walls and doors of the temple. Each cherub had the face of a man and of a lion, possibly to represent the humanity and kingship of the Messiah.

[21]The doorposts of the temple *were* square, *as was* the front of the sanctuary; their appearance was similar. [22]The altar *was* of wood, three cubits high, and its length two cubits. Its corners, its length, and its sides *were* of wood, and he said to me, "This *is* the table that *is* before the LORD."

[23]The temple and the sanctuary had two doors. [24]The doors had two panels *apiece,* two folding panels: two *panels* for one door and two panels for the other *door.* [25]Cherubim and palm trees *were* carved on the doors of the temple just as they *were* carved on the walls. A wooden canopy *was* on the front of the vestibule outside. [26]*There were* beveled window *frames* and palm trees on one side and on the other, on the sides of the vestibule—also on the side chambers of the temple and on the canopies.

The Chambers for the Priests

42 Then he brought me out into the outer court, by the way toward the north; and he brought me into the chamber which *was* opposite the separating courtyard, and which *was* opposite the building toward the north. [2]Facing the length, *which was* one hundred cubits (the width was fifty cubits), was the north door. [3]Opposite the inner court of twenty *cubits,* and opposite the pavement of the outer court, *was* gallery against gallery in three *stories.* [4]In front of the chambers, toward the inside, *was* a walk ten cubits wide, at a distance of one cubit; and their doors faced north. [5]Now the upper chambers *were* shorter, because the galleries took away *space* from them more than from the lower and middle stories of the building. [6]For they *were* in three *stories* and did not have pillars like the pillars of the courts; therefore *the upper level* was shortened more than the lower and middle levels from the ground up. [7]And a wall which *was* outside ran parallel to the chambers, at the front of the chambers, toward the outer court; its length *was* fifty cubits. [8]The length of the chambers toward the outer court *was* fifty cubits, whereas that facing the temple *was* one hundred cubits. [9]At the lower chambers *was* the entrance on the east side, as one goes into them from the outer court.

[10]Also *there were* chambers in the thick-

42:3 gallery against gallery. The priestly rooms described ran along the south, north, and west walls of the sanctuary and Most Holy Place, in three stories. The priests eat the holy offerings and dress there (see Lev. 2:3,10).

41:17 [a]Literally *house,* here *the Most Holy Place*

ness of the wall of the court toward the east, opposite the separating courtyard and opposite the building. ¹¹*There was* a walk in front of them also, and their appearance *was* like the chambers which *were* toward the north; they *were* as long and as wide as the others, and all their exits and entrances *were* according to plan. ¹²And corresponding to the doors of the chambers that *were* facing south, as one enters them, *there was* a door in front of the walk, the way directly in front of the wall toward the east.

¹³Then he said to me, "The north chambers *and* the south chambers, which *are* opposite the separating courtyard, *are* the holy chambers where the priests who approach the LORD shall eat the most holy offerings. There they shall lay the most holy offerings—the grain offering, the sin offering, and the trespass offering—for the place *is* holy. ¹⁴When the priests enter them, they shall not go out of the holy *chamber* into the outer court; but there they shall leave their garments in which they minister, for they *are* holy. They shall put on other garments; then they may approach *that* which *is* for the people."

Outer Dimensions of the Temple

¹⁵Now when he had finished measuring the inner temple, he brought me out through the gateway that faces toward the east, and measured it all around. ¹⁶He measured the east side with the measuring rod,ᵃ five hundred rods by the measuring rod all around. ¹⁷He measured the north side, five hundred rods by the measuring rod all around. ¹⁸He measured the south side, five hundred rods by the measuring rod. ¹⁹He came around to the west side *and* measured five hundred rods by the measuring rod. ²⁰He measured it on the four sides;

42:15–20 out through the gateway. The angel measured the height and thickness of the outside wall, then the outer court, then the inner court with the chambers, and finally the extent of all the temple buildings outside. The outer wall was approximately one mile on each of the four sides. Since this is much too large for Mount Moriah, it will require changes in the topography of Jerusalem, as Zechariah predicted (14:9–11).

it had a wall all around, five hundred *cubits* long and five hundred wide, to separate the holy areas from the common.

The Temple, the LORD's Dwelling Place

43 Afterward he brought me to the gate, the gate that faces toward the east. ²And behold, the glory of the God of Israel came from the way of the east. His voice *was* like the sound of many waters; and the earth shone with His glory. ³*It was* like the appearance of the vision which I saw—like the vision which I saw when Iᵃ came to destroy the city. The visions *were* like the vision which I saw by the River Chebar; and I fell on my face. ⁴And the glory of the LORD came into the temple by way of the gate which faces toward the east. ⁵The Spirit lifted me up and brought me into the inner court; and behold, the glory of the LORD filled the temple.

43:2 the glory of the God of Israel. In earlier chapters, emphasis was given to the departure of God's glory from the temple (see chaps. 8–11). Here, in the millennial temple, God's glory returns. His glory will be fully manifested in the future kingdom, after the Lord's Second Advent (Matt. 16:27). **came from...the east.** When God judged Israel, the glory departed to the E, so when He restores His people and their worship, it returns from the E.

⁶Then I heard *Him* speaking to me from the temple, while a man stood beside me. ⁷And He said to me, "Son of man, *this is* the place of My throne and the place of the soles of My feet, where I will dwell in the midst of the children of Israel forever. No more shall the house of Israel defile My holy name, they nor their kings, by their harlotry or with the carcasses of their kings on their high places. ⁸When they set their threshold by My threshold, and their doorpost by My doorpost, with a wall between them and Me, they defiled My holy name by the abominations which they committed; therefore I have consumed them in My anger. ⁹Now let them put their harlotry and the carcasses of their kings far away from Me, and I will dwell in their midst forever.

¹⁰"Son of man, describe the temple to the house of Israel, that they may be ashamed

---

42:16 ᵃCompare 40:5   43:3 ᵃSome Hebrew manuscripts and Vulgate read *He.*

of their iniquities; and let them measure the pattern. ¹¹And if they are ashamed of all that they have done, make known to them the design of the temple and its arrangement, its exits and its entrances, its entire design and all its ordinances, all its forms and all its laws. Write *it* down in their sight, so that they may keep its whole design and all its ordinances, and perform them. ¹²This *is* the law of the temple: The whole area surrounding the mountaintop *is* most holy. Behold, this *is* the law of the temple.

43:10–12 These glorious future plans show how much Israel forfeited by their sins. Every detail should lead Ezekiel's hearers and readers to repentance, which is the key to the vision of chapters 40–48.

Dimensions of the Altar

¹³"These are the measurements of the altar in cubits (the *cubit is* one cubit and a handbreadth): the base one cubit high and one cubit wide, with a rim all around its edge of one span. This *is* the height of the altar: ¹⁴from the base on the ground to the lower ledge, two cubits; the width of the ledge, one cubit; from the smaller ledge to the larger ledge, four cubits; and the width of the ledge, *one* cubit. ¹⁵The altar hearth *is* four cubits high, with four horns extending upward from the hearth. ¹⁶The altar hearth *is* twelve cubits long, twelve wide, square at its four corners; ¹⁷the ledge, fourteen *cubits* long and fourteen wide on its four sides, with a rim of half a cubit around it; its base, one cubit all around; and its steps face toward the east."

Consecrating the Altar

¹⁸And He said to me, "Son of man, thus says the Lord GOD: 'These *are* the ordinances for the altar on the day when it is made, for sacrificing burnt offerings on it, and for sprinkling blood on it. ¹⁹You shall give a young bull for a sin offering to the

43:19 a young bull for a sin offering. Exact offerings are literal here, as they were in Moses' day. They are of a memorial nature, pointing to the value of Christ's effective sacrifice, once for all (Heb. 9:28). Israel will finally offer acceptable sacrifices when they understand that these expressions of worship point to the Lamb of God. These sacrifices are tangible memorials of the glory of the Cross.

priests, the Levites, who are of the seed of Zadok, who approach Me to minister to Me,' says the Lord GOD. ²⁰You shall take some of its blood and put *it* on the four horns of the altar, on the four corners of the ledge, and on the rim around it; thus you shall cleanse it and make atonement for it. ²¹Then you shall also take the bull of the sin offering, and burn it in the appointed place of the temple, outside the sanctuary. ²²On the second day you shall offer a kid of the goats without blemish for a sin offering; and they shall cleanse the altar, as they cleansed *it* with the bull. ²³When you have finished cleansing *it*, you shall offer a young bull without blemish, and a ram from the flock without blemish. ²⁴When you offer them before the LORD, the priests shall throw salt on them, and they will offer them up *as* a burnt offering to the LORD. ²⁵Every day for seven days you shall prepare a goat *for* a sin offering; they shall also prepare a young bull and a ram from the flock, both without blemish. ²⁶Seven days they shall make atonement for the altar and purify it, and so consecrate *it*. ²⁷When these days are over it shall be, on the eighth day and thereafter, that the priests shall offer your burnt offerings and your peace offerings on the altar; and I will accept you,' says the Lord GOD."

The East Gate and the Prince

44 Then He brought me back to the outer gate of the sanctuary which faces toward the east, but it *was* shut. ²And the LORD said to me, "This gate shall be shut; it shall not be opened, and no man shall enter by it, because the LORD God of Israel has entered by it; therefore it shall be shut. ³*As for* the prince, *because* he *is* the prince, he may sit in it to eat bread before the LORD; he shall enter by way of the vestibule of the gateway, and go out the same way."

44:3 the prince...may sit in it. This prince is not the Lord Jesus Christ. He offers sacrifices for sins (45:22), he has sons (46:16–18), he cannot enter the E gate that the Lord used, he cannot perform priestly duties (45:19), and he must worship the Lord (46:2). He is most likely one who administrates the kingdom, representing the King and the princes who lead the 12 tribes. He may be a descendant of David.

Those Admitted to the Temple

⁴Also He brought me by way of the north gate to the front of the temple; so I looked, and behold, the glory of the LORD filled the house of the LORD; and I fell on my face. ⁵And the LORD said to me, "Son of man, mark well, see with your eyes and hear with your ears, all that I say to you concerning all the ordinances of the house of the LORD and all its laws. Mark well who may enter the house and all who go out from the sanctuary.

⁶"Now say to the rebellious, to the house of Israel, 'Thus says the Lord GOD: "O house of Israel, let Us have no more of all your abominations. ⁷When you brought in foreigners, uncircumcised in heart and uncircumcised in flesh, to be in My sanctuary to defile it—My house—and when you offered My food, the fat and the blood, then they broke My covenant because of all your abominations. ⁸And you have not kept charge of My holy things, but you have set *others* to keep charge of My sanctuary for you." ⁹Thus says the Lord GOD: "No foreigner, uncircumcised in heart or uncircumcised in flesh, shall enter My sanctuary, including any foreigner who *is* among the children of Israel.

44:5–9 Mark well who may enter. God will only allow the circumcised in heart to enter His temple (Deut. 30:6; Rom. 2:25–29). A circumcised heart is sincere about removing sin and being devoted to the Lord (see Jer. 29:13). In the Millennium, a Jew with an uncircumcised (sinful) heart will be considered a foreigner (rejecter of God). Many people besides Jews will enter God's kingdom during the Millennium because they have believed in Jesus Christ.

Laws Governing Priests

¹⁰"And the Levites who went far from Me, when Israel went astray, who strayed away from Me after their idols, they shall bear their iniquity. ¹¹Yet they shall be ministers in My sanctuary, *as* gatekeepers of the house and ministers of the house; they shall slay the burnt offering and the sacrifice for the people, and they shall stand before them to minister to them. ¹²Because they ministered to them before their idols and caused the house of Israel to fall into iniquity, therefore I have raised My hand in an oath against them," says the Lord GOD, "that they shall bear their iniquity. ¹³And

they shall not come near Me to minister to Me as priest, nor come near any of My holy things, nor into the Most Holy *Place*; but they shall bear their shame and their abominations which they have committed. ¹⁴Nevertheless I will make them keep charge of the temple, for all its work, and for all that has to be done in it.

¹⁵"But the priests, the Levites, the sons of Zadok, who kept charge of My sanctuary when the children of Israel went astray from Me, they shall come near Me to minister to Me; and they shall stand before Me to offer to Me the fat and the blood," says the Lord GOD. ¹⁶"They shall enter My sanctuary, and they shall come near My table to minister to Me, and they shall keep My charge. ¹⁷And it shall be, whenever they enter the gates of the inner court, that they shall put on linen garments; no wool shall come upon them while they minister within the gates of the inner court or within the house. ¹⁸They shall have linen turbans on their heads and linen trousers on their bodies; they shall not clothe themselves with *anything that causes* sweat. ¹⁹When they go out to the outer court, to the *outer* court to the people, they shall take off their garments in which they have ministered, leave them in the holy chambers, and put on other garments; and in their holy garments they shall not sanctify the people.

²⁰"They shall neither shave their heads, nor let their hair grow long, but they shall keep their hair well trimmed. ²¹No priest shall drink wine when he enters the inner court. ²²They shall not take as wife a widow or a divorced woman, but take virgins of the descendants of the house of Israel, or widows of priests.

²³"And they shall teach My people *the difference* between the holy and the unholy, and cause them to discern between the unclean and the clean. ²⁴In controversy they shall stand as judges, *and* judge it according to My judgments. They shall keep My laws and My statutes in all My appointed meetings, and they shall hallow My Sabbaths.

²⁵"They shall not defile *themselves* by coming near a dead person. Only for father or mother, for son or daughter, for brother or unmarried sister may they defile themselves. ²⁶After he is cleansed, they shall count seven days for him. ²⁷And on the day

that he goes to the sanctuary to minister in the sanctuary, he must offer his sin offering in the inner court," says the Lord GOD. [28]"It shall be, in regard to their inheritance, *that* I *am* their inheritance. You shall give them no possession in Israel, for I *am* their possession. [29]They shall eat the grain offering, the sin offering, and the trespass offering; every dedicated thing in Israel shall be theirs. [30]The best of all firstfruits of any kind, and every sacrifice of any kind from all your sacrifices, shall be the priest's; also you shall give to the priest the first of your ground meal, to cause a blessing to rest on your house. [31]The priests shall not eat anything, bird or beast, that died naturally or was torn *by wild beasts.*

44:28–31 I am their possession. The priests had no possessions in the Land when it was originally apportioned. In the future, God will be their portion.

The Holy District

45 "Moreover, when you divide the land by lot into inheritance, you shall set apart a district for the LORD, a holy section of the land; its length *shall be* twenty-five thousand *cubits,* and the width ten thousand. It *shall be* holy throughout its territory all around. [2]Of this there shall be a square plot for the sanctuary, five hundred by five hundred *rods,* with fifty cubits around it for an open space. [3]So this is the district you shall measure: twenty-five thousand *cubits* long and ten thousand wide; in it shall be the sanctuary, the Most Holy *Place.* [4]It shall be a holy *section* of the land, belonging to the priests, the ministers of the sanctuary, who come near to minister to the LORD; it shall be a place for their houses and a holy place for the sanctuary. [5]*An area* twenty-five thousand *cubits* long and ten thousand wide shall belong to the Levites, the ministers of the temple; they shall have twenty chambers as a possession.[a]

Properties of the City and the Prince

[6]"You shall appoint as the property of the city *an area* five thousand *cubits* wide and twenty-five thousand long, adjacent to the

district of the holy *section;* it shall belong to the whole house of Israel.

[7]"The prince shall have *a section* on one side and the other of the holy district and the city's property; and bordering on the holy district and the city's property, extending westward on the west side and eastward on the east side, the length *shall be* side by side with one of the *tribal* portions, from the west border to the east border. [8]The land shall be his possession in Israel; and My princes shall no more oppress My people, but they shall give *the rest of* the land to the house of Israel, according to their tribes."

45:8 My princes shall no more oppress. God promises that under the Messiah's rule, the leaders (the princes of each tribe) will not take advantage of the people by seizing their land (see 1 Kin. 21). No one will be deprived of his possessions.

Laws Governing the Prince

[9]Thus says the Lord GOD: "Enough, O princes of Israel! Remove violence and plundering, execute justice and righteousness, and stop dispossessing My people," says the Lord GOD. [10]"You shall have honest scales, an honest ephah, and an honest bath. [11]The ephah and the bath shall be of the same measure, so that the bath contains one-tenth of a homer, and the ephah one-tenth of a homer; their measure shall be according to the homer. [12]The shekel *shall be* twenty gerahs; twenty shekels, twenty-five shekels, *and* fifteen shekels shall be your mina.

45:9–12 The leaders of the land are warned to be honest in their commercial dealings, which signifies that sin can exist during the Millennium. The believing Jews who enter the 1,000 year reign of Christ and inherit the promised kingdom will be fully human and capable of sinning. Some children may not believe, as the final rebellion against the Messiah and His temple proves (see Rev. 20:7–9).

[13]"This *is* the offering which you shall offer: you shall give one-sixth of an ephah from a homer of wheat, and one-sixth of an ephah from a homer of barley. [14]The

---

45:5 [a]Following Masoretic Text, Targum, and Vulgate; Septuagint reads *a possession, cities of dwelling.*

ordinance concerning oil, the bath of oil, *is* one-tenth of a bath from a kor. A kor *is* a homer or ten baths, for ten baths *are* a homer. 15And one lamb shall be given from a flock of two hundred, from the rich pastures of Israel. These shall be for grain offerings, burnt offerings, and peace offerings, to make atonement for them," says the Lord GOD. 16"All the people of the land shall give this offering for the prince in Israel. 17Then it shall be the prince's part *to give* burnt offerings, grain offerings, and drink offerings, at the feasts, the New Moons, the Sabbaths, and at all the appointed seasons of the house of Israel. He shall prepare the sin offering, the grain offering, the burnt offering, and the peace offerings to make atonement for the house of Israel."

Keeping the Feasts

18'Thus says the Lord GOD: "In the first *month*, on the first *day* of the month, you shall take a young bull without blemish and cleanse the sanctuary. 19The priest shall take some of the blood of the sin offering and put *it* on the doorposts of the temple, on the four corners of the ledge of the altar, and on the gateposts of the gate of the inner court. 20And so you shall do on the seventh *day* of the month for everyone who has sinned unintentionally or in ignorance. Thus you shall make atonement for the temple.

21"In the first *month*, on the fourteenth day of the month, you shall observe the Passover, a feast of seven days; unleavened bread shall be eaten. 22And on that day the prince shall prepare for himself and for all the people of the land a bull *for* a sin offering. 23On the seven days of the feast he shall prepare a burnt offering to the LORD, seven bulls and seven rams without blemish, daily for seven days, and a kid of the goats daily *for* a sin offering. 24And he shall prepare a grain offering of one ephah for

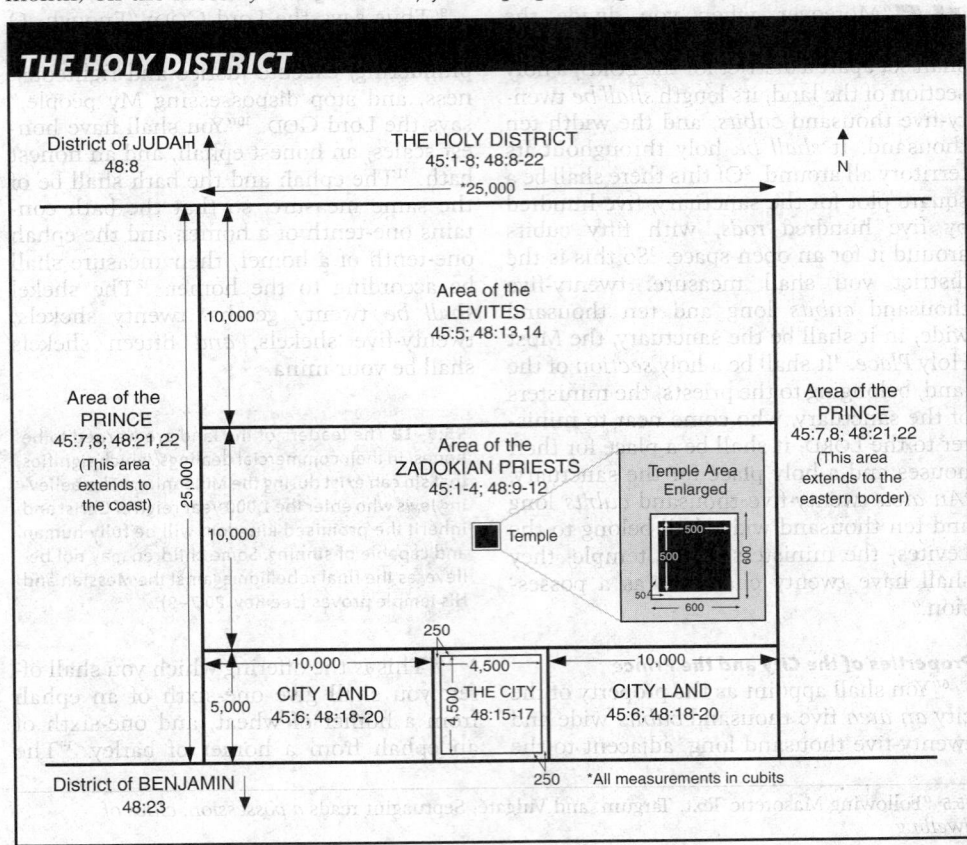

THE HOLY DISTRICT

District of JUDAH
48:8

THE HOLY DISTRICT
45:1-8; 48:8-22

*25,000

N

Area of the
LEVITES
45:5; 48:13,14

10,000

Area of the
PRINCE
45:7,8; 48:21,22
(This area
extends to
the coast)

25,000

Area of the
ZADOKIAN PRIESTS
45:1-4; 48:9-12

10,000

Area of the
PRINCE
45:7,8; 48:21,22
(This area
extends to the
eastern border)

Temple Area
Enlarged

Temple

500
500
600
500
600

250

5,000

10,000

4,500

CITY LAND
45:6; 48:18-20

4,500

THE CITY
48:15-17

10,000

CITY LAND
45:6; 48:18-20

District of BENJAMIN
48:23

250   *All measurements in cubits

each bull and one ephah for each ram, together with a hin of oil for each ephah.

²⁵"In the seventh *month*, on the fifteenth day of the month, at the feast, he shall do likewise for seven days, according to the sin offering, the burnt offering, the grain offering, and the oil."

The Manner of Worship

46 ¹Thus says the Lord GOD: "The gateway of the inner court that faces toward the east shall be shut the six working days; but on the Sabbath it shall be opened, and on the day of the New Moon it shall be opened. ²The prince shall enter by way of the vestibule of the gateway from the outside, and stand by the gatepost. The priests shall prepare his burnt offering and his peace offerings. He shall worship at the threshold of the gate. Then he shall go out, but the gate shall not be shut until evening. ³Likewise the people of the land shall worship at the entrance to this gateway before the LORD on the Sabbaths and the New Moons. ⁴The burnt offering that the prince offers to the LORD on the Sabbath day *shall be* six lambs without blemish, and a ram without blemish; ⁵and the grain offering *shall be one* ephah for a ram, and the grain offering for the lambs, as much as he wants to give, as well as a hin of oil with every ephah. ⁶On the day of the New Moon *it shall be* a young bull without blemish, six lambs, and a ram; they shall be without blemish. ⁷He shall prepare a grain offering of an ephah for a bull, an ephah for a ram, as much as he wants to give for the lambs, and a hin of oil with every ephah. ⁸When the prince enters, he shall go in by way of the vestibule of the gateway, and go out the same way.

⁹"But when the people of the land come before the LORD on the appointed feast days, whoever enters by way of the north gate to worship shall go out by way of the south gate; and whoever enters by way of the south gate shall go out by way of the north gate. He shall not return by way of the gate through which he came, but shall go out through the opposite gate. ¹⁰The prince shall then be in their midst. When they go in, he shall go in; and when they go out, he shall go out. ¹¹At the festivals and the appointed feast days the grain offering shall be an ephah for a bull, an ephah for a ram, as much as he wants to give for the lambs, and a hin of oil with every ephah.

¹²"Now when the prince makes a voluntary burnt offering or voluntary peace offering to the LORD, the gate that faces toward the east shall then be opened for him; and he shall prepare his burnt offering and his peace offerings as he did on the Sabbath day. Then he shall go out, and after he goes out the gate shall be shut.

¹³"You shall daily make a burnt offering to the LORD *of* a lamb of the first year without blemish; you shall prepare it every morning. ¹⁴And you shall prepare a grain offering with it every morning, a sixth of an ephah, and a third of a hin of oil to moisten the fine flour. This grain offering is a perpetual ordinance, to be made regularly to the LORD. ¹⁵Thus they shall prepare the lamb, the grain offering, and the oil, *as* a regular burnt offering every morning."

The Prince and Inheritance Laws

¹⁶'Thus says the Lord GOD: "If the prince gives a gift *of some* of his inheritance to any of his sons, it shall belong to his sons; it is their possession by inheritance. ¹⁷But if he gives a gift of some of his inheritance to one of his servants, it shall be his until the year of liberty, after which it shall return to the prince. But his inheritance shall belong to his sons; it shall become theirs. ¹⁸Moreover the prince shall not take any of the people's inheritance by evicting them from their property; he shall provide an inheritance for his sons from his own property, so that none of My people may be scattered from his property." ' "

How the Offerings Were Prepared

¹⁹Now he brought me through the entrance, which *was* at the side of the gate, into the holy chambers of the priests which

face toward the north; and there a place *was* situated at their extreme western end. ²⁰And he said to me, "This *is* the place where the priests shall boil the trespass offering and the sin offering, *and* where they shall bake the grain offering, so that they do not bring *them* out into the outer court to sanctify the people."

²¹Then he brought me out into the outer court and caused me to pass by the four corners of the court; and in fact, in every corner of the court *there was another* court. ²²In the four corners of the court *were* enclosed courts, forty *cubits* long and thirty wide; all four corners *were* the same size. ²³*There was* a row *of building stones* all around in them, all around the four of them; and cooking hearths were made under the rows of stones all around. ²⁴And he said to me, "These *are* the kitchens where the ministers of the temple shall boil the sacrifices of the people."

The Healing Waters and Trees

47 Then he brought me back to the door of the temple; and there was water, flowing from under the threshold of the temple toward the east, for the front of the temple faced east; the water was flowing from under the right side of the temple, south of the altar. ²He brought me out by way of the north gate, and led me around on the outside to the outer gateway that faces east; and there was water, running out on the right side.

³And when the man went out to the east with the line in his hand, he measured one thousand cubits, and he brought me through the waters; the water *came up to my* ankles. ⁴Again he measured one thousand and brought me through the waters; the water *came up to my* knees. Again he measured one thousand and brought me through; the water *came up to my* waist. ⁵Again he measured one thousand, *and it was* a river that I could not cross; for the water was too deep, water in which one must swim, a river that could not be crossed. ⁶He said to me, "Son of man, have you seen *this?*" Then he brought me and returned me to the bank of the river.

⁷When I returned, there, along the bank of the river, *were* very many trees on one side and the other. ⁸Then he said to me: "This water flows toward the eastern region, goes down into the valley, and enters the sea. *When it* reaches the sea, *its* waters are healed. ⁹And it shall be *that* every living thing that moves, wherever the rivers go, will live. There will be a very great multitude of fish, because these waters go there; for they will be healed, and everything will live wherever the river goes. ¹⁰It shall be *that* fishermen will stand by it from En Gedi to En Eglaim; they will be *places* for spreading their nets. Their fish will be of the same kinds as the fish of the Great Sea, exceedingly many. ¹¹But its swamps and marshes will not be healed; they will be

47:1–12 This section emphasizes that in the final kingdom, amazing physical and geographical changes will occur on earth, especially in Israel. This chapter deals mainly with changes in the water.

47:8 waters are healed. The water that flowed east and south into the Dead Sea could not support life because of its salt content (more than 6 times as salty as the sea). The Dead Sea is transformed into a "living sea" of fresh water.

MILLENNIAL FEASTS

Levitical	Millennial
1. N/A	1. New Year—Ezekiel 45:18–20
2. Passover—Leviticus 23:5	2. Passover—Ezekiel 45:21–24
3. Unleavened Bread—Leviticus 23:6–8	3. Unleavened Bread—Ezekiel 45:21–24
4. Pentecost—Leviticus 23:9–22	4. N/A
5. Trumpets—Leviticus 23:23–25	5. N/A
6. Atonement—Leviticus 23:26–32	6. N/A
7. Tabernacles—Leviticus 23:33–44	7. Tabernacles—Ezekiel 45:25

given over to salt. ¹²Along the bank of the river, on this side and that, will grow all *kinds of* trees used for food; their leaves will not wither, and their fruit will not fail. They will bear fruit every month, because their water flows from the sanctuary. Their fruit will be for food, and their leaves for medicine."

47:12 all *kinds of* trees. The scene describes the blessing of returning to Eden-like abundance (Gen. 2:8,9,16). **leaves...fruit.** The fruit is for food and the leaves are for medicinal purposes. The fruit is perpetual due to a continual supply of spring water from the temple.

Borders of the Land

¹³Thus says the Lord GOD: "These *are* the borders by which you shall divide the land as an inheritance among the twelve tribes of Israel. Joseph *shall have two* portions. ¹⁴You shall inherit it equally with one another; for I raised My hand in an oath to give it to your fathers, and this land shall fall to you as your inheritance.

47:13 Joseph...*two* portions. This follows the promise of Jacob to Joseph (Gen. 48:5,6,22; 49:22–26).

¹⁵"This *shall be* the border of the land on the north: from the Great Sea, *by* the road to Hethlon, as one goes to Zedad, ¹⁶Hamath, Berothah, Sibraim (which *is* between the border of Damascus and the border of Hamath), to Hazar Hatticon (which *is* on the border of Hauran). ¹⁷Thus the boundary shall be from the Sea to Hazar Enan, the border of Damascus; and as for the north, northward, it is the border of Hamath. *This is* the north side.

¹⁸"On the east side you shall mark out the border from between Hauran and Damascus, and between Gilead and the land of Israel, along the Jordan, and along the eastern side of the sea. *This is* the east side.

¹⁹"The south side, toward the South,[a] *shall be* from Tamar to the waters of Meribah by Kadesh, along the brook to the Great Sea. *This is* the south side, toward the South.

²⁰"The west side *shall be* the Great Sea, from the *southern* boundary until one comes to a point opposite Hamath. This *is* the west side.

²¹"Thus you shall divide this land among yourselves according to the tribes of Israel. ²²It shall be that you will divide it by lot as an inheritance for yourselves, and for the strangers who dwell among you and who bear children among you. They shall be to you as native-born among the children of Israel; they shall have an inheritance with you among the tribes of Israel. ²³And it shall be *that* in whatever tribe the stranger dwells, there you shall give *him* his inheritance," says the Lord GOD.

47:22 bear children. Children will be born all during the 1,000 year rule of the Messiah. Not all will believe and be saved, as evidenced by the final rebellion (see Rev. 20:8,9).

Division of the Land

48 "Now these *are* the names of the tribes: From the northern border along the road to Hethlon at the entrance of Hamath, to Hazar Enan, the border of Damascus northward, in the direction of Hamath, *there shall be* one *section for* Dan from its east to its west side; ²by the border of Dan, from the east side to the west, one *section for* Asher; ³by the border of Asher, from the east side to the west, one *section for* Naphtali; ⁴by the border of Naphtali, from the east side to the west, one *section for* Manasseh; ⁵by the border of Manasseh, from the east side to the west, one *section for* Ephraim; ⁶by the border of Ephraim, from the east side to the west, one *section for* Reuben; ⁷by the border of Reuben, from the east side to the west, one *section for* Judah; ⁸by the border of Judah, from the east side to the west, shall be the district which you shall set apart, twenty-five thousand *cubits* in width, and *in* length the same as one of the *other* portions, from the east side

48:1–7,23–29 the tribes. The land pledged to each tribe (47:13–23) fulfills God's promise to restore the Israelites to the Promised Land, just as they were scattered from it (28:25,26; Jer. 31:33). Dan, the first tribe mentioned, was omitted from the 144,000 in Rev. 7, most likely because of severe idolatry; but here Dan is graciously restored.

to the west, with the sanctuary in the center.

9"ThThe district that you shall set apart for the LORD *shall be* twenty-five thousand *cubits* in length and ten thousand in width. 10To these—to the priests—the holy district shall belong: on the north twenty-five thousand *cubits in length*, on the west ten thousand in width, on the east ten thousand in width, and on the south twenty-five thousand in length. The sanctuary of the LORD shall be in the center. 11*It shall be* for the priests of the sons of Zadok, who are sanctified, who have kept My charge, who did not go astray when the children of Israel went astray, as the Levites went astray. 12And *this* district of land that is set apart shall be to them a thing most holy by the border of the Levites.

13"Opposite the border of the priests, the Levites *shall have an area* twenty-five thousand *cubits* in length and ten thousand in width; its entire length *shall be* twenty-five thousand and its width ten thousand. 14And they shall not sell or exchange any of it; they may not alienate this best *part* of the land, for *it is* holy to the LORD.

15"The five thousand *cubits* in width that remain, along the edge of the twenty-five thousand, shall be for general use by the city, for dwellings and common-land; and the city shall be in the center. 16These *shall be* its measurements: the north side four thousand five hundred *cubits*, the south side four thousand five hundred, the east side four thousand five hundred, and the west side four thousand five hundred. 17The common-land of the city shall be: to the north two hundred and fifty *cubits*, to the south two hundred and fifty, to the east two hundred and fifty, and to the west two hundred and fifty. 18The rest of the length, alongside the district of the holy *section*, *shall be* ten thousand *cubits* to the east and ten thousand to the west. It shall be adjacent to the district of the holy *section*, and its produce shall be food for the workers of the city. 19The workers of the city, from all the tribes of Israel, shall cultivate it. 20The entire district *shall be* twenty-five thousand *cubits* by twenty-five thousand *cubits*, foursquare. You shall set

apart the holy district with the property of the city.

21"The rest *shall belong* to the prince, on one side and on the other of the holy district and of the city's property, next to the twenty-five thousand *cubits* of the *holy* district as far as the eastern border, and westward next to the twenty-five thousand as far as the western border, adjacent to the *tribal* portions; *it shall belong* to the prince. It shall be the holy district, and the sanctuary of the temple *shall be* in the center. 22Moreover, apart from the possession of the Levites and the possession of the city *which are* in the midst of what *belongs* to the prince, *the area* between the border of Judah and the border of Benjamin shall belong to the prince.

23"As for the rest of the tribes, from the east side to the west, Benjamin *shall have* one *section*; 24by the border of Benjamin, from the east side to the west, Simeon *shall have* one *section*; 25by the border of Simeon, from the east side to the west, Issachar *shall have* one *section*; 26by the border of Issachar, from the east side to the west, Zebulun *shall have* one *section*; 27by the border of Zebulun, from the east side to the west, Gad *shall have* one *section*; 28by the border of Gad, on the south side, toward the South,[a] the border shall be from Tamar *to* the waters of Meribah *by* Kadesh, along the brook to the Great Sea. 29This *is* the land which you shall divide by lot as an inheritance among the tribes of Israel, and these *are* their portions," says the Lord GOD.

The Gates of the City and Its Name

30"These *are* the exits of the city. On the north side, measuring four thousand five hundred *cubits* 31(the gates of the city *shall be* named after the tribes of Israel), the three gates northward: one gate for Reuben, one gate for Judah, and one gate for Levi;

> **48:30 four thousand five hundred *cubits*.** All four sides of Jerusalem totaled 18,000 cubits, which is nearly six miles around. Josephus, a Jewish historian, reported in the first century A.D. that Jerusalem was approximately four miles in perimeter.

48:28 [a]Hebrew *Negev*

[32]on the east side, four thousand five hundred *cubits*, three gates: one gate for Joseph, one gate for Benjamin, and one gate for Dan; [33]on the south side, measuring four thousand five hundred *cubits*, three gates: one gate for Simeon, one gate for Issachar, and one gate for Zebulun; [34]on the west side, four thousand five hundred *cubits* with their three gates: one gate for Gad, one gate for Asher, and one gate for Naphtali. [35]All the way around *shall be* eighteen thousand *cubits*; and the name of the city from *that* day *shall be*: THE LORD *IS* THERE."[a]

48:35 the name. The city is called YHWH Shammah, "The LORD is There." God's glory has returned, and His temple is the center of His kingdom. The Abrahamic Covenant (Gen. 12), the Levitic Covenant (Num. 25), the Davidic Covenant (2 Sam. 7), and the New Covenant (Jer. 31) have all been fulfilled. The returned presence of God is the consummation of Israel's history!

48:35 [a]Hebrew *YHWH Shammah*

DANIEL

Long before he faced down a den of lions, Daniel demonstrated courage, wisdom and integrity. He faced the loss of family and homeland with youthful dignity. He never used outside pressure or the humiliation of slavery to excuse a loss of personal standards. He served God and king without getting the two confused. When he emerged unscathed from the lion's den, the king knew Daniel had received God's protection. The king understood Daniel's ultimate loyalty. Daniel left a mark on history because he was a man of God.

AUTHOR AND DATE

Daniel was written by Daniel during his ministry, before 530 B.C.

Several internal references indicate that Daniel wrote this book (8:15,27; 9:2; 10:2,7; 12:4,5). Christ confirmed Daniel as the author (Matthew 24:15). Ezekiel called Daniel righteous and wise (Ezekiel 14:14,20; 28:3). The writer of Hebrews in the New Testament alluded to Daniel as one of ". . . the prophets: who through faith . . . stopped the mouths of lions" (Hebrews 11:32,33). The name Daniel means, "God is my Judge."

Daniel, a teenager from a noble Jewish family, was captured and taken from Israel to Babylon. He remained throughout the captivity (70 years) and probably died in Babylon. His background and apparent character earned him special attention in the court. Daniel made the most of his exile, successfully exalting God by his integrity and service. He quickly rose to the role of statesman by official royal appointment and served as an advisor to kings and a prophet of God in two world empires (Babylonian—2:48 and Medo-Persian—6:1,2).

Daniel lived beyond the date given as the third year of King Cyrus (Daniel 10:1), or about 536 B.C. The most likely date for Daniel's writing falls after this date. Interestingly, part of the book (2:46–7:28) was originally written in Aramaic, the contemporary language of international business.

BACKGROUND AND SETTING

The Book of Daniel opens in the heat and humiliation of Nebuchadnezzar's siege of Jerusalem in 605 B.C. With Israel's defeat, treasures from the temple and children from the best families were deported to Babylon. Among them were Daniel and three friends. Daniel's book continues to record the eventual demise of Babylon and the rise of the Medo-Persian Empire.

With the exception of the opening verses, the events recorded by Daniel occurred in Babylon. The captivity of the people of Judah had been prophesied by generations of God's servants. The group that included Daniel was exiled in the first of three major deportations from Judah to Babylon. The other two occurred in 597 B.C. and 586 B.C. The defeat came in stages. Eventually, Jerusalem and the beloved temple were destroyed. Daniel provides a description of life during the exile years.

Daniel was probably born during the reign of the last righteous King of Judah, Josiah (ca. 641–609 B.C.). He was captured following King Jehoiakim's defeat. He was old enough to remember his homeland. Writing 70 years later, Daniel's passion for Judah, particularly the temple in Jerusalem, still flowed from his pen.

HISTORICAL AND THEOLOGICAL THEMES

Prominent among the themes in Daniel is God's sovereign control over the affairs of all rulers and nations, and their eventual replacement by the True King and His everlasting Kingdom. The key verses that illustrate this theme are 2:20–22,44. In spite of Israel's fall, God had not suffered defeat. He was providentially working out His purposes and His plan. God allowed the Gentiles (Babylon, 605–539 B.C.; Medo-Persia, 539–331 B.C.; Greece, 331–146 B.C.; Rome, 146 B.C.–476 A.D. and all the way to the Second Advent of Christ) to dominate Israel as part of His sovereign plan.

> IN SPITE OF ISRAEL'S FALL, **GOD HAD NOT SUFFERED DEFEAT.** HE WAS PROVIDENTIALLY WORKING OUT **HIS PURPOSES** AND **HIS PLAN.**

Throughout Daniel, a picture of the character of the Messiah emerges. He is like a stone (chapter 2); like a son of man (chapter 7); the Anointed One (9:26). Chapter 9 provides a prophetic chronological framework from Daniel's day to Christ's kingdom.

Another significant theme woven into the fabric of Daniel is the display of God's power through miracles. Daniel credits his capacity to identify and interpret dreams completely to God. Other miracles included: (1) God's writing on the wall and Daniel's interpretation (chapter 5); (2) God's protection of the three men in a blazing furnace (chapter 3); (3) God's provision of safety for Daniel in the lions' den (chapter 6); and (4) Daniel's supernatural prophecies (chapters 2,7–12).

OUTLINE

Daniel and His Friends Obey God

1 In the third year of the reign of Jehoiakim king of Judah, Nebuchadnezzar king of Babylon came to Jerusalem and besieged it. ²And the Lord gave Jehoiakim king of Judah into his hand, with some of the articles of the house of God, which he carried into the land of Shinar to the house of his god; and he brought the articles into the treasure house of his god.

> **1:2 Shinar.** This is a term for Babylon. **his god.** This refers to Bel or Marduk (same as Merodach), one of many Babylonian gods. To conquer another nation's deity was thought to prove the superiority of the victor's god.

³Then the king instructed Ashpenaz, the master of his eunuchs, to bring some of the children of Israel and some of the king's descendants and some of the nobles, ⁴young men in whom *there was* no blemish, but good-looking, gifted in all wisdom, possessing knowledge and quick to understand, who *had* ability to serve in the king's palace, and whom they might teach the language and literature of the Chaldeans. ⁵And the king appointed for them a daily provision of the king's delicacies and of the wine which he drank, and three years of training for them, so that at the end of *that time*

AN OVERVIEW OF DANIEL'S KINGDOMS

I. Daniel 2/Daniel 7

A. Babylon	2:32,37,38; 7:4,17
B. Medo-Persia	2:32,39; 7:5,17
C. Greece	2:32,39; 7:6,17
D. Rome	2:33,40; 7:7,17,23
E. Revived Rome	2:33,41–43; 7:7,8,11, 24,25
F. Millennium	2:34,35,44,45; 7:13,14, 26,27

II. Daniel 8/Daniel 11

A. Medo-Persia	8:3–8,20,21; 10:20,21, 11:2–35
B. Greece	8:3–8,20,21; 10:20,21, 11:2–35
C. Revived Rome	8:9–12,23–26; 11:36–45.

they might serve before the king. ⁶Now from among those of the sons of Judah were Daniel, Hananiah, Mishael, and Azariah. ⁷To them the chief of the eunuchs gave names: he gave Daniel *the name* Belteshazzar; to Hananiah, Shadrach; to Mishael, Meshach; and to Azariah, Abed-Nego.

⁸But Daniel purposed in his heart that he would not defile himself with the portion of the king's delicacies, nor with the wine which he drank; therefore he requested of the chief of the eunuchs that he might not defile himself. ⁹Now God had brought Daniel into the favor and goodwill of the chief of the eunuchs. ¹⁰And the chief of the eunuchs said to Daniel, "I fear my lord the king, who has appointed your food and drink. For why should he see your faces looking worse than the young men who *are* your age? Then you would endanger my head before the king."

> **1:8 Daniel purposed.** Daniel "purposed in his heart" (see Prov. 4:23) not to indulge in the pagan food or drink, as it was offered to idols. To indulge would be to honor these deities, and Daniel would not compromise his commitment to God (see Dan. 1:12). God's law prohibited food that the pagans consumed (Lev. 1). Moses (Heb. 11:24–26), the psalmist (Ps. 119:115), and Jesus (Heb. 7:26) all took this stand.

¹¹So Daniel said to the steward[a] whom the chief of the eunuchs had set over Daniel, Hananiah, Mishael, and Azariah, ¹²"Please test your servants for ten days, and let them give us vegetables to eat and water to drink. ¹³Then let our appearance be examined before you, and the appearance of the young men who eat the portion of the king's delicacies; and as you see fit, *so* deal with your servants." ¹⁴So he consented with them in this matter, and tested them ten days.

¹⁵And at the end of ten days their features appeared better and fatter in flesh than all the young men who ate the portion of the king's delicacies. ¹⁶Thus the steward took away their portion of delicacies and the wine that they were to drink, and gave them vegetables.

> **1:15 fatter in flesh.** This indicates healthiness.

1:11 ᵃHebrew *Melzar*, also in verse 16

[17]As for these four young men, God gave them knowledge and skill in all literature and wisdom; and Daniel had understanding in all visions and dreams.

[18]Now at the end of the days, when the king had said that they should be brought in, the chief of the eunuchs brought them in before Nebuchadnezzar. [19]Then the king interviewed[a] them, and among them all none was found like Daniel, Hananiah, Mishael, and Azariah; therefore they served before the king. [20]And in all matters of wisdom *and* understanding about which the king examined them, he found them ten times better than all the magicians *and* astrologers who *were* in all his realm. [21]Thus Daniel continued until the first year of King Cyrus.

Nebuchadnezzar's Dream

2 Now in the second year of Nebuchadnezzar's reign, Nebuchadnezzar had dreams; and his spirit was *so* troubled that his sleep left him. [2]Then the king gave the command to call the magicians, the astrologers, the sorcerers, and the Chaldeans to tell the king his dreams. So they came and stood before the king. [3]And the king said to them, "I have had a dream, and my spirit is anxious to know the dream."

[4]Then the Chaldeans spoke to the king in Aramaic,[a] "O king, live forever! Tell your servants the dream, and we will give the interpretation."

2:4 Aramaic. This was the popular language of the Babylonian, Assyrian, and Persian areas and was useful in governmental and trade relations. Daniel switches to this language, which was written with an alphabet similar to Hebrew. Daniel 1:1–2:4a and 8:1–12:13 were written in Hebrew, as the focus was on Hebrew matters. Verses 2:4b–7:28 are in Aramaic because the content focuses on other nations.

[5]The king answered and said to the Chaldeans, "My decision is firm: if you do not make known the dream to me, and its interpretation, you shall be cut in pieces, and your houses shall be made an ash heap. [6]However, if you tell the dream and its interpretation, you shall receive from me gifts, rewards, and great honor. Therefore tell me the dream and its interpretation."

[7]They answered again and said, "Let the king tell his servants the dream, and we will give its interpretation."

[8]The king answered and said, "I know for certain that you would gain time, because you see that my decision is firm: [9]if you do not make known the dream to me, *there is only* one decree for you! For you have agreed to speak lying and corrupt words before me till the time has changed. Therefore tell me the dream, and I shall know that you can give me its interpretation."

[10]The Chaldeans answered the king, and said, "There is not a man on earth who can tell the king's matter; therefore no king, lord, or ruler has *ever* asked such things of any magician, astrologer, or Chaldean. [11]*It is* a difficult thing that the king requests, and there is no other who can tell it to the king except the gods, whose dwelling is not with flesh."

[12]For this reason the king was angry and very furious, and gave the command to destroy all the wise *men* of Babylon. [13]So the decree went out, and they began killing the wise *men*; and they sought Daniel and his companions, to kill *them*.

God Reveals Nebuchadnezzar's Dream

[14]Then with counsel and wisdom Daniel answered Arioch, the captain of the king's guard, who had gone out to kill the wise *men* of Babylon; [15]he answered and said to Arioch the king's captain, "Why is the decree from the king so urgent?" Then Arioch made the decision known to Daniel.

[16]So Daniel went in and asked the king to give him time, that he might tell the king the interpretation. [17]Then Daniel went to his house, and made the decision known to Hananiah, Mishael, and Azariah, his companions, [18]that they might seek mercies from the God of heaven concerning this secret, so that Daniel and his companions might not perish with the rest of the wise *men* of Babylon. [19]Then the secret was revealed to Daniel in a night vision. So Daniel blessed the God of heaven.

[20]Daniel answered and said:

"Blessed be the name of God forever
    and ever,

1:19 [a]Literally *talked with them*   2:4 [a]The original language of Daniel 2:4b through 7:28 is Aramaic.

For wisdom and might are His.
21 And He changes the times and the
        seasons;
    He removes kings and raises up kings;
    He gives wisdom to the wise
    And knowledge to those who have
        understanding.
22 He reveals deep and secret things;
    He knows what *is* in the darkness,
    And light dwells with Him.

23 "I thank You and praise You,
        O God of my fathers;
    You have given me wisdom and
        might,
    And have now made known to me
        what we asked of You,
    For You have made known to us the
        king's demand."

2:20–23 This praise to God sums up the theme of the whole book: God is the One who controls all things and grants all wisdom and might.

Daniel Explains the Dream

24Therefore Daniel went to Arioch, whom the king had appointed to destroy the wise *men* of Babylon. He went and said thus to him: "Do not destroy the wise *men* of Babylon; take me before the king, and I will tell the king the interpretation." 25Then Arioch quickly brought Daniel before the king, and said thus to him, "I have found a man of the captives*a* of Judah, who will make known to the king the interpretation." 26The king answered and said to Daniel, whose name *was* Belteshazzar, "Are you able to make known to me the dream which I have seen, and its interpretation?" 27Daniel answered in the presence of the king, and said, "The secret which the king has demanded, the wise *men*, the astrologers, the magicians, and the soothsayers cannot declare to the king. 28But there is a God in heaven who reveals secrets, and He has made known to King Nebuchadnezzar what will be in the latter days. Your dream, and the visions of your head upon your bed, were these: 29As for you, O king, thoughts came *to* your *mind while* on your bed,

about what would come to pass after this; and He who reveals secrets has made known to you what will be. 30But as for me, this secret has not been revealed to me because I have more wisdom than anyone living, but for *our* sakes who make known the interpretation to the king, and that you may know the thoughts of your heart. 31"You, O king, were watching; and behold, a great image! This great image, whose splendor *was* excellent, stood before you; and its form *was* awesome. 32This image's head *was* of fine gold, its chest and arms of silver, its belly and thighs*a* of bronze, 33its legs of iron, its feet partly of iron and partly of clay.*a* 34You watched while a stone was cut out without hands, which struck the image on its feet of iron and clay, and broke them in pieces. 35Then the iron, the clay, the bronze, the silver, and the gold were crushed together, and became like chaff from the summer threshing floors; the wind carried them away so that no trace of them was found. And the stone that struck the image became a great mountain and filled the whole earth.

2:36–45 we will tell the interpretation. Babylon, Medo-Persia, Greece, Rome and the later revived Rome would all rule over Israel. Each empire, pictured by parts of a statue, would rule differently, as indicated by the declining quality of the metal. A stone, picturing Christ (Luke 20:18) at His second coming, will destroy the final phase fourth empire (2:34,35,44,45). By shattering the Gentile power, Christ will establish His millennial kingdom (2:44; 7:27).

36"This *is* the dream. Now we will tell the interpretation of it before the king. 37You, O king, *are* a king of kings. For the God of heaven has given you a kingdom, power, strength, and glory; 38and wherever the children of men dwell, or the beasts of the field and the birds of the heaven, He has given *them* into your hand, and has made you ruler over them all—you *are* this head of gold. 39But after you shall arise another kingdom inferior to yours; then another, a third kingdom of bronze, which shall rule over all the earth. 40And the fourth kingdom shall be as strong as iron, inasmuch as

---

2:25 *a*Literally *of the sons of the captivity*   2:32 *a*Or *sides*   2:33 *a*Or *baked clay*, and so in verses 34, 35, and 42

iron breaks in pieces and shatters everything; and like iron that crushes, *that kingdom* will break in pieces and crush all the others. [41]Whereas you saw the feet and toes, partly of potter's clay and partly of iron, the kingdom shall be divided; yet the strength of the iron shall be in it, just as you saw the iron mixed with ceramic clay. [42]And *as* the toes of the feet *were* partly of iron and partly of clay, *so* the kingdom shall be partly strong and partly fragile. [43]As you saw iron mixed with ceramic clay, they will mingle with the seed of men; but they will not adhere to one another, just as iron does not mix with clay. [44]And in the days of these kings the God of heaven will set up a kingdom which shall never be destroyed; and the kingdom shall not be left to other people; it shall break in pieces and consume all these kingdoms, and it shall stand forever. [45]Inasmuch as you saw that the stone was cut out of the mountain without hands, and that it broke in pieces the iron, the bronze, the clay, the silver, and the gold—the great God has made known to the king what will come to pass after this. The dream is certain, and its interpretation is sure."

2:41–43 clay and...iron. The iron in the 10 toes (kings) represents the strength of the revived Roman Empire, prior to the second coming of Christ (see Rev. 13:4,5). The clay mixed in represents the vulnerability of the union of kings and nations due to human weakness.

Daniel and His Friends Promoted

[46]Then King Nebuchadnezzar fell on his face, prostrate before Daniel, and commanded that they should present an offering and incense to him. [47]The king answered Daniel, and said, "Truly your God *is* the God of gods, the Lord of kings, and a revealer of secrets, since you could reveal this secret." [48]Then the king promoted Daniel and gave him many great gifts; and he made him ruler over the whole province of Babylon, and chief administrator over all the wise *men* of Babylon. [49]Also Daniel petitioned the king, and he set Shadrach, Meshach, and Abed-Nego over the affairs of the province of Babylon; but Daniel *sat* in the gate[a] of the king.

The Image of Gold

3 Nebuchadnezzar the king made an image of gold, whose height *was* sixty cubits *and* its width six cubits. He set it up in the plain of Dura, in the province of Babylon. [2]And King Nebuchadnezzar sent *word* to gather together the satraps, the administrators, the governors, the counselors, the treasurers, the judges, the magistrates, and all the officials of the provinces, to come to the dedication of the image which King Nebuchadnezzar had set up. [3]So the satraps, the administrators, the governors, the counselors, the treasurers, the judges, the magistrates, and all the officials of the provinces gathered together for the dedication of the image that King Nebuchadnezzar had set up; and they stood before the image that Nebuchadnezzar had set up. [4]Then a herald cried aloud: "To you it is commanded, O peoples, nations, and languages, [5]*that* at the time you hear the sound of the horn, flute, harp, lyre, *and* psaltery, in symphony with all kinds of music, you shall fall down and worship the gold image that King Nebuchadnezzar has set up; [6]and whoever does not fall down and worship shall be cast immediately into the midst of a burning fiery furnace."

3:1 image of gold. Nebuchadnezzar arrogantly made the statue to represent himself and to reflect his dream in which he was the head of gold. It was not necessarily made of solid gold but was probably overlaid with gold. The image was about 90 feet high and 9 feet wide. This established the worship of Nebuchadnezzar and secured the nation under his power.

[7]So at that time, when all the people heard the sound of the horn, flute, harp, *and* lyre, in symphony with all kinds of music, all the people, nations, and languages fell down *and* worshiped the gold image which King Nebuchadnezzar had set up.

Daniel's Friends Disobey the King

[8]Therefore at that time certain Chaldeans came forward and accused the Jews.

2:49 [a]That is, the king's court

[9]They spoke and said to King Nebuchadnezzar, "O king, live forever! [10]You, O king, have made a decree that everyone who hears the sound of the horn, flute, harp, lyre, *and* psaltery, in symphony with all kinds of music, shall fall down and worship the gold image; [11]and whoever does not fall down and worship shall be cast into the midst of a burning fiery furnace. [12]There are certain Jews whom you have set over the affairs of the province of Babylon: Shadrach, Meshach, and Abed-Nego; these men, O king, have not paid due regard to you. They do not serve your gods or worship the gold image which you have set up."

[13]Then Nebuchadnezzar, in rage and fury, gave the command to bring Shadrach, Meshach, and Abed-Nego. So they brought these men before the king. [14]Nebuchadnezzar spoke, saying to them, "*Is it* true, Shadrach, Meshach, and Abed-Nego, *that* you do not serve my gods or worship the gold image which I have set up? [15]Now if you are ready at the time you hear the sound of the horn, flute, harp, lyre, *and* psaltery, in symphony with all kinds of music, and you fall down and worship the image which I have made, *good!* But if you do not worship, you shall be cast immediately into the midst of a burning fiery furnace. And who *is* the god who will deliver you from my hands?"

[16]Shadrach, Meshach, and Abed-Nego answered and said to the king, "O Nebuchadnezzar, we have no need to answer you in this matter. [17]If that *is the case,* our God whom we serve is able to deliver us from the burning fiery furnace, and He will deliver *us* from your hand, O king. [18]But if not, let it be known to you, O king, that we do not serve your gods, nor will we worship the gold image which you have set up."

> **3:16 we have no need to answer.** The three men meant no disrespect. They did not have a defense, nor did they need to reconsider their commitment, since they stood fast for their God. Their lives were in His hands, as they indicated in verses 17,18 (see Is. 43:1,2).

Saved in Fiery Trial

[19]Then Nebuchadnezzar was full of fury, and the expression on his face changed toward Shadrach, Meshach, and Abed-Nego. He spoke and commanded that they heat the furnace seven times more than it was usually heated. [20]And he commanded certain mighty men of valor who *were* in his army to bind Shadrach, Meshach, and Abed-Nego, *and* cast *them* into the burning fiery furnace. [21]Then these men were bound in their coats, their trousers, their turbans, and their *other* garments, and

Who was the fourth person in the fiery furnace of 3:19–25?

The delivery of Shadrach, Meshach, and Abednego from the flames was an astonishing, miraculous event. The furnace was real, and the flames were hot. The guards who carried the young men close enough to cast them in the furnace were killed. Why complicate this miracle with a fourth person in the furnace? Because the king himself noticed the discrepancy between the number he had thrown into the flames and the number he saw strolling about. The truth usually includes unexpected complications.

The king concluded the fourth person was a heavenly being. He identified the visitor in two different ways: (1) "like the Son of God" (3:25); (2) "angel" (3:28). When he commanded the three friends to exit the furnace, the king did not extend an invitation to God's special servant.

Viewed from the context of all of Scripture, the fourth person could possibly have been the second person of the Godhead (Jesus Christ) in a pre-incarnate appearance. For other similar Old Testament instances, see Exodus 3:2, Joshua 5:13–15, and Judges 6:11ff. While the term "angel" is used in these reports, the person had a special connection with the Lord. He wasn't an angel, but the Angel of the Lord. His presence may be startling but He does not have the stunning and awe-inspiring appearance of an angel. The king saw four men in the furnace. The one who appeared miraculously he identified as the Son of God. It may well have been an inspired exclamation.

were cast into the midst of the burning fiery furnace. ²²Therefore, because the king's command was urgent, and the furnace exceedingly hot, the flame of the fire killed those men who took up Shadrach, Meshach, and Abed-Nego. ²³And these three men, Shadrach, Meshach, and Abed-Nego, fell down bound into the midst of the burning fiery furnace.

²⁴Then King Nebuchadnezzar was astonished; and he rose in haste *and* spoke, saying to his counselors, "Did we not cast three men bound into the midst of the fire?"

They answered and said to the king, "True, O king."

²⁵"Look!" he answered, "I see four men loose, walking in the midst of the fire; and they are not hurt, and the form of the fourth is like the Son of God."*a*

Nebuchadnezzar Praises God

²⁶Then Nebuchadnezzar went near the mouth of the burning fiery furnace *and* spoke, saying, "Shadrach, Meshach, and Abed-Nego, servants of the Most High God, come out, and come *here*." Then Shadrach, Meshach, and Abed-Nego came from the midst of the fire. ²⁷And the satraps, administrators, governors, and the king's counselors gathered together, and they saw these men on whose bodies the fire had no power; the hair of their head was not singed nor were their garments affected, and the smell of fire was not on them.

²⁸Nebuchadnezzar spoke, saying, "Blessed be the God of Shadrach, Meshach, and Abed-Nego, who sent His Angel*a* and delivered His servants who trusted in Him, and they have frustrated the king's word, and yielded their bodies, that they should not serve nor worship any god except their own God! ²⁹Therefore I make a decree that any people, nation, or language which speaks anything amiss against the God of Shadrach, Meshach, and Abed-Nego shall be cut in pieces, and their houses shall be made an ash heap; because there is no other God who can deliver like this."

³⁰Then the king promoted Shadrach, Meshach, and Abed-Nego in the province of Babylon.

Nebuchadnezzar's Second Dream

4 Nebuchadnezzar the king,

To all peoples, nations, and languages that dwell in all the earth:

Peace be multiplied to you.

² I thought it good to declare the signs and wonders that the Most High God has worked for me.

³ How great *are* His signs,
And how mighty His wonders!
His kingdom *is* an everlasting kingdom,
And His dominion *is* from generation to generation.

⁴ I, Nebuchadnezzar, was at rest in my house, and flourishing in my palace. ⁵I saw a dream which made me afraid, and the thoughts on my bed and the visions of my head troubled me. ⁶Therefore I issued a decree to bring in all the wise *men* of Babylon before me, that they might make known to me the interpretation of the dream. ⁷Then the magicians, the astrologers, the Chaldeans, and the soothsayers came in, and I told them the dream; but they did not make known to me its interpretation. ⁸But at last Daniel came before me (his name *is* Belteshazzar, according to the name of my god; in him *is* the Spirit of the Holy God), and I told the dream before him, *saying:* ⁹"Belteshazzar, chief of the magicians, because I know that the Spirit of the Holy God *is* in you, and no secret troubles you, explain to me the visions of my dream that I have seen, and its interpretation.

¹⁰ "These *were* the visions of my head *while* on my bed:

I was looking, and behold,
A tree in the midst of the earth,
And its height was great.
¹¹ The tree grew and became strong;

3:25 *a*Or *a son of the gods*   3:28 *a*Or *angel*

Its height reached to the heavens,
And it could be seen to the ends of all
    the earth.
¹² Its leaves *were* lovely,
Its fruit abundant,
And in it *was* food for all.
The beasts of the field found shade
    under it,
The birds of the heavens dwelt in its
    branches,
And all flesh was fed from it.

4:10–17 A tree. This pictures Nebuchadnezzar after 605 B.C. (see 4:20–22). The creatures in verse 12 represent people under his rule. The fall of the tree represents the coming time of God's judgment on him (see 4:23–25).

¹³ "I saw in the visions of my head *while*
on my bed, and there was a watcher, a
holy one, coming down from heaven.
¹⁴He cried aloud and said thus:

'Chop down the tree and cut off its
    branches,
Strip off its leaves and scatter its fruit.
Let the beasts get out from under it,
And the birds from its branches.
¹⁵ Nevertheless leave the stump and
    roots in the earth,
Bound with a band of iron and bronze,
In the tender grass of the field.
Let it be wet with the dew of heaven,
And *let* him graze with the beasts
On the grass of the earth.
¹⁶ Let his heart be changed from *that of*
    a man,
Let him be given the heart of a beast,
And let seven times*ᵃ* pass over him.

4:16 heart of a beast. A form of the disease called lycanthropy, in which a person thinks he is an animal, caused him to eat grass, have thick nails and shaggy hair, and behave inhumanly. **seven times.** This probably refers to seven "years" (not "months," which is used in v. 29). Daniel uses the same term to mean "years" in 7:25.

¹⁷ 'This decision *is* by the decree of the
    watchers,
And the sentence by the word of the
    holy ones,

In order that the living may know
That the Most High rules in the
    kingdom of men,
Gives it to whomever He will,
And sets over it the lowest of men.'

¹⁸ "This dream I, King Nebuchadnezzar,
have seen. Now you, Belteshazzar,
declare its interpretation, since all the
wise *men* of my kingdom are not able
to make known to me the
interpretation; but you *are* able, for
the Spirit of the Holy God *is* in you."

Daniel Explains the Second Dream

¹⁹ Then Daniel, whose name was
Belteshazzar, was astonished for a
time, and his thoughts troubled him.
So the king spoke, and said,
"Belteshazzar, do not let the dream or
its interpretation trouble you."
Belteshazzar answered and said, "My
lord, *may* the dream concern those
who hate you, and its interpretation
concern your enemies!

²⁰ "The tree that you saw, which grew
and became strong, whose height
reached to the heavens and which
could be seen by all the earth, ²¹whose
leaves *were* lovely and its fruit
abundant, in which *was* food for all,
under which the beasts of the field
dwelt, and in whose branches the
birds of the heaven had their home—
²²it *is* you, O king, who have grown
and become strong; for your greatness
has grown and reaches to the
heavens, and your dominion to the
end of the earth.

²³ "And inasmuch as the king saw a
watcher, a holy one, coming down
from heaven and saying, 'Chop down
the tree and destroy it, but leave its
stump and roots in the earth, *bound*
with a band of iron and bronze in the
tender grass of the field; let it be wet
with the dew of heaven, and let him
graze with the beasts of the field, till
seven times pass over him'; ²⁴this is
the interpretation, O king, and this is

4:16 *ᵃ*Possibly *seven years*, and so in verses 23,25, and 32

the decree of the Most High, which has come upon my lord the king: 25They shall drive you from men, your dwelling shall be with the beasts of the field, and they shall make you eat grass like oxen. They shall wet you with the dew of heaven, and seven times shall pass over you, till you know that the Most High rules in the kingdom of men, and gives it to whomever He chooses.

26   "And inasmuch as they gave the command to leave the stump *and* roots of the tree, your kingdom shall be assured to you, after you come to know that Heaven rules. 27Therefore, O king, let my advice be acceptable to you; break off your sins by *being* righteous, and your iniquities by showing mercy to *the* poor. Perhaps there may be a lengthening of your prosperity."

4:27 break off your sins. Daniel called for a recognition of sin and repentance (see Is. 55:7). He was not presenting a works salvation, but he treated the issue of sin as Jesus did with the rich young ruler in Matt. 19:16–23. The king did not repent at this point.

Nebuchadnezzar's Humiliation

28   All *this* came upon King Nebuchadnezzar. 29At the end of the twelve months he was walking about the royal palace of Babylon. 30The king spoke, saying, "Is not this great Babylon, that I have built for a royal dwelling by my mighty power and for the honor of my majesty?"

31   While the word *was still* in the king's mouth, a voice fell from heaven: "King Nebuchadnezzar, to you it is spoken: the kingdom has departed from you! 32And they shall drive you from men, and your dwelling *shall be* with the beasts of the field. They shall make you eat grass like oxen; and seven times shall pass over you, until you know that the Most High rules in the kingdom of men, and gives it to whomever He chooses."

33   That very hour the word was fulfilled concerning Nebuchadnezzar; he was driven from men and ate grass like oxen; his body was wet with the dew of heaven till his hair had grown like eagles' *feathers* and his nails like birds' *claws*.

Nebuchadnezzar Praises God

34   And at the end of the time[a] I, Nebuchadnezzar, lifted my eyes to heaven, and my understanding returned to me; and I blessed the Most High and praised and honored Him who lives forever:

For His dominion *is* an everlasting
    dominion,
And His kingdom *is* from generation
    to generation.
35   All the inhabitants of the earth *are*
    reputed as nothing;
He does according to His will in the
    army of heaven
And *among* the inhabitants of the
    earth.
No one can restrain His hand
Or say to Him, "What have You
    done?"

36   At the same time my reason returned to me, and for the glory of my kingdom, my honor and splendor returned to me. My counselors and nobles resorted to me, I was restored to my kingdom, and excellent majesty was added to me. 37Now I, Nebuchadnezzar, praise and extol and honor the King of heaven, all of whose works *are* truth, and His ways justice. And those who walk in pride He is able to put down.

Belshazzar's Feast

5 Belshazzar the king made a great feast for a thousand of his lords, and drank wine in the presence of the thousand. 2While he tasted the wine, Belshazzar gave the command to bring the gold and silver vessels which his father Nebuchadnezzar had taken from the temple which *had been*

4:34 *a*Literally *days*

5:1 Belshazzar. This king, whose name (similar to Daniel's, see 4:8) means "Bel, protect the king," is about to be conquered by the Medo-Persian army. This occurred in 539 B.C., more than two decades after the death of his father, Nebuchadnezzar (about 563/62 B.C.).

in Jerusalem, that the king and his lords, his wives, and his concubines might drink from them. ³Then they brought the gold vessels that had been taken from the temple of the house of God which *had been* in Jerusalem; and the king and his lords, his wives, and his concubines drank from them. ⁴They drank wine, and praised the gods of gold and silver, bronze and iron, wood and stone.

⁵In the same hour the fingers of a man's hand appeared and wrote opposite the lampstand on the plaster of the wall of the king's palace; and the king saw the part of the hand that wrote. ⁶Then the king's countenance changed, and his thoughts troubled him, so that the joints of his hips were loosened and his knees knocked against each other. ⁷The king cried aloud to bring in the astrologers, the Chaldeans, and the soothsayers. The king spoke, saying to the wise *men* of Babylon, "Whoever reads this writing, and tells me its interpretation, shall be clothed with purple and *have* a chain of gold around his neck; and he shall be the third ruler in the kingdom." ⁸Now all the king's wise *men* came, but they could not read the writing, or make known to the king its interpretation. ⁹Then King Belshazzar was greatly troubled, his countenance was changed, and his lords were astonished.

¹⁰The queen, because of the words of the king and his lords, came to the banquet hall. The queen spoke, saying, "O king, live forever! Do not let your thoughts trouble you, nor let your countenance change. ¹¹There is a man in your kingdom in whom *is* the Spirit of the Holy God. And in the days of your father, light and understanding

5:10 The queen spoke. This queen was either a surviving wife of Nebuchadnezzar or one of his daughters. If the latter, she was a wife of Nabonidus, who co-ruled with Belshazzar. She, like Nebuchadnezzar in chapter 4, has confidence in Daniel (vv. 11,12).

and wisdom, like the wisdom of the gods, were found in him; and King Nebuchadnezzar your father—your father the king—made him chief of the magicians, astrologers, Chaldeans, *and* soothsayers. ¹²Inasmuch as an excellent spirit, knowledge, understanding, interpreting dreams, solving riddles, and explaining enigmas*ᵃ* were found in this Daniel, whom the king named Belteshazzar, now let Daniel be called, and he will give the interpretation."

The Writing on the Wall Explained

¹³Then Daniel was brought in before the king. The king spoke, and said to Daniel, "*Are* you that Daniel who is one of the captives*ᵃ* from Judah, whom my father the king brought from Judah? ¹⁴I have heard of you, that the Spirit of God *is* in you, and *that* light and understanding and excellent wisdom are found in you. ¹⁵Now the wise *men*, the astrologers, have been brought in before me, that they should read this writing and make known to me its interpretation, but they could not give the interpretation of the thing. ¹⁶And I have heard of you, that you can give interpretations and explain enigmas. Now if you can read the writing and make known to me its interpretation, you shall be clothed with purple and *have* a chain of gold around your neck, and shall be the third ruler in the kingdom."

¹⁷Then Daniel answered, and said before the king, "Let your gifts be for yourself, and give your rewards to another; yet I will read the writing to the king, and make known to him the interpretation. ¹⁸O king, the Most High God gave Nebuchadnezzar your father a kingdom and majesty, glory and honor. ¹⁹And because of the majesty that He gave him, all peoples, nations, and languages trembled and feared before him. Whomever he wished, he executed; whomever he wished, he kept alive; whomever he wished, he set up; and whomever he wished, he put down. ²⁰But when his heart was lifted up, and his spirit was hardened in pride, he was deposed from his kingly throne, and they took his glory from him. ²¹Then he was driven from the sons of men, his heart was made like the beasts, and his dwelling *was* with the wild donkeys. They

5:12 *ᵃ*Literally *untying knots*, and so in verse 16   5:13 *ᵃ*Literally *of the sons of the captivity*

fed him with grass like oxen, and his body was wet with the dew of heaven, till he knew that the Most High God rules in the kingdom of men, and appoints over it whomever He chooses.

22"But you his son, Belshazzar, have not humbled your heart, although you knew all this. 23And you have lifted yourself up against the Lord of heaven. They have brought the vessels of His house before you, and you and your lords, your wives and your concubines, have drunk wine from them. And you have praised the gods of silver and gold, bronze and iron, wood and stone, which do not see or hear or know; and the God who *holds* your breath in His hand and owns all your ways, you have not glorified. 24Then the fingers*a* of the hand were sent from Him, and this writing was written.

25"And this is the inscription that was written:

MENE,*a* MENE, TEKEL,*b* UPHARSIN.*c*

26This *is* the interpretation of *each* word. MENE: God has numbered your kingdom, and finished it; 27TEKEL: You have been weighed in the balances, and found wanting; 28PERES: Your kingdom has been divided, and given to the Medes and Persians."*a* 29Then Belshazzar gave the command, and they clothed Daniel with purple and *put* a chain of gold around his neck, and made a proclamation concerning him that he should be the third ruler in the kingdom.

5:25–29 MENE, MENE. This means "counted," or "appointed." It is doubled for stronger emphasis. *Tekel* means "weighed" or "assessed," by the God who weighs actions (1 Sam. 2:3). *Peres* means "divided," referring to the Medes and Persians. *Pharsin* is the plural of *peres*, possibly emphasizing the division. The "U" prefix on *pharsin* has the idea of the English "and."

Belshazzar's Fall

30That very night Belshazzar, king of the Chaldeans, was slain. 31And Darius the Mede received the kingdom, *being* about sixty-two years old.

The Plot Against Daniel

6 It pleased Darius to set over the kingdom one hundred and twenty satraps, to be over the whole kingdom; 2and over these, three governors, of whom Daniel *was* one, that the satraps might give account to them, so that the king would suffer no loss. 3Then this Daniel distinguished himself above the governors and satraps, because an excellent spirit *was* in him; and the king gave thought to setting him over the whole realm. 4So the governors and satraps sought to find *some* charge against Daniel concerning the kingdom; but they could find no charge or fault, because he *was* faithful; nor was there any error or fault found in him. 5Then these men said, "We shall not find any charge against this Daniel unless we find *it* against him concerning the law of his God."

6:3 an excellent spirit. Daniel, over 80, had enjoyed God's blessings throughout his life (see 1:20). **over the whole realm.** Cyrus favored Daniel because of his experience, wisdom, sense of history, leadership, good reputation, ability, attitude, and revelation from God. God placed Daniel in the position of influence to encourage and assist the Jews in their return to Judah (539–537 B.C.).

6So these governors and satraps thronged before the king, and said thus to him: "King Darius, live forever! 7All the governors of the kingdom, the administrators and satraps, the counselors and advisors, have consulted together to establish a royal statute and to make a firm decree, that whoever petitions any god or man for thirty days, except you, O king, shall be cast into the den of lions. 8Now, O king, establish the decree and sign the writing, so that it cannot be changed, according to the law of the Medes and Persians, which does not alter." 9Therefore King Darius signed the written decree.

Daniel in the Lions' Den

10Now when Daniel knew that the writing was signed, he went home. And in his upper room, with his windows open toward

---

5:24 *a*Literally *palm*   5:25 *a*Literally *a mina* (50 shekels) from the verb "to number"   *b*Literally *a shekel* from the verb "to weigh"   *c*Literally *and half-shekels* from the verb "to divide"
5:28 *a*Aramaic *Paras*, consonant with *Peres*

Jerusalem, he knelt down on his knees three times that day, and prayed and gave thanks before his God, as was his custom since early days.

¹¹Then these men assembled and found Daniel praying and making supplication before his God. ¹²And they went before the king, and spoke concerning the king's decree: "Have you not signed a decree that every man who petitions any god or man within thirty days, except you, O king, shall be cast into the den of lions?"

The king answered and said, "The thing *is* true, according to the law of the Medes and Persians, which does not alter."

¹³So they answered and said before the king, "That Daniel, who is one of the captives*ᵃ* from Judah, does not show due regard for you, O king, or for the decree that you have signed, but makes his petition three times a day."

¹⁴And the king, when he heard *these* words, was greatly displeased with himself, and set *his* heart on Daniel to deliver him; and he labored till the going down of the sun to deliver him. ¹⁵Then these men approached the king, and said to the king, "Know, O king, that *it is* the law of the Medes and Persians that no decree or statute which the king establishes may be changed."

¹⁶So the king gave the command, and they brought Daniel and cast *him* into the den of lions. *But* the king spoke, saying to Daniel, "Your God, whom you serve continually, He will deliver you." ¹⁷Then a stone was brought and laid on the mouth of the den, and the king sealed it with his own signet ring and with the signets of his lords, that the purpose concerning Daniel might not be changed.

Daniel Saved from the Lions

¹⁸Now the king went to his palace and spent the night fasting; and no musicians*ᵃ* were brought before him. Also his sleep went from him. ¹⁹Then the king arose very early in the morning and went in haste to the den of lions. ²⁰And when he came to the den, he cried out with a lamenting voice to Daniel. The king spoke, saying to Daniel, "Daniel, servant of the living God, has your

God, whom you serve continually, been able to deliver you from the lions?"

²¹Then Daniel said to the king, "O king, live forever! ²²My God sent His angel and shut the lions' mouths, so that they have not hurt me, because I was found innocent before Him; and also, O king, I have done no wrong before you."

> **6:22 His angel.** The angel was possibly the same person as the fourth person in the fiery furnace (see 3:25). **innocent before Him.** Daniel was innocent before God and unworthy of such a death.

²³Now the king was exceedingly glad for him, and commanded that they should take Daniel up out of the den. So Daniel was taken up out of the den, and no injury whatever was found on him, because he believed in his God.

Darius Honors God

²⁴And the king gave the command, and they brought those men who had accused Daniel, and they cast *them* into the den of lions—them, their children, and their wives; and the lions overpowered them, and broke all their bones in pieces before they ever came to the bottom of the den.

²⁵Then King Darius wrote:

To all peoples, nations, and languages that dwell in all the earth:

Peace be multiplied to you.

²⁶ I make a decree that in every
dominion of my kingdom *men must*
tremble and fear before the God of
Daniel.

For He *is* the living God,
And steadfast forever;
His kingdom *is the one* which shall
not be destroyed,
And His dominion *shall endure* to the
end.
²⁷ He delivers and rescues,
And He works signs and wonders
In heaven and on earth,
Who has delivered Daniel from the
power of the lions.

6:13 *ᵃLiterally of the sons of the captivity*　6:18 *ᵃExact meaning unknown*

²⁸So this Daniel prospered in the reign of Darius and in the reign of Cyrus the Persian.

Vision of the Four Beasts

7 In the first year of Belshazzar king of Babylon, Daniel had a dream and visions of his head *while* on his bed. Then he wrote down the dream, telling the main facts.*ª*

²Daniel spoke, saying, "I saw in my vision by night, and behold, the four winds of heaven were stirring up the Great Sea. ³And four great beasts came up from the sea, each different from the other. ⁴The first *was* like a lion, and had eagle's wings. I watched till its wings were plucked off; and it was lifted up from the earth and made to stand on two feet like a man, and a man's heart was given to it.

⁵"And suddenly another beast, a second, like a bear. It was raised up on one side, and *had* three ribs in its mouth between its teeth. And they said thus to it: 'Arise, devour much flesh!'

⁶"After this I looked, and there was another, like a leopard, which had on its back four wings of a bird. The beast also had four heads, and dominion was given to it.

⁷"After this I saw in the night visions, and behold, a fourth beast, dreadful and terrible, exceedingly strong. It had huge iron teeth; it was devouring, breaking in pieces, and trampling the residue with its feet. It *was* different from all the beasts that *were*

> **7:4–7 lion...wings.** The lion represents Babylon. Winged lions guarded the gates of the royal palaces of Babylon. Jeremiah, Ezekiel, and Habakkuk used this animal to describe Nebuchadnezzar. **a leopard.** This represents Greece. **fourth beast.** This is a unique beast representing the Roman Empire, which fell apart in A.D. 476. It will be restored in the time near Christ's second coming.

before it, and it had ten horns. ⁸I was considering the horns, and there was another horn, a little one, coming up among them, before whom three of the first horns were plucked out by the roots. And there, in this horn, *were* eyes like the eyes of a man, and a mouth speaking pompous words.

Vision of the Ancient of Days

⁹ "I watched till thrones were put in
       place,
   And the Ancient of Days was seated;
   His garment *was* white as snow,
   And the hair of His head *was* like
       pure wool.
   His throne *was* a fiery flame,
   Its wheels a burning fire;
¹⁰   A fiery stream issued
   And came forth from before Him.
   A thousand thousands ministered to
       Him;
   Ten thousand times ten thousand
       stood before Him.
   The court*ª* was seated,
   And the books were opened.

¹¹"I watched then because of the sound of the pompous words which the horn was speaking; I watched till the beast was slain, and its body destroyed and given to the burning flame. ¹²As for the rest of the beasts, they had their dominion taken away, yet their lives were prolonged for a season and a time.

> **7:11,12 the beast was slain.** This refers to the revived Roman Empire, headed up by the "little horn" or Antichrist. He will be destroyed at Christ's second coming (see Rev. 19:20; 20:10).

¹³ "I was watching in the night visions,
   And behold, *One* like the Son of Man,
   Coming with the clouds of heaven!
   He came to the Ancient of Days,
   And they brought Him near before
       Him.
¹⁴   Then to Him was given dominion and
       glory and a kingdom,
   That all peoples, nations, and
       languages should serve Him.
   His dominion *is* an everlasting
       dominion,
   Which shall not pass away,
   And His kingdom *the one*
   Which shall not be destroyed.

Daniel's Visions Interpreted

¹⁵"I, Daniel, was grieved in my spirit within *my* body, and the visions of my head troubled me. ¹⁶I came near to one of those

---

7:1 *ª*Literally *the head* (or *chief*) *of the words*   7:10 *ª*Or *judgment*

who stood by, and asked him the truth of all this. So he told me and made known to me the interpretation of these things: [17]"Those great beasts, which are four, *are* four kings[a] *which* arise out of the earth. [18]But the saints of the Most High shall receive the kingdom, and possess the kingdom forever, even forever and ever.'

> **7:15 grieved in my spirit.** Daniel was saddened by the coming judgment, as it meant that history to its end would be a story of sin and judgment.

[19]"Then I wished to know the truth about the fourth beast, which was different from all the others, exceedingly dreadful, *with* its teeth of iron and its nails of bronze, *which* devoured, broke in pieces, and trampled the residue with its feet; [20]and the ten horns that *were* on its head, and the other *horn* which came up, before which three fell, namely, that horn which had eyes and a mouth which spoke pompous words, whose appearance *was* greater than his fellows. [21]"I was watching; and the same horn was making war against the saints, and prevailing against them, [22]until the Ancient of Days came, and a judgment was made in

favor of the saints of the Most High, and the time came for the saints to possess the kingdom.

[23]"Thus he said:

'The fourth beast shall be
A fourth kingdom on earth,
Which shall be different from all
   other kingdoms,
And shall devour the whole earth,
Trample it and break it in pieces.
[24]   The ten horns *are* ten kings
Who shall arise from this kingdom.
And another shall rise after them;
He shall be different from the first
   ones,
And shall subdue three kings.
[25]   He shall speak *pompous* words
   against the Most High,
Shall persecute[a] the saints of the
   Most High,

> **7:25 time and times and half a time.** This refers to the 3 and one half years that are the last half of the 7-year period of the Antichrist's power, continuing on to Christ's second coming as the Judgment Stone and glorious Son of Man (see Rev. 11:2,3).

7:17 [a]Representing their kingdoms (compare verse 23)   7:25 [a]Literally *wear out*

How can those who believe in the miraculous nature of Daniel's prophecies and other miracles answer those skeptics who actually doubt Daniel's authorship and early date because the predictions are astonishingly accurate?

Confidence in the divine origin of Scripture does not rely on blind faith. There are reasonable explanations and acceptable corroborating evidence that point to the trustworthiness of the Bible. Daniel's use of what is now called Imperial Aramaic in writing the book points to an early date. The Dead Sea scrolls offer evidence that also pushes back the date for Daniel.

When accurate prophecy and possible miracles are discounted by definition as unacceptable, proving Daniel's value becomes challenging. But the problem has little to do with lack of evidence and much to do with willful unbelief. Skeptical interpreters, unwilling to acknowledge supernatural prophecies in Daniel that came to pass (over 100 in chapter 11 alone that were fulfilled) attempt to replace miraculous foresight with simple observation. They assume that the writer of Daniel was actually living in the time of Antiochus and reported current events in prophetic form. That is, the writer wrote as though he was predicting certain events, when, in reality, he was writing after the events had occurred. For scholars like these, no amount of fulfilled prophecy will be enough to convince them. They actually become a reminder to believers that people are not argued into the kingdom of God. The most compelling evidence as well as the most resistant people both need the assistance of God's Spirit in arriving at genuine faith.

And shall intend to change times and
   law.
Then *the saints* shall be given into his
   hand
For a time and times and half a time.

26 'But the court shall be seated,
    And they shall take away his
       dominion,
    To consume and destroy *it* forever.
27 Then the kingdom and dominion,
    And the greatness of the kingdoms
       under the whole heaven,
    Shall be given to the people, the
       saints of the Most High.
    His kingdom *is* an everlasting
       kingdom,
    And all dominions shall serve and
       obey Him.'

28"This *is* the end of the account.*a* As for
me, Daniel, my thoughts greatly troubled
me, and my countenance changed; but I
kept the matter in my heart."

Vision of a Ram and a Goat

8 In the third year of the reign of King
Belshazzar a vision appeared *to* me—to
me, Daniel—after the one that appeared to
me the first time. ²I saw in the vision, and it
so happened while I was looking, that I *was*
in Shushan, the citadel, which *is* in the
province of Elam; and I saw in the vision
that I was by the River Ulai. ³Then I lifted
my eyes and saw, and there, standing beside the river, was a ram which had two
horns, and the two horns *were* high; but
one *was* higher than the other, and the
higher *one* came up last. ⁴I saw the ram
pushing westward, northward, and southward, so that no animal could withstand
him; nor *was there any* that could deliver
from his hand, but he did according to his
will and became great.

⁵And as I was considering, suddenly a
male goat came from the west, across the
surface of the whole earth, without touching the ground; and the goat *had* a notable
horn between his eyes. ⁶Then he came to
the ram that had two horns, which I had
seen standing beside the river, and ran at
him with furious power. ⁷And I saw him

confronting the ram; he was moved with
rage against him, attacked the ram, and
broke his two horns. There was no power
in the ram to withstand him, but he cast
him down to the ground and trampled him;
and there was no one that could deliver the
ram from his hand.

⁸Therefore the male goat grew very great;
but when he became strong, the large horn
was broken, and in place of it four notable
ones came up toward the four winds of
heaven. ⁹And out of one of them came a little horn which grew exceedingly great toward the south, toward the east, and
toward the Glorious *Land.* ¹⁰And it grew up
to the host of heaven; and it cast down
some of the host and *some* of the stars to
the ground, and trampled them. ¹¹He even
exalted *himself* as high as the Prince of the
host; and by him the daily *sacrifices* were
taken away, and the place of His sanctuary
was cast down. ¹²Because of transgression,
an army was given over *to the horn* to oppose the daily *sacrifices*; and he cast truth
down to the ground. He did *all this* and
prospered.

8:3–9 The ram's horns stand for the Medes and the
Persians, who merged into one empire. The higher
horn represents Persia. The goat represents Greece,
with its great horn Alexander. The broken horn is
Alexander in his death, and the 4 horns are the generals who then became kings over the 4 sectors of
the Grecian empire. The small horn represents
Antiochus Epiphanes, who ruled the Syrian division
in 175–164 B.C.

¹³Then I heard a holy one speaking; and
another holy one said to that certain *one*
who was speaking, "How long *will* the vision *be, concerning* the daily *sacrifices* and
the transgression of desolation, the giving
of both the sanctuary and the host to be
trampled underfoot?"
¹⁴And he said to me, "For two thousand
three hundred days;*a* then the sanctuary
shall be cleansed."

Gabriel Interprets the Vision
¹⁵Then it happened, when I, Daniel, had
seen the vision and was seeking the meaning, that suddenly there stood before me
one having the appearance of a man. ¹⁶And

7:28 *a*Literally *the word*   8:14 *a*Literally *evening-mornings*

8:14 two thousand three hundred days. These are 2,300 evenings/mornings, which is about 6 and one half years of sacrificing a lamb twice a day, morning and evening (Ex.29:38,39). This was the time of Antiochus' persecution (about Sept. 6, 171 B.C. to Dec. 25, 165/64 B.C.). After his death, Jews celebrated the cleansing of their holy place in the Feast of Lights, or Hanukkah, in celebration of the restoration led by Judas Maccabeus.

I heard a man's voice between *the banks of* the Ulai, who called, and said, "Gabriel, make this *man* understand the vision." [17]So he came near where I stood, and when he came I was afraid and fell on my face; but he said to me, "Understand, son of man, that the vision *refers* to the time of the end."

[18]Now, as he was speaking with me, I was in a deep sleep with my face to the ground; but he touched me, and stood me upright. [19]And he said, "Look, I am making known to you what shall happen in the latter time of the indignation; for at the appointed time the end *shall be*. [20]The ram which you saw, having the two horns—*they are* the kings of Media and Persia. [21]And the male goat *is* the kingdom[a] of Greece. The large horn that *is* between its eyes *is* the first king. [22]As for the broken *horn* and the four that stood up in its place, four kingdoms shall arise out of that nation, but not with its power.

8:22 broken _horn_ and...four. Alexander died at age 33 in 323 B.C., leaving no heir ready to reign. After 22 years of fighting, 4 men ruled the 4 Grecian sectors. Cassander ruled Macedonia, Lysimachus ruled Thrace and Asia Minor, Seleucus ruled Syria and Babylonia, and Ptolemy ruled Egypt and Arabia. These are the 4 referred to in "toward the four winds" (v. 8). The phrase "not with its power" indicates they did not have Alexander's power or direct family lineage.

[23] "And in the latter time of their
    kingdom,
  When the transgressors have reached
    their fullness,
  A king shall arise,
  Having fierce features,
  Who understands sinister schemes.

[24] His power shall be mighty, but not by
    his own power;
  He shall destroy fearfully,
  And shall prosper and thrive;
  He shall destroy the mighty, and *also*
    the holy people.

[25] "Through his cunning
  He shall cause deceit to prosper under
    his rule;[a]
  And he shall exalt *himself* in his
    heart.
  He shall destroy many in *their*
    prosperity.
  He shall even rise against the Prince
    of princes;
  But he shall be broken without
    human means.[b]

[26] "And the vision of the evenings and
    mornings
  Which was told is true;
  Therefore seal up the vision,
  For *it refers* to many days *in the
    future*."

[27]And I, Daniel, fainted and was sick for days; afterward I arose and went about the king's business. I was astonished by the vision, but no one understood it.

Daniel's Prayer for the People

9 In the first year of Darius the son of Ahasuerus, of the lineage of the Medes, who was made king over the realm of the Chaldeans— [2]in the first year of his reign I, Daniel, understood by the books the number of the years *specified* by the word of the LORD through Jeremiah the prophet, that He would accomplish seventy years in the desolations of Jerusalem.

[3]Then I set my face toward the Lord God to make request by prayer and supplications,

9:2 seventy years. Daniel's study of the Old Testament scrolls focused on the years prophesied for the captivity (see Jer. 25:11,12; 29:10). The end of that time span was near, so he prayed for God's next move on behalf of Israel. The 70 years of exile were intended to restore the Sabbath rests that Israel had ignored for many years (see 2 Chr. 36:21).

8:21 [a]Literally *king,* representing his kingdom (compare 7:17,23)   8:25 [a]Literally *hand* [b]Literally *hand*

with fasting, sackcloth, and ashes. [4]And I prayed to the LORD my God, and made confession, and said, "O Lord, great and awesome God, who keeps His covenant and mercy with those who love Him, and with those who keep His commandments, [5]we have sinned and committed iniquity, we have done wickedly and rebelled, even by departing from Your precepts and Your judgments. [6]Neither have we heeded Your servants the prophets, who spoke in Your name to our kings and our princes, to our fathers and all the people of the land. [7]O Lord, righteousness *belongs* to You, but to us shame of face, as *it is* this day—to the men of Judah, to the inhabitants of Jerusalem and all Israel, those near and those far off in all the countries to which You have driven them, because of the unfaithfulness which they have committed against You.

[8]"O Lord, to us *belongs* shame of face, to our kings, our princes, and our fathers, because we have sinned against You. [9]To the Lord our God *belong* mercy and forgiveness, though we have rebelled against Him. [10]We have not obeyed the voice of the LORD our God, to walk in His laws, which He set before us by His servants the prophets. [11]Yes, all Israel has transgressed Your law, and has departed so as not to obey Your voice; therefore the curse and the oath written in the Law of Moses the servant of God have been poured out on us, because we have sinned against Him. [12]And He has confirmed His words, which He spoke against us and against our judges who judged us, by bringing upon us a great disaster; for under the whole heaven such has never been done as what has been done to Jerusalem.

[13]"As *it is* written in the Law of Moses, all this disaster has come upon us; yet we have not made our prayer before the LORD our God, that we might turn from our iniquities and understand Your truth. [14]Therefore the LORD has kept the disaster in mind, and brought it upon us; for the LORD our God *is* righteous in all the works which He does, though we have not obeyed His voice. [15]And now, O Lord our God, who brought Your people out of the land of Egypt with a mighty hand, and made Yourself a name, as

it is this day—we have sinned, we have done wickedly!

[16]"O Lord, according to all Your righteousness, I pray, let Your anger and Your fury be turned away from Your city Jerusalem, Your holy mountain; because for our sins, and for the iniquities of our fathers, Jerusalem and Your people *are* a reproach to all *those* around us. [17]Now therefore, our God, hear the prayer of Your servant, and his supplications, and for the Lord's sake cause Your face to shine on Your sanctuary, which is desolate. [18]O my God, incline Your ear and hear; open Your eyes and see our desolations, and the city which is called by Your name; for we do not present our supplications before You because of our righteous deeds, but because of Your great mercies. [19]O Lord, hear! O Lord, forgive! O Lord, listen and act! Do not delay for Your own sake, my God, for Your city and Your people are called by Your name."

The Seventy-Weeks Prophecy

[20]Now while I *was* speaking, praying, and confessing my sin and the sin of my people Israel, and presenting my supplication before the LORD my God for the holy mountain of my God, [21]yes, while I *was* speaking in prayer, the man Gabriel, whom I had seen in the vision at the beginning, being caused to fly swiftly, reached me about the time of the evening offering. [22]And he informed *me*, and talked with me, and said, "O Daniel, I have now come forth to give you skill to understand. [23]At the beginning of your supplications the command went out, and I have come to tell *you*, for you *are* greatly beloved; therefore consider the matter, and understand the vision:

9:21 the man Gabriel. This angel was called a "man" because he appeared in the form of a man. **the evening offering.** This was the second lamb of two offered daily (see 8:14). It was offered at 3 p.m., a common time for prayer (Ezra 9:5).

[24]   " Seventy weeks[a] are determined
      For your people and for your holy city,
      To finish the transgression,
      To make an end of[b] sins,

To make reconciliation for iniquity,
To bring in everlasting righteousness,
To seal up vision and prophecy,
And to anoint the Most Holy.

9:24 This complex, startlingly accurate prophecy gives the future of Israel in the end of the age. God promises to restrain Israel's long trend of apostasy, to judge sin with finality, and to cover sin by full atonement through the blood of the crucified Messiah. This three-fold promise is fulfilled in principle at Christ's first coming, in full at His return. At Christ's second coming, God will bring in righteousness, seal up vision (meaning His revelation will be complete), and anoint the Most Holy (meaning He will consecrate the new center of worship).

---

25   "Know therefore and understand,
        That from the going forth of the
            command
      To restore and build Jerusalem
      Until Messiah the Prince,
        There shall be seven weeks and sixty-
            two weeks;
      The street*ᵃ* shall be built again, and
            the wall,*ᵇ*
      Even in troublesome times.

26   "And after the sixty-two weeks
      Messiah shall be cut off, but not for
            Himself;
      And the people of the prince who is to
            come
      Shall destroy the city and the
            sanctuary.
      The end of it *shall be* with a flood,
      And till the end of the war desolations
            are determined.
27   Then he shall confirm a covenant
            with many for one week;
      But in the middle of the week
      He shall bring an end to sacrifice and
            offering.
      And on the wing of abominations
            shall be one who makes desolate,
      Even until the consummation, which
            is determined,
      Is poured out on the desolate."

Vision of the Glorious Man

10 In the third year of Cyrus king of Persia a message was revealed to Daniel, whose name was called Belteshazzar. The message *was* true, but the appointed time *was* long;*ᵃ* and he understood the message, and had understanding of the vision. ²In those days I, Daniel, was mourning three full weeks. ³I ate no pleasant food, no meat or wine came into my mouth, nor did I anoint myself at all, till three whole weeks were fulfilled.

⁴Now on the twenty-fourth day of the first month, as I was by the side of the great river, that *is*, the Tigris,*ᵃ* ⁵I lifted my eyes and looked, and behold, a certain man clothed in linen, whose waist *was* girded with gold of Uphaz! ⁶His body *was* like beryl, his face like the appearance of lightning, his eyes like torches of fire, his arms and feet like burnished bronze in color, and the sound of his words like the voice of a multitude.

10:6 His body...like beryl. The messenger whom Daniel sees in a vision (vv. 1,7) was distinct from the angel Michael, from whom he needed assistance (v. 13). Some believe he was Christ in a pre-incarnate appearance (see Josh. 5:13–15; Judg. 6:11–23). He is described almost identically to Christ (Rev. 1:13), and Daniel's reaction to him is similar to John's (Rev. 1:17).

---

⁷And I, Daniel, alone saw the vision, for the men who were with me did not see the vision; but a great terror fell upon them, so that they fled to hide themselves. ⁸Therefore I was left alone when I saw this great vision, and no strength remained in me; for my vigor was turned to frailty in me, and I retained no strength. ⁹Yet I heard the sound of his words; and while I heard the sound of his words I was in a deep sleep on my face, with my face to the ground.

Prophecies Concerning Persia and Greece

¹⁰Suddenly, a hand touched me, which made me tremble on my knees and *on the* palms of my hands. ¹¹And he said to me, "O Daniel, man greatly beloved, understand the words that I speak to you, and stand upright, for I have now been sent to you." While he was speaking this word to me, I stood trembling.

¹²Then he said to me, "Do not fear,

9:25 *ᵃ*Or *open square*   *ᵇ*Or *moat*   10:1 *ᵃ*Or *and of great conflict*   10:4 *ᵃ*Hebrew *Hiddekel*

Daniel, for from the first day that you set your heart to understand, and to humble yourself before your God, your words were heard; and I have come because of your words. [13]But the prince of the kingdom of Persia withstood me twenty-one days; and behold, Michael, one of the chief princes, came to help me, for I had been left alone there with the kings of Persia. [14]Now I have come to make you understand what will happen to your people in the latter days, for the vision *refers* to *many* days yet *to come.*"

[15]When he had spoken such words to me, I turned my face toward the ground and became speechless. [16]And suddenly, *one* having the likeness of the sons[a] of men touched my lips; then I opened my mouth and spoke, saying to him who stood before me, "My lord, because of the vision my sorrows have overwhelmed me, and I have retained no strength. [17]For how can this servant of my lord talk with you, my lord? As for me, no strength remains in me now, nor is any breath left in me."

[18]Then again, *the one* having the likeness of a man touched me and strengthened me. [19]And he said, "O man greatly beloved, fear not! Peace *be* to you; be strong, yes, be strong!"

So when he spoke to me I was strengthened, and said, "Let my lord speak, for you have strengthened me."

[20]Then he said, "Do you know why I have come to you? And now I must return to fight with the prince of Persia; and when I have gone forth, indeed the prince of Greece will come. [21]But I will tell you what is noted in the Scripture of Truth. (No one upholds me against these, except Michael your prince.

> **11:2–45** This prophecy begins with the history of Israel's spiritual conflict and ends with the tribulation, when Michael helps to deliver Israel. The accuracy of this prophecy has caused unbelieving critics to date this prophecy 400 years after Daniel, which would make the prophet a deceiver. In reality, the prophecy looks ahead from Daniel to the final Antichrist.

11 "Also in the first year of Darius the Mede, I, *even* I, stood up to confirm and strengthen him.) [2]And now I will tell you the truth: Behold, three more kings will arise in Persia, and the fourth shall be far richer than *them* all; by his strength, through his riches, he shall stir up all against the realm of Greece. [3]Then a mighty king shall arise, who shall rule with great dominion, and do according to his will. [4]And when he has arisen, his kingdom shall be broken up and divided toward the four winds of heaven, but not among his posterity nor according to his dominion with which he ruled; for his kingdom shall be uprooted, even for others besides these.

10:16 [a]Theodotion and Vulgate read *the son*; Septuagint reads *a hand.*

Why is the Book of Daniel often called the Old Testament equivalent of the New Testament Book of Revelation?

The Books of Daniel and Revelation complement one another in many ways. Written about 600 years apart, they both deal with God's plan in history. Though much of Daniel's prophetic vision had already come true by the time John wrote Revelation, there are two specific ways in which John's work complements Daniel's:

1. Both books deal in part with final events and offer parallel prophetic views of the closing days of the original universe and God's design of the new heaven, earth, and kingdom.

2. Revelation confirms the understanding of prophecy that suggests fulfillment can often happen in stages or waves. For instance, many of the prophecies given to Daniel were fulfilled to some degree in the historic events preceding the life of Christ, but will be ultimately and completely fulfilled in the final events of history.

Warring Kings of North and South

5"Also the king of the South shall become strong, as well as *one* of his princes; and he shall gain power over him and have dominion. His dominion *shall be* a great dominion. 6And at the end of *some* years they shall join forces, for the daughter of the king of the South shall go to the king of the North to make an agreement; but she shall not retain the power of her authority,*a* and neither he nor his authority*b* shall stand; but she shall be given up, with those who brought her, and with him who begot her, and with him who strengthened her in *those* times. 7But from a branch of her roots *one* shall arise in his place, who shall come with an army, enter the fortress of the king of the North, and deal with them and prevail. 8And he shall also carry their gods captive to Egypt, with their princes*a and* their precious articles of silver and gold; and he shall continue *more* years than the king of the North.

> **11:6 join forces.** In order to form a political alliance, Syria's King Antiochus II Theos (261–246 B.C.) divorced his wife and married Berenice, daughter of Egypt's Ptolemy II Philadelphus (285–246 B.C.). The divorced wife later murdered Berenice, Antiochus, and their baby son by poisoning them, thus bringing her own son, Seleucus II Callinicus, to the throne.

9"Also *the king of the North* shall come to the kingdom of the king of the South, but shall return to his own land. 10However his sons shall stir up strife, and assemble a multitude of great forces; and *one* shall certainly come and overwhelm and pass through; then he shall return to his fortress and stir up strife.

11"And the king of the South shall be moved with rage, and go out and fight with him, with the king of the North, who shall muster a great multitude; but the multitude shall be given into the hand of his *enemy.* 12When he has taken away the multitude, his heart will be lifted up; and he will cast down tens of thousands, but he will not prevail. 13For the king of the North will return and muster a multitude greater

than the former, and shall certainly come at the end of some years with a great army and much equipment.

14"Now in those times many shall rise up against the king of the South. Also, violent men*a* of your people shall exalt themselves in fulfillment of the vision, but they shall fall. 15So the king of the North shall come and build a siege mound, and take a fortified city; and the forces*a* of the South shall not withstand *him.* Even his choice troops *shall have* no strength to resist. 16But he who comes against him shall do according to his own will, and no one shall stand against him. He shall stand in the Glorious Land with destruction in his power.*a*

17"He shall also set his face to enter with the strength of his whole kingdom, and upright ones*a* with him; thus shall he do. And he shall give him the daughter of women to destroy it; but she shall not stand *with him,* or be for him. 18After this he shall turn his face to the coastlands, and shall take many. But a ruler shall bring the reproach against them to an end; and with the reproach removed, he shall turn back on him. 19Then he shall turn his face toward the fortress of his own land; but he shall stumble and fall, and not be found.

> **11:17 give...the daughter.** Antiochus felt pressure from Rome to make peace with Egypt, so he offered his daughter, Cleopatra, in marriage to Ptolemy V Epiphanes (about 192 B.C.). He hoped his daughter would help him weaken Egypt by spying, but Cleopatra instead favored her Egyptian husband.

20"There shall arise in his place one who imposes taxes *on* the glorious kingdom; but within a few days he shall be destroyed, but not in anger or in battle. 21And in his place shall arise a vile person, to whom they will not give the honor of royalty; but he shall come in peaceably, and seize the kingdom by intrigue. 22With the force*a* of a flood they shall be swept away from before him and be broken, and also the prince of the covenant. 23And after the league *is made* with him he shall act deceitfully, for he shall come up and become strong with a small *number of*

11:6 *a*Literally *arm* *b*Literally *arm*   11:8 *a*Or *molded images*   11:14 *a*Or *robbers,* literally *sons of breakage*   11:15 *a*Literally *arms*   11:16 *a*Literally *hand*   11:17 *a*Or *bring equitable terms*
11:22 *a*Literally *arms*

people. ²⁴He shall enter peaceably, even into the richest places of the province; and he shall do *what* his fathers have not done, nor his forefathers: he shall disperse among them the plunder, spoil, and riches; and he shall devise his plans against the strongholds, but *only* for a time.

> **11:24 enter peaceably.** Antiochus, pretending to be friendly, plundered wealthy places in Egypt. To gain support, he gave lavish gifts, possibly battle spoils. **devise his plans against the strongholds.** Antiochus formed a scheme to take over Egypt.

²⁵"He shall stir up his power and his courage against the king of the South with a great army. And the king of the South shall be stirred up to battle with a very great and mighty army; but he shall not stand, for they shall devise plans against him. ²⁶Yes, those who eat of the portion of his delicacies shall destroy him; his army shall be swept away, and many shall fall down slain. ²⁷Both these kings' hearts *shall be* bent on evil, and they shall speak lies at the same table; but it shall not prosper, for the end *will* still *be* at the appointed time. ²⁸While returning to his land with great riches, his heart shall be *moved* against the holy covenant; so he shall do *damage* and return to his own land.

> **11:31 defile the sanctuary.** Antiochus' soldiers guarded the temple, halting all worship, while others attacked the city on the Sabbath, slaughtering men, women, and children. They desecrated the temple, banned circumcision and daily sacrifices, and sacrificed a pig on the altar. The Syrians placed an idol statue in honor of the Olympian god, Zeus, in the temple. The Jews called all of this the "abomination of desolation."

The Northern King's Blasphemies

²⁹"At the appointed time he shall return and go toward the south; but it shall not be like the former or the latter. ³⁰For ships from Cyprus*ᵃ* shall come against him; therefore he shall be grieved, and return in rage against the holy covenant, and do *damage.*

"So he shall return and show regard for those who forsake the holy covenant. ³¹And forces*ᵃ* shall be mustered by him, and they shall defile the sanctuary fortress; then they shall take away the daily *sacrifices,* and place *there* the abomination of desolation. ³²Those who do wickedly against the covenant he shall corrupt with flattery; but the people who know their God shall be strong, and carry out *great exploits.* ³³And those of the people who understand shall instruct many; yet *for many* days they shall fall by sword and flame, by captivity and plundering. ³⁴Now when they fall, they shall be aided with a little help; but many shall join with them by intrigue. ³⁵And *some* of those of understanding shall fall, to refine them, purify *them,* and make *them* white, *until* the time of the end; because *it is* still for the appointed time.

³⁶"Then the king shall do according to his own will: he shall exalt and magnify himself above every god, shall speak blasphemies against the God of gods, and shall prosper till the wrath has been accomplished; for what has been determined shall be done. ³⁷He shall regard neither the God*ᵃ* of his fathers nor the desire of women, nor regard any god; for he shall exalt himself above *them* all. ³⁸But in their place he shall honor a god of fortresses; and a god which his fathers did not know he shall honor with gold and silver, with precious stones and pleasant things. ³⁹Thus he shall act against the strongest fortresses with a foreign god, which he shall acknowledge, *and* advance *its* glory; and he shall cause them to rule over many, and divide the land for gain.

> **11:37 God of his fathers.** The word for "God" here is "Elohim," which is plural. In this context, it could refer to gods. This king has no regard for any of the pagan gods. His only god is power. **desire of women.** This could mean that the Antichrist will be a homosexual. It surely means he has no normal interest in women.

The Northern King's Conquests

⁴⁰"At the time of the end the king of the South shall attack him; and the king of the North shall come against him like a whirlwind, with chariots, horsemen, and with many ships; and he shall enter the countries, overwhelm *them,* and pass through.

11:30 *ᵃ*Hebrew *Kittim,* western lands, especially Cyprus   11:31 *ᵃ*Literally *arms*   11:37 *ᵃ*Or *gods*

⁴¹He shall also enter the Glorious Land, and many *countries* shall be overthrown; but these shall escape from his hand: Edom, Moab, and the prominent people of Ammon. ⁴²He shall stretch out his hand against the countries, and the land of Egypt shall not escape. ⁴³He shall have power over the treasures of gold and silver, and over all the precious things of Egypt; also the Libyans and Ethiopians *shall follow* at his heels. ⁴⁴But news from the east and the north shall trouble him; therefore he shall go out with great fury to destroy and annihilate many. ⁴⁵And he shall plant the tents of his palace between the seas and the glorious holy mountain; yet he shall come to his end, and no one will help him.

Prophecy of the End Time

12 "At that time Michael shall stand up,

The great prince who stands *watch*
    over the sons of your people;
And there shall be a time of trouble,
Such as never was since there was a nation,
Even to that time.
And at that time your people shall be delivered,
Every one who is found written in the book.
2 And many of those who sleep in the
    dust of the earth shall awake,
Some to everlasting life,
Some to shame *and* everlasting contempt.
3 Those who are wise shall shine
Like the brightness of the firmament,
And those who turn many to righteousness
Like the stars forever and ever.

⁴"But you, Daniel, shut up the words, and seal the book until the time of the end; many shall run to and fro, and knowledge shall increase."

⁵Then I, Daniel, looked; and there stood two others, one on this riverbank and the other on that riverbank. ⁶And *one* said to the man clothed in linen, who *was* above

the waters of the river, "How long shall the fulfillment of these wonders *be*?"

⁷Then I heard the man clothed in linen, who *was* above the waters of the river, when he held up his right hand and his left hand to heaven, and swore by Him who lives forever, that *it shall be* for a time, times, and half *a time*; and when the power of the holy people has been completely shattered, all these *things* shall be finished.

⁸Although I heard, I did not understand. Then I said, "My lord, what *shall be* the end of these *things*?"

⁹And he said, "Go *your way*, Daniel, for the words *are* closed up and sealed till the time of the end. ¹⁰Many shall be purified, made white, and refined, but the wicked shall do wickedly; and none of the wicked shall understand, but the wise shall understand.

¹¹"And from the time *that* the daily *sacrifice* is taken away, and the abomination of desolation is set up, *there shall be* one thousand two hundred and ninety days. ¹²Blessed *is* he who waits, and comes to the one thousand three hundred and thirty-five days.

¹³"But you, go *your way* till the end; for you shall rest, and will arise to your inheritance at the end of the days."

HOSEA

Can you think of anything God asks you to do that seems hard or unfair? If you can't, you haven't been paying careful enough attention to God's Word. Start with some of Jesus' words: Love your enemies, bless those who curse you, do good to those who hate you . . ." (Matthew 5:44). God loves us so much that He gives us tough assignments, and then He helps us accomplish them. Hosea's life offers us a heart-wrenching example of just how hard God's instructions can be and just how great His love remains.

AUTHOR AND DATE

Hosea was written by Hosea during his ministry, approximately 755 to 710 B.C.

Our information about Hosea and his family comes entirely from this book. Hosea probably shares with Jonah the distinction of being the only two writing prophets from the northern kingdom of Israel. Most of the incidental historical, topographical, and political clues in the book of Hosea (cf. 4:15; 5:1,13; 6:8,9; 10:5; 12:11,12; 14:6) refer to the northern kingdom.

Hosea had a lengthy ministry of 45 years, spanning the reigns of 7 kings in Israel and 4 kings in Judah. Although his writing comes first in the Minor Prophets (called that for their length, not importance), he actually ministered after Jonah (793–753 B.C.) and Amos (760–750 B.C.) in Israel, and Obadiah (855–840 B.C.) and Joel (835–796 B.C.) in Judah. Both Isaiah and Micah were contemporaries of Hosea, though they only prophesied in Judah.

BACKGROUND AND SETTING

God called Hosea to be a prophet during the closing days of Jeroboam II. Although Israel was enjoying a time of political peace and material prosperity, the nation was also rife with moral corruption and spiritual bankruptcy. Jeroboam II's death ushered in anarchy and the nation rapidly declined. During the next 20 years leading up to the complete overthrow by Assyria, Israel experienced 6 short reigns, 4 of which were ended by assassination.

Hosea spoke for God during those chaotic times. His messages were filled with warnings against Israel's moral waywardness and her violation of the covenant relationship that she had with the Lord. His life illustrated the truth of his messages. Hosea announced the coming judgment.

The historical themes in Hosea remain in the background, while God's loyal love for His covenant people takes center stage. Under the spotlight of God's faithfulness, Israel's idolatry and unfaithfulness stand exposed.

Hosea has been called the St. John (the apostle of love) of the Old Testament. His book teaches and illustrates two central characteristics of God's true love: (1) the Lord's love is unending; and (2) the Lord's love will tolerate no rival.

> **THE LORD'S LOVE IS UNENDING, AND THE LORD'S LOVE WILL TOLERATE NO RIVAL.**

Although Hosea's message contains much condemnation, he also poignantly portrays the passionate love of God toward His people.

Hosea lived the theme of his message. God instructed him to marry a certain woman and experience with her a domestic life that dramatized the relationship between God and His people. The marital life of Hosea and Gomer provides the rich metaphor that clarifies the theological themes of this book: sin, judgment, and forgiving love.

OUTLINE

1 The word of the LORD that came to Hosea the son of Beeri, in the days of Uzziah, Jotham, Ahaz, *and* Hezekiah, kings of Judah, and in the days of Jeroboam the son of Joash, king of Israel.

The Family of Hosea

²When the LORD began to speak by Hosea, the LORD said to Hosea:

> "Go, take yourself a wife of harlotry
> And children of harlotry,
> For the land has committed great
>   harlotry
> *By departing* from the LORD."

> **1:4,6,9 Jezreel.** The name means "God will scatter" (see Zech. 10:9). It is given to the child as a prediction of judgment (see 2 Kin. 9:7–10:28). **Lo-Ruhamah.** This name, meaning "not pitied," is given to the daughter to symbolize God's bringing judgment on Israel, no longer extending His favor toward them. **Lo-Ammi.** This name, meaning "not My people," symbolizes God's rejection of Israel.

³So he went and took Gomer the daughter of Diblaim, and she conceived and bore him a son. ⁴Then the LORD said to him:

> "Call his name Jezreel,
> For in a little *while*
> I will avenge the bloodshed of Jezreel
>   on the house of Jehu,
> And bring an end to the kingdom of
>   the house of Israel.

5
> It shall come to pass in that day
> That I will break the bow of Israel in
>   the Valley of Jezreel."

⁶And she conceived again and bore a daughter. Then *God* said to him:

> "Call her name Lo-Ruhamah,ᵃ
> For I will no longer have mercy on the
>   house of Israel,
> But I will utterly take them away.ᵇ
7
> Yet I will have mercy on the house of
>   Judah,
> Will save them by the LORD their
>   God,
> And will not save them by bow,
> Nor by sword or battle,
> By horses or horsemen."

⁸Now when she had weaned Lo-Ruhamah, she conceived and bore a son. ⁹Then *God* said:

> "Call his name Lo-Ammi,ᵃ
> For you *are* not My people,
> And I will not be your *God.*

The Restoration of Israel

10 "Yet the number of the children of
>   Israel
> Shall be as the sand of the sea,
> Which cannot be measured or
>   numbered.
> And it shall come to pass

1:6 ᵃLiterally *No-Mercy* ᵇOr *That I may forgive them at all*   1:9 ᵃLiterally *Not-My-People*

Did God instruct Hosea to actually marry a prostitute?

Some interpreters try to ease the question by suggesting that the marital scenes in the first three chapters of Hosea are merely an allegory of God's relationship to His people. Nothing in the account encourages such an interpretation. Much of the impact of the lesson would have been lost if it had not been literal. Those who object usually do so on the grounds that too many negative moral implications arise if God did ask Hosea to marry such a woman.

The language of God's command in the original provides some support for the chastity of Gomer at the time of her marriage to Hosea. The words "take yourself a wife of harlotry" (1:2) can be understood prophetically (looking to the future). Thus, Gomer would have taken up immoral behavior after marriage. This explanation fits better with God's description of Israel coming out of Egypt as a young woman (2:15; 9:10), who then wandered away from God (11:1). The moral power behind Hosea's action in taking back Gomer after her adultery (chapter 3) depends on the purity of their original union, which she violated. Had Hosea married an acknowledged prostitute, he would have had no grounds for offense over her adultery.

In the place where it was said to
     them,
'You *are* not My people,'*a*
There it shall be said to them,
'*You are* sons of the living God.'

11 Then the children of Judah and the
     children of Israel
Shall be gathered together,
And appoint for themselves one head;
And they shall come up out of the
     land,
For great *will be* the day of Jezreel!

2 Say to your brethren, 'My people,'*a*
And to your sisters, 'Mercy*b* *is shown.*'

God's Unfaithful People

2   "Bring charges against your mother,
     bring charges;
For she *is* not My wife, nor *am* I her
     Husband!
Let her put away her harlotries from
     her sight,
And her adulteries from between her
     breasts;

> **2:2 Bring charges against your mother.** The physical immorality of Gomer represents the spiritual idolatry of Israel. This depicts a courtroom scene in which the Lord, as the plaintiff, brings charges against the defendant. The Israelites are commanded to bring charges against their mother, Israel, as a nation.

3   Lest I strip her naked
And expose her, as in the day she was
     born,
And make her like a wilderness,
And set her like a dry land,
And slay her with thirst.

4   "I will not have mercy on her
     children,
For they *are* the children of harlotry.
5   For their mother has played the
     harlot;
She who conceived them has behaved
     shamefully.
For she said, 'I will go after my lovers,
Who give *me* my bread and my water,
My wool and my linen,
My oil and my drink.'

6   "Therefore, behold,
I will hedge up your way with thorns,
And wall her in,
So that she cannot find her paths.
7   She will chase her lovers,
But not overtake them;
Yes, she will seek them, but not find
     them.
Then she will say,
'I will go and return to my first
     husband,
For then *it was* better for me than
     now.'
8   For she did not know
That I gave her grain, new wine, and
     oil,
And multiplied her silver and gold—
Which they prepared for Baal.

9   "Therefore I will return and take away
My grain in its time
And My new wine in its season,

> **2:8–13** God withheld rain and productivity to show Israel that the Canaanite god, Baal, did not control the rain or fertility.

1:10 *a*Hebrew *lo-ammi* (compare verse 9)   2:1 *a*Hebrew *Ammi* (compare 1:9,10)   *b*Hebrew *Ruhamah* (compare 1:6)

GOD'S LOVINGKINDNESS TO ISRAEL

	HOSEA and GOMER	GOD and ISRAEL
Betrothal	Hosea 1:2	Assumed; Jeremiah 2:2; Ezekiel 16:8
One Flesh	Hosea 1:3	Assumed; Jeremiah 3:1; Ezekiel 16:9–14
Adultery	Hosea 2:2; 3:1	Hosea 2:5; 4:12; Jeremiah 3:6; 5:7; Ezekiel 16:15–34
Divorce	Hosea 3:1	Hosea 2:2; Jeremiah 3:8–10,20; Ezekiel 16:35–59
Remarriage	Hosea 3:3–5	Hosea 1:10,11; 2:14–23; 14:4–9; Jeremiah 3:22–4:2; Ezekiel 16:60–63

And will take back My wool and My
   linen,
Given to cover her nakedness.
10 Now I will uncover her lewdness in
   the sight of her lovers,
And no one shall deliver her from My
   hand.
11 I will also cause all her mirth to
   cease,
Her feast days,
Her New Moons,
Her Sabbaths—
All her appointed feasts.

12 "And I will destroy her vines and her
   fig trees,
Of which she has said,
'These *are* my wages that my lovers
   have given me.'
So I will make them a forest,
And the beasts of the field shall eat
   them.
13 I will punish her
For the days of the Baals to which she
   burned incense.
She decked herself with her earrings
   and jewelry,
And went after her lovers;
But Me she forgot," says the LORD.

God's Mercy on His People
14 "Therefore, behold, I will allure her,
Will bring her into the wilderness,
And speak comfort to her.
15 I will give her her vineyards from
   there,
And the Valley of Achor as a door of
   hope;
She shall sing there,
As in the days of her youth,
As in the day when she came up from
   the land of Egypt.

16 "And it shall be, in that day,"
Says the LORD,
"*That* you will call Me 'My Husband,'*a*
And no longer call Me 'My Master,'*b*
17 For I will take from her mouth the
   names of the Baals,
And they shall be remembered by
   their name no more.

18 In that day I will make a covenant for
   them
With the beasts of the field,
With the birds of the air,
And *with* the creeping things of the
   ground.
Bow and sword of battle I will shatter
   from the earth,
To make them lie down safely.

19 "I will betroth you to Me forever;
Yes, I will betroth you to Me
In righteousness and justice,
In lovingkindness and mercy;
20 I will betroth you to Me in
   faithfulness,
And you shall know the LORD.

> **2:19,20 I will betroth you.** This term emphasizes the
> intensity of God's restoring love for the nation. Israel
> brings nothing to the marriage; God makes all the
> promises and provides the dowry. In a coming day,
> Israel will no longer be thought of as a prostitute who
> left the one true God for other gods. These verses are
> recited by orthodox Jews (see Deut. 11:18). The con-
> version of Israel is much like that of an individual
> (see 1 Cor. 5:16–19).

21 "It shall come to pass in that day
That I will answer," says the LORD;
"I will answer the heavens,
And they shall answer the earth.
22 The earth shall answer
With grain,
With new wine,
And with oil;
They shall answer Jezreel.*a*
23 Then I will sow her for Myself in the
   earth,
And I will have mercy on *her who had*
   not obtained mercy;*a*
Then I will say to *those who were* not
   My people,*b*
'You *are* My people!'
And they shall say, '*You are* my
   God!' "

Israel Will Return to God
3 Then the LORD said to me, "Go again,
love a woman *who is* loved by a lover*a*
and is committing adultery, just like the

2:16 *a*Hebrew *Ishi*   *b*Hebrew *Baali*   2:22 *a*Literally *God Will Sow*   2:23 *a*Hebrew *lo-ruhamah*
*b*Hebrew *lo-ammi*   3:1 *a*Literally *friend* or *husband*

love of the LORD for the children of Israel, who look to other gods and love *the* raisin cakes *of the pagans.*"

²So I bought her for myself for fifteen *shekels* of silver, and one and one-half homers of barley. ³And I said to her, "You shall stay with me many days; you shall not play the harlot, nor shall you have a man—so, too, *will I be* toward you."

⁴For the children of Israel shall abide many days without king or prince, without sacrifice or *sacred* pillar, without ephod or teraphim. ⁵Afterward the children of Israel shall return and seek the LORD their God and David their king. They shall fear the LORD and His goodness in the latter days.

God's Charge Against Israel

4 Hear the word of the LORD,
    You children of Israel,
For the LORD *brings* a charge against
    the inhabitants of the land:

  "There is no truth or mercy
  Or knowledge of God in the land.

4:1 the LORD *brings* a charge. Turning from the analogy of his own marriage, the prophet made the judicial charge in God's indictment against Israel.

²   *By* swearing and lying,
    Killing and stealing and committing
      adultery,
    They break all restraint,
    With bloodshed upon bloodshed.
³   Therefore the land will mourn;
    And everyone who dwells there will
      waste away
    With the beasts of the field
    And the birds of the air;
    Even the fish of the sea will be taken
      away.

⁴   "Now let no man contend, or rebuke
    another;
    For your people *are* like those who
      contend with the priest.
⁵   Therefore you shall stumble in the
    day;

    The prophet also shall stumble with
      you in the night;
    And I will destroy your mother.
⁶ My people are destroyed for lack of
    knowledge.
    Because you have rejected knowledge,
    I also will reject you from being priest
      for Me;
    Because you have forgotten the law of
      your God,
    I also will forget your children.

⁷   "The more they increased,
    The more they sinned against Me;
    I will change*ᵃ* their glory*ᵇ* into
      shame.
⁸   They eat up the sin of My people;
    They set their heart on their iniquity.
⁹   And it shall be: like people, like
      priest.
    So I will punish them for their ways,
    And reward them for their deeds.
¹⁰ For they shall eat, but not have
      enough;
    They shall commit harlotry, but not
      increase;
    Because they have ceased obeying the
      LORD.

The Idolatry of Israel

¹¹ "Harlotry, wine, and new wine enslave
    the heart.
¹² My people ask counsel from their
      wooden *idols,*
    And their staff informs them.
    For the spirit of harlotry has caused
      them to stray,
    And they have played the harlot
      against their God.
¹³ They offer sacrifices on the
      mountaintops,
    And burn incense on the hills,
    Under oaks, poplars, and terebinths,
    Because their shade *is* good.
    Therefore your daughters commit
      harlotry,
    And your brides commit adultery.
¹⁴ "I will not punish your daughters when
    they commit harlotry,

4:7 ᵃFollowing Masoretic Text, Septuagint, and Vulgate; scribal tradition, Syriac, and Targum read *They will change.* ᵇFollowing Masoretic Text, Septuagint, Syriac, Targum, and Vulgate; scribal tradition reads *My glory.*

Nor your brides when they commit
　　adultery;
For *the men* themselves go apart with
　　harlots,
And offer sacrifices with a ritual
　　harlot.*a*
Therefore people *who* do not
　　understand will be trampled.

> **4:14** God forbade punishing only the adulteresses and leaving the men who patronized them to go free. Instead, the heaviest punishment would be on the fathers and husbands who set such a bad example by their involvement with prostitutes.

15　"Though you, Israel, play the harlot,
　　Let not Judah offend.
　　Do not come up to Gilgal,
　　Nor go up to Beth Aven,
　　Nor swear an oath, *saying,* 'As the
　　　LORD lives'—
16　"For Israel is stubborn
　　Like a stubborn calf;
　　Now the LORD will let them forage
　　Like a lamb in open country.
17　"Ephraim *is* joined to idols,
　　Let him alone.
18　Their drink is rebellion,
　　They commit harlotry continually.
　　Her rulers dearly love dishonor.*a*
19　The wind has wrapped her up in its
　　　wings,
　　And they shall be ashamed because of
　　　their sacrifices.

Impending Judgment on Israel and Judah

5 "Hear this, O priests!
　　Take heed, O house of Israel!
　　Give ear, O house of the king!
　　For yours *is* the judgment,
　　Because you have been a snare to
　　　Mizpah
　　And a net spread on Tabor.
2　The revolters are deeply involved in
　　　slaughter,
　　Though I rebuke them all.
3　I know Ephraim,
　　And Israel is not hidden from Me;

For now, O Ephraim, you commit
　　harlotry;
Israel is defiled.

4　"They do not direct their deeds
　　Toward turning to their God,
　　For the spirit of harlotry is in their
　　　midst,
　　And they do not know the LORD.
5　The pride of Israel testifies to his
　　　face;
　　Therefore Israel and Ephraim stumble
　　　in their iniquity;
　　Judah also stumbles with them.

> **5:5 pride of Israel testifies to his face.** Israel's pride in idolatry provided self-incrimination.

6　"With their flocks and herds
　　They shall go to seek the LORD,
　　But they will not find *Him;*
　　He has withdrawn Himself from
　　　them.
7　They have dealt treacherously with
　　　the LORD,
　　For they have begotten pagan
　　　children.
　　Now a New Moon shall devour them
　　　and their heritage.

8　"Blow the ram's horn in Gibeah,
　　The trumpet in Ramah!
　　Cry aloud *at* Beth Aven,
　　'*Look* behind you, O Benjamin!'
9　Ephraim shall be desolate in the day
　　　of rebuke;
　　Among the tribes of Israel I make
　　　known what is sure.

10　"The princes of Judah are like those
　　　who remove a landmark;
　　I will pour out my wrath on them like
　　　water.

> **5:10 remove a landmark.** Boundaries, marked by stones, could be easily removed at night. Moving them, however, was equivalent to stealing land from a neighbor (see Deut. 19:14). This statement pictures Israel's leaders moving the spiritual boundaries that had been established by God.

4:14 *a*Compare Deuteronomy 23:18　4:18 *a*Hebrew is difficult; a Jewish tradition reads *Her rulers shamefully love, 'Give!'*

11 Ephraim is oppressed *and* broken in
   judgment,
   Because he willingly walked by
   human precept.
12 Therefore I *will be* to Ephraim like a
   moth,
   And to the house of Judah like
   rottenness.

13 "When Ephraim saw his sickness,
   And Judah *saw* his wound,
   Then Ephraim went to Assyria
   And sent to King Jareb;
   Yet he cannot cure you,
   Nor heal you of your wound.
14 For I *will be* like a lion to Ephraim,
   And like a young lion to the house of
   Judah.
   I, *even* I, will tear *them* and go away;
   I will take *them* away, and no one
   shall rescue.
15 I will return again to My place
   Till they acknowledge their offense.
   Then they will seek My face;
   In their affliction they will earnestly
   seek Me."

A Call to Repentance

6 Come, and let us return to the LORD;
   For He has torn, but He will heal us;
   He has stricken, but He will bind us
   up.
2 After two days He will revive us;
   On the third day He will raise us up,
   That we may live in His sight.

> **6:2 After two days...On the third day.** This refers to
> the quickness of the future healing of the nation's ill-
> ness and its restoration (see Job 5:19; Prov. 6:16).

3 Let us know,
   Let us pursue the knowledge of the
   LORD.
   His going forth is established as the
   morning;
   He will come to us like the rain,
   Like the latter *and* former rain to the
   earth.

Impenitence of Israel and Judah

4 "O Ephraim, what shall I do to you?
   O Judah, what shall I do to you?

For your faithfulness is like a morning
   cloud,
   And like the early dew it goes away.
5 Therefore I have hewn *them* by the
   prophets,
   I have slain them by the words of My
   mouth;
   And your judgments *are like* light *that*
   goes forth.
6 For I desire mercy and not sacrifice,
   And the knowledge of God more than
   burnt offerings.

7 "But like men[a] they transgressed the
   covenant;
   There they dealt treacherously with Me.
8 Gilead *is* a city of evildoers
   And defiled with blood.
9 As bands of robbers lie in wait for a
   man,
   So the company of priests murder on
   the way to Shechem;
   Surely they commit lewdness.
10 I have seen a horrible thing in the
   house of Israel:
   There *is* the harlotry of Ephraim;
   Israel is defiled.
11 Also, O Judah, a harvest is appointed
   for you,
   When I return the captives of My
   people.

7 "When I would have healed Israel,
   Then the iniquity of Ephraim was
   uncovered,
   And the wickedness of Samaria.
   For they have committed fraud;
   A thief comes in;
   A band of robbers takes spoil outside.
2 They do not consider in their hearts
   That I remember all their wickedness;
   Now their own deeds have
   surrounded them;
   They are before My face.
3 They make a king glad with their
   wickedness,
   And princes with their lies.

4 "They *are* all adulterers.
   Like an oven heated by a baker—
   He ceases stirring *the fire* after
   kneading the dough,

6:7 [a]Or *like Adam*

Until it is leavened.

5 In the day of our king
Princes have made *him* sick, inflamed
with wine;
He stretched out his hand with
scoffers.

6 They prepare their heart like an oven,
While they lie in wait;
Their baker[a] sleeps all night;
In the morning it burns like a flaming
fire.

7 They are all hot, like an oven,
And have devoured their judges;
All their kings have fallen.
None among them calls upon Me.

8 "Ephraim has mixed himself among
the peoples;
Ephraim is a cake unturned.

9 Aliens have devoured his strength,
But he does not know *it*;
Yes, gray hairs are here and there on
him,
Yet he does not know *it*.

> **7:8,9** Israel "mixed himself among the peoples" by inviting foreign nations to make debilitating inroads into its national and religious life. This was making the nation like "a cake unturned," burned on one side and raw on the other. Payment for this foreign assistance had "devoured his strength" (v. 9), making the nation like an old and feeble person who doesn't realize his strength is gone.

10 And the pride of Israel testifies to his
face,
But they do not return to the LORD
their God,
Nor seek Him for all this.

Futile Reliance on the Nations

11 "Ephraim also is like a silly dove,
without sense—
They call to Egypt,
They go to Assyria.

12 Wherever they go, I will spread My
net on them;

I will bring them down like birds of
the air;
I will chastise them
According to what their congregation
has heard.

13 "Woe to them, for they have fled from
Me!
Destruction to them,
Because they have transgressed
against Me!
Though I redeemed them,
Yet they have spoken lies against Me.

14 They did not cry out to Me with their
heart
When they wailed upon their beds.

"They assemble together for[a] grain and
new wine,
They rebel against Me;[b]

15 Though I disciplined *and*
strengthened their arms,
Yet they devise evil against Me;

16 They return, *but* not to the Most
High;[a]
They are like a treacherous bow.
Their princes shall fall by the sword
For the cursings of their tongue.
This *shall be* their derision in the
land of Egypt.

The Apostasy of Israel

8 "*Set* the trumpet[a] to your mouth!
He shall come like an eagle against
the house of the LORD,
Because they have transgressed My
covenant
And rebelled against My law.

2 Israel will cry to Me,
'My God, we know You!'

3 Israel has rejected the good;
The enemy will pursue him.

4 "They set up kings, but not by Me;
They made princes, but I did not
acknowledge *them*.
From their silver and gold
They made idols for themselves—

7:6 [a]Following Masoretic Text and Vulgate; Syriac and Targum read *Their anger*; Septuagint reads *Ephraim*.   7:14 [a]Following Masoretic Text and Targum; Vulgate reads *thought upon*; Septuagint reads *slashed themselves for* (compare 1 Kings 18:28).   [b]Following Masoretic Text, Syriac, and Targum; Septuagint omits *They rebel against Me*; Vulgate reads *They departed from Me*.   7:16 [a]Or *upward*   8:1 [a]Hebrew *shophar*, ram's horn

That they might be cut off.

5 Your calf is rejected, O Samaria!
My anger is aroused against them—
How long until they attain to
    innocence?

6 For from Israel *is* even this:
A workman made it, and it *is* not God;
But the calf of Samaria shall be
    broken to pieces.

7 "They sow the wind,
And reap the whirlwind.
The stalk has no bud;
It shall never produce meal.
If it should produce,
Aliens would swallow it up.

8 Israel is swallowed up;
Now they are among the Gentiles
Like a vessel in which *is* no pleasure.

9 For they have gone up to Assyria,
Like a wild donkey alone by itself;
Ephraim has hired lovers.

8:9 they have gone up to Assyria. This refers to the alliance Israel made with Assyria. Instead of depending on God, Israel had stubbornly pursued foreign assistance "like a wild donkey."

10 Yes, though they have hired among
    the nations,
Now I will gather them;
And they shall sorrow a little,[a]
Because of the burden[b] of the king of
    princes.

11 "Because Ephraim has made many
    altars for sin,
They have become for him altars for
    sinning.

12 I have written for him the great things
    of My law,
But they were considered a strange
    thing.

13 *For* the sacrifices of My offerings they
    sacrifice flesh and eat *it,*
But the LORD does not accept them.
Now He will remember their iniquity
    and punish their sins.
They shall return to Egypt.

14 "For Israel has forgotten his Maker,
And has built temples;[a]

Judah also has multiplied fortified
    cities;
But I will send fire upon his cities,
And it shall devour his palaces."

Judgment of Israel's Sin

9 Do not rejoice, O Israel, with joy like
    other peoples,
For you have played the harlot against
    your God.
You have made love *for* hire on every
    threshing floor.

2 The threshing floor and the winepress
Shall not feed them,
And the new wine shall fail in her.

3 They shall not dwell in the LORD's
    land,
But Ephraim shall return to Egypt,
And shall eat unclean *things* in
    Assyria.

4 They shall not offer wine *offerings* to
    the LORD,
Nor shall their sacrifices be pleasing
    to Him.
It shall be like bread of mourners to
    them;
All who eat it shall be defiled.
For their bread *shall be* for their *own*
    life;
It shall not come into the house of
    the LORD.

9:4 bread of mourners...defiled. Food eaten during the time of mourning was considered unclean, defiling anyone who ate it (see Deut. 26:12–15).

5 What will you do in the appointed
    day,
And in the day of the feast of the
    LORD?

6 For indeed they are gone because of
    destruction.
Egypt shall gather them up;
Memphis shall bury them.
Nettles shall possess their valuables
    of silver;
Thorns *shall be* in their tents.

7 The days of punishment have come;
The days of recompense have come.
Israel knows!

8:10 [a]Or *begin to diminish*   [b]Or *oracle*   8:14 [a]Or *palaces*

The prophet *is* a fool,
The spiritual man *is* insane,
Because of the greatness of your
    iniquity and great enmity.
8 The watchman of Ephraim *is* with my
    God;
But the prophet *is* a fowler's[a] snare in
    all his ways—
Enmity in the house of his God.
9 They are deeply corrupted,
As in the days of Gibeah.
He will remember their iniquity;
He will punish their sins.

10 "I found Israel
Like grapes in the wilderness;
I saw your fathers
As the firstfruits on the fig tree in its
    first season.
But they went to Baal Peor,
And separated themselves *to that*
    shame;
They became an abomination like the
    thing they loved.
11 *As for* Ephraim, their glory shall fly
    away like a bird—
No birth, no pregnancy, and no
    conception!
12 Though they bring up their children,
Yet I will bereave them to the last
    man.
Yes, woe to them when I depart from
    them!
13 Just as I saw Ephraim like Tyre,
    planted in a pleasant place,
So Ephraim will bring out his children
    to the murderer."

14 Give them, O LORD—
What will You give?
Give them a miscarrying womb
And dry breasts!

> **9:11–14** In the pattern of the imprecatory psalms,
> Hosea prayed that God would withdraw His blessing
> from His people. In this case, he asked God to with-
> hold the blessing of having and nurturing children.

15 "All their wickedness *is* in Gilgal,
For there I hated them.
Because of the evil of their deeds

I will drive them from My house;
I will love them no more.
All their princes *are* rebellious.
16 Ephraim is stricken,
Their root is dried up;
They shall bear no fruit.
Yes, were they to bear children,
I would kill the darlings of their
    womb."

17 My God will cast them away,
Because they did not obey Him;
And they shall be wanderers among
    the nations.

Israel's Sin and Captivity

10 Israel empties *his* vine;
He brings forth fruit for himself.
According to the multitude of his fruit
He has increased the altars;
According to the bounty of his land
They have embellished *his sacred*
    pillars.
2 Their heart is divided;
Now they are held guilty.
He will break down their altars;
He will ruin their *sacred* pillars.
3 For now they say,
"We have no king,
Because we did not fear the LORD.
And as for a king, what would he do
    for us?"
4 They have spoken words,
Swearing falsely in making a covenant.
Thus judgment springs up like
    hemlock in the furrows of the field.
5 The inhabitants of Samaria fear
Because of the calf[a] of Beth Aven.
For its people mourn for it,
And its priests shriek for it—
Because its glory has departed from it.
6 *The idol* also shall be carried to
    Assyria
As a present for King Jareb.
Ephraim shall receive shame,
And Israel shall be ashamed of his
    own counsel.

7 *As for* Samaria, her king is cut off
Like a twig on the water.

9:8 [a]That is, one who catches birds in a trap or snare   10:5 [a]Literally *calves*

8 Also the high places of Aven, the sin
　　of Israel,
Shall be destroyed.
The thorn and thistle shall grow on
　　their altars;
They shall say to the mountains,
　　"Cover us!"
And to the hills, "Fall on us!"

> **10:8 Cover us...Fall on us.** The captivity would be so severe that the people would pray for the mountains and hills to fall on them. This is similar to the events in the last days (see Luke 23:30; Rev. 6:16).

9 "O Israel, you have sinned from the
　　days of Gibeah;
There they stood.
The battle in Gibeah against the
　　children of iniquity[a]
Did not overtake them.
10 When *it is* My desire, I will chasten
　　them.
Peoples shall be gathered against
　　them
When I bind them for their two
　　transgressions.[a]
11 Ephraim *is* a trained heifer
That loves to thresh *grain;*
But I harnessed her fair neck,
I will make Ephraim pull *a plow.*
Judah shall plow;
Jacob shall break his clods."

12 Sow for yourselves righteousness;
Reap in mercy;
Break up your fallow ground,
For *it is* time to seek the LORD,
Till He comes and rains righteousness
　　on you.

13 You have plowed wickedness;
You have reaped iniquity.
You have eaten the fruit of lies,
Because you trusted in your own way,
In the multitude of your mighty men.
14 Therefore tumult shall arise among
　　your people,

And all your fortresses shall be
　　plundered
As Shalman plundered Beth Arbel in
　　the day of battle—
A mother dashed in pieces upon *her*
　　children.
15 Thus it shall be done to you, O
　　Bethel,
Because of your great wickedness.
At dawn the king of Israel
Shall be cut off utterly.

God's Continuing Love for Israel

11 "When Israel *was* a child, I loved
　　him,
And out of Egypt I called My son.
2 *As* they called them,[a]
So they went from them;[b]
They sacrificed to the Baals,
And burned incense to carved images.

3 "I taught Ephraim to walk,
Taking them by their arms;[a]
But they did not know that I healed
　　them.
4 I drew them with gentle cords,[a]
With bands of love,
And I was to them as those who take
　　the yoke from their neck.[b]
I stooped *and* fed them.

5 "He shall not return to the land of
　　Egypt;
But the Assyrian shall be his king,
Because they refused to repent.
6 And the sword shall slash in his
　　cities,
Devour his districts,
And consume *them,*
Because of their own counsels.
7 My people are bent on backsliding
　　from Me.
Though they call to the Most High,[a]
None at all exalt *Him.*

8 "How can I give you up, Ephraim?
How can I hand you over, Israel?

10:9 [a]So read many Hebrew manuscripts, Septuagint, and Vulgate; Masoretic Text reads *unruliness.*
10:10 [a]Or *in their two habitations*　11:2 [a]Following Masoretic Text and Vulgate; Septuagint reads *Just as I called them;* Targum interprets as *I sent prophets to a thousand of them.*　[b]Following Masoretic Text, Targum, and Vulgate; Septuagint reads *from My face.*　11:3 [a]Some Hebrew manuscripts, Septuagint, Syriac, and Vulgate read *My arms.*　11:4 [a]Literally *cords of a man*　[b]Literally *jaws*
11:7 [a]Or *upward*

How can I make you like Admah?
How can I set you like Zeboiim?
My heart churns within Me;
My sympathy is stirred.
9   I will not execute the fierceness of My
anger;
I will not again destroy Ephraim.
For I *am* God, and not man,
The Holy One in your midst;
And I will not come with terror.[a]

10 "They shall walk after the LORD.
He will roar like a lion.
When He roars,
Then *His* sons shall come trembling
from the west;

11:10 will roar like a lion. The Lord would roar as a lion against Israel in judgment (see Amos 1:2), but He would also roar to call, protect, and bless them (see Joel 3:16). **from the west.** Captives returning from Assyria and Babylon were from the east. This pictures Christ's return at the Second Advent to set up the millennial kingdom (see Is. 11:11,12), when He will call Israel from its dispersion and reverse the judgment of 9:17.

11 They shall come trembling like a bird
from Egypt,
Like a dove from the land of Assyria.
And I will let them dwell in their
houses,"
Says the LORD.

God's Charge Against Ephraim
12 "Ephraim has encircled Me with lies,
And the house of Israel with deceit;
But Judah still walks with God,
Even with the Holy One[a] *who is*
faithful.

12 "Ephraim feeds on the wind,
And pursues the east wind;
He daily increases lies and desolation.
Also they make a covenant with the
Assyrians,
And oil is carried to Egypt.

2   "The LORD also *brings* a charge against
Judah,
And will punish Jacob according to
his ways;

According to his deeds He will
recompense him.
3   He took his brother by the heel in the
womb,
And in his strength he struggled with
God.[a]
4   Yes, he struggled with the Angel and
prevailed;
He wept, and sought favor from Him.
He found Him *in* Bethel,
And there He spoke to us—
5   That is, the LORD God of hosts.
The LORD *is* His memorable name.
6   So you, by *the help of* your God,
return;
Observe mercy and justice,
And wait on your God continually.

12:3–6 Hosea exhorted the people to follow their father Jacob's persevering prayerfulness, which brought God's favor on him. Because God is unchanging, He would show the same favor to Jacob's offspring if they sought Him.

7   "A cunning Canaanite!
Deceitful scales *are* in his hand;
He loves to oppress.
8   And Ephraim said,
'Surely I have become rich,
I have found wealth for myself;
In all my labors
They shall find in me no iniquity that
is sin.'

9   "But I *am* the LORD your God,
Ever since the land of Egypt;
I will again make you dwell in tents,
As in the days of the appointed feast.
10 I have also spoken by the prophets,
And have multiplied visions;
I have given symbols through the
witness of the prophets."

11 Though Gilead *has* idols—
Surely they are vanity—
Though they sacrifice bulls in Gilgal,
Indeed their altars *shall be* heaps in
the furrows of the field.

12 Jacob fled to the country of Syria;
Israel served for a spouse,

11:9 [a]Or *I will not enter a city*   11:12 [a]Or *holy ones*   12:3 [a]Compare Genesis 32:28

And for a wife he tended *sheep*.
13 By a prophet the LORD brought Israel
    out of Egypt,
    And by a prophet he was preserved.
14 Ephraim provoked *Him* to anger most
    bitterly;
    Therefore his Lord will leave the guilt
        of his bloodshed upon him;
    And return his reproach upon him.

Relentless Judgment on Israel

13 When Ephraim spoke, trembling,
    He exalted *himself* in Israel;
    But when he offended through Baal
        worship, he died.

13:1 trembling. Early in Israel's history, Ephraim, the most powerful tribe, had authority that produced fear. **he died.** Ephraim died nationally and spiritually because of his sins.

2   Now they sin more and more,
    And have made for themselves
        molded images,
    Idols of their silver, according to their
        skill;
    All of it *is* the work of craftsmen.
    They say of them,
    "Let the men who sacrifice*a* kiss the
        calves!"
3   Therefore they shall be like the
        morning cloud
    And like the early dew that passes
        away,
    Like chaff blown off from a threshing
        floor
    And like smoke from a chimney.

4   "Yet I *am* the LORD your God
    Ever since the land of Egypt;
    And you shall know no God but Me;
    For *there is* no savior besides Me.
5   I knew you in the wilderness,
    In the land of great drought.
6   When they had pasture, they were
        filled;
    They were filled and their heart was
        exalted;
    Therefore they forgot Me.

7   "So I will be to them like a lion;
    Like a leopard by the road I will lurk;
8   I will meet them like a bear deprived
        of her cubs;
    I will tear open their rib cage,
    And there I will devour them like a
        lion.
    The wild beast shall tear them.

13:7,8 The lion, leopard, and bear are all native to Israel. God, her Protector, would now become to her as a wild beast, tearing and devouring (see Lev. 26:21,22).

9   "O Israel, you are destroyed,*a*
    But your help*b* *is* from Me.
10 I will be your King;*a*
    Where *is* any other,
    That he may save you in all your
        cities?
    And your judges to whom you said,
    'Give me a king and princes'?
11 I gave you a king in My anger,
    And took *him* away in My wrath.

12 "The iniquity of Ephraim *is* bound up;
    His sin *is* stored up.
13 The sorrows of a woman in childbirth
        shall come upon him.
    He *is* an unwise son,
    For he should not stay long where
        children are born.

14 "I will ransom them from the power of
        the grave;*a*
    I will redeem them from death.
    O Death, I will be your plagues!*b*
    O Grave,*c* I will be your destruction!*d*
    Pity is hidden from My eyes."

15 Though he is fruitful among *his*
        brethren,
    An east wind shall come;
    The wind of the LORD shall come up
        from the wilderness.
    Then his spring shall become dry,
    And his fountain shall be dried up.
    He shall plunder the treasury of every
        desirable prize.

13:2 *a*Or *those who offer human sacrifice*   13:9 *a*Literally *it* or *he destroyed you*   *b*Literally *in your help*   13:10 *a*Septuagint, Syriac, Targum, and Vulgate read *Where is your king?*   13:14 *a*Or *Sheol* *b*Septuagint reads *where is your punishment?*   *c*Or *Sheol*   *d*Septuagint reads *where is your sting?*

16 Samaria is held guilty,[a]
For she has rebelled against her God.
They shall fall by the sword,
Their infants shall be dashed in
        pieces,
And their women with child ripped
        open.

Israel Restored at Last

14 O Israel, return to the LORD your
        God,
For you have stumbled because of
        your iniquity;
2 Take words with you,
And return to the LORD.
Say to Him,
"Take away all iniquity;
Receive us graciously,
For we will offer the sacrifices[a] of our
        lips.
3 Assyria shall not save us,
We will not ride on horses,
Nor will we say anymore to the work
        of our hands, 'You are our gods.'
For in You the fatherless finds mercy."

4 "I will heal their backsliding,
I will love them freely,

For My anger has turned away from
        him.
5 I will be like the dew to Israel;
He shall grow like the lily,
And lengthen his roots like Lebanon.
6 His branches shall spread;
His beauty shall be like an olive
        tree,
And his fragrance like Lebanon.
7 Those who dwell under his shadow
        shall return;
They shall be revived like grain,
And grow like a vine.
Their scent[a] shall be like the wine of
        Lebanon.

8 "Ephraim shall say, 'What have I to do
        anymore with idols?'
I have heard and observed him.
I am like a green cypress tree;
Your fruit is found in Me."

9 Who is wise?
Let him understand these things.
Who is prudent?
Let him know them.
For the ways of the LORD are right;
The righteous walk in them,
But transgressors stumble in them.

14:4–8 Because Israel has not repented, the fulfillment of these blessings will occur in the millennium, during the end of the Great Tribulation (see Zech. 12:10–13:1). Yet the Lord continues to love His people. His love is described here as the dew, the lily, the cedars of Lebanon, and the olive tree.

14:9 Hosea concludes the prophecy by presenting the reader with two ways of living (see Deut. 30:19,20; Ps. 1). He calls the reader to be wise and choose the Lord's way, for His ways are right (see Ps. 107:43).

13:16 [a]Septuagint reads shall be disfigured   14:2 [a]Literally bull calves; Septuagint reads fruit.
14:7 [a]Literally remembrance

JOEL

The locusts struck like a firestorm. In their wake they left a devastated nation and a prophet speaking out the "word of the Lord" (1:1). Joel survived the plague of devouring insects and delivered a ringing message of explanation, a bold call to action, and a gift of hope. His timeless words still call those who believe in God to trust even when the waves of devastation and evil seem overwhelming. His message continues to inspire hope, "For day of the Lord is coming" (2:1).

AUTHOR AND DATE

Joel was written by Joel during his ministry, approximately 835 to 796 B.C.

The author identified himself only as "Joel, the son of Pethuel" (1:1). His father's name is not mentioned in the rest of the Old Testament. Even the internal evidence in the book provides little help in identifying Joel's background. Though tradition claims Joel was from the tribe of Reuben, his language and tone seem to indicate that he probably was from near Jerusalem.

The date for this book has been widely debated. The following three reasons support an early date for Joel: (1) the later world powers like Assyria, Babylon, and Persia are not mentioned; (2) Joel's style shares more similarities with Hosea and Amos than with the prophets who wrote after the Exile; (3) parallel concerns between Joel and Amos indicate they were responding to similar desperate times. These clues seem to place Joel and his writing in the years of King Joash (835–796 B.C.). While the date of this book cannot be determined with certainty, that issue has little impact on the interpretation of Joel's prophecies. The message of Joel is both timeless and effective in conveying doctrines with timely impact on any age.

BACKGROUND AND SETTING

Israel discovered that enemies come in many shapes and sizes. They were almost accustomed to the frequent raids by bandits from Tyre, Sidon, and Philistia (3:2). Suddenly, however, destruction came in a new form—swarms of locusts over-ran the land like an insatiable army. Judah, suffering the ravages of a long drought, now faced economic devastation (1:7–20).

The national disasters gave Joel a vivid illustration of God's judgment. Although the locusts were a severe judgment on sin, God's future judgments on the Day of the Lord will be far worse. In that day, God will judge His enemies and bless the faithful. Joel did not mention specific sins, but he called the people to

genuine repentance. He urged them to "rend your heart, and not your garments" (2:13).

Joel makes the Day of the Lord his central theme. It permeates every part of his message. Although eight other Old Testament authors mention the Day of the Lord, Joel offers the most sustained treatment of the term (1:15; 2:1,11,31; 3:14). The phrase does not refer to a specific date but to a general period of wrath and judgment uniquely focused on the Lord. The Day of the Lord will be a time during which God will unveil His character—mighty, powerful, and holy. God will terrify His enemies.

In general Old Testament usage, the Day of the Lord does not always refer to the final times. Ezekiel 13:5, for example, uses it to describe the meaning behind the Babylonian conquest and the destruction of Jerusalem. Characteristics associated with the Day of the Lord include seismic disturbances (2:1–11,31; 3:16), violent weather (Ezekiel 13:5), clouds and thick darkness (2:2), cosmic upheaval (2:3,30), and a "great and very terrible" (2:11) day that would "come as destruction from the Almighty" (1:15).

The latter half of Joel depicts the Day of the Lord as a prelude to promised hope. There will be a pouring out of the Spirit on all flesh, accompanied by prophetic utterances, dreams, and visions (2:28,29). The time will also be marked by the coming of Elijah, whose appearance will bring restoration and hope (Malachi 4:5,6). The Day of the Lord will result in physical blessings, fruitfulness, and prosperity (2:21ff; 3:16–21).

> THE DAY OF THE LORD WILL BE A TIME DURING WHICH GOD WILL UNVEIL HIS CHARACTER—MIGHTY, POWERFUL, AND HOLY.

OUTLINE

1 The word of the LORD that came to Joel the son of Pethuel.

The Land Laid Waste

2   Hear this, you elders,
    And give ear, all you inhabitants of
        the land!
    Has *anything like* this happened in
        your days,
    Or even in the days of your fathers?

3   Tell your children about it,
    Let your children *tell* their children,
    And their children another
        generation.

4   What the chewing locust[a] left, the
        swarming locust has eaten;
    What the swarming locust left, the
        crawling locust has eaten;
    And what the crawling locust left, the
        consuming locust has eaten.

5   Awake, you drunkards, and weep;
    And wail, all you drinkers of wine,
    Because of the new wine,
    For it has been cut off from your
        mouth.

6   For a nation has come up against My
        land,
    Strong, and without number;
    His teeth *are* the teeth of a lion,
    And he has the fangs of a fierce lion.

7   He has laid waste My vine,
    And ruined My fig tree;
    He has stripped it bare and thrown *it*
        away;
    Its branches are made white.

8   Lament like a virgin girded with
        sackcloth
    For the husband of her youth.

9   The grain offering and the drink
        offering
    Have been cut off from the house of
        the LORD;
    The priests mourn, who minister to
        the LORD.

10 The field is wasted,
    The land mourns;
    For the grain is ruined,
    The new wine is dried up,
    The oil fails.

11 Be ashamed, you farmers,
    Wail, you vinedressers,
    For the wheat and the barley;
    Because the harvest of the field has
        perished.

12 The vine has dried up,
    And the fig tree has withered;
    The pomegranate tree,
    The palm tree also,

1:4 [a]Exact identity of these locusts is unknown.

Does Joel's account mean the land of Israel was actually over-run with locusts?

Insect plagues such as the one reported by Joel are well known in many parts of the world. Joel described at length the different stages of life, or the different types of locusts (1:4). The vivid details included by Joel increase the usefulness of the event as a teaching tool, but they also emphasize the fact that the prophet saw before his eyes the devastated remains of his nation.

Joel's prophetic vision of the Day of the Lord elevated the tragedy of the locusts to become an illustration of the final devastation. In the prophet's similes, the locusts are "like the appearance of horses" (2:4) and "like mighty men" (2:7), but the underlying message announces the coming Day when real horses and men will arrive on the scene bringing God's judgment.

And the apple tree—
All the trees of the field are withered;
Surely joy has withered away from the
  sons of men.

1:12 All the trees...are withered. Even the deep roots of the trees could not withstand the destruction by the locusts, especially when accompanied by an extended drought. **joy has withered.** Despair replaced joy in all segments of society; everything was affected by the locusts.

Mourning for the Land

13 Gird yourselves and lament, you
      priests;
    Wail, you who minister before the
      altar;
    Come, lie all night in sackcloth,
    You who minister to my God;
    For the grain offering and the drink
      offering
    Are withheld from the house of your
      God.
14 Consecrate a fast,
    Call a sacred assembly;
    Gather the elders
    And all the inhabitants of the land
    Into the house of the LORD your God,
    And cry out to the LORD.

15 Alas for the day!
    For the day of the LORD *is* at hand;
    It shall come as destruction from the
      Almighty.
16 Is not the food cut off before our eyes,
    Joy and gladness from the house of
      our God?
17 The seed shrivels under the clods,

Storehouses are in shambles;
Barns are broken down,
For the grain has withered.
18 How the animals groan!
    The herds of cattle are restless,
    Because they have no pasture;
    Even the flocks of sheep suffer
      punishment.[a]

19 O LORD, to You I cry out;
    For fire has devoured the open
      pastures,
    And a flame has burned all the trees
      of the field.

1:19 to You I cry out. As the first to call for repentance, the prophet Joel had to be the first to heed the warning. He had to lead by example and motivate the people to respond. God's prophets often prayed for mercy and forgiveness in the midst of proclaiming judgment (see Ex. 32:11–14).

20 The beasts of the field also cry out to
      You,
    For the water brooks are dried up,
    And fire has devoured the open
      pastures.

The Day of the LORD

2 Blow the trumpet in Zion,
   And sound an alarm in My holy
     mountain!
   Let all the inhabitants of the land
     tremble;
   For the day of the LORD is coming,
   For it is at hand:
2   A day of darkness and gloominess,
     A day of clouds and thick darkness,

1:18 [a]Septuagint and Vulgate read *are made desolate.*

DAY OF THE LORD

NINETEEN EXPLICIT MENTIONS OF "DAY OF THE LORD" IN THE OLD TESTAMENT

1. Obadiah 15	6. Joel 3:14	11. Isaiah 13:6	16. Ezekiel 13:5
2. Joel 1:15	7. Amos 5:18	12. Isaiah 13:9	17. Ezekiel 30:3
3. Joel 2:1	8. Amos 5:18	13. Zephaniah 1:7	18. Zechariah 14:1
4. Joel 2:11	9. Amos 5:20	14. Zephaniah 1:14	19. Malachi 4:5
5. Joel 2:31	10. Isaiah 2:12	15. Zephaniah 1:1	

FOUR EXPLICIT MENTIONS OF "DAY OF THE LORD" IN THE NEW TESTAMENT

1. Acts 2:20	2. 1 Thessalonians 5:2	3. 2 Thessalonians 2:2	4. 2 Peter 3:10

Like the morning *clouds* spread over
 the mountains.
A people *come*, great and strong,
The like of whom has never been;
Nor will there ever be any *such* after
 them,
Even for many successive generations.

3 A fire devours before them,
And behind them a flame burns;
The land *is* like the Garden of Eden
 before them,
And behind them a desolate
 wilderness;
Surely nothing shall escape them.

4 Their appearance is like the
 appearance of horses;
And like swift steeds, so they run.

> **2:4 Their appearance is like...horses.** The resem-
> blance of the locust's head to that of a horse is strik-
> ing. Horses were used as military equipment in
> ancient times (Ex. 15:1; Deut. 20:1) and were greatly
> feared.

5 With a noise like chariots
Over mountaintops they leap,
Like the noise of a flaming fire that
 devours the stubble,
Like a strong people set in battle
 array.

6 Before them the people writhe in
 pain;

All faces are drained of color.[a]
7 They run like mighty men,
They climb the wall like men of war;
Every one marches in formation,
And they do not break ranks.
8 They do not push one another;
Every one marches in his own
 column.[a]
Though they lunge between the
 weapons,
They are not cut down.[b]
9 They run to and fro in the city,
They run on the wall;
They climb into the houses,
They enter at the windows like a
 thief.

10 The earth quakes before them,
The heavens tremble;
The sun and moon grow dark,
And the stars diminish their
 brightness.
11 The LORD gives voice before His
 army,
For His camp is very great;
For strong *is the One* who executes
 His word.
For the day of the LORD *is* great and
 very terrible;
Who can endure it?

A Call to Repentance

12 "Now, therefore," says the LORD,
"Turn to Me with all your heart,

2:6 [a]Septuagint, Targum, and Vulgate read *gather blackness*. 2:8 [a]Literally *his own highway* [b]That
is, they are not halted by losses

When Peter
quoted Joel 2:28–
32 at the begin-
ning of his sermon
in Acts 2:16–21,
how did his
interpretation
relate to the
ultimate fulfill-
ment of that
prophecy?

Some have viewed the events of Acts 2 and the destruction of
Jerusalem in 70 A.D. as the fulfillment of the Joel passage. Others
have reserved its ultimate fulfillment to the final Day of the
Lord. It appears likely that the initial pouring out of the Holy
Spirit at Pentecost was not a fulfillment but a preview and
sample of the Spirit's power and work. The full outpouring of
the Holy Spirit will come in the Messiah's kingdom after the Day
of the Lord. That was the ultimate vision in Joel's prophecy.

With fasting, with weeping, and with
    mourning."
13 So rend your heart, and not your
    garments;
Return to the LORD your God,
For He *is* gracious and merciful,
Slow to anger, and of great kindness;
And He relents from doing harm.
14 Who knows *if* He will turn and relent,
And leave a blessing behind Him—
A grain offering and a drink offering
For the LORD your God?

15 Blow the trumpet in Zion,
Consecrate a fast,
Call a sacred assembly;
16 Gather the people,
Sanctify the congregation,
Assemble the elders,
Gather the children and nursing
    babes;
Let the bridegroom go out from his
    chamber,
And the bride from her dressing
    room.
17 Let the priests, who minister to the
    LORD,
Weep between the porch and the altar;
Let them say, "Spare Your people,
    O LORD,
And do not give Your heritage to
    reproach,
That the nations should rule over
    them.
Why should they say among the
    peoples,
'Where *is* their God?' "

2:18–3:21 It is assumed that there is an interval of
time between v. 17 and v. 18 during which Israel repented. As a result, these verses focus on the physical, spiritual, and national restoration of Israel.

The Land Refreshed

18 Then the LORD will be zealous for His
    land,
And pity His people.
19 The LORD will answer and say to His
    people,
"Behold, I will send you grain and new
    wine and oil,
And you will be satisfied by them;

I will no longer make you a reproach
    among the nations.

20 "But I will remove far from you the
    northern *army*,
And will drive him away into a barren
    and desolate land,
With his face toward the eastern sea
And his back toward the western sea;
His stench will come up,
And his foul odor will rise,
Because he has done monstrous
    things."

21 Fear not, O land;
Be glad and rejoice,
For the LORD has done marvelous
    things!
22 Do not be afraid, you beasts of the
    field;
For the open pastures are springing
    up,
And the tree bears its fruit;
The fig tree and the vine yield their
    strength.
23 Be glad then, you children of Zion,
And rejoice in the LORD your God;
For He has given you the former rain
    faithfully,[a]
And He will cause the rain to come
    down for you—
The former rain,
And the latter rain in the first *month*.
24 The threshing floors shall be full of
    wheat,
And the vats shall overflow with new
    wine and oil.

25 "So I will restore to you the years that
    the swarming locust has eaten,
The crawling locust,
The consuming locust,
And the chewing locust,[a]
My great army which I sent among
    you.
26 You shall eat in plenty and be
    satisfied,
And praise the name of the LORD
    your God,
Who has dealt wondrously with you;
And My people shall never be put to
    shame.

2:23 [a]Or *the teacher of righteousness*   2:25 [a]Compare 1:4

27 Then you shall know that I *am* in the
     midst of Israel:
I *am* the LORD your God
And there is no other.
My people shall never be put to
     shame.

God's Spirit Poured Out

28 "And it shall come to pass afterward
     That I will pour out My Spirit on all
     flesh;
Your sons and your daughters shall
     prophesy,
Your old men shall dream dreams,
Your young men shall see visions.
29 And also on *My* menservants and on
     My maidservants
I will pour out My Spirit in those
     days.

30 "And I will show wonders in the
     heavens and in the earth:
Blood and fire and pillars of smoke.
31 The sun shall be turned into
     darkness,
And the moon into blood,
Before the coming of the great and
     awesome day of the LORD.
32 And it shall come to pass
That whoever calls on the name of
     the LORD
Shall be saved.
For in Mount Zion and in Jerusalem
     there shall be deliverance,
As the LORD has said,
Among the remnant whom the LORD
     calls.

God Judges the Nations

3 "For behold, in those days and at that
     time,
When I bring back the captives of
     Judah and Jerusalem,
2 I will also gather all nations,
And bring them down to the Valley of
     Jehoshaphat;
And I will enter into judgment with
     them there

On account of My people, My
     heritage Israel,
Whom they have scattered among the
     nations;
They have also divided up My land.

3 They have cast lots for My people,
Have given a boy *as payment* for a
     harlot,
And sold a girl for wine, that they
     may drink.

4 "Indeed, what have you to do with Me,
O Tyre and Sidon, and all the coasts
     of Philistia?
Will you retaliate against Me?
But if you retaliate against Me,
Swiftly and speedily I will return your
     retaliation upon your own head;
5 Because you have taken My silver and
     My gold,
And have carried into your temples
     My prized possessions.
6 Also the people of Judah and the
     people of Jerusalem
You have sold to the Greeks,
That you may remove them far from
     their borders.

7 "Behold, I will raise them
Out of the place to which you have
     sold them,
And will return your retaliation upon
     your own head.
8 I will sell your sons and your
     daughters
Into the hand of the people of Judah,
And they will sell them to the
     Sabeans,[a]

3:8 [a]Literally *Shebaites* (compare Isaiah 60:6 and Ezekiel 27:22)

To a people far off;
For the LORD has spoken."

9 Proclaim this among the nations:
   "Prepare for war!
   Wake up the mighty men,
   Let all the men of war draw near,
   Let them come up.
10 Beat your plowshares into swords
    And your pruning hooks into spears;
    Let the weak say, 'I *am* strong.' "
11 Assemble and come, all you nations,
    And gather together all around.
    Cause Your mighty ones to go down
        there, O LORD.

12 "Let the nations be wakened, and come
        up to the Valley of Jehoshaphat;
    For there I will sit to judge all the
        surrounding nations.
13 Put in the sickle, for the harvest is
        ripe.
    Come, go down;
    For the winepress is full,
    The vats overflow—
    For their wickedness *is* great."

14 Multitudes, multitudes in the valley
        of decision!
    For the day of the LORD *is* near in the
        valley of decision.
15 The sun and moon will grow dark,
    And the stars will diminish their
        brightness.
16 The LORD also will roar from Zion,
    And utter His voice from Jerusalem;
    The heavens and earth will shake;
    But the LORD will be a shelter for His
        people,
    And the strength of the children of
        Israel.

17 "So you shall know that I *am* the LORD
        your God,
    Dwelling in Zion My holy
        mountain.
    Then Jerusalem shall be holy,
    And no aliens shall ever pass through
        her again."

3:17 Zion My holy mountain. This will be the earthly location of God's presence in the millennial temple at Jerusalem (see Ezek. 40–48). **ever pass through her again.** God has promised a future time when His glory will remain on earth. This time of ultimate peace and prosperity will occur after Christ conquers the world and sets up His millennial kingdom (see Ezek. 37:24–28; Matt. 24,25).

God Blesses His People
18 And it will come to pass in that day
    That the mountains shall drip with
        new wine,
    The hills shall flow with milk,
    And all the brooks of Judah shall be
        flooded with water;
    A fountain shall flow from the house
        of the LORD
    And water the Valley of Acacias.

19 "Egypt shall be a desolation,
    And Edom a desolate wilderness,
    Because of violence *against* the people
        of Judah,
    For they have shed innocent blood in
        their land.
20 But Judah shall abide forever,
    And Jerusalem from generation to
        generation.
21 For I will acquit them of the guilt of
        bloodshed, whom I had not
        acquitted;
    For the LORD dwells in Zion."

AMOS

God finds people almost anywhere to serve Him. Most of the people we meet in the Bible had minimal formal religious training. God showed little interest in their occupations, positions, or successes in life. He looked for men and women with the right kind of heart. God simply met them wherever they were and gave them directions. We have God's Word because these men and women were faithful. Among the unusual people God called to be His prophets was a lowly shepherd named Amos.

AUTHOR AND DATE

Amos was written by Amos during his ministry, approximately 760 to 750 B.C.

Amos gave his readers two significant clues about himself: his hometown (Tekoa) and his occupation (sheep-breeder). He was the only prophet to report his occupation before receiving his divine commission. At one point he expressed some amazement that God called him to deliver a message. After all, he wrote, "I was no prophet, nor was I a son of a prophet, but I was a sheep-breeder and a tender of sycamore fruit" (7:14). Apparently, Amos also worked as seasonal help in the sycamore groves, preparing the fruit for harvest.

Among the prophets, Amos was a contemporary of Jonah, Hosea, and Isaiah. Amos wrote and prophesied during the reigns of Uzziah, king of Judah (790–739 B.C.) and Jeroboam II, king of Israel (793–753 B.C.). A further aid in dating Amos can be found in his mention of a great earthquake (1:1), also noted in Zechariah 14:5 and thought to have occurred in approximately 760 B.C.

BACKGROUND AND SETTING

Although Amos identified himself as a Judean prophet, God directed him to deliver a message intended for the northern tribes of Israel (7:15). Amos confronted Israel during a time of extended prosperity and security. King Jeroboam II had followed his father Joash's example and "restored the territory of Israel" (2 Kings 14:25). The widespread peace throughout the region was due in part to the subdued threat of Assyria following Nineveh's repentance under the preaching of Jonah. On the home front, Amos was called to confront the rampant corruption and moral decay that permeated his society.

Amos targeted Israel's two primary sins: (1) an absence of true worship; (2) a lack of justice. The people were content with religious rituals instead of pursuing the Lord with their whole hearts (4:4,5; 5:4–6). They had God's standards of justice in the Law, but they were not following it in the way they treated their neighbors (5:10–13; 6:12). The apostasy of the people was confirmed by their willful rejection of Amos' prophecy. Although Amos delivered the promise of divine judgment, he also reminded the people of God's faithfulness to His covenant and that He would not abandon them altogether, but would bring future restoration to a righteous remnant (9:7–15).

> **THE PEOPLE WERE CONTENT WITH RELIGIOUS RITUALS INSTEAD OF PURSUING THE LORD WITH THEIR WHOLE HEARTS.**

OUTLINE

I. JUDGMENT AGAINST THE NATIONS (1:1–2:16)

    A. Introduction (1:1–2)

    B. Against Israel's Enemies (1:3–2:3)

    C. Against Judah (2:4–5)

    D. Against Israel (2:6–16)

II. CONDEMNATIONS AGAINST ISRAEL (3:1–6:14)

    A. Sin of Irresponsibility (3:1–15)

    B. Sin of Idolatry (4:1–13)

    C. Sin of Moral/Ethical Decay (5:1–6:14)

III. VISIONS OF JUDGMENT AND RESTORATION (7:1–9:15)

    A. The Lord Will Spare (7:1–6)

        1. Vision of locusts (7:1–3)

        2. Vision of fire (7:4–6)

    B. The Lord Will No Longer Spare (7:7–9:10)

        1. Vision of the plumb line (7:7–9)

        2. Historical interlude (7:10–17)

        3. Vision of the fruit basket (8:1–14)

        4. Vision of the altar (9:1–10)

    C. The Lord Will Restore (9:11–15)

1 The words of Amos, who was among the sheepbreeders*a* of Tekoa, which he saw concerning Israel in the days of Uzziah king of Judah, and in the days of Jeroboam the son of Joash, king of Israel, two years before the earthquake.

²And he said:

> "The LORD roars from Zion,
> And utters His voice from Jerusalem;
> The pastures of the shepherds mourn,
> And the top of Carmel withers."

1:2 roars. In Joel 3:16, the Lord "roars" against the nations; here His wrath is directed toward Israel (see Jer. 25:30). Amos, a shepherd who protected his sheep from wild animals like lions, warned the people that they were in danger from a roaring lion, the Lord (see 3:8). **Carmel.** This means "fertility" or "garden land" and refers to the mountain range that runs east to west in northern Israel and juts out into the Mediterranean Sea (see 9:3).

Judgment on the Nations

³Thus says the LORD:

> "For three transgressions of Damascus, and for four,
> I will not turn away its *punishment*,
> Because they have threshed Gilead with implements of iron.

⁴ But I will send a fire into the house of Hazael,
> Which shall devour the palaces of Ben-Hadad.

⁵ I will also break the *gate* bar of Damascus,
> And cut off the inhabitant from the Valley of Aven,
> And the one who holds the scepter from Beth Eden.
> The people of Syria shall go captive to Kir,"
> Says the LORD.

⁶Thus says the LORD:

> "For three transgressions of Gaza, and for four,
> I will not turn away its *punishment*,
> Because they took captive the whole captivity

To deliver *them* up to Edom.

⁷ But I will send a fire upon the wall of Gaza,
> Which shall devour its palaces.

⁸ I will cut off the inhabitant from Ashdod,
> And the one who holds the scepter from Ashkelon;
> I will turn My hand against Ekron,
> And the remnant of the Philistines shall perish,"
> Says the Lord GOD.

⁹Thus says the LORD:

> "For three transgressions of Tyre, and for four,
> I will not turn away its *punishment*,
> Because they delivered up the whole captivity to Edom,
> And did not remember the covenant of brotherhood.

1:9 covenant of brotherhood. A longstanding brotherly relationship existed between Phoenicia and Israel, beginning with King Hiram's assistance to David and Solomon in the building of the temple (2 Sam. 5:11). It was later reinforced through Jezebel's marriage to Ahab (1 Kin. 16:31). No king of Israel ever made war against Phoenicia.

¹⁰ But I will send a fire upon the wall of Tyre,
> Which shall devour its palaces."

¹¹Thus says the LORD:

> "For three transgressions of Edom, and for four,
> I will not turn away its *punishment*,
> Because he pursued his brother with the sword,
> And cast off all pity;
> His anger tore perpetually,
> And he kept his wrath forever.

¹² But I will send a fire upon Teman,
> Which shall devour the palaces of Bozrah."

¹³Thus says the LORD:

> "For three transgressions of the people of Ammon, and for four,

I will not turn away its *punishment*,
Because they ripped open the women
　　with child in Gilead,
That they might enlarge their
　　territory.
14 But I will kindle a fire in the wall of
　　Rabbah,
And it shall devour its palaces,
Amid shouting in the day of battle,
And a tempest in the day of the
　　whirlwind.
15 Their king shall go into captivity,
He and his princes together,"
Says the LORD.

2 Thus says the LORD:

"For three transgressions of Moab, and
　　for four,
I will not turn away its *punishment*,
Because he burned the bones of the
　　king of Edom to lime.
2 But I will send a fire upon Moab,
And it shall devour the palaces of
　　Kerioth;
Moab shall die with tumult,
With shouting *and* trumpet sound.
3 And I will cut off the judge from its
　　midst,
And slay all its princes with him,"
Says the LORD.

Judgment on Judah

4 Thus says the LORD:

"For three transgressions of Judah, and
　　for four,
I will not turn away its *punishment*,
Because they have despised the law of
　　the LORD,
And have not kept His
　　commandments.
Their lies lead them astray,

2:4 Judah. After making the judgments against the nations, the prophet addressed Judah, moving closer to his ultimate target of Israel. **despised the law of the LORD.** The nations were judged for sinning against God's law, which was written in the heart and conscience (see Rom. 2:14,15). Judah and Israel were also judged for sinning against God's revealed, written law.

Lies which their fathers followed.
5 But I will send a fire upon Judah,
And it shall devour the palaces of
　　Jerusalem."

Judgment on Israel

6 Thus says the LORD:

"For three transgressions of Israel, and
　　for four,
I will not turn away its *punishment*,
Because they sell the righteous for
　　silver,
And the poor for a pair of sandals.
7 They pant after[a] the dust of the earth
　　which is on the head of the poor,
And pervert the way of the humble.
A man and his father go in to the
　　same girl,
To defile My holy name.
8 They lie down by every altar on
　　clothes taken in pledge,
And drink the wine of the
　　condemned *in* the house of their
　　god.

9 "Yet *it was* I *who* destroyed the
　　Amorite before them,
Whose height *was* like the height of
　　the cedars,
And he *was as* strong as the oaks;
Yet I destroyed his fruit above
And his roots beneath.
10 Also *it was* I *who* brought you up
　　from the land of Egypt,
And led you forty years through the
　　wilderness,
To possess the land of the Amorite.
11 I raised up some of your sons as
　　prophets,
And some of your young men as
　　Nazirites.
Is it not so, O you children of Israel?"
Says the LORD.
12 "But you gave the Nazirites wine to
　　drink,
And commanded the prophets saying,
　'Do not prophesy!'

13 "Behold, I am weighed down by you,
As a cart full of sheaves is weighed
　　down.

2:7 [a]Or *trample on*

¹⁴   Therefore flight shall perish from the
          swift,
     The strong shall not strengthen his
          power,
     Nor shall the mighty deliver himself;
¹⁵   He shall not stand who handles the
          bow,
     The swift of foot shall not escape,
     Nor shall he who rides a horse deliver
          himself.
¹⁶   The most courageous men of might
     Shall flee naked in that day,"
     Says the LORD.

Authority of the Prophet's Message

3 Hear this word that the LORD has spoken against you, O children of Israel,
against the whole family which I brought
up from the land of Egypt, saying:

²   "You only have I known of all the
          families of the earth;
     Therefore I will punish you for all
          your iniquities."

> **3:2 You only have I known.** This refers to God's in-
> timate relationship with Israel (see Gen. 4:1,17; Matt.
> 1:25). God's sovereign choice of Israel did not exempt
> her from punishment for disobedience, however.

³   Can two walk together, unless they
          are agreed?
⁴   Will a lion roar in the forest, when he
          has no prey?
     Will a young lion cry out of his den, if
          he has caught nothing?
⁵   Will a bird fall into a snare on the
          earth, where there is no trap for it?
     Will a snare spring up from the earth,
          if it has caught nothing at all?
⁶   If a trumpet is blown in a city, will
          not the people be afraid?
     If there is calamity in a city, will not
          the LORD have done it?

⁷   Surely the Lord GOD does nothing,
     Unless He reveals His secret to His
          servants the prophets.
⁸   A lion has roared!
     Who will not fear?
     The Lord GOD has spoken!
     Who can but prophesy?

> **3:3–8** The Lord posed a series of questions to show
> that nothing happens in Israel outside of His sover-
> eign will. The prophet spoke the Lord's word, and the
> people should have listened with trembling. Instead,
> they tried to silence the prophet (see 2:12).

Punishment of Israel's Sins

⁹   "Proclaim in the palaces at Ashdod,ᵃ
     And in the palaces in the land of
          Egypt, and say:
     'Assemble on the mountains of
          Samaria;
     See great tumults in her midst,
     And the oppressed within her.
¹⁰ For they do not know to do right,'
     Says the LORD,
     'Who store up violence and robbery in
          their palaces.' "

¹¹Therefore thus says the Lord GOD:

     "An adversary *shall be* all around the
          land;
     He shall sap your strength from you,
     And your palaces shall be plundered."

¹²Thus says the LORD:

     "As a shepherd takes from the mouth
          of a lion
     Two legs or a piece of an ear,
     So shall the children of Israel be taken
          out
     Who dwell in Samaria—
     In the corner of a bed and on the
          edgeᵃ of a couch!
¹³ Hear and testify against the house of
          Jacob,"
     Says the Lord GOD, the God of hosts,
¹⁴ "That in the day I punish Israel for
          their transgressions,
     I will also visit *destruction* on the
          altars of Bethel;
     And the horns of the altar shall be cut
          off
     And fall to the ground.
¹⁵ I will destroy the winter house along
          with the summer house;
     The houses of ivory shall perish,
     And the great houses shall have an
          end,"
     Says the LORD.

3:9 ᵃFollowing Masoretic Text; Septuagint reads *Assyria*.   3:12 ᵃThe Hebrew is uncertain.

4 Hear this word, you cows of Bashan,
    who *are* on the mountain of
      Samaria,
    Who oppress the poor,
    Who crush the needy,
    Who say to your husbands,*a* "Bring
      wine, let us drink!"

> **4:2,3 *through* broken *walls*...into Harmon.** Captives will be led out of the city through breaches in the walls, depicting a massive overthrow of the city. The location of Harmon is unknown.

2 The Lord GOD has sworn by His
     holiness:
  "Behold, the days shall come upon you
   When He will take you away with
     fishhooks,
   And your posterity with fishhooks.
3 You will go out *through* broken *walls*,
   Each one straight ahead of her,
   And you will be cast into Harmon,"
   Says the LORD.

4 "Come to Bethel and transgress,
   At Gilgal multiply transgression;
   Bring your sacrifices every morning,
   Your tithes every three days.*a*
5 Offer a sacrifice of thanksgiving with
     leaven,
   Proclaim *and* announce the freewill
     offerings;
   For this you love,
   You children of Israel!"
   Says the Lord GOD.

Israel Did Not Accept Correction
6 "Also I gave you cleanness of teeth in
     all your cities,
   And lack of bread in all your places;
   Yet you have not returned to Me,"
   Says the LORD.

> **4:6 cleanness of teeth.** This depicts the absence of food during a time of famine and drought sent by God as a warning to Israel (see Deut. 28:22–24,47,48).

7 "I also withheld rain from you,
   When *there were* still three months
     to the harvest.
   I made it rain on one city,

   I withheld rain from another city.
   One part was rained upon,
   And where it did not rain the part
     withered.
8 So two *or* three cities wandered to
     another city to drink water,
   But they were not satisfied;
   Yet you have not returned to Me,"
   Says the LORD.

9 "I blasted you with blight and mildew.
   When your gardens increased,
   Your vineyards,
   Your fig trees,
   And your olive trees,
   The locust devoured *them*;
   Yet you have not returned to Me,"
   Says the LORD.

10 "I sent among you a plague after the
     manner of Egypt;
   Your young men I killed with a sword,
   Along with your captive horses;
   I made the stench of your camps
     come up into your nostrils;
   Yet you have not returned to Me,"
   Says the LORD.

11 "I overthrew *some* of you,
   As God overthrew Sodom and
     Gomorrah,
   And you were like a firebrand plucked
     from the burning;
   Yet you have not returned to Me,"
   Says the LORD.

12 "Therefore thus will I do to you,
     O Israel;
   Because I will do this to you,
   Prepare to meet your God, O Israel!"

> **4:12 Prepare to meet your God.** This concept was first used when Israel was to prepare to receive the covenant at Sinai (Ex. 19:11,15). Here Israel is implored to prepare for God's judgment.

13 For behold,
   He who forms mountains,
   And creates the wind,
   Who declares to man what his*a*
     thought *is*,

4:1 *a*Literally *their lords* or *their masters*   4:4 *a*Or *years* (compare Deuteronomy 14:28)
4:13 *a*Or *His*

And makes the morning darkness,
Who treads the high places of the
    earth—
The LORD God of hosts *is* His name.

A Lament for Israel

5 Hear this word which I take up against
    you, a lamentation, O house of Israel:

2   The virgin of Israel has fallen;
     She will rise no more.
     She lies forsaken on her land;
     There is no one to raise her up.

3For thus says the Lord GOD:

    "The city that goes out by a thousand
    Shall have a hundred left,
    And that which goes out by a hundred
    Shall have ten left to the house of
        Israel."

A Call to Repentance
4For thus says the LORD to the house of
Israel:

    "Seek Me and live;
5   But do not seek Bethel,
     Nor enter Gilgal,
     Nor pass over to Beersheba;
     For Gilgal shall surely go into captivity,
     And Bethel shall come to nothing.
6   Seek the LORD and live,
     Lest He break out like fire *in* the
         house of Joseph,
     And devour *it*,
     With no one to quench *it* in Bethel—
7   You who turn justice to wormwood,
     And lay righteousness to rest in the
         earth!"

8   He made the Pleiades and Orion;
     He turns the shadow of death into
         morning
     And makes the day dark as night;
     He calls for the waters of the sea
     And pours them out on the face of the
         earth;
     The LORD *is* His name.
9   He rains ruin upon the strong,
     So that fury comes upon the fortress.

10   They hate the one who rebukes in the
         gate,

And they abhor the one who speaks
    uprightly.
11   Therefore, because you tread down
         the poor
     And take grain taxes from him,
     Though you have built houses of
         hewn stone,
     Yet you shall not dwell in them;
     You have planted pleasant vineyards,
     But you shall not drink wine from
         them.
12   For I know your manifold
         transgressions
     And your mighty sins:
     Afflicting the just *and* taking bribes;
     Diverting the poor *from justice* at the
         gate.
13   Therefore the prudent keep silent at
         that time,
     For it *is* an evil time.

5:10–13 The fabric of justice had been destroyed,
causing pervasive corruption "in the gates," the
place where justice was supposed to be administered (see Deut. 21:19).

14   Seek good and not evil,
     That you may live;
     So the LORD God of hosts will be with
         you,
     As you have spoken.
15   Hate evil, love good;
     Establish justice in the gate.
     It may be that the LORD God of hosts
     Will be gracious to the remnant of
         Joseph.

The Day of the LORD
16Therefore the LORD God of hosts, the
Lord, says this:

    "*There shall be* wailing in all streets,
    And they shall say in all the
        highways,
    'Alas! Alas!'
    They shall call the farmer to
        mourning,
    And skillful lamenters to wailing.
17 In all vineyards *there shall be* wailing,
    For I will pass through you,"
    Says the LORD.

18   Woe to you who desire the day of the
         LORD!

For what good *is* the day of the LORD
 to you?
It *will be* darkness, and not light.
19 It *will be* as though a man fled from a
 lion,
 And a bear met him!
 Or *as though* he went into the house,
 Leaned his hand on the wall,
 And a serpent bit him!
20 *Is* not the day of the LORD darkness,
 and not light?
 Is it not very dark, with no brightness
 in it?

21 "I hate, I despise your feast days,
 And I do not savor your sacred
 assemblies.
22 Though you offer Me burnt offerings
 and your grain offerings,
 I will not accept *them*,
 Nor will I regard your fattened peace
 offerings.
23 Take away from Me the noise of your
 songs,
 For I will not hear the melody of your
 stringed instruments.
24 But let justice run down like water,
 And righteousness like a mighty
 stream.

25 "Did you offer Me sacrifices and
 offerings
 In the wilderness forty years, O house
 of Israel?
26 You also carried Sikkuth*a* your king*b*
 And Chiun,*c* your idols,
 The star of your gods,
 Which you made for yourselves.

> **5:25,26** Israel worshiped other gods in the wilderness. Molech worship included the worship of Saturn and the host of heaven along with the sacrifice of children (2 Kin. 17:16,17). Israel was warned against Molech worship (Deut. 18:9–13), but the nation continued to worship this idol during the time of Solomon (1 Kin. 11:7) until Josiah (2 Kin. 23:10). Stephen recited Amos 5:25–27 when he recounted the sins of Israel (see Acts 7:42,43).

27 Therefore I will send you into
 captivity beyond Damascus,"

Says the LORD, whose name *is* the
 God of hosts.

Warnings to Zion and Samaria

6 Woe to you *who are* at ease in Zion,
 And trust in Mount Samaria,
 Notable persons in the chief nation,
 To whom the house of Israel comes!
2 Go over to Calneh and see;
 And from there go to Hamath the
 great;
 Then go down to Gath of the
 Philistines.
 Are you better than these kingdoms?
 Or is their territory greater than your
 territory?

3 *Woe to* you who put far off the day of
 doom,
 Who cause the seat of violence to
 come near;
4 Who lie on beds of ivory,
 Stretch out on your couches,
 Eat lambs from the flock
 And calves from the midst of the stall;
5 Who sing idly to the sound of stringed
 instruments,
 And invent for yourselves musical
 instruments like David;
6 Who drink wine from bowls,
 And anoint yourselves with the best
 ointments,
 But are not grieved for the affliction of
 Joseph.
7 Therefore they shall now go captive as
 the first of the captives,
 And those who recline at banquets
 shall be removed.

8 The Lord GOD has sworn by Himself,
 The LORD God of hosts says:
 "I abhor the pride of Jacob,
 And hate his palaces;
 Therefore I will deliver up *the* city
 And all that is in it."

9Then it shall come to pass, that if ten
men remain in one house, they shall die.
10And when a relative *of the dead*, with one
who will burn *the bodies*, picks up the
bodies*a* to take them out of the house, he

5:26 *a*A pagan deity   *b*Septuagint and Vulgate read *tabernacle of Moloch*.   *c*A pagan deity
6:10 *a*Literally *bones*

will say to one inside the house, "*Are there* any more with you?"

Then someone will say, "None."

And he will say, "Hold your tongue! For we dare not mention the name of the LORD."

> **6:10 one who will burn.** This could refer to cremation of dead bodies because of the excessive number killed and the fear of epidemics. With rare exceptions (see 1 Sam. 31:12), corpses were buried in ancient Israel, not burned.

11   For behold, the LORD gives a
     command:
    He will break the great house into
     bits,
    And the little house into pieces.

12   Do horses run on rocks?
    Does *one* plow *there* with oxen?
    Yet you have turned justice into gall,
    And the fruit of righteousness into
     wormwood,
13   You who rejoice over Lo Debar,*a*
    Who say, "Have we not taken
     Karnaim*b* for ourselves
    By our own strength?"

14   "But, behold, I will raise up a nation
     against you,
    O house of Israel,"
    Says the LORD God of hosts;
    "And they will afflict you from the
     entrance of Hamath
    To the Valley of the Arabah."

Vision of the Locusts

7 Thus the Lord GOD showed me: Behold, He formed locust swarms at the beginning of the late crop; indeed *it was* the late crop after the king's mowings. ²And so it was, when they had finished eating the grass of the land, that I said:

    "O Lord GOD, forgive, I pray!
     Oh, that Jacob may stand,

> **7:1–3** The first vision, symbolizing God's action, was of a king taking the first crops, and then a swarm of locusts devouring the people's portion of the later crops (see Joel. 1:2–12).

     For he *is* small!"
3   So the LORD relented concerning this.
    "It shall not be," said the LORD.

Vision of the Fire

⁴Thus the Lord GOD showed me: Behold, the Lord GOD called for conflict by fire, and it consumed the great deep and devoured the territory. ⁵Then I said:

    "O Lord GOD, cease, I pray!
     Oh, that Jacob may stand,
    For he *is* small!"
6   So the LORD relented concerning this.
    "This also shall not be," said the Lord
     GOD.

Vision of the Plumb Line

⁷Thus He showed me: Behold, the Lord stood on a wall *made* with a plumb line, with a plumb line in His hand. ⁸And the LORD said to me, "Amos, what do you see?"

And I said, "A plumb line."

Then the Lord said:

    "Behold, I am setting a plumb line
     In the midst of My people Israel;
    I will not pass by them anymore.
9   The high places of Isaac shall be
     desolate,
    And the sanctuaries of Israel shall be
     laid waste.
    I will rise with the sword against the
     house of Jeroboam."

> **7:4–9** The second vision is of a devastating drought, causing the underground water supplies to dry up and fields to become consumed by fire (see Deut. 32:22). In the third vision, Israel's spiritual nature is tested by God's plumb line of righteousness. The sword of judgment was to come from Assyria.

Amaziah's Complaint

¹⁰Then Amaziah the priest of Bethel sent to Jeroboam king of Israel, saying, "Amos has conspired against you in the midst of the house of Israel. The land is not able to bear all his words. ¹¹For thus Amos has said:

    'Jeroboam shall die by the sword,
    And Israel shall surely be led away
     captive
    From their own land.' "

6:13 *a*Literally *Nothing*   *b*Literally *Horns*, symbol of strength

¹²Then Amaziah said to Amos:

"Go, you seer!
Flee to the land of Judah.
There eat bread,
And there prophesy.
¹³   But never again prophesy at Bethel,
For it *is* the king's sanctuary,
And it *is* the royal residence."

¹⁴Then Amos answered, and said to Amaziah:

"I *was* no prophet,
Nor *was* I a son of a prophet,
But I *was* a sheepbreeder^a
And a tender of sycamore fruit.
¹⁵   Then the LORD took me as I followed
the flock,
And the LORD said to me,
'Go, prophesy to My people Israel.'
¹⁶   Now therefore, hear the word of the
LORD:
You say, 'Do not prophesy against
Israel,
And do not spout against the house of
Isaac.'

¹⁷"Therefore thus says the LORD:

'Your wife shall be a harlot in the
city;
Your sons and daughters shall fall by
the sword;
Your land shall be divided by *survey*
line;
You shall die in a defiled land;
And Israel shall surely be led away
captive
From his own land.' "

FIVE VISIONS OF AMOS

1. Vision of Locusts (7:1–3)
2. Vision of Fire (7:4–6)
3. Vision of the Plumb Line (7:7–9)
4. Vision of the Summer Fruit (8:1–14)
5. Vision of the Lord (9:1–10)

Vision of the Summer Fruit

8 Thus the Lord GOD showed me: Behold, a basket of summer fruit. ²And
He said, "Amos, what do you see?"
So I said, "A basket of summer fruit."
Then the LORD said to me:

"The end has come upon My people
Israel;
I will not pass by them anymore.

8:1 summer fruit. This fourth vision pictures Israel ripe for judgment, like fruit that is fully ripened by the summer sun.

³   And the songs of the temple
Shall be wailing in that day,"
Says the Lord GOD—
"Many dead bodies everywhere,
They shall be thrown out in silence."

⁴   Hear this, you who swallow up^a the
needy,
And make the poor of the land fail,

⁵Saying:

"When will the New Moon be past,
That we may sell grain?
And the Sabbath,
That we may trade wheat?
Making the ephah small and the
shekel large,
Falsifying the scales by deceit,
⁶   That we may buy the poor for silver,
And the needy for a pair of sandals—
Even sell the bad wheat?"

⁷   The LORD has sworn by the pride of
Jacob:
"Surely I will never forget any of their
works.
⁸   Shall the land not tremble for this,
And everyone mourn who dwells in
it?
All of it shall swell like the River,^a
Heave and subside
Like the River of Egypt.

⁹   "And it shall come to pass in that day,"
says the Lord GOD,

7:14 ^aCompare 2 Kings 3:4   8:4 ^aOr *trample on* (compare 2:7)   8:8 ^aThat is, the Nile; some Hebrew manuscripts, Septuagint, Syriac, Targum, and Vulgate read *River;* Masoretic Text reads *the light.*

"That I will make the sun go down at
noon,
And I will darken the earth in broad
daylight;
10 I will turn your feasts into mourning,
And all your songs into lamentation;
I will bring sackcloth on every waist,
And baldness on every head;
I will make it like mourning for an
only *son*,
And its end like a bitter day.

11 "Behold, the days are coming," says
the Lord GOD,
"That I will send a famine on the
land,
Not a famine of bread,
Nor a thirst for water,
But of hearing the words of the LORD.
12 They shall wander from sea to sea,
And from north to east;
They shall run to and fro, seeking the
word of the LORD,
But shall not find *it*.

13 "In that day the fair virgins
And strong young men
Shall faint from thirst.
14 Those who swear by the sin*a* of
Samaria,
Who say,
'As your god lives, O Dan!'

And, 'As the way of Beersheba lives!'
They shall fall and never rise again."

The Destruction of Israel

9 I saw the Lord standing by the altar,
and He said:

"Strike the doorposts, that the
thresholds may shake,
And break them on the heads of them
all.
I will slay the last of them with the
sword.
He who flees from them shall not get
away,
And he who escapes from them shall
not be delivered.

> **9:1** The fifth vision opens with the Lord standing beside the altar in Bethel, commanding that the temple be torn down, thus falling upon the worshipers. He would spare no one.

2 "Though they dig into hell,*a*
From there My hand shall take them;
Though they climb up to heaven,
From there I will bring them down;
3 And though they hide themselves on
top of Carmel,
From there I will search and take
them;

8:14 *a*Or *Ashima*, a Syrian goddess 9:2 *a*Or *Sheol*

Since Amos 9:11 was quoted as prophecy in the New Testament, to what degree has it been fulfilled?

This verse promises that the Lord "will raise up the tabernacle of David, which has fallen down." James quoted the same promise in Acts 15:15,16 during the first Jerusalem Council discussion. At stake was whether Gentiles should be allowed into the church without requiring circumcision. Peter had just reported that God had "visited the Gentiles to take out of them a people for His name" (Acts 15:14). James apparently thought of this passage because it makes the point that part of God's plan all along was to include the Gentiles.

Some, however, have concluded that James' usage indicates the complete fulfillment of Amos' prophecy. They assign the phrase above to Jesus as the greater Son of David, through whom the dynasty of David was reestablished.

It seems better, however, to see James's use as an illustration of Amos' words rather than a fulfillment. The original prophecy contains the key phrase "In that day" (9:11) indicating along with the details of the passage that the prophet was speaking of Messiah's return at the Second Advent to sit upon the throne of David. The establishment of the church by the apostles and the inclusion of the Gentiles set the stage for that eventual fulfillment.

Though they hide from My sight at
the bottom of the sea,
From there I will command the
serpent, and it shall bite them;
4 Though they go into captivity before
their enemies,
From there I will command the
sword,
And it shall slay them.
I will set My eyes on them for harm
and not for good."

5 The Lord GOD of hosts,
He who touches the earth and it
melts,
And all who dwell there mourn;
All of it shall swell like the River,*a*
And subside like the River of Egypt.
6 He who builds His layers in the sky,
And has founded His strata in the
earth;
Who calls for the waters of the sea,
And pours them out on the face of the
earth—
The LORD *is* His name.

7 "*Are* you not like the people of
Ethiopia to Me,
O children of Israel?" says the LORD.
"Did I not bring up Israel from the
land of Egypt,
The Philistines from Caphtor,
And the Syrians from Kir?

8 "Behold, the eyes of the Lord GOD *are*
on the sinful kingdom,
And I will destroy it from the face of
the earth;

THE ULTIMATE RESTORATION OF ISRAEL

1. Is. 27; 42–44; 65; 66	8. Obad. 17,21
2. Jer. 30–33	9. Micah 7:14–20
3. Ezek. 36; 37; 40–48	10. Zeph. 3:14–20
4. Dan. 9:20–27; 12:1–3	11. Hag. 2:20–23
5. Hosea 2:14–23; 14:4–7	12. Zech. 13;14
6. Joel 3:18–21	13. Mal. 4:1–3
7. Amos 9:11–15	

Yet I will not utterly destroy the
house of Jacob,"
Says the LORD.

9 "For surely I will command,
And will sift the house of Israel
among all nations,
As *grain* is sifted in a sieve;
Yet not the smallest grain shall fall to
the ground.
10 All the sinners of My people shall die
by the sword,
Who say, 'The calamity shall not
overtake nor confront us.'

> **9:11–15** The faithful remnant will be blessed in the millennium when the Messiah reigns in Jerusalem over all the nations. The Jews will never again be taken away from the land God had promised them.

Israel Will Be Restored

11 "On that day I will raise up
The tabernacle*a* of David, which has
fallen down,
And repair its damages;
I will raise up its ruins,
And rebuild it as in the days of old;
12 That they may possess the remnant
of Edom,*a*
And all the Gentiles who are called by
My name,"
Says the LORD who does this thing.

13 "Behold, the days are coming," says
the LORD,
"When the plowman shall overtake the
reaper,
And the treader of grapes him who
sows seed;
The mountains shall drip with sweet
wine,
And all the hills shall flow *with it.*
14 I will bring back the captives of My
people Israel;
They shall build the waste cities and
inhabit *them;*
They shall plant vineyards and drink
wine from them;
They shall also make gardens and eat
fruit from them.

9:5 *a*That is, the Nile   9:11 *a*Literally *booth,* figure of a deposed dynasty   9:12 *a*Septuagint reads *mankind.*

15　I will plant them in their land,
　　And no longer shall they be pulled up
　　From the land I have given them,"
　　Says the LORD your God.

9:15 no longer shall they be pulled up from the land. The ultimate fulfillment of God's promise to Abraham (see Gen. 12:7; 15:7) will occur during Christ's millennial reign on earth (see Joel 2:26,27).

OBADIAH

Edom ranks as God's least favored nation in the Old Testament. Eight different books devote space to words of God's condemnation and wrath on that nation. Among the most serious charges against Edom were those leveled by Obadiah, in this brief book that bears his name.

AUTHOR AND DATE

Obadiah was written by Obadiah during King Jehoram's reign in Judah, approximately 848 to 841 B.C.

Obadiah's brief writing contains few clues to indicate much about him. The name Obadiah appears frequently in the Old Testament, but none of those mentioned refer to the prophet. Geographic allusions seem to indicate that he was from the southern kingdom.

The internal evidence used in dating Obadiah centers on the prophet's description of an Edomite assault on Jerusalem (verses 10–14). Of the four possible Jerusalem attacks in the Old Testament, two fit the criteria included by Obadiah. One of these seems less likely because it involved the complete destruction of the city by Nebuchadnezzar and his allies. The treacherous attack by the Edomites that Obadiah had in mind probably occurred earlier, during the reign of King Jehoram in Judah (848–841 B.C.). In that case, Obadiah was a contemporary of Elijah and Elisha.

BACKGROUND AND SETTING

The Edomites traced their origin to Esau, the firstborn (twin) son of Isaac and Rebekah (Genesis 25:24–26). In the womb, Esau struggled with his brother Jacob (Genesis 25:22), and they struggled thereafter. Genesis 25:30 explains the origin of the nickname Edom. The term means "red" and refers to the "red stew" Esau chose in exchange for his birthright as the oldest son.

The tensions between Esau and Jacob became part of the heritage of the nations they fathered. Edom resented Israel and repeatedly tried to prevent God's chosen people from entering and keeping the Promised Land. God instructed Israel to be kind to Edom (Deuteronomy 23:7,8). Later, Obadiah was sent to confront Edom with their sins and to convey God's judgment on their nation for their treatment of Israel.

Edom had an ongoing role in biblical history even past the close of the New Testament. Herod the Great, one of Esau's descendants, tried to kill Jesus shortly

after he was born. The Edomites were eventually wiped out during the conquest and destruction of Jerusalem that occurred in 70 A.D. Their extinction fulfilled Obadiah's long-standing prophecies that they would be "cut off forever" (verse 10) and that "no survivor shall remain of the house of Esau" (verse 18).

HISTORICAL AND THEOLOGICAL THEMES

Obadiah can be used as a case study of God's faithfulness to His promises. God pledged in Genesis 12:1–3 to bless Israel and those who blessed her and to curse anyone who cursed her. God demonstrated His faithfulness in two ways: (1) Edom represented one of those nations that cursed Israel. God judged Edom because of her attitude of pride and because of her participation in Judah's downfall. (2) Judah continued to enjoy God's promised blessing in spite of disobedience and punishment because God remained faithful to His own promise. Judah would be preserved and restored.

> **OBADIAH** CAN BE USED AS A **CASE STUDY** OF **GOD'S FAITHFULNESS** TO **HIS PROMISES.**

OUTLINE

The Coming Judgment on Edom

¹The vision of Obadiah.

Thus says the Lord GOD concerning Edom
(We have heard a report from the LORD,
And a messenger has been sent among the nations, *saying,*
"Arise, and let us rise up against her for battle"):

² "Behold, I will make you small among the nations;
You shall be greatly despised.
³ The pride of your heart has deceived you,
You who dwell in the clefts of the rock,
Whose habitation is high;
You who say in your heart, 'Who will bring me down to the ground?'
⁴ Though you ascend *as* high as the eagle,
And though you set your nest among the stars,
From there I will bring you down,"
says the LORD.

> **3,4 Who will bring me down...I will bring you down.** Edom's capital city, Petra, was located in difficult mountain terrain, making the city virtually inaccessible to an enemy army that might want to attack by surprise. This gave Edom a sense of security and self-sufficiency. God used Edom's enemies to judge her pride (see Prov. 16:18; 1 Cor. 10:12).

⁵ "If thieves had come to you,
If robbers by night—
Oh, how you will be cut off!—
Would they not have stolen till they had enough?
If grape-gatherers had come to you,
Would they not have left *some* gleanings?

⁶ "Oh, how Esau shall be searched out!
How his hidden treasures shall be sought after!
⁷ All the men in your confederacy
Shall force you to the border;
The men at peace with you
Shall deceive you *and* prevail against you.
Th*ose who eat* your bread shall lay a trap*ᵃ* for you.
No one is aware of it.

⁸ "Will I not in that day," says the LORD,
"Even destroy the wise *men* from Edom,
And understanding from the mountains of Esau?
⁹ Then your mighty men, O Teman, shall be dismayed,
To the end that everyone from the mountains of Esau
May be cut off by slaughter.

Edom Mistreated His Brother

¹⁰ "For violence against your brother Jacob,
Shame shall cover you,
And you shall be cut off forever.
¹¹ In the day that you stood on the other side—
In the day that strangers carried captive his forces,
When foreigners entered his gates

---

7 *ᵃ*Or *wound,* or *plot*

The striking similarity between Obadiah 1–9 and Jeremiah 49:7–22 brings up the question: Who borrowed from whom?

Assuming there was not a third common source, it appears that Jeremiah borrowed, where appropriate, from Obadiah. This conclusion rests on the observation that the verses in question form a single unit in Obadiah, while in Jeremiah they are scattered among other verses.

And cast lots for Jerusalem—
Even you *were* as one of them.

12 "But you should not have gazed on the
day of your brother
In the day of his captivity;*a*
Nor should you have rejoiced over the
children of Judah
In the day of their destruction;
Nor should you have spoken
proudly
In the day of distress.
13 You should not have entered the gate
of My people
In the day of their calamity.
Indeed, you should not have gazed on
their affliction
In the day of their calamity,
Nor laid *hands* on their substance
In the day of their calamity.
14 You should not have stood at the
crossroads
To cut off those among them who
escaped;
Nor should you have delivered up
those among them who remained
In the day of distress.

15 "For the day of the LORD upon all the
nations *is* near;
As you have done, it shall be done to
you;

> **16 My holy mountain.** This is Zion, which refers to
> Jerusalem (see v. 17). **drink, and swallow.** This re-
> fers to God's wrath (see Zech. 12:2). Judah drank tem-
> porarily of judgment, but Edom would drink
> "continually."

Your reprisal shall return upon your
own head.
16 For as you drank on My holy
mountain,
So shall all the nations drink
continually;
Yes, they shall drink, and swallow,
And they shall be as though they had
never been.

Israel's Final Triumph

17 "But on Mount Zion there shall be
deliverance,
And there shall be holiness;
The house of Jacob shall possess their
possessions.
18 The house of Jacob shall be a fire,
And the house of Joseph a flame;
But the house of Esau *shall be*
stubble;
They shall kindle them and devour
them,
And no survivor shall *remain* of the
house of Esau,"
For the LORD has spoken.

19 The South*a* shall possess the
mountains of Esau,
And the Lowland shall possess
Philistia.
They shall possess the fields of
Ephraim
And the fields of Samaria.
Benjamin *shall possess* Gilead.
20 And the captives of this host of the
children of Israel
Shall possess the land of the
Canaanites
As far as Zarephath.

---

12 *a*Literally *on the day he became a foreigner*   19 *a*Hebrew *Negev*

Why did God include such a short book in Scripture?

First, Obadiah is not the shortest book in Scripture. Two others, in fact, are shorter: 2 John (13 verses) and 3 John (14 verses). These short books should not be overlooked because of their length. God manages to communicate a great deal in a small amount of space.

Second, Obadiah and his short companions offer highly concentrated views of single issues. The prophet may have had years of ministry and dozens of messages, but he had one vision. God gave him a powerful warning to deliver, and even the echoes of its truth can offer hope today. In Obadiah's closing words, "And the kingdom shall be the LORD's" (Obadiah 21b).

GOD'S JUDGMENT ON EDOM

More than any other nation mentioned in the OT, Edom is the supreme object of God's wrath.

- Pss. 83:5–18; 137:7
- Is. 11:14; 21:11,12; 34:5; 63:1–6
- Jer. 49:7–22
- Lam. 4:21,22
- Ezek. 25:12–14; 35:1–15
- Joel 3:19
- Amos 1:11,12; 9:11,12
- Mal. 1:2–5

The captives of Jerusalem who are in Sepharad
Shall possess the cities of the South.[a]
21 Then saviors[a] shall come to Mount Zion
To judge the mountains of Esau,
And the kingdom shall be the LORD's.

21 saviors shall…to judge. Just as the Lord raised up judges to deliver His people (see Neh. 9:27), so He will establish similar leaders to help rule in the millennial kingdom (see 1 Cor. 6:2). **the kingdom shall be the LORD's.** When the nations are judged in the Day of the Lord, He will set up His millennial kingdom and rule His people on earth (Zech. 14:4–9; Rev. 11:15).

---

20 [a]Hebrew *Negev*   21 [a]Or *deliverers*

JONAH

God often works through people in spite of themselves. Jonah was a reluctant prophet. He tried to run from his mission. He tried to hide from God. He even offered himself as a noble sacrifice. But he discovered that even attempted suicide couldn't get him out of God's plans. God offered him an opportunity to learn to love the people of Nineveh by having him preach a message that transformed the city. Jonah chose to hold on to his hatred. He resented the mercy God poured out on Nineveh because he didn't fully appreciate the mercy God poured out on him. Jonah's account ends with a haunting rhetorical question from God, "Should I not pity Nineveh?"

AUTHOR AND DATE

Jonah was written or told by Jonah during his ministry, approximately 793 to 758 B.C.

Although Jonah never spoke in the first person in this book, there are good reasons to think he was the author. First, the Old Testament offers other examples of authors writing in the third person (Moses—Exodus 11:3; Samuel—1 Samuel 12:11). Second, certain intimate autobiographical material in this book could only have come from Jonah himself. The fish held no other witnesses. Even the introductory verse that establishes the third person account is characteristic of most of the prophets' writings.

A reference to Jonah in 2 Kings 14:25 establishes his hometown as Gath-hepher, near Nazareth. His ministry years coincide with the reign of Jeroboam II (about 793–758 B.C.). Jonah preceded Amos as a prophet to the northern tribes of Israel.

BACKGROUND AND SETTING

Jonah represented God to the 10 northern tribes during a time of relative peace and prosperity. He and Amos shared very similar political and cultural conditions. Both Syria and Assyria were weak, allowing King Jeroboam II to enlarge the northern borders of Israel.

Spiritually, however, the nation was in poverty. Genuine faith in God had been forgotten and replaced by religious rituals. Idolatry had rapidly increased. Justice had become perverted and meaningless. Peacetime and wealth were being misused to bring about spiritual, moral and ethical bankruptcy.

God's judgment was devastating. He eventually allowed the Assyrians to bring destruction and captivity to the Northern Kingdom in 722 B.C., years after Jonah's ministry.

Jonah's mission to Nineveh probably occurred close to the end of his active years. It appears that God arranged for a couple of plagues (765 and 759 B.C.) and a solar eclipse (763 B.C.) that may have contributed to the softening of Nineveh for Jonah's message.

HISTORICAL AND THEOLOGICAL THEMES

Israel and Judah shared a long animosity toward Assyria. Nineveh, the capital of that cruel empire, was considered a particularly evil city. Jonah's reluctance to carry out God's command was not just a personal but a national attitude. Israel felt the threat of Assyria. They also felt spiritually superior because they were the people of God's special blessing. "Why should the God of Israel care for the Assyrians?", thought Jonah and his countrymen. God sent Jonah to Nineveh, in part, to shame Israel by the fact that a pagan city repented at the preaching of a stranger while Israel would not repent though preached to by many prophets.

This book reveals and illustrates God's sovereign rule over human beings and all creation. Jonah acknowledges God as Creator (1:9). In contrast to Jonah, creation instantly cooperates with God's command (1:4,17; 2:10; 4:6,7).

Jonah also provided Jesus with evidence to convict the Pharisees of his day for their unwillingness to repent (Matthew 12:38–41; Luke 11:29–32). He contrasted the eager repentance of Nineveh under the less-than-enthusiastic preaching of Jonah with the resistance of the Pharisees to the preaching of the greatest of all prophets, their Lord and Messiah. Jesus even used Jonah's journey in the great fish as an illustration of His own brief journey into death (Matthew 12:38–41; 16:4; Luke 11:29–32).

THIS BOOK REVEALS AND ILLUSTRATES GOD'S SOVEREIGN RULE OVER HUMAN BEINGS AND ALL CREATION.

OUTLINE

Jonah's Disobedience

1 Now the word of the LORD came to Jonah the son of Amittai, saying, ²"Arise, go to Nineveh, that great city, and cry out against it; for their wickedness has come up before Me." ³But Jonah arose to flee to Tarshish from the presence of the LORD. He went down to Joppa, and found a ship going to Tarshish; so he paid the fare, and went down into it, to go with them to Tarshish from the presence of the LORD.

> **1:2 Arise, go to Nineveh.** This is the only case of a prophet being sent to a foreign nation to deliver God's message against it. Nineveh was the capital of Assyria and possibly the largest city in the world at this time. This powerful city exerted much influence over the Middle East until its destruction by Nebuchadnezzar in 612 B.C. Jonah was sent to bring the message of salvation to the city, as well as to bring shame upon Israel. God wanted to rebuke the Jews who were reluctant to bring Gentiles to the true God.

The Storm at Sea

⁴But the LORD sent out a great wind on the sea, and there was a mighty tempest on the sea, so that the ship was about to be broken up.

⁵Then the mariners were afraid; and every man cried out to his god, and threw the cargo that *was* in the ship into the sea,

TEN MIRACLES IN JONAH

1. 1:4 "the LORD sent out a great wind on the sea"
2. 1:7 "the lot fell on Jonah"
3. 1:15 "the sea ceased from its raging"
4. 1:17 "the LORD had prepared a great fish"
5. 1:17 "to swallow Jonah (alive)"
6. 2:10 "the LORD spoke to the fish...it vomited Jonah onto dry *land*"
7. 3:10 "God saw their works...they turned from their evil way"
8. 4:6 "the LORD God prepared a plant"
9. 4:7 "God prepared a worm"
10. 4:8 "God prepared a vehement east wind"

to lighten the load.ᵃ But Jonah had gone down into the lowest parts of the ship, had lain down, and was fast asleep.

⁶So the captain came to him, and said to him, "What do you mean, sleeper? Arise, call on your God; perhaps your God will consider us, so that we may not perish."

⁷And they said to one another, "Come, let us cast lots, that we may know for whose cause this trouble *has come* upon us." So they cast lots, and the lot fell on Jonah. ⁸Then they said to him, "Please tell us! For whose cause *is* this trouble upon us? What is your occupation? And where do you come from? What is your country? And of what people are you?"

> **1:7 cast lots.** God could reveal His will by controlling the lots, which He did. This method of discernment (the exact procedure is unknown) was not forbidden in Israel (see Prov. 16:33).

⁹So he said to them, "I *am* a Hebrew; and I fear the LORD, the God of heaven, who made the sea and the dry *land*."

Jonah Thrown into the Sea

¹⁰Then the men were exceedingly afraid, and said to him, "Why have you done this?" For the men knew that he fled from the presence of the LORD, because he had told them. ¹¹Then they said to him, "What shall we do to you that the sea may be calm for us?"—for the sea was growing more tempestuous.

¹²And he said to them, "Pick me up and throw me into the sea; then the sea will become calm for you. For I know that this great tempest *is* because of me." ¹³Nevertheless the men rowed hard to return to land, but they could not, for the sea continued to grow more tempestuous against them. ¹⁴Therefore they cried out to the LORD and said, "We pray, O LORD, please do not let us perish for this man's life, and do not charge us with innocent blood; for You, O LORD, have done as it pleased You." ¹⁵So they picked up Jonah and threw him into the sea, and the sea ceased from its raging. ¹⁶Then the men feared the LORD exceedingly, and offered a sacrifice to the LORD and took vows.

1:5 ᵃLiterally *from upon them*

Jonah's Prayer and Deliverance

¹⁷Now the LORD had prepared a great fish to swallow Jonah. And Jonah was in the belly of the fish three days and three nights.

1:17 a great fish. The species of fish is uncertain; the Hebrew word for "whale" is not used here. God appointed a great fish to rescue Jonah. Apparently Jonah sank into the depth of the sea before the fish swallowed him.

---

2 Then Jonah prayed to the LORD his God from the fish's belly. ²And he said:

"I cried out to the LORD because of my affliction,
  And He answered me.

"Out of the belly of Sheol I cried,
  And You heard my voice.
³ For You cast me into the deep,
  Into the heart of the seas,
  And the floods surrounded me;
  All Your billows and Your waves
    passed over me.
⁴ Then I said, 'I have been cast out of
    Your sight;
  Yet I will look again toward Your holy
    temple.'
⁵ The waters surrounded me, *even* to
    my soul;
  The deep closed around me;
  Weeds were wrapped around my head.

⁶ I went down to the moorings of the
    mountains;
  The earth with its bars *closed* behind
    me forever;
  Yet You have brought up my life from
    the pit,
  O LORD, my God.

⁷ "When my soul fainted within me,
  I remembered the LORD;
  And my prayer went *up* to You,
  Into Your holy temple.

⁸ "Those who regard worthless idols
  Forsake their own Mercy.
⁹ But I will sacrifice to You
  With the voice of thanksgiving;
  I will pay what I have vowed.
  Salvation *is* of the LORD."

¹⁰So the LORD spoke to the fish, and it vomited Jonah onto dry *land*.

Jonah Preaches at Nineveh

3 Now the word of the LORD came to Jonah the second time, saying, ²"Arise, go to Nineveh, that great city, and preach to it the message that I tell you." ³So Jonah arose and went to Nineveh, according to the word of the LORD. Now Nineveh was an exceedingly great city, a three-day journey*a* in extent. ⁴And Jonah began to enter the city on the first day's walk. Then he cried

---

3:3 *a*Exact meaning unknown

Were Jonah's adventures some kind of mythical story, or did the prophet actually experience those amazing miracles?

Those who have some problems with the idea of miracles have great problems with Jonah. The miracles in that book happen on a grand scale: an implacable storm; survival inside a large fish; repentance by the leader of a recognized world power. These are not for the timid in faith. Some skeptics and critics simply deny Jonah's historical validity. Others attempt to offer substitute spiritual lessons by making parts of Jonah allegorical or interpreting the whole book as a parable.

Two factors speak strongly in favor of taking Jonah at face value: (1) The role of the miracles in Jonah offended the central character. Those miracles made him look cowardly, mean, and bitter. Given the constant tension between the prophet and the mission God had given to him, the greatest miracle of all is probably that Jonah eventually recorded these God-glorifying and prophet-humiliating historical events. (2) Jesus referred to Jonah several times as a historical person, not a parable (see Matthew 12:38–44; 16:4; Luke 11:29–32).

out and said, "Yet forty days, and Nineveh shall be overthrown!"

The People of Nineveh Believe

⁵So the people of Nineveh believed God, proclaimed a fast, and put on sackcloth, from the greatest to the least of them. ⁶Then word came to the king of Nineveh; and he arose from his throne and laid aside his robe, covered *himself* with sackcloth and sat in ashes. ⁷And he caused *it* to be proclaimed and published throughout Nineveh by the decree of the king and his nobles, saying,

> **3:5 the people...believed God.** The Ninevites paid attention to Jonah because of his experience with the fish. Their repentance was a miraculous work of God. Pagan sailors and a pagan city responded to the reluctant prophet, showing the power of God in spite of the weakness of His servant.

Let neither man nor beast, herd nor flock, taste anything; do not let them eat, or drink water. ⁸But let man and beast be covered with sackcloth, and cry mightily to God; yes, let every one turn from his evil way and from the violence that is in his hands. ⁹Who can tell *if* God will turn and relent, and turn away from His fierce anger, so that we may not perish?

¹⁰Then God saw their works, that they turned from their evil way; and God relented from the disaster that He had said He would bring upon them, and He did not do it.

Jonah's Anger and God's Kindness

4 But it displeased Jonah exceedingly, and he became angry. ²So he prayed to the LORD, and said, "Ah, LORD, was not this what I said when I was still in my country? Therefore I fled previously to Tarshish; for I know that You *are* a gracious and merciful God, slow to anger and abundant in lovingkindness, One who relents from doing harm. ³Therefore now, O LORD, please take my life from me, for *it is* better for me to die than to live!"

> **4:1,2** Jonah was not in favor of dealing with Gentiles, nor did he want their participation in salvation. That was why he had fled to Tarshish in the first place. Thus, Jonah was displeased with God's mercy toward the Ninevites. Jonah understood the gracious character of God (see 1 Tim. 2:4) because he himself had received God's pardon. But he didn't want Nineveh to experience God's mercy.

⁴Then the LORD said, "*Is it* right for you to be angry?"

⁵So Jonah went out of the city and sat on the east side of the city. There he made himself a shelter and sat under it in the shade, till he might see what would become of the city. ⁶And the LORD God prepared a plant[a] and made it come up over Jonah, that it might be shade for his head to deliver him from his misery. So Jonah was very grateful for the plant. ⁷But as morning dawned the next day God prepared a worm, and it *so* damaged the plant that it withered. ⁸And it happened, when the sun arose, that God prepared a vehement east wind; and the sun beat on Jonah's head, so

---

4:6 ᵃHebrew *kikayon*, exact identity unknown

Why did God care about what happened to Nineveh?

That was precisely Jonah's question. He certainly did not care about Nineveh. He hoped and prayed that God would carry out His intention to overthrow the city. But Jonah also knew that God usually gives warnings as opportunities. Jonah did not want Nineveh to have another chance.

Jonah hated Nineveh and their reputation. He resented the suffering that had befallen his own people through the rulers of Nineveh. He failed to identify with the people of Nineveh, however, seeing them simply as a faceless enemy. God offered Jonah a priceless lesson in compassion. He stirred up Jonah's sense of outrage through a plant and then explained to the prophet that He had the divine right to exercise compassion on the many thousands in Nineveh who were ignorant of their own condition (4:1–11).

that he grew faint. Then he wished death for himself, and said, *"It is* better for me to die than to live."

⁹Then God said to Jonah, *"Is it* right for you to be angry about the plant?"

And he said, *"It is* right for me to be angry, even to death!"

¹⁰But the LORD said, "You have had pity on the plant for which you have not labored, nor made it grow, which came up in a night and perished in a night. ¹¹And should I not pity Nineveh, that great city, in which are more than one hundred and twenty thousand persons who cannot discern between their right hand and their left—and much livestock?"

4:10,11 God's love for Nineveh is contrasted with Jonah's indifference to their damnation. If God was ready to spare Sodom for ten righteous people (see Gen. 18:22,23), wouldn't He spare Nineveh, which had 120,000 small children who could not discern the right hand from the left? With that many young children, the total population was most likely more than 600,000.

MICAH

"Order in the court!" The words have a powerful effect on a room full of people. The words demand attention. The judge is about to render judgment.

The book of Micah reads like a court document. Micah's prophecies record God's judgment on three groups of plaintiffs: (1) Samaria and Jerusalem; (2) the leaders of Israel and Judah; and (3) the people in Israel and Judah. God holds nations, leaders, and individuals responsible for their failure to acknowledge or obey Him. Micah's words ring with an urgency and truth that still apply today.

AUTHOR AND DATE

Micah was written by Micah, approximately 735 to 710 B.C.

The first verse names Micah as the author. Little else is known about this prophet of God, but his name (which means "Who is like the Lord?") suggests a godly heritage. Micah noted his hometown as Moresheth (1:1), a village about 25 miles southwest of Jerusalem. This scant information implies that Micah, like Amos, grew up in a rural area, removed from the powerful and influential. He, like Amos, had been chosen by God (3:8) to deliver a message of judgment to the princes and citizens of Jerusalem and Samaria.

Micah names the kings who reigned during his ministry: Jothan (750–731 B.C.), Ahaz (731–715 B.C.), and Hezekiah (715–686 B.C.). His prophecies clearly fit the times in which he lived. Micah's references to the imminent fall of Samaria (1:6) date at least part of his ministry before 722 B.C., when Samaria was crushed by Assyria.

BACKGROUND AND SETTING

The fact that Micah only mentions the names of the kings of Judah probably indicates the reality of Samaria's defeat in 722 B.C. The prophet did include the northern kingdom in some of his messages (1:5–7), but his attention was primarily directed toward the southern kingdom of Judah. Although Judah's days were also numbered, the nation outlasted her northern neighbor by several decades.

During Micah's lifetime, much of the economic prosperity and political influence that had marked the reign of Jeroboam II soon faded. Conditions between the northern and southern kingdoms rapidly deteriorated. Although Micah's ministry was directed at both houses of God's people, the divisions between them created constant hostility. At one point Israel and Syria invaded Judah and took wicked king Ahaz hostage for a while (2 Chronicles 28:5–16; Isaiah 7:1,2). After

the fall of the northern kingdom, God used Hezekiah, the good king of Judah, to lead Judah back to true worship.

Micah witnessed and influenced all of this. His message from God may not have turned the people away from coming judgment, but some listened. God's hopeful notes in Micah's words about the future (5:2) kept alive the hope of God's promise. Centuries later, when wisemen visited Jerusalem looking for a child born the King of the Jews, the priests knew right where to look in prophecy for the birthplace of God's Messiah (5:2).

HISTORICAL AND THEOLOGICAL THEMES

Similar to other prophets (Hosea 4:1; Amos 3:1), Micah presented his message in lawsuit/courtroom terminology (1:2; 6:1,2). The format emphasized to his audience the deadly seriousness of God's Word.

The prophecy is arranged in three oracles or cycles, each beginning with the announcement to "hear" (1:2; 3:1; 6:1). Each oracle follows a pattern, starting with doom and moving toward hope. The doom always refers to the consequences of breaking God's law. Hope comes only because of God's unchanging covenant with the people's forefathers (7:20).

> HOPE COMES ONLY BECAUSE OF GOD'S UNCHANGING COVENANT WITH THE PEOPLE'S FOREFATHERS.

In Micah the theme of the inevitability of divine judgment for sin is coupled together with God's immutable commitment to His covenant promises. The combination of God's (1) absolute consistence in judging sin and (2) unbending commitment to His covenant through the remnant of His people provides the reader with a clear disclosure of the character of the Sovereign of the universe.

OUTLINE

1 The word of the LORD that came to Micah of Moresheth in the days of Jotham, Ahaz, *and* Hezekiah, kings of Judah, which he saw concerning Samaria and Jerusalem.

> **1:2–7** The prophet summons all the nations of the world into court to hear charges against Samaria and Judah. Their destruction was to be a warning, showing God's judgment on all who sin against Him. God, sovereign over all creation, is assured of victory.

The Coming Judgment on Israel

2 Hear, all you peoples!
   Listen, O earth, and all that is in it!
   Let the Lord GOD be a witness against
      you,
   The Lord from His holy temple.

3 For behold, the LORD is coming out of
      His place;
   He will come down
   And tread on the high places of the
      earth.
4 The mountains will melt under Him,
   And the valleys will split
   Like wax before the fire,
   Like waters poured down a steep place.
5 All this is for the transgression of
      Jacob
   And for the sins of the house of Israel.
   What *is* the transgression of Jacob?
   Is it not Samaria?
   And what *are* the high places of
      Judah?
   Are they not Jerusalem?

6 "Therefore I will make Samaria a heap
      of ruins in the field,
   Places for planting a vineyard;
   I will pour down her stones into the
      valley,

   And I will uncover her foundations.
7 All her carved images shall be beaten
      to pieces,
   And all her pay as a harlot shall be
      burned with the fire;
   All her idols I will lay desolate,
   For she gathered *it* from the pay of a
      harlot,
   And they shall return to the pay of a
      harlot."

Mourning for Israel and Judah
8 Therefore I will wail and howl,
   I will go stripped and naked;
   I will make a wailing like the jackals
   And a mourning like the ostriches,
9 For her wounds *are* incurable.
   For it has come to Judah;
   It has come to the gate of My
      people—
   To Jerusalem.

10 Tell *it* not in Gath,
   Weep not at all;
   In Beth Aphrah[a]
   Roll yourself in the dust.
11 Pass by in naked shame, you
      inhabitant of Shaphir;
   The inhabitant of Zaanan[a] does not
      go out.
   Beth Ezel mourns;
   Its place to stand is taken away from
      you.

12 For the inhabitant of Maroth pined[a]
      for good,
   But disaster came down from the
      LORD
   To the gate of Jerusalem.
13 O inhabitant of Lachish,
   Harness the chariot to the swift
      steeds

1:10 [a]Literally *House of Dust*   1:11 [a]Literally *Going Out*   1:12 [a]Literally *was sick*

How is a book like Micah used in the New Testament?

Twice in the book of Matthew, passages from Micah play a significant part in events. In Matthew 2:6, the chief priests and scribes quote 5:2 in response to Herod's query about the birthplace of the Messiah. Later, in Matthew 10:35,36, Jesus quotes 7:6 while commissioning His disciples. The people in the New Testament were intimately familiar with the Old Testament prophets. Their writings and thinking were permeated with phrases as well as predictions that God had given to those messengers of old.

(She *was* the beginning of sin to the
daughter of Zion),
For the transgressions of Israel were
found in you.

14 Therefore you shall give presents to
Moresheth Gath;*a*
The houses of Achzib*b* *shall be* a lie to
the kings of Israel.
15 I will yet bring an heir to you,
O inhabitant of Mareshah;*a*
The glory of Israel shall come to
Adullam.
16 Make yourself bald and cut off your
hair,
Because of your precious children;
Enlarge your baldness like an eagle,
For they shall go from you into
captivity.

Woe to Evildoers

2 Woe to those who devise iniquity,
And work out evil on their beds!
At morning light they practice it,
Because it is in the power of their
hand.
2 They covet fields and take *them* by
violence,
Also houses, and seize *them*.
So they oppress a man and his house,
A man and his inheritance.

> **2:1–11** This chapter denounces the people's sins against one another. Micah pointed out the corrupt practices of the affluent. He also attacked the false prophets and those who would silence the true prophets.

³Therefore thus says the LORD:

"Behold, against this family I am
devising disaster,
From which you cannot remove your
necks;
Nor shall you walk haughtily,
For this *is* an evil time.
4 In that day *one* shall take up a
proverb against you,
And lament with a bitter lamentation,
saying:
'We are utterly destroyed!

He has changed the heritage of my
people;
How He has removed *it* from me!
To a turncoat He has divided our
fields.' "

5 Therefore you will have no one to
determine boundaries*a* by lot
In the assembly of the LORD.

Lying Prophets

6 "Do not prattle," *you say to those* who
prophesy.
So they shall not prophesy to you;*a*
They shall not return insult for
insult.*b*
7 *You who are* named the house of
Jacob:
"Is the Spirit of the LORD restricted?
Are these His doings?
Do not My words do good
To him who walks uprightly?
8 "Lately My people have risen up as an
enemy—
You pull off the robe with the garment
From those who trust *you*, as they
pass by,
Like men returned from war.
9 The women of My people you cast
out
From their pleasant houses;
From their children
You have taken away My glory forever.

10 "Arise and depart,
For this *is* not *your* rest;
Because it is defiled, it shall destroy,
Yes, with utter destruction.
11 If a man should walk in a false spirit
And speak a lie, *saying,*

> **2:6–11** The false prophets would not prophesy against the people's evil actions or confront them with the divine standard of holiness. Their false message had stopped the mouths of the true prophets and permitted the rulers to engage in social atrocities. The people, refusing to listen to the true prophets, were thus led to destruction. It is important to note that Micah speaks in v. 6, and God speaks in vv. 7–11.

1:14 *a*Literally *Possession of Gath*   *b*Literally *Lie*   1:15 *a*Literally *Inheritance*   2:5 *a*Literally *one casting a surveyor's line*   2:6 *a*Literally *to these*   *b*Vulgate reads *He shall not take shame.*

'I will prophesy to you of wine and
    drink,'
Even he would be the prattler of this
    people.

Israel Restored

12 "I will surely assemble all of you,
    O Jacob,
I will surely gather the remnant of
    Israel;
I will put them together like sheep of
    the fold,*a*
Like a flock in the midst of their
    pasture;
They shall make a loud noise because
    of *so many* people.
13 The one who breaks open will come
    up before them;
They will break out,
Pass through the gate,
And go out by it;
Their king will pass before them,
With the LORD at their head."

Wicked Rulers and Prophets

3 And I said:

"Hear now, O heads of Jacob,
    And you rulers of the house of Israel:
    Is it not for you to know justice?
2   You who hate good and love evil;
Who strip the skin from My people,*a*
And the flesh from their bones;
3   Who also eat the flesh of My people,
Flay their skin from them,
Break their bones,
And chop *them* in pieces
Like *meat* for the pot,
Like flesh in the caldron."

4   Then they will cry to the LORD,
But He will not hear them;
He will even hide His face from them
    at that time,

Because they have been evil in their
    deeds.

5   Thus says the LORD concerning the
    prophets
Who make my people stray;
Who chant "Peace"
While they chew with their teeth,
But who prepare war against him
Who puts nothing into their mouths:
6   "Therefore you shall have night
    without vision,
And you shall have darkness without
    divination;
The sun shall go down on the prophets,
And the day shall be dark for them.
7   So the seers shall be ashamed,
And the diviners abashed;
Indeed they shall all cover their lips;
For *there is* no answer from God."

8   But truly I am full of power by the
    Spirit of the LORD,
And of justice and might,
To declare to Jacob his transgression
And to Israel his sin.

9   Now hear this,
You heads of the house of Jacob
And rulers of the house of Israel,
Who abhor justice
And pervert all equity,
10 Who build up Zion with bloodshed
And Jerusalem with iniquity:
11 Her heads judge for a bribe,
Her priests teach for pay,
And her prophets divine for money.
Yet they lean on the LORD, and say,
"Is not the LORD among us?
No harm can come upon us."
12 Therefore because of you
Zion shall be plowed *like* a field,
Jerusalem shall become heaps of
    ruins,
And the mountain of the temple*a*
Like the bare hills of the forest.

3:5–7 False prophets stood guilty before the Judge because they misled the people, prophesying peace when they were fed but predicting war when they were not. They were motivated by greed. These false prophets would be struck with blindness because they had blinded others.

3:9–12 All the ruling classes were guilty: rulers judged for reward, priests taught for hire, and prophets divined for money. They were self-deceived, thinking the Lord would give them favor for identifying themselves with Him. As a result, the nation would be destroyed by Nebuchadnezzar in 586 B.C.

2:12 *a*Hebrew *Bozrah*   3:2 *a*Literally *them*   3:12 *a*Literally *house*

The Lord's Reign in Zion

4 Now it shall come to pass in the latter
days
That the mountain of the LORD's
house
Shall be established on the top of the
mountains,
And shall be exalted above the hills;
And peoples shall flow to it.
2   Many nations shall come and say,
"Come, and let us go up to the
mountain of the LORD,
To the house of the God of Jacob;
He will teach us His ways,
And we shall walk in His paths."
For out of Zion the law shall go forth,
And the word of the LORD from
Jerusalem.
3   He shall judge between many peoples,
And rebuke strong nations afar off;
They shall beat their swords into
plowshares,
And their spears into pruning hooks;
Nation shall not lift up sword against
nation,
Neither shall they learn war
anymore.*a*

4   But everyone shall sit under his vine
and under his fig tree,
And no one shall make *them* afraid;
For the mouth of the LORD of hosts
has spoken.
5   For all people walk each in the name
of his god,
But we will walk in the name of the
LORD our God
Forever and ever.

Zion's Future Triumph

6   "In that day," says the LORD,
"I will assemble the lame,
I will gather the outcast
And those whom I have afflicted;
7   I will make the lame a remnant,
And the outcast a strong nation;
So the LORD will reign over them in
Mount Zion
From now on, even forever.
8   And you, O tower of the flock,
The stronghold of the daughter of
Zion,

To you shall it come,
Even the former dominion shall
come,
The kingdom of the daughter of
Jerusalem."

9   Now why do you cry aloud?
Is there no king in your midst?
Has your counselor perished?
For pangs have seized you like a
woman in labor.
10   Be in pain, and labor to bring forth,
O daughter of Zion,
Like a woman in birth pangs.
For now you shall go forth from the
city,
You shall dwell in the field,
And to Babylon you shall go.
There you shall be delivered;
There the LORD will redeem you
From the hand of your enemies.

4:9,10 Judah would be taken captive to Babylon, but
the Lord would release them by the edict of Cyrus
(about 538 B.C.) and allow them to return to Jerusalem (see Ezra 1:2–4).

11   Now also many nations have gathered
against you,
Who say, "Let her be defiled,
And let our eye look upon Zion."
12   But they do not know the thoughts of
the LORD,
Nor do they understand His counsel;
For He will gather them like sheaves
to the threshing floor.

13   "Arise and thresh, O daughter of Zion;
For I will make your horn iron,
And I will make your hooves bronze;
You shall beat in pieces many
peoples;
I will consecrate their gain to the
LORD,
And their substance to the Lord of the
whole earth."

5 Now gather yourself in troops,
O daughter of troops;
He has laid siege against us;
They will strike the judge of Israel
with a rod on the cheek.

4:3 *a*Compare Isaiah 2:2–4

The Coming Messiah

2 "But you, Bethlehem Ephrathah,
   Though you are little among the
        thousands of Judah,
   Yet out of you shall come forth to Me
   The One to be Ruler in Israel,
   Whose goings forth *are* from of old,
   From everlasting."

> **5:2 Bethlehem Ephrathah.** This town, south of Jeru-
> salem, was the birthplace of David and, later, of Jesus
> Christ (1 Sam. 16; Matt. 2:5). Bethlehem means "house
> of bread" because the area was a grain-producing
> region. Ephrathah, known for vineyards and olive
> orchards, means "fruitful" and is different from the
> Galilean town by the same name. **from of old, From
> everlasting.** This refers to God's incarnation in the
> person of Jesus Christ and points to His millennial
> reign as King of kings (see Is. 9:6).

3 Therefore He shall give them up,
   Until the time *that* she who is in
        labor has given birth;
   Then the remnant of His brethren
   Shall return to the children of Israel.
4 And He shall stand and feed *His flock*
   In the strength of the LORD,
   In the majesty of the name of the
        LORD His God;
   And they shall abide,
   For now He shall be great
   To the ends of the earth;
5 And this *One* shall be peace.

Judgment on Israel's Enemies

   When the Assyrian comes into our
        land,
   And when he treads in our palaces,
   Then we will raise against him
   Seven shepherds and eight princely
        men.
6 They shall waste with the sword the
        land of Assyria,
   And the land of Nimrod at its
        entrances;
   Thus He shall deliver *us* from the
        Assyrian,
   When he comes into our land
   And when he treads within our
        borders.

7 Then the remnant of Jacob
   Shall be in the midst of many peoples,

   Like dew from the LORD,
   Like showers on the grass,
   That tarry for no man
   Nor wait for the sons of men.
8 And the remnant of Jacob
   Shall be among the Gentiles,
   In the midst of many peoples,
   Like a lion among the beasts of the
        forest,
   Like a young lion among flocks of
        sheep,
   Who, if he passes through,
   Both treads down and tears in pieces,
   And none can deliver.
9 Your hand shall be lifted against your
        adversaries,
   And all your enemies shall be cut off.

> **5:7–9** Israel's presence in the midst of many peoples
> would be a source of blessing to some (see Zech.
> 8:22,23), but a source of fear and destruction (like a
> lion) to others (see Is. 11:14).

10 "And it shall be in that day," says the
        LORD,
   "That I will cut off your horses from
        your midst
   And destroy your chariots.
11 I will cut off the cities of your land
   And throw down all your strongholds.
12 I will cut off sorceries from your
        hand,
   And you shall have no soothsayers.
13 Your carved images I will also cut off,
   And your sacred pillars from your
        midst;
   You shall no more worship the work
        of your hands;
14 I will pluck your wooden images*a*
        from your midst;
   Thus I will destroy your cities.

> **5:11–14 cut off the cities...strongholds.** Fortified
> cities were designed for strength, and people were
> tempted to put their trust in them rather than in God
> alone (see Ps. 27:1). The cities were associated with
> the pagan worship of Asherah, the Canaanite god-
> dess of fertility and war. All forms of reliance on war
> and gods will be removed, so that the nation must
> rely solely on Christ for deliverance and worship Him
> alone.

5:14 *a*Hebrew *Asherim*, Canaanite deities

15 And I will execute vengeance in anger
   and fury
   On the nations that have not heard."[a]

God Pleads with Israel

6 Hear now what the LORD says:

"Arise, plead your case before the
   mountains,
   And let the hills hear your voice.
2 Hear, O you mountains, the LORD's
   complaint,
   And you strong foundations of the
   earth;
   For the LORD has a complaint against
   His people,
   And He will contend with Israel.

3 "O My people, what have I done to you?
   And how have I wearied you?
   Testify against Me.
4 For I brought you up from the land of
   Egypt,
   I redeemed you from the house of
   bondage;
   And I sent before you Moses, Aaron,
   and Miriam.
5 O My people, remember now
   What Balak king of Moab counseled,
   And what Balaam the son of Beor
   answered him,
   From Acacia Grove[a] to Gilgal,
   That you may know the
   righteousness of the LORD."

6 With what shall I come before the
   LORD,
   And bow myself before the High God?
   Shall I come before Him with burnt
   offerings,
   With calves a year old?
7 Will the LORD be pleased with
   thousands of rams,
   Ten thousand rivers of oil?
   Shall I give my firstborn for my
   transgression,
   The fruit of my body for the sin of my
   soul?
8 He has shown you, O man, what is
   good;

And what does the LORD require of
   you
   But to do justly,
   To love mercy,
   And to walk humbly with your God?

6:8 The people should have known what was required of them. Spiritual blindness had led them to
offer everything to God except a true, spiritual commitment of their hearts (see Deut. 10:12–19; Matt.
22:37–39). This theme is presented in other places in
the Old Testament (see 1 Sam. 15:22; Jer. 7:21–23).

Punishment of Israel's Injustice

9 The LORD's voice cries to the city—
   Wisdom shall see Your name:

   "Hear the rod!
   Who has appointed it?
10 Are there yet the treasures of
   wickedness
   In the house of the wicked,
   And the short measure that is an
   abomination?
11 Shall I count pure those with the
   wicked scales,
   And with the bag of deceitful weights?
12 For her rich men are full of violence,
   Her inhabitants have spoken lies,
   And their tongue is deceitful in their
   mouth.
13 "Therefore I will also make you sick by
   striking you,
   By making you desolate because of
   your sins.
14 You shall eat, but not be satisfied;
   Hunger[a] shall be in your midst.
   You may carry some away,[b] but shall
   not save them;
   And what you do rescue I will give
   over to the sword.

15 "You shall sow, but not reap;
   You shall tread the olives, but not
   anoint yourselves with oil;
   And make sweet wine, but not drink
   wine.
16 For the statutes of Omri are kept;
   All the works of Ahab's house are
   done;

5:15 [a]Or obeyed 6:5 [a]Hebrew *Shittim* (compare Numbers 25:1; Joshua 2:1; 3:1) 6:14 [a]Or
Emptiness or *Humiliation* [b]Targum and Vulgate read *You shall take hold.*

And you walk in their counsels,
That I may make you a desolation,
And your inhabitants a hissing.
Therefore you shall bear the reproach
　　of My people."[a]

Sorrow for Israel's Sins

7 Woe is me!
For I am like those who gather
　　summer fruits,
Like those who glean vintage grapes;
There is no cluster to eat
Of the first-ripe fruit *which* my soul
　　desires.
2　The faithful *man* has perished from
　　the earth,
And *there is* no one upright among
　　men.
They all lie in wait for blood;
Every man hunts his brother with a net.

3　That they may successfully do evil
　　with both hands—
The prince asks *for gifts,*
The judge *seeks* a bribe,
And the great *man* utters his evil
　　desire;
So they scheme together.
4　The best of them *is* like a brier;
The most upright *is sharper* than a
　　thorn hedge;
The day of your watchman and your
　　punishment comes;
Now shall be their perplexity.

5　Do not trust in a friend;
Do not put your confidence in a
　　companion;
Guard the doors of your mouth
From her who lies in your bosom.
6　For son dishonors father,

Daughter rises against her mother,
Daughter-in-law against her mother-
　　in-law;
A man's enemies *are* the men of his
　　own household.
7　Therefore I will look to the LORD;
I will wait for the God of my
　　salvation;
My God will hear me.

Israel's Confession and Comfort

8　Do not rejoice over me, my enemy;
When I fall, I will arise;
When I sit in darkness,
The LORD *will be* a light to me.
9　I will bear the indignation of the
　　LORD,
Because I have sinned against Him,
Until He pleads my case
And executes justice for me.
He will bring me forth to the light;
I will see His righteousness.
10　Then *she who is* my enemy will see,
And shame will cover her who said to
　　me,
"Where is the LORD your God?"
My eyes will see her;
Now she will be trampled down
Like mud in the streets.

11　*In* the day when your walls are to be
　　built,
In that day the decree shall go far and
　　wide.[a]
12　*In* that day they[a] shall come to you
From Assyria and the fortified cities,[b]
From the fortress[c] to the River,[d]
From sea to sea,
And mountain *to* mountain.
13　Yet the land shall be desolate
Because of those who dwell in it,
And for the fruit of their deeds.

7:1–6 In his vain search for an upright person, Micah compared himself to the vinedresser who enters his vineyard late in the season and finds no fruit. He lamented the circumstances of his day: The leaders conspired together to get what they wanted, and no one could be trusted. Christ used v. 6 as an illustration when He commissioned the 12 disciples in Matthew 10:1,35,36.

7:14–17 Micah petitioned the Lord to shepherd, feed, and protect His people (see Ps. 23). The Lord replied that He would demonstrate His presence and power among them as He did in the Exodus from Egypt. As a result, the prideful nations would be humbled and would no longer listen to or engage in taunting His people (see Gen. 12:3; Is. 52:15).

6:16 [a]Following Masoretic Text, Targum, and Vulgate; Septuagint reads *of nations.*　7:11 [a]Or *the boundary shall be extended*　7:12 [a]Literally *he,* collective of the captives　[b]Hebrew *arey mazor,* possibly *cities of Egypt*　[c]Hebrew *mazor,* possibly *Egypt*　[d]That is, the Euphrates

God Will Forgive Israel

14 Shepherd Your people with Your staff,
The flock of Your heritage,
Who dwell solitarily *in* a woodland,
In the midst of Carmel;
Let them feed *in* Bashan and Gilead,
As in days of old.

15 "As in the days when you came out of
the land of Egypt,
I will show them[a] wonders."

16 The nations shall see and be ashamed
of all their might;
They shall put *their* hand over *their*
mouth;

Their ears shall be deaf.
17 They shall lick the dust like a serpent;
They shall crawl from their holes like
snakes of the earth.
They shall be afraid of the LORD our
God,
And shall fear because of You.
18 Who *is* a God like You,
Pardoning iniquity
And passing over the transgression of
the remnant of His heritage?

He does not retain His anger forever,
Because He delights *in* mercy.
19 He will again have compassion on us,
And will subdue our iniquities.

You will cast all our[a] sins
Into the depths of the sea.
20 You will give truth to Jacob
And mercy to Abraham,
Which You have sworn to our fathers
From days of old.

GOD'S FORGIVENESS OF SIN

1. God removes our sins as far as the east is
from the west (Ps. 103:12)
2. God completely cleanses us from the stain
of our sins (Is. 1:18)
3. God throws our sins behind His back
(Is. 38:17)
4. God remembers our sins no more
(Jer. 31:34)
5. God treads our sins underfoot (Mic. 7:19)
6. God casts our sins into the depths of the sea
(Mic. 7:19)

7:20 sworn to our fathers. In spite of Israel's unfaithfulness, the Lord intends to fulfill His promises in the Abrahamic and Davidic Covenants (see Gen. 12,15,17; 2 Sam. 7:8–16). Because of these covenants, Israel will again be restored as a nation to the land originally promised to Abraham. Jesus Christ, the ultimate descendant of David, will rule the world from Jerusalem as the King of kings and Lord of lords (see Rev. 17:14).

7:15 [a]Literally *him*, collective for the captives   7:19 [a]Literally *their*

NAHUM

God gave the ancient great city of Nineveh an extra 100 years of life. Jonah's reluctant missionary visit resulted in a genuine repentance by the city. She avoided destruction, but, unfortunately, the change wasn't lasting. The city and the empire she represented soon continued on their evil ways. A century later, God announced her final judgment through the prophet Nahum.

AUTHOR AND DATE

Nahum was written by Nahum, approximately 650 B.C.

As is true of most of the prophets, we know little about Nahum's life. This fact highlights the importance of their message. Their primary purpose was to speak for God, not about themselves. In Nahum's case, even the location of his hometown remains a mystery. He called himself an Elkoshite (1:1), but no location fitting that name has been clearly identified. Nahum could have been a survivor living in Judah or an exile living in Assyria.

Nahum did not include any of the usual clues that help to date an ancient writing (like the names of kings). The dating of this prophetic book must rely on comparing the external historical data to the content of Nahum's message. When the prophet wrote, Nineveh was still a powerful city. Nahum mentions the victory at No Amon (Thebes) in 663 B.C., a symbol of Nineveh's might. The turning point for Nineveh came with the death of Ashurbanipal in 626 B.C., and the great city was destroyed in 612 B.C. This points to a date in the middle of the seventh century B.C. for Nahum's prophecy.

BACKGROUND AND SETTING

A century after Nineveh repented at the preaching of Jonah, the Assyrian capital returned to idolatry, violence, and arrogance (3:1–4). Assyria was at the height of her power, quickly forgetting the humiliation of Sennacherib's defeat (701 B.C.) at Jerusalem (Isaiah 37:36–38). Assyria's borders extended all the way to Egypt. Conquered peoples were moved from the homelands to other places, making them easier to control. Samaria and Galilee were resettled by exiles in 670 B.C.

Assyria seemed like an unstoppable force, yet God announced to the world through Nahum and other prophets that the nation's days were numbered. Nineveh's destruction happened just as God had prophesied.

Nahum offers a sequel to the book of Jonah. They are literally the bookends of Nineveh's great century. Jonah recounts the withholding of God's promised judgment toward Nineveh, while Nahum records the eventual execution of God's judgment on the city.

Nineveh prided herself in her great defenses. Her 100 foot high walls and wide moat made her seem invincible, but Nahum declared the fact that the sovereign God (1:2–5) would bring vengeance upon those who violated His law (1:8,14; 3:5–7). Human weapons and protection could not deter God's justice, and He would, as promised, pour out His loving kindness upon the faithful (Nahum 1:7,12–15; 2:2). So the prophecy that announced God's judgment on Nineveh brought comfort to Judah and all who feared the cruel Assyrians.

> **NAHUM DECLARED** THE FACT THAT **THE SOVEREIGN GOD WOULD BRING VENGEANCE** UPON **THOSE** WHO **VIOLATED HIS LAW.**

Nahum described Nineveh's destruction as "an overflowing flood" (1:8). The accuracy of the prophet's words can be seen in the tactics of the Babylonians who invaded the city. They caused the Tigris River to overflow and destroy part of the mud walls, allowing their army to enter. Nahum also mentioned that the great city would be "hidden" (3:11). After its destruction in 612 B.C., the ruins of Nineveh were not discovered until 1842 A.D.

OUTLINE

1 The burden[a] against Nineveh. The book of the vision of Nahum the El-koshite.

God's Wrath on His Enemies

2 God *is* jealous, and the LORD avenges;
   The LORD avenges and *is* furious.
   The LORD will take vengeance on His
      adversaries,
   And He reserves *wrath* for His
      enemies;

1:2 jealous. This attribute, often used to describe God's burning zeal for His wife, Israel, emphasizes His passionate reaction against anyone guilty of spiritual adultery. The context here is either the captivity of the 10 northern tribes (722 B.C.) or the invasion of Sennacherib (701 B.C.).

---

3 The LORD *is* slow to anger and great
      in power,
   And will not at all acquit *the wicked.*

   The LORD has His way
   In the whirlwind and in the storm,
   And the clouds *are* the dust of His
      feet.
4 He rebukes the sea and makes it dry,
   And dries up all the rivers.
   Bashan and Carmel wither,
   And the flower of Lebanon wilts.
5 The mountains quake before Him,
   The hills melt,
   And the earth heaves[a] at His
      presence,
   Yes, the world and all who dwell in it.

GOD'S JUDGMENT AGAINST ASSYRIA/NINEVEH

IN RETROSPECT—Fulfilled	
1. Jer. 50:17,18	2. Ezek. 32:22,23

IN PROSPECT—Prophesied	
1. Is. 10:5	6. Mic. 5:5,6
2. Is. 10:24–27	7. Nah. 1:1
3. Is. 14:24,25	8. Nah. 2:8
4. Is. 30:31–33	9. Nah. 3:7,18
5. Is. 31:8,9	10. Zeph. 2:13–15

---

6 Who can stand before His
      indignation?
   And who can endure the fierceness of
      His anger?
   His fury is poured out like fire,
   And the rocks are thrown down by
      Him.

7 The LORD *is* good,
   A stronghold in the day of trouble;
   And He knows those who trust in
      Him.
8 But with an overflowing flood
   He will make an utter end of its place,
   And darkness will pursue His
      enemies.

1:9–15 After establishing God's power and sovereign right to judge, Nahum announced God's judgment upon Nineveh. Nahum also speaks of the blessing and hope for Israel, showing that the sovereign Judge not only punishes but also saves.

---

9 What do you conspire against the
      LORD?
   He will make an utter end *of it.*
   Affliction will not rise up a second
      time.
10 For while tangled *like* thorns,
   And while drunken *like* drunkards,
   They shall be devoured like stubble
      fully dried.
11 From you comes forth *one*
   Who plots evil against the LORD,
   A wicked counselor.

12 Thus says the LORD:

   "Though *they are* safe, and likewise
      many,
   Yet in this manner they will be cut
      down
   When he passes through.
   Though I have afflicted you,
   I will afflict you no more;
13 For now I will break off his yoke from
      you,
   And burst your bonds apart."

14 The LORD has given a command
      concerning you:

1:1 [a]Or *oracle*   1:5 [a]Targum reads *burns.*

"Your name shall be perpetuated no
    longer.
Out of the house of your gods
I will cut off the carved image and the
    molded image.
I will dig your grave,
For you are vile."

1:14 Three judgments were pronounced. First, the king of Assyria, representing the nation, would become destitute of descendants. Second, the gods by which the Assyrians received their authority would be destroyed. Third, the king would be put to death (note the fall of Nineveh in 612 B.C.).

15 Behold, on the mountains
    The feet of him who brings good
        tidings,
    Who proclaims peace!
O Judah, keep your appointed feasts,
    Perform your vows.
For the wicked one shall no more pass
        through you;
    He is utterly cut off.

The Destruction of Nineveh

2 He who scatters*a* has come up before
    your face.
Man the fort!
Watch the road!
Strengthen *your* flanks!
Fortify *your* power mightily.

2 For the LORD will restore the
    excellence of Jacob
    Like the excellence of Israel,
For the emptiers have emptied them
    out
And ruined their vine branches.

3 The shields of his mighty men *are*
    made red,
The valiant men *are* in scarlet.
The chariots *come* with flaming
    torches
In the day of his preparation,
And the spears are brandished.*a*
4 The chariots rage in the streets,
They jostle one another in the broad
    roads;

They seem like torches,
They run like lightning.
5 He remembers his nobles;
They stumble in their walk;
They make haste to her walls,
And the defense is prepared.
6 The gates of the rivers are opened,
And the palace is dissolved.
7 It is decreed:*a*
She shall be led away captive,
She shall be brought up;
And her maidservants shall lead *her*
    as with the voice of doves,
    Beating their breasts.

2:1–13 Nineveh's fall in 612 B.C. at the hands of Nebuchadnezzar of Babylon, though still future in Nahum's day, is described vividly in present tense terms.

8 Though Nineveh of old *was* like a
    pool of water,
Now they flee away.
"Halt! Halt!" *they cry;*
But no one turns back.
9 Take spoil of silver!
Take spoil of gold!
There is no end of treasure,
Or wealth of every desirable prize.
10 She is empty, desolate, and waste!
The heart melts, and the knees shake;
Much pain *is* in every side,
And all their faces are drained of
    color.*a*

11 Where *is* the dwelling of the lions,
And the feeding place of the young
    lions,
Where the lion walked, the lioness
    and lion's cub,
And no one made *them* afraid?
12 The lion tore in pieces enough for his
    cubs,
Killed for his lionesses,
Filled his caves with prey,
And his dens with flesh.

13"Behold, I *am* against you," says the
LORD of hosts, "I will burn your*a* chariots

2:1 *a*Vulgate reads *He who destroys.*   2:3 *a*Literally *the cypresses are shaken;* Septuagint and Syriac read *the horses rush about;* Vulgate reads *the drivers are stupefied.*   2:7 *a*Hebrew *Huzzab*
2:10 *a*Compare Joel 2:6   2:13 *a*Literally *her*

in smoke, and the sword shall devour your young lions; I will cut off your prey from the earth, and the voice of your messengers shall be heard no more."

2:11–13 Where is. Nahum is ridiculing Nineveh because of her fall from power and glory. Archaeologists have found a carving from a palace showing an Assyrian king on a lion hunt. Like a pride of lions, with plenty to eat, and in fear of no enemy, Nineveh tore her prey to pieces. But under God's sovereign direction, she herself will become prey for another nation.

3:8–10 Nineveh had not learned from No Amon. The city of No Amon (Thebes) was the capital of southern Egypt, 400 miles south of Cairo. It was renowned for its 100 gates, a temple 330 feet long and 170 feet wide, and its network of canals. That city fell to Ashurbanipal of Assyria in 663 B.C. Like No Amon, Nineveh enjoyed the security of conquered nations around her, but her end would be like that of No Amon.

The Woe of Nineveh

3 Woe to the bloody city!
It *is* all full of lies *and* robbery.
Its victim never departs.

2 The noise of a whip
And the noise of rattling wheels,
Of galloping horses,
Of clattering chariots!

3 Horsemen charge with bright sword
and glittering spear.
There is a multitude of slain,
A great number of bodies,
Countless corpses—
They stumble over the corpses—

4 Because of the multitude of harlotries
of the seductive harlot,
The mistress of sorceries,
Who sells nations through her
harlotries,
And families through her sorceries.

5 "Behold, I *am* against you," says the
LORD of hosts;
"I will lift your skirts over your face,
I will show the nations your
nakedness,
And the kingdoms your shame.

6 I will cast abominable filth upon you,
Make you vile,
And make you a spectacle.

7 It shall come to pass *that* all who look
upon you
Will flee from you, and say,
'Nineveh is laid waste!
Who will bemoan her?'
Where shall I seek comforters for
you?"

8 Are you better than No Amon[a]
That was situated by the River,[b]
That had the waters around her,
Whose rampart *was* the sea,
Whose wall *was* the sea?

9 Ethiopia and Egypt *were* her strength,
And *it was* boundless;
Put and Lubim were your[a] helpers.

10 Yet she *was* carried away,
She went into captivity;
Her young children also were dashed
to pieces
At the head of every street;
They cast lots for her honorable men,
And all her great men were bound in
chains.

11 You also will be drunk;
You will be hidden;
You also will seek refuge from the
enemy.

12 All your strongholds *are* fig trees with
ripened figs:
If they are shaken,
They fall into the mouth of the eater.

13 Surely, your people in your midst *are*
women!
The gates of your land are wide open
for your enemies;
Fire shall devour the bars of your *gates*.

14 Draw your water for the siege!
Fortify your strongholds!
Go into the clay and tread the mortar!
Make strong the brick kiln!

15 There the fire will devour you,
The sword will cut you off;
It will eat you up like a locust.

Make yourself many—like the locust!
Make yourself many—like the
swarming locusts!

3:8 [a]That is, ancient Thebes; Targum and Vulgate read *populous Alexandria.* [b]Literally *rivers,* that is, the Nile and the surrounding canals   **3:9** [a]Septuagint reads *her.*

16 You have multiplied your merchants
      more than the stars of heaven.
   The locust plunders and flies away.
17 Your commanders *are* like *swarming*
      locusts,
   And your generals like great
      grasshoppers,
   Which camp in the hedges on a cold
      day;
   When the sun rises they flee away,
   And the place where they *are* is not
      known.

18 Your shepherds slumber, O king of
      Assyria;

Your nobles rest *in the dust.*
Your people are scattered on the
   mountains,
And no one gathers them.
19 Your injury *has* no healing,
Your wound is severe.
All who hear news of you
Will clap *their* hands over you,
For upon whom has not your
   wickedness passed continually?

3:18,19 Nineveh's destiny was certain. Assyria had devastated many nations with her atrocities, but she would not recover from this death blow. All who would hear of the city's fall would rejoice.

HABAKKUK

"It's just not fair!" Arguments between friends, within families, and between nations often boil down to an issue of fairness. One of the unwritten basic assumptions about life is that it ought to be fair. The assumption ventures into its most dangerous territory when it comes between us and God.

The prophet Habakkuk asked God two very familiar questions about fairness:

1. Why aren't things fair, God?
2. Why don't you do something when things aren't fair, God?

God's answers and Habakkuk's conclusions make his book a valuable spiritual resource.

AUTHOR AND DATE

Habakkuk was written by Habakkuk, approximately 615 to 605 B.C.

As with most of the Minor Prophets, little is known about Habakkuk except minimal internal information in his book. His simple introduction as "the prophet Habakkuk" may imply that he was a well-known prophet of his day. Habakkuk was a contemporary of Jeremiah, Ezekiel, Daniel and Zephaniah.

The mention of the Chaldeans (1:6) immediately narrows the dating of the book to the late seventh century B.C. Habakkuk's bitter lament (1:2–4) may reflect a time period shortly after the death of Josiah (609 B.C.) when the godly king's reforms (2 Kings 23) were quickly overturned by his successor, Jehoiakim (Jeremiah 22:13–19).

BACKGROUND AND SETTING

Habakkuk prophesied during the final days of the Assyrian Empire and the beginning of the Babylonian domination of the world. The most recognizable world figure of his time was Nebuchadnezzar, prince and then king of Babylon. The Babylonians began their ascent to power in 626 B.C. and by 605 B.C. had defeated their primary enemies.

Judah got involved in this chapter of world events when King Josiah challenged Assyria's ally Egypt in the battle of Megiddo in 609 B.C. Josiah was killed during the fighting. Although Josiah had instituted significant spiritual reforms in Judah (2 Kings 22,23), his successors did not follow his godly direction. The nation quickly reverted to her evil ways (Jeremiah 22:13–19), causing Habakkuk to question God's silence and apparent lack of punitive action to purge His covenant people.

The opening verses allude to a historical situation similar to the days of Amos and Micah. Justice had all but disappeared from the land. Violence and wickedness seemed to rule unchecked. Facing those dark days, the prophet cried out for divine intervention (1:2–4).

God's response, that He was sending the Chaldeans to judge Judah (1:5–11), created an even greater theological dilemma for this sensitive prophet: Why didn't God directly purge His people and restore their righteousness? How could God use the evil Chaldeans to judge a people more righteous than they (1:12–2:1)? God's assurances that the Chaldeans would also suffer punishment did not satisfy Habakkuk's concerns. In his mind, the issue crying out for resolution was no longer God's righteous response toward evil (or lack thereof), but the vindication of God's character and covenant with His people (1:13). The prophet's unabashed argument with God turned out to be of great spiritual benefit. Ultimately, Habakkuk realized that God was not to be worshiped merely because of the temporal blessings He bestowed, but for His own sake (3:17–19).

THE **PROPHET'S** UNABASHED **ARGUMENT WITH GOD** TURNED OUT TO BE OF **GREAT SPIRITUAL BENEFIT.**

OUTLINE

1

The burden[a] which the prophet Habak-kuk saw.

The Prophet's Question

2   O LORD, how long shall I cry,
And You will not hear?
Even cry out to You, "Violence!"
And You will not save.

3   Why do You show me iniquity,
And cause *me* to see trouble?
For plundering and violence *are* before me;
There is strife, and contention arises.

4   Therefore the law is powerless,
And justice never goes forth.
For the wicked surround the righteous;
Therefore perverse judgment proceeds.

> **1:2–4.** Jealous for God's righteousness and knowing that a breach of the covenant required judgment (see Deut. 28), Habakkuk questioned God's wisdom in appearing indifferent to Judah's sin. The Jews had sinned by violence and injustice and should have been punished by the same.

The LORD's Reply

5   "Look among the nations and watch—
Be utterly astounded!
For *I will* work a work in your days
Which you would not believe, though it were told *you.*

6   For indeed I am raising up the Chaldeans,
A bitter and hasty nation
Which marches through the breadth of the earth,
To possess dwelling places *that are* not theirs.

7   They are terrible and dreadful;
Their judgment and their dignity proceed from themselves.

8   Their horses also are swifter than leopards,
And more fierce than evening wolves.
Their chargers charge ahead;
Their cavalry comes from afar;
They fly as the eagle *that* hastens to eat.

9   "They all come for violence;
Their faces are set *like* the east wind.
They gather captives like sand.

10   They scoff at kings,
And princes are scorned by them.
They deride every stronghold,
For they heap up earthen *mounds* and seize it.

11   Then *his* mind[a] changes, and he transgresses;
He commits offense,
Ascribing this power to his god."

The Prophet's Second Question

12   Are You not from everlasting,
O LORD my God, my Holy One?
We shall not die.
O LORD, You have appointed them for judgment;

> **1:12 O LORD my God...Holy One.** Habakkuk expressed complete trust in God, even though he did not comprehend His workings. He knew that Judah would not be completely destroyed (see Jer. 31:35–40). Under the faithful hand of God, the Chaldeans would come to correct, not annihilate. **O Rock.** This title expresses God's immovable and unshakeable character (see Ps. 18:2,31,46).

1:1 [a]Or *oracle*   1:11 [a]Literally *spirit* or *wind*

In what ways do God's answers to Habakkuk's deep questions offer help to modern people reading his book?

Habakkuk certainly expressed some of the most fundamental questions in all of life. God's answers provide crucial foundation stones on which to build a proper understanding of God's character and sovereign actions in history. Ultimately, Habakkuk demonstrates that life's meaning does not rest in finely argued intellectual answers, but in trusting God. The prophet echoes the theme of genuine holy living: "the just shall live by his faith" (2:4). Those who read the prophet today will find a fellow traveler who may well lead them to trusting the God he came to trust.

O Rock, You have marked them for
    correction.
13 *You are* of purer eyes than to behold
    evil,
And cannot look on wickedness.
Why do You look on those who deal
    treacherously,
And hold Your tongue when the
    wicked devours
A *person* more righteous than he?
14 *Why* do You make men like fish of the
    sea,
Like creeping things *that have* no
    ruler over them?

15 They take up all of them with a hook,
They catch them in their net,
And gather them in their dragnet.
Therefore they rejoice and are glad.
16 Therefore they sacrifice to their net,
And burn incense to their dragnet;
Because by them their share *is*
    sumptuous
And their food plentiful.
17 Shall they therefore empty their net,
And continue to slay nations without
    pity?

1:12–2:1 Habakkuk, in his reaction to the perplexing revelation, declared his confidence in the Lord. Then he voiced his second complaint, questioning how God could use a wicked nation (Chaldea/Babylonia, 1:6) to judge a nation more righteous than they (Judah, 1:13). The prophet then expressed his determination to wait for God's answer.

OTHER PSALMS

2 I will stand my watch
And set myself on the rampart,
And watch to see what He will say to
    me,
And what I will answer when I am
    corrected.

The Just Live by Faith
2 Then the LORD answered me and said:

"Write the vision
And make *it* plain on tablets,
That he may run who reads it.
3 For the vision *is* yet for an appointed
    time;
But at the end it will speak, and it
    will not lie.
Though it tarries, wait for it;
Because it will surely come,
It will not tarry.

4 "Behold the proud,
His soul is not upright in him;
But the just shall live by his faith.

2:4 the proud. This passage introduces the marks that distinguish the wicked from the righteous, regardless of ethnic origin. Two opposing characteristics are contrasted: The proud trusts in himself, but the just lives by faith. **the just shall live by his faith.** The just will be preserved through his faithfulness to God. This is the core of God's message through Habakkuk.

Woe to the Wicked
5 "Indeed, because he transgresses by
    wine,
He is a proud man,
And he does not stay at home.
Because he enlarges his desire as
    hell,*a*
And he *is* like death, and cannot be
    satisfied,
He gathers to himself all nations
And heaps up for himself all peoples.

6 "Will not all these take up a proverb
    against him,
And a taunting riddle against him,
    and say,
'Woe to him who increases
What is not his—how long?

2:5 *a* Or *Sheol*

And to him who loads himself with
many pledges'?[a]

7 Will not your creditors[a] rise up
suddenly?
Will they not awaken who oppress
you?
And you will become their booty.

8 Because you have plundered many
nations,
All the remnant of the people shall
plunder you,
Because of men's blood
And the violence of the land *and* the
city,
And of all who dwell in it.

9 "Woe to him who covets evil gain for
his house,
That he may set his nest on high,
That he may be delivered from the
power of disaster!

10 You give shameful counsel to your
house,
Cutting off many peoples,
And sin *against* your soul.

11 For the stone will cry out from the
wall,
And the beam from the timbers will
answer it.

12 "Woe to him who builds a town with
bloodshed,
Who establishes a city by iniquity!

13 Behold, *is it* not of the LORD of hosts
That the peoples labor to feed the
fire,[a]

And nations weary themselves in
vain?

14 For the earth will be filled
With the knowledge of the glory of the
LORD,
As the waters cover the sea.

> **2:6–20** Five woes, in the form of a taunting song,
> were pronounced upon the Chaldeans in anticipa-
> tion of their judgment. The first woe charged extor-
> tion, the second charged premeditated exploitation
> due to covetousness, the third charged ruthless des-
> pots, the fourth charged debauchery, and the fifth
> charged idolatry.

15 "Woe to him who gives drink to his
neighbor,
Pressing[a] *him* to your bottle,
Even to make *him* drunk,
That you may look on his nakedness!

16 You are filled with shame instead of
glory.
You also—drink!
And be exposed as uncircumcised![a]
The cup of the LORD's right hand *will
be* turned against you,
And utter shame *will be* on your
glory.

17 For the violence *done to* Lebanon will
cover you,
And the plunder of beasts *which*
made them afraid,
Because of men's blood
And the violence of the land *and* the
city,
And of all who dwell in it.

2:6 [a]Syriac and Vulgate read *thick clay.*   2:7 [a]Literally *those who bite you*   2:13 [a]Literally *for what
satisfies fire,* that is, for what is of no lasting value   2:15 [a]Literally *Attaching* or *Joining*   2:16 [a]Dead
Sea Scrolls and Septuagint read *And reel!;* Syriac and Vulgate read *And fall fast asleep!*

How does Habakkuk impact the New Testament?

The writers of the New Testament quoted Habakkuk in a way
that gave him significant importance. The writer of Hebrews
quoted 2:4 to amplify the believer's need to remain strong and
faithful in the midst of affliction and trials (Hebrews 10:38). The
apostle Paul, on the other hand, employed that same verse
twice (Romans 1:17; Galatians 3:11) to accentuate the doctrine
of justification by faith. Though these different usages might indicate an interpretive conflict,
such is not the case. All of these references point beyond a single act of faith to include the
continuity of faith. Faith in the Scriptures is not a one-time act but a way of life. The true
believer, declared righteous by God, will persevere in faith throughout his or her life
(Colossians 1:22,23; Hebrews 3:12–14). The believer will trust the sovereign God who only
does what is right.

18 "What profit is the image, that its
        maker should carve it,
    The molded image, a teacher of lies,
    That the maker of its mold should
        trust in it,
    To make mute idols?
19 Woe to him who says to wood,
        'Awake!'
    To silent stone, 'Arise! It shall teach!'
    Behold, it is overlaid with gold and
        silver,
    Yet in it there is no breath at all.

20 "But the LORD is in His holy temple.
    Let all the earth keep silence before
        Him."

3:1–19 The reference to "Habakkuk the prophet"
marks a transition from the argumentative tone of the
previous chapters to a plea for God's mercy, a review
of His power, and a chorus of praise for His grace and
sufficiency. Having been informed of God's plan of
judgment, Habakkuk returns to the matter of Judah's
judgment and pleads for mercy.

The Prophet's Prayer

3 A prayer of Habakkuk the prophet, on
    Shigionoth.[a]

2   O LORD, I have heard Your speech
        and was afraid;
    O LORD, revive Your work in the
        midst of the years!
    In the midst of the years make *it*
        known;
    In wrath remember mercy.

3   God came from Teman,
    The Holy One from Mount Paran.
                                    Selah

    His glory covered the heavens,
    And the earth was full of His praise.
4   *His* brightness was like the light;
    He had rays *flashing* from His hand,

3:3,4 The Shekinah glory, which protected and led
Israel from Egypt through the wilderness (see Ex.
40:34–38), was the physical manifestation of God's
presence. Like the sun, He spread His radiance
throughout the heavens and the earth.

    And there His power *was* hidden.
5   Before Him went pestilence,
    And fever followed at His feet.

6   He stood and measured the earth;
    He looked and startled the nations.
    And the everlasting mountains were
        scattered,
    The perpetual hills bowed.
    His ways *are* everlasting.
7   I saw the tents of Cushan in affliction;
    The curtains of the land of Midian
        trembled.

8   O LORD, were *You* displeased with the
        rivers,
    Was Your anger against the rivers,
    Was Your wrath against the sea,
    That You rode on Your horses,
    Your chariots of salvation?
9   Your bow was made quite ready;
    Oaths were sworn over *Your* arrows.[a]
                                    Selah

    You divided the earth with rivers.
10 The mountains saw You *and*
        trembled;
    The overflowing of the water passed
        by.
    The deep uttered its voice,
    And lifted its hands on high.
11 The sun and moon stood still in their
        habitation;
    At the light of Your arrows they went,
    At the shining of Your glittering spear.

3:11 sun and moon stood still. As prominent symbols of God's created order, the sun and moon are
subservient to His beckoning. The imagery here is
reminiscent of Israel's victory over the Amorites at
Gibeon (Josh. 10:12–14).

12 You marched through the land in
        indignation;
    You trampled the nations in anger.
13 You went forth for the salvation of
        Your people,
    For salvation with Your Anointed.
    You struck the head from the house of
        the wicked,
    By laying bare from foundation to
        neck.   Selah

3:1 [a]Exact meaning unknown   3:9 [a]Literally *rods* or *tribes* (compare verse 14)

¹⁴ You thrust through with his own
         arrows
     The head of his villages.
     They came out like a whirlwind to
         scatter me;
     Their rejoicing was like feasting on
         the poor in secret.

¹⁵ You walked through the sea with Your
         horses,
     Through the heap of great waters.

¹⁶ When I heard, my body trembled;
     My lips quivered at *the* voice;
     Rottenness entered my bones;
     And I trembled in myself,
     That I might rest in the day of
         trouble.
     When he comes up to the people,
     He will invade them with his troops.

A Hymn of Faith

¹⁷ Though the fig tree may not blossom,
     Nor fruit be on the vines;
     Though the labor of the olive may
         fail,

And the fields yield no food;
Though the flock may be cut off from
    the fold,
And there be no herd in the stalls—
¹⁸ Yet I will rejoice in the LORD,
I will joy in the God of my salvation.

¹⁹ The LORD God^a is my strength;
He will make my feet like deer's *feet*,
And He will make me walk on my
    high hills.

To the Chief Musician. With my stringed
instruments.

3:19 The LORD God is my strength. God promised divine wrath, favor, and hope in response to Habakkuk's perplexing questions. Security and hope were not based on temporal blessings but on the Lord Himself. This is the essence of "the just shall live by his faith" (2:4). **like deer's feet.** As the sure-footed deer scaled the precipitous mountain without slipping, so Habakkuk's faith in the Lord enabled him to endure hardships. **To the Chief Musician.** Habakkuk 3 possibly served as a psalm for temple worship.

3:19 ^aHebrew *YHWH Adonai*

ZEPHANIAH

Standing on a busy corner, the prophet lifts a rough sign inscribed with the short message: "Repent, for the end is near!" People rush by. They don't notice, or don't want to notice the message. God has become someone they can ignore.

Zephaniah's moment in history was an ancient version of that scene. He repeatedly warned the people: "The Day of the Lord is at hand!", using the expression more than any other prophet did. His work set the stage for a last minute revival under Josiah that proved to be short-lived. Within a few years, Judah was defeated and sent into exile. People who ignored God discovered they could not ignore the "Day of the Lord."

AUTHOR AND DATE

Zephaniah was written by Zephaniah during his ministry, approximately 635 to 625 B.C.

Among the few facts about Zephaniah included in Scripture, one stands out: the prophet claimed a place in the royal lineage. He appears to have been the only prophet descended from royal blood. Zephaniah was a contemporary of the prophet Jeremiah.

Zephaniah himself dates his message during the reign of Josiah (640–609 B.C.). Internal evidence indicates that the prophet wrote his book before the reform movement that started under King Josiah. Zephaniah includes no mention of the discovery of the Book of Law (622 B.C.), an event that had an explosive, though short-lived, effect on the people.

BACKGROUND AND SETTING

Zephaniah prophesied during a time of almost universal upheaval. The rise of the Babylonians and the fall of the Assyrians left much of the world between conquerors. Judah experienced relative freedom for the first time in 50 years. King Josiah was able to initiate certain reforms that eventually led to a brief spiritual revival in Judah.

The warnings of impending judgment voiced by Zephaniah probably found little response from the people. The effects of half a century of evil leadership left a nation steeped in sin, and King Josiah's reforms resulted in little more than surface changes. Even the discovery of the Law of God in the Temple rubble that occurred after Zephaniah, while it energized Josiah's efforts, had little long term effect on the attitudes of the people.

Zephaniah's central message focuses on the Day of the Lord. That phrase represents God's decisive action in history. The prophecies introduced an almost immediate fulfillment when God exercised divine judgment at the hands of Nebuchadnezzar, 605–586 B.C. But Zephaniah also holds out a hope and a hint that the Day of the Lord will be a final, concluding event in God's plan for the world.

> **ZEPHANIAH** ALSO **URGED** THE PEOPLE **TO SEEK GOD** FOR **SHELTER** DURING WRATH AND FOR **EVENTUAL SALVATION.**

In Zephaniah, the Day looms near (1:7). It is promised to be a time of wrath, trouble, distress, devastation, desolation, darkness, gloominess, clouds, thick darkness, trumpet sounds, and alarm (1:15,16). Among these descriptions of divine judgment, however, Zephaniah also urged the people to seek God for shelter during wrath and for eventual salvation (2:3,7; 3:9–20).

OUTLINE

1 The word of the LORD which came to Zephaniah the son of Cushi, the son of Gedaliah, the son of Amariah, the son of Hezekiah, in the days of Josiah the son of Amon, king of Judah.

The Great Day of the LORD

2 "I will utterly consume everything
From the face of the land,"
Says the LORD;
3 "I will consume man and beast;
I will consume the birds of the heavens,
The fish of the sea,
And the stumbling blocks[a] along with the wicked.
I will cut off man from the face of the land,"
Says the LORD.

4 "I will stretch out My hand against Judah,
And against all the inhabitants of Jerusalem.
I will cut off every trace of Baal from this place,
The names of the idolatrous priests[a] with the *pagan* priests—

> **1:4 cut off every trace of Baal.** The worship of Baal, the Canaanite god of fertility, was a constant temptation for Israel (see Num. 25:1–5). People tried worshiping Baal along with worshiping God (Jer. 7:9), and this became a cause for judgment (Hos. 2:8) that would forever remove the worship of Baal from Israel.

5 Those who worship the host of heaven on the housetops;
Those who worship and swear *oaths* by the LORD,
But who *also* swear by Milcom;[a]
6 Those who have turned back from *following* the LORD,
And have not sought the LORD, nor inquired of Him."

7 Be silent in the presence of the Lord GOD;
For the day of the LORD *is* at hand,

For the LORD has prepared a sacrifice;
He has invited[a] His guests.

> **1:7 Be silent.** The people had no defense against God's judgment, and they were left shocked and mute (see Hab. 2:20). **prepared a sacrifice...invited His guests.** God's judgment on Israel was viewed as His sacrifice. The guests were the Babylonians, who, as "priests," were invited to slay the sacrifice, which was Judah (see Is. 13:3; Jer. 46:10).

8 "And it shall be,
In the day of the LORD's sacrifice,
That I will punish the princes and the king's children,
And all such as are clothed with foreign apparel.
9 In the same day I will punish
All those who leap over the threshold,[a]
Who fill their masters' houses with violence and deceit.

10 "And there shall be on that day," says the LORD,
"The sound of a mournful cry from the Fish Gate,
A wailing from the Second Quarter,
And a loud crashing from the hills.
11 Wail, you inhabitants of Maktesh![a]
For all the merchant people are cut down;
All those who handle money are cut off.

"DAY OF THE LORD" FULFILLMENTS

Near	Far
Obadiah 1–14	Obadiah 15–21
Joel 1:15; 2:1,11	Joel 2:31 (3:1); 3:14
Amos 5:18–20	_____
_____	Isaiah 2:12
Isaiah 13:6	Isaiah 13:9
Zephaniah 1:7	Zephaniah 1:14
Ezekiel 13:5; 20:3	_____
_____	Zechariah 14:1
_____	Malachi 4:5

1:3 [a]Figurative of idols   1:4 [a]Hebrew *chemarim*   1:5 [a]Or *Malcam*, an Ammonite god, also called *Molech* (compare Leviticus 18:21)   1:7 [a]Literally *set apart, consecrated*   1:9 [a]Compare 1 Samuel 5:5   1:11 [a]Literally *Mortar*, a market district of Jerusalem

12 "And it shall come to pass at that time
That I will search Jerusalem with
    lamps,
And punish the men
Who are settled in complacency,*a*
Who say in their heart,
'The LORD will not do good,
Nor will He do evil.'
13 Therefore their goods shall become
    booty,
And their houses a desolation;
They shall build houses, but not
    inhabit *them*;
They shall plant vineyards, but not
    drink their wine."

14 The great day of the LORD *is* near;
It is near and hastens quickly.
The noise of the day of the LORD is
    bitter;
There the mighty men shall cry out.
15 That day *is* a day of wrath,
A day of trouble and distress,
A day of devastation and desolation,
A day of darkness and gloominess,
A day of clouds and thick darkness,
16 A day of trumpet and alarm
Against the fortified cities
And against the high towers.

17 "I will bring distress upon men,
And they shall walk like blind men,
Because they have sinned against the
    LORD;
Their blood shall be poured out like
    dust,
And their flesh like refuse."

18 Neither their silver nor their gold
Shall be able to deliver them
In the day of the LORD's wrath;
But the whole land shall be devoured
By the fire of His jealousy,
For He will make speedy riddance
Of all those who dwell in the land.

A Call to Repentance

2 Gather yourselves together, yes,
    gather together,
O undesirable*a* nation,
2 Before the decree is issued,

Or the day passes like chaff,
Before the LORD's fierce anger comes
    upon you,
Before the day of the LORD's anger
    comes upon you!
3 Seek the LORD, all you meek of the
    earth,
Who have upheld His justice.
Seek righteousness, seek humility.
It may be that you will be hidden
In the day of the LORD's anger.

2:4–15 God used the heathen nations to punish His people, but He did not leave those nations unpunished. To illustrate this, 4 representative nations were chosen from the 4 points of the compass.

Judgment on Nations

4 For Gaza shall be forsaken,
And Ashkelon desolate;
They shall drive out Ashdod at
    noonday,
And Ekron shall be uprooted.
5 Woe to the inhabitants of the
    seacoast,
The nation of the Cherethites!
The word of the LORD *is* against you,
O Canaan, land of the Philistines:
"I will destroy you;
So there shall be no inhabitant."

6 The seacoast shall be pastures,
With shelters*a* for shepherds and folds
    for flocks.
7 The coast shall be for the remnant of
    the house of Judah;
They shall feed *their* flocks there;
In the houses of Ashkelon they shall
    lie down at evening.
For the LORD their God will intervene
    for them,
And return their captives.

8 "I have heard the reproach of Moab,
And the insults of the people of
    Ammon,
With which they have reproached My
    people,
And made arrogant threats against
    their borders.
9 Therefore, as I live,"

1:12 *a*Literally *on their lees*, that is, settled like the dregs of wine   2:1 *a*Or *shameless*   2:6 *a*Literally *excavations*, either underground huts or cisterns

Says the LORD of hosts, the God of
    Israel,
"Surely Moab shall be like Sodom,
And the people of Ammon like
    Gomorrah—
Overrun with weeds and saltpits,
And a perpetual desolation.
The residue of My people shall
    plunder them,
And the remnant of My people shall
    possess them."

10 This they shall have for their pride,
Because they have reproached and
    made arrogant threats
Against the people of the LORD of
    hosts.
11 The LORD *will be* awesome to them,
For He will reduce to nothing all the
    gods of the earth;
People shall worship Him,
Each one from his place,
Indeed all the shores of the nations.

> **2:8–11** Moab and Ammon, nations descended from
> Lot by his daughters through incest (Gen. 19:30–38),
> had provoked God's wrath by reproaching and revil-
> ing His people (see Gen. 12:3). Like Sodom and Go-
> morrah, they too would come to ruin.

12 "You Ethiopians also,
You shall be slain by My sword."

13 And He will stretch out His hand
    against the north,
Destroy Assyria,
And make Nineveh a desolation,
As dry as the wilderness.
14 The herds shall lie down in her
    midst,
Every beast of the nation.
Both the pelican and the bittern
Shall lodge on the capitals *of* her
    pillars;
Their voice shall sing in the windows;
Desolation *shall be* at the threshold;
For He will lay bare the cedar work.
15 This is the rejoicing city
That dwelt securely,
That said in her heart,
"I *am it,* and *there is* none besides
    me."
How has she become a desolation,
A place for beasts to lie down!

Everyone who passes by her
Shall hiss and shake his fist.

The Wickedness of Jerusalem

3 Woe to her who is rebellious and
    polluted,
To the oppressing city!
2 She has not obeyed *His* voice,
She has not received correction;
She has not trusted in the LORD,
She has not drawn near to her God.

> **3:2 She has not received correction.** Jerusalem
> would soon learn that rejecting God's correction
> leads to destruction (Prov. 5:23). **She has not drawn**
> **near to her God.** The Lord had taken up residence
> in Jerusalem, making Him easily accessible (Deut.
> 4:7), yet the people refused to draw near to Him in
> proper worship.

3 Her princes in her midst *are* roaring
    lions;
Her judges *are* evening wolves
That leave not a bone till morning.
4 Her prophets are insolent,
    treacherous people;
Her priests have polluted the
    sanctuary,
They have done violence to the law.
5 The LORD *is* righteous in her midst,
He will do no unrighteousness.
Every morning He brings His justice
    to light;
He never fails,
But the unjust knows no shame.

6 "I have cut off nations,
Their fortresses are devastated;
I have made their streets desolate,
With none passing by.
Their cities are destroyed;
There is no one, no inhabitant.
7 I said, 'Surely you will fear Me,
You will receive instruction'—
So that her dwelling would not be cut
    off,
Despite everything for which I
    punished her.
But they rose early and corrupted all
    their deeds.

A Faithful Remnant
8 "Therefore wait for Me," says the
    LORD,

"Until the day I rise up for plunder;[a]
My determination *is* to gather the
    nations
To My assembly of kingdoms,
To pour on them My indignation,
All My fierce anger;
All the earth shall be devoured
With the fire of My jealousy.

> **3:9–20** The final section unveils the blessings of restoration for God's people and the nations.

9 "For then I will restore to the peoples a
        pure language,
    That they all may call on the name of
        the LORD,
    To serve Him with one accord.
10 From beyond the rivers of Ethiopia
        My worshipers,
    The daughter of My dispersed ones,
        Shall bring My offering.
11 In that day you shall not be shamed
        for any of your deeds
    In which you transgress against Me;
    For then I will take away from your
        midst
    Those who rejoice in your pride,
    And you shall no longer be haughty
    In My holy mountain.
12 I will leave in your midst

A meek and humble people,
And they shall trust in the name of
    the LORD.
13 The remnant of Israel shall do no
        unrighteousness
    And speak no lies,
    Nor shall a deceitful tongue be found
        in their mouth;
    For they shall feed *their* flocks and lie
        down,
    And no one shall make *them* afraid."

Joy in God's Faithfulness

14 Sing, O daughter of Zion!
    Shout, O Israel!
    Be glad and rejoice with all *your* heart,
    O daughter of Jerusalem!

> **3:15–17** Joy comes when Israel's judgment is past and her King is residing in her midst. His departure, just prior to Nebuchadnezzar's destruction of the temple, is depicted in Ezek. 8–11, but He will return as Lord and Messiah.

15 The LORD has taken away your
        judgments,
    He has cast out your enemy.
    The King of Israel, the LORD, *is* in
        your midst;
    You shall see[a] disaster no more.

3:8 [a]Septuagint and Syriac read *for witness;* Targum reads *for the day of My revelation for judgment;* Vulgate reads *for the day of My resurrection that is to come.*   **3:15** [a]Some Hebrew manuscripts, Septuagint, and Bomberg read *see;* Masoretic Text and Vulgate read *fear.*

Q How much validity can be given to the interpretation that takes Zephaniah's phrase "I will restore to the peoples a pure language" (3:9) as a prophetic anticipation of God's restoration of a universal language?

A Although some have taken this phrase to refer to an undoing of God's decision to confuse the languages at the Tower of Babel (Genesis 11:1–9), the context of the phrase does not lend much support to that interpretation. True, the word "language" in Zephaniah is identical to the one used in Genesis. The over-all context, however, indicates that Zephaniah had in mind a purification of heart and life (Zephaniah 3:13). Throughout the Old Testament, the word "language" is most often translated "lip." When combined with "pure," the reference to speech refers to an inward cleansing from sin (Isaiah 6:5), demonstrated in speech (Matthew 12:34). This kind of speech is purified by the removal of the names of false gods from their lips (Hosea 2:17). It is unlikely that Zephaniah had in mind a single world language.

16 In that day it shall be said to
  Jerusalem:
  "Do not fear;
  Zion, let not your hands be weak.
17 The LORD your God in your midst,
  The Mighty One, will save;
  He will rejoice over you with
    gladness,
  He will quiet *you* with His love,
  He will rejoice over you with singing."

18 "I will gather those who sorrow over
    the appointed assembly,
  Who are among you,
  To whom its reproach *is* a burden.
19 Behold, at that time
  I will deal with all who afflict you;
  I will save the lame,
  And gather those who were driven
    out;
  I will appoint them for praise and
    fame

In every land where they were put to
  shame.
20 At that time I will bring you back,
  Even at the time I gather you;
  For I will give you fame and praise
  Among all the peoples of the earth,
  When I return your captives before
    your eyes,"
  Says the LORD.

GOD'S "I WILLS" OF RESTORATION

Zephaniah 3:18–20

1. I will gather	3:18
2. I will deal	3:19
3. I will save	3:19
4. I will appoint	3:19
5. I will bring you back	3:20
6. I will give you	3:20

HAGGAI

Solomon said it well, "A time for every purpose under heaven" (Ecclesiastes 3:1). This rule applies particularly when the purpose at hand comes from God. His plans take precedence. Haggai prophesied to a people with an agenda of their own. They were procrastinating over God's instructions. The prophet's task was to convince the people of Israel that the time had come to carry out God's purposes.

AUTHOR AND DATE

Haggai was written by Haggai during his ministry, approximately 520 B.C.

This is the second shortest book in the Old Testament. Haggai's biography is even shorter, and neither his name nor his writing offer clues about his background and personality. Although Ezra mentions Haggai twice (Ezra 5:1; 6:14), he adds no details other than to identify Haggai as a prophet. Apparently Haggai and his companion Zechariah succeeded in their ministry, for Ezra reported that the people responded to their leadership and rebuilt the temple.

In contrast with information about himself, Haggai offers very specific notes about the dates of his writing. Haggai ties his prophecies to four dates in the reign of Persian King Darius (1:1; 2:1,10,20), approximately 520 B.C.

BACKGROUND AND SETTING

Eighteen years before Haggai prophesied (538 B.C.), Cyrus the Persian had allowed the exiled Jews to return from Babylon to their homeland (Ezra 1:1–4). About 50,000 Jews had returned under the civil leadership of Zerubbabel. External resistance from neighbor nations and internal indifference from the Jews themselves had brought the reconstruction work to a standstill (Ezra 3:1–4:24). Sixteen years later, Haggai and Zechariah were called by God to stir up the people to: (1) rebuild the temple, and (2) reorder their spiritual priorities (Ezra 5:1–6:22). The temple was completed 4 years later (about 516 B.C.). Haggai wrote his book about the process of motivating the people to work.

Haggai's central theme is God's call to His people to rebuild the temple. Solomon's magnificent original edifice had lain in ruins since its destruction by Nebuchadnezzar in 586 B.C. Haggai contains five divine messages in which Haggai exhorted the people to renew their efforts to rebuild the house of the Lord. He reminded the people that some of their hardships (droughts and crop failures) were consequences for disobedience to God (1:9–11).

> FOR HAGGAI, THE REBUILDING OF THE TEMPLE INVITED THE RETURN OF GOD'S PRESENCE AMONG THEM AS A PEOPLE.

A rebuilt temple, however, was not Haggai's ultimate objective. True, the temple would represent God's presence with His chosen people. God had allowed the destruction of the earlier temple because He no longer chose to call it His dwelling place. For Haggai, the rebuilding of the temple invited the return of God's presence among them as a people. Furthermore, using the immediate historical context as a springboard, the prophet reveled in the supreme glory of the ultimate messianic temple yet to come (2:7), encouraging the people with the promise of even greater peace (2:9), prosperity (2:19), divine rulership (2:21, 22), and national blessing (2:23) during the Millennium.

OUTLINE

The Command to Build God's House

1 In the second year of King Darius, in the sixth month, on the first day of the month, the word of the LORD came by Haggai the prophet to Zerubbabel the son of Shealtiel, governor of Judah, and to Joshua the son of Jehozadak, the high priest, saying, ²"Thus speaks the LORD of hosts, saying: 'This people says, "The time has not come, the time that the LORD's house should be built." ' "

> **1:1–11** Discouraged by the opposition of their neighbors (Ezra 4:1–5,24), the people had wrongly concluded that it was not yet time to rebuild the temple. The Lord reminded them that it was not right for them to live in paneled houses while the temple lay in ruins. He urged them to carefully consider the consequences of their indifference.

³Then the word of the LORD came by Haggai the prophet, saying, ⁴"*Is it* time for you yourselves to dwell in your paneled houses, and this temple*ᵃ to lie* in ruins?" ⁵Now therefore, thus says the LORD of hosts: "Consider your ways!

⁶ "You have sown much, and bring in little;
You eat, but do not have enough;
You drink, but you are not filled with drink;
You clothe yourselves, but no one is warm;
And he who earns wages,
Earns wages *to put* into a bag with holes."

⁷Thus says the LORD of hosts: "Consider your ways! ⁸Go up to the mountains and bring wood and build the temple, that I may take pleasure in it and be glorified," says the LORD. ⁹"*You* looked for much, but indeed *it came to* little; and when you brought it home, I blew it away. Why?" says the LORD of hosts. "Because of My house that *is in* ruins, while every one of you runs to his own house. ¹⁰Therefore the heavens above you withhold the dew, and the earth withholds its fruit. ¹¹For I called for a drought on the land and the mountains, on the grain and the new wine and the oil, on

> **1:8 Go up...bring wood...build.** The 70-year captivity allowed the forest to grow, so there was ample wood. The people were to use it to rebuild the house of the Lord, where He would be glorified. By putting God first, He would be honored in their worship and they would be blessed. Compare this project (Ezra 3:12; Hag. 2:3) with Solomon's first temple (see 1 Chr. 28,29).

whatever the ground brings forth, on men and livestock, and on all the labor of *your* hands."

The People's Obedience

¹²Then Zerubbabel the son of Shealtiel, and Joshua the son of Jehozadak, the high priest, with all the remnant of the people, obeyed the voice of the LORD their God, and the words of Haggai the prophet, as the LORD their God had sent him; and the people feared the presence of the LORD. ¹³Then Haggai, the LORD's messenger, spoke the LORD's message to the people, saying, "I *am* with you, says the LORD." ¹⁴So the LORD stirred up the spirit of Zerubbabel the son of Shealtiel, governor of Judah, and the spirit of Joshua the son of Jehozadak, the high priest, and the spirit of all the remnant of the people; and they came and worked on the house of the LORD of hosts, their God, ¹⁵on the twenty-fourth day of the sixth month, in the second year of King Darius.

The Coming Glory of God's House

2 In the seventh *month*, on the twenty-first of the month, the word of the LORD came by Haggai the prophet, saying: ²"Speak now to Zerubbabel the son of Shealtiel, governor of Judah, and to Joshua the son of Jehozadak, the high priest, and to the remnant of the people, saying: ³'Who is left among you who saw this temple*ᵃ in its former glory? And how do you see it now?

> **2:1–9** The Lord encouraged the people, especially the elderly who had seen Solomon's greater temple, during the building of this new, but less glorious, temple. He urged them to be courageous, assuring them of His presence and His faithfulness to His covenant promises. He promised a greater and more glorious temple in the future.

1:4 ᵃLiterally *house*, and so in verse 8   2:3 ᵃLiterally *house*, and so in verses 7 and 9

In comparison with it, *is this* not in your eyes as nothing? ⁴'Yet now be strong, Zerubbabel,' says the LORD; 'and be strong, Joshua, son of Jehozadak, the high priest; and be strong, all you people of the land,' says the LORD, 'and work; for I *am* with you,' says the LORD of hosts. ⁵*According to* the word that I covenanted with you when you came out of Egypt, so My Spirit remains among you; do not fear!'

⁶"For thus says the LORD of hosts: 'Once more (it *is* a little while) I will shake heaven and earth, the sea and dry land; ⁷and I will shake all nations, and they shall come to the Desire of All Nations,ᵃ and I will fill this temple with glory,' says the LORD of hosts. ⁸'The silver *is* Mine, and the gold *is* Mine,' says the LORD of hosts. ⁹'The glory of this latter temple shall be greater than the former,' says the LORD of hosts. 'And in this place I will give peace,' says the LORD of hosts."

> **2:7 Desire of All Nations.** This probably refers to the Messiah, for whom all the nations ultimately long. **I will fill this temple with glory.** No Scripture indicates that God's glory ever did come to Zerubbabel's temple, as the first temple was filled with the Shekinah glory (see 1 Kin. 8:10,11). Here, the context speaks of Christ's presence and glory in the temple during the millennial kingdom (Ezek. 43:5).

The People Are Defiled

¹⁰On the twenty-fourth *day* of the ninth *month*, in the second year of Darius, the word of the LORD came by Haggai the prophet, saying, ¹¹"Thus says the LORD of hosts: 'Now, ask the priests *concerning the* law, saying, ¹²"If one carries holy meat in the fold of his garment, and with the edge he touches bread or stew, wine or oil, or any food, will it become holy?" ' "

Then the priests answered and said, "No."

¹³And Haggai said, "If *one who is* unclean *because* of a dead body touches any of these, will it be unclean?"

So the priests answered and said, "It shall be unclean."

¹⁴Then Haggai answered and said, " 'So is this people, and so is this nation before Me,' says the LORD, 'and so is every work of their hands; and what they offer there is unclean.

> **2:11–14** The first question to the priests showed that ceremonial cleanness cannot be transferred. The second question showed that ceremonial uncleanness *can* be transferred. Even though the people had been bringing offerings, the offerings were not acceptable because the people were neglecting the rebuilding of the temple. Their sin caused their sacrifices to be contaminated. Their offerings could not transmit cleanness. Sin is contagious; righteousness is not (see 1 Sam. 15:22; Hos. 6:6).

Promised Blessing

¹⁵'And now, carefully consider from this day forward: from before stone was laid upon stone in the temple of the LORD— ¹⁶since those *days,* when *one* came to a heap of twenty ephahs, there were *but* ten; when *one* came to the wine vat to draw out fifty baths from the press, there were *but* twenty. ¹⁷I struck you with blight and mildew and hail in all the labors of your hands; yet you did not *turn* to Me,' says the LORD.

2:7 ᵃOr *the desire of all nations*

| What exactly did Haggai mean when he used the phrase "the Desire of All Nations" (2:7)? | A number of translations of the original phrase have been offered, but only two interpretations seem possible. Pointing to "The silver is Mine, and the gold is Mine" (2:8), as well as to references such as Isaiah 60:5 and Zechariah 14:14, some argue that Haggai had Jerusalem in mind, to which the wealth of the nations will be brought during the Millennium. The preferable interpretation, however, seems to be to see here a reference to the Messiah Himself, the Deliverer for whom all the nations ultimately long. Not only is this interpretation supported by the ancient rabbis and the early church, the mention of "glory" in the latter part of the verse suggests a personal reference to the Messiah (Isaiah 40:5; 60:1; Luke 2:32). |

18'Consider now from this day forward, from the twenty-fourth day of the ninth month, from the day that the foundation of the LORD's temple was laid—consider it: 19Is the seed still in the barn? As yet the vine, the fig tree, the pomegranate, and the olive tree have not yielded *fruit. But* from this day I will bless *you.*'"

THE TEMPLES OF THE BIBLE

Identification	Date	Description	References
The Tabernacle (mobile Temple)	about 1444 B.C.	Detailed plan received by Moses from the Lord Constructed by divinely appointed artisans Desecrated by Nadab and Abihu	Exodus 25–30; 35:30–40:38; Leviticus 10:1–7
Solomon's Temple	966–586 B.C.	Planned by David Constructed by Solomon Destroyed by Nebuchadnezzar	2 Samuel 7:1–29; 1 Kings 8:1–66; Jeremiah 32:28–44
Zerubbabel's Temple	516–169 B.C.	Envisioned by Zerubbabel Constructed by Zerubbabel and the elders of the Jews Desecrated by Antiochus Epiphanes	Ezra 6:1–22; 3:1–8; 4:1–14
Herod's Temple	19 B.C.–A.D. 70	Zerubbabel's temple restored by Herod the Great Destroyed by the Romans	Mark 13:2,4–23; Luke 1:11–20; 2:22–38; 2:42–51; 4:21–24; Acts 21:27–33
The Present Temple	Present Age	Found in the heart of the believer The body of the believer is the Lord's only temple until the Messiah returns	1 Corinthians 6:19,20; 2 Corinthians 6:16–18
The Temple of Revelation 11	Tribulation Period	To be constructed during the Tribulation by the Antichrist To be desecrated and destroyed	Daniel 9:2; Matthew 24:15; 2 Thessalonians 2:4; Revelation 17:1
Ezekiel's (Millennial) Temple	Millennium	Envisioned by the prophet Ezekiel To be built by the Messiah during His millennial reign	Ezekiel 40:1–42:20; Zechariah 6:12,13
The Eternal Temple of His Presence	The Eternal Kingdom	The greatest temple of all ("The Lord God Almighty and the Lamb are its temple") A spiritual temple	Revelation 21:22; 22:1–21

The temple (Gr. *hieron) is a* place of worship, a sacred or holy space built primarily for the national worship of God.

²⁰And again the word of the LORD came to Haggai on the twenty-fourth day of the month, saying, ²¹"Speak to Zerubbabel, governor of Judah, saying:

'I will shake heaven and earth.
²² I will overthrow the throne of
　　kingdoms;
　I will destroy the strength of the
　　Gentile kingdoms.

I will overthrow the chariots
And those who ride in them;
The horses and their riders shall
　come down,
Every one by the sword of his
　brother.

²³'In that day,' says the LORD of hosts, 'I will take you, Zerubbabel My servant, the son of Shealtiel,' says the LORD, 'and will make you like a signet *ring*; for I have chosen you,' says the LORD of hosts."

ZERUBBABEL

```
             ┌──── DAVID ────┐
             │               │
      SOLOMON                 NATHAN
             │               │
           ZERUBBABEL
   (Matt. 1:12)         (Luke 3:27)
             │               │
        JOSEPH              MARY
```

2:23 signet *ring*. This was a symbol of honor, authority, and power (see Song 8:6). As God's signet ring, Zerubbabel stands as the official representative of the Davidic dynasty, resuming the messianic line interrupted by the Exile. Possibly through a Levirate marriage, Zerubbabel appears in the line of Christ on both Joseph's side (Matt. 1:12) and Mary's side (Luke 3:27). He bypassed the curse on the lines of Jehoiakim and Jehoiachin (see Jer. 22:24–30; 36:27–32).

ZECHARIAH

When a team is losing, the coach's halftime talk holds special significance. The game isn't over, but the team may be discouraged, and they need an effective motivation to pursue victory.

Zechariah and his prophet-partner Haggai offered the people of Jerusalem some necessary halftime encouragement. They were losing the contest of wills to the opposition and had stopped rebuilding the temple. God's spokesmen described the benefits that would come if the people worked hard for God, who would ultimately gain the victory.

AUTHOR AND DATE

Zechariah was written by Zechariah during his ministry, from approximately 520 to 518 B.C., with another section written near 480 to 470 B.C.

Like Jeremiah and Ezekiel, Zechariah was also a priest (Nehemiah 12:12–16). Born in Babylon, he had joined his grandfather, Iddo, in the first group of exiles to return to Jerusalem under the leadership of Zerubbabel and Joshua the High-Priest (Nehemiah 12:4). Because Zechariah is sometimes called the son of Iddo (Ezra 5:1; 6:14; Nehemiah 12:16), scholars have concluded that Zechariah may have lost his father Berechiah at an early age and therefore had inherited the priesthood directly from his grandfather.

Ancient Jewish tradition also holds that Zechariah was a member of the Great Synagogue, a council of 120 originated by Nehemiah and presided over by Ezra. This council later developed into the ruling elders of the nation, referred to as the Sanhedrin in the New Testament.

The book begins with a reference to an historical marker, the second year of Darius I (520 B.C.). Zechariah's career followed closely after Haggai's, with their opening prophecies only two months apart. Because Zechariah is described as a young man (2:4), he was probably the younger of the two prophets. The first part of Zechariah's ministry lasted the same two years that Haggai was active (520–518 B.C.). Chapters 9–14 are generally thought to come later in his life, probably between 480 and 470 B.C.

Matthew 23:35 reports that the prophet Zechariah was murdered between the temple and the altar. Jesus said that the consequences for Zechariah's death would make up part of God's judgment on his own generation.

Zechariah and Haggai share the same historical background and setting. God had called both prophets into action sixteen years after the arrival of the original 50,000 Jewish exiles returning from Babylon in 538 B.C. At first the exiles had worked hard to rebuild the temple and repair the city, but opposition had eventually intimidated and discouraged them. All the work had stopped. In 520 B.C., however, Zechariah and Haggai served to spur the people back to action. Ezra 6:15 records that the temple was completed in four years (516 B.C.).

Zechariah joined Haggai in rousing the people from their indifference and discouragement. They both challenged the people to rebuild the temple. Though they addressed the same problems, however, the two prophets took different approaches. Haggai, who began the process, preached with a tone of rebuke for the people's indifference, sin, and lack of trust in God. His confrontational style started the spiritual revival. Zechariah arrived a little later as a re-enforcement, urging the people to keep working. He called them to repentance and reassured them about God's future blessings.

ZECHARIAH'S PROPHECY CENTERS ON **JESUS CHRIST,** FOCUSING ON **HIS COMING GLORY** AS **A MEANS** TO **COMFORT ISRAEL.**

Zechariah sought to encourage the people to build the temple based on the promise that someday Messiah would come to inhabit it. The building was meant to represent both immediate and future hope. That hope centered on the Savior.

This book is the most messianic, apocalyptic, and eschatological in the Old Testament. Zechariah's prophecy centers on Jesus Christ, focusing on His coming glory as a means to comfort Israel (1:13,17). While the book is filled with visions, prophecies, signs, celestial visitors, and the voice of God, it also deals with practical issues like repentance, divine care, salvation, and holy living. Prophetic voices would soon be silenced for 400 years until John the Baptist, so God used Zechariah to bring a rich, abundant outburst of promise about the future to sustain the faithful remnant through those silent years.

OUTLINE

A Call to Repentance

1 In the eighth month of the second year of Darius, the word of the LORD came to Zechariah the son of Berechiah, the son of Iddo the prophet, saying, ²"The LORD has been very angry with your fathers. ³Therefore say to them, 'Thus says the LORD of hosts: "Return to Me," says the LORD of hosts, "and I will return to you," says the LORD of hosts. ⁴"Do not be like your fathers, to whom the former prophets preached, saying, 'Thus says the LORD of hosts: "Turn now from your evil ways and your evil deeds." ' But they did not hear nor heed Me," says the LORD.

> **1:3 the LORD of hosts.** God is the commander of the armies of Israel (see 2 Chr.26:11), of the heathen nations (see Judg. 4:2), and of the heavenly inhabitants (see 1 Kin. 22:19). **Return to Me.** The prophet calls for repentance—he did not want God's chosen people to think they would be blessed regardless of their spiritual condition. God desires that His wayward people return to Him (see Gen. 17:7; 2 Cor. 6:16). Their relationship with Him is the constant condition for blessing.

⁵ "Your fathers, where *are* they?
    And the prophets, do they live forever?
⁶ Yet surely My words and My statutes,
    Which I commanded My servants the
       prophets,
    Did they not overtake your fathers?

"So they returned and said:

'Just as the LORD of hosts determined
    to do to us,
    According to our ways and according
      to our deeds,
    So He has dealt with us.' " ' "

Vision of the Horses

⁷On the twenty-fourth day of the eleventh month, which is the month Shebat, in the second year of Darius, the word of the LORD came to Zechariah the son of Berechiah, the son of Iddo the prophet: ⁸I saw by night, and behold, a man riding on a red horse, and it stood among the myrtle trees in the hollow; and behind him *were* horses: red, sorrel, and white. ⁹Then I said, "My lord, what *are* these?" So the angel who talked with me said to me, "I will show you what they *are*."

> **1:8 red, sorrel, and white.** The colors may speak of the riders' work: red represents bloodshed and judgment (see Is. 63:1,2), white represents victory (see Rev. 19:11), and sorrel (a brown) is possibly a combination of the others. A similar picture is found in Rev. 6:1–8. These horses are about to gain a victorious judgment. They are most likely angels acting as messengers of vengeance.

¹⁰And the man who stood among the myrtle trees answered and said, "These *are* the ones whom the LORD has sent to walk to and fro throughout the earth." ¹¹So they answered the Angel of the LORD, who stood among the myrtle trees, and said, "We have walked to and fro throughout the earth, and behold, all the earth is resting quietly."

The LORD Will Comfort Zion

¹²Then the Angel of the LORD answered and said, "O LORD of hosts, how long will You not have mercy on Jerusalem and on the cities of Judah, against which You were angry these seventy years?"

> **1:7–6:15** God gave Zechariah these visions to comfort the remnant of Israel who had been commissioned to return to the land promised to Abraham (see Gen. 12). They were to rebuild the temple (see 1 and 2 Chr.) and to anticipate the day of the Messiah's return. Some portions of the visions have been fulfilled, but most await the Second Advent of Jesus Christ.

¹³And the LORD answered the angel who talked to me, *with* good *and* comforting words. ¹⁴So the angel who spoke with me said to me, "Proclaim, saying, 'Thus says the LORD of hosts:

"I am zealous for Jerusalem
    And for Zion with great zeal.
¹⁵ I am exceedingly angry with the
      nations at ease;
    For I was a little angry,
    And they helped—*but* with evil
      intent."

¹⁶'Therefore thus says the LORD:

"I am returning to Jerusalem with
    mercy;

My house shall be built in it," says
    the LORD of hosts,
"And a *surveyor's* line shall be
    stretched out over Jerusalem." '

¹⁷"Again proclaim, saying, 'Thus says the
LORD of hosts:

"My cities shall again spread out
    through prosperity;
The LORD will again comfort Zion,
And will again choose Jerusalem." ' "

Vision of the Horns

¹⁸Then I raised my eyes and looked, and
there *were* four horns. ¹⁹And I said to the
angel who talked with me, "What *are*
these?"

So he answered me, "These *are* the horns
that have scattered Judah, Israel, and Jerusalem."

> **1:18 four horns.** Horns symbolized power and pride
> (see Ps. 75:10; Mic. 4:13). In the context of judgment,
> each symbolized either a nation or the head of that
> nation (see Dan. 7:21). Here the horns represent na-
> tions that attacked God's people, referring either to
> Egypt, Assyria, Babylonia, and Medo-Persia, or to the
> 4 world empires of Dan. 7:2–8 (Babylonia, Medo-
> Persia, Greece, and Rome).

²⁰Then the LORD showed me four crafts-
men. ²¹And I said, "What are these coming
to do?"

So he said, "These *are* the horns that
scattered Judah, so that no one could lift up
his head; but the craftsmen*ᵃ* are coming to
terrify them, to cast out the horns of the
nations that lifted up *their* horn against the
land of Judah to scatter it."

Vision of the Measuring Line

2 Then I raised my eyes and looked, and
behold, a man with a measuring line in
his hand. ²So I said, "Where are you going?"

And he said to me, "To measure Jerusalem, to see what *is* its width and what *is* its
length."

³And there *was* the angel who talked with
me, going out; and another angel was coming out to meet him, ⁴who said to him,
"Run, speak to this young man, saying: 'Je-

rusalem shall be inhabited *as* towns without walls, because of the multitude of men
and livestock in it. ⁵For I,' says the LORD,
'will be a wall of fire all around her, and I
will be the glory in her midst.' "

> **2:5 a wall of fire all around her.** Though without
> walls, Jerusalem would dwell securely because of
> divine protection. The phrase is reminiscent of the
> pillar of fire at the Exodus (see Ex. 13:21). **I will be the
> glory in her midst.** The glory depicts the Messiah's
> blessing and presence in His earthly kingdom (see Is.
> 4:2–6).

Future Joy of Zion and Many Nations

⁶"Up, up! Flee from the land of the
north," says the LORD; "for I have spread
you abroad like the four winds of heaven,"
says the LORD. ⁷Up, Zion! Escape, you who
dwell with the daughter of Babylon."

⁸For thus says the LORD of hosts: "He
sent Me after glory, to the nations which
plunder you; for he who touches you
touches the apple of His eye. ⁹For surely I
will shake My hand against them, and they
shall become spoil for their servants. Then
you will know that the LORD of hosts has
sent Me.

¹⁰"Sing and rejoice, O daughter of Zion!
For behold, I am coming and I will dwell in
your midst," says the LORD. ¹¹"Many nations shall be joined to the LORD in that
day, and they shall become My people. And
I will dwell in your midst. Then you will
know that the LORD of hosts has sent Me to
you. ¹²And the LORD will take possession of
Judah as His inheritance in the Holy Land,
and will again choose Jerusalem. ¹³Be silent, all flesh, before the LORD, for He is
aroused from His holy habitation!"

Vision of the High Priest

3 Then he showed me Joshua the high
priest standing before the Angel of the
LORD, and Satan standing at his right hand
to oppose him. ²And the LORD said to Satan, "The LORD rebuke you, Satan! The
LORD who has chosen Jerusalem rebuke
you! *Is* this not a brand plucked from the
fire?"

³Now Joshua was clothed with filthy gar-
ments, and was standing before the Angel.

1:21 *ᵃ*Literally *these*

3:1 Satan. This could also be translated "adversary," leaving this person's identity unknown. However, it seems he is Satan because of his accusations (see Job 1,2). The malicious adversary stands in the presence of the Lord to proclaim Israel's sins and her unworthiness of God's favor. If Joshua is vindicated, Israel is accepted. If Joshua is rejected, Israel is rejected. God's plan for Israel was revealed in the outcome.

⁴Then He answered and spoke to those who stood before Him, saying, "Take away the filthy garments from him." And to him He said, "See, I have removed your iniquity from you, and I will clothe you with rich robes."

⁵And I said, "Let them put a clean turban on his head."

So they put a clean turban on his head, and they put the clothes on him. And the Angel of the LORD stood by.

The Coming Branch

⁶Then the Angel of the LORD admonished Joshua, saying, ⁷"Thus says the LORD of hosts:

'If you will walk in My ways,
And if you will keep My command,
Then you shall also judge My house,
And likewise have charge of My
courts;
I will give you places to walk
Among these who stand here.

⁸ 'Hear, O Joshua, the high priest,
You and your companions who sit
before you,
For they are a wondrous sign;
For behold, I am bringing forth My
Servant the BRANCH.
⁹ For behold, the stone
That I have laid before Joshua:
Upon the stone are seven eyes.
Behold, I will engrave its inscription,'

3:8,9 My Servant the BRANCH. The phrase, "My Servant," is used by other prophets to refer to the Messiah (Is. 42:1; Ezek. 34:23,24) and His complete obedience and humility. "Branch" also points to the Messiah (see Is. 4:2; Jer. 23:5), denoting His rise from humble beginnings (Is. 11:1) and His fruitfulness (Is. 11:1). **the stone.** This is another reference to the Messiah (see Ps. 118:22,23; Dan. 2:35; 1 Pet. 2:6–8).

Says the LORD of hosts,
'And I will remove the iniquity of that
land in one day.
¹⁰ In that day,' says the LORD of hosts,
'Everyone will invite his neighbor
Under his vine and under his fig tree.' "

Vision of the Lampstand and Olive Trees

4 Now the angel who talked with me came back and wakened me, as a man who is wakened out of his sleep. ²And he said to me, "What do you see?"

So I said, "I am looking, and there is a lampstand of solid gold with a bowl on top of it, and on the stand seven lamps with seven pipes to the seven lamps. ³Two olive trees are by it, one at the right of the bowl and the other at its left." ⁴So I answered and spoke to the angel who talked with me, saying, "What are these, my lord?"

⁵Then the angel who talked with me answered and said to me, "Do you not know what these are?"

And I said, "No, my lord."

⁶So he answered and said to me:

"This is the word of the LORD to
Zerubbabel:
'Not by might nor by power, but by My
Spirit,'
Says the LORD of hosts.

4:6 Not by might...power, but by My Spirit. Neither human might, wealth, or physical stamina would be sufficient to complete the work. Only the power of the Holy Spirit would enable Zerubbabel to carry out the task of completing the temple, thus enabling Israel to be a light to the world in the Messiah's kingdom (see Ezek. 36:24).

⁷ 'Who are you, O great mountain?
Before Zerubbabel you shall become a
plain!
And he shall bring forth the capstone
With shouts of "Grace, grace to it!" ' "

⁸Moreover the word of the LORD came to me, saying:

⁹ "The hands of Zerubbabel
Have laid the foundation of this
temple;ᵃ

His hands shall also finish *it*.
Then you will know
That the LORD of hosts has sent Me
    to you.
10 For who has despised the day of small
        things?
For these seven rejoice to see
The plumb line in the hand of
    Zerubbabel.
They are the eyes of the LORD,
Which scan to and fro throughout the
    whole earth."

¹¹Then I answered and said to him, "What *are* these two olive trees—at the right of the lampstand and at its left?" ¹²And I further answered and said to him, "What *are these* two olive branches that *drip* into the receptacles*ᵃ* of the two gold pipes from which the golden *oil* drains?"

¹³Then he answered me and said, "Do you not know what these *are?*"

And I said, "No, my lord."

¹⁴So he said, "These *are* the two anointed ones, who stand beside the Lord of the whole earth."

Vision of the Flying Scroll

5 Then I turned and raised my eyes, and saw there a flying scroll.

²And he said to me, "What do you see?"

So I answered, "I see a flying scroll. Its length *is* twenty cubits and its width ten cubits."

³Then he said to me, "This *is* the curse that goes out over the face of the whole earth: 'Every thief shall be expelled,' according *to* this side of *the scroll;* and, 'Every perjurer shall be expelled,' according *to* that side of it."

⁴   "I will send out *the curse*," says the
        LORD of hosts;
    "It shall enter the house of the
        thief

> **5:1–4** This sixth vision of the flying scroll depicts the Word of God, which Israel and the world has disobeyed. It calls for God's righteous judgment of the sinner according to His standard found in His Word.

And the house of the one who swears
    falsely by My name.
It shall remain in the midst of his
    house
And consume it, with its timber and
    stones."

Vision of the Woman in a Basket

⁵Then the angel who talked with me came out and said to me, "Lift your eyes now, and see what this *is* that goes forth."

⁶So I asked, "What *is* it?" And he said, "It *is* a basket*ᵃ* that is going forth."

He also said, "This *is* their resemblance throughout the earth: ⁷Here *is* a lead disc lifted up, and this *is* a woman sitting inside the basket"; ⁸then he said, "This *is* Wickedness!" And he thrust her down into the basket, and threw the lead cover*ᵃ* over its mouth. ⁹Then I raised my eyes and looked, and there *were* two women, coming with the wind in their wings; for they had wings like the wings of a stork, and they lifted up the basket between earth and heaven.

> **5:9 two women...wind in their wings.** Because storks are unclean birds (Lev. 11:19), these must be agents of evil who set up the final evil world system. God allows them to set up that system, but He will destroy it when He returns (see Rev. 19:11–16).

¹⁰So I said to the angel who talked with me, "Where are they carrying the basket?"

¹¹And he said to me, "To build a house for it in the land of Shinar;*ᵃ* when it is ready, *the basket* will be set there on its base."

Vision of the Four Chariots

6 Then I turned and raised my eyes and looked, and behold, four chariots *were* coming from between two mountains, and the mountains *were* mountains of bronze. ²With the first chariot *were* red horses, with the second chariot black horses, ³with the third chariot white horses, and with the fourth chariot dappled horses—strong *steeds.* ⁴Then I answered and said to the angel who talked with me, "What *are* these, my lord?"

⁵And the angel answered and said to me, "These *are* four spirits of heaven, who go

---

4:12 *ᵃ*Literally *into the hands of*   5:6 *ᵃ*Hebrew *ephah,* a measuring container, and so elsewhere
5:8 *ᵃ*Literally *stone*   5:11 *ᵃ*That is, Babylon

out from *their* station before the Lord of all the earth. ⁶The one with the black horses is going to the north country, the white are going after them, and the dappled are going toward the south country." ⁷Then the strong *steeds* went out, eager to go, that they might walk to and fro throughout the earth. And He said, "Go, walk to and fro throughout the earth." So they walked to and fro throughout the earth. ⁸And He called to me, and spoke to me, saying, "See, those who go toward the north country have given rest to My Spirit in the north country."

The Command to Crown Joshua

⁹Then the word of the LORD came to me, saying: ¹⁰"Receive *the gift* from the captives—from Heldai, Tobijah, and Jedaiah, who have come from Babylon—and go the same day and enter the house of Josiah the son of Zephaniah. ¹¹Take the silver and gold, make an elaborate crown, and set *it* on the head of Joshua the son of Jehozadak, the high priest. ¹²Then speak to him, saying, 'Thus says the LORD of hosts, saying:

> "Behold, the Man whose name *is* the
>   BRANCH!
> From His place He shall branch out,
> And He shall build the temple of the
>   LORD;

> **6:12 the BRANCH.** Though the crown was placed on the head of Joshua, the High-Priest, the act symbolized the future crowning of the Messiah, the BRANCH. In Him, the offices of king and priest will be united.

> ¹³ Yes, He shall build the temple of the
>   LORD.
>   He shall bear the glory,
>   And shall sit and rule on His throne;
>   So He shall be a priest on His throne,
>   And the counsel of peace shall be
>   between them both." '

¹⁴"Now the elaborate crown shall be for a memorial in the temple of the LORD for Helem,ᵃ Tobijah, Jedaiah, and Hen the son of Zephaniah. ¹⁵Even those from afar shall come and build the temple of the LORD. Then you shall know that the LORD of hosts has sent Me to you. And *this* shall come to pass if you diligently obey the voice of the LORD your God."

Obedience Better than Fasting

7 Now in the fourth year of King Darius it came to pass *that* the word of the LORD came to Zechariah, on the fourth day of the ninth month, Chislev, ²when *the* peopleᵃ sent Sherezer,ᵇ with Regem-Melech and his men, *to* the house of God,ᶜ to pray before the LORD, ³*and* to ask the priests

> **7:3 weep in the fifth month and fast.** The Day of Atonement was the only annual fast required by God's law (Lev. 23:27). The fall of Jerusalem was remembered by 4 fasts (see 2 Kin. 25) in the fourth, fifth, seventh, and tenth months. Because the temple was burned in the fifth month (July-Aug.), that fast was the most serious, and the people continued it for "many years." However, that fast had become a wearisome ritual in light of their present prosperity.

who *were* in the house of the LORD of hosts, and the prophets, saying, "Should I weep in the fifth month and fast as I have done for so many years?"

⁴Then the word of the LORD of hosts came to me, saying, ⁵"Say to all the people of the land, and to the priests: 'When you fasted and mourned in the fifth and seventh *months* during those seventy years, did you really fast for Me—for Me? ⁶When you eat and when you drink, do you not eat and drink *for yourselves?* ⁷Should *you* not *have obeyed* the words which the LORD proclaimed through the former prophets when Jerusalem and the cities around it were inhabited and prosperous, and the Southᵃ and the Lowland were inhabited?' "

> **7:7 obeyed the words.** Obedience is more important than ritual. Obedience to God's Word brought joy, peace, and prosperity to Israel during the time of David and Solomon. If the people in Zechariah's time substituted ritual for obedience, they would lose their joy, peace, and prosperity.

6:14 ᵃFollowing Masoretic Text, Targum, and Vulgate; Syriac reads *for Heldai* (compare verse 10); Septuagint reads *for the patient ones.*   7:2 ᵃLiterally *they* (compare verse 5)   ᵇOr *Sar-Ezer*   ᶜHebrew *Bethel*   7:7 ᵃHebrew *Negev*

Disobedience Resulted in Captivity

⁸Then the word of the LORD came to Zechariah, saying, ⁹"Thus says the LORD of hosts:

'Execute true justice,
Show mercy and compassion
Everyone to his brother.
10 Do not oppress the widow or the
        fatherless,
The alien or the poor.
Let none of you plan evil in his heart
Against his brother.'

¹¹But they refused to heed, shrugged their shoulders, and stopped their ears so that they could not hear. ¹²Yes, they made their hearts like flint, refusing to hear the law and the words which the LORD of hosts had sent by His Spirit through the former prophets. Thus great wrath came from the LORD of hosts. ¹³Therefore it happened, *that* just as He proclaimed and they would not hear, so they called out and I would not listen," says the LORD of hosts. ¹⁴"But I scattered them with a whirlwind among all the nations which they had not known. Thus the land became desolate after them, so that no one passed through or returned; for they made the pleasant land desolate."

Jerusalem, Holy City of the Future

8 Again the word of the LORD of hosts came, saying, ²"Thus says the LORD of hosts:

'I am zealous for Zion with great zeal;
With great fervor I am zealous for
    her.'

8:2 zealous. God cannot bear to be separated from His chosen people due to their sin, nor can He tolerate Israel's enemies. His love for Israel is so great that He will again return to them and dwell with them. Ezekiel had the vision of God leaving Jerusalem (Ezek. 8–11) and of His presence returning (Ezek. 43:1–5). **Zion.** This is the mountain on which ancient Jerusalem was built, and it is also another name for the city.

³"Thus says the LORD:

'I will return to Zion,
And dwell in the midst of Jerusalem.

Jerusalem shall be called the City of
    Truth,
The Mountain of the LORD of hosts,
The Holy Mountain.'

⁴"Thus says the LORD of hosts:

'Old men and old women shall again
    sit
In the streets of Jerusalem,
Each one with his staff in his hand
Because of great age.
5 The streets of the city
Shall be full of boys and girls
Playing in its streets.'

⁶"Thus says the LORD of hosts:

'If it is marvelous in the eyes of the
    remnant of this people in these
    days,
Will it also be marvelous in My eyes?'
Says the LORD of hosts.

⁷"Thus says the LORD of hosts:

'Behold, I will save My people from
    the land of the east
And from the land of the west;
8 I will bring them *back,*
And they shall dwell in the midst of
    Jerusalem.
They shall be My people
And I will be their God,
In truth and righteousness.'

⁹"Thus says the LORD of hosts:

'Let your hands be strong,
You who have been hearing in these
    days
These words by the mouth of the
    prophets,
Who *spoke* in the day the foundation
    was laid
For the house of the LORD of hosts,
That the temple might be built.

8:9 the prophets. This refers to Haggai and Zechariah, and possibly some other non-writing prophets.

10 For before these days
There *were* no wages for man nor any
    hire for beast;

There *was* no peace from the enemy
   for whoever went out or came in;
For I set all men, everyone, against
   his neighbor.

11But now I *will* not *treat* the remnant of
this people as in the former days,' says the
LORD of hosts.

12   'For the seed *shall be* prosperous,
     The vine shall give its fruit,
     The ground shall give her increase,
     And the heavens shall give their
       dew—
     I will cause the remnant of this
       people
     To possess all these.
13   And it shall come to pass
     Th*at* just as you were a curse among
       the nations,
     O house of Judah and house of
       Israel,
     So I will save you, and you shall be a
       blessing.
     Do not fear,
     Let your hands be strong.'

OTHER NAMES FOR JERUSALEM

Lit. "The city of peace"

- The city of our God (Ps. 48:1)
- The city of the great King (Ps. 48:2)
- The city of the LORD of hosts (Ps. 48:8)
- Salem (Ps. 76:2)
- Zion (Ps. 76:2)
- The city of righteousness (Is. 1:26)
- The faithful city (Is. 1:26)
- Ariel, i.e., Lion of God (Is. 29:1)
- The holy city (Is. 52:1)
- City of the LORD (Is. 60:14)
- Hephzibah ["My delight is in her"] (Is. 62:4)
- The Throne of the LORD (Jer. 3:17)
- THE LORD OUR RIGHTEOUSNESS (Jer. 33:16)
- The perfection of beauty (Lam. 2:15)
- The joy of the whole earth (Lam. 2:15)
- THE LORD IS THERE [YHWH Shammah] (Ezek. 48:35)
- City of truth (Zech. 8:3)
- The Holy Mountain (Zech. 8:3)

14"For thus says the LORD of hosts:

'Just as I determined to punish you
   When your fathers provoked Me to
     wrath,'
   Says the LORD of hosts,
'And I would not relent,
15   So again in these days
   I am determined to do good
   To Jerusalem and to the house of
     Judah.
   Do not fear.
16   These *are* the things you shall do:
   Speak each man the truth to his
     neighbor;
   Give judgment in your gates for truth,
     justice, and peace;
17   Let none of you think evil in your*a*
     heart against your neighbor;
   And do not love a false oath.
   For all these *are things* that I hate,'
   Says the LORD."

18Then the word of the LORD of hosts
came to me, saying, 19"Thus says the LORD
of hosts:

'The fast of the fourth *month*,
   The fast of the fifth,
   The fast of the seventh,
   And the fast of the tenth,
   Shall be joy and gladness and cheerful
     feasts
   For the house of Judah.
   Therefore love truth and peace.'

8:18,19 The fourth and final response to the delegation from Bethel notes how national days of fasting and mourning will be transformed into joyous feasts. This answers the question in 7:3.

20"Thus says the LORD of hosts:

'Peoples shall yet come,
   Inhabitants of many cities;
21   The inhabitants of one *city* shall go to
     another, saying,
"Let us continue to go and pray before
     the LORD,
   And seek the LORD of hosts.
   I myself will go also."

8:17 *a*Literally *his*

22 Yes, many peoples and strong nations
Shall come to seek the LORD of hosts
in Jerusalem,
And to pray before the LORD.'

23 "Thus says the LORD of hosts: 'In those
days ten men from every language of the
nations shall grasp the sleeve of a Jewish
man, saying, "Let us go with you, for we
have heard that God is with you." ' "

> **9:1–8** This oracle is a series of judgments announced against the nations surrounding Israel, with deliverance promised for God's people. This is understood to be a prophecy of Alexander the Great's victories, given about 200 years before he marched through Palestine. It also pictures Christ returning to judge the nations and save Israel at the end of the Great Tribulation (see Matt. 24:21).

Israel Defended Against Enemies

9 The burden[a] of the word of the LORD
Against the land of Hadrach,
And Damascus its resting place
(For the eyes of men
And all the tribes of Israel
Are on the LORD);
2 Also against Hamath, which borders
on it,
And against Tyre and Sidon, though
they are very wise.

3 For Tyre built herself a tower,
Heaped up silver like the dust,
And gold like the mire of the streets.
4 Behold, the LORD will cast her out;
He will destroy her power in the sea,
And she will be devoured by fire.

5 Ashkelon shall see it and fear;
Gaza also shall be very sorrowful;
And Ekron, for He dried up her
expectation.
The king shall perish from Gaza,
And Ashkelon shall not be inhabited.

6 "A mixed race shall settle in Ashdod,
And I will cut off the pride of the
Philistines.
7 I will take away the blood from his
mouth,
And the abominations from between
his teeth.

But he who remains, even he shall be
for our God,
And shall be like a leader in Judah,
And Ekron like a Jebusite.
8 I will camp around My house
Because of the army,
Because of him who passes by and
him who returns.
No more shall an oppressor pass
through them,
For now I have seen with My eyes.

The Coming King

9 "Rejoice greatly, O daughter of Zion!
Shout, O daughter of Jerusalem!
Behold, your King is coming to you;
He is just and having salvation,
Lowly and riding on a donkey,
A colt, the foal of a donkey.

> **9:9 King...riding on a donkey.** Unlike Alexander the Great, this King comes riding on a donkey (see Jer. 17:25). This was fulfilled in Christ's triumphal entry into Jerusalem (Matt. 21:1–5). The Jews should have been looking for someone from the line of David (see 2 Sam. 7). This verse describes the Messiah as a King who is just, humble, and brings salvation.

10 I will cut off the chariot from
Ephraim
And the horse from Jerusalem;
The battle bow shall be cut off.
He shall speak peace to the nations;
His dominion shall be 'from sea to
sea,
And from the River to the ends of the
earth.'[a]

God Will Save His People

11 "As for you also,
Because of the blood of your
covenant,
I will set your prisoners free from the
waterless pit.
12 Return to the stronghold,
You prisoners of hope.
Even today I declare
That I will restore double to you.
13 For I have bent Judah, My bow,
Fitted the bow with Ephraim,
And raised up your sons, O Zion,
Against your sons, O Greece,

9:1 aOr oracle   9:10 aPsalm 72:8

And made you like the sword of a
mighty man."

14 Then the LORD will be seen over them,
And His arrow will go forth like
lightning.
The Lord GOD will blow the trumpet,
And go with whirlwinds from the
south.

15 The LORD of hosts will defend them;
They shall devour and subdue with
slingstones.
They shall drink *and* roar as if with
wine;
They shall be filled *with blood* like
basins,
Like the corners of the altar.

16 The LORD their God will save them in
that day,
As the flock of His people.
For they *shall be like* the jewels of a
crown,
Lifted like a banner over His land—

17 For how great is its*a* goodness
And how great its*b* beauty!
Grain shall make the young men
thrive,
And new wine the young women.

> **9:16,17** Abundant prosperity, such as the world has never seen, results in excessive rejoicing. Praise results from God "saving" Israel (see Deut. 33:28; Ps. 4:7,8).

Restoration of Judah and Israel

10 Ask the LORD for rain
In the time of the latter rain.*a*
The LORD will make flashing clouds;
He will give them showers of rain,
Grass in the field for everyone.

2 For the idols*a* speak delusion;
The diviners envision lies,
And tell false dreams;
They comfort in vain.
Therefore *the people* wend their way
like sheep;
They are in trouble because *there is*
no shepherd.

3 "My anger is kindled against the
shepherds,

And I will punish the goatherds.
For the LORD of hosts will visit His
flock,
The house of Judah,
And will make them as His royal
horse in the battle.

4 From him comes the cornerstone,
From him the tent peg,
From him the battle bow,
From him every ruler*a* together.

> **10:4 cornerstone.** This title for the Messiah (see Is. 28:16; Eph. 2:20) shows that Christ is the foundation on which His kingdom rests. **tent peg.** This may refer to a peg attached to the tent's center pole on which utensils and valuables were hung. The Messiah is the peg in the midst of His kingdom, where the glory of the kingdom will hang (see Is. 22:23,24). **battle bow...ruler.** These words also refer to the Messiah (Rev. 19:11–16).

5 They shall be like mighty men,
Who tread down *their enemies*
In the mire of the streets in the battle.
They shall fight because the LORD is
with them,
And the riders on horses shall be put
to shame.

6 "I will strengthen the house of Judah,
And I will save the house of Joseph.
I will bring them back,
Because I have mercy on them.
They shall be as though I had not cast
them aside;
For I *am* the LORD their God,
And I will hear them.

7 Th*ose of* Ephraim shall be like a
mighty man,
And their heart shall rejoice as if with
wine.
Yes, their children shall see *it* and be
glad;
Their heart shall rejoice in the LORD.

8 I will whistle for them and gather
them,
For I will redeem them;
And they shall increase as they once
increased.

9 "I will sow them among the peoples,
And they shall remember Me in far
countries;

9:17 *a*Or *His*   *b*Or *His*   10:1 *a*That is, spring rain   10:2 *a*Hebrew *teraphim*   10:4 *a*Or *despot*

They shall live, together with their children,
And they shall return.
10 I will also bring them back from the land of Egypt,
And gather them from Assyria.
I will bring them into the land of Gilead and Lebanon,
Until no *more room* is found for them.
11 He shall pass through the sea with affliction,
And strike the waves of the sea:
All the depths of the River[a] shall dry up.
Then the pride of Assyria shall be brought down,
And the scepter of Egypt shall depart.

12 "So I will strengthen them in the LORD,
And they shall walk up and down in His name,"
Says the LORD.

> **11:1–17** This passage presents an ugly picture of the rejection of the Messiah. The prophet turns from the glories of the accepted Messiah at His second coming to the national apostasy and rejection of Him at His first coming.

Desolation of Israel

11 Open your doors, O Lebanon,
That fire may devour your cedars.
2 Wail, O cypress, for the cedar has fallen,
Because the mighty *trees* are ruined.
Wail, O oaks of Bashan,
For the thick forest has come down.
3 There is the sound of wailing shepherds!
For their glory is in ruins.
There is the sound of roaring lions!
For the pride[a] of the Jordan is in ruins.

Prophecy of the Shepherds

4 Thus says the LORD my God, "Feed the flock for slaughter, 5 whose owners slaughter them and feel no guilt; those who sell

them say, 'Blessed be the LORD, for I am rich'; and their shepherds do not pity them. 6 For I will no longer pity the inhabitants of the land," says the LORD. "But indeed I will give everyone into his neighbor's hand and into the hand of his king. They shall attack the land, and I will not deliver *them* from their hand."

7 So I fed the flock for slaughter, in particular the poor of the flock.[a] I took for myself two staffs: the one I called Beauty,[b] and the other I called Bonds;[c] and I fed the flock. 8 I dismissed the three shepherds in one month. My soul loathed them, and their soul also abhorred me. 9 Then I said, "I will not feed you. Let what is dying die, and

> **11:7 the poor of the flock.** Only the poor believed in Jesus (see Matt. 11:5). They did not follow the pride of the priests, scribes, and Pharisees. **Beauty...Bonds.** Eastern shepherds often carried a rod to ward off wild beasts and a staff to guide and retrieve wayward sheep (see Ps. 23:4). The staff speaks of Christ, the Good Shepherd, who expressed God's love and grace by leading and protecting His people (Mark 6:34). The rod speaks of Him uniting the scattered house of Israel into one fold (see Matt. 15:24).

what is perishing perish. Let those that are left eat each other's flesh." 10 And I took my staff, Beauty, and cut it in two, that I might break the covenant which I had made with all the peoples. 11 So it was broken on that day. Thus the poor[a] of the flock, who were watching me, knew that it *was* the word of the LORD. 12 Then I said to them, "If it is agreeable to you, give *me* my wages; and if not, refrain." So they weighed out for my wages thirty *pieces* of silver.

13 And the LORD said to me, "Throw it to

> **11:12 thirty *pieces* of silver.** Zechariah symbolically pictured Jesus asking those He came to shepherd what they felt He was worth to them. The leaders mockingly offered 30 pieces of silver, the amount of compensation for a slave gored by an ox (see Ex. 21:32). This is what Judas Iscariot was paid to betray Jesus (Matt. 26:14–16). By paying this amount, the Jews of Jesus' day were saying He was worth no more than a common slave.

10:11 [a]That is, the Nile   11:3 [a]Or *floodplain, thicket*   11:7 [a]Following Masoretic Text, Targum, and Vulgate; Septuagint reads *for the Canaanites.*   [b]Or *Grace*, and so in verse 10   [c]Or *Unity*, and so in verse 14   11:11 [a]Following Masoretic Text, Targum, and Vulgate; Septuagint reads *the Canaanites.*

the potter"—that princely price they set on me. So I took the thirty *pieces* of silver and threw them into the house of the LORD for the potter. ¹⁴Then I cut in two my other staff, Bonds, that I might break the brotherhood between Judah and Israel.

¹⁵And the LORD said to me, "Next, take for yourself the implements of a foolish shepherd. ¹⁶For indeed I will raise up a shepherd in the land *who* will not care for those who are cut off, nor seek the young, nor heal those that are broken, nor feed those that still stand. But he will eat the flesh of the fat and tear their hooves in pieces.

¹⁷　"Woe to the worthless shepherd,
　　　Who leaves the flock!
　　　A sword *shall be* against his arm
　　　And against his right eye;
　　　His arm shall completely wither,
　　　And his right eye shall be totally
　　　　blinded."

> **11:17 His arm...right eye.** Zechariah condemned the worthless shepherd, noting that his strength ("arm") and his intelligence ("eye") would be taken away from him (see Dan. 7:9–14; 2 Thess. 2:8).

The Coming Deliverance of Judah

12 The burden*ᵃ* of the word of the LORD against Israel. Thus says the LORD, who stretches out the heavens, lays the foundation of the earth, and forms the spirit of man within him: ²"Behold, I will make Jerusalem a cup of drunkenness to all the surrounding peoples, when they lay siege against Judah and Jerusalem. ³And it shall happen in that day that I will make Jerusalem a very heavy stone for all peoples; all who would heave it away will surely be cut in pieces, though all nations of the earth are gathered against it. ⁴In that day," says the LORD, "I will strike every horse with confusion, and its rider with madness; I will open My eyes on the house of Judah, and will strike every horse of the peoples with blindness. ⁵And the governors of Judah shall say in their heart, 'The inhabitants of Jerusalem *are* my strength in the LORD of hosts, their God.' ⁶In that day I will make the governors of Judah like a

firepan in the woodpile, and like a fiery torch in the sheaves; they shall devour all the surrounding peoples on the right hand and on the left, but Jerusalem shall be inhabited again in her own place—Jerusalem.

⁷"The LORD will save the tents of Judah first, so that the glory of the house of David and the glory of the inhabitants of Jerusalem shall not become greater than that of Judah. ⁸In that day the LORD will defend the inhabitants of Jerusalem; the one who is feeble among them in that day shall be like David, and the house of David *shall be* like God, like the Angel of the LORD before them. ⁹It shall be in that day *that* I will seek to destroy all the nations that come against Jerusalem.

Mourning for the Pierced One

¹⁰"And I will pour on the house of David and on the inhabitants of Jerusalem the Spirit of grace and supplication; then they will look on Me whom they pierced. Yes, they will mourn for Him as one mourns for *his* only *son*, and grieve for Him as one grieves for a firstborn. ¹¹In that day there shall be a great mourning in Jerusalem, like the mourning at Hadad Rimmon in the plain of Megiddo.*ᵃ* ¹²And the land shall mourn, every family by itself: the family of the house of David by itself, and their wives by themselves; the family of the house of Nathan by itself, and their wives by themselves; ¹³the family of the house of Levi by itself, and their wives by themselves; the family of Shimei by itself, and their wives by themselves; ¹⁴all the families that remain, every family by itself, and their wives by themselves.

> **12:10 look on Me whom they pierced.** Israel will repent when they look to Jesus, the One they rejected and crucified (see Is. 53:5), at the Second Advent (Rom. 11:25–27). When God says they pierced "Me," He is affirming that Jesus is God.

Idolatry Cut Off

13 "In that day a fountain shall be opened for the house of David and for the inhabitants of Jerusalem, for sin and for uncleanness.

²"It shall be in that day," says the LORD of

hosts, *that* I will cut off the names of the idols from the land, and they shall no longer be remembered. I will also cause the prophets and the unclean spirit to depart from the land. ³It shall come to pass *that* if anyone still prophesies, then his father and mother who begot him will say to him, 'You shall not live, because you have spoken lies in the name of the LORD.' And his father and mother who begot him shall thrust him through when he prophesies.

⁴"And it shall be in that day *that* every prophet will be ashamed of his vision when he prophesies; they will not wear a robe of coarse hair to deceive. ⁵But he will say, 'I *am* no prophet, I *am* a farmer; for a man taught me to keep cattle from my youth.' ⁶And *one* will say to him, 'What are these wounds between your arms?'ᵃ Then he will answer, 'Th*ose* with which I was wounded in the house of my friends.'

The Shepherd Savior

⁷ " Awake, O sword, against My
  Shepherd,
  Against the Man who is My
   Companion,"
  Says the LORD of hosts.
 " Strike the Shepherd,
  And the sheep will be scattered;
  Then I will turn My hand against the
   little ones.

> **13:7 My Shepherd...the Man who is My Companion.** God identifies Jesus as His co-equal, affirming Jesus' deity (see John 1:1). **Strike the Shepherd.** The Good Shepherd's death was designed by God (see Is. 53:10). **sheep...scattered.** These are the disciples who defected from Jesus after His arrest (Matt. 26:33–35,56). **the little ones.** This refers to the Jews who were faithful to the Messiah after His crucifixion.

⁸ And it shall come to pass in all the
  land,"
  Says the LORD,
 " Th*at* two-thirds in it shall be cut off
  and die,
  But *one*-third shall be left in it:
⁹ I will bring the *one*-third through the
  fire,
  Will refine them as silver is refined,
  And test them as gold is tested.

They will call on My name,
 And I will answer them.
I will say, 'This *is* My people';
 And each one will say, 'The LORD *is*
  my God.' "

The Day of the LORD

14 Behold, the day of the LORD is
  coming,
 And your spoil will be divided in your
  midst.
² For I will gather all the nations to
  battle against Jerusalem;
 The city shall be taken,
 The houses rifled,
 And the women ravished.
 Half of the city shall go into captivity,
 But the remnant of the people shall
  not be cut off from the city.

> **14:1–21** Prior to Israel's conversion, the Jews will make a pact with the foolish shepherd, the Antichrist. In the middle of that 7-year pact, the Antichrist will break his treaty with them and require the worship of him alone (Dan. 9:24–27). Israel will refuse, the armies of the world will gather to fight, and these events will climax in the siege of Jerusalem and the Battle of Armageddon (Rev. 19). Israel's restoration will come following the Lord's victory (see Rev. 19:11–16).

³ Then the LORD will go forth
  And fight against those nations,
  As He fights in the day of battle.
⁴ And in that day His feet will stand on
  the Mount of Olives,
 Which faces Jerusalem on the east.
 And the Mount of Olives shall be
  split in two,
 From east to west,
 Making a very large valley;
 Half of the mountain shall move
  toward the north
 And half of it toward the south.
⁵ Then you shall flee *through* My
  mountain valley,
 For the mountain valley shall reach to
  Azal.
 Yes, you shall flee
 As you fled from the earthquake
 In the days of Uzziah king of Judah.

13:6 ᵃOr *hands*

Thus the LORD my God will come,
And all the saints with You.[a]

6 It shall come to pass in that day
Th*at* there will be no light;
The lights will diminish.
7 It shall be one day
Which is known to the LORD—
Neither day nor night.
But at evening time it shall happen
Th*at* it will be light.

8 And in that day it shall be
Th*at* living waters shall flow from
　　Jerusalem,
Half of them toward the eastern sea
And half of them toward the western
　　sea;
In both summer and winter it shall
　　occur.
9 And the LORD shall be King over all
　　the earth.
In that day it shall be—
"The LORD *is* one,"[a]
And His name one.

14:9 LORD *is* one...His name one. During the millennium, there will be only one religion in the world. Christ, ruling with a rod of iron (see Rev. 19:15), will do away with all false religions. The Abrahamic, Davidic, and New Covenants will be ultimately fulfilled in and by Jesus Christ.

[10]All the land shall be turned into a plain from Geba to Rimmon south of Jerusalem. *Jerusalem*[a] shall be raised up and inhabited in her place from Benjamin's Gate to the place of the First Gate and the Corner Gate, and *from* the Tower of Hananel to the king's winepresses.

11 The *people* shall dwell in it;
And no longer shall there be utter
　　destruction,
But Jerusalem shall be safely
　　inhabited.

[12]And this shall be the plague with which the LORD will strike all the people who fought against Jerusalem:

Their flesh shall dissolve while they
　　stand on their feet,
Their eyes shall dissolve in their
　　sockets,
And their tongues shall dissolve in
　　their mouths.

13 It shall come to pass in that day
Th*at* a great panic from the LORD will
　　be among them.
Everyone will seize the hand of his
　　neighbor,
And raise his hand against his
　　neighbor's hand;
14 Judah also will fight at Jerusalem.
And the wealth of all the surrounding
　　nations
Shall be gathered together:
Gold, silver, and apparel in great
　　abundance.

14:5 [a]Or *you;* Septuagint, Targum, and Vulgate read *Him.*　　14:9 [a]Compare Deuteronomy 6:4
14:10 [a]Literally *She*

Why is Zechariah sometimes called the "apocalypse of the Old Testament"?

Zechariah's message functions in much the same way as Revelation (The Apocalypse of the New Testament). His prophecies related both to Zechariah's immediate audience as well as to future generations. This conclusion is borne out in the structure of the prophecy itself. In each of the three major sections (1–6; 7,8; 9–14), the prophet begins historically and then moves forward to the time of the Second Advent, when Messiah returns to His temple to set up His earthly kingdom.
　　The prophet reminded the people that Messiah had both an immediate and long-term commitment to His people. Thus Zechariah's words were "good *and* comforting" (1:13), both to the exiles of his own day as well as to the remnant of God's chosen people in that future day. That dual function of speaking to the present and to the future has caused some to give Zechariah the title of "apocalypse of the Old Testament."

15 Such also shall be the plague
  On the horse *and* the mule,
  On the camel and the donkey,
  And on all the cattle that will be in
     those camps.
  So *shall* this plague *be*.

14:16–19 During the millennium, a remnant from heathen nations will make annual pilgrimages to Jerusalem to worship the Lord and celebrate the Feast of Tabernacles. The feast represented the last of the 3 major pilgrimage festivals (Lev. 23:34–36), marked the final harvest of the year, and provided a time of rejoicing. During the millennium, it will celebrate the Messiah's presence and the restoration of Israel. Those who refuse to go will experience drought and plague. Thousands of people, however, will reject Christ and be destroyed and cast into hell forever (see Rev. 20:7–15).

The Nations Worship the King

16And it shall come to pass *that* everyone who is left of all the nations which came against Jerusalem shall go up from year to year to worship the King, the LORD of hosts, and to keep the Feast of Tabernacles. 17And it shall be *that* whichever of the families of the earth do not come up to Jerusalem to worship the King, the LORD of hosts, on them there will be no rain. 18If the family of Egypt will not come up and enter in, they *shall have* no *rain;* they shall receive the plague with which the LORD strikes the nations who do not come up to keep the Feast of Tabernacles. 19This shall be the punishment of Egypt and the punishment of all the nations that do not come up to keep the Feast of Tabernacles.

20In that day "HOLINESS TO THE LORD" shall be *engraved* on the bells of the horses. The pots in the LORD's house shall be like the bowls before the altar. 21Yes, every pot in Jerusalem and Judah shall be holiness to the LORD of hosts.*a* Everyone who sacrifices shall come and take them and cook in them. In that day there shall no longer be a Canaanite in the house of the LORD of hosts.

14:21 Canaanite. This represents the morally and spiritually unclean people who will be excluded from entering the millennial temple. The evil Canaanites inhabited the Promised Land before Israel conquered it.

MALACHI

God's final words in the Old Testament include a promise: "I will send you Elijah the prophet" (Malachi 4:5). The next prophet to speak was born 400 years later. John the Baptist picked up the prophetic mantle and prepared the way for Jesus Christ. God's prophetic silence for four centuries certainly makes His final words worth our careful attention. God sent that message through the prophet Malachi.

AUTHOR AND DATE

Malachi was written by Malachi during his ministry, approximately 433 to 424 B.C.

Because the name Malachi means "my messenger" or "the LORD's messenger, some have suggested that the book may have been written anonymously. Only here is this phrase used as a personal name in the Old Testament. Since all other prophetic books consistently identify their authors in the introductory heading, however, there is good reason to identify the author of this last book as the prophet, Malachi. Ancient Jewish tradition numbers Malachi among the members of the Great Synagogue who collected and preserved the Scriptures.

The internal evidence available in Malachi indicates a date for this prophecy in the late fifth century B.C., probably during the years when Nehemiah was absent from Jerusalem back in Persia (433–424 B.C.). Conditions in the Promised Land seem consistent with the passage of almost a century since the ministry of Haggai and Zechariah. Although the temple had been rebuilt and in use for many years, the spiritual fires in the nation had long grown cold.

The time was ripe for the kind of message that Malachi had come to bring. Similar to Revelation 2,3, in which Christ writes about what He thinks of the conditions of the churches, here God writes through Malachi to impress upon Israel His thoughts about the nation.

BACKGROUND AND SETTING

During the first return, 50,000 exiles returned to Judah from Babylon (538–536 B.C.). By 516 B.C., the temple was rebuilt and back in use. Ezra returned to Jerusalem in 458 B.C., followed by Nehemiah in 445 B.C. The people's desire to return to their homeland had not translated into a desire to walk with God. As time passed, religious practices became meaningless routines, with little attention given to God's law. Into this chaos stepped the last of the Old Testament prophets. Malachi rebuked and condemned these abuses, forcefully indicting the people and calling them to repentance. Later, Nehemiah would return from almost a decade back in Persia

and add his stinging confrontation over their temple abuses, Sabbath violations, and the Jewish men's unlawful divorce of their Jewish wives in order to marry foreign women. God's people sank into anonymity among the lost and aimless nations of the world.

As over two millennia of Old Testament history since Abraham concluded, none of the glorious promises of the Abrahamic, Davidic, or New Covenants had been fulfilled in the ultimate sense. Despite a few high points in Israel's history, like Joshua, David, and Josiah, the Jews seemed determined to turn away from God's favor. Less than a century after returning from crushing captivity, they were again deeply mired in sin. The long anticipated Messiah had not arrived and did not seem to be in sight.

Malachi wrote the capstone prophecy of the Old Testament in which he delivered: (1) God's message of judgment on Israel for their continuing sin; and (2) God's promise that one day in the future, when the Jews would repent, Messiah would be revealed and God's covenant promises would be fulfilled.

HISTORICAL AND THEOLOGICAL THEMES

God's love for His people pervades the book. The Lord repeatedly refers to His covenant with Israel (2:4,5,8,10,14; 3:1). He reminds them, from the opening words, of their unfaithfulness to His love/marriage relationship with them (1:2–5). Apparently all promises God had given through the prophets had not led to faithful commitment on the part of Israel's leaders but, instead, to resolute complacency.

> GOD'S LOVE FOR HIS PEOPLE PERVADES THE BOOK. THE LORD REPEATEDLY REFERS TO HIS COVENANT WITH ISRAEL.

The people of Malachi's day were living as if God could be satisfied with superficial rituals. God answered that misunderstanding through his prophet by assaulting their corruption, wickedness, and false security. He directed His judgments at their hypocrisy, infidelity, compromise, divorce, false worship, and arrogance.

Malachi's prophecy is set in the form of a dispute. He leveled questions and demanded responses from the people. What he got in response were often cynical questions (1:2,6,7; 2:17; 3:7,8,13). Undaunted, Malachi indicted the priests and people on at least six counts of willful sin: (1) repudiating God's love (1:2–5); (2) refusing God His due honor (1:6–2:9); (3) rejecting God's faithfulness (2:10–16); (4) redefining God's righteousness (2:17–3:5); (5) robbing God's riches (3:6–12); and (6) reviling God's grace (3:13–15).

OUTLINE

1 The burden[a] of the word of the LORD to Israel by Malachi.

Israel Beloved of God

2 "I have loved you," says the LORD.
"Yet you say, 'In what way have You
      loved us?'
   Was not Esau Jacob's brother?"
   Says the LORD.
   "Yet Jacob I have loved;
3   But Esau I have hated,
   And laid waste his mountains and his
      heritage
   For the jackals of the wilderness."

> **1:3 Esau I have hated.** This love/hate language does not signify a comparative love in which God loved Jacob more and Esau less. The context here speaks of love as "choosing for intimate fellowship" and hate as "not choosing for intimate fellowship" in the realm of redemption.

4   Even though Edom has said,
   "We have been impoverished,
   But we will return and build the
      desolate places,"

Thus says the LORD of hosts:

   "They may build, but I will throw
      down;
   They shall be called the Territory of
      Wickedness,
   And the people against whom the
      LORD will have indignation forever.
5   Your eyes shall see,
   And you shall say,
   'The LORD is magnified beyond the
      border of Israel.'

Polluted Offerings

6   "A son honors *his* father,
   And a servant *his* master.
   If then I am the Father,
   Where *is* My honor?
   And if I *am* a Master,
   Where *is* My reverence?
   Says the LORD of hosts
   To you priests who despise My name.
   Yet you say, 'In what way have we
      despised Your name?'

7   "You offer defiled food on My altar,
   But say,

> **1:7 defiled food.** This refers to animal sacrifices. The priests were offering unclean or blemished sacrifices, which were strictly forbidden by God (see Lev. 22:20–25). They had contempt for the Lord because of His disapproval of their offerings. **table of the LORD.** This refers to the altar for sacrifices (see Ezek. 41:22).

1:1 [a]Or *oracle*

OLD TESTAMENT NAMES FOR GOD

1. Elohim, "God," i.e., His power and might	Genesis 1:1; Psalms 19:1
2. El-Elyon, "The most high God"	Genesis 14:17–20; Isaiah 14:13,14
3. El-Olam, "The everlasting God"	Isaiah 40:28–31
4. El-Roi, "The strong one who sees"	Genesis 16:12
5. El-Shaddai, "God Almighty"	Genesis 17:1; Psalms 91:1
6. Adonai, "Lord," i.e., the Lordship of God	Malachi 1:6
7. Jehovah (Yahweh), "The LORD," i.e., God's eternal nature	Genesis 2:4
8. Jehovah-Jireh, "The LORD will provide"	Genesis 22:13,14
9. Jehovah-Maccaddeshem, "The LORD your sanctifier"	Exodus 31:13
10. Jehovah-Nissi, "The LORD our banner"	Exodus 17:15
11. Jehovah-Rapha, "The LORD our healer"	Exodus 16:26
12. Jehovah-Rohi, "The LORD my shepherd"	Psalms 23:1
13. Jehovah-Sabbaoth, "The LORD of Hosts"	Isaiah 6:1–3
14. Jehovah-Shalom, "The LORD is peace"	Judges 6:24
15. Jehovah-Shammah, "The LORD who is present"	Ezekiel 48:35
16. Jehovah-Tsidkenu, "The LORD our righteousness"	Jeremiah 23:6

'In what way have we defiled You?'
By saying,
'The table of the LORD is
    contemptible.'
8 And when you offer the blind as a
    sacrifice,
Is it not evil?
And when you offer the lame and
    sick,
Is it not evil?
Offer it then to your governor!
Would he be pleased with you?
Would he accept you favorably?"
Says the LORD of hosts.

9 "But now entreat God's favor,
That He may be gracious to us.
While this is being *done* by your
    hands,
Will He accept you favorably?"
Says the LORD of hosts.
10 "Who *is there* even among you who
    would shut the doors,
So that you would not kindle fire *on*
    My altar in vain?
I have no pleasure in you,"
Says the LORD of hosts,
"Nor will I accept an offering from
    your hands.
11 For from the rising of the sun, even to
    its going down,
My name *shall be* great among the
    Gentiles;
In every place incense *shall be* offered
    to My name,
And a pure offering;
For My name shall be great among
    the nations,"
Says the LORD of hosts.

12 "But you profane it,
In that you say,
'The table of the LORD[a] is defiled;
And its fruit, its food, *is*
    contemptible.'

1:12,13 Tired of meeting the exact requirements of the sacrifices, the priests refused to lead the people to revere the Lord and to offer Him their best. Their attitude and actions were profaning the altar and insulting the Lord (see Is. 43:22–24), so He rejected their offerings.

13 You also say,
'Oh, what a weariness!'
And you sneer at it,"
Says the LORD of hosts.
"And you bring the stolen, the lame,
    and the sick;
Thus you bring an offering!
Should I accept this from your
    hand?"
Says the LORD.
14 "But cursed *be* the deceiver
Who has in his flock a male,
And takes a vow,
But sacrifices to the Lord what is
    blemished—
For I *am* a great King,"
Says the LORD of hosts,
"And My name *is to be* feared among
    the nations.

Corrupt Priests

2 "And now, O priests, this
    commandment is for you.
2 If you will not hear,
And if you will not take *it* to heart,
To give glory to My name,"
Says the LORD of hosts,
"I will send a curse upon you,
And I will curse your blessings.
Yes, I have cursed them already,
Because you do not take *it* to heart.

3 "Behold, I will rebuke your
    descendants
And spread refuse on your faces,
The refuse of your solemn feasts;
And *one* will take you away with it.
4 Then you shall know that I have sent
    this commandment to you,
That My covenant with Levi may
    continue,"
Says the LORD of hosts.

2:4,5 My covenant with Levi. God's relationship to the priesthood was set forth in the Levitic covenant (Num. 3:44–48). God expected reverence for Himself in exchange for life and peace for the priests. This covenant was made with Aaron (of Levi's line) and his descendants. The Jewish priests of Malachi's days had deceived themselves by claiming the privileges of the covenant, while neglecting the conditions of it.

1:12 [a]Following Bomberg; Masoretic Text reads *Lord.*

5 "My covenant was with him, *one* of
   life and peace,
   And I gave them to him *that he might*
   fear Me;
   So he feared Me
   And was reverent before My name.
6 The law of truth*a* was in his mouth,
   And injustice was not found on his
   lips.
   He walked with Me in peace and
   equity,
   And turned many away from iniquity.

7 "For the lips of a priest should keep
   knowledge,
   And *people* should seek the law from
   his mouth;
   For he is the messenger of the LORD
   of hosts.
8 But you have departed from the way;
   You have caused many to stumble at
   the law.
   You have corrupted the covenant of
   Levi,"
   Says the LORD of hosts.
9 "Therefore I also have made you
   contemptible and base
   Before all the people,
   Because you have not kept My ways
   But have shown partiality in the law."

Treachery of Infidelity

10 Have we not all one Father?
   Has not one God created us?
   Why do we deal treacherously with
   one another
   By profaning the covenant of the
   fathers?
11 Judah has dealt treacherously,
   And an abomination has been
   committed in Israel and in
   Jerusalem,
   For Judah has profaned

The LORD's holy *institution* which He
   loves:
He has married the daughter of a
   foreign god.
12 May the LORD cut off from the tents
   of Jacob
The man who does this, being awake
   and aware,*a*
Yet who brings an offering to the
   LORD of hosts!

13 And this is the second thing you do:
You cover the altar of the LORD with
   tears,
With weeping and crying;
So He does not regard the offering
   anymore,
Nor receive *it* with goodwill from your
   hands.
14 Yet you say, "For what reason?"
Because the LORD has been witness
Between you and the wife of your
   youth,
With whom you have dealt
   treacherously;
Yet she is your companion
And your wife by covenant.
15 But did He not make *them* one,
Having a remnant of the Spirit?
And why one?
He seeks godly offspring.
Therefore take heed to your spirit,
And let none deal treacherously with
   the wife of his youth.

16 "For the LORD God of Israel says
That He hates divorce,
For it covers one's garment with
   violence,"
Says the LORD of hosts.
"Therefore take heed to your spirit,
That you do not deal
   treacherously."

2:10,11 deal treacherously. The men were divorcing their Jewish wives and marrying foreign women.
Through intermarriage with idol worshipers, they
caused division from God, their Father (see Is. 43:1).
This violated the covenant God had made with their
ancestors to insure the maintenance of a people set
apart for Him (see Ex. 19:5; Lev. 20:24).

2:16 He hates divorce. God sees this unwarranted
divorce as a gross act of sin which, like blood splattered from a murder victim on the killer, leaves evidence of the evil deed. Though God hates divorce,
there are times when it is the lesser of the evils and
would prevent a future and even greater spiritual
catastrophe (see Matt. 5:32).

2:6 *a*Or *true instruction*   2:12 *a*Talmud and Vulgate read *teacher and student.*

17 You have wearied the LORD with your
     words;
     Yet you say,
 "In what way have we wearied *Him?*"
     In that you say,
 "Everyone who does evil
     Is good in the sight of the LORD,
     And He delights in them,"
     Or, "Where *is* the God of justice?"

The Coming Messenger

3 "Behold, I send My messenger,
     And he will prepare the way before Me.
     And the Lord, whom you seek,
     Will suddenly come to His temple,
     Even the Messenger of the covenant,
     In whom you delight.
     Behold, He is coming,"
     Says the LORD of hosts.

> **3:1 My messenger.** The name Malachi means "the
> LORD's messenger." It was customary for Near East-
> ern kings to send messengers before them to clear
> the way for their visit. God announced that He was
> sending one who would "prepare the way before
> Me." This is "the voice of one crying in the wilder-
> ness" (Is. 40:3) and the Elijah of 4:5 who comes before
> the Lord. The New Testament identifies him as John
> the Baptist (see Matt. 3:3; Mark 1:2).

2 "But who can endure the day of His
     coming?
     And who can stand when He appears?
     For He *is* like a refiner's fire
     And like launderers' soap.
3 He will sit as a refiner and a purifier
     of silver;
     He will purify the sons of Levi,
     And purge them as gold and silver,
     That they may offer to the LORD
     An offering in righteousness.

4 "Then the offering of Judah and
     Jerusalem
     Will be pleasant to the LORD,
     As in the days of old,
     As in former years.
5 And I will come near you for
     judgment;
     I will be a swift witness
     Against sorcerers,
     Against adulterers,
     Against perjurers,
     Against those who exploit wage
     earners and widows and orphans,

And against those who turn away an
     alien—
     Because they do not fear Me,"
     Says the LORD of hosts.

6 "For I *am* the LORD, I do not change;
     Therefore you are not consumed,
     O sons of Jacob.
7 Yet from the days of your fathers
     You have gone away from My
     ordinances
     And have not kept *them.*
     Return to Me, and I will return to
     you,"
     Says the LORD of hosts.
 "But you said,
     'In what way shall we return?'

Do Not Rob God

8 "Will a man rob God?
     Yet you have robbed Me!
     But you say,
     'In what way have we robbed You?'
     In tithes and offerings.
9 You are cursed with a curse,
     For you have robbed Me,
     Even this whole nation.
10 Bring all the tithes into the
     storehouse,
     That there may be food in My
     house,
     And try Me now in this,"
     Says the LORD of hosts,
 "If I will not open for you the windows
     of heaven
     And pour out for you *such* blessing
     That *there will* not *be room* enough
     to receive it.

11 "And I will rebuke the devourer for
     your sakes,
     So that he will not destroy the fruit of
     your ground,
     Nor shall the vine fail to bear fruit for
     you in the field,"
     Says the LORD of hosts;

> **3:10–12 try Me.** The people were invited to put God
> to the test (see Is. 7:11,12). If they would honor Him
> by reversing their robbery and show repentance by
> bringing what He required, He would shower them
> with excessive abundance (see Prov. 11:24,25), pro-
> tect them from locusts, and make them the delight of
> the nations (see Is. 62:4).

12   And all nations will call you blessed,
       For you will be a delightful land,"
       Says the LORD of hosts.

The People Complain Harshly
13   "Your words have been harsh against
          Me,"
       Says the LORD,
       "Yet you say,
       'What have we spoken against You?'
14   You have said,
       'It is useless to serve God;
       What profit *is it* that we have kept His
          ordinance,
       And that we have walked as
          mourners
       Before the LORD of hosts?
15   So now we call the proud blessed,
       For those who do wickedness are
          raised up;
       They even tempt God and go free.' "

A Book of Remembrance
16   Then those who feared the LORD
          spoke to one another,
       And the LORD listened and heard
          them;
       So a book of remembrance was
          written before Him
       For those who fear the LORD
       And who meditate on His name.

17   "They shall be Mine," says the LORD
       of hosts,

> **3:16 book of remembrance.** Judgment produced fear even in the hearts of those who loved and served God in Israel. Malachi encouraged the godly remnant by noting how the Lord had not forgotten those "who fear the Lord and who meditate on His name." The book may be the "book of life" in which the names of God's children are recorded (Ex. 32:32–34; Dan. 12:1). The Persians were known to record in books the acts of a person who should be rewarded in the future (Esth. 6:1,2).

       "On the day that I make them My
          jewels.[a]
       And I will spare them
       As a man spares his own son who
          serves him."
18   Then you shall again discern
       Between the righteous and the wicked,
       Between one who serves God
       And one who does not serve Him.

The Great Day of God
4   "For behold, the day is coming,
       Burning like an oven,
       And all the proud, yes, all who do
          wickedly will be stubble.
       And the day which is coming shall
          burn them up,"
       Says the LORD of hosts,
       "That will leave them neither root nor
          branch.
2   But to you who fear My name
       The Sun of Righteousness shall arise
       With healing in His wings;

3:17 [a]Literally *special treasure*

In what ways does John the Baptist fulfill Malachi's final prophecy in which God promises to send Elijah "before the coming of the great and dreadful day of the LORD" (4:5)?

The identity and meaning of Malachi's "Elijah" has been debated. Was this prophecy fulfilled in John the Baptist, or is it yet to be fulfilled? Could God have been announcing the reincarnation of Elijah? Evidence seems to weigh in favor of seeing Malachi's prophecy fulfilled by John the Baptist. Not only did the angel announce that John the Baptist would "go before Him in the spirit and power of Elijah" (Luke 1:17), but John himself stated that he was not Elijah (John 1:21). We conclude that John was like Elijah: (1) internally in "spirit and power"; and (2) externally in rugged independence and nonconformity. To the Jews who received the Messiah, John would be the Elijah spoken of (Matthew 11:14; 17:9–13). But, since the Jews as a whole refused the King, then another Elijah-like prophet would be sent in the future, perhaps as one of the two witnesses (Revelation 11:1–19).

And you shall go out
And grow fat like stall-fed calves.

3 You shall trample the wicked,
For they shall be ashes under the
    soles of your feet
On the day that I do *this*,"
Says the LORD of hosts.

4 "Remember the Law of Moses, My
    servant,
Which I commanded him in Horeb
    for all Israel,
With the statutes and judgments.

5 Behold, I will send you Elijah the
    prophet
Before the coming of the great and
    dreadful day of the LORD.

6 And he will turn
The hearts of the fathers to the
    children,
And the hearts of the children to their
    fathers,
Lest I come and strike the earth with
    a curse."

4:5 Elijah. One like Elijah was to announce the Messiah's arrival. John the Baptist was a type of Elijah at Christ's first advent (see Luke 1:17). Moses and Elijah appeared at the Mount of Transfiguration (see Matt. 17:14) and may be the two witnesses in the Great Tribulation (see Rev. 11:1–3). Most likely, this will be an Elijah-like person who will preach reconciliation to God so that souls can believe and be spared.

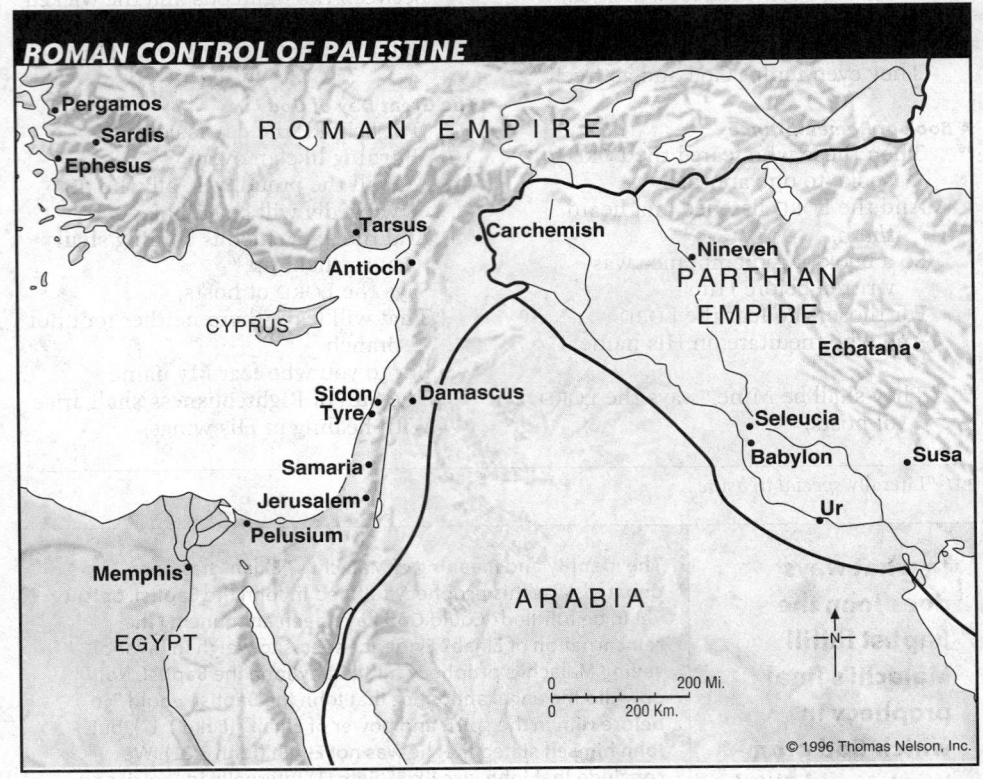

ROMAN CONTROL OF PALESTINE

Pergamos
Sardis
Ephesus
ROMAN EMPIRE
Tarsus
Carchemish
Antioch
Nineveh
PARTHIAN EMPIRE
CYPRUS
Ecbatana
Sidon
Damascus
Tyre
Seleucia
Babylon
Susa
Samaria
Jerusalem
Ur
Pelusium
Memphis
ARABIA
EGYPT

0   200 Mi.
0   200 Km.

© 1996 Thomas Nelson, Inc.

INTRODUCTION TO THE INTERTESTAMENTAL PERIOD

More than 400 years separated the final events (Neh. 13:4–30) and final prophecy (Mal. 1:1–4:6) recorded in the Old Testament from the beginning actions (Luke 1:5–25) narrated in the New Testament (about 424–26 B.C.). During this period, God gave no prophetic messages, causing this period to be called "the four hundred silent years." The history of these years followed the pattern predicted in Daniel (Dan. 2:24,45; 7:1–28; 8:1–27; 11:1–35) with exact precision. Though the voice of God was silent, the hand of God actively directed the course of events during these centuries.

JEWISH HISTORY

As Daniel had predicted, control of the land of Israel passed from the empire of Medo-Persia to Greece and then to Rome (Dan. 2:39,40; 7:5–7). For about 200 years, the Persian Empire ruled the Jews (539–332 B.C.). The Persians allowed the Jews to return to Jerusalem and rebuild the temple (2 Chr. 36:22,23; Ezra 1:1–4). For about 100 years after the close of the Old Testament canon, Judea remained a Persian territory under the governor of Syria, with the High Priest exercising a measure of civil authority. The Jews were allowed to worship without any official governmental interference.

Between 334 B.C. and 331 B.C., Alexander the Great defeated the Persian king, Darius III, in three decisive battles that gave him control of the lands of the Persian Empire. The land of Israel thus passed into Greek control in 332 B.C. (Dan. 8:5–7,20,21; 11:3). Alexander permitted the Jews to observe their laws. However, Alexander sought to bring Greek culture, or "Hellenism," to the lands he had conquered. He wished to create a world united by Greek language and thought. This enduring policy was as dangerous to the religion of Israel as the cult of Baal had been, because Hellenism was attractive and sophisticated but utterly ungodly.

When Alexander died in 323 B.C., his generals fought over the division of

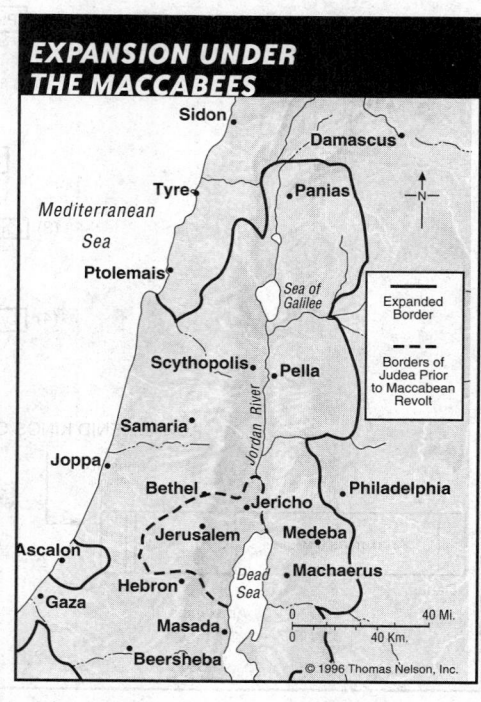

EXPANSION UNDER THE MACCABEES

CHRONOLOGY OF THE INTERTESTAMENTAL PERIOD

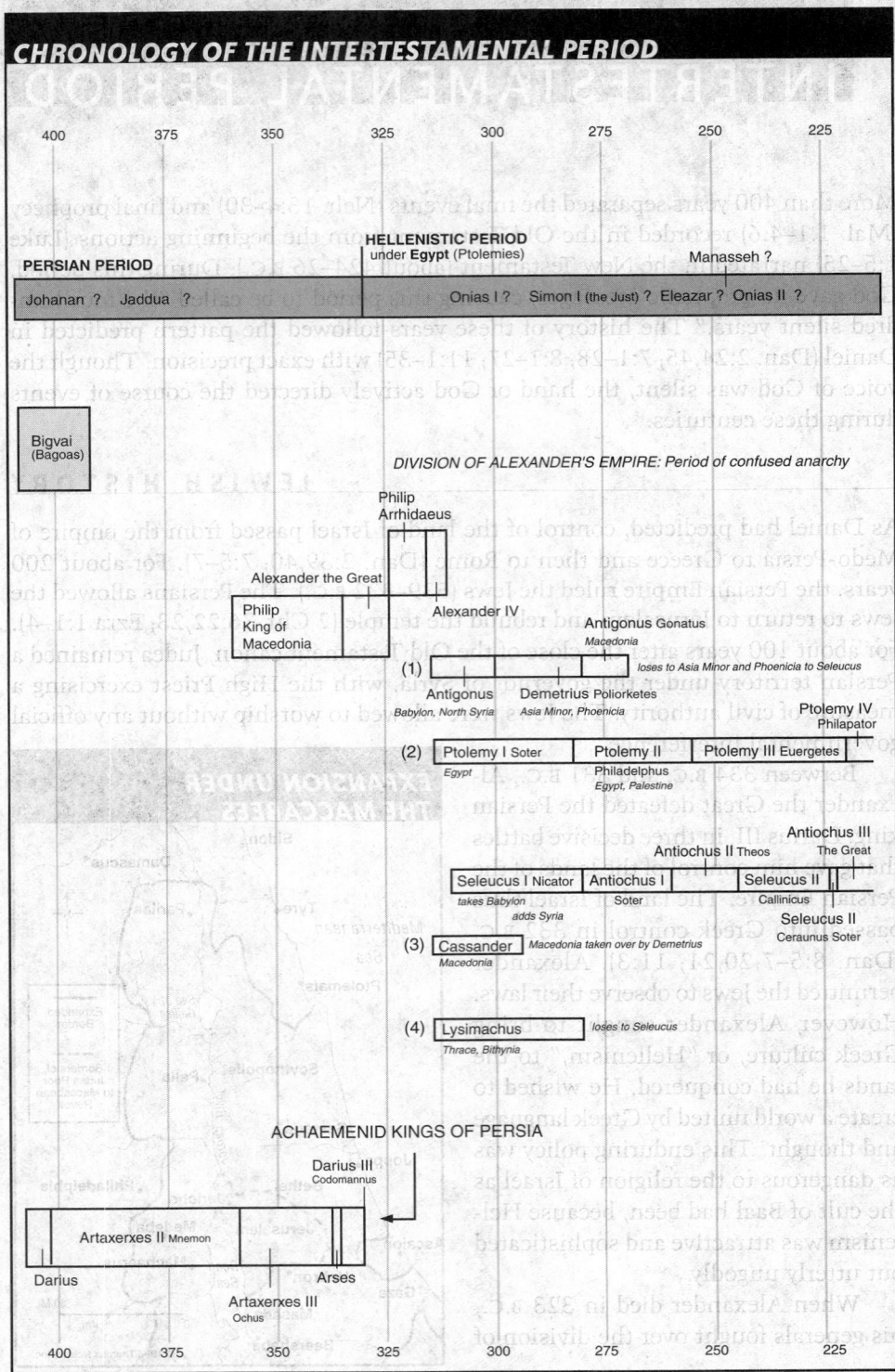

CHRONOLOGY OF THE INTERTESTAMENTAL PERIOD

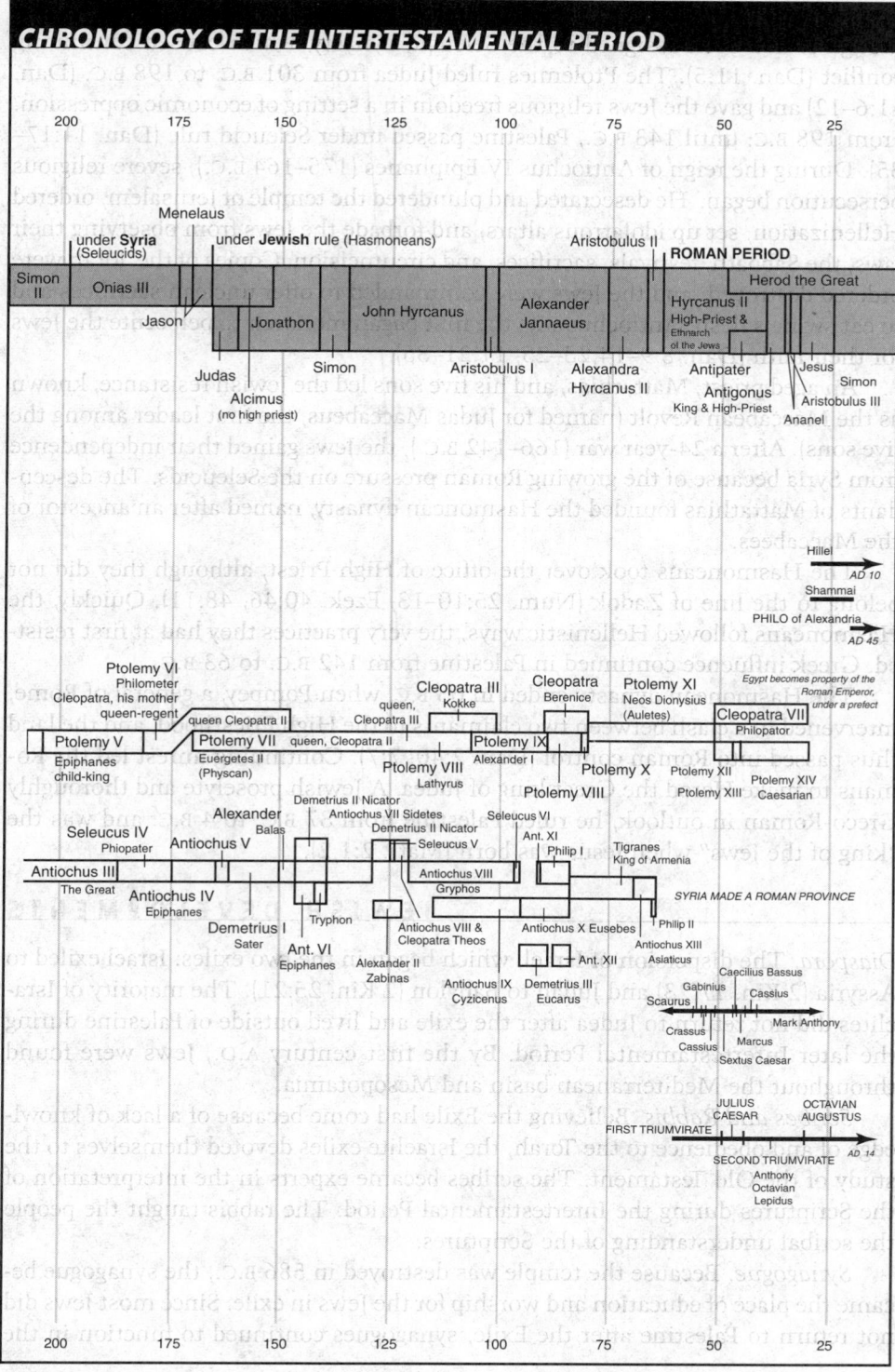

his empire (Dan. 8:22; 11:4). The Ptolemaic dynasty took control of Israel, even though it had been assigned to the Seleucid dynasty, which caused continuing conflict (Dan. 11:5). The Ptolemies ruled Judea from 301 B.C. to 198 B.C. (Dan. 11:6–12) and gave the Jews religious freedom in a setting of economic oppression. From 198 B.C. until 143 B.C., Palestine passed under Seleucid rule (Dan. 11:17–35). During the reign of Antiochus IV Epiphanes (175–164 B.C.), severe religious persecution began. He desecrated and plundered the temple of Jerusalem, ordered Hellenization, set up idolatrous altars, and forbade the Jews from observing their laws, the Sabbath, festivals, sacrifices, and circumcision. Copies of the Torah were ordered destroyed, and the Jews were commanded to offer unclean sacrifices and to eat swine's flesh. Antiochus was the first pagan monarch to persecute the Jews for their faith (Dan. 8:9–14,23–25; 11:21–35).

An aged priest, Mattathias, and his five sons led the Jewish resistance, known as the Maccabean Revolt (named for Judas Maccabeus, the first leader among the five sons). After a 24-year war (166–142 B.C.), the Jews gained their independence from Syria because of the growing Roman pressure on the Seleucids. The descendants of Mattathias founded the Hasmonean dynasty, named after an ancestor of the Maccabees.

The Hasmoneans took over the office of High Priest, although they did not belong to the line of Zadok (Num. 25:10–13; Ezek. 40:46; 48:11). Quickly, the Hasmoneans followed Hellenistic ways, the very practices they had at first resisted. Greek influence continued in Palestine from 142 B.C. to 63 B.C.

The Hasmonean dynasty ended in 63 B.C. when Pompey, a general of Rome, intervened in a clash between two claimants to the High Priesthood, and the land thus passed into Roman control (Dan. 2:40; 7:7). Continuing unrest led the Romans to make Herod the Great king of Judea. A Jewish proselyte and thoroughly Greco-Roman in outlook, he ruled Palestine from 37 B.C. to 4 B.C. and was the "king of the Jews" when Jesus was born (Matt. 2:1,2).

JEWISH DEVELOPMENTS

Diaspora. The dispersion of Israel, which began in the two exiles: Israel exiled to Assyria (2 Kin. 17:23) and Judah to Babylon (2 Kin. 25:21). The majority of Israelites did not return to Judea after the exile and lived outside of Palestine during the later Intertestamental Period. By the first century A.D., Jews were found throughout the Mediterranean basin and Mesopotamia.

Scribes and Rabbis. Believing the Exile had come because of a lack of knowledge of and obedience to the Torah, the Israelite exiles devoted themselves to the study of the Old Testament. The scribes became experts in the interpretation of the Scriptures during the Intertestamental Period. The rabbis taught the people the scribal understanding of the Scriptures.

Synagogue. Because the temple was destroyed in 586 B.C., the synagogue became the place of education and worship for the Jews in exile. Since most Jews did not return to Palestine after the Exile, synagogues continued to function in the

Diaspora and were also established in Palestine, even after the reconstruction of the temple by Zerubbabel in 516 B.C.

Septuagint. Hellenistic pressure caused the Jews of the Diaspora to become predominately Greek-speakers. According to Jewish legend, in ca. 250 B.C., Ptolemy Philadelphus brought together 72 scholars who translated the Old Testament into Greek in 72 days. The Latin word for 70, "Septuagint" (LXX), was the name attached to this translation. More likely translated over the period 250 B.C. to 125 B.C. in Alexandria, Egypt, the Septuagint was the most important and widely used Greek translation of the Old Testament.

Pharisees. This religious party probably began as the "holy ones" associated with the Maccabees and tried to rid the land of Hellenistic elements. When the Maccabees turned to Hellenism once they were in power, these holy ones "separated" from the official religious establishment. The Pharisees interpreted the law strictly, according to the developing oral tradition, and sought to enforce their understanding upon all Jews. Though few in number, they enjoyed the favor of the majority of the people in Palestine.

Sadducees. These Hellenized, aristocratic Jews became the guardians of the temple policy and practices. The Sadducees rejected the Old Testament as Scripture, except for the Torah (the first five books of the Old Testament); that is, they did not believe in the resurrection of the dead (Acts 23:6–8).

NEW TESTAMENT

The English word "gospel" derives from the Anglo-Saxon word *godspell*, which can mean either "a story about God," or "a good story." The latter meaning is in harmony with the Greek word translated "gospel," *euangellion*, which means "good news." The 4 gospels are the good news about the most significant events in all of history—the life, sacrificial death, and resurrection of Jesus of Nazareth.

The gospels are not full biographies, since they do not intend to present a complete life of Jesus (see John 20:30; 21:25). Apart from the birth narratives, they give little information about the first 30 years of Jesus' life. While Jesus' public ministry lasted over 3 years, the gospels focus much of their attention on the last week of His life (see John 12–20). Though they are completely accurate historically, and present important details of Jesus' life, the primary purposes of the gospels are theological and apologetic (John 20:31). They provide authoritative answers to questions about Jesus' life and ministry, and they strengthen believers' assurance regarding the reality of their faith (Luke 1:4).

Although other gospels were written, the church from earliest times has accepted only Matthew, Mark, Luke, and John as inspired Scripture. Matthew, Mark, and Luke share a common point of view and are known as the synoptic (from a Greek word meaning "to see together," or "to share a common point of view") gospels. Matthew, Mark, and Luke focus on Christ's Galilean ministry, while John focuses on His ministry in Judea. The synoptic gospels contain numerous parables, while John records none. All four gospels record only two common events (Jesus' walking on the water, and the feeding of the 5,000) prior to Passion Week. These differences between John and the synoptic gospels are not contradictory, but complementary.

Each gospel was written from a unique perspective, for a different audience. As a result, each gospel contains distinctive elements. Taken together, the 4 gospels form a complete testimony about Jesus Christ.

Matthew wrote primarily to a Jewish audience, presenting Jesus of Nazareth as Israel's long-awaited Messiah and rightful King. His genealogy, unlike Luke's, focuses on Jesus' royal bloodline from Israel's greatest king, David. Matthew interspersed Old Testament quotes showing Jesus' life and ministry as the fulfillment of Old Testament messianic prophecy. Only Matthew uses the phrase "kingdom of heaven" to avoid the parallel phrase "kingdom of God" because of its unbiblical connotations in first-century Jewish thought. Matthew wrote his gospel to strengthen the faith of Jewish Christians and to evangelize the Jews.

Mark targeted a Gentile audience, particularly the Romans (see Introduction to Mark: Background and Setting). Mark is the gospel of action; the frequent use of "immediately" and "then" moves his narrative rapidly along. Mark portrayed

Jesus as the Servant who came to suffer for the sins of many (see Mark 10:45). Mark's fast-paced approach appealed to the practical, action-oriented Romans.

Luke addressed a broader Gentile audience. As an educated Greek (see Introduction to Luke: Author and Date), he used the most sophisticated written Greek of any New Testament writer. He was a careful researcher (Luke 1:1–4) and an accurate historian. Luke portrays Jesus as the Son of Man (a title used 26 times), the answer to the needs and hopes of the human race, and the one who came to seek and save lost sinners (Luke 9:56; 19:10).

John, the last gospel written, emphasizes the deity of Jesus Christ (for example, 5:18; 8:58; 10:30–33; 14:9). John wrote to strengthen the faith of believers and to appeal to unbelievers. The apostle clearly stated his purpose for writing in 20:31: ". . . these are written that you may believe that Jesus is the Christ, the Son of God, and that believing you may have life in His name."

Taken together, the 4 gospels paint a complete portrait of the God-Man, Jesus of Nazareth. In Him were blended perfect humanity and deity, making Him the only sacrifice for the sins of the world and the worthy Lord of those who believe.

THE ROMAN EMPIRE IN THE NEW TESTAMENT ERA

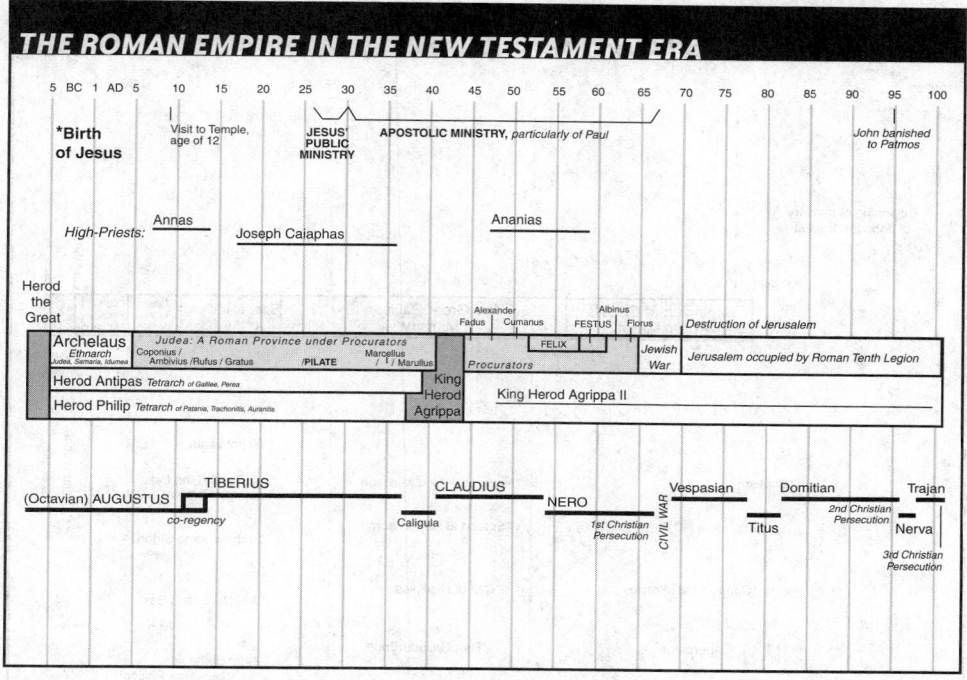

THE MINISTRIES OF THE APOSTLES

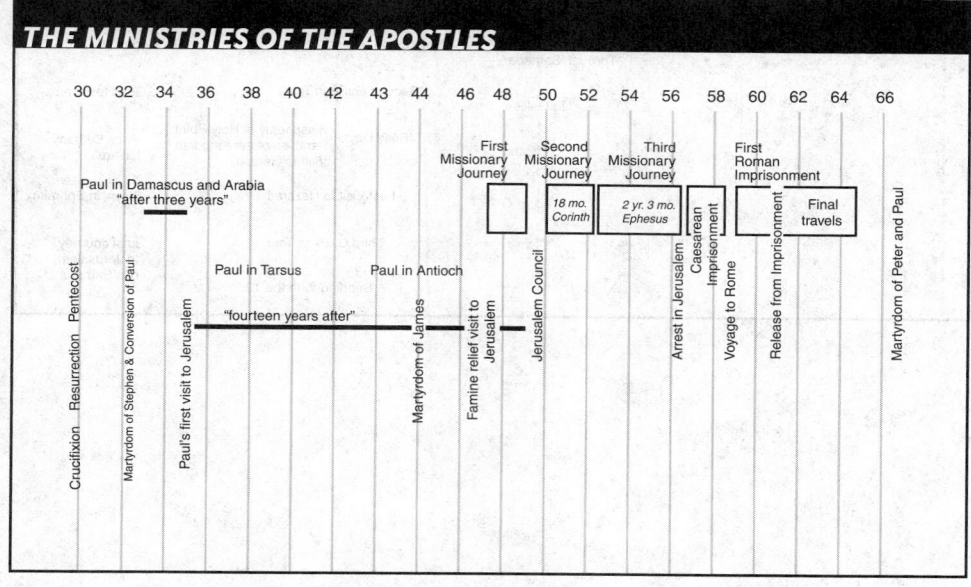

THE MINISTRIES OF JESUS CHRIST

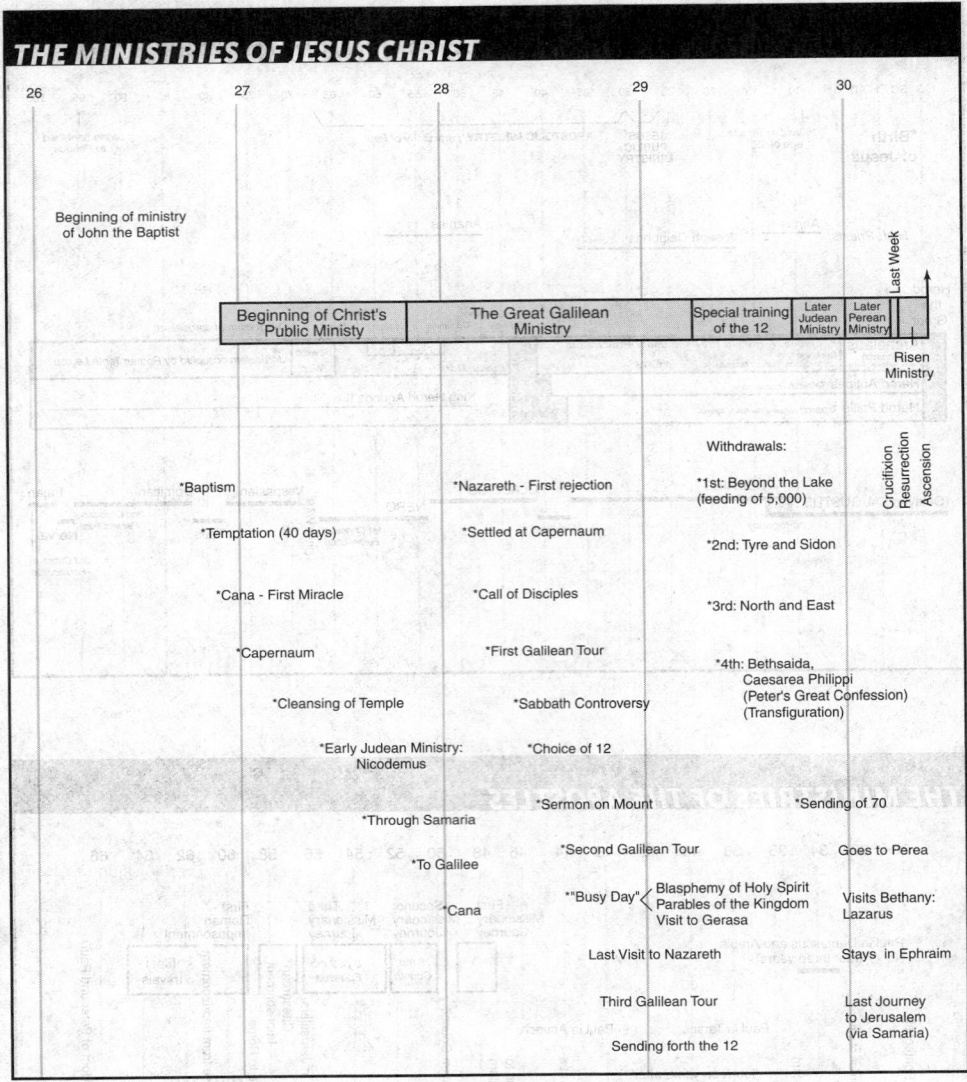

26	27	28	29	30

Beginning of ministry
of John the Baptist

| Beginning of Christ's Public Ministy | The Great Galilean Ministry | Special training of the 12 | Later Judean Ministry | Later Perean Ministry | Last Week |

Risen Ministry

Withdrawals:

*Baptism   *Nazareth - First rejection   *1st: Beyond the Lake
                                                                      (feeding of 5,000)

*Temptation (40 days)   *Settled at Capernaum

                                                                      *2nd: Tyre and Sidon

*Cana - First Miracle   *Call of Disciples

                                                                      *3rd: North and East

*Capernaum   *First Galilean Tour

                                                                      *4th: Bethsaida,
                                                                            Caesarea Philippi
*Cleansing of Temple   *Sabbath Controversy   (Peter's Great Confession)
                                                                            (Transfiguration)

*Early Judean Ministry: *Choice of 12
     Nicodemus

                                  *Sermon on Mount   *Sending of 70

*Through Samaria

                                  *Second Galilean Tour   Goes to Perea

     *To Galilee

                                  *"Busy Day" ⟨ Blasphemy of Holy Spirit   Visits Bethany:
          *Cana   Parables of the Kingdom   Lazarus
                                               Visit to Gerasa

                                  Last Visit to Nazareth   Stays in Ephraim

                                  Third Galilean Tour   Last Journey
                                                                      to Jerusalem
                                                                      (via Samaria)
                                       Sending forth the 12

Crucifixion
Resurrection
Ascension

A HARMONY OF
THE GOSPELS

Part Six: The Ministry of Christ in Galilee

	Matt.	Mark	Luke	John
Reaction of the multitudes	7:28–29			
GROWING FAME AND EMPHASIS ON REPENTANCE				
A certain centurion's faith and the healing of his servant		8:1,5–13		7:1–10
A widow's son raised at Nain			7:11–17	
John the Baptist's relationship to the kingdom	11:2–19		7:18–35	
Woes upon Chorazin and Bethsaida for failure to repent	11:20–30			
Christ's feet anointed by a sinful, but contrite, woman			7:36–50	
FIRST PUBLIC REJECTION BY JEWISH LEADERS				
A tour with the twelve and other followers			8:1–3	
Blasphemous accusation by the scribes and Pharisees	12:22–37	3:20–30		
Request for a sign refused	12:38–45			
Announcement of new spiritual ties	12:46–50	3:31–35	8:19–21	
PARABOLIC MYSTERIES ABOUT THE KINGDOM				
To the Crowds by the Sea				
The setting of the parables	13:1–3a	4:1–2	8:4	
The parable of the soils	13:3b–23	4:3–25	8:5–18	
The parable of the seed's spontaneous growth		4:26–29		
The parable of the tares	13:24–30			
The parable of the mustard tree		13:31–32	4:30–32	
The parable of the leavened loaf	13:33–35	4:33–34		
To the Disciples in the House				
The parable of the tares explained	13:36–43			
The parable of the hidden treasure	13:44			
The parable of the pearl of great price	13:45–46			
The parable of the dragnet	13:47–50			
The parable of the householder	13:51–52			
CONTINUING OPPOSITION				
Departure across the sea and calming the storm	13:53; 8:18,23–27	4:35–41	8:22–25	
Healing the Gerasene demoniacs and resultant opposition	8:28–34	5:1–20	8:26–39	
Return to Galilee, healing of woman who touched Christ's garment, and raising of Jairus' daughter	9:18–26	5:21–43	8:40–56	
Three miracles of healing and another blasphemous accusation	9:27–34			
Final visit to unbelieving Nazareth	13:54–58	6:1–6a		
FINAL GALILEAN CAMPAIGN				
Shortage of workers	9:35–38	6:6b		
Commissioning of the twelve	10:1–42	6:7–11	9:1–5	
Workers sent out	11:1	6:12–13	9:6	
Antipas' mistaken identification of Jesus	14:1–2	6:14–16	9:7–9	
Earlier imprisonment and beheading of John the Baptist	14:3–12	6:17–29		
Return of the workers		6:30	9:10a	

Part Seven: The Ministry of Christ Around Galilee

LESSON ON THE BREAD OF LIFE

	Matt.	Mark	Luke	John
Withdrawal from Galilee	14:13–14	6:31–34	9:10b–11	6:1–3
Feeding the 5,000	14:15–21	6:35–44	9:12–17	6:4–13
A premature attempt to make Jesus king blocked	14:22–23	6:45–46		6:14–15
Walking on the water during a storm at sea	14:24–33	6:47–52		6:16–21
Healings at Gennesaret	14:34–36	6:53–56		
Discourse on the true bread of life				6:22–59
Defection among the disciples				6:60–71

Part Eight: The Later Judean Ministry of Christ

Part Nine: The Ministry of Christ in and around Perea

Part Ten: The Formal Presentation of Christ to Israel and the Resulting Conflict

TRIUMPHAL ENTRY AND THE FIG TREE

OFFICIAL CHALLENGE OF CHRIST'S AUTHORITY

CHRIST'S RESPONSE TO HIS ENEMIES' CHALLENGES

Part Eleven: Prophecies in Preparation for the Death of Christ

THE OLIVET DISCOURSE: PROPHECIES ABOUT THE TEMPLE AND THE RETURN OF CHRIST

ARRANGEMENTS FOR BETRAYAL

THE LAST SUPPER

	Matt.	Mark	Luke	John
DISCOURSE AND PRAYERS FROM THE UPPER ROOM TO GETHSEMANE				
Questions about His destination, the Father, and the Holy Spirit answered				14:1–31
The Vine and the branches				15:1–17
Opposition from the world				15:18–16:4
Coming and ministry of the Spirit				16:5–15
Prediction of joy over His resurrection				16:16–22
Promise of answered prayer and peace				16:23–33
Jesus' prayer for His disciples and all who will believe				17:1–26
Second prediction of Peter's denial	16:30–35	14:26–31	22:39–40a	18:1
Jesus' 3 agonizing prayers in Gethsemane	26:36–46	14:32–42	22:40b–46	

Part Twelve: The Death of Christ

	Matt.	Mark	Luke	John
BETRAYAL AND ARREST				
Jesus betrayed, arrested, and forsaken	26:47–56	14:43–52	22:47–53	18:2–12
TRIAL				
First Jewish phase, before Anna				18:13–24
Second Jewish phase, before Caiaphas and the Sanhedrin	26:57–68	14:53–65	22:54	
Peter's denials	26:69–75	14:66–72	22:55–65	18:25–27
Third Jewish phase, before the Sanhedrin	27:1	15:1a	22:66–71	
Remorse and suicide of Judas Iscariot (Acts 1:18–19)	27:3–10			
First Roman phase, before Pilate	27:2,11–14	15:1b–5	23:1–5	18:28–38
Second Roman phase, before Herod Antipas			23:6–12	
Third Roman phase, before Pilate	27:15–26	15:6–15	23:13–25	18:39–19:16
CRUCIFIXION				
Mockery by the Roman soldiers	27:27–30	15:16–19		
Journey to Golgotha	27:31–34	15:20–23	23:26–33a	19:17
First 3 hours of crucifixion	27:35–44	15:24–32	23:33b–43	19:18–27
Last 3 hours of crucifixion	27:45–50	15:33–37	23:44–45a, 46	19:28–30
Witnesses of Jesus' death	27:51–56	15:38–41	23:45b,47–49	
BURIAL				
Certification of death and procurement of the body	27:57–58	15:42–45	23:50–52	19:31–38
Jesus' body placed in a tomb	27:59–60	15:46	23:53–54	19:39–42
Tomb watched by the women and guarded by the soldiers	27:61–66	15:47	23:55–56	

Part Thirteen: The Resurrection and Ascension of Christ

	Matt.	Mark	Luke	John
THE EMPTY TOMB				
The tomb visited by the women	28:1	16:1		
The stone rolled away	28:2–4			
The tomb found to be empty by the women	28:5–8	16:2–8	24:1–8	20:1
The tomb found the be empty by Peter and John			24:9–11, [12]	20:2–10
THE POST-RESURRECTION APPEARANCES				
Appearance to Mary Magdalene		[16:9–11]		20:11–18
Appearance to the other women	28:9–10			
Report of the soldiers to the Jewish authorities	28:11–15			
Appearance to two disciples traveling to Emmaus		[16:12–13]		24:13–32
Report of the two disciples to the rest (1 Cor. 15:5a)			24:33–35	
Appearance to the 10 assembled disciples		[16:14]	24:36–43	20:19–25

	Matt.	Mark	Luke	John
Appearance to the 11 assembled disciples (1 Cor. 15:5b)				20:26–31
Appearance to the 7 disciples while fishing				21:1–25
Appearance to the 11 in Galilee (1 Cor. 15:6)	28:16–20	[16:15–18]		
Appearance to James, His brother (1 Cor. 15:7)				
Appearance to the disciples in Jerusalem (Acts 1:3–8)			24:44–49	
THE ASCENSION				
Christ's parting blessing and departure (Acts 1:9–12)		[16:19–20]	24:50–53	

AN OVERVIEW OF CHRIST'S MINISTRY

26
winter

PUBLIC MINISTRY OF JOHN

spring

Baptism of Christ

summer

The temptation

fall
27
winter

END OF JOHN'S MINISTRY AND BEGINNING OF CHRIST'S

spring

First Passover in His public ministry

summer

Nicodemus' interview with Christ

fall

Challenge of a spiritual harvest

28
winter

Disciples called

spring

Second Passover (not mentioned in gospels)

summer

MINISTRY IN GALILEE
Feast of Tabernacles; Sabbath controversies

fall

Sermon on the Mount

29

First public rejection; parabolic ministry begun

winter

Final Galilean campaign
Third Passover

spring

The Bread of Life
MINISTRY AROUND GALILEE

summer

Lesson of Messiahship learned and confirmed
Feast of Tabernacles

Fall

LATER JUDEAN MINISTRY

30

Feast of Dedication

winter

MINISTRY IN AND AROUND PEREA

spring

PASSION WEEK
RESURRECTION AND ASCENSION

summer

CHRIST'S PASSION WEEK

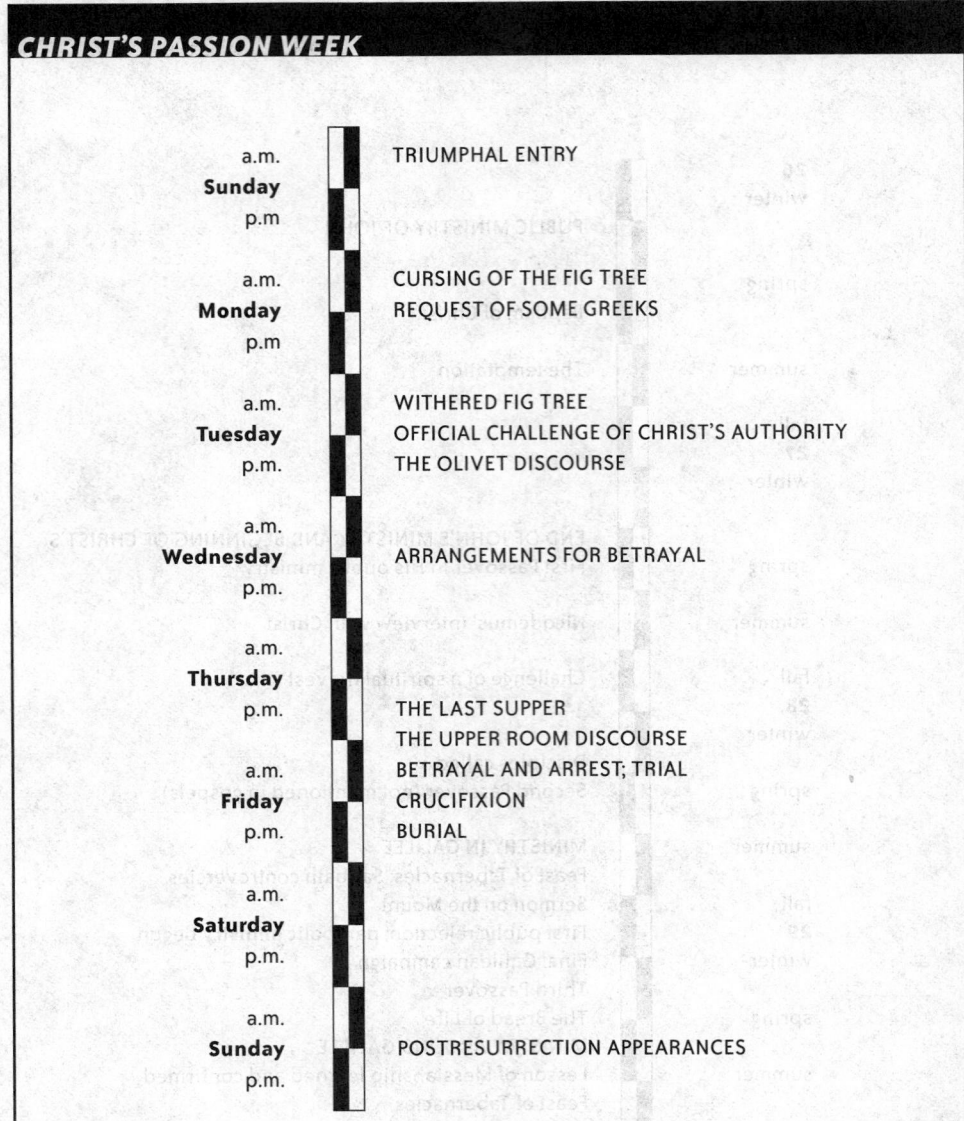

a.m.		TRIUMPHAL ENTRY
Sunday		
p.m		
a.m.		CURSING OF THE FIG TREE
Monday		REQUEST OF SOME GREEKS
p.m		
a.m.		WITHERED FIG TREE
Tuesday		OFFICIAL CHALLENGE OF CHRIST'S AUTHORITY
p.m.		THE OLIVET DISCOURSE
a.m.		
Wednesday		ARRANGEMENTS FOR BETRAYAL
p.m.		
a.m.		
Thursday		
p.m.		THE LAST SUPPER
		THE UPPER ROOM DISCOURSE
a.m.		BETRAYAL AND ARREST; TRIAL
Friday		CRUCIFIXION
p.m.		BURIAL
a.m.		
Saturday		
p.m.		
a.m.		
Sunday		POSTRESURRECTION APPEARANCES
p.m.		

MATTHEW

Although all the gospel writers had the same biography to write, each one approached the subject in a different way. For Matthew, Jesus was the promised King. Matthew backed up this claim by repeatedly pointing out the way that Jesus fulfilled the Old Testament prophecies concerning the Messiah. Matthew particularly focused on teaching his fellow Jews that their hopes had been answered in Jesus.

AUTHOR AND DATE

Matthew was written by Matthew, between A.D. 50 and 70.

One day near Capernaum, Jesus passed Matthew at his tax-collector's table and called him to follow. Matthew, also known as Levi, immediately left everything to join Jesus. But he took with him certain personal characteristics that impacted the gospel he would write. Thus, when writing, he approached his task with an accountant's mind. His version of Christ's life placed a higher priority on categories than on chronology. Consequently, parables, miracles, and sayings tend to be grouped by shared characteristics and not necessarily by when the events occurred.

Matthew also took pains to account for the claims of Christ. He frequently noted the ways that Jesus' words and actions fulfilled prophecy. This disciple put his tax-collecting experience to unique use in compiling one of the biographies of Jesus. Matthew's use of Greek is consistent with that of a Palestinian Jew writing to Hellenistic Jews elsewhere. He wrote as an eyewitness of many of the events he described, giving firsthand testimony about the words and works of Jesus of Nazareth.

This gospel was written at a relatively early date—prior to the destruction of the temple and Jerusalem in A.D. 70. Eusebius (about A.D. 265–339) quoted Origen (about A.D. 185–254) to establish the authorship and authority of Matthew's Gospel:

> Among the four Gospels, which are the only indisputable ones in the Church of God under heaven, I have learned by tradition that the first was written by Matthew, who was once a publican, but afterwards an apostle of Jesus Christ, and it was prepared for the converts from Judaism (*Ecclesiastical History*, 6:25).

BACKGROUND AND SETTING

The Jewish flavor of Matthew's gospel is remarkable. Even the opening genealogies only trace Jesus' lineage as far back as Abraham. In contrast, Luke, who aimed

to show Christ as the Redeemer, follows Jesus' family tree all the way back to Adam. Matthew's purpose was somewhat narrower: to demonstrate that Christ is the King and Messiah of Israel. This gospel quotes more than 60 times from Old Testament prophetic passages, emphasizing how Christ fulfilled all those promises.

The conclusion that Matthew's audience was predominantly Jewish also comes from several other facts: (1) Matthew usually mentions Jewish customs without explaining them, in contrast to the other gospels (see Mark 7:3; John 19:40); (2) Matthew consistently refers to Christ as "the Son of David" (1:1; 9:27; 12:23; 15:22; 20:30; 21:9,15; 22:42,45); (3) Matthew even respects Jewish sensibilities regarding the name of God by using the phrase "the kingdom of heaven" where the other evangelists write "the kingdom of God"; and (4) All the gospel's major themes are rooted in the Old Testament and interpreted in light of Israel's messianic expectations.

Matthew's purpose is clear: to demonstrate that Jesus is the Jewish nation's long-awaited Messiah. His frequent quoting of the Old Testament emphasizes the tie between the Messiah of promise and the Christ of history. This purpose is never out of focus for Matthew. He even points to incidental details from Old Testament prophecies as proofs of Jesus' messianic claims (2:17,18; 4:13–15; 13:35; 21:4,5; 27:9,10).

HISTORICAL AND THEOLOGICAL THEMES

One remarkable characteristic about the gospel of Matthew involves his signature phrase "the kingdom of heaven." It occurs in this gospel 32 times and nowhere else in all of Scripture. This usage emphasizes Matthew's central purpose to set forth Jesus as Messiah, the King of the Jews, whose unique kingdom was promised in the Old Testament.

The opening genealogy in Matthew documents Christ's credentials as Israel's king. The rest of the book underscores this claim. Matthew shows that Christ is the true heir of the kingly line. He demonstrates that Jesus fulfilled dozens of Old Testament prophecies regarding the king who would come. He offers fact after fact to validate Christ's kingly authority and privilege. All other themes in Matthew's gospel flow from this one.

> **MATTHEW'S CENTRAL PURPOSE** WAS TO SET FORTH **JESUS AS MESSIAH,** THE **KING** OF THE **JEWS.**

Among the secondary themes in Matthew, the rejection of the Messiah and the conflict between Jesus and the Pharisees take precedence. In no other gospel are the attacks against Jesus portrayed as strongly as here. From Herod's scheme to kill the newborn Christ (2:13–23), through the frequent clashes with the Pharisees, to the scene at the cross, Matthew paints a vivid portrayal of Christ's rejection by those He came to save. In his account of the crucifixion, for example, no thief repents, and no friends or loved ones are seen at the foot of the cross. Matthew even highlights the fact that God forsook Jesus in His death (27:46). The shadow of rejection is never lifted from the story.

OUTLINE

B. Narrative 4: The Jerusalem Ministry (19:1–23:39)
1. Some kingly lessons (19:1–20:28)
2. Some kingly deeds (20:29–21:27)
3. Some kingly parables (21:28–22:14)
4. Some kingly answers (22:15–46)
5. Some kingly pronouncements (23:1–39)

VI. THE KING'S ATONEMENT (24:1–28:15)

A. Discourse 5: The Olivet Discourse (24:1–25:46)
1. The destruction of the temple (24:1,2)
2. The signs of the times (24:3–31)
3. The parable of the fig tree (24:32–35)
4. The lesson of Noah (24:36–44)
5. The parable of the two servants (24:45–51)
6. The parable of the ten virgins (25:1–13)
7. The parable of the talents (25:14–30)
8. The judgment of the nations (25:31–46)

B. Narrative 5: The Crucifixion and Resurrection (26:1–28:15)
1. The plot to kill the King (26:1–5)
2. Mary's anointing (26:6–13)
3. Judas' betrayal (26:14–16)
4. The Passover (26:17–30)
5. The prophecy of Peter's denial (26:31–35)
6. Jesus' agony (26:36–46)
7. Jesus' arrest (26:47–56)
8. The trial before the Sanhedrin (26:57–68)
9. Peter's denial (26:69–75)
10. Judas' suicide (27:1–10)
11. The trial before Pilate (27:11–26)
12. The soldiers' mocking (27:27–31)
13. The crucifixion (27:32–56)
14. The burial (27:57–66)
15. The resurrection (28:1–15)

VII. (EPILOGUE) THE KING'S ASSIGNMENT (28:16–20)

The first three gospels share so many similarities even in wording. Who copied from whom?

The Problem

Even a cursory reading of Matthew, Mark, and Luke reveals many striking similarities. Compare, for example, Matthew 9:2–8, Mark 2:3–12, and Luke 5:18–26. Significant differences can also be found, however, in the way each writer views the life, ministry, and teaching of Jesus. The question about how to explain these similarities and differences is known as the "Synoptic Problem" (*syn* means "together" and *optic* means "seeing").

The modern solution—even among evangelicals—has been to assume that some form of literary dependence exists between the synoptic gospels. This means that there was some copying between the gospel writers. The most commonly accepted theory to explain such an alleged literary dependence is known as the "Two Source" theory. According to that theory, Mark was the first gospel written, and Matthew and Luke then used Mark as a source in writing their gospels. Proponents of this view suggest an extinct second source, labeled Q (from the German word *Quelle*, meaning "source"), and argue that this no-longer-available source must have supplied the material in Matthew and Luke that does not appear in Mark. They offer the following evidence to support their theory:

1. First, most of Mark is paralleled in Matthew and Luke. Since it is much shorter than Matthew and Luke, the latter must be expansions of Mark.

2. Second, the first three gospels follow the same general chronological outline, but when either Matthew or Luke departs from Mark's chronology, the other agrees with Mark. Put another way, Matthew and Luke do not both depart from Mark's chronology in the same places. That pattern, it is argued, shows that Matthew and Luke used Mark for their historical framework.

3. Third, in passages common to all three gospels, Matthew's and Luke's wording seldom agrees when it differs from Mark's. Proponents of the "Two-Source" theory see this as confirmation that Matthew and Luke used Mark's gospel as a source.

The Answer

The arguments above do not prove that Matthew and Luke used Mark's gospel as a source. In fact, the weight of all the evidence strongly resists such a theory:

1. The nearly unanimous testimony of the church until the nineteenth century was that Matthew was the first gospel written. Such a consistent and impressive chorus cannot be ignored.

2. Why would Matthew, an apostle and eyewitness to the events of Christ's life, depend on Mark (who was not an eyewitness)—even for the account of his own conversion?

3. A careful statistical analysis of the synoptic gospels has revealed that the parallels between them are far less extensive and the differences more significant than is commonly acknowledged. The differences, in particular, argue against literary dependence between gospel writers.

4. Since the gospels record actual historical events, it would be surprising if they did not follow the same general chronological sequence. For example, the fact that three books on American history all discuss the Revolutionary War, the Civil War, World War I, World War II, the Vietnam War, and the Gulf War in the same order would not prove that the authors had read each others' books. General agreement in content does not prove literary dependency.

5. The passages in which Matthew and Luke agree against Mark (see the third argument in favor of the "Two-Source" theory above) amount to about one-sixth of Matthew and one-sixth of Luke. If they used Mark's gospel as a source, there is no satisfactory explanation for why Matthew and Luke would so often both change Mark's wording in the same way.

6. The "Two-Source" theory cannot account for the important section in Mark's gospel (6:45–8:26) that Luke omits. That omission suggests that Luke had not seen Mark's gospel when he wrote.

7. No historical or manuscript evidence exists to confirm the Q document. It is purely a fabrication of modern skepticism and a way to possibly deny the verbal inspiration of the gospels.

8. The theories of literary dependence between the gospel writers are notorious for downplaying the significance of their personal contacts with each other. Mark and Luke were both companions of Paul (Philemon 24). The early church (including Matthew) met for a time in the home of Mark's mother (Acts 12:12). Luke may well have met Matthew during Paul's two year imprisonment at Caesarea. Such contacts make theories of mutual literary dependence unnecessary.

The simplest solution to the Synoptic Problem is that no such problem exists! Because critics cannot prove literary dependency between the gospel writers, there is no need to explain it. The traditional view that the gospel writers were inspired by God and wrote independently of each other—except that all three were moved by the same Holy Spirit (2 Peter 1:20)—remains the only plausible view.

The Genealogy of Jesus Christ

1 The book of the genealogy of Jesus Christ, the Son of David, the Son of Abraham:

²Abraham begot Isaac, Isaac begot Jacob, and Jacob begot Judah and his brothers. ³Judah begot Perez and Zerah by Tamar, Perez begot Hezron, and Hezron begot Ram. ⁴Ram begot Amminadab, Amminadab begot Nahshon, and Nahshon begot Salmon. ⁵Salmon begot Boaz by Rahab, Boaz begot Obed by Ruth, Obed begot Jesse, ⁶and Jesse begot David the king.

> **1:3 Tamar.** It was unusual to name women in genealogies, but Matthew mentioned five: Tamar (v. 3; Gen. 38:13–30), Rahab (v. 5; Josh. 2:1), Ruth (v. 5; Ruth 1:3), Bathsheba ("Uriah's wife," v. 6; 2 Sam. 11), and Mary (v. 16). Each of these women is an example of divine grace.

David the king begot Solomon by her *who had been the wife*ᵃ of Uriah. ⁷Solomon begot Rehoboam, Rehoboam begot Abijah, and Abijah begot Asa.ᵃ ⁸Asa begot Jehoshaphat, Jehoshaphat begot Joram, and Joram begot Uzziah. ⁹Uzziah begot Jotham, Jotham begot Ahaz, and Ahaz begot Hezekiah. ¹⁰Hezekiah begot Manasseh, Manasseh begot Amon,ᵃ and Amon begot Josiah. ¹¹Josiah begot Jeconiah and his brothers about the time they were carried away to Babylon.

> **1:8 Joram begot Uzziah.** Matthew skips over Ahaziah, Joash, and Amaziah between Joram and Uzziah (see 2 Chr. 3:10–12). This is genealogical shorthand used to make a symmetrical threefold division in v. 17.

¹²And after they were brought to Babylon, Jeconiah begot Shealtiel, and Shealtiel begot Zerubbabel. ¹³Zerubbabel begot Abiud, Abiud begot Eliakim, and Eliakim begot Azor. ¹⁴Azor begot Zadok, Zadok begot Achim, and Achim begot Eliud. ¹⁵Eliud begot Eleazar, Eleazar begot Matthan, and Matthan begot Jacob. ¹⁶And Jacob begot Joseph the husband of Mary, of whom was born Jesus who is called Christ.

¹⁷So all the generations from Abraham to David *are* fourteen generations, from David until the captivity in Babylon *are* fourteen generations, and from the captivity in Babylon until the Christ *are* fourteen generations.

Christ Born of Mary

¹⁸Now the birth of Jesus Christ was as follows: After His mother Mary was betrothed to Joseph, before they came together, she was found with child of the Holy Spirit. ¹⁹Then Joseph her husband, being a just *man*, and not wanting to make her a public example, was minded to put her away secretly. ²⁰But while he thought about these things, behold, an angel of the Lord appeared to him in a dream, saying, "Joseph, son of David, do not be afraid to take to you Mary your wife, for that which is conceived in her is of the Holy Spirit. ²¹And she will bring forth a Son, and you shall call His name JESUS, for He will save His people from their sins."

> **1:18 betrothed.** Jewish betrothal was as binding as a modern marriage and could only be broken through divorce. The betrothed couple was legally considered husband and wife, even though physical union had not yet taken place.

²²So all this was done that it might be fulfilled which was spoken by the Lord

---

1:6 ᵃWords in italic type have been added for clarity. They are not found in the original Greek.
1:7 ᵃNU-Text reads *Asaph*.　1:10 ᵃNU-Text reads *Amos*.

Why is Jesus' genealogy in Matthew different from the one in Luke?

The genealogies of Jesus recorded by Matthew and Luke have two significant differences: (1) Matthew's genealogy traces the line of descent through Joseph, while Luke's traces Jesus' ancestry through Mary; and (2) Matthew begins his genealogy with Abraham since his concern has to do with the Jewish connection with Christ and God's plan of salvation. Luke's genealogy begins with Adam and sees Christ's role in the salvation of people.

through the prophet, saying: [23]"*Behold, the virgin shall be with child, and bear a Son, and they shall call His name Immanuel,"* [a] which is translated, "God with us."

> **1:22 that it might be fulfilled.** Matthew often referred to places where OT scriptures were fulfilled (see 2:15,17,23). He quoted from the OT more than 60 times, more frequently than any other NT writer, except Paul in Romans.

[24]Then Joseph, being aroused from sleep, did as the angel of the Lord commanded him and took to him his wife, [25]and did not know her till she had brought forth her firstborn Son.[a] And he called His name JESUS.

Wise Men from the East

2 Now after Jesus was born in Bethlehem of Judea in the days of Herod the king, behold, wise men from the East came to Jerusalem, [2]saying, "Where is He who has been born King of the Jews? For we have seen His star in the East and have come to worship Him."

> **2:1 in the days of Herod the king.** Herod the Great was the first in a dynasty of rulers and is thought to be a descendant of Esau. A ruthless and cunning ruler, he saw the beginning of the rebuilding of the Jerusalem temple under his reign. **wise men from the East.** The number of men is not given, though the 3 gifts can be seen to represent one man each. These men were Magi—magicians and astrologers—not kings.

[3]When Herod the king heard *this*, he was troubled, and all Jerusalem with him. [4]And when he had gathered all the chief priests and scribes of the people together, he inquired of them where the Christ was to be born.

[5]So they said to him, "In Bethlehem of Judea, for thus it is written by the prophet:

[6]   '*But you, Bethlehem, in the land of Judah,*
         Are not the least among the rulers of Judah;

For out of you shall come a Ruler
Who will shepherd My people Israel.' " [a]

[7]Then Herod, when he had secretly called the wise men, determined from them what time the star appeared. [8]And he sent them to Bethlehem and said, "Go and search carefully for the young Child, and when you have found *Him*, bring back word to me, that I may come and worship Him also."

> **2:8 that I may come and worship Him.** Herod actually wanted to kill the Child (vv. 13–18) because he saw Him as a potential threat to his throne.

[9]When they heard the king, they departed; and behold, the star which they had seen in the East went before them, till it came and stood over where the young Child was. [10]When they saw the star, they rejoiced with exceedingly great joy. [11]And when they had come into the house, they saw the young Child with Mary His mother, and fell down and worshiped Him. And when they had opened their treasures, they presented gifts to Him: gold, frankincense, and myrrh. [12]Then, being divinely warned in a dream that they should not return to Herod, they departed for their own country another way.

The Flight into Egypt

[13]Now when they had departed, behold, an angel of the Lord appeared to Joseph in a dream, saying, "Arise, take the young Child and His mother, flee to Egypt, and stay there until I bring you word; for Herod will seek the young Child to destroy Him." [14]When he arose, he took the young Child and His mother by night and departed for Egypt, [15]and was there until the death of Herod, that it might be fulfilled which was spoken by the Lord through the prophet, saying, *"Out of Egypt I called My Son."* [a]

Massacre of the Innocents

[16]Then Herod, when he saw that he was deceived by the wise men, was exceedingly angry; and he sent forth and put to death all the male children who were in Bethlehem

---

1:23 *[a]Isaiah 7:14. Words in oblique type in the New Testament are quoted from the Old Testament.
1:25 [a]NU-Text reads *a Son*.   2:6 [a]Micah 5:2   2:15 [a]Hosea 11:1

and in all its districts, from two years old and under, according to the time which he had determined from the wise men. ¹⁷Then was fulfilled what was spoken by Jeremiah the prophet, saying:

18 "A voice was heard in Ramah,
    Lamentation, weeping, and great
       mourning,
    Rachel weeping for her children,
    Refusing to be comforted,
    Because they are no more." ᵃ

The Home in Nazareth

¹⁹Now when Herod was dead, behold, an angel of the Lord appeared in a dream to Joseph in Egypt, ²⁰saying, "Arise, take the young Child and His mother, and go to the land of Israel, for those who sought the young Child's life are dead." ²¹Then he arose, took the young Child and His mother, and came into the land of Israel.

²²But when he heard that Archelaus was reigning over Judea instead of his father Herod, he was afraid to go there. And being warned by God in a dream, he turned aside into the region of Galilee. ²³And he came and dwelt in a city called Nazareth, that it might be fulfilled which was spoken by the prophets, "He shall be called a Nazarene."

2:23 "He shall be called a Nazarene." Nazareth was an obscure town of lowly reputation; it is not mentioned in the OT. "Nazarene" may mean "branch" in Hebrew, as in Is. 11:1, but it also may be used to describe one who was detestable, as people from that region often were considered in those days (see John 1:46).

John the Baptist Prepares the Way

3 In those days John the Baptist came preaching in the wilderness of Judea, ²and saying, "Repent, for the kingdom of heaven is at hand!" ³For this is he who was spoken of by the prophet Isaiah, saying:

"The voice of one crying in the
    wilderness:
'Prepare the way of the LORD;
    Make His paths straight.'"ᵃ

⁴Now John himself was clothed in camel's hair, with a leather belt around his waist; and his food was locusts and wild honey. ⁵Then Jerusalem, all Judea, and all the region around the Jordan went out to him ⁶and were baptized by him in the Jordan, confessing their sins.

⁷But when he saw many of the Pharisees and Sadducees coming to his baptism, he said to them, "Brood of vipers! Who

2:18 ᵃJeremiah 31:15   3:3 ᵃIsaiah 40:3

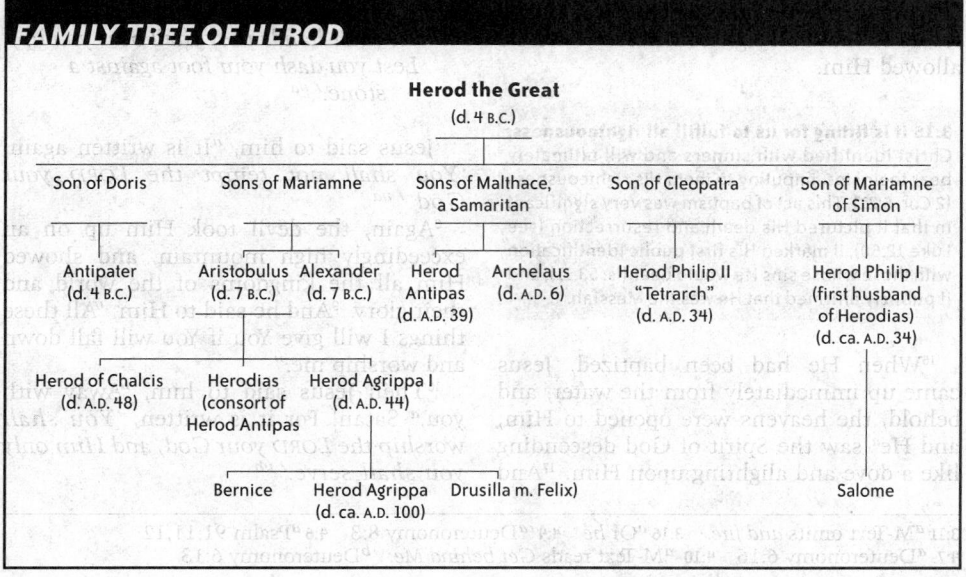

FAMILY TREE OF HEROD

Herod the Great
(d. 4 B.C.)

Son of Doris	Sons of Mariamne	Sons of Malthace, a Samaritan	Son of Cleopatra	Son of Mariamne of Simon
Antipater (d. 4 B.C.)	Aristobulus (d. 7 B.C.) Alexander (d. 7 B.C.)	Herod Antipas (d. A.D. 39) Archelaus (d. A.D. 6)	Herod Philip II "Tetrarch" (d. A.D. 34)	Herod Philip I (first husband of Herodias) (d. ca. A.D. 34)
	Herod of Chalcis (d. A.D. 48) Herodias (consort of Herod Antipas) Herod Agrippa I (d. A.D. 44)			
	Bernice Herod Agrippa (d. ca. A.D. 100) Drusilla m. Felix)			Salome

warned you to flee from the wrath to come? [8]Therefore bear fruits worthy of repentance, [9]and do not think to say to yourselves, 'We have Abraham as *our* father.' For I say to you that God is able to raise up children to Abraham from these stones. [10]And even now the ax is laid to the root of the trees. Therefore every tree which does not bear good fruit is cut down and thrown into the fire. [11]I indeed baptize you with water unto repentance, but He who is coming after me is mightier than I, whose sandals I am not worthy to carry. He will baptize you with the Holy Spirit and fire.[a] [12]His winnowing fan *is* in His hand, and He will thoroughly clean out His threshing floor, and gather His wheat into the barn; but He will burn up the chaff with unquenchable fire."

3:9 Abraham as *our* father. The Sadducees believed that merely being of Abraham's line and members of God's chosen race made them pleasing before God. Abraham's real descendants, however, are those who share his faith (see Rom. 4:16).

John Baptizes Jesus

[13]Then Jesus came from Galilee to John at the Jordan to be baptized by him. [14]And John *tried to* prevent Him, saying, "I need to be baptized by You, and are You coming to me?" [15]But Jesus answered and said to him, "Permit *it to be so* now, for thus it is fitting for us to fulfill all righteousness." Then he allowed Him.

3:15 it is fitting for us to fulfill all righteousness. Christ identified with sinners and will ultimately bear their sins, imputing to them His righteousness (2 Cor. 5:21). This act of baptism was very significant in that it pictured His death and resurrection (see Luke 12:50), it marked His first public identification with those whose sins He would bear (Is. 53:11), and it publicly affirmed that He was the Messiah.

[16]When He had been baptized, Jesus came up immediately from the water; and behold, the heavens were opened to Him, and He[a] saw the Spirit of God descending like a dove and alighting upon Him. [17]And suddenly a voice *came* from heaven, saying, "This is My beloved Son, in whom I am well pleased."

Satan Tempts Jesus

4 Then Jesus was led up by the Spirit into the wilderness to be tempted by the devil. [2]And when He had fasted forty days and forty nights, afterward He was hungry. [3]Now when the tempter came to Him, he said, "If You are the Son of God, command that these stones become bread."

[4]But He answered and said, "It is written, '*Man shall not live by bread alone, but by every word that proceeds from the mouth of God.*'"[a]

4:4 It is written. All 3 of Jesus' responses were taken from Deuteronomy. This reply, taken from Deut. 8:3, taught of God's ability to provide for His people. ***every word that proceeds from the mouth of God.*** God's Word nurtures our spiritual needs for eternal purposes and is more important than food.

[5]Then the devil took Him up into the holy city, set Him on the pinnacle of the temple, [6]and said to Him, "If You are the Son of God, throw Yourself down. For it is written:

'*He shall give His angels charge over you,*'

and,

'*In their hands they shall bear you up, Lest you dash your foot against a stone.*'"[a]

[7]Jesus said to him, "It is written again, '*You shall not tempt the LORD your God.*'"[a] [8]Again, the devil took Him up on an exceedingly high mountain, and showed Him all the kingdoms of the world and their glory. [9]And he said to Him, "All these things I will give You if You will fall down and worship me." [10]Then Jesus said to him, "Away with you,[a] Satan! For it is written, '*You shall worship the LORD your God, and Him only you shall serve.*'"[b]

3:11 [a]M-Text omits *and fire*.   3:16 [a]Or *he*   4:4 [a]Deuteronomy 8:3   4:6 [a]Psalm 91:11,12
4:7 [a]Deuteronomy 6:16   4:10 [a]M-Text reads *Get behind Me*.   [b]Deuteronomy 6:13

[11]Then the devil left Him, and behold, angels came and ministered to Him.

Jesus Begins His Galilean Ministry

[12]Now when Jesus heard that John had been put in prison, He departed to Galilee. [13]And leaving Nazareth, He came and dwelt in Capernaum, which is by the sea, in the regions of Zebulun and Naphtali, [14]that it might be fulfilled which was spoken by Isaiah the prophet, saying:

[15]   *"The land of Zebulun and the land of*
          Naphtali,
       By the way of the sea, beyond the
          Jordan,
       Galilee of the Gentiles:
[16]   *The people who sat in darkness have*
          seen a great light,
       And upon those who sat in the region
          and shadow of death
       Light has dawned." [a]

[17]From that time Jesus began to preach and to say, "Repent, for the kingdom of heaven is at hand."

> **4:17 From that time Jesus began to preach.** His public ministry began here with a message similar to John the Baptist's. **Repent, for the kingdom of heaven is at hand.** Repentance was a constant theme in Jesus' earthly ministry, from beginning to end (see Luke 24:47).

Four Fishermen Called as Disciples

[18]And Jesus, walking by the Sea of Galilee, saw two brothers, Simon called Peter, and Andrew his brother, casting a net into the sea; for they were fishermen. [19]Then He said to them, "Follow Me, and I will make you fishers of men." [20]They immediately left *their* nets and followed Him.

[21]Going on from there, He saw two other brothers, James *the son* of Zebedee, and John his brother, in the boat with Zebedee their father, mending their nets. He called them, [22]and immediately they left the boat and their father, and followed Him.

Jesus Heals a Great Multitude

[23]And Jesus went about all Galilee, teaching in their synagogues, preaching the gospel of the kingdom, and healing all kinds of sickness and all kinds of disease among the people. [24]Then His fame went throughout all Syria; and they brought to Him all sick people who were afflicted with various diseases and torments, and those who were demon-possessed, epileptics, and paralytics; and He healed them. [25]Great multitudes followed Him—from Galilee, and *from* Decapolis, Jerusalem, Judea, and beyond the Jordan.

The Beatitudes

5 And seeing the multitudes, He went up on a mountain, and when He was seated His disciples came to Him. [2]Then He opened His mouth and taught them, saying:

[3]   "Blessed *are* the poor in spirit,
          For theirs is the kingdom of
          heaven.
[4]   Blessed *are* those who mourn,

> **5:3 Blessed.** Jesus described the divine well-being that only belongs to the faithful. The Beatitudes describe how heavenly blessedness is antithetical to worldly standards; that blessedness provides a picture of true faith. **poor in spirit.** This means being able to recognize one's spiritual bankruptcy apart from God and the need for His grace (see Luke 18:13). **theirs is the kingdom of heaven.** Jesus taught that the kingdom is a gracious gift to those who sense their own poverty of spirit.

4:16 [a]Isaiah 9:1,2

Why are three similar gospels necessary?

Readers who examine the gospels carefully, noting the viewpoints of the authors and the details they include, make two important discoveries: (1) The differences between the gospels highlight their independence and their value as part of a complete picture; and (2) The similarities affirm their common subject and message. The accounts are never contradictory, but complementary. When seen together, they present a fuller understanding of Christ.

For they shall be comforted.

5 Blessed *are* the meek,
  For they shall inherit the earth.
6 Blessed *are* those who hunger and
    thirst for righteousness,
  For they shall be filled.
7 Blessed *are* the merciful,
  For they shall obtain mercy.
8 Blessed *are* the pure in heart,
  For they shall see God.
9 Blessed *are* the peacemakers,
  For they shall be called sons of
    God.
10 Blessed *are* those who are persecuted
    for righteousness' sake,
  For theirs is the kingdom of
    heaven.

11"Blessed are you when they revile and persecute you, and say all kinds of evil against you falsely for My sake. 12Rejoice and be exceedingly glad, for great *is* your reward in heaven, for so they persecuted the prophets who were before you.

Believers Are Salt and Light

13"You are the salt of the earth; but if the salt loses its flavor, how shall it be seasoned? It is then good for nothing but to be thrown out and trampled underfoot by men.

14"You are the light of the world. A city that is set on a hill cannot be hidden. 15Nor do they light a lamp and put it under a basket, but on a lampstand, and it gives light to all *who are* in the house. 16Let your light so shine before men, that they may see your good works and glorify your Father in heaven.

Christ Fulfills the Law

17"Do not think that I came to destroy the Law or the Prophets. I did not come to destroy but to fulfill. 18For assuredly, I say to you, till heaven and earth pass away, one jot or one tittle will by no means pass from the law till all is fulfilled. 19Whoever therefore breaks one of the least of these commandments, and teaches men so, shall be called least in the kingdom of heaven; but whoever does and teaches *them*, he shall be

called great in the kingdom of heaven. 20For I say to you, that unless your righteousness exceeds *the righteousness* of the scribes and Pharisees, you will by no means enter the kingdom of heaven.

> **5:20 unless your righteousness exceeds *the righteousness* of the scribes and Pharisees.** Jesus called His disciples to a deeper holiness that surpassed the standard of the day. Pharisees focused on the external appearance and not on the condition of their souls. Jesus challenged them to be internally and externally consistent in line with the spirit of the law. **will by no means enter the kingdom of heaven.** Because sinners are not able to live according to the law, only righteousness from God can provide the means to salvation.

Murder Begins in the Heart

21"You have heard that it was said to those of old, '*You shall not murder,*ᵃ *and whoever murders will be in danger of the judgment.*' 22But I say to you that whoever is angry with his brother without a causeᵃ shall be in danger of the judgment. And whoever says to his brother, 'Raca!' shall be in danger of the council. But whoever says, 'You fool!' shall be in danger of hell fire. 23Therefore if you bring your gift to the altar, and there remember that your brother has something against you, 24leave your gift there before the altar, and go your way. First be reconciled to your brother, and then come and offer your gift. 25Agree with your adversary quickly, while you are on the way with him, lest your adversary deliver you to the judge, the judge hand you over to the officer, and you be thrown into prison. 26Assuredly, I say to you, you will by no means get out of there till you have paid the last penny.

Adultery in the Heart

27"You have heard that it was said to those of old,ᵃ '*You shall not commit adultery.*' ᵇ 28But I say to you that whoever looks at a woman to lust for her has already committed adultery with her in his heart. 29If your right eye causes you to sin, pluck it out and cast *it* from you; for it is more profitable for you that one of your members perish, than for your whole body to be cast

5:21 ᵃExodus 20:13; Deuteronomy 5:17   5:22 ᵃNU-Text omits *without a cause.*   5:27 ᵃNU-Text and M-Text omit *to those of old.*   ᵇExodus 20:14; Deuteronomy 5:18

into hell. ³⁰And if your right hand causes you to sin, cut it off and cast *it* from you; for it is more profitable for you that one of your members perish, than for your whole body to be cast into hell.

Marriage Is Sacred and Binding

³¹"Furthermore it has been said, 'Whoever divorces his wife, let him give her a certificate of divorce.' ³²But I say to you that whoever divorces his wife for any reason except sexual immorality*ᵃ* causes her to commit adultery; and whoever marries a woman who is divorced commits adultery.

> **5:31** *it* **has been said.** The rabbis wrongly understood Deut. 24:1–4 to mean that divorce only required regulated paperwork and could be granted for anything that displeased a man. Moses provided this as a concession to protect the woman who was divorced, not to justify or legalize divorce under all circumstances.

Jesus Forbids Oaths

³³"Again you have heard that it was said to those of old, 'You shall not swear falsely, but shall perform your oaths to the Lord.' ³⁴But I say to you, do not swear at all: neither by heaven, for it is God's throne; ³⁵nor by the earth, for it is His footstool; nor by Jerusalem, for it is the city of the great King. ³⁶Nor shall you swear by your head, because you cannot make one hair white or black. ³⁷But let your 'Yes' be 'Yes,' and your 'No,' 'No.' For whatever is more than these is from the evil one.

Go the Second Mile

³⁸"You have heard that it was said, '*An eye for an eye and a tooth for a tooth.*'ᵃ ³⁹But I tell you not to resist an evil person. But whoever slaps you on your right cheek, turn the other to him also. ⁴⁰If anyone wants to sue you and take away your tunic, let him have *your* cloak also. ⁴¹And whoever compels you to go one mile, go with him two. ⁴²Give to him who asks you, and from him who wants to borrow from you do not turn away.

Love Your Enemies

⁴³"You have heard that it was said, '*You shall love your neighbor*ᵃ *and hate your enemy.*' ⁴⁴But I say to you, love your enemies, bless those who curse you, do good to those who hate you, and pray for those who spitefully use you and persecute you,*ᵃ* ⁴⁵that you may be sons of your Father in heaven; for He makes His sun rise on the evil and on the good, and sends rain on the just and on the unjust. ⁴⁶For if you love those who love you, what reward have you? Do not even the tax collectors do the same? ⁴⁷And if you greet your brethren*ᵃ* only, what do you do more *than others?* Do not even the tax collectors*ᵇ* do so? ⁴⁸Therefore you shall be perfect, just as your Father in heaven is perfect.

> **5:43** *love your neighbor* **and hate your enemy.** The law contains the first half of this statement (Lev. 19:18) and the Pharisees' explanation of the law was the latter part. Jesus' application is the opposite—we should even love our enemies.

Do Good to Please God

6 "Take heed that you do not do your charitable deeds before men, to be seen by them. Otherwise you have no reward from your Father in heaven. ²Therefore, when you do a charitable deed, do not sound a trumpet before you as the hypocrites do in the synagogues and in the streets, that they may have glory from men. Assuredly, I say to you, they have their reward. ³But when you do a charitable deed, do not let your left hand know what your right hand is doing, ⁴that your charitable deed may be in secret; and your Father who sees in secret will Himself reward you openly.*ᵃ*

The Model Prayer

⁵"And when you pray, you shall not be like the hypocrites. For they love to pray standing in the synagogues and on the corners of the streets, that they may be seen by men. Assuredly, I say to you, they have their reward. ⁶But you, when you pray, go

---

5:32 *ᵃ*Or *fornication*   **5:38** *ᵃ*Exodus 21:24; Leviticus 24:20; Deuteronomy 19:21   **5:43** *ᵃ*Compare Leviticus 19:18   **5:44** *ᵃ*NU-Text omits three clauses from this verse, leaving, "*But I say to you, love your enemies and pray for those who persecute you.*"   **5:47** *ᵃ*M-Text reads *friends.* *ᵇ*NU-Text reads *Gentiles.*   **6:4** *ᵃ*NU-Text omits *openly.*

into your room, and when you have shut your door, pray to your Father who *is* in the secret *place;* and your Father who sees in secret will reward you openly.[a] 7And when you pray, do not use vain repetitions as the heathen *do.* For they think that they will be heard for their many words.

8"Therefore do not be like them. For your Father knows the things you have need of before you ask Him. 9In this manner, therefore, pray:

> Our Father in heaven,
> Hallowed be Your name.

6:9 In this manner. This prayer is a model, not merely a liturgy. Of the 6 petitions, 3 are directed toward God (vv. 9–10) and 3 toward human needs (vv. 11–13).

10   Your kingdom come.
      Your will be done
      On earth as *it is* in heaven.
11   Give us this day our daily bread.
12   And forgive us our debts,
      As we forgive our debtors.
13   And do not lead us into temptation,
      But deliver us from the evil one.
      For Yours is the kingdom and the
            power and the glory forever.
            Amen.[a]

14"For if you forgive men their trespasses, your heavenly Father will also forgive you. 15But if you do not forgive men their trespasses, neither will your Father forgive your trespasses.

Fasting to Be Seen Only by God

16"Moreover, when you fast, do not be like the hypocrites, with a sad countenance. For they disfigure their faces that they may appear to men to be fasting. Assuredly, I say to you, they have their reward. 17But you, when you fast, anoint your

6:16,17 when you fast. This indicates that fasting is to be a normal part of one's spiritual life (see 1 Cor. 7:5). It is associated with sadness (9:14,15), charity (Is. 58:3–6), and seeking the Lord's will (Acts 13:2,3).

head and wash your face, 18so that you do not appear to men to be fasting, but to your Father who *is* in the secret *place;* and your Father who sees in secret will reward you openly.[a]

Lay Up Treasures in Heaven

19"Do not lay up for yourselves treasures on earth, where moth and rust destroy and where thieves break in and steal; 20but lay up for yourselves treasures in heaven, where neither moth nor rust destroys and where thieves do not break in and steal. 21For where your treasure is, there your heart will be also.

The Lamp of the Body

22"The lamp of the body is the eye. If therefore your eye is good, your whole body will be full of light. 23But if your eye is bad, your whole body will be full of darkness. If therefore the light that is in you is darkness, how great *is* that darkness!

You Cannot Serve God and Riches

24"No one can serve two masters; for either he will hate the one and love the other, or else he will be loyal to the one and despise the other. You cannot serve God and mammon.

Do Not Worry

25"Therefore I say to you, do not worry about your life, what you will eat or what you will drink; nor about your body, what you will put on. Is not life more than food and the body more than clothing? 26Look at the birds of the air, for they neither sow nor reap nor gather into barns; yet your heavenly Father feeds them. Are you not of more value than they? 27Which of you by worrying can add one cubit to his stature?

28"So why do you worry about clothing? Consider the lilies of the field, how they grow: they neither toil nor spin; 29and yet I say to you that even Solomon in all his glory was not arrayed like one of these. 30Now if God so clothes the grass of the field, which today is, and tomorrow is thrown into the oven, *will He* not much more *clothe* you, O you of little faith?

6:6 [a]NU-Text omits *openly.*   6:13 [a]NU-Text omits *For Yours* through *Amen.*   6:18 [a]NU-Text and M-Text omit *openly.*

³¹"Therefore do not worry, saying, 'What shall we eat?' or 'What shall we drink?' or 'What shall we wear?' ³²For after all these things the Gentiles seek. For your heavenly Father knows that you need all these things. ³³But seek first the kingdom of God and His righteousness, and all these things shall be added to you. ³⁴Therefore do not worry about tomorrow, for tomorrow will worry about its own things. Sufficient for the day *is* its own trouble.

Do Not Judge

7 "Judge not, that you be not judged. ²For with what judgment you judge, you will be judged; and with the measure you use, it will be measured back to you. ³And why do you look at the speck in your brother's eye, but do not consider the plank in your own eye? ⁴Or how can you say to your brother, 'Let me remove the speck from your eye'; and look, a plank *is* in your own eye? ⁵Hypocrite! First remove the plank from your own eye, and then you will see clearly to remove the speck from your brother's eye.

⁶"Do not give what is holy to the dogs; nor cast your pearls before swine, lest they trample them under their feet, and turn and tear you in pieces.

> **7:6 Do not give what is holy to the dogs.** Jesus did not perform miracles for unbelievers (13:58) because it would not have respected what was holy. The point is how to handle the gospel in the face of those who hate the truth.

Keep Asking, Seeking, Knocking

⁷"Ask, and it will be given to you; seek, and you will find; knock, and it will be opened to you. ⁸For everyone who asks receives, and he who seeks finds, and to him who knocks it will be opened. ⁹Or what man is there among you who, if his son asks for bread, will give him a stone? ¹⁰Or if he asks for a fish, will he give him a serpent? ¹¹If you then, being evil, know how to give good gifts to your children, how much more will your Father who is in heaven give good things to those who ask Him! ¹²Therefore, whatever you want men to do to you,

do also to them, for this is the Law and the Prophets.

> **7:12 do also to them.** Other traditional "Golden Rules" before this time were stated in the negative: "What is hateful to yourself do not do to someone else." Jesus made it a positive command and enriched its meaning by underscoring that this statement summarized the entire Law and the Prophets.

The Narrow Way

¹³"Enter by the narrow gate; for wide *is* the gate and broad *is* the way that leads to destruction, and there are many who go in by it. ¹⁴Because*ᵃ* narrow *is* the gate and difficult *is* the way which leads to life, and there are few who find it.

You Will Know Them by Their Fruits

¹⁵"Beware of false prophets, who come to you in sheep's clothing, but inwardly they are ravenous wolves. ¹⁶You will know them by their fruits. Do men gather grapes from thornbushes or figs from thistles? ¹⁷Even so, every good tree bears good fruit, but a bad tree bears bad fruit. ¹⁸A good tree cannot bear bad fruit, nor *can* a bad tree bear good fruit. ¹⁹Every tree that does not bear good fruit is cut down and thrown into the fire. ²⁰Therefore by their fruits you will know them.

I Never Knew You

²¹"Not everyone who says to Me, 'Lord, Lord,' shall enter the kingdom of heaven, but he who does the will of My Father in heaven. ²²Many will say to Me in that day, 'Lord, Lord, have we not prophesied in Your name, cast out demons in Your name, and done many wonders in Your name?' ²³And then I will declare to them, 'I never knew you; depart from Me, you who practice lawlessness!'

Build on the Rock

²⁴"Therefore whoever hears these sayings of Mine, and does them, I will liken him to a wise man who built his house on the rock: ²⁵and the rain descended, the floods came, and the winds blew and beat on that house; and it did not fall, for it was founded on the rock.

7:14 *ᵃ*NU-Text and M-Text read *How . . . !*

26"But everyone who hears these sayings of Mine, and does not do them, will be like a foolish man who built his house on the sand: 27and the rain descended, the floods came, and the winds blew and beat on that house; and it fell. And great was its fall."

28And so it was, when Jesus had ended these sayings, that the people were astonished at His teaching, 29for He taught them as one having authority, and not as the scribes.

> **7:24–28** The house represents a religious life, and the rain represents divine judgment. Only the one obedient to God's Word will stand. Only God's grace can save us, not anything we do on our own.

Jesus Cleanses a Leper

8 When He had come down from the mountain, great multitudes followed Him. 2And behold, a leper came and worshiped Him, saying, "Lord, if You are willing, You can make me clean."

3Then Jesus put out His hand and touched him, saying, "I am willing; be cleansed." Immediately his leprosy was cleansed.

4And Jesus said to him, "See that you tell no one; but go your way, show yourself to the priest, and offer the gift that Moses commanded, as a testimony to them."

Jesus Heals a Centurion's Servant

5Now when Jesus had entered Capernaum, a centurion came to Him, pleading with Him, 6saying, "Lord, my servant is lying at home paralyzed, dreadfully tormented."

7And Jesus said to him, "I will come and heal him."

8The centurion answered and said, "Lord, I am not worthy that You should come under my roof. But only speak a

> **8:8 I am not worthy that You should come under my roof.** Jewish tradition said that a person who entered a Gentile's house became ceremonially unclean (see John 18:28). The centurion most likely acted upon this knowledge and did not want Jesus to suffer such an inconvenience for his sake. He also had faith enough to trust in Jesus' power to heal by merely speaking a word.

word, and my servant will be healed. 9For I also am a man under authority, having soldiers under me. And I say to this one, 'Go,' and he goes; and to another, 'Come,' and he comes; and to my servant, 'Do this,' and he does it."

10When Jesus heard it, He marveled, and said to those who followed, "Assuredly, I say to you, I have not found such great faith, not even in Israel! 11And I say to you that many will come from east and west, and sit down with Abraham, Isaac, and Jacob in the kingdom of heaven. 12But the sons of the kingdom will be cast out into outer darkness. There will be weeping and gnashing of teeth." 13Then Jesus said to the centurion, "Go your way; and as you have believed, so let it be done for you." And his servant was healed that same hour.

Peter's Mother-in-Law Healed

14Now when Jesus had come into Peter's house, He saw his wife's mother lying sick with a fever. 15So He touched her hand, and the fever left her. And she arose and served them.a

Many Healed After Sabbath Sunset

16When evening had come, they brought to Him many who were demon-possessed. And He cast out the spirits with a word, and healed all who were sick, 17that it might be fulfilled which was spoken by Isaiah the prophet, saying:

> "He Himself took our infirmities
> And bore our sicknesses."a

The Cost of Discipleship

18And when Jesus saw great multitudes about Him, He gave a command to depart to the other side. 19Then a certain scribe came and said to Him, "Teacher, I will follow You wherever You go."

20And Jesus said to him, "Foxes have holes and birds of the air have nests, but the Son of Man has nowhere to lay His head."

21Then another of His disciples said to Him, "Lord, let me first go and bury my father."

22But Jesus said to him, "Follow Me, and let the dead bury their own dead."

8:15 aNU-Text and M-Text read Him.   8:17 aIsaiah 53:4

> **8:21 let me first go and bury my father.** This does not mean that the man's father was already dead. This phrase was a common figure of speech meaning, "Let me wait until I receive my inheritance."

Wind and Wave Obey Jesus

²³Now when He got into a boat, His disciples followed Him. ²⁴And suddenly a great tempest arose on the sea, so that the boat was covered with the waves. But He was asleep. ²⁵Then His disciples came to *Him* and awoke Him, saying, "Lord, save us! We are perishing!"

²⁶But He said to them, "Why are you fearful, O you of little faith?" Then He arose and rebuked the winds and the sea, and there was a great calm. ²⁷So the men marveled, saying, "Who can this be, that even the winds and the sea obey Him?"

Two Demon-Possessed Men Healed

²⁸When He had come to the other side, to the country of the Gergesenes,*a* there met Him two demon-possessed *men*, coming out of the tombs, exceedingly fierce, so that no one could pass that way. ²⁹And suddenly they cried out, saying, "What have we to do with You, Jesus, You Son of God? Have You come here to torment us before the time?"

> **8:29 to torment us before the time?** The demons not only recognized the deity of Jesus, but also knew there was a divinely appointed time for their judgment and that He would be their judge.

³⁰Now a good way off from them there was a herd of many swine feeding. ³¹So the demons begged Him, saying, "If You cast us out, permit us to go away*a* into the herd of swine."

³²And He said to them, "Go." So when they had come out, they went into the herd of swine. And suddenly the whole herd of swine ran violently down the steep place into the sea, and perished in the water. ³³Then those who kept *them* fled; and they went away into the city and told everything, including what *had happened* to the demon-possessed *men*. ³⁴And behold, the whole city came out to meet Jesus. And when they saw Him, they begged *Him* to depart from their region.

Jesus Forgives and Heals a Paralytic

9 So He got into a boat, crossed over, and came to His own city. ²Then behold, they brought to Him a paralytic lying on a bed. When Jesus saw their faith, He said to the paralytic, "Son, be of good cheer; your sins are forgiven you."

³And at once some of the scribes said within themselves, "This Man blasphemes!"

⁴But Jesus, knowing their thoughts, said, "Why do you think evil in your hearts? ⁵For which is easier, to say, '*Your* sins are forgiven you,' or to say, 'Arise and walk'? ⁶But that you may know that the Son of Man has power on earth to forgive sins"—then He said to the paralytic, "Arise, take up your bed, and go to your house." ⁷And he arose and departed to his house.

⁸Now when the multitudes saw *it*, they marveled*a* and glorified God, who had given such power to men.

Matthew the Tax Collector

⁹As Jesus passed on from there, He saw a man named Matthew sitting at the tax office. And He said to him, "Follow Me." So he arose and followed Him.

¹⁰Now it happened, as Jesus sat at the table in the house, *that* behold, many tax collectors and sinners came and sat down with Him and His disciples. ¹¹And when the Pharisees saw *it*, they said to His disciples, "Why does your Teacher eat with tax collectors and sinners?"

¹²When Jesus heard *that*, He said to them, "Those who are well have no need of a physician, but those who are sick. ¹³But go and learn what *this* means: '*I desire mercy and not sacrifice.*'*a* For I did not come to call the righteous, but sinners, to repentance."*b*

> **9:13 go and learn what *this* means.** This was a common rebuke for someone who did not know something that they should have known. Citing Hos. 6:6, Jesus emphasized the priority of the law's moral standards over the ceremonial requirements. He was challenging their focus on the external appearance of righteousness while maintaining an internal incongruity with the spirit of the law.

8:28 *a*NU-Text reads *Gadarenes.*   8:31 *a*NU-Text reads *send us.*   9:8 *a*NU-Text reads *were afraid.*   9:13 *a*Hosea 6:6   *b*NU-Text omits *to repentance.*

Jesus Is Questioned About Fasting

[14]Then the disciples of John came to Him, saying, "Why do we and the Pharisees fast often,[a] but Your disciples do not fast?"

[15]And Jesus said to them, "Can the friends of the bridegroom mourn as long as the bridegroom is with them? But the days will come when the bridegroom will be taken away from them, and then they will fast. [16]No one puts a piece of unshrunk cloth on an old garment; for the patch pulls away from the garment, and the tear is made worse. [17]Nor do they put new wine into old wineskins, or else the wineskins break, the wine is spilled, and the wineskins are ruined. But they put new wine into new wineskins, and both are preserved."

> **9:17 new wine into old wineskins.** Animal skins were used for fermentation of wine because of their elasticity. A previously stretched skin lacked elasticity and would rupture, ruining both the wine and the wineskin. This illustrated that the forms of old rituals were not fit for the New Covenant era (see Col. 2:17).

A Girl Restored to Life and a Woman Healed

[18]While He spoke these things to them, behold, a ruler came and worshiped Him, saying, "My daughter has just died, but come and lay Your hand on her and she will live." [19]So Jesus arose and followed him, and so did His disciples.

[20]And suddenly, a woman who had a flow of blood for twelve years came from behind and touched the hem of His garment. [21]For she said to herself, "If only I may touch His garment, I shall be made well." [22]But Jesus turned around, and when He saw her He said, "Be of good cheer, daughter; your faith has made you well." And the woman was made well from that hour.

[23]When Jesus came into the ruler's house, and saw the flute players and the noisy crowd wailing, [24]He said to them, "Make room, for the girl is not dead, but sleeping." And they ridiculed Him. [25]But when the crowd was put outside, He went in and took her by the hand, and the girl arose. [26]And the report of this went out into all that land.

Two Blind Men Healed

[27]When Jesus departed from there, two blind men followed Him, crying out and saying, "Son of David, have mercy on us!"

[28]And when He had come into the house, the blind men came to Him. And Jesus said to them, "Do you believe that I am able to do this?"

They said to Him, "Yes, Lord."

[29]Then He touched their eyes, saying, "According to your faith let it be to you." [30]And their eyes were opened. And Jesus sternly warned them, saying, "See that no one knows it." [31]But when they had departed, they spread the news about Him in all that country.

A Mute Man Speaks

[32]As they went out, behold, they brought to Him a man, mute and demon-possessed. [33]And when the demon was cast out, the mute spoke. And the multitudes marveled, saying, "It was never seen like this in Israel!"

[34]But the Pharisees said, "He casts out demons by the ruler of the demons."

The Compassion of Jesus

[35]Then Jesus went about all the cities and villages, teaching in their synagogues, preaching the gospel of the kingdom, and healing every sickness and every disease among the people.[a] [36]But when He saw the multitudes, He was moved with compassion for them, because they were weary[a] and scattered, like sheep having no shepherd. [37]Then He said to His disciples, "The harvest truly is plentiful, but the laborers are few. [38]Therefore pray the Lord of the harvest to send out laborers into His harvest."

The Twelve Apostles

10 And when He had called His twelve disciples to Him, He gave them power over unclean spirits, to cast them out, and to heal all kinds of sickness and all kinds of disease. [2]Now the names of the twelve apostles are these: first, Simon, who is called Peter, and Andrew his brother; James the son of Zebedee, and John his

---

9:14 [a]NU-Text brackets *often* as disputed.   9:35 [a]NU-Text omits *among the people.*   9:36 [a]NU-Text and M-Text read *harassed.*

brother; [3]Philip and Bartholomew; Thomas and Matthew the tax collector; James the *son* of Alphaeus, and Lebbaeus, whose surname was[a] Thaddaeus; [4]Simon the Cananite,[a] and Judas Iscariot, who also betrayed Him.

> **10:2 the names of the twelve apostles.** The 12 are always listed in a similar order (see Mark 12:16–19), and Peter is always named first. The list contains 3 groups of 4. The subgroups are always listed in the same order, and the first name of each subgroup is always the same. Judas Iscariot is always named last.

Sending Out the Twelve

[5]These twelve Jesus sent out and commanded them, saying: "Do not go into the way of the Gentiles, and do not enter a city of the Samaritans. [6]But go rather to the lost sheep of the house of Israel. [7]And as you go, preach, saying, 'The kingdom of heaven is at hand.' [8]Heal the sick, cleanse the lepers, raise the dead,[a] cast out demons. Freely you have received, freely give. [9]Provide neither gold nor silver nor copper in your money belts, [10]nor bag for *your* journey, nor two tunics, nor sandals, nor staffs; for a worker is worthy of his food.

> **10:8 Freely you have received, freely give.** Jesus gave them power to heal the sick and raise the dead. He instructed them not to use these gifts for monetary gain, but for their ministry. They were permitted to accept gifts from people for their daily needs.

[11]"Now whatever city or town you enter, inquire who in it is worthy, and stay there till you go out. [12]And when you go into a household, greet it. [13]If the household is worthy, let your peace come upon it. But if it is not worthy, let your peace return to you. [14]And whoever will not receive you nor hear your words, when you depart from that house or city, shake off the dust from

> **10:14 hear your words.** The priority was to preach that the King had come and that His kingdom was near. The signs and wonders were to authenticate this message.

your feet. [15]Assuredly, I say to you, it will be more tolerable for the land of Sodom and Gomorrah in the day of judgment than for that city!

Persecutions Are Coming

[16]"Behold, I send you out as sheep in the midst of wolves. Therefore be wise as serpents and harmless as doves. [17]But beware of men, for they will deliver you up to councils and scourge you in their synagogues. [18]You will be brought before governors and kings for My sake, as a testimony to them and to the Gentiles. [19]But when they deliver you up, do not worry about how or what you should speak. For it will be given to you in that hour what you should speak; [20]for it is not you who speak, but the Spirit of your Father who speaks in you.

[21]"Now brother will deliver up brother to death, and a father *his* child; and children will rise up against parents and cause them to be put to death. [22]And you will be hated by all for My name's sake. But he who endures to the end will be saved. [23]When they persecute you in this city, flee to another. For assuredly, I say to you, you will not have gone through the cities of Israel before the Son of Man comes.

[24]"A disciple is not above *his* teacher, nor a servant above his master. [25]It is enough for a disciple that he be like his teacher, and a servant like his master. If they have called the master of the house Beelzebub,[a] how much more *will they call* those of his household! [26]Therefore do not fear them. For there is nothing covered that will not be revealed, and hidden that will not be known.

Jesus Teaches the Fear of God

[27]"Whatever I tell you in the dark, speak in the light; and what you hear in the ear, preach on the housetops. [28]And do not fear those who kill the body but cannot kill the soul. But rather fear Him who is able to destroy both soul and body in hell. [29]Are not two sparrows sold for a copper coin? And not one of them falls to the ground apart from your Father's will. [30]But the very hairs

---

10:3 [a]NU-Text omits *Lebbaeus, whose surname was.*   10:4 [a]NU-Text reads *Cananaean.*
10:8 [a]NU-Text reads *raise the dead, cleanse the lepers;* M-Text omits *raise the dead.*   10:25 [a]NU-Text and M-Text read *Beelzebul.*

of your head are all numbered. ³¹Do not fear therefore; you are of more value than many sparrows.

Confess Christ Before Men

³²"Therefore whoever confesses Me before men, him I will also confess before My Father who is in heaven. ³³But whoever denies Me before men, him I will also deny before My Father who is in heaven.

Christ Brings Division

³⁴"Do not think that I came to bring peace on earth. I did not come to bring peace but a sword. ³⁵For I have come to *'set a man against his father, a daughter against her mother, and a daughter-in-law against her mother-in-law'*; ³⁶and *'a man's enemies will be those of his own household.'ᵃ* ³⁷He who loves father or mother more than Me is not worthy of Me. And he who loves son or daughter more than Me is not worthy of Me. ³⁸And he who does not take his cross and follow after Me is not worthy of Me. ³⁹He who finds his life will lose it, and he who loses his life for My sake will find it.

> **10:38 take his cross.** This is Jesus' first mention of the word "cross" to His disciples. He was demanding their total commitment—even to physical death. This is the same message that they were to include in their preaching to others. For those who come to Christ with self-renouncing faith, there will be true and eternal life (v. 39).

A Cup of Cold Water

⁴⁰"He who receives you receives Me, and he who receives Me receives Him who sent Me. ⁴¹He who receives a prophet in the name of a prophet shall receive a prophet's reward. And he who receives a righteous man in the name of a righteous man shall receive a righteous man's reward. ⁴²And whoever gives one of these little ones only a cup of cold *water* in the name of a disciple, assuredly, I say to you, he shall by no means lose his reward."

John the Baptist Sends Messengers to Jesus

11 Now it came to pass, when Jesus finished commanding His twelve disciples, that He departed from there to teach and to preach in their cities.

²And when John had heard in prison about the works of Christ, he sent two ofᵃ his disciples ³and said to Him, "Are You the Coming One, or do we look for another?"

⁴Jesus answered and said to them, "Go and tell John the things which you hear and see: ⁵*The* blind see and *the* lame walk; *the* lepers are cleansed and *the* deaf hear; *the* dead are raised up and *the* poor have the gospel preached to them. ⁶And blessed is he who is not offended because of Me."

⁷As they departed, Jesus began to say to the multitudes concerning John: "What did you go out into the wilderness to see? A reed shaken by the wind? ⁸But what did you go out to see? A man clothed in soft garments? Indeed, those who wear soft *clothing* are in kings' houses. ⁹But what did you go out to see? A prophet? Yes, I say to you, and more than a prophet. ¹⁰For this is *he* of whom it is written:

> *'Behold, I send My messenger before Your face,*
> *Who will prepare Your way before You.' ᵃ*

¹¹"Assuredly, I say to you, among those born of women there has not risen one greater than John the Baptist; but he who is least in the kingdom of heaven is greater than he. ¹²And from the days of John the Baptist until now the kingdom of heaven suffers violence, and the violent take it by force. ¹³For all the prophets and the law prophesied until John. ¹⁴And if you are willing to receive *it*, he is Elijah who is to come. ¹⁵He who has ears to hear, let him hear!

> **11:11 least...is greater than he.** John was greater than the OT prophets because he witnessed and participated in the fulfillment of their prophecies (see 1 Pet. 1:10,11). All believers after the cross are greater still because they participate in the actual atoning work of Christ.

¹⁶"But to what shall I liken this generation? It is like children sitting in the marketplaces and calling to their companions, ¹⁷and saying:

10:36 ᵃMicah 7:6   11:2 ᵃNU-Text reads *by* for *two of.*   11:10 ᵃMalachi 3:1

'We played the flute for you,
    And you did not dance;
We mourned to you,
    And you did not lament.'

[18]For John came neither eating nor drinking, and they say, 'He has a demon.' [19]The Son of Man came eating and drinking, and they say, 'Look, a glutton and a winebibber, a friend of tax collectors and sinners!' But wisdom is justified by her children."[a]

Woe to the Impenitent Cities

[20]Then He began to rebuke the cities in which most of His mighty works had been done, because they did not repent: [21]"Woe to you, Chorazin! Woe to you, Bethsaida! For if the mighty works which were done in you had been done in Tyre and Sidon, they would have repented long ago in sackcloth and ashes. [22]But I say to you, it will be more tolerable for Tyre and Sidon in the day of judgment than for you. [23]And you, Capernaum, who are exalted to heaven, will be[a] brought down to Hades; for if the mighty works which were done in you had been done in Sodom, it would have remained until this day. [24]But I say to you that it shall be more tolerable for the land of Sodom in the day of judgment than for you."

Jesus Gives True Rest

[25]At that time Jesus answered and said, "I thank You, Father, Lord of heaven and earth, that You have hidden these things from the wise and prudent and have revealed them to babes. [26]Even so, Father, for so it seemed good in Your sight. [27]All things have been delivered to Me by My Father, and no one knows the Son except the Father. Nor does anyone know the Father except the Son, and the one to whom the Son

> **11:28–30 Come to Me, all you who labor and are heavy laden.** The first Beatitude echoes in this passage. This invitation is phrased so that only those who recognize their spiritual bankruptcy and need for grace will respond. Humanity's stubborn rebellion requires God's awakening to see our spiritual need. That is why the work of salvation is described as the sovereign work of God (v. 27).

wills to reveal Him. [28]Come to Me, all you who labor and are heavy laden, and I will give you rest. [29]Take My yoke upon you and learn from Me, for I am gentle and lowly in heart, and you will find rest for your souls. [30]For My yoke is easy and My burden is light."

Jesus Is Lord of the Sabbath

12 At that time Jesus went through the grainfields on the Sabbath. And His disciples were hungry, and began to pluck heads of grain and to eat. [2]And when the Pharisees saw it, they said to Him, "Look, Your disciples are doing what is not lawful to do on the Sabbath!"

[3]But He said to them, "Have you not read what David did when he was hungry, he and those who were with him: [4]how he entered the house of God and ate the showbread which was not lawful for him to eat, nor for those who were with him, but only for the priests? [5]Or have you not read in the law that on the Sabbath the priests in the temple profane the Sabbath, and are blameless? [6]Yet I say to you that in this place there is One greater than the temple. [7]But if you had known what this means, ' I desire mercy and not sacrifice,'[a] you would not have condemned the guiltless. [8]For the Son of Man is Lord even[a] of the Sabbath."

> **12:3 He said.** Jesus pointed out that the Sabbath laws did not restrict deeds of necessity (vv. 3,4), service to God (vv. 5,6), or acts of mercy (vv. 7,8). He affirmed that the Sabbath was made for man's benefit and God's glory. It was never intended to be a yoke of bondage to God's people (Mark 2:27).

Healing on the Sabbath

[9]Now when He had departed from there, He went into their synagogue. [10]And behold, there was a man who had a withered hand. And they asked Him, saying, "Is it lawful to heal on the Sabbath?"—that they might accuse Him.

[11]Then He said to them, "What man is there among you who has one sheep, and if it falls into a pit on the Sabbath, will not lay hold of it and lift it out? [12]Of how much more value then is a man than a sheep?

11:19 [a]NU-Text reads works.   11:23 [a]NU-Text reads will you be exalted to heaven? No, you will be.
12:7 [a]Hosea 6:6   12:8 [a]NU-Text and M-Text omit even.

Therefore it is lawful to do good on the Sabbath." [13]Then He said to the man, "Stretch out your hand." And he stretched *it* out, and it was restored as whole as the other. [14]Then the Pharisees went out and plotted against Him, how they might destroy Him.

Behold, My Servant

[15]But when Jesus knew *it*, He withdrew from there. And great multitudes[a] followed Him, and He healed them all. [16]Yet He warned them not to make Him known, [17]that it might be fulfilled which was spoken by Isaiah the prophet, saying:

> **12:15 healed them all.** There had never before been a person who exhibited such extensive healing power. Christ chose these physical acts to display His deity, thus showing the Messiah's power over the spiritual and physical realms. He did this in a strikingly compassionate way toward those afflicted by sin.

[18]   *"Behold! My Servant whom I have chosen,*
    My Beloved in whom My soul is well pleased!
    I will put My Spirit upon Him,
    And He will declare justice to the Gentiles.
[19]   *He will not quarrel nor cry out,*
    Nor will anyone hear His voice in the streets.
[20]   *A bruised reed He will not break,*
    And smoking flax He will not quench,
    Till He sends forth justice to victory;
[21]   *And in His name Gentiles will trust."* [a]

A House Divided Cannot Stand

[22]Then one was brought to Him who was demon-possessed, blind and mute; and He healed him, so that the blind and[a] mute man both spoke and saw. [23]And all the multitudes were amazed and said, "Could this be the Son of David?"

[24]Now when the Pharisees heard *it* they said, "This *fellow* does not cast out demons except by Beelzebub,[a] the ruler of the demons."

[25]But Jesus knew their thoughts, and said to them: "Every kingdom divided against itself is brought to desolation, and every city or house divided against itself will not stand. [26]If Satan casts out Satan, he is divided against himself. How then will his kingdom stand? [27]And if I cast out demons by Beelzebub, by whom do your sons cast *them* out? Therefore they shall be your judges. [28]But if I cast out demons by the Spirit of God, surely the kingdom of God has come upon you. [29]Or how can one enter a strong man's house and plunder his goods, unless he first binds the strong man? And then he will plunder his house. [30]He who is not with Me is against Me, and he who does not gather with Me scatters abroad.

The Unpardonable Sin

[31]"Therefore I say to you, every sin and blasphemy will be forgiven men, but the blasphemy *against* the Spirit will not be forgiven men. [32]Anyone who speaks a word against the Son of Man, it will be forgiven him; but whoever speaks against the Holy Spirit, it will not be forgiven him, either in this age or in the *age* to come.

> **12:31 the blasphemy *against* the Spirit.** The sin Jesus confronted was the Pharisees' deliberate rejection of that which they knew to be of God (see John 11:48). They could not deny the reality of what the Spirit did through Jesus, so they attributed the acts to Satan (Mark 3:22).

A Tree Known by Its Fruit

[33]"Either make the tree good and its fruit good, or else make the tree bad and its fruit bad; for a tree is known by *its* fruit. [34]Brood of vipers! How can you, being evil, speak good things? For out of the abundance of the heart the mouth speaks. [35]A good man out of the good treasure of his heart[a] brings forth good things, and an evil man out of the evil treasure brings forth evil things. [36]But I say to you that for every idle word men may speak, they will give account of it in the day of judgment. [37]For by your words you will be justified, and by your words you will be condemned."

12:15 [a]NU-Text brackets *multitudes* as disputed.   12:21 [a]Isaiah 42:1–4   12:22 [a]NU-Text omits *blind and.*   12:24 [a]NU-Text and M-Text read *Beelzebul.*   12:35 [a]NU-Text and M-Text omit *of his heart.*

The Scribes and Pharisees Ask for a Sign

[38]Then some of the scribes and Pharisees answered, saying, "Teacher, we want to see a sign from You."

[39]But He answered and said to them, "An evil and adulterous generation seeks after a sign, and no sign will be given to it except the sign of the prophet Jonah. [40]For as Jonah was three days and three nights in the belly of the great fish, so will the Son of Man be three days and three nights in the heart of the earth. [41]The men of Nineveh will rise up in the judgment with this generation and condemn it, because they repented at the preaching of Jonah; and indeed a greater than Jonah *is* here. [42]The queen of the South will rise up in the judgment with this generation and condemn it, for she came from the ends of the earth to hear the wisdom of Solomon; and indeed a greater than Solomon *is* here.

An Unclean Spirit Returns

[43]"When an unclean spirit goes out of a man, he goes through dry places, seeking rest, and finds none. [44]Then he says, 'I will return to my house from which I came.' And when he comes, he finds *it* empty, swept, and put in order. [45]Then he goes and takes with him seven other spirits more wicked than himself, and they enter and dwell there; and the last *state* of that man is worse than the first. So shall it also be with this wicked generation."

> **12:45 the last *state* of that man is worse than the first.** The problem here is that the evil spirit found the house "empty" (v. 44). This describes someone who attempts moral reform without ever being indwelt by the Holy Spirit. Reform, without the help of the Holy Spirit, is not possible and will eventually yield once again to old ways and old habits.

Jesus' Mother and Brothers Send for Him

[46]While He was still talking to the multitudes, behold, His mother and brothers stood outside, seeking to speak with Him. [47]Then one said to Him, "Look, Your mother and Your brothers are standing outside, seeking to speak with You."

[48]But He answered and said to the one who told Him, "Who is My mother and who are My brothers?" [49]And He stretched out His hand toward His disciples and said,

"Here are My mother and My brothers! [50]For whoever does the will of My Father in heaven is My brother and sister and mother."

The Parable of the Sower

13 On the same day Jesus went out of the house and sat by the sea. [2]And great multitudes were gathered together to Him, so that He got into a boat and sat; and the whole multitude stood on the shore.

[3]Then He spoke many things to them in parables, saying: "Behold, a sower went out to sow. [4]And as he sowed, some *seed* fell by the wayside; and the birds came and devoured them. [5]Some fell on stony places, where they did not have much earth; and they immediately sprang up because they had no depth of earth. [6]But when the sun was up they were scorched, and because they had no root they withered away. [7]And some fell among thorns, and the thorns sprang up and choked them. [8]But others fell on good ground and yielded a crop: some a hundredfold, some sixty, some thirty. [9]He who has ears to hear, let him hear!"

> **13:3 parables.** Parables were a common form of teaching in Judaism; they are long analogies in story form. Jesus employed them to obscure the truth from unbelievers while making His teaching clear to His disciples (vv. 11,12). For the unbelievers, this was both an act of judgment and an act of mercy. It kept them in the darkness they loved (see John 3:19), but also spared them from greater condemnation for rejecting more truth than they already knew.

The Purpose of Parables

[10]And the disciples came and said to Him, "Why do You speak to them in parables?"

[11]He answered and said to them, "Because it has been given to you to know the mysteries of the kingdom of heaven, but to them it has not been given. [12]For whoever has, to him more will be given, and he will have abundance; but whoever does not

> **13:11 it has been given to you.** Here Jesus clearly affirmed that the ability to comprehend spiritual truth is a gracious gift of God, sovereignly given to the elect. The reprobate ones are passed over. They reap the natural consequences of their own unbelief and rebellion—spiritual blindness (v. 13).

have, even what he has will be taken away from him. ¹³Therefore I speak to them in parables, because seeing they do not see, and hearing they do not hear, nor do they understand. ¹⁴And in them the prophecy of Isaiah is fulfilled, which says:

'Hearing you will hear and shall not
    understand,
And seeing you will see and not
    perceive;
¹⁵ For the hearts of this people have
    grown dull.
Their ears are hard of hearing,
And their eyes they have closed,
Lest they should see with their eyes
    and hear with their ears,
Lest they should understand with their
    hearts and turn,
So that I should^a heal them.' ^b

¹⁶But blessed *are* your eyes for they see, and your ears for they hear; ¹⁷for assuredly, I say to you that many prophets and righteous *men* desired to see what you see, and did not see *it*, and to hear what you hear, and did not hear *it*.

The Parable of the Sower Explained

¹⁸"Therefore hear the parable of the sower: ¹⁹When anyone hears the word of the kingdom, and does not understand *it*, then the wicked *one* comes and snatches away what was sown in his heart. This is he who received seed by the wayside. ²⁰But he who received the seed on stony places, this is he who hears the word and immedi-

ately receives it with joy; ²¹yet he has no root in himself, but endures only for a while. For when tribulation or persecution arises because of the word, immediately he stumbles. ²²Now he who received seed among the thorns is he who hears the word, and the cares of this world and the deceitfulness of riches choke the word, and he becomes unfruitful. ²³But he who received seed on the good ground is he who hears the word and understands *it*, who indeed bears fruit and produces: some a hundredfold, some sixty, some thirty."

13:22 who received seed among the thorns. These people make superficial commitments without true repentance. They cannot break with the love of money and of the world (see James 4:4).

The Parable of the Wheat and the Tares

²⁴Another parable He put forth to them, saying: "The kingdom of heaven is like a man who sowed good seed in his field; ²⁵but while men slept, his enemy came and sowed tares among the wheat and went his way. ²⁶But when the grain had sprouted and produced a crop, then the tares also appeared. ²⁷So the servants of the owner came and said to him, 'Sir, did you not sow good seed in your field? How then does it have tares?' ²⁸He said to them, 'An enemy has done this.' The servants said to him, 'Do you want us then to go and gather them up?' ²⁹But he said, 'No, lest while you gather up the tares you also uproot the wheat with them. ³⁰Let both grow together until the harvest, and at the time of harvest I will

---

13:15 ^aNU-Text and M-Text read *would.* ^bIsaiah 6:9,10

Why are some events in Matthew in a different order from the order in Mark and Luke?

In general, Matthew presents a topical or thematic approach to the life of Christ. He groups Jesus' teaching into five major discourses:

1. The Sermon on the Mount (chapters 5–7)
2. The commissioning of the apostles (chapter 10)
3. The parables of the kingdom (chapter 13)
4. The childlikeness of the believer (chapter 18)
5. The discourse on His second coming (chapters 24,25).

Matthew makes no attempt to follow a strict chronology. A comparison of the synoptic gospels reveals that he freely placed things out of order. He was dealing with themes and broad concepts, not laying out a timeline. Mark's and Luke's gospels follow a chronological order more closely.

THE PARABLES OF JESUS

Parable	Matthew	Mark	Luke
1. Lamp Under a Basket	5:14–16	4:21,22	8:16,17; 11:33–36
2. A Wise Man Builds on Rock and a Foolish Man Builds on Sand	7:24–27		6:47–49
3. Unshrunk (New) Cloth on an Old Garment	9:16	2:21	5:36
4. New Wine in Old Wineskins	9:17	2:22	5:37,38
5. The Sower	13:3–23	4:2–20	8:4–15
6. The Tares (Weeds)	13:24–30		
7. The Mustard Seed	13:31,32	4:30–32	13:18,19
8. The Leaven	13:33		13:20,21
9. The Hidden Treasure	13:44		
10. The Pearl of Great Price	13:45,46		
11. The Dragnet	13:47–50		
12. The Lost Sheep	18:12–14		15:3–7
13. The Unforgiving Servant	18:23–35		
14. The Workers in the Vineyard	20:1–16		
15. The Two Sons	21:28–32		
16. The Wicked Vinedressers	21:33–45	12:1–12	20:9–19
17. The Wedding Feast	22:2–14		
18. The Fig Tree	24:32–44	13:28–32	21:29–33
19. The Wise and Foolish Virgins	25:1–13		
20. The Talents	25:14–30		
21. The Growing Seed		4:26–29	
22. The Absent Householder		13:33–37	
23. The Creditor and Two Debtors			7:41–43
24. The Good Samaritan			10:30–37
25. A Friend in Need			11:5–13
26. The Rich Fool			12:16–21
27. The Watchful Servants			12:35–40
28. The Faithful Servant and the Evil Servant			12:42–48
29. The Barren Fig Tree			13:6–9
30. The Great Supper			14:16–24
31. Building a Tower and a King Making War			14:25–35
32. The Lost Coin			15:8–10
33. The Lost Son			15:11–32
34. The Unjust Steward			16:1–13
35. The Rich Man and Lazarus			16:19–31
36. Unprofitable Servants			17:7–10
37. The Persistent Widow			18:1–8
38. The Pharisee and the Tax Collector			18:9–14
39. The Minas (Pounds)			19:11–27

John F. MacArthur, Jr., *The MacArthur Study Bible*, (Dallas: Word Publishing) 1997.

say to the reapers, "First gather together the tares and bind them in bundles to burn them, but gather the wheat into my barn." ' "

The Parable of the Mustard Seed

³¹Another parable He put forth to them, saying: "The kingdom of heaven is like a mustard seed, which a man took and sowed in his field, ³²which indeed is the least of all the seeds; but when it is grown it is greater than the herbs and becomes a tree, so that the birds of the air come and nest in its branches."

The Parable of the Leaven

³³Another parable He spoke to them: "The kingdom of heaven is like leaven, which a woman took and hid in three measures*a* of meal till it was all leavened."

Prophecy and the Parables

³⁴All these things Jesus spoke to the multitude in parables; and without a parable He did not speak to them, ³⁵that it might be fulfilled which was spoken by the prophet, saying:

"I will open My mouth in parables;
I will utter things kept secret from the
foundation of the world." *a*

The Parable of the Tares Explained

³⁶Then Jesus sent the multitude away and went into the house. And His disciples came to Him, saying, "Explain to us the parable of the tares of the field."

³⁷He answered and said to them: "He who sows the good seed is the Son of Man. ³⁸The field is the world, the good seeds are the sons of the kingdom, but the tares are the sons of the wicked *one*. ³⁹The enemy who sowed them is the devil, the harvest is the end of the age, and the reapers are the angels. ⁴⁰Therefore as the tares are gathered and burned in the fire, so it will be at the end of this age. ⁴¹The Son of Man will send out His angels, and they will gather out of His kingdom all things that offend, and those who practice lawlessness, ⁴²and will cast them into the furnace of fire. There

will be wailing and gnashing of teeth. ⁴³Then the righteous will shine forth as the sun in the kingdom of their Father. He who has ears to hear, let him hear!

The Parable of the Hidden Treasure

⁴⁴"Again, the kingdom of heaven is like treasure hidden in a field, which a man found and hid; and for joy over it he goes and sells all that he has and buys that field.

The Parable of the Pearl of Great Price

⁴⁵"Again, the kingdom of heaven is like a merchant seeking beautiful pearls, ⁴⁶who, when he had found one pearl of great price, went and sold all that he had and bought it.

13:44–46 Both of these parables picture salvation as something hidden from most people, but so valuable that those who understand are willing to give up all they have to possess it.

The Parable of the Dragnet

⁴⁷"Again, the kingdom of heaven is like a dragnet that was cast into the sea and gathered some of every kind, ⁴⁸which, when it was full, they drew to shore; and they sat down and gathered the good into vessels, but threw the bad away. ⁴⁹So it will be at the end of the age. The angels will come forth, separate the wicked from among the just, ⁵⁰and cast them into the furnace of fire. There will be wailing and gnashing of teeth."

⁵¹Jesus said to them,*a* "Have you understood all these things?"

They said to Him, "Yes, Lord."*b*

⁵²Then He said to them, "Therefore every scribe instructed concerning*a* the kingdom of heaven is like a householder who brings out of his treasure *things* new and old."

Jesus Rejected at Nazareth

⁵³Now it came to pass, when Jesus had finished these parables, that He departed from there. ⁵⁴When He had come to His own country, He taught them in their synagogue, so that they were astonished and said, "Where did this *Man* get this wisdom and *these* mighty works? ⁵⁵Is this not the

---

13:33 *a*Greek *sata*, approximately two pecks in all   13:35 *a*Psalm 78:2   13:51 *a*NU-Text omits *Jesus* said to them.   *b*NU-Text omits *Lord*.   13:52 *a*Or *for*

carpenter's son? Is not His mother called Mary? And His brothers James, Joses,[a] Simon, and Judas? ⁵⁶And His sisters, are they not all with us? Where then did this *Man* get all these things?" ⁵⁷So they were offended at Him.

> **13:57 A prophet...in his own country.** This is like the saying, "familiarity breeds contempt." Jesus was known as a boy from town, and the people concluded that He could not be anyone special.

But Jesus said to them, "A prophet is not without honor except in his own country and in his own house." ⁵⁸Now He did not do many mighty works there because of their unbelief.

John the Baptist Beheaded

14 At that time Herod the tetrarch heard the report about Jesus ²and said to his servants, "This is John the Baptist; he is risen from the dead, and therefore these powers are at work in him." ³For Herod had laid hold of John and bound him, and put *him* in prison for the sake of Herodias, his brother Philip's wife. ⁴Because John had said to him, "It is not lawful for you to have her." ⁵And although he wanted to put him to death, he feared the multitude, because they counted him as a prophet.

> **14:3 Herodias, his brother Philip's wife.** She was the daughter of Aristobulus, another son of Herod the Great; when she married Philip, she married her own father's brother. Herod Antipas (another of Herodias's uncles) talked Herodias into leaving her husband (his brother) in order to marry him (Mark 6:17)—thus compounding the incest. John the Baptist's outrage at this landed him in prison and eventually caused his execution.

⁶But when Herod's birthday was celebrated, the daughter of Herodias danced before them and pleased Herod. ⁷Therefore he promised with an oath to give her whatever she might ask.

⁸So she, having been prompted by her mother, said, "Give me John the Baptist's head here on a platter."

⁹And the king was sorry; nevertheless, because of the oaths and because of those who sat with him, he commanded *it* to be given to *her*. ¹⁰So he sent and had John beheaded in prison. ¹¹And his head was brought on a platter and given to the girl, and she brought *it* to her mother. ¹²Then his disciples came and took away the body and buried it, and went and told Jesus.

Feeding the Five Thousand

¹³When Jesus heard *it*, He departed from there by boat to a deserted place by Himself. But when the multitudes heard it, they followed Him on foot from the cities. ¹⁴And when Jesus went out He saw a great multitude; and He was moved with compassion for them, and healed their sick. ¹⁵When it was evening, His disciples came to Him, saying, "This is a deserted place, and the hour is already late. Send the multitudes away, that they may go into the villages and buy themselves food."

¹⁶But Jesus said to them, "They do not need to go away. You give them something to eat."

> **14:16 give them something to eat.** Jesus knew that His disciples did not have enough food to feed the crowd. He wanted the disciples to state it plainly so the record would be clear that a miracle occurred by His power (vv. 17,18).

¹⁷And they said to Him, "We have here only five loaves and two fish."

¹⁸He said, "Bring them here to Me." ¹⁹Then He commanded the multitudes to sit down on the grass. And He took the five loaves and the two fish, and looking up to heaven, He blessed and broke and gave the loaves to the disciples; and the disciples gave to the multitudes. ²⁰So they all ate and were filled, and they took up twelve baskets full of the fragments that remained. ²¹Now those who had eaten were about five thousand men, besides women and children.

Jesus Walks on the Sea

²²Immediately Jesus made His disciples get into the boat and go before Him to the other side, while He sent the multitudes away. ²³And when He had sent the multitudes away, He went up on the mountain by Himself to pray. Now when evening

---

13:55 ᵃNU-Text reads *Joseph.*

came, He was alone there. ²⁴But the boat was now in the middle of the sea,ᵃ tossed by the waves, for the wind was contrary.

²⁵Now in the fourth watch of the night Jesus went to them, walking on the sea. ²⁶And when the disciples saw Him walking on the sea, they were troubled, saying, "It is a ghost!" And they cried out for fear.

²⁷But immediately Jesus spoke to them, saying, "Be of good cheer! It is I; do not be afraid."

²⁸And Peter answered Him and said, "Lord, if it is You, command me to come to You on the water."

²⁹So He said, "Come." And when Peter had come down out of the boat, he walked on the water to go to Jesus. ³⁰But when he saw that the wind *was* boisterous,ᵃ he was afraid; and beginning to sink he cried out, saying, "Lord, save me!"

³¹And immediately Jesus stretched out *His* hand and caught him, and said to him, "O you of little faith, why did you doubt?" ³²And when they got into the boat, the wind ceased.

³³Then those who were in the boat came andᵃ worshiped Him, saying, "Truly You are the Son of God."

Many Touch Him and Are Made Well

³⁴When they had crossed over, they came to the land ofᵃ Gennesaret. ³⁵And when the men of that place recognized Him, they sent out into all that surrounding region, brought to Him all who were sick, ³⁶and begged Him that they might only touch the hem of His garment. And as many as touched *it* were made perfectly well.

Defilement Comes from Within

15 Then the scribes and Pharisees who were from Jerusalem came to Jesus, saying, ²"Why do Your disciples transgress the tradition of the elders? For they do not wash their hands when they eat bread."

³He answered and said to them, "Why do you also transgress the commandment of God because of your tradition? ⁴For God

commanded, saying, '*Honor your father and your mother*';ᵃ and, '*He who curses father or mother, let him be put to death.*'ᵇ ⁵But you say, 'Whoever says to his father or mother, "Whatever profit you might have received from me *is* a gift *to God*"— ⁶then he need not honor his father or mother.'ᵃ Thus you have made the commandmentᵇ of God of no effect by your tradition. ⁷Hypocrites! Well did Isaiah prophesy about you, saying:

⁸   '*These people draw near to Me with*
        their mouth,
      *And*ᵃ *honor Me with their lips,*
      But their heart is far from Me.
⁹   *And in vain they worship Me,*
        Teaching as doctrines the
        commandments of men.' "ᵃ

¹⁰When He had called the multitude to *Himself*, He said to them, "Hear and understand: ¹¹Not what goes into the mouth defiles a man; but what comes out of the mouth, this defiles a man."

> **15:11 what comes out of the mouth, this defiles a man.** Jesus distinguished between the law's ceremonial requirements and its sacred moral standard. Ceremonial defilement could be dealt with through ceremonial means, but moral defilement corrupts a person's soul.

¹²Then His disciples came and said to Him, "Do You know that the Pharisees were offended when they heard this saying?"

¹³But He answered and said, "Every plant which My heavenly Father has not planted will be uprooted. ¹⁴Let them alone. They are blind leaders of the blind. And if the blind leads the blind, both will fall into a ditch."

¹⁵Then Peter answered and said to Him, "Explain this parable to us."

¹⁶So Jesus said, "Are you also still without understanding? ¹⁷Do you not yet understand that whatever enters the mouth goes into the stomach and is eliminated? ¹⁸But

---

14:24 ᵃNU-Text reads *many furlongs away from the land.*   14:30 ᵃNU-Text brackets *that* and *boisterous* as disputed.   14:33 ᵃNU-Text omits *came and.*   14:34 ᵃNU-Text reads *came to land at.*   15:4 ᵃExodus 20:12; Deuteronomy 5:16   ᵇExodus 21:17   15:6 ᵃNU-Text omits *or mother.*   ᵇNU-Text reads *word.*   15:8 ᵃNU-Text omits *draw near to Me with their mouth, And.*   15:9 ᵃIsaiah 29:13

those things which proceed out of the mouth come from the heart, and they defile a man. [19]For out of the heart proceed evil thoughts, murders, adulteries, fornications, thefts, false witness, blasphemies. [20]These are *the things* which defile a man, but to eat with unwashed hands does not defile a man."

A Gentile Shows Her Faith

[21]Then Jesus went out from there and departed to the region of Tyre and Sidon. [22]And behold, a woman of Canaan came from that region and cried out to Him, saying, "Have mercy on me, O Lord, Son of David! My daughter is severely demon-possessed."

[23]But He answered her not a word.

And His disciples came and urged Him, saying, "Send her away, for she cries out after us."

[24]But He answered and said, "I was not sent except to the lost sheep of the house of Israel."

[25]Then she came and worshiped Him, saying, "Lord, help me!"

[26]But He answered and said, "It is not good to take the children's bread and throw *it* to the little dogs."

> **15:26 the children's bread.** The lost sheep of the house of Israel must be fed before the "little dogs" would be fed. Jesus' words are not to be understood as harsh or unfeeling. In fact, He was drawing from the woman an expression of her faith (v. 27).

[27]And she said, "Yes, Lord, yet even the little dogs eat the crumbs which fall from their masters' table."

[28]Then Jesus answered and said to her, "O woman, great *is* your faith! Let it be to you as you desire." And her daughter was healed from that very hour.

Jesus Heals Great Multitudes

[29]Jesus departed from there, skirted the Sea of Galilee, and went up on the mountain and sat down there. [30]Then great multitudes came to Him, having with them *the* lame, blind, mute, maimed, and many others; and they laid them down at Jesus' feet, and He healed them. [31]So the multitude marveled when they saw *the* mute speaking, *the* maimed made whole, *the* lame walking, and *the* blind seeing; and they glorified the God of Israel.

Feeding the Four Thousand

[32]Now Jesus called His disciples to *Himself* and said, "I have compassion on the multitude, because they have now continued with Me three days and have nothing to eat. And I do not want to send them away hungry, lest they faint on the way."

[33]Then His disciples said to Him, "Where could we get enough bread in the wilderness to fill such a great multitude?"

[34]Jesus said to them, "How many loaves do you have?"

And they said, "Seven, and a few little fish."

[35]So He commanded the multitude to sit down on the ground. [36]And He took the seven loaves and the fish and gave thanks, broke *them* and gave *them* to His disciples; and the disciples *gave* to the multitude. [37]So they all ate and were filled, and they took up seven large baskets full of the fragments that were left. [38]Now those who ate were four thousand men, besides women and children. [39]And He sent away the multitude, got into the boat, and came to the region of Magdala.[a]

The Pharisees and Sadducees Seek a Sign

16 Then the Pharisees and Sadducees came, and testing Him asked that He would show them a sign from heaven. [2]He answered and said to them, "When it is evening you say, '*It will be* fair weather, for the sky is red'; [3]and in the morning, '*It will be* foul weather today, for the sky is red and threatening.' Hypocrites![a] You know how to discern the face of the sky, but you cannot *discern* the signs of the times. [4]A wicked and adulterous generation seeks after a sign, and no sign shall be given to it except the sign of the prophet[a] Jonah." And He left them and departed.

The Leaven of the Pharisees and Sadducees

[5]Now when His disciples had come to the other side, they had forgotten to take bread. [6]Then Jesus said to them, "Take heed and

---

15:39 [a]NU-Text reads *Magadan*.   16:3 [a]NU-Text omits *Hypocrites*.   16:4 [a]NU-Text omits *the prophet*.

beware of the leaven of the Pharisees and the Sadducees."

> **16:6 the leaven of the Pharisees and Sadducees.**
> When Jesus warned of this dangerous influence, the disciples thought He was talking about bread. Again, He reminded them that the Lord provided plenty of bread, so they did not need the bread the Pharisees were offering. How soon the disciples forgot the miracles.

[7]And they reasoned among themselves, saying, "It is because we have taken no bread."

[8]But Jesus, being aware of it, said to them, "O you of little faith, why do you reason among yourselves because you have brought no bread?[a] [9]Do you not yet understand, or remember the five loaves of the five thousand and how many baskets you took up? [10]Nor the seven loaves of the four thousand and how many large baskets you took up? [11]How is it you do not understand that I did not speak to you concerning bread?—but to beware of the leaven of the Pharisees and Sadducees." [12]Then they understood that He did not tell them to beware of the leaven of bread, but of the doctrine of the Pharisees and Sadducees.

Peter Confesses Jesus as the Christ

[13]When Jesus came into the region of Caesarea Philippi, He asked His disciples, saying, "Who do men say that I, the Son of Man, am?"

[14]So they said, "Some say John the Baptist, some Elijah, and others Jeremiah or one of the prophets."

[15]He said to them, "But who do you say that I am?"

[16]Simon Peter answered and said, "You are the Christ, the Son of the living God."

[17]Jesus answered and said to him, "Blessed are you, Simon Bar-Jonah, for flesh and blood has not revealed this to you, but My Father who is in heaven. [18]And I also say to you that you are Peter, and on this rock I will build My church, and the gates of Hades shall not prevail against it. [19]And I will give you the keys of the kingdom of heaven, and whatever you bind on earth will be bound in heaven, and whatever you loose on earth will be loosed[a] in heaven."

> **16:17 flesh and blood has not revealed this to you.**
> Christ's messianic claims were always subtle allusions to OT prophecies and were coupled with miraculous works to substantiate those claims. Never before had He revealed His full identity to Peter and the apostles. God had opened Peter's spiritual eyes to see Jesus for who He truly is and the significance of this reality. Peter's confession was a statement of faith.

[20]Then He commanded His disciples that they should tell no one that He was Jesus the Christ.

Jesus Predicts His Death and Resurrection

[21]From that time Jesus began to show to His disciples that He must go to Jerusalem, and suffer many things from the elders and chief priests and scribes, and be killed, and be raised the third day.

[22]Then Peter took Him aside and began to rebuke Him, saying, "Far be it from You, Lord; this shall not happen to You!"

[23]But He turned and said to Peter, "Get behind Me, Satan! You are an offense to Me, for you are not mindful of the things of God, but the things of men."

> **16:23 "Get behind Me, Satan!"** Jesus suggested that Peter was being a mouthpiece for Satan. Jesus' death was part of His sovereign plan (Acts 2:23). Christ had come to die as an atonement for sin (John 12:27). Those who would thwart His mission were doing Satan's work.

Take Up the Cross and Follow Him

[24]Then Jesus said to His disciples, "If anyone desires to come after Me, let him deny himself, and take up his cross, and follow Me. [25]For whoever desires to save his life will lose it, but whoever loses his life for My sake will find it. [26]For what profit is it to a man if he gains the whole world, and loses his own soul? Or what will a man give in exchange for his soul? [27]For the Son of Man will come in the glory of His Father with His angels, and then He will reward each according to his works.

16:8 [a]NU-Text reads you have no bread.   **16:19** [a]Or will have been bound . . . will have been loosed

Jesus Transfigured on the Mount

[28]Assuredly, I say to you, there are some standing here who shall not taste death till they see the Son of Man coming in His kingdom."

17 Now after six days Jesus took Peter, James, and John his brother, led them up on a high mountain by themselves; [2]and He was transfigured before them. His face shone like the sun, and His clothes became as white as the light. [3]And behold, Moses and Elijah appeared to them, talking with Him. [4]Then Peter answered and said to Jesus, "Lord, it is good for us to be here; if You wish, let us[a] make here three tabernacles: one for You, one for Moses, and one for Elijah."

> **17:2,3 transfigured.** Christ underwent a dramatic change in appearance so the disciples could behold Him in His glory. **Moses and Elijah.** They represented the Law and the Prophets respectively. Both of them foretold Christ's death, and that is what Luke says the 3 of them were discussing (Luke 9:31).

[5]While he was still speaking, behold, a bright cloud overshadowed them; and suddenly a voice came out of the cloud, saying, "This is My beloved Son, in whom I am well pleased. Hear Him!" [6]And when the disciples heard *it*, they fell on their faces and were greatly afraid. [7]But Jesus came and touched them and said, "Arise, and do not be afraid." [8]When they had lifted up their eyes, they saw no one but Jesus only.

[9]Now as they came down from the mountain, Jesus commanded them, saying, "Tell the vision to no one until the Son of Man is risen from the dead."

[10]And His disciples asked Him, saying, "Why then do the scribes say that Elijah must come first?"

[11]Jesus answered and said to them, "Indeed, Elijah is coming first[a] and will restore all things. [12]But I say to you that Elijah has come already, and they did not know him but did to him whatever they wished. Likewise the Son of Man is also about to suffer at their hands." [13]Then the disciples understood that He spoke to them of John the Baptist.

A Boy Is Healed

[14]And when they had come to the multitude, a man came to Him, kneeling down to Him and saying, [15]"Lord, have mercy on my son, for he is an epileptic[a] and suffers severely; for he often falls into the fire and often into the water. [16]So I brought him to Your disciples, but they could not cure him."

[17]Then Jesus answered and said, "O faithless and perverse generation, how long shall I be with you? How long shall I bear with you? Bring him here to Me." [18]And Jesus rebuked the demon, and it came out of him; and the child was cured from that very hour.

[19]Then the disciples came to Jesus privately and said, "Why could we not cast it out?"

> **17:19 "Why could we not cast it out?"** Less than a year after being successful in similar missions to heal and cast out demons, these disciples failed in this attempt. Christ's explanation was that their faith was deficient (v. 20), not their confidence. The problem lay in their failure to make God—rather than their own gifts—the object of their confidence.

[20]So Jesus said to them, "Because of your unbelief;[a] for assuredly, I say to you, if you have faith as a mustard seed, you will say to this mountain, 'Move from here to there,' and it will move; and nothing will be impossible for you. [21]However, this kind does not go out except by prayer and fasting."[a]

Jesus Again Predicts His Death and Resurrection

[22]Now while they were staying[a] in Galilee, Jesus said to them, "The Son of Man is about to be betrayed into the hands of men, [23]and they will kill Him, and the third day He will be raised up." And they were exceedingly sorrowful.

Peter and His Master Pay Their Taxes

[24]When they had come to Capernaum,[a] those who received the *temple* tax came to

---

17:4 [a]NU-Text reads *I will.*   17:11 [a]NU-Text omits *first.*   17:15 [a]Literally *moonstruck*
17:20 [a]NU-Text reads *little faith.*   17:21 [a]NU-Text omits this verse.   17:22 [a]NU-Text reads *gathering together.*   17:24 [a]NU-Text reads *Capharnaum* (here and elsewhere).

Peter and said, "Does your Teacher not pay the *temple* tax?"

²⁵He said, "Yes."

And when he had come into the house, Jesus anticipated him, saying, "What do you think, Simon? From whom do the kings of the earth take customs or taxes, from their sons or from strangers?"

²⁶Peter said to Him, "From strangers."

Jesus said to him, "Then the sons are free. ²⁷Nevertheless, lest we offend them, go to the sea, cast in a hook, and take the fish that comes up first. And when you have opened its mouth, you will find a piece of money;ª take that and give it to them for Me and you."

Who Is the Greatest?

18 At that time the disciples came to Jesus, saying, "Who then is greatest in the kingdom of heaven?"

²Then Jesus called a little child to Him, set him in the midst of them, ³and said, "Assuredly, I say to you, unless you are converted and become as little children, you will by no means enter the kingdom of heaven. ⁴Therefore whoever humbles himself as this little child is the greatest in the kingdom of heaven. ⁵Whoever receives one little child like this in My name receives Me.

> **18:3 become as little children.** This is how Jesus characterized conversion. Faith is pictured as being the simple and trusting dependence of those who have no resources of their own. People of faith rely on God rather than on themselves.

Jesus Warns of Offenses

⁶"Whoever causes one of these little ones who believe in Me to sin, it would be better for him if a millstone were hung around his neck, and he were drowned in the depth of the sea. ⁷Woe to the world because of offenses! For offenses must come, but woe to that man by whom the offense comes!

⁸"If your hand or foot causes you to sin, cut it off and cast *it* from you. It is better for you to enter into life lame or maimed, rather than having two hands or two feet, to be cast into the everlasting fire. ⁹And if your eye causes you to sin, pluck it out and cast *it* from you. It is better for you to enter into life with one eye, rather than having two eyes, to be cast into hell fire.

The Parable of the Lost Sheep

¹⁰"Take heed that you do not despise one of these little ones, for I say to you that in heaven their angels always see the face of My Father who is in heaven. ¹¹For the Son of Man has come to save that which was lost.ª

¹²"What do you think? If a man has a hundred sheep, and one of them goes astray, does he not leave the ninety-nine and go to the mountains to seek the one that is straying? ¹³And if he should find it, assuredly, I say to you, he rejoices more over that *sheep* than over the ninety-nine that did not go astray. ¹⁴Even so it is not the will of your Father who is in heaven that one of these little ones should perish.

Dealing with a Sinning Brother

¹⁵"Moreover if your brother sins against you, go and tell him his fault between you and him alone. If he hears you, you have gained your brother. ¹⁶But if he will not hear, take with you one or two more, that *'by the mouth of two or three witnesses every word may be established.'ª* ¹⁷ And if he refuses to hear them, tell *it* to the church. But if he refuses even to hear the church, let him be to you like a heathen and a tax collector.

> **18:15** The prescription for church discipline in vv. 15–17 must be read in light of the parable of the lost sheep (vv. 12–14). The goal of this process is restoration. Step one is to privately confront the individual about his or her fault.

¹⁸"Assuredly, I say to you, whatever you bind on earth will be bound in heaven, and whatever you loose on earth will be loosed in heaven.

¹⁹"Again I sayª to you that if two of you agree on earth concerning anything that they ask, it will be done for them by My

---

17:27 ªGreek *stater*, the exact amount to pay the temple tax (didrachma) for two   18:11 ªNU-Text omits this verse.   18:16 ªDeuteronomy 19:15   18:19 ªNU-Text and M-Text read *Again, assuredly, I say.*

Father in heaven. ²⁰For where two or three are gathered together in My name, I am there in the midst of them."

The Parable of the Unforgiving Servant

²¹Then Peter came to Him and said, "Lord, how often shall my brother sin against me, and I forgive him? Up to seven times?"

> **18:21 Up to seven times.** Peter thought he was being generous. The rabbis, citing several verses from Amos (1:3,6,9,11,13), taught that God forgave Israel's enemies only 3 times. In that line of thinking it was presumptuous and unnecessary to forgive anyone more than 3 times.

²²Jesus said to him, "I do not say to you, up to seven times, but up to seventy times seven. ²³Therefore the kingdom of heaven is like a certain king who wanted to settle accounts with his servants. ²⁴And when he had begun to settle accounts, one was brought to him who owed him ten thousand talents. ²⁵But as he was not able to pay, his master commanded that he be sold, with his wife and children and all that he had, and that payment be made. ²⁶The servant therefore fell down before him, saying, 'Master, have patience with me, and I will pay you all.' ²⁷Then the master of that servant was moved with compassion, released him, and forgave him the debt.

²⁸"But that servant went out and found one of his fellow servants who owed him a hundred denarii; and he laid hands on him and took *him* by the throat, saying, 'Pay me what you owe!' ²⁹So his fellow servant fell down at his feet*ᵃ* and begged him, saying, 'Have patience with me, and I will pay you all.'*ᵇ* ³⁰And he would not, but went and threw him into prison till he should pay the debt. ³¹So when his fellow servants saw what had been done, they were very grieved, and came and told their master all that had been done. ³²Then his master, after he had called him, said to him, 'You wicked servant! I forgave you all that debt because you begged me. ³³Should you not also have had compassion on your fellow

servant, just as I had pity on you?' ³⁴And his master was angry, and delivered him to the torturers until he should pay all that was due to him.

³⁵"So My heavenly Father also will do to you if each of you, from his heart, does not forgive his brother his trespasses."*ᵃ*

Marriage and Divorce

19 Now it came to pass, when Jesus had finished these sayings, *that* He departed from Galilee and came to the region of Judea beyond the Jordan. ²And great multitudes followed Him, and He healed them there.

³The Pharisees also came to Him, testing Him, and saying to Him, "Is it lawful for a man to divorce his wife for *just* any reason?"

⁴And He answered and said to them, "Have you not read that He who made*ᵃ them* at the beginning 'made them male and female,' *ᵇ* ⁵and said, 'For this reason a man shall leave his father and mother and be joined to his wife, and the two shall become one flesh'?*ᵃ* ⁶So then, they are no longer two but one flesh. Therefore what God has joined together, let not man separate."

⁷They said to Him, "Why then did Moses command to give a certificate of divorce, and to put her away?"

> **19:7 Why then did Moses command to give a certificate of divorce?** The Pharisees misrepresented Deut. 24:1–4. It was not a "command" for divorce, but a limitation on remarriage in the event of divorce. Moses merely recognized the legitimacy of divorce for finding some uncleanness in one's wife (sexual sin by Jesus' interpretation, see v. 9). It is only a last resort to hard-hearted sexual immorality.

⁸He said to them, "Moses, because of the hardness of your hearts, permitted you to divorce your wives, but from the beginning it was not so. ⁹And I say to you, whoever divorces his wife, except for sexual immorality,*ᵃ* and marries another, commits adultery; and whoever marries her who is divorced commits adultery."

18:29 *ᵃ*NU-Text omits *at his feet.*   *ᵇ*NU-Text and M-Text omit *all.*   18:35 *ᵃ*NU-Text omits *his trespasses.* 19:4 *ᵃ*NU-Text reads *created.* *ᵇ*Genesis 1:27; 5:2   19:5 *ᵃ*Genesis 2:24   19:9 *ᵃ*Or *fornication*

¹⁰His disciples said to Him, "If such is the case of the man with *his* wife, it is better not to marry."

Jesus Teaches on Celibacy

¹¹But He said to them, "All cannot accept this saying, but only *those* to whom it has been given: ¹²For there are eunuchs who were born thus from *their* mother's womb, and there are eunuchs who were made eunuchs by men, and there are eunuchs who have made themselves eunuchs for the kingdom of heaven's sake. He who is able to accept *it*, let him accept *it*."

> **19:12 let him accept it.** Christ is making celibacy a matter of personal choice—except for those who are physically incapable to marry for any reason. Others may find pragmatic reasons not to marry. In no way did Christ suggest that celibacy is superior to marriage (see Gen. 2:18).

Jesus Blesses Little Children

¹³Then little children were brought to Him that He might put *His* hands on them and pray, but the disciples rebuked them. ¹⁴But Jesus said, "Let the little children come to Me, and do not forbid them; for of such is the kingdom of heaven." ¹⁵And He laid *His* hands on them and departed from there.

Jesus Counsels the Rich Young Ruler

¹⁶Now behold, one came and said to Him, "Good[a] Teacher, what good thing shall I do that I may have eternal life?" ¹⁷So He said to him, "Why do you call Me good?[a] No one is good but One, *that is*, God.[b] But if you want to enter into life, keep the commandments." ¹⁸He said to Him, "Which ones?"

Jesus said, " 'You shall not murder,' 'You shall not commit adultery,' 'You shall not steal,' 'You shall not bear false witness,' ¹⁹'Honor your father and your mother,'[a] and, 'You shall love your neighbor as yourself.' "[b] ²⁰The young man said to Him, "All these things I have kept from my youth.[a] What do I still lack?"

²¹Jesus said to him, "If you want to be perfect, go, sell what you have and give to the poor, and you will have treasure in heaven; and come, follow Me."

> **19:21 go, sell what you have and give to the poor.** Jesus was not setting forth terms for salvation, but rather exposing the young man's true heart. The man's refusal to obey revealed that he was guilty of the law he claimed to have kept. He loved himself and his possessions more than his neighbors and he lacked true faith in God. Jesus demanded that He be placed first above all, and the young man could not do this.

²²But when the young man heard that saying, he went away sorrowful, for he had great possessions.

With God All Things Are Possible

²³Then Jesus said to His disciples, "Assuredly, I say to you that it is hard for a rich man to enter the kingdom of heaven. ²⁴And again I say to you, it is easier for a camel to go through the eye of a needle than for a rich man to enter the kingdom of God." ²⁵When His disciples heard *it*, they were greatly astonished, saying, "Who then can be saved?" ²⁶But Jesus looked at *them* and said to them, "With men this is impossible, but with God all things are possible." ²⁷Then Peter answered and said to Him, "See, we have left all and followed You. Therefore what shall we have?" ²⁸So Jesus said to them, "Assuredly I say to you, that in the regeneration, when the Son of Man sits on the throne of His glory, you who have followed Me will also sit on twelve thrones, judging the twelve tribes of Israel. ²⁹And everyone who has left houses or brothers or sisters or father or mother or wife[a] or children or lands, for My name's sake, shall receive a hundredfold, and inherit eternal life. ³⁰But many *who are* first will be last, and the last first.

The Parable of the Workers in the Vineyard

20 "For the kingdom of heaven is like a landowner who went out early in the morning to hire laborers for his vine-

---

19:16 [a]NU-Text omits *Good*.   19:17 [a]NU-Text reads *Why do you ask Me about what is good?*
[b]NU-Text reads *There is One who is good*.   19:19 [a]Exodus 20:12–16; Deuteronomy 5:16–20
[b]Leviticus 19:18   19:20 [a]NU-Text omits *from my youth*.   19:29 [a]NU-Text omits *or wife*.

yard. ²Now when he had agreed with the laborers for a denarius a day, he sent them into his vineyard. ³And he went out about the third hour and saw others standing idle in the marketplace, ⁴and said to them, 'You also go into the vineyard, and whatever is right I will give you.' So they went. ⁵Again he went out about the sixth and the ninth hour, and did likewise. ⁶And about the eleventh hour he went out and found others standing idle,ᵃ and said to them, 'Why have you been standing here idle all day?' ⁷They said to him, 'Because no one hired us.' He said to them, 'You also go into the vineyard, and whatever is right you will receive.'ᵃ

⁸"So when evening had come, the owner of the vineyard said to his steward, 'Call the laborers and give them *their* wages, beginning with the last to the first.' ⁹And when those came who *were hired* about the eleventh hour, they each received a denarius. ¹⁰But when the first came, they supposed that they would receive more; and they likewise received each a denarius. ¹¹And when they had received *it*, they complained against the landowner, ¹²saying, 'These last *men* have worked *only* one hour, and you made them equal to us who have borne the burden and the heat of the day.' ¹³But he answered one of them and said, 'Friend, I am doing you no wrong. Did you not agree with me for a denarius? ¹⁴Take *what* is yours and go your way. I wish to give to this last man *the same* as to you. ¹⁵Is it not lawful for me to do what I wish with my own things? Or is your eye evil because I am good?' ¹⁶So the last will be first, and the first last. For many are called, but few chosen."ᵃ

> **20:13 I am doing you no wrong.** To their great surprise, everyone, no matter when he started working, received a full day's wage (vv. 9–11). The man's gracious act of paying even wages was not to slight or reward anyone unjustly. It was the man's privilege to extend the same generosity to all (see Rom. 9:15).

Jesus a Third Time Predicts His Death and Resurrection

¹⁷Now Jesus, going up to Jerusalem, took the twelve disciples aside on the road and said to them, ¹⁸"Behold, we are going up to Jerusalem, and the Son of Man will be betrayed to the chief priests and to the scribes; and they will condemn Him to death, ¹⁹and deliver Him to the Gentiles to mock and to scourge and to crucify. And the third day He will rise again."

Greatness Is Serving

²⁰Then the mother of Zebedee's sons came to Him with her sons, kneeling down and asking something from Him.

²¹And He said to her, "What do you wish?"

She said to Him, "Grant that these two sons of mine may sit, one on Your right hand and the other on the left, in Your kingdom."

²²But Jesus answered and said, "You do not know what you ask. Are you able to drink the cup that I am about to drink, and be baptized with the baptism that I am baptized with?"ᵃ

They said to Him, "We are able."

²³So He said to them, "You will indeed drink My cup, and be baptized with the baptism that I am baptized with;ᵃ but to sit on My right hand and on My left is not Mine to give, but *it is for those* for whom it is prepared by My Father."

> **20:23 You will indeed.** James was beheaded (Acts 12:2), and John was tortured and exiled to Patmos (Rev. 1:9) for the sake of Christ.

²⁴And when the ten heard *it*, they were greatly displeased with the two brothers. ²⁵But Jesus called them to *Himself* and said, "You know that the rulers of the Gentiles lord it over them, and those who are great exercise authority over them. ²⁶Yet it shall not be so among you; but whoever desires to become great among you, let him be your servant. ²⁷And whoever desires to be first among you, let him be your slave— ²⁸just as the Son of Man did not come to be served, but to serve, and to give His life a ransom for many."

20:6 ᵃNU-Text omits *idle*.   20:7 ᵃNU-Text omits the last clause of this verse.   20:16 ᵃNU-Text omits the last sentence of this verse.   20:22 ᵃNU-Text omits *and be baptized with the baptism that I am baptized with*.   20:23 ᵃNU-Text omits *and be baptized with the baptism that I am baptized with*.

Two Blind Men Receive Their Sight

²⁹Now as they went out of Jericho, a great multitude followed Him. ³⁰And behold, two blind men sitting by the road, when they heard that Jesus was passing by, cried out, saying, "Have mercy on us, O Lord, Son of David!"

³¹Then the multitude warned them that they should be quiet; but they cried out all the more, saying, "Have mercy on us, O Lord, Son of David!"

³²So Jesus stood still and called them, and said, "What do you want Me to do for you?" ³³They said to Him, "Lord, that our eyes may be opened." ³⁴So Jesus had compassion and touched their eyes. And immediately their eyes received sight, and they followed Him.

The Triumphal Entry

21 Now when they drew near Jerusalem, and came to Bethphage,ᵃ at the Mount of Olives, then Jesus sent two disciples, ²saying to them, "Go into the village opposite you, and immediately you will find a donkey tied, and a colt with her. Loose *them* and bring *them* to Me. ³And if anyone says anything to you, you shall say, 'The Lord has need of them,' and immediately he will send them."

⁴Allᵃ this was done that it might be fulfilled which was spoken by the prophet, saying:

5   "*Tell the daughter of Zion,*
      '*Behold, your King is coming to you,*
      Lowly, and sitting on a donkey,
      A colt, the foal of a donkey.'"ᵃ

> **21:5 A colt, the foal of a donkey.** This is an exact quotation from Zech. 9:9 (see Is. 62:11). The Jewish crowds recognized this, and they erupted with accolades and titles fit only for the Messiah.

⁶So the disciples went and did as Jesus commanded them. ⁷They brought the donkey and the colt, laid their clothes on them, and set *Him*ᵃ on them. ⁸And a very great multitude spread their clothes on the road; others cut down branches from the trees

and spread *them* on the road. ⁹Then the multitudes who went before and those who followed cried out, saying:

    "Hosanna to the Son of David!
    '*Blessed is He who comes in the name*
       of the LORD*!*' ᵃ
    Hosanna in the highest!"

> **21:9 Hosanna.** In the Hebrew this means "Save now" (see Ps. 118:25). **Blessed is He.** This is an exact quotation from Ps. 118:26. This, along with the title, "Son of David," makes it clear that the multitudes acknowledged Jesus as Messiah.

¹⁰And when He had come into Jerusalem, all the city was moved, saying, "Who is this?" ¹¹So the multitudes said, "This is Jesus, the prophet from Nazareth of Galilee."

Jesus Cleanses the Temple

¹²Then Jesus went into the temple of Godᵃ and drove out all those who bought and sold in the temple, and overturned the tables of the money changers and the seats of those who sold doves. ¹³And He said to them, "It is written, '*My house shall be called a house of prayer,*'ᵃ but you have made it a '*den of thieves.*' "ᵇ

¹⁴Then *the* blind and *the* lame came to Him in the temple, and He healed them. ¹⁵But when the chief priests and scribes saw the wonderful things that He did, and the children crying out in the temple and saying, "Hosanna to the Son of David!" they were indignant ¹⁶and said to Him, "Do You hear what these are saying?"

And Jesus said to them, "Yes. Have you never read,

      '*Out of the mouth of babes and*
         nursing infants
      You have perfected praise'?"ᵃ

> **21:16 Yes. Have you never read.** Jesus' reply amounted to an inescapable assertion of His deity. He quoted from Ps. 8:2, which speaks of "praise" offered to God. By employing that verse in defense of the worship God had ordained for Him, He was claiming the right to receive worship as God.

21:1 ᵃM-Text reads *Bethsphage*.   21:4 ᵃNU-Text omits *All*.   21:5 ᵃZechariah 9:9   21:7 ᵃNU-Text reads *and He sat*.   21:9 ᵃPsalm 118:26   21:12 ᵃNU-Text omits *of God*.   21:13 ᵃIsaiah 56:7 ᵇJeremiah 7:11   21:16 ᵃPsalm 8:2

¹⁷Then He left them and went out of the city to Bethany, and He lodged there.

The Fig Tree Withered

¹⁸Now in the morning, as He returned to the city, He was hungry. ¹⁹And seeing a fig tree by the road, He came to it and found nothing on it but leaves, and said to it, "Let no fruit grow on you ever again." Immediately the fig tree withered away.

The Lesson of the Withered Fig Tree

²⁰And when the disciples saw *it*, they marveled, saying, "How did the fig tree wither away so soon?"

²¹So Jesus answered and said to them, "Assuredly, I say to you, if you have faith and do not doubt, you will not only do what was done to the fig tree, but also if you say to this mountain, 'Be removed and be cast into the sea,' it will be done. ²²And whatever things you ask in prayer, believing, you will receive."

> **21:21 if you have faith and do not doubt.** This presupposes that what is requested is actually God's will—for only God-given faith is so free from doubt (see Mark 9:24). **it will be done.** The scribes and Pharisees wanted a cosmic-sized miracle to be performed, but Jesus always declined. Here Jesus spoke figuratively about the immeasurable power of God in the lives of those with true faith.

Jesus' Authority Questioned

²³Now when He came into the temple, the chief priests and the elders of the people confronted Him as He was teaching, and said, "By what authority are You doing these things? And who gave You this authority?"

²⁴But Jesus answered and said to them, "I also will ask you one thing, which if you tell Me, I likewise will tell you by what authority I do these things: ²⁵The baptism of John—where was it from? From heaven or from men?"

And they reasoned among themselves, saying, "If we say, 'From heaven,' He will say to us, 'Why then did you not believe him?' ²⁶But if we say, 'From men,' we fear the multitude, for all count John as a prophet." ²⁷So they answered Jesus and said, "We do not know."

And He said to them, "Neither will I tell you by what authority I do these things.

The Parable of the Two Sons

²⁸"But what do you think? A man had two sons, and he came to the first and said, 'Son, go, work today in my vineyard.' ²⁹He answered and said, 'I will not,' but afterward he regretted it and went. ³⁰Then he came to the second and said likewise. And he answered and said, 'I go, sir,' but he did not go. ³¹Which of the two did the will of *his* father?"

They said to Him, "The first."

Jesus said to them, "Assuredly, I say to you that tax collectors and harlots enter the kingdom of God before you. ³²For John came to you in the way of righteousness, and you did not believe him; but tax collectors and harlots believed him; and when you saw *it*, you did not afterward relent and believe him.

The Parable of the Wicked Vinedressers

³³"Hear another parable: There was a certain landowner who planted a vineyard and set a hedge around it, dug a winepress in it and built a tower. And he leased it to vinedressers and went into a far country. ³⁴Now when vintage-time drew near, he sent his servants to the vinedressers, that they might receive its fruit. ³⁵And the vinedressers took his servants, beat one, killed one, and stoned another. ³⁶Again he sent other servants, more than the first, and they did likewise to them. ³⁷Then last of all he sent his son to them, saying, 'They will respect my son.' ³⁸But when the vinedressers saw the son, they said among themselves, 'This is the heir. Come, let us kill him and seize his inheritance.' ³⁹So they took him and cast *him* out of the vineyard and killed *him*.

⁴⁰"Therefore, when the owner of the vineyard comes, what will he do to those vinedressers?"

⁴¹They said to Him, "He will destroy those wicked men miserably, and lease *his* vineyard to other vinedressers who will render to him the fruits in their seasons."

⁴²Jesus said to them, "Have you never read in the Scriptures:

'The stone which the builders rejected
Has become the chief cornerstone.

This was the LORD's doing,
And it is marvelous in our eyes'?ᵃ

> **21:42 The stone...rejected.** This refers to Jesus' crucifixion, while the restoration of "the chief cornerstone" anticipates the resurrection. **the chief cornerstone.** This phrase is taken from a messianic psalm (118:22,23). Jesus cited it to suggest that the Son who was killed and thrown out of the vineyard was also "the chief cornerstone" in God's redemptive plan.

⁴³"Therefore I say to you, the kingdom of God will be taken from you and given to a nation bearing the fruits of it. ⁴⁴And whoever falls on this stone will be broken; but on whomever it falls, it will grind him to powder."

⁴⁵Now when the chief priests and Pharisees heard His parables, they perceived that He was speaking of them. ⁴⁶But when they sought to lay hands on Him, they feared the multitudes, because they took Him for a prophet.

The Parable of the Wedding Feast

22 And Jesus answered and spoke to them again by parables and said: ²"The kingdom of heaven is like a certain king who arranged a marriage for his son, ³and sent out his servants to call those who were invited to the wedding; and they were not willing to come. ⁴Again, he sent out other servants, saying, 'Tell those who are invited, "See, I have prepared my dinner; my oxen and fatted cattle *are* killed, and all things *are* ready. Come to the wedding."' ⁵But they made light of it and went their ways, one to his own farm, another to his business. ⁶And the rest seized his servants, treated them spitefully, and killed *them*. ⁷But when the king heard *about it*, he was furious. And he sent out his armies, destroyed those murderers, and burned up their city. ⁸Then he said to his servants, 'The wedding is ready, but those who were invited were not worthy. ⁹Therefore go into the highways, and as many as you find, invite to the wedding.' ¹⁰So those servants went out into the highways and gathered together all whom they found, both bad and good. And the wedding *hall* was filled with guests.

¹¹"But when the king came in to see the guests, he saw a man there who did not have on a wedding garment. ¹²So he said to him, 'Friend, how did you come in here without a wedding garment?' And he was speechless. ¹³Then the king said to the servants, 'Bind him hand and foot, take him away, andᵃ cast *him* into outer darkness; there will be weeping and gnashing of teeth.'

> **22:11 a wedding garment.** The imagery seems to represent those who put on the external appearance of a Christian yet spurn the garment of righteousness Christ offers (see Rom. 10:3). Ashamed to admit their own spiritual poverty, they refuse the better garment that the King graciously offers, thus making them guilty of a horrible sin against His goodness.

¹⁴"For many are called, but few *are* chosen."

The Pharisees: Is It Lawful to Pay Taxes to Caesar?

¹⁵Then the Pharisees went and plotted how they might entangle Him in *His* talk. ¹⁶And they sent to Him their disciples with the Herodians, saying, "Teacher, we know that You are true, and teach the way of God in truth; nor do You care about anyone, for You do not regard the person of men. ¹⁷Tell us, therefore, what do You think? Is it lawful to pay taxes to Caesar, or not?"

¹⁸But Jesus perceived their wickedness, and said, "Why do you test Me, *you* hypocrites? ¹⁹Show Me the tax money."

So they brought Him a denarius.

²⁰And He said to them, "Whose image and inscription is this?"

²¹They said to Him, "Caesar's."

And He said to them, "Render therefore to Caesar the things that are Caesar's, and

> **22:21 Caesar's...God's.** Caesar's image is stamped on the coin; God's image is stamped on the person (Gen. 1:26,27). The Christian should obey Caesar in Caesar's realm (Rom. 13:1–7), but the things of God should be given only to God. Christ acknowledged Caesar's right to collect taxes and instructed Christians to pay them. Ultimately, all things are God's— even the realm under which any ruler exercises authority.

21:42 ᵃPsalm 118:22, 23   22:13 ᵃNU-Text omits *take him away, and.*

to God the things that are God's." ²²When they had heard *these words*, they marveled, and left Him and went their way.

The Sadducees: What About the Resurrection?

²³The same day the Sadducees, who say there is no resurrection, came to Him and asked Him, ²⁴saying: "Teacher, Moses said that if a man dies, having no children, his brother shall marry his wife and raise up offspring for his brother. ²⁵Now there were with us seven brothers. The first died after he had married, and having no offspring, left his wife to his brother. ²⁶Likewise the second also, and the third, even to the seventh. ²⁷Last of all the woman died also. ²⁸Therefore, in the resurrection, whose wife of the seven will she be? For they all had her."

²⁹Jesus answered and said to them, "You are mistaken, not knowing the Scriptures nor the power of God. ³⁰For in the resurrection they neither marry nor are given in marriage, but are like angels of God*ᵃ* in heaven. ³¹But concerning the resurrection of the dead, have you not read what was spoken to you by God, saying, ³²*I am the God of Abraham, the God of Isaac, and the God of Jacob'?ᵃ* God is not the God of the dead, but of the living." ³³And when the multitudes heard *this*, they were astonished at His teaching.

The Scribes: Which Is the First Commandment of All?

³⁴But when the Pharisees heard that He had silenced the Sadducees, they gathered together. ³⁵Then one of them, a lawyer, asked *Him a question*, testing Him, and saying, ³⁶"Teacher, which *is* the great commandment in the law?"

³⁷Jesus said to him, " '*You shall love the* LORD *your God with all your heart, with all your soul, and with all your mind.'ᵃ* ³⁸This is *the* first and great commandment. ³⁹And the second *is* like it: '*You shall love your neighbor as yourself.'ᵃ* ⁴⁰On these two commandments hang all the Law and the Prophets."

> **22:40 all the Law and the Prophets.** This refers to the whole OT. Jesus summarizes man's moral duty under two categories: love for God and love for one's neighbor. These same two categories differentiate the first 4 commandments from the last 6.

Jesus: How Can David Call His Descendant Lord?

⁴¹While the Pharisees were gathered together, Jesus asked them, ⁴²saying, "What do you think about the Christ? Whose Son is He?"

They said to Him, "*The Son* of David."

⁴³He said to them, "How then does David in the Spirit call Him '*Lord*,' saying:

⁴⁴ '*The* LORD *said to my Lord,*
" *Sit at My right hand,*
Till I make Your enemies Your
footstool" '?ᵃ

⁴⁵If David then calls Him '*Lord*,' how is He his Son?" ⁴⁶And no one was able to answer Him a word, nor from that day on did anyone dare question Him anymore.

> **22:45 David then calls Him 'Lord.'** Jesus was pointing out that the title "Son of David" did not begin to sum up all that is true about the Messiah, who is also the "Son of God" (Luke 22:70). The inescapable implication is that Jesus was declaring His deity.

Woe to the Scribes and Pharisees

23 Then Jesus spoke to the multitudes and to His disciples, ²saying: "The scribes and the Pharisees sit in Moses' seat. ³Therefore whatever they tell you to observe,*ᵃ* *that* observe and do, but do not do according to their works; for they say, and do not do. ⁴For they bind heavy burdens, hard to bear, and lay *them* on men's shoulders; but they *themselves* will not move them with one of their fingers. ⁵But all their works they do to be seen by men. They make their phylacteries broad and enlarge the borders of their garments. ⁶They love the best places at feasts, the best seats in the synagogues, ⁷greetings in the marketplaces, and to be called by men, 'Rabbi, Rabbi.' ⁸But you, do not be called

---

22:30 *ᵃ*NU-Text omits *of God.*   22:32 *ᵃ*Exodus 3:6,15   22:37 *ᵃ*Deuteronomy 6:5   22:39 *ᵃ*Leviticus 19:18   22:44 *ᵃ*Psalm 110:1   23:3 *ᵃ*NU-Text omits *to observe.*

23:5 phylacteries. These were leather boxes that contained parchments with four columns written on them. They were worn by men during prayer—one on the forehead and another on the left arm just above the elbow. This was done to fulfill an overly-literal interpretation of Ex. 13:9,10.

'Rabbi'; for One is your Teacher, the Christ,[a] and you are all brethren. [9]Do not call anyone on earth your father; for One is your Father, He who is in heaven. [10]And do not be called teachers; for One is your Teacher, the Christ. [11]But he who is greatest among you shall be your servant. [12]And whoever exalts himself will be humbled, and he who humbles himself will be exalted.

[13]"But woe to you, scribes and Pharisees, hypocrites! For you shut up the kingdom of heaven against men; for you neither go in *yourselves*, nor do you allow those who are entering to go in. [14]Woe to you, scribes and Pharisees, hypocrites! For you devour widows' houses, and for a pretense make long prayers. Therefore you will receive greater condemnation.[a]

[15]"Woe to you, scribes and Pharisees, hypocrites! For you travel land and sea to win one proselyte, and when he is won, you make him twice as much a son of hell as yourselves.

[16]"Woe to you, blind guides, who say, 'Whoever swears by the temple, it is nothing; but whoever swears by the gold of the temple, he is obliged *to perform it.*' [17]Fools and blind! For which is greater, the gold or the temple that sanctifies[a] the gold? [18]And, 'Whoever swears by the altar, it is nothing; but whoever swears by the gift that is on it, he is obliged *to perform it.*' [19]Fools and blind! For which is greater, the gift or the altar that sanctifies the gift? [20]Therefore he who swears by the altar, swears by it and by all things on it. [21]He who swears by the temple, swears by it and by Him who dwells[a] in it. [22]And he who swears by heaven, swears by the throne of God and by Him who sits on it.

[23]"Woe to you, scribes and Pharisees, hypocrites! For you pay tithe of mint and anise and cummin, and have neglected the weightier *matters* of the law: justice and mercy and faith. These you ought to have done, without leaving the others undone. [24]Blind guides, who strain out a gnat and swallow a camel!

[25]"Woe to you, scribes and Pharisees, hypocrites! For you cleanse the outside of the cup and dish, but inside they are full of extortion and self-indulgence.[a] [26]Blind Pharisee, first cleanse the inside of the cup and dish, that the outside of them may be clean also.

23:25 you cleanse the outside. The Pharisees' focus on the external righteousness lay at the heart of their error. Their souls' internal condition was compromised and ignored for the appearance of holiness. This was the basis of their hypocrisy, and Jesus repeatedly rebuked them for it.

[27]"Woe to you, scribes and Pharisees, hypocrites! For you are like whitewashed tombs which indeed appear beautiful outwardly, but inside are full of dead *men's* bones and all uncleanness. [28]Even so you also outwardly appear righteous to men, but inside you are full of hypocrisy and lawlessness.

[29]"Woe to you, scribes and Pharisees, hypocrites! Because you build the tombs of the prophets and adorn the monuments of the righteous, [30]and say, 'If we had lived in the days of our fathers, we would not have been partakers with them in the blood of the prophets.'

[31]"Therefore you are witnesses against yourselves that you are sons of those who murdered the prophets. [32]Fill up, then, the measure of your fathers' *guilt.* [33]Serpents, brood of vipers! How can you escape the condemnation of hell? [34]Therefore, indeed, I send you prophets, wise men, and scribes: *some* of them you will kill and crucify, and *some* of them you will scourge in your synagogues and persecute from city to city, [35]that on you may come all the righteous blood shed on the earth, from the blood of righteous Abel to the blood of Zechariah, son of Berechiah, whom you murdered between the temple and the altar. [36]Assuredly, I say to you, all these things will come upon this generation.

23:8 [a]NU-Text omits *the Christ.*   23:14 [a]NU-Text omits this verse.   23:17 [a]NU-Text reads *sanctified.*
23:21 [a]M-Text reads *dwelt.*   23:25 [a]M-Text reads *unrighteousness.*

Jesus Laments over Jerusalem

37"O Jerusalem, Jerusalem, the one who kills the prophets and stones those who are sent to her! How often I wanted to gather your children together, as a hen gathers her chicks under *her* wings, but you were not willing! 38See! Your house is left to you desolate; 39for I say to you, you shall see Me no more till you say, '*Blessed is He who comes in the name of the* LORD! ' "*a*

> **24:1–25:46** This is the last of the 5 discourses Matthew features. It is known as the Olivet Discourse, and it contains some of the most important prophetic material in all of Scripture.

Jesus Predicts the Destruction of the Temple

24 Then Jesus went out and departed from the temple, and His disciples came up to show Him the buildings of the temple. 2And Jesus said to them, "Do you not see all these things? Assuredly, I say to you, not *one* stone shall be left here upon another, that shall not be thrown down."

The Signs of the Times and the End of the Age

3Now as He sat on the Mount of Olives, the disciples came to Him privately, saying, "Tell us, when will these things be? And what *will be* the sign of Your coming, and of the end of the age?"

4And Jesus answered and said to them: "Take heed that no one deceives you. 5For many will come in My name, saying, 'I am the Christ,' and will deceive many. 6And you will hear of wars and rumors of wars.

See that you are not troubled; for all*a these things* must come to pass, but the end is not yet. 7For nation will rise against nation, and kingdom against kingdom. And there will be famines, pestilences,*a* and earthquakes in various places. 8All these *are* the beginning of sorrows.

9"Then they will deliver you up to tribulation and kill you, and you will be hated by all nations for My name's sake. 10And then many will be offended, will betray one another, and will hate one another. 11Then many false prophets will rise up and deceive many. 12And because lawlessness will abound, the love of many will grow cold. 13But he who endures to the end shall be saved. 14And this gospel of the kingdom will be preached in all the world as a witness to all the nations, and then the end will come.

> **24:13 endures to the end...be saved.** This does not suggest that our perseverance secures our salvation, but actually the opposite (1 Pet. 1:5). The guarantee is part of the New Covenant promise in Jer. 32:40. This does not mean that we remain passive in the process. Our faith is required to be active (see Heb. 10:23).

The Great Tribulation

15"Therefore when you see the '*abomination of desolation,*'*a* spoken of by Daniel the prophet, standing in the holy place" (whoever reads, let him understand), 16"then let those who are in Judea flee to the mountains. 17Let him who is on the housetop not go down to take anything out of his house. 18And let him who is in the field not

---

23:39 *a*Psalm 118:26   24:6 *a*NU-Text omits *all.*   24:7 *a*NU-Text omits *pestilences.*   24:15 *a*Daniel 11:31; 12:11

How should Jesus' prophetic statements, many of which are found in Matthew 24 and 25, be interpreted?

The prophetic passages present a particular challenge for those seeking to understand a correct interpretation of Jesus' words. The Olivet discourse (Matthew 24,25), for example, contains some details that evoke images of the violent destruction of Jerusalem in A.D. 70. Jesus' words in 24:34 have led some to conclude that all these things were fulfilled—albeit not literally—in the Roman conquest of that era. This view is known as "preterism." But this is a serious interpretive blunder, forcing the interpreter to read into these passages spiritualized, allegorical meanings unwarranted by normal exegetical study methods. The grammatical-historical hermeneutical approach to these passages is the approach to follow, and it yields a consistently futuristic interpretation of crucial prophecies.

go back to get his clothes. ¹⁹But woe to those who are pregnant and to those who are nursing babies in those days! ²⁰And pray that your flight may not be in winter or on the Sabbath. ²¹For then there will be great tribulation, such as has not been since the beginning of the world until this time, no, nor ever shall be. ²²And unless those days were shortened, no flesh would be saved; but for the elect's sake those days will be shortened.

²³"Then if anyone says to you, 'Look, here is the Christ!' or 'There!' do not believe it. ²⁴For false christs and false prophets will rise and show great signs and wonders to deceive, if possible, even the elect. ²⁵See, I have told you beforehand.

> **24:24 to deceive, if possible, even the elect.** This clearly implies that such deception is not possible (John 10:4,5).

²⁶"Therefore if they say to you, 'Look, He is in the desert!' do not go out; or 'Look, He is in the inner rooms!' do not believe it. ²⁷For as the lightning comes from the east and flashes to the west, so also will the coming of the Son of Man be. ²⁸For wherever the carcass is, there the eagles will be gathered together.

The Coming of the Son of Man

²⁹"Immediately after the tribulation of those days the sun will be darkened, and the moon will not give its light; the stars will fall from heaven, and the powers of the heavens will be shaken. ³⁰Then the sign of the Son of Man will appear in heaven, and then all the tribes of the earth will mourn, and they will see the Son of Man coming on the clouds of heaven with power and great glory. ³¹And He will send His angels with a great sound of a trumpet, and they will gather together His elect from the four winds, from one end of heaven to the other.

The Parable of the Fig Tree

³²"Now learn this parable from the fig tree: When its branch has already become tender and puts forth leaves, you know that summer *is* near. ³³So you also, when you see all these things, know that it*ᵃ* is near—at the doors! ³⁴Assuredly, I say to you, this generation will by no means pass away till all these things take place. ³⁵Heaven and earth will pass away, but My words will by no means pass away.

No One Knows the Day or Hour

³⁶"But of that day and hour no one knows, not even the angels of heaven,*ᵃ* but My Father only. ³⁷But as the days of Noah *were*, so also will the coming of the Son of Man be. ³⁸For as in the days before the flood, they were eating and drinking, marrying and giving in marriage, until the day that Noah entered the ark, ³⁹and did not know until the flood came and took them all away, so also will the coming of the Son of Man be. ⁴⁰Then two *men* will be in the field: one will be taken and the other left. ⁴¹Two *women will be* grinding at the mill: one will be taken and the other left. ⁴²Watch therefore, for you do not know what hour*ᵃ* your Lord is coming. ⁴³But know this, that if the master of the house had known what hour the thief would come, he would have watched and not allowed his house to be broken into. ⁴⁴Therefore you also be ready, for the Son of Man is coming at an hour you do not expect.

> **24:37 as the days of Noah *were*.** Jesus' emphasis was not on the extreme sinfulness of the day, but on the matters of everyday life. Being caught up in their daily activities played a role in the people's lack of concern for the warnings they were given leading up to the flood. As a result, they all suffered.

The Faithful Servant and the Evil Servant

⁴⁵"Who then is a faithful and wise servant, whom his master made ruler over his household, to give them food in due season? ⁴⁶Blessed *is* that servant whom his master, when he comes, will find so doing. ⁴⁷Assuredly, I say to you that he will make him ruler over all his goods. ⁴⁸But if that evil servant says in his heart, 'My master is delaying his coming,'*ᵃ* ⁴⁹and begins to beat *his* fellow servants, and to eat and drink with the drunkards, ⁵⁰the master of that

---

24:33 *ᵃ*Or *He*   24:36 *ᵃ*NU-Text adds *nor the Son.*   24:42 *ᵃ*NU-Text reads *day.*   24:48 *ᵃ*NU-Text omits *his coming.*

servant will come on a day when he is not looking for *him* and at an hour that he is not aware of, ⁵¹and will cut him in two and appoint *him* his portion with the hypocrites. There shall be weeping and gnashing of teeth.

> **25:1–13** The parable of the 10 virgins underscores the importance of being ready for Christ's imminent return—even if He appears delayed. When He does return, there will be no second chance for the unprepared.

The Parable of the Wise and Foolish Virgins

25 "Then the kingdom of heaven shall be likened to ten virgins who took their lamps and went out to meet the bridegroom. ²Now five of them were wise, and five *were* foolish. ³Those who *were* foolish took their lamps and took no oil with them, ⁴but the wise took oil in their vessels with their lamps. ⁵But while the bridegroom was delayed, they all slumbered and slept.

⁶"And at midnight a cry was *heard:* 'Behold, the bridegroom is coming;ᵃ go out to meet him!' ⁷Then all those virgins arose and trimmed their lamps. ⁸And the foolish said to the wise, 'Give us *some* of your oil, for our lamps are going out.' ⁹But the wise answered, saying, '*No,* lest there should not be enough for us and you; but go rather to those who sell, and buy for yourselves.' ¹⁰And while they went to buy, the bridegroom came, and those who were ready went in with him to the wedding; and the door was shut.

¹¹"Afterward the other virgins came also, saying, 'Lord, Lord, open to us!' ¹²But he answered and said, 'Assuredly, I say to you, I do not know you.'

¹³"Watch therefore, for you know neither the day nor the hourᵃ in which the Son of Man is coming.

> **25:14–30** The parable of the talents illustrates the tragedy of wasted opportunity. The man who goes on the journey represents Christ, and the servants represent professing believers given different levels of responsibility. The parable suggests that those who are faithful will be fruitful to some degree. There is no room in the kingdom for an unfaithful servant.

The Parable of the Talents

¹⁴"For *the kingdom of heaven is* like a man traveling to a far country, *who* called his own servants and delivered his goods to them. ¹⁵And to one he gave five talents, to another two, and to another one, to each according to his own ability; and immediately he went on a journey. ¹⁶Then he who had received the five talents went and traded with them, and made another five talents. ¹⁷And likewise he who *had received* two gained two more also. ¹⁸But he who had received one went and dug in the ground, and hid his lord's money. ¹⁹After a long time the lord of those servants came and settled accounts with them.

²⁰"So he who had received five talents came and brought five other talents, saying, 'Lord, you delivered to me five talents; look, I have gained five more talents besides them.' ²¹His lord said to him, 'Well *done,* good and faithful servant; you were faithful over a few things, I will make you ruler over many things. Enter into the joy of your lord.' ²²He also who had received two talents came and said, 'Lord, you delivered to me two talents; look, I have gained two more talents besides them.' ²³His lord said to him, 'Well *done,* good and faithful servant; you have been faithful over a few things, I will make you ruler over many things. Enter into the joy of your lord.'

²⁴"Then he who had received the one talent came and said, 'Lord, I knew you to be a hard man, reaping where you have not sown, and gathering where you have not scattered seed. ²⁵And I was afraid, and went and hid your talent in the ground. Look, *there* you have *what is* yours.'

²⁶"But his lord answered and said to him, 'You wicked and lazy servant, you knew that I reap where I have not sown, and gather where I have not scattered seed. ²⁷So you ought to have deposited my money with the bankers, and at my coming I would have received back my own with interest. ²⁸So take the talent from him, and give *it* to him who has ten talents.

²⁹'For to everyone who has, more will be given, and he will have abundance; but from him who does not have, even what he has will be taken away. ³⁰And cast the

---

25:6 ᵃNU-Text omits *is coming.*   25:13 ᵃNU-Text omits the rest of this verse.

unprofitable servant into the outer darkness. There will be weeping and gnashing of teeth.'

The Son of Man Will Judge the Nations

³¹"When the Son of Man comes in His glory, and all the holy*ᵃ* angels with Him, then He will sit on the throne of His glory. ³²All the nations will be gathered before Him, and He will separate them one from another, as a shepherd divides *his* sheep from the goats. ³³And He will set the sheep on His right hand, but the goats on the left. ³⁴Then the King will say to those on His right hand, 'Come, you blessed of My Father, inherit the kingdom prepared for you from the foundation of the world: ³⁵for I was hungry and you gave Me food; I was thirsty and you gave Me drink; I was a stranger and you took Me in; ³⁶I *was* naked and you clothed Me; I was sick and you visited Me; I was in prison and you came to Me.'

³⁷"Then the righteous will answer Him, saying, 'Lord, when did we see You hungry and feed *You*, or thirsty and give *You* drink? ³⁸When did we see You a stranger and take *You* in, or naked and clothe *You*? ³⁹Or when did we see You sick, or in prison, and come to You?' ⁴⁰And the King will answer and say to them, 'Assuredly, I say to you, inasmuch as you did *it* to one of the least of these My brethren, you did *it* to Me.'

⁴¹"Then He will also say to those on the left hand, 'Depart from Me, you cursed, into the everlasting fire prepared for the devil and his angels: ⁴²for I was hungry and you gave Me no food; I was thirsty and you gave Me no drink; ⁴³I was a stranger and you did not take Me in, naked and you did not clothe Me, sick and in prison and you did not visit Me.'

⁴⁴"Then they also will answer Him,*ᵃ* saying, 'Lord, when did we see You hungry or thirsty or a stranger or naked or sick or in prison, and did not minister to You?' ⁴⁵Then He will answer them, saying, 'Assuredly, I say to you, inasmuch as you did not do *it* to one of the least of these, you did not do *it* to Me.' ⁴⁶And these will go away into everlasting punishment, but the righteous into eternal life."

The Plot to Kill Jesus

26 Now it came to pass, when Jesus had finished all these sayings, *that* He said to His disciples, ²"You know that after two days is the Passover, and the Son of Man will be delivered up to be crucified."

³Then the chief priests, the scribes,*ᵃ* and the elders of the people assembled at the palace of the high priest, who was called Caiaphas, ⁴and plotted to take Jesus by trickery and kill *Him*. ⁵But they said, "Not during the feast, lest there be an uproar among the people."

The Anointing at Bethany

⁶And when Jesus was in Bethany at the house of Simon the leper, ⁷a woman came to Him having an alabaster flask of very costly fragrant oil, and she poured *it* on His head as He sat *at the table*. ⁸But when His disciples saw *it*, they were indignant, saying, "Why this waste? ⁹For this fragrant oil might have been sold for much and given to *the* poor."

¹⁰But when Jesus was aware of *it*, He said to them, "Why do you trouble the woman?

25:31 *ᵃ*NU-Text omits *holy.*   25:44 *ᵃ*NU-Text and M-Text omit *Him.*   26:3 *ᵃ*NU-Text omits *the scribes.*

For she has done a good work for Me. ¹¹For you have the poor with you always, but Me you do not have always. ¹²For in pouring this fragrant oil on My body, she did *it* for My burial. ¹³Assuredly, I say to you, wherever this gospel is preached in the whole world, what this woman has done will also be told as a memorial to her."

26:12 she did *it* for My burial. Mary probably did not know of the proximity of Jesus' death, so she was not aware of the significance of her action. This was an act of pure worship. Her heart was moved by God to perform a sacrificial and symbolic act.

Judas Agrees to Betray Jesus

¹⁴Then one of the twelve, called Judas Iscariot, went to the chief priests ¹⁵and said, "What are you willing to give me if I deliver Him to you?" And they counted out to him thirty pieces of silver. ¹⁶So from that time he sought opportunity to betray Him.

Jesus Celebrates Passover with His Disciples

¹⁷Now on the first *day of the Feast* of the Unleavened Bread the disciples came to Jesus, saying to Him, "Where do You want us to prepare for You to eat the Passover?" ¹⁸And He said, "Go into the city to a certain man, and say to him, 'The Teacher says, "My time is at hand; I will keep the Passover at your house with My disciples." ' " ¹⁹So the disciples did as Jesus had directed them; and they prepared the Passover.

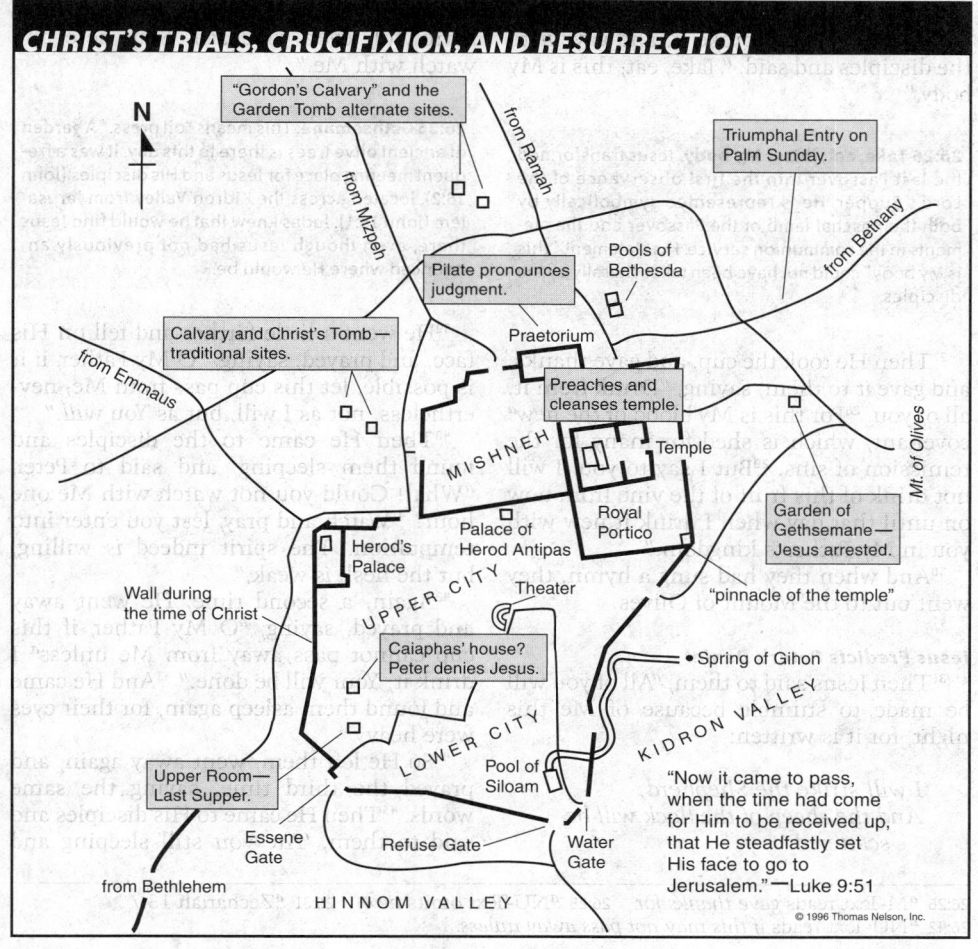

CHRIST'S TRIALS, CRUCIFIXION, AND RESURRECTION

N

"Gordon's Calvary" and the Garden Tomb alternate sites.

from Ramah

from Mizpeh

Triumphal Entry on Palm Sunday.

from Bethany

Pools of Bethesda

Pilate pronounces judgment.

Calvary and Christ's Tomb — traditional sites.

from Emmaus

Praetorium

Preaches and cleanses temple.

MISHNEH

Temple

Garden of Gethsemane — Jesus arrested.

Mt. of Olives

Palace of Herod Antipas

Royal Portico

Herod's Palace

UPPER CITY

Theater

"pinnacle of the temple"

Wall during the time of Christ

Caiaphas' house? Peter denies Jesus.

Spring of Gihon

KIDRON VALLEY

LOWER CITY

Upper Room— Last Supper.

Pool of Siloam

"Now it came to pass, when the time had come for Him to be received up, that He steadfastly set His face to go to Jerusalem."—Luke 9:51

Essene Gate

Refuse Gate

Water Gate

from Bethlehem

HINNOM VALLEY

© 1996 Thomas Nelson, Inc.

²⁰When evening had come, He sat down with the twelve. ²¹Now as they were eating, He said, "Assuredly, I say to you, one of you will betray Me."

²²And they were exceedingly sorrowful, and each of them began to say to Him, "Lord, is it I?"

²³He answered and said, "He who dipped *his* hand with Me in the dish will betray Me. ²⁴The Son of Man indeed goes just as it is written of Him, but woe to that man by whom the Son of Man is betrayed! It would have been good for that man if he had not been born."

²⁵Then Judas, who was betraying Him, answered and said, "Rabbi, is it I?"

He said to him, "You have said it."

Jesus Institutes the Lord's Supper

²⁶And as they were eating, Jesus took bread, blessed*ᵃ* and broke *it*, and gave *it* to the disciples and said, "Take, eat; this is My body."

> **26:26 Take, eat; this is My body.** Jesus transformed the last Passover into the first observance of the Lord's Supper. He is represented symbolically by both the paschal lamb of the Passover and the elements in the communion service. His statement, "this is My body" could not have been taken literally by the disciples.

²⁷Then He took the cup, and gave thanks, and gave *it* to them, saying, "Drink from it, all of you. ²⁸For this is My blood of the new*ᵃ* covenant, which is shed for many for the remission of sins. ²⁹But I say to you, I will not drink of this fruit of the vine from now on until that day when I drink it new with you in My Father's kingdom."

³⁰And when they had sung a hymn, they went out to the Mount of Olives.

Jesus Predicts Peter's Denial

³¹Then Jesus said to them, "All of you will be made to stumble because of Me this night, for it is written:

'I will strike the Shepherd,
And the sheep of the flock will be
   scattered.' *ᵃ*

³²But after I have been raised, I will go before you to Galilee."

³³Peter answered and said to Him, "Even if all are made to stumble because of You, I will never be made to stumble."

³⁴Jesus said to him, "Assuredly, I say to you that this night, before the rooster crows, you will deny Me three times."

³⁵Peter said to Him, "Even if I have to die with You, I will not deny You!"

And so said all the disciples.

The Prayer in the Garden

³⁶Then Jesus came with them to a place called Gethsemane, and said to the disciples, "Sit here while I go and pray over there." ³⁷And He took with Him Peter and the two sons of Zebedee, and He began to be sorrowful and deeply distressed. ³⁸Then He said to them, "My soul is exceedingly sorrowful, even to death. Stay here and watch with Me."

> **26:36 Gethsemane.** This means "oil press." A garden of ancient olive trees is there to this day. It was a frequent meeting place for Jesus and His disciples (John 18:2), located across the Kidron Valley from Jerusalem (John 18:1). Judas knew that he would find Jesus there, even though Jesus had not previously announced where He would be.

³⁹He went a little farther and fell on His face, and prayed, saying, "O My Father, if it is possible, let this cup pass from Me; nevertheless, not as I will, but as You *will*."

⁴⁰Then He came to the disciples and found them sleeping, and said to Peter, "What! Could you not watch with Me one hour? ⁴¹Watch and pray, lest you enter into temptation. The spirit indeed *is* willing, but the flesh *is* weak."

⁴²Again, a second time, He went away and prayed, saying, "O My Father, if this cup cannot pass away from Me unless*ᵃ* I drink it, Your will be done." ⁴³And He came and found them asleep again, for their eyes were heavy.

⁴⁴So He left them, went away again, and prayed the third time, saying the same words. ⁴⁵Then He came to His disciples and said to them, "Are *you* still sleeping and

---

26:26 *ᵃ*M-Text reads *gave thanks for.*   26:28 *ᵃ*NU-Text omits *new.*   26:31 *ᵃ*Zechariah 13:7
26:42 *ᵃ*NU-Text reads *if this may not pass away unless.*

resting? Behold, the hour is at hand, and the Son of Man is being betrayed into the hands of sinners. [46]Rise, let us be going. See, My betrayer is at hand."

Betrayal and Arrest in Gethsemane

[47]And while He was still speaking, behold, Judas, one of the twelve, with a great multitude with swords and clubs, came from the chief priests and elders of the people. [48]Now His betrayer had given them a sign, saying, "Whomever I kiss, He is the One; seize Him." [49]Immediately he went up to Jesus and said, "Greetings, Rabbi!" and kissed Him.

[50]But Jesus said to him, "Friend, why have you come?"

Then they came and laid hands on Jesus and took Him. [51]And suddenly, one of those who were with Jesus stretched out his hand and drew his sword, struck the servant of the high priest, and cut off his ear. [52]But Jesus said to him, "Put your sword in its place, for all who take the sword will perish[a] by the sword. [53]Or do you think that I cannot now pray to My Father, and He will provide Me with more than twelve legions of angels? [54]How then could the Scriptures be fulfilled, that it must happen thus?"

26:54 Scriptures be fulfilled. God Himself planned every detail of Jesus' death (Acts 2:23). Jesus submitted to the Father's will by dying. Jesus was in absolute control (John 10:17,18), but everyone around Him, including His enemies, had a part in fulfilling the OT prophecies. These events display His divine sovereignty.

---

[55]In that hour Jesus said to the multitudes, "Have you come out, as against a robber, with swords and clubs to take Me? I sat daily with you, teaching in the temple, and you did not seize Me. [56]But all this was done that the Scriptures of the prophets might be fulfilled."

Then all the disciples forsook Him and fled.

Jesus Faces the Sanhedrin

[57]And those who had laid hold of Jesus led Him away to Caiaphas the high priest, where the scribes and the elders were assembled. [58]But Peter followed Him at a distance to the high priest's courtyard. And he went in and sat with the servants to see the end.

[59]Now the chief priests, the elders,[a] and all the council sought false testimony against Jesus to put Him to death, [60]but found none. Even though many false witnesses came forward, they found none.[a] But at last two false witnesses[b] came forward [61]and said, "This fellow said, 'I am able to destroy the temple of God and to build it in three days.' "

[62]And the high priest arose and said to Him, "Do You answer nothing? What is it these men testify against You?" [63]But Jesus kept silent. And the high priest answered and said to Him, "I put You under oath by the living God: Tell us if You are the Christ, the Son of God!"

[64]Jesus said to him, "It is as you said. Nevertheless, I say to you, hereafter you will see the Son of Man sitting at the right hand of the Power, and coming on the clouds of heaven."

[65]Then the high priest tore his clothes, saying, "He has spoken blasphemy! What further need do we have of witnesses? Look, now you have heard His blasphemy! [66]What do you think?"

26:65 the high priest tore his clothes. Normally this was an expression of deep grief (2 Kin. 19:1). The High-Priest was forbidden to tear his clothes (Lev. 10:6), but the Talmud made an exception for High-Priests who witnessed a blasphemy. Caiaphas' supposed grief was as phony as the charge made against Jesus; he was gloating over having found something on which to base his charges.

They answered and said, "He is deserving of death." [67]Then they spat in His face and beat Him; and others struck Him with the palms of their hands, [68]saying, "Prophesy to us, Christ! Who is the one who struck You?"

Peter Denies Jesus, and Weeps Bitterly

⁶⁹Now Peter sat outside in the courtyard. And a servant girl came to him, saying, "You also were with Jesus of Galilee."

⁷⁰But he denied it before *them* all, saying, "I do not know what you are saying."

⁷¹And when he had gone out to the gateway, another *girl* saw him and said to those *who were* there, "This *fellow* also was with Jesus of Nazareth."

⁷²But again he denied with an oath, "I do not know the Man!"

⁷³And a little later those who stood by came up and said to Peter, "Surely you also are *one* of them, for your speech betrays you."

⁷⁴Then he began to curse and swear, *saying*, "I do not know the Man!"

Immediately a rooster crowed. ⁷⁵And Peter remembered the word of Jesus who had said to him, "Before the rooster crows, you will deny Me three times." So he went out and wept bitterly.

> **26:75 And Peter remembered.** Jesus made eye contact with Peter at this very moment, intensifying Peter's shame (Luke 22:61). Peter departed from Caiaphas' house and wept bitterly. The true Peter is seen, however, in his repentance. His account reminds us of our weakness and of the riches of divine grace (see John 21:15–19).

Jesus Handed Over to Pontius Pilate

27 When morning came, all the chief priests and elders of the people plotted against Jesus to put Him to death. ²And when they had bound Him, they led Him away and delivered Him to Pontius*ᵃ* Pilate the governor.

Judas Hangs Himself

³Then Judas, His betrayer, seeing that He had been condemned, was remorseful and brought back the thirty pieces of silver to the chief priests and elders, ⁴saying, "I have sinned by betraying innocent blood."

And they said, "What *is that* to us? You see *to it!*"

⁵Then he threw down the pieces of silver in the temple and departed, and went and hanged himself.

⁶But the chief priests took the silver pieces and said, "It is not lawful to put them into the treasury, because they are the price of blood." ⁷And they consulted together and bought with them the potter's field, to bury strangers in. ⁸Therefore that field has been called the Field of Blood to this day.

⁹Then was fulfilled what was spoken by Jeremiah the prophet, saying, "*And they took the thirty pieces of silver, the value of Him who was priced, whom they of the children of Israel priced,* ¹⁰*and gave them for the potter's field, as the* LORD *directed me.*"*ᵃ*

Jesus Faces Pilate

¹¹Now Jesus stood before the governor. And the governor asked Him, saying, "Are You the King of the Jews?"

Jesus said to him, "*It is as* you say." ¹²And while He was being accused by the chief priests and elders, He answered nothing.

¹³Then Pilate said to Him, "Do You not hear how many things they testify against You?" ¹⁴But He answered him not one word, so that the governor marveled greatly.

Taking the Place of Barabbas

¹⁵Now at the feast the governor was accustomed to releasing to the multitude one prisoner whom they wished. ¹⁶And at that time they had a notorious prisoner called Barabbas.*ᵃ* ¹⁷Therefore, when they had gathered together, Pilate said to them, "Whom do you want me to release to you? Barabbas, or Jesus who is called Christ?" ¹⁸For he knew that they had handed Him over because of envy.

¹⁹While he was sitting on the judgment seat, his wife sent to him, saying, "Have nothing to do with that just Man, for I have suffered many things today in a dream because of Him."

²⁰But the chief priests and elders persuaded the multitudes that they should ask for Barabbas and destroy Jesus. ²¹The governor answered and said to them, "Which of the two do you want me to release to you?"

They said, "Barabbas!"

²²Pilate said to them, "What then shall I do with Jesus who is called Christ?"

27:2 *ᵃ*NU-Text omits *Pontius.*   27:10 *ᵃ*Jeremiah 32:6–9   27:16 *ᵃ*NU-Text reads *Jesus Barabbas.*

They all said to him, "Let Him be crucified!"

²³Then the governor said, "Why, what evil has He done?"

But they cried out all the more, saying, "Let Him be crucified!"

²⁴When Pilate saw that he could not prevail at all, but rather *that* a tumult was rising, he took water and washed *his* hands before the multitude, saying, "I am innocent of the blood of this just Person.ᵃ You see *to it*."

²⁵And all the people answered and said, "His blood *be* on us and on our children."

²⁶Then he released Barabbas to them; and when he had scourged Jesus, he delivered *Him* to be crucified.

The Soldiers Mock Jesus

²⁷Then the soldiers of the governor took Jesus into the Praetorium and gathered the whole garrison around Him. ²⁸And they stripped Him and put a scarlet robe on Him. ²⁹When they had twisted a crown of thorns, they put *it* on His head, and a reed in His right hand. And they bowed the knee before Him and mocked Him, saying, "Hail, King of the Jews!" ³⁰Then they spat on Him, and took the reed and struck Him on the head. ³¹And when they had mocked Him, they took the robe off Him, put His

---

27:27 Praetorium. This was Pilate's residence in Jerusalem, located in the Antonia Fortress, adjacent to the NW corner of the temple. The soldiers, part of a garrison of 600 soldiers, were assigned to serve Pilate during his stay in Jerusalem.

---

own clothes on Him, and led Him away to be crucified.

The King on a Cross

³²Now as they came out, they found a man of Cyrene, Simon by name. Him they compelled to bear His cross. ³³And when they had come to a place called Golgotha, that is to say, Place of a Skull, ³⁴they gave Him sourᵃ wine mingled with gall to drink. But when He had tasted *it*, He would not drink.

³⁵Then they crucified Him, and divided His garments, casting lots,ᵃ that it might be fulfilled which was spoken by the prophet:

"*They divided My garments among
        them,
        And for My clothing they cast lots.*" ᵇ

³⁶Sitting down, they kept watch over Him there. ³⁷And they put up over His head the accusation written against Him:

        THIS IS JESUS THE KING
        OF THE JEWS.

³⁸Then two robbers were crucified with Him, one on the right and another on the left.

³⁹And those who passed by blasphemed Him, wagging their heads ⁴⁰and saying, "You who destroy the temple and build *it* in three days, save Yourself! If You are the Son of God, come down from the cross."

⁴¹Likewise the chief priests also, mocking with the scribes and elders,ᵃ said, ⁴²"He saved others; Himself He cannot save. If

---

27:24 ᵃNU-Text omits *just*.   27:34 ᵃNU-Text omits *sour*.   27:35 ᵃNU-Text and M-Text omit the rest of this verse.   ᵇPsalm 22:18   27:41 ᵃM-Text reads *with the scribes, the Pharisees, and the elders.*

Does Matthew include any material not found in the other gospels?

Matthew includes nine events in Jesus' life that are unique to his gospel:
1. Joseph's dream (1:20–24).
2. Visit of the wise men (2:1–12).
3. Flight into Egypt (2:13–15).
4. Herod kills the children (2:16–18).
5. Judas repents (27:3–10, but see Acts 1:18,19).
6. The dream of Pilate's wife (27:19).
7. Other resurrections (27:52).
8. The bribery of the soldiers (28:11–15).
9. The Great Commission (28:19,20).

27:40 destroy the temple and build *it* **in three days.** They missed Jesus' point. "He was speaking of the temple of His body" (John 2:21). He would not "come down from the cross," but not because He was powerless to do so (John 10:18). The proof that He was the Son of God came "in three days," when He returned with His body ("the temple") rebuilt.

He is the King of Israel,*a* let Him now come down from the cross, and we will believe Him.*b* 43He trusted in God; let Him deliver Him now if He will have Him; for He said, 'I am the Son of God.' "

44Even the robbers who were crucified with Him reviled Him with the same thing.

Jesus Dies on the Cross

45Now from the sixth hour until the ninth hour there was darkness over all the land. 46And about the ninth hour Jesus cried out with a loud voice, saying, "Eli, Eli, lama sabachthani?" that is, *"My God, My God, why have You forsaken Me?"* *a*

47Some of those who stood there, when they heard *that*, said, "This Man is calling for Elijah!" 48Immediately one of them ran and took a sponge, filled *it* with sour wine and put *it* on a reed, and offered it to Him to drink.

49The rest said, "Let Him alone; let us see if Elijah will come to save Him."

50And Jesus cried out again with a loud voice, and yielded up His spirit.

51Then, behold, the veil of the temple was torn in two from top to bottom; and the earth quaked, and the rocks were split, 52and the graves were opened; and many bodies of the saints who had fallen asleep were raised; 53and coming out of the graves after His resurrection, they went into the holy city and appeared to many.

54So when the centurion and those with him, who were guarding Jesus, saw the

27:51 the veil of the temple. This was the curtain that blocked the entrance to the Most Holy Place (Ex. 26:33). The tearing of the veil signified that the way into God's presence was now open to all through a new, living way (Heb. 10:19–22). The fact that it tore "from top to bottom" showed that only God could have split it.

earthquake and the things that had happened, they feared greatly, saying, "Truly this was the Son of God!"

55And many women who followed Jesus from Galilee, ministering to Him, were there looking on from afar, 56among whom were Mary Magdalene, Mary the mother of James and Joses,*a* and the mother of Zebedee's sons.

Jesus Buried in Joseph's Tomb

57Now when evening had come, there came a rich man from Arimathea, named Joseph, who himself had also become a disciple of Jesus. 58This man went to Pilate and asked for the body of Jesus. Then Pilate commanded the body to be given to him. 59When Joseph had taken the body, he wrapped it in a clean linen cloth, 60and laid it in his new tomb which he had hewn out of the rock; and he rolled a large stone against the door of the tomb, and departed. 61And Mary Magdalene was there, and the other Mary, sitting opposite the tomb.

27:57 Joseph. He was a member of the Sanhedrin (Mark 15:43; Luke 23:50,51). He had not agreed with the decision to condemn Christ. Joseph and Nicodemus (John 19:39), prominent Jewish leaders, buried Christ in Joseph's own "new tomb," thus fulfilling the prophecy of Is. 53:9. **Arimathea.** This was a town about 20 miles NW of Jerusalem.

Pilate Sets a Guard

62On the next day, which followed the Day of Preparation, the chief priests and Pharisees gathered together to Pilate, 63saying, "Sir, we remember, while He was still alive, how that deceiver said, 'After three days I will rise.' 64Therefore command that the tomb be made secure until the third day, lest His disciples come by night*a* and steal Him *away*, and say to the people, 'He has risen from the dead.' So the last deception will be worse than the first."

65Pilate said to them, "You have a guard; go your way, make *it* as secure as you know how." 66So they went and made the tomb secure, sealing the stone and setting the guard.

27:42 *a*NU-Text reads *He is the King of Israel!*   *b*NU-Text and M-Text read *we will believe in Him.*
27:46 *a*Psalm 22:1   27:56 *a*NU-Text reads *Joseph.*   27:64 *a*NU-Text omits *by night.*

He Is Risen

28 Now after the Sabbath, as the first *day* of the week began to dawn, Mary Magdalene and the other Mary came to see the tomb. ²And behold, there was a great earthquake; for an angel of the Lord descended from heaven, and came and rolled back the stone from the door,*a* and sat on it. ³His countenance was like lightning, and his clothing as white as snow. ⁴And the guards shook for fear of him, and became like dead *men*.

28:1 as the first day of the week began to dawn. Sabbath officially ended at sundown on Saturday. At that time the women could purchase and prepare spices (Luke 24:1). The event described here occurred at dawn on Sunday, the first day of the week. **other Mary.** She was the mother of James the Less.

---

⁵But the angel answered and said to the women, "Do not be afraid, for I know that you seek Jesus who was crucified. ⁶He is not here; for He is risen, as He said. Come, see the place where the Lord lay. ⁷And go quickly and tell His disciples that He is risen from the dead, and indeed He is going before you into Galilee; there you will see Him. Behold, I have told you."

⁸So they went out quickly from the tomb with fear and great joy, and ran to bring His disciples word.

The Women Worship the Risen Lord

⁹And as they went to tell His disciples,*a* behold, Jesus met them, saying, "Rejoice!" So they came and held Him by the feet and worshiped Him. ¹⁰Then Jesus said to them, "Do not be afraid. Go *and* tell My brethren to go to Galilee, and there they will see Me."

The Soldiers Are Bribed

¹¹Now while they were going, behold, some of the guard came into the city and reported to the chief priests all the things that had happened. ¹²When they had assembled with the elders and consulted together, they gave a large sum of money to the soldiers, ¹³saying, "Tell them, 'His disciples came at night and stole Him *away* while we slept.' ¹⁴And if this comes to the governor's ears, we will appease him and make you secure." ¹⁵So they took the money and did as they were instructed; and this saying is commonly reported among the Jews until this day.

The Great Commission

¹⁶Then the eleven disciples went away into Galilee, to the mountain which Jesus had appointed for them. ¹⁷When they saw Him, they worshiped Him; but some doubted.

¹⁸And Jesus came and spoke to them, saying, "All authority has been given to Me in heaven and on earth. ¹⁹Go therefore*a* and make disciples of all the nations, baptizing them in the name of the Father and of the Son and of the Holy Spirit, ²⁰teaching them to observe all things that I have commanded you; and lo, I am with you always, *even* to the end of the age." Amen.*a*

28:18 All authority. Absolute sovereign authority is handed to Christ "in heaven and on earth." This is proof of His deity. The time of His humiliation was at an end, and God had exalted Him above all (Phil. 2:9–11).

28:2 *a*NU-Text omits *from the door.*   28:9 *a*NU-Text omits the first clause of this verse.
28:19 *a*M-Text omits *therefore.*   28:20 *a*NU-Text omits *Amen.*

As the chilly shadows of evening lengthen into night, the travelers draw closer to the fire. Among them stands a storyteller, spotlighted by the flames. His story is vivid, colorful and full of action. His voice conveys a sense of conviction. Some in his audience find themselves deeply moved by the storyteller's account. It sounds to them like good news. If the story is true, then it is the best story ever shared, for it tells about God's personal visit to earth. That rapid, condensed, but fascinating storyteller's approach to the life of Jesus was used by Mark to record his gospel.

AUTHOR AND DATE

Mark was written by Mark, between A.D. 50 and 70.

Unlike the epistles, the gospels do not name their authors. The early church fathers, however, unanimously affirm that Mark wrote the second gospel. Among these witnesses are Papias, bishop of Hierapolis (about A.D. 140), Justin Martyr (about A.D. 150), and Irenaeus (about A.D. 185). Justin Martyr referred to the Gospel of Mark as "the memoirs of Peter." Irenaeus called Mark "the disciple and interpreter of Peter." Papias' statement about the authorship of Mark bears repeating at length.

And the presbyter [the Apostle John] said this: Mark having become the interpreter of Peter, wrote down accurately whatsoever he remembered. It was not, however, in exact order that he related the sayings or deeds of Christ. For he neither heard the Lord nor accompanied Him. But afterwards, as I said, he accompanied Peter, who accommodated his instructions to the necessities [of his hearers], but with no intention of giving a regular narrative of the Lord's sayings. Wherefore Mark made no mistake in thus writing some things as he remembered them. For of one thing he took especial care, not to omit anything he had heard, and not to put anything fictitious into the statements. [*From the Exposition of the Oracles of the Lord* (6)]

Evangelical scholars have suggested dates for the writing of Mark's gospel ranging from A.D. 50 to 70. The testimony of the church fathers differ as to whether this gospel was written before or after Peter's death (about A.D. 67–68). A date before the destruction of Jerusalem and the temple in A.D. 70 is required by the comment of Jesus in Mark 13:2. That, and the role played by Mark in the events recorded in Acts of the Apostles makes it likely, though not certain, that Mark

was written at an early date, possibly sometime in the A.D. 50's, but certainly later than Matthew.

BACKGROUND AND SETTING

In contrast to Matthew's Jewish audience, Mark seems to have targeted Roman believers, particularly Gentiles. When he employed Aramaic terms, Mark translated them for his readers (3:17; 5:4; 7:11,34; 10:46; 14:36; 15:22,34). Further, in some places he used Latin (Roman) expressions instead of their Greek equivalents (5:9; 6:27; 12:15,42; 15:16,39). Mark also used the Roman system when referring to time (6:48; 13:35), and he took care to explain Jewish customs (7:3,4; 14:12; 15:42). Some of Mark's omissions (primarily the genealogies) make sense if his audience had little interest in such material. This gospel also includes less references to the Old Testament and fewer instances that would be of particular interest to Jewish readers—such as details of the conflict between Jesus and the Pharisees and Sadducees. When mentioning Simon of Cyrene (15:21), however, Mark identifies him as the father of Rufus, a prominent member of the church at Rome (Romans 16:13). These details support the traditional view that Mark was written for a Gentile audience initially at Rome.

HISTORICAL AND THEOLOGICAL THEMES

Mark presents Jesus as the suffering Servant of the Lord (10:45). His focus is on the deeds of Jesus more than on His teachings. Mark emphasizes Jesus' service and sacrifice. He omits the lengthy discourses found in the other gospels, often relating only brief excerpts to give the gist of what Jesus taught. This gospel effectively presents the power and impact of Jesus' character with rapid strokes and few details. Mark was the vivid storyteller among the gospel writers.

MARK EMPHASIZES
JESUS' SERVICE AND **SACRIFICE.**

The Gospel of Mark demonstrates the humanity of Christ more clearly than the other evangelists, emphasizing (1) Christ's human emotions (1:41; 3:5; 6:34; 8:12; 9:36); (2) His human limitations (4:38; 11:12; 13:32); and (3) other details that highlight the human side of the Son of God (7:33,34; 8:12; 9:36; 10:13–16).

OUTLINE

John the Baptist Prepares the Way

1 The beginning of the gospel of Jesus Christ, the Son of God. ²As it is written in the Prophets:ª

> "Behold, I send My messenger before
>   Your face,
> Who will prepare Your way before
>   You."ᵇ

1:1 The beginning...the Son of God. This is Mark's title for his gospel. **gospel.** The 4 gospels are written records of the good news about the life, death, and resurrection of Jesus Christ. **Jesus Christ.** "Jesus," the Lord's human name (see Matt. 1:21), is the Greek form of the Hebrew name *Joshua* ("the LORD is salvation"); "Christ": ("anointed one") is the Greek equivalent of the Hebrew word *Messiah* and signifies His office as ruler of God's coming kingdom (Dan. 9:25,26).

³   "The voice of one crying in the
>   wilderness:
>   'Prepare the way of the LORD;
>   Make His paths straight.' " ª

⁴John came baptizing in the wilderness and preaching a baptism of repentance for the remission of sins. ⁵Then all the land of Judea, and those from Jerusalem, went out to him and were all baptized by him in the Jordan River, confessing their sins.

⁶Now John was clothed with camel's hair and with a leather belt around his waist, and he ate locusts and wild honey. ⁷And he preached, saying, "There comes One after me who is mightier than I, whose sandal strap I am not worthy to stoop down and loose. ⁸I indeed baptized you with water, but He will baptize you with the Holy Spirit."

1:6 camel's hair...leather belt. These traditional clothes of a wilderness dweller were sturdy, but not fashionable or comfortable. John's clothing would have reminded the people of Elijah (see 2 Kin. 1:8), whom they expected to come before the Messiah (Mal. 4:5). **locusts and wild honey.** John was a Nazirite, which his diet reflected (see Luke 1:15). The OT dietary regulations permitted the eating of "locusts" (Lev. 11:21,22). "Wild honey" could be found in the wilderness (Deut. 32:13).

John Baptizes Jesus

⁹It came to pass in those days *that* Jesus came from Nazareth of Galilee, and was baptized by John in the Jordan. ¹⁰And immediately, coming up fromª the water, He saw the heavens parting and the Spirit descending upon Him like a dove. ¹¹Then a voice came from heaven, "You are My beloved Son, in whom I am well pleased."

Satan Tempts Jesus

¹²Immediately the Spirit drove Him into the wilderness. ¹³And He was there in the wilderness forty days, tempted by Satan, and was with the wild beasts; and the angels ministered to Him.

1:12 immediately. Jesus' temptation came right after His baptism. **the Spirit drove Him.** Compelled by the Spirit, Jesus confronted Satan, taking the first step toward overthrowing his evil kingdom (see 1 John 3:8). God tempts no one (James 1:13), but He sometimes allows Satan to tempt His people (see Job). **the wilderness.** This may have been the same place where John lived, the desolate region farther south, or the Arabian desert.

Jesus Begins His Galilean Ministry

¹⁴Now after John was put in prison, Jesus came to Galilee, preaching the gospel of the kingdomª of God, ¹⁵and saying, "The time is fulfilled, and the kingdom of God is at hand. Repent, and believe in the gospel."

Four Fishermen Called as Disciples

¹⁶And as He walked by the Sea of Galilee, He saw Simon and Andrew his brother casting a net into the sea; for they were fishermen. ¹⁷Then Jesus said to them, "Follow Me, and I will make you become fishers of men." ¹⁸They immediately left their nets and followed Him.

¹⁹When He had gone a little farther from

1:16 Simon and Andrew. These brothers were fishermen. Because Andrew had been a follower of John the Baptist (John 1:40), Peter may have been also. They had already met and spent time with Jesus and here were called to follow Him permanently. **net.** This rope, forming a circle about 9 feet in diameter with a net attached, could be thrown by hand into the water and hauled in by a weighted rope attached to it.

1:2 ªNU-Text reads *Isaiah the prophet.* ᵇMalachi 3:1   1:3 ªIsaiah 40:3   1:10 ªNU-Text reads *out of.*
1:14 ªNU-Text omits *of the kingdom.*

there, He saw James the *son* of Zebedee, and John his brother, who also *were* in the boat mending their nets. ²⁰And immediately He called them, and they left their father Zebedee in the boat with the hired servants, and went after Him.

Jesus Casts Out an Unclean Spirit

²¹Then they went into Capernaum, and immediately on the Sabbath He entered the synagogue and taught. ²²And they were astonished at His teaching, for He taught them as one having authority, and not as the scribes.

²³Now there was a man in their synagogue with an unclean spirit. And he cried out, ²⁴saying, "Let *us* alone! What have we to do with You, Jesus of Nazareth? Did You come to destroy us? I know who You are— the Holy One of God!"

THE MIRACLES OF JESUS

Miracle	Matthew	Mark	Luke	John
1. Cleansing a Leper	8:2	1:40	5:12	
2. Healing a Centurion's Servant (of paralysis)	8:5		7:1	
3. Healing Peter's Mother-in-Law	8:14	1:30	4:38	
4. Healing the Sick at Evening	8:16	1:32	4:40	
5. Stilling the Storm	8:23	4:35	8:22	
6. Demons Entering a Herd of Swine	8:28	5:1	8:26	
7. Healing a Paralytic	9:2	2:3	5:18	
8. Raising the Ruler's Daughter	9:18,23	5:22,35	8:40,49	
9. Healing the Hemorrhaging Woman	9:20	5:25	8:43	
10. Healing Two Blind Men	9:27			
11. Curing a Demon-Possessed, Mute Man	9:32			
12. Healing a Man's Withered Hand	12:9	3:1	6:6	
13. Curing a Demon-Possessed, Blind and Mute Man	12:22		11:14	
14. Feeding the Five Thousand	14:13	6:30	9:10	6:1
15. Walking on the Sea	14:25	6:48		6:19
16. Healing the Gentile Woman's Daughter	15:21	7:24		
17. Feeding the Four Thousand	15:32	8:1		
18. Healing the Epileptic Boy	17:14	9:17	9:38	
19. Temple Tax in the Fish's Mouth	17:24			
20. Healing Two Blind Man	20:30	10:46	18:35	
21. Withering the Fig Tree	21:18	11:12		
22. Casting Out an Unclean Spirit		1:23	4:33	
23. Healing a Deaf-Mute		7:31		
24. Healing a Blind Man at Bethsaida		8:22		
25. Escape from the Hostile Multitude			4:30	
26. Catch of Fish			5:1	
27. Raising of a Widow's Son at Nain			7:11	
28. Healing the Infirm, Bent Woman			13:11	
29. Healing the Man with Dropsy			14:1	
30. Cleansing the Ten Lepers			17:11	
31. Restoring a Servant's Ear			22:51	
32. Turning Water into Wine				2:1
33. Healing the Nobleman's Son (of fever)				4:46
34. Healing an Infirm Man at Bethesda				5:1
35. Healing the Man Born Blind				9:1
36. Raising of Lazarus				11:43
37. Second Catch of Fish				21:1

1:22 authority. Jesus' authority came as the spoken Word of God. The people were familiar with scribes of the OT who based their authority on that of other rabbis. The people were astonished by Jesus' direct, personal, and forceful teaching (see Titus 2:15).

²⁵But Jesus rebuked him, saying, "Be quiet, and come out of him!" ²⁶And when the unclean spirit had convulsed him and cried out with a loud voice, he came out of him. ²⁷Then they were all amazed, so that they questioned among themselves, saying, "What is this? What new doctrine *is* this? For with authority*ᵃ* He commands even the unclean spirits, and they obey Him." ²⁸And immediately His fame spread throughout all the region around Galilee.

Peter's Mother-in-Law Healed

²⁹Now as soon as they had come out of the synagogue, they entered the house of Simon and Andrew, with James and John. ³⁰But Simon's wife's mother lay sick with a fever, and they told Him about her at once. ³¹So He came and took her by the hand and lifted her up, and immediately the fever left her. And she served them.

Many Healed After Sabbath Sunset

³²At evening, when the sun had set, they brought to Him all who were sick and those who were demon-possessed. ³³And the whole city was gathered together at the door. ³⁴Then He healed many who were sick with various diseases, and cast out many demons; and He did not allow the demons to speak, because they knew Him.

Preaching in Galilee

³⁵Now in the morning, having risen a long while before daylight, He went out and departed to a solitary place; and there He prayed. ³⁶And Simon and those *who were* with Him searched for Him. ³⁷When they found Him, they said to Him, "Everyone is looking for You."

³⁸But He said to them, "Let us go into the next towns, that I may preach there also, because for this purpose I have come forth." ³⁹And He was preaching in their synagogues throughout all Galilee, and casting out demons.

Jesus Cleanses a Leper

⁴⁰Now a leper came to Him, imploring Him, kneeling down to Him and saying to Him, "If You are willing, You can make me clean."

⁴¹Then Jesus, moved with compassion, stretched out *His* hand and touched him, and said to him, "I am willing; be cleansed." ⁴²As soon as He had spoken, immediately the leprosy left him, and he was cleansed. ⁴³And He strictly warned him and sent him away at once, ⁴⁴and said to him, "See that you say nothing to anyone; but go your way, show yourself to the priest, and offer for your cleansing those things which Moses commanded, as a testimony to them."

1:41 compassion. Only Mark records Jesus' emotional reaction to the leper's desperate situation. The Greek word appears only in the synoptic gospels and, apart from the parables, is used only in reference to Jesus.

⁴⁵However, he went out and began to proclaim *it* freely, and to spread the matter, so that Jesus could no longer openly enter the city, but was outside in deserted places; and they came to Him from every direction.

Jesus Forgives and Heals a Paralytic

2 And again He entered Capernaum after *some* days, and it was heard that He was in the house. ²Immediately*ᵃ* many gathered together, so that there was no

---

1:27 *ᵃ*NU-Text reads *What is this? A new doctrine with authority.*   2:2 *ᵃ*NU-Text omits *Immediately.*

What is the relationship of Mark to Luke and Matthew?

Even a cursory reading of the first three gospels reveals many striking similarities. Compare Mark 2:3-12, Matthew 9:2-8, and Luke 5:18-26. Significant differences can also be found, however, in the way each writer handles many details about Jesus. The question about how to explain these similarities and differences is known as the "Synoptic Problem" (*syn* means "together" and *optic* means "seeing"). See the discussion of the "Synoptic Problem" following the Introduction to Matthew.

longer room to receive *them*, not even near the door. And He preached the word to them. ³Then they came to Him, bringing a paralytic who was carried by four *men*. ⁴And when they could not come near Him because of the crowd, they uncovered the roof where He was. So when they had broken through, they let down the bed on which the paralytic was lying.

2:4 they uncovered the roof. The roof was made of slabs of burnt or dried clay that were placed on supporting beams which stretched from wall to wall. Fresh, wet clay was spread over the slabs to seal against rain. The paralytic's friends had to dig out the top coat of clay and remove several slabs until they made room to lower him down.

⁵When Jesus saw their faith, He said to the paralytic, "Son, your sins are forgiven you."

⁶And some of the scribes were sitting there and reasoning in their hearts, ⁷"Why does this *Man* speak blasphemies like this? Who can forgive sins but God alone?"

⁸But immediately, when Jesus perceived in His spirit that they reasoned thus within themselves, He said to them, "Why do you reason about these things in your hearts? ⁹Which is easier, to say to the paralytic, '*Your* sins are forgiven you,' or to say, 'Arise, take up your bed and walk'? ¹⁰But that you may know that the Son of Man has power on earth to forgive sins"—He said to the paralytic, ¹¹"I say to you, arise, take up your bed, and go to your house." ¹²Immediately he arose, took up the bed, and went out in the presence of them all, so that all were amazed and glorified God, saying, "We never saw *anything* like this!"

2:9 Which is easier. It is obviously easier to simply say the words, "Your sins are forgiven." No human can prove that it occurred, since the outcome is invisible. Commanding a paralytic to walk, however, is more difficult, for the truth of the statement will be immediately verified or shown to be false.

Matthew the Tax Collector

¹³Then He went out again by the sea; and all the multitude came to Him, and He taught them. ¹⁴As He passed by, He saw

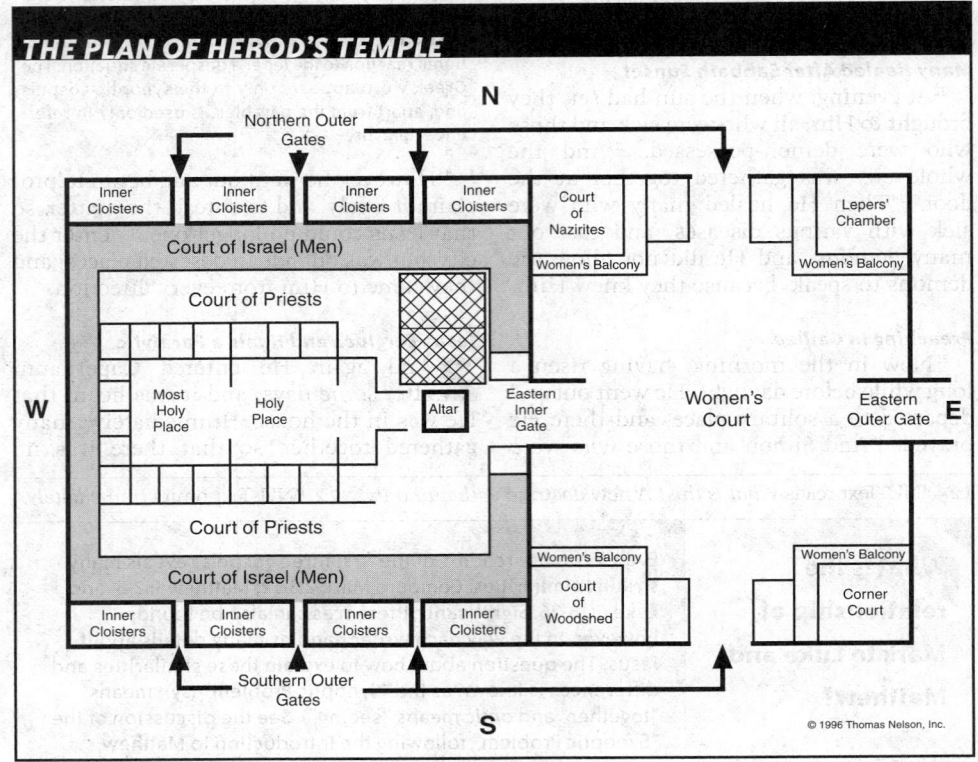

THE PLAN OF HEROD'S TEMPLE

© 1996 Thomas Nelson, Inc.

Levi the *son* of Alphaeus sitting at the tax office. And He said to him, "Follow Me." So he arose and followed Him.

¹⁵Now it happened, as He was dining in *Levi's* house, that many tax collectors and sinners also sat together with Jesus and His disciples; for there were many, and they followed Him. ¹⁶And when the scribes and*ᵃ* Pharisees saw Him eating with the tax collectors and sinners, they said to His disciples, "How *is it* that He eats and drinks with tax collectors and sinners?"

¹⁷When Jesus heard it, He said to them, "Those who are well have no need of a physician, but those who are sick. I did not come to call *the* righteous, but sinners, to repentance."*ᵃ*

Jesus Is Questioned About Fasting

¹⁸The disciples of John and of the Pharisees were fasting. Then they came and said to Him, "Why do the disciples of John and of the Pharisees fast, but Your disciples do not fast?"

¹⁹And Jesus said to them, "Can the friends of the bridegroom fast while the bridegroom is with them? As long as they have the bridegroom with them they cannot fast. ²⁰But the days will come when the bridegroom will be taken away from them, and then they will fast in those days. ²¹No one sews a piece of unshrunk cloth on an old garment; or else the new piece pulls away from the old, and the tear is made worse. ²²And no one puts new wine into old wineskins; or else the new wine bursts the wineskins, the wine is spilled, and the wineskins are ruined. But new wine must be put into new wineskins."

> **2:21,22** Jesus' two parables illustrate that His new and internal gospel of repentance from and forgiveness of sin could not be connected to or contained in the old and external traditions of self-righteousness and ritual. **new wineskins.** New, unused wineskins had the strength and elasticity to hold up as the wine fermented.

Jesus Is Lord of the Sabbath

²³Now it happened that He went through the grainfields on the Sabbath; and as they went His disciples began to pluck the heads of grain. ²⁴And the Pharisees said to Him, "Look, why do they do what is not lawful on the Sabbath?"

²⁵But He said to them, "Have you never read what David did when he was in need and hungry, he and those with him: ²⁶how he went into the house of God *in the days* of Abiathar the high priest, and ate the showbread, which is not lawful to eat except for the priests, and also gave some to those who were with him?"

²⁷And He said to them, "The Sabbath was made for man, and not man for the Sabbath. ²⁸Therefore the Son of Man is also Lord of the Sabbath."

> **2:27 The Sabbath was made for man.** God instituted the Sabbath to benefit man by giving him a day to rest from his labors and be a blessing to him. The Pharisees had turned it into a burden, making man a slave to regulations.

Healing on the Sabbath

3 And He entered the synagogue again, and a man was there who had a withered hand. ²So they watched Him closely, whether He would heal him on the Sabbath, so that they might accuse Him. ³And He said to the man who had the withered hand, "Step forward." ⁴Then He said to them, "Is it lawful on the Sabbath to do good or to do evil, to save life or to kill?" But they kept silent. ⁵And when He had looked around at them with anger, being grieved by the hardness of their hearts, He said to the man, "Stretch out your hand." And he stretched *it* out, and his hand was restored as whole as the other.*ᵃ* ⁶Then the Pharisees went out and immediately plotted with the Herodians against Him, how they might destroy Him.

A Great Multitude Follows Jesus

⁷But Jesus withdrew with His disciples to the sea. And a great multitude from Galilee followed Him, and from Judea ⁸and Jerusalem and Idumea and beyond the Jordan; and those from Tyre and Sidon, a great multitude, when they heard how many things He was doing, came to Him. ⁹So He

---

2:16 *ᵃ*NU-Text reads *of the.*   2:17 *ᵃ*NU-Text omits *to repentance.*   3:5 *ᵃ*NU-Text omits *as whole as the other.*

told His disciples that a small boat should be kept ready for Him because of the multitude, lest they should crush Him. ¹⁰For He healed many, so that as many as had afflictions pressed about Him to touch Him. ¹¹And the unclean spirits, whenever they saw Him, fell down before Him and cried out, saying, "You are the Son of God." ¹²But He sternly warned them that they should not make Him known.

The Twelve Apostles

¹³And He went up on the mountain and called to *Him* those He Himself wanted. And they came to Him. ¹⁴Then He appointed twelve,ᵃ that they might be with Him and that He might send them out to preach, ¹⁵and to have power to heal sicknesses andᵃ to cast out demons: ¹⁶Simon,ᵃ to whom He gave the name Peter; ¹⁷James the *son* of Zebedee and John the brother of James, to whom He gave the name Boanerges, that is, "Sons of Thunder"; ¹⁸Andrew, Philip, Bartholomew, Matthew, Thomas, James the *son* of Alphaeus, Thaddaeus, Simon the Cananite; ¹⁹and Judas Iscariot, who also betrayed Him. And they went into a house.

A House Divided Cannot Stand

²⁰Then the multitude came together again, so that they could not so much as eat bread. ²¹But when His own people heard *about this*, they went out to lay hold of Him, for they said, "He is out of His mind." ²²And the scribes who came down from Jerusalem said, "He has Beelzebub," and, "By the ruler of the demons He casts out demons."

²³So He called them to *Himself* and said to them in parables: "How can Satan cast out Satan? ²⁴If a kingdom is divided against itself, that kingdom cannot stand. ²⁵And if a house is divided against itself, that house cannot stand. ²⁶And if Satan has risen up against himself, and is divided, he cannot stand, but has an end. ²⁷No one can enter a strong man's house and plunder his goods, unless he first binds the strong man. And then he will plunder his house.

The Unpardonable Sin

²⁸"Assuredly, I say to you, all sins will be forgiven the sons of men, and whatever blasphemies they may utter; ²⁹but he who blasphemes against the Holy Spirit never has forgiveness, but is subject to eternal condemnation"—³⁰because they said, "He has an unclean spirit."

Jesus' Mother and Brothers Send for Him

³¹Then His brothers and His mother came, and standing outside they sent to Him, calling Him. ³²And a multitude was sitting around Him; and they said to Him, "Look, Your mother and Your brothersᵃ are outside seeking You."

³³But He answered them, saying, "Who is My mother, or My brothers?" ³⁴And He looked around in a circle at those who sat about Him, and said, "Here are My mother and My brothers! ³⁵For whoever does the will of God is My brother and My sister and mother."

3:14 ᵃNU-Text adds *whom He also named apostles.*   3:15 ᵃNU-Text omits *to heal sicknesses and.*
3:16 ᵃNU-Text reads *and He appointed the twelve: Simon. . . .*   3:32 ᵃNU-Text and M-Text add *and Your sisters.*

The Parable of the Sower

4 And again He began to teach by the sea. And a great multitude was gathered to Him, so that He got into a boat and sat *in it* on the sea; and the whole multitude was on the land facing the sea. [2]Then He taught them many things by parables, and said to them in His teaching:

[3]"Listen! Behold, a sower went out to sow. [4]And it happened, as he sowed, *that* some *seed* fell by the wayside; and the birds of the air[a] came and devoured it. [5]Some fell on stony ground, where it did not have much earth; and immediately it sprang up because it had no depth of earth. [6]But when the sun was up it was scorched, and because it had no root it withered away. [7]And some *seed* fell among thorns; and the thorns grew up and choked it, and it yielded no crop. [8]But other *seed* fell on good ground and yielded a crop that sprang up, increased and produced: some thirtyfold, some sixty, and some a hundred."

[9]And He said to them,[a] "He who has ears to hear, let him hear!"

The Purpose of Parables

[10]But when He was alone, those around Him with the twelve asked Him about the parable. [11]And He said to them, "To you it has been given to know the mystery of the kingdom of God; but to those who are outside, all things come in parables, [12]so that

'Seeing they may see and not perceive,
And hearing they may hear and not understand;
Lest they should turn,
And their sins be forgiven them.' "[a]

The Parable of the Sower Explained

[13]And He said to them, "Do you not understand this parable? How then will you understand all the parables? [14]The sower sows the word. [15]And these are the ones by the wayside where the word is sown. When they hear, Satan comes immediately and takes away the word that was sown in their hearts. [16]These likewise are the ones sown on stony ground who, when they hear the word, immediately receive it with gladness; [17]and they have no root in themselves, and so endure only for a time. Afterward, when tribulation or persecution arises for the word's sake, immediately they stumble. [18]Now these are the ones sown among thorns; *they are* the ones who hear the word, [19]and the cares of this world, the deceitfulness of riches, and the desires for other things entering in choke the word, and it becomes unfruitful. [20]But these are the ones sown on good ground, those who hear the word, accept *it*, and bear fruit: some thirtyfold, some sixty, and some a hundred."

4:17 no root. The gospel cannot take root and transform the life of someone whose heart is hard like the stony ground. **tribulation or persecution.** This refers to the suffering which results from one's association with God's Word. **stumble.** The superficial believer is offended, stumbles, and falls away when his faith is put to the test (see John 8:31).

Light Under a Basket

[21]Also He said to them, "Is a lamp brought to be put under a basket or under a bed? Is it not to be set on a lampstand? [22]For there is nothing hidden which will not be revealed, nor has anything been kept secret but that it should come to light. [23]If anyone has ears to hear, let him hear."

[24]Then He said to them, "Take heed what you hear. With the same measure you use, it will be measured to you; and to you who hear, more will be given. [25]For whoever has,

---

4:4 [a]NU-Text and M-Text omit *of the air.*   4:9 [a]NU-Text and M-Text omit *to them.*
4:12 [a]Isaiah 6:9,10

Q **Does Mark include any material not found in the other gospels?**

A Three passages found in Mark are only recorded in his gospel:

1. The parable of the growing seed (4:26–29).
2. A deaf and mute man is healed (7:31–37).
3. A blind man is healed (8:22–26).

to him more will be given; but whoever does not have, even what he has will be taken away from him."

The Parable of the Growing Seed

26And He said, "The kingdom of God is as if a man should scatter seed on the ground, 27and should sleep by night and rise by day, and the seed should sprout and grow, he himself does not know how. 28For the earth yields crops by itself: first the blade, then the head, after that the full grain in the head. 29But when the grain ripens, immediately he puts in the sickle, because the harvest has come."

The Parable of the Mustard Seed

30Then He said, "To what shall we liken the kingdom of God? Or with what parable shall we picture it? 31*It is* like a mustard seed which, when it is sown on the ground, is smaller than all the seeds on earth; 32but when it is sown, it grows up and becomes greater than all herbs, and shoots out large branches, so that the birds of the air may nest under its shade."

4:31 a mustard seed. This refers to the black mustard plant. The leaves were used as a vegetable and the seed as a condiment. It also was used for medicinal purposes. **smaller than all.** The mustard seed is not the smallest seed in existence, but it was the smallest in comparison to all the other seeds sowed in Palestine.

Jesus' Use of Parables

33And with many such parables He spoke the word to them as they were able to hear it. 34But without a parable He did not speak to them. And when they were alone, He explained all things to His disciples.

Wind and Wave Obey Jesus

35On the same day, when evening had come, He said to them, "Let us cross over to the other side." 36Now when they had left the multitude, they took Him along in the boat as He was. And other little boats were also with Him. 37And a great windstorm arose, and the waves beat into the boat, so that it was already filling. 38But He

was in the stern, asleep on a pillow. And they awoke Him and said to Him, "Teacher, do You not care that we are perishing?"

39Then He arose and rebuked the wind, and said to the sea, "Peace, be still!" And the wind ceased and there was a great calm. 40But He said to them, "Why are you so fearful? How *is it* that you have no faith?"a 41And they feared exceedingly, and said to one another, "Who can this be, that even the wind and the sea obey Him!"

4:41 they feared exceedingly. This is a reverence for the supernatural power Jesus had displayed. Having God in the boat was more terrifying than the storm itself. **Who can this be.** This statement betrayed the disciples' wonder at the true identity of Jesus.

A Demon-Possessed Man Healed

5 Then they came to the other side of the sea, to the country of the Gadarenes.a 2And when He had come out of the boat, immediately there met Him out of the tombs a man with an unclean spirit, 3who had *his* dwelling among the tombs; and no one could bind him,a not even with chains, 4because he had often been bound with shackles and chains. And the chains had been pulled apart by him, and the shackles broken in pieces; neither could anyone tame him. 5And always, night and day, he was in the mountains and in the tombs, crying out and cutting himself with stones.

6When he saw Jesus from afar, he ran and worshiped Him. 7And he cried out with a loud voice and said, "What have I to do with You, Jesus, Son of the Most High God? I implore You by God that You do not torment me."

8For He said to him, "Come out of the

5:9 "What *is* your name?" Jesus probably asked this in view of the demon's appeal to not be tortured. He did not need to know the demon's name in order to expel him. Rather, Jesus asked in order to bring the reality of the situation into the open. **Legion.** This Latin term, common to the Jews and Greeks, defined a Roman military unit of 6,000 infantrymen. The man was controlled by a large number of evil spirits.

4:40 aNU-Text reads *Have you still no faith?*   5:1 aNU-Text reads *Gerasenes.*   5:3 aNU-Text adds *anymore.*

man, unclean spirit!" ⁹Then He asked him, "What *is* your name?"

And he answered, saying, "My name *is* Legion; for we are many." ¹⁰Also he begged Him earnestly that He would not send them out of the country.

¹¹Now a large herd of swine was feeding there near the mountains. ¹²So all the demons begged Him, saying, "Send us to the swine, that we may enter them." ¹³And at once Jesus*ᵃ* gave them permission. Then the unclean spirits went out and entered the swine (there were about two thousand); and the herd ran violently down the steep place into the sea, and drowned in the sea.

¹⁴So those who fed the swine fled, and they told *it* in the city and in the country. And they went out to see what it was that had happened. ¹⁵Then they came to Jesus, and saw the one *who had been* demon-possessed and had the legion, sitting and clothed and in his right mind. And they were afraid. ¹⁶And those who saw it told them how it happened to him *who had been* demon-possessed, and about the swine. ¹⁷Then they began to plead with Him to depart from their region.

> **5:17 plead with Him to depart from their region.** The residents of the region were frightened and resentful toward Jesus because of what had happened. They may have been concerned about the disruption of their normal routine and loss of property. They were ungodly people who were frightened by Christ's display of spiritual power.

¹⁸And when He got into the boat, he who had been demon-possessed begged Him that he might be with Him. ¹⁹However, Jesus did not permit him, but said to him, "Go home to your friends, and tell them what great things the Lord has done for you, and how He has had compassion on you." ²⁰And he departed and began to proclaim in Decapolis all that Jesus had done for him; and all marveled.

A Girl Restored to Life and a Woman Healed

²¹Now when Jesus had crossed over again by boat to the other side, a great multitude gathered to Him; and He was by the sea. ²²And behold, one of the rulers of the synagogue came, Jairus by name. And when he saw Him, he fell at His feet ²³and begged Him earnestly, saying, "My little daughter lies at the point of death. Come and lay Your hands on her, that she may be healed, and she will live." ²⁴So *Jesus* went with him, and a great multitude followed Him and thronged Him.

²⁵Now a certain woman had a flow of blood for twelve years, ²⁶and had suffered many things from many physicians. She had spent all that she had and was no better, but rather grew worse. ²⁷When she heard about Jesus, she came behind *Him* in the crowd and touched His garment. ²⁸For she said, "If only I may touch His clothes, I shall be made well."

> **5:28 If only I may touch His clothes.** The woman's faith in Jesus' healing powers was so great that she believed even indirect contact with Him through His garments would be enough to heal her.

²⁹Immediately the fountain of her blood was dried up, and she felt in *her* body that she was healed of the affliction. ³⁰And Jesus, immediately knowing in Himself that power had gone out of Him, turned around in the crowd and said, "Who touched My clothes?"

³¹But His disciples said to Him, "You see the multitude thronging You, and You say, 'Who touched Me?' "

³²And He looked around to see her who had done this thing. ³³But the woman, fearing and trembling, knowing what had happened to her, came and fell down before Him and told Him the whole truth. ³⁴And He said to her, "Daughter, your faith has made you well. Go in peace, and be healed of your affliction."

³⁵While He was still speaking, *some* came from the ruler of the synagogue's *house* who said, "Your daughter is dead. Why trouble the Teacher any further?"

³⁶As soon as Jesus heard the word that was spoken, He said to the ruler of the synagogue, "Do not be afraid; only believe." ³⁷And He permitted no one to follow Him except Peter, James, and John the brother of James. ³⁸Then He came to the house of the ruler of the synagogue, and saw a tumult

---

5:13 *ᵃ*NU-Text reads *And He gave.*

and those who wept and wailed loudly. [39]When He came in, He said to them, "Why make this commotion and weep? The child is not dead, but sleeping."

[40]And they ridiculed Him. But when He had put them all outside, He took the father and the mother of the child, and those *who were* with Him, and entered where the child was lying. [41]Then He took the child by the hand, and said to her, "Talitha, cumi," which is translated, "Little girl, I say to you, arise." [42]Immediately the girl arose and walked, for she was twelve years *of age*. And they were overcome with great amazement. [43]But He commanded them strictly that no one should know it, and said that *something* should be given her to eat.

Jesus Rejected at Nazareth

6 Then He went out from there and came to His own country, and His disciples followed Him. [2]And when the Sabbath had come, He began to teach in the synagogue. And many hearing *Him* were astonished, saying, "Where *did* this Man *get* these things? And what wisdom *is* this which is given to Him, that such mighty works are performed by His hands! [3]Is this not the carpenter, the Son of Mary, and brother of James, Joses, Judas, and Simon? And are not His sisters here with us?" So they were offended at Him.

> **6:3 carpenter.** The people of Nazareth saw Jesus as a carpenter, like his father (see Matt. 13:55). The common earthly position of Jesus and His family caused the townspeople to stumble; they could not see Jesus as higher than themselves and would not accept Him as the Son of God and Messiah. **Son of Mary.** Jesus is called this only here. Normally, a son was identified by his father's name. Perhaps Joseph had already died or the people were recalling the rumors of Jesus' illegitimate birth and were trying to insult Him with this title.

[4]But Jesus said to them, "A prophet is not without honor except in his own country, among his own relatives, and in his own house." [5]Now He could do no mighty work there, except that He laid His hands on a few sick people and healed *them*. [6]And He marveled because of their unbelief. Then He went about the villages in a circuit, teaching.

Sending Out the Twelve

[7]And He called the twelve to *Himself*, and began to send them out two by two, and gave them power over unclean spirits. [8]He commanded them to take nothing for the journey except a staff—no bag, no bread, no copper in *their* money belts—[9]but to wear sandals, and not to put on two tunics.

[10]Also He said to them, "In whatever place you enter a house, stay there till you depart from that place. [11]And whoever[a] will not receive you nor hear you, when you depart from there, shake off the dust under your feet as a testimony against them.[b] Assuredly, I say to you, it will be more tolerable for Sodom and Gomorrah in the day of judgment than for that city!"

> **6:11 shake off the dust.** This was a symbolic act of renouncing further fellowship with someone. The disciples showed that since the people had rejected Jesus and the gospel, they would be rejected themselves by the disciples and by the Lord. **more tolerable for Sodom and Gomorrah.** People who reject Christ's gospel will be judged far worse than those judged in the two cities (see Gen. 19:24).

[12]So they went out and preached that *people* should repent. [13]And they cast out many demons, and anointed with oil many who were sick, and healed *them*.

John the Baptist Beheaded

[14]Now King Herod heard *of Him*, for His name had become well known. And he said, "John the Baptist is risen from the dead, and therefore these powers are at work in him."

[15]Others said, "It is Elijah."

And others said, "It is the Prophet, or[a] like one of the prophets."

[16]But when Herod heard, he said, "This is John, whom I beheaded; he has been raised from the dead!" [17]For Herod himself had sent and laid hold of John, and bound him in prison for the sake of Herodias, his brother Philip's wife; for he had married

---

6:11 [a]NU-Text reads *whatever place*. [b]NU-Text omits the rest of this verse.   6:15 [a]NU-Text and M-Text omit *or*.

her. [18]Because John had said to Herod, "It is not lawful for you to have your brother's wife."

[19]Therefore Herodias held it against him and wanted to kill him, but she could not; [20]for Herod feared John, knowing that he *was* a just and holy man, and he protected him. And when he heard him, he did many things, and heard him gladly.

[21]Then an opportune day came when Herod on his birthday gave a feast for his nobles, the high officers, and the chief *men* of Galilee. [22]And when Herodias' daughter herself came in and danced, and pleased Herod and those who sat with him, the king said to the girl, "Ask me whatever you want, and I will give *it* to you." [23]He also swore to her, "Whatever you ask me, I will give you, up to half my kingdom."

> **6:23 up to half my kingdom.** This was an exaggeration to enhance Herod's previous statement of generosity. As a Roman tetrarch, Herod had no "kingdom" to give.

[24]So she went out and said to her mother, "What shall I ask?"

And she said, "The head of John the Baptist!"

[25]Immediately she came in with haste to the king and asked, saying, "I want you to give me at once the head of John the Baptist on a platter."

[26]And the king was exceedingly sorry; *yet*, because of the oaths and because of those who sat with him, he did not want to refuse her. [27]Immediately the king sent an executioner and commanded his head to be brought. And he went and beheaded him in prison, [28]brought his head on a platter, and gave it to the girl; and the girl gave it to her mother. [29]When his disciples heard *of it*, they came and took away his corpse and laid it in a tomb.

Feeding the Five Thousand

[30]Then the apostles gathered to Jesus and told Him all things, both what they had done and what they had taught. [31]And He said to them, "Come aside by yourselves to a deserted place and rest a while." For there were many coming and going, and they did not even have time to eat. [32]So they departed to a deserted place in the boat by themselves.

[33]But the multitudes[a] saw them departing, and many knew Him and ran there on foot from all the cities. They arrived before them and came together to Him. [34]And Jesus, when He came out, saw a great multitude and was moved with compassion for them, because they were like sheep not having a shepherd. So He began to teach them many things. [35]When the day was now far spent, His disciples came to Him and said, "This is a deserted place, and already the hour *is* late. [36]Send them away, that they may go into the surrounding country and villages and buy themselves bread;[a] for they have nothing to eat."

> **6:34 sheep not having a shepherd.** This OT picture (see Num. 27:17) was used to describe the people as helpless and starving, lacking in spiritual guidance and protection.

[37]But He answered and said to them, "You give them something to eat."

And they said to Him, "Shall we go and buy two hundred denarii worth of bread and give them *something* to eat?"

[38]But He said to them, "How many loaves do you have? Go and see."

And when they found out they said, "Five, and two fish."

[39]Then He commanded them to make them all sit down in groups on the green grass. [40]So they sat down in ranks, in hundreds and in fifties. [41]And when He had taken the five loaves and the two fish, He looked up to heaven, blessed and broke the loaves, and gave *them* to His disciples to set before them; and the two fish He divided among *them* all. [42]So they all ate and were filled. [43]And they took up twelve baskets full of fragments and of the fish. [44]Now those who had eaten the loaves were about[a] five thousand men.

Jesus Walks on the Sea

[45]Immediately He made His disciples get into the boat and go before Him to the

---

6:33 [a]NU-Text and M-Text read *they*.   6:36 [a]NU-Text reads *something to eat* and omits the rest of this verse.   6:44 [a]NU-Text and M-Text omit *about*.

6:44 five thousand men. The Greek word for "men" means only males, so the estimated number did not include women and children (see Matt. 14:12). Traditionally, women and children sat apart from the men for meals. When everyone was added, there could have been at least 20,000 people.

other side, to Bethsaida, while He sent the multitude away. ⁴⁶And when He had sent them away, He departed to the mountain to pray. ⁴⁷Now when evening came, the boat was in the middle of the sea; and He *was* alone on the land. ⁴⁸Then He saw them straining at rowing, for the wind was against them. Now about the fourth watch of the night He came to them, walking on the sea, and would have passed them by. ⁴⁹And when they saw Him walking on the sea, they supposed it was a ghost, and cried out; ⁵⁰for they all saw Him and were troubled. But immediately He talked with them and said to them, "Be of good cheer! It is I; do not be afraid." ⁵¹Then He went up into the boat to them, and the wind ceased. And they were greatly amazed in themselves beyond measure, and marveled. ⁵²For they had not understood about the loaves, because their heart was hardened.

6:50 Be of good cheer! This command accompanies a situation of fear and apprehension in the gospels (see Matt. 9:2,22). It urged the disciples to have courage. **It is I.** This statement (literally "I AM") identified the figure as Jesus and not some phantom. It echoed the OT self-revelation of God (see Ex. 3:14).

Many Touch Him and Are Made Well

⁵³When they had crossed over, they came to the land of Gennesaret and anchored there. ⁵⁴And when they came out of the boat, immediately the people recognized Him, ⁵⁵ran through that whole surrounding region, and began to carry about on beds those who were sick to wherever they heard He was. ⁵⁶Wherever He entered, into villages, cities, or the country, they laid the sick in the marketplaces, and begged Him that they might just touch the hem of His garment. And as many as touched Him were made well.

Defilement Comes from Within

7 Then the Pharisees and some of the scribes came together to Him, having come from Jerusalem. ²Now when[a] they saw some of His disciples eat bread with defiled, that is, with unwashed hands, they found fault. ³For the Pharisees and all the Jews do not eat unless they wash *their* hands in a special way, holding the tradition of the elders. ⁴*When they come* from the marketplace, they do not eat unless they wash. And there are many other things which they have received and hold, *like* the washing of cups, pitchers, copper vessels, and couches.

⁵Then the Pharisees and scribes asked Him, "Why do Your disciples not walk according to the tradition of the elders, but eat bread with unwashed hands?"

⁶He answered and said to them, "Well did Isaiah prophesy of you hypocrites, as it is written:

> 'This people honors Me with their lips,
> But their heart is far from Me.
> ⁷ And in vain they worship Me,
> Teaching as doctrines the commandments of men.'[a]

7:6 did Isaiah prophesy. Isaiah 29:13 is quoted almost exactly from the Greek translation of the OT. Isaiah's prophecy fit the actions of the Pharisees and scribes. **hypocrites.** These spiritual phonies followed the traditions of men. Their teaching required only mechanical and thoughtless conformity without the need for pure hearts.

⁸For laying aside the commandment of God, you hold the tradition of men[a]—the washing of pitchers and cups, and many other such things you do."

⁹He said to them, "*All too* well you reject the commandment of God, that you may keep your tradition. ¹⁰For Moses said, 'Honor your father and your mother';[a] and, 'He who curses father or mother, let him be put to death.'[b] ¹¹But you say, 'If a man says to his father or mother, "Whatever profit you might have received from me *is* Corban"—' (that is, a gift *to God*),

---

7:2 [a]NU-Text omits *when* and *they found fault.*   7:7 [a]Isaiah 29:13   7:8 [a]NU-Text omits the rest of this verse.   7:10 [a]Exodus 20:12; Deuteronomy 5:16 [b]Exodus 21:17

[12]then you no longer let him do anything for his father or his mother, [13]making the word of God of no effect through your tradition which you have handed down. And many such things you do."

[14]When He had called all the multitude to *Himself*, He said to them, "Hear Me, everyone, and understand: [15]There is nothing that enters a man from outside which can defile him; but the things which come out of him, those are the things that defile a man. [16]If anyone has ears to hear, let him hear!"[a]

[17]When He had entered a house away from the crowd, His disciples asked Him concerning the parable. [18]So He said to them, "Are you thus without understanding also? Do you not perceive that whatever enters a man from outside cannot defile him, [19]because it does not enter his heart but his stomach, and is eliminated, *thus* purifying all foods?"[a] [20]And He said, "What comes out of a man, that defiles a man. [21]For from within, out of the heart of men, proceed evil thoughts, adulteries, fornica-tions, murders, [22]thefts, covetousness, wickedness, deceit, lewdness, an evil eye, blasphemy, pride, foolishness. [23]All these evil things come from within and defile a man."

A Gentile Shows Her Faith

[24]From there He arose and went to the region of Tyre and Sidon.[a] And He entered a house and wanted no one to know *it*, but He could not be hidden. [25]For a woman whose young daughter had an unclean spirit heard about Him, and she came and fell at His feet. [26]The woman was a Greek, a Syro-Phoenician by birth, and she kept asking Him to cast the demon out of her daughter. [27]But Jesus said to her, "Let the

> **7:27 first.** Jesus tested the woman's faith. His "first" responsibility was to preach to the Jews (see Rom. 1:16). There would come a time when Gentiles would also receive God's blessings. **the children's bread and throw *it* to the little dogs.** The "bread" refers to God's blessings offered to the Jews. The "little dogs" (Gentiles) had a place in the household of God, though not a prominent place.

7:16 [a]NU-Text omits this verse. 7:19 [a]NU-Text ends quotation with *eliminated,* setting off the final clause as Mark's comment that Jesus has declared all foods clean. 7:24 [a]NU-Text omits *and Sidon.*

How did Mark come to write one of the gospels if he wasn't one of the original disciples?

Although Mark was not one of the original Apostles of Jesus, he was involved in many of the events recorded in the New Testament. He traveled as a close companion of the Apostle Peter and appears repeatedly throughout the book of Acts, where he is known as "John whose surname was Mark" (Acts 12:12,25; 15:37,39). When Peter was miraculously freed from prison, his first action was to go to John Mark's mother's home in Jerusalem (Acts 12:12).

John Mark was also a cousin of Barnabas (Colossians 4:10), and he joined Paul and Barnabas on their first missionary journey (Acts 12:25; 13:5). But Mark deserted the mission team while in Perga and returned to Jerusalem (Acts 13:13). Later, when Barnabas wanted to give Mark another opportunity to travel with Paul's second missionary team, Paul refused. The resulting friction between Paul and Barnabas led to their separation (Acts 15:38–40).

Eventually, Mark's youthful vacillation gave way to great strength and maturity. In time, he proved himself even to the Apostle Paul. When Paul wrote to the Colossians, he told them that if John Mark came, they were to welcome him (Colossians 4:10). Paul even listed Mark as a fellow worker (Philemon 24). Later, Paul told Timothy to "Get Mark and bring him with you, for he is useful to me for ministry" (2 Timothy 4:11).

John Mark's restoration to useful ministry and preparation for writing his gospel was due, in part, to his extended close relationship with Peter (1 Peter 5:13). The older Apostle was no stranger to failure, and his influence on the younger man was no doubt instrumental. Mark grew out of the instability of his youth and into the strength and maturity he would need for the work to which God had called him. As is explained in the Introduction, Mark's gospel represents primarily Peter's version of the life of Jesus.

children be filled first, for it is not good to take the children's bread and throw *it* to the little dogs."

²⁸And she answered and said to Him, "Yes, Lord, yet even the little dogs under the table eat from the children's crumbs."

²⁹Then He said to her, "For this saying go your way; the demon has gone out of your daughter."

³⁰And when she had come to her house, she found the demon gone out, and her daughter lying on the bed.

Jesus Heals a Deaf-Mute

³¹Again, departing from the region of Tyre and Sidon, He came through the midst of the region of Decapolis to the Sea of Galilee. ³²Then they brought to Him one who was deaf and had an impediment in his speech, and they begged Him to put His hand on him. ³³And He took him aside from the multitude, and put His fingers in his ears, and He spat and touched his tongue. ³⁴Then, looking up to heaven, He sighed, and said to him, "Ephphatha," that is, "Be opened."

³⁵Immediately his ears were opened, and the impediment of his tongue was loosed, and he spoke plainly. ³⁶Then He commanded them that they should tell no one; but the more He commanded them, the more widely they proclaimed *it*. ³⁷And they were astonished beyond measure, saying, "He has done all things well. He makes both the deaf to hear and the mute to speak."

Feeding the Four Thousand

8 In those days, the multitude being very great and having nothing to eat, Jesus called His disciples *to Him* and said to them, ²"I have compassion on the multitude, because they have now continued with Me three days and have nothing to eat. ³And if I send them away hungry to their own houses, they will faint on the way; for some of them have come from afar."

⁴Then His disciples answered Him, "How can one satisfy these people with bread here in the wilderness?"

⁵He asked them, "How many loaves do you have?"

And they said, "Seven."

⁶So He commanded the multitude to sit down on the ground. And He took the seven loaves and gave thanks, broke *them* and gave *them* to His disciples to set before *them*; and they set *them* before the multitude. ⁷They also had a few small fish; and having blessed them, He said to set them also before *them*. ⁸So they ate and were filled, and they took up seven large baskets of leftover fragments. ⁹Now those who had eaten were about four thousand. And He sent them away, ¹⁰immediately got into the boat with His disciples, and came to the region of Dalmanutha.

The Pharisees Seek a Sign

¹¹Then the Pharisees came out and began to dispute with Him, seeking from Him a sign from heaven, testing Him. ¹²But He sighed deeply in His spirit, and said, "Why does this generation seek a sign? Assuredly, I say to you, no sign shall be given to this generation."

Beware of the Leaven of the Pharisees and Herod

¹³And He left them, and getting into the boat again, departed to the other side. ¹⁴Now the disciples*ᵃ* had forgotten to take bread, and they did not have more than one loaf with them in the boat. ¹⁵Then He charged them, saying, "Take heed, beware of the leaven of the Pharisees and the leaven of Herod."

¹⁶And they reasoned among themselves, saying, "*It is* because we have no bread."

¹⁷But Jesus, being aware of *it*, said to them, "Why do you reason because you have no bread? Do you not yet perceive nor understand? Is your heart still*ᵃ* hardened? ¹⁸Having eyes, do you not see? And having ears, do you not hear? And do you not remember? ¹⁹When I broke the five loaves for the five thousand, how many baskets full of fragments did you take up?"

They said to Him, "Twelve."

²⁰"Also, when I broke the seven for the four thousand, how many large baskets full of fragments did you take up?"

And they said, "Seven."

²¹So He said to them, "How *is it* you do not understand?"

8:14 *ᵃ*NU-Text and M-Text read *they*.   8:17 *ᵃ*NU-Text omits *still*.

A Blind Man Healed at Bethsaida

²²Then He came to Bethsaida; and they brought a blind man to Him, and begged Him to touch him. ²³So He took the blind man by the hand and led him out of the town. And when He had spit on his eyes and put His hands on him, He asked him if he saw anything.

> **8:23 spit on his eyes.** This action and Jesus' touching the blind man's eyes were meant to reassure him (who would naturally depend on his other senses, such as touch) that Jesus would heal his eyes (see John 9:6).

²⁴And he looked up and said, "I see men like trees, walking."

²⁵Then He put *His* hands on his eyes again and made him look up. And he was restored and saw everyone clearly. ²⁶Then He sent him away to his house, saying, "Neither go into the town, nor tell anyone in the town."ᵃ

Peter Confesses Jesus as the Christ

²⁷Now Jesus and His disciples went out to the towns of Caesarea Philippi; and on the road He asked His disciples, saying to them, "Who do men say that I am?"

²⁸So they answered, "John the Baptist; but some *say*, Elijah; and others, one of the prophets."

²⁹He said to them, "But who do you say that I am?"

Peter answered and said to Him, "You are the Christ."

³⁰Then He strictly warned them that they should tell no one about Him.

Jesus Predicts His Death and Resurrection

³¹And He began to teach them that the Son of Man must suffer many things, and be rejected by the elders and chief priests and scribes, and be killed, and after three days rise again. ³²He spoke this word openly. Then Peter took Him aside and began to rebuke Him. ³³But when He had turned around and looked at His disciples, He rebuked Peter, saying, "Get behind Me, Satan! For you are not mindful of the things of God, but the things of men."

Take Up the Cross and Follow Him

³⁴When He had called the people to *Himself*, with His disciples also, He said to them, "Whoever desires to come after Me, let him deny himself, and take up his cross, and follow Me. ³⁵For whoever desires to save his life will lose it, but whoever loses his life for My sake and the gospel's will save it. ³⁶For what will it profit a man if he gains the whole world, and loses his own soul? ³⁷Or what will a man give in exchange for his soul? ³⁸For whoever is ashamed of Me and My words in this adulterous and sinful generation, of him the Son of Man also will be ashamed when He comes in the glory of His Father with the holy angels."

> **8:33 Get behind Me, Satan!** Peter had just been praised for being God's spokesman (Matt. 16:17–19). Here he was condemned as Satan's mouthpiece. Jesus' death was God's plan (Acts 2:22,23), and anyone who opposed it was advocating Satan's work.

Jesus Transfigured on the Mount

9 And He said to them, "Assuredly, I say to you that there are some standing here who will not taste death till they see the kingdom of God present with power."

> **9:1 not taste death till they see the kingdom.** Jesus was most likely speaking of the Transfiguration, which provided a foretaste of His glory in His second coming. All 3 synoptic gospels place this promise immediately before the Transfiguration.

²Now after six days Jesus took Peter, James, and John, and led them up on a high mountain apart by themselves; and He was transfigured before them. ³His clothes became shining, exceedingly white, like snow, such as no launderer on earth can whiten them. ⁴And Elijah appeared to them with Moses, and they were talking with Jesus. ⁵Then Peter answered and said to Jesus, "Rabbi, it is good for us to be here; and let us make three tabernacles: one for You, one for Moses, and one for Elijah"— ⁶because he did not know what to say, for they were greatly afraid.

⁷And a cloud came and overshadowed them; and a voice came out of the cloud, saying, "This is My beloved Son. Hear

---

8:26 ᵃNU-Text reads *"Do not even go into the town."*

Him!" ⁸Suddenly, when they had looked around, they saw no one anymore, but only Jesus with themselves.

⁹Now as they came down from the mountain, He commanded them that they should tell no one the things they had seen, till the Son of Man had risen from the dead. ¹⁰So they kept this word to themselves, questioning what the rising from the dead meant.

¹¹And they asked Him, saying, "Why do the scribes say that Elijah must come first?"

¹²Then He answered and told them, "Indeed, Elijah is coming first and restores all things. And how is it written concerning the Son of Man, that He must suffer many things and be treated with contempt? ¹³But I say to you that Elijah has also come, and they did to him whatever they wished, as it is written of him."

A Boy Is Healed

¹⁴And when He came to the disciples, He saw a great multitude around them, and scribes disputing with them. ¹⁵Immediately, when they saw Him, all the people were greatly amazed, and running to *Him*, greeted Him. ¹⁶And He asked the scribes, "What are you discussing with them?"

¹⁷Then one of the crowd answered and said, "Teacher, I brought You my son, who has a mute spirit. ¹⁸And wherever it seizes

him, it throws him down; he foams at the mouth, gnashes his teeth, and becomes rigid. So I spoke to Your disciples, that they should cast it out, but they could not."

¹⁹He answered him and said, "O faithless generation, how long shall I be with you? How long shall I bear with you? Bring him to Me." ²⁰Then they brought him to Him. And when he saw Him, immediately the spirit convulsed him, and he fell on the ground and wallowed, foaming at the mouth.

²¹So He asked his father, "How long has this been happening to him?"

And he said, "From childhood. ²²And often he has thrown him both into the fire and into the water to destroy him. But if You can do anything, have compassion on us and help us."

²³Jesus said to him, "If you can believe,[a] all things *are* possible to him who believes."

²⁴Immediately the father of the child cried out and said with tears, "Lord, I believe; help my unbelief!"

²⁵When Jesus saw that the people came running together, He rebuked the unclean spirit, saying to it, "Deaf and dumb spirit, I command you, come out of him and enter him no more!" ²⁶Then *the spirit* cried out, convulsed him greatly, and came out of him. And he became as one dead, so that many said, "He is dead." ²⁷But Jesus took him by the hand and lifted him up, and he arose.

²⁸And when He had come into the house, His disciples asked Him privately, "Why could we not cast it out?"

²⁹So He said to them, "This kind can come out by nothing but prayer and fasting."[a]

Jesus Again Predicts His Death and Resurrection

³⁰Then they departed from there and passed through Galilee, and He did not

---

want anyone to know *it*. [31]For He taught His disciples and said to them, "The Son of Man is being betrayed into the hands of men, and they will kill Him. And after He is killed, He will rise the third day." [32]But they did not understand this saying, and were afraid to ask Him.

Who Is the Greatest?

[33]Then He came to Capernaum. And when He was in the house He asked them, "What was it you disputed among yourselves on the road?" [34]But they kept silent, for on the road they had disputed among themselves who *would be the* greatest. [35]And He sat down, called the twelve, and said to them, "If anyone desires to be first, he shall be last of all and servant of all." [36]Then He took a little child and set him in the midst of them. And when He had taken him in His arms, He said to them, [37]"Whoever receives one of these little children in My name receives Me; and whoever receives Me, receives not Me but Him who sent Me."

Jesus Forbids Sectarianism

[38]Now John answered Him, saying, "Teacher, we saw someone who does not follow us casting out demons in Your name, and we forbade him because he does not follow us." [39]But Jesus said, "Do not forbid him, for no one who works a miracle in My name can soon afterward speak evil of Me. [40]For he who is not against us is on our[a] side. [41]For whoever gives you a cup of water to drink in My name, because you belong to Christ, assuredly, I say to you, he will by no means lose his reward.

Jesus Warns of Offenses

[42]"But whoever causes one of these little ones who believe in Me to stumble, it would be better for him if a millstone were hung around his neck, and he were thrown into the sea. [43]If your hand causes you to sin, cut it off. It is better for you to enter into life maimed, rather than having two hands, to go to hell, into the fire that shall never be quenched— [44]where

> *'Their worm does not die*
> *And the fire is not quenched.'*[a]

> **9:42 whoever causes...to stumble.** "To stumble" means "to cause to fall." To entice, trap, or lead a believer into sin is very serious. **millstone.** This refers to a large, upper millstone so heavy that it had to be turned by a donkey. Even such a horrifying death (a Gentile form of execution) is preferable to leading a Christian into sin.

[45]And if your foot causes you to sin, cut it off. It is better for you to enter life lame, rather than having two feet, to be cast into hell, into the fire that shall never be quenched— [46]where

> *'Their worm does not die*
> *And the fire is not quenched.'*[a]

[47]And if your eye causes you to sin, pluck it out. It is better for you to enter the kingdom of God with one eye, rather than having two eyes, to be cast into hell fire— [48]where

> *'Their worm does not die*
> *And the fire is not quenched.'*[a]

Tasteless Salt Is Worthless

[49]"For everyone will be seasoned with fire,[a] and every sacrifice will be seasoned with salt. [50]Salt *is* good, but if the salt loses its flavor, how will you season it? Have salt in yourselves, and have peace with one another."

Marriage and Divorce

10 Then He arose from there and came to the region of Judea by the other side of the Jordan. And multitudes gathered to Him again, and as He was accustomed, He taught them again.

[2]The Pharisees came and asked Him, "Is it lawful for a man to divorce *his* wife?" testing Him.

9:40 [a]M-Text reads *against you is on your side.*   9:44 [a]NU-Text omits this verse.   9:46 [a]NU-Text omits the last clause of verse 45 and all of verse 46.   9:48 [a]Isaiah 66:24   9:49 [a]NU-Text omits the rest of this verse.

³And He answered and said to them, "What did Moses command you?"

⁴They said, "Moses permitted *a man* to write a certificate of divorce, and to dismiss *her.*"

⁵And Jesus answered and said to them, "Because of the hardness of your heart he wrote you this precept. ⁶But from the beginning of the creation, God '*made them male and female.*'ᵃ ⁷*For this reason a man shall leave his father and mother and be joined to his wife,* ⁸*and the two shall become one flesh';*ᵃ so then they are no longer two, but one flesh. ⁹Therefore what God has joined together, let not man separate."

> **10:7–9** Jesus presents arguments against divorce, taken from Gen. 2:24. God created only two humans, not a group of males and females who could switch partners as it suited them. "Be joined" means "to glue," which reflects the strength of the marriage bond. A married couple is "one flesh" in God's eyes. God ordains marriage, and thus it is not to be broken by man.

¹⁰In the house His disciples also asked Him again about the same *matter.* ¹¹So He said to them, "Whoever divorces his wife and marries another commits adultery against her. ¹²And if a woman divorces her husband and marries another, she commits adultery."

Jesus Blesses Little Children

¹³Then they brought little children to Him, that He might touch them; but the disciples rebuked those who brought *them.* ¹⁴But when Jesus saw *it,* He was greatly displeased and said to them, "Let the little children come to Me, and do not forbid them; for of such is the kingdom of God. ¹⁵Assuredly, I say to you, whoever does not

> **10:14 do not forbid them.** Jesus rebuked the disciples for attempting to prevent the children from seeing Him. They were not to decide who could have access to Jesus (see Matt. 15:23). **of such is the kingdom of God.** Most of these children would have been too young to exercise personal faith. Jesus' words imply that God graciously extends salvation to those too young or too mentally impaired to exercise faith.

receive the kingdom of God as a little child will by no means enter it." ¹⁶And He took them up in His arms, laid *His* hands on them, and blessed them.

Jesus Counsels the Rich Young Ruler

¹⁷Now as He was going out on the road, one came running, knelt before Him, and asked Him, "Good Teacher, what shall I do that I may inherit eternal life?"

¹⁸So Jesus said to him, "Why do you call Me good? No one *is* good but One, *that is,* God. ¹⁹You know the commandments: '*Do not commit adultery,*' '*Do not murder,*' '*Do not steal,*' '*Do not bear false witness,*' '*Do not defraud,*' '*Honor your father and your mother.*' "ᵃ

²⁰And he answered and said to Him, "Teacher, all these things I have kept from my youth."

²¹Then Jesus, looking at him, loved him, and said to him, "One thing you lack: Go your way, sell whatever you have and give to the poor, and you will have treasure in heaven; and come, take up the cross, and follow Me."

> **10:21 Jesus...loved him.** God loves the unsaved. **sell whatever you have.** Jesus does not make philanthropy or poverty a requirement for salvation. Unwillingness to acknowledge and repent of sin and submit to the Lordship of Christ is what kept the young man from eternal life. **treasure in heaven.** The treasure is salvation and all its benefits in this life and the life to come, given by the Father who dwells in heaven.

²²But he was sad at this word, and went away sorrowful, for he had great possessions.

With God All Things Are Possible

²³Then Jesus looked around and said to His disciples, "How hard it is for those who have riches to enter the kingdom of God!" ²⁴And the disciples were astonished at His words. But Jesus answered again and said to them, "Children, how hard it is for those who trust in riches ᵃ to enter the kingdom of God! ²⁵It is easier for a camel to go through the eye of a needle than for a rich man to enter the kingdom of God."

10:6 ᵃGenesis 1:27; 5:2   10:8 ᵃGenesis 2:24   10:19 ᵃExodus 20:12–16; Deuteronomy 5:16–20
10:24 ᵃNU-Text omits *for those who trust in riches.*

²⁶And they were greatly astonished, saying among themselves, "Who then can be saved?"

²⁷But Jesus looked at them and said, "With men *it is* impossible, but not with God; for with God all things are possible."

²⁸Then Peter began to say to Him, "See, we have left all and followed You."

²⁹So Jesus answered and said, "Assuredly, I say to you, there is no one who has left house or brothers or sisters or father or mother or wife[a] or children or lands, for My sake and the gospel's, ³⁰who shall not receive a hundredfold now in this time—houses and brothers and sisters and mothers and children and lands, with persecutions—and in the age to come, eternal life. ³¹But many *who are* first will be last, and the last first."

> **10:30 in this time...the age to come.** Following Jesus brings rewards in this present age and when the Messiah's glorious kingdom comes. **with persecutions.** Great trials often accompany great blessings.

Jesus a Third Time Predicts His Death and Resurrection

³²Now they were on the road, going up to Jerusalem, and Jesus was going before them; and they were amazed. And as they followed they were afraid. Then He took the twelve aside again and began to tell them the things that would happen to Him: ³³"Behold, we are going up to Jerusalem, and the Son of Man will be betrayed to the chief priests and to the scribes; and they will condemn Him to death and deliver Him to the Gentiles; ³⁴and they will mock Him, and scourge Him, and spit on Him, and kill Him. And the third day He will rise again."

Greatness Is Serving

³⁵Then James and John, the sons of Zebedee, came to Him, saying, "Teacher, we want You to do for us whatever we ask."

³⁶And He said to them, "What do you want Me to do for you?"

³⁷They said to Him, "Grant us that we may sit, one on Your right hand and the other on Your left, in Your glory."

³⁸But Jesus said to them, "You do not know what you ask. Are you able to drink the cup that I drink, and be baptized with the baptism that I am baptized with?"

³⁹They said to Him, "We are able."

So Jesus said to them, "You will indeed drink the cup that I drink, and with the baptism I am baptized with you will be baptized; ⁴⁰but to sit on My right hand and on My left is not Mine to give, but *it is for those* for whom it is prepared."

> **10:37–39 sit...on Your right...Your left.** This refers to the places of highest prominence and honor beside God's throne. **in Your glory.** This refers to the glorious majesty of His kingdom (see Matt. 20:21). **the cup...the baptism.** This refers to suffering and sin-bearing in death as Jesus would. James and John would suffer like their Master (see Acts 12:2; Rev. 1:9), but that would not earn them the honors they desired.

⁴¹And when the ten heard *it,* they began to be greatly displeased with James and John. ⁴²But Jesus called them to *Himself* and said to them, "You know that those who are considered rulers over the Gentiles lord it over them, and their great ones exercise authority over them. ⁴³Yet it shall not be so among you; but whoever desires to become great among you shall be your servant. ⁴⁴And whoever of you desires to be first shall be slave of all. ⁴⁵For even the Son of Man did not come to be served, but to serve, and to give His life a ransom for many."

Jesus Heals Blind Bartimaeus

⁴⁶Now they came to Jericho. As He went out of Jericho with His disciples and a great multitude, blind Bartimaeus, the son of Timaeus, sat by the road begging. ⁴⁷And when he heard that it was Jesus of Nazareth, he began to cry out and say, "Jesus, Son of David, have mercy on me!"

⁴⁸Then many warned him to be quiet; but he cried out all the more, "Son of David, have mercy on me!"

⁴⁹So Jesus stood still and commanded him to be called.

Then they called the blind man, saying to him, "Be of good cheer. Rise, He is calling you."

10:29 [a]NU-Text omits *or wife.*

⁵⁰And throwing aside his garment, he rose and came to Jesus.

⁵¹So Jesus answered and said to him, "What do you want Me to do for you?"

The blind man said to Him, "Rabboni, that I may receive my sight."

⁵²Then Jesus said to him, "Go your way; your faith has made you well." And immediately he received his sight and followed Jesus on the road.

> **10:52 your faith has made you well.** Bartimaeus' physical and spiritual eyes were likely opened at the same time. The outward healing reflected the inner comprehension and acceptance of salvation.

The Triumphal Entry

11 Now when they drew near Jerusalem, to Bethphage*ᵃ* and Bethany, at the Mount of Olives, He sent two of His disciples; ²and He said to them, "Go into the village opposite you; and as soon as you have entered it you will find a colt tied, on which no one has sat. Loose it and bring *it*. ³And if anyone says to you, 'Why are you doing this?' say, 'The Lord has need of it,' and immediately he will send it here."

⁴So they went their way, and found theᵃ colt tied by the door outside on the street, and they loosed it. ⁵But some of those who stood there said to them, "What are you doing, loosing the colt?"

⁶And they spoke to them just as Jesus had commanded. So they let them go. ⁷Then they brought the colt to Jesus and threw their clothes on it, and He sat on it. ⁸And many spread their clothes on the road, and others cut down leafy branches from the trees and spread *them* on the road. ⁹Then those who went before and those who followed cried out, saying:

> **11:8,9 spread their clothes.** This was part of the ancient practice of welcoming a new king. **branches.** Palm branches symbolized joy and salvation, picturing future royal tribute to Christ (Rev. 7:9). The crowd was excited and full of praise for the Messiah who taught with authority, healed the sick, and raised the dead (see John 12:12–18). **Hosanna.** This Hebrew prayer means "save now," but was probably used here to welcome Jesus.

"Hosanna!

'*Blessed is He who comes in the name of the LORD!* 'ᵃ

10   Blessed *is* the kingdom of our father David

That comes in the name of the Lord!ᵃ

Hosanna in the highest!"

¹¹And Jesus went into Jerusalem and into the temple. So when He had looked around at all things, as the hour was already late, He went out to Bethany with the twelve.

The Fig Tree Withered

¹²Now the next day, when they had come out from Bethany, He was hungry. ¹³And seeing from afar a fig tree having leaves, He went to see if perhaps He would find something on it. When He came to it, He found nothing but leaves, for it was not the season for figs. ¹⁴In response Jesus said to it, "Let no one eat fruit from you ever again."

And His disciples heard *it*.

> **11:14 "Let no one eat fruit from you ever again."** Jesus condemned the tree for its misleading appearance that suggested great productivity without providing it. The fig was often used in the OT to represent the Jewish nation (Hos. 9:10). Here Jesus used the tree to teach a lesson on Israel's spiritual hypocrisy and fruitlessness (see Is. 5:1–7).

Jesus Cleanses the Temple

¹⁵So they came to Jerusalem. Then Jesus went into the temple and began to drive out those who bought and sold in the temple, and overturned the tables of the money changers and the seats of those who sold doves. ¹⁶And He would not allow anyone to carry wares through the temple. ¹⁷Then He taught, saying to them, "Is it not written, '*My house shall be called a house of prayer for all nations*'?ᵃ But you have made it a '*den of thieves*.'ᵇ

¹⁸And the scribes and chief priests heard it and sought how they might destroy Him; for they feared Him, because all the people were astonished at His teaching. ¹⁹When evening had come, He went out of the city.

11:1 ᵃM-Text reads *Bethsphage*.   11:4 ᵃNU-Text and M-Text read *a*.   11:9 ᵃPsalm 118:26
11:10 ᵃNU-Text omits *in the name of the Lord*.   11:17 ᵃIsaiah 56:7   ᵇJeremiah 7:11

The Lesson of the Withered Fig Tree

²⁰Now in the morning, as they passed by, they saw the fig tree dried up from the roots. ²¹And Peter, remembering, said to Him, "Rabbi, look! The fig tree which You cursed has withered away."

²²So Jesus answered and said to them, "Have faith in God. ²³For assuredly, I say to you, whoever says to this mountain, 'Be removed and be cast into the sea,' and does not doubt in his heart, but believes that those things he says will be done, he will have whatever he says. ²⁴Therefore I say to you, whatever things you ask when you pray, believe that you receive *them*, and you will have *them*.

> **11:23 this mountain...into the sea.** This expression relates to a metaphor of that day, "rooter up of mountains," which was used to describe rabbis and spiritual leaders who could solve difficult problems. Jesus did not uproot mountains; He refused to do such spectacular miracles for the unbelieving Jewish leaders. If believers sincerely trust in God and in His power, they will see His mighty powers at work (see John 14:13,14).

Forgiveness and Prayer

²⁵"And whenever you stand praying, if you have anything against anyone, forgive him, that your Father in heaven may also forgive you your trespasses. ²⁶But if you do not forgive, neither will your Father in heaven forgive your trespasses."*a*

Jesus' Authority Questioned

²⁷Then they came again to Jerusalem. And as He was walking in the temple, the chief priests, the scribes, and the elders came to Him. ²⁸And they said to Him, "By what authority are You doing these things? And who gave You this authority to do these things?"

²⁹But Jesus answered and said to them, "I also will ask you one question; then answer Me, and I will tell you by what authority I do these things: ³⁰The baptism of John—was it from heaven or from men? Answer Me."

³¹And they reasoned among themselves, saying, "If we say, 'From heaven,' He will say, 'Why then did you not believe him?' ³²But if we say, 'From men' "—they feared

> **11:30 baptism of John.** Jesus made their evaluation of John's authority a test case for their evaluation of His own authority. **was it from heaven or from men?** Jesus gave the Jewish leaders two alternatives in judging the source of John's authority, and by implication, His own authority. **Answer Me.** This challenge, only found in Mark's account, implied that the Jews did not have the courage to answer His question honestly.

the people, for all counted John to have been a prophet indeed. ³³So they answered and said to Jesus, "We do not know."

And Jesus answered and said to them, "Neither will I tell you by what authority I do these things."

The Parable of the Wicked Vinedressers

12 Then He began to speak to them in parables: "A man planted a vineyard and set a hedge around *it*, dug *a place for* the wine vat and built a tower. And he leased it to vinedressers and went into a far country. ²Now at vintage-time he sent a servant to the vinedressers, that he might receive some of the fruit of the vineyard from the vinedressers. ³And they took *him* and beat him and sent *him* away empty-handed. ⁴Again he sent them another servant, and at him they threw stones,*a* wounded *him* in the head, and sent *him* away shamefully treated. ⁵And again he sent another, and him they killed; and many others, beating some and killing some. ⁶Therefore still having one son, his beloved, he also sent him to them last, saying, 'They will respect my son.' ⁷But those vinedressers said among themselves, 'This is the heir. Come, let us kill him, and the inheritance will be ours.' ⁸So they took him and killed *him* and cast *him* out of the vineyard.

⁹"Therefore what will the owner of the vineyard do? He will come and destroy the

> **12:9 destroy the vinedressers.** The owner of the vineyard will execute the vinedressers; this prophesied the destruction of Jerusalem (A.D. 70) and the nation of Israel. This verdict was echoed by the chief priests, scribes, and elders (see Matt. 21:41). **give the vineyard to others.** This was fulfilled in the establishment of the church and its leaders, who were mostly Gentiles.

11:26 *a*NU-Text omits this verse.   12:4 *a*NU-Text omits *and at him they threw stones.*

vinedressers, and give the vineyard to others. ¹⁰Have you not even read this Scripture:

'The stone which the builders rejected
Has become the chief cornerstone.
11   This was the LORD's doing,
And it is marvelous in our eyes'?"ᵃ

¹²And they sought to lay hands on Him, but feared the multitude, for they knew He had spoken the parable against them. So they left Him and went away.

The Pharisees: Is It Lawful to Pay Taxes to Caesar?

¹³Then they sent to Him some of the Pharisees and the Herodians, to catch Him in *His* words. ¹⁴When they had come, they said to Him, "Teacher, we know that You are true, and care about no one; for You do not regard the person of men, but teach the way of God in truth. Is it lawful to pay taxes to Caesar, or not? ¹⁵Shall we pay, or shall we not pay?"

But He, knowing their hypocrisy, said to them, "Why do you test Me? Bring Me a denarius that I may see *it*." ¹⁶So they brought *it*.

And He said to them, "Whose image and inscription *is* this?" They said to Him, "Caesar's."

¹⁷And Jesus answered and said to them, "Render to Caesar the things that are Caesar's, and to God the things that are God's."

And they marveled at Him.

The Sadducees: What About the Resurrection?

¹⁸Then *some* Sadducees, who say there is no resurrection, came to Him; and they asked Him, saying: ¹⁹"Teacher, Moses

12:18 Sadducees. These were the most wealthy, influential, and aristocratic of all the Jewish sects. They included the High-Priests, chief priests, and the majority of the Sanhedrin. They ignored the oral law, traditions, and scribal laws of the Pharisees, viewing only the Pentateuch as authoritative. **who say there is no resurrection.** This is the most distinctive aspect of the Sadducees' theology.

wrote to us that if a man's brother dies, and leaves *his* wife behind, and leaves no children, his brother should take his wife and raise up offspring for his brother. ²⁰Now there were seven brothers. The first took a wife; and dying, he left no offspring. ²¹And the second took her, and he died; nor did he leave any offspring. And the third likewise. ²²So the seven had her and left no offspring. Last of all the woman died also. ²³Therefore, in the resurrection, when they rise, whose wife will she be? For all seven had her as wife."

²⁴Jesus answered and said to them, "Are you not therefore mistaken, because you do not know the Scriptures nor the power of God? ²⁵For when they rise from the dead, they neither marry nor are given in marriage, but are like angels in heaven. ²⁶But concerning the dead, that they rise, have you not read in the book of Moses, in the *burning* bush *passage*, how God spoke to him, saying, '*I am the God of Abraham, the God of Isaac, and the God of Jacob*'?ᵃ ²⁷He is not the God of the dead, but the God of the living. You are therefore greatly mistaken."

12:26 book of Moses. This is the Pentateuch, the first 5 books of the OT. The Sadducees viewed this as the only authoritative Scriptures. **the *burning* bush *passage*.** This refers to Ex. 3:1–4:17, where God first appeared to Moses. **how God spoke to him, saying, '*I am*.'** Jesus emphasized the personal and perpetual covenantal relationship God established with the 3 patriarchs, who were experiencing eternal fellowship with Him in heaven.

The Scribes: Which Is the First Commandment of All?

²⁸Then one of the scribes came, and having heard them reasoning together, perceivingᵃ that He had answered them well, asked Him, "Which is the first commandment of all?"

²⁹Jesus answered him, "The first of all the commandments *is*: '*Hear, O Israel, the LORD our God, the LORD is one. ³⁰And you shall love the LORD your God with all your heart, with all your soul, with all your mind, and with all your strength.*'ᵃ This is

---

12:11 ᵃPsalm 118:22,23   12:26 ᵃExodus 3:6,15   12:28 ᵃNU-Text reads *seeing.*   12:30 ᵃDeuteronomy 6:4,5

the first commandment.*b* 31And the second, like *it*, is this: '*You shall love your neighbor as yourself.*'*a* There is no other commandment greater than these."

32So the scribe said to Him, "Well *said*, Teacher. You have spoken the truth, for there is one God, and there is no other but He. 33And to love Him with all the heart, with all the understanding, with all the soul,*a* and with all the strength, and to love one's neighbor as oneself, is more than all the whole burnt offerings and sacrifices."

34Now when Jesus saw that he answered wisely, He said to him, "You are not far from the kingdom of God."

But after that no one dared question Him.

Jesus: How Can David Call His Descendant Lord?

35Then Jesus answered and said, while He taught in the temple, "How *is it* that the scribes say that the Christ is the Son of David? 36For David himself said by the Holy Spirit:

'The LORD said to my Lord,
"Sit at My right hand,
Till I make Your enemies Your
footstool." ' *a*

> **12:36 David himself said by the Holy Spirit.** David used his own words, yet he wrote under the inspiration of the Holy Spirit (see 2 Sam. 23:2). **The LORD said to my Lord.** The first word for "LORD" is *Yahweh*, God's covenant name. The second word for "Lord" is a title the Jews used for God. Here David pictures God speaking to the Messiah, whom David calls his Lord. The religious leaders recognized this psalm as messianic.

37Therefore David himself calls Him '*Lord*'; how is He *then* his Son?"

And the common people heard Him gladly.

Beware of the Scribes

38Then He said to them in His teaching, "Beware of the scribes, who desire to go around in long robes, *love* greetings in the marketplaces, 39the best seats in the syna-

gogues, and the best places at feasts, 40who devour widows' houses, and for a pretense make long prayers. These will receive greater condemnation."

> **12:40 devour widows' houses.** Jesus exposed the greedy practices of the scribes. They often served as estate planners for widows and gave them the opportunity to serve God by supporting the temple or the scribes' own work. The scribes benefited monetarily from this arrangement, which basically amounted to robbing the widows. **long prayers.** Desiring reverence from the people, the Pharisees flaunted their prayers by praying for long periods.

The Widow's Two Mites

41Now Jesus sat opposite the treasury and saw how the people put money into the treasury. And many *who were* rich put in much. 42Then one poor widow came and threw in two mites,*a* which make a quadrans. 43So He called His disciples to *Himself* and said to them, "Assuredly, I say to you that this poor widow has put in more than all those who have given to the treasury; 44for they all put in out of their abundance, but she out of her poverty put in all that she had, her whole livelihood."

> **12:44 her whole livelihood.** The widow would not be able to eat until she had more money. She exemplified true sacrificial giving.

Jesus Predicts the Destruction of the Temple

13 Then as He went out of the temple, one of His disciples said to Him, "Teacher, see what manner of stones and what buildings *are here!*"

2And Jesus answered and said to him, "Do you see these great buildings? Not *one* stone shall be left upon another, that shall not be thrown down."

The Signs of the Times and the End of the Age

3Now as He sat on the Mount of Olives opposite the temple, Peter, James, John, and Andrew asked Him privately, 4"Tell us, when will these things be? And what *will be* the sign when all these things will be fulfilled?"

12:30 *b*NU-Text omits this sentence.　12:31 *a*Leviticus 19:18　12:33 *a*NU-Text omits *with all the soul.*
12:36 *a*Psalm 110:1　12:42 *a*Greek *lepta*, very small copper coins worth a fraction of a penny

⁵And Jesus, answering them, began to say: "Take heed that no one deceives you. ⁶For many will come in My name, saying, 'I am *He*,' and will deceive many. ⁷But when you hear of wars and rumors of wars, do not be troubled; for *such things* must happen, but the end *is* not yet. ⁸For nation will rise against nation, and kingdom against kingdom. And there will be earthquakes in various places, and there will be famines and troubles.ᵃ These *are* the beginnings of sorrows.

⁹"But watch out for yourselves, for they will deliver you up to councils, and you will be beaten in the synagogues. You will be broughtᵃ before rulers and kings for My sake, for a testimony to them. ¹⁰And the gospel must first be preached to all the nations. ¹¹But when they arrest *you* and deliver you up, do not worry beforehand, or premeditateᵃ what you will speak. But whatever is given you in that hour, speak that; for it is not you who speak, but the Holy Spirit. ¹²Now brother will betray brother to death, and a father *his* child; and children will rise up against parents and cause them to be put to death. ¹³And you will be hated by all for My name's sake. But he who endures to the end shall be saved.

The Great Tribulation

¹⁴"So when you see the '*abomination of desolation*,'ᵃ spoken of by Daniel the prophet,ᵇ standing where it ought not" (let the reader understand), "then let those who are in Judea flee to the mountains. ¹⁵Let him who is on the housetop not go down into the house, nor enter to take anything out of his house. ¹⁶And let him who is in the field not go back to get his clothes. ¹⁷But woe to those who are pregnant and to those

> **13:14 the 'abomination of desolation.'** This first referred to the desecration of the temple by Antiochus Epiphanes, the king of Syria, in the second century B.C., when he sacrificed a pig on the temple altar. Here, Jesus refers to the Antichrist's desecration when he sets up an image of himself in the temple during the Tribulation.

who are nursing babies in those days! ¹⁸And pray that your flight may not be in winter. ¹⁹For *in* those days there will be tribulation, such as has not been since the beginning of the creation which God created until this time, nor ever shall be. ²⁰And unless the Lord had shortened those days, no flesh would be saved; but for the elect's sake, whom He chose, He shortened the days.

> **13:20 shortened.** Jesus referred to God cutting short the period of time to only three and one half years (see Dan. 7:25). **the elect's sake.** The "elect" could refer to the nation of Israel (see Is. 45:4) or those who become Christians during the Tribulation (Rev. 17:14). In either case, God cuts short the days of horrible persecution for their benefit.

²¹"Then if anyone says to you, 'Look, here *is* the Christ!' or, 'Look, *He is* there!' do not believe it. ²²For false christs and false prophets will rise and show signs and wonders to deceive, if possible, even the elect. ²³But take heed; see, I have told you all things beforehand.

The Coming of the Son of Man

²⁴"But in those days, after that tribulation, the sun will be darkened, and the moon will not give its light; ²⁵the stars of heaven will fall, and the powers in the heavens will be shaken. ²⁶Then they will see the Son of Man coming in the clouds with great power and glory. ²⁷And then He will send His angels, and gather together His elect from the four winds, from the farthest part of earth to the farthest part of heaven.

The Parable of the Fig Tree

²⁸"Now learn this parable from the fig tree: When its branch has already become tender, and puts forth leaves, you know that summer is near. ²⁹So you also, when you see these things happening, know that itᵃ is near—at the doors! ³⁰Assuredly, I say to you, this generation will by no means pass away till all these things take place. ³¹Heaven and earth will pass away, but My words will by no means pass away.

13:8 ᵃNU-Text omits *and troubles.*   13:9 ᵃNU-Text and M-Text read *will stand.*   13:11 ᵃNU-Text omits *or premeditate.*   13:14 ᵃDaniel 11:31; 12:11   ᵇNU-Text omits *spoken of by Daniel the prophet.*   13:29 ᵃOr *He*

No One Knows the Day or Hour

³²"But of that day and hour no one knows, not even the angels in heaven, nor the Son, but only the Father. ³³Take heed, watch and pray; for you do not know when the time is. ³⁴*It is* like a man going to a far country, who left his house and gave authority to his servants, and to each his work, and commanded the doorkeeper to watch. ³⁵Watch therefore, for you do not know when the master of the house is coming—in the evening, at midnight, at the crowing of the rooster, or in the morning— ³⁶lest, coming suddenly, he find you sleeping. ³⁷And what I say to you, I say to all: Watch!"

> **13:32 that day and hour.** This refers to the exact day and time of Christ's return. **no one knows.** The time of Christ's return will not be revealed to any man. At this time, it was known only to God the Father. **angels.** The angels have no knowledge of the time of Christ's return. **nor the Son.** At this time, even Jesus did not know the day or time of His return. Although He was God, He voluntarily restricted the use of certain divine attributes when He became a man (see Phil. 2:6–8).

The Plot to Kill Jesus

14 After two days it was the Passover and *the Feast* of Unleavened Bread. And the chief priests and the scribes sought how they might take Him by trickery and put *Him* to death. ²But they said, "Not during the feast, lest there be an uproar of the people."

The Anointing at Bethany

³And being in Bethany at the house of Simon the leper, as He sat at the table, a woman came having an alabaster flask of very costly oil of spikenard. Then she broke the flask and poured *it* on His head. ⁴But there were some who were indignant

> **14:3 Simon the leper.** A leper was an outcast in Jewish society. This man was probably healed by Jesus and may have planned this meal for Jesus in gratitude. **a woman.** This is Mary, the sister of Martha and Lazarus who were also at the meal (John 12:3). **alabaster flask.** This long-necked bottle was probably made out of marble, a material that best preserved expensive perfumes and oils. **spikenard.** This expensive oil was derived from the nard plant, which is native to India.

among themselves, and said, "Why was this fragrant oil wasted? ⁵For it might have been sold for more than three hundred denarii and given to the poor." And they criticized her sharply.

⁶But Jesus said, "Let her alone. Why do you trouble her? She has done a good work for Me. ⁷For you have the poor with you always, and whenever you wish you may do them good; but Me you do not have always. ⁸She has done what she could. She has come beforehand to anoint My body for burial. ⁹Assuredly, I say to you, wherever this gospel is preached in the whole world, what this woman has done will also be told as a memorial to her."

Judas Agrees to Betray Jesus

¹⁰Then Judas Iscariot, one of the twelve, went to the chief priests to betray Him to them. ¹¹And when they heard *it*, they were glad, and promised to give him money. So he sought how he might conveniently betray Him.

> **14:10 Judas Iscariot.** The name "Iscariot" means "man of Kerioth," which was a small town in Judea. Judas was not a Galilean like the other disciples. He was attracted to Jesus because he expected Him to become a powerful religious and political leader and sought prestige through association with Him. Jesus chose him as one of the 12 so Scripture and God's plan of salvation would be fulfilled through his betrayal (Ps. 41:9; Zech. 11:12,13).

Jesus Celebrates the Passover with His Disciples

¹²Now on the first day of Unleavened Bread, when they killed the Passover *lamb*, His disciples said to Him, "Where do You want us to go and prepare, that You may eat the Passover?"

¹³And He sent out two of His disciples and said to them, "Go into the city, and a man will meet you carrying a pitcher of water; follow him. ¹⁴Wherever he goes in, say to the master of the house, 'The Teacher says, "Where is the guest room in which I may eat the Passover with My disciples?" ' ¹⁵Then he will show you a large upper room, furnished *and* prepared; there make ready for us."

¹⁶So His disciples went out, and came into the city, and found it just as He had

said to them; and they prepared the Passover.

¹⁷In the evening He came with the twelve. ¹⁸Now as they sat and ate, Jesus said, "Assuredly, I say to you, one of you who eats with Me will betray Me."

¹⁹And they began to be sorrowful, and to say to Him one by one, "Is it I?" And another *said*, "Is it I?"ᵃ

²⁰He answered and said to them, "*It is* one of the twelve, who dips with Me in the dish. ²¹The Son of Man indeed goes just as it is written of Him, but woe to that man by whom the Son of Man is betrayed! It would have been good for that man if he had never been born."

> **14:21 as it is written.** Jesus' betrayal by Judas was prophesied in the OT (Ps. 22; Is. 53). **good...if he had never been born.** The terror Judas would experience in hell would be great. This strong statement shows the human responsibility for believing in Jesus Christ and the great consequences of unbelief.

Jesus Institutes the Lord's Supper

²²And as they were eating, Jesus took bread, blessed and broke *it*, and gave *it* to them and said, "Take, eat;ᵃ this is My body."

²³Then He took the cup, and when He had given thanks He gave *it* to them, and they all drank from it. ²⁴And He said to them, "This is My blood of the newᵃ covenant, which is shed for many. ²⁵Assuredly, I say to you, I will no longer drink of the fruit of the vine until that day when I drink it new in the kingdom of God."

> **14:25 I will no longer drink.** This would be Jesus' last Passover. He would not drink wine with them again, as this was His last meal. Believers are to share this special meal of remembrance until the coming of the millennial kingdom. **drink it new.** The disciples were assured of Jesus' return and the establishment of His earthly, millennial kingdom. **kingdom of God.** This refers to the earthly millennial kingdom.

²⁶And when they had sung a hymn, they went out to the Mount of Olives.

Jesus Predicts Peter's Denial

²⁷Then Jesus said to them, "All of you will be made to stumble because of Me this night,ᵃ for it is written:

'I *will strike the Shepherd,*
*And the sheep will be scattered.'*ᵇ

²⁸"But after I have been raised, I will go before you to Galilee."

²⁹Peter said to Him, "Even if all are made to stumble, yet I *will* not *be*."

³⁰Jesus said to him, "Assuredly, I say to you that today, *even* this night, before the rooster crows twice, you will deny Me three times."

³¹But he spoke more vehemently, "If I have to die with You, I will not deny You!" And they all said likewise.

The Prayer in the Garden

³²Then they came to a place which was named Gethsemane; and He said to His disciples, "Sit here while I pray." ³³And He took Peter, James, and John with Him, and He began to be troubled and deeply distressed. ³⁴Then He said to them, "My soul is exceedingly sorrowful, *even* to death. Stay here and watch."

³⁵He went a little farther, and fell on the ground, and prayed that if it were possible, the hour might pass from Him. ³⁶And He said, "Abba, Father, all things *are* possible for You. Take this cup away from Me; nevertheless, not what I will, but what You *will*."

> **14:36 Abba.** This intimate Aramaic term is equivalent to the English word "Daddy" (see Rom 8:15). **all things *are* possible.** Jesus knew God could provide an alternate plan of salvation if He desired. **cup.** This was the cup of God's wrath referred to in the OT (Ps. 75:8; Jer. 49:12). Christ had to drink this cup in order to overcome sin, Satan, the power of death, and the guilt of iniquity. **not what I will, but what You will.** Jesus would do God's will.

³⁷Then He came and found them sleeping, and said to Peter, "Simon, are you sleeping? Could you not watch one hour? ³⁸Watch and pray, lest you enter into temptation. The spirit indeed *is* willing, but the flesh *is* weak."

14:19 ᵃNU-Text omits this sentence.   14:22 ᵃNU-Text omits *eat.*   14:24 ᵃNU-Text omits *new.*
14:27 ᵃNU-Text omits *because of Me this night.*   ᵇZechariah 13:7

[39]Again He went away and prayed, and spoke the same words. [40]And when He returned, He found them asleep again, for their eyes were heavy; and they did not know what to answer Him.

[41]Then He came the third time and said to them, "Are you still sleeping and resting? It is enough! The hour has come; behold, the Son of Man is being betrayed into the hands of sinners. [42]Rise, let us be going. See, My betrayer is at hand."

Betrayal and Arrest in Gethsemane

[43]And immediately, while He was still speaking, Judas, one of the twelve, with a great multitude with swords and clubs, came from the chief priests and the scribes and the elders. [44]Now His betrayer had given them a signal, saying, "Whomever I kiss, He is the One; seize Him and lead *Him* away safely."

14:44 kiss. A kiss was a sign of respect, affection, and homage in Middle Eastern culture. Judas chose to embrace Jesus and kiss His cheek, which signified intimate love and affection. Judas could not have chosen a more despicable way to identify Jesus.

[45]As soon as he had come, immediately he went up to Him and said to Him, "Rabbi, Rabbi!" and kissed Him. [46]Then they laid their hands on Him and took Him. [47]And one of those who stood by drew his sword and struck the servant of the high priest, and cut off his ear.

[48]Then Jesus answered and said to them, "Have you come out, as against a robber, with swords and clubs to take Me? [49]I was daily with you in the temple teaching, and you did not seize Me. But the Scriptures must be fulfilled."

[50]Then they all forsook Him and fled.

A Young Man Flees Naked

[51]Now a certain young man followed Him, having a linen cloth thrown around *his* naked *body*. And the young men laid hold of him, [52]and he left the linen cloth and fled from them naked.

Jesus Faces the Sanhedrin

[53]And they led Jesus away to the high priest; and with him were assembled all the chief priests, the elders, and the scribes.

[54]But Peter followed Him at a distance, right into the courtyard of the high priest. And he sat with the servants and warmed himself at the fire.

[55]Now the chief priests and all the council sought testimony against Jesus to put Him to death, but found none. [56]For many bore false witness against Him, but their testimonies did not agree.

14:56 The Jewish leaders could not convict Jesus except by relying on perjured testimony and perverted justice. They were intent on doing whatever necessary, even violating biblical and rabbinical rules, in order to get rid of Jesus. **did not agree.** The testimonies were inconsistent. The law, however, required exact agreement between two witnesses (Deut. 17:6).

[57]Then some rose up and bore false witness against Him, saying, [58]"We heard Him say, 'I will destroy this temple made with hands, and within three days I will build another made without hands.' " [59]But not even then did their testimony agree.

[60]And the high priest stood up in the midst and asked Jesus, saying, "Do You answer nothing? What *is it* these men testify against You?" [61]But He kept silent and answered nothing.

Again the high priest asked Him, saying to Him, "Are You the Christ, the Son of the Blessed?"

[62]Jesus said, "I am. And you will see the Son of Man sitting at the right hand of the Power, and coming with the clouds of heaven."

14:62 I am. In these two words, Jesus declared that He was and is the Messiah and the Son of God. **Son of Man.** Jesus used this title for Himself more than 80 times in the gospels. **right hand of the Power.** The "Power" refers to God. Jesus' glorified position is next to the throne of God.

[63]Then the high priest tore his clothes and said, "What further need do we have of witnesses? [64]You have heard the blasphemy! What do you think?"

And they all condemned Him to be deserving of death.

[65]Then some began to spit on Him, and to blindfold Him, and to beat Him, and to say to Him, "Prophesy!" And the officers

struck Him with the palms of their hands.[a]

Peter Denies Jesus, and Weeps

[66]Now as Peter was below in the courtyard, one of the servant girls of the high priest came. [67]And when she saw Peter warming himself, she looked at him and said, "You also were with Jesus of Nazareth."

[68]But he denied it, saying, "I neither know nor understand what you are saying." And he went out on the porch, and a rooster crowed.

[69]And the servant girl saw him again, and began to say to those who stood by, "This is one of them." [70]But he denied it again.

And a little later those who stood by said to Peter again, "Surely you are *one* of them; for you are a Galilean, and your speech shows *it*."[a]

[71]Then he began to curse and swear, "I do not know this Man of whom you speak!"

[72]A second time *the* rooster crowed. Then Peter called to mind the word that Jesus had said to him, "Before the rooster crows twice, you will deny Me three times." And when he thought about it, he wept.

Jesus Faces Pilate

15 Immediately, in the morning, the chief priests held a consultation with the elders and scribes and the whole council; and they bound Jesus, led *Him* away, and delivered *Him* to Pilate. [2]Then Pilate asked Him, "Are You the King of the Jews?"

He answered and said to him, "*It is as* you say."

[3]And the chief priests accused Him of many things, but He answered nothing.

15:2 Pilate asked. The Jewish leaders demanded that Pilate agree to the death sentence that they had already pronounced on Jesus (John 18:30). Pilate refused, and the Jewish leaders proceeded to present their false charges (Luke 23:2). Pilate questioned Jesus based on the false charges. **"Are You the King of the Jews?"** The only charge Pilate took seriously was that Jesus claimed to be a king, making Him guilty of rebellion against Rome.

---

[4]Then Pilate asked Him again, saying, "Do You answer nothing? See how many things they testify against You!"[a] [5]But Jesus still answered nothing, so that Pilate marveled.

Taking the Place of Barabbas

[6]Now at the feast he was accustomed to releasing one prisoner to them, whomever they requested. [7]And there was one named Barabbas, *who was* chained with his fellow rebels; they had committed murder in the rebellion. [8]Then the multitude, crying aloud,[a] began to ask *him to do* just as he had always done for them. [9]But Pilate answered them, saying, "Do you want me to release to you the King of the Jews?" [10]For he knew that the chief priests had handed Him over because of envy.

[11]But the chief priests stirred up the crowd, so that he should rather release Barabbas to them. [12]Pilate answered and said to them again, "What then do you want me to do *with Him* whom you call the King of the Jews?"

[13]So they cried out again, "Crucify Him!"

[14]Then Pilate said to them, "Why, what evil has He done?"

But they cried out all the more, "Crucify Him!"

[15]So Pilate, wanting to gratify the crowd, released Barabbas to them; and he delivered Jesus, after he had scourged *Him*, to be crucified.

15:15 scourged. Jesus was scourged with a whip (called a *flagellum*) that was made of a wooden handle with attached metal-tipped leather thongs. It ripped the flesh to the bone, causing severe bleeding. Many prisoners died from this beating. **crucified.** This was a common Roman execution of slaves and foreigners, described by the Roman writer Cicero as "the cruelest and most hideous punishment possible."

The Soldiers Mock Jesus

[16]Then the soldiers led Him away into the hall called Praetorium, and they called together the whole garrison. [17]And they clothed Him with purple; and they twisted a crown of thorns, put it on His *head*, [18]and began to salute Him, "Hail, King of the Jews!" [19]Then they struck Him on the head

---

14:65 [a]NU-Text reads *received Him with slaps.*   14:70 [a]NU-Text omits *and your speech shows it.*
15:4 [a]NU-Text reads *of which they accuse You.*   15:8 [a]NU-Text reads *going up.*

with a reed and spat on Him; and bowing the knee, they worshiped Him. ²⁰And when they had mocked Him, they took the purple off Him, put His own clothes on Him, and led Him out to crucify Him.

The King on a Cross

²¹Then they compelled a certain man, Simon a Cyrenian, the father of Alexander and Rufus, as he was coming out of the country and passing by, to bear His cross. ²²And they brought Him to the place Golgotha, which is translated, Place of a Skull. ²³Then they gave Him wine mingled with myrrh to drink, but He did not take *it.* ²⁴And when they crucified Him, they divided His garments, casting lots for them to determine what every man should take.

²⁵Now it was the third hour, and they crucified Him. ²⁶And the inscription of His accusation was written above:

THE KING OF THE JEWS.

15:26 inscription of His accusation. The crime for which a condemned man was executed was written on a wooden board that was fastened to the cross above his head. Jesus' inscription was written in Latin, Hebrew, and Greek (John 19:20). **THE KING OF THE JEWS.** Pilate ordered this inscription as an insult to the Jewish leaders who had given him so much trouble.

²⁷With Him they also crucified two robbers, one on His right and the other on His left. ²⁸So the Scripture was fulfilled*ᵃ* which says, *"And He was numbered with the transgressors."ᵇ*

²⁹And those who passed by blasphemed Him, wagging their heads and saying, "Aha! *You* who destroy the temple and build *it* in three days, ³⁰save Yourself, and come down from the cross!"

³¹Likewise the chief priests also, mocking among themselves with the scribes, said, "He saved others; Himself He cannot save. ³²Let the Christ, the King of Israel, descend now from the cross, that we may see and believe."*ᵃ*

Even those who were crucified with Him reviled Him.

Jesus Dies on the Cross

³³Now when the sixth hour had come, there was darkness over the whole land until the ninth hour. ³⁴And at the ninth hour Jesus cried out with a loud voice, saying, "Eloi, Eloi, lama sabachthani?" which is translated, *"My God, My God, why have You forsaken Me?"ᵃ*

³⁵Some of those who stood by, when they heard *that,* said, "Look, He is calling for Elijah!" ³⁶Then someone ran and filled a sponge full of sour wine, put *it* on a reed, and offered *it* to Him to drink, saying, "Let Him alone; let us see if Elijah will come to take Him down."

³⁷And Jesus cried out with a loud voice, and breathed His last.

³⁸Then the veil of the temple was torn in two from top to bottom. ³⁹So when the centurion, who stood opposite Him, saw that He cried out like this and breathed His last,*ᵃ* he said, "Truly this Man was the Son of God!"

15:39 centurion. He was the Roman officer in charge of the crucifixion. Centurions, the backbone of the Roman army, commanded 100 soldiers. **saw that He cried out like this.** The centurion had never seen a crucified victim with so much strength, which Jesus demonstrated with His loud cry. That, along with the earthquake that occurred (Matt. 27:51–54), convinced the centurion that Jesus truly was the Son of God, and he believed.

⁴⁰There were also women looking on from afar, among whom were Mary Magdalene, Mary the mother of James the Less and of Joses, and Salome, ⁴¹who also followed Him and ministered to Him when He was in Galilee, and many other women who came up with Him to Jerusalem.

Jesus Buried in Joseph's Tomb

⁴²Now when evening had come, because it was the Preparation Day, that is, the day before the Sabbath, ⁴³Joseph of Arimathea, a prominent council member, who was himself waiting for the kingdom of God, coming and taking courage, went in to Pilate and asked for the body of Jesus. ⁴⁴Pilate marveled that He was already dead; and

15:28 *ᵃ*Isaiah 53:12 *ᵇ*NU-Text omits this verse.   15:32 *ᵃ*M-Text reads *believe Him.*   15:34 *ᵃ*Psalm 22:1   15:39 *ᵃ*NU-Text reads *that He thus breathed His last.*

summoning the centurion, he asked him if He had been dead for some time. [45]So when he found out from the centurion, he granted the body to Joseph. [46]Then he bought fine linen, took Him down, and wrapped Him in the linen. And he laid Him in a tomb which had been hewn out of the rock, and rolled a stone against the door of the tomb. [47]And Mary Magdalene and Mary *the mother* of Joses observed where He was laid.

> **15:46 wrapped Him in the linen.** The Jews did not embalm corpses, but wrapped them in perfumed burial cloths. Nicodemus, another prominent member of the Sanhedrin (see John 7:50), helped Joseph of Arimathea care for Jesus' body (John 19:39,40). These men, who had kept their allegiance to Jesus a secret during His lifetime, came forward publicly to bury Him. The disciples, on the other hand, were hiding (John 20:19).

He Is Risen

16 Now when the Sabbath was past, Mary Magdalene, Mary *the mother* of James, and Salome bought spices, that they might come and anoint Him. [2]Very early in the morning, on the first *day* of the week, they came to the tomb when the sun had risen. [3]And they said among themselves, "Who will roll away the stone from the door of the tomb for us?" [4]But when they looked up, they saw that the stone had been rolled away—for it was very large. [5]And entering the tomb, they saw a young man clothed in a long white robe sitting on the right side; and they were alarmed.

[6]But he said to them, "Do not be alarmed. You seek Jesus of Nazareth, who was crucified. He is risen! He is not here. See the place where they laid Him. [7]But go, tell His disciples—and Peter—that He is going before you into Galilee; there you will see Him, as He said to you."

[8]So they went out quickly[a] and fled from the tomb, for they trembled and were

> **16:6 He is risen!** Christ's resurrection is a central truth of the Christian faith (1 Cor. 15:4) and the only reasonable explanation for the empty tomb. The Jewish leaders did not deny the empty tomb; they concocted the story that the disciples had stolen Jesus' body (Matt. 28:11–15). This story is absurd. Many other theories have been invented over the centuries to explain away the empty tomb, all of them equally futile.

16:8 [a]NU-Text and M-Text omit *quickly.*

Were the last 12 verses of chapter 16 originally part of Mark's gospel?

The external evidence strongly suggests that Mark 16:9–20 was not originally part of Mark's gospel. While the majority of Greek manuscripts contain these verses, the earliest and most reliable ones do not. A shorter ending also existed, but it is not included in this text. Further, some manuscripts that include the passage note that it was missing from older Greek copies, while others have scribal marks indicating that the passage was considered doubtful. The fourth-century church fathers Eusebius and Jerome noted that almost all Greek manuscripts available to them lacked verses 9–20.

The internal evidence from this passage also weighs heavily against Mark's authorship. The grammatical transition between verses 8 and 9 is abrupt and awkward. The vocabulary in these verses does not match the rest of Mark. Even the events and people mentioned in these verses appear in awkward fashion. For example, Mary Magdalene is introduced as if she were a new person on the scene rather than someone Mark had mentioned three times (v. 1; 15:40,47). Clearly, Mark 16:9–20 represents an early attempt to complete Mark's gospel.

While for the most part summarizing truths taught elsewhere in Scripture, these verses should always be compared with the rest of Scripture, and no doctrines should be formulated based solely on them. Further, in spite of all these considerations of the likely unreliability of this section, it is possible to be wrong on the issue. It is good to consider the meaning of this passage, therefore, and leave it in the text, just as is done with the other text with a similar history, John 7:53–8:11.

amazed. And they said nothing to anyone, for they were afraid.

Mary Magdalene Sees the Risen Lord

[9]Now when *He* rose early on the first *day* of the week, He appeared first to Mary Magdalene, out of whom He had cast seven demons. [10]She went and told those who had been with Him, as they mourned and wept. [11]And when they heard that He was alive and had been seen by her, they did not believe.

Jesus Appears to Two Disciples

[12]After that, He appeared in another form to two of them as they walked and went into the country. [13]And they went and told *it* to the rest, *but* they did not believe them either.

The Great Commission

[14]Later He appeared to the eleven as they sat at the table; and He rebuked their unbelief and hardness of heart, because they did not believe those who had seen Him after He had risen. [15]And He said to them, "Go into all the world and preach the gospel to every creature. [16]He who believes and is baptized will be saved; but he who does not believe will be condemned. [17]And these signs will follow those who believe: In My name they will cast out demons; they will speak with new tongues; [18]they[a] will take up serpents; and if they drink anything deadly, it will by no means hurt them; they will lay hands on the sick, and they will recover."

Christ Ascends to God's Right Hand

[19]So then, after the Lord had spoken to them, He was received up into heaven, and sat down at the right hand of God. [20]And they went out and preached everywhere, the Lord working with *them* and confirming the word through the accompanying signs. Amen.[a]

16:18 [a]NU-Text reads *and in their hands they will.*   16:20 [a]Verses 9–20 are bracketed in NU-Text as not original. They are lacking in Codex Sinaiticus and Codex Vaticanus, although nearly all other manuscripts of Mark contain them.

LUKE

People write biographies for different reasons. Usually, they are convinced the subject of their writing ought to be introduced to as many people as possible. An effective biographer uses good sources and interviews people who can give first-hand accounts of events, words, and habits from the subject's life. A good biographer presents an honest and full record of the subject's impact on others.

The gospel writer Luke approached his task with each of these objectives. His opening verses describe in detail how he gathered his materials and why he decided to compose his biography of Jesus Christ. Luke's Gospel could be sub-titled, *An Historian's View of the Lord Jesus.*

AUTHOR AND DATE

Luke was written by Luke, approximately A.D. 60.

The Gospel of Luke and the book of Acts clearly were written by the same individual (Luke 1:1–4; Acts 1:1). Although never identifying himself by name, the writer's use of "we" in many sections of Acts indicates that the author was a close companion of Paul (Acts 16:10–17; 20:5–15; 21:1–18; 27:1–28:16). Only Luke, among the colleagues whom Paul mentions in his own epistles (Colossians 4:14; 2 Timothy 4:11; Philemon 24), fits the profile of the author of these books. That agrees perfectly with the earliest tradition of the church, which unanimously attributed this gospel to Luke.

Luke and Acts appear to have been written at the same time. Combined, they give a sweeping history of the founding of Christianity, from the birth of Christ to Paul's imprisonment in Rome (Acts 28:30,31). One important factor in establishing the date for Luke's gospel involves the fact that he wrote his two books around the time of Paul's imprisonment in A.D. 60–62. Luke records Jesus' prophecy of the destruction of Jerusalem in A.D. 70 (19:42–44; 21:20–24) but makes no mention of the fulfillment of that prophecy in either of his books. This is significant because he did make it a point to record other such prophetic fulfillments (Acts 11:28). Thus, because Luke did not mention the destruction of Jerusalem in A.D. 70 or the great persecution of Christians under Emperor Nero in A.D. 64 or the martyrdom of James around A.D. 62, the most likely date for this gospel is A.D. 60 or 61.

BACKGROUND AND SETTING

Luke expressly stated that his knowledge of the events recorded in his gospel came from the reports of those who were eyewitnesses (1:1,2), strongly implying that

he personally was not an eyewitness. The prologue makes it clear that Luke's aim was to give an ordered account of the event of Jesus' life, but this does not mean that he always followed a strict chronological order in all instances.

Luke's acknowledgment that he compiled his account from various extant sources does not invalidate the claim of divine inspiration for his work. The process of inspiration never bypasses or overrides the personalities, vocabularies, and styles of the human authors of Scripture. The unique traits of the human authors are always indelibly stamped on the book of Scripture. Luke's research creates no exception to this rule. The research itself was orchestrated by divine Providence. Most importantly, when Luke wrote, he was moved by the Spirit of God (2 Peter 1:21). Therefore, his account is infallibly true.

The Apostle Paul referred to Luke as a physician (Colossians 4:14). This is helpful background for Luke's obvious interest in medical phenomena. He gave special emphasis to Jesus' healing ministry throughout his gospel (4:38–40; 5:15–25; 6:17–19; 7:11–15; 8:43–47,49–56; 9:2,6,11; 13:11–13; 14:2–4; 17:12–14; 22:50,51). Luke also displays a physician's sensitivity by including Jesus' compassion for Gentiles, Samaritans, women, children, tax collectors, sinners, and others often regarded as outcasts in Israel.

HISTORICAL AND THEOLOGICAL THEMES

As a general statement of historical themes, Luke provides the most thoroughly historical treatment of the life of Christ. He shows special awareness of the value of details that help identify the historical context of the events he described.

A running theme in Luke's gospel is Jesus' compassion for the poor and outcasts. Every time he mentions a tax collector (3:12; 5:27; 7:29; 15:1; 18:10–13; 19:2), it is in a positive sense. Even so, Luke did not ignore the salvation of those who were rich and respectable (23:50–53). From the outset of Jesus' public ministry (4:18) to the Lord's final words on the cross (23:40–43), Luke underscored Christ's care for the pariahs as well as the powerful of society. Again and again he showed how the Great Physician ministered to those most aware of their need (5:31,32; 15:4–7,31,32; 19:10).

> AGAIN AND AGAIN **LUKE SHOWED** HOW **THE GREAT PHYSICIAN MINISTERED** TO THOSE **MOST AWARE** OF THEIR NEED.

The high profile Luke accords to women is particularly significant. From the nativity account, in which Mary, Elizabeth, and Anna are given prominence (chapters 1 and 2), to the events of resurrection morning, in which women again are major participants (24:1,10), Luke emphasizes the central role of women in the life and ministry of our Lord (7:12–15, 37–50; 8:2,3,43–48; 10:38–42; 13:11–13; 21:2–4; 23:27–29,49,55,56).

Several other recurring themes form threads through Luke's gospel. Examples of these are human fear in the presence of God (1:12,30,65; 2:9,10; 5:10,26; 7:16; 8:25,37,50; 9:34,45; 23:40), forgiveness (3:3; 5:20–25; 6:37; 7:41–50; 11:4; 12:10;

17:3,4; 23:34; 24:47), joy (1:14,44,47,58; 2:10; 6:23; 8:13; 10:17–21; 13:17; 15:5–10,22–32; 19:6,37; 24:52), wonder at the mysteries of divine truth (1:21,63; 2:18,19,33,47,48; 4:22,36; 5:9; 8:25; 9:43–45; 11:14; 20:26; 24:12,41), the role of the Holy Spirit (1:15,35,41,67; 2:25–27; 3:16,22; 4:1,14,18; 10:21; 11:13; 12:10,12), the temple in Jerusalem (1:9–22; 2:27–38,46–49; 4:9–13; 18:10–14; 19:45–48; 20:1–21:6,37,38; 24:53), and Jesus' prayers (3:21; 5:16; 6:12; 9:18,28,29; 11:1; 22:32,40–46).

Beginning at 9:51, Luke devoted ten chapters to a travelogue of Jesus' final journey to Jerusalem. Much of the material in this section is unique to Luke. This is the heart of Luke's gospel, and it features a theme that Luke stressed throughout: Jesus' relentless progression toward the cross. This was the very purpose for which Christ had come to earth (9:22,23; 17:25; 18:31–33; 24:25,26,46), and He would not be deterred. The saving of sinners was His whole mission (19:10).

OUTLINE

Dedication to Theophilus

1 Inasmuch as many have taken in hand to set in order a narrative of those things which have been fulfilled[a] among us, [2]just as those who from the beginning were eyewitnesses and ministers of the word delivered them to us, [3]it seemed good to me also, having had perfect understanding of all things from the very first, to write to you an orderly account, most excellent Theophilus, [4]that you may know the certainty of those things in which you were instructed.

1:3 having had perfect understanding. Luke, more than anyone else in the early church, had the abilities and the opportunity to consult with eyewitnesses of Jesus' ministry. He spent more than two years (during Paul's imprisonment in Caesarea—Acts 24:26,27) meeting and interviewing apostles and other eyewitnesses. Luke's ultimate understanding, however, came from the divine revelation through the Holy Spirit (1 Tim. 3:16).

John's Birth Announced to Zacharias

[5]There was in the days of Herod, the king of Judea, a certain priest named Zacharias, of the division of Abijah. His wife was of the daughters of Aaron, and her name was Elizabeth. [6]And they were both righteous before God, walking in all the commandments and ordinances of the Lord blameless. [7]But they had no child, because Elizabeth was barren, and they were both well advanced in years.

[8]So it was, that while he was serving as priest before God in the order of his division, [9]according to the custom of the priesthood, his lot fell to burn incense when he went into the temple of the Lord. [10]And the whole multitude of the people was praying outside at the hour of incense. [11]Then an angel of the Lord appeared to him, standing on the right side of the altar of incense.

[12]And when Zacharias saw him, he was troubled, and fear fell upon him.

1:9 his lot fell to burn incense. This was a high honor (Ex. 30:7,8). Most priests would never be chosen for this duty, and no one was permitted to serve in this capacity twice. Zacharias regarded this as the supreme moment in his life as a priest. The incense was kept burning perpetually in front of the veil that divided the Holy Place from the Most Holy Place. Zacharias would offer the incense every morning and evening.

---

[13]But the angel said to him, "Do not be afraid, Zacharias, for your prayer is heard; and your wife Elizabeth will bear you a son, and you shall call his name John. [14]And you will have joy and gladness, and many will rejoice at his birth. [15]For he will be great in the sight of the Lord, and shall drink neither wine nor strong drink. He will also be filled with the Holy Spirit, even from his mother's womb. [16]And he will turn many of the children of Israel to the Lord their God. [17]He will also go before Him in the spirit and power of Elijah, 'to turn the hearts of the fathers to the children,'[a] and the disobedient to the wisdom of the just, to make ready a people prepared for the Lord."

1:17 in the spirit and power of Elijah. Elijah, like John the Baptist, was known for his uncompromising stand for the Word of God, even in the face of a ruthless monarch (see 1 Kin. 18:17–24). Mal. 4:5,6 promised the return of Elijah before the Day of the Lord. **to turn the hearts.** John the Baptist fulfilled the prophecy of Mal. 4:6. **make ready.** This is possibly an allusion to Is. 40:3–5.

---

[18]And Zacharias said to the angel, "How shall I know this? For I am an old man, and my wife is well advanced in years." [19]And the angel answered and said to

---

1:1 [a]Or are most surely believed   1:17 [a]Malachi 4:5,6

What is the relationship of Luke to Matthew and Mark?

Even a cursory reading of the first three gospels reveals many striking similarities. Compare Luke 5:18-26, Matthew 9:2-8, and Mark 2:3-12. Significant differences can also be found, however, in the way each writer handles many details about Jesus. The question about how to explain these similarities and differences is known as the "Synoptic Problem" (syn means "together" and optic means "seeing"). See the discussion of the "Synoptic Problem" following the Introduction to Matthew.

him, "I am Gabriel, who stands in the presence of God, and was sent to speak to you and bring you these glad tidings. ²⁰But behold, you will be mute and not able to speak until the day these things take place, because you did not believe my words which will be fulfilled in their own time."

²¹And the people waited for Zacharias, and marveled that he lingered so long in the temple. ²²But when he came out, he could not speak to them; and they perceived that he had seen a vision in the temple, for he beckoned to them and remained speechless.

> **1:21 marveled that he lingered so long.** Zacharias was only supposed to offer incense, then come out to pronounce the familiar blessing (Num. 6:23–27) on the people waiting in the temple court. The conversation with the angel would have taken additional time.

²³So it was, as soon as the days of his service were completed, that he departed to his own house. ²⁴Now after those days his wife Elizabeth conceived; and she hid herself five months, saying, ²⁵"Thus the Lord has dealt with me, in the days when He looked on *me*, to take away my reproach among people."

Christ's Birth Announced to Mary

²⁶Now in the sixth month the angel Gabriel was sent by God to a city of Galilee named Nazareth, ²⁷to a virgin betrothed to a man whose name was Joseph, of the house of David. The virgin's name *was* Mary. ²⁸And having come in, the angel said to her, "Rejoice, highly favored *one*, the Lord *is* with you; blessed *are* you among women!"*a*

²⁹But when she saw him,*a* she was trou-

1:28 *a*NU-Text omits *blessed are you among women.*   1:29 *a*NU-Text omits *when she saw him.*

NEW TESTAMENT WOMEN

Mary, the virgin mother of Jesus, has a place of honor among the women of the New Testament. She is an enduring example of faith, humility, and service (Luke 1:26–56). Other notable women of the New Testament include the following:

Name	Description	Biblical Reference
Anna	Recognized Jesus as the long-awaited Messiah	Luke 2:36–38
Bernice	Sister of Agrippa before whom Paul made his defense	Acts 25:13
Candace	A queen of Ethiopia	Acts 8:27
Chloe	Woman who knew of divisions in the church at Corinth	1 Cor. 1:11
Claudia	Christian of Rome	2 Tim. 4:21
Damaris	Woman of Athens converted under Paul's ministry	Acts 17:34
Dorcas (Tabitha)	Christian in Joppa who was raised from the dead by Peter	Acts 9:36–41
Drusilla	Wife of Felix, governor of Judea	Acts 24:24
Elizabeth	Mother of John the Baptist	Luke 1:5,13
Eunice	Mother of Timothy	2 Tim. 1:5
Herodias	Queen who demanded the execution of John the Baptist	Matt. 14:3–10
Joanna	Provided for the material needs of Jesus	Luke 8:3
Lois	Grandmother of Timothy	2 Tim. 1:5
Lydia	Converted under Paul's ministry in Philippi	Acts 16:14
Martha and Mary	Sisters of Lazarus; friends of Jesus	Luke 10:38–42
Mary Magdalene	Woman from whom Jesus cast out demons	Matt. 27:56–61; Mark 16:9
Phoebe	A servant, perhaps a deaconess, in the church at Cenchrea	Rom. 16:1,2
Priscilla	Wife of Aquila; laborer with Paul at Corinth and Ephesus	Acts 18:2,18,19
Salome	Mother of Jesus' disciples James and John	Matt. 20:20–24
Sapphira	Held back goods from the early Christian community	Acts 5:1
Susanna	Provided for the material needs of Jesus	Luke 8:3

1:27 a virgin. A correct view of the Incarnation hinges on the truth that Jesus was virgin-born. Both Luke and Matthew expressly state that Mary was a virgin when Jesus was conceived. The Holy Spirit wrought the conception through supernatural means. The nature of Christ's conception testifies both to His deity and His sinlessness.

bled at his saying, and considered what manner of greeting this was. ³⁰Then the angel said to her, "Do not be afraid, Mary, for you have found favor with God. ³¹And behold, you will conceive in your womb and bring forth a Son, and shall call His name JESUS. ³²He will be great, and will be called the Son of the Highest; and the Lord God will give Him the throne of His father David. ³³And He will reign over the house of Jacob forever, and of His kingdom there will be no end."

³⁴Then Mary said to the angel, "How can this be, since I do not know a man?"

³⁵And the angel answered and said to her, "*The* Holy Spirit will come upon you, and the power of the Highest will overshadow you; therefore, also, that Holy One who is to be born will be called the Son of God. ³⁶Now indeed, Elizabeth your relative has also conceived a son in her old age; and this is now the sixth month for her who was called barren. ³⁷For with God nothing will be impossible."

³⁸Then Mary said, "Behold the maidservant of the Lord! Let it be to me according to your word." And the angel departed from her.

1:38 Let it be to me according to your word. Mary was in an extremely embarrassing and difficult position. Betrothed to Joseph, she faced the stigma of being an unwed mother. Joseph would have obviously known that the child was not his. She knew she would be accused of adultery, which was punishable by stoning (Deut. 22:13–21). Yet, she willingly submitted to the will of God.

Mary Visits Elizabeth

³⁹Now Mary arose in those days and went into the hill country with haste, to a city of Judah, ⁴⁰and entered the house of Zacharias and greeted Elizabeth. ⁴¹And it happened, when Elizabeth heard the greeting of Mary, that the babe leaped in her womb; and Elizabeth was filled with the Holy Spirit.

⁴²Then she spoke out with a loud voice and said, "Blessed *are* you among women, and blessed *is* the fruit of your womb! ⁴³But why *is* this *granted* to me, that the mother of my Lord should come to me? ⁴⁴For indeed, as soon as the voice of your greeting sounded in my ears, the babe leaped in my womb for joy. ⁴⁵Blessed *is* she who believed, for there will be a fulfillment of those things which were told her from the Lord."

The Song of Mary

⁴⁶And Mary said:

"My soul magnifies the Lord,
⁴⁷   And my spirit has rejoiced in God my
        Savior.

1:47 my Savior. Mary referred to God as "Savior," indicating that she recognized her own need of a Savior and that she knew the true God as her Savior. Mary never thought of herself as "immaculate" (free from sin). Instead, she spoke as someone whose only hope for salvation was divine grace. Nothing in this passage supports the notion that Mary should be an object of adoration.

⁴⁸   For He has regarded the lowly state of
        His maidservant;
      For behold, henceforth all generations
        will call me blessed.
⁴⁹   For He who is mighty has done great
        things for me,
      And holy *is* His name.
⁵⁰   And His mercy *is* on those who fear
        Him
      From generation to generation.
⁵¹   He has shown strength with His arm;
      He has scattered *the* proud in the
        imagination of their hearts.
⁵²   He has put down the mighty from
        their thrones,
      And exalted *the* lowly.
⁵³   He has filled *the* hungry with good
        things,
      And *the* rich He has sent away
        empty.
⁵⁴   He has helped His servant Israel,
      In remembrance of *His* mercy,
⁵⁵   As He spoke to our fathers,
      To Abraham and to his seed forever."

⁵⁶And Mary remained with her about three months, and returned to her house.

Birth of John the Baptist

57Now Elizabeth's full time came for her to be delivered, and she brought forth a son. 58When her neighbors and relatives heard how the Lord had shown great mercy to her, they rejoiced with her.

Circumcision of John the Baptist

59So it was, on the eighth day, that they came to circumcise the child; and they would have called him by the name of his father, Zacharias. 60His mother answered and said, "No; he shall be called John."

61But they said to her, "There is no one among your relatives who is called by this name." 62So they made signs to his father—what he would have him called.

63And he asked for a writing tablet, and wrote, saying, "His name is John." So they all marveled. 64Immediately his mouth was opened and his tongue *loosed*, and he spoke, praising God. 65Then fear came on all who dwelt around them; and all these sayings were discussed throughout all the hill country of Judea. 66And all those who heard *them* kept *them* in their hearts, saying, "What kind of child will this be?" And the hand of the Lord was with him.

> **1:68–79** This passage is known as the *Benedictus*. It contains many OT quotations and allusions. When Zacharias had been struck mute in the temple, he was supposed to have delivered a benediction. So it is fitting that when his speech was restored, the first words out of his mouth were this inspired benediction.

Zacharias' Prophecy

67Now his father Zacharias was filled with the Holy Spirit, and prophesied, saying:

68   "Blessed *is* the Lord God of Israel,
        For He has visited and redeemed His
            people,
69   And has raised up a horn of salvation
            for us
        In the house of His servant David,
70   As He spoke by the mouth of His holy
            prophets,
        Who *have been* since the world
            began,

71   That we should be saved from our
            enemies
        And from the hand of all who hate us,
72   To perform the mercy *promised* to our
            fathers
        And to remember His holy covenant,
73   The oath which He swore to our
            father Abraham:
74   To grant us that we,
        Being delivered from the hand of our
            enemies,
        Might serve Him without fear,
75   In holiness and righteousness before
            Him all the days of our life.

76   "And you, child, will be called the
            prophet of the Highest;
        For you will go before the face of the
            Lord to prepare His ways,
77   To give knowledge of salvation to His
            people
        By the remission of their sins,
78   Through the tender mercy of our
            God,
        With which the Dayspring from on
            high has visited*a* us;
79   To give light to those who sit in
            darkness and the shadow of death,
        To guide our feet into the way of
            peace."

80So the child grew and became strong in spirit, and was in the deserts till the day of his manifestation to Israel.

Christ Born of Mary

2 And it came to pass in those days *that* a decree went out from Caesar Augustus that all the world should be registered. 2This census first took place while Quirinius was governing Syria. 3So all went to be registered, everyone to his own city.

4Joseph also went up from Galilee, out of

> **2:4 Nazareth...Bethlehem.** Both Joseph and Mary were descendants of David and, therefore, went to their tribal home in Judea to be registered. This was a difficult journey of more than 70 miles through mountainous terrain. Mary was on the verge of delivery, and perhaps she and Joseph were conscious that the baby's birth in Bethlehem would fulfill the prophecy in Mic. 5:2.

1:78 *a*NU-Text reads *shall visit.*

the city of Nazareth, into Judea, to the city of David, which is called Bethlehem, because he was of the house and lineage of David, [5]to be registered with Mary, his betrothed wife,[a] who was with child. [6]So it was, that while they were there, the days were completed for her to be delivered. [7]And she brought forth her firstborn Son, and wrapped Him in swaddling cloths, and laid Him in a manger, because there was no room for them in the inn.

Glory in the Highest

[8]Now there were in the same country shepherds living out in the fields, keeping watch over their flock by night. [9]And behold,[a] an angel of the Lord stood before them, and the glory of the Lord shone around them, and they were greatly afraid. [10]Then the angel said to them, "Do not be afraid, for behold, I bring you good tidings of great joy which will be to all people. [11]For there is born to you this day in the city of David a Savior, who is Christ the Lord. [12]And this *will be* the sign to you: You will find a Babe wrapped in swaddling cloths, lying in a manger."

> **2:11 City of David.** This is Bethlehem, the town where David was born (not the City of David, which was on the southern slope of Mount Zion in 2 Sam. 5:7–9). **a Savior.** This is one of only two places in the gospels where Christ is referred to as "Savior" (the other is in John 4:42). **Christ.** "Christ" is the Greek equivalent of "Messiah." **Lord.** This Greek word can mean "master," but here it translates the covenant name of God.

[13]And suddenly there was with the angel a multitude of the heavenly host praising God and saying:

[14] "Glory to God in the highest,
     And on earth peace, goodwill toward
       men!"[a]

[15]So it was, when the angels had gone away from them into heaven, that the shepherds said to one another, "Let us now go to Bethlehem and see this thing that has come to pass, which the Lord has made known to us." [16]And they came with haste and found Mary and Joseph, and the Babe lying in a manger. [17]Now when they had seen *Him,* they made widely[a] known the saying which was told them concerning this Child. [18]And all those who heard *it* marveled at those things which were told them by the shepherds. [19]But Mary kept all these things and pondered *them* in her heart. [20]Then the shepherds returned, glorifying and praising God for all the things that they had heard and seen, as it was told them.

Circumcision of Jesus

[21]And when eight days were completed for the circumcision of the Child,[a] His name was called JESUS, the name given by the angel before He was conceived in the womb.

Jesus Presented in the Temple

[22]Now when the days of her purification according to the law of Moses were completed, they brought Him to Jerusalem to present *Him* to the Lord [23](as it is written in the law of the Lord, *"Every male who opens the womb shall be called holy to the* LORD*"*),[a] [24]and to offer a sacrifice according to what is said in the law of the Lord, *"A pair of turtledoves or two young pigeons."*[a]

> **2:22 her purification.** A woman was ceremonially unclean for 40 days if she bore a son, 80 days if she bore a daughter (Lev. 12:2). After that period of time, she was to offer a yearling lamb and a dove or pigeon (Lev. 12:6), or two doves or pigeons if she was poor (Lev. 12:8). Mary's offering indicates that she and Joseph were poor. **to Jerusalem.** This was a journey of 6 miles from Bethlehem. **to present *Him* to the Lord.** The dedication of the firstborn son was required by Moses' law (see Ex. 13:2,12–15).

Simeon Sees God's Salvation

[25]And behold, there was a man in Jerusalem whose name was Simeon, and this man was just and devout, waiting for the Consolation of Israel, and the Holy Spirit was upon him. [26]And it had been revealed

---

2:5 [a]NU-Text omits *wife.*   2:9 [a]NU-Text omits *behold.*   2:14 [a]NU-Text reads *toward men of goodwill.*
2:17 [a]NU-Text omits *widely.*   2:21 [a]NU-Text reads *for His circumcision.*   2:23 [a]Exodus 13:2,12,15
2:24 [a]Leviticus 12:8

to him by the Holy Spirit that he would not see death before he had seen the Lord's Christ. [27]So he came by the Spirit into the temple. And when the parents brought in the Child Jesus, to do for Him according to the custom of the law, [28]he took Him up in his arms and blessed God and said:

[29] "Lord, now You are letting Your servant depart in peace,
According to Your word;

[30] For my eyes have seen Your salvation

[31] Which You have prepared before the face of all peoples,

[32] A light to *bring* revelation to the Gentiles,
And the glory of Your people Israel."

[33]And Joseph and His mother[a] marveled at those things which were spoken of Him. [34]Then Simeon blessed them, and said to Mary His mother, "Behold, this *Child* is destined for the fall and rising of many in Israel, and for a sign which will be spoken against [35](yes, a sword will pierce through your own soul also), that the thoughts of many hearts may be revealed."

Anna Bears Witness to the Redeemer

[36]Now there was one, Anna, a prophetess, the daughter of Phanuel, of the tribe of Asher. She was of a great age, and had lived with a husband seven years from her virginity; [37]and this woman *was* a widow of about eighty-four years,[a] who did not depart from the temple, but served *God* with fastings and prayers night and day. [38]And coming in that instant she gave thanks to the Lord,[a] and spoke of Him to all those who looked for redemption in Jerusalem.

2:37 a widow of about eighty-four years. This probably means she was an 84-year-old widow, not that she had been widowed that long. **not depart from the temple.** The widow lived on the temple grounds. There would have been several such dwelling places for priests in the outer court, and Anna must have been allowed to live there because of her status as a prophetess.

The Family Returns to Nazareth

[39]So when they had performed all things according to the law of the Lord, they returned to Galilee, to their *own* city, Nazareth. [40]And the Child grew and became strong in spirit,[a] filled with wisdom; and the grace of God was upon Him.

The Boy Jesus Amazes the Scholars

[41]His parents went to Jerusalem every year at the Feast of the Passover. [42]And when He was twelve years old, they went up to Jerusalem according to the custom of the feast. [43]When they had finished the days, as they returned, the Boy Jesus lingered behind in Jerusalem. And Joseph and His mother[a] did not know *it*; [44]but supposing Him to have been in the company, they went a day's journey, and sought Him among *their* relatives and acquaintances. [45]So when they did not find Him, they returned to Jerusalem, seeking Him. [46]Now so it was *that* after three days they found Him in the temple, sitting in the midst of the teachers, both listening to them and asking them questions. [47]And all who heard Him were astonished at His understanding and answers. [48]So when they saw Him, they were amazed; and His mother said to Him, "Son, why have You done this to us? Look, Your father and I have sought You anxiously."

[49]And He said to them, "Why did you seek Me? Did you not know that I must be about My Father's business?" [50]But they did not understand the statement which He spoke to them.

2:49 My Father's business. Jesus' reply reveals genuine amazement that His parents had not known where to look for Him. This also reveals that even at so young an age, He clearly understood His identity and mission.

Jesus Advances in Wisdom and Favor

[51]Then He went down with them and came to Nazareth, and was subject to them, but His mother kept all these things in her heart. [52]And Jesus increased in wisdom and stature, and in favor with God and men.

2:33 [a]NU-Text reads *And His father and mother.* 2:37 [a]NU-Text reads *a widow until she was eighty-four.* 2:38 [a]NU-Text reads *to God.* 2:40 [a]NU-Text omits *in spirit.* 2:43 [a]NU-Text reads *And His parents.*

John the Baptist Prepares the Way

3 Now in the fifteenth year of the reign of Tiberius Caesar, Pontius Pilate being governor of Judea, Herod being tetrarch of Galilee, his brother Philip tetrarch of Iturea and the region of Trachonitis, and Lysanias tetrarch of Abilene, ²while Annas and Caiaphas were high priests,ᵃ the word of God came to John the son of Zacharias in the wilderness. ³And he went into all the region around the Jordan, preaching a baptism of repentance for the remission of sins, ⁴as it is written in the book of the words of Isaiah the prophet, saying:

" The voice of one crying in the
      wilderness:
  'Prepare the way of the LORD;
   Make His paths straight.

> **3:4 Make His paths straight.** This is quoted from Is. 40:3–5. A monarch traveling in wilderness regions would have men go ahead to make sure the road was clear of obstructions and hazards. In a spiritual sense, John was calling the people of Israel to prepare their hearts for the coming of their Messiah.

5   Every valley shall be filled
       And every mountain and hill brought
          low;
       The crooked places shall be made
          straight
       And the rough ways smooth;
6   And all flesh shall see the salvation of
          God. ' "ᵃ

John Preaches to the People

⁷Then he said to the multitudes that came out to be baptized by him, "Brood of vipers! Who warned you to flee from the wrath to come? ⁸Therefore bear fruits wor-

> **3:8 children to Abraham.** Abraham's true children are those who share his faith, believing God's Word as he did (Rom. 4:11–16). To trust one's physical ancestry is to shift the focus of faith away from God, which is spiritually fatal (see John 8:39–44). **stones.** God can turn a heart of stone into a believing heart. He can raise up children to Abraham from inanimate objects or even from Gentiles if He chooses.

thy of repentance, and do not begin to say to yourselves, 'We have Abraham as our father.' For I say to you that God is able to raise up children to Abraham from these stones. ⁹And even now the ax is laid to the root of the trees. Therefore every tree which does not bear good fruit is cut down and thrown into the fire."

¹⁰So the people asked him, saying, "What shall we do then?"

¹¹He answered and said to them, "He who has two tunics, let him give to him who has none; and he who has food, let him do likewise."

¹²Then tax collectors also came to be baptized, and said to him, "Teacher, what shall we do?"

¹³And he said to them, "Collect no more than what is appointed for you."

¹⁴Likewise the soldiers asked him, saying, "And what shall we do?"

So he said to them, "Do not intimidate anyone or accuse falsely, and be content with your wages."

> **3:14 soldiers.** These were most likely members of the forces of Herod Antipas, stationed at Perea, perhaps, along with Judean police. **Do not intimidate anyone.** John demanded integrity and high character in the practical matters of everyday life, not a monastic lifestyle or a mystical asceticism (see James 1:27).

¹⁵Now as the people were in expectation, and all reasoned in their hearts about John, whether he was the Christ or not, ¹⁶John answered, saying to all, "I indeed baptize you with water; but One mightier than I is coming, whose sandal strap I am not worthy to loose. He will baptize you with the Holy Spirit and fire. ¹⁷His winnowing fan is in His hand, and He will thoroughly clean out His threshing floor, and gather the wheat into His barn; but the chaff He will burn with unquenchable fire."

¹⁸And with many other exhortations he preached to the people. ¹⁹But Herod the tetrarch, being rebuked by him concerning Herodias, his brother Philip's wife,ᵃ and for all the evils which Herod had done, ²⁰also

---

3:2 ᵃNU-Text and M-Text read in the high priesthood of Annas and Caiaphas.   3:6 ᵃIsaiah 40:3–5
3:19 ᵃNU-Text reads his brother's wife.

added this, above all, that he shut John up in prison.

John Baptizes Jesus

21When all the people were baptized, it came to pass that Jesus also was baptized; and while He prayed, the heaven was opened. 22And the Holy Spirit descended in bodily form like a dove upon Him, and a voice came from heaven which said, "You are My beloved Son; in You I am well pleased."

The Genealogy of Jesus Christ

23Now Jesus Himself began *His ministry at* about thirty years of age, being (as was supposed) *the* son of Joseph, *the* son of Heli, 24*the son* of Matthat,*a the* son of Levi, *the son* of Melchi, *the son* of Janna, *the son* of Joseph, 25*the son* of Mattathiah, *the son* of Amos, *the son* of Nahum, *the son* of Esli, *the son* of Naggai, 26*the son* of Maath, *the son* of Mattathiah, *the son* of Semei, *the son* of Joseph, *the son* of Judah, 27*the son* of Joannas, *the son* of Rhesa, *the son* of Zerubbabel, *the son* of Shealtiel, *the son* of Neri, 28*the son* of Melchi, *the son* of Addi, *the son* of Cosam, *the son* of Elmodam, *the son* of Er, 29*the son* of Jose, *the son* of Eliezer, *the son* of Jorim, *the son* of Matthat, *the son* of Levi, 30*the son* of Simeon, *the son* of Judah, *the son* of Joseph, *the son* of Jonan, *the son* of Eliakim, 31*the son* of Melea, *the son* of Menan, *the son* of Mattathah, *the son* of Nathan, *the son* of David, 32*the son* of Jesse, *the son* of Obed, *the son* of Boaz, *the son* of Salmon, *the son* of Nahshon, 33*the son* of Amminadab, *the*

son of Ram, *the son* of Hezron, *the son* of Perez, *the son* of Judah, 34*the son* of Jacob, *the son* of Isaac, *the son* of Abraham, *the son* of Terah, *the son* of Nahor, 35*the son* of Serug, *the son* of Reu, *the son* of Peleg, *the son* of Eber, *the son* of Shelah, 36*the son* of Cainan, *the son* of Arphaxad, *the son* of Shem, *the son* of Noah, *the son* of Lamech, 37*the son* of Methuselah, *the son* of Enoch, *the son* of Jared, *the son* of Mahalalel, *the son* of Cainan, 38*the son* of Enosh, *the son* of Seth, *the son* of Adam, *the son* of God.

Satan Tempts Jesus

4 Then Jesus, being filled with the Holy Spirit, returned from the Jordan and was led by the Spirit into*a* the wilderness, 2being tempted for forty days by the devil. And in those days He ate nothing, and afterward, when they had ended, He was hungry.

3And the devil said to Him, "If You are the Son of God, command this stone to become bread."

4But Jesus answered him, saying,*a* "It is written, '*Man shall not live by bread alone, but by every word of God.*' "*b*

5Then the devil, taking Him up on a high mountain, showed Him*a* all the kingdoms of the world in a moment of time. 6And the devil said to Him, "All this authority I will give You, and their glory; for *this* has been delivered to me, and I give it to whomever I wish. 7Therefore, if You will worship before me, all will be Yours."

8And Jesus answered and said to him, "Get behind Me, Satan!*a* For*b* it is written, '*You shall worship the Lord your God, and Him only you shall serve.*' "*c*

9Then he brought Him to Jerusalem, set Him on the pinnacle of the temple, and said to Him, "If You are the Son of God, throw Yourself down from here. 10For it is written:

> '*He shall give His angels charge over you,*
>   *To keep you,*'

3:23 about thirty years of age. This was an approximation, as 30 was the customary age for entering into the office of prophet (Ezek. 1:1), priest (Num. 4:3,35), or king (Gen. 41:46). **as was supposed.** Luke already established the fact of the virgin birth (1:34,35); here he made it clear again that Joseph was not Jesus' true father.

3:24 *a*This and several other names in the genealogy are spelled somewhat differently in the NU-Text. Since the New King James Version uses the Old Testament spelling for persons mentioned in the New Testament, these variations, which come from the Greek, have not been footnoted.   4:1 *a*NU-Text reads *in.*   4:4 *a*Deuteronomy 8:3   *b*NU-Text omits *but by every word of God.*   4:5 *a*NU-Text reads *And taking Him up, he showed Him.*   4:8 *a*NU-Text omits *Get behind Me, Satan.*   *b*NU-Text and M-Text omit *For.*   *c*Deuteronomy 6:13

[11]and,

> 'In their hands they shall bear you up,
> Lest you dash your foot against a
>   stone.' "[a]

[12]And Jesus answered and said to him, "It has been said, 'You shall not tempt the LORD your God.' "[a]

[13]Now when the devil had ended every temptation, he departed from Him until an opportune time.

Jesus Begins His Galilean Ministry

[14]Then Jesus returned in the power of the Spirit to Galilee, and news of Him went out through all the surrounding region. [15]And He taught in their synagogues, being glorified by all.

Jesus Rejected at Nazareth

[16]So He came to Nazareth, where He had been brought up. And as His custom was, He went into the synagogue on the Sabbath day, and stood up to read. [17]And He was handed the book of the prophet Isaiah. And when He had opened the book, He found the place where it was written:

[18]   " The Spirit of the LORD is upon Me,
> Because He has anointed Me
> To preach the gospel to the poor;
> He has sent Me to heal the
>   brokenhearted,[a]
> To proclaim liberty to the captives

> And recovery of sight to the blind,
> To set at liberty those who are
>   oppressed;
> [19] To proclaim the acceptable year of the
>   LORD."[a]

[20]Then He closed the book, and gave it back to the attendant and sat down. And the eyes of all who were in the synagogue were fixed on Him. [21]And He began to say to them, "Today this Scripture is fulfilled in your hearing." [22]So all bore witness to Him, and marveled at the gracious words which proceeded out of His mouth. And they said, "Is this not Joseph's son?"

> **4:21 this Scripture is fulfilled.** Jesus claimed that He was the Messiah who fulfilled the prophecy. The townspeople correctly understood His meaning but could not accept such lofty claims from One whom they knew as the carpenter's son (see Matt. 13:55).

[23]He said to them, "You will surely say this proverb to Me, 'Physician, heal yourself! Whatever we have heard done in Capernaum,[a] do also here in Your country.' " [24]Then He said, "Assuredly, I say to you, no prophet is accepted in his own country. [25]But I tell you truly, many widows were in Israel in the days of Elijah, when the heaven was shut up three years and six months, and there was a great famine throughout all the land; [26]but to none of them was Elijah sent except to Zarephath,[a]

4:11 [a]Psalm 91:11,12   4:12 [a]Deuteronomy 6:16   4:18 [a]NU-Text omits to heal the brokenhearted. 4:19 [a]Isaiah 61:1,2   4:23 [a]Here and elsewhere the NU-Text spelling is Capharnaum.   4:26 [a]Greek Sarepta

---

For whom did Luke write?

Luke shares some similarities with Mark, indicating that he intended his gospel for a Gentile readership. Luke took pains to identify locations that would have been familiar to all Jews (4:31; 23:51; 24:13), suggesting that he had in mind readers who did not have a knowledge of Palestinian geography. He usually preferred Greek terms over Hebrew ones; for example, "Calvary" instead of "Golgotha" (23:33). Luke avoided the use of Semitic terms such as "Abba" (Mark 14:36), "rabbi" (Matthew 23:7,8; John 1:38,49), and "hosanna" (Matthew 21:9; Mark 11:9,10; John 12:13).

The third gospel writer quoted the Old Testament more sparingly than Matthew. When citing Old Testament passages, Luke nearly always employed the Septuagint, a Greek translation of the Hebrew Scriptures. Furthermore, most of Luke's Old Testament references are actually allusions rather than direct quotations. They appear in Jesus' words rather than in Luke's narrative sections (2:23,24; 3:4–6; 4:4,8,10–12,18,19; 7:27; 10:27; 18:20; 19:46; 20:17,18,37,42,43; 22:37).

in the region of Sidon, to a woman *who was* a widow. 27And many lepers were in Israel in the time of Elisha the prophet, and none of them was cleansed except Naaman the Syrian."

28So all those in the synagogue, when they heard these things, were filled with wrath, 29and rose up and thrust Him out of the city; and they led Him to the brow of the hill on which their city was built, that they might throw Him down over the cliff. 30Then passing through the midst of them, He went His way.

> **4:30 passing through the midst of them.** This is the first of several similar incidents in which Jesus miraculously escaped a premature death at the hands of a mob (see John 7:30; 8:59; 10:39).

Jesus Casts Out an Unclean Spirit

31Then He went down to Capernaum, a city of Galilee, and was teaching them on the Sabbaths. 32And they were astonished at His teaching, for His word was with authority. 33Now in the synagogue there was a man who had a spirit of an unclean demon. And he cried out with a loud voice, 34saying, "Let *us* alone! What have we to do with You, Jesus of Nazareth? Did You come to destroy us? I know who You are—the Holy One of God!"

35But Jesus rebuked him, saying, "Be quiet, and come out of him!" And when the demon had thrown him in *their* midst, it came out of him and did not hurt him. 36Then they were all amazed and spoke among themselves, saying, "What a word this *is!* For with authority and power He commands the unclean spirits, and they come out." 37And the report about Him went out into every place in the surrounding region.

Peter's Mother-in-Law Healed

38Now He arose from the synagogue and entered Simon's house. But Simon's wife's mother was sick with a high fever, and they made request of Him concerning her. 39So He stood over her and rebuked the fever, and it left her. And immediately she arose and served them.

Many Healed After Sabbath Sunset

40When the sun was setting, all those who had any that were sick with various diseases brought them to Him; and He laid His hands on every one of them and healed them. 41And demons also came out of many, crying out and saying, "You are the Christ,*a* the Son of God!"

And He, rebuking *them*, did not allow them to speak, for they knew that He was the Christ.

Jesus Preaches in Galilee

42Now when it was day, He departed and went into a deserted place. And the crowd sought Him and came to Him, and tried to keep Him from leaving them; 43but He said to them, "I must preach the kingdom of God to the other cities also, because for this purpose I have been sent." 44And He was preaching in the synagogues of Galilee.*a*

Four Fishermen Called as Disciples

5 So it was, as the multitude pressed about Him to hear the word of God, that He stood by the Lake of Gennesaret, 2and saw two boats standing by the lake; but the fishermen had gone from them and were washing *their* nets. 3Then He got into one of the boats, which was Simon's, and asked him to put out a little from the land. And He sat down and taught the multitudes from the boat.

4When He had stopped speaking, He said to Simon, "Launch out into the deep and let down your nets for a catch."

5But Simon answered and said to Him, "Master, we have toiled all night and caught nothing; nevertheless at Your word I will let down the net." 6And when they had done this, they caught a great number of fish, and their net was breaking. 7So they signaled to *their* partners in the other boat to come and help them. And they came and filled both the boats, so that they began to sink. 8When Simon Peter saw *it*, he fell down at Jesus' knees, saying, "Depart from me, for I am a sinful man, O Lord!"

9For he and all who were with him were astonished at the catch of fish which they had taken; 10and so also *were* James and John, the sons of Zebedee, who were part-

---

4:41 *a*NU-Text omits *the Christ.*   4:44 *a*NU-Text reads *Judea.*

5:8 Depart from me. The miraculous catch of fish astonished the fishermen in Capernaum. Peter immediately realized that he was in the presence of the Holy One, and he was stricken with shame over his own sinfulness (see Ex. 20:19; Job 42:5,6).

5:20 your sins are forgiven. Christ ignored the paralysis and addressed the man's greater need first. In doing so, He asserted a prerogative that was God's alone (v. 21). Christ's subsequent healing of the man's paralysis was proof that He had authority to forgive sins as well.

ners with Simon. And Jesus said to Simon, "Do not be afraid. From now on you will catch men." [11]So when they had brought their boats to land, they forsook all and followed Him.

Jesus Cleanses a Leper

[12]And it happened when He was in a certain city, that behold, a man who was full of leprosy saw Jesus; and he fell on *his* face and implored Him, saying, "Lord, if You are willing, You can make me clean."

[13]Then He put out *His* hand and touched him, saying, "I am willing; be cleansed." Immediately the leprosy left him. [14]And He charged him to tell no one, "But go and show yourself to the priest, and make an offering for your cleansing, as a testimony to them, just as Moses commanded."

[15]However, the report went around concerning Him all the more; and great multitudes came together to hear, and to be healed by Him of their infirmities. [16]So He Himself *often* withdrew into the wilderness and prayed.

Jesus Forgives and Heals a Paralytic

[17]Now it happened on a certain day, as He was teaching, that there were Pharisees and teachers of the law sitting by, who had come out of every town of Galilee, Judea, and Jerusalem. And the power of the Lord was *present* to heal them.*a* [18]Then behold, men brought on a bed a man who was paralyzed, whom they sought to bring in and lay before Him. [19]And when they could not find how they might bring him in, because of the crowd, they went up on the housetop and let him down with *his* bed through the tiling into the midst before Jesus. [20]When He saw their faith, He said to him, "Man, your sins are forgiven you." [21]And the scribes and the Pharisees began to reason, saying, "Who is this who speaks

blasphemies? Who can forgive sins but God alone?"

[22]But when Jesus perceived their thoughts, He answered and said to them, "Why are you reasoning in your hearts? [23]Which is easier, to say, 'Your sins are forgiven you,' or to say, 'Rise up and walk'? [24]But that you may know that the Son of Man has power on earth to forgive sins"— He said to the man who was paralyzed, "I say to you, arise, take up your bed, and go to your house."

[25]Immediately he rose up before them, took up what he had been lying on, and departed to his own house, glorifying God. [26]And they were all amazed, and they glorified God and were filled with fear, saying, "We have seen strange things today!"

Matthew the Tax Collector

[27]After these things He went out and saw a tax collector named Levi, sitting at the tax office. And He said to him, "Follow Me." [28]So he left all, rose up, and followed Him.

[29]Then Levi gave Him a great feast in his own house. And there were a great number of tax collectors and others who sat down with them. [30]And their scribes and the Pharisees*a* complained against His disciples, saying, "Why do You eat and drink with tax collectors and sinners?"

5:30 eat and drink. Associating with outcasts was deplorable. Eating and drinking with them implied a friendship that was abhorrent to the Pharisees (see 7:34).

[31]Jesus answered and said to them, "Those who are well have no need of a physician, but those who are sick. [32]I have not come to call *the* righteous, but sinners, to repentance."

5:17 *a*NU-Text reads *present with Him to heal.*   5:30 *a*NU-Text reads *But the Pharisees and their scribes.*

Jesus Is Questioned About Fasting

[33]Then they said to Him, "Why do[a] the disciples of John fast often and make prayers, and likewise those of the Pharisees, but Yours eat and drink?"

[34]And He said to them, "Can you make the friends of the bridegroom fast while the bridegroom is with them? [35]But the days will come when the bridegroom will be taken away from them; then they will fast in those days."

[36]Then He spoke a parable to them: "No one puts a piece from a new garment on an old one;[a] otherwise the new makes a tear, and also the piece that was *taken* out of the new does not match the old. [37]And no one puts new wine into old wineskins; or else the new wine will burst the wineskins and be spilled, and the wineskins will be ruined. [38]But new wine must be put into new wineskins, and both are preserved.[a] [39]And no one, having drunk old *wine*, immediately[a] desires new; for he says, 'The old is better.' "[b]

Jesus Is Lord of the Sabbath

6 Now it happened on the second Sabbath after the first[a] that He went through the grainfields. And His disciples plucked the heads of grain and ate *them*, rubbing *them* in *their* hands. [2]And some of the Pharisees said to them, "Why are you doing what is not lawful to do on the Sabbath?"

[3]But Jesus answering them said, "Have you not even read this, what David did when he was hungry, he and those who were with him: [4]how he went into the house of God, took and ate the showbread, and also gave some to those with him, which is not lawful for any but the priests to eat?" [5]And He said to them, "The Son of Man is also Lord of the Sabbath."

Healing on the Sabbath

[6]Now it happened on another Sabbath, also, that He entered the synagogue and taught. And a man was there whose right hand was withered. [7]So the scribes and Pharisees watched Him closely, whether He would heal on the Sabbath, that they might find an accusation against Him. [8]But He knew their thoughts, and said to the man who had the withered hand, "Arise and stand here." And he arose and stood. [9]Then Jesus said to them, "I will ask you one thing: Is it lawful on the Sabbath to do good or to do evil, to save life or to destroy?"[a] [10]And when He had looked around at them all, He said to the man,[a] "Stretch out your hand." And he did so, and his hand was restored as whole as the other.[b] [11]But they were filled with rage, and discussed with one another what they might do to Jesus.

6:7 whether He would heal on the Sabbath. The scribes and Pharisees saw the man with the withered hand and immediately knew that this would be an occasion for Christ to heal him. In contrast to all other so-called healers, Christ was not selective: He healed all who came to Him (see Matt. 8:16).

The Twelve Apostles

[12]Now it came to pass in those days that He went out to the mountain to pray, and continued all night in prayer to God. [13]And when it was day, He called His disciples to *Himself*; and from them He chose twelve whom He also named apostles: [14]Simon, whom He also named Peter, and Andrew his brother; James and John; Philip and Bartholomew; [15]Matthew and Thomas; James the *son* of Alphaeus, and Simon called the Zealot; [16]Judas *the son* of James, and Judas Iscariot who also became a traitor.

Jesus Heals a Great Multitude

[17]And He came down with them and stood on a level place with a crowd of His disciples and a great multitude of people from all Judea and Jerusalem, and from the seacoast of Tyre and Sidon, who came to hear Him and be healed of their diseases, [18]as well as those who were tormented with

---

5:33 [a]NU-Text omits *Why do*, making the verse a statement.   5:36 [a]NU-Text reads *No one tears a piece from a new garment and puts it on an old one.*   5:38 [a]NU-Text omits *and both are preserved.* 5:39 [a]NU-Text omits *immediately.* [b]NU-Text reads *good.*   6:1 [a]NU-Text reads *on a Sabbath.* 6:9 [a]M-Text reads *to kill.*   6:10 [a]NU-Text and M-Text read *to him.* [b]NU-Text omits *as whole as the other.*

unclean spirits. And they were healed. ¹⁹And the whole multitude sought to touch Him, for power went out from Him and healed *them* all.

The Beatitudes

²⁰Then He lifted up His eyes toward His disciples, and said:

"Blessed *are you* poor,
  For yours is the kingdom of God.

> **6:20 you poor.** Christ's concern for the poor and outcasts is one of Luke's favorite themes. Luke uses the pronoun "you" to underscore the tender, personal sense of Christ's words. Matthew uses the article "the" (Matt. 5:3). A comparison of the two passages reveals that Christ was dealing with something more significant than material poverty or wealth. The poverty spoken of here refers to spiritual impoverishment.

²¹   Blessed *are you* who hunger now,
       For you shall be filled.
     Blessed *are you* who weep now,
       For you shall laugh.
²²   Blessed are you when men hate you,
       And when they exclude you,
       And revile *you*, and cast out your
         name as evil,
       For the Son of Man's sake.
²³   Rejoice in that day and leap for joy!
       For indeed your reward *is* great in
         heaven,
       For in like manner their fathers did
         to the prophets.

Jesus Pronounces Woes

²⁴   "But woe to you who are rich,
       For you have received your
         consolation.
²⁵   Woe to you who are full,
       For you shall hunger.
     Woe to you who laugh now,
       For you shall mourn and weep.
²⁶   Woe to you*ᵃ* when all*ᵇ* men speak well
         of you,
       For so did their fathers to the false
         prophets.

Love Your Enemies

²⁷"But I say to you who hear: Love your enemies, do good to those who hate you,

²⁸bless those who curse you, and pray for those who spitefully use you. ²⁹To him who strikes you on the *one* cheek, offer the other also. And from him who takes away your cloak, do not withhold *your* tunic either. ³⁰Give to everyone who asks of you. And from him who takes away your goods do not ask *them* back. ³¹And just as you want men to do to you, you also do to them likewise. ³²"But if you love those who love you, what credit is that to you? For even sinners love those who love them. ³³And if you do good to those who do good to you, what credit is that to you? For even sinners do the same. ³⁴And if you lend *to those* from whom you hope to receive back, what credit is that to you? For even sinners lend to sinners to receive as much back. ³⁵But love your enemies, do good, and lend, hoping for nothing in return; and your reward will be great, and you will be sons of the Most High. For He is kind to the unthankful and evil. ³⁶Therefore be merciful, just as your Father also is merciful.

> **6:35 sons of the Most High.** God is loving, gracious, and generous, even to His enemies. His children should bear the stamp of His moral character and be like Him.

Do Not Judge

³⁷"Judge not, and you shall not be judged. Condemn not, and you shall not be condemned. Forgive, and you will be forgiven. ³⁸Give, and it will be given to you: good measure, pressed down, shaken together, and running over will be put into your bosom. For with the same measure that you use, it will be measured back to you." ³⁹And He spoke a parable to them: "Can the blind lead the blind? Will they not both fall into the ditch? ⁴⁰A disciple is not above his teacher, but everyone who is perfectly trained will be like his teacher. ⁴¹And why do you look at the speck in your brother's eye, but do not perceive the plank in your own eye? ⁴²Or how can you say to your brother, 'Brother, let me remove the speck that *is* in your eye,' when you yourself do not see the plank that *is* in your own eye? Hypocrite! First remove the plank from

---

6:26 *ᵃ*NU-Text and M-Text omit *to you*. *ᵇ*M-Text omits *all*.

your own eye, and then you will see clearly to remove the speck that is in your brother's eye.

A Tree Is Known by Its Fruit

43"For a good tree does not bear bad fruit, nor does a bad tree bear good fruit. 44For every tree is known by its own fruit. For *men* do not gather figs from thorns, nor do they gather grapes from a bramble bush. 45A good man out of the good treasure of his heart brings forth good; and an evil man out of the evil treasure of his heart*a* brings forth evil. For out of the abundance of the heart his mouth speaks.

Build on the Rock

46"But why do you call Me 'Lord, Lord,' and not do the things which I say? 47Whoever comes to Me, and hears My sayings and does them, I will show you whom he is like: 48He is like a man building a house, who dug deep and laid the foundation on the rock. And when the flood arose, the stream beat vehemently against that house, and could not shake it, for it was founded on the rock.*a* 49But he who heard and did nothing is like a man who built a house on the earth without a foundation, against which the stream beat vehemently; and immediately it fell.*a* And the ruin of that house was great."

6:46 you call Me 'Lord, Lord.' It is not sufficient to give lip service to Christ's lordship. Genuine faith produces obedience. A tree is known by its fruit (v. 44).

Jesus Heals a Centurion's Servant

7 Now when He concluded all His sayings in the hearing of the people, He entered Capernaum. 2And a certain centurion's servant, who was dear to him, was sick and ready to die. 3So when he heard about Jesus, he sent elders of the Jews to Him, pleading with Him to come and heal his servant. 4And when they came to Jesus, they begged Him earnestly, saying that the one for whom He should do this was deserving, 5"for he loves our nation, and has built us a synagogue."

6Then Jesus went with them. And when He was already not far from the house, the centurion sent friends to Him, saying to Him, "Lord, do not trouble Yourself, for I am not worthy that You should enter under my roof. 7Therefore I did not even think myself worthy to come to You. But say the word, and my servant will be healed. 8For I also am a man placed under authority, having soldiers under me. And I say to one, 'Go,' and he goes; and to another, 'Come,' and he comes; and to my servant, 'Do this,' and he does *it*."

9When Jesus heard these things, He marveled at him, and turned around and said to the crowd that followed Him, "I say to you, I have not found such great faith, not even in Israel!" 10And those who were sent, returning to the house, found the servant well who had been sick.*a*

Jesus Raises the Son of the Widow of Nain

11Now it happened, the day after, *that* He went into a city called Nain; and many of His disciples went with Him, and a large crowd. 12And when He came near the gate of the city, behold, a dead man was being carried out, the only son of his mother; and she was a widow. And a large crowd from the city was with her. 13When the Lord saw her, He had compassion on her and said to her, "Do not weep." 14Then He came and touched the open coffin, and those who carried *him* stood still. And He said, "Young man, I say to you, arise." 15So he who was dead sat up and began to speak. And He presented him to his mother.

16Then fear came upon all, and they glorified God, saying, "A great prophet has risen up among us"; and, "God has visited His people." 17And this report about Him went throughout all Judea and all the surrounding region.

John the Baptist Sends Messengers to Jesus

18Then the disciples of John reported to him concerning all these things. 19And John, calling two of his disciples to *him*, sent *them* to Jesus,*a* saying, "Are You the Coming One, or do we look for another?" 20When the men had come to Him, they

---

6:45 *aNU-Text omits *treasure of his heart*.   6:48 *aNU-Text reads *for it was well built*.   6:49 *aNU-Text reads *collapsed*.   7:10 *aNU-Text omits *who had been sick*.   7:19 *aNU-Text reads *the Lord*.

7:19 Are You the Coming One. John was in prison, and Christ was encountering unbelief and hostility. Yet John's faith was not failing, and he had not lost confidence in Christ. He wanted reassurance from Christ, which he received (vv. 22,23).

said, "John the Baptist has sent us to You, saying, 'Are You the Coming One, or do we look for another?' " ²¹And that very hour He cured many of infirmities, afflictions, and evil spirits; and to many blind He gave sight.

²²Jesus answered and said to them, "Go and tell John the things you have seen and heard: that *the* blind see, *the* lame walk, *the* lepers are cleansed, *the* deaf hear, *the* dead are raised, *the* poor have the gospel preached to them. ²³And blessed is *he* who is not offended because of Me."

²⁴When the messengers of John had departed, He began to speak to the multitudes concerning John: "What did you go out into the wilderness to see? A reed shaken by the wind? ²⁵But what did you go out to see? A man clothed in soft garments? Indeed those who are gorgeously appareled and live in luxury are in kings' courts. ²⁶But what did you go out to see? A prophet? Yes, I say to you, and more than a prophet. ²⁷This is *he* of whom it is written:

'Behold, I send My messenger before
    Your face,
Who will prepare Your way before
    You.'ᵃ

²⁸For I say to you, among those born of women there is not a greater prophet than John the Baptist;ᵃ but he who is least in the kingdom of God is greater than he."

²⁹And when all the people heard *Him,* even the tax collectors justified God, having been baptized with the baptism of John. ³⁰But the Pharisees and lawyers rejected the will of God for themselves, not having been baptized by him.

³¹And the Lord said,ᵃ "To what then shall I liken the men of this generation, and what are they like? ³²They are like children sitting in the marketplace and calling to one another, saying:

'We played the flute for you,
    And you did not dance;
We mourned to you,
    And you did not weep.'

³³For John the Baptist came neither eating bread nor drinking wine, and you say, 'He has a demon.' ³⁴The Son of Man has come eating and drinking, and you say, 'Look, a glutton and a winebibber, a friend of tax collectors and sinners!' ³⁵But wisdom is justified by all her children."

7:34 eating and drinking. This refers to living an ordinary life. Jesus and John the Baptist had different methods of preaching the same message, which took away the Pharisees' excuses. They wanted to see rigid abstinence and a Spartan lifestyle from Jesus and his disciples—a lifestyle that had characterized John the Baptist's ministry. Yet the Pharisees had rejected John. Their problem was the corruption of their own hearts, not these men's lifestyles, but they would not acknowledge that.

A Sinful Woman Forgiven

³⁶Then one of the Pharisees asked Him to eat with him. And He went to the Pharisee's house, and sat down to eat. ³⁷And behold, a woman in the city who was a sinner, when she knew that *Jesus* sat at the table in the Pharisee's house, brought an alabaster flask of fragrant oil, ³⁸and stood at His feet behind *Him* weeping; and she began to wash His feet with her tears, and wiped *them* with the hair of her head; and she kissed His feet and anointed *them* with the fragrant oil. ³⁹Now when the Pharisee who had invited Him saw *this,* he spoke to himself, saying, "This Man, if He were a prophet, would know who and what manner of woman *this is* who is touching Him, for she is a sinner."

⁴⁰And Jesus answered and said to him, "Simon, I have something to say to you."

So he said, "Teacher, say it."

⁴¹"There was a certain creditor who had two debtors. One owed five hundred denarii, and the other fifty. ⁴²And when they had nothing with which to repay, he freely forgave them both. Tell Me, therefore, which of them will love him more?"

7:27 ᵃMalachi 3:1   7:28 ᵃNU-Text reads *there is none greater than John.*   7:31 ᵃNU-Text and M-Text omit *And the Lord said.*

[43]Simon answered and said, "I suppose the *one* whom he forgave more."

And He said to him, "You have rightly judged." [44]Then He turned to the woman and said to Simon, "Do you see this woman? I entered your house; you gave Me no water for My feet, but she has washed My feet with her tears and wiped *them* with the hair of her head. [45]You gave Me no kiss, but this woman has not ceased to kiss My feet since the time I came in. [46]You did not anoint My head with oil, but this woman has anointed My feet with fragrant oil. [47]Therefore I say to you, her sins, *which are* many, are forgiven, for she loved much. But to whom little is forgiven, *the same* loves little."

7:44 no water for My feet. Washing a guest's feet was an essential formality. To not offer a guest water for their feet was regarded as an insult.

[48]Then He said to her, "Your sins are forgiven."

[49]And those who sat at the table with Him began to say to themselves, "Who is this who even forgives sins?"

[50]Then He said to the woman, "Your faith has saved you. Go in peace."

Many Women Minister to Jesus

8 Now it came to pass, afterward, that He went through every city and village, preaching and bringing the glad tidings of the kingdom of God. And the twelve *were* with Him, [2]and certain women who had been healed of evil spirits and infirmities—Mary called Magdalene, out of whom had come seven demons, [3]and Joanna the wife of Chuza, Herod's steward, and Susanna, and many others who provided for Him[a] from their substance.

The Parable of the Sower

[4]And when a great multitude had gathered, and they had come to Him from every city, He spoke by a parable: [5]"A sower went out to sow his seed. And as he sowed, some fell by the wayside; and it was trampled down, and the birds of the air devoured it. [6]Some fell on rock; and as soon as it sprang up, it withered away because it lacked moisture. [7]And some fell among thorns, and the thorns sprang up with it and choked it. [8]But others fell on good ground, sprang up, and yielded a crop a hundredfold." When He had said these things He cried, "He who has ears to hear, let him hear!"

8:5 to sow his seed. Seed was sown by hand over plowed soil. While throwing seed toward the edges of a field, the sower would naturally throw some seed that would land on the hard beaten path where it could not penetrate the soil. This could refer to the hard, obstinate Jewish leaders.

The Purpose of Parables

[9]Then His disciples asked Him, saying, "What does this parable mean?"

[10]And He said, "To you it has been given to know the mysteries of the kingdom of God, but to the rest *it is given* in parables, that

> '*Seeing they may not see,*
> *And hearing they may not*
> *understand.*'[a]

The Parable of the Sower Explained

[11]"Now the parable is this: The seed is the word of God. [12]Those by the wayside are the ones who hear; then the devil comes and takes away the word out of their hearts, lest they should believe and be saved. [13]But the ones on the rock *are those* who, when they hear, receive the word with joy; and these have no root, who believe for a while and in time of temptation fall away. [14]Now the ones *that* fell among thorns are those who, when they have heard, go out and are choked with cares, riches, and pleasures of life, and bring no fruit to maturity. [15]But the ones *that* fell on the good ground are those who, having heard the word with a noble and good heart, keep *it* and bear fruit with patience.

8:15 heard...keep...bear fruit. This is evidence of true salvation. "Heard" refers to understanding and believing (John 8:31,47). "Keep" refers to ongoing obedience (11:28). "Fruit" is good works (Matt. 7:16–20).

8:3 [a]NU-Text and M-Text read *them*.   8:10 [a]Isaiah 6:9

The Parable of the Revealed Light

16"No one, when he has lit a lamp, covers it with a vessel or puts *it* under a bed, but sets *it* on a lampstand, that those who enter may see the light. 17For nothing is secret that will not be revealed, nor *anything* hidden that will not be known and come to light. 18Therefore take heed how you hear. For whoever has, to him *more* will be given; and whoever does not have, even what he seems to have will be taken from him."

Jesus' Mother and Brothers Come to Him

19Then His mother and brothers came to Him, and could not approach Him because of the crowd. 20And it was told Him *by some,* who said, "Your mother and Your brothers are standing outside, desiring to see You."

21But He answered and said to them, "My mother and My brothers are these who hear the word of God and do it."

Wind and Wave Obey Jesus

22Now it happened, on a certain day, that He got into a boat with His disciples. And He said to them, "Let us cross over to the other side of the lake." And they launched out. 23But as they sailed He fell asleep. And a windstorm came down on the lake, and they were filling *with water,* and were in jeopardy. 24And they came to Him and awoke Him, saying, "Master, Master, we are perishing!"

Then He arose and rebuked the wind and the raging of the water. And they ceased, and there was a calm. 25But He said to them, "Where is your faith?"

And they were afraid, and marveled, saying to one another, "Who can this be? For He commands even the winds and water, and they obey Him!"

A Demon-Possessed Man Healed

26Then they sailed to the country of the Gadarenes,*a* which is opposite Galilee. 27And when He stepped out on the land, there met Him a certain man from the city who had demons for a long time. And he wore no clothes,*a* nor did he live in a house but in the tombs. 28When he saw Jesus, he cried out, fell down before Him, and with a loud voice said, "What have I to do with You, Jesus, Son of the Most High God? I beg You, do not torment me!" 29For He had commanded the unclean spirit to come out of the man. For it had often seized him, and he was kept under guard, bound with chains and shackles; and he broke the bonds and was driven by the demon into the wilderness.

8:27 a certain man. Matthew reveals there were actually two men. Only one did the talking (see Matt. 8:28).

30Jesus asked him, saying, "What is your name?"

And he said, "Legion," because many demons had entered him. 31And they begged Him that He would not command them to go out into the abyss.

32Now a herd of many swine was feeding there on the mountain. So they begged Him that He would permit them to enter them. And He permitted them. 33Then the demons went out of the man and entered the swine, and the herd ran violently down the steep place into the lake and drowned.

34When those who fed *them* saw what had happened, they fled and told *it* in the city and in the country. 35Then they went out to see what had happened, and came to Jesus, and found the man from whom the demons had departed, sitting at the feet of Jesus, clothed and in his right mind. And they were afraid. 36They also who had seen *it* told them by what means he who had been demon-possessed was healed. 37Then the whole multitude of the surrounding region of the Gadarenes*a* asked Him to depart from them, for they were seized with great fear. And He got into the boat and returned.

38Now the man from whom the demons had departed begged Him that he might be with Him. But Jesus sent him away, saying, 39"Return to your own house, and tell what great things God has done for you." And he went his way and proclaimed throughout the whole city what great things Jesus had done for him.

A Girl Restored to Life and a Woman Healed

⁴⁰So it was, when Jesus returned, that the multitude welcomed Him, for they were all waiting for Him. ⁴¹And behold, there came a man named Jairus, and he was a ruler of the synagogue. And he fell down at Jesus' feet and begged Him to come to his house, ⁴²for he had an only daughter about twelve years of age, and she was dying.

But as He went, the multitudes thronged Him. ⁴³Now a woman, having a flow of blood for twelve years, who had spent all her livelihood on physicians and could not be healed by any, ⁴⁴came from behind and touched the border of His garment. And immediately her flow of blood stopped.

> **8:44 came from behind and touched.** Because of her affliction, she would normally render anyone she touched unclean. The effect here was precisely the opposite.

⁴⁵And Jesus said, "Who touched Me?" When all denied it, Peter and those with him*a* said, "Master, the multitudes throng and press You, and You say, 'Who touched Me?' "*b*
⁴⁶But Jesus said, "Somebody touched Me, for I perceived power going out from Me." ⁴⁷Now when the woman saw that she was not hidden, she came trembling; and falling down before Him, she declared to Him in the presence of all the people the reason she had touched Him and how she was healed immediately.

⁴⁸And He said to her, "Daughter, be of good cheer;*a* your faith has made you well. Go in peace."

⁴⁹While He was still speaking, someone came from the ruler of the synagogue's *house,* saying to him, "Your daughter is dead. Do not trouble the Teacher."*a*
⁵⁰But when Jesus heard *it,* He answered him, saying, "Do not be afraid; only believe, and she will be made well." ⁵¹When He came into the house, He permitted no one to go in*a* except Peter, James, and John,*b* and the father and mother of the girl. ⁵²Now all wept and mourned for her; but He said, "Do not weep; she is not dead, but sleeping." ⁵³And they ridiculed Him, knowing that she was dead.

⁵⁴But He put them all outside,*a* took her by the hand and called, saying, "Little girl, arise." ⁵⁵Then her spirit returned, and she arose immediately. And He commanded that she be given *something* to eat. ⁵⁶And her parents were astonished, but He charged them to tell no one what had happened.

Sending Out the Twelve

9 Then He called His twelve disciples together and gave them power and authority over all demons, and to cure diseases. ²He sent them to preach the kingdom of God and to heal the sick. ³And He said to them, "Take nothing for the journey, neither staffs nor bag nor bread nor money; and do not have two tunics apiece. ⁴"Whatever house you enter, stay there,

---

8:45 *a*NU-Text omits *and those with him.* *b*NU-Text omits *and You say, "Who touched Me?"*
8:48 *a*NU-Text omits *be of good cheer.* 8:49 *a*NU-Text adds *anymore.* 8:51 *a*NU-Text adds *with Him.* *b*NU-Text and M-Text read *Peter, John, and James.* 8:54 *a*NU-Text omits *put them all outside.*

What do we know about Luke himself?

Very little is actually known about Luke. According to tradition and limited internal evidence, Luke was a Gentile. The Apostle Paul seems to confirm this, distinguishing Luke from those who were "of the circumcision" (Colossians 4:11,14). That would make Luke the only Gentile to pen any books of Scripture.

Luke almost never included personal details about himself. Nothing definite is known about his background or his conversion. Both Eusebius and Jerome identified him as a native of Antioch, which may explain why so much of the book of Acts centers on Antioch (Acts 11:19–27; 13:1–3; 14:26; 15:22,23,30–35; 18:22,23).

Luke was a frequent companion of the Apostle Paul. They were apparently inseparable from the time of Paul's Macedonian vision (Acts 16:9,10) right up to the time of Paul's martyrdom (2 Timothy 4:11). Paul referred to Luke as a physician (Colossians 4:14). This explains Luke's interest in medical phenomena and the high profile he gave to Jesus' healing ministry.

and from there depart. ⁵And whoever will not receive you, when you go out of that city, shake off the very dust from your feet as a testimony against them."

⁶So they departed and went through the towns, preaching the gospel and healing everywhere.

Herod Seeks to See Jesus

⁷Now Herod the tetrarch heard of all that was done by Him; and he was perplexed, because it was said by some that John had risen from the dead, ⁸and by some that Elijah had appeared, and by others that one of the old prophets had risen again. ⁹Herod said, "John I have beheaded, but who is this of whom I hear such things?" So he sought to see Him.

> **9:7 Herod the tetrarch.** News of Christ reached to the highest levels of government. **John had risen from the dead.** This was not true, but Herod seemed gripped by guilty fear (see Mark 6:16).

Feeding the Five Thousand

¹⁰And the apostles, when they had returned, told Him all that they had done. Then He took them and went aside privately into a deserted place belonging to the city called Bethsaida. ¹¹But when the multitudes knew *it*, they followed Him; and He received them and spoke to them about the kingdom of God, and healed those who had need of healing. ¹²When the day began to wear away, the twelve came and said to Him, "Send the multitude away, that they may go into the surrounding towns and country, and lodge and get provisions; for we are in a deserted place here."

¹³But He said to them, "You give them something to eat."

And they said, "We have no more than five loaves and two fish, unless we go and buy food for all these people." ¹⁴For there were about five thousand men.

Then He said to His disciples, "Make them sit down in groups of fifty." ¹⁵And they did so, and made them all sit down.

¹⁶Then He took the five loaves and the two fish, and looking up to heaven, He blessed and broke *them*, and gave *them* to the disciples to set before the multitude.

¹⁷So they all ate and were filled, and twelve baskets of the leftover fragments were taken up by them.

Peter Confesses Jesus as the Christ

¹⁸And it happened, as He was alone praying, *that* His disciples joined Him, and He asked them, saying, "Who do the crowds say that I am?"

¹⁹So they answered and said, "John the Baptist, but some *say* Elijah; and others *say* that one of the old prophets has risen again."

²⁰He said to them, "But who do you say that I am?"

Peter answered and said, "The Christ of God."

Jesus Predicts His Death and Resurrection

²¹And He strictly warned and commanded them to tell this to no one, ²²saying, "The Son of Man must suffer many things, and be rejected by the elders and chief priests and scribes, and be killed, and be raised the third day."

Take Up the Cross and Follow Him

²³Then He said to *them* all, "If anyone desires to come after Me, let him deny himself, and take up his cross daily,ᵃ and follow Me. ²⁴For whoever desires to save his life will lose it, but whoever loses his life for My sake will save it. ²⁵For what profit is it to a man if he gains the whole world, and is himself destroyed or lost? ²⁶For whoever is ashamed of Me and My words, of him the Son of Man will be ashamed when He comes in His *own* glory, and *in His* Father's, and of the holy angels.

> **9:23 cross.** Jesus commonly spoke of self-denial to His disciples (see 14:26,27). The kind of self-denial He sought was not asceticism, but a willingness to obey His commandments, serve one another, suffer, and even die for His sake.

Jesus Transfigured on the Mount

²⁷But I tell you truly, there are some standing here who shall not taste death till they see the kingdom of God."

²⁸Now it came to pass, about eight days after these sayings, that He took Peter, John, and James and went up on the mountain

9:23 ᵃM-Text omits *daily*.

to pray. [29]As He prayed, the appearance of His face was altered, and His robe *became* white *and* glistening. [30]And behold, two men talked with Him, who were Moses and Elijah, [31]who appeared in glory and spoke of His decease which He was about to accomplish at Jerusalem. [32]But Peter and those with him were heavy with sleep; and when they were fully awake, they saw His glory and the two men who stood with Him. [33]Then it happened, as they were parting from Him, *that* Peter said to Jesus, "Master, it is good for us to be here; and let us make three tabernacles: one for You, one for Moses, and one for Elijah"—not knowing what he said.

[34]While he was saying this, a cloud came and overshadowed them; and they were fearful as they entered the cloud. [35]And a voice came out of the cloud, saying, "This is My beloved Son.[a] Hear Him!" [36]When the voice had ceased, Jesus was found alone. But they kept quiet, and told no one in those days any of the things they had seen.

A Boy Is Healed

[37]Now it happened on the next day, when they had come down from the mountain, that a great multitude met Him. [38]Suddenly a man from the multitude cried out, saying, "Teacher, I implore You, look on my son, for he is my only child. [39]And behold, a spirit seizes him, and he suddenly cries out; it convulses him so that he foams *at the mouth*; and it departs from him with great difficulty, bruising him. [40]So I implored Your disciples to cast it out, but they could not."

> **9:39 a spirit seizes him.** This was not a case of epilepsy; it was clearly demon possession. There is no reason to think that Luke, a physician, was merely accommodating the understanding of his readers. Jesus healed the boy by rebuking the demon (v. 42; see Mark 9:25).

[41]Then Jesus answered and said, "O faithless and perverse generation, how long shall I be with you and bear with you? Bring your son here." [42]And as he was still com-

ing, the demon threw him down and convulsed *him*. Then Jesus rebuked the unclean spirit, healed the child, and gave him back to his father.

Jesus Again Predicts His Death

[43]And they were all amazed at the majesty of God.

But while everyone marveled at all the things which Jesus did, He said to His disciples, [44]"Let these words sink down into your ears, for the Son of Man is about to be betrayed into the hands of men." [45]But they did not understand this saying, and it was hidden from them so that they did not perceive it; and they were afraid to ask Him about this saying.

Who Is the Greatest?

[46]Then a dispute arose among them as to which of them would be greatest. [47]And Jesus, perceiving the thought of their heart, took a little child and set him by Him, [48]and said to them, "Whoever receives this little child in My name receives Me; and whoever receives Me receives Him who sent Me. For he who is least among you all will be great."

> **9:49 because he does not follow with us.** It is ironic that John, "the apostle of love," would be the one to raise this objection. He came to see that the only legitimate tests of another person's ministry are the test of doctrine (1 John 4:1–3) and the test of fruit (1 John 2:4–6). This man would have passed both tests, but John was inclined to reject him because of his group affiliation. That is the error of sectarianism.

Jesus Forbids Sectarianism

[49]Now John answered and said, "Master, we saw someone casting out demons in Your name, and we forbade him because he does not follow with us."

[50]But Jesus said to him, "Do not forbid *him*, for he who is not against us[a] is on our[b] side."

A Samaritan Village Rejects the Savior

[51]Now it came to pass, when the time had come for Him to be received up, that He steadfastly set His face to go to Jerusalem,

---

9:35 [a]NU-Text reads *This is My Son, the Chosen One.*   9:50 [a]NU-Text reads *you.* [b]NU-Text reads *your.*

⁵²and sent messengers before His face. And as they went, they entered a village of the Samaritans, to prepare for Him. ⁵³But they did not receive Him, because His face was *set* for the journey to Jerusalem. ⁵⁴And when His disciples James and John saw *this*, they said, "Lord, do You want us to command fire to come down from heaven and consume them, just as Elijah did?"ᵃ

9:54 James and John. Jesus nicknamed these brothers "Boanerges," Sons of Thunder (Mark 3:17). This was John's second sin against charity in a short time (v. 49). Several years later, John journeyed through Samaria once again with Peter, this time preaching the gospel in Samaritan villages (Acts 8:25).

⁵⁵But He turned and rebuked them,ᵃ and said, "You do not know what manner of spirit you are of. ⁵⁶For the Son of Man did not come to destroy men's lives but to save *them*."ᵃ And they went to another village.

The Cost of Discipleship

⁵⁷Now it happened as they journeyed on the road, *that* someone said to Him, "Lord, I will follow You wherever You go."

⁵⁸And Jesus said to him, "Foxes have holes and birds of the air *have* nests, but the Son of Man has nowhere to lay His head."

⁵⁹Then He said to another, "Follow Me."

But he said, "Lord, let me first go and bury my father."

⁶⁰Jesus said to him, "Let the dead bury their own dead, but you go and preach the kingdom of God."

⁶¹And another also said, "Lord, I will follow You, but let me first go *and* bid them farewell who are at my house."

⁶²But Jesus said to him, "No one, having put his hand to the plow, and looking back, is fit for the kingdom of God."

The Seventy Sent Out

10 After these things the Lord appointed seventy others also,ᵃ and sent them two by two before His face into every city and place where He Himself was about to go. ²Then He said to them, "The harvest truly *is* great, but the laborers *are* few; therefore pray the Lord of the harvest to send out laborers into His harvest. ³Go your way; behold, I send you out as lambs among wolves. ⁴Carry neither money bag, knapsack, nor sandals; and greet no one along the road. ⁵But whatever house you enter, first say, 'Peace to this house.' ⁶And if a son of peace is there, your peace will rest on it; if not, it will return to you. ⁷And remain in the same house, eating and drinking such things as they give, for the laborer is worthy of his wages. Do not go from house to house. ⁸Whatever city you enter, and they receive you, eat such things as are set before you. ⁹And heal the sick there, and say to them, 'The kingdom of God has come near to you.' ¹⁰But whatever city you enter, and they do not receive you, go out into its streets and say, ¹¹'The very dust of your city which clings to usᵃ we wipe off against you. Nevertheless know this, that the kingdom of God has come near you.' ¹²Butᵃ I say to you that it will be more tolerable in that Day for Sodom than for that city.

Woe to the Impenitent Cities

¹³"Woe to you, Chorazin! Woe to you, Bethsaida! For if the mighty works which were done in you had been done in Tyre and Sidon, they would have repented long ago, sitting in sackcloth and ashes. ¹⁴But it will be more tolerable for Tyre and Sidon at the judgment than for you. ¹⁵And you, Capernaum, who are exalted to heaven, will be brought down to Hades.ᵃ ¹⁶He who hears you hears Me, he who rejects you rejects Me, and he who rejects Me rejects Him who sent Me."

The Seventy Return with Joy

¹⁷Then the seventyᵃ returned with joy, saying, "Lord, even the demons are subject to us in Your name." ¹⁸And He said to them, "I saw Satan fall like lightning from heaven. ¹⁹Behold, I give

---

9:54 ᵃNU-Text omits *just as Elijah did.*   9:55 ᵃNU-Text omits the rest of this verse.   9:56 ᵃNU-Text omits the first sentence of this verse.   10:1 ᵃNU-Text reads *seventy-two others.*   10:11 ᵃNU-Text reads *our feet.*   10:12 ᵃNU-Text and M-Text omit *But.*   10:15 ᵃNU-Text reads *will you be exalted to heaven? You will be thrust down to Hades!*   10:17 ᵃNU-Text reads *seventy-two.*

you the authority to trample on serpents and scorpions, and over all the power of the enemy, and nothing shall by any means hurt you. ²⁰Nevertheless do not rejoice in this, that the spirits are subject to you, but rather^a rejoice because your names are written in heaven."

10:20 do not rejoice in this. Rather than being enthralled with extraordinary manifestations such as power over demons and miracles, the 70 disciples should have realized that the greatest wonder of all is the reality of salvation. Salvation is the whole point of the gospel message.

Jesus Rejoices in the Spirit

²¹In that hour Jesus rejoiced in the Spirit and said, "I thank You, Father, Lord of heaven and earth, that You have hidden these things from *the* wise and prudent and revealed them to babes. Even so, Father, for so it seemed good in Your sight. ²²All^a things have been delivered to Me by My Father, and no one knows who the Son is except the Father, and who the Father is except the Son, and *the one* to whom the Son wills to reveal *Him.*"

²³Then He turned to *His* disciples and said privately, "Blessed *are* the eyes which see the things you see; ²⁴for I tell you that many prophets and kings have desired to see what you see, and have not seen *it*, and to hear what you hear, and have not heard *it.*"

The Parable of the Good Samaritan

²⁵And behold, a certain lawyer stood up and tested Him, saying, "Teacher, what shall I do to inherit eternal life?"

²⁶He said to him, "What is written in the law? What is your reading *of it?*"

²⁷So he answered and said, " '*You shall love the* LORD *your God with all your heart, with all your soul, with all your strength, and with all your mind,*'^a and '*your neighbor as yourself.*' "^b

²⁸And He said to him, "You have answered rightly; do this and you will live."

²⁹But he, wanting to justify himself, said to Jesus, "And who is my neighbor?"

³⁰Then Jesus answered and said: "A cer-

10:29 wanting to justify himself. This reveals the man's self-righteous character. **who is my neighbor?** The scribes and Pharisees saw only the righteous people as their neighbors. They hated Gentiles, especially Samaritans, because they saw them as the enemies of God. They used Ps. 139:21,22 to justify their position, where hatred of evil is the result of loving righteousness. Yet Jesus taught that godly hatred is marked by a broken-hearted grieving over the condition of the sinner and is tempered by genuine love (Matt. 5:44–48).

tain *man* went down from Jerusalem to Jericho, and fell among thieves, who stripped him of his clothing, wounded *him,* and departed, leaving *him* half dead. ³¹Now by chance a certain priest came down that road. And when he saw him, he passed by on the other side. ³²Likewise a Levite, when he arrived at the place, came and looked, and passed by on the other side. ³³But a certain Samaritan, as he journeyed, came where he was. And when he saw him, he had compassion. ³⁴So he went to *him* and bandaged his wounds, pouring on oil and wine; and he set him on his own animal, brought him to an inn, and took care of him. ³⁵On the next day, when he departed,^a he took out two denarii, gave *them* to the innkeeper, and said to him, 'Take care of him; and whatever more you spend, when I come again, I will repay you.' ³⁶So which of these three do you think was neighbor to him who fell among the thieves?"

³⁷And he said, "He who showed mercy on him."

Then Jesus said to him, "Go and do likewise."

Mary and Martha Worship and Serve

³⁸Now it happened as they went that He entered a certain village; and a certain woman named Martha welcomed Him into her house. ³⁹And she had a sister called Mary, who also sat at Jesus'^a feet and heard His word. ⁴⁰But Martha was distracted with much serving, and she approached Him and said, "Lord, do You not care that my sister has left me to serve alone? Therefore tell her to help me."

⁴¹And Jesus^a answered and said to her,

10:20 ^aNU-Text and M-Text omit *rather.*   10:22 ^aM-Text reads *And turning to the disciples He said,* "*All . . . .*   10:27 ^aDeuteronomy 6:5   ^bLeviticus 19:18   10:35 ^aNU-Text omits *when he departed.* 10:39 ^aNU-Text reads *the Lord's.*   10:41 ^aNU-Text reads *the Lord.*

"Martha, Martha, you are worried and troubled about many things. ⁴²But one thing is needed, and Mary has chosen that good part, which will not be taken away from her."

> **10:42 one thing...good part.** Jesus was not speaking of the number of dishes to be served. Mary exemplified the one necessary priority: an attitude of worship and meditation, listening with an open mind and heart to Jesus' words.

The Model Prayer

11 Now it came to pass, as He was praying in a certain place, when He ceased, *that* one of His disciples said to Him, "Lord, teach us to pray, as John also taught his disciples."

²So He said to them, "When you pray, say:

Our Father in heaven,*^a*
Hallowed be Your name.
Your kingdom come.*^b*
Your will be done
On earth as *it is* in heaven.
³ Give us day by day our daily bread.
⁴ And forgive us our sins,
For we also forgive everyone who is indebted to us.
And do not lead us into temptation,
But deliver us from the evil one." *^a*

A Friend Comes at Midnight

⁵And He said to them, "Which of you shall have a friend, and go to him at midnight and say to him, 'Friend, lend me three loaves; ⁶for a friend of mine has come to me on his journey, and I have nothing to set before him'; ⁷and he will answer from within and say, 'Do not trouble me; the door is now shut, and my children are with me in bed; I cannot rise and give to you'? ⁸I say to you, though he will not rise and give to him because he is his friend, yet because of his persistence he will rise and give him as many as he needs.

Keep Asking, Seeking, Knocking

⁹"So I say to you, ask, and it will be given to you; seek, and you will find; knock, and it will be opened to you. ¹⁰For everyone who asks receives, and he who seeks finds, and to him who knocks it will be opened. ¹¹If a son asks for bread*^a* from any father among you, will he give him a stone? Or if *he asks* for a fish, will he give him a serpent instead of a fish? ¹²Or if he asks for an egg, will he offer him a scorpion? ¹³If you then, being evil, know how to give good gifts to your children, how much more will *your* heavenly Father give the Holy Spirit to those who ask Him!"

A House Divided Cannot Stand

¹⁴And He was casting out a demon, and it was mute. So it was, when the demon had gone out, that the mute spoke; and the multitudes marveled. ¹⁵But some of them said, "He casts out demons by Beelzebub,*^a* the ruler of the demons."

¹⁶Others, testing *Him*, sought from Him a sign from heaven. ¹⁷But He, knowing their thoughts, said to them: "Every kingdom divided against itself is brought to desolation, and a house *divided* against a house falls. ¹⁸If Satan also is divided against himself, how will his kingdom stand? Because you say I cast out demons by Beelzebub. ¹⁹And if I cast out demons by Beelzebub, by whom do your sons cast *them* out? Therefore they will be your judges. ²⁰But if I cast out demons with the finger of God, surely the kingdom of God has come upon you. ²¹When a strong man, fully armed, guards his own palace, his goods are in peace. ²²But when a stronger than he comes upon him and overcomes him, he takes from him all his armor in which he trusted, and divides his spoils. ²³He who is not with Me is against Me, and he who does not gather with Me scatters.

> **11:20 with the finger of God.** In Ex. 8:19, the phony magicians of Egypt were forced to confess that Moses' miracles were works of God. Jesus made a similar comparison between His exorcisms and the work of the Jewish exorcists.

An Unclean Spirit Returns

²⁴"When an unclean spirit goes out of a man, he goes through dry places, seeking

---

11:2 *^a*NU-Text omits *Our* and *in heaven.* *^b*NU-Text omits the rest of this verse.   11:4 *^a*NU-Text omits *But deliver us from the evil one.*   11:11 *^a*NU-Text omits the words from *bread* through *for* in the next sentence.   11:15 *^a*NU-Text and M-Text read *Beelzebul.*

rest; and finding none, he says, 'I will return to my house from which I came.' [25]And when he comes, he finds *it* swept and put in order. [26]Then he goes and takes with *him* seven other spirits more wicked than himself, and they enter and dwell there; and the last *state* of that man is worse than the first."

Keeping the Word

[27]And it happened, as He spoke these things, that a certain woman from the crowd raised her voice and said to Him, "Blessed *is* the womb that bore You, and *the* breasts which nursed You!"

[28]But He said, "More than that, blessed *are* those who hear the word of God and keep it!"

11:28 More than that. While not denying the blessedness of Mary, Christ did not elevate Mary as an object of adoration. Mary's relationship to Him as His physical mother did not give her any greater honor than the blessedness of those who hear and obey God's Word.

Seeking a Sign

[29]And while the crowds were thickly gathered together, He began to say, "This is an evil generation. It seeks a sign, and no sign will be given to it except the sign of Jonah the prophet.[a] [30]For as Jonah became a sign to the Ninevites, so also the Son of Man will be to this generation. [31]The queen of the South will rise up in the judgment with the men of this generation and condemn them, for she came from the ends of the earth to hear the wisdom of Solomon; and indeed a greater than Solomon *is* here. [32]The men of Nineveh will rise up in the judgment with this generation and condemn it, for they repented at the preaching of Jonah; and indeed a greater than Jonah *is* here.

The Lamp of the Body

[33]"No one, when he has lit a lamp, puts *it* in a secret place or under a basket, but on a lampstand, that those who come in may see the light. [34]The lamp of the body is the eye. Therefore, when your eye is good, your whole body also is full of light. But when

your eye is bad, your body also *is* full of darkness. [35]Therefore take heed that the light which is in you is not darkness. [36]If then your whole body *is* full of light, having no part dark, *the* whole *body* will be full of light, as when the bright shining of a lamp gives you light."

11:34 The lamp of the body. Here the eye is the "lamp," the source of light for the body. **when your eye is bad.** The problem was people's perception, not a lack of light. They did not need a sign; they needed hearts to believe the display of divine power they had already seen.

Woe to the Pharisees and Lawyers

[37]And as He spoke, a certain Pharisee asked Him to dine with him. So He went in and sat down to eat. [38]When the Pharisee saw *it*, he marveled that He had not first washed before dinner.

[39]Then the Lord said to him, "Now you Pharisees make the outside of the cup and dish clean, but your inward part is full of greed and wickedness. [40]Foolish ones! Did not He who made the outside make the inside also? [41]But rather give alms of such things as you have; then indeed all things are clean to you.

[42]"But woe to you Pharisees! For you tithe mint and rue and all manner of herbs, and pass by justice and the love of God. These you ought to have done, without leaving the others undone. [43]Woe to you Pharisees! For you love the best seats in the synagogues and greetings in the marketplaces. [44]Woe to you, scribes and Pharisees, hypocrites![a] For you are like graves which are not seen, and the men who walk over *them* are not aware *of them*."

[45]Then one of the lawyers answered and said to Him, "Teacher, by saying these things You reproach us also."

[46]And He said, "Woe to you also, lawyers! For you load men with burdens hard to bear, and you yourselves do not touch the burdens with one of your fingers. [47]Woe to you! For you build the tombs of the prophets, and your fathers killed them. [48]In fact, you bear witness that you approve the deeds of your fathers; for they indeed killed them, and you build their tombs. [49]There-

---

11:29 [a]NU-Text omits *the prophet.*　　11:44 [a]NU-Text omits *scribes and Pharisees, hypocrites.*

fore the wisdom of God also said, 'I will send them prophets and apostles, and *some* of them they will kill and persecute,' [50]that the blood of all the prophets which was shed from the foundation of the world may be required of this generation, [51]from the blood of Abel to the blood of Zechariah who perished between the altar and the temple. Yes, I say to you, it shall be required of this generation.

[52]"Woe to you lawyers! For you have taken away the key of knowledge. You did not enter in yourselves, and those who were entering in you hindered."

> **11:52 the key of knowledge.** Ironically, the lawyers, experts in God's law, had locked up the truth and thrown away the key by imposing on God's Word their faulty interpretations and human traditions.

[53]And as He said these things to them,[a] the scribes and the Pharisees began to assail *Him* vehemently, and to cross-examine Him about many things, [54]lying in wait for Him, and seeking to catch Him in something He might say, that they might accuse Him.[a]

Beware of Hypocrisy

12 In the meantime, when an innumerable multitude of people had gathered together, so that they trampled one another, He began to say to His disciples first *of all*, "Beware of the leaven of the Pharisees, which is hypocrisy. [2]For there is nothing covered that will not be revealed, nor hidden that will not be known. [3]Therefore whatever you have spoken in the dark will be heard in the light, and what you have spoken in the ear in inner rooms will be proclaimed on the housetops.

Jesus Teaches the Fear of God

[4]"And I say to you, My friends, do not be afraid of those who kill the body, and after that have no more that they can do. [5]But I will show you whom you should fear: Fear Him who, after He has killed, has power to cast into hell; yes, I say to you, fear Him! [6]"Are not five sparrows sold for two cop-

per coins?[a] And not one of them is forgotten before God. [7]But the very hairs of your head are all numbered. Do not fear therefore; you are of more value than many sparrows.

Confess Christ Before Men

[8]"Also I say to you, whoever confesses Me before men, him the Son of Man also will confess before the angels of God. [9]But he who denies Me before men will be denied before the angels of God.

[10]"And anyone who speaks a word against the Son of Man, it will be forgiven him; but to him who blasphemes against the Holy Spirit, it will not be forgiven.

> **12:10 blasphemes against the Holy Spirit.** This cannot be done out of ignorance. This refers to deliberate hostility toward Christ, exemplified by the Pharisees in Matt. 12 when they attributed Christ's work to Satan (see 11:15).

[11]"Now when they bring you to the synagogues and magistrates and authorities, do not worry about how or what you should answer, or what you should say. [12]For the Holy Spirit will teach you in that very hour what you ought to say."

The Parable of the Rich Fool

[13]Then one from the crowd said to Him, "Teacher, tell my brother to divide the inheritance with me."

[14]But He said to him, "Man, who made Me a judge or an arbitrator over you?" [15]And He said to them, "Take heed and beware of covetousness,[a] for one's life does not consist in the abundance of the things he possesses."

[16]Then He spoke a parable to them, saying: "The ground of a certain rich man yielded plentifully. [17]And he thought within himself, saying, 'What shall I do, since I have no room to store my crops?' [18]So he said, 'I will do this: I will pull down my barns and build greater, and there I will store all my crops and my goods. [19]And I will say to my soul, "Soul, you have many goods laid up for many years; take your

---

11:53 [a]NU-Text reads *And when He left there.*   11:54 [a]NU-Text omits *and seeking* and *that they might accuse Him.*   12:6 [a]Greek *assarion,* a coin of very small value   12:15 [a]NU-Text reads *all covetousness.*

ease; eat, drink, *and* be merry." ' ²⁰But God said to him, 'Fool! This night your soul will be required of you; then whose will those things be which you have provided?'

²¹"So *is* he who lays up treasure for himself, and is not rich toward God."

Do Not Worry

²²Then He said to His disciples, "Therefore I say to you, do not worry about your life, what you will eat; nor about the body, what you will put on. ²³Life is more than food, and the body *is more* than clothing. ²⁴Consider the ravens, for they neither sow nor reap, which have neither storehouse nor barn; and God feeds them. Of how much more value are you than the birds? ²⁵And which of you by worrying can add one cubit to his stature? ²⁶If you then are not able to do *the* least, why are you anxious for the rest? ²⁷Consider the lilies, how they grow: they neither toil nor spin; and yet I say to you, even Solomon in all his glory was not arrayed like one of these. ²⁸If then God so clothes the grass, which today is in the field and tomorrow is thrown into the oven, how much more *will He clothe* you, O *you* of little faith?

²⁹"And do not seek what you should eat or what you should drink, nor have an anxious mind. ³⁰For all these things the nations of the world seek after, and your Father knows that you need these things. ³¹But seek the kingdom of God, and all these things*ᵃ* shall be added to you.

³²"Do not fear, little flock, for it is your Father's good pleasure to give you the kingdom. ³³Sell what you have and give alms; provide yourselves money bags which do not grow old, a treasure in the heavens that does not fail, where no thief approaches nor

moth destroys. ³⁴For where your treasure is, there your heart will be also.

The Faithful Servant and the Evil Servant

³⁵"Let your waist be girded and *your* lamps burning; ³⁶and you yourselves be like men who wait for their master, when he will return from the wedding, that when he comes and knocks they may open to him immediately. ³⁷Blessed *are* those servants whom the master, when he comes, will find watching. Assuredly, I say to you that he will gird himself and have them sit down *to eat*, and will come and serve them. ³⁸And if he should come in the second watch, or come in the third watch, and find *them* so, blessed are those servants. ³⁹But know this, that if the master of the house had known what hour the thief would come, he would have watched and*ᵃ* not allowed his house to be broken into. ⁴⁰Therefore you also be ready, for the Son of Man is coming at an hour you do not expect."

⁴¹Then Peter said to Him, "Lord, do You speak this parable *only* to us, or to all *people*?"

⁴²And the Lord said, "Who then is that faithful and wise steward, whom *his* master will make ruler over his household, to give *them their* portion of food in due season? ⁴³Blessed *is* that servant whom his master will find so doing when he comes. ⁴⁴Truly, I say to you that he will make him ruler over all that he has. ⁴⁵But if that servant says in his heart, 'My master is delaying his coming,' and begins to beat the male and female servants, and to eat and drink and be drunk, ⁴⁶the master of that servant will come on a day when he is not looking for *him*, and at an hour when he is not aware, and will cut him in two and appoint *him* his portion with the unbelievers. ⁴⁷And that servant who knew his master's will, and did not prepare *himself* or do according to his will, shall be beaten with many *stripes*. ⁴⁸But he who did not know, yet committed things deserving of stripes, shall be beaten with few. For everyone to whom much is given, from him much will be required; and to whom much has been committed, of him they will ask the more.

> **12:33 Sell what you have and give alms.** Those who thought their security lay in earthly possessions needed to lay up treasures in heaven instead. Believers in the early church sold their goods to meet the needs of poorer brethren (Acts 2:44,45). This commandment is not to be twisted into an absolute prohibition of all earthly possessions. Peter made it clear to Ananias in Acts 5:4 that selling possessions was optional.

12:31 *ᵃ*NU-Text reads *His kingdom, and these things.*　　12:39 *ᵃ*NU-Text reads *he would not have allowed.*

Christ Brings Division

49"I came to send fire on the earth, and how I wish it were already kindled! 50But I have a baptism to be baptized with, and how distressed I am till it is accomplished! 51Do *you* suppose that I came to give peace on earth? I tell you, not at all, but rather division. 52For from now on five in one house will be divided: three against two, and two against three. 53Father will be divided against son and son against father, mother against daughter and daughter against mother, mother-in-law against her daughter-in-law and daughter-in-law against her mother-in-law."

> **12:50 a baptism.** This is a baptism of suffering. Christ was referring to His death. Christian baptism symbolizes identification with Him in death, burial, and resurrection. **till it is accomplished.** Jesus was distressed about His coming death, but it was what He had come to accomplish.

Discern the Time

54Then He also said to the multitudes, "Whenever *you see* a cloud rising out of the west, immediately you say, 'A shower is coming'; and so it is. 55And when you see the south wind blow, you say, 'There will be hot weather'; and there is. 56Hypocrites! You can discern the face of the sky and of the earth, but how *is it* you do not discern this time?

Make Peace with Your Adversary

57"Yes, and why, even of yourselves, do you not judge what is right? 58When you go with your adversary to the magistrate, make every effort along the way to settle with him, lest he drag you to the judge, the judge deliver you to the officer, and the officer throw you into prison. 59I tell you, you shall not depart from there till you have paid the very last mite."

Repent or Perish

13 There were present at that season some who told Him about the Galileans whose blood Pilate had mingled with their sacrifices. 2And Jesus answered and said to them, "Do you suppose that these

> **13:1 Galileans whose blood Pilate had mingled with their sacrifices.** Some worshipers from Galilee, perhaps seditious zealots, had been in the process of offering a sacrifice when they were killed in the temple by Roman authorities. Such a killing was the most awful sort of blasphemy. Incidents like this caused the Jews to hate the Romans, which led to rebellion and the destruction of Jerusalem in A.D. 70.

Galileans were worse sinners than all *other* Galileans, because they suffered such things? 3I tell you, no; but unless you repent you will all likewise perish. 4Or those eighteen on whom the tower in Siloam fell and killed them, do you think that they were worse sinners than all *other* men who dwelt in Jerusalem? 5I tell you, no; but unless you repent you will all likewise perish."

The Parable of the Barren Fig Tree

6He also spoke this parable: "A certain *man* had a fig tree planted in his vineyard, and he came seeking fruit on it and found none. 7Then he said to the keeper of his vineyard, 'Look, for three years I have come seeking fruit on this fig tree and find none. Cut it down; why does it use up the ground?' 8But he answered and said to him, 'Sir, let it alone this year also, until I dig around it and fertilize *it*. 9And if it bears fruit, *well*. But if not, after that*a* you can cut it down.' "

A Spirit of Infirmity

10Now He was teaching in one of the synagogues on the Sabbath. 11And behold, there was a woman who had a spirit of infirmity eighteen years, and was bent over and could in no way raise *herself* up. 12But when Jesus saw her, He called *her* to *Him* and said to her, "Woman, you are loosed from your infirmity." 13And He laid *His* hands on her, and immediately she was made straight, and glorified God.

14But the ruler of the synagogue answered with indignation, because Jesus had healed on the Sabbath; and he said to the crowd, "There are six days on which men ought to work; therefore come and be healed on them, and not on the Sabbath day." 15The Lord then answered him and said, "Hypocrite!*a* Does not each one of you on

---

13:9 *a*NU-Text reads *And if it bears fruit after that, well. But if not, you can cut it down.* **13:15** *a*NU-Text and M-Text read *Hypocrites.*

the Sabbath loose his ox or donkey from the stall, and lead *it* away to water it? ¹⁶So ought not this woman, being a daughter of Abraham, whom Satan has bound—think of it—for eighteen years, be loosed from this bond on the Sabbath?" ¹⁷And when He said these things, all His adversaries were put to shame; and all the multitude rejoiced for all the glorious things that were done by Him.

13:15 loose his ox. Nothing in Scripture forbade the watering of an ox or the healing of the sick on the Sabbath. The Sabbath traditions had placed a higher value on animals than on people in distress, which corrupted the whole purpose of the Sabbath (Mark 2:27).

The Parable of the Mustard Seed

¹⁸Then He said, "What is the kingdom of God like? And to what shall I compare it? ¹⁹It is like a mustard seed, which a man took and put in his garden; and it grew and became a large*ᵃ* tree, and the birds of the air nested in its branches."

The Parable of the Leaven

²⁰And again He said, "To what shall I liken the kingdom of God? ²¹It is like leaven, which a woman took and hid in three measures*ᵃ* of meal till it was all leavened."

The Narrow Way

²²And He went through the cities and villages, teaching, and journeying toward Jerusalem. ²³Then one said to Him, "Lord, are there few who are saved?"

And He said to them, ²⁴"Strive to enter through the narrow gate, for many, I say to you, will seek to enter and will not be able. ²⁵When once the Master of the house has risen up and shut the door, and you begin to stand outside and knock at the door, saying, 'Lord, Lord, open for us,' and He will

13:24,25 many...will seek to enter. This refers to the judgment, when many will protest that they deserve entrance into heaven (see Matt. 7:21–23). **I do not know you.** Clearly, no relationship ever existed, though these people had deluded themselves into thinking they knew the owner of the house (Christ).

answer and say to you, 'I do not know you, where you are from,' ²⁶then you will begin to say, 'We ate and drank in Your presence, and You taught in our streets.' ²⁷But He will say, 'I tell you I do not know you, where you are from. Depart from Me, all you workers of iniquity.' ²⁸There will be weeping and gnashing of teeth, when you see Abraham and Isaac and Jacob and all the prophets in the kingdom of God, and yourselves thrust out. ²⁹They will come from the east and the west, from the north and the south, and sit down in the kingdom of God. ³⁰And indeed there are last who will be first, and there are first who will be last."

³¹On that very day*ᵃ* some Pharisees came, saying to Him, "Get out and depart from here, for Herod wants to kill You."

³²And He said to them, "Go, tell that fox, 'Behold, I cast out demons and perform cures today and tomorrow, and the third *day* I shall be perfected.' ³³Nevertheless I must journey today, tomorrow, and the *day* following; for it cannot be that a prophet should perish outside of Jerusalem.

13:32 that fox. Jesus, having divine authority, had every right to speak of Herod in such terms. Rabbinical writings often used "the fox" to signify someone who was crafty and worthless. The Pharisees, who trembled at Herod's power, must have been astonished by Christ's boldness. **be perfected.** This refers to the finishing of Christ's work through death (see Heb. 2:10). Herod was threatening to kill Jesus, but no one could kill Him before His time (John 10:17,18).

Jesus Laments over Jerusalem

³⁴"O Jerusalem, Jerusalem, the one who kills the prophets and stones those who are sent to her! How often I wanted to gather your children together, as a hen *gathers* her brood under *her* wings, but you were not willing! ³⁵See! Your house is left to you desolate; and assuredly,*ᵃ* I say to you, you shall not see Me until *the time* comes when you say, '*Blessed is He who comes in the name of the LORD!* '"*ᵇ*

A Man with Dropsy Healed on the Sabbath

14 Now it happened, as He went into the house of one of the rulers of the

---

13:19 *ᵃ*NU-Text omits *large*.   13:21 *ᵃ*Greek *sata*, approximately two pecks in all   13:31 *ᵃ*NU-Text reads *In that very hour.*   13:35 *ᵃ*NU-Text and M-Text omit *assuredly.*   *ᵇ*Psalm 118:26

Pharisees to eat bread on the Sabbath, that they watched Him closely. [2]And behold, there was a certain man before Him who had dropsy. [3]And Jesus, answering, spoke to the lawyers and Pharisees, saying, "Is it lawful to heal on the Sabbath?"[a]

> **14:3 lawyers.** These were the scribes. **Is it lawful.** Jesus repeatedly defended Sabbath healings, and His arguments consistently silenced the scribes (see 6:9). He questioned them about the legality of healing on the Sabbath, and still they could give no substantial reasons why they believed healing violated Sabbath laws (see v. 6).

[4]But they kept silent. And He took *him* and healed him, and let him go. [5]Then He answered them, saying, "Which of you, having a donkey[a] or an ox that has fallen into a pit, will not immediately pull him out on the Sabbath day?" [6]And they could not answer Him regarding these things.

Take the Lowly Place

[7]So He told a parable to those who were invited, when He noted how they chose the best places, saying to them: [8]"When you are invited by anyone to a wedding feast, do not sit down in the best place, lest one more honorable than you be invited by him; [9]and he who invited you and him come and say to you, 'Give place to this man,' and then you begin with shame to take the lowest place. [10]But when you are invited, go and sit down in the lowest place, so that when he who invited you comes he may say to you, 'Friend, go up higher.' Then you will have glory in the presence of those who sit at the table with you. [11]For whoever exalts himself will be humbled, and he who humbles himself will be exalted."

[12]Then He also said to him who invited Him, "When you give a dinner or a supper, do not ask your friends, your brothers, your relatives, nor rich neighbors, lest they also invite you back, and you be repaid. [13]But when you give a feast, invite *the* poor, *the* maimed, *the* lame, *the* blind. [14]And you will be blessed, because they cannot repay you; for you shall be repaid at the resurrection of the just."

The Parable of the Great Supper

[15]Now when one of those who sat at the table with Him heard these things, he said to Him, "Blessed *is* he who shall eat bread[a] in the kingdom of God!"

[16]Then He said to him, "A certain man gave a great supper and invited many, [17]and sent his servant at supper time to say to those who were invited, 'Come, for all things are now ready.' [18]But they all with one *accord* began to make excuses. The first said to him, 'I have bought a piece of ground, and I must go and see it. I ask you to have me excused.' [19]And another said, 'I have bought five yoke of oxen, and I am going to test them. I ask you to have me excused.' [20]Still another said, 'I have married a wife, and therefore I cannot come.' [21]So that servant came and reported these things to his master. Then the master of the house, being angry, said to his servant, 'Go out quickly into the streets and lanes of the city, and bring in here *the* poor and *the* maimed and *the* lame and *the* blind.' [22]And the servant said, 'Master, it is done as you commanded, and still there is room.' [23]Then the master said to the servant, 'Go out into the highways and hedges, and compel *them* to come in, that my house may be filled. [24]For I say to you that none of those men who were invited shall taste my supper.' "

Leaving All to Follow Christ

[25]Now great multitudes went with Him. And He turned and said to them, [26]"If anyone comes to Me and does not hate his father and mother, wife and children, brothers and sisters, yes, and his own life also, he cannot be My disciple. [27]And whoever does not bear his cross and come after Me cannot be My disciple. [28]For which of you, intending to build a tower, does not sit down first and count the cost, whether he has *enough* to finish *it*— [29]lest, after he has

> **14:25 great multitudes.** Christ did not aim to gather appreciative crowds. He desired to make true disciples and always plainly declared the high cost of discipleship. Here He made several bold demands that would discourage the half-hearted.

14:3 [a]NU-Text adds *or not.*   14:5 [a]NU-Text and M-Text read *son.*   14:15 [a]M-Text reads *dinner.*

laid the foundation, and is not able to finish, all who see *it* begin to mock him, ³⁰saying, 'This man began to build and was not able to finish.' ³¹Or what king, going to make war against another king, does not sit down first and consider whether he is able with ten thousand to meet him who comes against him with twenty thousand? ³²Or else, while the other is still a great way off, he sends a delegation and asks conditions of peace. ³³So likewise, whoever of you does not forsake all that he has cannot be My disciple.

Tasteless Salt Is Worthless

³⁴"Salt *is* good; but if the salt has lost its flavor, how shall it be seasoned? ³⁵It is neither fit for the land nor for the dunghill, *but* men throw it out. He who has ears to hear, let him hear!"

The Parable of the Lost Sheep

15 Then all the tax collectors and the sinners drew near to Him to hear Him. ²And the Pharisees and scribes complained, saying, "This Man receives sinners and eats with them." ³So He spoke this parable to them, saying:

⁴"What man of you, having a hundred sheep, if he loses one of them, does not

> **15:2 complained.** The complaints of the crowds prompted Christ to tell 3 parables to illustrate God's joy over the repentance of a sinner. The first two parables picture God as taking the initiative in seeking sinners. **This Man receives sinners.** This phrase is the key to the parables. Christ was not ashamed to be known as a "friend of tax collectors and sinners" (7:34).

leave the ninety-nine in the wilderness, and go after the one which is lost until he finds it? ⁵And when he has found *it*, he lays *it* on his shoulders, rejoicing. ⁶And when he comes home, he calls together *his* friends and neighbors, saying to them, 'Rejoice with me, for I have found my sheep which was lost!' ⁷I say to you that likewise there will be more joy in heaven over one sinner who repents than over ninety-nine just persons who need no repentance.

The Parable of the Lost Coin

⁸"Or what woman, having ten silver coins,ᵃ if she loses one coin, does not light a lamp, sweep the house, and search carefully until she finds *it?* ⁹And when she has found *it*, she calls *her* friends and neighbors together, saying, 'Rejoice with me, for I have found the piece which I lost!' ¹⁰Likewise, I say to you, there is joy in the pres-

---

15:8 ᵃGreek *drachma*, a valuable coin often worn in a ten-piece garland by married women

---

What about those who claim to see a wide gap between Luke's theology and Paul's theology?

Although Luke, more than any of the other gospel writers, highlighted the universal scope of the gospel invitation, some have questioned why a companion of Paul's would use so little of Paul's language in explaining the process of salvation. But a difference in vocabulary does not necessarily imply a difference in thought or underlying theology.

Luke certainly wrote with his own style. He was an astute observer and careful thinker. In writing the gospel, he was careful not to insert Pauline language back into the gospel account. The theology of Luke's record parallels Paul's exactly. Luke repeatedly related accounts of Gentiles, Samaritans, and other outcasts who found grace in Jesus' eyes. This emphasis not only records Jesus' appeal, but also proves to be precisely what we would expect from the close companion of the "apostle to the Gentiles" (Romans 11:13).

A compelling illustration of this parallel involves Luke's treatment of the centerpiece of Paul's doctrine—justification by faith. Luke highlighted and illustrated justification by faith in many of the incidents and parables he related in his gospel. For example, the account of the Pharisee and the publican (18:9–14), the familiar story of the Prodigal Son (15:11–32), the incident at Simon's house (7:36–50), and the salvation of Zacchaeus (19:1–10) all serve to demonstrate that Jesus taught justification by faith long before Paul wrote about it.

ence of the angels of God over one sinner who repents."

The Parable of the Lost Son

[11]Then He said: "A certain man had two sons. [12]And the younger of them said to *his* father, 'Father, give me the portion of goods that falls *to me.*' So he divided to them *his* livelihood. [13]And not many days after, the younger son gathered all together, journeyed to a far country, and there wasted his possessions with prodigal living. [14]But when he had spent all, there arose a severe famine in that land, and he began to be in want. [15]Then he went and joined himself to a citizen of that country, and he sent him into his fields to feed swine. [16]And he would gladly have filled his stomach with the pods that the swine ate, and no one gave him *anything.*

> **15:11,12** This most beloved of all Christ's parables has more than one lesson. The prodigal son illustrates sound repentance. The elder brother illustrates the wickedness of the Pharisees' self-righteousness, prejudice, and indifference toward repenting sinners. The father pictures God, eager to forgive and longing for the return of the sinner. The parable expresses God's joy and the celebrations in heaven when a sinner repents.

[17]"But when he came to himself, he said, 'How many of my father's hired servants have bread enough and to spare, and I perish with hunger! [18]I will arise and go to my father, and will say to him, "Father, I have sinned against heaven and before you, [19]and I am no longer worthy to be called your son. Make me like one of your hired servants."'

[20]"And he arose and came to his father. But when he was still a great way off, his father saw him and had compassion, and ran and fell on his neck and kissed him. [21]And the son said to him, 'Father, I have sinned against heaven and in your sight, and am no longer worthy to be called your son.'

[22]"But the father said to his servants, 'Bring[a] out the best robe and put *it* on him, and put a ring on his hand and sandals on *his* feet. [23]And bring the fatted calf here and

kill *it,* and let us eat and be merry; [24]for this my son was dead and is alive again; he was lost and is found.' And they began to be merry.

> **15:20 his father saw him.** The father had been waiting and watching for his son's return. **ran.** The father's eagerness and joy at his son's return are unmistakable. This is the magnificent attribute of God that sets Him apart from false gods. He is not indifferent or hostile, but a Savior longing to see sinners repent. From Gen. 3:8 (the fall) to Rev. 22:17 (the consummation), God has been and will be seeking to save sinners.

[25]"Now his older son was in the field. And as he came and drew near to the house, he heard music and dancing. [26]So he called one of the servants and asked what these things meant. [27]And he said to him, 'Your brother has come, and because he has received him safe and sound, your father has killed the fatted calf.'

[28]"But he was angry and would not go in. Therefore his father came out and pleaded with him. [29]So he answered and said to *his* father, 'Lo, these many years I have been serving you; I never transgressed your commandment at any time; and yet you never gave me a young goat, that I might make merry with my friends. [30]But as soon as this son of yours came, who has devoured your livelihood with harlots, you killed the fatted calf for him.'

[31]"And he said to him, 'Son, you are always with me, and all that I have is yours. [32]It was right that we should make merry and be glad, for your brother was dead and is alive again, and was lost and is found.' "

The Parable of the Unjust Steward

16 He also said to His disciples: "There was a certain rich man who had a steward, and an accusation was brought to him that this man was wasting his goods. [2]So he called him and said to him, 'What is this I hear about you? Give an account of your stewardship, for you can no longer be steward.'

[3]"Then the steward said within himself, 'What shall I do? For my master is taking the stewardship away from me. I cannot

---

15:22 [a]NU-Text reads *Quickly bring.*

dig; I am ashamed to beg. *I have resolved what to do, that when I am put out of the stewardship, they may receive me into their houses.'

[5]"So he called every one of his master's debtors to *him*, and said to the first, 'How much do you owe my master?' [6]And he said, 'A hundred measures[a] of oil.' So he said to him, 'Take your bill, and sit down quickly and write fifty.' [7]Then he said to another, 'And how much do you owe?' So he said, 'A hundred measures[a] of wheat.' And he said to him, 'Take your bill, and write eighty.' [8]So the master commended the unjust steward because he had dealt shrewdly. For the sons of this world are more shrewd in their generation than the sons of light.

> **16:8 the master commended the unjust steward.** The master's admiration for the evil steward's criminal genius shows that he, too, was a wicked man. It is natural for a fallen heart to admire a villain's craftiness (Ps. 49:18). All the characters in this parable are corrupt. **more shrewd.** Most unbelievers are wiser in the ways of the world than some believers are in the things of God.

[9]"And I say to you, make friends for yourselves by unrighteous mammon, that when you fail,[a] they may receive you into an everlasting home. [10]He who *is* faithful in *what is* least is faithful also in much; and he who is unjust in *what is* least is unjust also in much. [11]Therefore if you have not been faithful in the unrighteous mammon, who will commit to your trust the true *riches?* [12]And if you have not been faithful in what is another man's, who will give you what is your own?

[13]"No servant can serve two masters; for either he will hate the one and love the other, or else he will be loyal to the one and

> **16:13 You cannot serve God and mammon.** Many Pharisees taught that one could be devoted to money and to God at the same time. They believed that earthly riches signified divine blessings. Rich people were regarded as God's favorites. While not condemning wealth, Christ denounced both love of wealth and devotion to mammon.

despise the other. You cannot serve God and mammon."

The Law, the Prophets, and the Kingdom

[14]Now the Pharisees, who were lovers of money, also heard all these things, and they derided Him. [15]And He said to them, "You are those who justify yourselves before men, but God knows your hearts. For what is highly esteemed among men is an abomination in the sight of God.

[16]"The law and the prophets *were* until John. Since that time the kingdom of God has been preached, and everyone is pressing into it. [17]And it is easier for heaven and earth to pass away than for one tittle of the law to fail.

[18]"Whoever divorces his wife and marries another commits adultery; and whoever marries her who is divorced from *her* husband commits adultery.

The Rich Man and Lazarus

[19]"There was a certain rich man who was clothed in purple and fine linen and fared sumptuously every day. [20]But there was a certain beggar named Lazarus, full of sores, who was laid at his gate, [21]desiring to be fed with the crumbs which fell[a] from the rich man's table. Moreover the dogs came and licked his sores. [22]So it was that the beggar died, and was carried by the angels to Abraham's bosom. The rich man also died and was buried. [23]And being in torments in Hades, he lifted up his eyes and saw Abraham afar off, and Lazarus in his bosom.

> **16:22 Abraham's bosom.** This same expression (found only here in Scripture) was used in the Talmud as a figure for heaven. The idea was that Lazarus was given a place of high honor, reclining next to Abraham at the heavenly banquet.

[24]"Then he cried and said, 'Father Abraham, have mercy on me, and send Lazarus that he may dip the tip of his finger in water and cool my tongue; for I am tormented in this flame.' [25]But Abraham said, 'Son, remember that in your lifetime you received your good things, and likewise Lazarus evil things; but now he is comforted and you are

---

16:6 [a]Greek *batos,* eight or nine gallons each (Old Testament *bath*)   16:7 [a]Greek *koros,* ten or twelve bushels each (Old Testament *kor*)   16:9 [a]NU-Text reads *it fails.*   16:21 [a]NU-Text reads *with what fell.*

tormented. [26]And besides all this, between us and you there is a great gulf fixed, so that those who want to pass from here to you cannot, nor can those from there pass to us.'

[27]"Then he said, 'I beg you therefore, father, that you would send him to my father's house, [28]for I have five brothers, that he may testify to them, lest they also come to this place of torment.' [29]Abraham said to him, 'They have Moses and the prophets; let them hear them.' [30]And he said, 'No, father Abraham; but if one goes to them from the dead, they will repent.' [31]But he said to him, 'If they do not hear Moses and the prophets, neither will they be persuaded though one rise from the dead.' "

16:31 neither will they be persuaded. This speaks of the singular sufficiency of Scripture to overcome unbelief. The gospel itself is the power of God unto salvation (Rom. 1:16).

Jesus Warns of Offenses

17 Then He said to the disciples, "It is impossible that no offenses should come, but woe to him through whom they do come! [2]It would be better for him if a millstone were hung around his neck, and he were thrown into the sea, than that he should offend one of these little ones. [3]Take heed to yourselves. If your brother sins against you,[a] rebuke him; and if he repents, forgive him. [4]And if he sins against you seven times in a day, and seven times in a day returns to you,[a] saying, 'I repent,' you shall forgive him."

Faith and Duty

[5]And the apostles said to the Lord, "Increase our faith."

[6]So the Lord said, "If you have faith as a mustard seed, you can say to this mulberry tree, 'Be pulled up by the roots and be planted in the sea,' and it would obey you. [7]And which of you, having a servant plowing or tending sheep, will say to him when he has come in from the field, 'Come at once and sit down to eat'? [8]But will he not rather say to him, 'Prepare something for my supper, and gird yourself and serve me

till I have eaten and drunk, and afterward you will eat and drink'? [9]Does he thank that servant because he did the things that were commanded him? I think not.[a] [10]So likewise you, when you have done all those things which you are commanded, say, 'We are unprofitable servants. We have done what was our duty to do.' "

17:7–10 This parable shows that a servant should not expect a special reward for doing his duty. The demanding standards Christ set may have seemed too high to the disciples, but they represented only the minimal duties for a servant of Christ. Those who obey are not to think that their obedience deserves reward.

Ten Lepers Cleansed

[11]Now it happened as He went to Jerusalem that He passed through the midst of Samaria and Galilee. [12]Then as He entered a certain village, there met Him ten men who were lepers, who stood afar off. [13]And they lifted up their voices and said, "Jesus, Master, have mercy on us!"

[14]So when He saw them, He said to them, "Go, show yourselves to the priests." And so it was that as they went, they were cleansed.

[15]And one of them, when he saw that he was healed, returned, and with a loud voice glorified God, [16]and fell down on his face at His feet, giving Him thanks. And he was a Samaritan.

[17]So Jesus answered and said, "Were there not ten cleansed? But where are the nine? [18]Were there not any found who returned to give glory to God except this foreigner?" [19]And He said to him, "Arise, go your way. Your faith has made you well."

The Coming of the Kingdom

[20]Now when He was asked by the Pharisees when the kingdom of God would come, He answered them and said, "The kingdom of God does not come with observation; [21]nor will they say, 'See here!' or 'See there!'[a] For indeed, the kingdom of God is within you."

[22]Then He said to the disciples, "The days will come when you will desire to see

---

17:3 [a]NU-Text omits against you.   17:4 [a]M-Text omits to you.   17:9 [a]NU-Text ends verse with commanded; M-Text omits him.   17:21 [a]NU-Text reverses here and there.

17:20 when the kingdom of God would come. The Pharisees may have asked the question mockingly, having already concluded that Jesus was not the Messiah. **does not come with observation.** The Pharisees believed that the Messiah would come, overthrow Rome, and set up the millennial kingdom. Instead, Christ's kingdom would manifest itself by the rule of God in the hearts of men through faith in the Savior (see Rom. 14:17).

one of the days of the Son of Man, and you will not see it. ²³And they will say to you, 'Look here!' or 'Look there!'ᵃ Do not go after *them* or follow *them*. ²⁴For as the lightning that flashes out of one *part* under heaven shines to the other *part* under heaven, so also the Son of Man will be in His day. ²⁵But first He must suffer many things and be rejected by this generation. ²⁶And as it was in the days of Noah, so it will be also in the days of the Son of Man: ²⁷They ate, they drank, they married wives, they were given in marriage, until the day that Noah entered the ark, and the flood came and destroyed them all. ²⁸Likewise as it was also in the days of Lot: They ate, they drank, they bought, they sold, they planted, they built; ²⁹but on the day that Lot went out of Sodom it rained fire and brimstone from heaven and destroyed *them* all. ³⁰Even so will it be in the day when the Son of Man is revealed.

³¹"In that day, he who is on the housetop, and his goods *are* in the house, let him not come down to take them away. And likewise the one who is in the field, let him not

turn back. ³²Remember Lot's wife. ³³Whoever seeks to save his life will lose it, and whoever loses his life will preserve it. ³⁴I tell you, in that night there will be two *men* in one bed: the one will be taken and the other will be left. ³⁵Two *women* will be grinding together: the one will be taken and the other left. ³⁶Two *men* will be in the field: the one will be taken and the other left."ᵃ

³⁷And they answered and said to Him, "Where, Lord?"

So He said to them, "Wherever the body is, there the eagles will be gathered together."

The Parable of the Persistent Widow

18 Then He spoke a parable to them, that men always ought to pray and not lose heart, ²saying: "There was in a certain city a judge who did not fear God nor regard man. ³Now there was a widow in that city; and she came to him, saying, 'Get justice for me from my adversary.' ⁴And he would not for a while; but afterward he said within himself, 'Though I do not fear God nor regard man, ⁵yet because this widow troubles me I will avenge her, lest by her continual coming she weary me.'"

⁶Then the Lord said, "Hear what the un-

18:2 did not fear God nor regard man. This judge was wicked. If such an unjust man would respond to persistent pleas, would not God, who is just, loving, and merciful, more readily do so?

17:23 ᵃNU-Text reverses *here* and *there*.   17:36 ᵃNU-Text and M-Text omit verse 36.

What passages in Luke are unique to his gospel?

Luke included 12 events or major passages not found in the other gospels:

1. Events preceding the birth of John the Baptist and Jesus (1:5–80).
2. Scenes from Jesus' childhood (2:1–52).
3. Herod imprisons John the Baptist (3:19,20).
4. The people of Nazareth reject Jesus (4:16–30).
5. The first disciples are called (5:1–11).
6. A widow's son is raised (7:11–17).
7. A woman anoints Jesus' feet (7:36–50).
8. Certain women minister to Christ (8:1–3).
9. Events, teaching, and miracles during the months leading up to Christ's death (10:1–18:14).
10. Christ abides with Zacchaeus (19:1–27).
11. Herod tries Christ (23:6–12).
12. Some of Jesus' final words before his ascension (24:44–49).

just judge said. [7]And shall God not avenge His own elect who cry out day and night to Him, though He bears long with them? [8]I tell you that He will avenge them speedily. Nevertheless, when the Son of Man comes, will He really find faith on the earth?"

The Parable of the Pharisee and the Tax Collector

[9]Also He spoke this parable to some who trusted in themselves that they were righteous, and despised others: [10]"Two men went up to the temple to pray, one a Pharisee and the other a tax collector. [11]The Pharisee stood and prayed thus with himself, 'God, I thank You that I am not like other men—extortioners, unjust, adulterers, or even as this tax collector. [12]I fast twice a week; I give tithes of all that I possess.' [13]And the tax collector, standing afar off, would not so much as raise *his* eyes to heaven, but beat his breast, saying, 'God, be merciful to me a sinner!' [14]I tell you, this man went down to his house justified *rather* than the other; for everyone who exalts himself will be humbled, and he who humbles himself will be exalted."

18:9 This parable illustrates how a sinner may become righteous before God through an act of repentant faith. The parable is addressed to the Pharisees who trusted their own righteousness. Human righteousness falls short of the divine standard (Matt. 5:48). Scripture teaches that sinners are only justified through God's righteousness (see Gen. 15:6; Phil. 3:4–9), and it was only on that basis that the tax collector could be saved.

Jesus Blesses Little Children

[15]Then they also brought infants to Him that He might touch them; but when the disciples saw *it*, they rebuked them. [16]But Jesus called them to *Him* and said, "Let the little children come to Me, and do not forbid them; for of such is the kingdom of God. [17]Assuredly, I say to you, whoever does not receive the kingdom of God as a little child will by no means enter it."

Jesus Counsels the Rich Young Ruler

[18]Now a certain ruler asked Him, saying, "Good Teacher, what shall I do to inherit eternal life?"

[19]So Jesus said to him, "Why do you call Me good? No one *is* good but One, *that is,* God. [20]You know the commandments: '*Do not commit adultery,*' '*Do not murder,*' '*Do not steal,*' '*Do not bear false witness,*' '*Honor your father and your mother.*' "[a]

[21]And he said, "All these things I have kept from my youth."

[22]So when Jesus heard these things, He said to him, "You still lack one thing. Sell all that you have and distribute to the poor, and you will have treasure in heaven; and come, follow Me."

[23]But when he heard this, he became very sorrowful, for he was very rich.

With God All Things Are Possible

[24]And when Jesus saw that he became very sorrowful, He said, "How hard it is for those who have riches to enter the kingdom of God! [25]For it is easier for a camel to go through the eye of a needle than for a rich man to enter the kingdom of God."

[26]And those who heard it said, "Who then can be saved?"

[27]But He said, "The things which are impossible with men are possible with God."

[28]Then Peter said, "See, we have left all[a] and followed You."

[29]So He said to them, "Assuredly, I say to you, there is no one who has left house or parents or brothers or wife or children, for the sake of the kingdom of God, [30]who shall not receive many times more in this present time, and in the age to come eternal life."

Jesus a Third Time Predicts His Death and Resurrection

[31]Then He took the twelve aside and said to them, "Behold, we are going up to Jerusalem, and all things that are written by the prophets concerning the Son of Man will be accomplished. [32]For He will be delivered to the Gentiles and will be mocked and insulted and spit upon. [33]They will scourge Him and kill Him. And the third day He will rise again."

[34]But they understood none of these things; this saying was hidden from them, and they did not know the things which were spoken.

18:20 [a]Exodus 20:12–16; Deuteronomy 5:16–20   18:28 [a]NU-Text reads *our own.*

A Blind Man Receives His Sight

³⁵Then it happened, as He was coming near Jericho, that a certain blind man sat by the road begging. ³⁶And hearing a multitude passing by, he asked what it meant. ³⁷So they told him that Jesus of Nazareth was passing by. ³⁸And he cried out, saying, "Jesus, Son of David, have mercy on me!"

³⁹Then those who went before warned him that he should be quiet; but he cried out all the more, "Son of David, have mercy on me!"

⁴⁰So Jesus stood still and commanded him to be brought to Him. And when he had come near, He asked him, ⁴¹saying, "What do you want Me to do for you?"

He said, "Lord, that I may receive my sight."

⁴²Then Jesus said to him, "Receive your sight; your faith has made you well." ⁴³And immediately he received his sight, and followed Him, glorifying God. And all the people, when they saw it, gave praise to God.

Jesus Comes to Zacchaeus' House

19 Then *Jesus* entered and passed through Jericho. ²Now behold, *there was* a man named Zacchaeus who was a chief tax collector, and he was rich. ³And he sought to see who Jesus was, but could not because of the crowd, for he was of short stature. ⁴So he ran ahead and climbed up into a sycamore tree to see Him, for He was going to pass that *way.* ⁵And when Jesus came to the place, He looked up and saw him,ᵃ and said to him, "Zacchaeus, make haste and come down, for today I must stay at your house." ⁶So he made haste and came down, and received Him joyfully. ⁷But when they saw *it,* they all complained, saying, "He has gone to be a guest with a man who is a sinner."

19:2 chief tax collector. Zacchaeus was a wealthy man who oversaw a large tax district in Jericho. Earlier, Luke recorded the account of the rich young ruler and Jesus' statement about "how hard it is for those who have riches to enter the kingdom of God" (18:24). Here Jesus demonstrates that with God, nothing is impossible (see 18:27).

⁸Then Zacchaeus stood and said to the Lord, "Look, Lord, I give half of my goods to the poor; and if I have taken anything from anyone by false accusation, I restore fourfold."

⁹And Jesus said to him, "Today salvation has come to this house, because he also is a son of Abraham; ¹⁰for the Son of Man has come to seek and to save that which was lost."

19:8 I restore fourfold. Zacchaeus' willingness to make restitution proved that his conversion was genuine. It was the fruit, not the condition, of his salvation. The law required a penalty of one-fifth as restitution for money acquired by fraud (Lev. 6:5), so Zacchaeus was doing more than was required. He judged his own crime severely by giving half of his goods to the poor.

The Parable of the Minas

¹¹Now as they heard these things, He spoke another parable, because He was near Jerusalem and because they thought the kingdom of God would appear immediately. ¹²Therefore He said: "A certain nobleman went into a far country to receive for himself a kingdom and to return. ¹³So he called ten of his servants, delivered to them ten minas,ᵃ and said to them, 'Do business till I come.' ¹⁴But his citizens hated him, and sent a delegation after him, saying, 'We will not have this *man* to reign over us.'

¹⁵"And so it was that when he returned, having received the kingdom, he then commanded these servants, to whom he had given the money, to be called to him, that he might know how much every man had gained by trading. ¹⁶Then came the first, saying, 'Master, your mina has earned ten minas.' ¹⁷And he said to him, 'Well *done,*

19:17 faithful in a very little. Those with small gifts and opportunities are just as responsible to use them faithfully as those who are given more. **over ten cities.** The reward is greater than the 10 minas warranted. The rewards were apportioned according to the servants' diligence: the one who gained 10 minas was given 10 cities; the one who gained 5 minas, 5 cities, and so on.

19:5 ᵃNU-Text omits *and saw him.*   19:13 ᵃThe *mina* (Greek *mna,* Hebrew *minah*) was worth about three months' salary.

good servant; because you were faithful in a very little, have authority over ten cities.' ¹⁸And the second came, saying, 'Master, your mina has earned five minas.' ¹⁹Likewise he said to him, 'You also be over five cities.'

²⁰"Then another came, saying, 'Master, here is your mina, which I have kept put away in a handkerchief. ²¹For I feared you, because you are an austere man. You collect what you did not deposit, and reap what you did not sow.' ²²And he said to him, 'Out of your own mouth I will judge you, you wicked servant. You knew that I was an austere man, collecting what I did not deposit and reaping what I did not sow. ²³Why then did you not put my money in the bank, that at my coming I might have collected it with interest?'

²⁴"And he said to those who stood by, 'Take the mina from him, and give it to him who has ten minas.' ²⁵(But they said to him, 'Master, he has ten minas.') ²⁶'For I say to you, that to everyone who has will be given; and from him who does not have, even what he has will be taken away from him. ²⁷But bring here those enemies of mine, who did not want me to reign over them, and slay them before me.' "

The Triumphal Entry

²⁸When He had said this, He went on ahead, going up to Jerusalem. ²⁹And it came to pass, when He drew near to Bethphage*a* and Bethany, at the mountain called Olivet, that He sent two of His disciples, ³⁰saying, "Go into the village opposite you, where as you enter you will find a colt tied, on which no one has ever sat. Loose it and bring it here. ³¹And if anyone asks you, 'Why are you loosing it?' thus you shall say to him, 'Because the Lord has need of it.' "

³²So those who were sent went their way and found it just as He had said to them. ³³But as they were loosing the colt, the owners of it said to them, "Why are you loosing the colt?"

³⁴And they said, "The Lord has need of him." ³⁵Then they brought him to Jesus. And they threw their own clothes on the colt, and they set Jesus on him. ³⁶And as He

went, many spread their clothes on the road.

³⁷Then, as He was now drawing near the descent of the Mount of Olives, the whole multitude of the disciples began to rejoice and praise God with a loud voice for all the mighty works they had seen, ³⁸saying:

> " 'Blessed is the King who comes in the
>   name of the LORD!'*a*
> Peace in heaven and glory in the
>   highest!"

³⁹And some of the Pharisees called to Him from the crowd, "Teacher, rebuke Your disciples."

⁴⁰But He answered and said to them, "I tell you that if these should keep silent, the stones would immediately cry out."

> **19:40 the stones would immediately cry out.** This was a strong claim of deity and perhaps a reference to the words of Hab. 2:11. Scripture often speaks of inanimate nature praising God (see Ps. 96:11; Is. 55:12).

Jesus Weeps over Jerusalem

⁴¹Now as He drew near, He saw the city and wept over it, ⁴²saying, "If you had known, even you, especially in this your day, the things that make for your peace! But now they are hidden from your eyes. ⁴³For days will come upon you when your enemies will build an embankment around you, surround you and close you in on every side, ⁴⁴and level you, and your children within you, to the ground; and they will not leave in you one stone upon another, because you did not know the time of your visitation."

Jesus Cleanses the Temple

⁴⁵Then He went into the temple and began to drive out those who bought and sold in it,*a* ⁴⁶saying to them, "It is written, 'My house is*a* a house of prayer,'*b* but you have made it a 'den of thieves.' "*c*

⁴⁷And He was teaching daily in the temple. But the chief priests, the scribes, and the leaders of the people sought to destroy Him, ⁴⁸and were unable to do anything; for

---

19:29 *a*M-Text reads *Bethsphage.*   19:38 *a*Psalm 118:26   19:45 *a*NU-Text reads *those who were selling.*
19:46 *a*NU-Text reads *shall be.*   *b*Isaiah 56:7   *c*Jeremiah 7:11

all the people were very attentive to hear Him.

Jesus' Authority Questioned

20 Now it happened on one of those days, as He taught the people in the temple and preached the gospel, *that* the chief priests and the scribes, together with the elders, confronted *Him* ²and spoke to Him, saying, "Tell us, by what authority are You doing these things? Or who is he who gave You this authority?"

³But He answered and said to them, "I also will ask you one thing, and answer Me: ⁴The baptism of John—was it from heaven or from men?"

⁵And they reasoned among themselves, saying, "If we say, 'From heaven,' He will say, 'Why then*ᵃ* did you not believe him?' ⁶But if we say, 'From men,' all the people will stone us, for they are persuaded that John was a prophet." ⁷So they answered that they did not know where *it was* from.

> **20:5 'Why then did you not believe him?'** John clearly testified that Jesus was the Messiah. If John was a prophet whose words were true, they ought to believe his testimony about Christ. It would have been political folly for the Pharisees to deny the legitimacy and authority of John the Baptist, a prophet of God and a national hero. The Pharisees pleaded ignorance, as they did not want to question John's authority.

⁸And Jesus said to them, "Neither will I tell you by what authority I do these things."

The Parable of the Wicked Vinedressers

⁹Then He began to tell the people this parable: "A certain man planted a vineyard, leased it to vinedressers, and went into a far country for a long time. ¹⁰Now at vintage-time he sent a servant to the vinedressers, that they might give him some of the fruit of the vineyard. But the vinedressers beat him and sent *him* away empty-handed. ¹¹Again he sent another servant; and they beat him also, treated *him* shamefully, and sent *him* away empty-handed. ¹²And again he sent a third; and they wounded him also and cast *him* out.

¹³"Then the owner of the vineyard said, 'What shall I do? I will send my beloved son. Probably they will respect *him* when they see him.' ¹⁴But when the vinedressers saw him, they reasoned among themselves, saying, 'This is the heir. Come, let us kill him, that the inheritance may be ours.' ¹⁵So they cast him out of the vineyard and killed *him.* Therefore what will the owner of the vineyard do to them? ¹⁶He will come and destroy those vinedressers and give the vineyard to others."

And when they heard *it* they said, "Certainly not!"

> **20:16 destroy those vinedressers.** This probably refers to the destruction of Jerusalem. **Certainly not!** Only Luke recorded this hostile reaction from the crowd. The response suggests that they grasped the meaning of the parable.

¹⁷Then He looked at them and said, "What then is this that is written:

'*The stone which the builders rejected*
  Has become the chief cornerstone'?*ᵃ*

¹⁸Whoever falls on that stone will be broken; but on whomever it falls, it will grind him to powder."

¹⁹And the chief priests and the scribes that very hour sought to lay hands on Him, but they feared the people*ᵃ*—for they knew He had spoken this parable against them.

The Pharisees: Is It Lawful to Pay Taxes to Caesar?

²⁰So they watched *Him,* and sent spies who pretended to be righteous, that they might seize on His words, in order to deliver Him to the power and the authority of the governor. ²¹Then they asked Him, saying, "Teacher, we know that You say and teach rightly, and You do not show personal favoritism, but teach the way of God in truth: ²²Is it lawful for us to pay taxes to Caesar or not?"

²³But He perceived their craftiness, and said to them, "Why do you test Me?*ᵃ* ²⁴Show Me a denarius. Whose image and inscription does it have?"

20:5 *ᵃ*NU-Text and M-Text omit *then.*　　20:17 *ᵃ*Psalm 118:22　　20:19 *ᵃ*M-Text reads *but they were afraid.*　　20:23 *ᵃ*NU-Text omits *Why do you test Me?*

They answered and said, "Caesar's."

²⁵And He said to them, "Render therefore to Caesar the things that are Caesar's, and to God the things that are God's."

²⁶But they could not catch Him in His words in the presence of the people. And they marveled at His answer and kept silent.

> **20:25 Render therefore to Caesar.** Christ recognized that all citizens have duties to the secular state as well as duties to God. He also recognized a legitimate distinction between the two.

The Sadducees: What About the Resurrection?

²⁷Then some of the Sadducees, who deny that there is a resurrection, came to *Him* and asked Him, ²⁸saying: "Teacher, Moses wrote to us *that* if a man's brother dies, having a wife, and he dies without children, his brother should take his wife and raise up offspring for his brother. ²⁹Now there were seven brothers. And the first took a wife, and died without children. ³⁰And the second*ᵃ* took her as wife, and he died childless. ³¹Then the third took her, and in like manner the seven also; and they left no children,*ᵃ* and died. ³²Last of all the woman died also. ³³Therefore, in the resurrection, whose wife does she become? For all seven had her as wife."

³⁴Jesus answered and said to them, "The sons of this age marry and are given in marriage. ³⁵But those who are counted worthy to attain that age, and the resurrection from the dead, neither marry nor are given in marriage; ³⁶nor can they die anymore, for they are equal to the angels and are sons of God, being sons of the resurrection. ³⁷But even Moses showed in the *burning* bush *passage* that the dead are raised, when he called the Lord *'the God of Abraham, the God of Isaac, and the God of Jacob.'ᵃ* ³⁸For He is not the God of the dead but of the living, for all live to Him."

> **20:38 all live to Him.** Only Luke records this phrase. All people, whether departed from their earthly bodies or not, are still living and will live forever. No one is annihilated in death (see John 5:28–30).

³⁹Then some of the scribes answered and said, "Teacher, You have spoken well." ⁴⁰But after that they dared not question Him anymore.

Jesus: How Can David Call His Descendant Lord?

⁴¹And He said to them, "How can they say that the Christ is the Son of David? ⁴²Now David himself said in the Book of Psalms:

'The LORD said to my Lord,
 " Sit at My right hand,
⁴³   Till I make Your enemies Your
       footstool." 'ᵃ

⁴⁴Therefore David calls Him *'Lord';* how is He then his Son?"

Beware of the Scribes

⁴⁵Then, in the hearing of all the people, He said to His disciples, ⁴⁶"Beware of the scribes, who desire to go around in long robes, love greetings in the marketplaces, the best seats in the synagogues, and the best places at feasts, ⁴⁷who devour widows' houses, and for a pretense make long prayers. These will receive greater condemnation."

The Widow's Two Mites

21 And He looked up and saw the rich putting their gifts into the treasury, ²and He saw also a certain poor widow putting in two mites. ³So He said, "Truly I say to you that this poor widow has put in more than all; ⁴for all these out of their abundance have put in offerings for God,ᵃ but she out of her poverty put in all the livelihood that she had."

Jesus Predicts the Destruction of the Temple

⁵Then, as some spoke of the temple, how it was adorned with beautiful stones and donations, He said, ⁶"These things which you see—the days will come in which not *one* stone shall be left upon another that shall not be thrown down."

20:30 ᵃNU-Text ends verse 30 here.   20:31 ᵃNU-Text and M-Text read *the seven also left no children.*
20:37 ᵃExodus 3:6,15   20:43 ᵃPsalm 110:1   21:4 ᵃNU-Text omits *for God.*

21:5 donations. The wealthy gave gifts of golden sculptures, plaques, and other treasures to the temple. Herod had donated a golden vine with clusters of golden grapes nearly 6 feet tall. The gifts were displayed on the walls and suspended in the portico, showing an unimaginable collection of wealth. All these riches were looted by the Romans when the temple was destroyed.

The Signs of the Times and the End of the Age

⁷So they asked Him, saying, "Teacher, but when will these things be? And what sign *will there be* when these things are about to take place?"

⁸And He said: "Take heed that you not be deceived. For many will come in My name, saying, 'I am *He*,' and, 'The time has drawn near.' Therefore*ᵃ* do not go after them. ⁹But when you hear of wars and commotions, do not be terrified; for these things must come to pass first, but the end *will not come* immediately."

¹⁰Then He said to them, "Nation will rise against nation, and kingdom against kingdom. ¹¹And there will be great earthquakes in various places, and famines and pestilences; and there will be fearful sights and great signs from heaven. ¹²But before all these things, they will lay their hands on you and persecute *you*, delivering *you* up to the synagogues and prisons. You will be brought before kings and rulers for My name's sake. ¹³But it will turn out for you as an occasion for testimony. ¹⁴Therefore settle *it* in your hearts not to meditate beforehand on what you will answer; ¹⁵for I will give you a mouth and wisdom which all your adversaries will not be able to contradict or resist. ¹⁶You will be betrayed even by parents and brothers, relatives and friends; and they will put *some* of you to death. ¹⁷And you will be hated by all for My name's sake. ¹⁸But not a hair of your head shall be lost. ¹⁹By your patience possess your souls.

The Destruction of Jerusalem

²⁰"But when you see Jerusalem surrounded by armies, then know that its desolation is near. ²¹Then let those who are in Judea flee to the mountains, let those who are in the midst of her depart, and let not those who are in the country enter her. ²²For these are the days of vengeance, that all things which are written may be fulfilled. ²³But woe to those who are pregnant and to those who are nursing babies in those days! For there will be great distress in the land and wrath upon this people. ²⁴And they will fall by the edge of the sword, and be led away captive into all nations. And Jerusalem will be trampled by Gentiles until the times of the Gentiles are fulfilled.

The Coming of the Son of Man

²⁵"And there will be signs in the sun, in the moon, and in the stars; and on the earth distress of nations, with perplexity, the sea and the waves roaring; ²⁶men's hearts failing them from fear and the expectation of those things which are coming on the earth, for the powers of the heavens will be shaken. ²⁷Then they will see the Son of Man coming in a cloud with power and great glory. ²⁸Now when these things begin to happen, look up and lift up your heads, because your redemption draws near."

21:28 lift up your heads. The tribulations and signs that mark the last days will be cause for great expectation, joy, and triumph for believers. **redemption.** This refers to the final fullness of redemption, when the redeemed are united with Christ forever.

The Parable of the Fig Tree

²⁹Then He spoke to them a parable: "Look at the fig tree, and all the trees. ³⁰When they are already budding, you see and know for yourselves that summer is now near. ³¹So you also, when you see these things happening, know that the kingdom of God is near. ³²Assuredly, I say to you, this generation will by no means pass away till all things take place. ³³Heaven and earth will pass away, but My words will by no means pass away.

The Importance of Watching

³⁴"But take heed to yourselves, lest your hearts be weighed down with carousing, drunkenness, and cares of this life, and that Day come on you unexpectedly. ³⁵For it will come as a snare on all those who dwell on the face of the whole earth. ³⁶Watch there-

---

21:8 *ᵃ*NU-Text omits *Therefore*.

fore, and pray always that you may be counted worthy[a] to escape all these things that will come to pass, and to stand before the Son of Man."

37And in the daytime He was teaching in the temple, but at night He went out and stayed on the mountain called Olivet. 38Then early in the morning all the people came to Him in the temple to hear Him.

The Plot to Kill Jesus

22 Now the Feast of Unleavened Bread drew near, which is called Passover. 2And the chief priests and the scribes sought how they might kill Him, for they feared the people.

3Then Satan entered Judas, surnamed Iscariot, who was numbered among the twelve. 4So he went his way and conferred with the chief priests and captains, how he might betray Him to them. 5And they were glad, and agreed to give him money. 6So he promised and sought opportunity to betray Him to them in the absence of the multitude.

22:3 Satan entered. Satan possessed Judas on two occasions: once before Judas arranged his betrayal with the chief priests, and again during the Last Supper immediately before he was to betray Jesus (John 13:27).

Jesus and His Disciples Prepare the Passover

7Then came the Day of Unleavened Bread, when the Passover must be killed. 8And He sent Peter and John, saying, "Go and prepare the Passover for us, that we may eat."

9So they said to Him, "Where do You want us to prepare?"

10And He said to them, "Behold, when you have entered the city, a man will meet you carrying a pitcher of water; follow him into the house which he enters. 11Then you shall say to the master of the house, 'The Teacher says to you, "Where is the guest room where I may eat the Passover with My disciples?" ' 12Then he will show you a large, furnished upper room; there make ready."

13So they went and found it just as He had said to them, and they prepared the Passover.

Jesus Institutes the Lord's Supper

14When the hour had come, He sat down, and the twelve[a] apostles with Him. 15Then He said to them, "With *fervent* desire I have desired to eat this Passover with you before I suffer; 16for I say to you, I will no longer eat of it until it is fulfilled in the kingdom of God."

22:16 fulfilled. Christ's death fulfilled the symbolism of the Passover meal, which was a memorial of the deliverance from Egypt and a prophecy of the sacrifice of Christ that would set people free from their bondage to sin.

17Then He took the cup, and gave thanks, and said, "Take this and divide *it* among yourselves; 18for I say to you,[a] I will not drink of the fruit of the vine until the kingdom of God comes."

19And He took bread, gave thanks and broke *it,* and gave *it* to them, saying, "This is My body which is given for you; do this in remembrance of Me."

20Likewise He also *took* the cup after supper, saying, "This cup *is* the new covenant in My blood, which is shed for you. 21But behold, the hand of My betrayer *is* with Me on the table. 22And truly the Son of Man goes as it has been determined, but woe to that man by whom He is betrayed!"

22:22 as it has been determined. Every detail of the crucifixion of Christ was under the sovereign control of God, in accordance with His eternal purposes (see Acts 2:23). **but woe.** Judas' betrayal was part of God's plan, but it does not free him from the guilt of the crime he willfully committed. God's sovereignty is never an excuse for human guilt.

23Then they began to question among themselves, which of them it was who would do this thing.

The Disciples Argue About Greatness

24Now there was also a dispute among them, as to which of them should be considered the greatest. 25And He said to them,

---

21:36 [a]NU-Text reads *may have strength.*   22:14 [a]NU-Text omits *twelve.*   22:18 [a]NU-Text adds *from now on.*

"The kings of the Gentiles exercise lordship over them, and those who exercise authority over them are called 'benefactors.' [26]But not so *among* you; on the contrary, he who is greatest among you, let him be as the younger, and he who governs as he who serves. [27]For who *is* greater, he who sits at the table, or he who serves? *Is* it not he who sits at the table? Yet I am among you as the One who serves.

[28]"But you are those who have continued with Me in My trials. [29]And I bestow upon you a kingdom, just as My Father bestowed *one* upon Me, [30]that you may eat and drink at My table in My kingdom, and sit on thrones judging the twelve tribes of Israel."

Jesus Predicts Peter's Denial

[31]And the Lord said,[a] "Simon, Simon! Indeed, Satan has asked for you, that he may sift *you* as wheat. [32]But I have prayed for you, that your faith should not fail; and when you have returned to *Me*, strengthen your brethren."

> **22:32 I have prayed for you.** The pronoun "you" is singular. Although Jesus prayed for all of them (John 17:6–19), He personally assured Peter of His prayers and inspired Peter to be an encouragement to the others. **that your faith should not fail.** Peter failed miserably, but his faith was never overthrown (see John 21:18,19).

[33]But he said to Him, "Lord, I am ready to go with You, both to prison and to death." [34]Then He said, "I tell you, Peter, the rooster shall not crow this day before you will deny three times that you know Me."

Supplies for the Road

[35]And He said to them, "When I sent you without money bag, knapsack, and sandals, did you lack anything?"

So they said, "Nothing."

[36]Then He said to them, "But now, he who has a money bag, let him take *it*, and likewise a knapsack; and he who has no sword, let him sell his garment and buy one. [37]For I say to you that this which is written must still be accomplished in Me:

'And He was numbered with the transgressors.'[a] For the things concerning Me have an end."

[38]So they said, "Lord, look, here *are* two swords."

And He said to them, "It is enough."

The Prayer in the Garden

[39]Coming out, He went to the Mount of Olives, as He was accustomed, and His disciples also followed Him. [40]When He came to the place, He said to them, "Pray that you may not enter into temptation." [41]And He was withdrawn from them about a stone's throw, and He knelt down and prayed, [42]saying, "Father, if it is Your will, take this cup away from Me; nevertheless not My will, but Yours, be done." [43]Then an angel appeared to Him from heaven, strengthening Him. [44]And being in agony, He prayed more earnestly. Then His sweat became like great drops of blood falling down to the ground.[a]

> **22:44 like great drops of blood.** This suggests a dangerous condition called *hematidrosis*, the effusion of blood in one's perspiration. It can be caused by extreme anguish or physical strain. Subcutaneous capillaries dilate and burst, mingling blood with sweat. Christ stated that His distress had brought Him to the threshold of death.

[45]When He rose up from prayer, and had come to His disciples, He found them sleeping from sorrow. [46]Then He said to them, "Why do you sleep? Rise and pray, lest you enter into temptation."

Betrayal and Arrest in Gethsemane

[47]And while He was still speaking, behold, a multitude; and he who was called Judas, one of the twelve, went before them and drew near to Jesus to kiss Him. [48]But Jesus said to him, "Judas, are you betraying the Son of Man with a kiss?" [49]When those around Him saw what was going to happen, they said to Him, "Lord, shall we strike with the sword?" [50]And one of them struck the servant of the high priest and cut off his right ear. [51]But Jesus answered and said, "Permit

---

22:31 [a]NU-Text omits *And the Lord said.*   22:37 [a]Isaiah 53:12   22:44 [a]NU-Text brackets verses 43 and 44 as not in the original text.

even this." And He touched his ear and healed him.

⁵²Then Jesus said to the chief priests, captains of the temple, and the elders who had come to Him, "Have you come out, as against a robber, with swords and clubs? ⁵³When I was with you daily in the temple, you did not try to seize Me. But this is your hour, and the power of darkness."

Peter Denies Jesus, and Weeps Bitterly

⁵⁴Having arrested Him, they led *Him* and brought Him into the high priest's house. But Peter followed at a distance. ⁵⁵Now when they had kindled a fire in the midst of the courtyard and sat down together, Peter sat among them. ⁵⁶And a certain servant girl, seeing him as he sat by the fire, looked intently at him and said, "This man was also with Him."

⁵⁷But he denied Him,ᵃ saying, "Woman, I do not know Him."

⁵⁸And after a little while another saw him and said, "You also are of them."

But Peter said, "Man, I am not!"

⁵⁹Then after about an hour had passed, another confidently affirmed, saying, "Surely this *fellow* also was with Him, for he is a Galilean."

⁶⁰But Peter said, "Man, I do not know what you are saying!"

Immediately, while he was still speaking, the roosterᵃ crowed. ⁶¹And the Lord turned and looked at Peter. Then Peter remembered the word of the Lord, how He had said to him, "Before the rooster crows,ᵃ you will deny Me three times." ⁶²So Peter went out and wept bitterly.

> **22:61 the Lord turned and looked at Peter.** Only Luke records that Jesus made eye contact with Peter. The verb suggests an intent, fixed look. The fact that He could see Peter meant that Jesus had already been brought into the courtyard to be beaten.

Jesus Mocked and Beaten

⁶³Now the men who held Jesus mocked Him and beat Him. ⁶⁴And having blindfolded Him, they struck Him on the face and asked Him,ᵃ saying, "Prophesy! Who is the one who struck You?" ⁶⁵And many other things they blasphemously spoke against Him.

Jesus Faces the Sanhedrin

⁶⁶As soon as it was day, the elders of the people, both chief priests and scribes, came together and led Him into their council, saying, ⁶⁷"If You are the Christ, tell us."

But He said to them, "If I tell you, you will by no means believe. ⁶⁸And if I also ask *you*, you will by no means answer Me or let *Me* go.ᵃ ⁶⁹Hereafter the Son of Man will sit on the right hand of the power of God."

⁷⁰Then they all said, "Are You then the Son of God?"

So He said to them, "You *rightly* say that I am."

⁷¹And they said, "What further testimony do we need? For we have heard it ourselves from His own mouth."

Jesus Handed Over to Pontius Pilate

23 Then the whole multitude of them arose and led Him to Pilate. ²And they began to accuse Him, saying, "We found this *fellow* perverting theᵃ nation, and forbidding to pay taxes to Caesar, saying that He Himself is Christ, a King."

> **23:1 the whole multitude of them.** All 70 members of the Sanhedrin were present. At least one member of the council, Joseph of Arimathea, dissented from the decision to condemn Christ (vv. 50–52).

³Then Pilate asked Him, saying, "Are You the King of the Jews?"

He answered him and said, "*It is as* you say."

⁴So Pilate said to the chief priests and the crowd, "I find no fault in this Man."

⁵But they were the more fierce, saying, "He stirs up the people, teaching throughout all Judea, beginning from Galilee to this place."

Jesus Faces Herod

⁶When Pilate heard of Galilee,ᵃ he asked if the Man were a Galilean. ⁷And as soon as he knew that He belonged to Herod's

---

22:57 ᵃNU-Text reads *denied it.*   22:60 ᵃNU-Text and M-Text read *a rooster.*   22:61 ᵃNU-Text adds *today.*   22:64 ᵃNU-Text reads *And having blindfolded Him, they asked Him.*   22:68 ᵃNU-Text omits *also* and *Me or let Me go.*   23:2 ᵃNU-Text reads *our.*   23:6 ᵃNU-Text omits *of Galilee.*

jurisdiction, he sent Him to Herod, who was also in Jerusalem at that time. ⁸Now when Herod saw Jesus, he was exceedingly glad; for he had desired for a long *time* to see Him, because he had heard many things about Him, and he hoped to see some miracle done by Him. ⁹Then he questioned Him with many words, but He answered him nothing. ¹⁰And the chief priests and scribes stood and vehemently accused Him. ¹¹Then Herod, with his men of war, treated Him with contempt and mocked *Him*, arrayed Him in a gorgeous robe, and sent Him back to Pilate. ¹²That very day Pilate and Herod became friends with each other, for previously they had been at enmity with each other.

> **23:9 answered him nothing.** Herod was the only one to whom Jesus refused to speak (see Matt. 7:6). Herod had rejected the truth when he heard it from John the Baptist, so it would have been pointless for Jesus to answer him (see Is. 53:7; 1 Pet. 2:23).

Taking the Place of Barabbas

¹³Then Pilate, when he had called together the chief priests, the rulers, and the people, ¹⁴said to them, "You have brought this Man to me, as one who misleads the people. And indeed, having examined *Him* in your presence, I have found no fault in this Man concerning those things of which you accuse Him; ¹⁵no, neither did Herod, for I sent you back to him;ᵃ and indeed nothing deserving of death has been done by Him. ¹⁶I will therefore chastise Him and release *Him*" ¹⁷(for it was necessary for him to release one to them at the feast).ᵃ

¹⁸And they all cried out at once, saying, "Away with this *Man*, and release to us Barabbas"— ¹⁹who had been thrown into prison for a certain rebellion made in the city, and for murder.

²⁰Pilate, therefore, wishing to release Jesus, again called out to them. ²¹But they shouted, saying, "Crucify *Him*, crucify Him!"

²²Then he said to them the third time, "Why, what evil has He done? I have found no reason for death in Him. I will therefore chastise Him and let *Him* go."

²³But they were insistent, demanding with loud voices that He be crucified. And the voices of these men and of the chief priests prevailed.ᵃ ²⁴So Pilate gave sentence that it should be as they requested. ²⁵And he released to themᵃ the one they requested, who for rebellion and murder had been thrown into prison; but he delivered Jesus to their will.

The King on a Cross

²⁶Now as they led Him away, they laid hold of a certain man, Simon a Cyrenian, who was coming from the country, and on him they laid the cross that he might bear *it* after Jesus.

²⁷And a great multitude of the people followed Him, and women who also mourned and lamented Him. ²⁸But Jesus, turning to them, said, "Daughters of Jerusalem, do not weep for Me, but weep for yourselves and for your children. ²⁹For indeed the days are coming in which they will say, 'Blessed *are* the barren, wombs that never bore, and breasts which never nursed!' ³⁰Then they will begin *'to say to the mountains, "Fall on us!" and to the hills, "Cover us!"'* ᵃ ³¹For if they do these things in the green wood, what will be done in the dry?"

³²There were also two others, criminals, led with Him to be put to death. ³³And when they had come to the place called Calvary, there they crucified Him, and the criminals, one on the right hand and the other on the left. ³⁴Then Jesus said, "Father, forgive them, for they do not know what they do."ᵃ

> **23:34 forgive them.** This refers to Jesus' tormentors, both Jews and Romans (see Acts 7:60). Some of the fruit of this prayer can be found in the salvation of thousands of people in Jerusalem at Pentecost (Acts 2:41). **they do not know what they do.** They were not aware of the scope of their wickedness because they did not recognize Jesus as the Messiah (Acts 13:27,28). However, their ignorance did not excuse them, nor did it bring them forgiveness.

And they divided His garments and cast lots. ³⁵And the people stood looking on. But even the rulers with them sneered, saying,

---

23:15 ᵃNU-Text reads *for he sent Him back to us.*   23:17 ᵃNU-Text omits verse 17.   23:23 ᵃNU-Text omits *and of the chief priests.*   23:25 ᵃNU-Text and M-Text omit *to them.*   23:30 ᵃHosea 10:8   23:34 ᵃNU-Text brackets the first sentence as a later addition.

"He saved others; let Him save Himself if He is the Christ, the chosen of God."

36The soldiers also mocked Him, coming and offering Him sour wine, 37and saying, "If You are the King of the Jews, save Yourself."

38And an inscription also was written over Him in letters of Greek, Latin, and Hebrew:*a*

THIS IS THE KING OF THE JEWS.

39Then one of the criminals who were hanged blasphemed Him, saying, "If You are the Christ,*a* save Yourself and us."

40But the other, answering, rebuked him, saying, "Do you not even fear God, seeing you are under the same condemnation? 41And we indeed justly, for we receive the due reward of our deeds; but this Man has done nothing wrong." 42Then he said to Jesus, "Lord,*a* remember me when You come into Your kingdom."

> **23:42 Lord, remember me.** The thief's prayer reflected his belief that the soul lives after death, that Christ rules over the kingdom of the souls of men, and that Christ would soon enter His kingdom. The thief's request was a plea for mercy, demonstrating his faith.

43And Jesus said to him, "Assuredly, I say to you, today you will be with Me in Paradise."

Jesus Dies on the Cross

44Now it was*a* about the sixth hour, and there was darkness over all the earth until the ninth hour. 45Then the sun was darkened,*a* and the veil of the temple was torn in two. 46And when Jesus had cried out with a loud voice, He said, "Father, '*into Your hands I commit My spirit.*'"*a* Having said this, He breathed His last.

47So when the centurion saw what had happened, he glorified God, saying, "Certainly this was a righteous Man!"

48And the whole crowd who came together to that sight, seeing what had been

done, beat their breasts and returned. 49But all His acquaintances, and the women who followed Him from Galilee, stood at a distance, watching these things.

Jesus Buried in Joseph's Tomb

50Now behold, *there was* a man named Joseph, a council member, a good and just man. 51He had not consented to their decision and deed. *He was* from Arimathea, a city of the Jews, who himself was also waiting*a* for the kingdom of God. 52This man went to Pilate and asked for the body of Jesus. 53Then he took it down, wrapped it in linen, and laid it in a tomb *that was* hewn out of the rock, where no one had ever lain before. 54That day was the Preparation, and the Sabbath drew near.

55And the women who had come with Him from Galilee followed after, and they observed the tomb and how His body was laid. 56Then they returned and prepared spices and fragrant oils. And they rested on the Sabbath according to the commandment.

> **23:55 observed...how his body was laid.** Nicodemus and Joseph wrapped the body with linen and a hundred pounds of spices and aloes which Nicodemus had brought (John 19:39). The women from Galilee were determined to prepare Jesus' body for burial themselves. They were probably unfamiliar with Joseph and Nicodemus, who were Judeans and associated with the Jewish leaders who conspired against Jesus.

He Is Risen

24 Now on the first *day* of the week, very early in the morning, they, and certain *other women* with them,*a* came to the tomb bringing the spices which they had prepared. 2But they found the stone rolled away from the tomb. 3Then they went in and did not find the body of the Lord Jesus. 4And it happened, as they were greatly*a* perplexed about this, that behold, two men stood by them in shining garments. 5Then, as they were afraid and bowed *their* faces to the earth, they said to

---

23:38 *a*NU-Text omits *written* and *in letters of Greek, Latin, and Hebrew.*　23:39 *a*NU-Text reads *Are You not the Christ?*　23:42 *a*NU-Text reads *And he said, "Jesus, remember me.*　23:44 *a*NU-Text adds *already.*　23:45 *a*NU-Text reads *obscured.*　23:46 *a*Psalm 31:5　23:51 *a*NU-Text reads *who was waiting.*　24:1 *a*NU-Text omits *and certain other women with them.*　24:4 *a*NU-Text omits *greatly.*

them, "Why do you seek the living among the dead? ⁶He is not here, but is risen! Remember how He spoke to you when He was still in Galilee, ⁷saying, 'The Son of Man must be delivered into the hands of sinful men, and be crucified, and the third day rise again.' "

⁸And they remembered His words. ⁹Then they returned from the tomb and told all these things to the eleven and to all the rest. ¹⁰It was Mary Magdalene, Joanna, Mary *the mother* of James, and the other *women* with them, who told these things to the apostles. ¹¹And their words seemed to them like idle tales, and they did not believe them. ¹²But Peter arose and ran to the tomb; and stooping down, he saw the linen cloths lying*ᵃ* by themselves; and he departed, marveling to himself at what had happened.

The Road to Emmaus

¹³Now behold, two of them were traveling that same day to a village called Emmaus, which was seven miles*ᵃ* from Jerusalem. ¹⁴And they talked together of all these things which had happened. ¹⁵So it was, while they conversed and reasoned, that Jesus Himself drew near and went with them. ¹⁶But their eyes were restrained, so that they did not know Him.

> **24:13 two of them.** These were not any of the 11 disciples. According to v. 18, one was named Cleopas. **Emmaus.** This town, mentioned nowhere else in Scripture, may be the town known as Kubeibeh, which is 7 miles NW of Jerusalem.

¹⁷And He said to them, "What kind of conversation *is* this that you have with one another as you walk and are sad?"*ᵃ*

¹⁸Then the one whose name was Cleopas answered and said to Him, "Are You the only stranger in Jerusalem, and have You not known the things which happened there in these days?"

¹⁹And He said to them, "What things?"

So they said to Him, "The things concerning Jesus of Nazareth, who was a Prophet mighty in deed and word before God and all the people, ²⁰and how the chief priests and our rulers delivered Him to be condemned to death, and crucified Him. ²¹But we were hoping that it was He who was going to redeem Israel. Indeed, besides all this, today is the third day since these things happened. ²²Yes, and certain women of our company, who arrived at the tomb early, astonished us. ²³When they did not find His body, they came saying that they had also seen a vision of angels who said He was alive. ²⁴And certain of those *who were* with us went to the tomb and found *it* just as the women had said; but Him they did not see."

²⁵Then He said to them, "O foolish ones, and slow of heart to believe in all that the prophets have spoken! ²⁶Ought not the Christ to have suffered these things and to enter into His glory?" ²⁷And beginning at Moses and all the Prophets, He expounded to them in all the Scriptures the things concerning Himself.

The Disciples' Eyes Opened

²⁸Then they drew near to the village where they were going, and He indicated that He would have gone farther. ²⁹But they constrained Him, saying, "Abide with us, for it is toward evening, and the day is far spent." And He went in to stay with them.

³⁰Now it came to pass, as He sat at the table with them, that He took bread, blessed and broke *it*, and gave it to them. ³¹Then their eyes were opened and they knew Him; and He vanished from their sight.

> **24:31 their eyes were opened.** God kept these men from recognizing Jesus until it was time for Him to depart. His resurrection body was glorified, and so was altered from its previous appearance (see Rev. 1:13–16). Even Mary Magdalene had not recognized Him at first (see John 20:14–16). **He vanished from their sight.** Christ, in His glorified body, could disappear bodily (John 20:19,26). The fact that He ascended into heaven bodily showed that His resurrection body was already fit for heaven.

³²And they said to one another, "Did not our heart burn within us while He talked with us on the road, and while He opened

---

24:12 *ᵃ*NU-Text omits *lying*.   24:13 *ᵃ*Literally *sixty stadia*   24:17 *ᵃ*NU-Text reads *as you walk? And they stood still, looking sad.*

the Scriptures to us?" ³³So they rose up that very hour and returned to Jerusalem, and found the eleven and those *who were* with them gathered together, ³⁴saying, "The Lord is risen indeed, and has appeared to Simon!" ³⁵And they told about the things *that had happened* on the road, and how He was known to them in the breaking of bread.

Jesus Appears to His Disciples

³⁶Now as they said these things, Jesus Himself stood in the midst of them, and said to them, "Peace to you." ³⁷But they were terrified and frightened, and supposed they had seen a spirit. ³⁸And He said to them, "Why are you troubled? And why do doubts arise in your hearts? ³⁹Behold My hands and My feet, that it is I Myself. Handle Me and see, for a spirit does not have flesh and bones as you see I have."

⁴⁰When He had said this, He showed them His hands and His feet.ᵃ ⁴¹But while they still did not believe for joy, and marveled, He said to them, "Have you any food here?" ⁴²So they gave Him a piece of a broiled fish and some honeycomb.ᵃ ⁴³And He took *it* and ate in their presence.

The Scriptures Opened

⁴⁴Then He said to them, "These *are* the words which I spoke to you while I was still with you, that all things must be fulfilled which were written in the Law of Moses and *the* Prophets and *the* Psalms concerning Me." ⁴⁵And He opened their understanding, that they might comprehend the Scriptures.

> **24:45 opened their understanding.** Jesus taught the disciples from the OT, as He had taught the men on the road to Emmaus. Their minds were supernaturally opened to receive the truths He unfolded. Before, their understanding had been dull (9:45); here, however, they finally saw clearly (see Ps. 119:18; 2 Cor. 3:14–16).

The Ascension

⁴⁶Then He said to them, "Thus it is written, and thus it was necessary for the Christ to suffer and to riseᵃ from the dead the third day, ⁴⁷and that repentance and remission of sins should be preached in His name to all nations, beginning at Jerusalem. ⁴⁸And you are witnesses of these things. ⁴⁹Behold, I send the Promise of My Father upon you; but tarry in the city of Jerusalemᵃ until you are endued with power from on high."

⁵⁰And He led them out as far as Bethany, and He lifted up His hands and blessed them. ⁵¹Now it came to pass, while He blessed them, that He was parted from them and carried up into heaven. ⁵²And they worshiped Him, and returned to Jerusalem with great joy, ⁵³and were continually in the temple praising andᵃ blessing God. Amen.ᵇ

> **24:51,52 carried up into heaven.** Before, the resurrected Christ simply vanished (v. 31). This time, the believers saw Him ascend (see Acts 1:9–11). **they worshiped Him.** Now that they had understanding, they perceived the full truth of Christ's deity (see Matt. 28:9; John 20:28).

24:40 ᵃSome printed New Testaments omit this verse. It is found in nearly all Greek manuscripts. 24:42 ᵃNU-Text omits *and some honeycomb.* 24:46 ᵃNU-Text reads *written, that the Christ should suffer and rise.* 24:49 ᵃNU-Text omits *of Jerusalem.* 24:53 ᵃNU-Text omits *praising and.* ᵇNU-Text omits *Amen.*

When an exciting event happens, some people can't wait to talk about it. Others like to think about the reasons and details for a while before they offer their comments. One of the four biographies of Jesus fits this second category. John must have spoken many times about his experiences with Jesus, but he did not write down his Gospel until long after the other three writers had published theirs. The passage of time did not change the central character in John's account, but it allowed him to express some conclusions about Jesus that could best be made after lifelong reflections on the significance of God's visit to earth.

AUTHOR AND DATE

John was written by the Apostle John, approximately A.D. 80 to 90.

Although the author's name does not appear in the gospel, early church tradition strongly and consistently identifies him as the Apostle John. Ireneaus (about A.D. 130–200), who was a disciple of Polycarp (about A.D. 70–160), a disciple of the Apostle John, testified on Polycarp's authority that John wrote this gospel (*Against Heresies* 2.22.5; 3.1.1.). Subsequent to Ireneaus, all the church fathers assumed John to be the gospel's author. One of them, Clement of Alexandria (about A.D. 150–215), wrote that John, aware of the facts set forth in the other gospels, and being moved by the Holy Spirit, composed a "spiritual gospel" (see Eusebius' *Ecclesiastical History* 6.14.7).

Reinforcing early church tradition are significant internal characteristics of the gospel. While the synoptic gospels (Matthew, Mark, and Luke) frequently identify the Apostle John by name, he is not directly mentioned by name at all in the Gospel of John. Instead, the author prefers to identify himself as the disciple "whom Jesus loved" (13:23; 19:26; 20:2; 21:7,20). The absence of John's name is remarkable when one considers the important part played by other named disciples in this gospel. Yet, the recurring designation of himself as the disciple "whom Jesus loved," a deliberate avoidance by John of his personal name, reflects his humility and celebrates his relation to his Lord Jesus. John's authorship is established by conspicuous absence.

Two factors affect the traditional dating of John's gospel. The writings of some church fathers indicate that John was actively writing in his old age. They also note that John was aware of the synoptic gospels. These points cause many to date the gospel sometime after the composition of the synoptics, but prior to John's writing of 1, 2, and 3 John or Revelation. This means that John wrote his gospel about A.D. 80–90, about 50 years after he witnessed Jesus' earthly ministry.

John's gospel is the only one of the four that contains a precise statement regarding the author's purpose (20:30,31). He declares, "these are written that you may believe that Jesus is the Christ, the Son of God, and that believing you may have life in His name" (20:31). The motivating purposes for writing this book, therefore, are two–fold: evangelistic and apologetic.

John emphasized his evangelistic purpose by using the word "believe" approximately 100 times in the gospel—twice as often as the synoptics use the term. He composed his gospel to provide reasons for saving faith in his readers and, as a result, to assure them that they would receive the divine gift of eternal life (1:12).

John's apologetic purpose often overlapped his evangelistic purpose. He wrote to convince his readers of Jesus' true identity as the incarnate God-Man whose divine and human natures were perfectly united into one person who was the prophesied Christ ("Messiah") and Savior of the world (1:41; 3:16; 4:25,26; 8:58). John organized his gospel around eight "signs" or proofs (apart from the central sign of the resurrection itself) that reinforce Jesus' true identity leading to faith. Seven of the miraculous signs lead up to the resurrection and one follows it: (1) turning water into wine (2:1–11); (2) healing the royal official's son (4:46–54); (3) healing the lame man (5:1–18); (4) feeding multitudes (6:1–15); (5) walking on water (6:16–21); (6) healing the blind man (9:1–41); (7) raising Lazarus (11:1–57); and (8) catching fish miraculously (21:6–11).

When Ireneaus identified the Apostle John as the writer of this gospel, he added some background details. According to his ancient witness, John wrote the book while in residence in Ephesus, in Asia Minor, when he was advanced in age. Tradition adds that the aged Apostle was aware of the synoptic gospels. These facts make it apparent that John intended to make a unique contribution to the records of Jesus' life by supplementing and complementing the other three gospels. This gospel's unique characteristics reinforce John's intentions. First, John supplied a large amount of unique material not recorded in the other gospels. Second, his information often helps the understanding of the events in the synoptics. For example, while the synoptics begin with Jesus' ministry in Galilee, they imply that Jesus had a ministry prior to that time (Matthew 4:12; Mark 1:14). John fills this gap with information on Jesus' early ministry in Judea (chapter 3) and Samaria (chapter 4). Third, John is the most theological of the gospels. It contains, for example, a heavily theological prologue (1:1–18), larger amounts of didactic and discourse material in proportion to narrative, and the largest amount of teaching on the Holy Spirit (14:16,17,26; 16:7–14). Although John was aware of the synoptics and fashioned his gospel with them in mind, he did not depend upon them for information. Rather, under the inspiration of the Holy Spirit, he utilized his own memory as an eyewitness in composing the gospel (1:14; 19:35; 21:24).

John's evangelistic and apologetic purposes come together in the central theme of his gospel, found in 20:31: "Jesus is the Christ, the Son of God." The towering person and work of Christ form the center of the book. The titles and roles of Jesus make a supporting set of themes: (1) Jesus as the Word, the Messiah, the Son of God; (2) Jesus brings the gift of salvation to humankind; and (3) Jesus, the One accepted or rejected by humankind. John also includes seven emphatic "I AM" statements made by Jesus in his gospel that underscore Jesus' self-understanding as God and Messiah (6:35,48; 8:12; 10:7,9,10,11,14; 11:25; 14:6; 15:1,5).

Three predominant words—"signs," "believe," and "life"—found together in 20:30,31, appear throughout the gospel to enforce the theme of salvation in Christ. This pattern originates in the prologue (1:1–18) and appears throughout the gospel in various ways (6:35,48; 8:12; 10:7,9,11–14; 11:25; 14:6; 17:3). These key words also serve to emphasize the ways in which people responded to Jesus Christ and His offer of salvation.

THE **TOWERING PERSON** AND **WORK OF CHRIST** FORM THE **CENTER** OF **THE BOOK**.

John also includes certain contrastive sub-themes that reinforce his main theme. He uses dualism (life and death, light and darkness, love and hate, from above and from below) to convey vital information about the person and work of Christ and the need to believe in Him (1:4,5,12,13; 3:16–21; 12:44–46; 15:17–20).

OUTLINE

I. THE INCARNATION OF THE SON OF GOD (1:1–18)

   A. His Eternality (1:1,2)

   B. His Pre-incarnate Work (1:3–5)

   C. His Forerunner (1:6–8)

   D. His Rejection (1:9–11)

   E. His Reception (1:12,13)

   F. His Deity (1:14–18)

II. THE PRESENTATION OF THE SON OF GOD (1:19–4:54)

   A. Presentation by John the Baptist (1:19–34)

     1. To the religious leaders (1:19–28)

     2. At Christ's baptism (1:29–34)

   B. Presentation to John's Disciples (1:35–51)

     1. Andrew and Peter (1:35–42)

     2. Philip and Nathanael (1:43–51)

   C. Presentation in Galilee (2:1–12)

     1. First sign: water to wine (2:1–10)

     2. Disciples believe (2:11,12)

   D. Presentation in Judea (2:13–3:36)

     1. Cleansing the temple (2:13–25)

     2. Teaching Nicodemus (3:1–21)

     3. Preaching by John the Baptist (3:22–36)

   E. Presentation in Samaria (4:1–42)

     1. Witness to the Samaritan woman (4:1–26)

     2. Witness to the disciples (4:27–38)

     3. Witness to the Samaritans (4:39–42)

   F. Presentation in Galilee (4:43–54)

     1. Reception by the Galileans (4:43–45)

     2. Second sign: healing the nobleman's son (4:46–54)

III. THE OPPOSITION TO THE SON OF GOD (5:1–12:50)

   A. Opposition at the Feast in Jerusalem (5:1–47)

     1. Third sign: healing the paralytic (5:1–9)

     2. Rejection by the Jews (5:10–47)

   B. Opposition During Passover (6:1–71)

     1. Fourth sign: feeding the 5,000 (6:1–14)

     2. Fifth sign: walking on water (6:15–21)

     3. Bread of Life discourse (6:22–71)

C. Opposition at the Feast of Tabernacles (7:1–10:21)
    1. The opposition (7:1–8:59)
    2. Sixth sign: healing the man born blind (9:1–10:21)
D. Opposition at the Feast of Dedication (10:22–42)
E. Opposition at Bethany (11:1–12:11)
    1. Seventh sign: raising of Lazarus (11:1–44)
    2. Pharisees plot to kill Christ (11:45–57)
    3. Mary anointing Christ (12:1–11)
F. Opposition in Jerusalem (12:12–50)
    1. The triumphal entry (12:12–22)
    2. The discourse on faith and rejection (12:23–50)

IV. THE PREPARATION OF THE DISCIPLES BY THE SON OF GOD (13:1–17:26)
A. In the Upper Room (13:1–14:31)
    1. Washing feet (13:1–20)
    2. Announcing the betrayal (13:21–30)
    3. Discourse on Christ's departure (13:31–14:31)
B. On the Way to the Garden (15:1–17:26)
    1. Instructing the disciples (15:1–16:33)
    2. Interceding with the Father (17:1–26)

V. THE EXECUTION OF THE SON OF GOD (18:1–19:37)
A. The Rejection of Christ (18:1–19:16)
    1. His arrest (18:1–11)
    2. His trials (18:12–19:16)
B. The Crucifixion of Christ (19:17–37)

VI. THE RESURRECTION OF THE SON OF GOD (19:38–21:23)
A. The Burial of Christ (19:38–42)
B. The Resurrection of Christ (20:1–10)
C. The Appearances of Christ (20:11–21:23)
    1. To Mary Magdalene (20:11–18)
    2. To the disciples without Thomas (20:19–25)
    3. To the disciples with Thomas (20:26–29)
    4. Statement of purpose for the Gospel (20:30,31)
    5. To the disciples (21:1–14)
    6. To Peter (21:15–23)

VII. CONCLUSION (21:24,25)

The Eternal Word

1 In the beginning was the Word, and the Word was with God, and the Word was God. [2]He was in the beginning with God. [3]All things were made through Him, and without Him nothing was made that was made. [4]In Him was life, and the life was the light of men. [5]And the light shines in the darkness, and the darkness did not comprehend[a] it.

> **1:1 In the beginning.** This phrase parallels Gen. 1. **the Word.** John borrowed this term from both the OT (Gen. 1:3) and Greek philosophy and made it refer to Jesus. **the Word was with God.** The Word, being the Second Person of the Trinity, was in intimate fellowship with the Father throughout eternity. **was God.** The Word had all the essence and attributes of deity: Jesus was and is fully God. Though He became fully human, He did not lose any of His deity.

John's Witness: The True Light

[6]There was a man sent from God, whose name was John. [7]This man came for a witness, to bear witness of the Light, that all through him might believe. [8]He was not that Light, but was sent to bear witness of that Light. [9]That was the true Light which gives light to every man coming into the world.[a]

[10]He was in the world, and the world was made through Him, and the world did not know Him. [11]He came to His own,[a] and His own[b] did not receive Him. [12]But as many as received Him, to them He gave the right to become children of God, to those who believe in His name: [13]who were born, not of blood, nor of the will of the flesh, nor of the will of man, but of God.

The Word Becomes Flesh

[14]And the Word became flesh and dwelt among us, and we beheld His glory, the glory as of the only begotten of the Father, full of grace and truth.

[15]John bore witness of Him and cried out, saying, "This was He of whom I said, 'He who comes after me is preferred before me, for He was before me.' "

[16]And[a] of His fullness we have all received, and grace for grace. [17]For the law was given through Moses, but grace and truth came through Jesus Christ. [18]No one has seen God at any time. The only begotten Son,[a] who is in the bosom of the Father, He has declared Him.

> **1:14 the Word became flesh.** Christ became human; the infinite and eternal took on finite time and space. Christ did not cease to be God, but became God in human flesh. **dwelt.** We can compare this term to the OT tabernacle where God dwelt with Israel before the temple was constructed (Ex. 25:8). In the NT, God chose a more personal way to dwell among His people—the form of His Son.

A Voice in the Wilderness

[19]Now this is the testimony of John, when the Jews sent priests and Levites from Jerusalem to ask him, "Who are you?"

[20]He confessed, and did not deny, but confessed, "I am not the Christ."

[21]And they asked him, "What then? Are you Elijah?"

He said, "I am not."

"Are you the Prophet?"

And he answered, "No."

[22]Then they said to him, "Who are you, that we may give an answer to those who sent us? What do you say about yourself?"

[23]He said: "I am

'The voice of one crying in the wilderness:

"Make straight the way of the LORD," ' [a]

as the prophet Isaiah said."

> **1:23** John quoted and applied Is. 40:3 to himself (see Matt. 3:3). The words of Isaiah foreshadowed a time of Israel's return to their God from spiritual darkness and alienation through the redemption of their Messiah (see Rom. 12:25–27).

[24]Now those who were sent were from the Pharisees. [25]And they asked him, saying, "Why then do you baptize if you are not the Christ, nor Elijah, nor the Prophet?"

1:5 [a]Or overcome 1:9 [a]Or That was the true Light which, coming into the world, gives light to every man. 1:11 [a]That is, His own things or domain [b]That is, His own people 1:16 [a]NU-Text reads For. 1:18 [a]NU-Text reads only begotten God. 1:23 [a]Isaiah 40:3

²⁶John answered them, saying, "I baptize with water, but there stands One among you whom you do not know. ²⁷It is He who, coming after me, is preferred before me, whose sandal strap I am not worthy to loose."

²⁸These things were done in Bethabara[a] beyond the Jordan, where John was baptizing.

The Lamb of God

²⁹The next day John saw Jesus coming toward him, and said, "Behold! The Lamb of God who takes away the sin of the world! ³⁰This is He of whom I said, 'After me comes a Man who is preferred before me, for He was before me.' ³¹I did not know Him; but that He should be revealed to Israel, therefore I came baptizing with water."

1:29 The Lamb of God. The image of a lamb taking away sin was very familiar to the Jews, primarily through the sacrificial rituals and Passover celebration that had been instituted by God (Ex. 12:1–36; Lev. 14:12–21). John the Baptist, here, referred to the ultimate sacrifice of Jesus on the cross for the atonement of the world's sins.

³²And John bore witness, saying, "I saw the Spirit descending from heaven like a dove, and He remained upon Him. ³³I did not know Him, but He who sent me to baptize with water said to me, 'Upon whom you see the Spirit descending, and remaining on Him, this is He who baptizes with the Holy Spirit.' ³⁴And I have seen and testified that this is the Son of God."

1:34 the Son of God. John used this phrase as a title pointing to the unique oneness and intimacy that Jesus has with God the Father. The term is also used to denote His deity as the Messiah (v. 49).

The First Disciples

³⁵Again, the next day, John stood with two of his disciples. ³⁶And looking at Jesus as He walked, he said, "Behold the Lamb of God!"

³⁷The two disciples heard him speak, and they followed Jesus. ³⁸Then Jesus turned, and seeing them following, said to them, "What do you seek?"

They said to Him, "Rabbi" (which is to say, when translated, Teacher), "where are You staying?"

³⁹He said to them, "Come and see." They came and saw where He was staying, and remained with Him that day (now it was about the tenth hour).

⁴⁰One of the two who heard John *speak*, and followed Him, was Andrew, Simon Peter's brother. ⁴¹He first found his own brother Simon, and said to him, "We have found the Messiah" (which is translated, the Christ). ⁴²And he brought him to Jesus.

Now when Jesus looked at him, He said, "You are Simon the son of Jonah.[a] You shall be called Cephas" (which is translated, A Stone).

1:41 Messiah. Meaning "Anointed One," this title came to refer to the prophesied "Coming One" in His role as prophet, priest, and king. The term "Christ," a Greek word that comes from a verb meaning "to anoint," is used in translating the Hebrew term. The words "Messiah" and "Christ" are titles, not personal names, for Jesus.

Philip and Nathanael

⁴³The following day Jesus wanted to go to Galilee, and He found Philip and said to him, "Follow Me." ⁴⁴Now Philip was from Bethsaida, the city of Andrew and Peter. ⁴⁵Philip found Nathanael and said to him, "We have found Him of whom Moses in the law, and also the prophets, wrote—Jesus of Nazareth, the son of Joseph."

⁴⁶And Nathanael said to him, "Can anything good come out of Nazareth?"

Philip said to him, "Come and see."

⁴⁷Jesus saw Nathanael coming toward Him, and said of him, "Behold, an Israelite indeed, in whom is no deceit!"

⁴⁸Nathanael said to Him, "How do You know me?"

Jesus answered and said to him, "Before Philip called you, when you were under the fig tree, I saw you."

⁴⁹Nathanael answered and said to Him, "Rabbi, You are the Son of God! You are the King of Israel!"

⁵⁰Jesus answered and said to him, "Because I said to you, 'I saw you under the fig tree,' do you believe? You will see greater

---

1:28 [a]NU-Text and M-Text read *Bethany*.   1:42 [a]NU-Text reads *John*.

things than these." ⁵¹And He said to him, "Most assuredly, I say to you, hereafter*a* you shall see heaven open, and the angels of God ascending and descending upon the Son of Man."

Water Turned to Wine

2 On the third day there was a wedding in Cana of Galilee, and the mother of Jesus was there. ²Now both Jesus and His disciples were invited to the wedding. ³And when they ran out of wine, the mother of Jesus said to Him, "They have no wine."

⁴Jesus said to her, "Woman, what does your concern have to do with Me? My hour has not yet come."

⁵His mother said to the servants, "Whatever He says to you, do *it*."

⁶Now there were set there six waterpots of stone, according to the manner of purification of the Jews, containing twenty or thirty gallons apiece. ⁷Jesus said to them, "Fill the waterpots with water." And they filled them up to the brim. ⁸And He said to them, "Draw *some* out now, and take *it* to

the master of the feast." And they took *it*. ⁹When the master of the feast had tasted the water that was made wine, and did not know where it came from (but the servants who had drawn the water knew), the master of the feast called the bridegroom. ¹⁰And he said to him, "Every man at the beginning sets out the good wine, and when the *guests* have well drunk, then the inferior. You have kept the good wine until now!"

¹¹This beginning of signs Jesus did in Cana of Galilee, and manifested His glory; and His disciples believed in Him.

¹²After this He went down to Capernaum, He, His mother, His brothers, and His disciples; and they did not stay there many days.

Jesus Cleanses the Temple

¹³Now the Passover of the Jews was at hand, and Jesus went up to Jerusalem. ¹⁴And He found in the temple those who sold oxen and sheep and doves, and the money changers doing business. ¹⁵When He had made a whip of cords, He drove them all out of the temple, with the sheep and the oxen, and poured out the changers' money and overturned the tables. ¹⁶And He said to those who sold doves, "Take these things away! Do not make My Father's

1:51 *a*NU-Text omits *hereafter*.

THE SEVEN SIGNS

Turns water into wine (John 2:1–12) .... Jesus is the Source of life.
Heals a nobleman's son (John 4:46–54) .... Jesus is Master over distance.
Heals a lame man at the pool of Bethesda (John 5:1–17) .... Jesus is Master over time.
Feeds 5,000 (John 6:1–14) .... Jesus is the Bread of life.
Walks on water, stills a storm (John 6:15–21) .... Jesus is Master over nature.
Heals a man blind from birth (John 9:1–41) .... Jesus is the Light of the world.
Raises Lazarus from the dead (John 11:17–45) .... Jesus has power over death.

house a house of merchandise!" [17]Then His disciples remembered that it was written, *"Zeal for Your house has eaten[a] Me up."[b]*

[18]So the Jews answered and said to Him, "What sign do You show to us, since You do these things?"

[19]Jesus answered and said to them, "Destroy this temple, and in three days I will raise it up."

[20]Then the Jews said, "It has taken forty-six years to build this temple, and will You raise it up in three days?"

[21]But He was speaking of the temple of His body. [22]Therefore, when He had risen from the dead, His disciples remembered that He had said this to them;[a] and they believed the Scripture and the word which Jesus had said.

The Discerner of Hearts

[23]Now when He was in Jerusalem at the Passover, during the feast, many believed in His name when they saw the signs which He did. [24]But Jesus did not commit Himself to them, because He knew all *men*, [25]and had no need that anyone should testify of man, for He knew what was in man.

> **2:23,24 many believed in His name...But Jesus did not commit Himself.** This verse subtly revealed the true nature of belief from a biblical standpoint. Jesus made it His habit not to wholeheartedly "commit" Himself to the people because He knew their hearts. He looked for genuine conversion rather than enthusiasm for the miraculous.

The New Birth

3 There was a man of the Pharisees named Nicodemus, a ruler of the Jews. [2]This man came to Jesus by night and said to Him, "Rabbi, we know that You are a teacher come from God; for no one can do these signs that You do unless God is with him."

[3]Jesus answered and said to him, "Most

> **3:3 born again.** Jesus read Nicodemus' heart and his need for spiritual transformation through the Holy Spirit. New birth is an act of God whereby eternal life is given to the believer (2 Cor. 5:17).

assuredly, I say to you, unless one is born again, he cannot see the kingdom of God."

[4]Nicodemus said to Him, "How can a man be born when he is old? Can he enter a second time into his mother's womb and be born?"

[5]Jesus answered, "Most assuredly, I say to you, unless one is born of water and the Spirit, he cannot enter the kingdom of God. [6]That which is born of the flesh is flesh, and that which is born of the Spirit is spirit. [7]Do not marvel that I said to you, 'You must be born again.' [8]The wind blows where it wishes, and you hear the sound of it, but cannot tell where it comes from and where it goes. So is everyone who is born of the Spirit."

[9]Nicodemus answered and said to Him, "How can these things be?"

[10]Jesus answered and said to him, "Are you the teacher of Israel, and do not know these things? [11]Most assuredly, I say to you, We speak what We know and testify what We have seen, and you do not receive Our witness. [12]If I have told you earthly things and you do not believe, how will you believe if I tell you heavenly things? [13]No one has ascended to heaven but He who came down from heaven, *that is*, the Son of Man who is in heaven.[a] [14]And as Moses lifted up the serpent in the wilderness, even so must the Son of Man be lifted up, [15]that whoever believes in Him should not perish but[a] have eternal life. [16]For God so loved the world that He gave His only begotten Son, that whoever believes in Him should not perish but have everlasting life. [17]For God did not send His Son into the world to condemn the world, but that the world through Him might be saved.

> **3:14 so must the Son of Man be lifted up.** This is a veiled prediction of Jesus' death on a cross. Jesus refers to the story in Num. 21:5–9. The Israelites, plagued by snakebites, were instructed to look at a bronze serpent lifted up on Moses' staff and they would be healed. As Moses lifted up the snake on the pole so that those who looked upon it might live physically, so those who look to Christ, who was "lifted up" for the sins of the world, will live spiritually and eternally.

2:17 [a]NU-Text and M-Text read *will eat.*   [b]Psalm 69:9   2:22 [a]NU-Text and M-Text omit *to them.*
3:13 [a]NU-Text omits *who is in heaven.*   3:15 [a]NU-Text omits *not perish but.*

[18]"He who believes in Him is not condemned; but he who does not believe is condemned already, because he has not believed in the name of the only begotten Son of God. [19]And this is the condemnation, that the light has come into the world, and men loved darkness rather than light, because their deeds were evil. [20]For everyone practicing evil hates the light and does not come to the light, lest his deeds should be exposed. [21]But he who does the truth comes to the light, that his deeds may be clearly seen, that they have been done in God."

John the Baptist Exalts Christ

[22]After these things Jesus and His disciples came into the land of Judea, and there He remained with them and baptized. [23]Now John also was baptizing in Aenon near Salim, because there was much water there. And they came and were baptized. [24]For John had not yet been thrown into prison.

3:24 John had not yet been thrown into prison. This provides another indication that John supplemented the synoptic gospels (Matthew, Mark, and Luke) by giving additional information that helps one understand the movements of John the Baptist and Jesus. This phrase fills the slot between Jesus' baptism and temptation and John the Baptist's imprisonment.

[25]Then there arose a dispute between *some* of John's disciples and the Jews about purification. [26]And they came to John and said to him, "Rabbi, He who was with you beyond the Jordan, to whom you have testified—behold, He is baptizing, and all are coming to Him!"

[27]John answered and said, "A man can receive nothing unless it has been given to him from heaven. [28]You yourselves bear me witness, that I said, 'I am not the Christ,' but, 'I have been sent before Him.' [29]He who has the bride is the bridegroom; but the friend of the bridegroom, who stands and hears him, rejoices greatly because of the bridegroom's voice. Therefore this joy of mine is fulfilled. [30]He must increase, but I *must* decrease. [31]He who comes from above is above all; he who is of the earth is earthly and speaks of the earth. He who comes from heaven is above all. [32]And what

He has seen and heard, that He testifies; and no one receives His testimony. [33]He who has received His testimony has certified that God is true. [34]For He whom God has sent speaks the words of God, for God does not give the Spirit by measure. [35]The Father loves the Son, and has given all things into His hand. [36]He who believes in the Son has everlasting life; and he who does not believe the Son shall not see life, but the wrath of God abides on him."

3:29 bridegroom...friend of bridegroom. Here John gives his understanding of his own role through the use of a parable. The "friend" is the equivalent of the best man at a wedding. This friend found his greatest joy in watching the marriage ceremony proceed without problems. Most likely, John was alluding to OT passages where faithful Israel is depicted as the bride of the Lord (Is. 62:4,5).

A Samaritan Woman Meets Her Messiah

4 Therefore, when the Lord knew that the Pharisees had heard that Jesus made and baptized more disciples than John [2](though Jesus Himself did not baptize, but His disciples), [3]He left Judea and departed again to Galilee. [4]But He needed to go through Samaria.

[5]So He came to a city of Samaria which is called Sychar, near the plot of ground that Jacob gave to his son Joseph. [6]Now Jacob's well was there. Jesus therefore, being wearied from *His* journey, sat thus by the well. It was about the sixth hour.

[7]A woman of Samaria came to draw water. Jesus said to her, "Give Me a drink." [8]For His disciples had gone away into the city to buy food.

4:7 A woman of Samaria came to draw water. Women usually came in groups to collect water, either early or late in the day. The timing and nature of this woman's trip may indicate public shame (vv. 16–19). **"Give Me a drink."** It was a breach of social custom for a man to speak to a woman in public, let alone ask her for something. Further, a rabbi did not hold conversations with women of ill-repute (v. 18). Added to that, Jews and Samaritans generally treated one another with great animosity.

[9]Then the woman of Samaria said to Him, "How is it that You, being a Jew, ask a drink from me, a Samaritan woman?" For Jews have no dealings with Samaritans.

¹⁰Jesus answered and said to her, "If you knew the gift of God, and who it is who says to you, 'Give Me a drink,' you would have asked Him, and He would have given you living water."

¹¹The woman said to Him, "Sir, You have nothing to draw with, and the well is deep. Where then do You get that living water? ¹²Are You greater than our father Jacob, who gave us the well, and drank from it himself, as well as his sons and his livestock?"

¹³Jesus answered and said to her, "Whoever drinks of this water will thirst again, ¹⁴but whoever drinks of the water that I shall give him will never thirst. But the water that I shall give him will become in him a fountain of water springing up into everlasting life."

¹⁵The woman said to Him, "Sir, give me this water, that I may not thirst, nor come here to draw."

¹⁶Jesus said to her, "Go, call your husband, and come here."

¹⁷The woman answered and said, "I have no husband."

Jesus said to her, "You have well said, 'I have no husband,' ¹⁸for you have had five husbands, and the one whom you now have is not your husband; in that you spoke truly."

¹⁹The woman said to Him, "Sir, I perceive that You are a prophet. ²⁰Our fathers worshiped on this mountain, and you Jews say that in Jerusalem is the place where one ought to worship."

4:20 on this mountain. The Jews and Samaritans both recognized that God had commanded their forefathers to set apart a place to worship Him (Deut. 12:5). The Jews recognized the entire canon and chose Jerusalem (2 Sam. 7:5–13). The Samaritans, acknowledging only the Pentateuch, chose Mount Gerizim because it was the first place where Abraham built an altar to the Lord (Gen. 12:6,7).

²¹Jesus said to her, "Woman, believe Me, the hour is coming when you will neither on this mountain, nor in Jerusalem, worship the Father. ²²You worship what you do not know; we know what we worship, for salvation is of the Jews. ²³But the hour is coming, and now is, when the true worshipers will worship the Father in spirit and truth; for the Father is seeking such to worship Him. ²⁴God is Spirit, and those who worship Him must worship in spirit and truth."

4:24 in spirit and truth. Jesus' point is that a person must worship not just externally, through ceremonial practices, but also inwardly ("in spirit") with the proper heart attitude. This worship must be done in a way consistent with the revealed Scripture and centered on the "Word made flesh" who ultimately revealed His Father (14:6).

²⁵The woman said to Him, "I know that Messiah is coming" (who is called Christ). "When He comes, He will tell us all things."

²⁶Jesus said to her, "I who speak to you am He."

The Whitened Harvest

²⁷And at this point His disciples came, and they marveled that He talked with a woman; yet no one said, "What do You seek?" or, "Why are You talking with her?"

²⁸The woman then left her waterpot, went her way into the city, and said to the men, ²⁹"Come, see a Man who told me all things that I ever did. Could this be the Christ?" ³⁰Then they went out of the city and came to Him.

³¹In the meantime His disciples urged Him, saying, "Rabbi, eat."

³²But He said to them, "I have food to eat of which you do not know."

³³Therefore the disciples said to one another, "Has anyone brought Him anything to eat?"

³⁴Jesus said to them, "My food is to do the will of Him who sent Me, and to finish His work. ³⁵Do you not say, 'There are still four months and then comes the harvest'? Behold, I say to you, lift up your eyes and look at the fields, for they are already white for harvest! ³⁶And he who reaps receives wages, and gathers fruit for eternal life, that both he who sows and he who reaps may rejoice together. ³⁷For in this the saying is

4:36–38 The Lord's call to the disciples to do the work of evangelism contains promises of reward ("wages"), fruit that produces eternal joy, and a mutual partnership with shared privileges.

true: 'One sows and another reaps.' ³⁸I sent you to reap that for which you have not labored; others have labored, and you have entered into their labors."

The Savior of the World

³⁹And many of the Samaritans of that city believed in Him because of the word of the woman who testified, "He told me all that I *ever* did." ⁴⁰So when the Samaritans had come to Him, they urged Him to stay with them; and He stayed there two days. ⁴¹And many more believed because of His own word.

⁴²Then they said to the woman, "Now we believe, not because of what you said, for we ourselves have heard *Him* and we know that this is indeed the Christ,ᵃ the Savior of the world."

Welcome at Galilee

⁴³Now after the two days He departed from there and went to Galilee. ⁴⁴For Jesus Himself testified that a prophet has no honor in his own country. ⁴⁵So when He came to Galilee, the Galileans received Him, having seen all the things He did in Jerusalem at the feast; for they also had gone to the feast.

A Nobleman's Son Healed

⁴⁶So Jesus came again to Cana of Galilee where He had made the water wine. And there was a certain nobleman whose son was sick at Capernaum. ⁴⁷When he heard that Jesus had come out of Judea into Galilee, he went to Him and implored Him to come down and heal his son, for he was at the point of death. ⁴⁸Then Jesus said to him, "Unless you *people* see signs and wonders, you will by no means believe."

⁴⁹The nobleman said to Him, "Sir, come down before my child dies!"

> **4:47 implored Him.** The man repeatedly asked Jesus to heal his son. He approached Jesus out of desperation, but had little appreciation or understanding of who Jesus was. In light of v. 46, the nobleman's motivation was probably based on Jesus' reputation as a miracle worker, not on an understanding that Jesus was the Messiah.

⁵⁰Jesus said to him, "Go your way; your son lives." So the man believed the word that Jesus spoke to him, and he went his way. ⁵¹And as he was now going down, his servants met him and told *him*, saying, "Your son lives!"

⁵²Then he inquired of them the hour when he got better. And they said to him, "Yesterday at the seventh hour the fever left him." ⁵³So the father knew that *it was* at the same hour in which Jesus said to him, "Your son lives." And he himself believed, and his whole household.

⁵⁴This again *is* the second sign Jesus did when He had come out of Judea into Galilee.

A Man Healed at the Pool of Bethesda

5 After this there was a feast of the Jews, and Jesus went up to Jerusalem. ²Now there is in Jerusalem by the Sheep *Gate* a pool, which is called in Hebrew, Bethesda,ᵃ having five porches. ³In these lay a great multitude of sick people, blind, lame, paralyzed, waiting for the moving of the water. ⁴For an angel went down at a certain time into the pool and stirred up the water; then whoever stepped in first, after the stirring of the water, was made well of whatever disease he had.ᵃ ⁵Now a certain man was there who had an infirmity thirty-eight years. ⁶When Jesus saw him lying there, and knew that he already had been *in that condition* a long time, He said to him, "Do you want to be made well?"

⁷The sick man answered Him, "Sir, I have no man to put me into the pool when the water is stirred up; but while I am coming, another steps down before me."

⁸Jesus said to him, "Rise, take up your bed and walk." ⁹And immediately the man was made well, took up his bed, and walked.

And that day was the Sabbath. ¹⁰The Jews therefore said to him who was cured, "It is the Sabbath; it is not lawful for you to carry your bed."

¹¹He answered them, "He who made me well said to me, 'Take up your bed and walk.'"

¹²Then they asked him, "Who is the Man

4:42 ᵃNU-Text omits *the Christ*.   5:2 ᵃNU-Text reads *Bethzatha*.   5:4 ᵃNU-Text omits *waiting for the moving of the water* at the end of verse 3, and all of verse 4.

5:10,11 The OT had forbidden work on the Sabbath, but did not stipulate what activities were considered "work" (Ex. 20:8–11). Rabbinical oral tradition seems to have gone further than the assumption that work meant one's employment. The rabbis developed extra rules that included carrying anything from one place to another. This is the law that the man broke, not the OT law.

who said to you, 'Take up your bed and walk'?" [13]But the one who was healed did not know who it was, for Jesus had withdrawn, a multitude being in *that* place. [14]Afterward Jesus found him in the temple, and said to him, "See, you have been made well. Sin no more, lest a worse thing come upon you."

[15]The man departed and told the Jews that it was Jesus who had made him well.

Honor the Father and the Son

[16]For this reason the Jews persecuted Jesus, and sought to kill Him,[a] because He had done these things on the Sabbath. [17]But Jesus answered them, "My Father has been working until now, and I have been working."

5:17–47 These verses explain why Jesus confronted the Jews' religious hypocrisy. He declared His deity with 5 claims to equality with God: He is equal with God in person (5:17,18), in works (5:19), in power and sovereignty (5:20–23), in judgment (5:24–30), and in honor (5:31–47).

[18]Therefore the Jews sought all the more to kill Him, because He not only broke the Sabbath, but also said that God was His Father, making Himself equal with God. [19]Then Jesus answered and said to them, "Most assuredly, I say to you, the Son can do nothing of Himself, but what He sees the Father do; for whatever He does, the Son also does in like manner. [20]For the Father loves the Son, and shows Him all things that He Himself does; and He will show Him greater works than these, that you may marvel. [21]For as the Father raises the dead and gives life to *them*, even so the Son gives life to whom He will. [22]For the Father judges no one, but has committed all judgment to the Son, [23]that all should honor the Son just as they honor the Fa-

ther. He who does not honor the Son does not honor the Father who sent Him.

Life and Judgment Are Through the Son

[24]"Most assuredly, I say to you, he who hears My word and believes in Him who sent Me has everlasting life, and shall not come into judgment, but has passed from death into life. [25]Most assuredly, I say to you, the hour is coming, and now is, when the dead will hear the voice of the Son of God; and those who hear will live. [26]For as the Father has life in Himself, so He has granted the Son to have life in Himself,

5:24 passed from death into life. Jesus gives life to whomever He desires. Those who hear the Word and believe in the Father and the Son receive eternal life and will never be condemned (Rom.8:1).

[27]and has given Him authority to execute judgment also, because He is the Son of Man. [28]Do not marvel at this; for the hour is coming in which all who are in the graves will hear His voice [29]and come forth—those who have done good, to the resurrection of life, and those who have done evil, to the resurrection of condemnation. [30]I can of Myself do nothing. As I hear, I judge; and My judgment is righteous, because I do not seek My own will but the will of the Father who sent Me.

5:29 those who have done good...evil. Jesus taught that it is believing in the Son, thus receiving a new nature, that produces good works, not that good works earn salvation (James 2:14–20). The essence of doing evil is rejecting the Son, which leads to hatred of the light and evil deeds. One's works are merely indicative of the state of one's nature.

The Fourfold Witness

[31]"If I bear witness of Myself, My witness is not true. [32]There is another who bears witness of Me, and I know that the witness which He witnesses of Me is true. [33]You have sent to John, and he has borne witness to the truth. [34]Yet I do not receive testimony from man, but I say these things that you may be saved. [35]He was the burning and shining lamp, and you were willing for a time to rejoice in his light. [36]But I have a

5:16 [a]NU-Text omits *and sought to kill Him.*

greater witness than John's; for the works which the Father has given Me to finish—the very works that I do—bear witness of Me, that the Father has sent Me. [37]And the Father Himself, who sent Me, has testified of Me. You have neither heard His voice at any time, nor seen His form. [38]But you do not have His word abiding in you, because whom He sent, Him you do not believe. [39]You search the Scriptures, for in them you think you have eternal life; and these are they which testify of Me. [40]But you are not willing to come to Me that you may have life.

[41]"I do not receive honor from men. [42]But I know you, that you do not have the love of God in you. [43]I have come in My Father's name, and you do not receive Me; if another comes in his own name, him you will receive. [44]How can you believe, who receive honor from one another, and do not seek the honor that comes from the only God? [45]Do not think that I shall accuse you to the Father; there is one who accuses you—Moses, in whom you trust. [46]For if you believed Moses, you would believe Me; for he wrote about Me. [47]But if you do not believe his writings, how will you believe My words?"

> **6:1–14** This is the only miracle recorded in all 4 gospels (Matt. 14:13–23; Mark 6:30–46; Luke 9:10–17). This miracle demonstrated that Jesus was the Messiah and had incredible power. It also set the stage for Jesus to refer to Himself as the "bread of life" (vv. 22–40). Interestingly, this miracle of the bread, coupled with the turning of water into wine (2:1–10), speaks of the main elements in the Lord's supper (v. 53).

Feeding the Five Thousand

6 After these things Jesus went over the Sea of Galilee, which is the Sea of Tiberias. [2]Then a great multitude followed Him, because they saw His signs which He performed on those who were diseased. [3]And Jesus went up on the mountain, and there He sat with His disciples.

[4]Now the Passover, a feast of the Jews, was near. [5]Then Jesus lifted up His eyes, and seeing a great multitude coming toward Him, He said to Philip, "Where shall we buy bread, that these may eat?" [6]But

this He said to test him, for He Himself knew what He would do.

[7]Philip answered Him, "Two hundred denarii worth of bread is not sufficient for them, that every one of them may have a little."

[8]One of His disciples, Andrew, Simon Peter's brother, said to Him, [9]"There is a lad here who has five barley loaves and two small fish, but what are they among so many?"

[10]Then Jesus said, "Make the people sit down." Now there was much grass in the place. So the men sat down, in number about five thousand. [11]And Jesus took the loaves, and when He had given thanks He distributed them to the disciples, and the disciples[a] to those sitting down; and likewise of the fish, as much as they wanted. [12]So when they were filled, He said to His disciples, "Gather up the fragments that remain, so that nothing is lost." [13]Therefore they gathered them up, and filled twelve baskets with the fragments of the five barley loaves which were left over by those who had eaten. [14]Then those men, when they had seen the sign that Jesus did, said, "This is truly the Prophet who is to come into the world."

Jesus Walks on the Sea

[15]Therefore when Jesus perceived that they were about to come and take Him by force to make Him king, He departed again to the mountain by Himself alone.

> **6:15 take Him by force to make Him king.** Jesus dismissed the disciples and withdrew from the crowd because He, through supernatural knowledge, knew the crowd's intention to make Him king because He had healed and fed them. He knew that this was not God's will.

[16]Now when evening came, His disciples went down to the sea, [17]got into the boat, and went over the sea toward Capernaum. And it was already dark, and Jesus had not come to them. [18]Then the sea arose because a great wind was blowing. [19]So when they had rowed about three or four miles,[a] they saw Jesus walking on the sea and drawing near the boat; and they were afraid. [20]But

---

6:11 [a]NU-Text omits to the disciples, and the disciples.   6:19 [a]Literally twenty-five or thirty stadia

He said to them, "It is I; do not be afraid."
²¹Then they willingly received Him into the
boat, and immediately the boat was at the
land where they were going.

6:22–58 This is Jesus' famous discourse on the
Bread of life. This reinforces John's theme of Jesus
being the Messiah and Son of God (20:30,31). John
also is intentional about correctly defining Jesus as
the Son of God who came to save the world from sin
(3:16); He was not just a miracle worker.

The Bread from Heaven

²²On the following day, when the people
who were standing on the other side of the
sea saw that there was no other boat there,
except that one which His disciples had
entered,ᵃ and that Jesus had not entered
the boat with His disciples, but His disciples had gone away alone—²³however, other
boats came from Tiberias, near the place
where they ate bread after the Lord had giv-
en thanks—²⁴when the people therefore
saw that Jesus was not there, nor His disciples, they also got into boats and came to
Capernaum, seeking Jesus. ²⁵And when
they found Him on the other side of the
sea, they said to Him, "Rabbi, when did
You come here?"

²⁶Jesus answered them and said, "Most
assuredly, I say to you, you seek Me, not
because you saw the signs, but because you
ate of the loaves and were filled. ²⁷Do not
labor for the food which perishes, but for
the food which endures to everlasting life,
which the Son of Man will give you, because God the Father has set His seal on
Him."

²⁸Then they said to Him, "What shall we
do, that we may work the works of God?"

²⁹Jesus answered and said to them, "This
is the work of God, that you believe in Him
whom He sent."

³⁰Therefore they said to Him, "What sign
will You perform then, that we may see it
and believe You? What work will You do?
³¹Our fathers ate the manna in the desert;
as it is written, 'He gave them bread from
heaven to eat.' "ᵃ

³²Then Jesus said to them, "Most assuredly, I say to you, Moses did not give you

6:31 Our fathers ate the manna. The crowd seems
to say that Jesus' miracle was small compared to
what Moses had done in the desert. In order for them
to believe in Jesus, they would need to see Him feed
the nation of Israel as God had during the Exodus (Ex.
16:11–36). The blindness of the crowd caused them
not to see that Jesus was referring to Himself as spiritual bread. They thought He was talking about physical bread.

the bread from heaven, but My Father gives
you the true bread from heaven. ³³For the
bread of God is He who comes down from
heaven and gives life to the world."

³⁴Then they said to Him, "Lord, give us
this bread always."

³⁵And Jesus said to them, "I am the bread
of life. He who comes to Me shall never
hunger, and he who believes in Me shall
never thirst. ³⁶But I said to you that you
have seen Me and yet do not believe. ³⁷All
that the Father gives Me will come to Me,
and the one who comes to Me I will by no
means cast out. ³⁸For I have come down
from heaven, not to do My own will, but
the will of Him who sent Me. ³⁹This is the
will of the Father who sent Me, that of all
He has given Me I should lose nothing, but
should raise it up at the last day. ⁴⁰And this
is the will of Him who sent Me, that every-

THE "I AM" STATEMENTS

Twenty-three times in all we find our Lord's
meaningful "I AM" (ego eimi, Gr.) in the Greek
text of this gospel (4:26; 6:20,35,41,48,51;
8:12,18,24,28,58; 10:7,9,11,14; 11:25; 13:19; 14:6;
15:1,5; 18:5,6,8). In several of these, He joins
His "I AM" with seven tremendous metaphors
which are expressive of His saving relationship toward the world.

"I AM the Bread of life" (6:35,41,48,51).
"I AM the Light of the world" (8:12).
"I AM the Door of the sheep" (10:7,9).
"I AM the Good Shepherd" (10:11,14).
"I AM the Resurrection and the Life" (11:25).
"I AM the Way, the Truth, and the Life" (14:6).
"I AM the true Vine" (15:1,5).

6:22 ᵃNU-Text omits *that* and *which His disciples had entered.*   **6:31** ᵃExodus 16:4; Nehemiah 9:15;
Psalm 78:24

one who sees the Son and believes in Him may have everlasting life; and I will raise him up at the last day."

Rejected by His Own

⁴¹The Jews then complained about Him, because He said, "I am the bread which came down from heaven." ⁴²And they said, "Is not this Jesus, the son of Joseph, whose father and mother we know? How is it then that He says, 'I have come down from heaven'?"

> **6:41 The Jews.** In this gospel, "the Jews" often refers to those Jews who were hostile toward Christ (obviously, not all of the Jews were hostile). It is ironic that the very people who should have recognized and accepted Jesus were blind and hardened toward Him (see 12:37–40). **complained.** This reaction of the synagogue crowd was comparable to that of the Israelites in the wilderness when they were provided manna to eat (see Ex. 16:2,8,9).

⁴³Jesus therefore answered and said to them, "Do not murmur among yourselves. ⁴⁴No one can come to Me unless the Father who sent Me draws him; and I will raise him up at the last day. ⁴⁵It is written in the prophets, *'And they shall all be taught by God.'ᵃ* Therefore everyone who has heard and learnedᵇ from the Father comes to Me. ⁴⁶Not that anyone has seen the Father, except He who is from God; He has seen the Father. ⁴⁷Most assuredly, I say to you, he who believes in Meᵃ has everlasting life. ⁴⁸I am the bread of life. ⁴⁹Your fathers ate the manna in the wilderness, and are dead. ⁵⁰This is the bread which comes down from heaven, that one may eat of it and not die. ⁵¹I am the living bread which came down from heaven. If anyone eats of this bread, he will live forever; and the bread that I shall give is My flesh, which I shall give for the life of the world."

> **6:49,50** The manna had been sent from heaven, but it was still merely earthly bread that could not provide eternal life. The "Bread of life," however, came down from heaven in the person of Jesus to bring salvation to the world. The contrast centers on the irrefutable fact that all of the people who ate manna in the desert died.

⁵²The Jews therefore quarreled among themselves, saying, "How can this Man give us *His* flesh to eat?"

⁵³Then Jesus said to them, "Most assuredly, I say to you, unless you eat the flesh of the Son of Man and drink His blood, you have no life in you. ⁵⁴Whoever eats My flesh and drinks My blood has eternal life, and I will raise him up at the last day. ⁵⁵For My flesh is food indeed,ᵃ and My blood is drink indeed. ⁵⁶He who eats My flesh and drinks My blood abides in Me, and I in him. ⁵⁷As the living Father sent Me, and I live because of the Father, so he who feeds on Me will live because of Me. ⁵⁸This is the bread which came down from heaven—not as your fathers ate the manna, and are dead. He who eats this bread will live forever."

⁵⁹These things He said in the synagogue as He taught in Capernaum.

Many Disciples Turn Away

⁶⁰Therefore many of His disciples, when they heard *this*, said, "This is a hard saying; who can understand it?"

⁶¹When Jesus knew in Himself that His disciples complained about this, He said to them, "Does this offend you? ⁶²*What* then if you should see the Son of Man ascend where He was before? ⁶³It is the Spirit who gives life; the flesh profits nothing. The words that I speak to you are spirit, and *they* are life. ⁶⁴But there are some of you who do not believe." For Jesus knew from the beginning who they were who did not believe, and who would betray Him. ⁶⁵And He said, "Therefore I have said to you that no one can come to Me unless it has been granted to him by My Father."

⁶⁶From that *time* many of His disciples went back and walked with Him no more. ⁶⁷Then Jesus said to the twelve, "Do you also want to go away?"

⁶⁸But Simon Peter answered Him, "Lord, to whom shall we go? You have the words of eternal life. ⁶⁹Also we have come to believe and know that You are the Christ, the Son of the living God."ᵃ

⁷⁰Jesus answered them, "Did I not choose you, the twelve, and one of you is a devil?"

6:45 ᵃIsaiah 54:13 ᵇM-Text reads *hears and has learned.* 6:47 ᵃNU-Text omits *in Me.* 6:55 ᵃNU-Text reads *true food* and *true drink.* 6:69 ᵃNU-Text reads *You are the Holy One of God.*

[71]He spoke of Judas Iscariot, *the son* of Simon, for it was he who would betray Him, being one of the twelve.

6:70 Did I not choose you, the twelve. In response to Peter's comment, Jesus reminded them that they had been chosen by Him, not the other way around. **a devil.** God's prime adversary operates behind failing humans so that his malice becomes theirs (see Matt. 16:23). In this light, Judas can be understood as a tool of Satan doing unmitigated wickedness.

Jesus' Brothers Disbelieve

7 After these things Jesus walked in Galilee; for He did not want to walk in Judea, because the Jews[a] sought to kill Him. [2]Now the Jews' Feast of Tabernacles was at hand. [3]His brothers therefore said to Him, "Depart from here and go into Judea, that Your disciples also may see the works that You are doing. [4]For no one does anything in secret while he himself seeks to be known openly. If You do these things, show Yourself to the world." [5]For even His brothers did not believe in Him.

7:3 His brothers. Jesus' brothers were James, Joses, Simon, and Judas (Matt. 13:55). James authored the epistle that bears his name, and Judas wrote the epistle that bears his name (Jude). Because of the virgin birth, they were only half-brothers; Mary was their only common parent (Matt. 1:16).

[6]Then Jesus said to them, "My time has not yet come, but your time is always ready. [7]The world cannot hate you, but it hates Me because I testify of it that its works are evil. [8]You go up to this feast. I am not yet[a] going up to this feast, for My time has not yet fully come." [9]When He had said these things to them, He remained in Galilee.

The Heavenly Scholar

[10]But when His brothers had gone up, then He also went up to the feast, not openly, but as it were in secret. [11]Then the Jews sought Him at the feast, and said, "Where is He?" [12]And there was much complaining among the people concerning Him. Some said, "He is good"; others said, "No, on the contrary, He deceives the people." [13]However, no one spoke openly of Him for fear of the Jews.

[14]Now about the middle of the feast Jesus went up into the temple and taught. [15]And the Jews marveled, saying, "How does this Man know letters, having never studied?"

7:15 marveled. The people were amazed that someone who had never studied at a rabbinical center could display such profound mastery of the Scripture. The content and manner of His teaching was qualitatively different than any other teacher.

[16]Jesus[a] answered them and said, "My doctrine is not Mine, but His who sent Me. [17]If anyone wills to do His will, he shall know concerning the doctrine, whether it is from God or *whether* I speak on My own *authority*. [18]He who speaks from himself seeks his own glory; but He who seeks the glory of the One who sent Him is true, and no unrighteousness is in Him. [19]Did not Moses give you the law, yet none of you keeps the law? Why do you seek to kill Me?"

[20]The people answered and said, "You have a demon. Who is seeking to kill You?"

[21]Jesus answered and said to them, "I did one work, and you all marvel. [22]Moses therefore gave you circumcision (not that it is from Moses, but from the fathers), and you circumcise a man on the Sabbath. [23]If a man receives circumcision on the Sabbath, so that the law of Moses should not be broken, are you angry with Me because I made a man completely well on the Sabbath? [24]Do not judge according to appearance, but judge with righteous judgment."

7:23 on the Sabbath. The law required that circumcision occur on the eighth day after a boy's birth (Lev. 12:1–3). If the eighth day fell on a Sabbath, the Jews would still circumcise the child—thus effectively breaking their own Sabbath law. Their hypocrisy is evident. **I made a man completely well.** Jesus argued that if they allowed the ceremonial cleansing of one part of the body on the Sabbath, then they should permit healing of the entire body on the Sabbath.

Could This Be the Christ?

[25]Now some of them from Jerusalem said, "Is this not He whom they seek to

---

7:1 [a]That is, the ruling authorities   7:8 [a]NU-Text omits *yet*.   7:16 [a]NU-Text and M-Text read *So Jesus*.

kill? ²⁶But look! He speaks boldly, and they say nothing to Him. Do the rulers know indeed that this is truly*ᵃ* the Christ? ²⁷However, we know where this Man is from; but when the Christ comes, no one knows where He is from."

²⁸Then Jesus cried out, as He taught in the temple, saying, "You both know Me, and you know where I am from; and I have not come of Myself, but He who sent Me is true, whom you do not know. ²⁹But*ᵃ* I know Him, for I am from Him, and He sent Me."

³⁰Therefore they sought to take Him; but no one laid a hand on Him, because His hour had not yet come. ³¹And many of the people believed in Him, and said, "When the Christ comes, will He do more signs than these which this *Man* has done?"

Jesus and the Religious Leaders

³²The Pharisees heard the crowd murmuring these things concerning Him, and the Pharisees and the chief priests sent officers to take Him. ³³Then Jesus said to them,*ᵃ* "I shall be with you a little while longer, and *then* I go to Him who sent Me. ³⁴You will seek Me and not find *Me,* and where I am you cannot come."

> **7:32 Pharisees and the chief priests.** These two groups did not historically have good relationships with each other, either politically or religiously. John purposely links them together (see v. 45) to emphasize that their cooperation stemmed from their mutual hatred of Jesus. **officers.** These were temple guards of the line of Levi who were in charge of maintaining order in the temple area.

³⁵Then the Jews said among themselves, "Where does He intend to go that we shall not find Him? Does He intend to go to the Dispersion among the Greeks and teach the Greeks? ³⁶What is this thing that He said, 'You will seek Me and not find Me, and where I am you cannot come'?"

The Promise of the Holy Spirit

³⁷On the last day, that great *day* of the feast, Jesus stood and cried out, saying, "If anyone thirsts, let him come to Me and drink. ³⁸He who believes in Me, as the Scripture has said, out of his heart will flow rivers of living water." ³⁹But this He spoke concerning the Spirit, whom those believing*ᵃ* in Him would receive; for the Holy*ᵇ* Spirit was not yet *given,* because Jesus was not yet glorified.

Who Is He?

⁴⁰Therefore many*ᵃ* from the crowd, when they heard this saying, said, "Truly this is the Prophet." ⁴¹Others said, "This is the Christ."

But some said, "Will the Christ come out of Galilee? ⁴²Has not the Scripture said that the Christ comes from the seed of David and from the town of Bethlehem, where David was?" ⁴³So there was a division among the people because of Him. ⁴⁴Now some of them wanted to take Him, but no one laid hands on Him.

> **7:41 out of Galilee?** This shows the people's ignorance. They did not even know where Jesus had been born. He was born in Bethlehem, not Galilee (Mic. 5:2). This also exposes their lack of interest in messianic credentials.

Rejected by the Authorities

⁴⁵Then the officers came to the chief priests and Pharisees, who said to them, "Why have you not brought Him?"

⁴⁶The officers answered, "No man ever spoke like this Man!"

⁴⁷Then the Pharisees answered them, "Are you also deceived? ⁴⁸Have any of the rulers or the Pharisees believed in Him? ⁴⁹But this crowd that does not know the law is accursed."

⁵⁰Nicodemus (he who came to Jesus by night,*ᵃ* being one of them) said to them, ⁵¹"Does our law judge a man before it hears him and knows what he is doing?"

⁵²They answered and said to him, "Are

> **7:52 no prophet has arisen out of Galilee.** The arrogant Pharisees displayed their own ignorance by not researching where Jesus was actually born. While they accused the crowds of ignorance, they were also ignorant (v. 42).

7:26 *ᵃ*NU-Text omits *truly.*   7:29 *ᵃ*NU-Text and M-Text omit *But.*   7:33 *ᵃ*NU-Text and M-Text omit *to them.*   7:39 *ᵃ*NU-Text reads *who believed.*   *ᵇ*NU-Text omits *Holy.*   7:40 *ᵃ*NU-Text reads *some.*
7:50 *ᵃ*NU-Text reads *before.*

you also from Galilee? Search and look, for no prophet has arisen[a] out of Galilee."

An Adulteress Faces the Light of the World

[53]And everyone went to his *own* house.[a]

8 But Jesus went to the Mount of Olives. [2]Now early[a] in the morning He came again into the temple, and all the people came to Him; and He sat down and taught them. [3]Then the scribes and Pharisees brought to Him a woman caught in adultery. And when they had set her in the midst, [4]they said to Him, "Teacher, this woman was caught[a] in adultery, in the very act. [5]Now Moses, in the law, commanded[a] us that such should be stoned.[b] But what do You say?"[c] [6]This they said, testing Him, that they might have *something* of which to accuse Him. But Jesus stooped down and wrote on the ground with *His* finger, as though He did not hear.[a]

[7]So when they continued asking Him, He raised Himself up[a] and said to them, "He who is without sin among you, let him throw a stone at her first." [8]And again He stooped down and wrote on the ground. [9]Then those who heard *it*, being convicted by *their* conscience,[a] went out one by one, beginning with the oldest *even* to the last. And Jesus was left alone, and the woman standing in the midst. [10]When Jesus had raised Himself up and saw no one but the woman, He said to her,[a] "Woman, where are those accusers of yours?[b] Has no one condemned you?"

[11]She said, "No one, Lord."

And Jesus said to her, "Neither do I condemn you; go and[a] sin no more."

[12]Then Jesus spoke to them again, saying, "I am the light of the world. He who follows Me shall not walk in darkness, but have the light of life."

> **8:12 I am the light of the world.** The OT indicates that the coming of the Messiah would be a time when the Lord would be a Light for all His people (Is. 60:19–22), as well as for the whole earth (Is. 42:6). This further emphasizes Jesus as Messiah and Son of God. **He who follows Me.** To "follow" means to completely give oneself to the person being followed. This is a veiled reference to the Jews, for they had followed the cloud and pillar of fire in the wilderness (Ex. 13:21).

Jesus Defends His Self-Witness

[13]The Pharisees therefore said to Him, "You bear witness of Yourself; Your witness is not true."

[14]Jesus answered and said to them, "Even if I bear witness of Myself, My witness is true, for I know where I came from and where I am going; but you do not know where I come from and where I am going. [15]You judge according to the flesh; I judge no one. [16]And yet if I do judge, My judg-

---

7:52 [a]NU-Text reads *is to rise.*   7:53 [a]The words *And everyone* through *sin no more* (8:11) are bracketed by NU-Text as not original. They are present in over 900 manuscripts.   8:2 [a]M-Text reads *very early.*   8:4 [a]M-Text reads *we found this woman.*   8:5 [a]M-Text reads *in our law Moses commanded.*   [b]NU-Text and M-Text read *to stone such.*   [c]M-Text adds *about her.*   8:6 [a]NU-Text and M-Text omit *as though He did not hear.*   8:7 [a]M-Text reads *He looked up.*   8:9 [a]NU-Text and M-Text omit *being convicted by their conscience.*   8:10 [a]NU-Text omits *and saw no one but the woman;* M-Text reads *He saw her and said.*   [b]NU-Text and M-Text omit *of yours.*   8:11 [a]NU-Text and M-Text add *from now on.*

What makes the Gospel of John so different from the other three gospels?

One of the early church fathers, Clement of Alexandria (about A.D. 150–215), may have been the first to describe John's biography of Jesus as a "spiritual gospel." Apparently, John wrote his book in order to make a unique contribution to the records of the Lord's life and to be supplementary as well as complementary to Matthew, Mark, and Luke.

Because John wrote in such a clear and simple style, one might tend to underestimate the depth of his gospel. True to its description as a "spiritual gospel," however, the truths John conveys are profound. A reader must prayerfully and meticulously explore the book in order to discover the vast richness of the spiritual treasure that the apostle, under the guidance of the Holy Spirit, has lovingly deposited (14:26; 16:13).

ment is true; for I am not alone, but I *am* with the Father who sent Me. ¹⁷It is also written in your law that the testimony of two men is true. ¹⁸I am One who bears witness of Myself, and the Father who sent Me bears witness of Me."

¹⁹Then they said to Him, "Where is Your Father?"

Jesus answered, "You know neither Me nor My Father. If you had known Me, you would have known My Father also."

²⁰These words Jesus spoke in the treasury, as He taught in the temple; and no one laid hands on Him, for His hour had not yet come.

Jesus Predicts His Departure

²¹Then Jesus said to them again, "I am going away, and you will seek Me, and will die in your sin. Where I go you cannot come."

²²So the Jews said, "Will He kill Himself, because He says, 'Where I go you cannot come'?"

²³And He said to them, "You are from beneath; I am from above. You are of this world; I am not of this world. ²⁴Therefore I said to you that you will die in your sins; for if you do not believe that I am *He*, you will die in your sins."

> **8:24 If you do not believe.** The unforgivable, eternal sin is failure to believe that Jesus is the Messiah. All other sins can be forgiven. **I am He.** In the original language, this phrase means "I AM," which carries important theological significance (see Ex. 3:14; Is. 40–55). In this, Jesus referred to himself as God (Yahweh, the LORD) of the OT and directly claimed full deity for Himself.

²⁵Then they said to Him, "Who are You?"

And Jesus said to them, "Just what I have been saying to you from the beginning. ²⁶I have many things to say and to judge concerning you, but He who sent Me is true; and I speak to the world those things which I heard from Him."

²⁷They did not understand that He spoke to them of the Father.

²⁸Then Jesus said to them, "When you lift up the Son of Man, then you will know that I am *He*, and *that* I do nothing of Myself; but as My Father taught Me, I speak these things. ²⁹And He who sent Me is with Me. The Father has not left Me alone, for I always do those things that please Him." ³⁰As He spoke these words, many believed in Him.

The Truth Shall Make You Free

³¹Then Jesus said to those Jews who believed Him, "If you abide in My word, you are My disciples indeed. ³²And you shall know the truth, and the truth shall make you free."

³³They answered Him, "We are Abraham's descendants, and have never been in bondage to anyone. How *can* You say, 'You will be made free'?"

³⁴Jesus answered them, "Most assuredly, I say to you, whoever commits sin is a slave of sin. ³⁵And a slave does not abide in the house forever, *but* a son abides forever. ³⁶Therefore if the Son makes you free, you shall be free indeed.

> **8:34 whoever commits sin.** Jesus had in mind slavery to sin, not physical slavery (see Rom. 6:17,18). To "commit sin" means to practice sin habitually (1 John 3:4,8,9). This habitual rebellion against God is the ultimate bondage.

Abraham's Seed and Satan's

³⁷"I know that you are Abraham's descendants, but you seek to kill Me, because My word has no place in you. ³⁸I speak what I have seen with My Father, and you do what you have seen with*ᵃ* your father."

³⁹They answered and said to Him, "Abraham is our father."

Jesus said to them, "If you were Abraham's children, you would do the works of Abraham. ⁴⁰But now you seek to kill Me, a Man who has told you the truth which I heard from God. Abraham did not do this. ⁴¹You do the deeds of your father."

Then they said to Him, "We were not born of fornication; we have one Father—God."

> **8:41 We were not born of fornication.** The Jews may have been referring to the controversy surrounding Jesus' birth, thus implying that His birth was illegitimate (see Matt. 1:18–25).

8:38 *ᵃ*NU-Text reads *heard from*.

[42]Jesus said to them, "If God were your Father, you would love Me, for I proceeded forth and came from God; nor have I come of Myself, but He sent Me. [43]Why do you not understand My speech? Because you are not able to listen to My word. [44]You are of *your* father the devil, and the desires of your father you want to do. He was a murderer from the beginning, and does not stand in the truth, because there is no truth in him. When he speaks a lie, he speaks from his own *resources*, for he is a liar and the father of it. [45]But because I tell the truth, you do not believe Me. [46]Which of you convicts Me of sin? And if I tell the truth, why do you not believe Me? [47]He who is of God hears God's words; therefore you do not hear, because you are not of God."

Before Abraham Was, I AM

[48]Then the Jews answered and said to Him, "Do we not say rightly that You are a Samaritan and have a demon?"

[49]Jesus answered, "I do not have a demon; but I honor My Father, and you dishonor Me. [50]And I do not seek My *own* glory; there is One who seeks and judges. [51]Most assuredly, I say to you, if anyone keeps My word he shall never see death."

[52]Then the Jews said to Him, "Now we know that You have a demon! Abraham is dead, and the prophets; and You say, 'If anyone keeps My word he shall never taste death.' [53]Are You greater than our father Abraham, who is dead? And the prophets are dead. Who do You make Yourself out to be?"

[54]Jesus answered, "If I honor Myself, My honor is nothing. It is My Father who honors Me, of whom you say that He is your[a] God. [55]Yet you have not known Him, but I know Him. And if I say, 'I do not know Him,' I shall be a liar like you; but I do know Him and keep His word. [56]Your father Abraham rejoiced to see My day, and he saw *it* and was glad."

[57]Then the Jews said to Him, "You are not yet fifty years old, and have You seen Abraham?"

[58]Jesus said to them, "Most assuredly, I say to you, before Abraham was, I AM."

[59]Then they took up stones to throw at Him; but Jesus hid Himself and went out of the temple,[a] going through the midst of them, and so passed by.

> **8:59 they took up stones.** The Jews understood that Jesus was claiming to be God, so they followed the law in Lev. 24:16, which calls for anyone who falsely claims to be God to be stoned. **hid Himself...going through the midst of them.** Jesus again escaped arrest because His hour had not yet come.

A Man Born Blind Receives Sight

9 Now as *Jesus* passed by, He saw a man who was blind from birth. [2]And His disciples asked Him, saying, "Rabbi, who sinned, this man or his parents, that he was born blind?"

[3]Jesus answered, "Neither this man nor his parents sinned, but that the works of God should be revealed in him. [4]I[a] must work the works of Him who sent Me while it is day; *the* night is coming when no one can work. [5]As long as I am in the world, I am the light of the world."

[6]When He had said these things, He spat on the ground and made clay with the saliva; and He anointed the eyes of the blind man with the clay. [7]And He said to him, "Go, wash in the pool of Siloam" (which is translated, Sent). So he went and washed, and came back seeing.

[8]Therefore the neighbors and those who previously had seen that he was blind[a] said, "Is not this he who sat and begged?"

[9]Some said, "This is he." Others *said*, "He is like him."[a]

He said, "I am *he*."

[10]Therefore they said to him, "How were your eyes opened?"

[11]He answered and said, "A Man called Jesus made clay and anointed my eyes and said to me, 'Go to the pool of[a] Siloam and wash.' So I went and washed, and I received sight."

[12]Then they said to him, "Where is He?" He said, "I do not know."

8:54 [a]NU-Text and M-Text read *our*.   8:59 [a]NU-Text omits the rest of this verse.   9:4 [a]NU-Text reads *We*.   9:8 [a]NU-Text reads *a beggar*.   9:9 [a]NU-Text reads *"No, but he is like him."*   9:11 [a]NU-Text omits *the pool of*.

The Pharisees Excommunicate the Healed Man

¹³They brought him who formerly was blind to the Pharisees. ¹⁴Now it was a Sabbath when Jesus made the clay and opened his eyes. ¹⁵Then the Pharisees also asked him again how he had received his sight. He said to them, "He put clay on my eyes, and I washed, and I see."

¹⁶Therefore some of the Pharisees said, "This Man is not from God, because He does not keep the Sabbath."

Others said, "How can a man who is a sinner do such signs?" And there was a division among them.

¹⁷They said to the blind man again, "What do you say about Him because He opened your eyes?"

He said, "He is a prophet."

> **9:17 He is a prophet.** The blind man saw that Jesus was more than a mere man; but the sighted, obstinate Pharisees were spiritually blind to the truth (see v. 39). Blindness in the Bible is a metaphor for spiritual darkness (2 Cor. 4:3–6).

¹⁸But the Jews did not believe concerning him, that he had been blind and received his sight, until they called the parents of him who had received his sight. ¹⁹And they asked them, saying, "Is this your son, who you say was born blind? How then does he now see?"

²⁰His parents answered them and said, "We know that this is our son, and that he was born blind; ²¹but by what means he now sees we do not know, or who opened his eyes we do not know. He is of age; ask him. He will speak for himself." ²²His parents said these *things* because they feared the Jews, for the Jews had agreed already that if anyone confessed *that* He *was* Christ, he would be put out of the synagogue. ²³Therefore his parents said, "He is of age; ask him."

²⁴So they again called the man who was blind, and said to him, "Give God the glory! We know that this Man is a sinner."

²⁵He answered and said, "Whether He is a sinner *or not* I do not know. One thing I know: that though I was blind, now I see."

²⁶Then they said to him again, "What did He do to you? How did He open your eyes?"

²⁷He answered them, "I told you already, and you did not listen. Why do you want to hear *it* again? Do you also want to become His disciples?"

²⁸Then they reviled him and said, "You are His disciple, but we are Moses' disciples. ²⁹We know that God spoke to Moses; *as for* this *fellow*, we do not know where He is from."

³⁰The man answered and said to them, "Why, this is a marvelous thing, that you do not know where He is from; yet He has opened my eyes! ³¹Now we know that God does not hear sinners; but if anyone is a worshiper of God and does His will, He hears him. ³²Since the world began it has been unheard of that anyone opened the eyes of one who was born blind. ³³If this Man were not from God, He could do nothing."

³⁴They answered and said to him, "You were completely born in sins, and are you teaching us?" And they cast him out.

> **9:34 are you teaching us?** The Pharisees were furious with the man and failed to see the truth that this uneducated, healed man had demonstrated. They also showed their ignorance of Scripture, for the OT indicated that the coming of the messianic age would include the giving of sight to the blind (Is. 29:18).

True Vision and True Blindness

³⁵Jesus heard that they had cast him out; and when He had found him, He said to him, "Do you believe in the Son of God?"ᵃ

³⁶He answered and said, "Who is He, Lord, that I may believe in Him?"

³⁷And Jesus said to him, "You have both seen Him and it is He who is talking with you."

³⁸Then he said, "Lord, I believe!" And he worshiped Him.

³⁹And Jesus said, "For judgment I have come into this world, that those who do not see may see, and that those who see may be made blind."

⁴⁰Then *some* of the Pharisees who were with Him heard these words, and said to Him, "Are we blind also?"

⁴¹Jesus said to them, "If you were blind,

9:35 ᵃNU-Text reads *Son of Man.*

you would have no sin; but now you say, 'We see.' Therefore your sin remains.

Jesus the True Shepherd

10 "Most assuredly, I say to you, he who does not enter the sheepfold by the door, but climbs up some other way, the same is a thief and a robber. ²But he who enters by the door is the shepherd of the sheep. ³To him the doorkeeper opens, and the sheep hear his voice; and he calls his own sheep by name and leads them out. ⁴And when he brings out his own sheep, he goes before them; and the sheep follow him, for they know his voice. ⁵Yet they will by no means follow a stranger, but will flee from him, for they do not know the voice of strangers." ⁶Jesus used this illustration, but they did not understand the things which He spoke to them.

Jesus the Good Shepherd

⁷Then Jesus said to them again, "Most assuredly, I say to you, I am the door of the sheep. ⁸All who *ever* came before Me*ᵃ* are thieves and robbers, but the sheep did not hear them. ⁹I am the door. If anyone enters by Me, he will be saved, and will go in and out and find pasture. ¹⁰The thief does not come except to steal, and to kill, and to destroy. I have come that they may have life, and that they may have *it* more abundantly.

> **10:7–10 I am the door.** While in vv. 1–5 the Shepherd leads the sheep out of the pen, here He is the entrance to the pen that leads to the pasture. This echoes Jesus' words in 14:6 where He exclaims that He is the only way to the Father. This is the only way of salvation. As some Near Eastern shepherds slept in the gate to guard their sheep, Jesus here describes Himself as the Door.

¹¹"I am the good shepherd. The good shepherd gives His life for the sheep. ¹²But a hireling, *he who is* not the shepherd, one who does not own the sheep, sees the wolf coming and leaves the sheep and flees; and the wolf catches the sheep and scatters them. ¹³The hireling flees because he is a hireling and does not care about the sheep. ¹⁴I am the good shepherd; and I know My *sheep,* and am known by My own. ¹⁵As the Father knows Me, even so I know the Father; and I lay down My life for the sheep. ¹⁶And other sheep I have which are not of this fold; them also I must bring, and they will hear My voice; and there will be one flock *and* one shepherd.

¹⁷"Therefore My Father loves Me, because I lay down My life that I may take it again. ¹⁸No one takes it from Me, but I lay it down of Myself. I have power to lay it down, and I have power to take it again. This command I have received from My Father."

¹⁹Therefore there was a division again among the Jews because of these sayings. ²⁰And many of them said, "He has a demon and is mad. Why do you listen to Him?"

²¹Others said, "These are not the words of one who has a demon. Can a demon open the eyes of the blind?"

The Shepherd Knows His Sheep

²²Now it was the Feast of Dedication in Jerusalem, and it was winter. ²³And Jesus walked in the temple, in Solomon's porch. ²⁴Then the Jews surrounded Him and said to Him, "How long do You keep us in doubt? If You are the Christ, tell us plainly."

²⁵Jesus answered them, "I told you, and you do not believe. The works that I do in My Father's name, they bear witness of Me. ²⁶But you do not believe, because you are not of My sheep, as I said to you.*ᵃ* ²⁷My sheep hear My voice, and I know them, and they follow Me. ²⁸And I give them eternal life, and they shall never perish; neither shall anyone snatch them out of My hand. ²⁹My Father, who has given *them* to Me, is greater than all; and no one is able to snatch *them* out of My Father's hand. ³⁰I and *My* Father are one."

> **10:30 I and *My* Father are one.** This stressed the united purpose and action between the Father and the Son for both the security and safety of the flock. It also describes their unity of nature and essence (see 5:17–23).

Renewed Efforts to Stone Jesus

³¹Then the Jews took up stones again to stone Him. ³²Jesus answered them, "Many good works I have shown you from My Fa-

---

10:8 *ᵃ*M-Text omits *before Me.*   10:26 *ᵃ*NU-Text omits *as I said to you.*

ther. For which of those works do you stone Me?"

³³The Jews answered Him, saying, "For a good work we do not stone You, but for blasphemy, and because You, being a Man, make Yourself God."

³⁴Jesus answered them, "Is it not written in your law, 'I said, "You are gods" '?ᵃ ³⁵If He called them gods, to whom the word of God came (and the Scripture cannot be broken), ³⁶do you say of Him whom the Father sanctified and sent into the world, 'You are blaspheming,' because I said, 'I am the Son of God'? ³⁷If I do not do the works of My Father, do not believe Me; ³⁸but if I do, though you do not believe Me, believe the works, that you may know and believeᵃ that the Father is in Me, and I in Him." ³⁹Therefore they sought again to seize Him, but He escaped out of their hand.

> **10:38 believe the works.** Jesus expected that His words alone would not make everyone believe. Because He does the same things the Father does, His enemies should consider this in their evaluation of Him. The implication is that the people were so ignorant of God that they could not recognize the works of the Father or the One whom the Father sent (see 14:10,11).

The Believers Beyond Jordan

⁴⁰And He went away again beyond the Jordan to the place where John was baptizing at first, and there He stayed. ⁴¹Then many came to Him and said, "John performed no sign, but all the things that John spoke about this Man were true." ⁴²And many believed in Him there.

The Death of Lazarus

11 Now a certain man was sick, Lazarus of Bethany, the town of Mary and her sister Martha. ²It was that Mary who anointed the Lord with fragrant oil and wiped His feet with her hair, whose brother

> **11:1 Lazarus.** The resurrection is the capstone of Jesus' public ministry. It is more monumental than the previous 6 miracles recorded in this gospel. Lazarus had been dead for 4 days, and the process of decomposition had already started.

Lazarus was sick. ³Therefore the sisters sent to Him, saying, "Lord, behold, he whom You love is sick."

⁴When Jesus heard that, He said, "This sickness is not unto death, but for the glory of God, that the Son of God may be glorified through it."

⁵Now Jesus loved Martha and her sister and Lazarus. ⁶So, when He heard that he was sick, He stayed two more days in the place where He was. ⁷Then after this He said to the disciples, "Let us go to Judea again."

⁸The disciples said to Him, "Rabbi, lately the Jews sought to stone You, and are You going there again?"

⁹Jesus answered, "Are there not twelve hours in the day? If anyone walks in the day, he does not stumble, because he sees the light of this world. ¹⁰But if one walks in the night, he stumbles, because the light is not in him." ¹¹These things He said, and after that He said to them, "Our friend Lazarus sleeps, but I go that I may wake him up."

> **11:9,10** When the sun was up, most people did their work safely, and when darkness came they stopped working. While the Son performed the Father's will (during the daylight of His ministry), He was safe. "Night" would soon come when Jesus' earthly work would end. His point was that as long as He was doing the Father's will on this earth, even in dangerous surroundings, He would safely complete God's purposes.

¹²Then His disciples said, "Lord, if he sleeps he will get well." ¹³However, Jesus spoke of his death, but they thought that He was speaking about taking rest in sleep. ¹⁴Then Jesus said to them plainly, "Lazarus is dead. ¹⁵And I am glad for your sakes that I was not there, that you may believe. Nevertheless let us go to him."

¹⁶Then Thomas, who is called the Twin, said to his fellow disciples, "Let us also go, that we may die with Him."

I Am the Resurrection and the Life

¹⁷So when Jesus came, He found that he had already been in the tomb four days. ¹⁸Now Bethany was near Jerusalem, about two milesᵃ away. ¹⁹And many of the Jews

---

10:34 ᵃPsalm 82:6   10:38 ᵃNU-Text reads understand.   11:18 ᵃLiterally fifteen stadia

had joined the women around Martha and Mary, to comfort them concerning their brother.

²⁰Now Martha, as soon as she heard that Jesus was coming, went and met Him, but Mary was sitting in the house. ²¹Now Martha said to Jesus, "Lord, if You had been here, my brother would not have died. ²²But even now I know that whatever You ask of God, God will give You."

²³Jesus said to her, "Your brother will rise again."

²⁴Martha said to Him, "I know that he will rise again in the resurrection at the last day."

²⁵Jesus said to her, "I am the resurrection and the life. He who believes in Me, though he may die, he shall live. ²⁶And whoever lives and believes in Me shall never die. Do you believe this?"

> **11:25,26** With this statement, Jesus moved Martha from an abstract belief in a "last days" resurrection (5:28,29) to a personalized trust in the One who alone can raise the dead. No resurrection or eternal life exists outside the Son of God.

²⁷She said to Him, "Yes, Lord, I believe that You are the Christ, the Son of God, who is to come into the world."

Jesus and Death, the Last Enemy

²⁸And when she had said these things, she went her way and secretly called Mary her sister, saying, "The Teacher has come and is calling for you." ²⁹As soon as she heard *that*, she arose quickly and came to Him. ³⁰Now Jesus had not yet come into the town, but was*ᵃ* in the place where Martha met Him. ³¹Then the Jews who were with her in the house, and comforting her, when they saw that Mary rose up quickly and went out, followed her, saying, "She is going to the tomb to weep there."*ᵃ*

³²Then, when Mary came where Jesus was, and saw Him, she fell down at His feet, saying to Him, "Lord, if You had been here, my brother would not have died."

³³Therefore, when Jesus saw her weeping, and the Jews who came with her weeping, He groaned in the spirit and was troubled. ³⁴And He said, "Where have you laid him?"

They said to Him, "Lord, come and see."

³⁵Jesus wept. ³⁶Then the Jews said, "See how He loved him!"

> **11:35 Jesus wept.** He silently burst into tears here in contrast to the loud lament of the group. He was not mourning Lazarus' death, but rather grieving over the fallen world entangled in sin which caused sorrow and death.

³⁷And some of them said, "Could not this Man, who opened the eyes of the blind, also have kept this man from dying?"

Lazarus Raised from the Dead

³⁸Then Jesus, again groaning in Himself, came to the tomb. It was a cave, and a stone lay against it. ³⁹Jesus said, "Take away the stone."

Martha, the sister of him who was dead, said to Him, "Lord, by this time there is a stench, for he has been *dead* four days."

⁴⁰Jesus said to her, "Did I not say to you that if you would believe you would see the glory of God?" ⁴¹Then they took away the stone *from the place* where the dead man was lying.*ᵃ* And Jesus lifted up *His* eyes and said, "Father, I thank You that You have heard Me. ⁴²And I know that You always hear Me, but because of the people who are standing by I said *this*, that they may believe that You sent Me." ⁴³Now when He had said these things, He cried with a loud voice, "Lazarus, come forth!" ⁴⁴And he who had died came out bound hand and foot with graveclothes, and his face was wrapped with a cloth. Jesus said to them, "Loose him, and let him go."

The Plot to Kill Jesus

⁴⁵Then many of the Jews who had come to Mary, and had seen the things Jesus did, believed in Him. ⁴⁶But some of them went away to the Pharisees and told them the things Jesus did. ⁴⁷Then the chief priests and the Pharisees gathered a council and said, "What shall we do? For this Man works many signs. ⁴⁸If we let Him alone like this, everyone will believe in Him, and

---

11:30 *ᵃ*NU-Text adds *still*.　11:31 *ᵃ*NU-Text reads *supposing that she was going to the tomb to weep there*.　11:41 *ᵃ*NU-Text omits *from the place where the dead man was lying*.

the Romans will come and take away both our place and nation."

⁴⁹And one of them, Caiaphas, being high priest that year, said to them, "You know nothing at all, ⁵⁰nor do you consider that it is expedient for us*a* that one man should die for the people, and not that the whole nation should perish." ⁵¹Now this he did not say on his own *authority*; but being high priest that year he prophesied that Jesus would die for the nation, ⁵²and not for that nation only, but also that He would gather together in one the children of God who were scattered abroad.

> **11:51 he prophesied.** Caiaphas' blasphemous words ended up being used by God to express His heart and glorious plan of salvation (Acts 4:27,28). This displays how God can take evil intentions and use them for good. God used Caiaphas as a prophet because Caiaphas was the High-Priest. Originally the High-Priest was the one through whom God revealed His will (2 Sam. 15:27).

⁵³Then, from that day on, they plotted to put Him to death. ⁵⁴Therefore Jesus no longer walked openly among the Jews, but went from there into the country near the wilderness, to a city called Ephraim, and there remained with His disciples.

⁵⁵And the Passover of the Jews was near, and many went from the country up to Jerusalem before the Passover, to purify themselves. ⁵⁶Then they sought Jesus, and spoke among themselves as they stood in the temple, "What do you think—that He will not come to the feast?" ⁵⁷Now both the chief priests and the Pharisees had given a command, that if anyone knew where He was, he should report *it*, that they might seize Him.

The Anointing at Bethany

12 Then, six days before the Passover, Jesus came to Bethany, where Lazarus was who had been dead,*a* whom He had raised from the dead. ²There they made Him a supper; and Martha served, but Lazarus was one of those who sat at the table with Him. ³Then Mary took a pound of very costly oil of spikenard, anointed the feet of Jesus, and wiped His feet with her hair. And the house was filled with the fragrance of the oil.

⁴But one of His disciples, Judas Iscariot, Simon's *son*, who would betray Him, said, ⁵"Why was this fragrant oil not sold for three hundred denarii*a* and given to the poor?" ⁶This he said, not that he cared for the poor, but because he was a thief, and had the money box; and he used to take what was put in it.

> **12:6 a thief.** Judas' altruism was a front for his greediness. He was the treasurer for the apostles, so was able to secretly keep some of the money for his own desires.

⁷But Jesus said, "Let her alone; she has kept*a* this for the day of My burial. ⁸For the poor you have with you always, but Me you do not have always."

The Plot to Kill Lazarus

⁹Now a great many of the Jews knew that He was there; and they came, not for Jesus' sake only, but that they might also see Lazarus, whom He had raised from the dead. ¹⁰But the chief priests plotted to put Lazarus to death also, ¹¹because on account of him many of the Jews went away and believed in Jesus.

The Triumphal Entry

¹²The next day a great multitude that had come to the feast, when they heard that Jesus was coming to Jerusalem, ¹³took branches of palm trees and went out to meet Him, and cried out:

> **12:13 took branches of palm trees.** Beginning about two centuries earlier, the waving of palm branches was a national symbol signaling the fervent hope that a messianic liberator was arriving on the scene (6:14,15). **Hosanna!** This exclamation of praise means "give salvation now" and was familiar to the Jews through the Psalms and ceremonial traditions. The crowds also shouted Ps. 118:26, which may have been the pronouncement of blessing upon a Davidic king, thus bearing messianic implications.

11:50 *a*NU-Text reads you.   12:1 *a*NU-Text omits *who had been dead.*   12:5 *a*About one year's wages for a worker   12:7 *a*NU-Text reads *that she may keep.*

"Hosanna!
  'Blessed is He who comes in the name
    of the LORD!'*a*
  The King of Israel!"

14Then Jesus, when He had found a young donkey, sat on it; as it is written:

15 "Fear not, daughter of Zion;
    Behold, your King is coming,
    Sitting on a donkey's colt."*a*

16His disciples did not understand these things at first; but when Jesus was glorified, then they remembered that these things were written about Him and *that* they had done these things to Him. 17Therefore the people, who were with Him when He called Lazarus out of his tomb and raised him from the dead, bore witness. 18For this reason the people also met Him, because they heard that He had done this sign. 19The Pharisees therefore said among themselves, "You see that you are accomplishing nothing. Look, the world has gone after Him!"

The Fruitful Grain of Wheat

20Now there were certain Greeks among those who came up to worship at the feast. 21Then they came to Philip, who was from Bethsaida of Galilee, and asked him, saying, "Sir, we wish to see Jesus." 22Philip came and told Andrew, and in turn Andrew and Philip told Jesus. 23But Jesus answered them, saying, "The hour has come that the Son of Man should be glorified. 24Most assuredly, I say to you, unless a grain of wheat falls into the ground and dies, it remains alone; but if it dies, it produces much grain. 25He who loves his life will lose it, and he who hates his life in this world will keep it for eternal life. 26If anyone serves Me, let him follow Me; and where I am, there My servant will be also. If anyone serves Me, him *My* Father will honor.

Jesus Predicts His Death on the Cross

27"Now My soul is troubled, and what shall I say? 'Father, save Me from this hour'? But for this purpose I came to this hour. 28Father, glorify Your name."

Then a voice came from heaven, *saying,* "I have both glorified *it* and will glorify *it* again."

> **12:28 glorify Your name.** This request embodied the principle that Jesus lived by and would die by (see 7:18). **I have...and will glorify.** The Father answered the Son in an audible voice. This is only 1 of 3 instances in Jesus' ministry when this took place (see Matt. 3:17; 17:5).

29Therefore the people who stood by and heard *it* said that it had thundered. Others said, "An angel has spoken to Him." 30Jesus answered and said, "This voice did not come because of Me, but for your sake. 31Now is the judgment of this world; now the ruler of this world will be cast out. 32And I, if I am lifted up from the earth, will draw all *peoples* to Myself." 33This He said, signifying by what death He would die.

34The people answered Him, "We have heard from the law that the Christ remains forever; and how *can* You say, 'The Son of Man must be lifted up'? Who is this Son of Man?" 35Then Jesus said to them, "A little while longer the light is with you. Walk while you have the light, lest darkness overtake you; he who walks in darkness does not know where he is going. 36While you have the light, believe in the light, that you may become sons of light." These things Jesus spoke, and departed, and was hidden from them.

Who Has Believed Our Report?

37But although He had done so many signs before them, they did not believe in Him, 38that the word of Isaiah the prophet might be fulfilled, which he spoke:

> "Lord, who has believed our report?
>   And to whom has the arm of the LORD
>   been revealed?"*a*

39Therefore they could not believe, because Isaiah said again:

40 "He has blinded their eyes and
    hardened their hearts,
  Lest they should see with their eyes,

12:13 *a*Psalm 118:26   12:15 *a*Zechariah 9:9   12:38 *a*Isaiah 53:1

Lest they should understand with their
    hearts and turn,
So that I should heal them." ᵃ

⁴¹These things Isaiah said whenᵃ he saw
His glory and spoke of Him.

Walk in the Light

⁴²Nevertheless even among the rulers
many believed in Him, but because of the
Pharisees they did not confess *Him,* lest
they should be put out of the synagogue;
⁴³for they loved the praise of men more
than the praise of God.

> **12:42,43** While the people seemed to trust Jesus with
> much more openness and fervency, the leaders who
> believed in Him demonstrated inadequate faith. Al-
> though some of these leaders believed, they refused
> to take a position that would threaten their place of
> honor in the synagogue. They desired the praises of
> men more than of God.

⁴⁴Then Jesus cried out and said, "He who
believes in Me, believes not in Me but in
Him who sent Me. ⁴⁵And he who sees Me
sees Him who sent Me. ⁴⁶I have come *as* a
light into the world, that whoever believes
in Me should not abide in darkness. ⁴⁷And
if anyone hears My words and does not
believe,ᵃ I do not judge him; for I did not

come to judge the world but to save the
world. ⁴⁸He who rejects Me, and does not
receive My words, has that which judges
him—the word that I have spoken will
judge him in the last day. ⁴⁹For I have not
spoken on My own *authority;* but the Father who sent Me gave Me a command,
what I should say and what I should speak.
⁵⁰And I know that His command is everlasting life. Therefore, whatever I speak,
just as the Father has told Me, so I speak."

Jesus Washes the Disciples' Feet

13 Now before the Feast of the Passover, when Jesus knew that His hour
had come that He should depart from this
world to the Father, having loved His own
who were in the world, He loved them to
the end.

²And supper being ended,ᵃ the devil having already put it into the heart of Judas Iscariot, Simon's *son,* to betray Him, ³Jesus,
knowing that the Father had given all
things into His hands, and that He had
come from God and was going to God, ⁴rose
from supper and laid aside His garments,
took a towel and girded Himself. ⁵After
that, He poured water into a basin and began to wash the disciples' feet, and to wipe
them with the towel with which He was
girded. ⁶Then He came to Simon Peter. And

12:40 ᵃIsaiah 6:10   12:41 ᵃNU-Text reads *because.*   12:47 ᵃNU-Text reads *keep them.*   13:2 ᵃNU-
Text reads *And during supper.*

Q How do scholars conclude that the expression "whom Jesus loved" was John's way of referring to himself in the Gospel of John?

A Three obvious clues about John's gospel help identify the
unnamed disciple who called himself the disciple "whom Jesus
loved" (13:23; 19:26; 20:2; 21:7,20).

Early church fathers invariably identify the Apostle John as
the author of this gospel. John is frequently mentioned by the
other gospel writers as an active participant among the
disciples of Jesus, yet John's name is absent from the fourth
gospel.

If four people take a trip together and each carries a camera,
the group-shots each person takes will naturally not include
them. In fact, someone else could probably guess who took
which pictures by which member of the group was absent. The
Gospel of John functions this way—John's absence by name
shouts his presence.

As for his signature phrase, the words "whom Jesus loved" convey both a sense of the
apostle's humility and the depth of his relationship to Jesus. The phrase doesn't mean that
John thought of himself as the only disciple Jesus loved. It simply expresses with disarming
honesty the wonder of this disciple over the fact that the Lord loved him!

13:4,5 Foot washing was necessary due to the dusty conditions of the roads. This act was traditionally done by servants, not among peers except as an expression of great love. Jesus' washing of the disciples feet serves as a model of spiritual cleansing (vv. 6–9) and of Christian humility (vv. 12–17). Through this act, He taught His disciples about selfless service.

Peter said to Him, "Lord, are You washing my feet?"

[7]Jesus answered and said to him, "What I am doing you do not understand now, but you will know after this."

[8]Peter said to Him, "You shall never wash my feet!"

Jesus answered him, "If I do not wash you, you have no part with Me."

[9]Simon Peter said to Him, "Lord, not my feet only, but also *my* hands and *my* head!"

[10]Jesus said to him, "He who is bathed needs only to wash *his* feet, but is completely clean; and you are clean, but not all of you." [11]For He knew who would betray Him; therefore He said, "You are not all clean."

[12]So when He had washed their feet, taken His garments, and sat down again, He said to them, "Do you know what I have done to you? [13]You call Me Teacher and Lord, and you say well, for *so* I am. [14]If I then, *your* Lord and Teacher, have washed your feet, you also ought to wash one another's feet. [15]For I have given you an example, that you should do as I have done to you. [16]Most assuredly, I say to you, a servant is not greater than his master; nor is he who is sent greater than he who sent him. [17]If you know these things, blessed are you if you do them.

Jesus Identifies His Betrayer

[18]"I do not speak concerning all of you. I know whom I have chosen; but that the Scripture may be fulfilled, '*He who eats bread with Me[a] has lifted up his heel against Me.*'[b] [19]Now I tell you before it comes, that when it does come to pass, you may believe that I am *He.* [20]Most assuredly, I say to you, he who receives whomever I send receives Me; and he who receives Me receives Him who sent Me."

[21]When Jesus had said these things, He was troubled in spirit, and testified and said, "Most assuredly, I say to you, one of you will betray Me." [22]Then the disciples looked at one another, perplexed about whom He spoke.

[23]Now there was leaning on Jesus' bosom one of His disciples, whom Jesus loved. [24]Simon Peter therefore motioned to him to ask who it was of whom He spoke.

[25]Then, leaning back[a] on Jesus' breast, he said to Him, "Lord, who is it?"

[26]Jesus answered, "It is he to whom I shall give a piece of bread when I have dipped *it.*" And having dipped the bread, He gave *it* to Judas Iscariot, *the son* of Simon. [27]Now after the piece of bread, Satan entered him. Then Jesus said to him, "What you do, do quickly." [28]But no one at the table knew for what reason He said this to him. [29]For some thought, because Judas had the money box, that Jesus had said to him, "Buy *those things* we need for the feast," or that he should give something to the poor.

13:26 He gave *it* to Judas Iscariot. The host of a feast (in this case, Jesus) would dip into a bowl and pull out a morsel, passing it to a guest as a special mark of honor or friendship. Because Jesus passed the morsel to Judas, it has been suggested that Judas was sitting near the Lord in a place of honor. Jesus demonstrated a final gesture of love for Judas, even though Judas would soon betray Him.

[30]Having received the piece of bread, he then went out immediately. And it was night.

The New Commandment

[31]So, when he had gone out, Jesus said, "Now the Son of Man is glorified, and God is glorified in Him. [32]If God is glorified in Him, God will also glorify Him in Himself, and glorify Him immediately. [33]Little children, I shall be with you a little while longer. You will seek Me; and as I said to the Jews, 'Where I am going, you cannot come,' so now I say to you. [34]A new commandment I give to you, that you love one another; as I have loved you, that you also love one another. [35]By this all will know that you are My disciples, if you have love for one another."

13:18 [a]NU-Text reads *My bread.* [b]Psalm 41:9   13:25 [a]NU-Text and M-Text add *thus.*

Jesus Predicts Peter's Denial

[36]Simon Peter said to Him, "Lord, where are You going?"

Jesus answered him, "Where I am going you cannot follow Me now, but you shall follow Me afterward."

[37]Peter said to Him, "Lord, why can I not follow You now? I will lay down my life for Your sake."

[38]Jesus answered him, "Will you lay down your life for My sake? Most assuredly, I say to you, the rooster shall not crow till you have denied Me three times.

> **14:1–31** This chapter centers on the promise that Jesus is the One who gives the believer comfort, not only in His future return but also in the present through the ministry of the Holy Spirit. This was a particularly challenging time for the disciples, and Christ was comforting their hearts.

The Way, the Truth, and the Life

14 "Let not your heart be troubled; you believe in God, believe also in Me. [2]In My Father's house are many mansions;[a] if it were not so, I would have told you. I go to prepare a place for you.[b] [3]And if I go and prepare a place for you, I will come again and receive you to Myself; that where I am, there you may be also. [4]And where I go you know, and the way you know."

[5]Thomas said to Him, "Lord, we do not know where You are going, and how can we know the way?"

[6]Jesus said to him, "I am the way, the truth, and the life. No one comes to the Father except through Me.

The Father Revealed

[7]"If you had known Me, you would have known My Father also; and from now on you know Him and have seen Him."

[8]Philip said to Him, "Lord, show us the Father, and it is sufficient for us."

[9]Jesus said to him, "Have I been with you so long, and yet you have not known Me, Philip? He who has seen Me has seen the Father; so how can you say, 'Show us the

Father'? [10]Do you not believe that I am in the Father, and the Father in Me? The words that I speak to you I do not speak on My own *authority*; but the Father who dwells in Me does the works. [11]Believe Me that I *am* in the Father and the Father in Me, or else believe Me for the sake of the works themselves.

The Answered Prayer

[12]"Most assuredly, I say to you, he who believes in Me, the works that I do he will do also; and greater *works* than these he will do, because I go to My Father. [13]And whatever you ask in My name, that I will do, that the Father may be glorified in the Son. [14]If you ask[a] anything in My name, I will do *it*.

> **14:12 greater works than these he will do.** Jesus did not mean greater works in power, but in extent. The emphasis is on spiritual, not physical, miracles. The disciples would bring many to salvation because of the Comforter dwelling in them. **because I go to My Father.** After the Holy Spirit came, the disciples would be used by God to do these greater works. The Spirit would not come, however, until Jesus returned to the Father (7:39).

Jesus Promises Another Helper

[15]"If you love Me, keep[a] My commandments. [16]And I will pray the Father, and He will give you another Helper, that He may abide with you forever—[17]the Spirit of truth, whom the world cannot receive, because it neither sees Him nor knows Him; but you know Him, for He dwells with you and will be in you. [18]I will not leave you orphans; I will come to you.

Indwelling of the Father and the Son

[19]"A little while longer and the world will see Me no more, but you will see Me. Because I live, you will live also. [20]At that day you will know that I *am* in My Father, and you in Me, and I in you. [21]He who has My commandments and keeps them, it is he who loves Me. And he who loves Me will be loved by My Father, and I will love him and manifest Myself to him."

14:2 [a]Literally *dwellings*   [b]NU-Text adds a word which would cause the text to read either *if it were not so, would I have told you that I go to prepare a place for you?* or *if it were not so I would have told you; for I go to prepare a place for you.*   14:14 [a]NU-Text adds *Me.*   14:15 [a]NU-Text reads *you will keep.*

²²Judas (not Iscariot) said to Him, "Lord, how is it that You will manifest Yourself to us, and not to the world?"

²³Jesus answered and said to him, "If anyone loves Me, he will keep My word; and My Father will love him, and We will come to him and make Our home with him. ²⁴He who does not love Me does not keep My words; and the word which you hear is not Mine but the Father's who sent Me.

The Gift of His Peace

²⁵"These things I have spoken to you while being present with you. ²⁶But the Helper, the Holy Spirit, whom the Father will send in My name, He will teach you all things, and bring to your remembrance all things that I said to you. ²⁷Peace I leave with you, My peace I give to you; not as the world gives do I give to you. Let not your heart be troubled, neither let it be afraid. ²⁸You have heard Me say to you, 'I am going away and coming back to you.' If you loved Me, you would rejoice because I said,ᵃ 'I am going to the Father,' for My Father is greater than I.

> **14:27 Peace I leave...not as the world gives.** This peace, unknown to the unsaved, secures composure in difficult trouble (see v. 1), dissolves fear (Phil. 4:7), and rules in the hearts of God's people to maintain harmony (see Col. 3:15). The greatest reality of this peace will be in the messianic kingdom (Num. 6:26).

²⁹"And now I have told you before it comes, that when it does come to pass, you may believe. ³⁰I will no longer talk much with you, for the ruler of this world is coming, and he has nothing in Me. ³¹But that the world may know that I love the Father, and as the Father gave Me commandment, so I do. Arise, let us go from here.

> **15:1–17** Israel was commonly symbolized in the OT as a vine (Ps. 80:9–16). Jesus specifically referred to Himself as the "true vine" and the Father as the "vinedresser," or caretaker, of the vine. The branches that bear fruit are the believers whose profession of faith is genuine. The fruitless branches are those who claim to be believers, but whose faith is not genuine.

The True Vine

15 "I am the true vine, and My Father is the vinedresser. ²Every branch in Me that does not bear fruit He takes away;ᵃ and every branch that bears fruit He prunes, that it may bear more fruit. ³You are already clean because of the word which I have spoken to you. ⁴Abide in Me, and I in you. As the branch cannot bear fruit of itself, unless it abides in the vine, neither can you, unless you abide in Me.

⁵"I am the vine, you are the branches. He who abides in Me, and I in him, bears much fruit; for without Me you can do nothing. ⁶If anyone does not abide in Me, he is cast out as a branch and is withered; and they gather them and throw them into the fire, and they are burned. ⁷If you abide in Me, and My words abide in you, you willᵃ ask what you desire, and it shall be done for you. ⁸By this My Father is glorified, that you bear much fruit; so you will be My disciples.

Love and Joy Perfected

⁹"As the Father loved Me, I also have loved you; abide in My love. ¹⁰If you keep My commandments, you will abide in My love, just as I have kept My Father's commandments and abide in His love.

> **15:9,10 abide in My love.** This is not emotional or mystical abiding, but is defined in v. 10 as obedience. We are to follow Jesus' model of obedience to the Father by being obedient to the Son.

¹¹"These things I have spoken to you, that My joy may remain in you, and that your joy may be full. ¹²This is My commandment, that you love one another as I have loved you. ¹³Greater love has no one than this, than to lay down one's life for his friends. ¹⁴You are My friends if you do whatever I command you. ¹⁵No longer do I call you servants, for a servant does not know what his master is doing; but I have called you friends, for all things that I heard from My Father I have made known to you. ¹⁶You did not choose Me, but I chose you and appointed you that you should go and bear fruit, and that your fruit should remain, that whatever you ask the Father in

---

14:28 ᵃNU-Text omits I said.   15:2 ᵃOr lifts up   15:7 ᵃNU-Text omits you will.

My name He may give you. ¹⁷These things I command you, that you love one another.

The World's Hatred

¹⁸"If the world hates you, you know that it hated Me before *it hated* you. ¹⁹If you were of the world, the world would love its own. Yet because you are not of the world, but I chose you out of the world, therefore the world hates you. ²⁰Remember the word that I said to you, 'A servant is not greater than his master.' If they persecuted Me, they will also persecute you. If they kept My word, they will keep yours also. ²¹But all these things they will do to you for My name's sake, because they do not know Him who sent Me. ²²If I had not come and spoken to them, they would have no sin, but now they have no excuse for their sin. ²³He who hates Me hates My Father also. ²⁴If I had not done among them the works which no one else did, they would have no sin; but now they have seen and also hated both Me and My Father. ²⁵But *this happened* that the word might be fulfilled which is written in their law, '*They hated Me without a cause.*'ᵃ

The Coming Rejection

²⁶"But when the Helper comes, whom I shall send to you from the Father, the Spirit of truth who proceeds from the Father, He will testify of Me. ²⁷And you also will bear witness, because you have been with Me from the beginning.

16 "These things I have spoken to you, that you should not be made to stumble. ²They will put you out of the synagogues; yes, the time is coming that whoever kills you will think that he offers God service. ³And these things they will do to youᵃ because they have not known the Fa-

ther nor Me. ⁴But these things I have told you, that when theᵃ time comes, you may remember that I told you of them.

"And these things I did not say to you at the beginning, because I was with you.

The Work of the Holy Spirit

⁵"But now I go away to Him who sent Me, and none of you asks Me, 'Where are You going?' ⁶But because I have said these things to you, sorrow has filled your heart. ⁷Nevertheless I tell you the truth. It is to your advantage that I go away; for if I do not go away, the Helper will not come to you; but if I depart, I will send Him to you. ⁸And when He has come, He will convict the world of sin, and of righteousness, and of judgment: ⁹of sin, because they do not believe in Me; ¹⁰of righteousness, because I go to My Father and you see Me no more; ¹¹of judgment, because the ruler of this world is judged.

¹²"I still have many things to say to you, but you cannot bear *them* now. ¹³However, when He, the Spirit of truth, has come, He will guide you into all truth; for He will not speak on His own *authority*, but whatever He hears He will speak; and He will tell you things to come. ¹⁴He will glorify Me, for He will take of what is Mine and declare *it* to you. ¹⁵All things that the Father has *are* Mine. Therefore I said that He will take of Mine and declare *it* to you.ᵃ

Sorrow Will Turn to Joy

¹⁶"A little while, and you will not see Me; and again a little while, and you will see Me, because I go to the Father."

¹⁷Then *some* of His disciples said among themselves, "What is this that He says to us, 'A little while, and you will not see Me; and again a little while, and you will see Me'; and, 'because I go to the Father'?" ¹⁸They said therefore, "What is this that He says, 'A little while'? We do not know what He is saying."

¹⁹Now Jesus knew that they desired to ask Him, and He said to them, "Are you inquiring among yourselves about what I said, 'A little while, and you will not see Me; and again a little while, and you will see Me'? ²⁰Most assuredly, I say to you that you will weep and lament, but the world will rejoice; and you will be sorrowful, but your sorrow will be turned into joy. ²¹A woman, when she is in labor, has sorrow because her hour has come; but as soon as she has given birth to the child, she no longer remembers the anguish, for joy that a human being has been born into the world. ²²Therefore you now have sorrow; but I will see you again and your heart will rejoice, and your joy no one will take from you.

²³"And in that day you will ask Me nothing. Most assuredly, I say to you, whatever you ask the Father in My name He will give you. ²⁴Until now you have asked nothing in My name. Ask, and you will receive, that your joy may be full.

Jesus Christ Has Overcome the World

²⁵"These things I have spoken to you in figurative language; but the time is coming when I will no longer speak to you in figurative language, but I will tell you plainly about the Father. ²⁶In that day you will ask in My name, and I do not say to you that I shall pray the Father for you; ²⁷for the Father Himself loves you, because you have loved Me, and have believed that I came forth from God. ²⁸I came forth from the Father and have come into the world. Again, I leave the world and go to the Father."

²⁹His disciples said to Him, "See, now You are speaking plainly, and using no fig-ure of speech! ³⁰Now we are sure that You know all things, and have no need that anyone should question You. By this we believe that You came forth from God."

> **16:26–28 I do not say.** Jesus clarified what he meant by praying in His name. He meant that the Father loves Christ's own: the ones whom the Father sent the Son to redeem. Asking in Jesus' name simply means asking on the basis of Christ's merit for whatever would honor and glorify Him so as to build His kingdom.

³¹Jesus answered them, "Do you now believe? ³²Indeed the hour is coming, yes, has now come, that you will be scattered, each to his own, and will leave Me alone. And yet I am not alone, because the Father is with Me. ³³These things I have spoken to you, that in Me you may have peace. In the world you will*ᵃ* have tribulation; but be of good cheer, I have overcome the world."

Jesus Prays for Himself

17 Jesus spoke these words, lifted up His eyes to heaven, and said: "Father, the hour has come. Glorify Your Son, that Your Son also may glorify You, ²as You have given Him authority over all flesh, that He should*ᵃ* give eternal life to as many as You have given Him. ³And this is eternal life, that they may know You, the only true God, and Jesus Christ whom You have sent. ⁴I have glorified You on the earth. I have finished the work which You have given Me to do. ⁵And now, O Father, glorify Me together with Yourself, with the glory which I had with You before the world was.

Jesus Prays for His Disciples

⁶"I have manifested Your name to the men whom You have given Me out of the world. They were Yours, You gave them to Me, and they have kept Your word. ⁷Now

> **17:6–10 They were Yours.** Jesus emphasized that those who believe in Him have been given to Him by the Father. This is also an assertion that even before their conversion, they belonged to God (see 6:37). See Acts 18:10 where God says that He had many people in Corinth who belonged to Him but had not yet believed.

16:33 *ᵃ*NU-Text and M-Text omit *will*.   17:2 *ᵃ*M-Text reads *shall*.

they have known that all things which You have given Me are from You. ⁸For I have given to them the words which You have given Me; and they have received *them*, and have known surely that I came forth from You; and they have believed that You sent Me.

⁹"I pray for them. I do not pray for the world but for those whom You have given Me, for they are Yours. ¹⁰And all Mine are Yours, and Yours are Mine, and I am glorified in them. ¹¹Now I am no longer in the world, but these are in the world, and I come to You. Holy Father, keep through Your name those whom You have given Me,ᵃ that they may be one as We *are*. ¹²While I was with them in the world,ᵃ I kept them in Your name. Those whom You gave Me I have kept;ᵇ and none of them is lost except the son of perdition, that the Scripture might be fulfilled. ¹³But now I come to You, and these things I speak in the world, that they may have My joy fulfilled in themselves. ¹⁴I have given them Your word; and the world has hated them because they are not of the world, just as I am not of the world. ¹⁵I do not pray that You should take them out of the world, but that You should keep them from the evil one. ¹⁶They are not of the world, just as I am not of the world. ¹⁷Sanctify them by Your truth. Your word is truth. ¹⁸As You sent Me into the world, I also have sent them into the world. ¹⁹And for their sakes I sanctify Myself, that they also may be sanctified by the truth.

> **17:17 Sanctify.** Sanctification is the setting apart of something for a particular use. Accordingly, believers are set apart for God and His purposes alone so that they do only what God wants and hate what God hates (Lev. 11:44,45). Sanctification is accomplished by truth, the revelation that the Son gave regarding all that the Father commanded Him. That truth is now contained in the Scriptures (see Eph. 5:26).

Jesus Prays for All Believers

²⁰"I do not pray for these alone, but also for those who willᵃ believe in Me through their word; ²¹that they all may be one, as You, Father, *are* in Me, and I in You; that they also may be one in Us, that the world

may believe that You sent Me. ²²And the glory which You gave Me I have given them, that they may be one just as We are one: ²³I in them, and You in Me; that they may be made perfect in one, and that the world may know that You have sent Me, and have loved them as You have loved Me.

²⁴"Father, I desire that they also whom You gave Me may be with Me where I am, that they may behold My glory which You have given Me; for You loved Me before the foundation of the world. ²⁵O righteous Father! The world has not known You, but I have known You; and these have known that You sent Me. ²⁶And I have declared to them Your name, and will declare *it*, that the love with which You loved Me may be in them, and I in them."

> **18:1–40** John's purpose was to present Jesus as the Messiah and Son of God, so he produced evidence to substantiate this throughout the account of Jesus' passion. He showed that Jesus' righteous response to all of the debasing and shameful acts that were directed at Him only provided further confirmation for who He was and why He had come.

Betrayal and Arrest in Gethsemane

18 When Jesus had spoken these words, He went out with His disciples over the Brook Kidron, where there was a garden, which He and His disciples entered. ²And Judas, who betrayed Him, also knew the place; for Jesus often met there with His disciples. ³Then Judas, having received a detachment *of troops*, and officers from the chief priests and Pharisees, came there with lanterns, torches, and weapons. ⁴Jesus therefore, knowing all things that would come upon Him, went forward and said to them, "Whom are you seeking?"

⁵They answered Him, "Jesus of Nazareth."

Jesus said to them, "I am *He*." And Judas, who betrayed Him, also stood with them. ⁶Now when He said to them, "I am *He*," they drew back and fell to the ground.

⁷Then He asked them again, "Whom are you seeking?"

17:11 ᵃNU-Text and M-Text read *keep them through Your name which You have given Me.*
17:12 ᵃNU-Text omits *in the world.* ᵇNU-Text reads *in Your name which You gave Me. And I guarded them;* (or *it;*).   17:20 ᵃNU-Text and M-Text omit *will.*

And they said, "Jesus of Nazareth."

⁸Jesus answered, "I have told you that I am *He*. Therefore, if you seek Me, let these go their way," ⁹that the saying might be fulfilled which He spoke, "Of those whom You gave Me I have lost none."

¹⁰Then Simon Peter, having a sword,

drew it and struck the high priest's servant, and cut off his right ear. The servant's name was Malchus.

¹¹So Jesus said to Peter, "Put your sword into the sheath. Shall I not drink the cup which My Father has given Me?"

Before the High Priest

¹²Then the detachment *of troops* and the captain and the officers of the Jews arrested Jesus and bound Him. ¹³And they led Him away to Annas first, for he was the father-in-law of Caiaphas who was high priest

> **18:4–8 "Whom are you seeking?"** By twice asking this question, Jesus forced the group to acknowledge that they had no authority to take His disciples. Instead, He powerfully and authoritatively declared that He was the one they were seeking.

The timing of events in parts of the Gospel of John seems to differ from the other gospels. How can we explain those apparent differences?

The chronological reckoning between John's gospel and the synoptics (the first three gospels) does present a challenge in the accounts of the Last Supper (13:2). While the synoptics portray the disciples and the Lord at the Last Supper as eating the Passover meal on Thursday evening (Nisan 14) and Jesus being crucified on Friday, John's gospel states that the Jews did not enter into the Praetorium "lest they should be defiled, but that they might eat the Passover" (18:28). So, the disciples had eaten the Passover on Thursday evening, but the Jews had not. In fact, John (19:14) states that Jesus' trial and crucifixion were on the day of Preparation for the Passover and not after the eating of the Passover. This means that because the trial and crucifixion occurred on Friday, Christ was actually sacrificed at the same time the Passover lambs were being slain (19:14). The question then becomes, "Why did the disciples eat the Passover meal on Thursday?"

The answer lies in the fact that there were two distinct ways the Jews in Jesus' day reckoned the beginning and ending of days. Jews in northern Palestine calculated days from sunrise to sunrise. At least one non-regional group, the Pharisees, used that system of time-keeping. But the Jews in southern Israel, which centered in Jerusalem, calculated the day from sunset to sunset. In contrast to the Pharisees, the priests and Sadducees, who for the most part lived around Jerusalem, followed the southern scheme.

In spite of the confusion that these two calendars must have created at times, they were kept for practical reasons. During the Passover season, for instance, it allowed for the feast to be celebrated legitimately on two adjoining days. This also permitted the temple sacrifices to be made over a total of four hours rather than two. The size of the population made this process complicated. By lengthening the time for sacrifices, the double calendar had the effect of reducing both regional and religious clashes between the different regional groups.

The double calendar easily explains the apparent contradictions in the gospel accounts. Being Galileans (northerners), Jesus and the disciples considered Passover day to have started at sunrise on Thursday and end at sunrise on Friday. The Jewish leaders who arrested and tried Jesus, being mostly priests and Sadducees, considered the Passover day to begin at sunset on Thursday and end at sunset on Friday. This explains how Jesus could thereby legitimately celebrate the last Passover meal with His disciples and yet still be sacrificed on Passover day.

In these meticulous details, one can see how God sovereignly and marvelously provided for the precise fulfillment of His redemptive plan. Jesus was anything but a victim of wicked human schemes, much less of blind circumstance. Every word He spoke and every action He took were divinely directed and secured. Even the words and actions by others against Him were divinely controlled (11:49–52; 19:11).

that year. [14]Now it was Caiaphas who advised the Jews that it was expedient that one man should die for the people.

Peter Denies Jesus

[15]And Simon Peter followed Jesus, and so did another[a] disciple. Now that disciple was known to the high priest, and went with Jesus into the courtyard of the high priest. [16]But Peter stood at the door outside. Then the other disciple, who was known to the high priest, went out and spoke to her who kept the door, and brought Peter in. [17]Then the servant girl who kept the door said to Peter, "You are not also one of this Man's disciples, are you?"

He said, "I am not."

> **18:15 another disciple...that disciple.** Traditionally this person has been identified as the "beloved disciple" (13:23,24). This was John the apostle who authored this gospel, but he never mentioned his own name.

[18]Now the servants and officers who had made a fire of coals stood there, for it was cold, and they warmed themselves. And Peter stood with them and warmed himself.

Jesus Questioned by the High Priest

[19]The high priest then asked Jesus about His disciples and His doctrine.

[20]Jesus answered him, "I spoke openly to the world. I always taught in synagogues and in the temple, where the Jews always meet,[a] and in secret I have said nothing. [21]Why do you ask Me? Ask those who have heard Me what I said to them. Indeed they know what I said."

[22]And when He had said these things, one of the officers who stood by struck Jesus with the palm of his hand, saying, "Do You answer the high priest like that?"

[23]Jesus answered him, "If I have spoken evil, bear witness of the evil; but if well, why do you strike Me?"

[24]Then Annas sent Him bound to Caiaphas the high priest.

Peter Denies Twice More

[25]Now Simon Peter stood and warmed himself. Therefore they said to him, "You

are not also one of His disciples, are you?"

He denied it and said, "I am not!"

[26]One of the servants of the high priest, a relative of him whose ear Peter cut off, said, "Did I not see you in the garden with Him?" [27]Peter then denied again; and immediately a rooster crowed.

In Pilate's Court

[28]Then they led Jesus from Caiaphas to the Praetorium, and it was early morning. But they themselves did not go into the Praetorium, lest they should be defiled, but that they might eat the Passover. [29]Pilate then went out to them and said, "What accusation do you bring against this Man?"

[30]They answered and said to him, "If He were not an evildoer, we would not have delivered Him up to you."

[31]Then Pilate said to them, "You take Him and judge Him according to your law."

Therefore the Jews said to him, "It is not lawful for us to put anyone to death," [32]that the saying of Jesus might be fulfilled which He spoke, signifying by what death He would die.

[33]Then Pilate entered the Praetorium again, called Jesus, and said to Him, "Are You the King of the Jews?"

[34]Jesus answered him, "Are you speaking for yourself about this, or did others tell you this concerning Me?"

[35]Pilate answered, "Am I a Jew? Your own nation and the chief priests have delivered You to me. What have You done?"

[36]Jesus answered, "My kingdom is not of this world. If My kingdom were of this world, My servants would fight, so that I should not be delivered to the Jews; but now My kingdom is not from here."

> **18:36 My kingdom is not of this world.** Jesus meant that His kingdom is not connected to political or national entities, nor does it have its origin in the evil world system that rebels against God. God's kingdom exists in the lives of His people, those who have allowed the Son to conquer their sin. His kingdom will overcome the evil world system at the second coming.

[37]Pilate therefore said to Him, "Are You a king then?"

18:15 [a]M-Text reads the other.   18:20 [a]NU-Text reads where all the Jews meet.

Jesus answered, "You say *rightly* that I am a king. For this cause I was born, and for this cause I have come into the world, that I should bear witness to the truth. Everyone who is of the truth hears My voice."

³⁸Pilate said to Him, "What is truth?" And when he had said this, he went out again to the Jews, and said to them, "I find no fault in Him at all.

Taking the Place of Barabbas

³⁹"But you have a custom that I should release someone to you at the Passover. Do you therefore want me to release to you the King of the Jews?"

⁴⁰Then they all cried again, saying, "Not this Man, but Barabbas!" Now Barabbas was a robber.

The Soldiers Mock Jesus

19 So then Pilate took Jesus and scourged *Him*. ²And the soldiers twisted a crown of thorns and put *it* on His head, and they put on Him a purple robe. ³Then they said,ᵃ "Hail, King of the Jews!" And they struck Him with their hands.

> **19:1 scourged.** Pilate appears to have flogged Jesus as a strategy to set Him free (vv. 4–6). He hoped that the Jews would be appeased by this action and that sympathy for Jesus' suffering would result in their desire to release Him (see Luke 23:13–16). This torture entailed the victim being stripped, tied to a post, and beaten by several soldiers. The body would be torn or lacerated to such an extent that the muscles, veins, or bones were exposed. This was meant to weaken and dehumanize the victim prior to execution.

⁴Pilate then went out again, and said to them, "Behold, I am bringing Him out to you, that you may know that I find no fault in Him."

Pilate's Decision

⁵Then Jesus came out, wearing the crown of thorns and the purple robe. And *Pilate* said to them, "Behold the Man!"

⁶Therefore, when the chief priests and officers saw Him, they cried out, saying, "Crucify *Him*, crucify *Him*!"

Pilate said to them, "You take Him and crucify *Him*, for I find no fault in Him."

⁷The Jews answered him, "We have a law, and according to ourᵃ law He ought to die, because He made Himself the Son of God."

⁸Therefore, when Pilate heard that saying, he was the more afraid, ⁹and went again into the Praetorium, and said to Jesus, "Where are You from?" But Jesus gave him no answer.

¹⁰Then Pilate said to Him, "Are You not speaking to me? Do You not know that I have power to crucify You, and power to release You?"

¹¹Jesus answered, "You could have no power at all against Me unless it had been given you from above. Therefore the one who delivered Me to you has the greater sin."

> **19:11** Jesus' response indicates that even the worst evil cannot escape the sovereignty of God. Pilate had no real control, yet still stood as a responsible moral agent for his own actions. **the one who delivered Me to you has the greater sin.** This could refer to either Judas or Caiaphas. The identity of the person is not critical, but the identity of guilt reveals the cold, calculated nature of the act of the Jews turning Jesus over to Pilate, a Gentile.

¹²From then on Pilate sought to release Him, but the Jews cried out, saying, "If you let this Man go, you are not Caesar's friend. Whoever makes himself a king speaks against Caesar."

¹³When Pilate therefore heard that saying, he brought Jesus out and sat down in the judgment seat in a place that is called *The* Pavement, but in Hebrew, Gabbatha. ¹⁴Now it was the Preparation Day of the Passover, and about the sixth hour. And he said to the Jews, "Behold your King!"

¹⁵But they cried out, "Away with *Him*, away with *Him*! Crucify Him!"

Pilate said to them, "Shall I crucify your King?"

The chief priests answered, "We have no king but Caesar!"

¹⁶Then he delivered Him to them to be crucified. Then they took Jesus and led *Him* away.ᵃ

19:3 ᵃNU-Text reads *And they came up to Him and said.*   19:7 ᵃNU-Text reads *the law.*   19:16 ᵃNU-Text omits *and led Him away.*

The King on a Cross

[17]And He, bearing His cross, went out to a place called *the Place* of a Skull, which is called in Hebrew, Golgotha, [18]where they crucified Him, and two others with Him, one on either side, and Jesus in the center. [19]Now Pilate wrote a title and put *it* on the cross. And the writing was:

JESUS OF NAZARETH,
THE KING OF THE JEWS.

[20]Then many of the Jews read this title, for the place where Jesus was crucified was near the city; and it was written in Hebrew, Greek, *and* Latin.

19:18 crucified Him. Jesus was made to lie down on the ground while his arms were nailed to the horizontal beam. Once the beam was fastened to the vertical beam, He was hoisted up with His feet also nailed into the wood. To breathe, it was necessary to push with the legs and pull with the arms, creating excruciating pain. Since collapse meant asphyxiation, the struggle for life continued.

[21]Therefore the chief priests of the Jews said to Pilate, "Do not write, 'The King of the Jews,' but, 'He said, "I am the King of the Jews." ' "

[22]Pilate answered, "What I have written, I have written."

[23]Then the soldiers, when they had crucified Jesus, took His garments and made four parts, to each soldier a part, and also the tunic. Now the tunic was without seam, woven from the top in one piece. [24]They said therefore among themselves, "Let us not tear it, but cast lots for it, whose it shall be," that the Scripture might be fulfilled which says:

" *They divided My garments among them,
And for My clothing they cast lots.*"[a]

Therefore the soldiers did these things.

Behold Your Mother

[25]Now there stood by the cross of Jesus His mother, and His mother's sister, Mary the *wife* of Clopas, and Mary Magdalene.

[26]When Jesus therefore saw His mother, and the disciple whom He loved standing by, He said to His mother, "Woman, behold your son!" [27]Then He said to the disciple, "Behold your mother!" And from that hour that disciple took her to his own *home*.

It Is Finished

[28]After this, Jesus, knowing[a] that all things were now accomplished, that the Scripture might be fulfilled, said, "I thirst!" [29]Now a vessel full of sour wine was sitting there; and they filled a sponge with sour wine, put *it* on hyssop, and put *it* to His mouth. [30]So when Jesus had received the sour wine, He said, "It is finished!" And bowing His head, He gave up His spirit.

Jesus' Side Is Pierced

[31]Therefore, because it was the Preparation *Day*, that the bodies should not remain on the cross on the Sabbath (for that Sabbath was a high day), the Jews asked Pilate that their legs might be broken, and *that* they might be taken away. [32]Then the soldiers came and broke the legs of the first and of the other who was crucified with Him. [33]But when they came to Jesus and saw that He was already dead, they did not break His legs. [34]But one of the soldiers pierced His side with a spear, and immediately blood and water came out. [35]And he who has seen has testified, and his testimony is true; and he knows that he is telling the truth, so that you may believe. [36]For these things were done that the Scripture should be fulfilled, *"Not one of His bones shall be broken."*[a] [37]And again another Scripture says, *" They shall look on Him whom they pierced."*[a]

19:31 Preparation Day. This refers to Friday, the day before, or "the preparation" day for, the Sabbath. **should not remain on the cross on the Sabbath.** Whereas Roman culture was to leave crucified bodies up on the cross until dead and eaten by vultures, the Mosaic law insisted that anyone being impaled (usually after execution) should not remain there overnight (Deut. 21:22,23). Such a person was under God's curse, and leaving him exposed would be to desecrate the land.

19:24 [a]Psalm 22:18   19:28 [a]M-Text reads *seeing.*   19:36 [a]Exodus 12:46; Numbers 9:12; Psalm 34:20
19:37 [a]Zechariah 12:10

19:36,37 These quotes, taken from Ex. 12:46 or Num. 9:12, specify that no bone of the Passover lamb may be broken. Since the NT portrays Jesus as the Passover Lamb that takes away the sin of the world (1 Cor. 5:7), these verses have special prophetic significance.

Jesus Buried in Joseph's Tomb

³⁸After this, Joseph of Arimathea, being a disciple of Jesus, but secretly, for fear of the Jews, asked Pilate that he might take away the body of Jesus; and Pilate gave *him* permission. So he came and took the body of Jesus. ³⁹And Nicodemus, who at first came to Jesus by night, also came, bringing a mixture of myrrh and aloes, about a hundred pounds. ⁴⁰Then they took the body of Jesus, and bound it in strips of linen with the spices, as the custom of the Jews is to bury. ⁴¹Now in the place where He was crucified there was a garden, and in the garden a new tomb in which no one had yet been laid. ⁴²So there they laid Jesus, because of the Jews' Preparation *Day*, for the tomb was nearby.

The Empty Tomb

20 Now the first *day* of the week Mary Magdalene went to the tomb early, while it was still dark, and saw *that* the stone had been taken away from the tomb. ²Then she ran and came to Simon Peter, and to the other disciple, whom Jesus loved, and said to them, "They have taken away the Lord out of the tomb, and we do not know where they have laid Him."

20:1 first day of the week. This was Sunday. From then on, believers set aside Sunday to meet and remember the marvelous resurrection of the Lord (see Acts 20:7). It became known as the Lord's Day (Rev. 1:10). **Mary Magdalene went to the tomb early, while it was still dark.** She came to finish the preparation of Jesus' body for burial by bringing more spices to anoint the corpse (Luke 24:1).

³Peter therefore went out, and the other disciple, and were going to the tomb. ⁴So they both ran together, and the other disciple outran Peter and came to the tomb first. ⁵And he, stooping down and looking in, saw the linen cloths lying *there*; yet he did not go in. ⁶Then Simon Peter came, following him, and went into the tomb; and he saw the linen cloths lying *there*, ⁷and the handkerchief that had been around His head, not lying with the linen cloths, but folded together in a place by itself. ⁸Then the other disciple, who came to the tomb first, went in also; and he saw and believed. ⁹For as yet they did not know the Scripture, that He must rise again from the dead. ¹⁰Then the disciples went away again to their own homes.

Mary Magdalene Sees the Risen Lord

¹¹But Mary stood outside by the tomb weeping, and as she wept she stooped down *and looked* into the tomb. ¹²And she saw two angels in white sitting, one at the head and the other at the feet, where the body of Jesus had lain. ¹³Then they said to her, "Woman, why are you weeping?"

She said to them, "Because they have taken away my Lord, and I do not know where they have laid Him."

¹⁴Now when she had said this, she turned around and saw Jesus standing *there*, and did not know that it was Jesus. ¹⁵Jesus said to her, "Woman, why are you weeping? Whom are you seeking?"

She, supposing Him to be the gardener, said to Him, "Sir, if You have carried Him away, tell me where You have laid Him, and I will take Him away."

¹⁶Jesus said to her, "Mary!"

She turned and said to Him,ᵃ "Rabboni!" (which is to say, Teacher).

¹⁷Jesus said to her, "Do not cling to Me, for I have not yet ascended to My Father; but go to My brethren and say to them, 'I am ascending to My Father and your Father, and *to* My God and your God.' "

20:17 Do not cling to Me, for I have not yet ascended. Mary desired to hold on to Jesus' physical presence for fear that she would again lose Him. Jesus' statement refers to the temporary length of His time with them physically. He would leave them after 40 days and send the Holy Spirit in His place to guide them. **My brethren.** The disciples had been called "servants" and "friends" (15:15), but not "brothers" until here. This new relationship with Christ was only made possible by His work on the cross.

20:16 ᵃNU-Text adds *in Hebrew.*

[18]Mary Magdalene came and told the disciples that she had seen the Lord,[a] and *that* He had spoken these things to her.

The Apostles Commissioned

[19]Then, the same day at evening, being the first *day* of the week, when the doors were shut where the disciples were assembled,[a] for fear of the Jews, Jesus came and stood in the midst, and said to them, "Peace *be* with you." [20]When He had said this, He showed them *His* hands and His side. Then the disciples were glad when they saw the Lord.

[21]So Jesus said to them again, "Peace to you! As the Father has sent Me, I also send you." [22]And when He had said this, He breathed on *them*, and said to them, "Receive the Holy Spirit. [23]If you forgive the sins of any, they are forgiven them; if you retain the *sins* of any, they are retained."

Seeing and Believing

[24]Now Thomas, called the Twin, one of the twelve, was not with them when Jesus came. [25]The other disciples therefore said to him, "We have seen the Lord."

So he said to them, "Unless I see in His hands the print of the nails, and put my finger into the print of the nails, and put my hand into His side, I will not believe."

[26]And after eight days His disciples were again inside, and Thomas with them. Jesus came, the doors being shut, and stood in the midst, and said, "Peace to you!" [27]Then He said to Thomas, "Reach your finger here, and look at My hands; and reach your hand *here*, and put *it* into My side. Do not be unbelieving, but believing."

[28]And Thomas answered and said to Him, "My Lord and my God!"

20:28 "My Lord and my God!" With these words, Thomas declared his firm belief in the resurrection and the deity of Jesus as the Messiah and Son of God (Titus 2:13). Thomas' confession serves as the fitting capstone of John's purpose in writing (see vv. 30,31).

---

[29]Jesus said to him, "Thomas,[a] because you have seen Me, you have believed.

Blessed *are* those who have not seen and *yet* have believed."

That You May Believe

[30]And truly Jesus did many other signs in the presence of His disciples, which are not written in this book; [31]but these are written that you may believe that Jesus is the Christ, the Son of God, and that believing you may have life in His name.

Breakfast by the Sea

21 After these things Jesus showed Himself again to the disciples at the Sea of Tiberias, and in this way He showed *Himself:* [2]Simon Peter, Thomas called the Twin, Nathanael of Cana in Galilee, the *sons* of Zebedee, and two others of His disciples were together. [3]Simon Peter said to them, "I am going fishing."

21:3 "I am going fishing." The most reasonable explanation for Peter and the others going to Galilee in order to fish was that they went in obedience to the Lord's command that they meet Him in Galilee (Matt. 28:16). Peter and the others occupied their time with their former livelihood while they awaited Jesus' appearance.

They said to him, "We are going with you also." They went out and immediately[a] got into the boat, and that night they caught nothing. [4]But when the morning had now come, Jesus stood on the shore; yet the disciples did not know that it was Jesus. [5]Then Jesus said to them, "Children, have you any food?"

They answered Him, "No."

[6]And He said to them, "Cast the net on the right side of the boat, and you will find *some*." So they cast, and now they were not able to draw it in because of the multitude of fish.

[7]Therefore that disciple whom Jesus loved said to Peter, "It is the Lord!" Now when Simon Peter heard that it was the Lord, he put on *his* outer garment (for he had removed it), and plunged into the sea. [8]But the other disciples came in the little boat (for they were not far from land, but about two hundred cubits), dragging the net

---

20:18 [a]NU-Text reads disciples, "I have seen the Lord," . . .   20:19 [a]NU-Text omits *assembled.*
20:29 [a]NU-Text and M-Text omit *Thomas.*   21:3 [a]NU-Text omits *immediately.*

with fish. ⁹Then, as soon as they had come to land, they saw a fire of coals there, and fish laid on it, and bread. ¹⁰Jesus said to them, "Bring some of the fish which you have just caught."

¹¹Simon Peter went up and dragged the net to land, full of large fish, one hundred and fifty-three; and although there were so many, the net was not broken. ¹²Jesus said to them, "Come *and* eat breakfast." Yet none of the disciples dared ask Him, "Who are You?"—knowing that it was the Lord. ¹³Jesus then came and took the bread and gave it to them, and likewise the fish.

¹⁴This *is* now the third time Jesus showed Himself to His disciples after He was raised from the dead.

Jesus Restores Peter

¹⁵So when they had eaten breakfast, Jesus said to Simon Peter, "Simon, *son* of Jonah,ᵃ do you love Me more than these?"

He said to Him, "Yes, Lord; You know that I love You."

He said to him, "Feed My lambs."

¹⁶He said to him again a second time, "Simon, *son* of Jonah,ᵃ do you love Me?"

He said to Him, "Yes, Lord; You know that I love You."

He said to him, "Tend My sheep."

¹⁷He said to him the third time, "Simon, *son* of Jonah,ᵃ do you love Me?" Peter was grieved because He said to him the third time, "Do you love Me?"

> **21:15–17** Two meanings of "love" are emphasized here. Jesus first asked Peter if he loved Him with total commitment. Peter responded that he loved Jesus, but did not use the word that meant total commitment. This may have been because Peter's past denial of Jesus made him feel unqualified to claim that level of love. Jesus then asked if Peter loved him supremely. Jesus' purpose was to relay the message that He demands total commitment from His followers.

And he said to Him, "Lord, You know all things; You know that I love You."

Jesus said to him, "Feed My sheep. ¹⁸Most assuredly, I say to you, when you were younger, you girded yourself and walked where you wished; but when you are old, you will stretch out your hands, and another will gird you and carry *you* where you do not wish." ¹⁹This He spoke, signifying by what death he would glorify God. And when He had spoken this, He said to him, "Follow Me."

The Beloved Disciple and His Book

²⁰Then Peter, turning around, saw the disciple whom Jesus loved following, who also had leaned on His breast at the supper, and said, "Lord, who is the one who betrays You?" ²¹Peter, seeing him, said to Jesus, "But Lord, what *about* this man?"

²²Jesus said to him, "If I will that he remain till I come, what *is that* to you? You follow Me."

²³Then this saying went out among the brethren that this disciple would not die. Yet Jesus did not say to him that he would not die, but, "If I will that he remain till I come, what *is that* to you?"

²⁴This is the disciple who testifies of these things, and wrote these things; and we know that his testimony is true.

> **21:24 the disciple who testifies.** John was a personal witness to the truth of the events that he recorded. The "we" most likely is an editorial device referring only to John (see 1:14), or it may include the collective witness of his fellow apostles.

²⁵And there are also many other things that Jesus did, which if they were written one by one, I suppose that even the world itself could not contain the books that would be written. Amen.

21:15 ᵃNU-Text reads *John*.   21:16 ᵃNU-Text reads *John*.   21:17 ᵃNU-Text reads *John*.

ACTS

Everyone underestimated the possibility and the power of the resurrection of Jesus Christ. Even those who had advanced warning were taken by surprise. The truth of His victory over death transformed the lives of His followers. They became living witnesses to Jesus' resurrection. That good news spread like wildfire.

Those first disciples were filled with more than a message, however; they were also filled with a Motivator—the Holy Spirit. Their travels, trials, and triumphs changed the course of history. Led by the Holy Spirit, the Apostles carried the gospel throughout the world. In fact, this book that describes the early years of the Christian Church could most properly be called "The Acts of the Holy Spirit through the Apostles." The Holy Spirit's directing, controlling, and empowering ministry strengthened the church and caused it to grow in numbers, spiritual power, and influence. The second half of Luke's masterpiece, Acts, records the story.

AUTHOR AND DATE

Acts was written by Luke, approximately A.D. 60 to 62.

The opening verses of Luke and Acts strongly suggest that both books had the same writer because both are addressed to Theophilus. The writer of Acts specifically claims to have written an earlier book to this mystery person named Theophilus (Acts 1:1) about the life and teaching of Jesus. Early church Fathers such as Irenaeus, Clement of Alexandria, Tertullian, Origen, Eusebius, and Jerome all affirmed Luke's authorship in their writings. So does the Muratorian Canon (about A.D. 170). Because Luke is a relatively obscure figure, mentioned only three times in the New Testament (Colossians 4:14; 2 Timothy 4:11; Philemon 24), it is unlikely that anyone would have forged a work to make it appear to be his. A forger surely would have attributed his work to a more prominent person, such as one of the original twelve disciples or Paul.

Some believe that Luke wrote Acts after the fall of Jerusalem (A.D. 70). He probably lived until about A.D. 85, but he probably wrote much earlier, before the end of Paul's first Roman imprisonment (about A.D. 60–62). That date best explains the abrupt ending of Acts, which leaves Paul awaiting trial before Caesar. Luke's silence about significant pre-A.D. 70 events such as: (1) the outcome of Paul's trial; (2) Paul's further ministry; (3) Paul's second imprisonment (2 Timothy 4:11); (4) Paul's death; (5) the death of James, head of the Jerusalem Church (A.D. 62); (6) the persecution under Nero (A.D. 64); and (7) the fall of Jerusalem itself (A.D. 70), all point to an earlier date of composition. Surely Luke would have mentioned these events if he had been writing after they occurred.

Luke's purposes in writing the Gospel of Luke and the Acts of the Apostles form a powerful parallel. Luke sought to write "an orderly account" (Luke 1:3) of what Jesus had accomplished during His earthly ministry. Acts simply extended the effort, offering "an orderly account" of what Jesus had accomplished through the early church.

Beginning with Christ's ascension (His rise into heaven), through the birth of the church on the Day of Pentecost and to Paul's preaching in Rome, Acts chronicles the spread of the gospel and the growth of the church (see 1:15; 2:41,47; 4:4; 5:14; 6:7; 9:31; 12:24; 13:49; 16:5; 19:20). It also tells of the mounting opposition to the gospel (see 2:13; 4:1–22; 5:17–42; 6:9–8:4; 12:1–5; 13:6–12,45–50; 14:2–6,19–24; 16:19,20; 17:5–9; 19:23–41; 21:27–36; 23:12–21; 28:24).

Like the Gospel of Luke, Acts begins with a dedication to Theophilus, whose name means "lover of God." The name has no history apart from Luke's use in his two books. Whether this was a believer whom Luke was instructing or a pagan whom Luke was seeking to convert is unknown. Luke's positive salutation, "most excellent Theophilus" (Luke 1:3), suggests that the recipient was a Roman official of some importance. Examples of this kind of greeting can be found in 24:3 and 26:25.

Acts begins in Jerusalem and ends in Rome. Luke's account captures the geographical spread of the gospel throughout the Roman Empire. He provides the story of how God "opened the door of faith to the Gentiles" (14:27).

HISTORICAL AND THEOLOGICAL THEMES

As the first work of church history ever penned, Acts records the initial response to the Great Commission (Matthew 28:19,20). It provides information about the first three decades of the church's existence—material found nowhere else in the New Testament.

Although not primarily a doctrinal work, Acts nonetheless emphasizes several key doctrines: (1) Jesus of Nazareth is Israel's long-awaited Messiah; (2) the gospel is offered to all people (not merely the Jews); and (3) the work of the Holy Spirit (mentioned more than 50 times). Luke accurately recorded how the early Jewish believers used the Old Testament as their biblical authority in taking the gospel into the world.

> AS THE **FIRST WORK** OF **CHURCH HISTORY** EVER PENNED, **ACTS RECORDS** THE **INITIAL RESPONSE** TO THE **GREAT COMMISSION.**

The following passages illustrate their method: 2:17–21 (Joel 2:28–32); 2:25–28 (Psalm 16:8–11); 2:35 (Psalm 110:1); 4:11 (Psalm 118:22); 4:25,26 (Psalm 2:1,2); 7:49,50 (Isaiah 66:1,2); 8:32,33 (Isaiah 53:7,8); 28:26,27 (Isaiah 6:9,10).

Acts abounds in transitions: (1) from the ministry of Jesus to that of the apostles; (2) from the Old Covenant to the New Covenant; and (3) from Israel as God's witness nation to the church (composed of both Jews and Gentiles) as God's wit-

ness people. While the book of Hebrews sets forth the theology of the transition from the Old Covenant to the New, Acts depicts the New Covenant's practical outworking in the life of the church.

OUTLINE

Prologue

1 The former account I made, O The-ophilus, of all that Jesus began both to do and teach, ²until the day in which He was taken up, after He through the Holy Spirit had given commandments to the apostles whom He had chosen, ³to whom He also presented Himself alive after His suffering by many infallible proofs, being seen by them during forty days and speak-ing of the things pertaining to the kingdom of God.

1:3 presented Himself...by many infallible proofs. To give the apostles confidence to present His mes-sage, Jesus showed them His wounds (Luke 24:39) and ate and drank with them (Luke 24:41–43). **forty days.** Forty days passed between Jesus' death and ascension, during which He appeared at intervals to the apostles and others (1 Cor. 15:5–8). **kingdom of God.** This refers to God's rule over believers' hearts (see Col. 1:13) and was the dominant theme during Christ's earthly ministry (see Matt. 4:23).

The Holy Spirit Promised

⁴And being assembled together with *them*, He commanded them not to depart from Jerusalem, but to wait for the Promise of the Father, "which," *He said*, "you have heard from Me; ⁵for John truly baptized with water, but you shall be baptized with the Holy Spirit not many days from now." ⁶Therefore, when they had come together, they asked Him, saying, "Lord, will You at this time restore the kingdom to Israel?" ⁷And He said to them, "It is not for you to know times or seasons which the Father has put in His own authority. ⁸But you shall receive power when the Holy Spirit has come upon you; and you shall be witnesses

---

1:8 The Holy Spirit empowered the apostles so they could fulfill their mission of spreading the gospel. History was altered as the gospel message reached all parts of the earth (Matt. 28:19,20). **receive power.** Soon the apostles would receive the Holy Spirit's in-dwelling presence empowering them to be Christ's witnesses. **witnesses.** These are people who tell the truth about Jesus Christ (see John 14:26). **Judea.** Je-rusalem was in this region. **Samaria.** This was the region north of Judea.

---

to Me*ᵃ* in Jerusalem, and in all Judea and Samaria, and to the end of the earth."

Jesus Ascends to Heaven

⁹Now when He had spoken these things, while they watched, He was taken up, and a cloud received Him out of their sight. ¹⁰And while they looked steadfastly toward heav-en as He went up, behold, two men stood by them in white apparel, ¹¹who also said, "Men of Galilee, why do you stand gazing up into heaven? This *same* Jesus, who was taken up from you into heaven, will so come in like manner as you saw Him go into heaven."

The Upper Room Prayer Meeting

¹²Then they returned to Jerusalem from the mount called Olivet, which is near Je-rusalem, a Sabbath day's journey. ¹³And when they had entered, they went up into the upper room where they were staying: Peter, James, John, and Andrew; Philip and Thomas; Bartholomew and Matthew; James *the son* of Alphaeus and Simon the Zealot; and Judas *the son* of James. ¹⁴These all continued with one accord in prayer and supplication,*ᵃ* with the women and Mary the mother of Jesus, and with His brothers.

Matthias Chosen

¹⁵And in those days Peter stood up in the midst of the disciples*ᵃ* (altogether the num-ber of names was about a hundred and twenty), and said, ¹⁶"Men *and* brethren, this Scripture had to be fulfilled, which the Holy Spirit spoke before by the mouth of David concerning Judas, who became a guide to those who arrested Jesus; ¹⁷for he was numbered with us and obtained a part in this ministry."

1:17 obtained a part in this ministry. Judas Iscari-ot had been a member of the 12, but he was never truly saved. He was called "the son of perdition" (John 17:12).

---

¹⁸(Now this man purchased a field with the wages of iniquity; and falling headlong, he burst open in the middle and all his en-trails gushed out. ¹⁹And it became known

---

1:8 *ᵃ*NU-Text reads *My witnesses.*   1:14 *ᵃ*NU-Text omits *and supplication.*   1:15 *ᵃ*NU-Text reads *brethren.*

to all those dwelling in Jerusalem; so that field is called in their own language, Akel Dama, that is, Field of Blood.)

²⁰"For it is written in the Book of Psalms:

'Let his dwelling place be desolate,
    And let no one live in it';^a

and,

'Let^b another take his office.'^c

²¹"Therefore, of these men who have accompanied us all the time that the Lord Jesus went in and out among us, ²²beginning from the baptism of John to that day when He was taken up from us, one of these must become a witness with us of His resurrection."

²³And they proposed two: Joseph called Barsabas, who was surnamed Justus, and Matthias. ²⁴And they prayed and said, "You, O Lord, who know the hearts of all, show which of these two You have chosen

²⁵to take part in this ministry and apostleship from which Judas by transgression fell, that he might go to his own place." ²⁶And they cast their lots, and the lot fell on Matthias. And he was numbered with the eleven apostles.

1:23 Barsabas...Justus. Barsabas means "son of the Sabbath." Justus ("the righteous") was Joseph's Latin name. Many Jews in the Roman Empire had equivalent Gentile names. **Matthias.** The name means "gift of God." The ancient historian Eusebius maintains that Matthias was among the 70 followers sent out in Luke 10:1.

Coming of the Holy Spirit

2 When the Day of Pentecost had fully come, they were all with one accord^a in one place. ²And suddenly there came a sound from heaven, as of a rushing mighty wind, and it filled the whole house where they were sitting. ³Then there appeared to them divided tongues, as of fire, and one sat upon each of them. ⁴And they were all

1:20 ^aPsalm 69:25   ^bPsalm 109:8   ^cGreek *episkopen, position of overseer*   2:1 ^aNU-Text reads *together.*

What can we learn about the Holy Spirit's special role from the Book of Acts?

One of the cautions we must exercise in studying and teaching from the Book of Acts has to do with the difference between *description* and *prescription*. The difference plays an important role in interpreting the historical biblical books. The Bible's description of an event does not imply that the event or action can, should, or will be repeated.

The role of the Holy Spirit in His arrival as the promised Helper (John 14:17), which Acts describes as a startling audiovisual event (2:1–13), had some partial and selected repetitions (8:14–19, 10:44–48, 19:1–7). These were special cases in which believers are reported to have received or been filled with the Holy Spirit. In each of these cases, the sound is of a rushing mighty wind and the tongues as of fire that were present in the original event (2:1–13) were absent, but the people spoke in tongues they did not know (but others recognized). These events should not be taken as the basis for teaching that believers today should expect the same tongue-evidence to accompany the filling of the Holy Spirit. Even in Acts itself, genuine conversions did not necessarily lead to extraordinary filling by the Holy Spirit. For example, a crowd of three thousand people believed and were baptized on the same Day of Pentecost (2:41) that started so dramatically, yet there is no mention of tongues. So, why in some cases did tongues accompany the confirmation of faith? That this actually occurred likely demonstrated that believers were being drawn from very different groups into the church. Each new group received a special welcome from the Holy Spirit. Thus, Samaritans (8:14–19), Gentiles (10:44–48), and believers from the Old Covenant (19:1–7) were added to the church, and the unity of the church was established. To demonstrate that unity, it was imperative to have some replication in each instance of what had occurred at Pentecost with the believing Jews, such as the presence of the apostles and the coming of the Spirit, manifestly indicated through speaking in the languages of Pentecost.

filled with the Holy Spirit and began to speak with other tongues, as the Spirit gave them utterance.

2:4 all. These were the apostles and the 120 other believers (see Joel 2:28–32). **filled with the Holy Spirit.** The filling of the Spirit is a repeated reality that God commands believers to maintain so that their behavior is pleasing to Him. **with other tongues.** These were known languages, not ecstatic utterances, which were given by the Holy Spirit as a sign of judgment to unbelieving Israel. God's people would come from all nations.

The Crowd's Response

⁵And there were dwelling in Jerusalem Jews, devout men, from every nation under heaven. ⁶And when this sound occurred, the multitude came together, and were confused, because everyone heard them speak in his own language. ⁷Then they were all amazed and marveled, saying to one another, "Look, are not all these who speak Galileans? ⁸And how *is it that* we hear, each in our own language in which we were born? ⁹Parthians and Medes and Elamites, those dwelling in Mesopotamia, Judea and Cappadocia, Pontus and Asia, ¹⁰Phrygia and Pamphylia, Egypt and the parts of Libya adjoining Cyrene, visitors from Rome, both Jews and proselytes, ¹¹Cretans and Arabs— we hear them speaking in our own tongues the wonderful works of God." ¹²So they were all amazed and perplexed, saying to one another, "Whatever could this mean?"

¹³Others mocking said, "They are full of new wine."

2:9–11 The list of specific countries and ethnic groups proves that the utterances were known human languages.

Peter's Sermon

¹⁴But Peter, standing up with the eleven, raised his voice and said to them, "Men of Judea and all who dwell in Jerusalem, let this be known to you, and heed my words. ¹⁵For these are not drunk, as you suppose, since it is *only* the third hour of the day. ¹⁶But this is what was spoken by the prophet Joel:

---

¹⁷ 'And it shall come to pass in the last days, says God,
   That I will pour out of My Spirit on all flesh;
   Your sons and your daughters shall prophesy,
   Your young men shall see visions,
   Your old men shall dream dreams.

2:17 visions...dreams. Visions and dreams were primarily reserved for prophets and apostles (see Num. 12:6) and were apocalyptic in nature. While frequent in the OT (see Gen. 15:1; Dan. 7:1), they were rare in the NT. In Acts, the visions were given either to Peter (chaps. 10,11) or Paul (chaps. 9,18). They were not considered normal in biblical times, nor should they be considered so now. God will use visions and dreams during the Tribulation period (see Joel 2:28–32).

---

¹⁸ And on My menservants and on My maidservants
   I will pour out My Spirit in those days;
   And they shall prophesy.
¹⁹ I will show wonders in heaven above
   And signs in the earth beneath:
   Blood and fire and vapor of smoke.
²⁰ The sun shall be turned into darkness,
   And the moon into blood,
   Before the coming of the great and awesome day of the LORD.
²¹ And it shall come to pass
   That whoever calls on the name of the LORD
   Shall be saved.'ᵃ

²²"Men of Israel, hear these words: Jesus of Nazareth, a Man attested by God to you by miracles, wonders, and signs which God did through Him in your midst, as you yourselves also know—²³Him, being delivered by the determined purpose and foreknowledge of God, you have takenᵃ by

---

2:23 by the determined purpose and foreknowledge of God. From eternity past (2 Tim. 1:9), God determined that Jesus would die an atoning death. **lawless hands, have crucified.** This is an indictment against the unbelieving Jews who instigated Jesus' death, even though the actual crucifixion was carried out by the Romans. God predetermined the crucifixion, but that did not absolve the guilt of those who caused it.

2:21 ᵃJoel 2:28–32   2:23 ᵃNU-Text omits *have taken*.

lawless hands, have crucified, and put to death; [24]whom God raised up, having loosed the pains of death, because it was not possible that He should be held by it. [25]For David says concerning Him:

> 'I foresaw the LORD always before my
>   face,
> For He is at my right hand, that I may
>   not be shaken.
>
> [26] Therefore my heart rejoiced, and my
>   tongue was glad;
> Moreover my flesh also will rest in
>   hope.
> [27] For You will not leave my soul in
>   Hades,
> Nor will You allow Your Holy One to
>   see corruption.
> [28] You have made known to me the ways
>   of life;
> You will make me full of joy in Your
>   presence.'[a]

[29]"Men and brethren, let me speak freely to you of the patriarch David, that he is both dead and buried, and his tomb is with us to this day. [30]Therefore, being a prophet, and knowing that God had sworn with an oath to him that of the fruit of his body, according to the flesh, He would raise up the Christ to sit on his throne,[a] [31]he, foreseeing this, spoke concerning the resurrection of the Christ, that His soul was not left in Hades, nor did His flesh see corruption. [32]This Jesus God has raised up, of which we are all witnesses. [33]Therefore being exalted to the right hand of God, and having received from the Father the promise of the Holy Spirit, He poured out this which you now see and hear. [34]"For David did not ascend into the heavens, but he says himself:

> 'The LORD said to my Lord,
>   "Sit at My right hand,

2:28 [a]Psalm 16:8–11   2:30 [a]NU-Text omits *according to the flesh, He would raise up the Christ* and completes the verse with *He would seat one on his throne.*

MINISTRIES OF THE HOLY SPIRIT

- Baptismal Medium .... 1 Corinthians 12:13
- Calls to Ministry .... Acts 13:2–4
- Channel of Divine Revelation .... 2 Samuel 23:2; Nehemiah 9:30; Zechariah 7:12; John 14:17
- Empowers .... Exodus 31:1,2; Judges 13:25; Acts 1:8
- Fills .... Luke 4:1; Acts 2:4; Ephesians 5:18
- Guarantees .... 2 Corinthians 1:22; 5:5; Ephesians 1:14
- Guards .... 2 Timothy 1:14
- Helps .... John 14:16,26; 15:26; 16:7
- Illuminates .... 1 Corinthians 2:10–13
- Indwells .... Romans 8:9–11; 1 Corinthians 3:16; 6:19
- Intercedes .... Romans 8:26,27
- Produces Fruit .... Galatians 5:22,23
- Provides Spiritual Character ..... Galatians 5:16,18,25
- Regenerates .... John 3:5,6,8
- Restrains/Convicts of Sin .... Genesis 6:3; John 16:8–10; Acts 7:51
- Sanctifies .... Romans 15:16; 1 Corinthians 6:11; 2 Thessalonians 2:13
- Seals .... 2 Corinthians 1:22; Ephesians 1:14; 4:30
- Selects Overseers .... Acts 20:28
- Source of Fellowship .... 2 Corinthians 13:14; Philippians 2:1
- Source of Liberty .... 2 Corinthians 3:17,18
- Source of Power .... Ephesians 3:16
- Source of Unity .... Ephesians 4:3,4
- Source of Spiritual Gifts .... 1 Corinthians 12:4–11
- Teaches .... John 14:26; Acts 15:28; 1 John 2:20,27

35 *Till I make Your enemies Your
footstool."* ' ᵃ

36"Therefore let all the house of Israel
know assuredly that God has made this
Jesus, whom you crucified, both Lord and
Christ."

37Now when they heard *this*, they were
cut to the heart, and said to Peter and the
rest of the apostles, "Men *and* brethren,
what shall we do?"

38Then Peter said to them, "Repent, and
let every one of you be baptized in the name
of Jesus Christ for the remission of sins;
and you shall receive the gift of the Holy
Spirit. 39For the promise is to you and to
your children, and to all who are afar off, as
many as the Lord our God will call."

A Vital Church Grows

40And with many other words he testified
and exhorted them, saying, "Be saved from
this perverse generation." 41Then those
who gladlyᵃ received his word were baptized; and that day about three thousand
souls were added *to them.* 42And they continued steadfastly in the apostles' doctrine
and fellowship, in the breaking of bread,
and in prayers. 43Then fear came upon every soul, and many wonders and signs were
done through the apostles. 44Now all who
believed were together, and had all things in
common, 45and sold their possessions and
goods, and divided them among all, as anyone had need.

2:42 apostles' doctrine. Scripture (at that time the
spoken words of the apostles) is the foundational
content for believers' spiritual growth. **fellowship.**
This means "partnership" or "sharing." Christians
are partners with Jesus Christ and other believers
(1 John 1:3), and it is their spiritual duty to encourage one another in righteousness and obedience
(see Rom. 12:10). **breaking of bread.** The Lord's
Table is mandatory for all Christians to observe (see
1 Cor. 11:24–29).

46So continuing daily with one accord in
the temple, and breaking bread from house
to house, they ate their food with gladness
and simplicity of heart, 47praising God and
having favor with all the people. And the

Lord added to the churchᵃ daily those who
were being saved.

A Lame Man Healed

3 Now Peter and John went up together
to the temple at the hour of prayer, the
ninth *hour.* 2And a certain man lame from
his mother's womb was carried, whom
they laid daily at the gate of the temple
which is called Beautiful, to ask alms from
those who entered the temple; 3who, seeing
Peter and John about to go into the temple,
asked for alms. 4And fixing his eyes on him,
with John, Peter said, "Look at us." 5So he
gave them his attention, expecting to receive something from them. 6Then Peter
said, "Silver and gold I do not have, but
what I do have I give you: In the name of
Jesus Christ of Nazareth, rise up and
walk." 7And he took him by the right hand
and lifted *him* up, and immediately his feet
and ankle bones received strength. 8So he,
leaping up, stood and walked and entered
the temple with them—walking, leaping,
and praising God. 9And all the people saw
him walking and praising God. 10Then they
knew that it was he who sat begging alms at
the Beautiful Gate of the temple; and they
were filled with wonder and amazement at
what had happened to him.

Preaching in Solomon's Portico

11Now as the lame man who was healed
held on to Peter and John, all the people ran
together to them in the porch which is
called Solomon's, greatly amazed. 12So
when Peter saw *it,* he responded to the people: "Men of Israel, why do you marvel at
this? Or why look so intently at us, as
though by our own power or godliness we
had made this man walk? 13The God of
Abraham, Isaac, and Jacob, the God of our

3:13 The God of Abraham, Isaac, and Jacob. Peter
used this description of God because it was familiar
to his Jewish audience (see Ex. 3:6,15) and would
show that he declared the same God and Messiah
whom the prophets had proclaimed. **Servant Jesus.**
Peter depicted Jesus as God's personal representative. This is an unusual NT title for Jesus, but it is
a familiar OT name for the Messiah (see Is. 42:1–4,19).

2:35 ᵃPsalm 110:1   2:41 ᵃNU-Text omits *gladly.*   2:47 ᵃNU-Text omits *to the church.*

fathers, glorified His Servant Jesus, whom you delivered up and denied in the presence of Pilate, when he was determined to let *Him* go. ¹⁴But you denied the Holy One and the Just, and asked for a murderer to be granted to you, ¹⁵and killed the Prince of life, whom God raised from the dead, of which we are witnesses. ¹⁶And His name, through faith in His name, has made this man strong, whom you see and know. Yes, the faith which *comes* through Him has given him this perfect soundness in the presence of you all.

¹⁷"Yet now, brethren, I know that you did *it* in ignorance, as *did* also your rulers. ¹⁸But those things which God foretold by the mouth of all His prophets, that the Christ would suffer, He has thus fulfilled. ¹⁹Repent therefore and be converted, that your sins may be blotted out, so that times of refreshing may come from the presence of the Lord, ²⁰and that He may send Jesus Christ, who was preached to you before,*ᵃ* ²¹whom heaven must receive until the times of restoration of all things, which God has spoken by the mouth of all His holy prophets since the world began. ²²For Moses truly said to the fathers, 'The LORD *your God will raise up for you a Prophet like me from your brethren. Him you shall hear in all things, whatever He says to you.* ²³*And it shall be that every soul who will not hear that Prophet shall be utterly destroyed from among the people.'ᵃ* ²⁴Yes, and all the prophets, from Samuel and those who follow, as many as have spoken, have also foretold*ᵃ* these days. ²⁵You are sons of the prophets, and of the covenant which God made with our fathers, saying to Abraham, '*And in your seed all the families of the earth shall be blessed.'ᵃ* ²⁶To you first, God,

---

3:19–21 times of refreshing...times of restoration of all things. "Times" means era or season. Two descriptions are given of the coming era of the millennial kingdom. They refer to Jesus Christ as being sent from God to bring about those times. Peter points to Christ's earthly reign (see Rom. 11:26) that will be marked by all kinds of blessing and renewal (see Is. 11:6–10; Rev. 19:1–10).

---

having raised up His Servant Jesus, sent Him to bless you, in turning away every one *of you* from your iniquities."

Peter and John Arrested

4 Now as they spoke to the people, the priests, the captain of the temple, and the Sadducees came upon them, ²being greatly disturbed that they taught the people and preached in Jesus the resurrection from the dead. ³And they laid hands on them, and put *them* in custody until the next day, for it was already evening. ⁴However, many of those who heard the word believed; and the number of the men came to be about five thousand.

4:3 already evening. The Jews detained Peter and John overnight in jail because Jewish law did not permit trials at night. It was too late to convene the Sanhedrin that afternoon, so the apostles would face a hearing the next day.

Addressing the Sanhedrin

⁵And it came to pass, on the next day, that their rulers, elders, and scribes, ⁶as well as Annas the high priest, Caiaphas, John, and Alexander, and as many as were of the family of the high priest, were gathered together at Jerusalem. ⁷And when they had set them in the midst, they asked, "By what power or by what name have you done this?"

⁸Then Peter, filled with the Holy Spirit, said to them, "Rulers of the people and elders of Israel: ⁹If we this day are judged for a good deed *done* to a helpless man, by what means he has been made well, ¹⁰let it be known to you all, and to all the people of Israel, that by the name of Jesus Christ of Nazareth, whom you crucified, whom God raised from the dead, by Him this man stands here before you whole. ¹¹This is the '*stone which was rejected by you builders, which has become the chief cornerstone.'ᵃ* ¹²Nor is there salvation in any other, for there is no other name under heaven given among men by which we must be saved."

3:20 *ᵃ*NU-Text and M-Text read *Christ Jesus, who was ordained for you before.*   **3:23** *ᵃ*Deuteronomy 18:15,18,19   **3:24** *ᵃ*NU-Text and M-Text read *proclaimed.*   **3:25** *ᵃ*Genesis 22:18; 26:4; 28:14
4:11 *ᵃ*Psalm 118:22

4:12 no other name. This refers to salvation only by faith in Jesus Christ. There are only two religious paths: the broad way of attempting to be saved by good works—which leads to eternal death, or the narrow way of faith in Jesus—which leads to eternal life (Matt. 7:13,14). Sadly, many of the Jewish religious leaders and their followers were on the first path.

The Name of Jesus Forbidden

[13]Now when they saw the boldness of Peter and John, and perceived that they were uneducated and untrained men, they marveled. And they realized that they had been with Jesus. [14]And seeing the man who had been healed standing with them, they could say nothing against it. [15]But when they had commanded them to go aside out of the council, they conferred among themselves, [16]saying, "What shall we do to these men? For, indeed, that a notable miracle has been done through them is evident to all who dwell in Jerusalem, and we cannot deny it. [17]But so that it spreads no further among the people, let us severely threaten them, that from now on they speak to no man in this name."

[18]So they called them and commanded them not to speak at all nor teach in the name of Jesus. [19]But Peter and John answered and said to them, "Whether it is right in the sight of God to listen to you more than to God, you judge. [20]For we cannot but speak the things which we have seen and heard." [21]So when they had further threatened them, they let them go, finding no way of punishing them, because of the people, since they all glorified God for what had been done. [22]For the man was over forty years old on whom this miracle of healing had been performed.

4:19 to listen to you more than to God. Christians should obey governmental authority (Rom. 13:1–7) as long as the government decrees are not contrary to God's Word (see Ex. 1:15–17).

Prayer for Boldness

[23]And being let go, they went to their own companions and reported all that the chief priests and elders had said to them. [24]So when they heard that, they raised their voice to God with one accord and said: "Lord, You are God, who made heaven and earth and the sea, and all that is in them, [25]who by the mouth of Your servant David[a] have said:

4:24 Lord. The Greek word, meaning "absolute master" (Luke 2:29), is an uncommon NT title for God. It represented the disciples' recognition of God's sovereignty.

'Why did the nations rage,
    And the people plot vain things?
26   The kings of the earth took their
        stand,
    And the rulers were gathered together
    Against the LORD and against His
        Christ.' [a]

[27]"For truly against Your holy Servant Jesus, whom You anointed, both Herod and Pontius Pilate, with the Gentiles and the people of Israel, were gathered together [28]to do whatever Your hand and Your purpose determined before to be done. [29]Now, Lord, look on their threats, and grant to Your servants that with all boldness they may speak Your word, [30]by stretching out Your hand to heal, and that signs and wonders may be done through the name of Your holy Servant Jesus."

[31]And when they had prayed, the place where they were assembled together was shaken; and they were all filled with the Holy Spirit, and they spoke the word of God with boldness.

Sharing in All Things

[32]Now the multitude of those who believed were of one heart and one soul; neither did anyone say that any of the things he possessed was his own, but they had all things in common. [33]And with great power the apostles gave witness to the resurrection of the Lord Jesus. And great grace was upon them all. [34]Nor was there anyone among them who lacked; for all who were possessors of lands or houses sold them, and brought the proceeds of the things that were sold, [35]and laid them at the apostles'

4:25 [a]NU-Text reads who through the Holy Spirit, by the mouth of our father, Your servant David.
4:26 [a]Psalm 2:1,2

feet; and they distributed to each as anyone had need.

³⁶And Joses,ᵃ who was also named Barnabas by the apostles (which is translated Son of Encouragement), a Levite of the country of Cyprus, ³⁷having land, sold *it*, and brought the money and laid *it* at the apostles' feet.

Lying to the Holy Spirit

5 But a certain man named Ananias, with Sapphira his wife, sold a possession. ²And he kept back *part* of the proceeds, his wife also being aware *of it*, and brought a certain part and laid *it* at the apostles' feet. ³But Peter said, "Ananias, why has Satan filled your heart to lie to the Holy Spirit and keep back *part* of the price

> **5:2 he kept back *part* of the proceeds.** This was not a sin in itself. However, they had said that they were giving the full sale amount to the Lord. Their outward sin was lying about how much they were giving to the church. The more devastating sin was their spiritual hypocrisy and selfishness.

of the land for yourself? ⁴While it remained, was it not your own? And after it was sold, was it not in your own control? Why have you conceived this thing in your heart? You have not lied to men but to God."

⁵Then Ananias, hearing these words, fell down and breathed his last. So great fear came upon all those who heard these things. ⁶And the young men arose and wrapped him up, carried *him* out, and buried *him*.

4:36 ᵃNU-Text reads *Joseph.*

MAJOR SERMONS IN ACTS

Sermon	Theme	Reference
Peter to crowds at Pentecost	Peter's explanation of the meaning of Pentecost	Acts 2:14–40
Peter to crowds at the temple	The Jewish people should repent for crucifying the Messiah	Acts 3:12–26
Peter to the Sanhedrin	Testimony that a helpless man was healed by the power of Jesus	Acts 4:5–12
Stephen to the Sanhedrin	Stephen's rehearsal of Jewish history, accusing the Jews of killing the Messiah	Acts 7:2–53
Peter to Gentiles	Gentiles can be saved in the same manner as Jews	Acts 10:28–47
Peter to church at Jerusalem	Peter's testimony of his experiences at Joppa and a defense of his ministry to the Gentiles	Acts 11:4–18
Paul to synagogue at Antioch	Jesus was the Messiah in fulfillment of Old Testament prophecies	Acts 13:16–41
Peter to Jerusalem Council	Salvation by grace available to all	Acts 15:7–11
James to Jerusalem Council	Gentile converts do not require circumcision	Acts 15:13–21
Paul to Ephesian elders	Remain faithful in spite of false teachers and persecution	Acts 20:17–35
Paul to crowd at Jerusalem	Paul's statement of his conversion and his mission to the Gentiles	Acts 22:1–21
Paul to Sanhedrin	Paul's defense, declaring himself a Pharisee and a Roman citizen	Acts 23:1–6
Paul to King Agrippa	Paul's statement of his conversion and his zeal for the gospel	Acts 26:2–23
Paul to Jewish leaders at Rome	Paul's statement about his Jewish heritage	Acts 28:17–20

[7]Now it was about three hours later when his wife came in, not knowing what had happened. [8]And Peter answered her, "Tell me whether you sold the land for so much?"

She said, "Yes, for so much."

[9]Then Peter said to her, "How is it that you have agreed together to test the Spirit of the Lord? Look, the feet of those who have buried your husband *are* at the door, and they will carry you out." [10]Then immediately she fell down at his feet and breathed her last. And the young men came in and found her dead, and carrying *her* out, buried *her* by her husband. [11]So great fear came upon all the church and upon all who heard these things.

Continuing Power in the Church

[12]And through the hands of the apostles many signs and wonders were done among the people. And they were all with one accord in Solomon's Porch. [13]Yet none of the rest dared join them, but the people esteemed them highly. [14]And believers were increasingly added to the Lord, multitudes of both men and women, [15]so that they brought the sick out into the streets and laid *them* on beds and couches, that at least the shadow of Peter passing by might fall on some of them. [16]Also a multitude gathered from the surrounding cities to Jerusalem, bringing sick people and those who were tormented by unclean spirits, and they were all healed.

> **5:15 shadow of Peter.** The people believed that Peter had divine healing power and that somehow it would extend to them through his shadow. Scripture does not say that Peter's shadow ever healed anyone. The obvious outpouring of healing power, however, was an answer to the prayer in 4:29,30.

Imprisoned Apostles Freed

[17]Then the high priest rose up, and all those who *were* with him (which is the sect of the Sadducees), and they were filled with indignation, [18]and laid their hands on the apostles and put them in the common prison. [19]But at night an angel of the Lord opened the prison doors and brought them out, and said, [20]"Go, stand in the temple and speak to the people all the words of this life."

[21]And when they heard *that,* they entered the temple early in the morning and taught. But the high priest and those with him came and called the council together, with all the elders of the children of Israel, and sent to the prison to have them brought.

Apostles on Trial Again

[22]But when the officers came and did not find them in the prison, they returned and reported, [23]saying, "Indeed we found the prison shut securely, and the guards standing outside[a] before the doors; but when we opened them, we found no one inside!" [24]Now when the high priest,[a] the captain of the temple, and the chief priests heard these things, they wondered what the outcome would be. [25]So one came and told them, saying,[a] "Look, the men whom you put in prison are standing in the temple and teaching the people!"

[26]Then the captain went with the officers and brought them without violence, for they feared the people, lest they should be stoned. [27]And when they had brought them, they set *them* before the council. And the high priest asked them, [28]saying, "Did we not strictly command you not to teach in this name? And look, you have filled Jerusalem with your doctrine, and intend to bring this Man's blood on us!"

[29]But Peter and the *other* apostles answered and said: "We ought to obey God rather than men. [30]The God of our fathers raised up Jesus whom you murdered by hanging on a tree. [31]Him God has exalted to His right hand *to be* Prince and Savior, to give repentance to Israel and forgiveness of sins. [32]And we are His witnesses to these things, and *so* also *is* the Holy Spirit whom God has given to those who obey Him."

Gamaliel's Advice

[33]When they heard *this,* they were furious and plotted to kill them. [34]Then one in the council stood up, a Pharisee named Gamaliel, a teacher of the law held in respect by

---

5:23 [a]NU-Text and M-Text omit *outside.*   5:24 [a]NU-Text omits *the high priest.*   5:25 [a]NU-Text and M-Text omit *saying.*

5:34 Gamaliel. Gamaliel was the most noted rabbi of his time; he led the liberal faction of the Pharisees. His most famous student was the Apostle Paul.

all the people, and commanded them to put the apostles outside for a little while. ³⁵And he said to them: "Men of Israel, take heed to yourselves what you intend to do regarding these men. ³⁶For some time ago Theudas rose up, claiming to be somebody. A number of men, about four hundred, joined him. He was slain, and all who obeyed him were scattered and came to nothing. ³⁷After this man, Judas of Galilee rose up in the days of the census, and drew away many people after him. He also perished, and all who obeyed him were dispersed. ³⁸And now I say to you, keep away from these men and let them alone; for if this plan or this work is of men, it will come to nothing; ³⁹but if it is of God, you cannot overthrow it—lest you even be found to fight against God."

⁴⁰And they agreed with him, and when they had called for the apostles and beaten *them*, they commanded that they should not speak in the name of Jesus, and let them go. ⁴¹So they departed from the presence of the council, rejoicing that they were counted worthy to suffer shame for His*ᵃ* name. ⁴²And daily in the temple, and in every house, they did not cease teaching and preaching Jesus *as* the Christ.

Seven Chosen to Serve

6 Now in those days, when *the number of* the disciples was multiplying, there arose a complaint against the Hebrews by the Hellenists,*ᵃ* because their widows were neglected in the daily distribution. ²Then the twelve summoned the multitude of the disciples and said, "It is not desirable that we should leave the word of God and serve tables. ³Therefore, brethren, seek out from among you seven men of *good* reputation, full of the Holy Spirit and wisdom, whom we may appoint over this business; ⁴but we will give ourselves continually to prayer and to the ministry of the word."

⁵And the saying pleased the whole multitude. And they chose Stephen, a man full of

faith and the Holy Spirit, and Philip, Prochorus, Nicanor, Timon, Parmenas, and Nicolas, a proselyte from Antioch, ⁶whom they set before the apostles; and when they had prayed, they laid hands on them.

6:6 prayed...laid hands on them. This expression was used of Jesus when He healed (Mark 6:5). Sometimes it indicated being taken prisoner (Mark 14:46). In the OT, people laid their hands on the heads of the animals being sacrificed as an expression of identification (Lev. 8:14). Symbolically, laying on of hands signified affirmation, support, and identification with someone and his ministry (see Num. 27:23).

⁷Then the word of God spread, and the number of the disciples multiplied greatly in Jerusalem, and a great many of the priests were obedient to the faith.

Stephen Accused of Blasphemy

⁸And Stephen, full of faith*ᵃ* and power, did great wonders and signs among the people. ⁹Then there arose some from what is called the Synagogue of the Freedmen (Cyrenians, Alexandrians, and those from Cilicia and Asia), disputing with Stephen. ¹⁰And they were not able to resist the wisdom and the Spirit by which he spoke. ¹¹Then they secretly induced men to say, "We have heard him speak blasphemous words against Moses and God." ¹²And they stirred up the people, the elders, and the scribes; and they came upon *him*, seized him, and brought *him* to the council. ¹³They also set up false witnesses who said, "This man does not cease to speak blasphemous*ᵃ* words against this holy place and the law; ¹⁴for we have heard him say that this Jesus of Nazareth will destroy this place and change the customs which Moses delivered to us." ¹⁵And all who sat in the council, looking steadfastly at him, saw his face as the face of an angel.

Stephen's Address: The Call of Abraham

7 Then the high priest said, "Are these things so?"

²And he said, "Brethren and fathers, listen: The God of glory appeared to our father Abraham when he was in Mesopota-

---

5:41 *ᵃ*NU-Text reads *the name;* M-Text reads *the name of Jesus.*　6:1 *ᵃ*That is, Greek-speaking Jews　6:8 *ᵃ*NU-Text reads *grace.*　6:13 *ᵃ*NU-Text omits *blasphemous.*

mia, before he dwelt in Haran, ³and said to him, 'Get out of your country and from your relatives, and come to a land that I will show you.'ᵃ ⁴Then he came out of the land of the Chaldeans and dwelt in Haran. And from there, when his father was dead, He moved him to this land in which you now dwell. ⁵And God gave him no inheritance in it, not even enough to set his foot on. But even when Abraham had no child, He promised to give it to him for a possession, and to his descendants after him. ⁶But God spoke in this way: that his descendants would dwell in a foreign land, and that they would bring them into bondage and oppress them four hundred years. ⁷'And the nation to whom they will be in bondage I will judge,'ᵃ said God, 'and after that they shall come out and serve Me in this place.'ᵇ ⁸Then He gave him the covenant of circumcision; and so Abraham begot Isaac and circumcised him on the eighth day; and Isaac begot Jacob, and Jacob begot the twelve patriarchs.

The Patriarchs in Egypt

⁹"And the patriarchs, becoming envious, sold Joseph into Egypt. But God was with him ¹⁰and delivered him out of all his troubles, and gave him favor and wisdom in the presence of Pharaoh, king of Egypt; and he made him governor over Egypt and all his house. ¹¹Now a famine and great trouble came over all the land of Egypt and Canaan, and our fathers found no sustenance. ¹²But when Jacob heard that there was grain in Egypt, he sent out our fathers first. ¹³And the second time Joseph was made known to his brothers, and Joseph's family became known to the Pharaoh. ¹⁴Then Joseph sent and called his father Jacob and all his relatives to him, seventy-fiveᵃ people. ¹⁵So Jacob went down to Egypt; and he died, he and our fathers. ¹⁶And they were carried back to Shechem and laid in the tomb that Abraham bought for a sum of money from the sons of Hamor, the father of Shechem.

God Delivers Israel by Moses

¹⁷"But when the time of the promise drew near which God had sworn to Abraham,

the people grew and multiplied in Egypt ¹⁸till another king arose who did not know Joseph. ¹⁹This man dealt treacherously with our people, and oppressed our forefathers, making them expose their babies, so that they might not live. ²⁰At this time Moses was born, and was well pleasing to God; and he was brought up in his father's house for three months. ²¹But when he was set out, Pharaoh's daughter took him away and brought him up as her own son. ²²And Moses was learned in all the wisdom of the Egyptians, and was mighty in words and deeds.

²³"Now when he was forty years old, it came into his heart to visit his brethren, the children of Israel. ²⁴And seeing one of them suffer wrong, he defended and avenged him who was oppressed, and struck down the Egyptian. ²⁵For he supposed that his brethren would have understood that God would deliver them by his hand, but they did not understand. ²⁶And the next day he appeared to two of them as they were fighting, and tried to reconcile them, saying, 'Men, you are brethren; why do you wrong one another?' ²⁷But he who did his neighbor wrong pushed him away, saying, 'Who made you a ruler and a judge over us? ²⁸Do you want to kill me as you did the Egyptian yesterday?'ᵃ ²⁹Then, at this saying, Moses fled and became a dweller in the land of Midian, where he had two sons.

> **7:23 he was forty years old.** Moses' life can be divided into three 40-year periods. The first 40 years encompassed his birth and life in Pharaoh's court, the second his exile in Midian, and the third included the events of the Exodus and the years of wandering in the wilderness.

³⁰"And when forty years had passed, an Angel of the Lordᵃ appeared to him in a flame of fire in a bush, in the wilderness of Mount Sinai. ³¹When Moses saw it, he marveled at the sight; and as he drew near to observe, the voice of the Lord came to him, ³²saying, 'I am the God of your fathers—the God of Abraham, the God of Isaac, and the God of Jacob.'ᵃ And Moses trembled and dared not look. ³³'Then the LORD said to

---

7:3 ᵃGenesis 12:1   7:7 ᵃGenesis 15:14   ᵇExodus 3:12   7:14 ᵃOr seventy (compare Exodus 1:5)
7:28 ᵃExodus 2:14   7:30 ᵃNU-Text omits of the Lord.   7:32 ᵃExodus 3:6,15

him, "Take your sandals off your feet, for the place where you stand is holy ground. [34]I have surely seen the oppression of My people who are in Egypt; I have heard their groaning and have come down to deliver them. And now come, I will send you to Egypt." ' [a]

[35]"This Moses whom they rejected, saying, 'Who made you a ruler and a judge?'[a] is the one God sent to be a ruler and a deliverer by the hand of the Angel who appeared to him in the bush. [36]He brought them out, after he had shown wonders and signs in the land of Egypt, and in the Red Sea, and in the wilderness forty years.

Israel Rebels Against God

[37]"This is that Moses who said to the children of Israel,[a] 'The LORD your God will raise up for you a Prophet like me from your brethren. Him you shall hear.'[b]

[38]"This is he who was in the congregation in the wilderness with the Angel who spoke to him on Mount Sinai, and with our fathers, the one who received the living oracles to give to us, [39]whom our fathers would not obey, but rejected. And in their hearts they turned back to Egypt, [40]saying to Aaron, 'Make us gods to go before us; as for this Moses who brought us out of the land of Egypt, we do not know what has become of him.'[a] [41]And they made a calf in those days, offered sacrifices to the idol, and rejoiced in the works of their own hands. [42]Then God turned and gave them up to worship the host of heaven, as it is written in the book of the Prophets:

> 'Did you offer Me slaughtered animals
>   and sacrifices during forty years in
>   the wilderness,
>   O house of Israel?
> [43] You also took up the tabernacle of
>   Moloch,

> And the star of your god Remphan,
> Images which you made to worship;
> And I will carry you away beyond
>   Babylon.'[a]

God's True Tabernacle

[44]"Our fathers had the tabernacle of witness in the wilderness, as He appointed, instructing Moses to make it according to the pattern that he had seen, [45]which our fathers, having received it in turn, also brought with Joshua into the land possessed by the Gentiles, whom God drove out before the face of our fathers until the days of David, [46]who found favor before God and asked to find a dwelling for the God of Jacob. [47]But Solomon built Him a house.

[48]"However, the Most High does not dwell in temples made with hands, as the prophet says:

> [49] 'Heaven is My throne,
>   And earth is My footstool.
>   What house will you build for Me?
>   says the LORD,
>   Or what is the place of My rest?
> [50] Has My hand not made all these
>   things?'[a]

Israel Resists the Holy Spirit

[51]"You stiff-necked and uncircumcised in heart and ears! You always resist the Holy Spirit; as your fathers did, so do you. [52]Which of the prophets did your fathers not persecute? And they killed those who foretold the coming of the Just One, of whom you now have become the betrayers and murderers, [53]who have received the law by the direction of angels and have not kept it."

> **7:2–53** Stephen's response does not seem to answer the High-Priest's question. Instead, he gave a detailed defense of the Christian faith from the OT and concluded by condemning the Jewish leaders for rejecting Jesus.

Stephen the Martyr

[54]When they heard these things they were cut to the heart, and they gnashed at

> **7:42 God...gave them up.** This is quoted from Amos 5:25–27. God abandoned the people to their sin and idolatry (see Hos. 4:17). **the host of heaven.** Israel's idolatrous worship of the sun, moon, and stars began in the wilderness and lasted through the Babylonian captivity (see Deut. 4:19; 2 Chr. 33:3,5).

7:34 [a]Exodus 3:5,7,8,10   7:35 [a]Exodus 2:14   7:37 [a]Deuteronomy 18:15   [b]NU-Text and M-Text omit *Him you shall hear.*   7:40 [a]Exodus 32:1,23   7:43 [a]Amos 5:25–27   7:50 [a]Isaiah 66:1,2

him with *their* teeth. ⁵⁵But he, being full of the Holy Spirit, gazed into heaven and saw the glory of God, and Jesus standing at the right hand of God, ⁵⁶and said, "Look! I see the heavens opened and the Son of Man standing at the right hand of God!"

⁵⁷Then they cried out with a loud voice, stopped their ears, and ran at him with one accord; ⁵⁸and they cast *him* out of the city and stoned *him*. And the witnesses laid down their clothes at the feet of a young man named Saul. ⁵⁹And they stoned Stephen as he was calling on *God* and saying, "Lord Jesus, receive my spirit." ⁶⁰Then he knelt down and cried out with a loud voice, "Lord, do not charge them with this sin." And when he had said this, he fell asleep.

> **7:58 laid down their clothes...Saul.** This is Paul's first appearance in Scripture. He was involved in Stephen's death, near enough to be holding the cloaks of Stephen's killers.

Saul Persecutes the Church

8 Now Saul was consenting to his death. At that time a great persecution arose against the church which was at Jerusalem; and they were all scattered throughout the regions of Judea and Samaria, except the apostles. ²And devout men carried Stephen *to his burial,* and made great lamentation over him.

³As for Saul, he made havoc of the church, entering every house, and dragging off men and women, committing *them* to prison.

Christ Is Preached in Samaria

⁴Therefore those who were scattered went everywhere preaching the word. ⁵Then Philip went down to the*ᵃ* city of Samaria and preached Christ to them. ⁶And

> **8:5 Philip.** He was the first missionary named in Scripture and the first to be called an "evangelist." **the city of Samaria.** This was the ancient capital of the northern kingdom of Israel, which fell to the Assyrians in 722 B.C. after over 200 years of idolatry and rebellion against God. The Assyrians relocated Gentiles from other areas into the region, and the interracial descendants of these Jews and Gentiles became known as Samaritans.

the multitudes with one accord heeded the things spoken by Philip, hearing and seeing the miracles which he did. ⁷For unclean spirits, crying with a loud voice, came out of many who were possessed; and many who were paralyzed and lame were healed. ⁸And there was great joy in that city.

The Sorcerer's Profession of Faith

⁹But there was a certain man called Simon, who previously practiced sorcery in the city and astonished the people of Samaria, claiming that he was someone great, ¹⁰to whom they all gave heed, from the least to the greatest, saying, "This man is the great power of God." ¹¹And they heeded him because he had astonished them with his sorceries for a long time. ¹²But when they believed Philip as he preached the things concerning the kingdom of God and the name of Jesus Christ, both men and women were baptized. ¹³Then Simon himself also believed; and when he was baptized he continued with Philip, and was amazed, seeing the miracles and signs which were done.

The Sorcerer's Sin

¹⁴Now when the apostles who were at Jerusalem heard that Samaria had received the word of God, they sent Peter and John to them, ¹⁵who, when they had come down, prayed for them that they might receive the Holy Spirit. ¹⁶For as yet He had fallen upon none of them. They had only been baptized in the name of the Lord Jesus. ¹⁷Then they laid hands on them, and they received the Holy Spirit.

> **8:16 as yet...upon none of them.** Confirmation by the apostles was necessary to verify the inclusion of the Samaritans into the church. Because of the animosity between the Samaritans and the Jews, it was essential that the Samaritans receive the Spirit in the presence of the leaders of Jerusalem in order to maintain a unified church. The delay revealed the Samaritans' need to come under apostolic authority.

¹⁸And when Simon saw that through the laying on of the apostles' hands the Holy Spirit was given, he offered them money, ¹⁹saying, "Give me this power also, that

anyone on whom I lay hands may receive the Holy Spirit."

20But Peter said to him, "Your money perish with you, because you thought that the gift of God could be purchased with money! 21You have neither part nor portion in this matter, for your heart is not right in the sight of God. 22Repent therefore of this your wickedness, and pray God if perhaps the thought of your heart may be forgiven you. 23For I see that you are poisoned by bitterness and bound by iniquity."

24Then Simon answered and said, "Pray to the Lord for me, that none of the things which you have spoken may come upon me."

25So when they had testified and preached the word of the Lord, they returned to Jerusalem, preaching the gospel in many villages of the Samaritans.

Christ Is Preached to an Ethiopian

26Now an angel of the Lord spoke to Philip, saying, "Arise and go toward the south along the road which goes down from Jerusalem to Gaza." This is desert. 27So he arose and went. And behold, a man of Ethiopia, a eunuch of great authority under Candace the queen of the Ethiopians, who had charge of all her treasury, and had come to Jerusalem to worship, 28was returning. And sitting in his chariot, he was reading Isaiah the prophet. 29Then the Spirit said to Philip, "Go near and overtake this chariot."

> **8:27 eunuch.** This could refer to a man who has been emasculated, but it may also have been a title for a government official. Both may have been true because Luke refers to him both as a eunuch and as one who held a position of authority in the queen's court. As a physical eunuch, he would have been denied access to the temple (Deut. 23:1) and not have been able to become a proselyte to Judaism. **Candace.** This was probably an official title given to the queen mothers in that land.

30So Philip ran to him, and heard him reading the prophet Isaiah, and said, "Do you understand what you are reading?"

31And he said, "How can I, unless someone guides me?" And he asked Philip to come up and sit with him. 32The place in the Scripture which he read was this:

> "He was led as a sheep to the slaughter;
> And as a lamb before its shearer is
>   silent,
> So He opened not His mouth.
> 33   In His humiliation His justice was
>   taken away,
> And who will declare His generation?
> For His life is taken from the earth."a

34So the eunuch answered Philip and said, "I ask you, of whom does the prophet say this, of himself or of some other man?" 35Then Philip opened his mouth, and beginning at this Scripture, preached Jesus to him. 36Now as they went down the road, they came to some water. And the eunuch said, "See, here is water. What hinders me from being baptized?"

37Then Philip said, "If you believe with all your heart, you may."

And he answered and said, "I believe that Jesus Christ is the Son of God."a

38So he commanded the chariot to stand still. And both Philip and the eunuch went down into the water, and he baptized him. 39Now when they came up out of the water, the Spirit of the Lord caught Philip away, so that the eunuch saw him no more; and he went on his way rejoicing. 40But Philip was found at Azotus. And passing through, he preached in all the cities till he came to Caesarea.

The Damascus Road: Saul Converted

9 Then Saul, still breathing threats and murder against the disciples of the Lord, went to the high priest 2and asked letters from him to the synagogues of Damascus, so that if he found any who were of the

> **9:1 Saul.** The Apostle Paul was originally named Saul, after the first king of Israel. He was born a Jew, studied in Jerusalem under Gamaliel, and became a Pharisee. He was a Roman citizen, a right he inherited from his father. Verses 1–19 record the external details of his conversion. Philippians 3:1–14 record his internal spiritual conversion.

8:33 aIsaiah 53:7,8   8:37 aNU-Text and M-Text omit this verse. It is found in Western texts, including the Latin tradition.

Way, whether men or women, he might bring them bound to Jerusalem.

³As he journeyed he came near Damascus, and suddenly a light shone around him from heaven. ⁴Then he fell to the ground, and heard a voice saying to him, "Saul, Saul, why are you persecuting Me?"

⁵And he said, "Who are You, Lord?"

Then the Lord said, "I am Jesus, whom you are persecuting.ᵃ It *is* hard for you to kick against the goads."

⁶So he, trembling and astonished, said, "Lord, what do You want me to do?"

Then the Lord *said* to him, "Arise and go into the city, and you will be told what you must do."

⁷And the men who journeyed with him stood speechless, hearing a voice but seeing no one. ⁸Then Saul arose from the ground, and when his eyes were opened he saw no one. But they led him by the hand and brought *him* into Damascus. ⁹And he was three days without sight, and neither ate nor drank.

Ananias Baptizes Saul

¹⁰Now there was a certain disciple at Damascus named Ananias; and to him the Lord said in a vision, "Ananias."

And he said, "Here I am, Lord."

¹¹So the Lord *said* to him, "Arise and go to the street called Straight, and inquire at the house of Judas for *one* called Saul of Tarsus, for behold, he is praying. ¹²And in a vision he has seen a man named Ananias coming in and putting *his* hand on him, so that he might receive his sight."

¹³Then Ananias answered, "Lord, I have heard from many about this man, how much harm he has done to Your saints in Jerusalem. ¹⁴And here he has authority from the chief priests to bind all who call on Your name."

¹⁵But the Lord said to him, "Go, for he is a chosen vessel of Mine to bear My name before Gentiles, kings, and the children of Israel. ¹⁶For I will show him how many things he must suffer for My name's sake."

¹⁷And Ananias went his way and entered the house; and laying his hands on him he said, "Brother Saul, the Lord Jesus,ᵃ who

> **9:15 chosen vessel.** This means "a vessel of election." God chose Paul to convey His grace to all men (Gal. 1:1). **before Gentiles, kings, and the children of Israel.** Paul began his ministry preaching to the Jews, but his primary calling was to the Gentiles (Rom. 11:13). God also called him to minister to kings such as Agrippa (25:23–26:32) and Caesar (see 2 Tim. 4:16,17).

appeared to you on the road as you came, has sent me that you may receive your sight and be filled with the Holy Spirit." ¹⁸Immediately there fell from his eyes *something* like scales, and he received his sight at once; and he arose and was baptized. ¹⁹So when he had received food, he was strengthened. Then Saul spent some days with the disciples at Damascus.

Saul Preaches Christ

²⁰Immediately he preached the Christᵃ in the synagogues, that He is the Son of God.

²¹Then all who heard were amazed, and said, "Is this not he who destroyed those who called on this name in Jerusalem, and has come here for that purpose, so that he might bring them bound to the chief priests?"

²²But Saul increased all the more in strength, and confounded the Jews who dwelt in Damascus, proving that this *Jesus* is the Christ.

Saul Escapes Death

²³Now after many days were past, the Jews plotted to kill him. ²⁴But their plot became known to Saul. And they watched the gates day and night, to kill him. ²⁵Then the disciples took him by night and let *him* down through the wall in a large basket.

> **9:23 after many days were past.** This was a period of 3 years in which he ministered in Nabatean Arabia, an area encompassing Damascus and south to the Sinai peninsula.

Saul at Jerusalem

²⁶And when Saul had come to Jerusalem, he tried to join the disciples; but they were all afraid of him, and did not believe that he was a disciple. ²⁷But Barnabas took him and

---

9:5 ᵃNU-Text and M-Text omit the last sentence of verse 5 and begin verse 6 with *But arise and go.*
9:17 ᵃM-Text omits *Jesus.*   9:20 ᵃNU-Text reads *Jesus.*

brought *him* to the apostles. And he declared to them how he had seen the Lord on the road, and that He had spoken to him, and how he had preached boldly at Damascus in the name of Jesus. [28]So he was with them at Jerusalem, coming in and going out. [29]And he spoke boldly in the name of the Lord Jesus and disputed against the Hellenists, but they attempted to kill him. [30]When the brethren found out, they brought him down to Caesarea and sent him out to Tarsus.

The Church Prospers

[31]Then the churches[a] throughout all Judea, Galilee, and Samaria had peace and were edified. And walking in the fear of the Lord and in the comfort of the Holy Spirit, they were multiplied.

Aeneas Healed

[32]Now it came to pass, as Peter went through all *parts of the country*, that he also came down to the saints who dwelt in Lydda. [33]There he found a certain man named Aeneas, who had been bedridden eight years and was paralyzed. [34]And Peter said to him, "Aeneas, Jesus the Christ heals you. Arise and make your bed." Then he arose immediately. [35]So all who dwelt at Lydda and Sharon saw him and turned to the Lord.

Dorcas Restored to Life

[36]At Joppa there was a certain disciple named Tabitha, which is translated Dorcas. This woman was full of good works and charitable deeds which she did. [37]But it happened in those days that she became sick and died. When they had washed her, they laid *her* in an upper room. [38]And since Lydda was near Joppa, and the disciples had heard that Peter was there, they sent two men to him, imploring *him* not to delay in coming to them. [39]Then Peter arose and went with them. When he had come, they brought *him* to the upper room. And all the widows stood by him weeping, showing the tunics and garments which Dorcas had made while she was with them. [40]But Peter put them all out, and knelt down and

prayed. And turning to the body he said, "Tabitha, arise." And she opened her eyes, and when she saw Peter she sat up. [41]Then he gave her *his* hand and lifted her up; and when he had called the saints and widows, he presented her alive. [42]And it became known throughout all Joppa, and many believed on the Lord. [43]So it was that he stayed many days in Joppa with Simon, a tanner.

> **9:43 Simon, a tanner.** Peter broke down a cultural barrier by staying with a tanner, an occupation despised by Jews because a tanner worked with the skins of dead animals. The local synagogue probably shunned Peter.

Cornelius Sends a Delegation

10 There was a certain man in Caesarea called Cornelius, a centurion of what was called the Italian Regiment, [2]a devout *man* and one who feared God with all his household, who gave alms generously to the people, and prayed to God always. [3]About the ninth hour of the day he saw clearly in a vision an angel of God coming in and saying to him, "Cornelius!"

[4]And when he observed him, he was afraid, and said, "What is it, lord?"

So he said to him, "Your prayers and your alms have come up for a memorial before God. [5]Now send men to Joppa, and send for Simon whose surname is Peter. [6]He is lodging with Simon, a tanner, whose house is by the sea.[a] He will tell you what you must do." [7]And when the angel who spoke to him had departed, Cornelius called two of his household servants and a devout soldier from among those who waited on him continually. [8]So when he had explained all *these* things to them, he sent them to Joppa.

Peter's Vision

[9]The next day, as they went on their journey and drew near the city, Peter went up on the housetop to pray, about the sixth hour. [10]Then he became very hungry and wanted to eat; but while they made ready, he fell into a trance [11]and saw heaven opened and an object like a great sheet bound at the four corners, descending to

---

9:31 [a]NU-Text reads *church . . . was edified.*   10:6 [a]NU-Text and M-Text omit the last sentence of this verse.

him and let down to the earth. [12]In it were all kinds of four-footed animals of the earth, wild beasts, creeping things, and birds of the air. [13]And a voice came to him, "Rise, Peter; kill and eat."

[14]But Peter said, "Not so, Lord! For I have never eaten anything common or unclean."

[15]And a voice spoke to him again the second time, "What God has cleansed you must not call common." [16]This was done three times. And the object was taken up into heaven again.

10:15 God has cleansed. God had set specific dietary restrictions regarding the eating of animals in order to keep the Israelites separate from their idolatrous neighbors (see Lev. 11:25,26). God ended these restrictions with the coming of the New Covenant and the calling of the church (see Mark 7:19). Unity was made possible in the church for both Jews (symbolized in the vision by the clean animals) and Gentiles (symbolized by the unclean animals) through the death of Christ.

Summoned to Caesarea

[17]Now while Peter wondered within himself what this vision which he had seen meant, behold, the men who had been sent from Cornelius had made inquiry for Simon's house, and stood before the gate. [18]And they called and asked whether Simon, whose surname was Peter, was lodging there.

[19]While Peter thought about the vision, the Spirit said to him, "Behold, three men are seeking you. [20]Arise therefore, go down

and go with them, doubting nothing; for I have sent them."

[21]Then Peter went down to the men who had been sent to him from Cornelius,[a] and said, "Yes, I am he whom you seek. For what reason have you come?"

[22]And they said, "Cornelius the centurion, a just man, one who fears God and has a good reputation among all the nation of the Jews, was divinely instructed by a holy angel to summon you to his house, and to hear words from you." [23]Then he invited them in and lodged them.

On the next day Peter went away with them, and some brethren from Joppa accompanied him.

Peter Meets Cornelius

[24]And the following day they entered Caesarea. Now Cornelius was waiting for them, and had called together his relatives and close friends. [25]As Peter was coming in, Cornelius met him and fell down at his feet and worshiped him. [26]But Peter lifted him up, saying, "Stand up; I myself am also a man." [27]And as he talked with him, he went in and found many who had come together. [28]Then he said to them, "You know how unlawful it is for a Jewish man to keep company with or go to one of another nation. But God has shown me that I should not call any man common or unclean. [29]Therefore I came without objection as soon as I was sent for. I ask, then, for what reason have you sent for me?"

10:21 [a]NU-Text and M-Text omit who had been sent to him from Cornelius.

How does the baptism with the Holy Spirit (1 Corinthians 12:13) relate to the Holy Spirit's activities in the Book of Acts?

Acts describes a number of occasions in which the Holy Spirit "fell on" or "filled" or "came upon" people (2:4; 10:44; 19:6). Peter identifies these actions by God as a fulfillment of Joel's prophecy (Joel 2:28–32). Viewed from the perspective of the entire New Testament, these experiences were neither the same nor replacements for what John the Baptist (Mark 1:8) and Paul described as the baptism with the Holy Spirit (1 Corinthians 12:13). The baptism with the Spirit is the one time act by which God places believers into His body. The filling is a repeated reality of Spirit-controlled behavior that God commands believers to maintain (Ephesians 5:18). Peter and others who experienced that special filling on Pentecost Day (2:4) were filled with the Spirit again (4:8,31; 6:5; 7:55) and so boldly spoke the Word of God. That was just the beginning. The fullness of the Spirit affects all areas of life, not just speaking boldly (Ephesians 5:18–33).

³⁰So Cornelius said, "Four days ago I was fasting until this hour; and at the ninth hour*a* I prayed in my house, and behold, a man stood before me in bright clothing, ³¹and said, 'Cornelius, your prayer has been heard, and your alms are remembered in the sight of God. ³²Send therefore to Joppa and call Simon here, whose surname is Peter. He is lodging in the house of Simon, a tanner, by the sea.*a* When he comes, he will speak to you.' ³³So I sent to you immediately, and you have done well to come. Now therefore, we are all present before God, to hear all the things commanded you by God."

Preaching to Cornelius' Household

³⁴Then Peter opened *his* mouth and said: "In truth I perceive that God shows no partiality. ³⁵But in every nation whoever fears Him and works righteousness is accepted by Him. ³⁶The word which *God* sent to the children of Israel, preaching peace through Jesus Christ—He is Lord of all—³⁷that word you know, which was proclaimed throughout all Judea, and began from Galilee after the baptism which John preached: ³⁸how God anointed Jesus of Nazareth with the Holy Spirit and with power, who went about doing good and healing all who were oppressed by the devil, for God was with Him. ³⁹And we are witnesses of all things which He did both in the land of the Jews and in Jerusalem, whom they*a* killed by hanging on a tree. ⁴⁰Him God raised up on the third day, and showed Him openly, ⁴¹not to all the people, but to witnesses chosen before by God, *even* to us who ate and drank with Him after He arose from the dead. ⁴²And He commanded us to preach to the people, and to testify that it is He who was ordained by God *to be* Judge of the living and the dead. ⁴³To Him all the prophets witness that, through His name, whoever believes in Him will receive remission of sins."

The Holy Spirit Falls on the Gentiles

⁴⁴While Peter was still speaking these words, the Holy Spirit fell upon all those who heard the word. ⁴⁵And those of the circumcision who believed were astonished, as many as came with Peter, because the gift of the Holy Spirit had been poured out on the Gentiles also. ⁴⁶For they heard them speak with tongues and magnify God.

Then Peter answered, ⁴⁷"Can anyone forbid water, that these should not be baptized who have received the Holy Spirit just as we *have*?" ⁴⁸And he commanded them to be baptized in the name of the Lord. Then they asked him to stay a few days.

Peter Defends God's Grace

11 Now the apostles and brethren who were in Judea heard that the Gentiles had also received the word of God. ²And when Peter came up to Jerusalem, those of the circumcision contended with him, ³saying, "You went in to uncircumcised men and ate with them!"

> **11:3 ate with them!** The Jewish believers were outraged over such a blatant breach of Jewish custom. It was difficult for them to understand that Jesus could be equally Lord of Gentile believers.

⁴But Peter explained *it* to them in order from the beginning, saying: ⁵"I was in the city of Joppa praying; and in a trance I saw a vision, an object descending like a great sheet, let down from heaven by four corners; and it came to me. ⁶When I observed it intently and considered, I saw four-footed animals of the earth, wild beasts, creeping things, and birds of the air. ⁷And I heard a voice saying to me, 'Rise, Peter; kill and eat.' ⁸But I said, 'Not so, Lord! For nothing common or unclean has at any time entered my mouth.' ⁹But the voice answered me again from heaven, 'What God has cleansed you must not call common.' ¹⁰Now this was done three times, and all were drawn up again into heaven. ¹¹At that very moment, three men stood before the house where I was, having been sent to me from Caesarea. ¹²Then the Spirit told me to go with them, doubting nothing. Moreover these six brethren accompanied me, and we entered the man's house. ¹³And he told us how he had seen an angel standing in his house, who said to him, 'Send men to Jop-

---

10:30 *a*NU-Text reads *Four days ago to this hour, at the ninth hour.* 10:32 *a*NU-Text omits the last sentence of this verse. 10:39 *a*NU-Text and M-Text add *also.*

pa, and call for Simon whose surname is Peter, ¹⁴who will tell you words by which you and all your household will be saved.' ¹⁵And as I began to speak, the Holy Spirit fell upon them, as upon us at the beginning. ¹⁶Then I remembered the word of the Lord, how He said, 'John indeed baptized with water, but you shall be baptized with the Holy Spirit.' ¹⁷If therefore God gave them the same gift as *He gave* us when we believed on the Lord Jesus Christ, who was I that I could withstand God?"

> **11:15 at the beginning.** God attested to the reality of the salvation of Gentiles with the same phenomenon that occurred at Pentecost.

¹⁸When they heard these things they became silent; and they glorified God, saying, "Then God has also granted to the Gentiles repentance to life."

Barnabas and Saul at Antioch

¹⁹Now those who were scattered after the persecution that arose over Stephen traveled as far as Phoenicia, Cyprus, and Antioch, preaching the word to no one but the Jews only. ²⁰But some of them were men from Cyprus and Cyrene, who, when they had come to Antioch, spoke to the Hellenists, preaching the Lord Jesus. ²¹And the hand of the Lord was with them, and a great number believed and turned to the Lord.

²²Then news of these things came to the ears of the church in Jerusalem, and they sent out Barnabas to go as far as Antioch. ²³When he came and had seen the grace of God, he was glad, and encouraged them all that with purpose of heart they should continue with the Lord. ²⁴For he was a good man, full of the Holy Spirit and of faith. And a great many people were added to the Lord.

²⁵Then Barnabas departed for Tarsus to seek Saul. ²⁶And when he had found him, he brought him to Antioch. So it was that for a whole year they assembled with the church and taught a great many people. And the disciples were first called Christians in Antioch.

Relief to Judea

²⁷And in these days prophets came from Jerusalem to Antioch. ²⁸Then one of them, named Agabus, stood up and showed by the Spirit that there was going to be a great famine throughout all the world, which also happened in the days of Claudius Caesar. ²⁹Then the disciples, each according to his ability, determined to send relief to the brethren dwelling in Judea. ³⁰This they also did, and sent it to the elders by the hands of Barnabas and Saul.

Herod's Violence to the Church

12 Now about that time Herod the king stretched out *his* hand to harass some from the church. ²Then he killed James the brother of John with the sword. ³And because he saw that it pleased the Jews, he proceeded further to seize Peter also. Now it was *during* the Days of Unleavened Bread. ⁴So when he had arrested him, he put *him* in prison, and delivered *him* to four squads of soldiers to keep him, intending to bring him before the people after Passover.

> **12:2 James.** He was the first of the apostles to be martyred. **with the sword.** The manner of his execution indicates that James was accused of leading people to follow false gods (see Deut. 13:12–15). *during* **the Days of Unleavened Bread.** This was the week-long feast that followed the Passover.

Peter Freed from Prison

⁵Peter was therefore kept in prison, but constant*ᵃ* prayer was offered to God for him by the church. ⁶And when Herod was about to bring him out, that night Peter was sleeping, bound with two chains between two soldiers; and the guards before the door were keeping the prison. ⁷Now behold, an angel of the Lord stood by *him*, and a light shone in the prison; and he struck Peter on the side and raised him up, saying, "Arise quickly!" And his chains fell off *his* hands. ⁸Then the angel said to him, "Gird yourself and tie on your sandals"; and so he did. And he said to him, "Put on your garment and follow me." ⁹So he went out and followed him, and did not know that what was done by the angel was real, but thought

---

12:5 *ᵃ*NU-Text reads *constantly* (or *earnestly*).

he was seeing a vision. ¹⁰When they were past the first and the second guard posts, they came to the iron gate that leads to the city, which opened to them of its own accord; and they went out and went down one street, and immediately the angel departed from him.

¹¹And when Peter had come to himself, he said, "Now I know for certain that the Lord has sent His angel, and has delivered me from the hand of Herod and *from* all the expectation of the Jewish people."

¹²So, when he had considered *this*, he came to the house of Mary, the mother of John whose surname was Mark, where many were gathered together praying. ¹³And as Peter knocked at the door of the gate, a girl named Rhoda came to answer. ¹⁴When she recognized Peter's voice, because of *her* gladness she did not open the gate, but ran in and announced that Peter stood before the gate. ¹⁵But they said to her, "You are beside yourself!" Yet she kept insisting that it was so. So they said, "It is his angel."

¹⁶Now Peter continued knocking; and when they opened *the door* and saw him, they were astonished. ¹⁷But motioning to them with his hand to keep silent, he declared to them how the Lord had brought him out of the prison. And he said, "Go, tell these things to James and to the brethren." And he departed and went to another place.

> **12:17 James.** He was the Lord's brother, now head of the Jerusalem church. **he departed.** Except for a brief appearance in chap. 15, Peter fades from the scene as the rest of Acts revolves around Paul and his ministry.

¹⁸Then, as soon as it was day, there was no small stir among the soldiers about what had become of Peter. ¹⁹But when Herod had searched for him and not found him, he examined the guards and commanded that *they* should be put to death.

And he went down from Judea to Caesarea, and stayed *there*.

Herod's Violent Death

²⁰Now Herod had been very angry with the people of Tyre and Sidon; but they came to him with one accord, and having made Blastus the king's personal aide their friend, they asked for peace, because their country was supplied with food by the king's *country*.

²¹So on a set day Herod, arrayed in royal apparel, sat on his throne and gave an oration to them. ²²And the people kept shouting, "The voice of a god and not of a man!" ²³Then immediately an angel of the Lord struck him, because he did not give glory to God. And he was eaten by worms and died.

²⁴But the word of God grew and multiplied.

Barnabas and Saul Appointed

²⁵And Barnabas and Saul returned from*ᵃ* Jerusalem when they had fulfilled *their* ministry, and they also took with them John whose surname was Mark.

13 Now in the church that was at Antioch there were certain prophets and teachers: Barnabas, Simeon who was called Niger, Lucius of Cyrene, Manaen who had been brought up with Herod the tetrarch, and Saul. ²As they ministered to the Lord and fasted, the Holy Spirit said, "Now separate to Me Barnabas and Saul for the work to which I have called them." ³Then, having fasted and prayed, and laid hands on them, they sent *them* away.

> **13:2 ministered.** This is from a Greek word used in Scripture to describe priestly service. Serving in leadership in the church is an act of worship, consisting of offering sacrifices to God such as prayer, oversight of the flock, and preaching the Word. **fasted.** This is often connected with vigilant, passionate prayer (see Neh. 1:4). It includes either a loss of desire for food or the purposeful setting aside of eating to concentrate on spiritual issues.

Preaching in Cyprus

⁴So, being sent out by the Holy Spirit, they went down to Seleucia, and from there they sailed to Cyprus. ⁵And when they arrived in Salamis, they preached the word of God in the synagogues of the Jews. They also had John as *their* assistant.

⁶Now when they had gone through the island*ᵃ* to Paphos, they found a certain sorcerer, a false prophet, a Jew whose name *was* Bar-Jesus, ⁷who was with the procon-

---

12:25 *ᵃ*NU-Text and M-Text read *to*.   13:6 *ᵃ*NU-Text reads *the whole island*.

sul, Sergius Paulus, an intelligent man. This man called for Barnabas and Saul and sought to hear the word of God. ⁸But Elymas the sorcerer (for so his name is translated) withstood them, seeking to turn the proconsul away from the faith. ⁹Then Saul, who also *is called* Paul, filled with the Holy Spirit, looked intently at him ¹⁰and said, "O full of all deceit and all fraud, *you* son of the devil, *you* enemy of all righteousness, will you not cease perverting the straight ways of the Lord? ¹¹And now, indeed, the hand of the Lord *is* upon you, and you shall be blind, not seeing the sun for a time."

And immediately a dark mist fell on him, and he went around seeking someone to lead him by the hand. ¹²Then the proconsul believed, when he saw what had been done, being astonished at the teaching of the Lord.

At Antioch in Pisidia

¹³Now when Paul and his party set sail from Paphos, they came to Perga in Pamphylia; and John, departing from them, returned to Jerusalem. ¹⁴But when they departed from Perga, they came to Antioch in Pisidia, and went into the synagogue on the Sabbath day and sat down. ¹⁵And after the reading of the Law and the Prophets, the rulers of the synagogue sent to them, saying, "Men *and* brethren, if you have any word of exhortation for the people, say on."

¹⁶Then Paul stood up, and motioning with *his* hand said, "Men of Israel, and you who fear God, listen: ¹⁷The God of this people Israel*ᵃ* chose our fathers, and exalted the people when they dwelt as strangers in the land of Egypt, and with an uplifted arm He brought them out of it. ¹⁸Now for a time of about forty years He put up with their ways in the wilderness. ¹⁹And when He had destroyed seven nations in the land of Ca-

naan, He distributed their land to them by allotment.

²⁰"After that He gave *them* judges for about four hundred and fifty years, until Samuel the prophet. ²¹And afterward they asked for a king; so God gave them Saul the son of Kish, a man of the tribe of Benjamin, for forty years. ²²And when He had removed him, He raised up for them David as king, to whom also He gave testimony and said, '*I have found Davidᵃ* the *son* of Jesse, *a man after My own heart,* who will do all My will.'*ᵇ* ²³From this man's seed, according to *the* promise, God raised up for Israel a Savior—Jesus—*ᵃ* ²⁴after John had first preached, before His coming, the baptism of repentance to all the people of Israel. ²⁵And as John was finishing his course, he said, 'Who do you think I am? I am not *He.* But behold, there comes One after me, the sandals of whose feet I am not worthy to loose.'

13:22 *a man after My own heart.* Some would question this designation for David, for he proved to be such a sinner at times (see 1 Sam. 11:1–4; 12:9). No man after God's own heart is perfect; yet he will recognize sin and repent of it, as David did (see Ps. 32). Paul quoted from 1 Sam. 13:14 and Ps. 89:20.

²⁶"Men *and* brethren, sons of the family of Abraham, and those among you who fear God, to you the word of this salvation has been sent. ²⁷For those who dwell in Jerusalem, and their rulers, because they did not know Him, nor even the voices of the Prophets which are read every Sabbath, have fulfilled *them* in condemning *Him.* ²⁸And though they found no cause for death *in Him,* they asked Pilate that He should be put to death. ²⁹Now when they had fulfilled all that was written concerning Him, they

13:15 reading of the Law and the Prophets. This is the reading of Scripture. It occupied the third part of the liturgy of the synagogue, after the recitation of the *shema* (Deut. 6:4) and further prayers, but before the teaching. **rulers of the synagogue.** These men had general oversight of the synagogue and designated who would read from the Scriptures.

13:29,30 tree...tomb...God raised. The OT predicted the crucifixion of Christ on a cross (Ps. 22; Deut. 21) at the time when this form of execution was not used. His burial in a "tomb" was also prophesied (Is. 53:9), yet victims of crucifixions were commonly tossed into mass graves. Jesus fulfilled specific OT prophecies. The climax of Paul's message was the resurrection of Christ, the ultimate proof that He is the Messiah.

13:17 *ᵃ*M-Text omits *Israel.*   13:22 *ᵃ*Psalm 89:20   *ᵇ*1 Samuel 13:14   13:23 *ᵃ*M-Text reads *for Israel salvation.*

took *Him* down from the tree and laid *Him* in a tomb. ³⁰But God raised Him from the dead. ³¹He was seen for many days by those who came up with Him from Galilee to Jerusalem, who are His witnesses to the people. ³²And we declare to you glad tidings—that promise which was made to the fathers. ³³God has fulfilled this for us their children, in that He has raised up Jesus. As it is also written in the second Psalm:

'You are My Son,
Today I have begotten You.'ᵃ

³⁴And that He raised Him from the dead, no more to return to corruption, He has spoken thus:

'I will give you the sure mercies of David.'ᵃ

³⁵Therefore He also says in another *Psalm:*

'You will not allow Your Holy One to see corruption.'ᵃ

³⁶"For David, after he had served his own generation by the will of God, fell asleep, was buried with his fathers, and saw corruption; ³⁷but He whom God raised up saw no corruption. ³⁸Therefore let it be known to you, brethren, that through this Man is preached to you the forgiveness of sins; ³⁹and by Him everyone who believes is justified from all things from which you could not be justified by the law of Moses. ⁴⁰Beware therefore, lest what has been spoken in the prophets come upon you:

⁴¹ 'Behold, you despisers,
Marvel and perish!
For I work a work in your days,
A work which you will by no means
believe,
Though one were to declare it to
you.' 'ᵃ

Blessing and Conflict at Antioch

⁴²So when the Jews went out of the synagogue,ᵃ the Gentiles begged that these words might be preached to them the next Sabbath. ⁴³Now when the congregation had broken up, many of the Jews and devout proselytes followed Paul and Barnabas, who, speaking to them, persuaded them to continue in the grace of God.

⁴⁴On the next Sabbath almost the whole city came together to hear the word of God. ⁴⁵But when the Jews saw the multitudes, they were filled with envy; and contradicting and blaspheming, they opposed the things spoken by Paul. ⁴⁶Then Paul and Barnabas grew bold and said, "It was necessary that the word of God should be spoken to you first; but since you reject it, and judge yourselves unworthy of everlasting life, behold, we turn to the Gentiles. ⁴⁷For so the Lord has commanded us:

'I have set you as a light to the
Gentiles,
That you should be for salvation to
the ends of the earth.' "ᵃ

⁴⁸Now when the Gentiles heard this, they were glad and glorified the word of the Lord. And as many as had been appointed to eternal life believed.

⁴⁹And the word of the Lord was being spread throughout all the region. ⁵⁰But the Jews stirred up the devout and prominent women and the chief men of the city, raised up persecution against Paul and Barnabas, and expelled them from their region. ⁵¹But they shook off the dust from their feet against them, and came to Iconium. ⁵²And the disciples were filled with joy and with the Holy Spirit.

> **13:51 shook off the dust from their feet.** The Jews' antagonism toward Gentiles extended to their unwillingness to even bring Gentile dust into Israel. That Paul and Barnabas shook the dust from their feet after dealing with Jews shows that they considered the Jews at Antioch no better than the heathen. There could have been no stronger condemnation.

At Iconium

14 Now it happened in Iconium that they went together to the synagogue

---

13:33 ᵃPsalm 2:7   13:34 ᵃIsaiah 55:3   13:35 ᵃPsalm 16:10   13:41 ᵃHabakkuk 1:5   13:42 ᵃOr *And when they went out of the synagogue of the Jews;* NU-Text reads *And when they went out of the synagogue, they begged.*   13:47 ᵃIsaiah 49:6

of the Jews, and so spoke that a great multitude both of the Jews and of the Greeks believed. [2]But the unbelieving Jews stirred up the Gentiles and poisoned their minds against the brethren. [3]Therefore they stayed there a long time, speaking boldly in the Lord, who was bearing witness to the word of His grace, granting signs and wonders to be done by their hands.

[4]But the multitude of the city was divided: part sided with the Jews, and part with the apostles. [5]And when a violent attempt was made by both the Gentiles and Jews, with their rulers, to abuse and stone them, [6]they became aware of it and fled to Lystra and Derbe, cities of Lycaonia, and to the surrounding region. [7]And they were preaching the gospel there.

Idolatry at Lystra

[8]And in Lystra a certain man without strength in his feet was sitting, a cripple from his mother's womb, who had never walked. [9]*This* man heard Paul speaking. Paul, observing him intently and seeing that he had faith to be healed, [10]said with a loud voice, "Stand up straight on your feet!" And he leaped and walked. [11]Now when the people saw what Paul had done, they raised their voices, saying in the Lycaonian *language*, "The gods have come down to us in the likeness of men!" [12]And Barnabas they called Zeus, and Paul, Hermes, because he was the chief speaker. [13]Then the priest of Zeus, whose temple was in front of their city, brought oxen and garlands to the gates, intending to sacrifice with the multitudes.

14:11–13. According to tradition, the gods Zeus and Hermes had at one time visited Lystra in disguise, asking for food and lodging. All turned them away except for a peasant, Philemon, and his wife, Baucis. The gods took vengeance by drowning everyone, but they turned Philemon's cottage into a temple where he and his wife served as priest and priestess. The people of Lystra believed Barnabas to be Zeus and Paul to be Hermes, and they did not want to repeat their ancestors' mistake.

[14]But when the apostles Barnabas and Paul heard this, they tore their clothes and ran in among the multitude, crying out [15]and saying, "Men, why are you doing these things? We also are men with the same nature as you, and preach to you that you should turn from these useless things to the living God, who made the heaven, the earth, the sea, and all things that are in them, [16]who in bygone generations allowed all nations to walk in their own ways. [17]Nevertheless He did not leave Himself without witness, in that He did good, gave us rain from heaven and fruitful seasons, filling our hearts with food and gladness." [18]And with these sayings they could scarcely restrain the multitudes from sacrificing to them.

Stoning, Escape to Derbe

[19]Then Jews from Antioch and Iconium came there; and having persuaded the multitudes, they stoned Paul *and* dragged *him* out of the city, supposing him to be dead. [20]However, when the disciples gathered around him, he rose up and went into the city. And the next day he departed with Barnabas to Derbe.

Strengthening the Converts

[21]And when they had preached the gospel to that city and made many disciples, they returned to Lystra, Iconium, and Antioch, [22]strengthening the souls of the disciples, exhorting *them* to continue in the faith, and *saying*, "We must through many tribulations enter the kingdom of God." [23]So when they had appointed elders in every church, and prayed with fasting, they commended them to the Lord in whom they had believed. [24]And after they had passed through Pisidia, they came to Pamphylia. [25]Now when they had preached the word in Perga, they went down to Attalia. [26]From there they sailed to Antioch, where they had been commended to the grace of God for the work which they had completed.

[27]Now when they had come and gathered the church together, they reported all that God had done with them, and that He had opened the door of faith to the Gentiles. [28]So they stayed there a long time with the disciples.

Conflict over Circumcision

15 And certain *men* came down from Judea and taught the brethren, "Unless you are circumcised according to the

15:1–30 There were 7 ecumenical councils in the church's early history, where church leaders met to settle doctrinal issues. The most important council was the first one, the Jerusalem Council, described in these verses. That Council established the answer to the most vital doctrinal question: "What must a person do to be saved?" The apostles affirmed that salvation is by grace through faith in Jesus Christ alone.

custom of Moses, you cannot be saved." [2]Therefore, when Paul and Barnabas had no small dissension and dispute with them, they determined that Paul and Barnabas and certain others of them should go up to Jerusalem, to the apostles and elders, about this question.

[3]So, being sent on their way by the church, they passed through Phoenicia and Samaria, describing the conversion of the Gentiles; and they caused great joy to all the brethren. [4]And when they had come to Jerusalem, they were received by the church and the apostles and the elders; and they reported all things that God had done with them. [5]But some of the sect of the Pharisees who believed rose up, saying, "It is necessary to circumcise them, and to command *them* to keep the law of Moses."

The Jerusalem Council

[6]Now the apostles and elders came together to consider this matter. [7]And when there had been much dispute, Peter rose up and said to them: "Men and brethren, you know that a good while ago God chose among us, that by my mouth the Gentiles should hear the word of the gospel and believe. [8]So God, who knows the heart, ac-

15:7 Peter rose up. Peter gave the first of 3 speeches at the Council that amount to one of the strongest defenses of salvation by grace through faith alone contained in Scripture. He spoke of how God saved Gentiles in the early days of the church without a requirement of circumcision, law keeping, or ritual (10:44–48; 11:17,18). If God did not require any additional qualifications for salvation, neither should the legalists.

knowledged them by giving them the Holy Spirit, just as *He did* to us, [9]and made no distinction between us and them, purifying their hearts by faith. [10]Now therefore, why do you test God by putting a yoke on the neck of the disciples which neither our fathers nor we were able to bear? [11]But we believe that through the grace of the Lord Jesus Christ[a] we shall be saved in the same manner as they."

[12]Then all the multitude kept silent and listened to Barnabas and Paul declaring how many miracles and wonders God had worked through them among the Gentiles. [13]And after they had become silent, James answered, saying, "Men *and* brethren, listen to me: [14]Simon has declared how God at the first visited the Gentiles to take out of them a people for His name. [15]And with this the words of the prophets agree, just as it is written:

[16]   'After this I will return
     And will rebuild the tabernacle of
       David, which has fallen down;
     I will rebuild its ruins,
     And I will set it up;
[17]   So that the rest of mankind may seek
       the LORD,
     Even all the Gentiles who are called by
       My name,
     Says the LORD who does all these
       things.'[a]

[18]"Known to God from eternity are all His works.[a] [19]Therefore I judge that we should not trouble those from among the Gentiles who are turning to God, [20]but that we write to them to abstain from things polluted by idols, *from* sexual immorality,[a] *from* things strangled, and *from* blood. [21]For

15:20 James and the other leaders did not want the Gentiles' freedom in Christ to cause the Jewish believers to follow that same liberty and violate their consciences. James proposed that the Gentiles abstain from 4 pagan, idolatrous practices so as not to offend the Jews: things polluted by idols, sexual immorality, things strangled, and drinking blood.

15:11 [a]NU-Text and M-Text omit *Christ*.   15:17 [a]Amos 9:11,12   15:18 [a]NU-Text (combining with verse 17) reads *Says the Lord, who makes these things known from eternity (of old)*.   15:20 [a]Or *fornication*

Moses has had throughout many generations those who preach him in every city, being read in the synagogues every Sabbath."

The Jerusalem Decree

²²Then it pleased the apostles and elders, with the whole church, to send chosen men of their own company to Antioch with Paul and Barnabas, *namely,* Judas who was also named Barsabas,ᵃ and Silas, leading men among the breathren.

²³They wrote this *letter* by them:

The apostles, the elders, and the brethren,

To the brethren who are of the Gentiles in Antioch, Syria, and Cilicia:

Greetings.

²⁴ Since we have heard that some who went out from us have troubled you with words, unsettling your souls, saying, *"You must* be circumcised and keep the law"ᵃ—to whom we gave no *such* commandment—²⁵it seemed good to us, being assembled with one accord, to send chosen men to you with our beloved Barnabas and Paul, ²⁶men who have risked their lives for the name of our Lord Jesus Christ. ²⁷We have therefore sent Judas and Silas, who will also report the same things by word of mouth. ²⁸For it seemed good to the Holy Spirit, and to us, to lay upon you no greater burden than these necessary things: ²⁹that you abstain from things offered to idols, from blood, from things strangled, and from sexual immorality.ᵃ If you keep yourselves from these, you will do well.

Farewell.

Continuing Ministry in Syria

³⁰So when they were sent off, they came to Antioch; and when they had gathered the multitude together, they delivered the letter. ³¹When they had read it, they rejoiced over its encouragement. ³²Now Judas and Silas, themselves being prophets also, exhorted and strengthened the brethren with many words. ³³And after they had stayed *there* for a time, they were sent back with greetings from the brethren to the apostles.ᵃ

³⁴However, it seemed good to Silas to remain there.ᵃ ³⁵Paul and Barnabas also remained in Antioch, teaching and preaching the word of the Lord, with many others also.

Division over John Mark

³⁶Then after some days Paul said to Barnabas, "Let us now go back and visit our brethren in every city where we have preached the word of the Lord, *and see* how they are doing." ³⁷Now Barnabas was determined to take with them John called Mark. ³⁸But Paul insisted that they should not take with them the one who had departed from them in Pamphylia, and had not gone with them to the work. ³⁹Then the contention became so sharp that they parted from one another. And so Barnabas took Mark and sailed to Cyprus; ⁴⁰but Paul chose Silas and departed, being commended by the brethren to the grace of God. ⁴¹And he went through Syria and Cilicia, strengthening the churches.

15:39 contention...parted. This was not an amicable parting; Paul and Barnabas were in serious disagreement over John Mark. They eventually reconciled (1 Cor. 9:6), and Paul and Mark also reconciled (2 Tim. 4:11).

Timothy Joins Paul and Silas

16 Then he came to Derbe and Lystra. And behold, a certain disciple was there, named Timothy, *the* son of a certain Jewish woman who believed, but his father *was* Greek. ²He was well spoken of by the brethren who were at Lystra and Iconium. ³Paul wanted to have him go on with him. And he took *him* and circumcised him because of the Jews who were in that region, for they all knew that his father was Greek.

15:22 ᵃNU-Text and M-Text read *Barsabbas.*   15:24 ᵃNU-Text omits *saying, "You must be circumcised and keep the law."*   15:29 ᵃOr *fornication*   15:33 ᵃNU-Text reads *to those who had sent them.*
15:34 ᵃNU-Text and M-Text omit this verse.

⁴And as they went through the cities, they delivered to them the decrees to keep, which were determined by the apostles and elders at Jerusalem. ⁵So the churches were strengthened in the faith, and increased in number daily.

The Macedonian Call

⁶Now when they had gone through Phrygia and the region of Galatia, they were forbidden by the Holy Spirit to preach the word in Asia. ⁷After they had come to Mysia, they tried to go into Bithynia, but the Spirit*ᵃ* did not permit them. ⁸So passing by Mysia, they came down to Troas. ⁹And a vision appeared to Paul in the night. A man of Macedonia stood and pleaded with him, saying, "Come over to Macedonia and help us." ¹⁰Now after he had seen the vision, immediately we sought to go to Macedonia, concluding that the Lord had called us to preach the gospel to them.

> **16:10 we.** A change from the third person pronoun to the first person indicates that Luke, the author, joined Paul, Silas, and Timothy.

Lydia Baptized at Philippi

¹¹Therefore, sailing from Troas, we ran a straight course to Samothrace, and the next *day* came to Neapolis, ¹²and from there to Philippi, which is the foremost city of that part of Macedonia, a colony. And we were staying in that city for some days. ¹³And on the Sabbath day we went out of the city to the riverside, where prayer was customarily made; and we sat down and spoke to the women who met *there*. ¹⁴Now a certain woman named Lydia heard *us*. She was a seller of purple from the city of Thyatira, who worshiped God. The Lord opened her

> **16:14 Lydia...from the city of Thyatira.** Her home city was in the Roman province of Lydia. The name "Lydia" was probably associated with her place of origin. **seller of purple.** Purple dye was extremely expensive, and purple garments were usually worn by royalty and the wealthy. Lydia had a good business, which enabled her to have a large enough house to accommodate the missionaries and, later, the church at Philippi.

heart to heed the things spoken by Paul. ¹⁵And when she and her household were baptized, she begged *us*, saying, "If you have judged me to be faithful to the Lord, come to my house and stay." So she persuaded us.

Paul and Silas Imprisoned

¹⁶Now it happened, as we went to prayer, that a certain slave girl possessed with a spirit of divination met us, who brought her masters much profit by fortune-telling. ¹⁷This girl followed Paul and us, and cried out, saying, "These men are the servants of the Most High God, who proclaim to us the way of salvation." ¹⁸And this she did for many days.

But Paul, greatly annoyed, turned and said to the spirit, "I command you in the name of Jesus Christ to come out of her." And he came out that very hour. ¹⁹But when her masters saw that their hope of profit was gone, they seized Paul and Silas and dragged *them* into the marketplace to the authorities.

²⁰And they brought them to the magistrates, and said, "These men, being Jews, exceedingly trouble our city; ²¹and they teach customs which are not lawful for us, being Romans, to receive or observe." ²²Then the multitude rose up together against them; and the magistrates tore off their clothes and commanded *them* to be beaten with rods. ²³And when they had laid many stripes on them, they threw *them* into prison, commanding the jailer to keep them securely. ²⁴Having received such a charge, he put them into the inner prison and fastened their feet in the stocks.

The Philippian Jailer Saved

²⁵But at midnight Paul and Silas were praying and singing hymns to God, and the prisoners were listening to them. ²⁶Suddenly there was a great earthquake, so that the foundations of the prison were shaken; and immediately all the doors were opened and everyone's chains were loosed. ²⁷And the keeper of the prison, awaking from sleep and seeing the prison doors open, supposing the prisoners had fled, drew his sword and was about to kill himself. ²⁸But Paul

---

16:7 *ᵃ*NU-Text adds *of Jesus.*

called with a loud voice, saying, "Do yourself no harm, for we are all here."

> **16:27 prison doors open...about to kill himself.** If he let a prisoner escape, a Roman soldier would pay with his life (12:19; 27:42). Instead of waiting to face humiliation and execution for letting a prisoner (in this case, many prisoners) escape, this Philippian jailer decided to kill himself.

²⁹Then he called for a light, ran in, and fell down trembling before Paul and Silas. ³⁰And he brought them out and said, "Sirs, what must I do to be saved?"

³¹So they said, "Believe on the Lord Jesus Christ, and you will be saved, you and your household." ³²Then they spoke the word of the Lord to him and to all who were in his house. ³³And he took them the same hour of the night and washed *their* stripes. And immediately he and all his family were baptized. ³⁴Now when he had brought them into his house, he set food before them; and he rejoiced, having believed in God with all his household.

Paul Refuses to Depart Secretly

³⁵And when it was day, the magistrates sent the officers, saying, "Let those men go."

³⁶So the keeper of the prison reported these words to Paul, saying, "The magistrates have sent to let you go. Now therefore depart, and go in peace."

³⁷But Paul said to them, "They have beaten us openly, uncondemned Romans, *and* have thrown *us* into prison. And now do they put us out secretly? No indeed! Let them come themselves and get us out."

> **16:37 Romans.** It was a serious crime to inflict corporal punishment on a Roman citizen, and it was more so since Paul and Silas had not received a trial. The magistrates faced the possibility of being removed from office and having Philippi's privileges as a Roman colony revoked.

³⁸And the officers told these words to the magistrates, and they were afraid when they heard that they were Romans. ³⁹Then they came and pleaded with them and brought *them* out, and asked *them* to de-

part from the city. ⁴⁰So they went out of the prison and entered *the house of* Lydia; and when they had seen the brethren, they encouraged them and departed.

Preaching Christ at Thessalonica

17 Now when they had passed through Amphipolis and Apollonia, they came to Thessalonica, where there was a synagogue of the Jews. ²Then Paul, as his custom was, went in to them, and for three Sabbaths reasoned with them from the Scriptures, ³explaining and demonstrating that the Christ had to suffer and rise again from the dead, and *saying,* "This Jesus whom I preach to you is the Christ." ⁴And some of them were persuaded; and a great multitude of the devout Greeks, and not a few of the leading women, joined Paul and Silas.

Assault on Jason's House

⁵But the Jews who were not persuaded, becoming envious,ᵃ took some of the evil men from the marketplace, and gathering a mob, set all the city in an uproar and attacked the house of Jason, and sought to bring them out to the people. ⁶But when they did not find them, they dragged Jason and some brethren to the rulers of the city, crying out, "These who have turned the world upside down have come here too. ⁷Jason has harbored them, and these are all acting contrary to the decrees of Caesar, saying there is another king—Jesus." ⁸And they troubled the crowd and the rulers of the city when they heard these things. ⁹So when they had taken security from Jason and the rest, they let them go.

Ministering at Berea

¹⁰Then the brethren immediately sent Paul and Silas away by night to Berea. When they arrived, they went into the synagogue of the Jews. ¹¹These were more fairminded than those in Thessalonica, in that they received the word with all readiness, and searched the Scriptures daily *to find out* whether these things were so. ¹²Therefore many of them believed, and also not a few of the Greeks, prominent women as well as men. ¹³But when the Jews from

---

17:5 ᵃNU-Text omits *who were not persuaded;* M-Text omits *becoming envious.*

Thessalonica learned that the word of God was preached by Paul at Berea, they came there also and stirred up the crowds. ¹⁴Then immediately the brethren sent Paul away, to go to the sea; but both Silas and Timothy remained there. ¹⁵So those who conducted Paul brought him to Athens; and receiving a command for Silas and Timothy to come to him with all speed, they departed.

The Philosophers at Athens

¹⁶Now while Paul waited for them at Athens, his spirit was provoked within him when he saw that the city was given over to idols. ¹⁷Therefore he reasoned in the synagogue with the Jews and with the *Gentile* worshipers, and in the marketplace daily with those who happened to be there. ¹⁸Then[a] certain Epicurean and Stoic philosophers encountered him. And some said, "What does this babbler want to say?"

Others said, "He seems to be a proclaimer of foreign gods," because he preached to them Jesus and the resurrection.

¹⁹And they took him and brought him to the Areopagus, saying, "May we know what this new doctrine *is* of which you speak? ²⁰For you are bringing some strange things to our ears. Therefore we want to know what these things mean." ²¹For all the Athenians and the foreigners who were there spent their time in nothing else but either to tell or to hear some new thing.

Addressing the Areopagus

²²Then Paul stood in the midst of the Areopagus and said, "Men of Athens, I perceive that in all things you are very religious; ²³for as I was passing through and considering the objects of your worship, I even found an altar with this inscription:

TO THE UNKNOWN GOD.

Therefore, the One whom you worship without knowing, Him I proclaim to you: ²⁴God, who made the world and everything in it, since He is Lord of heaven and earth, does not dwell in temples made with hands. ²⁵Nor is He worshiped with men's

> **17:23,24 TO THE UNKNOWN GOD.** The Athenians believed in the existence of someone beyond their ability to understand who had made all things. Because of this, Paul could introduce them to the Creator who could be known (Deut. 4:35). When evangelizing pagans, Paul started with creation, the general revelation of God. When evangelizing the Jews, he started from the OT.

hands, as though He needed anything, since He gives to all life, breath, and all things. ²⁶And He has made from one blood[a] every nation of men to dwell on all the face of the earth, and has determined their preappointed times and the boundaries of their dwellings, ²⁷so that they should seek the Lord, in the hope that they might grope for Him and find Him, though He is not far from each one of us; ²⁸for in Him we live and move and have our being, as also some of your own poets have said, 'For we are also His offspring.' ²⁹Therefore, since we are the offspring of God, we ought not to think that the Divine Nature is like gold or silver or stone, something shaped by art and man's devising. ³⁰Truly, these times of ignorance God overlooked, but now commands all men everywhere to repent, ³¹because He has appointed a day on which He will judge the world in righteousness by the Man whom He has ordained. He has given assurance of this to all by raising Him from the dead."

³²And when they heard of the resurrection of the dead, some mocked, while others said, "We will hear you again on this *matter*." ³³So Paul departed from among them. ³⁴However, some men joined him and believed, among them Dionysius the Areopagite, a woman named Damaris, and others with them.

Ministering at Corinth

18 After these things Paul departed from Athens and went to Corinth. ²And he found a certain Jew named Aquila, born in Pontus, who had recently come from Italy with his wife Priscilla (because Claudius had commanded all the Jews to depart from Rome); and he came to them. ³So, because he was of the same trade, he stayed with them and worked; for by occu-

---

17:18 [a]NU-Text and M-Text add *also*.   17:26 [a]NU-Text omits *blood*.

pation they were tentmakers. ⁴And he reasoned in the synagogue every Sabbath, and persuaded both Jews and Greeks.

⁵When Silas and Timothy had come from Macedonia, Paul was compelled by the Spirit, and testified to the Jews *that* Jesus *is* the Christ. ⁶But when they opposed him and blasphemed, he shook *his* garments and said to them, "Your blood *be* upon your *own* heads; I *am* clean. From now on I will go to the Gentiles." ⁷And he departed from there and entered the house of a certain *man* named Justus,ᵃ one who worshiped God, whose house was next door to the synagogue. ⁸Then Crispus, the ruler of the synagogue, believed on the Lord with all his household. And many of the Corinthians, hearing, believed and were baptized.

> **18:2 Aquila...Priscilla.** Paul was close friends with this married couple who risked their lives for him (Rom. 16:3,4). They appear 5 more times in Scripture, where Priscilla's name is listed first. This may imply that she had a higher social rank than Aquila, or that she was more prominent in the church. They probably were Christians when Paul met them, having come from Rome where a church already existed (Rom. 1:7,8).

⁹Now the Lord spoke to Paul in the night by a vision, "Do not be afraid, but speak, and do not keep silent; ¹⁰for I am with you, and no one will attack you to hurt you; for I have many people in this city." ¹¹And he continued *there* a year and six months, teaching the word of God among them.

¹²When Gallio was proconsul of Achaia, the Jews with one accord rose up against Paul and brought him to the judgment seat, ¹³saying, "This *fellow* persuades men to worship God contrary to the law."

¹⁴And when Paul was about to open *his* mouth, Gallio said to the Jews, "If it were a

> **18:13 contrary to the law.** Judaism was not an official religion, but it was tolerated by the Roman world. Christianity was viewed as a sect of Judaism. The Jews in Corinth claimed that Paul's teaching was external to Judaism and, therefore, should be banned. If Gallio had ruled in the Jews' favor, Christianity could have been outlawed throughout the Empire.

matter of wrongdoing or wicked crimes, O Jews, there would be reason why I should bear with you. ¹⁵But if it is a question of words and names and your own law, look *to it* yourselves; for I do not want to be a judge of such *matters*." ¹⁶And he drove them from the judgment seat. ¹⁷Then all the Greeksᵃ took Sosthenes, the ruler of the synagogue, and beat *him* before the judgment seat. But Gallio took no notice of these things.

Paul Returns to Antioch

¹⁸So Paul still remained a good while. Then he took leave of the brethren and sailed for Syria, and Priscilla and Aquila *were* with him. He had *his* hair cut off at Cenchrea, for he had taken a vow. ¹⁹And he came to Ephesus, and left them there; but he himself entered the synagogue and reasoned with the Jews. ²⁰When they asked *him* to stay a longer time with them, he did not consent, ²¹but took leave of them, saying, "I must by all means keep this coming feast in Jerusalem;ᵃ but I will return again to you, God willing." And he sailed from Ephesus.

> **18:18 He had *his* hair cut off...he had taken a vow.** Paul took this Nazirite vow to show God his gratitude for helping him in Corinth. The vow generally lasted a specific period of time, although Samson (Judg. 13:5), Samuel (1 Sam. 1:11), and John the Baptist (Luke 1:15) were Nazirites for life. In Paul's day, if someone made the vow while away from Jerusalem, he had to shave his head at the end of his vow and afterwards present the shorn hair at the temple within 30 days.

²²And when he had landed at Caesarea, and gone up and greeted the church, he went down to Antioch. ²³After he had spent some time *there*, he departed and went over the region of Galatia and Phrygia in order, strengthening all the disciples.

Ministry of Apollos

²⁴Now a certain Jew named Apollos, born at Alexandria, an eloquent man *and* mighty in the Scriptures, came to Ephesus. ²⁵This man had been instructed in the way of the Lord; and being fervent in spirit, he spoke and taught accurately the things of the Lord, though he knew only the baptism of

---

18:7 ᵃNU-Text reads *Titius Justus.*   18:17 ᵃNU-Text reads *they all.*   18:21 ᵃNU-Text omits *I must* through *Jerusalem.*

> **18:25 the way of the Lord.** This phrase is used in the OT to describe the spiritual and moral standards God requires of His people (Gen. 18:19; Judg. 2:22). **baptism of John.** Apollos acknowledged John's baptism and Jesus as Israel's Messiah. But he did not understand the significance of Christ's death and resurrection, the ministry of the Holy Spirit, and the church as God's witness. He was a redeemed OT believer.

John. 26So he began to speak boldly in the synagogue. When Aquila and Priscilla heard him, they took him aside and explained to him the way of God more accurately. 27And when he desired to cross to Achaia, the brethren wrote, exhorting the disciples to receive him; and when he arrived, he greatly helped those who had believed through grace; 28for he vigorously refuted the Jews publicly, showing from the Scriptures that Jesus is the Christ.

Paul at Ephesus

19 And it happened, while Apollos was at Corinth, that Paul, having passed through the upper regions, came to Ephesus. And finding some disciples 2he said to them, "Did you receive the Holy Spirit when you believed?"

So they said to him, "We have not so much as heard whether there is a Holy Spirit."

> **19:2 "Did you receive the Holy Spirit when you believed?"** Paul was uncertain about their spiritual status. Because all Christians receive the Holy Spirit at the moment of salvation, their answer revealed that they were not yet saved. Also, they had not yet received Christian baptism.

3And he said to them, "Into what then were you baptized?"

So they said, "Into John's baptism."

4Then Paul said, "John indeed baptized with a baptism of repentance, saying to the people that they should believe on Him who would come after him, that is, on Christ Jesus."

5When they heard this, they were baptized in the name of the Lord Jesus. 6And when Paul had laid hands on them, the Holy Spirit came upon them, and they spoke with tongues and prophesied. 7Now the men were about twelve in all.

8And he went into the synagogue and spoke boldly for three months, reasoning and persuading concerning the things of the kingdom of God. 9But when some were hardened and did not believe, but spoke evil of the Way before the multitude, he departed from them and withdrew the disciples, reasoning daily in the school of Tyrannus. 10And this continued for two years, so that all who dwelt in Asia heard the word of the Lord Jesus, both Jews and Greeks.

Miracles Glorify Christ

11Now God worked unusual miracles by the hands of Paul, 12so that even handkerchiefs or aprons were brought from his body to the sick, and the diseases left them and the evil spirits went out of them. 13Then some of the itinerant Jewish exorcists took it upon themselves to call the name of the Lord Jesus over those who had evil spirits, saying, "We*a* exorcise you by the Jesus whom Paul preaches." 14Also there were seven sons of Sceva, a Jewish chief priest, who did so.

15And the evil spirit answered and said, "Jesus I know, and Paul I know; but who are you?"

16Then the man in whom the evil spirit was leaped on them, overpowered*a* them, and prevailed against them,*b* so that they fled out of that house naked and wounded. 17This became known both to all Jews and Greeks dwelling in Ephesus; and fear fell on them all, and the name of the Lord Jesus was magnified. 18And many who had believed came confessing and telling their deeds. 19Also, many of those who had practiced magic brought their books together and burned *them* in the sight of all. And they counted up the value of them, and *it* totaled fifty thousand *pieces* of silver. 20So the word of the Lord grew mightily and prevailed.

The Riot at Ephesus

21When these things were accomplished, Paul purposed in the Spirit, when he had passed through Macedonia and Achaia, to go to Jerusalem, saying, "After I have been

---

19:13 *a*NU-Text reads *I.*   19:16 *a*M-Text reads *and they overpowered.*   *b*NU-Text reads *both of them.*

there, I must also see Rome." ²²So he sent into Macedonia two of those who ministered to him, Timothy and Erastus, but he himself stayed in Asia for a time.

19:21 I must also see Rome. Paul had not visited Rome yet, but he needed to go because of the strategic importance of the church there. He intended to use Rome in order to begin ministry in the region of Spain (Rom. 15:22–24). This declaration marked a turning point in Acts: Rome became Paul's goal. He would ultimately arrive there as a Roman prisoner (28:16).

²³And about that time there arose a great commotion about the Way. ²⁴For a certain man named Demetrius, a silversmith, who made silver shrines of Diana,ᵃ brought no small profit to the craftsmen. ²⁵He called them together with the workers of similar occupation, and said: "Men, you know that we have our prosperity by this trade. ²⁶Moreover you see and hear that not only at Ephesus, but throughout almost all Asia, this Paul has persuaded and turned away many people, saying that they are not gods which are made with hands. ²⁷So not only is this trade of ours in danger of falling into disrepute, but also the temple of the great goddess Diana may be despised and her magnificence destroyed,ᵃ whom all Asia and the world worship."

²⁸Now when they heard *this*, they were full of wrath and cried out, saying, "Great *is* Diana of the Ephesians!" ²⁹So the whole city was filled with confusion, and rushed into the theater with one accord, having seized Gaius and Aristarchus, Macedonians, Paul's travel companions. ³⁰And when Paul wanted to go in to the people, the disciples would not allow him. ³¹Then some of the officials of Asia, who were his friends, sent to him pleading that he would not venture into the theater. ³²Some therefore cried one thing and some another, for the assembly was confused, and most of them did not know why they had come together. ³³And they drew Alexander out of the multitude, the Jews putting him forward. And Alexander motioned with his hand, and wanted to make his defense to the people. ³⁴But when

they found out that he was a Jew, all with one voice cried out for about two hours, "Great *is* Diana of the Ephesians!"

19:31 officials of Asia. These members of the aristocracy, known as "Asiarchs," were dedicated to promoting Roman interests. Only one Asiarch ruled at a time, but they bore the title for life. These influential men were Paul's friends. This shows that they did not regard him or his message as criminal, so there was no legitimate cause for the riot. Naturally, they were concerned for Paul's safety.

³⁵And when the city clerk had quieted the crowd, he said: "Men of Ephesus, what man is there who does not know that the city of the Ephesians is temple guardian of the great goddess Diana, and of the *image* which fell down from Zeus? ³⁶Therefore, since these things cannot be denied, you ought to be quiet and do nothing rashly. ³⁷For you have brought these men here who are neither robbers of temples nor blasphemers of yourᵃ goddess. ³⁸Therefore, if Demetrius and his fellow craftsmen have a case against anyone, the courts are open and there are proconsuls. Let them bring charges against one another. ³⁹But if you have any other inquiry to make, it shall be determined in the lawful assembly. ⁴⁰For we are in danger of being called in question for today's uproar, there being no reason which we may give to account for this disorderly gathering." ⁴¹And when he had said these things, he dismissed the assembly.

Journeys in Greece

20 After the uproar had ceased, Paul called the disciples to *himself*, embraced *them*, and departed to go to Macedonia. ²Now when he had gone over that region and encouraged them with many words, he came to Greece ³and stayed three months. And when the Jews plotted against him as he was about to sail to Syria, he decided to return through Macedonia. ⁴And Sopater of Berea accompanied him to Asia—also Aristarchus and Secundus of the Thessalonians, and Gaius of Derbe, and Timothy, and Tychicus and Trophimus of Asia. ⁵These men, going ahead, waited

---

19:24 ᵃGreek *Artemis*   19:27 ᵃNU-Text reads *she be deposed from her magnificence.*   19:37 ᵃNU-Text reads *our.*

20:3 Jews plotted against him. The Jews in Corinth hated Paul because of their humiliation before Gallio (18:12–17) and the conversions of two of their prominent leaders, Crispus and Sosthenes. The Jews plotted to murder Paul during his voyage to Palestine. Paul canceled his plans to sail from Greece to Syria. He was unable to reach Palestine in time for Passover, but he hurried to be there for Pentecost (v. 16).

for us at Troas. 6But we sailed away from Philippi after the Days of Unleavened Bread, and in five days joined them at Troas, where we stayed seven days.

Ministering at Troas

7Now on the first *day* of the week, when the disciples came together to break bread, Paul, ready to depart the next day, spoke to them and continued his message until midnight. 8There were many lamps in the upper room where they*a* were gathered together. 9And in a window sat a certain young man named Eutychus, who was sinking into a deep sleep. He was overcome by sleep; and as Paul continued speaking, he fell down from the third story and was taken up dead. 10But Paul went down, fell on him, and embracing *him* said, "Do not trouble yourselves, for his life is in him." 11Now when he had come up, had broken bread and eaten, and talked a long while, even till daybreak, he departed. 12And they brought the young man in alive, and they were not a little comforted.

20:10 his life is in him. This does not mean that he had not died, but that his life had been restored. As a physician, Luke knew when someone died, as he plainly stated had been the case with Eutychus (v. 9).

From Troas to Miletus

13Then we went ahead to the ship and sailed to Assos, there intending to take Paul on board; for so he had given orders, intending himself to go on foot. 14And when he met us at Assos, we took him on board and came to Mitylene. 15We sailed from there, and the next *day* came opposite Chios. The following *day* we arrived at Samos and stayed at Trogyllium. The next *day* we came to Miletus. 16For Paul had decided to sail past Ephesus, so that he would not have to spend time in Asia; for he was hurrying to be at Jerusalem, if possible, on the Day of Pentecost.

The Ephesian Elders Exhorted

17From Miletus he sent to Ephesus and called for the elders of the church. 18And when they had come to him, he said to them: "You know, from the first day that I came to Asia, in what manner I always lived among you, 19serving the Lord with all humility, with many tears and trials which happened to me by the plotting of the Jews; 20how I kept back nothing that was helpful, but proclaimed it to you, and taught you publicly and from house to house, 21testifying to Jews, and also to Greeks, repentance toward God and faith toward our Lord Jesus Christ. 22And see, now I go bound in the spirit to Jerusalem, not knowing the things that will happen to me there, 23except that the Holy Spirit testifies in every city, saying that chains and tribulations await me. 24But none of these things move me; nor do I count my life dear to myself,*a* so that I may finish my race with joy, and the ministry which I received from the Lord Jesus, to testify to the gospel of the grace of God.

25"And indeed, now I know that you all, among whom I have gone preaching the kingdom of God, will see my face no more. 26Therefore I testify to you this day that I *am* innocent of the blood of all *men*. 27For I have not shunned to declare to you the whole counsel of God. 28Therefore take heed to yourselves and to all the flock, among which the Holy Spirit has made you overseers, to shepherd the church of God*a* which He purchased with His own blood. 29For I know this, that after my departure savage wolves will come in among you, not sparing the flock. 30Also from among yourselves men will rise up, speaking perverse things, to draw away the disciples after themselves. 31Therefore watch, and remember that for three years I did not cease to warn everyone night and day with tears.

32"So now, brethren, I commend you to God and to the word of His grace, which is able to build you up and give you an inheri-

---

20:8 *a*NU-Text and M-Text read *we.*   20:24 *a*NU-Text reads *But I do not count my life of any value or dear to myself.*   20:28 *a*M-Text reads *of the Lord and God.*

tance among all those who are sanctified. [33]I have coveted no one's silver or gold or apparel. [34]Yes,[a] you yourselves know that these hands have provided for my necessities, and for those who were with me. [35]I have shown you in every way, by laboring like this, that you must support the weak. And remember the words of the Lord Jesus, that He said, 'It is more blessed to give than to receive.' "

20:34 these hands...provided for my necessities. Paul had the right to earn his living from preaching the gospel (1 Cor. 9:3–14) and he sometimes accepted support (2 Cor. 11:8,9). But he often worked to support himself so he could "present the gospel of Christ without charge" (1 Cor. 9:18).

---

[36]And when he had said these things, he knelt down and prayed with them all. [37]Then they all wept freely, and fell on Paul's neck and kissed him, [38]sorrowing most of all for the words which he spoke, that they would see his face no more. And they accompanied him to the ship.

Warnings on the Journey to Jerusalem

21 Now it came to pass, that when we had departed from them and set sail, running a straight course we came to Cos, the following *day* to Rhodes, and from there to Patara. [2]And finding a ship sailing over to Phoenicia, we went aboard and set sail. [3]When we had sighted Cyprus, we passed it on the left, sailed to Syria, and landed at Tyre; for there the ship was to unload her cargo. [4]And finding disciples,[a] we stayed there seven days. They told Paul through the Spirit not to go up to Jerusalem. [5]When we had come to the end of those days, we departed and went on our

---

21:4 disciples. The church in Tyre was founded by Christians who had fled Jerusalem after Stephen's martyrdom, which Paul himself had instigated. **told Paul...not to go.** The Spirit had revealed to the believers at Tyre that Paul would face suffering in Jerusalem, so they tried to dissuade him from going. But Paul's mission to Jerusalem was given to him by the Lord, and the Spirit would never command him to abandon it.

---

way; and they all accompanied us, with wives and children, till *we were* out of the city. And we knelt down on the shore and prayed. [6]When we had taken our leave of one another, we boarded the ship, and they returned home.

[7]And when we had finished *our* voyage from Tyre, we came to Ptolemais, greeted the brethren, and stayed with them one day. [8]On the next *day* we who were Paul's companions[a] departed and came to Caesarea, and entered the house of Philip the evangelist, who was *one* of the seven, and stayed with him. [9]Now this man had four virgin daughters who prophesied. [10]And as we stayed many days, a certain prophet named Agabus came down from Judea. [11]When he had come to us, he took Paul's belt, bound his *own* hands and feet, and said, "Thus says the Holy Spirit, 'So shall the Jews at Jerusalem bind the man who owns this belt, and deliver *him* into the hands of the Gentiles.' "

21:9 virgin daughters. The virgins may have been called by God for special ministry (see 1 Cor. 7:34). The early church regarded these women as important sources of information on early church history. **prophesied.** They may have had ongoing prophecy, or they may have prophesied only once. Women are not to be teachers or preachers in the church (1 Cor. 14:34–36), so they probably ministered to individuals.

---

[12]Now when we heard these things, both we and those from that place pleaded with him not to go up to Jerusalem. [13]Then Paul answered, "What do you mean by weeping and breaking my heart? For I am ready not only to be bound, but also to die at Jerusalem for the name of the Lord Jesus." [14]So when he would not be persuaded, we ceased, saying, "The will of the Lord be done."

Paul Urged to Make Peace

[15]And after those days we packed and went up to Jerusalem. [16]Also some of the disciples from Caesarea went with us and brought with them a certain Mnason of Cyprus, an early disciple, with whom we were to lodge.

20:34 [a]NU-Text and M-Text omit *Yes.*   21:4 [a]NU-Text reads *the disciples.*   21:8 [a]NU-Text omits *who were Paul's companions.*

¹⁷And when we had come to Jerusalem, the brethren received us gladly. ¹⁸On the following *day* Paul went in with us to James, and all the elders were present. ¹⁹When he had greeted them, he told in detail those things which God had done among the Gentiles through his ministry. ²⁰And when they heard *it,* they glorified the Lord. And they said to him, "You see, brother, how many myriads of Jews there are who have believed, and they are all zealous for the law; ²¹but they have been informed about you that you teach all the Jews who are among the Gentiles to forsake Moses, saying that they ought not to circumcise *their* children nor to walk according to the customs. ²²What then? The assembly must certainly meet, for they will*ᵃ* hear that you have come. ²³Therefore do what we tell you: We have four men who have taken a vow. ²⁴Take them and be purified with them, and pay their expenses so that they may shave *their* heads, and that all may know that those things of which they were informed concerning you are nothing, but *that* you yourself also walk orderly and keep the law. ²⁵But concerning the Gentiles who believe, we have written *and* decided that they should observe no such thing,*ᵃ* except that they should keep themselves from *things* offered to idols, from blood, from things strangled, and from sexual immorality."

21:18 James. This is the brother of Jesus, the head of the Jerusalem church. **all the elders.** The apostles, often away on evangelistic work, turned the running of the Jerusalem church over to the elders. Some say there were 70 elders, paralleling the Sanhedrin. There were at least that many, as the Jerusalem church was very large. God had decreed that after the apostles were gone, the elders were to rule the church (14:23; 1 Tim. 5:17).

Arrested in the Temple

²⁶Then Paul took the men, and the next day, having been purified with them, entered the temple to announce the expiration of the days of purification, at which time an offering should be made for each one of them.

²⁷Now when the seven days were almost ended, the Jews from Asia, seeing him in the temple, stirred up the whole crowd and laid hands on him, ²⁸crying out, "Men of Israel, help! This is the man who teaches all *men* everywhere against the people, the law, and this place; and furthermore he also brought Greeks into the temple and has defiled this holy place." ²⁹(For they had previously*ᵃ* seen Trophimus the Ephesian with him in the city, whom they supposed that Paul had brought into the temple.)

21:28 the people, the law, and this place. Paul's enemies falsely charged him with teaching Jews to forsake their heritage, oppose the law, and defile the temple. **brought Greeks into the temple.** The Asian Jews accused Paul of bringing Trophimus into the part of the temple where Gentiles were forbidden. Paul would never have risked his friend's life by doing this (Gentiles who defiled the temple were executed).

³⁰And all the city was disturbed; and the people ran together, seized Paul, and dragged him out of the temple; and immediately the doors were shut. ³¹Now as they were seeking to kill him, news came to the commander of the garrison that all Jerusalem was in an uproar. ³²He immediately took soldiers and centurions, and ran down to them. And when they saw the commander and the soldiers, they stopped beating Paul. ³³Then the commander came near and took him, and commanded *him* to be bound with two chains; and he asked who he was and what he had done. ³⁴And some among the multitude cried one thing and some another.

So when he could not ascertain the truth because of the tumult, he commanded him to be taken into the barracks. ³⁵When he reached the stairs, he had to be carried by the soldiers because of the violence of the mob. ³⁶For the multitude of the people followed after, crying out, "Away with him!"

Addressing the Jerusalem Mob

³⁷Then as Paul was about to be led into the barracks, he said to the commander, "May I speak to you?"

21:22 *ᵃ*NU-Text reads *What then is to be done? They will certainly.* 21:25 *ᵃ*NU-Text omits *that they should observe no such thing, except.* 21:29 *ᵃ*M-Text omits *previously.*

He replied, "Can you speak Greek? ³⁸Are you not the Egyptian who some time ago stirred up a rebellion and led the four thousand assassins out into the wilderness?"

> **21:37 "Can you speak Greek?"** Paul's use of the language of educated people startled Lysias, who assumed his prisoner was an uncultured criminal.

³⁹But Paul said, "I am a Jew from Tarsus, in Cilicia, a citizen of no mean city; and I implore you, permit me to speak to the people."

⁴⁰So when he had given him permission, Paul stood on the stairs and motioned with his hand to the people. And when there was a great silence, he spoke to *them* in the Hebrew language, saying,

22 "Brethren and fathers, hear my defense before you now." ²And when they heard that he spoke to them in the Hebrew language, they kept all the more silent.

Then he said: ³"I am indeed a Jew, born in Tarsus of Cilicia, but brought up in this city at the feet of Gamaliel, taught according to the strictness of our fathers' law, and was zealous toward God as you all are today. ⁴I persecuted this Way to the death, binding and delivering into prisons both men and women, ⁵as also the high priest bears me witness, and all the council of the elders, from whom I also received letters to the brethren, and went to Damascus to bring in chains even those who were there to Jerusalem to be punished.

> **22:3 I am indeed a Jew.** This was a response to the false charges raised by the Asian Jews. **Cilicia.** Tarsus was the chief city of Cilicia. **brought up in this city.** Paul was born among the Hellenistic Jews of the Diaspora, but he had been brought up in Jerusalem. **father's law.** As a student of Gamaliel, Paul had received training in OT law and in the rabbinic traditions. The charge that Paul opposed the law was ridiculous.

⁶"Now it happened, as I journeyed and came near Damascus at about noon, suddenly a great light from heaven shone around me. ⁷And I fell to the ground and heard a voice saying to me, 'Saul, Saul, why are you persecuting Me?' ⁸So I answered, 'Who are You, Lord?' And He said to me, 'I am Jesus of Nazareth, whom you are persecuting.'

⁹"And those who were with me indeed saw the light and were afraid,ᵃ but they did not hear the voice of Him who spoke to me. ¹⁰So I said, 'What shall I do, Lord?' And the Lord said to me, 'Arise and go into Damascus, and there you will be told all things which are appointed for you to do.' ¹¹And since I could not see for the glory of that light, being led by the hand of those who were with me, I came into Damascus.

¹²"Then a certain Ananias, a devout man according to the law, having a good testimony with all the Jews who dwelt *there*, ¹³came to me; and he stood and said to me, 'Brother Saul, receive your sight.' And at that same hour I looked up at him. ¹⁴Then he said, 'The God of our fathers has chosen you that you should know His will, and see the Just One, and hear the voice of His mouth. ¹⁵For you will be His witness to all men of what you have seen and heard. ¹⁶And now why are you waiting? Arise and be baptized, and wash away your sins, calling on the name of the Lord.'

¹⁷"Now it happened, when I returned to Jerusalem and was praying in the temple, that I was in a trance ¹⁸and saw Him saying to me, 'Make haste and get out of Jerusalem quickly, for they will not receive your testimony concerning Me.' ¹⁹So I said, 'Lord, they know that in every synagogue I imprisoned and beat those who believe on You. ²⁰And when the blood of Your martyr Stephen was shed, I also was standing by consenting to his death,ᵃ and guarding the clothes of those who were killing him.' ²¹Then He said to me, 'Depart, for I will send you far from here to the Gentiles.' "

Paul's Roman Citizenship

²²And they listened to him until this word, and *then* they raised their voices and said, "Away with such a *fellow* from the earth, for he is not fit to live!" ²³Then, as they cried out and tore off *their* clothes and threw dust into the air, ²⁴the commander

---

22:9 ᵃNU-Text omits *and were afraid.*   22:20 ᵃNU-Text omits *to his death.*

ordered him to be brought into the barracks, and said that he should be examined under scourging, so that he might know why they shouted so against him. ²⁵And as they bound him with thongs, Paul said to the centurion who stood by, "Is it lawful for you to scourge a man who is a Roman, and uncondemned?"

²⁶When the centurion heard *that,* he went and told the commander, saying, "Take care what you do, for this man is a Roman."

> **22:26 "Take care...this man is a Roman."** The centurion informed Lysias of Paul's citizenship, cautioning him against an act that could have ended his military career and possibly his life.

²⁷Then the commander came and said to him, "Tell me, are you a Roman?"

He said, "Yes."

²⁸The commander answered, "With a large sum I obtained this citizenship."

And Paul said, "But I was born *a citizen.*"

²⁹Then immediately those who were about to examine him withdrew from him; and the commander was also afraid after he found out that he was a Roman, and because he had bound him.

The Sanhedrin Divided

³⁰The next day, because he wanted to know for certain why he was accused by the Jews, he released him from *his* bonds, and commanded the chief priests and all their council to appear, and brought Paul down and set him before them.

23 Then Paul, looking earnestly at the council, said, "Men *and* brethren, I have lived in all good conscience before God until this day." ²And the high priest Ananias commanded those who stood by him to strike him on the mouth. ³Then Paul said to him, "God will strike you, *you* whitewashed wall! For you sit to judge me according to the law, and do you command me to be struck contrary to the law?"

⁴And those who stood by said, "Do you revile God's high priest?"

⁵Then Paul said, "I did not know, breth-

> **23:3 contrary to the law.** Paul was angered by the High-Priest's violation of Jewish law. When Jesus was similarly struck in violation of the law, He reacted by calmly asking the reason for the blow (John 18:23). Paul admitted that his reaction was wrong. Ananias, although an evil man, held a God-ordained office and was to be respected.

ren, that he was the high priest; for it is written, *'You shall not speak evil of a ruler of your people.' "^a*

⁶But when Paul perceived that one part were Sadducees and the other Pharisees, he cried out in the council, "Men *and* brethren, I am a Pharisee, the son of a Pharisee; concerning the hope and resurrection of the dead I am being judged!"

⁷And when he had said this, a dissension arose between the Pharisees and the Sadducees; and the assembly was divided. ⁸For Sadducees say that there is no resurrection—and no angel or spirit; but the Pharisees confess both. ⁹Then there arose a loud outcry. And the scribes of the Pharisees' party arose and protested, saying, "We find no evil in this man; but if a spirit or an angel has spoken to him, let us not fight against God."^a

> **23:7 a dissension arose.** There were major social, political, and theological differences between the Sadducees and Pharisees. Paul raised the issue of resurrection, appealing to the Pharisees for support on perhaps the most important theological difference. Paul meant to divide the Sanhedrin over the resurrection of Christ, which is the central theme of Christianity.

¹⁰Now when there arose a great dissension, the commander, fearing lest Paul might be pulled to pieces by them, commanded the soldiers to go down and take him by force from among them, and bring *him* into the barracks.

The Plot Against Paul

¹¹But the following night the Lord stood by him and said, "Be of good cheer, Paul; for as you have testified for Me in Jerusalem, so you must also bear witness at Rome."

¹²And when it was day, some of the Jews

23:5 ^aExodus 22:28   23:9 ^aNU-Text omits last clause and reads *what if a spirit or an angel has spoken to him?*

banded together and bound themselves under an oath, saying that they would neither eat nor drink till they had killed Paul. [13]Now there were more than forty who had formed this conspiracy. [14]They came to the chief priests and elders, and said, "We have bound ourselves under a great oath that we will eat nothing until we have killed Paul. [15]Now you, therefore, together with the council, suggest to the commander that he be brought down to you tomorrow,*a* as though you were going to make further inquiries concerning him; but we are ready to kill him before he comes near."

[16]So when Paul's sister's son heard of their ambush, he went and entered the barracks and told Paul. [17]Then Paul called one of the centurions to *him* and said, "Take this young man to the commander, for he has something to tell him." [18]So he took him and brought *him* to the commander and said, "Paul the prisoner called me to *him* and asked *me* to bring this young man to you. He has something to say to you."

> **23:16 Paul's sister's son.** This is the only clear reference in Scripture to Paul's family. We do not know why Paul's nephew was in Jerusalem, away from his family in Tarsus. Nor is it evident why he would want to warn his uncle, for Paul's family possibly disinherited him when he became a Christian (Phil. 3:8). **entered the barracks and told Paul.** Paul was able to receive visitors because he was in protective custody and not under arrest.

[19]Then the commander took him by the hand, went aside, and asked privately, "What is it that you have to tell me?" [20]And he said, "The Jews have agreed to ask that you bring Paul down to the council tomorrow, as though they were going to inquire more fully about him. [21]But do not yield to them, for more than forty of them lie in wait for him, men who have bound themselves by an oath that they will neither eat nor drink till they have killed him; and now they are ready, waiting for the promise from you."

[22]So the commander let the young man depart, and commanded *him*, "Tell no one that you have revealed these things to me."

Sent to Felix

[23]And he called for two centurions, saying, "Prepare two hundred soldiers, seventy horsemen, and two hundred spearmen to go to Caesarea at the third hour of the night; [24]and provide mounts to set Paul on, and bring *him* safely to Felix the governor." [25]He wrote a letter in the following manner:

[26]   Claudius Lysias,

To the most excellent governor Felix:

Greetings.

[27]   This man was seized by the Jews and was about to be killed by them. Coming with the troops I rescued him, having learned that he was a Roman. [28]And when I wanted to know the reason they accused him, I brought him before their council. [29]I found out that he was accused concerning questions of their law, but had nothing charged against him deserving of death or chains. [30]And when it was told me that the Jews lay in wait for the man,*a* I sent him immediately to you, and also commanded his accusers to state before you the charges against him.

Farewell.

[31]Then the soldiers, as they were commanded, took Paul and brought *him* by night to Antipatris. [32]The next day they left the horsemen to go on with him, and returned to the barracks. [33]When they came to Caesarea and had delivered the letter to the governor, they also presented Paul to him. [34]And when the governor had read *it*, he asked what province he was from. And when he understood that *he was* from Cilicia, [35]he said, "I will hear you when your accusers also have come." And he commanded him to be kept in Herod's Praetorium.

Accused of Sedition

24 Now after five days Ananias the high priest came down with the elders and a certain orator *named* Tertullus.

23:15 *a*NU-Text omits *tomorrow.*   23:30 *a*NU-Text reads *there would be a plot against the man.*

These gave evidence to the governor against Paul.

²And when he was called upon, Tertullus began his accusation, saying: "Seeing that through you we enjoy great peace, and prosperity is being brought to this nation by your foresight, ³we accept *it* always and in all places, most noble Felix, with all thankfulness. ⁴Nevertheless, not to be tedious to you any further, I beg you to hear, by your courtesy, a few words from us. ⁵For we have found this man a plague, a creator of dissension among all the Jews throughout the world, and a ringleader of the sect of the Nazarenes. ⁶He even tried to profane the temple, and we seized him,*ᵃ* and wanted to judge him according to our law. ⁷But the commander Lysias came by and with great violence took *him* out of our hands, ⁸commanding his accusers to come to you. By examining him yourself you may ascertain all these things of which we accuse him." ⁹And the Jews also assented,*ᵃ* maintaining that these things were so.

24:3 Felix. Felix was a former slave whose brother (a favorite of Emperor Claudius) obtained for him the position of governor of Judea from A.D. 52 to 59. He accomplished little and was not highly regarded by the influential Romans of his day. He defeated the Egyptian and his followers (see 21:38), but his brutality angered the Jews and led to his overthrow by Emperor Nero two years after Paul's hearing.

The Defense Before Felix

¹⁰Then Paul, after the governor had nodded to him to speak, answered: "Inasmuch as I know that you have been for many years a judge of this nation, I do the more cheerfully answer for myself, ¹¹because you may ascertain that it is no more than twelve days since I went up to Jerusalem to worship. ¹²And they neither found me in the temple disputing with anyone nor incit-

24:10 many years a judge. Paul reminded Felix of his acquaintance with Jewish laws, customs, and beliefs due to his years as governor and service under the governor of Samaria. Felix was bound to give a just verdict.

ing the crowd, either in the synagogues or in the city. ¹³Nor can they prove the things of which they now accuse me. ¹⁴But this I confess to you, that according to the Way which they call a sect, so I worship the God of my fathers, believing all things which are written in the Law and in the Prophets. ¹⁵I have hope in God, which they themselves also accept, that there will be a resurrection of *the* dead,*ᵃ* both of *the* just and *the* unjust. ¹⁶This *being* so, I myself always strive to have a conscience without offense toward God and men.

¹⁷"Now after many years I came to bring alms and offerings to my nation, ¹⁸in the midst of which some Jews from Asia found me purified in the temple, neither with a mob nor with tumult. ¹⁹They ought to have been here before you to object if they had anything against me. ²⁰Or else let those who are *here* themselves say if they found any wrongdoing*ᵃ* in me while I stood before the council, ²¹unless *it is* for this one statement which I cried out, standing among them, 'Concerning the resurrection of the dead I am being judged by you this day.' "

Felix Procrastinates

²²But when Felix heard these things, having more accurate knowledge of *the* Way, he adjourned the proceedings and said, "When Lysias the commander comes down, I will make a decision on your case." ²³So he commanded the centurion to keep Paul and to let *him* have liberty, and told him not to forbid any of his friends to provide for or visit him.

²⁴And after some days, when Felix came with his wife Drusilla, who was Jewish, he sent for Paul and heard him concerning the faith in Christ. ²⁵Now as he reasoned about righteousness, self-control, and the judgment to come, Felix was afraid and answered, "Go away for now; when I have a convenient time I will call for you." ²⁶Meanwhile he also hoped that money would be given him by Paul, that he might release him.*ᵃ* Therefore he sent for him more often and conversed with him.

24:6 *ᵃ*NU-Text ends the sentence here and omits the rest of verse 6, all of verse 7, and the first clause of verse 8.   24:9 *ᵃ*NU-Text and M-Text read *joined the attack.*   24:15 *ᵃ*NU-Text omits *of the dead.*
24:20 *ᵃ*NU-Text and M-Text read *say what wrongdoing they found.*   24:26 *ᵃ*NU-Text omits *that he might release him.*

24:25 righteousness, self-control, and the judgment. God demands righteousness of all men because of His holy nature (Matt. 5:48). This requires self-control. The result of failing to demonstrate self-control and to conform to God's righteous standard is judgment. **Felix was afraid.** Felix realized that he faced judgment for living with a woman he had lured away from her husband, so he hastily dismissed Paul. **when I have a convenient time.** Felix passed up his opportunity to repent (see 2 Cor. 6:2).

27But after two years Porcius Festus succeeded Felix; and Felix, wanting to do the Jews a favor, left Paul bound.

Paul Appeals to Caesar

25 Now when Festus had come to the province, after three days he went up from Caesarea to Jerusalem. 2Then the high priest*a* and the chief men of the Jews informed him against Paul; and they petitioned him, 3asking a favor against him, that he would summon him to Jerusalem—while *they* lay in ambush along the road to kill him. 4But Festus answered that Paul should be kept at Caesarea, and that he himself was going *there* shortly. 5"Therefore," he said, "let those who have authority among you go down with *me* and accuse this man, to see if there is any fault in him."

6And when he had remained among them more than ten days, he went down to Caesarea. And the next day, sitting on the judgment seat, he commanded Paul to be brought. 7When he had come, the Jews who had come down from Jerusalem stood about and laid many serious complaints against Paul, which they could not prove, 8while he answered for himself, "Neither against the law of the Jews, nor against the temple, nor against Caesar have I offended in anything at all."

25:6 the judgment seat. This signified that this hearing was an official Roman trial (see Matt. 27:19).

9But Festus, wanting to do the Jews a favor, answered Paul and said, "Are you willing to go up to Jerusalem and there be judged before me concerning these things?"

10So Paul said, "I stand at Caesar's judgment seat, where I ought to be judged. To the Jews I have done no wrong, as you very well know. 11For if I am an offender, or have committed anything deserving of death, I do not object to dying; but if there is nothing in these things of which these men accuse me, no one can deliver me to them. I appeal to Caesar."

12Then Festus, when he had conferred with the council, answered, "You have appealed to Caesar? To Caesar you shall go!"

25:13 King Agrippa. This is Herod Agrippa II, son of the Herod who killed James and imprisoned Peter. He was the last of the Herods who played a prominent role in NT history. Though not the ruler of Judea, Agrippa was well versed in Jewish affairs. **Bernice.** This was Agrippa's consort and sister. She became the mistress of Emperor Vespasian, then of his son, Titus, but she always returned to her brother.

Paul Before Agrippa

13And after some days King Agrippa and Bernice came to Caesarea to greet Festus. 14When they had been there many days, Festus laid Paul's case before the king, saying: "There is a certain man left a prisoner by Felix, 15about whom the chief priests and the elders of the Jews informed *me*, when I was in Jerusalem, asking for a judgment against him. 16To them I answered, 'It is not the custom of the Romans to deliver any man to destruction*a* before the accused meets the accusers face to face, and has opportunity to answer for himself concerning the charge against him.' 17Therefore when they had come together, without any delay, the next day I sat on the judgment seat and commanded the man to be brought in. 18When the accusers stood up, they brought no accusation against him of such things as I supposed, 19but had some questions against him about their own religion and about a certain Jesus, who had died, whom Paul affirmed to be alive. 20And because I was uncertain of such questions, I asked whether he was willing to go to Jerusalem and there be judged concerning these matters. 21But when Paul appealed to be reserved for the decision of Augustus, I commanded him to be kept till I could send him to Caesar."

25:2 *a*NU-Text reads *chief priests.*   25:16 *a*NU-Text omits *to destruction,* although it is implied.

25:21 Augustus...Caesar. "Augustus," meaning "revered" or "worshiped one," was a title given to the emperor. The "Caesar" ruling at this time was Nero.

²²Then Agrippa said to Festus, "I also would like to hear the man myself."

"Tomorrow," he said, "you shall hear him."

²³So the next day, when Agrippa and Bernice had come with great pomp, and had entered the auditorium with the commanders and the prominent men of the city, at Festus' command Paul was brought in. ²⁴And Festus said: "King Agrippa and all the men who are here present with us, you see this man about whom the whole assembly of the Jews petitioned me, both at Jerusalem and here, crying out that he was not fit to live any longer. ²⁵But when I found that he had committed nothing deserving of death, and that he himself had appealed to Augustus, I decided to send him. ²⁶I have nothing certain to write to my lord concerning him. Therefore I have brought him out before you, and especially before you, King Agrippa, so that after the examination has taken place I may have something to write. ²⁷For it seems to me unreasonable to send a prisoner and not to specify the charges against him."

25:26 I have nothing certain. Festus did not understand the nature of the charges against Paul, so he did not know what to write in his official report to Nero. For a provincial governor to send a prisoner to the emperor with no clear charges was foolish and dangerous. **especially before you, King Agrippa.** Festus hoped Herod's expertise in Jewish affairs would enable him to make sense of the charges against Paul.

Paul's Early Life

26 Then Agrippa said to Paul, "You are permitted to speak for yourself."

So Paul stretched out his hand and answered for himself: ²"I think myself happy, King Agrippa, because today I shall answer for myself before you concerning all the things of which I am accused by the Jews, ³especially because you are expert in all customs and questions which have to do with the Jews. Therefore I beg you to hear me patiently.

⁴"My manner of life from my youth, which was spent from the beginning among my own nation at Jerusalem, all the Jews know. ⁵They knew me from the first, if they were willing to testify, that according to the strictest sect of our religion I lived a Pharisee. ⁶And now I stand and am judged for the hope of the promise made by God to our fathers. ⁷To this *promise* our twelve tribes, earnestly serving *God* night and day, hope to attain. For this hope's sake, King Agrippa, I am accused by the Jews. ⁸Why should it be thought incredible by you that God raises the dead?

⁹"Indeed, I myself thought I must do many things contrary to the name of Jesus of Nazareth. ¹⁰This I also did in Jerusalem, and many of the saints I shut up in prison, having received authority from the chief priests; and when they were put to death, I cast my vote against *them*. ¹¹And I punished them often in every synagogue and compelled *them* to blaspheme; and being exceedingly enraged against them, I persecuted *them* even to foreign cities.

Paul Recounts His Conversion

¹²"While thus occupied, as I journeyed to Damascus with authority and commission from the chief priests, ¹³at midday, O king, along the road I saw a light from heaven, brighter than the sun, shining around me and those who journeyed with me. ¹⁴And when we all had fallen to the ground, I heard a voice speaking to me and saying in the Hebrew language, 'Saul, Saul, why are you persecuting Me? *It is* hard for you to kick against the goads.' ¹⁵So I said, 'Who are You, Lord?' And He said, 'I am Jesus, whom you are persecuting. ¹⁶But rise and stand on your feet; for I have appeared to you for this purpose, to make you a minister and a witness both of the things which you have seen and of the things which I will yet reveal to you. ¹⁷I will deliver you from the *Jewish* people, as well as *from* the Gentiles, to whom I now*ᵃ* send you, ¹⁸to open their eyes, *in order* to turn *them* from darkness to light, and *from* the power of Satan to God, that they may receive forgiveness of sins and an inheritance among those who are sanctified by faith in Me.'

26:17 *ᵃ*NU-Text and M-Text omit *now*.

Paul's Post-Conversion Life

¹⁹"Therefore, King Agrippa, I was not disobedient to the heavenly vision, ²⁰but declared first to those in Damascus and in Jerusalem, and throughout all the region of Judea, and *then* to the Gentiles, that they should repent, turn to God, and do works befitting repentance. ²¹For these reasons the Jews seized me in the temple and tried to kill *me*. ²²Therefore, having obtained help from God, to this day I stand, witnessing both to small and great, saying no other things than those which the prophets and Moses said would come—²³that the Christ would suffer, that He would be the first to rise from the dead, and would proclaim light to the *Jewish* people and to the Gentiles."

Agrippa Parries Paul's Challenge

²⁴Now as he thus made his defense, Festus said with a loud voice, "Paul, you are beside yourself! Much learning is driving you mad!"

> **26:24 you are beside yourself!** Festus was astonished that a learned scholar like Paul could believe in resurrection, something no intelligent Roman would accept. He interrupted the proceedings, shouting that Paul's tremendous learning had driven him insane (see Mark 3:21).

²⁵But he said, "I am not mad, most noble Festus, but speak the words of truth and reason. ²⁶For the king, before whom I also speak freely, knows these things; for I am convinced that none of these things escapes his attention, since this thing was not done in a corner. ²⁷King Agrippa, do you believe the prophets? I know that you do believe." ²⁸Then Agrippa said to Paul, "You almost persuade me to become a Christian." ²⁹And Paul said, "I would to God that not only you, but also all who hear me today, might become both almost and altogether such as I am, except for these chains." ³⁰When he had said these things, the king stood up, as well as the governor and Bernice and those who sat with them; ³¹and when they had gone aside, they talked among themselves, saying, "This man is doing nothing deserving of death or chains." ³²Then Agrippa said to Festus, "This

man might have been set free if he had not appealed to Caesar."

The Voyage to Rome Begins

27 And when it was decided that we should sail to Italy, they delivered Paul and some other prisoners to *one* named Julius, a centurion of the Augustan Regiment. ²So, entering a ship of Adramyttium, we put to sea, meaning to sail along the coasts of Asia. Aristarchus, a Macedonian of Thessalonica, was with us. ³And the next *day* we landed at Sidon. And Julius treated Paul kindly and gave *him* liberty to go to his friends and receive care. ⁴When we had put to sea from there, we sailed under *the shelter of* Cyprus, because the winds were contrary. ⁵And when we had sailed over the sea which is off Cilicia and Pamphylia, we came to Myra, *a city* of Lycia. ⁶There the centurion found an Alexandrian ship sailing to Italy, and he put us on board.

> **27:1 we.** The use of the pronoun "we" marks the return of Luke, who has been absent since 21:18. He had likely been living near Caesarea so he could care for Paul during his imprisonment. Now he joined Paul for the journey to Rome. **centurion of the Augustan Regiment.** This regiment was stationed in Palestine during the reign of Agrippa II. Julius may have been on duty escorting important prisoners.

⁷When we had sailed slowly many days, and arrived with difficulty off Cnidus, the wind not permitting us to proceed, we sailed under *the shelter of* Crete off Salmone. ⁸Passing it with difficulty, we came to a place called Fair Havens, near the city *of* Lasea.

Paul's Warning Ignored

⁹Now when much time had been spent, and sailing was now dangerous because the Fast was already over, Paul advised them, ¹⁰saying, "Men, I perceive that this voyage will end with disaster and much loss, not only of the cargo and ship, but also our lives." ¹¹Nevertheless the centurion was

> **27:10 end with disaster.** Because of the lateness of the season and the difficulties they had already experienced, Paul wisely counseled them to spend the winter at Fair Havens.

more persuaded by the helmsman and the owner of the ship than by the things spoken by Paul. ¹²And because the harbor was not suitable to winter in, the majority advised to set sail from there also, if by any means they could reach Phoenix, a harbor of Crete opening toward the southwest and northwest, *and* winter *there.*

In the Tempest

¹³When the south wind blew softly, supposing that they had obtained *their* desire, putting out to sea, they sailed close by Crete. ¹⁴But not long after, a tempestuous head wind arose, called Euroclydon.*ª* ¹⁵So when the ship was caught, and could not head into the wind, we let *her* drive. ¹⁶And running under *the shelter of* an island called Clauda,*ª* we secured the skiff with difficulty. ¹⁷When they had taken it on board, they used cables to undergird the ship; and fearing lest they should run aground on the Syrtis*ª Sands,* they struck sail and so were driven. ¹⁸And because we were exceedingly tempest-tossed, the next *day* they lightened the ship. ¹⁹On the third *day* we threw the ship's tackle overboard with our own hands. ²⁰Now when neither sun nor stars appeared for many days, and no small tempest beat on *us,* all hope that we would be saved was finally given up.

²¹But after long abstinence from food, then Paul stood in the midst of them and said, "Men, you should have listened to me, and not have sailed from Crete and incurred this disaster and loss. ²²And now I urge you to take heart, for there will be no loss of life among you, but only of the ship. ²³For there stood by me this night an angel of the God to whom I belong and whom I serve, ²⁴saying, 'Do not be afraid, Paul; you must be brought before Caesar; and indeed God has granted you all those who sail with you.' ²⁵Therefore take heart, men, for I believe God that it will be just as it was told me. ²⁶However, we must run aground on a certain island."

²⁷Now when the fourteenth night had come, as we were driven up and down in the Adriatic *Sea,* about midnight the sailors sensed that they were drawing near some land. ²⁸And they took soundings and found *it* to be twenty fathoms; and when they had gone a little farther, they took soundings

---

27:14 *ª*NU-Text reads *Euraquilon.*   27:16 *ª*NU-Text reads *Cauda.*   27:17 *ª*M-Text reads *Syrtes.*

How can Luke's authorship of Acts of the Apostles be defended when his own name is not mentioned in the book?

Lack of the author's name is not an unusual challenge in establishing the authorship of a Bible book. Many books of the Bible come to us without obvious human authorship. In most cases, however, internal and external clues lead us to reasonable confidence in identifying the author. One benefit created by initial anonymity involves recognizing that the Bible books originated by the inspiration of the Holy Spirit. It may take some effort to discover whom God used in writing one of those books, but the original Author is not in question.

The Gospel of Luke and Acts of the Apostles share numerous marks of common human authorship. They are addressed to the same person—Theophilus (Luke 1:3; Acts 1:1). They are parallel in style. The second book claims to be an extension of the first.

Luke was in a unique position to record Acts of the Apostles. He was Paul's close friend, traveling companion, and personal physician (Colossians 4:14). His work indicates that he was a careful researcher (Luke 1:1–4) and an accurate historian, displaying an intimate knowledge of Roman laws and customs. His records of the geography of Palestine, Asia Minor, and Italy offer flawless details.

In writing Acts, Luke drew on written sources (15:23–29; 23:26–30). He also, no doubt, interviewed key figures, such as Peter, John, and others in the Jerusalem church. Paul's two year imprisonment at Caesarea (24:27) gave Luke ample opportunity to interview Philip and his daughters (important sources of information on the early days of the church). Finally, Luke's frequent use of the first person plural pronouns "we" and "us" (16:10–17; 20:5–21:18; 27:1–28:16) reveals that he was an eyewitness to many of the events recorded in Acts.

again and found *it* to be fifteen fathoms. ²⁹Then, fearing lest we should run aground on the rocks, they dropped four anchors from the stern, and prayed for day to come. ³⁰And as the sailors were seeking to escape from the ship, when they had let down the skiff into the sea, under pretense of putting out anchors from the prow, ³¹Paul said to the centurion and the soldiers, "Unless these men stay in the ship, you cannot be saved." ³²Then the soldiers cut away the ropes of the skiff and let it fall off.

³³And as day was about to dawn, Paul implored *them* all to take food, saying, "Today is the fourteenth day you have waited and continued without food, and eaten nothing. ³⁴Therefore I urge you to take nourishment, for this is for your survival, since not a hair will fall from the head of any of you." ³⁵And when he had said these things, he took bread and gave thanks to God in the presence of them all; and when he had broken *it* he began to eat. ³⁶Then they were all encouraged, and also took food themselves. ³⁷And in all we were two hundred and seventy-six persons on the ship. ³⁸So when they had eaten enough, they lightened the ship and threw out the wheat into the sea.

27:34 not a hair will fall. This was a common Jewish saying, referring to absolute protection (1 Sam. 14:45; Luke 21:18).

Shipwrecked on Malta

³⁹When it was day, they did not recognize the land; but they observed a bay with a beach, onto which they planned to run the ship if possible. ⁴⁰And they let go the anchors and left *them* in the sea, meanwhile loosing the rudder ropes; and they hoisted the mainsail to the wind and made for shore. ⁴¹But striking a place where two seas met, they ran the ship aground; and the prow stuck fast and remained immovable, but the stern was being broken up by the violence of the waves.

⁴²And the soldiers' plan was to kill the prisoners, lest any of them should swim away and escape. ⁴³But the centurion, wanting to save Paul, kept them from *their* purpose, and commanded that those who could swim should jump *overboard* first and get to land, ⁴⁴and the rest, some on boards and some on *parts* of the ship. And so it was that they all escaped safely to land.

Paul's Ministry on Malta

28 Now when they had escaped, they then found out that the island was called Malta. ²And the natives showed us unusual kindness; for they kindled a fire and made us all welcome, because of the rain that was falling and because of the cold. ³But when Paul had gathered a bundle of sticks and laid *them* on the fire, a viper came out because of the heat, and fastened on his hand. ⁴So when the natives saw the creature hanging from his hand, they said to one another, "No doubt this man is a murderer, whom, though he has escaped the sea, yet justice does not allow to live." ⁵But he shook off the creature into the fire and suffered no harm. ⁶However, they were expecting that he would swell up or suddenly fall down dead. But after they had looked for a long time and saw no harm come to him, they changed their minds and said that he was a god.

⁷In that region there was an estate of the leading citizen of the island, whose name was Publius, who received us and entertained us courteously for three days. ⁸And it happened that the father of Publius lay sick of a fever and dysentery. Paul went in to him and prayed, and he laid his hands on him and healed him. ⁹So when this was done, the rest of those on the island who had diseases also came and were healed. ¹⁰They also honored us in many ways; and when we departed, they provided such things as were necessary.

28:8 sick of a fever and dysentery. This gastric fever (caused by a microbe in goat's milk) was common on Malta. Dysentery, often the result of poor sanitation, was widespread in the ancient world.

Arrival at Rome

¹¹After three months we sailed in an Alexandrian ship whose figurehead was the Twin Brothers, which had wintered at the island. ¹²And landing at Syracuse, we stayed three days. ¹³From there we circled round and reached Rhegium. And after one day the south wind blew; and the next day we came to Puteoli, ¹⁴where we found

brethren, and were invited to stay with them seven days. And so we went toward Rome. [15]And from there, when the brethren heard about us, they came to meet us as far as Appii Forum and Three Inns. When Paul saw them, he thanked God and took courage.

[16]Now when we came to Rome, the centurion delivered the prisoners to the captain of the guard; but Paul was permitted to dwell by himself with the soldier who guarded him.

Paul's Ministry at Rome

[17]And it came to pass after three days that Paul called the leaders of the Jews together. So when they had come together, he said to them: "Men *and* brethren, though I have done nothing against our people or the customs of our fathers, yet I was delivered as a prisoner from Jerusalem into the hands of the Romans, [18]who, when they had examined me, wanted to let *me* go, because there was no cause for putting me to death. [19]But when the Jews[a] spoke against *it*, I was compelled to appeal to Caesar, not that I had anything of which to accuse my nation. [20]For this reason therefore I have called for you, to see *you* and speak with *you*, because for the hope of Israel I am bound with this chain."

[21]Then they said to him, "We neither received letters from Judea concerning you, nor have any of the brethren who came reported or spoken any evil of you. [22]But we desire to hear from you what you think; for concerning this sect, we know that it is spoken against everywhere."

[23]So when they had appointed him a day, many came to him at *his* lodging, to whom he explained and solemnly testified of the kingdom of God, persuading them concerning Jesus from both the Law of Moses and the Prophets, from morning till evening. [24]And some were persuaded by the things which were spoken, and some disbelieved. [25]So when they did not agree among themselves, they departed after Paul had said one word: "The Holy Spirit spoke rightly through Isaiah the prophet to our[a] fathers, [26]saying,

'Go to this people and say:
"Hearing you will hear, and shall not
    understand;
And seeing you will see, and not
    perceive;
[27] For the hearts of this people have
    grown dull.
Their ears are hard of hearing,
And their eyes they have closed,
Lest they should see with their eyes
    and hear with their ears,
Lest they should understand with their
    hearts and turn,
So that I should heal them." ' [a]

[28]"Therefore let it be known to you that the salvation of God has been sent to the Gentiles, and they will hear it!" [29]And when he had said these words, the Jews departed and had a great dispute among themselves.[a]

[30]Then Paul dwelt two whole years in his own rented house, and received all who came to him, [31]preaching the kingdom of God and teaching the things which concern the Lord Jesus Christ with all confidence, no one forbidding him.

> **28:30,31** The best explanation for this abrupt ending is that Luke wrote Acts before Paul's release from his first Roman imprisonment.

28:19 [a]That is, the ruling authorities   28:25 [a]NU-Text reads *your*.   28:27 [a]Isaiah 6:9,10   28:29 [a]NU-Text omits this verse.

ROMANS

Romans stands out among Paul's many books, not simply because it is first in line and length, but because it offers the most complete summary of Paul's thought. It was neither Paul's earliest nor latest writing. He composed Romans as a mature reflection, under the guidance of the Holy Spirit, on the central themes of the gospel. The study of the Epistle to the Romans remains a required course in the school of Christian discipleship.

AUTHOR AND DATE

Romans was written by the Apostle Paul, approximately A.D. 56.

No one disputes that the apostle Paul wrote Romans. Raised as both a Roman citizen and a devout Jew, Paul benefited from the finest education available in his time. He grew up as a Pharisee (Acts 23:6), a member of the strictest Jewish sect (Philippians 3:5). In the months following the resurrection of Jesus, Paul gained a reputation as a ruthless enemy of the followers of Jesus Christ.

Miraculously converted while on his way to Damascus (about A.D. 33–34) to arrest Christians in that city, Paul immediately began proclaiming the gospel message (Acts 9:30). After narrowly escaping from Damascus with his life (Acts 9:23–25; 2 Corinthians 11:32,33), Paul spent three years in Nabatean Arabia, south and east of the Dead Sea (Galatians 1:11,12). During that time, he received much of his doctrine as direct revelation from the Lord (Galatians 1:11,12).

More than any other individual, Paul was responsible for the spread of Christianity throughout the Roman Empire. He made three missionary journeys through much of the Mediterranean world, tirelessly preaching the gospel he had once sought to destroy (Acts 26:9). He eventually suffered martyrdom at Rome in about A.D. 65–67 (2 Timothy 4:6). (For more on Paul the apostle, see the FAQ, "Who was Paul?")

Paul wrote Romans from Corinth. References to Corinthian people (Phoebe, 16:1; Gaius, 16:23; Erastus, 16:23) and places (Cenchrea, 16:1) make this conclusion reasonable. The apostle wrote the letter toward the close of his third missionary journey (most likely in A.D. 56), as he prepared to leave Corinth for Palestine with an offering for the suffering church in Jerusalem (15:25). Phoebe was entrusted to deliver the letter to the Roman believers (16:1,2).

BACKGROUND AND SETTING

Rome was the capital and most important city of the Roman Empire. It was founded in 753 B.C. but is not mentioned in Scripture until New Testament times. In Paul's

day, the city had a population of over one million people, many of whom were slaves. Rome boasted magnificent buildings, such as the Emperor's palace, the Circus Maximus, and the Forum, but the slums that surrounded and infiltrated the city marred its beauty. According to tradition, Paul was martyred outside Rome on the Ostian Way during Nero's reign (A.D. 54–68).

Some of those converted on the Day of Pentecost in Jerusalem probably returned to Rome and founded the church (Acts 2:10). Paul had long wanted to visit the Roman church but had been prevented from doing so (1:13). As an example of God's providence, Paul's inability to visit Rome in person resulted in the universal gift of this inspired masterpiece of gospel doctrine.

Paul's primary purpose in writing Romans was to teach the great truths of the gospel of grace to believers who had never received apostolic instruction. The letter also introduced him to a church where he was personally unknown. Paul still hoped to visit for several important reasons: (1) to edify the believers (1:11); (2) to preach the gospel (1:15); and (3) to get to know the Roman Christians. He also anticipated their ministry to him by encouragement (1:12; 15:32); by prayer (15:30); and by help with his planned ministry in Spain (15:28).

Unlike some of his other epistles, Paul's purpose for writing Romans was not to correct aberrant theology or rebuke ungodly living. The Roman church was doctrinally sound but, like all churches, needed the rich doctrinal and practical instruction that this letter provides.

HISTORICAL AND THEOLOGICAL THEMES

Since Romans is primarily a work of doctrine, the book contains little historical material. It does use such familiar Old Testament people as Abraham (chapter 4), David (4:6–8), Adam (5:12–21), Sarah (9:9), Rebekah (9:10), Jacob and Esau (9:10–13), and Pharaoh (9:17) as illustrations. Paul also recounts some of Israel's history (chapters 9–11). Chapter 16 provides insightful glimpses into the nature and character of the first-century church and its members.

THE **OVERARCHING THEME** OF **ROMANS EXPLAINS** AND **EXPOUNDS** THE **RIGHTEOUSNESS** THAT COMES **FROM GOD.**

The overarching theme of Romans explains and expounds the righteousness that comes from God: the glorious truth that God justifies guilty, condemned sinners by grace alone through faith in Christ alone. Chapters 1–11 present the theological truths of that doctrine, while chapters 12–16 detail its practical outworking in the lives of individual believers and the life of the whole church.

Paul also teaches several other specific theological topics: (1) principles of spiritual leadership (1:8–15); (2) God's wrath against sinful human beings (1:18–32); (3) principles of divine judgment (2:1–16); (4) universality of sin (3:9–20); (5) an exposition and defense of justification by faith alone (3:21–4:25); (6) the security of salvation (5:1–11); (7) the transference of Adam's sin (5:12–21); (8) sanctification (chapters 6–8); (9) sovereign election (chapter 9); (10) God's plan for Israel

(chapter 11); (11) spiritual gifts and practical godliness (chapter 12); (12) the believer's responsibility to human government (chapter 13); and (13) principles of Christian liberty (14:1–15:12).

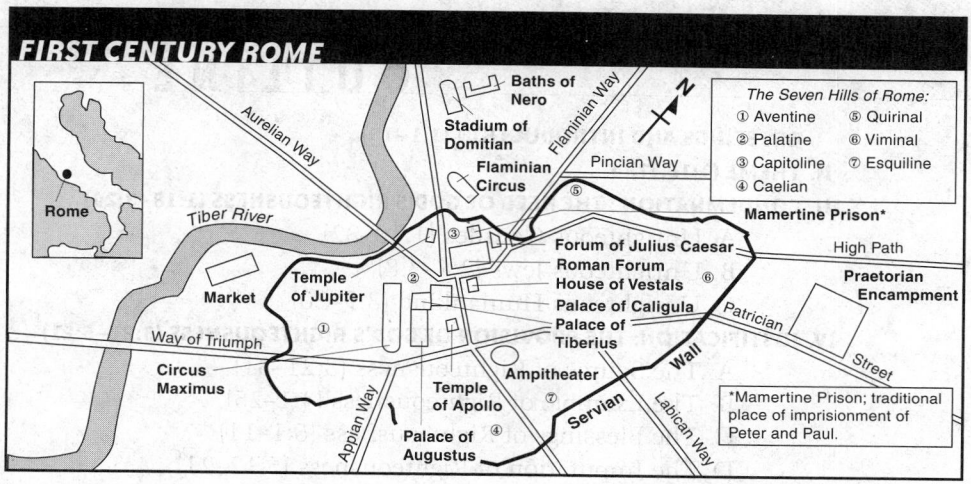

FIRST CENTURY ROME

- Baths of Nero
- Stadium of Domitian
- Flaminian Circus
- Aurelian Way
- Flaminian Way
- Pincian Way

The Seven Hills of Rome:
① Aventine   ⑤ Quirinal
② Palatine   ⑥ Viminal
③ Capitoline ⑦ Esquiline
④ Caelian

- Rome
- Tiber River
- Market
- Temple of Jupiter
- Way of Triumph
- Circus Maximus
- Appian Way
- Temple of Apollo
- Palace of Augustus

- Mamertine Prison*
- High Path
- Forum of Julius Caesar
- Roman Forum
- House of Vestals
- Palace of Caligula
- Palace of Tiberius
- Ampitheater
- Praetorian Encampment
- Patrician
- Wall
- Servian
- Labican Way
- Street

*Mamertine Prison; traditional place of imprisionment of Peter and Paul.

OUTLINE

Greeting

1 Paul, a bondservant of Jesus Christ, called *to be* an apostle, separated to the gospel of God ²which He promised before through His prophets in the Holy Scriptures, ³concerning His Son Jesus Christ our Lord, who was born of the seed of David according to the flesh, ⁴*and* declared *to be* the Son of God with power according to the Spirit of holiness, by the resurrection from the dead. ⁵Through Him we have received grace and apostleship for obedience to the faith among all nations for His name, ⁶among whom you also are the called of Jesus Christ;

> **1:1 bondservant.** In Greek culture, this usually referred to a slave who served involuntarily, but Paul used it in its Hebrew sense to describe a servant who willingly commits himself to serve a master he loves (Ex. 21:5; Gal. 1:10). **apostle.** The Greek word means "one who is sent." In the NT, it primarily refers to the 12 men Christ chose to accompany Him (Mark 3:13–19), plus Matthias (who replaced Judas, Acts 1:15–26), as well as Paul, Barnabas, and a few select others.

⁷To all who are in Rome, beloved of God, called *to be* saints:

Grace to you and peace from God our Father and the Lord Jesus Christ.

Desire to Visit Rome

⁸First, I thank my God through Jesus Christ for you all, that your faith is spoken of throughout the whole world. ⁹For God is my witness, whom I serve with my spirit in the gospel of His Son, that without ceasing I make mention of you always in my prayers, ¹⁰making request if, by some means, now at last I may find a way in the will of God to come to you. ¹¹For I long to see you, that I may impart to you some

> **1:8 I thank my God.** Paul usually began his letters by expressing gratitude for those who received his letters. **your faith.** This referred to the genuineness of their salvation. The testimony of the church in Rome was so strong that in A.D. 49 the emperor, Claudius, expelled all the Jews because of the influence of "Chrestus," referring to Christ (see Acts 18:2).

spiritual gift, so that you may be established—¹²that is, that I may be encouraged together with you by the mutual faith both of you and me.

¹³Now I do not want you to be unaware, brethren, that I often planned to come to you (but was hindered until now), that I might have some fruit among you also, just as among the other Gentiles. ¹⁴I am a debtor both to Greeks and to barbarians, both to wise and to unwise. ¹⁵So, as much as is in me, *I am* ready to preach the gospel to you who are in Rome also.

The Just Live by Faith

¹⁶For I am not ashamed of the gospel of Christ,*ᵃ* for it is the power of God to salvation for everyone who believes, for the Jew first and also for the Greek. ¹⁷For in it the righteousness of God is revealed from faith to faith; as it is written, *"The just shall live by faith."ᵃ*

> **1:16** Paul had been imprisoned in Philippi (Acts 16:23,24), chased out of Thessalonica (Acts 17:10), smuggled out of Berea (Acts 17:14), laughed at in Athens (Acts 17:32), regarded as a fool in Corinth (1 Cor. 1:18,23), and stoned in Galatia (Acts 14:19). Yet he remained eager to preach the gospel in Rome, the center of political power and pagan religion. Nothing could curb Paul's boldness; he knew that the omnipotence of God accompanied the gospel.

God's Wrath on Unrighteousness

¹⁸For the wrath of God is revealed from heaven against all ungodliness and unrighteousness of men, who suppress the truth in unrighteousness, ¹⁹because what may be known of God is manifest in them, for God has shown *it* to them. ²⁰For since the creation of the world His invisible *attributes*

> **1:20 by the things that are made.** The creation speaks of God's person (see Ps. 19:1–8). **His eternal power.** The Creator, who made everything, must be a being of awesome power. **Godhead.** This refers to God's divine nature, which includes faithfulness (Gen. 8:21,22), kindness, and graciousness (Acts 14:17). **they are without excuse.** God reveals Himself to all through His creation. If a person responds to this revelation, God will provide a means for that person to hear the gospel (see Acts 8:26–39).

1:16 *ᵃ*NU-Text omits *of Christ.*   1:17 *ᵃ*Habakkuk 2:4

are clearly seen, being understood by the things that are made, *even* His eternal power and Godhead, so that they are without excuse, ²¹because, although they knew God, they did not glorify *Him* as God, nor were thankful, but became futile in their thoughts, and their foolish hearts were darkened. ²²Professing to be wise, they became fools, ²³and changed the glory of the incorruptible God into an image made like corruptible man—and birds and four-footed animals and creeping things.

²⁴Therefore God also gave them up to uncleanness, in the lusts of their hearts, to dishonor their bodies among themselves, ²⁵who exchanged the truth of God for the lie, and worshiped and served the creature rather than the Creator, who is blessed forever. Amen.

> **1:24 God also gave them up.** This is a judicial term in Greek, used for handing a prisoner over to begin serving his sentence. When men consistently abandon God, He will abandon them (see Judg. 10:13) by removing His restraint and allowing their sin to run its course, as well as by acts of divine judgment and punishment. **uncleanness.** Here this refers to sexual immorality (2 Cor. 12:21), which begins in the heart and moves to the actions of the body.

²⁶For this reason God gave them up to vile passions. For even their women exchanged the natural use for what is against nature. ²⁷Likewise also the men, leaving the natural use of the woman, burned in their lust for one another, men with men committing what is shameful, and receiving in themselves the penalty of their error which was due.

²⁸And even as they did not like to retain God in *their* knowledge, God gave them over to a debased mind, to do those things which are not fitting; ²⁹being filled with all unrighteousness, sexual immorality,ᵃ wickedness, covetousness, maliciousness; full of envy, murder, strife, deceit, evil-mindedness; *they are* whisperers, ³⁰backbiters, haters of God, violent, proud, boasters, inventors of evil things, disobedient to parents, ³¹undiscerning, untrustworthy, unloving, unforgiving,ᵃ unmerciful;

³²who, knowing the righteous judgment of God, that those who practice such things are deserving of death, not only do the same but also approve of those who practice them.

God's Righteous Judgment

2 Therefore you are inexcusable, O man, whoever you are who judge, for in whatever you judge another you condemn yourself; for you who judge practice the same things. ²But we know that the judgment of God is according to truth against those who practice such things. ³And do you think this, O man, you who judge those practicing such things, and doing the same, that you will escape the judgment of God? ⁴Or do you despise the riches of His goodness, forbearance, and longsuffering, not knowing that the goodness of God leads you to repentance? ⁵But in accordance with your hardness and your impenitent heart you are treasuring up for yourself wrath in the day of wrath and revelation of the righteous judgment of God, ⁶who *"will render to each one according to his deeds"*:ᵃ ⁷eternal life to those who by patient continuance in doing good seek for glory, honor, and immortality; ⁸but to those who are self-seeking and do not obey the truth, but obey unrighteousness—indignation and wrath, ⁹tribulation and anguish, on every soul of man who does evil, of the Jew first and also of the Greek; ¹⁰but glory, honor, and peace to everyone who works what is good, to the Jew first and also to the Greek. ¹¹For there is no partiality with God.

> **2:6–10** Scripture teaches that salvation is not based on works, but that God's judgment is always based on man's actions (Is. 3:10,11; 1 Cor. 3:8). Paul described the works of the redeemed as the evidence of their salvation. They are not perfect, but there is evidence of righteousness in their lives.

¹²For as many as have sinned without law will also perish without law, and as many as have sinned in the law will be judged by the law ¹³(for not the hearers of the law *are* just in the sight of God, but the doers of the law will be justified; ¹⁴for when Gentiles,

---

1:29 ᵃNU-Text omits *sexual immorality.*   1:31 ᵃNU-Text omits *unforgiving.*   2:6 ᵃPsalm 62:12; Proverbs 24:12

who do not have the law, by nature do the things in the law, these, although not having the law, are a law to themselves, [15]who show the work of the law written in their hearts, their conscience also bearing witness, and between themselves *their* thoughts accusing or else excusing *them*) [16]in the day when God will judge the secrets of men by Jesus Christ, according to my gospel.

2:15 conscience. This means "with knowledge." Conscience is the instinctive sense of right and wrong that produces guilt when violated. Men are aware of God's laws and have a warning system that activates when they choose to ignore or disobey them. Paul urged believers not to violate their own consciences or cause others to (1 Cor. 8:7) because repeatedly ignoring the conscience desensitizes it and eventually silences it (1 Tim. 4:2).

The Jews Guilty as the Gentiles

[17]Indeed[a] you are called a Jew, and rest on the law, and make your boast in God, [18]and know *His* will, and approve the things that are excellent, being instructed out of the law, [19]and are confident that you yourself are a guide to the blind, a light to those who are in darkness, [20]an instructor of the foolish, a teacher of babes, having the form of knowledge and truth in the law. [21]You, therefore, who teach another, do you not teach yourself? You who preach that a man should not steal, do you steal? [22]You who say, "Do not commit adultery," do you commit adultery? You who abhor idols, do you rob temples? [23]You who make your boast in the law, do you dishonor God through breaking the law? [24]For *"the name of God is blasphemed among the Gentiles because of you,"[a]* as it is written.

Circumcision of No Avail

[25]For circumcision is indeed profitable if you keep the law; but if you are a breaker of the law, your circumcision has become uncircumcision. [26]Therefore, if an uncircumcised man keeps the righteous requirements of the law, will not his uncircumcision be counted as circumcision? [27]And will not the physically uncircumcised, if he fulfills the law, judge you who, *even* with *your* written

code and circumcision, *are* a transgressor of the law? [28]For he is not a Jew who *is one* outwardly, nor *is* circumcision that which is outward in the flesh; [29]but *he is* a Jew who *is one* inwardly; and circumcision *is that* of the heart, in the Spirit, not in the letter; whose praise *is* not from men but from God.

2:29 *he is* a Jew. He is a true child of God, the true spiritual seed of Abraham (see Gal. 3:29). **circumcision *is that* of the heart.** The outward act is of value only if the inner heart is separated from sin (see Deut. 10:16). **Spirit...letter.** Salvation results from the work of God's Spirit in the heart, not mere external efforts to conform to His law.

God's Judgment Defended

3 What advantage then has the Jew, or what *is* the profit of circumcision? [2]Much in every way! Chiefly because to them were committed the oracles of God. [3]For what if some did not believe? Will their unbelief make the faithfulness of God without effect? [4]Certainly not! Indeed, let God be true but every man a liar. As it is written:

> "That You may be justified in Your
> words,
> And may overcome when You are
> judged."[a]

[5]But if our unrighteousness demonstrates the righteousness of God, what shall we say? *Is* God unjust who inflicts wrath? (I speak as a man.) [6]Certainly not! For then how will God judge the world? [7]For if the truth of God has increased through my lie to His glory, why am I also still judged as a sinner? [8]And *why* not *say,* "Let us do evil that good may come"?—as we are slanderously reported and as some affirm that we say. Their condemnation is just.

All Have Sinned

[9]What then? Are we better *than they?* Not at all. For we have previously charged both Jews and Greeks that they are all under sin. [10]As it is written:

2:17 [a]NU-Text reads *But if.*   2:24 [a]Isaiah 52:5; Ezekiel 36:22   3:4 [a]Psalm 51:4

"*There is none righteous, no, not one;*
11 *There is none who understands;*
There is none who seeks after God.
12 *They have all turned aside;*
They have together become unprofitable;
There is none who does good, no, not one."[a]
13 "*Their throat is an open tomb;*
With their tongues they have practiced deceit";[a]
"*The poison of asps is under their lips*";[b]
14 "*Whose mouth is full of cursing and bitterness.*"[a]
15 "*Their feet are swift to shed blood;*
16 *Destruction and misery are in their ways;*
17 *And the way of peace they have not known.*"[a]
18 "*There is no fear of God before their eyes.*"[a]

19Now we know that whatever the law says, it says to those who are under the law, that every mouth may be stopped, and all the world may become guilty before God. 20Therefore by the deeds of the law no flesh will be justified in His sight, for by the law *is* the knowledge of sin.

God's Righteousness Through Faith

21But now the righteousness of God apart from the law is revealed, being witnessed by the Law and the Prophets, 22even the righ-teousness of God, through faith in Jesus Christ, to all and on all[a] who believe. For there is no difference; 23for all have sinned and fall short of the glory of God, 24being justified freely by His grace through the redemption that is in Christ Jesus, 25whom God set forth *as* a propitiation by His blood, through faith, to demonstrate His righteousness, because in His forbearance God had passed over the sins that were previously committed, 26to demonstrate at the present time His righteousness, that He might be just and the justifier of the one who has faith in Jesus.

Boasting Excluded

27Where *is* boasting then? It is excluded. By what law? Of works? No, but by the law of faith. 28Therefore we conclude that a man is justified by faith apart from the deeds of the law. 29Or *is He* the God of the Jews only? *Is He* not also the God of the Gentiles? Yes, of the Gentiles also, 30since *there is* one God who will justify the circumcised by faith and the uncircumcised through faith. 31Do we then make void the law through faith? Certainly not! On the contrary, we establish the law.

Abraham Justified by Faith

4 What then shall we say that Abraham our father has found according to the flesh?[a] 2For if Abraham was justified by

works, he has *something* to boast about, but not before God. ³For what does the Scripture say? *"Abraham believed God, and it was accounted to him for righteousness."* ᵃ ⁴"Now to him who works, the wages are not counted as grace but as debt.

David Celebrates the Same Truth

⁵But to him who does not work but believes on Him who justifies the ungodly, his faith is accounted for righteousness, ⁶just as David also describes the blessedness of the man to whom God imputes righteousness apart from works:

7   *"Blessed are those whose lawless deeds*
           are forgiven,
        And whose sins are covered;
8   *Blessed is the man to whom the LORD*
           shall not impute sin."ᵃ

Abraham Justified Before Circumcision

⁹*Does* this blessedness then *come* upon the circumcised *only*, or upon the uncircumcised also? For we say that faith was accounted to Abraham for righteousness. ¹⁰How then was it accounted? While he was circumcised, or uncircumcised? Not while circumcised, but while uncircumcised. ¹¹And he received the sign of circumcision, a seal of the righteousness of the faith which *he had while still* uncircumcised, that he might be the father of all those who believe, though they are uncircumcised, that righteousness might be imputed to them also, ¹²and the father of circumcision to those who not only *are* of the circumcision, but who also walk in the steps of the faith which our father Abraham *had while still* uncircumcised.

4:10 Not while...but while uncircumcised. The chronology of Genesis proved Paul's case that Abraham had been declared righteous *before* he was circumcised. Abraham was 86 when Ishmael was born (Gen. 16:16), and he was 99 when he was circumcised. God had declared Abraham righteous before Ishmael had even been conceived (Gen. 15:6), which was at least 14 years before Abraham's circumcision.

The Promise Granted Through Faith

¹³For the promise that he would be the heir of the world *was* not to Abraham or to his seed through the law, but through the righteousness of faith. ¹⁴For if those who are of the law *are* heirs, faith is made void and the promise made of no effect, ¹⁵because the law brings about wrath; for where there is no law *there is* no transgression.

¹⁶Therefore *it is* of faith that *it might be* according to grace, so that the promise might be sure to all the seed, not only to those who are of the law, but also to those who are of the faith of Abraham, who is the father of us all ¹⁷(as it is written, *"I have made you a father of many nations"ᵃ*) in the presence of Him whom he believed—God, who gives life to the dead and calls those things which do not exist as though they did; ¹⁸who, contrary to hope, in hope believed, so that he became the father of many nations, according to what was spoken, *"So shall your descendants be."ᵃ* ¹⁹And not being weak in faith, he did not consider his own body, already dead (since he was about a hundred years old), and the deadness of Sarah's womb. ²⁰He did not waver at the promise of God through unbelief, but was strengthened in faith, giving glory to God, ²¹and being fully convinced that what He had promised He was also able to perform. ²²And therefore *"it was accounted to him for righteousness."ᵃ*

4:17 calls those things which do not exist as though they did. This refers to the nature of justification. God can declare believing sinners to be righteous, even though they are not, by imputing His righteousness to them—just as He had made Jesus "sin" and punished Him, though Jesus was not a sinner. Those whom God justifies, He will conform to the image of His Son.

²³Now it was not written for his sake alone that it was imputed to him, ²⁴but also for us. It shall be imputed to us who believe in Him who raised up Jesus our Lord from the dead, ²⁵who was delivered up because of our offenses, and was raised because of our justification.

4:3 *ᵃ*Genesis 15:6   4:8 *ᵃ*Psalm 32:1,2   4:17 *ᵃ*Genesis 17:5   4:18 *ᵃ*Genesis 15:5   4:22 *ᵃ*Genesis 15:6

Faith Triumphs in Trouble

5 Therefore, having been justified by faith, we have[a] peace with God through our Lord Jesus Christ, [2]through whom also we have access by faith into this grace in which we stand, and rejoice in hope of the glory of God. [3]And not only *that*, but we also glory in tribulations, knowing that tribulation produces perseverance; [4]and perseverance, character; and character, hope. [5]Now hope does not disappoint, because the love of God has been poured out in our hearts by the Holy Spirit who was given to us.

> **5:2 access.** This word refers to the believer's access to God through Jesus Christ. What was unthinkable to the OT Jew (see Ex. 19:9,20) is now available to all who believe (Heb. 4:16). **stand.** Believers have a secure position in God's grace (see John 6:37). **hope of the glory of God.** This hope speaks of something that is certain, but not yet realized. The believer's hope in sharing God's glory (John 17:22) will be realized because Christ Himself secures it (1 Tim. 1:1). The basis for hope is found in the Word of God (Ps. 119:81).

Christ in Our Place

[6]For when we were still without strength, in due time Christ died for the ungodly. [7]For scarcely for a righteous man will one die; yet perhaps for a good man someone would even dare to die. [8]But God demonstrates His own love toward us, in that while we were still sinners, Christ died for us. [9]Much more then, having now been justified by His blood, we shall be saved from wrath through Him. [10]For if when we were enemies we were reconciled to God through the death of His Son, much more, having been reconciled, we shall be saved by His life. [11]And not only *that*, but we also rejoice in God through our Lord Jesus Christ, through whom we have now received the reconciliation.

Death in Adam, Life in Christ

[12]Therefore, just as through one man sin entered the world, and death through sin, and thus death spread to all men, because all sinned—[13](For until the law sin was in the world, but sin is not imputed when

> **5:12 just as...sin entered.** The inherent propensity to sin entered the human realm through Adam, who passed the sinful nature to all his descendants because of his first disobedience. That sinful nature is present from the moment of conception (Ps. 51:5), making it impossible for man to live in a way that pleases God. Satan, the father of sin (1 John 3:8), first brought temptation to Adam and Eve (Gen. 3:1–7).

5:1 [a]Another ancient reading is, *let us have peace.*

When Paul writes in Romans 5:12 that "through one man sin entered the world, and death through sin, and thus death spread to all men, because all sinned," what does he mean?

Paul's discussion of the perpetuation of Adam's sin (5:12–21) is one of the deepest, most significant theological passages in all of Scripture. It establishes the basis for Paul's teaching that one man's (Christ's) death can provide salvation for many. To prove his point, he uses Adam to develop the principle that it is possible for one man's actions to inexorably affect many other people.

In this passage, the word "sin" does not refer to a particular sin, but to the inherent propensity to sin that invaded the human realm through Adam. People become sinners by nature. Adam passed on to all his descendants that inherent sinful nature he possessed as a result of his first disobedience. He caught the infection; the rest of us inherit it. The sin nature is present from the moment of conception (Psalm 51:5), making it impossible for any person to live in a way that pleases God.

When Adam sinned, his sin transformed his inner nature and brought spiritual death and depravity which was then passed on seminally to his posterity. Because all humanity existed in the loins of Adam, and have through procreation inherited his fallenness and depravity, it can be said that all sinned in him. Therefore, humans are not sinners because they sin, but, rather, they sin because they are sinners.

there is no law. [14]Nevertheless death reigned from Adam to Moses, even over those who had not sinned according to the likeness of the transgression of Adam, who is a type of Him who was to come. [15]But the free gift *is* not like the offense. For if by the one man's offense many died, much more the grace of God and the gift by the grace of the one Man, Jesus Christ, abounded to many. [16]And the gift *is* not like *that which came* through the one who sinned. For the judgment *which came* from one *offense resulted* in condemnation, but the free gift *which came* from many offenses *resulted* in justification. [17]For if by the one man's offense death reigned through the one, much more those who receive abundance of grace and of the gift of righteousness will reign in life through the One, Jesus Christ.)

[18]Therefore, as through one man's offense *judgment* came to all men, resulting in condemnation, even so through one Man's righteous act *the free gift came* to all men, resulting in justification of life. [19]For as by one man's disobedience many were made sinners, so also by one Man's obedience many will be made righteous.

[20]Moreover the law entered that the offense might abound. But where sin abounded, grace abounded much more, [21]so that as sin reigned in death, even so grace might reign through righteousness to eternal life through Jesus Christ our Lord.

> **5:20 the law entered.** Although the Mosaic law is not flawed, its presence caused man's sin to increase because it made men aware of their own sinfulness and inability to keep God's perfect standard (Gal. 3:21,22). But it also served as a tutor, driving them to Christ (Gal. 3:24).

Dead to Sin, Alive to God

6 What shall we say then? Shall we continue in sin that grace may abound? [2]Certainly not! How shall we who died to sin live any longer in it? [3]Or do you not

> **6:3 baptized into Christ Jesus.** This does not refer to water baptism. Paul described someone who places faith in Christ as being immersed into the person of Christ—being united and identified with Him (see 1 Cor. 6:17). **into His death.** Believers are immersed specifically in Christ's death and resurrection.

know that as many of us as were baptized into Christ Jesus were baptized into His death? [4]Therefore we were buried with Him through baptism into death, that just as Christ was raised from the dead by the glory of the Father, even so we also should walk in newness of life.

[5]For if we have been united together in the likeness of His death, certainly we also shall be *in the likeness* of *His* resurrection, [6]knowing this, that our old man was crucified with *Him*, that the body of sin might be done away with, that we should no longer be slaves of sin. [7]For he who has died has been freed from sin. [8]Now if we died with Christ, we believe that we shall also live with Him, [9]knowing that Christ, having been raised from the dead, dies no more. Death no longer has dominion over Him. [10]For *the death* that He died, He died to sin once for all; but *the life* that He lives, He lives to God. [11]Likewise you also, reckon yourselves to be dead indeed to sin, but alive to God in Christ Jesus our Lord.

[12]Therefore do not let sin reign in your mortal body, that you should obey it in its lusts. [13]And do not present your members *as* instruments of unrighteousness to sin, but present yourselves to God as being alive from the dead, and your members *as* instruments of righteousness to God. [14]For sin shall not have dominion over you, for you are not under law but under grace.

> **6:13 present.** This refers to a decision of the will. Before sin can have power over a believer, it must first pass through his will (see Phil. 2:12,13). **your members.** These are the parts of the physical body from which sin operates in the believer (see 1 Cor. 9:27). **instruments of unrighteousness.** These are tools for accomplishing that which violates God's holy will and law.

From Slaves of Sin to Slaves of God

[15]What then? Shall we sin because we are not under law but under grace? Certainly not! [16]Do you not know that to whom you present yourselves slaves to obey, you are that one's slaves whom you obey, whether of sin *leading* to death, or of obedience *leading* to righteousness? [17]But God be thanked that *though* you were slaves of sin, yet you obeyed from the heart that form of doctrine to which you were delivered. [18]And having

been set free from sin, you became slaves of righteousness. ¹⁹I speak in human *terms* because of the weakness of your flesh. For just as you presented your members *as* slaves of uncleanness, and of lawlessness *leading* to *more* lawlessness, so now present your members *as* slaves *of* righteousness for holiness.

²⁰For when you were slaves of sin, you were free in regard to righteousness. ²¹What fruit did you have then in the things of which you are now ashamed? For the end of those things *is* death. ²²But now having been set free from sin, and having become slaves of God, you have your fruit to holiness, and the end, everlasting life. ²³For the wages of sin *is* death, but the gift of God *is* eternal life in Christ Jesus our Lord.

> **6:22 holiness.** The benefit of being slaves to God is sanctification, the process of becoming holy. The outcome of sanctification is eternal life.

Freed from the Law

7 Or do you not know, brethren (for I speak to those who know the law), that the law has dominion over a man as long as he lives? ²For the woman who has a husband is bound by the law to *her* husband as long as he lives. But if the husband dies, she is released from the law of *her* husband. ³So then if, while *her* husband lives, she marries another man, she will be called an adulteress; but if her husband dies, she is free from that law, so that she is no adulter-

ess, though she has married another man. ⁴Therefore, my brethren, you also have become dead to the law through the body of Christ, that you may be married to another—to Him who was raised from the dead, that we should bear fruit to God. ⁵For when we were in the flesh, the sinful passions which were aroused by the law were at work in our members to bear fruit to death. ⁶But now we have been delivered from the law, having died to what we were held by, so that we should serve in the newness of the Spirit and not *in* the oldness of the letter.

Sin's Advantage in the Law

⁷What shall we say then? *Is* the law sin? Certainly not! On the contrary, I would not have known sin except through the law. For I would not have known covetousness unless the law had said, *"You shall not covet."*ᵃ ⁸But sin, taking opportunity by the commandment, produced in me all *manner of evil* desire. For apart from the law sin *was* dead. ⁹I was alive once without the law, but when the commandment came, sin re-

> **7:8 opportunity by the commandment.** "Opportunity" describes a starting point. Sin uses the specific requirements of the law as a starting point for its evil work. Confronted by God's law, the sinner's rebellious nature finds the forbidden thing more attractive because it provides the opportunity to assert one's self-will. **sin was dead.** This means it was dormant. When the law comes, sin becomes fully active, overwhelming the sinner.

7:7 ᵃExodus 20:17; Deuteronomy 5:21

In verses like Romans 5:12 and 6:23, to what kind of death is Paul referring?

The word "death" has three distinct manifestations in biblical terminology: (1) spiritual death or separation from God (Ephesians 1:1,2,4,18); (2) physical death (Hebrews 9:27); and (3) eternal death (also called the second death), which includes not only eternal separation from God, but eternal torment in the lake of fire (Revelation 20:11–15).

When sin entered the human race through Adam, all these aspects of death came with it. Adam was not originally subject to death, but through his sin, death became a grim certainty for him and his posterity. The "death" referred to in Romans 6:23 includes the first and third descriptions above. That verse establishes two inexorable absolutes: (1) spiritual death and eternal separation from God make up the paycheck for every person's slavery to sin; and (2) eternal life is a free gift God gives undeserving sinners who believe in His Son (Ephesians 2:8,9).

vived and I died. ¹⁰And the commandment, which *was* to *bring* life, I found to *bring* death. ¹¹For sin, taking occasion by the commandment, deceived me, and by it killed *me*. ¹²Therefore the law *is* holy, and the commandment holy and just and good.

Law Cannot Save from Sin

¹³Has then what is good become death to me? Certainly not! But sin, that it might appear sin, was producing death in me through what is good, so that sin through the commandment might become exceedingly sinful. ¹⁴For we know that the law is spiritual, but I am carnal, sold under sin.

> **7:14 the law is spiritual.** The law reflects God's holy character. **carnal.** This means "of flesh." It refers to being earthbound, mortal, and incarcerated in unredeemed humanness. Paul does not say he is still "in the flesh," but that the flesh is in him. **sold under sin.** Sin no longer controls the whole man, but it does hold captive his fleshly body. Sin contaminates him and frustrates his inner desire to obey the will of God.

¹⁵For what I am doing, I do not understand. For what I will to do, that I do not practice; but what I hate, that I do. ¹⁶If, then, I do what I will not to do, I agree with the law that *it is* good. ¹⁷But now, *it is* no longer I who do it, but sin that dwells in me. ¹⁸For I know that in me (that is, in my flesh) nothing good dwells; for to will is present with me, but *how* to perform what is good I do not find. ¹⁹For the good that I will *to do*, I do not do; but the evil I will not *to do*, that I practice. ²⁰Now if I do what I will not *to do*, it is no longer I who do it, but sin that dwells in me.

²¹I find then a law, that evil is present with me, the one who wills to do good. ²²For I delight in the law of God according to the inward man. ²³But I see another law in my members, warring against the law of my mind, and bringing me into captivity to the law of sin which is in my members. ²⁴O wretched man that I am! Who will deliver me from this body of death? ²⁵I thank God—through Jesus Christ our Lord!

In Romans 7:7–25, what is Paul's actual perspective? Is he describing his own experience as a believer or unbeliever, or is his style simply a literary device?

Paul uses the personal pronoun "I" throughout this passage, using his own experience as an example of what is true of unredeemed humanity (7:7–12) and of true Christians (7:13–25). Some interpret this chronicle of Paul's inner conflict as describing his life before Christ. They point out that Paul describes the person as "sold under sin" (7:14), as having "nothing good" in him (7:18), and as a "wretched man" trapped in a "body of death" (7:24). Those descriptions seem to contradict Paul's earlier description of the believer (6:2,6,7,11,17,18,22).

It is correct, however, to understand Paul here to be speaking about a believer. This person desires to obey God's law and hates sin (7:15,19,21). He is humble, recognizing that nothing good dwells in his humanness (7:18). He sees sin in himself, but not as all that is there (7:17,20–22). And he serves Jesus Christ with his mind (7:25). Paul has already established that none of those attitudes ever describe the unsaved (1:18–21,32; 3:10–20). Paul's use of the present tense verbs in 7:14–25 strongly supports the idea that he was describing his current experience as a Christian.

Even those who agree that Paul was speaking as a genuine believer, however, still find room for disagreement. Some see a carnal, fleshly Christian under the influence of old habits. Others see a legalistic Christian, frustrated by his feeble attempts in his own power to please God by keeping the Mosaic law. But the personal pronoun "I" refers to the apostle Paul, a standard of spiritual health and maturity. This leads to the conclusion that Paul, in 7:7–25, must be describing all Christians—even the most spiritual and mature—who, when they honestly evaluate themselves against the righteous standard of God's law, realize how far short they fall. Notice, particularly, Paul's honesty and transparency in the four laments (7:14–17,18–20,21–23,24–25).

So then, with the mind I myself serve the law of God, but with the flesh the law of sin.

> **7:24 wretched man.** In frustration and grief, Paul laments his sin (see Ps. 38:14). A believer perceives his own sinfulness in direct proportion to how clearly he sees the holiness of God and the perfection of His law. **deliver.** This means "to rescue from danger." Paul longed to be rescued from his sinful flesh. **body of death.** This refers to unredeemed humanness, which is found in the body.

Free from Indwelling Sin

8 *There is* therefore now no condemnation to those who are in Christ Jesus,[a] who do not walk according to the flesh, but according to the Spirit. ²For the law of the Spirit of life in Christ Jesus has made me free from the law of sin and death. ³For what the law could not do in that it was weak through the flesh, God *did* by sending His own Son in the likeness of sinful flesh, on account of sin: He condemned sin in the flesh, ⁴that the righteous requirement of the law might be fulfilled in us who do not walk according to the flesh but according to the Spirit. ⁵For those who live according to the flesh set their minds on the things of the flesh, but those *who live* according to the Spirit, the things of the Spirit. ⁶For to be carnally minded *is* death, but to be spiritually minded *is* life and peace. ⁷Because the carnal mind *is* enmity against God; for it is not subject to the law of God, nor indeed can be. ⁸So then, those who are in the flesh cannot please God.

> **8:3 what the law could not do.** The law could not deliver sinners from its penalty (Acts 13:38) or make them righteous (Gal. 3:21). **weak...the flesh.** The law was powerless to produce righteousness because of the sinful corruption of men (Gal. 3:21). **in the likeness of sinful flesh.** Christ took only the outward appearance of sinful flesh in His incarnation because He was completely without sin (Heb. 4:15). **condemned sin in the flesh.** God's condemnation against sin was fully poured out on Christ (Is. 53:4–8).

⁹But you are not in the flesh but in the Spirit, if indeed the Spirit of God dwells in you. Now if anyone does not have the Spirit of Christ, he is not His. ¹⁰And if Christ *is* in you, the body *is* dead because of sin, but the Spirit *is* life because of righteousness. ¹¹But if the Spirit of Him who raised Jesus from the dead dwells in you, He who raised Christ from the dead will also give life to your mortal bodies through His Spirit who dwells in you.

> **8:9 dwells.** This refers to being in one's own home. The Spirit of God makes His home in every person who trusts in Jesus Christ (see 1 Cor. 6:19,20). When there is no evidence of His presence by the fruit He produces (Gal. 5:22,23), a person has no legitimate claim to Christ as Savior and Lord.

Sonship Through the Spirit

¹²Therefore, brethren, we are debtors—not to the flesh, to live according to the flesh. ¹³For if you live according to the flesh you will die; but if by the Spirit you put to death the deeds of the body, you will live. ¹⁴For as many as are led by the Spirit of God, these are sons of God. ¹⁵For you did not receive the spirit of bondage again to fear, but you received the Spirit of adoption by whom we cry out, "Abba, Father." ¹⁶The Spirit Himself bears witness with our spirit that we are children of God, ¹⁷and if children, then heirs—heirs of God and joint heirs with Christ, if indeed we suffer with *Him*, that we may also be glorified together.

> **8:15 spirit of bondage...to fear.** Because of their sin, unsaved people are slaves to their fears of death (Heb. 2:14,15) and final punishment (1 John 4:18). **Spirit of adoption.** This refers to the Spirit-produced awareness that God has made us His children, and we can come before Him without fear or hesitation because He is our Father. **Abba.** This informal Aramaic term for Father (English, "Daddy") connotes tenderness, dependence, and a relationship free of fear or anxiety (see Mark 14:36).

From Suffering to Glory

¹⁸For I consider that the sufferings of this present time are not worthy *to be compared* with the glory which shall be revealed in us. ¹⁹For the earnest expectation of the creation eagerly waits for the revealing of the sons of God. ²⁰For the creation was subjected to futility, not willingly, but because of Him who subjected *it* in hope; ²¹because the creation itself also will be delivered from the bond-

---

8:1 [a]NU-Text omits the rest of this verse.

age of corruption into the glorious liberty of the children of God. ²²For we know that the whole creation groans and labors with birth pangs together until now. ²³Not only *that,* but we also who have the firstfruits of the Spirit, even we ourselves groan within ourselves, eagerly waiting for the adoption, the redemption of our body. ²⁴For we were saved in this hope, but hope that is seen is not hope; for why does one still hope for what he sees? ²⁵But if we hope for what we do not see, we eagerly wait for *it* with perseverance.

> **8:26 Likewise.** The Spirit, along with the creation and believers, groans for ultimate restoration. **groanings which cannot be uttered.** These are divine articulations within the Trinity that cannot be expressed in words. They carry profound appeals for the welfare of every believer (see 1 Cor. 2:11). This word of the Holy Spirit parallels the high priestly work of intercession by Jesus on behalf of believers (see Heb. 2:17).

²⁶Likewise the Spirit also helps in our weaknesses. For we do not know what we should pray for as we ought, but the Spirit Himself makes intercession for us*ᵃ* with groanings which cannot be uttered. ²⁷Now He who searches the hearts knows what the mind of the Spirit *is,* because He makes intercession for the saints according to *the will of* God.

²⁸And we know that all things work together for good to those who love God, to those who are the called according to *His* purpose. ²⁹For whom He foreknew, He also predestined *to be* conformed to the image of His Son, that He might be the firstborn among many brethren. ³⁰Moreover whom He predestined, these He also called; whom He called, these He also justified; and whom He justified, these He also glorified.

God's Everlasting Love

³¹What then shall we say to these things? If God *is* for us, who *can be* against us? ³²He who did not spare His own Son, but delivered Him up for us all, how shall He not with Him also freely give us all things? ³³Who shall bring a charge against God's elect? *It is* God who justifies. ³⁴Who *is* he

who condemns? *It is* Christ who died, and furthermore is also risen, who is even at the right hand of God, who also makes intercession for us. ³⁵Who shall separate us from the love of Christ? *Shall* tribulation, or distress, or persecution, or famine, or nakedness, or peril, or sword? ³⁶As it is written:

> *"For Your sake we are killed all day*
> *   long;*
> *We are accounted as sheep for the*
> *   slaughter."ᵃ*

> **8:35 the love of Christ.** This is Christ's love for us (John 13:1), specifically as He demonstrated it in salvation (1 John 4:9,10). **tribulation.** This probably refers to adversity common to all men. **distress.** This refers to being confined in a narrow, difficult place or being helplessly hemmed in by one's circumstances. **persecution.** This is the suffering inflicted on us by men because of our relationship with Christ (Matt. 5:10–12).

³⁷Yet in all these things we are more than conquerors through Him who loved us. ³⁸For I am persuaded that neither death nor life, nor angels nor principalities nor powers, nor things present nor things to come, ³⁹nor height nor depth, nor any other created thing, shall be able to separate us from the love of God which is in Christ Jesus our Lord.

Israel's Rejection of Christ

9 I tell the truth in Christ, I am not lying, my conscience also bearing me witness in the Holy Spirit, ²that I have great sorrow and continual grief in my heart. ³For I could wish that I myself were accursed from Christ for my brethren, my countrymen*ᵃ* according to the flesh, ⁴who are Israelites, to whom *pertain* the adoption, the glory, the covenants, the giving of the law, the service *of God,* and the promises; ⁵of whom *are* the fathers and from whom, according to the flesh, Christ *came,* who is over all, *the* eternally blessed God. Amen.

Israel's Rejection and God's Purpose

⁶But it is not that the word of God has taken no effect. For they *are* not all Israel who *are* of Israel, ⁷nor *are they* all children

---

8:26 *ᵃ*NU-Text omits *for us.*   8:36 *ᵃ*Psalm 44:22   9:3 *ᵃ*Or *relatives*

9:6 word of God. This refers to the privileges and promises God had revealed to Israel (see Is. 55:11). **not all Israel who are of Israel.** Not all of the physical descendants of Abraham are true heirs of the promise.

because they are the seed of Abraham; but, *"In Isaac your seed shall be called."ᵃ* ⁸That is, those who *are* the children of the flesh, these *are* not the children of God; but the children of the promise are counted as the seed. ⁹For this *is* the word of promise: *"At this time I will come and Sarah shall have a son."ᵃ*

¹⁰And not only *this*, but when Rebecca also had conceived by one man, *even* by our father Isaac ¹¹(for *the children* not yet being born, nor having done any good or evil, that the purpose of God according to election might stand, not of works but of Him who calls), ¹²it was said to her, *" The older shall serve the younger."ᵃ* ¹³As it is written, *"Jacob I have loved, but Esau I have hated."ᵃ*

Israel's Rejection and God's Justice

¹⁴What shall we say then? *Is there* unrighteousness with God? Certainly not! ¹⁵For He says to Moses, *"I will have mercy on whomever I will have mercy, and I will have compassion on whomever I will have compassion."ᵃ* ¹⁶So then *it is* not of him who wills, nor of him who runs, but of God who shows mercy. ¹⁷For the Scripture says to the Pharaoh, *"For this very purpose I have raised you up, that I may show My power in you, and that My name may be declared in all the earth."ᵃ* ¹⁸Therefore He has mercy on whom He wills, and whom He wills He hardens.

9:15 Paul quotes from Ex. 33:19 in response to the accusation that such a teaching about God's sovereign election is inconsistent with His fairness. This OT text clearly indicates that God is absolutely sovereign and elects who will be saved without violating His other attributes. He determines who receives mercy.

9:7 ᵃGenesis 21:12   9:9 ᵃGenesis 18:10,14   9:12 ᵃGenesis 25:23   9:13 ᵃMalachi 1:2,3   9:15 ᵃExodus 33:19   9:17 ᵃExodus 9:16

Explain the process Paul refers to in Romans 8:28–30 and 9:6–29. What do words like "called," "foreknew," "predestined," and "elect" tell us about our standing with God?

With these words, God reveals in human terms His divine role in the process of salvation. Paul's description offends the human spirit because it minimizes our role. Yet only those who see their own helplessness in the face of sin can come to see how gracious God has been in acting and choosing ahead of time. We never surprise God; He always anticipates us! "But God demonstrates His own love toward us, in that while we were still sinners, Christ died for us" (Romans 5:8).

The term "foreknew" (8:29) does not simply refer to God's omniscience—that in eternity past He knew who would come to Christ. Rather, it speaks of a predetermined choice by God to set His love on us and establish an intimate relationship. The term "election" (9:11) refers to the same action on God's part (1 Peter 1:1,2,20). Salvation is not initiated by human choice. Even faith is a gift of God (Romans 1:16; John 6:37; Ephesians 2:8,9).

The term "predestined" (8:29) literally means "to mark out, appoint, or determine beforehand." Those God chooses, He destines for His chosen end—that is, likeness to His Son (Ephesians 1:4,5,11). The goal of God's predestined purpose for His own is that they would be made like Jesus Christ.

The reality and security of our standing with God rests ultimately in His character and decision, not ours. Paul summarized his teaching about the believer's security in Christ with a thundering litany of questions and answers that haunt believers. They reach their peak with "Who shall separate us from the love of Christ?" (8:35). Paul's answer is an almost poetic expression of praise for God's grace in bringing salvation to completion for all who are chosen and believe—it is a hymn of security.

¹⁹You will say to me then, "Why does He still find fault? For who has resisted His will?" ²⁰But indeed, O man, who are you to reply against God? Will the thing formed say to him who formed *it*, "Why have you made me like this?" ²¹Does not the potter have power over the clay, from the same lump to make one vessel for honor and another for dishonor?

²²*What* if God, wanting to show *His* wrath and to make His power known, endured with much longsuffering the vessels of wrath prepared for destruction, ²³and that He might make known the riches of His glory on the vessels of mercy, which He had prepared beforehand for glory, ²⁴*even* us whom He called, not of the Jews only, but also of the Gentiles?

> **9:22 wanting.** The Greek word speaks of divine intention, not passive resignation. **endured.** God could justly destroy sinners the first time they sin by immediately giving them eternal punishment, but He patiently endures their rebellion. **vessels of wrath.** This refers to those whom God has not chosen for salvation and who will receive the just penalty of God's wrath for their sin. **prepared for destruction.** God does not make men who reject Him sinful; He leaves them in the sin they have chosen.

²⁵As He says also in Hosea:

"I will call them My people, who were
    not My people,
And her beloved, who was not
    beloved."ᵃ
²⁶ "And it shall come to pass in the place
    where it was said to them,
  'You are not My people,'
  There they shall be called sons of the
    living God."ᵃ

²⁷Isaiah also cries out concerning Israel:ᵃ

"Though the number of the children of
    Israel be as the sand of the sea,
The remnant will be saved.
²⁸ For He will finish the work and cut it
    short in righteousness,

Because the LORD will make a short
    work upon the earth."ᵃ

²⁹And as Isaiah said before:

"Unless the LORD of Sabaothᵃ had left
    us a seed,
We would have become like Sodom,
And we would have been made like
    Gomorrah." ᵇ

Present Condition of Israel

³⁰What shall we say then? That Gentiles, who did not pursue righteousness, have attained to righteousness, even the righteousness of faith; ³¹but Israel, pursuing the law of righteousness, has not attained to the law of righteousness.ᵃ ³²Why? Because *they did* not *seek it* by faith, but as it were, by the works of the law.ᵃ For they stumbled at that stumbling stone. ³³As it is written:

"Behold, I lay in Zion a stumbling
    stone and rock of offense,
And whoever believes on Him will not
    be put to shame."ᵃ

> **9:30–32** Paul reminded his readers that although God chooses some to receive His mercy, those who receive His judgment do so not because of something God has done to them, but because of their own unwillingness to believe the gospel (see 1 Thess. 2:10). Sinners are condemned for their personal sin—the supreme sin being rejection of God and Christ (see John 8:21–24).

Israel Needs the Gospel

10 Brethren, my heart's desire and prayer to God for Israelᵃ is that they may be saved. ²For I bear them witness that they have a zeal for God, but not according to knowledge. ³For they being ignorant of God's righteousness, and seeking to establish their own righteousness, have not submitted to the righteousness of God. ⁴For Christ *is* the end of the law for righteousness to everyone who believes.

⁵For Moses writes about the righteousness

---

which is of the law, "*The man who does those things shall live by them.*"*a* ⁶But the righteousness of faith speaks in this way, "*Do not say in your heart, 'Who will ascend into heaven?'*"*a* (that is, to bring Christ down *from above*) ⁷or, "*'Who will descend into the abyss?'*"*a* (that is, to bring Christ up from the dead). ⁸But what does it say? "*The word is near you, in your mouth and in your heart*"*a* (that is, the word of faith which we preach): ⁹that if you confess with your mouth the Lord Jesus and believe in your heart that God has raised Him from the dead, you will be saved. ¹⁰For with the heart one believes unto righteousness, and with the mouth confession is made unto salvation. ¹¹For the Scripture says, "*Whoever believes on Him will not be put to shame.*"*a* ¹²For there is no distinction between Jew and Greek, for the same Lord over all is rich to all who call upon Him. ¹³For "*whoever calls on the name of the LORD shall be saved.*"*a*

Israel Rejects the Gospel

¹⁴How then shall they call on Him in whom they have not believed? And how shall they believe in Him of whom they have not heard? And how shall they hear without a preacher? ¹⁵And how shall they preach unless they are sent? As it is written:

"*How beautiful are the feet of those who preach the gospel of peace,*a* Who bring glad tidings of good things!*"*b*

¹⁶But they have not all obeyed the gospel. For Isaiah says, "*LORD, who has believed our report?*"*a* ¹⁷So then faith *comes* by hearing, and hearing by the word of God.

¹⁸But I say, have they not heard? Yes indeed:

"*Their sound has gone out to all the earth, And their words to the ends of the world.*"*a*

¹⁹But I say, did Israel not know? First Moses says:

"*I will provoke you to jealousy by those who are not a nation, I will move you to anger by a foolish nation.*"*a*

²⁰But Isaiah is very bold and says:

"*I was found by those who did not seek Me; I was made manifest to those who did not ask for Me.*"*a*

²¹But to Israel he says:

"*All day long I have stretched out My hands To a disobedient and contrary people.*"*a*

Israel's Rejection Not Total

11 I say then, has God cast away His people? Certainly not! For I also am an Israelite, of the seed of Abraham, *of* the tribe of Benjamin. ²God has not cast away His people whom He foreknew. Or do you not know what the Scripture says of Elijah, how he pleads with God against Israel, saying, ³"*LORD, they have killed Your prophets and torn down Your altars, and I alone

---

10:5 *ᵃLeviticus 18:5   10:6 *ᵃDeuteronomy 30:12   10:7 *ᵃDeuteronomy 30:13   10:8 *ᵃDeuteronomy 30:14   10:11 *ᵃIsaiah 28:16   10:13 *ᵃJoel 2:32   10:15 *ᵃNU-Text omits *preach the gospel of peace, Who.* *ᵇIsaiah 52:7; Nahum 1:15   10:16 *ᵃIsaiah 53:1   10:18 *ᵃPsalm 19:4   10:19 *ᵃDeuteronomy 32:21 10:20 *ᵃIsaiah 65:1   10:21 *ᵃIsaiah 65:2

am left, and they seek my life"? [a] [4]"But what does the divine response say to him? *"I have reserved for Myself seven thousand men who have not bowed the knee to Baal."* [a] [5]Even so then, at this present time there is a remnant according to the election of grace. [6]And if by grace, then *it is* no longer of works; otherwise grace is no longer grace. [a] But if *it is* of works, it is no longer grace; otherwise work is no longer work.

> **11:5 a remnant.** Although the nation had rejected Jesus, thousands of Jews had come to faith in Him (see Acts 2:41). **election of grace.** God chose this remnant because of His grace (see Deut. 7:7,8), not because of their faith, good works, spiritual worthiness, or racial descent.

[7]What then? Israel has not obtained what it seeks; but the elect have obtained it, and the rest were blinded. [8]Just as it is written:

> *"God has given them a spirit of stupor,*
> *Eyes that they should not see*
> *And ears that they should not hear,*
> *To this very day."* [a]

[9]And David says:

> *"Let their table become a snare and a trap,*
> *A stumbling block and a recompense to them.*
> [10] *Let their eyes be darkened, so that they do not see,*
> *And bow down their back always."* [a]

Israel's Rejection Not Final

[11]I say then, have they stumbled that they should fall? Certainly not! But through their fall, to provoke them to jealousy, sal-

> **11:11 stumbled...fall.** The form of Paul's question and response confirms that Israel's blindness, hardening, and apostasy can be reversed. **their fall.** This was Israel's rejection of Jesus Christ. **provoke...to jealousy.** God intends to use His offer of salvation to the Gentiles to draw Israel back to Him. **salvation...to the Gentiles.** The OT had long prophesied this (see Gen. 12:3; Is. 49:6).

vation *has come* to the Gentiles. [12]Now if their fall *is* riches for the world, and their failure riches for the Gentiles, how much more their fullness!

[13]For I speak to you Gentiles; inasmuch as I am an apostle to the Gentiles, I magnify my ministry, [14]if by any means I may provoke to jealousy *those who are* my flesh and save some of them. [15]For if their being cast away *is* the reconciling of the world, what *will* their acceptance *be* but life from the dead?

[16]For if the firstfruit *is* holy, the lump *is* also *holy;* and if the root *is* holy, so *are* the branches. [17]And if some of the branches were broken off, and you, being a wild olive tree, were grafted in among them, and with them became a partaker of the root and fatness of the olive tree, [18]do not boast against the branches. But if you do boast, *remember that* you do not support the root, but the root supports you.

> **11:17 branches were broken off.** Some of the branches of Israel were removed, but God always preserved a believing remnant. **a wild olive tree...grafted in.** The old, unproductive branches (Israel) were broken off, and branches from a wild olive tree (Gentiles) were grafted in. **the root and fatness.** Once grafted in, Gentiles partake in God's covenant blessings as the spiritual heirs of Abraham. **the olive tree.** This refers to God's covenant with Abraham (Gen. 12:1–3).

[19]You will say then, "Branches were broken off that I might be grafted in." [20]Well *said.* Because of unbelief they were broken off, and you stand by faith. Do not be haughty, but fear. [21]For if God did not spare the natural branches, He may not spare you either. [22]Therefore consider the goodness and severity of God: on those who fell, severity; but toward you, goodness, [a] if you continue in *His* goodness. Otherwise you also will be cut off. [23]And they also, if they do not continue in unbelief, will be grafted in, for God is able to graft them in again. [24]For if you were cut out of the olive tree which is wild by nature, and were grafted contrary to nature into a cultivated olive tree, how much more will these, who *are*

11:3 [a]1 Kings 19:10,14　11:4 [a]1 Kings 19:18　11:6 [a]NU-Text omits the rest of this verse.
11:8 [a]Deuteronomy 29:4; Isaiah 29:10　11:10 [a]Psalm 69:22,23　11:22 [a]NU-Text adds *of God.*

natural *branches*, be grafted into their own olive tree?

²⁵For I do not desire, brethren, that you should be ignorant of this mystery, lest you should be wise in your own opinion, that blindness in part has happened to Israel until the fullness of the Gentiles has come in. ²⁶And so all Israel will be saved,ᵃ as it is written:

> "The Deliverer will come out of Zion,
> And He will turn away ungodliness
>   from Jacob;
> ²⁷ For this is My covenant with them,
>   When I take away their sins."ᵃ

²⁸Concerning the gospel *they are* enemies for your sake, but concerning the election *they are* beloved for the sake of the fathers. ²⁹For the gifts and the calling of God *are* irrevocable. ³⁰For as you were once disobedient to God, yet have now obtained mercy through their disobedience, ³¹even so these also have now been disobedient, that through the mercy shown you they also may obtain mercy. ³²For God has committed them all to disobedience, that He might have mercy on all.

³³Oh, the depth of the riches both of the wisdom and knowledge of God! How unsearchable *are* His judgments and His ways past finding out!

> ³⁴ "For who has known the mind of the
>   LORD?
>   Or who has become His counselor?"ᵃ
> ³⁵ "Or who has first given to Him
>   And it shall be repaid to him?"ᵃ

³⁶For of Him and through Him and to Him *are* all things, to whom *be* glory forever. Amen.

Living Sacrifices to God

12 I beseech you therefore, brethren, by the mercies of God, that you present your bodies a living sacrifice, holy, acceptable to God, *which is* your reasonable service. ²And do not be conformed to this world, but be transformed by the renewing of your mind, that you may prove what *is* that good and acceptable and perfect will of God.

> **12:1 present your bodies a living sacrifice.** Under the Old Covenant, God accepted the sacrifices of animals. The OT sacrifices are no longer effective because of Christ's ultimate sacrifice (Heb. 9:11,12). For those in Christ, the only acceptable worship is to offer themselves completely to God. **reasonable service.** "Reasonable" is from the Greek for "logic." Since believers enjoy the fruit of God's mercies (Rom. 11:33,36), it logically follows that they owe God their highest form of service.

Serve God with Spiritual Gifts

³For I say, through the grace given to me, to everyone who is among you, not to think of *himself* more highly than he ought to think, but to think soberly, as God has dealt to each one a measure of faith. ⁴For as we have many members in one body, but all the members do not have the same function, ⁵so we, *being* many, are one body in Christ, and individually members of one another. ⁶Having then gifts differing according to the grace that is given to us, *let us use them:* if prophecy, *let us prophesy* in proportion to our faith; ⁷or ministry, *let us use it* in *our* ministering; he who teaches, in teaching; ⁸he who exhorts, in exhortation; he who gives, with liberality; he who leads, with diligence; he who shows mercy, with cheerfulness.

Behave Like a Christian

⁹*Let* love *be* without hypocrisy. Abhor what is evil. Cling to what is good. ¹⁰*Be* kindly affectionate to one another with brotherly love, in honor giving preference to one another; ¹¹not lagging in diligence, fervent in spirit, serving the Lord; ¹²rejoicing in hope, patient in tribulation, continuing steadfastly in prayer; ¹³distributing to the needs of the saints, given to hospitality. ¹⁴Bless those who persecute you; bless and do not curse. ¹⁵Rejoice with those who rejoice, and weep with those who weep.

> **12:9 love.** This is the supreme NT virtue, which centers on the needs and welfare of the one loved and does whatever necessary to meet those needs (see Matt. 22:37–39). **hypocrisy.** Christian love is to be shown purely and sincerely, without self-centeredness or guile.

11:26 ᵃOr *delivered*   11:27 ᵃIsaiah 59:20,21   11:34 ᵃIsaiah 40:13; Jeremiah 23:18   11:35 ᵃJob 41:11

[16]Be of the same mind toward one another. Do not set your mind on high things, but associate with the humble. Do not be wise in your own opinion.

[17]Repay no one evil for evil. Have regard for good things in the sight of all men. [18]If it is possible, as much as depends on you, live peaceably with all men. [19]Beloved, do not avenge yourselves, but *rather* give place to wrath; for it is written, "*Vengeance is Mine, I will repay,*" [a] says the Lord. [20]Therefore

> "*If your enemy is hungry, feed him;*
> *If he is thirsty, give him a drink;*
> *For in so doing you will heap coals of*
> *fire on his head.*" [a]

[21]Do not be overcome by evil, but overcome evil with good.

Submit to Government

13 Let every soul be subject to the governing authorities. For there is no authority except from God, and the authorities that exist are appointed by God. [2]Therefore whoever resists the authority resists the ordinance of God, and those who resist will bring judgment on themselves. [3]For rulers are not a terror to good works, but to evil. Do you want to be unafraid of the authority? Do what is good, and you will have praise from the same. [4]For he is God's minister to you for good. But if you do evil, be afraid; for he does not bear the sword in vain; for he is God's minister, an avenger to *execute* wrath on him who practices evil. [5]Therefore *you* must be subject, not only because of wrath but also for conscience' sake. [6]For because of this you also pay taxes, for they are God's ministers attending continually to this very thing.

> **13:1 be subject.** This Greek word was used of a soldier's absolute obedience to his superior officer. Scripture makes the exception to this command when obedience to civil authority requires disobedience to God's Word (Ex. 1:17). **appointed.** Human government's authority derives from and is defined by God. He instituted human government to reward good and to restrain sin in a fallen world.

[7]Render therefore to all their due: taxes to whom taxes *are due*, customs to whom customs, fear to whom fear, honor to whom honor.

Love Your Neighbor

[8]Owe no one anything except to love one another, for he who loves another has fulfilled the law. [9]For the commandments, "*You shall not commit adultery,*" "*You shall not murder,*" "*You shall not steal,*" "*You shall not bear false witness,*" [a] "*You shall not covet,*" [b] and if *there is* any other commandment, are *all* summed up in this saying, namely, "*You shall love your neighbor as yourself.*" [c] [10]Love does no harm to a neighbor; therefore love *is* the fulfillment of the law.

Put on Christ

[11]And *do* this, knowing the time, that now *it is* high time to awake out of sleep; for now our salvation *is* nearer than when we *first* believed. [12]The night is far spent, the day is at hand. Therefore let us cast off the works of darkness, and let us put on the armor of light. [13]Let us walk properly, as in the day, not in revelry and drunkenness, not in lewdness and lust, not in strife and envy. [14]But put on the Lord Jesus Christ, and make no provision for the flesh, to *fulfill its* lusts.

> **13:11 time.** The Greek word views time as a period, era, or age (see Matt. 16:3). **sleep.** This refers to spiritual apathy or lethargy. **our salvation.** This is the final feature of our redemption, which is glorification. **is nearer.** Jesus' return, when we will be glorified, draws closer every day. The Bible frequently uses the return of Jesus to motivate believers to holy living (Titus 2:11–13).

The Law of Liberty

14 Receive one who is weak in the faith, *but* not to disputes over doubtful things. [2]For one believes he may eat all things, but he who is weak eats *only* vegetables. [3]Let not him who eats despise him who does not eat, and let not him who does not eat judge him who eats; for God has received him. [4]Who are you to judge another's servant? To his own master he

---

12:19 [a]Deuteronomy 32:35   12:20 [a]Proverbs 25:21,22   13:9 [a]NU-Text omits "*You shall not bear false witness.*" [b]Exodus 20:13–15,17; Deuteronomy 5:17–19,21   [c]Leviticus 19:18

14:1 Receive. This refers to personal and willing acceptance of another. **weak in the faith.** This characterizes believers who are unable to let go of the religious ceremonies and rituals of their past. The weak Jewish believer had difficulty abandoning the rites and prohibitions of the Old Covenant. The weak Gentile believer had been involved in pagan idolatry and felt that any contact with anything related to his past would taint him with sin.

stands or falls. Indeed, he will be made to stand, for God is able to make him stand.

5One person esteems *one* day above another; another esteems every day *alike*. Let each be fully convinced in his own mind. 6He who observes the day, observes *it* to the Lord;*a* and he who does not observe the day, to the Lord he does not observe *it*. He who eats, eats to the Lord, for he gives God thanks; and he who does not eat, to the Lord he does not eat, and gives God thanks. 7For none of us lives to himself, and no one dies to himself. 8For if we live, we live to the Lord; and if we die, we die to the Lord. Therefore, whether we live or die, we are the Lord's. 9For to this end Christ died and rose*a* and lived again, that He might be Lord of both the dead and the living. 10But why do you judge your brother? Or why do you show contempt for your brother? For we shall all stand before the judgment seat of Christ.*a* 11For it is written:

" *As I live, says the LORD,*
  Every knee shall bow to Me,
  And every tongue shall confess to
    God." a

14:5 esteems *one* day. Though it was no longer required by God, the weak Jewish believer felt compelled to observe the Sabbath and other special days associated with Judaism (see Ga. 4:9,10). The weak Gentile believer, on the other hand, wanted to separate himself from the special days of festivities associated with his former paganism. **esteems every day alike.** The mature believers were unaffected by those concerns.

12So then each of us shall give account of himself to God. 13Therefore let us not judge one another anymore, but rather resolve this, not to put a stumbling block or a cause to fall in *our* brother's way.

The Law of Love

14I know and am convinced by the Lord Jesus that *there is* nothing unclean of itself; but to him who considers anything to be unclean, to him *it is* unclean. 15Yet if your brother is grieved because of *your* food, you are no longer walking in love. Do not destroy with your food the one for whom Christ died. 16Therefore do not let your good be spoken of as evil; 17for the kingdom of God is not eating and drinking, but righteousness and peace and joy in the Holy Spirit. 18For he who serves Christ in these things*a* *is* acceptable to God and approved by men.

14:14 I know and am convinced by the Lord Jesus. This truth was the product of divine revelation (see Gal. 1:12). **unclean.** The Greek word originally meant "common" but came to mean "impure" or "evil." **to him who considers...to him *it is* unclean.** If a believer is convinced that a certain behavior is sin, he should not do it. If he does, he will violate his conscience, experience guilt (see 1 Cor. 8:4–7), and perhaps be driven back into deeper legalism.

19Therefore let us pursue the things *which make* for peace and the things by which one may edify another. 20Do not destroy the work of God for the sake of food. All things indeed *are* pure, but *it is* evil for the man who eats with offense. 21*It is* good neither to eat meat nor drink wine nor *do anything* by which your brother stumbles or is offended or is made weak.*a* 22Do you have faith?*a* Have *it* to yourself before God. Happy *is* he who does not condemn himself in what he approves. 23But he who doubts is condemned if he eats, because *he does* not *eat* from faith; for whatever *is* not from faith is sin.*a*

14:22 Have *it* to yourself before God. This is better translated, "have as your own conviction before God." Paul urged the strong believer to understand his liberty, enjoy it, and keep it between God and himself. **what he approves.** The strong believer has a healthy conscience because he does not cause a weak believer to stumble.

14:6 *a*NU-Text omits the rest of this sentence.   14:9 *a*NU-Text omits *and rose*.   14:10 *a*NU-Text reads *of God.*   14:11 *a*Isaiah 45:23   14:18 *a*NU-Text reads *this.*   14:21 *a*NU-Text omits *or is offended or is made weak.*   14:22 *a*NU-Text reads *The faith which you have—have.*   14:23 *a*M-Text puts Romans 16:25–27 here.

Bearing Others' Burdens

15 We then who are strong ought to bear with the scruples of the weak, and not to please ourselves. ²Let each of us please *his* neighbor for *his* good, leading to edification. ³For even Christ did not please Himself; but as it is written, *" The reproaches of those who reproached You fell on Me."* ᵃ ⁴For whatever things were written before were written for our learning, that we through the patience and comfort of the Scriptures might have hope. ⁵Now may the God of patience and comfort grant you to be like-minded toward one another, according to Christ Jesus, ⁶that you may with one mind *and* one mouth glorify the God and Father of our Lord Jesus Christ.

Glorify God Together

⁷Therefore receive one another, just as Christ also received us,ᵃ to the glory of God. ⁸Now I say that Jesus Christ has become a servant to the circumcision for the truth of God, to confirm the promises *made* to the fathers, ⁹and that the Gentiles might glorify God for *His* mercy, as it is written:

> *"For this reason I will confess to You among the Gentiles,*
> *And sing to Your name."* ᵃ

¹⁰And again he says:

> *"Rejoice, O Gentiles, with His people!"* ᵃ

¹¹And again:

> *"Praise the LORD, all you Gentiles! Laud Him, all you peoples!"* ᵃ

¹²And again, Isaiah says:

> *"There shall be a root of Jesse;*
> *And He who shall rise to reign over the Gentiles,*
> *In Him the Gentiles shall hope."* ᵃ

15:3 ᵃPsalm 69:9   15:7 ᵃNU-Text and M-Text read *you*.   15:9 ᵃ2 Samuel 22:50; Psalm 18:49
15:10 ᵃDeuteronomy 32:43   15:11 ᵃPsalm 117:1   15:12 ᵃIsaiah 11:10

Who was Paul the apostle and why does he seem to have two names?

Paul (Greek name) the apostle was also known as Saul, which was his Hebrew name. Along with his double name, Paul was also able to exercise dual citizenship as a Jewish descendant from the tribe of Benjamin (Philippians 3:5) and as a Roman (Acts 16:37; 22:25). Paul was born about the time of Christ's birth, in Tarsus, located in modern Turkey (Acts 9:11).

Young Saul spent much of his early life in Jerusalem as a student of the celebrated rabbi (teacher) Gamaliel (Acts 22:3). Like his father before him, Paul was a Pharisee (Acts 23:6), a member of the strictest Jewish sect (Philippians 3:5). He actively resisted those who followed Jesus. His first appearance in Scripture occurs in Acts 7:58 as he observed the martyrdom of Stephen.

Miraculously converted while on his way to Damascus (about A.D. 33–34) to persecute Christians, Paul immediately began proclaiming the gospel (Acts 9:20). After narrowly escaping Damascus (Acts 9:23–25; 2 Corinthians 11:32,33), Paul spent three years in the wilderness (Galatians 1:17,18). During those years, he received much of his doctrine as direct revelation from the Lord (Galatians 1:11,12).

More than any other individual, Paul was responsible for the spread of Christianity throughout the Roman Empire. He made three missionary journeys along the north side of the Mediterranean Sea, tirelessly preaching the gospel he had once tried to destroy (Acts 26:9). Eventually he was arrested in Jerusalem (Acts 21:27–31), appealed for a hearing before Caesar, and finally reached Rome (chapters 27,28). Later, he was released for a short time of ministry then arrested again and martyred at Rome in about A.D. 65–67.

Though physically unimpressive (2 Corinthians 10:10; Galatians 4:14), Paul possessed an inner strength granted him through the Holy Spirit's power (Philippians 4:13). The grace of God proved sufficient to provide for his every need (2 Corinthians 12:9,10), enabling this noble servant of Christ to successfully finish his spiritual race (2 Timothy 4:7).

¹³Now may the God of hope fill you with all joy and peace in believing, that you may abound in hope by the power of the Holy Spirit.

15:14–22 Paul did not want to jeopardize his relationship with the believers in Rome by seeming to be insensitive, presumptuous, or unloving. Here he explains how he could write such a forthright letter to a church that he had not founded and had never visited.

From Jerusalem to Illyricum

¹⁴Now I myself am confident concerning you, my brethren, that you also are full of goodness, filled with all knowledge, able also to admonish one another.ᵃ ¹⁵Nevertheless, brethren, I have written more boldly to you on *some* points, as reminding you, because of the grace given to me by God, ¹⁶that I might be a minister of Jesus Christ to the Gentiles, ministering the gospel of God, that the offering of the Gentiles might be acceptable, sanctified by the Holy Spirit. ¹⁷Therefore I have reason to glory in Christ Jesus in the things *which pertain* to God. ¹⁸For I will not dare to speak of any of those things which Christ has not accomplished through me, in word and deed, to make the Gentiles obedient—¹⁹in mighty signs and wonders, by the power of the Spirit of God, so that from Jerusalem and round about to Illyricum I have fully preached the gospel of Christ. ²⁰And so I have made it my aim to preach the gospel, not where Christ was named, lest I should build on another man's foundation, ²¹but as it is written:

> "To whom He was not announced,
>   they shall see;
> And those who have not heard shall
>   understand."ᵃ

15:20 another man's foundation. Paul's goal was to reach those who had never heard the gospel, which is the primary function of a NT evangelist (Eph. 4:11). A pastor's ministry was to build on the foundation laid by an evangelist (see 1 Cor. 3:6).

Plan to Visit Rome

²²For this reason I also have been much hindered from coming to you. ²³But now no longer having a place in these parts, and having a great desire these many years to come to you, ²⁴whenever I journey to Spain, I shall come to you.ᵃ For I hope to see you on my journey, and to be helped on my way there by you, if first I may enjoy your *company* for a while. ²⁵But now I am going to Jerusalem to minister to the saints. ²⁶For it pleased those from Macedonia and Achaia to make a certain contribution for the poor among the saints who are in Jerusalem. ²⁷It pleased them indeed, and they are their debtors. For if the Gentiles have been partakers of their spiritual things, their duty is also to minister to them in material things. ²⁸Therefore, when I have performed this and have sealed to them this fruit, I shall go by way of you to Spain. ²⁹But I know that when I come to you, I shall come in the fullness of the blessing of the gospelᵃ of Christ.

³⁰Now I beg you, brethren, through the Lord Jesus Christ, and through the love of the Spirit, that you strive together with me in prayers to God for me, ³¹that I may be delivered from those in Judea who do not believe, and that my service for Jerusalem may be acceptable to the saints, ³²that I may come to you with joy by the will of God, and may be refreshed together with you. ³³Now the God of peace *be* with you all. Amen.

16:1–27 In this chapter, Paul expressed his love and affection for other believers and co-workers. He provides insights into the lives of ordinary first-century Christians and gives an inside look at the nature and character of the early church.

Sister Phoebe Commended

16 I commend to you Phoebe our sister, who is a servant of the church in Cenchrea, ²that you may receive her in the Lord in a manner worthy of the saints, and assist her in whatever business she has need of you; for indeed she has been a helper of many and of myself also.

Greeting Roman Saints

³Greet Priscilla and Aquila, my fellow workers in Christ Jesus, ⁴who risked their

---

own necks for my life, to whom not only I give thanks, but also all the churches of the Gentiles. ⁵Likewise *greet* the church that is in their house.

Greet my beloved Epaenetus, who is the firstfruits of Achaia*ᵃ* to Christ. ⁶Greet Mary, who labored much for us. ⁷Greet Andronicus and Junia, my countrymen and my fellow prisoners, who are of note among the apostles, who also were in Christ before me.

⁸Greet Amplias, my beloved in the Lord. ⁹Greet Urbanus, our fellow worker in Christ, and Stachys, my beloved. ¹⁰Greet Apelles, approved in Christ. Greet those who are of the *household* of Aristobulus. ¹¹Greet Herodion, my countryman.*ᵃ* Greet those who are of the *household* of Narcissus who are in the Lord.

¹²Greet Tryphena and Tryphosa, who have labored in the Lord. Greet the beloved Persis, who labored much in the Lord. ¹³Greet Rufus, chosen in the Lord, and his mother and mine. ¹⁴Greet Asyncritus, Phlegon, Hermas, Patrobas, Hermes, and the brethren who are with them. ¹⁵Greet Philologus and Julia, Nereus and his sister, and Olympas, and all the saints who are with them.

¹⁶Greet one another with a holy kiss. The*ᵃ* churches of Christ greet you.

> **16:16 holy kiss.** Kissing between friends on the forehead, cheek, or beard was common in the OT. The Jews in the NT church carried on the practice. To new believers who often had been rejected by their families because of their faith, this was a precious sign of spiritual kinship.

Avoid Divisive Persons

¹⁷Now I urge you, brethren, note those who cause divisions and offenses, contrary to the doctrine which you learned, and avoid them. ¹⁸For those who are such do not serve our Lord Jesus*ᵃ* Christ, but their own belly, and by smooth words and flattering speech deceive the hearts of the simple. ¹⁹For your obedience has become known to all. Therefore I am glad on your behalf; but I want you to be wise in what is good, and simple concerning evil. ²⁰And the God of peace will crush Satan under your feet shortly.

The grace of our Lord Jesus Christ *be* with you. Amen.

Greetings from Paul's Friends

²¹Timothy, my fellow worker, and Lucius, Jason, and Sosipater, my countrymen, greet you.

²²I, Tertius, who wrote *this* epistle, greet you in the Lord.

²³Gaius, my host and *the host* of the whole church, greets you. Erastus, the treasurer of the city, greets you, and Quartus, a brother. ²⁴The grace of our Lord Jesus Christ *be* with you all. Amen.*ᵃ*

Benediction

²⁵Now to Him who is able to establish you according to my gospel and the preaching of Jesus Christ, according to the revelation of the mystery kept secret since the world began ²⁶but now made manifest, and by the prophetic Scriptures made known to all nations, according to the commandment of the everlasting God, for obedience to the faith—²⁷to God, alone wise, *be* glory through Jesus Christ forever. Amen.*ᵃ*

> **16:25–27** The letter concludes with a beautiful doxology that praises God for His work through Jesus Christ, thereby summarizing the major themes in this letter to the Romans (see Matt. 6:13; Heb. 13:20,21).

16:5 *ᵃ*NU-Text reads *Asia.*   16:11 *ᵃ*Or *relative*   16:16 *ᵃ*NU-Text reads *All the churches.*   16:18 *ᵃ*NU-Text and M-Text omit *Jesus.*   16:24 *ᵃ*NU-Text omits this verse.   16:27 *ᵃ*M-Text puts Romans 16:25–27 after Romans 14:23.

1 CORINTHIANS

Who will settle the argument? When people can't agree on an answer, sometimes they will agree to an arbitrator. One New Testament church became famous for its conflicts and questions—the church in Corinth. Fortunately, they had the Apostle Paul for an arbitrator. First Corinthians was one of several letters that Paul wrote to instruct this struggling church.

AUTHOR AND DATE

First Corinthians was written by the Apostle Paul, about A.D. 55.

The first verse of this letter credits the Apostle Paul as the writer. His authorship cannot be seriously questioned, and the church has maintained that position since the first century. The letter repeatedly identifies its author (1:1,13; 3:4–6; 4:15; 16:21). External evidence for Pauline authorship includes the witness of Clement of Rome (A.D. 95) in a letter to the same Corinthian church. Other early Christian leaders also authenticated Paul as the author: Ignatius (about A.D. 110), Polycarp (about A.D. 135), and Tertullian (about A.D. 200).

This letter was most likely written in the first half of A.D. 55 from Ephesus (16:8,9,19) while Paul was on his third missionary journey. The apostle intended to remain in Ephesus to complete his 3-year stay (Acts 20:31) until Pentecost (May/June) of A.D. 55 (16:8). Then he hoped to winter (A.D. 55–56) in Corinth (16:6; Acts 2:20). He was anticipating his departure for Corinth even as he was writing this letter (4:19; 11:34; 16:8).

BACKGROUND AND SETTING

Corinth was located in southern Greece, in what was the Roman province of Achaia, about 45 miles west from Athens. Corinth sat on a narrow isthmus which not only funneled land traffic through its gates, but also controlled a portage for ships transported overland from the Gulf of Corinth on the West to the Saronic Gulf on the East. The city grew prosperous from all the trade traffic.

Although officially famous as the host-city of the Isthmian games (rivaled in their time only by the Olympian games), Corinth was infamous for its depravity. Even by the pagan standards of the time, Corinth was so morally corrupt that its very name became synonymous with debauchery and moral depravity. In 6:9,10, Paul lists some of the specific sins for which the city was noted and which formerly had characterized many believers in the church there. Tragically, some of the worst sins were still found among church members. One of those sins, incest, was condemned even by most pagan Gentiles (5:1).

Like most ancient Greek cities, Corinth had an acropolis (high city) which rose 2,000 feet and was used both for defense and for pagan worship. Corinth boasted of a temple to Aphrodite, the Greek goddess of love. The temple and the city employed more than 1,000 priestesses, who were "religious" prostitutes. Sexual immorality was rampant throughout Corinth.

Paul founded the church in Corinth on his second missionary journey (Acts 18:1ff). As usual, his ministry began among the Jews in the synagogue but then shifted to the Gentiles after his countrymen rejected the gospel. During the year and a half that Paul worked in Corinth he was assisted by Priscilla and Aquilla, two Jewish believers, and by Paul's associates Silas and Timothy.

The most serious problem of the Corinthian church was worldliness, an unwillingness to divorce the culture around them. Most of the believers did not consistently separate themselves from their old, selfish, immoral, and pagan ways. Paul decided it was necessary for him to write to correct these patterns with disciplinary directions (5:9–13).

Before writing *this* inspired letter, Paul had exchanged other correspondence with the church (5:9), also corrective in nature. Because a copy of that letter has never been discovered, it has been referred to as the "lost epistle." Another non-canonical letter followed 1 Corinthians, usually called "the severe letter" (2 Corinthians 2:4).

HISTORICAL AND THEOLOGICAL THEMES

The major thrust of this epistle aims to correct behavior rather than offer instruction. Nevertheless, Paul includes significant teaching on many doctrines directly related to matters of sin and righteousness. In one way or another, wrong living always stems from wrong belief. Sexual sins, for example, are inevitably related to disobeying God's plan for marriage and family (7:1–40). Proper worship flows from such things as recognition of God's holy character (3:17), the spiritual identity of the church (12:12–27), and pure partaking of the Lord's Supper (11:17–34). The church cannot grow in faith or effectiveness unless believers understand and exercise their spiritual gifts (12:1–14:40).

> PAUL OFFERED HIS READERS THE **TRUTHFUL BUILDING MATERIALS** FOR **GODLY LIVING.**

Chapter 15 makes a brilliant and extended argument for the importance of the doctrine of the resurrection. This doctrine cannot be overestimated because if there is no resurrection of the dead, then Christ is not risen. And if Christ is not risen, then preaching is empty and so is faith (15:13,14).

Paul also touched on the following themes: (1) God's judgment of believers, the right understanding of which would produce right motives for godly living (3:13–15); (2) the right understanding of idols and of false gods which would help immature Christians think maturely about such practices as eating meat that had been sacrificed to idols (8:1–11:1); and (3) the right understanding and expression of genuine, godly love which was mandatory to right use of the gifts and even to

right knowledge about all the things of God (13:1–13). Paul offered his readers the truthful building materials for godly living, necessary for constructing a life capable of standing the fiery test (3:11–15).

OUTLINE

Greeting

1 Paul, called *to be* an apostle of Jesus Christ through the will of God, and Sosthenes *our* brother,

> **1:1 apostle.** This means "a sent one." Paul needed to establish his authority as an emissary of Jesus by God's appointment (see Acts 9:3–6) because so much of this epistle is corrective. Because Paul was delegated by God to speak and write, if the people resisted his message, they were resisting God. **Sosthenes.** He was probably Paul's secretary, a former leader of the Corinthian synagogue who had become a believer. He was once beaten for bringing Paul before the civil court at Corinth (Acts 18:12–17).

²To the church of God which is at Corinth, to those who are sanctified in Christ Jesus, called *to be* saints, with all who in every place call on the name of Jesus Christ our Lord, both theirs and ours:

³Grace to you and peace from God our Father and the Lord Jesus Christ.

Spiritual Gifts at Corinth

⁴I thank my God always concerning you for the grace of God which was given to you by Christ Jesus, ⁵that you were enriched in everything by Him in all utterance and all knowledge, ⁶even as the testimony of Christ was confirmed in you, ⁷so that you come short in no gift, eagerly waiting for the revelation of our Lord Jesus Christ, ⁸who will also confirm you to the end, *that you may be* blameless in the day of our Lord Jesus Christ. ⁹God *is* faithful, by whom you were called into the fellowship of His Son, Jesus Christ our Lord.

> **1:9 God *is* faithful.** Because of God's sovereign and unchangeable promise, believers are assured future glory at Christ's appearing (Eph. 5:26,27). **by whom you were called.** This is an effectual call that saves. God, who calls to salvation and heaven, will be faithful to give the grace needed to fulfill that call.

Sectarianism Is Sin

¹⁰Now I plead with you, brethren, by the name of our Lord Jesus Christ, that you all speak the same thing, and *that* there be no divisions among you, but *that* you be perfectly joined together in the same mind and in the same judgment. ¹¹For it has been declared to me concerning you, my brethren, by those of Chloe's *household*, that there are contentions among you. ¹²Now I say this, that each of you says, "I am of Paul," or "I am of Apollos," or "I am of Cephas," or "I am of Christ." ¹³Is Christ divided? Was Paul crucified for you? Or were you baptized in the name of Paul?

¹⁴I thank God that I baptized none of you except Crispus and Gaius, ¹⁵lest anyone should say that I had baptized in my own name. ¹⁶Yes, I also baptized the household of Stephanas. Besides, I do not know whether I baptized any other. ¹⁷For Christ did not send me to baptize, but to preach the gospel, not with wisdom of words, lest the cross of Christ should be made of no effect.

> **1:17** This verse does not mean that people should not be baptized (see Acts 2:38). Paul was explaining that he had been called to preach the gospel and bring people to oneness in Christ, not to start a private cult of people personally baptized by him (see Acts 26:16–18).

Christ the Power and Wisdom of God

¹⁸For the message of the cross is foolishness to those who are perishing, but to us who are being saved it is the power of God. ¹⁹For it is written:

> "I will destroy the wisdom of the wise,
> And bring to nothing the
>   understanding of the prudent."ᵃ

²⁰Where *is* the wise? Where *is* the scribe? Where *is* the disputer of this age? Has not God made foolish the wisdom of this world? ²¹For since, in the wisdom of God, the world through wisdom did not know God, it pleased God through the foolishness of the message preached to save those who believe. ²²For Jews request a sign, and Greeks seek after wisdom; ²³but we preach Christ crucified, to the Jews a stumbling block and to the Greeksᵃ foolishness, ²⁴but to those who are called, both Jews and Greeks, Christ the power of God and the wisdom of God. ²⁵Because the foolishness of God is wiser than men, and the weakness of God is stronger than men.

1:19 ᵃIsaiah 29:14   1:23 ᵃNU-Text reads *Gentiles*.

Glory Only in the Lord

²⁶For you see your calling, brethren, that not many wise according to the flesh, not many mighty, not many noble, *are called.* ²⁷But God has chosen the foolish things of the world to put to shame the wise, and God has chosen the weak things of the world to put to shame the things which are mighty; ²⁸and the base things of the world and the things which are despised God has chosen, and the things which are not, to bring to nothing the things that are, ²⁹that no flesh should glory in His presence. ³⁰But of Him you are in Christ Jesus, who became for us wisdom from God—and righteousness and sanctification and redemption—³¹that, as it is written, *"He who glories, let him glory in the Lord."ᵃ*

Christh Crucified

2 And I, brethren, when I came to you, did not come with excellence of speech or of wisdom declaring to you the testimonyᵃ of God. ²For I determined not to know anything among you except Jesus Christ and Him crucified. ³I was with you in weakness, in fear, and in much trembling. ⁴And my speech and my preaching *were* not with persuasive words of humanᵃ wisdom, but in demonstration of the Spirit and of power, ⁵that your faith should not be in the wisdom of men but in the power of God.

Spiritual Wisdom

⁶However, we speak wisdom among those who are mature, yet not the wisdom of this age, nor of the rulers of this age, who are coming to nothing. ⁷But we speak the wisdom of God in a mystery, the hidden *wisdom* which God ordained before the ages for our glory, ⁸which none of the rulers of this age knew; for had they known, they would not have crucified the Lord of glory.

⁹But as it is written:

> *"Eye has not seen, nor ear heard,*
> *Nor have entered into the heart of*
> *man*
> *The things which God has prepared*
> *for those who love Him."ᵃ*

¹⁰But God has revealed *them* to us through His Spirit. For the Spirit searches all things, yes, the deep things of God. ¹¹For what man knows the things of a man except the spirit of the man which is in him? Even so no one knows the things of God except the Spirit of God. ¹²Now we have received, not the spirit of the world, but the Spirit who is from God, that we might know the things that have been freely given to us by God.

¹³These things we also speak, not in words which man's wisdom teaches but which the Holyᵃ Spirit teaches, comparing spiritual things with spiritual. ¹⁴But the natural man does not receive the things of the Spirit of God, for they are foolishness to him; nor can he know *them,* because they are spiritually discerned. ¹⁵But he who is spiritual judges all things, yet he himself is *rightly* judged by no one. ¹⁶For *"who has known the mind of the Lord that he may instruct Him?"ᵃ* But we have the mind of Christ.

Sectarianism Is Carnal

3 And I, brethren, could not speak to you as to spiritual *people* but as to carnal, as to babes in Christ. ²I fed you with milk and not with solid food; for until now you were not able *to receive it,* and even now you are still not able; ³for you are still carnal. For where *there are* envy, strife, and divisions among you, are you not carnal and

---

1:31 ᵃJeremiah 9:24   2:1 ᵃNU-Text reads *mystery.*   2:4 ᵃNU-Text omits *human.*   2:9 ᵃIsaiah 64:4
2:13 ᵃNU-Text omits *Holy.*   2:16 ᵃIsaiah 40:13

3:2 milk. This refers to the easily digestible truths of doctrine that were given to new believers. **solid food.** This refers to the deeper features of the doctrines of Scripture. The difference is not the kind of food, but the degree of depth. Spiritual immaturity disables one to receive the richest truths.

behaving like *mere* men? [4]For when one says, "I am of Paul," and another, "I *am* of Apollos," are you not carnal?

Watering, Working, Warning

[5]Who then is Paul, and who *is* Apollos, but ministers through whom you believed, as the Lord gave to each one? [6]I planted, Apollos watered, but God gave the increase. [7]So then neither he who plants is anything, nor he who waters, but God who gives the increase. [8]Now he who plants and he who waters are one, and each one will receive his own reward according to his own labor.

[9]For we are God's fellow workers; you are God's field, *you are* God's building. [10]According to the grace of God which was given to me, as a wise master builder I have laid the foundation, and another builds on it. But let each one take heed how he builds on it. [11]For no other foundation can anyone lay than that which is laid, which is Jesus Christ. [12]Now if anyone builds on this foundation *with* gold, silver, precious stones, wood, hay, straw, [13]each one's work will become clear; for the Day will declare it, because it will be revealed by fire; and the fire will test each one's work, of what sort it is. [14]If anyone's work which he has built on *it* endures, he will receive a reward. [15]If anyone's work is burned, he will suffer loss; but he himself will be saved, yet so as through fire.

3:12 if anyone builds. This first refers to evangelists and pastors, and then to all believers who are called to build the church through faithful ministry. **gold, silver, precious stones.** These quality materials represent dedicated, spiritual service to build the church. **wood, hay, straw.** Inferior materials imply shallow activity with no eternal value. They do not imply evil activities.

[16]Do you not know that you are the temple of God and *that* the Spirit of God dwells in you? [17]If anyone defiles the temple of God, God will destroy him. For the temple of God is holy, which *temple* you are.

Avoid Worldly Wisdom

[18]Let no one deceive himself. If anyone among you seems to be wise in this age, let him become a fool that he may become wise. [19]For the wisdom of this world is foolishness with God. For it is written, *"He catches the wise in their own craftiness";*[a] [20]and again, *" The Lord knows the thoughts of the wise, that they are futile."*[a] [21]Therefore let no one boast in men. For all things are yours: [22]whether Paul or Apollos or Cephas, or the world or life or death, or things present or things to come—all are yours. [23]And you *are* Christ's, and Christ *is* God's.

Stewards of the Mysteries of God

4 Let a man so consider us, as servants of Christ and stewards of the mysteries of God. [2]Moreover it is required in stewards that one be found faithful. [3]But with me it is a very small thing that I should be judged by you or by a human court.[a] In fact, I do not even judge myself. [4]For I know of nothing against myself, yet I am not justified by this; but He who judges me is the Lord. [5]Therefore judge nothing before the time, until the Lord comes, who will both bring to light the hidden things of darkness and reveal the counsels of the hearts. Then each one's praise will come from God.

4:1 so consider us. Paul wanted everyone to view him and his fellow ministers as the humble messengers God had ordained them to be (see 3:9,22). **servants.** This word refers to the lowest galley slaves who rowed on the bottom tier of a ship (see Luke 1:2). **stewards.** Paul defines his responsibilities as an apostle by using a word originally referring to a person in charge of his master's entire household. **mysteries of God.** Here "mystery" is used to describe God's full revealed truth in the NT.

Fools for Christ's Sake

[6]Now these things, brethren, I have figuratively transferred to myself and Apollos for your sakes, that you may learn in us not to think beyond what is written, that none

of you may be puffed up on behalf of one against the other. [7]For who makes you differ *from another?* And what do you have that you did not receive? Now if you did indeed receive *it,* why do you boast as if you had not received *it?*

> **4:6 these things.** Paul was referring to the analogies he used to depict those who minister for the Lord, including himself and Apollos. **your sakes.** Paul's example of humility was meant to teach the believers not to exalt the apostles and preachers (see Gen. 18:27). **what is written.** God's servants are to be treated with respect only within the bounds of what is scriptural (1 Thess. 5:12). **puffed up.** Pride and arrogance were problems in the Corinthian church.

[8]You are already full! You are already rich! You have reigned as kings without us—and indeed I could wish you did reign, that we also might reign with you! [9]For I think that God has displayed us, the apostles, last, as men condemned to death; for we have been made a spectacle to the world, both to angels and to men. [10]We *are* fools for Christ's sake, but you *are* wise in Christ! We *are* weak, but you *are* strong! You *are* distinguished, but we *are* dishonored! [11]To the present hour we both hunger and thirst, and we are poorly clothed, and beaten, and homeless. [12]And we labor, working with our own hands. Being reviled, we bless; being persecuted, we endure; [13]being defamed, we entreat. We have been made as the filth of the world, the offscouring of all things until now.

> **4:13 filth...offscouring.** Paul used the scum and dregs scraped from a dirty dish or garbage pot—a description used for the most degraded criminals who were sacrificed in pagan sacrifices—to describe himself and his fellow preachers. This was a rebuke of the proud, carnal Corinthians who saw themselves at the top, while the humble apostle considered himself at the bottom.

Paul's Paternal Care

[14]I do not write these things to shame you, but as my beloved children I warn *you.* [15]For though you might have ten thousand instructors in Christ, yet *you do* not *have* many fathers; for in Christ Jesus I have be-

gotten you through the gospel. [16]Therefore I urge you, imitate me. [17]For this reason I have sent Timothy to you, who is my beloved and faithful son in the Lord, who will remind you of my ways in Christ, as I teach everywhere in every church.

[18]Now some are puffed up, as though I were not coming to you. [19]But I will come to you shortly, if the Lord wills, and I will know, not the word of those who are puffed up, but the power. [20]For the kingdom of God *is* not in word but in power. [21]What do you want? Shall I come to you with a rod, or in love and a spirit of gentleness?

Immorality Defiles the Church

5 It is actually reported *that there is* sexual immorality among you, and such sexual immorality as is not even named[a] among the Gentiles—that a man has his father's wife! [2]And you are puffed up, and have not rather mourned, that he who has done this deed might be taken away from among you. [3]For I indeed, as absent in body but present in spirit, have already judged (as though I were present) him who has so done this deed. [4]In the name of our Lord Jesus Christ, when you are gathered together, along with my spirit, with the power of our Lord Jesus Christ, [5]deliver such a one to Satan for the destruction of the flesh, that his spirit may be saved in the day of the Lord Jesus.[a]

[6]Your glorying *is* not good. Do you not know that a little leaven leavens the whole lump? [7]Therefore purge out the old leaven, that you may be a new lump, since you truly are unleavened. For indeed Christ, our Passover, was sacrificed for us.[a] [8]Therefore let us keep the feast, not with old leaven, nor with the leaven of malice and wickedness, but with the unleavened *bread* of sincerity and truth.

> **5:6 glorying.** This means "boasting." The Corinthian believers' proud sense of satisfaction had blinded them to their duty regarding blatant sin that was devastating the church. **leaven.** In Scripture, leaven usually represents evil influence (see Ex. 13:3,7; although in Matt. 13:33 it refers to the good influence of the kingdom of heaven). **whole lump.** Sin, if tolerated, will permeate and corrupt the whole local church.

5:1 [a]NU-Text omits *named.*   5:5 [a]NU-Text omits *Jesus.*   5:7 [a]NU-Text omits *for us.*

Immorality Must Be Judged

⁹I wrote to you in my epistle not to keep company with sexually immoral people. ¹⁰Yet I certainly *did* not *mean* with the sexually immoral people of this world, or with the covetous, or extortioners, or idolaters, since then you would need to go out of the world. ¹¹But now I have written to you not to keep company with anyone named a brother, who is sexually immoral, or covetous, or an idolater, or a reviler, or a drunkard, or an extortioner—not even to eat with such a person.

¹²For what *have* I *to do* with judging those also who are outside? Do you not judge those who are inside? ¹³But those who are outside God judges. Therefore *"put away from yourselves the evil person."*ᵃ

Do Not Sue the Brethren

6 Dare any of you, having a matter against another, go to law before the unrighteous, and not before the saints? ²Do you not know that the saints will judge the world? And if the world will be judged by you, are you unworthy to judge the smallest matters? ³Do you not know that we shall judge angels? How much more, things that pertain to this life? ⁴If then you have judgments concerning things pertaining to this life, do you appoint those who are least esteemed by the church to judge? ⁵I say this to your shame. Is it so, that there is not a wise man among you, not even one, who will be able to judge between his brethren?

6:4 When Christians have earthly quarrels and disputes among themselves, it is inconceivable that they would turn to those least qualified (unbelievers) to resolve the matters. The most legally untrained believers, who know the Word of God and are obedient to the Spirit, are far more competent to settle disagreements between believers than the most experienced unbeliever.

⁶But brother goes to law against brother, and that before unbelievers!

⁷Now therefore, it is already an utter failure for you that you go to law against one another. Why do you not rather accept wrong? Why do you not rather *let yourselves* be cheated? ⁸No, you yourselves do wrong and cheat, and *you do* these things *to your* brethren! ⁹Do you not know that the unrighteous will not inherit the kingdom of God? Do not be deceived. Neither fornicators, nor idolaters, nor adulterers, nor homosexuals,ᵃ nor sodomites, ¹⁰nor thieves, nor covetous, nor drunkards, nor revilers, nor extortioners will inherit the kingdom of God. ¹¹And such were some of

6:9 not inherit the kingdom. The kingdom of God is the spiritual sphere of salvation where God rules as King over all who belong to Him by faith. All believers are in that spiritual kingdom, yet are waiting to enter into the full inheritance of it in the age to come. People who are characterized by these iniquities are not saved. Believers can and do commit these sins, but they resent their sins and seek to gain victory over them (see Rom. 7:14–25).

5:13 ᵃDeuteronomy 17:7; 19:19; 22:21,24; 24:7   6:9 ᵃThat is, catamites

---

What factors made it difficult for the gospel to take root in a healthy way in the city of Corinth?

The mindset of the Corinthians made it almost impossible for the church to fully break with the surrounding culture. The congregation continually behaved in a factional way, showing its carnality and immaturity. After the gifted Apollos had ministered in the church for a while, some of his admirers established a clique that had little to do with the rest of the church. Another group, loyal to Paul, developed; another claimed special allegiance to Peter (Cephas), and still another to Christ alone (1:10–13; 3:1–9). Instead of the church having a significant impact on the city, the city had too much impact on the church.

Paul knew that this church would never become a faithful witness for Christ until they understood that those who claimed church participation but who continued to be disobedient and unrepentant before God must be removed from the local body (5:9–13). The Corinthians seem to have been unwilling to pay the price of obedience.

you. But you were washed, but you were sanctified, but you were justified in the name of the Lord Jesus and by the Spirit of our God.

Glorify God in Body and Spirit

[12]All things are lawful for me, but all things are not helpful. All things are lawful for me, but I will not be brought under the power of any. [13]Foods for the stomach and the stomach for foods, but God will destroy both it and them. Now the body *is* not for sexual immorality but for the Lord, and the Lord for the body. [14]And God both raised up the Lord and will also raise us up by His power.

[15]Do you not know that your bodies are members of Christ? Shall I then take the members of Christ and make *them* members of a harlot? Certainly not! [16]Or do you not know that he who is joined to a harlot is one body *with her?* For "the two," He says, "*shall become one flesh.*"[a] [17]But he who is joined to the Lord is one spirit *with Him.*

[18]Flee sexual immorality. Every sin that a man does is outside the body, but he who commits sexual immorality sins against his own body. [19]Or do you not know that your body is the temple of the Holy Spirit *who is* in you, whom you have from God, and you are not your own? [20]For you were bought at a price; therefore glorify God in your body[a] and in your spirit, which are God's.

> **6:18 Every sin…is outside.** Sexual sin destroys a person like no other sin because it is so intimate and entangling, corrupting on the deepest human level. No sin has greater potential to destroy the body. Paul is probably alluding here to venereal disease, which was prevalent in his day, just as it is today.

Principles of Marriage

7 Now concerning the things of which you wrote to me:

It is good for a man not to touch a woman. [2]Nevertheless, because of sexual immorality, let each man have his own wife, and let each woman have her own husband. [3]Let the husband render to his wife the affection due her, and likewise also the wife

to her husband. [4]The wife does not have authority over her own body, but the husband *does.* And likewise the husband does not have authority over his own body, but the wife *does.* [5]Do not deprive one another except with consent for a time, that you may give yourselves to fasting and prayer; and come together again so that Satan does not tempt you because of your lack of self-control. [6]But I say this as a concession, not as a commandment. [7]For I wish that all men were even as I myself. But each one has his own gift from God, one in this manner and another in that.

> **7:5 deprive.** This command may indicate that deprivation was going on among believing spouses as a reaction to the sexual sins of their past and the desire to leave all that behind. Paul said that husbands and wives could abstain temporarily from sexual activity, but only when they mutually agree to do so as part of their fasting. **so that Satan does not tempt.** After the agreed-upon time of abstinence, sexual desires intensify, and a spouse becomes more vulnerable to sinful desire (see 1 Thess. 3:5).

[8]But I say to the unmarried and to the widows: It is good for them if they remain even as I am; [9]but if they cannot exercise self-control, let them marry. For it is better to marry than to burn *with passion.*

Keep Your Marriage Vows

[10]Now to the married I command, *yet* not I but the Lord: A wife is not to depart from *her* husband. [11]But even if she does depart, let her remain unmarried or be reconciled to *her* husband. And a husband is not to divorce *his* wife.

[12]But to the rest I, not the Lord, say: If any brother has a wife who does not believe, and she is willing to live with him, let him not divorce her. [13]And a woman who has a husband who does not believe, if he is willing to live with her, let her not divorce him. [14]For the unbelieving husband is sanctified by the wife, and the unbelieving wife is sanctified by the husband; otherwise your children would be unclean, but now they are holy. [15]But if the unbeliever departs, let him depart; a brother or a sister is not under bondage in such *cases.* But God has called us to peace. [16]For how do you

6:16 [a]Genesis 2:24   6:20 [a]NU-Text ends the verse at *body.*

7:15 let him depart. This refers to divorce. When an unbelieving spouse cannot tolerate the partner's faith and wants a divorce, it is best to let it happen to preserve peace in the family (see Rom. 12:18). The bond of marriage is broken only by death (Rom. 7:2), adultery (Matt. 19:9), or an unbeliever's leaving. **not under bondage.** When a bond is broken in any of those ways, a Christian is free to marry another believer.

know, O wife, whether you will save *your* husband? Or how do you know, O husband, whether you will save *your* wife?

Live as You Are Called

[17]But as God has distributed to each one, as the Lord has called each one, so let him walk. And so I ordain in all the churches. [18]Was anyone called while circumcised? Let him not become uncircumcised. Was anyone called while uncircumcised? Let him not be circumcised. [19]Circumcision is noth-

ing and uncircumcision is nothing, but keeping the commandments of God *is what matters*. [20]Let each one remain in the same calling in which he was called. [21]Were you called *while* a slave? Do not be concerned about it; but if you can be made free, rather use *it.* [22]For he who is called in the Lord *while* a slave is the Lord's freedman. Likewise he who is called *while* free is Christ's slave. [23]You were bought at a price; do not become slaves of men. [24]Brethren, let each one remain with God in that *state* in which he was called.

To the Unmarried and Widows

[25]Now concerning virgins: I have no commandment from the Lord; yet I give judgment as one whom the Lord in His mercy *has made* trustworthy. [26]I suppose therefore that this is good because of the present distress—that *it is* good for a man to remain as he is; [27]Are you bound to a wife? Do not

---

How does Paul address the issue of divorce for the Corinthian church?

Paul taught about divorce in the context of answering a number of questions that the church had sent to him. The first of those questions had to do with marriage, an area of trouble due to the moral corruption of the surrounding culture that tolerated fornication, adultery, homosexuality, polygamy, and concubinage.

The apostle reminded the believers that his teaching was based on what Jesus had already made clear during His earthly ministry (Matthew 5:31,32; 19:5–8). Jesus Himself based His teaching on the previously revealed Word of God (Genesis 2:24; Malachi 2:16).

Paul's departure point for teaching affirmed God's prohibition of divorce. He wrote that in cases where a Christian has already divorced another Christian except for adultery (7:10,11), neither partner is free to marry another person. They should reconcile or at least remain unmarried.

Paul then added some helpful direction on the issue of marital conflicts created in cases where one spouse becomes a believer (7:12–16). First, the believing spouse lives under orders to make the best of the marriage, seeking to win his or her spouse to Christ. If the unbelieving spouse decides to end the marriage, Paul's response is "let him depart" (7:15). This term refers to divorce (7:10,11). When an unbelieving spouse cannot tolerate the partner's faith and wants a divorce, it is best to let that happen in order to preserve peace in the family (Romans 12:18). Therefore, the bond of marriage is broken only by death (Romans 7:2), adultery (Matthew 19:9), or an unbeliever's departure.

When the bond of marriage is broken in any of those ways, a Christian is free to marry another believer (7:15). Throughout Scripture, whenever legitimate divorce occurs, remarriage is an assumed option. When divorce is permitted, so is remarriage.

In general, conversion and obedience to Christ should lead us to greater faithfulness and commitment in every relationship. This extended passage (7:1–24) plainly repeats the basic principle that Christians should willingly accept the marital condition and social situations into which God has placed them and be content to serve Him there until He leads them elsewhere.

seek to be loosed. Are you loosed from a wife? Do not seek a wife. ²⁸But even if you do marry, you have not sinned; and if a virgin marries, she has not sinned. Nevertheless such will have trouble in the flesh, but I would spare you.

> **7:28 marry, you have not sinned.** Marriage is a fully legitimate and godly option for both the divorced (on biblical grounds) and virgins. **trouble in the flesh.** "Trouble" means "pressed together" or "under pressure." Marriage involves many conflicts and adjustments that singleness does not. Marriage presses two fallen people into intimate life that leads to inevitable trouble. The troubles of singleness may be exceeded by the conflicts of marriage.

²⁹But this I say, brethren, the time *is* short, so that from now on even those who have wives should be as though they had none, ³⁰those who weep as though they did not weep, those who rejoice as though they did not rejoice, those who buy as though they did not possess, ³¹and those who use this world as not misusing *it.* For the form of this world is passing away.

³²But I want you to be without care. He who is unmarried cares for the things of the Lord—how he may please the Lord. ³³But he who is married cares about the things of the world—how he may please *his* wife. ³⁴There is*ᵃ* a difference between a wife and a virgin. The unmarried woman cares about the things of the Lord, that she may be holy both in body and in spirit. But she who is married cares about the things of the world—how she may please *her* husband. ³⁵And this I say for your own profit, not that I may put a leash on you, but for what is proper, and that you may serve the Lord without distraction.

³⁶But if any man thinks he is behaving improperly toward his virgin, if she is past the flower of youth, and thus it must be, let

> **7:36 his virgin.** This refers to a man's daughter. In Corinth, some of the fathers, intending devotion to God, dedicated their young daughters to the Lord as permanent virgins. **past the flower of youth.** This refers to a mature woman capable of child-bearing. **it must be.** When daughters became of marriageable age and insisted on being married, their fathers were free to break the vow and let them marry.

him do what he wishes. He does not sin; let them marry. ³⁷Nevertheless he who stands steadfast in his heart, having no necessity, but has power over his own will, and has so determined in his heart that he will keep his virgin,*ᵃ* does well. ³⁸So then he who gives *herᵃ* in marriage does well, but he who does not give *her* in marriage does better.

³⁹A wife is bound by law as long as her husband lives; but if her husband dies, she is at liberty to be married to whom she wishes, only in the Lord. ⁴⁰But she is happier if she remains as she is, according to my judgment—and I think I also have the Spirit of God.

Be Sensitive to Conscience

8 Now concerning things offered to idols: We know that we all have knowledge. Knowledge puffs up, but love edifies. ²And if anyone thinks that he knows anything, he knows nothing yet as he ought to know. ³But if anyone loves God, this one is known by Him.

> **8:1 things offered to idols.** The Greeks and Romans worshiped many gods and believed in many evil spirits. They believed evil spirits invaded human beings by attaching themselves to food and that they could only be removed by sacrificing the food to a god. The food which was not burned was served at pagan feasts and sold in the market. After conversion, believers resented eating such food bought in the markets.

⁴Therefore concerning the eating of things offered to idols, we know that an idol *is* nothing in the world, and that *there is* no other God but one. ⁵For even if there are so-called gods, whether in heaven or on earth (as there are many gods and many lords), ⁶yet for us *there is* one God, the Father, of whom *are* all things, and we for Him; and one Lord Jesus Christ, through whom *are* all things, and through whom we *live.*

⁷However, *there is* not in everyone that knowledge; for some, with consciousness of the idol, until now eat *it* as a thing offered to an idol; and their conscience, being weak, is defiled. ⁸But food does not com-

---

7:34 *ᵃ*M-Text adds *also.*   7:37 *ᵃ*Or *virgin daughter*   7:38 *ᵃ*NU-Text reads *his own virgin.*

mend us to God; for neither if we eat are we the better, nor if we do not eat are we the worse.

⁹But beware lest somehow this liberty of yours become a stumbling block to those who are weak. ¹⁰For if anyone sees you who have knowledge eating in an idol's temple, will not the conscience of him who is weak be emboldened to eat those things offered to idols? ¹¹And because of your knowledge shall the weak brother perish, for whom Christ died? ¹²But when you thus sin against the brethren, and wound their weak conscience, you sin against Christ. ¹³Therefore, if food makes my brother stumble, I will never again eat meat, lest I make my brother stumble.

A Pattern of Self-Denial

9 Am I not an apostle? Am I not free? Have I not seen Jesus Christ our Lord? Are you not my work in the Lord? ²If I am not an apostle to others, yet doubtless I am to you. For you are the seal of my apostleship in the Lord.

³My defense to those who examine me is this: ⁴Do we have no right to eat and drink? ⁵Do we have no right to take along a believing wife, as do also the other apostles, the brothers of the Lord, and Cephas? ⁶Or is it only Barnabas and I who have no right to refrain from working? ⁷Who ever goes to war at his own expense? Who plants a vineyard and does not eat of its fruit? Or who tends a flock and does not drink of the milk of the flock?

> **9:6 working.** Paul, a tentmaker (Acts 18:3), let the Corinthians know that he and Barnabas had as much right as others to receive full financial support from their work. They paid their own expenses voluntarily, but accepted help from a few churches (Phil. 4:15,16).

⁸Do I say these things as a *mere* man? Or does not the law say the same also? ⁹For it is written in the law of Moses, *"You shall not muzzle an ox while it treads out the grain."ᵃ* Is it oxen God is concerned about? ¹⁰Or does He say *it* altogether for our sakes? For our sakes, no doubt, *this* is written, that

he who plows should plow in hope, and he who threshes in hope should be partaker of his hope. ¹¹If we have sown spiritual things for you, *is it* a great thing if we reap your material things? ¹²If others are partakers of *this* right over you, *are* we not even more? Nevertheless we have not used this right, but endure all things lest we hinder the gospel of Christ. ¹³Do you not know that those who minister the holy things eat *of the things* of the temple, and those who serve at the altar partake of *the offerings of* the altar? ¹⁴Even so the Lord has commanded that those who preach the gospel should live from the gospel.

¹⁵But I have used none of these things, nor have I written these things that it should be done so to me; for it *would be* better for me to die than that anyone should make my boasting void. ¹⁶For if I preach the gospel, I have nothing to boast of, for necessity is laid upon me; yes, woe is me if I do not preach the gospel! ¹⁷For if I do this willingly, I have a reward; but if against my will, I have been entrusted with a stewardship. ¹⁸What is my reward then? That when I preach the gospel, I may present the gospel of Christᵃ without charge, that I may not abuse my authority in the gospel.

> **9:15 none of these things.** This refers to the 6 reasons given in vv. 1–14 that include Paul's right to financial support. **nor have I written.** He did not want the Corinthians to feel obligated to pay him (2 Cor. 11:8,9). **better...to die.** He would rather die than have anyone think he ministered with a financial motive (see Acts 20:33–35). **make my boasting void.** "Boast" refers to sincere joy, not pride (see Rom. 15:17). Paul was genuinely overjoyed for the privilege of serving the Lord and did not want material support to rob him of it in any way.

Serving All Men

¹⁹For though I am free from all *men*, I have made myself a servant to all, that I might win the more; ²⁰and to the Jews I became as a Jew, that I might win Jews; to those *who are* under the law, as under the law,ᵃ that I might win those *who are* under the law; ²¹to those *who are* without law, as without law (not being without law toward God,ᵃ but under law toward Christᵇ), that I

9:9 ᵃDeuteronomy 25:4   9:18 ᵃNU-Text omits *of Christ.*   9:20 ᵃNU-Text adds *though not being myself under the law.*   9:21 ᵃNU-Text reads *God's law.*   ᵇNU-Text reads *Christ's law.*

might win those *who are* without law; [22]to the weak I became as[a] weak, that I might win the weak. I have become all things to all *men*, that I might by all means save some. [23]Now this I do for the gospel's sake, that I may be partaker of it with *you*.

> **9:22 weak.** He stooped to make the gospel clear to the Corinthians who had a lower level of comprehension. **all things...all means.** Paul would not change Scripture or compromise the truth; in order not to offend the Jew, Gentile, or those weak in understanding, however, he would condescend in ways that could lead to salvation.

Striving for a Crown

[24]Do you not know that those who run in a race all run, but one receives the prize? Run in such a way that you may obtain *it*. [25]And everyone who competes *for the prize* is temperate in all things. Now they *do it* to obtain a perishable crown, but we *for* an imperishable *crown*. [26]Therefore I run thus: not with uncertainty. Thus I fight: not as *one who* beats the air. [27]But I discipline my body and bring *it* into subjection, lest, when I have preached to others, I myself should become disqualified.

> **9:27 discipline.** This comes from a term that means to hit under the eye. Paul knocked out the bodily impulses to keep them from preventing him from his mission of winning souls to Christ. **disqualified.** This metaphor from the athletic games refers to a contestant who failed to meet basic training requirements. Paul may have been referring to fleshly sins that disqualify a man from preaching and leading the church.

Old Testament Examples

10 Moreover, brethren, I do not want you to be unaware that all our fathers were under the cloud, all passed through the sea, [2]all were baptized into Moses in the cloud and in the sea, [3]all ate the same spiritual food, [4]and all drank the same spiritual drink. For they drank of that spiritual Rock that followed them, and that Rock was Christ. [5]But with most of them God was not well pleased, for *their bodies* were scattered in the wilderness.

[6]Now these things became our examples, to the intent that we should not lust after evil things as they also lusted. [7]And do not become idolaters as *were* some of them. As it is written, " *The people sat down to eat and drink, and rose up to play.*"[a] [8]Nor let us commit sexual immorality, as some of them did, and in one day twenty-three thousand fell; [9]nor let us tempt Christ, as some of them also tempted, and were destroyed by serpents; [10]nor complain, as some of them also complained, and were destroyed by the destroyer. [11]Now all[a] these things happened to them as examples, and they were written for our admonition, upon whom the ends of the ages have come.

[12]Therefore let him who thinks he stands take heed lest he fall. [13]No temptation has overtaken you except such as is common to man; but God *is* faithful, who will not allow you to be tempted beyond what you are able, but with the temptation will also make the way of escape, that you may be able to bear *it*.

Flee from Idolatry

[14]Therefore, my beloved, flee from idolatry. [15]I speak as to wise men; judge for yourselves what I say. [16]The cup of blessing which we bless, is it not the communion of the blood of Christ? The bread which we break, is it not the communion of the body of Christ? [17]For we, *though* many, are one bread *and* one body; for we all partake of that one bread.

> **10:16 communion.** This means "to have in common, to participate, and have partnership with" (see 2 Cor. 8:4). Commemorating the Lord's Supper was a regular and cherished practice in the early church, by which believers remembered their Savior's death and celebrated their common salvation and eternal life.

[18]Observe Israel after the flesh: Are not those who eat of the sacrifices partakers of the altar? [19]What am I saying then? That an idol is anything, or what is offered to idols is anything? [20]Rather, that the things which the Gentiles sacrifice they sacrifice to demons and not to God, and I do not want you to have fellowship with demons. [21]You cannot drink the cup of the Lord and the

---

9:22 [a]NU-Text omits *as*. 10:7 [a]Exodus 32:6 10:11 [a]NU-Text omits *all*.

cup of demons; you cannot partake of the Lord's table and of the table of demons. ²²Or do we provoke the Lord to jealousy? Are we stronger than He?

All to the Glory of God

²³All things are lawful for me,ᵃ but not all things are helpful; all things are lawful for me,ᵇ but not all things edify. ²⁴Let no one seek his own, but each one the other's *well-being.*

²⁵Eat whatever is sold in the meat market, asking no questions for conscience' sake; ²⁶for *"the earth is the Lord's, and all its fullness."* ᵃ

²⁷If any of those who do not believe invites you *to dinner,* and you desire to go, eat whatever is set before you, asking no question for conscience' sake. ²⁸But if anyone says to you, "This was offered to idols," do not eat it for the sake of the one who told you, and for conscience' sake;ᵃ for *"the earth is the Lord's, and all its fullness."* ᵇ ²⁹"Conscience," I say, not your own, but that of the other. For why is my liberty judged by another *man's* conscience? ³⁰But if I partake with thanks, why am I evil spoken of for *the food* over which I give thanks?

³¹Therefore, whether you eat or drink, or whatever you do, do all to the glory of God. ³²Give no offense, either to the Jews or to the Greeks or to the church of God, ³³just as I also please all *men* in all *things,* not seeking my own profit, but the *profit* of many, that they may be saved.

11 Imitate me, just as I also *imitate* Christ.

Head Coverings

²Now I praise you, brethren, that you remember me in all things and keep the traditions just as I delivered *them* to you. ³But I want you to know that the head of every man is Christ, the head of woman *is* man, and the head of Christ *is* God. ⁴Every man praying or prophesying, having *his* head covered, dishonors his head. ⁵But every woman who prays or prophesies with *her* head uncovered dishonors her head, for that is one and the same as if her head were

> **11:5 woman who prays or prophesies.** Women are not to lead or speak in services of the church (see 1 Tim. 2:12). They may pray and proclaim the truth to unbelievers and teach children and other women (see 1 Tim. 5:16) while maintaining a proper distinction from men. **uncovered.** In Corinth, a woman covered her head while ministering to signify a subordinate relationship to her husband. There is nothing spiritual about wearing or not wearing a covering. Symbols of male and female roles are to be genuinely honored in every culture.

shaved. ⁶For if a woman is not covered, let her also be shorn. But if it is shameful for a woman to be shorn or shaved, let her be covered. ⁷For a man indeed ought not to cover *his* head, since he is the image and glory of God; but woman is the glory of man. ⁸For man is not from woman, but woman from man. ⁹Nor was man created for the woman, but woman for the man. ¹⁰For this reason the woman ought to have *a symbol of* authority on *her* head, because of the angels. ¹¹Nevertheless, neither *is* man independent of woman, nor woman independent of man, in the Lord. ¹²For as woman *came* from man, even so man also *comes* through woman; but all things are from God.

¹³Judge among yourselves. Is it proper for a woman to pray to God with her head uncovered? ¹⁴Does not even nature itself teach you that if a man has long hair, it is a dishonor to him? ¹⁵But if a woman has long hair, it is a glory to her; for *her* hair is given to herᵃ for a covering. ¹⁶But if anyone seems to be contentious, we have no such custom, nor *do* the churches of God.

> **11:17–34** The early church love feasts (see Jude 12) usually closed with observance of the Lord's Supper. The worldly Corinthian church had turned those sacred meals into gluttonous, drunken revelries (see 2 Pet. 2:13). Wealthy believers brought food and drink for themselves but refused to share, letting their poorer brethren go away hungry.

Conduct at the Lord's Supper

¹⁷Now in giving these instructions I do not praise *you,* since you come together not for the better but for the worse. ¹⁸For first of

---

10:23 ᵃNU-Text omits *for me.* ᵇNU-Text omits *for me.*   10:26 ᵃPsalm 24:1   10:28 ᵃNU-Text omits the rest of this verse. ᵇPsalm 24:1   11:15 ᵃM-Text omits *to her.*

all, when you come together as a church, I hear that there are divisions among you, and in part I believe it. ¹⁹For there must also be factions among you, that those who are approved may be recognized among you. ²⁰Therefore when you come together in one place, it is not to eat the Lord's Supper. ²¹For in eating, each one takes his own supper ahead of *others*; and one is hungry and another is drunk. ²²What! Do you not have houses to eat and drink in? Or do you despise the church of God and shame those who have nothing? What shall I say to you? Shall I praise you in this? I do not praise *you*.

Institution of the Lord's Supper

²³For I received from the Lord that which I also delivered to you: that the Lord Jesus on the *same* night in which He was betrayed took bread; ²⁴and when He had given thanks, He broke *it* and said, "Take, eat;ᵃ this is My body which is brokenᵇ for you; do this in remembrance of Me." ²⁵In the same manner *He* also *took* the cup after supper, saying, "This cup is the new covenant in My blood. This do, as often as you drink *it*, in remembrance of Me."

> **11:25 new covenant in My blood.** The Old Covenant was practiced repeatedly by men shedding the blood of animals as atonement for their sins; the New Covenant has been ratified once and for all by the death of Christ (see Heb. 9:28). **in remembrance of Me.** Jesus transformed the third cup of the Passover into the cup of remembrance of His offering.

²⁶For as often as you eat this bread and drink this cup, you proclaim the Lord's death till He comes.

Examine Yourself

²⁷Therefore whoever eats this bread or drinks *this* cup of the Lord in an unworthy manner will be guilty of the body and bloodᵃ of the Lord. ²⁸But let a man examine himself, and so let him eat of the bread and drink of the cup. ²⁹For he who eats and drinks in an unworthy mannerᵃ eats and drinks judgment to himself, not discerning the

Lord'sᵇ body. ³⁰For this reason many *are* weak and sick among you, and many sleep. ³¹For if we would judge ourselves, we would not be judged. ³²But when we are judged, we

> **11:30 sleep.** This means "are dead." The offense was so serious that God put the worst offenders to death, an extreme but effective form of church purification (see Luke 13:1–5).

are chastened by the Lord, that we may not be condemned with the world.

³³Therefore, my brethren, when you come together to eat, wait for one another. ³⁴But if anyone is hungry, let him eat at home, lest you come together for judgment. And the rest I will set in order when I come.

Spiritual Gifts: Unity in Diversity

12 Now concerning spiritual *gifts*, brethren, I do not want you to be ignorant: ²You know thatᵃ you were Gentiles, carried away to these dumb idols, however you were led. ³Therefore I make known to you that no one speaking by the Spirit of God calls Jesus accursed, and no one can say that Jesus is Lord except by the Holy Spirit.

⁴There are diversities of gifts, but the same Spirit. ⁵There are differences of ministries, but the same Lord. ⁶And there are diversities of activities, but it is the same God who works all in all. ⁷But the manifestation of the Spirit is given to each one for the profit *of all:* ⁸for to one is given the word of wisdom through the Spirit, to another the word of knowledge through the same Spirit, ⁹to another faith by the same Spirit, to another gifts of healings by the sameᵃ

> **12:4 gifts.** These gifts are sovereignly and supernaturally bestowed by the Holy Spirit on all believers, enabling them to spiritually edify each other effectively and honor the Lord. The gifts fall into two categories: speaking and serving (see Rom. 12:6–8). These are permanent gifts that will operate throughout the church age. Miracles, healing, languages, and the interpretation of languages were temporary sign gifts limited to the apostolic age and have, therefore, ceased.

11:24 ᵃNU-Text omits *Take, eat.* ᵇNU-Text omits *broken.* 11:27 ᵃNU-Text and M-Text read *the blood.* 11:29 ᵃNU-Text omits *in an unworthy manner.* ᵇNU-Text omits *Lord's.* 12:2 ᵃNU-Text and M-Text add *when.* 12:9 ᵃNU-Text reads *one.*

Spirit, ¹⁰to another the working of miracles, to another prophecy, to another discerning of spirits, to another *different* kinds of tongues, to another the interpretation of tongues. ¹¹But one and the same Spirit works all these things, distributing to each one individually as He wills.

Unity and Diversity in One Body

¹²For as the body is one and has many members, but all the members of that one body, being many, are one body, so also *is* Christ. ¹³For by one Spirit we were all bap-

> **12:13 baptized.** The church is formed as believers are immersed by Christ with the Holy Spirit. Christ is the baptizer who immerses each believer with the Spirit into unity with all other believers. Paul was not writing of water baptism, which depicts the believer's union with Christ in His death and resurrection. He is emphasizing the unity of believers. Believers have all been Spirit-baptized, and thus are all in one body.

tized into one body—whether Jews or Greeks, whether slaves or free—and have all been made to drink into*ᵃ* one Spirit. ¹⁴For in fact the body is not one member but many.

¹⁵If the foot should say, "Because I am not a hand, I am not of the body," is it therefore not of the body? ¹⁶And if the ear should say, "Because I am not an eye, I am not of the body," is it therefore not of the body? ¹⁷If the whole body *were* an eye, where *would be* the hearing? If the whole *were* hearing, where *would be* the smelling? ¹⁸But now God has set the members, each one of them, in the body just as He pleased. ¹⁹And if they *were* all one member, where *would* the body *be?*

²⁰But now indeed *there are* many members, yet one body. ²¹And the eye cannot say to the hand, "I have no need of you"; nor again the head to the feet, "I have no need of you." ²²No, much rather, those members of the body which seem to be weaker are

12:13 *ᵃ*NU-Text omits *into.*

How does Paul's teaching in 1 Corinthians help resolve the controversy over the sign gifts discussed in chapters 12–14?

Three chapters in this letter are devoted to the subject of spiritual gifts in the church. Paul knew that the subject was controversial but vital to a healthy church. The atmosphere of false religions that abounded in Corinth caused counterfeit spiritual manifestations that had to be confronted. Paul informed the church and challenged the believers in Corinth to regulate their behavior by the truth and the Spirit.

The categories of giftedness in these verses do not refer to natural talents, skills, or abilities. Believers and unbelievers alike possess such resources. No, these gifts are sovereignly and supernaturally bestowed by the Holy Spirit on all believers (12:7,11), enabling them to spiritually edify each other effectively and thus honor the Lord.

The varieties of spiritual gifts fall roughly into two general types: (1) speaking gifts, and (2) serving gifts (12:8–10; Romans 12:6–8; 1 Peter 4:10,11). The speaking or verbal gifts (prophecy, knowledge, wisdom, teaching, and exhortation) and the serving, nonverbal gifts (leadership, helps, giving, mercy, faith, and discernment) are all permanent and will operate throughout the church age. Their purpose is to build up the church and glorify God. The list here and in Romans 12:3–8 is best seen as representative of categories of giftedness from which the Holy Spirit draws to give each believer whatever kind or combination of kinds He chooses (12:11). Some believers may be gifted in similar ways to others but are personally unique because the Spirit suits each grace gift to the individual.

A special category made up of miracles, healing, languages, and the interpretation of languages, served as a set of temporary sign gifts limited to the apostolic age and have, therefore, ceased. Their purpose was to authenticate the apostles and their message as the true Word of God. Once God's Word was complete and became self-authenticating, they were no longer required.

necessary. ²³And those *members* of the body which we think to be less honorable, on these we bestow greater honor; and our unpresentable *parts* have greater modesty, ²⁴but our presentable *parts* have no need. But God composed the body, having given greater honor to that *part* which lacks it, ²⁵that there should be no schism in the body, but *that* the members should have the same care for one another. ²⁶And if one member suffers, all the members suffer with *it*; or if one member is honored, all the members rejoice with *it*.

> **12:21 no need.** Some in Corinth were complaining of not having public gifts, while those who had them were belittling those with the less prominent gifts. The "eye" and "head" represent the people with public gifts. They were indifferent and self-sufficient, disdaining those whom they perceived as less gifted and less significant.

²⁷Now you are the body of Christ, and members individually. ²⁸And God has appointed these in the church: first apostles, second prophets, third teachers, after that miracles, then gifts of healings, helps, administrations, varieties of tongues. ²⁹*Are* all apostles? *Are* all prophets? *Are* all teachers? *Are* all workers of miracles? ³⁰Do all have gifts of healings? Do all speak with tongues? Do all interpret? ³¹But earnestly desire the best*ᵃ* gifts. And yet I show you a more excellent way.

> **13:1–13** Spiritual gifts and right doctrine were present in Corinth, but love was absent. This led to quarrels, selfishness, and pride within the church, especially in the area of spiritual gifts. Believers should love each other instead of selfishly desiring showy spiritual gifts. **love.** Self-giving love is more concerned with giving than receiving (see Matt. 5:44,45). Unless the Corinthians' speech was done with love, it was no better than the gibberish of pagan ritual.

The Greatest Gift

13 Though I speak with the tongues of men and of angels, but have not love, I have become sounding brass or a clanging cymbal. ²And though I have *the gift of* prophecy, and understand all mysteries and all knowledge, and though I have all faith, so that I could remove mountains, but have not love, I am nothing. ³And though I bestow all my goods to feed *the poor*, and though I give my body to be burned,*ᵃ* but have not love, it profits me nothing.

⁴Love suffers long *and* is kind; love does not envy; love does not parade itself, is not puffed up; ⁵does not behave rudely, does not seek its own, is not provoked, thinks no evil; ⁶does not rejoice in iniquity, but rejoices in the truth; ⁷bears all things, believes all things, hopes all things, endures all things.

⁸Love never fails. But whether *there are* prophecies, they will fail; whether *there are* tongues, they will cease; whether *there is* knowledge, it will vanish away. ⁹For we know in part and we prophesy in part. ¹⁰But when that which is perfect has come, then that which is in part will be done away.

¹¹When I was a child, I spoke as a child, I understood as a child, I thought as a child; but when I became a man, I put away childish things. ¹²For now we see in a mirror, dimly, but then face to face. Now I know in part, but then I shall know just as I also am known.

¹³And now abide faith, hope, love, these three; but the greatest of these *is* love.

> **13:13 love.** The objects of faith and hope will be fulfilled and perfectly realized in heaven, but love, the God-like virtue, is everlasting (see 1 John 4:8). Heaven will be the place for the expression of nothing but perfect love toward God and each other.

Prophecy and Tongues

14 Pursue love, and desire spiritual *gifts*, but especially that you may prophesy. ²For he who speaks in a tongue does not speak to men but to God, for no one understands *him*; however, in the spirit he speaks mysteries. ³But he who prophesies speaks edification and exhortation and comfort to men. ⁴He who speaks in a tongue edifies himself, but he who prophesies edifies the church. ⁵I wish you all spoke with tongues, but even more that you prophesied; for*ᵃ* he who prophesies *is* greater than he who speaks with tongues, unless indeed he interprets, that the church may receive edification.

12:31 *ᵃ*NU-Text reads *greater.*   13:3 *ᵃ*NU-Text reads *so I may boast.*   14:5 *ᵃ*NU-Text reads *and.*

Tongues Must Be Interpreted

[6]But now, brethren, if I come to you speaking with tongues, what shall I profit you unless I speak to you either by revelation, by knowledge, by prophesying, or by teaching? [7]Even things without life, whether flute or harp, when they make a sound, unless they make a distinction in the sounds, how will it be known what is piped or played? [8]For if the trumpet makes an uncertain sound, who will prepare for battle? [9]So likewise you, unless you utter by the tongue words easy to understand, how will it be known what is spoken? For you will be speaking into the air. [10]There are, it may be, so many kinds of languages in the world, and none of them *is* without significance. [11]Therefore, if I do not know the meaning of the language, I shall be a foreigner to him who speaks, and he who speaks *will be* a foreigner to me. [12]Even so you, since you are zealous for spiritual *gifts, let it be* for the edification of the church *that* you seek to excel.

14:6 if I come to you...what shall I profit? An apostle who spoke in tongues did not spiritually benefit a congregation unless his words were interpreted so that they could be understood clearly. This gift could not be used privately because it was a sign to unbelievers; it must have a translator to have meaning, and it must edify the church.

[13]Therefore let him who speaks in a tongue pray that he may interpret. [14]For if I pray in a tongue, my spirit prays, but my understanding is unfruitful. [15]What is *the conclusion* then? I will pray with the spirit, and I will also pray with the understanding. I will sing with the spirit, and I will also sing with the understanding. [16]Otherwise, if you bless with the spirit, how will he who occupies the place of the uninformed say "Amen" at your giving of thanks, since he does not understand what you say? [17]For you indeed give thanks well, but the other is not edified.

[18]I thank my God I speak with tongues more than you all; [19]yet in the church I would rather speak five words with my understanding, that I may teach others also, than ten thousand words in a tongue.

14:20–25 This passage deals with the gift of languages. Such speaking was not something given to all believers, it was not connected to the baptism with the Holy Spirit, and it was not a sign of superior spirituality. Because of the corruption of the real gift by the Corinthians, Paul gave the principles for its proper and limited operation as a sign.

Tongues a Sign to Unbelievers

[20]Brethren, do not be children in understanding; however, in malice be babes, but in understanding be mature.

[21]In the law it is written:

> "With men of other tongues and other
>   lips
> I will speak to this people;
> And yet, for all that, they will not hear
>   Me," [a]

says the Lord.

[22]Therefore tongues are for a sign, not to those who believe but to unbelievers; but prophesying is not for unbelievers but for those who believe. [23]Therefore if the whole church comes together in one place, and all speak with tongues, and there come in *those who are* uninformed or unbelievers, will they not say that you are out of your mind? [24]But if all prophesy, and an unbeliever or an uninformed person comes in, he is convinced by all, he is convicted by all. [25]And thus[a] the secrets of his heart are revealed; and so, falling down on *his* face, he will worship God and report that God is truly among you.

Order in Church Meetings

[26]How is it then, brethren? Whenever you come together, each of you has a psalm, has a teaching, has a tongue, has a revelation, has an interpretation. Let all things be done for edification. [27]If anyone speaks in a tongue, *let there be* two or at the most three, *each* in turn, and let one interpret.

14:27,28 This gift could only be exercised when two or three other speaking persons were in a service, when they were only speaking one at a time, and only if there was an interpreter. Without those conditions, one was to meditate and pray silently.

14:21 [a]Isaiah 28:11,12   14:25 [a]NU-Text omits *And thus.*

²⁸But if there is no interpreter, let him keep silent in church, and let him speak to himself and to God. ²⁹Let two or three prophets speak, and let the others judge. ³⁰But if *anything* is revealed to another who sits by, let the first keep silent. ³¹For you can all prophesy one by one, that all may learn and all may be encouraged. ³²And the spirits of the prophets are subject to the prophets. ³³For God is not *the author* of confusion but of peace, as in all the churches of the saints.

> **14:33 confusion.** The worshiping church should reflect God's character and nature because He is a God of peace, harmony, order, and clarity—not strife and confusion (see Rom. 15:33). **as in all the churches.** This phrase belongs at the beginning of v. 34 as a logical introduction to a universal principle for churches.

³⁴Let your*ᵃ* women keep silent in the churches, for they are not permitted to speak; but *they are* to be submissive, as the law also says. ³⁵And if they want to learn something, let them ask their own husbands at home; for it is shameful for women to speak in church.

³⁶Or did the word of God come *originally* from you? Or *was it* you only that it reached? ³⁷If anyone thinks himself to be a prophet or spiritual, let him acknowledge that the things which I write to you are the commandments of the Lord. ³⁸But if anyone is ignorant, let him be ignorant.*ᵃ*

³⁹Therefore, brethren, desire earnestly to prophesy, and do not forbid to speak with tongues. ⁴⁰Let all things be done decently and in order.

The Risen Christ, Faith's Reality

15 Moreover, brethren, I declare to you the gospel which I preached to you, which also you received and in which you stand, ²by which also you are saved, if you hold fast that word which I preached to you—unless you believed in vain.

³For I delivered to you first of all that which I also received: that Christ died for our sins according to the Scriptures, ⁴and that He was buried, and that He rose again the third day according to the Scriptures,

⁵and that He was seen by Cephas, then by the twelve. ⁶After that He was seen by over five hundred brethren at once, of whom the greater part remain to the present, but some have fallen asleep. ⁷After that He was seen by James, then by all the apostles. ⁸Then last of all He was seen by me also, as by one born out of due time.

⁹For I am the least of the apostles, who am not worthy to be called an apostle, because I persecuted the church of God. ¹⁰But by the grace of God I am what I am, and His grace toward me was not in vain; but I labored more abundantly than they all, yet not I, but the grace of God *which was* with me. ¹¹Therefore, whether *it was* I or they, so we preach and so you believed.

> **15:12 some among you say.** Some Corinthian Christians could not understand the resurrection of believers. Their confusion came from their experiences with pagan philosophies and religions. One such philosophy, dualism, taught that everything physical was intrinsically evil; thus, for many, the idea of a resurrected body was repulsive (Acts 17:32). In addition, some Jewish Christians may have been influenced by the Sadducees, who did not believe in the resurrection.

The Risen Christ, Our Hope

¹²Now if Christ is preached that He has been raised from the dead, how do some among you say that there is no resurrection of the dead? ¹³But if there is no resurrection of the dead, then Christ is not risen. ¹⁴And if Christ is not risen, then our preaching *is* empty and your faith *is* also empty. ¹⁵Yes, and we are found false witnesses of God, because we have testified of God that He raised up Christ, whom He did not raise up—if in fact the dead do not rise. ¹⁶For if *the* dead do not rise, then Christ is not risen. ¹⁷And if Christ is not risen, your faith *is* futile; you are still in your sins! ¹⁸Then also those who have fallen asleep in Christ have perished. ¹⁹If in this life only we have

> **15:19 most pitiable.** This is because of the sacrifices believers make in this life in light of their hope in the life to come. If there is no life to come, we would be better "to eat, drink and be merry" before we die.

14:34 *ᵃ*NU-Text omits *your.*   14:38 *ᵃ*NU-Text reads *if anyone does not recognize this, he is not recognized.*

hope in Christ, we are of all men the most pitiable.

The Last Enemy Destroyed

20But now Christ is risen from the dead, *and* has become the firstfruits of those who have fallen asleep. 21For since by man *came* death, by Man also *came* the resurrection of the dead. 22For as in Adam all die, even so in Christ all shall be made alive. 23But each one in his own order: Christ the firstfruits, afterward those *who are* Christ's at His coming. 24Then *comes* the end, when He delivers the kingdom to God the Father, when He puts an end to all rule and all authority and power. 25For He must reign till He has put all enemies under His feet. 26The last enemy *that* will be destroyed *is* death. 27For *"He has put all things under His feet."*[a] But when He says "all things are put under *Him,"* *it is* evident that He who put all things under Him is excepted. 28Now when all things are made subject to Him, then the Son Himself will also be subject to Him who put all things under Him, that God may be all in all.

> **15:24 Then comes the end.** The third aspect of the resurrection involves the restoration of the earth to the rule of Christ. "End" can refer to what is over and to what is complete and fulfilled. **He delivers the kingdom of God.** After Christ's 1,000 year reign, all things will be returned to the way they were designed by God to be, revealed in the sinless glory of the new heaven and new earth (see Rev. 21,22).

Effects of Denying the Resurrection

29Otherwise, what will they do who are baptized for the dead, if the dead do not rise at all? Why then are they baptized for the dead? 30And why do we stand in jeopardy every hour? 31I affirm, by the boasting in you which I have in Christ Jesus our Lord, I die daily. 32If, in the manner of men, I have fought with beasts at Ephesus, what advantage *is it* to me? If *the* dead do not rise, *"Let us eat and drink, for tomorrow we die!"* [a]

> **15:29** This verse does not teach that a dead person can be saved by another person being baptized on his behalf, because baptism has no part in a person's salvation (Eph. 2:8). It is possible that this refers to living believers who were baptized in water because they had been drawn to Christ by the witness of believers who had subsequently died. Paul's point is that if there is no resurrection, then why would people come to Christ to follow the hope of those who had died?

33Do not be deceived: "Evil company corrupts good habits." 34Awake to righteousness, and do not sin; for some do not have the knowledge of God. I speak *this* to your shame.

A Glorious Body

35But someone will say, "How are the dead raised up? And with what body do they come?" 36Foolish one, what you sow is not made alive unless it dies. 37And what you sow, you do not sow that body that shall be, but mere grain—perhaps wheat or some other *grain.* 38But God gives it a body as He pleases, and to each seed its own body.

39All flesh *is* not the same flesh, but *there is* one *kind of* flesh[a] of men, another flesh of animals, another of fish, *and* another of birds.

40*There are* also celestial bodies and ter-

15:27 [a]Psalm 8:6   15:32 [a]Isaiah 22:13   15:39 [a]NU-Text and M-Text omit *of flesh.*

Does 1 Corinthians 15:22 actually teach universalism—the idea that all people will eventually be saved?

Some people, under a misguided notion of fairness and a woefully inadequate view of God, attempt to see in this verse a basis for their belief in universalism (salvation of everyone without regard to faith). The two "alls" in 15:22 are alike only in the sense that they both apply to descendants. The second "all" applies only to believers. The immediate context (verse 23) limits the second "all" to "those who are Christ's." Many other passages clearly teach against universalism by affirming the eternal punishment of unbelievers (Matthew 5:29; 10:28; 25:41,46; Luke 16:23; 2 Thessalonians 1:9; Revelation 20:15).

restrial bodies; but the glory of the celestial *is* one, and the *glory* of the terrestrial *is* another. ⁴¹*There is* one glory of the sun, another glory of the moon, and another glory of the stars; for *one* star differs from *another* star in glory.

⁴²So also *is* the resurrection of the dead. *The body* is sown in corruption, it is raised in incorruption. ⁴³It is sown in dishonor, it is raised in glory. It is sown in weakness, it is raised in power. ⁴⁴It is sown a natural body, it is raised a spiritual body. There is a natural body, and there is a spiritual body. ⁴⁵And so it is written, "*The first man Adam became a living being.*"ᵃ The last Adam *became* a life-giving spirit.

⁴⁶However, the spiritual is not first, but the natural, and afterward the spiritual. ⁴⁷The first man *was* of the earth, *made* of dust; the second Man *is* the Lordᵃ from heaven. ⁴⁸As *was* the *man* of dust, so also *are* those *who are made* of dust; and as *is* the heavenly *Man*, so also *are* those *who are* heavenly. ⁴⁹And as we have borne the image of the *man* of dust, we shall also bearᵃ the image of the heavenly *Man*.

> **15:45–49** Adam was created with a natural body, not perfect, but good in every way (Gen. 3:1). The "last Adam" is Jesus Christ (Rom. 5:19,21). Through the first Adam, we receive our natural bodies; through the last Adam, we will receive our spiritual bodies in resurrection. As we have borne the image of Adam's body on earth, believers will bear the image of Christ's body fit for heaven (Acts 1:11).

Our Final Victory

⁵⁰Now this I say, brethren, that flesh and blood cannot inherit the kingdom of God; nor does corruption inherit incorruption. ⁵¹Behold, I tell you a mystery: We shall not all sleep, but we shall all be changed—⁵²in a moment, in the twinkling of an eye, at the last trumpet. For the trumpet will sound, and the dead will be raised incorruptible, and we shall be changed. ⁵³For this corruptible must put on incorruption, and this mortal *must* put on immortality. ⁵⁴So when this corruptible has put on incorruption, and this mortal has put on immortality, then shall be brought to pass the saying

that is written: "*Death is swallowed up in victory.*"ᵃ

⁵⁵   "*O Death, where is your sting?*ᵃ
         O Hades, where is your victory?"ᵇ

⁵⁶The sting of death *is* sin, and the strength of sin *is* the law. ⁵⁷But thanks *be* to God, who gives us the victory through our Lord Jesus Christ.

⁵⁸Therefore, my beloved brethren, be steadfast, immovable, always abounding in the work of the Lord, knowing that your labor is not in vain in the Lord.

Collection for the Saints

16 Now concerning the collection for the saints, as I have given orders to the churches of Galatia, so you must do also: ²On the first *day* of the week let each one of you lay something aside, storing up as he may prosper, that there be no collections when I come. ³And when I come, whomever you approve by *your* letters I will send to bear your gift to Jerusalem. ⁴But if it is fitting that I go also, they will go with me.

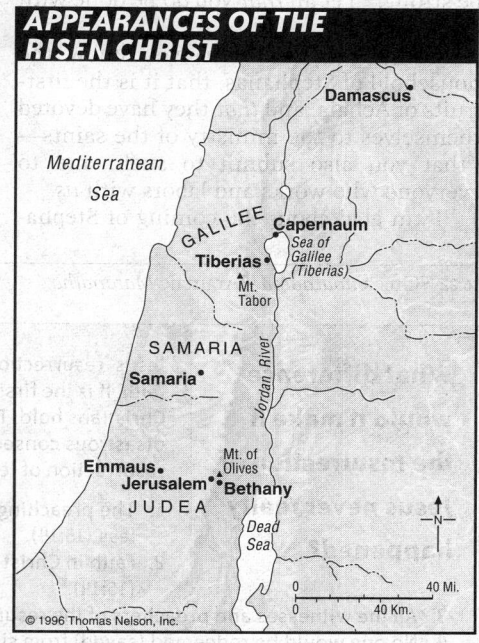

APPEARANCES OF THE RISEN CHRIST

Damascus

Mediterranean Sea

GALILEE
Capernaum
Tiberias
Sea of Galilee (Tiberias)
Mt. Tabor

SAMARIA
Samaria

Jordan River

Emmaus
Mt. of Olives
Jerusalem   Bethany
JUDEA
Dead Sea

—N→

0   40 Mi.
0   40 Km.

© 1996 Thomas Nelson, Inc.

15:45 ᵃGenesis 2:7   15:47 ᵃNU-Text omits *the Lord*.   15:49 ᵃM-Text reads *let us also bear*.
15:54 ᵃIsaiah 25:8   15:55 ᵃHosea 13:14   ᵇNU-Text reads *O Death, where is your victory? O Death, where is your sting?*

⁵Now I will come to you when I pass through Macedonia (for I am passing through Macedonia). ⁶And it may be that I will remain, or even spend the winter with you, that you may send me on my journey, wherever I go. ⁷For I do not wish to see you now on the way; but I hope to stay a while with you, if the Lord permits.

⁸But I will tarry in Ephesus until Pentecost. ⁹For a great and effective door has opened to me, and *there are* many adversaries.

¹⁰And if Timothy comes, see that he may be with you without fear; for he does the work of the Lord, as I also *do*. ¹¹Therefore let no one despise him. But send him on his journey in peace, that he may come to me; for I am waiting for him with the brethren.

¹²Now concerning *our* brother Apollos, I strongly urged him to come to you with the brethren, but he was quite unwilling to come at this time; however, he will come when he has a convenient time.

Final Exhortations

¹³Watch, stand fast in the faith, be brave, be strong. ¹⁴Let all *that* you *do* be done with love.

¹⁵I urge you, brethren—you know the household of Stephanas, that it is the firstfruits of Achaia, and *that* they have devoted themselves to the ministry of the saints— ¹⁶that you also submit to such, and to everyone who works and labors with *us*.

¹⁷I am glad about the coming of Stepha-

> **16:15,17 firstfruits.** The members of the household of Stephanas were among the first converts in Corinth. Stephanas was one of the Corinthian believers Paul had baptized; he was visiting with Paul in Ephesus at the time this epistle was written. With Fortunatus and Achaicus, he probably delivered the earlier letter from Corinth mentioned in 7:1.

nas, Fortunatus, and Achaicus, for what was lacking on your part they supplied. ¹⁸For they refreshed my spirit and yours. Therefore acknowledge such men.

Greetings and a Solemn Farewell

¹⁹The churches of Asia greet you. Aquila and Priscilla greet you heartily in the Lord, with the church that is in their house. ²⁰All the brethren greet you.

Greet one another with a holy kiss.

²¹The salutation with my own hand— Paul's.

²²If anyone does not love the Lord Jesus Christ, let him be accursed.*ᵃ* O Lord, come!*ᵇ*

²³The grace of our Lord Jesus Christ *be* with you. ²⁴My love *be* with you all in Christ Jesus. Amen.

> **16:22 accursed.** This means devoted to destruction. **O Lord, come!** Paul was appealing for the Lord to take away the nominal, false Christians who threatened the spiritual well-being of the church. This was also an expression of eagerness for the Lord's return (see Rev. 22:20). The Aramaic words are transliterated "Maranatha."

16:22 ᵃGreek *anathema* ᵇAramaic *Maranatha*

What difference would it make if the resurrection of Jesus never really happened?

Jesus' resurrection is the least optional part of the Christian faith. It is the first essential among the essential beliefs Christians hold. The Apostle Paul identified at least six disastrous consequences that would be unavoidable if the resurrection of Jesus proved to be a hoax:

1. The preaching of Christ would be senseless and meaningless (15:14).
2. Faith in Christ would be useless since He would still be dead (15:14).
3. All the witnesses and preachers of the resurrection would be liars (15:15).
4. No one would be redeemed (saved) from sin (15:17).
5. All former believers would have died as fools (15:18).
6. Christians would be the most pitiable people in the world (15:19).

At the center of Christianity stands the risen Christ, victorious, and coming again.

2 CORINTHIANS

In ancient times, letters were significant. They offered just about the only form of long distance communication. In a world without electronics or even printing, a handwritten letter was a powerful tool, and only the person or their personal representative carried greater authority. When God revealed Himself in written form, He chose letters as one of His tools.

The letters written by the Apostle Paul were the result of the inspiration of the Holy Spirit. Thus, they are God's Word. They also reveal to us a great deal about their human author. Paul's concern and his compassion became part of the permanent record. The last letter he wrote to the Corinthians conveys to us Paul's heart and God's Word to a struggling church.

AUTHOR AND DATE

Second Corinthians was written by Paul, approximately A.D. 55 to 56.

That the Apostle Paul wrote 2 Corinthians is uncontested. The lack of any motive for a forger to write this highly personal and biographical epistle has led even the most critical scholars to affirm Paul as its author.

The dating of 2 Corinthians offers an interesting example of the way in which scholars assign dates to biblical books. Historical details become crucial clues. For example, Acts 18:12–17 records Paul's trial before Gallio the Roman proconsul in Corinth. Extrabiblical sources indicate that Gallio probably took office in July, A.D. 51. His legal encounter with Paul took place shortly thereafter. These events occurred during Paul's founding visit among the Corinthians while on his second missionary journey.

The sequence and timing of Paul's travels (Acts 18:18; 19:8,10) and the internal clues in his letters (1 Corinthians 4:17; 16:8–11) help point to late A.D. 55 or early A.D. 56 as the most likely date for 2 Corinthians.

BACKGROUND AND SETTING

Paul's association with the important city of Corinth began during his second missionary journey (Acts 18:1–18). He spent 18 months in Corinth planting and tending a new church. In the years that followed, Paul wrote at least four letters and visited the church twice. Second Corinthians was Paul's fourth letter to the Corinthian Christians.

The church in Corinth experienced almost continuous spiritual struggles from internal and external problems. Paul had to deal with rampant immorality and

divisiveness within the church itself. He also had to confront outside influences in the form of self-styled false apostles (11:5–15).

In order to create a platform to teach their false gospel, the false prophets began assaulting Paul's character. They wanted to take advantage of the tension between the apostle and the church. If they could convince the people to turn from Paul, the congregation would then be completely vulnerable to their own demonic doctrines. The situation became so critical that Paul intervened personally. He referred to that episode as the "painful visit" (2:1). The tension in the church had broken out into public and personal attacks (2:5–8,10; 7:12). Paul, realizing he had done what he could, left the city but followed up his visit with what he called the "severe letter" (2:4) that Titus carried to Corinth on Paul's behalf (7:5–16).

Sometime later, anxious for news about Corinth, Paul traveled to meet Titus (2:13). His younger associate gave Paul the news that the majority of the Corinthians had repented of their rebellion against him (7:7). When Paul wrote this letter (2 Corinthians), he was intent on rejoicing for the church (7:8–16), warning them about dangers ahead by confronting the false apostles (chapters 10–13), and, particularly, re-establishing his reputation and authority among them by defending his apostleship (chapters 1–7). Paul also encouraged the Corinthians to resume preparations for the collection for the poor at Jerusalem (chapters 8,9), which he planned to collect on his next visit (12:14; 13:1,2). The Corinthians' participation in the Jerusalem offering (Romans 15:26) implies that Paul's third visit to that church was successful.

HISTORICAL AND THEOLOGICAL THEMES

Second Corinthians complements the historical record of Paul's dealings with the Corinthian church recorded in Acts and 1 Corinthians. The letter also contains important biographical data on Paul.

Although intensely personal, written by Paul in the heat of battle against those attacking his credibility, this letter includes several significant theological themes. It portrays God the Father as a merciful comforter (1:3; 7:6), the Creator (4:6), the One who raised Jesus from the dead (4:14; 13:4), and the One who will raise believers as well (1:9). It reminds the Corinthians that Jesus Christ is the One who suffered (1:5), who fulfilled God's promises (1:20), who was proclaimed Lord (4:5), who

SECOND CORINTHIANS PRESENTS THE **CLEAREST, MOST CONCISE SUMMARY** OF THE **SUBSTITUTIONARY ATONEMENT** OF **CHRIST.**

manifested God's glory (4:6), and who in His incarnation became poor for believers (8:9; see Philippians 2:5–8). The letter portrays the Holy Spirit as God (3:17,18) and the guarantee of believers' salvation (1:22; 5:5).

Paul's other themes in 2 Corinthians include: (1) an exposé of Satan, who is identified as the "god of this age" (4:4; see 1 John 5:19), a deceiver (11:14), and the leader of human and angelic deceivers (11:15); (2) insight into the end times

regarding the believer's glorification (4:16–5:8) and his judgment (5:10); (3) the glorious truth of God's sovereignty in salvation (5:14–21); (4) the necessary response by human beings to God's offer of salvation—genuine repentance (7:9,10); and (5) a definition of the mission of the church—to proclaim reconciliation (5:18–20).

Second Corinthians also presents the clearest, most concise summary of the substitutionary atonement of Christ to be found anywhere in Scripture (5:21; see Isaiah 53). The nature of the New Covenant receives its fullest exposition outside the book of Hebrews (3:6–16).

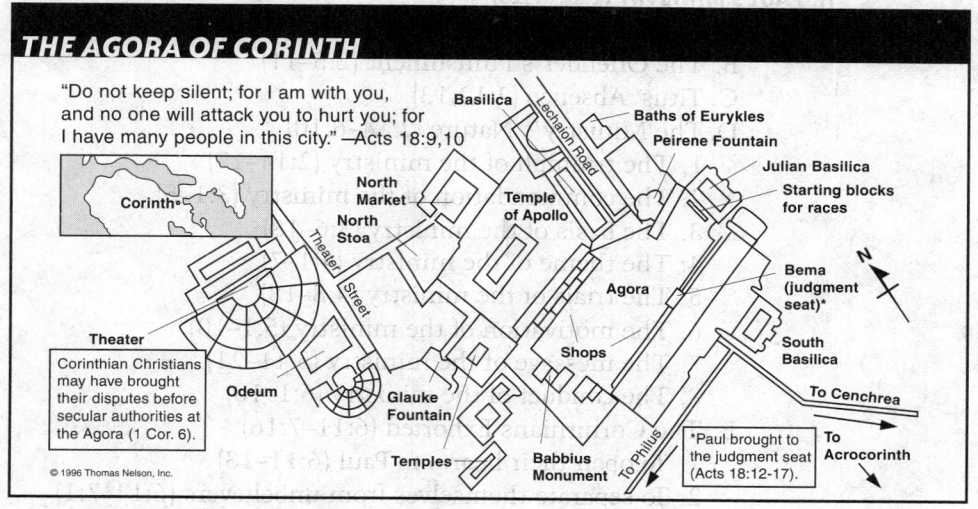

THE AGORA OF CORINTH

"Do not keep silent; for I am with you, and no one will attack you to hurt you; for I have many people in this city." —Acts 18:9,10

Corinth

Basilica
Baths of Eurykles
Peirene Fountain
Julian Basilica
Starting blocks for races

North Market
North Stoa
Temple of Apollo
Lechaion Road

Theater Street

Theater
Corinthian Christians may have brought their disputes before secular authorities at the Agora (1 Cor. 6).

Odeum

Glauke Fountain

Temples
Babbius Monument

Agora
Shops

Bema (judgment seat)*
South Basilica

To Cenchrea
To Acrocorinth
To Philus

*Paul brought to the judgment seat (Acts 18:12-17).

To Acrocorinth

© 1996 Thomas Nelson, Inc.

OUTLINE

Greeting

1 Paul, an apostle of Jesus Christ by the will of God, and Timothy *our* brother,

To the church of God which is at Corinth, with all the saints who are in all Achaia:

> **1:1 apostle.** This refers to Paul's position as a messenger sent by Christ. **by the will of God.** Paul's credentials were by divine appointment, and his letter reflected the words of Christ. **Timothy *our* brother.** Timothy was Paul's son in the faith and a dominant person in Paul's life and ministry. Paul first met Timothy in Lystra on his second missionary journey (Acts 16:1–4). Timothy was with him during the founding of the church in Corinth (Acts 18:1–5).

²Grace to you and peace from God our Father and the Lord Jesus Christ.

Comfort in Suffering

³Blessed *be* the God and Father of our Lord Jesus Christ, the Father of mercies and God of all comfort, ⁴who comforts us in all our tribulation, that we may be able to comfort those who are in any trouble, with the comfort with which we ourselves are comforted by God. ⁵For as the sufferings of Christ abound in us, so our consolation also abounds through Christ. ⁶Now if we are afflicted, *it is* for your consolation and salvation, which is effective for enduring the same sufferings which we also suffer. Or if we are comforted, *it is* for your consolation and salvation. ⁷And our hope for you *is* steadfast, because we know that as you are partakers of the sufferings, so also *you will partake* of the consolation.

> **1:7 partakers of the sufferings.** Many people in the church at Corinth were suffering for righteousness, as Paul was. Although the church had caused him much pain and concern, Paul saw its members as partners to be helped because of their mutual suffering.

Delivered from Suffering

⁸For we do not want you to be ignorant, brethren, of our trouble which came to us in Asia: that we were burdened beyond measure, above strength, so that we despaired even of life. ⁹Yes, we had the sentence of death in ourselves, that we should not trust in ourselves but in God who raises the dead, ¹⁰who delivered us from so great a death, and does*ᵃ* deliver us; in whom we trust that He will still deliver *us*, ¹¹you also helping together in prayer for us, that thanks may be given by many persons on our*ᵃ* behalf for the gift *granted* to us through many.

Paul's Sincerity

¹²For our boasting is this: the testimony of our conscience that we conducted ourselves in the world in simplicity and godly sincerity, not with fleshly wisdom but by the grace of God, and more abundantly toward you. ¹³For we are not writing any other things to you than what you read or understand. Now I trust you will understand, even to the end ¹⁴(as also you have understood us in part), that we are your boast as you also *are* ours, in the day of the Lord Jesus.

> **1:16 come again.** Paul had planned to leave Ephesus, stop at Corinth on the way to Macedonia, and return again to Corinth (see 1 Cor. 16:5–7). For some reason his plans were changed, and he was unable to stop in Corinth the first time. The false apostles in the church used Paul's honest change of schedule to accuse him of being untrustworthy.

Sparing the Church

¹⁵And in this confidence I intended to come to you before, that you might have a second benefit— ¹⁶to pass by way of you to Macedonia, to come again from Macedonia to you, and be helped by you on my way to Judea. ¹⁷Therefore, when I was planning this, did I do it lightly? Or the things I plan, do I plan according to the flesh, that with me there should be Yes, Yes, and No, No? ¹⁸But *as* God *is* faithful, our word to you was not Yes and No. ¹⁹For the Son of God, Jesus Christ, who was preached among you by us—by me, Silvanus, and Timothy—was not Yes and No, but in Him was Yes. ²⁰For all the promises of God in Him *are* Yes, and in Him Amen, to the glory of God through us. ²¹Now He who establishes us with you in Christ and has anointed us *is* God, ²²who

---

1:10 *ᵃ*NU-Text reads *shall.*   1:11 *ᵃ*M-Text reads *your behalf.*

also has sealed us and given us the Spirit in our hearts as a guarantee.

²³Moreover I call God as witness against my soul, that to spare you I came no more to Corinth. ²⁴Not that we have dominion over your faith, but are fellow workers for your joy; for by faith you stand.

> **1:23 to spare you.** Paul explained that he could not come earlier because he wanted them to have time to repent of and correct their sinful behavior. He waited for a report from Titus before taking further action, hoping he would not have to come again to face their rebellion.

2 But I determined this within myself, that I would not come again to you in sorrow. ²For if I make you sorrowful, then who is he who makes me glad but the one who is made sorrowful by me?

Forgive the Offender

³And I wrote this very thing to you, lest, when I came, I should have sorrow over those from whom I ought to have joy, having confidence in you all that my joy is *the joy* of you all. ⁴For out of much affliction and anguish of heart I wrote to you, with many tears, not that you should be grieved, but that you might know the love which I have so abundantly for you.

⁵But if anyone has caused grief, he has not grieved me, but all of you to some extent—not to be too severe. ⁶This punishment which *was inflicted* by the majority *is* sufficient for such a man, ⁷so that, on the contrary, you *ought* rather to forgive and comfort *him,* lest perhaps such a one be swallowed up with too much sorrow. ⁸Therefore I urge you to reaffirm *your* love to him. ⁹For to this end I also wrote, that I might put you to the test, whether you are obedient in all things. ¹⁰Now whom you forgive anything, I also *forgive.* For if indeed I

> **2:7 to forgive.** It was time to grant forgiveness so the man's joy would be restored (see Ps. 51:12,14). Paul knew there was no place in the church for man-made limits on God's grace, mercy, and forgiveness toward repentant sinners. Such restrictions could only rob the fellowship of the joy of unity (see Matt. 18:34,35).

have forgiven anything, I have forgiven that one*ᵃ* for your sakes in the presence of Christ, ¹¹lest Satan should take advantage of us; for we are not ignorant of his devices.

Triumph in Christ

¹²Furthermore, when I came to Troas to *preach* Christ's gospel, and a door was opened to me by the Lord, ¹³I had no rest in my spirit, because I did not find Titus my brother; but taking my leave of them, I departed for Macedonia.

¹⁴Now thanks *be* to God who always leads us in triumph in Christ, and through us diffuses the fragrance of His knowledge in every place. ¹⁵For we are to God the fragrance of Christ among those who are being saved and among those who are perishing. ¹⁶To the one *we are* the aroma of death *leading* to death, and to the other the aroma of life *leading* to life. And who *is* sufficient for these things? ¹⁷For we are not, as so many,*ᵃ* peddling the word of God; but as of sincerity, but as from God, we speak in the sight of God in Christ.

> **2:15 to God the fragrance of Christ.** Paul was further thankful for the privilege of pleasing God. Paul pictured God as the emperor at the end of the Triumph who smells the pervasive fragrance and is pleased with the victorious efforts it represents. Wherever God's servant is faithful and is an influence for the gospel, God is pleased (see Matt. 25:21).

Christ's Epistle

3 Do we begin again to commend ourselves? Or do we need, as some *others,* epistles of commendation to you or *letters* of commendation from you? ²You are our epistle written in our hearts, known and read by all men; ³clearly *you are* an epistle of Christ, ministered by us, written not with ink but by the Spirit of the living God,

> **3:2 written in our hearts.** This is an affirmation of Paul's affection for the believers in Corinth. **known and read by all men.** The transformed lives of the Corinthians were like an open letter that could be seen and read by all men as a testimony to Paul's faithfulness and the truth of his message.

2:10 *ᵃ*NU-Text reads *For indeed, what I have forgiven, if I have forgiven anything, I did it.*
2:17 *ᵃ*M-Text reads *the rest.*

not on tablets of stone but on tablets of flesh, *that is,* of the heart.

The Spirit, Not the Letter

⁴And we have such trust through Christ toward God. ⁵Not that we are sufficient of ourselves to think of anything as *being* from ourselves, but our sufficiency *is* from God, ⁶who also made us sufficient as ministers of the new covenant, not of the letter but of the Spirit;*ª* for the letter kills, but the Spirit gives life.

Glory of the New Covenant

⁷But if the ministry of death, written *and* engraved on stones, was glorious, so that the children of Israel could not look steadily at the face of Moses because of the glory of his countenance, which *glory* was passing away, ⁸how will the ministry of the Spirit not be more glorious? ⁹For if the ministry of condemnation *had* glory, the ministry of righteousness exceeds much more in glory. ¹⁰For even what was made glorious had no glory in this respect, because of the glory that excels. ¹¹For if what is passing away *was* glorious, what remains *is* much more glorious.

> **3:8,9 ministry of the Spirit...exceeds much more in glory.** The "ministry of the Spirit" is Paul's description of the New Covenant. Paul argued that if such glory attended the giving of the law under the ministry that brought death, how much more glorious will be the ministry of the Spirit in the New Covenant which brings righteousness. The law pointed to the superior New Covenant, and thus a glory that must also be superior.

¹²Therefore, since we have such hope, we use great boldness of speech—¹³unlike Moses, *who* put a veil over his face so that the children of Israel could not look steadily at the end of what was passing away. ¹⁴But their minds were blinded. For until this day the same veil remains unlifted in the reading of the Old Testament, because the *veil* is taken away in Christ. ¹⁵But even to this day, when Moses is read, a veil lies on their heart. ¹⁶Nevertheless when one turns to the Lord, the veil is taken away. ¹⁷Now the Lord is the Spirit; and where the Spirit of the Lord *is,* there *is* liberty. ¹⁸But we all, with unveiled face, beholding as in a mirror the glory of the Lord, are being transformed into the same image from glory to glory, just as by the Spirit of the Lord.

> **3:14 the *veil* is taken away in Christ.** Without Christ, the OT is unintelligible. When a person comes to Christ, however, the veil is lifted and his spiritual perception is no longer impaired (Is. 25:68). With the veil removed, believers can see the glory of God revealed in Christ (John 1:14). They understand that the law was never given to save them, but to lead them to the One who would.

The Light of Christ's Gospel

4 Therefore, since we have this ministry, as we have received mercy, we do not lose heart. ²But we have renounced the hidden things of shame, not walking in craftiness nor handling the word of God deceitfully, but by manifestation of the truth commending ourselves to every man's conscience in the sight of God. ³But even if our gospel is veiled, it is veiled to those who are perishing, ⁴whose minds the god of this age has blinded, who do not believe, lest the light of the gospel of the glory of Christ, who is the image of God, should shine on them. ⁵For we do not preach ourselves, but Christ Jesus the Lord, and ourselves your bondservants for Jesus' sake. ⁶For it is the God who commanded light to shine out of darkness, who has shone in our hearts to *give* the light of the knowledge of the glory of God in the face of Jesus Christ.

Cast Down but Unconquered

⁷But we have this treasure in earthen vessels, that the excellence of the power may be of God and not of us. ⁸*We are* hardpressed on every side, yet not crushed; *we*

> **4:7 earthen vessels.** The Greek word means "baked clay" and refers to clay pots that were cheap and breakable, but served necessary household functions. They were sometimes used to store valuables or important documents, but they were mostly used for holding garbage and human waste. The latter use is what Paul had in mind, and it was how he viewed himself (see 2 Tim. 2:20,21).

are perplexed, but not in despair; ⁹persecuted, but not forsaken; struck down, but not destroyed—¹⁰always carrying about in the body the dying of the Lord Jesus, that the life of Jesus also may be manifested in our body. ¹¹For we who live are always delivered to death for Jesus' sake, that the life of Jesus also may be manifested in our mortal flesh. ¹²So then death is working in us, but life in you.

¹³And since we have the same spirit of faith, according to what is written, *"I believed and therefore I spoke,"ª* we also believe and therefore speak, ¹⁴knowing that He who raised up the Lord Jesus will also raise us up with Jesus, and will present *us* with you. ¹⁵For all things *are* for your sakes, that grace, having spread through the many, may cause thanksgiving to abound to the glory of God.

Seeing the Invisible

¹⁶Therefore we do not lose heart. Even though our outward man is perishing, yet the inward *man* is being renewed day by day. ¹⁷For our light affliction, which is but for a moment, is working for us a far more exceeding *and* eternal weight of glory, ¹⁸while we do not look at the things which are seen, but at the things which are not seen. For the things which are seen *are* temporary, but the things which are not seen *are* eternal.

4:16 our outward man is perishing. Paul was referring to the normal aging process, but he emphasized that his lifestyle sped up the process. While not an old man, Paul wore himself out in ministry—in the effort and pace he maintained, plus the number of beatings and attacks he received from his enemies. **inward man.** This is the soul of every believer (see Eph. 4:24). **being renewed.** While the physical body is decaying, the inner self of the believer continues to become more and more like Christ (see Eph. 3:16–20).

Assurance of the Resurrection

5 For we know that if our earthly house, *this* tent, is destroyed, we have a building from God, a house not made with hands, eternal in the heavens. ²For in this we groan, earnestly desiring to be clothed with our habitation which is from heaven, ³if indeed, having been clothed, we shall

not be found naked. ⁴For we who are in *this* tent groan, being burdened, not because we want to be unclothed, but further clothed, that mortality may be swallowed up by life. ⁵Now He who has prepared us for this very thing *is* God, who also has given us the Spirit as a guarantee.

5:1 earthly house...tent. This is Paul's metaphor for the physical body (see 2 Pet. 1:13,14). Like a temporary tent, man's earthly existence is fragile, insecure, and lowly (see 1 Pet. 2:11). **a building from God.** This pictured the believer's resurrected, glorified body (see 1 Cor. 15:35–50). Just as the Israelites replaced the tabernacle with the temple, so believers ought to long to exchange their earthly bodies for glorified ones. **a house...in the heavens.** This is the heavenly, eternal body for which Paul longed.

⁶So *we are* always confident, knowing that while we are at home in the body we are absent from the Lord. ⁷For we walk by faith, not by sight. ⁸We are confident, yes, well pleased rather to be absent from the body and to be present with the Lord.

5:6 at home in the body...absent from the Lord. While a believer is alive on earth, he is away from the fullness of God's presence. He has contact with God through prayer, the indwelling of the Holy Spirit, and fellowship through the Word. Paul was expressing a strong yearning to be at home with his Lord (see Ps. 73:25).

The Judgment Seat of Christ

⁹Therefore we make it our aim, whether present or absent, to be well pleasing to Him. ¹⁰For we must all appear before the judgment seat of Christ, that each one may receive the things *done* in the body, according to what he has done, whether good or bad. ¹¹Knowing, therefore, the terror of the Lord, we persuade men; but we are well known to God, and I also trust are well known in your consciences.

Be Reconciled to God

¹²For we do not commend ourselves again to you, but give you opportunity to boast on our behalf, that you may have *an answer* for those who boast in appearance and not in heart. ¹³For if we are beside ourselves, *it*

4:13 ªPsalm 116:10

is for God; or if we are of sound mind, *it is* for you. [14]For the love of Christ compels us, because we judge thus: that if One died for all, then all died; [15]and He died for all, that those who live should live no longer for themselves, but for Him who died for them and rose again.

[16]Therefore, from now on, we regard no one according to the flesh. Even though we have known Christ according to the flesh, yet now we know *Him thus* no longer. [17]Therefore, if anyone *is* in Christ, *he is* a new creation; old things have passed away; behold, all things have become new. [18]Now all things *are* of God, who has reconciled us to Himself through Jesus Christ, and has given us the ministry of reconciliation, [19]that is, that God was in Christ reconciling the world to Himself, not imputing their trespasses to them, and has committed to us the word of reconciliation.

[20]Now then, we are ambassadors for Christ, as though God were pleading through us: we implore *you* on Christ's behalf, be reconciled to God. [21]For He made Him who knew no sin *to be* sin for us, that we might become the righteousness of God in Him.

Marks of the Ministry

6 We then, *as* workers together *with Him* also plead with *you* not to receive the grace of God in vain. [2]For He says:

> "In an acceptable time I have heard
>   you,
> And in the day of salvation I have
>   helped you." [a]

5:17 in Christ. These words signify the believer's security in Christ, his acceptance in Him, his future assurance in the inheritance in heaven, and his participation in the divine nature of Christ who is the everlasting Word (see 2 Pet. 1:4). **new creation.** This refers to regeneration or the new birth (see John 3:3). **old things have passed away.** After a person is regenerate, old value systems, priorities, beliefs, loves, and plans are gone. **all things...new.** The believer lives for eternity, not for temporal things.

6:1 to receive the grace of God in vain. Most in the Corinthian church were saved, but some were hindered by legalistic teachings regarding sanctification. Others who were not truly saved had been deceived by a gospel of works, which was being taught by false teachers (see Gal. 5:4). Both cases prevented the people from assuming any "ministry of reconciliation." Paul was concerned that his months of ministry in Corinth had been for nothing.

6:2 [a]Isaiah 49:8

What does Paul mean when he writes about being "in Christ" and someone being "a new creation" (5:17)?

Paul uses the term "in Christ" when he writes about various aspects of our relationship with Jesus Christ as Lord and Savior. These two words comprise a brief but profound statement of the inexhaustible significance of the believer's redemption (salvation), which includes the following:

1. The believer's security in Christ, who bore in His body God's judgment against sin.
2. The believer's acceptance in (through) Christ with whom God alone is well pleased.
3. The believer's future assurance in Him who is the resurrection to eternal life and the sole guarantor of the believer's inheritance in heaven.
4. The believer's participation in the divine nature of Christ, the everlasting Word (2 Peter 1:4).

All of the changes that Christ brings to the believer's life result in a state that can be rightly called "a new creation." The terms describe something created at a qualitatively new level of excellence. They parallel other biblical concepts like regeneration and new birth (John 3:3; Ephesians 2:1–3; Titus 3:5; 1 Peter 1:23; 1 John 2:29; 3:9; 5:4). The expression includes the Christian's forgiveness of sins paid for in Christ's substitutionary death (Galatians 6:15; Ephesians 4:24).

Behold, now *is* the accepted time; behold, now *is* the day of salvation.

³We give no offense in anything, that our ministry may not be blamed. ⁴But in all *things* we commend ourselves as ministers of God: in much patience, in tribulations, in needs, in distresses, ⁵in stripes, in imprisonments, in tumults, in labors, in sleeplessness, in fastings; ⁶by purity, by knowledge, by longsuffering, by kindness, by the Holy Spirit, by sincere love, ⁷by the word of truth, by the power of God, by the armor of righteousness on the right hand and on the left, ⁸by honor and dishonor, by evil report and good report; as deceivers, and *yet* true; ⁹as unknown, and *yet* well known; as dying, and behold we live; as chastened, and *yet* not killed; ¹⁰as sorrowful, yet always rejoicing; as poor, yet making many rich; as having nothing, and *yet* possessing all things.

> **6:7 by the armor of righteousness.** Paul did not fight Satan's kingdom with human resources, but with spiritual virtue. **the right hand...the left.** Paul had both offensive weapons (such as the sword of the Spirit) and defensive weapons (such as the shield of faith and the helmet of salvation) at his disposal.

Be Holy

¹¹O Corinthians! We have spoken openly to you, our heart is wide open. ¹²You are not restricted by us, but you are restricted by your *own* affections. ¹³Now in return for the same (I speak as to children), you also be open.

¹⁴Do not be unequally yoked together with unbelievers. For what fellowship has righteousness with lawlessness? And what communion has light with darkness? ¹⁵And what accord has Christ with Belial? Or what part has a believer with an unbeliever? ¹⁶And what agreement has the temple of God with idols? For you*ᵃ* are the temple of the living God. As God has said:

> **6:14 unequally yoked together.** Paul used OT prohibitions to Israel regarding the work-related joining together of two different kinds of livestock as an analogy to teach that believers should not join together spiritually with unbelievers.

"I will dwell in them
  And walk among them.
I will be their God,
  And they shall be My people." *ᵇ*

¹⁷Therefore

"Come out from among them
  And be separate, says the Lord.
Do not touch what is unclean,
  And I will receive you."*ᵃ*
¹⁸ "I will be a Father to you,
  And you shall be My sons and
    daughters,
  Says the LORD Almighty."*ᵃ*

7 Therefore, having these promises, beloved, let us cleanse ourselves from all filthiness of the flesh and spirit, perfecting holiness in the fear of God.

The Corinthians' Repentance

²Open *your hearts* to us. We have wronged no one, we have corrupted no one, we have cheated no one. ³I do not say *this* to condemn; for I have said before that you are in our hearts, to die together and to live together. ⁴Great *is* my boldness of speech toward you, great *is* my boasting on your behalf. I am filled with comfort. I am exceedingly joyful in all our tribulation.

⁵For indeed, when we came to Macedonia, our bodies had no rest, but we were troubled on every side. Outside *were* conflicts, inside *were* fears. ⁶Nevertheless God, who comforts the downcast, comforted us by the coming of Titus, ⁷and not only by his coming, but also by the consolation with which he was comforted in you, when he told us of your earnest desire, your mourning, your zeal for me, so that I rejoiced even more.

⁸For even if I made you sorry with my letter, I do not regret it; though I did regret it. For I perceive that the same epistle made you sorry, though only for a while. ⁹Now I rejoice, not that you were made sorry, but that your sorrow led to repentance. For you were made sorry in a godly manner, that you might suffer loss from us in nothing. ¹⁰For godly sorrow produces repentance

---

6:16 *ᵃ*NU-Text reads *we.* *ᵇ*Leviticus 26:12; Jeremiah 32:38; Ezekiel 37:27   6:17 *ᵃ*Isaiah 52:11; Ezekiel 20:34, 41   6:18 *ᵃ*2 Samuel 7:14

leading to salvation, not to be regretted; but the sorrow of the world produces death. ¹¹For observe this very thing, that you sorrowed in a godly manner: What diligence it produced in you, *what* clearing *of yourselves, what* indignation, *what* fear, *what* vehement desire, *what* zeal, *what* vindication! In all *things* you proved yourselves to be clear in this matter. ¹²Therefore, although I wrote to you, *I did* not *do it* for the sake of him who had done the wrong, nor for the sake of him who suffered wrong, but that our care for you in the sight of God might appear to you.

> **7:10 godly sorrow produces repentance *leading* to salvation.** "Godly sorrow" refers to sorrow that is according to the will of God and produced by the Holy Spirit. Repentance cannot occur without genuine sorrow over one's sin. **sorrow of the world produces death.** Human sorrow is merely the wounded pride of getting caught in sin and leads to guilt, shame, despair, self-pity, depression, and hopelessness. Such sorrow does not lead to repentance, but only to death (see Ps. 32:3,4).

The Joy of Titus

¹³Therefore we have been comforted in your comfort. And we rejoiced exceedingly more for the joy of Titus, because his spirit has been refreshed by you all. ¹⁴For if in anything I have boasted to him about you, I am not ashamed. But as we spoke all things to you in truth, even so our boasting to Titus was found true. ¹⁵And his affections are greater for you as he remembers the obedience of you all, how with fear and trembling you received him. ¹⁶Therefore I rejoice that I have confidence in you in everything.

> **8:1—9:15** This section specifically deals with Paul's instruction to the Corinthians about a particular collection for the saints in Jerusalem. It also provides the richest, most detailed model of Christian giving in the NT.

Excel in Giving

8 Moreover, brethren, we make known to you the grace of God bestowed on the churches of Macedonia: ²that in a great trial of affliction the abundance of their joy and their deep poverty abounded in the riches of their liberality. ³For I bear witness that according to *their* ability, yes, and beyond *their* ability, *they were* freely willing, ⁴imploring us with much urgency that we would receive*ᵃ* the gift and the fellowship of the ministering to the saints. ⁵And not *only* as we had hoped, but they first gave themselves to the Lord, and *then* to us by the will of God. ⁶So we urged Titus, that as he had begun, so he would also complete this grace in you as well. ⁷But as you abound in everything—in faith, in speech, in knowledge, in all diligence, and in your love for us—*see* that you abound in this grace also.

> **8:3** The Macedonians gave proportionately, sacrificially, and voluntarily. These traits sum up the concept of freewill giving, which has always been God's plan (see Gen. 4:2–4; Ex. 1,2). Freewill giving is not to be confused with tithing, which related to the national taxation system of Israel and is paralleled in the NT and the present by paying taxes.

Christ Our Pattern

⁸I speak not by commandment, but I am testing the sincerity of your love by the diligence of others. ⁹For you know the grace of our Lord Jesus Christ, that though He was rich, yet for your sakes He became poor, that you through His poverty might become rich.

> **8:9 though He was rich.** As the second person of the Trinity, Christ is rich as God is rich. He owns everything and possesses all power, authority, sovereignty, glory, honor, and majesty (see Is. 9:6). **He became poor.** This refers to Christ's incarnation (see John 1:14). He left His place with God, took on human form, and died on a cross like a criminal (Phil. 2:5–8). **that you...might become rich.** Believers become spiritually rich through the sacrifice and impoverishment of Christ (Phil. 2:5–8).

¹⁰And in this I give advice: It is to your advantage not only to be doing what you began and were desiring to do a year ago; ¹¹but now you also must complete the doing *of it;* that as *there was* a readiness to desire *it,* so *there* also *may be* a completion out of what *you* have. ¹²For if there is first a willing mind, *it is* accepted according to what

---

8:4 *ᵃ*NU-Text and M-Text omit *that we would receive,* thus changing text to *urgency for the favor and fellowship* . . . .

one has, *and* not according to what he does not have.

¹³For *I do* not *mean* that others should be eased and you burdened; ¹⁴but by an equality, *that* now at this time your abundance *may supply* their lack, that their abundance also may supply your lack—that there may be equality. ¹⁵As it is written, *"He who gathered much had nothing left over, and he who gathered little had no lack."ᵃ*

Collection for the Judean Saints

¹⁶But thanks *be* to God who putsᵃ the same earnest care for you into the heart of Titus. ¹⁷For he not only accepted the exhortation, but being more diligent, he went to you of his own accord. ¹⁸And we have sent with him the brother whose praise *is* in the gospel throughout all the churches, ¹⁹and not only *that*, but who was also chosen by the churches to travel with us with this gift, which is administered by us to the glory of the Lord Himself and *to show* your ready mind, ²⁰avoiding this: that anyone should blame us in this lavish gift which is administered by us— ²¹providing honorable things, not only in the sight of the Lord, but also in the sight of men.

> **8:19 chosen by the churches.** To protect Paul and Titus from false accusations regarding the mishandling of the money, the churches picked an unbiased brother as their representative to lend accountability. **to the glory of the Lord Himself.** Paul desired careful scrutiny as protection against bringing dishonor to Christ for any misappropriation of the money. He wanted to avoid criticisms and accusations.

²²And we have sent with them our brother whom we have often proved diligent in many things, but now much more diligent, because of the great confidence which *we have* in you. ²³If *anyone inquires* about Titus, *he is* my partner and fellow worker concerning you. Or if our brethren *are inquired about, they are* messengers of the churches, the glory of Christ. ²⁴Therefore show to them, andᵃ before the churches the proof of your love and of our boasting on your behalf.

Administering the Gift

9 Now concerning the ministering to the saints, it is superfluous for me to write to you; ²for I know your willingness, about which I boast of you to the Macedonians, that Achaia was ready a year ago; and your zeal has stirred up the majority. ³Yet I have sent the brethren, lest our boasting of you should be in vain in this respect, that, as I said, you may be ready; ⁴lest if *some* Macedonians come with me and find you unprepared, we (not to mention you!) should be ashamed of this confident boasting.ᵃ ⁵Therefore I thought it necessary to exhort the brethren to go to you ahead of time, and prepare your generous gift beforehand, which *you had* previously promised, that it may be ready as *a matter of* generosity and not as a grudging obligation.

The Cheerful Giver

⁶But this *I say:* He who sows sparingly will also reap sparingly, and he who sows bountifully will also reap bountifully. ⁷*So let* each one *give* as he purposes in his heart, not grudgingly or of necessity; for God loves a cheerful giver. ⁸And God *is* able to make all grace abound toward you, that you, always having all sufficiency in all *things*, may have an abundance for every good work. ⁹As it is written:

> *"He has dispersed abroad,*
>   *He has given to the poor;*
>   *His righteousness endures forever."ᵃ*

> **9:6** This principle teaches that the harvest is directly proportionate to the amount of seed sown (see Prov. 11:24,25). **bountifully.** This is from the Greek word from which we get the word "eulogy" ("blessing"). When a generous believer gives by faith and trust in God, with a desire to produce a great blessing, he will receive that kind of a harvest of blessing (see Mal. 3:10). God gives a return on the amount one invests with Him.

¹⁰Now mayᵃ He who supplies seed to the sower, and bread for food, supply and multiply the seed you have *sown* and increase the fruits of your righteousness,

---

¹¹while *you are* enriched in everything for all liberality, which causes thanksgiving through us to God. ¹²For the administration of this service not only supplies the needs of the saints, but also is abounding through many thanksgivings to God, ¹³while, through the proof of this ministry, they glorify God for the obedience of your confession to the gospel of Christ, and for *your* liberal sharing with them and all *men*, ¹⁴and by their prayer for you, who long for you because of the exceeding grace of God in you. ¹⁵Thanks *be* to God for His indescribable gift!

The Spiritual War

10 Now I, Paul, myself am pleading with you by the meekness and gentleness of Christ—who in presence *am* lowly among you, but being absent am bold toward you. ²But I beg *you* that when I am present I may not be bold with that confidence by which I intend to be bold against some, who think of us as if we walked according to the flesh. ³For though we walk in the flesh, we do not war according to the flesh. ⁴For the weapons of our warfare *are* not carnal but mighty in God for pulling down strongholds, ⁵casting down arguments and every high thing that exalts

9:12 administration of this service. This is a priestly word from which we get "liturgy." Paul viewed the collection as a spiritual, worshipful offering to God that would glorify Him. **supplies the needs of the saints.** Many members of the Jerusalem church had gone to Jerusalem to celebrate Pentecost, had been converted, and had remained in the city without adequate finances. Many in Jerusalem had lost their jobs due to persecution. However, the Corinthians, who had not yet suffered persecution, were wealthy enough to help meet the needs of those in Jerusalem.

10:3 walk in the flesh. Paul's opponents in Corinth had wrongly accused him of walking in the flesh in a moral sense (see Rom. 8:4). Paul affirmed that he did walk in the flesh in a physical sense. Although he possessed the power and authority of an apostle of Christ, he was still a human being. **war according to the flesh.** Paul did not fight the spiritual battle for men's souls using human ingenuity, worldly wisdom, or clever methodologies (see 1 Cor. 1:17–25). Those weapons are powerless in bringing men to Christ.

Why does the tone of 2 Corinthians change so abruptly between 9:15 and 10:1?

Even a casual reader usually notices the sudden change in tone that occurs between the ninth and tenth chapters of 2 Corinthians. This apparent difference has prompted various explanations of the relationship between chapters 1–9 and 10–13.

Some have argued that chapters 10–13 were actually part of the "severe letter" that Paul mentions in 2:4. Based on this theory, these four chapters belong chronologically before chapters 1–9. Chapters 10–13 cannot, however, have been written before chapters 1–9 because they refer to Titus' visit as a past event (see 8:6; 12:18). Further, the offender whose defiance prompted Paul's "severe letter" (2:5–8) is nowhere mentioned in chapters 10–13.

Others agree that chapters 10–13 belong after chapters 1–9 but suggest that they form a separate letter. They assume that Paul, after sending chapters 1–9 to the Corinthians, received reports of new trouble at Corinth and wrote chapters 10–13 in response. A variation of this view proposes that Paul paused after writing chapters 1–9, then heard bad news from Corinth before he resumed writing chapters 10–13. Although this view preserves the unity of 2 Corinthians, Paul gives no indication in the last four chapters that he received fresh news from Corinth.

The best interpretation sees 2 Corinthians as a unified letter with two distinct sections. Chapters 1–9 are addressed to the repentant majority (see 2:6) and chapters 10–13 to the minority still influenced by the false teachers. The following facts support this view: (1) no ancient authorities (Greek manuscripts, early church fathers, or early translations) indicate that chapters 10–13 ever circulated as a separate letter; (2) the over-all differences in tone between the two sections have been exaggerated (compare 6:11; 7:2 with 11:11; 12:14); and (3) chapters 10–13 do form a logical conclusion to chapters 1–9 as Paul prepared the Corinthians for his promised visit (1:15,16; 2:1–3).

itself against the knowledge of God, bringing every thought into captivity to the obedience of Christ, ⁶and being ready to punish all disobedience when your obedience is fulfilled.

Reality of Paul's Authority

⁷Do you look at things according to the outward appearance? If anyone is convinced in himself that he is Christ's, let him again consider this in himself, that just as he *is* Christ's, even so we *are* Christ's.ᵃ ⁸For even if I should boast somewhat more about our authority, which the Lord gave usᵃ for edification and not for your destruction, I shall not be ashamed— ⁹lest I seem to terrify you by letters. ¹⁰"For *his* letters," they say, "*are* weighty and powerful, but *his* bodily presence *is* weak, and *his* speech contemptible." ¹¹Let such a person consider this, that what we are in word by letters when we are absent, such *we will* also *be* in deed when we are present.

> **10:8** The debate with the false apostles had forced Paul to emphasize his authority more than he cared to—Paul's claims for his authority normally were restrained by his humility. But no matter how much he said about his authority, Paul would never be ashamed. The Lord gave Paul his authority to strengthen and edify the church, which he had done at Corinth. The false apostles only brought confusion and turmoil to the church, proving that their authority was not from the Lord.

Limits of Paul's Authority

¹²For we dare not class ourselves or compare ourselves with those who commend themselves. But they, measuring themselves by themselves, and comparing themselves among themselves, are not wise. ¹³We, however, will not boast beyond measure, but within the limits of the sphere which God appointed us—a sphere which especially includes you. ¹⁴For we are not overextending ourselves (as though *our authority* did not extend to you), for it was to you that we came with the gospel of Christ; ¹⁵not boasting of things beyond measure, *that is,* in other men's labors, but having hope, *that* as your faith is increased, we

shall be greatly enlarged by you in our sphere, ¹⁶to preach the gospel in the *regions* beyond you, *and* not to boast in another man's sphere of accomplishment.

¹⁷But *"he who glories, let him glory in the* LORD.*"ᵃ* ¹⁸For not he who commends himself is approved, but whom the Lord commends.

Concern for Their Faithfulness

11 Oh, that you would bear with me in a little folly—and indeed you do bear with me. ²For I am jealous for you with godly jealousy. For I have betrothed you to one husband, that I may present *you as* a chaste virgin to Christ. ³But I fear, lest somehow, as the serpent deceived Eve by his craftiness, so your minds may be corrupted from the simplicityᵃ that is in Christ. ⁴For if he who comes preaches another Jesus whom we have not preached, or *if* you receive a different spirit which you have not received, or a different gospel which you have not accepted—you may well put up with it!

> **11:2 I am jealous for you.** Paul was concerned for the Corinthians to the point of jealousy for their spiritual purity. **godly jealousy.** This jealousy is inspired by zeal for God's causes, as God is jealous for His name and His people's loyalty (see Ex. 20:5). **I have betrothed you to one husband.** As their spiritual father (see 1 Cor. 4:15), Paul portrayed the Corinthians like a daughter, whom he had betrothed to Jesus Christ. **chaste virgin.** Paul wanted the Corinthians to be pure until the marriage day finally arrived (see Rev. 19:7).

Paul and False Apostles

⁵For I consider that I am not at all inferior to the most eminent apostles. ⁶Even though *I am* untrained in speech, yet *I am* not in knowledge. But we have been thoroughly manifestedᵃ among you in all things.

⁷Did I commit sin in humbling myself that you might be exalted, because I preached the gospel of God to you free of charge? ⁸I robbed other churches, taking wages *from them* to minister to you. ⁹And when I was present with you, and in need, I was a burden to no one, for what I lacked

---

10:7 ᵃNU-Text reads *even as we are.*　10:8 ᵃNU-Text omits *us.*　10:17 ᵃJeremiah 9:24　11:3 ᵃNU-Text adds *and purity.*　11:6 ᵃNU-Text omits *been.*

the brethren who came from Macedonia supplied. And in everything I kept myself from being burdensome to you, and so I will keep *myself.* ¹⁰As the truth of Christ is in me, no one shall stop me from this boasting in the regions of Achaia. ¹¹Why? Because I do not love you? God knows!

> **11:7 free of charge.** Greek culture measured the importance of a teacher by the fee he could command. The false apostles accused Paul of being a counterfeit, since he refused to charge for his services (see 1 Cor. 9:1–15). They convinced the Corinthians to be offended by Paul's refusal to accept their support. Paul's resort to manual labor (Acts 18:1–3) embarrassed the Corinthians, who felt such work was beneath an apostle. Paul had humbled himself so they could be exalted (lifted out of their sin and idolatry).

¹²But what I do, I will also continue to do, that I may cut off the opportunity from those who desire an opportunity to be regarded just as we are in the things of which they boast. ¹³For such *are* false apostles, deceitful workers, transforming themselves into apostles of Christ. ¹⁴And no wonder! For Satan himself transforms himself into an angel of light. ¹⁵Therefore *it is* no great thing if his ministers also transform themselves into ministers of righteousness, whose end will be according to their works.

> **11:13–15** Paul directly exposed the false apostles as emissaries of Satan. Not only was their claim to apostleship false, so was their doctrine. As satanic purveyors of false teaching, they were under the curse of Gal. 1:8,9. Paul's forceful language expressed the godly jealousy he felt for the Corinthians. He was unwilling to sacrifice truth for the sake of unity (see 1 Tim. 4:12).

Reluctant Boasting

¹⁶I say again, let no one think me a fool. If otherwise, at least receive me as a fool, that I also may boast a little. ¹⁷What I speak, I speak not according to the Lord, but as it were, foolishly, in this confidence of boasting. ¹⁸Seeing that many boast according to the flesh, I also will boast. ¹⁹For you put up with fools gladly, since you *yourselves* are wise! ²⁰For you put up with it if one brings you into bondage, if one devours *you,* if one takes *from you,* if one exalts himself, if one

strikes you on the face. ²¹To *our* shame I say that we were too weak for that! But in whatever anyone is bold—I speak foolishly— I am bold also.

Suffering for Christ

²²Are they Hebrews? So *am* I. Are they Israelites? So *am* I. Are they the seed of Abraham? So *am* I. ²³Are they ministers of Christ?—I speak as a fool—I *am* more: in labors more abundant, in stripes above measure, in prisons more frequently, in deaths often. ²⁴From the Jews five times I received forty *stripes* minus one. ²⁵Three times I was beaten with rods; once I was stoned; three times I was shipwrecked; a night and a day I have been in the deep; ²⁶*in* journeys often, *in* perils of waters, *in* perils of robbers, *in* perils of *my own* countrymen, *in* perils of the Gentiles, *in* perils in the city, *in* perils in the wilderness, *in* perils in the sea, *in* perils among false brethren; ²⁷in weariness and toil, in sleeplessness often, in hunger and thirst, in fastings often, in cold and nakedness— ²⁸besides the other things, what comes upon me daily: my deep concern for all the churches. ²⁹Who is weak, and I am not weak? Who is made to stumble, and I do not burn *with indignation?*

> **11:24 forty *stripes* minus one.** Deuteronomy 25:1–3 set 40 as the maximum number of beatings that could legally be administered; in Paul's day the Jews reduced that number by one to avoid accidentally going over the maximum. Jesus warned that His followers would receive such beatings (Matt. 10:17).

³⁰If I must boast, I will boast in the things which concern my infirmity. ³¹The God and Father of our Lord Jesus Christ, who is blessed forever, knows that I am not lying. ³²In Damascus the governor, under Aretas the king, was guarding the city of the Damascenes with a garrison, desiring to arrest me; ³³but I was let down in a basket through a window in the wall, and escaped from his hands.

The Vision of Paradise

12 It is doubtless*ᵃ* not profitable for me to boast. I will come to visions and

---

12:1 *ᵃ*NU-Text reads *necessary, though not profitable,* to boast.

revelations of the Lord: ²I know a man in Christ who fourteen years ago—whether in the body I do not know, or whether out of the body I do not know, God knows—such a one was caught up to the third heaven. ³And I know such a man—whether in the body or out of the body I do not know, God knows— ⁴how he was caught up into Paradise and heard inexpressible words, which it is not lawful for a man to utter. ⁵Of such a one I will boast; yet of myself I will not boast, except in my infirmities. ⁶For though I might desire to boast, I will not be a fool; for I will speak the truth. But I refrain, lest anyone should think of me above what he sees me *to be* or hears from me.

> **12:2–4** This vision probably took place between Paul's return to Tarsus from Jerusalem (Acts 9:30) and the start of his missionary journeys (Acts 13:1–3). **caught up to the third heaven...caught up into Paradise.** The "third heaven" and "Paradise" are the same place (see Rev. 2:7; 22:14). The first heaven is the earth's atmosphere (Gen. 8:2); the second is interplanetary and interstellar space (Gen. 15:5); and the third is the abode of God (1 Kin. 8:30).

The Thorn in the Flesh

⁷And lest I should be exalted above measure by the abundance of the revelations, a thorn in the flesh was given to me, a mes-senger of Satan to buffet me, lest I be exalted above measure. ⁸Concerning this thing I pleaded with the Lord three times that it might depart from me. ⁹And He said to me, "My grace is sufficient for you, for My strength is made perfect in weakness." Therefore most gladly I will rather boast in my infirmities, that the power of Christ may rest upon me. ¹⁰Therefore I take pleasure in infirmities, in reproaches, in needs, in persecutions, in distresses, for Christ's sake. For when I am weak, then I am strong.

> **12:7 a thorn in the flesh...a messenger of Satan.** This thorn was sent to Paul by God to keep him humble. As with Job, Satan was the immediate cause, but God was the ultimate cause. Paul's use of the word "messenger" from Satan suggests the "thorn in the flesh" was a demon, not a physical illness. This demon was possibly indwelling the leader of the false apostles in Corinth, who were tearing up the church.

Signs of an Apostle

¹¹I have become a fool in boasting;ᵃ you have compelled me. For I ought to have been commended by you; for in nothing was I behind the most eminent apostles, though I am nothing. ¹²Truly the signs of an apostle were accomplished among you with all perseverance, in signs and wonders and

---

12:11 ᵃNU-Text omits *in boasting.*

To what was Paul referring by the term "thorn in the flesh" (12:7)?

Paul began his account about the "thorn in the flesh" by indicating the reason it was given to him—"lest I should be exalted"—to keep him humble. As with Job, Satan was the immediate cause, but God was the ultimate cause behind Paul's thorn. This is why the thorn was not removed even though Paul pleaded (12:8). God had a purpose in allowing Paul to suffer in this way—to show Paul that "My grace is sufficient for you" (12:9).

Paul's use of the word "messenger" (Greek, *angellos*, or angel) from Satan suggests the "thorn in the flesh" (literally, "a stake for the flesh") was a demon, not a physical illness. Of the 188 uses of the Greek word *angellos* in the New Testament, at least 180 refer to angels. This particular angel was from Satan, a demon afflicting Paul.

Possibly, the best explanation for this demon is that he was indwelling the ringleader of the Corinthian conspiracy, the leader of the false apostles. Through them he was tearing apart Paul's beloved church and thus driving a painful stake through Paul. Added support for this view comes from the context of chapters 10–13, in which Paul engages his enemies (the false prophets). The verb translated "buffet" always refers to ill treatment from other people (Matthew 26:67; Mark 14:65; 1 Corinthians 4:11; 1 Peter 2:20). Finally, the Old Testament frequently describes Israel's enemies as thorns (Numbers 33:55; Joshua 23:13; Judges 2:3; Ezekiel 28:24).

mighty deeds. ¹³For what is it in which you were inferior to other churches, except that I myself was not burdensome to you? Forgive me this wrong!

> **12:12 the signs of an apostle.** The purpose of miraculous signs was to authenticate the apostles as God's messengers (see Acts 2:22,43).

Love for the Church

¹⁴Now *for* the third time I am ready to come to you. And I will not be burdensome to you; for I do not seek yours, but you. For the children ought not to lay up for the parents, but the parents for the children. ¹⁵And I will very gladly spend and be spent for your souls; though the more abundantly I love you, the less I am loved.

¹⁶But be that *as it may,* I did not burden you. Nevertheless, being crafty, I caught you by cunning! ¹⁷Did I take advantage of you by any of those whom I sent to you? ¹⁸I urged Titus, and sent our brother with *him.* Did Titus take advantage of you? Did we not walk in the same spirit? Did *we* not *walk* in the same steps?

¹⁹Again, do you think*ᵃ* that we excuse ourselves to you? We speak before God in Christ. But *we do* all things, beloved, for your edification. ²⁰For I fear lest, when I come, I shall not find you such as I wish, and *that* I shall be found by you such as you do not wish; lest *there be* contentions, jealousies, outbursts of wrath, selfish ambitions, backbitings, whisperings, conceits, tumults; ²¹lest, when I come again, my God will humble me among you, and I shall mourn for many who have sinned before and have not repented of the uncleanness, fornication, and lewdness which they have practiced.

Coming with Authority

13 This *will be* the third *time* I am coming to you. *"By the mouth of two or three witnesses every word shall be established."ᵃ* ²I have told you before, and foretell as if I were present the second time, and now being absent I write*ᵃ* to those who have sinned before, and to all the rest, that if I come again I will not spare— ³since you seek a proof of Christ speaking in me, who is not weak toward you, but mighty in you. ⁴For though He was crucified in weakness, yet He lives by the power of God. For we also are weak in Him, but we shall live with Him by the power of God toward you.

> **13:3 a proof of Christ speaking in me.** Those Corinthians still seeking proof of Paul's genuine apostleship would have it when he arrived. Paul was going to use his authority and power to deal with any sin and rebellion he found there. **who is not weak.** Christ's power was to be revealed through Paul against the sinning Corinthians (see 1 Cor. 11:30–32). By rebelling against Paul, they were rebelling against Christ.

⁵Examine yourselves *as to* whether you are in the faith. Test yourselves. Do you not know yourselves, that Jesus Christ is in you?—unless indeed you are disqualified. ⁶But I trust that you will know that we are not disqualified.

Paul Prefers Gentleness

⁷Now I*ᵃ* pray to God that you do no evil, not that we should appear approved, but that you should do what is honorable, though we may seem disqualified. ⁸For we can do nothing against the truth, but for the truth. ⁹For we are glad when we are weak and you are strong. And this also we pray, that you may be made complete. ¹⁰Therefore I write these things being absent, lest being present I should use sharpness, according to the authority which the Lord has given me for edification and not for destruction.

Greetings and Benediction

¹¹Finally, brethren, farewell. Become complete. Be of good comfort, be of one mind, live in peace; and the God of love and peace will be with you. ¹²Greet one another with a holy kiss. ¹³All the saints greet you.

¹⁴The grace of the Lord Jesus Christ, and the love of God, and the communion of the Holy Spirit *be* with you all. Amen.

12:19 *ᵃ*NU-Text reads *You have been thinking for a long time.* . . . 13:1 *ᵃ*Deuteronomy 19:15
13:2 *ᵃ*NU-Text omits *I write.*   13:7 *ᵃ*NU-Text reads *we.*

GALATIANS

Paul's epistle to the Galatians bears two significant distinctions. First, it represents the earliest of his many letters written under the inspiration of the Holy Spirit. Second, Galatians is the only one of Paul's messages targeted for a region, a group of churches, rather than a specific local church. First and always, Paul preached the gospel as the ultimate freedom found in Christ through justification by faith.

AUTHOR AND DATE

Galations was written by Paul, about A.D. 50.

There is no compelling reason to question the internal claims that the apostle Paul wrote Galatians (1:1; 5:2). Further, Paul was familiar with this region, having been born in Tarsus, a city in the neighboring province of Cilicia. He also visited the southern area of Galatia and planted churches there during his first missionary journey. He would have had good reasons to follow up those visits with a letter, particularly in the light of news that struggling young churches needed to hear about the Jerusalem Council (Acts 15). (For more on Paul, see the Introduction to Romans and the FAQ "Who Was Paul?")

The most important dating fact for Galatians is the timing of the Jerusalem Council (Acts 15). Paul based part of his letter on that event (2:1). Since most scholars date the Jerusalem Council about A.D. 49, the most likely date for Galatians is shortly thereafter.

BACKGROUND AND SETTING

In Paul's day, the word *Galatia* had two distinct meanings: ethnic and political. In a strict ethnic sense, Galatia was the region of central Asia Minor (today's Turkey) inhabited by a transplanted group called Galatians. They were a Celtic people who migrated to that region from Gaul (today's France) in the third century B.C. The Romans conquered the Galatians in 189 B.C. but allowed them a measure of independence until 25 B.C., when Galatia became a Roman province.

When establishing the boundaries of the province of Galatia, Rome included some regions not populated by ethnic Galatians. This broader term was the primary meaning by the time of the New Testament.

Paul founded churches in the southern Galatian cities of Antioch, Iconium, Lystra, and Derbe (Acts 13:14–14:23). These were cities in the Roman province, but they were not inhabited by ethnic Galatians. Although Acts notes two brief

visits by Paul into ethnic Galatia (Acts 16:6; 18:23), it makes no mention of any churches founded in that region.

Despite suggestions that Paul might have written his letter to the northern regions he had not visited, his concerns and the needs of the southern Galatian churches make them more likely recipients of the letter. The apostle received word that the churches he had recently founded were under assault by Judaizing false teachers who were undermining the central New Testament doctrine of justification by faith. Ignoring the express decree of the Jerusalem Council (Acts 15:23–29), these teachers were insisting that Gentiles must first become Jewish proselytes and submit to all the Mosaic law before they could become Christians (1:7; 4:17,21; 5:2–12; 6:12,13). Shocked by the Galatians' openness to that damning heresy (1:6), Paul wrote this letter to defend justification by faith and to warn these churches of the dire consequences of abandoning that essential doctrine. Galatians is the only Pauline letter without an opening commendation for its readers. That obvious omission reflects the urgency he felt about confronting the possible defection and defending the essential doctrine of justification.

HISTORICAL AND THEOLOGICAL THEMES

Galatians provides valuable historical information about Paul's background (chapters 1 and 2). This includes his 3-year stay in Nabatean Arabia (1:17,18) which Acts does not mention; his 15-day visit with Peter after his stay in Arabia (1:18,19), his trip to the Jerusalem Council (2:1–10), and his confrontation of Peter in Antioch (2:11–21).

THE CENTRAL THEOLOGICAL THEME OF GALATIANS IS JUSTIFICATION BY FAITH.

The central theological theme of Galatians (like that of Romans) is justification by faith. Paul defends that doctrine (that is the heart of the gospel) both in its theological (chapters 3 and 4) and practical (chapters 5 and 6) ramifications.

Other theological themes in Galatians also parallel Romans:
1. The law cannot justify (2:16, and Romans 3:20)
2. Believers are dead to the law (2:19, and Romans 7:14)
3. Believers are crucified with Christ (2:20, and Romans 6:6)
4. Abraham was justified by faith (3:6, and Romans 4:3)
5. Believers are Abraham's spiritual children (3:7, and Romans 4:10,11) and therefore blessed (3:9, and Romans 4:23,24)
6. The law brings not salvation but God's wrath (3:10, and Romans 4:15)
7. The just shall live by faith (3:11, and Romans 1:17)
8. Sin is universally pervasive (3:22, and Romans 11:32)
9. Believers are spiritually baptized into Christ (3:27, and Romans 6:3)
10. Believers are adopted as God's spiritual children (4:5–7, and Romans 8:14–17)
11. Love fulfills the law (5:14, and Romans 13:8–10)

12. Believers should walk in the Spirit (5:16, and Romans 8:4)

13. The flesh wars against the Spirit (5:17, and Romans 7:23,25)

14. Believers should bear one another's burdens (6:2, and Romans 15:1).

Paul also defends his position as an apostle (chapters 1 and 2). As in Corinth, the false teachers in Galatia had attempted to gain a hearing for their heretical teaching by undermining Paul's credibility.

OUTLINE

Greeting

1 Paul, an apostle (not from men nor through man, but through Jesus Christ and God the Father who raised Him from the dead), ²and all the brethren who are with me,

To the churches of Galatia:

> **1:2 churches of Galatia.** These are the churches Paul founded at Antioch of Pisidia, Iconium, Lystra, and Derbe during his first missionary journey (Acts 13:14–14:23).

³Grace to you and peace from God the Father and our Lord Jesus Christ, ⁴who gave Himself for our sins, that He might deliver us from this present evil age, according to the will of our God and Father, ⁵to whom *be* glory forever and ever. Amen.

Only One Gospel

⁶I marvel that you are turning away so soon from Him who called you in the grace of Christ, to a different gospel, ⁷which is not another; but there are some who trouble you and want to pervert the gospel of Christ. ⁸But even if we, or an angel from heaven, preach any other gospel to you than what we have preached to you, let him be accursed. ⁹As we have said before, so now I say again, if anyone preaches any other gospel to you than what you have received, let him be accursed.

¹⁰For do I now persuade men, or God? Or do I seek to please men? For if I still pleased

> **1:8 we, or an angel from heaven.** Paul calls on himself and holy angels as the most unlikely examples for false teaching. The Galatians should receive no messenger, regardless of how impeccable his credentials, if his doctrine of salvation differed even slightly from God's truth revealed through Christ and the apostles. **accursed.** The Greek word *anathema* refers to devoting someone to destruction in hell (see Rom. 9:3).

men, I would not be a bondservant of Christ.

Call to Apostleship

¹¹But I make known to you, brethren, that the gospel which was preached by me is not according to man. ¹²For I neither received it from man, nor was I taught *it*, but *it came* through the revelation of Jesus Christ.

¹³For you have heard of my former conduct in Judaism, how I persecuted the church of God beyond measure and *tried to* destroy it. ¹⁴And I advanced in Judaism beyond many of my contemporaries in my own nation, being more exceedingly zealous for the traditions of my fathers.

¹⁵But when it pleased God, who separated me from my mother's womb and called *me* through His grace, ¹⁶to reveal His Son in me, that I might preach Him among the Gentiles, I did not immediately confer with flesh and blood, ¹⁷nor did I go up to Jerusalem to those *who were* apostles before me; but I went to Arabia, and returned again to Damascus.

How do the events mentioned in Galatians match the chronology of Acts?

A comparison of the references in Acts (11:27–30; 15:2,12,22,35) and Galatians (1:18; 2:1–10) seems to indicate at least three visits by Paul to Jerusalem, including his role in the Jerusalem council. Other visits occurred after the Council (Acts 18:18–22; 21:15–17). The visit mentioned in Galatians 1:18 records Paul's first direct contact with the apostles in Jerusalem after his own conversion. Chapter 2:1 mentions a fourteen year gap, after which Paul returned again to Jerusalem, most likely as a participant in the Jerusalem Council (Acts 15), called to resolve the issue of Gentile salvation.

Linguistically, the word "again" (2:1) need not refer to the next visit; it can just as easily mean "once again" or "another time" without respect to how many visits took place in-between. And in fact, Paul did visit Jerusalem at least once during that 14-year period to deliver famine relief to the church there (Acts 11:27–30; 12:24,25). He simply did not mention that intervening visit in Galatians probably because it was not significant in his defense of his apostolic authority.

1:16 reveal His Son in me. Not only was Christ revealed *to* Paul on the Damascus Road, but *in* him as God gave him the life, light, and faith to believe in Him. **preach Him among the Gentiles.** Paul was called to proclaim the gospel to the non-Jews. **confer with flesh and blood.** Paul did not look to Ananias or other Christians at Damascus for clarification of or addition to the revelation he had received from Christ (Acts 9:19,20).

Contacts at Jerusalem

[18]Then after three years I went up to Jerusalem to see Peter,[a] and remained with him fifteen days. [19]But I saw none of the other apostles except James, the Lord's brother. [20](Now *concerning* the things which I write to you, indeed, before God, I do not lie.)

[21]Afterward I went into the regions of Syria and Cilicia. [22]And I was unknown by face to the churches of Judea which *were* in Christ. [23]But they were hearing only, "He who formerly persecuted us now preaches the faith which he once *tried to* destroy." [24]And they glorified God in me.

Defending the Gospel

2 Then after fourteen years I went up again to Jerusalem with Barnabas, and also took Titus with *me*. [2]And I went up by revelation, and communicated to them that gospel which I preach among the Gentiles, but privately to those who were of reputation, lest by any means I might run, or had run, in vain. [3]Yet not even Titus who *was* with me, being a Greek, was compelled to be circumcised. [4]And *this occurred* because of false brethren secretly brought in (who came in by stealth to spy out our liberty which we have in Christ Jesus, that they might bring us into bondage), [5]to whom we

2:3 compelled to be circumcised. The Judaizers were teaching that there could be no salvation without circumcision (Acts 15:1,5,24). Paul and the apostles denied that, and the conflict was settled at the Jerusalem Council (Acts 15:1–22). As a true believer, Titus was proof that circumcision and the Mosaic regulations were not prerequisites of salvation. The apostles refused to require that Titus be circumcised, verifying their rejection of the Judaizers' doctrine (see Acts 16:1–3).

did not yield submission even for an hour, that the truth of the gospel might continue with you.

[6]But from those who seemed to be something—whatever they were, it makes no difference to me; God shows personal favoritism to no man—for those who seemed *to be something* added nothing to me. [7]But on the contrary, when they saw that the gospel for the uncircumcised had been committed to me, as *the gospel* for the circumcised *was* to Peter [8](for He who worked effectively in Peter for the apostleship to the circumcised also worked effectively in me toward the Gentiles), [9]and when James, Cephas, and John, who seemed to be pillars, perceived the grace that had been given to me, they gave me and Barnabas the right hand of fellowship, that we *should go* to the Gentiles and they to the circumcised. [10]*They desired* only that we should remember the poor, the very thing which I also was eager to do.

2:9 James, Cephas, and John. This James was Jesus' half-brother, who had a prominent role in the Jerusalem church. Cephas (Peter) and John (the brother of James, the apostle, martyred in Acts 12:2), were two of Christ's closest companions and became the main apostles in the Jerusalem church. **pillars.** This emphasizes the role of James, Peter, and John in establishing and supporting the church.

No Return to the Law

[11]Now when Peter[a] had come to Antioch, I withstood him to his face, because he was to be blamed; [12]for before certain men came from James, he would eat with the Gentiles; but when they came, he withdrew and separated himself, fearing those who were of the circumcision. [13]And the rest of the Jews also played the hypocrite with him, so that even Barnabas was carried away with their hypocrisy.

[14]But when I saw that they were not straightforward about the truth of the gospel, I said to Peter before *them* all, "If you, being a Jew, live in the manner of Gentiles and not as the Jews, why do you[a] compel Gentiles to live as Jews?[b] [15]We *who are* Jews by nature, and not sinners of the Gentiles,

---

1:18 [a]NU-Text reads *Cephas*.   2:11 [a]NU-Text reads *Cephas*.   2:14 [a]NU-Text reads how can you.
[b]Some interpreters stop the quotation here.

16knowing that a man is not justified by the works of the law but by faith in Jesus Christ, even we have believed in Christ Jesus, that we might be justified by faith in Christ and not by the works of the law; for by the works of the law no flesh shall be justified.

2:16 works...faith. Paul declared that salvation is only through faith in Christ and not by law. **justified.** This Greek word describes a judge declaring an accused person innocent before the law. In Scripture, it refers to God declaring a sinner not guilty and righteous before Him, attributing man's sin to Christ for punishment. **works of the law.** The law served as a mirror to reveal sin; it was not a cure for it.

17"But if, while we seek to be justified by Christ, we ourselves also are found sinners, is Christ therefore a minister of sin? Certainly not! 18For if I build again those things which I destroyed, I make myself a transgressor. 19For I through the law died to the law that I might live to God. 20I have been crucified with Christ; it is no longer I who live, but Christ lives in me; and the *life* which I now live in the flesh I live by faith

2:20 I have been crucified with Christ. When a person trusts in Christ for salvation, he spiritually participates with the Lord in His crucifixion and His victory over sin and death. **no longer I who live, but Christ lives in me.** The believer's old self is dead, having been crucified with Christ (Rom. 6:3,5). The believer's new man has the indwelling of Christ empowering him and living through him.

in the Son of God, who loved me and gave Himself for me. 21I do not set aside the grace of God; for if righteousness *comes* through the law, then Christ died in vain."

Justification by Faith

3 O foolish Galatians! Who has bewitched you that you should not obey the truth,[a] before whose eyes Jesus Christ was clearly portrayed among you[b] as crucified? 2This only I want to learn from you: Did you receive the Spirit by the works of the law, or by the hearing of faith? 3Are you so foolish? Having begun in the Spirit, are you now being made perfect by the flesh? 4Have you suffered so many things in vain—if indeed *it was* in vain?

5Therefore He who supplies the Spirit to you and works miracles among you, *does He do it* by the works of the law, or by the hearing of faith?—6just as Abraham *"believed God, and it was accounted to him for righteousness."* [a] 7Therefore know that *only* those who are of faith are sons of Abraham. 8And the Scripture, foreseeing that God would justify the Gentiles by faith, preached the gospel to Abraham beforehand, *saying, "In you all the nations shall be blessed."* [a] 9So then those who *are* of faith are blessed with believing Abraham.

The Law Brings a Curse

10For as many as are of the works of the law are under the curse; for it is written, *"Cursed is everyone who does not continue*

3:1 [a]NU-Text omits *that you should not obey the truth.* [b]NU-Text omits *among you.*
3:6 [a]Genesis 15:6   3:8 [a]Genesis 12:3; 18:18; 22:18; 26:4; 28:14

Galatians 3:27 seems to read as if baptism is necessary for salvation. What did Paul mean in that verse?

Paul's use of the term "baptized" in this verse does not refer to water baptism, which cannot save. Paul used the word here in a metaphorical manner to speak of being "immersed," or "placed into" Christ. The larger context here refers to faith and the spiritual miracle of union with Him in His death and resurrection, not an outward ceremony. The phrase that immediately follows, "put on Christ," pictures the result of the believer's spiritual union with Christ. Paul was emphasizing the fact that we have been united with Christ through salvation. Positionally before God, we have put on Christ, His death, resurrection, and righteousness. Practically we need to "put on Christ" before our family, friends, neighbors, and co-workers, in our conduct (Romans 13:14).

in all things which are written in the book of the law, to do them." [a] [11]But that no one is justified by the law in the sight of God is evident, for "the just shall live by faith." [a] [12]Yet the law is not of faith, but "the man who does them shall live by them." [a]

[13]Christ has redeemed us from the curse of the law, having become a curse for us (for it is written, "Cursed is everyone who hangs on a tree" [a]), [14]that the blessing of Abraham might come upon the Gentiles in Christ Jesus, that we might receive the promise of the Spirit through faith.

> **3:13 Christ has redeemed us from the curse of the law.** The Greek word "redeemed" was often used to speak of buying a slave's freedom. Through His death, Christ purchased believers from slavery to sin and from the sentence of eternal death (Titus 2:14). **having become a curse for us.** By bearing God's wrath for believer's sins on the cross (see Heb. 9:28), Christ took upon Himself the curse pronounced on those who disobeyed the law.

The Changeless Promise

[15]Brethren, I speak in the manner of men: Though it is only a man's covenant, yet if it is confirmed, no one annuls or adds to it. [16]Now to Abraham and his Seed were the promises made. He does not say, "And to seeds," as of many, but as of one, "And to your Seed," [a] who is Christ. [17]And this I say, that the law, which was four hundred and thirty years later, cannot annul the covenant that was confirmed before by God in Christ, [a] that it should make the promise of no effect. [18]For if the inheritance is of the law, it is no longer of promise; but God gave it to Abraham by promise.

Purpose of the Law

[19]What purpose then does the law serve? It was added because of transgressions, till the Seed should come to whom the promise was made; and it was appointed through angels by the hand of a mediator. [20]Now a mediator does not mediate for one only, but God is one.

> **3:19 was added because of transgressions.** The purpose of the law was to reveal man's sinfulness, inability to save himself, and need of a Savior. It was never intended to be the way of salvation. **through angels.** Angels were involved in the giving of the law (see Acts 7:53), but their precise role is unknown.

[21]Is the law then against the promises of God? Certainly not! For if there had been a law given which could have given life, truly righteousness would have been by the law. [22]But the Scripture has confined all under sin, that the promise by faith in Jesus Christ might be given to those who believe. [23]But before faith came, we were kept under guard by the law, kept for the faith which would afterward be revealed. [24]Therefore the law was our tutor to bring us to Christ, that we might be justified by faith. [25]But after faith has come, we are no longer under a tutor.

Sons and Heirs

[26]For you are all sons of God through faith in Christ Jesus. [27]For as many of you as were baptized into Christ have put on Christ. [28]There is neither Jew nor Greek, there is neither slave nor free, there is neither male nor female; for you are all one in

---

3:10 [a]Deuteronomy 27:26   3:11 [a]Habakkuk 2:4   3:12 [a]Leviticus 18:5   3:13 [a]Deuteronomy 21:23
3:16 [a]Genesis 12:7; 13:15; 24:7   3:17 [a]NU-Text omits in Christ.

How does Paul's statement about gender, race, and status equality in 3:28 affect other biblical teachings about roles?

This passage is sometimes quoted by those who wish to challenge the traditional concepts of authority and submission, particularly as it affects marriage. This verse does not deny that God's plan has included certain racial, social, and sexual distinctions among Christians, but it affirms that those do not imply spiritual inequality before God. In other words, the great doctrine of spiritual equality is not incompatible with the God-ordained roles of headship and submission in the church, society, and at home. Even Jesus Christ, though fully equal with the Father, assumed a submissive role during His incarnation (Philippians 2:5–8).

3:27 baptized into Christ. Paul used the word "baptized" to speak of being "immersed," or "placed into" Christ by the union with Him in His death and resurrection. **put on Christ.** This is the result of the believer's spiritual union with Christ. We have been united with Christ through salvation.

Christ Jesus. ²⁹And if you *are* Christ's, then you are Abraham's seed, and heirs according to the promise.

4 Now I say *that* the heir, as long as he is a child, does not differ at all from a slave, though he is master of all, ²but is under guardians and stewards until the time appointed by the father. ³Even so we, when we were children, were in bondage under the elements of the world. ⁴But when the fullness of the time had come, God sent forth His Son, born*ᵃ* of a woman, born under the law, ⁵to redeem those who were under the law, that we might receive the adoption as sons.

4:4 the fullness of the time. Jesus came into the world when the exact religious, cultural, and political conditions demanded by God's perfect plan were in place. **born of a woman.** This emphasizes Jesus' full humanity (Is. 7:14). He had to be fully God for His sacrifice to atone for sin, and He had to be fully man so He could take upon Himself the penalty of sin as the substitute for man. **under the law.** Jesus, like all men, was obligated to obey God's law. He perfectly obeyed that law (John 8:46), making Him the unblemished sacrifice for sins.

⁶And because you are sons, God has sent forth the Spirit of His Son into your hearts, crying out, "Abba, Father!" ⁷Therefore you are no longer a slave but a son, and if a son, then an heir of*ᵃ* God through Christ.

Fears for the Church
⁸But then, indeed, when you did not know God, you served those which by nature are not gods. ⁹But now after you have known God, or rather are known by God, how *is it that* you turn again to the weak and beggarly elements, to which you desire again to be in bondage? ¹⁰You observe days and months and seasons and years. ¹¹I am afraid for you, lest I have labored for you in vain.

¹²Brethren, I urge you to become like me, for I *became* like you. You have not injured me at all. ¹³You know that because of physical infirmity I preached the gospel to you at the first. ¹⁴And my trial which was in my flesh you did not despise or reject, but you received me as an angel of God, *even* as Christ Jesus. ¹⁵What*ᵃ* then was the blessing you *enjoyed?* For I bear you witness that, if possible, you would have plucked out your own eyes and given them to me. ¹⁶Have I therefore become your enemy because I tell you the truth?

4:12 become like me, for I *became* like you. Paul had been a proud Pharisee, trusting in his own righteousness to save him (see Phil. 3:4–6). When he came to Christ, he abandoned all efforts to save himself and trusted in God's grace (Phil. 3:7–9). He urged the Galatians to follow his example and avoid the legalism of the Judaizers. **You have not injured me.** Though the Jews persecuted him when he first went to Galatia, the Galatian believers had not harmed Paul but had received him when he preached to them (see Acts 13:42–50).

¹⁷They zealously court you, *but* for no good; yes, they want to exclude you, that you may be zealous for them. ¹⁸But it is good to be zealous in a good thing always, and not only when I am present with you. ¹⁹My little children, for whom I labor in birth again until Christ is formed in you, ²⁰I would like to be present with you now and to change my tone; for I have doubts about you.

4:19 until Christ is formed in you. In contrast to the evil motives of the Judaizers, Paul sought to bring the Galatians to Christlikeness. This is the goal of salvation.

Two Covenants
²¹Tell me, you who desire to be under the law, do you not hear the law? ²²For it is written that Abraham had two sons: the one by a bondwoman, the other by a freewoman. ²³But he *who was* of the bondwoman was born according to the flesh, and he of the freewoman through promise, ²⁴which things are symbolic. For these are the*ᵃ* two covenants: the one from Mount Sinai

---

4:4 *ᵃ*Or made   4:7 *ᵃ*NU-Text reads *through God* and omits *through Christ*.   4:15 *ᵃ*NU-Text reads *Where*.   4:24 *ᵃ*NU-Text and M-Text omit *the*.

which gives birth to bondage, which is Hagar—[25]for this Hagar is Mount Sinai in Arabia, and corresponds to Jerusalem which now is, and is in bondage with her children—[26]but the Jerusalem above is free, which is the mother of us all. [27]For it is written:

> "Rejoice, O barren,
> You who do not bear!
> Break forth and shout,
> You who are not in labor!
> For the desolate has many more
>   children
> Than she who has a husband." [a]

[28]Now we, brethren, as Isaac was, are children of promise. [29]But, as he who was born according to the flesh then persecuted him who was born according to the Spirit, even so it is now. [30]Nevertheless what does the Scripture say? "Cast out the bondwoman and her son, for the son of the bondwoman shall not be heir with the son of the freewoman."[a] [31]So then, brethren, we are not children of the bondwoman but of the free.

Christian Liberty

5 Stand fast therefore in the liberty by which Christ has made us free,[a] and do not be entangled again with a yoke of bondage. [2]Indeed I, Paul, say to you that if you become circumcised, Christ will profit you nothing. [3]And I testify again to every man who becomes circumcised that he is a debt-

or to keep the whole law. [4]You have become estranged from Christ, you who attempt to be justified by law; you have fallen from grace. [5]For we through the Spirit eagerly wait for the hope of righteousness by faith. [6]For in Christ Jesus neither circumcision nor uncircumcision avails anything, but faith working through love.

> **5:1 Stand fast.** Paul urged the believers to stay where they were because of the benefit of being free from law and the flesh as a way of salvation, as well as because of the fullness of blessing by grace. **free.** When a sinner, under the curse of the law by striving to achieve his own righteousness, embraces Christ and receives salvation by grace, he is delivered. **yoke of bondage.** The law was a yoke of slavery for those who pursued it for salvation.

> **5:6 neither circumcision nor uncircumcision avails anything.** Nothing done or not done in the flesh makes any difference in one's relationship to God. The external is immaterial and worthless, unless it reflects genuine internal righteousness (see Rom. 2:25–29). **faith working through love.** Faith proves its character by works of love. The one who lives by faith is motivated by love for God and Christ (see Matt. 22:37–40).

Love Fulfills the Law

[7]You ran well. Who hindered you from obeying the truth? [8]This persuasion does not come from Him who calls you. [9]A little leaven leavens the whole lump. [10]I have confidence in you, in the Lord, that you will have no other mind; but he who

---

4:27 [a]Isaiah 54:1   4:30 [a]Genesis 21:10   5:1 [a]NU-Text reads For freedom Christ has made us free; stand fast therefore.

What does the phrase "you have fallen from grace" (5:4) mean in relation to the doctrine of eternal security?

Paul uses two terms in this verse that imply separation, loss, and breakdown: "estranged from Christ" and "fallen from grace." The Greek word for "estranged" means "to be separated" or "to be severed." The word for "fallen" means "to lose one's grasp of something." The context clarifies Paul's meaning. Any attempt to be justified by the law equates to a rejection of salvation by grace alone through faith alone. Those once exposed to the gracious truth of the gospel, who then turn their backs on Christ (Hebrews 6:4–6) and seek to be justified by the law, are separated from Christ and lose all prospects of God's gracious salvation. Their desertion of Christ and the gospel only proves that their faith was never genuine (Luke 8:13,14; 1 John 2:19).

troubles you shall bear his judgment, whoever he is.

[11]And I, brethren, if I still preach circumcision, why do I still suffer persecution? Then the offense of the cross has ceased. [12]I could wish that those who trouble you would even cut themselves off!

[13]For you, brethren, have been called to liberty; only do not *use* liberty as an opportunity for the flesh, but through love serve one another. [14]For all the law is fulfilled in one word, *even* in this: *"You shall love your neighbor as yourself."* [a] [15]But if you bite and devour one another, beware lest you be consumed by one another!

Walking in the Spirit

[16]I say then: Walk in the Spirit, and you shall not fulfill the lust of the flesh. [17]For the flesh lusts against the Spirit, and the Spirit against the flesh; and these are contrary to one another, so that you do not do the things that you wish. [18]But if you are led by the Spirit, you are not under the law.

5:16 Walk in the Spirit. All believers have the presence of the indwelling Holy Spirit (see Rom. 8:9) as the personal power for living to please God. "Walk" implies a habitual lifestyle and progress. **the flesh.** This refers to the physical body, as well as to the mind, will, and emotions which are all subject to sin. "Flesh" refers to our unredeemed humanness.

[19]Now the works of the flesh are evident, which are: adultery,[a] fornication, uncleanness, lewdness, [20]idolatry, sorcery, hatred, contentions, jealousies, outbursts of wrath, selfish ambitions, dissensions, heresies, [21]envy, murders,[a] drunkenness, revelries, and the like; of which I tell you beforehand, just as I also told *you* in time past, that those who practice such things will not inherit the kingdom of God.

[22]But the fruit of the Spirit is love, joy, peace, longsuffering, kindness, goodness, faithfulness, [23]gentleness, self-control. Against such there is no law. [24]And those *who are* Christ's have crucified the flesh with its passions and desires. [25]If we live in the Spirit, let us also walk in the Spirit. [26]Let us not become conceited, provoking one another, envying one another.

5:22 fruit of the Spirit. This refers to godly attitudes that characterize the lives of those who belong to God by faith in Christ. The Spirit produces fruit which consists of 9 attitudes that are linked with each other and are commanded of believers throughout the New Testament. **love.** This is *agape* love, the love of choice. It refers to respect, devotion, and affection that leads to willing, self-sacrificial service (John 15:13).

Bear and Share the Burdens

6 Brethren, if a man is overtaken in any trespass, you who *are* spiritual restore such a one in a spirit of gentleness, considering yourself lest you also be tempted. [2]Bear one another's burdens, and so fulfill the law of Christ. [3]For if anyone thinks himself to be something, when he is nothing, he deceives himself. [4]But let each one examine his own work, and then he will have rejoicing in himself alone, and not in another. [5]For each one shall bear his own load.

Be Generous and Do Good

[6]Let him who is taught the word share in all good things with him who teaches.

[7]Do not be deceived, God is not mocked; for whatever a man sows, that he will also reap. [8]For he who sows to his flesh will of the flesh reap corruption, but he who sows to the Spirit will of the Spirit reap everlasting life. [9]And let us not grow weary while doing good, for in due season we shall reap if we do not lose heart. [10]Therefore, as we have opportunity, let us do good to all, especially to those who are of the household of faith.

6:7 whatever a man sows...reap. This agricultural principle, applied metaphorically to the moral and spiritual realm, is universally true (see Job 4:8). This law is a form of God's wrath.

Glory Only in the Cross

[11]See with what large letters I have written to you with my own hand! [12]As many as desire to make a good showing in the flesh, these *would* compel you to be circumcised, only that they may not suffer persecution for the cross of Christ. [13]For not even those who are circumcised keep the law, but they

---

5:14 [a]Leviticus 19:18   5:19 [a]NU-Text omits *adultery*.   5:21 [a]NU-Text omits *murders*.

6:11 with what large letters. This could refer to Paul's poor eyesight forcing him to use large letters; it may also refer to large, block letters (used in public notices) emphasizing the letter's content rather than its form. It contrasted Paul's concern for the content of the gospel with the Judaizer's concern for appearances. **I have written...my own hand.** Paul wrote this letter himself in order to personalize it and to make sure the Galatians knew he was writing it.

6:14 boast except in the cross. The Greek word for "boast" is an expression of praise. Paul rejoices in the sacrifice of Jesus Christ (see Rom. 8:1–3). **the world.** This refers to the evil, Satanic system. **crucified to me, and I to the world.** The world is spiritually dead to believers, and they are dead to the world (see Phil. 3:20,21).

desire to have you circumcised that they may boast in your flesh. ¹⁴But God forbid that I should boast except in the cross of our Lord Jesus Christ, by whom^a the world has been crucified to me, and I to the world. ¹⁵For in Christ Jesus neither circumcision nor uncircumcision avails anything, but a new creation.

Blessing and a Plea

¹⁶And as many as walk according to this rule, peace and mercy *be* upon them, and upon the Israel of God.

¹⁷From now on let no one trouble me, for I bear in my body the marks of the Lord Jesus.

¹⁸Brethren, the grace of our Lord Jesus Christ *be* with your spirit. Amen.

6:14 ^a Or *by which* (the cross)

EPHESIANS

The church in the city of Ephesus received two letters recorded in Scripture. One came from the Apostle Paul, the other from Jesus (Revelation 2:1–6). When Jesus appeared to John and had him write letters to seven churches, he began with Ephesus. Both Jesus and Paul used the church in Ephesus as an example of the challenges and benefits of growing into an authentic living and loving Body of Christ in this world.

AUTHOR AND DATE

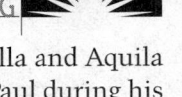

Ephesians was written by Paul, between A.D. 60 to 62.

No compelling evidence indicates that the authorship of Paul should be in question. His name appears in the opening salutation (1:1; 3:1). Parallel themes, context, and tone have made Ephesians one of the "prison epistles" (along with Philippians, Colossians, and Philemon). This group of letters were written while Paul awaited his trial in Rome (Acts 28:16–31).

The origin of this letter also establishes a historical time frame during which it was written, for Paul's Roman imprisonment occurred between A.D. 60 and 62.

BACKGROUND AND SETTING

The church in Ephesus probably began under the ministry of Priscilla and Aquila (Acts 18:26), an exceptionally gifted couple who were left there by Paul during his second missionary journey (Acts 18:18,19). Later, Paul visited Ephesus during his third missionary journey (Acts 19) and spent three years establishing the fledgling church. After Paul's departure, Timothy pastored the congregation for perhaps a year and a half, providing corrective instruction against the false teaching of a few influential men who were probably elders in the congregation (1 Timothy 1:3,20).

Located at the mouth of the Cayster River, on the east shore of the Aegean Sea, Ephesus was perhaps best known for its temple of Artemis, or Diana. That magnificent structure was one of the seven wonders of the ancient world. Ephesus also served as an important political, educational, and commercial center—a great city in its time.

The letter to the Ephesians follows Paul's pattern of emphasizing doctrine in the early chapters (1–3) and encouraging practical, Christian behavior in the later ones (chapters 4–6). The key theme of the letter is the "mystery" (meaning a heretofore unrevealed truth) of the church. In his explanation of the mystery Paul wrote, "that the Gentiles should be fellow heirs, of the same body, and partakers of His promise in Christ through the gospel" (3:6), a truth completely hidden from the Old Testament saints (3:5,9). The mystery becomes revealed in the truth that all believers in Jesus Christ, the Messiah, are equal before the Lord as His children and as citizens of His eternal kingdom. Only believers in this present age possess this marvelous truth. Paul also wrote of the mystery of the church as the bride of Christ (5:32; see Revelation 21:9).

This letter also emphasizes the further truth of the church as Christ's present spiritual, earthly body, a distinct and formerly unrevealed truth about God's people. This metaphor depicts the church, not as an organization, but as a living organism composed of mutually related and interdependent parts. Christ is Head of the body, and the Holy Spirit is its lifeblood. The body functions and grows as its members faithfully use their various spiritual gifts, sovereignly and uniquely given by the Holy Spirit to each believer.

> ## ALL BELIEVERS IN JESUS CHRIST, THE MESSIAH, ARE EQUAL BEFORE THE LORD AS HIS CHILDREN AND AS CITIZENS OF HIS ETERNAL KINGDOM.

Other major themes revolve around the immeasurable riches and fullness of blessing that believers possess through Jesus Christ. Paul wrote of the "riches of [God's] grace" (1:7), "the unsearchable riches of Christ" (3:8), and "the riches of His glory" (3:16). These priceless benefits in Christ are based on His grace (1:2,6,7; 2:7), peace (1:2), will (1:5), pleasure and purpose (1:9), glory (1:12,14), calling and inheritance (1:18), power and strength (1:19; 6:10), love (2:4), workmanship (2:10), Holy Spirit (3:16), offering and sacrifice (5:2), and armor (6:11,13). The word "riches" appears five times in this brief letter; "grace" 12 times; "glory" eight times, "fullness" or "filled" six times. The key phrase "in Christ" (or "in Him") appears 12 times.

Despite, and partly because of, a Christian's great blessings in Jesus Christ, he or she is sure to be tempted by Satan to self-satisfaction and complacency. For this reason, Paul concluded this letter by reminding believers of the full and sufficient armor supplied to them through God's Word and by His Spirit (6:10–17). Paul insisted on the crucial role of vigilant and persistent prayer (6:18).

OUTLINE

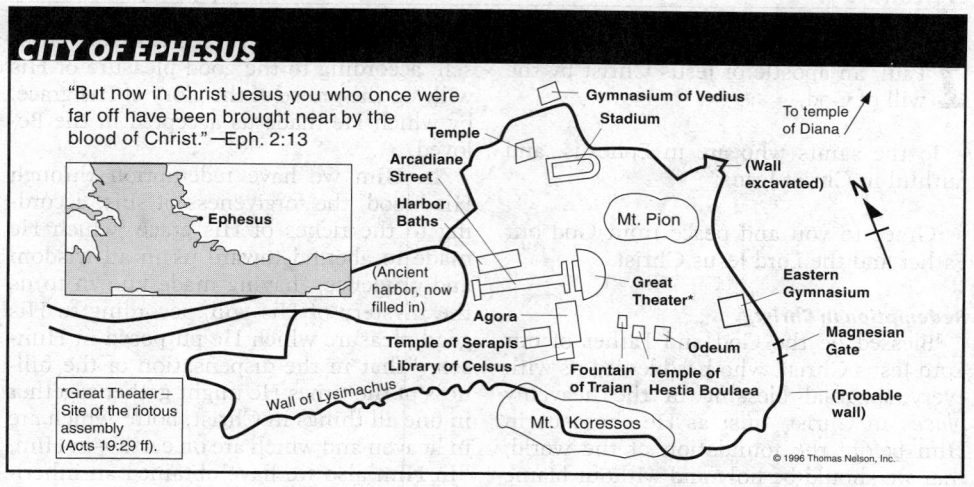

CITY OF EPHESUS

"But now in Christ Jesus you who once were far off have been brought near by the blood of Christ."—Eph. 2:13

Ephesus

(Ancient harbor, now filled in)

Harbor Baths

Arcadiane Street

Temple

Gymnasium of Vedius

Stadium

To temple of Diana

(Wall excavated)

N

Mt. Pion

Great Theater*

Eastern Gymnasium

Agora

Magnesian Gate

Temple of Serapis

Odeum

Library of Celsus

Fountain of Trajan

Temple of Hestia Boulaea

(Probable wall)

Wall of Lysimachus

Mt. Koressos

*Great Theater—
Site of the riotous assembly
(Acts 19:29 ff).

© 1996 Thomas Nelson, Inc.

Greeting

1 Paul, an apostle of Jesus Christ by the will of God,

To the saints who are in Ephesus, and faithful in Christ Jesus:

²Grace to you and peace from God our Father and the Lord Jesus Christ.

Redemption in Christ

³Blessed *be* the God and Father of our Lord Jesus Christ, who has blessed us with every spiritual blessing in the heavenly *places* in Christ, ⁴just as He chose us in Him before the foundation of the world, that we should be holy and without blame before Him in love, ⁵having predestined us

---

1:4,5 He chose us. The form of the Greek verb behind "chose" indicates that God chose *by* Himself and *for* Himself to the praise of His own glory. His election does not nullify man's responsibility to believe in Jesus as Lord and Savior (see Matt. 3:1,2). **having predestined us to adoption as sons.** God makes those who have trusted in Christ to be His children, made in the image of His Son. He gives them Christ's riches and blessings, along with His very nature (see John 15:15).

---

to adoption as sons by Jesus Christ to Himself, according to the good pleasure of His will, ⁶to the praise of the glory of His grace, by which He made us accepted in the Beloved.

⁷In Him we have redemption through His blood, the forgiveness of sins, according to the riches of His grace ⁸which He made to abound toward us in all wisdom and prudence, ⁹having made known to us the mystery of His will, according to His good pleasure which He purposed in Himself, ¹⁰that in the dispensation of the fullness of the times He might gather together in one all things in Christ, both*ᵃ* which are in heaven and which are on earth—in Him. ¹¹In Him also we have obtained an inheritance, being predestined according to the purpose of Him who works all things according to the counsel of His will, ¹²that we who first trusted in Christ should be to the praise of His glory.

¹³In Him you also *trusted,* after you heard the word of truth, the gospel of your salvation; in whom also, having believed, you were sealed with the Holy Spirit of promise, ¹⁴who*ᵃ* is the guarantee of our inheritance until the redemption of the purchased possession, to the praise of His glory.

1:10 *ᵃ*NU-Text and M-Text omit *both.*   1:14 *ᵃ*NU-Text reads *which.*

Why does Paul use the word "mystery" so often in his letter to the Ephesians?

Paul actually uses the word "mystery" six times in this letter (1:9; 3:3,4,9; 5:32; 6:19). By comparison, the word appears twice in Romans, once in 1 Corinthians, four times in Colossians, once in 1 Timothy, and nowhere else. Contrary to our use of mystery as a series of clues to be figured out, Paul's use of the word points to mystery as a heretofore unrevealed truth that has been made clear. The word "mystery" preserves the sense that the revealed truth has such awesome implications that it continues to amaze and humble those who accept it.

Ephesians introduces various aspects of the "mystery." Paul explained his use of the word in 3:4-6 by saying, "that the Gentiles should be fellow heirs, of the same body, and partakers of the His promise in Christ through the gospel." When the unsearchable riches of Christ are preached among the Gentiles, one result is an understanding of the "fellowship of the mystery" (3:9). And when God's plan for human marriage is used to explain the unique relationship between Christ and His bride, the church, Paul reminded his readers that the real subject is a great mystery (5:32). And finally, Paul asked the Ephesians to pray for him that he would be able "boldly to make known the mystery of the gospel" (6:19). The gospel is not mysterious because it is hard to understand. It is mysterious because it is unexpected, unmerited, and free. Though Paul didn't use the word in this passage, his summary of the mystery for the Ephesians can be found in 2:8,9: "For by grace you have been saved through faith, and that not of yourselves; it is the gift of God, not of works, lest anyone should boast."

Prayer for Spiritual Wisdom

[15]Therefore I also, after I heard of your faith in the Lord Jesus and your love for all the saints, [16]do not cease to give thanks for you, making mention of you in my prayers: [17]that the God of our Lord Jesus Christ, the Father of glory, may give to you the spirit of wisdom and revelation in the knowledge of Him, [18]the eyes of your understanding*a* being enlightened; that you may know what is the hope of His calling, what are the riches of the glory of His inheritance in the saints, [19]and what *is* the exceeding greatness of His power toward us who believe, according to the working of His mighty power [20]which He worked in Christ when He raised Him from the dead and seated *Him* at His right hand in the heavenly *places*, [21]far above all principality and power and might and dominion, and every name that is named, not only in this age but also in that which is to come. [22]And He put all *things* under His feet, and gave Him *to be* head over all *things* to the church, [23]which is His body, the fullness of Him who fills all in all.

By Grace Through Faith

2And you *He made alive,* who were dead in trespasses and sins, [2]in which you once walked according to the course of this world, according to the prince of the power of the air, the spirit who now works in the sons of disobedience, [3]among whom also we all once conducted ourselves in the lusts of our flesh, fulfilling the desires of the flesh and of the mind, and were by nature children of wrath, just as the others.

[4]But God, who is rich in mercy, because of His great love with which He loved us, [5]even when we were dead in trespasses, made us alive together with Christ (by grace you have been saved), [6]and raised *us* up together, and made *us* sit together in the heavenly *places* in Christ Jesus, [7]that in the ages to come He might show the exceeding riches of His grace in *His* kindness toward us in Christ Jesus. [8]For by grace you have been saved through faith, and that not of yourselves; *it is* the gift of God, [9]not of works, lest anyone should boast. [10]For we are His workmanship, created in Christ Jesus for good works, which God prepared beforehand that we should walk in them.

Brought Near by His Blood

[11]Therefore remember that you, once Gentiles in the flesh—who are called Uncircumcision by what is called the Circumcision made in the flesh by hands—[12]that at that time you were without Christ, being aliens from the commonwealth of Israel

How do grace, faith, and works make up the process of salvation that Paul describes in 2:8–10?

Paul describes the effective process of salvation as something God graciously accomplishes through faith. The word "that" in verse 8—"and that not of yourselves"—refers to the entire previous statement of salvation, not only the grace but also the faith. Although individuals are required to believe for salvation, even that faith is part of the gift of God that saves and cannot be exercised by one's own power. God's grace accomplishes the crucial action in every aspect of salvation.

Even "works," which cannot produce salvation, are also part of God's gift. As with salvation, a believer's sanctification and good works are ordained before time. Opportunities, strength, and will to do good works are subsequent and resultant God empowered fruits and evidences of grace having accomplished salvation through faith (see John 15:8; Philippians 2:12,13; 2 Timothy 3:17; Titus 2:14; James 2:16–26).

and strangers from the covenants of promise, having no hope and without God in the world. ¹³But now in Christ Jesus you who once were far off have been brought near by the blood of Christ.

Christ Our Peace

¹⁴For He Himself is our peace, who has made both one, and has broken down the middle wall of separation, ¹⁵having abolished in His flesh the enmity, *that is,* the law of commandments *contained* in ordinances, so as to create in Himself one new man *from* the two, *thus* making peace, ¹⁶and that He might reconcile them both to God in one body through the cross, thereby putting to death the enmity. ¹⁷And He came and preached peace to you who were afar off and to those who were near. ¹⁸For through Him we both have access by one Spirit to the Father.

> **2:15 abolished in His flesh the enmity.** Through His death, Christ abolished OT ceremonial laws, feasts, and sacrifices that separated Jews from Gentiles. God's moral law was encompassed in the New Covenant because it reflects His holy nature (Matt. 5:17–19). **one new man.** "New" refers to something completely unlike what it was before. Spiritually, a person in Christ is no longer Jew or Gentile, but a Christian (see Rom. 10:12,13).

Christ Our Cornerstone

¹⁹Now, therefore, you are no longer strangers and foreigners, but fellow citizens with the saints and members of the household of God, ²⁰having been built on the foundation of the apostles and prophets, Jesus Christ Himself being the chief cornerstone, ²¹in whom the whole building, being fitted together, grows into a holy temple in the Lord, ²²in whom you also are being built together for a dwelling place of God in the Spirit.

> **2:20 the foundation of the apostles and prophets.** The divine revelation, taught authoritatively by the apostles before the completion of the NT, provided the foundation for the church (see Rom. 15:20). **cornerstone.** This stone set the foundation and squared the building.

The Mystery Revealed

3 For this reason I, Paul, the prisoner of Christ Jesus for you Gentiles—²if indeed you have heard of the dispensation of the grace of God which was given to me for you, ³how that by revelation He made known to me the mystery (as I have briefly written already, ⁴by which, when you read, you may understand my knowledge in the mystery of Christ), ⁵which in other ages was not made known to the sons of men, as it has now been revealed by the Spirit to His holy apostles and prophets: ⁶that the Gentiles should be fellow heirs, of the same body, and partakers of His promise in Christ through the gospel, ⁷of which I became a minister according to the gift of the grace of God given to me by the effective working of His power.

> **3:4 the mystery of Christ.** There were many truths hidden and later revealed in the NT that are called mysteries. One mystery is that the Jew and Gentile were brought together in one body in the Messiah, which is what Paul explained and clarified. Paul realized that spiritual knowledge must precede practical application.

Purpose of the Mystery

⁸To me, who am less than the least of all the saints, this grace was given, that I should preach among the Gentiles the unsearchable riches of Christ, ⁹and to make all see what *is* the fellowship*ª* of the mystery, which from the beginning of the ages has been hidden in God who created all things through Jesus Christ;*ᵇ* ¹⁰to the intent that now the manifold wisdom of God might be made known by the church to the principalities and powers in the heavenly *places,* ¹¹according to the eternal purpose which He accomplished in Christ Jesus our Lord, ¹²in whom we have boldness and access with confidence through faith in Him. ¹³Therefore I ask that you do not lose heart at my tribulations for you, which is your glory.

Appreciation of the Mystery

¹⁴For this reason I bow my knees to the Father of our Lord Jesus Christ,*ª* ¹⁵from

---

3:9 *ª*NU-Text and M-Text read *stewardship* (dispensation). *ᵇ*NU-Text omits *through Jesus Christ.*
3:14 *ª*NU-Text omits *of our Lord Jesus Christ.*

whom the whole family in heaven and earth is named, ¹⁶that He would grant you, according to the riches of His glory, to be strengthened with might through His Spirit in the inner man, ¹⁷that Christ may dwell in your hearts through faith; that you, being rooted and grounded in love, ¹⁸may be able to comprehend with all the saints what *is* the width and length and depth and height— ¹⁹to know the love of Christ which passes knowledge; that you may be filled with all the fullness of God.

²⁰Now to Him who is able to do exceedingly abundantly above all that we ask or think, according to the power that works in us, ²¹to Him *be* glory in the church by Christ Jesus to all generations, forever and ever. Amen.

3:19 to know the love of Christ. This is the love of and from Christ that He places in the hearts of believers before they can truly love Him or anyone else (Rom. 5:5). **which passes knowledge.** Knowledge of Christ's love is only known by those who are God's children (see Phil. 4:7). **filled with all the fullness of God.** This means to be so strong spiritually that one is totally dominated by the Lord, with nothing left of self.

Walk in Unity

4 I, therefore, the prisoner of the Lord, beseech you to walk worthy of the calling with which you were called, ²with all lowliness and gentleness, with longsuffering, bearing with one another in love, ³endeavoring to keep the unity of the Spirit in the bond of peace. ⁴*There is* one body and one Spirit, just as you were called in one

---

Paul describes a number of leadership roles in 4:11. How do we understand these roles in the church today?

Christ possesses the authority and sovereignty to assign the spiritual gifts (4:7,8) to those He has called into service in His church. He gives not only gifts but also gifted people. This passage uses five terms to describe these roles: apostles, prophets, evangelists, pastors, and teachers.

"Apostles" is the New Testament term used particularly of the 12 disciples who had seen the risen Christ (Acts 1:22), including Matthias, who replaced Judas. Later, Paul was uniquely set apart as the apostle to the Gentiles (Galatians 1:15–17). Those apostles were chosen directly by Christ, so as to be called "apostles of Christ" (Galatians 1:1; 1 Peter 1:1). They were given three basic responsibilities: (1) to lay the foundation of the church (2:20); (2) to receive, declare, and write God's Word (3:5; Acts 11:28; 21:10,11); and (3) to confirm that Word through signs, wonders, and miracles (Acts 8:6,7; 2 Corinthians 12:12; Hebrews 2:3,4). The term "apostle" is used in more general ways of others in the early church, including Barnabas (Acts 14:4), Silas, and Timothy (1 Thessalonians 2:6), and others (Romans 16:7; Philippians 2:25).

"Prophets" were not ordinary believers who had the gift of prophecy but those who had been especially commissioned by the early church. The office of prophet seems to have been exclusively for work within local congregations. They sometimes spoke practical direct revelation for a church about God (Acts 11:21–28), or they expounded revelation already given (implied in Acts 13:1). Since the offices of apostle and prophet ceased with the completion of the New Testament, the ongoing leadership needs of the church have been met by other offices.

"Evangelists" proclaimed the good news of salvation in Jesus Christ to unbelievers (Acts 21:8; 2 Timothy 4:5). The related verb translated "to preach the gospel" is used 54 times and the related noun translated "gospel" is used 76 times in the New Testament.

The phrase "pastors and teachers" is best understood in context as a single office of leadership in the church. The Greek word translated "and" can mean "in particular" (1 Timothy 5:17). Pastor is the equivalent of "shepherd," so the words, pastor-teacher, and the two functions together define the teaching shepherd. This person is identified as one who is under the "great Pastor" Jesus (Hebrews 13:20,21; 1 Peter 2:25). One who holds this office is also called an "elder" and "bishop" (Acts 20:28; 1 Timothy 3:1–7; Titus 1:5–9; 1 Peter 5:1,2).

4:2 lowliness. "Humility" is a term not found in the Roman or Greek vocabularies of Paul's day. It was coined by Christians to describe a quality for which no other word was available. Humility, the most foundational Christian virtue (James 4:6), is the quality of character commanded in the first beatitude (Matt. 5:3) and describes the grace of Christ (Phil. 2:7,8).

hope of your calling; [5]one Lord, one faith, one baptism; [6]one God and Father of all, who *is* above all, and through all, and in you[a] all.

Spiritual Gifts

[7]But to each one of us grace was given according to the measure of Christ's gift. [8]Therefore He says:

> "When He ascended on high,
> He led captivity captive,
> And gave gifts to men."[a]

[9](Now this, *"He ascended"*—what does it mean but that He also first[a] descended into the lower parts of the earth? [10]He who descended is also the One who ascended far above all the heavens, that He might fill all things.)
[11]And He Himself gave some *to be* apostles, some prophets, some evangelists, and some pastors and teachers, [12]for the equipping of the saints for the work of ministry, for the edifying of the body of Christ, [13]till we all come to the unity of the faith and of the knowledge of the Son of God, to a perfect man, to the measure of the stature of the fullness of Christ; [14]that we should no longer be children, tossed to and fro and carried about with every wind of doctrine, by the trickery of men, in the cunning craftiness of deceitful plotting, [15]but, speaking the truth in love, may grow up in all things

4:12 equipping. This refers to leading Christians from sin to obedience. Scripture is the key to this process. **saints.** These are all who believe in Jesus Christ. **the work of ministry.** This is the spiritual service required of every Christian, not just of church leaders (see 1 Cor. 15:58). **the edifying of the body of Christ.** This refers to the spiritual edification, nurturing, and development of the church (see Acts 20:32).

into Him who is the head—Christ—[16]from whom the whole body, joined and knit together by what every joint supplies, according to the effective working by which every part does its share, causes growth of the body for the edifying of itself in love.

The New Man

[17]This I say, therefore, and testify in the Lord, that you should no longer walk as the rest of[a] the Gentiles walk, in the futility of their mind, [18]having their understanding darkened, being alienated from the life of God, because of the ignorance that is in them, because of the blindness of their heart; [19]who, being past feeling, have given themselves over to lewdness, to work all uncleanness with greediness.

4:17 the futility of their mind. Unbelievers are intellectually unproductive. As far as spiritual and moral issues are concerned, their rational processes are distorted and inadequate, failing to produce godly understanding or moral living. Their lives are empty, vain, and without meaning (see Rom. 1:21–28).

[20]But you have not so learned Christ, [21]if indeed you have heard Him and have been taught by Him, as the truth is in Jesus: [22]that you put off, concerning your former conduct, the old man which grows corrupt according to the deceitful lusts, [23]and be renewed in the spirit of your mind, [24]and that you put on the new man which was created according to God, in true righteousness and holiness.

Do Not Grieve the Spirit

[25]Therefore, putting away lying, *"Let each one of you speak truth with his neighbor,"*[a] for we are members of one another. [26]*"Be angry, and do not sin"*:[a] do not let the

4:26 Be angry, and do not sin. This is quoted from Ps. 4:4. By NT standards, anger can be either good or bad, depending on motive and purpose. Anger that hates any kind of evil is unselfish; anger based on love for God and others is permissible and commanded. **sun go down.** Even righteous anger can turn to bitterness, so it should be set aside by the end of the day.

4:6 [a]NU-Text omits *you;* M-Text reads *us.*   4:8 [a]Psalm 68:18   4:9 [a]NU-Text omits *first.*   4:17 [a]NU-Text omits *the rest of.*   4:25 [a]Zechariah 8:16   4:26 [a]Psalm 4:4

sun go down on your wrath, ²⁷nor give place to the devil. ²⁸Let him who stole steal no longer, but rather let him labor, working with *his* hands what is good, that he may have something to give him who has need. ²⁹Let no corrupt word proceed out of your mouth, but what is good for necessary edification, that it may impart grace to the hear-

ers. ³⁰And do not grieve the Holy Spirit of God, by whom you were sealed for the day of redemption. ³¹Let all bitterness, wrath, anger, clamor, and evil speaking be put away from you, with all malice. ³²And be kind to one another, tenderhearted, forgiving one another, even as God in Christ forgave you.

4:30 do not grieve the Holy Spirit of God. God is grieved when His children refuse to change the old ways of sin for those righteous ways of the new life. The Holy Spirit's response indicates He is a person. Other indications of His personhood include personal pronouns (John 14:17), His intellect (1 Cor. 2:11), feelings (Rom. 8:27), will (1 Cor. 12:11), speaking (Acts 13:2), convicting (John 16:8–11), interceding (Rom. 8:26), guiding (John 16:13), glorifying Christ (John 16:14), and serving God (Acts 16:6,7).

Walk in Love

5 Therefore be imitators of God as dear children. ²And walk in love, as Christ also has loved us and given Himself for us, an offering and a sacrifice to God for a sweet-smelling aroma.

³But fornication and all uncleanness or covetousness, let it not even be named among you, as is fitting for saints; ⁴neither filthiness, nor foolish talking, nor coarse jesting, which are not fitting, but rather

---

How do the principles of submission and love establish God's expectation of Christian marriage as described in 5:21–33?

The section that begins with a call to wise living (5:15) leads up to Paul's general counsel about submission (5:21). This last verse serves to introduce the next section (5:22–6:9) which spells out the godly expectations for various relationships. Here Paul stated unequivocally that every spirit filled Christian is to be a humble, submissive Christian. This is foundational to all the relationships in this section. No believer is inherently superior to any other believer. In their standing before God, all believers are equal in every way (3:28).

Having established the foundational principle of submission (5:21), Paul applied it first to the wife. The command is unqualified and applicable to every Christian wife, no matter what her own abilities, education, knowledge of Scripture, spiritual maturity, or any other qualities might be in relation to those of her husband. The submission is not the husband's to command but for the wife to willingly and lovingly offer. The phrase "your own husband" limits the wife's submission to the one man that God has placed over her.

The Spirit filled wife recognizes that her husband's role in giving leadership is not only God ordained but also a reflection of Christ's own loving, authoritative headship of the church. As the Lord delivered His church from the dangers of sin, death, and hell, so the husband provides for, protects, preserves, and loves his wife, leading her to blessing as she submits (Titus 1:4; 2:13; 3:6).

Paul has much more to say to the man who has been placed in the role of authority within marriage. That authority comes with supreme responsibilities for husbands in regard to their wives. Husbands are to love their wives with the same sacrificial love that Christ has for His church. Christ gave everything He had, including His own life, for the sake of His church, and that is the standard of sacrifice for a husband's love of his wife.

The clarity of God's guidelines makes it certain that problems in marriage must always be traced in both directions so that each partner clearly understands his or her roles and responsibilities. Failure to love is just as often the source of marital trouble as failure to submit.

giving of thanks. [5]For this you know,[a] that no fornicator, unclean person, nor covetous man, who is an idolater, has any inheritance in the kingdom of Christ and God. [6]Let no one deceive you with empty words, for because of these things the wrath of God comes upon the sons of disobedience. [7]Therefore do not be partakers with them.

Walk in Light

[8]For you were once darkness, but now *you are* light in the Lord. Walk as children of light [9](for the fruit of the Spirit[a] *is* in all goodness, righteousness, and truth), [10]finding out what is acceptable to the Lord. [11]And have no fellowship with the unfruitful works of darkness, but rather expose *them.* [12]For it is shameful even to speak of those things which are done by them in secret. [13]But all things that are exposed are made manifest by the light, for whatever makes manifest is light. [14]Therefore He says:

> "Awake, you who sleep,
> Arise from the dead,
> And Christ will give you light."

> **5:11 no fellowship with...darkness.** Paul instructs Christians to faithfully live in righteousness and purity, having nothing to do with the evil ways of Satan and the world. **but rather expose *them.*** The Christian is also responsible for exposing and opposing darkness wherever it is found, especially when it is found in the church.

Walk in Wisdom

[15]See then that you walk circumspectly, not as fools but as wise, [16]redeeming the time, because the days are evil.

[17]Therefore do not be unwise, but understand what the will of the Lord *is.* [18]And do not be drunk with wine, in which is dissipation; but be filled with the Spirit, [19]speaking to one another in psalms and hymns and spiritual songs, singing and making melody in your heart to the Lord, [20]giving thanks always for all things to God the Father in the name of our Lord Jesus Christ, [21]submitting to one another in the fear of God.[a]

> **5:18 And do not be drunk with wine.** Although Scripture consistently condemns all drunkenness, the context here suggests that Paul is speaking about the drunken orgies commonly associated with pagan worship ceremonies of that day. Such festivities were supposed to induce some ecstatic communion with the deities. Paul referred to such as the "cup of demons." (1Cor. 10:20,21) **but be filled with the Spirit.** True communion with God is induced by the Holy Spirit. Being filled with the Spirit is the same as walking with the Spirit (see Gal. 5:16–23).

Marriage—Christ and the Church

[22]Wives, submit to your own husbands, as to the Lord. [23]For the husband is head of the wife, as also Christ is head of the church; and He is the Savior of the body. [24]Therefore, just as the church is subject to Christ, so *let* the wives *be* to their own husbands in everything.

[25]Husbands, love your wives, just as Christ also loved the church and gave Himself for her, [26]that He might sanctify and cleanse her with the washing of water by the word, [27]that He might present her to Himself a glorious church, not having spot or wrinkle or any such thing, but that she should be holy and without blemish. [28]So husbands ought to love their own wives as their own bodies; he who loves his wife loves himself. [29]For no one ever hated his own flesh, but nourishes and cherishes it, just as the Lord *does* the church. [30]For we are members of His body,[a] of His flesh and of His bones. [31]*For this reason a man shall leave his father and mother and be joined to his wife, and the two shall become one flesh."* [a] [32]This is a great mystery, but I speak concerning Christ and the church. [33]Nevertheless let each one of you in particular so love his own wife as himself, and let the wife *see* that she respects *her* husband.

> **5:28 as their own bodies.** A Christian husband is to care for his wife with the same devotion that he naturally manifests as he cares for himself. His self-sacrificing love causes him to put her first (see Phil. 2:1–4). **loves his wife loves himself.** A husband who loves his wife in these ways brings blessing to himself from her and from the Lord.

5:5 [a]NU-Text reads *For know this.*   5:9 [a]NU-Text reads *light.*   5:21 [a]NU-Text reads *Christ.*
5:30 [a]NU-Text omits the rest of this verse.   5:31 [a]Genesis 2:24

Children and Parents

6 Children, obey your parents in the Lord, for this is right. [2]*"Honor your father and mother,"* which is the first commandment with promise: [3]*"that it may be well with you and you may live long on the earth."* [a]

[4]And you, fathers, do not provoke your children to wrath, but bring them up in the training and admonition of the Lord.

Bondservants and Masters

[5]Bondservants, be obedient to those who are your masters according to the flesh, with fear and trembling, in sincerity of heart, as to Christ; [6]not with eyeservice, as men-pleasers, but as bondservants of Christ, doing the will of God from the heart, [7]with goodwill doing service, as to the Lord, and not to men, [8]knowing that whatever good anyone does, he will receive the same from the Lord, whether *he is* a slave or free.

[9]And you, masters, do the same things to

6:6 eyeservice. This refers to working well only when being watched by the boss. **men-pleasers.** This is working only to promote one's welfare, rather than to honor the employer and the Lord.

6:3 [a]Deuteronomy 5:16

Why does Paul insist in 6:10–17 that Christians must be prepared for spiritual battle?

The true believer described in chapters 1–3, who lives the Spirit controlled life described in 4:1–6:9, can be sure to encounter spiritual warfare. So, Paul closed his letter with warnings about upcoming battles and instructions about victorious living. The Lord provides His saints with sufficient armor to combat and defeat the adversary. Ephesians 6:10–13 briefly sets forth the basic truths regarding the believer's necessary spiritual preparation as well as truths about the enemy, the battle, and the victory. Verses 14–17 specify the six most necessary pieces of spiritual armor with which God equips His children to resist and overcome Satan's assaults.

The spiritual equipment parallels the standard military equipment worn by soldiers in Paul's day:

1. Belt of truth—The soldier wore a tunic of loose-fitting clothing. Since ancient combat was largely hand-to-hand, the tunic was a potential hindrance and danger. The belt cinched up the loose material. The belt that pulls together all the spiritual loose ends is "truth" or, better, "truthfulness."

2. Breastplate of righteousness—A tough, sleeveless piece of leather or heavy material covered the soldier's full torso, protecting his heart and other vital organs. Because righteousness, or holiness, is such a distinctive characteristic of God Himself, it is easy to understand why it is the Christian's chief protection against Satan and his schemes.

3. Boots of the gospel—Roman soldiers wore boots with nails in them to grip the ground in combat. The gospel of peace pertains to the good news that through Christ believers are at peace with God, and He is on their side (Romans 5:6–10).

4. Shield of faith—This Greek word usually refers to the large shield that protected the soldier's entire body. The believer's continual trust in God's Word and promise is "above all" absolutely necessary to protect him or her from temptations to every sort of sin.

5. Helmet of salvation—The helmet protected the head, always a major target in battle. This passage is speaking to those who are already saved; therefore, it does not refer to attaining salvation. Rather, since Satan seeks to destroy a believer's assurance of salvation with his weapons of doubt and discouragement, the believer must be as conscious of his or her confident status in Christ as he or she would be aware of a helmet on the head.

6. Sword of the Spirit—A sword was the soldier's only weapon. In the same way, God's Word is the only weapon that a believer needs, infinitely more powerful than any of Satan's devices.

them, giving up threatening, knowing that your own Master also[a] is in heaven, and there is no partiality with Him.

The Whole Armor of God

[10]Finally, my brethren, be strong in the Lord and in the power of His might. [11]Put on the whole armor of God, that you may be able to stand against the wiles of the devil. [12]For we do not wrestle against flesh and blood, but against principalities, against powers, against the rulers of the darkness of this age,[a] against spiritual *hosts* of wickedness in the heavenly *places*. [13]Therefore take up the whole armor of God, that you may be able to withstand in the evil day, and having done all, to stand.

6:12 wrestle. This term is used of hand-to-hand combat. It features the kind of deception that Satan and his hosts use when they attack God's people. Coping with deceptive temptation requires truth and righteousness. The 4 designations describe the different rankings of those demons and the evil empire in which they operate. Satan's forces of darkness are highly structured for the most destructive purposes (see Col. 2:15). **spiritual *hosts* of wickedness.** This possibly refers to extreme sexual perversions, occultism, and Satan worship.

[14]Stand therefore, having girded your waist with truth, having put on the breastplate of righteousness, [15]and having shod your feet with the preparation of the gospel of peace; [16]above all, taking the shield of faith with which you will be able to quench all the fiery darts of the wicked one. [17]And take the helmet of salvation, and the sword of the Spirit, which is the word of God; [18]praying always with all prayer and supplication in the Spirit, being watchful to this end with all perseverance and supplication for all the saints—[19]and for me, that utterance may be given to me, that I may open my mouth boldly to make known the mystery of the gospel, [20]for which I am an ambassador in chains; that in it I may speak boldly, as I ought to speak.

A Gracious Greeting

[21]But that you also may know my affairs *and* how I am doing, Tychicus, a beloved brother and faithful minister in the Lord, will make all things known to you; [22]whom I have sent to you for this very purpose, that you may know our affairs, and *that* he may comfort your hearts.

[23]Peace to the brethren, and love with faith, from God the Father and the Lord Jesus Christ. [24]Grace *be* with all those who love our Lord Jesus Christ in sincerity. Amen.

6:9 [a]NU-Text reads *He who is both their Master and yours.*   6:12 [a]NU-Text reads *rulers of this darkness.*

PHILIPPIANS

If people were to search for joy, they probably would not think to look in prison. But that is where Paul wrote this marvelous letter about joy. Through Paul, the Holy Spirit taught that circumstances don't dictate the quality of joy believers have in Christ. How did Paul find joy in prison? He didn't. He took joy in Christ into jail with him; therefore, joy was his continual companion.

AUTHOR AND DATE

Philippians was written by Paul, approximately A.D. 61.

The unanimous testimony of the early church was that the Apostle Paul wrote Philippians. The question of when this letter was written cannot be separated from where. The traditional view is that Philippians, along with the other Prison Epistles (Ephesians, Colossians, Philemon), was written during Paul's first imprisonment at Rome, about A.D. 60–62. Other views concerning where Paul wrote the Prison Epistles face significant internal textual difficulties. In the light of those difficulties, there is no reason to reject the traditional view that Paul wrote the Prison Epistles—including this one—from Rome. The most natural understanding of the references to the "palace guard" (1:13) and the "saints . . . of Caesar's household" (4:22) is that Paul was in Rome, where the emperor lived.

Paul's stated belief that his case would soon be decided (2:23,24) points to a writing date toward the close of the apostle's two year Roman imprisonment (about A.D. 61).

BACKGROUND AND SETTING

In New Testament times, Philippi was known primarily as the site of one of the most famous events in Roman history. In 42 B.C., the forces of Antony and Octavian defeated those of Brutus and Cassius at the Battle of Philippi, thus ending the Roman Republic and ushering in the Empire. After that battle, Philippi became a Roman colony (Acts 16:12), and many veterans of the Roman army settled there.

As a colony, Philippi had autonomy from the provincial government and the same rights granted to cities in Italy, including the use of Roman law, exemption from certain taxes, and Roman citizenship for its residents (Acts 16:21). Recognition as a colony provided a source for much civic pride for the Philippians, who used Latin as their official language, adopted Roman customs, and modeled their city government after that of Italian cities.

The church at Philippi, the first one founded by Paul in Europe, dates from the apostle's second missionary journey (Acts 16:12–40). Among the early con-

verts were Lydia, a wealthy merchant dealing in expensive purple dyed goods (Acts 16:14), and the jailer whose prison housed Paul and Silas until an earthquake set them free and opened his own heart to the gospel.

Paul apparently visited Philippi twice during his third missionary journey, once at the beginning (2 Corinthians 8:1-5) and again near the end (Acts 20:6). About four or five years later, while a prisoner in Rome, Paul received a delegation from the Philippian church. They presented the apostle with some funds (4:10) and offered to leave Epaphroditus behind to minister to his needs. Because Epaphroditus had suffered a near-fatal illness (2:26,27) however, Paul decided to send him back to Philippi (2:25,26), along with this letter for the church.

Both Acts and the letter to the Philippians reflect Philippi's status as a Roman colony. Paul's description of Christians as citizens of heaven (3:20) would have been particularly meaningful to the Philippians' pride over being citizens of Rome (Acts 16:21). Some of the retired veterans in Philippi may well have been former members of the elite palace guard (1:13) and part of Caesar's household (4:22).

Paul revealed several purposes behind his decision to write to the Philippian church. First, he wanted to express in writing his thanks for the Philippians' gift (4:10–18). Second, he wanted the Philippians to know why he had decided to return Epaphroditus to them, so they would not think his service to Paul had been unsatisfactory (2:25,26). Third, he wanted to inform them about his circumstances at Rome (1:12–26). Fourth, he wrote to exhort them to unity (2:1,2; 4:2). Finally, he wrote to warn them against false teachers (3:1–4:1).

HISTORICAL AND THEOLOGICAL THEMES

The most notable historical material in the letter to the Philippians can be found in the summary of Paul's spiritual autobiography (3:4–7). Just as 2:5–11 describes what Jesus gave up in order to accomplish God's saving plan, 3:4–7 describes what Paul "counted loss for Christ."

Paul also complimented the believers' pattern of generosity. They had supported Paul in the past (4:15,16), and they contributed generously for the needy in Jerusalem (2 Corinthians 8:1–4). And when they heard about Paul's imprisonment, they sent both personal and financial encouragement to him (4:10). Their actions offer a fine example of Christian generosity.

OUT OF THAT **UNDERSTANDING** OF **CHRIST COMES** THE **ENCOURAGEMENT** TO **PURSUE CHRISTLIKENESS.**

Among the theological themes, Paul's hymn about Christ's character (2:5–11) contains some of the most profound and crucial teaching about the Lord Jesus Christ in the entire Bible. Out of that understanding of Christ comes the encouragement to pursue Christlikeness (2:5; 3:12–14), a continual emphasis in Paul's ministry. Beyond these, it bears repeating that the dominant tone of this letter is joyful.

OUTLINE

Greeting

1 Paul and Timothy, bondservants of Jesus Christ,

To all the saints in Christ Jesus who are in Philippi, with the bishops*ᵃ* and deacons:

²Grace to you and peace from God our Father and the Lord Jesus Christ.

Thankfulness and Prayer

³I thank my God upon every remembrance of you, ⁴always in every prayer of mine making request for you all with joy, ⁵for your fellowship in the gospel from the first day until now, ⁶being confident of this very thing, that He who has begun a good work in you will complete *it* until the day of Jesus Christ; ⁷just as it is right for me to think this of you all, because I have you in my heart, inasmuch as both in my chains and in the defense and confirmation of the gospel, you all are partakers with me of grace. ⁸For God is my witness, how greatly I long for you all with the affection of Jesus Christ.

> **1:6 He...will complete it.** When God begins a work of salvation in a person, He finishes and perfects that work. The verb "will complete" points to the eternal security of the Christian. **day of Jesus Christ.** This is the day of final salvation, reward, and glorification of believers (see 1 Cor. 3:10).

⁹And this I pray, that your love may abound still more and more in knowledge and all discernment, ¹⁰that you may approve the things that are excellent, that you may be sincere and without offense till the day of Christ, ¹¹being filled with the fruits of righteousness which *are* by Jesus Christ, to the glory and praise of God.

Christ Is Preached

¹²But I want you to know, brethren, that the things *which happened* to me have actually turned out for the furtherance of the gospel, ¹³so that it has become evident to the whole palace guard, and to all the rest, that my chains are in Christ; ¹⁴and most of the brethren in the Lord, having become confident by my chains, are much more bold to speak the word without fear.

¹⁵Some indeed preach Christ even from envy and strife, and some also from good-

> **1:13 evident...chains are in Christ.** People around Paul recognized that he was no criminal; he had become a prisoner because of preaching Jesus Christ and the gospel (see Eph. 6:20). **whole palace guard.** This refers to either a special building or the group of men in the Imperial guard. Because Paul was in a private house in Rome, "palace guard" probably refers to the members of the Imperial guard who guarded Paul day and night.

will: ¹⁶The former*ᵃ* preach Christ from selfish ambition, not sincerely, supposing to add affliction to my chains; ¹⁷but the latter out of love, knowing that I am appointed for the defense of the gospel. ¹⁸What then? Only *that* in every way, whether in pretense or in truth, Christ is preached; and in this I rejoice, yes, and will rejoice.

To Live Is Christ

¹⁹For I know that this will turn out for my deliverance through your prayer and the supply of the Spirit of Jesus Christ, ²⁰according to my earnest expectation and hope that in nothing I shall be ashamed, but with all boldness, as always, so now also Christ will be magnified in my body, whether by life or by death. ²¹For to me, to live *is* Christ, and to die *is* gain. ²²But if *I* live on in the flesh, this *will mean* fruit from *my* labor; yet what I shall choose I cannot tell. ²³For*ᵃ* I am hard-pressed between the two, having a desire to depart and be with Christ, *which is* far better. ²⁴Nevertheless to remain in the flesh *is* more needful for you. ²⁵And being confident of this, I know that I shall remain and continue with you all for your progress and joy of faith, ²⁶that your rejoicing for me may be more abundant in Jesus Christ by my coming to you again.

> **1:22 the flesh.** This refers to physical life. **fruit.** Paul knew that the only reason to remain in this world was to bring souls to Christ and build up believers to do the same.

1:1 *ᵃ*Literally *overseers*   1:16 *ᵃ*NU-Text reverses the contents of verses 16 and 17.   1:23 *ᵃ*NU-Text and M-Text read *But.*

Striving and Suffering for Christ

²⁷Only let your conduct be worthy of the gospel of Christ, so that whether I come and see you or am absent, I may hear of your affairs, that you stand fast in one spirit, with one mind striving together for the faith of the gospel, ²⁸and not in any way terrified by your adversaries, which is to them a proof of perdition, but to you of salvation,ᵃ and that from God. ²⁹For to you it has been granted on behalf of Christ, not only to believe in Him, but also to suffer for His sake, ³⁰having the same conflict which you saw in me and now hear *is* in me.

> **1:28 proof of perdition.** When believers willingly suffer without being "terrified," it is a sign that God's enemies will be destroyed and eternally lost.

Unity Through Humility

2 Therefore if *there is* any consolation in Christ, if any comfort of love, if any fellowship of the Spirit, if any affection and mercy, ²fulfill my joy by being like-minded, having the same love, *being* of one accord, of one mind. ³*Let* nothing *be done* through selfish ambition or conceit, but in lowliness of mind let each esteem others better than himself. ⁴Let each of you look out not only for his own interests, but also for the interests of others.

> **2:3 selfish ambition.** This is the pride that prompts people to push for their own way. **conceit.** This word refers to the pursuit of personal glory, which is the motivation for selfish ambition. **lowliness of mind.** Paul and other NT writers coined this term. It was a term of derision, with the idea of being low, shabby, and humble (see 1 Cor. 15:9). **esteem others better than himself.** This is true humility (see Rom. 12:10).

The Humbled and Exalted Christ

⁵Let this mind be in you which was also in Christ Jesus, ⁶who, being in the form of God, did not consider it robbery to be equal with God, ⁷but made Himself of no reputation, taking the form of a bondservant, *and* coming in the likeness of men. ⁸And being found in appearance as a man, He humbled Himself and became obedient to *the point of* death, even the death of the cross. ⁹Therefore God also has highly exalted

Him and given Him the name which is above every name, ¹⁰that at the name of Jesus every knee should bow, of those in heaven, and of those on earth, and of those under the earth, ¹¹and *that* every tongue should confess that Jesus Christ *is* Lord, to the glory of God the Father.

> **2:8 in appearance as a man.** Christ's humanity is described from the viewpoint of those who saw Him. Although He outwardly looked like a man, there was much more to Him (His deity) than many people recognized (see John 6:42). **He humbled Himself.** Jesus humbled Himself in the incarnation, as well as in His willingness to be subjected to persecution at the hands of unbelievers (see Is. 53:7).

Light Bearers

¹²Therefore, my beloved, as you have always obeyed, not as in my presence only, but now much more in my absence, work out your own salvation with fear and trembling; ¹³for it is God who works in you both to will and to do for *His* good pleasure.

¹⁴Do all things without complaining and disputing, ¹⁵that you may become blameless and harmless, children of God without fault in the midst of a crooked and perverse generation, among whom you shine as lights in the world, ¹⁶holding fast the word of life, so that I may rejoice in the day of Christ that I have not run in vain or labored in vain.

¹⁷Yes, and if I am being poured out *as a drink offering* on the sacrifice and service of your faith, I am glad and rejoice with you all. ¹⁸For the same reason you also be glad and rejoice with me.

Timothy Commended

¹⁹But I trust in the Lord Jesus to send Timothy to you shortly, that I also may be encouraged when I know your state. ²⁰For I have no one like-minded, who will sincerely care for your state. ²¹For all seek their

> **2:20 I have no one like-minded.** Timothy was one in thought, feeling, and spirit with Paul in love for the church. He was unique in being Paul's protégé (see 1 Tim. 1:2). Paul had no other like Timothy because many others were devoted to their own purposes rather than Christ's.

1:28 ᵃNU-Text reads *of your salvation.*

own, not the things which are of Christ Jesus. ²²But you know his proven character, that as a son with *his* father he served with me in the gospel. ²³Therefore I hope to send him at once, as soon as I see how it goes with me. ²⁴But I trust in the Lord that I myself shall also come shortly.

Epaphroditus Praised

²⁵Yet I considered it necessary to send to you Epaphroditus, my brother, fellow worker,

and fellow soldier, but your messenger and the one who ministered to my need; ²⁶since he was longing for you all, and was distressed because you had heard that he was sick. ²⁷For indeed he was sick almost unto death; but God had mercy on him, and not only on him but on me also, lest I should have sorrow upon sorrow. ²⁸Therefore I sent him the more eagerly, that when you see him again you may rejoice, and I may be less sorrowful. ²⁹Receive him therefore

---

What can we learn about Jesus from the great eulogy in 2:6–11?

This is the classic Christological passage in the New Testament, summarizing the divinity, character, and incarnation of Jesus Christ. It stands so clearly as a unit that it was probably sung as a hymn in the early church.

This meditation begins by focusing on the eternal nature of Christ (2:6). The usual Greek term for "being" is not used here. Instead, Paul chose another term that stresses the essence of a person's nature—his or her continuous state or condition. Also, of the two Greek words for "form," Paul chose the one that specifically denotes the essential, unchanging character of something—what it is in and of itself. The fundamental doctrine of the deity of Christ has always included these crucial characteristics (see also John 1:1,3,4,14; 8:58; Colossians 1:15–17; Hebrews 1:3). Although Christ had all the rights, privileges, and honors of deity—for which He was eternally and continually worthy—His attitude was not to cling to His position but to willingly give it up for a time.

Next, the passage describes the process that Christ underwent in order to carry out the incarnation. First, He "made Himself of no reputation" or better, "emptied Himself" (2:7). The Greek root word used here, *kenosis*, is now used as the theological term for the doctrine of Christ's self—emptying in His incarnation. This step did not mean that Jesus emptied Himself of deity. Jesus did, however, renounce or set aside His privileges in several areas: (1) heavenly glory (John 17:5); (2) independent authority—during His incarnation Christ completely submitted Himself to the will of His Father (Matthew 26:39; John 5:30; Hebrews 5:8); (3) divine prerogatives—Christ set aside the voluntary display of His divine attributes and submitted Himself to the Spirit's direction (Matthew 24:36; John 1:45–49); (4) eternal riches (2 Corinthians 8:9); (5) a favorable relationship with God—Christ felt the Father's wrath for human sin while on the cross (Matthew 27:46).

Next, Christ took on the "form of a bondservant" and the "likeness of men" (2:7). The same Greek word for "form" occurs here as in verse 6. Christ became more than just God in a human body; He took on all the essential attributes of humanity (Luke 2:52; Galatians 4:4; Colossians 1:22), even to the extent that he identified with basic human needs and weaknesses (Hebrews 2:14,17; 4:15). He became the God-Man: fully divine and fully human.

Next, Christ carried out the full purposes and implications of His divine action. He experienced every aspect of life as a human being. This included the ultimate obedience of dying as a criminal, following God's plan for Him (Matthew 26:39; Acts 2:23).

Christ's utter humiliation (2:5–8) is causally and inseparably linked to his exaltation by God (2:9–11). Jesus was honored in at least six distinct ways: (1) His resurrection; (2) His coronation (His position at the right hand of God); (3) His role as intercessor for believers (Acts 2:32,33; 5:30,31; Ephesians 1:20,21; Hebrews 4:15; 7:25,26); (4) His ascension (Hebrews 4:14); (5) His acknowledged role as the ultimate and perfect substitute for sin; (6) His given title and name as Lord, which identifies Him fully as the divine and sovereign ruler (Isaiah 45:21–23; Mark 15:2; Luke 2:11; John 13:13; 18:37; 20:28; Acts 2:36; 10:36; Romans 14:9–11; 1 Corinthians 8:6; 15:57; Revelation 17:14; 19:16). Scripture affirms throughout Jesus' rightful title and name as Lord, which identifies Him fully as the divine and sovereign ruler

2:25 Epaphroditus...messenger. Little is known of this Philippian believer named Epaphroditus. His name originally meant "favorite of Aphrodite," but later it came to mean "loving." He was a leader of the church of Philippi, sent to Paul with monetary love gifts. He was to remain and serve Paul as he could. Paul's sending him back to the church with this letter needed an explanation, lest the believers think that Epaphroditus had not served Paul well.

in the Lord with all gladness, and hold such men in esteem; [30]because for the work of Christ he came close to death, not regarding his life, to supply what was lacking in your service toward me.

All for Christ

3 Finally, my brethren, rejoice in the Lord. For me to write the same things to you *is* not tedious, but for you *it is* safe.

[2]Beware of dogs, beware of evil workers, beware of the mutilation! [3]For we are the circumcision, who worship God in the Spirit,[a] rejoice in Christ Jesus, and have no confidence in the flesh, [4]though I also might have confidence in the flesh. If anyone else thinks he may have confidence in the flesh, I more so: [5]circumcised the

3:5 the eighth day. Paul was circumcised on the prescribed day (Gen. 17:12). **of Israel.** All true Jews were direct descendants of Abraham, Isaac, and Jacob. Paul's Jewish heritage was pure. **Hebrew of the Hebrews.** Paul was born to Hebrew parents and maintained the Hebrew tradition and language, even while living in a pagan city (see Acts 21:40). **a Pharisee.** Paul may have come from a line of Pharisees (see Acts 23:6), legalistic fundamentalists of Judaism, whose devotion to the OT Scriptures led to a complex system of tradition and works righteousness.

eighth day, of the stock of Israel, *of* the tribe of Benjamin, a Hebrew of the Hebrews; concerning the law, a Pharisee; [6]concerning zeal, persecuting the church; concerning the righteousness which is in the law, blameless.

[7]But what things were gain to me, these I have counted loss for Christ. [8]Yet indeed I also count all things loss for the excellence of the knowledge of Christ Jesus my Lord, for whom I have suffered the loss of all things, and count them as rubbish, that I may gain Christ [9]and be found in Him, not having my own righteousness, which *is* from the law, but that which *is* through faith in Christ, the righteousness which is from God by faith; [10]that I may know Him and the power of His resurrection, and the fellowship of His sufferings, being conformed to His death, [11]if, by any means, I may attain to the resurrection from the dead.

3:11 by any means. Paul longed for death and for the fulfillment of his salvation in his resurrection body (see Rom. 8:23). **the resurrection from the dead.** This refers to the resurrection which accompanies the rapture of the church (1 Thess. 4:13–17).

Pressing Toward the Goal

[12]Not that I have already attained, or am already perfected; but I press on, that I may lay hold of that for which Christ Jesus has also laid hold of me. [13]Brethren, I do not count myself to have apprehended; but one thing *I do,* forgetting those things which are behind and reaching forward to those things which are ahead, [14]I press toward the goal for the prize of the upward call of God in Christ Jesus.

[15]Therefore let us, as many as are ma-

3:3 [a]NU-Text and M-Text read *who worship in the Spirit of God.*

To whom is Paul referring by the term "enemies of the cross" in 3:18?

As he had done in many of his contacts with churches he had founded (Acts 20:28–31), Paul warned the Philippians about the dangers of false teachers. Paul's language implies that these teachers did not openly claim to oppose Christ, His work on the cross, or salvation by grace alone through faith alone, but they did not pursue Christlikeness through godly living. Their faith was a fraud. Apparently, they had been posing as friends of Christ and possibly had even reached positions of leadership in the church. Their lives displayed their true allegiance.

ture, have this mind; and if in anything you think otherwise, God will reveal even this to you. [16]Nevertheless, to *the degree* that we have already attained, let us walk by the same rule,[a] let us be of the same mind.

Our Citizenship in Heaven

[17]Brethren, join in following my example, and note those who so walk, as you have us for a pattern. [18]For many walk, of whom I have told you often, and now tell you even weeping, *that they are* the enemies of the cross of Christ: [19]whose end *is* destruction, whose god *is their* belly, and *whose* glory *is* in their shame—who set their mind on earthly things. [20]For our citizenship is in heaven, from which we also eagerly wait for the Savior, the Lord Jesus Christ, [21]who will transform our lowly body that it may be conformed to His glorious body, according to the working by which He is able even to subdue all things to Himself.

4 Therefore, my beloved and longed-for brethren, my joy and crown, so stand fast in the Lord, beloved.

Be United, Joyful, and in Prayer

[2]I implore Euodia and I implore Syntyche to be of the same mind in the Lord. [3]And[a] I urge you also, true companion, help these women who labored with me in the gospel, with Clement also, and the rest of my fellow workers, whose names *are* in the Book of Life.

> **4:2 Euodia...Syntyche.** These two women were prominent church members who may have been among the women meeting for prayer when Paul first preached the gospel in Philippi (Acts 16:13). They were leading two opposing factions in the church, most likely over a personal conflict. **the same mind.** Spiritual stability depends on mutual love, harmony, and peace between believers. The disunity in the Philippian church was about to destroy its testimony.

[4]Rejoice in the Lord always. Again I will say, rejoice!

[5]Let your gentleness be known to all men. The Lord *is* at hand.

[6]Be anxious for nothing, but in everything by prayer and supplication, with thanksgiving, let your requests be made known to God; [7]and the peace of God, which surpasses all understanding, will guard your hearts and minds through Christ Jesus.

Meditate on These Things

[8]Finally, brethren, whatever things are true, whatever things *are* noble, whatever things *are* just, whatever things *are* pure, whatever things *are* lovely, whatever things *are* of good report, if *there is* any virtue and if *there is* anything praiseworthy—meditate on these things. [9]The things which you learned and received and heard and saw in me, these do, and the God of peace will be with you.

3:16 [a]NU-Text omits *rule* and the rest of the verse.   4:3 [a]NU-Text and M-Text read *Yes.*

How do the words "joy" and "rejoice" capture Paul's central message to this group of believers?

Paul uses the word "joy" four times in this letter (1:4,25; 2:2; 4:1). The word "rejoice" appears in the text 9 times (1:18 twice, 26; 2:17,18; 3:1; 4:4 twice, 10). In the early chapters, these terms are used primarily to describe Paul's own experience of life in Christ. The beginning of chapter 3, however, is a transition point, shifting to a section of spiritual direction. Paul's expression "rejoice in the Lord" (3:1) is the first time in this letter for the phrase "in the Lord," signifying the reason and the sphere in which the believers' joy exists. Unrelated to the circumstances of life, the believer's joy flows from an unassailable, unchanging relationship to the sovereign Lord.

The theme of joy reaches a peak in 4:4 with the double command, "Rejoice in the Lord always. Again I will say, rejoice!" The verses that follow spell out the external behavior and the internal attitudes that characterize a person whose joy is genuine. Paul also included God's promise to supply both His presence and His peace to those who live rejoicing in the Lord.

Philippian Generosity

¹⁰But I rejoiced in the Lord greatly that now at last your care for me has flourished again; though you surely did care, but you lacked opportunity. ¹¹Not that I speak in regard to need, for I have learned in whatever state I am, to be content: ¹²I know how to be abased, and I know how to abound. Everywhere and in all things I have learned both to be full and to be hungry, both to abound and to suffer need. ¹³I can do all things through Christ*a* who strengthens me.

> **4:10 at last...you lacked opportunity.** About 10 years had passed since the Philippians first had given a gift to Paul, helping meet his needs during his first visit to Thessalonica. Paul was aware of their desire to continue to help, but he realized, within God's providence, that they had not had the "opportunity" (season) to help.

¹⁴Nevertheless you have done well that you shared in my distress. ¹⁵Now you Philippians know also that in the beginning of the gospel, when I departed from Macedonia, no church shared with me concerning giving and receiving but you only. ¹⁶For even in Thessalonica you sent *aid* once and again for my necessities. ¹⁷Not that I seek the gift, but I seek the fruit that abounds to your account. ¹⁸Indeed I have all and abound. I am full, having received from Epaphroditus the things *sent* from you, a

> **4:15 in the beginning of the gospel.** This refers to when Paul first preached the gospel in Philippi (Acts 16:13). **when I departed.** This was when Paul first left Philippi approximately 10 years before (Acts 16:40). **concerning giving and receiving.** Paul was a faithful steward of God's resources and kept careful records of what he received and spent. **but you only.** Only the Philippians had sent Paul provisions to meet his needs.

sweet-smelling aroma, an acceptable sacrifice, well pleasing to God. ¹⁹And my God shall supply all your need according to His riches in glory by Christ Jesus. ²⁰Now to our God and Father *be* glory forever and ever. Amen.

Greeting and Blessing

²¹Greet every saint in Christ Jesus. The brethren who are with me greet you. ²²All the saints greet you, but especially those who are of Caesar's household.

²³The grace of our Lord Jesus Christ be with you all.*a* Amen.

> **4:22 Caesar's household.** This refers to many people, not limited to Caesar's family, such as courtiers, princes, judges, accountants, stablemen, food-tasters, cooks, musicians, soldiers, and builders. Within that large group, Paul had in mind those who had been saved prior to his coming. Newly added to their number were those led to Christ by Paul himself, including the soldiers who were chained to him while he was a prisoner.

4:13 *a*NU-Text reads *Him who.*   4:23 *a*NU-Text reads *your spirit.*

COLOSSIANS

How does Christianity spread and grow? The church of Jesus in the city of Colosse began as a second-generation church. Paul and his team planted a church in Ephesus. Epaphras, who probably became a Christian in Ephesus, carried the gospel to Colosse and planted a new church. Later, when Paul heard that the Colossian believers were experiencing troubles, he wrote them this letter, a condensed handbook of the Christian faith.

AUTHOR AND DATE

Colossians was written by Paul, approximately A.D. 60 to 62.

The opening verse identifies Paul as the author of this letter (1:1,23; 4:18). The early church, represented by Irenaeus, Clement of Alexandria, Tertullian, Origen, and Eusebius, confirms the genuineness of Paul's authorship. Additional evidence comes from the book's close parallels with Philemon, which is universally accepted as having been written by Paul.

Like Philemon and the other Prison Epistles (Ephesians and Philippians), Colossians was written during A.D. 60–62 while Paul was a prisoner in Rome.

BACKGROUND AND SETTING

Colosse was a city in Phrygia, in the Roman province of Asia (part of modern Turkey), about 100 miles east of Ephesus. An ancient city, Colosse prospered through the marketing of black wool and dyes. Until New Testament times, the city had served as an important regional crossroads. By Paul's day, however, the main road had been rerouted through nearby Laodicea, causing Colosse to gradually decline in importance. Although the population of Colosse consisted mainly of Gentiles, a sizable Jewish settlement had existed for several hundred years.

The church at Colosse began during Paul's 3-year ministry at Ephesus (Acts 19). Epaphras, who probably had been saved during a visit to Ephesus, had returned home with such good news that the new church had sprung from his testimony. Several years after the founding of the Colossian church, a dangerous heresy arose to attack it. The threat to the church was real because the false teaching had elements that appealed to both the pagan and Jewish backgrounds of the church members. Epaphras was so concerned about this heresy that he made the long journey from Colosse to Rome (4:12,13) to consult with Paul who was a prisoner there. As a result, Paul composed this letter to warn the Colossians against the heresy. Epaphras stayed in Rome with Paul, but the letter was delivered by Tych-

icus, who was accompanied by Onesimus, the runaway slave returning to his master, Philemon, a member of the Colossian church (4:7–9, Philemon 23).

Colossians contains teaching on several key areas of theology: (1) the deity of Christ (1:15–20; 2:2–10); (2) reconciliation (1:20–23); (3) redemption (1:13,14; 2:13,14; 3:9–11); (4) election (3:12); (5) forgiveness (3:13); and (6) the nature of the church (1:18,24, 25; 2:19; 3:11,15).

> **THE HERESY PAUL ATTACKED** IN HIS LETTER WAS A **DISORGANIZED COLLECTION OF ERRORS** THAT LATER BECAME KNOWN AS **GNOSTICISM.**

The heresy Paul attacked in his letter was a disorganized collection of errors that later became a powerful system of destructive teaching known as Gnosticism. The following elements represent aspects of the heresy that appealed to both the pagan and Jewish backgrounds of the church:

1. God is good, but matter is evil—leading to a belief that the incarnation is impossible as well as to the twisted thinking that immoral behavior was acceptable since matter is evil anyway

2. Jesus Christ was merely one of a series of emanations descending from God and being less than God (leading them to deny Christ's full divinity and true humanity)

3. a secret, higher knowledge above Scripture is necessary for enlightenment and salvation

4. aspects of Jewish legalism—the necessity of circumcision and the observance of the ceremonial rituals of the Old Testament law—were promoted

5. rigid asceticism

6. worship of angels

7. mystical experiences

This odd mixture of beliefs created the confusion that Paul refuted and corrected in his letter.

OUTLINE

THE GLORIES OF CHRIST

"Not that we are sufficient of ourselves to think of anything as *being* from ourselves, but our sufficiency is from God…" (2 Cor. 3:5)

One of the great tenets of Scripture is the claim that Jesus Christ is completely sufficient for all matters of life and godliness (2 Pet. 1:3,4)! He is sufficient for creation (Col. 1:16,17), salvation (Heb. 10:10–12), sanctification (Eph. 5:26,27), and glorification (Rom. 8:30). So pure is He that there is no blemish, stain, spot of sin, defilement, lying, deception, corruption, error, or imperfection (1 Pet. 1:18–20).

So complete is He that there is no other God besides Him (Is. 45:5); He is the only begotten Son (John 1:14,18); all the treasures of wisdom and knowledge are in Him (Col. 2:3); the fullness of the Godhead dwells bodily in Him (Col. 2:9); He is heir of all things (Heb. 1:2); He created all things and all things were made by Him, through Him, and for Him (Col. 1:16); He upholds all things by the word of His power (Col. 1:17; Heb. 1:3); He is the firstborn of all creation (Col. 1:15); He is the exact representation of God (Heb. 1:3).

He is the only Mediator between God and man; He is the Sun that enlightens; the Physician that heals; the Wall of Fire that defends; the Friend that comforts; the Pearl that enriches; the Ark that supports; and the Rock to sustain under the heaviest of pressures; He is seated at the right hand of the throne of the Majesty on high (Heb. 1:3; 8:1); He is better than the angels (Heb. 1:4–14); better than Moses; better than Aaron; better than Joshua; better than Melchizedek; better than all the prophets; greater than Satan (Luke 4:1–12); and stronger than death (1 Cor. 15:55).

He has no beginning and no end (Rev. 1:17,18); He is the spotless Lamb of God; He is our Peace (Eph. 2:14); He is our Hope (1 Tim. 1:1); He is our Life (Col. 3:4); He is the living and true Way (John 14:6); He is the Strength of Israel (1 Sam. 15:29); He is the Root and Offspring of David, the Bright and Morning Star (Rev. 22:16); He is Faithful and True (Rev. 19:11); He is the Author and Finisher of our faith (Heb. 12:1,2); He is the Captain of our Salvation (Heb. 2:10); He is the Champion; He is the Elect One (Is. 42:1); He is the Apostle and High-Priest of our confession (Heb. 3:1); He is the Righteous Servant (Is. 53:11).

He is the Lord of Hosts, the Redeemer—the Holy One of Israel, the God of the whole earth (Is. 54:5); He is the Man of Sorrows (Is. 53:3); He is the Light; He is the Son of Man (Matt. 20:28); He is the Vine; He is the Bread of Life; He is the Door; He is Lord (Phil. 2:10–13); He is Prophet, Priest and King (Heb. 1:1–3); He is our Sabbath rest (Heb. 4:9); He is our Righteousness (Jer. 23:6); He is the Wonderful Counselor, the Mighty God, the Everlasting Father, the Prince of Peace (Is. 9:6); He is the Chief Shepherd (1 Pet. 5:4); He is Lord God of hosts; He is Lord of the nations; He is the Lion of Judah; the Living Word; the Rock of Salvation; the Eternal Spirit; He is the Ancient of Days; Creator and Comforter; Messiah; and He is the great I AM (John 8:58)!

Greeting

1 Paul, an apostle of Jesus Christ by the will of God, and Timothy our brother,

²To the saints and faithful brethren in Christ *who are* in Colosse:

Grace to you and peace from God our Father and the Lord Jesus Christ.*ᵃ*

> **1:2 saints.** This refers to those who have been separated from sin and set apart to God. **faithful.** This word is used in the NT exclusively for believers. **Colosse.** This was one of three cities in the Lycus River valley in the region of Phyrgia, in the Roman province of Asia (part of modern Turkey), about 100 miles east of Ephesus. **Grace...and peace.** This is Paul's greeting in all 13 of his epistles.

Their Faith in Christ

³We give thanks to the God and Father of our Lord Jesus Christ, praying always for you, ⁴since we heard of your faith in Christ Jesus and of your love for all the saints; ⁵because of the hope which is laid up for you in heaven, of which you heard before in the word of the truth of the gospel, ⁶which has come to you, as *it has* also in all the world, and is bringing forth fruit,*ᵃ* as *it is* also among you since the day you heard and

knew the grace of God in truth; ⁷as you also learned from Epaphras, our dear fellow servant, who is a faithful minister of Christ on your behalf, ⁸who also declared to us your love in the Spirit.

Preeminence of Christ

⁹For this reason we also, since the day we heard it, do not cease to pray for you, and to ask that you may be filled with the knowledge of His will in all wisdom and spiritual understanding; ¹⁰that you may walk worthy of the Lord, fully pleasing *Him*, being fruitful in every good work and increasing in the knowledge of God; ¹¹strengthened with all might, according to His glorious power, for all patience and longsuffering with joy; ¹²giving thanks to the Father who has qualified us to be partakers of the inheritance of

> **1:12 qualified us.** Apart from God's grace through Jesus Christ, all people would be qualified only to receive His wrath. **inheritance.** Each believer will receive his own individual portion of the total divine inheritance. **in the light.** Scripture represents "light" intellectually as divine truth (Ps. 119:130) and morally as divine purity (Eph. 5:8–14). The saints' inheritance exists in the spiritual realm of truth and purity where God dwells (1 Tim. 6:16). Light is a synonym for God's kingdom (see John 8:12).

1:2 *ᵃ*NU-Text omits *and the Lord Jesus Christ.* 1:6 *ᵃ*NU-Text and M-Text add *and growing.*

How does a passage like 1:15–20, which describes Christ as the "firstborn over all creation," fit with the biblical doctrine of Christ's deity?

This passage, 1:15–20, includes a powerful defense of Christ's deity. Apparently, a central component of the heresy that threatened the Colossian church was the denial of the deity of Christ. Ironically, throughout the centuries some cults have used the phrase "firstborn over all creation" (1:15) to undermine Christ's deity. The assumption is that if Jesus was born at creation, then He is more like us than He is God.

The Greek word for "firstborn" can refer to one who was born first chronologically, but it most often refers to preeminence in position or rank (Hebrews 1:6; Romans 8:9). Firstborn in this context clearly means highest in rank, not first created (Psalm 89:27; Revelation 1:5) for several reasons: (1) Christ cannot be both "first begotten" and "only begotten" (see John 1:14,18; 3:16,18; 1 John 4:9); (2) when the "firstborn" is one of a class, the class is in the plural form (1:18; Romans 8:29), but "creation," the class here, is in a singular form; (3) if Paul were teaching that Christ was a created being, he would be agreeing with the heresy that he was writing to refute; and (4) it is impossible for Christ to be both created and the Creator of everything (1:16). Thus, Jesus is the firstborn in the sense that He has the preeminence (1:18) and that he possesses the right of inheritance "over all creation" (Hebrews 1:2; Revelation 5:1–7,13).

the saints in the light. [13]He has delivered us from the power of darkness and conveyed *us* into the kingdom of the Son of His love, [14]in whom we have redemption through His blood,[a] the forgiveness of sins.

[15]He is the image of the invisible God, the firstborn over all creation. [16]For by Him all things were created that are in heaven and that are on earth, visible and invisible, whether thrones or dominions or principalities or powers. All things were created through Him and for Him. [17]And He is before all things, and in Him all things consist. [18]And He is the head of the body, the church, who is the beginning, the firstborn from the dead, that in all things He may have the preeminence.

> **1:18 head of the body.** Paul uses the human body as a metaphor for the church, of which Christ serves as the "head." **the beginning.** The church had its origins in Jesus (Eph. 1:4), and He gave life to the church through His death and resurrection. **the firstborn from the dead.** Jesus was the first chronologically to be resurrected, never to die again. Of all who have been or ever will be raised from the dead, Christ is supreme.

Reconciled in Christ

[19]For it pleased *the Father that* in Him all the fullness should dwell, [20]and by Him to reconcile all things to Himself, by Him, whether things on earth or things in heaven, having made peace through the blood of His cross.

[21]And you, who once were alienated and enemies in your mind by wicked works, yet now He has reconciled [22]in the body of His flesh through death, to present you holy, and blameless, and above reproach in His sight— [23]if indeed you continue in the faith, grounded and steadfast, and are not moved away from the hope of the gospel which you heard, which was preached to every creature under heaven, of which I, Paul, became a minister.

Sacrificial Service for Christ

[24]I now rejoice in my sufferings for you, and fill up in my flesh what is lacking in the afflictions of Christ, for the sake of His body, which is the church, [25]of which I became a minister according to the stewardship from God which was given to me for you, to fulfill the word of God, [26]the mystery which has been hidden from ages and from generations, but now has been revealed to His saints. [27]To them God willed to make known what are the riches of the glory of this mystery among the Gentiles: which[a] is Christ in you, the hope of glory.

> **1:24 my sufferings.** Paul refers to his present imprisonment (Acts 28:16,30). **fill up...what is lacking.** Christ's enemies had not gotten their fill of persecuting Him. They turned their hatred on those who preached the gospel (see John 15:18,24). Paul filled up what was lacking in Christ's afflictions. **the sake of His body.** Paul endured suffering to benefit and build Christ's church.

1:14 [a]NU-Text and M-Text omit *through His blood.*   1:27 [a]M-Text reads *who.*

What does the conditional statement "if indeed you continue in the faith" (1:22,23) have to do with whether or not believers can lose their salvation?

The Christian doctrine that deals with this question is often called "the perseverance of the saints." Scripture, as here, sometimes calls us to hold fast to our faith (Hebrews 10:23; Revelation 3:11) or warns us against falling away (Hebrews 10:26–29). Such admonitions do not negate the many promises that true believers will persevere (John 10:28,29; Romans 8:38,39; 1 Corinthians 1:8,9; Philippians 1:6). Rather, the warnings and pleas are among the means God uses to secure our perseverance in the faith. Conditional statements like the one in 1:22,23 simply underscore the point that those who do fall away from Christ give conclusive proof that they were never truly believers to begin with (1 John 2:19). To say that God secures our perseverance is not to say that we are passive in the process, however. God keeps us "through faith" (1 Peter 1:5)—our faith.

²⁸Him we preach, warning every man and teaching every man in all wisdom, that we may present every man perfect in Christ Jesus. ²⁹To this *end* I also labor, striving according to His working which works in me mightily.

Not Philosophy but Christ

2 For I want you to know what a great conflict I have for you and those in Laodicea, and *for* as many as have not seen my face in the flesh, ²that their hearts may be encouraged, being knit together in love, and *attaining* to all riches of the full assurance of understanding, to the knowledge of the mystery of God, both of the Father and*ᵃ* of Christ, ³in whom are hidden all the treasures of wisdom and knowledge.

> **2:3 all the treasures.** The false teachers claimed to possess a secret wisdom and transcendent knowledge available only to the spiritual elite. Paul declared that all the richness of truth necessary for either salvation, sanctification, or glorification is found in Jesus Christ, who Himself is God revealed (see John 1:14).

⁴Now this I say lest anyone should deceive you with persuasive words. ⁵For though I am absent in the flesh, yet I am with you in spirit, rejoicing to see your *good* order and the steadfastness of your faith in Christ.

⁶As you therefore have received Christ Jesus the Lord, so walk in Him, ⁷rooted and built up in Him and established in the faith, as you have been taught, abounding in it*ᵃ* with thanksgiving.

⁸Beware lest anyone cheat you through philosophy and empty deceit, according to the tradition of men, according to the basic principles of the world, and not according to Christ. ⁹For in Him dwells all the fullness of the Godhead bodily; ¹⁰and you are complete in Him, who is the head of all principality and power.

Not Legalism but Christ

¹¹In Him you were also circumcised with the circumcision made without hands, by putting off the body of the sins*ᵃ* of the flesh,

> **2:11,12 circumcision made without hands.** Circumcision symbolized man's need for cleansing of the heart (see Deut. 10:16) and was the outward sign of that cleansing of sin that comes by faith in God (Rom. 4:11). At salvation, believers undergo a spiritual circumcision "by putting off the body of the sins of the flesh" (see Rom. 6:6). This is the new birth. The believer's baptism by water has become the outward affirmation of that inner transformation (Acts 2:38).

by the circumcision of Christ, ¹²buried with Him in baptism, in which you also were raised with *Him* through faith in the working of God, who raised Him from the dead. ¹³And you, being dead in your trespasses and the uncircumcision of your flesh, He has made alive together with Him, having forgiven you all trespasses, ¹⁴having wiped out the handwriting of requirements that was against us, which was contrary to us. And He has taken it out of the way, having nailed it to the cross. ¹⁵Having disarmed principalities and powers, He made a public spectacle of them, triumphing over them in it.

¹⁶So let no one judge you in food or in drink, or regarding a festival or a new moon or sabbaths, ¹⁷which are a shadow of things to come, but the substance is of Christ. ¹⁸Let no one cheat you of your reward, taking delight in *false* humility and worship of angels, intruding into those things which he has not*ᵃ* seen, vainly puffed up by his fleshly mind, ¹⁹and not holding fast to the Head, from whom all the body, nourished and knit together by joints and ligaments, grows with the increase *that is* from God.

> **2:16 food...drink.** The false teachers sought to impose dietary regulations, probably based on the Mosaic law (see Lev. 11). Since they were under the New Covenant, the Colossians were not obligated to observe the OT dietary restrictions (see Mark 7:14–19). **new moon.** This was the monthly sacrifice offered on the first day of each month (Num. 10:10).

²⁰Therefore,*ᵃ* if you died with Christ from the basic principles of the world, why, as *though* living in the world, do you subject yourselves to regulations— ²¹"Do not

---

2:2 *ᵃ*NU-Text omits *both of the Father and.*   2:7 *ᵃ*NU-Text omits *in it.*   2:11 *ᵃ*NU-Text omits *of the sins.*   2:18 *ᵃ*NU-Text omits *not.*   2:20 *ᵃ*NU-Text and M-Text omit *Therefore.*

touch, do not taste, do not handle," ²²which all concern things which perish with the using—according to the commandments and doctrines of men? ²³These things indeed have an appearance of wisdom in self-imposed religion, *false* humility, and neglect of the body, *but are* of no value against the indulgence of the flesh.

Not Carnality but Christ

3 If then you were raised with Christ, seek those things which are above, where Christ is, sitting at the right hand of God. ²Set your mind on things above, not on things on the earth. ³For you died, and your life is hidden with Christ in God.

> **3:1 you were raised.** Because of their union with Christ, believers spiritually entered His death and resurrection at the moment of their conversion and have been and are now alive in Him. They understand spiritual truths, realities, blessings, and the will of God. **sitting at the right hand of God.** This is the position of honor and majesty (see Ps. 110:1) that Christ enjoys as the exalted Son of God.

⁴When Christ *who is* our life appears, then you also will appear with Him in glory.

⁵Therefore put to death your members which are on the earth: fornication, uncleanness, passion, evil desire, and covetousness, which is idolatry. ⁶Because of these things the wrath of God is coming upon the sons of disobedience, ⁷in which you yourselves once walked when you lived in them.

> **3:6 wrath of God.** This is God's constant reaction against sin. **sons of disobedience.** This expression designates unbelievers as bearing the very nature and character of the disobedient, rebellious sinfulness they love.

⁸But now you yourselves are to put off all these: anger, wrath, malice, blasphemy, filthy language out of your mouth. ⁹Do not lie to one another, since you have put off the old man with his deeds, ¹⁰and have put on the new *man* who is renewed in knowledge according to the image of Him who created him, ¹¹where there is neither Greek

TITLES OF CHRIST

Name or Title	Significance	Biblical Reference
Adam, Last Adam	First of the new race of the redeemed	1 Corinthians 15:45
Alpha and Omega	The beginning and ending of all things	Revelation 21:6
Bread of Life	The one essential food	John 6:35
Chief Cornerstone	A sure foundation for life	Ephesians 2:20
Chief Shepherd	Protector, sustainer, and guide	1 Peter 5:4
Firstborn from the Dead	Leads us into resurrection and eternal life	Colossians 1:18
Good Shepherd	Provider and caretaker	John 10:11
Great Shepherd of the Sheep	Trustworthy guide and protector	Hebrews 13:20
High Priest	A perfect sacrifice for our sins	Hebrews 3:1
Holy One of God	Sinless in His nature	Mark 1:24
Immanuel (God With Us)	Stands with us in all life's circumstances	Matthew 1:23
King of Kings, Lord of Lords	The Almighty, before whom every knee will bow	Revelation 19:16
Lamb of God	Gave His life as a sacrifice on our behalf	John 1:29
Light of the World	Brings hope in the midst of darkness	John 9:5
Lord of Glory	The power and presence of the living God	1 Corinthians 2:8
Mediator between God and Men	Brings us into God's presence redeemed and forgiven	1 Timothy 2:5
Only Begotten of the Father	The unique, one-of-a-kind Son of God	John 1:14
Prophet	Faithful proclaimer of the truths of God	Acts 3:22
Savior	Delivers from sin and death	Luke 1:47
Seed of Abraham	Mediator of God's covenant	Galatians 3:16
Son of Man	Identifies with us in our humanity	Matthew 18:11
The Word	Present with God at the creation	John 1:1

nor Jew, circumcised nor uncircumcised, barbarian, Scythian, slave *nor* free, but Christ *is* all and in all.

> **3:11** The church must destroy old barriers that separate people (see Gal. 3:28). **Greek.** This is a Gentile, or a non-Jew. **Jew.** This is a descendant of Abraham through Isaac. **Scythian.** These were ancient nomadic and warlike people who invaded the Fertile Crescent in the seventh century B.C. and were known for their savagery. **slave *nor* free.** A social barrier had always existed between slaves and freemen. Faith in Christ removed the separation (1 Cor. 12:13).

Character of the New Man

¹²Therefore, as *the* elect of God, holy and beloved, put on tender mercies, kindness, humility, meekness, longsuffering; ¹³bearing with one another, and forgiving one another, if anyone has a complaint against another; even as Christ forgave you, so you also *must do.* ¹⁴But above all these things put on love, which is the bond of perfection. ¹⁵And let the peace of God rule in your hearts, to which also you were called in one body; and be thankful. ¹⁶Let the word of Christ dwell in you richly in all wisdom, teaching and admonishing one another in psalms and hymns and spiritual songs, singing with grace in your hearts to the Lord. ¹⁷And *whatever* you do in word or deed, *do* all in the name of the Lord Jesus, giving thanks to God the Father through Him.

> **3:17 *do all in the name of the Lord Jesus.*** This simply means to act consistently with who Christ is and what He wants.

The Christian Home

¹⁸Wives, submit to your own husbands, as is fitting in the Lord. ¹⁹Husbands, love your wives and do not be bitter toward them. ²⁰Children, obey your parents in all things, for this is well pleasing to the Lord. ²¹Fathers, do not provoke your children, lest they become discouraged.

What were the Prison Epistles and what prison was Paul in when he wrote them?

Four of Paul's letters are grouped as the Prison Epistles: Ephesians, Philippians, Colossians, and Philemon. Each of them includes clear internal references to the writer's prison surroundings (Ephesians 3:1; 4:1; 6:20; Philippians 1:7,13,14,17; Colossians 4:3,10,18; Philemon 1,9,10,13,23). The similarities between the details of Paul's imprisonment given in Acts and in the Prison Epistles support the traditional position that the letters were written from Rome. Among these details are: (1) Paul was guarded by soldiers (Acts 28:16; Philippians 1:13,14); (2) Paul was permitted to receive visitors (Acts 28:30; Philippians 4:18); and (3) Paul had the opportunity to preach the gospel (Acts 28:31; Ephesians 6:18–20; Philippians 1:12–14; Colossians 4:2-4).

Caesarea and Ephesus have also been suggested as Paul's possible location when he wrote at least some of these letters. Paul was imprisoned in Caesarea for two years (Acts 24:27), but his opportunities to receive visitors and proclaim the gospel were severely limited during that time (Acts 23:35). The Prison Epistles express Paul's hope for a favorable verdict (Philippians 1:25; 2:24; Philemon 23). In Caesarea, however, Paul's only hope for release was either to bribe Felix (Acts 24:26), or agree to stand trial at Jerusalem under Festus (Acts 25:9). In the Prison Epistles, Paul expected the decision in his case to be final (Philippians 1:20–23; 2:17,23). That could not have been true at Caesarea, since Paul could and did appeal his case to the emperor.

Ephesus has been the other suggested location. Most of the same difficulties faced by the Caesarea suggestion face those who support Ephesus. The most telling argument against Ephesus as the point of origin for the Prison Epistles, however, is that there is no evidence that Paul was ever imprisoned at Ephesus.

In light of the serious difficulties faced by both the Caesarean and Ephesian views, no reason remains for rejecting the traditional view that Paul wrote the Prison Epistles from Rome while awaiting a hearing before the emperor on his appeal for justice as a Roman citizen.

²²Bondservants, obey in all things your masters according to the flesh, not with eyeservice, as men-pleasers, but in sincerity of heart, fearing God. ²³And whatever you do, do it heartily, as to the Lord and not to men, ²⁴knowing that from the Lord you will receive the reward of the inheritance; for*a* you serve the Lord Christ. ²⁵But he who does wrong will be repaid for what he has done, and there is no partiality.

4 Masters, give your bondservants what is just and fair, knowing that you also have a Master in heaven.

Christian Graces

²Continue earnestly in prayer, being vigilant in it with thanksgiving; ³meanwhile praying also for us, that God would open to us a door for the word, to speak the mystery of Christ, for which I am also in chains, ⁴that I may make it manifest, as I ought to speak.

⁵Walk in wisdom toward those *who are* outside, redeeming the time. ⁶*Let* your speech always *be* with grace, seasoned with salt, that you may know how you ought to answer each one.

Final Greetings

⁷Tychicus, a beloved brother, faithful minister, and fellow servant in the Lord, will tell you all the news about me. ⁸I am sending him to you for this very purpose, that he*a* may know your circumstances and comfort your hearts, ⁹with Onesimus, a faithful and beloved brother, who is *one* of

> **4:9 Onesimus.** He is the runaway slave whose return to his master was the basis for Paul's letter to Philemon.

you. They will make known to you all things which *are happening* here.

¹⁰Aristarchus my fellow prisoner greets you, with Mark the cousin of Barnabas (about whom you received instructions: if he comes to you, welcome him), ¹¹and Jesus who is called Justus. These *are my* only fellow workers for the kingdom of God who are of the circumcision; they have proved to be a comfort to me.

¹²Epaphras, who is *one* of you, a bondservant of Christ, greets you, always laboring fervently for you in prayers, that you may stand perfect and complete*a* in all the will of God. ¹³For I bear him witness that he has a great zeal*a* for you, and those who are in Laodicea, and those in Hierapolis. ¹⁴Luke the beloved physician and Demas greet you. ¹⁵Greet the brethren who are in Laodicea, and Nymphas and the church that *is* in his*a* house.

> **4:14 Luke.** He was Paul's personal physician and close friend who traveled frequently with him on his missionary journeys. He wrote the Gospel of Luke and Acts. **Demas.** This man demonstrated commitment to the Lord's work before the attraction of the world led him to abandon Paul and the ministry (2 Tim. 4:9,10).

Closing Exhortations and Blessing

¹⁶Now when this epistle is read among you, see that it is read also in the church of the Laodiceans, and that you likewise read the epistle from Laodicea. ¹⁷And say to Archippus, "Take heed to the ministry which you have received in the Lord, that you may fulfill it."

¹⁸This salutation by my own hand—Paul. Remember my chains. Grace *be* with you. Amen.

3:24 *a*NU-Text omits *for.*   4:8 *a*NU-Text reads *you may know our circumstances and he may.*
4:12 *a*NU-Text reads *fully assured.*   4:13 *a*NU-Text reads *concern.*   4:15 *a*NU-Text reads *Nympha . . . her house.*

1 THESSALONIANS

Christians were dying, and Christ hadn't returned. When the gospel was first preached to the Thessalonians, a strong part of the message focused on the expectation of Christ's return. Several years later, the death of some of the believers raised questions in the church. How long would Christ delay? What about those who died in the meantime? How should Christians live? In response to these questions, and other concerns, Paul sent the Thessalonians a letter.

AUTHOR AND DATE

First Thessalonians was written by Paul, about A.D. 51.

As was his custom, Paul identified himself as the author of this letter (1:1; 2:18). This has not been questioned until recently by radical critics. Their attempts to undermine Pauline authorship have failed in light of the combined weight of evidence favoring the traditional view such as: (1) direct assertions of Paul's authorship; (2) the letter's perfect correlation with Paul's travels in Acts 16–18; (3) the multitude of intimate details concerning Paul; and (4) the confirmation by multiple, early historical witnesses starting with Marcion's canon in A.D. 140.

Based in part on the archeological evidence verifying the dates of Gallio's service as proconsul in Achaia as A.D. 51–52 (Acts 18:12–17), the first letter to the Thessalonians is dated about A.D. 51. This makes 1 Thessalonians second only to Galatians in the chronological order of Paul's letters.

BACKGROUND AND SETTING

Thessalonica (modern Salonica) stood at the northern end of the Thermaic Gulf in the Aegean Sea. The city became the capital of Macedonia (about 168 B.C.) and enjoyed the status of a "free city" (one ruled by its own citizenry) under the Roman Empire (Acts 17:6). Thessalonica served as a key commercial and political hub on the Via Egnatia, the primary east-west Roman highway in the region. The population in Paul's day reached 200,000 people.

Paul's original visit to Thessalonica during his second missionary journey (A.D. 50—Acts 16:1–18:22) was brief but effective. A church was planted there before the apostle and his companions were evicted (Acts 17:1–9). Within a year, Paul sent Timothy back into the region to obtain a report on the new churches at Berea and Thessalonica. Timothy's good news prompted Paul to write his first letter. At that point the apostle was in Corinth, where he remained long enough to write his second letter to the church.

Timothy's report about Thessalonica must have included details that delighted and some that concerned Paul. Some of these became the purposes behind his letter: (1) to encourage the church (1:2–10); (2) to answer false allegations (2:1–12); (3) to comfort a persecuted flock (2:13–16); (4) to express his joy in their faith (2:17–3:13); (5) to remind them of the importance of moral purity (4:1–8); (6) to condemn the sluggard lifestyle (4:9–12); (7) to correct a wrong understanding of prophetic events (4:13-5:11); (8) to defuse tensions within the church (5:12–15); and (9) to exhort the church in the basics of Christian living (5:16–22).

HISTORICAL AND THEOLOGICAL THEMES

Both letters to Thessalonica have been referred to as "the eschatological epistles" (having to do with last things). In light of their more extensive focus on the church, however, they would better be categorized as "the ecclesiological (or church) epistles." Five major themes are woven together throughout 1 Thessalonians:

> BOTH LETTERS TO THESSALONICA WOULD BETTER BE CATEGORIZED AS 'THE ECCLESIOLOGICAL (OR CHURCH) EPISTLES.'

1. an apologetic theme with the historical correlation between Acts and 1 Thessalonians
2. an ecclesiastical theme with the portrayal of a healthy, growing church
3. a pastoral theme with the example of shepherding activities and attitudes
4. an eschatological theme with the focus on future events as the church's hope
5. a missionary theme with the emphasis on gospel proclamation and church planting.

OUTLINE

Greeting

1 Paul, Silvanus, and Timothy,

To the church of the Thessalonians in God the Father and the Lord Jesus Christ:

Grace to you and peace from God our Father and the Lord Jesus Christ.[a]

Their Good Example

[2]We give thanks to God always for you all, making mention of you in our prayers, [3]remembering without ceasing your work of faith, labor of love, and patience of hope in our Lord Jesus Christ in the sight of our God and Father, [4]knowing, beloved brethren, your election by God. [5]For our gospel did not come to you in word only, but also in power, and in the Holy Spirit and in much assurance, as you know what kind of men we were among you for your sake.

1:4 your election by God. The church is commonly called "the elect" (see Rom. 8:33). Salvation is initiated by God's will, not man's (see John 1:13). Humans participate by responding to God's promptings. Paul makes this clear when he says later that the Thessalonians received the Word, and they turned to God from idols. These two responses describe faith and repentance, to which God repeatedly calls sinners throughout Scripture (see Acts 20:21).

---

[6]And you became followers of us and of the Lord, having received the word in much affliction, with joy of the Holy Spirit, [7]so that you became examples to all in Macedonia and Achaia who believe. [8]For from you the word of the Lord has sounded forth, not only in Macedonia and Achaia, but also in every place. Your faith toward God has gone out, so that we do not need to say anything. [9]For they themselves declare con-

---

1:10 to wait. This is a recurring theme in the Thessalonian letters. These passages show that they expected the deliverance was near; it was something that Paul felt could happen in their lifetime. **delivers us from the wrath to come.** This emphasizes Christ's work of salvation, to save us from sin and to deliver us from the eternal wrath of God in hell (see also 1 Thess. 5:9).

---

cerning us what manner of entry we had to you, and how you turned to God from idols to serve the living and true God, [10]and to wait for His Son from heaven, whom He raised from the dead, *even* Jesus who delivers us from the wrath to come.

Paul's Conduct

2 For you yourselves know, brethren, that our coming to you was not in vain. [2]But even[a] after we had suffered before and were spitefully treated at Philippi, as you know, we were bold in our God to speak to you the gospel of God in much conflict. [3]For our exhortation *did* not *come* from error or uncleanness, nor *was it* in deceit.

[4]But as we have been approved by God to be entrusted with the gospel, even so we speak, not as pleasing men, but God who tests our hearts. [5]For neither at any time did we use flattering words, as you know, nor a cloak for covetousness—God *is* witness. [6]Nor did we seek glory from men, either from you or from others, when we might have made demands as apostles of Christ. [7]But we were gentle among you, just as a nursing *mother* cherishes her own children. [8]So, affectionately longing for you, we were well pleased to impart to you not only the gospel of God, but also our own lives, because you had become dear to us. [9]For you remember, brethren, our labor and toil; for laboring night and day, that we might not be a burden to any of you, we preached to you the gospel of God.

2:5,6 flattering words. Paul affirms the purity of his motives for ministry. He denies being a smooth-talking preacher. He never pretended to be poor so that he could work to grow rich through the ministry. He did not use his honored position as an apostle to seek personal glory.

---

[10]You *are* witnesses, and God *also*, how devoutly and justly and blamelessly we

---

2:10 you are witnesses. Old Testament law required two or more witnesses to verify the truth (Num. 35:30). Here Paul called on both the Thessalonians and God as witnesses to affirm his holy conduct in the ministry (see 2 Cor. 1:12).

1:1 [a]NU-Text omits *from God our Father and the Lord Jesus Christ.*   2:2 [a]NU-Text and M-Text omit *even.*

behaved ourselves among you who believe; [11]as you know how we exhorted, and comforted, and charged[a] every one of you, as a father *does* his own children, [12]that you would walk worthy of God who calls you into His own kingdom and glory.

Their Conversion

[13]For this reason we also thank God without ceasing, because when you received the word of God which you heard from us, you welcomed *it* not *as* the word of men, but as it is in truth, the word of God, which also effectively works in you who believe. [14]For you, brethren, became imitators of the churches of God which are in Judea in Christ Jesus. For you also suffered the same things from your own countrymen, just as they *did* from the Judeans, [15]who killed both the Lord Jesus and their own prophets, and have persecuted us; and they do not please God and are contrary to all men, [16]forbidding us to speak to the Gentiles that they may be saved, so as always to fill up *the measure of* their sins; but

wrath has come upon them to the uttermost.

Longing to See Them

[17]But we, brethren, having been taken away from you for a short time in presence, not in heart, endeavored more eagerly to see your face with great desire. [18]Therefore we wanted to come to you—even I, Paul, time and again—but Satan hindered us. [19]For what *is* our hope, or joy, or crown of rejoicing? *Is it* not even you in the presence of our Lord Jesus Christ at His coming? [20]For you are our glory and joy.

> **2:17 having been taken away.** Paul had been forcedly separated from his spiritual children (see Acts 17:5–9). His parental instincts had been dealt a severe blow. The Thessalonians had been orphaned by Paul's forced departure.

Concern for Their Faith

3 Therefore, when we could no longer endure it, we thought it good to be left in Athens alone, [2]and sent Timothy, our

2:11 [a]NU-Text and M-Text read *implored.*

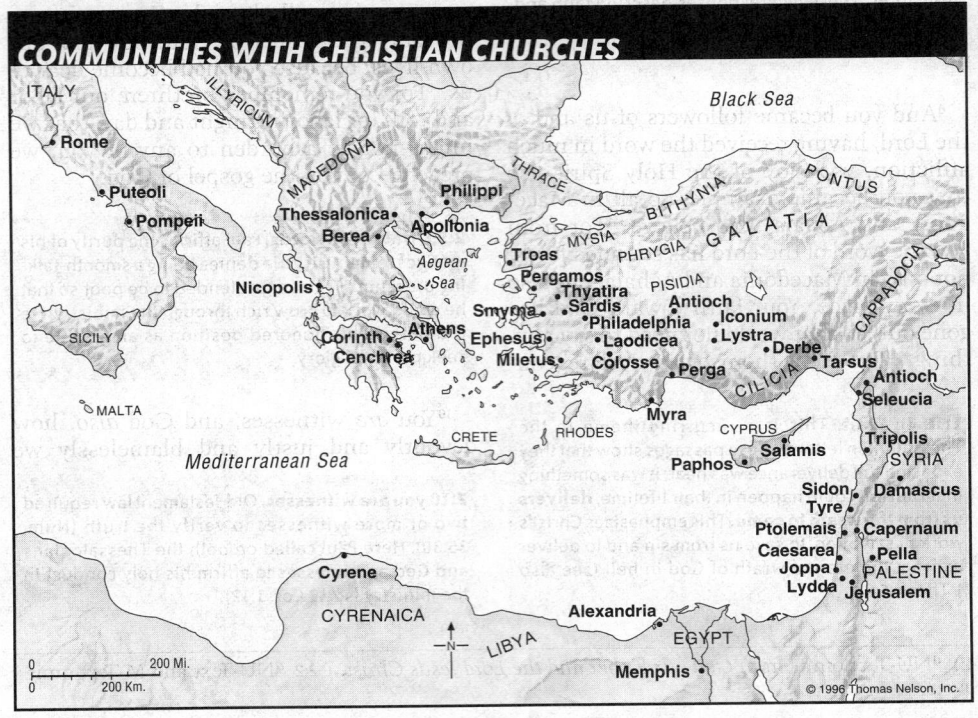

COMMUNITIES WITH CHRISTIAN CHURCHES

© 1996 Thomas Nelson, Inc.

brother and minister of God, and our fellow laborer in the gospel of Christ, to establish you and encourage you concerning your faith, ³that no one should be shaken by these afflictions; for you yourselves know that we are appointed to this. ⁴For, in fact, we told you before when we were with you that we would suffer tribulation, just as it happened, and you know. ⁵For this reason, when I could no longer endure it, I sent to know your faith, lest by some means the tempter had tempted you, and our labor might be in vain.

3:5 the tempter. Satan is characterized as a tempter, for he tries and tests people in order to cause them to fail (see Matt. 4:3). Paul was neither ignorant of Satan's schemes (2 Cor. 2:11) nor vulnerable to his methods (Eph. 6:11). He took action to counterattack Satan's expected maneuver and to assure that all his efforts were not useless.

Encouraged by Timothy

⁶But now that Timothy has come to us from you, and brought us good news of your faith and love, and that you always have good remembrance of us, greatly desiring to see us, as we also *to see* you— ⁷therefore, brethren, in all our affliction and distress we were comforted concerning you by your faith. ⁸For now we live, if you stand fast in the Lord.

⁹For what thanks can we render to God for you, for all the joy with which we rejoice for your sake before our God, ¹⁰night and day praying exceedingly that we may see your face and perfect what is lacking in your faith?

Prayer for the Church

¹¹Now may our God and Father Himself, and our Lord Jesus Christ, direct our way to you. ¹²And may the Lord make you increase and abound in love to one another and to all, just as we *do* to you, ¹³so that He may establish your hearts blameless in holiness before our God and Father at the coming of our Lord Jesus Christ with all His saints.

Plea for Purity

4 Finally then, brethren, we urge and exhort in the Lord Jesus that you should abound more and more, just as you received from us how you ought to walk and to please God; ²for you know what commandments we gave you through the Lord Jesus.

³For this is the will of God, your sanctification: that you should abstain from sexual immorality; ⁴that each of you should know how to possess his own vessel in sanctification and honor, ⁵not in passion of lust, like the Gentiles who do not know God; ⁶that no one should take advantage of and defraud his brother in this matter, because the Lord *is* the avenger of all such, as we also forewarned you and testified. ⁷For God did not call us to uncleanness, but in holiness. ⁸Therefore he who rejects *this* does not reject man, but God, who has also given*ᵃ* us His Holy Spirit.

4:7 call us. Whenever the epistles refer to the "call" of God, it refers to His effective, saving call for a person to be saved, never to a general plea. It is linked to justification (see Rom. 8:30).

A Brotherly and Orderly Life

⁹But concerning brotherly love you have no need that I should write to you, for you yourselves are taught by God to love one another; ¹⁰and indeed you do so toward all the brethren who are in all Macedonia. But we urge you, brethren, that you increase more and more; ¹¹that you also aspire to lead a quiet life, to mind your own business, and to work with your own hands, as we commanded you, ¹²that you may walk properly toward those who are outside, and *that* you may lack nothing.

The Comfort of Christ's Coming

¹³But I do not want you to be ignorant, brethren, concerning those who have fallen asleep, lest you sorrow as others who have no hope. ¹⁴For if we believe that Jesus died and rose again, even so God will bring with Him those who sleep in Jesus.*ᵃ*

¹⁵For this we say to you by the word of the Lord, that we who are alive *and* remain until the coming of the Lord will by no means precede those who are asleep. ¹⁶For the Lord Himself will descend from heaven with a

4:8 *ᵃ*NU-Text reads *who also gives.* 4:14 *ᵃ*Or *those who through Jesus sleep*

shout, with the voice of an archangel, and with the trumpet of God. And the dead in Christ will rise first. ¹⁷Then we who are alive *and* remain shall be caught up together with them in the clouds to meet the Lord in the air. And thus we shall always be with the Lord. ¹⁸Therefore comfort one another with these words.

The Day of the Lord

5 But concerning the times and the seasons, brethren, you have no need that I

How did Paul answer the Thessalonians' concerns about the fate of those Christians who had already died?

The statement in 4:13–18 provides an enduring and powerful answer to some of the recurring questions that trouble Christians when they face the death of loved ones in Christ. The Thessalonians had the same practical concerns. Even though Paul's ministry in Thessalonica was brief, it is clear that the people came to believe in and hope for the reality of their Savior's return (1:3,9,10; 2:19; 5:1,2; 2 Thessalonians 2:1,5). They were living in expectation of that coming, eagerly awaiting Christ. They knew that His return was the climactic event in redemptive history and anticipated their participation in it. Verse 13 (see also 2 Thessalonians 2:1–3) indicates that the believers were agitated about those who might miss Christ's return. Based on Paul's answers, their major questions seem to have been: "What happens to the Christians who die before He comes? Do they miss His return?

Clearly, the Thessalonians had an imminent view of Christ's return. Evidently they had interpreted Paul's teaching to mean that Christ would definitely come back very soon, during their lifetime. Quite naturally, therefore they became confused as they were being persecuted, an experience from which they assumed they would be delivered by the Lord's return.

Paul's answer begins with a note about grief. It does not say that Christians shouldn't "sorrow" over the death of another Christian. Instead, Paul's point is that sorrow for the Christian is hopeful, not hopeless. Then the letter offers a series of promises that affect those who "fall asleep in Christ"—believers who die:

1. As Jesus died and rose again, so too will those who have died in Christ (4:14 and John 14:1–3; 1 Corinthians 15:51–58). These texts describe the rapture of the church (including dead Christians) which will occur when Jesus comes to collect His redeemed and take them back to heaven.

2. Those who are alive and those who have died will experience the Lord's return at the same time (4:15). Apparently, the Thessalonians were informed fully about the Day of the Lord judgment (5:1,2), but not the preceding event—the rapture of the church. Until Paul revealed it as the revelation from God to him, it had been a secret, with the only prior mention being Jesus' teaching in John 14:1–3. Because Paul didn't know God's timing, he lived and spoke as if this event could happen in his lifetime. As with all early Christians, he believed it was near (Romans 13:11; 1 Corinthians 6:14; 10:11; 16:22; Philippians 3:20,21; 1 Timothy 6:14; Titus 2:13).

3. "The Lord Himself will descend" (4:16). This fulfills the pledge by Jesus in John 14:1–3. Until then, He remains in heaven (1:10; Hebrews 1:1–3).

4. Believers who have died will rise first, in time to participate in Christ's return (4:16; 1 Corinthians 15:52).

5. Those alive at the Rapture will accompany those dead who rise first (4:17) and "meet the Lord in the air."

Paul assured the Thessalonians, and all believers, that Jesus will not have any of His own miss out on His return. The final verse of the chapter reveals Paul's central intent in the passage—to encourage those Christians whose loved ones have died. The comfort here is based on the following: (1) the dead will be resurrected and will participate in the Lord's coming for His own; (2) when Christ comes the living will be reunited forever with their loved ones; and (3) all believers, both the living and the dead, will be with the Lord eternally (4:17,18).

4:17 caught up. The spirits of those who had already died have been with the Lord and will now be joined to new, resurrected bodies. After they come forth, the living Christians will be raptured (see John 10:28). The Rapture occurs 7 years before Christ's second coming, when He comes in judgment. The Rapture involves the complete transformation of believers (see 1 Cor. 15:51,52) and their eternal union with Christ.

should write to you. ²For you yourselves know perfectly that the day of the Lord so comes as a thief in the night. ³For when they say, "Peace and safety!" then sudden destruction comes upon them, as labor pains upon a pregnant woman. And they shall not escape. ⁴But you, brethren, are not in darkness, so that this Day should overtake you as a thief. ⁵You are all sons of light and sons of the day. We are not of the night nor of darkness. ⁶Therefore let us not sleep, as others *do*, but let us watch and be sober. ⁷For those who sleep, sleep at night, and those who get drunk are drunk at night. ⁸But let us who are of the day be sober, putting on the breastplate of faith and love, and *as* a helmet the hope of salvation. ⁹For God did not appoint us to wrath, but to ob-

5:4 But you, brethren. Because the church will be raptured before the judgment on the Day of the Lord, believers will not be present on earth to experience the terror and destruction. **not in darkness.** Believers have no part in the Day of the Lord because they have been delivered from the domain of darkness and transferred to the kingdom of light (Col. 1:13). Believing in Jesus saves a person from spiritual darkness (John 8:12).

tain salvation through our Lord Jesus Christ, ¹⁰who died for us, that whether we wake or sleep, we should live together with Him.

¹¹Therefore comfort each other and edify one another, just as you also are doing.

Various Exhortations

¹²And we urge you, brethren, to recognize those who labor among you, and are over you in the Lord and admonish you, ¹³and to esteem them very highly in love for their work's sake. Be at peace among yourselves.

5:13 esteem. In addition to knowing their pastors personally, congregations are to think rightly of them and to treat them lovingly, not because of their charm or personality, but because they work for the Chief Shepherd as His special servants (see 1 Pet. 5:2–4). In addition, they should submit to pastoral leadership so that "peace" prevails in the church.

¹⁴Now we exhort you, brethren, warn those who are unruly, comfort the fainthearted, uphold the weak, be patient with all. ¹⁵See that no one renders evil for evil to anyone, but always pursue what is good both for yourselves and for all.

¹⁶Rejoice always, ¹⁷pray without ceasing, ¹⁸in everything give thanks; for this is the will of God in Christ Jesus for you.

¹⁹Do not quench the Spirit. ²⁰Do not

5:19 quench. The fire of God's Spirit is not to be doused with sin. Believers are also instructed to not grieve the Holy Spirit (Eph. 4:30), but to be controlled by the Holy Spirit (Eph. 5:18) and to walk by the Holy Spirit (Gal. 5:16).

What did Paul mean by the "times and seasons" (5:1) and why did he find no need to write the church about them?

Chapter 5 begins with Paul shifting the specific subject from his discussion of the blessings of the rapture of believers (4:13–18) to the judgment of unbelievers (5:1–11). The two terms "times and seasons" refer to the measurement of time and the character of the times respectively (Daniel 2:21; Acts 1:7). Instead of writing to them about this subject, Paul needed only to remind them of what they had already been taught.

Apparently, the Thessalonians knew all God intended believers to know about coming judgment, and once Paul had taught them what they needed to know about the Rapture (4:13–18), his remaining duty was to encourage. Paul exhorted them to live godly lives in the light of coming judgment on the world, rather than to be distracted by probing into issues of prophetic timing. They could not know the timing of God's final judgment, but they knew well that it would come unexpectedly (5:2).

despise prophecies. ²¹Test all things; hold fast what is good. ²²Abstain from every form of evil.

Blessing and Admonition

²³Now may the God of peace Himself sanctify you completely; and may your whole spirit, soul, and body be preserved blameless at the coming of our Lord Jesus Christ. ²⁴He who calls you *is* faithful, who also will do *it*.

²⁵Brethren, pray for us.

²⁶Greet all the brethren with a holy kiss.

²⁷I charge you by the Lord that this epistle be read to all the holy*ᵃ* brethren.

²⁸The grace of our Lord Jesus Christ *be* with you. Amen.

5:26 holy kiss. This gesture of affection is commanded five times in the NT and refers to the cultural hug and kiss greeting common in the first century. For Christians, this should be done righteously, in recognition that believers are brothers and sisters in the family of God.

5:27 *ᵃ*NU-Text omits *holy.*

How does Paul add his voice to the rest of Scripture in using the expression "day of the Lord" (5:2)?

Nineteen indisputable uses of "the Day of the Lord" occur in the Old Testament and four in the New Testament (Acts 2:20; 1 Thessalonians 5:2; 2 Thessalonians 2:2; 2 Peter 3:10). The Old Testament prophets used "Day of the Lord" to describe: (1) near historical judgments (Isaiah 13:6–12; Ezekiel 30:2–19; Joel 1:15; 3:14; Amos 5:18–20; Zephaniah 1:14–18); and (2) far eschatological divine judgments (Joel 2:30–32; Zechariah 14:1; Malachi 4:1,5). Six times it is referred to as the "day of doom" and four times "day of vengeance."

The New Testament calls it a day of "wrath," day of "visitation," and the "Great Day of God Almighty" (Revelation 16:4).

These are terrifying judgments from God (Joel 2:30,31; 2 Thessalonians 1:7) for the overwhelming sinfulness of the world. The future "Day of the Lord" which unleashes God's wrath, falls into two parts: the end of the 7 year tribulation period (Revelation 19:11–21) and the end of the Millennium. These two are actually 1,000 years apart. Peter refers to the end of the 1,000 year period in connection with the final "Day of the Lord" (2 Peter 3:10; Revelation 20:7–15).

Here the reference to the "Day of the Lord" refers to the conclusion of the tribulation period. The descriptive phrase "a thief in the night" is never used in Scripture to refer to the rapture of the church. It is used of Christ's coming in judgment on the Day of the Lord at the end of the 7 year tribulation that is distinct from the rapture of the church (4:15) which occurs immediately prior to this 7 year period. It is also used of the judgment that concludes the Millennium (2 Peter 3:10). As a thief comes unexpectedly and without warning, so will the Day of the Lord come in both its final phases.

2 THESSALONIANS

No one can accuse the apostle Paul of lacking in persistence. If one of his letters didn't accomplish its goal, he simply would write another one. Within a short time of writing his first letter to the church in Thessalonica, Paul wrote a second time. As before, his primary purpose was to encourage those believers. He saw in them a persistent need for encouragement that matched his own persistent need to minister.

AUTHOR AND DATE

Second Thessalonians was written by Paul, about late A.D. 51 or early A.D. 52.

As with 1 Thessalonians and most of his letters, Paul identified himself twice as the author of this letter (1:1; 3:17). Evidence, both within this letter and with regard to vocabulary, style, and doctrinal content, strongly supports Pauline authorship.

The time of this writing was surely a few months after the first epistle, while Paul was still in Corinth with Silas and Timothy (1:1; Acts 18:5) in late A.D. 51 or early A.D. 52.

BACKGROUND AND SETTING

For background information on Thessalonica, see the Introduction to 1 Thessalonians. Some have suggested that Paul penned this letter from Ephesus (Acts 18:18–21), but his 18-month stay in Corinth provided ample time for him to write both the Thessalonian letters.

Paul apparently managed to stay apprised of the happenings in Thessalonica. Perhaps the bearer of the first letter had returned with an update on the condition of the church. Paul was aware of the maturity and expansion of that church (1:3), but he also knew of their suffering under pressure and persecution. There were signs of danger in the seeds of false teaching about the Lord that were being sown, as well as in the disorderly behavior of some people.

As Paul took up his pen, he had the following picture of the church in his mind: (1) discouraged by persecution and needing incentive to persevere; (2) deceived by false teachers who confused them about the Lord's return; and (3) disobedient to divine commands, particularly by refusing to work. For each of these, Paul had this to offer: (1) comfort for the persecuted believers (1:3–12); (2) correction for falsely taught and frightened believers (2:1–15); and (3) confrontation for the disobedient and undisciplined believers (3:6–15).

Although the first two chapters contain much prophetic material, the overall tone still makes this primarily a "pastoral letter." Paul's response to the false teachers and their false teaching is characterized by pastoral concern for the church. The emphasis is on how to maintain a healthy church with an effective testimony in proper response to sound eschatology and obedience to the truth.

> **PAUL'S RESPONSE TO THE FALSE TEACHERS AND THEIR FALSE TEACHING IS CHARACTERIZED BY PASTORAL CONCERN FOR THE CHURCH.**

Eschatology dominates the theological issues in this letter. One of the clearest statements of personal eschatological consequences for unbelievers is found in 1:9. Church discipline is the major focus of 3:6–15. Paul understood that truthful doctrine and faithful righteous living would lead to peace in the Lord (3:16) and ongoing health for the church in Thessalonica and everywhere.

OUTLINE

Greeting

1 Paul, Silvanus, and Timothy,

To the church of the Thessalonians in God our Father and the Lord Jesus Christ:

²Grace to you and peace from God our Father and the Lord Jesus Christ.

God's Final Judgment and Glory

³We are bound to thank God always for you, brethren, as it is fitting, because your faith grows exceedingly, and the love of every one of you all abounds toward each other, ⁴so that we ourselves boast of you among the churches of God for your patience and faith in all your persecutions and tribulations that you endure, ⁵*which is* manifest evidence of the righteous judgment of God, that you may be counted worthy of the kingdom of God, for which you also suffer; ⁶since *it is* a righteous thing with God to repay with tribulation those who trouble you, ⁷and to *give* you who are troubled rest with us when the Lord Jesus is revealed from heaven with His mighty angels, ⁸in flaming fire taking vengeance on those who do not know God, and on those who do not obey the gospel of our Lord Jesus Christ. ⁹These shall be punished with everlasting destruction from the presence of the Lord and from the glory of His power, ¹⁰when He comes, in that Day, to be glorified in His saints and to be admired among all those who believe,ᵃ because our testimony among you was believed.

> **1:8 in flaming fire.** Fire symbolizes judgment (see Ex. 3:2). **taking vengeance.** Meaning, "to give full punishment." **do not know God.** Those who lack a personal relationship with God through Jesus Christ do not know Him (see John 17:3). They are punished, not because they persecuted Christians, but because they did not obey God's command to believe (see Acts 17:30,31) and to call upon the name of the Lord to be saved from their sin (Rom. 10:9–13).

¹¹Therefore we also pray always for you that our God would count you worthy of *this* calling, and fulfill all the good pleasure of *His* goodness and the work of faith with

power, ¹²that the name of our Lord Jesus Christ may be glorified in you, and you in Him, according to the grace of our God and the Lord Jesus Christ.

The Great Apostasy

2 Now, brethren, concerning the coming of our Lord Jesus Christ and our gathering together to Him, we ask you, ²not to be soon shaken in mind or troubled, either by spirit or by word or by letter, as if from us, as though the day of Christᵃ had come. ³Let no one deceive you by any means; for *that Day will not come* unless the falling away comes first, and the man of sinᵃ is revealed, the son of perdition, ⁴who opposes and exalts himself above all that is called God or that is worshiped, so that he sits as Godᵃ in the temple of God, showing himself that he is God.

⁵Do you not remember that when I was still with you I told you these things? ⁶And now you know what is restraining, that he may be revealed in his own time. ⁷For the mystery of lawlessness is already at work; only Heᵃ who now restrains *will do so* until Heᵇ is taken out of the way. ⁸And then the lawless one will be revealed, whom the Lord will consume with the breath of His mouth and destroy with the brightness of His coming. ⁹The coming of the *lawless one* is according to the working of Satan, with all power, signs, and lying wonders, ¹⁰and with all unrighteous deception among those who perish, because they did not receive the love of the truth, that they might be saved. ¹¹And for this reason God will send them strong delusion, that they should believe the lie, ¹²that they all may be condemned who did not believe the truth but had pleasure in unrighteousness.

> **2:7 the mystery of lawlessness.** This is the spirit of lawlessness that is already prevalent in society (see 1 John 3:4). The mystery will be revealed in the one who blasphemously assumes the place of God on earth, which God has reserved for Jesus Christ. The spirit of such a man is already in operation (see 1 John 2:18), but the man who fully embodies that spirit has not yet come.

1:10 ᵃNU-Text and M-Text read *have believed.*   2:2 ᵃNU-Text reads *the Lord.*   2:3 ᵃNU-Text reads *lawlessness.*   2:4 ᵃNU-Text omits *as God.*   2:7 ᵃOr *he* ᵇOr *he*

Stand Fast

¹³But we are bound to give thanks to God always for you, brethren beloved by the Lord, because God from the beginning chose you for salvation through sanctification by the Spirit and belief in the truth, ¹⁴to which He called you by our gospel, for the obtaining of the glory of our Lord Jesus Christ. ¹⁵Therefore, brethren, stand fast and hold the traditions which you were taught, whether by word or our epistle.

¹⁶Now may our Lord Jesus Christ Himself, and our God and Father, who has loved us and given *us* everlasting consolation and good hope by grace, ¹⁷comfort your hearts and establish you in every good word and work.

Pray for Us

3 Finally, brethren, pray for us, that the word of the Lord may run *swiftly* and be glorified, just as *it is* with you, ²and that we

may be delivered from unreasonable and wicked men; for not all have faith.

> **3:2 unreasonable and wicked men.** These were Paul's enemies at Corinth, where he ministered when he wrote, who were perverse and unrighteous, aggressively opposing Paul and the Gospel (see Acts 18:9–17).

³But the Lord is faithful, who will establish you and guard *you* from the evil one. ⁴And we have confidence in the Lord concerning you, both that you do and will do the things we command you.

⁵Now may the Lord direct your hearts into the love of God and into the patience of Christ.

Warning Against Idleness

⁶But we command you, brethren, in the name of our Lord Jesus Christ, that you withdraw from every brother who walks

---

How does Paul expand on some of his teaching about the Day of the Lord in 2:1–5?

The Christians in Thessalonica had a persistent problem with the tension between an attitude of expectation for the Lord's soon return and the realities of daily living that required hard work and commitment. False teachers were fanning the flames of confusion. The idea that the Day of the Lord had already arrived conflicted with what Paul had previously taught them about the Rapture. Whoever was telling them they were already in the Day of the Lord claimed that the message had come from Paul. Thus the lie was given supposed apostolic authority. The results were shock, fear, and alarm. This error, which so upset the Thessalonians, Paul corrected in 2:1–12. He showed that the Day of the Lord hadn't come and couldn't come until certain realities were in place, most especially, "the man of sin" (verse 3).

The same verse refers to "the falling away." The language indicates a specific event, not general apostasy that exists now and always will. Rather, Paul had in mind *the* apostasy. This is a clearly and specifically identifiable unique event, the consummate act of rebellion, an event of final magnitude. The key to identifying the event depends on the identity of the main person involved. Paul calls him the "man of sin." This figure is also called "the prince who is to come" (Daniel 9:26) and "the little horn" (Daniel 7:8). John calls him "the beast" (Revelation 13:2–10,18), but most know him as the Antichrist.

This statement is referring to the very act of ultimate apostasy that reveals the final Antichrist and sets the course for the events that usher in the Day of the Lord. Apparently, he will be seen as supportive of religion so that God and Christ will not appear as his enemies until the apostasy. He exalts himself and opposes God by moving into the temple, the place for worship of God, declaring himself to be God and demanding the world's worship (verse 4). In this act of Satanic, self-deification, he commits the great apostasy in defiance of God. The seven-year Tribulation that follows under the reign of Antichrist (Daniel 7:25; 11:36–39; Matthew 24:15–21; Revelation 13:1–8) culminates with the Day of the Lord.

This section of Paul's letter continues to emphasize that the Thessalonians did not need to be agitated or troubled, thinking they had missed the rapture and thus were in the Day of Judgment. They were destined for glory, not judgment and would not be included with those deceived and judged in that Day.

3:6 we command you. Paul's directions were not mere suggestions but commands, carrying the weight and authority of a judge's court order that the apostle delivered and enforced. He required obedient Christians to separate from habitually disobedient believers and to stop fellowship with them. **the tradition.** There were false (Mark 7:2–13) and true traditions. Paul's traditions were the inspired teachings he had given.

disorderly and not according to the tradition which he*a* received from us. ⁷For you yourselves know how you ought to follow us, for we were not disorderly among you; ⁸nor did we eat anyone's bread free of charge, but worked with labor and toil night and day, that we might not be a burden to any of you, ⁹not because we do not have authority, but to make ourselves an example of how you should follow us.

¹⁰For even when we were with you, we commanded you this: If anyone will not work, neither shall he eat. ¹¹For we hear that there are some who walk among you in a disorderly manner, not working at all, but are busybodies. ¹²Now those who are such we command and exhort through our Lord Jesus Christ that they work in quietness and eat their own bread.

¹³But *as for* you, brethren, do not grow weary *in* doing good. ¹⁴And if anyone does not obey our word in this epistle, note that person and do not keep company with him, that he may be ashamed. ¹⁵Yet do not count *him* as an enemy, but admonish *him* as a brother.

Benediction

¹⁶Now may the Lord of peace Himself give you peace always in every way. The Lord *be* with you all.

¹⁷The salutation of Paul with my own hand, which is a sign in every epistle; so I write.

¹⁸The grace of our Lord Jesus Christ *be* with you all. Amen.

3:6 *a*NU-Text and M-Text read *they.*

How does Paul's teaching on church discipline in 3:6–15 fit with other major passages of Scripture on this subject?

Paul addressed a particular issue of church discipline with the Thessalonians in 3:6–15. Helpful parallel passages that should be consulted in studying this one include Matthew 18:15–20, 1 Corinthians 5:1–13, Galatians 6:1–5, and 1 Timothy 5:19,20.

This passage (3:6–15) gives specific direction on the nature of the church's response to someone who deliberately refuses to follow God' Word, expecting to benefit from fellowship with God's people while being unwilling to participate in a meaningful way. In Paul's words, "If anyone will not work, neither shall he eat" (3:10). These were fellow-believers acting in a parasitic way, sapping the generosity of other believers. Paul had already addressed this pattern in his first letter (1 Thessalonians 4:11).

This passage offers an emphatic command, a personal confrontation, and a compassionate caution. First, verses 6 and 14 instruct the rest of the church to "withdraw" and "not keep company" with such a person. In other words, Paul was commanding the church to disfellowship blatantly disobedient Christians in order to produce shame (verse 14) and, hopefully, repentance. Second, Paul was giving the sluggards a direct command to "work in quietness and eat their own bread" (verse 12), removing any excuse that they had not been warned about discipline. Third, Paul added two crucial words of caution. He reminded the believers that genuinely needy people deserved help. He urged them, "do not grow weary in doing good" (verse 13). He also cautioned them to limit their disciplinary withdrawal. "Yet do not count him as an enemy, but admonish him as a brother" (verse 15). While an unrepentant pattern of sin should be handled decisively, they should continually remember that the person being disciplined is a brother or sister in the Lord. All further warnings to this person about his or her sin should be done with love and concern, praying for this fellow believer's restoration.

1 TIMOTHY

The Apostle Paul surrounded himself with some amazing friends. Among Paul, Timothy, Luke, Mark, Titus, and Philemon they wrote or received 16 out of 27 books in the New Testament. Three of these friends Paul called "sons in the faith"—Timothy, Titus, and Onesimus. Paul honored his friends by writing them powerful letters. This one to young Timothy reflects the unique accountability and friendship that grew between Paul and his protégé.

AUTHOR AND DATE

First Timothy was written by Paul, about A.D. 62 to 64.

Many modernist critics deny that Paul wrote the Pastoral Epistles (1 Timothy, 2 Timothy, and Titus). To do so, they must dismiss the testimony of the letters themselves (1:1; 2 Timothy 1:1; Titus 1:1). They must also ignore the testimony of the early church, which is as strong in favor of Pauline authorship of the Pastoral Epistles as for any of the letters, except for Romans and 1 Corinthians (which enjoys impregnable support). These critics maintain that a devout follower of Paul wrote the Pastoral Epistles in the second century. They offer extensive, but refutable, support for their argument. And, since the "latest evidence" often turns out to be flawed, and Scripture repeatedly turns out to be right, it is best in this case to maintain the straightforward scriptural claim of Pauline authorship for the Pastoral Epistles. (For a detailed analysis of the arguments see the FAQ on the authorship of the Pastoral Epistles).

The evidence seems clear that Paul wrote 1 Timothy and Titus shortly after his release from his first Roman imprisonment (about A.D. 62–64) and 2 Timothy from prison during his second Roman imprisonment (about A.D. 66–67), shortly before his death.

BACKGROUND AND SETTING

Timothy was from Lystra (Acts 16:1–3), a city in the Roman province of Galatia. Paul had led Timothy to Christ (1:2,18; 1 Corinthians 4:17; 2 Timothy 1:2), undoubtedly during his ministry in Lystra on his first missionary journey (Acts 14:6–23). Timothy would be Paul's disciple, friend, and co-laborer for the rest of the apostle's life, ministering with him in Berea (Acts 17:4), Athens (Acts 17:15), and Corinth (Acts 18:5; 2 Corinthians 1:19) and accompanying him on his trip to Jerusalem (Acts 20:4). He was with Paul in his first Roman imprisonment, and he went to Philippi (Philippians 2:19–23) after Paul's release. In addition, Paul's

epistles frequently mention Timothy (Romans 16:21; 2 Corinthians 1:1; Philippians 1:1; Colossians 1:1; 1 Thessalonians 1:1; 2 Thessalonians 1:1; Philemon 1). Paul often would send Timothy to churches as his representative (1 Corinthians 4:17; 16:10; Philippians 2:19; 1 Thessalonians 3:2); thus this letter finds him on another assignment, serving as pastor of the church at Ephesus (1:3).

After being released from his first Roman imprisonment (Acts 28:30), Paul revisited several of the cities in which he had previously ministered, including Ephesus. He left Timothy in Ephesus to deal with problems that had arisen in the church there, such as false doctrine (1:3–7; 4:1–3; 6:3–5), disorder in worship (2:1–15), the lack of qualified leaders (3:1–14), and materialism (6:6–19). Paul continued on to Macedonia, from where he wrote Timothy this letter to help him carry out his task in the church (3:14,15).

HISTORICAL AND THEOLOGICAL THEMES

This is a practical letter containing pastoral instructions from Paul to Timothy (3:14,15). Because this young pastor was well versed in Paul's theology, the apostle devoted little space to doctrinal instruction. The epistle does, however, imply or allude to many important theological truths, such as the proper function of the law (1:5–11); salvation (1:14–16; 2:4–6); the attributes of God (1:17); the Fall (2:13,14); the Person of Christ (3:16; 6:15,16); election (6:12); the second coming of Christ (6:14,15).

> **THIS IS A PRACTICAL LETTER CONTAINING PASTORAL INSTRUCTIONS FROM PAUL TO TIMOTHY.**

OUTLINE

I. **GREETING (1:1,2)**

II. **INSTRUCTIONS CONCERNING FALSE DOCTRINE (1:3–20)**
    A. The False Doctrine at Ephesus (1:3–11)
    B. The True Doctrine of Paul (1:12–17)
    C. The Exhortation to Timothy (1:18–20)

III. **INSTRUCTIONS CONCERNING THE CHURCH (2:1–3:16)**
    A. The Importance of Prayer (2:1–8)
    B. The Role of Women (2:9–15)
    C. The Qualifications for Leaders (3:1–13)
    D. The Reason for Paul's Letter (3:14–16)

IV. **INSTRUCTIONS CONCERNING FALSE TEACHERS (4:1–16)**
    A. The Description of False Teachers (4:1–5)
    B. The Description of True Teachers (4:6–16)

V. **INSTRUCTIONS CONCERNING PASTORAL RESPONSIBILITIES (5:1–6:2)**
    A. The Responsibility to Sinning Members (5:1,2)
    B. The Responsibility to Widows (5:3–16)
    C. The Responsibility to Elders (5:17–25)
    D. The Responsibility to Slaves (6:1,2)

VI. **INSTRUCTIONS CONCERNING THE MAN OF GOD (6:3–21)**
    A. The Peril of False Teaching (6:3–5)
    B. The Peril of Loving Money (6:6–10)
    C. The Proper Character and Motivation of a Man of God (6:11–16)
    D. The Proper Handling of Treasure (6:17–19)
    D. The Proper Handling of Truth (6:20,21)

Greeting

1 Paul, an apostle of Jesus Christ, by the commandment of God our Savior and the Lord Jesus Christ, our hope,

²To Timothy, a true son in the faith:

Grace, mercy, *and* peace from God our Father and Jesus Christ our Lord.

> **1:2 true son in the faith.** Only Timothy (2 Tim. 1:2) and Titus (1:4) received this special expression of Paul's favor. The Greek word for "son" is better translated "child," which emphasizes Paul's role as spiritual father to Timothy. "True" speaks of Timothy's genuine faith (see 2 Tim. 1:5). Timothy was Paul's most cherished pupil and protégé (1 Cor. 4:17).

No Other Doctrine

³As I urged you when I went into Macedonia—remain in Ephesus that you may charge some that they teach no other doctrine, ⁴nor give heed to fables and endless genealogies, which cause disputes rather than godly edification which is in faith. ⁵Now the purpose of the commandment is love from a pure heart, *from* a good conscience, and *from* sincere faith, ⁶from which some, having strayed, have turned aside to idle talk, ⁷desiring to be teachers of the law, understanding neither what they say nor the things which they affirm.

> **1:7 desiring to be teachers.** The false teachers wanted the kind of prestige that the Jewish rabbis had, but they were not concerned about truly learning the law and teaching it to others (see Matt. 23:5–7). Instead, they imposed on the believers in Ephesus legalistic, false teachings that offered salvation by works.

⁸But we know that the law *is* good if one uses it lawfully, ⁹knowing this: that the law is not made for a righteous person, but for *the* lawless and insubordinate, for *the* ungodly and for sinners, for *the* unholy and profane, for murderers of fathers and murderers of mothers, for manslayers, ¹⁰for fornicators, for sodomites, for kidnappers, for liars, for perjurers, and if there is any other thing that is contrary to sound doctrine, ¹¹according to the glorious gospel of the blessed God which was committed to my trust.

Glory to God for His Grace

¹²And I thank Christ Jesus our Lord who has enabled me, because He counted me faithful, putting *me* into the ministry, ¹³although I was formerly a blasphemer, a persecutor, and an insolent man; but I obtained mercy because I did *it* ignorantly in unbelief. ¹⁴And the grace of our Lord was exceedingly abundant, with faith and love which are in Christ Jesus. ¹⁵This *is* a faithful saying and worthy of all acceptance, that Christ Jesus came into the world to save sinners, of whom I am chief. ¹⁶However, for this reason I obtained mercy, that in me first Jesus Christ might show all longsuffering, as a pattern to those who are going to believe on Him for everlasting life.

> **1:13 a blasphemer, a persecutor, and an insolent man.** Paul had been a "blasphemer," violating the first half of the Ten Commandments, through his overt attacks against Christ (see Acts 9:4,5; 22:7,8). As a "persecutor" and an "insolent man," Paul violated the second half of the Ten Commandments through his attacks on believers.

When Paul writes, "This is a faithful saying," is he quoting other Scripture?

Paul used this phrase a number of times in the Pastoral Epistles (1:15; 3:1; 4:9; 2 Timothy 2:11; Titus 3:8). The statement that follows in each case summarizes a key doctrine. The added phrase "worthy of all acceptance" gives the statement added emphasis. Apparently, these sayings were well known in the churches as concise expressions of cardinal gospel truth. In their travels together, Timothy and Titus would have heard Paul expand on these statements many times.

These "sayings" do not quote other Scripture directly but summarize biblical teaching. For example, the saying in 1:15 "that Christ Jesus came into the world to save sinners" is based on Jesus' statements recorded in Matthew 9:13 and Luke 19:10. Naturally, their usage by Paul under the inspiration of the Holy Spirit confirmed that these "sayings" were God's Word.

¹⁷Now to the King eternal, immortal, invisible, to God who alone is wise,[a] *be* honor and glory forever and ever. Amen.

Fight the Good Fight

¹⁸This charge I commit to you, son Timothy, according to the prophecies previously made concerning you, that by them you may wage the good warfare, ¹⁹having faith and a good conscience, which some having rejected, concerning the faith have suffered shipwreck, ²⁰of whom are Hymenaeus and Alexander, whom I delivered to Satan that they may learn not to blaspheme.

> **1:18 prophecies previously made concerning you.** A series of prophecies had been given about Timothy in connection with his receiving his spiritual gift. These prophecies specifically and supernaturally called Timothy into God's service. **wage the good warfare.** Paul urged Timothy to fight the battle against the enemies of Christ and the Gospel (see 2 Cor. 10:3–5).

Pray for All Men

2 Therefore I exhort first of all that supplications, prayers, intercessions, *and* giving of thanks be made for all men, ²for kings and all who are in authority, that we may lead a quiet and peaceable life in all godliness and reverence. ³For this *is* good and acceptable in the sight of God our Savior, ⁴who desires all men to be saved and to come to the knowledge of the truth. ⁵For *there is* one God and one Mediator between God and men, *the* Man Christ Jesus, ⁶who gave Himself a ransom for all, to be testified in due time, ⁷for which I was appointed a preacher and an apostle—I am speaking the truth in Christ[a] *and* not lying—a teacher of the Gentiles in faith and truth.

Men and Women in the Church

⁸I desire therefore that the men pray everywhere, lifting up holy hands, without wrath and doubting; ⁹in like manner also, that the women adorn themselves in modest apparel, with propriety and moderation,

---

1:17 [a]NU-Text reads *to the only God.*   2:7 [a]NU-Text omits *in Christ.*

If 2:4–6 states that God "desires all men to be saved," why isn't everyone saved? How far does salvation extend?

The Greek word for "desires" is not the one usually used to express God's will of decree (His sovereign eternal purpose). Rather, it expresses God's will of desire. There is a distinction between God's desire and His eternal saving purpose, which must transcend His desires. God does not want people to sin. He hates sin with all His being (see Psalm 5:4; 45:7). Thus, He hates its consequences—eternal wickedness in hell. God does not want people to remain wicked forever in eternal remorse and hatred of Him. Yet God, for His own glory, and to manifest that glory in wrath, chose to endure "vessels . . . prepared for destruction" for the supreme fulfillment of His will (see Romans 9:22). In His eternal purpose, He chose only the elect out of the world (see John 17:6) and passed over the rest, leaving them to the consequences of their sin, unbelief, and rejection of Christ (see Romans 1:18–32). Ultimately, God's choices and action are determined by His sovereign, eternal purpose, not His desires.

Paul describes Christ's role in salvation with the phrase, "a ransom for all" (verse 6). Jesus Himself used similar wording when he described his purpose to be "a ransom for many" (Matthew 20:28). The "all" is qualified by the "many." Not all will be ransomed (though His death would be sufficient), but only the many who believe by the work of the Holy Spirit and for whom the actual atonement was made. The "for all" should be taken in two senses: (1) temporal benefits of the atonement that accrue to people universally (for example, daily experiences of God's compassion and grace); and (2) Christ's death was sufficient to cover the sins of all people. Yet the substitutionary aspect of His death is applied to the elect alone. Christ's death is therefore unlimited in its sufficiency but limited in its application. The fact that not all are saved has no bearing on Christ's ability to save but rather rests in humanity's profound sinfulness and God's sovereign plan.

not with braided hair or gold or pearls or costly clothing, ¹⁰but, which is proper for women professing godliness, with good works. ¹¹Let a woman learn in silence with all submission. ¹²And I do not permit a woman to teach or to have authority over a man, but to be in silence. ¹³For Adam was formed first, then Eve. ¹⁴And Adam was not deceived, but the woman being deceived, fell into transgression. ¹⁵Nevertheless she will be saved in childbearing if they continue in faith, love, and holiness, with self-control.

2:11 Let a woman learn. Women were not to be public teachers when the church assembled, but they were to be fully included in the learning process. Paul commands that women be taught in the church, which was a novel concept, since neither first century Judaism nor Greek culture held women in high esteem. Some women may have taken advantage of this by seeking dominant roles of leadership.

Qualifications of Overseers

3 This *is* a faithful saying: If a man desires the position of a bishop,[a] he desires a good work. ²A bishop then must be blameless, the husband of one wife, temperate, sober-minded, of good behavior, hospitable, able to teach; ³not given to wine, not violent, not greedy for money,[a] but gentle, not quarrelsome, not covetous; ⁴one who rules his own house well, having *his* children in submission with all reverence ⁵(for if a man does not know how to rule his own house, how will he take care of the church of God?); ⁶not a novice, lest being puffed up with pride he fall into the *same* condemnation as the devil. ⁷Moreover he must have a good testimony among those who are outside, lest he fall into reproach and the snare of the devil.

3:1 desires...desires. The first means, "to reach out after." The second means "a strong passion." Both describe the type of man who pursues the ministry because he is driven by a strong internal desire. **bishop.** The word means "overseer" and identifies the men who are responsible to lead the church (see 1 Thess. 5:12). Bishops (pastors, overseers, elders) are responsible to lead, preach, help the spiritually weak, care for the church, and ordain other leaders.

3:5 take care of the church of God. An elder must first prove in the intimacy of his own home his ability to lead others to salvation and sanctification. There he proves that God has gifted him uniquely to spiritually set the example of virtue, to serve others, resolve conflict, build unity, and maintain love. If he cannot do those essential things in his own home, he will not be able to do them in the church.

Qualifications of Deacons

⁸Likewise deacons *must be* reverent, not double-tongued, not given to much wine, not greedy for money, ⁹holding the mystery of the faith with a pure conscience. ¹⁰But let these also first be tested; then let them serve as deacons, being *found* blameless. ¹¹Likewise, *their* wives *must be* reverent, not slanderers, temperate, faithful in all things. ¹²Let deacons be the husbands of one wife, ruling *their* children and their own houses well. ¹³For those who have served well as deacons obtain for themselves a good standing and great boldness in the faith which is in Christ Jesus.

3:11 *their* wives. Paul is likely referring to the women who serve as deacons. Since Paul gave no requirements for elders' wives, there is no reason to assume there would be qualifications for deacons' wives. **not slanderers.** "Slanderers" is the plural form of *diabolos*, a title frequently given to Satan (Matt. 4:5,8,11). **faithful in all things.** Women who serve in the church must be trustworthy in all aspects of their lives and ministries.

The Great Mystery

¹⁴These things I write to you, though I hope to come to you shortly; ¹⁵but if I am delayed, *I write* so that you may know how you ought to conduct yourself in the house of God, which is the church of the living God, the pillar and ground of the truth. ¹⁶And without controversy great is the mystery of godliness:

God[a] was manifested in the flesh,
Justified in the Spirit,
Seen by angels,
Preached among the Gentiles,
Believed on in the world,
Received up in glory.

3:1 [a]Literally *overseer*   3:3 [a]NU-Text omits *not greedy for money.*   3:16 [a]NU-Text reads *Who.*

The Great Apostasy

4 Now the Spirit expressly says that in latter times some will depart from the faith, giving heed to deceiving spirits and doctrines of demons, ²speaking lies in hypocrisy, having their own conscience seared with a hot iron, ³forbidding to marry, *and commanding* to abstain from foods which God created to be received with thanksgiving by those who believe and know the truth. ⁴For every creature of God *is* good, and nothing is to be refused if it is received with thanksgiving; ⁵for it is sanctified by the word of God and prayer.

4:2 speaking lies in hypocrisy. These are the false teachers who spread demon doctrine (see 1 John 4:1). **seared.** This is a medical term for burning and deadening. False teachers can teach their hypocritical lies because their consciences have been desensitized (see Eph. 4:19), as if all the nerves for feeling had been destroyed and turned into scar tissue by the burning of demonic deception.

A Good Servant of Jesus Christ

⁶If you instruct the brethren in these things, you will be a good minister of Jesus Christ, nourished in the words of faith and of the good doctrine which you have carefully followed. ⁷But reject profane and old wives' fables, and exercise yourself toward godliness. ⁸For bodily exercise profits a little, but godliness is profitable for all things, having promise of the life that now is and of that which is to come. ⁹This *is* a faithful saying and worthy of all acceptance. ¹⁰For to this *end* we both labor and suffer reproach,ᵃ because we trust in the living God, who is *the* Savior of all men, especially of those who believe. ¹¹These things command and teach.

Take Heed to Your Ministry

¹²Let no one despise your youth, but be an example to the believers in word, in conduct, in love, in spirit,ᵃ in faith, in purity. ¹³Till I come, give attention to reading, to exhortation, to doctrine. ¹⁴Do not neglect

---

4:10 ᵃNU-Text reads *we labor and strive.*   4:12 ᵃNU-Text omits *in spirit.*

What specific instructions did Paul give Timothy that would apply to a young person?

A young person seeking to live as a disciple of Jesus Christ can find essential guidelines in 4:12–16, where Paul listed five areas (verse 12) in which Timothy was to be an example to the church:

1. In "word" or speech—see also Matthew 12:34–37; Ephesians 4:25,29,31.
2. In "conduct" or righteous living—see also Titus 2:10; 1 Peter 1:15; 2:12; 3:16.
3. In "love" or self—sacrificial service for others—see also John 15:13.
4. In "faith" or faithfulness or commitment, not belief—see also 1 Corinthians 4:2.
5. In "purity" and particularly sexual purity—see also 4:2.

The verses that follow hold several other building blocks to a life of discipleship:
1. Timothy was to be involved in the public reading, study, and application of Scripture (verse 13).
2. Timothy was to diligently use his spiritual gift that others had confirmed and affirmed in a public way (verse 14).
3. Timothy was to be committed to a process of progress in his walk with Christ (verse 15).
4. Timothy was to "take heed" to pay careful attention to "yourself and to the doctrine" (verse 16).

The priorities of a godly leader should be summed up in Timothy's personal holiness and public teaching. All of Paul's exhortations in verses 6–16 fit into one or the other of those two categories. By careful attention to his own godly life and faithful preaching of the Word, Timothy would continue to be the human instrument God would use to bring the gospel and to save some who heard him. Though salvation is God's work, it is His pleasure to do it through human instruments.

the gift that is in you, which was given to you by prophecy with the laying on of the hands of the eldership. [15]Meditate on these things; give yourself entirely to them, that your progress may be evident to all. [16]Take heed to yourself and to the doctrine. Continue in them, for in doing this you will save both yourself and those who hear you.

> **4:12 Let no one despise your youth.** Greek culture placed great value on age and experience. Since Timothy was still in his thirties, which was young by cultural standards, he would have to earn respect through his godly example. Because he had been with Paul since he was a young teenager, Timothy had much experience to mature him. Disrespecting him because he was young was inexcusable.

Treatment of Church Members

5 Do not rebuke an older man, but exhort *him* as a father, younger men as brothers, [2]older women as mothers, younger women as sisters, with all purity.

> **5:1 rebuke.** An older, sinning believer is to be respected by not being addressed harshly (see 2 Tim. 2:24,25). **an older man.** Timothy was instructed to confront sinning, older men with honor, based on OT principles (see Lev. 19:32). **exhort.** This Greek word, which is related to a title for the Holy Spirit, refers to helping someone. We are to strengthen our fellow believers (see Gal. 6:1,2).

Honor True Widows

[3]Honor widows who are really widows. [4]But if any widow has children or grandchildren, let them first learn to show piety at home and to repay their parents; for this is good and[a] acceptable before God. [5]Now she who is really a widow, and left alone, trusts in God and continues in supplications and prayers night and day. [6]But she who lives in pleasure is dead while she lives. [7]And these things command, that they may be blameless. [8]But if anyone does not provide for his own, and especially for those of his household, he has denied the faith and is worse than an unbeliever.

[9]Do not let a widow under sixty years old be taken into the number, *and not unless* she has been the wife of one man, [10]well reported for good works: if she has brought up children, if she has lodged strangers, if she has washed the saints' feet, if she has relieved the afflicted, if she has diligently followed every good work.

> **5:9 under sixty.** In New Testament culture, 60 was considered retirement age. By that age, older women would have completed their child-rearing and would have the time, maturity, and character to devote their lives in service to God and the church. At 60, widows would likely not remarry. **be taken into the number.** This was a list of widows eligible for special church ministry (see Titus 2:3–5).

[11]But refuse *the* younger widows; for when they have begun to grow wanton against Christ, they desire to marry, [12]having condemnation because they have cast off their first faith. [13]And besides they learn *to be* idle, wandering about from house to house, and not only idle but also gossips and busybodies, saying things which they ought not. [14]Therefore I desire that *the* younger *widows* marry, bear children, manage the house, give no opportunity to the adversary to speak reproachfully. [15]For some have already turned aside after Satan. [16]If any believing man or[a] woman has widows, let them relieve them, and do not let the church be burdened, that it may relieve those who are really widows.

> **5:14 bear children.** The younger widows were still of childbearing age and thus had the potential blessing of remarrying and having children. **manage the house.** The Greek term denotes all aspects of household administration. The home is the domain where a married woman fulfills herself in God's design.

Honor the Elders

[17]Let the elders who rule well be counted worthy of double honor, especially those who labor in the word and doctrine. [18]For the Scripture says, *"You shall not muzzle an ox while it treads out the grain,"[a]* and, *"The laborer is worthy of his wages."[b]* [19]Do not receive an accusation against an elder except from two or three witnesses. [20]Those who are sinning rebuke in the presence of all, that the rest also may fear.

5:4 [a]NU-Text and M-Text omit *good and.*   5:16 [a]NU-Text omits *man or.*   5:18 [a]Deuteronomy 25:4   [b]Luke 10:7

²¹I charge *you* before God and the Lord Jesus Christ and the elect angels that you observe these things without prejudice, doing nothing with partiality. ²²Do not lay hands on anyone hastily, nor share in other people's sins; keep yourself pure.

> **5:22 Do not lay hands on...hastily.** The laying on of hands affirmed a man's suitability for and acceptance into public ministry as an elder/pastor/overseer. This began with the Old Testament practice of laying hands on a sacrificial animal to identify with it (Ex. 29:10,15,19). Laying hands on hastily would be to affirm a leader without thorough investigation and preparation to determine the man's qualifications.

²³No longer drink only water, but use a little wine for your stomach's sake and your frequent infirmities.

²⁴Some men's sins are clearly evident, preceding *them* to judgment, but those of some *men* follow later. ²⁵Likewise, the good works *of some* are clearly evident, and those that are otherwise cannot be hidden.

Honor Masters

6 Let as many bondservants as are under the yoke count their own masters worthy of all honor, so that the name of God and *His* doctrine may not be blasphemed.

> **6:2 believing masters.** The tendency might be for a servant to assume equality in Christ with a Christian master and thus disdain the master's authority. Instead, working for a Christian should produce more loyal, diligent service, out of love. **exhort.** To strongly direct and insist on obedience to the principles for correct behavior in the workplace.

²And those who have believing masters, let them not despise *them* because they are brethren, but rather serve *them* because those who are benefited are believers and beloved. Teach and exhort these things.

Error and Greed

³If anyone teaches otherwise and does not consent to wholesome words, *even* the words of our Lord Jesus Christ, and to the doctrine which accords with godliness, ⁴he is proud, knowing nothing, but is obsessed with disputes and arguments over words, from which come envy, strife, reviling, evil suspicions, ⁵useless wranglings*ᵃ* of men of corrupt minds and destitute of the truth, who suppose that godliness is a *means of* gain. From such withdraw yourself.*ᵇ*

⁶Now godliness with contentment is great gain. ⁷For we brought nothing into *this* world, *and it is* certain*ᵃ* we can carry nothing out. ⁸And having food and clothing, with these we shall be content. ⁹But those who desire to be rich fall into temptation and a snare, and *into* many foolish and harmful lusts which drown men in destruction and perdition. ¹⁰For the love of money is a root of all *kinds of* evil, for which some have strayed from the faith in their greediness, and pierced themselves through with many sorrows.

> **6:10 love of money.** In this context, this sin applies to false teachers, but the principle is true universally. Money itself is not evil; it is a gift from God (Deut. 8:18). Paul does not condemn money but the love of it (see Matt. 6:24). **strayed from the faith.** These sinners have replaced God with gold and have turned from Him to pursue money.

6:5 *ᵃ*NU-Text and M-Text read *constant friction.* *ᵇ*NU-Text omits this sentence.   6:7 *ᵃ*NU-Text omits *and it is certain.*

What are the characteristics of a false teacher?

Paul provided for Timothy a helpful profile of false teachers by identifying three primary characteristics in 6:3. False teachers reveal themselves in these ways: (1) they "teach otherwise"—a different doctrine, or any teaching that contradicts God's revelation in Scripture (see Galatians 1:6–9); (2) they do "not consent to wholesome words"—they do not agree with sound, healthy teaching, specifically the teaching contained in Scripture (see 2 Peter 3:16); and (3) they reject "doctrine which accords with godliness"—teaching not based on Scripture will always result in an unholy life. Instead of godliness, the lives of false teachers will be marked by sin (see 2 Peter 2:10–22; Jude 4,8–16).

The Good Confession

[11]But you, O man of God, flee these things and pursue righteousness, godliness, faith, love, patience, gentleness. [12]Fight the good fight of faith, lay hold on eternal life, to which you were also called and have confessed the good confession in the presence of many witnesses. [13]I urge you in the sight of God who gives life to all things, and *before* Christ Jesus who witnessed the good confession before Pontius Pilate, [14]that you keep *this* commandment without spot, blameless until our Lord Jesus Christ's appearing, [15]which He will manifest in His own time, *He who is* the blessed and only Potentate, the King of kings and Lord of lords, [16]who alone has immortality, dwelling in unapproachable light, whom no man has seen or can see, to whom *be* honor and everlasting power. Amen.

6:15 in His own time. The time for Christ to return is known only by God (Mark 13:32). **Potentate.** Meaning, "Sovereign." **King of kings and Lord of lords.** A title for Christ (Rev. 17:14) used here for God the Father. Paul probably used this title for God to confront the cult of emperor worship, intending to show that only God is sovereign and worthy of worship.

Instructions to the Rich

[17]Command those who are rich in this present age not to be haughty, nor to trust in uncertain riches but in the living God, who gives us richly all things to enjoy. [18]Let *them* do good, that they be rich in good works, ready to give, willing to share, [19]storing up for themselves a good foundation for the time to come, that they may lay hold on eternal life.

Guard the Faith

[20]O Timothy! Guard what was committed to your trust, avoiding the profane *and* idle babblings and contradictions of what is falsely called knowledge—[21]by professing it some have strayed concerning the faith.

Grace *be* with you. Amen.

6:20 what was committed to your trust. Meaning "deposit." The deposit with which Timothy was entrusted was the truth, the divine revelation. Every Christian has that sacred trust to guard the revelation of God (see 1 Cor. 4:1). **what is falsely called knowledge.** This refers to false doctrine. False teachers claim to have superior knowledge and to know transcendent secrets, but they are actually ignorant in their understanding.

NAMES OF SATAN

1.	Abaddon	Destruction	Revelation 9:11
2.	Accuser	Opposes believers before God	Revelation 12:10
3.	Adversary	Against God	1 Peter 5:8
4.	Apollyon	Destroyer	Revelation 9:11
5.	Beelzebub	Lord of the fly	Matthew 12:24
6.	Belial	Worthless	2 Corinthians 6:15
7.	Devil	Slanderer	Matthew 4:1
8.	Dragon	Destructive	Revelation 12:3,7,9
9.	Enemy	Opponent	Matthew 13:28
10.	Evil one	Intrinsically evil	John 17:15
11.	God of this age	Influences thinking of world	2 Corinthians 4:4
12.	Liar	Perverts the truth	John 8:44
13.	Murderer	Leads people to eternal death	John 8:44
14.	Prince of the power of the air	Control of unbelievers	Ephesians 2:2
15.	Roaring lion	One who destroys	1 Peter 5:8
16.	Ruler of demons	Leader of fallen angels	Mark 3:22
17.	Ruler of this world	Rules in world system	John 12:31
18.	Satan	Adversary	1 Timothy 5:15
19.	Serpent of old	Deceiver in garden	Revelation 12:9; 20:2
20.	Tempter	Solicits people to sin	1 Thessalonians 3:5

What directions did Paul give Timothy about dealing with people who are wealthy?

Paul counseled Timothy (6:17–19) concerning what to teach those who are rich in material possessions—that is, those who have more than the mere essentials of food, clothing, and shelter. Paul had already made the case (6:6–8) that Christians should be satisfied and sufficient, and not to seek for more than what God has already given them, for He is the source of true contentment. Instead of condemning wealthy people or commanding them to get rid of their wealth, Paul called them to be good stewards of their God-given resources (see also Deuteronomy 8:18; 1 Samuel 2:7; 1 Chronicles 29:12; 2 Corinthians 3:5; 9:8; Philippians 4:11–13,19).

Those who have an abundance face a constant temptation to look down on others and act superior—haughty (6:17). Paul reminded Timothy that riches and pride often go together; thus, the wealthier a person becomes, the more he or she is tempted to be proud (see Proverbs 18:23; 28:11; James 2:1–4). If fact, those who have much tend to trust in their wealth (see Proverbs 23:4,5). But God provides far more security than any earthly investment can ever give (see Ecclesiastes 5:18–20; Matthew 6:19–21).

2 TIMOTHY

Last words often carry special significance. The Apostle Paul saw that the end of life was near, so he wrote to share some final thoughts with his "son in the faith," Timothy. Paul's words take the form of a powerful, Spirit inspired last will and testament. The letter also expresses a tribute to the Lord Jesus Christ, of whom Paul could say, "I know whom I have believed and am persuaded that He is able to keep what I have committed to Him until that Day" (2 Timothy 1:12).

AUTHOR AND DATE

Second Timothy was written by Paul, in about A.D. 66 to 67.

Paul's authorship is claimed by the first word in the first verse of this letter. Suggestions to the contrary are discussed in the FAQ *Did Paul Write the Pastoral Epistles?* Scripture and tradition attest that Paul wrote 2 Timothy, the last of his inspired letters, shortly before his martyrdom in about A.D. 66–67. For more biographical information on Timothy, see the introduction to 1 Timothy.

BACKGROUND AND SETTING

Paul was released from his first Roman imprisonment for a short period of ministry. During that time, he wrote the epistles, 1 Timothy and Titus. By the time he wrote this letter, however, he was imprisoned again (1:16; 2:9). His re-arrest probably occurred during Nero's persecution of Christians. Unlike Paul's confident hope of release during his earlier imprisonment (Philippians 1:19,25,26; 2:24; Philemon 22), this time he had no such hopes (4:6–8). In his first imprisonment in Rome (about A.D. 60–62), before Nero began aggressively persecuting believers (A.D. 64), Paul was only under house arrest and enjoyed much interaction and ministry with people (Acts 28:16–31). Five or six years later when he wrote 2 Timothy (about A.D. 66–67), however, the apostle was in a cold cell (4:13), in chains (2:9), and with no hope of deliverance (4:6). Fearful of their own persecution, nearly all those close to Paul had abandoned him (1:15; 4:9–12,16). So facing imminent execution, Paul wrote to Timothy, urging him to hurry to Rome for one last visit (4:9,21). History does not report whether Timothy made it there before Paul's death. According to tradition, Paul remained in Roman custody until he suffered the martyrdom that he had foreseen (4:6).

In this letter, Paul, aware that the end was near, passed the mantle of ministry to Timothy (2:2). The older disciple challenged the younger one in the following areas. He exhorted Timothy: (1) to continue faithful in his duties (1:6); (2) to hold

on to sound doctrine (1:13,14); (3) to avoid error (2:15–18); (4) to accept persecution for the gospel (2:3,4; 3:10–12); and (5) to put his confidence in the Scripture, and preach it relentlessly (3:15–4:5).

HISTORICAL AND THEOLOGICAL THEMES

Paul's second letter to Timothy seems to indicate he had reason to fear that Timothy was in danger of weakening spiritually. This would have been a grave concern for Paul because he had entrusted Timothy with significant ministry responsibilities (2:2). This concern can be seen, for example, in Paul's exhortation to "stir up" his gift (1:6), to replace fear with power, love, and a sound mind (1:7), to not be ashamed of Paul and the Lord but willingly suffer for the gospel (1:8), and to hold on to the truth (1:13,14). Further, some of Paul's expressions seem aimed at the possibility that Timothy might be weakening under the pressure of the church and the persecution of the world. Paul called him to generally "be strong" (2:11), the key exhortation of the first part of the letter, and to continue to "preach the word" (4:2), the central admonition of the last part. These final words to Timothy include few commendations but many commands.

> **PAUL CALLED HIM** TO GENERALLY **'BE STRONG'** AND TO CONTINUE TO **'PREACH THE WORD.'**

Since Timothy was well versed in Paul's theology, the apostle offered few doctrinal instructions. He did, however, allude to several important doctrines, including: (1) salvation by God's sovereign grace (1:9,10; 2:10); (2) the person of Christ (2:8; 4:1,8); (3) perseverance (2:11–13); and (4) the inspiration of Scripture (3:16,17)—the most pointed and crucial text in the New Testament on this doctrine.

A COMPARISON OF PAUL'S TWO ROMAN IMPRISONMENTS

First Imprisonment	Second Imprisonment
Acts 28—Wrote the Prison Epistles	2 Timothy
Accused by Jews of heresy and sedition	Persecuted by Rome and arrested as a criminal against the Empire
Local sporadic persecutions (A.D. 60–63)	Neronian persecution (A.D. 64–68)
Decent living conditions in a rented house (Acts 28:30,31)	Poor conditions, in a cold, dark dungeon
Many friends visited him	Virtually alone (only Luke with him)
Many opportunities for Christian witness were available	Opportunities for witness were restricted
Was optimistic for release and freedom (Philippians 1:24–26)	Anticipated his execution (2 Timothy 4:6)

OUTLINE

Greeting

1 Paul, an apostle of Jesus Christ*a* by the will of God, according to the promise of life which is in Christ Jesus,

²To Timothy, a beloved son:

Grace, mercy, *and* peace from God the Father and Christ Jesus our Lord.

Timothy's Faith and Heritage

³I thank God, whom I serve with a pure conscience, as *my* forefathers *did,* as without ceasing I remember you in my prayers night and day, ⁴greatly desiring to see you, being mindful of your tears, that I may be filled with joy, ⁵when I call to remembrance the genuine faith that is in you, which

> **1:6 stir up the gift of God.** This seems to indicate that Paul was unsatisfied with Timothy's current level of faithfulness. "Stir up" means "to keep the fire alive," to keep Timothy's spiritual gift alive and burning. Paul reminds Timothy that he should not let his gift for preaching, teaching, and evangelizing fall into disuse. **laying on of my hands.** Paul might have done this at the time of Timothy's conversion, when he received his spiritual gift.

dwelt first in your grandmother Lois and your mother Eunice, and I am persuaded is in you also. ⁶Therefore I remind you to stir up the gift of God which is in you through the laying on of my hands. ⁷For God has not given us a spirit of fear, but of power and of love and of a sound mind.

Not Ashamed of the Gospel

⁸Therefore do not be ashamed of the testimony of our Lord, nor of me His prisoner, but share with me in the sufferings for the gospel according to the power of God, ⁹who has saved us and called *us* with a holy calling, not according to our works, but according to His own purpose and grace which was given to us in Christ Jesus before time began, ¹⁰but has now been revealed by the appearing of our Savior Jesus Christ, *who* has abolished death and brought life and immortality to light through the gospel, ¹¹to which I was appointed a preacher, an apostle, and a teacher of the Gentiles.*a* ¹²For this reason I also suffer these things; nevertheless I am not ashamed, for I know whom I have believed and am persuaded that He is able to keep what I have committed to Him until that Day.

1:1 *a*NU-Text and M-Text read *Christ Jesus.*   1:11 *a*NU-Text omits *of the Gentiles.*

Q In 1:7, to what or whom does the term "spirit" refer?

A This statement is contrasting two attitudes rather than describing the Holy Spirit, whose presence (1:14) produces the second of the two "spirits" mentioned here. The spirit of fear that could be translated "timidity" denotes a cowardly, shameful fear caused by a weak, selfish character. Since this is not a by-product of God's presence, it must be coming from somewhere else.

The threat of Roman persecution, which was escalating under Nero, the hostility of those in the Ephesian church who resented Timothy's leadership, and the assaults of false teachers with their sophisticated systems of deception may have been overwhelming Timothy. But if he was fearful, his fear didn't come from God.

As an antidote to fear, Paul reminded Timothy of the resources God does supply. God has already given believers all the spiritual resources they need for every trial and threat (see Matthew 10:19,20). First, divine "power"—effective, productive spiritual energy belongs to believers (see Ephesians 1:18–20; 3:20; Zechariah 4:6). Second, God provides "love." This love centers on pleasing God and seeking other's welfare before one's own (see Romans 14:8; Galatians 5:22,25; Ephesians 3:19; 1 Peter 1:22; 1 John 4:18). Third, God promotes a "sound mind." This refers to a disciplined, self-controlled, and properly prioritized mind. This is the opposite of fear and cowardice that causes disorder and confusion. Focusing on the sovereign nature and perfect purposes of our eternal God allows believers to control their lives with godly wisdom and confidence in every situation (see Romans 12:3; 1 Timothy 3:2; Titus 1:8; 2:2).

1:12 I am not ashamed. Paul had no fear of the hostile persecution and possible death he faced from preaching the gospel. He was confident that God had sealed his future glory and blessing. **know whom I have believed.** "Know" describes the certainty of Paul's saving knowledge. **what I have committed.** Paul's life in time and eternity had been given to his Lord. **that Day.** The "Day of Christ," when believers will stand before the judgment seat and will be rewarded.

Be Loyal to the Faith

¹³Hold fast the pattern of sound words which you have heard from me, in faith and love which are in Christ Jesus. ¹⁴That good thing which was committed to you, keep by the Holy Spirit who dwells in us.

¹⁵This you know, that all those in Asia have turned away from me, among whom are Phygellus and Hermogenes. ¹⁶The Lord grant mercy to the household of Onesiphorus, for he often refreshed me, and was not ashamed of my chain; ¹⁷but when he arrived in Rome, he sought me out very zealously and found *me.* ¹⁸The Lord grant to him that he may find mercy from the Lord in that Day—and you know very well how many ways he ministered *to me*[a] at Ephesus.

Be Strong in Grace

2 You therefore, my son, be strong in the grace that is in Christ Jesus. ²And the things that you have heard from me among many witnesses, commit these to faithful men who will be able to teach others also. ³You therefore must endure[a] hardship as a

good soldier of Jesus Christ. ⁴No one engaged in warfare entangles himself with the affairs of *this* life, that he may please him who enlisted him as a soldier. ⁵And also if anyone competes in athletics, he is not crowned unless he competes according to the rules. ⁶The hardworking farmer must be first to partake of the crops. ⁷Consider what I say, and may[a] the Lord give you understanding in all things.

2:4 entangles himself. Just as a soldier called to duty is completely severed from the normal affairs of civilian life, so also the soldier of Jesus Christ must refuse to allow the things of the world to distract him (see James 4:4).

⁸Remember that Jesus Christ, of the seed of David, was raised from the dead according to my gospel, ⁹for which I suffer trouble as an evildoer, *even* to the point of chains; but the word of God is not chained. ¹⁰Therefore I endure all things for the sake of the elect, that they also may obtain the salvation which is in Christ Jesus with eternal glory.

¹¹*This is* a faithful saying:

> For if we died with *Him,*
>> We shall also live with *Him.*
> 12 If we endure,
>> We shall also reign with *Him.*
> If we deny *Him,*
>> He also will deny us.
> 13 If we are faithless,
>> He remains faithful;
>> He cannot deny Himself.

1:18 [a]*To me* is from the Vulgate and a few Greek manuscripts.   2:3 [a]NU-Text reads *You must share.*
2:7 [a]NU-Text reads *the Lord will give you.*

How many generations of discipleship does 2:2 include?

As Paul directed Timothy in the process of transmitting the gospel message, he mentioned four generations of lives transformed by the grace of Christ. The first mentioned was his own generation. He reminded Timothy that the source of his message for others was the countless hours of preaching and teaching he had heard the apostle deliver "among many witnesses." The next generation was Timothy's. What he had heard, he was charged to deliver to others. These others would be the next generation. Not a random audience, but "faithful" believers with teaching abilities. These in turn would teach the next generation about the "grace that is in Christ Jesus." The process of spiritual reproduction, which began in the early church, is to continue until the Lord returns.

Approved and Disapproved Workers

[14]Remind *them* of these things, charging *them* before the Lord not to strive about words to no profit, to the ruin of the hearers. [15]Be diligent to present yourself approved to God, a worker who does not need to be ashamed, rightly dividing the word of truth. [16]But shun profane *and* idle babblings, for they will increase to more ungodliness. [17]And their message will spread like cancer. Hymenaeus and Philetus are of this sort, [18]who have strayed concerning the truth, saying that the resurrection is already past; and they overthrow the faith of some. [19]Nevertheless the solid foundation of God stands, having this seal: "The Lord knows those who are His," and, "Let everyone who names the name of Christ[a] depart from iniquity."

[20]But in a great house there are not only vessels of gold and silver, but also of wood and clay, some for honor and some for dishonor. [21]Therefore if anyone cleanses himself from the latter, he will be a vessel for honor, sanctified and useful for the Master, prepared for every good work. [22]Flee also youthful lusts; but pursue righteousness, faith, love, peace with those who call on the Lord out of a pure heart. [23]But avoid foolish and ignorant disputes, knowing that they generate strife. [24]And a servant of the Lord must not quarrel but be gentle to all, able to teach, patient, [25]in humility correcting those who are in opposition, if God perhaps will grant them repentance, so that they may know the truth, [26]and *that* they may come to their senses *and escape* the snare of the devil, having been taken captive by him to *do* his will.

> **2:15 Be diligent.** This word denotes zealous persistence in accomplishing a goal. Timothy should strive to impart God's Word completely, accurately, and clearly. **rightly dividing.** Just as trades such as carpentry, masonry, and Paul's trade of leather working and tentmaking demanded exactness, biblical interpretation demands the highest level of precision and accuracy. Anything less is shameful.

Perilous Times and Perilous Men

3 But know this, that in the last days perilous times will come: [2]For men will be

> **3:1 the last days.** The time following the first coming of the Lord Jesus, the age in which we live. **perilous times.** "Perilous" describes the savage nature of two demon-possessed men (Matt. 8:28). "Times" refers to eras. Such savage eras will increase in frequency and severity as the return of Christ approaches. The church age is filled with these dangerous movements, which accumulate strength as the end nears (see Matt. 7:15).

lovers of themselves, lovers of money, boasters, proud, blasphemers, disobedient to parents, unthankful, unholy, [3]unloving, unforgiving, slanderers, without self-control, brutal, despisers of good, [4]traitors, headstrong, haughty, lovers of pleasure rather than lovers of God, [5]having a form of godliness but denying its power. And from such people turn away! [6]For of this sort are those who creep into households and make captives of gullible women loaded down with sins, led away by various lusts, [7]always learning and never able to come to the knowledge of the truth. [8]Now as Jannes and Jambres resisted Moses, so do these also resist the truth: men of corrupt minds, disapproved concerning the faith; [9]but they will progress no further, for their folly will be manifest to all, as theirs also was.

> **3:6 gullible women.** Weak in virtue and their knowledge of the truth, weighed down with emotional and spiritual guilt, these women were easy prey for the deceitful, false teachings.

The Man of God and the Word of God

[10]But you have carefully followed my doctrine, manner of life, purpose, faith, longsuffering, love, perseverance, [11]persecutions, afflictions, which happened to me at Antioch, at Iconium, at Lystra—what persecutions I endured. And out of *them* all the Lord delivered me. [12]Yes, and all who desire to live godly in Christ Jesus will suffer persecution. [13]But evil men and impostors will grow worse and worse, deceiving and being deceived. [14]But you must continue in the things which you have learned and been assured of, knowing from whom you have learned *them*, [15]and that from childhood you have known the Holy Scriptures, which are able to make you wise for

---

2:19 [a]NU-Text and M-Text read *the Lord.*

salvation through faith which is in Christ Jesus.

¹⁶All Scripture *is* given by inspiration of God, and *is* profitable for doctrine, for reproof, for correction, for instruction in righteousness, ¹⁷that the man of God may be complete, thoroughly equipped for every good work.

3:16 All Scripture. Both Old Testament and New Testament Scripture are included. **given by inspiration of God.** Sometimes God told the writers of the Bible the exact words to write (Jer. 1:9), but more often He used their minds, vocabularies, and experiences to produce His own perfect Word. Inspiration applies only to Scripture, not to the writers; there are no inspired writers, only inspired Scripture.

Did Paul write the Pastoral Epistles (1 Timothy, 2 Timothy, and Titus)?

The question implies that Pauline authorship has been debated. It has. Many modernist critics, who seem to delight in attacking the plain statement of Scripture, deny that Paul wrote these three letters called the Pastoral Epistles. Despite the internal evidence (1 Timothy 1:1; 2 Timothy 1:1; Titus 1:1) and the ancient testimony of the early church, these critics maintain that a devout follower of Paul wrote these letters in the second century.

As proof of their assertions, these critics offer five lines of supposed evidence against Pauline authorship:

1. The historical references in the Pastoral Epistles cannot be harmonized with the chronology of Paul's life recorded in Acts.
2. The false teaching described in the Pastoral Epistles is the fully-developed Gnosticism of the second century.
3. The church organizational structure in the Pastoral Epistles is that of the second century and is too well developed for Paul's day.
4. The Pastoral Epistles do not contain the great themes of Paul's theology.
5. The Greek vocabulary of the Pastoral Epistles contains many words not found in Paul's other letters, nor in the rest of the New Testament.

In reply to the critic's arguments, the following facts refute each of their points of evidence:
1. The suggestion of historical incompatibility proves valid only if Paul never left his Roman imprisonment recorded in Acts. But he was released. Acts does not record Paul's execution, and Paul himself expected to be released (see Philippians 1:19,25,26; 2:24; Philemon 22). The historical events mentioned in these letters fall after the close of the book of Acts.
2. While similarities exist between the heresy of the Pastoral Epistles and second-century Gnosticism, so do important differences. Unlike second-century Gnosticism, the false teachers faced by Timothy were still within the church (1:3–7), and their teaching was based on Judaistic legalism (1:7; Titus 1:10,14; 3:9).
3. The church organizational structure mentioned in the Pastoral Epistles is, in fact, consistent with that established elsewhere by Paul (see Acts 14:23; Philippians 1:1).
4. The Pastoral Epistles do mention the central themes of Paul's theology, including the inspiration of Scripture (3:15–17), election (1:9; Titus 1:1,2), salvation (Titus 3:5–7), the deity of Christ (Titus 2:13), Christ's mediatorial work (1 Timothy 2:5), and substitutionary atonement (2:6).
5. The different subject matter in the Pastoral Epistles required a different vocabulary from that in Paul's other epistles.

The idea that a "pious forger" wrote the Pastoral Epistles faces several further difficulties: (1) The early church did not approve of such practices. (2) Why forge three letters that include similar material and deviant doctrine? (3) If a counterfeit, why not invent an itinerary for Paul that would have harmonized with Acts? (4) Would a later, devoted follower of Paul have put the words of 1:13,15 into his master's mouth? (5) Why would he include warnings against deceivers (3:13; Titus 1:10) if he himself were one?

Pauline authorship of the Pastoral Epistles continues to be the most reasonable, defendable, and, certainly, biblical position.

Preach the Word

4 I charge *you* therefore before God and the Lord Jesus Christ, who will judge the living and the dead at*[a]* His appearing and His kingdom: [2]Preach the word! Be ready in season *and* out of season. Convince, rebuke, exhort, with all longsuffering and teaching. [3]For the time will come when they will not endure sound doctrine, but according to their own desires, *because* they have itching ears, they will heap up for themselves teachers; [4]and they will turn *their* ears away from the truth, and be turned aside to fables. [5]But you be watchful in all things, endure afflictions, do the work of an evangelist, fulfill your ministry.

> **4:3 their own desires...itching ears.** Professing to be Christians, nominal believers will follow their own desires and will listen to preachers who tell them that they can have God's blessings apart from His forgiveness. Their ears itch for easy teachings that will make them feel good about themselves. They want men to preach "according to their own desires," what they want to hear rather than what God reveals in His Word.

Paul's Valedictory

[6]For I am already being poured out as a drink offering, and the time of my departure is at hand. [7]I have fought the good fight, I have finished the race, I have kept the faith. [8]Finally, there is laid up for me the crown of righteousness, which the Lord, the righteous Judge, will give to me on that Day, and not to me only but also to all who have loved His appearing.

The Abandoned Apostle

[9]Be diligent to come to me quickly; [10]for Demas has forsaken me, having loved this present world, and has departed for Thessalonica—Crescens for Galatia, Titus for Dalmatia. [11]Only Luke is with me. Get Mark and bring him with you, for he is useful to me for ministry. [12]And Tychicus I have sent to Ephesus. [13]Bring the cloak that I left with Carpus at Troas when you come—and the books, especially the parchments.

> **4:8 the crown of righteousness.** The Greek word for "crown" means "surrounding" and describes the plaited wreaths placed on the heads of victorious military officials or athletes. In this context, the crown represents eternal righteousness. Believers receive Christ's righteousness as their own when they are saved (Rom. 4:6,11). The Holy Spirit sanctifies believers throughout their lifetimes, making them righteous, even though they still struggle with sin (Rom. 6:13,19). Believers receive Christ's full, perfect righteousness when they are glorified in heaven.

> **4:13 the books, especially the parchments.** The books to which Paul was referring were papyrus scrolls, possibly OT books. Parchments were expensive, vellum sheets made of treated animal hides. They may have been copies of Paul's letters or blank sheets for writing new letters. Because Paul did not have these shows that he may have been arrested in Troas and had not had an opportunity to retrieve them.

[14]Alexander the coppersmith did me much harm. May the Lord repay him according to his works. [15]You also must beware of him, for he has greatly resisted our words.

[16]At my first defense no one stood with me, but all forsook me. May it not be charged against them.

4:1 *[a]*NU-Text omits *therefore* and reads *and by* for *at.*

What is a valedictory, and why did Paul include one in his second letter to Timothy?

A valedictory is a speech or action done in parting. It is a farewell message. While hints of Paul's mood appear throughout the letter, 4:6–8 centers on Paul's self-evaluation. Nearing the end of his life, Paul was able to look back without regret or remorse. In these verses, he examined his life from three perspectives: (1) the present reality of the approaching end of his life, for which he was ready (verse 6); (2) the past, when he had been faithful (verse 7); and (3) the future, as he anticipated his heavenly reward (verse 8).

The Lord Is Faithful

¹⁷But the Lord stood with me and strengthened me, so that the message might be preached fully through me, and *that* all the Gentiles might hear. Also I was delivered out of the mouth of the lion. ¹⁸And the Lord will deliver me from every evil work and preserve *me* for His heavenly kingdom. To Him *be* glory forever and ever. Amen!

Come Before Winter

¹⁹Greet Prisca and Aquila, and the household of Onesiphorus. ²⁰Erastus stayed in Corinth, but Trophimus I have left in Miletus sick.

²¹Do your utmost to come before winter.

Eubulus greets you, as well as Pudens, Linus, Claudia, and all the brethren.

Farewell

²²The Lord Jesus Christ*ᵃ* be with your spirit. Grace be with you. Amen.

4:18 will deliver me from every evil work. Based on the present, when the Lord continued to strengthen Paul and stand with him, Paul had a firm hope for the Lord's future work. He knew that God would deliver him from all temptations and plots against him (2 Cor. 1:8–10). **preserve *me* for His heavenly kingdom.** Paul knew the completion of his own salvation was nearer than when he had first believed (see Rom. 13:11).

4:22 *ᵃ*NU-Text omits *Jesus Christ.*

TITUS

The apostle Paul often would extend his ministry by sending letters. He also would send people. Titus served as one of Paul's trusted messengers. He went where Paul could not go. When Paul was imprisoned, men like Titus and Timothy carried on his ministry. Even when he was free, Paul found that the work far exceeded his personal reach. Titus allowed Paul to expand his impact. Then Paul used this letter to instruct and encourage Titus on his mission for the gospel.

AUTHOR AND DATE

Titus was written by Paul, around A.D. 62 to 64.

The letter to Titus (along with 1 and 2 Timothy) is the third of the Pastoral Epistles. Authorship by the Apostle Paul (1:1) is essentially uncontested (See the FAQ *Did Paul Write the Pastoral Epistles?*). Paul wrote Titus sometime between A.D. 62–64 while he ministered in Macedonia between his first and second Roman imprisonments.

BACKGROUND AND SETTING

Although Titus is not mentioned by name in the book of Acts, it seems probable that he, a Gentile (Galatians 2:3), was led to faith in Christ by Paul (1:4) before or during the apostle's first missionary journey. Titus then accompanied Paul and Barnabas to the Council of Jerusalem (Acts 15; Galatians 2:1–5), where he witnessed the debate over the way in which new Gentile believers would be treated and welcomed into the church. As a Gentile, Titus would have been particularly sensitive to the impact of the Judaizers, false teachers in the church, who among other things insisted that all Christians, Gentiles as well as Jews, were bound by the Mosaic law.

Titus traveled with Paul during the third missionary journey, making his presence felt, especially in Corinth. Paul later mentioned him nine times in 2 Corinthians (2:13; 7:6,13,14; 8:6,16,23; 12:18). Paul considered Titus to be a "brother" (2 Corinthians 2:13), "my partner and fellow worker" (2 Corinthians 8:23), and "a true son" (Titus 1:4).

Later, Titus ministered for a while with Paul on the Island of Crete and was left behind to continue and strengthen the work (1:5) in much the same way as Paul left Timothy in Ephesus (1 Timothy 1:3). Paul indicated that he intended to send Artemas or Tychicus (3:12) to relieve Titus in the ministry on Crete. The apostle wanted Titus to join him in Nicopolis, in the Grecian province of Achaia

for the winter months (3:12). Paul's letter informed Titus of the upcoming plans and offered him direction for his ongoing ministry in Crete.

HISTORICAL AND THEOLOGICAL THEMES

As in Paul's two letters to Timothy, this letter gives personal encouragement and counsel to a young pastor. Titus, though well-trained and faithful, faced continuing opposition from ungodly people within the churches where he ministered. Titus was to pass on that encouragement and counsel to the leaders that Paul instructed him to appoint in the Cretan churches (1:5).

In contrast to most of Paul's letters, this one devotes little space to explaining or defending doctrine. Paul had full confidence in Titus's theological understanding and convictions, evidenced by the fact that he entrusted Titus with such a demanding ministry. Except for the warning about false teachers and Judaizers, the letter gives no theological correction, strongly suggesting that Paul also had confidence in the doctrinal grounding of most of the church members there, despite the fact that the majority were new believers. Nevertheless, this letter affirms the following key doctrines: (1) God's sovereign election of believers (1:1,2); (2) God's saving grace (2:11; 3:5); (3) Christ's deity and second coming (2:13); (4) Christ's substitutionary atonement (2:14); and (5) the Holy Spirit's regeneration and renewing of believers (3:5).

> THIS **LETTER GIVES PERSONAL ENCOURAGEMENT** AND **COUNSEL** TO A **YOUNG PASTOR.**

These general themes appear throughout Titus: (1) work(s) (1:16; 2:7,14; 3:1,5,8,14); (2) soundness in faith and doctrine (1:4,9,13; 2:1,2,7,8,10; 3:15); and (3) salvation (1:3,4; 2:10,13; 3:4,6).

OUTLINE

Greeting

1 Paul, a bondservant of God and an apostle of Jesus Christ, according to the faith of God's elect and the acknowledgment of the truth which accords with godliness, ²in hope of eternal life which God, who cannot lie, promised before time began, ³but has in due time manifested His word through preaching, which was committed to me according to the commandment of God our Savior;

> **1:2 hope.** This is divinely promised to all believers, providing endurance and patience (see John 6:37–40). **cannot lie.** Because God is truth and is the source of truth, it is impossible for Him to lie (John 14:6,17). **before time began.** Even before Creation, God had a plan of salvation to redeem sinful humanity. The promise was made to God the Son, Jesus Christ.

⁴To Titus, a true son in *our* common faith:

Grace, mercy, *and* peace from God the Father and the Lord Jesus Christ*ᵃ* our Savior.

Qualified Elders

⁵For this reason I left you in Crete, that you should set in order the things that are lacking, and appoint elders in every city as I commanded you— ⁶if a man is blameless, the husband of one wife, having faithful children not accused of dissipation or insubordination. ⁷For a bishop*ᵃ* must be blameless, as a steward of God, not self-willed, not quick-tempered, not given to wine, not violent, not greedy for money, ⁸but hospitable, a lover of what is good, sober-minded, just, holy, self-controlled, ⁹holding fast the faithful word as he has been taught, that he may be able, by sound

> **1:7 steward.** A steward manages someone else's properties for the well being of those under the master's care. Here it refers to one who manages spiritual truths, who lives on God's behalf, and who is wholly accountable to Him. Elders are accountable to God for the way they lead His church (Heb. 13:17). **greedy.** Some men became pastors in order to gain wealth (see 1 Pet. 5:3).

doctrine, both to exhort and convict those who contradict.

The Elders' Task

¹⁰For there are many insubordinate, both idle talkers and deceivers, especially those of the circumcision, ¹¹whose mouths must be stopped, who subvert whole households, teaching things which they ought not, for the sake of dishonest gain. ¹²One of them, a prophet of their own, said, "Cretans *are* always liars, evil beasts, lazy gluttons." ¹³This testimony is true. Therefore rebuke them sharply, that they may be sound in the faith, ¹⁴not giving heed to Jewish fables and commandments of men who turn from the truth. ¹⁵To the pure all things are pure, but to those who are defiled and unbelieving nothing is pure; but even their mind and conscience are defiled. ¹⁶They profess to know God, but in works they deny Him, being abominable, disobedient, and disqualified for every good work.

> **1:14 fables and commandments of men.** Most of the false teachers were Jewish. They taught the same kind of unscriptural laws and external traditions that both Isaiah and Jesus had attacked (Is. 29:13; Matt. 15:1–9).

Qualities of a Sound Church

2 But as for you, speak the things which are proper for sound doctrine: ²that the older men be sober, reverent, temperate, sound in faith, in love, in patience; ³the older women likewise, that they be reverent in behavior, not slanderers, not given to much wine, teachers of good things—⁴that they admonish the young women to love their husbands, to love their children, ⁵to be discreet, chaste, homemakers, good, obedient to their own husbands, that the word of God may not be blasphemed.

⁶Likewise, exhort the young men to be sober-minded, ⁷in all things showing yourself *to be* a pattern of good works; in doctrine *showing* integrity, reverence, incorruptibility,*ᵃ* ⁸sound speech that cannot be condemned, that one who is an opponent may be ashamed, having nothing evil to say of you.*ᵃ*

1:4 *ᵃ*NU-Text reads *and Christ Jesus.*   1:7 *ᵃ*Literally *overseer*   2:7 *ᵃ*NU-Text omits *incorruptibility.*
2:8 *ᵃ*NU-Text and M-Text read *us.*

⁹*Exhort* bondservants to be obedient to their own masters, to be well pleasing in all *things,* not answering back, ¹⁰not pilfering, but showing all good fidelity, that they may adorn the doctrine of God our Savior in all things.

> **2:10 not pilfering.** Referring to embezzlement. **all good fidelity.** Loyalty. **adorn the doctrine.** The supreme purpose of a virtuous life is to make attractive the teaching that God saves sinners.

Trained by Saving Grace

¹¹For the grace of God that brings salvation has appeared to all men, ¹²teaching us that, denying ungodliness and worldly lusts, we should live soberly, righteously, and godly in the present age, ¹³looking for the blessed hope and glorious appearing of our great God and Savior Jesus Christ, ¹⁴who gave Himself for us, that He might

> **2:14 redeem...purify.** To "redeem" is to release someone held captive, on the payment of a ransom. The price was Christ's blood paid to satisfy God's justice. **special people.** These people are special because of God's decree and because they are confirmed by the grace of salvation that they have embraced. **zealous.** Good works are the product, not the means, of salvation (see Eph. 2:10).

redeem us from every lawless deed and purify for Himself *His* own special people, zealous for good works.

¹⁵Speak these things, exhort, and rebuke with all authority. Let no one despise you.

Graces of the Heirs of Grace

3 Remind them to be subject to rulers and authorities, to obey, to be ready for every good work, ²to speak evil of no one, to be peaceable, gentle, showing all humility to all men. ³For we ourselves were also once foolish, disobedient, deceived, serving various lusts and pleasures, living in malice and envy, hateful and hating one another. ⁴But when the kindness and the love of God our Savior toward man appeared, ⁵not by works of righteousness which we have done, but according to His mercy He saved us, through the washing of regeneration and renewing of the Holy Spirit, ⁶whom He poured out on us abundantly through Jesus Christ our Savior, ⁷that having been justified by His grace we should become

> **3:3 ourselves.** Before salvation, every life is characterized by such sins. This realization should make believers humble when they deal with the unsaved. Without God's saving grace, all would be wicked.

In what ways does Paul's letter to his disciple Titus indicate that the message was intended for more than just Titus and the Christians on Crete?

Titus 2:11–13 presents the heart of Paul's letter to Titus. The apostle had already emphasized God's sovereign purpose in calling out elders as leaders (1:5) and in commanding His people to live righteously (2:1–10). That purpose is to provide the witness that brings God's plan and purpose of salvation to fulfillment. As always, the apostle had a larger audience in mind. The gospel has a universal scope. Here Paul condensed the saving plan of God into three realities: (1) salvation from the penalty of sin (verse 11); (2) salvation from the power of sin (verse 12); and (3) salvation from the presence of sin (verse 13).

As he described the "grace of God that brings salvation" (verse 11), Paul was not simply referring to the divine attribute of grace but to Jesus Christ Himself, grace incarnate, God's supremely gracious gift to fallen humankind (see John 1:14). The term "all men" (verse 11), in spite of efforts to make it a proof text for universalism, does not, in fact provide support for that error. "All men" is translated as "man" in 3:4, to refer to humanity in general, as a category, not to every individual. Jesus Christ made a sufficient offering to cover the sins of every one who believes (see John 3:16–18; 1 Timothy 2:5,6; 4:10; 1 John 2:2). The opening words of this letter to Titus make it clear that salvation becomes effective only through "the faith of God's elect" (1:1). Paul was well aware that the gospel had universal implications. Out of all humanity, only those who believe will be saved (see John 1:12; 3:16; 5:24,38,40; 6:40; 10:9; Romans 10:9–17).

heirs according to the hope of eternal life.

⁸This is a faithful saying, and these things I want you to affirm constantly, that those who have believed in God should be careful to maintain good works. These things are good and profitable to men.

Avoid Dissension

⁹But avoid foolish disputes, genealogies, contentions, and strivings about the law;

> **3:9 foolish disputes.** Paul warns believers not to be involved in senseless discussions with the many false teachers on the island of Crete, especially the Judaizers, who argued that a Christian must obey the Mosaic law. Their position contradicted the doctrine of justification by grace through faith alone. Proclaiming the truth, not arguing, is the biblical way to evangelize.

for they are unprofitable and useless. ¹⁰Reject a divisive man after the first and second admonition, ¹¹knowing that such a person is warped and sinning, being self-condemned.

Final Messages

¹²When I send Artemas to you, or Tychicus, be diligent to come to me at Nicopolis, for I have decided to spend the winter there. ¹³Send Zenas the lawyer and Apollos on their journey with haste, that they may lack nothing. ¹⁴And let our *people* also learn to maintain good works, to *meet* urgent needs, that they may not be unfruitful.

Farewell

¹⁵All who *are* with me greet you. Greet those who love us in the faith.

Grace *be* with you all. Amen.

How does 3:1–11 make a case for the value of evangelism?

Throughout this letter, Paul made it clear that Titus had a larger role than simply to maintain the existing church in Crete. Paul's purpose was evangelistic. He wanted Titus' work to result in more people coming to faith in Christ. In order for this to occur, Paul's directions focused on equipping the churches of Crete for effective evangelism. Even Paul's standards for leadership required godly leaders who would not only shepherd believers under their care (1:5–9) but also equip those Christians for evangelizing their pagan neighbors. Paul's consistent pattern is best described in 2 Timothy 2:2.

Paul's closing remarks admonish Titus to remind believers under his care of their attitudes toward: (1) the unsaved rulers (3:1) and people in general (3:2); (2) their previous state as unbelievers lost in sin (3:3); (3) of their gracious salvation through Jesus Christ (3:4–7); (4) of their righteous testimony to the unsaved world (3:8); and (5) of their responsibility to oppose false teachers and factious members within the church (3:9–11). All these matters prove essential to effective evangelism. A humble and compassionate witness by a well-ordered body of believers offers the most compelling message of the gospel.

PHILEMON

Philemon owned a slave who ran away. His slave, Onesimus, eventually met the Apostle Paul and became a Christian. Paul sent Onesimus back to Philemon with this letter of explanation. The letter provides an insightful look into the realities of slavery in the ancient world, and how Christ lifted the value of slaves from being property to being "a beloved brother" (verse 16).

AUTHOR AND DATE

Philemon was written by Paul while in prison, about A.D. 60 to 62.

This letter to Philemon, along with the epistles to the Ephesians, Philippians, and Colossians, completes the group called the Prison Epistles (For more on this, see the FAQ *Did Paul Write the Prison Epistles?*). Paul's authorship is based on internal evidence (verses 1,9,19) as well as the testimony of early church fathers (Jerome, Chrysostom, and Theodore of Mopsuestia) and the Muratorian canon (about A.D. 170). For biographical information on Paul, see the FAQ *Who was Paul?*

Because of this letter's close ties with the letter to the Colossians, Philemon is dated about A.D. 60–62. Both letters were written and sent at the same time, during Paul's first Roman imprisonment.

BACKGROUND AND SETTING

Philemon was a prominent member of the Colossian church. He had been saved under Paul's ministry, probably in Ephesus (verse 19). Wealthy enough to have a large house (verse 2), Philemon also owned at least one slave, a man named Onesimus.

Onesimus was not a believer when he stole money (verse 18) from Philemon and ran away. Like thousands of other runaway slaves, Onesimus fled to Rome, seeking to lose himself in the Imperial city's teeming population. Through circumstances not recorded in Scripture, Onesimus met Paul in Rome and became a Christian.

The apostle grew to love the runaway slave (verses 12,16) and considered keeping Onesimus with him in Rome (verses 11,13). But by stealing and running away from Philemon, Onesimus had broken Roman law and defrauded his master. Paul knew those issues had to be dealt with, and decided to send Onesimus back to Colosse. It was too hazardous for him to make the trip alone (because of the danger of slave-catchers), so Paul sent him back with Tychicus. The two of them carried Paul's letters to Philemon and the church at Colosse (Colossians 4:7–9). Paul's

beautiful epistle to Philemon urged the master to forgive the slave and welcome him back into service as a brother in Christ (verses 15–17).

HISTORICAL AND THEOLOGICAL THEMES

Philemon provides valuable historical insights into the early church's relationship to the institution of slavery. Widespread in the Roman Empire, slavery was an accepted part of daily life. According to some estimates, slaves constituted at least a third of the population. In Paul's day, slavery had virtually eclipsed free labor. Slaves could be doctors, musicians, teachers, artists, librarians, or accountants. Almost all jobs could be and were filled by slaves.

Slaves were not legally considered persons, but were the tools of their masters. They represented property. They could be bought, sold, inherited, exchanged, or seized to pay their master's debt. The master had almost unlimited power over a slave's life.

By the time of the New Testament, however, slavery was beginning to change. Realizing that contented slaves were more productive, masters tended to treat them more leniently. In A.D. 20 the Roman Senate granted slaves accused of crimes the right to a trial. But they did not grant them status as persons.

The New Testament nowhere directly attacks slavery. Instead, Christianity undermined the evils of slavery by changing the hearts of slaves and masters. By stressing the spiritual equality of master and slave (verse 16; Galatians 3:28; Ephesians 6:9; Colossians 4:1; 1 Timothy 6:1,2), the Bible did away with slavery's abuses.

> **CHRISTIANITY UNDERMINED THE EVILS OF SLAVERY BY CHANGING THE HEARTS OF SLAVES AND MASTERS.**

The rich theological theme that dominates this letter is forgiveness (Matthew 6:12–15; 18:21–35; Ephesians 4:32; Colossians 3:13). Paul's instruction to Philemon provides a biblical definition of forgiveness without ever using the word.

OUTLINE

Greeting

[1]Paul, a prisoner of Christ Jesus, and Timothy *our* brother,

To Philemon our beloved *friend* and fellow laborer, [2]to the beloved[a] Apphia, Archippus our fellow soldier, and to the church in your house:

> **1 prisoner of Christ Jesus.** At the time of writing, Paul was imprisoned in Rome for the sake of Christ (see Eph. 3:1). A reminder of Paul's severe hardships was bound to influence Philemon to obey Paul's upcoming request. **Timothy.** He was not the co-author of this letter, but he was probably with Paul when he wrote it. **Philemon.** He was a wealthy member of the Colossian church, which met in his house.

[3]Grace to you and peace from God our Father and the Lord Jesus Christ.

Philemon's Love and Faith

[4]I thank my God, making mention of you always in my prayers, [5]hearing of your love and faith which you have toward the Lord Jesus and toward all the saints, [6]that the sharing of your faith may become effective by the acknowledgment of every good thing which is in you[a] in Christ Jesus. [7]For we have[a] great joy[b] and consolation in your love, because the hearts of the saints have been refreshed by you, brother.

The Plea for Onesimus

[8]Therefore, though I might be very bold in Christ to command you what is fitting, [9]yet for love's sake I rather appeal *to you*— being such a one as Paul, the aged, and now also a prisoner of Jesus Christ— [10]I appeal to you for my son Onesimus, whom I have begotten *while* in my chains, [11]who once was unprofitable to you, but now is profitable to you and to me.

> **10 my son Onesimus.** To Paul, he was a son in the faith. **begotten...in my chains.** While in prison in Rome, Paul had led him to faith in Christ.

[12]I am sending him back.[a] You therefore receive him, that is, my own heart, [13]whom I wished to keep with me, that on your behalf he might minister to me in my chains for the gospel. [14]But without your consent I wanted to do nothing, that your good deed might not be by compulsion, as it were, but voluntary. [15]For perhaps he departed for a while for this *purpose*, that you might receive him forever, [16]no longer as a slave but more than a slave—a beloved brother, especially to me but how much more to you, both in the flesh and in the Lord.

Philemon's Obedience Encouraged

[17]If then you count me as a partner, receive him as *you would* me. [18]But if he has

---

2 [a]NU-Text reads *to our sister Apphia.*   6 [a]NU-Text and M-Text read *us.*   7 [a]NU-Text reads *had.* [b]M-Text reads *thanksgiving.*   12 [a]NU-Text reads *back to you in person, that is, my own heart.*

Who was Onesimus, and why did Paul write a letter to Philemon about him?

Onesimus was a slave owned by Philemon, a prominent member of the church at Colosse. Through happy and divine coincidence, Onesimus met up with Paul after running away from Philemon. At the time, Onesimus was a double lawbreaker, on the run as a thief and an escaped slave. Shortly after meeting Paul, Onesimus became a Christian.

Although Onesimus was providing useful service to Paul, the apostle decided to send him back to Philemon. With him, he sent both Tychicus as an escort and a personal cover letter as an explanation to Philemon. The wealthy Colossian owed Paul much as the messenger who brought him the gospel, and Paul didn't hesitate to mention that debt to awaken Philemon's awareness of the importance of welcoming and forgiving his vagabond slave.

Paul's letter to Philemon provides an insightful glimpse of the New Testament's handling of slavery. Rather than a direct attack on this terrible practice, Christianity disarmed the institution from within by radically changing the relationship between slaves and masters. See the Introduction to this letter for more on this subject.

wronged you or owes anything, put that on my account. ¹⁹I, Paul, am writing with my own hand. I will repay—not to mention to you that you owe me even your own self besides. ²⁰Yes, brother, let me have joy from you in the Lord; refresh my heart in the Lord.

²¹Having confidence in your obedience, I write to you, knowing that you will do even more than I say. ²²But, meanwhile, also prepare a guest room for me, for I trust that through your prayers I shall be granted to you.

Farewell

²³Epaphras, my fellow prisoner in Christ Jesus, greets you, ²⁴*as do* Mark, Aristarchus, Demas, Luke, my fellow laborers.

²⁵The grace of our Lord Jesus Christ *be* with your spirit. Amen.

---

21 even more than I say. Paul urged Philemon not only to forgive Onesimus, but also either to welcome him back enthusiastically (see Luke 15:22–24), to permit Onesimus to minister spiritually with him, or to forgive any others who might have wronged him. Whichever Paul intended, he was not subtly urging Philemon to grant Onesimus freedom.

How did Paul intervene with Philemon on Onesimus' behalf?

Paul re-introduced the slave Onesimus to the master Philemon as his own son in the faith (verse 10). Paul had led the slave to Christ while in prison at Rome. Since Onesimus was a common slave name meaning "useful," Paul offered a play on words as a tribute to Onesimus' new life in Christ. Paul's description (verse 11) basically means, "Useful—formerly was useless, but now really is useful." Onesimus had been radically transformed by God's grace.

Although Paul did not challenge Onesimus' existing legal standing with Philemon as a slave (verse 16), he challenged Philemon to a new relationship with Onesimus. Paul did not call for the slave's freedom (1 Corinthians 7:20–22) but that the master would receive his slave now as a fellow-believer in Christ (see Ephesians 6:9; Colossians 4:1; 1 Timothy 6:2). Paul's effort here did not aim at abolishing slavery but rather to make a relationship within this institution just and kind. The master and the slave were to enjoy spiritual oneness and fellowship as they worshiped and ministered together.

Paul also recognized that Philemon's forgiveness would involve a cost. The original theft as well as the loss due to Onesimus's absence were justifiable concerns that Paul was willing to address. If Philemon felt the need for restitution, Paul declared that he would pay Onesimus' debt. He also gently hinted, however, that Philemon might consider what he owed Paul as he was reckoning his losses.

HEBREWS

All 39 books of the Old Testament were originally given to the Jews. Only one New Testament book was aimed specifically at their needs. That single epistle was Hebrews. This certainly does not mean that God had forgotten the Jews. Other books, like Matthew, Romans, and Galatians have Jewish believers much in mind. All the New Testament books with the exception of Luke and Acts were given by the Holy Spirit's inspiration through Jews. But one book, Hebrews, brings the richness of the Old Testament background into the world of the New Testament church.

AUTHOR AND DATE

Hebrews was written by an unknown author, around A.D. 67 to 69.

The author of Hebrews is unknown. Paul, Barnabas, Silas, Apollos, Luke, Philip, Priscilla, Aquila, and Clement of Rome have been suggested by different scholars. The epistle's history, vocabulary, style, and various literary characteristics, however, do not clearly support any particular authorship claim. It is significant that the writer includes himself among those people who had received confirmation of Christ's message from others (2:3). That would seem to rule out someone like Paul who claimed that he had received such confirmation directly from God and not from any human being (Galatians 1:12). Regardless of his identity, the author preferred citing Old Testament references from the Greek Old Testament (LXX) rather than the Hebrew text.

Even the early church expressed various opinions on authorship. Current scholarship admits the puzzle still has no solution. Therefore, it seems best to accept the epistle's anonymity. The ultimate author, of course, was the Holy Spirit.

The use of the present tense in passages like 5:1–4 and 7:21,23,27,28 and others suggest that the Levitical priesthood and sacrificial system were still in operation when the epistle was composed. Because the temple in Jerusalem was destroyed in A.D. 70, this book must have been written prior to that date. References to Timothy's imprisonment (13:23) and growing persecution (10:32–39; 12:4; 13:3) suggest a date for the epistle around A.D. 67–69.

BACKGROUND AND SETTING

Extensive use of the Old Testament, an emphasis on the Levitical priesthood and on sacrifices, as well as the absence of any reference to the Gentiles, support the conclusion that a community of Hebrews was the original recipient of the epistle. Although these Jews were primarily converts to Christ, probably a number of

unbelievers were in their midst, attracted to various degrees by the message of salvation but who had not yet made a full commitment of faith in Christ.

The contents of the epistle make it clear that this community of Hebrews was facing the possibility of intensified persecution (10:32–39; 12:4). Under this pressure, the Hebrews were tempted to cast aside any identification with Christ. They may have considered demoting Christ from God's Son to a mere angel. Others had certainly done so. These kinds of doctrinal aberrations would explain the emphasis in Hebrews on the superiority of Christ over angels.

Phrases and clues have given rise to a number of suggestions about the location of the original recipients of the letter to the Hebrews. At one time or another, Palestine, Egypt, Italy, Asia Minor, and Greece have all had their defenders. Each offers an inconclusive possibility.

The generation of Hebrews who received this letter had practiced the Levitical sacrifices at the temple in Jerusalem. This was not unusual. Jews living on foreign soil made regular pilgrimages to the temple. These were practitioners of ancient traditions. The writer of Hebrews emphasized the superiority of Christianity over Judaism and the superiority of Christ's once-for-all sacrifice over the repeated and imperfect Levitical sacrifices observed in the temple.

HISTORICAL AND THEOLOGICAL THEMES

Because this book is grounded in the work of the Levitical priesthood, an understanding of Leviticus is essential to properly understanding Hebrews. In the Old Testament, God graciously established a system of sacrifices that symbolically addressed the recurring sins of the people by picturing inner repentance of sinners and God's divine forgiveness. But the need for sacrifices never ended because the people and priests continued to sin. All people needed a perfect priest and a perfect sacrifice that would once and for all actually remove sin. God's provision for the perfect priest and sacrifice in Christ is the central message of Hebrews.

> **GOD'S PROVISION** FOR THE **PERFECT PRIEST** AND **SACRIFICE** IN **CHRIST IS** THE **CENTRAL MESSAGE** OF **HEBREWS.**

Hebrews offers a study in contrasts between the Old Covenant given under Moses and the New Covenant offered by the perfect High-Priest, God's only Son and the Messiah, Jesus Christ. Included in the "greater and better" provisions are: a better hope, testament, promise, sacrifice, substance, country, and resurrection. Those who belong to the New Covenant dwell in a completely new and heavenly atmosphere; they worship a heavenly Savior, have a heavenly calling, receive a heavenly gift, are citizens of a heavenly country, look forward to a heavenly Jerusalem, and have their very names written in heaven.

One of the key theological themes in Hebrews is that all believers now have direct access to God under the New Covenant and, therefore, may approach the throne of God boldly (4:16; 10:22). One's hope is in the very presence of God, into which he or she follows the Savior (6:19,20; 10:19,20). The book of Hebrews may

be summarized in these words: Believers in Jesus Christ, as God's perfect sacrifice for sin, have the perfect High-Priest through whose ministry everything is new and better than under the covenant of law.

OUTLINE

God's Supreme Revelation

1 God, who at various times and in various ways spoke in time past to the fathers by the prophets, ²has in these last days spoken to us by *His* Son, whom He has appointed heir of all things, through whom also He made the worlds; ³who being the brightness of *His* glory and the express image of His person, and upholding all things by the word of His power, when He had by Himself*ᵃ* purged our*ᵇ* sins, sat down at the right hand of the Majesty on high, ⁴having become so much better than the angels, as He has by inheritance obtained a more excellent name than they.

1:2 last days. Jews understood the "last days" as the time when the Messiah would come (see Num. 24:14). When Christ came, the messianic prophecies were fulfilled. Christians understood that the "last days" are the time since Christ came (see 1 Cor. 10:11). **heir.** Everything that exists will eventually come under the Messiah's control (see Ps. 2:8,9). **worlds.** This refers to time, space, energy, and matter—everything that is a part of the universe (see John 1:3).

The Son Exalted Above Angels

⁵For to which of the angels did He ever say:

> "You are My Son,
> Today I have begotten You"?*ᵃ*

And again:

> "I will be to Him a Father,
> And He shall be to Me a Son"?*ᵇ*

⁶But when He again brings the firstborn into the world, He says:

> "Let all the angels of God worship Him." *ᵃ*

⁷And of the angels He says:

1:7 of the angels. The angels are subservient to the Son of God (Ps. 104:4). This is the only one of the 7 OT quotations in chap. 1 that has no connection to the Davidic Covenant. The quote simply defines the primary nature and purpose of angels.

1:3 *ᵃ*NU-Text omits *by Himself.* *ᵇ*NU-Text omits *our.* 1:5 *ᵃ*Psalm 2:7 *ᵇ*2 Samuel 7:14
1:6 *ᵃ*Deuteronomy 32:43 (Septuagint, Dead Sea Scrolls); Psalm 97:7

To which Hebrews was this book written?

Although the author and the original recipients of this letter are unknown, the title, dating as early as the second century A.D., has been "To the Hebrews." The title certainly fits the content. The epistle exudes a Jewish mindset. References to Hebrew history and religion abound. And since no particular Gentile or pagan practice gains any attention in the book, the church has kept the traditional title.

A proper interpretation of Hebrews, however, requires the recognition that it addresses three distinct groups of Jews:

1. Hebrew Christians formed the primary addressees. These had already suffered rejection and persecution by fellow Jews (10:23–34) although none had yet been martyred (12:4). They were an immature group of believers who were tempted to hold on to the symbolic and spiritually powerless rituals and traditions of Judaism. This letter was written to give them encouragement and confidence in Christ, their Messiah and High-Priest.

2. Jewish unbelievers who were intellectually convinced of the gospel. They gave mental assent to the truth of the gospel but had not placed their faith in Jesus Christ as their Savior and Lord. They were intellectually persuaded but spiritually uncommitted. These unbelievers are addressed in such passages as 2:1–3; 6:4–6; 10:26–29; 12:15–17.

3. Jewish unbelievers who were attracted by the gospel and the person of Christ but who had reached no final conviction about Him. Chapter 9 of Hebrews speaks specifically to this group (particularly verses 11,14,15,27,28).

Failure to acknowledge these groups will lead to interpretations that are inconsistent with the rest of Scripture.

"Who makes His angels spirits
And His ministers a flame of fire."[a]

[8]But to the Son He says:

"Your throne, O God, is forever and
ever;
A scepter of righteousness is the
scepter of Your kingdom.
[9] You have loved righteousness and
hated lawlessness;
Therefore God, Your God, has
anointed You
With the oil of gladness more than
Your companions."[a]

[10]And:

"You, LORD, in the beginning laid the
foundation of the earth,
And the heavens are the work of Your
hands.
[11] They will perish, but You remain;
And they will all grow old like a
garment;
[12] Like a cloak You will fold them up,
And they will be changed.
But You are the same,
And Your years will not fail." [a]

[13]But to which of the angels has He ever
said:

"Sit at My right hand,
Till I make Your enemies Your
footstool" ?[a]

[14]Are they not all ministering spirits sent
forth to minister for those who will inherit
salvation?

Do Not Neglect Salvation

2 Therefore we must give the more earnest heed to the things we have heard,
lest we drift away. [2]For if the word spoken
through angels proved steadfast, and every
transgression and disobedience received a
just reward, [3]how shall we escape if we neglect so great a salvation, which at the first
began to be spoken by the Lord, and was
confirmed to us by those who heard Him,

2:1 earnest heed...drift away. Both phrases have
nautical connotations. The first refers to tying a ship
up at the dock, and the second describes a ship that
had been allowed to drift past the harbor. The warning is to secure oneself to the truth of the gospel, being careful not to pass by the only "harbor" of
salvation.

[4]God also bearing witness both with signs
and wonders, with various miracles, and
gifts of the Holy Spirit, according to His
own will?

The Son Made Lower than Angels

[5]For He has not put the world to come, of
which we speak, in subjection to angels.
[6]But one testified in a certain place, saying:

"What is man that You are mindful of
him,
Or the son of man that You take care
of him?
[7] You have made him a little lower than
the angels;
You have crowned him with glory and
honor,[a]
And set him over the works of Your
hands.
[8] You have put all things in subjection
under his feet." [a]

For in that He put all in subjection under
him, He left nothing that is not put under
him. But now we do not yet see all things
put under him. [9]But we see Jesus, who was
made a little lower than the angels, for the
suffering of death crowned with glory and
honor, that He, by the grace of God, might
taste death for everyone.

2:8 subjection. Despite the superiority of angels
over humans, God originally placed the administration of the earth into the hands of humanity (Gen.
1:26–28). Because of the Fall, people are incapable of
fulfilling that divinely ordained position (Gen. 3).

Bringing Many Sons to Glory

[10]For it was fitting for Him, for whom are
all things and by whom are all things, in
bringing many sons to glory, to make the
captain of their salvation perfect through

1:7 [a]Psalm 104:4   1:9 [a]Psalm 45:6,7   1:12 [a]Psalm 102:25–27   1:13 [a]Psalm 110:1   2:7 [a]NU-Text
and M-Text omit the rest of verse 7.   2:8 [a]Psalm 8:4–6

sufferings. [11]For both He who sanctifies and those who are being sanctified *are* all of one, for which reason He is not ashamed to call them brethren, [12]saying:

> "I will declare Your name to My
>   brethren;
> In the midst of the assembly I will
>   sing praise to You." [a]

[13]And again:

> "I will put My trust in Him." [a]

And again:

> "Here am I and the children whom
>   God has given Me." [b]

[14]Inasmuch then as the children have partaken of flesh and blood, He Himself likewise shared in the same, that through death He might destroy him who had the power of death, that is, the devil, [15]and release those who through fear of death were all their lifetime subject to bondage. [16]For indeed He does not give aid to angels, but He does give aid to the seed of Abraham. [17]Therefore, in all things He had to be made like *His* brethren, that He might be a merci-

2:16 give aid. In this context, the phrase means "to take on the nature of," as Christ identified with humanity and took upon Himself a human nature. **seed of Abraham.** Christ is that promised seed. Since the readers are Hebrews, they would identify themselves with this description. The Messiah had been born in the line of Abraham, in fulfillment of the Old Testament prophecies (Matt. 1:1).

ful and faithful High Priest in things *pertaining* to God, to make propitiation for the sins of the people. [18]For in that He Himself has suffered, being tempted, He is able to aid those who are tempted.

The Son Was Faithful

3 Therefore, holy brethren, partakers of the heavenly calling, consider the Apostle and High Priest of our confession, Christ Jesus, [2]who was faithful to Him who appointed Him, as Moses also *was faithful* in all His house. [3]For this One has been counted worthy of more glory than Moses, inasmuch as He who built the house has

3:3,4 He who built. Moses was only a part of God's household of faith, whereas Jesus was the Creator of that household (see 2 Sam. 7:13). Therefore, He is greater than Moses and equal to God.

2:12 [a]Psalm 22:22 2:13 [a]2 Samuel 22:3; Isaiah 8:17 [b]Isaiah 8:18

What are the central warnings for believers in the Book of Hebrews?

Beyond its value as a doctrinal treatise, this book is intensely practical in its application to everyday living. The writer even refers to this letter as a "word of exhortation" (13:22). Exhortations designed to stir the readers into action are found throughout the text. Those exhortations take the form of six distinct warnings:

1. Warning against drifting from "the things we have heard" (2:1–4)
2. Warning against disbelieving the "voice" of God (3:7–14)
3. Warning against digressing from "the elementary principles of Christ" (5:11–6:20)
4. Warning against despising "the knowledge of truth" (10:26–39)
5. Warning against devaluing "the grace of God" (12:15–17)
6. Warning against departing from Him "who speaks" (12:25–29)

For example, when the writer warns of the danger of drifting (2:1), he uses some vivid nautical terms. The phrase "earnest heed" refers to mooring a ship by securing it to a dock. The second phrase "drifting away" was often used of a ship that had been allowed to drift past the harbor. The warning is to secure oneself to the truth of the gospel in such as way as to not pass by the only harbor of salvation. The alternate tendency towards apathy points to those who make a shipwreck of their lives (see 6:19 and 1 Timothy 1:18).

more honor than the house. [4]For every house is built by someone, but He who built all things *is* God. [5]And Moses indeed *was* faithful in all His house as a servant, for a testimony of those things which would be spoken *afterward*, [6]but Christ as a Son over His own house, whose house we are if we hold fast the confidence and the rejoicing of the hope firm to the end.[a]

Be Faithful

[7]Therefore, as the Holy Spirit says:

> "Today, if you will hear His voice,
> [8] Do not harden your hearts as in the rebellion,
> In the day of trial in the wilderness,
> [9] Where your fathers tested Me, tried Me,
> And saw My works forty years.
> [10] Therefore I was angry with that generation,
> And said, 'They always go astray in their heart,
> And they have not known My ways.'
> [11] So I swore in My wrath,
> 'They shall not enter My rest.' "[a]

> **3:11 My rest.** Because they rebelled against God, an entire generation of Israelites was prohibited from entering into physical rest in the Promised Land (see Deut. 28:65). The application is to spiritual rest in the Lord. At salvation, every believer enters true rest, spiritual rest, never again laboring to please God through personal effort.

[12]Beware, brethren, lest there be in any of you an evil heart of unbelief in departing from the living God; [13]but exhort one another daily, while it is called *"Today,"* lest any of you be hardened through the deceitfulness of sin. [14]For we have become partakers of Christ if we hold the beginning of our confidence steadfast to the end, [15]while it is said:

> "Today, if you will hear His voice,
> Do not harden your hearts as in the rebellion."[a]

Failure of the Wilderness Wanderers

[16]For who, having heard, rebelled? Indeed, *was it* not all who came out of Egypt, *led* by Moses? [17]Now with whom was He angry forty years? *Was it* not with those who sinned, whose corpses fell in the wilderness? [18]And to whom did He swear that they would not enter His rest, but to those who did not obey? [19]So we see that they could not enter in because of unbelief.

The Promise of Rest

4 Therefore, since a promise remains of entering His rest, let us fear lest any of

> **4:1 promise.** This is the first use of this word in Hebrews. The content of this promise is defined as "entering His rest." **His rest.** For believers, God's rest includes peace, confidence of salvation, reliance on His strength, and assurance of a future heavenly home (see Matt. 11:29).

3:6 [a]NU-Text omits *firm to the end.*   3:11 [a]Psalm 95:7–11   3:15 [a]Psalm 95:7,8

How does the writer of Hebrews use the Old Testament as a basis for teaching?

This book provides many examples of clear exposition of Old Testament Scriptures. The writer proves to be a skilled expositor of the Word of God. His handling of God's Word remains an instructive model for preachers and teachers.

Eight passages in Hebrews offer expositions (explanatory teaching) on Old Testament passages:

1.	1:1–2:4	Exposition of Deuteronomy 32, 2 Samuel 7, and several passages from Psalms
2.	2:5–18	Exposition of Psalm 8:4–6
3.	3:1–4:13	Exposition of Psalm 95:7–11
4.	4:14–7:28	Exposition of Psalm 110:4
5.	8:1–10:18	Exposition of Jeremiah 31:31–34
6.	10:32–12:3	Exposition of Habakkuk 2:3,4
7.	12:4–13	Exposition of Proverbs 3:11,12
8.	12:18–29	Exposition of Exodus 19,20

you seem to have come short of it. ²For indeed the gospel was preached to us as well as to them; but the word which they heard did not profit them,ᵃ not being mixed with faith in those who heard it. ³For we who have believed do enter that rest, as He has said:

> "So I swore in My wrath,
> 'They shall not enter My rest,' "ᵃ

although the works were finished from the foundation of the world. ⁴For He has spoken in a certain place of the seventh *day* in this way: "And God rested on the seventh day from all His works";ᵃ ⁵and again in this place: "They shall not enter My rest." ᵃ

⁶Since therefore it remains that some *must* enter it, and those to whom it was first preached did not enter because of disobedience, ⁷again He designates a certain day, saying in David, "Today," after such a long time, as it has been said:

> "Today, if you will hear His voice,
> Do not harden your hearts."ᵃ

⁸For if Joshua had given them rest, then He would not afterward have spoken of another day. ⁹There remains therefore a rest for the people of God. ¹⁰For he who has entered His rest has himself also ceased from his works as God *did* from His.

The Word Discovers Our Condition

¹¹Let us therefore be diligent to enter that rest, lest anyone fall according to the same example of disobedience. ¹²For the word of God *is* living and powerful, and sharper than any two-edged sword, piercing even to the division of soul and spirit, and of joints and marrow, and is a discerner of the thoughts and intents of the heart. ¹³And there is no creature hidden from His sight, but all things *are* naked and open to the eyes of Him to whom we *must give* account.

4:12 two-edged sword. The Word of God is not only comforting and nourishing to those who believe but is also a tool of judgment and execution for those who do not believe. Some of the Hebrews were merely going through the motions of following Christ and were not committed to God. His Word would expose their shallow beliefs and false intentions (see 1 Sam. 16:7). **division of soul and spirit.** These words do not imply that soul and spirit are two separate entities but instead express fullness (see Luke 10:27), describing the whole, eternal, inner person.

Our Compassionate High Priest

¹⁴Seeing then that we have a great High Priest who has passed through the heavens, Jesus the Son of God, let us hold fast *our* confession. ¹⁵For we do not have a High Priest who cannot sympathize with our weaknesses, but was in all *points* tempted as *we are, yet* without sin. ¹⁶Let us therefore come boldly to the throne of grace, that we may obtain mercy and find grace to help in time of need.

Qualifications for High Priesthood

5 For every high priest taken from among men is appointed for men in things per-

---

4:2 ᵃNU-Text and M-Text read *profit them, since they were not united by faith with those who heeded it.*   4:3 ᵃPsalm 95:11   4:4 ᵃGenesis 2:2   4:5 ᵃPsalm 95:11   4:7 ᵃPsalm 95:7,8

What does 4:14–16 teach about prayer?

This passage offers two very personal benefits which come to those who have trusted in Jesus the Son of God, as the great High-Priest: (1) Someone who can "sympathize with our weaknesses" because He "was in all points tempted as we are, yet without sin" (verse 15); and (2) confident access to the "throne of grace" (verse 16) because Someone knows our need.

Christian prayer accepts God's invitation to enjoy the access provided through Christ.

The Christian's unique access to God was a radical idea in the ancient world. Most ancient rulers were unapproachable by anyone but their highest advisers. In contrast, the Holy Spirit calls for all to come confidently before God's throne to receive mercy and grace through Jesus Christ (see 7:25; 10:22; Matthew 27:51). It was at the throne of God that Christ made atonement for sins, and it is there that grace is dispensed to believers for all the issues of life (see 2 Corinthians 4:15; 9:8; 12:9; Ephesians 1:7; 2:7).

taining to God, that he may offer both gifts and sacrifices for sins. ²He can have compassion on those who are ignorant and going astray, since he himself is also subject to weakness. ³Because of this he is required as for the people, so also for himself, to offer *sacrifices* for sins. ⁴And no man takes this honor to himself, but he who is called by God, just as Aaron *was.*

> **5:1–4** No angel with supernatural power could serve as the High-Priest. Only someone with human weaknesses could be the High-Priest. In the Levitical system, the position of High-Priest was by appointment only. The use of the present tense in these verses indicates that the Levitical system was still being practiced at the time of this epistle.

A Priest Forever

⁵So also Christ did not glorify Himself to become High Priest, *but it* was He who said to Him:

"You are My Son,
Today I have begotten You." *ᵃ*

⁶As *He* also *says* in another *place:*

"You *are* a priest forever
According to the order of
Melchizedek"; *ᵃ*

⁷who, in the days of His flesh, when He had offered up prayers and supplications, with vehement cries and tears to Him who was able to save Him from death, and was heard because of His godly fear, ⁸though He was a Son, *yet* He learned obedience by the things which He suffered. ⁹And having been perfected, He became the author of eternal salvation to all who obey Him, ¹⁰called by God as High Priest "*according to*

> **5:8 learned obedience.** Christ did not need to suffer in order to conquer disobedience. As the incarnate Lord, He humbled Himself to learn obedience for the same reason that He bore temptations: to confirm His humanity and to experience human suffering to the fullest. His obedience was necessary so that He could fulfill all righteousness (Matt. 5:13), proving that He was the perfect sacrifice in the place of sinners (1 Pet. 3:18).

the order of Melchizedek," ¹¹of whom we have much to say, and hard to explain, since you have become dull of hearing.

Spiritual Immaturity

¹²For though by this time you ought to be teachers, you need *someone* to teach you again the first principles of the oracles of God; and you have come to need milk and not solid food. ¹³For everyone who partakes *only* of milk *is* unskilled in the word of righteousness, for he is a babe. ¹⁴But solid food belongs to those who are of full age, *that is,* those who by reason of use have their senses exercised to discern both good and evil.

> **5:12,13 milk.** By rejecting saving faith, the Hebrews regressed in their understanding concerning the Messiah. They had been exposed to the Gospel long enough to be teaching it to others, but they were too much like babies, unable to comprehend, let alone teach, the truth of God.

The Peril of Not Progressing

6 Therefore, leaving the discussion of the elementary *principles* of Christ, let us go on to perfection, not laying again the foundation of repentance from dead works and of faith toward God, ²of the doctrine of baptisms, of laying on of hands, of resurrection of the dead, and of eternal judgment. ³And this we will*ᵃ* do if God permits.

⁴For *it is* impossible for those who were once enlightened, and have tasted the heavenly gift, and have become partakers of the Holy Spirit, ⁵and have tasted the good word of God and the powers of the age to come, ⁶if they fall away,*ᵃ* to renew them again to repentance, since they crucify again for themselves the Son of God, and put *Him* to an open shame.

> **6:4 tasted the heavenly gift.** In the NT, tasting refers to consciously experiencing something momentarily or continually. All people experience the goodness of God, but that does not mean they are all saved (see Matt. 5:45). Many Jews experienced Jesus' blessings when He healed them, delivered them from demons, and miraculously fed them. But having an experience with Christ is not equivalent to salvation.

5:5 *ᵃ*Psalm 2:7   5:6 *ᵃ*Psalm 110:4   6:3 *ᵃ*M-Text reads *let us do.*   6:6 *ᵃ*Or *and have fallen away*

[7]For the earth which drinks in the rain that often comes upon it, and bears herbs useful for those by whom it is cultivated, receives blessing from God; [8]but if it bears thorns and briers, *it is* rejected and near to being cursed, whose end *is* to be burned.

A Better Estimate

[9]But, beloved, we are confident of better things concerning you, yes, things that accompany salvation, though we speak in this manner. [10]For God *is* not unjust to forget your work and labor of[a] love which you have shown toward His name, *in that* you have ministered to the saints, and do minister. [11]And we desire that each one of you show the same diligence to the full assurance of hope until the end, [12]that you do not become sluggish, but imitate those who through faith and patience inherit the promises.

> **6:11 you.** The author is speaking to unbelievers and distinguishes between this group and those in vv. 4–6, who are in danger of being impossible to restore. **diligence.** Eagerness or haste. The author pleads for unbelieving Jews to come to Christ immediately. Salvation should not be postponed.

God's Infallible Purpose in Christ

[13]For when God made a promise to Abraham, because He could swear by no one greater, He swore by Himself, [14]saying, *"Surely blessing I will bless you, and multiplying I will multiply you."* [a] [15]And so, after he had patiently endured, he obtained the promise. [16]For men indeed swear by the greater, and an oath for confirmation *is* for them an end of all dispute. [17]Thus God, determining to show more abundantly to the heirs of promise the immutability of His counsel, confirmed *it* by an oath, [18]that by two immutable things, in which it *is* impossible for God to lie, we might[a] have strong consolation, who have fled for refuge to lay hold of the hope set before *us.*

> **6:18 two immutable things.** These are God's promise and His oath. The Greek term for "immutable" refers to a legal will, which could only be changed by the maker of the will. **fled for refuge.** The Greek word is used in the Old Testament for the cities of refuge, which were places of safety that God provided for anyone who accidentally killed another person, to protect him from a rash avenger (Num. 35:9–34). **hope.** Hope for the fulfillment of salvation keeps the believer secure during troubled times.

[19]This *hope* we have as an anchor of the soul, both sure and steadfast, and which enters the *Presence* behind the veil, [20]where the forerunner has entered for us, *even* Jesus, having become High Priest forever according to the order of Melchizedek.

6:10 [a]NU-Text omits *labor of.*   6:14 [a]Genesis 22:17   6:18 [a]M-Text omits *might.*

To whom is 6:4–6, and particularly the phrase "once enlightened" directed?

The phrase, "once enlightened" is often taken to refer to Christians. The accompanying warning, then, is taken to indicate the danger of losing their salvation if they "fall away" and "crucify again for themselves the Son of God." But the immediate context has no mention of their being saved. They are not described with any terms that apply only to believers (such as holy, born again, righteous, or saints).

The interpretive problem arises from inaccurately identifying the spiritual condition of the ones being addressed. In this case, they were unbelievers who had been exposed to God's redemptive truth and, perhaps, had made a profession of faith but had not exercised genuine saving faith. Another passage (10:26) addresses the same issue. The subject here is people who come in contact with the gospel but are spiritually unchanged by it. Apostate Christians are Christians in name only, not genuine believers who are often incorrectly thought to lose their salvation because of their sins.

There is no possibility of these verses referring to someone losing salvation. Many Scripture passages make unmistakably clear that salvation is eternal (see, for example, John 10:27–29; Romans 8:35,38,39; Philippians 1:6; 1 Peter 1:4,5). Those who want to make this passage mean that believers can lose salvation will have to admit that it would then also make the point that one could never get it back again.

The King of Righteousness

7 For this Melchizedek, king of Salem, priest of the Most High God, who met Abraham returning from the slaughter of the kings and blessed him, ²to whom also Abraham gave a tenth part of all, first being translated "king of righteousness," and then also king of Salem, meaning "king of peace," ³without father, without mother, without genealogy, having neither beginning of days nor end of life, but made like the Son of God, remains a priest continually.

⁴Now consider how great this man *was*, to whom even the patriarch Abraham gave a tenth of the spoils. ⁵And indeed those who are of the sons of Levi, who receive the priesthood, have a commandment to receive tithes from the people according to the law, that is, from their brethren, though they have come from the loins of Abraham; ⁶but he whose genealogy is not derived from them received tithes from Abraham and blessed him who had the promises. ⁷Now beyond all contradiction the lesser is blessed by the better. ⁸Here mortal men receive tithes, but there he *receives them*, of whom it is witnessed that he lives. ⁹Even Levi, who receives tithes, paid tithes through Abraham, so to speak, ¹⁰for he was still in the loins of his father when Melchizedek met him.

Need for a New Priesthood

¹¹Therefore, if perfection were through the Levitical priesthood (for under it the people received the law), what further need *was there* that another priest should rise according to the order of Melchizedek, and not be called according to the order of Aaron? ¹²For the priesthood being changed, of necessity there is also a change of the law. ¹³For He of whom these things are spoken belongs to another tribe, from which no man has officiated at the altar.

> **7:11 perfection.** Throughout Hebrews, the term refers to complete reconciliation with and access to God through salvation. The Levitical system and its priesthood could not save people from their sins.

¹⁴For *it is* evident that our Lord arose from Judah, of which tribe Moses spoke nothing concerning priesthood.*ᵃ* ¹⁵And it is yet far more evident if, in the likeness of Melchizedek, there arises another priest ¹⁶who has come, not according to the law of a fleshly commandment, but according to the power of an endless life. ¹⁷For He testifies:*ᵃ*

7:14 *ᵃ*NU-Text reads *priests*.   7:17 *ᵃ*NU-Text reads *it is testified*.

Who was Melchizedek and why was he so important?

Melchizedek shows up abruptly and briefly in the Old Testament, but his special role in Abraham's life makes him a significant figure. He is mentioned again in Psalm 110:4, the passage under consideration in 4:14–7:28. As the king of Salem and priest of the Most High God in the time of Abraham, Melchizedek offered a historical precedent for the role of king-priest (Genesis 14:18–20), filled perfectly by Jesus Christ.

By using the two Old Testament references to Melchizedek, the writer (7:1–28) explains the superiority of Christ's priesthood by reviewing Melchizedek's unique role as a type of Christ and his superiority to the Levitical High Priesthood. The Levitical priesthood was hereditary, but Melchizedek's was not. Through Abraham's honor, Melchizedek's rightful role was established. The major ways in which the Melchizedekan priesthood was superior to the Levitical priesthood are these:

1. the receiving of tithes (7:2–10), as when Abraham the ancestor of the Levites gave Melchizedek a tithe of the spoils
2. the giving of the blessing (7:1,6,7), as when Abraham accepted Melchizedek's blessing
3. the continual replacement of the Levitical priesthood (7:11–19), which passed down from father to son
4. the perpetuity of the Melchizedekan priesthood (7:3,8,16,17,20–28), since the record about his priesthood does not record his death.

"*You are a priest forever*
According to the order of
Melchizedek."[b]

[18]For on the one hand there is an annulling of the former commandment because of its weakness and unprofitableness, [19]for the law made nothing perfect; on the other hand, *there is the* bringing in of a better hope, through which we draw near to God.

> **7:18 annulling.** The law was weak in that it could not save or bring about inward change in a person (see Rom. 8:3).

Greatness of the New Priest

[20]And inasmuch as *He was* not *made* priest without an oath [21](for they have become priests without an oath, but He with an oath by Him who said to Him:

> "*The LORD has sworn*
> *And will not relent,*
> '*You are a priest forever*[a]
> *According to the order of*
> *Melchizedek*'*"*),[b]

[22]by so much more Jesus has become a surety of a better covenant.

[23]Also there were many priests, because they were prevented by death from continuing. [24]But He, because He continues forever, has an unchangeable priesthood. [25]Therefore He is also able to save to the uttermost those who come to God through Him, since He always lives to make intercession for them.

> **7:25 intercession.** The act of mediating, or intervening, on behalf of another. It referred to bringing a petition to a king on behalf of someone else. Since rabbis assigned intercessory powers to angels, perhaps the people were treating angels as intercessors. Only Christ is the Intercessor (see 1 Tim. 2:5).

[26]For such a High Priest was fitting for us, *who is* holy, harmless, undefiled, separate from sinners, and has become higher than the heavens; [27]who does not need daily, as those high priests, to offer up sacrifices, first for His own sins and then for the people's, for this He did once for all when He offered up Himself. [28]For the law appoints as high priests men who have weakness, but the word of the oath, which came after the law, *appoints* the Son who has been perfected forever.

The New Priestly Service

8 Now *this is* the main point of the things we are saying: We have such a High Priest, who is seated at the right hand of the throne of the Majesty in the heavens, [2]a Minister of the sanctuary and of the true tabernacle which the Lord erected, and not man.

[3]For every high priest is appointed to offer both gifts and sacrifices. Therefore *it is* necessary that this One also have something to offer. [4]For if He were on earth, He would not be a priest, since there are priests who offer the gifts according to the law; [5]who serve the copy and shadow of the heavenly things, as Moses was divinely instructed when he was about to make the tabernacle. For He said, "*See that you make all things according to the pattern shown you on the mountain.*"[a] [6]But now He has obtained a more excellent ministry, inasmuch as He is also Mediator of a better covenant, which was established on better promises.

> **8:6 Mediator.** The word describes a go-between or an arbitrator, in this case between people and God (see Gal. 3:19,20). **better covenant...better promises.** This covenant is identified as the "new covenant" in verses 8,13; 9:15.

A New Covenant

[7]For if that first *covenant* had been faultless, then no place would have been sought for a second. [8]Because finding fault with them, He says: "*Behold, the days are coming, says the LORD, when I will make a new covenant with the house of Israel and with the house of Judah—* [9]*not according to the covenant that I made with their fathers in the day when I took them by the hand to lead them out of the land of Egypt; because they did not continue in My covenant, and I disregarded them, says the LORD.* [10]*For this is the covenant that I will make with the house of Israel after those days, says the*

7:17 [b]Psalm 110:4   7:21 [a]NU-Text ends the quotation here. [b]Psalm 110:4   8:5 [a]Exodus 25:40

LORD: *I will put My laws in their mind and write them on their hearts; and I will be their God, and they shall be My people.* [11]*None of them shall teach his neighbor, and none his brother, saying, 'Know the Lord,' for all shall know Me, from the least of them to the greatest of them.* [12]*For I will be merciful to their unrighteousness, and their sins and their lawless deeds[a] I will remember no more."* [b]

[13]In that He says, *"A new covenant,"* He has made the first obsolete. Now what is becoming obsolete and growing old is ready to vanish away.

The Earthly Sanctuary

9 Then indeed, even the first *covenant* had ordinances of divine service and the earthly sanctuary. [2]For a tabernacle was prepared: the first *part,* in which *was* the lampstand, the table, and the showbread, which is called the sanctuary; [3]and behind the second veil, the part of the tabernacle which is called the Holiest of All, [4]which had the golden censer and the ark of the covenant overlaid on all sides with gold, in which *were* the golden pot that had the manna, Aaron's rod that budded, and the tablets of the covenant; [5]and above it were the cherubim of glory overshadowing the mercy seat. Of these things we cannot now speak in detail.

Limitations of the Earthly Service

[6]Now when these things had been thus prepared, the priests always went into the first part of the tabernacle, performing *the services.* [7]But into the second part the high priest *went* alone once a year, not without blood, which he offered for himself and *for* the people's sins *committed* in ignorance; [8]the Holy Spirit indicating this, that the

> **9:7 not without blood.** The first of many references to the blood of sacrifice, a central theme in 9:1–10:18. The deaths of OT sacrifices are identified with Christ's death. However, the shedding of blood by itself is an insufficient sacrifice. Christ had not only to shed His blood but also to die. He gave His body as the sacrificial offering; thus His blood had saving value.

way into the Holiest of All was not yet made manifest while the first tabernacle was still standing. [9]It *was* symbolic for the present time in which both gifts and sacrifices are offered which cannot make him who performed the service perfect in regard to the conscience— [10]concerned only with foods and drinks, various washings, and fleshly ordinances imposed until the time of reformation.

The Heavenly Sanctuary

[11]But Christ came *as* High Priest of the good things to come,[a] with the greater and more perfect tabernacle not made with hands, that is, not of this creation. [12]Not with the blood of goats and calves, but with His own blood He entered the Most Holy Place once for all, having obtained eternal redemption. [13]For if the blood of bulls and goats and the ashes of a heifer, sprinkling the unclean, sanctifies for the purifying of the flesh, [14]how much more shall the blood of Christ, who through the eternal Spirit offered Himself without spot to God, cleanse your conscience from dead works to serve the living God? [15]And for this reason He is the Mediator of the new covenant, by means of death, for the redemption of the transgressions under the first covenant, that those who are called may receive the promise of the eternal inheritance.

> **9:12 goats and calves.** Only one of each was sacrificed on the Day of Atonement (see Lev. 16:5–10). The plural here represents the numbers sacrificed year after year. **with His own blood.** Nothing indicates that Christ carried His actual physical blood with Him into the heavenly sanctuary. The Sacrificer was also the Sacrifice. **eternal redemption.** This word for redemption, found only here and in Luke 1:68, 2:38, was originally used for the release of slaves by payment of a ransom.

The Mediator's Death Necessary

[16]For where there *is* a testament, there must also of necessity be the death of the testator. [17]For a testament *is* in force after men are dead, since it has no power at all while the testator lives. [18]Therefore not even the first *covenant* was dedicated without blood. [19]For when Moses had spoken

---

every precept to all the people according to the law, he took the blood of calves and goats, with water, scarlet wool, and hyssop, and sprinkled both the book itself and all the people, ²⁰saying, *"This is the blood of the covenant which God has commanded you."* ᵃ ²¹Then likewise he sprinkled with blood both the tabernacle and all the vessels of the ministry. ²²And according to the law almost all things are purified with blood, and without shedding of blood there is no remission.

9:19 water, scarlet wool, and hyssop. These items were used at the Passover in Egypt (Ex. 12:22) for the sprinkling of blood, in the ritual cleansing for lepers (Lev. 14:4), and in the red heifer ceremony (Num. 19:6). **the book...the people.** The consecration of Aaron and his sons to the priesthood is the only other occasion in the OT when any persons were sprinkled with blood (Ex. 29:21). Sprinkling the book with blood is not recorded in the Exodus account.

Greatness of Christ's Sacrifice

²³Therefore *it was* necessary that the copies of the things in the heavens should be purified with these, but the heavenly things themselves with better sacrifices than these. ²⁴For Christ has not entered the holy places made with hands, *which are* copies of the true, but into heaven itself, now to appear in the presence of God for us; ²⁵not that He should offer Himself often, as the high priest enters the Most Holy Place every year with blood of another—²⁶He then would have had to suffer often since the foundation of the world; but now, once at the end of the ages, He has appeared to put away sin by the sacrifice of Himself. ²⁷And as it is appointed for men to die once, but after this the judgment, ²⁸so Christ was offered once to bear the sins of many. To those who eagerly wait for Him He will appear a second time, apart from sin, for salvation.

9:28 second time. On the Day of Atonement, the people eagerly waited for the High-Priest to come back out of the Holy of Holies. When he appeared, they knew the sacrifice on their behalf had been accepted by God. When Christ appears at His second coming, it will confirm that the Father has been fully satisfied with the Son's sacrifice on behalf of believers. At this point, salvation will be completed (see 1 Pet. 1:3–5).

9:20 ᵃExodus 24:8

Why does Hebrews have so much about blood, including a statement like "without the shedding of blood there is no remission" (9:22)?

Beginning with 9:7, the writer examined the significance of the blood of sacrifice. This term is especially central to 9:1–10:18 where the passage identifies the deaths of Old Testament sacrifices with the death of Christ (9:12–14). Note however, that this shedding of blood in and of itself was an insufficient sacrifice. Christ had not only to shed His blood, but he also had to die—10:10 indicates that He gave His body as a sacrificial offering. Without His death, His blood had no saving value.

The expression, then, "blood of Christ" (9:14) refers not simply to the fluid but to the whole atoning sacrificial work of Christ in His death. Blood is used as a substitute word for death (see, for example, Matthew 23:30,35; 27:6,8,24,25; John 6:54–56; Acts 18:6; 20:26). By reviewing the significance of the blood sacrifices in the Old Testament, the writer was pointing to a pattern of lessons that prepared the world to understand the necessity of Christ's death. The emphatic phrase, "without the shedding of blood there is no remission" (9:22) simply repeats the lesson that sin creates a debt that must be paid by someone. "It is the blood that makes atonement for the soul" (Leviticus 17:11). The phraseology is reminiscent of Christ's words, "For this is my blood of the new covenant, which is shed for many for the remission of sins" (Matthew 26:28). Remission means forgiveness in these verses—forgiveness for the sinner and payment of the debt. Christ's death (blood) provides the remission.

Animal Sacrifices Insufficient

10 For the law, having a shadow of the good things to come, *and* not the very image of the things, can never with these same sacrifices, which they offer continually year by year, make those who approach perfect. ²For then would they not have ceased to be offered? For the worshipers, once purified, would have had no more consciousness of sins. ³But in those *sacrifices there is* a reminder of sins every year. ⁴For *it is* not possible that the blood of bulls and goats could take away sins.

Christ's Death Fulfills God's Will

⁵Therefore, when He came into the world, He said:

"Sacrifice and offering You did not desire,
But a body You have prepared for Me.
⁶ In burnt offerings and sacrifices for sin You had no pleasure.

10:5,6 You did not desire. God was not pleased with sacrifices given out of an insincere heart (see Ps. 51:17). To sacrifice only as a ritual, without obedience, was a mockery and worse than no sacrifice at all (see Is. 1:11–18).

⁷ Then I said, 'Behold, I have come—
In the volume of the book it is written of Me—
To do Your will, O God.' "ᵃ

⁸Previously saying, "Sacrifice and offering, burnt offerings, and offerings for sin You did not desire, nor had pleasure in them" (which are offered according to the law), ⁹then He said, "Behold, I have come to do Your will, O God."ᵃ He takes away the first that He may establish the second. ¹⁰By that will we have been sanctified through the offering of the body of Jesus Christ once *for all.*

Christ's Death Perfects the Sanctified

¹¹And every priest stands ministering daily and offering repeatedly the same sacrifices, which can never take away sins. ¹²But this Man, after He had offered one sacrifice for sins forever, sat down at the right hand of God, ¹³from that time waiting till His enemies are made His footstool. ¹⁴For by one offering He has perfected forever those who are being sanctified.

10:13 footstool. This refers to Ps. 110:1. This prediction will be fulfilled when Christ returns and all creation acknowledges His lordship by bowing at His feet (Phil. 2:10).

¹⁵But the Holy Spirit also witnesses to us; for after He had said before,

¹⁶"This is the covenant that I will make with them after those days, says the LORD: I will put My laws into their hearts, and in their minds I will write them,"ᵃ ¹⁷then He adds, "Their sins and their lawless deeds I

10:7 ᵃPsalm 40:6–8   10:9 ᵃNU-Text and M-Text omit *O God.*   10:16 ᵃJeremiah 31:33

What significance can be found in the statement, "And as it is appointed for men to die once, but after this the judgment" (9:27)?

First, this passage offers a direct answer to those tempted to flirt with any form of re-incarnation. Second, it states the general rule for all humankind, with very rare and only partial exceptions. Lazarus and the multitudes who were resuscitated at Christ's resurrection had to die again (see Matthew 27:51–53; John 14:43,44). Those, like Lazarus, who were raised from the dead by a miraculous act of our Lord were not resurrected to a glorified body and unending life. They only experienced resuscitation. Another exception will be those who don't die even once, but who will be "caught up . . . to meet the Lord in the air" (1 Thessalonians 4:17). Enoch (Genesis 5:24) and Elijah (2 Kings 2:11) are also part of this last group.

The general rule for all human beings includes another shared event—judgment. The "judgment" noted here refers to the judgment of all people, believers (2 Corinthians 5:10) and unbelievers (Revelation 20:11–15).

will remember no more." *a* 18Now where there is remission of these, *there is* no longer an offering for sin.

Hold Fast Your Confession

19Therefore, brethren, having boldness to enter the Holiest by the blood of Jesus, 20by a new and living way which He consecrated for us, through the veil, that is, His flesh, 21and *having* a High Priest over the house of God, 22let us draw near with a true heart in full assurance of faith, having our hearts sprinkled from an evil conscience and our bodies washed with pure water. 23Let us hold fast the confession of *our* hope without wavering, for He who promised *is* faithful. 24And let us consider one another in order to stir up love and good works, 25not forsaking the assembling of ourselves together, as *is* the manner of some, but exhorting *one another*, and so much the more as you see the Day approaching.

> **10:20 veil...flesh.** The temple veil, which symbolically separated men from God's presence, tore when Jesus' flesh was torn at His crucifixion (Matt. 27:51). When the High-Priest entered the Holy of Holies on the Day of Atonement, the people waited outside for him to return. When Christ entered the heavenly temple, He did not return. Instead, He opened the curtain and exposed the Holy of Holies so that we could follow Him.

The Just Live by Faith

26For if we sin willfully after we have received the knowledge of the truth, there no longer remains a sacrifice for sins, 27but a certain fearful expectation of judgment, and fiery indignation which will devour the adversaries. 28Anyone who has rejected Moses' law dies without mercy on the testimony of two or three witnesses. 29Of how much worse punishment, do you suppose,

> **10:27 fearful expectation.** The judgment is certain to happen, so it causes fear. **judgment and fiery indignation.** The description is similar to that in Is. 26:11 and Zeph. 1:18 (see 2 Thess. 1:7–9). Such judgment means eternity in the lake of fire (see Matt. 13:38–42,49,50). **adversaries.** This refers to opposition against God and toward God's plan of salvation.

will he be thought worthy who has trampled the Son of God underfoot, counted the blood of the covenant by which he was sanctified a common thing, and insulted the Spirit of grace? 30For we know Him who said, *"Vengeance is Mine, I will repay,"* *a* says the Lord.*b* And again, *"The LORD will judge His people."* *c* 31It is a fearful thing to fall into the hands of the living God.

32But recall the former days in which, after you were illuminated, you endured a great struggle with sufferings: 33partly while you were made a spectacle both by reproaches and tribulations, and partly while you became companions of those who were so treated; 34for you had compassion on me*a* in my chains, and joyfully accepted the plundering of your goods, knowing that you have a better and an enduring possession for yourselves in heaven.*b* 35Therefore do not cast away your confidence, which has great reward. 36For you have need of endurance, so that after you have done the will of God, you may receive the promise:

> **10:33 a spectacle.** This verse alludes to the theater and the actors being placed on a stage where they can be observed by everyone. In the context, the idea is exposure to disgrace and ridicule (see 1 Cor. 4:9). **companions.** These unconverted Hebrews associated with believers and were thus exposed to persecution, and their property was seized because of their relationships with believers. They had not turned away because they were interested in the prospects of heaven.

37 "For yet a little while,
   And He*a* who is coming will come and
      will not tarry.
38 Now the*a* just shall live by faith;
   But if anyone draws back,
   My soul has no pleasure in him." *b*

39But we are not of those who draw back to perdition, but of those who believe to the saving of the soul.

By Faith We Understand

11 Now faith is the substance of things hoped for, the evidence of

---

10:39 draw back to perdition. Believing readers ("we") will not be counted among "those" who fall away to destruction. Apostates will draw back from Christ, but some are near to believing who can be pulled "out of the fire" (see Jude 23). "Perdition" is often used in the New Testament to describe the everlasting judgment of unbelievers (see Matt. 7:13).

things not seen. ²For by it the elders obtained a *good* testimony.

³By faith we understand that the worlds were framed by the word of God, so that the things which are seen were not made of things which are visible.

Faith at the Dawn of History

⁴By faith Abel offered to God a more excellent sacrifice than Cain, through which he obtained witness that he was righteous, God testifying of his gifts; and through it he being dead still speaks.

⁵By faith Enoch was taken away so that he did not see death, *"and was not found, because God had taken him"*;ᵃ for before he was taken he had this testimony, that he pleased God. ⁶But without faith *it is* impossible to please *Him,* for he who comes to God must believe that He is, and *that* He is a rewarder of those who diligently seek Him.

⁷By faith Noah, being divinely warned of things not yet seen, moved with godly fear, prepared an ark for the saving of his house-

11:6 impossible to please. Enoch pleased God because he had faith. Without faith it is impossible for anyone to please God. **He is.** Genuine faith believes that the God of Scripture is the only God who exists. Not believing He exists is equivalent to calling Him a liar (see 1 John 5:10). **rewarder.** A person must not only believe that God exists but also believe that He will reward faith in Him with forgiveness and righteousness (see Gen. 15:1).

hold, by which he condemned the world and became heir of the righteousness which is according to faith.

Faithful Abraham

⁸By faith Abraham obeyed when he was called to go out to the place which he would receive as an inheritance. And he went out, not knowing where he was going. ⁹By faith he dwelt in the land of promise as *in* a foreign country, dwelling in tents with Isaac and Jacob, the heirs with him of the same promise; ¹⁰for he waited for the city which has foundations, whose builder and maker *is* God.

¹¹By faith Sarah herself also received strength to conceive seed, and she bore a childᵃ when she was past the age, because she judged Him faithful who had promised. ¹²Therefore from one man, and him as good as dead, were born *as many* as the stars of the sky in multitude—innumerable as the sand which is by the seashore.

11:5 ᵃGenesis 5:24   11:11 ᵃNU-Text omits *she bore a child.*

Why are so many Old Testament people listed in chapter 11?

The eleventh chapter of Hebrews offers a moving account of faithful Old Testament saints who remain models of faith. The chapter has received such titles as "The Saint's Hall of Fame," "The Honor Roll of Old Testament Saints," and "Heroes of the Faith." Their lives attest to the value of living by faith. They compose the "cloud of witnesses" (12:1) who give powerful testimony to the Hebrews that they should come to faith in Christ.

This passage begins with an emphatic statement about the nature of faith. Faith involves the most solid possible conviction—the God-given present assurance of a future reality. True faith is not based on empirical evidence but on divine assurance and is a gift of God (Ephesians 2:8).

The names, accomplishments and sufferings described in this chapter illustrate the range of faithfulness in the lives of saints. Some experienced great success in this world; whereas others suffered great affliction. The point is that they all courageously and uncompromisingly followed God, regardless of the earthly outcome. They placed their trust in Him and in His promises (see 6:12; 2 Timothy 3:12).

The Heavenly Hope

¹³These all died in faith, not having received the promises, but having seen them afar off were assured of them,^a embraced *them* and confessed that they were strangers and pilgrims on the earth. ¹⁴For those who say such things declare plainly that they seek a homeland. ¹⁵And truly if they had called to mind that *country* from which they had come out, they would have had opportunity to return. ¹⁶But now they desire a better, that is, a heavenly *country*. Therefore God is not ashamed to be called their God, for He has prepared a city for them.

11:13 These all. This refers only to Abraham, Isaac, and Jacob. The promises began with Abraham (see Acts 7:17) and were passed on to Isaac (Gen. 26:2–5,24) and Jacob (Gen. 28:10–15). They did not know when they would inherit the promise. They lived in the land but did not possess it.

The Faith of the Patriarchs

¹⁷By faith Abraham, when he was tested, offered up Isaac, and he who had received the promises offered up his only begotten son, ¹⁸of whom it was said, *"In Isaac your seed shall be called,"* ^a ¹⁹concluding that God *was* able to raise *him* up, even from the dead, from which he also received him in a figurative sense.

²⁰By faith Isaac blessed Jacob and Esau concerning things to come.

²¹By faith Jacob, when he was dying, blessed each of the sons of Joseph, and worshiped, *leaning* on the top of his staff.

²²By faith Joseph, when he was dying, made mention of the departure of the children of Israel, and gave instructions concerning his bones.

The Faith of Moses

²³By faith Moses, when he was born, was hidden three months by his parents, be-

11:23 beautiful child. This means divinely favored (Acts 7:20). The faith described here was exercised by Moses' parents, although it is unclear as to how much they understood about God's plan for their child.

cause they saw *he was* a beautiful child; and they were not afraid of the king's command.

²⁴By faith Moses, when he became of age, refused to be called the son of Pharaoh's daughter, ²⁵choosing rather to suffer affliction with the people of God than to enjoy the passing pleasures of sin, ²⁶esteeming the reproach of Christ greater riches than the treasures in^a Egypt; for he looked to the reward.

²⁷By faith he forsook Egypt, not fearing the wrath of the king; for he endured as seeing Him who is invisible. ²⁸By faith he kept the Passover and the sprinkling of blood, lest he who destroyed the firstborn should touch them.

²⁹By faith they passed through the Red Sea as by dry *land, whereas* the Egyptians, attempting *to do* so, were drowned.

By Faith They Overcame

³⁰By faith the walls of Jericho fell down after they were encircled for seven days. ³¹By faith the harlot Rahab did not perish with those who did not believe, when she had received the spies with peace.

³²And what more shall I say? For the time would fail me to tell of Gideon and Barak and Samson and Jephthah, also *of* David and Samuel and the prophets: ³³who through faith subdued kingdoms, worked righteousness, obtained promises, stopped the mouths of lions, ³⁴quenched the violence of fire, escaped the edge of the sword, out of weakness were made strong, became valiant in battle, turned to flight the armies of the aliens. ³⁵Women received their dead raised to life again.

Others were tortured, not accepting de-

11:35 Women received their dead. This refers to the widow of Zarephath (1 Kin. 17:22) and the woman of Shunem (2 Kin. 4:34). **tortured.** They were beaten to death while strapped to some sort of rack. **better resurrection.** The deliverance from certain death or near death would be like returning from the dead, but it would not be the promised resurrection. Those who had died and were raised experienced resuscitation, not the true and glorious final resurrection (Dan. 12:2).

11:13 ^aNU-Text and M-Text omit *were assured of them.*   11:18 ^aGenesis 21:12   11:26 ^aNU-Text and M-Text read *of.*

liverance, that they might obtain a better resurrection. ³⁶Still others had trial of mockings and scourgings, yes, and of chains and imprisonment. ³⁷They were stoned, they were sawn in two, were tempted,ᵃ were slain with the sword. They wandered about in sheepskins and goatskins, being destitute, afflicted, tormented—³⁸of whom the world was not worthy. They wandered in deserts and mountains, *in* dens and caves of the earth.

³⁹And all these, having obtained a good testimony through faith, did not receive the promise, ⁴⁰God having provided something better for us, that they should not be made perfect apart from us.

The Race of Faith

12 Therefore we also, since we are surrounded by so great a cloud of witnesses, let us lay aside every weight, and the sin which so easily ensnares *us*, and let us run with endurance the race that is set before us, ²looking unto Jesus, the author and finisher of *our* faith, who for the joy that was set before Him endured the cross, despising the shame, and has sat down at the right hand of the throne of God.

> **12:1 witnesses.** The runner is motivated by the godly examples that the deceased saints set during their lives. The great crowd consists of those whose past lives of faith encourage others to live with faith. **every weight.** This refers to the legalism of the Levitical system that was weighing down the Hebrews.

The Discipline of God

³For consider Him who endured such hostility from sinners against Himself, lest you become weary and discouraged in your souls. ⁴You have not yet resisted to bloodshed, striving against sin. ⁵And you have forgotten the exhortation which speaks to you as to sons:

"My son, do not despise the chastening
　of the LORD,
Nor be discouraged when you are
　rebuked by Him;
⁶　For whom the LORD loves He
　chastens,

And scourges every son whom He
　receives."ᵃ

⁷Ifᵃ you endure chastening, God deals with you as with sons; for what son is there whom a father does not chasten? ⁸But if you are without chastening, of which all have become partakers, then you are illegitimate and not sons. ⁹Furthermore, we have had human fathers who corrected *us*, and we paid *them* respect. Shall we not much more readily be in subjection to the Father of spirits and live? ¹⁰For they indeed for a few days chastened *us* as seemed *best* to them, but He for *our* profit, that *we* may be partakers of His holiness. ¹¹Now no chastening seems to be joyful for the present, but painful; nevertheless, afterward it yields the peaceable fruit of righteousness to those who have been trained by it.

> **12:8 illegitimate.** The word is found only here in the NT, but it is used elsewhere in Greek literature of those born to slaves or concubines. This could imply reference to Hagar and Ishmael (Gen. 16), Abraham's concubine and his illegitimate son.

Renew Your Spiritual Vitality

¹²Therefore strengthen the hands which hang down, and the feeble knees, ¹³and make straight paths for your feet, so that what is lame may not be *dislocated*, but rather be healed.

¹⁴Pursue peace with all *people*, and holiness, without which no one will see the Lord: ¹⁵looking carefully lest anyone fall short of the grace of God; lest any root of bitterness springing up cause trouble, and by this many become defiled; ¹⁶lest there *be* any fornicator or profane person like Esau, who for one morsel of food sold his birthright. ¹⁷For you know that afterward, when he wanted to inherit the blessing, he was rejected, for he found no place for repentance, though he sought it diligently with tears.

The Glorious Company

¹⁸For you have not come to the mountain thatᵃ may be touched and that burned with fire, and to blackness and darknessᵇ and

---

11:37 ᵃNU-Text omits *were tempted.*　12:6 ᵃProverbs 3:11,12　12:7 ᵃNU-Text and M-Text read *It is for discipline that you endure; God . . . .*　12:18 ᵃNU-Text reads *to that which.*　ᵇNU-Text reads *gloom.*

tempest, [19]and the sound of a trumpet and the voice of words, so that those who heard *it* begged that the word should not be spoken to them anymore. [20](For they could not endure what was commanded: *"And if so much as a beast touches the mountain, it shall be stoned[a] or shot with an arrow." [b]* [21]And so terrifying was the sight *that* Moses said, *"I am exceedingly afraid and trembling."[a])*

[22]But you have come to Mount Zion and to the city of the living God, the heavenly Jerusalem, to an innumerable company of angels, [23]to the general assembly and church of the firstborn *who are* registered in heaven, to God the Judge of all, to the spirits of just men made perfect, [24]to Jesus the Mediator of the new covenant, and to the blood of sprinkling that speaks better things than *that of* Abel.

12:23 general assembly. This describes the attitude of the innumerable angels in heaven in a festal gathering around the throne of God. **church of the firstborn.** The firstborn is Jesus Christ. The "church" is comprised of believers who are fellow heirs with Christ (Rom. 8:17,29). **just men made perfect.** These are the OT saints, separate from the "church of the firstborn," who are the NT believers.

Hear the Heavenly Voice

[25]See that you do not refuse Him who speaks. For if they did not escape who refused Him who spoke on earth, much more *shall we not escape* if we turn away from

Him who *speaks* from heaven, [26]whose voice then shook the earth; but now He has promised, saying, *"Yet once more I shake[a] not only the earth, but also heaven." [b]* [27]Now this, *"Yet once more,"* indicates the removal of those things that are being shaken, as of things that are made, that the things which cannot be shaken may remain.

[28]Therefore, since we are receiving a kingdom which cannot be shaken, let us have grace, by which we may[a] serve God acceptably with reverence and godly fear. [29]For our God *is* a consuming fire.

12:29 consuming fire. God's law given at Sinai (see Deut. 4:24) prescribed many severe punishments, but the punishment is far worse for those who reject His offer of salvation through His Son, Jesus Christ (see Luke 3:16,17).

Concluding Moral Directions

13 Let brotherly love continue. [2]Do not forget to entertain strangers, for by so *doing* some have unwittingly entertained angels. [3]Remember the prisoners as if chained with them—those who are mistreated—since you yourselves are in the body also.

[4]Marriage *is* honorable among all, and the bed undefiled; but fornicators and adulterers God will judge.

[5]*Let your* conduct *be* without covetousness; *be* content with such things as you have. For He Himself has said, *"I will never*

12:20 [a]NU-Text and M-Text omit the rest of this verse. [b]Exodus 19:12,13 12:21 [a]Deuteronomy 9:19 12:26 [a]NU-Text reads *will shake.* [b]Haggai 2:6 12:28 [a]M-Text omits *may.*

Did the writer of Hebrews actually think Christians might entertain angels (13:2)?

This verse primarily highlights the importance of extending love to strangers (Romans 13:3; 1 Timothy 3:2). Hospitality in the ancient world would often include putting up a guest overnight or longer. This is most difficult when experiencing a time of persecution. The Hebrews would not know whether a guest would prove to be a spy, a lost sinner needing Christ, or a fellow believer being pursued.

The possibility of an angelic visit was not mentioned as the ultimate motivation for hospitality but to reveal that one never knows how far-reaching an act of kindness might be (Matthew 25:40,45). The writer was appealing to historical precedents that his Jewish readers would have known well. Angels certainly had visited and had been entertained by Abraham and Sarah (Genesis 18:1-3), Lot (Genesis 19:1,2), Gideon (Judges 6:11-24), and Manoah (Judges 13:6-20).

leave you nor forsake you." *a* ⁶So we may boldly say:

"The LORD is my helper;
I will not fear.
What can man do to me?" *a*

Concluding Religious Directions

⁷Remember those who rule over you, who have spoken the word of God to you, whose faith follow, considering the outcome of *their* conduct. ⁸Jesus Christ *is* the same yesterday, today, and forever. ⁹Do not be carried about*a* with various and strange doctrines. For *it is* good that the heart be established by grace, not with foods which have not profited those who have been occupied with them.

> **13:9 various and strange doctrines.** Any teaching contrary to God's Word. The NT contains many warnings against false teaching and false teachers (see Acts 20:29,30; 2 Cor. 10:4,5). **established by grace.** Those who experience God's grace in Christ have stable hearts and minds. **foods.** For Christians, the Mosaic law and its regulations (Lev. 11) have been nullified (Acts 10:9–16).

¹⁰We have an altar from which those who serve the tabernacle have no right to eat. ¹¹For the bodies of those animals, whose blood is brought into the sanctuary by the high priest for sin, are burned outside the camp. ¹²Therefore Jesus also, that He might sanctify the people with His own blood, suffered outside the gate. ¹³Therefore let us go forth to Him, outside the camp, bearing His reproach. ¹⁴For here we have no continuing city, but we seek the one to come. ¹⁵Therefore by Him let us continually offer the sacrifice of praise to God, that is, the fruit of *our* lips, giving thanks to His name. ¹⁶But do not forget to do good and to share, for with such sacrifices God is well pleased.

¹⁷Obey those who rule over you, and be submissive, for they watch out for your souls, as those who must give account. Let them do so with joy and not with grief, for that would be unprofitable for you.

> **13:17 rule over you.** The pastors/elders of the church exercise the very authority of Christ when they preach, teach, and apply Scripture. They serve the church on behalf of Christ and must give Him an account of their faithfulness. These also include secular rulers. Those who do not know God are still ordained and used by Him (see Rom. 13:1,4). **joy.** The church must help its leaders do their work with satisfaction and delight.

Prayer Requested

¹⁸Pray for us; for we are confident that we have a good conscience, in all things desiring to live honorably. ¹⁹But I especially urge *you* to do this, that I may be restored to you the sooner.

13:5 *a*Deuteronomy 31:6,8; Joshua 1:5   13:6 *a*Psalm 118:6   13:9 *a*NU-Text and M-Text read *away*.

Does the letter to the Hebrews contain any practical teaching?

The doctrine of salvation is the ultimate practical teaching. The significance of every other application flows from the reality of a right relationship with God through Christ. Once that is established, many other responses follow. Chapter 13 focuses on some of the essential practical ethics of Christian living. These ethics help portray the true gospel to the world, encourage others to believe in Christ, and bring glory to God.

The chapter begins with the primary ethical application: love (see John 13:35). Although the immediate reference would be to Christians, the writer probably had emotions similar to those of the Apostle Paul when it come to considering his fellow Hebrews (see Romans 9:3,4). After this, the book specifically mentions strangers and imprisoned fellow Christians.

Marriage and general relationships among Christians also receive special attention. Verses 7–17 highlight the role of leaders and the submission required from believers. The chapter then concludes with a request for prayer, a benediction, and final greetings. In short, a careful reading of Hebrews, particularly the last chapter, will yield a wealth of godly direction for living.

Benediction, Final Exhortation, Farewell

20Now may the God of peace who brought up our Lord Jesus from the dead, that great Shepherd of the sheep, through the blood of the everlasting covenant, 21make you complete in every good work to do His will, working in youᵃ what is well pleasing in His sight, through Jesus Christ, to whom *be* glory forever and ever. Amen.

22And I appeal to you, brethren, bear with the word of exhortation, for I have written to you in few words. 23Know that *our* brother Timothy has been set free, with whom I shall see you if he comes shortly.

24Greet all those who rule over you, and all the saints. Those from Italy greet you.

25Grace *be* with you all. Amen.

13:24 Those from Italy. The group to whom the author wrote may have been in Italy, or he might have meant that the Italian Christians who were with him sent their greetings. The use of similar phrases elsewhere is ambiguous since some clearly refer to people still in their location (Acts 10:23) and those who were away from their homes (Acts 21:27).

13:21 ᵃNU-Text and M-Text read *us.*

Jesus had four half-brothers—James, Joses, Judas, and Simon. The Bible makes it clear that after Jesus' miraculous birth, Mary and Joseph had other children (Mark 6:3). Eventually, Jude and James came to believe in their brother Jesus as Lord. But neither James (Mark 6:3), nor Jude (Matthew 13:55) were early followers. James had at first rejected Jesus as Messiah (John 7:5), but he later believed (1 Corinthians 15:7). James became one of the leaders in the Jerusalem church, and authored this very practical handbook of Christian living that bears his name.

AUTHOR AND DATE

James was written by James the half-brother of Jesus, between A.D. 44 and 49.

James was a common name in New Testament times. At least four men with that name participated in Jesus' ministry and the early years of the church. Although some have suggested James the son of Zebedee and brother of John as a likely candidate as the author of this book, he was martyred too early to have written it (Acts 12:2). Only James, the oldest half-brother of Jesus, fits the profile of the author of this book that bears his name.

After James believed in Christ (1 Corinthians 15:7), he became the key leader in the Jerusalem church (Acts 12:17; 15:13; 21:18; Galatians 2:12). He was called one of the "pillars" of the church (Galatians 2:9).

Textual evidence from a comparison between James' vocabulary in the letter that he authored after the Jerusalem council (Acts 15) and this letter further corroborates his authorship.

The brief samples offer at least six common vocabulary words: "greetings" (Acts 15:23; James 1:1); "beloved" (Acts 15:25; James 1:16,19; 2:5); "your souls" (Acts 15:24,26; James 1:21; 5:20); "visit" (Acts 15:14; James 1:27); "keep" (Acts 15:24; James 2:10); "turn" (Acts 15:19; James 5:19,20). James wrote with the authority of one who had personally seen the resurrected Christ (1 Corinthians 15:7), who was a recognized associate of the apostles (Galatians 1:19), and who was the leader of the Jerusalem church.

James most likely wrote this epistle following the dispersion recorded in Acts 12 (about A.D. 44). Since there is no mention of the Council of Jerusalem (Acts 15) which occurred about A.D. 49, the date of composition was probably earlier. Therefore, James can be reliably dated between A.D. 44–49, making it the earliest written book in the New Testament.

The recipients of this letter were Jewish believers who were scattered (1:1), possibly as a result of Stephen's martyrdom (Acts 7; A.D. 31–34), but more likely due to the persecution under Herod Agrippa I (Acts 12; about A.D. 44). The author refers to his audience as "brethren" 15 times (1:2,16,19; 2:1,5,14; 3:1,10,12; 4:11; 5:7,9,10,12,19), which was a common epithet among the first century Jews. Not surprisingly, then, James displays a distinct Jewish flavor in style and content. His letter contains more than 40 allusions to the Old Testament and more than 20 to the Sermon on the Mount (Matthew 5–7).

HISTORICAL AND THEOLOGICAL THEMES

James, with its devotion to direct, pungent statements of wise living, bears strong similarities to the book of Proverbs. It has a practical emphasis, stressing godly behavior more than theological knowledge. James wrote with a passionate desire for his reader to be uncompromisingly obedient to the Word of God. He used at least 30 references to nature in a manner similar to his half-brother Jesus and as one who

> **JAMES WROTE** WITH A **PASSIONATE DESIRE** FOR **HIS READER** TO BE **UNCOMPROMISINGLY OBEDIENT** TO THE **WORD OF GOD.**

spent a great deal of time outdoors. His approach complements Paul's emphasis on justification by faith with his own emphasis on spiritual fruitfulness demonstrating true faith.

OUTLINE

Greeting to the Twelve Tribes

1 James, a bondservant of God and of the Lord Jesus Christ,

To the twelve tribes which are scattered abroad:

Greetings.

1:1 James. He was the half-brother of Jesus. **twelve tribes.** This refers to the Jews (see Matt. 19:28). When the kingdom split after Solomon's reign, 10 tribes comprised the northern tribes, called Israel. The two tribes of Benjamin and Judah combined to form the southern kingdom, called Judah. After the fall of Israel to Assyria (722 B.C.), some of the remnant of those 10 tribes filtered down into Judah, thus preserving all 12 tribes in Judah's land.

Profiting from Trials

²My brethren, count it all joy when you fall into various trials, ³knowing that the testing of your faith produces patience. ⁴But let patience have *its* perfect work, that you may be perfect and complete, lacking nothing. ⁵If any of you lacks wisdom, let him ask of God, who gives to all liberally and without reproach, and it will be given to him. ⁶But let him ask in faith, with no doubting, for he who doubts is like a wave of the sea driven and tossed by the wind. ⁷For let not that man suppose that he will receive anything from the Lord; ⁸*he is a* double-minded man, unstable in all his ways.

1:8 double-minded man. This describes someone whose mind or soul is divided between God and the world. This person is a hypocrite and an unbeliever, who occasionally believes in God but fails to trust Him when trials come.

The Perspective of Rich and Poor

⁹Let the lowly brother glory in his exaltation, ¹⁰but the rich in his humiliation, because as a flower of the field he will pass away. ¹¹For no sooner has the sun risen with a burning heat than it withers the grass; its flower falls, and its beautiful appearance perishes. So the rich man also will fade away in his pursuits.

Loving God Under Trials

¹²Blessed *is* the man who endures temptation; for when he has been approved, he will receive the crown of life which the Lord has promised to those who love Him. ¹³Let no one say when he is tempted, "I am tempted by God"; for God cannot be tempted by evil, nor does He Himself tempt anyone. ¹⁴But each one is tempted when he is drawn away by his own desires and enticed. ¹⁵Then, when desire has conceived, it gives birth to sin; and sin, when it is full-grown, brings forth death.

¹⁶Do not be deceived, my beloved brethren. ¹⁷Every good gift and every perfect gift is from above, and comes down from the Father of lights, with whom there is no variation or shadow of turning. ¹⁸Of His own will He brought us forth by the word of

---

How can James expect Christians to somehow "count it all joy" when they face difficulties and trials (1:2)?

The Greek word for "count" may also be translated "consider" or "evaluate." The natural human response to hardships and difficulties rarely considers rejoicing as an option; therefore, the believer must make a conscious commitment to face trials with joy. Trials, then, should be reminders to rejoice (Philippians 3:1).

"Trials" translates a Greek word that connotes trouble, or something that breaks the pattern of peace, comfort, joy, and happiness in a person's life. The verb form of this word means "to put someone or something to the test," with the purpose of discovering that person's nature or that thing's quality. God brings such tests to prove—and increase—the strength and quality of one's faith and to demonstrate its validity (verses 2–12). Every trial becomes a test of faith designed to strengthen; if the believer fails the test by wrongly responding, that test then becomes a temptation, or a solicitation to evil. The choice to rejoice avoids greater trouble later.

truth, that we might be a kind of firstfruits of His creatures.

> **1:17 Every good...perfect gift is from above.** Two different Greek words for "gift" emphasize the perfection and inclusiveness of God's graciousness. The first denotes the act of giving; the second denotes the object given. **Father of lights.** This is an ancient Jewish expression for God as the Creator. "Lights" refers to the sun, moon, and stars (see Gen. 1:14–19). **no variation or shadow of turning.** God is changeless; He does not vary in movement, rotation, intensity, and shadow as do the celestial bodies (see Mal. 3:6).

Qualities Needed in Trials

[19]So then,[a] my beloved brethren, let every man be swift to hear, slow to speak, slow to wrath; [20]for the wrath of man does not produce the righteousness of God.

Doers—Not Hearers Only

[21]Therefore lay aside all filthiness and overflow of wickedness, and receive with meekness the implanted word, which is able to save your souls.

[22]But be doers of the word, and not hearers only, deceiving yourselves. [23]For if anyone is a hearer of the word and not a doer, he is like a man observing his natural face

> **1:23,24 mirror.** First century mirrors were made of bronze, silver, or gold. The image they reflected was adequate, but not perfect (see 1 Cor. 13:12). **forgets what kind of man he was.** Unless professing Christians act promptly after they hear the Word, they will forget the changes and improvements that their reflections showed them they need to make.

in a mirror; [24]for he observes himself, goes away, and immediately forgets what kind of man he was. [25]But he who looks into the perfect law of liberty and continues in it, and is not a forgetful hearer but a doer of the work, this one will be blessed in what he does.

[26]If anyone among you[a] thinks he is religious, and does not bridle his tongue but deceives his own heart, this one's religion is useless. [27]Pure and undefiled religion before God and the Father is this: to visit orphans and widows in their trouble, *and* to keep oneself unspotted from the world.

Beware of Personal Favoritism

2 My brethren, do not hold the faith of our Lord Jesus Christ, *the Lord* of glory, with partiality. [2]For if there should come into your assembly a man with gold rings, in fine apparel, and there should also come in a poor man in filthy clothes, [3]and you pay attention to the one wearing the fine clothes and say to him, "You sit here in a good place," and say to the poor man, "You stand there," or, "Sit here at my footstool," [4]have you not shown partiality among yourselves, and become judges with evil thoughts?

[5]Listen, my beloved brethren: Has God

> **2:4 shown partiality.** This is the true nature of the sin in this passage, not the wealth of the rich man. **judges with evil thoughts.** James feared that his readers would behave just like the sinful world by catering to the rich and prominent while shunning the poor and common.

1:19 [a]NU-Text reads *Know this* or *This you know.*   1:26 [a]NU-Text omits *among you.*

When the Bible says "the perfect law of liberty," what do the terms "law" and "liberty", that appear to be contradictory, really mean (1:25)?

In both the Old Testament and the New Testament, God's revealed, inerrant, sufficient, and comprehensive Word is called "law" (Psalm 19:7). The presence of God's grace does not mean the absence of moral law or code of conduct for believers to obey. Believers are enabled by the Spirit to keep God's standards.

True liberty is not the license to do what we want but the assistance to do what we ought. The law of liberty frees us from sin (2:12,13). It liberates us when we have sinned by showing us a gracious God and directs us away from sin as we obey Him. As the Holy Spirit applies the principles of Scripture to believers' hearts, they are freed from sin's bondage and enabled to live in true freedom (John 8:34–36).

not chosen the poor of this world *to be* rich in faith and heirs of the kingdom which He promised to those who love Him? [6]But you have dishonored the poor man. Do not the rich oppress you and drag you into the courts? [7]Do they not blaspheme that noble name by which you are called?

[8]If you really fulfill *the* royal law according to the Scripture, *"You shall love your neighbor as yourself,"* [a] you do well; [9]but if you show partiality, you commit sin, and are convicted by the law as transgressors. [10]For whoever shall keep the whole law, and yet stumble in one *point,* he is guilty of all. [11]For He who said, *"Do not commit adultery,"* [a] also said, *"Do not murder."* [b] Now if you do not commit adultery, but you do murder, you have become a transgressor of the law. [12]So speak and so do as those who will be judged by the law of liberty. [13]For judgment is without mercy to the one who has shown no mercy. Mercy triumphs over judgment.

2:13 A person who shows no mercy and compassion for people in need demonstrates that he has never responded to the mercy of God. Unredeemed people will receive judgment in eternal hell (see Matt. 5:7). **Mercy triumphs over judgment.** The person whose life is characterized by mercy is ready for the day of judgment and will escape all charges because of God's mercy.

Faith Without Works Is Dead

[14]What *does it* profit, my brethren, if someone says he has faith but does not have works? Can faith save him? [15]If a brother or sister is naked and destitute of daily food, [16]and one of you says to them, "Depart in peace, be warmed and filled," but you do not give them the things which are needed for the body, what *does it* profit? [17]Thus also faith by itself, if it does not have works, is dead.

[18]But someone will say, "You have faith, and I have works." Show me your faith without your[a] works, and I will show you my faith by my[b] works. [19]You believe that there is one God. You do well. Even the demons believe—and tremble! [20]But do you want to know, O foolish man, that faith without works is dead?[a] [21]Was not Abraham our father justified by works when he offered Isaac his son on the altar? [22]Do you see that faith was working together with his works, and by works faith was made perfect? [23]And the Scripture was fulfilled which says, *"Abraham believed God, and it was accounted to him for righteousness."* [a] And he was called the friend of God. [24]You see then that a man is justified by works, and not by faith only.

[25]Likewise, was not Rahab the harlot also justified by works when she received the messengers and sent *them* out another way?

[26]For as the body without the spirit is dead, so faith without works is dead also.

The Untamable Tongue

3 My brethren, let not many of you become teachers, knowing that we shall

2:8 [a]Leviticus 19:18   2:11 [a]Exodus 20:14; Deuteronomy 5:18   [b]Exodus 20:13; Deuteronomy 5:17
2:18 [a]NU-Text omits *your.* [b]NU-Text omits *my.*   2:20 [a]NU-Text reads *useless.*   2:23 [a]Genesis 15:6

What is the "royal law" (2:8)?

The phrase "royal law" translates better as "sovereign law." The idea is that this law is supreme or binding. James was quoting the second half of what Jesus had taught was the whole of the sovereign law. "Love your neighbor as yourself" (Leviticus 19:18; Mark 12:31), when combined with the command to love God (Deuteronomy 6:4,5), summarizes all the Law and the Prophets (Matthew 22:36–40; Romans 13:8–10).

James already alluded to the first part of the great commandment (2:5). This passage focuses on the theme of this section, which is human relationships. James was not advocating some kind of emotional affection for oneself—self-love is clearly a sin (2 Timothy 3:2). Rather, the command is to meet the physical health and spiritual well-being needs of our neighbors with the same intensity and concern that we naturally have for ourselves (Philippians 2:3,4), while never forgetting that we are under royal law to do so.

3:1 stricter judgment. The unbelieving false teacher will be judged at the second coming (Jude 14,15), and the believer will be rewarded before Christ (1 Cor. 4:3–5). This is meant to warn the prospective teacher of the role's seriousness (see Ezek. 3:17,18).

receive a stricter judgment. ²For we all stumble in many things. If anyone does not stumble in word, he *is* a perfect man, able also to bridle the whole body. ³Indeed,*ᵃ* we put bits in horses' mouths that they may obey us, and we turn their whole body. ⁴Look also at ships: although they are so large and are driven by fierce winds, they are turned by a very small rudder wherever the pilot desires. ⁵Even so the tongue is a little member and boasts great things.

See how great a forest a little fire kindles! ⁶And the tongue *is* a fire, a world of iniquity. The tongue is so set among our members that it defiles the whole body, and sets on fire the course of nature; and it is set on fire by hell. ⁷For every kind of beast and bird, of reptile and creature of the sea, is tamed and has been tamed by mankind. ⁸But no man can tame the tongue. *It is* an unruly evil, full of deadly poison. ⁹With it we bless our God and Father, and with it we curse men, who have been made in the similitude of God. ¹⁰Out of the same mouth proceed blessing and cursing. My brethren, these things ought not to be so. ¹¹Does a spring send forth fresh *water* and bitter from the same opening? ¹²Can a fig tree, my brethren, bear olives, or a grapevine bear figs? Thus no spring yields both salt water and fresh.*ᵃ*

3:6 tongue *is* a fire. Like fire, the tongue's sinful words can spread destruction rapidly. As smoke, those words can permeate and ruin everything around it. **defiles.** "To pollute or contaminate" (see Mark 7:20). **the course of nature.** The tongue's evil can extend beyond the individual to affect everything around him. **hell.** "Hell" is the translated word for the valley of Hinnom, a valley used as the city dump that was always burning. Jesus used that place to symbolize the eternal place of punishment and torment (see Mark 9:43,45).

Heavenly Versus Demonic Wisdom

¹³Who *is* wise and understanding among you? Let him show by good conduct *that* his works *are done* in the meekness of wisdom. ¹⁴But if you have bitter envy and self-seeking in your hearts, do not boast and lie against the truth. ¹⁵This wisdom does not descend from above, but *is* earthly, sensual, demonic. ¹⁶For where envy and self-seeking *exist*, confusion and every evil thing *are*

3:16 confusion. This is the disorder that results from the instability and chaos of human wisdom. **every evil thing.** This denotes things that are not necessarily intrinsically evil but are simply good for nothing.

3:3 *ᵃ*NU-Text reads *Now if.*   3:12 *ᵃ*NU-Text reads *Neither can a salty spring produce fresh water.*

If salvation is by faith in Christ alone, how can James write "faith without works is dead" (2:14–26)?

This passage comes within a longer section that provides readers with a series of tests they can use to evaluate whether their faith is living, or dead. Here is the central test–the one that pulls the others together: the test of works or righteous behavior. James defined this behavior as obeying God's Word and manifesting a godly nature (1:22–25).

The point here is not that a person is saved by works. The Bible strongly and clearly asserts that salvation is a gracious gift from God (1:17,18; Ephesians 2:8,9). Rather, James' concern was to show that a kind of apparent faith is dead and does not save (2:14,17,20,24,26). His teaching parallels the rest of Scripture (Matthew 3:7,8; 5:16; 7:21; 13:18–23; John 8:30,31; 15:6). Quite possibly, James was writing to Jews who had turned away from the works righteousness of Judaism and had then embraced another mistaken notion: since righteous works and obedience to God were not efficacious for salvation, then they were not necessary at all. Thus, they had reduced faith to a mere mental assent to the facts about Christ. To refute this, James rightly declared that such faith is, in fact, dead.

there. [17]But the wisdom that is from above is first pure, then peaceable, gentle, willing to yield, full of mercy and good fruits, without partiality and without hypocrisy. [18]Now the fruit of righteousness is sown in peace by those who make peace.

Pride Promotes Strife

4 Where do wars and fights *come* from among you? Do *they* not *come* from your *desires for* pleasure that war in your members? [2]You lust and do not have. You murder and covet and cannot obtain. You fight and war. Yet[a] you do not have because you do not ask. [3]You ask and do not receive, because you ask amiss, that you may spend *it* on your pleasures. [4]Adulterers and[a] adulteresses! Do you not know that friendship with the world is enmity with God? Whoever therefore wants to be a friend of the world makes himself an enemy of God. [5]Or do you think that the Scripture says in

vain, "The Spirit who dwells in us yearns jealously"?

[6]But He gives more grace. Therefore He says:

> "God resists the proud,
> But gives grace to the humble." [a]

Humility Cures Worldliness

[7]Therefore submit to God. Resist the devil and he will flee from you. [8]Draw near to God and He will draw near to you. Cleanse *your* hands, *you* sinners; and purify *your* hearts, *you* double-minded. [9]Lament and mourn and weep! Let *your* laughter be turned to mourning and *your* joy to gloom. [10]Humble yourselves in the sight of the Lord, and He will lift you up.

4:1 wars and fights...among you. This refers to conflicts between people in the church. Discord in the church is not by God's design (John 13:34,35). It results from the mix of false believers and redeemed people that make up the church. **desires.** This word always has a negative connotation in the NT. The desires for worldly pleasures that mark unbelievers (Eph. 2:3) are the internal source of the external conflict in the church.

4:9 Lament. This is the state of affliction and misery of those who are truly broken over their sin. **mourn.** God will not turn away a heart that repents of sin (Ps. 51:17). Mourning is the inner response to such brokenness. **weep.** This is the outward manifestation of inner sorrow over sin (see Mark 14:72). **laughter.** This word, used only here in the NT, signifies the flippant laughter of those foolishly indulging in worldly pleasures. James calls these people to mourn over their sin (see Luke 18:13,14).

Do Not Judge a Brother

[11]Do not speak evil of one another, brethren. He who speaks evil of a brother and

---

4:2 [a]NU-Text and M-Text omit *Yet*.   4:4 [a]NU-Text omits *Adulterers and*.   4:6 [a]Proverbs 3:34

How does James explain the difference between the two kinds of wisdom in the world (3:13–18)?

The term "wise" in verse 13 is the common Greek word for speculative knowledge and philosophy. The Hebrews, particularly when they used it in the Old Testament, infused this word with the much richer meaning of skillfully applying knowledge to produce practical living. This passage points out that two groups of people can be called wise, but in each case the source of wisdom and the character of the "wise" are entirely opposite.

Wisdom from above (verse 17) includes the following characteristics: (1) meekness (power under control, verse 13); (2) purity (verse 17); (3) peace-loving (verse 17); (4) willingness to yield (verse 17); (5) full of mercy and good fruits (verse 17); (6) without partiality (verse 17); and (7) without hypocrisy (verse 17).

In contrast to godly wisdom, the wisdom from below has its own characteristics: (1) bitterness and envy (verse 14); and (2) self-seeking attitude (verse 14). James describes human wisdom as: (1) limited to earth; (2) characterized by humanness, frailty, an unsanctified heart, and an unredeemed spirit; and (3) generated by Satan's forces (verse 15 and 1 Corinthians 2:14; 2 Corinthians 11:14,15).

judges his brother, speaks evil of the law and judges the law. But if you judge the law, you are not a doer of the law but a judge. [12]There is one Lawgiver,[a] who is able to save and to destroy. Who[b] are you to judge another?[c]

Do Not Boast About Tomorrow

[13]Come now, you who say, "Today or tomorrow we will[a] go to such and such a city, spend a year there, buy and sell, and make a profit"; [14]whereas you do not know what will happen tomorrow. For what is your life? It is even a vapor that appears for a little time and then vanishes away. [15]Instead you ought to say, "If the Lord wills, we shall

> **4:15 If the Lord wills.** The true Christian submits personal plans to the lordship of Christ (see Prov. 19:21).

live and do this or that." [16]But now you boast in your arrogance. All such boasting is evil.

[17]Therefore, to him who knows to do good and does not do it, to him it is sin.

Rich Oppressors Will Be Judged

5 Come now, you rich, weep and howl for your miseries that are coming upon you! [2]Your riches are corrupted, and your garments are moth-eaten. [3]Your gold and silver are corroded, and their corrosion will be a witness against you and will eat your flesh like fire. You have heaped up treasure in the last days. [4]Indeed the wages of the laborers who mowed your fields, which you kept back by fraud, cry out; and the cries of the reapers have reached the ears of the Lord of Sabaoth.[a] [5]You have lived on the earth in pleasure and luxury; you have fattened your hearts as[a] in a day of slaughter.

4:12 [a]NU-Text adds and Judge. [b]NU-Text and M-Text read But who. [c]NU-Text reads a neighbor.
4:13 [a]M-Text reads let us. 5:4 [a]Literally, in Hebrew, Hosts 5:5 [a]NU-Text omits as.

What do the 10 commands that fill 4:7–10 have to do with grace?

These verses contain a series of 10 commands that prepare a person to receive saving grace. These commands delineate a person's response to God's gracious offer of salvation and reveal what it means to be humble. Each command uses a Greek imperative to define the expected action:

1. Submit to God (verse 7)—James used the phrase to describe a willing, conscious submission to God's authority as sovereign ruler of the universe (Matthew 10:38).

2. Resist the devil (verse 7)—Those who consciously "take their stand against" Satan and transfer their allegiance to God will find that Satan "will flee from" them; he is a defeated foe (John 8:44; Ephesians 2:2; 1 John 3:8; 5:19).

3. Draw near to God (verse 8)—Pursue an intimate relationship with God (Philippians 3:10).

4. Cleanse your hands (verse 8)—The added term "sinners" addresses the unbeliever's need to recognize and confess his or her sin (5:20).

5. Purify your hearts (verse 8)—Cleansing the hands symbolizes external behavior; this phrase refers to the inner thoughts, motives, and desires of the heart (Psalm 24:3,4; Jeremiah 4:4; 1 Timothy 1:5; 2 Timothy 2:22; 1 Peter 1:22).

6. Lament (verse 9)—To be afflicted, wretched and miserable. This is the state of those truly broken over their sin (Matthew 5:3).

7. Mourn (verse 9)—The internal experience of brokenness over sin (Psalm 51:17; Matthew 5:4).

8. Weep (verse 9)—The outward manifestation of inner sorrow over sin (Mark 14:72).

9. Grieve without laughter or joy (verse 9)—The signs of denial; the flippant laughter of those foolishly indulging in worldly pleasures without regard to God, life, death, sin, judgment or holiness.

10. Humble yourself (verse 10)—This final command sums up the preceding nine. The word humble means, "to make oneself low." Those conscious of being in the presence of the majestic, infinitely holy God are humbled (Isaiah 6:5).

⁶You have condemned, you have murdered the just; he does not resist you.

Be Patient and Persevering

⁷Therefore be patient, brethren, until the coming of the Lord. See *how* the farmer waits for the precious fruit of the earth, waiting patiently for it until it receives the early and latter rain. ⁸You also be patient. Establish your hearts, for the coming of the Lord is at hand.

> **5:7 the early and latter rain.** The "early" rain falls in Israel during October and November and softens the ground for planting. The "latter" rain falls in March and April before the spring harvest. Just as the farmer waits patiently for the crop to ripen, so Christians must patiently wait for the Lord's return (see Gal. 6:9).

⁹Do not grumble against one another, brethren, lest you be condemned.*ᵃ* Behold, the Judge is standing at the door! ¹⁰My brethren, take the prophets, who spoke in the name of the Lord, as an example of suffering and patience. ¹¹Indeed we count them blessed who endure. You have heard of the perseverance of Job and seen the end *intended by* the Lord—that the Lord is very compassionate and merciful.

¹²But above all, my brethren, do not swear, either by heaven or by earth or with any other oath. But let your "Yes" be "Yes," and *your* "No," "No," lest you fall into judgment.*ᵃ*

> **5:12 do not swear...any other oath.** James condemned the Jewish practice of swearing false, deceptive oaths by everything other than the name of the Lord, which alone was considered binding. **"Yes" be "Yes."** James called for straightforward, honest, plain speech. To speak otherwise is to invite God's judgment.

Meeting Specific Needs

¹³Is anyone among you suffering? Let him pray. Is anyone cheerful? Let him sing psalms. ¹⁴Is anyone among you sick? Let him call for the elders of the church, and let them pray over him, anointing him with oil in the name of the Lord. ¹⁵And the prayer of faith will save the sick, and the Lord will raise him up. And if he has committed sins, he will be forgiven. ¹⁶Confess *your* trespasses*ᵃ* to one another, and pray for one another, that you may be healed. The effective, fervent prayer of a righteous man avails much. ¹⁷Elijah was a man with a nature like ours, and he prayed earnestly that

---

5:9 *ᵃ*NU-Text and M-Text read *judged.*   5:12 *ᵃ*M-Text reads *hypocrisy.*   5:16 *ᵃ*NU-Text reads *Therefore confess your sins.*

What does James mean by the closing words of his letter, "he who turns a sinner from the error of his way will save a soul from death and cover a multitude of sins" (5:20)?

The language used by James makes it clear that the "sinner" he had in mind was someone whose faith was dead (2:14–26) not a believer who had sinned. The term is used throughout Scripture to describe those outside of Christ and unregenerate (Proverbs 11:31; 13:6,22; Matthew 9:13; Luke 7:37,39; 15:7,10; 18:13; Romans 5:8; 1 Timothy 1:9,15; 1 Peter 4:18).

A person who wanders from the truth and never allows it to transform him or her puts his or her soul in jeopardy. The "death" in view is not physical death, but eternal death–eternal separation from God and eternal punishment in hell (Isaiah 66:24; Daniel 12:2; Matthew 13:40,42,50; 25:41,46; Mark 9:43–49; 2 Thessalonians 1:8,9; Romans 6:23; Revelation 20:11–15; 21:8). Knowing the height of the stakes should motivate Christians to aggressively pursue such people.

Since even one sin is enough to condemn a person to hell, the word "multitude" emphasizes the hopeless condition of lost, unregenerate sinners. The good news of the gospel is that God's forgiving grace, which is greater than any sin (Romans 5:20), is available to those who turn from their sins and exercise faith in the Lord Jesus Christ (Ephesians 2:8,9).

it would not rain; and it did not rain on the land for three years and six months. [18]And he prayed again, and the heaven gave rain, and the earth produced its fruit.

Bring Back the Erring One

[19]Brethren, if anyone among you wanders from the truth, and someone turns him back, [20]let him know that he who turns a sinner from the error of his way will save a soul[a] from death and cover a multitude of sins.

> **5:19 if anyone among you.** This refers to professing believers who have strayed from the truth. **wanders from the truth.** These people reject the truth they once professed (see Heb. 5:12–6:9). They are in grave danger, and the church must call them back to true faith.

5:20 [a]NU-Text reads *his soul*.

1 PETER

Among the disciples of Jesus, Peter remains the most recognizable name. He was probably the first of those Jesus specifically called to follow Him (Mark 1:16,17). Jesus' last recorded words to Peter had the same theme, "You follow Me" (John 21:22). Along the way, Christ replaced his name Simon with Peter (Greek) or Cephas (Aramaic), both words meaning "stone" or "rock."

The Lord clearly singled out Peter for special lessons throughout the gospels (Matthew 10; 16:13–21; 17:1–9; 24:1–7; 26:31–33; John 6:6; 21:3–7,15–17). He was the spokesman for the Twelve, articulating their thoughts and questions as well as his own. He was probably the primary source for Mark's gospel. Eventually, he wrote two canonical (inspired) letters himself of which this is the first.

AUTHOR AND DATE

First Peter was written by Peter, about A.D. 64 to 65.

The opening verse of the epistle claims Peter as the author. He was clearly the leader among the apostles. The gospel writers emphasize this by placing his name at the head of each list of the apostles (Matthew 10; Mark 3; Luke 6; Acts 1), and including more information about him in the four gospels than any person other than Christ.

Because of his unique prominence, the early church had many documents falsely claiming to be written by Peter. That the Apostle Peter is the author of this letter, however, is certain. The material bears definite resemblance to Peter's messages in the book of Acts. Compare 2:7,8 with Acts 4:10,11, both which have Peter teaching that Christ is the Stone rejected by the builders. Similarly, 1:17 and Acts 10:34 point out that Christ is no respecter of persons. In addition to these and other internal evidences, it is noteworthy that the early Christians universally recognized the letter as the work of Peter.

The only significant doubt to be mentioned about Peter's authorship arises from the rather classical style of Greek employed in the letter. (For more on this see the FAQ, *How did a fisherman like Peter write such a literary masterpiece like 1 Peter?*) The difference between writing and speaking, along with Peter's use of an amanuensis (secretary), provide enough reasonable confidence to maintain his authorship.

First Peter was most likely written just before or shortly after July, A.D. 64, when the city of Rome burned. For this reason, the letter receives a composition date of A.D. 64–65.

Peter's audience of believers was facing increasing signs of persecution through-out the Roman Empire. Conditions were ripe for the tactics used by Nero to de-flect blame for burning Rome from himself to the Christians. Once Nero spread the word that Christians had set the fires, the accusation stuck because the Chris-tians were already hated as those who associated with Jews and who also were hostile to Roman culture. The vicious persecution that ensued touched the far corners of the empire, reaching the very places mentioned by Peter's salutation (1:1).

The general addressees of the letter and the ambiguous location of the writer (Babylon—5:13) underscore the tension of the times. Believers established under-ground networks that would have directed Peter's letter and his envoy to the nec-essary places. It is likely that Babylon was an alias for Rome. Peter was protecting his own companions in the way he identified his location. Nevertheless, the Apostle realized the scattered and battered Christians needed spiritual strengthening be-cause of the sufferings. Under the inspiration of the Holy Spirit, Peter wrote this epistle to encourage them.

HISTORICAL AND THEOLOGICAL THEMES

Since the believers addressed were suffering escalating persecution (1:6; 2:12,19–21; 3:9,13–18; 4:1,12–16,19), the purpose of this letter was to teach them how to live victoriously in the midst of that hostility: (1) without losing hope; (2) without becoming bit-ter; (3) while trusting in their Lord; and (4) while looking for His second coming. Peter wished to impress on his readers that by living an obedient, victorious life under duress, a Christian can actually evangelize his hostile world (1:14; 2:1,12,15; 3:1–6,13–17; 4:2; 5:8,9).

> THE **PURPOSE** OF **THIS LETTER** WAS **TO TEACH THEM** HOW TO **LIVE VICTORIOUSLY** IN THE **MIDST** OF THAT **HOSTILITY.**

This epistle emphasizes two categories of truth. The first category is positive and includes a long list of blessings bestowed by God on Christians. As he wrote about the identity of Christians and what it means to know Christ, Peter men-tioned one privilege and blessing after another. Alongside and interwoven into the list of privileges, he also included a catalog of suffering. This category of truth reminds Christians that though they are greatly privileged, they should also know that the world will treat them unjustly. Their citizenship is in heaven, and they are strangers in a hostile, Satan-energized world. Thus the Christian life can be summed up as a call to victory and glory through the path of suffering.

The most basic question that this epistle answers is, How should Christians deal with animosity? Peter's answer features practical truths and focuses on Jesus Christ as the model of one who maintained a triumphant attitude in the midst of hostility.

OUTLINE

Greeting to the Elect Pilgrims

1 Peter, an apostle of Jesus Christ,

To the pilgrims of the Dispersion in Pontus, Galatia, Cappadocia, Asia, and Bithynia, ²elect according to the foreknowledge of God the Father, in sanctification of the Spirit, for obedience and sprinkling of the blood of Jesus Christ:

Grace to you and peace be multiplied.

> **1:1 pilgrims.** These were strangers dispossessed, in a land not their own, as temporary residents or foreigners. Like all believers, they were residents of an eternal city (Phil. 3:20). **the Dispersion.** Here this refers to spiritual pilgrims, aliens to the earth, whether Jews or Gentiles (the church). **Pontus...Bithynia.** Peter's letter is addressed to churches in provinces located in modern-day Turkey, which were part of the Roman Empire.

A Heavenly Inheritance

³Blessed *be* the God and Father of our Lord Jesus Christ, who according to His abundant mercy has begotten us again to a living hope through the resurrection of Jesus Christ from the dead, ⁴to an inheritance incorruptible and undefiled and that does not fade away, reserved in heaven for you, ⁵who are kept by the power of God through faith for salvation ready to be revealed in the last time.

⁶In this you greatly rejoice, though now for a little while, if need be, you have been grieved by various trials, ⁷that the genuineness of your faith, *being* much more pre-

> **1:5 kept by the power of God.** God's supreme power, knowledge, and sovereignty keep each believer's inheritance secure. No one can steal the Christian's treasure, and no one can disqualify the believer from receiving it. **through faith.** The Christian's response to God's election and the Spirit's conviction is faith, but even faith is empowered by God. The Christian's continued faith is evidence of God's keeping power.

cious than gold that perishes, though it is tested by fire, may be found to praise, honor, and glory at the revelation of Jesus Christ, ⁸whom having not seen[a] you love. Though now you do not see *Him*, yet believing, you rejoice with joy inexpressible and full of glory, ⁹receiving the end of your faith—the salvation of *your* souls.

¹⁰Of this salvation the prophets have inquired and searched carefully, who prophesied of the grace *that would come* to you, ¹¹searching what, or what manner of time, the Spirit of Christ who was in them was indicating when He testified beforehand the sufferings of Christ and the glories that would follow. ¹²To them it was revealed that, not to themselves, but to us[a] they were ministering the things which now have been reported to you through those who have preached the gospel to you by the Holy Spirit sent from heaven—things which angels desire to look into.

Living Before God Our Father

¹³Therefore gird up the loins of your mind, be sober, and rest *your* hope fully upon the grace that is to be brought to you

---

1:8 [a]M-Text reads *known.*   1:12 [a]NU-Text and M-Text read *you.*

Why does Peter call his readers "elect" (1:2)?

The term used here in Greek also connotes "called out ones." The word means "to pick out" or "to select." In the Old Testament, the word was used of Israel (Deuteronomy 7:6), indicating that God had sovereignly chosen Israel from among all the nations of the world to believe in and belong to Him (Deuteronomy 14:12; Psalm 105:43; 135:4). In this book, the word is used for Christians, those chosen by God for salvation (Romans 8:33; Colossians 3:12; 2 Timothy 2:10). The word is also used for those who receive Christ during the tribulation time (Matthew 24:22,24), and holy, unfallen angels (1 Timothy 5:21). To be reminded that they were elected by God was a great comfort to those persecuted Christians.

By using this and other terms of ownership, Peter was establishing the basis from which he would encourage believers not to see their suffering as evidence of a different standing with God. Their ultimate security, even in the face of persecution and suffering, was in God's hands.

at the revelation of Jesus Christ; [14]as obedient children, not conforming yourselves to the former lusts, *as* in your ignorance; [15]but as He who called you *is* holy, you also be holy in all *your* conduct, [16]because it is written, *"Be holy, for I am holy."* [a]

[17]And if you call on the Father, who without partiality judges according to each one's work, conduct yourselves throughout the time of your stay *here* in fear; [18]knowing that you were not redeemed with corruptible things, *like* silver or gold, from your aimless conduct *received* by tradition from your fathers, [19]but with the precious blood of Christ, as of a lamb without blemish and without spot. [20]He indeed was foreordained before the foundation of the world, but was manifest in these last times for you [21]who through Him believe in God, who raised Him from the dead and gave Him glory, so that your faith and hope are in God.

The Enduring Word

[22]Since you have purified your souls in obeying the truth through the Spirit[a] in sincere love of the brethren, love one another fervently with a pure heart, [23]having been born again, not of corruptible seed but incorruptible, through the word of God which lives and abides forever,[a] [24]because

> *"All flesh is as grass,*
> *And all the glory of man[a] as the flower*
> *   of the grass.*
> *The grass withers,*
> *And its flower falls away,*
> [25] *But the word of the LORD endures*
> *   forever."* [a]

Now this is the word which by the gospel was preached to you.

2 Therefore, laying aside all malice, all deceit, hypocrisy, envy, and all evil speaking, [2]as newborn babes, desire the pure milk of the word, that you may grow thereby,[a] [3]if indeed you have tasted that the Lord *is* gracious.

The Chosen Stone and His Chosen People

[4]Coming to Him *as to* a living stone, rejected indeed by men, but chosen by God *and* precious, [5]you also, as living stones, are being built up a spiritual house, a holy priesthood, to offer up spiritual sacrifices acceptable to God through Jesus Christ.

1:16 [a]Leviticus 11:44, 45; 19:2; 20:7   1:22 [a]NU-Text omits *through the Spirit.*   1:23 [a]NU-Text omits *forever.*   1:24 [a]NU-Text reads *all its glory.*   1:25 [a]Isaiah 40:6–8   2:2 [a]NU-Text adds *up to salvation.*

What is the "pure milk of the word" (2:2)?

The Scriptures frequently use startling but clear, figurative language to teach spiritual truth. Daily life often mirrors heavenly realities. God's Word offers pure spiritual nourishment. Spiritual growth is always marked by a craving for and delight in God's Word with the same intensity with which a baby craves milk (Job 23:12; Psalm 1:1,2; 19:7–11; 119:16,24,35, 47,48,72,92,97,103,111,113,127,159,167,174; Jeremiah 15:16). That initial by-product of spiritual rebirth ought to be a consistent part of the Christian's life.

A Christian develops and maintains a desire for the truth of God's Word by: (1) remembering his or her life's source (1:25; Isaiah 55:10,11; John 15:3; Hebrews 4:12); (2) eliminating sin from his or her life (2:1); (3) admitting his or her need for God's truth (2:2, "as newborn babes"; Matthew 4:4); (4) pursuing spiritual growth (2:2, "that you may grow thereby"); and (5) surveying his or her blessings (2:3, "the Lord is gracious").

2:4 Coming to Him. This means to remain in Christ's presence with intimate fellowship (see John 15:5–15). **a living stone.** This Old Testament phrase emphasizes that Christ, the "cornerstone," is alive from the dead and has a living relationship with believers (see 1 Cor. 15:45). **rejected...but chosen.** Jesus' messianic credentials were rejected by the religious leaders (see Matt. 12:22–24). But Jesus Christ was God's elect Son, ultimately authenticated through His resurrection from the dead (see Ps. 2:10).

⁶Therefore it is also contained in the Scripture,

> "Behold, I lay in Zion
> A chief cornerstone, elect, precious,
> And he who believes on Him will by
>   no means be put to shame."ᵃ

⁷Therefore, to you who believe, *He is* precious; but to those who are disobedient,ᵃ

> "The stone which the builders rejected
> Has become the chief cornerstone," ᵇ

⁸and

> "A stone of stumbling
> And a rock of offense." ᵃ

They stumble, being disobedient to the word, to which they also were appointed.
⁹But you *are* a chosen generation, a royal priesthood, a holy nation, His own special

people, that you may proclaim the praises of Him who called you out of darkness into His marvelous light; ¹⁰who once *were* not a people but *are* now the people of God, who had not obtained mercy but now have obtained mercy.

2:9 a chosen generation. In contrast to the disobedient, who are appointed by God to wrath, Christians are chosen by God to salvation. **a royal priesthood.** Israel temporarily forfeited this privilege because of their apostasy (Ex. 19:6) and because their leaders executed the Messiah. Presently, the church is a royal priesthood united with the royal Priest, Jesus Christ. A royal priesthood belongs to and serves the king, and it also exercises rule.

Living Before the World

¹¹Beloved, I beg *you* as sojourners and pilgrims, abstain from fleshly lusts which war against the soul, ¹²having your conduct honorable among the Gentiles, that when they speak against you as evildoers, they may, by *your* good works which they observe, glorify God in the day of visitation.

Submission to Government

¹³Therefore submit yourselves to every ordinance of man for the Lord's sake, whether to the king as supreme, ¹⁴or to governors, as to those who are sent by him for the punishment of evildoers and *for the* praise of those who do good. ¹⁵For this is the will of God, that by doing good you may put

---

2:6 ᵃIsaiah 28:16   2:7 ᵃNU-Text reads *to those who disbelieve.*   ᵇPsalm 118:22   2:8 ᵃIsaiah 8:14

Do Christians need a priesthood to intercede for them with God (2:9)?

Along with "royal priesthood," Peter used several Old Testament concepts to emphasize the privileges of New Testament Christians (Deuteronomy 7:6–8). This phrase gave rise to the theological expression "the priesthood of believers." For believers, the need for a representative priest has been met by Jesus Christ, the ultimate royal priest (Hebrews 4:14–9:15). The role of priest is not eliminated but altered. This verse indicates that a central role of the priesthood of all believers is to "proclaim the praises of Him who called you out of darkness into His marvelous light."

The concept of a kingly priesthood is drawn from Exodus 19:6. Israel temporarily forfeited this privilege because of its apostasy and because its wicked leaders executed the Messiah. At the present time, the church is a royal priesthood united with the royal priest, Jesus Christ. A royal priesthood is not only a priesthood that belongs to and serves the king; it is also a priesthood that exercises rule. This will ultimately be fulfilled in Christ's future kingdom (1 Corinthians 6:1–4; Revelation 5:10; 20:6).

to silence the ignorance of foolish men—
[16]as free, yet not using liberty as a cloak for
vice, but as bondservants of God. [17]Honor
all *people*. Love the brotherhood. Fear God.
Honor the king.

> **2:14 governors.** Christians are to obey every institu-
> tion of civil and social order on earth. This includes
> obedience to the national government, the state gov-
> ernment, the police, and judges. A Christian should
> refuse to submit only when the government requires
> disobedience to God (see Acts 4:18–20).

Submission to Masters

[18]Servants, *be* submissive to *your* masters with all fear, not only to the good and
gentle, but also to the harsh. [19]For this *is*
commendable, if because of conscience toward God one endures grief, suffering
wrongfully. [20]For what credit *is it* if, when
you are beaten for your faults, you take it
patiently? But when you do good and suffer,
if you take it patiently, this *is* commendable
before God. [21]For to this you were called,
because Christ also suffered for us,[a] leaving
us[b] an example, that you should follow His
steps:

[22]   "Who committed no sin,
      Nor was deceit found in His mouth";[a]

> **2:19,20 commendable before God.** Favor with God
> is found when a worker, treated unjustly, accepts the
> poor treatment with faith in God's sovereign care,
> rather than responding in anger, hostility, discon-
> tentment, pride, or rebellion (see Matt. 5:11).

[23]who, when He was reviled, did not revile
in return; when He suffered, He did not
threaten, but committed *Himself* to Him
who judges righteously; [24]who Himself bore
our sins in His own body on the tree, that
we, having died to sins, might live for righteousness—by whose stripes you were
healed. [25]For you were like sheep going
astray, but have now returned to the Shepherd and Overseer[a] of your souls.

Submission to Husbands

3 Wives, likewise, *be* submissive to your
own husbands, that even if some do

> **3:1 be submissive.** Peter insisted that if Christians
> are to be a witness for their Lord, they must submit
> to the civil and social orders that God had designed.
> **own husbands.** Women are not inferior to men, but
> the role of a wife is to submit to the headship of her
> husband, as commanded by the Lord. **some do not
> obey the word.** This refers to a non-Christian hus-
> band. Peter did not urge the Christian wife to leave
> her husband (see 1 Cor. 7:13–16), preach to him, or
> demand her rights, but instead to evangelize him
> through her loving, gracious submission.

not obey the word, they, without a word,
may be won by the conduct of their wives,
[2]when they observe your chaste conduct *accompanied* by fear. [3]Do not let your adorn-
ment be *merely* outward—arranging the
hair, wearing gold, or putting on *fine* apparel—[4]rather *let it be* the hidden person of
the heart, with the incorruptible *beauty* of
a gentle and quiet spirit, which is very precious in the sight of God. [5]For in this manner, in former times, the holy women who
trusted in God also adorned themselves,
being submissive to their own husbands,
[6]as Sarah obeyed Abraham, calling him
lord, whose daughters you are if you do
good and are not afraid with any terror.

A Word to Husbands

[7]Husbands, likewise, dwell with *them*
with understanding, giving honor to the
wife, as to the weaker vessel, and as *being*
heirs together of the grace of life, that your
prayers may not be hindered.

> **3:7 Husbands, likewise.** Christian husbands are
> also commanded to submit (see Eph. 5:21). The hus-
> band must submit to the loving duty of being sensi-
> tive to his wife's needs, fears, and feelings. **weaker
> vessel.** The woman is fully equal in Christ and not
> inferior spiritually. She is physically weaker and in
> need of protection, provision, and strength from her
> husband. **heirs together of the grace of life.** This
> "grace of life" refers to marriage, the best relation-
> ship that earthly life offers.

Called to Blessing

[8]Finally, all *of you be* of one mind, having
compassion for one another; love as brothers, *be* tenderhearted, *be* courteous;[a] [9]not

---

2:21 [a]NU-Text reads *you*. [b]NU-Text and M-Text read *you*.   2:22 [a]Isaiah 53:9   2:25 [a]Greek *Episkopos*
3:8 [a]NU-Text reads *humble*.

returning evil for evil or reviling for reviling, but on the contrary blessing, knowing that you were called to this, that you may inherit a blessing. ¹⁰For

"He who would love life
   And see good days,
   Let him refrain his tongue from evil,
   And his lips from speaking deceit.
¹¹ Let him turn away from evil and do
     good;
   Let him seek peace and pursue it.
¹² For the eyes of the LORD are on the
     righteous,
   And His ears are open to their
     prayers;
   But the face of the LORD is against
     those who do evil." ᵃ

Suffering for Right and Wrong

¹³And who is he who will harm you if you become followers of what is good? ¹⁴But even if you should suffer for righteousness' sake, you are blessed. "And do not be afraid of their threats, nor be troubled." ᵃ ¹⁵But sanctify the Lord Godᵃ in your hearts, and always be ready to give a defense to everyone who asks you a reason for the hope that is in you, with meekness and fear; ¹⁶having a good conscience, that when they defame you as evildoers, those who revile your good conduct in Christ may be ashamed. ¹⁷For it is better, if it is the will of God, to suffer for doing good than for doing evil.

3:15 sanctify the Lord God in your hearts. The heart is the sanctuary in which Christ prefers to be worshiped. **always be ready to give a defense.** The English word "apologetics," the defense of the Christian faith, comes from the Greek word translated "defense." Believers must understand what they believe and why they are Christians, and they must be able to articulate personal beliefs humbly, thoughtfully, reasonably, and biblically.

3:12 ᵃPsalm 34:12–16   3:14 ᵃIsaiah 8:12   3:15 ᵃNU-Text reads Christ as Lord.

How does Peter use familiar terms like "spirit," "abyss," "flood," and "baptism" in 3:18–22?

This passage proves to be one of the most difficult texts in the New Testament to translate and interpret. The line between Old Testament allusions and New Testament applications gets blurred. Peter's overall purpose of this passage, which was to encourage his readers in their suffering, must be kept in mind during interpretation. The apostle repeatedly reminded them that even Christ suffered unjustly because it was God's will (verses 17,18) and accomplished God's purposes.

Therefore, although Jesus experienced a violent physical execution that terminated His earthly life when He was "put to death in the flesh" (verse 18; Hebrews 5:7), nevertheless He was "made alive by the Spirit" (verse 18). This is not a reference to the Holy Spirit, but to Jesus' true inner life, His own spirit. Contrasted with His flesh (humanness) which was dead for three days, His spirit (deity) remained alive, literally "in spirit" (Luke 23:46).

Part of God's purpose in Christ's death involved His activities between His death and resurrection. His living spirit went to the demon spirits bound in the Abyss and proclaimed victory in spite of death. Peter further explained that the Abyss is inhabited by bound demons that have been there since the time of Noah. They were sent there because they overstepped the limits of God's tolerance with their wickedness. Not even 120 years of Noah's example and preaching had stemmed the tide of wickedness in his time (Genesis 6:1–8). Thus God bound these demons permanently in the Abyss until their final sentencing.

Peter's analogy spotlights the ministry of Jesus Christ in saving us as surely as the ark saved Noah's family. He is not referring to water baptism here but to a figurative immersion in Christ that keeps us safe from the flood of God's sure judgment. The resurrection of Christ demonstrates God's acceptance of Christ's substitutionary death for the sins of those who believer (Acts 2:30,31; Romans 1:4). God's judgment fell on Christ just as the judgment of the floodwaters fell on the ark. The believer who is in Christ is thus in the ark of safety that will sail over the waters of judgment into eternal glory (Romans 6:1–4).

Christ's Suffering and Ours

¹⁸For Christ also suffered once for sins, the just for the unjust, that He might bring us^a to God, being put to death in the flesh but made alive by the Spirit, ¹⁹by whom also He went and preached to the spirits in prison, ²⁰who formerly were disobedient, when once the Divine longsuffering waited^a in the days of Noah, while *the* ark was being prepared, in which a few, that is, eight souls, were saved through water. ²¹There is also an antitype which now saves us—baptism (not the removal of the filth of the flesh, but the answer of a good conscience toward God), through the resurrection of Jesus Christ, ²²who has gone into heaven and is at the right hand of God, angels and authorities and powers having been made subject to Him.

4 Therefore, since Christ suffered for us^a in the flesh, arm yourselves also with the same mind, for he who has suffered in the flesh has ceased from sin, ²that he no longer should live the rest of *his* time in the flesh for the lusts of men, but for the will of God. ³For we *have spent* enough of our past lifetime^a in doing the will of the Gentiles— when we walked in lewdness, lusts, drunkenness, revelries, drinking parties, and abominable idolatries. ⁴In regard to these, they think it strange that you do not run with *them* in the same flood of dissipation, speaking evil of *you*. ⁵They will give an account to Him who is ready to judge the living and the dead. ⁶For this reason the

---

3:21 baptism...through the resurrection of Jesus Christ. Peter is not referring to water baptism but to a figurative baptism into union with Christ, as an ark of safety from the judgment of God. Judgment fell on Christ just as the judgment of the flood fell on the ark. The believer who is in Christ is in the ark of safety that will sail safely over the waters of judgment into eternal glory (see Rom. 6:1–4).

4:4 they think it strange. The former friends are surprised and offended and resent the Christian's lack of interest in ungodly pleasures. **the same flood of dissipation.** "Dissipation" refers to the state of evil in which a person thinks about nothing else. This image is of a large crowd running together in a mad, wild race to pursue sin.

3:18 ^aNU-Text and M-Text read *you*.   3:20 ^aNU-Text and M-Text read *when the longsuffering of God waited patiently.*   4:1 ^aNU-Text omits *for us.*   4:3 ^aNU-Text reads *time.*

How did a fisherman like Peter write a masterpiece like this book?

Some have argued that Peter, being an uneducated fisherman (Acts 4:13), could not have written in the kind of sophisticated Greek style employed in the writing of 1 Peter. The less formal Greek of 2 Peter is then placed into evidence as proof that one person could not have written both letters.

Though superficially persuasive, these arguments do not stand up to careful scrutiny. In the first place, the fact that Peter was "unlearned" (a conclusion drawn by those who had ulterior motives in minimizing the apostle's authority), does not mean he was illiterate, but only that he was without formal, rabbinical training in the Scriptures. Moreover, though Aramaic may have been Peter's primary language, there's no particular reason to believe that he could not speak Greek, which was a widely spoken second language in Palestine. It is also apparent that at least some of the authors of the New Testament, though not highly educated, could read the Greek of the Old Testament Septuagint (Acts 15:14–18 records James quoting the LXX).

Beyond these evidences of Peter's own ability in Greek, another linguistic factor underscores Peter's authorship. He notes in 5:13 that he wrote this letter "by Silvanus," also known as Silas. The implication of this statement is that Silvanus served as his secretary, or amanuensis. Dictation was common in the ancient Roman world, and secretaries often aided with syntax and grammar. There is evidence that Paul used a similar method (Romans 16:22). Christians have long held, therefore, that Peter, under the superintendence of the Spirit of God, dictated this letter to Sylvanus. Then Sylvanus, in turn, who also was a prophet (Acts 15:32), may have aided in some of the composition of the more classical Greek.

gospel was preached also to those who are dead, that they might be judged according to men in the flesh, but live according to God in the spirit.

Serving for God's Glory

⁷But the end of all things is at hand; therefore be serious and watchful in your prayers. ⁸And above all things have fervent love for one another, for *"love will cover a multitude of sins."* ᵃ ⁹*Be* hospitable to one another without grumbling. ¹⁰As each one has received a gift, minister it to one another, as good stewards of the manifold grace of God. ¹¹If anyone speaks, *let him speak* as the oracles of God. If anyone ministers, *let him do it* as with the ability which God supplies, that in all things God may be glorified through Jesus Christ, to whom belong the glory and the dominion forever and ever. Amen.

Suffering for God's Glory

¹²Beloved, do not think it strange concerning the fiery trial which is to try you, as though some strange thing happened to you; ¹³but rejoice to the extent that you partake of Christ's sufferings, that when His glory is revealed, you may also be glad with exceeding joy. ¹⁴If you are reproached for the name of Christ, blessed *are you*, for the Spirit of glory and of God rests upon you.ᵃ On their part He is blasphemed, but on your part He is glorified. ¹⁵But let none of you suffer as a murderer, a thief, an evildoer, or as a busybody in other people's matters. ¹⁶Yet if *anyone suffers* as a Christian, let him not be ashamed, but let him glorify God in this matter.ᵃ

¹⁷For the time *has come* for judgment to begin at the house of God; and if *it begins*

with us first, what will *be* the end of those who do not obey the gospel of God? ¹⁸Now

> *"If the righteous one is scarcely saved,*
> *Where will the ungodly and the sinner*
> *appear?"* ᵃ

¹⁹Therefore let those who suffer according to the will of God commit their souls *to Him* in doing good, as to a faithful Creator.

Shepherd the Flock

5 The elders who are among you I exhort, I who am a fellow elder and a witness of the sufferings of Christ, and also a partaker of the glory that will be revealed: ²Shepherd the flock of God which is among you, serving as overseers, not by compulsion but willingly,ᵃ not for dishonest gain but eagerly; ³nor as being lords over those entrusted to you, but being examples to the flock; ⁴and when the Chief Shepherd appears, you will receive the crown of glory that does not fade away.

5:2 Shepherd the flock of God. Shepherding involves feeding and protecting. The flock belongs to God, not to the pastor. God entrusts some of His flock to a pastor to lead, nurture, and feed (teach). **not by compulsion but willingly.** Peter may be warning the elders against laziness. The divine calling should prevent laziness and indifference (see 2 Cor. 9:7).

Submit to God, Resist the Devil

⁵Likewise you younger people, submit yourselves to *your* elders. Yes, all of *you* be submissive to one another, and be clothed with humility, for

> *"God resists the proud,*
> *But gives grace to the humble."* ᵃ

⁶Therefore humble yourselves under the mighty hand of God, that He may exalt you in due time, ⁷casting all your care upon Him, for He cares for you.

⁸Be sober, be vigilant; becauseᵃ your adversary the devil walks about like a roaring lion, seeking whom he may devour. ⁹Resist him, steadfast in the faith, knowing that

---

4:12 the fiery trial. Peter probably wrote this letter shortly before or after the burning of Rome and at the beginning of a 200-year period of Christian persecution. He explains that in order for Christians to be triumphant in persecution, they must expect it, rejoice in it, evaluate its cause, and entrust it to God. **some strange thing happened.** God allows persecution to test, purge, and cleanse the believer.

4:8 ᵃProverbs 10:12   4:14 ᵃNU-Text omits the rest of this verse.   4:16 ᵃNU-Text reads *name.*
4:18 ᵃProverbs 11:31   5:2 ᵃNU-Text adds *according to God.*   5:5 ᵃProverbs 3:34   5:8 ᵃNU-Text and M-Text omit *because.*

5:7 casting all your care upon Him. This verse partly quotes and partly interprets Ps. 55:22. To cast is to throw something upon something else. Christians are to cast their discontentment, discouragement, despair, and suffering on the Lord and to trust Him and His plan for their lives (see 1 Sam. 1:10–18). Along with submission and humility, trust in God is the third attitude necessary for victorious Christian living.

the same sufferings are experienced by your brotherhood in the world. [10]But may[a] the God of all grace, who called us[b] to His eternal glory by Christ Jesus, after you have suffered a while, perfect, establish, strengthen, and settle *you.* [11]To Him *be* the glory and the dominion forever and ever. Amen.

Farewell and Peace

[12]By Silvanus, our faithful brother as I consider him, I have written to you briefly, exhorting and testifying that this is the true grace of God in which you stand.

[13]She who is in Babylon, elect together with *you,* greets you; and *so does* Mark my son. [14]Greet one another with a kiss of love.

Peace to you all who are in Christ Jesus. Amen.

5:13 She who is in Babylon. This refers to a church in Rome (see 2 John 1,13; Rev. 17,18). **Mark my son.** Mark, called John Mark, was Peter's spiritual son. Tradition indicates that Peter helped him write the Gospel of Mark (see Acts 12:12). This is the same Mark who once failed Paul (Acts 13:13), but he later was restored into valuable ministry (2 Tim. 4:11).

5:10 [a]NU-Text reads *But the God of all grace . . . will perfect, establish, strengthen, and settle you.* [b]NU-Text and M-Text read *you.*

2 PETER

Peter's last written message has much of the warmth, concern and passion that fills the pages of Paul's final letter (2 Timothy). These great men of the faith knew their days were numbered. Peter was keenly aware of the warfare between good and evil that would outlast his life (1:12–15). He wanted to leave a strong dose of equipping and encouraging for those believers who would remain. The hope of Christ's coming consistently shines through in the background of his letter. Among his closing thoughts were these words: "Therefore, beloved, looking forward to these things, be diligent to be found by Him in peace, without spot and blameless" (3:14).

AUTHOR AND DATE

Second Peter was written by Peter, about A.D. 67 to 68.

A number of internal references point to authorship of this letter by the Apostle Peter. The first verse of the epistle states the claim. In 1:14, he refers to the Lord's unique prediction of his own death (John 21:18,19). In 1:16–18, the author claims to have been present at the Transfiguration of Christ (Matthew 17:1–4). Later, in 3:1, Peter refers to his earlier letter (1 Peter).

It must be noted, however, that critics have generated more controversy over 2 Peter's authorship and rightful place in the canon of Scripture than over any other New Testament book. True, the church fathers were slow in giving the letter their acceptance. No church father refers to 2 Peter by name until Origen near the beginning of the third century. The ancient church historian Eusebius grouped 2 Peter with several other disputed books: James, Jude, 2 John, and 3 John. To this it must be responded that 2 Peter has not been questioned about the orthodoxy of its contents. There was no shortage in the early church of documents falsely claiming to be written by Peter. It is not surprising that even a genuine epistle from the apostle received added scrutiny.

Much has been made over the differences in style between 1 Peter and 2 Peter. Most of these difficulties can be resolved by recognizing a difference in themes and methods of composition for each letter. First Peter was written to help suffering Christians; 2 Peter aimed at exposing false teachers. The earlier was admittedly written with the aid of a secretary (amanuensis; 1 Peter 5:12); the later used a different secretary or was written by Peter himself. The two letters contain significant vocabulary similarities. For more details about the differences between the two letters, see the FAQ entitled *"How can two letters (1 and 2 Peter) from the same author be so different in style?"*

Finally, it appears irrational that a false teacher would spuriously write a letter against false teachers. No unusual, new, or false doctrines appear in this book, so if it were a forgery, it would be a forgery written by a fool for no reason at all. This is too much to believe. The conclusion to the question of authorship is that when the writer introduced the letter and referred to himself as Peter, he was writing the truth.

Nero died in A.D. 68, and tradition says Peter died during Nero's persecution. The epistle may have been written shortly before his death (1:14; around A.D. 67–68).

BACKGROUND AND SETTING

Since writing and sending his first letter, Peter had become increasingly concerned about false teachers who were infiltrating the churches in Asia Minor. Though these false teachers had already caused trouble, Peter expected that their heretical doctrines and immoral life-styles would result in more damage in the future. Thus Peter, in an almost last will and testament (1:13–15), wrote to warn the beloved believers in Christ about the doctrinal dangers they would facing. Although Peter mentioned no specific recipients in the salutation of the letter, later reference to his earlier letter (3:2) indicates he was writing to the same people who had received his earlier letter.

Peter does not explicitly say where he was when he wrote this letter, as he does in 1 Peter (1 Peter 5:13). But the consensus seems to be that he wrote this letter from prison in Rome, where he was facing imminent death. Shortly after writing this letter, Peter was martyred, according to reliable tradition, by being crucified upside down.

HISTORICAL AND THEOLOGICAL THEMES

Second Peter was written for the purpose of exposing, thwarting, and defeating the invasion of false teachers into the church. Peter intended to instruct Christians in how to defend themselves against these false teachers and their deceptive lies. This book is the most graphic and penetrating exposé of false teachers in Scripture, comparable only to Jude.

THIS BOOK IS THE MOST GRAPHIC AND PENETRATING EXPOSÉ OF FALSE TEACHERS IN SCRIPTURE.

Other encouraging themes can be discerned in the midst of Peter's polemic against the false teachers:

1. He wanted to motivate his readers to continue to develop their Christian character (1:5–11).

2. He reminded his readers how a believer can have assurance of salvation (1:5–11).

3. He wanted to persuade the believers about the divine character of the apostolic writings (1:12–21).

4. He presented reasons for the delay in Christ's second coming (3:1–13).

One key word in the epistle is "knowledge." That word appears in some form sixteen times in these three short chapters. It is not too much to say that Peter's primary solution to false teaching is knowledge of true doctrine.

OUTLINE

I. **SALUTATION (1:1,2)**

II. **KNOW YOUR SALVATION (1:3–11)**
- A. Sustained by God's Power (1:3,4)
- B. Confirmed by Christian Graces (1:5–7)
- C. Honored by Abundant Reward (1:8–11)

III. **KNOW YOUR SCRIPTURES (1:12–21)**
- A. Certified by Apostolic Witness (1:12–18)
- B. Inspired by the Holy Spirit (1:19–21)

IV. **KNOW YOUR ADVERSARIES (2:1–22)**
- A. Deceptive in Their Infiltration (2:1–3)
- B. Doomed by Their Iniquity (2:4–10a)
- C. Disdainful in Their Impurity (2:10b–17)
- D. Devastating in Their Impact (2:18–22)

V. **KNOW YOUR PROPHECY (3:1–18)**
- A. The Sureness of the Day of the Lord (3:1–10)
- B. The Sanctification of God's People (3:11–18)

Greeting the Faithful

1 Simon Peter, a bondservant and apostle of Jesus Christ,

To those who have obtained like precious faith with us by the righteousness of our God and Savior Jesus Christ:

[2]Grace and peace be multiplied to you in the knowledge of God and of Jesus our Lord, [3]as His divine power has given to us all things that *pertain* to life and godliness, through the knowledge of Him who called us by glory and virtue, [4]by which have been given to us exceedingly great and precious promises, that through these you may be partakers of the divine nature, having escaped the corruption *that is* in the world through lust.

> **1:4 exceedingly great and precious promises.** These are the promises of abundant, eternal life. **partakers of the divine nature.** Because of the precious promises of salvation, we can become God's children in the present age (John 1:12) and thus share in His nature and eternal life. Christians will partake of the divine nature even more when they receive their glorified bodies, like Jesus Christ (Phil. 3:20,21).

Fruitful Growth in the Faith

[5]But also for this very reason, giving all diligence, add to your faith virtue, to virtue knowledge, [6]to knowledge self-control, to self-control perseverance, to perseverance godliness, [7]to godliness brotherly kindness, and to brotherly kindness love. [8]For if these things are yours and abound, *you will be* neither barren nor unfruitful in the knowledge of our Lord Jesus Christ. [9]For he who lacks these things is shortsighted, even to blindness, and has forgotten that he was cleansed from his old sins.

> **1:8 neither barren.** To be barren is to be inactive, lazy, and useless (see Titus 1:12). A Christian will not be barren if the virtues of vv. 5–7 are displayed in his life. **nor unfruitful.** When these qualities are absent from a believer's life, he will be indistinguishable from an evildoer or superficial believer. But when these qualities increase in a Christian's life, the "divine nature" is manifested in him.

[10]Therefore, brethren, be even more diligent to make your call and election sure, for if you do these things you will never stumble; [11]for so an entrance will be supplied to you abundantly into the everlasting kingdom of our Lord and Savior Jesus Christ.

Peter's Approaching Death

[12]For this reason I will not be negligent to remind you always of these things, though you know and are established in the present truth. [13]Yes, I think it is right, as long as I am in this tent, to stir you up by reminding *you,* [14]knowing that shortly I *must* put off my tent, just as our Lord Jesus Christ showed me. [15]Moreover I will be careful to ensure that you always have a reminder of these things after my decease.

The Trustworthy Prophetic Word

[16]For we did not follow cunningly devised fables when we made known to you the power and coming of our Lord Jesus Christ,

> **1:16 cunningly devised fables.** Fables are mythical stories about gods and miracles (see 1 Tim. 1:4). Peter gave evidences in the following verses to prove that he wrote the truth of God, because he knew that the false leaders and their followers would try to discredit his letter. Most likely, he had already been accused of concocting fables and myths in order to get people to follow him.

Q What does Peter mean by the counsel to "make your call and election sure" (2 Peter 1:10)?

A This phrase hits the theological bull's-eye at which Peter was aiming in 1:5–9. Though God is "sure" who His elect are and has given them an eternally secure salvation (1 Peter 1:1–5; Romans 8:31–39), the Christian might not always have inward assurance of personal salvation. Security is the fact revealed by the Holy Spirit that salvation lasts forever. Assurance is one's confidence that he possesses that eternal salvation. In other words, the believer who pursues the spiritual qualities mentioned in the context of this phrase will guarantee to himself by spiritual fruit that he was called (Romans 8:30; 1 Peter 2:21) and chosen (1 Peter 1:2) by God to salvation.

but were eyewitnesses of His majesty. [17]For He received from God the Father honor and glory when such a voice came to Him from the Excellent Glory: "This is My beloved Son, in whom I am well pleased." [18]And we heard this voice which came from heaven when we were with Him on the holy mountain.

[19]And so we have the prophetic word confirmed,[a] which you do well to heed as a light that shines in a dark place, until the day dawns and the morning star rises in your hearts; [20]knowing this first, that no prophecy of Scripture is of any private interpretation,[a] [21]for prophecy never came by the will of man, but holy men of God[a] spoke *as they were* moved by the Holy Spirit.

> **1:20 private interpretation.** The Greek word for "interpretation" has connotations of "loosing," and in this context Peter is saying that no Scripture came from any man privately "untying" and "loosing" the truth. Peter focuses on how Scripture originated and on its original source. The false prophets untied and loosed their own ideas. But no part of God's revelation came from an unaided human source, but from God Himself.

1:19 [a]Or *We also have the more sure prophetic word.*   1:20 [a]Or *origin*   1:21 [a]NU-Text reads *but men spoke from God.*

How does Peter explain the doctrine of the inspiration of Scripture (2 Peter 1:19–21)?

This particular section of 2 Peter provides crucial insights regarding the nature and authenticity of Scripture. Even the apostle expected his readers to provide a reasonable defense for their confidence in the Scriptures. He realized that false teachers would attempt to discredit his letter as well as his past ministry, and he countered their arguments. He knew they would accuse him of concocting fables and myths as a way to manipulate his audience. (This charge by the false teachers actually revealed their own approach and purpose.) So, Peter gave evidence in this passage to prove that he wrote the truth of God as a genuinely inspired writer.

He begins by reporting his role with the other disciples as "eyewitnesses of His majesty" (verse 16). This general claim becomes specific when Peter describes his own participation in the Transfiguration of Christ (Matthew 16:28). In that event, God not only confirmed the divine nature of His Son, but also confirmed the Old Testament Scriptures as accurate in their prophetic statements and by extension provided the disciples with the authoritative source for their teaching. Peter implied that there was no reason to believe the false teachers who denied the majesty and second coming of Christ, since they were not on the Mount of Transfiguration to see the preview of the kingdom and glory of Christ, as were he, James and John.

Peter then comes to the details of the process of inspiration. Scripture, claims Peter, is not of human origin. Neither is Scripture the result of human will (1:21). The emphasis in this phrase is that no part of Scripture was produced solely because men wanted it so. The Bible is not the product of sheer human effort. The prophets, in fact, often wrote what they could not understand (1 Peter 1:10,11), but were nevertheless faithful to write what God revealed to them.

Instead of relying on their own purposes, men were "moved by the Holy Spirit" (1:21) to write. Grammatically, this means that they were continually carried or borne along by the Spirit of God (Luke 1:70; Acts 27:15,17). Thus the Holy Spirit is the divine author and originator, the producer of the Scriptures. In the Old Testament alone, the human writers refer to their writings as the words of God over 3800 times (Jeremiah 1:4; 3:2; Romans 3:2; 1 Corinthians 2:10). Though the human writers were active rather than passive in the process of writing Scripture, God the Holy Spirit superintended them so that, using their own individual personalities, thought processes, and vocabulary, they composed and recorded without error the exact words God wanted written. The original documents of Scripture are therefore inspired (God-breathed; 2 Timothy 3:16), and inerrant (without error; John 10:34,35; 17:17; Titus 1:2). Peter here has described the process of inspiration that created an inerrant original text (Proverbs 30:5; 1 Corinthians 14:36; 1 Thessalonians 2:13).

Destructive Doctrines

2 But there were also false prophets among the people, even as there will be false teachers among you, who will secretly bring in destructive heresies, even denying the Lord who bought them, *and* bring on themselves swift destruction. ²And many will follow their destructive ways, because of whom the way of truth will be blasphemed. ³By covetousness they will exploit you with deceptive words; for a long time their judgment has not been idle, and their destruction does*ᵃ* not slumber.

Doom of False Teachers

⁴For if God did not spare the angels who sinned, but cast *them* down to hell and delivered *them* into chains of darkness, to be

2:4 the angels who sinned. Referring to the fallen angels before the flood and before the destruction of Sodom and Gomorrah (see Gen. 6:1–3; 19). **chains of darkness.** The demons feared going there and begged Jesus not to send them there (see Matt. 8:29). Not all demons are bound. Many roam the heavens and the earth (see Rev. 12:7–9).

reserved for judgment; ⁵and did not spare the ancient world, but saved Noah, *one of* eight *people,* a preacher of righteousness, bringing in the flood on the world of the ungodly; ⁶and turning the cities of Sodom and Gomorrah into ashes, condemned *them* to destruction, making *them* an example to those who afterward would live ungodly; ⁷and delivered righteous Lot, *who was* oppressed by the filthy conduct of the

How can two letters (1 and 2 Peter) from the same author be so different in style?

The differences between 1 Peter and 2 Peter fall in three areas: (1) style; (2) vocabulary; and (3) theme. These differences must be resolved, for the author of 2 Peter clearly claims to also have been the author of 1 Peter (2 Peter 3:2).

Questions about the difference in Greek style between the two letters can be satisfactorily answered. Peter reported that he used a secretary (amanuensis), Silvanus, in writing 1 Peter (5:12). When he wrote 2 Peter, the apostle either used a different secretary, or took up a pen himself. These methods of composition were not unusual in ancient times. Paul occasionally used an amanuensis (Romans 16:22). The role of a secretary or scribe did not cast doubt on the origin of the contents of writing.

Alongside the questions about style in these two letters come queries about differences in vocabulary. The doubts raised seem strained. Most of the vocabulary differences can be easily answered by noting the difference in themes between the two letters. But beyond this, the very questions seem contrived. There are remarkable similarities in vocabulary and usage between the two epistles. The salutation, "grace to you and peace be multiplied," is essentially the same in each book. The author uses such words as "precious," "virtue," "putting off," and "eyewitness," to name just a few examples, in both letters. Certain rather unusual words found in 2 Peter are also found in Peter's speeches in Acts. These include "obtained" (1:2; Acts 1:17), "godliness" (1:3,6,7; 3:11; Acts 3:12), and "wages of iniquity" (2:13,15; Acts 1:18). Both letters also refer to the same Old Testament event (1 Peter 3:18–20; 2 Peter 2:5). Some scholars have pointed out that there are as many similarities and differences in vocabulary between 1 and 2 Peter as there are between 1 Timothy and Titus, two letters almost universally believed to have been written by Paul.

The differences in theme also explain many of the differences between 1 and 2 Peter. One letter emphasizes that the second coming is near, while the other points to its possible delay. First Peter, ministering especially to suffering Christians, focuses on the imminency of Christ as a means of encouraging the Christians. Second Peter, dealing with scoffers, emphasizes the reasons why that imminent return of Christ has not yet occurred. Other proposed differences, such as the supposed contradiction between the Resurrection of Christ in one letter and the Transfiguration of Christ in the other, seem invented by critics to validate their determination to doubt.

wicked [8](for that righteous man, dwelling among them, tormented *his* righteous soul from day to day by seeing and hearing *their* lawless deeds)—[9]*then* the Lord knows how to deliver the godly out of temptations and to reserve the unjust under punishment for the day of judgment, [10]and especially those who walk according to the flesh in the lust of uncleanness and despise authority. *They are* presumptuous, self-willed. They are not afraid to speak evil of dignitaries, [11]whereas angels, who are greater in power and might, do not bring a reviling accusation against them before the Lord.

2:9 to deliver the godly out of temptations. The Greek word for "temptations" can mean, "to attack with intent to destroy" (see Mark 8:11). It refers to severe, divine judgment. God's plan is to rescue the godly before His judgment falls on the wicked. **to reserve the unjust.** The wicked are kept like prisoners awaiting the sentence that will send them to their eternal prison. The final judgment on them is called the Great White Throne Judgment (Rev. 20:11–15).

Depravity of False Teachers

[12]But these, like natural brute beasts made to be caught and destroyed, speak evil of the things they do not understand, and will utterly perish in their own corruption, [13]*and* will receive the wages of unrighteousness, *as* those who count it pleasure to carouse in the daytime. *They are* spots and blemishes, carousing in their own decep-

tions while they feast with you, [14]having eyes full of adultery and that cannot cease from sin, enticing unstable souls. *They have* a heart trained in covetous practices, *and are* accursed children. [15]They have forsaken the right way and gone astray, following the way of Balaam the *son* of Beor, who loved the wages of unrighteousness; [16]but he was rebuked for his iniquity: a dumb donkey speaking with a man's voice restrained the madness of the prophet.

[17]These are wells without water, clouds[a] carried by a tempest, for whom is reserved the blackness of darkness forever.[b]

2:17 wells without water. A well without water would be a great disappointment in the hot, dry Middle East. Likewise, false teachers have a pretense of spiritual water to quench the thirsty soul, but they actually have nothing to offer. **clouds carried by a tempest.** Clouds seem to promise rain, but the land remains hot and dry when the storm blows them past. The false teachers seemed to promise spiritual refreshment, but they had no substance (see Jude 12). **the blackness of darkness.** This is hell (see Matt. 8:12).

Deceptions of False Teachers

[18]For when they speak great swelling *words* of emptiness, they allure through the lusts of the flesh, through lewdness, the ones who have actually escaped[a] from those who live in error. [19]While they promise them liberty, they themselves are slaves

2:17 [a]NU-Text reads *and mists.* [b]NU-Text omits *forever.*   2:18 [a]NU-Text reads *are barely escaping.*

Who were the false teachers in the early church that Peter addressed in 2 Peter?

Second Peter offers the most graphic and penetrating exposé of false teachers in Scripture, comparable only to Jude. Peter does not identify a specific false religion, cult, or system of teaching. He is more concerned with general principles of recognizing and resisting false instruction in the church.

In his broadest characterization of false teachers, Peter points out that they teach destructive heresies. They deny Christ and twist the Scriptures. They bring true faith into disrepute. They mock the second coming of Christ. It is not too much to claim that Peter's primary response to false teaching is knowledge of true doctrine. Falsehoods may come in a variety of shades, but they stand revealed as wrong when compared with the truth.

Peter was just as concerned to show the immoral character of false teachers as he was to expose their teaching. He describes them in more detail than their doctrine. He knows the quality of fruit reveals the soundness of the tree. Wickedness is not the product of sound doctrine, but of "destructive heresies" (2:1). Instead, Peter urges Christians to pursue a deliberate plan of spiritual growth (1:5–9), allowing a life of integrity to expose what is false.

of corruption; for by whom a person is overcome, by him also he is brought into bondage. ²⁰For if, after they have escaped the pollutions of the world through the knowledge of the Lord and Savior Jesus Christ, they are again entangled in them and overcome, the latter end is worse for them than the beginning. ²¹For it would have been better for them not to have known the way of righteousness, than having known *it*, to turn from the holy commandment delivered to them. ²²But it has happened to them according to the true proverb: *"A dog returns to his own vomit,"*ᵃ and, *"a sow, having washed, to her wallowing in the mire."*

God's Promise Is Not Slack

3 Beloved, I now write to you this second epistle (in *both of* which I stir up your pure minds by way of reminder), ²that you may be mindful of the words which were spoken before by the holy prophets, and of the commandment of us,ᵃ the apostles of the Lord and Savior, ³knowing this first: that scoffers will come in the last days,

> **3:2 holy prophets.** The Old Testament prophets were holy in contrast to the false teachers. Those prophets wrote God's Word and warned of the approaching judgment and the coming of the Lord (see Is. 13:10–13; Zech. 14:1–9). **the commandment of us.** Peter is referring to the warnings that he and the other apostles had written concerning judgment (Jude 17).

walking according to their own lusts, ⁴and saying, "Where is the promise of His coming? For since the fathers fell asleep, all things continue as *they were* from the beginning of creation." ⁵For this they willfully forget: that by the word of God the heavens were of old, and the earth standing out of water and in the water, ⁶by which the world *that* then existed perished, being flooded with water. ⁷But the heavens and the earth *which* are now preserved by the same word, are reserved for fire until the day of judgment and perdition of ungodly men.

> **3:7 are now preserved by the same word.** The heavens and the earth will be judged in the future, destroyed by fire. Just as God initiated the creation and the flood with a word, so He will speak the future heavens and earth into existence after the judgment. **reserved for fire.** In the future, God will destroy the heavens and the earth by fire (see Is. 66:15). The whole creation is a potential fire bomb due to its atomic structure.

⁸But, beloved, do not forget this one thing, that with the Lord one day *is* as a thousand years, and a thousand years as one day. ⁹The Lord is not slack concerning *His* promise, as some count slackness, but is longsuffering toward us,ᵃ not willing that any should perish but that all should come to repentance.

The Day of the Lord

¹⁰But the day of the Lord will come as a thief in the night, in which the heavens will

---

2:22 ᵃProverbs 26:11   3:2 ᵃNU-Text and M-Text read *commandment of the apostles of your Lord and Savior* or *commandment of your apostles of the Lord and Savior.*   3:9 ᵃNU-Text reads *you.*

How does the phrase "with the Lord one day is as a thousand years, and a thousand years as one day" (2 Peter 3:8) affect our understanding of God's plan?

God understands time much differently from man. From man's viewpoint, Christ's coming seems like a long time away (Psalm 90:4). From God's viewpoint, it will not be long. Peter reminds his readers of this fact before pointing out that any delay in Christ's return from the human perspective should never be taken as an indication that God is loitering or late. The passage of time actually is a clearer signal of God's immense capacity for patience before He breaks forth in judgment (Joel 2:13; Luke 15:20; Romans 9:22; 1 Peter 3:15).

Beyond that general frame of reference, this text may be a specific indication of the fact that there are actually 1,000 years between the first phase of the Day of the Lord at the end of the Tribulation (Revelation 6:17), and the second phase 1,000 years later at the end of the millennial kingdom when the Lord creates the new heaven and new earth.

pass away with a great noise, and the elements will melt with fervent heat; both the earth and the works that are in it will be burned up.*ᵃ* ¹¹Therefore, since all these things will be dissolved, what manner *of persons* ought you to be in holy conduct and godliness, ¹²looking for and hastening the coming of the day of God, because of which the heavens will be dissolved, being on fire, and the elements will melt with fervent heat? ¹³Nevertheless we, according to His promise, look for new heavens and a new earth in which righteousness dwells.

> **3:12 looking for and hastening.** Expectation is a motive for holy and godly living. Christians are not to fear the future day of God, but to eagerly hope for it (see 1 Cor. 1:7). **the day of God.** Different from the "Day of the Lord," which is the day of judgment, "the day of God" refers to the eternal state, after the heavens and earth have been burned and the new creation is in place. When the day of God comes, the universe that Satan and humans have corrupted will have been judged and destroyed.

Be Steadfast

¹⁴Therefore, beloved, looking forward to these things, be diligent to be found by Him in peace, without spot and blameless; ¹⁵and consider *that* the longsuffering of our Lord *is* salvation—as also our beloved brother Paul, according to the wisdom given to him, has written to you, ¹⁶as also in all his epistles, speaking in them of these things, in which are some things hard to understand, which untaught and unstable *people* twist to their own destruction, as *they do* also the rest of the Scriptures.

¹⁷You therefore, beloved, since you know *this* beforehand, beware lest you also fall from your own steadfastness, being led away with the error of the wicked; ¹⁸but grow in the grace and knowledge of our Lord and Savior Jesus Christ.

To Him *be* the glory both now and forever. Amen.

> **3:17 know this beforehand.** Since Christians know that there will be false teachers who will twist and distort the Scriptures, they should be on their guard. **beware lest you also fall.** Anytime a believer listens to a false teacher, he runs the risk of being led astray (see 2 Tim. 2:14–18).

3:10 *ᵃ*NU-Text reads *laid bare* (literally *found*).

If the Lord is "not willing that any should perish" (2 Peter 3:9), why does it appear that many will have that very end?

The "any" in this passage must refer to those whom the Lord has chosen and will call to complete the redeemed, the "us" mentioned above in the same verse. Since the whole passage is about God's destroying the wicked, His patience is not so He can save all of them, but so that He can receive all of His own. He can't be waiting for everyone to be saved, since the emphasis is that He will destroy the world and the ungodly. Those who do perish and go to hell, go because they are depraved and worthy only of hell. They have rejected the only remedy, Jesus Christ, not because they were created for hell and predetermined to go there. The path to damnation is the path of a non-repentant heart; it is the path of one who rejects the person and provision of Jesus Christ and holds on to sin (Isaiah 55:1; Jeremiah 13:17; Ezekiel 18:32; Matthew 11:28; 13:37; Luke 13:3; John 3:16; 8:21,24; 1 Timothy 2:3,4; Revelation 22:17).

The "all" which begins the next phrase, "but that all should come to repentance," must refer to all who are God's people who will come to Christ to make up the full number of the people of God. The reason for the delay in Christ's coming and the attendant judgments is not because He is slow to keep His promise, or because He wants to judge more of the wicked, or because He is impotent in the face of wickedness. He delays His coming because He is patient and desires the time for His people to repent.

What do Peter's comments about Paul's writings mean (2 Peter 3:15,16)?

In the final thoughts of his letter, Peter turns for biblical support to the writings of Paul. Since Paul had (by the time Peter wrote) written all his letters and died, the readers of 2 Peter would have already received letters about future events from Paul. Some of Paul's explanations were difficult (but not impossible) to interpret. Nevertheless, Peter does not hesitate to use Paul as a support for his own teaching.

Peter then goes on to add a word of caution in pointing out that there were those willing to "twist" (3:16) and pervert the apostolic teaching about the future. The fact that distorting Paul's writings leads to eternal damnation proves that God inspired Paul's writings. Peter's further addition of the phrase, "the rest of the Scriptures" (3:16), offers one of the most clear-cut statements in the Bible to affirm that the writings of Paul are Scripture. Peter's testimony is that Paul wrote Scripture, but the false teachers distorted it. The New Testament apostles were aware that they spoke and wrote the Word of God (1 Thessalonians 2:13) as surely as did the Old Testament prophets. Peter affirmed that the New Testament writers compiled the divine truth that completed the Bible (1 Peter 1:10–12).

1 JOHN

The Apostle John made a significant contribution to the New Testament with five books (Gospel of John, 1, 2, and 3 John, and Revelation). His writing represents a wider variety than that of any of the other authors. He composed a gospel, three letters and a lengthy prophetic work. The purpose of John's gospel was "that you may believe that Jesus is the Christ, the Son of God, and that believing you may have life in His name" (John 20:31). First John serves like a cover letter for the Gospel of John, filled with practical ways to live out the Christian life that begins by believing in Jesus.

AUTHOR AND DATE

First John was written by John in about A.D. 90 to 95.

The epistle does not identify the author, but the strong, consistent, and earliest testimony of the church ascribes it to John the disciple and apostle (Luke 6:13,14). This anonymity strongly affirms the early church's identification of the epistle as John's, for only someone with his well-known and preeminent status as an apostle would be able to write with such unmistakable authority. The author expected complete obedience from his readers even without clearly identifying himself (4:6). He and his message were so well known to the readers that he didn't need to mention his own name.

John and James, his older brother (Acts 12:2), were known as "the sons of Zebedee" (Matthew 10:2–4). Jesus also called them "Sons of Thunder" (Mark 3:17). John was one of the three most intimate associates of Jesus (along with Peter and James—Matthew 17:1; 26:37). He was an eyewitness and participant in Jesus' earthly ministry from the start, which explains the intimate tone of the opening of this letter (1:1–4). In addition to the three epistles, John also authored the fourth gospel, in which he identified himself as the disciple "whom Jesus loved" and as the one who reclined on Jesus' breast during the Last Supper (John 13:23; 19:26; 20:2; 21:7,20). He also wrote the book of Revelation (Revelation 1:1).

Precise dating is difficult because 1 John includes no clear historical indications to assist that process. Church tradition maintains that John was alive and actively writing from Ephesus in Asia Minor in the latter part of the first century. Similarities in vocabulary and tone have led many to suggest that John's Gospel and this letter were written about the same time. Since no mention is made of the persecution under Emperor Domitian, which began about A.D. 95, it seems reasonable to assign a date for the composition of 1 John of about A.D. 90–95.

Although he was advanced in age when he penned this epistle, John was still actively ministering to churches in and around Ephesus in Asia Minor. By then, he was the sole remaining apostolic survivor who had an intimate, eyewitness association with Jesus throughout His earthly ministry, death, resurrection, and ascension. The church fathers indicate that John eventually settled in Ephesus. There he gave oversight to many churches, conducted an extensive evangelistic program, and wrote much of his contribution to the New Testament. One church father (Papias), who had direct contact with John, described him as a "living and abiding voice." As the last remaining apostle, John's testimony was highly authoritative among Christians at the end of the first century.

Ephesus (Acts 19:10) lay within the intellectual center of Asia Minor. As predicted years before by the Apostle Paul (Acts 20:28–31), false teachers had risen from within the church's own ranks. These leaders, saturated with the prevailing climate of philosophical trends, began infecting the church with false doctrine, perverting fundamental apostolic teaching. These false teachers advocated new ideas that eventually became known as "Gnosticism" (from the Greek work "knowledge"). Second only to the battle over the influence of legalistic Judaism in the early church, Gnosticism was the most dangerous heresy that threatened the church during the first three centuries. Most likely, John was combating the early strains of that virulent heresy. Since even the primitive forms of this false teaching were spiritually lethal, John took action. With gentleness and love, but with unquestionable apostolic authority, he sent this letter to churches in his sphere of influence to stem this spreading plague of false doctrine. For more on Gnosticism, see the FAQ entitled *"How does 1 John help us understand some of the destructive teaching that attacked Christianity in the first century?"*

In light of the circumstances of the epistle, the central theme of 1 John is "a recall to the fundamentals of the faith" or "back to the basics of Christianity." The apostle deals with certainties, not opinions or conjecture. He expresses the absolute character of Christianity in simple, clear, and unmistakable terms. He leaves no doubt as to the fundamental nature of those truths.

> JOHN EXPRESSES THE ABSOLUTE CHARACTER OF CHRISTIANITY IN SIMPLE, CLEAR, AND UNMISTAKABLE TERMS.

The tone of First John is pastoral, written from the heart of a pastor who has concerns for his people. As a shepherd, John used a warm, conversational, and loving approach to communicate to his flock. He imparted vitally essential principles regarding the basics of the faith. He desired them to have a joyful certainty in their faith rather than being upset by the false teaching and current defections of some (1:4).

John's letter also includes a strong dose of positive and negative polemics. He refutes the defectors with sound doctrine, exhibiting no tolerance for those who pervert divine truth. He labels those departing from the truth as "false prophets" (4:1), "those who try to deceive" (2:26; 3:7), and "antichrists" (2:18). He pointedly identifies the ultimate source of all such defection from sound doctrine as demonic (4:1–7).

A continuous repetition of three sub-themes reinforces the central theme regarding faithfulness to the basics of Christianity: (1) happiness (1:4); (2) holiness (2:1); and (3) security (5:13). Faithfulness to the basics will yield these three results. The basics are also summarized by a three-part cycle of true spirituality in 1 John: (1) a proper belief in Jesus produces (2) obedience to His commands, which in turn produces (3) love for God and fellow believers (3:23,24). When these three (sound faith, obedience, love) operate in concert, they result in happiness, holiness and assurance. They constitute the evidence, the litmus test of a true Christian.

OUTLINE

What Was Heard, Seen, and Touched

1 That which was from the beginning, which we have heard, which we have seen with our eyes, which we have looked upon, and our hands have handled, concerning the Word of life—²the life was manifested, and we have seen, and bear witness, and declare to you that eternal life which was with the Father and was manifested to us—³that which we have seen and heard we declare to you, that you also may have fellowship with us; and truly our fellowship *is* with the Father and with His Son Jesus Christ. ⁴And these things we write to you that your*ᵃ* joy may be full.

> **1:1 from the beginning.** This phrase refers to the beginnings of the gospel preaching, when the readers first heard about Jesus. It also emphasizes the stability of the gospel message; its content never changes, and it is not affected by worldly fads or philosophical thinking. **we have heard...we have seen...we have looked upon...our hands have handled.** John, 60 years later, is remembering the person of Jesus.

Fellowship with Him and One Another

⁵This is the message which we have heard from Him and declare to you, that God is light and in Him is no darkness at all. ⁶If we say that we have fellowship with Him, and walk in darkness, we lie and do not practice the truth. ⁷But if we walk in the light as He is in the light, we have fellowship with one another, and the blood of Jesus Christ His Son cleanses us from all sin.

⁸If we say that we have no sin, we deceive ourselves, and the truth is not in us. ⁹If we confess our sins, He is faithful and just to forgive us *our* sins and to cleanse us from all unrighteousness. ¹⁰If we say that we have not sinned, we make Him a liar, and His word is not in us.

> **1:10 make Him a liar.** Since God has said that all people are sinners, to deny that fact is to blaspheme God and to defame His name (see Ps. 14:3; Rom. 3:10–19,23).

2 My little children, these things I write to you, so that you may not sin. And if anyone sins, we have an Advocate with the Father, Jesus Christ the righteous. ²And He Himself is the propitiation for our sins, and not for ours only but also for the whole world.

The Test of Knowing Him

³Now by this we know that we know Him, if we keep His commandments. ⁴He who says, "I know Him," and does not keep His commandments, is a liar, and the truth is not in him. ⁵But whoever keeps His word, truly the love of God is perfected in him. By this we know that we are in Him. ⁶He who says he abides in Him ought himself also to walk just as He walked.

What does confession have to do with gaining forgiveness in 1 John 1:9?

The false teachers that John was resisting shared a characteristic with many modern people. They walked in spiritual darkness (sin) but went so far as to deny the existence of a sin nature in their lives. If someone never admits to being a sinner, salvation cannot result (see Matthew 19:16–22 for the account of the young man who refused to recognize his sin). Confession (admission of sin) is like opening a hand to release an object; once the spirit opens, it can now receive forgiveness.

Continual confession of sin is an indication of genuine salvation. While the false teachers would not admit their sin, the genuine Christians admitted and forsook it (Psalm 32:3–5; Proverbs 28:13). The term "confess" means to say the same thing about sin that God says, to acknowledge His perspective on sin. Confession of sin characterizes genuine Christians, and God continually cleanses those who are confessing. Rather than focusing on confession for every single sin as necessary, John refers especially to a settled recognition and acknowledgment that one is a sinner who needs cleansing and forgiveness (Ephesians 4:32; Colossians 2:13).

> **2:6 abides.** This is one of John's favorite terms for salvation. **just as He walked.** Jesus' life of obedience is the Christian's pattern. Those who claim to be Christians ought to live as He did, since they possess His Spirit (see John 6:38).

7 Brethren,[a] I write no new commandment to you, but an old commandment which you have had from the beginning. The old commandment is the word which you heard from the beginning.[b] 8 Again, a new commandment I write to you, which thing is true in Him and in you, because the darkness is passing away, and the true light is already shining.

9 He who says he is in the light, and hates his brother, is in darkness until now. 10 He who loves his brother abides in the light, and there is no cause for stumbling in him. 11 But he who hates his brother is in darkness and walks in darkness, and does not know where he is going, because the darkness has blinded his eyes.

Their Spiritual State

12   I write to you, little children,
      Because your sins are forgiven you
         for His name's sake.
13   I write to you, fathers,
      Because you have known Him *who is* from the beginning.
   I write to you, young men,

2:7 [a]NU-Text reads *Beloved.* [b]NU-Text omits *from the beginning.*

How does 1 John help us understand some of the destructive teaching that attacked Christianity in the first century?

Paul, Peter, and John all faced early forms of a system of false teaching that later became known as Gnosticism. That term (derived from the Greek word "knowledge") refers to the habit that gnostics had of claiming an elevated knowledge, a higher truth known only to those in on the deep things. Those initiated into this mystical knowledge of truth had a higher internal authority than Scripture. This resulted in a chaotic situation in which the gnostics tried to judge divine revelation by human ideas rather than judging human ideas by divine revelation (1 John 2:15–17).

Philosophically, the heresy relied on a distortion of Platonism. It advocated a dualism in which matter was inherently evil and spirit was good. One of the direct errors of this heresy involved attributing some form of deity to Christ but denying his true humanity, supposedly to preserve Him from evil (which they concluded He would be if He actually came in the flesh). Such a view destroys not only the true humanity of Jesus, but also the atonement work of Christ. Jesus must not only have been truly God, but also the truly human (physically real) man who actually suffered and died upon the cross in order to be the acceptable substitutionary sacrifice for sin (Hebrews 2:14–17). The biblical view of Jesus affirms His complete humanity as well as His full deity.

The Gnostic heresy, even in John's day, featured two basic forms: (1) Docetism; and (2) the error of Cerinthus. Docetism (from a Greek word that means, "to appear") asserted that Jesus' physical body was not real but only "seemed" to be physical. John forcefully and repeatedly affirmed the physical reality of Jesus. He reminded his readers that he was an eyewitness to Him ("heard," "seen," "handled," "Jesus Christ has come in the flesh"; 1 John 1:1–4; 4:2,3). The other form of early Gnosticism was traced back to Cerinthus by the early church apologist Irenaeus. Cerinthus taught that Christ's "spirit" descended on the human Jesus at His baptism but left Him shortly before His crucifixion. John asserted that the Jesus who was baptized at the beginning of His ministry was the same person who was crucified on the cross (1 John 5:6).

John does not directly specify the early gnostic beliefs, but his arguments offer clear clues about his targets. Further, John's wisdom was to avoid direct attacks on rapidly shifting heresies, but to provide a timely, positive restatement of the fundamentals of the faith that would provide timeless truth and answers for later generations of Christians.

Because you have overcome the
wicked one.
I write to you, little children,
Because you have known the
Father.
14 I have written to you, fathers,
Because you have known Him *who
is* from the beginning.
I have written to you, young men,
Because you are strong, and the
word of God abides in you,
And you have overcome the wicked
one.

> **2:13,14 fathers...young men...little children.** This describes 3 stages of spiritual growth. "Fathers," the most mature, have a deep knowledge of God. The pinnacle of spiritual maturity is to know God in His fullness (see Phil. 3:10). "Young men" are those who know the Word and stand strong against sin. "Little children" are those who have only the basic awareness of God and still need to grow.

Do Not Love the World

15Do not love the world or the things in the world. If anyone loves the world, the love of the Father is not in him. 16For all that *is* in the world—the lust of the flesh, the lust of the eyes, and the pride of life—is not of the Father but is of the world. 17And the world is passing away, and the lust of it; but he who does the will of God abides forever.

Deceptions of the Last Hour

18Little children, it is the last hour; and as you have heard that the*a* Antichrist is coming, even now many antichrists have come, by which we know that it is the last hour.

> **2:18 the Antichrist.** The term "antichrist" first occurs here and is found only in John's epistles. The Antichrist is the final, world ruler who will try to replace and oppose the true Christ (Dan. 8:9–11). **many antichrists have come.** The plural form of "antichrist" refers to false teachers who troubled John's congregations with their false doctrines that opposed Christ (Matt. 24:24). The term refers to the evil that lies within in men who oppose God (see 2 Cor. 10:4,5).

19They went out from us, but they were not of us; for if they had been of us, they would have continued with us; but *they went out* that they might be made manifest, that none of them were of us.

20But you have an anointing from the Holy One, and you know all things.*a* 21I have not written to you because you do not know the truth, but because you know it, and that no lie is of the truth.

22Who is a liar but he who denies that Jesus is the Christ? He is antichrist who denies the Father and the Son. 23Whoever denies the Son does not have the Father either; he who acknowledges the Son has the Father also.

Let Truth Abide in You

24Therefore let that abide in you which you heard from the beginning. If what you heard from the beginning abides in you, you also will abide in the Son and in the Father. 25And this is the promise that He has promised us—eternal life.

26These things I have written to you concerning those who *try to* deceive you. 27But the anointing which you have received from Him abides in you, and you do not need that anyone teach you; but as the

---

2:18 *a*NU-Text omits *the*.   2:20 *a*NU-Text reads *you all know*.

Why are we not to love the world (1 John 2:15)?

Although John often repeats the importance of love and that God is love (4:7,8), he also reveals that God hates a certain type of love: love of the world (John 15:18–20). An absence of love for the world must habitually characterize the love life of those considered born again. Conversely, Christians love God and their fellow Christians.

"Love" here signifies affection and devotion. God, not the world, must have the first place in the Christian's life (Matthew 10:37–39; Philippians 3:20). The term "world" is not a reference to the physical, material world but to the invisible, spiritual system of evil—dominated by Satan and all that it offers in opposition to God, His Word, and His people (5:19; John 12:31; 1 Corinthians 1:21; 2 Corinthians 4:4; James 4:4; 2 Peter 1:4).

same anointing teaches you concerning all things, and is true, and is not a lie, and just as it has taught you, you will[a] abide in Him.

> **2:27 anointing.** Although gifted teachers are important in the church, John indicates that neither the teachers nor the believers are dependent on human wisdom or on human opinion for the truth. The Holy Spirit guards and guides believers into truth. **abide in Him.** The task of the believer is to "walk in the truth," persevering in faithfulness and sound doctrine (see 2 John 4).

The Children of God

²⁸And now, little children, abide in Him, that when[a] He appears, we may have confidence and not be ashamed before Him at His coming. ²⁹If you know that He is righteous, you know that everyone who practices righteousness is born of Him.

3 Behold what manner of love the Father has bestowed on us, that we should be

> **3:1 Therefore the world does not know us.** The real aliens in the world are Christians. They display a nature and lifestyle like their Savior's. This nature seems totally foreign to the unsaved (1 Cor. 2:15,16). Thus believers are described as pilgrims, sojourners, and strangers in this world. The Lord Jesus had a heavenly origin, as do those who are born again. Our true transformed lives have not yet been manifested.

called children of God![a] Therefore the world does not know us,[b] because it did not know Him. ²Beloved, now we are children of God; and it has not yet been revealed what we shall be, but we know that when He is revealed, we shall be like Him, for we shall see Him as He is. ³And everyone who has this hope in Him purifies himself, just as He is pure.

Sin and the Child of God

⁴Whoever commits sin also commits lawlessness, and sin is lawlessness. ⁵And you know that He was manifested to take

2:27 [a]NU-Text reads *you abide.*   2:28 [a]NU-Text reads *if.*   3:1 [a]NU-Text adds *And we are.* [b]M-Text reads *you.*

What four reasons does John give for why true Christians cannot habitually practice sin (1 John 3:4–10)?

This passage begins with the phrase "Whoever commits sin" (verse 4). "Commits" translates a Greek verb that conveys the idea of habitual practice. Although genuine Christians have a sin nature (1:8), and do behave sinfully, their confession of sin (1:9; 2:1) and acceptance of forgiveness prevent sin from becoming the unbroken pattern of their lives (John 8:31,34–36; Romans 6:11; 2 John 9). God builds a certain growing awareness about sin that provides four effective reasons why true Christians cannot habitually practice sin:

1. Genuine Christians cannot practice sin because sin is incompatible with the law of God, which they love (3:4; Psalm 119:34,77,97; Romans 7:12,22); whereas habitual sin betrays the ultimate sense of rebellion—living as if there were no law or ignoring what laws exist (James 4:17)—in short, lawlessness.

2. Genuine Christians cannot practice sin because sin is incompatible with the work of Christ (3:5). Christ died to sanctify (make holy) the believer (2 Corinthians 5:21; Ephesians 5:25–27). Habitual sin contradicts Christ's work of breaking the dominion of sin in the believer's life (Romans 6:1–15).

3. Genuine Christians cannot practice sin because Christ came to destroy the works of the arch-sinner, Satan (3:8). The devil is still operating, but he has been defeated, and in Christ we escape his tyranny. The day will come when all of Satan's activity will cease in the universe, and he will be sent to hell forever (Revelation 20:10).

4. Genuine Christians cannot practice sin because sin is incompatible with the ministry of the Holy Spirit, who has imparted a new nature to the believer (3:9; John 3:5–8). This new nature shuns sin and exhibits the habitual character of righteousness produced by the Holy Spirit (Galatians 5:22–24).

away our sins, and in Him there is no sin. ⁶Whoever abides in Him does not sin. Whoever sins has neither seen Him nor known Him.

> **3:4–10** These verses deal with the Christian's incompatibility with sin. The false teachers discounted the significance of sin and the need for obedience. They followed a kind of thinking called philosophical dualism, that taught that matter is inherently bad, and as a result, any sins committed in the physical realm were regarded as inconsequential. In this section, John gives four reasons why Christians habitually practice sin (John 8:31,34–36).

⁷Little children, let no one deceive you. He who practices righteousness is righteous, just as He is righteous. ⁸He who sins is of the devil, for the devil has sinned from the beginning. For this purpose the Son of God was manifested, that He might destroy the works of the devil. ⁹Whoever has been born of God does not sin, for His seed remains in him; and he cannot sin, because he has been born of God.

> **3:9 born of God.** God makes Christians new creatures with new natures (2 Cor. 5:17), which bear a righteousness produced by the Holy Spirit (Gal. 5:22–24). **His seed.** The new birth involves the acquisition of a seed, which refers to the principle of life of God imparted to the believer at salvation. **remains.** The new birth is permanent and irreversible. **he cannot sin.** This refers to habitual sinning.

The Imperative of Love

¹⁰In this the children of God and the children of the devil are manifest: Whoever does not practice righteousness is not of God, nor *is* he who does not love his brother. ¹¹For this is the message that you heard from the beginning, that we should love one another, ¹²not as Cain *who* was of the wicked one and murdered his brother. And why did he murder him? Because his works were evil and his brother's righteous.

¹³Do not marvel, my brethren, if the world hates you. ¹⁴We know that we have passed from death to life, because we love the brethren. He who does not love *his* brother*ᵃ* abides in death. ¹⁵Whoever hates his brother is a murderer, and you know that no murderer has eternal life abiding in him.

The Outworking of Love

¹⁶By this we know love, because He laid down His life for us. And we also ought to lay down *our* lives for the brethren. ¹⁷But whoever has this world's goods, and sees his brother in need, and shuts up his heart from him, how does the love of God abide in him?

> **3:17 whoever has this world's goods...and shuts up his heart.** True love is not limited to supreme sacrifices, but shows up in lesser ones. Christian love expresses itself in sacrificial giving to other Christians' needs. A practical love is motivated by helping others (1 Tim. 6:17–19).

3:14 *ᵃ*NU-Text omits *his brother.*

What are the non-negotiable basics of the faith that John spells out in 1 John?

John presents the basics or fundamentals of the Christian life in absolute, non-relative terms. Unlike Paul, who often included exceptions when discussing spiritual principles, John does not deal with the "what if I fail" issues. John does recognize the importance of forgiveness and Christ's role as Advocate when we fail (1:8,9; 2:1), but most of his letter presents truths in black and white rather than shades of gray. His stark contrasts allow little room for compromise: light versus darkness (1:5,7; 2:8-11); truth versus lies (2:21,22; 4:1); children of God versus children of the devil (3:10).

Those who claim to be Christians must absolutely display the characteristics of genuine Christians: sound doctrine, obedience, and love. Those who are truly born again have been given a new nature, which gives evidence of itself. Those who do not display characteristics of the new nature do not have it, so were never truly born again. The issues do not center (as much of Paul's writing does) on maintaining temporal or daily fellowship with God but on the application of basic tests to one's life to confirm that salvation has truly occurred. Such absolute distinctions were also characteristic of John's gospel.

¹⁸My little children, let us not love in word or in tongue, but in deed and in truth. ¹⁹And by this we know*ᵃ* that we are of the truth, and shall assure our hearts before Him. ²⁰For if our heart condemns us, God is greater than our heart, and knows all things. ²¹Beloved, if our heart does not condemn us, we have confidence toward God. ²²And whatever we ask we receive from Him, because we keep His commandments and do those things that are pleasing in His sight. ²³And this is His commandment: that we should believe on the name of His Son Jesus Christ and love one another, as He gave us*ᵃ* commandment.

The Spirit of Truth and the Spirit of Error

²⁴Now he who keeps His commandments abides in Him, and He in him. And by this we know that He abides in us, by the Spirit whom He has given us.

4 Beloved, do not believe every spirit, but test the spirits, whether they are of God; because many false prophets have

4:1 do not believe every spirit. Demonic spirits exist and produce false prophets and teachers to spread false doctrine. Christians are to have a healthy skepticism regarding any teaching. They are to be like the Bereans, who examined the Scriptures to determine truth and error (Acts 17:11,12). **test.** Christians must test any teaching by comparing it to the Scripture to determine its value.

gone out into the world. ²By this you know the Spirit of God: Every spirit that confesses that Jesus Christ has come in the flesh is of God, ³and every spirit that does not confess that*ᵃ* Jesus Christ has come in the flesh is not of God. And this is the *spirit* of the Antichrist, which you have heard was coming, and is now already in the world.

⁴You are of God, little children, and have overcome them, because He who is in you is greater than he who is in the world. ⁵They are of the world. Therefore they speak *as* of the world, and the world hears them. ⁶We are of God. He who knows God

---

3:19 *ᵃ*NU-Text reads *we shall know.*   3:23 *ᵃ*M-Text omits *us.*   4:3 *ᵃ*NU-Text omits *that* and *Christ has come in the flesh.*

John's letter includes five specific reasons why Christians love (1 John 4:7–21). What are they?

In stark contrast to the self-centered and destructive philosophies and practices of the false teachers, John unfolds the powerful reasons why Christians practice love. In 1 John 4:7–21, the apostle includes 5 such reasons:

1. Christians habitually practice love because God, who indwells them, is the essence of love. The gnostics believed that God was immaterial spirit and light, but never defined the source of love as coming from His inmost being. As God is spirit (John 4:24), light (1:5), and a consuming fire (Hebrews 12:9), so He is love (4:7,8). Love is inherent in all He is and does. Even His judgment and wrath are perfectly harmonized with His love.

2. Christians habitually practice love because they desire to imitate the supreme example of God's sacrificial love in sending His Son for us (4:9).

3. Christians habitually practice love because love is the heart of Christian witness (4:12). Nobody can see God loving since He is invisible. Jesus no longer is in the world to manifest the love of God. The only demonstration of God's love in this age is the church. That testimony is critical (John 13:35; 2 Corinthians 5:18–20).

4. Christians habitually practice love because love is the Christian's assurance (4:13–16; 3:21). Love banishes self-condemnation. When a Christian recognizes in his life the manifestation of love in actions, it results in confidence about his relationship with God.

5. Christians habitually practice love because love is the Christian's confidence in judgment (4:17–20; 3:16–23). Confidence is a sign that love is mature. This is not to suggest sinless perfection in a Christian's life, but rather a habitual practice of love marked by confidence in the face of judgment. Christians love, not in order to escape judgment, but because they have escaped judgment.

hears us; he who is not of God does not hear us. By this we know the spirit of truth and the spirit of error.

> **4:6 By this we know the spirit of truth and the spirit of error.** The Old and New Testaments are the sole standards by which all teaching is to be tested. In contrast, demonically inspired teachers either reject the teaching of God's Word or add elements to it (2 Cor. 4:2).

Knowing God Through Love

[7]Beloved, let us love one another, for love is of God; and everyone who loves is born of God and knows God. [8]He who does not love does not know God, for God is love. [9]In this the love of God was manifested toward us, that God has sent His only begotten Son into the world, that we might live through Him. [10]In this is love, not that we loved God, but that He loved us and sent His Son *to be* the propitiation for our sins. [11]Beloved, if God so loved us, we also ought to love one another.

Seeing God Through Love

[12]No one has seen God at any time. If we love one another, God abides in us, and His love has been perfected in us. [13]By this we know that we abide in Him, and He in us, because He has given us of His Spirit. [14]And we have seen and testify that the Father has sent the Son *as* Savior of the world. [15]Whoever confesses that Jesus is the Son of God, God abides in him, and he in God. [16]And we have known and believed the love that God has for us. God is love, and he who abides in love abides in God, and God in him.

The Consummation of Love

[17]Love has been perfected among us in this: that we may have boldness in the day of judgment; because as He is, so are we in this world. [18]There is no fear in love; but perfect love casts out fear, because fear involves torment. But he who fears has not been made perfect in love. [19]We love Him[a] because He first loved us.

Obedience by Faith

[20]If someone says, "I love God," and hates his brother, he is a liar; for he who does not love his brother whom he has seen, how can[a] he love God whom he has not seen? [21]And this commandment we have from Him: that he who loves God *must* love his brother also.

> **4:21** This verse summarizes chapter 4. One cannot love God without first loving fellow believers. A claim to love God is a lie if it is not accompanied by unselfish love for other Christians.

5 Whoever believes that Jesus is the Christ is born of God, and everyone who loves Him who begot also loves him who is begotten of Him. [2]By this we know that we love the children of God, when we love God and keep His commandments. [3]For this is the love of God, that we keep His commandments. And His commandments are not burdensome. [4]For whatever is born of God overcomes the world. And this is the victory that has overcome the world—our[a] faith. [5]Who is he who overcomes the world, but he who believes that Jesus is the Son of God?

> **5:4 overcomes.** Overcomers are those who believe that Jesus is God's Son. The word for "overcomer" comes from a Greek word meaning "to conquer" or "to have victory." The word reflects a superiority that leads to success. The victory is demonstrable; it involves overthrowing the enemy so that the victory is evident to all. Because of believers' union with Christ, they partake in His victory (Rom. 8:37).

The Certainty of God's Witness

[6]This is He who came by water and blood—Jesus Christ; not only by water, but by water and blood. And it is the Spirit who bears witness, because the Spirit is truth. [7]For there are three that bear witness in heaven: the Father, the Word, and the Holy Spirit; and these three are one. [8]And there are three that bear witness on earth:[a] the Spirit, the water, and the blood; and these three agree as one.

[9]If we receive the witness of men, the wit-

4:19 [a]NU-Text omits *Him.*   4:20 [a]NU-Text reads *he cannot.*   5:4 [a]M-Text reads *your.*   5:8 [a]NU-Text and M-Text omit the words from *in heaven* (verse 7) through *on earth* (verse 8). Only four or five very late manuscripts contain these words in Greek.

ness of God is greater; for this is the witness of God which[a] He has testified of His Son. ¹⁰He who believes in the Son of God has the witness in himself; he who does not believe God has made Him a liar, because he has not believed the testimony that God has given of His Son. ¹¹And this is the testimony: that God has given us eternal life, and this life is in His Son. ¹²He who has the Son has life; he who does not have the Son of God does not have life. ¹³These things I have written to you who believe in the name of the Son of God, that you may know that you have eternal life,[a] and that you may *continue to* believe in the name of the Son of God.

5:13 that you may know that you have eternal life. John wrote this epistle to give believers confidence that they possessed eternal life. The false brethren's departure left the congregation shaken. He assured those who remained that since they adhered to the faith, their salvation was sure. **eternal life.** Eternal life is not related to a period of time but to a relationship with Jesus Christ, who shares His nature with believers.

Confidence and Compassion in Prayer

¹⁴Now this is the confidence that we have in Him, that if we ask anything according to His will, He hears us. ¹⁵And if we know that He hears us, whatever we ask, we know that we have the petitions that we have asked of Him.

¹⁶If anyone sees his brother sinning a sin *which does* not *lead* to death, he will ask, and He will give him life for those who commit sin not *leading* to death. There is sin *leading* to death. I do not say that he should pray about that. ¹⁷All unrighteousness is sin, and there is sin not *leading* to death.

Knowing the True—Rejecting the False

¹⁸We know that whoever is born of God does not sin; but he who has been born of God keeps himself,[a] and the wicked one does not touch him.

¹⁹We know that we are of God, and the whole world lies *under the sway of* the wicked one.

5:18 wicked one. This refers to Satan. **does not touch him.** The word suggests "to grasp" in order to harm. Because the believer belongs to God, Satan must operate under God's authority and cannot function beyond what God allows. God protects His children and places limits on Satan's influence and power (John 10:28).

²⁰And we know that the Son of God has come and has given us an understanding, that we may know Him who is true; and we are in Him who is true, in His Son Jesus Christ. This is the true God and eternal life.

²¹Little children, keep yourselves from idols. Amen.

5:9 [a]NU-Text reads *God, that.*   5:13 [a]NU-Text omits the rest of this verse.   5:18 [a]NU-Text reads *him.*

Why are there so many seemingly repeated thoughts in 1 John?

In a unique fashion, John challenges his readers and interpreters by his repetition of similar themes over and over to emphasize the basic truths about genuine Christianity. Some have likened John's repetitive style to a spiral that moves outward, becoming larger and larger, each cycle spreading the same truth over a wider territory and encompassing a larger area of life. Others have seen the spirals moving inward, penetrating deeper and deeper into the same themes while expanding on his thoughts. However one views the spiraling pattern, John clearly uses repetition of basic truths as a means to accentuate their importance and to help his readers understand and remember them.

2 JOHN

Even a memo from one of the original disciples has great value—particularly if it was inspired by the Holy Spirit. This shortest of the New Testament books fits on a single sheet of papyrus. It is also the only letter specifically addressed to a woman. In it, John includes only crucial encouragement and warnings. There was much more to say, but he hoped to visit soon (verse 12).

AUTHOR AND DATE

Second John was written by the Apostle John in about A.D. 90 to 95.

The author describes himself in 2 John 1 as "The Elder." It fits the apostle's pattern of not using his own name in his writings. In the Gospel of John he called himself the disciple "whom Jesus loved" (John 13:23; 19:26; 20:2; 21:7,20). "The Elder" conveys the advanced age of the apostle, his authority, and his status during the foundational period of Christianity.

The precise date of this epistle cannot be determined. Since the wording, subject matter, and circumstances of 2 John closely approximate 1 John (for example, compare verse 5 to 1 John 2:7; 3:11 and verse 9 to 1 John 2:23), it is likely that the two letters were composed at about the same time, around A.D. 90–95.

BACKGROUND AND SETTING

The primary difference between 1 and 2 John has to do with the audience. First John is addressed in a general way to Christians. Second John is written to a particular person and a particular church (verse 1). Both letters warn of the dangers of those false teachers who, influenced by early Gnostic thought, were threatening the church.

Based on the internal evidence, John was concerned that the individual addressed in the greeting (verse 1) inadvertently or unwisely may have shown these false prophets hospitality (verses 10,11). Apparently, false teachers were conducting an itinerant ministry among John's congregations, seeking to make converts, and taking advantage of Christian hospitality to advance their cause. That apostle urgently warned his readers against showing hospitality to such deceivers (verses 10,11). Although his exhortation may appear on the surface to be harsh or unloving, the acutely dangerous nature of the false teaching justified such actions, especially since it threatened to destroy the very foundations of the faith (verse 9).

Second John echoes 1 John's theme of a "recall to the fundamentals of the faith" or "back to the basics of Christianity" (verses 4–6). For John, the basics of Christianity are summarized by adherence to the truth (verse 4), love (verse 5), and obedience (verse 6).

The personal nature of this letter, however, allows the apostle to convey an additional but related theme in 2 John: "the biblical guidelines for hospitality."

> THE **BASIS** OF **HOSPITALITY** MUST BE **COMMON LOVE** OF OR **INTEREST** IN THE **TRUTH.**

Not only are Christians to adhere to the fundamentals of the faith, but the gracious hospitality that is commanded of them (Romans 12:13) must be discriminating. The basis of hospitality must be common love of or interest in the truth. Christians must share their love within the confines of those guidelines. Hospitality and kindness must be focused on those who are adhering to the fundamentals of the faith. Otherwise, Christians may actually aid those who are attempting to destroy those basic truths of the faith. Sound doctrine must serve as the test of fellowship and the basis of separation between those who profess to be Christians and those who actually are (verses 10,11; Romans 16:17; Galatians 1:8,9; 2 Thessalonians 3:6,14; Titus 3:10).

OUTLINE

Greeting the Elect Lady

The Elder,

[1] To the elect lady and her children, whom I love in truth, and not only I, but also all those who have known the truth, [2] because of the truth which abides in us and will be with us forever:

> **1 The Elder.** John uses this title to emphasize his advanced age, his spiritual authority over the congregations in Asia Minor, and the strength of his own personal, eyewitness testimony to the life of Jesus and all that He taught. **the elect lady and her children.** This probably refers to a particular woman and her children who were well known to John. **whom I love in truth.** Because truth is the necessary condition for unity, it is also the basis for Christian hospitality.

[3] Grace, mercy, *and* peace will be with you[a] from God the Father and from the Lord Jesus Christ, the Son of the Father, in truth and love.

Walk in Christ's Commandments

[4] I rejoiced greatly that I have found *some* of your children walking in truth, as we received commandment from the Father. [5] And now I plead with you, lady, not as though I wrote a new commandment to you, but that which we have had from the beginning: that we love one another. [6] This is love, that we walk according to His commandments. This is the commandment, that as you have heard from the beginning, you should walk in it.

> **7 many deceivers.** John sets limits for Christian hospitality. Since Satan comes as an angel of light (2 Cor. 11:13–15), believers must know the truth intimately to guard against error. **who do not confess Jesus Christ as coming in the flesh.** Jesus Christ's nature was both fully God and fully human. The fundamental error in false religions is the denial of Jesus' true nature, that He was equally, fully, simultaneously both God and man.

Beware of Antichrist Deceivers

[7] For many deceivers have gone out into the world who do not confess Jesus Christ *as* coming in the flesh. This is a deceiver and an antichrist. [8] Look to yourselves, that we[a] do not lose those things we worked for, but *that* we[b] may receive a full reward.

[9] Whoever transgresses[a] and does not

---

3 [a]NU-Text and M-Text read *us.*   8 [a]NU-Text reads *you.*   [b]NU-Text reads *you.*   9 [a]NU-Text reads *goes ahead.*

Why was it so important to John to "confess Jesus Christ as coming in the flesh" (2 John 7)?

John's purpose was to strengthen Christians to resist the tide of heresy that was rising against the church. Much of this false teaching was an early form of Gnosticism. For more on the heresy itself, see the FAQ "How does 1 John help us understand some of the destructive teaching that attacked Christianity in the first century?"

The gnostic idea that matter was evil and only spirit was good led to the idea that either the body should be treated harshly, a form of asceticism (Colossians 2:21–23), or that sin committed in the body had no connection or effect on one's spirit. In other words, the false teaching sought to drive a wedge between body and soul. This is why it often maintained that Jesus could not have been God and man at the same time.

The result of this error in teaching was compounded when some, including John's opponents, concluded that sins committed in the physical body did not matter. Absolute indulgence in immorality was permissible. One could deny sin even existed (1 John 1:8-10) and disregard God's law (1 John 3:4).

As a bulwark against this heresy, John lifted the confession that "Jesus Christ came in the flesh" (verse 7). What Christians do in their physical life is directly connected with what they do in their spiritual life. John emphasized the need for obedience to God's laws, for he defined the true love for God as obedience to His commandments (1 John 5:3). Jesus, in His human living, offered the perfect example of that kind of love.

abide in the doctrine of Christ does not have God. He who abides in the doctrine of Christ has both the Father and the Son. [10]If anyone comes to you and does not bring this doctrine, do not receive him into your house nor greet him; [11]for he who greets him shares in his evil deeds.

John's Farewell Greeting

[12]Having many things to write to you, I did not wish *to do so* with paper and ink;

> **11 shares in his evil deeds.** Hospitality to such leaders aids the spread of their heresy, and it gives the impression that believers are sanctioning the false teachings of these antichrists (see 1 John 2:22). Supreme loyalty to God and His Word alone must characterize the actions of every true believer.

but I hope to come to you and speak face to face, that our joy may be full.

[13]The children of your elect sister greet you. Amen.

How does John's teaching about truth and love affect the discussions about Christian unity today (2 John 4–6)?

John's teaching stands in direct antithesis to the frequent cry for ecumenism and Christian unity among believers. Love and truth are inseparable in Christianity. Truth must always guide the exercise of love (Ephesians 4:5). Love must stand the test of truth. The main lesson of John's second letter is that truth determines the bounds of love, and as a consequence, the bounds of unity. Therefore, truth must exist before love can unite, for truth generates love (1 Peter 1:22). When someone compromises the truth, true Christian love and unity are destroyed. Only shallow sentimentalism exists where truth is not the foundation of unity.

3 JOHN

Like Second John, 3 John is marked by brevity. It will fit on a single sheet of papyrus. In it, the Apostle announces his intention to visit soon. John's note to a leader named Gaius challenges and encourages him by using the behavior of two other leaders as negative and positive examples of effective spiritual leadership. John hoped to add much more teaching when he arrived.

AUTHOR AND DATE

Third John was written by the Apostle John about A.D. 90 to 95.

John used the same identifying term that he used in 2 John. In both letters, he referred to himself as "The Elder." The term conveys the advanced age of the apostle, as well as his authority and his privileged role as one of the remaining eyewitnesses of Jesus' ministry.

The precise date of the epistle cannot be determined. Since the structure, style, and vocabulary closely approximate 2 John, most likely John composed the letters at the same time, around A.D. 90–95. Compare the following passages for those similarities: verse 1 to 2 John 2; verse 4 to 2 John 4; verse 13 to 2 John 12; verse 14 to 2 John 12. As with 1 and 2 John, the apostle probably wrote this letter during his ministry at Ephesus near the end of his life.

BACKGROUND AND SETTING

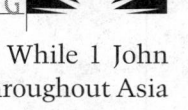

Third John is perhaps the most personal of John's three epistles. While 1 John appears to be a general letter addressed to congregations scattered throughout Asia Minor, and 2 John was sent to a lady and her family (2 John 1), in 3 John the apostle clearly names the sole recipient as "the beloved Gaius" (verse 1). The name Gaius was common in the first century, and men bearing it appear in a number of New Testament passages (Acts 19:29; 20:4; Romans 16:23; 1 Corinthians 1:14). Beyond this letter, however, no other specific identity for Gaius has been found.

The composition of this letter was motivated by those who returned from Gaius with a report of the hospitality and support they had received from him as a brother in Christ. Meanwhile, others, like Diotrephes (verse 9), had refused to extend a welcome to visiting teachers from John. The apostle followed up those reports with this note of gratitude and encouragement for Gaius.

As with 2 John, 3 John focuses on the theme of hospitality, but from a different perspective. While 2 John warns against showing hospitality to false teachers (2 John 7–11), 3 John commends appropriate hospitality shown to faithful ministers of the Word by Gaius (verses 5–8). He also condemns the behavior of Diotrephes, who set a bad example by domineering a local congregation and by refusing to welcome visiting ministers (verse 9). Diotrephes went even further, for he also verbally slandered the Apostle John with malicious accusations and excluded anyone from the assembly who dared challenge him (verse 10).

THIRD JOHN COMMENDS APPROPRIATE HOSPITALITY SHOWN TO FAITHFUL MINISTERS OF THE WORD BY GAIUS.

OUTLINE

Greeting to Gaius

The Elder,

¹To the beloved Gaius, whom I love in truth:

> **1 Gaius.** Nothing is known of Gaius beyond the mention of his name here. The name was one of the 18 common names Roman parents chose for a son. Gaius was held in the highest esteem for his Christian walk by John, fellow believers, and even strangers to whom he extended hospitality. He was probably a member of a church in Asia Minor that was under John's influence.

²Beloved, I pray that you may prosper in all things and be in health, just as your soul prospers. ³For I rejoiced greatly when brethren came and testified of the truth *that is* in you, just as you walk in the truth. ⁴I have no greater joy than to hear that my children walk in truth.[a]

Gaius Commended for Generosity

⁵Beloved, you do faithfully whatever you do for the brethren and[a] for strangers, ⁶who have borne witness of your love before the church. *If* you send them forward on their journey in a manner worthy of God, you will do well, ⁷because they went forth for His name's sake, taking nothing from the Gentiles. ⁸We therefore ought to receive[a] such, that we may become fellow workers for the truth.

Diotrephes and Demetrius

⁹I wrote to the church, but Diotrephes, who loves to have the preeminence among them, does not receive us. ¹⁰Therefore, if I come, I will call to mind his deeds which he does, prating against us with malicious words. And not content with that, he himself does not receive the brethren, and forbids those who wish to, putting *them* out of the church.

> **6 who have borne witness of your love before the church.** Gaius' reputation for hospitality and kindness was well known throughout the churches in the region. **in a manner worthy of God.** The phrase carries the connotation of treating people as God would treat them (see Matt. 10:40), which is how hospitality should be practiced (Matt. 25:40–45). **you will do well.** John encouraged Gaius to keep practicing hospitality, especially because Diotrephes was campaigning against it.

¹¹Beloved, do not imitate what is evil, but what is good. He who does good is of God, but[a] he who does evil has not seen God.

> **11 do not imitate what is evil, but what is good.** Gaius was to imitate Demetrius as the correct role model for his actions. **He who does good is of God, but he who does evil has not seen God.** Diotrephes' actions proved that he was never a Christian. This is a practical application of the moral test (see 1 John 5:2,3).

¹²Demetrius has a *good* testimony from all, and from the truth itself. And we also bear witness, and you know that our testimony is true.

Farewell Greeting

¹³I had many things to write, but I do not wish to write to you with pen and ink; ¹⁴but

---

4 [a]NU-Text reads *the truth.*   5 [a]NU-Text adds *especially.*   8 [a]NU-Text reads *support.*
11 [a]NU-Text and M-Text omit *but.*

What guidelines about Christian hospitality are found in 3 John?

John offers both encouragement and counsel regarding hospitality. He certainly believed that Christians should practice the kind of hospitality that could be judged in a "manner worthy of God" (verse 6). First, Christians must show hospitality to those who have pure motives. He described these as itinerant missionaries who went out "for the sake of the name" (verse 7, Romans 1:5). They must be doing ministry for God's glory, not for their own. Second, Christians must show hospitality to those who are not in ministry for money. Since these missionaries were "taking nothing from the Gentiles" (verse 7), the church was their only means of support. Third, when Christians practice hospitality, they become participants in the ministry of those to whom they extend a welcome (verse 8).

I hope to see you shortly, and we shall speak face to face.

Peace to you. Our friends greet you. Greet the friends by name.

In his third letter, why was John so upset about this person called Diotrephes?

John mentioned Diotrephes to Gaius as an example of the kind of negative effect caused by a leader who contradicts Jesus' teaching on servant-leadership in the church (Matthew 20:20–28; Philippians 2:5–11; 1 Timothy 3:3; 1 Peter 5:3), and who violates the standards of hospitality required of Christians. John noted at least six errors in Diotrephes' behavior that form helpful warnings to others: (1) he loved to have preeminence (the desire to be first, verse 9); (2) he rejected John's authority and therefore the authority of God's Word by refusing to receive John's letter (verse 9); (3) John charged Diotrephes with "prating against us" (a term that conveys the idea of someone talking nonsense, verse 10); (4) Diotrephes acted "with malicious words" (his false accusations against John were also evil, verse 10); (5) he "does not receive the brethren" (his hostility extended to other Christians, verse 10); and (6) he was even "putting them out of the church" (he was excommunicating those who resisted his authority, verse 10).

JUDE

Jude was the second half-brother of Jesus (James was the first) to write a New Testament letter (Matthew 13:55; Mark 6:3). Although Jude had earlier rejected Jesus as Messiah (John 7:1–9), he, along with other half-brothers of our Lord, was converted after Christ's resurrection (Acts 1:14). Like his brother James, Jude became a significant leader in the church in Jerusalem following Jesus' death, resurrection, and ascension into heaven. He was also active on missionary journeys with other brothers (1 Corinthians 9:5).

AUTHOR AND DATE

Jude was written by Jude about A.D. 68 to 70.

Although Jude (Judas) was a common name in Palestine (at least eight men by that name are mentioned in the New Testament), the author of Jude generally has been accepted as Jude, Christ's half-brother. Three internal clues reinforce this conclusion: (1) Jude's appeal to being the "brother of James," the leader of the Jerusalem Council (Acts 15) and another half-brother of Jesus (verse 1; Galatians 1:19); (2) The similarities between Jude's and James' salutations (verse 1; James 1:1); and (3) Jude's not identifying himself as an apostle (verse 1), but rather distinguishing himself from them (verse 17). These clues negate the other main candidate for authorship, the Apostle Judas (not Judas Iscariot), the son of James (Luke 6:16; Acts 1:13).

Early questions about the canonicity of Jude revolve around its relationship with 2 Peter. Jude quotes directly from 2 Peter 3:3 and acknowledges that it is from an apostle (verses 17,18). If Peter had quoted Jude, there would have been no question about canonicity, since Peter would thereby have given Jude apostolic affirmation. The authenticity of Jude, however, was attested by Clement of Rome (about A.D. 96) and Clement of Alexandria (about A.D. 200).

Since no mention of Jerusalem's destruction in A.D. 70 was included by Jude, and though Jude most likely came after 2 Peter (A.D. 67–68), the former fits into the same narrow time frame as the latter. Jude was probably written about A.D. 68–70.

BACKGROUND AND SETTING

Jude lived at a time when Christianity was under severe political pressure from Rome and aggressive spiritual infiltration from gnostic-like apostates who sowed abundant seed for a gigantic harvest of doctrinal error. The exact audience of be-

lievers with whom Jude corresponded is unknown but seems to be Jewish in light of Jude's illustrations. He undoubtedly wrote to a region recently plagued by false teachers.

Except for John, who lived until the close of the first century, all the other apostles had likely been martyred by the time Jude wrote. Christianity was thought to be extremely vulnerable. Thus, Jude called the church to fight, in the midst of intense spiritual warfare, for the truth.

HISTORICAL AND THEOLOGICAL THEMES

Jude is the only New Testament book devoted exclusively to confronting "apostasy," meaning defection from the true, biblical faith (verses 3,17). Apostates are described elsewhere in 2 Thessalonians 2:10; Hebrews 10:29; 2 Peter 2:1–22; 1 John 2:18–23). Jude wrote to condemn the apostates and to urge believers to contend for the faith.

His writing vividly described apostates in terms of their character and unscrupulous activities (verses 4,8,10,16,18,19). Additionally, he borrowed from nature to illustrate the futility of their teaching (verses 12,13). While Jude never commented on the specific content of apostate teaching, he clearly demonstrated from their degenerate personal lives and fruitless ministries the ultimate tragedy of attempting to teach error as though it were truth. This emphasis on character repeats the constant theme regarding false teachers—their personal corruption. While their teaching

> JUDE WROTE TO CONDEMN THE APOSTATES AND TO URGE BELIEVERS TO CONTEND FOR THE FAITH.

may be clever, subtle, deceptive, enticing, and delivered in myriads of forms, the common way to recognize them is to look behind their false spiritual fronts and see their wicked lives (2 Peter 2:10,12,18,19).

Jude is replete with historical illustrations from the Old Testament which include: (1) the Exodus (verse 5); (2) Satan's rebellion (verse 6); (3) Sodom and Gomorrah (verse 7); (4) Moses' death (verse 9); (5) Cain (verse 11); (6) Balaam (verse 11); (7) Korah (verse 11); (8) Enoch (verses 14,15); and (9) Adam (verse 14).

OUTLINE

Greeting to the Called

¹Jude, a bondservant of Jesus Christ, and brother of James,

To those who are called, sanctified*ᵃ* by God the Father, and preserved in Jesus Christ:

²Mercy, peace, and love be multiplied to you.

Contend for the Faith

³Beloved, while I was very diligent to write to you concerning our common salvation, I found it necessary to write to you exhorting you to contend earnestly for the faith which was once for all delivered to the saints. ⁴For certain men have crept in unnoticed, who long ago were marked out for this condemnation, ungodly men, who turn the grace of our God into lewdness and deny the only Lord God*ᵃ* and our Lord Jesus Christ.

Old and New Apostates

⁵But I want to remind you, though you once knew this, that the Lord, having saved the people out of the land of Egypt, afterward destroyed those who did not believe. ⁶And the angels who did not keep their proper domain, but left their own abode, He has reserved in everlasting chains under darkness for the judgment of the great day; ⁷as Sodom and Gomorrah, and the cities around them in a similar manner to these, having given themselves over to sexual immorality and gone after strange flesh, are set forth as an example, suffering the vengeance of eternal fire.

⁸Likewise also these dreamers defile the flesh, reject authority, and speak evil of dignitaries. ⁹Yet Michael the archangel, in contending with the devil, when he disputed about the body of Moses, dared not bring against him a reviling accusation, but said, "The Lord rebuke you!" ¹⁰But these speak evil of whatever they do not know; and whatever they know naturally, like brute beasts, in these things they corrupt them-

---

3 I found it necessary. Jude had originally intended to write a letter about salvation as the common blessing enjoyed by all believers. But instead, he was compelled to write a call to battle for the truth, in light of the arrival of apostate (false) teachers. **contend earnestly.** The salvation of those to whom he wrote was not in jeopardy, but false teachers were misleading those who needed to hear the true gospel. Jude wrote this letter to encourage the believers to fight strenuously for the truth.

8 these dreamers. This refers to a confused state of the soul or abnormal imagination, producing delusions and sensual confusion. These men's minds were numb to the truth of God's Word, causing them to fantasize wicked, perverted things. Perhaps they falsely claimed these were visions from God. **defile the flesh.** Apostates have few, if any, moral restraints and are frequently characterized by immoral lifestyles (see Titus 1:15).

---

1 *ᵃ*NU-Text reads *beloved.*   4 *ᵃ*NU-Text omits *God.*

What does Jude mean by the phrase "the faith which was once . . . delivered to the saints"

Jude is referring to the whole body of revealed salvation truth contained in the Scriptures (Galatians 1:23; Ephesians 4:5,13; Philippians 1:27; 1 Timothy 4:1). Here, and later in verse 20, Jude is describing a fixed body of spiritual revelation that can be known as sound doctrine (Ephesians 4:14; Colossians 3:16; 1 Peter 2:2; 1 John 2:12–14), used in discerning and sorting out truth from error (1 Thessalonians 5:20–22), and effective in confronting and attacking error (2 Corinthians 10:3–5; Philippians 1:17,27; 1 Timothy 1:18; 6:12; 2 Timothy 1:13; 4:7,8; Titus 1:13).

God's revelation was delivered once as a unit, at the completion of the Scripture, and is not to be edited by either deletion or addition (Deuteronomy 4:2; 12:32; Proverbs 30:6; Revelation 22:18,19). Scripture is complete, sufficient, and finished; therefore it is fixed for all time. Nothing is to be added to the body of the inspired Word (2 Timothy 3:16,17; 2 Peter 1:19–21) because nothing else is needed.

selves. [11]Woe to them! For they have gone in the way of Cain, have run greedily in the error of Balaam for profit, and perished in the rebellion of Korah.

Apostates Depraved and Doomed

[12]These are spots in your love feasts, while they feast with you without fear, serving *only* themselves. *They are* clouds without water, carried about[a] by the winds; late autumn trees without fruit, twice dead, pulled up by the roots; [13]raging waves of the sea, foaming up their own shame; wandering stars for whom is reserved the blackness of darkness forever.

> **13 raging waves.** Apostates promise powerful ministry but are quickly exposed as wreakers of havoc and workers of worthless shame (see Is. 57:20). **wandering stars.** This most likely refers to a meteor or shooting star that has an uncontrolled moment of brilliance and then fades away forever into nothing. Apostates promise enduring spiritual direction, but they deliver a brief, worthless message.

PROFILE OF AN APOSTATE

1. Ungodly (v. 4)
2. Morally perverted (v. 4)
3. Deny Christ (v. 4)
4. Defile the flesh (v. 8)
5. Rebellious (v. 8)
6. Revile holy angels (v. 8)
7. Dreamers (v. 10)
8. Ignorant (v. 10)
9. Corrupted (v. 10)
10. Grumblers (v. 16)
11. Fault finders (v. 16)
12. Self seeking (v. 16)
13. Arrogant speakers (v. 16)
14. Flatterers (v. 16)
15. Mockers (v. 18)
16. Cause division (v. 19)
17. Worldly minded (v. 19)
18. Without the Spirit (v. 19)[1]

[1]John F. MacArthur, Jr., *The MacArthur Study Bible*, (Dallas: Word Publishing) 1997.

[14]Now Enoch, the seventh from Adam, prophesied about these men also, saying, "Behold, the Lord comes with ten thousands of His saints, [15]to execute judgment on all, to convict all who are ungodly among them of all their ungodly deeds which they have committed in an ungodly way, and of all the harsh things which ungodly sinners have spoken against Him."

Apostates Predicted

[16]These are grumblers, complainers, walking according to their own lusts; and they mouth great swelling *words*, flattering people to gain advantage. [17]But you, beloved, remember the words which were spoken before by the apostles of our Lord Jesus Christ: [18]how they told you that there would be mockers in the last time who would walk according to their own ungodly lusts. [19]These are sensual persons, who cause divisions, not having the Spirit.

Maintain Your Life with God

[20]But you, beloved, building yourselves up on your most holy faith, praying in the

---

12 [a]NU-Text and M-Text read *along.*

Since Jude quotes from books that are not in the Bible, does this give those other books a special value?

Jude quoted specifically from two extra-biblical books: (1) 1 Enoch (verse 14); and (2) Assumption of Moses (verse 9). The authors of these books are unknown. Jude referred to them to support and illustrate his points.

Christians have held that Jude was writing under the inspiration of the Holy Spirit (2 Timothy 3:16; 2 Peter 1:20,21) and included material that was accurate and true in its affirmations. His use of extra-biblical material was selective and not meant to extend any special authority to those texts. Paul followed the same pattern in quoting or referring to non-biblical authors (Acts 17:28; 1 Corinthians 15:33; Titus 1:12).

19 sensual persons. Apostate teachers advertise themselves as having the highest spiritual knowledge, but they are actually attracted to the lowest levels of life (see James 3:15). **cause divisions.** They fractured the church rather than united it (see Eph. 4:4–6). **not having the Spirit.** To not have the Spirit is to be an unbeliever.

Holy Spirit, ²¹keep yourselves in the love of God, looking for the mercy of our Lord Jesus Christ unto eternal life.

22 compassion. The victims of the apostate teachers need mercy and patience because they have not yet reached a firm conclusion about Christ and eternal life. They remain doubters who could possibly be swayed to the truth.

²²And on some have compassion, making a distinction;*^a* ²³but others save with fear, pulling *them* out of the fire,*^a* hating even the garment defiled by the flesh.

Glory to God

²⁴   Now to Him who is able to keep you*^a*
        from stumbling,
        And to present *you* faultless
        Before the presence of His glory with
        exceeding joy,

²⁵   To God our Savior,*^a*
        Who alone is wise,*^b*
        Be glory and majesty,
        Dominion and power,*^c*
        Both now and forever.
        Amen.

---

22 *^a*NU-Text reads *who are doubting* (or *making distinctions*).   23 *^a*NU-Text adds *and on some have mercy with fear* and omits *with fear* in first clause.   24 *^a*M-Text reads *them.*   25 *^a*NU-Text reads *To the only God our Savior.*   *^b*NU-Text omits *Who . . . is wise* and adds *Through Jesus Christ our Lord.* *^c*NU-Text adds *Before all time.*

Why are the last verses in Jude called a "doxology?"

The word itself is not found in the Bible, but is an ancient term referring to special passages that express high praise to God. The first part of the word comes from the Greek word "doxa," which means "glory." The second part of the word comes from the Greek word "logos" which means "word." These words in Jude express in the most exalted terms the glory of God. They stand alongside other splendid examples in the New Testament (Romans 11:33–36; 16:25–27; 2 Corinthians 13:14; Hebrews 13:20,21).

Jude's doxology includes Christians in a powerful way, highlighting what God can do for them that no one else can do. Jude re-emphasized his theme of salvation and bolstered the courage of the believers to know that Christ would protect them from the present apostasy.

REVELATION

God made sure His Word had a grand finale. What opened with the overture of Genesis comes to a dramatic conclusion in Revelation. Unlike most books of the Bible, Revelation contains its own title: "The Revelation of Jesus Christ" (1:1). In all its uses, "revelation" refers to something or someone, once hidden, becoming visible. What this book reveals or unveils is Jesus Christ in glory. Truths about Him and His final victory, that the rest of Scripture merely allude to, become visible through this expanded revelation about Jesus Christ.

AUTHOR AND DATE

Revelation was written by the Apostle John in about A.D. 94 to 96.

Four times the author identifies himself as John (1:1,4,9; 22:8). Early tradition unanimously identifies him as John the apostle, author of the fourth gospel and three epistles. Important second century witnesses to the Apostle John's authorship include Justin Martyr, Irenaeus, Clement of Alexandria, and Tertullian. Many of the book's original readers were still alive during the lifetimes of Justin Martyr and Irenaeus—both of whom held to apostolic authorship.

There are differences in style between Revelation and John's other writings, but they are insignificant considering the radical difference in subject matter and setting. There are, however, some striking parallels between Revelation and John's other works. In the New Testament, only John's gospel and Revelation refer to Jesus Christ as the Word (19:13; John 1:1). Revelation (1:7) and John's gospel (19:37) translate Zechariah 12:10 differently from the Septuagint (the Greek Old Testament), but in agreement with each other. Further, only Revelation and the Gospel of John describe Jesus as the "Lamb" (5:6,8; John 1:29) and as a "witness" (1:5; John 5:31,32).

Revelation was written in the last decade of the first century (about A.D. 94–96), near the end of Emperor Domitian's reign (A.D. 81–96). Although some date it during Nero's reign, (A.D. 54–68), their arguments are unconvincing and conflict with the view of the early church. Writing in the second century, Irenaeus declared that Revelation had been written toward the end of Domitian's reign. Other early writers, Clement of Alexandria, Origen, Victorinus (who wrote one of the earliest commentaries on Revelation), Eusebius, and Jerome affirm the Domitian date.

The spiritual decline of the seven churches (chapters 2,3) also argues for the later date. Those churches were strong and spiritually healthy in the mid-60s, when

Paul last ministered in Asia Minor. The brief time between Paul's ministry there and the end of Nero's reign was too short for such a decline to have occurred. The longer time gap also explains the rise of the heretical sect known as the Nicolaitans (2:6,15), who are not mentioned in Paul's letters. Finally, dating Revelation during Nero's reign does not allow time for John's ministry in Asia Minor to reach the point at which the authorities would have felt the need to exile him.

BACKGROUND AND SETTING

Revelation begins with John, the last surviving apostle and an old man, in exile on the small, barren island of Patmos, located in the Aegean Sea southwest of Ephesus. The Roman authorities had banished him there because of his faithful preaching of the gospel (1:9). While on Patmos, John received a series of visions that laid out the future history of the world.

When he was arrested, John was in Ephesus, ministering to the church there and in surrounding cities. Although he could no longer minister to those congregations in person, John received a divine command to address Revelation to them (1:4,11). Those churches had begun to feel the effects of violent persecution. At least one man—probably a pastor—had already been martyred (2:13). John himself had been exiled. But the storm of persecution was about to break in full fury upon the seven churches so dear to the apostle's heart (2:10). To those churches, Revelation provided a message of hope: God is in sovereign control of all the events of human history, and though evil often seems pervasive and wicked men powerful, their ultimate doom is certain. Christ will come in glory to judge and rule.

HISTORICAL AND THEOLOGICAL THEMES

Since it is primarily prophetic, Revelation contains little contemporary historical material aside from chapters 1–3. The seven churches to whom the letter was addressed were existing churches in Asia Minor (modern Turkey). Apparently, they were singled out because John had ministered in them.

> **REVELATION IS FIRST AND FOREMOST A REVELATION ABOUT JESUS CHRIST.**

Revelation is first and foremost a revelation about Jesus Christ (1:1). The book uses numerous roles and titles to describe His unique and divine position: (1) the glorified Son of God ministering among the churches (1:10; 2:18); (2) "the Alpha and Omega, the Beginning and the End" (1:8); (3) the One "who is and who was and who is to come, the Almighty" (1:8); (4) the First and the Last (1:11); (5) the Son of Man (1:13); (6) the One who was dead, but now is alive forevermore (1:18); (7) the One who is holy and true (3:7); (8) the "Amen, the Faithful and True Witness, the Beginning of the creation of God" (3:14); (9) the Lion of the tribe of Judah (5:5), (10) the Lamb in heaven, on the throne (6:1; 7:17); (11) the Messiah who will reign forever (11:15); (12) the Word of God (19:13); (13) the majestic King of kings and Lord of lords (19:11); and (14) the "Root and the Offspring of David, the Bright and Morning Star" (22:16).

Many other rich theological themes find expression in Revelation. The church is warned about sin and exhorted to holiness. John's vivid pictures of worship in heaven encourage and instruct believers. The ministry of angels is prominent.

Revelation's primary theological contribution is to eschatology—the doctrine of the last things. The book includes: (1) the final political setup of the world; (2) the last battle of human history; (3) the career and ultimate defeat of the Antichrist; (4) Christ's 1,000-year earthly kingdom; (5) the glories of heaven and the eternal state; and (6) the final state of the wicked and the righteous. Finally, only Daniel rivals this book in declaring that God providentially rules over the kingdoms of men and will accomplish His sovereign purposes regardless of human or demonic opposition.

OUTLINE

Introduction and Benediction

1 The Revelation of Jesus Christ, which God gave Him to show His servants— things which must shortly take place. And He sent and signified *it* by His angel to His servant John, ²who bore witness to the word of God, and to the testimony of Jesus Christ, to all things that he saw. ³Blessed *is* he who reads and those who hear the words of this prophecy, and keep those things which are written in it; for the time *is* near.

> **1:3 Blessed.** This is the only biblical book that comes with a blessing for the one who listens to it being read and explained and then responds in obedience. **time is near.** "Time" refers to epochs, eras, or seasons. The next great era of God's redemptive history is near. Christ's return may be delayed long enough so that people begin to doubt if He will ever come (see Matt. 24:36–39).

Greeting the Seven Churches

⁴John, to the seven churches which are in Asia:

Grace to you and peace from Him who is and who was and who is to come, and from the seven Spirits who are before His throne, ⁵and from Jesus Christ, the faithful witness, the firstborn from the dead, and the ruler over the kings of the earth.

To Him who loved us and washed*ᵃ* us from our sins in His own blood, ⁶and has made us kings*ᵃ* and priests to His God and Father, to Him *be* glory and dominion forever and ever. Amen.

⁷Behold, He is coming with clouds, and every eye will see Him, even they who pierced Him. And all the tribes of the earth will mourn because of Him. Even so, Amen.

⁸"I am the Alpha and the Omega, *the* Beginning and *the* End,"*ᵃ* says the Lord,*ᵇ* "who is and who was and who is to come, the Almighty."

Vision of the Son of Man

⁹I, John, both*ᵃ* your brother and companion in the tribulation and kingdom and patience of Jesus Christ, was on the island that is called Patmos for the word of God and for the testimony of Jesus Christ. ¹⁰I was in the Spirit on the Lord's Day, and I heard behind me a loud voice, as of a trumpet, ¹¹saying, "I am the Alpha and the Omega, the First and the Last," and,*ᵃ* "What you see, write in a book and send *it* to the seven churches which are in Asia:*ᵇ* to Ephesus, to Smyrna, to Pergamos, to Thyatira, to Sardis, to Philadelphia, and to Laodicea."

> **1:8 Alpha and the Omega.** These are the first and last letters of the Greek alphabet. An alphabet is an ingenious method of communication, able to hold and convey all knowledge. Christ is the supreme, sovereign alphabet; there is nothing outside His knowledge. **the Almighty.** This underscores that God's power is supreme over all the cataclysmic events recorded in Revelation. His sovereignty extends over all people, objects, and events.

¹²Then I turned to see the voice that spoke with me. And having turned I saw seven golden lampstands, ¹³and in the midst of the seven lampstands *One* like the Son of Man, clothed with a garment down to the feet and girded about the chest with a golden band. ¹⁴His head and hair *were* white like wool, as white as snow, and His eyes like a flame of fire; ¹⁵His feet *were* like fine brass, as if refined in a furnace, and His voice as the sound of many waters; ¹⁶He had in His right hand seven stars, out of His mouth went a sharp two-edged sword, and His countenance *was* like the sun shining in its strength. ¹⁷And when I saw Him, I fell at His feet as dead. But He laid His right hand on me, saying to me,*ᵃ* "Do not be afraid; I am the First and the Last. ¹⁸I *am* He who lives, and was dead, and behold, I am alive forevermore. Amen. And I have the keys of Hades and of Death.

> **1:16 seven stars.** These are the human messengers who represented the 7 churches. They are pictured here in Christ's hand, meaning that He controls the church and its leaders. **a sharp two-edged sword.** This signifies judgment on those who attack His people and destroy His church (see 2:16).

1:5 *ᵃ*NU-Text reads *loves us and freed*; M-Text reads *loves us and washed.* 1:6 *ᵃ*NU-Text and M-Text read *a kingdom.* 1:8 *ᵃ*NU-Text and M-Text omit *the Beginning and the End.* *ᵇ*NU-Text and M-Text add *God.* 1:9 *ᵃ*NU-Text and M-Text omit *both.* 1:11 *ᵃ*NU-Text and M-Text omit *I am* through third *and.* *ᵇ*NU-Text and M-Text omit *which are in Asia.* 1:17 *ᵃ*NU-Text and M-Text omit *to me.*

¹⁹Write*a* the things which you have seen, and the things which are, and the things which will take place after this. ²⁰The mystery of the seven stars which you saw in My right hand, and the seven golden lampstands: The seven stars are the angels of the seven churches, and the seven lampstands which you saw*a* are the seven churches.

The Loveless Church

2 "To the angel of the church of Ephesus write,

'These things says He who holds the seven stars in His right hand, who walks in the midst of the seven golden lampstands: ²"I know your works, your labor, your patience, and that you cannot bear those who are evil. And you have tested those who say they are apostles and are not, and have found them liars; ³and you have persevered and have patience, and have labored for My name's sake and have not become weary. ⁴Nevertheless I have *this* against you, that

you have left your first love. ⁵Remember therefore from where you have fallen; repent and do the first works, or else I will come to you quickly and remove your lampstand from its place—unless you repent. ⁶But this you have, that you hate the deeds of the Nicolaitans, which I also hate.

⁷"He who has an ear, let him hear what the Spirit says to the churches. To him who overcomes I will give to eat from the tree of life, which is in the midst of the Paradise of God." '

The Persecuted Church

⁸"And to the angel of the church in Smyrna write,

'These things says the First and the Last, who was dead, and came to life: ⁹"I know your works, tribulation, and poverty (but you are rich); and *I know* the blasphemy of those who say they are Jews and are not, but *are* a synagogue of Satan. ¹⁰Do not fear any of those things which you are about to suffer. Indeed, the devil is about to throw

---

2:4 left your first love. To be a Christian is to love Jesus (John 14:21). The Ephesians' passion and fervor for Christ had become cold, mechanical orthodoxy. Their doctrinal and moral purity, their undiminished zeal for truth, and their disciplined service were no substitute for the love of Christ they had forsaken.

2:9 who say they are Jews. Although they were Jews physically, they were not true Jews, but pseudo-spiritual pagans (see Rom. 2:28) who allied with other pagans in putting Christians to death as they attempted to stamp out the Christian faith. **synagogue of Satan.** Judaism becomes as much a tool of Satan as emperor worship when the Messiah is rejected.

1:19 *a*NU-Text and M-Text read *Therefore, write.*   1:20 *a*NU-Text and M-Text omit *which you saw.*

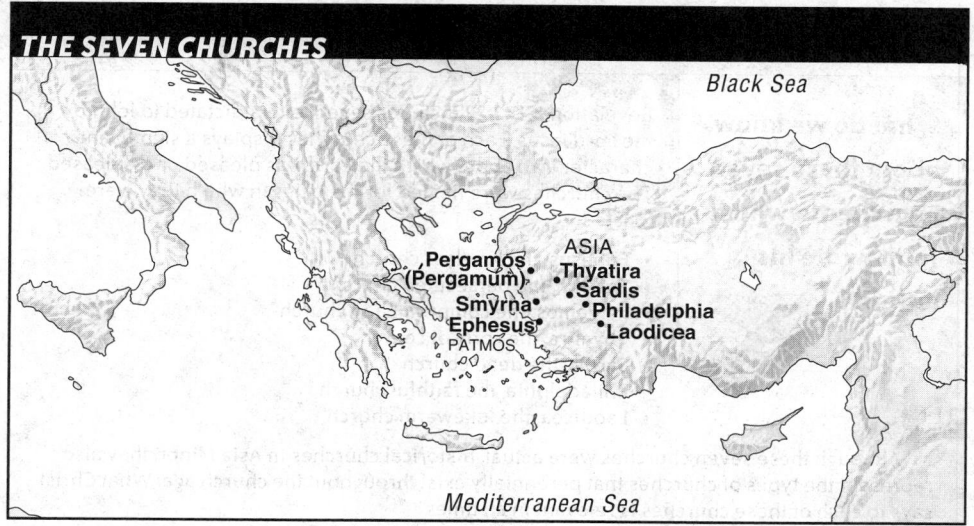

THE SEVEN CHURCHES

Black Sea

ASIA
Pergamos (Pergamum)
Thyatira
Sardis
Smyrna
Philadelphia
Ephesus
Laodicea
PATMOS

Mediterranean Sea

some of you into prison, that you may be tested, and you will have tribulation ten days. Be faithful until death, and I will give you the crown of life.

[11]"He who has an ear, let him hear what the Spirit says to the churches. He who overcomes shall not be hurt by the second death."'

The Compromising Church

[12]"And to the angel of the church in Pergamos write,

'These things says He who has the sharp two-edged sword: [13]"I know your works, and where you dwell, where Satan's throne *is*. And you hold fast to My name, and did not deny My faith even in the days in which Antipas *was* My faithful martyr, who was killed among you, where Satan dwells. [14]But I have a few things against you, because you have there those who hold the doctrine of Balaam, who taught Balak to put a stumbling block before the children of Israel, to eat things sacrificed to idols, and to commit sexual immorality. [15]Thus you also have those who hold the doctrine of the Nicolaitans, which thing I hate.[a] [16]Repent, or else I will come to you quickly and will fight against them with the sword of My mouth.

[17]"He who has an ear, let him hear what the Spirit says to the churches. To him who overcomes I will give some of the hidden manna to eat. And I will give him a white stone, and on the stone a new name written which no one knows except him who receives *it*."'

> **2:17 hidden manna.** Just as God provided Israel with promised manna, so will He give the true believer the spiritual bread the unbelieving world cannot see: Jesus Christ (see John 6:51). **white stone.** As part of a prize, an athlete was given a white stone that was an admission pass to the winner's celebration afterwards. This is an image of the moment when the believer will receive his ticket to an eternal victory celebration.

The Corrupt Church

[18]"And to the angel of the church in Thyatira write,

'These things says the Son of God, who has eyes like a flame of fire, and His feet like fine brass: [19]"I know your works, love, service, faith,[a] and your patience; and *as for* your works, the last *are* more than the first. [20]Nevertheless I have a few things against you, because you allow[a] that woman[b] Jezebel, who calls herself a prophetess, to teach and seduce[c] My servants to commit sexual immorality and eat things sacrificed to idols. [21]And I gave her time to repent of her sexual immorality, and she did not repent.[a] [22]Indeed I will cast her into a sickbed, and those who commit adultery with her into

---

2:15 [a]NU-Text and M-Text read *likewise* for *which thing I hate.*　2:19 [a]NU-Text and M-Text read *faith, service.*　2:20 [a]NU-Text and M-Text read *I have against you that you tolerate.*　[b]M-Text reads *your wife Jezebel.*　[c]NU-Text and M-Text read *and teaches and seduces.*　2:21 [a]NU-Text and M-Text read *time to repent, and she does not want to repent of her sexual immorality.*

What do we know about these seven churches to which John wrote his letters?

Revelation 2:1–3:22 includes seven letters dictated to John by the Lord Jesus. Each of these churches displays a significant character trait about which the Lord was pleased or displeased. The churches were named for the cities in which they were located:

- Ephesus, the loveless church
- Smyrna, the persecuted church
- Pergamos, the compromising church
- Thyatira, the corrupt church
- Sardis, the dead church
- Philadelphia, the faithful church
- Laodicea, the lukewarm church

Although these seven churches were actual, historical churches in Asia Minor, they also represent the types of churches that perennially exist throughout the church age. What Christ says to each of these churches is relevant in all times.

great tribulation, unless they repent of their*a* deeds. ²³I will kill her children with death, and all the churches shall know that I am He who searches the minds and hearts. And I will give to each one of you according to your works.

²⁴"Now to you I say, and*a* to the rest in Thyatira, as many as do not have this doctrine, who have not known the depths of Satan, as they say, I will*b* put on you no other burden. ²⁵But hold fast what you have till I come. ²⁶And he who overcomes, and keeps My works until the end, to him I will give power over the nations—

²⁷ *'He shall rule them with a rod of iron;*
     They shall be dashed to pieces like the
         *potter's vessels'*ᵃ —

as I also have received from My Father; ²⁸and I will give him the morning star.

²⁹"He who has an ear, let him hear what the Spirit says to the churches." '

> **2:28 the morning star.** John later reveals Christ to be the "morning star." Although He has already dawned in our hearts (2 Pet. 1:19), someday we will have Him in His fullness.

The Dead Church

3 "And to the angel of the church in Sardis write,

'These things says He who has the seven Spirits of God and the seven stars: "I know your works, that you have a name that you are alive, but you are dead. ²Be watchful, and strengthen the things which remain, that are ready to die, for I have not found your works perfect before God.*a* ³Remember therefore how you have received and heard; hold fast and repent. Therefore if you will not watch, I will come upon you as a thief, and you will not know what hour I will come upon you. ⁴You*a* have a few names even in Sardis who have not defiled their garments; and they shall walk with Me in white, for they are worthy. ⁵He who overcomes shall be clothed in white gar-

ments, and I will not blot out his name from the Book of Life; but I will confess his name before My Father and before His angels.

⁶"He who has an ear, let him hear what the Spirit says to the churches." '

The Faithful Church

⁷"And to the angel of the church in Philadelphia write,

'These things says He who is holy, He who is true, *"He who has the key of David, He who opens and no one shuts, and shuts and no one opens"*:*a* ⁸"I know your works. See, I have set before you an open door, and no one can shut it;*a* for you have a little strength, have kept My word, and have not denied My name. ⁹Indeed I will make *those* of the synagogue of Satan, who say they are Jews and are not, but lie—indeed I will make them come and worship before your feet, and to know that I have loved you. ¹⁰Because you have kept My command to persevere, I also will keep you from the hour of trial which shall come upon the whole world, to test those who dwell on the earth. ¹¹Behold,*a* I am coming quickly! Hold fast what you have, that no one may take your crown. ¹²He who overcomes, I will make him a pillar in the temple of My God, and he shall go out no more. I will write on him the name of My God and the name of the city of My God, the New Jerusalem, which comes down out of heaven from My God. And *I will write on him* My new name.

> **3:10 keep you from the hour of trial.** This must refer to the Tribulation, a 7 year period before Christ's earthly kingdom begins, when the divine wrath will be unleashed in judgments described as seals, trumpets, and bowls. The wording of this verse supports the pretribulational rapture of the church, the idea that believers will be taken away from earth before the Tribulation begins. This period is the same as Daniel's 70th week and "the time of Jacob's trouble."

¹³"He who has an ear, let him hear what the Spirit says to the churches." '

2:22 *a*NU-Text and M-Text read *her.*   2:24 *a*NU-Text and M-Text omit *and.*   *b*NU-Text and M-Text omit *will.*   2:27 *a*Psalm 2:9   3:2 *a*NU-Text and M-Text read *My God.*   3:4 *a*NU-Text and M-Text read *Nevertheless you have a few names in Sardis.*   3:7 *a*Isaiah 22:22   3:8 *a*NU-Text and M-Text read *which no one can shut.*   3:11 *a*NU-Text and M-Text omit *Behold.*

The Lukewarm Church

[14]"And to the angel of the church of the Laodiceans[a] write,

'These things says the Amen, the Faithful and True Witness, the Beginning of the creation of God: [15]"I know your works, that you are neither cold nor hot. I could wish you were cold or hot. [16]So then, because you are lukewarm, and neither cold nor hot,[a] I will vomit you out of My mouth. [17]Because you say, 'I am rich, have become wealthy, and have need of nothing'—and do not know that you are wretched, miserable, poor, blind, and naked—[18]I counsel you to buy from Me gold refined in the fire, that you may be rich; and white garments, that you may be clothed, *that* the shame of your nakedness may not be revealed; and anoint your eyes with eye salve, that you may see. [19]As many as I love, I rebuke and chasten. Therefore be zealous and repent. [20]Behold, I stand at the door and knock. If anyone hears My voice and opens the door, I will come in to him and dine with him, and he with Me. [21]To him who overcomes I will grant to sit with Me on My throne, as I also overcame and sat down with My Father on His throne.

> **3:14 the Amen.** This is a common biblical expression signifying certainty and truthfulness (see Is. 65:16, "the God of truth"). According to 2 Cor. 1:20, all of God's promises are fulfilled in the person and work of Jesus Christ. **Beginning of the creation.** This corrects a heresy apparently in Laodicea and Colosse that stated that Christ was a created being (see Col. 1:15–20). As a human He had a beginning, but in His essence as God He was the beginning.

[22]"He who has an ear, let him hear what the Spirit says to the churches." ' "

The Throne Room of Heaven

4 After these things I looked, and behold, a door *standing* open in heaven. And the first voice which I heard *was* like a trumpet speaking with me, saying, "Come up here, and I will show you things which must take place after this."

> **4:1 Come up here.** This is not a veiled reference to the rapture of the church, but a command for John to be temporarily transported to heaven "in the Spirit" to receive revelation about future events. **things which must take place after this.** This begins the third and final section of the book, describing the events that will follow the church age.

[2]Immediately I was in the Spirit; and behold, a throne set in heaven, and *One* sat on the throne. [3]And He who sat there was[a] like a jasper and a sardius stone in appearance; and *there was* a rainbow around the throne, in appearance like an emerald. [4]Around the throne *were* twenty-four thrones, and on the thrones I saw twenty-four elders sitting, clothed in white robes; and they had crowns[a] of gold on their heads. [5]And from the throne proceeded lightnings, thunderings, and voices.[a] Seven lamps of fire *were* burning before the throne, which are the[b] seven Spirits of God.

[6]Before the throne *there was*[a] a sea of glass, like crystal. And in the midst of the throne, and around the throne, *were* four living creatures full of eyes in front and in back. [7]The first living creature *was* like a

---

3:14 [a]NU-Text and M-Text read *in Laodicea.*   3:16 [a]NU-Text and M-Text read *hot nor cold.*
4:3 [a]M-Text omits *And He who sat there was* (which makes the description in verse 3 modify the throne rather than God).   4:4 [a]NU-Text and M-Text read *robes, with crowns.*   4:5 [a]NU-Text and M-Text read *voices, and thunderings.*   [b]M-Text omits *the.*   4:6 [a]NU-Text and M-Text add *something like.*

Q Does Revelation 3:20 mean that Christ is standing at each person's life, knocking to come in?

A Rather than allowing for the common interpretation of Christ's knocking on a person's heart, the context demands to say that Christ was seeking to enter this church that bore His name but lacked a single true believer. The poignant letter to the church in Laodicea was Christ's knocking. If one member would recognize his spiritual bankruptcy and respond in saving faith, Christ would enter the church.

lion, the second living creature like a calf, the third living creature had a face like a man, and the fourth living creature *was* like a flying eagle. [8]*The* four living creatures, each having six wings, were full of eyes around and within. And they do not rest day or night, saying:

> "Holy, holy, holy,[a]
> Lord God Almighty,
> Who was and is and is to come!"

> **4:7 first...like a lion.** John compares these 4 beings with 4 of God's earthly creations. The likeness to a lion symbolizes strength and power. **second...like a calf.** The calf symbolizes these beings' humble service to God. **third...face like a man.** Their likeness to man shows that they are rational beings. **fourth...like a flying eagle.** The cherubim serve God with swiftness as if on eagles' wings.

[9]Whenever the living creatures give glory and honor and thanks to Him who sits on the throne, who lives forever and ever, [10]the twenty-four elders fall down before Him who sits on the throne and worship Him who lives forever and ever, and cast their crowns before the throne, saying:

[11] "You are worthy, O Lord,[a]
> To receive glory and honor and power;
> For You created all things,
> And by Your will they exist[b] and were
>   created."

The Lamb Takes the Scroll

5 And I saw in the right *hand* of Him who sat on the throne a scroll written inside and on the back, sealed with seven seals. [2]Then I saw a strong angel proclaiming with a loud voice, "Who is worthy to open the scroll and to loose its seals?" [3]And no one in heaven or on the earth or under the earth was able to open the scroll, or to look at it. [4]So I wept much, because no one was found worthy to open and read[a] the scroll, or to look at it. [5]But one of the elders said to me, "Do not weep. Behold, the Lion of the tribe of Judah, the Root of David, has prevailed to open the scroll and to loose[a] its seven seals."

> **5:5 the Lion of the tribe of Judah.** This is one of the earliest titles for the Messiah and describes His fierceness and strength, which do not appear in their fullness until the moment anticipated here. **the Root of David.** This is another messianic title, which signifies His being a descendant of David. Christ will compel the wicked of the earth to succumb to His authority.

[6]And I looked, and behold,[a] in the midst of the throne and of the four living creatures, and in the midst of the elders, stood a Lamb as though it had been slain, having seven horns and seven eyes, which are the seven Spirits of God sent out into all the earth. [7]Then He came and took the scroll out of the right hand of Him who sat on the throne.

Worthy Is the Lamb

[8]Now when He had taken the scroll, the four living creatures and the twenty-four elders fell down before the Lamb, each having a harp, and golden bowls full of incense, which are the prayers of the saints. [9]And they sang a new song, saying:

> "You are worthy to take the scroll,
> And to open its seals;
> For You were slain,
> And have redeemed us to God by Your
>   blood
> Out of every tribe and tongue and
>   people and nation,
[10] And have made us[a] kings[b] and priests
>   to our God;
> And we[c] shall reign on the earth."

[11]Then I looked, and I heard the voice of many angels around the throne, the living creatures, and the elders; and the number of them was ten thousand times ten thousand, and thousands of thousands, [12]saying with a loud voice:

4:8 [a]M-Text has *holy* nine times.   4:11 [a]NU-Text and M-Text read *our Lord and God.*   [b]NU-Text and M-Text read *existed.*   5:4 [a]NU-Text and M-Text omit *and read.*   5:5 [a]NU-Text and M-Text omit *to loose.*   5:6 [a]NU-Text and M-Text read *I saw in the midst . . . a Lamb standing.*   5:10 [a]NU-Text and M-Text read *them.*   [b]NU-Text reads *a kingdom.*   [c]NU-Text and M-Text read *they.*

"Worthy is the Lamb who was slain
To receive power and riches and
   wisdom,
And strength and honor and glory and
   blessing!"

[13]And every creature which is in heaven and on the earth and under the earth and such as are in the sea, and all that are in them, I heard saying:

"Blessing and honor and glory and
   power
Be to Him who sits on the throne,
And to the Lamb, forever and ever!"[a]

[14]Then the four living creatures said, "Amen!" And the twenty-four[a] elders fell down and worshiped Him who lives forever and ever.[b]

First Seal: The Conqueror

6 Now I saw when the Lamb opened one of the seals;[a] and I heard one of the four living creatures saying with a voice like thunder, "Come and see." [2]And I looked, and behold, a white horse. He who sat on it had a bow; and a crown was given to him, and he went out conquering and to conquer.

> **6:1 the seals.** As Christ, the only One found worthy to open the scroll, breaks the 7 seals, each seal unleashes a new demonstration of God's judgment on the earth in the future tribulation period. The 7th seal contains the 7 trumpets, and the 7th trumpet contains the 7 bowls.

Second Seal: Conflict on Earth

[3]When He opened the second seal, I heard the second living creature saying, "Come and see."[a] [4]Another horse, fiery red, went out. And it was granted to the one who sat on it to take peace from the earth, and that *people* should kill one another; and there was given to him a great sword.

Third Seal: Scarcity on Earth

[5]When He opened the third seal, I heard the third living creature say, "Come and

see." So I looked, and behold, a black horse, and he who sat on it had a pair of scales in his hand. [6]And I heard a voice in the midst of the four living creatures saying, "A quart[a] of wheat for a denarius,[b] and three quarts of barley for a denarius; and do not harm the oil and the wine."

Fourth Seal: Widespread Death on Earth

[7]When He opened the fourth seal, I heard the voice of the fourth living creature saying, "Come and see." [8]So I looked, and behold, a pale horse. And the name of him who sat on it was Death, and Hades followed with him. And power was given to them over a fourth of the earth, to kill with sword, with hunger, with death, and by the beasts of the earth.

Fifth Seal: The Cry of the Martyrs

[9]When He opened the fifth seal, I saw under the altar the souls of those who had been slain for the word of God and for the testimony which they held. [10]And they cried with a loud voice, saying, "How long, O Lord, holy and true, until You judge and avenge our blood on those who dwell on the earth?" [11]Then a white robe was given to each of them; and it was said to them that they should rest a little while longer, until both *the number of* their fellow servants and their brethren, who would be killed as they *were*, was completed.

Sixth Seal: Cosmic Disturbances

[12]I looked when He opened the sixth seal, and behold,[a] there was a great earthquake; and the sun became black as sackcloth of hair, and the moon[b] became like blood. [13]And the stars of heaven fell to the earth, as a fig tree drops its late figs when it is shaken by a mighty wind. [14]Then the sky receded as a scroll when it is rolled up, and every mountain and island was moved out of its place. [15]And the kings of the earth, the great men, the rich men, the commanders,[a] the mighty men, every slave and every free man, hid themselves in the caves and in

---

5:13 [a]M-Text adds *Amen.*   5:14 [a]NU-Text and M-Text omit *twenty-four.*   [b]NU-Text and M-Text omit *Him who lives forever and ever.*   6:1 [a]NU-Text and M-Text read *seven seals.*   6:3 [a]NU-Text and M-Text omit *and see.*   6:6 [a]Greek *choinix;* that is, approximately one quart   [b]This was approximately one day's wage for a worker.   6:12 [a]NU-Text and M-Text omit *behold.*   [b]NU-Text and M-Text read *the whole moon.*   6:15 [a]NU-Text and M-Text read *the commanders, the rich men.*

6:14 sky receded as a scroll. The earth's atmosphere will be somehow dramatically affected, and the sky as we know it will disappear (see Is. 34:4). **every mountain and island was moved.** The global earthquake will cause the earth's plates to shift and slip, realigning whole continents.

7:4 One hundred *and* forty-four thousand. These are redeemed Jews who are instrumental in the salvation of many Jews and Gentiles during the Tribulation (vv. 9–17). They will be the firstfruits of a new redeemed Israel (Zech. 12:10). **all the tribes of the children of Israel.** By sovereign election, God will seal 12,000 Jews from each of the 12 tribes, promising to protect them while they accomplish their mission.

the rocks of the mountains, [16]and said to the mountains and rocks, "Fall on us and hide us from the face of Him who sits on the throne and from the wrath of the Lamb! [17]For the great day of His wrath has come, and who is able to stand?"

The Sealed of Israel

7 After these things I saw four angels standing at the four corners of the earth, holding the four winds of the earth, that the wind should not blow on the earth, on the sea, or on any tree. [2]Then I saw another angel ascending from the east, having the seal of the living God. And he cried with a loud voice to the four angels to whom it was granted to harm the earth and the sea, [3]saying, "Do not harm the earth, the sea, or the trees till we have sealed the servants of our God on their foreheads." [4]And I heard the number of those who were sealed. One hundred *and* forty-four thousand of all the tribes of the children of Israel *were* sealed:

[5]   of the tribe of Judah twelve thousand
            were sealed;[a]

of the tribe of Reuben twelve
        thousand *were* sealed;
of the tribe of Gad twelve thousand
        were sealed;
[6]   of the tribe of Asher twelve thousand
        were sealed;
of the tribe of Naphtali twelve
        thousand *were* sealed;
of the tribe of Manasseh twelve
        thousand *were* sealed;
[7]   of the tribe of Simeon twelve
        thousand *were* sealed;
of the tribe of Levi twelve thousand
        were sealed;
of the tribe of Issachar twelve
        thousand *were* sealed;
[8]   of the tribe of Zebulun twelve
        thousand *were* sealed;
of the tribe of Joseph twelve thousand
        were sealed;
of the tribe of Benjamin twelve
        thousand *were* sealed.

A Multitude from the Great Tribulation

[9]After these things I looked, and behold, a great multitude which no one could

7:5 [a]In NU-Text and M-Text *were sealed* is stated only in verses 5a and 8c; the words are understood in the remainder of the passage.

What is the "tribulation" and where does it fit in the Book of Revelation?

The Tribulation refers to that 7-year time period immediately following the removal of the church from the earth (John 14:1–3; 1 Thessalonians 4:13–18), when the righteous judgments of God will be poured out upon an unbelieving world (Jeremiah 30:7; Daniel 9:27; 12:1; 2 Thessalonians 2:7–12; Revelation 16). These judgments will be climaxed by the return of Christ in glory to the earth (Matthew 24:27–31; 25:31–46; 2 Thessalonians 2:7–12).

In the Book of Revelation, the lengthy section between 6:1–19:21 details the judgments and events of the time of tribulation from its beginning with the opening of the first seal through the seventh seal, trumpet, and bowl judgments of God, to the return of Christ to destroy the ungodly (19:11–21). The passage of time during this period is tracked in Revelation (11:2,3; 12:6,14; 13:5). The second half of the 7 year period is specifically called in Revelation 7:14 "the great tribulation."

number, of all nations, tribes, peoples, and tongues, standing before the throne and before the Lamb, clothed with white robes, with palm branches in their hands, ¹⁰and crying out with a loud voice, saying, "Salvation *belongs* to our God who sits on the throne, and to the Lamb!" ¹¹All the angels stood around the throne and the elders and the four living creatures, and fell on their faces before the throne and worshiped God, ¹²saying:

> "Amen! Blessing and glory and
>   wisdom,
> Thanksgiving and honor and power
>   and might,
> *Be* to our God forever and ever.
> Amen."

¹³Then one of the elders answered, saying to me, "Who are these arrayed in white robes, and where did they come from?"

¹⁴And I said to him, "Sir,*ᵃ* you know."

So he said to me, "These are the ones who come out of the great tribulation, and washed their robes and made them white in the blood of the Lamb. ¹⁵Therefore they are before the throne of God, and serve Him day and night in His temple. And He who sits on the throne will dwell among them. ¹⁶They shall neither hunger anymore nor thirst anymore; the sun shall not strike them, nor any heat; ¹⁷for the Lamb who is in the midst of the throne will shepherd them and lead them to living fountains of waters.*ᵃ* And God will wipe away every tear from their eyes."

> **7:14 the great tribulation.** These people did not go with the raptured church, since they were not yet saved. During the 7 year period they will be saved, martyred, and brought to heaven. Compared to other time periods, both God's judgment and His grace will be unparalleled during this time.

Seventh Seal: Prelude to the Seven Trumpets

8 When He opened the seventh seal, there was silence in heaven for about half an hour. ²And I saw the seven angels who stand before God, and to them were given seven trumpets. ³Then another angel,

> **8:2 seven trumpets.** In Revelation, trumpets primarily announce impending judgment. They are more intense than the seals, but not as destructive as the final bowl judgments. The first 4 trumpets announce the divine destruction of earth's ecology (vv. 6–12), while the final 3 involve demonic devastation of the earth's inhabitants (9:1–21).

having a golden censer, came and stood at the altar. He was given much incense, that he should offer *it* with the prayers of all the saints upon the golden altar which was before the throne. ⁴And the smoke of the incense, with the prayers of the saints, ascended before God from the angel's hand. ⁵Then the angel took the censer, filled it with fire from the altar, and threw *it* to the earth. And there were noises, thunderings, lightnings, and an earthquake.

⁶So the seven angels who had the seven trumpets prepared themselves to sound.

First Trumpet: Vegetation Struck

⁷The first angel sounded: And hail and fire followed, mingled with blood, and they were thrown to the earth.*ᵃ* And a third of the trees were burned up, and all green grass was burned up.

Second Trumpet: The Seas Struck

⁸Then the second angel sounded: And *something* like a great mountain burning with fire was thrown into the sea, and a third of the sea became blood. ⁹And a third of the living creatures in the sea died, and a third of the ships were destroyed.

Third Trumpet: The Waters Struck

¹⁰Then the third angel sounded: And a great star fell from heaven, burning like a torch, and it fell on a third of the rivers and on the springs of water. ¹¹The name of the star is Wormwood. A third of the waters became wormwood, and many men died from the water, because it was made bitter.

Fourth Trumpet: The Heavens Struck

¹²Then the fourth angel sounded: And a third of the sun was struck, a third of the moon, and a third of the stars, so that a third of them were darkened. A third of the

---

7:14 *ᵃ*NU-Text and M-Text read *My lord*.   7:17 *ᵃ*NU-Text and M-Text read *to fountains of the waters of life*.   8:7 *ᵃ*NU-Text and M-Text add *and a third of the earth was burned up*.

day did not shine, and likewise the night.

¹³And I looked, and I heard an angel*a* flying through the midst of heaven, saying with a loud voice, "Woe, woe, woe to the inhabitants of the earth, because of the remaining blasts of the trumpet of the three angels who are about to sound!"

Fifth Trumpet: The Locusts from the Bottomless Pit

9 Then the fifth angel sounded: And I saw a star fallen from heaven to the earth. To him was given the key to the bottomless pit. ²And he opened the bottomless pit, and smoke arose out of the pit like the smoke of a great furnace. So the sun and the air were darkened because of the smoke of the pit. ³Then out of the smoke locusts came upon the earth. And to them was given power, as the scorpions of the earth have power. ⁴They were commanded not to harm the grass of the earth, or any green thing, or any tree, but only those men who do not have the seal of God on their foreheads. ⁵And they were not given *authority* to kill them, but to torment them *for* five months. Their torment *was* like the torment of a scorpion when it strikes a man. ⁶In those days men will seek death and will not find it; they will desire to die, and death will flee from them.

> **9:1 a star fallen from heaven.** This star will be an angelic being (see v. 2), and will likely be Satan himself (v. 4).

⁷The shape of the locusts was like horses prepared for battle. On their heads were crowns of something like gold, and their faces *were* like the faces of men. ⁸They had hair like women's hair, and their teeth were like lions' *teeth.* ⁹And they had breastplates like breastplates of iron, and the sound of their wings *was* like the sound of chariots with many horses running into battle. ¹⁰They had tails like scorpions, and there were stings in their tails. Their power *was* to hurt men five months. ¹¹And they had as king over them the angel of the bottomless pit, whose name in Hebrew *is* Abaddon, but in Greek he has the name Apollyon.

¹²One woe is past. Behold, still two more woes are coming after these things.

Sixth Trumpet: The Angels from the Euphrates

¹³Then the sixth angel sounded: And I heard a voice from the four horns of the golden altar which is before God, ¹⁴saying to the sixth angel who had the trumpet, "Release the four angels who are bound at the great river Euphrates." ¹⁵So the four angels, who had been prepared for the hour and day and month and year, were released to kill a third of mankind. ¹⁶Now the number of the army of the horsemen *was* two hundred million; I heard the number of them. ¹⁷And thus I saw the horses in the vision: those who sat on them had breastplates of fiery red, hyacinth blue, and sulfur yellow; and the heads of the horses *were* like the heads of lions; and out of their mouths came fire, smoke, and brimstone. ¹⁸By these three *plagues* a third of mankind was killed—by the fire and the smoke and the brimstone which came out of their mouths. ¹⁹For their power*a* is in their mouth and in their tails; for their tails *are* like serpents, having heads; and with them they do harm.

> **9:14 four angels.** Scripture never refers to holy angels being bound. These are fallen angels and another segment of Satan's force that has been temporarily bound by God, but who will eventually be freed to accomplish His judgment through their horsemen (vv. 15–19). Demons are bound and freed at God's command. **Euphrates.** This is one of 4 rivers that flowed through the Garden of Eden. Beginning with Babel, this region has spawned many of the world's pagan religions.

²⁰But the rest of mankind, who were not killed by these plagues, did not repent of the works of their hands, that they should not worship demons, and idols of gold, silver, brass, stone, and wood, which can neither see nor hear nor walk. ²¹And they did not repent of their murders or their sorceries*a* or their sexual immorality or their thefts.

The Mighty Angel with the Little Book

10 I saw still another mighty angel coming down from heaven, clothed

---

8:13 *a*NU-Text and M-Text read *eagle.*   9:19 *a*NU-Text and M-Text read *the power of the horses.*
9:21 *a*NU-Text and M-Text read *drugs.*

10:1–11:14 These verses serve as an interlude between the 6th and 7th trumpets. God's intention is to encourage and comfort His people in the midst of the Tribulation and to remind them that they will be victorious in the end.

with a cloud. And a rainbow *was* on his head, his face *was* like the sun, and his feet like pillars of fire. ²He had a little book open in his hand. And he set his right foot on the sea and *his* left *foot* on the land, ³and cried with a loud voice, as *when* a lion roars. When he cried out, seven thunders uttered their voices. ⁴Now when the seven thunders uttered their voices,*ᵃ* I was about to write; but I heard a voice from heaven saying to me,*ᵇ* "Seal up the things which the seven thunders uttered, and do not write them."

⁵The angel whom I saw standing on the sea and on the land raised up his hand*ᵃ* to heaven ⁶and swore by Him who lives forever and ever, who created heaven and the things that are in it, the earth and the things that are in it, and the sea and the things that are in it, that there should be delay no longer, ⁷but in the days of the sounding of the seventh angel, when he is about to sound, the mystery of God would be finished, as He declared to His servants the prophets.

John Eats the Little Book

⁸Then the voice which I heard from heaven spoke to me again and said, "Go, take the little book which is open in the hand of the angel who stands on the sea and on the earth."

10:4 *ᵃ*NU-Text and M-Text read *sounded.*   *ᵇ*NU-Text and M-Text omit *to me.*   10:5 *ᵃ*NU-Text and M-Text read *right hand.*

What are the different ways in which the Book of Revelation can be interpreted?

No other New Testament book poses more interpretive challenges than Revelation. The book's vivid imagery and striking symbolism have produced four main interpretive approaches:

1. The *preterist* approach interprets Revelation as a description of first century events in the Roman Empire. This view conflicts with the book's own repeated claim to be prophecy (1:3; 22:7,10,18,19). It is impossible to see all the events in Revelation as already fulfilled. The Second Coming of Christ, for example, obviously did not take place in the first century.

2. The *historicist* approach views Revelation as a panoramic description of church history from apostolic times to the present—seeing in the symbolism such events as the barbarian invasions of Rome, the rise of the Roman Catholic Church, the emergence of Islam, and the French Revolution. This interpretive method, however, robs Revelation of any meaning for those to whom it was originally written. It also ignores the time limitations the book itself places on the unfolding event (11:2; 12:6,14; 13:5). Historicism has produced many different—and often conflicting—interpretations of the actual historical events contained in Revelation.

3. The *idealist* approach interprets Revelation as a timeless depiction of the cosmic struggle between the forces of good and evil. In this view, the book contains neither historical allusions nor predictive prophecy. Since this view ignores Revelation's stated prophetic character, however, it tends to sever the book from any connection with actual historical events. Revelation then becomes merely a collection of stories designed to teach spiritual truth.

4. The *futurist* approach insists that the events recorded in chapters 6–22 are yet future, and that those chapters literally and symbolically depict actual people and events yet to appear on the world scene. The chapters describe the events surrounding the Second Coming of Jesus Christ (chapters 6–19), the Millenium and final judgment (chapter 20), and the eternal state (chapters 21,22). Only this view does justice to Revelation's claim to be prophecy and interprets the entire book by the consistent grammatical-historical method used for the rest of Scripture.

⁹So I went to the angel and said to him, "Give me the little book."

And he said to me, "Take and eat it; and it will make your stomach bitter, but it will be as sweet as honey in your mouth."

> **10:9 Take and eat it.** John's physical reactions display the believer's proper response to God's judgment (see Ezek. 3:1): the sweet anticipation of God's glory and our victory coupled with the bitterness of seeing God's wrath poured out on those who reject Christ.

¹⁰Then I took the little book out of the angel's hand and ate it, and it was as sweet as honey in my mouth. But when I had eaten it, my stomach became bitter. ¹¹And he*ᵃ* said to me, "You must prophesy again about many peoples, nations, tongues, and kings."

The Two Witnesses

11 Then I was given a reed like a measuring rod. And the angel stood,*ᵃ* saying, "Rise and measure the temple of God, the altar, and those who worship there. ²But leave out the court which is outside the temple, and do not measure it, for it has been given to the Gentiles. And they will tread the holy city underfoot *for* forty-two months. ³And I will give *power* to my two witnesses, and they will prophesy one thousand two hundred and sixty days, clothed in sackcloth."

> **11:3 two witnesses.** Individuals were granted power and authority by God to preach judgment and salvation during the second half of the Tribulation. The OT required two or more witnesses to confirm testimony (see Deut. 17:6). **sackcloth.** Wearing garments made from goat or camel hair expressed penitence, humility, and mourning (see Gen. 37:34). The witnesses were mourning over the wickedness of the world, God's judgment on it, and the desecration of the temple and holy city by the Antichrist.

⁴These are the two olive trees and the two lampstands standing before the God*ᵃ* of the earth. ⁵And if anyone wants to harm them, fire proceeds from their mouth and devours their enemies. And if anyone wants to harm them, he must be killed in this manner. ⁶These have power to shut heaven, so that no rain falls in the days of their prophecy; and they have power over waters to turn them to blood, and to strike the earth with all plagues, as often as they desire.

The Witnesses Killed

⁷When they finish their testimony, the beast that ascends out of the bottomless pit will make war against them, overcome them, and kill them. ⁸And their dead bodies *will lie* in the street of the great city which spiritually is called Sodom and Egypt, where also our*ᵃ* Lord was crucified. ⁹Then *those* from the peoples, tribes, tongues, and nations will see their dead bodies three-and-a-half days, and not allow*ᵃ* their dead bodies to be put into graves. ¹⁰And those who dwell on the earth will rejoice over them, make merry, and send gifts to one another, because these two prophets tormented those who dwell on the earth.

The Witnesses Resurrected

¹¹Now after the three-and-a-half days the breath of life from God entered them, and they stood on their feet, and great fear fell on those who saw them. ¹²And they*ᵃ* heard a loud voice from heaven saying to them, "Come up here." And they ascended to heaven in a cloud, and their enemies saw them. ¹³In the same hour there was a great earthquake, and a tenth of the city fell. In the earthquake seven thousand people were killed, and the rest were afraid and gave glory to the God of heaven.

> **11:12 ascended to heaven in a cloud.** Some may wonder why God will not allow them to preach, assuming their message would have more force following their resurrection. But that ignores Christ's clear statement to the contrary (Luke 16:31). **enemies saw them.** Those who hated and dishonored the two witnesses will watch their vindication.

¹⁴The second woe is past. Behold, the third woe is coming quickly.

10:11 *ᵃ*NU-Text and M-Text read *they*.   11:1 *ᵃ*NU-Text and M-Text omit *And the angel stood*. 11:4 *ᵃ*NU-Text and M-Text read *Lord*.   11:8 *ᵃ*NU-Text and M-Text read *their*.   11:9 *ᵃ*NU-Text and M-Text read *nations see . . . and will not allow*.   11:12 *ᵃ*M-Text reads *I*.

Seventh Trumpet: The Kingdom Proclaimed

¹⁵Then the seventh angel sounded: And there were loud voices in heaven, saying, "The kingdoms^a of this world have become *the kingdoms* of our Lord and of His Christ, and He shall reign forever and ever!" ¹⁶And the twenty-four elders who sat before God on their thrones fell on their faces and worshiped God, ¹⁷saying:

"We give You thanks, O Lord God Almighty,
　The One who is and who was and who is to come,^a
　Because You have taken Your great power and reigned.
¹⁸　The nations were angry, and Your wrath has come,
　And the time of the dead, that they should be judged,
　And that You should reward Your servants the prophets and the saints,
　And those who fear Your name, small and great,
　And should destroy those who destroy the earth."

¹⁹Then the temple of God was opened in heaven, and the ark of His covenant^a was seen in His temple. And there were lightnings, noises, thunderings, an earthquake, and great hail.

> **11:19 temple of God...heaven.** God's throne is the heavenly Holy of Holies. John has seen the throne, the altar, and the Holy of Holies. **ark of His covenant.** This symbolized God's presence, atonement, and covenant with His people in the OT. The earthly ark was only a picture of this heavenly one (see Heb. 9:23). **lightnings, noises, thunderings, an earthquake, and great hail.** These terrifying events occur as part of the 7th bowl and are the climax of the 7th trumpet.

The Woman, the Child, and the Dragon

12 Now a great sign appeared in heaven: a woman clothed with the sun, with the moon under her feet, and on her head a garland of twelve stars. ²Then being with child, she cried out in labor and in pain to give birth.

³And another sign appeared in heaven: behold, a great, fiery red dragon having seven heads and ten horns, and seven diadems on his heads. ⁴His tail drew a third of the stars of heaven and threw them to the earth. And the dragon stood before the woman who was ready to give birth, to devour her Child as soon as it was born. ⁵She bore a male Child who was to rule all nations with a rod of iron. And her Child was caught up to God and His throne. ⁶Then the woman fled into the wilderness, where she has a place prepared by God, that they should feed her there one thousand two hundred and sixty days.

> **12:3 great, fiery red dragon.** The woman's mortal enemy is Satan, who appears as a dragon 13 times in this book. Red symbolizes bloodshed (see John 8:44). **seven heads...ten horns...seven diadems.** This depicts Satan's domination of 7 past worldly kingdoms and 10 future kingdoms (see Dan. 7:7,20,24). Satan has and will rule the world until the 7th trumpet blows. He has inflicted pain on the woman, Israel (Dan. 8:24), desiring to kill her before she could bring forth the Child that would destroy him.

Satan Thrown Out of Heaven

⁷And war broke out in heaven: Michael and his angels fought with the dragon; and the dragon and his angels fought, ⁸but they did not prevail, nor was a place found for them^a in heaven any longer. ⁹So the great dragon was cast out, that serpent of old, called the Devil and Satan, who deceives the whole world; he was cast to the earth, and his angels were cast out with him.

¹⁰Then I heard a loud voice saying in heaven, "Now salvation, and strength, and the kingdom of our God, and the power of His Christ have come, for the accuser of our brethren, who accused them before our God day and night, has been cast down. ¹¹And they overcame him by the blood of the Lamb and by the word of their testimony, and they did not love their lives to the death. ¹²Therefore rejoice, O heavens, and you who dwell in them! Woe to the inhabitants of the earth and the sea! For the devil has come down to you, having great wrath, because he knows that he has a short time."

11:15 ^aNU-Text and M-Text read *kingdom . . . has become.*　　11:17 ^aNU-Text and M-Text omit *and who is to come.*　　11:19 ^aM-Text reads *the covenant of the Lord.*　　12:8 ^aM-Text reads *him.*

The Woman Persecuted

¹³Now when the dragon saw that he had been cast to the earth, he persecuted the woman who gave birth to the male *Child.* ¹⁴But the woman was given two wings of a great eagle, that she might fly into the wilderness to her place, where she is nourished for a time and times and half a time, from the presence of the serpent. ¹⁵So the serpent spewed water out of his mouth like a flood after the woman, that he might cause her to be carried away by the flood. ¹⁶But the earth helped the woman, and the earth opened its mouth and swallowed up the flood which the dragon had spewed out of his mouth. ¹⁷And the dragon was enraged with the woman, and he went to make war with the rest of her offspring, who keep the commandments of God and have the testimony of Jesus Christ.*a*

> **12:14 a time and times and half a time.** This is three and one-half years, the second half of the Tribulation.

The Beast from the Sea

13 Then I*a* stood on the sand of the sea. And I saw a beast rising up out of the sea, having seven heads and ten horns,*b* and on his horns ten crowns, and on his heads a blasphemous name. ²Now the beast which I saw was like a leopard, his feet were like *the feet of* a bear, and his mouth like the mouth of a lion. The dragon gave him his power, his throne, and great authority. ³And *I saw* one of his heads as if it had been mortally wounded, and his deadly wound was healed. And all the world marveled and followed the beast. ⁴So they worshiped the dragon who gave authority to the beast; and they worshiped beast, saying, "Who *is* like the beast? Who is able to make war with him?"

> **13:3 his deadly wound was healed.** This could refer to one of the kingdoms that was destroyed and revived, or it could refer to a fake death and resurrection enacted by the Antichrist. **world marveled.** People in the world will be fascinated when the Antichrist appears to rise from the dead. They will follow him unquestioningly (see 2 Thess. 2:8–12).

⁵And he was given a mouth speaking great things and blasphemies, and he was given authority to continue*a* for forty-two months. ⁶Then he opened his mouth in blasphemy against God, to blaspheme His name, His tabernacle, and those who dwell in heaven. ⁷It was granted to him to make war with the saints and to overcome them. And authority was given him over every tribe,*a* tongue, and nation. ⁸All who dwell on the earth will worship him, whose names have not been written in the Book of Life of the Lamb slain from the foundation of the world.

⁹If anyone has an ear, let him hear. ¹⁰He

12:17 *a*NU-Text and M-Text omit *Christ.*   13:1 *a*NU-Text reads *he.*   *b*NU-Text and M-Text read *ten horns and seven heads.*   13:5 *a*M-Text reads *make war.*   13:7 *a*NU-Text and M-Text add *and people.*

Why does the number 666 get so much attention?

Numbers are important in Scripture in two ways: (1) they speak to God's exactness; and (2) they represent certain recurring ideas. The number 666 is mentioned in Revelation 13:18. The significance of the number itself is not emphasized, so speculation about the meaning must be cautious and limited.

The number 666 represents the essential number of a man. The number 6 falls one short of God's perfect number, 7, and thus points to human imperfection. The Antichrist, the most powerful human the world will ever know, will still be a man— a 6. The ultimate in human and demonic power is a 6, not perfect, as God is. The three-fold repetition of the number is intended to emphasize man's identity. He is emphatically imperfect, not almost perfect. When the Antichrist is finally revealed, there will be some way to identify him with this basic number of a man, or his name may have the numerical equivalent of 666. In many languages, including Hebrew, Greek, and Latin, letters from the alphabet were used to represent numbers.

Beyond these basic observations, the text reveals very little about the meaning of 666. It is unwise, therefore, to speculate beyond what God's Word gives us.

who leads into captivity shall go into captivity; he who kills with the sword must be killed with the sword. Here is the patience and the faith of the saints.

> **13:12 exercises all the authority of the first beast.** The false prophet exercises the same kind of satanic power as the Antichrist, because he is empowered by the same source. He will also have worldwide influence as a miracle worker and speaker.

The Beast from the Earth

[11]Then I saw another beast coming up out of the earth, and he had two horns like a lamb and spoke like a dragon. [12]And he exercises all the authority of the first beast in his presence, and causes the earth and those who dwell in it to worship the first beast, whose deadly wound was healed. [13]He performs great signs, so that he even makes fire come down from heaven on the earth in the sight of men. [14]And he deceives those[a] who dwell on the earth by those signs which he was granted to do in the sight of the beast, telling those who dwell on the earth to make an image to the beast who was wounded by the sword and lived. [15]He was granted *power* to give breath to the image of the beast, that the image of the beast should both speak and cause as many as would not worship the image of the beast to be killed. [16]He causes all, both small and great, rich and poor, free and slave, to receive a mark on their right hand or on their foreheads, [17]and that no one may buy or sell except one who has the mark or[a] the name of the beast, or the number of his name.

[18]Here is wisdom. Let him who has un-

> **13:17 buy or sell.** The Antichrist's mark will allow people to engage in daily commerce. Without the identifying mark, individuals will be cut off from purchasing the necessities of life. **number of his name.** The beast (Antichrist) will have a name somehow tied to a numbering system, though it is not clear from the text what this name and number system will be or what its significance will be. Because the text reveals very little about this, it is unwise to speculate beyond what is said.

derstanding calculate the number of the beast, for it is the number of a man: His number *is* 666.

The Lamb and the 144,000

14 Then I looked, and behold, a[a] Lamb standing on Mount Zion, and with Him one hundred *and* forty-four thousand, having[b] His Father's name written on their foreheads. [2]And I heard a voice from heaven, like the voice of many waters, and like the voice of loud thunder. And I heard the sound of harpists playing their harps. [3]They sang as it were a new song before the throne, before the four living creatures, and the elders; and no one could learn that song except the hundred *and* forty-four thousand who were redeemed from the earth. [4]These are the ones who were not defiled with women, for they are virgins. These are the ones who follow the Lamb wherever He goes. These were redeemed[a] from *among* men, *being* firstfruits to God and to the Lamb. [5]And in their mouth was found no deceit,[a] for they are without fault before the throne of God.[b]

The Proclamations of Three Angels

[6]Then I saw another angel flying in the midst of heaven, having the everlasting gospel to preach to those who dwell on the earth—to every nation, tribe, tongue, and people—[7]saying with a loud voice, "Fear God and give glory to Him, for the hour of His judgment has come; and worship Him who made heaven and earth, the sea and springs of water."

[8]And another angel followed, saying, "Babylon[a] is fallen, is fallen, that great city,

> **14:8 Babylon is fallen.** Babylon refers to the entire worldwide political, economic, and religious kingdom of the Antichrist (see 16:17–19). The original city of Babylon was the birthplace of idolatry with the Tower of Babel, a monument to rebellion and false religion. This idolatry then spread when God confused human language and scattered people around the world (see Gen. 11:1–9).

13:14 [a]M-Text reads *my own people.*   13:17 [a]NU-Text and M-Text omit *or.*   14:1 [a]NU-Text and M-Text read *the.*   [b]NU-Text and M-Text add *His name and.*   14:4 [a]M-Text adds *by Jesus.*
14:5 [a]NU-Text and M-Text read *falsehood.*   [b]NU-Text and M-Text omit *before the throne of God.*
14:8 [a]NU-Text reads *Babylon the great is fallen, is fallen, which has made;* M-Text reads *Babylon the great is fallen. She has made.*

because she has made all nations drink of the wine of the wrath of her fornication."

⁹Then a third angel followed them, saying with a loud voice, "If anyone worships the beast and his image, and receives *his* mark on his forehead or on his hand, ¹⁰he himself shall also drink of the wine of the wrath of God, which is poured out full strength into the cup of His indignation. He shall be tormented with fire and brimstone in the presence of the holy angels and in the presence of the Lamb. ¹¹And the smoke of their torment ascends forever and ever; and they have no rest day or night, who worship the beast and his image, and whoever receives the mark of his name."

¹²Here is the patience of the saints; here *are* those*ᵃ* who keep the commandments of God and the faith of Jesus.

¹³Then I heard a voice from heaven saying to me,*ᵃ* "Write: 'Blessed *are* the dead who die in the Lord from now on.' "

"Yes," says the Spirit, "that they may rest from their labors, and their works follow them."

Reaping the Earth's Harvest

¹⁴Then I looked, and behold, a white cloud, and on the cloud sat *One* like the Son of Man, having on His head a golden crown, and in His hand a sharp sickle. ¹⁵And another angel came out of the temple, crying with a loud voice to Him who sat on the cloud, "Thrust in Your sickle and reap, for the time has come for You*ᵃ* to reap, for the harvest of the earth is ripe." ¹⁶So He who sat on the cloud thrust in His sickle on the earth, and the earth was reaped.

> **14:15 harvest of the earth.** The grain is representative of the ungodly people who are ready to be gathered up and judged.

Reaping the Grapes of Wrath

¹⁷Then another angel came out of the temple which is in heaven, he also having a sharp sickle.

¹⁸And another angel came out from the altar, who had power over fire, and he cried with a loud cry to him who had the sharp sickle, saying, "Thrust in your sharp sickle and gather the clusters of the vine of the earth, for her grapes are fully ripe." ¹⁹So the angel thrust his sickle into the earth and gathered the vine of the earth, and threw *it* into the great winepress of the wrath of God. ²⁰And the winepress was trampled outside the city, and blood came out of the winepress, up to the horses' bridles, for one thousand six hundred furlongs.

> **15:1–8** Chap. 15 introduces the 7 bowls of wrath, God's final judgment at the end of the 7 year Tribulation period. The 7 bowls come in rapid succession, each one increasing in intensity.

Prelude to the Bowl Judgments

15 Then I saw another sign in heaven, great and marvelous: seven angels having the seven last plagues, for in them the wrath of God is complete.

²And I saw *something* like a sea of glass mingled with fire, and those who have the victory over the beast, over his image and over his mark*ᵃ* *and* over the number of his name, standing on the sea of glass, having harps of God. ³They sing the song of Moses, the servant of God, and the song of the Lamb, saying:

"Great and marvelous *are* Your works,
Lord God Almighty!
Just and true *are* Your ways,
O King of the saints!*ᵃ*
⁴ Who shall not fear You, O Lord, and
glorify Your name?
For *You* alone *are* holy.
For all nations shall come and
worship before You,
For Your judgments have been
manifested."

⁵After these things I looked, and behold,*ᵃ* the temple of the tabernacle of the testimony in heaven was opened. ⁶And out of the temple came the seven angels having the seven plagues, clothed in pure bright linen, and having their chests girded with golden

---

14:12 *ᵃ*NU-Text and M-Text omit *here are those.*   14:13 *ᵃ*NU-Text and M-Text omit *to me.*
14:15 *ᵃ*NU-Text and M-Text omit *for You.*   15:2 *ᵃ*NU-Text and M-Text omit *over his mark.*
15:3 *ᵃ*NU-Text and M-Text read *nations.*   15:5 *ᵃ*NU-Text and M-Text omit *behold.*

bands. ⁷Then one of the four living creatures gave to the seven angels seven golden bowls full of the wrath of God who lives forever and ever. ⁸The temple was filled with smoke from the glory of God and from His power, and no one was able to enter the temple till the seven plagues of the seven angels were completed.

> **15:7 seven golden bowls.** These are shallow saucers that were often associated with various functions of the temple worship (1 Kin. 7:50), such as wine (Amos 6:6) and blood sacrifice (Ex. 27:3). Their flat shallowness is significant because it enables one to understand how God's judgments will be poured out. The bowls will be emptied instantly, rather than being slowly poured, drowning those who refused to drink the cup of salvation.

16

Then I heard a loud voice from the temple saying to the seven angels, "Go and pour out the bowls*a* of the wrath of God on the earth."

First Bowl: Loathsome Sores

²So the first went and poured out his bowl upon the earth, and a foul and loathsome sore came upon the men who had the mark of the beast and those who worshiped his image.

Second Bowl: The Sea Turns to Blood

³Then the second angel poured out his bowl on the sea, and it became blood as of a dead *man*; and every living creature in the sea died.

Third Bowl: The Waters Turn to Blood

⁴Then the third angel poured out his bowl on the rivers and springs of water, and they became blood. ⁵And I heard the angel of the waters saying:

"You are righteous, O Lord,*a*
The One who is and who was and
    who is to be,*b*
Because You have judged these
    things.
6   For they have shed the blood of saints
    and prophets,

And You have given them blood to
    drink.
For*a* it is their just due."

> **16:6 given them blood to drink.** The thick, blood-like substance, which the fresh waters have become, is all that is available to drink. **For it is their just due.** God is not too harsh. The generation during this period will shed more blood than any other before it, including that of the saints (6:9) and prophets (11:7–10). God's judgment is fair and proper (see Ex. 21:25–27).

⁷And I heard another from*a* the altar saying, "Even so, Lord God Almighty, true and righteous *are* Your judgments."

Fourth Bowl: Men Are Scorched

⁸Then the fourth angel poured out his bowl on the sun, and power was given to him to scorch men with fire. ⁹And men were scorched with great heat, and they blasphemed the name of God who has power over these plagues; and they did not repent and give Him glory.

Fifth Bowl: Darkness and Pain

¹⁰Then the fifth angel poured out his bowl on the throne of the beast, and his kingdom became full of darkness; and they gnawed their tongues because of the pain. ¹¹They blasphemed the God of heaven because of their pains and their sores, and did not repent of their deeds.

Sixth Bowl: Euphrates Dried Up

¹²Then the sixth angel poured out his bowl on the great river Euphrates, and its water was dried up, so that the way of the kings from the east might be prepared. ¹³And I saw three unclean spirits like frogs *coming* out of the mouth of the dragon, out of the mouth of the beast, and out of the mouth of the false prophet. ¹⁴For they are

> **16:13 the dragon...the beast...the false prophet.** This is sometimes referred to as the "unholy trinity," and is composed of Satan (the dragon), the Antichrist (the beast), and the Antichrist's associate (the false prophet). This group spews out this plague.

16:1 *a*NU-Text and M-Text read *seven bowls.*   16:5 *a*NU-Text and M-Text omit *O Lord.*   *b*NU-Text and M-Text read *who was, the Holy One.*   16:6 *a*NU-Text and M-Text omit *For.*   16:7 *a*NU-Text and M-Text omit *another from.*

spirits of demons, performing signs, *which* go out to the kings of the earth and*a* of the whole world, to gather them to the battle of that great day of God Almighty.

¹⁵"Behold, I am coming as a thief. Blessed *is* he who watches, and keeps his garments, lest he walk naked and they see his shame."

¹⁶And they gathered them together to the place called in Hebrew, Armageddon.*a*

Seventh Bowl: The Earth Utterly Shaken

¹⁷Then the seventh angel poured out his bowl into the air, and a loud voice came out of the temple of heaven, from the throne, saying, "It is done!" ¹⁸And there were noises and thunderings and lightnings; and there was a great earthquake, such a mighty and great earthquake as had not occurred since men were on the earth. ¹⁹Now the great city was divided into three parts, and the cities of the nations fell. And great Babylon was remembered before God, to give her the cup of the wine of the fierceness of His wrath. ²⁰Then every island fled away, and the mountains were not found. ²¹And great hail from heaven fell upon men, *each hailstone* about the weight of a talent. Men blasphemed God because of the plague of the hail, since that plague was exceedingly great.

16:19 the great city. Jerusalem will be split into 3 parts, not as a judgment, but as an improvement. The additional water supply and topographical changes will prepare the city for its central place in the millennial kingdom. Jerusalem is the only city to be spared the judgment and will be made more beautiful because of her repentance (see 11:13; 1 Chr. 23:25; Ps. 48:2; Zech. 14:4–8).

The Scarlet Woman and the Scarlet Beast

17 Then one of the seven angels who had the seven bowls came and talked with me, saying to me,*a* "Come, I will show you the judgment of the great harlot who sits on many waters, ²with whom the kings of the earth committed fornication, and the inhabitants of the earth were made drunk with the wine of her fornication."

³So he carried me away in the Spirit into the wilderness. And I saw a woman sitting on a scarlet beast *which was* full of names of blasphemy, having seven heads and ten horns. ⁴The woman was arrayed in purple and scarlet, and adorned with gold and precious stones and pearls, having in her hand a golden cup full of abominations and the filthiness of her fornication.*a* ⁵And on her forehead a name *was* written:

MYSTERY,
BABYLON THE GREAT,
THE MOTHER OF HARLOTS
AND OF THE
ABOMINATIONS OF THE EARTH.

17:5 forehead. Roman prostitutes customarily wore headbands with their names on them (see Jer. 3:3), parading their wretchedness for all to see. The harlot's forehead is emblazoned with a 3-fold title descriptive of the world's false religious system. **MYSTERY.** Spiritual Babylon's true identity is yet to be revealed. Thus, the precise details of how it will be manifested in the world are not yet known. **BABYLON THE GREAT.** This Babylon is distinct from the Babylon of John's day. The details of John's vision cannot be applied to any historical city. **MOTHER OF HARLOTS.** All false religious systems ultimately stem from Babel, or Babylon (see Gen. 11).

⁶I saw the woman, drunk with the blood of the saints and with the blood of the martyrs of Jesus. And when I saw her, I marveled with great amazement.

The Meaning of the Woman and the Beast

⁷But the angel said to me, "Why did you marvel? I will tell you the mystery of the woman and of the beast that carries her, which has the seven heads and the ten horns. ⁸The beast that you saw was, and is not, and will ascend out of the bottomless pit and go to perdition. And those who dwell on the earth will marvel, whose names are not written in the Book of Life from the foundation of the world, when they see the beast that was, and is not, and yet is.*a*

⁹"Here *is* the mind which has wisdom: The seven heads are seven mountains on

---

16:14 *a*NU-Text and M-Text omit *of the earth and.* 16:16 *a*M-Text reads *Megiddo.* 17:1 *a*NU-Text and M-Text omit *to me.* 17:4 *a*M-Text reads *the filthiness of the fornication of the earth.* 17:8 *a*NU-Text and M-Text read *and shall be present.*

which the woman sits. [10]There are also seven kings. Five have fallen, one is, *and* the other has not yet come. And when he comes, he must continue a short time. [11]The beast that was, and is not, is himself also the eighth, and is of the seven, and is going to perdition.

[12]"The ten horns which you saw are ten kings who have received no kingdom as yet, but they receive authority for one hour as kings with the beast. [13]These are of one mind, and they will give their power and authority to the beast. [14]These will make war with the Lamb, and the Lamb will overcome them, for He is Lord of lords and King of kings; and those *who are* with Him *are* called, chosen, and faithful."

17:12 ten kings. These kings rule the 10 administrative districts under the Antichrist (see Dan. 2:41,42). **no kingdom as yet.** The kings cannot be identified with any historical figures. **one hour.** This is symbolic of the brief 3½-year period of time.

[15]Then he said to me, "The waters which you saw, where the harlot sits, are peoples, multitudes, nations, and tongues. [16]And the ten horns which you saw on[a] the beast, these will hate the harlot, make her desolate and naked, eat her flesh and burn her with fire. [17]For God has put it into their hearts to fulfill His purpose, to be of one mind, and to give their kingdom to the beast, until the words of God are fulfilled. [18]And the woman whom you saw is that great city which reigns over the kings of the earth."

The Fall of Babylon the Great

18 After these things I saw another angel coming down from heaven, having great authority, and the earth was illuminated with his glory. [2]And he cried mightily[a] with a loud voice, saying, "Babylon the great is fallen, is fallen, and has become a dwelling place of demons, a prison for every foul spirit, and a cage for every unclean and hated bird! [3]For all the nations have drunk of the wine of the wrath of her fornication, the kings of the earth have

committed fornication with her, and the merchants of the earth have become rich through the abundance of her luxury."

[4]"And I heard another voice from heaven saying, "Come out of her, my people, lest you share in her sins, and lest you receive of her plagues. [5]For her sins have reached[a] to heaven, and God has remembered her iniquities. [6]Render to her just as she rendered to you,[a] and repay her double according to her works; in the cup which she has mixed, mix double for her. [7]In the measure that she glorified herself and lived luxuriously, in the same measure give her torment and sorrow; for she says in her heart, 'I sit *as* queen, and am no widow, and will not see sorrow.' [8]Therefore her plagues will come in one day—death and mourning and famine. And she will be utterly burned with fire, for strong *is* the Lord God who judges[a] her.

18:4 Come out of her, my people. God will call His own to abandon the evil system before it is destroyed (see 2 Cor. 6:17). The judgment of God on that society living in sin can be avoided (see Is. 48:20; Jer. 50:8).

The World Mourns Babylon's Fall

[9]"The kings of the earth who committed fornication and lived luxuriously with her will weep and lament for her, when they see the smoke of her burning, [10]standing at a distance for fear of her torment, saying, 'Alas, alas, that great city Babylon, that mighty city! For in one hour your judgment has come.'

[11]"And the merchants of the earth will weep and mourn over her, for no one buys their merchandise anymore: [12]merchandise of gold and silver, precious stones and pearls, fine linen and purple, silk and scarlet, every kind of citron wood, every kind of object of ivory, every kind of object of most precious wood, bronze, iron, and marble; [13]and cinnamon and incense, fragrant oil and frankincense, wine and oil, fine flour and wheat, cattle and sheep, horses and chariots, and bodies and souls of men. [14]The fruit that your soul longed for has

---

17:16 [a]NU-Text and M-Text read *saw, and the beast.*   18:2 [a]NU-Text and M-Text omit *mightily.*
18:5 [a]NU-Text and M-Text read *have been heaped up.*   18:6 [a]NU-Text and M-Text omit *to you.*
18:8 [a]NU-Text and M-Text read *has judged.*

gone from you, and all the things which are rich and splendid have gone from you,[a] and you shall find them no more at all. [15]The merchants of these things, who became rich by her, will stand at a distance for fear of her torment, weeping and wailing, [16]and saying, 'Alas, alas, that great city that was clothed in fine linen, purple, and scarlet, and adorned with gold and precious stones and pearls! [17]For in one hour such great riches came to nothing.' Every shipmaster, all who travel by ship, sailors, and as many as trade on the sea, stood at a distance [18]and cried out when they saw the smoke of her burning, saying, 'What *is* like this great city?'

[19]"They threw dust on their heads and cried out, weeping and wailing, and saying, 'Alas, alas, that great city, in which all who had ships on the sea became rich by her wealth! For in one hour she is made desolate.'

[20]"Rejoice over her, O heaven, and *you* holy apostles[a] and prophets, for God has avenged you on her!"

Finality of Babylon's Fall

[21]Then a mighty angel took up a stone like a great millstone and threw *it* into the sea, saying, "Thus with violence the great city Babylon shall be thrown down, and shall not be found anymore. [22]The sound of harpists, musicians, flutists, and trumpeters shall not be heard in you anymore. No craftsman of any craft shall be found in you anymore, and the sound of a millstone

shall not be heard in you anymore. [23]The light of a lamp shall not shine in you anymore, and the voice of bridegroom and bride shall not be heard in you anymore. For your merchants were the great men of the earth, for by your sorcery all the nations were deceived. [24]And in her was found the blood of prophets and saints, and of all who were slain on the earth."

> **18:22,23** The fall of Babylon ends all normalcy in the world, after all the seals, trumpets, and bowls. There will be no more music, no industry, no preparing food ("millstone"), nor more power for light, and no more weddings because God will destroy the deceivers and deceived. The end will be near.

Heaven Exults over Babylon

19 After these things I heard[a] a loud voice of a great multitude in heaven, saying, "Alleluia! Salvation and glory and honor and power *belong* to the Lord[b] our God! [2]For true and righteous *are* His judgments, because He has judged the great harlot who corrupted the earth with her fornication; and He has avenged on her the blood of His servants *shed* by her." [3]Again they said, "Alleluia! Her smoke rises up forever and ever!" [4]And the twenty-four elders and the four living creatures fell down and worshiped God who sat on the throne, saying, "Amen! Alleluia!" [5]Then a voice came from the throne, saying, "Praise our God, all you His servants and those who fear Him, both[a] small and great!"

[6]And I heard, as it were, the voice of a

18:14 [a]NU-Text and M-Text read *been lost to you.*   18:20 [a]NU-Text and M-Text read *saints and apostles.*   19:1 [a]NU-Text and M-Text add *something like.*   [b]NU-Text and M-Text omit *the Lord.* 19:5 [a]NU-Text and M-Text omit *both.*

Why does the great multitude in Revelation 19:1–6 keep saying "Alleluia"?

The term is a transliterated Hebrew word that appears only four times in the New Testament, all in this chapter (verses 1,3,4,6). This exclamation, meaning "Praise the Lord," occurs frequently in the Old Testament (Psalms 104:35; 105:45; 106:1; 111:1; 112:1; 113:1; 117:1; 135:1; 146:1).

In the case of this great multitude gathered in heaven, they have five reasons for repeatedly shouting, "Alleluia—Praise the Lord!" (1) They praise God for delivering His people from their enemies (verses 1,2). (2) They praise God for meeting out justice (verse 2). (3) They praise God for permanently crushing man's rebellion (verse 3). (4) They praise God for His sovereignty (verse 6). (5) They praise God for communing (being) with His people (verse 7).

great multitude, as the sound of many waters and as the sound of mighty thunderings, saying, "Alleluia! For the[a] Lord God Omnipotent reigns! [7]Let us be glad and rejoice and give Him glory, for the marriage of the Lamb has come, and His wife has made herself ready." [8]And to her it was granted to be arrayed in fine linen, clean and bright, for the fine linen is the righteous acts of the saints.

19:7 marriage of the Lamb. Hebrew weddings consisted of betrothal, presentation (the festivities that preceded the ceremony), and the ceremony. The church was betrothed to Christ by His sovereign choice in eternity past (Eph. 1:4) and will be presented to Him at the Rapture (John 14:1–3). The final supper, signifying the end of the ceremony, will occur at the establishment of the millennial kingdom and will last throughout the 1,000-year period. "Bride" refers to the church here, but will ultimately expand to include all the redeemed of all ages in time.

[9]Then he said to me, "Write: 'Blessed *are* those who are called to the marriage supper of the Lamb!' " And he said to me, "These are the true sayings of God." [10]And I fell at his feet to worship him. But he said to me, "See *that you do* not *do that!* I am your fellow servant, and of your brethren who have the testimony of Jesus. Worship God! For the testimony of Jesus is the spirit of prophecy."

Christ on a White Horse

[11]Now I saw heaven opened, and behold, a white horse. And He who sat on him *was* called Faithful and True, and in righteousness He judges and makes war. [12]His eyes *were* like a flame of fire, and on His head *were* many crowns. He had[a] a name written that no one knew except Himself. [13]He *was* clothed with a robe dipped in blood,

19:11 heaven opened. Christ will return to take back the earth from the usurper and to establish His kingdom. This is an event marked by judgment, in which Christ will accompany His own to earth. It is preceded by blackness then lightning and blinding glory as Jesus comes. It differs from the Rapture, when Christ meets His own in the air.

and His name is called The Word of God. [14]And the armies in heaven, clothed in fine linen, white and clean,[a] followed Him on white horses. [15]Now out of His mouth goes a sharp[a] sword, that with it He should strike the nations. And He Himself will rule them with a rod of iron. He Himself treads the winepress of the fierceness and wrath of Almighty God. [16]And He has on *His* robe and on His thigh a name written:

KING OF KINGS
AND LORD OF LORDS.

The Beast and His Armies Defeated

[17]Then I saw an angel standing in the sun; and he cried with a loud voice, saying to all the birds that fly in the midst of heaven, "Come and gather together for the supper of the great God,[a] [18]that you may eat the flesh of kings, the flesh of captains, the flesh of mighty men, the flesh of horses and of those who sit on them, and the flesh of all *people*, free[a] and slave, both small and great."

19:17–21 These verses depict the Battle of Armageddon, the pinnacle of the Day of the Lord. In this battle, Jesus kills the remaining rebels. This Day of the Lord was seen by Isaiah (66:15,16), Joel (3:12–21), Ezekiel (39:1–4,17–20), Paul (2 Thess. 1:6; 2:8), and our Lord (Matt. 25:31–46).

[19]And I saw the beast, the kings of the earth, and their armies, gathered together to make war against Him who sat on the horse and against His army. [20]Then the beast was captured, and with him the false prophet who worked signs in his presence, by which he deceived those who received the mark of the beast and those who worshiped his image. These two were cast alive into the lake of fire burning with brimstone. [21]And the rest were killed with the sword which proceeded from the mouth of Him who sat on the horse. And all the birds were filled with their flesh.

Satan Bound 1000 Years

20 Then I saw an angel coming down from heaven, having the key to the

---

20:1–22:21 The events of chap. 20 include the binding of Satan, Christ's 1,000-year earthly kingdom, Satan's final rebellion, and the Great White Throne Judgment. These events fit chronologically between the close of the Tribulation (chap. 19) and the creation of the new heaven and the new earth described in chaps. 21 and 22.

bottomless pit and a great chain in his hand. ²He laid hold of the dragon, that serpent of old, who is *the* Devil and Satan, and bound him for a thousand years; ³and he cast him into the bottomless pit, and shut him up, and set a seal on him, so that he should deceive the nations no more till the thousand years were finished. But after these things he must be released for a little while.

The Saints Reign with Christ 1000 Years

⁴And I saw thrones, and they sat on them, and judgment was committed to them. Then *I saw* the souls of those who had been beheaded for their witness to Jesus and for the word of God, who had not worshiped the beast or his image, and had not received *his* mark on their foreheads or on their hands. And they lived and reigned with Christ for a*ᵃ* thousand years. ⁵But the rest of the dead did not live again until the thousand years were finished. This *is* the first resurrection. ⁶Blessed and holy *is* he who has part in the first resurrection. Over such the second death has no power, but they shall be priests of God and of Christ, and shall reign with Him a thousand years.

Satanic Rebellion Crushed

⁷Now when the thousand years have expired, Satan will be released from his prison ⁸and will go out to deceive the nations which are in the four corners of the earth, Gog and Magog, to gather them together to battle, whose number *is* as the sand of the sea. ⁹They went up on the breadth of the

20:7 Satan...released. He is loosed to bring cohesive leadership to the rebels and to reveal the character of Christ-rejecting sinners who are brought into judgment for the last time.

20:4 *ᵃ*M-Text reads *the.*

What is the "millennium" and where does it fit in Revelation?

Revelation 20 includes 6 mentions of a kingdom that will last 1,000 years (verses 2,3,4,5,6,7). There are 3 main views regarding the nature and duration of this period:

1. *Premillennialism* sees this as a literal 1,000-year period during which Jesus Christ, in fulfillment of numerous Old Testament prophecies (2 Samuel 7:12–16; Psalm 2; Isaiah 11:6–12; 24:23; Hosea 3:4,5; Joel 3:9–21; Amos 9:8–15; Micah 4:1–8; Zephaniah 3:14–20; Zechariah 14:1–11) and Jesus' own teaching (Matthew 24:29–31,36–44), will reign on the earth. Using the same general principles of interpretation for both prophetic and non-prophetic passages leads most naturally to Premillennialism. This view is also strongly supported by the fact that so many biblical prophecies have already been literally fulfilled and therefore suggests that future prophecies will likewise be fulfilled literally.

2. *Postmillennialism* understands the reference to a 1,000-year period as only symbolic of a golden age of righteousness and spiritual prosperity. It will be ushered in by the spread of the gospel during the present church age and brought to completion when Christ returns. According to this view, references to Christ's reign on earth primarily describe His spiritual reign in the hearts of believers in the church.

3. *Amillennialism* understands the 1,000 years to be merely symbolic of a long period of time. This view interprets Old Testament prophecies of a Millennium as being fulfilled spiritually now in the church (either on earth or in heaven), or as references to the eternal state.

In summary, nothing in the text leads directly to the conclusion that "a thousand years" is symbolic. Never in Scripture when the term "year" is used with a number is its meaning nonliteral. The weight of biblical evidence points to the premillennialist position.

earth and surrounded the camp of the saints and the beloved city. And fire came down from God out of heaven and devoured them. [10]The devil, who deceived them, was cast into the lake of fire and brimstone where[a] the beast and the false prophet *are*. And they will be tormented day and night forever and ever.

The Great White Throne Judgment

[11]Then I saw a great white throne and Him who sat on it, from whose face the earth and the heaven fled away. And there was found no place for them. [12]And I saw the dead, small and great, standing before God,[a] and books were opened. And another book was opened, which is *the Book* of Life. And the dead were judged according to their works, by the things which were written in the books. [13]The sea gave up the dead who were in it, and Death and Hades delivered up the dead who were in them. And they were judged, each one according to his works. [14]Then Death and Hades were cast into the lake of fire. This is the second death.[a] [15]And anyone not found written in the Book of Life was cast into the lake of fire.

20:12 standing before God. Since all the sinners have been killed and all the believers glorified, at this point no living sinners remain. **books.** These books record every thought, word, and deed of sinful people. They will provide evidence for eternal condemnation. **Book of Life.** It contains the names of all the redeemed (Dan. 12:1). **judged according to their works.** Their thoughts, words, and actions will be compared to God's perfect, holy standard. This implies that hell has different degrees of punishment (see Matt. 10:14,15).

All Things Made New

21 Now I saw a new heaven and a new earth, for the first heaven and the first earth had passed away. Also there was no more sea. [2]Then I, John,[a] saw the holy city, New Jerusalem, coming down out of heaven from God, prepared as a bride

21:2 New Jerusalem. This is the capital city of heaven, a place of perfect holiness. It descends into the new heavens and new earth from its place on high. This is where the saints will live (see John 14:1–3). **bride.** Believers (the bride) in the New Jerusalem come to meet Christ (the bridegroom) in the final ceremony of redemptive history. God has brought home a bride for His Son, and all the saints live with Christ in the Father's house.

adorned for her husband. [3]And I heard a loud voice from heaven saying, "Behold, the tabernacle of God *is* with men, and He will dwell with them, and they shall be His people. God Himself will be with them *and be* their God. [4]And God will wipe away every tear from their eyes; there shall be no more death, nor sorrow, nor crying. There shall be no more pain, for the former things have passed away."

[5]Then He who sat on the throne said, "Behold, I make all things new." And He said to me,[a] "Write, for these words are true and faithful."

[6]And He said to me, "It is done![a] I am the Alpha and the Omega, the Beginning and the End. I will give of the fountain of the water of life freely to him who thirsts. [7]He who overcomes shall inherit all things,[a] and I will be his God and he shall be My son. [8]But the cowardly, unbelieving,[a] abominable, murderers, sexually immoral, sorcerers, idolaters, and all liars shall have their part in the lake which burns with fire and brimstone, which is the second death."

The New Jerusalem

[9]Then one of the seven angels who had the seven bowls filled with the seven last plagues came to me[a] and talked with me, saying, "Come, I will show you the bride, the Lamb's wife."[b] [10]And he carried me away in the Spirit to a great and high mountain, and showed me the great city, the holy[a] Jerusalem, descending out of heaven from God, [11]having the glory of God. Her light *was* like a most precious

---

20:10 [a]NU-Text and M-Text add *also*.   20:12 [a]NU-Text and M-Text read *the throne*.   20:14 [a]NU-Text and M-Text add *the lake of fire*.   21:2 [a]NU-Text and M-Text omit *John*.   21:5 [a]NU-Text and M-Text omit *to me*.   21:6 [a]M-Text omits *It is done*.   21:7 [a]M-Text reads *overcomes, I shall give him these things*.   21:8 [a]M-Text adds *and sinners*.   21:9 [a]NU-Text and M-Text omit *to me*.   [b]M-Text reads *I will show you the woman, the Lamb's bride*.   21:10 [a]NU-Text and M-Text omit *the great* and read *the holy city, Jerusalem*.

stone, like a jasper stone, clear as crystal. [12]Also she had a great and high wall with twelve gates, and twelve angels at the gates, and names written on them, which are *the names* of the twelve tribes of the children of Israel: [13]three gates on the east, three gates on the north, three gates on the south, and three gates on the west.

[14]Now the wall of the city had twelve foundations, and on them were the names[a] of the twelve apostles of the Lamb. [15]And he who talked with me had a gold reed to measure the city, its gates, and its wall. [16]The city is laid out as a square; its length is as great as its breadth. And he measured the city with the reed: twelve thousand furlongs. Its length, breadth, and height are equal. [17]Then he measured its wall: one hundred *and* forty-four cubits, *according* to the measure of a man, that is, of an angel. [18]The construction of its wall was *of* jasper; and the city *was* pure gold, like clear glass. [19]The foundations of the wall of the city *were* adorned with all kinds of precious stones: the first foundation *was* jasper, the second sapphire, the third chalcedony, the fourth emerald, [20]the fifth sardonyx, the sixth sardius, the seventh chrysolite, the eighth beryl, the ninth topaz, the tenth chrysoprase, the eleventh jacinth, and the twelfth amethyst. [21]The twelve gates *were* twelve pearls: each individual gate was of one pearl. And the street of the city *was* pure gold, like transparent glass.

> **21:16 twelve thousand furlongs.** This would be nearly 1,400 miles cubed or over two million square miles, offering plenty of room for all the glorified saints to live.

The Glory of the New Jerusalem

[22]But I saw no temple in it, for the Lord God Almighty and the Lamb are its temple. [23]The city had no need of the sun or of the moon to shine in it,[a] for the glory[b] of God illuminated it. The Lamb *is* its light. [24]And the nations of those who are saved[a] shall walk in its light, and the kings of the earth bring their glory and honor into it.[b] [25]Its gates shall not be shut at all by day (there shall be no night there). [26]And they shall bring the glory and the honor of the nations into it.[a] [27]But there shall by no means enter it anything that defiles, or causes[a] an abomination or a lie, but only those who are written in the Lamb's Book of Life.

> **21:22 no temple.** There is no temple in eternity because the Temple is not a building; it is the Lord God Himself. There is no need for a temple since God will be the Temple in which everything exists. The presence of God fills the entire new heaven and new earth. Going to heaven will be entering the limitless presence of the Lord (see John 14:3).

The River of Life

22 And he showed me a pure[a] river of water of life, clear as crystal, proceeding from the throne of God and of the Lamb. [2]In the middle of its street, and on either side of the river, *was* the tree of life, which bore twelve fruits, each *tree* yielding its fruit every month. The leaves of the tree *were* for the healing of the nations. [3]And there shall be no more curse, but the throne of God and of the Lamb shall be in it, and His servants shall serve Him. [4]They shall see His face, and His name *shall be* on their foreheads. [5]There shall be no night there: They need no lamp nor light of the sun, for the Lord God gives them light. And they shall reign forever and ever.

> **22:3 no more curse.** The curse laid on humanity and the earth as a whole, which began after Adam and Eve's disobedience (Gen. 3:16–19), will be totally finished. God will never have to judge sin again since it will never exist in the new heaven and new earth.

The Time Is Near

[6]Then he said to me, "These words *are* faithful and true." And the Lord God of the holy[a] prophets sent His angel to show His servants the things which must shortly take place.

[7]"Behold, I am coming quickly! Blessed *is*

---

he who keeps the words of the prophecy of this book."

⁸Now I, John, saw and heard*a* these things. And when I heard and saw, I fell down to worship before the feet of the angel who showed me these things.

⁹Then he said to me, "See *that you do* not *do that.* For*a* I am your fellow servant, and of your brethren the prophets, and of those who keep the words of this book. Worship God." ¹⁰And he said to me, "Do not seal the words of the prophecy of this book, for the time is at hand. ¹¹He who is unjust, let him be unjust still; he who is filthy, let him be filthy still; he who is righteous, let him be righteous*a* still; he who is holy, let him be holy still."

Jesus Testifies to the Churches

¹²"And behold, I am coming quickly, and My reward *is* with Me, to give to every one according to his work. ¹³I am the Alpha and the Omega, *the* Beginning and *the* End, the First and the Last."*a*

¹⁴Blessed *are* those who do His commandments,*a* that they may have the right to the tree of life, and may enter through the gates into the city. ¹⁵But*a* outside *are* dogs and sorcerers and sexually immoral and murderers and idolaters, and whoever loves and practices a lie.

¹⁶"I, Jesus, have sent My angel to testify to you these things in the churches. I am the Root and the Offspring of David, the Bright and Morning Star."

¹⁷And the Spirit and the bride say, "Come!" And let him who hears say, "Come!" And let him who thirsts come. Whoever desires, let him take the water of life freely.

A Warning

¹⁸For*a* I testify to everyone who hears the words of the prophecy of this book: If anyone adds to these things, God will add*b* to him the plagues that are written in this book; ¹⁹and if anyone takes away from the words of the book of this prophecy, God shall take away*a* his part from the Book*b* of Life, from the holy city, and *from* the things which are written in this book.

> **22:18,19** These are not the first of such warnings (see Deut. 4:2). These warnings against altering the biblical text represent the close of the NT canon. Attempting to falsify, diminish, alter, or misinterpret the truth of the scriptures will result in the judgments described in these verses.

I Am Coming Quickly

²⁰He who testifies to these things says, "Surely I am coming quickly."

Amen. Even so, come, Lord Jesus!

²¹The grace of our Lord Jesus Christ *be* with you all.*a* Amen.

22:8 *a*NU-Text and M-Text read *am the one who heard and saw.*   22:9 *a*NU-Text and M-Text omit *For.*   22:11 *a*NU-Text and M-Text read *do right.*   22:13 *a*NU-Text and M-Text read *the First and the Last, the Beginning and the End.*   22:14 *a*NU-Text reads *wash their robes.*   22:15 *a*NU-Text and M-Text omit *But.*   22:18 *a*NU-Text and M-Text omit *For.*   *b*M-Text reads *may God add.*   22:19 *a*M-Text reads *may God take away.*   *b*NU-Text and M-Text read *tree of life.*   22:21 *a*NU-Text reads *with all;* M-Text reads *with all the saints.*

ACCESS TO GOD.

Is of God. Ps 65:4.

Is by Christ. John 10:7,9; 14:6; Rom 5:2; Eph 2:13; 3:12; Heb 7:25; 10:19; 1 Pet 3:18.

Is by the Holy Spirit. Eph 2:18.

Obtained through faith. Acts 14:27; Rom 5:2; Eph 3:12; Heb 11:6.

Follows upon reconciliation to God. Col 1:21,22.

In prayer. See Prayer. Deut 4:7; Matt 6:6; 1 Pet 1:17.

In His temple. Ps 15:1; 27:4; 43:3; 65:4.

To obtain mercy and grace. Heb 4:16.

A privilege of believers. Deut 4:7; Ps 15:1; 23:6; 24:3,4.

Believers have, with confidence. Eph 3:12; Heb 4:16; 10:19,20.

Vouchsafed to repenting sinners. See Repentance. Hos 14:2; Joel 2:12.

Believers earnestly seek. Ps 27:4; 42:1,2; 43:3; 84:1,2.

The wicked commanded to seek. Is 55:6,7; James 4:8.

Urge others to seek. Is 2:3; Jer 31:6.

Promises connected with. Ps 145:18; Is 55:3; Matt 6:6; James 4:8.

Blessedness connected with. Ps 16:11; 65:4; 73:28.

ADOPTION.

Explained. 2 Cor 6:18.

Is according to promise. Rom 9:8; Gal 3:29.

Is by faith. Gal 3:7,26.

Is of God's grace. Ezek 16:3–6; Rom 4:16,17; Eph 1:5,6,11.

Is through Christ. John 1:12; Gal 4:4,5; Eph 1:5; Heb 2:10,13.

Believers predestinated to. Rom 8:29; Eph 1:5,11.

Of Gentiles, predicted. Hos 2:23; Rom 9:24–26; Eph 3:6.

The adopted are gathered together in one by Christ. John 11:52.

New birth connected with. John 1:12,13.

The Holy Spirit is a witness of. Rom 8:16.

Being led by the Spirit is an evidence of. Rom 8:14.

Believers receive the Spirit of. Rom 8:15; Gal 4:6.

A privilege of believers. John 1:12; 1 John 3:1.

Believers become brethren of Christ by. Heb 2:11,12.

Believers wait for final consummation of. Rom 8:19,23; 1 John 3:2.

Subjects believers to the fatherly discipline of God. Deut 8:5; 2 Sam 7:14; Prov 3:11,12; Heb 12:5–11.

God is long-suffering and merciful towards the partakers of. Jer 31:1,9,20.

Should lead to holiness. 2 Cor 6:17,18; 7:1; Phil 2:15; 1 John 3:2,3.

Should produce

Likeness to God. Matt 5:44,45,48; Eph 5:1.

Child-like confidence in God. Matt 6:25–34.

A desire for God's glory. Matt 5:16.

A spirit of prayer. Matt 7:7–11.

A love of peace. Matt 5:9.

A forgiving spirit. Matt 6:14.

A merciful spirit. Luke 6:35,36.

An avoidance of ostentation. Matt 6:1–4,6,18.

Safety of those who receive. Prov 14:26.

Confers a new name. See Titles of Believers. Num 6:27; Is 62:2; Acts 15:17.

Entitles to an inheritance. Rom 8:17; Gal 3:29; 4:7; Eph 3:6.

Is to be pleaded in prayer. Is 63:16; Matt 6:9.

AFFLICTIONS.

God appoints. 2 Kin 6:33; Job 5:6,17; Ps 66:11; Amos 3:6; Mic 6:9.

God dispenses, as He will. Job 11:10; Is 10:15; 45:7.

God regulates the measure of. Ps 80:5; Is 9:1; Jer 46:28.

God determines the continuance of. Gen 15:13,14; Num 14:33; Is 10:25; Jer 29:10.

God does not willingly send. Lam 3:33.

Man is born to. Job 5:6,7; 14:1.

Believers appointed to. 1 Thess 3:3.

Consequent upon the fall. Gen 3:16–19.

Sin produces. Job 4:8; 20:11; Prov 1:31.

Sin visited with. 2 Sam 12:14; Ps 89:30–32; Is 57:17; Acts 13:10,11.

Often severe. Job 16:7–16; Ps 42:7; 66:12; Jon 2:3; Rev 7:14.

Always less than we deserve. Ezra 9:13; Ps 103:10.

Frequently terminate in good. Gen 50:20; Ex 1:11,12; Deut 8:15,16; Jer 24:5,6; Ezek 20:37.

Tempered with mercy. Ps 78:38,39; 106:43–46; Is 30:18–21; Lam 3:32; Mic 7:7–9; Nah 1:12.

Believers are to expect. John 16:33; Acts 14:22.

Of believers, are comparatively light. Acts 20:23,24; Rom 8:18; 2 Cor 4:17.

Of believers, are but temporary. Ps 30:5; 103:9; Is 54:7,8; John 16:20; 1 Pet 1:6; 5:10.

Believers have joy under. Job 5:17; James 5:11.

Of believers, end in joy and blessedness. Ps 126:5,6; Is 61:2,3; Matt 5:4; 1 Pet 4:13,14.

Often arise from the profession of the gospel. Matt 24:9; John 15:21; 2 Tim 3:11,12.

Exhibit the love and faithfulness of God. Deut 8:5; Ps 119:75; Prov 3:12; 1 Cor 11:32; Heb 12:6,7; Rev 3:19.

AFFLICTIONS MADE BENEFICIAL.

In promoting the glory of God. John 9:1–3; 11:3,4; 21:18,19.

In exhibiting the power and faithfulness of God. Ps 34:19,20; 2 Cor 4:8–11.

In teaching us the will of God. Ps 119:71; Is 26:9.

In turning us to God. Deut 4:30,31; Neh 1:8,9; Ps 78:34; Is 10:20,21; Hos 2:6,7.

In keeping us from again departing from God. Job 34:31,32; Is 10:20; Ezek 14:10,11.

In leading us to seek God in prayer. Judg 4:3; Jer 31:18; Lam 2:17–19; Hos 5:14,15; Jon 2:1.

In convincing us of sin. Job 36:8,9; Ps 119:67; Luke 15:16–18.

In leading us to confession of sin. Num 21:7; Ps 32:5; 51:3,5.

In testing and exhibiting our sincerity. Job 23:10; Ps 66:10; Prov 17:3.

In trying our faith and obedience. Gen 22:1,2; Ex 15:23–25; Deut 8:2,16; Heb 11:17; 1 Pet 1:7; Rev 2:10.

In humbling us. Deut 8:3,16; 2 Chr 7:13,14; Lam 3:19,20; 2 Cor 12:7.

In purifying us. Eccl 7:2,3; Is 1:25,26; 48:10; Jer 9:6,7; Zech 13:9; Mal 3:2,3.

In exercising our patience. Ps 40:1; Rom 5:3; James 1:3; 1 Pet 2:20.

In rendering us fruitful in good works. John 15:2; Heb 12:10,11.

In furthering the gospel. Acts 8:3,4; 11:19–21; Phil 1:12; 2 Tim 2:9,10; 4:16,17.

ALTARS.

Designed for sacrifice. Ex 20:24.

To be made of earth, or unhewn stone. Ex 20:24,25; Deut 27:5,6.

Of brick, hateful to God. Is 65:3.

Natural rocks sometimes used as. Judg 6:19–21; 13:19,20.

Were not to have steps up to them. Ex 20:26.

For idolatrous worship, often erected on roofs of houses. 2 Kin 23:12; Jer 19:13; 32:29.

Idolaters planted groves near. Judg 6:30; 1 Kin 16:32,33; 2 Kin 21:3.

The Jews not to plant groves near. Deut 16:21.

For idolatrous worship, to be destroyed. Ex 34:13; Deut 7:5.

Probable origin of inscriptions on. Deut 27:8.

Mentioned in Scripture

Of Noah. Gen 8:20.

Of Abraham. Gen 12:7,8; 13:18; 22:9.

Of Isaac. Gen 26:25.

Of Jacob. Gen 33:20; 35:1,3,7.

Of Moses. Ex 17:15; 24:4.

Of Balaam. Num 23:1,14,29.

Of Joshua. Josh 8:30,31.

Of the temple of Solomon. 2 Chr 4:1,19.

Of the second temple. Ezra 3:2,3.

Of Reubenites, etc. east of Jordan. Josh 22:10.

Of Gideon. Judg 6:26,27.

Of the people of Israel. Judg 21:4.

Of Samuel. 1 Sam 7:17.

Of David. 2 Sam 24:21,25.

Of Jeroboam at Bethel. 1 Kin 12:33.

Of Ahaz. 2 Kin 16:10–12.

Of the Athenians. Acts 17:23.

For burnt offering. Ex 27:1–8.

For incense. Ex 30:1–6.

Protection afforded by. 1 Kin 1:50,51.

Afforded no protection to murderers. Ex 21:14; 1 Kin 2:18–34.

AMBITION.

God condemns. Gen 11:7; Is 5:8.

Christ condemns. Matt 18:1,3,4; 20:25,26; 23:11,12.

Believers avoid. Ps 131:1,2.

Vanity of. Job 20:5–9; 24:24; Ps 49:11–20.

Leads to strife and contention. James 4:1,2.

Punishment of. Prov 17:19; Is 14:12–15; Ezek 31:10,11; Obad 3,4.

Connected with

Pride. Hab 2:5.

Covetousness. Hab 2:8,9.

Cruelty. Hab 2:12.

ANGELS.

Created by God and Christ. Neh 9:6; Col 1:16.

Worship God and Christ. Neh 9:6; Phil 2:9–11; Heb 1:6.

Are ministering spirits. 1 Kin 19:5; Ps 104:4; Luke 16:22; Acts 12:7–11; 27:23; Heb 1:7,14.

Communicate the will of God and Christ. Dan 8:16,17; 9:21–23; 10:11; 12:6,7; Matt 2:13,20; Luke 1:19,28; Acts 5:20; 8:26; 10:5; 27:23; Rev 1:1.

Obey the will of God. Ps 103:20; Matt 6:10.

Execute the purposes of God. Num 22:22; Ps 103:21; Matt 13:39–42; 28:2; John 5:4; Rev 5:2.

Execute the judgments of God. 2 Sam 24:16; 2 Kin 19:35; Ps 35:5,6; Acts 12:23; Rev 16:1.

Celebrate the praises of God. Job 38:7; Ps 148:2; Is 6:3; Luke 2:13,14; Rev 5:11,12; 7:11,12.

The law given by the ministration of. Acts 7:53; Heb 2:2.

Announced
  The conception of Christ. Matt 1:20,21; Luke 1:31.
  The birth of Christ. Luke 2:10–12.
  The resurrection of Christ. Matt 28:5–7; Luke 24:23.
  The ascension and second coming of Christ. Acts 1:11.
  The conception of John the Baptist. Luke 1:13,36.

Minister to Christ. Matt 4:11; Luke 22:43; John 1:51.

Are subject to Christ. Eph 1:21; Col 1:16; 2:10; 1 Pet 3:22.

Shall execute the purposes of Christ. Matt 13:41; 24:31.

Shall attend Christ at his second coming. Matt 16:27; 25:31; Mark 8:38; 2 Thess 1:7.

Know and delight in the gospel of Christ. Eph 3:9,10; 1 Tim 3:16; 1 Pet 1:12.

Rejoice over every repentant sinner. Luke 15:7,10.

Have charge over the children of God. Ps 34:7; 91:11,12; Dan 6:22; Matt 18:10.

Are of different orders. 1 Pet 3:22; Jude 1:9; Rev 12:7.

Not to be worshipped. Col 2:18; Rev 19:10; 22:9.

Are examples of meekness. 2 Pet 2:11; Jude 1:9.

Are wise. 2 Sam 14:20.

Are mighty. Ps 103:20.

Are holy. Matt 25:31.

Are elect. 1 Tim 5:21.

Are innumerable. Job 25:3; Heb 12:22.

ANGER.

Forbidden. Eccl 7:9; Matt 5:22; Rom 12:19.

A work of the flesh. Gal 5:20.

A characteristic of fools. Prov 12:16; 14:29; 27:3; Eccl 7:9.

Connected with
  Pride. Prov 21:24.
  Cruelty. Gen 49:7; Prov 27:3,4.
  Clamour and evil-speaking. Eph 4:31.
  Malice and blasphemy. Col 3:8.
  Strife and contention. Prov 21:19; 29:22; 30:33.

Brings its own punishment. Job 5:2; Prov 19:19; 25:28.

Grievous words stir up. Judg 12:4; 2 Sam 19:43; Prov 15:1.

Should not betray us into sin. Ps 37:8; Eph 4:26.

In prayer be free from. 1 Tim 2:8.

May be averted by wisdom. Prov 29:8.

Meekness pacifies. Prov 15:1; Eccl 10:4.

Children should not be provoked to. Eph 6:4; Col 3:21.

Be slow to. Prov 15:18; 16:32; 19:11; Titus 1:7; James 1:19.

Avoid those given to. Gen 49:6; Prov 22:24.

ANGER OF GOD, THE.

Averted by Christ. Luke 2:11,14; Rom 5:9; 2 Cor 5:18,19; Eph 2:14,17; Col 1:20; 1 Thess 1:10.

Is averted from them that believe. John 3:14–18; Rom 3:25; 5:1.

Is averted upon confession of sin and repentance. Job 33:27,28; Ps 106:43–45; Jer 3:12,13; 18:7,8; 31:18–20; Joel 2:12–14.

Is slow. Ps 103:8; Is 48:9; Jon 4:2; Nah 1:3.

Is righteous. Ps 58:10,11; Lam 1:18; Rom 2:6,8; 3:5,6; Rev 16:6,7.

The justice of, not to be questioned. Rom 9:18,20,22.

Manifested in terrors. Ex 14:24; Ps 76:6–8; Jer 10:10; Lam 2:20–22.

Manifested in judgments and afflictions. Job 21:17; Ps 78:49–51; 90:7; Is 9:19; Jer 7:20; Ezek 7:19; Heb 3:17.

Cannot be resisted. Job 9:13; 14:13; Ps 76:7; Nah 1:6.

Aggravated by continual provocation. Num 32:14.

Specially reserved for the day of wrath. Zeph 1:14–18; Matt 25:41; Rom 2:5; 2 Thess 1:8; Rev 6:17; 11:18; 19:15.

Against
  The wicked. Ps 7:11; 21:8,9; Is 3:8; 13:9; Nah 1:2,3; Rom 1:18; 2:8; Eph 5:6; Col 3:6.
  Those who forsake Him. Ezra 8:22; Is 1:4.
  Unbelief. Ps 78:21,22; Heb 3:18,19; John 3:36.
  Impenitence. Ps 7:12; Prov 1:30,31; Is 9:13,14; Rom 2:5.
  Apostasy. Heb 10:26,27.
  Idolatry. Deut 29:20,27,28; 32:19–22; Josh 23:16; 2 Kin 22:17; Ps 78:58,59; Jer 44:3.
  Sin, in believers. Ps 89:30–32; 90:7–9; 99:8; 102:9,10; Is 47:6.

Extreme, against those who oppose the gospel. Ps 2:2,3,5; 1 Thess 2:16.

Folly of provoking. Jer 7:19; 1 Cor 10:22.

To be dreaded. Ps 2:12; 76:7; 90:11; Matt 10:28.

Removal of, should be prayed for. Ps 39:10; 79:5; 80:4; Dan 9:16; Hab 3:2.

Tempered with mercy to believers. Ps 30:5; Is 26:20; 54:8; 57:15,16; Jer 30:11; Mic 7:11.

To be borne with submission. 2 Sam 24:17; Lam 3:39; Mic 7:9.

Should lead to repentance. Is 42:24,25; Jer 4:8.

ANOINTING.

With oil. Ps 92:10.

With ointment. John 11:2.

Was used for
  Decorating the person. Ruth 3:3.
  Refreshing the body. 2 Chr 28:15.
  Purifying the body. Esth 2:12; Is 57:9.
  Curing the sick. Mark 6:13.
  Healing wounds. Is 1:6; Luke 10:34.
  Preparing weapons for war. Is 21:5.
  Preparing the dead for burial. Matt 26:12; Mark 16:1; Luke 23:56.

The Jews were very fond of. Prov 27:9; Amos 6:6.

Was applied to
  The head. Ps 23:5; Eccl 9:8.
  The face. Ps 104:15.
  The feet. Luke 7:38,39; John 12:3.
  The eyes. Rev 3:18.

Ointment for
  Richly perfumed. Song 4:10; John 12:3.
  Most expensive. 2 Kin 20:13; Amos 6:6; John 12:3,5.
  Prepared by the apothecary. Eccl 10:1.
  An article of commerce. Ezek 27:17; Rev 18:13.
  Neglected in times of affliction. 2 Sam 12:20; 14:2; Dan 10:3.

Neglect of, to guests, a mark of disrespect. Luke 7:46.

A token of joy. Eccl 9:7,8.

Deprivation of, threatened as a punishment. Deut 28:40; Mic 6:15.

Why recommended by Christ in times of fasting. Matt 6:17,18.

ANTICHRIST.

Denies the Father and the Son. 1 John 2:22.

Denies the incarnation of Christ. 1 John 4:3; 2 John 7.

Prevalent in apostolic times. 1 John 2:18.

Deceit, a characteristic of. 2 John 7.

APOSTLES, THE.

Christ pre-eminently called "The Apostle." Heb 3:1.

Ordained by Christ. Mark 3:14; John 15:16.

Received their title from Christ. Luke 6:13.

Called by
  God. 1 Cor 1:1; 12:28; Gal 1:1,15,16.
  Christ. Matt 10:1; Mark 3:13; Acts 20:24; Rom 1:5.
  The Holy Spirit. Acts 20:24; Rom 1:5.

Some were unlearned men. Acts 4:13.

Selected from obscure stations. Matt 4:18.

Sent first to the house of Israel. Matt 10:5,6; Luke 24:47; Acts 13:46.

Sent to preach the gospel to all nations. Matt 28:19,20; Mark 16:15; 2 Tim 1:11.

Christ always present with. Matt 28:20.

Warned against a timid profession of Christ. Matt 10:27–33.

The Holy Spirit given to. John 20:22; Acts 2:1–4; 9:17.

Guided by the Spirit into all truth. John 14:26; 15:26; 16:13.

Instructed by the Spirit to answer adversaries. Matt 10:19,20; Luke 12:11,12.

Specially devoted to the office of the ministry. Acts 6:4; 20:27.

Humility urged upon. Matt 20:26,27; Mark 9:33–37; Luke 22:24–30.

Self-denial urged upon. Matt 10:37–39.

Mutual love urged upon. John 15:17.

Equal authority given to each of. Matt 16:19; 18:18; 2 Cor 11:5.

Were not of the world. John 15:19; 17:16.

Were hated by the world. Matt 10:22; 24:9; John 15:18.

Persecutions and sufferings of. Matt 10:16,18; Luke 21:16; John 15:20; 16:2.

Saw Christ in the flesh. Luke 1:2; Acts 1:22; 1 Cor 9:1; 1 John 1:1.

Witnesses of the resurrection and ascension of Christ. Luke 24:33–41,51; Acts 1:2–9; 10:40,41; 1 Cor 15:8.

Empowered to work miracles. Matt 10:1,8; Mark 16:20; Luke 9:1; Acts 2:43.

ASCENSION OF CHRIST, THE.

Prophecies respecting.Ps 68:18; Eph 4:7,8.
Foretold by Himself. John 6:62; 7:33; 14:28; 16:5; 20:17.
Forty days after His resurrection. Acts 1:3.
Described. Acts 1:9.
From Mount Olivet. Mark 11:1; Luke 24:50; Acts 1:12.
While blessing His disciples. Luke 24:50.
When He had atoned for sin. Heb 9:12; 10:12.
Was triumphant. Ps 68:18.
Was to supreme power and dignity. Luke 24:26; Eph 1:20,21; 1 Pet 3:22.
As the forerunner of His people. Heb 6:20.
To intercede. Rom 8:34; Heb 9:24.
To send the Holy Spirit. John 16:7; Acts 2:33.
To receive gifts for men. Ps 68:18; Eph 4:8,11.
To prepare a place for His people. John 14:2.
His second coming shall be in like manner as. Acts 1:10,11.
Typified. Lev 16:15; Heb 6:20; 9:7,9,12.

ASSURANCE.

Produced by faith. Eph 3:12; 2 Tim 1:12; Heb 10:22.
Made full by hope. Heb 6:11,19.
Confirmed by love. 1 John 3:14,19; 4:18.
Is abundant in the understanding of the gospel. Col 2:2; 1 Thess 1:5.
Believers privileged to have, of
Their election. Ps 4:3; 1 Thess 1:4.
Their redemption. Job 19:25.
Their adoption. Rom 8:16; 1 John 3:2.
Their salvation. Is 12:2.
Eternal life. 1 John 5:13.
The unalienable love of God. Rom 8:38,39.
Union with God and Christ. 1 Cor 6:15; 2 Cor 13:5; Eph 5:30; 1 John 2:5; 4:13.
Peace with God by Christ. Rom 5:1.
Preservation. Ps 3:6,8; 27:3–5; 46:1–3.
Answers to prayer. 1 John 3:22; 5:14,15.
Continuance in grace. Phil 1:6.
Comfort in affliction. Ps 73:26; Luke 4:18,19; 2 Cor 4:8-10,16–18.
Support in death. Ps 23:4.
A glorious resurrection. Job 19:26; Ps 17:15; Phil 3:21; 1 John 3:2.
A kingdom. Heb 12:28; Rev 5:10.
A crown. 2 Tim 4:7,8; James 1:12.
Give diligence to attain to. 2 Pet 1:10,11.
Strive to maintain. Heb 3:14,18.
Confident hope in God restores. Ps 42:11.

ATONEMENT, THE.

Explained. Rom 5:8–11; 2 Cor 5:18,19; Gal 1:4; 1 John 2:2; 4:10.
Foreordained. Rom 3:25; 1 Pet 1:11,20; Rev 13:8.
Foretold. Is 53:4–6,8–12; Dan 9:24–27; Zech 13:1,7; John 11:50,51.
Effected by Christ alone. John 1:29,36; Acts 4:10,12; 1 Thess 1:10; 1 Tim 2:5,6; Heb 2:9; 1 Pet 2:24.
Was voluntary. Ps 40:6–8; John 10:11,15,17,18;Heb 10:5–9.
Exhibits the
Grace and mercy of God. Rom 8:32; Eph 2:4,5,7; 1 Tim 2:4; Heb 2:9.
Love of God. Rom 5:8; 1 John 4:9,10.

Love of Christ. John 15:13; Gal 2:20; Eph 5:2,25; Rev 1:5.
Reconciles the justice and mercy of God. Is 45:21; Rom 3:25,26.
Necessity for. Is 59:16; Luke 19:10; Heb 9:22.
Made but once. Heb 7:27; 9:24–28; 10:10,12,14; 1 Pet 3:18.
Acceptable to God. Eph 5:2.
Reconciliation to God effected by. Rom 5:10; 2 Cor 5:18–20; Eph 2:13–16; Col 1:20–22; Heb 2:17; 1 Pet 3:18.
Access to God by. Heb 10:19,20.
Remission of sins by. John 1:29; Rom 3:25; Eph 1:7; 1 John 1:7; Rev 1:5.
Justification by. Rom 5:9; 2 Cor 5:21.
Sanctification by. 2 Cor 5:15; Eph 5:26,27; Titus 2:14; Heb 10:10; 13:12.
Redemption by. Matt 20:28; Acts 20:28; 1 Tim 2:6; Heb 9:12; Rev 5:9.
Has delivered believers from the
Power of sin. Rom 8:3; 1 Pet 1:18,19.
Power of the World. Gal 1:4; 6:14.
Power of the devil. Col 2:15; Heb 2:14,15.
Believers glorify God for. 1 Cor 6:20; Gal 2:20; Phil 1:20,21.
Believers rejoice in God for. Rom 5:11.
Believers praise God for. Rev 5:9–13.
Faith in, indispensable. Rom 3:25; Gal 3:13,14.
Commemorated in the Lord's Supper. Matt 26:26–28; 1 Cor 11:23–26.
Ministers should fully set forth. Acts 5:29–31,42; 1 Cor 15:3; 2 Cor 5:18–21.
Typified. Gen 4:4; Heb 11:4; Gen 22:2; Heb 11:17,19; Ex 12:5,11,14; 1 Cor 5:7; Ex 24:8; Heb 9:20; Lev 16:30,34; Heb 9:7,12,28; Lev 17:11; Heb 9:22.

ATONEMENT, THE DAY OF.

Tenth day of seventh month. Lev 23:26,27.
A day of humiliation. Lev 16:29,31; 23:27.
Observed as a sabbath. Lev 23:28,32.
Offerings to be made on. Lev 16:3,5–15.
The high priest entered into the holy place on. Lev 16:2,3; Heb 9:7.
Atonement made on
For the holy place. Ex 30:10; Lev 16:15,16.
For the high priest. Lev 16:11; Heb 9:7.
For the whole congregation. Lev 16:17,24; Heb 9:7.
The sins of the people borne off by the scapegoat on. Lev 16:21.
Punishment for not observing. Lev 23:29,30.
Year of Jubilee commenced on. Lev 25:9.
Typical. Heb 9:8,24.

BACKSLIDING.

Is turning from God. 1 Kin 11:9.
Is leaving the first love. Rev 2:4.
Is departing form the simplicity of the gospel. 2 Cor 11:3; Gal 3:1–3; 5:4,7.
God is displeased at. Ps 78:57,59.
Warnings against. Ps 85:8; 1 Cor 10:12.
Guilt and consequences of. Num 14:43; Ps 125:5; Is 59:2,9–11; Jer 5:6; 8:5,13; 15:6; Luke 9:62.
Brings its own punishment. Prov 14:14; Jer 2:19.
A haughty spirit leads to. Prov 16:18.
Proneness to. Prov 24:16; Hos 11:7.
Liable to continue and increase. Jer 8:5; 14:7.
Exhortations to return from. 2 Chr 30:6; Is 31:6; Jer 3:12,14,22; Hos 6:1.
Pray to be restored from. Ps 80:3; 85:4; Lam 5:21.

Punishment of tempting others to the sin of. Prov 28:10; Matt 18:6.
Not hopeless. Ps 37:24; Prov 24:16.
Endeavour to bring back those guilty of. Gal 6:1; James 5:19,20.
Sin of, to be confessed. Is 59:12–14; Jer 3:13,14; 14:7–9.
Pardon of, promised. 2 Chr 7:14; Jer 3:12; 31:20; 36:3.
Healing of, promised. Jer 3:22; Hos 14:4.
Afflictions sent to heal. Hos 5:15.
Blessedness of those who keep from. Prov 28:14; Is 26:3,4; Col 1:21–23.
Hateful to believers. Ps 101:3.
Exemplified
Israel. Ex 32:8; Neh 9:26; Jer 3:11; Hos 4:16.
Saul. 1 Sam 15:11.
Solomon. 1 Kin 11:3,4.
Peter. Matt 26:70–74.

BAPTISM.

As administered by John. Matt 3:5–12; John 3:23; Acts 13:24; 19:4.
Sanctioned by Christ's submission to it. Matt 3:13–15; Luke 3:21.
Adopted by Christ. John 3:22; 4:1,2.
Appointed an ordinance of the Christian church. Matt 28:19,20; Mark 16:15,16.
To be administered in the name of the Father, Son, and Holy Spirit. Matt 28:19.
Water, the outward and visible sign in. Acts 8:36; 10:47.
Remission of sins, signified by. Acts 2:38; 22:16.
Unity of the Church effected by. 1 Cor 12:13; Gal 3:27,28.
Confession of sin necessary to. Matt 3:6.
Repentance necessary to. Acts 2:38.
Faith necessary to. Acts 8:37; 18:8.
There is but one. Eph 4:5.
Administered to
Individuals. Acts 8:38; 9:18.
Households. Acts 16:15; 1 Cor 1:16.
Only to professing believers. Acts 2:38; Matt 3:6; Mark 16:16; Acts 8:12,36,37; 10:47,48.
Administered by immersing the whole body of the person in water. Matt 3:16; Acts 8:38,39.
Emblematic of the influences of the Holy Spirit. Matt 3:11; Titus 3:5.
Typified. 1 Cor 10:2; 1 Pet 3:20,21.

BELIEVERS, COMPARED TO.

The sun. Judg 5:31; Matt 13:43.
Stars. Dan 12:3.
Lights. Matt 5:14; Phil 2:15.
Mount Zion. Ps 125:1,2.
Lebanon. Hos 14:5–7.
Treasure. Ex 19:5; Ps 135:4.
Jewels. Mal 3:17.
Gold. Job 23:10; Lam 4:2.
Vessels of gold and silver. 2 Tim 2:20.
Jewels of a crown. Zech 9:16.
Living stones. 1 Pet 2:5.
Babes. Matt 11:25; 1 Pet 2:2.
Little children. Matt 18:3; 1 Cor 14:20.
Obedient children. 1 Pet 1:14.
Members of the body. 1 Cor 12:20,27.
Soldiers. 2 Tim 2:3,4.
Runners in a race. 1 Cor 9:24; Heb 12:1.
Wrestlers. 2 Tim 2:5.
Good servants. Matt 25:21.
Strangers and pilgrims. 1 Pet 2:11.
Sheep. Ps 78:52; Matt 25:33; John 10:4.
Lambs. Is 40:11; John 21:15.
Calves of the stall. Mal 4:2.
Lions. Prov 28:1; Mic 5:8.

Eagles. Ps 103:5; Is 40:31.
Doves. Ps 68:13; Is 60:8.
Thirsting deer. Ps 42:1.
Good fish. Matt 13:48.
Dew and showers. Mic 5:7.
Watered gardens. Is 58:11.
Unfailing springs. Is 58:11.
Vines. Hos 14:7.
Branches of a vine. John 15:2,4,5.
Good figs. Jer 24:2–7.
Lilies. Hos 14:5.
Willows by the water courses. Is 44:4.
Trees planted by rivers. Ps 1:3.
Cedars in Lebanon. Ps 92:12.
Palm trees. Ps 92:12.
Green olive trees. Ps 52:8; Hos 14:6.
Fruitful trees. Ps 1:3; Jer 17:8.
Grain. Hos 14:7.
Wheat. Matt 3:12; 13:29,30.
Salt. Matt 5:13.

BLASPHEMY.

Christ assailed with. Matt 10:25; Luke
  22:64,65; 1 Pet 4:14.
Charged upon Christ. Matt 9:2,3;
  26:64,65; John 10:33,36.
Charged upon believers. Acts 6:11,13.
Proceeds from the heart. Matt 15:19.
Forbidden. Ex 20:7; Col 3:8.
The wicked practice it. Ps 74:18; Is 52:5;
  2 Tim 3:2.
Idolatry counted as. Is 65:7; Ezek
  20:27,28.
Hypocrisy counted as. Rev 2:9.
Believers grieved to hear. Ps 44:15,16;
  74:10,18,22.
Believers give no occasion for. 2 Sam
  12:14; 1 Tim 6:1.
Against the Holy Spirit, unpardonable.
  Matt 12:31,32.
Connected with folly and pride. 2 Kin
  19:22; Ps 74:18.
Punishment of. Lev 24:16; Is 65:7; Ezek
  20:27–33; 35:11,12.
Exemplified
  The Danite. Lev 24:11.
  Sennacherib. 2 Kin 19:4,10,22.
  The Jews. Luke 22:65.
  Hymenaeus. 1 Tim 1:20.

BLINDNESS, SPIRITUAL.

Explained. 1 Cor 2:14.
The effect of sin. Is 29:10; Matt 6:23;
  John 3:19,20.
The effect of Unbelief. Rom 11:8; 2 Cor
  4:3,4.
A proof of a lack of love. 1 John 2:9,11.
A work of the devil. 2 Cor 4:4.
Leads to all evil. Eph 4:17–19.
Is inconsistent with communion with
  God. 1 John 1:6,7.
Of ministers, fatal to themselves and to
  the people. Matt 15:14.
The wicked are in. Ps 82:5; Jer 5:21.
The self-righteous are in. Matt 23:19,26;
  Rev 3:17.
Judicially inflicted. Ps 69:23; Is 29:10;
  44:18; Matt 13:13,14; John 12:40.
Pray for the removal of. Ps 13:3; 119:18.
Christ appointed to remove. Is 42:7; Luke
  4:18; John 8:12; 9:39; 2 Cor 4:6.
Christ's ministers are lights to remove.
  Matt 5:14; Acts 26:18.
Believers are delivered from. John 8:12;
  Eph 5:8; Col 1:13; 1 Thess 5:4,5; 1 Pet
  2:9.
Removal of, illustrated. John 9:7,11,25;
  Acts 9:18; Rev 3:18.

BLOOD.

The life of animals. Gen 9:4; Lev
  17:11,14.

Of all men the same. Acts 17:26.
Eating of, forbidden
  Man after the flood. Gen 9:4.
  The Israelites under the law. Lev 3:17;
    17:10,12.
  The early Christians. Acts 15:20,29.
The Jews often guilty of eating. Ezek
  33:25.
Of animals slain for good to be poured on
  the earth and covered. Lev 17:13; Deut
  12:16,24.
Birds of prey delight in. Job 39:30.
Beasts of prey delight in. Num 23:24; Ps
  68:23.
Shedding of human
  Forbidden. Gen 9:5.
  Hateful to God. Prov 6:16,17.
  Defiling to the land. Ps 106:38.
  Defiling to the person. Is 59:3.
  Jews often guilty of. Jer 22:17; Ezek
    22:4.
  Always punished. Gen 9:6.
  Mode of clearing those accused of.
    Deut 21:1–9.
The price of, not to be consecrated. Matt
  27:6.
Of legal sacrifices
  For atonement. Ex 30:10; Lev 17:11.
  For purification. Heb 9:13,19–22.
  How disposed of. Ex 29:12; Lev 4:7.
  Not offered with leaven. Ex 23:18;
    34:25.
  Ineffectual to remove sin. Heb 10:4.
Idolaters made drink offerings of. Ps 16:4.
Water turned into, as a sign. Ex 4:9.
Waters of Egypt turned into, as a
  judgment. Ex 7:17–21.

BONDAGE, SPIRITUAL.

Is to the devil. 2 Tim 2:26.
Is to the fear of death. Heb 2:14,15.
Is to sin. John 8:34; Acts 8:23; Rom 6:16;
  7:23; Gal 4:3; 2 Pet 2:19.
Deliverance from, promised. Is 42:6,7.
Christ delivers from. Luke 4:18,21; John
  8:36; Rom 7:24,24; Eph 4:8.
The gospel, the instrument of deliverance
  from. John 8:32; Rom 8:2.
Believers are delivered from. Rom 6:18,22.
Typified
  Israel in Egypt. Ex 1:13,14.

BURNT OFFERING, THE.

To be offered only to the Lord. Judg 13:16.
Specially acceptable. Gen 8:21; Lev
  1:9,13,17.
The most ancient of all sacrifices. Gen
  4:4; 8:20; 22:2,13; Job 1:5.
Offered by the Jews before the law. Ex
  10:25; 24:5.
To be taken from
  The flock or herd. Lev 1:2.
  The birds. Lev 1:14.
Was an atonement for sin. Lev 9:7.
Guilt transferred to, by imposition of
  hands. Lev 1:4; Num 8:12.
Required to be
  Killed, if a beast, by the person who
    brought it. Lev 1:5,11.
  Killed, if a bird, by the priest.
    Lev 1:15.
  For the people at large, killed and
    prepared by the Levites. Ezek 44:11.
  A male without blemish. Lev 1:3;
    22:19.
  Voluntary. Lev 1:3; 22:18,19.
  Presented at the door of the tabernacle.
    Lev 1:3; Deut 12:6,11,14.
  Offered by priests only. Lev 1:9; Ezek
    44:15.
  Offered in righteousness. Ps 51:19.

Entirely burned. Lev 1:8,9,12,13; 6:9.
Blood of, sprinkled round about upon the
  altar. Lev 1:5,11.
If a bird, the blood was wrung out at the
  side of the altar. Lev 1:15.
Ashes of, collected at foot of the altar, and
  conveyed without the camp. Lev 6:11.
Skin of, given to the priests for clothing.
  Gen 3:21; Lev 7:8.
Was offered
  Every morning and evening. Ex 29:38–
    42.
  Every Sabbath day. Num 28:9,10.
  The first day of every month. Num
    28:11.
  The seven days of unleavened bread.
    Num 28:19,24.
  The Day of Atonement. Lev 16:3,5;
    Num 29:8.
  At consecration of Levites. Num 8:12.
  At consecration priests. Lev 9:2,12–
    14.
  At consecration of kings. 1 Chr 29:21–
    23.
  At purification of women. Lev 12:6.
  For Nazirites after defilement, or at
    the end of their vow. Num 6:11,14.
  For the healed leper. Lev 14:13,19,20.
  At dedication of sacred places. Num
    7:15; 1 Kin 8:64.
  After great mercies. 1 Sam 6:14;
    2 Sam 24:22,25.
  Before going to war. 1 Sam 7:9.
  With sounds of trumpets at feasts.
    Num 10:10.
The fat, etc. of all peace offerings laid on,
  and consumed with the daily. Lev 3:5;
  6:12.
Of the wicked, not accepted by God. Is
  1:10,11; Jer 6:19,20; Amos 5:22.
Obedience better than. 1 Sam 15:22; Jer
  7:21–23.
Knowledge of God better than. Hos 6:6.
Love of God better than. Mark 12:33.
Abraham tried by the command to offer
  Isaac as. Gen 22:1–24.
Incapable of removing sin, and reconciling
  to God. Ps 40:6; 50:8; Heb 10:6.
The most costly, no adequate tribute to
  God. Is 40:16; Ps 50:9–13.
Guilt of unauthorised persons offering.
  1 Sam 13:12,13.
Guilt of offering, except in the place
  appointed. Lev 17:8,9.
Of human victims execrated. Deut 12:31;
  2 Kin 3:27; Jer 7:31; 19:5.
Illustrative of
  The offering of Christ. Eph 5:2; Heb
    10:8–10.
  Devotedness to God. Rom 12:1.

BUSY-BODIES.

The idle are. 2 Thess 3:11; 1 Tim 5:13.
Are mischievous tale-bearers. 1 Tim 5:13.
Bring mischief upon themselves. 2 Kin
  14:10; Prov 26:17.
Christians must not be. 1 Pet 4:15.

CANAANITES, THE.

Descended from Ham. Gen 10:6.
An accursed race. Gen 9:25,26.
Different families of. Gen 10:15–18.
Included seven distinct nations. Deut 7:1.
Borders of their country. Gen 10:19.
Country of, fertile. Ex 3:17; Num 13:27.
Described as
  Great and mighty. Num 13:28; Deut
    7:1.
  Idolatrous. Deut 29:17.
  Superstitious. Deut 18:9–11.
  Profane and wicked. Lev 18:27.

Had many strong cities. Num 13:28; Deut 1:28.

Expelled for wickedness. Deut 9:4; 18:12.

Abraham

Called to dwell amongst. Gen 12:1–5.

Was promised the country of, of inheritance. Gen 13:14–17; 15:18; 17:8.

Kind to the patriarchs. Gen 14:13; 23:6.

Israel commanded

To make no covenant with. Deut 7:2; Judg 2:2.

Not to intermarry with. Deut 7:3; Josh 23:12.

Not to follow idols of. Ex 23:24; Deut 7:25.

Not to follow customs of. Lev 18:26,27.

To destroy, without mercy. Deut 7:2,24.

To destroy all vestiges of their idolatry. Ex 23:24; Deut 7:5,25.

Not to fear. Deut 7:17,18; 31:7.

Terrified at the approach of Israel. Ex 15:15,16; Josh 2:9–11; 5:1.

Partially subdued by Israel. Josh 10:1– 11:23; Judg 1:1–36.

Part of their country left

To try Israel. Judg 2:21,22; 3:1–4.

To chastise Israel. Num 33:55; Judg 4:2.

Israel ensnared by. Judg 2:3,19; Ps 106:36– 38.

Some descendants of, in our Lord's time. Matt 15:22; Mark 7:26.

CHARACTER OF BELIEVERS.

Attentive to Christ's voice. John 10:3,4.

Blameless and harmless. Phil 2:15.

Bold. Prov 28:1; Rom 13:3.

Contrite. Is 57:15; 66:2.

Devout. Acts 8:2; 22:12.

Faithful. Rev 17:14.

Following Christ. John 10:4,27.

Godly. Ps 4:3; 2 Pet 2:9.

Guileless. John 1:47.

Holy. Deut 7:6; 14:2; Col 3:12.

Humble. Ps 34:2; 1 Pet 5:5.

Hungering after righteousness. Matt 5:6.

Just. Gen 6:9; Hab 2:4; Luke 2:25.

Led by the Spirit. Rom 8:14.

Liberal. Is 32:8; 2 Cor 9:13.

Loving. Col 1:4; 1 Thess 4:9.

Lowly. Prov 16:19.

Meek. Is 29:19; Matt 5:5.

Merciful. Ps 37:26; Matt 5:7.

New creatures. 2 Cor 5:17; Eph 2:10.

Obedient. Rom 16:19; 1 Pet 1:14.

Poor in spirit. Ps 51:17; Matt 5:3.

Prudent. Prov 16:21.

Pure in heart. Matt 5:8; 1 John 3:3.

Righteous. Is 60:21; Luke 1:6.

Sincere. 2 Cor 1:12; 2:17.

Steadfast. Acts 2:42; Col 2:5.

Taught of God. Is 54:13; 1 John 2:27.

True. 2 Cor 6:8.

Undefiled. Ps 119:1.

Upright. 1 Kin 3:6; Ps 15:2.

Watchful. Luke 12:37.

Zealous of good works. Titus 2:14; 3:8.

CHARACTER OF THE WICKED.

Abominable. Rev 21:8.

Alienated from God. Eph 4:18; Col 1:21.

Blasphemous. Luke 22:65; Rev 16:9.

Blinded. 2 Cor 4:4; Eph 4:18.

Boastful. Ps 10:3; 49:6.

Conspiring against God's people. Neh 4:8; 6:2; Ps 38:12.

Covetous. Mic 2:2; Rom 1:29.

Deceitful. Ps 5:6; Rom 3:13.

Delighting in the iniquity of others. Prov 2:14; Rom 1:32.

Despising the works of the faithful. Neh 2:19; 4:2; 2 Tim 3:3,4.

Destructive. Is 59:7.

Disobedient. Neh 9:26; Titus 3:3; 1 Pet 2:7.

Enticing to evil. Prov 1:10–14; 2 Tim 3:6.

Envious. Neh 2:10; Titus 3:3.

Fearful. Prov 28:1; Rev 21:8.

Fierce. Prov 16:29; 2 Tim 3:3.

Foolish. Deut 32:6; Ps 5:5.

Forgetting God. Job 8:13.

Fraudulent. Ps 37:21; Mic 6:11.

Glorying in their shame. Phil 3:19.

Hard-hearted. Ezek 3:7.

Hating the light. Job 24:13; John 3:20.

Heady and high-minded. 2 Tim 3:4.

Hostile to God. Rom 8:7; Col 1:21.

Hypocritical. Is 29:13; 2 Tim 3:5.

Ignorant of God. Hos 4:1; 2 Thess 1:8.

Impudent. Ezek 2:4.

Infidel. Ps 10:4; 14:1.

Loathsome. Prov 13:5.

Lovers of pleasure more than of God. 2 Tim 3:4.

Lying. Ps 58:3; 62:4; Is 59:4.

Mischievous. Prov 24:8; Mic 7:3.

Murderous. Ps 10:8; 94:6; Rom 1:29.

Prayerless. Job 21:15; Ps 53:4.

Persecuting. Ps 69:26; 109:16.

Perverse. Deut 32:5.

Proud. Ps 59:12; Obad 3; 2 Tim 3:2.

Rejoicing in the affliction of believers. Ps 35:15.

Reprobate. 2 Cor 13:5; 2 Tim 3:8; Titus 1:16.

Selfish. 2 Tim 3:2.

Sensual. Phil 3:19; Jude 19.

Sold under sin. 1 Kin 21:20; 2 Kin 17:17.

Stiff-necked. Ex 33:5; Acts 7:51.

Uncircumcised in heart. Jer 9:26; Acts 7:51.

Unjust. Prov 11:7; Is 26:10.

Unmerciful. Rom 1:31.

Ungodly. Prov 16:27.

Unholy. 2 Tim 3:2.

Unprofitable. Matt 25:30; Rom 3:12.

Unruly. Titus 1:10.

Unwise. Deut 32:6.

CHARITY.

Explained. 1 Cor 13:4–7.

Enjoined. See "Love to man." Col 3:14.

CHASTITY.

Commanded. Ex 20:14; Prov 31:3; Acts 15:20; Rom 13:13; Col 3:5; 1 Thess 4:3.

Required in vision. Job 31:1; Matt 5:28.

Required in heart. Prov 6:25.

Required in speech. Eph 5:3.

Keep the body in. 1 Cor 6:13,15–18.

Preserved by wisdom. Prov 2:10,11,16; 7:1–5.

Believers are kept in. Eccl 7:26.

Advantages of. 1 Pet 3:1,2.

Shun those devoid of. 1 Cor 5:11; 1 Pet 4:3.

The wicked are devoid of. Rom 1:29; Eph 4:19; 2 Pet 2:14; Jude 1:8.

Dangerous to deviate from. 2 Sam 11:2–4.

Consequences of associating with those devoid of. Prov 7:25–27; 22:14.

Lack of, excludes from heaven. Gal 5:19– 21.

Drunkenness destructive to. Prov 23:31– 33.

Breach of, punished. 1 Cor 3:16,17; Eph 5:5,6; Heb 13:4; Rev 22:15.

Motives for. 1 Cor 6:19; 1 Thess 4:7.

CHILDREN.

Christ was an example to. Luke 2:51.

Are a gift from God. Gen 33:5; Ps 127:3.

Are capable of glorifying God. Ps 8:2; 148:12,13; Matt 21:15,16.

Should be

Brought to Christ. Mark 10:13–16.

Brought early to the house of God. 1 Sam 1:24.

Instructed in the ways of God. Deut 31:12,13; Prov 22:6.

Judiciously trained. Prov 22:15; 29:17; Eph 6:4.

Should

Fear and obey God. Deut 30:2; Prov 24:21; Eccl 12:1.

Attend to parental teaching. Prov 1:8,9.

Honor parents. Ex 20:12; Heb 12:9.

Obey parents. Prov 6:20; Eph 6:1.

Take care of parents. 1 Tim 5:4.

Honor the aged. Lev 19:32; 1 Pet 5:5.

Not imitate bad parents. Ezek 20:18.

An heritage from the Lord. Ps 113:9; 127:3.

Not to have

Considered an affliction. Gen 15:2,3; Jer 22:30.

A reproach in Israel. 1 Sam 1:6,7; Luke 1:25.

Anxiety of the Jews for. Gen 30:1; 1 Sam 1:5,8.

Often prayed for. 1 Sam 1:10,11; Luke 1:13.

Often given in answer to prayer. Gen 25:21; 1 Sam 1:27; Luke 1:13.

Mostly nursed by the mothers. 1 Sam 1:22; 1 Kin 3:21; Ps 22:9; Song 8:1.

Weaning of, a time of joy and feasting. Gen 21:8; 1 Sam 1:24.

Circumcised on the eighth day. Phil 3:5.

Named at circumcision. Luke 1:59; 2:21.

Were named

After relatives. Luke 1:59,61.

From circumstances connected with their birth. Gen 25:25,26; 35:18; 1 Chr 4:9.

Often by God. Is 8:3; Hos 1:4,6,9.

Often numerous. 2 Kin 10:1; 1 Chr 4:27.

Numerous, considered an especial blessing. Ps 115:14; 127:4,5.

Sometimes born when parents were old. Gen 15:3,6; 17:17; Luke 1:18.

Male

If firstborn, belonged to God and were redeemed. Ex 13:12,13,15.

Birth of, announced to the father by a messenger. Jer 20:15.

Under the care of tutors, till they came of age. 2 Kin 10:1; Gal 4:1,2.

Inherited the possessions of their father. Deut 21:16,17; Luke 12:13,14.

Received the blessing of their father before his death. Gen 27:1–4; 48:15; 49:1–33.

Female

Taken care of by nurses. Gen 35:8.

Inherited property in default of sons. Num 27:1–8; Josh 17:1–6.

Fondness and care of mothers for. Ex 2:2– 10; 1 Sam 2:19; 1 Kin 3:27; Is 49:15; 1 Thess 2:7,8.

Of God's people, holy. Ezra 9:2; 1 Cor 7:14.

Of God's people, interested in the promises. Deut 29:29; Acts 2:39.

Prosperity of, greatly depended on obedience of parents. Deut 4:40; 12:25,28; Ps 128:1–3.

Frequently bore the curse of parents. Ex 20:5; Ps 109:9,10.

To submit to discipline. Prov 29:17; Heb 12:9.

Mode of giving public instruction to. Luke 2:46; Acts 22:3.

Power of parents over, during the patriarchal age. Gen 9:24,25; 21:14; 38:24.

Rebellious, punished by the civil power. Ex 21:15–17; Deut 21:18–21.

Sometimes devoted their property to avoid supporting parents. Matt 15:5; Mark 7:11,12.

Casting out of weak, etc. alluded to. Ezek 16:5.

Sometimes offered to idols. 2 Kin 17:31; 2 Chr 28:3; 33:6.

Illegitimate
Had no inheritance. Gen 21:10,14; Gal 4:30.

Not cared for by the father. Heb 12:8.

Excluded from the congregation. Deut 23:2.

Sometimes sent away with gifts. Gen 25:6.

Despised by their brethren. Judg 11:2.

Grief occasioned by loss of. Gen 37:35; 44:27–29; 2 Sam 13:37; Jer 6:26; 31:15.

Resignation manifested at loss of. Lev 10:19,20; 2 Sam 12:18–23; Job 1:19–21.

CHRIST, CHARACTER OF.

Holy. Luke 1:35; Acts 4:27; Rev 3:7.
Righteous. Is 53:11; Heb 1:9.
Good. Matt 19:16.
Faithful. Is 11:5; 1 Thess 5:24.
True. John 1:14; 7:18; 1 John 5:20.
Just. Zech 9:9; John 5:30; Acts 22:14.
Sinless. Is 53:9; Matt 4:1–10; 27:4; John 8:46; 2 Cor 5:21; Heb 7:26; 1 Pet 1:19; 2:22.
Obedient to God the Father. Ps 40:8; John 4:34; 15:10.
Zealous. Luke 2:49; John 2:17; 8:29.
Humble. Is 53:7; Zech 9:9; Matt 11:29.
Merciful. Heb 2:17.
Patient. Is 53:7; Matt 27:14; 1 Tim 1:16.
Compassionate. Is 40:11; Matt 4:23,24; Luke 19:41; Acts 10:38.
Loving. John 13:1; 15:13.
Self-denying. Matt 8:20; 2 Cor 8:9.
Humble. Luke 22:27; Phil 2:8.
Forgiving. Luke 23:34.
Subject to His parents. Luke 2:51.
Believers are conformed to. Rom 8:29.

CHRIST IS GOD.

As Jehovah. Is 40:3; Matt 3:3.
As Jehovah of glory. Ps 24:7,10; 1 Cor 2:8; James 2:1.
As Jehovah, our Righteousness. Jer 23:5,6; 1 Cor 1:30.
As Jehovah, above all. Ps 97:9; John 3:31.
As Jehovah, the First and the Last. Is 44:6; Rev 1:17; Is 48:12–16; Rev 22:13.
As Jehovah's Fellow and Equal. Zech 13:7; Phil 2:6.
As Jehovah of Hosts. Is 6:1–3; John 12:41; Is 8:13,14; 1 Pet 2:8.
As Jehovah, the Shepherd. Is 40:11; Heb 13:20.
As Jehovah, for whose glory all things were created. Prov 16:4; Col 1:16.
As Jehovah, the Messenger of the covenant. Mal 3:1; Mark 1:2; Luke 2:27.
Invoked as Jehovah. Joel 2:32; Acts 2:21; 1 Cor 1:2.

As the Eternal God and Creator. Ps 102:24–27; Heb 1:8,10–12.
As the mighty God. Is 9:6.
As the Great God and Savior. Hos 1:7; Titus 2:13.
As God over all. Ps 45:6,7; Rom 9:5.
As the true God. Jer 10:10; 1 John 5:20.
As God the Word. John 1:1.
As God the Judge. Eccl 12:14; 1 Cor 4:5; 2 Cor 5:10; 2 Tim 4:1.
As Emmanuel. Is 7:14; Matt 1:23.
As King of kings and Lord of lords. Dan 10:17; Rev 1:5; 17:14.
As the Holy One. 1 Sam 2:2; Acts 3:14.
As the Lord from heaven. 1 Cor 15:47.
As Lord of the Sabbath. Gen 2:3; Matt 12:8.
As Lord of all. Acts 10:36; Rom 10:11–13.
As Son of God. Matt 26:63–67.
As the Only-begotten Son of the Father. John 1:14,18; 3:16,18; 1 John 4:9.
His blood is called the blood of God. Acts 20:28.
As one with the Father. John 10:30,38; 12:45; 14:7–10; 17:10.
As sending the Spirit, equally with the Father. John 14:16; 15:26.
As entitled to equal honor with the Father. John 5:23.
As Owner of all things, equally with the Father. John 16:15.
As unrestricted by the law of the Sabbath, equally with the Father. John 5:17.
As the Source of grace, equally with the Father. 1 Thess 3:11; 2 Thess 2:16,17.
As unsearchable, equally with the Father. Prov 30:4; Matt 11:27.
As Creator of all things. Is 40:28; John 1:3; Col 1:16; Heb 1:2.
As Supporter and Preserver of all things. Neh 9:6; Col 1:17; Heb 1:3.
As possessed of the fullness of the God head. Col 2:9; Heb 1:3.
As raising the dead. John 5:21; 6:40,54.
As raising Himself from the dead. John 2:19,21; 10:18.
As Eternal. Is 9:6; Mic 5:2; John 1:1; Col 1:17; Heb 1:8–10; Rev 1:8.
As Omnipresent. Matt 18:20; 28:20; John 3:13.
As Omnipotent. Ps 45:3; Phil 3:21; Rev 1:8.
As Omniscient. John 16:30; 21:17.
As discerning the thoughts of the heart. 1 Kin 8:39; Luke 5:22; Ezek 11:5; John 2:24,25; Rev 2:23.
As unchangeable. Mal 3:6; Heb 1:12; 13:8.
As having power to forgive sins. Col 3:13; Mark 2:7,10.
As Giver of pastors to the Church. Jer 3:15; Eph 4:11–13.
As Husband of the Church. Is 54:5; Eph 5:25–32; Is 62:5; Rev 21:2,9.
As the object of divine worship. Acts 7:59; 2 Cor 12:8,9; Heb 1:6; Rev 5:12.
As the object of faith. Ps 2:12; 1 Pet 2:6; Jer 17:5,7; John 14:1.
As God, He redeems and purifies the Church to himself. Rev 5:9; Titus 2:14.
As God, He presents the Church to Himself. Eph 5:27; Jude 24,25.
Believers live to Him as God. Rom 6:11; Gal 2:19; 2 Cor 5:15.
Acknowledged by His apostles. John 20:28.
Acknowledged by the Old Testament believers. Gen 17:1; 48:15,16; 32:24–30; Hos 12:3–5; Judg 6:22–24; 13:21,22; Job 19:25–27.

CHRIST, THE KING.

Foretold. Num 24:17; Ps 2:6; Is 9:7; Jer 23:5; Mic 5:2.

Glorious. Ps 24:7–10; 1 Cor 2:8; James 2:1.
Supreme. Ps 89:27; Rev 1:5; 19:16.
His throne. Rev 3:21.
In the line of David. Is 9:7; Ezek 37:24,25; Luke 1:32; Acts 2:30.
Rules Zion. Ps 2:6; Is 52:7; Zech 9:9; Matt 21:5; John 12:12–15.
Has a righteous kingdom. Ps 45:6; Is 32:1; Jer 23:5; Heb 1:8,9.
Has an everlasting kingdom. Dan 2:44; 7:14; Luke 1:33.
Has an universal kingdom. Ps 2:8; 72:8; Zech 14:9; Rev 11:15.
Has a spiritual kingdom. John 18:36.
Believers are subjects of His Kingdom. Luke 22:29,30; Col 1:13; Heb 12:28; Rev 15:3.
Acknowledged by
The wise men from the East. Matt 2:2.
Nathanael. John 1:49.
His followers. Luke 19:38; John 12:13.
Declared by Himself. Matt 25:34; John 18:37.
Written on His cross. John 19:19.
The Jews shall seek to. Hos 3:5.
Believers shall behold. Is 33:17; Rev 22:3,4.
Kings shall pay homage to. Ps 72:10; Is 49:7.
Shall overcome all His enemies. Ps 110:1; Mark 12:36; 1 Cor 15:25; Rev 17:14.

CHRIST, THE MEDIATOR.

Through His death. Eph 2:13–18; Heb 9:15.
The only one between God and man. 1 Tim 2:5.
Of the gospel covenant. Heb 8:6; 12:24.

CHRIST, THE SHEPHERD.

Foretold. Gen 49:24; Is 40:11; Ezek 34:23; 37:24.
The chief. 1 Pet 5:4.
The good. John 10:11,14.
The great. Mic 5:4; Heb 13:20.
His sheep
He knows. John 10:14,27.
He calls. John 10:3.
He guides. Ps 23:3; John 10:3,4.
He feeds. John 10:9.
He laid down His life for. Zech 13:7; Matt 26:31; John 10:11,15; Acts 20:28.
He gives eternal life to. John 10:28.

CHURCH, THE.

Belongs to God. 1 Tim 3:15.
The body of Christ. Eph 1:23; Col 1:24.
Christ, the foundation-stone of. 1 Cor 3:11; Eph 2:20; 1 Pet 2:4,5.
Christ, the head of. Eph 1:22; 5:23.
Loved by Christ. Eph 5:25.
Purchased by the blood of Christ. Acts 20:28; Eph 5:25; Heb 9:12.
Sanctified. Eph 5:26,27.
Subject to Christ. Rom 7:4; Eph 5:24.
The object of the grace of God. 2 Cor 8:1.
Displays the wisdom of God. Eph 3:10.
God defends. Matt 16:18.
God provides ministers for. Eph 4:11,12.
Glory to be ascribed to God by. Eph 3:21.
Elect. 1 Pet 5:13.
Glorious. Eph 5:27.
Clothed in righteousness. Rev 19:8.
Believers continually added to, by the Lord. Acts 2:27; 5:14; 11:24.
Unity of. Rom 12:5; 1 Cor 10:17; 12:12; Gal 3:28.
Believers baptised into, by one Spirit. 1 Cor 12:13.

Ministers commanded to feed. Acts 20:28.
Is edified by the Word. 1 Cor 14:4,13; Eph 4:15,16.
The wicked persecute. Acts 8:1–3; 1 Thess 2:14,15.
Not to be despised. 1 Cor 11:22.

CIRCUMCISION.

Instituted by God. Gen 17:9,10.
Described. Gen 17:11; Ex 4:25.
Enforced by the law. Lev 12:3; John 7:22.
Called the
Covenant of circumcision. Acts 7:8.
Circumcision in the flesh. Eph 2:11.
A painful and bloody rite. Ex 4:26; Josh 5:8.
Promises to Abraham previous to. Rom 4:9,13.
A seal of the covenant. Gen 17:11; Rom 4:11.
Spiritual significance of. Rom 2:28–29.
Necessary to enjoying the privileges of the Jewish State. Ex 12:48; Ezek 44:7.
Was performed
On males home-born and bought. Gen 17:12,13.
On the eighth day. Gen 17:12; Lev 12:3.
Even on the sabbath day. John 7:22,23.
With knives of flint. Ex 4:25; Josh 5:3.
By the heads of families. Gen 17:23; Ex 4:25.
By persons in authority. Josh 5:3.
In the presence of the family, etc. Luke 1:58–61.
Accompanied with naming the child. Gen 21:3,4; Luke 1:59; 2:21.
First performed on Abraham and his family. Gen 17:24–27.
Not performed in the wilderness. Josh 5:5.
Performed by Joshua at Gilgal. Josh 5:2,7.
Punishment for neglecting. Gen 17:14; Ex 4:24,26.
Without faith, vain. Rom 3:30; Gal 5:6.
Without obedience, vain. Rom 2:25; 1 Cor 7:19.
The Jews
Identified by. Acts 10:45; Gal 2:9.
Held it unlawful to intermarry with the uncircumcision. Gen 34:14; Judg 14:3.
Held no interaction with those not of the. Acts 10:28; 11:3; Gal 2:12.
Despised as unclean those not of the. 1 Sam 14:6; 17:26; Matt 15:26,27; Eph 2:11,15.
Sometimes performed on slain enemies. 1 Sam 18:25–27; 2 Sam 3:14.
Abolished by the gospel. Eph 2:11,15; Col 3:11.
Performed on Timothy as a matter or expediency because of the Jews. Acts 16:3.
Necessity of, denied by Paul. Gal 2:3–5.
Necessity of, asserted by false teachers. Acts 15:24; Gal 6:12; Titus 1:10.
Trusting to, a denial of Christ. Gal 3:3,4; 5:3,4.
Paul denounced for opposing. Acts 21:21.
Illustrative of
Readiness to hear and obey. Jer 6:10.
Purity of heart. Deut 10:16; 30:6.
Purity of speech. Ex 6:12.

COMMUNICATION.

Communication
The power of words. Prov 11:9; 12:18; 15:4; 18:21; Matt 12:37; James 3:1–8.
The value of words. Prov 20:15; 25:11–14.
The source of words. Prov 6:12; 15:28; 16:23,24; Matt 12:34.
Communication Guidelines
By listening. Prov 18:13; 19:20; James 1:19.
Do not talk too much. Prov 10:19; 13:2,3; 17:27,28; Eccl 10:12–14; Col 4:6.
Do not nag. Prov 21:19; 26:21.
Do not meddle. Prov 26:27.
Do not gossip. Prov 11:13; 20:19; 26:20.
Do not brag. Prov 14:23; 27:2.
Be slow to speak. Prov 15:28; 29:20; James 1:19.
Be wise in timing. Prov 15:23; Eph 4:29.
Admit wrongs. Prov 29:23; James 5:16.
Do not lie. Ps 34:13; Prov 12:19,22; 26:18,19; Eph 4:15,25.
Do not respond in anger. Prov 15:1; Eph 4:26.
Avoid quarrels. Prov 17:14; 20:3.
Set a guard over my lips. Ps 141:3.
Deliver me from lying lips. Ps 120:3.
May my lips offer up a sacrifice of praise. Heb 13:15.
Let me speak encouragingly. Eph 4:29.
Bridle my tongue. James 1:26.

COMMUNION WITH GOD.

Is communion with the Father. 1 John 1:3.
Is communion with the Son. 1 Cor 1:9; 1 John 1:3; Rev 3:20.
Is communion with the Holy Spirit. 1 Cor 12:13; 2 Cor 13:14; Phil 2:1.
Holiness essential to. 2 Cor 6:14–16.
Promised to the obedient. John 14:23.
Believers
Desire. Ps 42:1; Phil 1:23.
Have, in meditation. Ps 63:5,6.
Have, in prayer. Phil 4:6; Heb 4:16.
Have, in the Lord's Supper. 1 Cor 10:16.
Should always enjoy. Ps 16:8; John 14:16–18.

CONDEMNATION.

Inseparable consequence of sin. Prov 12:2; Matt 25:41; Rom 5:12,16,18; 6:23.
Increased by
Impenitence. Matt 11:20–24.
Unbelief. John 3:18,19.
Pride. 1 Tim 3:6.
Oppression. James 5:1–5.
Hypocrisy. Matt 23:14.
Conscience testifies to the justice of. Job 9:20; Rom 2:1; Titus 3:11.
The law testifies to the justice of. Rom 3:19.
According to men's deserts. Matt 12:37; 2 Cor 11:15.
Believers are delivered from, by Christ. John 3:18; 5:24; Rom 8:1,33,34.
Of the wicked, an example. 2 Pet 2:7; Jude 7.
Chastisements are designed to rescue us from. Ps 94:12,13; 1 Cor 11:32.
The law is the ministration of. 2 Cor 3:9.

CONFESSING CHRIST.

Influences of the Holy Spirit necessary to. 1 Cor 12:3; 1 John 4:2.
Evidence of salvation. 1 John 2:23; 4:2,3,15.
Necessary to salvation. Rom 10:9,10.
Ensures his confessing us. Matt 10:32.
The fear of man prevents. John 7:13; 12:42,43.
Persecution should not prevent us from. Mark 8:35; 2 Tim 2:12.
Must be connected with faith. Rom 10:9.
Consequences of not. Matt 10:33.

CONFESSION OF SIN.

God regards. Job 33:27,28; Dan 9:20–23.
Exhortation to. Josh 7:19; Jer 3:13; James 5:16.
Promises to. Lev 26:40–42; Prov 28:13.
Should be accompanied with
Prayer for forgiveness. 2 Sam 24:10; Ps 25:11; 51:1; Jer 14:7–9,20.
Self-abasement. Is 64:5,6; Jer 3:25.
Godly sorrow. Ps 38:18; Lam 1:20.
Forsaking sin. Prov 28:13.
Restitution. Num 5:6,7.
Should be full and unreserved. Ps 32:5; 51:3; 106:6.
Followed by pardon. Ps 32:5; 1 John 1:9.

CONSCIENCE.

Witnesses in man. Prov 20:27; Rom 2:15.
Accuses of sin. Gen 42:21; 2 Sam 24:10; Matt 27:3; Acts 2:37.
We should have the approval of. Job 27:6; Acts 24:16; Rom 9:1; 14:22.
The blood of Christ alone can purify. Heb 9:14; 10:2–10,22.
Walk obediently for the sake of. Rom 13:5; 1 Tim 1:19; 3:9; 1 Pet 2:19.
Of believers, pure and good. Heb 13:18; 1 Pet 3:16,21.
Testimony of, a source of joy. 2 Cor 1:12; 1 John 3:21.
Of others, not to be offended. Rom 14:21; 1 Cor 10:28–32.
Ministers should commend themselves to that of their people. 2 Cor 4:2; 5:11.
Of the wicked unbelievers. 1 Tim 4:2; Titus 1:15.

CONTENTMENT.

Believers should exhibit
In their respective callings. 1 Cor 7:20.
With appointed wages. Luke 3:14.
With what things they have. Heb 13:5.
With food and raiment. 1 Tim 6:8.
God's promises should lead to. Heb 13:5.
The wicked lack. Eccl 5:10; Is 5:8.

CONVERSION.

Divine origin of. 1 Kin 18:37; Prov 1:23; John 6:44; Acts 3:26; 21:19; Rom 15:18.
Is of grace. Acts 11:21,23.
Follows repentance. Acts 3:19; 26:20.
Is the result of faith. Acts 11:21.
Through the instrumentality of
The Scriptures. Ps 19:7.
Ministers. Acts 26:18; 1 Thess 1:9.
Self-examination. Ps 119:59; Lam 3:40.
Affliction. Ps 78:34.
Of sinners, a cause of joy
To God. Ezek 18:23; Luke 15:32.
To believers. Acts 15:3; Gal 1:23,24.
Is necessary. Matt 18:3.
Exhortations to. Prov 1:23; Is 31:6; 55:7; Jer 3:7; Ezek 33:11.
Promises connected with. Neh 1:9; Is 1:27; Jer 3:14; Ezek 18:27.
Pray for. Ps 80:7; 85:4; Jer 31:18; Lam 5:21.
Is accompanied by confession of sin, and prayer. 1 Kin 8:35.
Danger of neglecting. Ps 7:12; Jer 44:5,11; Ezek 3:19.
Duty of leading sinners to. Ps 51:13.
Encouragement for leading sinners to. Dan 12:3; James 5:19,20.
Of Gentiles, predicted. Is 2:2; 11:10; 60:5; 66:12.
Of Israel, predicted. Ezek 36:25–27.

COVENANTS.

Agreements between two parties. Gen 26:28; Dan 11:6.
Designed for
  Establishing friendship. 1 Sam 18:3.
  Procuring assistance in war. 1 Kin 15:18,19.
  Mutual protection. Gen 26:28,29; 31:50–52.
  Establishing peace. Josh 9:15,16.
  Promoting commerce. 1 Kin 5:6–11.
  Selling land. Gen 23:14–16.
Conditions of
  Clearly specified. 1 Sam 11:1,2.
  Confirmed by oath. Gen 21:23,31; 26:31.
  Witnessed. Gen 23:17,18; Ruth 4:9–11.
  Written and sealed. Neh 9:38; 10:1.
God often called to witness. Gen 31:50,53.
When confirmed, unalterable. Gal 3:15.
Made by passing between the pieces of the divided sacrifices. Gen 15:9–17; Jer 34:18,19.
Salt a sign of perpetuity in. Num 18:19; 2 Chr 13:5.
Ratified by joining hands. Prov 11:21; Ezek 17:18.
Followed by a feast. Gen 26:30; 31:54.
Presents given as tokens. Gen 21:27–30; 1 Sam 18:3,4.
Pillars raised in token of. Gen 31:45,46.
Names given to places where made. Gen 21:31; 31:47–49.
The Jews
  Forbidden to make, with idolatrous nations. Ex 23:32; Deut 7:2.
  Frequently made with other nations. 1 Kin 5:12; 2 Kin 17:4.
  Condemned for making, with idolatrous nations. Is 30:2–5; Hos 12:1.
  Regarded, as sacred. Josh 9:16–19; Ps 15:4.

COVETOUSNESS.

Heart is origin of. Ezek 33:31; Mark 7:22,23; 2 Peter 2:14.
Is idolatry. Eph 5:5; Col 3:5.
Is never satisfied. Eccl 5:10; Hab 2:5.
Is vanity. Ps 39:6; Eccl 4:8.
Is inconsistent for believers. Eph 5:3; 1 Tim 3:3; Heb 13:5.
Leads to
  Injustice and oppression. Prov 28:20; Mic 2:2.
  Foolish and hurtful lusts. 1 Tim 6:9.
  Departure from the faith. 1 Tim 6:10.
  Lying. 2 Kin 5:22–25.
  Murder. Prov 1:18,19; Ezek 22:12.
  Theft. Josh 7:21.
  Poverty. Prov 28:22.
  Domestic troubles. Prov 15:27.
Forbidden. Ex 20:17.
A characteristic of the wicked. Ps 10:3; Prov 21:26; Rom 1:29.
Hated by believers. Ex 18:21; Acts 20:33.
To be mortified by believers. Col 3:5.
Prophets denounced. Is 5:8; Hab 2:9.
Punishment of. Job 20:15; Is 57:17; Jer 22:17–19; Mic 2:2,3.
Avoid. Ps 119:36; Luke 12:15; 1 Cor 5:11.
Reward of those who hate. Prov 28:16.
Shall abound in the last days. 2 Tim 3:2; 2 Pet 2:1–3.

CREATION.

The formation of things which had no previous existence. Rom 4:17; Heb 11:3.
Effected
  By God. Gen 1:1; 2:4,5; Prov 26:10.

By Christ. John 1:3,10; Col 1:16.
By the Holy Spirit. Job 26:13; Ps 104:30.
By the command of God. Ps 33:9; Heb 11:3.
In the beginning. Gen 1:1; Matt 24:21.
In six normal days. Ex 20:11; 31:17.
According to God's purpose. Ps 135:6.
For God's pleasure. Prov 16:4; Rev 4:11.
For Christ. Col 1:16.
By faith we believe, to be God's work. Heb 11:3.
Order of
  First day, making light and dividing it from darkness. Gen 1:3–5; 2 Cor 4:6.
  Second day, making the firmament or atmosphere, and separating the waters. Gen 1:6–8.
  Third day, separating the land from the water, and making it fruitful. Gen 1:9–13.
  Fourth day, placing the sun, moon, and stars to give light, etc. Gen 1:14–19.
  Fifth day, making birds, insects, and fishes. Gen 1:20–23.
  Sixth day, making beasts of the earth, and man. Gen 1:24,28.
God rested from, on the seventh day. Gen 2:2,3.
Exhibits
  The deity of God. Rom 1:20.
  The power of God. Is 40:26,28; Rom 1:20.
  The glory and handiwork of God. Ps 19:1.
  The wisdom of God. Ps 104:24; 136:5.
  The goodness of God. Ps 33:5.
  God as the sole object of worship. Is 45:16,18; Acts 17:24,27.
Glorifies God. Ps 145:10; 148:5.
God to be praised for. Neh 9:6; Ps 146:5,6.
Leads to confidence. Ps 124:8; 146:5,6.
Insignificance of man seen from. Ps 8:3,4; Is 40:12,17.
Groans because of sin. Rom 8:22.

DARKNESS.

Created by God. Ps 104:20; Is 45:7.
Originally covered the earth. Gen 1:2.
Separated from the light. Gen 1:4.
Called night. Gen 1:5.
Occurred after sunset. Gen 15:17; John 6:17.
Inexplicable nature of. Job 38:19,20.
Exhibits God's power and greatness. Job 38:8,9.
Degrees of, mentioned
  Great. Gen 15:12.
  That may be felt. Ex 10:21.
  Thick. Deut 5:22; Joel 2:2.
  Dense. Jer 13:16.
  Outer or extreme. Matt 8:12.
Effects of
  Keeps us from seeing objects. Ex 10:23.
  Causes us to go astray. John 12:35; 1 John 2:11.
  Causes us to stumble. Is 59:10.
Sometimes a synonym for night. Ps 91:6.
Cannot hide us from God. Ps 139:11,12.
The wicked
  The children of. 1 Thess 5:5.
  Live in. Ps 107:10.
  Walk in. Ps 82:5.
  Perpetuate their designs in. Job 24:16.
  Are full of. Matt 6:23.
Miraculous
  On Mount Sinai. Ex 19:16; Heb 12:18.

Over the land of Egypt. Ex 10:21,22.
At the death of Christ. Matt 27:45.
Before the destruction of Jerusalem. Matt 24:29.

DEATH OF CHRIST, THE.

Foretold. Is 53:8; Dan 9:26; Zech 13:7.
Appointed by God. Is 53:6,10; Acts 2:23.
Necessary for the redemption of man. Luke 24:46; Acts 17:3.
Acceptable, as a sacrifice to God. Matt 20:28; Eph 5:2; 1 Thess 5:10.
Was voluntary. Is 53:12; Matt 26:53; John 10:17,18.
Was undeserved. Is 53:9.
Mode of
  Foretold by Christ. Matt 20:18,19; John 12:32,33.
  Prefigured. Num 21:8; John 3:14.
  Ignominious. Heb 12:2.
  Accursed. Gal 3:13.
  Exhibited His humility. Phil 2:8.
  A stumbling block to Jews. 1 Cor 1:23.
  Foolishness to Gentiles. 1 Cor 1:18,23.
Demanded by the Jews. Matt 27:22,23.
Inflicted by the Gentiles. Matt 27:26–35.
In the company of transgressors. Is 53:12; Matt 27:38.
Accompanied by supernatural signs. Matt 27:45,51–53.
Signified death to sin. Rom 6:3–8; Gal 2:20.
Commemorated in the ordinance of the Lord's Supper. Luke 22:19,20; 1 Cor 11:26–29.

DEATH OF BELIEVERS, THE.

Asleep in Christ. 1 Cor 15:18; 1 Thess 4:14.
Is blessed. Rev 14:13.
Is gain. Phil 1:21.
Is full of
  Faith. Heb 11:13.
  Peace. Is 57:2.
  Hope. Prov 14:32.
Sometimes desired. Job 14:14; Luke 2:29.
Met with resignation. Gen 50:24; Josh 23:14; 1 Kin 2:2.
Met without fear. 1 Cor 15:55.
Precious in God's sight. Ps 116:15.
God is with them in. Ps 23:4; 48:14.
Removes from coming evil. 2 Kin 22:20; Is 57:1.
Leads to
  Rest. Job 3:17; 2 Thess 1:7.
  Comfort. Luke 16:25.
  Christ's presence. 2 Cor 5:8; Phil 1:23.
  A crown of life. 2 Tim 4:8; Rev 2:10.
  A joyful resurrection. Is 26:19; Dan 12:2.
Disregarded by the wicked. Is 57:1.
Survivors consoled by. 1 Thess 4:13–18.
The wicked wish theirs to resemble. Num 23:10.
Illustrated. Luke 16:22.

DEATH, SPIRITUAL.

Alienation from God is. Eph 4:18.
Carnal-mindedness is. Rom 8:6.
Walking in trespasses and sins is. Eph 2:1; Col 2:13.
Spiritual ignorance is. Is 9:2; Matt 4:16; Luke 1:79; Eph 4:18.
Unbelief is. John 3:36; 1 John 5:12.
Living in pleasure is. 1 Tim 5:6.
Hypocrisy is. Rev 3:1,2.
Is a consequence of the Fall. Rom 5:15.
Is the state of all men by nature. Rom 6:13; 8:6.

The fruits of, are dead works. Heb 6:1; 9:14.

A call to arise from. Eph 5:14.

Deliverance from, is through Christ. John 5:24,25; Eph 2:5; 1 John 5:12.

Believers are raised from. Rom 6:13.

Love of the brethren, a proof of being raised from. 1 John 3:14.

Illustrated. Ezek 37:2,3; Luke 15:24.

DECEIT.

Is falsehood. Ps 119:118.

The tongue, the instrument of. Rom 3:13.

Comes from the heart. Mark 7:22.

Characteristic of the heart. Jer 17:9.

God abhors. Ps 5:6.

Forbidden. Prov 24:28; 1 Pet 3:10.

Christ was perfectly free from. Is 53:9; 1 Pet 2:22.

Believers

Free from. Ps 24:4; Zeph 3:13; Rev 14:5.

Purposed against. Job 27:4.

Avoid. Job 31:5.

Shun those addicted to. Ps 101:7.

Pray for deliverance from those who use. Ps 43:1; 120:2.

Should beware of those who teach. Eph 5:6; Col 2:8.

Should lay aside, in seeking truth. 1 Pet 2:1.

The wicked

Are full of. Rom 1:29.

Devise. Ps 35:20; 38:12; Prov 12:5.

Utter. Ps 10:7; 36:3.

Work. Prov 11:18.

Increase in. 2 Tim 3:13.

Use, to each other. Jer 9:5.

Use, to themselves. Jer 37:9; Obad 3:7.

Delight in. Prov 20:17.

False teachers

Are workers of. 2 Cor 11:13.

Preach. Jer 14:14; 23:26.

Impose on others by. Rom 16:18; Eph 4:14.

Entertain themselves with. 2 Pet 2:13.

Hypocrites devise. Job 15:35.

Hypocrites practice. Hos 11:12.

False witnesses use. Prov 12:17; 14:5.

A characteristic of Antichrist. 2 John 7.

A characteristic of end times. 2 Thess 2:10.

Evil of

Keeps from knowledge of God. Jer 9:6.

Keeps from turning to God. Jer 8:5.

Leads to pride and oppression. Jer 5:27,28.

Leads to lying. Prov 14:25.

Often accompanied by fraud and injustice. Ps 10:7; 43:1.

Hatred often concealed by. Prov 26:24–28.

The folly of fools is. Prov 14:8.

The kisses of an enemy are. Prov 27:6.

Blessedness of being free from. Ps 24:4,5; 32:2.

Punishment of. Ps 55:23; Jer 9:7–9.

DECISION.

Necessary to the service of God. Luke 9:62.

Exhortations to. Josh 24:14,15.

Exhibited in

Seeking God with the heart. 2 Chr 15:12.

Keeping the commandments of God. Neh 10:29.

Being on the Lord's side. Ex 32:26.

Following God fully. Num 14:24; 32:12; Josh 14:8.

Serving God. Is 56:6.

Loving God perfectly. Deut 6:5.

Blessedness of. Josh 1:7.

Opposed to

A divided service. Matt 6:24.

Doublemindedness. James 1:8.

Halting between two opinions. 1 Kin 18:21.

Turning to the right or left. Deut 5:32.

Not setting the heart aright. Ps 78:8,37.

DENIAL OF CHRIST.

In doctrine. Mark 8:38; 2 Tim 1:8.

In practice. Phil 3:10,18; Titus 1:16.

A characteristic of false teachers. 2 Pet 2:1; Jude 1:4.

Is the spirit of Antichrist. 1 John 2:22,23; 4:3.

Christ will deny those guilty of. Matt 10:33; 2 Tim 2:12.

Leads to destruction. 2 Pet 2:1; Jude 4,15.

DESPAIR.

Produced in the wicked by divine judgments. Deut 28:34,67; Rev 9:6; 16:10.

Leads to

Continuing in sin. Jer 2:25; 18:12.

Blasphemy. Is 8:21; Rev 16:10,11.

Shall seize upon the wicked at the appearing of Christ. Rev 6:16.

Believers sometimes tempted to. Job 7:6; Lam 3:18.

Believers enabled to overcome. 2 Cor 4:8,9.

Trust in God, a preservative against. Ps 42:5,11.

DEVIL, THE.

Sinned against God. 2 Pet 2:4; 1 John 3:8.

Cast out of heaven. Luke 10:18.

Cast down to hell. 2 Pet 2:4; Jude 6.

The author of the fall. Gen 3:1,6,14,24.

Tempted Christ. Matt 4:3–10.

Perverts the Scripture. Ps 91:11,12; Matt 4:6.

Opposes God's work. Zech 3:1; 1 Thess 2:18.

Works lying wonders. 2 Thess 2:9; Rev 16:14.

Assumes the form of an angel of light. 2 Cor 11:14.

The wicked

Are the children of. Matt 13:38; Acts 13:10; 1 John 3:10.

Turn aside after. 1 Tim 5:15.

Do the lusts of. John 8:44.

Possessed by. Luke 22:3; Acts 5:3; Eph 2:2.

Blinded by. 2 Cor 4:4.

Deceived by. 1 Kin 22:21,22; Rev 20:7,8.

Ensnared by. 1 Tim 3:7; 2 Tim 2:26.

Troubled by. 1 Sam 16:14.

Punished, together with. Matt 25:41.

Believers

Afflicted by, only as God permits. Job 1:12; 2:4–7.

Tempted by. 1 Chr 21:1; 1 Thess 3:5.

Sifted by. Luke 22:31.

Should resist. James 4:7; 1 Pet 5:9.

Should be armed against. Eph 6:11–16.

Should be watchful against. 2 Cor 2:11.

Overcome. 1 John 2:13; Rev 12:10,11.

Shall finally triumph over. Rom 16:20.

Triumph over, by Christ

Predicted. Gen 3:15.

In resisting His temptations. Matt 4:11.

In casting out the spirits of. Luke 11:20; 13:32.

In empowering His disciples to cast out. Matt 10:1; Mark 16:17.

In destroying the works of. 1 John 3:8.

Completed by His death. Col 2:15; Heb 2:14.

Illustrated. Luke 11:21,22.

Character of

Presumptuous. Job 1:6; Matt 4:5,6.

Proud. 1 Tim 3:6.

Powerful. Eph 2:2; 6:12.

Wicked. 1 John 2:13.

Cynical. Job 1:9; 2:4.

Crafty. Gen 3:1; 2 Cor 11:3.

Deceitful. 2 Cor 11:14; Eph 6:11.

Fierce and cruel. Luke 8:29; 9:39,42; 1 Pet 5:8.

Cowardly. James 4:7.

The AntiChrist is of. 2 Thess 2:9.

Shall be condemned at the judgment. Jude 6; Rev 20:10.

Everlasting fire is prepared for. Matt 25:41.

Compared to

A fowler. Ps 91:3.

Birds. Matt 13:4.

A sower of tares. Matt 13:25,28.

A wolf. John 10:12.

A roaring lion. 1 Pet 5:8.

A serpent. Rev 12:9; 20:2.

DEVOTION TO GOD.

A characteristic of believers. Job 23:12.

Christ, an example of. John 4:34; 17:4.

Grounded upon

The mercies of God. Rom 12:1.

The goodness of God. 1 Sam 12:24.

The call of God. 1 Thess 2:12.

The death of Christ. 2 Cor 5:15.

Our creation. Ps 86:9.

Our preservation. Is 46:4.

Our redemption. 1 Cor 6:19,20.

Should be

With our spirit. 1 Cor 6:20; 1 Pet 4:6.

With our bodies. Rom 12:1; 1 Cor 6:20.

With our members. Rom 6:12,13; 1 Pet 4:2.

With our substance. Ex 22:29; Prov 3:9.

Unreserved. Matt 6:24; Luke 14:33.

Abounding. 1 Thess 4:1.

Persevering. Luke 1:74,75; 9:62.

In life and death. Rom 14:8; Phil 1:20.

Should be exhibited in

Loving God. Deut 6:5; Luke 10:27.

Serving God. 1 Sam 12:24; Rom 12:11.

Walking worthy of God. 1 Thess 2:12.

Doing all to God's glory. 1 Cor 10:31.

Bearing the cross. Mark 8:34.

Self-denial. Mark 8:34.

Living to Christ. 2 Cor 5:15.

Giving up all for Christ. Matt 19:21,28,29.

Lack of, condemned. Rev 3:16.

DILIGENCE.

Christ, an example. Mark 1:35; Luke 2:49.

Required by God in

Seeking Him. 1 Chr 22:19; Heb 11:6.

Obeying Him. Deut 6:17; 11:13.

Listening to Him. Is 55:2.

Pursuing sanctification. Phil 3:13,14; 2 Pet 1:5..

Keeping the souls. Deut 4:9.

Keeping the heart. Prov 4:23.

Labors of love. Heb 6:10–12.

Following every good work. 1 Tim 5:10.

Guarding against defilement. Heb 12:15.

Seeking to be found spotless. 2 Pet 3:14.
Making our call, etc., sure. 2 Pet 1:10.
Self-examination. Ps 77:6.
Lawful business. Prov 27:23; Eccl 9:10.
Teaching religion. 2 Tim 4:2; Jude 3.
Instructing children. Deut 11:19.
Discharging official duties. Deut 19:18.
Believers should abound in. 2 Cor 8:7.
In the service of God
  Should be preserved in. Gal 6:9.
  Is not in vain. 1 Cor 15:58.
  Preserves from evil. Ex 15:26.
  Leads to assured hope. Heb 6:11.
God rewards. Deut 11:14; Heb 11:6.
In temporal matters, leads to
  Favor. Prov 11:27.
  Prosperity. Prov 10:4; 13:4.
  Honor. Prov 12:24; 22:29.

DISOBEDIENCE TO GOD.

Provokes His anger. Ps 78:10,40; Is 3:8.
Forfeits His favor. 1 Sam 13:14.
Forfeits His promised blessings. Josh 5:6; 1 Sam 2:30; Jer 18:10.
Brings a curse. Deut 11:28; 28:15.
A characteristic of the wicked. Eph 2:2; Titus 1:16; 3:3.
The wicked persevere in. Jer 2:21.
Heinousness of, illustrated. Jer 35:14.
Men prone to excuse. Gen 3:12,13.
Shall be punished. Is 42:24,25; Heb 2:2.
Acknowledge the punishment of, to be just. Neh 9:32,33; Dan 9:10,11,14.
Warnings against. 1 Sam 12:15; Jer 12:17.
Bitter results of, illustrated. Jer 9:13,15.

DIVORCE.

Law of marriage against. Gen 2:24; Matt 19:6.
Recognized
  By the Mosaic law. Deut 24:1.
  On account of hardness of heart. Matt 19:8.
Often sought by the Jews. Mic 2:9; Mal 2:14.
Sought on slight grounds. Matt 5:31; 19:3.
Not allowed to those who falsely accused their wives. Deut 22:18,19.
Women
  Could marry after. Deut 24:2.
  Responsible for vows after. Num 30:9.
  Married after, could not return to first husband. Deut 24:3,4; Jer 3:1.
  Afflicted by. Is 54:4,6.
Priests not to marry women after. Lev 21:14.
Of servants, regulated by law. Ex 21:7,11.
Of captives, regulated by law. Deut 21:13,14.
Forced on those who had idolatrous wives. Ezra 10:2–17; Neh 13:23,30.
Jews condemned for love of. Mal 2:14–16.
Forbidden by Christ except for adultery. Matt 5:32; 19:9.
Prohibition of, offended the Jews. Matt 19:10.
Illustrative of God's casting off of the Jewish church. Is 50:1; Jer 3:8.

DOCTRINES, FALSE.

Destructive to faith. 2 Tim 2:18.
Hateful to God. Rev 2:14,15.
Unprofitable and vain. Titus 3:9; Heb 13:9.
Should be avoided by
  Ministers. 1 Tim 1:4; 6:20.
  Believers. Eph 4:14; Col 2:8.
  All men. Jer 23:16; 29:8.

The wicked love. 2 Tim 4:3,4.
The wicked given up to believe. 2 Thess 2:11.
Teachers of
  Not to be countenanced. 2 John 10.
  Should be avoided. Rom 16:17,18.
  Bring reproach on religion. 2 Pet 2:2.
  Speak perverse things. Acts 20:30.
  Deceive many. Matt 24:5.
  Shall abound in the latter days. 1 Tim 4:1.
  Pervert the gospel of Christ. Gal 1:6,7.
  Shall be exposed. 2 Tim 3:9.
Teachers of, are described as
  Cruel. Acts 20:29.
  Deceitful. 2 Cor 11:13.
  Covetous. Titus 1:11; 2 Pet 2:3.
  Ungodly. Judg 1:4,8.
  Proud and ignorant. 1 Tim 6:3,4.
  Corrupt and reprobate. 2 Tim 3:8.
Try, by Scripture. Is 8:20; 1 John 4:1.
Curse on those who teach. Gal 1:8,9.
Punishment on those who teach. Mic 3:6,7; 2 Pet 2:1,3.

DREAMS.

Visions in sleep. Job 33:15; Dan 2:28.
Often imaginary. Job 20:8; Is 29:8.
Excess of business frequently leads to. Eccl 5:3.
God's will often revealed in. Num 12:6; Job 33:15.
False prophets
  Pretend to. Jer 23:25–28; 29:8.
  Not to be regarded in. Deut 13:1–3; Jer 27:9.
  Condemned for pretending to. Jer 23:32.
Vanity of trusting to natural. Eccl 5:7.
The ancients
  Put great faith in. Judg 7:15.
  Often perplexed by. Gen 40:6; 41:8; Job 7:14; Dan 2:1; 4:5.
  Anxious to have, explained. Gen 40:8; Dan 2:3.
  Consulting magicians on. Gen 41:8; Dan 2:2–4.
God the only interpreter of. Gen 40:8; 41:16; Dan 2:27–30; 7:16.
Mentioned in Scripture
  Abimelech. Gen 20:3–7.
  Jacob. Gen 28:12; 31:10.
  Laban. Gen 31:24.
  Joseph. Gen 37:5–9.
  Pharaoh's butler and baker. Gen 40:5–19.
  Pharaoh. Gen 41:1–7.
  Midianite. Judg 7:13–15.
  Solomon. 1 Kin 3:5–15.
  Nebuchadnezzar. Dan 2:1,31; 4:5,8.
  Daniel. Dan 7:1–28.
  Joseph. Matt 1:20,21; 2:13,19,20.
  Wise men. Matt 2:11,12.
  Pilate's wife. Matt 27:19.

DRUNKENNESS.

Forbidden. Eph 5:18.
Caution against. Luke 21:34.
Is a work of the flesh. Gal 5:21.
Is debasing. Is 28:8.
Is inflaming. Is 5:11.
Enslaves the heart. Luke 21:34.
Takes away the heart. Hos 4:11.
Leads to
  Poverty. Prov 21:17; 23:21.
  Strife. Prov 23:29,30.
  Woe and sorrow. Prov 23:29,30.
  Error. Is 28:7.
  Contempt of God's works. Is 5:12.
  Scorning. Hos 7:5.

Revelry and lust. Rom 13:13.
The wicked addicted to. Dan 5:1–4.
False teachers often addicted to. Is 56:12.
Folly of yielding to. Prov 20:1.
Avoid those given to. Prov 23:20; 1 Cor 5:11.
Denunciations against
  Those given to. Is 5:11,12; 28:1–3.
  Those who encourage. Hab 2:15.
Excludes from heaven. 1 Cor 6:10; Gal 5:21.
Punishment of. Deut 21:20; Joel 1:5,6; Amos 6:6,7; Matt 24:49–51.

EARTH, THE.

The world in general. Gen 1:2.
The dry land as divided from waters. Gen 1:10.
God
  Created. Gen 1:1; Neh 9:6.
  Laid the foundation of. Job 38:4; Ps 102:25.
  Formed. Ps 90:2.
  Spread abroad. Is 42:5; 44:24.
  Suspended in space. Job 26:7.
  Supports. Ps 75:3.
  Establishes. Ps 78:69; 119:90.
  Enlightens. Gen 1:14–16; Jer 33:25.
  Waters. Ps 65:9; 147:8.
  Makes fruitful. Gen 1:11; 27:28.
  Inspects. Zech 4:10.
  Governs supremely. Job 34:13; Ps 135:6.
  Reigns in. Ex 8:22; Ps 97:1.
  Shall be exalted in. Ps 46:10.
Is the Lord's. Ex 9:29; 1 Cor 10:26.
Created to be inhabited. Is 45:18.
First division of. Gen 10:25.
Ideas of the ancients respecting the form of. Job 11:9; 38:18; Prov 25:3.
Diversified by hills and mountains. Hab 3:6.
Full of minerals. Deut 8:9; Job 28:1–5,15–19.
Described as
  God's footstool. Is 66:1; Matt 5:35.
  Full of God's goodness. Ps 33:5.
  Full of God's riches. Ps 104:24.
  Full of God's mercy. Ps 119:64.
  Full of God's glory. Num 14:21; Is 6:3.
  Shining with God's glory. Ezek 43:2.
  Trembling before God. Ps 68:8; Jer 10:10.
  Melting at God's voice. Ps 46:6.
  Burning at God presence. Nah 1:5.
Man
  Formed out of. Gen 2:7; Ps 103:14.
  Given dominion over. Gen 1:26; Ps 115:16.
  By nature is of. 1 Cor 15:47–48.
  By nature minds the thing of. Phil 3:19.
  Brought a curse on. Gen 3:17.
  Shall return to. Gen 3:19; Ps 146:4.
Subject to God's judgments. Ps 46:8; Is 11:4.
Corrupted by sin. Gen 6:11,12; Is 24:5.
Made barren by sin. Deut 28:23; Ps 107:34.
Made to mourn and languish by sin. Is 24:4; Jer 4:28; 12:4; Hos 4:3.
Satan goes to and fro in. Job 1:7; 1 Pet 5:8.
Shall be filled with the knowledge of God. Is 11:9; Hab 2:14.
Once inundated. Gen 7:17–24.
Not to be again inundated. Gen 9:11; 2 Pet 3:6,7.
To be dissolved by fire. 2 Pet 3:7,10,12.
To be renewed. Is 65:17; 2 Pet 3:13.
Believers shall inherit. Ps 25:13; Matt 5:5.

ELECTION.

Of Christ, as Messiah. Is 42:1; 1 Pet 2:6.
Of good angels. 1 Tim 5:21.
Of Israel. Deut 7:6; Is 45:5.
Of ministers. Luke 6:13; Acts 9:15.
Of churches. 1 Pet 5:13.
Of believers, is
  Of God. 1 Thess 1:4; Titus 1:1.
  By Christ. John 13:18; 15:16.
  In Christ. Eph 1:4.
  Personal. Matt 20:16; John 6:44; Acts
    22:14; 2 John 13.
  According to the purpose of God. Rom
    9:11; Eph 1:11.
  According to the foreknowledge of
    God. Rom 8:29; 1 Pet 1:2.
  Eternal. Eph 1:4.
  Sovereign. Rom 9:15,16; 1 Cor 1:27;
    Eph 1:11.
  Irrespective of merit. Rom 9:11.
  Of grace. Rom 11:5.
  Recorded in heaven. Luke 10:20.
  For the glory of God. Eph 1:6.
  Through faith. 2 Thess 2:13.
  Through sanctification of the Spirit.
    1 Pet 1:2.
  To adoption. Eph 1:5.
  To salvation. 2 Thess 2:13.
  To conformity with Christ. Rom 8:29.
  To good works. Eph 2:10.
  To spiritual warfare. 2 Tim 2:4.
  To eternal glory. Rom 9:23.
Ensures to believers
  Effectual calling. Rom 8:30.
  Divine teaching. John 17:6.
  Belief in Christ. Acts 13:48.
  Acceptance with God. Rom 11:7.
  Protection. Mark 13:20.
  Vindication of their wrongs. Luke
    18:7.
  Working of all things for good. Rom
    8:28.
  Blessedness. Ps 33:12; 65:4.
  The inheritance. Is 65:9; 1 Pet 1:4,5.
Should lead to cultivation of graces. Col
  3:12.
Should be evidenced by diligence. 2 Pet
  1:10.
Believers may have assurance of. 1 Thess
  1:4.

ENEMIES.

Christ prayed for His. Luke 23:34.
The lives of, to be spared. 1 Sam 24:10;
  2 Sam 16:10,11.
The goods of, to be taken care of. Ex
  23:4,5.
Should be
  Loved. Matt 5:44.
  Prayed for. Acts 7:60.
  Assisted. Prov 25:21; Rom 12:20.
  Overcome by kindness. 1 Sam 26:21.
Rejoice not at the misfortunes of. Job
  31:29.
Rejoice not at the failings of. Prov 24:17.
Desire not the death of. 1 Kin 3:11.
Curse them not. Job 31:30.
Be affectionately concerned for. Ps 35:13.
The friendship of, deceitful. 2 Sam
  20:9,10; Prov 26:26; 27:6; Matt
  26:48,49.
God defends against. Ps 59:9; 61:3.
God delivers from. 1 Sam 12:11; Ezra
  8:31; Ps 18:48.
Made to be at peace with believers. Prov
  16:7.
Pray for deliverance from. 1 Sam 12:10; Ps
  17:9; 59:1; 64:1.
Of believers, God will destroy. Ps 60:12.
Praise God for deliverance from. Ps
  136:24.

ENVY.

Forbidden. Prov 3:31; Rom 13:13.
Produced by foolish disputation. 1 Tim
  6:4.
Excited by good deeds of others. Eccl 4:4.
A work of the flesh. Gal 5:21; James 4:5.
Harmful to the health. Job 5:2; Prov
  14:30.
None can stand before. Prov 27:4.
A proof of carnal-mindedness. 1 Cor 3:1,3.
Inconsistent with the gospel. James 3:14.
Hinders growth in grace. 1 Pet 2:1,2.
The wicked
  Are full of. Rom 1:29.
  Live in. Titus 3:3.
Leads to every evil work. James 3:16.
Prosperity of the wicked should not excite.
  Ps 37:1,35; 73:3,17–20.
Punishment of. Is 26:11.
Exemplified
  Cain. Gen 4:5.
  Philistines. Gen 26:14.
  Laban's sons. Gen 31:1.
  Joseph's brethren. Gen 37:11.
  Joshua. Num 11:28,29.
  Aaron, etc. Num 12:2.
  Korah, etc. Num 16:3; Ps 106:16.
  Saul. 1 Sam 18:8.
  Sanballat, etc. Neh 2:10.
  Haman. Esth 5:13.
  Edomites. Ezek 35:11.
  Princes of Babylon. Dan 6:3,4.
  Chief Priests. Mark 15:10.
  Jews. Acts 13:45; 17:5.

EXAMPLE OF CHRIST, THE.

Is perfect. Heb 7:26.
Conformity to, required in
  Holiness. 1 Pet 1:15,16; Rom 1:6.
  Righteousness. 1 John 2:6.
  Purity. 1 John 3:3.
  Love. John 13:34; Eph 5:2; 1 John
    3:16.
  Humility. Luke 22:27; Phil 2:5,7.
  Meekness. Matt 11:29.
  Obedience. John 15:10.
  Self-denial. Matt 16:24.
  Ministering to others. Matt 20:28;
    John 13:14,15.
  Benevolence. Acts 20:35; 2 Cor 8:7,9.
  Forgiving injuries. Col 3:13.
  Overcoming the world. John 16:33;
    1 John 5:4.
  Being not of the world. John 17:16.
  Being without deceit. 1 Pet 2:21–22.
  Suffering wrongfully. 1 Pet 2:21–23.
  Suffering for righteousness. Heb
    12:3,4.
Believers predestinated to follow. Rom
  8:29.
Conformity to, progressive. 2 Cor 3:18.

FAITH.

Is the substance of things hoped for. Heb
  11:1.
Is the evidence of things not seen. Heb
  11:1.
Commanded. Matt 11:22; 1 John 3:23.
The objects of, are
  God. John 14:1.
  Christ. John 6:29; Acts 20:21.
  Writings of Moses. John 5:46; Acts
    24:14.
  Writings of the prophets. 2 Chr 20:20;
    Acts 26:27.
  The gospel. Mark 1:15.
  Promises of God. Rom 4:21; Heb
    11:13.
In Christ is
  The gift of God. Rom 12:3; Eph 2:8;
    6:23; Phil 1:29.

The work of God. Acts 11:21; 1 Cor
  2:5.
Precious. 2 Pet 1:1.
Most holy. Jude 20.
Fruitful. 1 Thess 1:3.
Accompanied by repentance. Mark
  1:15; Luke 24:47.
Followed by conversion. Acts 11:21.
Christ is the Author and Finisher of. Heb
  12:2.
Is a gift of the Holy Spirit. 1 Cor 12:9.
The Scriptures designed to produce. John
  20:31; 2 Tim 3:15.
Preaching designed to produce. John
  17:20; Acts 8:12; Rom 10:14,15,17;
  1 Cor 3:5.
Through it is
  Remission of sins. Acts 10:43; Rom
    3:25.
  Justification. Acts 13:39; Rom
    3:21,22,28,30; 5:1; Gal 2:16.
  Salvation. Mark 16:16; Acts 16:31.
  Sanctification. Acts 15:9; 26:18.
  Spiritual light. John 12:36,46.
  Spiritual life. John 20:31; Gal 2:20.
  Eternal life. John 3:15,16; 6:40,47.
  Rest in heaven. Heb 4:3.
  Edification. 1 Tim 1:4; Jude 20.
  Preservation. 1 Pet 1:5.
  Adoption. John 1:12; Gal 3:26.
  Access to God. Rom 5:2; Eph 3:12.
  Inheritance of the promises. Gal 3:22;
    Heb 6:12.
  The gift of the Holy Spirit. Acts
    11:15–17; Gal 3:14; Eph 1:13.
Impossible to please God without. Heb
  11:6.
Justification is by, to be of grace. Rom
  4:16.
Essential to the profitable reception of the
  gospel. Heb 4:2.
Necessary in the Christian warfare. 1 Tim
  1:18,19; 6:12.
The Word effectual in those who have.
  1 Thess 2:13.
Excludes self-justification. Rom 10:3,4.
Excludes boasting. Rom 3:27.
Works by love. Gal 5:6; 1 Tim 1:5;
  Philem 5.
Produces
  Hope. Rom 5:2.
  Joy. Acts 16:34; 1 Pet 1:8.
  Peace. Rom 15:13.
  Confidence. Is 28:16; 1 Pet 2:6.
  Boldness in preaching. Ps 116:10;
    2 Cor 4:13.
Christ is precious to those having. Eph
  3:17; 1 Pet 2:7.
Necessary in prayer. Matt 21:22; James
  1:6.
Unbelievers have not. John 10:26,27.
An evidence of the new birth. 1 John 5:1.
By it believers
  Live. Gal 2:20.
  Stand. Rom 11:20; 2 Cor 1:24.
  Walk. Rom 4:12; 2 Cor 5:7.
  Obtain a good report. Heb 11:2.
  Overcome the world. 1 John 5:4,5.
  Resist the devil. 1 Pet 5:9.
  Overcome the devil. Eph 6:16.
  Are supported. Ps 27:13; 1 Tim 4:10.
Believers die in. Heb 11:13.
Believers should
  Be sincere in. 1 Tim 1:5; 2 Tim 1:5.
  Abound in. 2 Cor 8:7.
  Continue in. Acts 14:22; Col 1:23.
  Be strong in. Rom 4:20–24.
  Stand fast in. 1 Cor 16:13.
  Be grounded and settled in. Col 1:23.
  Hold, with a good conscience. 1 Tim
    1:19.

Pray for the increase of. Luke 17:5.
Have full assurance of. 2 Tim 1:12;
Heb 10:22.
True, evidenced by its fruits. James
2:17,20,26.
Examine whether you be in. 2 Cor 13:5.
All difficulties overcome by. Matt 17:20;
21:21; Mark 9:23.
All things should be done in. Rom 14:22.
Whatever is not of, is sin. Rom 14:23.
Often tried by affliction. 1 Pet 1:6,7.
Trial of, works patience. James 1:3.
The wicked often profess. Acts 8:13,21.
The wicked destitute of. John 10:25;
12:37; Acts 19:9; 2 Thess 3:2.

FAITHFULNESS.

A characteristic of believers. Eph 1:1; Col
1:2; 1 Tim 6:2; Rev 17:14.
Exhibited in
The service of God. Matt 24:45.
Declaring the Word of God. Jer 23:28;
2 Cor 2:17; 4:2.
The care of dedicated things. 2 Chr
31:12.
Helping the brethren. 3 John 5.
Bearing witness. Prov 14:5.
Reproving others. Ps 141:5; Prov 27:6.
Situations of trust. 2 Kin 12:15; Neh
13:13; Acts 6:1–3.
Doing work. 2 Chr 34:12.
Keeping secrets. Prov 11:13.
Conveying messages. Prov 13:17;
25:13.
All things. 1 Tim 3:11.
The smallest matters. Luke 16:10–12.
Should be to death. Rev 2:10.
Especially required in
Ministers. 1 Cor 4:2; 2 Tim 2:2.
The wives of ministers. 1 Tim 3:11.
The children of ministers. Titus 1:6.
Difficulty of finding. Prov 20:6.
The wicked devoid of. Ps 5:9.
Associate with those who exhibit. Ps
101:6.
Blessedness of. 1 Sam 26:23; Prov 28:20.
Blessedness of, illustrated. Matt 24:45,46;
25:21,23.

FAITHFULNESS OF GOD, THE.

Is part of His character. Is 49:7; 1 Cor 1:9;
1 Thess 5:24.
Declared to be
Great. Lam 3:23.
Established. Ps 89:2.
Incomparable. Ps 89:8.
Unfailing. Ps 89:33; 2 Tim 2:13.
Infinite. Ps 36:5.
Everlasting. Ps 119:90; 146:6.
Should be pleaded in prayer. Ps 143:1.
Should be proclaimed. Ps 40:10; 89:1.
Manifested
In His counsels. Is 25:1.
In afflicting His believers. Ps 119:75.
In fulfilling His promises. 1 Kin 8:20;
Ps 132:11; Mic 7:20; Heb 10:23.
In keeping His covenant. Deut 7:9; Ps
111:5.
In executing His judgments. Jer 23:20;
51:29.
In forgiving sins. 1 John 1:9.
To His believers. Ps 89:24; 2 Thess 3:3.
Believers encouraged to depend on.
1 Pet 4:19.
Will be praised. Ps 89:5; 92:2.

FALL OF MAN, THE.

By the disobedience of Adam. Gen
3:6,11,12; Rom 5:12,15,19.
Through temptation of the devil. Gen 3:1–
5; 2 Cor 11:3; 1 Tim 2:14.

Man in consequence of
Made in the image of Adam. Gen 5:3;
1 Cor 15:48,49.
Born in sin. Job 15:14; 25:4; Ps 51:5;
Is 48:8; John 3:6.
A child of wrath. Eph 2:3.
Evil in heart. Gen 6:5; 8:21; Jer 16:12;
Matt 15:19.
Blinded in heart. Eph 4:18.
Corrupt and perverse in his ways. Gen
6:12; Rom 3:12–16.
Depraved in mind. Rom 8:5–7; Eph
4:17; Col 1:21; Titus 1:15.
Without understanding. Ps 14:2,3;
Rom 1:31; 3:11.
Receives not the things of God. 1 Cor
2:14.
Comes short of God's glory. Rom 3:23.
Defiled in conscience. Titus 1:15; Heb
10:22.
Intractable. Job 11:12.
Estranged from God. Gen 3:8; Ps 58:3;
Eph 4:18; Col 1:21.
In bondage to sin. Rom 6:19; 7:5,23;
Gal 5:17; Titus 3:3.
In bondage to the devil. 2 Tim 2:26;
Heb 2:14,15.
Constant in evil. Ps 10:5; 2 Pet 2:14.
Conscious of guilt. Gen 3:7,8,10.
Unrighteous. Eccl 7:20; Rom 3:10.
Completely corrupt. Job 15:16; Ps 14:3.
Turned to his own way. Is 53:6.
Loves darkness. John 3:19.
Corrupt, etc. in speech. Rom 3:13,14.
Devoid of the fear of God. Rom 3:18.
Totally depraved. Gen 6:5; Rom 7:18.
Dead in sin. Eph 2:1; Col 2:13.
All men partake of the effects of. 1 Kin
8:46; Gal 3:22; 1 John 1:8; 5:19.
Punishment consequent upon
Banishment from Paradise. Gen 3:24.
Condemnation to labor and sorrow.
Gen 3:16,19; 5:6,7.
Temporal death. Gen 3:19; Rom 5:12;
1 Cor 15:22.
Eternal death. Job 21:30; Rom
5:18,21; 6:23.
Cannot be remedied by man. Prov 20:9;
Jer 2:22; 13:23.
Remedy for, provided by God. Gen 3:15;
John 3:16.

FAMILIES.

Of believers blessed. Ps 128:3–6.
Should
Be taught the Scriptures. Deut 4:9,10.
Worship God together. 1 Cor 16:19.
Be duly regulated. Prov 31:27; 1 Tim
3:4,5,12.
Live in unity. Gen 45:24; Ps 133:1.
Members forgive one another. Gen
50:17–21; Matt 18:21,22.
Rejoice together before God. Deut
14:26.
Deceivers and liars should be removed
from. Ps 101:7.
Warning against departing from God. Deut
29:18.
Punishment of unbelieving ones. Jer 10:25.

FAMINE.

Sent by God. Ps 10:16.
Often on account of sin. Lev 26:21,26;
Lam 4:4–6.
One of God's four sore judgments. Ezek
14:21.
Caused by
God's blessing withheld. Hos 2:8,9;
Hag 1:6.
Want of seasonable rain. 1 Kin 17:1;
Jer 14:1–4; Amos 4:7.

Rotting of the seed in the ground. Joel
1:17.
Swarms of locusts. Deut 28:38,42; Joel
1:4.
Blight and mildew. Amos 4:9; Hag
2:17.
Devastation by enemies. Deut
28:33,51.
Often long continued. Gen 41:27; 2 Kin
8:1,2.
Often severe. Gen 12:10; 1 Kin 18:2; Jer
52:6.
Expressed by
Taking away the supply of bread, etc.
Is 3:1.
Cleanness of teeth. Amos 4:6.
The arrows of famine. Ezek 5:16.
Often accompanied by war. Jer 14:15;
29:18.
Often followed by pestilence. Jer 42:17;
Ezek 7:15; Matt 24:7.
Things eaten during
Wild herbs. 2 Kin 4:39,40.
Donkey's flesh. 2 Kin 6:25.
Dung. 2 Kin 6:25.
Human flesh. Lev 26:29; 2 Kin
6:28,29.
Provisions sold by weight during. Ezek
4:16.
Suffering of brute creation from. Jer
14:5,6.
Caused
Burning and fever. Deut 32:24.
Damaged skin. Lam 4:8; 5:10.
Grief and mourning. Joel 1:11–13.
Faintness. Gen 47:13.
Wasting of the body. Lam 4:8; Ezek
4:17.
Death. 2 Kin 7:4; Jer 11:22.
God provided for His people during. 1 Kin
17:4,9; Job 5:20; Ps 33:19; 37:19.
Instances of, in Scripture
In the days of Abraham. Gen 12:10.
In the days of Isaac. Gen 26:1.
In the days of Joseph. Gen 41:53–56.
In the days of the Judges. Ruth 1:1.
In the reign of David. 2 Sam 21:1.
In the reign of Ahab. 1 Kin 17:1; 18:5.
In the time of Elisha. 2 Kin 4:38.
During the siege of Samaria. 2 Kin 6:25.
Of seven years foretold by Elisha.
2 Kin 8:1.
In the time of Jeremiah. Jer 14:1.
During the siege of Jerusalem. 2 Kin
25:3.
After the captivity. Neh 5:3.
In the reign of Claudius Caesar. Acts
11:28.
Before destruction of Jerusalem. Matt
24:7.
The Jews in their restored state not to be
afflicted by. Ezek 36:29,30.

FASTING.

Spirit of, explained. Is 58:6,7.
Not to be made a subject of display. Matt
6:16–18.
Should be to God. Zech 7:5; Matt 6:18.
For the chastening of the soul. Ps 69:10.
For the humbling of the soul. Ps 35:13.
Observed on occasions of
Judgments of God. Joel 1:14; 2:12.
Public calamities. 2 Sam 1:12.
Afflictions of the Church. Luke 5:33–
35.
Afflictions of others. Ps 35:13; Dan
6:18.
Private afflictions. 2 Sam 12:16.
Approaching danger. Esth 4:16.
Ordination of ministers. Acts 13:3;
14:23.

Accompanied by
　Prayer. Ezra 8:23; Dan 9:3.
　Confession of sin. 1 Sam 7:6; Neh
　　9:1,2.
　Mourning. Joel 2:12.
　Humiliation. Deut 9:18; Neh 9:1.
Promises connected with. Is 58:8–12;
　Matt 6:18.
Of hypocrites
　Described. Is 58:4,5.
　Ostentatious. Matt 6:16.
　Boasted of, before God. Luke 18:12.
　Rejected. Is 58:3; Jer 14:12.

FATHERLESS.

Find mercy in God. Hos 14:3.
God will
　Be a father of. Ps 68:5.
　Be a helper of. Ps 10:14.
　Hear the cry of. Ex 22:23.
　Execute the judgment of. Deut 10:18;
　　Ps 10:18.
　Punish those who oppress. Ex 22:24;
　　Is 10:1–3; Mal 3:5.
　Punish those who judge not. Jer
　　5:28,29.
Visit in affliction. James 1:27.
Let them share in our blessings. Deut
　14:29.
Defend. Ps 82:3; Is 1:17.
Wrong not, in judgment. Deut 24:17.
Defraud not. Prov 23:10.
Afflict not. Ex 22:22.
Oppress not. Zech 7:10.
Do no violence to. Jer 22:3.
Blessedness of taking care of. Deut 14:29;
　Job 29:12,13; Jer 7:6,7.
The wicked
　Rob. Is 10:2.
　Overwhelm. Job 6:27.
　Mistreat. Ezek 22:7.
　Oppress. Job 24:3.
　Murder. Ps 94:6.
　Judge not for. Is 1:23; Jer 5:28.
A curse on those who oppress. Deut
　27:19.
Promises with respect to. Jer 49:11.
A type of Zion in affliction. Lam 5:3.

FEAR, GODLY.

God is the object of. Is 8:13.
God is the author of. Jer 32:39,40.
Searching the Scriptures gives the
　understanding of. Prov 2:3–5.
Described as
　Hatred of evil. Prov 8:13.
　Wisdom. Job 28:28; Ps 111:10.
　A treasure to believers. Prov 15:16; Is
　　33:6.
　A fountain of life. Prov 14:27.
　Sanctifying. Ps 19:9.
　Filial and reverential. Heb 12:9,28.
Commanded. Deut 13:4; Ps 22:23; Eccl
　12:13; 1 Pet 2:17.
Motives to
　The holiness of God. Rev 15:4.
　The greatness of God. Deut 10:12,17.
　The goodness of God. 1 Sam 12:24.
　The forgiveness of God. Ps 130:4.
　Wondrous works of God. Josh 4:23,24.
　Judgments of God. Rev 14:7.
A characteristic of believers. Mal 3:16.
Should accompany the joy of believers. Ps
　2:11.
Necessary to
　The worship of God. Ps 5:7; 89:7.
　The service of God. Ps 2:11; Heb 12:28.
　Avoiding of sin. Ex 20:20.
　Righteous government. 2 Sam 23:3.
　Impartial administration of justice.
　　2 Chr 19:6–9.

Perfecting holiness. 2 Cor 7:1.
Those who have
　Give pleasure to God. Ps 147:11.
　Are pitied by God. Ps 103:13.
　Are accepted of God. Acts 10:35.
　Receive mercy from God. Ps
　　103:11,17; Luke 1:50.
　Are blessed. Ps 112:1; 115:13.
　Confide in God. Ps 115:11; Prov
　　14:26.
　Depart from evil. Prov 16:6.
　Converse together of holy things. Mal
　　3:16.
　Should not fear man. Is 8:12,13; Matt
　　10:28.
　Desires of, fulfilled by God. Ps 145:19.
　Days of, prolonged. Prov 10:27.
Should be
　Prayed for. Ps 86:11.
　Exhibited in our callings. Col 3:22.
　Exhibited in giving a reason for our
　　hope. 1 Pet 3:15.
　Constantly maintained. Deut 14:23;
　　Josh 4:24; Prov 23:17.
　Taught to others. Ps 34:11.
Advantages of. Prov 15:16; 19:23; Eccl
　8:12,13.
The wicked destitute of. Ps 36:1; Prov
　1:29; Jer 2:19; Rom 3:18.

FEAR, UNHOLY.

A characteristic of the wicked. Rev 21:8.
Is described as
　A fear of idols. 2 Kin 17:38.
　A fear of man. 1 Sam 15:24; John
　　9:22.
　A fear of judgments. Is 2:19; Luke
　　21:26; Rev 6:16,17.
　A fear of future punishment. Heb
　　10:27.
　Overwhelming. Ex 15:16; Job
　　15:21,24.
　Consuming. Ps 73:19.
A guilty conscience leads to. Gen 3:8,10;
　Ps 53:5; Prov 28:1.
Seizes the wicked. Job 15:24; 18:11.
Surprises the hypocrite. Is 33:14,18.
The wicked judicially filled with. Lev
　26:16,17; Deut 28:65–67; Jer 49:5.
Shall be realised. Prov 1:27; 10:24.
God mocks. Prov 1:26.
Believers sometimes tempted to. Ps 55:5.
Believers delivered from. Prov 1:33; Is
　14:3.
Trust in God, a preservative from. Ps 27:1.
Exhortations against. Is 8:12; John 14:27.

FELLOWSHIP OF BELIEVERS, THE

Is with
　God. 1 John 1:3.
　Believers in heaven. Heb 12:22–24.
　Each other. Gal 2:9; 1 John 1:3,7.
Christ is present in. Matt 18:20.
In public and social worship. Acts 1:14;
　Heb 10:25.
In the Lord's Supper. 1 Cor 10:17.
In prayer for each other. 2 Cor 1:11; Eph
　6:18.
In exhortation. Col 3:16; Heb 10:25.
In mutual comfort and edification.
　1 Thess 4:18; 5:11.
In mutual sympathy and kindness. Rom
　12:15; Eph 4:32.
Delight of. Rom 15:32.
Exhortation to. Eph 4:1–3.
Opposed to communion with the wicked.
　2 Cor 6:14–17; Eph 5:11.
Exemplified
　Apostles. Acts 1:14.
　The Church. Acts 2:42; 5:12.
　Paul. Acts 20:36–38.

FIRSTBORN, THE.

Of man and beast dedicated to God. Ex
　13:2,12; 22:29.
Dedicated to commemorate the Passover.
　Ex 13:15; Num 3:13; 8:17.
Of clean beasts
　Not to labor. Deut 15:19.
　Not shorn. Deut 15:19.
　Not taken from the mother for seven
　　days. Ex 22:30; Lev 22:27.
　Offered in sacrifice. Num 18:17.
　Could not be a free-will offering. Lev
　　27:26.
　Antiquity of offering. Gen 4:4.
　Flesh of, the priest's portion. Num
　　18:18.
Of clean beasts
　To be redeemed. Num 18:15.
　Law of redemption for. Num 18:16.
Of the donkey to be redeemed with lamb
　or its neck broken. Ex 13:13; 34:20.
Of Israel
　Tribe of Levi taken for. Num 3:12,40–
　　43; 8:18.
　To be redeemed. Ex 34:20; Num
　　18:15.
　Price of redemption for. Num 3:46,47.
　Price of, given to the priests. Num
　　3:48–51.
Laws respecting, restored after the
　captivity. Neh 10:36.
Laws respecting, observed at Christ's
　birth. Luke 2:22,23.
The beginning of strength and excellency
　of power. Gen 49:3; Deut 21:17.
Precious and valuable. Mic 6:7; Zech
　12:10.
Objects of special love. Gen 25:28; Jer
　31:9,20.
Privileges of
　Precedence in the family. Gen
　　48:13,14.
　Authority over the younger children.
　　Gen 27:29; 1 Sam 20:29.
　Special blessing by the father. Gen
　　27:4,35.
　The father's title and power. 2 Chr
　　21:3.
　A double portion of inheritance. Deut
　　21:17.
　In case of death the next brother to
　　raise up seed to. Deut 25:5,6; Matt
　　22:24–28.
　Not to be alienated by parents through
　　caprice. Deut 21:15,16.
　Could be forfeited by misconduct. Gen
　　49:3,4,8; 1 Chr 5:1.
　Could be sold. Gen 25:31,33; Heb
　　12:16,17.
Instances of, superseded
　Cain. Gen 4:4,5.
　Japheth. Gen 10:21.
　Ishmael. Gen 17:19–21.
　Esau. Gen 25:23; Rom 9:12,13.
　Manasseh. Gen 48:15–20.
　Reuben, etc. 1 Chr 5:1,2.
　Aaron. Ex 7:1,2; Num 12:2,8.
　David's brothers. 1 Sam 16:6–12.
　Adonijah. 1 Kin 2:15,22.

FLATTERY.

Believers should not use. Job 32:21,22.
Ministers should not use. 1 Thess 2:5.
The wicked use, to
　Others. Ps 5:9; 12:2.
　Themselves. Ps 36:2.
Hypocrites use, to
　God. Ps 78:36.
　Those in authority. Dan 11:34.
False prophets and teachers use. Ezek
　12:24; Rom 16:18.

Wisdom, a preservative against. Prov 4:5.
Worldly advantage obtained by. Dan 11:21,22.
Seldom gains respect. Prov 28:23.
Avoid those given to. Prov 20:19.
Danger of. Prov 7:21–23; 20:5.
Punishment of. Job 17:5; Ps 12:3.

FOOLS.

All men are, without the knowledge of God. Titus 3:3.
Deny God. Ps 14:1; 53:1.
Blaspheme God. Ps 74:18.
Reproach God. Ps 74:22.
Mock at sin. Prov 14:9.
Despise instruction. Prov 1:7; 15:5.
Hate knowledge. Prov 1:22.
Delight not in understanding. Prov 18:2.
Sport themselves in mischief. Prov 10:23.
Walk in darkness. Eccl 2:14.
Hate to depart from evil. Prov 13:19.
Worship of, evil to God. Eccl 5:1.
Are
    Corrupt and abominable. Ps 14:1.
    Self-sufficient. Prov 12:15; Rom 1:22.
    Self-confident. Prov 14:16.
    Self-deceivers. Prov 14:8.
    Mere professors of religion. Matt 25:2–12.
    Full of words. Eccl 10:14.
    Given to quarreling. Prov 20:3.
    Slanderers. Prov 10:18.
    Liars. Prov 10:18.
    Slothful. Eccl 4:5.
    Angry. Eccl 7:9.
    Contentious. Prov 18:6.
    A grief to parents. Prov 17:25; 19:13.
Come to shame. Prov 3:35.
Destroy themselves by their speech. Prov 10:8,14; Eccl 10:12.
The company of, ruinous. Prov 13:20.
Lips of, a snare to the soul. Prov 18:7.
Cling to their folly. Prov 26:11; 27:22.
Worship idols. Jer 10:8; Rom 1:22,23.
Trust to their own hearts. Prov 28:26.
Depend upon their wealth. Luke 12:20.
Hear the gospel and obey it not. Matt 7:26.
The mouth of, pours out folly. Prov 15:2.
Honor is unbecoming for. Prov 26:1,8.
God has no pleasure in. Eccl 5:4.
Shall not stand in the presence of God. Ps 5:5.
Believers should avoid them. Prov 9:6; 14:7.
Exhorted to seek wisdom. Prov 8:5.
Punishment of. Ps 107:17; Prov 19:29; 26:10.

FORGIVENESS.

Christ set an example of. Luke 23:34.
Commanded. Mark 11:25; Rom 12:19.
To be unlimited. Matt 18:22; Luke 17:4.
A characteristic of believers. Ps 7:4.
Motives to
    The mercy of God. Luke 6:36.
    Our need of forgiveness. Mark 11:25.
    God's forgiveness of us. Eph 4:32.
    Christ's forgiveness of us. Col 3:13.
A glory to believers. Prov 19:11.
Should be accompanied by
    Forbearance. Col 3:13.
    Kindness. Gen 45:5–11; Rom 12:20.
    Blessing and prayer. Matt 5:44.
Promises for. Matt 6:14; Luke 6:37.
Must be extended to be received. Matt 6:15; James 2:13.
Illustrated. Matt 18:23–35.
Exemplified
    Joseph. Gen 50:20,21.
    David. 1 Sam 24:7; 2 Sam 18:5; 19:23.

Solomon. 1 Kin 1:53.
Stephen. Acts 7:60.
Paul. 2 Tim 4:16.

FORSAKING GOD.

Idolaters guilty of. 1 Sam 8:8; 1 Kin 11:33.
The wicked guilty of. Deut 28:20.
Backsliders guilty of. Jer 15:6.
Is forsaking
    His house. 2 Chr 29:6.
    His covenant. Deut 29:25; 1 Kin 19:10; Jer 22:9; Dan 11:30.
    His commandments. Ezra 9:10.
    The right way. 2 Pet 2:15.
Trusting in man is. Jer 17:5.
Leads men to follow their own devices. Jer 2:13.
Prosperity tempts to. Deut 31:20; 32:15.
Wickedness of. Jer 2:13; 5:7.
Unreasonableness and ingratitude of. Jer 2:5,6.
Brings confusion. Jer 17:13.
Followed by remorse. Ezek 6:9.
Brings down his wrath. Ezra 8:22.
Provokes God to forsake men. Judg 10:13; 2 Chr 15:2; 24:20,24.
People's resolve against. Josh 24:16; Neh 10:29–39.
Curse pronounced upon. Jer 17:5.
Sin of, to be confessed. Ezra 9:10.
Warnings against. Josh 24:20; 1 Chr 28:9.
Punishment for. Deut 28:20; 2 Kin 22:16,17; Is 1:28; Jer 1:16; 5:19.

GENEROSITY.

Pleasing to God. 2 Cor 9:7; Heb 13:16.
God never forgets. Heb 6:10.
Christ set an example of. 2 Cor 8:9.
Characteristic of believers. Ps 112:9; Is 32:8.
Unprofitable, without love. 1 Cor 13:3.
Should be exercised
    In the service of God. Ex 35:21–29.
    Toward believers. Rom 12:13; Gal 6:10.
    Toward servants. Deut 15:12–14.
    Toward the poor. Deut 15:11; Is 58:7.
    Toward strangers. Lev 25:35.
    Toward enemies. Prov 25:21.
    Toward all men. Gal 6:10.
    In leading to those in want. Matt 5:42.
    In giving alms. Luke 12:33.
    In relieving the destitute. Is 58:7.
    In supporting missions. Phil 4:14–16.
    In rendering personal services. Phil 2:30.
    Without ostentation. Matt 6:1–3.
    With simplicity. Rom 12:8.
    According to ability. Deut 16:10,17; 1 Cor 16:2.
    Willingly. Ex 25:2; 2 Cor 8:12.
    Abundantly. 2 Cor 8:7; 9:11–13.
Exercise of, provokes others to. 2 Cor 9:2.
Labor to make possible. Acts 20:35; Eph 4:28.
Lack of
    Brings many a curse. Prov 28:27.
    A proof of not loving God. 1 John 3:17.
    A proof of not having faith. James 2:14–16.
Blessings connected with. Ps 41:1; Prov 22:9; Acts 20:35.
Promises to. Ps 112:9; Prov 11:25; 28:27; Eccl 11:1,2; Is 58:10.
Exhortations to. Luke 3:11; 11:41; Acts 20:35; 1 Cor 16:1; 1 Tim 6:17,18.

GENTILES.

Includes all nations except the Jews. Rom 2:9; 3:9; 9:24.

Called
    Heathen. Ps 2:1; Gal 3:8.
    Nations. Ps 9:20; 22:28; Is 9:1.
    Uncircumcised. Is 14:6; 52:1.
    Uncircumcision. Rom 2:26.
    Greeks. Rom 1:16; 10:12.
    Strangers. Is 14:1; 60:10.
Ruled by God. 2 Chr 20:6; Ps 47:8.
Chastised by God. Ps 9:5; 94:10.
Counsel of, brought to nothing. Ps 33:10.
Characterised as
    Ignorant of God. Rom 1:21; 1 Thess 4:5.
    Refusing to know God. Rom 1:28.
    Without the law. Rom 2:14.
    Idolatrous. Rom 1:23,25; 1 Cor 12:2.
    Superstitious. Deut 18:14.
    Depraved and wicked. Rom 1:28–32; Eph 4:19.
    Blasphemous and reproachful. Neh 5:9.
    Loyal to their false gods. Jer 2:11.
Hated and despised the Jews. Esth 9:1,5; Ps 44:13,14; 123:3.
Often ravaged and defiled the holy land and sanctuary. Ps 79:1; Lam 1:10.
The Jews
    Not to follow the ways of. Lev 18:3; Jer 10:2.
    Not to intermarry with. Deut 7:3.
    Permitted to have, as servants. Lev 25:44.
    Despised, as if dogs. Matt 15:26.
    Never associated with. Acts 10:28; 11:2,3.
    Often corrupted by. 2 Kin 17:7,8.
    Dispersed amongst. John 7:35.
Excluded from Israel's privileges. Eph 2:11,12.
Not allowed to enter the temple. Acts 21:28,29.
Outer court of temple for. Eph 2:14; Rev 11:2.
Given to Christ as His inheritance. Ps 2:8.
Christ given as a light to. Is 42:6; Luke 2:32.
Conversion of, predicted. Is 2:2; 11:10.
United with the Jews against Christ. Acts 4:27.
The gospel not to be preached to, till preached to the Jews. Matt 10:5; Luke 24:47; Acts 13:46.
First special introduction of the gospel to. Acts 10:34–45; 15:14.
First general introduction of the gospel to. Acts 13:48,49,52; 15:12.
Paul the apostle of. Acts 9:15; Gal 2:7,8.
Jerusalem trodden down by, etc. Luke 21:24.
Israel rejected till the fullness of. Rom 11:25.

GIFT OF THE HOLY SPIRIT, THE.

By the Father. Luke 11:13.
By the Son. John 20:22.
To Christ without measure. John 3:34.
Given
    According to promise. Acts 2:38,39.
    Upon the exaltation. John 7:39.
    Through the intercession of Christ. John 14:16.
    In answer to prayer. Luke 11:13; Eph 1:16,17.
    For instruction. John 16:13.
    For comfort of believers. John 14:16.
    To those who repent and believe. Acts 2:38.
    To those who obey God. Acts 5:32.
    To the Gentiles. Acts 10:44,45; 11:17; 15:8.
Is abundant. John 7:38,39.

Is permanent. 1 Pet 4:14.
Is fruit bearing. Gal 5:22,23..
Received through faith. Gal 3:14.
An evidence of union with Christ. 1 John 3:24; 4:13.
An earnest of the inheritance of the believers. 2 Cor 1:22; 5:5; Eph 1:14.

GLORIFYING GOD.

Commanded. 1 Chr 16:28; Ps 22:23; Is 42:12.
Due to Him. 1 Chr 16:29.
For His
  Holiness. Ps 99:9; Rev 15:4.
  Mercy and truth. Ps 115:1; Rom 15:9.
  Faithfulness and truth. Is 25:1.
  Wondrous works. Matt 15:31; Acts 4:21.
  Judgments. Is 25:3; Ezek 28:22; Rev 14:7.
  Deliverance. Ps 50:15.
  Grace to others. Acts 11:18; 2 Cor 9:13; Gal 1:24.
Obligation of believers to. 1 Cor 6:20.
Is acceptable through Christ. Phil 1:11; 1 Pet 4:11.
Christ, an example of. John 17:4.
Accomplished by
  Relying on His promises. Rom 4:20.
  Praising Him. Ps 50:23.
  Doing all to Him. 1 Cor 10:31.
  Dying for Him. John 21:19.
  Confessing Christ. Phil 2:11.
  Suffering for Christ. 1 Pet 4:14,16.
  Glorifying Christ. Acts 19:17; 2 Thess 1:12.
  Bringing forth fruits of righteousness. John 15:8; Phil 1:11.
  Patience in affliction. Is 24:15.
  Faithfulness. 1 Pet 4:11.
Required in body and spirit. 1 Cor 6:20.
Shall be universal. Ps 86:9; Rev 5:13.
Believers should
  Resolve to. Ps 69:30; 118:28.
  Unite in. Ps 34:3; Rom 15:6.
  Persevere in. Ps 86:12.
All the blessings of God are designed to lead to. Is 60:21; 61:3.
The holy example of believers may lead others to. Matt 5:16; 1 Pet 2:12.
All, by nature, fail in. Rom 3:23.
The wicked averse to. Dan 5:23; Rom 1:21.
Punishment for not. Dan 5:23,30; Mal 2:2; Acts 12:23; Rom 1:21.
Heavenly host engaged in. Rev 4:11.

GLORY.

God is, to His people. Ps 3:3; Zech 2:5.
Christ is, to His people. Is 60:1; Luke 2:32.
The gospel ordained to be, to believers. 1 Cor 2:7.
Of the gospel, exceeds that of the law. 2 Cor 3:9,10.
The joy of believers is full of. 1 Pet 1:8.
Spiritual
  Is given by God. Ps 84:11.
  Is given by Christ. John 17:22.
  Is the work of the Holy Spirit. 2 Cor 3:18.
Eternal
  Procured by the death of Christ. Heb 2:10.
  Accompanies salvation by Christ. 2 Tim 2:10.
  Inherited by believers. 1 Sam 2:8; Ps 73:24; Prov 3:35; Col 3:4; 1 Pet 5:10.
  Believers called to. 2 Thess 2:14; 1 Pet 5:10.
  Believers called to. Rom 9:23.

Enhanced by present afflictions. 2 Cor 4:17.
Present afflictions not worthy to be compared with. Rom 8:18.
The bodies of believers shall be raised in. 1 Cor 15:43; Phil 3:21.
Believers shall be, of their ministers. 1 Thess 2:19,20.
Temporal
  Is given by God. Dan 2:37.
  Passes away. 1 Pet 1:24.
  The devil tries to seduce by. Matt 4:8.
Of hypocrites turned to shame. Hos 4:7.
Seek not, from man. Matt 6:2; 1 Thess 2:6.
Of the wicked
  Is in their shame. Is 5:14; Phil 3:19.

GLORY OF GOD, THE.

Exhibited in Christ. John 1:14; 2 Cor 4:6; Heb 1:3.
Exhibited in
  His name. Deut 28:58; Neh 9:5.
  His majesty. Job 37:22; Ps 93:1; 104:1; 145:5,12; Is 2:10.
  His power. Ex 15:1,6; Rom 6:4.
  His works. Ps 19:1; 111:3.
  His holiness. Ex 15:11.
Described as
  Great. Ps 138:5.
  Eternal. Ps 104:31.
  Rich. Eph 3:16.
  Highly exalted. Ps 8:1; 113:4.
Exhibited to
  Moses. Ex 33:18–23; 34:5–7.
  Stephen. Acts 7:55.
Believers desire to behold. Ps 63:2; 90:16.
God is jealous. Is 42:8.
Reverence. Is 59:19.
Plead in prayer. Ps 79:9.
Declare. 1 Chr 16:24; Ps 145:5,11.
Magnify. Ps 57:5.
The earth is full of. Is 6:3.
The knowledge of, shall fill the earth. Hab 2:14.

GLUTTONY.

Christ was falsely accused of. Matt 11:19.
The wicked addicted to. Phil 3:19; Jude 12.
Leads to
  Carnal security. Is 22:13; 1 Cor 15:32; Luke 12:19.
  Poverty. Prov 23:21.
Of princes, ruinous to their people. Eccl 10:16,17.
Is inconsistent in believers. 1 Pet 4:3.
Caution against. Prov 23:2,3; Luke 21:34; Rom 13:13,14.
Pray against temptations to. Ps 141:4.
Punishment of. Num 11:33,34; Deut 21:21; Ps 78:31; Amos 6:4,7.

GOD.

Is a spirit. John 4:24; 2 Cor 3:17.
Is declared to be
  Light. Is 60:19; James 1:17; 1 John 1:5.
  Love. 1 John 4:8,16.
  Invisible. Job 23:8,9; John 1:18; 5:37; Col 1:15; 1 Tim 1:17.
  Unsearchable. Job 11:7; 37:23; Ps 145:3; Is 40:28; Rom 11:33.
  Incorruptible. Rom 1:23.
  Eternal. Deut 33:27; Ps 90:2; Rev 4:8–10.
  Immortal. 1 Tim 1:17; 6:16.
  Omnipotent. Gen 17:1; Ex 6:3.
  Omniscient. Ps 139:1–6; Prov 5:21.
  Omnipresent. Ps 139:7; Jer 23:23.
  Immutable. Ps 102:26,27; James 1:17.

Alone is wise. Rom 16:27; 1 Tim 1:17.
Glorious. Ex 15:11; Ps 145:5.
Most High. Ps 83:18; Acts 7:48.
Perfect. Matt 5:48.
Holy. Ps 99:9; Is 5:16.
Just. Deut 32:4; Is 45:21.
True. Jer 10:10; John 17:3.
Upright. Ps 25:8; 92:15.
Righteous. Ezra 9:15; Ps 145:17.
Good. Ps 25:8; 119:68.
Great. 2 Chr 2:5; Ps 86:10.
Gracious. Ex 34:6; Ps 116:5.
Faithful. 1 Cor 10:13; 1 Pet 4:19.
Merciful. Ex 34:6,7; Ps 86:5.
Long-suffering. Num 14:18; Mic 7:1.
Jealous. Josh 24:19; Nah 1:2.
Compassionate. 2 Kin 13:23.
A consuming fire. Heb 12:29.
None equal to Him. Deut 4:35; Is 43:10; 44:6.
None like to Him. Ex 9:14; Deut 33:26; 2 Sam 7:22; Is 46:5,9; Jer 10:6.
None good but He. Matt 19:17.
Fills heaven and earth. 1 Kin 8:27; Jer 23:24.
Should be worshipped in spirit and in truth. John 4:24.

GOD, FAVOR OF.

Christ the special object of. Luke 2:52.
Is the source of
  Mercy. Is 60:10.
  Spiritual life. Ps 30:5.
Spiritual wisdom leads to. Prov 8:35.
Mercy and truth lead to. Prov 3:3,4.
Believers
  Obtain. Prov 12:2.
  Surrounded by. Ps 5:12.
  Strengthened by. Ps 30:7.
  Victorious through. Ps 44:3.
  Preserved through. Job 10:12.
  Exalted in. Ps 89:17.
  Sometimes tempted to doubt. Ps 77:7.
Domestic blessings traced to. Prov 18:22.
Disappointment of enemies an assured evidence of. Ps 41:11.
Given in answer to prayer. Job 33:26.
Pray for. Ps 106:4; 119:58.
Plead, in prayer. Ex 33:12; Num 11:15.
To be acknowledged. Ps 85:1.
The wicked
  Uninfluenced by. Is 26:10.
  Do not obtain. Is 27:11; Jer 16:13.
Exemplified
  Naphtali. Deut 33:23.
  Samuel. 1 Sam 2:26.
  Job. Job 10:12.
  The Virgin Mary. Luke 1:28,30.
  David. Acts 7:46.

GOODNESS OF GOD, THE.

Is part of His character. Ps 25:8; Nah 1:7; Matt 19:17.
Declared to be
  Great. Neh 9:35; Zech 9:17.
  Rich. Ps 104:24; Rom 2:4.
  Abundant. Ex 34:6; Ps 33:5.
  Satisfying. Ps 65:4; Jer 31:12,14.
  Enduring. Ps 23:6; 52:1.
  Universal. Ps 145:9; Matt 5:45.
Manifested
  In doing good. Ps 119:68; 145:9.
  In supplying temporal wants. Acts 14:17.
  In providing for the poor. Ps 68:10.
  In forgiving sins. 2 Chr 30:18; Ps 86:5.
Leads to repentance. Rom 2:4.
Recognize, in His dealings. Ezra 8:18; Neh 2:18.
Pray for the manifestation of. 2 Thess 1:11.

Despise not. Rom 2:4.
Reverence. Jer 33:9; Hos 3:5.
Magnify. Ps 107:8; Jer 33:11.
Urge others to confide in. Ps 34:8.
The wicked disregard. Neh 9:35.

GOSPEL, THE.

Is good tidings of great joy for all people. Luke 2:10,11,31,32.
Foretold. Is 41:27; 52:7; 61:1–3; Mark 1:15.
Preached under the Old Testament. Heb 4:2.
Exhibits the grace of God. Acts 14:3; 20:32.
The knowledge of the glory of God is by. 2 Cor 4:4,6.
Brings life and immortality. 2 Tim 1:10.
Is the power of God to salvation. Rom 1:16; 1 Cor 1:18; 1 Thess 1:5.
Is glorious. 2 Cor 4:4.
Is everlasting. 1 Pet 1:25; Rev 14:6.
Preached by Christ. Matt 4:23; Mark 1:14.
Ministers have a stewardship to preach. 1 Cor 9:17.
Preached beforehand to Abraham. Gen 22:18; Gal 3:8.
Preached to
  The Jews first. Luke 24:47; Acts 13:46.
  The Gentiles. Mark 13:10; Gal 2:2,9.
  The poor. Matt 11:5; Luke 4:18.
  Every creature. Mark 16:15; Col 1:23.
Must be believed. Mark 1:15; Heb 4:2.
Brings peace. Luke 2:10,14; Eph 6:15.
Produces hope. Col 1:23.
Believers have fellowship in. Phil 1:5.
There is fulness of blessing in. Rom 15:29.
Those who receive, should
  Adhere to the truth of. Gal 1:6,7; 2:14; 2 Tim 1:13.
  Not be ashamed of. Rom 1:16; 2 Tim 1:8.
  Live in subjection to. 2 Cor 9:13.
  Conform their conduct to. Phil 1:27.
  Earnestly contend for the faith of. Phil 1:17,27; Jude 3.
  Sacrifice everything. Matt 8:35; 10:37.
Profession of, attended by afflictions. 2 Tim 3:12.
Promises to sufferers. Mark 8:35; 10:30.
Be careful not to hinder. 1 Cor 9:12.
Is hid to them that are lost. 2 Cor 4:3.
Testifies to the final judgment. Rom 2:16.
Let him who preached another, be accursed. Gal 1:8.
Awful consequences of not obeying. 2 Thess 1:8,9.
Is called the
  Gospel of peace. Eph 6:15.
  Gospel of God. Rom 1:1; 1 Thess 2:8; 1 Pet 4:17.
  Gospel of Christ. Rom 1:9,16; 2 Cor 2:12; 1 Thess 3:2.
  Gospel of the grace of God. Acts 20:24.
  Gospel of the kingdom. Matt 24:14.
  Gospel of salvation. Eph 1:13.
  Glorious gospel of Jesus Christ. 2 Cor 4:4.
  Preaching of Jesus Christ. Rom 16:25.
  Mystery of the gospel. Eph 6:19.
  Word of God. 1 Thess 2:13.
  Word of Christ. Col 3:16.
  Word of grace. Acts 14:3; 20:32.
  Word of salvation. Acts 13:26.
  Word of reconciliation. 2 Cor 5:19.
  Word of truth. Eph 1:13; James 1:18.
  Word of faith. Rom 10:8.
  Word of life. Phil 2:16.
  Ministration of the Spirit. 2 Cor 3:8.

  Doctrine which accords godliness. 1 Tim 6:3.
  Pattern of sound words. 2 Tim 1:13.
Rejection of, by many, foretold. Is 53:1; Rom 10:15,16.
Rejection of, by the Jews, a means of blessing to the Gentiles. Rom 11:28.

GRACE.

God is the source of all. Ps 84:11; James 1:17; 1 Pet 5:10.
God's throne, the throne of. Heb 4:16.
The Holy Spirit is the Spirit of. Zech 12:10; Heb 10:29.
Was upon Christ. Luke 2:40; John 3:24.
Christ spoke with. Ps 45:2; Luke 4:22.
Christ was full of. John 1:14.
Came by Christ. John 1:17; Rom 5:15.
Given by Christ. 1 Cor 1:4.
Foretold by the prophets. 1 Pet 1:10.
Riches of, exhibited in God's kindness through Christ. Eph 2:7.
Glory of, exhibited in our acceptance in Christ. Eph 1:6.
Is described as
  Great. Acts 4:33.
  Sovereign. Rom 5:21.
  Rich. Eph 1:7; 2:7.
  Exceeding. 2 Cor 9:14.
  Manifold. 1 Pet 4:10.
  All-sufficient. 2 Cor 12:9.
  All-abundant. Rom 5:15,17,20.
  Glorious. Eph 1:6.
The gospel, a declaration of. Acts 20:24,32.
Is the source of
  Election. Rom 11:5.
  The call of God. Gal 1:15.
  Justification. Rom 3:24; Titus 3:7.
  Faith. Acts 18:27.
  Forgiveness of sins. Eph 1:7.
  Salvation. Acts 15:11; Eph 2:5,8.
  Consolation. 2 Thess 2:16.
  Hope. 2 Thess 2:16.
Necessary to the service of God. Heb 12:28.
God's work completed in believers by. 2 Thess 1:11,12.
The success and completion of the work of God to be attributed to. Zech 4:7.
Inheritance of the promises by. Rom 4:16.
Justification by, opposed to that by works. Rom 4:4,5; 11:6; Gal 5:4.
Believers
  Are heirs of. 1 Pet 3:7.
  Are under. Rom 6:14.
  Receive, from Christ. John 1:16.
  Are what they are by. 1 Cor 15:10; 2 Cor 1:12.
  Abound in gifts of. Acts 4:33; 2 Cor 8:1; 9:8,14.
  Should be established in. Heb 13:9.
  Should be strong in. 2 Tim 2:1.
  Should grow in. 2 Pet 3:18.
  Should speak with. Eph 4:29; Col 4:6.
Specially given
  To ministers. Rom 12:3,6; 15:15; 1 Cor 3:10; Gal 2:9; Eph 3:7.
  To the humble. Prov 3:34; James 4:6.
  To those who walk uprightly. Ps 84:11.
Not to be received in vain. 2 Cor 6:1.
Pray for
  For yourselves. Heb 4:16.
  For others. 2 Cor 13:14; Eph 6:24.
Beware lest you fail of. Heb 12:15.
Manifestation of, in others, a cause of gladness. Acts 11:23; 1 John 1:3,4.
Special manifestation of, at the second coming of Christ. 1 Pet 1:13.
Not to be abused. Rom 3:8; 6:1,15.
Lawlwss men will abuse. Jude 4.

HATRED.

Forbidden. Lev 19:17; Col 3:8.
Is murder. 1 John 3:15.
A work of the flesh. Gal 5:20.
Often cloaked by deceit. Prov 10:18; 26:26.
Leads to deceit. Prov 26:24,25.
Stirs up strife. Prov 10:12.
Embitters life. Prov 15:17.
Inconsistent with
  The knowledge of God. 1 John 2:9,11.
  The love of God. 1 John 4:20.
  Liars prone to. Prov 26:28.
The wicked exhibit
  Towards God. Rom 1:30.
  Towards believers. Ps 25:19; Prov 29:10.
  Towards each other. Titus 3:3.
Christ experienced. Ps 35:19; John 7:7; 15:18,24,25.
Believers should
  Expect. Matt 10:22; John 15:18,19.
  Not marvel at. 1 John 3:13.
  Return good for. Ex 23:5; Matt 5:44.
  Not rejoice in the calamities of those who exhibit. Job 31:29,30; Ps 35:13,14.
  Give no cause for. Prov 25:17.
Punishment of. Ps 34:21; 44:7; 89:23; Amos 1:11.
We should exhibit against
  False ways. Ps 119:104,128.
  Lying. Ps 119:163.
  Evil. Ps 97:10; Prov 8:13.
  Backsliding. Ps 101:3.
  Hatred and opposition to God. Ps 139:21,22.

HEART, THE.

Issues of life are out of. Prov 4:23.
God
  Tries. 1 Chr 29:17; Jer 12:3.
  Knows. Ps 44:21; Jer 20:12.
  Searches. 1 Chr 28:9; Jer 17:10.
  Understands the thoughts of. 1 Chr 28:9; Ps 139:2.
  Ponders. Prov 21:2; 24:12.
  Influences. 1 Sam 10:26; Ezra 6:22; 7:27; Prov 21:1; Jer 20:9.
  Creates a new. Ps 51:10; Ezek 36:26.
  Prepares. 1 Chr 29:18; Prov 16:1.
  Opens. Acts 16:14.
  Enlightens. 2 Cor 4:6; Eph 1:18.
  Strengthens. Ps 27:14.
  Establishes. Ps 112:8; 1 Thess 3:13.
Should be
  Dedicated to God. 1 Sam 7:3; Prov 23:26.
  Perfect with God. 1 Kin 8:61.
  Applied to wisdom. Ps 90:12; Prov 2:2.
  Guided in the right. Prov 23:19.
  Purified. James 4:8.
  Single. Eph 6:5; Col 3:22.
  Tender. Eph 4:32.
  Kept with diligence. Prov 4:23.
We should
  Believe with. Acts 8:37; Rom 10:10.
  Serve God with all. Deut 11:13.
  Keep God's statutes with all. Deut 26:16.
  Walk before God with all. 1 Kin 2:4.
  Trust in God with all. Prov 3:5.
  Love God with all. Matt 22:37.
  Return to God with all. Deut 30:2.
  Do the will of God from. Eph 6:6.
  Sanctify God in. 1 Pet 3:15.
  Love one another with a pure. 1 Pet 1:22.
No man can cleanse. Prov 20:9.
Faith, the means of purifying. Acts 15:9.
Renewal of, promised under the gospel.

Ezek 11:19; 36:26; Heb 3:10.
When broken and contrite, not despised by
God. Ps 51:17.
The pure in, shall see God. Matt 5:8.
Pray that it may be
Cleansed. Ps 51:10.
Inclined to God's testimonies. Ps
119:36.
United to fear God. Ps 86:11.
Directed into the love of God. 2 Thess
3:5.
Harden not, against God. Ps 95:8; Heb
4:7.
Harden not, against the poor. Deut 15:7.
Regard not iniquity in. Ps 66:18.
Take heed lest it be deceived. Deut 11:16.
Know the plague of. 1 Kin 8:38.
He that trusts in, is a fool. Prov 28:26.

HEAVEN.

Created by God. Gen 1:1; Rev 10:6.
Everlasting. Ps 89:29; 2 Cor 5:1.
Immeasurable. Jer 31:37.
High. Ps 103:11; Is 57:15.
Holy. Deut 26:15; Ps 20:6; Is 57:15.
God's dwelling-place. 1 Kin 8:30; Matt
6:9.
God's throne. Is 66:1; Acts 7:49.
God
Is the Lord of. Dan 5:23; Matt 11:25.
Reigns in. Ps 11:4; 135:6; Dan 4:35.
Fills. 1 Kin 8:27; Jer 23:24.
Answers His people from. 1 Chr 21:26;
2 Chr 7:14; Neh 9:27; Ps 20:6.
Sends His judgments from. Gen 19:24;
1 Sam 2:10; Dan 4:13,14; Rom
1:18.
Christ
As Mediator, entered into. Acts 3:21;
Heb 6:20; 9:12,24.
Is all-powerful in. Matt 28:18; 1 Pet
3:22.
Angels are in. Matt 18:10; 24:36.
Believers rewarded in. Matt 5:12; Luke
10:20; Heb 12:23; 1 Pet 1:4.
Repentance occasions joy in. Luke 15:7.
Lay up treasure in. Matt 6:20; Luke 12:33.
Flesh and blood cannot inherit. 1 Cor
15:50.
Happiness of, described. Rev 7:16,17.
Is called
A barn. Matt 3:12.
The kingdom of Christ and of God.
Eph 5:5.
The Father's house. John 14:2.
A heavenly country. Heb 11:16.
A rest. Heb 4:9.
Paradise. Luke 23:43; 2 Cor 12:2,4.
Contained place of rest, Abraham's
bosom. Luke 16:23.
The wicked excluded from. Gal 5:21; Eph
5:5; Rev 22:15.
Enoch and Elijah were translated into.
Gen 5:24; 2 Kin 2:11; Heb 11:5.

HELL.

The place of disembodied spirits
Acts 2:31.
Which Christ visited. Acts 2:31; 1 Pet
3:19.
And a place of torment. Luke 16:23.
The place of future punishment
Destruction from the presence of God.
2 Thess 1:9.
Described as
Everlasting punishment. Matt 25:46.
Everlasting fire. Matt 25:41.
Everlasting burnings. Is 33:14.
A furnace of fire. Matt 13:42,50.
A lake of fire. Rev 20:15.
Fire and brimstone. Rev 14:10.

Unquenchable fire. Matt 3:12.
Devouring fire. Is 33:14.
Prepared for the devil. Matt 25:41.
Devils are confined in, until the judgment
day. 2 Pet 2:4; Jude 6.
Punishment of, is eternal. Is 33:14; Rev
20:10.
The wicked shall be turned into. Ps 9:17.
Human power cannot preserve from. Ezek
32:27.
The body suffers in. Matt 5:29; 10:28.
The soul suffers in. Matt 10:28.
The wise avoid. Prov 15:24.
Endeavour to keep others from. Prov
23:14; Jude 23.
The society of the wicked leads to. Prov
5:5; 9:18.
The beast, false prophets, and the devil
shall be cast into. Rev 19:20; 20:10.
The powers of, cannot prevail against the
Church. Matt 16:18.

HOLINESS.

Commanded. Lev 11:45; 20:7; Rom 12:1;
Eph 5:8; Col 3:12.
Christ
Desires, for His people. John 17:17.
Effects, in His people. Eph 5:25–27.
An example of. Heb 7:26; 1 Pet
2:21,22.
The character of God, the standard of. Lev
19:2; Eph 5:1; 1 Pet 1:15,16.
The character of Christ, the standard of.
Rom 8:29; Phil 2:5; 1 John 2:6
The gospel the way of. Is 35:8.
None shall see God without. Ps 24:3,4;
Eph 5:5; Heb 12:14.
Believers
Elected to. Rom 8:29; Eph 1:4.
Called to. 1 Thess 4:7; 2 Tim 1:9.
New man created in. Eph 4:24.
Possess. 1 Cor 3:17; Heb 3:1.
Have their fruit to. Rom 6:22.
Should follow after. Heb 12:14.
Should serve God in. Luke 1:74,75.
Should yield their members as
instruments of. Rom 6:13,19.
Should present their bodies to God in.
Rom 12:1.
Should have their conversation in.
1 Pet 1:15; 2 Pet 3:11.
Should continue in. Luke 1:75.
Should seek perfection in. 2 Cor 7:1.
Shall be presented to God in. Col 1:22;
1 Thess 3:13.
Shall continue in, for ever. Rev 22:11.
Behavior of aged women should be as
becomes. Titus 2:3.
Promise to women who continue in.
1 Tim 2:15.
The Word of God the means of producing.
John 17:17; 2 Tim 3:16,17.
Is the result of
The manifestation of God's grace.
Titus 2:3,11,12.
Subjection to God. Rom 6:22.
God's keeping. John 17:15.
Union with Christ. John 15:4,5; 17:9.
Required in prayer. 1 Tim 2:8.
Ministers should
Possess. Titus 1:8.
Avoid everything inconsistent with.
Lev 21:6; Is 52:11.
Be examples of. 1 Tim 4:12.
Exhort to. Heb 12:14; 1 Pet 1:14–16.
Motives to
The glory of God. John 15:8; Phil 1:11.
The love of Christ. 2 Cor 5:14,15.
The mercies of God. Rom 12:1,2.
The dissolution of all things. 2 Pet
3:11.

Chastisements are intended to produce, in
believers. Heb 12:10; James 1:2,3.
Should lead to separation from the wicked.
Num 16:21,26; 2 Cor 6:17,18.
The wicked are without. 1 Tim 1:9; 2 Tim
3:2.
Exemplified
David. Ps 86:2.
Israel. Jer 2:3.
John the Baptist. Mark 6:20.
Prophets. Luke 1:70.
Paul. 1 Thess 2:10.
Wives of patriarchs. 1 Pet 3:5.

HOLINESS OF GOD, THE.

Is incomparable. Ex 15:11; 1 Sam 2:2.
Exhibited in His
Character. Ps 22:3; John 17:11.
Name. Is 57:15; Luke 1:49.
Words. Ps 60:6; Jer 23:9.
Works. Ps 145:17.
Kingdom. Ps 47:8; Matt 13:41; 1 Cor
6:9,10; Rev 21:27.
Is pledged for the fulfilment of
His promises. Ps 89:35.
His judgments. Amos 4:2.
Believers are commanded to imitate. Lev
11:44; 1 Pet 1:15,16.
Believers should praise. Ps 30:4.
Should produce reverential fear. Rev 15:4.
Heavenly hosts adore. Is 6:3; Rev 4:8.
Should be magnified. 1 Chr 16:10; Ps
48:1; 99:3,5; Rev 15:4.

HOLY SPIRIT, ANOINTING OF THE.

Is from God. 2 Cor 1:21.
That Christ should receive
Foretold. Is 61:1; Dan 9:24.
Fulfilled. Luke 4:18,21; Acts 4:27;
10:38; Heb 1:9.
God preserves those who receive. Ps 18:50;
20:6; 89:20–23.
Believers receive. 1 John 2:20.
Is abiding in believers. 1 John 2:27.
Guides into all truth. 1 John 2:27.

HOLY SPIRIT, BAPTISM WITH THE.

Is through Christ. Titus 3:6.
Christ administered. Matt 3:11; John
1:33.
Promised to believers. Acts 1:5; 2:38,39;
11:16.
All believers partake of. 1 Cor 12:13.
Necessity for. John 3:5; Acts 19:2–6.
Renews and cleanses the soul. Titus 3:5;
1 Pet 3:20,21.
The Word of God instrumental to. Acts
10:44; Eph 5:26.
Typified. Acts 2:1–4.

HOLY SPIRIT, THE COMFORTER, THE.

Given
By the Father. John 14:16.
By Christ. Is 61:3.
Through Christ's intercession. John
14:16.
Sent in the name of Christ. John 14:26.
Sent by Christ from the Father. John
15:26; 16:7.
As such He
Communicates joy to believers. Rom
14:17; Gal 5:22; 1 Thess 1:6.
Edifies the Church. Acts 9:31.
Testifies of Christ. John 15:26.
Imparts the love of God. Rom 5:3–5.
Imparts hope. Rom 15:13; Gal 5:5.
Teaches believers. John 14:26.
Dwells with, and in believers. John
14:17.
Abides for ever with believers. John
14:16.

Is known by believers. John 14:17.
The world cannot receive. John 14:17.

HOLY SPIRIT, THE, IS GOD.

As Lord. Ex 17:7; Heb 3:7–9; Num 12:6; 2 Pet 1:21.
As Lord of hosts. Is 6:3,8–10; Acts 28:25.
As Lord, Most High. Ps 78:17,21; Acts 7:51.
Being invoked as Lord. Luke 2:26–29; Acts 1:16,20; 4:23–25; 2 Thess 3:5.
As called God. Acts 5:3,4.
As joined with the Father and the Son in the baptismal formula. Matt 28:19.
As eternal. Heb 9:14.
As omnipresent. Ps 139:7–13.
As omniscient. 1 Cor 2:10.
As omnipotent. Luke 1:35; Rom 15:19.
As the Spirit of glory and of God. 1 Pet 4:14.
As Creator. Gen 1:26,27; Job 33:4.
As equal to, and one with the Father. Matt 28:19; 2 Cor 13:14.
As Sovereign Disposer of all things. Dan 4:35; 1 Cor 12:6,11.
As Author of the new birth. John 3:5,6; 1 John 5:4.
As raising Christ from the dead. Acts 2:24; Rom 1:4; Heb 13:20; 1 Pet 3:18;.
As inspiring Scripture. 2 Tim 3:16; 2 Pet 1:21.
As the source of wisdom. 1 Cor 12:8; Is 11:2; John 14:26; 16:13.
As the source of miraculous power. Matt 12:28; Luke 11:20; Acts 19:11; Rom 15:19.
As appointing and sending ministers. Acts 13:2; 9:38; 20:28.
As directing where the gospel should be preached. Acts 16:6,7,10.
As dwelling in believers. John 14:17; 1 Cor 3:16; 6:19;14:25.
As Comforter of the Church. Acts 9:31; 2 Cor 1:3.
As sanctifying the Church. Rom 15:16.
As the Witness. Heb 10:15; 1 John 5:9.
As convincing of sin, of righteousness, and of judgment. John 16:8–11.

HOLY SPIRIT, THE PERSONALITY OF.

He creates and gives life. Job 33:4.
He appoints and commissions ministers. Is 48:16; Acts 13:2; 20:28.
He directs ministers where to preach. Acts 8:29; 10:19,20.
He directs ministers where not to preach. Acts 16:6,7.
He instructs ministers what to preach. 1 Cor 2:13.
He spoke in, and by, the prophets. Acts 1:16; 1 Pet 1:11,12; 2 Pet 1:21.
He strives with sinners. Gen 6:3.
He reproves. John 16:8.
He comforts. Acts 9:31.
He helps our infirmities. Rom 8:26.
He teaches. John 14:26; 1 Cor 12:3.
He guides. John 16:13.
He sanctifies. Rom 15:16; 1 Cor 6:11.
He testifies of Christ. John 15:26.
He glorifies Christ. John 16:14.
He has a power of his own. Rom 15:13.
He searches all things. Rom 11:33,34; 1 Cor 2:10,11.
He works according to his own will. 1 Cor 12:11.
He dwells with believers. John 14:17.
He can be grieved. Eph 4:30.
He can be vexed. Is 63:10.
He can be resisted. Acts 7:51.
He can be tested. Acts 5:9.

HOPE.

In God. Ps 39:7; 1 Pet 1:21.
In Christ. 1 Cor 15:19; 1 Tim 1:1.
In God's promises. Acts 26:6,7; Titus 1:2.
In the mercy of God. Ps 33:18.
Is the work of the Holy Spirit. Rom 15:13; Gal 5:5.
Obtained through
　Grace. 2 Thess 2:16.
　The word. Ps 119:81.
　Patience and comfort of the Scriptures. Rom 15:4.
　The gospel. Col 1:5,23.
　Faith. Rom 5:1,2; Gal 5:5.
The result of character. Rom 5:4.
A better hope brought in by Christ. Heb 7:19.
Described as
　Good. 2 Thess 2:16.
　Living. 1 Pet 1:3.
　Sure and steadfast. Heb 6:19.
　Gladdening. Prov 10:28.
　Blessed. Titus 2:13.
Does not disappoint. Rom 5:5.
Triumphs over difficulties. Rom 4:18.
Is an encouragement to boldness in preaching. 2 Cor 3:12.
Believers
　Are called to. Eph 4:4.
　Rejoice in. Rom 5:2; 12:12.
　Have all, the same. Eph 4:4.
　Have, in death. Prov 14:32.
　Should abound in. Rom 15:13.
　Should look for the object of. Titus 2:13.
　Should not be ashamed of. Ps 119:16.
　Should hold fast. Heb 3:6.
　Should not be moved from. Col 1:23.
　Should continue in. Ps 71:14; 1 Pet 1:13.
Connected with faith and love. 1 Cor 13:13.
Objects of
　Salvation. 1 Thess 5:8.
　Righteousness. Gal 5:5.
　Christ's glorious appearing. Titus 2:13.
　A resurrection. Acts 23:6; 24:15.
　Eternal life. Titus 1:2; 3:7.
　Glory. Rom 5:2; Col 1:27.
Leads to purity. 1 John 3:3.
Leads to patience. Rom 8:25; 1 Thess 1:3.
Seek for full assurance of. Heb 6:11.
Be ready to give an answer concerning. 1 Pet 3:15.
Encouragement to. Hos 2:15; Zech 9:12.
Encourage others to. Ps 130:7.
Happiness of. Ps 146:5.
Life is the season of. Eccl 9:4; Is 38:18.
The wicked have no ground for. Eph 2:12.
Of the wicked
　Is in their worldly possessions. Job 31:24.
　Shall make them ashamed. Is 20:5,6; Zech 9:5.
　Shall perish. Job 8:13; 11:20; Prov 10:28.
　Shall be extinguished in death. Job 27:8.

HOSPITALITY.

Commanded. Rom 12:13; 1 Pet 4:9.
Required in ministers. 1 Tim 3:2; Titus 1:8.
A test of Christian character. 1 Tim 5:10.
Specially to be shown to
　Strangers. Heb 13:2.
　The poor. Is 58:7; Luke 14:13.
　Enemies. 2 Kin 6:22,23; Rom 12:20.
Encouragement to. Luke 14:14; Heb 13:2.

HUMAN NATURE OF CHRIST, THE.

Was necessary to His mediatorial office. Gal 4:4,5; 1 Cor 15:21; Rom 6:15,19; 1 Tim 2:5; Heb 2:17.
Is proved by His
　Conception in the Virgin's womb. Matt 1:18; Luke 1:31.
　Birth. Matt 1:16,25; 2:2; Luke 2:7,11.
　Partaking of flesh and blood. John 1:14; Heb 2:14.
　Having a human soul. Matt 26:38; Luke 23:46; Acts 2:31.
　Circumcision. Luke 2:21.
　Increase in wisdom and stature. Luke 2:52.
　Weeping. Luke 19:41; John 11:35.
　Hungering. Matt 4:2; 21:18.
　Thirsting. John 4:7; 19:28.
　Sleeping. Matt 8:24; Mark 4:38.
　Being subject to weariness. John 4:6.
　Being a man of sorrows. Is 53:3,4; Luke 22:44; John 11:33; 12:27.
　Being buffeted. Matt 26:67; Luke 22:64.
　Enduring indignities. Luke 23:11.
　Being scourged. Matt 27:26; Luke 22:64.
　Being nailed to the cross. Ps 22:16; Luke 23:33.
　Death. John 19:30.
　Side being pierced. John 19:34.
　Burial. Matt 27:59,60; Mark 15:46.
　Resurrection. Acts 3:15; 2 Tim 2:8.
Was like our own in all things except sin. Acts 3:22; Phil 2:7,8; Heb 2:17.
Was without sin. John 8:46; 18:38; Heb 4:15; 7:26,28; 1 Pet 2:22; 1 John 3:5.
Verified by the senses. Luke 24:39; John 20:27; 1 John 1:1,2.
Was of the seed of
　The woman. Gen 3:15; Is 7:4; Jer 31:22; Luke 1:31; Gal 4:4.
　Abraham. Gen 22:18; Gal 3:16; Heb 2:16.
　David. 2 Sam 7:12,16; Ps 89:35,36; Jer 23:5; Matt 22:42; Mark 10:47; Acts 2:30; 13:23; Rom 1:3.
Genealogy of. Matt 1:1–17; Luke 3:23–38.
Attested by himself. Matt 8:20; 16:13.
Confession of, a test of belonging to God. John 4:2.
Acknowledged by men. Mark 6:3; John 7:27; 19:5; Acts 22:2.
Denied by Antichrist. 1 John 4:3; 2 John 7.

HUMILITY.

Necessary to the service of God. Mic 6:8.
Christ an example of. Matt 11:29; John 13:14,15; Phil 2:5–8.
A characteristic of believers. Ps 34:2.
Those who have
　Regarded by God. Ps 138:6; Is 66:2.
　Heard by God. Ps 9:12; Is 10:17.
　Enjoy the presence of God. Is 57:15.
　Delivered by God. Job 22:29.
　Lifted up by God. James 4:10.
　Exalted by God. Luke 14:11; 18:14.
　Are greatest in Christ's kingdom. Matt 18:4; 20:26–28.
　Receive more grace. Prov 3:34; James 4:6.
　Upheld by honor. Prov 18:12; 29:23.
Is before honor. Prov 15:33.
Leads to riches, honor, and life. Prov 22:4.
Believers should
　Put on. Col 3:12.
　Be clothed with. 1 Pet 5:5.
　Walk with. Eph 4:1,2.
　Beware of false. Col 2:18,23.
Afflictions intended to produce. Lev 26:41; Deut 8:3; Lam 3:20.

Lack of, condemned. 2 Chr 33:23; 36:12; Jer 44:10; Dan 5:22.
Temporal judgments averted by. 2 Chr 7:14; 12:6,7.
Excellency of. Prov 16:19.
Blessedness of. Matt 5:3.

HUMILITY OF CHRIST, THE.

Declared by Himself. Matt 11:29.
Exhibited in His
Taking our nature. Phil 2:7; Heb 2:16.
Birth. Luke 2:4–7.
Subjection to His parents. Luke 2:51.
Station in life. Matt 13:55; John 9:29.
Poverty. Luke 9:58; 2 Cor 8:9.
Partaking of our infirmities. Heb 4:15; 5:7.
Submitting to ordinances. Matt 3:13–15.
Becoming a servant. Matt 20:28; Luke 22:27; Phil 2:7.
Associating with the despised. Matt 9:10,11; Luke 15:1,2.
Refusing honors. John 5:41; 6:15.
Entry into Jerusalem. Zech 9:9; Matt 21:5,7.
Washing His disciples' feet. John 13:5.
Obedience. John 6:38; Heb 10:9.
Submitting to sufferings. Is 50:6; 53:7; Matt 26:37–39; Acts 8:32.
Exposing Himself to reproach and contempt. Ps 22:6; 69:9; Rom 15:3; Is 53:3.
Death. John 10:15,17,18; Phil 2:8; Heb 12:2.
Believers should imitate. Phil 2:5–8.
On account of, He was despised. Mark 6:3; John 9:29.
His exaltation, the result of. Phil 2:9.

HUSBANDS.

Should have but one wife. Gen 2:24; Mark 10:6–8; 1 Cor 7:2–4.
Have authority over their wives. Gen 3:16; 1 Cor 11:3; Eph 5:23.
Duty of, to wives
To respect them. 1 Pet 3:7.
To love them. Eph 5:25–33; Col 3:19.
To regard them as themselves. Gen 2:23; Matt 19:5.
To be faithful to them. Prov 5:19; Mal 2:14,15.
To dwell with them for life. Gen 2:24; Matt 19:3–9.
To comfort them. 1 Sam 1:8.
To consult with them. Gen 31:4–7.
Not to leave them, though unbelieving. 1 Cor 7:11,12,14,16.
Duties of, not to interfere with their duties to Christ. Matt 19:29; Luke 14:26.

HYPOCRITES.

God knows and detects. Is 29:15,16.
Christ knew and detected. Matt 22:18.
God has no pleasure in. Is 9:17.
Shall not come before God. Job 13:16.
Described as
Willfully blind. Matt 23:17,19,26.
Vile. Is 32:6.
Self-righteous. Is 65:5; Luke 18:11.
Covetous. Ezek 33:31; 2 Pet 2:3.
Ostentatious. Matt 15:2,5,16; 23:5.
Censorious. Matt 7:3–5; Luke 13:14,15.
Regarding tradition more than the word of God. Matt 15:1–3.
Exact in minor, but neglecting important duties. Matt 23:23,24.
Having but a form of godliness. 2 Tim 3:5.

Seeking only outward purity. Luke 11:39.
Professing but not practicing. Ezek 33:31,32; Matt 23:3; Rom 2:17–23.
Using mere lip-worship. Is 29:13; Matt 15:8.
Glorying in appearance only. 2 Cor 5:12.
Trusting in privileges. Jer 7:4; Matt 3:9.
Apparently zealous in the things of God. Is 58:2.
Zealous in making proselytes. Matt 23:15.
Devouring widows' houses. Matt 23:14.
Loving pre-eminence. Matt 23:6,7.
Worship of, not acceptable to God. Is 1:11–15; 58:3–5; Matt 15:9.
Joy of, but for a moment. Job 20:5.
Hope of perishes. Job 8:13; 27:8,9.
Heap up wrath. Job 36:13.
Fearfulness shall surprise. Is 33:14.
Destroy others by slander. Prov 11:9.
In power, are a snare. Job 34:30.
The last days to abound with. 1 Tim 4:2.
Beware the principles of. Luke 12:1.
Spirit of, hinders growth in grace. 1 Pet 2:1.
Woe to. Is 29:15; Matt 23:13.
Punishment of. Job 15:34; Is 10:6; Jer 42:20,22; Matt 24:51.

IDLENESS.

Forbidden. Rom 12:11; Heb 6:12.
Produce apathy. Prov 12:27; 26:15.
Akin to extravagance. Prov 18:9.
Accompanied by conceit. Prov 26:16.
Lead to
Poverty. Prov 10:4; 20:13.
Want. Prov 20:4; 24:34.
Hunger. Prov 19:15; 20:13.
Bondage. Prov 12:24.
Disappointment. Prov 13:4; 21:25.
Ruin. Prov 24:30,31; Eccl 10:18.
Tattling and meddling. 1 Tim 5:13.
Effects of, afford instruction to others. Prov 24:30–32.
Remonstrance against. Prov 6:6,9.
False excuses for. Prov 20:4; 22:13.

IDOLATRY.

Forbidden. Ex 20:2,3; Deut 5:7.
Consists in
Bowing down to images. Ex 20:5; Deut 5:9.
Worshiping images. Is 44:17; Dan 3:5,10,15.
Sacrificing to images. Ps 106:38; Acts 7:41.
Worshiping other gods. Deut 30:17; Ps 81:9.
Swearing by other gods. Ex 23:13; Josh 23:7.
Walking after other gods. Deut 8:19.
Speaking in the name of other gods. Deut 18:20.
Looking to other gods. Hos 3:1.
Serving other gods. Deut 7:4; Jer 5:19.
Fearing other gods. 2 Kin 17:35.
Sacrificing to other gods. Ex 22:20.
Worshiping the true God by an image, etc. Ex 32:4–6; Ps 106:19,20.
Worshiping angels. Col 2:18.
Worshiping the host of heaven. Deut 4:19; 17:3.
Worshiping demons. Matt 4:9,10; Rev 9:20.
Worshiping dead men. Ps 106:28.
Setting up idols in the heart. Ezek 14:3,4.

Covetousness. Eph 5:5; Col 3:5.
Sensuality. Phil 3:19.
Is changing the glory of God into an image. Rom 1:23; Acts 17:29.
Is changing the truth of God into a lie. Is 44:20; Rom 1:25.
Is a work of the flesh. Gal 5:19,20.
Incompatible with the service of God. Gen 35:2,3; Josh 24:23; 1 Sam 7:3; 1 Kin 18:21; 2 Cor 6:15,16.
Described as
An abomination to God. Deut 7:25.
Hateful to God. Deut 16:22; Jer 44:4.
Vain and foolish. Ps 115:4–8; Is 44:19; Jer 10:3.
Bloody. Ezek 23:39.
Abominable. 1 Pet 4:3.
Unprofitable. Judg 10:14; Is 46:7.
Irrational. Acts 17:29; Rom 1:21–23.
Defiling. Ezek 20:7; 36:18.
They who practice
Forget God. Deut 8:19; Jer 18:15.
Go astray from God. Ezek 44:10.
Profane the name of God. Ezek 20:39.
Defile the sanctuary of God. Ezek 5:11.
Are estranged from God. Ezek 14:5.
Forsake God. 2 Kin 22:17; Jer 16:11.
Hate God. 2 Chr 19:2,3.
Provoke God. Deut 31:20; Is 65:3; Jer 25:6.
Are ignorant and foolish. Rom 1:21,22.
Inflame themselves. Is 57:5.
Hold fast their deceit. Jer 8:5.
Are carried away by it. 1 Cor 12:2.
Go after it in heart. Ezek 20:16.
Are insane about it. Jer 50:38.
Boast of it. Ps 97:7.
Have fellowship with devils. Hos 4:12.
Look to idols for deliverance. Is 44:17; 45:20.
Swear by their idols. Amos 8:14.
Objects of, numerous. 1 Cor 8:5.
Objects of described as
Strange gods. Gen 35:2,4; Josh 24:20.
Other gods. Judg 2:12,17; 1 Kin 14:9.
New gods. Deut 32:17; Judg 5:8.
Gods that cannot save. Is 45:20.
Gods that have not made the heavens. Jer 10:11.
No gods. Jer 5:7; Gal 4:8.
Molten gods. Ex 34:17; Lev 19:4.
Molten images. Deut 27:15; Hab 2:18.
Graven images. Is 45:20; Hos 11:2.
Senseless idols. Deut 4:28; Ps 115:5,7.
Dumb idols. Hab 2:18.
Dumb stones. Hab 2:19.
Wood and stone. Jer 3:9; Hos 4:12.
Abominations. Is 44:19; Jer 32:34.
Images of abomination. Ezek 7:20.
Idols of abomination. Ezek 16:36.
Stumbling blocks. Ezek 14:3.
Teachers of lies. Hab 2:18.
Wind and confusion. Is 41:29.
Nothing. Is 41:24; 1 Cor 8:4.
Helpless. Jer 10:5.
Vanity. Jer 18:15.
Vanities of the Gentiles. Jer 14:22.
Making idols for the purpose of, described and ridiculed. Is 44:10–20.
Obstinate sinners judicially given up to. Deut 4:28; 28:64; Hos 4:17.
Warnings against. Deut 4:15–19.
Exhortations to turn from. Ezek 14:6; 20:7; Acts 14:15.
Renounced on conversion. 1 Thess 1:9.
Led to abominable sins. Acts 15:20; Rom 1:26–32.
Believers should
Keep from. Josh 23:7; 1 John 5:21.

Flee from. 1 Cor 10:14.
Not have anything connected with in their houses. Deut 7:26.
Not partake of any thing connected with. 1 Cor 10:19,20.
Not have close relationship with those who practice. Josh 23:7; 1 Cor 5:11.
Not covenant with those who practice. Ex 34:12,15; Deut 7:2.
Not intermarry with those who practice. Ex 34:16; Deut 7:3.
Testify against. Acts 14:15; 19:26.
Refuse to engage in, though threatened with death. Dan 3:18.
Believes preserved by God from. 1 Kin 19:18; Rom 11:4.
Believers refuse to receive the worship of. Acts 10:25,26; 14:11-15.
Angels refuse to receive the worship of. Rev 22:8,9.
Destruction of, promised. Ezek 36:25; Zech 13:2.
Everything connected with, should be destroyed. Ex 34:13; Deut 7:5; 2 Sam 5:21; 2 Kin 23:14.
God condemns. Deut 27:15; Hab 2:19.
Punishment of
  Judicial death. Deut 17:2-5.
  Dreadful judgments which end in death. Jer 8:2; 16:1-11.
  Banishment. Jer 8:3; Hos 8:5-8; Amos 5:26,27.
  Exclusion from heaven. 1 Cor 6:9,10; Eph 5:5; Rev 22:15.
  Eternal torments. Rev 14:9-11; 21:8.
All forms of, forbidden by the law of Moses. Ex 20:4,5.
All heathen nations given up to. Ps 96:5; Rom 1:23,25; 1 Cor 12:2.
Led the heathen to think that their gods visited the earth in bodily shapes. Acts 14:11.
Led the heathen to consider their gods to have but a local influence. 1 Kin 20:23; 2 Kin 17:26.
Temples built for. Hos 8:14.
Altars raised for. 1 Kin 18:26; Hos 8:11.
Accompanied by feasts. 2 Kin 10:20; 1 Cor 10:27,28.
Objects of, worshipped
  With sacrifices. Num 22:40; 2 Kin 10:24.
  With libations. Is 57:6; Jer 19:13.
  With incense. Jer 48:35.
  With prayer. 1 Kin 18:26; Is 44:17.
  With singing and dancing. Ex 32:18,19; 1 Kin 18:26; 1 Cor 10:7.
  By bowing to them. 1 Kin 19:18; 2 Kin 5:18.
  By kissing them. 1 Kin 19:18; Hos 13:2.
  By kissing the hand to them. Job 31:26,27.
  By cutting the flesh. 1 Kin 18:28.
  By burning children. Deut 12:31; 2 Chr 33:6; Jer 19:4,5; Ezek 16:21.
  In temples. 2 Kin 5:18.
  On high places. Num 22:41; Jer 2:20.
  In groves. Ex 34:13.
  Under trees. Is 57:5; Jer 2:20.
  In private houses. Judg 17:4,5.
  On the tops of houses. 2 Kin 23:12; Zeph 1:5.
  In secret places. Is 57:8.
  Rites of, obscene and impure. Ex 32:25; Num 25:1-3; 2 Kin 17:9; Is 57:6,8,9; 1 Pet 4:3.
Divination connected with. 2 Chr 33:6.
Victims sacrificed in, often adorned with garlands. Acts 14:13.
Idols, mentioned in Scripture
  Adrammelech. 2 Kin 17:31.
  Anammelech. 2 Kin 17:31.

  Ashima. 2 Kin 17:30.
  Ashtoreth. Judg 2:13; 1 Kin 11:33.
  Baal. Judg 2:11-13; 6:25.
  Baal-berith. Judg 8:33; 9:4,46.
  Baal-peor. Num 25:1-3.
  Baalzebub. 2 Kin 1:2,16.
  Baal-zephon. Ex 14:2.
  Bel. Jer 50:2; 51:44.
  Chemosh. Num 21:29; 1 Kin 11:33.
  Chiun. Amos 5:26.
  Dagon. Judg 16:23; 1 Sam 5:1-3.
  Diana. Acts 19:24,27.
  Molech or Milcom. Lev 18:21; 1 Kin 11:5,33.
  Merodach. Jer 50:2.
  Nergal. 2 Kin 17:30.
  Nebo. Is 46:1.
  Nibhaz and Tartak. 2 Kin 17:31.
  Nisroch. 2 Kin 19:37.
  Queen of heaven. Jer 44:17,25.
  Remphan. Acts 7:43.
  Rimmon. 2 Kin 5:18.
  Succothbenoth. 2 Kin 17:30.
  Tammuz. Ezek 8:14.
Objects of, carried in procession. Is 46:7; Amos 5:26; Acts 7:43.
Early notice of, amongst God's professing people. Gen 31:19,30; 35:1-4; Josh 24:2.
The Jews
  Practiced, in Egypt. Josh 24:14; Ezek 23:3,19.
  Brought out of Egypt with them. Ezek 23:8; Acts 7:39-41.
  Forbidden to practice. Ex 20:1-5; 23:24.
  Often mixed up, with true worship. Ex 32:1-5; 1 Kin 12:27,28.
  Followed the Canaanites in. Judg 2:11-13; 1 Chr 5:25.
  Followed the Moabites in. Num 25:1-3.
  Followed the Assyrians in. Ezek 16:28-30; 23:5-7.
  Followed the Syrians in. Judg 10:6.
Adopted by Solomon. 1 Kin 11:5-8.
Adopted by the wicked kings. 1 Kin 21:26; 2 Kin 21:21; 2 Chr 28:2-4; 33:3,7.
Example of the kings encouraged Israel in. 1 Kin 12:30; 2 Kin 21:11; 2 Chr 33:9.
Great prevalence of, in Israel. Is 2:8; Jer 2:28; Ezek 8:10.
Meant they forsook God. Jer 2:9-13.
The good kings of Judah endeavoured to destroy. 2 Chr 15:16; 34:7.
Captivity of Israel on account of. 2 Kin 17:6-18.
Captivity of Judah on account of. 2 Kin 17:19-23.

INDWELLING OF THE HOLY SPIRIT, THE.

In His Church, as His temple. 1 Cor 3:16.
In the body of believers, as His temple. 1 Cor 6:19; 2 Cor 6:16.
Believers filled with. Acts 6:5; Eph 5:18; 2 Tim 1:14.
Is the means of
  Receiving life. Rom 8:11; 1 John 2:27.
  Guiding. John 16:13; 34:7.
  Fruit bearing. Gal 5:22.
A proof of being Christ's. Rom 8:9; 1 John 4:13.
A proof of adoption. Rom 8:15; Gal 4:5.
Those who have not
  Are sensual. Jude 19.
  Are without Christ. Rom 8:9.
Opposed by the carnal nature. Gal 5:17.

INGRATITUDE.

A characteristic of the wicked. Ps 38:20; 2 Tim 3:2.

Often exhibited
  By relations. Job 19:14.
  By servants. Job 19:15,16.
  To benefactors. Ps 109:5; Eccl 9:15.
  To friends in distress. Ps 38:11.
Believers should avoid the guilt of. Ps 7:4,5.
Should be met with
  Prayers. Ps 35:12,13; 109:4.
  Faithfulness. Gen 31:38-42.
  Persevering love. 2 Cor 12:15.
Punishment of. Prov 17:13; Jer 18:20,21.

INJUSTICE.

Forbidden. Lev 19:15,35; Deut 16:19.
Specially to be avoided toward
  The poor. Ex 23:6; Prov 22:16,22,23.
  The stranger and fatherless. Ex 22:21,22; Deut 24:17; Jer 22:3.
  Servants. Job 31:13,14; Deut 24:14; Jer 22:13.
Of the least kind, condemned. Luke 16:10.
God
  Regards. Eccl 5:8.
  Approves not of. Prov 17:15; 20:10; Lam 3:35,36.
  Hears the cry of those who suffer. James 5:4.
  Provoked to avenge. Ps 12:5.
Brings a curse. Deut 27:17,19.
A bad example leads to. Ex 23:2.
Intemperance leads to. Prov 31:5.
Covetousness leads to. Jer 6:13; Ezek 22:12; Mic 2:2.
Believers should
  Hate. Prov 29:27.
  Testify against. Ps 58:1,2; Mic 3:8,9.
  Bear, patiently. 1 Cor 6:7.
  Take no vengeance for. Matt 5:39.
The wicked
  Deal with. Is 26:10.
  Judge with. Ps 82:2; Eccl 3:16; Hab 1:4.
  Practice, without shame. Jer 6:13,15; Zeph 3:5.
Punishment of. Prov 11:7; 28:8; Amos 5:11,12; 8:5,8; 1 Thess 4:6.

INSPIRATION OF THE HOLY SPIRIT, THE.

Foretold. Joel 2:28; Acts 2:16-18.
All Scripture given by. 2 Sam 23:2; 2 Tim 3:16; 2 Pet 1:21.
Design of
  To reveal future events. Acts 1:16; 28:25; 1 Pet 1:11.
  To reveal the mysteries of God. Amos 3:7; 1 Cor 2:10.
  To give power to ministers. Mic 3:8; Acts 1:8.
  To direct ministers. Ezek 3:24-27; Acts 11:12; 13:2.
  To control ministers. Acts 16:6.
  To testify against sin. 2 Kin 17:13; Neh 9:30; Mic 3:8; John 16:8,9.
Modes of
  Various. Heb 1:1.
  By secret impulse. 2 Pet 1:21.
  By a voice. Is 6:8; Acts 8:29.
  By visions. Num 12:6; Ezek 11:24.
  By dreams. Num 12:6; Dan 7:1.
Necessary to prophesying. Num 11:25-27; 2 Chr 20:14-17.
Is irresistible. Amos 3:8.
  Despisers of, punished. 2 Chr 36:15,16; Zech 7:12.

JEHOVAH, THE ONLY TRUE GOD.

Jehovah is "Alpha and Omega" and "the First and the Last." Rev 1:7,8; 22:12,13,20; Is 48:12,13.
Death and life of "the First and the Last."

Rev 2:8; 1:17,18; Matt 28:5,6.
There is only one true God, Jehovah. Is 43:10,11; John 1:1.

JERUSALEM.

The ancient Salem. Gen 14:18; Ps 76:2.
The ancient Jebusi or Jebus. Josh 15:8; 18:28; Judg 19:10.
The king of, defeated and slain by Joshua. Josh 10:5–23.
Allotted to the tribe of Benjamin. Josh 18:28.
Partly taken and burned by Judah. Judg 1:8.
The Jebusites
  Formerly dwelt in. Judg 19:10,11.
  Held possession of, with Judah and Benjamin. Josh 15:63; Judg 1:21.
  Finally dispossessed of, by David. 2 Sam 5:6–8.
Made the royal city. 2 Sam 5:9; 20:3.
Specially chosen by God. 2 Chr 6:6; Ps 135:21.
The seat of government under the Romans for a time. Matt 27:2,19.
Roman government transferred from, to Caesarea. Acts 23:23,24; 25:1–13.
Called
  City of God. Ps 46:4; 48:1.
  City of the Lord. Is 60:14.
  City of Judah. 2 Chr 25:28.
  City of the great king. Ps 48:2; Matt 5:5.
  City of appointed feasts. Is 33:20.
  City of righteousness. Is 1:26.
  City of truth. Zech 8:3.
  A city not forsaken. Is 62:12.
  Faithful city. Is 1:21,26.
  Holy city. Neh 11:1; Is 48:2; Matt 4:5.
  Throne of the Lord. Jer 3:17.
  Zion. Ps 48:12; Is 33:20.
  Zion of the Holy One of Israel. Is 60:14.
Surrounded by mountains. Ps 125:2.
Surrounded by a wall. 1 Kin 3:1.
Protected by forts and bulwarks. Ps 48:12,13.
Entered by gates. Ps 122:2; Jer 17:19–21.
Hezekiah made an aqueduct for. 2 Kin 20:20.
Spoils of war placed in. 1 Sam 17:54; 2 Sam 8:7.
Described as
  Beautiful in elevation. Ps 48:2.
  Compact. Ps 122:3.
  Lovely. Song 6:4.
  The perfection of beauty. Lam 2:15.
  Joy of the whole earth. Ps 48:2; Lam 2:15.
  Princess among the provinces. Lam 1:1.
  Great. Jer 22:8.
  Populous. Lam 1:1.
  Wealth, etc. in the time of Solomon. 1 Kin 10:26,27.
Protected by God. Is 31:5.
Instances of God's care and protection of. 2 Sam 24:16; 2 Kin 19:32–34; 2 Chr 12:7.
The temple built in. 2 Chr 3:1; Ps 68:29.
The Jews
  Went up to, at the feasts. Ps 122:4; Luke 2:42.
  Loved. Ps 137:5,6.
  Lamented the affliction of. Neh 1:2–4.
  Prayed for the prosperity of. Ps 51:18; 122:6.
  Prayed toward. 1 Kin 8:41; Dan 6:10.
Wickedness of. Is 1:1–4; Jer 5:1–5; Mic 3:10.
Idolatry of. 2 Chr 28:4; Ezek 8:7–10.

Wickedness of, the cause of its calamities. 2 Kin 21:12–15; 2 Chr 24:18; Lam 1:8; Ezek 5:5–8.
Was the tomb of the prophets. Luke 13:33,34.
Christ
  Preached in. Luke 21:37,38; John 18:20.
  Did many miracles in. John 4:45.
  Publicly entered, as king. Matt 21:9,10.
  Lamented over. Matt 23:37; Luke 19:41.
  Put to death at. Luke 9:31; Acts 13:27,29.
Gospel first preached at. Luke 24:47; Acts 2:14.
Miraculous gift of the Holy Spirit first given at. Acts 1:4; 2:1–5.
Persecution of the Christian church commenced at. Acts 4:1; 8:1.
First Christian council held at. Acts 15:4,6.
Calamities of, mentioned
  Taken and plundered by Shishak. 1 Kin 14:25,26; 2 Chr 12:1–4.
  Taken and plundered by Jehoash king of Israel. 2 Kin 14:13,14.
  Besieged but not taken by Rezin and Pekah. Is 7:1; 2 Kin 16:5.
  Besieged but not taken by Sennacherib. 2 Kin 18:17; 19:1–37.
  Taken and made tributary by Pharaoh-Necho. 2 Kin 23:33–35.
  Besieged by Nebuchadnezzar. 2 Kin 24:10,11.
  Taken and burned by Nebuchadnezzar. 2 Kin 25:1–30; Jer 39:1–8.
  Threatened by Sanballat. Neh 4:7,8.
Rebuilt after the captivity by order of Cyrus. Ezra 1:1–4.
Prophecies respecting
  To be taken by king of Babylon. Jer 20:5.
  To be made a heap of ruins. Jer 9:11; 26:18.
  To be a wilderness. Is 64:10.
  To be rebuilt by Cyrus. Is 44:26–28.
  To be a quiet habitation. Is 33:20.
  To be a terror to her enemies. Zech 12:2,3.
  Christ to enter, as king. Zech 9:9.
  The gospel to go forth from. Is 2:3; 40:9.
  To be destroyed by the Romans. Luke 19:42–44.
  Its destruction accompanied by severe calamities. Matt 24:21,29; Luke 21:23,24.
  Signs preceding its destruction. Matt 24:6–15; Luke 21:7–11,25,28.

JOY.

God gives. Eccl 2:26; Ps 4:7.
Christ appointed to give. Is 61:3.
Is a fruit of the Spirit. Gal 5:22.
The gospel, good tidings of. Luke 2:10,11.
God's word affords. Neh 8:12; Jer 15:16.
The gospel to be received with. 1 Thess 1:6.
Promised to believers. Ps 132:16; Is 35:10; 55:12; 56:7.
Prepared for believers. Ps 97:11.
Commanded to believers. Ps 32:11; Phil 3:1.
Fullness of, in God's presence. Ps 16:11.
Vanity of seeking, from earthly things. Eccl 2:10,11; 11:8.
Experienced by
  Believers. Luke 24:52; Acts 16:34.
  Peace-makers. Prov 12:20.

The just. Prov 21:15.
The wise, and discreet. Prov 15:23.
Parents of wise children. Prov 23:24.
Increased to the meek. Is 29:19.
Of believers is
  In God. Ps 89:16; 149:2; Hab 3:18; Rom 5:11.
  In Christ. Luke 1:47; Phil 3:3.
  In the Holy Spirit. Rom 14:17.
  For election. Luke 10:20.
  For salvation. Ps 21:1; Is 61:10.
  For deliverance from bondage. Ps 105:43; Jer 31:10–13.
  For manifestation of goodness. 2 Chr 7:10.
  For temporal blessings. Joel 2:23,24.
  For supplies of grace. Is 12:3.
  For divine protection. Ps 5:11; 16:8,9.
  For divine support. Ps 28:7; 63:7.
  For the victory of Christ. John 16:33.
  For the hope of glory. Rom 5:2.
  For the success of the gospel. Acts 15:3.
Of believers should be
  Great. Zech 9:9; Acts 8:8.
  Abundant. 2 Cor 8:2.
  Exceeding. Ps 21:6; 68:3.
  Animated. Ps 32:11; Luke 6:23.
  Unspeakable. 1 Pet 1:8.
  Full of glory. 1 Pet 1:8.
  Constant. 2 Cor 6:10; Phil 4:4.
  For evermore. 1 Thess 5:16.
  With awe. Ps 2:11.
  In hope. Rom 12:12.
  In sorrow. 2 Cor 6:10.
  Under trials. James 1:2; 1 Pet 1:6.
  Under persecutions. Matt 5:11,12; Luke 6:22,23; Heb 10:34.
  Under calamities. Hab 3:17,18.
  Expressed in hymns. Eph 5:19; James 5:13.
Afflictions of believers succeeded by. Ps 30:5; 126:5; Is 35:10; John 16:20.
Pray for restoration of. Ps 51:8,12; 85:6.
Promote, in the afflicted. Job 29:13.
Of believers, made full by
  The favor of God. Acts 2:28.
  Faith in Christ. Rom 15:13.
  Abiding in Christ. John 15:10,11.
  The word of Christ. John 17:13.
  Answers to prayer. John 16:24.
  Communion of believers. 2 Tim 1:4; 1 John 1:3,4; 2 John 12.
Believers should afford, to their ministers. Phil 2:2; Philem 20.
Ministers should
  Esteem their people as their. Phil 4:1; 1 Thess 2:20.
  Promote, in their people. 2 Cor 1:24; Phil 1:25.
  Pray for, for their people. Rom 15:13.
  Have, in the faith and holiness of their people. 2 Cor 7:4; 1 Thess 3:9; 3 John 4.
  Come to their people with. Rom 15:32.
  Finish their course with. Acts 20:24.
  Desire to render an account with. Phil 2:16; Heb 13:17.
Serve God with. Ps 100:2.
Generosity in God's service should cause. 1 Chr 29:9,17.
Believers should engage in all religious services with. Ezra 6:22; Ps 42:4.
Believers should have, in all their undertakings. Deut 12:18.
Believers shall be presented to God with exceeding. 1 Pet 4:13; Jude 1:24.
The coming of Christ will afford to believers, exceeding. 1 Pet 4:13.
Shall be the final reward of believers at the judgment day. Matt 25:21.

Of the wicked
Is derived from earthly pleasures. Eccl 2:10; 11:9.
Is derived from folly. Prov 15:21.
Is delusive. Prov 14:13.
Is short-lived. Job 20:5; Eccl 7:6.
Should be turned into mourning. James 4:9.
Shall be taken away. Is 16:10.

JUDGMENT, THE.
Predicted in the Old Testament. 1 Chr 16:33; Ps 9:7; 96:13; Eccl 3:17.
A first principle of the gospel. Heb 6:2.
A day appointed for. Acts 17:31; Rom 2:16.
Time of, unknown to us. Mark 13:32.
Called the
Day of wrath. Rom 2:5; Rev 6:17.
Revelation of the righteous judgment of God. Rom 2:5.
Day of judgment and perdition of ungodly men. 2 Pet 3:7.
Day of destruction. Job 21:30.
Judgment of the great day. Jude 6.
Shall be administered by Christ. John 5:22,27; Acts 10:42; Rom 14:10; 2 Cor 5:10.
Believers shall sit with Christ in. 1 Cor 6:2; Rev 20:4.
Shall take place at the coming of Christ. Matt 25:31; 2 Tim 4:1.
Of unbelievers, by the law of conscience. Rom 2:12,14,15.
Of Jews, by the law of Moses. Rom 2:12.
Of Christians, by the gospel. James 2:12.
Shall involve
All nations. Matt 25:32.
All men. Heb 9:27; 12:23.
Small and great. Rev 20:12.
The righteous and wicked. Eccl 3:17.
Quick and dead. 2 Tim 4:1; 1 Pet 4:5.
Shall be in righteousness. Ps 98:9; Acts 17:31.
The books shall be opened at. Dan 7:10.
Shall be of all
Actions. Eccl 11:9; 12:14; Rev 20:13.
Words. Matt 12:36,37; Jude 15.
Thoughts. Eccl 12:14; 1 Cor 4:5.
None, by nature can stand in. Ps 130:3; 143:2; Rom 3:19.
Believers shall, through Christ, be enabled to stand in. Rom 8:33,34.
Christ will acknowledge believers at. Matt 25:34–40; Rev 3:5.
Perfect love will give boldness in. 1 John 4:17.
Believers shall be rewarded at. 2 Tim 4:8; Rev 11:18.
The wicked shall be condemned in. Matt 7:22,23; 25:41.
Final punishment of the wicked will succeed. Matt 13:40–42; 25:46.
The word of Christ shall be a witness against the wicked in. John 12:48.
The certainty of, a motive to
Repentance. Acts 17:30,31.
Faith. Is 28:16,17.
Holiness. 2 Cor 5:9,10; 2 Pet 3:11,14.
Prayer and watchfulness. Mark 13:33.
Warn the wicked of. Acts 24:25; 2 Cor 5:11.
The wicked dread. Acts 24:25; Heb 10:27.
Neglected advantages increase condemnation at. Matt 11:20–24; Luke 11:31,32.
Devils shall be condemned at. 2 Pet 2:4; Jude 6.

JUSTICE.
Commanded. Deut 16:20; Is 56:1.

Christ, an example of. Ps 98:9; Is 11:4; Jer 23:5.
Specially required in rulers. 2 Sam 23:3; Ezek 45:9.
To be done
In executing judgment. Deut 16:18; Jer 21:12.
In buying and selling. Lev 19:36; Deut 25:15.
To the poor. Prov 29:14; 31:9.
To the fatherless and widows. Is 1:17.
To servants. Col 4:1.
Bribes impede. Ex 23:8.
God
Requires. Mic 6:8.
Sets the highest value on. Prov 2:13.
Delights in. Prov 11:1.
Gives wisdom to execute. 1 Kin 3:11,12; Prov 2:6,9.
Displeased with the lack of. Eccl 5:8.
Brings its own reward. Jer 22:15.
Believers should
Study the principles of. Phil 4:8.
Receive instruction in. Prov 1:3.
Pray for wisdom to execute. 1 Kin 3:9.
Always do. Ps 119:121; Ezek 18:8,9.
Take pleasure in doing. Prov 21:15.
Teach others to do. Gen 18:19.
Promises concerning. Is 33:15,16; Jer 7:5,7.
The wicked
Scorn. Prov 19:28.
Abhor. Mic 3:9.
Call not for. Is 59:4.
Pass over. Luke 11:42.
Afflict those who act with. Job 12:4; Amos 5:12.

JUSTICE OF GOD, THE.
Is a part of his character. Deut 32:4; Is 45:21.
Declared to be
Plenteous. Job 37:23.
Incomparable. Job 4:17.
Incorruptible. Deut 10:17; 2 Chr 19:7.
Impartial. Jer 32:19.
Unfailing. Zeph 3:5.
Undeviating. Job 8:3; 34:12.
Without respect of persons. Rom 2:11; Col 3:25; 1 Pet 1:17.
The habitation of His throne. Ps 89:14.
Not to be sinned against. Jer 50:7.
Denied by the ungodly. Ezek 33:17,20.
Exhibited in
Forgiving sins. 1 John 1:9.
Redemption. Rom 3:26.
His government. Ps 9:4; Jer 9:24.
His judgments. Gen 18:25; Rev 19:2.
All His ways. Ezek 18:25,29.
The final judgment. Acts 17:31.
Acknowledgement of. Ps 51:4; Rom 3:4.
Magnify. Ps 98:9; 99:3,4.

JUSTIFICATION BEFORE GOD.
Promised in Christ. Is 45:25; 53:11.
Is the act of God. Is 50:8; Rom 8:33.
Under law
Requires perfect obedience. Lev 18:5; Rom 2:13; 10:5; James 2:10.
Man cannot attain to. Job 9:2,3,20; 25:4; Ps 130:3; 143:2; Rom 3:20; 9:31,32.
Under the gospel
Is not of works. Acts 13:39; Rom 8:3; Gal 2:16; 3:11.
Is not of faith and works united. Acts 15:1–29; Rom 3:28; 11:6; Gal 2:14–21; 5:4.
Is by faith alone. John 5:24; Acts 13:39; Rom 3:30; 5:1; Gal 2:16.
Is of grace. Rom 3:24; 4:16; 5:17–21.
In the name of Christ. 1 Cor 6:11.

By imputation of Christ's righteousness. Is 61:10; Jer 23:6; Rom 3:22; 5:18; 1 Cor 1:30; 2 Cor 5:21.
By the blood of Christ. Rom 5:9.
By the resurrection of Christ. Rom 4:25; 1 Cor 15:17.
Blessedness of. Ps 32:1,2; Rom 4:6–8.
Frees from condemnation. Is 50:8,9; 54:17; Rom 8:33,34.
Entitles to an inheritance. Titus 3:7.
Ensures glorification. Rom 8:30.
The wicked shall not attain to. Ex 23:7.
By faith
Revealed under the Old Testament age. Hab 2:4; Rom 1:17.
Excludes boasting. Rom 3:27; 4:2; 1 Cor 1:29,31.
Typified. Zech 3:4,5.
Illustrated. Luke 18:14.
Exemplified
Abraham. Gen 15:6.
Paul. Phil 3:8,9.

LAMB, THE.
The young of the flock. Ex 12:5; Ezek 45:15.
Described as
Patient. Is 53:7.
Playful. Ps 114:4,6.
Exposed to danger from wild beasts. 1 Sam 17:34.
The shepherd's care for. Is 40:11.
Used for
Food. Deut 32:14; 2 Sam 12:4.
Clothing. Prov 27:26.
Sacrifice. 1 Chr 29:21; 2 Chr 29:32.
Considered a great delicacy. Amos 6:4.
Offered in sacrifice
Males. Ex 12:5.
Females. Num 6:14.
While sucking. 1 Sam 7:9.
At a year old. Ex 12:5; Num 6:14.
From the earliest times. Gen 4:4; 22:7,8.
Every morning and evening. Ex 29:38,39; Num 28:3,4.
At the Passover. Ex 12:3,6,7.
By the wicked not accepted. Is 1:11; 66:3.
Numbers of, given by Josiah to the people for sacrifice. 2 Chr 35:7.
The firstborn of an ass to be redeemed with. Ex 13:13; 34:20.
An extensive commerce in. Ezra 7:17; Ezek 27:21.
Tribute often paid in. 2 Kin 3:4; Is 16:1.
Human covenants confirmed by gift of. Gen 21:28–30.
The image of, was on money. Gen 33:19; Josh 24:32.

LAW OF GOD, THE.
Is absolute and perpetual. Matt 5:18.
Given
To Adam. Gen 2:16,17.
To Noah. Gen 9:6.
To the Israelites. Ex 20:2–17; Ps 78:5.
Through Moses. Ex 31:18; John 7:19.
Through the ministration of angels. Acts 7:53; Gal 3:19; Heb 2:2.
Described as
Pure. Ps 19:8.
Spiritual. Rom 7:14.
Holy, just, and good. Rom 7:12.
Exceeding broad. Ps 119:96.
Perfect. Ps 19:7; Rom 12:2.
Truth. Ps 119:142.
Not burdensome. 1 John 5:3.
Requires obedience of the heart. Deut 27:26; Ps 51:6; Matt 5:28; 22:37; Gal 3:10; James 2:10.

Love is the fulfilling of. Rom 13:8,10.
Man, by nature, not in subjection to. Rom 7:5; 8:7.
Man cannot render perfect obedience to. 1 Kin 8:46; Eccl 7:20; Rom 3:10.
Sin is a transgression of. 1 John 3:4.
All men have transgressed. Rom 3:9,19.
Man cannot be justified by. Acts 13:39; Rom 3:20,28; Gal 2:16; 3:11.
Gives the knowledge of sin. Rom 3:20; 7:7.
Works wrath. Rom 4:15.
Conscience testifies to. Rom 2:15.
Designed to lead to Christ. Gal 3:24.
Blessedness of keeping. Ps 119:1; Matt 5:19; Rev 22:14.
Christ
  Came to fulfil. Matt 5:17.
  Magnified. Is 42:21.
  Explained. Matt 7:12; 22:37–40.
The love of, produces peace. Ps 119:165.
Believers
  Freed from the bondage of. Rom 6:14; 7:4,6; Gal 3:13.
  Freed from the curse of. Gal 3:13.
  Have, written on their hearts. Jer 31:33; Heb 8:10.
  Love. Ps 119:97,113.
  Delight in. Ps 119:77; Rom 7:22.
  Prepare their hearts to seek. Ezra 7:10.
  Pledge themselves to walk in. Neh 10:29.
  Keep. Ps 119:55.
  Pray to understand. Ps 119:18.
  Pray for power to keep. Ps 119:34.
  Should remember. Mal 4:4.
  Should make the subject of their conversation. Ex 13:9.
  Lament over the violation of, by others. Ps 119:136.
The wicked
  Despise. Amos 2:4.
  Forget. Hos 4:6.
  Forsake. 2 Chr 12:1; Jer 9:13.
  Refuse to hear. Is 30:9; Jer 6:19.
  Refuse to walk in. Ps 78:10.
  Cast away. Is 5:24.
  Punishment for disobeying. Neh 9:26,27; Is 65:11–13; Jer 9:13–16.

LIBERTY, CHRISTIAN.

Foretold. Is 42:7; 61:1.
Conferred
  By God. Col 1:13.
  By Christ. Gal 4:3–5; 5:1.
  By the Holy Spirit. Rom 8:15; 2 Cor 3:17.
Confirmed by Christ. John 8:36.
Proclaimed by Christ. Luke 4:18.
The service of Christ is. 1 Cor 7:22.
Is freedom from
  The law. Rom 7:6; 8:2.
  The curse of the law. Gal 3:13.
  The fear of death. Heb 2:15.
  Sin. Rom 6:7,18.
  Corruption. Rom 8:21.
  Bondage of man. 1 Cor 9:19.
  Jewish ordinances. Gal 4:3; Col 2:20.
Called the glorious liberty of the children of God. Rom 8:21.
Believers should
  Praise God for. Ps 116:16,17.
  Assert. 1 Cor 10:29.
  Walk in. Ps 119:45.
  Stand fast in. Gal 2:5; 5:1.
  Not abuse. Gal 5:13; 1 Pet 2:16.
  Not offend others by. 1 Cor 8:9; 10:29,32.
Portrait of a new life. James 1:25; 2:12.
False teachers
  Promise, to others. 2 Pet 2:19.

Abuse. Jude 4.
Try to destroy. Gal 2:4.
The wicked, devoid of. John 8:34; Rom 6:20.

LIFE, ETERNAL.

Christ is. 1 John 1:2; 5:20.
Revealed by Christ. John 6:68; 2 Tim 1:10.
To know God and Christ is. John 17:3.
Given
  By God. Ps 133:3; Rom 6:23.
  By Christ. John 6:27; 10:28.
  In Christ. 1 John 5:11.
  Through Christ. Rom 5:21; 6:23.
  To all given to Christ. John 17:2.
  To those who believe in God. John 5:24.
  To those who believe in Christ. John 3:15,16; 6:40,47.
  To those who hate life for Christ. John 12:25.
  In answer to prayer. Ps 21:4.
Revealed in the Scriptures. John 5:39.
Results from
  Drinking the water of life. John 4:14.
  Eating the bread of life. John 6:50–58.
  Eating of the tree of life. Rev 2:7.
They who are ordained to, believe the gospel. Acts 13:48.
Believers
  Have promises of. 1 Tim 4:8; 2 Tim 1:1; Titus 1:2; 1 John 2:25.
  Have hope of. Titus 1:2; 3:7.
  May have assurance of. 2 Cor 5:1; 1 John 5:13.
  Shall reap, through the Spirit. Gal 6:8.
  Shall inherit. Matt 19:29.
  Look for the mercy of the Lord Jesus Christ. Jude 21.
  Should lay hold of. 1 Tim 6:12,19.
  Are preserved to. John 10:28,29.
  Shall rise to. Dan 12:2; John 5:29.
  Shall go into. Matt 25:46.
  Shall reign in. Dan 7:18; Rom 5:17.
Cannot be inherited by works. Rom 2:7; 3:10–19.
The wicked
  Have not. 1 John 3:15.
  Judge themselves unworthy of. Acts 13:46.
Exhortation to seek. John 6:27.

LIFE, SPIRITUAL.

God is the Author of. Ps 36:9; Col 2:13.
Christ is the Author of. John 5:21,25; 6:33,51–53; 14:6; 1 John 4:9.
The Holy Spirit is the Author of. Ezek 37:14; Rom 8:9–13.
The Word of God is the instrument of. Is 55:3; 1 Pet 4:6.
Is hidden with Christ. Col 3:3.
The fear of God is. Prov 14:27; 19:23.
Life and peace is. Rom 8:6.
Is maintained by
  Christ. John 6:57; 1 Cor 10:3,4.
  Faith. Gal 2:20.
  The word of God. Deut 8:3; Matt 4:4.
  Prayer. Ps 69:32.
Has its origin in the new-birth. John 3:3–8.
Has its infancy. Luke 10:21; 1 Cor 3:1,2; 1 John 2:12.
Has its youth. 1 John 2:13,14.
Has its maturity. Eph 4:13; 1 John 2:13,14.
Revived by God. Ps 85:6; Hos 6:2.
Evidenced by love to the brethren. 1 John 3:14.
All believers have. Eph 2:1,5; Col 2:13.
Should animate the services of believers.

Rom 12:1; 1 Cor 14:15.
Believers praise God for. Ps 119:175.
Seek to grow in. Eph 4:15; 1 Pet 2:2.
Pray for the increase of. Ps 119:25; 143:11.
The wicked alienated from. Eph 4:18.
Lovers of pleasure destitute of. 1 Tim 5:6.
Hypocrites destitute of. Jude 12; Rev 3:1.

LIGHT.

God the only source of. James 1:17.
Created by God. Gen 1:3; Is 45:7.
Separated from darkness. Gen 1:4.
Sun, moon, and stars appointed to communicate to the earth. Gen 1:14–17; Jer 31:35.
Divided into
  Natural. Job 24:14; Is 5:30.
  Extraordinary or miraculous. Ex 14:20; Ps 78:14; Acts 9:3; 12:7.
  Artificial. Jer 25:10; Acts 16:29.
Communicated to the body through the eye. Prov 15:30; Matt 6:22.
Described as
  White and pure. Matt 17:2.
  Bright. Job 37:21.
  Shining. 2 Sam 23:4; Job 41:18.
  Diffusive. Job 25:3; 36:30.
  Useful and precious. Eccl 2:13.
  Manifesting objects. John 3:20,21; Eph 5:13.
The theory of, beyond man's comprehension. Job 38:19,20,24.

LONG-SUFFERING OF GOD, THE.

Is part of his character. Ex 34:6; Num 14:18; Ps 86:15.
Salvation, the object of. 2 Pet 3:15.
Should lead to repentance. Rom 2:4; 2 Pet 3:9.
An encouragement to repent. Joel 2:13.
Exercised toward
  His people. Is 30:18; Ezek 20:17.
  The wicked. Rom 9:22; 1 Pet 3:20.
Plead in prayer. Jer 15:15.
Limits set to. Gen 6:3; Jer 44:22.
The wicked
  Abuse. Eccl 8:11; Matt 24:48,49.
  Despise. Rom 2:4.
  Punished for despising. Neh 9:30; Matt 24:48–51; Rom 2:5.

LORD'S SUPPER, THE.

Prefigured. Ex 12:21–28; 1 Cor 5:7,8.
Instituted. Matt 26:26; 1 Cor 11:23.
Purpose and character of. Matt 26:27; Luke 22:19; 1 Cor 5:7,8; 10:16,21; 11:24,26,28,30.
Was continually partaken of, by the Church. Acts 2:42; 20:7.
Unworthy partakers of
  Are guilty of the body and blood of Christ. 1 Cor 11:27.
  Discern not the Lord's body. 1 Cor 11:29.
  Are visited with judgments. 1 Cor 11:30.

LOVE OF CHRIST, THE.

To the Father. Ps 91:14; John 14:31.
To His church. Eph 5:24.
To those who love Him. Prov 8:17; John 14:21.
Manifested in His
  Coming to seek the lost. Luke 19:10.
  Praying for His enemies. Luke 23:34.
  Giving Himself for us. Gal 2:20.
  Dying for us. John 15:13; 1 John 3:16.
  Washing away our sins. Rev 1:5.
  Interceding for us. Heb 7:25; 9:24.
  Sending the Spirit. John 16:7.

Rebukes and chastisements. Rev 3:19.

Passes knowledge. Eph 3:19.

To be imitated. John 13:34; 15:12; Eph 5:2; 1 John 3:16.

To believers, is

Constraining. 2 Cor 5:14.

Unchangeable. John 13:1.

Indissoluble. Rom 8:35.

Obedient believers abide in. John 15:10.

Believers obtain victory through. Rom 8:37.

Is the ground of his believers love to Him. Luke 7:47.

To believers, shall be acknowledge even by enemies. Rev 3:9.

LOVE OF GOD, THE.

Is a part of His character. 2 Cor 13:11; 1 John 4:8.

Christ, the special object of. John 15:9; 17:26.

Christ abides in. John 15:10.

Described as

Sovereign. Deut 7:8; 10:15.

Great. Eph 2:4.

Abiding. Zeph 3:17.

Unfailing. Is 49:15,16.

Unalienable. Rom 8:39.

Constraining. Hos 11:4.

Everlasting. Jer 31:3.

Irrespective of merit. Deut 7:7; Job 7:17.

Manifested towards

Perishing sinners. John 3:16; Titus 3:4.

His believers. John 16:27; 17:23; 2 Thess 2:16; 1 John 4:16.

The destitute. Deut 10:18.

The cheerful giver. 2 Cor 9:7.

LOVE TO CHRIST.

Exhibited by God. Matt 17:5; John 5:20.

Exhibited by believers. 1 Pet 1:8.

His love to us a motive to. 2 Cor 5:14.

Manifested in

Obeying Him. John 14:15,21,23.

Ministering to Him. Matt 25:40; 27:55.

Preferring Him to all others. Matt 10:37.

Taking up the cross for Him. Matt 10:38.

An evidence of adoption. John 8:42.

Should be

Sincere. Eph 6:24.

In proportion to our mercies. Luke 7:47.

Supreme. Matt 10:37.

Even to death. Acts 21:13; Rev 12:11.

Promises to. 2 Tim 4:8; James 1:12.

Increase of, to be prayed for. Phil 1:9.

Pray for grace to those who have. Eph 6:24.

They who have

Are loved by the Father. John 14:21,23; 16:27.

Are loved by Christ. Prov 8:17; John 14:21.

Enjoy communion with God and Christ. John 14:23.

Decrease of, rebuked. Rev 2:4.

Want of, denounced. 1 Cor 16:22.

The wicked, destitute of. John 15:18,25.

LOVE TO GOD.

Commanded. Deut 11:1; Josh 22:5.

The first great commandment. Matt 22:38.

With all the heart. Deut 6:5; Matt 22:37.

Better than all sacrifices. Mark 12:33.

Produced by

The Holy Spirit. Gal 5:22; 2 Thess 3:5.

The love of God to us. 1 John 4:19.

Answers to prayer. Ps 116:1.

Exhibited by Christ. John 14:31.

A characteristic of believers. Ps 5:11.

Should produce

Joy. Ps 5:11.

Love to believers. 1 John 5:1.

Hatred of sin. Ps 97:10.

Obedience to God. Deut 30:20; 1 John 5:3.

Perfected in obedience. 1 John 2:5.

Perfected, gives boldness. 1 John 4:17,18.

They who have

Are known of Him. 1 Cor 8:3.

Are preserved by Him. Ps 145:20.

Are delivered by Him. Ps 91:14.

Partake of his mercy. Ex 20:6; Deut 7:9.

Have all things working for their good. Rom 8:28.

Persevere in. Jude 21.

Exhort one another to. Ps 31:23.

The love of the world is a proof of not having. 1 John 2:15.

They who love not others, are without. 1 John 4:20.

Hypocrites, without. Luke 11:42; John 5:42.

The uncharitable, without. 1 John 3:17.

God tries the sincerity of. Deut 13:3.

Promises connected with. Deut 11:13–15; Ps 69:36; Is 56:6,7; James 1:12.

LOVE TO MAN.

Is of God. 1 John 4:7.

Commanded by God. 1 John 4:21.

Commanded by Christ. John 13:34; 15:12; 1 John 3:23.

After the example of Christ. John 13:34; 15:12; Eph 5:2.

Taught by God. 1 Thess 4:9.

Faith works by. Gal 5:6.

A fruit of the Spirit. Gal 5:22; Col 1:8.

Purity of heart leads to. 1 Pet 1:22.

Explained. 1 Cor 13:4–7.

Is an active principle. 1 Thess 1:3; Heb 6:10.

Is an abiding principle. 1 Cor 13:8,13.

Is the second great commandment. Matt 22:37–39.

Is the purpose of the commandment. 1 Tim 1:5.

Supernatural gifts are nothing without. 1 Cor 13:1,2.

The greatest sacrifices are nothing without. 1 Cor 13:3.

Especially enjoined upon ministers. 1 Tim 4:12; 2 Tim 2:22.

Believers should

Put on. Col 3:14.

Follow after. 1 Cor 14:1.

Abound in. Phil 1:9; 1 Thess 3:12.

Continue in. 1 Tim 2:15; Heb 13:1.

Provoke each other to. 2 Cor 8:7; 9:2; Heb 10:24.

Be sincere in. Rom 12:9; 2 Cor 6:6; 8:8; 1 John 3:18.

Be unselfish in. 1 Cor 10:24; 13:5; Phil 2:4.

Be fervent in. 1 Pet 1:22; 4:8.

All things should be done with. 1 Cor 16:14.

Should be exhibited, toward

Believers. 1 Pet 2:17; 1 John 5:1.

Ministers. 1 Thess 5:13.

Our families. Eph 5:25; Titus 2:4.

Fellow-countrymen. Ex 32:32; Rom 9:2,3; 10:1.

Strangers. Lev 19:34; Deut 10:19.

Enemies. Ex 23:4,5; 2 Kin 6:22; Matt 5:44; Rom 12:14,20; 1 Pet 3:9.

All men. Gal 6:10.

Should be exhibited, in

Ministering to the wants of others. Matt 25:35; Heb 6:10.

Loving each other. Gal 5:13.

Relieving strangers. Lev 25:35; Matt 25:36.

Clothing the naked. Is 58:7; Matt 25:36.

Visiting the sick, etc. Job 31:16–22; James 1:27.

Sympathizing. Rom 12:15; 1 Cor 12:26.

Supporting the weak. Gal 6:2; 1 Thess 5:14.

Covering the faults of others. Prov 10:12; 1 Pet 4:8.

Forgiving insults. Eph 4:32; Col 3:13.

Forbearing. Eph 4:2.

Rebuking. Lev 19:17; Matt 18:15.

The love of God is a motive to. John 13:34; 1 John 4:11.

An evidence of

Being in the light. 1 John 2:10.

Discipleship with Christ. John 13:35.

Spiritual life. 1 John 3:14.

Is the fulfilling of the law. Rom 13:8–10; Gal 5:14; James 2:8.

Love to self is the measure of. Mark 12:33.

Is good and pleasant. Ps 133:1,2.

Is a bond of union. Col 2:2.

Is the bond of perfectness. Col 3:14.

Hypocrites, devoid of. 1 John 2:9,11; 4:20.

The wicked devoid of. 1 John 3:10.

LOVINGKINDNESS OF GOD, THE.

Is through Christ. Eph 2:7; Titus 3:4–6.

Described as

Great. Neh 9:17.

Excellent. Ps 36:7.

Good. Ps 69:16.

Marvellous. Ps 17:7; 31:21.

Abundant. Is 63:7.

Everlasting. Is 54:8.

Merciful. Ps 117:2.

Better than life. Ps 63:3.

Consideration of the dealings of God gives a knowledge of. Ps 107:43.

Believers

Betrothed in. Hos 2:19.

Drawn by. Jer 31:3.

Preserved by. Ps 40:11.

Revived by. Ps 119:88.

Comforted by. Ps 119:76.

Look for mercy through. Ps 51:1.

Receive mercy through. Is 54:8.

Are heard according to. Ps 119:149.

Are ever mindful of. Ps 26:3; 48:9.

Should expect, in affliction. Ps 42:7,8.

Crowned with. Ps 103:4.

Never utterly taken from believers. Ps 89:33; Is 54:10.

Former manifestations of, to be pleaded in prayer. Ps 25:6; 89:49.

Pray for the

Exhibition of. Ps 17:7; 143:8.

Continuance of. Ps 36:10.

Extension of. Gen 24:12; 2 Sam 2:6.

Praise God for. Ps 92:2; 138:2.

Proclaim. Ps 40:10.

LYING.

Forbidden. Lev 19:11; Col 3:9.

An abomination to God. Prov 6:16–19; 12:22.

A hindrance to prayer. Is 59:2,3.

The devil, the father of. John 8:44.

The devil prompts men to. 1 Kin 22:22; Acts 5:3.

Believers

Hate. Ps 119:163; Prov 13:5.

Avoid. Is 63:8; Zeph 3:13.
Reject those who practice. Ps 101:7.
Pray to be preserved from. Ps 119:29;
   Prov 30:8.
Unbecoming in rulers. Prov 17:7.
The evil of rulers listening to. Prov 29:12.
False prophets addicted to. Jer 23:14; Ezek
   22:28.
False witnesses addicted to. Prov 14:5,25.
Antinomians guilty of. 1 John 1:6; 2:4.
Hypocrites addicted to. Hos 11:12.
Hypocrites, a seed of. Is 57:4.
The wicked
   Addicted to, from their infancy. Ps
      58:3.
   Love. Ps 52:3.
   Delight in. Ps 62:4.
   Seek after. Ps 4:2.
   Prepare their tongues for. Jer 9:3,5.
   Bring forth. Ps 7:14.
   Give heed to. Prov 17:4.
A characteristic of the Apostasy. 2 Thess
   2:9; 1 Tim 4:2.
Leads to
   Hatred. Prov 26:28.
   Love of impure conversation. Prov
      17:4.
Often accompanied by gross crimes. Hos
   4:1,2.
Folly of concealing hatred by. Prov 10:18.
Vanity of getting riches by. Prov 21:6.
Shall be detected. Prov 12:19.
Poverty preferable to. Prov 19:22.
Excludes from heaven. Rev 21:27; 22:15.
They who are guilty of, shall be cast into
   hell. Rev 21:8.
Punishment for. Ps 5:6; 120:3,4; Prov
   19:5; Jer 50:36.

MALICE.

Springs from an evil heart. Matt 15:19,20;
   Gal 5:19.
Forbidden. 1 Cor 14:20; Eph 4:26,27; Col
   3:8.
A hindrance to growth in grace. 1 Pet
   2:1,2.
Incompatible with the worship of God.
   1 Cor 5:7,8.
Believers avoid. Job 31:29,30; Ps 35:12–
   14.
The wicked
   Speak with. 3 John 10.
   Live in. Titus 3:3.
   Conceive. Ps 7:14.
   Filled with. Rom 1:29.
   Visit believers with. Ps 83:3; Matt
      22:6.
Pray for those who injure you through.
   Matt 5:44.
Brings its own punishment. Ps 7:15,16.
God repays. Ps 10:14; Ezek 36:5.
Punishment of. Amos 1:11,12; Obad 10–
   15.

MARRIAGE.

Divinely instituted. Gen 2:24.
Designed for
   The happiness of man. Gen 2:18.
   Increasing the human population. Gen
      1:28; 9:1.
   Raising up godly seed. Mal 2:15.
   Preventing fornication. 1 Cor 7:2.
The expectation of the promised seed of
   the woman an incentive to, in the early
   age. Gen 3:15; 4:1.
Lawful in all. 1 Cor 7:2,28; 1 Tim 5:14.
Honorable for all. Heb 13:4.
Should be only in the Lord. 1 Cor 7:39.
Expressed by
   Joining together. Matt 19:6.
   Making affinity. 1 Kin 3:1.

Taking to wife. Ex 2:1.
Giving daughters to sons, and sons to
   daughters. Deut 7:3; Ezra 9:12.
Indissoluble during the joint lives of the
   parties. Matt 19:6; Rom 7:2,3; 1 Cor
   7:39.
Early introduction of polygamy. Gen 4:19.
Contracted in patriarchal age with near
   relations. Gen 20:12; 24:24; 28:2.
Often contracted by parents for children.
   Gen 24:49–51; 34:6,8.
Should be with consent of parents. Gen
   28:8; Judg 14:2,3.
Consent of the parties necessary to. Gen
   24:57,58; 1 Sam 18:20; 25:41.
Parents might refuse to give their children
   in. Ex 22:17; Deut 7:3.
The Jews
   Forbidden to contract, with their near
      relations. Lev 18:6.
   Forbidden to contract with idolaters.
      Deut 7:3,4; Josh 23:12; Ezra 9:11,12.
   Often contracted with foreigners.
      1 Kin 11:1; Neh 13:23.
   Sometimes guilty of polygamy. 1 Kin
      11:1,3.
   Careful in contracting for their
      children. Gen 24:2,3; 28:1,2.
   Betrothed themselves some time
      before. Deut 20:7; Judg 14:1,2,8;
      Matt 1:18.
   Contracted when young. Prov 2:17;
      Joel 1:8.
   Often contracted, in their own tribe.
      Ex 2:1; Num 36:6–13; Luke 1:5,27.
   Obliged to contract with a brother's
      wife who died without seed. Deut
      25:5; Matt 22:24.
   Considered being prevented from, a
      reproach. Is 4:1.
   Considered being prevented from, a
      cause of grief. Judg 11:38.
   Often punished by being prevented
      from. Jer 7:34; 16:9; 25:10.
   Were allowed divorce from, because of
      hardness of their hearts. Deut 24:1;
      Matt 19:7,8.
   Exempted from going to war
      immediately after. Deut 20:7.
Priest not to contract, with divorced or
   improper persons. Lev 21:7.
The high priest not to contract, with a
   widow or a divorced or profane person.
   Lev 21:14.
Contracted at the gate and before
   witnesses. Ruth 4:1,10,11.
Modes of demanding women in. Gen
   24:3,4; 34:6,8; 1 Sam 25:39,40.
Elder daughters usually given in, before the
   younger. Gen 29:26.
A dowry given to the woman's parents
   before. Gen 29:18; 34:12; 1 Sam
   18:27,28; Hos 3:2.
Celebrated
   With great rejoicing. Jer 33:11; John
      3:29.
   With feasting. Gen 29:22; Judg 14:10;
      Matt 22:2,3; John 2:1–10.
   For seven days. Judg 14:12.
A benediction pronounced after. Gen
   24:60; Ruth 4:11,12.
The bride
   Received presents before. Gen 24:53.
   Given a handmaid at. Gen 24:59;
      29:24,29.
   Adorned with jewels for. Is 49:18;
      61:10.
   Gorgeously apparelled. Ps 45:13,14.
   Attended by bridesmaids. Ps 45:9.
   Stood on the right of bridegroom. Ps
      45:9.

Called to forget her father's house. Ps
   45:10.
The bridegroom
   Adorned with ornaments. Is 61:10.
   Attended by many friends. Judg 14:11;
      John 3:29.
   Crowned with garlands. Song 3:11.
   Rejoiced over the bride. Is 62:5.
   Returned with the bride to his house
      at night. Matt 25:1–6.
Infidelity of those contracted in, punished
   as if married. Deut 22:23,24; Matt
   1:19.

MARTYRDOM.

Is death endured for the word of God, and
   testimony of Christ. Rev 6:9; 20:4.
Believers
   Forewarned of. Matt 10:21; 24:9; John
      16:2.
   Should not fear. Matt 10:28; Rev 2:10.
   Should be prepared for. Matt 16:24,25;
      Acts 21:13.
   Should resist sin to. Heb 12:4.
Reward of. Rev 2:10; 6:11.
Inflicted at the instigation of the devil. Rev
   2:10,13.
The Apostasy guilty of inflicting. Rev 17:6;
   18:24.
Of believers, shall be avenged. Luke
   11:50,51; Rev 18:20–24.

MEEKNESS.

Christ set an example of. Ps 45:4; Is 53:7;
   Matt 11:29; 21:5; 2 Cor 10:1; 1 Pet
   2:21–23.
His teaching. Matt 5:38–45.
A fruit of the Spirit. Gal 5:22,23.
Believers should
   Seek. Zeph 2:3.
   Put on. Col 3:12–13.
   Receive the word of God with. James
      1:21.
   Exhibit, in conduct, etc. James 3:13.
   Answer for their hope with. 1 Pet 3:15.
   Show to all men. Titus 3:2.
   Restore the erring with. Gal 6:1.
Precious in the sight of God. 1 Pet 3:4.
Ministers should
   Follow after. 1 Tim 6:11.
   Instruct opposers with. 2 Tim 2:24,25.
   Urge, on their people. Titus 3:1,2.
A characteristic of wisdom. James 3:17.
Necessary to a Christian walk. 1 Cor 6:7;
   Eph 4:1,2.
Those who are gifted with
   Are preserved. Ps 76:9.
   Are exalted. Ps 147:6; Matt 23:12.
   Are guided and taught. Ps 25:9.
   Are richly provided for. Ps 22:26.
   Are beautified with salvation. Ps
      149:4.
   Increase their joy. Is 29:19.
   Shall inherit the earth. Ps 37:11.
The gospel to be preached to those who
   possess. Is 61:1.
Blessedness of. Matt 5:5.

MERCY.

After the example of God. Luke 6:36.
Enjoined. 2 Kin 6:21–23; Hos 12:6; Rom
   12:20,21; Col 3:12.
To be engraved on the heart. Prov 3:3.
Characteristic of believers. Ps 37:26; Is
   57:1.
Should be shown
   With cheerfulness. Rom 12:8.
   To our brethren. Zech 7:9.
   To those that are in distress. Luke
      10:37.
   To the poor. Prov 14:31; Dan 4:27.

To backsliders. Luke 15:18–20; 2 Cor 2:6–8.

To animals. Prov 12:10.

Upholds the throne of kings. Prov 20:28.

Beneficial to those who exercise. Prov 11:17.

Blessedness of showing. Prov 14:21; Matt 5:7.

Hypocrites devoid of. Matt 23:23.

Denunciations against those devoid of. Hos 4:1,3; Matt 18:23–25; James 2:13.

MERCY OF GOD, THE.

Is part of His character. Ex 34:6,7; Neh 9:17; Ps 62:12; Jon 4:2,10,11; 2 Cor 1:3.

Described as

Great. Num 14:18; Is 54:7.

Rich. Eph 2:4.

Manifold. Neh 9:27; Lam 3:32.

Plenteous. Ps 86:5,15; 103:8.

Abundant. 1 Pet 1:3.

Sure. Is 55:3; Mic 7:20.

Everlasting. 1 Chr 16:34; Ps 89:28; 106:1; 107:1; 136:1–26.

Tender. Ps 25:6; 103:4; Luke 1:78.

New every morning. Lam 3:23.

High as heaven. Ps 36:5; 103:11.

Filling the earth. Ps 119:64.

Over all His works. Ps 145:9.

Manifested

In the sending of Christ. Luke 1:78.

In salvation. Titus 3:5.

In long-suffering. Lam 3:22; Dan 9:9.

To His people. Deut 32:43; 1 Kin 8:23.

To them that fear Him. Ps 103:17; Luke 1:50.

To returning backsliders. Jer 3:12; Hos 14:4; Joel 2:13.

To repentant sinners. Ps 32:5; Prov 28:13; Is 55:7; Luke 15:18–20.

To the afflicted. Is 49:13; 54:7.

To the fatherless. Hos 14:3.

To whom He will. Hos 2:23; Rom 9:15,18.

With everlasting kindness. Is 54:8.

A ground of hope. Ps 130:7; 147:11.

A ground of trust. Ps 52:8.

Should be

Sought for ourselves. Ps 6:2.

Sought for others. Gal 6:16; 1 Tim 1:2; 2 Tim 1:18.

Pleaded in prayer. Ps 6:4; 25:6; 51:1.

Rejoiced in. Ps 31:7.

Magnified. 1 Chr 16:34; Ps 115:1; 118:1–4,29; Jer 33:11.

MIRACLES.

Described as

Marvellous things. Ps 78:12.

Marvellous works. Ps 105:5; Is 29:14.

Signs and wonders. Jer 32:21; John 4:48; 2 Cor 12:12.

Manifest

The glory of God. John 11:4.

The glory of Christ. John 2:11; 11:4.

The works of God. John 9:3.

Were evidences of a divine commission. Ex 4:1–5; Mark 16:20.

Performed by Christ.. Matt 4:23–25; 11:2–6; 14:35,36; Luke 7:20–22; John 5:36; 6:2,26; 7:31; 12:18; Acts 2:22.

A gift of the Holy Spirit. 1 Cor 12:10.

Were performed

By the power of God. Ex 8:19; Acts 14:3; 15:12; 19:11.

By the power of Christ. Matt 10:1.

By the power of the Holy Spirit. Matt 12:28; Rom 15:19.

In the name of Christ. Matt 16:17; Acts 3:16; 4:30.

First preaching of the gospel confirmed by. Mark 16:20; Heb 2:4.

Should produce obedience. Deut 11:1–3; 29:2,3,9.

Instrumental to the early propagation of the gospel. Acts 8:6; Rom 15:18,19.

Faith required in

Those who performed. Matt 17:20; 21:21; John 2:23;14:12; Acts 3:16; 6:8.

Those for whom they were performed. Matt 9:28; 13:58; Mark 9:22–24; John 20:30,31; Acts 14:9.

Should be remembered. 1 Chr 16:12; Ps 105:5.

Should be told to future generations. Ex 10:2; Judg 6:13.

Insufficient of themselves, to produce conversion. Luke 16:31.

The wicked

Desire to see. Matt 27:42; Luke 11:29; 23:8.

Often acknowledge. John 11:47; Acts 4:16.

Do not understand. Ps 106:7.

Do not consider. Mark 6:52.

Forget. Neh 9:17; Ps 78:1,11.

Guilt of rejecting the evidence afforded by. Num 14:22; Matt 11:20–24; John 12:37; 15:24.

MIRACLES OF CHRIST, THE.

Water turned to wine. John 2:6–10.

Nobleman's son healed. John 4:46–53.

Centurion's servant healed. Matt 9:5–13.

Catches of fish. Luke 5:4–6; John 21:6.

Demons cast out. Matt 8:28–32; 9:32,33; 15:22–28; 17:14–18; Mark 1:23–27.

Peter's mother-in-law healed. Matt 8:14,15.

Lepers cleansed. Matt 8:3; Luke 17:14.

Paralytic healed. Mark 2:3–12.

Withered hand restored. Matt 12:10–13.

Handicapped man healed. John 5:5–9.

The dead raised to life. Matt 9:18; 19:23–25; Luke 7:12–15; John 11:11–44.

Flow of blood stopped. Matt 9:20–22.

The blind restored to sight. Matt 9:27–30; Mark 8:22–25; John 9:1–7.

The deaf and mute cured. Mark 7:32–35.

The multitude fed. Matt 14:15–21; 15:32–38.

His walking on the sea. Matt 14:25–27.

His allowing Peter to walk on the sea. Matt 14:29.

Tempest stilled. Matt 8:23–26; 14:32.

Sudden arrival of the ship. John 6:21.

Tribute money. Matt 17:27.

Woman healed of infirmity. Luke 13:11–13.

Dropsy cured. Luke 14:2–4.

Fig tree blighted. Matt 21:19.

Malchus healed. Luke 22:50,51.

Performed before the messengers of John the Baptist. Luke 7:21,22.

Many and different diseases healed. Matt 4:23,24; 14:14; 15:30; Mark 1:34; Luke 6:17–19.

His transfiguration. Matt 17:1–8.

His resurrection. Luke 24:6; John 10:18.

His appearance to His disciples, the doors being shut. John 20:19.

His ascension. Acts 1:9.

MIRACLES THROUGH EVIL AGENTS.

Performed through the power of Satan. 2 Thess 2:9; Rev 16:14.

Performed

In support of false religions. Deut 13:1–2.

By false christs. Matt 24:24.

By false prophets. Matt 24:24; Rev 19:20.

A mark of the end times. 2 Thess 2:3,9; Rev 13:13.

Not to be regarded. Deut 13:3.

Deceive the ungodly. 2 Thess 2:10–12; Rev 13:14; 19:20.

MIRACLES WROUGHT THROUGH SERVANTS OF GOD.

Moses and Aaron

Rod turned into a serpent. Ex 4:3; 7:10.

Rod restored. Ex 4:4.

Hand made leprous. Ex 4:6.

Hand healed. Ex 4:7.

Water turned into blood. Ex 4:9,30.

River turned into blood. Ex 7:20.

Frogs brought. Ex 8:6.

Frogs removed. Ex 8:13.

Lice brought. Ex 8:17.

Flies brought. Ex 8:21–24.

Flies removed. Ex 8:31.

Pestilence of stock. Ex 9:3–6.

Boils and sores brought. Ex 9:10,11.

Hail brought. Ex 9:23.

Hail removed. Ex 9:33.

Locusts brought. Ex 10:13.

Locusts removed. Ex 10:19.

Darkness brought. Ex 10:22.

The firstborn destroyed. Ex 12:29.

The Red Sea divided. Ex 14:21,22.

Egyptians overwhelmed. Ex 14:26–28.

Water sweetened. Ex 15:25.

Water from rock in Horeb. Ex 17:6.

Amalek defeated. Ex 17:11–13.

Destruction of Korah. Num 16:28–32.

Water from rock in Kadesh. Num 20:11.

Healing by bronze serpent. Num 21:8,9.

Joshua

Waters of Jordan divided. Josh 3:10–17.

Jordan restored to its course. Josh 4:18.

Jericho taken. Josh 6:6–20.

The sun and moon stopped. Josh 10:12–14.

Gideon

Midianites destroyed. Judg 7:16–22.

Samson

A lion killed. Judg 14:6.

Philistines killed. Judg 14:19; 15:15.

The gates of Gaza carried away. Judg 16:3.

Dagon's house pulled down. Judg 16:30.

Samuel

Thunder and rain in harvest. 1 Sam 12:18.

The prophet of Judah

Jeroboam's hand withered. 1 Kin 13:4.

The altar split. 1 Kin 13:5.

The withered hand restored. 1 Kin 13:6.

Elijah

Drought caused. 1 Kin 17:1; James 5:17.

Meal and oil multiplied. 1 Kin 17:14–16.

A child restored to life. 1 Kin 17:22,23.

Sacrifice consumed by fire. 1 Kin 18:36,38.

Men destroyed by fire. 2 Kin 1:10–12.

Rain brought. 1 Kin 18:41–45; James 5:18.

Waters of Jordan divided. 2 Kin 2:8.

Taken to heaven. 2 Kin 2:11.

Elisha

Waters of Jordan divided. 2 Kin 2:14.

Waters healed. 2 Kin 2:21,22.
Children torn by bears. 2 Kin 2:24.
Oil multiplied. 2 Kin 4:1–7.
Child restored to life. 2 Kin 4:32–35.
Naaman healed. 2 Kin 5:10,14.
Gehazi struck with leprosy. 2 Kin 5:27.
Axe head floats. 2 Kin 6:6.
Syrians smitten with blindness. 2 Kin 6:20.
Syrians restored to sight. 2 Kin 6:20.
A man restored to life. 2 Kin 13:21.
Isaiah
Hezekiah healed. 2 Kin 20:7.
Shadow put back on the dial. 2 Kin 20:11.
The seventy disciples
Various miracles. Luke 10:9,17.
The apostles
Many miracles. Acts 2:43; 5:12.
Peter
Lame man cured. Acts 3:7.
Death of Ananias. Acts 5:5.
Death of Sapphira. Acts 5:10.
The sick healed. Acts 5:15,16.
Aeneas made whole. Acts 9:34.
Tabitha restored to life. Acts 9:40.
Stephen
Great miracles. Acts 6:8.
Philip
Various miracles. Acts 8:6,7,13.
Paul
Elymas smitten with blindness. Acts 13:11.
Lame man cured. Acts 14:10.
An unclean spirit cast out. Acts 16:18.
Special miracles. Acts 19:11,12.
Eutychus restored to life. Acts 20:10–12.
Viper's bite made harmless. Acts 28:5.
Father of Publius healed. Acts 28:8.
Paul and Barnabas
Various miracles. Acts 14:3.

MISSIONARIES, ALL CHRISTIANS SHOULD BE AS.

After the example of Christ. Acts 10:38.
Women and children as well as men. Ps 8:2; Prov 31:26; Matt 21:15,16; Phil 4:3; 1 Tim 5:10; Titus 2:3–5; 1 Pet 3:1.
The zeal of idolaters should provoke to. Jer 7:18.
The zeal of hypocrites should provoke to. Matt 23:15.
An imperative duty. Judg 5:23; Luke 19:40.
The principle on which. 2 Cor 5:14,15.
However weak they may be. 1 Cor 1:27.
From their calling as believers. Ex 19:6; 1 Pet 2:9.
As faithful stewards. 1 Pet 4:10,11.
In youth. Ps 71:17; 148:12,13.
In old age. Deut 32:7; Ps 71:18.
In the family. Deut 6:7; Ps 78:5–8; Is 38:19; 1 Cor 7:16.
In their intercourse with the world. Matt 5:16; Phil 2:15,16; 1 Pet 2:12.
In first giving their own selves to the Lord. 2 Cor 8:5.
In declaring what God has done for them. Ps 66:16; 116:16–19.
In hating life for Christ. Luke 14:26.
In openly confessing Christ. Matt 10:32.
In following Christ. Luke 14:27; 18:22.
In preferring Christ above all relations. Luke 14:26; 1 Cor 2:2.
In joyfully suffering for Christ. Heb 10:34.
In forsaking all for Christ. Luke 5:11.
In a holy example. Matt 5:16; Phil 2:15; 1 Thess 1:7.
In holy conduct. 1 Pet 2:12.

In holy boldness. Ps 119:46.
In dedicating themselves to the service of God. Josh 24:15; Ps 27:4.
In devoting all property to God. 1 Chr 29:2,3,14,16; Eccl 11:1; Matt 6:19,20; Mark 12:44; Luke 12:33; 18:22,28; Acts 2:45; 4:32–34.
In holy conservation. Ps 37:30; Prov 10:31; 15:7; Eph 4:29; Col 4:6.
In talking of God and His works. Ps 71:24; 77:12; 119:27; 145:11,12.
In showing forth God's praises. Is 43:21.
In inviting forth God's praises. Is 43:21.
In inviting others to embrace the gospel. Ps 34:8; Is 2:3; John 1:46; 4:29.
In seeking the edification of others. Rom 14:19; 15:2; 1 Thess 5:11.
In admonishing others. 1 Thess 5:14; 2 Thess 3:15.
In reproving others. Lev 19:17; Eph 5:11.
In teaching and exhorting. Ps 34:11; 51:13; Col 3:16; Heb 3:13; 10:25.
In interceding for others. Col 4:3; Heb 13:18; James 5:16.
In aiding ministers in their labors. Rom 16:3,9; 2 Cor 11:9; Phil 4:14–16; 3 John 6.
In giving a reason for their faith. Ex 12:26,27; Deut 6:20,21; 1 Pet 3:15.
In encouraging the weak. Is 35:3,4; Rom 14:1; 15:1; 1 Thess 5:14.
In visiting and relieving the poor, the sick, etc. Lev 25:35; Ps 112:9; 2 Cor 9:9; Matt 25:36; Acts 20:35; James 1:27.
With a willing heart. Ex 35:29; 1 Chr 29:9,14.
With a superabundant liberality. Ex 36:5–7; 2 Cor 8:3.
Encouragement to. Prov 11:25,30; 1 Cor 1:27; James 5:19,20.
Blessedness of. Dan 12:3.

MONEY.

Gold and silver used as. Gen 13:2; Num 22:18.
Copper introduced as, by the Romans. Matt 10:9.
Units of, referred to by weight or piece. Gen 23:15; 33:19.
Of the Romans, stamped with the image of Caesar. Matt 22:20,21.
Usually taken by weight. Gen 23:16; Jer 32:10.
Pieces of mentioned
Talent of gold. 1 Kin 9:14; 2 Kin 23:23.
Talent of silver. 1 Kin 16:24; 2 Kin 5:22,23.
Shekel of silver. Judg 17:10; 2 Kin 15:20.
Half shekel or bekah. Ex 30:15.
Third of a shekel. Neh 10:32.
Fourth of a shekel. 1 Sam 9:8.
Gerah the twentieth of a shekel. Num 3:47.
Minah. Luke 19:13.
Denarius. Matt 20:2; Mark 6:37.
Penny. Matt 5:26; Luke 12:6.
Mite. Mark 12:42; Luke 21:2.
Of the Jews regulated by the standard of sanctuary. Lev 5:15; Num 3:47.
Was current with the merchants. Gen 23:16.
Jews forbidden to take usury for. Lev 25:37.
Changing of, a trade. Matt 21:12; John 2:15.
Uses of
For lands. Gen 23:9; Acts 4:37.
For slaves. Gen 37:28; Ex 21:21.
For merchandise. Gen 43:12; Deut 2:6.

For tribute. 2 Kin 23:33; Matt 22:19.
As wages. Ezra 3:7; Matt 20:2; James 5:4.
As offerings. 2 Kin 12:7–9; Neh 10:32.
As alms. 1 Sam 2:36; Acts 3:3,6.
As gifts within families. Job 42:11.
Power and usefulness of. Eccl 7:12; 10:19.
Love of, the root of all evil. 1 Tim 6:10.

MURDER.

Forbidden by Mosaic law. Ex 20:13; Deut 5:17.
The law made to restrain. 1 Tim 1:9.
Described as killing
With premeditation. Ex 21:14.
From hatred. Num 35:20,21; Deut 19:11.
By lying in wait. Num 35:20; Deut 19:11.
By an instrument of iron. Num 35:16.
By the blow of a stone. Num 35:17.
By a hand weapon of wood. Num 35:18.
Killing a thief in the day, counted as. Ex 22:3.
First mention of. Gen 4:8.
Represented as a sin crying to heaven. Gen 4:10; Heb 12:24; Rev 6:10.
The Jews often guilty of. Is 1:21.
Persons guilty of
Fearful and cowardly. Gen 4:14.
Wanderers and vagabonds. Gen 4:14.
Flee from God's presence. Gen 4:16.
Not protected in refuge cities. Deut 19:11,12.
Had no protection from altars. Ex 21:14.
Not to be pitied or spared. Deut 19:13.
Often committed by night. Neh 6:10; Job 24:14.
Imputed to the nearest city when the murderer was unknown. Deut 21:1–3.
Mode of clearing those suspected of. Deut 21:3–9; Matt 27:24.
To be proved by two witnesses at least. Num 35:30; Deut 19:11,15.
Punishment for
The curse of God. Gen 4:11.
Death. Gen 9:5,6; Ex 21:12; Num 35:16.
Not to be commuted. Num 35:32.
Inflicted by the nearest of kin. Num 35:19,21.
Forbidden. Gen 9:6; Ex 20:13; Deut 5:17; Rom 13:9.
Explained as anger. Matt 5:21,22.
Hatred is. 1 John 3:15.
Is a work for the flesh. Gal 5:21.
Comes from the heart. Matt 15:19.
Defiles the
Hands. Is 59:3.
Person and garments. Lam 4:13,14.
Land. Num 35:33; Ps 106:38.
Not concealed from God. Is 26:21; Jer 2:34.
Cries for vengeance. Gen 4:10.
God
Abominates. Prov 6:16,17.
Makes inquisition for. Ps 9:12.
Will avenge. Deut 32:43; 1 Kin 21:19; Hos 1:4.
Requires blood for. Gen 9:5; Num 35:33; 1 Kin 2:32.
Rejects the prayers of those guilty of. Is 1:15; 59:2,3.
Curses those guilty of. Gen 4:11.
Believers
Specially warned against. 1 Pet 4:15.
Want to avoid. Ps 51:14.

Should warn others against. Gen 37:22; Jer 26:15.
Connected with idolatry. Ezek 22:3,4; 2 Kin 3:27.
The wicked
  Filled with. Rom 1:29.
  Conspire. Gen 27:41; 37:18.
  Intent on. Jer 22:17.
  Lie in wait to commit. Ps 10:8–10.
  Swift to commit. Prov 1:16; Rom 3:15.
  Perpetrate. Job 24:14; Ezek 22:3.
  Have hands full of. Is 1:15.
  Encourage others to commit. 1 Kin 21:8–10; Prov 1:11.
Characteristic of the devil. John 8:44.
Punishment of. Gen 4:12–15; 9:6; Num 35:30; 2 Kin 9:36,37; Jer 19:4–9.
Punishment of, not commuted under the Law. Num 35:31.
Of believers, specially avenged. Deut 32:43; Matt 23:35; Rev 18:20,24.
Excludes from heaven. Gal 5:21; Rev 22:15.

MURMURING.

Forbidden. 1 Cor 10:10; Phil 2:14.
Against
  The sovereignty of God. Prov 19:3; Rom 9:19,20.
  The service of God. Mal 3:14.
  Christ. Luke 5:30; 15:2; 19:7; John 6:41–43,52.
  Ministers of God. Ex 17:3; Num 16:41.
  Disciples of Christ. Matt 7:2; Luke 5:30; 6:2.
Unreasonableness of. Lam 3:39.
Tempts God. Ex 17:2.
Provokes God. Num 14:2,11; Deut 9:8,22.
Believers cease from. Is 29:23,24.
Characteristic of the wicked. Jude 16.
Guilt of encouraging others in. Num 13:31–33; 14:36,37.
Punishment of. Num 11:1; 14:27–29; 16:45,46; Ps 106:25,26.

MUSIC.

Divided into
  Vocal. 2 Sam 19:35; Acts 16:25.
  Instrumental. Dan 6:18.
Designed to promote joy. Eccl 2:8,10.
Secular is vanity. Eccl 2:8,11.
Considered emotionally soothing. 1 Sam 16:14–17,23.
Effects produced on the prophets of old by. 1 Sam 10:5,6; 2 Kin 3:15.
Instruments of
  Cymbals. 1 Chr 16:5; Ps 150:5.
  Lyre. Dan 3:5.
  Flute. 1 Kin 1:40; Jer 48:36; Dan 3:5.
  Harp. Gen 4:21; Ps 137:2; Ezek 26:13.
  Pipe. Is 5:12;.
  Psaltery. Ps 33:2; 71:22.
  Tamborine. 1 Sam 10:5; Is 24:8.
  Timbrel. Ex 15:20; Ps 68:25.;150:4.
  Trumpet. 2 Kin 11:14; 2 Chr 29:27; Ps 98:6; Hos 5:8.
  Stringed intsruments. Is 14:11; Amos 5:23.
  Made of fir wood. 2 Sam 6:5.
  Made of almug wood. 1 Kin 10:12.
  Made of brass. 1 Cor 13:1.
  Made of silver. Num 10:2.
  Made of horns of animals. Josh 6:8.
  Many, with strings. Ps 33:2; 150:4.
  Early invention of. Gen 4:21.
  Invented by David. 1 Chr 23:5; 2 Chr 7:6.
The Jews celebrated for inventing. Amos 6:5.
Often expensively ornamented. Ezek 28:13.

Great diversity of. Eccl 2:8.
Appointed to be used in the temple. 1 Chr 16:4–6; 23:5,6; 25:1; 2 Chr 29:25.
Custom of sending away friends with. Gen 31:27.
The Jews used
  In sacred processions. 2 Sam 6:4,5,15; 1 Chr 13:6–8; 15:27,28.
  At laying foundation of temple. Ezra 3:9,10.
  At consecration of temple. 2 Chr 5:11–13.
  At coronation of kings. 2 Chr 23:11,13.
  At dedication of city walls. Neh 12:27,28.
  To celebrate victories. Ex 15:20; 1 Sam 18:6,7.
  In religious feasts. 2 Chr 30:21.
  In private entertainments. Is 5:12; Amos 6:5.
  In dances. Matt 11:17; Luke 15:25.
  In funeral ceremonies. Matt 9:23.
  In commemorating great men. 2 Chr 35:25.
Used in idol worship. Dan 3:5.
The movements of armies regulated by. Josh 6:8; 1 Cor 14:8.
Generally put aside in times of affliction. Ps 137:2–4; Dan 6:18.

NEW BIRTH, THE.

The corruption of human nature requires. John 3:6; Rom 8:7,8.
None can enter heaven without. John 3:3.
Effected by
  God. John 1:13; 1 Pet 1:3.
  Christ. 1 John 2:29.
  The Holy Spirit. John 3:6; Titus 3:5.
Through the instrumentality of
  The Word of God. James 1:18; 1 Pet 1:23.
  The resurrection of Christ. 1 Pet 1:3.
  The ministry of the gospel. 1 Cor 4:15.
Is of the will of God. James 1:18.
Is of the mercy of God. Titus 3:5.
Described as
  A new creation. 2 Cor 5:17; Gal 6:15; Eph 2:10.
  Newness of life. Rom 6:4.
  A spiritual resurrection. Rom 6:4–6; Eph 2:1,5; Col 2:12; 3:1.
  A new heart. Ezek 36:26.
  A new spirit. Ezek 11:19; Rom 7:6.
  Putting on the new man. Eph 4:24.
  The inward man. Rom 7:22; 2 Cor 4:16.
  Circumcision of the heart. Deut 30:6; Rom 2:29; Col 2:11.
  Partaking of the divine nature. 2 Pet 1:4.
  The washing of regeneration. Titus 3:5.
All believers partake of. Rom 8:16,17; 1 Pet 2:2; 1 John 5:1.
Produces
  Likeness to God. Eph 4:24; Col 3:10.
  Likeness to Christ. Rom 8:29; 2 Cor 3:18; 1 John 3:2.
  Knowledge of God. Col 3:10.
  Hatred of sin. 1 John 3:9; 5:18.
  Victory over the world. 1 John 5:4.
  Delight in God's law. Rom 7:22.
Evidenced by
  Faith in Christ. 1 John 5:1.
  Righteousness. 1 John 2:29.
  Brotherly love. 1 John 4:7.
Connected with adoption. John 1:12,13.
Manner of effecting—Illustrated. John 3:8.
  Preserves from Satan's devices. 1 John 5:18.

NEW COVENANT, THE.

Christ, the substance of. Is 42:6; 49:8.
Christ, the Mediator of. Heb 8:6; 9:15; 12:24.
Christ, the Messenger of. Mal 3:1.
God's making of. Jer 31:31–33; Rom 11:27; Heb 8:8–10,13.
Fulfilled in Christ. Luke 1:68–79.
Confirmed in Christ. Gal 3:17.
Ratified by the blood of Christ. Heb 9:11–14,16–23.
Is a covenant of peace. Is 54:9,10; Ezek 34:25; 37:26.
Is unalterable. Ps 89:34; Is 54:10; 59:21.
Is everlasting. Is 55:3; 61:8; Ezek 16:60–63; Heb 13:20.
All believers interested in. Heb 8:10.
The wicked have no interest in. Eph 2:12.
Punishment for despising. Heb 10:29,30.

OATHS.

The lawful purpose of, explained. Heb 6:16.
Antiquity of. Gen 14:22; 24:3,8.
Used for
  Confirming covenants. Gen 26:28; 31:44,53; 1 Sam 20:16,17.
  Deciding controversies in courts of law. Ex 22:11; Num 5:19; 1 Kin 8:31.
  Pledging allegiance to sovereigns. 2 Kin 11:4; Eccl 8:2.
  Binding to performance of sacred duties. Num 30:2; 2 Chr 15:14,15; Neh 10:29; Ps 132:2.
  Binding to performance of any particular act. Gen 24:3,4; 50:25; Josh 2:12.
Judicial form of administering. 1 Kin 22:16; Matt 26:63.
Often accompanied by raising up the hand. Gen 14:22; Dan 12:7; Rev 10:5,6.
Often accompanied by placing the hand under the thigh of the person sworn to. Gen 24:2,9; 47:29.
To be taken in fear and reverence. Eccl 9:2.
The Jews
  Forbidden to take, in name of idols. Josh 23:7.
  Forbidden to take, in the name of any created thing. Matt 5:34–36; James 5:12.
  Forbidden to take false. Lev 6:3; Zech 8:17.
  Forbidden to take rash, or unholy. Lev 5:4.
  To use God's name alone in. Deut 6:13; 10:20; Is 65:16.
  To take, in truth, judgment, etc. Jer 4:2.
  Generally respected the obligation of. Josh 9:19,20; 2 Sam 21:7; Ps 15:4; Matt 14:9.
  Fell into many errors respecting. Matt 23:16–22.
  Often guilty of rashly taking. Judg 21:7; Matt 14:7; 26:72.
  Often guilty of falsely taking. Lev 6:3; Jer 5:2; 7:9.
  Condemned for false. Zech 5:4; Mal 3:5.
  Condemned for profane. Jer 23:10; Hos 4:2.
Instances of rash
  Joshua, etc. Josh 9:15,16.
  Jephthah. Judg 11:30–36.
  Saul. 1 Sam 14:27,44.
  Herod. Matt 14:7–9.
  The Jews who sought to kill Paul. Acts 23:21.

Custom of swearing by the life of the king. Gen 42:15,16.

Expressions used as
By the fear of Isaac. Gen 31:53.
As the Lord lives. Judg 8:19; Ruth 3:13.
The Lord do so to me, and more also. Ruth 1:17.
God do so to thee, and more also. 1 Sam 3:17.
By the Lord. 2 Sam 19:7; 1 Kin 2:42.
Before God I lie not. Gal 1:20.
I call God for a witness. 2 Cor 1:23.
God is witness. 1 Thess 2:5.
I charge you by the Lord. 1 Thess 5:27.
As your soul lives. 1 Sam 1:26; 25:26.
God used, to show the immutability of his counsel. Gen 22:16; Num 6:17; 14:28.

OBEDIENCE TO GOD.

Commanded. Deut 13:4.
Without faith, is impossible. Heb 11:6.
Includes
Obeying His voice. Ex 19:5; Jer 7:23.
Obeying His law. Deut 11:27; Is 42:24.
Obeying Christ. Ex 23:21; 2 Cor 10:5.
Obeying the gospel. Rom 1:5; 6:17; 10:16,17.
Keeping His commandments. Eccl 12:13.
Submission to higher powers. Rom 13:1.
Better than sacrifice. 1 Sam 15:22.
Justification obtained by that of Christ. Rom 5:19.
Christ, an example of. Matt 3:15; John 15:20; Phil 2:5-8; Heb 5:8.
Angels engaged in. Ps 103:20.
A characteristic of believers. 1 Pet 1:14.
Believers elected to. 1 Pet 1:2.
Obligations to. Acts 4:19,20; 5:29.
Exhortations to. Jer 26:13; 38:20.
Should be
From the heart. Deut 11:13; Rom 6:17.
With willingness. Ps 18:44; Is 1:19.
Unreserved. Josh 22:2,3.
With resolve. Deut 28:14.
Constant. Phil 2:12.
Resolve upon. Ex 24:7; Josh 24:24.
Confess your failure in. Dan 9:10.
Prepare the heart for. 1 Sam 7:3; Ezra 7:10.
Pray to be taught. Ps 119:35; 143:10.
Promises to. Ex 23:22; 1 Sam 12:14; Is 1:19; Jer 7:23.
To be universal in the latter days. Dan 7:27.
Blessedness of. Deut 11:27; 28:1-13; Luke 11:28; James 1:25.
The wicked refuse. Ex 5:2; Neh 9:17.
Punishment of refusing. Deut 11:28; 28:15-68; Josh 5:6; Is 1:20.
Exemplified
Noah. Gen 6:22.
Abram. Gen 12:1-4; 22:3,12; Heb 11:8.
Israelites. Ex 12:28; 24:7.
Caleb, etc. Num 32:12.
Asa. 1 Kin 15:11.
Elijah. 1 Kin 17:5.
Hezekiah. 2 Kin 18:6.
Josiah. 2 Kin 22:2.
David. Ps 119:106.
Zerubbabel. Hag 1:12.
Joseph. Matt 1:24.
Wise men. Matt 2:12.
Zacharias, etc. Luke 1:6.
Paul. Acts 26:19.
Believers of Rome. Rom 16:19.

OFFENSE.

Occasions of, must arrive. Matt 18:7.
Occasions of, forbidden. 1 Cor 10:32; 2 Cor 6:3.
Persecution, a cause of, to mere professors. Matt 13:21; 24:10; 26:31.
The wicked take, at
The low station of Christ. Is 53:1-3; Matt 13:54-57.
Christ, as the stumbling stone. Is 8:14; Rom 9:33; 1 Pet 2:8.
Christ, as the bread of life. John 6:58-61.
Christ crucified. 1 Cor 1:23; Gal 5:11.
The righteousness of faith. Rom 9:32.
The necessity of inward purity. Matt 15:11,12.
Blessedness of not taking, at Christ. Matt 11:6.
Believers warned against taking. John 16:1.
Believers should
Be without. Phil 1:10.
Be cautious of giving. Ps 73:15; Rom 14:13; 1 Cor 8:9.
Have a conscience void of. Acts 24:16.
Cut off what causes, to themselves. Matt 5:29,30; Mark 9:43-47.
Not let their liberty cause for, to others. 1 Cor 8:9.
Use self-denial rather than cause. Rom 14:21; 1 Cor 8:13.
Avoid those who cause. Rom 16:17.
Reprove those who cause. Ex 32:21; 1 Sam 2:24.
Ministers should
Be cautious of giving. 2 Cor 6:3.
Remove that which causes. Is 57:14.
All things that cause, shall be gathered out of Christ's kingdom. Matt 13:41.
Denunciation against those who cause. Matt 18:7; Mark 9:42.
Punishment because of. Ezek 44:12; Mal 2:8,9; Matt 18:6,7.

OFFENSES AGAINST THE HOLY SPIRIT.

Exhortations against. Eph 4:30; 1 Thess 5:19.
Exhibited in
Tempting Him. Acts 5:9.
Vexing Him. Is 63:10.
Grieving Him. Eph 4:30.
Quenching Him. 1 Thess 5:19.
Lying to Him. Acts 5:3,4.
Resisting Him. Acts 7:51.
Undervaluing His gifts. Acts 8:19,20.
Danger of trifling with the Holy Spirit. Heb 6:4-6.
Doing despite to Him. Heb 10:29.
Disregarding His testimony. Neh 9:30.
Blasphemy against Him, unpardonable. Matt 12:31,32; 1 John 5:16.

OFFERINGS.

To be made to God alone. Ex 22:20; Judg 13:16.
Antiquity of. Gen 4:3,4.
Different kinds of
Burnt. Lev 1:3-17; Ps 66:15.
Sin. Lev 4:3-35; 6:25; 10:17.
Trespass. Lev 5:16-19; 6:6; 7:1.
Peace. Lev 3:1-17; 7:11.
Heave. Ex 7:14; 29:27,28; Num 15:19.
Wave. Ex 29:26; Lev 7:30.
Grain. Lev 2:1-16; Num 15:4.
Drink. Gen 35:14; Ex 29:40; Num 15:5.
Thank. Lev 7:12; 22:29; Ps 50:14.
Freewill. Lev 23:38; Deut 16:10; 23:23.
Incense. Ex 30:8; Mal 1:11; Luke 1:9.

Firstfruits. Ex 22:29; Deut 18:4.
Tithe. Lev 27:30; Num 18:21; Deut 14:22.
Gifts. Ex 35:22; Num 7:2-88.
Jealousy. Num 5:15.
Personal, for redemption. Ex 30:13,15.
Declared to be most holy. Num 18:9.
Required to be
Perfect. Lev 22:21.
The best of their kind. Mal 1:14.
Offered willingly. Lev 22:19.
Offered in righteousness. Mal 3:3.
Offered inclear conscience. Matt 5:23,24.
Brought in a clean vessel. Is 66:20.
Brought to the place appointed of God. Deut 12:6; Ps 27:6; Heb 9:9.
Laid before the altar. Matt 5:23,24.
Presented by the priest. Heb 5:1.
Brought without delay. Ex 22:29,30.
Unacceptable, without gratitude. Ps 50:8,14.
Could not make the offerer perfect. Heb 9:9.
Things forbidden as
The image of a harlot. Deut 23:18.
The price of a dog. Deut 23:18.
Whatever was blemished. Lev 22:20.
Whatever was imperfect. Lev 22:24.
Whatever was unclean. Lev 27:11,27.
Laid up in the temple. 2 Chr 31:12; Neh 10:37.
Hezekiah prepared chambers for. 2 Chr 31:11.
The Jews often
Slow in presenting. Neh 13:10-12.
Robbed God of. Mal 3:8.
Gave the worst they had as. Mal 1:8,13.
Rejected in, because of sin. Is 1:13; Mal 1:10.
Abhorred, on account of the sins of the priests. 1 Sam 2:17.
Presented to idols. Ezek 20:28.
Made by strangers, to be the same as by the Jews. Num 15:14-16.
Some offenses under the law, beyond the efficacy of. 1 Sam 3:14; Ps 51:16.

OFFERING, SIN.

Probable origin of. Gen 4:4,7.
Was offered
For unintentional. Lev 4:2,13,22,27.
At the consecration of priests. Ex 29:10,14; Lev 8:14.
At the consecration of Levites. Num 8:8.
At the expiration of a Nazarite's vow. Num 6:14.
On the day of atonement. Lev 16:3,9.
Was a most holy sacrifice. Lev 6:25,29.
Consisted of
A young bull for priests. Lev 4:3; 9:2,8; 16:3,6.
A young bull or he-goat for the congregation. Lev 4:14; 16:9; 2 Chr 29:23.
A male kid for a ruler. Lev 4:23.
A female kid or female lamb for a private person. Lev 4:28,32.
Sins of the offerer transferred to, by laying on of hands. Lev 4:4,15,24,29; 2 Chr 29:23.
Was killed in the same place as the burnt offering. Lev 4:24; 6:25.
The blood of
Brought by the priest into the tabernacle. Lev 4:5,16.
Sprinkled seven times before the Lord, outside the veil. Lev 4:6,17.
Put upon the horns of the altar of burnt offering. Lev 4:25,30.

Poured at the foot of the altar of burnt offering. Lev 4:7; 18:25,30; 9:9.

Fat of the inside, kidneys, burned on the altar of burnt offering. Lev 4:8–10, 19,26,31; 9:10.

When for a priest or the congregation, the flesh and hide, burned outside the camp. Lev 4:11,12,21; 6:30; 9:11.

Was eaten by the priests in a holy place, when its blood had not been brought into the tabernacle. Lev 6:26,29,30.

Aaron, etc. rebuked for burning and not eating that of the congregation. Lev 10:16–18; 9:9,15.

Whatever touched the flesh of, was rendered holy. Lev 6:27.

Garments sprinkled with the blood of, to be washed. Lev 6:27.

Laws respecting the vessels used for boiling the flesh of. Lev 6:28.

Was typical of Christ's sacrifice. 2 Cor 5:21; Heb 13:11–13.

PARABLES.

Remarkable parables of the Old Testament. Judg 9:8–15; 2 Sam 12:1–4; 14:5–7.

Parables of Christ

Wise and foolish builders. Matt 7:24–27.

Friends of the bridegroom. Matt 9:15.

New cloth and old garment. Matt 9:16.

New wine and old wineskins. Matt 9:17.

Unclean spirit. Matt 12:43.

Sower. Matt 13:3–23; Luke 8:5–15.

Tares. Matt 13:24–30,36–43.

Mustard seed. Matt 13:31,32; Luke 13:19.

Leaven. Matt 13:33.

Treasure hid in a field. Matt 13:44.

Pearl of great price. Matt 13:45,46.

Net cast into the sea. Matt 13:47–50.

What defiles a person. Matt 15:10–15.

Unmerciful servant. Matt 18:23–35.

Laborers hired. Matt 20:1–16.

Two sons. Matt 21:28–32.

Wicked vinedressers. Matt 21:33–45.

Marriage-feast. Matt 22:2–14.

Fig tree. Matt 24:32–34.

Master of the house watching. Matt 24:43.

Faithful, and evil servants. Matt 24:45–51.

Ten virgins. Matt 25:1–13.

Talents. Matt 25:14–30.

Kingdom, divided against itself. Mark 3:24.

House, divided against itself. Mark 3:25.

Strong man armed. Mark 3:27; Luke 11:21.

Seed growing secretly. Mark 4:26–29.

Lighted lamp. Mark 4:21; Luke 11:33–36.

Man taking a far journey. Mark 13:34–37.

Blind leading the blind. Luke 6:39.

Plank and speck. Luke 6:41,42.

Tree and its fruit. Luke 6:43–45.

Creditor and debtors. Luke 7:41–47.

Good Samaritan. Luke 10:30–37.

Persistent friend. Luke 11:5–9.

Rich fool. Luke 12:16–21.

Cloud and wind. Luke 12:54–57.

Barren fig tree. Luke 13:6–9.

Men invited to a feast. Luke 14:7–11.

Builder of a tower. Luke 14:28–30,33.

King going to war. Luke 14:31–33.

Seasoning of salt. Luke 14:34,35.

Lost sheep. Luke 15:3–7.

Lost piece of silver. Luke 15:8–10.

Prodigal son. Luke 15:11–32.

Unjust steward. Luke 16:1–8.

Rich man and Lazarus. Luke 16:19–31.

Persistent widow. Luke 18:1–8.

Pharisee and tax collector. Luke 18:9–14.

Minas. Luke 19:12–27.

Good Shepherd. John 10:1–6.

Vine and branches. John 15:1–5.

PARDON.

Promised. Is 1:18; Jer 31:34; 50:20; Heb 8:12

None without shedding of blood. Lev 17:11; Heb 9:22.

Legal sacrifices, ineffectual for. Heb 10:4.

Outward purifications, ineffectual for. Job 9:30,31; Jer 2:22.

Is granted

By God alone. Dan 9:9; Mark 2:7.

By Christ. Mark 2:5; Luke 7:48.

Through Christ. Luke 1:69,77; Acts 5:31; 13:38.

Through the blood of Christ. Matt 26:28; Rom 3:25; Col 1:14.

For the name's sake of Christ. 1 John 2:12.

According to the riches of grace. Eph 1:7.

On the exaltation of Christ. Acts 5:31.

Freely. Is 43:25.

Readily. Neh 9:17; Ps 86:5.

Abundantly. Is 55:7; Rom 5:20.

To those who confess their sins. 2 Sam 12:13; Ps 32:5; 1 John 1:9.

To those who repent. Acts 2:38.

To those who believe. Acts 10:43.

Should be preached in the name of Christ. Luke 24:47.

Exhibits the

Compassion of God. Mic 7:18,19.

Grace of God. Rom 5:15,16.

Mercy of God. Ex 34:7; Ps 51:1.

Goodness of God. 2 Chr 30:18; Ps 86:5.

Forbearance of God. Rom 3:25.

Lovingkindness of God. Ps 51:1.

Justice of God. 1 John 1:9.

Faithfulness of God. 1 John 1:9.

Expressed by

Forgiving transgression. Ps 32:1.

Removing transgression. Ps 103:12.

Blotting out transgression. Is 44:22.

Covering sin. Ps 32:1.

Casting sins into the sea. Mic 7:19.

Not imputing sin. Rom 4:8.

Not mentioning transgression. Ezek 18:22.

Remembering sins no more. Heb 10:17.

All believers enjoy. Col 2:13; 1 John 2:12.

Blessedness of. Ps 32:1; Rom 4:7.

Should lead to

Returning to God. Is 44:22.

Loving God. Luke 7:47.

Fearing God. Ps 130:4.

Praising God. Ps 103:2,3.

Ministers are appointed to proclaim. Is 40:1,2; 2 Cor 5:19.

Pray for

Yourselves. Ps 25:11,18; 51:1; Matt 6:12; Luke 11:4.

Others. James 5:15; 1 John 5:16.

Encouragement to pray for. 2 Chr 7:14.

Withheld from

The unforgiving. Mark 11:26; Luke 6:37.

The unbelieving. John 8:21,24.

The impenitent. Luke 13:2–5.

Blasphemers against the Holy Spirit. Matt 12:32; Mark 3:28,29.

Apostates. Heb 10:26,27.

PARENTS.

Receive their children from God. Gen 33:5; 1 Sam 1:27; Ps 127:3.

Their duty to their children is

To love them. Titus 2:4.

To bring them to Christ. Matt 19:13,14.

To train them up for God. Prov 22:6; Eph 6:4.

To instruct them in God's Word. Deut 4:9; 11:19; Is 38:19.

To tell them of God's judgments. Joel 1:3.

To tell them of the miraculous works of God. Ex 10:2; Ps 78:4.

To command them to obey God. Deut 32:46; 1 Chr 28:9.

To bless them. Gen 48:15; Heb 11:20.

To pity them. Ps 103:13.

To provide for them. Job 42:15; 2 Cor 12:14; 1 Tim 5:8.

To rule them. 1 Tim 3:4,12.

To correct them. Prov 13:24; 19:18; 23:13; 29:17; Heb 12:7.

Not to provoke them. Eph 6:4; Col 3:21.

Not to make unholy marriages for them. Gen 24:1–4; 28:1,2.

Wicked children, a cause of grief to. Prov 10:1; 17:25.

Should pray for their children

For their spiritual welfare. Gen 17:18; 1 Chr 29:19.

When in temptation. Job 1:5.

When in sickness. 2 Sam 12:16; Mark 5:23; John 4:46,49.

When faithful

Are blessed by their children. Prov 31:28.

Leave a blessing to their children. Ps 112:2; Prov 11:21; Is 65:23.

Sins of, visited on their children. Ex 20:5; Is 14:20; Lam 5:7.

Negligence of, sorely punished. 1 Sam 3:13.

When wicked

Instruct their children in evil. Jer 9:14; 1 Pet 1:18.

Set a bad example to their children. Ezek 20:18; Amos 2:4.

PATIENCE.

God, is the God of. Rom 15:5.

Christ, an example of. Is 53:7; Matt 27:14; Acts 8:32.

Commanded. Titus 2:2; 2 Pet 1:6.

Should have its perfect work. James 1:4.

Trials of believers lead to. Rom 5:3; James 1:3.

Produces

Hope. Rom 15:4.

Suffering with, for well-doing, is acceptable with God. 1 Pet 2:20.

To be exercised

Running the race set before us. Heb 12:1.

Bringing forth fruits. Luke 8:15.

Well-doing. Rom 2:7; Gal 6:9.

Waiting for God. Ps 37:7; 40:1.

Waiting for Christ. 1 Cor 1:7; 2 Thess 3:5.

Waiting for the hope of the gospel. Rom 8:25; Gal 5:5.

Waiting for God's salvation. Lam 3:26.

Bearing the yoke. Lam 3:27.

In tribulation. Luke 21:19; Rom 12:12.

Necessary to the inheritance of the promises. Heb 6:12; 10:36.

They who are in authority, should exercise. Matt 18:26; Acts 26:3.

Ministers should follow after. 1 Tim 6:11.

Ministers approved by. 2 Cor 6:4.

Should be accompanied by
Godliness. 2 Pet 1:6.
Faith. 2 Thess 1:4; Heb 6:12; Rev 13:10.
Self-control. 2 Pet 1:6.
Long-suffering. Col 1:11.
Joyfulness. Col 1:11.

Believers strengthened to all. Col 1:11.

Commended. Eccl 7:8; Rev 2:2,3.

PEACE.

God is the Author of. Ps 147:14; Is 45:7; 1 Cor 14:33.

Results from
Heavenly wisdom. James 3:17.
The government of Christ. Is 2:4.
Praying for rulers. 1 Tim 2:2.
Seeking the peace of those with whom we dwell. Jer 29:7.

Necessary to the enjoyment of life. Ps 34:12,14; 1 Pet 3:10,11.

God bestows upon those who
Obey him. Lev 26:6.
Please him. Ps 16:7.
Endure his chastisements. Job 5:17,23,24.

The fruit of righteousness should be sown in. James 3:18.

Believers should
Love. Zech 8:19.
Seek. Ps 34:14; 1 Pet 3:11.
Follow. 2 Tim 2:22.
Follow the things which make for. Rom 14:19.
Cultivate. Ps 120:7.
Speak. Esth 10:3.
Live in. 2 Cor 13:11.
Have, with each other. Mark 9:50; 1 Thess 5:13.
Endeavour to have with all men. Rom 12:18; Heb 12:14.

Exhort others to. Gen 45:24.

Ministers should exhort to. 2 Thess 3:12.

Advantages of. Prov 17:1; Eccl 4:6.

Blessedness of. Ps 133:1.

Blessedness of promoting. Matt 5:9.

The wicked
Hypocritically speak. Ps 28:3.
Speak not. Ps 35:20.
Enjoy not. Is 48:22; Ezek 7:25.
Opposed to. Ps 120:7.
Hate. Ps 120:6.

Shall abound in the latter days. Is 2:4; 11:13; 32:18.

PEACE, SPIRITUAL.

God is the God of. Rom 15:33; 2 Cor 13:11; 1 Thess 5:23; Heb 13:20.

God ordains. Is 26:12.

God speaks, to His believers. Ps 85:8.

Christ is the Lord of. 2 Thess 3:16.

Christ is the Prince of. Is 9:6.

Christ gives. 2 Thess 3:16.

Christ guides into the way of. Luke 1:79.

Christ is our. Eph 2:14.

Is through the atonement of Christ. Is 53:5; Eph 2:14,15; Col 1:20.

Granted by Christ. John 14:27.

Preached
By Christ. Eph 2:17.
Through Christ. Acts 10:36.
By ministers. Is 52:7; Rom 10:15.

Announced by angels. Luke 2:14.

Follows upon justification. Rom 5:1.

A fruit of the Spirit. Rom 14:17; Gal 5:22.

Divine wisdom is the way of. Prov 3:17.

Accompanies
Faith. Rom 15:13.
Righteousness. Is 32:17.
Acquaintance with God. Job 22:21.
The love of God's law. Ps 119:165.
Spiritual-mindedness. Rom 8:6.

Established by covenant. Is 54:10; Ezek 34:25; Mal 2:5.

Promised to
The Gentiles. Zech 9:10.
Believers. Ps 72:3,7; Is 55:12.
The meek. Ps 37:11.
Those who confide in God. Is 26:3.
Returning backsliders. Is 57:18,19.

We should love. Zech 8:19.

Believers
Have in Christ. John 16:33.
Have, with God. Is 27:5; Rom 5:1.
Enjoy. Ps 119:165.
Rest in. Ps 4:8.
Blessed with. Ps 29:11.
Kept in perfect. Is 26:3.
Ruled by. Col 3:15.
Guarded by. Phil 4:7.
Die in. Ps 37:37; Luke 2:29.
Wish, to each other. Gal 6:16; Phil 1:2; Col 1:2; 1 Thess 1:1.

Of believers
Great. Ps 119:165; Is 54:13.
Abundant. Ps 72:7; Jer 33:6.
Secure. Job 34:29.
Passes all understanding. Phil 4:7.
Consummated after death. Is 57:2.

The gospel is good tidings of. Rom 10:15.

The wicked
Know not the way of. Is 57:2; Rom 3:17.
Know not the things of. Luke 19:42.
Promise, to themselves. Deut 29:19.
Are promised, by false teachers. Jer 6:14.
There is none for. Is 48:22; 57:21.

Supports under trials. John 14:27; 16:33.

PERFECTION.

Is of God. Ps 18:32; 138:8.

All believers have, in Christ. 1 Cor 2:6; Phil 3:15; Col 2:10.

God's perfection the standard of. Matt 5:48.

Implies
Entire devotedness. Matt 19:21.
Purity and holiness in speech. James 3:2.

Believers commanded to aim at. Gen 17:1; Deut 18:13.

Believers claim not. Job 9:20; Phil 3:12.

Believers follow after. Prov 4:18; Phil 3:12.

Ministers appointed to lead believers to. Eph 4:12; Col 1:28.

Exhortation to. 2 Cor 7:1; 13:11.

Impossibility of attaining to. 2 Chr 6:36; Ps 119:96.

The Word of God is
The rule of. James 1:25.
Designed to lead us to. 2 Tim 3:16,17.

Love is the bond of. Col 3:14.

Patience leads to. James 1:4.

Pray for. Heb 13:20,21; 1 Pet 5:10.

The Church shall attain to. John 17:23; Eph 4:13.

Blessedness of. Ps 37:37; Prov 2:21.

PERSECUTION.

Christ suffered. Ps 69:26; John 5:16.

Christ voluntarily submitted to. Is 50:6.

Christ was patient under. Is 53:7.

Believers may expect. Mark 10:30; Luke 21:12; John 15:20.

Believers suffer, for the sake of God. Jer 15:15.

Of believers, is a persecution of Christ. Zech 2:8; Acts 9:4,5.

All that live godly in Christ, shall suffer. 2 Tim 3:12.

Originates
Hatred to God and Christ. John 15:20,24.
Hatred to the gospel. Matt 13:21.
Pride. Ps 10:2.
Mistaken zeal. Acts 13:50; 26:9–11.

Is inconsistent with the spirit of the gospel. Matt 26:52.

Men by nature addicted to. Gal 4:29.

Preacher of the gospel subject to. Gal 5:11.

Is sometimes to death. Acts 22:4.

God forsakes not His believers under. 2 Cor 4:9.

God delivers out of. Dan 3:25,28; 2 Cor 1:10; 2 Tim 3:11.

Cannot be separated from Christ. Rom 8:35.

Lawful means may be used to escape. Matt 2:13; 10:23; 12:14,15.

Believers suffering, should
Commit themselves to God. 1 Pet 4:19.
Exhibit patience. 1 Cor 4:12.
Rejoice. Matt 5:12; 1 Pet 4:13.
Glorify God. 1 Pet 4:16.
Pray for deliverance. Ps 7:1; 119:86.
Pray for those who inflict. Matt 5:44.
Return blessing for. Rom 12:14.

The hope of future blessedness supports under. 1 Cor 15:19,32; Heb 10:34,35.

Blessedness of enduring, for Christ's sake. Matt 5:10; Luke 6:22.

Pray for those suffering. 2 Thess 3:2.

Hypocrites cannot endure. Matt 4:17.

False teachers shrink from. Gal 6:12.

The wicked
Addicted to. Ps 10:2; 69:26.
Active in. Ps 143:3; Lam 4:19.
Encourage each other in. Ps 71:11.
Rejoice in its success. Ps 13:4; Rev 11:10.
Punishment for. Ps 7:13; 2 Thess 1:6.
Illustrated. Matt 21:33–39.

Spirit of—Exemplified
Pharaoh, etc. Ex 1:8–14.
Saul. 1 Sam 26:18.
Jezebel. 1 Kin 19:2.
Zedekiah, etc. Jer 38:4–6.
Chaldeans. Dan 3:8–30.
Pharisees. Matt 12:14.
Jews. John 5:16; 1 Thess 2:15.
Herod. Acts 12:1.
Gentiles. Acts 14:5.
Paul. Phil 3:6; 1 Tim 1:13.

Suffering of—Exemplified
Micaiah. 1 Kin 22:27.
David. Ps 119:161.
Jeremiah. Jer 32:2.
Daniel. Dan 6:5–17.
Peter, etc. Acts 4:3.
Apostles. Acts 5:18.
The Prophets. Acts 7:52.
The Church. Acts 8:1.
Paul and Barnabas. Acts 13:50.
Paul and Silas. Acts 16:23.
Hebrews. Heb 10:33.
Believers of old. Heb 11:36.

PERSEVERANCE.

An evidence of reconciliation with God. Col 1:21–23.

An evidence of belonging to Christ. John 8:31; Heb 3:6,14.

A characteristic of believers. Prov 4:18.

To be manifested in
Seeking God. 1 Chr 16:11.
Waiting upon God. Hos 12:6.
Prayer. Rom 12:12; Eph 6:18.
Well-doing. Rom 2:7; 2 Thess 3:13.
Continuing in the faith. Acts 14:22;
Col 1:23; 2 Tim 4:7.
Holding fast hope. Heb 3:6.
Maintained through
The power of God. Ps 37:24; Phil 1:6.
The power of Christ. John 10:28.
The intercession of Christ. Luke
22:31,32; John 17:11.
The fear of God. Jer 32:40.
Faith. 1 Pet 1:5.
Promised to believers. Job 17:9.
Leads to increase of knowledge. John
8:31,32.
In well-doing
Leads to assurance of hope. Heb
6:10,11.
Is not in vain. 1 Cor 15:58; Gal 6:9.
Ministers should exhort to. Acts 13:43;
14:22.
Encouragement to. Heb 12:2,3.
Promises to. Matt 10:22; 24:13; Rev 2:26–
28.
Blessedness of. James 1:25.
Lack of
Excludes from the benefits of the
gospel. Heb 6:4–6.
Punished. John 15:6; Rom 11:22.

PHARISEES, THE.

A sect of the Jews. Acts 15:5.
The strictest observers of the Mosaic
ritual. Acts 26:5.
By descent, especially esteemed.
Acts 23:6.
Character of
Zealous of the law. Acts 15:5; Phil 3:5.
Zealous of tradition. Mark 7:3,5–8;
Gal 1:14.
Outwardly moral. Luke 18:11; Phil
3:5,6.
Rigid in fasting. Luke 5:33; 18:12.
Active in proselytising. Matt 23:15.
Self-righteous. Luke 16:15; 18:9.
Avaricious. Matt 23:14; Luke 16:14.
Ambitious of precedence. Matt 23:6.
Fond of public salutations. Matt 23:7.
Fond of distinguished titles. Matt
23:7–10.
Particular in paying all dues. Matt
23:23.
Oppressive. Matt 23:4.
Cruel in persecuting. Acts 9:1,2.
Believed in the resurrection, etc. Acts
23:8.
Made broad their phylacteries. Matt 23:5.
Their opinions, a standard for others. John
7:48.
Many priests and Levites were of. John
1:19,24.
Many rulers, lawyers, and scribes were of.
John 3:1; Acts 5:34; 23:9.
Had disciples. Luke 5:33; Acts 22:3.
Some came to John for baptism. Matt 3:7.
As a body, rejected John's baptism. Luke
7:30.
Christ
Often invited by. Luke 7:36; 11:37.
Condemned by, for associating with
sinners. Matt 9:11; Luke 7:39;
15:1,2.
Asked for signs by. Matt 12:38; 16:1.
Tested by, with questions about the
law. Matt 19:3; 22:15,16,35.
Watched by, for evil. Luke 6:7.
Offended, by His doctrine. Matt 15:12;
21:45; Luke 16:14.

Declared the imaginary righteousness
of, to be insufficient for salvation.
Matt 5:20.
Declared the doctrines of, to be
hypocrisy. Matt 16:6,11,12; Luke
12:1.
Denounced woes against. Matt 23:13–
33.
Called, an evil and adulterous
generation. Matt 12:39.
Called, serpents and generation of
vipers. Matt 23:33.
Called, fools and blind guides. Matt
23:17,24.
Compared, to whited sepulchres. Matt
23:27.
Compared, to graves that appear not.
Luke 11:44.
Left Judea for a time on account of.
John 4:1–3.
Imputed Christ's miracles to Satan's
power. Matt 9:34; 12:24.
Sent officers to apprehend Christ. John
7:32,45.
Often sought to destroy Christ. Matt
12:14; 21:46; John 11:47,53,57.

POOR, THE.

Made by God. Job 34:19; Prov 22:2.
Are such by God's appointment. 1 Sam
2:7; Job 1:21.
Condition of, often results from
Sloth. Prov 20:13.
Bad company. Prov 28:19.
Drunkenness and gluttony. Prov
23:21.
God
Regards equally with the rich. Job
34:19.
Forgets not. Ps 9:18.
Hears. Ps 69:33; Is 41:17.
Maintains the right of. Ps 140:12.
Delivers. Job 36:15; Ps 35:10.
Protects. Ps 12:5; 109:31.
Exalts. 1 Sam 2:8; Ps 107:41.
Provides for. Ps 68:10; 146:7.
Despises not the prayer of. Ps 102:17.
Is the refuge of. Ps 14:6.
Will slways exist. Deut 15:11; Zeph 3:12;
Matt 26:11.
May be
Rich in faith. James 2:5.
Generous. Mark 12:42; 2 Cor 9:12.
Wise. Prov 28:11.
Upright. Prov 19:1.
Christ lived as one of. Matt 8:20.
Christ preached to. Luke 4:18.
Christ delivers. Ps 72:12.
Offerings of, acceptable to God. Mark
12:42–44; 2 Cor 8:2,12.
Should
Rejoice in God. Is 29:19.
Hope in God. Job 5:16.
Commit themselves to God. Ps 10:14.
When converted, rejoice in their
exaltation. James 1:9.
Provided for under the Law. Ex 23:11;
Lev 19:9,10.
Neglect towards is
A neglect of Christ. Matt 25:42–45.
Inconsistent with love to God. 1 John
3:17.
A proof of unbelief. James 2:15–17.
Rob not. Prov 22:22.
Be not unjust toward. Ex 23:6.
Take no usury from. Lev 25:36.
Harden not the heart against. Deut 15:7.
Do not withhold generosity. Deut 15:7.
Oppress not. Lev 25:39,43; Deut 24:14;
Zech 7:10.
Despise not. Prov 14:21; James 2:2–4.

Relieve. Lev 25:35; Matt 19:21.
Defend. Ps 82:3,4.
Do justice to. Ps 82:3; Jer 22:3,16.
A care for
Is characteristic of believers. Ps 112:9;
2 Cor 9:9.
Is a fruit of repentance. Luke 3:11.
Should be urged. 2 Cor 8:7,8; Gal
2:10.
Give to
Not grudgingly. Deut 15:10; 2 Cor 9:7.
Generoulsy. Deut 14:29; 15:8,11.
Cheerfully. 2 Cor 8:12; 9:7.
Without ostentation. Matt 6:1.
Specially if believers. Rom 12:13; Gal
6:10.
Pray for. Ps 74:19,21.
They who in faith, relieve
Are happy. Prov 14:21.
Are blessed. Deut 15:10; Ps 41:1; Prov
22:9; Acts 20:35.
Have the favor of God. Heb 13:16.
Have promises. Prov 28:27; Luke
14:13,14.
By oppressing, God is reproached. Prov
14:31.
By mocking, God is reproached. Prov 17:5.
The wicked
Care not for. John 12:6.
Oppress. Job 24:4–10; Ezek 18:12.
Regard not the cause of. Prov 29:7.
Sell. Amos 2:6.
Crush. Amos 4:1.
Tread down. Amos 5:11.
Grind the faces of. Is 3:15.
Devour. Hab 3:14.
Persecute. Ps 10:2.
Defraud. Amos 8:5,6.
Despise the counsel of. Ps 14:6.
Guilt of defrauding. James 5:4.
Punishment for
Oppressing. Prov 22:16; Ezek
22:29,31.
Spoiling. Is 3:13–15; Ezek 18:13.
Refusing to assist. Job 22:7,10; Prov
21:13.
Acting unjustly towards. Job 20:19,29;
22:6,10; Is 10:1–3; Amos 5:11,12.

POWER OF CHRIST, THE.

As the Son of God, is the power of God.
John 5:17–19; 10:28–30.
As man, is from the Father. Acts 10:38.
Described as
Supreme. Eph 1:20,21; 1 Pet 3:22.
Unlimited. Matt 28:18.
Over all flesh. John 17:2.
Over all things. John 3:35; Eph 1:22.
Glorious. 2 Thess 1:9.
Everlasting. 1 Tim 6:16.
Is able to subdue all things. Phil 3:21.
Exhibited in
Creation. John 1:3,10; Col 1:16.
Upholding all things. Col 1:17; Heb
1:3.
Salvation. Is 63:1; Heb 7:25.
His teaching. Matt 7:28,29; Luke 4:32.
Working miracles. Matt 8:27; Luke
5:17.
Enabling others to work miracles.
Matt 10:1; Mark 16:17,18; Luke
10:17.
Forgiving sins. Matt 9:6; Acts 5:31.
Giving spiritual life. John 5:21,25,26.
Giving eternal life. John 17:2.
Raising the dead. John 5:28,29.
Raising Himself from the dead. John
2:19–21; 10:18.
Overcoming the world. John 16:33.
Overcoming Satan. Col 2:15; Heb
2:14.

Destroying the works of Satan. 1 John
3:8.
Ministers should make known. 2 Pet 1:16.
Believers
Made willingly by. Ps 110:3.
Helped by. Heb 2:18.
Strengthened by. Phil 4:13; 2 Tim 4:17.
Preserved by. 2 Tim 1:12; 4:18.
Bodies of, shall be changed by. Phil
3:21.
Rests upon believers. 2 Cor 12:9.
Present in the assembly of believers. 1 Cor
5:4.
Shall be specially manifested at his second
coming. Mark 13:26; 2 Pet 1:16.
Shall subdue all power. 1 Cor 15:24.
The wicked shall be destroyed by. Ps 2:9;
Is 11:4; 63:3; 2 Thess 1:9.

POWER OF GOD, THE.

Is one of His attributes. Ps 62:11.
Expressed by the
Voice of God. Ps 29:3,5; 68:33.
Finger of God. Ex 8:19; Ps 8:3.
Hand of God. Ex 9:3,15; Is 48:13.
Arm of God. Job 40:9; Is 52:10.
Thunder of His power. Job 26:14.
Described as
Great. Ps 79:11; Nah 1:3.
Strong. Ps 89:13; 136:12.
Glorious. Ex 15:6; Is 63:12.
Mighty. Job 9:4; Ps 89:13.
Everlasting. Is 26:4; Rom 1:20.
Sovereign. Rom 9:21.
Effectual. Is 43:13; Eph 3:7.
Irresistible. Deut 32:39; Dan 4:35.
Incomparable. Ex 15:11,12; Deut 3:24;
Job 40:9; Ps 89:8.
Unsearchable. Job 5:9; 9:10.
Incomprehensible. Job 26:14; Eccl
3:11.
Can accomplish anything. Gen 18:14; Jer
32:27; Matt 19:26.
Can save by many or by few. 1 Sam 14:6.
Is the source of all strength. 1 Chr 29:12;
Ps 68:35.
Exhibited in
Creation. Ps 102:25; Jer 10:12.
Establishing and governing all things.
Ps 65:6; 66:7.
The miracles of Christ. Luke 11:20.
The resurrection of Christ. 2 Cor 13:4;
Col 2:12.
The resurrection of believers. 1 Cor
6:14.
Making the gospel effectual. Rom
1:16; 1 Cor 1:18,24.
Delivering His people. Ps 106:8.
The destruction of the wicked. Ex
9:16; Rom 9:22.
Believers
Long for exhibitions. Ps 63:1,2.
Have confidence in. Jer 20:11.
Receive increase of grace by. 2 Cor 9:8.
Strengthened by. Eph 6:10; Col 1:11.
Upheld by. Ps 37:17; Is 41:10.
Supported in affliction by. 2 Cor 6:7;
2 Tim 1:8.
Delivered by. Neh 1:10; Dan 3:17.
Exalted by. Job 36:22.
Kept by, to salvation. 1 Pet 1:5.
Exerted on their behalf. 2 Cor 16:9; 2 Cor
13:4; Eph 1:19; 3:20.
The faith of believers stands in. 1 Cor 2:5.
Should be
Acknowledged. 1 Chr 29:11; Is 33:13.
Pleaded in prayer. Ps 79:11; Matt 6:13.
Feared. Jer 5:22; Matt 10:28.
Magnified. Ps 21:13; Jude 25.
Efficiency of ministers is through. 1 Cor
3:6–8; Gal 2:8; Eph 3:7.

The wicked
Know not. Matt 22:29.
Have against them. Ezra 8:22.
Shall be destroyed by. Luke 12:5.
The heavenly host magnify. Rev 4:11;
5:13; 11:17.

POWER OF THE HOLY SPIRIT, THE.

Is the power of God. Matt 12:28; Luke
11:20.
Christ commenced His ministry in. Luke
4:14.
Christ wrought His miracles by. Matt
12:28.
Exhibited in
Creation. Gen 1:2; Job 26:13; Ps
104:30.
The conception of Christ. Luke 1:35.
Raising Christ from the dead. 1 Pet
3:18.
Giving spiritual life. Ezek 37:11–14;
Rom 8:11.
Working miracles. Rom 15:19.
Making the gospel efficacious. 1 Cor
2:4; 1 Thess 1:5.
Overcoming all difficulties. Zech
4:6,7.
Believers
Upheld by. Ps 51:12.
Strengthened by. Eph 3:16.
Enable to speak the truth boldly by.
Mic 3:8; Acts 6:5,10; 2 Tim 1:7,8.
Helped in prayer by. Rom 8:26.
Abound in hope by. Rom 15:13.
Qualifies ministers. Luke 24:49; Acts 1:8.
God's Word the instrument of. Eph 6:17.

PRAISE.

God is worthy of. 2 Sam 22:4.
Christ is worthy of. Rev 5:12.
God is glorified by. Ps 22:23; 50:23.
Offered to Christ. John 12:13.
Acceptable through Christ. Heb 13:15.
Is due to God on account of
His majesty. Ps 96:1,6; Is 24:14.
His glory. Ps 138:5; Ezek 3:12.
His excellency. Ex 15:7; Ps 148:13.
His greatness. 1 Chr 16:25; Ps 145:3.
His holiness. Ps 15:11; Is 6:3.
His wisdom. Dan 2:20; Jude 25.
His power. Ps 21:13.
His goodness. Ps 107:8; 118:1; 136:1;
Jer 33:11.
His mercy. 2 Chr 20:21; Ps 89:1;
118:1–4; 136:1–26.
His lovingkindness and truth. Ps
138:2.
His faithfulness and truth. Is 25:1.
His salvation. Ps 18:46; Is 35:10;
61:10; Luke 1:68,69.
His wonderful works. Ps 89:5; 150:2;
Is 25:1.
His consolation. Ps 42:5; Is 12:1.
His judgment. Ps 101:1.
His counsel. Ps 16:7; Jer 32:19.
Fulfilling of His promises. 1 Kin 8:56.
Pardon of sin. Ps 103:1–3; Hos 14:2.
Spiritual health. Ps 103:3.
Constant preservation. Ps 71:6–8.
Deliverance. Ps 40:1–3; 124:6.
Protection. Ps 28:7; 59:17.
Answering prayer. Ps 28:6; 118:21.
The hope of glory. 1 Pet 1:3,4.
All spiritual blessings. Ps 103:2; Eph
1:3.
All temporal blessings. Ps 104:1,14;
136:25.
The continuance of blessings. Ps
68:19.
Is obligatory upon
Angels. Ps 103:20; 148:2.

Believers. Ps 30:4; 149:5.
Gentiles. Ps 117:1; Rom 15:11.
Children. Ps 8:2; Matt 21:16.
Those in heaven and on earth.
Ps 148:1,11.
Young and old. Ps 148:1,12.
Small and great. Rev 19:5.
All creation. Ps 148:1–10; 150:6.
Is good and pleasant. Ps 33:1; 147:1.
Should be offered
With understanding. Ps 47:7; 1 Cor
14:15.
With the soul. Ps 103:1; 104:1,35.
With the whole heart. Ps 9:1; 111:1;
138:1.
With uprightness of heart. Ps 119:7.
With the lips. Ps 63:3; 119:171.
With the mouth. Ps 51:15; 63:5.
With joy. Ps 63:5; 98:4.
With gladness. 2 Chr 29:30; Jer 33:11.
With thankfulness. 1 Chr 16:4; Neh
12:24; Ps 147:7.
Continually. Ps 35:28; 71:6.
During life. Ps 104:33.
More and more. Ps 71:14.
Day and night. Rev 4:8.
Day by day. 2 Chr 30:21.
For ever and ever. Ps 145:1,2.
Throughout the world. Ps 113:3.
In psalms and hymns, etc. Ps 105:2;
Eph 5:19; Col 3:16.
Accompanied with musical instruments.
1 Chr 16:41,42; Ps 150:3,5.
Is a part of public worship. Ps 9:14; 100:4;
118:19,20; Heb 2:12.
Believers should
Show forth. Is 43:21; 1 Pet 2:9.
Be endued with the spirit of. Is 61:3.
Render, under affliction. Acts 16:25.
Glory in. 1 Chr 16:35.
Triumph in. Ps 106:47.
Express their joy by. James 5:13.
Declare. Is 42:12.
Invite others to. Ps 34:3; 95:1.
Pray for ability to offer. Ps 51:15;
119:175.
Jews offered, while standing.. 1 Chr
23:30; Neh 9:5.
Called the
Fruit of the lips. Heb 13:15.
Voice of praise. Ps 66:8.
Voice of triumph. Ps 47:1.
Voice of melody. Is 51:3.
Voice of a psalm. Ps 98:5.
Garment of praise. Is 61:3.
Sacrifice of praise. Heb 13:15.
Sacrifices of joy. Ps 27:6.
Sacrifices of the lips. Hos 14:2.
The heavenly host engage in. Is 6:3; Luke
2:13; Rev 4:9–11; 5:12.

PRAYER.

Commanded. Is 55:6; Matt 7:7; Phil 4:6.
To be offered
To God. Ps 5:2; Matt 4:10.
To Christ. Luke 23:42; Acts 7:59.
Through Christ. Eph 2:18; Heb 10:19.
God hears. Ps 10:17; 65:2.
God answers. Ps 99:6; Is 58:9.
Is described as
Bowing the knees. Eph 3:14.
Looking up. Ps 5:3.
Lifting up the soul. Ps 25:1.
Lifting up the heart. Lam 3:41.
Pouring out the heart. Ps 62:8.
Pouring out the soul. 1 Sam 1:15.
Calling upon the name of the Lord.
Gen 12:8; Ps 116:4; Acts 22:16.
Crying to God. Ps 27:7; 34:6.
Drawing near to God. Ps 73:28; Heb
10:22.

Crying to heaven. 2 Chr 32:20.
Pleading with the Lord. Ex 32:11.
Seeking God. Job 8:5.
Seeking the face of the Lord. Ps 27:8.
Making supplication. Job 8:5; Jer 36:7.
Acceptable through Christ. John 14:13,14;
15:16; 16:23,24.
Ascends to heaven. 2 Chr 30:27; Rev 5:8.
Quickening grace necessary to. Ps 80:18.
The Holy Spirit
Promised as a Spirit of. Zech 12:10.
As the Spirit of adoptions, leads to.
Rom 8:15; Gal 4:6.
Helps our infirmities in. Rom 8:26.
An evidence of conversion. Acts 9:11.
Of the righteous, avails much. James
5:16.
Of the upright, a delight to God. Prov
15:8.
Should be offered up
In the Holy Spirit. Eph 6:18; Jude 20.
In faith. Matt 21:22; James 1:6; Heb
10:22.
In a forgiving spirit. Matt 6:12.
With the heart. Jer 29:13; Lam 3:41.
With the whole heart. Ps 119:58,145.
With preparation of heart. Job 11:13.
With a true heart. Heb 10:22.
With the soul. Ps 42:4.
With the spirit and understanding.
John 4:22–24; 1 Cor 14:15.
With confidence in God. Ps 56:9; 86:7;
1 John 5:14.
With submission to God. Luke 22:42.
With sincere lips. Ps 17:1.
With deliberation. Eccl 5:2.
With holiness. 1 Tim 2:8.
With humility. 2 Chr 7:14; 33:12.
With truth. Ps 145:18; John 4:24.
With desire to be heard. Neh 1:6; Ps
17:1; 55:1,2; 61:1.
With desire to be answered. Ps 27:7;
102:2; 108:6; 143:1.
With boldness. Heb 4:16.
With earnestness. 1 Thess 3:10; James
5:17.
With persistence. Gen 32:26; Luke
11:8,9; 18:1–7.
Night and day. 1 Tim 5:5.
All the time. 1 Thess 5:17.
Everywhere. 1 Tim 2:8.
In everything. Phil 4:6.
For temporal blessings. Gen 28:20; Prov
30:8; Matt 6:11.
For spiritual blessings. Matt 6:33.
For mercy and grace to help in time of
need. Heb 4:16.
Model for. Matt 6:9–13.
Model to avoid. Matt 6:5,7.
Accompanied with
Repentance. 1 Kin 8:33; Jer 36:7.
Confession. Neh 1:4,7; Dan 9:4–11.
Weeping. Jer 31:9; Hos 12:4.
Fasting. Neh 1:4; Dan 9:3; Acts 13:3.
Watchfulness. Luke 21:36; 1 Pet 4:7.
Praise. Ps 66:17.
Thanksgiving. Phil 4:6; Col 4:2.
Plead in the
Promises of God. Gen 32:9–12; Ex
32:13; 1 Kin 8:26; Ps 119:49.
Covenant of God. Jer 14:21.
Faithfulness of God. Ps 143:1.
Mercy of God. Ps 51:1; Dan 9:18.
Righteousness of God. Dan 9:16.
Rise early for. Ps 5:3; 119:147.
Seek divine teaching for. Luke 11:1.
Avoid hindrances in. 1 Pet 3:7.
Suitable in affliction. Is 26:16; James 5:13.
Shortness of time a motive to. 1 Pet 4:7.
Postures in
Standing. 1 Kin 8:22; Mark 11:25.

Bowing down. Ps 95:6.
Kneeling. 2 Chr 6:13; Ps 95:6; Luke
22:41; Acts 20:36.
Falling on the face. Num 16:22; Josh
5:14; 1 Chr 21:16; Matt 26:39.
Spreading forth the hands. Is 1:15.
Lifting up the hands. Ps 28:2; Lam
2:19; 1 Tim 2:8.
The promises of God encourage to. Is
65:24; Amos 5:4; Zech 13:9.
The promises of Christ encourage to. Luke
11:9,10; John 14:13,14.
Experience of past mercies an incentive to.
Ps 4:1; 112:2.

PRAYER, ANSWERS TO.

God gives. Ps 99:6; 118:5; 138:3.
Christ gives. John 4:10,14; 14:14.
Christ received. John 11:42; Heb 5:7.
Granted
Through the grace of God. Is 30:19.
Sometimes immediately. Is 65:24; Dan
9:21,23; 10:12.
Sometimes after delay. Luke 18:7.
Sometimes differently from our desire.
2 Cor 12:8,9.
Beyond expectation. Jer 33:3; Eph
3:20.
Promised. Is 58:9; Jer 29:12; Matt 7:7.
Promised especially in times of trouble. Ps
50:15; 91:15.
Received by those who
Seek God. Ps 34:4.
Seek God with all the heart. Jer
29:12,13.
Wait upon God. Ps 40:1.
Return to God. 2 Chr 7:14; Job
22:23,27.
Ask in faith. Matt 21:11; James 5:15.
Ask in the name of Christ. John
14:13.
Ask according to God's will. 1 John
5:14.
Call upon God in truth. Ps 145:18.
Fear God. Ps 145:19.
Set their love upon God. Ps 91:14,15.
Keep God's commandments. 1 John
3:22.
Call upon God under oppression. Is
19:20.
Call upon God under affliction. Ps
18:6; 106:44; Is 30:19,20.
Abide in Christ. John 15:7.
Humble themselves. 2 Chr 7:14; Ps
9:12.
Are righteous. Ps 34:15; James 5:16.
Are poor and needy. Is 41:17.
Believers
Are assured of. 1 John 5:15.
Love God for. Ps 116:1.
Bless God for. Ps 66:20.
Praise God for. Ps 116:17; 118:21.
A motive for continued prayer. Ps 116:2.
Denied to those who
Ask amiss. James 4:3.
Live in sin. Ps 66:18; Is 59:2; John
9:31.
Offer unworthy service to God. Mal
1:7–9.
Forsake God. Jer 14:10,12.
Reject the call of God. Prov 1:24,25,28.
Hear not the law. Prov 28:9; Zech 7:11–
13.
Are deaf to the cry of the poor. Prov
21:13.
Are blood shedders. Is 1:15; 59:3.
Are idolaters. Jer 11:11–14; Ezek 8:15–
18.
Are wavering. James 1:6,7.
Are hypocrites. Job 27:8,9.
Are proud. Job 35:12,13.

Are self-righteous. Luke 18:11,12,14.
Are the enemies of believers. Ps
18:40,41.
Cruelly oppress believers. Mic 3:2–4.

PRAYER, INTERCESSORY.

Christ set an example of. Luke 22:32;
23:34; John 17:9–24.
Commanded. 1 Tim 2:1; James 5:14,16.
Should be offered up for
All in authority. 1 Tim 2:2.
Ministers. 2 Cor 1:11; Phil 1:19.
All believers. Eph 6:18.
All men. 1 Tim 2:1.
Masters. Gen 24:12–14.
Servants. Luke 7:2,3.
Children. Gen 17:18; Matt 15:22.
Friends. Job 42:8.
Fellow-countrymen. Rom 10:1.
The sick. James 5:14.
Persecutors. Matt 5:44.
Enemies among whom we dwell. Jer
29:7.
Those who envy us. Num 12:13.
Those who forsake us. 2 Tim 4:16.
Those who murmur against God.
Num 11:1,2; 14:13,19.
By ministers for their people. Eph 1:16;
3:14–19; Phil 1:4.
Encouragement to. James 5:16; 1 John
5:16.
Beneficial to the offerer. Job 42:10.
Sin of neglecting. 1 Sam 12:23.
Believers should ask for. 1 Sam 12:19; Heb
13:18.
Unavailing for the unbelievers. Jer 7:13–
16; 14:10,11.

PRAYER, PRIVATE.

Christ was constant in. Matt 14:23;
26:36,39; Mark 1:35; Luke 9:18,29.
Commanded. Matt 6:6.
Should be offered
At evening, morning, and noon. Ps
55:17.
Day and night. Ps 88:1.
Without ceasing. 1 Thess 5:17.
Shall be heard. Job 22:27.
Rewarded openly. Matt 6:6.
An evidence of conversion. Acts 9:11.
Nothing should hinder. Dan 6:10.

PRAYER, PUBLIC.

Acceptable to God. Is 56:7.
God promises to hear. 2 Chr 7:14,16.
God promises to bless in. Ex 20:24.
Christ
Sanctifies by His presence. Matt 18:20.
Attended. Matt 12:9; Luke 4:16.
Promises answers to. Matt 18:19.
Instituted form of. Luke 11:2.
Should not be made in an unknown
language. 1 Cor 14:14–16.
Believers delight in. Ps 42:4; 122:1.
Exhortation to. Heb 10:25.
Urge others to join in. Ps 95:6; Zech 8:21.

PRESUMPTION.

A characteristic of the wicked. 2 Pet 2:10.
A characteristic of Antichrist. 2 Thess 2:4.
Exhibited in
Opposing God. Job 15:25,26.
Wilful commission of sin. Rom 1:32.
Self-righteousness. Hos 12:8; Rev
3:17.
Spiritual pride. Is 65:5; Luke 18:11.
Esteeming our own ways right. Prov
12:15.
Seeking precedence. Luke 14:7–11.
Planning for the future. Luke 12:18;
James 4:13.

Pretending to prophesy. Deut 18:22.
Pray to be kept from sins of. Ps 19:13.
Believers should avoid. Ps 131:1.
Punishment for. Num 15:30; Rev 18:7,8.

PRIDE.

Is sin. Prov 21:4.
Hateful to God. Prov 6:16,17; 16:5.
Hateful to Christ. Prov 8:12,13.
Often originates in
   Self-righteousness. Luke 18:11,12.
   Religious privileges. Zeph 3:11.
   Unsanctified knowledge. 1 Cor 8:1.
   Inexperience. 1 Tim 3:6.
   Possession of power. Lev 26:19; Ezek 30:6.
   Possession of wealth. 2 Kin 20:13.
Forbidden. 1 Sam 2:3; Rom 12:3,16.
Defiles a man. Mark 7:20,22.
Hardens the mind. Dan 5:20.
Believers
   Give not away. Ps 131:1.
   Respect not, in others. Ps 40:4.
   Mourn over, in others. Jer 13:17.
   Hate, in others. Ps 101:5.
A hindrance to seeking God. Ps 10:4; Hos 7:10.
A hindrance to improvement. Prov 26:12.
A characteristic
   The devil. 1 Tim 3:6.
   The world. 1 John 2:16.
   False teachers. 1 Tim 6:3,4.
   The wicked. Hab 2:4,5; Rom 1:30.
Comes from the heart. Mark 7:21–23.
The wicked encompassed with. Ps 73:6.
Leads men to
   Contempt and rejection of God's Word and ministers. Jer 43:2.
   A persecuting spirit. Ps 10:2.
   Wrath. Prov 21:24.
   Contention. Prov 13:10; 28:25.
   Self-deception. Jer 49:16; Obad 3.
Exhortation against. Jer 13:15.
Is followed by
   Shame. Prov 11:2.
   Debasement. Prov 29:23; Is 28:3.
   Destruction. Prov 16:18; 18:12.
Shall abound in the last days. 2 Tim 3:2.
Woe to. Is 28:1,3.
They who are guilty of, shall be
   Resisted. James 4:6.
   Brought into contempt. Is 23:9.
   Recompensed. Ps 31:23.
   Ruined. Jer 13:9.
   Subdued. Ex 18:11; Is 13:11.
   Brought low. Ps 18:27; Is 2:12.
   Abased. Dan 4:37; Matt 23:12.
   Scattered. Luke 1:51.
   Punished. Zeph 2:10,11; Mal 4:1.

PROCRASTINATION.

Condemned by Christ. Luke 9:59–62.
Believers avoid. Ps 27:8; 119:60.
To be avoided in
   Listening to God. Ps 95:7,8; Heb 3:7,8.
   Seeking God. Is 55:6.
   Glorifying God. Jer 13:16.
   Keeping God's commandments. Ps 119:60.
   Making offerings to God. Ex 22:29.
   Performance of vows. Deut 23:21; Eccl 5:4.
Motives for avoiding
   The present the best time. Eccl 12:1; 2 Cor 6:2.
   The uncertainty of life. Prov 27:1.

PROMISES OF GOD, THE.

Contained in the Scriptures. Rom 1:2.
Made in Christ. Eph 3:6; 2 Tim 1:1.

Made to
   Christ. Gal 3:16,19.
   Abraham. Gen 12:3,7; Gal 3:16.
   Isaac. Gen 26:3,4.
   Jacob. Gen 28:14.
   David. 2 Sam 7:12; Ps 89:3,4,35,36.
   The Israelites. Rom 9:4.
   The Fathers. Acts 13:32; 26:6,7.
   All who are called of God. Acts 2:39.
   Those who love Him. James 1:12; 2:5.
Confirmed by an oath. Ps 89:3,4; Heb 8:6.
Covenant established upon. Heb 8:6.
God is faithful to. Titus 1:2; Heb 10:23.
God remembers. Ps 105:42; Luke 1:54,55.
Are
   Good. 1 Kin 8:56.
   Holy. Ps 105:42.
   Exceedingly great and precious. 2 Pet 1:4.
   Confirmed in Christ. Rom 15:8.
   Certain in Christ. 2 Cor 1:20.
   Fulfilled in Christ. Acts 13:23; Luke 1:69–73.
   Through the righteousness of faith. Rom 4:13,16.
   Obtained through faith. Heb 11:33.
   Given to those who believe. Gal 3:22.
   Inherited through faith and patience. Heb 6:12,15; 10:36.
   Performed in due season. Jer 33:14; Acts 7:17; Gal 4:4.
Not one shall fail. Josh 23:14; 1 Kin 8:56.
The law not against. Gal 3:21.
The law could not annul. Gal 3:17.
Subjects of
   Christ. 2 Sam 7:12,13; Acts 13:22,23.
   The Holy Spirit. Acts 2:33; Eph 1:13.
   The gospel. Rom 1:1,2.
   Life in Christ. 2 Tim 1:1.
   A crown of life. James 1:12.
   Eternal life. Titus 1:2; 1 John 2:25.
   The life that now is. 1 Tim 4:8.
   Adoption. 2 Cor 6:18; 7:1.
   Preservation in affliction. Is 43:2.
   Blessing. Deut 1:11.
   Forgiveness of sins. Is 1:18; Heb 8:12.
   Putting the law into the heart. Jer 31:33; Heb 8:10.
   Second coming of Christ. 2 Pet 3:4.
   New heavens and earth. 2 Pet 3:13.
   Entering into rest. Josh 22:4; Heb 4:1.
Should lead to perfecting holiness. 2 Cor 7:1.
The inheritance of the believers is of. Rom 4:13; Gal 3:18.
Believers
   Children of. Rom 9:8; Gal 4:28.
   Heirs of. Gal 3:29; Heb 6:17; 11:9.
   Waver not at. Rom 4:20.
   Have implicit confidence in. Heb 11:11.
   Expect the performance of. Luke 1:38,45; 2 Pet 3:13.
   Sometimes, through infirmity, tempted to doubt. Ps 77:8,10.
   Plead in prayer. Gen 32:9,12; 1 Chr 17:23,26; Is 43:26.
Should wait for the performance of. Acts 1:4.
Gentiles shall be partakers of. Eph 3:6.
Man, by nature, has no interest in. Eph 2:12.
Scoffers despise. 2 Pet 3:3,4.
Fear, lest they come short of. Heb 4:1.

PROPHECIES RESPECTING CHRIST.

As the Son of God. Ps 2:7.
   Fulfilled. Luke 1:32,35.
As the seed of the woman. Gen 3:15.
   Fulfilled. Gal 4:4.

As the seed of Abraham. Gen 17:7; 22:18.
   Fulfilled. Gal 3:16.
As the seed of Isaac. Gen 21:12.
   Fulfilled. Heb 11:17–19.
As the seed of David. Ps 132:11; Jer 23:5.
   Fulfilled. Acts 13:23; Rom 1:3.
His coming at a set time. Gen 49:10; Dan 9:24,25.
   Fulfilled. Luke 2:1.
His being born of a virgin. Is 7:14.
   Fulfilled. Matt 1:22,23; Luke 2:7.
His being called Immanuel. Is 7:14.
   Fulfilled. Matt 1:22,23.
His being born in Bethlehem of Judea. Mic 5:2.
   Fulfilled. Matt 2:1; Luke 2:4–6.
Great persons coming to adore him. Ps 72:10.
   Fulfilled. Matt 2:1–11.
The slaying of the children of Bethlehem. Jer 31:15.
   Fulfilled. Matt 2:16–18.
His being called out of Egypt. Hos 11:1.
   Fulfilled. Matt 2:15.
His being preceded by John the Baptist. Is 40:3; Mal 3:1.
   Fulfilled. Matt 3:1,3; Luke 1:17.
His being anointed with the Spirit. Ps 45:7; Is 11:2; 61:1.
   Fulfilled. Matt 3:16; John 3:34; Acts 10:38.
His being a Prophet like to Moses. Deut 18:15–18.
   Fulfilled. Acts 3:20–22.
His being a Priest after the order of Melchizedek. Ps 110:4.
   Fulfilled. Heb 5:5,6.
His entering on His public ministry. Is 61:1,2.
   Fulfilled. Luke 4:16–21,43.
His ministry commencing in Galilee. Is 9:1,2.
   Fulfilled. Matt 4:12–16,23.
His entering publicly into Jerusalem. Zech 9:9.
   Fulfilled. Matt 21:1–5.
His coming into the temple. Hag 2:7,9; Mal 3:1.
   Fulfilled. Matt 21:12; Luke 2:27–32; John 2:13–16.
His poverty. Is 53:2.
   Fulfilled. Mark 6:3; Luke 9:58.
His meekness and want of ostentatious. Is 42:2.
   Fulfilled. Matt 12:15,16,19.
His tenderness and compassion. Is 40:11; 42:3.
   Fulfilled. Matt 12:15,20; Heb 4:15.
His being without deceit. Is 53:9.
   Fulfilled. 1 Pet 2:22.
His zeal. Ps 69:9.
   Fulfilled. John 2:17.
His preaching by parables. Ps 78:2.
   Fulfilled. Matt 13:34,35.
His working miracles. Is 35:5,6.
   Fulfilled. Matt 11:4–6; John 11:47.
His bearing reproach. Ps 22:6; 69:7,9,20.
   Fulfilled. Rom 15:3.
His being rejected by His brethren. Ps 69:8; Is 63:3.
   Fulfilled. John 1:11; 7:3.
His being a stone of stumbling to the Jews. Is 8:14.
   Fulfilled. Rom 9:32; 1 Pet 2:8.
His being hated by the Jews. Ps 69:4; Is 49:7.
   Fulfilled. John 15:24,25.
His being rejected by the Jewish rulers. Ps 118:22.
   Fulfilled. Matt 21:42; John 7:48.

That the Jews and Gentiles should combine against Him. Ps 2:1,2.
Fulfilled. Luke 23:12; Acts 4:27.
His being betrayed by a friend. Ps 41:9; 55:12–14.
Fulfilled. John 13:18,21.
His disciples forsaking Him. Zech 13:7.
Fulfilled. Matt 26:31,56.
His being sold for thirty pieces silver. Zech 11:12.
Fulfilled. Matt 26:15.
His price being given for the potter's field. Zech 11:13.
Fulfilled. Matt 27:7.
The intensity of His sufferings. Ps 22:14,15.
Fulfilled. Luke 22:42,44.
His sufferings being for others. Is 53:4–6,12; Dan 9:26.
Fulfilled. Matt 20:28.
His patience and silence under suffering. Is 53:7.
Fulfilled. Matt 26:63; 27:12–14.
His being struck on the cheek. Mic 5:1.
Fulfilled. Matt 27:30.
His visage being marred. Is 52:14; 53:3.
Fulfilled. John 19:5.
His being spit on and scourged. Is 50:6.
Fulfilled. Mark 14:65; John 19:1.
His hands and feet being nailed to the cross. Ps 22:16.
Fulfilled. John 19:18; 20:25.
His being forsaken by God. Ps 22:1.
Fulfilled. Matt 27:46.
His being mocked. Ps 22:7,8.
Fulfilled. Matt 27:39–44.
Gall and vinegar being given Him to drink. Ps 69:21.
Fulfilled. Matt 27:34.
His garments being parted, and lots cast for His clothing. Ps 22:18.
Fulfilled. Matt 27:35.
His being numbered with the transgressors. Is 53:12.
Fulfilled. Mark 15:28.
His intercession for His murderers. Is 53:12.
Fulfilled. Luke 23:34.
His death. Is 53:12.
Fulfilled. Matt 27:50.
That a bone of Him should not be broken. Ex 12:46; Ps 34:20.
Fulfilled. John 19:33,36.
His being pierced. Zech 12:10.
Fulfilled. John 19:34,37.
His being buried with the rich. Is 53:9.
Fulfilled. Matt 27:57–60.
His flesh not seeing corruption. Ps 16:10.
Fulfilled. Acts 2:31.
His resurrection. Ps 16:10; Is 26:19.
Fulfilled. Luke 24:6,31,34.
His ascension. Ps 68:18.
Fulfilled. Luke 24:51; Acts 1:9.
His sitting on the right hand of God. Ps 110:1.
Fulfilled. Heb 1:3.
His exercising the priestly office in heaven. Zech 6:13.
Fulfilled. Rom 8:34.
His being the chief corner-stone of the Church. Is 28:16.
Fulfilled. 1 Pet 2:6,7.
His being King in Zion. Ps 2:6.
Fulfilled. Luke 1:32; John 18:33–37.
The conversion of the Gentiles to Him. Is 11:10; 42:1.
Fulfilled. Matt 1:17,21; John 10:16; Acts 10:45,47.
His righteous government. Ps 45:6,7.
Fulfilled. John 5:30; Rev 19:11.
His universal dominion. Ps 72:8; Dan 7:14.

Fulfilled. Phil 2:9,11.
The perpetuity of His kingdom. Is 9:7; Dan 7:14.
Fulfilled. Luke 1:32,33.

PROPHECY.

Is sometimes the foretelling of future events. Gen 49:1; Num 24:14.
God is the Author of. Is 44:7; 45:21.
God gives, through Christ. Rev 1:1.
A gift of Christ. Eph 4:11; Rev 11:3.
A gift of the Holy Spirit. 1 Cor 12:10.
Came not by the will of man. 2 Pet 1:21.
Given from the beginning. Luke 1:70.
Is a sure word. 2 Pet 1:19.
They who uttered
    Raised up by God. Amos 2:11.
    Ordained by God. 1 Sam 3:20; Jer 1:5.
    Sent by God. 2 Chr 36:15; Jer 7:25.
    Sent by Christ. Matt 23:34.
    Controlled by the Holy Spirit. Luke 1:67.
    Moved by the Holy Spirit. 2 Pet 1:21.
    Spoke by the Holy Spirit. Acts 1:16; 11:28; 28:25.
    Spoke in the name of the Lord. 2 Chr 33:18; James 5:10.
    Spoke with authority. 1 Kin 17:1.
God accomplishes. Is 44:26; Acts 3:18.
Christ the great subject of. Acts 3:22–24; 10:43; 1 Pet 1:10,11.
Fulfilled respecting Christ. Luke 24:44.
Gift of, promised. Joel 2:28; Acts 2:16,17.
Is for our benefit. 1 Pet 1:12.
Is a light in dark place. 2 Pet 1:19.
Is not of private interpretation. 2 Pet 1:20.
Despise not. 1 Thess 5:20.
Listen. 2 Pet 1:19.
Receive in faith. 2 Chr 20:20; Luke 24:25.
Blessedness of reading, hearing, and keeping. Rev 1:3; 22:7.
Sin of pretending to the gift of. Jer 14:14; 23:13,14; Ezek 13:2,3.
Punishment for
    Not giving ear to. Neh 9:30.
    Adding to, or taking from. Rev 22:18,19.
    Pretending to the gift of. Deut 18:20; Jer 14:15; 23:15.
Gift of, sometimes possessed by unconverted men. Num 24:2–9; 1 Sam 19:20,23; Matt 7:22; John 11:49–51; 1 Cor 13:2.
How tested. Deut 13:1–3; 18:22.

PROPHETS.

God spoke of old by. Hos 12:10; Heb 1:1.
The messengers of God. 2 Chr 36:15; Is 44:26.
The servants of God. Jer 35:15.
The watchmen of Israel. Ezek 3:17.
Were called
    Men of God. 1 Sam 9:6.
    Prophets of God. Ezra 5:2.
    Holy prophets. Luke 1:70; Rev 18:20; 22:6.
    Holy men of God. 2 Pet 1:21.
    Seers. 1 Sam 9:9.
Were esteemed as holy men. 2 Kin 4:9.
Women sometimes endowed as. Joel 2:28.
God communicated to them
    His secret things. Amos 3:7.
    At various times and in different ways. Heb 1:1.
    By an audible voice. Num 12:8; 1 Sam 3:4–14.
    By angels. Dan 8:15–26; Rev 22:8,9.
    By dreams and visions. Num 12:6; Joel 2:28.
Spoken by of the Holy Spirit while prophesying. Luke 1:67; 2 Pet 1:21.

Spoke in the name of the Lord. 2 Chr 33:18; Ezek 3:11; James 5:10.
Frequently spoke in parables and riddles. 2 Sam 12:1–6; Is 5:1–7; Ezek 17:2–10.
Frequently used actions, and objects as signs. Is 20:2–4; Jer 19:1,10,11; 27:2,3; 43:9; 51:63; Ezek 4:1–13; 5:1–4; 7:23; 12:3–7; 21:6,7; 24:1–24; Hos 1:2–9.
Frequently left without divine communication on account of sins of the people. 1 Sam 28:6; Lam 2:9; Ezek 7:26.
Were required
    To be bold and undaunted. Ezek 2:6; 3:8,9.
    To be vigilant and faithful. Ezek 3:17–21.
    To receive with attention all God's communications. Ezek 3:10.
    Not to speak anything but what they received from God. Deut 18:20.
    To declare everything that the Lord commanded. Jer 26:2.
Words sometimes uttered under great bodily and mental excitement. Jer 23:9; Ezek 3:14,15; Dan 7:28; 10:8; Hab 3:2,16.
Sometimes spoke in verse. Deut 32:44; Is 5:1.
Often accompanied by music while predicting. 1 Sam 10:5; 2 Kin 3:15.
Often committed their predictions to writing. 2 Chr 21:12; Jer 36:2.
Writings of, read in the synagogues. Luke 4:17; Acts 13:15.
Ordinary ones
    Numerous in Israel. 1 Sam 10:5; 1 Kin 18:4.
    Trained up and instructed in schools. 2 Kin 2:3,5; 1 Sam 19:20.
    The sacred poets of the Jews. Ex 15:20,21; 1 Sam 10:5,10; 1 Chr 25:1.
Extraordinary ones
    Specially raised up on occasions of emergency. 1 Sam 3:19–21; Is 6:8,9; Jer 1:5.
    Often endued with miraculous power. Ex 4:1–4; 1 Kin 17:23; 2 Kin 5:3–8.
Frequently married men. 2 Kin 4:1; Ezek 24:18.
Wore hair-cloth. 2 Kin 1:8; Zech 13:4; Matt 3:4; Rev 11:3.
Often led a wandering and unsettled life. 1 Kin 18:10–12; 19:3,8,15; 2 Kin 4:10.
Simple in their manner of life. Matt 3:4.
The historians of Israel. 1 Chr 29:29; 2 Chr 9:29.
The interpreters of dreams. Dan 1:17.
Were consulted in all difficulties. 1 Sam 9:6; 28:15; 1 Kin 14:2–4; 22:7.
Presented with gifts by those who consulted them. 1 Sam 9:7,8; 1 Kin 14:3.
Sometimes thought it right to reject presents. 2 Kin 5:15,16.
Were sent to
    Reprove the wicked and exhort to repentance. 2 Kin 17:13; 2 Chr 24:19; Jer 25:4,5.
    Denounce the wickedness of kings. 1 Sam 15:10,16–19; 2 Sam 12:7–12; 1 Kin 18:18; 21:17–22.
    Exhort to faithfulness and constancy in God's service. 2 Chr 15:1,2,7.
    Predict the coming of Christ. Luke 24:44; John 1:45; Acts 3:24; 10:43.
    Predict the downfall of nations. Is 15:1; 17:1; Jer 47:1–51:64.

Felt deeply on account of the calamities which they predicted. Is 16:9–11; Jer 9:1–7.

Predictions of

Frequently proclaimed at the gate of the Lord's house. Jer 7:2.

Proclaimed in the cities and streets. Jer 11:6.

Written on tables for the public. Hab 2:2.

Written on rolls and read to the people. Is 8:1; Jer 36:2.

Were all fulfilled. 2 Kin 10:10; Is 44:26; Acts 3:18; Rev 10:7.

Assisted the Jews in their great national undertakings. Ezra 5:2.

One generally attached to the king's household. 2 Sam 24:11; 2 Chr 29:25; 35:15.

The Jews

Required to hear and believe. Deut 18:15; 2 Chr 20:20.

Often tried to make them speak smooth things. 1 Kin 22:13; Is 30:10; Amos 2:12.

Persecuted them. 2 Chr 36:16; Matt 5:12.

Often imprisoned them. 1 Kin 22:27; Jer 32:2; 37:15,16.

Often put them to death. 1 Kin 18:13; 19:10; Matt 23:34–37.

Often left without, on account of sin. 1 Sam 3:1; Ps 74:9; Amos 8:11,12.

Were mighty through faith. Heb 11:32–40.

Great patience of, under suffering. James 5:10.

God avenged all injuries done to. 2 Kin 9:7; 1 Chr 16:21,22; Matt 23:35–38; Luke 11:50.

Christ exercised the office of, as predicted. Deut 18:15; Matt 24:1–25:46; Mark 10:32–34; Acts 3:22.

PROPHETS, FALSE.

Pretended to be sent by God. Jer 23:17,18,31.

Not sent or commissioned by God. Jer 14:14; 23:21; 29:31.

Used by God to test Israel. Deut 13:3.

Described as

Light and treacherous. Zeph 3:4.

Covetous. Mic 3:11.

Crafty. Matt 7:15.

Drunken. Is 28:7.

Immoral and profane. Jer 23:11,14.

Women sometimes acted as. Neh 6:14; Rev 2:20.

Called foolish prophets. Ezek 13:2.

Compared to foxes in the desert. Ezek 13:4.

Compared to wind. Jer 5:13.

Influenced by evil spirits. 1 Kin 22:21,22.

Prophesied

Falsely. Jer 5:31.

Lies in the name of the Lord. Jer 14:14.

Out of their own heart. Jer 23:16,26; Ezek 13:2.

In the name of false gods. Jer 2:8.

Peace, when there was no peace. Jer 6:14; 23:17; Ezek 13:10; Mic 3:5.

Often practiced divination and witchcraft. Jer 14:14; Ezek 22:28; Acts 13:6.

Often pretended to dream. Jer 23:28,32.

Often deceived by God as a judgment. Ezek 14:9.

The people

Led into error. Jer 23:13; Mic 3:5.

Made to forget God's name by. Jer 23:27.

Deprived of God's Word by. Jer 23:30.

Taught profaneness and sin by. Jer 23:14,15.

Oppressed and defrauded by. Ezek 22:25.

Warned not to listen to. Deut 13:3; Jer 23:16; 27:9,15,16.

Encouraged and praised by. Jer 5:31; Luke 6:26.

Mode of trying and detecting. Deut 13:1,2; 18:21,22; 1 John 4:1–3.

Predicted to arise

Before destruction of Jerusalem. Matt 24:11,24.

In the latter times. 2 Pet 2:1.

Judgments pronounced against. Jer 8:1,2; 14:15; 28:16,17; 29:32.

Involved the people in their own ruin. Is 9:15,16; Jer 20:6; Ezek 14:10.

PROTECTION.

God is able to afford. 1 Pet 1:5; Jude 24.

God is faithful to afford. 1 Thess 5:23,24; 2 Thess 3:3.

Of God is

Indispensable. Ps 127:1.

Timely. Ps 46:1.

Certain. Deut 31:6; Josh 1:5.

Effectual. John 10:28–30; 2 Cor 12:9.

Uninterrupted. Ps 121:3.

Encouraging. Is 41:10; 50:7.

Perpetual. Ps 121:8.

Often afforded through weak means. Judg 7:7; 1 Sam 17:45,50; 2 Chr 14:11.

Is afforded to

Those who listen to God. Prov 1:33.

Returning sinners. Job 22:23,25.

The loyal in heart. 2 Chr 16:9.

The poor. Ps 14:6; 72:12–14.

The oppressed. Ps 9:9.

Israel. Ps 48:3; Zech 2:4,5.

Is promised to believers in

Preserving them. Ps 145:20.

Strengthening them. 2 Tim 4:17.

Upholding them. Ps 37:17,24; 63:8.

Guarding their feet. 1 Sam 2:9; Prov 3:26.

Keeping them from evil. 2 Thess 3:3.

Keeping them from falling. Jude 24.

Keeping them in the way. Ex 23:20.

Keeping them from temptation. Rev 3:10.

Providing a refuge for them. Prov 14:26; Is 4:6; 32:2.

Defending them against their enemies. Deut 20:1–4; 33:27; Is 59:19.

Defeating the counsels of enemies. Is 8:10.

Temptation. 1 Cor 10:13; 2 Pet 2:9.

Persecution. Luke 21:18.

Calamities. Ps 57:1; 59:16.

All dangers. Ps 91:3–7.

All places. Gen 28:15; 2 Chr 16:9.

Sleep. Ps 3:5; 4:8; Prov 3:24.

Death. Ps 23:4.

Believers

Acknowledge God as their. Ps 18:2; 62:2; 89:18.

Pray for. Ps 17:5,8; Is 51:9.

Praise God for. Ps 5:11.

Withdrawn from the

Disobedient. Lev 26:14–17.

Backsliding. Josh 23:12,13; Judg 10:13.

Presumptuous. Num 14:40–45.

Unbelieving. Is 7:9.

Obstinately impenitent. Matt 23:38.

Not to be found in

Idols. Deut 32:37–39; Is 46:7.

Man. Ps 146:3; Is 30:7.

Riches. Prov 11:4,28; Zeph 1:18.

Hosts. Josh 11:4–8; Ps 33:16.

Horses. Ps 33:17; Prov 21:31.

PROVIDENCE OF GOD, THE.

Is His care over his works. Ps 145:9.

Is exercised in

Preserving His creatures. Neh 9:6; Ps 36:6; Matt 10:29.

Providing for His creatures. Ps 104:27,28; 136:25; 147:9; Matt 6:26.

The special preservation and protection of believers. Ps 37:28; 91:11; Matt 10:30.

Prospering believers. Gen 24:48,56.

Protecting believers. Ps 91:4; 140:7.

Delivering believers. Ps 91:3; Is 31:5.

Leading believers. Deut 8:2,15; Is 31:5; 63:12.

Bringing His words to pass. Num 26:65; Josh 21:45; Luke 21:32,33.

Ordaining the lives of men. Prov 16:9; 19:21; 20:24; 1 Sam 2:7,8; Ps 75:6,7.

Determining the period of human life. Ps 31:15; 39:5; Acts 17:26.

Defeating wicked designs. Ex 15:9–19; 2 Sam 17:14,15; Ps 33:10.

Overruling wicked designs for good. Gen 45:5–7; 50:20; Phil 1:12.

Preserving the course of nature. Gen 8:22; Job 26:10; Ps 104:5–9.

Directing all events. Josh 7:14; 1 Sam 6:7–10,12; Prov 16:33; Is 44:7; Acts 1:26.

Ruling the elements. Job 37:9–13; Is 50:2; John 1:4,15; Nah 1:4.

Ordering the minutest matters. Matt 10:29,30; Luke 21:18.

Is righteous. Ps 145:17; Dan 4:37.

Is ever watchful. Ps 121:4; Is 27:3.

Is all pervading. Ps 139:1–5.

Sometimes dark and mysterious. Ps 36:6; 73:16; 77:19; Rom 11:33.

All things are ordered by

For His glory. Is 63:14.

For good to believers. Rom 8:28.

The wicked sometimes made to further. Is 10:5–12; Acts 3:17,18.

To be acknowledged

In prosperity. Deut 8:18; 1 Chr 29:12.

In adversity. Job 1:21; Ps 119:15.

In public calamities. Amos 3:6.

In our daily support. Gen 48:15.

In all things. Prov 3:6.

Cannot be defeated. 1 Kin 22:30,34; Prov 21:30.

Man's efforts are useless without. Ps 127:1,2; Prov 21:31.

Believers should

Trust in. Matt 6:33,34; 10:9,29–31.

Have full confidence in. Ps 16:8; 139:10.

Commit their works to. Prov 16:3.

Encourage themselves with. 1 Sam 30:6.

Pray in dependence upon. Acts 12:5.

Pray to be guided by. Gen 24:12–14; 28:20,21; Acts 1:24.

Result of depending upon. Luke 22:35.

Connected with the use of means. 1 Kin 21:19; 22:37,38; Mic 5:2; Luke 2:1–4; Acts 27:22,31,32.

Danger of denying. Is 10:13–17; Ezek 28:2–10; Dan 4:29–31; Hos 2:8,9.

PUNISHMENT OF THE WICKED, THE.

Is from God. Lev 26:18; Is 13:11.

On account of their

Sin. Lam 3:39.

Iniquity. Jer 36:31; Ezek 3:17,18; 18:4,13,20; Amos 3:2.

Idolatry. Lev 26:30; Is 10:10,11.
Rejection of the law of God. 1 Sam 15:23; Hos 4:6–9.
Disobedience of God. 2 Thess 1:8.
Evil ways and doings. Jer 21:14; Hos 4:9; 12:2.
Pride. Is 10:12; 24:21; Luke 14:11.
Unbelief. Mark 16:16; Rom 11:20; Heb 3:18,19; 4:2.
Covetousness. Is 57:17; Jer 51:13.
Oppression. Is 49:26; Jer 30:16,20.
Persecuting. Jer 11:21,22; Matt 23:34–36.
Disobeying God. Neh 9:26,27; Eph 5:6.
Disobeying the gospel. 2 Thess 1:8.
Is the fruit of their sin. Job 4:8; Prov 22:8; Rom 6:21; Gal 6:8.
Is the reward of their sins. Ps 91:8; Is 3:11; Jer 16:18; Rom 6:23; Heb 2:2.
Often brought about by their evil designs. Esth 7:10; Ps 37:15; 57:6.
Often begins on earth. Prov 11:31.
In this life by
Sickness. Lev 26:16; Ps 78:50.
Famine. Lev 26:19,20,26,29; Ps 107:34.
Wild beasts. Lev 26:22.
War. Lev 26:25,32,33; Jer 6:4.
Deliverance to enemies. Neh 9:27.
Fear. Lev 26:36,37; Job 18:11.
Reprobate mind. Rom 1:28.
Being put in slippery places. Ps 73:3–19.
Trouble and distress. Is 8:22; Zeph 1:15.
Being cut off. Ps 94:23.
Bringing down their pride. Is 13:11.
Future, shall be awarded by Christ. Matt 16:27; 25:31,41.
Future described as
Hell. Ps 9:17; Matt 5:29; Luke 12:5; 16:23.
Darkness. Matt 8:12; 2 Pet 2:17.
Death. Rom 5:12–17; 6:23.
Resurrection of damnation. John 5:29.
Rising to shame and everlasting contempt. Dan 12:2.
Everlasting destruction. Ps 52:5; 92:7; 2 Thess 1:9.
Everlasting fire. Matt 25:41; Jude 7.
Second death. Rev 2:11; 21:8.
Damnation of hell. Matt 23:33.
Eternal condemnation. Mark 3:29.
Blackness of darkness. 2 Pet 2:17; Jude 13.
Everlasting burnings. Is 33:14.
The wrath of God. John 3:36.
Wine of the wrath of God. Rev 14:10.
Torment with fire. Rev 14:10.
Torment for ever and ever. Rev 14:11.
The righteousness of God requires. 2 Thess 1:6.
Often sudden and unexpected. Ps 35:8; 64:7; Prov 29:1; Luke 12:20; 1 Thess 5:3.
Shall be
According to their deeds. Matt 16:27; Rom 2:6,9; 2 Cor 5:10.
According to the knowledge possessed by them. Luke 12:47,48.
Increased by neglect of privileges. Matt 11:21–24; Luke 10:13–15.
Relentless. Luke 16:23–26.
Accompanied by remorse. Is 66:24; Mark 9:44.
No combination avails against. Prov 11:21.
Deferred, emboldens them in sin. Eccl 8:11.
Should be a warning to others. Num 26:10; 1 Cor 10:6–11; Jude 7.
Consummated at the day of judgment. Matt 25:31,46; Rom 2:5,16; 2 Pet 2:9.

REBELLION AGAINST GOD.

Forbidden. Num 14:9; Josh 22:19.
Provokes God. Num 16:30; Neh 9:26.
Provokes Christ. Ex 23:20,21; 1 Cor 10:9.
Grieves the Holy Spirit. Is 63:10.
Exhibited in
Unbelief. Deut 9:23; Ps 106:24,25.
Rejecting His government. 1 Sam 8:7; 15:23.
Revolting from Him. Is 1:5; 31:6.
Despising His law. Neh 9:26.
Despising His counsels. Ps 107:11.
Distrusting His power. Ezek 17:15.
Murmuring against Him. Num 20:3,10.
Refusing to listen to Him. Deut 9:23; Ezek 20:8; Zech 7:11.
Departing from Him. Is 59:13.
Rebellion against governors appointed by Him. Dan 9:5; Josh 1:18.
Departing from His instituted worship. Ex 32:8,9; Josh 22:16–19.
Sinning against light. Job 24:13; John 15:22; Acts 13:41.
Walking after our own thoughts. Is 65:2.
Connected with
Stubbornness. Deut 31:27.
Injustice and corruption. Is 1:23.
Contempt of God. Ps 107:11.
Man is prone to. Deut 31:27; Rom 7:14–18.
The heart is the seat of. Jer 5:23; Matt 15:18,19; Heb 3:12.
They who are guilty of
Aggravate their sin by. Job 34:27.
Practice hypocrisy to hide. Hos 7:14.
Persevere in. Deut 9:7,24.
Increase in, though chastised. Is 1:5.
Warned not to exalt themselves. Ps 66:7.
Denounced. Is 30:1.
Have God as their enemy. Is 63:10.
Have God's hand against them. 1 Sam 12:15; Ps 106:26,27.
Impoverished for. Ps 68:6.
Brought low for. Ps 107:11,12.
Delivered into the hands of enemies on account of. Neh 9:26,27.
Cast out because of it. Ps 5:10; Ezek 20:38.
Restored through Christ alone. Ps 68:18.
Heinousness of. 1 Sam 15:23.
Guilt of
Aggravated by God's fatherly care. Is 1:2; 65:2.
To be avoided. Josh 22:29.
To be confessed. Lam 1:18,20; Dan 9:5.
God alone can forgive. Dan 9:9.
God is ready to forgive. Neh 9:17.
Religious instruction designed to prevent. Ps 78:5,8.
Promises to those who avoid. Deut 28:1–13; 1 Sam 12:14.
Forgiven upon repentance. Neh 9:26,27.
Ministers
Cautioned against. Ezek 2:8.
Sent to those guilty of. Ezek 2:3–7; 3:4–9; Mark 12:4–8.
Should testify against. Num 14:9; Is 30:8,9; Ezek 17:12; 44:6.
Should remind their people of past. Deut 9:7; 31:27.
Punishment for. Lev 26:14–39; 1 Sam 12:15; Is 1:20; Jer 4:16–18; Jer 28:16; Ezek 20:8,38.
Ingratitude of—Illustrated. Is 1:2,3.

REBUKE.

God gives, to his own children. 2 Sam 7:14; Job 5:17; Ps 94:12; 119:67,71,75; Heb 12:6,7.
God gives, to the wicked. Ps 50:21; Is 51:20.
Christ sent to give. Is 2:4; 11:3.
The Holy Spirit gives. John 16:7,8.
Christ gives, in love. Rev 3:19.
On account of
Impenitence. Matt 11:20–24.
Not understanding. Matt 16:9,11; Mark 7:18; Luke 24:25; John 8:43; 13:7,8.
Hardness of heart. Mark 8:17; 16:14.
Fearfulness. Mark 4:40; Luke 24:37,38.
Unbelief. Matt 17:17,20; Mark 16:14.
Vain boasting. Luke 22:34.
Hypocrisy. Matt 15:7; 23:13.
Reviling Christ. Luke 23:40.
Unruly conduct. 1 Thess 5:14.
Oppressing our brethren. Neh 5:7.
Sinful practices. Matt 21:13; Luke 3:19; John 2:16.
The Scriptures are profitable for. Ps 19:7–11; 2 Tim 3:16.
When from God
Is for correction. Ps 39:11.
Is despised by the wicked. Prov 1:30.
Should not discourage believers. Heb 12:5.
Pray that it be not be in anger. Ps 6:1.
Should be accompanied by exhortation to repentance. 1 Sam 12:20–25.
Declared to be
Better than secret love. Prov 27:5.
Better than the praise of fools. Eccl 7:5.
An excellent oil. Ps 141:5.
More profitable to believers, than blows to a fool. Prov 17:10.
A proof of faithful friendship. Prov 27:6.
Leads to
Understanding. Prov 15:32.
Knowledge. Prov 19:25.
Wisdom. Prov 15:31; 29:15.
Honor. Prov 13:18.
Happiness. Prov 6:23.
Eventually brings more respect than flattery. Prov 28:23.
Of those who offend, a warning to others. Lev 19:17; Acts 5:3,4,9; 1 Tim 5:20; Titus 1:10,13.
Hypocrites not qualified to give. Matt 7:5.
Ministers are sent to give. Jer 44:4; Ezek 3:17.
Ministers are empowered to give. Mic 3:8.
Ministers should give
Openly. 1 Tim 5:20.
Fearlessly. Ezek 2:3–7.
With all authority. Titus 2:15.
With longsuffering, etc. 2 Tim 4:2.
Unreservedly. Is 58:1.
Sharply, if necessary. Titus 1:13.
With Christian love. 2 Thess 3:15.
They who give, are hated by scoffers. Prov 9:8; 15:12.
Hatred of, a proof of stupidity. Prov 12:1.
Hatred of, leads to destruction. Prov 15:10; 29:1.
Contempt of, leads to remorse. Prov 5:12.
Rejection of, leads to error. Prov 10:17.
Believers should
Administer. Lev 19:17; Eph 5:11.
Give no occasion for. Phil 2:15.
Receive kindly. Ps 141:5.
Love those who give. Prov 9:8.
Delight in those who give. Prov 24:25.

RECONCILIATION WITH GOD.

Predicted. Dan 9:24; Is 53:5.

Proclaimed by angels at the birth of Christ. Luke 2:14.

Blotting out the hand-legalistic requirements is necessary to. Eph 2:16; Col 2:14.

Effected for men

By God in Christ. 2 Cor 5:19.

By Christ as High Priest. Heb 2:17.

By the death of Christ. Rom 5:10; Eph 2:16; Col 1:21,22.

By the blood of Christ. Eph 2:13; Col 1:20.

While alienated from God. Col 1:21.

Without strength. Rom 5:6.

Yet sinners. Rom 5:8.

While enemies to God. Rom 5:10.

The ministry of committed to ministers. 2 Cor 5:18,19.

Ministers, in Christ's stead, should beseech men to seek. 2 Cor 5:20.

Effects of

Peace of God. Rom 5:1; Eph 2:16,17.

Access to God. Rom 5:2; Eph 2:18.

Union of Jews and Gentiles. Eph 2:14.

Union of things in heaven and earth. Eph 1:10; Col 1:20;

A pledge of final salvation. Rom 5:10.

REDEMPTION.

Defined. 1 Cor 6:20; 7:23.

Is of God. Is 44:21–23; 43:1; Luke 1:68.

Is by Christ and His blood. Matt 20:28; Acts 20:28; 1 Cor 1:30; Gal 3:13; 4:4,5; Heb 9:12; 1 Pet 1:19; Rev 5:9.

Is from

The bondage of the law. Gal 4:5.

The curse of the law. Gal 3:13.

The power of sin. Rom 6:18,22.

The power of the grave and death. Ps 49:15; Hos 13:14.

All troubles. Ps 25:22.

All iniquity. Ps 130:8; Titus 2:14.

All evil. Gen 48:16.

The present evil age. Gal 1:4.

Aimless conduct. 1 Pet 1:18.

Enemies. Ps 106:10,11; Jer 15:21.

Destruction. Ps 103:4.

Man cannot effect. Ps 49:7.

Corruptible things cannot purchase. 1 Pet 1:18.

Procures for us

Justification. Rom 3:24.

Forgiveness of sin. Eph 1:7; Col 1:14.

Adoption. Gal 4:4,5.

Purification. Titus 2:14.

The present life, the only season for. Job 36:18,19.

Described as

Precious. Ps 49:8.

Abundant. Ps 130:7.

Eternal. Heb 9:12.

Subjects of

The soul. Ps 49:8.

The body. Rom 8:23.

The life. Ps 103:4; Lam 3:58.

The inheritance. Eph 1:14.

Manifests the

Power of God. Is 50:2.

Grace of God. Is 52:3.

Love and pity of God. Is 63:9; John 3:16; Rom 6:8; 1 John 4:10.

A subject for praise. Is 44:22,23; 51:11.

Old Testament believers partakers of. Heb 9:15.

They who partake of

Are the property of God. Is 43:1; 1 Cor 6:20.

Are firstfruits to God. Rev 14:4.

Are a special people. 2 Sam 7:23; Titus 2:14; 1 Pet 2:9.

Have assurance of. Job 19:25; Ps 31:5.

Are sealed to the day of. Eph 4:30.

Are zealous for good works. Eph 2:10; Titus 2:14; 1 Pet 2:9.

Walk safely in holiness. Is 35:8,9.

Shall return to Zion with joy. Is 35:10.

Alone can learn the songs of heaven. Rev 14:3,4.

Commit themselves to God. Ps 31:5.

Have a guarantee of the completion of. Eph 1:14; 2 Cor 1:22.

Wait for the completion of. Rom 8:23; Phil 3:20,21; Titus 2:11–13.

Pray for the completion of. Ps 26:11; 44:26.

Praise God for. Ps 71:23; 103:4; Rev 5:9.

Should glorify God for. 1 Cor 6:20.

Should be without fear. Is 43:1.

REPENTANCE.

What it is. Is 45:22; Acts 14:15; 2 Cor 5:17; Col 3:2; 1 Thess 1:9.

Commanded to all by God. Ezek 18:30–32; Acts 17:30.

Commanded by Christ. Rev 2:5,16; 3:3.

Given by God. Acts 11:18; 2 Tim 2:25.

Christ came to call sinners to. Matt 9:13.

Christ exalted to give. Acts 5:31.

By the operation of the Holy Spirit. Zech 12:10.

Called repentance to life. Acts 11:18.

Called repentance to salvation. 2 Cor 7:10.

We should be led to, by

The long-suffering of God. Gen 6:3; 1 Pet 3:20; 2 Pet 3:9.

The goodness of God. Rom 2:4.

The chastisements of God. 1 Kin 8:47; Rev 3:19.

Godly sorrow. 2 Cor 7:10.

Necessary to the pardon of sin. Acts 2:38; 3:19; 8:22.

Conviction of sin necessary to. 1 Kin 8:38; Prov 28:13; Acts 2:37,38; 19:18.

Preached

By Christ. Matt 4:17; Mark 1:15.

By John the Baptist. Matt 3:2.

By the apostles. Mark 6:12; Acts 20:21.

In the name of Christ. Luke 24:47.

Not to be regretted of. 2 Cor 7:10.

Now is the time for. Ps 95:7,8; Prov 27:1; Is 55:6; 2 Cor 6:2; Heb 3:7,8; 4:7.

There is joy in heaven over one sinner brought to. Luke 15:7,10.

Ministers should rejoice over their people on their. 2 Cor 7:9.

Should be evidenced by fruits. Is 1:16,17; Dan 4:27; Matt 3:8; Acts 26:20.

Should be accompanied by

Humility. 2 Chr 7:14; James 4:9,10.

Shame and confusion. Ezra 9:6–15; Jer 31:19; Ezek 16:61,63; Dan 9:7,8.

Self-abhorrence. Job 42:6.

Confession. Lev 26:40; Job 33:27.

Faith. Matt 21:32; Mark 1:15; Acts 20:21.

Prayer. 1 Kin 8:33; Acts 8:22.

Conversion. Acts 3:19; 26:20.

Turning from sin. 2 Chr 6:26.

Turning from idolatry. Ezek 14:6; 1 Thess 1:9.

Greater zeal in the path of duty. 2 Cor 7:11.

Exhortations to. Ezek 14:6; 18:30; Acts 2:38; 3:19.

The wicked

Averse to. Jer 8:6; Matt 21:32.

Not led to by the judgments of God. Rev 9:20,21; 16:9.

Not led to, by miraculous intervemtion. Luke 16:30,31.

Neglect the opportunity for. Rev 2:21.

Condemned for neglecting. Matt 11:20.

Danger of neglecting. Matt 11:20–24; Luke 13:3,5; Rev 2:22.

Neglect of, followed by swift judgment. Rev 2:5,16.

Denied to apostates. Heb 6:4–6.

RESURRECTION, THE.

A doctrine of the Old Testament. Job 19:26; Ps 16:10; 49:15; Is 26:19; Dan 12:2; Hos 13:14.

A first principle of the gospel. 1 Cor 15:13,14; Heb 6:1,2.

Expected by the Jews. John 11:24; Heb 11:35.

Denied by the Sadducees. Matt 22:23; Luke 20:27; Acts 23:8.

Explained away by false teachers. 2 Tim 2:18.

Called in question by some in the church. 1 Cor 15:12.

Is not contrary to reason. Mark 12:24; John 12:24; Acts 26:8; 1 Cor 15:35–49.

Assumed and proved by our Lord. Matt 22:29–32; Luke 14:14; John 5:28,29.

Preached by the apostles. Acts 4:2; 17:18; 24:15.

Credibility of, shown by the resurrection of individuals. Matt 9:25; 27:53; Luke 7:14; John 11:44; Heb 11:35.

Certainty of, proved by the resurrection of Christ. 1 Cor 15:12–20.

Effected by the power of

God. Matt 22:29.

Christ. John 5:28,29; 6:39,40,44.

The Holy Spirit. Rom 8:11.

Shall be of all the dead. John 5:28; Acts 24:15; Rev 20:13.

Believers in, shall

Rise through Christ. John 11:25; Acts 4:2; 1 Cor 15:21,22.

Rise first. 1 Cor 15:23; 1 Thess 4:16.

Rise to eternal life. Dan 12:2; John 5:29.

Be glorified with Christ. Col 3:4.

Be as the angels. Matt 22:30.

Have incorruptible bodies. 1 Cor 15:42.

Have glorious bodies. 1 Cor 15:43.

Have powerful bodies. 1 Cor 15:43.

Have spiritual bodies. 1 Cor 15:44.

Have bodies like Christ's. Phil 3:21; 1 John 3:2.

Be recompensed. Luke 14:14.

Believers should look forward to. Dan 12:13; Phil 3:11; 2 Cor 5:1.

Of believers shall be followed by the change of those then alive. 1 Cor 15:51; 1 Thess 4:17.

The preaching of, caused

Mocking. Acts 17:32.

Persecution. Acts 23:6; 24:11–15.

Blessedness of those who have part in the first. Rev 20:6.

Of the wicked, shall be to

Shame and everlasting contempt. Dan 12:2.

Damnation. John 5:29.

RESURRECTION OF CHRIST, THE.

Foretold by the prophets. Ps 16:10; Is 26:19; Acts 13:34,35.

Foretold by Himself. Matt 20:19; Mark 9:9; 14:28; John 2:19–22.

Was necessary for

The fulfilment of Scripture. Luke 24:45,46.

Forgiveness of sins. 1 Cor 15:17.

Justification. Rom 4:25; 8:34.

Hope. 1 Cor 15:19.

The efficacy of preaching. 1 Cor 15:14.

The efficacy of faith. 1 Cor 15:14,17.

A proof of His being the Son of God. Ps 2:7; Acts 13:33; Rom 1:4.

Effected by

The power of God. Acts 2:24; 3:15; Rom 8:11; Eph 1:20; Col 2:12.

His own power. John 2:19; 10:18.

The power of the Holy Spirit. 1 Pet 3:18.

On the first day of the week. Mark 16:9.

On the third day after His death. Luke 24:46; Acts 10:40; 1 Cor 15:4.

The apostles

At first did not understand the predictions respecting. Mark 9:10; John 20:9.

Very slow to believe. Mark 16:13; Luke 24:9,11,37,38.

Rebuked for their unbelief of. Mark 16:14.

He appeared after to

Mary Magdalene. Mark 16:9; John 20:18.

The women. Matt 28:9.

Simon Peter. Luke 24:34.

Two disciples. Luke 24:13–31.

Apostles, except Thomas. John 20:19,24.

Apostles, Thomas being present. John 20:26.

Apostles at the sea of Tiberias. John 21:1.

Apostles in Galilee. Matt 28:16,17.

About five hundred brethren. 1 Cor 15:6.

James. 1 Cor 15:7.

All the apostles. Luke 24:51; Acts 1:9; 1 Cor 15:7.

Paul. 1 Cor 15:8.

Fraud impossible in. Matt 27:63–66.

He gave many infallible proofs of. Luke 24:35,39,43; John 20:20,27; Acts 1:3.

Was attested by

Angels. Matt 28:5–7; Luke 24:4–7,23.

Apostles. Acts 1:22; 2:32; 3:15; 4:33.

His enemies. Matt 28:11–15.

Asserted and preached by the Apostles. Acts 25:19; 26:23.

Believers

Begotten to a living hope. 1 Pet 1:3, 21.

Desire to know the power of. Phil 3:10.

Should keep, in remembrance. 2 Tim 2:8.

Shall rise in the likeness of. Rom 6:5; 1 Cor 15:49; Phil 3:21.

Is an emblem of the new birth. Rom 6:4; Col 2:12.

The firstfruits of our resurrection. Acts 26:23; 1 Cor 15:20,23.

Followed by His exaltation. Acts 4:10,11; Rom 8:34; Eph 1:20; Phil 2:9,10; Rev 1:18.

An assurance of the judgment. Acts 17:31.

REVENGE.

Forbidden by God. Lev 19:18; Prov 24:17,29; Matt 5:39–41; Rom 12:17,19; 1 Thess 5:15; 1 Pet 3:9.

Christ an example of forbearing. Is 53:7; 1 Pet 2:23.

Rebuked by Christ. Luke 9:54,55.

Inconsistent with Christian spirit. Luke 9:55.

Proceeds from a spiteful heart. Ezek 25:15.

Instead of taking, we should

Trust in God. Prov 20:22; Rom 12:16.

Exhibit love. Lev 19:18; Luke 6:35.

Give place to wrath. Rom 12:19.

Exercise forbearance. Matt 5:38–41.

Bless. Rom 12:14.

Overcome others by kindness. Prov 25:21,22; Rom 12:20.

Keep others from taking. 1 Sam 24:10; 25:24–31; 26:9.

The wicked are eager for. Jer 20:10.

Punishment for. Ezek 25:15–17; Amos 1:11,12.

REWARD OF BELIEVERS, THE.

Is from God. Rom 2:7; Col 3:24; Heb 11:6.

Is of grace, through faith alone. Rom 4:4,5,16; 11:6.

Is of God's good pleasure. Matt 20:14,15; Luke 12:32.

Prepared by Christ. John 14:2.

As servants of Christ. Col 3:24.

Described as

Being with Christ. John 12:26; 14:3; Phil 1:23; 1 Thess 4:17.

Beholding the face of God. Ps 17:15; Matt 5:8; Rev 22:4.

Beholding the glory of Christ. John 17:24.

Being glorified with Christ. Rom 8:17,18; Phil 3:21; Col 3:4; 1 John 3:2.

Sitting in judgment with Christ. Dan 7:22; Matt 19:28; Luke 22:30; 1 Cor 6:2.

Reigning with Christ. 2 Tim 2:12; Rev 3:21; 5:10; 20:4; Rev 22:5.

A crown of righteousness. 2 Tim 4:8.

A crown of glory. 1 Pet 5:4.

A crown of life. James 1:12; Rev 2:10.

An incorruptible crown. 1 Cor 9:25.

Joint heir with Christ. Rom 8:17.

An inheritance of all things. Acts 20:32; 26:18; Col 1:12; Heb 9:15; 1 Pet 1:4; Rev 21:7.

A kingdom. Matt 25:34; Luke 22:29; Heb 12:28.

Shining as the stars. Dan 12:3.

Everlasting light. Is 60:19.

Everlasting life. Luke 18:30; John 6:40; 17:2,3; Rom 2:7; 6:23; 1 John 5:11.

An enduring substance. Heb 10:34.

A house eternal in the heavens. 2 Cor 5:1.

A city which had foundation. Heb 11:10.

Entering into the joy of the Lord. Matt 25:21; Heb 12:2.

Rest. Heb 4:9; Rev 14:13.

Fullness of joy. Ps 16:11.

The prize of the upward call of God in Christ. Phil 3:14.

Treasure in heaven. Matt 19:21; Luke 12:33.

An eternal weight of glory. 2 Cor 4:17.

Is great. Matt 5:12; Luke 6:35; Heb 10:35.

Is full. 2 John 8.

Is sure. Prov 11:18.

Is satisfying. Ps 17:15.

Is inestimable. Is 64:4; 1 Cor 2:9.

Believers may feel confident of. Ps 73:24; Is 25:8,9; 2 Cor 5:1; 2 Tim 4:8.

Hope of, a cause of rejoicing. Rom 5:2.

Be careful not to lose. 2 John 8.

The prospect of, should lead to

Diligence. 2 John 8.

Pressing forward. Phil 3:14.

Enduring suffering for Christ. 2 Cor 4:16–18; Heb 11:26.

Faithfulness to death. Rev 2:10.

Present afflictions not to be compared with. Rom 8:18; 2 Cor 5:17.

Shall be given at the second coming of Christ. Matt 16:27; Rev 22:12.

RICHES.

The true riches. 1 Cor 1:30; Eph 3:8; Col 2:3; 1 Pet 2:7.

God gives. 1 Sam 2:7; Eccl 5:19.

To God belongs this world's riches. Hag 2:8.

God gives power to obtain. Deut 8:18.

The blessing of the Lord brings. Prov 10:22.

Give worldly power. Prov 22:7.

Described as

Temporary. Prov 27:24.

Uncertain. 1 Tim 6:17.

Unsatisfying. Eccl 4:8; 5:10.

Corruptible. James 5:2; 1 Pet 1:18.

Fleeting. Prov 23:5; Rev 18:16,17.

Deceitful. Matt 13:22.

Liable to be stolen. Matt 6:19.

Perishable. Jer 48:36.

Often an obstruction to the gospel. Matt 13:22; Mark 10:23–25.

The love of, the root of all evil. 1 Tim 6:10.

Often lead to

Pride. Ezek 28:5; Hos 12:8.

Forgetting God. Deut 8:13,14.

Denying God. Prov 30:8,9.

Forsaking God. Deut 32:15.

Rebelling against God. Neh 9:25,26.

Rejecting Christ. Matt 10:22; 19:22.

Self-sufficiency. Prov 28:11.

Anxiety. Eccl 5:12.

An overbearing spirit. Prov 18:23.

Violence. Mic 6:12.

Oppression. James 2:6.

Fraud. James 5:4.

Sensual indulgence. Luke 16:19; James 5:5.

Be not over-anxious for. Prov 30:8.

Labor not for. Prov 23:4.

They who covet

Fall into temptation and hurtful lusts. 1 Tim 6:9.

Err from the faith. 1 Tim 6:10.

Use unlawful means to acquire. Prov 28:20.

Bring trouble on themselves. 1 Tim 6:10.

Bring trouble on their families. Prov 15:27.

Cannot secure prosperity. James 1:11.

Cannot redeem the soul. Ps 49:6–9; 1 Pet 1:18.

Cannot deliver in the day of God's wrath. Prov 11:4; Zeph 1:18; Rev 6:15–17.

They who possess, should

Ascribe them to God. 1 Chr 29:12.

Not trust in them. Job 31:24; 1 Tim 6:17.

Not set the heart on them. Ps 62:10.

Not boast of obtaining them. Deut 8:17.

Not glory in them. Jer 9:23.

Not hoard them up. Matt 6:19.

Devote them to God's service. 1 Chr 29:3; Mark 12:42–44.

Give of them to the poor. Matt 19:21; 1 John 3:17.

Use them in promoting the salvation of others. Luke 16:9.

Be liberal in all things. 1 Chr 29:14; 1 Tim 6:18.

Not to be high-minded. 1 Tim 6:17.
When converted, rejoice in being
humbled. James 1:9,10.
Heavenly treasures superior to. Matt
6:19,20.
Of the wicked stored up for the just. Prov
13:22.
The wicked
Often increase in. Ps 73:12.
Often spend their day in. Job 21:13.
Swallow down. Job 20:15.
Trust in the abundance of. Ps 52:7.
Heap up. Job 27:16; Ps 39:6; Eccl 2:26.
Keep, to their hurt. Eccl 5:13.
Boast about their. Ps 49:6; 52:7.
Profit not by. Prov 11:4; 13:7; Eccl
5:11.
Have trouble with. Prov 15:6; 1 Tim
6:9,10.
Must leave, to others. Ps 49:10.
Vanity of heaping up. Ps 39:6; Eccl
5:10,11.
Guilt of trusting in. Job 31:24,28; Ezek
28:4,5,8.
Denunciations against those who
Get, dishonestly. Prov 13:11; 21:6; Jer
17:11.
Increase, by oppression. Prov 22:16;
Hab 2:6–8; Mic 2:2,3.
Hoard up. Eccl 5:13,14; James 5:3.
Trust in. Prov 11:28; Luke 6:24.
Abuse. James 5:1,5.
Spend, upon their appetite. Job 20:15–
17.
Folly and danger of trusting to—
Illustrated. Luke 12:16–21.
Danger of misusing—Illustrated. Luke
16:19–25.

RIGHTEOUSNESS.

Is obedience to God's law. Deut 6:25; Ps
1:2; Rom 10:5; Luke 1:6.
God loves. Ps 11:7.
God looks for. Is 5:7.
Christ
Is the "sun" of. Mal 4:2.
Loves. Ps 45:7; Heb 1:9.
Was girded with. Is 11:5.
Put on, as breastplate. Is 59:17.
Was sustained by. Is 59:16.
Preached. Ps 40:9.
Fulfilled all. Matt 3:15.
Became. 1 Cor 1:30.
Is the end of the law for. Rom 10:4.
Has brought in everlasting. Dan 9:24.
Shall judge with. Ps 72:2; Is 11:4; Acts
17:31; Rev 19:11.
Shall reign in. Ps 45:6; Is 32:1; Heb
1:8.
Shall execute. Ps 99:4; Jer 23:6.
None, by nature have. Job 15:14; Ps 14:3;
Rom 3:10.
Cannot come by the law. Gal 2:21; 3:21.
No salvation by works of. Rom 3:20;
9:31,32; Gal 2:16; Eph 2:8,9; 2 Tim
1:9; Titus 3:5.
Unregenerate man seeks justification by
works of. Luke 18:9; Rom 10:3.
The blessing of God is not to be attributed
to our works of. Deut 9:5.
Believers
Have, in Christ. Is 45:24; 54:17; 2 Cor
5:21.
Have, imputed. Rom 4:11,22.
Are covered with the robe of. Is 61:10.
Receive, from God. Ps 24:5.
Are renewed in. Eph 4:24.
Are led in the paths of. Ps 23:3.
Are servants of. Rom 6:16,18.
Characterized by. Gen 18:25; Ps 1:5,6.
Know. Is 51:7.

Do. 1 John 2:29; 3:7.
Work, by faith. Heb 11:33.
Follow after. Is 51:1.
Put on. Job 29:14.
Wait for the hope of. Gal 5:5.
Pray for the spirit of. Ps 51:10.
Hunger and thirst after. Matt 5:6.
Walk before God in. 1 Kin 3:6.
Offer the sacrifice of. Ps 4:5; 51:19.
Put no trust in their own. Phil 3:6–8.
Count their own, as filthy rags. Is
64:6.
Should seek. Zeph 2:3.
Should live in. Titus 2:12; 1 Pet 2:24.
Should serve God in. Luke 1:75.
Should yield their members to. Rom
6:13,19.
Should have on the breastplate of. Eph
6:14.
Shall receive a crown of. 2 Tim 4:8.
Shall see God's face in. Ps 17:15.
Of believers endures forever. Ps 112:3,9;
2 Cor 9:9.
An evidence of the new birth. 1 John 2:29.
The kingdom of God is. Rom 14:17.
The fruit of the Spirit is in all. Eph 5:9.
The Scriptures instruct in. 2 Tim 3:16.
Judgments designed to lead to. Is 26:9.
Chastisements yield the fruit of. Heb
12:11.
Has no fellowship with unrighteousness.
2 Cor 6:14.
Ministers should
Be preachers of. 2 Pet 2:5.
Reason about. Acts 24:25.
Follow after. 1 Tim 6:11; 2 Tim 2:22.
Be clothed with. Ps 132:9.
Be armed with. 2 Cor 6:7.
Pray for the fruit of, in their people.
2 Cor 9:10; Phil 1:11.
Keep believers in the right way. Prov 11:5;
13:6.
Judgment should be executed in. Lev
19:15.
They who walk in, and follow
Are righteous. 1 John 3:7.
Are the excellent of the earth. Ps 16:3;
Prov 12:26.
Are loved by God. Ps 5:12;146:8; Prov
15:9; Luke 18:7; Acts 10:35; James
5:16.
Are objects of God's watchful care. Job
36:7; Ps 34:15; Prov 10:3; 1 Pet
3:12.
Are tried by God. Ps 11:5.
Are exalted by God. Job 36:7.
Dwell in security. Is 33:15,16.
Are bold as a lion. Prov 28:1.
Are delivered out of all troubles. Ps
34:19; Prov 11:8.
Are never forsaken by God. Ps 37:25.
Are abundantly provided for. Ps 112:3;
Prov 13:25; 15:6; Matt 6:25–33.
Think and desire good. Prov 11:23;
12:5.
Know the secret of the Lord. Ps 25:14;
Prov 3:32.
Have their prayers heard. Ps 34:17;
Prov 15:29; 1 Pet 3:12.
Have their desires granted. Prov 10:24.
Find it with life and honor. Prov 21:21.
Shall hold to their way. Job 17:9.
Shall never be moved. Ps 15:2,5;
55:22; Prov 10:30; 12:3.
Shall be remembered. Ps 112:6.
Shall flourish as a branch. Prov 11:28.
Shall be glad in the Lord. Ps 64:10.
Brings its own reward. Prov 11:18; Is 3:10.
Leads to life. Prov 11:19; 12:28.
The work of, shall be peace. Is 32:17.
Is a crown of glory to the aged. Prov 16:31.

The wicked
Are far from. Ps 119:150; Is 46:12.
Are free from. Rom 6:20.
Are enemies of. Acts 13:10.
Leave off. Amos 5:7; Ps 36:3.
Follow not after. Rom 9:30.
Do not. 1 John 3:10.
Do not obey. Rom 2:8; 2 Thess 2:12.
Love lying rather than. Ps 52:3.
Make mention of God, not it. Is 48:1.
Do not take opportunities to learn. Is
26:10; Ps 106:43.
Hate those who follow. Ps 31:18;
34:21; Matt 27:39–44..
Slay those who follow. Ps 37:32;
1 John 3:12; Matt 23:35.
Should break off their sins by. Dan
4:27.
Should awake to. 1 Cor 15:34.
Should sow to themselves in. Hos
10:12.
Vainly wish to die as those who follow.
Num 23:10.
The throne of kings established by. Prov
16:12; 25:5.
Nations exalted by. Prov 14:34.
Blessedness of
Having imputed, without works. Rom
4:6.
Doing. Ps 106:3.
Hungering and thirsting after. Matt
5:6.
Suffering for. 1 Pet 3:14.
Being persecuted for. Matt 5:10.
Turning others to. Dan 12:3.

RIGHTEOUSNESS IMPUTED.

Predicted. Is 56:1; Ezek 16:14.
Revealed in the gospel. Rom 1:17.
Is of the Lord. Is 54:17.
Described as
The righteousness of faith. Rom 4:13;
9:30; 10:6.
The righteousness of God, apart from
the law. Rom 3:21.
The righteousness of God by faith in
Christ. Rom 3:22.
Christ being made righteousness to us.
1 Cor 1:30.
Our being made the righteousness of
God, in Christ. 2 Cor 5:21.
Christ is the end of the law for. Rom 10:4.
Christ called "The Lord our righteous-
ness." Jer 23:6.
Christ brings in an everlasting
righteousness. Dan 9:24.
Is a free gift. Rom 5:17.
God's righteousness never to be abolished.
Is 5:16.
The promises made through. Rom 4:13.
Believers
Receive, on believing. Rom 4:5,11,24.
Clothed with the robe of righteous-
ness. Is 61:10.
Exalted in righteousness. Ps 89:16.
Desire to be found in. Phil 3:9.
Glory in having. Is 45:24,25.
Exhortation to seek righteousness. Matt
6:33.
The Gentiles attained to. Rom 9:30.
The Jews
Ignorant of. Rom 10:3.
Stumble at righteousness by faith.
Rom 9:32.
Submit not to. Rom 10:3.

RIGHTEOUSNESS OF GOD, THE.

Is part of His character. Ps 7:9; 116:5;
119:137.
Described as
Very high. Ps 71:19.

Abundant. Ps 48:10.
Beyond computation. Ps 71:15.
Everlasting. Ps 119:142.
Enduring for ever. Ps 111:3.
The habitation of His throne. Ps 97:2.
Christ acknowledged. John 17:25.
Christ committed His cause to. 1 Pet 2:23.
Angels acknowledge. Rev 16:5.
Exhibited in
His testimonies. Ps 119:138,144.
His commandments. Deut 4:8; Ps 119:172.
His judgments. Ps 19:9; 119:7,62.
His Word. Ps 119:123.
His ways. Ps 145:17.
His acts. Judg 5:11; 1 Sam 12:7.
His government. Ps 96:13; 98:9.
The gospel. Ps 85:10; Rom 3:25,26.
The final judgment. Acts 17:31.
The punishment of the wicked. Rom 2:5; 2 Thess 1:6; Rev 16:7; 19:2.
Shown to the posterity of believers. Ps 103:17.
Shown openly before the heathen. Ps 98:2.
God delights in the exercise of. Jer 9:24.
The heavens shall declare. Ps 50:6; 97:6.
Believers
Ascribe, to Him. Job 36:3; Dan 9:7.
Acknowledge, in His dealings. Ezra 9:15.
Acknowledge, though the wicked prosper. Ps 73:12–17; Jer 12:1.
Recognize, in the fulfilment of His promises. Neh 9:8.
Confident of beholding. Mic 7:9.
Upheld by. Is 41:10.
Do not conceal. Ps 40:10.
Mention, only. Ps 71:16.
Talk of. Ps 35:28; 71:15,24.
Declare to others. Ps 22:31.
Magnify. Ps 7:17; 51:14; 145:7.
Plead in prayer. Ps 143:11; Dan 9:16.
Leads God to love righteousness. Ps 11:7.
We should pray
To be led in. Ps 5:8.
To be revived in. Ps 119:40.
To be delivered in. Ps 31:1; 71:2.
To be answered in. Ps 143:1.
To be judged according to. Ps 35:24.
For its continued manifestation. Ps 36:10.
Redemption of His people designed to teach. Mic 6:4,5.
The wicked have no interest in. Ps 69:27.

SABBATH, THE.

Instituted by God. Gen 2:3.
Grounds of its institution. Gen 2:2,3; Ex 20:11.
The seventh day observed as. Ex 20:9–11.
Made for man. Mark 2:27.
God
Blessed. Gen 2:3; Ex 20:11.
Sanctified. Gen 2:3; Ex 31:15.
Hallowed. Ex 20:11.
Commanded, its observance. Ex 20:8; Lev 19:3,30.
Will have His goodness commemorated in the observance of. Deut 5:15.
Shows favor in appointing. Ex 23:12; Neh 9:14.
A sign of the covenant. Ex 31:13,17.
A type of the heavenly rest. Heb 4:4,9.
Christ
Is Lord of. Mark 2:28.
Was accustomed to observe. Luke 4:16.
Taught on. Luke 4:31; 6:6.
Servants and cattle should be allowed to rest upon. Ex 20:10; Deut 5:14.
No manner of work to be done on. Ex 20:10; Lev 23:3.

No purchases to be made on. Neh 10:31; 13:15–17.
No burdens to be carried on. Neh 13:19; Jer 17:21.
Divine worship to be celebrated on. Ezek 46:3; Acts 16:13.
The Scriptures to be read on. Acts 13:27; 15:21.
The Word of God to be preached on. Acts 13:14,15,44; 17:2; 18:4.
Works connected with religious service lawful on. Num 28:9; Matt 12:5; John 7:23.
Works of mercy lawful on. Matt 12:12; 13:16; John 9:14.
Necessary wants may be supplied. Matt 12:1; Luke 13:15; 14:1.
Called
The Sabbath of the Lord. Ex 20:10; Lev 23:3; Deut 5:14.
The Sabbath of rest. Ex 31:15.
A holy sabbath to the Lord. Ex 16:23.
God's holy day. Is 58:13.
Old Testaments believers were to
Observe. Neh 13:22.
Honor God in observing. Is 58:13.
Rejoice in. Ps 118:24; Is 58:13.
Testify against those who desecrate. Neh 13:15,20,21.
Blessedness of honoring. Is 58:13,14.
Blessedness of keeping. Is 56:2,6.
Denunciations against those who profane. Neh 13:18; Jer 17:27.
Punishment of those who profane. Ex 31:14,15; Num 15:32–36.
The wicked
Pollute. Is 56:2; Ezek 20:13,16.
Profane. Neh 13:17; Ezek 22:8.
Wearied by. Amos 8:5.
Hide their eyes from. Ezek 22:26.
Do their own pleasure on. Is 58:13.
Do work and business on. Neh 10:31; 13:15,16.
Sometimes pretend to be zealous for. Luke 13:14; John 9:16.
May be judicially deprived of. Lam 2:6; Hos 2:11.

SACRIFICES.

Divine institution of. Gen 3:21; 1:29; 9:3; 4:4,5; Heb 11:4.
To be offered to God alone as supreme. Ex 22:20; Judg 13:16; 2 Kin 5:17; 17:36.; Jon 1:16.
Consisted of
Clean animals or bloody sacrifices. Gen 8:20.
The fruits of the earth or sacrifices without blood. Gen 4:4; Lev 2:1.
Always offered upon altars. Ex 20:24.
The offering of, an acknowledgment of sin. Heb 10:3.
Were offered
From the earliest age. Gen 4:3,4.
By the patriarchs. Gen 22:2,13; 31:54; 46:1; Job 1:5.
After the departure of Israel from Egypt. Ex 5:3,17; 18:12; 24:5.
Under the Mosaic age. Lev 1:1–7:38; Heb 10:1–3.
Daily. Ex 29:38,39; Num 28:3,4.
Weekly. Num 28:9,10.
Monthly. Num 28:11.
Yearly. Lev 16:3; 1 Sam 1:3,21; 20:6.
At all the feasts. Num 10:10.
For the whole nation. Lev 16:15–30; 1 Chr 29:21.
For individuals. Lev 1:2; 17:8.
In faith of a coming Savior. Heb 11:4,17,28.

Required to be perfect and without blemish. Lev 22:19; Deut 15:21; 17:1; Mal 1:8,14.
Generally the best of their kind. Gen 4:4; 1 Sam 15:22; Ps 66:15; Is 1:11.
Different kinds of
Burnt offering wholly consumed by fire. Lev 1:1–17; 1 Kin 18:38.
Sin offering for sins of ignorance. Lev 4:1–35.
Trespass offering for intentional sins. Lev 6:1–7; 7:1–7.
Peace offering. Lev 3:1–17.
To be brought to the place appointed by God. Deut 12:6; 2 Chr 7:12.
Were bound to the horns of the altar. Ps 118:27.
Were seasoned with salt. Lev 2:13; Mark 9:49.
Often consumed by fire from heaven. Lev 9:24; 1 Kin 18:38; 2 Chr 7:1.
When bloody, accompanied with meat and drink offering. Num 15:3–12.
No leaven offered with, except for peace offering. Ex 23:18; Lev 7:13.
Fat of, not to remain until morning. Ex 23:8.
The priests
Appointed to offer. 1 Sam 2:28; Ezek 44:11,15; Heb 5:1; 8:3.
Had a portion of, and lived by. Ex 29:27,28; Deut 18:3; Josh 13:14; 1 Cor 9:13.
Were typical of Christ's sacrifice. 1 Cor 5:7; Eph 5:2; Heb 10:1,11,12.
Were accepted when offered in sincerity and faith. Gen 4:4; 8:21; Heb 11:4.
Imparted a legal purification. Heb 9:13,22.
Could not take away sin. Ps 40:6; Heb 9:9; 10:1–11.
Without obedience, worthless. 1 Sam 15:22; Prov 21:3; Mark 12:33.
The covenants of God confirmed by. Gen 15:9–17; Ex 24:5–8; Ps 50:5; Heb 9:19,20.
The Jews
Condemned for not treating with respect. 1 Sam 2:29; Mal 1:12.
Condemned for bringing defective and blemished. Mal 1:13,14.
Condemned for not offering. Is 43:23,24.
Unaccepted in, on account of sin. Is 1:11,15; 66:3; Hos 8:13.
Condemned for offering, to idols. 2 Chr 34:25; Is 65:3,7; Ezek 20:28,31.
Offered to false gods, are offered to devils. Lev 17:7; Deut 32:17; Ps 106:37; 1 Cor 10:20.
On great occasions, very numerous. 2 Chr 5:6; 7:5.
For public use often provided by the state. 2 Chr 31:3.

SALVATION.

Is of God. Ps 3:8; 37:39; Jer 3:23.
Is of the purpose of God. 2 Tim 1:9.
Is of the appointment of God. 1 Thess 5:9.
God is willing to give. 1 Tim 2:4.
Is by Christ. Is 63:9; Eph 5:23.
Is by Christ alone. Is 45:21,22; 59:16; Acts 4:12.
Announced after the fall. Gen 3:15.
Of Israel, predicted. Is 35:4; 45:17; Zech 9:16; Rom 11:26.
Of the Gentiles, predicted. Is 45:22; 49:6; 52:10.
Revealed in the gospel. Eph 1:13; 2 Tim 1:10.

Came to the Gentiles through the fall of
the Jews. Rom 11:11.

Christ

The Captain of. Heb 2:10.
The Author of. Heb 5:9.
Appointed for. Is 49:6.
Raised up for. Luke 1:69.
Has. Zech 9:9.
Brings, with Him. Is 62:11; Luke 19:9.
Mighty to effect. Is 63:1; Heb 7:25.
Came to effect. Matt 18:11; 1 Tim
1:15.
Died to effect. John 3:14,15; Gal 1:4.
Exalted to give. Acts 5:31.

Is not by works. Rom 11:6; Eph 2:9; 2 Tim
1:9; Titus 3:5.
Is of grace. Eph 2:5,8; 2 Tim 1:9; Titus
2:11.
Is of love. Rom 5:8; 1 John 4:9,10.
Is of mercy. Ps 6:4; Titus 3:5.
Is of the long-suffering of God. 2 Pet 3:15.
Is through faith in Christ. Mark 16:16;
Acts 16:31; Rom 10:9; Eph 2:8; 1 Pet
1:5.
Reconciliation to God, a pledge of. Rom
5:10.
Is deliverance from
Sin. Matt 1:21; 1 John 3:5.
Uncleanness. Ezek 36:29.
The devil. Col 2:15; Heb 2:14,15.
Wrath. Rom 5:9; 1 Thess 1:10.
This present evil world. Gal 1:4.
Enemies. Luke 1:71,74.
Eternal death. John 3:16,17.
Confession of Christ necessary to. Rom
10:10.
Regeneration necessary to. John 3:3.
Final perseverance necessary to. Matt
10:22.
Described as
Great. Heb 2:3.
Glorious. 2 Tim 2:10.
Common. Jude 1:3.
From generation to generation. Is
51:8.
To the uttermost. Heb 7:25.
Eternal. Is 45:17; 51:6; Heb 5:9.
Searched into and exhibited by the
prophets. 1 Pet 1:10.
The gospel is the power of God to. Rom
1:16; 1 Cor 1:18.
Preaching the word is the appointed
means of. 1 Cor 1:21.
The Scriptures are able to make wise to.
2 Tim 3:15; James 1:21.
Now is the day of. Is 49:8; 2 Cor 6:2.
From sin, to be worked out with fear and
trembling. Phil 2:12.
Believers
Appointed to obtain. 1 Thess 5:9;
2 Thess 2:13; 2 Tim 1:9.
Are heirs of. Heb 1:14.
Have, through grace. Acts 15:11.
Have a token of, in their patient
suffering for Christ. Phil 1:28,29.
Kept by the power of God to. 1 Pet 1:5.
Beautified with. Ps 149:4.
Clothed with. Is 61:10.
Satisfied by. Luke 2:30.
Love. Ps 40:16.
Hope for. Lam 3:26; Rom 8:24.
Wait for. Gen 49:18; Lam 3:26.
Long for. Ps 119:81,174.
Earnestly look for. Ps 119:123.
Daily approach nearer to. Rom 13:11.
Receive, as the end of their faith. 1 Pet
1:9.
Welcome the news of. Is 52:7; Rom
10:15.
Pray to be visited with. Ps 85:7; 106:4;
119:41.

Pray for the assurance of. Ps 35:3.
Pray for a joyful sense of. Ps 51:12.
Evidence, by works. Heb 6:9,10.
Ascribe, to God. Ps 25:5; Is 12:2.
Praise God for. 1 Chr 16:23; Ps 96:2;
116:12.
Rejoice in. Ps 9:14; 21:1; Is 25:9.
Glory in. 1 Cor 1:31; Gal 6:14.
Declare. Ps 40:10; 71:15.
Godly sorrow works repentance to. 2 Cor
7:10.
All the earth shall see. Is 52:10; Luke 3:6.
Ministers
Give the knowledge of. Luke 1:77.
Show the way of. Acts 16:17.
Should exhort to. Ezek 3:18,19; Acts
2:40.
Should labor to lead others to. Rom
11:14.
Should be clothed in. 2 Chr 6:41; Ps
132:16.
Should use self-denial to lead others
to. 1 Cor 9:22.
Should endure suffering that the elect
may obtain. 2 Tim 2:10.
Are a fragrance of Christ to God, in
those who obtain. 2 Cor 2:15.
The heavenly host ascribe, to God. Rev
7:10; 19:1.
Sought in vain from
Idols. Is 45:20; Jer 2:28.
Earthly power. Jer 3:23.
No escape for those who neglect. Heb 2:3.
Is far off from the wicked. Ps 119:155; Is
59:11.

SANCTIFICATION.

Is separation to the service of God. Ps 4:3;
2 Cor 6:17.
Effected by
God. Ezek 37:28; 1 Thess 5:23;
Jude 1.
Christ. Heb 2:11; 13:12.
The Holy Spirit. Rom 15:16; 1 Cor
6:11.
In Christ. 1 Cor 1:2.
Through the atonement of Christ. Heb
10:10; 13:12.
Through the Word of God. John 17:17,19;
Eph 5:26.
Christ made, of God, to us. 1 Cor 1:30.
Effected by the Holy Spirit. 2 Thess 2:13;
1 Pet 1:2.
All believers are in a state of. Acts 20:32;
26:18; 1 Cor 6:11.
The Church made glorious by. Eph
5:26,27.
Should lead to
Mortification of sin. 1 Thess 4:3,4.
Holiness. Rom 6:22; Eph 5:7-9.
Offering up of believers acceptable
through. Rom 15:16.
Believers fitted for the service of God by.
2 Tim 2:21.
Leads to mortification of sin. 1 Thess 4:3.
Ministers
Set apart to God's service by. Jer 1:5.
Should pray that their people enjoy
complete. 1 Thess 5:23.
Should exhort their people to walk in.
1 Thess 4:1,3.
None can inherit the kingdom of God
without. 1 Cor 6:9-11.
Typified. Gen 2:3; Ex 13:2; 19:14; 40:9-
15; Lev 27:14-16.

SCRIPTURES, THE.

Given by inspiration of God. 2 Tim 3:16.
Given by inspiration of the Holy Spirit.
Acts 1:16; Heb 3:7; 2 Pet 1:21.
Christ sanctioned, by appealing to them.

Matt 4:4; Mark 12:10; John 7:42.
Christ taught out of. Luke 24:27.
Are called the
Word. James 1:21-23; 1 Pet 2:2.
Word of God. Luke 11:28; Heb 4:12.
Word of Christ. Col 3:16.
Word of truth. James 1:18.
Holy Scriptures. Rom 1:2; 2 Tim 3:15.
Scripture of truth. Dan 10:21.
Book. Ps 40:7; Rev 22:19.
Book of the Lord. Is 34:16.
Book of the Law. Neh 8:3; Gal 3:10.
Law of the Lord. Ps 1:2; Is 30:9.
Sword of the Spirit. Eph 6:17.
Oracles of God. Rom 3:2; 1 Pet 4:11.
Contain the promises of the gospel. Rom
1:2.
Reveal the laws, statutes, and judgments
of God. Ex 24:3,4; Deut 4:5,14.
Record divine prophecies. 2 Pet 1:19-21.
Testify of Christ. John 5:39; Acts 10:43;
18:28; 1 Cor 15:3.
Are full and sufficient. Luke 16:29,31.
Are an unerring guide. Prov 6:23; 2 Pet
1:19.
Instruction about salvation. 2 Tim 3:15.
Are profitable both for doctrine and
practice. 2 Tim 3:16,17.
Described as
Pure. Ps 12:6; 119:140; Prov 30:5.
True. Ps 119:160; John 17:17.
Perfect. Ps 19:7.
Precious. Ps 19:10.
Living and powerful. Heb 4:12.
Written for our instruction. Rom 15:4.
Intended for the use of all men. Rom
16:26.
Nothing to be taken from, or added to.
Deut 4:2; 12:32.
One portion of, to be compared with
another. 1 Cor 2:13.
Designed for
Regenerating. James 1:18; 1 Pet 1:23.
Giving life. Ps 119:50,93.
Illuminating. Ps 119:130.
Converting the soul. Ps 19:7.
Making wise the simple. Ps 19:7.
Sanctifying. John 17:17; Eph 5:26.
Producing faith. John 20:31.
Producing hope. Ps 119:49; Rom 15:4.
Producing obedience. Deut 17:19,20.
Cleansing the heart. John 15:3; Eph
5:26.
Cleansing the ways. Ps 119:9.
Keeping from destructive paths. Ps
17:4.
Supporting life. Deut 8:3; Matt 4:4.
Promoting growth in grace. 1 Pet 2:2.
Building up in the faith. Acts 20:32.
Admonishing. Ps 19:11; 1 Cor 10:11.
Comforting. Ps 119:82; Rom 15:4.
Rejoicing the heart. Ps 19:8; 119:111.
Work effectually in them that believe.
1 Thess 2:13.
The letter of, without the Spirit, kills. John
6:63; 2 Cor 3:6.
Ignorance of, a source of error. Matt 22:29;
Acts 13:27.
Christ enables us to understand. Luke
24:45.
The Holy Spirit enables us to understand.
John 16:13; 1 Cor 2:10-14.
No prophecy of, is of any private
interpretation. 2 Pet 1:20.
Everything should be tried by. Is 8:20; Acts
17:11.
Should be
The standard of teaching. 1 Pet 4:11.
Believed. John 2:22.
Appealed to. 1 Cor 1:31; 1 Pet 1:16.
Read. Deut 17:19; Is 34:16.

Read publicly to all. Deut 31:11–13;
Neh 8:3; Jer 36:6; Acts 13:15.
Known. 2 Tim 3:15.
Received, not as the word of men, but
as the word of God. 1 Thess 2:13.
Received with meekness. James 1:21.
Searched. John 5:39; 7:52; Acts 17:11.
Laid up in the heart. Job 11:18.
Taught to children. Deut 6:7; 11:19;
2 Tim 3:15.
Taught to all. 2 Chr 17:7–9; Neh
8:7,8.
Talked of continually. Deut 6:7.
Not handled deceitfully. 2 Cor 4:2.
Not only heard, but obeyed. Matt 7:24;
Luke 11:28; James 1:22.
Used to answer spiritual enemies.
Matt 4:4,7,10; Eph 6:11,17.
All should desire to hear. Neh 8:1.
Advantage of possessing. Rom 3:2.
Believers
Love exceedingly. Ps
119:97,113,159,167.
Delight in. Ps 1:2.
Regard, as sweet. Ps 119:103.
Esteem, above all things. Job 23:12.
Long after. Ps 119:82.
Stand in awe of. Ps 119:161; Is 66:2.
Keep, in remembrance. Ps 119:16.
Grieve when men disobey. Ps 119:158.
Hide, in their hearts. Ps 119:11.
Hope in. Ps 119:74,81,147.
Meditate in. Ps 1:2; 119:99,148.
Rejoice in. Ps 119:162; Jer 15:16.
Trust in. Ps 119:42.
Obey. Ps 119:67; Luke 8:21; John 17:6.
Speak of. Ps 119:172.
Esteem, as a light. Ps 119:105.
Pray to be taught. Ps 119:12,13,33,66.
Pray to be conformed to. Ps 119:133.
Plead the promises of, in prayer. Ps
119:25,28,41,76,169.
Those who search, are truly noble. Acts
17:11.
Blessedness of hearing and obeying. Luke
11:28; James 1:25.
Let them dwell richly in you. Col 3:16.
The wicked
Corrupt. 2 Cor 2:17.
Make, of none effect through their
traditions. Mark 7:9–13.
Reject. Jer 8:9.
Stumble at. 1 Pet 2:8.
Obey not. Ps 119:158.
Frequently twist, to their own
destruction. 2 Pet 3:16.
Consequences for. Jer 36:29–31; Rev
22:18,19.

SEALING OF THE HOLY SPIRIT.

Christ received. John 6:27.
Believers receive. 2 Cor 1:22; Eph 1:13.
Is to the day of redemption. Eph 4:30.
The wicked do not receive. Rev 9:4.
Judgment suspended until all believers
receive. Rev 7:3.

SECOND COMING OF CHRIST, THE.

Time of, unknown. Matt 24:36; Mark
13:32.
Called the
Times of restitution of all things. Acts
3:21; Rom 8:21.
Last time. 1 Pet 1:5.
Appearing of Jesus Christ. 1 Pet 1:7.
Revelation of Jesus Christ. 1 Pet 1:13.
Glorious appearing of our God and
Savior. Titus 2:13.
Coming of the day of God. 2 Pet 3:12.
Day of our Lord Jesus Christ. 1 Cor
1:8.

Foretold by
Prophets. Dan 7:13; Jude 14.
Himself. Matt 25:31; John 14:3.
Apostles. Acts 3:20; 1 Tim 6:14.
Angels. Acts 1:10,11.
Signs preceding. Matt 24:3–51.
The Manner of
In clouds. Matt 24:30; 26:64; Rev 1:7.
In the glory of His Father. Matt 16:27.
In His own glory. Matt 25:31.
In flaming fire. 2 Thess 1:8.
With power and great glory. Matt
24:30.
As He ascended. Acts 1:9,11.
Accompanied by angels. Matt 16:27;
25:31; Mark 8:38; 2 Thess 1:7.
Suddenly. Mark 13:36.
Unexpectedly. Matt 24:44; Luke 12:40.
As a thief in the night. 1 Thess 5:2;
2 Pet 3:10; Rev 16:15.
As the lightning. Matt 24:27.
Is not to make atonement. Rom 6:9,10;
Heb 9:28;10:14.
The purposes of, are to
Complete the salvation of believers.
Heb 9:28; 1 Pet 1:5.
Be glorified in His believers. 2 Thess
1:10.
Bring to light the hidden things of
darkness. 1 Cor 4:5.
Judge. Ps 50:3,4; John 5:22; 2 Tim 4:1;
Jude 15.
Reign. Is 24:23; Dan 7:14; Rev 11:15.
Destroy death. 1 Cor 15:25,26.
Every eye shall see Him at. Rev 1:7.
Should be always considered as at hand.
Rom 13:12; Phil 4:5; 1 Pet 4:7.
Blessedness of being prepared for. Matt
24:46; Luke 12:37,38.
Believers
Assured of. Job 19:25,26.
Love. 2 Tim 4:8.
Look for. Phil 3:20; Titus 2:13.
Wait for. 1 Cor 1:7; 1 Thess 1:10.
Haste to. 2 Pet 3:12.
Pray for. Rev 22:20.
Should be ready for. Matt 24:44; Luke
12:40.
Should watch for. Matt 24:42; Mark
13:35–37; Luke 21:36.
Should be patient to. 2 Thess 3:5;
James 5:7,8.
Shall be preserved to. Phil 1:6; 2 Tim 4:18;
1 Pet 1:5; Jude 24.
Shall not be ashamed at. 1 John 2:28;
4:17.
Shall be blameless at. 1 Cor 1:8; 1 Thess
3:13; 5:23; Jude 24.
Shall be like Him at. Phil 3:21; 1 John 3:2.
Shall see Him as he is, at. 1 John 3:2.
Shall appear with Him in glory at. Col 3:4.
Shall receive a crown of glory at. 2 Tim
4:8; 1 Pet 5:4.
Shall reign with Him at. Dan 7:27; 2 Tim
2:12; Rev 5:10; 20:6; 22:5.
Faith of, shall be found to praise at. 1 Pet
1:7.
The wicked
Scoff at. 2 Pet 3:3,4.
Presume upon the delay of. Matt
24:48.
Shall be surprised by. Matt 24:37–39;
1 Thess 5:3; 2 Pet 3:10.
Shall be punished at. 2 Thess 1:8,9.
The lawless one to be destroyed at.
2 Thess 2:8.

SEEKING GOD.

Commanded. Is 55:6; Matt 7:7.
Includes seeking
His Name. Ps 83:16.

His word. Is 34:16.
His face. Ps 27:8; 105:4.
His strength. 1 Chr 16:11; Ps 105:4.
His commandments. 1 Chr 28:8; Mal
2:7.
His precepts. Ps 119:45,94.
His kingdom. Matt 6:33; Luke 12:31.
His righteousness. Matt 6:33.
Christ. Mal 3:1; Luke 2:15,16.
Honor which comes from Him. John
5:44.
Justification by Christ. Gal 2:16,17.
The city which God has prepared. Heb
11:10,16; 13:14.
By prayer. Job 8:5; Dan 9:3.
In His house. Deut 12:5; Ps 27:4.
Should be
Immediate. Hos 10:12.
Evermore. Ps 105:4.
While He may be found. Is 55:6.
With diligence. Heb 11:6.
With the heart. Deut 4:29; 1 Chr
22:19.
In the day of trouble. Ps 77:2.
Ensures
His being found. Deut 4:29; 1 Chr
28:9; Prov 8:17; Jer 29:13.
His favor. Lam 3:25.
His protection. Ezra 8:22.
His not forsaking us. Ps 9:10.
Life. Ps 69:32; Amos 5:4,6.
Prosperity. Job 8:5,6; Ps 34:10.
Being heard of Him. Ps 34:4.
Understanding all things. Prov 28:5.
Gifts of righteousness. Hos 10:12.
Imperative upon all. Is 8:19.
Afflictions designed to lead to. Ps
78:33,34; Hos 5:15.
None, by nature, are found to be engaged
in. Ps 14:2; Rom 3:11; Luke 12:23,30.
Believers
Specially exhorted to. Zeph 2:3.
Desirous of. Job 5:8.
Purpose, in heart. Ps 27:8.
Prepare their hearts for. 2 Chr 30:19.
Set their hearts to. 2 Chr 11:16.
Engage in, with the whole heart. 2 Chr
15:12; Ps 119:10.
Early in. Ps 63:1; Is 26:9.
Earnest in. Job 8:5; Song 3:2,4.
Characterised by. Ps 24:6.
Is never in vain. Is 45:19.
Blessedness of. Ps 119:2.
Leads to joy. Ps 70:4; 105:3.
Ends in praise. Ps 22:26.
Promise connected with. Ps 69:32.
Shall be rewarded. Heb 11:6.
The wicked
Are gone out of the way of. Ps 14:2,3;
Rom 3:11,12.
Prepare not their hearts for. 2 Chr
12:14.
Refuse, through pride. Ps 10:4.
Not led to, by affliction. Is 9:13.
Sometimes pretend to. Ezra 4:2; Is
58:2.
Rejected, when too late in. Prov 1:28.
They who neglect denounced. Is 31:1.
Punishment of those who neglect. Zeph
1:4–6.

SELF-DELUSION.

A characteristic of the wicked. Ps 49:18.
Prosperity frequently leads to. Ps 30:6;
Hos 12:8; Luke 12:17–19.
Obstinate sinners often given up to. Ps
81:11,12; Hos 4:17; 2 Thess 2:10,11.
Exhibited in thinking that
Our own ways are right. Prov 14:12.
We should adhere to established
wicked practices. Jer 44:17.

We are pure. Prov 30:12.

We are better than others. Luke 18:11.

We are rich in spiritual things. Rev 3:17.

We may have peace while in sin. Deut 29:19.

We are above adversity. Ps 10:6.

Gifts entitle us to heaven. Matt 7:21,22.

Privileges entitle us to heaven. Matt 3:9; Luke 13:25,26.

God will not punish our sins. Ps 10:11; Jer 5:12.

Christ shall not come to judge. 2 Pet 3:4.

Our lives shall be prolonged. Is 56:12; Luke 12:19; James 4:13.

Frequently preserved in, to the last. Matt 7:22; 25:11,12; Luke 13:24,25.

Fatal consequences of. Matt 7:23; 24:48–51; Luke 12:20; 1 Thess 5:3.

SELF-DENIAL.

Christ examplified. Matt 4:8–10; 8:20; John 6:38; Rom 15:3; Phil 2:6–8.

Necessary

In following Christ. Matt 10:37,38; Luke 9:23,24; 14:27–33.

In the warfare of believers. 2 Tim 2:4.

To the triumph of believers. 1 Cor 9:25–27.

Ministers especially called to exercise. 2 Cor 6:4,5.

Should be exercised in

Denying ungodliness and worldly lusts. Rom 6:12; Titus 2:12.

Controlling the appetite. Prov 23:2.

Abstaining from fleshly lusts. 1 Pet 2:11.

No longer living to lusts of men. 1 Pet 4:2.

Mortifying sinful lusts. Mark 9:43; Col 3:5.

Mortifying deeds of the body. Rom 8:13.

Not pleasing ourselves. Rom 15:1–3.

Not seeking out own profit. 1 Cor 10:24,33; 13:5; Phil 2:4.

Preferring the profit of others. Rom 14:20,21; 1 Cor 10:24,33.

Assisting others. Luke 3:11.

Even lawful things. 1 Cor 10:23.

Forsaking all. Luke 14:33.

Taking up the cross and following Christ. Matt 10:38; 16:24.

Crucifying the flesh. Gal 5:24.

Being crucified with Christ. Rom 6:6.

Being crucified to the world. Gal 6:14.

Putting off the old man which is corrupt. Eph 4:22; Col 3:9.

Preferring Christ to all earthly relations. Matt 8:21,22; Luke 14:26.

Becomes strangers and pilgrims. Heb 11:13–15; 1 Pet 2:11.

Danger of neglecting. Matt 16:25,26; 1 Cor 9:27.

Reward of. Matt 19:28,29; Rom 8:13.

Happy result. 2 Pet 1:4.

SELF-EXAMINATION.

Enjoined. 2 Cor 13:5.

Necessary before the Lord's table. 1 Cor 11:28.

A difficult process. Jer 17:9.

Should be engaged in

With holy awe. Ps 4:4.

With diligent search. Ps 77:6; Lam 3:40.

With prayer for divine searching. Ps 26:2; 139:23,24.

With purpose of amendment. Ps 119:59; Lam 3:40.

Advantages of. 1 Cor 11:31; Gal 6:4; 1 John 3:20–22.

SELFISHNESS.

Contrary to the law of God. Lev 19:18; Matt 22:39; James 2:8.

The example of Christ condemns. John 4:34; Rom 15:3; 2 Cor 8:9.

God hates. Mal 1:10.

Inconsistent with Christian love. 1 Cor 13:5.

Inconsistent with fellowship of believers. Rom 12:4,5; 1 Cor 12:12–27.

Especially forbidden to believers. 1 Cor 10:24; Phil 2:4.

The love of Christ should constrain us to avoid. 2 Cor 5:14,15.

Ministers should be devoid of. 1 Cor 9:19–23; 10:33.

All men addicted to. Eph 2:3; Phil 2:21.

Believers sometimes falsely accused of. Job 1:9–11.

Characteristic of the last days. 2 Tim 3:1,2.

SELF-RIGHTEOUSNESS.

Man is prone to. Prov 20:6; 30:12.

Hateful to God. Luke 16:15.

Is useless because our righteousness is

But external. Matt 23:25–28; Luke 11:39–44.

But partial. Matt 23:25; Luke 11:44.

No better than filthy rags. Is 64:6.

Ineffectual for salvation. Job 9:30,31; Matt 5:20; Rom 3:20.

Unprofitable. Is 57:12.

Is boastful. Matt 23:30.

They who are given to

Audaciously approach God. Luke 18:11.

Seek to justify themselves. Luke 10:29; 16:15.

Reject the righteousness of God. Rom 10:3.

Condemn others. Matt 9:11–13; Luke 7:39.

Consider their own way right. Prov 21:2.

Despise others. Is 65:5; Luke 18:9.

Proclaim their own goodness. Prov 20:6.

Are pure in their own eyes. Prov 30:12.

Are abominable before God. Is 65:5.

Folly of. Job 9:20.

Believers renounce. Phil 3:7–10.

Warnings against. Deut 9:4.; Matt 23:27,28.

Illustrated. Luke 18:10–12.

SELF-WILL AND STUBBORNNESS.

Forbidden. 2 Chr 30:8; Ps 75:5; 95:8.

Proceed from

Unbelief. 2 Kin 17:14.

Pride. Neh 9:16,29.

An evil heart. Jer 7:24.

God knows. Is 48:4.

Exhibited in

Refusing to listen to God. Prov 1:24.

Refusing to listen to the messengers of God. 1 Sam 8:19; Jer 44:16; Zech 7:11.

Refusing to walk in the ways of God. Neh 9:17; Ps 78:10; Is 42:24; Jer 6:16.

Refusing to listen to parents. Deut 21:18,19.

Refusing to receive correction. Deut 21:18; Jer 5:3; 7:28.

Rebelling against God. Deut 31:27; Ps 78:8.

Resisting the Holy Spirit. Acts 7:51.

Walking in the counsels of an evil heart. Jer 7:24; 23:17.

Hardening the neck. Neh 9:16.

Hardening the heart. 2 Chr 36:13.

Going backward and not forward. Jer 7:24.

Heinousness of. 1 Sam 15:23.

Ministers should

Be without. Titus 1:7.

Warn their people against. Heb 3:7–12.

Pray that their people may be forgiven for. Ex 34:9; Deut 9:27.

Characteristic of the wicked. Prov 7:11; 2 Pet 2:10.

The wicked cease not from. Judg 2:19.

Punishment for. Deut 21:21; Prov 29:1.

SERVANTS.

Early mention of. Gen 9:25,26.

Divided into

Male. Gen 24:34; 32:5.

Female. Gen 16:6; 32:5.

Bond. Gen 43:18; Lev 25:46.

Hired. Mark 1:20; Luke 15:17.

Persons devoted to the service of another. Ps 119:49; Is 56:6.

The subjects of a prince or king. Ex 9:20; 11:8.

Persons of low condition. Eccl 10:7.

Persons devoted to God. Ps 119:49; Is 56:6; Rom 1:1.

The term often used to express humility. Gen 18:3; 33:5; 1 Sam 20:7; 1 Kin 20:32.

Hired

Called hirelings. Job 7:1; John 10:12,13.

Engaged by the year. Lev 25:53; Is 16:14.

Engaged by the day. Matt 20:2.

Not to be oppressed. Deut 24:14.

To be paid without delay at the expiration of their service. Lev 19:13; Deut 24:15.

To be esteemed worthy of their wages. Luke 10:7.

To partake of the produce of the land in the sabbatical year. Lev 25:6.

If foreigners not allowed to partake of the Passover or holy things. Ex 12:45; Lev 22:10.

Anxiety of, for the end of their daily toil, alluded to. Job 7:2.

Hebrew slaves serving their brethren to be treated as. Lev 25:39,40.

Hebrew slaves serving strangers to be treated as. Lev 25:47,53.

Often stood in the market place waiting for employment. Matt 20:1–3.

Often well fed. Luke 15:17.

Often oppressed and their wages kept back. Mal 3:5; James 5:4.

Slaves or servants

Joseph's brothers willing to be. Gen 43:18; 44:9.

Some served from birth. Gen 14:14; Ps 116:16; Jer 2:14.

Some purchased. Gen 17:27; 37:36.

Captives taken in war often kept as. Deut 20:14; 2 Kin 5:2.

Strangers dwelling in Israel might be purchased as. Lev 25:45.

Foreigners might be purchased as. Lev 25:44.

Persons unable to pay their debts liable to be sold as. 2 Kin 4:1; Neh 5:4,5; Matt 18:25.

Thieves unable to make restitution were sold as. Ex 22:3.

Slaves more valuable than hired servants. Deut 15:18.

When Israelites not to be treated harshly. Lev 25:39,40,46.

When Israelites to have their liberty after six years service. Ex 21:2; Deut 15:12.

Israelites sold as, refusing their liberty, to have their ears bored to the door. Ex 21:5,6; Deut 15:16,17.

Israelites sold to strangers as, might be redeemed by their nearest of kin. Lev 25:47–55.

All Israelites sold as, to be free at the Jubilee. Lev 25:10,40,41,54.

Could not when set free demand wives or children procured during servitude. Ex 21:3,4.

To be furnished liberally, when their servitude expired. Deut 15:13,14.

When foreigners to be circumcised. Gen 17:13,27; Ex 12:44.

To be allowed to rest on the Sabbath. Ex 20:10.

To participate in all national rejoicings. Deut 12:18; 16:11,14.

Persons of distinction had many. Gen 14:14; Eccl 2:7.

Engaged in the most menial offices. 1 Sam 25:41; John 13:4,5.

Maimed or injured by masters to have their freedom. Ex 21:26,27.

Masters to be recompensed for injury done to. Ex 21:32.

Laws respecting the killing of. Ex 21:20,21.

Of others not to be coveted or enticed away. Ex 20:17; Deut 5:21.

Seeking protection not to be delivered up to masters. Deut 23:15.

Custom of branding, alluded to. Gal 6:17.

Sometimes rose to higher position. Eccl 10:7.

Sometimes intermarried with their master's family. 1 Chr 2:34,35.

Laws respecting marriage with female. Ex 21:7–11.

Seizing and stealing of men for, condemned and punished by the law. Ex 21:16; Deut 24:7; 1 Tim 1:10.

Bond, Illustrative

Of Christ. Ps 40:6; Phil 2:7,8; Heb 10:5.

Of believers. 1 Cor 6:20; 7:23.

Of the wicked. 2 Pet 2:19; Rom 6:16,19.

Christ condescended to the office of. Matt 20:28; Luke 22:27; John 13:5; Phil 2:7.

Are inferior to their masters. Luke 22:27.

Should follow Christ's example. 1 Pet 2:21.

Duties of, to masters

To pray for them. Gen 24:12.

To honor them. Mal 1:6; 1 Tim 6:1.

To revere them the more, when they are believers. 1 Tim 6:2.

To submit and obey them. Eph 6:5; Titus 2:9; 1 Pet 2:18.

To attend to their call. Ps 123:2.

To please them well in all things. Titus 2:9.

To sympathize with them. 2 Sam 12:18.

To prefer their business to their own food. Gen 24:33.

To bless God for mercies shown to them. Gen 24:27,48.

To be faithful to them. Luke 16:10–12; 1 Cor 4:2; Titus 2:10.

To be profitable to them. Luke 19:15,16,18; Philem 11.

To be concerned for their welfare. 1 Sam 25:14–17; 2 Kin 5:2,3.

To be earnest in transacting their business. Gen 24:54–56.

To be prudent in the management of their affairs. Gen 24:34–49.

To be industrious in laboring for them. Neh 4:16,23.

To be kind and attentive to their guests. Gen 43:23,24.

To be submissive even to the harsh. Gen 16:6,9; 1 Pet 2:18.

Not to answer them rudely. Titus 2:9.

Not to serve them with eyeservice, as men-pleasers. Eph 6:6; Col 3:22.

Not to defraud them. Titus 2:10.

Should be contented in their situation. 1 Cor 7:20,21.

Should be compassionate to their fellow servants. Matt 18:33.

Should serve

For conscience towards God. 1 Pet 2:19.

In the fear of God. Eph 6:5; Col 3:22.

As the servants of Christ. Eph 6:5,6.

Heartily, as to the Lord, and not to men. Eph 6:7; Col 3:23.

As doing the will of God from the heart. Eph 6:6.

In singleness of heart. Eph 6:5; Col 3:22.

When patient under suffering are acceptable to God. 1 Pet 2:19,20.

When good

Are the servants of Christ. Col 3:24.

Are brethren beloved in the Lord. Philem 16.

Are the Lord's freemen. 1 Cor 7:22.

Are partakers of gospel privileges. 1 Cor 12:13; Gal 3:28; Eph 6:8; Col 3:11.

Deserve the confidence of their masters. Gen 24:2,4,10; 39:4.

Often exalted. Gen 41:40; Prov 17:2.

Often advanced by master. Gen 39:4,5.

To be honored. Gen 24:31; Prov 27:18.

Bring God's blessing upon their masters. Gen 30:27,30; 39:3.

Adorn the doctrine of God their Savior in all things. Titus 2:10.

Have God with them. Gen 31:42; 39:21; Acts 7:9,10.

Are prospered by God. Gen 39:3.

Are protected by God. Gen 31:7.

Are guided by God. Gen 24:7,27.

Are blessed by God. Matt 24:46.

Are mourned over after death. Gen 35:8.

Shall be rewarded. Eph 6:8; Col 3:24.

The property of masters increased by faithful. Gen 30:29,30.

Characteristics of wicked, unbelieving servants

Men-pleasers. Eph 6:6; Col 3:22.

Deceit. 2 Sam 19:26; Ps 101:6,7.

Quarrelsome. Gen 13:7; 26:20.

Covetous. 2 Kin 5:20.

Lying. 2 Kin 5:22,24.

Stealing. Titus 2:10.

Violence and greed. Matt 24:49.

Unmerciful to their fellow servants. Matt 18:30.

Will not submit to correction. Prov 29:19.

Do not rule graciously. Prov 30:21,22; Is 3:5.

Shall be punished. Matt 24:50.

Good—Exemplified

Eliezer. Gen 24:1–67.

Deborah. Gen 24:59; 35:8.

Jacob. Gen 31:36–40.

Joseph. Gen 39:3; Acts 7:10.

Servants of Boaz. Ruth 2:4.

Jonathan's armour bearer. 1 Sam 14:6,7.

David's servants. 2 Sam 12:18.

Captive young girl. 2 Kin 5:2–4.

Servants of Naaman. 2 Kin 5:13.

Servants of Centurion. Matt 8:9.

Servants of Cornelius. Acts 10:7.

Onesimus after his conversion. Philem 11.

Bad—Exemplified

Servants of Abraham and Lot. Gen 13:7.

Servants of Abimelech. Gen 21:25.

Absalom's servants. 2 Sam 13:28,29; 14:30.

Ziba. 2 Sam 16:1–4.

Servants of Shimei. 1 Kin 2:39.

Jeroboam. 1 Kin 11:26.

Zimri. 1 Kin 16:9.

Gehazi. 2 Kin 5:20.

Servants of Amon. 2 Kin 21:23.

Job's servants. Job 19:16.

Servants of the High Priest. Mark 14:65.

Onesimus before his conversion. Philem 11.

SICKNESS.

Sent by God. Deut 28:59–61; 32:39; 2 Sam 12:15; Acts 12:23.

The devil sometimes permitted to inflict. Job 2:6,7; Luke 9:39; 13:16.

Often brought on by intemperance. Hos 7:5.

Often sent as a punishment of sin. Lev 26:14–16; 2 Chr 21:12–15; 1 Cor 11:30.

One of God's four harsh judgments on a guilty land. Ezek 14:19–21.

God

Promises to heal. Ex 23:25; 2 Kin 20:5.

Heals. Deut 32:39; Ps 103:3; Is 38:5,9.

Exhibits His mercy in healing. Phil 2:27.

Exhibits His power in healing. Luke 5:17.

Exhibits His love in healing. Is 38:17.

Often manifests saving grace to sinners during. Job 33:19–24; Ps 107:17–21.

Permits believers to be tried by. Job 2:5,6.

Strengthens believers in. Ps 41:3.

Comforts believers in. Ps 41:3.

Hears the prayers of those in. Ps 30:2; 107:18–20.

Abandons the wicked to. Jer 34:17.

Persecutes the wicked by. Jer 29:18.

Healing of, lawful on the Sabbath. Luke 13:14–16.

Christ compassionate toward those in. Is 53:4; Matt 8:16,17.

Christ healed by

Being present. Mark 1:31; Matt 4:23.

Not being present. Matt 8:13.

By laying on of hands. Mark 6:5; Luke 13:13.

Touch. Matt 8:3.

The touch of his garment. Matt 14:35,36; Mark 5:27–34.

A word. Matt 8:8,13.

Faith required in those healed of, by Christ. Matt 9:28,29; Mark 5:34; 10:52.

Often incurable by human means. Deut 28:27; 2 Chr 21:18.

The Apostles were endued with power to heal. Matt 10:1; Mark 16:18,20.

The power of healing

One of the miraculous gifts bestowed on the early Church. 1 Cor 12:9,30; James 5:14,15.

Believers
Acknowledge that it comes from God. Ps 31:1–8; Is 38:12,15.
Are resigned under. Job 2:10.
Mourn under, with prayer. Is 38:14.
Pray for recovery from. Is 38:2,3.
Ascribe recovery from, to God. Is 38:20.
Praise God for recovery from. Ps 103:1–3; Is 38:19; Luke 17:15.
Thank God publicly for recovery from. Is 38:20; Acts 3:8.
Feel for others in. Ps 35:13.
Visit those in. Matt 25:36.
Visiting those in, an evidence of belonging to Christ. Matt 25:34,36,40.
Pray for those afflicted with. Acts 28:8; James 5:14,15.
God's aid should be sought in. 2 Chr 16:12.
The wicked
Have much sorrow, with. Eccl 5:17.
Forsake those in. 1 Sam 30:13.
Visit not those in. Matt 25:43.
Not visiting those in, an evidence of not belonging to Christ. Matt 25:43,45.

SIMPLICITY.

Is opposed to fleshly wisdom. 2 Cor 1:12.
Necessity for. Matt 18:2,3.
Should be exhibited
In preaching the gospel. 1 Thess 2:3–7.
In acts of benevolence. Rom 12:8.
In all our conduct. 2 Cor 1:12.
Concerning our own wisdom. 1 Cor 3:18.
Concerning evil. Rom 16:19.
Concerning malice. 1 Cor 14:20.
Exhortation to. Rom 16:19; 1 Pet 2:2.
They who have the grace of
Are made wise by God. Matt 11:25.
Are made wise by the Word of God. Ps 19:7; 119:130.
Are preserved by God. Ps 116:6.
Made circumspect by instruction. Prov 1:4.
Profit by the correction of others. Prov 19:25; 21:11.
Beware of being corrupted from that, which is in Christ. 2 Cor 11:3.

SIN.

Is the transgression of the law. 1 John 3:4.
Is of the devil. 1 John 3:8; John 8:44.
All unrighteousness is. 1 John 5:17.
Is the omission of what we know to be good. James 4:17.
Whatever is not of faith is. Rom 14:23.
The thought of foolishness is. Prov 24:9.
All the imaginations of the unrenewed heart are. Gen 6:5; 8:21.
Described as
Coming from the heart. Matt 15:19.
The fruit of lust. James 1:15.
The sting of death. 1 Cor 15:56.
Rebellion against God. Deut 9:7; Josh 1:18.
Works of darkness. Eph 5:11.
Dead works. Heb 6:1; 9:14.
An abomination to God. Prov 15:9; Jer 44:4,11.
Reproaching the Lord. Num 15:30; Ps 74:18.
Defiling. Prov 30:12; Is 59:3.
Deceitful. Heb 3:13.
A reproach. Prov 14:34.
Often very great. Ex 32:20; 1 Sam 2:17.
Often mighty. Amos 5:12.

Often manifold. Amos 5:12.
Often presumptuous. Ps 19:13.
Sometimes open and manifest. 1 Tim 5:24.
Sometimes secret. Ps 90:8; 1 Tim 5:24.
Besetting. Heb 12:1.
Like scarlet and crimson. Is 1:18.
Reaching to heaven. Rev 18:5.
Entered into the world by Adam. Gen 3:6,7; Rom 5:12.
All men are conceived and born in. Gen 5:3; Job 15:14; 25:4; Ps 51:5.
Scripture concludes all under. Gal 3:22.
No man is without. 1 Kin 8:46; Eccl 7:20.
Christ alone was without. 2 Cor 5:21; Heb 4:15; 7:26; 1 John 3:5.
God
Abominates. Deut 25:16; Prov 6:16–19.
Marks. Job 10:14.
Remembers. Rev 18:5.
Is provoked to jealousy by. 1 Kin 14:22.
Is provoked to anger by. 1 Kin 16:2.
Alone can forgive. Ex 34:7; Dan 9:9; Mic 7:18; Mark 2:7.
Recompenses those who live in. Jer 16:18; Rev 18:6.
Punishes. Is 13:11; Amos 3:2.
The Law
Is transgressed by every act of. James 2:10,11; 1 John 3:4.
Gives knowledge of. Rom 3:20; 7:7.
Shows exceeding sinfulness of. Rom 7:13.
Made to restrain. 1 Tim 1:9,10.
Arouses tendency toward. Rom 7:5,8,11.
Is the strength of. 1 Cor 15:56.
Curses those guilty of. Gal 3:10.
No man can atone for. Job 9:30,31; Prov 20:9; Jer 2:22; Mic 6:7.
God has opened a fountain for cleansing from. Zech 13:1.
Christ was manifested to take away. John 1:29; 1 John 3:5.
Christ's blood redeems and cleanses from. Eph 1:7; 1 John 1:7.
Believers
Made free from. Rom 6:18.
Dead to. Rom 6:2,11; 1 Pet 2:24.
Profess to have ceased from. 1 Pet 4:1.
Cannot live in. 1 John 3:9; 5:18.
Resolve against. Job 34:32.
Ashamed of having committed. Rom 6:21.
Abhor themselves on account of. Job 42:6; Ezek 20:43.
Have yet the remains of, in them. Rom 7:17,23; Gal 5:17.
The fear of God restrains. Ex 20:20; Ps 4:4; Prov 16:6.
The Word of God keeps from. Ps 17:4; 119:11.
The Holy Spirit convinces of. John 16:8,9.
If we say that we have no, we make God a liar. 1 John 1:10.
Shame belongs to those guilty of. Dan 9:7,8.
Should be
Confessed. Job 33:27; Prov 28:13.
Mourned over. Ps 38:18; Jer 3:21.
Hated. Ps 97:10; Prov 8:13; Amos 5:15; Rom 12:9.
Put away. Job 11:14.
Departed from. Ps 34:14; 2 Tim 2:19.
Avoided even in appearance. 1 Thess 5:22.
Guarded against. Ps 4:4; 39:1.
Striven against. Heb 12:4.

Mortified. Rom 8:13; Col 3:5.
Wholly destroyed. Rom 6:6.
Specially strive against besetting. Heb 12:1.
Aggravated by neglecting advantages. Luke 12:47; John 15:22.
Guilt concerning. Job 31:33; Prov 28:13.
We should pray to God
To search for, in our hearts. Ps 139:23,24.
To make us know our. Job 13:23.
To forgive our. Ex 34:9; Luke 11:4.
To keep us from. Ps 19:13.
To deliver us from. Matt 6:13.
To cleanse us from. Ps 51:2.
Prayer hindered by. Ps 66:18; Is 59:2.
Blessings withheld on account of. Jer 5:25.
The wicked
Servants to. John 8:34; Rom 6:16.
Dead in. Eph 2:1.
Guilty of, in everything they do. Prov 21:4; Ezek 21:24.
Plead necessity for. 1 Sam 13:11,12.
Excuse. Gen 3:12,13; 1 Sam 15:13–15.
Encourage themselves in. Ps 64:5.
Defy God in committing. Is 5:18,19.
Boast of. Is 3:9.
Mock. Prov 14:9.
Expect impunity in. Ps 10:11; 50:21; 94:7.
Cannot cease from. 2 Pet 2:14.
Commit more and more. Ps 78:17; Is 30:1.
Encouraged in, by prosperity. Job 21:7–15; Prov 10:16.
Led by despair to continue in. Jer 2:25; 18:12.
Try to conceal, from God. Gen 3:8,10; Job 31:33.
Throw the blame of, on God. Gen 3:12; Jer 7:10.
Throw the blame of, on others. Gen 3:12,13; Ex 32:22–24.
Tempt others to. Gen 3:6; 1 Kin 16:2; 21:25; Prov 1:10–14.
Delight in those who commit. Ps 10:3; Hos 7:3; Rom 1:32.
Shall bear the shame of. Ezek 16:52.
Shall find out the wicked. Num 32:23.
Ministers should warn the wicked to forsake. Ezek 33:9; Dan 4:27.
Leads to
Shame. Rom 6:21.
Disquiet. Ps 38:3.
Disease. Job 20:11.
Toil and sorrow originated in. Gen 3:16,17,19; Job 14:1.
Excludes from heaven. 1 Cor 6:9,10; Gal 5:19–21; Eph 5:5; Rev 21:27.
When finished brings forth death. James 1:15.
Death, the wages of. Rom 6:23.
Death, the punishment of. Gen 2:17; Ezek 18:4.

SINCERITY.

Christ was an example of. 1 Pet 2:22.
Ministers should be examples of. Titus 2:7.
Opposed to fleshly wisdom. 2 Cor 1:12.
Should characterise
Our love to God. 2 Cor 8:8,24.
Our love to Christ. Eph 6:24.
Our service to God. Josh 24:14; John 4:3,24.
Our faith. 1 Tim 1:5.
Our love to one another. Rom 12:9; 1 Pet 1:22; 1 John 3:18.
Our whole conduct. 2 Cor 1:12.
The preaching of the gospel. 2 Cor 2:17; 1 Thess 2:3–5.

A characteristic of the doctrines of the gospel. 1 Pet 2:2.
The gospel sometimes preached without. Phil 1:16.
The wicked devoid of. Ps 5:9; 55:21.
Exhortations to. Ps 34:13; 1 Cor 5:8; 1 Pet 2:1.
Pray for, on behalf of others. Phil 1:10.
Blessedness of. Ps 32:2.

SLANDER.

An abomination to God. Prov 6:16,19.
Forbidden. Ex 23:1; Eph 4:31; James 4:11.
Includes
  Whispering. Rom 1:29; 2 Cor 12:20.
  Backbiting. Rom 1:30; 2 Cor 12:20.
  Evil surmising. 1 Tim 6:4.
  Talebearing. Lev 19:16.
  Babbling. Eccl 10:11.
  Tattling. 1 Tim 5:13.
  Evil speaking. Ps 41:5; 109:20.
  Defaming. Jer 20:10; 1 Cor 4:13.
  Bearing false witness. Ex 20:16; Deut 5:20; Luke 3:14.
  Judging uncharitably. James 4:11,12.
  Circulating false reports. Ex 23:1.
  Repeating matters. Prov 17:9.
Is a deceitful work. Ps 52:2.
Comes from the evil heart. Matt 15:19; Luke 6:45.
Often arises from hatred. Ps 41:7; 109:3.
Idleness leads to. 1 Tim 5:13.
The wicked addicted to. Ps 50:20; Prov 11:9; Jer 6:28; 9:4.
A characteristic of the devil. Rev 12:10.
The wicked love. Ps 52:4.
They who indulge in, are fools. Prov 10:18.
They who indulge in, not to be trusted. Jer 9:4.
Women warned against. Titus 2:3.
Minister's wives should avoid. 1 Tim 3:11.
Christ was exposed to. Ps 35:11; Matt 26:60.
Authorities exposed to. 2 Pet 2:10; Jude 8.
Ministers exposed to. Rom 3:8; 2 Cor 6:8.
The nearest relations exposed to. Ps 50:20.
Believers exposed to. Ps 38:12; 109:2; 1 Pet 4:4.
Believers
  Should keep their tongue from. Ps 34:13; 1 Pet 3:10.
  Should lay aside. Eph 4:31; 1 Pet 2:1.
  Should be warned against. Titus 3:1,2.
  Should give no occasion for. 1 Pet 2:12; 3:16.
  Should return good for. 1 Cor 4:13.
  Blessed in enduring. Matt 5:11.
  Characterised as avoiding. Ps 15:1,3.
Should not be listened to. 1 Sam 24:9.
Should deserve frowning disapproval. Prov 25:23.
Effects of
  Separating friends. Prov 16:28; 17:9.
  Produces wounds. Prov 18:8; 26:22.
  Strife. Prov 26:20.
  Discord among brethren. Prov 6:19.
  Murder. Ps 31:13; Ezek 22:9.
The tongue of, is a scourge. Job 5:21.
Is venomous. Ps 140:3; Eccl 10:11.
Is destructive. Prov 11:9.
End of, is mischievous madness. Eccl 10:13.
Men shall give account for. Matt 12:36; James 1:26.
Punishment for. Deut 19:16–21; Ps 101:5.

SOBRIETY.

Commanded. 1 Pet 1:13; 5:8.

The gospel designed to teach. Titus 2:11,12.
With watchfulness. 1 Thess 5:6.
With prayer. 1 Pet 4:7.
Required in
  Ministers. 1 Tim 3:2,3; Titus 1:8.
  Wives of ministers. 1 Tim 3:11.
  Aged men. Titus 2:2.
  Young men. Titus 2:6.
  Young women. Titus 2:4.
  All believers. 1 Thess 5:6,8.
Women should exhibit, in dress. 1 Tim 2:9.
We should estimate our character and talents with. Rom 12:3.
Motives to. 1 Pet 4:7; 5:8.

STEADFASTNESS.

Exhibited by God. Num 23:19; Dan 6:26; James 1:17.
Commanded. Phil 4:1; 2 Thess 2:15; James 1:6–8.
Godliness necessary to. Job 11:13–15.
Secured by
  The power of God. Ps 55:22; 62:2; 1 Pet 1:5; Jude 24.
  The presence of God. Ps 16:8.
  Trust in God. Ps 26:1.
  The intercession of Christ. Luke 22:31,32.
A characteristic of believers. Job 17:9; John 8:31.
Should be manifested
  In cleaving to God. Deut 10:20; Acts 11:23.
  In the work of the Lord. 1 Cor 15:58.
  In continuing in the Apostles' doctrine. Acts 2:42.
  In holding fast our profession. Heb 4:14; 10:23.
  In holding fast the confidence and rejoicing of the hope. Heb 3:6,14.
  In keeping the faith. Col 2:5; 1 Pet 5:9.
  In standing fast in the faith. 1 Cor 16:13.
  In holding fast what is good. 1 Thess 5:21.
  In maintaining Christian liberty. Gal 5:1.
  In striving for the faith of the gospel. Phil 1:27; Jude 3.
  Even under affliction. Ps 44:17–19; Rom 8:35–37; 1 Thess 3:3.
Believers pray for. Ps 17:5; 116:8.
Ministers
  Exhorted to. 2 Tim 1:13,14; Titus 1:9.
  Should exhort others to. Acts 13:43; 14:22.
  Should pray for, in their people. 1 Thess 3:13; 2 Thess 2:17.
  Encouraged by, in their people. 1 Thess 3:8.
  Rejoiced to see, in their people. Col 2:5.
The wicked devoid of. Ps 78:8,37.
Principle of—Illustrated. Matt 7:24,25; John 15:4; Col 2:7.

SWEARING FALSELY.

Forbidden. Lev 19:12; Num 30:2; Matt 5:33.
Hateful to God. Zech 8:17.
We should not love. Zech 8:17.
Fraud often leads to. Lev 6:2,3.
Believers abstain from. Josh 9:20; Ps 15:4.
Blessedness of abstaining from. Ps 24:4,5.
The wicked
  Addicted to the practice of. Jer 5:2; Hos 10:4.
  Plead excuses for. Jer 7:9,10.

Shall be judged on account of. Mal 3:5.
Shall be cut off for. Zech 5:3.
Shall have a curse upon their houses for. Zech 5:4.
False witnesses guilty of. Deut 19:16,18.

SWEARING, PROFANE.

Of all kinds. Ex 20:7; Matt 5:34–36; 23:21,22; James 5:12.
The wicked
  Addicted to. Ps 10:7; Rom 3:14.
  Love. Ps 109:17.
  Clothe themselves with. Ps 109:18.
Guilt of. Ex 20:7; Deut 5:11.
Woe pronounced against. Matt 23:16.
Nations visited for. Jer 23:10; Hos 4:1–3.
Punishment for. Lev 24:16,23; Ps 59:12; 109:17,18.

TEMPTATION.

Does not come from God. James 1:13.
Comes from
  Lusts. James 1:14.
  Covetousness. Prov 28:20; 1 Tim 6:9,10.
The devil is the author of. 1 Chr 21:1; Matt 4:1; John 13:2; 1 Thess 3:5.
Evil associates, the instruments of. Prov 1:10; 7:6; 16:29.
Often arises through
  Poverty. Prov 30:9; Matt 4:2,3.
  Prosperity. Prov 30:9; Matt 4:8.
  Worldly glory. Num 22:17; Dan 4:30; 5:2; Matt 4:8.
To distrust God's providence. Matt 4:3.
Presumption. Matt 4:6.
Worshiping the god of this world. Matt 4:9.
Often strengthened by the perversion of God's Word. Matt 4:6.
Permitted as a trial of
  Faith. 1 Pet 1:7; James 1:2,3.
  Dedication. Job 1:9–12.
Always conformable to the nature of man. 1 Cor 10:13.
Often ends in sin and death. 1 Tim 6:9; James 1:15.
Christ
  Endured, from the devil. Mark 1:13.
  Endured, from the wicked. Matt 16:1; 22:18; Luke 10:25.
  Resisted by the Word of God. Matt 4:4,7,10.
  Overcame. Matt 4:11.
  Sympathizes with those under. Heb 4:15.
  Is able to help those under. Heb 2:18.
  Intercedes for His people under. Luke 22:31,32; John 17:15.
God will not suffer believers to be exposed to, beyond their powers to bear. 1 Cor 10:13.
God will make a way for believers to escape out of. 1 Cor 10:13.
God enables the believers to bear. 1 Cor 10:13.
God knows how to deliver believers out of. 2 Pet 2:9.
Christ keeps faithful believers from the hour of. Rev 3:10.
Believers may be in heaviness through. 1 Pet 1:6.
Believers should
  Should resist, in faith. Eph 6:16; 1 Pet 5:9.
  Should watch against. Matt 26:41; 1 Pet 5:8.
  Should pray to be kept from. Matt 6:13; 26:41.
  Should not cause for others. Rom 14:13.

Should restore those overcome by. Gal 6:1.

Should avoid the way of. Prov 4:14,15.

The devil will renew. Luke 4:13.

Weakness of the flesh makes it stronger. Matt 26:41.

Nominal Christians fall away in time of. Luke 8:13.

Blessedness of those who meet and overcome. James 1:2–4,12.

THANKSGIVING.

Christ set an example of. Matt 11:25; 26:27; John 6:11; 11:41.

The heavenly host engaged in. Rev 4:9; 7:11,12; 11:16,17.

Commanded. Ps 50:14; Phil 4:6.

Is a good thing. Ps 92:1.

Should be offered
To God. Ps 50:14.
To Christ. 1 Tim 1:12.
Through Christ. Rom 1:8; Col 3:17; Heb 13:15.
In the name of Christ. Eph 5:20.
In behalf of ministers. 2 Cor 1:11.
In private worship. Dan 6:10.
In public worship. Ps 35:18.
In everything. 1 Thess 5:18.
Upon the completion of great undertakings. Neh 12:31,40.
Before taking food. John 6:11; Acts 27:35.
Always. Eph 1:16; 5:20; 1 Thess 1:2.
At the remembrance of God's holiness. Ps 30:4; 97:12.
For the goodness and mercy of God. Ps 106:1; 107:1; 136:1–3.
For the gift of Christ. 2 Cor 9:15.
For Christ's power and reign. Rev 11:17.
For the reception and effectual working of the word of God in others. 1 Thess 2:13.
For deliverance through Christ from in-dwelling sin. Rom 7:23–25.
For victory over death and the grave. 1 Cor 15:57.
For wisdom and might. Dan 2:23.
For the triumph of the gospel. 2 Cor 2:14.
For the conversion of others. Rom 6:17.
For faith exhibited by others. Rom 1:8; 2 Thess 1:3.
For love exhibited by others. 2 Thess 1:3.
For the grace bestowed on others. 1 Cor 1:4; Phil 1:3–5; Col 1:3–6.
For the zeal exhibited by others. 2 Cor 8:16.
For the nearness of God's presence. Ps 75:1.
For appointment to the ministry. 1 Tim 1:12.
For willingness to offer our property for God's service. 1 Chr 29:6–14.
For the supply of our bodily wants. Rom 14:6,7; 1 Tim 4:3,4.
For all men. 1 Tim 2:1.

Should be accompanied by intercession for others. 1 Tim 2:1; 2 Tim 1:3; Philem 4.

Should always accompany prayer. Neh 11:17; Phil 4:6; Col 4:2.

Should always accompany praise. Ps 92:1; Heb 13:15.

Expressed in psalms. 1 Chr 16:7.

Ministers appointed to offer, in public. 1 Chr 16:4,7; 23:30; 2 Chr 31:2.

Believers
Exhorted to. Ps 105:1; Col 3:15.
Resolved to offer. Ps 18:49; 30:12.

Habitually offer. Dan 6:10.

Offer sacrifices of. Ps 116:17.

Abound in the faith with. Col 2:7.

Magnify God by. Ps 69:30.

Come before God with. Ps 95:2.

Should enter God's gate with. Ps 100:4.

Of hypocrites, full of boasting. Luke 18:11.

The wicked averse to. Rom 1:21.

THEFT.

Is an abomination. Jer 7:9,10.

Forbidden. Ex 20:15; Mark 10:19; Rom 13:9.

From the poor specially forbidden. Prov 22:2.

Includes fraud in general. Lev 19:13.

Includes fraud concerning wages. Lev 19:13; Mal 3:5; James 5:4.

Proceeds from the heart. Matt 15:19.

Defiles a man. Matt 15:20.

The wicked
Addicted to. Ps 119:61.
Store up the fruits of. Amos 3:10.
Lie in wait to commit. Hos 6:9.
Commit, under shelter of the night. Job 24:14; Obad 5.
Join those who commit. Ps 50:18.
Associate with those who commit. Is 1:23.
May, for a season, prosper in. Job 12:6.
Plead excuses for. Jer 7:9,10.
Repent not of. Rev 9:21.
Destroy themselves by. Prov 21:7.

Connected with murder. Jer 7:9; Hos 4:2.

Shame follows the detection of. Jer 2:26.

Brings a curse on those who commit it. Hos 4:2,3; Zech 5:3,4; Mal 3:5.

Brings the wrath of God upon those who commit it. Ezek 22:29,31.

Excludes from heaven. 1 Cor 6:10.

They who connive at
Hate their own souls. Prov 29:24.
Shall be reproved of God. Ps 50:18,21.

Mosaic law respecting. Ex 22:1–8.

Believers
Warned against. Eph 4:28; 1 Pet 4:15.

All earthly treasure exposed to. Matt 6:19.

Heavenly treasure secure from. Matt 6:20; Luke 12:33.

Woe pronounced against. Is 10:2; Nah 3:1.

TITHE.

The tenth of anything. 1 Sam 8:15,17.

Antiquity of the custom of giving one to God's ministers. Gen 14:20; Heb 7:6.

Considered a just return to God for his blessings. Gen 28:22.

Under the law belonged to God. Lev 27:30.

Various forms of
Of all the produce of the land. Lev 27:30.
Of all cattle. Lev 27:32.
Of holy things dedicated. 2 Chr 31:6.

Given by God to the Levites for their services. Num 18:21,24; Neh 10:37.

The tenth of, offered by the Levites as an heave offering to God. Num 18:26,27.

The tenth of, given by the Levites to the priests as their portion. Num 18:26,28; Neh 10:38.

Reasonableness of appointing, for the Levites. Num 18:20,23,24; Josh 13:33.

When redeemed for a fifth part of the value added. Lev 27:31.

Punishment for changing. Lev 27:33.

The Jews slow in giving. Neh 13:10.

The Jews reproved for withholding. Mal 3:8.

The pious rulers of Israel caused the

payment of. 2 Chr 31:5; Neh 13:11,12.

Treasurers appointed over, for distributing. 2 Chr 31:12; Neh 13:13.

The Pharisees scrupulous in paying. Luke 11:42; 18:12.

A second
Its value yearly brought to the tabernacle and eaten before the Lord. Deut 12:6,7,17–19; 14:22–27.
To be consumed at home every third year to promote hospitality and charity. Deut 14:28,29; 26:12–15.

TITLES AND NAMES OF CHRIST.

Almighty. Rev 1:18.

Amen. Rev 3:14.

Alpha and Omega. Rev 1:8; 22:13.

Advocate. 1 John 2:1.

Angel. Gen 48:16; Ex 23:20,21.

Angel of the Lord. Ex 3:2; Judg 13:15–18.

Angel of God's presence. Is 63:9.

Apostle. Heb 3:1.

Arm of the Lord. Is 51:9; 53:1.

Author and Finisher or our faith. Heb 12:2.

Blessed and only Potentate. 1 Tim 6:15.

Beginning of the creation of God. Rev 3:14.

Branch. Jer 23:5; Zech 3:8; 6:12.

Bread of Life. John 6:35,48.

Commander of the army of the Lord. Josh 5:14,15.

Captain of salvation. Heb 2:10.

Chief Shepherd. 1 Pet 5:4.

Christ of God. Luke 9:20.

Consolation of Israel. Luke 2:25.

Chief Cornerstone. Eph 2:20; 1 Pet 2:6.

Commander. Is 55:4.

Counsellor. Is 9:6.

David. Jer 30:9; Ezek 34:23.

Dayspring. Luke 1:78.

Deliverer. Rom 11:26.

Desire of all nations. Hag 2:7.

Door. John 10:7.

Elect One. Is 42:1.

Emmanuel. Is 7:14; Matt 1:23.

Eternal life. 1 John 1:2; 5:20.

Everlasting Father. Is 9:6.

Faithful witness. Rev 1:5; 3:14.

First and Last. Rev 1:17; 2:8.

First born from the dead. Rev 1:5.

Firstborn over all creation. Col 1:15.

Forerunner. Heb 6:20.

God. Is 40:9; John 20:28.

God's companion. Zech 13:7.

Glory of the Lord. Is 40:5.

Good Shepherd. John 10:14.

Great High Priest. Heb 4:14.

Governor. Matt 2:6.

Head of the Church. Eph 5:23; Col 1:18.

Heir of all things. Heb 1:2.

Holy One. Ps 16:10; Acts 2:27,31.

Holy One of God. Mark 1:24.

Holy One of Israel. Is 41:14.

Horn of salvation. Luke 1:69.

I AM. Ex 3:14; John 8:58.

Jehovah. Is 26:4.

Jesus. Matt 1:21; 1 Thess 1:10.

Judge of Israel. Mic 5:1.

Just One. Acts 7:52.

King. Zech 9:9; Matt 21:5.

King of Israel. John 1:49.

King of the Jews. Matt 2:2.

King of the saints. Rev 15:3.

King of kings. 1 Tim 6:15; Rev 17:14.

Law giver. Is 33:22.

Lamb. Rev 5:6,12; 13:8; 21:22; 22:3.

Lamb of God. John 1:29,36.

Leader. Is 55:4.

Life. John 14:6; Col 3:4; 1 John 1:2.

Light of the world. John 8:12.

Lion of the tribe of Judah. Rev 5:5.
Lord of glory. 1 Cor 2:8.
Lord of all. Acts 10:36.
Lord our righteousness. Jer 23:6.
Lord God of the holy prophets. Rev 22:6.
Lord God Almighty. Rev 15:3.
Mediator. 1 Tim 2:5.
Messenger of the covenant. Mal 3:1.
Messiah. Dan 9:25; John 1:41.
Mighty God. Is 9:6.
Mighty One of Jacob. Is 60:16.
Morning star. Rev 22:16.
Nazarene. Matt 2:23.
Offspring of David. Rev 22:16.
Only begotten. John 1:14.
Our Passover. 1 Cor 5:7.
Prince of life. Acts 3:15.
Prince of peace. Is 9:6.
Prophet. Luke 24:19; John 7:40.
Ransom. 1 Tim 2:6.
Redeemer. Job 19:25; Is 59:20; 60:16.
Resurrection and life. John 11:25.
Rock. 1 Cor 10:4.
Root of David. Rev 22:16.
Root of Jesse. Is 11:10.
Ruler in Israel. Mic 5:2.
Savior. 2 Pet 2:20; 3:18.
Servant. Is 42:1; 52:13.
Shepherd and Overseer of souls. 1 Pet 2:25.
Shiloh. Gen 49:10.
Son of the Blessed. Mark 14:61.
Son of God. Luke 1:35; John 1:49.
Son of the Highest. Luke 1:32.
Son of David. Matt 9:27.
Son of Man. John 5:27; 6:37.
Star. Num 24:17.
Sun of righteousness. Mal 4:2.
Surety. Heb 7:22.
True God. 1 John 5:20.
True Light. John 1:9.
True Vine. John 15:1.
Truth. John 14:6.
Way. John 14:6.
Wisdom. Prov 8:12.
Witness. Is 55:4.
Wonderful. Is 9:6.
Word. John 1:1; 5:7.
Word of God. Rev 19:13.
Word of Life. 1 John 1:1.

TITLES AND NAMES OF THE CHURCH.

Body of Christ. Eph 1:22,23; Col 1:24.
Bride of Christ. Rev 21:9.
Church of God. Acts 20:28.
Church of the Living God. 1 Tim 3:15.
Church of the firstborn. Heb 12:23.
Family in heaven and earth. Eph 3:15.
Flock of God. 1 Pet 5:2.
Fold of Christ. John 10:16.
General assembly of the firstborn. Heb 12:23.
Golden candlestick. Rev 1:20.
God's building. 1 Cor 3:9.
God's husbandry. 1 Cor 3:9.
God's heritage. 1 Pet 5:3.
Habitation of God. Eph 2:22.
Heavenly of Jerusalem. Gal 4:26; Heb 12:22.
Holy city. Rev 21:2.
House of God. 1 Tim 3:15; Heb 10:21.
House of Christ. Heb 3:6.
Household of God. Eph 2:19.
Lamb's wife. Rev 19:7; 21:9.
Pillar and ground of the truth. 1 Tim 3:15.
Spiritual house. 1 Pet 2:5.
Temple of God. 1 Cor 3:16,17.
Temple of the Living God. 2 Cor 6:16.

TITLES AND NAMES OF THE DEVIL.

Accuser of our brethren. Rev 12:10.
Adversary. 1 Pet 5:8.

Beelzebub. Matt 12:24.
Belial. 2 Cor 6:15.
Crooked serpent. Is 27:1.
Dragon. Is 27:1; Rev 20:2.
Enemy. Matt 13:39.
Evil spirit. 1 Sam 16:14.
Father of lies. John 8:44.
Great red dragon. Rev 12:3.
Liar. John 8:44.
Lying spirit. 1 Kin 22:22.
Murderer. John 8:44.
Old serpent. Rev 12:9; 20:2.
Piercing serpent. Is 27:1.
Power of darkness. Col 1:13.
Prince of this world. John 14:30.
Prince of the devils. Matt 12:24.
Prince of the power of the air. Eph 2:2.
Ruler of the darkness of this world. Eph 6:12.
Satan. 1 Chr 21:1; Job 1:6.
Serpent. Gen 3:4,16; 2 Cor 11:3.
Spirit that works in the children of disobedience. Eph 2:2.
Tempter. Matt 4:3; 1 Thess 3:5.
The god of this world. 2 Cor 4:4.
Wicked one. Matt 13:19,38.

TITLES AND NAMES OF BELIEVERS.

Believers. Acts 5:14; 1 Tim 4:12.
Beloved of God. Rom 1:7.
Beloved brethren. 1 Cor 15:58; James 2:5.
Blessed of the Lord. Gen 24:31; 26:29.
Blessed of the Father. Matt 25:34.
Brethren. Matt 23:8; Acts 12:17.
Called of Jesus Christ. Rom 1:6.
Children of the Lord. Deut 14:1.
Children of God. John 11:52; 1 John 3:10.
Sons of the Living God. Rom 9:26.
Sons of the Father. Matt 5:45.
Sons of the Highest. Luke 6:35.
Sons of Abraham. Gal 3:7.
Children of Jacob. Ps 105:6.
Children of promise. Rom 9:8; Gal 4:28.
Children of the free woman. Gal 4:31.
Children of the kingdom. Matt 13:38.
Children of Zion. Ps 149:2; Joel 2:23.
Friends of the bridegroom. Matt 9:15.
Sons of light. Luke 16:8; Eph 5:8; 1 Thess 5:5.
Sons of the day. 1 Thess 5:5.
Sons of the resurrection. Luke 20:36.
Chosen generation. 1 Pet 2:9.
Chosen ones. 1 Chr 16:13.
Chosen vessels. Acts 9:15.
Christians. Acts 11:26; 26:28.
Dear children. Eph 5:1.
Disciples of Christ. John 8:31; 15:8.
Elect of God. Col 3:12; Titus 1:1.
Epistles of Christ. 2 Cor 3:3.
Excellent ones, The. Ps 16:3.
Faithful brethren in Christ. Col 1:2.
Faithful, The. Ps 12:1.
Faithful of the land. Ps 101:6.
Fellow citizens with the saints. Eph 2:19.
Fellow heirs. Eph 3:6.
Fellow servants. Rev 6:11.
Friends of God. 2 Chr 20:7; James 2:23.
Friends of Christ. John 15:15.
Godly, The. Ps 4:3; 2 Pet 2:9.
Heirs of God. Rom 8:17; Gal 4:7.
Heirs of the grace of life. 1 Pet 3:7.
Heirs of the kingdom. James 2:5.
Heirs of promise. Heb 6:17; Gal 3:29.
Heirs of salvation. Heb 1:14.
Holy brethren. 1 Thess 5:27; Heb 3:1.
Holy nation. Ex 19:6; 1 Pet 2:9.
Holy people. Deut 26:19; Is 62:12.
Holy priesthood. 1 Pet 2:5.
Joint heirs with Christ. Rom 8:17.
Just, The. Hab 2:4.

Kings and priests to God. Rev 1:6.
Kingdom of priests. Ex 19:6.
Lambs. Is 40:11; John 21:15.
Lights of the world. Matt 5:14.
Little children. John 13:33; 1 John 2:1.
Living stones. 1 Pet 2:5.
Members of Christ. 1 Cor 6:15; Eph 5:30.
Men of God. Deut 33:1; 1 Tim 6:11; 2 Tim 3:17.
Obedient children. 1 Pet 1:14.
Special people. Deut 14:2; Titus 2:14; 1 Pet 2:9.
Special treasure. Ex 19:5; Ps 135:4.
People of God. Heb 4:9; 1 Pet 2:10.
People near to God. Ps 148:14.
People saved by the Lord. Deut 33:29.
Pillars in the temple of God. Rev 3:12.
Redeemed of the Lord. Is 51:11.
Royal priesthood. 1 Pet 2:9.
Salt of the earth. Matt 5:13.
Servants of Christ. 1 Cor 7:22; Eph 6:6.
Slaves of righteousness. Rom 6:18.
Sheep of Christ. John 10:1–16; 21:16.
Sojourners with God. Lev 25:23; Ps 39:12.
The Lord's freemen. 1 Cor 7:22.
Trees of righteousness. Is 61:3.
Vessels to honor. 2 Tim 2:21.
Vessels of mercy. Rom 9:23.
Witnesses for God. Is 44:8.

TRINITY, THE.

Doctrine of proved from Scripture. Matt 3:16,17; 28:19; Rom 8:9; 1 Cor 12:3–6; 2 Cor 13:14; Eph 4:4–6; 1 Pet 1:2; Jude 20,21; Rev 1:4,5.
Divine titles applied to the three persons in. Ex 20:2; John 20:28; Acts 5:3,4.
Each person in, described as
    Eternal. Rom 16:26; Heb 9:14; Rev 22:13;
    Holy. Acts 3:14; 1 John 2:20; Rev 4:8; 15:4.
    True. John 7:28; Rev 3:7.
    Omnipresent. Ps 139:7; Jer 23:24; Eph 1:23.
    Omnipotent. Gen 17:1; Jer 32:17; Luke 1:35; Rom 15:19; Heb 1:3; Rev 1:8.
    Omniscient. Acts 15:18; John 21:17; 1 Cor 2:10,11.
    Creator. Gen 1:1; Job 26:13; 33:4; Ps 148:5; John 1:3; Col 1:16.
    Sanctifier. Heb 2:11; 1 Pet 1:2; Jude 1;
    Author of all spiritual operations. 1 Cor 12:11; Col 1:29; Heb 13:21.
    Source of eternal life. John 10:28; Rom 6:23; Gal 6:8.
    Teacher. Is 48:17; 54:13; Luke 21:15; John 14:26; Gal 1:12; 1 John 2:20.
    Raising Christ from the dead. 1 Cor 6:14; John 2:19; 1 Pet 3:18.
    Inspiring the prophets, etc. Mark 13:11; 2 Cor 13:3; Heb 1:1.
    Supplying ministers to the Church. Jer 3:15; Eph 4:11; Jer 26:5; Matt 10:5; Acts 13:2; 20:28.
Salvation the work of. 2 Thess 2:13,14; Titus 3:4–6; 1 Pet 1:2.
Baptism administered in name of. Matt 28:19.
Benediction given in name of. 2 Cor 13:14.

TRUST.

God is the true object of. Ps 65:5.
The fear of God leads to. Prov 14:26.
Encouragements to
    The everlasting strength of God. Is 26:4.
    The goodness of God. Nah 1:7.

The lovingkindness of God. Ps 36:7.
The rich bounty of God. 1 Tim 6:17.
The care of God for us. 1 Pet 5:7.
Previous deliverances. Ps 9:10; 2 Cor
  1:10.
Should be with the whole heart. Prov 3:5.
Should be from youth up. Ps 71:5.
Of believers is
  Not in the flesh. Phil 3:3,4.
  Not in themselves. 2 Cor 1:9.
  Not in carnal weapons. 1 Sam
    17:38,39,45; Ps 44:6; 2 Cor 10:4.
  In God. Ps 11:1; 31:14; 2 Cor 1:9.
  In the Word of God. Ps 119:42.
  In the mercy of God. Ps 13:5; 52:8.
  In Christ. Eph 3:12.
  Through Christ. 2 Cor 3:4.
  Grounded in God's covenant. 2 Sam
    23:5.
  Strong in the prospect of death. Ps
    23:4.
  Fixed. Job 13:15; 2 Sam 22:3; Ps
    112:7.
  Despised by the wicked. Is 36:4,7.
  For ever. Ps 52:8; 62:8; Is 26:4.
Believers plead, in prayer. Ps 25:20; 31:1;
  141:8.
The Lord knows those who have. Nah 1:7.
Exhortations to. Ps 4:5; 115:9–11.
Leads to
  Being compassed with mercy. Ps
    32:10.
  Enjoyment of perfect peace. Is 26:3.
  Enjoyment of all temporal and
    spiritual blessings. Is 57:13.
  Enjoyment of happiness. Prov 16:20.
  Rejoicing in God. Ps 5:11; 33:21.
  Fulfillment of all holy desires. Ps 37:5.
  Deliverance from enemies. Ps 37:40.
  Safety in times of danger. Prov 29:25.
  Stability. Ps 125:1.
  Prosperity. Prov 28:25.
Keeps from
  Fear. Ps 56:11; Is 12:2; Heb 13:6.
  Slipping. Ps 26:1.
  Condemnation. Ps 34:22.
To be accompanied by doing good. Ps 37:3.
Blessedness of placing, in God. Ps 2:12;
  34:8; 40:4; Jer 17:7.
Of the wicked
  Is not in God. Ps 78:22; Zeph 3:2.
  Is in idols. Is 42:17; Hab 2:18.
  Is in man. Judg 9:26; Ps 118:8,9.
  Is in their own heart. Prov 28:26.
  Is in their own righteousness. Luke
    18:9,12.
  Is in futile things. Job 15:31; Is 59:4.
  Is in falsehood. Is 28:15; Jer 13:25.
  Is in earthly alliances. Is 30:2; Ezek
    17:15.
  Is in wealth. Ps 49:6; 52:7; Prov 11:28;
    Jer 48:7; Mark 10:24.
  Is vain and delusive. Is 30:7; Jer 2:37.
  Shall make them ashamed. Is 20:5;
    30:3,5; Jer 48:13.
  Shall be destroyed. Job 18:14; Is 28:18.
Woe and curse of false. Is 30:1,2; 31:1–3;
  Jer 17:5.
Of believers—Illustrated. Ps 91:12; Prov
  18:10.
Of the wicked—Illustrated. 2 Kin 18:21;
  Job 8:14.
Of believers—Exemplified
  David. 1 Sam 17:45; 30:6.
  Hezekiah. 2 Kin 18:5.
  Jehoshaphat. 2 Chr 20:12.
  Shadrach etc. Dan 3:28.
  Paul. 2 Tim 1:12.
Of the wicked—Exemplified
  Goliath. 1 Sam 17:43–45.
  Benhadad. 1 Kin 20:10.

Sennacherib. 2 Chr 32:8.
Israelites. Is 31:1.

TRUTH.

God is a God of. Deut 32:4; Ps 31:15.
Christ is. John 14:6; 7:18.
Christ was full of. John 1:14.
Christ spoke. John 8:45.
The Holy Spirit is the Spirit of. John
  14:17.
The Holy Spirit guides into all. John
  16:13.
The Word of God is. Dan 10:21; John
  17:17.
God regards, with favor. Jer 5:3.
The judgments of God are according to. Ps
  96:13; Rom 2:2.
Believers should
  Worship God in. John 4:24; Ps 145:18.
  Serve God in. Josh 24:14; 1 Sam
    12:24.
  Walk before God in. 1 Kin 2:4; 2 Kin
    20:3.
  Keep religious feasts with. 1 Cor 5:8.
  Esteem, as priceless. Prov 23:23.
  Rejoice in. 1 Cor 13:6.
  Speak, to one another. Zech 8:16; Eph
    4:25.
  Meditate upon. Phil 4:8.
  Write upon the tablet of the heart.
    Prov 3:3.
God desires in the heart. Ps 51:6.
The fruit of the Spirit is in. Eph 5:9.
Ministers should
  Speak. 2 Cor 12:6; Gal 4:16.
  Teach in. 1 Tim 2:7.
  Approve themselves by. 2 Cor 4:2;
    6:7,8; 7:14.
Magistrates should be men of. Ex 18:21.
Kings are preserved by. Prov 20:28.
They who speak
  Show forth righteousness. Prov 12:17.
  Shall be established. Prov 12:19.
  Are the delight of God. Prov 12:22.
The wicked
  Destitute of. Hos 4:1.
  Speak not. Jer 9:5.
  Uphold not. Is 59:14,15.
  Plead not for. Is 59:4.
  Are not valiant for. Jer 9:3.
  Punished for lack of. Jer 9:5,9; Hos 4:1.
The gospel as
  Came by Christ. John 1:17.
Christ bears witness to. John 18:37.
Is in Christ. Rom 9:1; 1 Tim 2:7.
John bears witness to. John 5:33.
Is according to godliness. Titus 1:1.
Is sanctifying. John 17:17,19.
Is purifying. 1 Pet 1:22.
Is part of Christian armor. Eph 6:14.
Is available to believers. Jer 33:6; 2 John 2.
Should be acknowledged. 2 Tim 2:25.
Should be believed. 2 Thess 2:12,13;
  1 Tim 4:3.
Should be obeyed. Rom 2:8; Gal 3:1.
Should be loved. 2 Thess 2:10.
Should be manifested. 2 Cor 4:2.
Should be rightly divided. 2 Tim 2:15.
The wicked opposed to. 1 Tim 6:5; 2 Tim
  3:8; 4:4.
The church is the pillar and ground of.
  1 Tim 3:15.
The devil is devoid of. John 8:44.

TRUTH OF GOD, THE.

Is one of His attributes. Deut 32:4; Is
  65:16.
Always goes before His face. Ps 89:14.
He keeps, for ever. Ps 146:6.
Described as
  Great. Ps 57:10.

Plenteous. Ps 86:15.
Abundant. Ex 34:6.
Inviolable. Num 23:19; Titus 1:2.
Enduring to all generations. Ps 100:5.
United with mercy in redemption. Ps
  85:10.
Exhibited in his
  Counsels of old. Is 25:1.
  Ways. Rev 15:3.
  Works. Ps 33:4; 11:7; Dan 4:37.
  Judgments. Ps 19:9; 96:13.
  Word. Ps 119:160; John 17:17.
  Fulfillment of promises in Christ.
    2 Cor 1:20.
  Fulfillment of his covenant. Mic 7:20.
  Dealings with believers. Ps 25:10.
  Deliverance of believers. Ps 57:3.
Remembered toward believers. Ps 98:3.
Is a shield and buckler to believers. Ps
  9:14.
Believers should
  Confide in. Ps 31:5; Titus 1:2.
  Plead, in prayer. Ps 89:49.
  Pray for its manifestation to ourselves.
    2 Chr 6:17.
  Pray for its exhibition to others. 2 Sam
    2:6.
  Make known to others. Is 38:19.
  Magnify. Ps 71:22; 138:2.
Is denied by
  The devil. Gen 3:4,5.
  The self-righteous. 1 John 1:10.
  Unbelievers. 1 John 5:10.

TYPES OF CHRIST.

Adam. Rom 5:14; 1 Cor 15:45.
Abel. Gen 4:8,10; Heb 12:24.
Abraham. Gen 17:5; Eph 3:15.
Aaron. Ex 28:1; Lev 16:15; Heb 5:4,5;
  9:7,24.
Ark. Gen 7:16; 1 Pet 3:20,21.
Bronze serpent. Num 21:9; John 3:14,15.
Bronze altar. Ex 27:1,2; Heb 13:10.
Burnt offering. Lev 1:2,4; Heb 10:10.
Cities of refuge. Num 35:6; Heb 6:18.
David. 2 Sam 8:15; Ps 89:19,20; Ezek
  37:24; Phil 2:9.
Eliakim. Is 22:20–22; Rev 3:7.
Firstfruits. Ex 22:29; 1 Cor 15:20.
Gold lampstand. Ex 25:31; John 8:12.
Golden altar. Ex 40:5,26,27; Heb 13:15;
  Rev 8:3.
Isaac. Gen 22:1,2; Heb 11:17–19.
Jacob. Gen 32:28; John 11:42; Heb 7:25.
Jacob's ladder. Gen 28:12; John 1:51.
Joseph. Gen 50:19,20.
Joshua. Josh 1:5,6; 11:23; Acts 20:32; Heb
  4:8,9;
Jonah. Jon 1:17; Matt 12:40.
Laver of bronze. Ex 30:18–20; Zech 13:1;
  Eph 5:26,27.
Leper's offering. Lev 14:4–7; Rom 4:25.
Manna. Ex 16:11–15; John 6:32–35.
Melchizedek. Gen 14:18–20; Heb 7:1–17.
Mercy seat. Ex 25:17–22; Rom 3:25; Heb
  4:16.
Morning and evening sacrifices. Ex 29:38–
  41; John 1:29,36.
Moses. Num 12:7; Deut 18:15; Acts 3:20–
  22; Heb 3:2.
Noah. Gen 5:29; 2 Cor 1:5.
Passover lamb. Ex 12:3–6,46; John 19:36;
  1 Cor 5:7.
Peace offerings. Lev 3:1; Eph 2:14,16.
Red heifer. Num 19:2–6; Heb 9:13,14.
Rock of Horeb. Ex 17:6; 1 Cor 10:4.
Samson. Judg 16:30; Col 2:14,15.
Scapegoat. Lev 16:20–22; Is 53:6,12.
Sin offering. Lev 4:2,3,12; Heb 13:11,12.
Solomon. 2 Sam 7:12,13; Luke 1:32,33;
  1 Pet 2:5.

Tabernacle. Ex 40:2,34; Col 2:9;
Heb 9:11.
Table and showbread. Ex 25:23–30; John
1:16; 6:48.
Temple. 1 Kin 6:1,38; John 2:19,21.
Tree of life. Gen 2:9; John 1:4; Rev 22:2.
Trespass offering. Lev 6:1–7; Is 53:10.
Vail of the tabernacle and temple. Ex
40:21; 2 Chr 3:14; Heb 10:20.
Zerubbabel. Zech 4:7–9; Heb 12:2,3.

UNBELIEF.

Is sin. John 16:9.
Defilement inseparable from. Titus 1:15.
All, by nature, concluded in. Rom 11:32.
Proceeds from
An evil heart. Heb 3:12.
Slowness of heart. Luke 24:25.
Hardness of heart. Mark 16:14; Acts
19:9.
Not listening to the truth. John
8:45,46.
Judicial blindness. John 12:39,40.
Not being Christ's sheep. John 10:26.
The devil blinding the mind. Luke 8:12;
2 Cor 4:4.
Seeking honor from men. John 5:44.
Make God a liar. 1 John 5:10.
Exhibited in
Rejecting Christ. John 16:9.
Rejecting the Word of God. Ps 106:24.
Rejecting the gospel. Is 53:1; John
12:38.
Rejecting evidence of miracles. John
12:37.
Departing from God. Heb 3:12.
Questioning the power of God. 2 Kin
7:2; Ps 78:19,20.
Not believing the works of God. Ps
78:32.
Staggering at the promise of God. Rom
4:20.
Rebuked by Christ. Matt 17:17; John
20:27.
Was an impediment to the performance of
miracles. Matt 17:20; Mark 6:5.
Miracles designed to convince those in.
John 10:37,38; 1 Cor 14:22.
The Jews rejected for. Rom 11:20.
Believers should hold no fellowship with
those in. 2 Cor 6:14.
They who are guilty of
Have not the Word of God in them.
John 5:38.
Cannot please God. Heb 11:6.
Malign the gospel. Acts 19:9.
Persecute the ministers of God. Rom
15:31.
Excite others against believers. Acts
14:2.
Persevere in it. John 12:37.
Stiffen their necks. 2 Kin 17:14.
Are condemned already. John 3:18.
Have the wrath of God abiding upon.
John 3:36.
Shall not be established. Is 7:9.
Shall die in their sins. John 8:24.
Shall not enter rest. Heb 3:19; 4:11.
Shall be condemned. Mark 16:16;
2 Thess 2:12.
Shall be destroyed. Jude 5.
Shall be cast into the lake of fire. Rev
21:8.
Warnings against. Heb 3:12; 4:11.
Prayer for help against. Mark 9:24.
The portion of, awarded to all unfaithful
servants. Luke 12:46.

UNION WITH CHRIST.

As Head of the Church. Eph 1:22,23;
4:15,16; Col 1:18.

Christ prayed that all believers might
have. John 17:21,23.
Described as
Christ being in us. Eph 3:17; Col 1:27.
Our being in Christ. 2 Cor 12:2;
1 John 5:20.
Includes union with the Father. John
17:21; 1 John 2:24.
Is of God. 1 Cor 1:30.
Maintained by
Faith. Gal 2:20; Eph 3:17.
Abiding in Him. John 15:4,7.
His Word abiding in us. John 15:7;
1 John 2:24; 2 John 9.
Feeding on Him. John 6:56.
Obeying Him. 1 John 3:24.
The Holy Spirit witnesses. 1 John 3:24.
The gift of the Holy Spirit is an evidence
of. 1 John 4:13.
Believers
Have, in mind. 1 Cor 2:16; Phil 2:5.
Have, in spirit. 1 Cor 6:17.
Have, in love. Song 2:16; 7:10.
Have, in sufferings. Phil 3:10; 2 Tim
2:12.
Have, in His death. Rom 6:3–8; Gal
2:20.
Have assurance of. John 14:20.
Enjoy, in the Lord's Supper. 1 Cor
10:16,17.
Identified with Christ by. Matt
25:40,45; Acts 9:4; 8:1.
Are complete through. Col 2:10.
Exhorted to maintain. John 15:4; Acts
11:23; Col 2:7.
Necessary to growth in grace. Eph 4:15,16;
Col 2:19.
Necessary for fruitfulness. John 15:4,5.
Beneficial results of
Righteousness imputed. 2 Cor 5:21;
Phil 3:9.
Freedom from condemnation. Rom 8:1.
Freedom from dominion of sin. 1 John
3:6.
Being created anew. 2 Cor 5:17.
The spirit alive to righteousness. Rom
8:10.
Confidence at His coming. 1 John
2:28.
Abundant fruitfulness. John 15:5.
Answers to prayer. John 15:7.
They who have, ought to walk as He
walked. 1 John 2:6.
False teachers have not. Col 2:18,19.
Is indissoluble. Rom 8:35.
Punishment of those who have not. John
15:6.

UNITY OF GOD.

A ground for obeying Him exclusively.
Deut 4:39,40.
A ground for loving Him supremely. Deut
6:4,5; Mark 12:29,30.
Asserted by
God Himself. Is 44:6,8; 45:18,21.
Christ. Mark 12:29; John 17:3.
Moses. Deut 4:39; 6:4.
Apostles. 1 Cor 8:4,6; Eph 4:6; 1 Tim
2:5.
Consistent with the deity of Christ and of
the Holy Spirit. John 10:30; John 14:9–
11; 1 John 5:7.
Exhibited in
His greatness and wonderful works.
2 Sam 7:22; Ps 86:10.
His works of creation and providence.
Is 44:24; 45:5–8.
His exclusive fore-knowledge. Is 46:9–
11.
His exercise of uncontrolled
sovereignty. Deut 32:39.

His being the sole object of worship in
heaven and earth. Neh 9:6; Matt
4:10.
His being alone good. Matt 19:17.
His being the only Savior. Is 45:21,22.
His being the only source of pardon.
Mic 7:18; Mark 2:7.
His unparalleled election and care of
His people. Deut 4:32–35.
The knowledge of, necessary to eternal
life. John 17:3.
All believers acknowledge, in worshiping
Him. 2 Sam 7:22; 2 Kin 19:15; 1 Chr
17:20.
All should know and acknowledge. Deut
4:35; Ps 83:18.
May be acknowledged without saving
faith. James 2:19,20.

VANITY.

A consequence of the fall. Rom 8:20.
Every man is. Ps 39:11.
Every state of man is. Ps 62:9.
Man at his best estate is. Ps 39:5.
Man is like to. Ps 144:4.
The thoughts of man are. Ps 94:11.
The days of man witness. Job 7:16; Eccl
6:12.
Childhood and youth are. Eccl 11:10.
The beauty of man is. Ps 39:11; Prov
31:30.
The help of man in. Ps 60:11; Lam 4:17.
Man's own righteousness is. Is 57:12.
Worldly wisdom is. Eccl 2:15,21; 1 Cor
3:20.
Worldly pleasure is. Eccl 2:1.
Worldly truth attests to. Ps 39:6; 127:2.
Worldly labor is. Eccl 4:4.
Worldly enjoyment is. Eccl 2:3,10,11.
Worldly possessions are. Eccl 2:4–11.
Treasures of wickedness are. Prov 10:2.
Concern for wealth is a reflection of. Eccl
2:26; 4:8.
Love of riches is. Eccl 5:10.
Unblessed riches are. Eccl 6:2.
Riches gotten by falsehood are. Prov 21:6.
All earthly things are. Eccl 1:2.
Foolish questions, etc. are. 1 Tim 1:6,7;
6:20; 2 Tim 2:14,16; Titus 3:9.
The conduct of the ungodly is. 1 Pet 1:18.
The religion of hypocrites is. James 1:26.
The worship of the wicked is. Is 1:13;
Matt 6:7.
Lying words are. Jer 7:8.
False teaching is but. Jer 23:32.
Mere external religion is. 1 Tim 4:8; Heb
13:9.
Alms giving without charity is. 1 Cor
13:3.
Faith without works is. James 2:14.
Actions of unbelievers prove it. 2 Kin
17:15; Ps 31:6; Is 44:9,10; Jer 10:8;
18:15.
Believers
Hate the thoughts of. Ps 119:113.
Pray to be kept from. Ps 119:37; Prov
30:8.
Avoid. Ps 24:4.
Avoid those given to. Ps 26:4.
The wicked
Especially characterised by. Job 11:11.
Though full of, affect to be wise. Job
11:12.
Love. Ps 4:2.
Imagine. Ps 2:1; Acts 4:25; Rom 1:21.
Devise. Ps 36:4.
Speak. Ps 10:7; 12:2; 41:6.
Count God's service as. Job 21:15; Mal
3:14.
Allure others by words of. 2 Pet 2:18.
Walk after. Jer 2:5.

Walk in. Ps 39:6; Eph 4:17.
Inherit. Jer 16:19.
Reap. Prov 22:8; Jer 12:13.
Judicially given up to. Ps 78:33; Is 57:13.
Fools follow those given to. Prov 12:11.
Following those given to, leads to poverty. Prov 28:19.
They who trust in, rewarded with. Job 15:31.

WAITING UPON GOD.

As the God of providence. Jer 14:22.
As the God of salvation. Ps 25:5.
As the Giver of all temporal blessings. Ps 104:27,28; Ps 145:15,16.
The objects of
  Mercy. Ps 123:2.
  Pardon. Ps 39:7,8.
  The consolation of Israel. Luke 2:25.
  Salvation. Gen 49:18; Ps 62:1,2.
  Guidance and teaching. Ps 25:5.
  Protection. Ps 33:20; 59:9,10.
  The fulfillment of His Word. Hab 2:3.
  The fulfillment of His promises. Acts 1:4.
  Hope of righteous by faith. Gal 5:5.
  Coming of Christ. 1 Cor 1:7; 1 Thess 1:10.
Is good. Ps 52:9.
God calls us to. Zeph 3:8.
Exhortations and encouragements to. Ps 27:14; 37:7; Hos 12:6.
Should be
  With the soul. Ps 62:1,5.
  With earnest desire. Ps 130:6.
  With patience. Ps 37:7; 40:1.
  With resignation. Lam 3:26.
  With hope in His Word. Ps 130:5.
  With full confidence. Mic 7:7.
  Continually. Hos 12:6.
  All the day. Ps 25:5.
  Especially in adversity. Ps 59:1–9; Is 8:17.
  In the way of His judgments. Is 26:8.
Believers resolve to. Ps 52:9; 59:9.
Believers have expectation from. Ps 62:5.
Believers plead, in prayer. Ps 25:21; Is 33:2.
The patience of believers often tried in. Ps 69:3.
They who engage in
  Are heard. Ps 40:1.
  Are blessed. Is 30:18; Dan 12:12.
  Experience His goodness. Lam 3:25.
  Shall not be ashamed. Ps 25:3; Is 49:23.
  Shall renew their strength. Is 40:31.
  Shall inherit the earth. Ps 37:9.
  Shall be saved. Prov 20:22; Is 25:9.
  Shall rejoice in salvation. Is 25:9.
  Shall receive the glorious things prepared by God for them. Is 64:4.
Predicted of the Gentiles. Is 42:4; 60:9.

WARFARE OF BELIEVERS.

Is not after the flesh. 2 Cor 10:3.
Is called good. 1 Tim 1:18,19.
Called the good fight of faith. 1 Tim 6:12.
Is against
  The devil. Gen 3:15; 2 Cor 2:11; Eph 6:12; James 4:7; 1 Pet 5:8; Rev 12:17.
  The flesh. Rom 7:23; 1 Cor 9:25–27; 2 Cor 12:7; Gal 5:17; 1 Pet 2:11.
  Enemies. Ps 38:19; 56:2; 59:3.
  The world. John 16:33; 1 John 5:4,5.
  Death. 1 Cor 15:26; Heb 2:14,15.
Often arises from the opposition of friends or relatives. Mic 7:6; Matt 10:35,36.

To be carried on
  Under Christ, as our captain. Heb 2:10.
  Under the Lord's banner. Ps 60:4.
  With faith. 1 Tim 1:18,19.
  With a good conscience. 1 Tim 1:18,19.
  With steadfastness in the faith. 1 Cor 16:13; Heb 10:23; 1 Pet 5:9.
  With earnestness. Jude 3.
  With watchfulness. 1 Cor 16:13; 1 Pet 5:8.
  With sobriety. 1 Thess 5:6; 1 Pet 5:8.
  With endurance. 2 Tim 2:3,10.
  With self-denial. 1 Cor 9:25–27.
  With confidence in God. Ps 27:1–3.
  With prayer. Ps 35:1–3; Eph 6:18.
  Without earthly entanglements. 2 Tim 2:4.
Mere professors do not maintain. Jer 9:3.
Believers
  Are all engaged in. Phil 1:30.
  Must stand firm in. Eph 6:13,14.
  Exhorted to diligence. 1 Tim 6:12; Jude 3.
  Encouraged in. Is 41:11,12; 51:12; Mic 7:8; 1 John 4:4.
  Helped by God in. Ps 118:13; Is 41:13,14.
  Protected by God in. Ps 140:7.
  Comforted by God in. 2 Cor 7:5,6.
  Strengthened by God in. Ps 20:2; 27:14; Is 41:10.
  Strengthened by Christ in. 2 Cor 12:9; 2 Tim 4:17.
  Delivered by Christ in. 2 Tim 4:18.
  Thank God for victory in. Rom 7:25; 1 Cor 15:57.
Armor for
  Girdle of truth. Eph 6:14.
  Breastplate of righteousness. Eph 6:14.
  Preparation of the gospel. Eph 6:15.
  Shield of faith. Eph 6:16.
  Helmet of salvation. Eph 6:17; 1 Thess 5:8.
  Sword of the Spirit. Eph 6:17.
  Called armor of God. Eph 6:11.
  Called armor of righteousness. 2 Cor 6:7.
  Called armor of light. Rom 13:12.
  Not carnal. 2 Cor 10:4.
  Mighty through God. 2 Cor 10:4,5.
  The whole, is required. Eph 6:13.
Victory in, is
  Through Christ. Rom 7:25; 1 Cor 15:27; 2 Cor 12:9; Rev 12:11.
  By faith. Heb 11:33–37; 1 John 5:4,5.
  Over the devil. Rom 16:20; 1 John 2:14.
  Over the flesh. Rom 7:24,25; Gal 5:24.
  Over the world. 1 John 5:4,5.
  Over all that exalts itself. 2 Cor 10:5.
  Over death and the grave. Is 25:8; 26:19; Hos 13:14; 1 Cor 15:54,55.
  All encompassing. Rom 8:37; 2 Cor 10:5.
They who overcome in, shall
  Eat of the hidden manna. Rev 2:17.
  Eat of the tree of life. Rev 2:7.
  Be clothed in white raiment. Rev 3:5.
  Be pillars in the temple of God. Rev 3:12.
  Sit with Christ on His throne. Rev 3:21.
  Have a white stone, and, in it a new name written. Rev 2:17.
  Have power over the nations. Rev 2:26.
  Have the name of God written upon them by Christ. Rev 3:12.
  Have God as their God. Rev 21:7.
  Have the morning star. Rev 2:28.

  Inherit all things. Rev 21:7.
  Be confessed by Christ before God the Father. Rev 3:5.
  Be sons of God. Rev 21:7.
  Not be hurt by the second death. Rev 2:11.
  Not have their names blotted out of the Book of Life. Rev 3:5.

WATCHFULNESS.

Christ an example of. Matt 26:38,40; Luke 6:12.
Commanded. Mark 13:37; Rev 3:2.
Exhortations to. 1 Thess 5:6; 1 Pet 4:7.
God especially requires in ministers. Ezek 3:17; Is 62:6; Mark 13:34.
Ministers exhorted to. Acts 20:31; 2 Tim 4:5.
Faithful ministers exercise. Heb 13:17.
Faithful ministers approved by. Matt 24:45,46; Luke 12:41–44.
Should be
  With prayer. Luke 21:36; Eph 6:18.
  With thanksgiving. Col 4:2.
  With steadfastness in the faith. 1 Cor 16:13.
  With heedfulness. Mark 13:33.
  With sobriety. 1 Thess 5:6; 1 Pet 4:7.
  At all times. Prov 8:34.
  In all things. 2 Tim 4:5.
Believers pray to be kept in a state of. Ps 141:3.
Motives to
  Expected direction from God. Hab 2:1.
  Uncertain time of the coming of Christ. Matt 24:42; 25:13; Mark 13:35,36.
  Incessant assaults of the devil. 1 Pet 5:8.
  Liability to temptation. Matt 26:41.
Blessedness of. Luke 12:37; Rev 16:15.
Unfaithful ministers devoid of. Is 56:10.
The wicked averse to. 1 Thess 5:7.
Danger of remissness in. Matt 24:48–51; 25:5,8,12; Rev 3:3.

WIDOWS.

Character of true. Luke 2:37; 1 Tim 5:5,10.
God
  Surely hears the cry of. Ex 22:23.
  Judges for. Deut 10:18; Ps 68:5.
  Relieves. Ps 146:9.
  Establishes the border of. Prov 15:25.
  Will witness against oppressors of. Mal 3:5.
Exhorted to trust in God. Jer 49:11.
Should not be
  Afflicted. Ex 22:22.
  Oppressed. Jer 7:6; Zech 7:10.
  Treated with violence. Jer 22:3.
  Deprived of garment in pledge. Deut 24:17.
Should be
  Pleaded for. Is 1:17.
  Honored, if widows indeed. 1 Tim 5:3.
  Relieved by their friends. 1 Tim 5:4,16.
  Relieved by the church. Acts 6:1; 1 Tim 5:9.
  Visited in affliction. James 1:27.
  Allowed to share in our blessings. Deut 14:29; 16:11,14; 24:19–21.
Though poor, may be generous. Mark 12:42,43.
Believers
  Sympathize with. Acts 9:39.
  Cause joy to. Job 29:13.
  Disappoint not. Job 31:16.
The wicked
  Do no good to. Job 24:21.

Send, away empty. Job 22:9.
Take pledges from. Job 24:3.
Reject the cause of. Is 1:23.
Mistreat. Ezek 22:7.
Make a prey of. Is 10:2; Matt 23:14.
Slay. Ps 94:6.
Curse for perverting judgment of. Deut 27:19.
Woe to those who oppress. Is 10:1,2.
Blessings on those who relieve. Deut 14:29.
A type of Zion in affliction. Lam 5:3.
Were released from all obligation to former husbands. Rom 7:3.
Were clothed in mourning after the decease of husbands. Gen 38:14,19; 2 Sam 14:2,5.
Reproach connected with. Is 54:4.
Increase of, threatened as a punishment. Ex 22:24; Jer 15:8; 18:21.
Laws respecting
Not to be oppressed. Ex 22:22; Deut 27:19.
Garment of, not to be taken in pledge by creditors. Deut 24:17.
Bound to perform their vows. Num 30:9.
Not to intermarry with priests. Lev 21:14.
To be allowed to glean in fields and vineyards. Deut 24:19.
To have a share of the triennial tithe. Deut 14:28,29; 26:12,13.
To share in public rejoicings. Deut 16:11,14.
When daughters of priests and childless to partake of the holy things. Lev 22:13.
When left childless, to be married by their husband's male relative. Deut 25:5,6; Ruth 3:10–13; 4:4,5; Matt 22:24–26.
Allowed to marry again. Rom 7:3.
Intermarrying with, of kings considered treason. 1 Kin 2:21–24.
Lack of mourning, considered a great calamity. Job 27:15; Ps 78:64.
Were under the special protection of God. Deut 10:18; Ps 68:5.
Were frequently oppressed and persecuted. Job 24:3; Ezek 22:7.
Specially taken care of by the Church. Acts 6:1; 1 Tim 5:9.
Often devoted themselves entirely to God's service. Luke 2:37; 1 Tim 5:10.
Instances of great genorsity in. 1 Kin 17:9–15; Mark 12:42,43.
Illustrative of
A desolate condition. Is 47:8,9.
Zion in captivity. Lam 1:1.

WISDOM OF GOD, THE.

Is one of His attributes. 1 Sam 2:3; Job 9:4.
Described as
Perfect. Job 36:4; 37:16.
Mighty. Job 36:5.
Universal. Job 28:24; Dan 2:22; Acts 15:18.
Infinite. Ps 147:5; Rom 11:33.
Unsearchable. Is 40:28; Rom 11:33.
Beyond human comprehension. Ps 139:6.
Incomparable. Is 44:7; Jer 10:7.
Underived. Job 21:22; Is 40:14.
The gospel contains treasures of. 1 Cor 2:7.
Wisdom of believers is derived from. Ezra 7:25.
All human wisdom derived from. Dan 2:1.

Believers ascribe to Him. Dan 2:20.
Exhibited in
His works. Job 37:16; Ps 104:24; 136:5; Prov 3:19; Jer 10:12.
His counsels. Is 28:29; Jer 32:19.
His foreshadowing events. Is 42:9; 46:10.
Redemption. 1 Cor 1:24; Eph 1:8; 3:10.
Searching the heart. 1 Chr 28:9; Rev 2:23.
Understanding the thoughts. 1 Chr 28:9; Ps 139:2.
Exhibited in knowing
The heart. Ps 44:21; Prov 15:11; Luke 16:15.
The actions. Job 34:21; Ps 139:2,3.
The words. Ps 139:4.
Those who are His. 2 Sam 7:20; 2 Tim 2:19.
The way of believers. Job 23:10; Ps 1:6.
The needs of believers. Deut 2:7; Matt 6:8.
The afflictions of believers. Ex 3:7; Ps 142:3.
The frailties of believers. Ps 103:14.
The minutest matters. Matt 10:29,30.
The most secret things. Matt 6:18.
The time of judgment. Matt 24:36.
The wicked. Neh 9:10; Job 11:11.
The works, etc. of the wicked. Is 66:18.
Nothing is concealed from. Ps 139:12.
The wicked question. Ps 73:11; Is 47:10.
Should be magnified. Rom 16:27; Jude 1:25.

WIVES.

Not to be selected from among the ungodly. Gen 24:3; 26:34,35; 28:1.
Duties of, to their husbands
To love them. Titus 2:4.
To reverence them. Eph 5:33.
To be faithful to them. 1 Cor 7:3–5,10.
To be subject to them. Gen 3:16; Eph 5:22,24; 1 Pet 3:1.
To obey them. 1 Cor 14:34; Titus 2:5.
To remain with them for life. Rom 7:2,3.
Should be adorned
Not with ornaments. 1 Tim 2:9; 1 Pet 3:3.
With modesty and sobriety. 1 Tim 2:9.
With a meek and quiet spirit. 1 Pet 3:4,5.
With good works. 1 Tim 2:10; 5:10.
Good ones
Are from the Lord. Prov 19:14.
Are a token of the favor of God. Prov 18:22.
Are a blessing to husbands. Prov 12:4; 31:10,12.
Bring honor on husbands. Prov 31:23.
Secure confidence of husbands. Prov 31:11.
Are praised by husbands. Prov 31:28.
Are diligent and prudent. Prov 31:13–27.
Are benevolent to the poor. Prov 31:20.
Duty of, to unbelieving husbands. 1 Cor 7:13,14,16; 1 Pet 3:1,2.
Should be silent in the Churches. 1 Cor 14:34.
Should seek religious instruction from their husbands. 1 Cor 14:35.
Of ministers should be exemplary. 1 Tim 3:11.

WOMAN.

Origin and cause of the name. Gen 2:23.
Originally made
By God in His own image. Gen 1:27.
From one of Adam's ribs. Gen 2:21,22.
For man. 1 Cor 11:9.
To be a helper for man. Gen 2:18,20.
Subordinate to man. 1 Cor 11:3.
To be the glory of man. 1 Cor 11:7.
Deceived by Satan. Gen 3:1–6; 2 Cor 11:3; 1 Tim 2:14.
Led man to disobey God. Gen 3:6,11,12.
Curse pronounced on. Gen 3:16.
Salvation promised through the seed of. Gen 3:15; Is 7:14.
Safety in childbirth promised to the faithful and holy. 1 Tim 2:15.
Characterized as
Weaker than man. 1 Pet 3:7.
Timid. Is 19:16; Jer 50:37; 51:30; Nah 3:13.
Loving and affectionate. 2 Sam 1:26.
Tender and constant to her offspring. Is 49:15; Lam 4:10.
To wear her hair long as a covering. 1 Cor 11:15.
Good and virtuous, described. Prov 31:10–28.
Virtuous, held in high estimation. Ruth 3:11; Prov 31:10,30.
Frequently
Fond of self-indulgence. Is 32:9–11.
Subtle and deceitful. Prov 7:10; Eccl 7:26.
Gullible and easily led into error. 2 Tim 3:6.
Zealous in promoting superstition and idolatry. Jer 7:18; Ezek 13:17,23.
Active in instigating to sin. Num 31:15,16; 1 Kin 21:25; Neh 13:26.
Generally wore a veil in the presence of the other sex. Gen 24:65.
Generally lived in a separate apartment or tent. Gen 18:9; 24:67; Esth 2:9,11.
Submissive and respectful to husbands. Gen 18:12; 1 Pet 3:6.
Of distinction
Fair and graceful. Gen 12:11; 24:16; Song 1:8; Amos 8:13.
Haughty. Is 3:16.
Fond of dress and ornaments. Is 3:17–23.
Wore their hair braided and adorned with gold and pearls. Is 3:24; 1 Tim 2:9.
Of the poorer classes tanned from exposure to the sun. Song 1:5,6.
Young
Called maiden or girl. Ex 2:8; Luke 8:51,52.
Called virgins. Gen 24:16; Lam 1:4.
Happy and rejoicing. Judg 11:34; 21:21; Jer 31:13; Zech 9:17.
Kind and courteous to strangers. Gen 24:17.
Fond of ornaments. Jer 2:32.
Required to learn from and imitate their elders. Titus 2:4.
Inherited parents' property when there was no male heir. Num 27:8.
Could not marry without consent of parents. Gen 24:3,4; 34:6; Ex 22:17.
Not to be given in marriage considered a calamity. Judg 11:37; Ps 78:63; Is 4:1.
Sometimes taken captive. Lam 1:18; Ezek 30:17,18.
Punishment for seducing, when betrothed. Deut 22:23–27.

Punishment for seducing when not
betrothed. Ex 22:16,17; Deut
22:28,29.

Often treated with great cruelty in war.
Deut 32:25; Lam 2:21; 5:11.

Of distinction, dressed in robes of
various colors. 2 Sam 13:18; Ps
45:14.

Were required to hear and obey the law.
Josh 8:35.

Had a court of the tabernacle assigned to
them. Ex 38:8; 1 Sam 2:2.

Allowed to join in the temple-music from
the time of David. 1 Chr 25:5,6; Ezra
2:65; Neh 7:67.

Forms of employment
Household work. Gen 18:6; Prov
31:15.

Agriculture. Ruth 2:8; Song 1:6.

Tending sheep. Gen 29:9; Ex 2:16.

Drawing and carrying water. Gen
24:11,13,15,16; 1 Sam 9:11; John
4:7.

Grinding grain. Matt 24:41; Luke
17:35.

Spinning. Prov 31:13,14.

Embroidery. Prov 31:22.

Celebrating the victories of the nation.
Ex 15:20,21; Judg 11:34; 1 Sam
18:6,7.

Attending funerals as mourners. Jer
9:17,20.

Vows of, when married not binding upon
the husband. Num 30:6–8.

Unfaithfulness of, when married
discovered by the waters of jealousy.
Num 5:14–28.

Punishment for injuring, when with child.
Ex 21:22–25.

To be governed by, considered a calamity
by the Jews. Is 3:12.

To be slain by, considered a great disgrace.
Judg 9:54.

Considered a valuable captive in war. Deut
20:14; 1 Sam 30:2.

Often treated with great cruelty in war.
2 Kin 8:12; Lam 5:11; Ezek 9:6; Hos
13:16.

WORKS, GOOD.

Christ, an example of. John 10:32; Acts
10:38.

Called
Good fruits. James 3:17.

Fruits worthy of repentance. Matt 3:8.

Fruits of righteousness. Phil 1:11.

Works and labors of love. Heb 6:10.

Are by Jesus Christ to the glory and praise
of God. Phil 1:11.

They alone, who abide in Christ can
perform. John 15:4,5.

Wrought by God in us. Is 26:12; Phil 2:13.

The Scripture designed to lead us to.
2 Tim 3:16,17; James 1:25.

To be performed in Christ's name. Col
3:17.

Heavenly wisdom is full of. James 3:17.

Justification unattainable by. Rom 3:20;
Gal 2:16.

Salvation unattainable by. Eph 2:8,9;
2 Tim 1:9; Titus 3:5.

Believers
Created in Christ to. Eph 2:10.

Exhorted to put on. Col 3:12–14.

Are full of. Acts 9:36.

Are zealous of. Titus 2:14.

Should be furnished to all. 2 Tim 3:17.

Should be rich in. 1 Tim 6:18.

Should be careful to maintain. Titus
3:8,14.

Should be established in. 2 Thess 2:17.

Should be fruitful in. Col 1:10.

Should be perfect in. Heb 13:21.

Should be prepared to all. 2 Tim 2:21.

Should abound to all. 2 Cor 9:8.

Should be ready to all. Titus 3:1.

Should manifest, with meekness.
James 3:13.

Should provoke each other. Heb 10:24.

Should avoid ostentation in. Matt 6:1–
18.

Bring to the light their. John 3:21.

Followed into rest by their. Rev 14:13.

Holy women should manifest. 1 Tim 2:10;
5:10.

God remembers. Neh 13:14; Heb 6:9,10.

Shall be brought into the judgment. Eccl
12:14; 2 Cor 5:10.

In the judgment, will be an evidence of
faith. Matt 25:34–40; James 2:14–20.

ZEAL.

Christ an example of. Ps 69:9; John 2:17.

Godly sorrow leads to. 2 Cor 7:10,11.

Of believers, ardent. Ps 119:139.

Provokes others to do good. 2 Cor 9:2.

Should be exhibited
In spirit. Rom 12:11.

In well-doing. Gal 4:18; Titus 2:14.

In desiring the salvation of others.
Acts 26:29; Rom 10:1.

In contending for the faith. Jude:3.

In missionary labors. Rom 15:19,23.

For the glory of God. Num 25:11,13.

For the welfare of believers. Col 4:13.

Against idolatry. 2 Kin 23:4–14.

Sometimes wrongly directed. 2 Sam 21:2;
Acts 22:3,4; Phil 3:6.

Sometimes not according to knowledge.
Rom 10:2; Gal 1:14; Acts 21:20.

Ungodly men sometimes pretend to. 2 Kin
10:16; Matt 23:15.

Exhortation to. Rom 12:11; Rev 3:19.

THE BIBLE SAMPLER

100 select passages to overview the Bible.

☐ The Creation	Genesis 1:1–2:7
☐ The Fall	Genesis 3:1–24
☐ The Flood	Genesis 6:5–7:24
☐ Noah and the Ark	Genesis 8:1–9:17
☐ Tower of Babel	Genesis 11:1–9
☐ Abraham's Call	Genesis 12:1–9
☐ Abraham's Test	Genesis 22:1–19
☐ Jacob and Esau	Genesis 27:1–46
☐ Joseph Sold	Genesis 37:1–36
☐ Pharaoh's Dreams	Genesis 41:1–57
☐ Joseph Revealed	Genesis 45:1–28
☐ Birth of Moses	Exodus 1:8–2:10
☐ The Burning Bush	Exodus 3:1–22
☐ The Passover	Exodus 12:1–33
☐ Red Sea Parting	Exodus 14:1–31
☐ Manna	Exodus 16:1–36
☐ Ten Commandments	Exodus 20:1–21
☐ Spies into Canaan	Numbers 13:1–14:4, 26–38
☐ Battle of Jericho	Joshua 6:1–27
☐ Samson and Delilah	Judges 16:4–31
☐ Samuel's Prophecy	1 Samuel 3:21
☐ Saul Anointed King	1 Samuel 10:1–27
☐ David Anointed King	1 Samuel 16:1–13
☐ David and Goliath	1 Samuel 17:1–58
☐ David and Bathsheba	2 Samuel 11:1–27
☐ Nathan's Parable	2 Samuel 12:1–25
☐ Solomon's Wisdom	1 Kings 3:1–28
☐ Elijah's Victory	1 Kings 18:17–46
☐ Elijah Ascends to Heaven	2 Kings 2:1–18
☐ Elijah Raises Woman's Son	2 Kings 4:8–37
☐ The Fall of Jerusalem	2 Chronicles 36:1–23
☐ Esther Becomes Queen	Esther 2:1–23
☐ Esther Saves the Jews	Esther 6:1–7:10
☐ Satan Attacks Job	Job 1:1–22
☐ Job's Restoration	Job 42:1–17
☐ The Lord Is My Shepherd	Psalm 23
☐ David's Prayer of Repentance	Psalm 51
☐ Psalms of Thanksgiving	Psalm 99–100
☐ Praise for His Mercies	Psalm 103
☐ God Knows You	Psalm 139
☐ The Virtuous Wife	Proverbs 31:10–31
☐ Seek God in Early Life	Ecclesiastes 11:9–12:14
☐ Isaiah's Calling	Isaiah 6
☐ Christ the Servant	Isaiah 53
☐ Daniel Obeys God	Daniel 1:1–21
☐ The Fiery Furnace	Daniel 3:1–30
☐ Daniel in the Lions' Den	Daniel 6:1–28
☐ Jonah in the Fish	Jonah 1:1–2:10
☐ Ninevah Saved	Jonah 3:1–4:11
☐ Give God Your Best	Malachi 3:1–18

☐ The Birth of Christ	Matthew 1:18–2:23
☐ Sermon on the Mount	Matthew 5
☐ Jesus' Teachings	Matthew 6:1–7:14
☐ Jesus Feeds the 5000	Matthew 14:13–36
☐ The Triumphal Entry	Matthew 21:1–22
☐ The Lord's Supper	Matthew 26:17–75
☐ The Crucifixion	Matthew 27:1–66
☐ The Resurrection	Matthew 28:1–20
☐ Jesus Heals Jairus' Daughter	Mark 5:21–43
☐ Gabriel Visits Mary	Luke 1:26–56
☐ Christ Is Born	Luke 2:1–20
☐ The Good Samaritan	Luke 10:25–42
☐ The Prodigal Son	Luke 15:1–32
☐ The Deity of Christ	John 1:1–18
☐ To Be Born Again	John 3:1–21
☐ The Woman at the Well	John 4:1–42
☐ Woman Caught in Adultery	John 8:1–11
☐ Christ Raises Lazarus	John 11:1–44
☐ Washing the Disciples' Feet	John 13:1–20
☐ Christ Comforts His Disciples	John 14:1–31
☐ I Am the Vine	John 15:1–27
☐ Jesus' Arrest and Trial	John 18:1–27
☐ Christ Reinstates Peter	John 21:1–25
☐ Pentecost	Acts 2:1–47
☐ Boldness for Christ	Acts 4:1–31
☐ Stephen, the First Martyr	Acts 6:8–7:8; 7:44–8:3
☐ Philip and the Ethiopian	Acts 8:26–40
☐ Saul's Conversion	Acts 9:1–31
☐ Salvation for the Gentiles	Acts 11:1–18
☐ Paul and Silas Imprisoned	Acts 16:11–40
☐ All Have Sinned	Romans 3:1–26
☐ Christ in Our Place	Romans 5:1–11
☐ Freedom in Christ	Romans 8:1–39
☐ Living Sacrifices to God	Romans 12:1–21
☐ On Love	1 Corinthians 13
☐ The Fruit of the Spirit	Galatians 5:1–26
☐ By Grace Through Faith	Ephesians 2:1–22
☐ The Armor of God	Ephesians 5:10–20
☐ Humility	Philippians 2:1–18
☐ Paul's Admonitions	Philippians 3:1–4:9
☐ Set Your Mind on Christ	Colossians 3:1–4:1
☐ Plea for Purity	1 Thessalonians 4:1–18
☐ On Faith	Hebrews 11
☐ Run the Race	Hebrews 12:1–24
☐ The Test of Perseverance	James 1:2–27
☐ Taming the Tongue	James 3:1–18
☐ A Heavenly Inheritance	1 Peter 1:3–25
☐ The God of Love	1 John 3:16–4:19
☐ All Things Made New	Revelation 21:1–22:5
☐ Jesus Is Coming Soon	Revelation 22:6–21

THE CHARACTER OF GENUINE SAVING FAITH

Second Corinthians 13:5 says, "Examine yourselves as to whether you are in the faith. Test yourselves. Do you not know yourselves, that Jesus Christ is in you? —unless indeed you are disqualified." No one can judge another person's heart except the Lord. The Bible encourages us to examine ourselves to test our own faith.

The qualities given in the first list are often mistaken as proof of salvation; in reality, they are not solid proof.

EVIDENCES THAT NEITHER PROVE NOR DISPROVE ONE'S FAITH
Visible Morality: Matthew 19:16–21,23–27
Intellectual Knowledge: Romans 1:21; 2:17–24
Religious Involvement: Matthew 25:1–10
Active Ministry: Matthew 7:21–24
Conviction of Sin: Acts 24:25
Assurance: Matthew 23
Time of Decision: Luke 8:13,14

THE FRUIT/PROOF OF AUTHENTIC/GENUINE CHRISTIANITY
Love for God: Psalm 42:1–11; 73:25; Luke 10:27; Romans 8:7
Repentance from Sin: Psalm 32:5, Proverbs 28:13; Romans 7:14–25;
2 Corinthians 7:10; 1 John 1:8–10
Genuine Humility: Psalm 51:17; Matthew 5:1–12; James 4:6–10
Devotion to God's Glory: Psalm 105:3; 115:1; Isaiah 43:7; 48:10,11;
Jeremiah 9:23,24; 1 Corinthians 10:31
Continual Prayer: Luke 18:1; Ephesians 6:18–20; Philippians 4:6–9;
1 Timothy 2:1–4; James 5:16–18
Selfless Love: 1 John 2:9–17; 3:14; 4:7–21
Separation from the World: 1 Corinthians 2:12; James 4:4–17; 1 John 2:15–17; 5:5
Spiritual Growth: Luke 8:15; John 15:1–6; Ephesians 4:12–16
Obedient Living: Matthew 7:21; John 15:14–27; 1 Peter 1:2,22; 1 John 2:3–5

The qualities given in the second list are true, conclusive evidence of the Christian faith. If the first list is true of a person but the second list is false, there is cause to question the validity of one's profession of faith. If the second list is true, then the first list will be true also.

INDEX OF FAMOUS EVENTS AND TEACHINGS

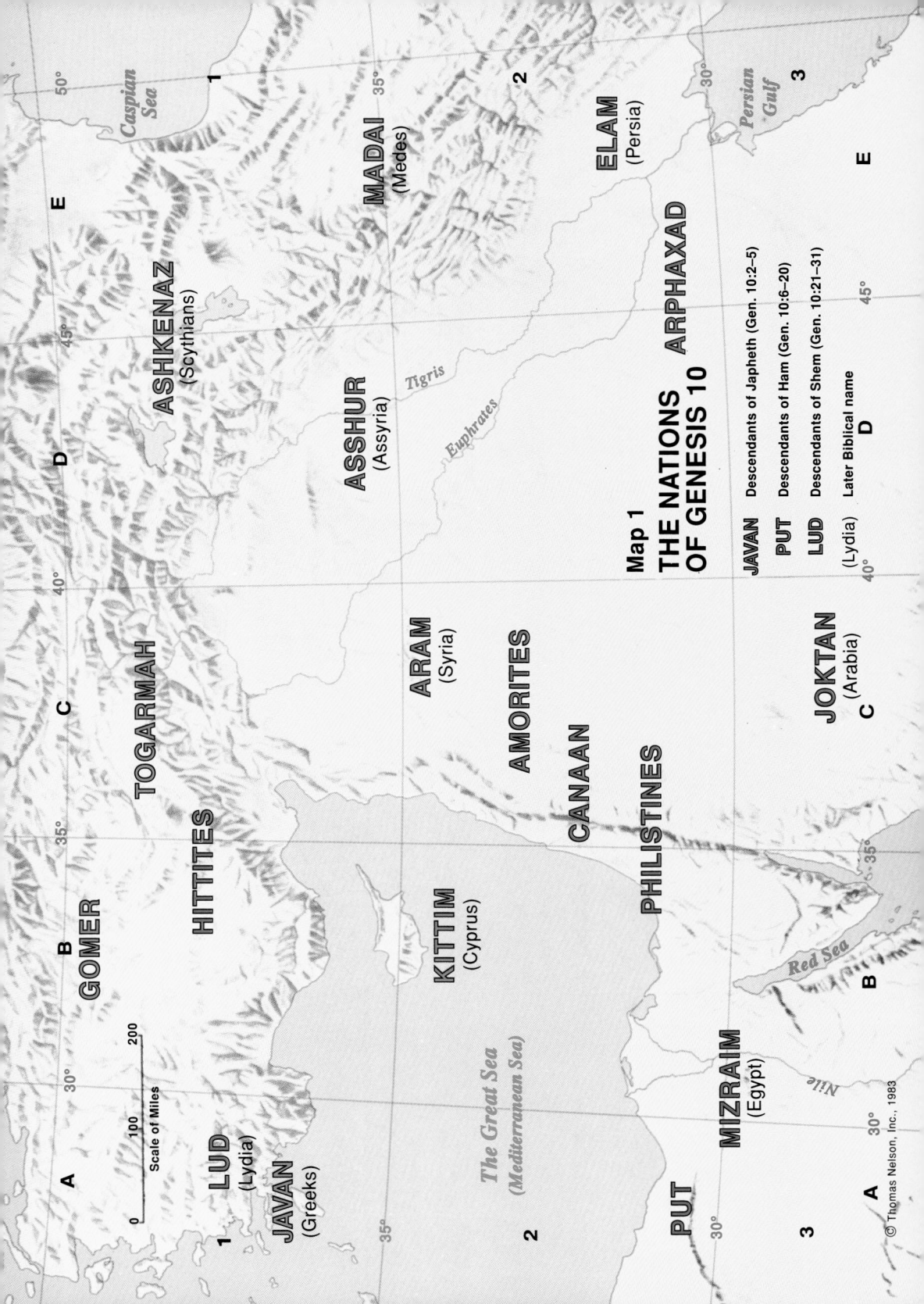

Map 1

THE NATIONS OF GENESIS 10

JAVAN   Descendants of Japheth (Gen. 10:2–5)
PUT   Descendants of Ham (Gen. 10:6–20)
LUD   Descendants of Shem (Gen. 10:21–31)
(Lydia)   Later Biblical name

GOMER
TOGARMAH
HITTITES
ASHKENAZ
(Scythians)
MADAI
(Medes)
ASSHUR
(Assyria)
Tigris
Euphrates
ELAM
(Persia)
ARPHAXAD
LUD
(Lydia)
JAVAN
(Greeks)
KITTIM
(Cyprus)
ARAM
(Syria)
AMORITES
CANAAN
PHILISTINES
JOKTAN
(Arabia)
PUT
MIZRAIM
(Egypt)
Nile
The Great Sea
(Mediterranean Sea)
Red Sea
Caspian Sea
Persian Gulf

Scale of Miles
0   100   200

© Thomas Nelson, Inc., 1983

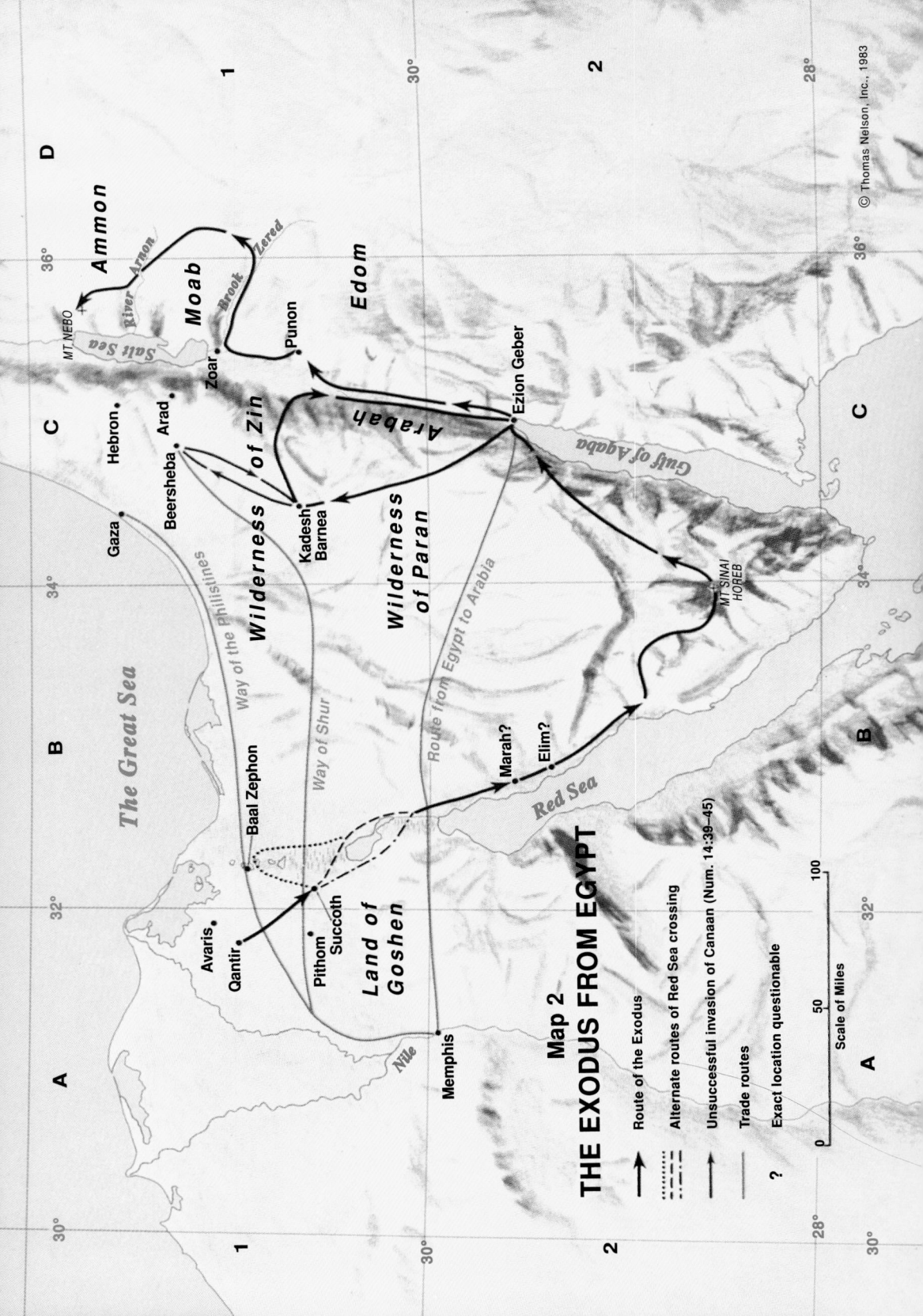

Map 2
THE EXODUS FROM EGYPT

Route of the Exodus
Alternate routes of Red Sea crossing
Unsuccessful invasion of Canaan (Num. 14:39–45)
Trade routes
? Exact location questionable

Scale of Miles
0   50   100

The Great Sea

Ammon
Moab
Edom
Arnon River
Brook Zered
MT. NEBO
Salt Sea
Zoar
Punon
Hebron
Arad
Beersheba
Gaza
Wilderness of Zin
Kadesh Barnea
Arabah
Ezion Geber
Gulf of Aqaba
Wilderness of Paran
MT. SINAI HOREB
Way of the Philistines
Way of Shur
Route from Egypt to Arabia
Baal Zephon
Avaris
Qantir
Pithom
Succoth
Land of Goshen
Memphis
Nile
Marah?
Elim?
Red Sea

© Thomas Nelson, Inc., 1983

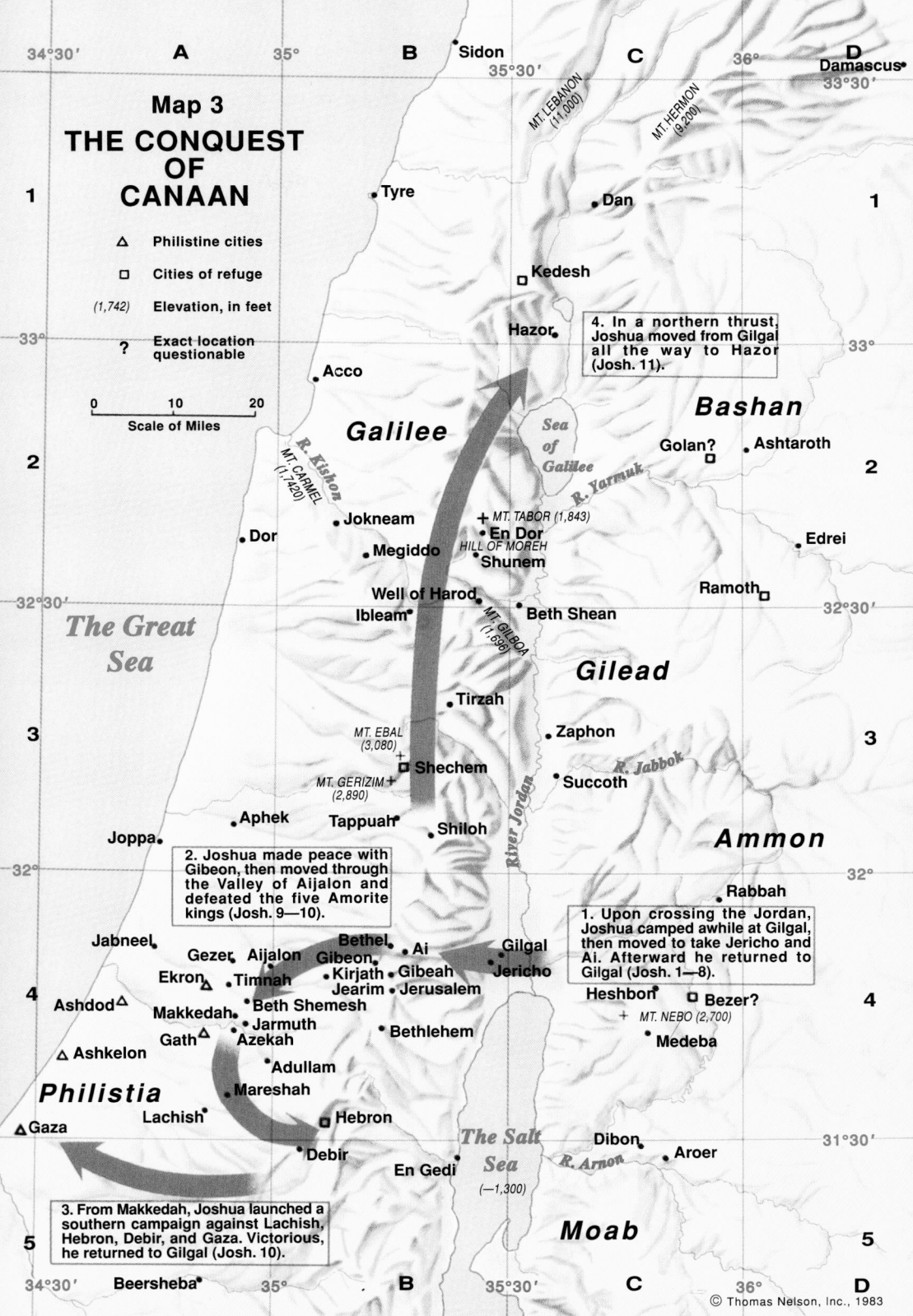

Map 3
THE CONQUEST OF CANAAN

△ Philistine cities

□ Cities of refuge

(1,742) Elevation, in feet

? Exact location questionable

Scale of Miles
0　　10　　20

1. Upon crossing the Jordan, Joshua camped awhile at Gilgal, then moved to take Jericho and Ai. Afterward he returned to Gilgal (Josh. 1—8).

2. Joshua made peace with Gibeon, then moved through the Valley of Aijalon and defeated the five Amorite kings (Josh. 9—10).

3. From Makkedah, Joshua launched a southern campaign against Lachish, Hebron, Debir, and Gaza. Victorious, he returned to Gilgal (Josh. 10).

4. In a northern thrust, Joshua moved from Gilgal all the way to Hazor (Josh. 11).

The Great Sea

The Salt Sea (−1,300)

Sidon

Damascus•

MT. LEBANON (11,000)

MT. HERMON (9,200)

Tyre•

Dan•

Kedesh □

Hazor•

Acco•

Galilee

Sea of Galilee

Bashan

Golan? □　Ashtaroth•

R. Kishon
MT. CARMEL (1,420)

Dor•

Jokneam•

Megiddo•

+ MT. TABOR (1,843)
En Dor•
HILL OF MOREH
Shunem•

Edrei•

Well of Harod•
Ibleam•

MT. GILBOA (1,696)

Beth Shean•

R. Yarmuk

Ramoth □

Gilead

Tirzah•

Zaphon•

MT. EBAL (3,080) +
+ Shechem•
MT. GERIZIM (2,890) +

Succoth•

R. Jabbok

Joppa•

Aphek•

Tappuah•

Shiloh•

River Jordan

Ammon

Rabbah•

Jabneel•

Bethel•　•Ai

Gilgal

Gezer•　Aijalon
Ekron △　Timnah•
Gibeon•　Kirjath Jearim•　Gibeah•

Jericho•

Jerusalem•

Heshbon □　Bezer?•

+ MT. NEBO (2,700)

Ashdod △

Makkedah•
Gath △　Jarmuth•
Azekah•

Beth Shemesh•

Bethlehem•

Medeba•

Ashkelon △

Adullam•

Philistia

Mareshah•

Lachish•

Hebron □

En Gedi•

Dibon•　Aroer•

△ Gaza

Debir•

R. Arnon

Moab

Beersheba•

© Thomas Nelson, Inc., 1983

Map 4
THE KINGDOM YEARS

Probable extent of Israelite control during the Kingdom of Solomon, c. 950 B.C.

The Kingdoms of Israel and Judah, c. 860 B.C.

- - - Boundary between Israel and Judah

? Exact location questionable

0   25   50
Scale of Miles

1

Riblah

Zobah

Byblos

2

Sidon
Zarephath

Phoenicia

MT. LEBANON

Damascus

MT. HERMON

Tyre

Dan

Kedesh

Syria

Hazor

3

The Great Sea

Acco

Sea of Chinnereth

Ashtaroth

MT. CARMEL

R. Yarmuk

Golan?

Dor

Jokneam

Megiddo

Ramoth Gilead

Taanach

Jezreel

MT. GILBOA

Jabesh Gilead

Dothan

Tirzah

Zaphon

Jordan R.

Samaria

Succoth

Shechem

R. Jabbok

Aphek

Shiloh

Ammon

Joppa

ISRAEL

Rabbah

Mizpah

Bethel

Jabneh

Gezer

Philistia

Ramah

Heshbon

Beth Shemesh

Jerusalem

Ashkelon

Bethlehem

Medeba

Gaza

Eglon?

Adullam

Tekoa

Dibon

Hebron

The Salt Sea

Aroer

Ziklag?

Debir

R. Arnon

Beersheba

Arad

Moab

Kir Hareseth

Zoar

R. Zered

JUDAH

Bozrah

Kadesh Barnea

Edom

5

Teman

6

Brook of Egypt

Note: Other place names significant during the time of the Kingdoms are found on Map 3.

Ezion Geber

Elath

© Thomas Nelson, Inc., 1983

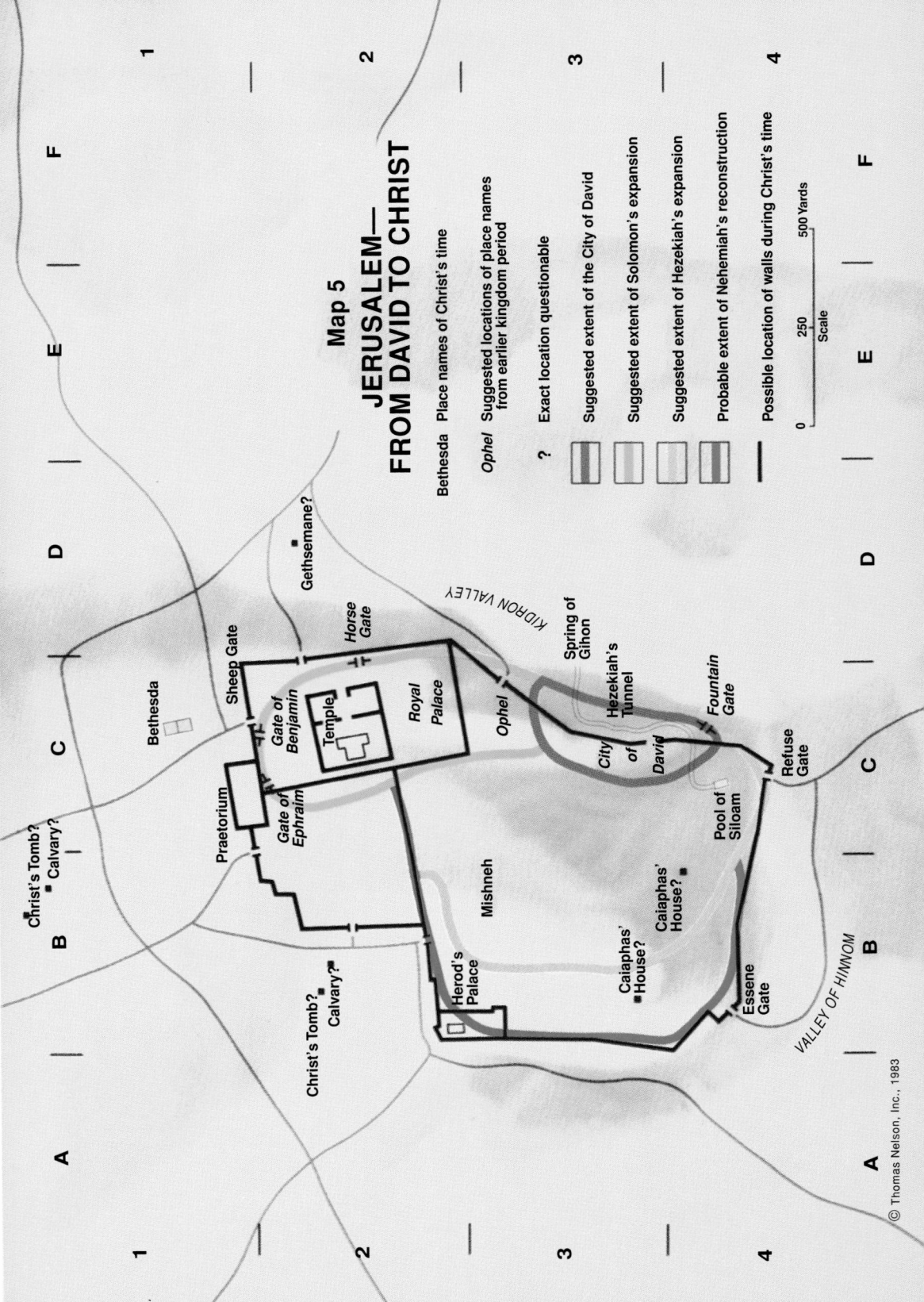

Map 5
JERUSALEM—
FROM DAVID TO CHRIST

Bethesda   Place names of Christ's time

Ophel   Suggested locations of place names
from earlier kingdom period

?   Exact location questionable

Suggested extent of the City of David

Suggested extent of Solomon's expansion

Suggested extent of Hezekiah's expansion

Probable extent of Nehemiah's reconstruction

Possible location of walls during Christ's time

Scale

0   250   500 Yards

Sheep Gate

Bethesda

Gate of Benjamin

Temple

Horse Gate

Gethsemane?

Royal Palace

Gate of Ephraim

Praetorium

Christ's Tomb?   Calvary?

Christ's Tomb?   Calvary?

Herod's Palace

Mishneh

Caiaphas' House?

Caiaphas' House?

Ophel

Spring of Gihon

KIDRON VALLEY

Hezekiah's Tunnel

City of David

Fountain Gate

Pool of Siloam

Refuse Gate

Essene Gate

VALLEY OF HINNOM

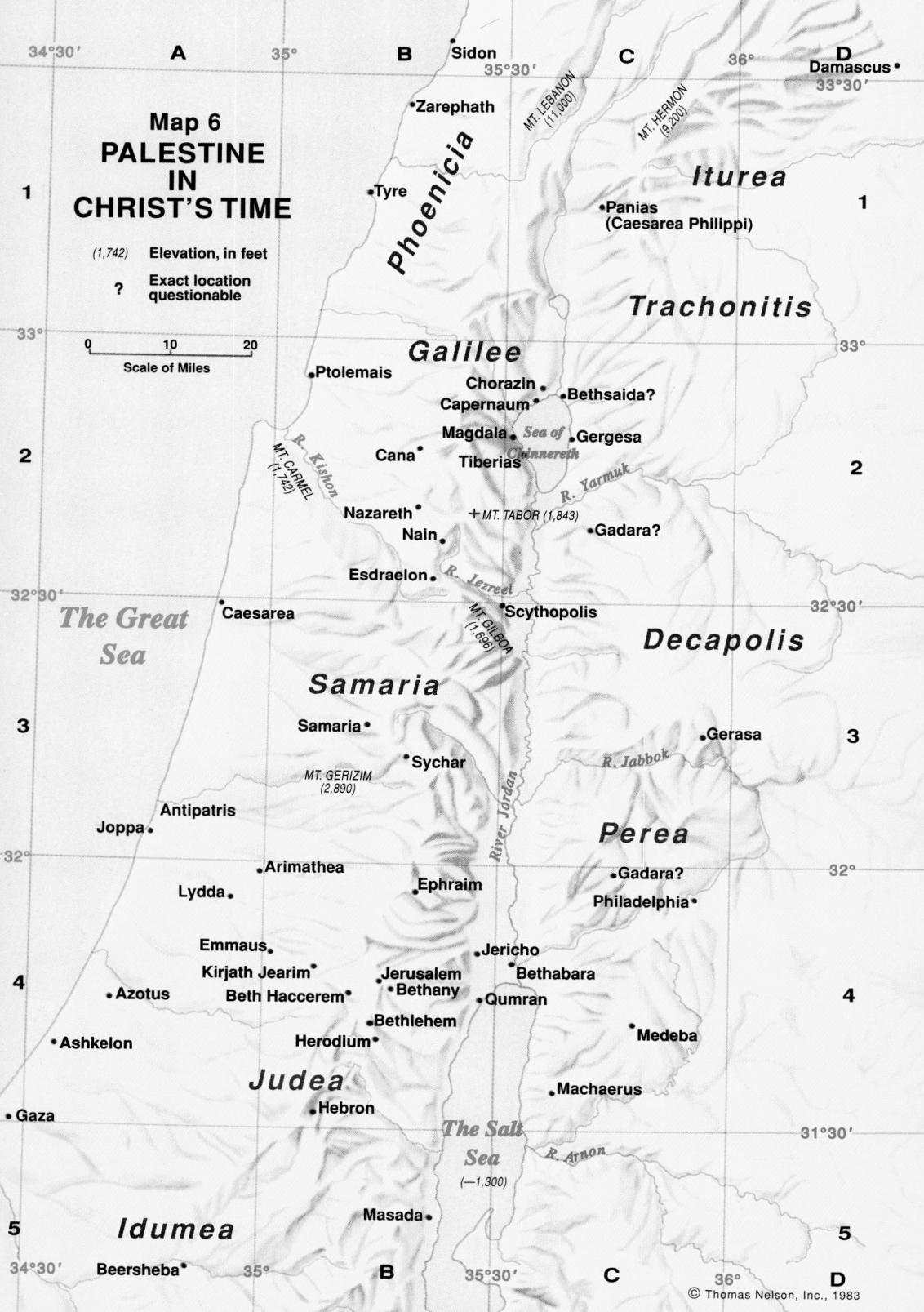

Map 6
PALESTINE
IN
CHRIST'S TIME

(1,742)   Elevation, in feet

?   Exact location
questionable

0   10   20
Scale of Miles

Sidon

34°30′   A   35°   B   35°30′   C   36°   D

Damascus •

33°30′

•Zarephath

Phoenicia

MT. LEBANON
(11,000)

MT. HERMON
(9,200)

Iturea

1   •Tyre   •Panias
(Caesarea Philippi)   1

Trachonitis

33°   *Galilee*   33°

•Ptolemais

Chorazin
•Capernaum   •**Bethsaida?**

R. Kishon

MT. CARMEL
(1,742)

•Magdala   *Sea of Chinnereth*   •Gergesa

2   •Cana   •Tiberias   R. Yarmuk   2

•Nazareth   + MT. TABOR (1,843)

•Nain   •Gadara?

•Esdraelon   R. Jezreel

32°30′   •Caesarea   MT. GILBOA
(1,696)   •Scythopolis   32°30′

*The Great
Sea*

Decapolis

Samaria

3   •Samaria   •Gerasa   3

•Sychar   R. Jabbok

MT. GERIZIM
(2,890)

•Antipatris

Joppa•   River Jordan

Perea

32°   •Arimathea   •Gadara?   32°

•Ephraim   •Philadelphia

•Lydda

•Emmaus
•Kirjath Jearim   •Jericho
•Jerusalem   •Bethabara

4   •Azotus   •Beth Haccerem   •Bethany   •Qumran   4

•Bethlehem   •Medeba

•Ashkelon   •Herodium

Judea

•Machaerus

•Gaza   •Hebron

*The Salt
Sea*
(−1,300)

R. Arnon

5   *Idumea*   •Masada   5

34°30′   Beersheba•   35°   B   35°30′   C   36°   D

© Thomas Nelson, Inc., 1983

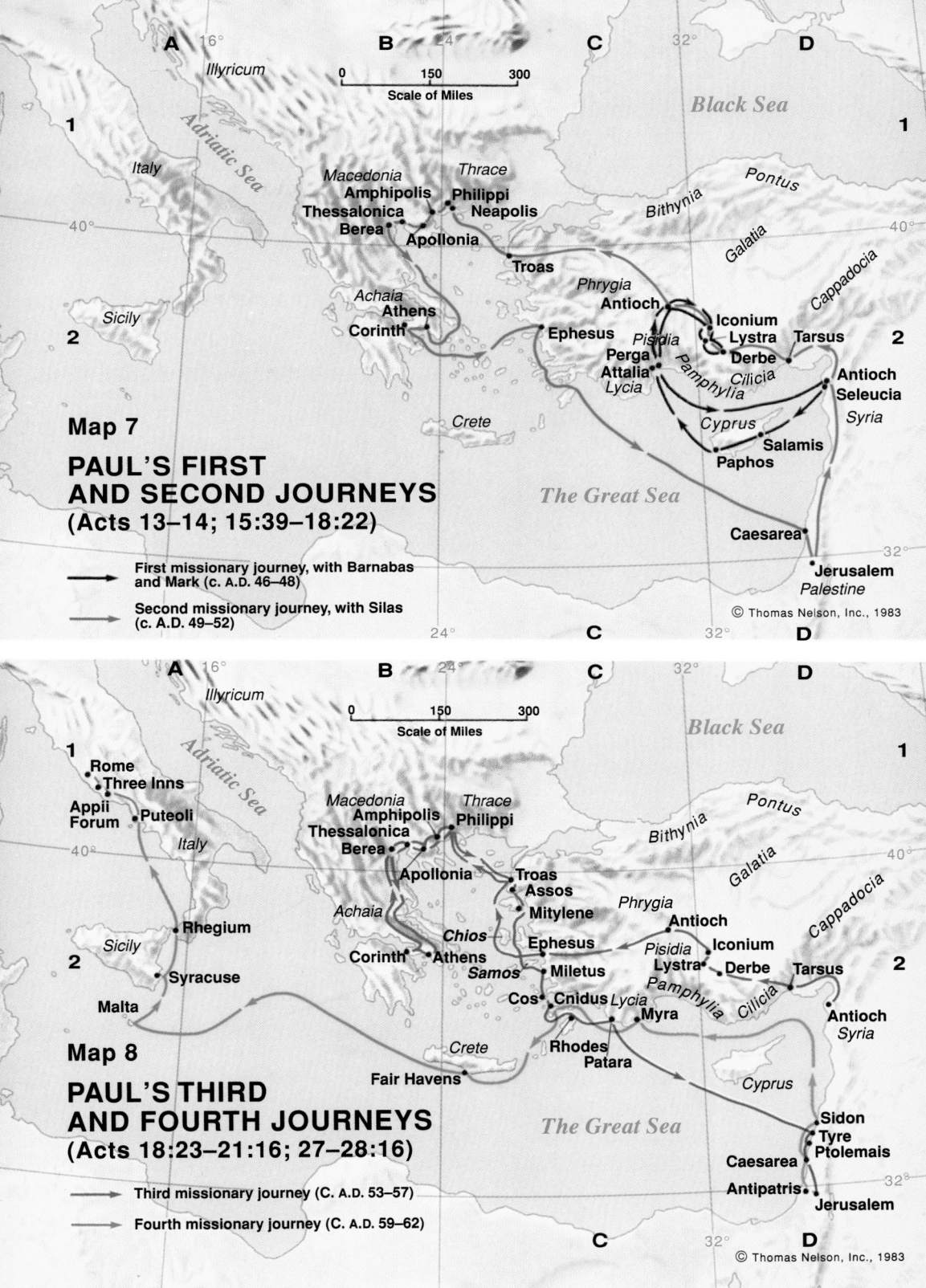

Map 7

PAUL'S FIRST AND SECOND JOURNEYS
(Acts 13–14; 15:39–18:22)

→ First missionary journey, with Barnabas and Mark (c. A.D. 46–48)

→ Second missionary journey, with Silas (c. A.D. 49–52)

© Thomas Nelson, Inc., 1983

Map 8

PAUL'S THIRD AND FOURTH JOURNEYS
(Acts 18:23–21:16; 27–28:16)

→ Third missionary journey (C. A.D. 53–57)

→ Fourth missionary journey (C. A.D. 59–62)

© Thomas Nelson, Inc., 1983

Map 9

THE HOLY LAND
IN MODERN TIMES

Area occupied by Israel
since June, 1967

0   25   50
Scale of Miles

LEBANON

Tripoli

Beirut

BEKAA VALLEY

Sidon

LEBANON MTS.

ANTI-LEBANON MTS.

Damascus

Tyre

Dan

U.N. Buffer Zone
1973 Line

SYRIA

Qiryat
Shemona

Quneitra
1967 Cease-Fire Line

Nahariyya

Safad

*Sea of
Galilee*

Golan
Heights

Akko

Haifa

Tiberias

Dera

Nazareth

Afula

Ramtha

Mediterranean Sea

Beth Shean

Hadera

Jarash

Netanya

Tulkarm

Jordan River

Herzliyya

Nablus

Tel Aviv
Yafo

Petah
Tiqwa

*West
Bank*

Amman

Rishon le Zion

Lod

Ramla

Ramalah

Ashdod

Jericho

Ashqelon

Jerusalem
Bethlehem

Madaba

Gaza

Qiryat
Gat

Hebron

*Dead
Sea*

Dhiban

En Gedi

Beersheba

JORDAN

Al-Arish

Karak

ISRAEL

EGYPT

Negev

Arabah

Sinai

Elat
Aqaba

© Thomas Nelson, Inc., 1983